GOULD'S
PENAL CODE
HANDBOOK
OF CALIFORNIA

—Including—

Penal Code
and Related Statutes from
Business and Professions Code, Evidence Code,
Health and Safety Code, Rules of Court, Vehicle Code &
Welfare and Institutions Code

1992 EDITION

GOULD PUBLICATIONS, INC.
107 Orange Blossom Circle
Altamonte Springs, Florida 32714

Copyright © 1984 through 1992
by J., B. & L. Gould
Printed in the U.S.A.

Published by
GOULD PUBLICATIONS, INC.
107 Orange Blossom Circle
Altamonte Springs, Fla. 32714
(800) 847-6502

ISBN 0-87526-268-6

All rights reserved. No part of this book may be used or reproduced in any manner whatsoever without written permission except in the case of brief quotations embodied in critical articles and reviews.

Every attempt has been made to ensure the accuracy and the completeness of the law contained herein. No express or implied guarantees or warranties are made.

Since laws change very often and vary from jurisdiction to jurisdiction, it is very important to check the timeliness and applicability of the laws contained herein.

PREFACE

The material presented herewith in convenient form is the **Gould's California Penal Code Handbook**, as currently amended to include the enactments of the 1991 Legislative Session through chapter 1231, for use in 1992. All changes have been incorporated in text, and effective dates have been added where applicable. This handbook contains the following:

1. Penal Code *(Complete Law)*
2. Business and Professions Code *(Selected Sections)*
3. Evidence Code *(Complete Law)*
4. Health and Safety Code *(Selected Sections)*
5. Rules of Court *(Selected Rules)*
6. Vehicle Code *(Selected Sections)*
7. Welfare and Institutions Code *(Selected Sections)*

A complete, up-to-date, integrated index is also included.

At the end of this volume is Gould's handy "Quick Find Locator" which helps you find the law you need.

Annual editions will incorporate changes as enacted. Please return the "IMPORTANT" subscription card at the front of this volume to ensure that you receive the latest changes contained herein.

Comments from users of this book and ways to improve its use would be appreciated by the publisher.

This page intentionally left blank.

© 1992 by J., B. & L. Gould
Printed in the U.S.A. **EP**

1991 Legislative Changes to the
CALIFORNIA PENAL CODE HANDBOOK
(for use in 1992)

PENAL CODE

Section	Change	Chapter	Effective Date
19.8	Amend	638(1)	1/1/92
115.2	New	1051(2)	1/1/92
146e	Amend	579(1)	1/1/92
148.1	Amend	503(1)	1/1/92
150	Amend	910(3)	1/1/92
186.2	Amend	1049(2)	1/1/92
186.2	Amend	1049(3)	1/1/92
186.10	Amend	1049(4)	1/1/92
186.22	Amend	201(1)	1/1/92
186.22	Amend	661(1)	1/1/92
186.22	Amend	661(2)	1/1/92
186.22a	Amend	260(1)	1/1/92
186.27	Amend	201(2)	1/1/92
193.7	Amend	1091(117)	1/1/92
243.4	Amend	149(1)	1/1/92
243.8	New	575(1)	1/1/92
258 to 260	Repeal	186(2)	1/1/92
264.2	New	999(1)	1/1/92
270h	Amend	1091(118)	1/1/92
273.88	New	483(1)	1/1/92
277	Amend	400(1)	1/1/92
286	Amend	144(1)	1/1/92
287	Repeal	144(2)	1/1/92
289.5	New	293(1)	1/1/92
308.2	New	1231(1)	1/1/92
318	Amend	684(2)	1/1/92
330	Amend	71(1)	1/1/92
332	Amend	684(3)	1/1/92
374.8	New	1120(1)	1/1/92
417	Amend	1202(3)	1/1/92
417.2	Amend	950(1.5)	1/1/92
422.6	Amend	1184(1.5)	1/1/92
422.7	Amend	1184(2.5)	1/1/92
422.75	New	607(7)	1/1/92
422.8	Amend	839(4)	1/1/92
422.95	New	607(8)	1/1/92
459	Amend	942(14)	1/1/92
460	Amend	942(15)	1/1/92
487g	Amend	490(2)	1/1/92
490.1	New	638(2)	1/1/92
549	New	116(35)	1/1/92
549	Amend	934(18)	1/1/92
602.1	New	673(1)	1/1/92

(continued)

© 1992 by J., B. & L. Gould
Printed in the U.S.A. **EP**

PENAL CODE
(Continued)

Section	Change	Chapter	Effective Date
602.3	Amend	930(1)	1/1/92
626.9	Amend	1202(4)	1/1/92
636.5	Amend	515(1)	1/1/92
640.5	Amend	556(1)	1/1/92
640.6	New	556(2)	1/1/92
650	Repeal	186(3)	1/1/92
650.5	Repeal	186(4)	1/1/92
667.5	Amend	451(1)	1/1/92
778a	Amend	635(1)	1/1/92
784a	Repeal	186(5)	1/1/92
802	Amend	129(1)	1/1/92
830.3	Amend	877(2)	1/1/92
830.3	Amend	910(5)	1/1/92
830.55	Amend	1100(1)	1/1/92
830.6	Amend	509(1)	1/1/92
830.7	Amend	229(1)	1/1/92
830.7	Amend	910(6)	1/1/92
831	Amend	1100(2)	1/1/92
831.5	Amend	265(1)	1/1/92
831.5	Amend	1100(3)	1/1/92
832	Amend	509(2)	1/1/92
836.6	New	171(1)	1/1/92
853.6	Amend	453(1)	1/1/92
853.6a	Amend	1202(5)	1/1/92
859a	Amend	613(6)	1/1/92
868.5	Amend	336(1)	1/1/92
904.4	New	1109(1)	1/1/92
904.5	Repeal	464(1)	10/2/91
904.6	Amend	464(2)	10/2/91
904.7	Repeal	464(3)	10/2/91
904.8	Repeal	464(4)	10/2/91
904.9	Repeal	464(5)	10/2/91
964	Repeal	186(6)	1/1/92
969f	New	249(1)	1/1/92
977.2	Amend	179(1)	1/1/92
1000	Amend	469(2)	1/1/92
1018	Amend	421(1)	1/1/92
1026.2	Amend	183(1)	1/1/92
1026.5	Amend	183(2)	1/1/92
1125	Repeal	186(7)	1/1/92
1126	Amend	186(8)	1/1/92
1170.75	Amend	607(9)	1/1/92
1170.75	Amend	1184(3.5)	1/1/92
1170.78	New	602(7)	1/1/92

(continued)

© 1992 by J., B. & L. Gould
Printed in the U.S.A. **EP**

Section	Change	Chapter	Effective Date
1203m	Amend	124(2)	1/1/92
1203.073	Amend	224(1)	1/1/92
1203.096	New	552(1)	1/1/92
1203.1e	Repeal	437(1)	9/19/91
1203.1e	New	437(2)	9/19/91
1203.1f	Amend	437(3)	9/19/91
1203.1f	New	437(4)	9/19/91
1203.1h	Amend	377(1)	1/1/92
1203.3	Amend	655(2)	1/1/92
1203.9	Amend	1202(6)	1/1/92
1203.11	New	866(5)	1/1/92
1205.1	New	90(24)	6/30/91
1205.1	Amend	189(15)	7/29/91
1205.1	Repeal	1168(4.7)	10/14/91
1208.2	New	437(5)	9/19/91
1208.3	New	437(6)	9/19/91
1208.5	Amend	437(7)	9/19/91
1208.5	New	437(8)	9/19/91
1214.3	Amend	1103(1)	1/1/92
1276.5	New	838(1)	1/1/92
1306	Amend	90(25)	6/30/91
1306	Amend	613(7)	1/1/92
1328	Amend	315(1)	1/1/92
1347	Amend	948(1)	1/1/92
1382	Amend	655(3)	1/1/92
1387	Amend	400(2)	1/1/92
1462	Amend	613(8)	1/1/92
1462.3	New	189(16)	7/29/91
1462.3	Amend	1168(5)	10/14/91
1463	Amend	90(26)	6/30/91
1463	Repeal	189(17)	7/29/91
1463	New	189(18)	7/29/91
1463.001	New	189(19)	7/29/91
1463.001	Amend	1168(6)	10/14/91
1463.002	New	189(20)	7/29/91
1463.003	New	189(21)	7/29/91
1463.003	Amend	1168(7)	10/14/91
1463.004	New	189(22)	7/29/91
1463.005	New	1168(7.5)	10/14/91
1463.006	New	189(23)	7/29/91
1463.009	New	189(24)	7/29/91
1463.02	Repeal	90(27)	6/30/91
1463.03	Repeal	90(28)	6/30/91
1463.04	Repeal	90(29)	6/30/91

(continued)

© 1992 by J., B. & L. Gould
Printed in the U.S.A. **EP**

PENAL CODE
(Continued)

Section	Change	Chapter	Effective Date
1463.04	New	189(25)	7/29/91
1463.05	Repeal	90(30)	6/30/91
1463.06	Repeal	90(31)	6/30/91
1463.2	Repeal	90(32)	6/30/91
1463.3	Repeal	90(33)	6/30/91
1463.4	Repeal	90(34)	6/30/91
1463.5a	Repeal	90(35)	6/30/91
1463.6	Repeal	90(36)	6/30/91
1463.7	Repeal	90(37)	6/30/91
1463.7	New	189(26)	7/29/91
1463.8	Repeal	90(38)	6/30/91
1463.9	Repeal	90(39)	6/30/91
1463.9	New	189(27)	7/29/91
1463.10	Repeal	90(40)	6/30/91
1463.11	Repeal	90(41)	6/30/91
1463.12	Repeal	90(42)	6/30/91
1463.13	Repeal	90(43)	6/30/91
1463.14	Repeal	90(44)	6/30/91
1463.14	New	189(28)	7/29/91
1463.15	Repeal	90(45)	6/30/91
1463.16	Repeal	90(46)	6/30/91
1463.16	New	189(29)	7/29/91
1463.17	Repeal	90(47)	6/30/91
1463.18	Repeal	90(48)	6/30/91
1463.18	New	189(30)	7/29/91
1463.19	Repeal	90(49)	6/30/91
1463.20	Repeal	90(50)	6/30/91
1463.21	Repeal	90(51)	6/30/91
1463.22	Repeal	90(52)	6/30/91
1463.22	New	189(31)	7/29/91
1463.23	Repeal	90(53)	6/30/91
1463.23	New	189(32)	7/29/91
1463.24	Repeal	90(54)	6/30/91
1463.25	Repeal	90(55)	6/30/91
1463.25	New	189(33)	7/29/91
1463.26	Repeal	90(56)	6/30/91
1463.26	New	189(34)	7/29/91
1463.27	Repeal	90(57)	6/30/91
1463.28	Amend	90(58)	6/30/91
1463.29	Amend	38(1)	1/1/92
1463.29	Repeal	90(59)	6/30/91
1464	Amend	90(60)	6/30/91
1464	Amend	189(35)	7/29/91
1464	Amend	613(9)	1/1/92

(continued)

© 1992 by J., B. & L. Gould
Printed in the U.S.A. **EP**

PENAL CODE
(Continued)

Section	Change	Chapter	Effective Date
1464.5	Repeal	189(36)	7/29/91
1464.8	New	90(61)	6/30/91
1464.8	Amend	189(37)	7/29/91
1465	Repeal	189(38)	7/29/91
1465.5	Amend	430(1)	9/19/91
1605	Amend	435(1)	1/1/92
2625	Amend	820(1)	1/1/92
2813.5	Amend	1157(1)	1/1/92
2900.5	Amend	437(9)	9/19/91
2900.5	New	437(10)	9/19/91
2910.5	Amend	1100(4)	1/1/92
2962	Amend	435(2)	1/1/92
2964	Amend	435(3)	1/1/92
2970	Amend	435(4)	1/1/92
2976	Amend	435(5)	1/1/92
3004	New	215(1)	1/1/92
3042	Amend	1017(1)	1/1/92
3088	Amend	229(2)	1/1/92
3089	New	229(3)	1/1/92
3417	Amend	820(2)	1/1/92
3601	Amend	1016(1)	1/1/92
4419.5	New	652(16)	1/1/92
4489.5	New	652(17)	1/1/92
4496.43	New	652(18)	1/1/92
4532	Amend	1162(1)	1/1/92
4572	Repeal	186(9)	1/1/92
6025.6	New	1017(2)	1/1/92
6031.2	Amend	1017(3)	1/1/92
6031.5	Amend	1100(5)	1/1/92
6035	Amend	1100(6)	1/1/92
6242	Amend	1100(7)	1/1/92
6242.6	Amend	1017(4)	1/1/92
7309.5	New	652(19)	1/1/92
7409.5	New	652(20)	1/1/92
7500 to 7504	Amend	768(1)	10/10/91
7510 to 7519	Amend	768(1)	10/10/91
7511	Amend	768(2)	10/10/91
7514	Change	768(3)	10/10/91
7520 to 7523	Amend	768(1)	10/10/91
7530	Repeal	768(1)	10/10/91
7531	Amend	768(1)	10/10/91
7540	Amend	768(1)	10/10/91
7550 to 7553	Amend	768(1)	10/10/91
7554	Amend	768(4)	10/10/91

(continued)

PENAL CODE
(Continued)

Section	Change	Chapter	Effective Date
7555	New	768(5)	10/10/91
11105.3	Amend	937(5)	1/1/92
11106	Amend	951(1)	1/1/92
11165.7	Amend	132(1)	1/1/92
11165.14	New	1102(5)	1/1/92
11166.5	Amend	132(2)	1/1/92
11400 to 11402	Repeal	186(10)	1/1/92
11411	Amend	605(1)	1/1/92
12001	Amend	950(2)	1/1/92
12001	Amend	955(1.1)	1/1/92
12001.1	Repeal	950(4)	1/1/92
12021	Amend	953(4)	10/14/91
12021	Amend	955(3)	1/1/92
12022.2	Amend	584(1)	1/1/92
12022.3	Amend	512(1)	1/1/92
12026.2	Amend	951(2)	1/1/92
12027	Amend	952(1)	1/1/92
12027.1	Amend	952(2)	1/1/92
12028	Amend	961(3)	1/1/92
12028.5	Amend	866(6)	1/1/92
12031	Amend	952(3)	1/1/92
12031	Amend	1022(1.1)	1/1/92
12031.5	New	1022(2)	1/1/92
12035	New	956(2)	1/1/92
12070	Amend	951(3)	1/1/92
12070	Amend	955(4.1)	1/1/92
12071	Amend	950(5)	1/1/92
12071	Amend	955(5)	1/1/92
12071	Amend	956(3)	1/1/92
12071.1	New	955(6)	1/1/92
12072	Amend	950(13)	1/1/92
12072	Amend	951(4.1)	1/1/92
12073	Amend	951(5)	1/1/92
12076	Amend	951(6)	1/1/92
12076	Amend	953(5)	10/14/91
12076	Amend	954(1.7)	1/1/92
12076.1	Repeal	953(6)	10/14/91
12077	Amend	951(6.5)	1/1/92
12077	Amend	955(7.1)	1/1/92
12078	Amend	951(7)	1/1/92
12078	Amend	955(8.1)	1/1/92
12080	Amend	950(17)	1/1/92
12081	Amend	950(18)	1/1/92
12082	Amend	955(9)	1/1/92

(continued)

© 1992 by J., B. & L. Gould
Printed in the U.S.A. **EP**

PENAL CODE
(Continued)

Section	Change	Chapter	Effective Date
12084	New	951(8.1)	1/1/92
12084	Amend	950(19)	1/1/92
12100	Amend	165(1)	1/1/92
12276	Amend	954(2)	1/1/92
12276.5	Amend	954(3)	1/1/92
12280	Amend	952(4)	1/1/92
12280	Amend	954(4.5)	1/1/92
12285	Amend	954(5)	1/1/92
12289	New	954(6)	1/1/92
12800 to 12809	New	950(20)	1/1/92
13508	New	1074(2)	1/1/92
13510	Amend	910(7)	1/1/92
13519	Amend	912(1)	1/1/92
13701	Amend	999(2)	1/1/92
13823.95	Amend	824(1)	1/1/92
14000 et seq.	Repeal	1091(120)	1/1/92
14165	Amend	1049(5)	1/1/92
14167	Amend	1049(6)	1/1/92

BUSINESS AND PROFESSIONS CODE

Section	Change	Chapter	Effective Date
123	Amend	647(1)	1/1/92
25658.4	New	726(4)	1/1/92

EVIDENCE CODE

Section	Change	Chapter	Effective Date
754	Amend	883(1)	1/1/92
755	New	883(2)	1/1/92
1103	Amend	16(1)	3/18/91
1107	New	812(1)	1/1/92
1560	Amend	1090(14)	1/1/92

HEALTH AND SAFETY CODE

Section	Change	Chapter	Effective Date
199.21	Amend	963(2)	1/1/92

(continued)

© 1992 by J., B. & L. Gould
Printed in the U.S.A.   EP

HEALTH AND SAFETY CODE
(Continued)

Section	Change	Chapter	Effective Date
7191	Repeal	895(1)	1/1/92
7191	New	895(2)	1/1/92
7194	Repeal	895(1)	1/1/92
11056	Amend	294(1)	1/1/92
11164	Amend	592(1)	1/1/92
11200	Amend	592(2)	1/1/92
11215	Amend	176(1)	1/1/92
11216	Repeal	176(2)	1/1/92
11350	Amend	257(1)	1/1/92
11364.7	Amend	573(1)	1/1/92
11365	Amend	551(1)	1/1/92
11366	Amend	492(1)	1/1/92
11369	Amend	573(2)	1/1/92
11370.1	Amend	469(1)	1/1/92
11377	Amend	294(2)	1/1/92
11378	Amend	294(3)	1/1/92
11379	Amend	294(4)	1/1/92
11379.2	New	294(5)	1/1/92
11489	Amend	641(2), (14)	1/1/92
11489	New	641(3)	1/1/92
11489	New	641(4)	1/1/92
11571	Amend	572(1), (2)	1/1/92
11571	Amend	1196(7)	1/1/92
11573.5	Amend	247(1)	1/1/92
11581	Amend	247(2)	1/1/92
11581	Amend	572(3)	1/1/92
11581	New	572(4)	1/1/92
11642	Amend	929(1)	1/1/92
25163	Amend	1084(1)	1/1/92
25163	New	1084(2)	1/1/92

RULES OF COURT

Rule	Change	Effective Date
31(c)	Amend	1/1/92
33(a)	Amend	1/1/92
33.5(a)	Amend	1/1/92
34.5	Amend	1/1/91
35(b)	Amend	1/1/92
39.1(f)	New	1/1/92
39.2(a)	Amend	1/1/92
185.5	New	7/1/91
425	Amend	1/1/91

(continued)

© 1992 by J., B. & L. Gould
Printed in the U.S.A.   **EP**

1991 Legislative Changes to the
CALIFORNIA PENAL CODE HANDBOOK
(Continued)

VEHICLE CODE

Section	Change	Chapter	Effective Date
2800.3	Amend	656(1)	1/1/92
4463	Amend	630(1)	1/1/92
10751	Amend	13(25)	2/13/91
12810	Amend	13(29)	2/13/91
12810	Amend	1223(2)	1/1/92
12810.5	Amend	928(20)	10/14/91
12810.5	New	928(21)	10/14/91
13201	Amend	656(2)	1/1/92
13350	Amend	656(3)	1/1/92
13350.5	Amend	656(4)	1/1/92
13351	Amend	656(5)	1/1/92
13352	Amend	209(1)	1/1/92
13353.4	Amend	990(1)	10/14/91
14602	Amend	1048(2)	1/1/92
20002	Amend	1103(2)	1/1/92
20003	Amend	1103(3)	1/1/92
22651	Amend	90(68)	6/30/91
22651	Amend	189(40)	7/29/91
22651.4	New	707(1)	1/1/92
22651.5	Amend	928(29)	10/14/91
22651.7	Amend	90(69)	6/30/91
22651.7	Amend	189(41)	7/29/91
22651.8	New	587(2)	1/1/92
22658	Amend	711(3)	1/1/92
22658	Amend	1004(4)	1/1/92
23103	Amend	928(30.5)	10/14/91
23161	Amend	19(1)	4/1/91
23166	Amend	209(2)	1/1/92
23171	Amend	990(2)	10/14/91
23175	Amend	1091(160)	1/1/92
23176	Amend	990(3)	10/14/91
23186	Amend	990(4)	10/14/91
23190	Amend	1091(161)	1/1/92
23191	Amend	209(3)	1/1/92
40802	Amend	459(1)	1/1/92
40802	Repeal	459(2)	1/1/92
40803	Amend	459(3)	1/1/92
42001	Amend	13(66)	2/13/91
42001.5	Amend	630(2)	1/1/92

(continued)

© 1992 by J., B. & L. Gould
Printed in the U.S.A. **EP**

WELFARE AND INSTITUTIONS CODE

Section	Change	Chapter	Effective Date
207.1	Amend	721(1)	1/1/92
224	New	91(10)	6/30/91
225.05	New	91(11)	6/30/91
225.05	Amend	611(7)	10/7/91
256	Amend	493(1)	1/1/92
256	Amend	1202(8)	1/1/92
256.5	New	1202(9)	1/1/92
257	Amend	493(2)	1/1/92
257	Amend	1202(10)	1/1/92
258	Amend	1202(11)	1/1/92
259	Repeal	1202(12)	1/1/92
259.1	Repeal	1202(13)	1/1/92
300	Amend	1203(1.5)	1/1/92
300	Repeal	1203(2)	1/1/92
301	Amend, Renum.	1203(4)	1/1/92
302	Amend, Renum.	1203(3)	1/1/92
340.5	New	980(1)	1/1/92
358	Amend	1203(5)	1/1/92
360	Amend	1203(6)	1/1/92
361.5	Amend	820(3)	1/1/92
366.22	Amend	820(4)	1/1/92
366.26	Amend	820(5)	1/1/92
601.3	Amend	1202(14)	1/1/92
650	Amend	1202(15)	1/1/92
653	Amend	1202(16)	1/1/92
654	Amend	1202(17)	1/1/92
655	Amend	1202(18)	1/1/92
707	Amend	303(1)	1/1/92
727.5	New	1202(19)	1/1/92
729.11	New	482(2)	10/4/91
740	Amend	1202(20)	1/1/92
741	Amend	482(3)	10/4/91
800	Amend	649(1)	1/1/92
827	Amend	1202(21)	1/1/92
841	Amend	155(1)	1/1/92
881.5	New	91(12)	6/30/91
903	Amend	110(19)	1/1/92
903	Amend	137(1)	1/1/92
1152	Amend	687(1)	1/1/92
1732.4	Repeal	721(2)	1/1/92
8100	Amend	951(9)	1/1/92
8100	Amend	952(5)	1/1/92
8102	Amend	866(8)	1/1/92
8103	Amend	955(10)	1/1/92
8105	Amend	951(10)	1/1/92

(continued)

© 1992 by J., B. & L. Gould
Printed in the U.S.A. **EP**

1991 Legislative Changes to the
CALIFORNIA PENAL CODE HANDBOOK
(Continued)

WELFARE AND INSTITUTIONS CODE
(Continued)

Section	Change	Chapter	Effective Date
prec. 15610	Amend	774(1)	1/1/92
15610	Amend	197(1)	1/1/92

This page intentionally left blank.

© 1992 by J., B. & L. Gould
Printed in the U.S.A. **EP**

TABLE OF CONTENTS

PENAL CODE HANDBOOK
OF CALIFORNIA

© 1992 by J., B. & L. Gould
Printed in the U.S.A. **EP**

This page intentionally left blank.

© 1992 by J., B. & L. Gould
Printed in the U.S.A.

PENAL CODE OF CALIFORNIA
Table of Contents

© 1992 by J., B. & L. Gould
Printed in the U.S.A. **EP**

© 1992 by J., B. & L. Gould
Printed in the U.S.A.   **EP**

© 1992 by J., B. & L. Gould
Printed in the U.S.A. **EP**

© 1992 by J., B. & L. Gould
Printed in the U.S.A. **EP**

Section(s)

© 1992 by J., B. & L. Gould
Printed in the U.S.A.   **EP**

© 1992 by J., B. & L. Gould
Printed in the U.S.A. **EP**

This page intentionally left blank.

© 1992 by J., B. & L. Gould
Printed in the U.S.A.　　**EP**

THE PENAL CODE OF CALIFORNIA

AN ACT
TO ESTABLISH A PENAL CODE
(Approved February 14, 1872)

The People of the State of California, represented in Senate and Assembly, do enact as follows:

TITLE OF THE ACT

Part
Preliminary Provisions. (Secs. 2—25)
1. Of Crimes and Punishments. (Secs. 26—679.03)
2. Of Criminal Procedure. (Secs. 681—1620)
3. Of Imprisonment and the Death Penalty. (Secs. 2000—10005)
4. Of Prevention of Crimes and Apprehension of Criminals. (Secs. 11006—14213)
5. Peace Officers' Memorial. (Secs. 15001, 15003)

TITLE OF THE ACT

§1. Title and divisions.
This Act shall be known as THE PENAL CODE OF CALIFORNIA, and is divided into four parts, as follows:
  I. OF CRIMES AND PUNISHMENTS.
  II. OF CRIMINAL PROCEDURE.
  III. OF THE STATE PRISON AND COUNTY JAILS.*
  IV. OF PREVENTION OF CRIMES AND APPREHENSION OF CRIMINALS. *(Amended by Stats 1985 ch 367 §1.)*
(Repealed by Stats 1941 ch 98. Present Part III "Of Imprisonment and the Death Penalty" added by Stats 1941 ch 106.)

PRELIMINARY PROVISIONS

§2. When this Act takes effect.
This Code takes effect at twelve o'clock, noon, on the first day of January, eighteen hundred and seventy-three.

§3. Not retroactive.
No part of it is retroactive, unless expressly so declared.

§4. Construction of the Penal Code.
The rule of the common law, that penal statutes are to be strictly construed, has no application to this Code. All its provisions are to be construed according to the fair import of their terms, with a view to effect its objects and to promote justice.

§5. Provisions similar to existing laws, how construed.
The provisions of this Code, so far as they are substantially the same as existing statutes, must be construed as continuations thereof, and not as new enactments.

§6. Effect of Code upon past offenses.
No act or omission, commenced after twelve o'clock noon of the day on which this Code takes effect as a law, is criminal or punishable, except as prescribed or authorized by this Code, or by some of the statutes which it specifies as continuing in force and as not affected by its provisions, or by some ordinance, municipal, county, or township regulation, passed or adopted, under such statutes and in force when this Code takes effect. Any act or omission commenced prior to that time may be inquired of, prosecuted, and punished in the same manner as if this code had not been passed.

§7. Definitions.
Words used in this code in the present tense include the future as well as the present; words used in the masculine gender include the feminine and neuter; the singular number includes the plural, and the plural the singular; the word "person" includes a corporation as well as a natural person; the word "county" includes "city and county"; writing includes printing and typewriting; oath includes affirmation or declaration; and every mode of oral statement, under oath or affirmation, is embraced by the term "testify," and every written one in the term "depose"; signature or subscription includes mark, when the person cannot write, his or her name being written near it, by a person who writes his or her own name as a witness; provided, that when a signature is made by mark it must, in order that the same may be acknowledged or serve as the signature to any sworn statement, be witnessed by two persons who must subscribe their own names as witnesses thereto.
The following words have in this code the signification attached to them in this section, unless otherwise apparent from the context:
1. The word "willfully," when applied to the intent with which an act is done or omitted, implies simply a purpose or willingness to commit the act, or make the omission referred to. It does not require any intent to violate law, or to injure another, or to acquire any advantage.
2. The words "neglect," "negligence," "negligent," and "negligently" import a want of such attention to the nature or probable consequences of the act or omission as a prudent man ordinarily bestows in acting in his own concerns.
3. The word "corruptly" imports a wrongful design to acquire or cause some pecuniary or other advantage to the person guilty of the act or omission referred to, or to some other person.
4. The words "malice" and "maliciously" import a wish to vex, annoy, or injure another person, or an intent to do a wrongful act, established either by proof or presumption of law.
5. The word "knowingly" imports only a knowledge that the facts exist which bring the act or omission within the provisions of this code. It does not require any knowledge of the unlawfulness of such act or omission.
6. The word "bribe" signifies anything of value or advantage, present or prospective, or any promise or undertaking to give any, asked, given, or accepted, with a corrupt intent to influence, unlawfully, the person to whom it is given, in his or her action, vote, or opinion, in any public or official capacity.
7. The word "vessel," when used with reference to shipping, includes ships of all kinds, steamboats, canalboats, barges, and every structure adapted to be navigated from place to place for the transportation of merchandise or persons, except that, as used in Sections 192.5 and 193.5, the word "vessel" means a vessel as defined in subdivision (c) of Section 651 of the Harbors and Navigation Code.

8. The words "peace officer" signify any one of the officers mentioned in Chapter 4.5 (commencing with Section 830) of Title 3 of Part 2.

9. The word "magistrate" signifies any one of the officers mentioned in Section 808.

10. The word "property" includes both real and personal property.

11. The words "real property" are coextensive with lands, tenements, and hereditaments.

12. The words "personal property" include money, goods, chattels, things in action, and evidences of debt.

13. The word "month" means a calendar month, unless otherwise expressed; the word "daytime" means the period between sunrise and sunset, and the word "nighttime" means the period between sunset and sunrise.

14. The word "will" includes codicil.

15. The word "writ" signifies an order or precept in writing, issued in the name of the people, or of a court or judicial officer, and the word "process" a writ or summons issued in the course of judicial proceedings.

16. Words and phrases must be construed according to the context and the approved usage of the language; but technical words and phrases, and such others as may have acquired a peculiar and appropriate meaning in law, must be construed according to such peculiar and appropriate meaning.

17. Words giving a joint authority to three or more public officers or other persons, are construed as giving such authority to a majority of them, unless it is otherwise expressed in the act giving the authority.

18. When the seal of a court or public officer is required by law to be affixed to any paper, the word "seal" includes an impression of such seal upon the paper alone, or upon any substance attached to the paper capable of receiving a visible impression. The seal of a private person may be made in like manner, or by the scroll of a pen, or by writing the word "seal" against his or her name.

19. The word "state," when applied to the different parts of the United States, includes the District of Columbia and the territories, and the words "United States" may include the district and territories.

20. The word "section," whenever herein-after employed, refers to a section of this code, unless some other code or statute is expressly mentioned.

21. To "book" signifies the recordation of an arrest in official police records, and the taking by the police of fingerprints and photographs of the person arrested, or any of these acts following an arrest. *(Amended by Stats 1987 ch 828 §1.)*

§8. What intent to defraud is sufficient.

Whenever, by any of the provisions of this Code, an intent to defraud is required in order to constitute any offense, it is sufficient if an intent appears to defraud any person, association, or body politic or corporate, whatever.

§9. Civil remedies preserved.

The omission to specify or affirm in this Code any liability to damages, penalty, forfeiture, or other remedy imposed by law and allowed to be recovered or enforced in any civil action or proceeding, for any act or omission declared punishable herein, does not affect any right to recover or enforce the same.

§10. Proceedings to impeach or remove officers and others preserved.

The omission to specify or affirm in this Code any ground of forfeiture of a public office, or other trust or special authority conferred by law, or any power conferred by law to impeach, remove, depose, or suspend any public officer or other person holding any trust, appointment, or other special authority, conferred by law, does not affect such forfeiture or power, or any proceeding authorized by law to carry into effect such impeachment, removal, deposition, or suspension.

§11. Power of military authority.

This code does not affect any power conferred by law upon any court-martial, or other military authority or officer, to impose or inflict punishment upon offenders; nor, except as provided in Section 19.2 of this code, any power conferred by law upon any public body, tribunal, or officer, to impose or inflict punishment for a contempt. *(Amended by Stats 1989 ch 897 §4, eff. 1/1/90.)*

§12. Of sections declaring crimes punishable. Duty of Court.

The several sections of this Code which declare certain crimes to be punishable as therein mentioned, devolve a duty upon the Court authorized to pass sentence, to determine and impose the punishment prescribed.

§13. Punishments, how determined.

Whenever in this Code the punishment for a crime is left undetermined between certain limits, the punishment to be inflicted in a particular case must be determined by the Court authorized to pass sentence, within such limits as may be prescribed by this Code.

§14. Witness' testimony may be read against him on prosecution for perjury.

The various sections of this Code which declare that evidence obtained upon the examination of a person as a witness cannot be received against him in any criminal proceeding, do not forbid such evidence being proved against such person upon any proceedings founded upon a charge of perjury committed in such examination.

§15. "Crime" and "public offense" defined.

A crime or public offense is an act committed or omitted in violation of a law forbidding or commanding it, and to which is annexed, upon conviction, either of the following punishments:

1. Death;
2. Imprisonment;
3. Fine;
4. Removal from office; or,
5. Disqualification to hold and enjoy any office of honor, trust, or profit in this State.

§16. Kinds of crimes.

Crimes and public offenses include:

1. Felonies;
2. Misdemeanors; and
3. Infractions.

§17. Classification of crimes.

(a) A felony is a crime which is punishable with death or by imprisonment in the state prison. Every

© 1992 by J., B. & L. Gould
Printed in the U.S.A.   EP

other crime or public offense is a misdemeanor except those offenses that are classified as infractions.

(b) When a crime is punishable, in the discretion of the court, by imprisonment in the state prison or by fine or imprisonment in the county jail, it is a misdemeanor for all purposes under the following circumstances:

(1) After a judgment imposing a punishment other than imprisonment in the state prison.

(2) When the court, upon committing the defendant to the Youth Authority, designates the offense to be a misdemeanor.

(3) When the court grants probation to a defendant without imposition of sentence and at the time of granting probation, or on application of the defendant or probation officer thereafter, the court declares the offense to be a misdemeanor.

(4) When the prosecuting attorney files in a court having jurisdiction over misdemeanor offenses a complaint specifying that the offense is a misdemeanor, unless the defendant at the time of his or her arraignment or plea objects to the offense being made a misdemeanor, in which event the complaint shall be amended to charge the felony and the case shall proceed on the felony complaint.

(5) When, at or before the preliminary examination or prior to filing an order pursuant to Section 872, the magistrate determines that the offense is a misdemeanor, in which event the case shall proceed as if the defendant had been arraigned on a misdemeanor complaint.

(c) When a defendant is committed to the Youth Authority for a crime punishable, in the discretion of the court, by imprisonment in the state prison or by fine or imprisonment in the county jail, the offense shall, upon the discharge of the defendant from the Youth Authority, thereafter be deemed a misdemeanor for all purposes.

(d) A violation of any code section listed in Section 19.8 is an infraction subject to the procedures described in Sections 19.6 and 19.7 when:

(1) The prosecutor files a complaint charging the offense as an infraction unless the defendant, at the time he or she is arraigned, after being informed of his or her rights, elects to have the case proceed as a misdemeanor, or;

(2) The court, with the consent of the defendant, determines that the offense is an infraction in which event the case shall proceed as if the defendant had been arraigned on an infraction complaint. *(Amended by Stats 1989 ch 897 §5, eff. 1/1/90.)*

§18. Punishment for felonies.

Except in cases where a different punishment is prescribed by any law of this state, every offense declared to be a felony, or to be punishable by imprisonment in a state prison, is punishable by imprisonment in any of the state prisons for 16 months, or two or three years; provided, however, every offense which is prescribed by any law of the state to be a felony punishable by imprisonment in any of the state prisons or by a fine, but without an alternate sentence to the county jail, may be punishable by imprisonment in the county jail not exceeding one year or by a fine, or by both.

§19. Misdemeanor; punishment.

Except in cases where a different punishment is prescribed by any law of this state, every offense

declared to be a misdemeanor is punishable by imprisonment in the county jail not exceeding six months, or by fine not exceeding one thousand dollars ($1,000), or by both.

§19b. *Repealed by Stats 1989 ch 897 §7, eff. 1/1/90.*

§19.2. Misdemeanor; maximum punishment.

In no case shall any person sentenced to confinement in a county or city jail, or in a county or joint county penal farm, road camp, work camp, or other county adult detention facility, or committed to the sheriff for placement in any county adult detention facility, on conviction of a misdemeanor, or as a condition of probation upon conviction of either a felony or a misdemeanor, or upon commitment for civil contempt, or upon default in the payment of a fine upon conviction of either a felony or a misdemeanor, or for any reason except upon conviction of more than one offense when consecutive sentences have been imposed, be committed for a period in excess of one year; provided, however, that the time allowed on parole shall not be considered as a part of the period of confinement. *(Amended and renumbered from §19a by Stats 1989 ch 897 §6, eff. 1/1/90.)*

§19.4. Misdemeanor as punishment for unclassified offenses.

When an act or omission is declared by a statute to be a public offense and no penalty for the offense is prescribed in any statute, the act or omission is punishable as a misdemeanor. *(Added by Stats 1989 ch 897 §11, eff. 1/1/90.)*

§19.6. Infraction; punishment.

An infraction is not punishable by imprisonment. A person charged with an infraction shall not be entitled to a trial by jury. A person charged with an infraction shall not be entitled to have the public defender or other counsel appointed at public expense to represent him or her unless he or she is arrested and not released on his or her written promise to appear, his or her own recognizance, or a deposit of bail. *(Amended and renumbered from §19c by Stats 1989 ch 897 §8, eff. 1/1/90.)*

§19.7. Misdemeanor provisions; applicability.

Except as otherwise provided by law, all provisions of law relating to misdemeanors shall apply to infractions including, but not limited to powers of peace officers, jurisdiction of courts, periods for commencing action and for bringing a case to trial and burden of proof. *(Amended and renumbered from §19d by Stats 1989 ch 897 §9, eff. 1/1/90.)*

§19.8. Offenses constituting infractions.

The following offenses are subject to subdivision (d) of Section 17: Sections 330, 415, 485, 555, and 853.7, of this code; subdivision (m) of Section 602 of this code; subdivision (b) of Section 25658 and Sections 25658.5, 25661, and 25662 of the Business and Professions Code; subdivision (c) of Section 23109 and Sections 12500, 14601.1, 27150.1, 40508, and 42005 of the Vehicle Code, and any other offense which the Legislature makes subject to subdivision (d) of Section 17. Except where a lesser maximum fine is expressly provided for violation of any of those sections, any violation which is an infraction is punishable by a fine not exceeding two hundred fifty dollars ($250).

Except for the violations enumerated in subdivision (d) of Section 13202.5 of the Vehicle Code, and Section 14601.1 of the Vehicle Code based upon failure to appear, a conviction for any offense made an infraction under subdivision (d) of Section 17 is not grounds for the suspension, revocation, or denial of any license, or for the revocation of probation or parole of the person convicted. *(Amended by Stats 1991 ch 638 §1, eff. 1/1/92.)*

§20. To constitute crime there must be unity of act and intent.

In every crime or public offense there must exist a union, or joint operation of act and intent, or criminal negligence.

§21. Intent; evidence of.

(a) The intent or intention is manifested by the circumstances connected with the offense.

(b) In the guilt phase of a criminal action or a juvenile adjudication hearing, evidence that the accused lacked the capacity or ability to control his conduct for any reason shall not be admissible on the issue of whether the accused actually had any mental state with respect to the commission of any crime. This subdivision is not applicable to Section 26.

§21a. Attempt to commit crime; two elements.

An attempt to commit a crime consists of two elements: a specific intent to commit the crime, and a direct but ineffectual act done toward its commission. *(Added by Stats 1986 ch 519 §1.)*

§22. Voluntary intoxication.

(a) No act committed by a person while in a state of voluntary intoxication is less criminal by reason of his having been in such condition. Evidence of voluntary intoxication shall not be admitted to negate the capacity to form any mental states for the crimes charged, including, but not limited to, purpose, intent, knowledge, premeditation, deliberation or malice aforethought, with which the accused committed the act.

(b) Evidence of voluntary intoxication is admissible solely on the issue of whether or not the defendant actually formed a required specific intent, premeditated, deliberated, or harbored malice aforethought, when a specific intent crime is charged.

(c) Voluntary intoxication includes the voluntary ingestion, injection, or taking by any other means of any intoxicating liquor, drug, or other substance.

§23. Proceeding against person holding business or professional license.

In any criminal proceeding against a person who has been issued a license to engage in a business or profession by a state agency pursuant to provisions of the Business and Professions Code or the Education Code, the state agency which issued the license may voluntarily appear to furnish pertinent information, make recommendations regarding specific conditions of probation, or provide any other assistance necessary to promote the interests of justice and protect the interests of the public, or may be ordered by the court to do so, if the crime charged is substantially related to the qualifications, functions, or duties of a licensee.

For purposes of this section, the term "license" shall include a permit or a certificate issued by a state agency.

For purposes of this section, the term "state agency" shall include any state board, commission, bureau, or division created pursuant to the provisions of the Business and Professions Code or the Education Code to license and regulate individuals who engage in certain businesses and professions. *(Amended by Stats 1989 ch 388 §6, eff. 1/1/90.)*

§24. This Act, how cited.

This Act, whenever cited, enumerated, referred to, or amended, may be designated simply as The Penal Code, adding, when necessary, the number of the section.

§25. Diminished capacity; insanity.

(a) The defense of diminished capacity is hereby abolished. In a criminal action, as well as any juvenile court proceeding, evidence concerning an accused person's intoxication, trauma, mental illness, disease, or defect shall not be admissible to show or negate capacity to form the particular purpose, intent, motive, malice aforethought, knowledge, or other mental state required for the commission of the crime charged.

(b) In any criminal proceeding, including any juvenile court proceeding, in which a plea of not guilty by reason of insanity is entered, this defense shall be found by the trier of fact only when the accused person proves by a preponderance of the evidence that he or she was incapable of knowing or understanding the nature and quality of his or her act and of distinguishing right from wrong at the time of the commission of the offense.

(c) Notwithstanding the foregoing, evidence of diminished capacity or of a mental disorder may be considered by the court only at the time of sentencing or other disposition or commitment.

(d) The provisions of this section shall not be amended by the Legislature except by statute passed in each house by rollcall vote entered in the journal, two-thirds of the membership concurring, or by a statute that becomes effective only when approved by the electors.

PART 1

OF CRIMES AND PUNISHMENTS

TITLE 1

OF PERSONS LIABLE TO PUNISHMENT FOR CRIME

§26. Criminal capability.

All persons are capable of committing crimes except those belonging to the following classes:

One—Children under the age of 14, in the absence of clear proof that at the time of committing the act charged against them, they knew its wrongfulness.

Two—Idiots.

Three—Persons who committed the act or made the omission charged under an ignorance or mistake of fact, which disproves any criminal intent.

Four—Persons who committed the act charged without being conscious thereof.

Five—Persons who committed the act or made the omission charged through misfortune or by accident, when it appears that there was no evil design, intention, or culpable negligence.

© 1992 by J., B. & L. Gould
Printed in the U.S.A.   **EP**

Six—Persons (unless the crime be punishable with death) who committed the act or made the omission charged under threats or menaces sufficient to show that they had reasonable cause to and did believe their lives would be endangered if they refused.

§27. Persons liable to punishment under state laws.

(a) The following persons are liable to punishment under the laws of this state:

1. All persons who commit, in whole or in part, any crime within this state;

2. All who commit any offense without this state which, if committed within this state, would be larceny, robbery, or embezzlement under the laws of this state, and bring the property stolen or embezzled, or any part of it, or are found with it, or any part of it, within this state;

3. All who, being without this state, cause or aid, advise or encourage, another person to commit a crime within this state, and are afterwards found therein.

(b) Perjury, in violation of Section 118, is punishable also when committed outside of California to the extent provided in Section 118.

§28. Mental disease.

(a) Evidence of mental disease, mental defect, or mental disorder shall not be admitted to show or negate the capacity to form any mental state, including, but not limited to, purpose, intent, knowledge, premeditation, deliberation, or malice aforethought, with which the accused committed the act. Evidence of mental disease, mental defect, or mental disorder is admissible solely on the issue of whether or not the accused actually formed a required specific intent, premeditated, deliberated, or harbored malice aforethought, when a specific intent crime is charged.

(b) As a matter of public policy there shall be no defense of diminished capacity, diminished responsibility, or irresistible impulse in a criminal action or juvenile adjudication hearing.

(c) This section shall not be applicable to an insanity hearing pursuant to Section 1026 or 1429.5.

(d) Nothing in this section shall limit a court's discretion, pursuant to the Evidence Code, to exclude psychiatric or psychological evidence on whether the accused had a mental disease, mental defect, or mental disorder at the time of the alleged offense.

§29. Testimony as to mental illness.

In the guilt phase of a criminal action, any expert testifying about a defendant's mental illness, mental disorder, or mental defect shall not testify as to whether the defendant had or did not have the required mental states, which include, but are not limited to, purpose, intent, knowledge, or malice aforethought, for the crimes charged. The question as to whether the defendant had or did not have the required mental states shall be decided by the trier of fact.

TITLE 2

OF PARTIES TO CRIME

§30. Classification of parties to crime.

The parties to crimes are classified as:
1. Principals; and,
2. Accessories.

§31. Who are principals.

All persons concerned in the commission of a crime, whether it be felony or misdemeanor, and whether they directly commit the act constituting the offense, or aid and abet in its commission, or, not being present, have advised and encouraged its commission, and all persons counseling, advising, or encouraging children under the age of fourteen years, lunatics or idiots, to commit any crime, or who, by fraud, contrivance, or force, occasion the drunkenness of another for the purpose of causing him to commit any crime, or who, by threats, menaces, command, or coercion, compel another to commit any crime, are principals in any crime so committed.

§32. Accessories.

Every person who, after a felony has been committed, harbors, conceals or aids a principal in such felony, with the intent that said principal may avoid or escape from arrest, trial, conviction or punishment, having knowledge that said principal has committed such felony or has been charged with such felony or convicted thereof, is an accessory to such felony.

§33. Punishment of accessories.

Except in cases where a different punishment is prescribed, an accessory is punishable by a fine not exceeding five thousand dollars ($5,000), or by imprisonment in the state prison, or in a county jail not exceeding one year, or by both such fine and imprisonment.

TITLE 3

OF OFFENSES AGAINST THE SOVEREIGNTY OF THE STATE

§37. Treason.

(a) Treason against this state consists only in levying war against it, adhering to its enemies, or giving them aid and comfort, and can be committed only by persons owing allegiance to the state. The punishment of treason shall be death or life imprisonment without possibility of parole. The penalty shall be determined pursuant to Sections 190.3 and 190.4.

(b) Upon a trial for treason, the defendant cannot be convicted unless upon the testimony of two witnesses to the same overt act, or upon confession in open court; nor, except as provided in Sections 190.3 and 190.4, can evidence be admitted of an overt act not expressly charged in the indictment or information; nor can the defendant be convicted unless one or more overt acts be expressly alleged therein. (*Amended by Stats 1989 ch 897 §12, eff. 1/1/90.*)

§38. Misprision of treason.

Misprision of treason is the knowledge and concealment of treason, without otherwise assenting to or participating in the crime. It is punishable by imprisonment in the state prison.

TITLE 5

OF CRIMES BY AND AGAINST THE EXECUTIVE POWER OF THE STATE

§67. Bribing executive officers.

Every person who gives or offers any bribe to any executive officer in this state, with intent to influence him in respect to any act, decision, vote, opinion, or other proceeding as such officer, is punishable by imprisonment in the state prison for two, three or four years, and is disqualified from holding any office in this state.

§67.5. Bribing public officers or employees.

(a) Every person who gives or offers as a bribe to any ministerial officer, employee, or appointee of the State of California, county or city therein, or political subdivision thereof, any thing the theft of which would be petty theft is guilty of a misdemeanor.

(b) If the theft of the thing given or offered would be grand theft the offense is a felony. *(Amended by Stats 1990 ch 350 §8, eff. 1/1/91.)*

§68. Bribes received by public officers or employees; punishment.

Every executive or ministerial officer, employee or appointee of the State of California, county or city therein or political subdivision thereof, who asks, receives, or agrees to receive, any bribe, upon any agreement or understanding that his vote, opinion, or action upon any matter then pending, or which may be brought before him in his official capacity, shall be influenced thereby, is punishable by imprisonment in the state prison for two, three or four years; and, in addition thereto, forfeits his office, and is forever disqualified from holding any office in this state.

§69. Resisting executive officers; punishment.

Every person who attempts, by means of any threat or violence, to deter or prevent an executive officer from performing any duty imposed upon such officer by law, or who knowingly resists, by the use of force or violence, such officer, in the performance of his duty, is punishable by a fine not exceeding ten thousand dollars ($10,000), or by imprisonment in the state prison, or in a county jail not exceeding one year, or by both such fine and imprisonment.

§70. Bribery or acceptance by public officers or employees.

(a) Every executive or ministerial officer, employee, or appointee of the State of California, or any county or city therein, or any political subdivision thereof, who knowingly asks, receives, or agrees to receive any emolument, gratuity, or reward, or any promise thereof excepting such as may be authorized by law for doing an official act, is guilty of a misdemeanor.

(b) This section does not prohibit deputy registrars of voters from receiving compensation when authorized by local ordinance from any candidate, political committee, or statewide political organization for securing the registration of voters.

(c) Nothing in this section precludes a peace officer, as defined in Chapter 4.5 (commencing with Section 830) of Title 3 of Part 2, from engaging in, or being employed in, casual or part-time employment as a private security guard or patrolman for a public entity while off duty from his or her principal employment and outside his or her regular employment as a peace officer of a state or local agency, and exercising the powers of a peace officer concurrently with that employment, provided that the peace officer is in a police uniform and is subject to reasonable rules and regulations of the agency for which he or she is a peace officer and within the provisions of subdivisions (k)

and (*l*) of Section 7522 of the Business and Professions Code. Notwithstanding the above provisions, any and all civil and criminal liability arising out of the secondary employment of any peace officer pursuant to this subdivision shall be borne by the officer's secondary employer.

It is the intent of the Legislature by this subdivision to abrogate the holdings in People v. Corey, 21 Cal. 3d 738, and Cervantez v. J.C. Penney Co., 24 Cal. 3d 579, to reinstate prior judicial interpretations of this section as they relate to criminal sanctions for battery on peace officers who are employed, on a part-time or casual basis, by a public entity, while wearing a police uniform as private security guards or patrolmen, and to allow the exercise of peace officer powers concurrently with that employment.

(d) Nothing in this section precludes a peace officer, as defined in Chapter 4.5 (commencing with Section 830) of Title 3 of Part 2, from engaging in, or being employed in, casual or part-time employment as a private security guard or patrolman by a private employer while off duty from his or her principal employment and outside his or her regular employment as a peace officer, and exercising the powers of a peace officer concurrently with that employment, provided that all of the following are true:

(1) The peace officer is in his or her police uniform.

(2) The casual or part-time employment as a private security guard or patrolman is approved by the county board of supervisors with jurisdiction over the principal employer or by the board's designee or by the city council with jurisdiction over the principal employer or by the council's designee.

(3) The wearing of uniforms and equipment is approved by the principal employer.

(4) The peace officer is subject to reasonable rules and regulations of the agency for which he or she is a peace officer and within the provisions of subdivisions (k) and (*l*) of Section 7522 of the Business and Professions Code.

Notwithstanding the above provisions, a peace officer while off duty from his or her principal employment and outside his or her regular employment as a peace officer of a state or local agency shall not exercise the powers of a police officer if employed by a private employer as a security guard during a strike, lockout, picketing, or other physical demonstration of a labor dispute at the site of the strike, lockout, picketing, or other physical demonstration of a labor dispute. The issue of whether or not casual or part-time employment as a private security guard or patrolman pursuant to this subdivision is to be approved shall not be a subject for collective bargaining. Any and all civil and criminal liability arising out of the secondary employment of any peace officer pursuant to this subdivision shall be borne by the officer's principal employer. The principal employer may require the secondary employer to enter into an indemnity agreement as a condition of approving casual or part-time employment pursuant to this subdivision.

It is the intent of the Legislature by this subdivision to abrogate the holdings in People v. Corey, 21 Cal. 3d 738, and Cervantez v. J.C. Penney Co., 24 Cal. 3d 579, to reinstate prior judicial interpretations of this section as they relate to criminal sanctions for battery on peace officers who are employed, on a part-time or casual basis, while wearing a police uniform approved by the principal employer, as private security guards

© 1992 by J., B. & L. Gould
Printed in the U.S.A.   **EP**

or patrolmen, and to allow the exercise of peace officer powers concurrently with that employment.

§70.5. Fees accepted by commissioner of civil marriages or deputy.

Every commissioner of civil marriages or every deputy commissioner of civil marriages who accepts any money or other thing of value for performing any marriage pursuant to Section 4205.1 of the Civil Code, including any money or thing of value voluntarily tendered by the persons about to be married or who have been married by the commissioner of civil marriages or deputy commissioner of civil marriages, other than a fee expressly imposed by law for performance of a marriage, whether the acceptance occurs before or after performance of the marriage and whether or not performance of the marriage is conditioned on the giving of such money or the thing of value by the persons being married, is guilty of a misdemeanor.

It is not a necessary element of the offense described by this section that the acceptance of the money or other thing of value be committed with intent to commit extortion or with other criminal intent.

This section does not apply to the request or acceptance by any retired commissioner of civil marriages of a fee for the performance of a marriage.

The provisions of this section are inapplicable to the acceptance of a fee for the performance of a marriage on Saturday, Sunday, or a legal holiday. *(Amended by Stats 1987 ch 753 §1.)*

§71. Threatening education employees; punishment.

Every person who, with intent to cause, attempts to cause, or causes, any officer or employee of any public or private educational institution or any public officer or employee to do, or refrain from doing, any act in the performance of his duties, by means of a threat, directly communicated to such person, to inflict an unlawful injury upon any person or property, and it reasonably appears to the recipient of the threat that such threat could be carried out, is guilty of a public offense punishable as follows:

(1) Upon a first conviction, such person is punishable by a fine not exceeding ten thousand dollars ($10,000), or by imprisonment in the state prison, or in a county jail not exceeding one year, or by both such fine and imprisonment.

(2) If such person has been previously convicted of a violation of this section, such previous conviction shall be charged in the accusatory pleading, and if such previous conviction is found to be true by the jury, upon a jury trial, or by the court, upon a court trial, or is admitted by the defendant, he is punishable by imprisonment in the state prison.

As used in this section, "directly communicated" includes, but is not limited to, a communication to the recipient of the threat by telephone, telegraph, or letter.

§72. False claims.

Every person who, with intent to defraud, presents for allowance or for payment to any state board or officer, or to any county, city, or district board or officer, authorized to allow or pay the same if genuine, any false or fraudulent claim, bill, account, voucher, or writing, is punishable either by imprisonment in the county jail for a period of not more than one year, by a fine of not exceeding one thousand dollars ($1,000), or by both such imprisonment and fine, or by imprisonment in the state prison, by a fine of not exceeding ten thousand dollars ($10,000), or by both such imprisonment and fine.

As used in this section "officer" includes a "carrier," as defined in subdivision (a) of Section 14124.70 of the Welfare and Institutions Code, authorized to act as an agent for a state board or officer or a county, city, or district board or officer, as the case may be. *(Amended by Stats 1987 ch 828 §3.)*

§72.5. Claims for reimbursement of expenses incurred for political functions.

(a) Every person who, knowing a claim seeks public funds for reimbursement of costs incurred in attending a political function organized to support or oppose any political party or political candidate, presents such a claim for allowance or for payment to any state board or officer, or to any county, city, or district board or officer authorized to allow or pay such claims, is punishable either by imprisonment in the county jail for a period of not more than one year, by a fine of not exceeding one thousand dollars ($1,000), or by both such imprisonment and fine, or by imprisonment in the state prison, by a fine of not exceeding ten thousand dollars ($10,000), or by both such imprisonment and fine.

(b) Every person who, knowing a claim seeks public funds for reimbursement of costs incurred to gain admittance to a political function expressly organized to support or oppose any ballot measure, presents such a claim for allowance or for payment to any state board or officer, or to any county, city, or district board or officer authorized to allow or pay such claims is punishable either by imprisonment in the county jail for a period of not more than one year, by a fine of not exceeding one thousand dollars ($1,000), or by both such imprisonment and fine, or by imprisonment in the state prison, by a fine of not exceeding ten thousand dollars ($10,000), or by both such imprisonment and fine.

§73. Buying appointments to office.

Every person who gives or offers any gratuity or reward, in consideration that he or any other person shall be appointed to any public office, or shall be permitted to exercise or discharge the duties thereof, is guilty of a misdemeanor.

§74. Bribery for appointment to office.

Every public officer who, for any gratuity or reward, appoints another person to a public office, or permits another person to exercise or discharge any of the duties of his office, is punishable by a fine not exceeding ten thousand dollars ($10,000), and, in addition thereto, forfeits his office and is forever disqualified from holding any office in this state.

§76. Threatening state officials; punishment.

Every person who knowingly and willingly threatens the life of any elected state official, exempt appointee of the Governor, or judge with the intent, and the apparent ability, to carry out that threat, is guilty of a public offense, punishable as follows:

(1) Upon a first conviction, the offense is punishable by a fine not exceeding five thousand dollars ($5,000), or by imprisonment in the state prison, or in

a county jail not exceeding one year, or by both fine and imprisonment.

(2) If the person has been previously convicted of a violation of this section, the previous conviction shall be charged in the accusatory pleading, and if the previous conviction is found to be true by the jury, upon a jury trial, or by the court, upon a court trial, or is admitted by the defendant, the offense is punishable by imprisonment in the state prison.

Any law enforcement agency which has knowledge of a violation of this section shall immediately report that information to the California State Police.

§77. Application preceding sections.

The various provisions of this title, except Section 76, apply to administrative and ministerial officers, in the same manner as if they were mentioned therein.

TITLE 6

OF CRIMES AGAINST THE LEGISLATIVE POWER

§85. Bribing members of the Legislature.

Every person who gives or offers to give a bribe to any Member of the Legislature, or to another person for him, or attempts by menace, deceit, suppression of truth, or any corrupt means, to influence a member in giving or withholding his vote, or in not attending the house or any committee of which he is a member, is punishable by imprisonment in the state prison for two, three or four years.

§86. Bribes received by members of the legislature.

Every member of either of the houses composing the Legislature of this state who asks, receives or agrees to receive, any bribe, upon any understanding that his official vote, opinion, judgment or action shall be influenced thereby, or shall give, in any particular manner, or upon any particular side of any question or matter upon which he may be required to act in his official capacity, or gives, or offers or promises to give, any official vote in consideration that another Member of the Legislature shall give any such vote either upon the same or another question, is punishable by imprisonment in the state prison for two, three or four years.

§88. Members of the Legislature, in addition to other penalties, to forfeit office and be disqualified, etc.

Every member of the Legislature convicted of any crime defined in this Chapter*, in addition to the punishment prescribed, forfeits his office and is forever disqualified from holding any office in this State.

*So in original. Probably should be "Title".

TITLE 7

OF CRIMES AGAINST PUBLIC JUSTICE

CHAPTER 1

BRIBERY AND CORRUPTION

§92. Bribing judges, jurors, referees, arbitrator, or umpire.

Every person who gives or offers to give a bribe to any judicial officer, juror, referee, arbitrator, or umpire, or to any person who may be authorized by law to hear or determine any question or controversy, with intent to influence his vote, opinion, or decision upon any matter or question which is or may be brought before him for decision, is punishable by imprisonment in the state prison for two, three or four years.

§93. Bribes received by judicial officer, juror, referee, arbitrator, or umpire.

Every judicial officer, juror, referee, arbitrator, or umpire, and every person authorized by law to hear or determine any question or controversy, who asks, receives, or agrees to receive, any bribe, upon any agreement or understanding that his vote, opinion, or decision upon any matters or question which is or may be brought before him for decision, shall be influenced thereby, is punishable by imprisonment in the state prison for two, three or four years.

§94. Extortion.

Every judicial officer who asks or receives any emolument, gratuity, or reward, or any promise thereof, except such as may be authorized by law, for doing any official act, is guilty of a misdemeanor. Every judicial officer who shall ask or receive the whole or any part of the fees allowed by law to any stenographer or reporter appointed by him, or any other person, to record the proceedings of any Court or investigation held by him, shall be guilty of a misdemeanor, and upon conviction thereof shall forfeit his office. Any stenographer or reporter, appointed by any judicial officer in this State, who shall pay, or offer to pay, the whole or any part of the fees allowed him by law, for his appointment or retention in office, shall be guilty of a misdemeanor, and upon conviction thereof shall be forever disqualified from holding any similar office in the courts of this State.

§94.5. Judges or commissioners receiving money or value for performance of marriage.

Every judge, justice, commissioner, or assistant commissioner of a court of this state who accepts any money or other thing of value for performing any marriage, including any money or thing of value voluntarily tendered by the persons about to be married or who have been married by such judge, justice, commissioner, or assistant commissioner, whether the acceptance occurs before or after performance of the marriage and whether or not performance of the marriage is conditioned on the giving of such money or the thing of value by the persons being married, is guilty of a misdemeanor.

It is not a necessary element of the offense described by this section that the acceptance of the money or other thing of value be committed with intent to commit extortion or with other criminal intent.

© 1992 by J., B. & L. Gould
Printed in the U.S.A.   EP

This section does not apply to the request for or acceptance of a fee expressly imposed by law for performance of a marriage or to the request or acceptance by any retired judge, retired justice, or retired commissioner of a fee for the performance of a marriage. For the purposes of this section, a retired judge or retired justice sitting on assignment in court shall not be deemed to be a retired judge or retired justice.

This section does not apply to an acceptance of a fee for performing a marriage on Saturday, Sunday, or a legal holiday. *(Amended by Stats 1987 ch 753 §2.)*

§95. Attempt to improperly influence juror, arbitrator, or referee.

Every person who corruptly attempts to influence a juror, or any person summoned or drawn as a juror, or chosen as an arbitrator or umpire, or appointed a referee, in respect to his or her verdict in, or decision of, any cause or proceeding, pending, or about to be brought before him or her, is punishable by a fine not exceeding ten thousand dollars ($10,000), or by imprisonment in the state prison, if it is by means of any of the following:

(a) Any oral or written communication with him or her except in the regular course of proceedings.

(b) Any book, paper, or instrument exhibited, otherwise than in the regular course of proceedings.

(c) Any threat, intimidation, persuasion, or entreaty.

(d) Any promise, or assurance of any pecuniary or other advantage. *(Amended by Stats 1990 ch 350 §9, eff. 1/1/91.)*

§95.1. Intimidation of juror.

Every person who threatens a juror with respect to a criminal proceeding in which a verdict has been rendered and who has the intent and apparent ability to carry out the threat so as to cause the target of the threat to reasonably fear for his or her safety or the safety of his or her immediate family, is guilty of a misdemeanor. *(Added by Stats 1987 ch 762 §1.)*

§96. Misconduct.

Every juror, or person drawn or summoned as a juror, or chosen arbitrator or umpire, or appointed referee, who either:

One—Makes any promise or agreement to give a verdict or decision for or against any party; or,

Two—Willfully and corruptly permits any communication to be made to him, or receives any book, paper, instrument, or information relating to any cause or matter pending before him, except according to the regular course of proceedings, is punishable by fine not exceeding ten thousand dollars ($10,000), or by imprisonment in the state prison.

§97. Purchasing judgments.

Every judge of a justice court or constable of the same judicial district who purchases or is interested in the purchase of any judgment or part thereof on the docket of, or on any docket in possession of such judge, is guilty of a misdemeanor.

§98. Officers to forfeit and be disqualified from holding office.

Every officer convicted of any crime defined in this Chapter, in addition to the punishment prescribed, forfeits his office and is forever disqualified from holding any office in this State.

§99. Superintendent of State Printing; interest in contracts.

The Superintendent of State Printing shall not, during his continuance in office, have any interest, either directly or indirectly, in any contract in any way connected with his office as Superintendent of State Printing; nor shall he, during said period, be interested, either directly or indirectly, in any state printing, binding, engraving, lithographing, or other state work of any kind connected with his said office; nor shall he, directly or indirectly, be interested in any contract for furnishing paper, or other printing stock or material, to or for use in his said office; and any violations of these provisions shall subject him, on conviction before a court of competent jurisdiction, to imprisonment in the state prison and to a fine of not less than one thousand dollars ($1,000) nor more than ten thousand dollars ($10,000), or by both such fine and imprisonment.

§100. Superintendent of State Printing; penalty for collusion.

If the Superintendent of State Printing corruptly colludes with any person or persons furnishing paper or materials, or bidding therefor, or with any other person or persons, or has any secret understanding with him or them, by himself or through others, to defraud the state, or by which the state is defrauded or made to sustain a loss, contrary to the true intent and meaning of this chapter, he, upon conviction thereof, forfeits his office, and is subject to imprisonment in the state prison, and to a fine of not less than one thousand dollars ($1,000) nor more than ten thousand dollars ($10,000), or both such fine and imprisonment.

CHAPTER 2

RESCUES

§102. Retaking goods from custody of officer.

Every person who willfully injures or destroys, or takes or attempts to take, or assists any person in taking or attempting to take, from the custody of any officer or person, any personal property which such officer or person has in charge under any process of law, is guilty of a misdemeanor.

CHAPTER 3

ESCAPES AND AIDING THEREIN

§107. Felony prisoners escaping from places of detention.

Every prisoner charged with or convicted of a felony who is an inmate of any public training school or reformatory or county hospital who escapes or attempts to escape from such public training school or reformatory or county hospital is guilty of a felony and is punishable by imprisonment in the state prison, or by a fine not exceeding ten thousand dollars ($10,000), or by both such fine and imprisonment.

§109. Escapes from public training schools; assistance.

Any person who willfully assists any inmate of any public training school or reformatory to escape, or in an attempt to escape from such public training school or reformatory is punishable by imprisonment in the state prison, and fine not exceeding ten thousand dollars ($10,000).

§110. Furnishing escape tools.

Every person who carries or sends into a public training school, or reformatory, anything useful to aid a prisoner or inmate in making his escape, with intent thereby to facilitate the escape of any prisoner or inmate confined therein, is guilty of a felony.

CHAPTER 4

FORGING, STEALING, MUTILATING, AND FALSIFYING JUDICIAL AND PUBLIC RECORDS AND DOCUMENTS

§115. Offering false or forged instruments to be filed or recorded.

(a) Every person who knowingly procures or offers any false or forged instrument to be filed, registered, or recorded in any public office within this state, which instrument, if genuine, might be filed, registered, or recorded under any law of this state or of the United States, is guilty of a felony.

(b) Each instrument which is procured or offered to be filed, registered, or recorded in violation of subdivision (a) shall constitute a separate violation of this section.

(c) Except in unusual cases where the interests of justice would best be served if probation is granted, probation shall not be granted to, nor shall the execution or imposition of sentence be suspended for, any of the following persons:

(1) Any person with a prior conviction under this section who is again convicted of a violation of this section in a separate proceeding.

(2) Any person who is convicted of more than one violation of this section in a single proceeding, with intent to defraud another, and where the violations resulted in a cumulative financial loss exceeding one hundred thousand dollars ($100,000).

(d) For purposes of prosecution under this section, each act of procurement or of offering a false or forged instrument to be filed, registered, or recorded shall be considered a separately punishable offense.

§115.1. Election campaign advertising; penalties.

(a) The Legislature finds and declares that the voters of California are entitled to accurate representations in materials which are directed to them in efforts to influence how they vote.

(b) No person shall publish or cause to be published, with intent to deceive, any campaign advertisement containing a signature which the person knows to be unauthorized.

(c) For purposes of this section, "campaign advertisement" means any communication directed to voters by means of a mass mailing as defined in Section 82041.5 of the Government Code, a paid television, radio, or newspaper advertisement, an outdoor advertisement, or any other printed matter, if the expenditures for that communication are required to be reported by Chapter 4 (commencing with Section 84100) of Title 9 of the Government Code.

(d) For purposes of this section, an authorization to use a signature shall be oral or written.

(e) Nothing in this section shall be construed to prohibit a person from publishing or causing to be published a reproduction of all or part of a document containing an actual or authorized signature, provided that the signature so reproduced shall not, with the intent to deceive, be incorporated into another document in a manner that falsely suggests that the person whose signature is reproduced has signed the other document.

(f) Any violation of this section is a public offense punishable by imprisonment in the state prison or in the county jail, or by a fine not to exceed fifty thousand dollars ($50,000), or both.

(g) As used in this section, "signature" means a handwritten or mechanical signature, or a copy thereof. *(Added by Stats 1990 ch 1590 §2, eff. 9/30/90.)*

§115.2. False depictions in campaign advertisement.

(a) No person shall publish or cause to be published, with actual knowledge, and intent to deceive, any campaign advertisement containing false or fraudulent depictions, or false or fraudulent representations, of official public documents or purported official public documents.

(b) For purposes of this section, "campaign advertisement" means any communication directed to voters by means of a mass mailing as defined in Section 82041.5 of the Government Code, a paid newspaper advertisement, an outdoor advertisement, or any other printed matter, if the expenditures for that communication are required to be reported by Chapter 4 (commencing with Section 84100) of Title 9 of the Government Code.

(c) Any violation of this section is a misdemeanor punishable by imprisonment in the county jail, or by a fine not to exceed fifty thousand dollars ($50,000), or both. *(Added by Stats 1991 ch 1051 §2, eff. 1/1/92.)*

§115.3. Altering certified copies of official records.

Any person who alters a certified copy of an official record, or knowingly furnishes an altered certified copy of an official record, of this state, including the executive, legislative, and judicial branches thereof, or of any city, county, city and county, district, or political subdivision thereof, is guilty of a misdemeanor.

§115.5. Filing false or forged documents or instruments.

(a) Every person who files any false or forged document or instrument with the county recorder which affects title to, places an encumbrance on, or places an interest secured by a mortgage or deed of trust on, real property consisting of a single-family residence containing not more than four dwelling units, with knowledge that the document is false or forged, is punishable, in addition to any other punishment, by a fine not exceeding seventy-five thousand dollars ($75,000).

(b) Every person who makes a false sworn statement to a notary public, with knowledge that the statement is false, to induce the notary public to perform an improper notarial act on an instrument or document affecting title to, or placing an encumbrance on, real property consisting of a single-family residence containing not more than four dwelling units is guilty of a felony.

© 1992 by J., B. & L. Gould
Printed in the U.S.A.   **EP**

§116. Jury list tampering.

Every person who adds any names to the list of persons selected to serve as jurors for the county, either by placing the names in the jury box or otherwise, or extracts any name therefrom, or destroys the jury box or any of the pieces of paper containing the names of jurors, or mutilates or defaces the names so that they cannot be read, or changes the names on the pieces of paper, except in cases allowed by law, is guilty of a felony. *(Amended by Stats 1989 ch 1360 §104, eff. 1/1/90.)*

§117. Falsifying jury lists, etc.

Every officer or person required by law to certify to the list of persons selected as jurors who maliciously, corruptly, or willfully certifies to a false or incorrect list, or a list containing other names than those selected, or who, being required by law to write down the names placed on the certified lists on separate pieces of paper, does not write down and place in the jury box the same names that are on the certified list, and no more and no less than are on such list, is guilty of a felony.

CHAPTER 5

PERJURY AND SUBORNATION OF PERJURY

§118. Perjury defined.

(a) Every person who, having taken an oath that he or she will testify, declare, depose, or certify truly before any competent tribunal, officer, or person, in any of the cases in which the oath may by law of the State of California be administered, willfully and contrary to the oath, states as true any material matter which he or she knows to be false, and every person who testifies, declares, deposes, or certifies under penalty of perjury in any of the cases in which the testimony, declarations, depositions, or certification is permitted by law of the State of California under penalty of perjury and willfully states as true any material matter which he or she knows to be false, is guilty of perjury.

This subdivision is applicable whether the statement, or the testimony, declaration, deposition, or certification is made or subscribed within or without the State of California.

(b) No person shall be convicted of perjury where proof of falsity rests solely upon contradiction by testimony of a single person other than the defendant. Proof of falsity may be established by direct or indirect evidence. *(Amended by Stats 1990 ch 950 §2, eff. 1/1/91.)*

§118a. False affidavits.

Any person who, in any affidavit taken before any person authorized to administer oaths, swears, affirms, declares, deposes, or certifies that he will testify, declare, depose, or certify before any competent tribunal, officer, or person, in any case then pending or thereafter to be instituted, in any particular manner, or to any particular fact, and in such affidavit willfully and contrary to such oath states as true any material matter which he knows to be false, is guilty of perjury. In any prosecution under this section, the subsequent testimony of such person, in any action involving the matters in such affidavit contained, which is contrary to any of the matters in such affidavit contained, shall be prima facie evidence that the matters in such affidavit were false.

§118.1. Peace officer filing false report; penalties.

Every peace officer who files any report with the agency which employs him or her regarding the commission of any crime or any investigation of any crime, if he or she knowingly and intentionally makes any statement regarding any material matter the report which the officer knows to be false, whether or not the statement is certified or otherwise expressly reported as true, is guilty of filing a false report punishable by imprisonment in the county jail for up to one year, or in the state prison for one, two, or three years. This subdivision shall not apply to the contents of any statement which the peace officer attributes in the report to any other person. *(Added by Stats 1990 ch 950 §3, eff. 1/1/91.)*

§119. Oath defined.

The term "oath," as used in the last two sections, includes an affirmation and every other mode authorized by law of attesting the truth of that which is stated.

§120. Oath of office.

So much of an oath of office as relates to the future performance of official duties is not such an oath as is intended by the two preceding sections.

§121. Administering oath; irregularity.

It is no defense to a prosecution for perjury that the oath was administered or taken in an irregular manner, or that the person accused of perjury did not go before, or was not in the presence of, the officer purporting to administer the oath, if such accused caused or procured such officer to certify that the oath had been taken or administered.

§122. Incompetency of witness no defense.

It is no defense to a prosecution for perjury that the accused was not competent to give the testimony, deposition, or certificate of which falsehood is alleged. It is sufficient that he did give such testimony or make such deposition or certificate.

§123. Witness' knowledge of materiality of his testimony not necessary.

It is no defense to a prosecution for perjury that the accused did not know the materiality of the false statement made by him; or that it did not, in fact, affect the proceeding in or for which it was made. It is sufficient that it was material, and might have been used to affect such proceeding.

§124. Deposition deemed complete.

The making of a deposition, affidavit or certificate is deemed to be complete, within the provisions of this chapter, from the time when it is delivered by the accused to any other person, with the intent that it be uttered or published as true.

§125. Statement of that which one does not know to be true.

An unqualified statement of that which one does not know to be true is equivalent to a statement of that which one knows to be false.

§126. Perjury; punishment.

Perjury is punishable by imprisonment in the state prison for two, three or four years.

§127. Subornation of perjury.

Every person who willfully procures another person to commit perjury is guilty of subornation of perjury, and is punishable in the same manner as he would be if personally guilty of the perjury so procured.

§128. Procuring execution of innocent person.

Every person who, by willful perjury or subornation of perjury procures the conviction and execution of any innocent person, is punishable by death or life imprisonment without possibility of parole. The penalty shall be determined pursuant to Sections 190.3 and 190.4.

§129. False statement under oath.

Every person who, being required by law to make any return, statement, or report, under oath, willfully makes and delivers any such return, statement, or report, purporting to be under oath, knowing the same to be false in any particular, is guilty of perjury, whether such oath was in fact taken or not.

CHAPTER 6

FALSIFYING EVIDENCE, AND BRIBING, INFLUENCING, INTIMIDATING OR THREATENING WITNESSES
(Amended by Stats 1985 ch 962 §2.)

§132. Offering false evidence.

Every person who upon any trial, proceeding, inquiry, or investigation whatever, authorized or permitted by law, offers in evidence, as genuine or true, any book, paper, document, record, or other instrument in writing, knowing the same to have been forged or fraudulently altered or antedated, is guilty of felony.

§133. Deceiving a witness.

Every person who practices any fraud or deceit, or knowingly makes or exhibits any false statement, representation, token, or writing, to any witness or person about to be called as a witness upon any trial, proceeding, inquiry, or investigation whatever, authorized by law, with intent to affect the testimony of such witness, is guilty of a misdemeanor.

§134. Preparing false evidence.

Every person guilty of preparing any false or antedated book, paper, record, instrument in writing, or other matter or thing, with intent to produce it, or allow it to be produced for any fraudulent or deceitful purpose, as genuine or true, upon any trial, proceeding, or inquiry whatever, authorized by law, is guilty of felony.

§135. Destroying evidence.

Every person who, knowing that any book, paper, record, instrument in writing, or other matter or thing, is about to be produced in evidence upon any trial, inquiry, or investigation whatever, authorized by law, willfully destroys or conceals the same, with intent thereby to prevent it from being produced, is guilty of a misdemeanor.

§136. Definitions.

As used in this chapter:

(1) "Malice" means an intent to vex, annoy, harm, or injure in any way another person, or to thwart or interfere in any manner with the orderly administration of justice.

(2) "Witness" means any natural person, (i) having knowledge of the existence or nonexistence of facts relating to any crime, or (ii) whose declaration under oath is received or has been received as evidence for any purpose, or (iii) who has reported any crime to any peace officer, prosecutor, probation or parole officer, correctional officer or judicial officer, or (iv) who has been served with a subpoena issued under the authority of any court in the state, or of any other state or of the United States, or (v) who would be believed by any reasonable person to be an individual described in subparagraphs (i) to (iv), inclusive.

(3) "Victim" means any natural person with respect to whom there is reason to believe that any crime as defined under the laws of this state or any other state or of the United States is being or has been perpetrated or attempted to be perpetrated.

§136 1/2. *Repealed by Stats 1987 ch 828.*

§136.1. Dissuading or preventing witness or victim from testifying.

(a) Except as provided in subdivision (c), any person who does any of the following is guilty of a misdemeanor:

(1) Knowingly and maliciously prevents or dissuades any witness or victim from attending or giving testimony at any trial, proceeding, or inquiry authorized by law.

(2) Knowingly and maliciously attempts to prevent or dissuade any witness or victim from attending or giving testimony at any trial, proceeding, or inquiry authorized by law.

(b) Except as provided in subdivision (c), every person who attempts to prevent or dissuade another person who has been the victim of a crime or who is witness to a crime from doing any of the following is guilty of a misdemeanor:

(1) Making any report of such victimization to any peace officer or state or local law enforcement officer or probation or parole or correctional officer or prosecuting agency or to any judge.

(2) Causing a complaint, indictment, information, probation or parole violation to be sought and prosecuted, and assisting in the prosecution thereof.

(3) Arresting or causing or seeking the arrest of any person in connection with such victimization.

(c) Every person doing any of the acts described in subdivision (a) or (b) knowingly and maliciously under any one or more of the following circumstances, is guilty of a felony punishable by imprisonment in the state prison for two, three, or four years under any of the following circumstances:

(1) Where the act is accompanied by force or by an express or implied threat of force or violence, upon a witness or victim or any third person or the property of any victim, witness, or any third person.

(2) Where the act is in furtherance of a conspiracy.

(3) Where the act is committed by any person who has been convicted of any violation of this section, any predecessor law hereto or any federal statute or statute of any other state which, if the act prosecuted

© 1992 by J., B. & L. Gould
Printed in the U.S.A.   EP

was committed in this state, would be a violation of this section.

(4) Where the act is committed by any person for pecuniary gain or for any other consideration acting upon the request of any other person. All parties to such a transaction are guilty of a felony.

(d) Every person attempting the commission of any act described in subdivisions (a), (b), and (c) is guilty of the offense attempted without regard to success or failure of such attempt. The fact that no person was injured physically, or in fact intimidated, shall be no defense against any prosecution under this section.

(e) Nothing in this section precludes the imposition of an enhancement for great bodily injury where the injury inflicted is significant or substantial.

(f) The use of force during the commission of any offense described in subdivision (c) shall be considered a circumstance in aggravation of the crime in imposing a term of imprisonment under subdivision (b) of Section 1170. *(Amended by Stats 1990 ch 350 §10, eff. 1/1/91.)*

§136.2. Orders of court.

Upon a good cause belief that intimidation or dissuasion of a victim or witness has occurred or is reasonably likely to occur, any court with jurisdiction over a criminal matter may issue orders including, but not limited to, the following:

(a) An order that a defendant shall not violate any provision of Section 136.1.

(b) An order that a person before the court other than a defendant, including, but not limited to, a subpoenaed witness or other person entering the courtroom of the court, shall not violate any provisions of Section 136.1.

(c) An order that any person described in this section shall have no communication whatsoever with any specified witness or any victim, except through an attorney under such reasonable restrictions as the court may impose.

(d) An order calling for a hearing to determine if an order as described in subdivisions (a) to (c), inclusive, should be issued.

(e) An order that a particular law enforcement agency within the jurisdiction of the court provide protection for a victim or a witness, or both, or for immediate family members of a victim or a witness who reside in the same household as the victim or witness or within reasonable proximity of the victim's or witness's household, as determined by the court. The order shall not be made without the consent of the law enforcement agency except for limited and specified periods of time and upon an express finding by the court of a clear and present danger of harm to the victim or witness or immediate family members of the victim or witness.

For purposes of this subdivision, "immediate family members" include the spouse, children, or parents of the victim or witness.

(f) Any order protecting victims of violent crime from contact, with the intent to annoy, harass, threaten, or commit acts of violence, by the defendant.

Any person violating any order made pursuant to subdivisions (a) to (f), inclusive, may be punished for any substantive offense described in Section 136.1, or for a contempt of the court making the order. No finding of contempt shall be a bar to prosecution for a violation of Section 136.1. However, any person so held in contempt shall be entitled to credit for any punishment imposed therein against any sentence imposed upon conviction of an offense described in Section 136.1. Any conviction or acquittal for any substantive offense under Section 136.1 shall be a bar to a subsequent punishment for contempt arising out of the same act.

(g) In all cases where the defendant is charged with a crime of domestic violence, as defined in Section 13700, the court shall consider issuing the above-described orders on its own motion. In order to facilitate this, the court's records of all criminal cases involving domestic violence shall be marked to clearly alert the court to this issue.

(h) On or before July 1, 1991, the Judicial Council shall adopt forms for orders under this section. *(Amended by Stats 1990 ch 935 §6, eff. 1/1/91.)*

§136.5. Intimidation of victim or witness with a deadly weapon.

Any person who has upon his person a deadly weapon with the intent to use such weapon to commit a violation of Section 136.1 is guilty of an offense punishable by imprisonment in the county jail for not more than one year, or in the state prison.

§136.7. Intimidation of victim or witness through fellow prisoner.

Every person imprisoned in a county jail or the state prison who has been convicted of a sexual offense, including, but not limited to, a violation of Section 243.4, 261, 261.5, 262, 264.1, 266, 266a, 266b, 266c, 266f, 285, 286, 288, 288a, or 289, who knowingly reveals the name and address of any witness or victim to that offense to any other prisoner with the intent that the other prisoner will intimidate or harass the witness or victim through the initiation of unauthorized correspondence with the witness or victim, is guilty of a public offense, punishable by imprisonment in the county jail not to exceed one year, or by imprisonment in the state prison.

Nothing in this section shall prevent the interviewing of witnesses. *(Added by Stats 1987 ch 520.)*

§137. Inducing or influencing testimony.

(a) Every person who gives or offers, or promises to give, to any witness, person about to be called as a witness, or person about to give material information pertaining to a crime to a law enforcement official, any bribe, upon any understanding or agreement that the testimony of such witness or information given by such person shall be thereby influenced is guilty of a felony.

(b) Every person who attempts by force or threat of force or by the use of fraud to induce any person to give false testimony or withhold true testimony or to give false material information pertaining to a crime to, or withhold true material information pertaining to a crime from, a law enforcement official is guilty of a felony, punishable by imprisonment in the state prison for two, three, or four years.

As used in this subdivision, "threat of force" means a credible threat of unlawful injury to any person or damage to the property of another which is communicated to a person for the purpose of inducing him to give false testimony or withhold true testimony or to give false material information pertaining to a crime to, or to withhold true material information pertaining to a crime from, a law enforcement official.

(c) Every person who knowingly induces another person to give false testimony or withhold true testimony not privileged by law or to give false material information pertaining to a crime to, or to withhold true material information pertaining to a crime from, a law enforcement official is guilty of a misdemeanor.

(d) At the arraignment, on a showing of cause to believe this section may be violated, the court, on motion of a party, shall admonish the person who there is cause to believe may violate this section and shall announce the penalties and other provisions of this section.

(e) As used in this section "law enforcement official" includes any district attorney, deputy district attorney, city attorney, deputy city attorney, the Attorney General or any deputy attorney general, or any peace officer included in Chapter 4.5 (commencing with Section 830) of Title 3 of Part 2.

(f) The provisions of subdivision (c) shall not apply to an attorney advising a client or to a person advising a member of his or her family.

§138. Offering or taking bribes by witnesses.

(a) Every person who gives or offers or promises to give to any witness or person about to be called as a witness, any bribe upon any understanding or agreement that the person shall not attend upon any trial or other judicial proceeding, or every person who attempts by means of any offer of a bribe to dissuade any person from attending upon any trial or other judicial proceeding, is guilty of a felony.

(b) Every person who is a witness, or is about to be called as such, who receives, or offers to receive, any bribe, upon any understanding that his or her testimony shall be influenced thereby, or that he or she will absent himself or herself from the trial or proceeding upon which his or her testimony is required, is guilty of a felony. *(Amended by Stats 1987 ch 828 §5.)*

§139. Threatening witnesses and families.

(a) Except as provided in Sections 71 and 136.1, any person who has been convicted of any felony offense specified in Section 12021.1 who willfully and maliciously communicates to a witness to, or a victim of, the crime for which the person was convicted, a credible threat to use force or violence upon that person or that person's immediate family, shall be punished by imprisonment in the county jail not exceeding one year or by imprisonment in the state prison for two, three, or four years.

(b) Any person who is convicted of violating subdivision (a) who subsequently is convicted of making a credible threat, as defined in subdivision (c), which constitutes a threat against the life of, or a threat to cause great bodily injury to, a person described in subdivision (a), shall be sentenced to consecutive terms of imprisonment as prescribed in Section 1170.13.

(c) As used in this section, "a credible threat" is a threat made with the intent and the apparent ability to carry out the threat so as to cause the target of the threat to reasonably fear for his or her safety or the safety of his or her immediate family.

(d) The present incarceration of the person making the threat shall not be a bar to prosecution under this section.

(e) As used in this section, "malice," "witness," and "victim" have the meanings given in Section 136. *(Amended by Stats 1990 ch 80 §1, eff. 1/1/91.)*

§140. Threatening a crime witness.

Except as provided in Section 139, every person who willfully threatens to use force or violence upon the person of a witness to, or a victim of, a crime or any other person, or to take, damage, or destroy any property of any witness, victim, or any other person, because the witness, victim, or informant has provided any assistance or information to a law enforcement officer, or to a public prosecutor in a criminal proceeding or juvenile court proceeding, shall be punished by imprisonment in the county jail not exceeding one year, or by imprisonment in the state prison for two, three, or four years. *(Amended by Stats 1990 ch 80 §2, eff. 1/1/91.)*

CHAPTER 7

OTHER OFFENSES AGAINST PUBLIC JUSTICE

§142. Peace officer refusing to receive or arrest parties charged with crime; penalty.

(a) Any peace officer who has the authority to receive or arrest a person charged with a criminal offense and willfully refuses to receive or arrest such person shall be punished by a fine not exceeding ten thousand dollars ($10,000), or by imprisonment in the state prison, or in a county jail not exceeding one year, or by both such fine and imprisonment.

(b) Notwithstanding subdivision (a), the sheriff may determine whether any jail, institution, or facility under his direction shall be designated as a reception, holding, or confinement facility, or shall be used for several of such purposes, and may designate the class of prisoners for which such facility shall be used.

§145. Delaying to take person arrested before a magistrate.

Every public officer or other person, having arrested any person upon a criminal charge, who willfully delays to take such person before a magistrate having jurisdiction, to take his examination, is guilty of a misdemeanor.

§146. Making arrests, etc., without lawful authority.

Every public officer, or person pretending to be a public officer, who, under the pretense or color of any process or other legal authority, does any of the following, without a regular process or other lawful authority, is guilty of a misdemeanor:

(a) Arrests any person or detains that person against his or her will.

(b) Seizes or levies upon any property.

(c) Dispossesses any one of any lands or tenements. *(Amended by Stats 1990 ch 350 §11, eff. 1/1/91.)*

§146a. Impersonating an officer; penalty.

Any person who falsely represents himself or herself to be a public officer, or investigator, inspector, deputy, or clerk in any state department and who, in that assumed character, does any of the following is guilty of a misdemeanor and upon conviction is punishable by imprisonment in a county jail, not exceeding six months, or by a fine, not exceeding two thousand five hundred dollars ($2,500), or by both that fine and imprisonment:

(a) Arrests or detains or threatens to arrest or detain any person.

© 1992 by J., B. & L. Gould
Printed in the U.S.A.   EP

(b) Otherwise intimidates any person.

(c) Searches any person, building, or other property of any person.

(d) Obtains money, or property, or other thing of value. *(Amended by Stats 1990 ch 350 §12, eff. 1/1/91.)*

§146b. False governmental communication.

Every person who, with intent to lead another to believe that a request or demand for information is being made by the State, a county, city, or other governmental entity, when such is not the case, sends to such other person a written or printed form or other communication which reasonably appears to be such request or demand by such governmental entity, is guilty of a misdemeanor.

§146c. Use of officer term in name of nongovernmental organization.

Every person who designates any nongovernmental organization by any name, including, but not limited to any name which incorporates the term "peace officer," "police," or "law enforcement," which would reasonably be understood to imply that the organization is composed of law enforcement personnel, when, in fact, less than 90 percent of the voting members of the organization are law enforcement personnel or firemen, active or retired, is guilty of a misdemeanor.

Every person who solicits another to become a member of any organization so named, of which less than 90 percent of the voting members are law enforcement personnel or firemen, or to make a contribution thereto or subscribe to or advertise in a publication of the organization, or who sells or gives to another any badge, pin, membership card, or other article indicating membership in the organization, knowing that less than 90 percent of the voting members are law enforcement personnel or firemen, active or retired, is guilty of a misdemeanor.

As used in this section, "law enforcement personnel" includes those mentioned in Chapter 4.5 (commencing with Section 830) of Title 3 of Part 2, plus any other officers in any segment of law enforcement who are employed by the state or any of its political subdivisions.

§146d. Gift or sale of membership cards where law enforcement toward recipient will be less rigorous.

Every person who sells or gives to another a membership card, badge, or other device, where it can be reasonably inferred by the recipient that display of the device will have the result that the law will be enforced less rigorously as to such person than would otherwise be the case is guilty of a misdemeanor.

§146e. Unauthorized revealing of address or telephone number of peace officer or family.

Every person who maliciously, and with the intent to obstruct justice or the due administration of the laws, publishes, disseminates, or otherwise discloses the residence address or telephone number of any peace officer or nonsworn police dispatcher, or that of the spouse or children of these persons, whether living with them or not, while designating the peace officer or nonsworn police dispatcher or relative of these persons as such, without the authorization of the employing agency, is guilty of a misdemeanor. *(Amended by Stats 1991 ch 579 §1, eff. 1/1/92.)*

§146f. Inmates prohibited access to peace officer personnel information records.

No inmate under the control or supervision of the Department of Corrections or the Department of the Youth Authority shall be permitted to work with records or files containing peace officer personnel information or be allowed access to the immediate area where that information is normally stored, except for maintenance services and only after those records or files have been secured and locked.

§147. Inhumanity to prisoners.

Every officer who is guilty of willful inhumanity or oppression toward any prisoner under his care or in his custody, is punishable by fine not exceeding four thousand dollars ($4,000), and by removal from office.

§148. Resisting public or peace officers or medical technicians in the discharge of their duties.

(a) Every person who willfully resists, delays, or obstructs any public officer, peace officer, or an emergency medical technician, as defined in Division 2.5 (commencing with Section 1797) of the Health and Safety Code, in the discharge or attempt to discharge any duty of his or her office or employment, when no other punishment is prescribed, is punishable by a fine not exceeding one thousand dollars ($1,000), or by imprisonment in a county jail not exceeding one year, or by both such fine and imprisonment.

(b) Every person who, during the commission of any offense described in subdivision (a), removes or takes any weapon, other than a firearm, from the person of, or immediate presence of, a public officer or peace officer is punishable by imprisonment in the county jail not to exceed one year, or in the state prison.

(c) Every person who, during the commission of any offense described in subdivision (a), removes or takes a firearm from the person of, or immediate presence of, a public officer or peace officer is guilty of a felony.

(d) Every person who, during the commission of any offense described in subdivision (a), attempts to remove or take a firearm from the person of, or immediate presence of, a public officer or peace officer is guilty of a public offense, punishable by imprisonment in a county jail not to exceed one year or in the state prison.

In order to prove a violation of this subdivision, the prosecution shall establish that the defendant had the specific intent to remove or take the firearm by demonstrating that any of the following direct, but ineffectual, acts occurred:

(1) The officer's holster strap was unfastened by the defendant.

(2) The firearm was partially removed from the officer's holster by the defendant.

(3) The firearm safety was released by the defendant.

(4) An independent witness corroborates that the defendant stated that he or she intended to remove the firearm and the defendant actually touched the firearm.

(5) An independent witness corroborates that the defendant actually had his or her hand on the firearm and tried to take the firearm away from the officer who was holding it.

(6) The defendant's fingerprint was found on the firearm or holster.

(7) Physical evidence authenticated by a scientifically verifiable procedure established that the defendant touched the firearm.

(8) In the course of any struggle, the officer's firearm fell and the defendant attempted to pick it up.

(e) A person may not be convicted of a violation of subdivision (a) in addition to a conviction of a violation of subdivision (b), (c), or (d) when the resistance, delay, or obstruction was committed against the same public officer, peace officer, or emergency medical technician. Multiple convictions under this section may take place when more than one public officer, peace officer, or emergency medical technician are victims. *(Amended by Stats 1990 ch 1181 §1, eff. 1/1/91.)*

§148.1. False report of secreted bomb.

(a) Any person who reports to any peace officer listed in Section 830.1 or 830.2, employee of a fire department or fire service, district attorney, newspaper, radio station, television station, deputy district attorney, employees of the Department of Justice, employees of an airline, employees of an airport, employees of a railroad or busline, an employee of a telephone company, occupants of a building or a news reporter in the employ of a newspaper or radio or television station, that a bomb or other explosive has been or will be placed or secreted in any public or private place knowing that the report is false, is guilty of a crime punishable by imprisonment in the state prison, or imprisonment in the county jail not to exceed one year.

(b) Any person who reports to any other peace officer defined in Chapter 4.5 (commencing with Section 830) of Title 3 of Part 2 that a bomb or other explosive has been or will be placed or secreted in any public or private place, knowing that the report is false, is guilty of a crime punishable by imprisonment in the state prison or in the county jail not to exceed one year if (1) the false information is given while the peace officer is engaged in the performance of his or her duties as a peace officer, and (2) the person providing the false information knows or should have known that the person receiving the information is a peace officer.

(c) Any person who maliciously informs any other person that a bomb or other explosive has been or will be placed or secreted in any public or private place, knowing that the information is false, is guilty of a crime punishable by imprisonment in the state prison, or imprisonment in the county jail not to exceed one year.

(d) Any person who maliciously gives, mails, sends, or causes to be sent any false or facsimile bomb to another person, or places, causes to be placed, or maliciously possesses any false or facsimile bomb, with the intent to cause another to fear for his or her personal safety or the safety of others, is guilty of a crime punishable by imprisonment in the state prison, or imprisonment in the county jail not to exceed one year. *(Amended by Stats 1991 ch 503 §1, eff. 1/1/92.)*

§148.2. Interference with firemen or emergency rescue personnel at fire.

Every person who willfully commits any of the following acts at the burning of a building or at any other time and place where any fireman or firemen or emergency rescue personnel are discharging or attempting to discharge an official duty, is guilty of a misdemeanor:

1. Resists or interferes with the lawful efforts of any fireman or firemen or emergency rescue personnel in the discharge or attempt to discharge an official duty.

2. Disobeys the lawful orders of any fireman or public officer.

3. Engages in any disorderly conduct which delays or prevents a fire from being timely extinguished.

4. Forbids or prevents others from assisting in extinguishing a fire or exhorts another person, as to whom he has no legal right or obligation to protect or control, from assisting in extinguishing a fire.

§148.3. Falsely reporting an emergency.

(a) Any individual who reports, or causes any report to be made, to any city, county, city and county, or state department, district, agency, division, commission, or board, that an "emergency" exists, knowing that such report is false, is guilty of a misdemeanor and, upon conviction thereof, shall be punishable by imprisonment in the county jail, not exceeding one year, or by a fine, not exceeding one thousand dollars ($1,000), or by both such fine and imprisonment.

(b) Any individual who reports, or causes any report to be made, to any city, county, city and county, or state department, district, agency, division, commission, or board, that an "emergency" exists, knowing that such report is false, and great bodily injury or death is sustained by any person as a result of such false report, is guilty of a felony and upon conviction thereof shall be punishable by imprisonment in the state prison, or by a fine of not more than ten thousand dollars ($10,000), or by both such fine and imprisonment.

(c) "Emergency" as used in this section means any condition which results in, or which could result in, the response of a public official in an authorized emergency vehicle, or any condition which jeopardizes or could jeopardize public safety and results in, or could result in, the evacuation of any area, building, structure, vehicle or of any other place which any individual may enter.

§148.4. Malicious acts with fire protection equipment; false alarms.

(a) Any person who does any of the following is guilty of a misdemeanor and upon conviction is punishable by imprisonment in a county jail, not exceeding one year, or by a fine, not exceeding one thousand dollars ($1,000), or by both that fine and imprisonment:

(1) Willfully and maliciously tampers with, molests, injures, or breaks any fire protection equipment, fire protection installation, fire alarm apparatus, wire, or signal.

(2) Willfully and maliciously sends, gives, transmits, or sounds any false alarm of fire, by means of any fire alarm system or signal or by any other means or methods.

(b) Any person who willfully and maliciously sends, gives, transmits, or sounds any false alarm of fire, by means of any fire alarm system or signal, or by any other means or methods, is guilty of a felony and upon conviction is punishable by imprisonment in the state prison or by a fine of not less than five hundred dollars ($500) nor more than ten thousand dollars ($10,000), or by both that fine and imprisonment, if any person sustains as a result thereof, any of the following:

(1) Great bodily injury.

(2) Death. *(Amended by Stats 1990 ch 350 §13, eff. 1/1/91.)*

© 1992 by J., B. & L. Gould
Printed in the U.S.A.   EP

§148.5. Knowingly providing false report of a crime.

(a) Every person who reports to any peace officer listed in Section 830.1 or 830.2, district attorney, or deputy district attorney that a felony or misdemeanor has been committed, knowing the report to be false, is guilty of a misdemeanor.

(b) Every person who reports to any other peace officer, as defined in Chapter 4.5 (commencing with Section 830) of Title 3 of Part 2, that a felony or misdemeanor has been committed, knowing the report to be false, is guilty of a misdemeanor if (1) the false information is given while the peace officer is engaged in the performance of his or her duties as a peace officer and (2) the person providing the false information knows or should have known that the person receiving the information is a peace officer.

(c) Except as provided in subdivisions (a) and (b), every person who reports to any employee who is assigned to accept reports from citizens, either directly or by telephone, and who is employed by a state or local agency which is designated in Section 830.1, 830.2, subdivision (e) of 830.3, Section 830.31, 830.32, 830.33, 830.34, 830.35, 830.36, 830.37, 830.38, or 830.4, that a felony or misdemeanor has been committed, knowing the report to be false, is guilty of a misdemeanor if (1) the false information is given while the employee is engaged in the performance of his or her duties as an agency employee and (2) the person providing the false information knows or should have known that the person receiving the information is an agency employee engaged in the performance of the duties described in this subdivision.

(d) Every person who makes a report to a grand jury that a felony or misdemeanor has been committed, knowing the report to be false, is guilty of a misdemeanor. This subdivision shall not be construed as prohibiting or precluding a charge of perjury or contempt for any report made under oath in an investigation or proceeding before a grand jury.

(e) This section does not apply to reports made by persons who are required by statute to report known or suspected instances of child abuse, dependent adult abuse, or elder abuse. (*Amended by Stats 1990 ch 675 §8; ch 1700 §2, eff. 1/1/91.*)

§148.7. Impersonating another in order to serve a sentence.

Every person who, for the purpose of serving in any county or city jail, industrial farm or road camp, or other local correctional institution any part or all of the sentence of another person, or any part or all of a term of confinement that is required to be served by another person as a condition of probation, represents to any public officer or employee that he is such other person, is guilty of a misdemeanor.

§148.9. False representation of identity to peace officer.

(a) Any person who falsely represents or identifies himself or herself as another person or as a fictitious person to any peace officer listed in Section 830.1 or 830.2, upon a lawful detention or arrest of the person, either to evade the process of the court, or to evade the proper identification of the person by the investigating officer is guilty of a misdemeanor.

(b) Any person who falsely represents or identifies himself or herself as another person or as a fictitious person to any other peace officer defined in Chapter 4.5 (commencing with Section 830) of Title 3 of Part 2, upon lawful detention or arrest of the person, either to evade the process of the court, or to evade the proper identification of the person by the arresting officer is guilty of a misdemeanor if (1) the false information is given while the peace officer is engaged in the performance of his or her duties as a peace officer, and (2) the person providing the false information knows or should have known that the person receiving the information is a peace officer.

§148.10. Resisting peace officer in discharge of duties: killing or injuring officer.

(a) Every person who willfully resists a peace officer in the discharge or attempt to discharge any duty of his or her office or employment and the willful resistance of the person proximately causes death or serious bodily injury to a peace officer, shall be punished by imprisonment in the state prison for two, three, or four years, or a fine of not less than one thousand dollars ($1,000) or more than ten thousand dollars ($10,000), or both the fine and imprisonment, or by imprisonment in the county jail for not more than one year, or by a fine of not more than one thousand dollars ($1,000), or by both the fine and imprisonment.

(b) For purposes of subdivision (a), the following facts shall be found by the trier of fact:

(1) That the peace officer's action was reasonable based on the facts or circumstances confronting the officer at the time.

(2) That the detention and arrest was lawful and there existed probable cause or reasonable cause to detain.

(3) That the person who willfully resisted, any peace officer knew or reasonably should have known that the other person was a peace officer engaged in the performance of his or her duties.

(c) This section shall not apply to conduct which occurs during labor picketing, demonstrations, or disturbing the peace.

(d) For purposes of this section, "serious bodily injury" is defined in paragraph (5) of subdivision (f) of Section 243. (*Added by Stats 1990 ch 1155 §1, eff. 1/1/91.*)

§149. Assaults by public officers.

Every public officer who, under color of authority, without lawful necessity, assaults or beats any person, is punishable by a fine not exceeding ten thousand dollars ($10,000), or by imprisonment in the state prison, or in a county jail not exceeding one year, or by both such fine and imprisonment.

§150. Refusal of aid to officers in arrest.

Every able-bodied person above 18 years of age who neglects or refuses to join the posse comitatus or power of the county, by neglecting or refusing to aid and assist in taking or arresting any person against whom there may be issued any process, or by neglecting to aid and assist in retaking any person who, after being arrested or confined, may have escaped from arrest or imprisonment, or by neglecting or refusing to aid and assist in preventing any breach of the peace, or the commission of any criminal offense, being thereto lawfully required by any uniformed peace officer, or by any peace officer described in Section 830.1 or in subdivision (a), (b), (c), (d), (e), or (f) of Section 830.2 of the Penal Code who identifies himself or herself with a badge or identification card issued by the officer's employing agency, or by any judge, is punishable by fine of not less than fifty dollars ($50) nor more than one thousand dollars ($1,000). *(Amended by Stats 1991 ch 910 §3, eff. 1/1/92.)*

§151. Advocating the killing or injuring of peace officer.

(a) Any person who advocates the willful and unlawful killing or injuring of a peace officer, with the specific intent to cause the willful and unlawful killing or injuring of a peace officer, and such advocacy is done at a time, place, and under circumstances in which the advocacy is likely to cause the imminent willful and unlawful killing or injuring of a peace officer is guilty of (1) a misdemeanor if such advocacy does not cause the unlawful and willful killing or injuring of a peace officer, or (2) a felony if such advocacy causes the unlawful and willful killing or injuring of a peace officer.

(b) As used in this section, "advocacy" means the direct incitement of others to cause the imminent willful and unlawful killing or injuring of a peace officer, and not the mere abstract teaching of a doctrine.

§153. Concealing or compounding crimes.

Every person who, having knowledge of the actual commission of a crime, takes money or property of another, or any gratuity or reward, or any engagement, or promise thereof, upon any agreement or understanding to compound or conceal such crime, or to abstain from any prosecution thereof, or to withhold any evidence thereof, except in the cases provided for by law, in which crimes may be compromised by leave of court, is punishable as follows:

1. By imprisonment in the state prison, or in a county jail not exceeding one year, where the crime was punishable by death or imprisonment in the state prison for life;

2. By imprisonment in the state prison, or in the county jail not exceeding six months, where the crime was punishable by imprisonment in the state prison for any other term than for life;

3. By imprisonment in the county jail not exceeding six months, or by fine not exceeding one thousand dollars ($1,000), where the crime was a misdemeanor.

§154. Fraudulently removing property by debtor.

(a) Every debtor who fraudulently removes his or her property or effects out of this state, or who fraudulently sells, conveys, assigns or conceals his or her property with intent to defraud, hinder or delay his or her creditors of their rights, claims, or demands, is punishable by imprisonment in the county jail not exceeding one year, or by fine not exceeding one thousand dollars ($1,000), or by both that fine and imprisonment.

(b) Where the property so removed, sold, conveyed, assigned, or concealed consists of a stock in trade, or a part thereof, of a value exceeding one hundred dollars ($100), the offense shall be a felony and punishable as such. *(Amended by Stats 1990 ch 350 §14, eff. 1/1/91.)*

§155. Defendant fraudulently concealing his property.

(a) Every person against whom an action is pending, or against whom a judgment has been rendered for the recovery of any personal property, who

fraudulently conceals, sells, or disposes of that property, with intent to hinder, delay, or defraud the person bringing the action or recovering the judgment, or with such intent removes that property beyond the limits of the county in which it may be at the time of the commencement of the action or the rendering of the judgment, is punishable by imprisonment in a county jail not exceeding one year, or by fine not exceeding one thousand dollars ($1,000), or by both that fine and imprisonment.

(b) Where the property so concealed, sold, disposed of, or removed consists of a stock in trade, or a part thereof, of a value exceeding one hundred dollars ($100), the offenses shall be a felony and punishable as such. *(Amended by Stats 1990 ch 350 §15, eff. 1/1/91.)*

§155.5. Disposal of property to avoid fine or restitution.

(a) Any defendant who enters a plea of guilty or nolo contendere, or against whom a judgment of guilty is entered, for the commission of a misdemeanor and who after such plea or judgment and prior to sentencing, sells, conveys, assigns, or conceals his or her property with the intent to lessen or impair his or her financial ability to pay in full any fine or restitution which he or she may lawfully be ordered to pay or to avoid forfeiture of assets pursuant to the California Control of Profits of Organized Crime Act (Chapter 9 (commencing with Section 186) of this title) is guilty of a misdemeanor.

(b) Any defendant who enters a plea of guilty or nolo contendere, or against whom a judgment of guilty is entered for the commission of a felony and prior to sentencing for the same felony offense, sells, conveys, assigns, or conceals his or her property with the intent to lessen or impair his or her financial ability to pay in full any fine or restitution which he or she may lawfully be ordered to pay or to avoid forfeiture of assets derived from either criminal profiteering pursuant to Chapter 9 (commencing with Section 186) of this title or trafficking in controlled substances pursuant to Chapter 8 (commencing with Section 11470) of Division 10 of the Health and Safety Code is guilty of a felony. *(Added by Stats 1986 ch 650 §1.)*

§156. Fraudulently producing an infant.

Every person who fraudulently produces an infant, falsely pretending it to have been born of any parent whose child would be entitled to inherit any real estate or to receive a share of any personal estate, with intent to intercept the inheritance of any such real estate, or the distribution of any such personal estate from any person lawfully entitled thereto, is punishable by imprisonment in the state prison for two, three or four years.

§157. Substituting children.

Every person to whom an infant has been confided for nursing, education, or any other purpose, who, with intent to deceive any parent or guardian of such child, substitutes or produces to such parent or guardian another child in the place of the one so confided, is punishable by imprisonment in the state prison for two, three or four years.

§158. Common barratry defined; punishment.

Common barratry is the practice of exciting groundless judicial proceedings, and is punishable by

© 1992 by J., B. & L. Gould
Printed in the U.S.A.　　**EP**

imprisonment in the county jail not exceeding six months and by fine not exceeding one thousand dollars ($1,000).

§159. What proof is required.

No person can be convicted of common barratry except upon proof that he has excited suits or proceedings at law in at least three instances, and with a corrupt or malicious intent to vex and annoy.

§165. Bribing supervisors, councilmen, or trustees.

Every person who gives or offers a bribe to any member of any common council, board of supervisors, or board of trustees of any county, city and county, city, or public corporation, with intent to corruptly influence such member in his action on any matter or subject pending before, or which is afterward to be considered by, the body of which he is a member, and every member of any of the bodies mentioned in this section who receives, or offers or agrees to receive any bribe upon any understanding that his official vote, opinion, judgment, or action shall be influenced thereby, or shall be given in any particular manner or upon any particular side of any question or matter, upon which he may be required to act in his official capacity, is punishable by imprisonment in the state prison for two, three or four years, and upon conviction thereof shall, in addition to said punishment, forfeit his office, and forever be disfranchised and disqualified from holding any public office or trust.

§166. Criminal contempts.

Every person guilty of any contempt of Court, of either of the following kinds, is guilty of a misdemeanor:

1. Disorderly, contemptuous, or insolent behavior committed during the sitting of any court of justice, in immediate view and presence of the court, and directly tending to interrupt its proceedings or to impair the respect due to its authority;

2. Behavior of the like character committed in the presence of any referee, while actually engaged in any trial or hearing, pursuant to the order of any court, or in the presence of any jury while actually sitting for the trial of a cause, or upon any inquest or other proceedings authorized by law;

3. Any breach of the peace, noise, or other disturbance directly tending to interrupt the proceedings of any Court;

4. Willful disobedience of any process or order lawfully issued by any Court;

5. Resistance willfully offered by any person to the lawful order or process of any Court;

6. The contumacious and unlawful refusal of any person to be sworn as a witness; or, when so sworn, the like refusal to answer any material question;

7. The publication of a false or grossly inaccurate report of the proceedings of any court;

8. Presenting to any Court having power to pass sentence upon any prisoner under conviction, or to any member of such Court, any affidavit or testimony or representation of any kind, verbal or written, in aggravation or mitigation of the punishment to be imposed upon such prisoner, except as provided in this Code.

§167. Unauthorized recording.

Every person who, by any means whatsoever, willfully and knowingly, and without knowledge and con-

sent of the jury, records, or attempts to record, all or part of the proceedings of any trial jury while it is deliberating or voting, or listens to or observes, or attempts to listen to or observe, the proceedings of any trial jury of which he is not a member while such jury is deliberating or voting is guilty of a misdemeanor.

This section is not intended to prohibit the taking of notes by a trial juror in connection with and solely for the purpose of assisting him in the performance of his duties as such juror.

§168. Disclosing search warrant or warrant of arrest prior to execution.

(a) Every district attorney, clerk, judge or peace officer who, except by issuing or in executing a search warrant or warrant of arrest for a felony, wilfully discloses the fact of the warrant prior to execution for the purpose of preventing the search or seizure of property or the arrest of any person shall be punished by imprisonment in the state prison or in the county jail for not exceeding one year.

(b) Nothing in this section shall prohibit disclosures made for the sole purpose of securing voluntary compliance with the warrant. (Amended by Stats 1986 ch 536 §1.)

§169. Repealed by Stats 1990 ch 216 §88, eff. 1/1/91.

§170. Maliciously procuring search warrant.

Every person who maliciously and without probable cause procures a search warrant or warrant of arrest to be issued and executed, is guilty of a misdemeanor.

§171. Interference with reformatories.

Every person, not authorized by law, who, without the permission of the officer in charge of any reformatory in this State, communicates with any person detained therein, or brings therein or takes therefrom any letter, writing, literature, or reading matter to or from any person confined therein, is guilty of a misdemeanor.

§171b. Possession of weapon in courtroom.

Any person, except a person who possesses or transports weapons to be used as evidence in a court of law, a duly appointed peace officer as defined in Chapter 4.5 (commencing with Section 830) of Title 3 of Part 2, a full-time paid peace officer of another state or the federal government who is carrying out official duties while in California, any person summoned by any such officer to assist in making arrests or preserving the peace while he or she is actually engaged in assisting the officer, a person holding a valid license to carry the firearm pursuant to Article 3 (commencing with Section 12050) of Chapter 1 of Title 2 of Part 4, or a person holding a valid tear gas weapon card pursuant to Section 12403.7 allowing that person to carry the tear gas, who brings or possesses, within any courtroom or building designated as a courthouse or court building in this state or at any meeting required to be open to the public pursuant to Chapter 9 (commencing with Section 54950) of Part 1 of Division 2 of Title 5 of, or Article 9 (commencing with Section 11120) of Chapter 1 of Part 1 of Division 3 of Title 2 of, the Government Code, any of the following, unless permission to possess that weapon is granted in writing by a duly authorized official or officials, is guilty of a public offense punishable by imprisonment in a county jail for not more than one year, or in the state prison:

(a) Any firearm.

(b) Any deadly weapon described in Section 653k or 12020.

(c) Any knife with a blade length in excess of four inches, the blade of which is fixed or is capable of being fixed in an unguarded position by the use of one or two hands.

(d) Any tear gas weapon, as defined in Sections 12401 and 12402.

(e) Any taser or stun gun, as defined in Section 244.5. *(Amended by Stats 1990 ch 350 §16, eff. 1/1/91.)*

§171c. Bringing loaded firearm in state capitol or state offices.

Any person, except a duly appointed peace officer as defined in Chapter 4.5 (commencing with Section 830) of Title 3 of Part 2, a full-time paid peace officer of another state or the federal government who is carrying out official duties while in California, any person summoned by any such officer to assist in making arrests or preserving the peace while he is actually engaged in assisting such officer, a member of the military forces of this state or the United States engaged in the performance of his duties, or a person holding a valid license to carry the firearm pursuant to Article 3 (commencing with Section 12050) of Chapter 1 of Title 2 of Part 4, who brings a loaded firearm into, or possesses a loaded firearm within, the State Capitol, any legislative office, any office of the Governor or other constitutional officer, or any hearing room in which any committee of the Senate or Assembly is conducting a hearing, or upon the grounds of the State Capitol, which is bounded by 10th, L, 15th, and N Streets in the City of Sacramento, shall be punished by imprisonment in the county jail for a period of not more than one year, a fine of not more than one thousand dollars ($1,000), or both such imprisonment and fine, or by imprisonment in the state prison.

§171d. Possession of loaded firearm in residence of elected official.

Any person, except a duly appointed peace officer as defined in Chapter 4.5 (commencing with Section 830) of Title 3 of Part 2, full-time paid peace officer of another state or the federal government who is carrying out official duties while in California, or any person summoned by any such officer to assist in making arrests or preserving the peace while he is actually engaged in assisting such officer, or a member of the military forces of this state or of the United States engaged in the performance of his duties, a person holding a valid license to carry the firearm pursuant to Article 3 (commencing with Section 12050) of Chapter 1 of Title 2 of Part 4 of the Penal Code, or the Governor or a member of his immediate family or a person acting with his permission with respect to the Governor's Mansion or any other residence of the Governor, any other constitutional officer or a member of his immediate family or a person acting with his permission with respect to such officer's residence, or a Member of the Legislature or a member of his immediate family or a person acting with his permission with respect to such legislator's residence, shall be punished by imprisonment in the county jail for not more than one year, or by fine of not more than one thousand dollars ($1,000), or by both such fine and

imprisonment, or by imprisonment in the state prison, if he does any of the following:

1. Brings a loaded firearm into, or possesses a loaded firearm within, the Governor's Mansion, or any other residence of the Governor, the residence of any other constitutional officer, or the residence of any Member of the Legislature.

2. Brings a loaded firearm upon, or possesses a loaded firearm upon, the grounds of the Governor's Mansion or any other residence of the Governor, the residence of any other constitutional officer, or the residence of any Member of the Legislature.

§171e. Loaded firearm defined.

A firearm shall be deemed loaded for the purposes of Sections 171c and 171d whenever both the firearm and unexpended ammunition capable of being discharged from such firearm are in the immediate possession of the same person.

In order to determine whether or not a firearm is loaded for the purpose of enforcing Section 171c or 171d, peace officers are authorized to examine any firearm carried by anyone on his person or in a vehicle while in any place or on the grounds of any place in or on which the possession of a loaded firearm is prohibited by Section 171c or 171d. Refusal to allow a peace officer to inspect a firearm pursuant to the provisions of this section constitutes probable cause for arrest for violation of Section 171c or 171d.

§171f. Unauthorized entry or conduct in State Capitol.

No person or group of persons shall willfully and knowingly:

1. Enter or remain within or upon any part of the chamber of either house of the Legislature unless authorized, pursuant to rules adopted or permission granted by either such house, to enter or remain within or upon a part of the chamber of either such house;

2. Engage in any conduct within the State Capitol which disrupts the orderly conduct of official business.

A violation of this section is a misdemeanor.

As used in this section, "State Capitol" means the building which is intended primarily for use of the legislative department and situated in the area bounded by 10th, L, 15th, and N Streets in the City of Sacramento.

Nothing in this section shall forbid any act of any Member of the Legislature, or any employee of a Member of the Legislature, any officer or employee of the Legislature or any committee or subcommittee thereof, or any officer or employee of either house of the Legislature or any committee or subcommittee thereof, which is performed in the lawful discharge of his official duties.

§172. Liquor sales near certain institutions.

(a) Every person who, within one-half mile of the land belonging to this state upon which any state prison, or within 1,900 feet of the land belonging to this state upon which any Youth Authority institution is situated, or within one mile of the grounds belonging to the University of California, at Berkeley, or within one mile of the grounds belonging to the University of California at Santa Barbara, as such grounds existed as of January 1, 1961, or within one mile of the grounds belonging to Fresno State College, as such grounds existed as of January 1, 1959, or within three

© 1992 by J., B. & L. Gould
Printed in the U.S.A.   EP

miles of the University Farm at Davis, or within 1½ miles of any building actually occupied as a home, retreat, or asylum for ex-soldiers, sailors, and marines of the Army and Navy of the United States, established or to be established by this state, or by the United States within this state, or within the State Capitol, or within the limits of the grounds adjacent and belonging thereto, sells or exposes for sale, any intoxicating liquor, is guilty of a misdemeanor, and upon conviction thereof shall be punished by a fine of not less than one hundred dollars ($100), or by imprisonment for not less than 50 days or by both such fine and imprisonment, in the discretion of the court.

(b) The provision of subdivision (a) of this section prohibiting the sale or exposure for sale of any intoxicating liquor within 1,900 feet of the land belonging to this state upon which any Youth Authority institution is situated shall not apply with respect to the Fred C. Nelles School for Boys.

(c) Except within the State Capitol or the limits of the grounds adjacent and belonging thereto, as mentioned in subdivision (a) of this section, the provisions of this section shall not apply to the sale or exposing or offering for sale of ale, porter, wine, similar fermented malt or vinous liquor or fruit juice containing one-half of 1 percent or more of alcohol by volume and not more than 3.2 percent of alcohol by weight nor the sale or exposing or offering for sale of beer.

(d) Distances provided in this section shall be measured not by airline but by following the shortest highway or highways as defined in Section 360 of the Vehicle Code connecting the points in question. In measuring distances from the Folsom State Prison and the eastern facilities of the California Institution for Men at Chino and Youth Training School, the measurement shall start at the entrance gate.

(e) The provision of subdivision (a) of this section prohibiting the sale or exposure for sale of any intoxicating liquor within 1½ miles of any building actually occupied as a home, retreat, or asylum for ex-soldiers, sailors, and marines of the Army and Navy of the United States shall not apply to the Veterans' Home at Yountville, Napa County, California.

§172a. Liquor sales near university.

Every person who, within one and one-half miles of the university grounds or campus, upon which are located the principal administrative offices of any university having an enrollment of more than 1,000 students, more than 500 of whom reside or lodge upon such university grounds or campus, sells or exposes for sale, any intoxicating liquor, is guilty of a misdemeanor; provided, however, that the provisions of this section shall not apply to nor prohibit the sale of any of said liquors by any regularly licensed pharmacist who shall maintain a fixed place of business in said territory, upon the written prescription of a physician regularly licensed to practice medicine under the laws of the State of California when such prescription is dated by the physician issuing it, contains the name of the person for whom the prescription is written, and is filled for such person only and within 48 hours of its date; provided further, that the provisions of this section shall not apply to nor prohibit the sale of any of said liquors for chemical or mechanical purposes; provided further, that the provisions of this section shall not apply to nor prohibit the sale or exposing or offering for sale of ale, porter, wine, similar fermented malt, or vinous liquor or fruit juice

containing one-half of 1 percent or more of alcohol by volume and not more than 3.2 percent of alcohol by weight nor the sale or exposing or offering for sale of beer.

In measuring distances from the university grounds or campus of any such university, such distances shall not be measured by airline but by following the shortest road or roads connecting the points in question. With respect to Leland Stanford Junior University measurements from the university grounds or campus shall be by airline measurement.

Any license issued and in effect in the City and County of San Francisco on the effective date of the amendment of this section enacted at the 1961 Regular Session of the Legislature may be transferred to any location in the City and County of San Francisco.

§172b. Liquor sales near UCLA campus.

1. Every person who, within one and one-half miles of the boundaries of the grounds belonging to the University of California at Los Angeles on which the principal administrative offices of the university are located, as such boundaries were established as of July 1, 1959, sells or exposes for sale any intoxicating liquor, is guilty of a misdemeanor, and upon conviction thereof shall be punished by a fine of not less than one hundred dollars ($100), or by imprisonment for not less than 50 days, or by both such fine and imprisonment, in the discretion of the court.

2. The provisions of this section shall not apply to the sale or exposing or offering for sale of ale, porter, wine, similar fermented malt or vinous liquor or fruit juice containing one-half of 1 percent or more of alcohol by volume and not more than 3.2 percent of alcohol by weight nor the sale or exposing or offering for sale of beer.

3. Distances provided in this section shall be measured not by airline but by following the shortest road or roads connecting the points in question.

§172c. Liquor sales at California Museum of Science and Industry.

The provisions of Section 172a shall not apply to the sale at auction of alcoholic beverages by a nonprofit organization at the California Museum of Science and Industry premises located at Exposition Park, Los Angeles, California.

§172d. Liquor sales near university; Riverside campus.

1. Every person who, within one mile of that portion of the grounds at Riverside (hereinafter described) belonging to the University of California, that will be used by the College of Letters and Sciences, sells, or exposes for sale, any intoxicating liquor, is guilty of a misdemeanor, and upon conviction thereof shall be punished by a fine of not less than one hundred dollars ($100), or by imprisonment for not less than 50 days or by both such fine and imprisonment in the discretion of the court.

2. The provisions of this section shall not apply to the sale or exposing or offering for sale of ale, porter, wine, similar fermented malt or vinous liquor or fruit juice containing one-half of 1 percent or more of alcohol by volume and not more than 3.2 percent of alcohol by weight nor the sale or exposing or offering for sale of beer.

3. Distances provided in this section shall be measured not by air line but by following the shortest vehicular road or roads connecting the points in question.

4. The portion of the grounds of the University of California referred to in paragraph 1 are situated in the County of Riverside and more particularly described as follows: beginning at the intersection of Canyon Crest Drive and U.S. Highway 60, thence southeasterly along said highway to a point opposite the intersection of said U.S. Highway 60 and Pennsylvania Avenue, thence northeasterly following centerline of present drive into University campus, thence continuing north along said centerline of drive on west side of Citrus Experiment Station buildings to a point intersecting the present east-west road running east from intersection of Canyon Crest Drive and U.S. Highway 60, thence east 500 feet more or less, thence north 1,300 feet more or less, thence east to intersection of east boundary of the Regents of the University of California property (Valencia Hill Drive), thence north along said east boundary to the north boundary of the Regents of the University of California property (Linden Street), thence west along said north boundary to the west boundary of the Regents of the University of California property (Canyon Crest Drive) thence south along said west boundary to the point of beginning.

§172e. Liquor sales near certain institutions.

The provisions of Sections 172, 172a, 172b, 172d, and 172g of this code shall not apply to the sale or the exposing or offering for sale of alcoholic beverages by an on-sale licensee under the Alcoholic Beverage Control Act within premises licensed as a bona fide public eating place as provided in the Constitution and as defined in the Alcoholic Beverage Control Act (commencing at Section 23000, Business and Professions Code), or within premises licensed as a club as defined in Articles 4 and 5 of Chapter 3 of the Alcoholic Beverage Control Act, provided that such club shall have been in existence for not less than 5 years, have a membership of 300 or more, and serves meals daily to its members, or by the holder of a caterer's permit under the provisions of Section 23399 of the Business and Professions Code in connection with the serving of bona fide meals as defined in Section 23038 of the Business and Professions Code, and the provisions of such sections shall not be construed so as to preclude the Department of Alcoholic Beverage Control from issuing licenses for bona fide public eating places within the areas prescribed by the sections. The provisions of this section shall not permit the issuance of licenses to fraternities, sororities, or other student organizations.

§172f. Inapplicability of provisions to liquor sales in certain existing licensed premises.

The provisions of Sections 172, 172a, 172b, 172d, and 172g of this code shall not apply to the sale or the exposing or offering for sale of any intoxicating liquor in any premises within the areas prescribed by said sections for which a license was issued under the Alcoholic Beverage Control Act (Division 9 (commencing with Section 23000), Business and Professions Code) and is in effect on the effective date of this section or on the effective date of any amendment to Section 172g specifying an additional institution, or in any licensed premises which may become included in

such a prescribed area because of the extension of the boundaries of any of the institutions mentioned in said sections or because of the increased enrollment or number of resident students at any of such institutions.

Any such licenses may be transferred from person to person, and may be transferred from premises to premises if the premises to which the license is transferred are not located nearer to the boundaries of the institution, as they exist on the date of the transfer, than the premises from which the license is transferred, except that such license may be transferred once from premises to premises located nearer by not more than 300 feet to the boundaries of the institution as they exist on the date of transfer than the premises from which the license is transferred. If a license is transferred pursuant to this section from premises to premises located nearer by not more than 300 feet to the boundaries of the institution as they exist on the date of the transfer than the premises from which the license is transferred, such license shall not be thereafter transferred to any other premises located nearer to the boundaries of the institution as they exist on the date of the transfer than the premises from which the license is transferred.

§172g. Liquor sales near La Sierra College, Loma Linda University, or University of Santa Clara.

1. Every person who, within one mile by air line from the intersection of Sierra Vista, Pierce, and Campus Drive streets at the entrance to La Sierra College in the City of Riverside, or within one mile of the grounds or campus of Loma Linda University in the County of San Bernardino, or within one mile of the grounds of the University of Santa Clara in the City of Santa Clara, sells, or exposes for sale, any intoxicating liquor, is guilty of a misdemeanor, and upon conviction thereof shall be punished by a fine of not less than one hundred dollars ($100), or by imprisonment in the county jail of not less than 50 days nor more than one year, or by both such fine and imprisonment in the discretion of the court.

2. The provisions of this section shall not apply to the sale or exposing or offering for sale of ale, porter, wine, similar fermented malt or vinous liquor or fruit juice containing one-half of 1 percent or more of alcohol by volume and not more than 3.2 percent of alcohol by weight nor the sale or exposing or offering for sale of beer.

3. Distances provided in this section shall be measured not by air line but by following the shortest road or roads connecting the points in question except those applying to La Sierra College.

§172h. Liquor sales exception for subsequent dormitory construction.

The provisions of Sections 172, 172a, 172b, 172d and 172g of this code shall not be applied to prohibit the sale or the exposing or offering for sale of any intoxicating liquor in, or the issuance of an alcoholic beverage license for, any premises because a university has constructed and occupied since January 1, 1960, or in the future constructs, dormitories for its students which has resulted or results in the premises being prohibited by the foregoing sections from selling, exposing or offering such liquor for sale because the premises are or become thereby within the area prescribed by these sections.

© 1992 by J., B. & L. Gould
Printed in the U.S.A.   EP

§172j. Liquor sales exception for off-sale licensees.

The provisions of Sections 172, 172a, 172b, 172d, and 172g shall not apply to the sale or exposing for sale of any intoxicating liquor on the premises of, and by the holder or agent of, a holder of a retail package off-sale general license or retail package off-sale beer and wine license issued under the Alcoholic Beverage Control Act (Division 9 (commencing with Section 23000), Business and Professions Code).

§172l. Liquor sales near Claremont Colleges.

The provisions of Section 172a shall not apply to the sale or offering for sale of any intoxicating liquor on the premises of, and by the holder or agent of a holder of, a retail off-sale license, as defined in Section 23394 of the Business and Professions Code, outside one mile of the closest building of the Claremont Colleges to these premises; nor shall the provisions of Section 172a apply to the sale or offering for sale of any beer, or wine, or both, on the premises of, and by the holder or agent of a holder of, a retail package off-sale beer and wine license, as defined in Section 23393 of the Business and Professions Code, outside 2,000 feet of the closest building of the Claremont Colleges to these premises.

Distance provided in this section shall be measured not by air line but by following the shortest road or roads connecting the points in question.

§172m. Liquor sales near Leland Stanford Junior University.

The provisions of Section 172a shall not apply to the sale or the exposing or offering for sale of alcoholic beverages at premises licensed under any type of on-sale license issued pursuant to Division 9 (commencing with Section 23000) of the Business and Professions Code, which premises are located off of the grounds or campus of Leland Stanford Junior University near the City of Palo Alto.

§172n. Liquor sales near UCLA campus.

The provisions of Sections 172a and 172b shall not apply to the sale or exposing or offering for sale of alcoholic beverages by any off-sale licensee under the Alcoholic Beverage Control Act situated more than 2,000 feet from the boundaries of the grounds belonging to the University of California at Los Angeles on which the principal administrative offices of the university are located, as such boundaries were established as of July 1, 1959, provided the licensee has conducted a retail grocery business and has held an off-sale beer and wine license at the same location for at least 15 years.

Distances provided in this section shall be measured not by airline but by following the shortest road or road connecting the points in question.

§172o. Wine sales for off-premises consumption.

The provisions of Sections 172, 172a, 172b, 172d, and 172g shall not apply to the sale of wine for consumption off the premises where sold when the wine is sold at a bona fide public eating place by the holder of an on-sale general alcoholic beverage license or an on-sale beer and wine license issued under the Alcoholic Beverage Control Act (Division 9 (commencing with Section 23000) of the Business and Professions Code). *(Added by Stats 1985 ch 267 §1.)*

§172.1. Wine possession on college premises.

No provision of law shall prevent the possession or use of wine on any state university, state college or community college premises solely for use in experimentation in or instruction of viticulture, enology, domestic science or home economics.

§172.3. Liquor sales near University of Redlands.

The provisions of Section 172a shall not apply to the sale or exposing or offering for sale of any alcoholic beverages on the premises of, and by the holder or agent of a holder of, any off-sale license situated within 1½ miles from the grounds of the University of Redlands.

§172.5. Liquor sales near university; Berkeley campus.

The provisions of Sections 172 and 172a of this code shall not apply to the sale or exposing or offering for sale of alcoholic beverages by a licensee under the Alcoholic Beverage Control Act within the premises occupied by any bona fide club which is situated within one mile of the grounds belonging to the University of California at Berkeley, if the club meets all of the following requirements:

(a) The membership in the club shall be limited to male American citizens over the age of 21 years.

(b) The club shall have been organized and have existed in the City of Berkeley for not less than 35 years continuously.

(c) The club shall have a bona fide membership of not less than 500 members.

(d) The premises occupied by the club are owned by the club, or by a corporation, at least 75 percent of whose capital stock is owned by the club, and have a value of not less than one hundred thousand dollars ($100,000).

§172.6. Liquor sales or gifts near San Quentin Prison.

The provisions of Section 172 of this code shall not apply to the sale, gift, or exposing or offering for sale of alcoholic beverages by a licensee under the Alcoholic Beverage Control Act within the premises occupied by any bona fide club which is situated within 2,000 feet of San Quentin Prison in Marin County, provided the club meets all the following requirements:

(a) The club shall have been organized and have existed in the County of Marin for not less than 25 years continuously.

(b) The club shall have a bona fide membership of not less than 1,000 persons.

(c) The premises occupied by the club are owned by the club or by club members.

§172.7. Liquor sales near Whittier College or Leland Stanford Junior University.

The provisions of Section 172a shall not apply to the sale, gift, or exposing or offering for sale of alcoholic beverages by a licensee under the Alcoholic Beverage Control Act within the premises occupied by any bona fide club which is situated within one mile of the campus of Whittier College in the City of Whittier, or one mile or more from the campus of Leland Stanford Junior University near the City of Palo Alto, provided the club meets all the following requirements:

(a) The club shall have been organized and have existed for not less than 10 years continuously.

(b) The club shall have a bona fide membership of not less than 350 persons.

(c) The club shall own the building which it occupies.

§172.8. Liquor sales near California Institute of Technology.

The provisions of Section 172a shall not apply to the sale of alcoholic beverages for consumption on the premises, by a nonprofit organization at a municipally owned conference center located more than one but less than 1½ miles from the California Institute of Technology in Pasadena.

§172.9. University defined.

The word "university," when used in this chapter with reference to the sale, exposing or offering for sale, of alcoholic beverages, means an institution which has the authority to grant an academic graduate degree.

§172.95. Liquor sales to wholesalers or retailers.

Sections 172 to 172.9, inclusive, do not apply to sales to wholesalers or retailers by licensed wine-growers, brandy manufacturers, beer manufacturers, distilled spirits manufacturers' agents, distilled spirits manufacturers, or wholesalers.

§173. Importing foreign convicts.

Every captain, master of a vessel, or other person, who willfully imports, brings, or sends, or causes or procures to be brought or sent, into this state, any person who is a foreign convict of any crime which, if committed within this state, would be punishable therein (treason and misprision of treason excepted), or who is delivered or sent to him from any prison or place of confinement in any place without this state, is guilty of a misdemeanor.

§175. Importing foreign convicts; separate prosecution.

Every individual person of the classes referred to in Section 173, brought to or landed within this state contrary to the provisions of such section, renders the person bringing or landing liable to a separate prosecution and penalty.

§177. Offenses punishable as misdemeanors.

When an act or omission is declared by a statute to be a public offense, and no penalty for the offense is prescribed in any statute, the act or omission is punishable as a misdemeanor. (*Amended by Stats 1989 ch 897 §14, 1360 §105, eff. 1/1/90.*)

§181. Slavery.

Every person who holds, or attempts to hold, any person in involuntary servitude, or assumes, or attempts to assume, rights of ownership over any person, or who sells, or attempts to sell, any person to another, or receives money or anything of value, in consideration of placing any person in the custody, or under the power or control of another, or who buys, or attempts to buy, any person, or pays money, or delivers anything of value, to another, in consideration of having any person placed in his custody, or under his power or control, or who knowingly aids or assists in any manner any one thus offending, is punishable by imprisonment in the state prison for two, three or four years.

CHAPTER 8

CONSPIRACY

§182. Criminal conspiracy.

(a) If two or more persons conspire:

(1) To commit any crime.

(2) Falsely and maliciously to indict another for any crime, or to procure another to be charged or arrested for any crime.

(3) Falsely to move or maintain any suit, action or proceeding.

(4) To cheat and defraud any person of any property, by any means which are in themselves criminal, or to obtain money or property by false pretenses or by false promises with fraudulent intent not to perform such promises.

(5) To commit any act injurious to the public health, to public morals, or to pervert or obstruct justice, or the due administration of the laws.

(6) To commit any crime against the person of the President or Vice President of the United States, the governor of any state or territory, any United States justice or judge, or the secretary of any of the executive departments of the United States.

They are punishable as follows:

When they conspire to commit any crime against the person of any official specified in paragraph (6), they are guilty of a felony and are punishable by imprisonment in the state prison for five, seven, or nine years.

When they conspire to commit any other felony, they shall lie punishable in the same manner and to the same extent as is provided for the punishment of the that* felony. If the felony is one for which different punishments are prescribed for different degrees, the jury or court which finds the defendant guilty, thereof shall determine the degree of the felony defendant conspired to commit. If the degree is not so determined, the punishment for conspiracy to commit the felony shall be that prescribed for the lesser degree, except in the case of conspiracy to commit murder, in which case the punishment shall be that prescribed for murder in the first degree.

So in original.

If the felony is conspiracy to commit two or more felonies which have different punishments and the commission of those felonies constitute but one offense of conspiracy, the penalty shall be that prescribed for the felony which has the greater maximum term.

When they conspire to do an act described in paragraph (4), they shall be punishable by imprisonment in the state prison, or by imprisonment in the county jail for not more than one year, or by a fine not exceeding ten thousand dollars ($10,000), or both.

When they conspire to do any of the other acts described in this section, they shall be punishable by imprisonment in the county jail for not more than one year, or in the state prison, or by a fine not exceeding ten thousand dollars ($10,000) or both.

All cases of conspiracy may be prosecuted and tried in the superior court of any county in which any overt act tending to effect such conspiracy shall be done.

(b) Upon a trial for conspiracy, in a case where an overt act is necessary to constitute the offense, the defendant cannot be convicted unless one or more overt acts are expressly alleged in the indictment or information, nor unless one of the acts alleged is proved; but other overt acts not alleged may be given

© 1992 by J., B. & L. Gould
Printed in the U.S.A.   **EP**

in evidence. *(Amended by Stats 1989 ch 897 §15, eff. 1/1/90.)*

§183. No other conspiracies punishable criminally.

No conspiracies, other than those enumerated in the preceding section, are punishable criminally.

§184. Overt act necessary.

No agreement amounts to a conspiracy, unless some act, beside such agreement, be done within this state to effect the object thereof, by one or more of the parties to such agreement and the trial of cases of conspiracy may be had in any county in which any such act be done.

§185. Wearing disguise or mask for evasion.

It shall be unlawful for any person to wear any mask, false whiskers, or any personal disguise (whether complete or partial) for the purpose of:

One. Evading or escaping discovery, recognition, or identification in the commission of any public offense.

Two. Concealment, flight, or escape, when charged with, arrested for, or convicted of, any public offense. Any person violating any of the provisions of this section shall be deemed guilty of a misdemeanor.

CHAPTER 9

CRIMINAL PROFITEERING

§186. Title.

This act may be cited as the "California Control of Profits of Organized Crime Act."

§186.1. Legislative intent.

The Legislature hereby finds and declares that an effective means of punishing and deterring criminal activities of organized crime is through the forfeiture of profits acquired and accumulated as a result of such criminal activities. It is the intent of the Legislature that the "California Control of Profits of Organized Crime Act" be used by prosecutors to punish and deter only such activities.

§186.2. Definitions.

For purposes of the application of this chapter, the following definitions shall govern:

(a) "Criminal profiteering activity" means any act committed or attempted or any threat made for financial gain or advantage, which act or threat may be charged as a crime under any of the following sections:

(1) Arson, as defined in Section 451.

(2) Bribery, as defined in Sections 67, 67.5, and 68.

(3) Child pornography or exploitation, as defined in subdivision (b) of Section 311.2, or Section 311.3 or 311.4, which may be prosecuted as a felony.

(4) Felonious assault, as defined in Section 245.

(5) Embezzlement, as defined in Sections 424 and 503.

(6) Extortion, as defined in Section 518.

(7) Forgery, as defined in Section 470.

(8) Gambling, as defined in Sections 337a to 337f, inclusive, and Section 337i, except the activities of a person who participates solely as an individual bettor.

(9) Kidnapping, as defined in Section 207.

(10) Mayhem, as defined in Section 203.

(11) Murder, as defined in Section 187.

(12) Pimping and pandering, as defined in Section 266.

(13) Receiving stolen property, as defined in Section 496.

(14) Robbery, as defined in Section 211.

(15) Solicitation of crimes, as defined in Section 653f.

(16) Grand theft, as defined in Section 487.

(17) Theft or taking of any motor vehicle, trailer, or vessel as described in Section 487h of this code or any vehicle as described in Section 10851 of the Vehicle Code.

(18) Trafficking in controlled substances, as defined in Sections 11351, 11352, and 11353 of the Health and Safety Code.

(19) Violation of the laws governing corporate securities, as defined in Section 25541 of the Corporations Code.

(20) Any of the offenses contained in Chapter 7.5 (commencing with Section 311) of Title 9, relating to obscene matter, or in Chapter 7.6 (commencing with Section 313) of Title 9, relating to harmful matter which may be prosecuted as a felony.

(21) Presentation of a false or fraudulent claim, as defined in Section 556 of the Insurance Code.

(22) Money laundering, as defined in Section 186.10.

(23) Conspiracy to commit any of the crimes listed above, as defined in Section 182.

(b) "Pattern of criminal profiteering activity" means engaging in at least two incidents of criminal profiteering, as defined by this act, which meet the following requirements:

(1) Have the same or a similar purpose, result, principals, victims or methods of commission, or are otherwise interrelated by distinguishing characteristics.

(2) Are not isolated events.

(3) Were committed as a criminal activity of organized crime.

Acts which would constitute a "pattern of criminal profiteering activity" may not be used by a prosecuting agency to seek the remedies provided by this chapter unless the underlying offense occurred after the effective date of this chapter and the prior act occurred within 10 years, excluding any period of imprisonment, of the commission of the underlying offense. A prior act may not be used by a prosecuting agency to seek remedies provided by this chapter if a prosecution for that act resulted in an acquittal.

(c) "Prosecuting agency" means the Attorney General or the district attorney of any county.

(d) "Organized crime" means crime which is of a conspiratorial and (1) organized nature and which seeks to supply illegal goods and services such as narcotics, prostitution, loan sharking, gambling, and pornography or, (2) through planning and coordination of individual efforts, to conduct the illegal activities of arson for profit, hijacking, insurance fraud, smuggling, operating vehicle theft rings, or systematically encumbering the assets of a business for the purpose of defrauding creditors.

(e) "Underlying offense" means an offense enumerated in subdivision (a) for which the defendant is being prosecuted.

(f) This section shall remain in effect only until January 1, 1993, and as of that date is repealed, unless a later enacted statute, which is enacted before January 1, 1993, deletes or extends that date. *(Amended by Stats 1991 ch 1049 §2, eff. 1/1/92 only until 1/1/93. See other section 186.2 below.)*

§186.2. Definitions.

For purposes of the application of this chapter, the following definitions shall govern:

(a) "Criminal profiteering activity" means any act committed or attempted or any threat made for financial gain or advantage, which act or threat may be charged as a crime under any of the following sections:

(1) Arson, as defined in Section 451.

(2) Bribery, as defined in Sections 67, 67.5, and 68.

(3) Child pornography or exploitation, as defined in subdivision (b) of Section 311.2, or Section 311.3 or 311.4, which may be prosecuted as a felony.

(4) Felonious assault, as defined in Section 245.

(5) Embezzlement, as defined in Sections 424 and 503.

(6) Extortion, as defined in Section 518.

(7) Forgery, as defined in Section 470.

(8) Gambling, as defined in Sections 337a to 337f, inclusive, and Section 337i, except the activities of a person who participates solely as an individual bettor.

(9) Kidnapping, as defined in Section 207.

(10) Mayhem, as defined in Section 203.

(11) Murder, as defined in Section 187.

(12) Pimping and pandering, as defined in Section 266.

(13) Receiving stolen property, as defined in Section 496.

(14) Robbery, as defined in Section 211.

(15) Solicitation of crimes, as defined in Section 653f.

(16) Grand theft, as defined in Section 487.

(17) Trafficking in controlled substances, as defined in Sections 11351, 11352, and 11353 of the Health and Safety Code.

(18) Violation of the laws governing corporate securities, as defined in Section 25541 of the Corporations Code.

(19) Any of the offenses contained in Chapter 7.5 (commencing with Section 311) of Title 9, relating to obscene matter, or in Chapter 7.6 (commencing with Section 313) of Title 9, relating to harmful matter which may be prosecuted as a felony.

(20) Presentation of a false or fraudulent claim, as defined in Section 556 of the Insurance Code.

(21) Money laundering, as defined in Section 186.10.

(22) Conspiracy to commit any of the crimes listed above, as defined in Section 182.

(b) "Pattern of criminal profiteering activity" means engaging in at least two incidents of criminal profiteering, as defined by this act, which meet the following requirements:

(1) Have the same or a similar purpose, result, principals, victims or methods of commission, or are otherwise interrelated by distinguishing characteristics.

(2) Are not isolated events.

(3) Were committed as a criminal activity of organized crime.

Acts which would constitute a "pattern of criminal profiteering activity" may not be used by a prosecuting agency to seek the remedies provided by this chapter unless the underlying offense occurred after the effective date of this chapter and the prior act occurred within 10 years, excluding any period of imprisonment, of the commission of the underlying offense. A prior act may not be used by a prosecuting agency to seek remedies provided by this chapter if a prosecution for that act resulted in an acquittal.

(c) "Prosecuting agency" means the Attorney General or the district attorney of any county.

(d) "Organized crime" means crime which is of a conspiratorial and (1) organized nature and which seeks to supply illegal goods and services such as narcotics, prostitution, loan sharking, gambling, and pornography or, (2) through planning and coordination of individual efforts, to conduct the illegal activities of arson for profit, hijacking, insurance fraud, smuggling, operating vehicle theft rings, or systematically encumbering the assets of a business for the purpose of defrauding creditors.

(e) "Underlying offense" means an offense enumerated in subdivision (a) for which the defendant is being prosecuted.

This section shall become operative on January 1, 1993. *(Amended by Stats 1991 ch 1049 §3, eff. 1/1/92, oper. 1/1/93. See other section 186.2 above.)*

§186.3. Criminal profiteering.

(a) In any case in which a person is alleged to have been engaged in a pattern of criminal profiteering activity, upon a conviction of the underlying offense, the assets listed in subdivisions (b) and (c) shall be subject to forfeiture upon proof of the provisions of subdivision (d) of Section 186.5.

(b) Any property interest whether tangible or intangible, acquired through a pattern of criminal profiteering activity.

(c) All proceeds of a pattern of criminal profiteering activity, which property shall include all things of value that may have been received in exchange for the proceeds immediately derived from the pattern of criminal profiteering activity.

§186.4. Petition of forfeiture.

(a) The prosecuting agency shall, in conjunction with the criminal proceeding, file a petition of forfeiture with the superior court of the county in which the defendant has been charged with the underlying criminal offense, which shall allege that the defendant has engaged in a pattern of criminal profiteering activity, including the acts or threats chargeable as crimes and the property forfeitable pursuant to Section 186.3. The prosecuting agency shall make service of process of a notice regarding that petition upon every individual who may have a property interest in the alleged proceeds, which notice shall state that any interested party may file a verified claim with the superior court stating the amount of their claimed interest and an affirmation or denial of the prosecuting agency's allegation. If the notices cannot be given by registered mail or personal delivery, the notices shall be published for at least three successive weeks in a newspaper of general circulation in the county where the property is located. If the property alleged to be subject to forfeiture is real property, the prosecuting agency shall, at the time of filing the petition of forfeiture, record a lis pendens in each county in which the real property is situated which specifically identifies the real property alleged to be subject to forfeiture. The judgment of forfeiture shall not affect the interest in real property of any third party which was acquired prior to the recording of the lis pendens.

(b) All notices shall set forth the time within which a claim of interest in the property seized is required to be filed pursuant to Section 186.5.

© 1992 by J., B. & L. Gould
Printed in the U.S.A.   **EP**

§186.5. Claims to forfeited property.

(a) Any person claiming an interest in the property or proceeds may, at any time within 30 days from the date of the first publication of the notice of seizure, or within 30 days after receipt of actual notice, file with the superior court of the county in which the action is pending a verified claim stating his or her interest in the property or proceeds. A verified copy of the claim shall be given by the claimant to the Attorney General or district attorney, as appropriate.

(b) (1) If, at the end of the time set forth in subdivision (a), an interested person, other than the defendant, has not filed a claim, the court, upon motion, shall declare that the person has defaulted upon his or her alleged interest, and it shall be subject to forfeiture upon proof of the provisions of subdivision (d).

(2) The defendant may admit or deny that the property is subject to forfeiture pursuant to the provisions of this chapter. If the defendant fails to admit or deny or to file a claim of interest in the property or proceeds, the court shall enter a response of denial on behalf of the defendant.

(c) (1) The forfeiture proceeding shall be set for hearing in the superior court in which the underlying criminal offense will be tried.

(2) If the defendant is found guilty of the underlying offense, the issue of forfeiture shall be promptly tried, either before the same jury or before a new jury in the discretion of the court, unless waived by the consent of all parties.

(d) At the forfeiture hearing, the prosecuting agency shall have the burden of establishing beyond a reasonable doubt that the defendant was engaged in a pattern of criminal profiteering activity and that the property alleged in the petition comes within the provisions of subdivision (b) or (c) of Section 186.3.

§186.6. Pendente lite orders.

(a) Concurrent with, or subsequent to, the filing of the petition, the prosecuting agency may move the superior court for the following pendente lite orders to preserve the status quo of the property alleged in the petition of forfeiture:

(1) An injunction to restrain all interested parties and enjoin them from transferring, encumbering, hypothecating or otherwise disposing of that property.

(2) Appointment of a receiver to take possession of, care for, manage, and operate the assets and properties so that such property may be maintained and preserved.

(b) No preliminary injunction may be granted or receiver appointed without notice to the interested parties and a hearing to determine that such an order is necessary to preserve the property, pending the outcome of the criminal proceedings, and that there is probable cause to believe that the property alleged in the forfeiture proceedings are proceeds or property interests forfeitable under Section 186.3. However, a temporary restraining order may issue pending that hearing pursuant to the provisions of Section 527 of the Code of Civil Procedure.

(c) Notwithstanding any other provision of law, the court in granting these motions may order a surety bond or undertaking to preserve the property interests of the interested parties.

(d) The court shall, in making its orders, seek to protect the interests of those who may be involved in the same enterprise as the defendant, but who were not involved in the commission of the criminal profiteering activity.

§186.7. Determining forfeiture petition.

(a) If the trier of fact at the forfeiture hearing finds that the alleged property or proceeds is forfeitable pursuant to Section 186.3 and the defendant was engaged in a pattern of criminal profiteering activity, the court shall declare that property or proceeds forfeited to the state or local governmental entity, subject to distribution as provided in Section 186.8. No property solely owned by a bona fide purchaser for value shall be subject to forfeiture.

(b) If the trier of fact at the forfeiture hearing finds that the alleged property is forfeitable pursuant to Section 186.3 but does not find that a person holding a valid lien, mortgage, security interest, or interest under a conditional sales contract acquired that interest with actual knowledge that the property was to be used for a purpose for which forfeiture is permitted, and the amount due to that person is less than the appraised value of the property, that person may pay to the state or the local governmental entity which initiated the forfeiture proceeding, the amount of the registered owner's equity, which shall be deemed to be the difference between the appraised value and the amount of the lien mortgage, security interest, or interest under a conditional sales contract. Upon that payment, the state or local governmental entity shall relinquish all claims to the property. If the holder of the interest elects not to make that payment to the state or local governmental entity, the property shall be deemed forfeited to the state or local governmental entity and the ownership certificate shall be forwarded. The appraised value shall be determined as of the date judgment is entered either by agreement between the legal owner and the governmental entity involved, or if they cannot agree, then by a court-appointed appraiser for the county in which the action is brought. A person holding a valid lien, mortgage, security interest, or interest under a conditional sales contract shall be paid the appraised value of his or her interest.

(c) If the amount due to a person holding a valid lien, mortgage, security interest, or interest under a conditional sales contract is less than the value of the property and the person elects not to make payment to the governmental entity, the property shall be sold at public auction by the Department of General Services or by the local governmental entity which shall provide notice of that sale by one publication in a newspaper published and or circulated in the city, community, or locality where the sale is to take place.

§186.8. Distribution of proceeds from forfeiture sale.

Notwithstanding that no response or claim has been filed pursuant to Section 186.5, in all cases where property is forfeited pursuant to this chapter and, where necessary, sold by the Department of General Services or local governmental entity, the money forfeited or the proceeds of sale shall be distributed by the state or local governmental entity as follows:

(a) To the bona fide or innocent purchaser, conditional sales vendor, or holder of a valid lien, mortgage or security interest, if any, up to the amount of his or her interest in the property or proceeds, when the court declaring the forfeiture orders a distribution to that person. The court shall endeavor to discover all such lienholders and protect their interests and may, at its discretion, order the proceeds placed in escrow for up to an additional 60 days to ensure that all valid claims are received and processed.

(b) To the Department of General Services or local governmental entity for all expenditures made or incurred by it in connection with the sale of the property, including expenditures for any necessary repairs, storage, or transportation of any property seized under this chapter.

(c) To the general fund of the state or local governmental entity, whichever prosecutes.

(d) In any case involving a violation of subdivision (b) of Section 311.2, or Section 311.3 or 311.4, in lieu of the distribution of the proceeds provided for by subdivisions (b) and (c), the proceeds shall be deposited in the county children's trust fund, established pursuant to Section 18966 of the Welfare and Institutions Code, of the county which filed the petition of forfeiture. If the county does not have a children's trust fund, the funds shall be deposited in the State Children's Trust Fund, established pursuant to section 18969 of the Welfare and Institutions Code. *(Amended by Stats 1985 ch 1099 §3.)*

CHAPTER 10

MONEY LAUNDERING
(Added by Stats 1986 ch 1039 §2, eff. only until 1/1/97.)

§186.9. Terms defined.

As used in this chapter:

(a) "Conducts" includes, but is not limited to, initiating, concluding, or participating in conducting, initiating, or concluding a transaction.

(b) "Financial institution" means, when located or doing business in this state, any national bank or banking association, state bank or banking association, commercial bank or trust company organized under the laws of the United States or any state, any private bank, industrial savings bank, savings bank or thrift institution, savings and loan association, or building and loan association organized under the laws of the United States or any state, any insured institution as defined in Section 401 of the National Housing Act (12 U.S.C. Sec. 1724(a)), any credit union organized under the laws of the United States or any state, any national banking association or corporation acting under Chapter 6 (commencing with Section 601) of Title 12 of the United States Code, any agency, agent or branch of a foreign bank, any currency dealer or exchange, any person or business engaged primarialy in the cashing of checks, any person or business who regularly engages in the issuing, selling or redeeming of traveler's checks, money orders, or similar instruments, any broker or dealer in securities registered or required to be registered with the Securities and Exchange Commission under the Securities Exchange Act of 1934 or with the Commissioner of Corporations under Part 3 (commencing with Section 25200) of Division 1 of Title 4 of the Corporations Code, any licensed transmitter of funds or other person or business regularly engaged in transmitting funds to a foreign nation for others, any investment banker or investment company, any insurer, any dealer in gold, silver, or platinum bullion or coins, diamonds, emeralds, rubies, or sapphires, any pawnbroker, any telegraph company, any personal property broker, any person or business acting as a real property securities

dealer within the meaning of Section 10237 of the Business and Professions Code, whether licensed to do so or not, any person or business acting within the meaning and scope of subdivisions (d) and (e) of Section 10131 and Section 10131.1 of the Business and Professions Code, whether licensed to do so or not, and any person or business defined as a "bank," "financial agency," or "financial institution" by Section 5312 of Title 31 of the United States Code and Section 103.11 of Title 31 of the Code of Federal Regulations and any successor provisions thereto.

(c) "Transaction" includes the deposit, withdrawal, transfer, bailment, loan, pledge, payment, or exchange of currency, or a monetary instrument, as defined by subdivision (d), by, through, or to, a financial institution as defined by subdivision (b).

(d) "Monetary instrument" means United States currency and coin; the currency and coin of any foreign country; any bank check, cashier's check, traveler's check, money order, stock, investment security, or negotiable instrument in bearer form or otherwise in such form that title thereto passes upon delivery; gold, silver, or platinum bullion or coins; and diamonds, emeralds, rubies, or sapphires. "Monetary instrument" does not include bank checks, cashier's checks, traveler's checks, or money orders made payable to the order of a named party which have not been endorsed or which bear restrictive endorsements.

(e) "Criminal activity" means a criminal offense punishable under the laws of this state by death or imprisonment in the state prison or from a criminal offense committed in another jurisdiction punishable under the laws of that jurisdiction by death or imprisonment for a term exceeding one year. *(Amended by Stats 1987 ch 828 §7.5, eff. only until 1/1/97.)*

§186.10. Money laundering.

(a) Any person who conducts or attempts to conduct a transaction involving a monetary instrument or instruments of a value exceeding five thousand dollars ($5,000) through a financial institution (1) with the intent to promote, manage, establish, carry on, or facilitate the promotion, management, establishment, or carrying on of any criminal activity, or (2) knowing that the monetary instrument represents the proceeds of, or is derived directly or indirectly from the proceeds of, criminal activity, is guilty of the crime of money laundering. In consideration of the constitutional right to counsel afforded by the Sixth Amendment to the United States Constitution and Section 15 of Article 1 of the California Constitution, when a case involves an attorney who accepts a fee for representing a client in a criminal investigation or proceeding, the prosecution shall additionally be required to prove that the monetary instrument was accepted by the attorney with the intent to disguise or aid in disguising the source of the funds or the nature of the criminal activity.

A violation of this section shall be punished by imprisonment in the county jail for not more than one year or in the state prison, by a fine of not more than two hundred fifty thousand dollars ($250,000) or twice the value of the property transacted, whichever is greater, or by both that imprisonment and fine. However, for a second or subsequent conviction for a violation of this section, the maximum fine that may be imposed is five hundred thousand dollars ($500,000) or five times the value of the property transacted, whichever is greater.

© 1992 by J., B. & L. Gould
Printed in the U.S.A.   EP

(b) Notwithstanding any other provision of law, for purposes of this section, each individual transaction conducted shall constitute a separate, punishable offense.

(c) This chapter shall remain in effect until January 1, 1997, and as of that date is repealed. *(Amended by Stats 1991 ch 1049 §4, eff. 1/1/92 only until 1/1/97.)*

CHAPTER 11

STREET TERRORISM ENFORCEMENT AND PREVENTION ACT
(Added by Stats 1988 ch 1242 §1, 1256 §1, eff. 9/23/88 only until 1/1/97.)

§186.20. Title.
This chapter shall be known and may be cited as the "California Street Terrorism Enforcement and Prevention Act." *(Added by Stats 1988 ch 1242 §1, 1256 §1, eff. 9/23/88 only until 1/1/97.)*

§186.21. Legislative findings.
The Legislature hereby finds and declares that it is the right of every person, regardless of race, color, creed, religion, national origin, sex, age, sexual orientation, or handicap, to be secure and protected from fear, intimidation, and physical harm caused by the activities of violent groups and individuals. It is not the intent of this chapter to interfere with the exercise of the constitutionally protected rights of freedom of expression and association. The Legislature hereby recognizes the constitutional right of every citizen to harbor and express beliefs on any lawful subject whatsoever, to lawfully associate with others who share similar beliefs, to petition lawfully constituted authority for a redress of perceived grievances, and to participate in the electoral process.

The Legislature, however, further finds that the State of California is in a state of crisis which has been caused by violent street gangs whose members threaten, terrorize, and commit a multitude of crimes against the peaceful citizens of their neighborhoods. These activities, both individually and collectively, present a clear and present danger to public order and safety and are not constitutionally protected. The Legislature finds that there are nearly 600 criminal street gangs operating in California, and that the number of gang-related murders is increasing. The Legislature also finds that in Los Angeles County alone there were 328 gang-related murders in 1986, and that gang homicides in 1987 have increased 80 percent over 1986. It is the intent of the Legislature in enacting this chapter to seek the eradication of criminal activity by street gangs by focusing upon patterns of criminal gang activity and upon the organized nature of street gangs, which together, are the chief source of terror created by street gangs. The Legislature further finds that an effective means of punishing and deterring the criminal activities of street gangs is through forfeiture of the profits, proceeds, and instrumentalities acquired, accumulated, or used by street gangs. *(Added by Stats 1988 ch 1242 §1, 1256 §1, eff. 9/23/88 only until 1/1/97.)*

§186.22. Participating in a criminal street gang.
(a) Any person who actively participates in any criminal street gang with knowledge that its members engage in or have engaged in a pattern of criminal gang activity, and who willfully promotes, furthers, or assists in any felonious criminal conduct by members of that gang, shall be punished by imprisonment in the county jail for a period not to exceed one year, or by imprisonment in the state prison for one, two, or three years.

(b) (1) Except as provided in paragraph (2), any person who is convicted of a felony which is committed for the benefit of, at the direction of, or in association with any criminal street gang, with the specific intent to promote, further, or assist in any criminal conduct by gang members, shall, upon conviction of that felony, in addition and consecutive to the punishment prescribed for the felony or attempted felony of which he or she has been convicted, be punished by an additional term of one, two, or three years at the court's discretion. However, if the underlying felony is committed on the grounds of, or within 1,000 feet of, a public or private elementary, vocational, junior high, or high school, during hours in which the facility is open for classes or school related programs or when minors are using the facility, the additional term shall be two, three, or four years, at the court's discretion. The court shall order the imposition of the middle term of the sentence enhancement, unless there are circumstances in aggravation or mitigation. The court shall state the reasons for its choice of sentence enhancements on the record at the time of the sentencing.

(2) Any person who violates this subdivision in the commission of a felony punishable by imprisonment in the state prison for life, shall not be paroled until a minimum of 15 calendar years have been served.

(c) Any person who is convicted of a public offense punishable as a felony or a misdemeanor, which is committed for the benefit of, at the direction of, or in association with, any criminal street gang, with the specific intent to promote, further, or assist in any criminal conduct by gang members, shall be punished by imprisonment in the county jail not to exceed one year, or by imprisonment in the state prison for one, two, or three years, provided that any person sentenced to imprisonment in the county jail shall be imprisoned for a period not to exceed one year, but not less than 180 days, and shall not be eligible for release upon completion of sentence, parole, or any other basis, until he or she has served 180 days. If the court grants probation or suspends the execution of sentence imposed upon the defendant, it shall require as a condition thereof that the defendant serve 180 days in the county jail.

(d) Notwithstanding any other provision of law, the court may strike the additional punishment for the enhancements provided in this section or refuse to impose the minimum jail sentence for misdemeanors in an unusual case where the interests of justice would best be served, if the court specifies on the record and enters into the minutes the circumstances indicating that the interests of justice would best be served by that disposition.

(e) As used in this chapter, "pattern of criminal gang activity" means the commission, attempted commission, or solicitation of two or more of the following offenses, provided at least one of those offenses occurred after the effective date of this chapter and the last of those offenses occurred within three years after a prior offense, and the offenses are committed on separate occasions, or by two or more persons:

(1) Assault with a deadly weapon or by means of force likely to produce great bodily injury, as defined in Section 245.

(2) Robbery, as defined in Chapter 4 (commencing with Section 211) of Title 8 of Part 1.

(3) Unlawful homicide or manslaughter, as defined in Chapter 1 (commencing with Section 187) of Title 8 of Part 1.

(4) The sale, possession for sale, transportation, manufacture, offer for sale, or offer to manufacture controlled substances as defined in Sections 11054, 11055, 11056, 11057, and 11058 of the Health and Safety Code.

(5) Shooting at an inhabited dwelling or occupied motor vehicle, as defined in Section 246.

(6) Arson, as defined in Chapter 1 (commencing with Section 450) of Title 13.

(7) The intimidation of witnesses and victims, as defined in Section 136.1.

(8) Grand theft of any vehicle, trailer, or vessel as described in Section 487h.

(f) As used in this chapter, "criminal street gang" means any ongoing organization, association, or group of three or more persons, whether formal or informal, having as one of its primary activities the commission of one or more of the criminal acts enumerated in paragraphs (1) to (8), inclusive, of subdivision (e), which has a common name or common identifying sign or symbol, whose members individually or collectively engage in or have engaged in a pattern of criminal gang activity.

(g) This section shall remain in effect only until January 1, 1993, and as of that date is repealed, unless a later enacted statute, which is enacted before January 1, 1993, deletes or extends that date. *(Amended by Stats 1991 ch 661 §1, eff. 1/1/92 only until 1/1/93. See other section 186.22 below.)*

§186.22. Participating in a criminal street gang.

(a) Any person who actively participates in any criminal street gang with knowledge that its members engage in or have engaged in a pattern of criminal gang activity, and who willfully promotes, furthers, or assists in any felonious criminal conduct by members of that gang, shall be punished by imprisonment in the county jail for a period not to exceed one year, or by imprisonment in the state prison for one, two, or three years.

(b) (1) Except as provided in paragraph (2), any person who is convicted of a felony which is committed for the benefit of, at the direction of, or in association with any criminal street gang, with the specific intent to promote, further, or assist in any criminal conduct by gang members, shall, upon conviction of that felony, in addition and consecutive to the punishment prescribed for the felony or attempted felony of which he or she has been convicted, be punished by an additional term of one, two, or three years at the court's discretion. However, if the underlying felony is committed on the grounds of, or within 1,000 feet of, a public or private elementary, vocational, junior high, or high school, during hours in which the facility is open for classes or school related programs or when minors are using the facility, the additional term shall be two, three, or four years, at the court's discretion. The court shall order the imposition of the middle term of the sentence enhancement, unless there are circumstances in aggravation or mitigation. The court shall

state the reasons for its choice of sentence enhancements on the record at the time of the sentencing.

(2) Any person who violates this subdivision in the commission of a felony punishable by imprisonment in the state prison for life, shall not be paroled until a minimum of 15 calendar years have been served.

(c) Any person who is convicted of a public offense punishable as a felony or a misdemeanor, which is committed for the benefit of, at the direction of, or in association with, any criminal street gang, with the specific intent to promote, further, or assist in any criminal conduct by gang members, shall be punished by imprisonment in the county jail not to exceed one year, or by imprisonment in the state prison for one, two, or three years, provided that any person sentenced to imprisonment in the county jail shall be imprisoned for a period not to exceed one year, but not less than 180 days, and shall not be eligible for release upon completion of sentence, parole, or any other basis, until he or she has served 180 days. If the court grants probation or suspends the execution of sentence imposed upon the defendant, it shall require as a condition thereof that the defendant serve 180 days in the county jail.

(d) Notwithstanding any other provision of law, the court may strike the additional punishment for the enhancements provided in this section or refuse to impose the minimum jail sentence for misdemeanors in an unusual case where the interests of justice would best be served, it the court specifies on the record and enters into the minutes the circumstances indicating that the interests of justice would best be served by that disposition.

(e) As used in this chapter, "pattern of criminal gang activity" means the commission, attempted commission, or solicitation of two or more of the following offenses, provided at least one of those offenses occurred after the effective date of this chapter and the last of those offenses occurred within three years after a prior offense, and the offenses are committed on separate occasions, or by two or more persons:

(1) Assault with a deadly weapon or by means of force likely to produce great bodily injury, as defined in Section 245.

(2) Robbery, as defined in Chapter 4 (commencing with Section 211) of Title 8 of Part 1.

(3) Unlawful homicide or manslaughter, as defined in Chapter 1 (commencing with Section 187) of Title 8 of Part 1.

(4) The sale, possession for sale, transportation, manufacture, offer for sale, or offer to manufacture controlled substances as defined in Sections 11054, 11055, 11056, 11057, and 11058 of the Health and Safety Code.

(5) Shooting at an inhabited dwelling or occupied motor vehicle, as defined in Section 246.

(6) Arson, as defined in Chapter 1 (commencing with Section 450) of Title 13.

(7) The intimidation of witnesses and victims, as defined in Section 136.1.

(f) As used in this chapter, "criminal street gang" means any ongoing organization, association, or group of three or more persons, whether formal or informal, having as one of its primary activities the commission of one or more of the criminal acts enumerated in paragraphs (1) to (7), inclusive, of subdivision (e), which has a common name or common identifying sign or symbol, whose members individually or collectively

© 1992 by J., B. & L. Gould
Printed in the U.S.A.   EP

engage in or have engaged in a pattern of criminal gang activity.

(g) This section shall become operative on January 1, 1993.

(h) This section shall remain in effect only until January 1, 1997, and on that date is repealed, unless a later enacted statute which is enacted before January 1, 1997, deletes or extends that date. *(Amended by Stats 1991 ch 661 §2, 201 §1, eff. 1/1/92, oper. 1/1/93 only until 1/1/97 See other section 186.22 above.)*

§186.22a. Buildings or places used by street gangs.

(a) Every building or place used by members of a criminal street gang for the purpose of the commission of the offenses listed in subdivision (c) of Section 186.22 or any offense involving dangerous or deadly weapons, burglary, or rape, and every building or place wherein or upon which that criminal conduct by gang members takes place, is a nuisance which shall be enjoined, abated, and prevented, and for which damages may be recovered, whether it is a public or private nuisance.

(b) Any action for injunction or abatement filed pursuant to subdivision (a) shall proceed according to the provisions of Article 3 (commencing with Section 11570) of Chapter 10 of Division 10 of the Health and Safety Code, except that all of the following shall apply:

(1) The court shall not assess a civil penalty against any person unless that person knew or should have known of the unlawful acts.

(2) No order of eviction or closure may be entered.

(3) All injunctions issued shall be limited to those necessary to protect the health and safety of the residents or the public or those necessary to prevent further criminal activity.

(4) Suit may not be filed until 30-day notice of the unlawful use or criminal conduct has been provided to the owner by mail, return receipt requested, postage prepaid, to the last known address.

(c) No nonprofit or charitable organization which is conducting its affairs with ordinary care or skill, and no governmental entity, shall be abated pursuant to subdivisions (a) and (b).

(d) Nothing in this chapter shall preclude any aggrieved person from seeking any other remedy provided by law.

(e) (1) Any firearm, ammunition which may be used with the firearm, or any deadly or dangerous weapon which is owned or possessed by a member of a criminal street gang for the purpose of the commission of any of the offenses listed in subdivision (c) of Section 186.22, or the commission of any burglary or rape, may be confiscated by any law enforcement agency or peace officer.

(2) In those cases where a law enforcement agency believes that the return of the firearm, ammunition, or deadly weapon confiscated pursuant to this subdivision, is or will be used in criminal street gang activity or that the return of the item would be likely to result in endangering the safety of others, the law enforcement agency shall initiate a petition in the superior court to determine if the item confiscated should be returned or declared a nuisance.

(3) No firearm, ammunition, or deadly weapon shall be sold or destroyed unless reasonable notice is given to its lawful owner if his or her identity and address can be reasonably ascertained. The law enforcement agency shall inform the lawful owner, at that person's last known address by registered mail, that he or she has 30 days from the date of receipt of the notice to respond to the court clerk to confirm his or her desire for a hearing and that the failure to respond shall result in a default order forfeiting the confiscated firearm, ammunition, or deadly weapon as a nuisance.

(4) If the person requests a hearing, the court clerk shall set a hearing no later than 30 days from receipt of that request. The court clerk shall notify the person, the law enforcement agency involved, and the district attorney of the date, time, and place of the hearing.

(5) At the hearing, the burden of proof is upon the law enforcement agency or peace officer to show by a preponderance of the evidence that the seized item is or will be used in criminal street gang activity or that return of the item would be likely to result in endangering the safety of others. All returns of firearms shall be subject to subdivision (d) of Section 12072.

(6) If the person does not request a hearing within 30 days of the notice or the lawful owner cannot be ascertained, the law enforcement agency may file a petition that the confiscated firearm, ammunition, or deadly weapon be declared a nuisance. If the items are declared to be a nuisance, the law enforcement agency shall dispose of the items as provided in Section 12028. *(Amended by Stats 1991 ch 260 §1, eff. 1/1/92 only until 1/1/97.)*

§186.23. Exempt organizations.

This chapter does not apply to employees engaged in concerted activities for their mutual aid and protection, or the activities of labor organizations or their members or agents. *(Added by Stats 1988 ch 1242 §1, 1256 §1, eff. 9/23/88 only until 1/1/97.)*

§186.24. Severability.

If any part or provision of this chapter, or the application thereof to any person or circumstance, is held invalid, the remainder of the chapter, including the application of that part or provision to other persons or circumstances, shall not be affected thereby and shall continue in full force and effect. To this end, the provisions of this chapter are severable. *(Added by Stats 1988 ch 1242 §1, 1256 §1, eff. 9/23/88 only until 1/1/97.)*

§186.25. Additional laws.

Nothing in this chapter shall prevent a local governing body from adopting and enforcing laws consistent with this chapter relating to gangs and gang violence. Where local laws duplicate or supplement this chapter, this chapter shall be construed as providing alternative remedies and not as preempting the field. *(Added by Stats 1988 ch 1242 §1, 1256 §1, eff. 9/23/88 only until 1/1/97.)*

§186.27. Repeal.

This chapter shall remain in effect only until January 1, 1997, and as of that date is repealed, unless a later enacted statute, which is chaptered before January 1, 1997, deletes or extends that date. *(Amended by Stats 1991 ch 201 §2, eff. 1/1/92 only until 1/1/97.)*

TITLE 8

OF CRIMES AGAINST THE PERSON

CHAPTER 1

HOMICIDE

§187. Murder defined.

(a) Murder is the unlawful killing of a human being, or a fetus, with malice aforethought.

(b) This section shall not apply to any person who commits an act which results in the death of a fetus if any of the following apply:

(1) The act complied with the Therapeutic Abortion Act, Chapter 11 (commencing with Section 25950) of Division 20 of the Health and Safety Code.

(2) The act was committed by a holder of a physician's and surgeon's certificate, as defined in the Business and Professions Code, in a case where, to a medical certainty, the result of childbirth would be death of the mother of the fetus or where her death from childbirth, although not medically certain, would be substantially certain or more likely than not.

(3) The act was solicited, aided, abetted, or consented to by the mother of the fetus.

(c) Subdivision (b) shall not be construed to prohibit the prosecution of any person under any other provision of law.

§188. Malice defined.

Such malice may be express or implied. It is express when there is manifested a deliberate intention unlawfully to take away the life of a fellow creature. It is implied, when no considerable provocation appears, or when the circumstances attending the killing show an abandoned and malignant heart.

When it is shown that the killing resulted from the intentional doing of an act with express or implied malice as defined above, no other mental state need be shown to establish the mental state of malice aforethought. Neither an awareness of the obligation to act within the general body of laws regulating society nor acting despite such awareness is included within the definition of malice.

§189. Murder; degrees of.

All murder which is perpetrated by means of a destructive device or explosive, knowing use of ammunition designed primarily to penetrate metal or armor, poison, lying in wait, torture, or by any other kind of willful, deliberate, and premeditated killing, or which is committed in the perpetration of, or attempt to perpetrate, arson, rape, robbery, burglary, mayhem, kidnapping, train wrecking, or any act punishable under Section 286, 288, 288a, or 289, is murder of the first degree; and all other kinds of murders are of the second degree.

As used in this section, "destructive device" shall mean any destructive device as defined in Section 12301, and "explosive" shall mean any explosive as defined in Section 12000 of the Health and Safety Code.

To prove the killing was "deliberate and premeditated," it shall not be necessary to prove the defendant maturely and meaningfully reflected upon the gravity of his or* act. (*Amended by Initiative Measure, Prop 115 §9, approved 6/5/90.*)

*So in original. Probably should be "his or her".

§189.5. Murder trial, burden of proving mitigating circumstances.

(a) Upon a trial for murder, the commission of the homicide by the defendant being proved, the burden of proving circumstances of mitigation, or that justify or excuse it, devolves upon the defendant, unless the proof on the part of the prosecution tends to show that the crime committed only amounts to manslaughter, or that the defendant was justifiable or excusable.

(b) Nothing in this section shall apply to or affect any proceeding under Section 190.3 or 190.4. (*Added by Stats 1989 ch 897 §16, eff. 1/1/90.*)

§190. Murder; punishment for.

(a) Every person guilty of murder in the first degree shall suffer death, confinement in state prison for life without possibility of parole, or confinement in the state prison for a term of 25 years to life. The penalty to be applied shall be determined as provided in Sections 190.1, 190.2, 190.3, 190.4, and 190.5.

Except as provided in subdivision (b), every person guilty of murder in the second degree shall suffer confinement in the state prison for a term of 15 years to life.

The provisions of Article 2.5 (commencing with Section 2930) of Chapter 7 of Title 1 of Part 3 of the Penal Code shall apply to reduce any minimum term of 25 or 15 years in a state prison imposed pursuant to this section, but such person shall not otherwise be released on parole prior to such time.

(b) Every person guilty of murder in the second degree shall suffer confinement in the state prison for a term of 25 years to life if the victim was a peace officer, as defined in subdivision (a) of Section 830.1, subdivision (a) or (b) of Section 830.2, or Section 830.5, who was killed while engaged in the performance of his or her duties, and the defendant knew or reasonably should have known that the victim was such a peace officer engaged in the performance of his or her duties.

The provisions of Article 2.5 (commencing with Section 2930) of Chapter 7 of Title 1 of Part 3 of the Penal Code shall not apply to reduce any minimum term of 25 years in state prison when the person is guilty of murder in the second degree and the victim was a peace officer, as defined in this subdivision, and such person shall not be released prior to serving 25 years confinement. (*Amended by Stats 1987 ch 1006 §1.*)

§190.05. Murder penalty; second conviction.

(a) The penalty for a defendant found guilty of murder in the second degree, who has served a prior prison term for murder in the first or second degree, shall be confinement in the state prison for a term of life without the possibility of parole or confinement in the state prison for a term of 15 years to life. For purposes of this section, a prior prison term for murder of the first or second degree is that time period in which a defendant has spent actually incarcerated for his or her offense prior to release on parole.

(b) A prior prison term for murder for purposes of this section includes either of the following:

(1) A prison term served in any state prison or federal penal institution, including confinement in a hospital or other institution or facility credited as service of prison time in the jurisdiction of confinement, as punishment for the commission of an offense

© 1992 by J., B. & L. Gould
Printed in the U.S.A.   EP

which includes all of the elements of murder in the first or second degree as defined under California law.

(2) Incarceration at a facility operated by the Youth Authority for murder of the first or second degree when the person was subject to the custody, control, and discipline of the Director of Corrections.

(c) The fact of a prior prison term for murder in the first or second degree shall be alleged in the accusatory pleading, and either admitted by the defendant in open court, or found to be true by the jury trying the issue of guilt or by the court where guilt is established by a plea of guilty or nolo contendere or by trial by the court sitting without a jury.

(d) In case of a reasonable doubt as to whether the defendant served a prior prison term for murder in the first or second degree, the defendant is entitled to a finding that the allegation is not true.

(e) If the trier of fact finds that the defendant has served a prior prison term for murder in the first or second degree, there shall be a separate penalty hearing before the same trier of fact, except as provided in subdivision (f).

(f) If the defendant was convicted by the court sitting without a jury, the trier of fact at the penalty hearing shall be a jury unless a jury is waived by the defendant and the people, in which case the trier of fact shall be the court. If the defendant was convicted by a plea of guilty or nolo contendere, the trier of fact shall be a jury unless a jury is waived by the defendant and the people.

If the trier of fact is a jury and has been unable to reach a unanimous verdict as to what the penalty shall be, the court shall dismiss the jury and shall order a new jury impaneled to try the issue as to what the penalty shall be. If the new jury is unable to reach a unanimous verdict as to what the penalty shall be, the court in its discretion shall either order a new jury or impose a punishment of confinement in the state prison for a term of 15 years to life.

(g) Evidence presented at any prior phase of the trial, including any proceeding under a plea of not guilty by reason of insanity pursuant to Section 1026, shall be considered at any subsequent phase of the trial, if the trier of fact of the prior phase is the same trier of fact at the subsequent phase.

(h) In the proceeding on the question of penalty, evidence may be presented by both the people and the defendant as to any matter relevant to aggravation, mitigation, and sentence, including, but not limited to, the nature and circumstances of the present offense, any prior felony conviction or convictions whether or not such conviction or convictions involved a crime of violence, the presence or absence of other criminal activity by the defendant which involved the use or attempted use of force or violence or which involved the express or implied threat to use force or violence, and the defendant's character, background, history, mental condition, and physical condition.

However, no evidence shall be admitted regarding other criminal activity by the defendant which did not involve the use or attempted use of force or violence or which did not involve the express or implied threat to use force or violence. As used in this section, criminal activity does not require a conviction.

However, in no event shall evidence of prior criminal activity be admitted for an offense for which the defendant was prosecuted and acquitted. The restriction on the use of this evidence is intended to apply only to proceedings pursuant to this section and is not intended to affect statutory or decisional law allowing such evidence to be used in any other proceedings.

Except for evidence in proof of the offense or the prior prison term for murder of the first or second degree which subjects a defendant to the punishment of life without the possibility of parole, no evidence may be presented by the prosecution in aggravation unless notice of the evidence to be introduced has been given to the defendant within a reasonable period of time as determined by the court, prior to trial. Evidence may be introduced without such notice in rebuttal to evidence introduced by the defendant in mitigation.

In determining the penalty, the trier of fact shall take into account any of the following factors if relevant:

(1) The circumstances of the crime of which the defendant was convicted in the present proceeding and the existence of the prior prison term for murder.

(2) The presence or absence of criminal activity by the defendant which involved the use or attempted use of force or violence or the express or implied threat to use force or violence.

(3) The presence or absence of any prior felony conviction.

(4) Whether or not the offense was committed while the defendant was under the influence of extreme mental or emotional disturbance.

(5) Whether or not the victim was a participant in the defendant's homicidal conduct or consented to the homicidal act.

(6) Whether or not the offense was committed under circumstances which the defendant reasonably believed to be a moral justification or extenuation for his or her conduct.

(7) Whether or not the defendant acted under extreme duress or under the substantial domination of another person.

(8) Whether or not at the time of the offense the ability of the defendant to appreciate the criminality of his or her conduct or to conform his or her conduct to the requirements of law was impaired as a result of mental disease or defect, or the effects of intoxication.

(9) The age of the defendant at the time of the crime.

(10) Whether or not the defendant was an accomplice to the offense and his or her participation in the commission of the offense was relatively minor.

(11) Any other circumstance which extenuates the gravity of the crime even though it is not a legal excuse for the crime.

After having heard and received all of the evidence, and after having heard and considered the arguments of counsel, the trier of fact shall consider, take into account, and be guided by the aggravating and mitigating circumstances referred to in this section, and shall impose a sentence of life without the possibility of parole if the trier of fact concludes that the aggravating circumstances outweigh the mitigating circumstances. If the trier of fact determines that the mitigating circumstances outweigh the aggravating circumstances, the trier of fact shall impose a sentence of confinement in the state prison for 15 years to life.

(i) Nothing in this section shall be construed to prohibit the charging of finding of any special circumstance pursuant to Sections 190.1, 190.2, 190.3, 190.4, and 190.5. (Added by Stats 1985 ch 1510 §1.)

§190.1. Procedure involving death penalty.

A case in which the death penalty may be imposed pursuant to this chapter shall be tried in separate phases as follows:

(a) The question of the defendant's guilt shall be first determined. If the trier of fact finds the defendant guilty of first degree murder, it shall at the same time determine the truth of all special circumstances charged as enumerated in Section 190.2 except for a special circumstance charged pursuant to paragraph (2) of subdivision (a) of Section 190.2 where it is alleged that the defendant had been convicted in a prior proceeding of the offense of murder in the first or second degree.

(b) If the defendant is found guilty of first degree murder and one of the special circumstances is charged pursuant to paragraph (2) of subdivision (a) of Section 190.2 which charges that the defendant had been convicted in a prior proceeding of the offense of murder of the first or second degree, there shall thereupon be further proceedings on the question of the truth of such special circumstance.

(c) If the defendant is found guilty of first degree murder and one or more special circumstances as enumerated in Section 190.2 has been charged and found to be true, his sanity on any plea of not guilty by reason of insanity under Section 1026 shall be determined as provided in Section 190.4. If he is found to be sane, there shall thereupon be further proceedings on the question of the penalty to be imposed. Such proceedings shall be conducted in accordance with the provisions of Sections 190.3 and 190.4.

§190.2. Mandatory penalty.

(a) The penalty for a defendant found guilty of murder in the first degree shall be death or confinement in a state prison for a term of life without the possibility of parole in any case in which one or more of the following special circumstances has been charged and specially found under Section 190.4, to be true:

(1) The murder was intentional and carried out for financial gain.

(2) The defendant was previously convicted of murder in the first degree or second degree. For the purpose of this paragraph an offense committed in another jurisdiction which if committed in California would be punishable as first or second degree murder shall be deemed murder in the first or second degree.

(3) The defendant has in this proceeding been convicted of more than one offense of murder in the first or second degree.

(4) The murder was committed by means of a destructive device, bomb, or explosive planted, hidden or concealed in any place, area, dwelling, building or structure, and the defendant knew or reasonably should have known that his or her act or acts would create a great risk of death to a human being or human beings.

(5) The murder was committed for the purpose of avoiding or preventing a lawful arrest or to perfect, or attempt to perfect an escape from lawful custody.

(6) The murder was committed by means of a destructive device, bomb, or explosive that the defendant mailed or delivered, attempted to mail or deliver, or cause to be mailed or delivered and the defendant knew or reasonably should have known that his or her act or acts would create a great risk of death to a human being or human beings.

(7) The victim was a peace officer as defined in Section 830.1, 830.2, 830.3, 830.31, 830.32, 830.33, 830.34, 830.35, 830.36, 830.37, 830.4, 830.5, 830.6, 830.10, 830.11 or 830.12, who, while engaged in the course of the performance of his or her duties was intentionally killed, and the defendant knew or reasonably should have known that the victim was a peace officer engaged in the performance of his or her duties; or the victim was a peace officer as defined in the above enumerated sections of the Penal Code, or a former peace officer under any of such sections, and was intentionally killed in retaliation for the performance of his or her official duties.

(8) The victim was a federal law enforcement officer or agent, who, while engaged in the course of the performance of his or her duties was intentionally killed, and the defendant knew or reasonably should have known that the victim was a federal law enforcement officer or agent, engaged in the performance of his or her duties; or the victim was a federal law enforcement officer or agent, and was intentionally killed in retaliation for the performance of his or her official duties.

(9) The victim was a firefighter as defined in Section 245.1, who while engaged in the course of the performance of his or her duties was intentionally killed, and the defendant knew or reasonably should have known that the victim was a firefighter engaged in the performance of his or her duties.

(10) The victim was a witness to a crime who was intentionally killed for the purpose of preventing his or her testimony in any criminal proceeding, and the killing was not committed during the commission, or attempted commission of the crime to which he or she was a witness; or the victim was a witness to a crime and was intentionally killed in retaliation for his or her testimony in any criminal proceeding.

(11) The victim was a prosecutor or assistant prosecutor or a former prosecutor or assistant prosecutor of any local or state prosecutor's office in this state or any other state, or a federal prosecutor's office and the murder was carried out in retaliation for or to prevent the performance of the victim's official duties.

(12) The victim was a judge or former judge of any court of record in the local, state or federal system in the State of California or in any other state of the United States and the murder was carried out in retaliation for or to prevent the performance of the victim's official duties.

(13) The victim was an elected or appointed official or former official of the Federal Government, a local or State government of California, or of any local or state government of any other state in the United States and the killing was intentionally carried out in retaliation for or to prevent the performance of the victim's official duties.

(14) The murder was especially heinous, atrocious, or cruel, manifesting exceptional depravity. As utilized in this section, the phrase especially heinous, atrocious or cruel manifesting exceptional depravity means a conscienceless, or pitiless crime which is unnecessarily torturous to the victim.

(15) The defendant intentionally killed the victim while lying in wait.

(16) The victim was intentionally killed because of his or her race, color, religion, nationality or country of origin.

© 1992 by J., B. & L. Gould
Printed in the U.S.A.   **EP**

(17) The murder was committed while the defendant was engaged in or was an accomplice in the commission of attempted commission of, or the immediate flight after committing or attempting to commit the following felonies:

(i) Robbery in violation of Section 211.

(ii) Kidnapping in violation of Sections 207 and 209.

(iii) Rape in violation of Section 261.

(iv) Sodomy in violation of Section 286.

(v) The performance of a lewd or lascivious act upon person of a child under the age of 14 in violation of Section 288.

(vi) Oral copulation in violation of Section 255a.

(vii) Burglary in the first or second degree in violation of Section 460.

(viii) Arson in violation of Section 447.

(ix) Train wrecking in violation of Section 219.

(18) The murder was intentional and involved the infliction of torture. For the purpose of this section torture requires proof of the infliction of extreme physical pain no matter how long its duration.

(19) The defendant intentionally killed the victim by the administration of poison.

(b) Every person whether or not the actual killer found guilty of intentionally aiding, abetting, counseling, commanding, inducing, soliciting, requesting, or assisting any actor in the commission of murder in the first degree shall suffer death or confinement in state prison for a term of life without the possibility of parole, in any case in which one or more of the special circumstances enumerated in paragraph (1), (3), (4), (5), (6), (7), (8), (9), (10), (11), (12), (13), (14), (15), (16), (17), (18), or (19) of subdivision (a) of this section has been charged and specially found under Section 190.4 to be true.

The penalty shall be determined as provided in Sections 190.1, 190.2, 190.3, 190.4, and 190.5. *(Amended by Stats 1989 ch 1165 §16; by Initiative Measure, Prop 114 §16, approved 6/5/90. See other section 190.2 below.)*

§190.2. Mandatory penalty.

(a) The penalty for a defendant found guilty of murder in the first degree shall be death or confinement in a state prison for a term of life without the possibility of parole in any case in which one or more of the following special circumstances has been found under Section 190.4, to be true:

(1) The murder was intentional and carried out for financial gain.

(2) The defendant was previously convicted of murder in the first degree or second degree. For the purpose of this paragraph an offense committed in another jurisdiction which if committed in California would be punishable as first or second degree murder shall be deemed murder in the first or second degree.

(3) The defendant has in this proceeding been convicted of more than one offense of murder in the first or second degree.

(4) The murder was committed by means of a destructive device, bomb, or explosive planted, hidden or concealed in any place, area, dwelling, building or structure, and the defendant knew or reasonably should have known that his or her act or acts would create a great risk of death to a human being or human beings.

(5) The murder was committed for the purpose of avoiding or preventing a lawful arrest or to perfect, or attempt to perfect an escape from lawful custody.

(6) The murder was committed by means of a destructive device, bomb, or explosive that the defendant mailed or delivered, attempted to mail or deliver, or cause to be mailed or delivered and the defendant knew or reasonably should have known that his or her act or acts would create a great risk of death to a human being or human beings.

(7) The victim was a peace officer as defined in Section 830.1, 830.2, 830.3, 830.31, 830.35, 830.36, 830.4, 830.5, 830.5a, 830.6, 830.10, 830.11 or 830.12, who, while engaged in the course of the performance of his or her duties was intentionally killed, and the defendant knew or reasonably should have known that the victim was a peace officer engaged in the performance of his or her duties; or the victim was a peace officer as defined in the above enumerated sections of the Penal Code, or a former peace officer under any of such sections, and was intentionally killed in retaliation for the performance of his or her official duties.

(8) The victim was a federal law enforcement officer or agent, who, while engaged in the course of the performance of his or her duties was intentionally killed, and the defendant knew or reasonably should have known that the victim was a federal law enforcement officer or agent, engaged in the performance of his or her duties; or the victim was a federal law enforcement officer or agent, and was intentionally killed in retaliation for the performance of his or her official duties.

(9) The victim was a fireman as defined in Section 245.1, who while engaged in the course of the performance of his or her duties was intentionally killed, and such defendant knew or reasonably should have known that the victim was a fireman engaged in the performance of his or her duties.

(10) The victim was a witness to a crime who was intentionally killed for the purpose of preventing his or her testimony in any criminal or juvenile proceeding, and the killing was not committed during the commission, or attempted commission of the crime to which he or she was a witness; or the victim was a witness to a crime and was intentionally killed in retaliation for his or her testimony in any criminal or juvenile proceeding brought pursuant to Section 602 or 707 of the Welfare and Institutions Code.

(11) The victim was a prosecutor or assistant prosecutor or a former prosecutor or assistant prosecutor of any local or state prosecutor's office in this state or any other state, or a federal prosecutor's office and the murder was intentionally carried out in retaliation for or to prevent the performance of the victim's official duties.

(12) The victim was a judge or former judge of any court of record in the local, state or federal system in the State of California or in any other state of the United States and the murder was intentionally carried out in retaliation for or to prevent the performance of the victim's official duties.

(13) The victim was an elected or appointed official or former official of the federal government, a local or state government of California, or of any local or state government of any other state in the United States and the killing was intentionally carried out in retaliation for or to prevent the performance of the victim's official duties.

(14) The murder was especially heinous, atrocious, or cruel, manifesting exceptional depravity. As utilized in this section, the phrase especially heinous,

atrocious or cruel manifesting exceptional depravity means a conscienceless, or pitiless crime which is unnecessarily torturous to the victim.

(15) The defendant intentionally killed the victim while lying in wait.

(16) The victim was intentionally killed because of his or her race, color, religion, nationality or country of origin.

(17) The murder was committed while the defendant was engaged in or was an accomplice in the commission of, attempted commission of, or the immediate flight after committing or attempting to commit the following felonies:

(i) Robbery in violation of Section 211 or 212.5.

(ii) Kidnapping in violation of Section 207 or 209.

(iii) Rape in violation of Section 261.

(iv) Sodomy in violation of Section 286.

(v) The performance of a lewd or lascivious act upon person of a child under the age of 14 in violation of Section 288.

(vi) Oral copulation in violation of Section 288a.

(vii) Burglary in the first or second degree in violation of Section 460.

(viii) Arson in violation of subdivision (b) of Section 451.

(ix) Train wrecking in violation of Section 219.

(x) Mayhem in violation of Section 203.

(xi) Rape by instrument in violation of Section 289.

(18) The murder was intentional and involved the infliction of torture.

(19) The defendant intentionally killed the victim by the administration of poison.

(b) Unless an intent to kill is specifically required under subdivision (a) for a special circumstance enumerated therein, an actual killer as to whom such special circumstance has been found to be true under Section 190.4 need not have had any intent to kill at the time of the commission of the offense which is the basis of the special circumstance in order to suffer death or confinement in state prison for a term of life without the possibility of parole.

(c) Every person not the actual killer who, with the intent to kill, aids, abets, counsels, commands, induces, solicits, requests, or assists any actor in the commission of murder in the first degree shall suffer death or confinement in state prison for a term of life without the possibility of parole, in any case in which one or more of the special circumstances enumerated in subdivision (a) of this section has been found to be true under Section 190.4

(d) Notwithstanding subdivision (c), every person not the actual killer, who, with reckless indifference to human life and as a major participant, aids, abets, counsels, commands, induces, solicits, requests, or assists in the commission of a felony enumerated in paragraph (17) of subdivision (a), which felony results in the death of some person or persons, who is found guilty of murder in the first degree therefor, shall suffer death or confinement in state prison for life without the possibility of parole, in any case in which a special circumstance enumerated in paragrpah (17) of subdivision (a) of this section has been found to be true under Section 190.4.

(e) The penalty shall be determined as provided in Sections 190.1, 190.2, 190.3, 190.4, and 190.5. *(Amended by Initiative Measure, Prop 115 §10, approved 6/5/90. See other section 190.2 above.)*

§190.25. Murder of transportation worker; penalty.

(a) The penalty for a defendant found guilty of murder in the first degree shall be confinement in state prison for a term of life without the possibility of parole in any case in which any of the following special circumstances has been charged and specially found under Section 190.4, to be true: the victim was the operator or driver of a bus, taxicab, streetcar, cable car, trackless trolley, or other motor vehicle operated on land, including a vehicle operated on stationary rails or on a track or rail suspended in the air, used for the transportation of persons for hire, or the victim was a station agent or ticket agent for the entity providing such transportation, who, while engaged in the course of the performance of his or her duties was intentionally killed, and such defendant knew or reasonably should have known that such victim was the operator or driver of a bus, taxicab, streetcar, cable car, trackless trolley, or other motor vehicle operated on land, including a vehicle operated on stationary rails or on a track or rail suspended in the air, used for the transportation of persons for hire, or was a station agent or ticket agent for the entity providing such transportation, engaged in the performance of his or her duties.

(b) Every person whether or not the actual killer found guilty of intentionally aiding, abetting, counseling, commanding, inducing, soliciting, requesting, or assisting any actor in the commission of murder in the first degree shall suffer confinement in state prison for a term of life without the possibility of parole, in any case in which one or more of the special circumstances enumerated in subdivision (a) of this section has been charged and specially found under Section 190.4 to be true.

(c) Nothing in this section shall be construed to prohibit the charging or finding of any special circumstance pursuant to Sections 190.1, 190.2, 190.3, 190.4, and 190.5.

§190.3. Death penalty or life imprisonment determination upon finding of special circumstances.

If the defendant has been found guilty of murder in the first degree, and a special circumstance has been charged and found to be true, or if the defendant may be subject to the death penalty after having been found guilty of violating subdivision (a) of Section 1672 of the Military and Veterans Code or Sections 37, 128, 219 or 4500 of this code, the trier of fact shall determine whether the penalty shall be death or confinement in state prison for a term of life without the possibility of parole. In the proceedings on the question of penalty, evidence may be presented by both the people and the defendant as to any matter relevant to aggravation, mitigation, and sentence including, but not limited to, the nature and circumstances of the present offense, any prior felony conviction or convictions whether or not such conviction or convictions involved a crime of violence, the presence or absence of other criminal activity by the defendant which involved the use or attempted use of force or violence or which involved the express or implied threat to use force or violence, and the defendant's character, background, history, mental condition and physical condition.

However, no evidence shall be admitted regarding other criminal activity by the defendant which did not involve the use or attempted use of force or violence or

© 1992 by J., B. & L. Gould
Printed in the U.S.A.   EP

which did not involve the express or implied threat to use force or violence. As used in this section, criminal activity does not require a conviction.

However, in no event shall evidence of prior criminal activity be admitted for an offense for which the defendant was prosecuted and acquitted. The restriction on the use of this evidence is intended to apply only to proceedings pursuant to this section and is not intended to affect statutory or decisional law allowing such evidence to be used in any other proceedings.

Except for evidence in proof of the offense or special circumstances which subject a defendant to the death penalty, no evidence may be presented by the prosecution in aggravation unless notice of the evidence to be introduced has been given to the defendant within a reasonable period of time as determined by the court, prior to trial. Evidence may be introduced without such notice in rebuttal to evidence introduced by the defendant in mitigation.

The trier of fact shall be instructed that a sentence of confinement to state prison for a term of life without the possibility of parole may in future after sentence is imposed, be commuted or modified to a sentence that includes the possibility of parole by the Governor of the State of California.

In determining the penalty, the trier of fact shall take into account any of the following factors if relevant:

(a) The circumstances of the crime of which the defendant was convicted in the present proceeding and the existence of any special circumstances found to be true pursuant to Section 190.1.

(b) The presence or absence of criminal activity by the defendant which involved the use or attempted use of force or violence or the express or implied threat to use force or violence.

(c) The presence or absence of any prior felony conviction.

(d) Whether or not the offense was committed while the defendant was under the influence of extreme mental or emotional disturbance.

(e) Whether or not the victim was a participant in the defendant's homicidal conduct or consented to the homicidal act.

(f) Whether or not the offense was committed under circumstances which the defendant was reasonably believed to be a moral justification or extenuation for his conduct.

(g) Whether or not defendant acted under extreme duress or under the substantial domination of another person.

(h) Whether or not at the time of the offense the capacity of the defendant to appreciate the criminality of his conduct or to conform his conduct to the requirements of law was impaired as a result of mental disease or defect, or the effects of intoxication.

(i) The age of the defendant at the time of the crime.

(j) Whether or not the defendant was an accomplice to the offense and his participation in the commission of the offense was relatively minor.

(k) Any other circumstance which extenuates the gravity of the crime even though it is not a legal excuse for the crime.

After having heard and received all of the evidence, and after having heard and considered the arguments of counsel, the trier of fact shall consider, take into account and be guided by the aggravating and mitigating circumstances referred to in this section, and shall impose a sentence of death if the trier of fact concludes that the aggravating circumstances outweigh the mitigating circumstances. If the trier of fact determines that the mitigating circumstances outweigh the aggravating circumstances the trier of fact shall impose a sentence of confinement in state prison for a term of life without the possibility of parole.

§190.4. Special circumstances finding.

(a) Whenever special circumstances as enumerated in Section 190.2 are alleged and the trier of fact finds the defendant guilty of first degree murder, the trier of fact shall also make a special finding on the truth of each alleged special circumstance. The determination of the truth of any or all of the special circumstances shall be made by the trier of fact on the evidence presented at the trial or at the hearing held pursuant to Subdivision (b) of Section 190.1.

In case of a reasonable doubt as to whether a special circumstance is true, the defendant is entitled to a finding that is not true. The trier of fact shall make a special finding that each special circumstance charged is either true or not true. Whenever a special circumstance requires proof of the commission or attempted commission of a crime, such crime shall be charged and proved pursuant to the general law applying to the trial and conviction of the crime.

If the defendant was convicted by the court sitting without a jury, the trier of fact shall be a jury unless a jury is waived by the defendant and by the people, in which case the trier of fact shall be the court. If the defendant was convicted by a plea of guilty, the trier of fact shall be a jury unless a jury is waived by the defendant and by the people.

If the trier of fact finds that any one or more of the special circumstances enumerated in Section 190.2 as charged is true, there shall be a separate penalty hearing, and neither the finding that any of the remaining special circumstances charged is not true, nor if the trier of fact is a jury, the inability of the jury to agree on the issue of the truth or untruth of any of the remaining special circumstances charged, shall prevent the holding of a separate penalty hearing.

In any case in which the defendant has been found guilty by a jury, and the jury has been unable to reach a unanimous verdict that one or more of the special circumstances charged are true, and does not reach a unanimous verdict that all the special circumstances charged are not true, the court shall dismiss the jury and shall order a new jury impaneled to try the issues, but the issue of guilt shall not be tried by such jury, nor shall such jury retry the issue of the truth of any of the special circumstances which were found by a unanimous verdict of the previous jury to be untrue. If such new jury is unable to reach the unanimous verdict that one or more of the special circumstances it is trying are true, the court shall dismiss the jury and in the court's discretion shall either order a new jury impaneled to try the issues the previous jury was unable to reach the unanimous verdict on, or impose a punishment of confinement in state prison for a term of 25 years.

(b) If defendant was convicted by the court sitting without a jury the trier of fact at the penalty hearing shall be a jury unless a jury is waived by the defendant and the people, in which case the trier of fact shall be the court. If the defendant was convicted by a plea of guilty, the trier of fact shall be a jury unless a jury is waived by the defendant and the people.

If the trier of fact is a jury and has been unable to reach a unanimous verdict as to what the penalty shall be, the court shall dismiss the jury and shall order a new jury impaneled to try the issue as to what the penalty shall be. If such new jury is unable to reach a unanimous verdict as to what the penalty shall be, the court in its discretion shall either order a new jury or impose a punishment of confinement in state prison for a term of life without the possibility of parole.

(c) If the trier of fact which convicted the defendant of a crime for which he may be subject to the death penalty was a jury, the same jury shall consider any plea of not guilty by reason of insanity pursuant to Section 1026, the truth of any special circumstances which may be alleged, and the penalty to be applied, unless for good cause shown the court discharges that jury in which case a new jury shall be drawn. The court shall state facts in support of the finding of good cause upon the record and cause them to be entered into the minutes.

(d) In any case in which the defendant may be subject to the death penalty, evidence presented at any prior phase of the trial, including any proceeding under a plea of not guilty by reason of insanity pursuant to Section 1026 shall be considered at any subsequent phase of the trial, if the trier of fact of the prior phase is the same trier of fact at the subsequent phase.

(e) In every case in which the trier of fact has returned a verdict or finding imposing the death penalty, the defendant shall be deemed to have made an application for modification of such verdict or finding pursuant to Subdivision 7 of Section 11.* In ruling on the application, the judge shall review the evidence, consider, take into account, and be guided by the aggravating and mitigating circumstances referred to in Section 190.3, and shall make a determination as to whether the jury's findings and verdicts that the aggravating circumstances outweigh the mitigating circumstances are contrary to law or the evidence presented. The judge shall state on the record the reasons for his findings.

*So in original. Probably should be "Section 1181".

The judge shall set forth the reasons for his ruling on the application and direct that they be entered on the Clerk's minutes. The denial of the modification of the death penalty verdict pursuant to subdivision (7) of Section 1181 shall be reviewed on the defendant's automatic appeal pursuant to subdivision (b) of Section 1239. The granting of the application shall be reviewed on the People's appeal pursuant to paragraph (6).

§190.41. Corpus delicti; felony-based special cirsumstance.

Notwithstanding Section 190.4 or any other provision of law, the corpus delicti of a felony-based special circumstance enumerated in paragraph (17) of subdivision (a) of Section 190.2 need not be proved independently of a defendant's extrajudicial statement. *(Added by Initiative Measure, Prop 115 §11, approved 6/5/90.)*

§190.5. Death penalty prohibited for persons under 18.

(a) Notwithstanding any other provision of law, the death penalty shall not be imposed upon any person who is under the age of 18 at the time of the commission of the crime. The burden of proof as to the age of such person shall be upon the defendant.

(b) The penalty for a defendant found guilty of murder in the first degree, in any case in which one or more special circumstances enumerated in Section 190.2 or 190.25 has been found to be true under Section 190.4, who was 16 years of age or older and under the age of 18 years at the time of the commission of the crime, shall be confinement in the state prison for life without the possibility of parole or, at the discretion of the court, 25 years to life.

(c) The trier of fact shall determine the existence of any special circumstance pursuant to the procedure set forth in Section 190.4. *(Amended by Initiative Measure, Prop 115 §12, approved 6/5/90.)*

§190.6. Capital cases expeditiously carried out.

The Legislature finds that the imposition of sentence in all capital cases should be expeditiously carried out.

Therefore, in all cases in which a sentence of death has been imposed, the appeal to the State Supreme Court must be decided and an opinion reaching the merits must be filed within 150 days of certification of the entire record by the sentencing court. In any case in which this time requirement is not met, the Chief Justice of the Supreme Court shall state on the record the extraordinary and compelling circumstances causing the delay and the facts supporting these circumstances. A failure to comply with the time requirements of this section shall not be grounds for precluding the ultimate imposition of the death penalty.

§190.7. Referral to entire record.

The "entire record" referred to in Section 190.6 shall include, but not be limited to, the following:

(a) The normal and additional record prescribed in the rules adopted by the Judicial Council pertaining to an appeal taken by the defendant from a judgment of conviction.

(b) A copy of any other paper or record on file or lodged with the superior court and a transcript of any other oral proceeding reported in the superior court pertaining to the trial of the cause.

Nothing contained in this section shall preclude a court from ordering that the entire record include municipal court or settlement proceedings pertaining to the case.

Notwithstanding this section, the Judicial Council may adopt rules, not inconsistent with the purpose of Section 190.6, specifically pertaining to the content, preparation and certification of the record on appeal when a judgment of death has been pronounced.

§190.8. Imposition of death sentence; certification.

In any case in which a death sentence has been imposed, the record on appeal shall be expeditiously certified. If the record has not been certified within 60 days of the date it is delivered to the parties or their counsel, the trial court shall monitor the preparation of the record monthly to expedite certification and report the status of the record to the California Supreme Court.

Corrections to the record shall not be required to include simple typographical errors that cannot conceivably cause confusion.

© 1992 by J., B. & L. Gould
Printed in the U.S.A.　　EP

§190.9. Imposition of death sentence; proceedings.

(a) In any case in which a death sentence may be imposed, all proceedings conducted in the justice, municipal, and superior courts, including proceedings in chambers, shall be conducted on the record with a court reporter present. The court reporter shall prepare and certify a daily transcript of these proceedings.

The court shall assign a court reporter who uses computer-aided transcription equipment to report all proceedings under this section. Failure to comply with the requirements of this section relating to the assignment of court reporters who use computer-aided transcription equipment shall not be a ground for reversal.

(b) This section shall become operative on July 1, 1990. *(Amended by Stats 1989 ch 379 §2, eff. 1/1/90, oper. 7/1/90.)*

§191. Petit treason abolished.

The rules of the common law distinguishing the killing of a master by his servant, and of a husband by his wife, as petit treason, are abolished, and these offenses are homicides, punishable in the manner prescribed by this Chapter.

§191.5. Gross vehicular manslaughter while intoxicated.

(a) Gross vehicular manslaughter while intoxicated is the unlawful killing of a human being without malice aforethought, in the driving of a vehicle, where the driving was in violation of Section 23152 or 23153 of the Vehicle Code, and the killing was either the proximate result of the commission of an unlawful act, not amounting to a felony, and with gross negligence, or the proximate result of the commission of a lawful act which might produce death, in an unlawful manner, and with gross negligence.

(b) Gross vehicular manslaughter while intoxicated also includes operating a vessel in violation of subdivision (b), (c), (d), or (e) of Section 655 of the Harbors and Navigation Code, and in the commission of an unlawful act, not amounting to felony, and with gross negligence; or operating a vessel in violation of subdivision (b), (c), (d), or (e) of Section 655 of the Harbors and Navigation Code, and in the commission of a lawful act which might produce death, in an unlawful manner, and with gross negligence.

(c) Gross vehicular manslaughter while intoxicated is punishable by imprisonment in the state prison for 4, 6, or 10 years.

(d) This section shall not be construed as prohibiting or precluding a charge of murder under Section 188 upon facts exhibiting wantonness and a conscious disregard for life to support a finding of implied malice, or upon facts showing malice consistent with the holding of the California Supreme Court in People v. Watson, 30 Cal. 3d 290.

(e) This section shall not be construed as making any homicide in the driving of a vehicle or the operation of a vessel punishable which is not a proximate result of the commission of an unlawful act, not amounting to felony, or of the commission of a lawful act which might produce death, in an unlawful manner.

(f) This section shall remain in effect only until January 1, 1992, and as of that date is repealed. *(Amended by Stats 1990 ch 1698 §3, eff. 1/1/91 only until 1/1/92. See other section 191.5 below.)*

§191.5. Gross vehicular manslaughter while intoxicated.

(a) Gross vehicular manslaughter while intoxicated is the unlawful killing of a human being without malice aforethought, in the driving of a vehicle, where the driving was in violation of Section 23152 or 23153 of the Vehicle Code, and the killing was either the proximate result of the commission of an unlawful act, not amounting to a felony, and with gross negligence, or the proximate result of the commission of a lawful act which might produce death, in an unlawful manner, and with gross negligence.

(b) Gross vehicular manslaughter while intoxicated also includes operating a vessel in violation of subdivision (b), (c), (d), (e), or (f) of Section 655 of the Harbors and Navigation Code, and in the commission of an unlawful act, not amounting to felony, and with gross negligence; or operating a vessel in violation of subdivision (b), (c), (d), (e), or (f) of Section 655 of the Harbors and Navigation Code, and in the commission of a lawful act which might produce death, in an unlawful manner, and with gross negligence.

(c) Gross vehicular manslaughter while intoxicated is punishable by imprisonment in the state prison for 4, 6, or 10 years.

(d) This section shall not be construed as prohibiting or precluding a charge of murder under Section 188 upon facts exhibiting wantonness and a conscious disregard for life to support a finding of implied malice, or upon facts showing malice consistent with the holding of the California Supreme Court in People v. Watson, 30 Cal. 3d 290.

(e) This section shall not be construed as making any homicide in the driving of a vehicle or the operation of a vessel punishable which is not a proximate result of the commission of an unlawful act, not amounting to felony, or of the commission of a lawful act which might produce death, in an unlawful manner.

(f) This section shall become operative on January 1, 1992. *(Added by Stats 1990 ch 1698 §4, eff. 1/1/91, oper. 1/1/92. See other section 191.5 above.)*

§192. Manslaughter defined; kinds.

Manslaughter is the unlawful killing of a human being without malice. It is of three kinds:

(a) Voluntary—upon a sudden quarrel or heat of passion.

(b) Involuntary—in the commission of an unlawful act, not amounting to felony; or in the commission of a lawful act which might produce death, in an unlawful manner, or without due caution and circumspection. This subdivision shall not apply to acts committed in the driving of a vehicle.

(c) Vehicular—

(1) Except as provided in Section 191.5, driving a vehicle in the commission of an unlawful act, not amounting to felony, and with gross negligence; or driving a vehicle in the commission of a lawful act which might produce death, in an unlawful manner, and with gross negligence.

(2) Except as provided in paragraph (3), driving a vehicle in the commission of an unlawful act, not amounting to felony, but without gross negligence; or driving a vehicle in the commission of a lawful act which might produce death, in an unlawful manner, but without gross negligence.

(3) Driving a vehicle in violation of Section 23152 or 23153 of the Vehicle Code and in the commission of

an unlawful act, not amounting to felony, but without gross negligence; or driving a vehicle in violation of Section 23152 or 23153 of the Vehicle Code and in the commission of a lawful act which might produce death, in an unlawful manner, but without gross negligence.

This section shall not be construed as making any homicide in the driving of a vehicle punishable which is not a proximate result of the commission of an unlawful act, not amounting to felony, or of the commission of a lawful act which might produce death, in an unlawful manner.

"Gross negligence", as used in this section, shall not be construed as prohibiting or precluding a charge of murder under Section 188 upon facts exhibiting wantonness and a conscious disregard for life to support a finding of implied malice, or upon facts showing malice, consistent with the holding of the California Supreme Court in People v. Watson 30 Cal. 3d 290. *(Amended by Stats 1986 ch 1106 §3.)*

§192.5. Vehicular manslaughter when operating a vessel.

Vehicular manslaughter pursuant to subdivision (c) of Section 192 includes:

(a) Except as provided in subdivision (b) of Section 191.5, operating a vessel in the commission of an unlawful act, not amounting to felony, and with gross negligence; or operating a vessel in the commission of a lawful act which might produce death, in an unlawful manner, and with gross negligence.

(b) Except as provided in subdivision (c), operating a vessel in the commission of an unlawful act, not amounting to felony, but without gross negligence; or operating a vessel in the commission of a lawful act which might produce death, in an unlawful manner, but without gross negligence.

(c) Operating a vessel in violation of subdivision (b), (c), (d), or (e) of Section 655 of the Harbors and Navigation Code, and in the commission of an unlawful act, not amounting to felony, but without gross negligence; or operating a vessel in violation of subdivision (b), (c), (d), or (e) of Section 655 of the Harbors and Navigation Code, and in the commission of a lawful act which might produce death, in an unlawful manner, but without gross negligence.

(d) This section shall remain in effect only until January 1, 1992, and as of that date is repealed. *(Amended by Stats 1990 ch 1698 §5, eff. 1/1/91 only until 1/1/92. See other section 192.5 below.)*

§192.5. Vehicular manslaughter when operating a vessel.

Vehicular manslaughter pursuant to subdivision (c) of Section 192 includes:

(a) Except as provided in subdivision (b) of Section 191.5, operating a vessel in the commission of an unlawful act, not amounting to felony, and with gross negligence; or operating a vessel in the commission of a lawful act which might produce death, in an unlawful manner, and with gross negligence.

(b) Except as provided in subdivision (c), operating a vessel in the commission of an unlawful act, not amounting to felony, but without gross negligence; or operating a vessel in the commission of a lawful act which might produce death, in an unlawful manner, but without gross negligence.

(c) Operating a vessel in violation of subdivision (b), (c), (d), (e), or (f) of Section 655 of the Harbors and Navigation Code, and in the commission of an unlaw-

ful act, not amounting to felony, but without gross negligence; or operating a vessel in violation of subdivision (b), (c), (d), (e), or (f) of Section 655 of the Harbors and Navigation Code, and in the commission of a lawful act which might produce death, in an unlawful manner, but without gross negligence.

(d) This section shall become operative on January 1, 1992. *(Added by Stats 1990 ch 1698 §6, eff. 1/1/91, oper. 1/1/92. See other section 192.5 above.)*

§193. Manslaughter; punishment.

(a) Voluntary manslaughter is punishable by imprisonment in the state prison for three, six, or eleven years.

(b) Involuntary manslaughter is punishable by imprisonment in the state prison for two, three, or four years.

(c) Vehicular manslaughter is punishable as follows:

(1) A violation of paragraph (1) of subdivision (c) of Section 192 is punishable either by imprisonment in the county jail for not more than one year or by imprisonment in the state prison for two, four, or six years.

(2) A violation of paragraph (2) of subdivision (c) of Section 192 is punishable by imprisonment in the county jail for not more than one year.

(3) A violation of paragraph (3) of subdivision (c) of Section 192 is punishable either by imprisonment in the county jail for not more than one year or by imprisonment in the state prison for 16 months or two or four years. *(Amended by Stats 1986 ch 1106 §4.)*

§193.5. Manslaughter when operating a vessel; punishment.

Manslaughter committed during the operation of a vessel is punishable as follows:

(a) A violation of subdivision (a) of Section 192.5 is punishable either by imprisonment in the county jail for not more than one year or by imprisonment in the state prison for two, four, or six years.

(b) A violation of subdivision (b) of Section 192.5 is punishable by imprisonment in the county jail for not more than one year.

(c) A violation of subdivision (c) of Section 192.5 is punishable either by imprisonment in the county jail for not more than one year or by imprisonment in the state prison for 16 months or two or four years. *(Amended by Stats 1988 ch 216 §5, eff. 6/29/88.)*

§193.7. Habitual traffic offender: designation.

Any person convicted of a violation of paragraph (3) of subdivision (c) of Section 192 which occurred within seven years of two or more separate violations of Section 23103, as specified in Section 23103.5, of, or Section 23152 or 23153 of, the Vehicle Code, or any combination thereof, which resulted in convictions, shall be designated as an habitual traffic offender subject to paragraph (3) of subdivision (e) of Section 14601.3 of the Vehicle Code, for a period of three years, subsequent to the conviction. The person shall be advised of this designation pursuant to subdivision (b) of Section 13350 of the Vehicle Code. *(Amended by Stats 1991 ch 1091 §117, eff. 1/1/92.)*

§194. Murder and manslaughter; computation of time of death.

To make the killing either murder or manslaughter, it is requisite that the party die within

© 1992 by J., B. & L. Gould
Printed in the U.S.A.   **EP**

three years and a day after the stroke received or the cause of death administered. In the computation of such time, the whole of the day on which the act was done shall be reckoned the first.

§195. Excusable homicide.

Homicide is excusable in the following cases:

1. When committed by accident and misfortune, or in doing any other lawful act by lawful means, with usual and ordinary caution, and without any unlawful intent.

2. When committed by accident and misfortune, in the heat of passion, upon any sudden and sufficient provocation, or upon a sudden combat, when no undue advantage is taken, nor any dangerous weapon used, and when the killing is not done in a cruel or unusual manner.

§196. Justifiable homicide by public officers.

Homicide is justifiable when committed by public officers and those acting by their command in their aid and assistance, either—

1. In obedience to any judgment of a competent Court; or,

2. When necessarily committed in overcoming actual resistance to the execution of some legal process, or in the discharge of any other legal duty; or,

3. When necessarily committed in retaking felons who have been rescued or have escaped, or when necessarily committed in arresting persons charged with felony, and who are fleeing from justice or resisting such arrest.

§197. Justifiable homicide by private citizens.

Homicide is also justifiable when committed by any person in any of the following cases:

1. When resisting any attempt to murder any person, or to commit a felony, or to do some great bodily injury upon any person; or,

2. When committed in defense of habitation, property, or person, against one who manifestly intends or endeavors, by violence or surprise, to commit a felony, or against one who manifestly intends and endeavors, in a violent, riotous or tumultuous manner, to enter the habitation of another for the purpose of offering violence to any person therein; or,

3. When committed in the lawful defense of such person, or of a wife or husband, parent, child, master, mistress, or servant of such person, when there is reasonable ground to apprehend a design to commit a felony or to do some great bodily injury, and imminent danger of such design being accomplished; but such person, or the person in whose behalf the defense was made, if he was the assailant or engaged in mutual combat, must really and in good faith have endeavored to decline any further struggle before the homicide was committed; or,

4. When necessarily committed in attempting, by lawful ways and means, to apprehend any person for any felony committed, or in lawfully suppressing any riot, or in lawfully keeping and preserving the peace.

§198. Bare fear not to justify killing.

A bare fear of the commission of any of the offenses mentioned in subdivisions 2 and 3 of Section 197, to prevent which homicide may be lawfully committed, is not sufficient to justify it. But the circumstances must be sufficient to excite the fears of a reasonable person, and the party killing must have acted under the influence of such fears alone. *(Amended by Stats 1987 ch 828 §8.)*

§198.5. Justifiable homicide within a person's home.

Any person using force intended or likely to cause death or great bodily injury within his or her residence shall be presumed to have held a reasonable fear of imminent peril of death or great bodily injury to self, family, or a member of the household when that force is used against another person, not a member of the family or household, who unlawfully and forcibly enters or has unlawfully and forcibly entered the residence and the person using the force knew or had reason to believe that an unlawful and forcible entry occurred.

As used in this section, great bodily injury means a significant or substantial physical injury.

§199. Justifiable and excusable homicide not punishable.

The homicide appearing to be justifiable or excusable, the person indicted must, upon his trial, be fully acquitted and discharged.

CHAPTER 2

MAYHEM

§203. Mayhem defined.

Every person who unlawfully and maliciously deprives a human being of a member of his body, or disables, disfigures, or renders it useless, or cuts or disables the tongue, or puts out an eye, or slits the nose, ear, or lip, is guilty of mayhem. *(Amended by Stats 1989 ch 1360 §106, eff. 1/1/90.)*

§204. Punishment for mayhem, a felony.

Mayhem is punishable by imprisonment in the state prison for two, four, or eight years. *(Amended by Stats 1986 ch 1424 §1.)*

§205. Aggravated mayhem, a felony.

A person is guilty of aggravated mayhem when he or she unlawfully, under circumstances manifesting extreme indifference to the physical or psychological well-being of another person, intentionally causes permanent disability or disfigurement of another human being or deprives a human being of a limb, organ, or member of his or her body. For purposes of this section, it is not necessary to prove an intent to kill. Aggravated mayhem is a felony punishable by imprisonment in the state prison for life with the possibility of parole. *(Added by Stats 1987 ch 785 §1.)*

§206. Torture defined.

Every person who, with the intent to cause cruel or extreme pain and suffering for the purpose of revenge, extortion, persuasion, or for any sadistic purpose, inflicts great bodily injury as defined in Section 12022.7 upon the person of another, is guilty of torture.

The crime of torture does not require any proof that the victim suffered pain. *(Added by Initiative Measure, Prop 115 §13, approved 6/5/90.)*

§206.1. Punishment for torture.

Torture is punishable by imprisonment in the state prison for a term of life. *(Added by Initiative Measure, Prop 115 §14, approved 6/5/90.)*

CHAPTER 3

KIDNAPPING

§207. Kidnapping defined.

(a) Every person who forcibly, or by any other means of instilling fear, steals or takes, or holds, detains, or arrests any person in this state, and carries the person into another country, state, or county, or into another part of the same county, is guilty of kidnapping.

(b) Every person, who for the purpose of committing any act defined in Section 288, hires, persuades, entices, decoys, or seduces by false promises, misrepresentations, or the like, any child under the age of 14 years to go out of this country, state, or county, or into another part of the same county, is guilty of kidnapping.

(c) Every person who forcibly, or by any other means of instilling fear, takes or holds, detains, or arrests any person, with a design to take the person out of this state, without having established a claim, according to the laws of the United States, or of this state, or who hires, persuades, entices, decoys, or seduces by false promises, misrepresentations, or the like, any person to go out of this state, or to be taken or removed therefrom, for the purpose and with the intent to sell that person into slavery or involuntary servitude, or otherwise to employ that person for his or her own use, or to the use of another, without the free will and consent of that persuaded person, is guilty of kidnapping.

(d) Every person who, being out of this state, abducts or takes by force or fraud any person contrary to the law of the place where that act is committed, and brings, sends, or conveys that person within the limits of this state, and is afterwards found within the limits thereof, is guilty of kidnapping.

(e) Subdivisions (a) to (d), inclusive, do not apply to any of the following:

(1) To any person who steals, takes, entices away, detains, conceals, or harbors any child under the age of 14 years, if that act is taken to protect the child from danger of imminent harm.

(2) To any person acting under Section 834 or 837. *(Amended by Stats 1990 ch 55 §1, eff. 1/1/91.)*

§208. Kidnapping; punishment.

(a) Kidnapping is punishable by imprisonment in the state prison for three, five, or eight years.

(b) If the person kidnapped is under 14 years of age at the time of the commission of the crime, the kidnapping is punishable by imprisonment in the state prison for 5, 8, or 11 years. This subdivision is not applicable to the taking, detaining, or concealing, of a minor child by a biological parent, a natural father, as specified in subdivision (a) of Section 7004 of the Civil Code, an adoptive parent, or a person who has been granted access to the minor child by a court order.

(c) In all cases in which probation is granted, the court shall, except in unusual cases where the interests of justice would best be served by a lesser penalty, require as a condition of the probation that the person be confined in the county jail for 12 months. If the court grants probation without requiring the defendant to be confined in the county jail for 12 months, it shall specify its reason or reasons for imposing a lesser penalty.

(d) If the person is kidnapped with the intent to commit rape, oral copulation, sodomy, or rape by instrument, the kidnapping is punishable by imprisonment in the state prison for 5, 8, or 11 years. *(Amended by Stats 1990 ch 55 §2; ch 1560 §1, eff. 1/1/91.)*

§209. Punishment of kidnapping for ransom, reward.

(a) Any person who seizes, confines, inveigles, entices, decoys, abducts, conceals, kidnaps or carries away another person by any means whatsoever with intent to hold or detain, or who holds or detains, that person for ransom, reward or to commit extortion or to exact from another person any money or valuable thing, or any person who aids or abets any such act, is guilty of a felony, and upon conviction thereof, shall be punished by imprisonment in the state prison for life without possibility of parole in cases in which any person subjected to any such act suffers death or bodily harm, or is intentionally confined in a manner which exposes such person to a substantial likelihood of death, or shall be punished by imprisonment in the state prison for life with the possibility of parole in cases where no such person suffers death or bodily harm.

(b) Any person who kidnaps or carries away any individual to commit robbery shall be punished by imprisonment in the state prison for life with possibility of parole.

(c) In all cases in which probation is granted, the court shall, except in unusual cases where the interests of justice would best be served by a lesser penalty, require as a condition of the probation that the person be confined in the county jail for 12 months. If the court grants probation without requiring the defendant to be confined in the county jail for 12 months, it shall specify its reason or reasons for imposing a lesser penalty. *(Amended by Stats 1990 ch 55 §3, eff. 1/1/91.)*

§210. Posing as kidnapper.

Every person who for the purpose of obtaining any ransom or reward, or to extort or exact from any person any money or thing of value, poses as, or in any manner represents himself to be a person who has seized, confined, inveigled, enticed, decoyed, abducted, concealed, kidnapped or carried away any person, or who poses as, or in any manner represents himself to be a person who holds or detains such person, or who poses as, or in any manner represents himself to be a person who has aided or abetted any such act, or who poses as or in any manner represents himself to be a person who has the influence, power, or ability, to obtain the release of such person so seized, confined, inveigled, enticed, decoyed, abducted, concealed, kidnapped or carried away, is guilty of a felony and upon conviction thereof shall be punished by imprisonment for two, three or four years.

Nothing in this section prohibits any person who, in good faith believes that he can rescue any person who has been seized, confined, inveigled, enticed, decoyed, abducted, concealed, kidnapped or carried away, and who has had no part in, or connection with, such confinement, inveigling, decoying, abducting, concealing, kidnapping, or carrying away, from offering to rescue or obtain the release of such person for a monetary consideration or other thing of value.

© 1992 by J., B. & L. Gould
Printed in the U.S.A.   EP

CHAPTER 3.5

HOSTAGES
(Added by Stats 1987 ch 580 §1.)

§210.5. Taking of hostages.
Every person who commits the offense of false imprisonment, as defined in Section 236, against a person for purposes of protection from arrest, which substantially increases the risk of harm to the victim, or for purposes of using the person as a shield is punishable by imprisonment in the state prison for three, five, or eight years. *(Added by Stats 1987 ch 580 §1.)*

CHAPTER 4

ROBBERY

§211. Robbery defined.
Robbery is the felonious taking of personal property in the possession of another, from his person or immediate presence, and against his will, accomplished by means of force or fear.

§211a. *Repealed by Stats 1986 ch 1428.*

§212. Fear of unlawful injury.
The fear mentioned in Section 211 may be either:
1. The fear of an unlawful injury to the person or property of the person robbed, or of any relative of his or member of his family; or,
2. The fear of an immediate and unlawful injury to the person or property of anyone in the company of the person robbed at the time of the robbery.

§212.5. Robbery of the first degree.
(a) Every robbery of any person who is performing his or her duties as an operator of any bus, taxicab, cable car, streetcar, trackless trolley, or other vehicle, including a vehicle operated on stationary rails or on a track or rail suspended in the air, and used for the transportation of persons for hire, every robbery of any passenger which is perpetrated on any of these vehicles, and every robbery which is perpetrated in an inhabited dwelling house, a vessel, as defined in Section 21 of the Harbors and Navigation Code, which is inhabited and designed for habitation, or a trailer coach, as defined in the Vehicle Code, which is inhabited, or the inhabited portion of any other building, is robbery of the first degree.

(b) All kinds of robbery other than those listed in subdivision (a) are of the second degree. *(Amended by Stats 1989 ch 361 §1, eff. 1/1/90.)*

§213. Robbery; how punishable.
(a) Robbery is punishable as follows:
(1) Robbery of the first degree: by imprisonment in the state prison for three, four, or six years.
(2) Robbery of the second degree: by imprisonment in the state prison for two, three, or five years.
(b) Notwithstanding Section 664, attempted robbery is punishable by imprisonment in the state prison. *(Added by Stats 1986 ch 1428 §4.)*

§213.5. *Repealed by Stats 1986 ch 1428.*

§214. Train robbery.
Every person who goes upon or boards any railroad train, car or engine, with the intention of robbing any passenger or other person on such train, car or engine, of any personal property thereon in the possession or care or under the control of any such passenger or other person, or who interferes in any manner with any switch, rail, sleeper, viaduct, culvert, embankment, structure or appliance pertaining to or connected with any railroad, or places any dynamite or other explosive substance or material upon or near the track of any railroad, or who sets fire to any railroad bridge or trestle, or who shows, masks, extinguishes or alters any light or other signal, or exhibits or compels any other person to exhibit any false light or signal, or who stops any such train, car or engine, or slackens the speed thereof, or who compels or attempts to compel any person in charge or control thereof to stop any such train, car or engine, or slacken the speed thereof, with the intention of robbing any passenger or other person on such train, car or engine, of any personal property thereon in the possession or charge or under the control of any such passenger or other person, is guilty of a felony.

CHAPTER 5

ATTEMPTS TO KILL

§217.1. Attempted murder or assault upon governmental officers.
(a) Every person who commits any assault upon the President or Vice President of the United States, the Governor of any state or territory, any justice or judge of the United States or any state or territory, the secretary or director of any executive agency or department of the United States or any state or territory, or any other official of the United States or any state or territory holding elective office, any mayor, city council member, county supervisor, sheriff, district attorney, public defender, or the chief of police of any municipal police department, in retaliation for or to prevent the performance of the victim's official duties, shall be punished by imprisonment in the county jail not exceeding one year or by imprisonment in the state prison.

(b) Every person who attempts to commit murder against any person listed in subdivision (a) in retaliation for or to prevent the performance of the victim's official duties, shall be confined in the state prison for a term of 15 years to life. The provisions of Article 2.5 (commencing with Section 2930) of Chapter 7 of Title 1 of Part 3 shall apply to reduce any minimum term of 15 years in a state prison imposed pursuant to this section, but such person shall not otherwise be released on parole prior to such time. *(Amended by Stats 1986 ch 616 §1.)*

§218. Train wrecking.
Every person who unlawfully throws out a switch, removes a rail, or places any obstruction on any railroad with the intention of derailing any passenger, freight or other train, car or engine, or who unlawfully places any dynamite or other explosive material or any other obstruction upon or near the track of any railroad with the intention of blowing up or derailing any such train, car or engine, or who unlawfully sets fire to any railroad bridge or trestle, over which any such train, car or engine must pass with the intention of

wrecking such train, car or engine, is guilty of a felony, and shall be punished by imprisonment in the state prison for life without possibility of parole.

§219. Acts resulting in train wrecking; penalty.

Every person who unlawfully throws out a switch, removes a rail, or places any obstruction on any railroad with the intention of derailing any passenger, freight or other train, car or engine and thus derails the same, or who unlawfully places any dynamite or other explosive material or any other obstruction upon or near the track of any railroad with the intention of blowing up or derailing any such train, car or engine and thus blows up or derails the same, or who unlawfully sets fire to any railroad bridge or trestle over which any such train, car or engine must pass with the intention of wrecking such train, car or engine, and thus wrecks the same, is guilty of a felony and punishable with death or imprisonment in the state prison for life without possibility of parole in cases where any person suffers death as a proximate result thereof, or imprisonment in the state prison for life with the possibility of parole, in cases where no person suffers death as a proximate result thereof. The penalty shall be determined pursuant to Sections 190.3 and 190.4.

§219.1. Throwing objects at vehicles.

Every person who unlawfully throws, hurls or projects at a vehicle operated by a common carrier, while such vehicle is either in motion or stationary, any rock, stone, brick, bottle, piece of wood or metal or any other missile of any kind or character, or does any unlawful act, with the intention of wrecking such vehicle and doing bodily harm, and thus wrecks the same and causes bodily harm, is guilty of a felony and punishable by imprisonment in the state prison for two, four, or six years.

§219.2. Throwing objects or missiles at vehicle or watercraft.

Every person who willfully throws, hurls, or projects a stone or other hard substance, or shoots a missile, at a train, locomotive, railway car, caboose, cable railway car, street railway car, or bus or at a steam vessel or watercraft used for carrying passengers or freight on any of the waters within or bordering on this state, is punishable by imprisonment in the county jail not exceeding one year, or in a state prison, or by fine not exceeding two thousand dollars ($2,000), or by both such fine and imprisonment.

§219.3. Throwing objects from toll bridge.

Any person who wilfully drops or throws any object or missile from any toll bridge is guilty of a misdemeanor.

CHAPTER 6

ASSAULTS WITH INTENT TO COMMIT FELONY, OTHER THAN ASSAULTS WITH INTENT TO MURDER

§220. Assault with intent to commit mayhem or sex crimes.

Every person who assaults another with intent to commit mayhem, rape, sodomy, oral copulation, or any violation of Section 264.1, 288 or 289 is punishable by imprisonment in the state prison for two, four, or six years.

§222. Administering stupefying drugs.

Every person guilty of administering to another any chloroform, ether, laudanum, or any controlled substance, anaesthetic, or intoxicating agent, with intent thereby to enable or assist himself or herself or any other person to commit a felony, is guilty of a felony.

CHAPTER 7

DUELS AND CHALLENGES

§225. Duel defined.

A duel is any combat with deadly weapons, fought between two or more persons, by previous agreement or upon a previous quarrel.

§226. Punishment for fighting a duel when death results.

Every person guilty of fighting any duel, from which death ensues within a year and a day, is punishable by imprisonment in the state prison for two, three or four years.

§227. Punishment for fighting a duel.

Every person who fights a duel, or who sends or accepts a challenge to fight a duel is punishable by imprisonment in the state prison, or in the county jail not exceeding one year.

§228. Persons fighting duels etc., with deadly weapons disqualified from public office, suffrage.

Any citizen of this state who shall fight a duel with deadly weapons, or send or accept a challenge to fight a duel with deadly weapons, either within this state or out of it, or who shall act as second, or knowingly aid or assist in any manner those thus offending, shall not be allowed to hold any office of profit, or to enjoy the right of suffrage, and shall be declared so disqualified in the judgment, upon conviction.

§229. Posting for not fighting.

Every person who posts or publishes another for not fighting a duel, or for not sending or accepting a challenge to fight a duel, or who uses any reproachful or contemptuous language, verbal, written, or printed, to or concerning another, for not sending or accepting a challenge to fight a duel, or with intent to provoke a duel, is guilty of a misdemeanor.

§230. Penalty for non-prevention of duels.

Every judge, sheriff, or other officer bound to preserve the public peace, who has knowledge of the intention on the part of any person to fight a duel, and who does not exert his official authority to arrest the party and prevent the duel, is punishable by fine not exceeding one thousand dollars ($1,000).

§231. Leaving the State with intent to evade laws against dueling.

Every person who leaves this state with intent to evade any of the provisions of this Chapter, and to commit any act out of this State such as is prohibited by this Chapter, and who does any act, although out of this State, which would be punishable by such provisions if committed within this State, is punishable in the same manner as he would have been in case such act had been committed within this State.

© 1992 by J., B. & L. Gould
Printed in the U.S.A. EP

§232. Persons fighting duels, etc., disqualified from public office, suffrage.

Any person who fights a duel, or sends or accepts a challenge to fight a duel, either within this state or out of it, or who shall act as a second, or knowingly aid or assist in any manner those thus offending, shall not be allowed to hold any office of profit, or to enjoy the right of suffrage.

CHAPTER 8

FALSE IMPRISONMENT

§236. False imprisonment defined.

False imprisonment is the unlawful violation of the personal liberty of another.

§237. Punishment for false imprisonment.

False imprisonment is punishable by fine not exceeding one thousand dollars ($1,000), or by imprisonment in the county jail not more than one year, or by both. If such false imprisonment be effected by violence, menace, fraud, or deceit, it shall be punishable by imprisonment in the state prison.

CHAPTER 9

ASSAULT AND BATTERY

§240. Assault defined.

An assault is an unlawful attempt, coupled with a present ability, to commit a violent injury on the person of another.

§241. Punishment for assault.

(a) An assault is punishable by a fine not exceeding one thousand dollars ($1,000), or by imprisonment in the county jail not exceeding six months, or by both the fine and imprisonment.

(b) When an assault is committed against the person of a peace officer, firefighter, emergency medical technician, mobile intensive care paramedic, lifeguard, process server, traffic officer, or animal control officer engaged in the performance of his or her duties, or a physician or nurse engaged in rendering emergency medical care outside a hospital, clinic, or other health care facility, and the person committing the offense knows or reasonably should know that the victim is a peace officer, firefighter, emergency medical technician, mobile intensive care paramedic, lifeguard, process server, traffic officer, or animal control officer engaged in the performance of his or her duties, or a physician or nurse engaged in rendering emergency medical care, the assault is punishable by a fine not exceeding two thousand dollars ($2,000), or by imprisonment in the county jail not exceeding one year, or by both the fine and imprisonment.

(c) As used in this section, the following definitions apply:

(1) Peace officer means any person defined in Chapter 4.5 (commencing with Section 830) of Title 3 of Part 2.

(2) "Emergency medical technician" means a person possessing a valid course completion certificate from a program approved by the State Department of Health Services for the medical training and education of ambulance personnel, and who meets the standards of Division 2.5 (commencing with Section 1797) of the Health and Safety Code.

(3) "Mobile intensive care paramedic" refers to those persons who meet the standards set forth in Division 2.5 (commencing with Section 1797) of the Health and Safety Code.

(4) "Nurse" means a person who meets the standards of Division 2.5 (commencing with Section 1797) of the Health and Safety Code.

(5) "Lifeguard" means a person who is:

(A) Employed as a lifeguard by the state, a county, or a city, and is designated by local ordinance as a public officer who has a duty and responsibility to enforce local ordinances and misdemeanors through the issuance of citations.

(B) Wearing distinctive clothing which includes written identification of the person's status as a lifeguard and which clearly identifies the employing organization.

(6) "Process server" means any person who meets the standards or is expressly exempt from the standards set forth in Section 22350 of the Business and Professions Code.

(7) "Traffic officer" means any person employed by a county or city to monitor and enforce state laws and local ordinances relating to parking and the operation of vehicles.

(8) "Animal control officer" means any person employed by a county or city for purposes of enforcing animal control laws or regulations. *(Amended by Stats 1988 ch 160 §126; ch 816 §1, eff. 1/1/89.)*

§241.1. Assault upon custodial officer.

When an assault is committed against the person of a custodial officer as defined in Section 831 or 831.5, and the person committing the offense knows or reasonably should know that such victim is such a custodial officer engaged in the performance of his duties, the offense shall be punished by imprisonment in the county jail not exceeding one year or by imprisonment in the state prison.

§241.2. Assault on school property.

(a) When an assault is committed on school or park property against any person, the assault is punishable by a fine not exceeding two thousand dollars ($2,000), or by imprisonment in the county jail not exceeding one year, or by both such fine and imprisonment.

(b) "School," as used in this section, means any elementary school, junior high school, four-year high school, senior high school, adult school or any branch thereof, opportunity school, continuation high school, regional occupational center, evening high school, technical school, or community college.

(c) "Park," as used in this section, means any publicly maintained or operated park. It does not include any facility when used for professional sports or commercial events. *(Amended by Stats 1989 ch 394 §1, eff. 1/1/90.)*

§241.3. Assault against transportation worker.

When an assault is committed against the person of an operator, driver, or passenger on a bus, taxicab, streetcar, cable car, trackless trolley, or other motor vehicle, including a vehicle operated on stationary rails or on a track or rail suspended in the air, used for the transportation of persons for hire, or against a schoolbus driver, or against the person of a station agent or ticket agent for the entity providing such transportation, and the person who commits the offense knows or reasonably should know that the victim, in the case of an operator, driver, or agent, is engaged in the performance of his or her duties, or is a passenger, the offense shall be punished by a fine not exceeding two thousand dollars ($2,000), or by imprisonment in the county jail not exceeding one year, or by both such fine and imprisonment. *(Amended by Stats 1987 ch 801 §2.)*

§241.4. Assault against school district peace officer.

An assault is punishable by fine not exceeding one thousand dollars ($1,000), or by imprisonment in the county jail not exceeding six months, or by both. When the assault is committed against the person of a peace officer engaged in the performance of his or her duties as a member of a police department of a school district pursuant to Section 39670 of the Education Code, and the person committing the offense knows or reasonably should know that the victim is a peace officer engaged in the performance of his or her duties, the offense shall be punished by imprisonment in the county jail not exceeding one year or by imprisonment in the state prison.

§241.6. Assault committed against school employee.

When an assault is committed against a school employee in retaliation for an act performed in the course of his or her duties, whether on or off campus, during the schoolday or at any other time, and the person committing the offense knows or reasonably should know the victim is a school employee, the assault is punishable by imprisonment in the county jail not exceeding one year, or by a fine not exceeding two thousand dollars ($2,000), or by both such fine and imprisonment.

For purposes of this section, "school employee" has the same meaning as defined in subdivision (d) of Section 245.5.

This section shall not apply to conduct arising during the course of an otherwise lawful labor dispute. *(Added by Stats 1989 ch 1306 §3, eff. 1/1/90.)*

§241.7. Assault against jurors.

Any person who is a party to a civil or criminal action in which a jury has been selected to try the case and who, while the legal action is pending or after the conclusion of the trial, commits an assault against any juror or alternate juror who was selected and sworn in that legal action, shall be punished by a fine not to exceed two thousand dollars ($2,000), or by imprisonment in the county jail not exceeding one year, or by both such fine and imprisonment, or by imprisonment in the state prison. *(Added by Stats 1986 ch 616 §2.)*

§242. Battery defined.

A battery is any willful and unlawful use of force or violence upon the person of another.

§243. Punishment for battery.

(a) A battery is punishable by a fine of not exceeding two thousand dollars ($2,000), or by imprisonment in the county jail not exceeding six months, or by both such fine and imprisonment.

(b) When a battery is committed against the person of a peace officer, custodial officer, firefighter, emergency medical technician, mobile intensive care paramedic, lifeguard, process server, traffic officer, or animal control officer engaged in the performance of

his or her duties, whether on or off duty, including when the peace officer is in a police uniform and is concurrently performing the duties required of him or her as a peace officer while also employed in a private capacity as a part-time or casual private security guard or patrolman, or a physician or nurse engaged in rendering emergency medical care outside a hospital, clinic, or other health care facility, and the person committing the offense knows or reasonably should know that the victim is a peace officer, custodial officer, firefighter, emergency medical technician, mobile intensive care paramedic, lifeguard, process server, traffic officer, or animal control officer engaged in the performance of his or her duties, or a physician or nurse engaged in rendering emergency medical care, the battery is punishable by a fine not exceeding two thousand dollars ($2,000), or by imprisonment in the county jail not exceeding one year, or by both such fine and imprisonment.

(c) When a battery is committed against a peace officer, custodial officer, firefighter, emergency medical technician, mobile intensive care paramedic, lifeguard, process server, traffic officer, or animal control officer engaged in the performance of his or her duties, whether on or off duty, including when the peace officer is in a police uniform and is concurrently performing the duties required of him or her as a peace officer while also employed in a private capacity as a part-time or casual private security guard or patrolman, or a physician or nurse engaged in rendering emergency medical care outside a hospital, clinic, or other health care facility, and the person committing the offense knows or reasonably should know that the victim is a peace officer, custodial officer, firefighter, emergency medical technician, mobile intensive care paramedic, lifeguard, process server, traffic officer, or animal control officer engaged in the performance of his or her duties, or a physician or nurse engaged in rendering emergency medical care, and an injury is inflicted on that victim, the battery is punishable by imprisonment in the county jail for a period of not more than one year, or by a fine of not more than two thousand dollars ($2,000), or by imprisonment in the state prison for 16 months, or two or three years.

(d) When a battery is committed against any person and serious bodily injury is inflicted on the person, the battery is punishable by imprisonment in the county jail for a period of not more than one year or imprisonment in the state prison for two, three, or four years.

(e) When a battery is committed against a non-cohabitating former spouse, fiancé, fiancée, or a person with whom the defendant currently has, or has previously had, a dating relationship, the battery is punishable by a fine not exceeding two thousand dollars ($2,000), or by imprisonment in the county jail for a period of not more than one year, or by both. If probation is granted, or the execution or imposition of the sentence is suspended, it shall be a condition thereof that the defendant participate in, for no less than one year, and successfully complete, a batterer's treatment program, or if none is available, in another appropriate counseling program designated by the court; however, this provision shall not be construed as requiring a city, a county, or a city and county to provide a new program or higher level of service as contemplated by Section 6 of Article XIII B of the California Constitution.

© 1992 by J., B. & L. Gould
Printed in the U.S.A.   EP

The Legislature finds and declares that these specified crimes merit special consideration when imposing a sentence so as to display society's condemnation for such crimes of violence upon victims with whom a close relationship has been formed.

(f) As used in this section:

(1) "Peace officer" means any person defined in Chapter 4.5 (commencing with Section 830) of Title 3 of Part 2.

(2) "Emergency medical technician" means a person possessing a valid course completion certificate from a program approved by the State Department of Health Services for the medical training and education of ambulance personnel, and who meets the standards of Division 2.5 (commencing with Section 1797) of the Health and Safety Code.

(3) "Mobile intensive care paramedic" means any person who meets the standards set forth in Section 1797.84 of, and Division 2.5 (commencing with Section 1797) of, the Health and Safety Code.

(4) "Nurse" means a person who meets the standards of Division 2.5 (commencing with Section 1797) of the Health and Safety Code.

(5) "Serious bodily injury" means a serious impairment of physical condition, including, but not limited to, the following: loss of consciousness; concussion; bone fracture; protracted loss or impairment of function of any bodily member or organ; a wound requiring extensive suturing; and serious disfigurement.

(6) "Injury" means any physical injury which requires professional medical treatment.

(7) "Custodial officer" means any person who has the responsibilities and duties described in Section 831 and who is employed by a law enforcement agency of any city or county or who performs those duties as a volunteer.

(8) "Lifeguard" means a person defined in paragraph (5) of subdivision (c) of Section 241.

(9) "Traffic officer" means any person employed by a city, county, or city and county, to monitor and enforce state laws and local ordinances relating to parking and the operation of vehicles.

(10) "Animal control officer" means any person employed by a city, county, or city and county for purposes of enforcing animal control laws or regulations.

(11) "Dating relationship" means frequent, intimate associations primarily characterized by the expectation of affectional or sexual involvement independent of financial considerations.

It is the intent of the Legislature by amendments to this section at the 1981-82 and 1983-84 Regular Sessions to abrogate the holdings in cases such as People v. Corey, 21 Cal. 3d 738, and Cervantez v. J.C. Penney Co., 24 Cal. 3d 579, and to reinstate prior judicial interpretations of this section as they relate to criminal sanctions for battery on peace officers who are employed, on a part-time or casual basis, while wearing a police uniform as private security guards or patrolmen and to allow the exercise of peace officer powers concurrently with that employment. *(Amended by Stats 1989 ch 191 §2, eff. 1/1/90.)*

§243.1. Battery against custodial officer.

When a battery is committed against the person of a custodial officer as defined in Section 831 of the Penal Code, and the person committing the offense knows or reasonably should know that such victim is a custodial officer engaged in the performance of his duties, and such custodial officer is engaged in the performance of his duties, the offense shall be punished by imprisonment in the state prison.

§243.2. Battery on school property.

(a) Except as otherwise provided in Section 243.6, when a battery is committed on school property or park property against any person, the battery is punishable by a fine not exceeding two thousand dollars ($2000), or by imprisonment in the county jail not exceeding one year, or by both such fine and imprisonment.

(b) "School," as used in this section, means any elementary school, junior high school, four-year high school, senior high school, adult school or any branch thereof, opportunity school, continuation high school, regional occupational center, evening high school, technical school, or community college.

(c) "Park," as used in this section, means any publicly maintained or operated park. It does not include any facility when used for professional sports or commercial events.

This section shall not apply to conduct arising during the course of an otherwise lawful labor dispute. *(Amended by Stats 1989 ch 394 §2, 1306 §4.5, eff. 1/1/90.)*

§243.3. Battery on a public conveyance.

When a battery is committed against the person of an operator, driver, or passenger on a bus, taxicab, streetcar, cable car, trackless trolley, or other motor vehicle, including a vehicle operated on stationary rails or on a track or rail suspended in the air, used for the transportation of persons for hire, or against a schoolbus driver, or against the person of a station agent or ticket agent for the entity providing such transportation, and the person who commits the offense knows or reasonably should know that the victim, in the case of an operator, driver, or agent, is engaged in the performance of his or her duties, or is a passenger the offense shall be punished by a fine not exceeding two thousand dollars ($2,000), or by imprisonment in the county jail not exceeding one year, or by both such fine and imprisonment. If an injury is inflicted on that victim, the offense shall be punished by imprisonment in the county jail for a period of not more than one year, or by a fine of not more than two thousand dollars ($2,000), or by imprisonment in the state prison for 16 months, or two or three years. *(Amended by Stats 1987 ch 801 §3.)*

§243.4. Punishment for sexual battery.

(a) Any person who touches an intimate part of another person while that person is unlawfully restrained by the accused or an accomplice, and if the touching is against the will of the person touched and is for the purpose of sexual arousal, sexual gratification, or sexual abuse, is guilty of sexual battery. Such an act is punishable by imprisonment in a county jail for not more than one year, and by a fine not exceeding two thousand dollars ($2,000); or by imprisonment in the state prison for two, three, or four years, and by a fine not exceeding ten thousand dollars ($10,000).

(b) Any person who touches an intimate part of another person who is institutionalized for medical treatment and who is seriously disabled or medically incapacitated, if the touching is against the will of the person touched, and if the touching is for the purpose of sexual arousal, sexual gratification, or sexual abuse, is guilty of sexual battery. Such an act is punishable by imprisonment in a county jail for not more than one year, and by a fine not exceeding two thousand dollars ($2,000); or by imprisonment in the state prison for two, three, or four years, and by a fine not exceeding ten thousand dollars ($10,000).

(c) Any person who, for the purpose of sexual arousal, sexual gratification, or sexual abuse, causes another, against that person's will while that person is unlawfully restrained either by the accused or an accomplice, or is institutionalized for medical treatment and is seriously disabled or medically incapacitated, to masturbate or touch an intimate part of either of those persons or a third person, is guilty of sexual battery. Such an act is punishable by imprisonment in a county jail for not more than one year, and by a fine not exceeding two thousand dollars ($2,000); or by imprisonment in the state prison for two, three, or four years, and by a fine not exceeding ten thousand dollars ($10,000).

(d) Any person who touches an intimate part of another person, if the touching is against the will of the person touched, and is for the specific purpose of sexual arousal, sexual gratification, or sexual abuse, is guilty of misdemeanor sexual battery, punishable by a fine not exceeding two thousand dollars ($2,000), or by imprisonment in a county jail not exceeding six months, or by both that fine and imprisonment. As used in this subdivision, "touches" means physical contact with another person, whether accomplished directly, through the clothing of the person committing the offense, or through the clothing of the victim.

(e) As used in subdivisions (a), (b), and (c), "touches" means physical contact with the skin of another person whether accomplished directly or through the clothing of the person committing the offense.

(f) As used in this section, the following terms have the following meanings:

(1) "Intimate part" means the sexual organ, anus, groin, or buttocks of any person, and the breast of a female.

(2) "Sexual battery" does not include the crimes defined in Section 261 or 289.

(3) "Seriously disabled" means a person with severe physical or sensory disabilities.

(4) "Medically incapacitated" means a person who is incapacitated as a result of prescribed sedatives, anesthesia, or other medication.

(5) "Institutionalized" means a person who is located voluntarily or involuntarily in a hospital, medical treatment facility, nursing home, acute care facility, or mental hospital.

(g) This section shall not be construed to limit or prevent prosecution under any other law which also proscribes a course of conduct that also is proscribed by this section. (Amended by Stats 1991 ch 149 §1, eff. 1/1/92.)

§243.5. Assault or battery on school premises.

(a) When a person commits an assault or battery on school property during hours when school activities are being conducted, a peace officer may, without a warrant, notwithstanding subdivision (2) or (3) of Section 836, arrest the person who commits the assault or battery:

(1) Whenever the person has committed the assault or battery, although not in the peace officer's presence.

(2) Whenever the peace officer has reasonable cause to believe that the person to be arrested has committed the assault or battery, whether or not it has in fact been committed.

(b) "School," as used in this section, means any elementary school, junior high school, four-year high school, senior high school, adult school or any branch thereof, opportunity school, continuation high school, regional occupational center, evening high school, technical school, or community college. (Amended by Stats 1987 ch 828 §13.)

§243.6. Battery committed against school employee.

When a battery is committed against a school employee in retaliation for an act performed in the course of his or her duties, whether on or off campus, during the school day or at any other time, and the person committing the offense knows or reasonably should know that the victim is a school employee, the battery is punishable by imprisonment in the county jail not exceeding one year, or by a fine not exceeding two thousand dollars ($2,000), or by both such fine and imprisonment. However, if an injury is inflicted on the victim, the battery shall be punishable by imprisonment in the county jail for not more than one year, or by a fine of not more than two thousand dollars ($2,000), or by imprisonment in the state prison for 16 months, or two or three years.

For purposes of this section, "school employee" has the same meaning as defined in subdivision (d) of Section 245.5.

This section shall not apply to conduct arising during the course of an otherwise lawful labor dispute. (Added by Stats 1989 ch 1306 §5, eff. 1/1/90.)

§243.7. Battering a juror, punishment.

Any person who is a party to a civil or criminal action in which a jury has been selected to try the case and who, while the legal action is pending or after the conclusion of the trial commits a battery against any juror or alternate juror who was selected and sworn in that legal action shall be punished by a fine not to exceed five thousand dollars ($5,000), or by imprisonment in the county jail not exceeding one year, or by both such fine and imprisonment, or by the imprisonment in the state prison for 16 months, or for two or three years.

§243.8. Battering a sports official.

(a) When a battery is committed against a sports official immediately prior to, during, or immediately following an interscholastic, intercollegiate, or any other organized amateur or professional athletic contest in which the sports official is participating, and the person who commits the offense knows or reasonably should know that the victim is engaged in the performance of his or her duties, the offense shall be punishable by a fine not exceeding two thousand dollars ($2,000), or by imprisonment in the county jail not exceeding one year, or by both that fine and imprisonment.

(b) For purposes of this section, "sports official" means any individual who serves as a referee, umpire, linesman, or who serves in a similar capacity but may be known by a different title or name and is duly registered by, or a member of, a local, state, regional, or national organization engaged in part in providing education and training to sports officials. (Added by Stats 1991 ch 575 §1, eff. 1/1/92.)

48

© 1992 by J., B. & L. Gould
Printed in the U.S.A.   EP

§244. Punishment for assaults with caustic chemicals.

Every person who willfully and maliciously places or throws, or causes to be placed or thrown, upon the person of another, any vitriol, corrosive acid, or caustic chemical of any nature, with the intent to injure the flesh or disfigure the body of such person, is punishable by imprisonment in the state prison for two, three or four years.

§244.5. Punishment for assault by infliction of electrical charge.

(a) As used in this section, "stun gun" means any item, except a taser, used or intended to be used as either an offensive or defensive weapon that is capable of temporarily immobilizing a person by the infliction of an electrical charge.

(b) Every person who commits an assault upon the person of another with a stun gun or taser shall be punished by imprisonment in a county jail for a term not exceeding one year, or by imprisonment in the state prison for 16 months, two, or three years.

(c) Every person who commits an assault upon the person of a peace officer or firefighter with a stun gun or taser, who knows or reasonably should know that the person is a peace officer or firefighter engaged in the performance of his or her duties, when the peace officer or firefighter is engaged in the performance of his or her duties, shall be punished by imprisonment in the county jail for a term not exceeding one year, or by imprisonment in the state prison for two, three, or four years.

(d) This section shall not be construed to preclude or in any way limit the applicability of Section 245 in any criminal prosecution. *(Amended by Stats 1988 ch 1113 §1, eff. 1/1/89.)*

§245. Punishment for assault with deadly weapon or instrument.

(a) (1) Every person who commits an assault upon the person of another with a deadly weapon or instrument other than a firearm or by any means of force likely to produce great bodily injury is punishable by imprisonment in the state prison for two, three or four years, or in a county jail not exceeding one year, or by fine not exceeding ten thousand dollars ($10,000), or by both such fine and imprisonment.

(2) Every person who commits an assault upon the person of another with a firearm is punishable by imprisonment in the state prison for two, three, or four years, or in a county jail for a term of not less than six months and not exceeding one year, or by both a fine not exceeding ten thousand dollars ($10,000) and imprisonment.

(3) Every person who commits an assault upon the person of another with a machinegun, as defined in Section 12200, or an assault weapon, as defined in Section 12276, shall be punished by imprisonment in the state prison for 4, 8, or 12 years.

(b) Every person who commits an assault upon the person of another with a semiautomatic rifle shall be punished by imprisonment in the state prison for three, six, or nine years.

(c) Every person who commits an assault with a deadly weapon or instrument, other than a firearm, or by any means likely to produce great bodily injury upon the person of a peace officer or fireman, and who knows or reasonably should know that the victim is a peace officer or fireman engaged in the performance of his or her duties, when such peace officer or fireman is engaged in the performance of his or her duties shall be punished by imprisonment in the state prison for three, four, or five years.

(d) (1) Every person who commits an assault with a firearm upon the person of a peace officer or firefighter, and who knows or reasonably should know that the victim is a peace officer or firefighter engaged in the performance of his or her duties, when the peace officer or firefighter is engaged in the performance of his or her duties shall be punished by imprisonment in the state prison for four, six, or eight years.

(2) Every person who commits an assault upon the person of a peace officer or firefighter with a semiautomatic rifle and who knows or reasonably should know that the victim is a peace officer or firefighter, who is engaged in the performance of his or her duties, when such peace officer or firefighter is engaged in the performance of his or her duties, shall be punished by imprisonment in the state prison for five, seven, or nine years.

(3) Every person who commits an assault with a machinegun, as defined in Section 1220, or an assault weapon, as defined in Section 12276, upon the person of a peace officer or firefighter, and who knows or reasonably should know that the victim is a peace officer or firefighter engaged in the performance of his or her duties, shall be punished by imprisonment in the state prison for 6, 9, or 12 years.

(e) When a person is convicted of a violation of this section, in a case involving use of a deadly weapon or instrument or firearm, and the weapon or instrument or firearm is owned by that person, the court shall order that the weapon or instrument or firearm be deemed a nuisance and it shall be confiscated and disposed of in the manner provided by Section 12028.

(f) As used in this section, "peace officer" refers to any person designated as a peace officer in Chapter 4.5 (commencing with Section 830) of Title 3 of Part 2. *(Amended by Stats 1989 ch 18, 19 §1, 1167 §1, eff. 1/1/90.)*

§245.1. Firemen and emergency rescue personnel defined.

As used in Sections 148.2, 241, 243, 244.5, and 245, "fireman" or "firefighter" includes any person who is an officer, employee or member of a fire department or fire protection or firefighting agency of the federal government, the State of California, a city, county, city and county, district, or other public or municipal corporation or political subdivision of this state, whether such person is a volunteer or partly paid or fully paid, while he or she is actually engaged in firefighting, fire supervision, fire suppression, fire prevention, or fire investigation.

As used in Section 148.2, "emergency rescue personnel" means any person who is an officer, employee or member of a fire department or fire protection or firefighting agency of the federal government, the State of California, a city, county, city and county, district, or other public or municipal corporation or political subdivision of this state, whether such person is a volunteer or partly paid or fully paid, while he or she is actually engaged in the on-the-site rescue of persons or property during an emergency as defined by subdivision (c) of Section 148.3.

§245.2. Punishment for assault against transportation personnel or passenger.

Every person who commits an assault with a deadly weapon or instrument or by any means of force likely to produce great bodily injury upon the person of an operator, driver, or passenger on a bus, taxicab, streetcar, cable car, trackless trolley, or other motor vehicle, including a vehicle operated on stationary rails or on a track or rail suspended in the air, used for the transportation of persons for hire, or upon the person of a station agent or ticket agent for the entity providing such transportation, when the driver, operator, or agent is engaged in the performance of his or her duties, and where the person who commits the assault knows or reasonably should know that the victim is engaged in the performance of his or her duties, or is a passenger, shall be punished by imprisonment in the state prison for three, four, or five years. *(Amended by Stats 1987 ch 801 §4.)*

§245.3. Assault upon custodial officer.

Every person who commits an assault with a deadly weapon or instrument or by any means likely to produce great bodily injury upon the person of a custodial officer as defined in Section 831 or 831.5, and who knows or reasonably should know that such victim is such a custodial officer engaged in the performance of his duties, shall be punished by imprisonment in the state prison for three, four, or five years.

When a person is convicted of a violation of this section in a case involving use of a deadly weapon or instrument, and such weapon or instrument is owned by such person, the court may, in its discretion, order that the weapon or instrument be deemed a nuisance and shall be confiscated and destroyed in the manner provided by Section 12028.

§245.5. Assault upon school employee.

(a) Every person who commits an assault with a deadly weapon or instrument, other than a firearm, or by any means likely to produce great bodily injury upon the person of a school employee, and who knows or reasonably should know that the victim is a school employee engaged in the performance of his or her duties, when that school employee is engaged in the performance of his or her duties, shall be punished by imprisonment in the state prison for three, four or five years, or in the county jail not exceeding one year.

(b) Every person who commits an assault with a firearm upon the person of a school employee, and who knows or reasonably should know that the victim is a school employee engaged in the performance of his or her duties, when the school employee is engaged in the performance of his or her duties, shall be punished by imprisonment in the state prison for four, six, or eight years, or in the county jail for a term of not less than six months and not exceeding one year.

(c) Every person who commits an assault upon the person of a school employee with a stun gun or taser, and who knows or reasonably should know that the person is a school employee engaged in the performance of his or her duties, when the school employee is engaged in the performance of his or her duties, shall be punished by imprisonment in the county jail for a term not exceeding one year or by imprisonment in the state prison for two, three or four years.

This subdivision shall not be construed to preclude or in any way limit the applicability of Section 245 in any criminal prosecution.

(d) As used in the section "school employee" means any person employed as a permanent or probationary certificated or classified employee of a school district on a part-time or full-time basis, including a substitute teacher. "School employee" as used in this section also includes a student teacher. "School" as used in this section has the same meaning as that term is defined in Section 626. *(Added by Stats 1988 ch 1113 §2, eff. 1/1/89.)*

§246. Discharge of firearm at inhabited place.

Any person who shall maliciously and willfully discharge a firearm at an inhabited dwelling house, occupied building, occupied motor vehicle, occupied aircraft, inhabited housecar, as defined in Section 362 of the Vehicle Code, or inhabited camper, as defined in Section 243 of the Vehicle Code, is guilty of a felony, and upon conviction shall be punished by imprisonment in the state prison for three, five, or seven years, or by imprisonment in the county jail for a term of not less than six months and not exceeding one year.

As used in this section, "inhabited" means currently being used for dwelling purposes, whether occupied or not. *(Amended by Stats 1988 ch 911 §1, eff. 9/15/88.)*

§246.1. Forfeiture of vehicle used in offense.

(a) Except as provided in subdivision (f), upon the conviction of any person found guilty of murder in the first or second degree, manslaughter, attempted murder, assault with a deadly weapon, or the unlawful discharge or brandishing of a firearm from or at an occupied vehicle where the victim was killed, attacked, or assaulted from or in a motor vehicle by the use of a firearm on a public street or highway, the court shall order a vehicle used in the commission of that offense sold.

Any vehicle ordered to be sold pursuant to this subdivision shall be surrendered to the sheriff of the county or the chief of police of the city in which the violation occurred. The officer to whom the vehicle is surrendered shall promptly ascertain from the Department of Motor Vehicles the names and addresses of all legal and registered owners of the vehicle and within five days of receiving that information, shall send by certified mail a notice to all legal and registered owners of the vehicle other than the defendant, at the addresses obtained from the department, informing them that the vehicle has been declared a nuisance and will be sold or otherwise disposed of pursuant to this section, and of the approximate date and location of the sale or other disposition. The notice shall also inform any legal owner of its right to conduct the sale pursuant to subdivision (b).

(b) Any legal owner which in the regular course of its business conducts sales of repossessed or surrendered motor vehicles may take possession and conduct the sale of the vehicle if it notifies the officer to whom the vehicle is surrendered of its intent to conduct the sale within 15 days of the mailing of the notice pursuant to subdivision (a). Sale of the vehicle pursuant to this subdivision may be conducted at the time, in the manner, and on the notice usually given by the legal owner for the sale of repossessed or surrendered vehicles. The proceeds of any sale conducted by the legal owner shall be disposed of as provided in subdivision (d).

(c) If the legal owner does not notify the officer to whom the vehicle is surrendered of its intent to con-

© 1992 by J., B. & L. Gould
Printed in the U.S.A.   **EP**

duct the sale as provided in subdivision (b), the officer shall offer the vehicle for sale at public auction within 60 days of receiving the vehicle. At least 10 days but not more than 20 days prior to the sale, not counting the day of sale, the officer shall give notice of the sale by advertising once in a newspaper of general circulation published in the city or county, as the case may be, in which the vehicle is located, which notice shall contain a description of the make, year, model, identification number, and license number of the vehicle, and the date, time, and location of the sale. For motorcycles, the engine number shall also be included. If there is no newspaper of general circulation published in the county, notice shall be given by posting a notice of sale containing the information required by this subdivision in three of the most public places in the city or county in which the vehicle is located and at the place where the vehicle is to be sold for 10 consecutive days prior to and including the day of the sale.

(d) The proceeds of a sale conducted pursuant to this section shall be disposed of in the following priority:

(1) To satisfy the costs of the sale, including costs incurred with respect to the taking and keeping of the vehicle pending sale.

(2) To the legal owner in an amount to satisfy the indebtedness owed to the legal owner remaining as of the date of sale, including accrued interest or finance charges and delinquency charges.

(3) To the holder of any subordinate lien or encumbrance on the vehicle to satisfy any indebtedness so secured if written notification of demand is received before distribution of the proceeds is completed. The holder of a subordinate lien or encumbrance, if requested, shall reasonably furnish reasonable proof of its interest, and unless it does so on request is not entitled to distribution pursuant to this paragraph.

(4) To any other person who can establish an interest in the vehicle, including a community property interest, to the extent of his or her provable interest.

(5) The balance, if any, to the city or county in which the violation occurred, to be deposited in a special account in its general fund to be used exclusively to pay the costs or a part of the costs of providing services or education to prevent juvenile violence.

The person conducting the sale shall disburse the proceeds of the sale as provided in this subdivision, and provide a written accounting regarding the disposition to all persons entitled to or claiming a share of the proceeds, within 15 days after the sale is conducted.

(e) If the vehicle to be sold under this section is not of the type that can readily be sold to the public generally, the vehicle shall be destroyed or donated to an eleemosynary institution.

(f) No vehicle may be sold pursuant to this section in either of the following circumstances:

(1) The vehicle is stolen, unless the identity of the legal and registered owners of the vehicle cannot be reasonably ascertained.

(2) The vehicle is owned by another, or there is a community property interest in the vehicle owned by a person other than the defendant and the vehicle is the only vehicle available to the defendant's immediate family which may be operated on the highway with a class 3 or class 4 driver's license.

(g) A vehicle is used in the commission of a violation of the offenses enumerated in subdivision (a) if a firearm is discharged either from the vehicle at another person or by an occupant of a vehicle other than the vehicle in which the victim is an occupant. *(Added by Stats 1987 ch 1147 §1.)*

§246.3. Discharging firearm in negligent manner.

Except as otherwise authorized by law, any person who willfully discharges a firearm in a grossly negligent manner which could result in injury or death to a person is guilty of a public offense and shall be punished by imprisonment in the county jail not exceeding one year, or by imprisonment in the state prison. *(Added by Stats 1988 ch 1275 §1, eff. 9/24/88.)*

§247. Discharging firearm at unoccupied aircraft or motor vehicles.

(a) Any person who willfully and maliciously discharges a firearm at an unoccupied aircraft is guilty of a felony.

(b) Any person who discharges a firearm at an unoccupied motor vehicle or an uninhabited building or dwelling house is guilty of a public offense punishable by imprisonment in the county jail for not more than one year or in the state prison. This subdivision does not apply to shooting at an abandoned vehicle, unoccupied vehicle, uninhabited building, or dwelling house with the permission of the owner.

As used in this section and Section 246 "aircraft" means any contrivance intended for and capable of transporting persons through the airspace. *(Amended by Stats 1988 ch 911 §2, eff. 9/15/88.)*

§247.5. Discharging laser at aircraft.

Any person who willfully and maliciously discharges a laser at an aircraft, whether in motion or in flight, while occupied, is guilty of a violation of this section, which shall be punishable as either a misdemeanor by imprisonment in the county jail for not more than one year or by a fine of one thousand dollars ($1,000), or a felony by imprisonment in the state prison for 16 months, two years, or three years, or by a fine of two thousand dollars ($2,000). This section does not apply to the conduct of laser development activity by or on behalf of the United States Armed Forces.

As used in this section, "aircraft" means any contrivance intended for and capable of transporting persons through the airspace.

As used in this section, "laser" means a device that utilizes the natural oscillations of atoms or molecules between energy levels for generating coherent electromagnetic radiation in the ultraviolet, visible, or infrared region of the spectrum, and when discharged exceeds one milliwatt continuous wave. *(Added by Stats 1986 ch 790 §1.)*

CHAPTER 10

LIBEL
(Repealed by Stats 1986 ch 141.)

§§248-257. *Repealed by Stats 1986 ch 141.*

CHAPTER 11

SLANDER
(Repealed by Stats 1991 ch 186 §2, eff. 1/1/92.)

§§258-260. *Repealed by Stats 1991 ch 186 §2, eff. 1/1/92.*

© 1992 by J., B. & L. Gould
Printed in the U.S.A. **EP**

TITLE 9

OF CRIMES AGAINST THE PERSON INVOLVING SEXUAL ASSAULT, AND CRIMES AGAINST PUBLIC DECENCY AND GOOD MORALS

CHAPTER 1

RAPE, ABDUCTION, CARNAL ABUSE OF CHILDREN, AND SEDUCTION

§261. Rape defined.

(a) Rape is an act of sexual intercourse accomplished with a person not the spouse of the perpetrator, under any of the following circumstances:

(1) Where a person is incapable, because of a mental disorder or developmental or physical disability, of giving legal consent, and this is known or reasonably should be known to the person committing the act. Notwithstanding the existence of a conservatorship pursuant to the provisions of the Lanterman-Petris-Short Act (Part 1 (commencing with Section 5000) of Division 5 of the Welfare and Institutions Code), the prosecuting attorney shall prove, as an element of the crime, that a mental disorder or developmental or physical disability rendered the alleged victim incapable of giving consent.

(2) Where it is accomplished against a person's will by means of force, violence, duress, menace, or fear of immediate and unlawful bodily injury on the person or another.

(3) Where a person is prevented from resisting by any intoxicating or anesthetic substance, or any controlled substance, administered by or with the privity of the accused.

(4) Where a person is at the time unconscious of the nature of the act, and this is known to the accused.

(5) Where a person submits under the belief that the person committing the act is the victim's spouse, and this belief is induced by any artifice, pretense, or concealment practiced by the accused, with intent to induce the belief.

(6) Where the act is accomplished against the victim's will by threatening to retaliate in the future against the victim or any other person, and there is a reasonable possibility that the perpetrator will execute the threat. As used in this paragraph "threatening to retaliate" means a threat to kidnap or falsely imprison, or to inflict extreme pain, serious bodily injury, or death.

(7) Where the act is accomplished against the victim's will by threatening to use the authority of a public official to incarcerate, arrest, or deport the victim or another, and the victim has a reasonable belief that the perpetrator is a public official. As used in this paragraph, "public official" means a person employed by a governmental agency who has the authority, as part of that position, to incarcerate, arrest, or deport another. The perpetrator does not actually have to be a public official.

(b) As used in this section, "duress" means a direct or implied threat of force, violence, danger, hardship, or retribution sufficient to coerce a reasonable person of ordinary susceptibilities to perform an act which otherwise would not have been performed, or acquiesce in an act to which one otherwise would not have submitted. The total circumstances, including the age of the victim, and his or her relationship to the defendant, are factors to consider in appraising the existence of duress.

(c) As used in this section, "menace" means any threat, declaration, or act which shows an intention to inflict an injury upon another. (*Amended by Stats 1990 ch 630 §1, eff. 1/1/91.*)

§261.5. Unlawful sexual intercourse.

Unlawful sexual intercourse is an act of sexual intercourse accomplished with a female not the wife of the perpetrator, where the female is under the age of 18 years.

§261.6. Consent defined.

In prosecutions under Section 261, 286, 288a, or 289, in which consent is at issue, "consent" shall be defined to mean positive cooperation in act or attitude pursuant to an exercise of free will. The person must act freely and voluntarily and have knowledge of the nature of the act or transaction involved.

A current or previous dating relationship shall not be sufficient to constitute consent where consent is at issue in a prosecution under Section 261, 286, 288a, or 289.

Nothing in this section shall affect the admissibility of evidence or the burden of proof on the issue of consent. (*Amended by Stats 1990 ch 271 §1, eff. 1/1/91.*)

§262. Rape of spouse.

(a) Rape of a person who is the spouse of a perpetrator is an act of sexual intercourse accomplished against the will of the spouse by means of force or fear of immediate and unlawful bodily injury on the spouse or another, or where the act is accomplished against the victim's will by threatening to retaliate in the future against the victim or any other person, and there is a reasonable possibility that the perpetrator will execute the threat. As used in this subdivision "threatening to retaliate" means a threat to kidnap or falsely imprison, or to inflict extreme pain, serious bodily injury, or death.

(b) The provisions of Section 800 shall apply to this section; however, there shall be no arrest or prosecution under this section unless the violation of this section is reported to a peace officer having the power to arrest for a violation of this section or to the district attorney of the county in which the violation occurred, within 90 days after the day of the violation.

§263. Sufficiency of penetration.

The essential guilt of rape consists in the outrage to the person and feelings of the victim of the rape. Any sexual penetration, however slight, is sufficient to complete the crime.

§264. Punishment for rape or unlawful sexual intercourse.

(a) Rape, as defined in Section 261, is punishable by imprisonment in the state prison for three, six, or eight years. Rape, as defined in Section 262, is punishable either by imprisonment in the county jail for not more than one year or in the state prison for three, six, or eight years. Unlawful sexual intercourse, as defined in Section 261.5, is punishable either by imprisonment in the county jail for not more than one year or in the state prison.

(b) In addition to any punishment imposed under this section, the judge may assess a fine not to exceed

© 1992 by J., B. & L. Gould
Printed in the U.S.A.   EP

seventy dollars ($70) against any person who violates Section 261, 261.5 or 262 with the proceeds of this fine to be used in accordance with Section 1463.23. The court shall, however, take into consideration the defendant's ability to pay, and no defendant shall be denied probation because of his or her inability to pay the fine permitted under this subdivision. *(Amended by Stats 1988 ch 1243 §5, eff. 1/1/89.)*

§264.1. Aiding or abetting rape.

The provisions of Section 264 notwithstanding, in any case in which the defendant, voluntarily acting in concert with another person, by force or violence and against the will of the victim, committed an act described in Section 261 or 289, either personally or by aiding and abetting the other person, that fact shall be charged in the indictment or information and if found to be true by the jury, upon a jury trial, or if found to be true by the court, upon a court trial, or if admitted by the defendant, the defendant shall suffer confinement in the state prison for five, seven, or nine years.

§264.2. Sex offense victims: law enforcement agency responsibilities.

(a) Whenever there is an alleged violation of Section 261, 261.5, 262, 286, 288a, or 289, the law enforcement officer assigned to the case shall immediately provide the victim of the crime with the "Victims of Domestic Violence" card, as specified in paragraph (5) of subdivision (i) of Section 13701 of the Penal Code.

(b) The law enforcement officer, or his or her agency, shall immediately notify the local rape victim counseling center whenever a victim of an alleged violation of Section 261, 261.5, 262, 286, 288a, or 289 is transported to a hospital for examination, and the victim approves of that notification. Should there be more than one rape victim counseling center in the local area, the victim shall select the center to be notified. *(Added by Stats 1991 ch 999 §1, eff. 1/1/92.)*

§265. Abduction of women.

Every person who takes any woman unlawfully, against her will, and by force, menace or duress, compels her to marry him, or to marry any other person, or to be defiled, is punishable by imprisonment in the state prison.

§266. Seduction for purposes of prostitution.

Every person who inveigles or entices any unmarried female, of previous chaste character, under the age of 18 years, into any house of ill fame, or of assignation, or elsewhere, for the purpose of prostitution, or to have illicit carnal connection with any man; and every person who aids or assists in such inveiglement or enticement; and every person who, by any false pretenses, false representation, or other fraudulent means, procures any female to have illicit carnal connection with any man, is punishable by imprisonment in the state prison, or by imprisonment in a county jail not exceeding one year, or by a fine not exceeding two thousand dollars ($2,000), or by both such fine and imprisonment.

§266a. Abduction or procurement for prostitution.

Every person who, within this state, takes any person against his or her will and without his or her consent, or with his or her consent procured by fraudulent inducement or misrepresentation, for the purpose of prostitution, as defined in subdivision (b) of Section 647, is punishable by imprisonment in the state prison, and a fine not exceeding two thousand dollars ($2,000).

§266b. Forcing illicit relationship.

Every person who takes any other person unlawfully, and against his or her will, and by force, menace, or duress, compels him or her to live with such person in an illicit relation, against his or her consent, or to so live with any other person, is punishable by imprisonment in the state prison.

§266c. Consent by false or fraudulent pretense.

Every person who induces any other person, except the spouse of the perpetrator, to engage in sexual intercourse, penetration of the genital or anal openings by a foreign object, substance, instrument, or device, oral copulation, or sodomy when his or her consent is procured by false or fraudulent representation or pretense that is made with the intent to create fear, and which does induce fear, and that would cause a reasonable person in like circumstances to act contrary to the person's free will, and does cause the victim to so act, is punishable by imprisonment in either the county jail for not more than one year or in the state prison for two, three, or four years.

As used in this section, "fear" means the fear of unlawful physical injury or death to the person or to any relative of the person or member of the person's family. *(Amended by Stats 1986 ch 1299 §2.)*

§266d. Receiving money for causing cohabitation.

Any person who receives any money or other valuable thing for or on account of placing in custody any other person for the purpose of causing the other person to cohabit with any person to whom the other person is not married, is guilty of a felony.

§266e. Paying a prostitute.

Every person who purchases, or pays any money or other valuable thing for, any person for the purpose of prostitution as defined in subdivision (b) of Section 647, or for the purpose of placing such person, for immoral purposes, in any house or place against his or her will, is guilty of a felony.

§266f. Person sold for immoral purposes.

Every person who sells any person or receives any money or other valuable thing for or on account of his or her placing in custody, for immoral purposes, any person, whether with or without his or her consent, is guilty of a felony.

§266g. Placing or permitting placement of one's wife in house of prostitution.

Every man who, by force, intimidation, threats, persuasion, promises, or any other means, places or leaves, or procures any other person or persons to place or leave, his wife in a house of prostitution, or connives at or consents to, or permits the placing or leaving of his wife in a house of prostitution, or allows or permits her to remain therein, is guilty of a felony and punishable by imprisonment in the state prison for two, three or four years; and in all prosecutions under this section a wife is a competent witness against her husband.

§266h. Pimping; punishment.

Any person who, knowing another person is a prostitute, lives or derives support or maintenance in whole or in part from the earnings or proceeds of the person's prostitution, or from money loaned or advanced to or charged against that person by any keeper or manager or inmate of a house or other place where prostitution is practiced or allowed, or who solicits or receives compensation for soliciting for the person, is guilty of pimping, a felony, and is punishable by imprisonment in the state prison for three, four, or six years, or, where the person engaged in prostitution is under 16 years of age, is punishable by imprisonment in the state prison for three, six, or eight years.

§266i. Pandering; punishment.

Any person who: (a) procures another person for the purpose of prostitution; or (b) by promises, threats, violence, or by any device or scheme, causes, induces, persuades or encourages another person to become a prostitute; or (c) procures for another person a place as inmate in a house of prostitution or as an inmate of any place in which prostitution is encouraged or allowed within this state; or (d) by promises, threats, violence or by any device or scheme, causes, induces, persuades or encourages an inmate of a house of prostitution, or any other place in which prostitution is encouraged or allowed, to remain therein as an inmate; or (e) by fraud or artifice, or by duress of person or goods, or by abuse of any position of confidence or authority, procures another person for the purpose of prostitution, or to enter any place in which prostitution is encouraged or allowed within this state, or to come into this state or leave this state for the purpose of prostitution; or (f) receives or gives, or agrees to receive or give, any money or thing of value for procuring, or attempting to procure, another person for the purpose of prostitution, or to come into this state or leave this state for the purpose of prostitution, is guilty of pandering, a felony, and is punishable by imprisonment in the state prison for three, four, or six years, or, where the other person is under 16 years of age, is punishable by imprisonment in the state prison for three, six, or eight years.

§266j. Lewd acts with children.

Any person who intentionally gives, transports, provides, or makes available, or who offers to give, transport, provide, or make available to another person, a child under the age of 16 for the purpose of any lewd or lascivious act as defined in Section 288, or who causes, induces, or persuades a child under the age of 16 to engage in such an act with another person, is guilty of a felony and shall be imprisoned in the state prison for a term of three, six, or eight years, and by a fine not to exceed fifteen thousand dollars ($15,000). *(Amended by Stats 1987 ch 1068 §1.)*

§266k. Additional fine on conviction.

(a) Upon the conviction of any person for a violation of Section 266h, 266i, or 266j, the court may, in addition to any other penalty or fine imposed, order the defendant to pay an additional fine not to exceed five thousand dollars ($5,000). In setting the amount of the fine, the court shall consider any relevant factors including, but not limited to, the seriousness and gravity of the offense and the circumstances of its commission, whether the defendant derived any economic gain as the result of the crime, and the extent to which the victim suffered losses as a result of the crime. Every fine imposed and collected under this section shall be deposited in the Victim-Witness Assistance Fund to be available for appropriation to fund child sexual exploitation and child sexual abuse victim counseling centers and prevention programs under Section 13837.

(b) If the court orders a fine to be imposed pursuant to this section, the actual administrative cost of collecting that fine, not to exceed 2 percent of the total amount paid, may be paid into the general fund of the county treasury for the use and benefit of the county. *(Added by Stats 1987 ch 1068 §2.)*

§267. Punishment for abduction of person under 18 for purpose of prostitution.

Every person who takes away any other person under the age of 18 years from the father, mother, guardian, or other person having the legal charge of the other person, without their consent, for the purpose of prostitution, is punishable by imprisonment in the state prison, and a fine not exceeding two thousand dollars ($2,000).

§269. *Repealed by Stats 1989 ch 897 §17, 1360 §107, eff. 1/1/90.*

CHAPTER 2

ABANDONMENT AND NEGLECT OF CHILDREN

§270. Child neglect; punishment.

If a parent of a minor child willfully omits, without lawful excuse, to furnish necessary clothing, food, shelter or medical attendance, or other remedial care for his or her child, he or she is guilty of a misdemeanor punishable by a fine not exceeding two thousand dollars ($2,000), or by imprisonment in the county jail not exceeding one year, or by both such fine and imprisonment. If a court of competent jurisdiction has made a final adjudication in either a civil or a criminal action that a person is the parent of a minor child and the person has notice of such adjudication and he or she then willfully omits, without lawful excuse, to furnish necessary clothing, food, shelter, medical attendance or other remedial care for his or her child, this conduct is punishable by imprisonment in the county jail not exceeding one year or in a state prison for a determinate term of one year and one day, or by a fine not exceeding two thousand dollars ($2,000), or by both such fine and imprisonment. This statute shall not be construed so as to relieve such parent from the criminal liability defined herein for such omission merely because the other parent of such child is legally entitled to the custody of such child nor because the other parent of such child or any other person or organization voluntarily or involuntarily furnishes such necessary food, clothing, shelter or medical attendance or other remedial care for such child or undertakes to do so.

Proof of abandonment or desertion of a child by such parent, or the omission by such parent to furnish necessary food, clothing, shelter or medical attendance or other remedial care for his or her child is prima facie evidence that such abandonment or desertion or omission to furnish necessary food, clothing, shelter or medical attendance or other remedial care is willful and without lawful excuse.

© 1992 by J., B. & L. Gould
Printed in the U.S.A.

EP

The court, in determining the ability of the parent to support his or her child, shall consider all income, including social insurance benefits and gifts.

The provisions of this section are applicable whether the parents of such child are or were ever married or divorced, and regardless of any decree made in any divorce action relative to alimony or to the support of the child. A child conceived but not yet born is to be deemed an existing person insofar as this section is concerned.

The husband of a woman who bears a child as a result of artificial insemination shall be considered the father of that child for the purpose of this section, if he consented in writing to the artificial insemination.

If a parent provides a minor with treatment by spiritual means through prayer alone in accordance with the tenets and practices of a recognized church or religious denomination, by a duly accredited practitioner thereof, such treatment shall constitute "other remedial care", as used in this section.

§270a. Refusal to provide support for spouse.

Every individual who has sufficient ability to provide for his or her spouse's support, or who is able to earn the means of such spouse's support, who willfully abandons and leaves his or her spouse in a destitute condition, or who refuses or neglects to provide such spouse with necessary food, clothing, shelter, or medical attendance, unless by such spouse's conduct the individual was justified in abandoning such spouse, is guilty of a misdemeanor.

§270b. Bond for support.

After arrest and before plea or trial, or after conviction or plea of guilty and before sentence under either Section 270 or 270a, if the defendant shall appear before the court and enter into an undertaking with sufficient sureties to the people of the State of California in such penal sum as the court may fix, to be approved by the court, and conditioned that the defendant will pay to the person having custody of such child or to such spouse, such sum per month as may be fixed by the court in order to thereby provide such minor child or such spouse as the case may be, with necessary food, shelter, clothing, medical attendance, or other remedial care, then the court may suspend proceedings or sentence therein; and such undertaking is valid and binding for two years, or such lesser time which the court shall fix; and upon the failure of defendant to comply with such undertaking, the defendant may be ordered to appear before the court and show cause why further proceedings should not be had in such action or why sentence should not be imposed, whereupon the court may proceed with such action, or pass sentence, or for good cause shown may modify the order and take a new undertaking and further suspend proceedings or sentence for a like period.

§270c. Support of indigent parents.

Except as provided in Section 206.5 of the Civil Code, every adult child who, having the ability so to do, fails to provide necessary food, clothing, shelter, or medical attendance for an indigent parent, is guilty of a misdemeanor.

§270d. Disposition of fines.

In any case where there is a conviction and sentence under the provisions of either Section 270 or Section 270a, should a fine be imposed, such fine shall be directed by the court to be paid in whole or in part to the spouse of the defendant or guardian or custodian of the child or children of such defendant, except as follows:

If the children are receiving public assistance, all fines, penalties or forfeitures imposed and all funds collected from the defendant shall be paid to the county department. Money so paid shall be applied first to support for the calendar month following its receipt by the county department and any balance remaining shall be applied to future needs, or be treated as reimbursement for past support furnished from public assistance funds.

§270e. Proof of marriage or parenthood.

No other evidence shall be required to prove marriage of husband and wife, or that a person is the lawful father or mother of a child or children, than is or shall be required to prove such facts in a civil action. In all prosecutions under either Section 270a or 270 of this code, Sections 970, 971, and 980 of the Evidence Code do not apply, and both husband and wife shall be competent to testify to any and all relevant matters, including the fact of marriage and the parentage of a child or children. Proof of the abandonment and nonsupport of a spouse, or of the omission to furnish necessary food, clothing, shelter, or of medical attendance for a child or children is prima facie evidence that such abandonment and nonsupport or omission to furnish necessary food, clothing, shelter or medical attendance is willful. In any prosecution under Section 270, it shall be competent for the people to prove nonaccess of husband to wife or any other fact establishing nonpaternity of a husband. In any prosecution pursuant to Section 270, the final establishment of paternity or nonpaternity in another proceeding shall be admissible as evidence of paternity or nonpaternity.

§270f. Investigation of a non-support report.

Where, under the provisions of this chapter, a report is filed by a parent of a child with the district attorney averring:

(1) That the other parent has failed to provide necessary support and

(2) That neither the child in need of assistance nor another on his behalf is receiving public assistance, the district attorney shall immediately investigate the verity of such report and determine the defaulting parent's location and financial ability to provide the needed support, and upon a finding that the report is true shall immediately take all steps necessary to obtain support for the child in need of assistance.

§270g. Review of non-support report.

A review of each report filed with the district attorney under Section 270f shall be made at 90-day intervals unless the support payments have been legally terminated, the parties involved are permanently located beyond county jurisdiction, or the defaulting parent is complying with the provisions of this chapter.

§270h. Support order.

In any case where there is a conviction under either Section 270 or 270a and there is an order granting probation which includes an order for support, the court may:

(a) Issue an execution on the order for the support payments that accrue during the time the probation

© 1992 by J., B. & L. Gould
Printed in the U.S.A. **EP**

order is in effect, in the same manner as on a judgment in a civil action for support payments. This remedy shall apply only when there is no existing civil order of this state or a foreign court order that has been reduced to a judgment of this state for support of the same person or persons included in the probation support order.

(b) Require assignment of wages pursuant to Chapter 5 (commencing with Section 4390) of Title 1.5 of Part 5 of Division 4 of the Civil Code as a condition of probation. This remedy shall apply only when there is no existing civil order for support of the same person or persons included in the probation support order upon which an order of assignment has been entered pursuant to Chapter 5 (commencing with Section 4390) of Title 1.5 of Part 5 of Division 4 of the Civil Code.

These remedies are in addition to any other remedies available to the court. *(Amended by Stats 1991 ch 1091 §118, eff. 1/1/92.)*

§270.5. Parent's failure to provide home for minor child.

(a) Every parent who refuses, without lawful excuse, to accept his or her minor child into the parent's home, or, failing to do so, to provide alternative shelter, upon being requested to do so by a child protective agency and after being informed of the duty imposed by this statute to do so, is guilty of a misdemeanor and shall be punished by a fine of not more than five hundred dollars ($500).

(b) For purposes of this section, "child protective agency" means a police or sheriff's department, a county probation department, or a county welfare department.

(c) For purposes of this section, "lawful excuse" shall include, but not be limited to, a reasonable fear that the minor child's presence in the home will endanger the safety of the parent or other persons residing in the home.

§271. Punishment for willful desertion of child under 14 years.

Every parent of any child under the age of 14 years, and every person to whom any such child has been confided for nurture, or education, who deserts such child in any place whatever with intent to abandon it, is punishable by imprisonment in the state prison or in the county jail not exceeding one year or by fine not exceeding one thousand dollars ($1,000) or by both.

§271a. Willful abandonment or nonsupport of child under 14 years.

Every person who knowingly and willfully abandons, or who, having ability so to do, fails or refuses to maintain his or her minor child under the age of 14 years, or who falsely, knowing the same to be false, represents to any manager, officer or agent of any orphan asylum or charitable institution for the care of orphans, that any child for whose admission into such asylum or institution application has been made is an orphan, is punishable by imprisonment in the state prison, or in the county jail not exceeding one year, or by fine not exceeding one thousand dollars ($ 1,000), or by both.

§272. Punishment for contributing to the delinquency of a minor.

Every person who commits any act or omits the performance of any duty, which act or omission causes or tends to cause or encourage any person under the age of 18 years to come within the provisions of Sections 300, 601, or 602 of the Welfare and Institutions Code or which act or omission contributes thereto, or any person who, by any act or omission; or by threats, commands, or persuasion, induces or endeavors to induce any person under the age of 18 years or any ward or dependent child of the juvenile court to fail or refuse to conform to a lawful order of the juvenile court, or to do or to perform any act or to follow any course of conduct or to so live as would cause or manifestly tend to cause any such person to become or to remain a person within the provisions of Sections 300, 601, or 602 of the Welfare and Institutions Code, is guilty of a misdemeanor and upon conviction thereof shall be punished by a fine not exceeding two thousand five hundred dollars ($2,500), or by imprisonment in the county jail for not more than one year, or by both such fine and imprisonment in a county jail, or may be released on probation for a period not exceeding five years. For purposes of this section, a parent or legal guardian to any person under the age of 18 years shall have the duty to exercise reasonable care, supervision, protection, and control over their minor child. *(Amended by Stats 1988 ch 1256 §2, eff. 9/23/88.)*

§273. Payments to parent for placing child for adoption.

(a) It is a misdemeanor for any person or agency to offer to pay money or anything of value, or to pay money or anything of value, to a parent for the placement for adoption, for the consent to an adoption, or for cooperation in the completion of an adoption of his or her child.

(b) This section does not make it unlawful to pay the maternity-connected medical or hospital and necessary living expenses of the mother preceding and during confinement as an act of charity, as long as the payment is not contingent upon placement of the child for adoption, consent to the adoption, or cooperation in the completion of the adoption.

(c) It is a misdemeanor punishable by incarceration in the county jail for six months or a fine not exceeding two thousand five hundred dollars ($2,500) for any parent to obtain the financial benefits set forth in subdivision (b) with the intent to receive those financial benefits where there is an intent to do either of the following:

(1) Not complete the adoption.

(2) Not consent to the adoption.

(d) It is a misdemeanor punishable by incarceration in the county jail for six months or a fine not exceeding two thousand five hundred dollars ($2,500) for any parent to obtain the financial benefits set forth in subdivision (b) from two or more prospective adopting families or persons if either parent does both of the following:

(1) Knowingly fails to disclose to those families or persons that there are other prospective adopting families or persons interested in adopting the child, with knowledge that there is an obligation to disclose that information.

(2) Knowingly accepts the financial benefits set forth in subdivision (b) if the aggregate amount exceeds the reasonable maternity-connected medical or hospital and necessary living expenses of the mother preceding and during the pregnancy.

(e) Any person who has been previously convicted of an offense described in subdivision (c) or (d), who is separately tried and convicted of a subsequent viola-

© 1992 by J., B. & L. Gould
Printed in the U.S.A.   **EP**

tion of subdivision (c) or (d), is guilty of a public offense punishable by imprisonment in the county jail or in state prison. *(Amended by Stats 1990 ch 1492 §1, eff. 1/1/91.)*

§273a. Willful cruelty to children.

(1) Any person who, under circumstances or conditions likely to produce great bodily harm or death, willfully causes or permits any child to suffer, or inflicts thereon unjustifiable physical pain or mental suffering, or having the care or custody of any child, willfully causes or permits the person or health of such child to be injured, or willfully causes or permits such child to be placed in such situation that its person or health is endangered, is punishable by imprisonment in the county jail not exceeding one year, or in the state prison for 2, 4, or 6 years.

(2) Any person who, under circumstances or conditions other than those likely to produce great bodily harm or death, willfully causes or permits any child to suffer, or inflicts thereon unjustifiable physical pain or mental suffering, or having the care or custody of any child, willfully causes or permits the person or health of such child to be injured, or willfully causes or permits such child to be placed in such situation that its person or health may be endangered, is guilty of a misdemeanor.

§273b. Confinement of child with adult convicted of crime.

No child under the age of 16 years shall be placed in any courtroom, or in any vehicle for transportation to any place, in company with adults charged with or convicted of crime, except in the presence of a proper official. *(Amended by Stats 1987 ch 828 §13.5.)*

§273c. Disposition of fines.

All fines, penalties, and forfeitures imposed and collected under the provisions of Sections 270, 271, 271a, 273a, and 273b, or under the provisions of any law relating to, or affecting, children, in every case where the prosecution is instituted or conducted by a society incorporated under the laws of this state for the prevention of cruelty to children, inure to such society in aid of the purposes for which it is incorporated. *(Amended by Stats 1987 ch 828 §14.)*

§273d. Inflicting corporal punishment upon child.

Any person who willfully inflicts upon any child any cruel or inhuman corporal punishment or injury resulting in a traumatic condition is guilty of a felony, and upon conviction thereof shall be punished by imprisonment in the state prison for 2, 4, or 6 years, or in the county jail for not more than one year, or by a fine of up to six thousand dollars ($6,000) or by both.

In any case in which a person is convicted of violating this section and probation is granted, the court shall require supervised counseling as a condition of probation unless, considering all of the facts and circumstances, the court finds counseling inappropriate for the defendant. *(Amended by Stats 1987 ch 415 §1.)*

§273e. Minors not to be messengers to or from immoral places.

Every telephone, special delivery company or association, and every other corporation or person engaged in the delivery of packages, letters, notes, messages, or other matter, and every manager, super-intendent, or other agent of such person, corporation, or association, who sends any minor in the employ or under the control of any such person, corporation, association, or agent, to the keeper of any house of prostitution, variety theater, or other place of questionable repute, or to any person connected with, or any inmate of, such house, theater, or other place, or who permits such minor to enter such house, theater, or other place, is guilty of a misdemeanor.

§273f. Sending minors to immoral places.

Any person, whether as parent, guardian, employer, or otherwise, and any firm or corporation, who as employer or otherwise, shall send, direct, or cause to be sent or directed to any saloon, gambling house, house of prostitution, or other immoral place, any minor, is guilty of a misdemeanor.

§273g. Habitual drunkenness or immoral practices in presence of children.

Any person who in the presence of any child indulges in any degrading, lewd, immoral or vicious habits or practices, or who is habitually drunk in the presence of any child in his care, custody or control, is guilty of a misdemeanor.

§273h. Sentence to work on public roads.

In all prosecutions under the provisions of either section 270, section 270a, section 270b, section 271 or section 271a, of this code where a conviction is had and sentence of imprisonment in the county jail or in the city jail is imposed, the court may direct that the person so convicted shall be compelled to work upon the public roads or highways, or any other public work, in the county or in the city where such conviction is had, during the term of such sentence. And it shall be the duty of the board of supervisors of the county where such person is imprisoned in the county jail, and of the city council of the city where such person is imprisoned in the city jail, where such conviction and sentence are had and where such work is performed by a person under sentence to the county jail or to the city jail, to allow and order the payment out of any funds available, to the wife or to the guardian, or to the custodian of a child or children, or to an organization, or to an individual, appointed by the court as trustee, at the end of each calendar month, for the support of such wife or children, a sum not to exceed two dollars for each day's work of such person so imprisoned.

§273.5. Inflicting corporal injury.

(a) Any person who willfully inflicts upon his or her spouse, or any person who willfully inflicts upon any person of the opposite sex with whom he or she is cohabiting, or any person who willfully inflicts upon any person who is the mother or father of his or her child, corporal injury resulting in a traumatic condition, is guilty of a felony, and upon conviction thereof shall be punished by imprisonment in the state prison for 2, 3 or 4 years, or in the county jail for not more than one year, or by a fine of up to six thousand dollars ($6,000) or by both.

(b) Holding oneself out to be the husband or wife of the person with whom one is cohabiting is not necessary to constitute cohabitation as the term is used in this section.

(c) As used in this section, "traumatic condition" means a condition of the body, such as a wound or external or internal injury, whether of a minor or serious nature, caused by a physical force.

(d) For the purpose of this section, a person shall be considered the father or mother of another person's child if the alleged male parent is presumed the natural father as set forth in Section 7004 of the Civil Code.

(e) In any case in which a person is convicted of violating this section and probation is granted, the court shall require participation in a batterer's treatment program as a condition of probation unless, considering all of the facts and the circumstances, the court finds participation in a batterer's treatment program inappropriate for the defendant.

(f) If probation is granted, or the execution or imposition of a sentence is suspended, for any person convicted under subdivision (a) who previously has been convicted under subdivision (a) for an offense that occurred within seven years of the offense of the second conviction, it shall be a condition thereof that he or she be imprisoned in the county jail for not less than 96 hours and that he or she participate in for no less than one year, and successfully complete, a batterer's treatment program, as designated by the court. However, the court, upon a showing of good cause, may find that the mandatory minimum imprisonment, or the participation in a batterer's treatment program, or both the mandatory minimum imprisonment and participation in a batterer's treatment program, as required by this subdivision, shall not be imposed and grant probation or the suspension of the execution or imposition of a sentence.

(g) If probation is granted, or the execution or imposition of a sentence is suspended, for any person convicted under subdivision (a) who previously has been convicted of two or more violations of subdivision (a) for offenses that occurred within seven years of the most recent conviction, it shall be a condition thereof that he or she be imprisoned in the county jail for not less than 30 days and that he or she participate in for no less than one year, and successfully complete, a batterer's treatment program as designated by the court. However, the court, upon a showing of good cause, may find that the mandatory minimum imprisonment, or the participation in a batterer's treatment program, or both the mandatory minimum imprisonment and participation in a batterer's treatment program, as required by this subdivision, shall not be imposed and grant probation or the suspension of the execution or imposition of a sentence. *(Amended by Stats 1990 ch 680 §1, eff. 1/1/91.)*

§273.6. Domestic violence; violation of orders.

(a) Any willful and knowing violation of any of the court orders set forth in this subdivision, when obtained pursuant to Section 4359, 4458, 4516, 7020, or 7021 of the Civil Code, Section 412.21 or 527.6 of the Code of Civil Procedure, or Chapter 4 (commencing with Section 540) of Title 7 of Part 2 of the Code of Civil Procedure shall be a misdemeanor punishable by a fine of not more than one thousand dollars ($1,000), or by imprisonment in the county jail for not more than one year or by both the fine and imprisonment.

(b) In the event of a violation of subdivision (a) which results in a physical injury, the person shall be imprisoned in the county jail for at least 48 hours, whether a fine or imprisonment is imposed, or the sentence is suspended.

(c) Subdivisions (a) and (b) shall apply to the following court orders:

(1) An order enjoining any party from molesting, attacking, striking, threatening, sexually assaulting, battering, harassing, or disturbing the peace of the other party, or other named family and household members.

(2) An order excluding one party from the family dwelling or from the dwelling of the other.

(3) An order enjoining a party from specified behavior which the court determined was necessary to effectuate the orders under subdivision (a) or (d).

(d) A second or subsequent conviction for a violation of an order issued pursuant to subdivision (a) occurring within seven years of a prior conviction for a violation of such an order and involving an act of violence or "a credible threat" of violence as defined in subdivision (b) of Section 139 is punishable by imprisonment in the county jail not to exceed one year, or in the state prison for 16 months or two or three years.

(e) The prosecuting agency of each county shall have the primary responsibility for the enforcement of orders issued pursuant to the provisions listed in subdivisions (a), (b), and (d). *(Amended by Stats 1990 ch 411 §8, eff. 7/25/90.)*

§273.7. Disclosure of location of domestic violence shelters.

(a) Any person who maliciously publishes, disseminates or otherwise discloses the location of any domestic violence shelter or any place designated as a domestic violence shelter, without the authorization of that domestic violence shelter, is guilty of a misdemeanor.

(b) (1) For purposes of this section, "domestic violence shelter" means a confidential location which provides emergency housing on a 24-hour basis for victims of sexual assault, spouse abuse, or both, and their families.

(2) Sexual assault, spousal abuse, or both, includes but is not limited to, those crimes described in Sections 240, 242, 243.4, 261, 261.5, 264.1, 266, 266a, 266b, 266c, 266f, 273.5, 273.6, 285, 288 and 289.

(c) Nothing in this section shall apply to confidential communications between an attorney and his or her client. *(Added by Stats 1988 ch 840 §1, eff. 1/1/89.)*

CHAPTER 2.5

SPOUSAL ABUSERS
(Added by Stats 1985 ch 1122 §1.)

§273.8. Legislative intent.

The Legislature hereby finds that spousal abusers present a clear and present danger to the mental and physical well-being of the citizens of the State of California. The Legislature further finds that the concept of vertical prosecution, in which a specially trained deputy district attorney or prosecution unit is assigned to a case from its filing to its completion, is a proven way of demonstrably increasing the likelihood of convicting spousal abusers and ensuring appropriate sentences for those offenders. In enacting this chapter, the Legislature intends to support increased efforts by district attorneys' offices to prosecute spousal abusers through organizational and operational techniques that have already proven their effectiveness in selected counties in this and other states. *(Added by Stats 1985 ch 1122 §1.)*

© 1992 by J., B. & L. Gould
Printed in the U.S.A.   **EP**

§273.81. Spousal Abuser Prosecution Program.

(a) There is hereby established in the Office of Criminal Justice Planning a program of financial and technical assistance for district attorneys' offices, designated the Spousal Abuser Prosecution Program. All funds appropriated to the Office of Criminal Justice Planning for the purposes of this chapter shall be administered and disbursed by the executive director of that office, and shall to the greatest extent feasible, be coordinated or consolidated with any federal or local funds that may be made available for these purposes.

The Office of Criminal Justice Planning shall establish guidelines for the provision of grant awards to proposed and existing programs prior to the allocation of funds under this chapter. These guidelines shall contain the criteria for the selection of agencies to receive funding and the terms and conditions upon which the Office of Criminal Justice Planning is prepared to offer grants pursuant to statutory authority. The guidelines shall not constitute rules, regulations, orders, or standards of general application.

(b) The executive director is authorized to allocate and award funds to counties in which spousal abuser prosecution units are established or are proposed to be established in substantial compliance with the policies and criteria set forth in this chapter.

(c) The allocation and award of funds shall be made upon application executed by the county's district attorney or by the city's attorney and approved by the county board of supervisors or by the city council. Funds disbursed under this chapter shall not supplant local funds that would, in the absence of the California Spousal Abuser Prosecution Program, be made available to support the prosecution of spousal abuser felony cases. Local grant awards made under this program shall not be subject to review as specified in Section 10295 of the Public Contract Code.

(d) Local government recipients shall provide 20 percent matching funds for every grant awarded under this program. *(Amended by Stats 1987 ch 828 §15.)*

§273.82. Prosecution of spouse abusers.

Spousal abuser prosecution units receiving funds under this chapter shall concentrate enhanced prosecution efforts and resources upon individuals identified under selection criteria set forth in Section 273.83. Enhanced prosecution efforts and resources shall include, but not be limited to, all of the following:

(a) (1) Vertical prosecutorial representation, whereby the prosecutor who, or prosecution unit which, makes the initial filing or appearance in a case performs all subsequent court appearances on that particular case through its conclusion, including the sentencing phase.

(2) Vertical counselor representation, whereby a trained domestic violence counselor maintains liaison from initial court appearances through the case's conclusion, including the sentencing phase.

(b) The assignment of highly qualified investigators and prosecutors to spousal abuser cases. "Highly qualified" for the purposes of this chapter means: (1) individuals with one year of experience in the investigation and prosecution of felonies, (2) individuals whom the district attorney has selected to receive training as set forth in Section 13836, or (3) individuals who have attended a program providing equivalent training as approved by the Office of Criminal Justice Planning.

(c) A significant reduction of caseloads for investigators and prosecutors assigned to spousal abuser cases.

(d) Coordination with local rape victim counseling centers, spousal abuse services programs, and victim-witness assistance programs. That coordination shall include, but not be limited to: referrals of individuals to receive client services; participation in local training programs; membership and participation in local task forces established to improve communication between criminal justice system agencies and community service agencies; and cooperating with individuals serving as liaison representatives of local rape victim counseling centers, spousal abuse victim programs, and victim-witness assistance programs. *(Amended by Stats 1987 ch 828 §16.)*

§273.83. Spousal abuser selection criteria.

(a) An individual shall be the subject of a spousal abuser prosecution effort who is under arrest for any act or omission described in subdivisions (a) and (b) of Section 13700.

(b) In applying the spousal abuser selection criteria set forth in subdivision (a), a district attorney shall not reject cases for filing exclusively on the basis that there is a family or personal relationship between the victim and the alleged offender.

(c) In exercising the prosecutorial discretion granted by Section 273.85, the district attorney shall consider the number and seriousness of the offenses currently charged against the defendant. *(Added by Stats 1985 ch 1122 §1.)*

§273.84. Policies for spousal abuser cases.

Subject to the provisions of Chapter 2.6 (commencing with Section 1000.6) of Title 6 of Part 2, each district attorney's office establishing a spousal abuser prosecution unit and receiving state support under this chapter shall adopt and pursue the following policies for spousal abuser cases:

(a) All reasonable prosecutorial efforts will be made to resist the pretrial release of a charged defendant meeting spousal abuser selection criteria.

(b) All reasonable prosecutorial efforts will be made to persuade the court to impose the most severe authorized sentence upon a person convicted after prosecution as a spousal abuser. In the prosecution of an intrafamily sexual abuse case, discretion may be exercised as to the type and nature of sentence recommended to the court.

(c) All reasonable prosecutorial efforts will be made to reduce the time between arrest and disposition of charge against an individual meeting spousal abuser criteria. *(Added by Stats 1985 ch 1122 §1.)*

§273.85. Adherence to selection criteria.

(a) The selection criteria set forth in Section 273.84 shall be adhered to for each spousal abuser case unless, in the reasonable exercise of prosecutor's discretion, extraordinary circumstances require departure from such policies in order to promote the general purposes and intent of this chapter.

(b) Each district attorney's office establishing a spousal abuser prosecution unit and receiving state support under this chapter shall submit the following information, on a quarterly basis, to the Office of Criminal Justice Planning:

(1) The number of spousal abuser cases referred to the district attorney's office for possible filing.

(2) The number of spousal abuser cases filed for felony prosecution.

(3) The number of spousal abuser cases taken to trial.

(4) The number of spousal abuser cases tried which resulted in conviction. *(Added by Stats 1985 ch 1122 §1.)*

§273.86. Characterization of defendant as a spousal abuser.

The characterization of a defendant as a "spousal abuser" as defined by this chapter shall not be communicated to the trier of fact. *(Added by Stats 1985 ch 1122 §1.)*

§273.87. Utilization of VOCA funds or other federal funds.

The Office of Criminal Justice Planning is encouraged to utilize Federal Victims of Crimes Act (VOCA) funds or any other federal funds which may become available in order to implement the provisions of this chapter. *(Added by Stats 1985 ch 1122 §1.)*

§273.88. Spousal abuser reports: pilot project.

(a) It is the Legislature's intent that the Office of Criminal Justice Planning conduct a pilot project to collect statistics on domestic violence prosecution from three counties which have established a vertical prosecution program for spousal abusers pursuant to this chapter.

(b) The Office of Criminal Justice Planning shall establish a pilot project, pursuant to this section, to operate in the Counties of Sacramento, Los Angeles, and Humboldt.

(c) Each law enforcement agency in the Counties of Sacramento and Humboldt shall submit to the Office of Criminal Justice Planning, on a quarterly basis, the following information:

(1) Number of domestic violence reports made and written.

(2) Total number of domestic violence felony and misdemeanor arrests.

(3) Number of domestic violence calls which involved a restraining order.

(4) Number of referrals made by law enforcement relating to domestic violence.

(5) Number of domestic violence training programs law enforcement participates in, including, but not limited to, training of domestic violence counselors at local shelters and attendance and participation in Office of Criminal Justice Planning, Department of Justice, and Peace Officer Standards and Training statewide training conferences.

(d) With regard to Los Angeles County, the Los Angeles County Sheriff's Office shall identify three stations that are representative of the county's ethnic and socioeconomic breakdown of the population and the crime ratio for domestic violence for the purposes of this section. The Los Angeles County Sheriff's Office shall submit to the Office of Criminal Justice Planning, on a quarterly basis, the information outlined in subdivision (c), as obtained with regard to the three stations identified as representative pursuant to this subdivision.

(e) Each district attorney's office or city attorney's office having misdemeanor jurisdiction in the counties specified in subdivision (b) shall submit to the Office of Criminal Justice Planning, on a quarterly basis, the following information:

(1) Number of spousal abuse cases referred to that office for possible filing.

(2) Number of spousal abuse cases filed for felony prosecution.

(3) Number of spousal abuse cases filed for misdemeanor prosecution.

(4) Number of spousal abuse cases sent to diversion.

(5) Number of spousal abuse cases tried which were dismissed and number of defendants acquitted.

(6) Number of spousal abuse cases resulting in conviction.

(7) Number of repeat spousal abuse offenders.

(8) Number of protective order violations where the protective order was the result of a spousal abuse case.

(9) Number of homicides where the victim was a spouse, cohabitant, girlfriend, ex-spouse, ex-cohabitant, or ex-girlfriend.

(10) Number of homicides where the victim had a protective order against the defendant.

(11) Number of referrals by that office to local victim counseling centers, spousal abuse programs, and victim witness assistance programs.

(12) Number of domestic violence training programs in which that office participates, including, but not limited to, training of domestic violence counselors at local shelters and attendance and participation in Office of Criminal Justice Planning, Department of Justice, and Peace Officer Standards and Training statewide training conferences.

(f) The Office of Criminal Justice Planning shall work with the counties specified in subdivision (b) to develop a format to collect the information required pursuant to subdivisions (c) and (d).

(g) The Office of Criminal Justice Planning shall submit a report to the Legislature regarding the accomplishments of the pilot project. The report shall include, but not be limited to, a program evaluation and recommendations on the vertical prosecution program for spousal abusers pursuant to this chapter. The program evaluation shall include specific data on the number of domestic violence reports received and written, number of domestic violence felony and misdemeanor arrests, and prosecutions and convictions for those crimes as measured by the pilot project. The project shall be considered to have met its objectives if the arrest and conviction rate has increased 10 percent in one year. A statewide analysis and needs assessment shall be part of the report. The report shall be submitted on or before January 1, 1993.

(h) This section shall remain in effect until January 30, 1993, and as of that date is repealed. *(Added by Stats 1991 ch 483 §1, eff. 1/1/92 only until 1/30/93.)*

CHAPTER 3

ABORTIONS

§274. Employing means to procure miscarriage.

Every person who provides, supplies, or administers to any woman, or procures any woman to take any medicine, drug, or substance, or uses or employs any instrument or other means whatever, with intent thereby to procure the miscarriage of such woman, except as provided in the Therapeutic Abortion Act, Chapter 11 (commencing with Section 25950) of Division 20 of the Health and Safety Code, is punishable by imprisonment in the state prison.

© 1992 by J., B. & L. Gould
Printed in the U.S.A.   EP

§275. Submitting to an attempt to procure miscarriage.

Every woman who solicits of any person any medicine, drug, or substance whatever, and takes the same, or who submits to any operation, or to the use of any means whatever, with intent thereby to procure a miscarriage, except as provided in the Therapeutic Abortion Act, Chapter 11 (commencing with Section 25950) of Division 20 of the Health and Safety Code, is punishable by imprisonment in the state prison.

§276. Solicitation for operation to procure miscarriage.

Every person who solicits any woman to submit to any operation, or to the use of any means whatever, to procure a miscarriage, except as provided in the Therapeutic Abortion Act, Chapter 11 (commencing with Section 25950) of Division 20 of the Health and Safety Code, is punishable by imprisonment in the county jail not longer than one year or in the state prison, or by fine of not more than ten thousand dollars ($10,000). Such offense must be proved by the testimony of two witnesses, or of one witness and corroborating circumstances.

CHAPTER 4

CHILD ABDUCTION

§277. Abduction with intent to deprive right of custody.

In the absence of a court order determining rights of custody or visitation to a minor child, every person having a right of custody of the child who maliciously takes, detains, conceals, or entices away that child within or without the state, without good cause, and with the intent to deprive the custody right of another person or a public agency also having a custody right to that child, shall be punished by imprisonment in the county jail for a period of not more than one year, a fine of one thousand dollars ($1,000), or both, or by imprisonment in the state prison for 16 months, or two or three years, a fine of not more than ten thousand dollars ($10,000), or both.

A subsequently obtained court order for custody or visitation shall not affect the application of this section.

As used in this section, "good cause" means a good faith and reasonable belief that the taking, detaining, concealing, or enticing away of the child is necessary to protect the child from immediate bodily injury or emotional harm. "Good cause" also includes the good faith and reasonable belief by a person with a right of custody of the child who has been the victim of domestic violence by another person with a right of custody of the child, that the child, if left with the other person, will suffer immediate bodily injury or emotional harm. The person who takes, detains, or conceals the child shall file a report with the district attorney's office of his or her action, and shall file a request for custody, within a reasonable time in the jurisdiction where the child had been living, setting forth the basis for the immediate bodily injury or emotional harm to the child. The address of the parent, or a person who has been granted access to the minor child by a court order, who takes, detains, or conceals the child, with good cause, shall remain confidential until released by court order.

As used in this section:

(a) "Domestic violence" means abuse perpetrated against any of the following persons:

(1) A spouse, former spouse, cohabitant, former cohabitant, any other adult person related by consanguinity or affinity within the second degree, or a person with whom the respondent has had a dating or engagement relationship.

(2) A person who is the parent of a child and the presumption applies that the male parent is the father of any child of the female parent pursuant to the Uniform Parentage Act (Part 7 (commencing with Section 7000) of Division 4 of the Civil Code).

(b) "Emotional harm" includes having a parent who has committed domestic violence against the parent who is taking and concealing the child. *(Amended by Stats 1991 ch 400 §1, eff. 1/1/92.)*

§278. Unlawful detention or concealment of minor child.

Every person, not having a right of custody, who maliciously takes, detains, conceals, or entices away, any minor child with intent to detain or conceal that child from a person, guardian, or public agency having the lawful charge of the child shall be punished by imprisonment in the state prison for two, three or four years, a fine of not more than ten thousand dollars ($10,000), or both, or imprisonment in a county jail for a period of not more than one year, a fine of not more than one thousand dollars ($1,000), or both.

§278.5. Violation of custody or provisions.

Every person who has a right to physical custody of or visitation with a child pursuant to an order, judgment, or decree of any court which grants another person, guardian, or public agency right to physical custody of or visitation with that child, and who within or without the state detains, conceals, takes, or entices away that child with the intent to deprive the other person of that right to custody or visitation shall be punished by imprisonment in the state prison for 16 months, or two or three years, a fine of not more than ten thousand dollars ($10,000), or both; or by imprisonment in a county jail for a period of not more than one year, a fine of not more than one thousand dollars ($1,000), or both. *(Amended by Stats 1989 ch 1428 §4, eff. 1/1/90.)*

§279. Protective custody.

(a) A peace officer investigating a report of a violation of Section 277, 278, or 278.5 may take a minor child into protective custody if it reasonably appears to the officer that any person unlawfully will flee the jurisdictional territory with the minor child.

(b) A child who has been detained or concealed shall be returned to the person, guardian, or public agency having lawful charge of the child, or to the court in which a custody proceeding is pending, or to the probation department of the juvenile court in the county in which the victim resides. Notwithstanding any other provision of law, when a person is arrested for an alleged violation of Section 277, 278, or 278.5 the court shall, at the time of the arraignment, impose the condition that the child shall be returned to the person or public agency having lawful charge of the child, and the court shall specify the date by which the child shall be returned. If conflicting custodial orders exist within this state, or between this state and a foreign state, the court shall set a hearing within five court days to determine which court has jurisdiction under the laws of this state, if the conflicting custodial orders are within this state, or if the conflict exists between this state and a foreign state; the court shall determine which state has subject matter jurisdiction to issue a custodial order under the laws of this state, the Uniform Child Custody Jurisdiction Act (Title 9 (commencing with Section 5150) of Part 5 of the Civil Code), or federal law, if applicable. At the conclusion of the hearing, the court shall enter an order as to which custody order is valid and is to be enforced. If the child has not been returned at the conclusion of the hearing, the court shall set a date within a reasonable time by which the child shall be returned to the person or agency having lawful charge of the child, and order the defendant to comply by this date, or to show cause on that date why he or she has not returned the child as directed. The court shall only enforce its order, or any subsequent orders for the return of the child, under subdivision (a) of Section 1219 of the Code of Civil procedure, to ensure that the child is promptly placed with the person or agency having lawful charge of the child. An order adverse to either the prosecution or defense is reviewable by a writ of mandate or prohibition addressed to the appropriate court.

(c) The offenses enumerated in Sections 277, 278, and 278.5 are continuous in nature, and continue for so long as the minor child is concealed or detained.

(d) Any expenses incurred in returning the child shall be reimbursed as provided in Section 4605 of the Civil Code. Those expenses, and costs reasonably incurred by the victim, shall be assessed against any defendant convicted of a violation of Section 277, 278, or 278.5.

(e) Pursuant to Sections 27 and 778, violation of Section 277, 278, or 278.5 is punishable in California, whether the intent to commit the offense is formed within or without the state, if the child was a resident of California or present in California at the time of the taking, if the child thereafter is found in California, or if one of the parents, or a person granted access to the minor child by a court order is a resident of California at the time of the alleged violation of Section 277, 278, or 278.5 by a person who was not a resident of or present in California at the time of the alleged offense.

(f) For purposes of Sections 277, 278, and 278.5:

(1) "A person having a right of custody" means the legal guardian of the child, a person who has a parent and child relationship with the child pursuant to Section 197 of the Civil Code, or a person or an agency that has been granted custody of the child pursuant to a court order.

(2) A "right of custody" means the right to physical custody of the child. In the absence of a court order to the contrary, a parent loses his or her right of custody of the child to the other parent if the parent having the right of custody is dead, is unable or refuses to take the custody, or has abandoned his or her family. *(Amended by Stats 1989 ch 1428 §5, eff. 1/1/90.)*

§280. Concealment or removal of child pending adoption proceeding.

Every person who willfully causes or permits the removal or concealment of any child in violation of Section 222.50, 224.33, or 226.40 of the Civil Code is punishable as follows:

(a) By imprisonment in the county jail for not more than one year if the child is concealed within the county in which the adoption proceeding is pending or in which the child has been placed for adoption, or is removed from that county to a place within this state; or

(b) By imprisonment in the state prison, or by imprisonment in the county jail for not more than one year if the child is removed from that county to a place outside of this state. *(Amended by Stats 1990 ch 1363 §14, eff. 1/1/91, oper. 7/1/91.)*

CHAPTER 5

BIGAMY, INCEST, AND THE CRIME AGAINST NATURE

§281. Bigamy defined.

(a) Every person having a husband or wife living, who marries any other person, except in the cases specified in Section 282, is guilty of bigamy.

(b) Upon a trial for bigamy, it is not necessary to prove either of the marriages by the register, certificate, or other record evidence thereof, but the marriages may be proved by evidence which is admissible to prove a marriage in other cases; and when the second marriage took place out of this state, proof of that fact, accompanied with proof of cohabitation thereafter in this state, is sufficient to sustain the charge. *(Amended by Stats 1989 ch 897 §18, eff. 1/1/90.)*

§282. Exceptions.

Section 281 does not extend to any of the following:

(a) To any person by reason of any former marriage whose husband or wife by such marriage has been absent for five successive years without being known to such person within that time to be living.

(b) To any person by reason of any former marriage which has been pronounced void, annulled, or dissolved by the judgment of a competent court.

§283. Punishment for bigamy.

Bigamy is punishable by a fine not exceeding ten thousand dollars ($10,000) or by imprisonment in a county jail not exceeding one year or in the state prison.

§284. Knowingly marrying another's husband or wife.

Every person who knowingly and willfully marries the husband or wife of another, in any case in which such husband or wife would be punishable under the provisions of this chapter, is punishable by fine not less than five thousand dollars ($5,000), or by imprisonment in the state prison.

§285. Punishment for incest.

Persons being within the degrees of consanguinity within which marriages are declared by law to be incestuous and void, who intermarry with each other, or who commit fornication or adultery with each other, are punishable by imprisonment in the state prison.

§286. Punishment for unlawful sodomy.

(a) Sodomy is sexual conduct consisting of contact between the penis of one person and the anus of another person. Any sexual penetration, however slight, is sufficient to complete the crime of sodomy.

(b) (1) Except as provided in Section 288, any person who participates in an act of sodomy with another person who is under 18 years of age shall be punished by imprisonment in the state prison, or in a county jail for not more than one year.

© 1992 by J., B. & L. Gould
Printed in the U.S.A.   **EP**

(2) Except as provided in Section 288, any person over the age of 21 years who participates in an act of sodomy with another person who is under 16 years of age shall be guilty of a felony.

(c) Any person who participates in an act of sodomy with another person who is under 14 years of age and more than 10 years younger than he or she, or when the act is accomplished against the victim's will by means of force, violence, duress, menace, or fear of immediate and unlawful bodily injury on the victim or another person or where the act is accomplished against the victim's will by threatening to retaliate in the future against the victim or any other person, and there is a reasonable possibility that the perpetrator will execute the threat shall be punished by imprisonment in the state prison for three, six, or eight years.

(d) Any person who, while voluntarily acting in concert with another person, either personally or aiding and abetting that other person, commits an act of sodomy when the act is accomplished against the victim's will by means of force or fear of immediate and unlawful bodily injury on the victim or another person or where the act is accomplished against the victim's will by threatening to retaliate in the future against the victim or any other person, and there is a reasonable possibility that the perpetrator will execute the threat shall be punished by imprisonment in the state prison for five, seven, or nine years.

(e) Any person who participates in an act of sodomy with any person of any age while confined in any state prison, as defined in Section 4504, or in any local detention facility as defined in Section 6031.4 shall be punished by imprisonment in the state prison, or in a county jail for not more than one year.

(f) Any person who commits an act of sodomy, and the victim is at the time unconscious of the nature of the act and this is known to the person committing the act, shall be punished by imprisonment in the state prison for three, six, or eight years.

(g) Except as provided in subdivision (h), a person who commits an act of sodomy, and the victim is at the time incapable, because of a mental disorder or developmental or physical disability, of giving legal consent, and this is known or reasonably should be known to the person committing the act, shall be punished by imprisonment in the state prison for three, six, or eight years. Notwithstanding the existence of a conservatorship pursuant to the Lanterman-Petris-Short Act (Part 1 (commencing with,Section 5000) of Division 5 of the Welfare and Institutions Code), the prosecuting attorney shall prove, as an element of the crime, that a mental disorder or developmental or physical disability rendered the alleged victim incapable of giving legal consent.

(h) Any person who commits an act of sodomy, and the victim is at the time incapable, because of a mental disorder or developmental or physical disability, of giving legal consent, and this is known or reasonably should be known to the person committing the act, and both the defendant and the victim are at the time confined in a state hospital for the care and treatment of the mentally disordered or in any other public or private facility for the care and treatment of the mentally disordered approved by a county mental health director, shall be punished by imprisonment in the state prison, or in a county jail for not more than one year. Notwithstanding the existence of a conservatorship pursuant to the Lanterman-Petris-Short Act (Part 1 (commencing with Section 5000) of Division 5

of the Welfare and Institutions Code), the prosecuting attorney shall prove, as an element of the crime, that a mental disorder or developmental or physical disability rendered the alleged victim incapable of giving legal consent.

(i) Any person who commits an act of sodomy, where the victim is prevented from resisting by an intoxicating or anesthetic substance, or any controlled substance, administered by or with the privity of the accused, shall be punished by imprisonment in the state prison for three, six, or eight years.

(j) Any person who commits an act of sodomy, where the victim submits under the belief that the person committing the act is the victim's spouse, and this belief is induced by any artifice, pretense, or concealment practiced by the accused, with intent to induce the belief, shall be punished by imprisonment in the state prison for three, six, or eight years.

(k) Any person who commits an act of sodomy, where the act is accomplished against the victim's will by threatening to use the authority of a public official to incarcerate, arrest, or deport the victim or another, and the victim has a reasonable belief that the perpetrator is a public official, shall be punished by imprisonment in the state prison for three, six, or eight years.

As used in this subdivision, "public official" means a person employed by a governmental agency who has the authority, as part of that position, to incarcerate, arrest, or deport another. The perpetrator does not actually have to be a public official.

(l) As used in subdivisions (c) and (d), "threatening to retaliate" means a threat to kidnap or falsely imprison, or inflict extreme pain, serious bodily injury, or death.

(m) In addition to any punishment imposed under this section, the judge may assess a fine not to exceed seventy dollars ($70) against any person who violates this section, with the proceeds of this fine to be used in accordance with Section 1463.23. The court, however, shall take into consideration the defendant's ability to pay, and no defendant shall be denied probation because of his or her inability to pay the fine permitted under this subdivision. *(Amended by Stats 1991 ch 144 §1, eff. 1/1/92.)*

§286.5. Assaulting animal sexually.

Any person who sexually assaults any animal protected by Section 597f for the purpose of arousing or gratifying the sexual desire of the person is guilty of a misdemeanor.

§287. *Repealed by Stats 1991 ch 144 §2, eff. 1/1/92. See now §286 above.*

§288. Lewd or lascivious acts or crimes against children.

(a) Any person who shall willfully and lewdly commit any lewd or lascivious act including any of the acts constituting other crimes provided for in Part 1 of this code upon or with the body, or any part or member thereof, of a child under the age of 14 years, with the intent of arousing, appealing to, or gratifying the lust or passions or sexual desires of that person or of the child, shall be guilty of a felony and shall be imprisoned in the state prison for a term of three, six, or eight years.

(b) Any person who commits an act described in subdivision (a) by use of force, violence, duress, menace, or fear of immediate and unlawful bodily injury on the victim or another person, shall be guilty of a felony and shall be imprisoned in the state prison for a term of three, six, or eight years.

(c) Any person who commits an act described in subdivision (a) with the intent described in that subdivision, and the victim is a child of 14 or 15 years, and the defendant is at least 10 years older than the child, shall be guilty of a public offense and shall be imprisoned in the state prison for one, two, or three years, or by imprisonment in the county jail for not more than one year.

(d) In any arrest or prosecution under this section or under Section 258.5 the peace officer, the district attorney, and the court shall consider the needs of the child victim and shall do whatever is necessary, within existing budgetary resources, and constitutionally permissible to prevent psychological harm to the child victim.

(e) Upon the conviction of any person for a violation of subdivision (a) or (b), the court may, in addition to any other penalty or fine imposed, order the defendant to pay an additional fine not to exceed five thousand dollars ($5,000). In setting the amount of the fine, the court shall consider any relevant factors including, but not limited to, the seriousness and gravity of the offense, and the circumstances of its commission, whether the defendant derived any economic gain as a result of the crime, and the extent to which the victim suffered economic losses as a result of the crime. Every fine imposed and collected under this section shall be deposited in the Victim-Witness Assistance Fund to be available for appropriation to fund child sexual exploitation and child sexual abuse victim counseling centers and prevention programs pursuant to Section 13837.

If the court orders a fine to be imposed pursuant to this subdivision, the actual administrative cost of collecting that fine, not to exceed 2 percent of the total amount paid, may be paid into the general fund of the county treasury for the use and benefit of the county. *(Amended by Stats 1989 ch 1402 §3, eff. 1/1/90.)*

§288a. Punishment for unlawful oral copulation.

(a) Oral copulation is the act of copulating the mouth of one person with the sexual organ or anus of another person.

(b) (1) Except as provided in Section 288, any person who participates in an act of oral copulation with another person who is under 18 years of age shall be punished by imprisonment in the state prison, or in a county jail for a period of not more than one year.

(2) Except as provided in Section 288, any person over the age of 21 years who participates in an act of oral copulation with another person who is under 16 years of age is guilty of a felony.

(c) Any person who participates in an act of oral copulation with another person who is under 14 years of age and more than 10 years younger than he or she, or when the act is accomplished against the victim's will by means of force, violence, duress, menace, or fear of immediate and unlawful bodily injury on the victim or another person or where the act is accomplished against the victim's will by threatening to retaliate in the future against the victim or any other person, and there is a reasonable possibility that the perpetrator will execute the threat shall be punished by imprisonment in the state prison for three, six, or eight years.

(d) Any person who, while voluntarily acting in concert with another person, either personally or by aiding and abetting that other person, commits an act of oral copulation (1) when the act is accomplished against the victim's will by means of force or fear of immediate and unlawful bodily injury on the victim or another person, or (2) where the act is accomplished against the victim's will by threatening to retaliate in the future against the victim or any other person, and there is a reasonable possibility that the perpetrator will execute the threat, or (3) where the victim is at the time incapable, because of a mental disorder or developmental or physical disability, of giving legal consent, and this is known or reasonably should be known to the person committing the act shall be punished by imprisonment in the state prison for five, seven, or nine years. Notwithstanding the appointment of a conservator with respect to the victim pursuant to the provisions of the Lanterman-Petris-Short Act (Part 1 (commencing with Section 5000) of Division 5 of the Welfare and Institutions Code), the prosecuting attorney shall prove, as an element of the crime described under paragraph (3), that a mental disorder or developmental or physical disability rendered the alleged victim incapable of giving legal consent.

(e) Any person who participates in an act of oral copulation while confined in any state prison, as defined in Section 4504 or in any local detention facility as defined in Section 6031.4, shall be punished by imprisonment in the state prison, or in a county jail for a period of not more than one year.

(f) Any person who commits an act of oral copulation, and the victim is at the time unconscious of the nature of the act and this is known to the person committing the act, shall be punished by imprisonment in the state prison for a period of three, six, or eight years.

(g) Except as provided in subdivision (h), any person who commits an act of oral copulation, and the victim is at the time incapable, because of a mental disorder or developmental or physical disability, of giving legal consent, and this is known or reasonably should be known to the person committing the act, shall be punished by imprisonment in the state prison, for three, six, or eight years. Notwithstanding the existence of a conservatorship pursuant to the provisions of the Lanterman-Petris-Short Act (Part 1 (commencing with Section 5000) of Division 5 of the Welfare and Institutions Code), the prosecuting attorney shall prove, as an element of the crime, that a mental disorder or developmental or physical disability rendered the alleged victim incapable of giving legal consent.

(h) Any person who commits an act of oral copulation, and the victim is at the time incapable, because of a mental disorder or developmental or physical disability, of giving legal consent, and this is known or reasonably should be known to the person committing the act, and both the defendant and the victim are at the time confined in a state hospital for the care and treatment of the mentally disordered or in any other public or private facility for the care and treatment of the mentally disordered approved by a county mental health director, shall be punished by imprisonment in the state prison, or in a county jail for a period of not more than one year. Notwithstanding the existence of a conservatorship pursuant to the provisions of the Lanterman-Petris-Short Act (Part 1 (commencing with

© 1992 by J., B. & L. Gould
Printed in the U.S.A.   **EP**

Section 5000) of Division 5 of the Welfare and Institutions Code), the prosecuting attorney shall prove, as an element of the crime, that a mental disorder or developmental or physical disability rendered the alleged victim incapable of giving legal consent.

(i) Any person who commits an act of oral copulation, where the victim is prevented from resisting by any intoxicating or anesthetic substance, or any controlled substance, administered by or with the privity of the accused, shall be punished by imprisonment in the state prison for a period of three, six, or eight years.

(j) Any person who commits an act of oral copulation, where the victim submits under the belief that the person committing the act is the victim's spouse, and this belief is induced by any artifice, pretense, or concealment practiced by the accused, with intent to induce the belief, shall be punished by imprisonment in the state prison for a period of three, six, or eight years.

(k) Any person who commits an act of oral copulation, where the act is accomplished against the victim's will by threatening to use the authority of a public official to incarcerate, arrest, or deport the victim or another, and the victim has a reasonable belief that the perpetrator is a public official, shall be punished by imprisonment in the state prison for a period of three, six, or eight years.

As used in this subdivision, "public official" means a person employed by a governmental agency who has the authority, as part of that position, to incarcerate, arrest, or deport another. The perpetrator does not actually have to be a public official.

(l) As used in subdivisions (c) and (d) "threatening to retaliate" means a threat to kidnap or falsely imprison, or to inflict extreme pain, serious bodily injury, or death.

(m) In addition to any punishment imposed under this section, the judge may assess a fine not to exceed seventy dollars ($70) against any person who violates this section, with the proceeds of this fine to be used in accordance with Section 1463.23. The court shall, however, take into consideration the defendant's ability to pay, and no defendant shall be denied probation because of his or her inability to pay the fine permitted under this subdivision. (Amended by Stats 1988 ch 1243 §7, eff. 1/1/89.)

§288.1. Report required prior to suspension of sentence.

Any person convicted of committing any lewd or lascivious act including any of the acts constituting other crimes provided for in Part 1 of this code upon or with the body, or any part or member thereof, of a child under the age of 14 years shall not have his sentence suspended until the court obtains a report from a reputable psychiatrist, or from a reputable psychologist who meets the standards set forth in Section 1027, as to the mental condition of that person.

§288.2. Minors, pornographic phone messages and other harmful matter.

(a) Every person who, with knowledge that a person is a minor, or who fails to exercise reasonable care in ascertaining the true age of a minor, knowingly distributes, sends, causes to be sent, exhibits, or offers to distribute or exhibit by any means, including, but not limited to, live or recorded telephone messages, any harmful matter, as defined in Section 313, to a minor with the intent of arousing, appealing to, or

gratifying the lust or passions or sexual desires of that person or of the minor, with the intent, or for the purpose of seducing the minor, is guilty of a public offense punishable by imprisonment in the state prison or in the county jail.

Upon the second and each subsequent conviction for a violation of this subdivision, a person so convicted is guilty of a felony.

(b) It shall be a defense to any prosecution under this section that a parent or guardian committed the act charged in aid of legitimate sex education.

(c) It shall be a defense in any prosecution under this section that the act charged was committed in aid of legitimate scientific or educational purposes.

(d) It does not constitute a violation of this section for a telephone corporation, as defined by Section 234 of the Public Utilities Code, to carry or transmit messages described in this section or perform related activities in providing telephone services. (Added by Stats 1989 ch 1316 §1, eff. 1/1/90.)

§288.5. Continual sexual abuse of a minor under 14 years of age.

(a) Any person who either resides in the same home with the minor child or has recurring access to the child, who over a period of time, not less than three months in duration, engages in three or more acts of substantial sexual conduct with a child under the age of 14 years at the time of the commission of the offense, as defined in subdivision (b) of Section 1203.066, or three or more acts of lewd or lascivious conduct under Section 288, with a child under the age of 14 years at the time of the commission of the offense is guilty of the offense of continuous sexual abuse of a child and shall be punished by imprisonment in the state prison for a term of 6, 12, or 16 years.

(b) To convict under this section the trier of fact, if a jury, need unanimously agree only that the requisite number of acts occurred not on which acts constitute the requisite number.

(c) No other felony sex offense involving the same victim may be charged in the same proceeding with a charge under this section unless the other charged offense occurred outside the time period charged under this section or the other offense is charged in the alternative. A defendant may be charged with only one count under this section unless more than one victim is involved in which case a separate count may be charged for each victim. (Added by Stats 1989 ch 1402 §4, eff. 1/1/90.)

§289. Penetration of genital or anal openings.

(a) Every person who causes the penetration, however slight, of the genital or anal openings of any person or causes another person to so penetrate the defendant's or another person's genital or anal openings for the purpose of sexual arousal, gratification, or abuse by any foreign object, substance, instrument, or device when the act is accomplished against the victim's will by means of force, violence, duress, menace, or fear of immediate and unlawful bodily injury on the victim or another person or where the act is accomplished against the victim's will by threatening to retaliate in the future against the victim or any other person, and there is a reasonable possibility that the perpetrator will execute the threat, shall be punished by imprisonment in the state prison for three, six, or eight years.

(b) Except as provided in subdivision (c), every person who causes the penetration, however slight, of the genital or anal openings of any person or causes another person to so penetrate the defendant's or another person's genital or anal openings for the purpose of sexual arousal, gratification, or abuse by any foreign object, substance, instrument, or device, and the victim is at the time incapable, because of a mental disorder or developmental or physical disability, of giving legal consent, and this is known or reasonably should be known to the person committing the act or causing the act to be committed, shall be punished by imprisonment in the state prison for three, six, or eight years. Notwithstanding the appointment of a conservator with respect to the victim pursuant to the provisions of the Lanterman-Petris-Short Act (Part 1 (commencing with Section 5000) of Division 5 of the Welfare and Institutions Code), the prosecuting attorney shall prove, as an element of crime, that a mental disorder or developmental or physical disability rendered the alleged victim incapable of giving legal consent.

(c) Every person who causes the penetration, however slight, of the genital or anal openings of any person or causes another person to so penetrate the defendant's or another person's genital or anal openings for the purpose of sexual arousal, gratification, or abuse by any foreign object, substance, instrument, or device, and the victim is at the time incapable, because of a mental disorder or developmental or physical disability, of giving legal consent, and this is known or reasonably should be known to the person committing the act or causing the act to be committed and both the defendant and the victim are at the time confined in a state hospital for the care and treatment of the mentally disordered or in any other public or private facility for the care and treatment of the mentally disordered approved by a county mental health director, shall be punished by imprisonment in the state prison, or in a county jail for a period of not more than one year. Notwithstanding the existence of a conservatorship pursuant to the provisions of the Lanterman-Petris-Short Act (Part 1 (commencing with Section 5000) of Division 5 of the Welfare and Institutions Code), the prosecuting attorney shall prove, as an element of the crime, that a mental disorder or developmental or physical disability rendered the alleged victim incapable of giving legal consent.

(d) Every person who causes the penetration, however slight, of the genital or anal openings of any person or causes another person to so penetrate the defendant's or another person's genital or anal openings for the purpose of sexual arousal, gratification, or abuse by any foreign object, substance, instrument, or device, and the victim is at the time unconscious of the nature of the act and this is known to the person committing the act or causing the act to be committed, shall be punished by imprisonment in the state prison for three, six, or eight years.

(e) Every person who causes the penetration, however slight, of the genital or anal openings of any person or causes another person to so penetrate the defendant's or another person's genital or anal openings for the purpose of sexual arousal, gratification, or abuse by any foreign object, substance, instrument, or device, where the victim is prevented from resisting by any intoxicating or anesthetic substance, or any controlled substance, administered by or with the privity of the accused, shall be punished by imprisonment in the state prison for a period of three, six, or eight years.

(f) Every person who causes the penetration, however slight, of the genital or anal openings of any person or causes another person to so penetrate the defendant's or another person's genital or anal openings for the purpose of sexual arousal, gratification, or abuse by any foreign object, substance, instrument, or device, where the victim submits under the belief that the person committing the act or causing the act to be committed is the victim's spouse, and this belief is induced by any artifice, pretense, or concealment practiced by the accused, with intent to induce the belief, shall be punished by imprisonment in the state prison for a period of three, six, or eight years.

(g) Every person who causes the penetration, however slight, of the genital or anal openings of any person or causes another person to so penetrate the defendant's or another person's genital or anal openings for the purpose of sexual arousal, gratification, or abuse by any foreign object, substance, instrument, or device, where the act is accomplished against the victim's will by threatening to use the authority of a public official to incarcerate, arrest, or deport the victim or another, and the victim has a reasonable belief that the perpetrator is a public official, shall be punished by imprisonment in the state prison for a period of three, six, or eight years.

As used in this subdivision, "public official" means a person employed by a governmental agency who has the authority, as part of that position, to incarcerate, arrest, or deport another. The perpetrator does not actually have to be a public official.

(h) Except as provided in Section 288, any person who participates in an act of penetration of genital or anal openings with a foreign object, substance, instrument, or device of a person who is under 18 years of age or causes another person under 18 years of age to so penetrate the defendant's or another person's genital or anal openings for the purpose of sexual arousal, gratification, or abuse, shall be punished by imprisonment in the state prison or in the county jail for a period of not more than one year.

(i) Except as provided in Section 288, any person over the age of 21 years who participates in an act of penetration of the genital or anal openings with a foreign object, substance, instrument, or device of another person who is under 16 years of age or causes another person under 16 years of age to so penetrate the defendant's or another person's genital or anal openings for the purpose of sexual arousal, gratification, or abuse, shall be guilty of a felony.

(j) Any person who participates in an act of penetration of the genital or anal openings with a foreign object, instrument, or device of another person who is under 14 years of age and who is more than 10 years younger than he or she or causes another person who is under 14 years of age and who is more than 10 years younger than the defendant to so penetrate the defendant's or another person's genital or anal openings for the purpose of sexual arousal, gratification, or abuse, shall be punished by imprisonment in the state prison for three, six, or eight years.

(k) As used in this section, "foreign object, substance, instrument, or device" shall include any part of the body, except a sexual organ.

(l) As used in subdivision (a) "threatening to retaliate" means a threat to kidnap or falsely im-

© 1992 by J., B. & L. Gould
Printed in the U.S.A.   EP

prison, or inflict extreme pain, serious bodily injury or death.

(m) As used in this section, "victim" includes any person who the defendant causes to penetrate the genital or anal openings of the defendant or another person or whose genital or anal openings are caused to be penetrated by the defendant or another person and who otherwise qualifies as a victim under the requirements of this section. *(Amended by Stats 1988 ch 404 §1, eff. 1/1/89.)*

§289.5. Punishment for penetration of genital or anal openings.

Whenever a person causes the penetration, however slight, of the genital or anal openings of any person or causes another person to so penetrate any person's genital or anal openings by a penis or by any foreign object, substance, instrument, or device, as defined in subdivision (k) of Section 289, under any circumstances set forth in Section 289, and it cannot be established whether penetration was by a penis or by a foreign object, substance, instrument, or device, the person shall be punished by imprisonment in the state prison for three, six, or eight years. However, if the penetration occurs under the circumstances set forth in subdivision (c), (h) or (i) of Section 289, the punishment set forth in those subdivisions shall apply. *(Added by Stats 1991 ch 293 §1, eff. 1/1/92.)*

§290. Registering sex offenders.

(a) Any person who, since July 1, 1944, has been or is hereafter convicted in this state of the offense of assault with intent to commit rape or sodomy under Section 220, or of any offense defined in subdivisions (1), (2), (3), (4), and (6) of Section 261, or of any offense defined in Section 264.1, 266, 267, 285, 286, 288, 288a 288.5, 289, or 647.6 or former Section 647a, subdivision (d) of Section 647, or subdivision 1 or 2 of Section 314, or of any offense involving lewd and lascivious conduct under Section 272, or any felony violation of Section 288.2; or any person who since that date has been or is hereafter convicted of the attempt to commit any of the above-mentioned offenses; or any person who since that date or at any time hereafter is discharged or paroled from a penal institution where he or she was confined because of the commission or attempt to commit one of the above-mentioned offenses; or any person who since that date or at any time hereafter is determined to be a mentally disordered sex offender under Article 1 (commencing with Section 6300) of Chapter 2 of Part 2 of Division 6 of the Welfare and Institutions Code; or any person who has been since that date or is hereafter convicted in any other state of any offense which, if committed or attempted in this state, would have been punishable as one or more of the above-mentioned offenses, shall, within 30 days after the effective date of this section or within 14 days of coming into any county, city, or city and county in which he or she temporarily resides or is domiciled for that length of time register with the chief of police of the city in which he or she is domiciled or the sheriff of the county if he or she is domiciled in an unincorporated area, and, additionally, with the chief of police of a campus of the University of California or the California State University if he or she is domiciled upon the campus or in any of its facilities.

(b) Any person who, after August 1, 1950, is discharged or paroled from a jail, prison, school, road camp, or other institution where he or she was con-

fined because of the commission or attempt to commit one of the above-mentioned offenses or is released from a state hospital to which he or she was committed as a mentally disordered sex offender under Article 1 (commencing with Section 6300) of Chapter 2 of Part 2 of Division 6 of the Welfare and Institutions Code shall, prior to discharge, parole, or release, be informed of his or her duty to register under this section by the official in charge of the place of confinement or hospital and the official shall require the person to read and sign such form as may be required by the Department of Justice, stating that the duty of the person to register under this section has been explained to the person. The official in charge of the place of confinement or hospital shall obtain the address where the person expects to reside upon his or her discharge, parole, or release and shall report the address to the Department of Justice. The official in charge of the place of confinement or hospital shall give one copy of the form to the person, and shall send one copy to the Department of Justice and one copy to the appropriate law enforcement agency or agencies having jurisdiction over the place the person expects to reside upon discharge, parole, or release. If the conviction which makes the person subject to this section is a felony conviction, the official in charge shall, not later than 45 days prior to the scheduled release of the person, send one copy to the appropriate law enforcement agency or agencies having local jurisdiction where the person expects to reside upon discharge, parole, or release; one copy to the prosecuting agency which prosecuted the person; and one copy to the Department of Justice. The official in charge of the place of confinement shall retain one copy. All such forms shall, if the conviction which makes the person subject to this section is a felony conviction, be transmitted within such times as to be received by the local law enforcement agency or agencies, and prosecuting agency 30 days prior to the discharge, parole, or release of the person.

(c) Any person who, after August 1, 1950, is convicted in this state of the commission or attempt to commit any of the above-mentioned offenses and who is released on probation or discharged upon payment of a fine shall, prior to release or discharge, be informed of the duty to register under this section by the court in which the person has been convicted and the court shall require the person to read and sign such form as may be required by the Department of Justice, stating that the duty of the person to register under this section has been explained to him or her. The court shall obtain the address where the person expects to reside upon release or discharge and shall report within three days the address to the Department of Justice. The court shall give one copy of the form to the person, and shall send one copy to the Department of Justice, and shall forward one copy to the appropriate law enforcement agency or agencies having local jurisdiction where the person expects to reside upon his or her discharge, parole, or release.

(d) (1) Any person who, on or after January 1, 1986, is discharged or paroled from the Youth Authority to the custody of which he or she was committed after having been adjudicated a ward of the court pursuant to Section 602 of the Welfare and Institutions Code because of the commission or attempted commission of the following offenses shall be subject to registration under the procedures of this section: assault with intent to commit rape, sodomy, or oral copulation, or any violation of Section 264.1, 288, 288.5, or 289 under Section 220; or any offense defined in Section 288, paragraph (1) of subdivision (b) or subdivision (c) or (d) of Section 286, paragraph (1) of subdivision (b) or subdivision (c) or (d) of Section 288a, subdivision (2) of Section 261, or subdivision (a) of Section 289; or any offense under Section 264.1 involving rape in concert with force or fear of bodily injury or penetration by any foreign object in concert with force or fear of bodily injury.

(2) Any person who is discharged or paroled from the Youth Authority to the custody of which he or she was committed after having been adjudicated a ward of the court pursuant to Section 602 of the Welfare and Institutions Code because of the commission or attempted commission of the offense set forth in Section 647.6, occurring on or after January 1, 1988, shall be subject to registration under the procedures of this section.

(3) Prior to discharge or parole from the Youth Authority, all persons subject to registration shall be informed of the duty to register under the procedures set forth in this section. Youth Authority officials shall transmit the required forms and information to the Department of Justice.

(4) The duty to register under this section for offenses adjudicated by a juvenile court shall terminate when a person reaches the age of 25.

(5) All records specifically relating to the registration in the custody of the Department of Justice, law enforcement agencies, and other agencies or public officials shall be destroyed when the person required to register attains the age of 25 or has his or her records sealed under the procedures set forth in Section 781 of the Welfare and Institutions Code, whichever event occurs first. This subdivision shall not be construed as requiring the destruction of other criminal offender or juvenile records relating to the case which are maintained by the Department of Justice, law enforcement agencies, the juvenile court, or other agencies and public officials unless ordered by a court under Section 781 of the Welfare and Institutions Code.

(e) The registration shall consist of (1) a statement in writing signed by the person, giving such information as may be required by the Department of Justice, and (2) the fingerprints and photograph of the person. Within three days thereafter, the registering law enforcement agency or agencies shall forward the statement, fingerprints, and photograph to the Department of Justice.

(f) If any person required to register pursuant to this section changes his or her residence address, the person shall inform, in writing within 10 days, the law enforcement agency or agencies with whom he or she last registered of the new address. The law enforcement agency or agencies shall, within three days after receipt of this information, forward it to the Department of Justice. The Department of Justice shall forward appropriate registration data to the law enforcement agency or agencies having local jurisdiction of the new place of residence.

(g) (1) Any person required to register under this section who violates any of its provisions is guilty of a misdemeanor. Any person who has been convicted of assault with intent to commit rape, oral copulation, or sodomy, or of any violation of Section 261, 264.1, 286, 288, 288a, 288.5, or 289, and who is required to register under this section who willfully violates any

of the provisions of this section is guilty of a misdemeanor and shall be sentenced to serve a term of not less than 90 days nor more than one year in the county jail. In no event does the court have the power to absolve a person who willfully violates this section from the obligation of spending at least 90 days of confinement in the county jail and of completing probation of at least one year.

(2) Any person who has two prior convictions for the offense of failing to register under this section and who subsequently and willfully commits that offense is, upon each subsequent conviction, guilty of a public offense punishable by imprisonment in the county jail not exceeding one year, or by imprisonment in state prison for 16 months, or two or three years.

The existence of any fact which would bring a person under this paragraph shall be alleged in the information or indictment and either admitted by the defendant in open court, or found to be true by the jury trying the issue of guilt or by the court where guilt is established by plea of guilty or nolo contendere or by trial by the court sitting without a jury.

(h) Whenever any person is released on parole or probation and is required to register under this section but fails to do so within the time prescribed, the Board of Prison Terms, the Youthful Offender Parole Board, or the court, as the case may be, shall order the parole or probation of the person revoked.

(i) The statements, photographs, and fingerprints herein required shall not be open to inspection by the public or by any person other than a regularly employed peace or other law enforcement officer.

(j) In any case in which a person who would be required to register pursuant to this section for a felony conviction is to be temporarily sent outside the institution where he or she is confined on any assignment within a city or county including fire fighting, disaster control, or of whatever nature the assignment may be, the local law enforcement agency having jurisdiction over the place or places where the assignment shall occur shall be notified within a reasonable time prior to removal from the institution. This provision does not apply to any person temporarily released under guard from the institution where he or she is confined.

(k) As used in this section, "mentally disordered sex offender" includes any person who has been determined to be a sexual psychopath or a mentally disordered sex offender under any provision which, on or before January 1, 1976, was contained in Division 6 (commencing with Section 6000) of the Welfare and Institutions Code.

(l) Every person who, prior to January 1, 1985, is required to register under this section, shall be notified whenever he or she next reregisters of the reduction of the registration period from 30 to 14 days. This notice shall be provided in writing by the registering agency or agencies. Failure to receive this notification shall be a defense against the penalties prescribed by subdivision (f) if the person did not register within 30 days. *(Amended by Stats 1989 ch 1316 §2, 1402 §5.5, 1407 §4, eff. 1/1/90.)*

§290.1. Registration requirement; exemption.

Notwithstanding Section 1203.4 and except as provided in Section 290.5, a person convicted of a felony sex offense shall not be relieved from the duty to register under Section 290.

© 1992 by J., B. & L. Gould
Printed in the U.S.A.   **EP**

§290.2. Specimens from sex offenders.

(a) Any person who is required to register under Section 290 because of the commission of, or the attempt to commit, a felony offense specified in Section 290, or who is convicted of murder in violation of Section 190 or 190.05, or who is convicted of a felony offense of assault or battery in violation of Section 217.1, 220, 241.1, 243, 243.1, 243.3, 243.4, 243.7, 244, 245, 245.2, 245.3, or 245.5, and who is discharged or paroled from a state prison, county jail, or any institution under the jurisdiction of the Youth Authority where he or she was confined, or is granted probation, or is released from a state hospital to which he or she was committed as a mentally disordered sex offender under the provisions of Article 1 (commencing with Section 6300) of Chapter 2 of Part 2 of Division 6 of the Welfare and Institutions Code, shall, prior to discharge, parole, the granting of probation or release, be required to provide two specimens of blood and a saliva sample to that institution or, in the case of a person granted probation, to a person and at a location within the county designated for testing. The county shall make every effort to utilize one location for testing a person under this section.

The withdrawal of blood shall be performed in a medically approved manner. Only a physician, registered nurse, licensed vocational nurse, duly licensed clinical laboratory technologist, or clinical laboratory bioanalyst may withdraw the blood specimens for purposes of this section.

(b) The Department of Justice shall provide all blood specimen vials, mailing tubes, labels, and instructions for the collection of the blood specimens and saliva samples. The specimens and samples shall thereafter be forwarded to the Department of Justice for analysis of deoxyribonucleic acid (DNA) and other genetic typing analysis at the department's DNA laboratory.

The Department of Justice shall perform DNA analysis and other genetic typing analysis only for law enforcement purposes.

(c) The Department of Justice DNA laboratory shall perform genetic typing only for those markers having value for law enforcement purposes.

For purposes of this subdivision, "marker" shall have the meaning generally ascribed to it by members of the scientific community experienced in the use of DNA technology.

(d) The DNA and other genetic typing information shall be filed with the offender's file maintained by the Sex Registration Unit of the Department of Justice or in a computerized data bank system, and shall not be included in the state summary criminal history information.

The computerized data bank system shall be limited to containing information only on individuals convicted of crimes specified in subdivision (a), or evidence accumulated from crime scenes during ongoing investigations and believed to have been left by a person suspected of having committed a violent felony specified in subdivision (c) of Section 667.5 or an offense specified in Section 290. Evidence accumulated pursuant to this provision from any crime scene with respect to a particular person shall be stricken from the data bank when it is determined that the person is no longer a suspect in the case.

(e) The DNA and other genetic typing information shall be released only to law enforcement agencies and district attorneys' offices, at the request of the agency, except as specified in this section. Dissemination of this information to law enforcement agencies and district attorneys' offices outside the state shall be done in conformity with the provisions of this section.

(f) Any person who knowingly discloses DNA or other genetic typing information developed pursuant to this section to unauthorized individuals or agencies, or for other than law enforcement purposes, shall be guilty of a misdemeanor.

(g) Furnishing DNA or other genetic typing information to defense counsel for criminal defense purposes in compliance with discovery is not a violation of this section.

(h) It is not a violation of this section to disseminate statistical or research information obtained from the offender's file or the computerized data bank system, provided that the subject of the file is not identified and cannot be identified from the information disclosed. It is also not a violation of this section to include information obtained from a file as follows: (1) in a transcript or record of a judicial proceeding, or (2) in any other public record when the inclusion of the information in the public record is authorized by a court, statute, or decisional law.

(i) The Department of Justice shall make public the methodology and procedures to be used in its DNA program prior to the commencement of DNA testing in its laboratories. The Department of Justice shall review and consider on an ongoing basis the findings and results of any peer review and validation studies submitted to te department by members of the relevant scientific community experienced in the use of DNA technology. (Amended by Stats 1989 ch 1304 §1.5, eff. 1/1/90.)

§290.3. Fine for failure to register.

Every person convicted of a violation of any offense listed in subdivision (a) of Section 290 shall, in addition to any imprisonment or fine, or both, imposed for violation of the underlying offense, be punished by a fine of one hundred dollars ($100) upon the first conviction or a fine of two hundred dollars ($200) upon the second and each subsequent conviction, unless the court determines that the defendant does not have the ability to pay the fine.

Out of the moneys deposited with the county treasurer pursuant to this section, there shall be transferred, once a month to the Controller for deposit in the General Fund, an amount equal to all fines collected during the preceding month upon conviction of, or upon the forfeiture of bail by, any person arrested or convicted of, an offense listed in Section 290. Moneys deposited in the General Fund pursuant to this section shall, when appropriated by the Legislature and until July 1, 1994, be used for the purposes of Chapter 10 (commencing with Section 13890) of Title 6 of Part 4. (Added by Stats 1988 ch 1134 §1, eff. 1/1/89 only until 7/1/94.)

§290.5. Certificate of rehabilitation.

A person required to register under Section 290 may initiate a proceeding under Chapter 3.5 (commencing with Section 4852.01) of Title 6 of Part 3 of this code, and upon obtaining a certificate of rehabilitation, shall be relieved of any further duty to register under Section 290. Such certificate shall not relieve petitioner of the duty to register under Section 290 for any offense subject to that section of which he is convicted in the future.

§291. Notice of arrest of public school employee.

Every sheriff or chief of police, upon the arrest for any of the offenses enumerated in Section 290 or in subdivision 1 of Section 261, or Section 44010 of the Education Code of any school employee, shall do either of the following:

(a) If the school employee is a teacher in any of the public schools of this state, he or she shall immediately notify by telephone the superintendent of schools of the school district employing the teacher and shall immediately give written notice of the arrest to the Commission for Teacher Preparation and Licensing and to the superintendent of schools in the county wherein the person is employed. Upon receipt of the notice, the county superintendent of schools shall immediately notify the governing board of the school district employing the person.

(b) If the school employee is a nonteacher in any of the public schools of this state, he or she shall immediately notify by telephone the superintendent of schools of the school district employing the nonteacher and shall immediately give written notice of the arrest to the governing board of the school district employing the person. *(Amended by Stats 1989 ch 388 §7, eff. 1/1/90.)*

§291.1. Notice of arrest to private schools.

Every sheriff or chief of police, upon the arrest for any of the offenses enumerated in Section 290 of any person who is employed as a teacher in any private school of this state, shall immediately give written notice of the arrest to the private school authorities employing the teacher. The sheriff or chief of police shall immediately notify by telephone the private school authorities employing such teacher.

§291.5. Notice of arrest of community college teacher.

Every sheriff or chief of police, upon the arrest for any of the offenses enumerated in Section 290 or in subdivision (1) of Section 261 of any teacher or instructor employed in any community college district shall immediately notify by telephone the superintendent of the community college district employing the teacher or instructor and shall immediately give written notice of the arrest to the Office of the Chancellor of the California Community Colleges. Upon receipt of such notice, the district superintendent shall immediately notify the governing board of the community college district employing the person.

§292. Clarification of violation deemed to be felony offense.

It is the intention of the Legislature in enacting this section to clarify that for the purposes of subdivisions (b) and (c) of Section 12 of Article 1 of the California Constitution, a violation of subdivision (2) or (6) of Section 261, Section 264.1, subdivision (c) or (d) of Section 286, subdivision (b) of Section 288, subdivision (c) or (d) of Section 288a, or subdivision (a) of Section 289, shall be deemed to be a felony offense involving an act of violence and a felony offense involving great bodily harm.

CHAPTER 6

VIOLATING SEPULTURE AND THE REMAINS OF THE DEAD
(Repealed by Stats 1937 ch 60.)

CHAPTER 7

OF CRIMES AGAINST RELIGION AND CONSCIENCE, AND OTHER OFFENSES AGAINST GOOD MORALS

§302. Disturbance of religious meetings.

(a) Every person who willfully disturbs or disquiets any assemblage of people met for religious worship at a tax-exempt place of worship, by profane discourse, rude or indecent behavior, or by any unnecessary noise, either within the place where the meeting is held, or so near it as to disturb the order and solemnity of the meeting, is guilty of a misdemeanor punishable by a fine not exceeding one thousand dollars ($1,000), or by imprisonment in the county jail for a period not exceeding six months, or by both that fine and imprisonment.

(b) A court may require performance of community service of not less than 20 hours and not exceeding 40 hours as an alternative to imprisonment or fine.

(c) In addition to the penalty set forth in subdivision (a), a person who has suffered a previous conviction of a violation of this section or Section 403, shall be required to perform community service of not less than 40 hours and not exceeding 80 hours.

(d) In addition to the penalty set forth in subdivision (a), a person who has suffered two or more previous convictions of violations of this section or Section 403, shall perform community service of not less than 80 hours and not exceeding 120 hours.

(e) The existence of any fact which would bring a person under subdivision (c) or (d) shall be alleged in the complaint, information, or indictment and either:

(1) Admitted by the defendant in open court.

(2) Found to be true by a jury trying the issue of guilt.

(3) Found to be true by the court where guilt is established by a plea of guilty or nolo contendere.

(4) Found to be true by trial by the court sitting without a jury.

(f) Upon conviction of any person under this section for disturbances of religious worship, the court may, in accordance with the performance of community service imposed under this section, consistent with public safety interests and with the victim's consent, order the defendant to perform a portion of, or all of, the required community service at the place where the disturbance of religious worship occurred.

(g) The court may waive the mandatory minimum requirements for community service whenever it is in the interest of justice to do so. When a waiver is granted, the court shall state on the record all reasons supporting the waiver. *(Amended by Stats 1990 ch 822 §1, eff. 1/1/91.)*

§303. Unlawfully employing a person to procure sale of alcoholic beverages.

It shall be unlawful for any person engaged in the sale of alcoholic beverages, other than in the original package, to employ upon the premises where the alcoholic beverages are sold any person for the purpose of procuring or encouraging the purchase or sale of

70

such beverages, or to pay any person a percentage or commission on the sale of such beverages for procuring or encouraging such purchase or sale. Violation of this section shall be a misdemeanor.

§303a. Begging or soliciting purchase of alcoholic beverages.

It shall be unlawful, in any place of business where alcoholic beverages are sold to be consumed upon the premises, for any person to loiter in or about said premises for the purpose of begging or soliciting any patron or customer of, or visitor in, such premises to purchase any alcoholic beverage for the one begging or soliciting. Violation of this section shall be a misdemeanor.

§307. Selling candy containing alcohol to person under 21.

Every person, firm, or corporation which sells or gives or in any way furnishes to another person, who is in fact under the age of 21 years, any candy, cake, cookie, or chewing gum which contains alcohol in excess of ½ of 1 percent by weight, is guilty of a misdemeanor. *(Amended by Stats 1985 ch 934 §4.)*

§308. Selling tobacco products or paraphernalia for smoking to minor.

(a) Every person, firm or corporation which knowingly sells, gives, or in any way furnishes to another person who is under the age of 18 years any tobacco, cigarette, or cigarette papers, or any other preparation of tobacco, or any other instrument or paraphernalia that is designed for the smoking or ingestion of tobacco, products prepared from tobacco, or any controlled substance, is subject to either a criminal action for a misdemeanor or to a civil action brought by a city attorney, a county counsel, or a district attorney, punishable by a fine of two hundred dollars ($200) for the first offense, five hundred dollars ($500) for the second offense, and one thousand dollars ($1,000) for the third offense.

Notwithstanding Section 1404 or any other provision of law, 25 percent of each civil and criminal penalty collected pursuant to this subdivision shall be paid to the office of the city attorney, county counsel, or district attorney, whoever is responsible for bringing the successful action, and 25 percent of each civil and criminal penalty collected pursuant to this subdivision shall be paid to the city or county for the administration and cost of the community service work component provided in subdivision (b).

Proof that a defendant, or his or her employee or agent, demanded, was shown, and reasonably relied upon evidence of majority shall be defense to any action brought pursuant to this subdivision. Evidence of majority of a person is a facsimile of or a reasonable likeness of a document issued by a federal, state, county, or municipal government, or subdivision or agency thereof, including, but not limited to, a motor vehicle operator's license, a registration certificate issued under the Federal Selective Service Act, or an identification card issued to a member of the armed forces.

For purposes of this section, the person liable for selling or furnishing tobacco products to minors by a tobacco vending machine shall be the person authorizing the installation or placement of the tobacco vending machine upon premises he or she manages or otherwise controls and under circumstances in which he or she has knowledge, or should otherwise have grounds for knowledge, that the tobacco vending machine will be utilized by minors.

(b) Every person under the age of 18 years who purchases or receives any tobacco, cigarette, or cigarette papers, or any other preparation of tobacco, or any other instrument or paraphernalia that is designed for the smoking of tobacco, products prepared from tobacco, or any controlled substance shall, upon conviction, be punished by a fine of fifty dollars ($50) or 25 hours of community service work.

(c) Every person, firm or corporation which sells, or deals in tobacco or any preparation thereof, shall post conspicuously and keep so posted in his, her, or their place of business a copy of this act, and any such person failing to do so shall upon conviction be punished by a fine of ten dollars ($10) for the first offense and fifty dollars ($50) for each succeeding violation of this provision, or by imprisonment for not more than 30 days.

The Secretary of State is hereby authorized to have printed sufficient copies of this act to enable him or her to furnish dealers in tobacco with copies thereof upon their request for the same.

(d) For purposes of determining the liability of persons, firms, or corporations controlling franchises or business operations in multiple locations for the second and subsequent violations of this section, each individual franchise or business location shall be deemed a separate entity.

(e) It is the Legislature's intent to regulate the subject matter of this section. As a result, no city, county, or city and county shall adopt any ordinance or regulation inconsistent with this section.

(f) Notwithstanding any other provision of this section, the Director of Corrections may sell or supply tobacco and tobacco products, including cigarettes and cigarette papers, to any person confined in any institution or facility under his, her, or its jurisdiction who has attained the age of 16 years, if the parent or guardian of the person consents thereto, and may permit smoking by any such person in any such institution or facility. No officer or employee of the Department of Corrections shall be considered to have violated this section by any act authorized by this subdivision. *(Amended by Stats 1989 ch 223 §1, eff. 1/1/90.)*

§308a. Repealed by Stats 1989 ch 223 §2, eff. 1/1/90.

§308b. Distribution of unsolicited tobacco products.

(a) Except as provided in subdivision (b), every person who knowingly delivers or causes to be delivered to any residence in this state any tobacco products unsolicited by any person residing therein is guilty of a misdemeanor.

(b) It is a defense to a violation of this section that the recipient of the tobacco products is personally known to the defendant at the time of the delivery.

(c) The distribution of unsolicited tobacco products to residences in violation of this section is a nuisance within the meaning of Section 3479 of the Civil Code.

(d) Nothing in this section shall be construed to impose any liability on any employee of the United States Postal Service for actions performed in the scope of his employment by the United States Postal Service.

§308.2. Selling cigarettes in unsealed package.

(a) Every person who sells one or more cigarettes, other than in a sealed and properly labeled package, is guilty of an infraction.

(b) "A sealed and properly labeled package," as used in this section, means the original packaging or sanitary wrapping of the manufacturer or importer which conforms to federal labeling requirements, including the federal warning label. *(Added by Stats 1991 ch 1231 §1, eff. 1/1/92.)*

§308.5. Advertising alcohol or tobacco products in video games.

(a) No person or business shall sell, lease, rent, or provide, or offer to sell, lease, rent, or otherwise offer to the public or to public establishments in this state, any video game intended for either private use or for use in a public establishment and intended primarily for use by any person under the age of 18 years, which contains, in its design and in the on-screen presentation of the video game, any paid commercial advertisement of alcoholic beverage or tobacco product containers or other forms of consumer packaging, particular brand names, trademarks, or copyrighted slogans of alcoholic beverages or tobacco products.

(b) As used in this section, "video game" means any electronic amusement device that utilizes a computer, microprocessor, or similar electronic circuitry and its own cathode ray tube, or is designed to be used with a television set or a monitor, that interacts with the user of the device.

(c) A violation of this section is a misdemeanor. *(Added by Stats 1990 ch 639 §1, eff. 1/1/91.)*

§309. Minor kept or admitted in house of prostitution.

Any proprietor, keeper, manager, conductor, or person having the control of any house of prostitution, or any house or room resorted to for the purpose of prostitution, who shall admit or keep any minor of either sex therein; or any parent or guardian of any such minor, who shall admit or keep such minor, or sanction, or connive at the admission or keeping thereof, into, or in any such house, or room, shall be guilty of a misdemeanor.

§310. Minors excluded from prizefights and cockfights.

Any minor under the age of 16 years who visits or attends any prizefight, cockfight, or place where any prizefight, or cockfight, is advertised to take place, and any owner, lessee, or proprietor, or the agent of any owner, lessee, or proprietor of any place where any prizefight or cockfight is advertised or represented to take place who admits any minor to a place where any prizefight or cockfight is advertised or represented to take place or who admits, sells or gives to any such minor a ticket or other paper by which such minor may be admitted to a place where a prizefight or cockfight is advertised to take place, is guilty of a misdemeanor, and is punishable by a fine of not exceeding one hundred dollars ($100) or by imprisonment in the county jail for not more than 25 days.

§310.2. Athletic supervisors furnishing minors with medication for nonmedical purposes.

(a) Any coach, trainer, or other person acting in an official or nonofficial capacity as an adult supervisor for an athletic team consisting of minors under the age of 18 who sells, gives, or otherwise furnishes to any member of that team a diuretic, diet pill, or laxative with the intent that it be consumed, injected, or administered for any nonmedical purpose such as loss of weight or altering the body in any way related to participation on the team or league, is guilty of a misdemeanor.

(b) Subdivision (a) does not apply to a minor's parent or guardian, or any person acting at the written direction of, or with the written consent of, the parent or guardian, if that person is in fact acting with that authority. Subdivision (a) does not apply to a physician. *(Added by Stats 1987 ch 999 §1.)*

CHAPTER 7.5

OBSCENE MATTER

§311. Definitions.

As used in this chapter, the following definitions shall control the meaning of the respective terms:

(a) "Obscene matter" means matter taken as a whole, which to the average person, applying contemporary statewide standards, appeals to the prurient interest, and is matter which, taken as a whole, depicts or describes in a patently offensive way sexual conduct; and which, taken as a whole, lacks serious literary, artistic, political, or scientific value.

(1) When it appears from the nature of the matter or the circumstances of its dissemination, distribution or exhibition that it is designed for clearly defined deviant sexual groups, the appeal of the matter shall be judged with reference to its intended recipient group.

(2) In prosecutions under this chapter, where circumstances of production, presentation, sale, dissemination, distribution, or publicity indicate that matter is being commercially exploited by the defendant for the sake of its prurient appeal, such evidence is probative with respect to the nature of the matter and can justify the conclusion that the matter lacks serious literary, artistic, political, or scientific value.

(3) In determining whether the matter taken as a whole lacks serious literary, artistic, political, or scientific value in description or representation of such matters, the fact that the defendant knew that the matter depicts persons under the age of 16 years engaged in sexual conduct, as defined in subdivision (c) of Section 311.4, is a factor which can be considered in making that determination.

(b) "Matter" means any book, magazine, newspaper or other printed or written material or any picture, drawing, photograph, motion picture, or other pictorial representation or any statue or other figure, or any recording, transcription or mechanical, chemical or electrical reproduction or any other articles, equipment, machines or materials. "Matter" also means live or recorded telephone messages when transmitted, disseminated, or distributed as part of a commercial transaction.

(c) "Person" means any individual, partnership, firm, association, corporation, or other legal entity.

(d) "Distribute" means to transfer possession of, whether with or without consideration.

(e) "Knowingly" means being aware of the character of the matter or live conduct.

(f) "Exhibit" means to show.

(g) "Obscene live conduct" means any physical human body activity, whether performed or engaged

© 1992 by J., B. & L. Gould
Printed in the U.S.A. **EP**

in alone or with other persons, including but not limited to singing, speaking, dancing, acting, simulating, or pantomiming, taken as a whole, which to the average person, applying contemporary statewide standards to the prurient interest and is conduct which, taken as a whole, depicts or describes in a patently offensive way sexual conduct and which, taken as a whole, lacks serious literary, artistic, political, or scientific value.

(1) When it appears from the nature of the conduct or the circumstances of its production, presentation or exhibition that it is designed for clearly defined deviant sexual groups, the appeal of the conduct shall be judged with reference to its intended recipient group.

(2) In prosecutions under this chapter, where circumstances of production, presentation advertising, or exhibition indicate that live conduct is being commercially exploited by the defendant for the sake of its prurient appeal, that evidence is probative with respect to the nature of the conduct and can justify the conclusion that the conduct lacks serious literary, artistic, political, or scientific value.

(3) In determining whether the live conduct taken as a whole lacks serious literary, artistic, political, or scientific value in description or representation of such matters, the fact that the defendant knew that the live conduct depicts persons under the age of 16 years engaged in sexual conduct, as defined in subdivision (c) of Section 311.4, is a factor which can be considered in making that determination. *(Amended by Stats 1988 ch 1378 §1; ch 1392 §2, eff. 1/1/89.)*

§311.2. Sale or distribution of obscene matter.

(a) Every person who knowingly sends or causes to be sent, or brings or causes to be brought, into this state for sale or distribution, or in this state possesses, prepares, publishes, or prints, with intent to distribute or to exhibit to others, or who offers to distribute, distributes, or exhibits to others, any obscene matter is for a first offense, guilty of a misdemeanor. If the person has previously been convicted of any violation of this section, the court may, in addition to the punishment authorized in Section 311.9, impose a fine not exceeding fifty thousand dollars ($50,000).

(b) Every person who knowingly sends or causes to be sent, or brings or causes to be brought, into this state for sale or distribution, or in this state possesses, prepares, publishes, develops, duplicates, or prints, with intent to distribute or to exhibit to, or to exchange with, others for commercial consideration, or who offers to distribute, distributes, or exhibits to, or exchanges with, others for commercial consideration, any obscene matter, knowing that the matter depicts a person under the age of 18 years personally engaging in or personally simulating sexual conduct, as defined in Section 311.4, is guilty of a felony and shall be punished by imprisonment in state prison for two, three, or six years, or by a fine not exceeding one hundred thousand dollars ($100,000), in the absence of a finding that the defendant would be incapable of paying such a fine, or by both such fine and imprisonment.

(c) Every person who knowingly sends or causes to be sent, or brings or causes to be brought, into this state for sale or distribution, or in this state possesses, prepares, publishes, develops, duplicates, or prints, with intent to distribute or to exhibit to, or to exchange with, a person 18 years of age or older, or who offers to distribute, distributes, or exhibits to, or exchanges with, a person 18 years of age or older any matter, knowing that the matter depicts a person under the age of 17 years personally engaging in or personally simulating sexual conduct, as defined in Section 311.4, is guilty of a misdemeanor and shall be punished by imprisonment in the county jail for up to one year, or by a fine not exceeding two thousand dollars ($2,000), or by both such fine and imprisonment. It is not necessary to prove commercial consideration or that the matter is obscene in order to establish a violation of this subdivision. If a person has been previously convicted of a violation of this subdivision, he or she is guilty of a felony.

(d) Every person who knowingly sends or causes to be sent, or brings or causes to be brought, into this state for sale or distribution, or in this state possesses, prepares, publishes, develops, duplicates, or prints, with intent to distribute or to exhibit to, or to exchange with, a person under 18 years of age, or who offers to distribute, distributes, or exhibits to, or exchanges with, a person under 18 years of age any matter, knowing that the matter depicts a person under the age of 17 years personally engaging in or personally simulating sexual conduct, as defined in Section 311.4, is guilty of a felony. It is not necessary to prove commercial consideration or that the matter is obscene in order to establish a violation of this subdivision.

(e) Subdivisions (a) to (d), inclusive, shall not apply to the activities of law enforcement and prosecuting agencies in the investigation and prosecution of criminal offenses or to legitimate medical, scientific, or educational activities, or to lawful conduct between spouses.

(f) This section shall not apply to matter which depicts a child under the age of 18, which child is legally emancipated, including lawful conduct between spouses when one or both are under the age of 18.

(g) It does not constitute a violation of this section for a telephone corporation, as defined by Section 234 of the Public Utilities Code, to carry or transmit messages described in this chapter or perform related activities in providing telephone services. *(Amended by Stats 1988 ch 1392 §3, eff. 1/1/89.)*

§311.3. Sexual exhibition of children.

(a) A person is guilty of sexual exploitation of a child when he or she knowingly develop, duplicate, print, or exchange any film, photograph, video tape, negative, or slide in which a person under the age of 14 years engaged in an act of sexual conduct.

(b) As used in this section "sexual conduct" means any of the following:

(1) Sexual intercourse, including genital-genital, oral-genital, anal-genital, or oral-anal, whether between persons of the same or opposite sex or between humans and animals.

(2) Penetration of the vagina or rectum by any object.

(3) Masturbation, for the purpose of sexual stimulation of the viewer.

(4) Sadomasochistic abuse for the purpose of sexual stimulation of the viewer.

(5) Exhibition of the genitals, pubic or rectal areas of any person for the purpose of sexual stimulation of the viewer.

(6) Defecation or urination for the purpose of sexual stimulation of the viewer.

© 1992 by J., B. & L. Gould
Printed in the U.S.A. **EP**

(c) Subdivision (a) shall not apply to the activities of law enforcement and prosecution agencies in the investigation and prosecution of criminal offenses or to legitimate medical, scientific, or educational activities, or to lawful conduct between spouses.

(d) Every person who violates subdivision (a) is punishable by a fine of not more than two thousand dollars ($2,000) or by imprisonment in the county jail for not more than one year, or by both such fine and imprisonment. If such person has been previously convicted of a violation of subdivision (a) or any section of this chapter, he or she is punishable by imprisonment in the state prison.

(e) The provisions of this section shall not apply to an employee of a commercial film developer who is acting within the scope of his employment and in accordance with the instructions of his employer, provided that the employee has no financial interest in the commercial developer by which he is employed.

§311.4. Employment of minor to perform prohibited acts.

(a) Every person who, with knowledge that a person is a minor, or who, while in possession of any facts on the basis of which he or she should reasonably know that the person is a minor, hires, employs, or uses the minor to do or assist in doing any of the acts described in Section 311.2, is, for a first offense, guilty of a misdemeanor. If the person has previously been convicted of any violation of this section, the court may, in addition to the punishment authorized in Section 311.9, impose a fine not exceeding fifty thousand dollars ($50,000).

(b) Every person who, with knowledge that a person is a minor under the age of 17 years, or who, while in possession of any facts on the basis of which he or she should reasonably know that the person is a minor under the age of 17 years, knowingly promotes, employs, uses, persuades, induces, or coerces a minor under the age of 17 years, or any parent or guardian of a minor under the age of 17 years under his or her control who knowingly permits the minor, to engage in or assist others to engage in either posing or modeling alone or with others for purposes of preparing a film, photograph, negative, slide, or live performance involving sexual conduct by a minor under the age of 17 years alone or with other persons or animals, for commercial purposes, is guilty of a felony and shall be punished by imprisonment in the state prison for three, six, or eight years.

(c) Every person who, with knowledge that a person is a minor under the age of 17 years, or who, while in possession of any facts on the basis of which he or she should reasonably know that the person is a minor under the age of 17 years, knowingly promotes, employs, uses, persuades, induces, or coerces a minor under the age of 17 years, or any parent or guardian of a minor under the age of 17 years under his or her control who knowingly permits the minor, to engage in or assist others to engage in either posing or modeling alone or with others for purposes of preparing a film, photograph, negative, slide, or live performance involving sexual conduct by a minor under the age of 17 years alone or with other persons or animals, is guilty of a felony. It shall not be necessary to prove commercial purposes in order to establish a violation of this subdivision.

(d) As used in subdivisions (b) and (c), "sexual conduct" means any of the following, whether actual or simulated: sexual intercourse, oral copulation, anal intercourse, anal oral copulation, masturbation, bestiality, sexual sadism, sexual masochism, penetration of the vagina or rectum by any object in a lewd or lascivious manner, exhibition of the genitals, pubic, or rectal area for the purpose of sexual stimulation of the viewer, any lewd or lascivious sexual act as defined in Section 288, or excretory functions performed in a lewd or lascivious manner, whether or not any of the above conduct is performed alone or between members of the same or opposite sex or between humans and animals. An act is simulated when it gives the appearance of being sexual conduct.

(e) This section shall not apply where the minor is legally emancipated, including lawful conduct between spouses when one or both are under the age of 17.

(f) In every prosecution under this section involving a minor under the age of 14 years at the time of the offense, the age of the victim shall be pled and proven for the purpose of the enhanced penalty provided in Section 647a. Failure to plead and prove that the victim was under the age of 14 years at the time of the offense shall not be a bar to prosecution under this section if it is proven that the victim was under the age of 18 years at the time of the offense. (*Amended by Stats 1987 ch 1394 §5.*)

§311.5. Promotion of obscene material.

Every person who writes, creates, or solicits the publication or distribution of advertising or other promotional material, or who in any manner promotes, the sale, distribution, or exhibition of matter represented or held out by him to be obscene, is guilty of a misdemeanor.

§311.6. Participation in obscene live conduct.

Every person who knowingly engages or participates in, manages, produces, sponsors, presents or exhibits obscene live conduct to or before an assembly or audience consisting of at least one person or spectator in any public place or in any place exposed to public view, or in any place open to the public or to a segment thereof, whether or not an admission fee is charged, or whether or not attendance is conditioned upon the presentation of a membership card or other token, is guilty of a misdemeanor.

§311.7. Sale conditioned on receipt of obscene matter.

Every person who, knowingly, as a condition to a sale, allocation, consignment, or delivery for resale of any paper, magazine, book, periodical, publication or other merchandise, requires that the purchaser or consignee receive any obscene matter or who denies or threatens to deny a franchise, revokes or threatens to revoke, or imposes any penalty, financial or otherwise, by reason of the failure of any person to accept obscene matter, or by reason of the return of such obscene matter, is guilty of a misdemeanor.

§311.8. Defenses defined.

(a) It shall be a defense in any prosecution for a violation of this chapter that the act charged was committed in aid of legitimate scientific or educational purposes.

(b) It shall be a defense in any prosecution for a violation of this chapter by a person who knowingly distributed any obscene matter by the use of telephones or telephone facilities to any person under

© 1992 by J., B. & L. Gould
Printed in the U.S.A.   EP

the age of 18 years that the defendant has taken either of the following measures to restrict access to the obscene matter by persons under 18 years of age:

(1) Required the person receiving the obscene matter to use an authorized access or identification code, as provided by the information provider, before transmission of the obscene matter begins, where the defendant has previously issued the code by mailing it to the applicant therefor after taking reasonable measures to ascertain that the applicant was 18 years of age or older and has established a procedure to immediately cancel the code of any person after receiving notice, in writing or by telephone, that the code has been lost, stolen, or used by persons under the age of 18 years or that the code is no longer desired.

(2) Required payment by credit card before transmission of the matter.

(c) Any list of applicants or recipients compiled or maintained by an information-access service provider for purposes of compliance with subdivision (b) is confidential and shall not be sold or otherwise disseminated except upon order of the court. *(Amended by Stats 1987 ch 1101 §1.)*

§311.9. Punishments.

(a) Every person who violates Section 311.2 or 311.5, except subdivision (b) of Section 311.2, is punishable by fine of not more than one thousand dollars ($1,000) plus five dollars ($5) for each additional unit of material coming within the provisions of this chapter, which is involved in the offense, not to exceed ten thousand dollars ($10,000), or by imprisonment in the county jail for not more than six months plus one day for each additional unit of material coming within the provisions of this chapter, and which is involved in the offense, such basic maximum and additional days not to exceed 360 days in the county jail, or by both such fine and imprisonment. If such person has previously been convicted of any offense in this chapter, or of a violation of Section 313.1, a violation of Section 311.2 or 311.5, except subdivision (b) of Section 311.2, is punishable as a felony.

(b) Every person who violates Section 311.4 is punishable by fine of not more than two thousand dollars ($2,000) or by imprisonment in the county jail for not more than one year, or by both such fine and such imprisonment. If such person has been previously convicted of a violation of former Section 311.3 or Section 311.4, he is punishable by imprisonment in the state prison.

(c) Every person who violates Section 311.7 is punishable by fine of not more than one thousand dollars ($1,000) or by imprisonment in the county jail for not more than six months, or by both such fine and imprisonment. For a second and subsequent offense he shall be punished by a fine of not more than two thousand dollars ($2,000), or by imprisonment in the county jail for not more than one year, or by both such fine and imprisonment. If such person has been twice convicted of a violation of this chapter, a violation of Section 311.7 is punishable as a felony.

§311.10. Advertising obscene matter.

(a) Any person who advertises for sale or distribution any obscene matter knowing that it depicts a person under the age of 18 years personally engaging in or personally simulating sexual conduct, as defined in Section 311.4, is guilty of a felony and is punishable by imprisonment in the state prison for two, three, or four years, or in a county jail not exceeding one year, or by a fine not exceeding fifty thousand dollars ($50,000), or by both such fine and imprisonment.

(b) Subdivision (a) shall not apply to the activities of law enforcement and prosecution agencies in the investigation and prosecution of criminal offenses. *(Added by Stats 1985 ch 1550 §1.)*

§311.11. Possessing child pornography.

(a) Every person who knowingly possesses or controls any matter, the production of which involves the use of a person under the age of 14 years, knowing that the matter depicts a person under the age of 14 years personally engaging in or simulating sexual conduct, as defined in subdivision (d) of Section 311.4, is guilty of a public offense and shall be punished by imprisonment in the county jail for up to one year, or by a fine not exceeding two thousand five hundred dollars ($2,500), or by both the fine and imprisonment.

(b) If a person has been previously convicted of a violation of this section, he or she is guilty of a felony and shall be punished by imprisonment of two, four, or six years.

(c) It is not necessary to prove that the matter is obscene in order to establish a violation of this section.

(d) For purposes of this section, matter as defined in subdivision (b) of Section 311, also includes developed or undeveloped film, negatives, photocopies, filmstrips, slides, and videotapes, the production of which involves the use of a child under the age of 14 years. This section shall not apply to drawings, figurines, statues, or any film rated by the Motion Picture Association of America, nor shall it apply to live or recorded telephone messages when transmitted, disseminated, or distributed as part of a commercial transaction. *(Added by Stats 1989 ch 1180 §2, eff. 1/1/90.)*

§312. Destruction of obscene material upon conviction.

Upon the conviction of the accused, the court may, when the conviction becomes final, order any matter or advertisement, in respect whereof the accused stands convicted, and which remains in the possession or under the control of the district attorney or any law enforcement agency, to be destroyed, and the court may cause to be destroyed any such material in its possession or under its control.

§312.1. Expert witness testimony.

In any prosecution for a violation of the provisions of this chapter or of Chapter 7.6 (commencing with Section 313), neither the prosecution nor the defense shall be required to introduce expert witness testimony concerning the obscene or harmful character of the matter or live conduct which is the subject of any such prosecution. Any evidence which tends to establish contemporary community standards of appeal to prurient interest or of customary limits of candor in the description or representation of nudity, sex or excretion, or which bears upon the question of significant literary, artistic, political, educational, or scientific value shall, subject to the provisions of the Evidence Code, be admissible when offered by either the prosecution or by the defense. *(Amended by Stats 1986 ch 51 §3.)*

§312.3. Forfeiture of obscene matter.

(a) Matter which depicts a person under the age of 17 years personally engaging in or personally simulating sexual conduct as defined in Section 311.4 and which is in the possession of any city, county, city and county, or state official or agency is subject to forfeiture pursuant to this section.

(b) An action to forfeit matter described in subdivision (a) may be brought by the Attorney General, the district attorney, county counsel, or the city attorney. Proceedings shall be initiated by a petition of forfeiture filed in the superior court of the county in which the matter is located.

(c) The prosecuting agency shall make service of process of a notice regarding that petition upon every individual who may have a property interest in the alleged proceeds, which notice shall state that any interested party may file a verified claim with the superior court stating the amount of their claimed interest and an affirmation or denial of the prosecuting agency's allegation. If the notices cannot be given by registered mail or personal delivery, the notice shall be published for at least three successive weeks in a newspaper of general circulation in the county where the property is located. All notices shall set forth the time within which a claim of interest in the property seized is required to be filed.

(d) (1) Any person claiming an interest in the property or proceeds may, at any time within 30 days from the date of the first publication of the notice of seizure, or within 30 days after receipt of actual notice, file with the superior court of the county in which the action is pending a verified claim stating his or her interest in the property or proceeds. A verified copy of the claim shall be given by the claimant to the Attorney General or district attorney, county counsel, or city attorney, as appropriate.

(2) If, at the end of the time set forth in paragraph (1), an interested person has not filed a claim, the court, upon motion, shall declare that the person has defaulted upon his or her alleged interest, and it shall be subject to forfeiture upon proof of compliance with subdivision (c).

(e) The burden shall be on the petitioner to prove beyond a reasonable doubt that matter is subject to forfeiture pursuant to this section.

(f) It shall not be necessary to seek or obtain a criminal conviction prior to the entry of an order for the destruction of matter pursuant to this section. Any matter described in subdivision (a) which is in the possession of any city, county, city and county, or state official or agency, including found property, or property obtained as the result of a case in which no trial was had or which has been disposed of by way of dismissal or otherwise than by way of conviction may be ordered destroyed.

(g) A court order for destruction of matter described in subdivision (a) may be carried out by a police or sheriff's department or by the Department of Justice. The court order shall specify the agency responsible for the destruction.

(h) As used in this section, "matter" means any book, magazine, newspaper, or other printed or written material or any picture, drawing, photograph, motion picture, or other pictorial representation, or any statue or other figure, or any recording, transcription or mechanical, chemical or electrical reproduction, or any other articles, equipment, machines, or materials.

(i) This section shall not apply where the minor depicted is lawfully emancipated, including lawful conduct between spouses when one or more are under the age of 17.

(j) It shall be a defense in any forfeiture proceeding that the matter seized was lawfully possessed in aid of legitimate scientific or educational purposes. *(Added by Stats 1985 ch 880 §1.)*

§312.5. Severability.

If any phrase, clause, sentence, section or provision of this chapter or application thereof to any person or circumstance is held invalid, such invalidity shall not affect any other phrase, clause, sentence, section, provision or application of this chapter, which can be given effect without the invalid phrase, clause, sentence, section, provision or application and to this end the provisions of this chapter are declared to be severable.

CHAPTER 7.6

HARMFUL MATTER

§313. Terms defined.

As used in this chapter:

(a) "Harmful matter" means matter, taken as a whole, which to the average person, applying contemporary statewide standards, appeals to the prurient interest, and is matter which, taken as a whole, depicts or describes in a patently offensive way sexual conduct and which, taken as a whole, lacks serious literary, artistic, political, or scientific value for minors.

(1) When it appears from the nature of the matter or the circumstances of its dissemination, distribution or exhibition that it is designed for clearly defined deviant sexual groups, the appeal of the matter shall be judged with reference to its intended recipient group.

(2) In prosecutions under this chapter, where circumstances of production, presentation, sale, dissemination, distribution or publicity indicate that matter is being commercially exploited by the defendant for the sake of its prurient appeal, that evidence is probative with respect to the nature of the matter and can justify the conclusion that the matter lacks serious literary, artistic, political, or scientific value for minors.

(b) "Matter" means any book, magazine, newspaper, video recording, or other printed or written material or any picture, drawing, photograph, motion picture, or other pictorial representation or any statue or other figure, or any recording, transcription, or mechanical, chemical, or electrical reproduction or any other articles, equipment, machines, or materials. "Matter" also includes live or recorded telephone messages when transmitted, disseminated, or distributed as part of a commercial transaction.

(c) "Person" means any individual, partnership, firm, association, corporation, or other legal entity.

(d) "Distribute" means to transfer possession of, whether with or without consideration.

(e) "Knowingly" means being aware of the character of the matter.

(f) "Exhibit" means to show.

(g) "Minor" means any natural person under 18 years of age. *(Amended by Stats 1989 ch 1058 §2, eff. 1/1/90.)*

§313.1. Distribution of harmful matter to minor.

(a) Every person who, with knowledge that a person is a minor, or who fails to exercise reasonable care

© 1992 by J., B. & L. Gould
Printed in the U.S.A.   EP

in ascertaining the true age of a minor, knowingly sells, rents, distributes, sends, causes to be sent, exhibits, or offers to distribute or exhibit by any means, including, but not limited to, live or recorded telephone messages, any harmful matter to the minor shall be punished as specified in Section 313.4.

It does not constitute a violation of this section for a telephone corporation, as defined by Section 234 of the Public Utilities Code, to carry or transmit messages described in this chapter or perform related activities in providing telephone services.

(b) Every person who misrepresents himself or herself to be the parent or guardian of a minor and thereby causes the minor to be admitted to an exhibition of any harmful matter shall be punished as specified in Section 313.4.

(c) Any person who knowingly displays, sells, or offers to sell in any coin- or slug-operated vending machine or mechanically or electronically controlled vending machine which is located in a public place, other than a public place from which minors are excluded, any harmful matter displaying to the public view photographs or pictorial representations of the commission of any of the following acts shall be punished as specified in Section 313.4: sodomy, oral copulation, sexual intercourse, masturbation, bestiality, or a photograph of an exposed penis in an erect and turgid state.

(d) Nothing in this section invalidates or prohibits the adoption of an ordinance by a city, county, or city and county which restricts the display of material which is harmful to minors, as defined in this chapter, in a public place, other than a public place from which minors are excluded, by requiring the placement of devices commonly known as blinder racks in front of the material, so that the lower two-thirds of the material is not exposed to view.

(e) Any person who sells or rents video recordings of harmful matter shall create an area within his or her business establishment for the placement of video recordings of harmful matter and for any material which advertises the sale or rental of these video recordings. This area shall be labeled "adults only." The failure to create and label the area is an infraction, and is punishable by a fine not to exceed one hundred dollars ($100). The failure to place a video recording or advertisement, regardless of its content, in this area shall not constitute an infraction. Any person who sells or distributes video recordings of harmful matter to others for resale purposes shall inform the purchaser of the requirements of this section. This subdivision shall not apply to public libraries as defined in Section 18710 of the Education Code.

(f) It shall be a defense in any prosecution for a violation of subdivision (a) by a person who knowingly distributed any harmful matter by the use of telephones or telephone facilities to any person under the age of 18 years that the defendant has taken either of the following measures to restrict access to the harmful matter by persons under 18 years of age:

(1) Required the person receiving the harmful matter to use an authorized access or identification code, as provided by the information provider, before transmission of the harmful matter begins, where the defendant has previously issued the code by mailing it to the applicant after taking reasonable measures to ascertain that the applicant was 18 years of age or older and has established a procedure to immediately cancel the code of any person after receiving notice, in writing or by telephone, that the code has been lost, stolen, or used by persons under the age of 18 years or that the code is no longer desired.

(2) Required payment by credit card before transmission of the matter.

(g) Any list of applicants or recipients compiled or maintained by an information-access service provider for purposes of compliance with paragraph (1) of subdivision (f) is confidential and shall not be sold or otherwise disseminated except upon order of the court. *(Amended by Stats 1990 ch 877 §1, eff. 1/1/91.)*

§313.2. Parental distribution of harmful material to child.

(a) Nothing in this chapter shall prohibit any parent or guardian from distributing any harmful matter to his child or ward or permitting his child or ward to attend an exhibition of any harmful matter if the child or ward is accompanied by him.

(b) Nothing in this chapter shall prohibit any person from exhibiting any harmful matter to any of the following:

(1) A minor who is accompanied by his parent or guardian.

(2) A minor who is accompanied by an adult who represents himself to be the parent or guardian of the minor and whom the person, by the exercise of reasonable care, does not have reason to know is not the parent or guardian of the minor.

§313.3. Defense.

It shall be a defense in any prosecution for a violation of this chapter that the act charged was committed in aid of legitimate scientific or educational purposes.

§313.4. Punishment.

Every person who violates Section 313.1, other than subdivision (e), is punishable by fine of not more than two thousand dollars ($2,000), by imprisonment in the county jail for not more than one year, or by both that fine and imprisonment. However, if the person has been previously convicted of a violation of Section 313.1, other than subdivision (e), or of any section of Chapter 7.5 (commencing with Section 311) of Title 9 of Part 1 of this code, the person shall be punished by imprisonment in the state prison. *(Amended by Stats 1989 ch 1058 §4, eff. 1/1/90.)*

§313.5. Severability.

If any phrase, clause, sentence, section or provision of this chapter or application thereof to any person or circumstance is held invalid, such invalidity shall not affect any other phrase, clause, sentence, section, provision or application of this chapter, which can be given effect without the invalid phrase, clause, sentence, section, provision or application and to this end the provisions of this chapter are declared to be severable.

CHAPTER 8

INDECENT EXPOSURE, OBSCENE EXHIBITIONS, AND BAWDY AND OTHER DISORDERLY HOUSES

§314. Indecent exposure; assisting another to indecent exposure.

Every person who willfully and lewdly, either:

1. Exposes his person, or the private parts thereof, in any public place, or in any place where there are present other persons to be offended or annoyed thereby; or,

2. Procures, counsels, or assists any person so to expose himself or take part in any model artist exhibition, or to make any other exhibition of himself to public view, or the view of any number of persons, such as is offensive to decency, or is adapted to excite to vicious or lewd thoughts or acts, is guilty of a misdemeanor.

Every person who violates subdivision 1 of this section after having entered, without consent, an inhabited dwelling house, or trailer coach as defined in Section 635 of the Vehicle Code, or the inhabited portion of any other building, is punishable by imprisonment in the state prison, or in the county jail not exceeding one year.

Upon the second and each subsequent conviction under subdivision 1 of this section, or upon a first conviction under subdivision 1 of this section after a previous conviction under Section 288, every person so convicted is guilty of a felony, and is punishable by imprisonment in state prison.

§315. Keeping or willfully residing in house of ill-fame.

Every person who keeps a house of ill-fame in this state, resorted to for the purposes of prostitution or lewdness, or who willfully resides in such house, is guilty of a misdemeanor; and in all prosecutions for keeping or resorting to such a house common repute may be received as competent evidence of the character of the house, the purpose for which it is kept or used, and the character of the women inhabiting or resorting to it.

§316. Keeping disorderly house which disturbs peace of neighborhood.

Every person who keeps any disorderly house, or any house for the purpose of assignation or prostitution, or any house of public resort, by which the peace, comfort, or decency of the immediate neighborhood is habitually disturbed, or who keeps any inn in a disorderly manner; and every person who lets any apartment or tenement, knowing that it is to be used for the purpose of assignation or prostitution, is guilty of a misdemeanor. *(Amended by Stats 1989 ch 1360 §108, eff. 1/1/90.)*

§318. Prevailing upon person to visit place of gambling or prostitution.

Whoever, through invitation or device, prevails upon any person to visit any room, building, or other places kept for the purpose of illegal gambling or prostitution, is guilty of a misdemeanor, and, upon conviction thereof, shall be confined in the county jail not exceeding six months, or fined not exceeding five hundred dollars ($500), or be punished by both that fine and imprisonment. *(Amended by Stats 1991 ch 684 §2, eff. 1/1/92.)*

§318.5. Exposure of private parts in food and beverage establishments.

Nothing in this code shall invalidate an ordinance of, or be construed to prohibit the adoption of an ordinance by, a county or city, if such ordinance directly regulates the exposure of the genitals or buttocks of or the breasts of any person who acts as a waiter, waitress, or entertainer, whether or not the owner of the establishment in which the activity is performed employs or pays any compensation to such person to perform such activity, in an establishment which serves food, beverages, or food and beverages, including, but not limited to, alcoholic beverages, for consumption on the premises of such establishment.

The provisions of this section shall not apply to a theater, concert hall, or similar establishment which is primarily devoted to theatrical performances.

This section shall be known and may be cited as the "Quimby-Walsh Act."

§318.6. Topless and bottomless exhibitions in public places.

Nothing in this code shall invalidate an ordinance of, or be construed to prohibit the adoption of an ordinance by, a city or county, if such ordinance relates to any live acts, demonstrations, or exhibitions which occur in public places, places open to the public, or places open to public view and involve the exposure of the private parts or buttocks of any participant or the breasts of any female participant, and if such ordinance prohibits an act or acts which are not expressly authorized or prohibited by this code.

The provisions of this section shall not apply to a theater, concert hall, or similar establishment which is primarily devoted to theatrical performances.

CHAPTER 9

LOTTERIES

§319. Lottery defined.

A lottery is any scheme for the disposal or distribution of property by chance, among persons who have paid or promised to pay any valuable consideration for the chance of obtaining such property or a portion of it, or for any share or any interest in such property, upon any agreement, understanding, or expectation that it is to be distributed or disposed of by lot or chance, whether called a lottery, raffle, or gift enterprise, or by whatever name the same may be known.

§319.5. Use of reverse vending machine.

Neither this chapter nor Chapter 10 (commencing with Section 330) applies to the possession or operation of a reverse vending machine. As used in this section a reverse vending machine is a machine in which empty beverage containers are deposited for recycling and which provides a payment of money, merchandise, vouchers, or other incentives at a frequency less than upon each deposit. The pay out of a reverse vending machine is made on a deposit selected at random within the designated number of required deposits.

The deposit of an empty beverage container in a reverse vending machine does not constitute consideration within the definition of lottery in Section 319.

§320. Punishment for drawing lottery.

Every person who contrives, prepares, sets up, proposes, or draws any lottery, is guilty of a misdemeanor.

§321. Punishment for selling lottery tickets.

Every person who sells, gives, or in any manner whatever, furnishes or transfers to or for any other person any ticket, chance, share, or interest, or any

© 1992 by J., B. & L. Gould
Printed in the U.S.A.   EP

paper, certificate, or instrument purporting or understood to be or to represent any ticket, chance, share, or interest in, or depending upon the event of any lottery, is guilty of a misdemeanor.

§322. Aiding lotteries.

Every person who aids or assists, either by printing, writing, advertising, publishing, or otherwise in setting up, managing, or drawing any lottery, or in selling or disposing of any ticket, chance, or share therein, is guilty of a misdemeanor.

§323. Lottery offices; advertising lottery offices.

Every person who opens, sets up, or keeps, by himself or by any other person, any office or other place for the sale of, or for registering the number of any ticket in any lottery, or who, by printing, writing, or otherwise, advertises or publishes the setting up, opening, or using of any such office, is guilty of a misdemeanor.

§324. Insuring lottery tickets.

Every person who insures or receives any consideration for insurance for or against the drawing of any ticket in any lottery whatever, whether drawn or to be drawn within this state or not, or who receives any valuable consideration upon any agreement to repay any sum, or deliver the same, or any other property, if any lottery ticket or number of any ticket in any lottery shall prove fortunate or unfortunate, or shall be drawn or not be drawn, at any particular time or in any particular order, or who promises or agrees to pay any sum of money, or to deliver any goods, things in action, or property, or to forbear to do anything for the benefit of any person, with or without consideration, upon any event or contingency dependent on the drawing of any ticket in any lottery, or who publishes any notice or proposal of any of the purposes aforesaid, is guilty of a misdemeanor.

§325. Forfeiture of money and property in lotteries.

All moneys and property offered for sale or distribution in violation of any of the provisions of this chapter are forfeited to the state, and may be recovered by information filed, or by an action brought by the Attorney General, or by any district attorney, in the name of the state. Upon the filing of the information or complaint, the clerk of the court must issue an attachment against the property mentioned in the complaint or information, which attachment has the same force and effect against such property, and is issued in the same manner as attachments issued from the superior courts in civil cases.

§326. Letting building for lottery purposes.

Every person who lets, or permits to be used, any building or vessel, or any portion thereof, knowing that it is to be used for setting up, managing, or drawing any lottery, or for the purpose of selling, or disposing of lottery tickets, is guilty of a misdemeanor.

§326.5. Bingo games.

(a) Neither this chapter nor Chapter 10 (commencing with Section 330) applies to any bingo game which is conducted in a city, county, or city and county pursuant to an ordinance enacted under Section 19 of Article IV of the State Constitution, provided that such ordinance allows games to be conducted only by organizations exempted from the payment of the bank and corporation tax by Sections 23701a, 23701b, 23701d, 23701e, 23701f, 23701g, and 23701l of the Revenue and Taxation Code and by mobile home park associations and senior citizens organizations; and provided that the receipts of such games are used only for charitable purposes.

(b) It is a misdemeanor for any person to receive or pay a profit, wage, or salary from any bingo game authorized by Section 19 of Article IV of the State Constitution. Security personnel employed by the organization conducting the bingo game may be paid from the revenues of bingo games as provided in subdivisions (j) and (k).

(c) A violation of subdivision (b) of this section shall be punishable by a fine not to exceed ten thousand dollars ($10,000), which fine shall be deposited in the general fund of the city, county, or city and county which enacted the ordinance authorizing the bingo game. A violation of any provision of this section, other than subdivision (b), is a misdemeanor.

(d) The city, county, or city and county which enacted the ordinance authorizing the bingo game may bring an action to enjoin a violation of this section.

(e) No minors shall be allowed to participate in any bingo game.

(f) An organization authorized to conduct bingo games pursuant to subdivision (a) shall conduct a bingo game only on property owned or leased by it, or property whose use is donated to the organization, and which property is used by such organization for an office or for performance of the purposes for which the organization is organized. Nothing in this subdivision shall be construed to require that the property owned or leased by or whose use is donated to the organization be used or leased exclusively by or donated exclusively to such organization.

(g) All bingo games shall be open to the public, not just to the members of the authorized organization.

(h) A bingo game shall be operated and staffed only by members of the authorized organization which organized it. Such members shall not receive a profit, wage, or salary from any bingo game. Only the organization authorized to conduct a bingo game shall operate such game, or participate in the promotion, supervision, or any other phase of such game. This subdivision does not preclude the employment of security personnel who are not members of the authorized organization at such bingo game by the organization conducting the game.

(i) No individual, corporation, partnership, or other legal entity except the organization authorized to conduct a bingo game shall hold a financial interest in the conduct of such bingo game.

(j) With respect to organizations exempt from payment of the bank and corporation tax by Section 23701d of the Revenue and Taxation Code, all profits derived from a bingo game shall be kept in a special fund or account and shall not be commingled with any other fund or account. Such profits shall be used only for charitable purposes.

(k) With respect to other organizations authorized to conduct bingo games pursuant to this section, all proceeds derived from a bingo game shall be kept in a special fund or account and shall not be commingled with any other fund or account. Proceeds are the receipts of bingo games conducted by organizations not within subdivision (j). Such proceeds shall be used only for charitable purposes, except as follows:

(1) Such proceeds may be used for prizes.

(2) A portion of such proceeds, not to exceed 20 percent of the proceeds before the deduction for prizes, or one thousand dollars ($1,000) per month, whichever is less, may be used for rental of property, overhead, including the purchase of bingo equipment, administrative expenses, security equipment, and security personnel.

(3) Such proceeds may be used to pay license fees.

(4) A city, county, or city and county which enacts an ordinance permitting bingo games may specify in such ordinance that if the monthly gross receipts from bingo games of an organization within this subdivision exceed five thousand dollars ($5,000), a minimum percentage of the proceeds shall be used only for charitable purposes not relating to the conducting of bingo games and that the balance shall be used for prizes, rental of property, overhead, administrative expenses and payment of license fees. The amount of proceeds used for rental of property, overhead, and administrative expenses is subject to the limitations specified in paragraph (2) of this subdivision.

(*l*) (1) A city, county, or city and county may impose a license fee on each organization which it authorizes to conduct bingo games. The fee, whether for the initial license or renewal, shall not exceed fifty dollars ($50) annually, except as provided in paragraph (2). If an application for a license is denied, one-half of any license fee paid shall be refunded to the organization.

(2) In lieu of the license fee permitted under paragraph (1), a city, county, or city and county may impose a license fee of fifty dollars ($50) paid upon application. If an application for a license is denied, one-half of the application fee shall be refunded to the organization. An additional fee of 1 percent of the monthly gross receipts over five thousand dollars ($5,000) derived from bingo games shall be collected monthly by the city, county, or city and county issuing the license.

(m) No person shall be allowed to participate in a bingo game, unless the person is physically present at the time and place in which the bingo game is being conducted.

(n) The total value of prizes awarded during the conduct of any bingo games shall not exceed two hundred fifty dollars ($250) in cash or kind, or both, for each separate game which is held.

(o) As used in this section "bingo" means a game of chance in which prizes are awarded on the basis of designated numbers or symbols on a card which conform to numbers or symbols selected at random. Notwithstanding Section 330c, as used in this section, the game of bingo shall include cards having numbers or symbols which are concealed and preprinted in a manner providing for distribution of prizes. The winning cards shall not be known prior to the game by any person participating in the playing or operation of the bingo game. All such preprinted cards shall bear the legend, "for sale or use only in a bingo game authorized under California law and pursuant to local ordinance." It is the intention of the Legislature that bingo as defined in this subdivision applies exclusively to this section and shall not be applied in the construction or enforcement of any other provision of law.

§327. Endless chain scheme.

Every person who contrives, prepares, sets up, proposes, or operates any endless chain is guilty of a public offense, and is punishable by imprisonment in the county jail not exceeding one year or in state prison for 16 months, two, or three years.

As used in this section, an "endless chain" means any scheme for the disposal or distribution of property whereby a participant pays a valuable consideration for the chance to receive compensation for introducing one or more additional persons into participation in the scheme or for the chance to receive compensation when a person introduced by the participant introduces a new participant. Compensation, as used in this section, does not mean or include payment based upon sales made to persons who are not participants in the scheme and who are not purchasing in order to participate in the scheme. *(Amended by Stats 1989 ch 436 §2, eff. 1/1/90.)*

§328. Production or printing services for lotteries.

Nothing in this chapter shall make unlawful the printing or other production of any advertisements for, or any ticket, chance, or share in a lottery conducted in any other state or nation where such lottery is not prohibited by the laws of such state or nation; or the sale of such materials by the manufacturer thereof to any person or entity conducting or participating in the conduct of such a lottery in any such state or nation. This section does not authorize any advertisement within California relating to lotteries, or the sale or resale within California of lottery tickets, chances, or shares to individuals, or acts otherwise in violation of any laws of the state.

§329. Lotteries, existence thereof.

Upon a trial for the violation of any of the provisions of this chapter, it is not necessary to prove the existence of any lottery in which any lottery ticket purports to have been issued, or to prove the actual signing of any such ticket or share, or pretended ticket or share, of any pretended lottery, nor that any lottery ticket, share, or interest was signed or issued by the authority of any manager, or of any person assuming to have authority as manager; but in all cases proof of the sale, furnishing, bartering, or procuring of any ticket, share, or interest therein, or of any instrument purporting to be a ticket, or part or share of any such ticket, is evidence that such share or interest was signed and issued according to the purport thereof. *(Added by Stats 1989 ch 897 §19, eff. 1/1/90.)*

CHAPTER 10

GAMING

§330. Punishment for gaming.

Every person who deals, plays, or carries on, opens, or causes to be opened, or who conducts, either as owner or employee, whether for hire or not, any game of faro, monte, roulette, lansquenet, rouge et noire, rondo, tan, fan-tan, seven-and-a-half, twenty-one, hokey-pokey, or any banking or percentage game played with cards, dice, or any device, for money, checks, credit, or other representative of value, and every person who plays or bets at or against any of those prohibited games, is guilty of a misdemeanor, and shall be punishable by a fine not less than one hundred dollars ($100) nor more than one thousand dollars ($1,000), or by imprisonment in the county jail not exceeding six months, or by both the fine and imprisonment. *(Amended by Stats 1991 ch 71 §1, eff. 1/1/92.)*

© 1992 by J., B. & L. Gould
Printed in the U.S.A.　　EP

§330a. Unlawful card dice or slot or card machines.

Every person, who has in his possession or under his control, either as owner, lessee, agent, employee, mortgagee, or otherwise, or who permits to be placed, maintained or kept, in any room, space, inclosure or building owned, leased or occupied by him, or under his management or control, any slot or card machine, contrivance, appliance or mechanical device, upon the result of action of which money or other valuable thing is staked or hazarded, and which is operated, or played, by placing or depositing therein any coins, checks, slugs, balls, or other articles or device, or in any other manner and by means whereof, or as a result of the operation of which any merchandise, money, representative or articles of value, checks, or tokens, redeemable in, or exchangeable for money or any other thing of value, is won or lost, or taken from or obtained from such machine, when the result of action or operation of such machine, contrivance, appliance, or mechanical device is dependent upon hazard or chance, and every person, who has in his possession or under his control, either as owner, lessee, agent, employee, mortgagee, or otherwise, or who permits to be placed, maintained or kept, in any room, space, inclosure or building, owned, leased or occupied by him, or under his management or control, any card dice, or any dice having more than six faces or bases each, upon the result of action of which any money or other valuable thing is staked or hazarded, or as a result of the operation of which any merchandise, money, representative or article of value, check or token, redeemable in or exchangeable for money or any other thing of value, is won or lost or taken, when the result of action or operation of such dice is dependent upon hazard or chance, is guilty of a misdemeanor, and shall be punishable by a fine not less than one hundred dollars ($100) nor more than one thousand dollars ($1,000), or by imprisonment in the county jail not exceeding six months, or by both such fine and imprisonment.

§330b. Possession of slot machines or devices.

(1) It is unlawful for any person to manufacture, repair, own, store, possess, sell, rent, lease, let on shares, lend or give away, transport, or expose for sale or lease, or to offer to repair, sell, rent, lease, let on shares, lend or give away, or to permit the operation of, or for any person to permit to be placed, maintained or kept in any place, room, space or building owned, leased or occupied by him or under his management or control, any slot machine or device as hereinafter defined, or to make or to permit to be made with any person any agreement with reference to any slot machine or device, as hereinafter defined, pursuant to which the user thereof, as a result of any element of hazard or chance or other outcome unpredictable by him, may become entitled to receive any money, credit, allowance, or thing of value or additional chance or right to use such slot machine or device, or to receive any check, slug, token or memorandum entitling the holder to receive any money, credit, allowance or thing of value; provided, however, that this section, insofar as it relates to owning storing, possessing, or transporting any slot machine or device as hereinafter defined, shall not apply to any slot machine or device as hereinafter defined, located upon or being transported by any vessel regularly operated and engaged in interstate or foreign commerce, so long as

such slot machine or device is located in a locked compartment of the vessel, is not accessible for use and is not used or operated within the territorial jurisdiction of this State.

(2) Any machine, apparatus or device is a slot machine or device within the provisions of this section if it is one that is adapted, or may readily be converted into one that is adapted, for use in such a way that, as a result of the insertion of any piece of money or coin or other object, or by any other means, such machine or device is caused to operate or may be operated, and by reason of any element of hazard or chance or of other outcome of such operation unpredictable by him, the user may receive or become entitled to receive any piece of money, credit, allowance or thing of value or additional chance or right to use such slot machine or device, or any check, slug, token or memorandum, whether of value or otherwise, which may be exchanged for any money, credit, allowance or thing of value, or which may be given in trade, irrespective of whether it may, apart from any element of hazard or chance or unpredictable outcome of such operation, also sell, deliver or present some merchandise, indication of weight, entertainment or other thing of value.

(3) Every person who violates this section is guilty of a misdemeanor.

(4) It is expressly provided that with respect to the provisions of Section 330b only of this code, pin ball, and other amusement machines or devices which are predominantly games of skill, whether affording the opportunity of additional chances or free plays or not, are not intended to be and are not included within the term slot machine or device as defined in said Section 330b of this code.

§330c. Punchboard defined.

A punchboard as hereinafter defined is hereby declared to be a slot machine or device within the meaning of Section 330b of this code and shall be subject to the provisions thereof. For the purposes of this section, a punchboard is any card, board or other device which may be played or operated by pulling, pressing, punching out or otherwise removing any slip, tab, paper or other substance therefrom to disclose any concealed number, name or symbol.

§330.1. Possession, manufacture or disposition of slot machines or devices.

Every person who manufactures, owns, stores, keeps, possesses, sells, rents, leases, lets on shares, lends or gives away, transports or exposes for sale or lease or offers to sell, rent, lease, let on shares, lend or give away or who permits the operation of or permits to be placed, maintained, used or kept in any room, space or building owned, leased or occupied by him or under his management or control, any slot machine or device as hereinafter defined, and every person who makes or permits to be made with any person any agreement with reference to any slot machine or device as hereinafter defined, pursuant to which agreement the user thereof, as a result of any element of hazard or chance, may become entitled to receive anything of value or additional chance or right to use such slot machine or device, or to receive any check, slug, token or memorandum, whether of value or otherwise, entitling the holder to receive anything of value, is guilty of a misdemeanor and shall be punishable by a fine of not more than one thousand dollars ($1,000) or by imprisonment in the county jail not

© 1992 by J., B. & L. Gould
Printed in the U.S.A. EP

exceeding six months or by both such fine and imprisonment. A slot machine or device within the meaning of Sections 330.1 to 330.5, inclusive, of this code is one that is, or may be, used or operated in such a way that, as a result of the insertion of any piece of money or coin or other object such machine or device is caused to operate or may be operated or played, mechanically, electrically, automatically or manually, and by reason of any element of hazard or chance, the user may receive or become entitled to receive anything of value or any check, slug, token or memorandum, whether of value or otherwise, which may be given in trade, or the user may secure additional chances or rights to use such machine or device, irrespective of whether it may, apart from any element of hazard or chance also sell, deliver or present some merchandise, indication of weight, entertainment or other thing of value.

§330.2. Thing of value defined.

As used in Sections 330.1 to 330.5, inclusive, of this code a "thing of value" is defined to be any money, coin, currency, check, chip, allowance, token, credit, merchandise, property, or any representative of value.

§330.3. Seizure of slot machines.

In addition to any other remedy provided by law any slot machine or device may be seized by any of the officers designated by Sections 335 and 335a of the Penal Code, and in such cases shall be disposed of, together with any and all money seized in or in connection with such machine or device, as provided in Section 335a of the Penal Code.

§330.4. Permitting placement of slot machines.

It is specifically declared that the mere possession or control, either as owner, lessee, agent, employee, mortgagor, or otherwise of any slot machine or device, as defined in Section 330.1 of this code, is prohibited and penalized by the provisions of Sections 330.1 to 330.5, inclusive, of this code.

It is specifically declared that every person who permits to be placed, maintained or kept in any room, space, enclosure, or building owned, leased or occupied by him, or under his management or control, whether for use or operation or for storage, bailment, safekeeping or deposit only, any slot machine or device, as defined in Section 330.1 of this code, is guilty of a misdemeanor and punishable as provided in Section 330.1 of this code.

It is further declared that the provisions of this section specifically render any slot machine or device as defined in Section 330.1 of this code subject to confiscation as provided in Section 335a of this code.

§330.5. Music and food vending machines exempt.

It is further expressly provided that Sections 330.1 to 330.4, inclusive, of this code shall not apply to music machines, weighing machines and machines which vend cigarettes, candy, ice cream, food, confections or other merchandise, in which there is deposited an exact consideration and from which in every case the customer obtains that which he purchases; and it is further expressly provided that with respect to the provisions of Sections 330.1 to 330.4, inclusive, only, of this code, pin ball, and other amusement machines or devices which are predominantly games of skill, whether affording the opportunity of additional chances or free plays or not, are not intended to be and

are not included within the term slot machine or device as defined within Sections 330.1 to 330.4, inclusive, of this code.

§330.6. Transporting slot machines.

The provisions of Sections 330.1 to 330.5, inclusive, of this code, with respect to owning, storing, keeping, possessing, or transporting any slot machine or device as therein defined, shall not apply to any slot machine or device as therein defined, located upon or being transported by any vessel regularly operated and engaged in interstate or foreign commerce, so long as such slot machine or device is located in a locked compartment of the vessel, is not accessible for use and is not used or operated within the territorial jurisdiction of this State.

§330.7. Protecting the collection and restoration of antique slot machines.

(a) It shall be a defense to any prosecution under this chapter relating to slot machines, as defined in subdivision (2) of Section 330b, if the defendant shows that the slot machine is an antique slot machine and was not operated for gambling purposes while in the defendant's possession. For the purposes of this section, the term "antique slot machine" means a slot machine manufactured in the United States of which two-thirds or more, by count, of the visible exterior metal components (excluding fasteners) are original equipment manufactured prior to 1956; provided, however, that if the machine has a front or top casting, or both, the front casting or the top casting must have been manufactured prior to 1956.

(b) Notwithstanding Section 335a, whenever the defense provided by subdivision (a) is offered, no slot machine seized from any defendant shall be destroyed or otherwise altered until after a final court determination that such defense is not applicable. If the defense is applicable, any such slot machine shall be returned pursuant to provisions of law providing for the return of property.

(c) It is the purpose of this section to protect the collection and restoration of antique slot machines not presently utilized for gambling purposes because of their aesthetic interest and importance in California history. *(Amended by Stats 1985 ch 677 §1.)*

§330.8. Authorization for sale, transportation, storage and manufacture of gambling devices.

Notwithstanding Sections 330a, 330b, and 330.1 to 330.5, inclusive, the sale, transportation, storage, and manufacture of gambling devices, as defined in Section 330.1, including the acquisition of essential parts therefor and the assembly of such parts, is permitted, provided those devices are sold, transported, stored, and manufactured only for subsequent transportation in interstate or foreign commerce when that transportation is not prohibited by any applicable federal law. Those activities may be conducted only by persons who have registered with the United States government pursuant to Chapter 24 (commencing with Section 1171) of Title 15 of the United States Code, as amended. Those gambling devices shall not be displayed to the general public or sold for use in California regardless of where purchased, nor held nor manufactured in violation of any applicable federal law. A violation of this section is a misdemeanor. *(Amended by Stats 1987 ch 828 §18.5.)*

© 1992 by J., B. & L. Gould
Printed in the U.S.A. **EP**

§331. Gambling permitted in house by owner or tenant.

Every person who knowingly permits any of the games mentioned in Sections 330 and 330a to be played, conducted, or dealt in any house owned or rented by such person, in whole or in part, is punishable as provided in Sections 330 and 330a. *(Amended by Stats 1987 ch 828 §19.)*

§332. Winning by fraudulent game or trick.

(a) Every person who by the game of "three card monte," so-called, or any other game, device, sleight of hand, pretensions to fortune telling, trick, or other means whatever, by use of cards or other implements or instruments, or while betting on sides or hands of any play or game, fraudulently obtains from another person money or property of any description, shall be punished as in case of larceny of property of like value.

(b) For the purposes of this section, "fraudulently obtains" includes, but is not limited to, cheating, including, for example, gaining an unfair advantage for any player in any game through a technique or device not sanctioned by the rules of the game.

(c) For the purposes of establishing the value of property under this section, poker chips, tokens, or markers have the monetary value assigned to them by the players in any game. *(Amended by Stats 1991 ch 684 §3, eff. 1/1/92.)*

§333. Witnesses neglecting or refusing to attend trial.

Every person duly summoned as a witness for the prosecution, on any proceedings had under this Chapter, who neglects or refuses to attend, as required, is guilty of a misdemeanor.

§334. Concession stands; frauds and cheats; razzle-dazzle.

(a) Every person who owns or operates any concession, and who fraudulently obtains money from another by means of any hidden mechanical device or obstruction with intent to diminish the chance of any patron to win a prize, or by any other fraudulent means, shall be punished as in the case of theft of property of like value.

(b) Any person who manufactures or sells any mechanical device or obstruction for a concession which he knows or reasonably should know will be fraudulently used to diminish the chance of any patron to win a prize is guilty of a misdemeanor.

(c) Any person who owns or operates any game, at a fair or carnival of a type known as razzle-dazzle is guilty of a misdemeanor.

As used in this subdivision, "razzle-dazzle" means a series of games of skill or chance in which the player pays money or other valuable consideration in return for each opportunity to make successive attempts to obtain points by the use of dice, darts, marbles or other implements, and where such points are accumulated in successive games by the player toward a total number of points, determined by the operator, which is required for the player to win a prize or other valuable consideration.

(d) As used in this section, "concession" means any game or concession open to the public and operated for profit in which the patron pays a fee for participating and may receive a prize upon a later happening.

(e) Nothing in this section shall be construed to prohibit or preempt more restrictive regulation of any concession at a fair or carnival by any local governmental entity.

§335. Duties of district attorneys, police officers, and others.

Every District Attorney, Sheriff, Constable, or police officer must inform against and diligently prosecute persons whom they have reasonable cause to believe offenders against the provisions of this Chapter, and every such officer refusing or neglecting so to do, is guilty of a misdemeanor.

§335a. Seizure and destruction of gambling devices.

In addition to any other remedy provided by law any machine or other device the possession or control of which is penalized by the laws of this State prohibiting lotteries or gambling may be seized by any peace officer, and a notice of intention summarily to destroy such machine or device as provided in this section must be posted in a conspicuous place upon the premises in or upon which such machine or device was seized. Such machine or device shall be held by such officer for 30 days after such posting, and if no action is commenced to recover possession of such machine or device, within such time, the same shall be summarily destroyed by such officer, or if such machine or device shall be held by the court, in any such action, to be in violation of such laws, or any of them, the same shall be summarily destroyed by such officer immediately after the decision of the court has become final.

The superior court shall have jurisdiction of any such actions or proceedings commenced to recover the possession of such machine or device or any money seized in connection therewith.

Any and all money seized in or in connection with such machine or device shall, immediately after such machine or device has been so destroyed, be paid into the treasury of the city or county, as the case may be, where seized, said money to be deposited in the general fund.

§336. Permitting minors to gamble in saloon.

Every owner, lessee, or keeper of any house used in whole, or in part, as a saloon or drinking place, who knowingly permits any person under 18 years of age to play at any game of chance therein, is guilty of a misdemeanor.

§337. Assisting violator.

Every state, county, city, city and county, town, or judicial district officer, or other person who shall ask for, receive, or collect any money, or other valuable consideration, either for his own or the public use, for and with the understanding that he will aid, exempt, or otherwise assist any person from arrest or conviction for a violation of Section 330 of the Penal Code; or who shall issue, deliver, or cause to be given or delivered to any person or persons, any license, permit, or other privilege, giving, or pretending to give, any authority or right to any person or persons to carry on, conduct, open, or cause to be opened, any game or games which are forbidden or prohibited by Section 330 of said code; and any of such officer or officers who shall vote for the passage of any ordinance or by-law, giving, granting, or pretending to give or grant to any person or persons any authority or privilege to open, carry on, conduct, or cause to be opened, carried on, or

© 1992 by J., B. & L. Gould
Printed in the U.S.A. **EP**

conducted, any game or games prohibited by said Section 330 of the Penal Code, is guilty of a felony.

§337a. Pool selling or bookmaking.

Every person,

1. Who engages in pool selling or bookmaking, with or without writing, at any time or place; or

2. Who, whether for gain, hire, reward, or gratuitously, or otherwise, keeps or occupies, for any period of time whatsoever, any room, shed, tenement, tent, booth, building, float, vessel, place, stand or enclosure, of any kind, or any part thereof, with a book or books, paper or papers, apparatus, device or paraphernalia, for the purpose of recording or registering any bet or bets, or any purported bet or bets, or wager or wagers, or any purported wager or wagers, or of selling pools, or purported pools, upon the result, or purported result, of any trial, or purported trial, or contest, or purported contest, of skill, speed or power of endurance of man or beast, or between men, beasts, or mechanical apparatus, or upon the result, or purported result, of any lot, chance, casualty, unknown or contingent event whatsoever; or

3. Who, whether for gain, hire, reward, or gratuitously, or otherwise, receives, holds, or forwards, or purports or pretends to receive, hold, or forward, in any manner whatsoever, any money, thing or consideration of value, or the equivalent or memorandum thereof, staked, pledged, bet or wagered, or to be staked, pledged, bet or wagered, or offered for the purpose of being staked, pledged, bet or wagered, upon the result, or purported result, of any trial, or purported trial, or contest, or purported contest, of skill, speed or power of endurance of man or beast, or between men, beasts, or mechanical apparatus, or upon the result, or purported result, of any lot, chance, casualty, unknown or contingent event whatsoever; or

4. Who, whether for gain, hire, reward, or gratuitously, or otherwise, at any time or place, records, or registers any bet or bets, wager or wagers, upon the result, or purported result, of any trial, or purported trial, or contest, or purported contest, of skill, speed or power of endurance of man or beast, or between men, beasts, or mechanical apparatus, or upon the result, or purported result, of any lot, chance, casualty, unknown or contingent event whatsoever; or

5. Who, being the owner, lessee or occupant of any room, shed, tenement, tent, booth, building, float, vessel, place, stand, enclosure or grounds, or any part thereof, whether for gain, hire, reward, or gratuitously, or otherwise, permits the same to be used or occupied for any purpose, or in any manner prohibited by subdivision 1, 2, 3 or 4 of this section; or

6. Who lays, makes, offers or accepts any bet or bets, or wager or wagers, upon the result, or purported result, of any trial, or purported trial, or contest, or purported contest, of skill, speed or power of endurance of man or beast, or between men, beasts, or mechanical apparatus, is punishable by imprisonment in the county jail for a period of not more than one year or in the state prison.

(a) In any accusatory pleading charging a violation of this section, if the defendant has been once previously convicted of a violation of any subdivision of this section, the previous conviction shall be charged in the accusatory pleading, and, if the previous conviction is found to be true by the jury, upon a jury trial, or by the court, upon a court trial, or is admitted by the defendant, the defendant shall, if he is not imprisoned in the state prison, be imprisoned in the county jail for a period of not more than one year or pay a fine of not less than five hundred dollars ($500) nor more than five thousand dollars ($5,000), or be punished by both such fine and imprisonment. Nothing in this paragraph shall prohibit a court from placing such a person on probation, provided, however, that such person shall be required to pay a fine of not less than five hundred dollars ($500) nor more than five thousand dollars ($5,000) or to be imprisoned in the county jail for a period of not more than one year as a condition thereof. In no event does the court have the power to absolve a person convicted hereunder from either being imprisoned or from paying a fine of not less than five hundred dollars ($500).

(b) In any accusatory pleading charging a violation of this section, if the defendant has been previously convicted two or more times of a violation of any subdivision of this section, each such previous conviction shall be charged in the accusatory pleadings; and if two or more of such previous convictions are found to be true by the jury, upon a jury trial, or by the court, upon a court trial, or are admitted by the defendant, the defendant shall, if he is not imprisoned in the state prison, be imprisoned in the county jail for a period of not more than one year or pay a fine of not less than one thousand dollars ($1,000) nor more than five thousand dollars ($5,000), or be punished by both such fine and imprisonment. Nothing in this paragraph shall prohibit a court from placing such a person on probation, provided, however, that such person shall be required to pay a fine of not less than one thousand dollars ($1,000) nor more than five thousand dollars ($5,000) or to be imprisoned in the county jail for a period of not more than one year as a condition thereof. In no event does the court have the power to absolve a person convicted hereunder from either being imprisoned or from paying a fine of not less than one thousand dollars ($1,000).

Except where the existence of a previous conviction of any subdivision of this section was not admitted or not found to be true pursuant to this section, or the court finds that a prior conviction was invalid, the court shall not strike or dismiss any prior convictions alleged in the information or indictment.

This section shall apply not only to persons who may commit any of the acts designated in subdivisions 1 to 6 inclusive of this section, as a business or occupation, but shall also apply to every person or persons who may do in a single instance any one of the acts specified in said subdivisions 1 to 6 inclusive.

§337b. Corrupt sporting practices.

Any person who gives, or offers or promises to give, or attempts to give or offer, any money, bribe, or thing of value, to any participant or player, or to any prospective participant or player, in any sporting event, contest, or exhibition of any kind whatsoever, except a wrestling exhibition as defined in Section 18626 of the Business and Professions Code, and specifically including, but without being limited to, such sporting events, contests, and exhibitions as baseball, football, basketball, boxing, horseracing, and wrestling matches, with the intention or understanding or agreement that such participant or player or such prospective participant or player shall not use his or her best efforts to win such sporting event, contest, or exhibition, or shall so conduct himself or

© 1992 by J., B. & L. Gould
Printed in the U.S.A.   EP

herself in such sporting event, contest, or exhibition that any other player, participant or team of players or participants shall thereby be assisted or enabled to win such sporting event, contest, or exhibition, or shall so conduct himself or herself in such sporting event, contest, or exhibition as to limit his or her or his or her team's margin of victory in such sporting event, contest, or exhibition, is guilty of a felony, and shall be punished by imprisonment in the state prison, or by a fine not exceeding five thousand dollars ($5,000), or by both such fine and imprisonment. *(Amended by Stats 1987 ch 828 §20.)*

§337c. Acceptance of bribe.

Any person who accepts, or attempts to accept, or offers to accept, or agrees to accept, any money, bribe or thing of value, with the intention or understanding or agreement that he or she will not use his or her best efforts to win any sporting event, contest, or exhibition of any kind whatsoever, except a wrestling exhibition as defined in Section 18626 of the Business and Professions Code, and specifically including, but without being limited to, such sporting events, contests, or exhibitions as baseball, football, basketball, boxing, horseracing, and wrestling matches, in which he or she is playing or participating or is about to play or participate in, or will so conduct himself or herself in such sporting event, contest, or exhibition that any other player or participant or team of players or participants shall thereby be assisted or enabled to win such sporting event, contest, or exhibition, or will so conduct himself or herself in such sporting event, contest, or exhibition as to limit his or her or his or her team's margin of victory in such sporting event, contest, or exhibition, is guilty of a felony, and shall be punished by imprisonment in the state prison, or by a fine not exceeding five thousand dollars ($5,000), or by both such fine and imprisonment. *(Amended by Stats 1987 ch 828 §21.)*

§337d. Bribing officials.

Any person who gives, or offers to give, or promises to give, or attempts to give, any money, bribe or thing of value to any person who is umpiring, managing, directing, refereeing, supervising, judging, presiding or officiating at, or who is about to umpire, manage, direct, referee, supervise, judge, preside or officiate at any sporting event, contest, or exhibition of any kind whatsoever, and specifically including, but without being limited to, such sporting events, contests, and exhibitions as baseball, football, boxing, horseracing, and wrestling matches, with the intention or agreement or understanding that such person shall corruptly or dishonestly umpire, manage, direct, referee, supervise, judge, preside, or officiate at, any such sporting event, contest, or exhibition, or the players or participants thereof, with the intention or purpose that the result of the sporting event, contest, or exhibition will be affected or influenced thereby, is guilty of a felony and shall be punished by imprisonment in the state prison, or by a fine not exceeding five thousand dollars ($5,000), or by both such fine and imprisonment.

§337e. Punishment for bribing officials.

Any person who as umpire, manager, director, referee, supervisor, judge, presiding officer or official receives or agrees to receive, or attempts to receive any money, bribe or thing of value, with the understanding or agreement that such umpire, manager, director, referee, supervisor, judge, presiding officer, or official shall corruptly conduct himself or shall corruptly umpire, manage, direct, referee, supervise, judge, preside, or officiate at, any sporting event, contest, or exhibition of any kind whatsoever, and specifically including, but without being limited to, such sporting events, contests, and exhibitions as baseball, football, boxing, horseracing, and wrestling matches, or any player or participant thereof, with the intention or purpose that the result of the sporting event, contest, or exhibition will be affected or influenced thereby, is guilty of a felony and shall be punished by imprisonment in the state prison, or by a fine not exceeding five thousand dollars ($5,000), or by both such fine and imprisonment.

§337f. Drugging race horses.

Any person: (a) Who influences, or induces, or conspires with, any owner, jockey, groom or other person associated with or interested in any stable, horse, or race in which a horse participates, to affect the result of such race by stimulating or depressing a horse through the administration of any drug to such horse, or by the use of any electrical device or any electrical equipment or by any mechanical or other device not generally accepted as regulation racing equipment, or

(b) Who so stimulates or depresses a horse, or

(c) Who knowingly enters any horse in any race within a period of 24 hours after any drug has been administered to such horse for the purpose of increasing or retarding the speed of such horse, is punishable by a fine not exceeding five thousand dollars ($5,000), or by imprisonment in the state prison, or in a county jail not exceeding one year, or by both such fine and imprisonment, or

(d) Who willfully or unjustifiably enters or races any horse in any running or trotting race under any name or designation other than the name or designation assigned to such horse by and registered with the Jockey Club or the United States Trotting Association or who willfully sets on foot, instigates, engages in or in any way furthers any act by which any horse is entered or raced in any running or trotting race under any name or designation other than the name or designation duly assigned by and registered with the Jockey Club or the United States Trotting Association is guilty of a felony and punishable by imprisonment in the state prison, or by a fine not exceeding five thousand dollars ($5,000) or by both such fine and imprisonment.

The term "drug" includes all substances recognized as having the power of stimulating or depressing the central nervous system, respiration, or blood pressure of an animal, such as narcotics, hypnotics, benzedrine or its derivatives, but shall not include recognized vitamins or supplemental feeds approved by the veterinarian representing the California Racing Board.

§337g. Possession, transport or use of local anaesthetic within racing inclosure.

The possession, transport or use of any local anaesthetic of the cocaine group, including but not limited to natural or synthetic drugs of this group, such as allocaine, apothesine, alypine, benzyl carbinol, butyn, procaine, nupercaine, betaeucaine, novol or anestubes, within the racing inclosure is prohibited, except upon a bona fide veterinarian's prescription with complete statement of uses and purposes of same on the container. A copy of such prescription shall be filed with the stewards, and such substances may be used only with approval of the stewards and under the supervision of the veterinarian representing the board.

§337h. Tampering with racing animals.

Any person who, except for medicinal purposes, administers any poison, drug, medicine, or other noxious substance, to any horse, stud, mule, ass, mare, horned cattle, meat cattle, gelding, colt, filly, dog, animals, or other livestock, entered or about to be entered in any race or upon any race course, or entered or about to be entered at or with any agricultural park, or association, race course, or corporation, or other exhibition for competition for prize, reward, purse, premium, stake, sweepstakes, or other reward, or who exposes any poison, drug, medicine, or noxious substance, with intent that it shall be taken, inhaled, swallowed, or otherwise received by any of these animals or other livestock, with intent to impede or affect its speed, endurance, sense, health, physical condition, or other character or quality, or who causes to be taken by or placed upon or in the body of any of these animals or other livestock, entered or about to be entered in any race or competition described in this section any sponge, wood, or foreign substance of any kind, with intent to impede or affect its speed, endurance, sense, health, or physical condition, is guilty of a misdemeanor.

§337i. Transmittal of racing information to gamblers.

Every person who knowingly transmits information as to the progress or results of a horserace, or information as to wagers, betting odds, changes in betting odds, post or off times, jockey or player changes in any contest or trial, or purported contest or trial, involving humans, beasts, or mechanical apparatus by any means whatsoever including, but not limited to telephone, telegraph, radio, and semaphore when such information is transmitted to or by a person or persons engaged in illegal gambling operations, is punishable by imprisonment in the county jail for a period of not more than one year or in the state prison.

This section shall not be construed as prohibiting a newspaper from printing such results or information as news, or any television or radio station from telecasting or broadcasting such results or information as news. This section shall not be so construed as to place in jeopardy any common carrier or its agents performing operations within the scope of a public franchise, or any gambling operation authorized by law.

§337s. Draw poker in counties with population exceeding 4,000,000.

(a) This section applies only in counties with a population exceeding 4,000,000.

(b) Every person who deals, plays, or carries on, opens, or causes to be opened, or who conducts, either as owner or employee, whether for hire or not, any game of draw poker, including lowball poker, is guilty of a misdemeanor.

(c) Subdivision (b) shall become operative in a county only if the board of supervisors thereof by resolution directs that there be placed on the ballot at a designated county election the question whether draw poker, including lowball poker, shall be prohibited in the county and a majority of electors

voting thereon vote affirmatively. Such question shall appear on the ballot in substantially the following form:

"Shall draw poker, including lowball poker, be prohibited in _____ County? Yes __ No __"

If a majority of electors voting thereon vote affirmatively, draw poker shall be prohibited in both incorporated and unincorporated territory in the county.

(d) Any county or city ordinances in any county prohibiting, restricting, or regulating the playing of draw poker and other acts relating to draw poker shall not be superseded until, pursuant to subdivision (c), the electorate of the county determines that subdivision (b) shall be operative in the county.

(e) The Legislature finds that in counties with a large, concentrated population, problems incident to the playing of draw poker are, in part, qualitatively, as well as quantitatively, different from the problems in smaller counties.

The Legislature finds that counties with a population exceeding 4,000,000 constitute a special problem, and it is reasonable classification to adopt prohibitory legislation applicable only to such counties.

(f) If any provision of this section is held invalid, the entire section shall be invalid. The provisions of this section are not severable.

CHAPTER 10.5

HORSE RACING

§337.1. Tout.

Any person, who knowingly and designedly by false representation attempts to, or does persuade, procure or cause another person to wager on a horse in a race to be run in this state or elsewhere, and upon which money is wagered in this state, and who asks or demands compensation as a reward for information or purported information given in such case is a tout, and is guilty of touting. *(Amended by Stats 1987 ch 828 §22.)*

§337.2. Punishment of tout.

Any person who is a tout, or who attempts or conspires to commit touting, is guilty of a misdemeanor and is punishable by a fine of not more than five hundred dollars ($500) or by imprisonment in the county jail for not more than six months, or by both such fine and imprisonment. For a second offense in this State, he shall be imprisoned.

§337.3. False use of official's name.

Any person who in the commission of touting falsely uses the name of any official of the California Horse Racing Board, its inspectors or attaches, or of any official of any race track association, or the names of any owner, trainer, jockey or other person licensed by the California Horse Racing Board as the source of any information or purported information is guilty of a felony and is punishable by a fine of not more than five thousand dollars ($5,000) or by imprisonment in the state prison or by both such fine and imprisonment.

§337.4. Touting as grand theft.

Any person who in the commission of touting obtains money in excess of four hundred dollars ($400) may, in addition to being prosecuted for the violation of any provision of this chapter, be prosecuted for the violation of Section 487 of this code.

© 1992 by J., B. & L. Gould
Printed in the U.S.A.   EP

§337.5. Exclusion of tout from race track.

Any person who has been convicted of touting, and the record of whose conviction on such charge is on file in the office of the California Horse Racing Board or in the State Bureau of Criminal Identification and Investigation or of the Federal Bureau of Investigation, or any person who has been ejected from any racetrack of this or any other state for touting or practices inimical to the public interest shall be excluded from all racetracks in this State. Any such person who refuses to leave such track when ordered to do so by inspectors of the California Horse Racing Board, or by any peace officer, or by an accredited attache of a race track or association is guilty of a misdemeanor.

§337.6. Misused credential or license.

Any credential or license issued by the California Horse Racing Board to licensees, if used by the holder thereof for a purpose other than identification and in the performance of legitimate duties on a race track, shall be automatically revoked whether so used on or off a race track.

§337.7. Use of another's or forged credential.

Any person other than the lawful holder thereof who has in his possession any credential or license issued by the California Horse Racing Board to licensees and any person who has a forged or simulated credential or license of said board in his possession, and who uses such credential or license for the purpose of misrepresentation, fraud or touting is guilty of a felony and shall be punished by a fine of five thousand dollars ($5,000) or by imprisonment in the state prison, or by both such fine and imprisonment. If he has previously been convicted of any offense under this chapter, he shall be imprisoned.

§337.8. Credentials used for touting.

Any person who uses any credential, other than a credential or license issued by the California Horse Racing Board, for the purpose of touting is guilty of touting, and if the credential has been forged shall be imprisoned as provided in this chapter, whether the offense was committed on or off a race track.

§337.9. Coordination of policy for enforcement.

The secretary and chief investigator of the California Horse Racing Board shall coordinate a policy for the enforcement of this chapter with all other enforcement bureaus in the State in order to insure prosecution of all persons who commit any offense against the horse racing laws of this State. For such purposes the secretary and chief investigator are peace officers and have all the powers thereof.

CHAPTER 11

PAWNBROKERS

§343. Failure to produce register, pledged articles or account of sales.

Every person who purchases gold bullion, gold bars or gold quartz or mineral containing gold, who fails, refuses, or neglects to produce for inspection his register, or to exhibit all articles received by him in pledge, or his account of sales, to any officer holding a warrant authorizing him to search for personal property or to any person appointed by the sheriff or head of the police department of any city, city and county or town, or an order of a committing magistrate directing such officer to inspect such register, or examine such articles or account of sales, is guilty of a misdemeanor.

§344. *Repealed by Stats 1987 ch 828.*

CHAPTER 12

OTHER INJURIES TO PERSONS

§346. Unauthorized sale of tickets for admission to entertainment event.

Any person who, without the written permission of the owner or operator of the property on which an entertainment event is to be held or is being held, sells a ticket of admission to the entertainment event, which was obtained for the purpose of resale, at any price which is in excess of the price that is printed or endorsed upon the ticket, while on the grounds of or in the stadium, arena, theater, or other place where an event for which admission tickets are sold is to be held or is being held, is guilty of a misdemeanor.

§347. Poisoning or adulterating food, drink, etc.

(a) Every person who willfully mingles any poison or harmful substance with any food, drink, medicine, or pharmaceutical product or who willfully places any poison or harmful substance in any spring, well, reservoir, or public water supply, where the person knows or should have known that the same would be taken by any human being to his or her injury, is guilty of a felony punishable by imprisonment in the state prison for two, four, or five years.

Any violation of this subdivision involving the use of a poison or harmful substance which may cause death if ingested or which causes the infliction of great bodily injury on any person shall be punished by an additional term of three years.

(b) Any person who maliciously informs any other person that a poison or other harmful substance has been or will be placed in any food, drink, medicine, pharmaceutical product, or public water supply, knowing that such report is false, is guilty of a crime punishable by imprisonment in the state prison, or by imprisonment in the county jail not to exceed one year.

(c) The court may impose the maximum fine for each item tampered with in violation of subdivision (a). *(Amended by Stats 1986 ch 379 §1.)*

§347b. Manufacturing poisonous solutions.

It shall be unlawful for any person, firm or corporation to manufacture, sell, furnish, or give away, or offer to manufacture, sell, furnish, or give away any alcoholic solution of a potable nature containing any deleterious or poisonous substance, and the burden of proof shall be upon the person, firm, or corporation manufacturing, selling, furnishing, or giving away, or offering to manufacture, sell, furnish, or give away, any such alcoholic solution of a potable nature containing any deleterious or poisonous substance, to show that such alcoholic solution of a potable nature did not contain any deleterious or poisonous substance. Every person who violates any of the provisions of this section is guilty of a misdemeanor, and shall be punished by a fine not exceeding two thousand five hundred dollars ($2,500), or by imprisonment in a county jail not exceeding one year, or by both such fine and imprisonment.

© 1992 by J., B. & L. Gould
Printed in the U.S.A. **EP**

§350. Manufacture or sale of counterfeit trademark.

(a) Any person who, without the consent of the registrant, willfully manufactures, or intentionally sells any counterfeit of a mark registered with the Secretary of State and registrable under Section 1052 of Title 15 of the United States Code or incontestable under Section 1065 of Title 15 of the United States Code, shall upon conviction, if such person is an individual, be fined not more than five thousand dollars ($5,000) or imprisoned in the county jail for not more than one year, or both, or if such person is a corporation, be fined not more than one hundred thousand dollars ($100,000).

(b) Any person who has been convicted of a violation of subdivision (a) shall upon subsequent conviction, if such person is an individual, be fined not more than fifty thousand dollars ($50,000) or imprisoned in the county jail for not more than one year or the state prison, or both, or if such person is a corporation, be fined not more than two hundred thousand dollars ($200,000).

(c) Any person who has been convicted of a violation of subdivision (a) and who, by virtue of the conduct which was the basis of the conviction, has directly and foreseeably caused death or great bodily injury to another through reliance on the counterfeited item for its intended purpose shall, if the person is an individual, be fined not more than fifty thousand dollars ($50,000) or imprisoned in the state prison for two, three, or four years, or both, or, if that person is a corporation, be fined not more than two hundred thousand dollars ($200,000).

(d) If, in any action brought under this section, the court determines that a mark is counterfeit, the court may order the destruction of all such marks, all means of making the marks, and all goods, articles, or other matter bearing the marks, which are in the possession or control of the court or of the defendant; or, after obliteration of the counterfeit mark, the court may dispose of those materials by ordering their transfer to the State of California, an eleemosynary institution, or the owner of the registered service marks or trademarks.

(e) For purposes of this section, the term "counterfeit mark" means a spurious mark which is identical with, or substantially indistinguishable from, a registered mark and which is used on or in connection with the same type of goods or services for which the genuine mark is registered.

(f) This section shall not be enforced against any party who has adopted and lawfully used the same or confusingly similar mark in the rendition of like services or the manufacture or sale of like goods in this state from a date prior to the effective date of registration of the service mark or trademark pursuant to Chapter 2 (commencing with Section 14200) of Division 6 of the Business and Professions Code. (*Amended by Stats 1987 ch 828 §23.3.*)

§351a. Falsely representing goods.

Any person who sells, attempts to sell, offers for sale or assists in the sale of any goods, product or output, and who willfully and falsely represents such goods, product or output to be the goods, product or output of any dealer, manufacturer or producer, other than the true dealer, manufacturer or producer, or any member of a firm or any officer of a corporation, who knowingly permits any employee of such firm or corporation to sell, offer for sale or assist in the sale of any goods, product or output or to falsely represent such goods, product or output to be the goods, product or output of any dealer, manufacturer or producer, other than the true dealer, manufacturer or producer, is guilty of a misdemeanor and punishable by a fine of not less than one hundred dollars ($100) or more than six hundred dollars ($600), or by imprisonment in the county jail for not less than 20 or more than 90 days, or both. This section shall not apply to any person who sells or offers for sale under his own name or brand the product or output of another manufacturer or producer with the written consent of such manufacturer or producer.

§355. Defacing marks upon wrecked property and destroying bills of lading.

Every person who defaces or obliterates the marks upon wrecked property, or in any manner disguises the appearance thereof, with intent to prevent the owner from discovering its identity, or who destroys or suppresses any invoice, bill of lading, or other document tending to show the ownership, is guilty of a misdemeanor.

§356. Defacing marks upon logs, lumber, or wood.

Every person who cuts out, alters, or defaces any mark made upon any log, lumber, or wood, or puts a false mark thereon with intent to prevent the owner from discovering its identity, is guilty of a misdemeanor.

§359. Contracting or solemnizing incestuous or forbidden marriages.

Every person authorized to solemnize marriage, who willfully and knowingly solemnizes any incestuous or other marriage forbidden by law, is punishable by fine of not less than one hundred nor more than one thousand dollars, or by imprisonment in the county jail not less than three months nor more than one year, or by both.

§360. Solemnizing marriage without license.

Every person authorized to solemnize any marriage, who solemnizes a marriage without first being presented with the marriage license, as required by Section 4207 of the Civil Code; or who solemnizes a marriage pursuant to Section 4213 of the Civil Code without the authorization required by that section; or who willfully makes a false return of any marriage or pretended marriage to the recorder or clerk; or who, having solemnized a marriage, fails for more than 30 days, to file with the recorder or clerk the marriage license with the certificate indorsed thereon, as required by Section 4208 of the Civil Code; or who having solemnized a marriage pursuant to Section 4213 of the Civil Code, fails for more than 30 days to file the certificate required to be filed by that section, and every person who willfully makes a false record of any marriage return, is guilty of a misdemeanor.

§361. *Repealed by Stats 1987 ch 828.*

§362. Refusing to issue or obey writ of habeas corpus.

Every officer or person to whom a writ of habeas corpus may be directed, who, after service thereof,

© 1992 by J., B. & L. Gould
Printed in the U.S.A.   EP

neglects or refuses to obey the command thereof, is guilty of a misdemeanor.

§363. Reconfining persons discharged upon writ of habeas corpus.

Every person who either solely or as a member of a court, knowingly and unlawfully recommits, imprisons, or restrains of his liberty, for the same cause, any person who has been discharged upon a writ of habeas corpus, is guilty of a misdemeanor.

§364. Concealing persons entitled to benefit of habeas corpus.

Every person having in his custody, or under his restraint or power, any person for whose relief a writ of habeas corpus has been issued, who, with the intent to elude the service of such writ or to avoid the effect thereof, transfers such person to the custody of another, or places him under the power or control of another, or conceals or changes the place of his confinement or restraint, or removes him without the jurisdiction of the court or judge issuing the writ, is guilty of a misdemeanor.

§365. Innkeepers and carriers refusing to receive guests and passengers.

Every person, and every agent or officer of any corporation carrying on business as an innkeeper, or as a common carrier of passengers, who refuses, without just cause or excuse to receive and entertain any guest, or to receive and carry any passenger, is guilty of a misdemeanor.

§365.5. Physically disabled persons' dogs; full and equal access.

(a) Any blind person, deaf person, or physically disabled person who is a passenger on any common carrier, airplane, motor vehicle, railway train, motorbus, streetcar, boat, or any other public conveyance or mode of transportation operating within this state, shall be entitled to have with him or her a specially trained guide dog, signal dog, or service dog.

(b) No blind person, deaf person, or physically disabled person and his or her specially trained guide dog, signal dog, or service dog shall be denied admittance to hotels, restaurants, lodging places, places of public accommodation, amusement, or resort or other places to which the general public is invited within this state because of that guide dog, signal dog, or service dog.

(c) Any person, firm, association, or corporation, or the agent of any person, firm, association, or corporation, who prevents a blind person, deaf person, or physically disabled person from exercising the rights specified in this section is guilty of an infraction, punishable by a fine not exceeding two hundred fifty dollars ($250).

(d) As used in this section, "guide dog" means any guide dog or seeing-eye dog which was trained by a person licensed under Chapter 9.5 (commencing with Section 7200) of Division 3 of the Business and Professions Code.

(e) As used in this section, "signal dog" means any dog trained to alert a deaf person, or a person whose hearing is impaired, to intruders or sounds.

(f) As used in this section "service dog" means any dog individually trained to do work or perform tasks to meet the requirements of a physically disabled person, including, but not limited to, minimal protec-tion work, rescue work, pulling a wheelchair, or fetching dropped items.

(g) Nothing in this section is intended to affect any civil remedies available for a violation of this section. *(Added by Stats 1986 ch 765 §1.)*

§366. Counterfeiting quicksilver stamps.

Every person who counterfeits, or who willfully uses the counterfeited seal or stamp of any person engaged in manufacturing or selling quicksilver, is guilty of a felony.

§367. Selling debased quicksilver.

Every person who willfully sells, or offers for sale as pure, any debased or adulterated quicksilver, is guilty of a misdemeanor.

§367f. Buying or selling human organs.

(a) Except as provided in subdivisions (d) and (e), it shall be unlawful for any person to knowingly acquire, receive, sell, promote the transfer of, or otherwise transfer any human organ, for purposes of transplantation, for valuable consideration.

(b) Except as provided in subdivisions (d), (e), and (f), it shall be unlawful to remove or transplant any human organ with the knowledge that the organ has been acquired or will be transferred or sold for valuable consideration in violation of subdivision (a).

(c) For purposes of this section, the following definitions apply:

(1) "Human organ" includes, but is not limited to, a human kidney, liver, heart, lung, pancreas, or any other human organ or nonrenewable or nonregenerative tissue except plasma and sperm.

(2) "Valuable consideration" means financial gain or advantage, but does not include the reasonable costs associated with the removal, storage, transportation, and transplantation of a human organ, or reimbursement for those services, or the expenses of travel, housing, and lost wages incurred by the donor of a human organ in connection with the donation of the organ.

(d) No act respecting the nonsale donation of organs or other nonsale conduct pursuant to or in the furtherance of the purposes of the Uniform Anatomical Gift Act, Chapter 3.5 (commencing with Section 7150) Part 1 of Division 7 of the Health and Safety Code, including acts pursuant to anatomical gifts offered under Section 12811 of the Vehicle Code, shall be made unlawful by this section.

(e) This section shall not apply to the person from whom the organ is removed, nor to the person who receives the transplant, or those persons' next-of-kin who assisted in obtaining the organ for purposes of transplantations.

(f) A licensed physician and surgeon who transplants a human organ in violation of subdivision (b) shall not be criminally liable under that subdivision if the act is performed under emergency and life-threatening conditions.

(g) Any person who violates subdivision (a) or (b) shall be punished by a fine not to exceed fifty thousand dollars ($50,000), or by imprisonment in the state prison for three, four, or five years, or both.

§368. Infliction of physical pain or mental suffering on dependent adult.

(a) Any person who, under circumstances or conditions likely to produce great bodily harm or death, willfully causes or permits any elder or dependent adult, with knowledge that he or she is an elder or a dependent adult, to suffer, or inflicts thereon unjustifiable physical pain or mental suffering, or having the care or custody of any elder or dependent adult, willfully causes or permits the person or health of the elder or dependent adult to be injured, or willfully causes or permits the elder or dependent adult to be placed in a situation such that his or her person or health is endangered is punishable by imprisonment in the county jail not exceeding one year, or in the state prison for two, three, or four years.

(b) Any person who, under circumstances or conditions other than those likely to produce great bodily harm or death, willfully causes or permits any elder or dependent adult, with knowledge that he or she is an elder or a dependent adult, to suffer, or inflicts thereon unjustifiable physical pain or mental suffering, or having the care or custody of any elder or dependent adult, willfully causes or permits the person or health of the elder or dependent adult to be injured or willfully causes or permits the elder or dependent adult to be placed in a situation such that his or her person or health may be endangered, is guilty of a misdemeanor.

(c) Any caretaker of an elder or a dependent adult who violates any provision of law proscribing theft or embezzlement, with respect to the property of that elder or dependent adult, is punishable by imprisonment in the county jail not exceeding one year, or in the state prison for two, three, or four years when the money, labor, or real or personal property taken is of a value exceeding four hundred dollars ($400), and by fine not exceeding one thousand dollars ($1,000) or by imprisonment in the county jail not exceeding one year, or both, when the money, labor, or real or personal property taken is of a value not exceeding four hundred dollars ($400).

(d) As used in this section, "elder" means any person who is 65 years of age or older.

(e) As used in this section, "dependent adult" means any person who is between the ages of 18 and 64, who has physical or mental limitations which restrict his or her ability to carry out normal activities or to protect his or her rights, including, but not limited to, persons who have physical or developmental disabilities or whose physical or mental abilities have diminished because of age. "Dependent adult" includes any person between the ages of 18 and 64 who is admitted as an inpatient to a 24-hour health facility, as defined in Sections 1250, 1250.2, and 1250.3 of the Health and Safety Code.

(f) As used in this section, "caretaker" means any person who has the care, custody, or control of or who stands in a position of trust with, an elder or a dependent adult. (Amended by Stats 1986 ch 769 §1.2.)

TITLE 10

OF CRIMES AGAINST THE PUBLIC HEALTH AND SAFETY

§369d. Failure to close bars or gates at railroad crossings.

Any person who enters upon or crosses any railroad, at any private passway which is inclosed by bars or gates, and neglects to leave the same securely closed after him, is guilty of a misdemeanor.

§369g. Driving along railroad track.

Any person who rides, drives, or propels any vehicle upon and along the track of any railroad, through or over its private right of way, without the authorization of its superintendent or other officer in charge thereof, is guilty of a misdemeanor.

§369h. Installing confusing signs for railroads.

Any person, partnership, firm or corporation installing, setting up, maintaining or operating upon public or private property, any sign or light in line of vision along any main line track of any railroad in this State of such type or in such form or manner that it may be mistaken for any fixed or standard railroad signal when viewed from an approaching locomotive cab, railway car, or train, by the operators or employees upon such locomotive cab, railway car, or train, so as to hinder the safe and efficient operation of such locomotive, railway car or train, and endanger the safety of persons or property upon such locomotive, railway car, or train, shall be guilty of maintaining a public nuisance. No sign, signal, flare or light placed within the right of way of any street or highway by public authorities in charge thereof, considered necessary by them to direct or warn highway traffic, shall be deemed to violate this section.

§369i. Trespass on railroad property.

Any person who enters or remains upon the property of any railroad without the permission of the owner of such land, his agent or the person in lawful possession and whose entry or presence or conduct upon such property interferes with, interrupts, or hinders, or which, if allowed to continue, would interfere with, interrupt, or hinder the safe and efficient operation of any locomotive, railway car or train is guilty of a misdemeanor.

As used in this section, "property of any railroad" means any land owned, leased, or possessed by a railroad upon which is placed a railroad track and the land immediately adjacent thereto, to the distance of 20 feet on either side of the track, which is owned, leased or possessed by a railroad.

This section does not prohibit picketing in such immediately adjacent area or any lawful activity by which the public is informed of the existence of an alleged labor dispute.

§370. Public nuisance defined.

Anything which is injurious to health, or is indecent, or offensive to the senses, or an obstruction to the free use of property, so as to interfere with the comfortable enjoyment of life or property by an entire community or neighborhood, or by any considerable number of persons, or unlawfully obstructs the free passage or use, in the customary manner, of any navigable lake, or river, bay, stream, canal, or basin, or any public park, square, street, or highway, is a public nuisance.

§371. Unequal annoyance or damage from a public nuisance.

An act which affects an entire community or neighborhood, or any considerable number of persons, as specified in the last section, is not less a nuisance because the extent of the annoyance or damage inflicted upon individuals is unequal. (Amended by Stats 1989 ch 1360 §109, eff. 1/1/90.)

© 1992 by J., B. & L. Gould
Printed in the U.S.A.   EP

§372. Maintaining a nuisance, a misdemeanor.

Every person who maintains or commits any public nuisance, the punishment for which is not otherwise prescribed, or who willfully omits to perform any legal duty relating to the removal of a public nuisance, is guilty of a misdemeanor.

§373a. Public nuisance; continuance after notice to abate.

Every person who maintains, permits, or allows a public nuisance to exist upon his or her property or premises, and every person occupying or leasing the property or premises of another who maintains, permits or allows a public nuisance to exist thereon, after reasonable notice in writing from a health officer or district attorney or city attorney or prosecuting attorney to remove, discontinue or abate the same has been served upon such person, is guilty of a misdemeanor, and shall be punished accordingly; and the existence of such nuisance for each and every day after the service of such notice shall be deemed a separate and distinct offense, and it is hereby made the duty of the district attorney, or the city attorney of any city the charter of which imposes the duty upon the city attorney to prosecute state misdemeanors, to prosecute all persons guilty of violating this section by continuous prosecutions until the nuisance is abated and removed.

§374. Littering and waste matter defined.

(a) Littering means the willful or negligent throwing, dropping, placing, depositing, or sweeping, or causing any such acts, of any waste matter on land or water in other than appropriate storage containers or areas designated for such purposes.

(b) Waste matter means discarded, used, or left over substance including, but not limited to, a lighted or nonlighted cigarette, cigar, match, or any flaming or glowing material, or any garbage, trash, refuse, paper, container, packaging or construction material, carcass of a dead animal, any nauseous or offensive matter of any kind, or any object likely to injure any person or create a traffic hazard.

§374a. Reward for information of persons littering or shooting upon highways.

Every person giving information leading to the arrest and conviction of any person for a violation of Section 374b or 374c is entitled to a reward therefor.

The amount of the reward for each such arrest and conviction shall be 50 percent of the fine levied against and collected from the person who violated Section 374b or 374c and shall be paid by the court. If the reward is payable to two or more persons, it shall be divided equally. The amount of collected fine to be paid under this section shall be paid prior to any distribution of the fine that may be prescribed by any other section, including Section 1463.9, with respect to the same fine.

§374b. *Amended and renumbered to section 374.3 by Stats 1987 ch 133 §2.*

§374b.5. *Amended and renumbered to section 374.4 by Stats 1987 ch 133 §3.*

§374c. Shooting from or upon public roads.

Every person who shoots any firearm from or upon a public road or highway is guilty of a misdemeanor.

§374d. Carcass of dead animal put on public road or highway.

Every person who knowingly allows the carcass of any dead animal which belonged to him at the time of its death to be put, or to remain, within 100 feet of any street, alley, public highway, or road in common use, and every person who puts the carcass of any dead animal within 100 feet of any street, alley, highway, or road in common use is guilty of a misdemeanor.

§374e. *Amended and renumbered to section 374.7 by Stats 1987 ch 133 §4.*

§374.2. Disposal of substance harmful to public sewer facility.

(a) It is unlawful for any person to maliciously discharge, dump, release, place, drop, pour, or otherwise deposit, or to maliciously cause to be discharged, dumped, released, placed, dropped, poured, or otherwise deposited, any substance capable of causing substantial damage or harm to the operation of a public sewer sanitary facility, or to deposit in commercial quantities any other substance, into a manhole, cleanout, or other sanitary sewer facility, not intended for use as a point of deposit for sewage, which is connected to a public sanitary sewer system, without possessing a written authorization therefor granted by the public entity which is charged with the administration of the use of the affected public sanitary sewer system or the affected portion of the public sanitary sewer system.

As used in this section, "maliciously" means an intent to do a wrongful act.

(b) For the purposes of this section "person" means an individual, trust, firm, partnership, joint stock company, or corporation, and "deposited in commercial quantities" refers to any substance deposited or otherwise discharged in any amount greater than for normal domestic sewer use.

(c) Lack of specific knowledge that the facility into which the prohibited discharge or release occurred is connected to a public sanitary sewer system shall not constitute a defense to a violation charged under this section.

(d) Any person who violates this section shall be punished by imprisonment in the county jail for not more than one year, or by a fine of up to twenty-five thousand dollars ($25,000), or by both a fine and imprisonment. If the conviction is for a second or subsequent violation, the person shall be punished by imprisonment in the county jail for not more than one year, or imprisonment in the state prison for 16, 20, or 24 months, and by a fine of not less than five thousand dollars ($5,000) or more than twenty-five thousand dollars ($25,000). *(Added by Stats 1988 ch 1057 §1, eff. 1/1/89.)*

§374.3. Unlawful dumping of waste.

(a) It is unlawful to dump or cause to be dumped any waste matter in or upon any public or private highway or road, including any portion of the right-of-way thereof, or in or upon any private property into or upon which the public is admitted by easement or license, or upon any private property without the consent of the owner, or in or upon any public park or other public property other than property designated or set aside for that purpose by the governing board or body having charge of that property.

(b) It is unlawful to place, deposit, or dump, or cause to be placed, deposited, or dumped, any rocks or dirt in or upon any private highway or road, including any portion of the right-of-way thereof, or any private property, without the consent of the owner, or in or upon any public park or other public property, without the consent of the state or local agency having jurisdiction over the highway, road, or property.

(c) Any person, firm, or corporation violating this section is guilty of an infraction. Each day that waste placed, deposited, or dumped in violation of this section remains is a separate violation.

(d) This section does not restrict a private owner in the use of his or her own private property, unless the placing, depositing, or dumping of the waste matter on the property creates a public health and safety hazard, a public nuisance, or a fire hazard, as determined by a local health department, local fire department or district providing fire protection services, or the Department of Forestry and Fire Protection, in which case this section applies.

(e) A person convicted of a violation of this section shall be punished by a mandatory fine of not less than one hundred dollars ($100) nor more than one thousand dollars ($1,000) upon a first conviction, by a mandatory fine of not less than five hundred dollars ($500) nor more than one thousand dollars ($1,000) upon a second conviction, and by a mandatory fine of not less than seven hundred fifty dollars ($750) nor more than one thousand dollars ($1,000) upon a third or subsequent conviction. If the court finds that the waste matter placed, deposited, or dumped was used tires, the fine prescribed in this subdivision shall be doubled.

(f) The court may require, in addition to any fine imposed upon a conviction, that, as a condition of probation and in addition to any other condition of probation, a person convicted under this section remove, or pay the cost of removing, any waste matter which the convicted person dumped or caused to be dumped upon public or private property.

(g) Except when the court requires the convicted person to remove waste matter which he or she is responsible for dumping as a condition of probation, the court may, in addition to the fine imposed upon a conviction, require as a condition of probation, in addition to any other condition of probation, that any person convicted of a violation of this section pick up waste matter at a time and place within the jurisdiction of the court for not less than eight hours. *(Amended by Stats 1989 ch 974 §3, eff. 1/1/90.)*

§374.4. Person, firm, or corporation littering on public or private property.

(a) It is unlawful to litter or cause to be littered in or upon any public or private property. Any person, firm, or corporation violating this section is guilty of an infraction.

(b) This section does not restrict a private owner in the use of his or her own property, unless the littering of waste matter on the property creates a public health and safety hazard, a public nuisance, or a fire hazard, as determined by a local health department, local fire department or district providing fire protection services, or the Department of Forestry and Fire Protection, in which case this section applies.

(c) As used in this section, "litter" means the discarding, dropping, or scattering of small quantities of waste matter ordinarily carried on or about the person, including, but not limited to, beverage containers and closures, packaging, wrappers, wastepaper, newspapers, and magazines, in a place other than a place

or container for the proper disposal thereof, and including waste matter which escapes or is allowed to escape from a container, receptacle, or package.

(d) A person, firm, or corporation convicted of a violation of this section shall be punished by a mandatory fine of not less than one hundred dollars ($100) nor more than one thousand dollars ($1,000) upon a first conviction, by a mandatory fine of not less than five hundred dollars ($500) nor more than one thousand dollars ($1,000) upon a second conviction, and by a mandatory fine of not less than seven hundred fifty dollars ($750) nor more than one thousand dollars ($1,000) upon a third or subsequent conviction.

(e) The court may, in addition to the fine imposed upon a conviction, require as a condition of probation, in addition to any other condition of probation, that any person convicted of a violation of this section pick up litter at a time and place within the jurisdiction of the court for not less than eight hours. *(Amended and renumbered from section 374b.5 by Stats 1987 ch 133 §3.)*

§374.7. Littering or dumping waste matter in waters.

(a) Every person who litters or causes to be littered, or dumps or causes to be dumped, any waste matter into any bay, lagoon, channel, river, creek, slough, canal, lake, or reservoir, or other stream or body of water, or upon a bank, beach, or shore within 150 feet of the high water mark of any stream or body of water, is guilty of a misdemeanor.

(b) Every person convicted of a violation of subdivision (a) shall be punished by a mandatory fine of not less than one hundred dollars ($100) nor more than one thousand dollars ($1,000) upon a first conviction, by a mandatory fine of not less than five hundred dollars ($500) nor more than one thousand dollars ($1,000) upon a second conviction, and by a mandatory fine of not less than seven hundred fifty dollars ($750) nor more than one thousand dollars ($1,000) upon a third or subsequent conviction.

(c) The court may, in addition to the fine imposed upon a conviction, require as a condition of probation, in addition to any other condition of probation, that any person convicted of a violation of subdivision (a), pick up litter at a time and place within the jurisdiction of the court for not less than eight hours. *(Amended and renumbered from section 374e by Stats 1987 ch 133 §4.)*

§374.8. Dumping hazardous substances.

(a) In any prosecution under this section, proof of the elements of the offense shall not be dependent upon the requirements of Title 22 of the California Code of Regulations.

(b) Any person who knowingly causes any hazardous substance to be deposited into or upon any road, street, highway, alley, or railroad right-of-way, or upon the land of another, without the permission of the owner, or into the waters of this state is punishable by imprisonment in the county jail for not more than one year or by imprisonment in the state prison for a term of 16 months, 2, or 3 years, or by a fine of not less than fifty dollars ($50) nor more than ten thousand dollars ($10,000), or by both the fine and imprisonment, unless the deposit occurred as a result of an emergency that the person promptly reported to the appropriate regulatory authority.

© 1992 by J., B. & L. Gould
Printed in the U.S.A.　**EP**

(c) For purposes of this section, "hazardous substance" means either of the following:

(1) Any material that, because of its quantity, concentration, or physical or chemical characteristics, poses a significant present or potential hazard to human health and safety or to the environment if released into the environment, including, but not limited to, hazardous waste and any material which the administering agency or a handler as defined in Chapter 6.91 (commencing with Section 25410) of Division 20 of the Health and Safety Code, has a reasonable basis for believing would be injurious to the health and safety of persons or harmful to the environment if released into the environment.

(2) Any substance or chemical product for which one of the following applies.

(A) The manufacturer or producer is required to prepare a MSDS, as defined in Section 6374 of the Labor Code, for the substance or product pursuant to the Hazardous Substances Information Training Act (Chapter 2.5 (commencing with Section 6360) of Part 1 of Division 5 of the Labor Code) or pursuant to any applicable federal law or regulation.

(B) The substance is described as a radioactive material in Chapter 1 of Title 10 of the Code of Federal Regulations maintained and updated by the nuclear Regulatory Commission.

(C) The substance is designated by the Secretary of Transportation in Chapter 27 (commencing with Section 1801) of the appendix to Title 49 of the United States Code and taxed as a radioactive substance or material.

(D) The materials listed in subdivision (b) of Section 6382 of the Labor Code. *(Added by Stats 1991 ch 1120 §1, eff. 1/1/92.)*

§375. Offensive substance in place of public assemblage.

(a) It shall be unlawful to throw, drop, pour, deposit, release, discharge or expose, or to attempt to throw, drop, pour, deposit, release, discharge or expose in, upon or about any theater, restaurant, place of business, place of amusement or any place of public assemblage, any liquid, gaseous or solid substance or matter of any kind which is injurious to person or property, or is nauseous, sickening, irritating or offensive to any of the senses.

(b) It shall be unlawful to manufacture or prepare, or to possess any liquid, gaseous, or solid substance or matter of any kind which is injurious to person or property, or is nauseous, sickening, irritating or offensive, to any of the senses with intent to throw, drop, pour, deposit, release, discharge or expose the same in, upon or about any theater, restaurant, place of business, place of amusement, or any other place of public assemblage.

(c) Any person violating any of the provisions hereof shall be punished by imprisonment in the county jail for not less than three months and not more than one year, or by a fine of not less than five hundred dollars ($500) and not more than two thousand dollars ($2,000), or by both such fine and imprisonment.

(d) Any person who, in violating any of the provisions of subdivision (a), willfully employs or uses any liquid, gaseous or solid substance which may produce serious illness or permanent injury through being vaporized or otherwise disbursed in the air or who, in violating any of the provisions of subdivision (a), willfully employs or uses any tear gas, mustard gas or any of the combinations or compounds thereof, or willfully employs or uses acid or explosives, shall be guilty of a felony and shall be punished by imprisonment in the state prison.

§377. False personation to obtain prescription.

Every person who, in order to obtain for himself or another any drug that can be lawfully dispensed by a pharmacist only on prescription, falsely represents himself to be a physician or other person who can lawfully prescribe such drug, or falsely represents that he is acting on behalf of a person who can lawfully prescribe such drug, in a telephone communication with a pharmacist, is guilty of a misdemeanor.

§380. Distributing, dispensing, or selling toluene.

(a) Every person who sells, dispenses or distributes toluene, or any substance or material containing toluene, to any person who is less than 18 years of age shall be guilty of a misdemeanor, and upon conviction shall be fined in a sum of not less than one thousand dollars ($1,000), nor more than two thousand five hundred dollars ($2,500), or by imprisonment for not less than six months nor more than one year.

(b) The court shall order the suspension of the business license, for a period of one year, of a person who knowingly violates any of the provisions of this section after having been previously convicted of a violation of this section unless the owner of such business license can demonstrate a good faith attempt to prevent illegal sales or deliveries by employees. The provisions of this subdivision shall become operative on July 1, 1980.

(c) The provisions of this section shall apply to, but are not limited to, the sale or distribution of glue, cement, dope, paint thinners, paint, and any combination of hydrocarbons either alone or in combination with any substance or material including, but not limited to, paint, paint thinners, shellac thinners, and solvents which, when inhaled, ingested or breathed, can cause a person to be under the influence of, or intoxicated from, any such combination of hydrocarbons.

This section shall not prohibit the sale of gasoline or other motor vehicle fuels to persons less than 18 years of age.

(d) This section shall not apply to any glue or cement which has been certified by the State Department of Health Services as containing a substance which makes such glue or cement malodorous or causes such glue or cement to induce sneezing, nor shall this section apply where the glue or cement is sold, delivered, or given away simultaneously with or as part of a kit used for the construction of model airplanes, model boats, model automobiles, model trains, or other similar models or used for the assembly or creation of hobby craft items using such components as beads, tiles, tiffany glass, ceramics, clay, or other craft-related components.

§381. Possession of toluene or substances containing toluene.

(a) Any person who possesses toluene or any substance or material containing toluene, including, but not limited to, glue, cement, dope, paint thinner, paint and any combination of hydrocarbons, either alone or in combination with any substance or material includ-

© 1992 by J., B. & L. Gould
Printed in the U.S.A. **EP**

ing but not limited to paint, paint thinner, shellac thinner, and solvents, with the intent to breathe, inhale or ingest for the purpose of causing a condition of intoxication, elation, euphoria, dizziness, stupefaction, or dulling of the senses or for the purpose of, in any manner, changing, distorting or disturbing the audio, visual, or mental processes, or who knowingly and with the intent to do so is under the influence of toluene or any material containing toluene, or any combination of hydrocarbons is guilty of a misdemeanor.

(b) Any person who possesses any substance or material, which the State Department of Health Services has determined by regulations adopted pursuant to the Administrative Procedures Act (Chapter 3.5 (commencing with Section 11340) of Part 1 of Division 3 of Title 2 of the Government Code) has toxic qualities similar to toluene, with the intent to breathe, inhale, or ingest for the purpose of causing a condition of intoxication, elation, euphoria, dizziness, excitement, irrational behavior, exhilaration, satisfaction, stupefaction, or dulling of the senses or for the purpose of, in any manner, changing, distorting or disturbing the audio, visual, or mental processes, or who is under the influence of such substance or material is guilty of a misdemeanor.

§381a. Using inaccurate machines for testing dairy products.

Any person, or persons, whether as principals, agents, managers, or otherwise, who buy or sell dairy products, or deal in milk, cream or butter, and who buy or sell the same upon the basis of their richness or weight or the percentage of cream, or butter-fat contained therein, who use any apparatus, test bottle or other appliance, or who use the "Babcock test" or machine of like character for testing such dairy products, cream or butter, which is not accurate and correct, or which gives wrong or false percentages, or which is calculated in any way to defraud or injure the person with whom he deals, is guilty of a misdemeanor, and upon conviction shall be fined not more than one thousand dollars ($1,000) or imprisoned in the county jail not more than six (6) months.

§381b. Possession of nitrous oxide or any substance containing nitrous oxide.

Any person who possesses nitrous oxide or any substance containing nitrous oxide, with the intent to breathe, inhale, or ingest for the purpose of causing a condition of intoxication, elation, euphoria, dizziness, stupefaction, or dulling of the senses or for the purpose of, in any manner, changing, distorting, or disturbing the audio, visual, or mental processes, or who knowingly and with the intent to do so is under the influence of nitrous oxide or any material containing nitrous oxide is guilty of a misdemeanor. This section shall not apply to any person who is under the influence of nitrous oxide or any material containing nitrous oxide pursuant to an administration for the purpose of medical, surgical, or dental care by a person duly licensed to administer such an agent.

§382. Adulteration of food, drugs and liquors.

Every person who adulterates or dilutes any article of food, drink, drug, medicine, spirituous or malt liquor, or wine, or any article useful in compounding them, with the fraudulent intent to offer the same, or cause or permit it to be offered for sale as unadul-

terated or undiluted; and every person who fraudulently sells, or keeps or offers for sale the same, as unadulterated or undiluted, or who, in response to an inquiry for any article of food, drink, drug, medicine, spirituous or malt liquor, or wine, sells or offers for sale, a different article, or an article of a different character or manufacture, without first informing such purchaser of such difference, is guilty of a misdemeanor; provided, that no retail dealer shall be convicted under the provisions of this section if he shall prove a written guaranty of purity obtained from the person from whom he purchased such adulterated or diluted goods.

§382.4. Administration of succinylcholine to dog or cat.

No person, other than a licensed veterinarian, shall administer succinylcholine, also known as sucostrin, to any dog or cat.

Violation of this section shall constitute a misdemeanor.

§382.5. Prescription, administration or sale of dinitrophenol.

Every person who sells, dispenses, administers or prescribes dinitrophenol for any purpose shall be guilty of a felony, punishable by a fine not less than one thousand dollars ($1,000) nor more than ten thousand dollars ($10,000), or by imprisonment in the state prison, or by both such fine and imprisonment.

This section shall not apply to dinitrophenol manufactured or sold as an economic poison registered under the provision of Section 12811 of the Food and Agricultural Code nor to sales for use in manufacturing or for scientific purposes, and not for human consumption. *(Amended by Stats 1987 ch 828 §24.)*

§382.6. Administration or sale of chemicals for dyeing eyebrows and eyelashes.

Every person who sells, dispenses, administers or prescribes preparations containing diphenylamine, paraphenylenediamine, or paratoluylenediamine, or a derivative of any such chemicals, to be used as eyebrow and eyelash dye, shall be guilty of a felony, punishable by a fine not less than one thousand dollars ($1,000) nor more than ten thousand dollars ($10,000), or by imprisonment in the state prison, or by both such fine and imprisonment.

§382.7. Dispensing or prescribing liquid silicone.

Every person who knowingly prescribes, dispenses, administers, or furnishes any liquid silicone substance for the purpose of injection into a human breast or mammary is guilty of a misdemeanor.

§383. Sale of unwholesome food, drink or drugs.

Every person who knowingly sells, or keeps or offers for sale, or otherwise disposes of any article of food, drink, drug, or medicine, knowing that the same is adulterated or has become tainted, decayed, spoiled, or otherwise unwholesome or unfit to be eaten or drunk, with intent to permit the same to be eaten or drunk, is guilty of a misdemeanor, and must be fined not exceeding one thousand dollars ($1,000), or imprisoned in the county jail not exceeding six months, or both, and may, in the discretion of the court, be adjudged to pay, in addition, all the necessary expenses, not exceeding one thousand dollars ($1,000),

© 1992 by J., B. & L. Gould
Printed in the U.S.A.   EP

incurred in inspecting and analyzing such articles. The term "drug," as used herein, includes all medicines for internal or external use, antiseptics, disinfectants, and cosmetics. The term "food," as used herein, includes all articles used for food or drink by man, whether simple, mixed, or compound. Any article is deemed to be adulterated within the meaning of this section:

(a) In case of drugs: (1) if, when sold under or by a name recognized in the United States Pharmacopoeia, it differs materially from the standard of strength, quality, or purity laid down therein; (2) if, when sold under or by a name not recognized in the United States Pharmacopoeia, but which is found in some other pharmacopoeia or other standard work on materia medica, it differs materially from the standard of strength, quality, or purity laid down in such work; (3) if its strength, quality, or purity falls below the professed standard under which it is sold.

(b) In the case of food: (1) if any substance or substances have been mixed with it, so as to lower or depreciate, or injuriously affect its quality, strength, or purity; (2) if any inferior or cheaper substance or substances have been substituted wholly or in part for it; (3) if any valuable or necessary constituent or ingredient has been wholly or in part abstracted from it; (4) if it is an imitation of, or is sold under the name of, another article; (5) if it consists wholly, or in part, of a diseased, decomposed, putrid, infected, tainted, or rotten animal or vegetable substance or article, whether manufactured or not; or in the case of milk, if it is the produce of a diseased animal; (6) if it is colored, coated, polished, or powdered, whereby damage or inferiority is concealed, or if by any means it is made to appear better or of greater value than it really is; (7) if it contains any added substance or ingredient which is poisonous or injurious to health.

§383a. Possession or sale of process or renovated butter without proper label.

Any person, firm, or corporation, who sells or offers for sale, or has in his or its possession for sale, any butter manufactured by boiling, melting, deodorizing, or renovating, which is the product of stale, rancid, or decomposed butter, or by any other process whereby stale, rancid, or decomposed butter is manufactured to resemble or appear like creamery or dairy butter, unless the same is plainly stenciled or branded upon each and every package, barrel, firkin, tub, pail, square, or roll, in letters not less than one half inch in length, "process butter," or "renovated butter," in such a manner as to advise the purchaser of the real character of such "process" or "renovated" butter, is guilty of a misdemeanor.

§383b. Sale of misrepresented kosher meats.

Every person who with intent to defraud, sells or exposes for sale any meat or meat preparations, and falsely represents the same to be kosher, whether such meat or meat preparations be raw or prepared for human consumption, or as having been prepared under and from a product or products sanctioned by the orthodox Hebrew religious requirements; or falsely represents any food product, or the contents of any package or container, to be so constituted and prepared, by having or permitting to be inscribed thereon the words "kosher" in any language; or sells or exposes for sale in the same place of business both kosher and nonkosher meat or meat preparations,

either raw or prepared for human consumption, who fails to indicate on his window signs in all display advertising in block letters at least four inches in height "kosher and nonkosher meats sold here"; or who exposes for sale in any show window or place of business as both kosher and nonkosher meat preparations, either raw or prepared for human consumption, who fails to display over each kind of meat or meat preparation so exposed a sign in block letters at least four inches in height, reading "kosher meat" or "nonkosher meat" as the case may be; or sells or exposes for sale in any restaurant or any other place where food products are sold for consumption on the premises, any article of food or food preparations and falsely represents the same to be kosher, or as having been prepared in accordance with the orthodox Hebrew religious requirements; or sells or exposes for sale in such restaurant, or such other place, both kosher and nonkosher food or food preparations for consumption on the premises, not prepared in accordance with the Jewish ritual, or not sanctioned by the Hebrew orthodox religious requirements, and who fails to display on his window signs in all display advertising, in block letters at least four inches in height "kosher and nonkosher food served here" is guilty of a misdemeanor and upon conviction thereof be punishable by a fine of not less than one hundred dollars ($100), nor more than six hundred dollars ($600), or imprisonment in the county jail of not less than 30 days, nor more than 90 days, or both such fine and imprisonment.

The word "kosher" is here defined to mean a strict compliance with every Jewish law and custom pertaining and relating to the killing of the animal or fowl from which the meat is taken or extracted, the dressing, treatment and preparation thereof for human consumption, and the manufacture, production, treatment and preparation of such other food or foods in connection wherewith Jewish laws and customs obtain and to the use of tools, implements, vessels, utensils, dishes and containers that are used in connection with the killing of such animals and fowls and the dressing, preparation, production, manufacture and treatment of such meats and other products, foods and foodstuffs.

§384. Party lines; refusal to relinquish.

(a) Any person who shall wilfully refuse to immediately relinquish a party line when informed that such line is needed for an emergency call, and in fact such line is needed for an emergency call, to a fire department or police department or for medical aid or ambulance service, or any person who shall secure the use of a party line by falsely stating that such line is needed for an emergency call, shall be guilty of a misdemeanor.

(b) "Party line" as used in this section means a subscribers' line telephone circuit, consisting of two or more main telephone stations connected therewith, each station with a distinctive ring or telephone number. "Emergency" as used in this section means a situation in which property or human life is in jeopardy and the prompt summoning of aid is essential.

(c) Every telephone directory hereafter published and distributed to the members of the general public in this State or in any portion thereof which lists the calling numbers of telephones of any telephone exchange located in this State shall contain a notice which explains the offense provided for in this section,

© 1992 by J., B. & L. Gould
Printed in the U.S.A.

such notice to be printed in type which is not smaller than any other type on the same page and to be preceded by the word "warning" printed in type at least as large as the largest type on the same page; provided, that the provisions of this subdivision shall not apply to those directories distributed solely for business advertising purposes, commonly known as classified directories, nor to any telephone directory heretofore distributed to the general public. Any person, firm or corporation providing telephone service which distributes or causes to be distributed in this State copies of a telephone directory which is subject to the provisions of this section and which do not contain the notice herein provided for shall be guilty of a misdemeanor.

§384a. Destroying highway vegetation.

Every person who within the State of California willfully or negligently cuts, destroys, mutilates, or removes any tree or shrub, or fern or herb or bulb or cactus or flower, or huckleberry or redwood greens, or portion of any tree or shrub, or fern or herb or bulb or cactus or flower, or huckleberry or redwood greens, growing upon state or county highway rights-of-way, or who removes leaf mold thereon; provided, however, that the provisions of this section shall not be construed to apply to any employee of the state or of any political subdivision thereof engaged in work upon any state, county, or public road or highway while performing work under the supervision of the state or of any political subdivision thereof, and every person who willfully or negligently cuts, destroys, mutilates, or removes any tree or shrub, or fern or herb or bulb or cactus or flower, or huckleberry or redwood greens, or portions of any tree or shrub, or fern or herb or bulb or cactus or flower, or huckleberry or redwood greens, growing upon public land or upon land not his or her own, or leaf mold on the surface of public land, or upon land not his or her own, without a written permit from the owner of the land signed by the owner or the owner's authorized agent, and every person who knowingly sells, offers, or exposes for sale, or transports for sale, any tree or shrub, or fern or herb or bulb or cactus or flower, or huckleberry or redwood greens, or portion of any tree or shrub, or fern or herb or bulb or cactus or flower, or huckleberry or redwood greens, or leaf mold, so cut or removed from state or county highway rights-of-way, or removed from public land or from land not owned by the person who cut or removed the same without the written permit from the owner of the land, signed by the owner or the owner's authorized agent, is guilty of a misdemeanor and upon conviction thereof shall be punished by a fine of not more than one thousand dollars ($1,000) or by imprisonment in a county jail for not more than six months or by both fine and imprisonment.

The written permit required under this section shall be signed by the landowner, or the landowner's authorized agent, and acknowledged before a notary public, or other person authorized by law to take acknowledgments. The permit shall contain the number and species of trees and amount of shrubs or ferns or herbs or bulbs or cacti or flowers, or huckleberry or redwood greens, or portions of any tree or shrub and shall contain the legal description of the real property as usually found in deeds and conveyances of the land on which cutting or removal, or both, shall take place. One copy of the permit shall be filed in the office of the sheriff of the county in which the land described in the

permit is located. The permit shall be filed prior to commencement of cutting of the trees or shrub or fern or herb or bulb or cactus or flower or huckleberry or redwood green or portions of any tree or shrub authorized by the permit. The permit required by this section need not be notarized or filed with the office of the sheriff of the county where trees are to be removed when five or less trees or five or less pounds of shrubs or boughs are to be cut or removed.

Any county or state firewarden, or personnel of the Department of Forestry as designated by the Director of Forestry, and personnel of the United States Forest Service as designated by the Regional Forester, Region 5, of the United States Forest Service, or any peace officer of the State of California, may enforce the provisions hereof and may confiscate any and all such shrubs, trees, ferns or herbs or bulbs or cacti or flowers, or huckleberry or redwood greens or leaf mold, or parts thereof unlawfully cut or removed or knowingly sold, offered, or exposed or transported for sale as provided in this section.

The provisions of this section do not apply to any tree or shrub, or fern or herb or bulb or cactus or flower, or greens declared by law to be a public nuisance.

The provisions of this section do not apply to the necessary cutting or trimming of any trees, shrubs, or ferns or herbs or bulbs or cacti or flowers, or greens if done for the purpose of protecting or maintaining an electric powerline, telephone line, or other property of a public utility.

The provisions of this section do not apply to persons engaged in logging operations, or in suppressing fires.

§384b. Transportation of shrubs, boughs, or trees on public roads.

For the purposes of Sections 384c through 384f, inclusive, unless the context otherwise requires, the definitions contained in this section shall govern the construction of such sections. "Person" shall include an employee with wages as his sole compensation and "permit" means a permit as required by Section 384a.

(a) "Tree" means any evergreen tree or top thereof which is harvested without having the limbs and foliage removed.

(b) "Shrub" means any toyon or Christmas redberry shrub or any of the following native desert plants: all species of the family Cactaceae (cactus family); and Agave deserti (desert agave), Agave utahensis (Utah agave), Nolina bigelovii, Nolina parryi (Parry nolina), Nolina wolfii, Yucca baccata, Yucca brevifolia (Joshua tree), Yucca schidigera (Mohave yucca), Yucca whipplei (Whipple yucca), Cercidium floridum (blue palo verde), Cercidium microphyllum (little leaf palo verde), Dalea spinosa (smoke tree), Olneya tesota (ironwood tree), and Fouquieria splendens (ocotillo), or any part thereof, except the fruit thereof, which is harvested without having the limbs and foliage removed.

(c) "Bough" means any limb or foliage removed from an evergreen tree.

(d) "Peace officer" means any county or state firewarden, personnel of the California Department of Forestry as designated by the Director of Forestry, personnel of the U.S. Forest Service as designated by the Regional Forester, Region 5 of the U.S. Forest Service, personnel of the U.S. Department of the Interior as designated by them, or any peace officer of the State of California.

© 1992 by J., B. & L. Gould
Printed in the U.S.A.   EP

(e) "Harvest" means to remove or cut and remove from the place where grown.

(f) "Harvester" means a person who harvests a tree, shrub or bough.

§384c. Limitation on transportation of trees, shrubs by purchaser; transportation tags.

Persons purchasing trees, shrubs, or boughs from harvesters thereof shall not transport more than five trees or more than five pounds of shrubs or boughs on the public roads or highways without obtaining from the seller of the trees, shrubs, or boughs and having validated as provided in Section 384d a transportation tag for each load of the trees, shrubs, or boughs.

Unless a valid transportation tag issued in California for a tree, shrub, or bough has already been obtained, persons who harvest trees, shrubs, or boughs from their own land or the land of another or who are in possession of trees, shrubs, or boughs shall, before transporting on the public roads or highways or selling or consigning for removal and transportation over the public roads and highways more than five trees or more than five pounds of other shrubs or boughs, file with the sheriff of each county in which the trees, shrubs, or boughs are to be harvested an application for transportation tags and obtain a supply of these transportation tags sufficient to provide one tag for each load of trees, shrubs, or boughs to be so transported or sold.

No person shall knowingly make any false statement on any application for the transportation tags and the application shall contain, but is not limited to, the following information:

(a) The name and address of the applicant.

(b) The amount and species of trees, shrubs, or boughs to be transported.

(c) The name of the county from which the trees, shrubs, or boughs are to be removed.

(d) A legal description of the real property from which the trees, shrubs, or boughs are to be removed.

(e) The name or names of the owner of the real property from which the trees, shrubs, or boughs are to be removed.

(f) The applicant's timber operator permit number, if the harvesting of the trees, shrubs, or boughs is subject to the Z'berg-Nejedly Forest Practice Act of 1973 (Chapter 8 (commencing with Section 4511) of Part 2 of Division 4 of the Public Resources Code).

(g) The destination of the trees, shrubs, or boughs.

(h) The proposed date or dates of the transportation.

Every applicant shall, at the time of application, show to the sheriff his or her permit or proof of ownership of the trees, shrubs, or boughs. The application forms and transportation tags shall be printed and distributed by the sheriff of each county.

§384d. Issuance of transportation tags by sheriff's office.

Upon the filing of an application containing the information required by Section 384c, and the presentation of a permit or proof of ownership as required by Section 384c, the county sheriff's office shall issue to persons who harvest or have in their possession, trees, shrubs or boughs within the county sufficient transportation tags stamped with the county seal and identified by the applicant's timber operator permit number, if any, to enable the person transporting any of the trees, shrubs or boughs harvested within the county by the applicant to have a tag accompany each and every load of such trees, shrubs or boughs. Harvesters of trees, shrubs or boughs, when selling from stockpile location, shall furnish to the purchaser of trees, shrubs or boughs a bill of sale and a transportation tag for each load or part thereof bearing the harvester's timber operator permit number, if any, and other information as hereinafter required.

The purchaser of harvested trees, shrubs or boughs or the harvester when transporting his own trees, shrubs or boughs shall have the transportation tag validated by a peace officer in the county of purchase or harvest or by the nearest peace officer in an adjacent county when the transportation route used does not pass an office of a peace officer in the county of purchase or harvest. The validated transportation tag or tags shall remain with the load to the marketing area.

The transportation tags shall be in two parts; one to be retained by the transporting party; one to be retained by the validating peace officer and forwarded to the county sheriff. The transportation tag shall be validated and in force only for the proposed date or dates of transportation as specified in the application for the transportation tags. The transportation tags will be validated without fee and each shall contain the following information: name and address of the person obtaining and using the tag; number or amount of each species of trees, shrubs and boughs in the load; make, model and license number of the transporting vehicle; the county of origin and county of destination; the specified period of time during which the transportation tag is in force; date and validating signature and title of a peace officer.

§384e. Presentation of transportation tag.

(a) The transportation tag described in Section 384d shall be presented to any peace officer upon demand.

(b) Failure to produce a transportation tag properly filled out and validated upon demand of any peace officer shall constitute sufficient grounds to hold in protective custody the entire load of trees, shrubs or boughs, until proof of legal right to transport is furnished.

§384f. Violation of tree and shrub transportation requirements.

Any person violating any of the provisions of Sections 384b through 384f shall be guilty of a misdemeanor and upon conviction thereof shall be punished by a fine of not more than one thousand dollars ($1,000) or by imprisonment in the county jail not exceeding six months or by both such fine and imprisonment.

§384g. *Repealed by Stats 1987 ch 828.*

§384h. Willfully or negligently wounding domestic animals.

Every person who willfully or negligently, while hunting upon the inclosed lands of another, kills, maims or wounds an animal, the property of another, is guilty of a misdemeanor.

§384i. Exceptions to application of §§384a-384f.

(a) Sections 384a to 384f, inclusive, shall not apply to maintenance and construction activities of public agencies and their employees.

© 1992 by J., B. & L. Gould
Printed in the U.S.A. EP

(b) Sections 384b to 384f, inclusive, shall not apply to native desert plants described in subdivision (b) of Section 384b, that have been propagated and cultivated by human beings and which are being transported under Section 6922 or 6923 of the Food and Agricultural Code, pursuant to a valid nursery stock certificate.

(c) Sections 384a to 384f, inclusive, shall not apply to any act regulated by the provisions of Division 23 (commencing with Section 80001) of the Food and Agricultural Code. *(Amended by Stats 1987 ch 828 §25.)*

§384.5. Minor forest products; removal and transport.

(a) (1) Any person who removes any minor forest products from the property where the products were cut and transports the products upon any public road or highway shall have in the person's possession a valid bill of sale for the products or a written permit issued by the owner of the property from which the products were removed authorizing the removal and transport.

(2) Any such permit or bill of sale shall include, but is not limited to, all of the following:

(A) The name, address, and signature of the landowner, and phone number, if available.

(B) The name, address, and signature of the permittee or purchaser.

(C) The amount, species, and type of minor forest products to be removed and transported.

(D) A description sufficient to identify the property from which the minor forest products are to be removed.

(E) The date of issuance of the permit or bill of sale and the duration of the period of time within which the minor forest products may be removed.

(F) Any conditions or additional information which the landowner may impose or include.

(3) Any permit for the removal of minor forest products from public lands that is issued by the United States Forest Service or the Bureau of Land Management is sufficient for the purposes of this subdivision, regardless of whether such permit conforms to the specific requirements as to content set forth in paragraph (2).

(4) For the purposes of this subdivision, "minor forest products" means firewood, posts, shakeboards, shake and shingle bolts, or split products, in quantities exceeding 20 cubic feet in volume, and burlwood or stumps, in quantities of two or more.

(b) This section shall not apply to the transport of any minor forest products carried in a passenger vehicle, as defined in Section 465 of the Vehicle Code.

(c) Violation of subdivision (a) is a misdemeanor punishable by a fine of not more than one thousand dollars ($1,000) or by imprisonment in a county jail for not more than six months or by both that fine and imprisonment. *(Amended by Stats 1988 ch 225 §1, eff. 1/1/89.)*

§385. Operation of tools near high voltage conductors.

(a) The term "high voltage" as used in this section means a voltage in excess of 750 volts, measured between conductors or measured between the conductor and the ground.

The term "overhead conductor" as used in this section means any electrical conductor (either bare or insulated) installed above the ground except such conductors as are enclosed in iron pipe or other metal covering of equal strength.

(b) Any person who either personally or through an employee or agent, or as an employee or agent of another, operates, places, erects or moves any tools, machinery, equipment, material, building or structure within six feet of a high voltage overhead conductor is guilty of a misdemeanor.

(c) It shall be a misdemeanor to own, operate or to employ any person to operate, any crane, derrick, power shovel, drilling rig, hay loader, hay stacker, pile driver, or similar apparatus, any part of which is capable of vertical, lateral or swinging motion, unless there is posted and maintained in plain view of the operator thereof, a durable warning sign legible at 12 feet, reading: "Unlawful to operate this equipment within six feet of high voltage lines."

Each day's failure to post or maintain such sign shall constitute a separate violation.

(d) The provisions of this section shall not apply to (1) the construction, reconstruction, operation or maintenance of any high voltage overhead conductor, or its supporting structures or appurtenances by persons authorized by the owner, or (2) the operation of standard rail equipment which is normally used in the transportation of freight or passengers, or the operation of relief trains or other emergency railroad equipment by persons authorized by the owner, or (3) any construction, reconstruction, operation or maintenance of any overhead structures covered by the rules for overhead line construction prescribed by the Public Utilities Commission of the State of California.

§386. Installation of inoperable fire-protection system.

(a) Any person who willfully or maliciously constructs or maintains a fire-protection system in any structure with the intent to install a fire protection system which is known to be inoperable or to impair the effective operation of a system, so as to threaten the safety of any occupant or user of the structure in the event of a fire, shall be subject to imprisonment in the state prison for two, three, or four years.

(b) A violation of subdivision (a) which proximately results in great bodily injury or death is a felony punishable by imprisonment in the state prison for five, six, or seven years.

(c) As used in this section, "fire-protection system" includes, but is not limited to, an automatic fire sprinkler system, standpipe system, automatic fixed fire extinguishing system, and fire alarm system.

(d) For purposes of this section, the following definitions shall control:

(1) "Automatic fire sprinkler system" means an integrated system of underground and overhead piping designed in accordance with fire protection engineering standards. The portion of the sprinkler system above ground is a network of specially sized or hydraulically designed piping installed in a building, structure, or area, generally overhead, and to which sprinklers are attached in a systematic pattern. The valve controlling each system riser is located in the system riser or its supply piping. Each sprinkler system riser includes a device for activating an alarm when the system is in operation. The system is normally activated by heat from a fire, and it discharges water over the fire area.

© 1992 by J., B. & L. Gould
Printed in the U.S.A.   EP

(2) "Standpipe system" means an arrangement of piping, valves, and hose connectors and allied equipment installed in a building or structure with the hose connectors located in a manner that water can be discharged in streams or spray patterns through attached hose and nozzles. The purpose of the system is to extinguish a fire, thereby protecting a building or structure and its contents and occupants. This system relies upon connections to water supply systems or pumps, tanks, and other equipment necessary to provide an adequate supply of water to the hose connectors.

(3) "Automatic fixed fire extinguishing system" means either of the following:

(A) An engineered fixed extinguishing system which is custom designed for a particular hazard, using components which are approved or listed only for their broad performance characteristics. Components may be arranged into a variety of configurations. These systems shall include, but not be limited to, dry chemical systems, carbon dioxide systems, halogenated agent systems, steam systems, high expansion foam systems, foam extinguishing systems, and liquid agent systems.

(B) A pre-engineered fixed extinguishing system is a system where the number of components and their configurations are included in the description of the system's approval and listing. These systems include, but are not limited to, dry chemical systems, carbon dioxide systems, halogenated agent systems, and liquid agent systems.

(4) "Fire alarm system" means a control unit and a combination of electrical interconnected devices designed and intended to cause an alarm or warning of fire in a building or structure by either manual or automatic activation, or by both, and includes the systems installed throughout any building or portion thereof.

(5) "Structure" means any building, whether private, commercial, or public, or any bridge, tunnel, or powerplant. *(Added by Stats 1987 ch 246 §1.)*

§387. Notification of serious concealed danger; penalties.

(a) Any corporation, or person who is a manager with respect to a product, facility, equipment, process, place of employment, or business practice, is guilty of a public offense punishable by imprisonment in the county jail for a term not exceeding one year, or by a fine not exceeding ten thousand dollars ($10,000), or by both that fine and imprisonment; or by imprisonment in the state prison for 16 months, two, or three years, or by a fine not exceeding twenty-five thousand dollars ($25,000); or by both that fine and imprisonment, but if the defendant is a corporation the fine shall not exceed one million dollars ($1,000,000), if that corporation or person does all of the following:

(1) Has actual knowledge of a serious concealed danger that is subject to the regulatory authority of an appropriate agency and is associated with that product or a component of that product or business practice.

(2) Knowingly fails during the period ending 15 days after the actual knowledge is acquired, or if there is imminent risk of great bodily harm or death, immediately, to do both of the following:

(A) Inform the Division of Occupational Safety and Health in the Department of Industrial Relations in writing, unless the corporation or manager has actual knowledge that the division has been so informed.

Where the concealed danger reported pursuant to this paragraph is subject to the regulatory authority of an agency other than the Division of Occupational Safety and Health in the Department of Industrial Relations, it shall be the responsibility of the Division of Occupational Safety and Health in the Department of Industrial Relations, within 24 hours of receipt of the information, to telephonically notify the appropriate government agency of the hazard, and promptly forward any written notification received.

(B) Warn its affected employees in writing, unless the corporation or manager has actual knowledge that the employees have been so warned.

The requirement for disclosure is not applicable if the hazard is abated within the time prescribed for reporting, unless the appropriate regulatory agency nonetheless requires disclosure by regulation.

Where the Division of Occupational Safety and Health in the Department of Industrial Relations was not notified, but the corporation or manager reasonably and in good faith believed that they were complying with the notification requirements of this section by notifying another government agency, as listed in paragraph (8) of subdivision (d), no penalties shall apply.

(b) As used in this section:

(1) "Manager" means a person having both of the following:

(A) Management authority in or as a business entity.

(B) Significant responsibility for any aspect of a business which includes actual authority for the safety of a product or business practice or for the conduct of research or testing in connection with a product or business practice.

(2) "Product" means an article of trade or commerce or other item of merchandise which is a tangible or an intangible good, and includes services.

(3) "Actual knowledge," used with respect to a serious concealed danger, means has information that would convince a reasonable person in the circumstances in which the manager is situated that the serious concealed danger exists.

(4) "Serious concealed danger," used with respect to a product or business practice, means that the normal or reasonably foreseeable use of, or the exposure of an individual to, the product or business practice creates a substantial probability of death, great bodily harm, or serious exposure to an individual, and the danger is not readily apparent to an individual who is likely to be exposed.

(5) "Great bodily harm" means a significant or substantial physical injury.

(6) "Serious exposure" means any exposure to a hazardous substance, when the exposure occurs as a result of an incident or exposure over time and to a degree or in an amount sufficient to create a substantial probability that death or great bodily harm in the future would result from the exposure.

(7) "Warn its affected employees" means give sufficient description of the serious concealed danger to all individuals working for or in the business entity who are likely to be subject to the serious concealed danger in the course of that work to make those individuals aware of that danger.

(8) "Appropriate government agency" means an agency on the following list that has regulatory au-

thority with respect to the product or business practice and serious concealed dangers of the sort discovered:

(A) The Division of Occupational Safety and Health in the Department of Industrial Relations.

(B) State Department of Health Services.

(C) Department of Agriculture.

(D) County departments of health.

(E) The United States Food and Drug Administration.

(F) The United States Environmental Protection Agency.

(G) The National Highway Traffic Safety Administration.

(H) The Federal Occupation Safety and Health Administration.

(I) The Nuclear Regulatory Commission.

(J) The Consumer Product Safety Commission.

(K) The Federal Aviation Administration.

(L) The Federal Mine Safety and Health Review Commission.

(c) Notification received pursuant to this section shall not be used against any manager in any criminal case, except a prosecution for perjury or for giving a false statement. *(Added by Stats 1990 ch 1616 §2, eff. 1/1/91.)*

§395. Frauds practiced intended to affect the market price.

Every person who willfully makes or publishes any false statement, spreads any false rumor, or employs any other false or fraudulent means or device, with intent to affect the market price of any kind of property, is guilty of a misdemeanor.

§396.5. Food stamps; unlawful use.

It shall be unlawful for any retail food store or wholesale food concern, as defined in Section 3(k) of the federal Food Stamp Act of 1977 (Public Law 95-113) (7 U.S.C. Sec. 2012(k)), or any person, to sell, furnish or give away any goods or services, other than those items authorized by the Food Stamp Act of 1964, as amended (Public Law 88-525) (Chapter 51 (commencing with Section 2011) of Title 7 of the United States Code), in exchange for food stamps issued pursuant to Chapter 10 (commencing with Section 18900), Part 6, Division 9 of the Welfare and Institutions Code.

Any violator of this section is guilty of a misdemeanor and shall be punished by a fine of not more than five thousand dollars ($5,000) or by imprisonment in the county jail not exceeding 90 days, or by both that fine and imprisonment. *(Amended by Stats 1987 ch 828 §25.5.)*

§397. Furnishing liquor to drunkard or incompetent.

Every person who sells or furnishes, or causes to be sold or furnished, intoxicating liquors to any habitual or common drunkard, or to any person who has been adjudged legally incompetent or insane by any court of this State and has not been restored to legal capacity, knowing such person to have been so adjudged, is guilty of a misdemeanor.

§398. *Repealed by Stats 1987 ch 828.*

§399. Death from mischievous animals.

If the owner of a mischievous animal, knowing its propensities, willfully suffers it to go at large, or keeps it without ordinary care, and such animal, while so at large, or while not kept with ordinary care, kills any human being who has taken all the precautions which the circumstances permitted, or which a reasonable person would ordinarily take in the same situation, is guilty of a felony.

§399.5. Owning or having custody or control of trained attack dogs.

(a) Any person owning or having custody or control of a dog trained to fight, attack, or kill is guilty of a misdemeanor punishable by imprisonment in the county jail not exceeding six months, or by fine not exceeding one thousand dollars ($1,000), or by both, if, as a result of that person's failure to exercise ordinary care, the dog bites a human being, on two separate occasions or on one occasion causing substantial physical injury. No person shall be criminally liable under this section, however, unless he or she knew or reasonably should have known of the vicious or dangerous nature of the dog, or if the victim failed to take all the precautions that a reasonable person would ordinarily take in the same situation.

(b) Following the conviction of an individual for a violation of this section, the court shall hold a hearing to determine whether conditions of the treatment or confinement of the dog or other circumstances existing at the time of the bite or bites have changed so as to remove the danger to other persons presented by the animal. The court, after hearing, may make any order it deems appropriate to prevent the recurrence of such an incident, including, but not limited to, the removal of the animal from the area or its destruction if necessary.

(c) Nothing in this section shall authorize the bringing of an action pursuant to subdivision (a) based on a bite or bites inflicted upon a trespasser, upon a person who has provoked the dog or contributed to his or her own injuries, or by a dog used in military or police work if the bite or bites occurred while the dog was actually performing in that capacity. As used in this subdivision, "provocation" includes, but is not limited to, situations where a dog held on a leash by its owner or custodian reacts in a protective manner to a person or persons who approach the owner or custodian in a threatening manner.

(d) Nothing in this section shall be construed to affect the liability of the owner of a dog under Section 399 or any other provision of law.

§401. Aiding suicide.

Every person who deliberately aids, or advises, or encourages another to commit suicide, is guilty of a felony.

§402. Sightseeing at scene of emergency.

(a) Every person who goes to the scene of an emergency, or stops at the scene of an emergency, for the purpose of viewing the scene or the activities of police officers, firefighters, emergency medical, or other emergency personnel, or military personnel coping with the emergency in the course of their duties during the time it is necessary for emergency vehicles or those personnel to be at the scene of the emergency or to be moving to or from the scene of the emergency for the purpose of protecting lives or property, unless it is part of the duties of that person's employment to view that scene or activities, and thereby impedes police officers, firefighters, emergency medical, or other emergency personnel or military personnel, in the performance of

© 1992 by J., B. & L. Gould
Printed in the U.S.A.   EP

their duties in coping with the emergency, is guilty of a misdemeanor.

(b) Every person who knowingly resists or interferes with the lawful efforts of a lifeguard in the discharge or attempted discharge of an official duty in an emergency situation, when the person knows or reasonably should know that the lifeguard is engaged in the performance of his or her official duty, is guilty of a misdemeanor.

(c) For the purposes of this section, an emergency includes a condition or situation involving injury to persons, damage to property, or peril to the safety of persons or property, which results from a fire, an explosion, an airplane crash, flooding, windstorm damage, a railroad accident, a traffic accident, a power plant accident, a toxic chemical or biological spill, or any other natural or human-caused event. *(Amended by Stats 1989 ch 214 §1, eff. 1/1/90.)*

§402a. Adulterated candy.

Every person who adulterates candy by using in its manufacture terra-alba or other deleterious substances, or who sells or keeps for sale any candy or candies adulterated with terra-alba, or any other deleterious substance, knowing the same to be adulterated, is guilty of a misdemeanor.

§402b. Discarding or abandoning appliances in place accessible to children.

Any person who discards or abandons or leaves in any place accessible to children any refrigerator, icebox, deep-freeze locker, clothes dryer, washing machine, or other appliance, having a capacity of one and one-half cubic feet or more, which is no longer in use, and which has not had the door removed or the hinges and such portion of the latch mechanism removed to prevent latching or locking of the door, is guilty of a misdemeanor. Any owner, lessee, or manager who knowingly permits such a refrigerator, icebox, deep-freeze locker, clothes dryer, washing machine, or other appliance to remain on premises under his control without having the door removed or the hinges and such portion of the latch mechanism removed to prevent latching or locking of the door, is guilty of a misdemeanor. Guilt of a violation of this section shall not, in itself, render one guilty of manslaughter, battery or other crime against a person who may suffer death or injury from entrapment in such a refrigerator, icebox, deep-freeze locker, clothes dryer, washing machine, or other appliance.

The provisions of this section shall not apply to any vendor or seller of refrigerators, iceboxes, deep-freeze lockers, clothes dryers, washing machines, or other appliances, who keeps or stores them for sale purposes, if the vendor or seller takes reasonable precautions to effectively secure the door of any such refrigerator, icebox, deep-freeze locker, clothes dryer, washing machine, or other appliance so as to prevent entrance by children small enough to fit therein.

§402c. Integral locks required for new refrigerators.

On and after January 1, 1970, any person who sells a new refrigerator, icebox, or deep-freeze locker not equipped with an integral lock in this state, having a capacity of two cubic feet or more, which cannot be opened from the inside by the exertion of 15 pounds of force against the latch edge of the closed door is guilty of a misdemeanor.

TITLE 11

OF CRIMES AGAINST THE PUBLIC PEACE

§403. Willful disturbance of public assembly or meeting.

Every person who, without authority of law, willfully disturbs or breaks up any assembly or meeting, not unlawful in its character, other than such as is mentioned in Section 302 of the Penal Code and Section 29440 of the Elections Code, is guilty of a misdemeanor.

§404. Riots defined.

(a) Any use of force or violence, disturbing the public peace, or any threat to use such force or violence, if accompanied by immediate power of execution, by two or more persons acting together, and without authority of law, is a riot.

(b) As used in this section, disturbing the public peace may occur in any place of confinement. Place of confinement means any state prison, county jail, industrial farm, or road camp, or any city jail, industrial farm, or road camp.

§404.6. Intent to cause a riot.

Every person who with the intent to cause a riot does an act or engages in conduct which urges a riot, or urges others to commit acts of force or violence, or the burning or destroying of property, and at a time and place and under circumstances which produce a clear and present and immediate danger of acts of force or violence or the burning or destroying of property, is guilty of a misdemeanor.

This section shall not apply to, nor in any way affect, restrain, or interfere with, otherwise lawful activity engaged in by or on behalf of a labor organization or organizations by its members, agents or employees.

§405. Punishment of participant in riot.

Every person who participates in any riot is punishable by a fine not exceeding one thousand dollars, or by imprisonment in a county jail not exceeding one year, or by both such fine and imprisonment.

§405a. Lynching defined.

The taking by means of a riot of any person from the lawful custody of any peace officer is a lynching.

§405b. Punishment of participant in lynching.

Every person who participates in any lynching is punishable by imprisonment in the state prison for two, three or four years.

§406. Rout defined.

Whenever two or more persons, assembled and acting together, make any attempt or advance toward the commission of an act which would be a riot if actually committed, such assembly is a rout.

§407. Unlawful assembly defined.

Whenever two or more persons assemble together to do an unlawful act, or do a lawful act in a violent, boisterous, or tumultuous manner, such assembly is an unlawful assembly.

§408. Punishment of rout and unlawful assembly.

Every person who participates in any rout or unlawful assembly is guilty of a misdemeanor.

© 1992 by J., B. & L. Gould
Printed in the U.S.A.   **EP**

§409. Remaining present at place of riot, etc., after warning to disperse.

Every person remaining present at the place of any riot, rout, or unlawful assembly, after the same has been lawfully warned to disperse, except public officers and persons assisting them in attempting to disperse the same, is guilty of a misdemeanor.

§409.3. Management of accident scene by appropriate authority.

Whenever law enforcement officers and emergency medical technicians are at the scene of an accident, management of the scene of the accident shall be vested in the appropriate law enforcement agency, whose representative shall consult with representatives of other response agencies at the scene to ensure that all appropriate resources are properly utilized. However, authority for patient care management at the scene of an accident shall be determined in accordance with Section 1798.6 of the Health and Safety Code.

For purposes of this section, "management of the scene of an accident" means the coordination of operations which occur at the location of an accident. *(Amended by Stats 1987 ch 1058 §6.)*

§409.5. Power of peace officers to close areas during emergencies.

(a) Whenever a menace to the public health or safety is created by a calamity such as flood, storm, fire, earthquake, explosion, accident, or other disaster, officers of the California Highway Patrol, California State Police Division, police departments, marshal's office or sheriff's office, any officer or employee of the Department of Forestry and Fire Protection designated a peace officer by subdivision (h) of Section 830.2, any officer or employee of the Department of Parks and Recreation designated a peace officer by subdivision (g) of Section 830.2, any officer or employee of the Department of Fish and Game designated a peace officer under subdivision (f) of Section 830.2, and any publicly employed full-time lifeguard or publicly employed full-time marine safety officer while acting in a supervisory position in the performance of his or her official duties, may close the area where the menace exists for the duration thereof by means of ropes, markers, or guards to any and all persons not authorized by the lifeguard or officer to enter or remain within the enclosed area. If the calamity creates an immediate menace to the public health, the local health officer may close the area where the menace exists pursuant to the conditions set forth in this section.

(b) Officers of the California Highway Patrol, California State Police Division, police departments, marshal's office or sheriff's office, officers of the Department of Fish and Game designated as peace officers by subdivision (f) of Section 830.2, or officers of the Department of Forestry and Fire Protection designated as peace officers by subdivision (h) of Section 830.2 may close the immediate area surrounding any emergency field command post or any other command post activated for the purpose of abating any calamity enumerated in this section or any riot or other civil disturbance to any and all unauthorized persons pursuant to the conditions set forth in this section whether or not the field command post or other command post is located near to the actual calamity or riot or other civil disturbance.

(c) Any unauthorized person who willfully and knowingly enters an area closed pursuant to subdivision (a) or (b) and who willfully remains within the area after receiving notice to evacuate or leave shall be guilty of a misdemeanor.

(d) Nothing in this section shall prevent a duly authorized representative of any news service, newspaper, or radio or television station or network from entering the areas closed pursuant to this section. *(Amended by Stats 1990 ch 82 §6, eff. 5/3/90; ch 1695 §8, eff. 1/1/91.)*

§409.6. Power of peace officers to close area after an avalanche.

(a) Whenever a menace to the public health or safety is created by an avalanche, officers of the California Highway Patrol, California State Police, police departments or sheriff's office, any officer or employee of the Department of Forestry designated a peace officer by subdivision (h) of Section 830.2, and any officer or employee of the Department of Parks and Recreation designated a peace officer by subdivision (g) of Section 830.2, may close the area where the menace exists for the duration thereof by means of ropes, markers or guards to any and all persons not authorized by such officer to enter or remain within the closed area. If an avalanche creates an immediate menace to the public health, the local health officer may close the area where the menace exists pursuant to the conditions which are set forth above in this section.

(b) Officers of the California Highway Patrol, California State Police, police departments, or sheriff's office or officers of the Department of Forestry designated as peace officers by subdivision (h) of Section 830.2 may close the immediate area surrounding any emergency field command post or any other command post activated for the purpose of abating hazardous conditions created by an avalanche to any and all unauthorized persons pursuant to the conditions which are set forth in this section whether or not such field command post or other command post is located near the avalanche.

(c) Any unauthorized person who willfully and knowingly enters an area closed pursuant to subdivision (a) or (b) and who willfully remains within such area, or any unauthorized person who willfully remains within an area closed pursuant to subdivision (a) or (b), after receiving notice to evacuate or leave from a peace officer named in subdivision (a) or (b) shall be guilty of a misdemeanor. If necessary, a peace officer named in subdivision (a) or (b) may use reasonable force to remove from the closed area any unauthorized person who willfully remains within such area after receiving notice to evacuate or leave.

(d) Nothing in this section shall prevent a duly authorized representative of any news service, newspaper, or radio or television station or network from entering the areas closed pursuant to this section. *(Amended by Stats 1989 ch 1165 §18, eff. 1/1/90.)*

§410. Magistrates neglecting or refusing to disperse rioters.

If a magistrate or officer, having notice of an unlawful or riotous assembly, mentioned in this chapter, neglects to proceed to the place of assembly, or as near thereto as he can with safety, and to exercise the authority with which he is invested for suppressing

© 1992 by J., B. & L. Gould
Printed in the U.S.A.   EP

the same and arresting the offenders, he is guilty of a misdemeanor.

§412. Prize-fighting.

Any person, who, within this state, engages in, or instigates, aids, encourages, or does any act to further, a pugilistic contest, or fight, or ring or prize-fight, or sparring or boxing exhibition, taking or to take place either within or without this state, between two or more persons, with or without gloves, for any price, reward, or compensation, directly or indirectly, or who goes into training preparatory to such pugilistic contest, or fight, or ring or prize-fight, or sparring or boxing exhibition, or acts as aider, abettor, backer, umpire, referee, trainer, second, surgeon, or assistant, at such pugilistic contest, or fight, or ring or prize-fight, or sparring or boxing exhibition, or who sends or publishes a challenge or acceptance of a challenge, or who knowingly carries or delivers such challenge or acceptance, or who gives or takes or receives any tickets, tokens, prize, money, or thing of value, from any person or persons, for the purpose of seeing or witnessing any such pugilistic contest, or fight, or ring or prize-fight, or sparring or boxing exhibition, or who, being the owner, lessee, agent, or occupant of any vessel, building, hotel, room, enclosure or ground, or any part thereof, whether for gain, hire, reward or gratuitously or otherwise, permits the same to be used or occupied for such a pugilistic contest, or fight, or ring or prize-fight, or sparring or boxing exhibition, or who lays, makes, offers or accepts, a bet or bets, or wager or wagers, upon the result or any feature of any pugilistic contest, or fight, or ring or prize fight, or sparring or boxing exhibition, or acts as stakeholder of any such bet or bets, or wager or wagers, shall be guilty of a misdemeanor, and upon conviction thereof, shall be fined not less than one hundred dollars nor more than one thousand dollars and be imprisoned in the county jail not less than thirty days nor exceeding one year. Provided, however, that amateur boxing exhibitions may be held within this state, of a limited number of rounds, not exceeding four of the duration of three minutes each; the interval between each round shall be one minute, and the contestants weighing one hundred and forty-five pounds or over shall wear gloves of not less than eight ounces each in weight, and contestants weighing under one hundred and forty-five pounds may wear gloves of not less than six ounces each in weight. All gloves used by contestants in such amateur boxing exhibitions shall be so constructed, as that the soft padding between the outside coverings shall be evenly distributed over the back of said gloves and cover the knuckles and back of the hands. And no bandages of any kind shall be used on the hands or arms of the contestants. For the purpose of this statute an amateur boxing exhibition shall be and is hereby defined as one in which no contestant has received or shall receive in any form, directly or indirectly, any money, prize, reward or compensation either for the expenses of training for such contest or for taking part therein, except as herein expressly provided. Nor shall any person appear as contestant in such amateur exhibition who prior thereto has received any compensation or reward in any form for displaying, exercising or giving any example of his skill in or knowledge of athletic exercises, or for rendering services of any kind to any athletic organization or to any person or persons as trainer, coach, instructor or otherwise, or who shall have been employed in any manner professionally by reason of his athletic skill or knowledge, provided, however, that a medal or trophy may be awarded to each contestant in such amateur boxing exhibitions, not to exceed in value the sum of $35.00 each, which such medal or trophy must have engraved thereon the name of the winner and the date of the event; but no portion of any admission fee or fees charged or received for any amateur boxing exhibition shall be paid or given to any contestant in such amateur boxing exhibition, either directly or indirectly, nor shall any gift be given to or received by such contestants for participating in such boxing exhibition, except said medal or trophy. At every amateur boxing exhibition held in this state and permitted by this section of the Penal Code, any sheriff, constable, marshal, policeman or other peace officer of the city, county or other political subdivision, where such exhibition is being held, shall have the right to, and it is hereby declared to be his duty to stop such exhibition, whenever it shall appear to him that the contestants are so unevenly matched or for any other reason, the said contestants have been, or either of them, has been seriously injured or there is danger that said contestants, or either of them, will be seriously injured if such contest continues, and he may call to his assistance in enforcing his order to stop said exhibition, as many peace officers or male citizens of the state as may be necessary for that purpose. Provided, further, that any contestant who shall continue to participate in such exhibition after an order to stop such exhibition shall have been given by such peace officer, or who shall violate any of the regulations herein prescribed, for governing amateur boxing exhibitions, shall be deemed guilty of violating this section of the Penal Code and subject to the punishment herein provided.

Nothing in this section contained shall be construed to prevent any county, city and county, or incorporated city or town from prohibiting, by ordinance, the holding or conducting of any boxing exhibition, or any person from engaging in any such boxing exhibition therein.

§413. Presence at prohibited prize-fight.

Every person willfully present as spectator at any fight or contention prohibited in the preceding section, is guilty of a misdemeanor.

An information may be laid before any of the magistrates mentioned in section eight hundred and eight of this code, that a person has taken steps toward promoting or participating in a contemplated pugilistic contest, or fight, or ring or prize-fight, or sparring or boxing exhibition, prohibited under the provision of section four hundred and twelve of this code, or is about to commit an offense under said section four hundred and twelve. When said information is laid before said magistrate, he must examine, on oath, the informer, and any witness or witnesses he may produce, and must take their depositions in writing and cause them to be subscribed by the parties making them. If it appears from the deposition that there is just reason to fear the commission of the offense contemplated by the person so informed against, the magistrate must issue a warrant directed generally to the sheriff of the county, or any constable, marshal, or policeman in the state, reciting the substance of the information and commanding the officer forthwith to arrest the person informed against and bring him before the magistrate. When the person informed against is brought before the magistrate, if the charge be controverted, the magistrate must take testimony in relation thereto. The evidence must be reduced to writing and subscribed by the witnesses. If it appears there is no just reason to fear the commission of the offense alleged to have been contemplated, the person complained against must be discharged. If, however, there is just reason to fear the commission of the offense, the person complained of must be required to enter into an undertaking in such sum, not less than three thousand dollars, as the magistrate may direct, with one or more sufficient sureties, conditioned that such person will not, for a period of one year thereafter, commit any such contemplated offense.

§414. Leaving the state to engage in prize fights.

Every person who leaves this state with intent to evade any of the provisions of Section 412 or 413, and to commit any act out of this state such as is prohibited by them, and who does any act which would be punishable under these provisions if committed within this state, is punishable in the same manner as he or she would have been in case such act had been committed within this state. *(Amended by Stats 1987 ch 828 §27.)*

§414a. Boxing witnesses; self-incrimination.

No person, otherwise competent as a witness, is disqualified from testifying as such, concerning any offense under this act, on the ground that such testimony may incriminate himself, but no prosecution can afterwards be had against him for any offense concerning which he testified. The provisions of section 1111 of the Penal Code of this state are not applicable to any prosecutions brought under the provisions of this act.

§415. Disturbing the peace.

Any of the following persons shall be punished by imprisonment in the county jail for a period of not more than 90 days, a fine of not more than four hundred dollars ($400), or both such imprisonment and fine:

(1) Any person who unlawfully fights in a public place or challenges another person in a public place to fight.

(2) Any person who maliciously and willfully disturbs another person by loud and unreasonable noise.

(3) Any person who uses offensive words in a public place which are inherently likely to provoke an immediate violent reaction.

§415.5. Disturbance of peace of school, community or state college or state university.

(a) Any person who (1) unlawfully fights within any building or upon the grounds of any school, community college, university, or state university or challenges another person within any building or upon the grounds to fight, or (2) maliciously and willfully disturbs another person within any of these buildings or upon the grounds by loud and unreasonable noise, or (3) uses offensive words within any of these buildings or upon the grounds which are inherently likely to provoke an immediate violent reaction is guilty of a misdemeanor punishable by a fine not exceeding four hundred dollars ($400) or by imprisonment in the county jail for a period of not more than 90 days, or both.

(b) If the defendant has been previously convicted once of a violation of this section or of any offense defined in Chapter 1 (commencing with Section 626) of Title 15 of Part 1, the defendant shall be sentenced to imprisonment in the county jail for a period of not less than 10 days or more than six months, or by both that imprisonment and a fine of not exceeding one thousand dollars ($1,000), and shall not be released on probation, parole, or any other basis until not less than 10 days of imprisonment has been served.

(c) If the defendant has been previously convicted two or more times of a violation of this section or of any offense defined in Chapter 1 (commencing with Section 626) of Title 15 of Part 1, the defendant shall be sentenced to imprisonment in the county jail for a period of not less than 90 days or more than six months, or by both that imprisonment and a fine of not exceeding one thousand dollars ($1,000), and shall not be released on probation, parole, or any other basis until not less than 90 days of imprisonment has been served.

(d) For the purpose of determining the penalty to be imposed pursuant to this section, the court may consider a written report from the Department of Justice containing information from its records showing prior convictions; and the communication is prima facie evidence of such convictions, if the defendant admits them, regardless of whether or not the complaint commencing the proceedings has alleged prior convictions.

(e) As used in this section "state university," "university," "community college," and "school" have the same meaning as these terms are given in Section 626.

(f) This section shall not apply to any person who is a registered student of the school, or to any person who is engaged in any otherwise lawful employee concerted activity. *(Amended by Stats 1988 ch 1113 §3, eff. 1/1/89.)*

§416. Refusing to disperse upon lawful command.

(a) If two or more persons assemble for the purpose of disturbing the public peace, or committing any unlawful act, and do not disperse on being desired or commanded so to do by a public officer, the persons so offending are severally guilty of a misdemeanor.

(b) Any person who, as a result of violating subdivision (a), personally causes damage to real or personal property, which is either publicly or privately owned, shall make restitution for the damage he or she caused, including, but not limited to, the costs of cleaning up, repairing, replacing, or restoring the property. Any restitution required to be paid pursuant to this subdivision shall be paid directly to the victim. If the court determines that the defendant is unable to pay restitution, the court shall order the defendant to perform community service, as the court deems appropriate, in lieu of the direct restitution payment.

(c) This section shall not preclude the court from imposing restitution in the form of a penalty assessment pursuant to Section 1464 if the court, in its discretion, deems that additional restitution appropriate.

(d) The burden of proof on the issue of whether any defendant or defendants personally caused any property damage shall rest with the prosecuting agency or claimant. In no event shall the burden of proof on this issue shift to the defendant or any of several defendants to prove that he or she was not responsible

© 1992 by J., B. & L. Gould
Printed in the U.S.A. **EP**

for the property damage. *(Amended by Stats 1989 ch 572 §1, eff. 1/1/90.)*

§417. Drawing, exhibiting, or using deadly weapon.

(a) (1) Every person who, except in self-defense, in the presence of any other person, draws or exhibits any deadly weapon whatsoever, other than a firearm, in a rude, angry, or threatening manner, or who in any manner, unlawfully uses the same in any fight or quarrel is guilty of a misdemeanor punishable by imprisonment in the county jail for a term of not less than 30 days.

(2) Every person who, except in self-defense, in the presence of any other person, draws or exhibits any firearm, whether loaded or unloaded, in a rude, angry, or threatening manner, or who in any manner, unlawfully uses the same in any fight or quarrel is guilty of a misdemeanor punishable by imprisonment in the county jail for a term of not less than three months.

(b) Every person who, except in self-defense, in the presence of any other person, draws or exhibits any loaded firearm in a rude, angry, or threatening manner, or who, in any manner, unlawfully uses any loaded firearm in any fight or quarrel upon the grounds of any day care center, as defined in Section 1596.76 of the Health and Safety Code, or any facility where programs, including day care programs or recreational programs, are being conducted for persons under 18 years of age, including programs conducted by a nonprofit organization, during the hours in which the center or facility is open for use, shall be punished by imprisonment in the state prison for one, two, or three years, or by imprisonment in a county jail for a term of not less than three months, nor more than one year.

(c) Every person who, in the immediate presence of a peace officer, draws or exhibits any firearm, whether loaded or unloaded, in a rude, angry, or threatening manner, and who knows or reasonably should know that the victim is a peace officer engaged in the performance of his or her duties, and that peace officer is engaged in the performance of his or her duties is guilty of a felony punishable by imprisonment in the county jail for a term of not less than nine months and not to exceed one year, or in the state prison.

As used in this section, "peace officers" refers to any person designated as a peace officer by Section 830.1, Section 830.2, subdivision (a) of Section 830.3, or Section 830.5. *(Amended by Stats 1991 ch 1202 §3, eff. 1/1/92.)*

§417.1. Exhibiting firearm in presence of reserve peace officer.

Every person who, in the immediate presence of a peace officer, draws or exhibits any firearm, whether loaded or unloaded, in a rude, angry or threatening manner, and who knows or reasonably should know that the victim is a peace officer engaged in the performance of his or her duties, and the peace officer is engaged in the performance of his or her duties, is guilty of a felony punishable by imprisonment in the county jail not to exceed one year, or in the state prison.

As used in this section, "peace officer" refers to any person designated as a reserve or auxiliary sheriff or city police officer, or a deputy sheriff, pursuant to Section 830.6.

§417.2. Exhibiting replica of firearm in threatening manner.

(a) Every person who, except in self-defense, draws or exhibits a replica of a firearm in a threatening manner against another in such a way as to cause a reasonable person apprehension or fear of bodily harm is guilty of a misdemeanor punishable by imprisonment in the county jail for a term of not less than 30 days. As used in this subdivision, "a replica of a firearm" means any device with the apparent capability of expelling a projectile by the force of air or an explosion and which is reasonably perceived by the person against whom the device is drawn or exhibited to be an actual firearm, including starter pistols and air guns.

(b) Commencing January 1, 1989, any person who sells, manufactures, or distributes an imitation firearm in violation of this section shall be liable for a civil fine in an action brought by the city attorney of the city or the district attorney of the county of not more than ten thousand dollars ($10,000) for each violation.

As used in this section, "imitation firearm" means a replica of a firearm which is so substantially similar in physical properties to an existing firearm as to lead a reasonable person to conclude that the replica is a firearm.

The manufacture, sale, or distribution of imitation firearms is permitted if the device is manufactured, sold, or distributed (1) solely for export in interstate or foreign commerce, (2) solely for lawful use in theatrical productions, including motion picture, television, and stage productions, (3) for use in a certified or regulated athletic event or competition, (4) for use in military or civil defense activities, or (5) for public displays authorized by public or private schools.

(c) As used in this section, "imitation firearm" does not include (1) a nonfiring collector's replica of an antique firearm which was designed prior to 1898, is historically significant, and is offered for sale in conjunction with a wall plaque or presentation case; (2) a nonfiring collector's replica of a firearm which was designed after 1898, is historically significant, was issued as a commemorative by a nonprofit organization, and is offered for sale in conjunction with a wall plaque or presentation case; or (3) a device, as defined in subdivision (g) of Section 12001. *(Amended by Stats 1991 ch 950 §1.5, eff. 1/1/92.)*

§417.3. Firearm drawn at occupant of a motor vehicle.

Every person who, except in self-defense, in the presence of any other person who is an occupant of a motor vehicle proceeding on a public street or highway, draws or exhibits any firearm, whether loaded or unloaded, in a threatening manner against another person in such a way as to cause a reasonable person apprehension or fear of bodily harm is guilty of a felony punishable by imprisonment in the state prison for 16 months or two or three years or by imprisonment for 16 months or two or three years and a three thousand dollar ($3,000) fine.

Nothing in this section shall preclude or prohibit prosecution under any other statute. *(Added by Stats 1987 ch 1433 §1.)*

§417.6. Serious bodily injury in commission of specified weapons offense.

(a) If, in the commission of a violation of Section 417, 417.1, or 417.8, serious bodily injury is intentionally inflicted by the person drawing or exhibiting the firearm or deadly weapon, the offense shall be punished by imprisonment in the county jail not exceeding one year or by imprisonment in the state prison. As used in this section, "serious bodily injury" means a serious impairment of physical condition, including, but not limited to, the following: loss of consciousness; concussion; bone fracture; protracted loss or impairment of function of any bodily member or organ; a wound requiring extensive suturing; and serious disfigurement.

(b) When a person is convicted of a violation of Section 417, 417.1, or 417.8 and the deadly weapon or firearm used by the person is owned by that person, the court shall order that the weapon or firearm be deemed a nuisance and disposed of in the manner provided by Section 12028.

§417.8. Exhibiting deadly weapon with intent to resist arrest.

Every person who draws or exhibits any firearm, whether loaded or unloaded, or other deadly weapon, with the intent to resist or prevent the arrest or detention of himself or another by a peace officer shall be imprisoned in the state prison for two, three, or four years.

§418. Forcible entry and detainer.

Every person using or procuring, encouraging or assisting another to use, any force or violence in entering upon or detaining any lands or other possessions of another, except in the cases and in the manner allowed by law, is guilty of a misdemeanor.

§419. Returning to take possession of lands after being removed by legal proceedings.

Every person who has been removed from any lands by process of law, or who has removed from any lands pursuant to the lawful adjudication or direction of any court, tribunal, or officer, and who afterwards unlawfully returns to settle, reside upon, or take possession of such lands, is guilty of a misdemeanor.

§420. Preventing entry upon public lands.

Every person who unlawfully prevents, hinders, or obstructs any person from peaceably entering upon or establishing a settlement or residence on any tract of public land of the United States within the State of California, subject to settlement or entry under any of the public land laws of the United States; or who unlawfully hinders, prevents, or obstructs free passage over or through the public lands of the United States within the State of California, for the purpose of entry, settlement, or residence, as aforesaid, is guilty of a misdemeanor.

TITLE 11.5

TERRORIST THREATS
(Added by Stats 1988 ch 1256 §4, eff. 9/23/88. Former Title 11.5 repealed by Stats 1987 ch 828.)

§422. Punishment for threats to commit crime.

Any person who willfully threatens to commit a crime which will result in death or great bodily injury to another person, with the specific intent that the statement is to be taken as a threat, even if there is no intent of actually carrying it out, which, on its face and under the circumstances in which it is made, is so unequivocal, unconditional, immediate, and specific as to convey to the person threatened, a gravity of purpose and an immediate prospect of execution of the threat, and thereby causes that person reasonably to be in sustained fear for his or her own safety or for his or her immediate family's safety, shall be punished by imprisonment in the county jail not to exceed one year, or by imprisonment in the state prison.

For the purposes of this section, "immediate family" means any spouse, whether by marriage or not, parent, child, any person related by consanguinity or affinity within the second degree, or any other person who regularly resides in the household, or who, within the prior six months, regularly resided in the household. *(Amended by Stats 1989 ch 1135 §1, eff. 1/1/90.)*

TITLE 11.6

CIVIL RIGHTS
(Added by Stats 1987 ch 1277 §4.)

§422.6. Interfering with person's civil rights.

(a) No person, whether or not acting under color of law, shall by force or threat of force, willfully injure, intimidate, interfere with, oppress, or threaten any other person in the free exercise or enjoyment of any right or privilege secured to him or her by the constitution or laws of this state or by the Constitution or laws of the United States because of the other person's race, color, religion, ancestry, national origin, disability, gender, or sexual orientation.

(b) No person, whether or not acting under color of law, shall knowingly deface, damage, or destroy the real or personal property of any other person for the purpose of intimidating or interfering with the free exercise or enjoyment of any right or privilege secured to the other person by the constitution or laws of this state or by the Constitution or laws of the United States, because of the other person's race, color, religion, ancestry, national origin, disability, gender, or sexual orientation.

(c) Any person convicted of violating subdivision (a) or (b) shall be punished by imprisonment in a county jail not to exceed one year, or by a fine not to exceed five thousand dollars ($5,000), or by both that imprisonment and fine. However, no person shall be convicted of violating subdivision (a) based upon speech alone, except upon a showing that the speech itself threatened violence against a specific person or group of persons and that the defendant had the apparent ability to carry out the threat. *(Amended by Stats 1991 ch 607, 1184 §1.5, eff. 1/1/92.)*

§422.7. Punishment for violation of a person's civil rights.

Except in the case of a person punished under Section 422.6, any crime which is not made punishable by imprisonment in the state prison shall be punishable by imprisonment in the state prison or in a county jail not to exceed one year, by a fine not to exceed ten thousand dollars ($10,000), or by both that imprisonment and fine, if the crime is committed against the person or property of another for the purpose of intimidating or interfering with that other person's free

© 1992 by J., B. & L. Gould
Printed in the U.S.A.   EP

exercise or enjoyment of any right secured to him or her by the constitution or laws of this state or by the Constitution or laws of the United States and because of the other person's race, color, religion, ancestry, national origin, disability, gender, or sexual orientation, under any of the following circumstances, which shall be charged in the accusatory pleading:

(a) The crime against the person of another either includes the present ability to commit a violent injury or causes actual physical injury.

(b) The crime against property causes damage in excess of five hundred dollars ($500).

(c) The person charged with a crime under this section has been convicted previously of a violation of subdivision (a) or (b) of Section 422.6, or has been convicted previously of a conspiracy to commit a crime described in subdivision (a) or (b) of Section 422.6. *(Amended by Stats 1991 ch 607, 1184 §2.5, eff. 1/1/92.)*

§422.75. Punishment for violation of a person's civil rights; additional term.

(a) Except in the case of a person punished under Section 422.7, a person who commits a felony or attempts to commit a felony because of the victim's race, color, religion, nationality, country of origin, ancestry, or sexual orientation shall receive an additional term of one, two, or three years in state prison at the court's discretion.

(b) Except in the case of a person punished under Section 422.7 or subdivision (a) of this section, any person who commits a felony or attempts to commit a felony because of the victim's race, color, religion, nationality, country of origin, ancestry, disability, or sexual orientation and who voluntarily acted in concert with another person either personally or by aiding and abetting another person shall receive an additional two, three, or four years in state prison, at the court's discretion.

(c) A person who is punished pursuant to subdivision (a) or (b) shall also receive an additional term of one year in state prison for each prior felony conviction on charges brought and tried separately in which it was found by the trier of the fact or admitted by the defendant that the crime was committed because of the victim's race, color, religion, nationality, country of origin, ancestry, disability, or sexual orientation. This additional term shall only apply where a sentence enhancement is not imposed pursuant to Section 667 or 667.5.

(d) The additional term in subdivisions (a), (b), and (c) shall not be imposed unless the allegation is charged in the accusatory pleading and admitted by the defendant or found to be true by the trier of fact.

(e) The additional term in subdivisions (a), (b), and (c) shall be in addition to any other punishment provided by law.

(f) Notwithstanding any other law, the court may strike the additional term in subdivisions (a), (b), and (c) if the court determines that there are mitigating circumstances and states on the record the reasons for striking the additional punishment. *(Added by Stats 1991 ch 607 §7, eff. 1/1/92.)*

§422.8. Limitation of prosecutions.

Except as otherwise required by law, nothing in this title shall be construed to prevent or limit the prosecution of any person pursuant to any provision of law. *(Amended by Stats 1991 ch 839 §4, eff. 1/1/92.)*

§422.9. Violations punishable as misdemeanors.

(a) Any willful and knowing violation of any order issued pursuant to subdivision (a) or (b) of Section 52.1 of the Civil Code shall be a misdemeanor punishable by a fine of not more than one thousand dollars ($1,000), or by imprisonment in the county jail for not more than six months, or by both the fine and imprisonment.

(b) A person who has previously been convicted one or more times of violating an order issued pursuant to subdivision (a) or (b) of Section 52.1 of the Civil Code upon charges separately brought and tried shall be imprisoned in the county jail for not more than one year. Subject to the discretion of the court, the prosecution shall have the opportunity to present witnesses and relevant evidence at the time of the sentencing of a defendant pursuant to this subdivision.

(c) The prosecuting agency of each county shall have the primary responsibility for the enforcement of orders issued pursuant to Section 52.1 of the Civil Code. *(Added by Stats 1987 ch 1277 §4.)*

§422.95. Racial or ethnic sensitivity training; condition of probation.

(a) In the case of any person who is granted probation for any offense defined in Section 422.6, 422.7, or 422.75, the court may order that the defendant complete a class or program on racial or ethnic sensitivity, or other similar training in the area of civil rights, if such class, program, or training is available, as a condition of probation.

(b) It is the intent of the Legislature to encourage counties, cities, and school districts to establish education and training programs to prevent violations of civil rights and hate crimes. *(Added by Stats 1991 ch 607 §8, eff. 1/1/92.)*

TITLE 12

OF CRIMES AGAINST THE REVENUE AND PROPERTY OF THIS STATE

§424. Embezzlement and falsification of accounts by public officers.

Each officer of this state, or of any county, city, town, or district of this state, and every other person charged with the receipt, safekeeping, transfer, or disbursement of public moneys, who either:

1. Without authority of law, appropriates the same, or any portion thereof, to his own use, or to the use of another; or,

2. Loans the same or any portion thereof; makes any profit out of, or uses the same for any purpose not authorized by law; or,

3. Knowingly keeps any false account, or makes any false entry or erasure in any account of or relating to the same; or,

4. Fraudulently alters, falsifies, conceals, destroys, or obliterates any such account; or,

5. Willfully refuses or omits to pay over, on demand, any public moneys in his hands, upon the presentation of a draft, order, or warrant drawn upon such moneys by competent authority; or,

6. Willfully omits to transfer the same, when such transfer is required by law; or,

7. Willfully omits or refuses to pay over to any officer or person authorized by law to receive the same,

any money received by him under any duty imposed by law so to pay over the same;—

Is punishable by imprisonment in the state prison for two, three or four years, and is disqualified from holding any office in this state.

As used in this section, "public moneys" includes the proceeds derived from the sale of bonds or other evidence of indebtedness authorized by the legislative body of any city, county, district, or public agency.

§425. Officers neglecting to pay over public moneys.

Every officer charged with the receipt, safe keeping, or disbursement of public moneys, who neglects or fails to keep and pay over the same in the manner prescribed by law is guilty of a felony.

§426. Public moneys defined.

The phrase "public moneys," as used in sections 424 and 425, includes all bonds and evidence of indebtedness, and all moneys belonging to the state, or any city, county, town, district, or public agency therein, and all moneys, bonds, and evidences of indebtedness received or held by state, county, district, city, town, or public agency officers in their official capacity. *(Amended by Stats 1987 ch 828 §29.)*

§428. Obstructing officer in collecting revenues.

Every person who willfully obstructs or hinders any public officer from collecting any revenue, taxes, or other sums of money in which the people of this State are interested, and which such officer is by law empowered to collect, is guilty of a misdemeanor.

§429. Failure of telephone companies to collect or remit fees.

Any provider of telecommunications services in this state that intentionally fails to collect or remit, as may be required, the annual fee imposed pursuant to Section 431 of the Public Utilities Code, the universal telephone service surcharge imposed pursuant to Section 879 or 879.5 of the Public Utilities Code, the fee for filing an application for a certificate of public convenience and necessity as provided in Section 1904 of the Public Utilities Code, or the surcharge imposed pursuant to subdivision (d) of Section 2881 of the Public Utilities Code, whether imposed on the provider or measured by the provider's service charges, is guilty of a misdemeanor. *(Added by Stats 1990 ch 390 §2, eff. 1/1/91.)*

§431. Delivering receipts for poll taxes, other than prescribed by law, or collecting poll taxes, etc., without giving the receipt prescribed by law.

Every person who uses or gives any receipt, except that prescribed by law, as evidence of the payment of any poll-tax, road-tax, or license of any kind, or who receives payment of such tax or license without delivering the receipt prescribed by law, or who inserts the name of more than one person therein, is guilty of a misdemeanor.

§432. Having blank receipts for licenses, etc., other than those prescribed by law.

Every person who has in his possession, with intent to circulate or sell, any blank licenses or poll tax receipts other than those furnished by the controller of state or county auditor, is guilty of felony.

§436. Unlawfully acting as auctioneer.

Every person who acts as an auctioneer in violation of the laws of this state relating to auctions and auctioneers, is guilty of a misdemeanor.

§439. Effecting insurance on account of foreign companies that have not complied with the laws of this State.

Every person who in this State procures, or agrees to procure, any insurance for a resident of this State, from any insurance company not incorporated under the laws of this State, unless such company or its agent has filed the bond required by the laws of this State relating to insurance, is guilty of a misdemeanor.

§440. Officer charged with collection, etc., of revenue, refusing to permit inspection of his books.

Every officer charged with the collection, receipt, or disbursement of any portion of the revenue of this state, who, upon demand, fails or refuses to permit the controller or attorney general to inspect his books, papers, receipts, and records pertaining to his office, is guilty of a misdemeanor.

TITLE 13

OF CRIMES AGAINST PROPERTY

CHAPTER 1

ARSON

§450. Terms defined.

In this chapter, the following terms have the following meanings:

(a) "Structure" means any building, or commercial or public tent, bridge, tunnel, or powerplant.

(b) "Forest land" means any brush covered land, cut-over land, forest, grasslands, or woods.

(c) "Property" means real property or personal property, other than a structure or forest land.

(d) "Inhabited" means currently being used for dwelling purposes whether occupied or not. "Inhabited structure" and "inhabited property" do not include the real property on which an inhabited structure or an inhabited property is located.

(e) "Maliciously" imports a wish to vex, defraud, annoy, or injure another person, or an intent to do a wrongful act, established either by proof or presumption of law.

(f) "Recklessly" means a person is aware of and consciously disregards a substantial and unjustifiable risk that his or her act will set fire to, burn, or cause to burn a structure, forest land, or property. The risk shall be of such nature and degree that disregard thereof constitutes a gross deviation from the standard of conduct that a reasonable person would observe in the situation. A person who creates such a risk but is unaware thereof solely by reason of voluntary intoxication also acts recklessly with respect thereto.

§451. Punishment for arson.

A person is guilty of arson when he or she willfully and maliciously sets fire to or burns or causes to be burned or who aids, counsels, or procures the burning of, any structure, forest land, or property.

© 1992 by J., B. & L. Gould
Printed in the U.S.A.   EP

(a) Arson that causes great bodily injury is a felony punishable by imprisonment in the state prison for five, seven, or nine years.

(b) Arson that causes an inhabited structure or inhabited property to burn is a felony punishable by imprisonment in the state prison for three, five, or eight years.

(c) Arson of a structure or forest land is a felony punishable by imprisonment in the state prison for two, four, or six years. However, in addition to any enhancement imposed pursuant to Section 667, if the person was previously convicted of arson of a structure or forest land and the prior conviction is charged in the accusatory pleading and admitted by the defendant or found to be true by the trier of fact, in addition and consecutive to the punishment prescribed for the felony of which he or she has been convicted the person shall be punished by an additional term of imprisonment in the state prison for one, two, or three years.

(d) Arson of property is a felony punishable by imprisonment in the state prison for 16 months, two, or three years. For purposes of this paragraph, arson of property does not include one burning or causing to be burned his or her own personal property unless there is an intent to defraud or there is injury to another person or another person's structure, forest land, or property.

(e) In the case of any person convicted of violating this section while confined in a state prison, prison road camp, prison forestry camp, or other prison camp or prison farm, or while confined in a county jail while serving a term of imprisonment for a felony or misdemeanor conviction, any sentence imposed shall be consecutive to the sentence for which the person was then confined. (Amended by Stats 1990 ch 63 §1, eff. 5/1/90.)

§452. Punishment for unlawfully causing a fire.

A person is guilty of unlawfully causing a fire when he recklessly sets fire to or burns or causes to be burned, any structure, forest land or property.

(a) Unlawfully causing a fire that causes great bodily injury is a felony punishable by imprisonment in the state prison for two, four or six years, or by imprisonment in the county jail for not more than one year, or by a fine, or by both such imprisonment and fine.

(b) Unlawfully causing a fire that causes an inhabited structure or inhabited property to burn is a felony punishable by imprisonment in the state prison for two, three or four years, or by imprisonment in the county jail for not more than one year, or by a fine, or by both such imprisonment and fine.

(c) Unlawfully causing a fire of a structure or forest land is a felony punishable by imprisonment in the state prison for 16 months, two or three years, or by imprisonment in the county jail for not more than six months, or by a fine, or by both such imprisonment and fine.

(d) Unlawfully causing a fire of property is a misdemeanor. For purposes of this paragraph, unlawfully causing a fire of property does not include one burning or causing to be burned his own personal property unless there is injury to another person or to another person's structure, forest land or property.

(e) In the case of any person convicted of violating this section while confined in a state prison, prison road camp, prison forestry camp, or other prison camp or prison farm, or while confined in a county jail while serving a term of imprisonment for a felony or misdemeanor conviction, any sentence imposed shall be consecutive to the sentence for which the person was then confined.

§453. Possession of flammable or explosive material.

(a) Every person who possesses any flammable, explosive or combustible material or substance, or any device in an arrangement or preparation, with intent to willfully and maliciously use such material, substance or device to set fire to or burn any structure, forest land or property, is punishable by imprisonment in the state prison, or in the county jail, not exceeding one year.

(b) Every person who possesses, manufactures or disposes of a firebomb is guilty of a felony.

For the purposes of this subdivision, "disposes of" means to give, give away, loan, offer, offer for sale, sell, or transfer.

For the purposes of this subdivision, a "firebomb" is a breakable container containing a flammable liquid with a flashpoint of 150 degrees Fahrenheit or less, having a wick or similar device capable of being ignited, but no device commercially manufactured primarily for the purpose of illumination shall be deemed to be a firebomb for the purposes of this subdivision.

(c) Subdivisions (a) and (b) of this section shall not prohibit the authorized use or possession of any material, substance or device described therein by a member of the armed forces of the United States or by firemen, police officers, peace officers, or law enforcement officers authorized by the properly constituted authorities; nor shall those subdivisions prohibit the use or possession of any material, substance or device described therein when used solely for scientific research, or educational purposes, or for disposal of brush under permit as provided for in Section 4494 of the Public Resources Code, or for any other lawful burning. Subdivision (b) of this section shall not prohibit the manufacture or disposal of a firebomb for the parties or purposes described in this subdivision.

§454. Violation during state of emergency.

Every person who violates any of the provisions of Section 451 or 452 during and within an area of a:

(a) State of insurrection pursuant to Section 143 of the Military and Veterans Code, or

(b) State of emergency pursuant to Section 8625 of the Government Code, when proclaimed by the Governor is punishable by imprisonment in the state prison for three, five or seven years.

§455. Acts preliminary to arson.

Any person who willfully and maliciously attempts to set fire to or attempts to burn or to aid, counsel or procure the burning of any structure, forest land or property, or who commits any act preliminary thereto, or in furtherance thereof, is punishable by imprisonment in the state prison for 16 months, two or three years.

The placing or distributing of any flammable, explosive or combustible material or substance, or any device in or about any structure, forest land or property in an arrangement or preparation with intent to eventually willfully and maliciously set fire to or burn same, or to procure the setting fire to or burning of the same shall, for the purposes of this act constitute an attempt to burn such structure, forest land or property.

§456. Fine upon conviction.

(a) Upon conviction for any felony violation of this chapter, in addition to the penalty prescribed, the court may impose a fine not to exceed fifty thousand dollars ($50,000) unless a greater amount is provided by law.

(b) When any person is convicted of a violation of any provision of this chapter and the reason he committed the violation was for pecuniary gain, in addition to the penalty prescribed and instead of the fine provided in subdivision (a), the court may impose a fine of twice the anticipated or actual gross gain.

§457. Submitting to psychiatric or psychological examination before sentencing.

Upon conviction of any person for a violation of any provision of this chapter, the court may order that such person, for the purpose of sentencing, submit to a psychiatric or psychological examination.

§457.1. Registration requirement for arsonist.

(a) As used in this section, "arson" means a violation of Section 451 or 453.

(b) Upon a conviction of the offense of arson or attempted arson, the court may impose, in addition to any other penalty prescribed by law, a requirement that the person shall register with the chief of police of the city in which he or she resides, or with the sheriff of the county if he or she resides in an unincorporated area, within 30 days of coming into any county or city in which he or she expects to reside or is temporarily domiciled for at least 30 days. The court may require the person to register under this subdivision only if it finds any of the following:

(1) The person committing the offense has previously been convicted of a violation of Section 451 or 453.

(2) The person is convicted of multiple counts of Section 451 or 453, relating to different events or occurrences.

(3) The person in committing the offense exhibited compulsive behavior.

The court shall state on the record the reasons for its findings and the reasons for requiring or not requiring registration.

(c) Any person required to register pursuant to this section who is discharged or paroled from a jail, prison, school, road camp, or other institution where he or she was confined because of the commission or attempted commission of arson shall, prior to the discharge, parole, or release, be informed of his or her duty to register under this section by the official in charge of the place of confinement. The official shall require the person to read and sign such form as may be required by the Department of Justice, stating that the duty of the person to register under this section has been explained to him or her. The official in charge of the place of confinement shall obtain the address where the person expects to reside upon his or her discharge, parole, or release and shall report the address to the Department of Justice. The official in charge of the place of confinement shall give one copy of the form to the person, and shall, not later than 45 days prior to the scheduled release of the person, send one copy to the appropriate law enforcement agency having local jurisdiction where the person expects to reside upon

his or her discharge, parole, or release; one copy to the prosecuting agency which prosecuted the person; and one copy to the Department of Justice. The official in charge of the place of confinement shall retain one copy. All forms shall be transmitted within such times as to be received by the local law enforcement agency and prosecuting agency 30 days prior to the discharge, parole, or release of the person.

(d) Any person who is required to register pursuant to this section who is released on probation or discharged upon payment of a fine shall, prior to the release or discharge, be informed of his or her duty to register under this section by the court in which he or she has been convicted, and the court shall require the person to read and sign such form as may be required by the Department of Justice, stating that the duty of the person to register under this section has been explained to him or her. The court shall obtain the address where the person expects to reside upon his or her release or discharge and shall report within three days the address to the Department of Justice. The court shall give one copy of the form to the person, and shall send two copies to the Department of Justice, which, in turn, shall forward one copy to the appropriate law enforcement agency having local jurisdiction where the person expects to reside upon his or her discharge, parole, or release.

(e) The registration shall consist of (1) a statement in writing signed by the person, giving the information as may be required by the Department of Justice, and (2) the fingerprints and photograph of the person. Within three days thereafter, the registering law enforcement agency shall forward the statement, fingerprints, and photograph to the Department of Justice.

(f) If any person required to register by this section changes his or her residence address, he or she shall inform, in writing within 10 days, the law enforcement agency with whom he or she last registered of his or her new address. The law enforcement agency shall, within three days after receipt of the information, forward it to the Department of Justice. The Department of Justice shall forward appropriate registration data to the law enforcement agency having local jurisdiction of the new place of residence.

(g) In the case of a person convicted for the first time of arson, the person shall be required to comply with the requirements of this section only for a period of five years after the discharge from prison, release from jail, or termination of probation or parole of the person convicted.

(h) Any person required to register under this section who violates any of the provisions thereof is guilty of a misdemeanor. Any person who has been convicted of arson or attempted arson and who is required to register under this section who willfully violates any of the provisions thereof is guilty of a misdemeanor and shall be sentenced to serve a term of not less than 90 days nor more than one year in the county jail. In no event does the court have the power to absolve a person who willfully violates this section from the obligation of spending at least 90 days of confinement in the county jail and of completing probation of at least one year.

(i) Whenever any person is released on parole or probation and is required to register under this section but fails to do so within the time prescribed, the Board of Prison Terms, the Department of the Youth Author-

© 1992 by J., B. & L. Gould
Printed in the U.S.A.   EP

ity, or the court, as the case may be, shall order the parole or probation of that person revoked.

(j) The statements, photographs, and fingerprints required by this section shall not be open to inspection by the public or by any person other than a regularly employed peace or other law enforcement officer.

(k) In any case in which a person who would be required to register pursuant to this section is to be temporarily sent outside the institution where he or she is confined on any assignment within a city or county, including firefighting, disaster control, or of whatever nature the assignment may be, the local law enforcement agency having jurisdiction over the place or places where that assignment shall occur shall be notified within a reasonable time prior to removal from the institution. This subdivision shall not apply to any person temporarily released under guard from the institution where he or she is confined.

(*l*) Nothing in this section shall be construed to conflict with Section 1203.4 concerning termination of probation and release from penalties and disabilities of probation.

A person required to register under this section may initiate a proceeding under Chapter 3.5 (commencing with Section 4852.01) of Title 6 of Part 3, and upon obtaining a certificate of rehabilitation, shall be relieved of any further duty to register under this section. This certificate shall not relieve the petitioner of the duty to register under this section for any offense subject to this section of which he or she is convicted in the future. *(Amended by Stats 1989 ch 311 §1, eff. 7/1/90.)*

CHAPTER 2

BURGLARY

§458. Cargo container defined.

As used in this chapter, the term "cargo container" means a receptacle with all of the following characteristics:

(a) Of a permanent character and accordingly strong enough to be suitable for repeated use.

(b) Specially designed to facilitate the carriage of goods, by one or more modes of transport, one of which shall be by vessels, without intermediate reloading.

(c) Fitted with devices permitting its ready handling, particularly its transfer from one mode of transport to another.

(d) So designed to be easy to fill and empty.

(e) Having a cubic displacement of 1,000 cubic feet or more.

§459. Burglary.

Every person who enters any house, room, apartment, tenement, shop, warehouse, store, mill, barn, stable, outhouse or other building, tent, vessel, as defined in Section 21 of the Harbors and Navigation Code, floating home, as defined in subdivision (d) of Section 18075.55 of the Health and Safety Code, railroad car, locked or sealed cargo container, whether or not mounted on a vehicle, trailer coach, as defined in Section 635 of the Vehicle Code, any house car, as defined in Section 362 of the Vehicle Code, inhabited camper, as defined in Section 243 of the Vehicle Code, vehicle as defined by the Vehicle Code, when the doors are locked, aircraft as defined by Section 21012 of the Public Utilities Code, or mine or any underground portion thereof, with intent to commit grand or petit

larceny or any felony is guilty of burglary. As used in this chapter, "inhabited" means currently being used for dwelling purposes, whether occupied or not. A house, trailer, vessel designed for habitation, or portion of a building is currently being used for dwelling purposes if, at the time of the burglary, it was not occupied solely because a natural or other disaster caused the occupants to leave the premises. *(Amended by Stats 1991 ch 942 §14, eff. 1/1/92.)*

§460. Degrees of burglary.

(a) Every burglary of an inhabited dwelling house, vessel, as defined in the Harbors and Navigation Code, which is inhabited and designed for habitation, floating home, as defined in subdivision (d) of Section 18075.55 of the Health and Safety Code, or trailer coach, as defined by the Vehicle Code, or the inhabited portion of any other building, is burglary of the first degree.

(b) All other kinds of burglary are of the second degree.

(c) This section shall not be construed to supersede or affect Section 464 of the Penal Code. *(Amended by Stats 1991 ch 942 §15, eff. 1/1/92.)*

§461. Punishment for burglary.

Burglary is punishable as follows:

1. Burglary in the first degree: by imprisonment in the state prison for two, four, or six years.

2. Burglary in the second degree: by imprisonment in the county jail not exceeding one year or in the state prison.

§462. Probation.

(a) Except in unusual cases where the interests of justice would best be served if the person is granted probation, probation shall not be granted to any person who is convicted of a burglary of an inhabited dwelling house or trailer coach, as defined in Section 635 of the Vehicle Code, or the inhabited portion of any other building.

(b) If the court grants probation under subdivision (a), it shall specify the reason or reasons for such order on the court record.

§462.5. Custodial institution burglary; probation.

(a) Except in unusual cases where the interests of justice would best be served if the person is granted probation, probation shall not be granted to any person who is convicted of a felony custodial institution burglary. In any case in which a person is convicted of a misdemeanor custodial institution burglary, such person shall be confined in the county jail for not less than 90 days nor more than one year except in unusual cases where the interests of justice would best be served by the granting of probation.

(b) As used in this section, "custodial institution burglary" shall mean a violation of Section 459 on the grounds of any jail or correctional institution with the intent to steal items to use or convert for use as weapons, escape tools, or intoxicating drugs.

(c) If the court grants probation under subdivision (a), it shall specify the reason or reasons for such order on the court record.

(d) Any person convicted of custodial institution burglary shall serve his or her sentence, including enhancements, consecutive to any other sentence in effect or pending. The felony sentence shall be calculated under Section 1170.1.

§463. Looting or petit theft during "state emergency".

(a) Every person who violates Section 459, punishable as a second degree burglary pursuant to subdivision 2 of Section 461, during and within an affected county in a "state of emergency" or a "local emergency" resulting from an earthquake or a flood shall be guilty of the crime of looting punishable by imprisonment in a county jail for one year or in the state prison. Any person convicted under this subdivision who is eligible for probation and who is granted probation shall, as a condition thereof, be confined in a county jail for at least 180 days, except that the court may, in the case where the interest of justice would best be served, reduce or eliminate that mandatory jail sentence, if the court specifies on the record and enters into the minutes the circumstances indicating that the interests of justice would best be served by that disposition.

(b) Every person who commits the crime of grand theft, as defined in Section 487, during and within an affected county in a "state of emergency" or a "local emergency" resulting from an earthquake or a flood shall be guilty of the crime of looting punishable by imprisonment in a county jail for one year or in the state prison. Any person convicted under this subdivision who is eligible for probation and who is granted probation shall, as a condition thereof, be confined in a county jail for at least 180 days, except that the court may, in the case where the interest of justice would best be served, reduce or eliminate that mandatory jail sentence, if the court specifies on the record and enters into the minutes the circumstances indicating that the interests of justice would best be served by that disposition.

(c) Every person who commits the crime of petty theft, as defined in Section 488, during and within an affected county in a "state of emergency" or a "local emergency" resulting from an earthquake or a flood shall be guilty of a misdemeanor punishable by imprisonment in a county jail for six months. Any person convicted under this subdivision who is eligible for probation and who is granted probation shall, as a condition thereof, be confined in a county jail for at least 90 days, except that the court may, in the case where the interest of justice would best be served, reduce or eliminate that mandatory minimum jail sentence, if the court specifies on the record and enters into the minutes the circumstances indicating that the interests of justice would best be served by that disposition.

(d) (1) For purposes of this section, "state of emergency" means conditions which, by reason of their magnitude, are or are likely to be beyond the control of the services, personnel, equipment, and facilities of any single county, city and county, or city and require the combined forces of a mutual aid region or regions to combat.

(2) For purposes of this section, "local emergency" means conditions which, by reason of their magnitude, are or are likely to be beyond the control of the services, personnel, equipment, and facilities of any single county, city and county, or city and require the combined forces of a mutual aid region or regions to combat.

(3) For purposes of this section, a "state of emergency" shall exist from the time of the proclamation of the condition of the emergency until three days thereafter. For purposes of this section only, a "local emergency" shall exist from the time of the proclamation of the condition of the emergency by the local governing body pursuant to Section 8630 of the Government Code until three days thereafter.

(4) Consensual entry into a commercial structure with the intent to commit a violation of Section 470, 476, 476a, 484f, or 484g of the Penal Code, shall not be charged as a violation under this section. (Added by Stats 1990 ch 1126 §1, eff. 1/1/91.)

§464. Use of burning device or explosive.

Any person who, with intent to commit crime, enters, either by day or by night, any building, whether inhabited or not, and opens or attempts to open any vault, safe, or other secure place by use of acetylene torch or electric arc, burning bar, thermal lance, oxygen lance, or any other similar device capable of burning through steel, concrete, or any other solid substance, or by use of nitroglycerine, dynamite, gunpowder, or any other explosive, is guilty of a felony and, upon conviction, shall be punished by imprisonment in the state prison for a term of three, five, or seven years.

CHAPTER 3

BURGLARIOUS AND LARCENOUS INSTRUMENTS AND DEADLY WEAPONS

§466. Possessing burglary tools.

Every person having upon him or her in his or her possession a picklock, crow, keybit, crowbar, screwdriver, vice grip pliers, water-pump pliers, slidehammer, slim jim, tension bar, lock pick gun, tubular lock pick, floor-safe door puller, master key, or other instrument or tool with intent feloniously to break or enter into any building, railroad car, aircraft, or vessel, trailer coach, or vehicle as defined in the Vehicle Code, or who shall knowingly make or alter, or shall attempt to make or alter, any key or other instrument above named so that the same will fit or open the lock of a building, railroad car, aircraft, or vessel, trailer coach, or vehicle as defined in the Vehicle Code, without being requested so to do by some person having the right to open the same, or who shall make, alter, or repair any instrument or thing, knowing or having reason to believe that it is intended to be used in committing a misdemeanor or felony, is guilty of misdemeanor. Any of the structures mentioned in Section 459 shall be deemed to be a building within the meaning of this section.

§466.1. Sale of burglary tools.

Any person who knowingly and willfully sells or provides a lock pick, a tension bar, a lock pick gun, a tubular lock pick, or a floor-safe door puller, to another, whether or not for compensation, shall obtain the name, address, telephone number, if any, date of birth, and driver's license number or identification number, if any, of the person to whom the device is sold or provided. This information, together with the date the device was sold or provided and the signature of the person to whom the device was sold or provided, shall be set forth on a bill of sale or receipt. A copy of each bill of sale or receipt shall be retained for one year and shall be open to inspection by any peace officer during business hours.

Any person who violates any provision of this section is guilty of a misdemeanor.

© 1992 by J., B. & L. Gould
Printed in the U.S.A.   EP

§466.3. Tools for breaking coin-operated machine.

(a) Whoever possesses a key, tool, instrument, explosive, or device, or a drawing, print, or mold of a key, tool, instrument, explosive, or device, designed to open, break into, tamper with, or damage a coin-operated machine as defined in subdivision (b), with intent to commit a theft from such machine, is punishable by imprisonment in the county jail for not more than one year, or by fine of not more than one thousand dollars ($1,000), or by both.

(b) As used in this section, the term "coin-operated machine" shall include any automatic vending machine or any part thereof, parking meter, coin telephone, coin laundry machine, coin dry cleaning machine, amusement machine, music machine, vending machine dispensing goods or services, or money-changer.

§466.5. Master keys.

(a) Every person who, with the intent to use it in the commission of an unlawful act, possesses a motor vehicle master key or a motor vehicle wheel lock master key is guilty of a misdemeanor.

(b) Every person who, with the intent to use it in the commission of an unlawful act, uses a motor vehicle master key to open a lock or operate the ignition switch of any motor vehicle or uses a motor vehicle wheel lock master key to open a wheel lock on any motor vehicle is guilty of a misdemeanor.

(c) Every person who knowingly manufactures for sale, advertises for sale, offers for sale, or sells a motor vehicle master key or a motor vehicle wheel lock master key, except to persons who use such keys in their lawful occupations or businesses, is guilty of a misdemeanor.

(d) As used in this section:

(1) "Motor vehicle master key" means a key which will operate all the locks or ignition switches, or both the locks and ignition switches, in a given group of motor vehicle locks or motor vehicle ignition switches, or both motor vehicle locks and motor vehicle ignition switches, each of which can be operated by a key which will not operate one or more of the other locks or ignition switches in such group.

(2) "Motor vehicle wheel lock" means a device attached to a motor vehicle wheel for theft protection purposes which can be removed only by a key unit unique to the wheel lock attached to a particular motor vehicle.

(3) "Motor vehicle wheel lock master key" means a key unit which will operate all the wheel locks in a given group of motor vehicle wheel locks, each of which can be operated by a key unit which will not operate any of the other wheel locks in the group.

§466.6. Making of motor vehicle key other than by duplication.

(a) Any person who makes a key capable of operating the ignition of a motor vehicle for another by any method other than by the duplication of an existing key, whether or not for compensation, shall obtain the name, address, telephone number, if any, date of birth, and driver's license number or identification number of the person requesting or purchasing the key; and the registration or identification number, license number, year, make, model, color, and vehicle identification number of the vehicle for which the key is to be made. Such information, together with the date the key was made and the signature of the person for whom the key was made, shall be set forth on a work order. A copy of each such work order shall be retained for one year and shall be open to inspection by any peace officer during business hours.

Any person who violates any provision of this subdivision is guilty of a misdemeanor.

(b) The provisions of this section shall include, but are not limited to, the making of a key from key codes or impressions.

(c) Nothing contained in this section shall be construed to prohibit the duplication of any key for a motor vehicle from another such key.

§466.7. Key made without consent of owner.

Every person who, with the intent to use it in the commission of an unlawful act, possesses a motor vehicle key with knowledge that such key was made without the consent of either the registered or legal owner of the motor vehicle or of a person who is in lawful possession of the motor vehicle, is guilty of a misdemeanor.

§466.8. Onsite making of residence key.

(a) Any person who knowingly and willfully makes a key capable of opening any door or other means of entrance to any residence for another by any method involving an onsite inspection of such door or entrance, whether or not for compensation, shall obtain, together with the date the key was made, the street address of the residence, and the signature of the person for whom the key was made, on a work order form, the following information regarding the person requesting or purchasing the key:

(1) Name.

(2) Address.

(3) Telephone number, if any.

(4) Date of birth.

(5) Driver's license number or identification number, if any.

A copy of each such work order shall be retained for one year and shall be open to inspection by any peace officer during business hours.

Any person who violates any provision of this subdivision is guilty of a misdemeanor.

(b) Nothing contained in this section shall be construed to prohibit the duplication of any key for a residence from another such key.

§467. Having possession of deadly weapons with intent to commit an assault.

Every person having upon him any deadly weapon with intent to assault another, is guilty of a misdemeanor.

§468. Sniperscopes.

Any person who knowingly buys, sells, receives, disposes of, conceals, or has in his possession a sniperscope shall be guilty of a misdemeanor, punishable by a fine not to exceed one thousand dollars ($1,000) or by imprisonment in the county jail for not more than one year, or by both such fine and imprisonment.

As used in this section, sniperscope means any attachment, device or similar contrivance designed for or adaptable to use on a firearm which, through the use of a projected infrared light source and electronic telescope, enables the operator thereof to visually determine and locate the presence of objects during the nighttime.

This section shall not prohibit the authorized use or possession of such sniper scope by a member of the armed forces of the United States or by police officers, peace officers, or law enforcement officers authorized by the properly constituted authorities for the enforcement of law or ordinances; nor shall this section prohibit the use or possession of such sniperscope when used solely for scientific research or educational purposes.

§469. Duplication of key to public building.

Any person who knowingly makes, duplicates, causes to be duplicated, or uses, or attempts to make, duplicate, cause to be duplicated, or use, or has in his possession any key to a building or other area owned, operated, or controlled by the State of California, any state agency, board, or commission, a county, city, or any public school or community college district without authorization from the person in charge of such building or area or his designated representative and with knowledge of the lack of such authorization is guilty of a misdemeanor.

CHAPTER 4

FORGERY AND COUNTERFEITING

§470. Forgery of legal instruments.

(a) Every person who, with intent to defraud, signs the name of another person, or a fictitious person, knowing that he or she has no authority so to do, to, or falsely makes, alters, forges, or counterfeits, any charter, letters patent, deed, lease, indenture, writing obligatory, will, testament, codicil, bond, covenant, bank bill or note, post note, check, draft, bill of exchange, contract, promissory note, due bill for the payment of money or property, receipt for money or property, passage ticket, lottery ticket or share purporting to be issued under the California State Lottery Act of 1984, trading stamp, power of attorney, certificate of ownership or other document evidencing ownership of a vehicle or undocumented vessel, or any certificate of any share, right, or interest in the stock of any corporation or association, or any controller's warrant for the payment of money at the treasury, county order or warrant, or request for the payment of money, or the delivery of goods or chattels of any kind, or for the delivery of any instrument of writing, or acquittance, release, or receipt for money or goods, or any acquittance, release, or discharge of any debt, account, suit, action, demand, or other thing, real or personal, or any transfer or assurance of money, certificate of shares of stock, goods, chattels, or other property whatever, or any letter of attorney, or other power to receive money, or to receive or transfer certificates of shares of stock or annuities, or to let, lease, dispose of, alien, or convey any goods, chattels, lands, or tenements, or other estate, real or personal, or any acceptance or endorsement of any bill of exchange, promissory note, draft, order, or any assignment of any bond, writing obligatory, promissory note, or other contract for money or other property; or counterfeits or forges the seal or handwriting of another; or utters, publishes, passes, or attempts to pass, as true and genuine, any of the above-named false, altered, forged, or counterfeited matters, as above specified and described, knowing the same to be false, altered, forged, or counterfeited, with intent to prejudice, damage, or defraud any person; or who, with intent to defraud, alters, corrupts, or falsifies any record of any will, codicil, conveyance, or other instrument, the record of which is by law evidence, or any record of any judgment of a court or the return of any officer to any process of any court, is guilty of forgery.

(b) Upon a trial for forging any bill or note purporting to be the bill or note of an incorporated company or bank, or for passing, or attempting to pass, or having in possession with intent to pass, any forged bill or note, it is not necessary to prove the incorporation of the bank or company by charter or act of incorporation, but it may be proved by general reputation; and persons of skill are competent witnesses to prove that the bill or note is forged or counterfeited. *(Amended by Stats 1989 ch 897 §20, eff. 1/1/90.)*

§470a. Falsification or reproduction of identification card or driver's license.

Every person who alters, falsifies, forges, duplicates or in any manner reproduces or counterfeits any driver's license or identification card issued by a governmental agency with the intent that such driver's license or identification card be used to facilitate the commission of any forgery, is punishable by imprisonment in the state prison, or by imprisonment in the county jail for not more than one year.

§470b. Displaying reproduced or false identification.

Every person who displays or causes or permits to be displayed or has in his possession any driver's license or identification card of the type enumerated in Section 470a with the intent that such driver's license or identification card be used to facilitate the commission of any forgery, is punishable by imprisonment in the state prison, or by imprisonment in the county jail for not more than one year.

§471. Making false entries in records or returns.

Every person who, with intent to defraud another, makes, forges, or alters any entry in any book of records, or any instrument purporting to be any record or return specified in the preceding section, is guilty of forgery.

§471.5. Alerting or modifying medical records.

Any person who alters or modifies the medical record of any person, with fraudulent intent, or who, with fraudulent intent, creates any false medical record, is guilty of a misdemeanor.

§472. Forgery of public and corporate seals.

Every person who, with intent to defraud another, forges, or counterfeits the seal of this state, the seal of any public officer authorized by law, the seal of any court of record, or the seal of any corporation, or any other public seal authorized or recognized by the laws of this state, or of any other state, government, or country, or who falsely makes, forges, or counterfeits any impression purporting to be an impression of any such seal, or who has in his possession any such counterfeited seal or impression thereof, knowing it to be counterfeited, and willfully conceals the same, is guilty of forgery.

§473. Punishment for forgery.

Forgery is punishable by imprisonment in the state prison, or by imprisonment in the county jail for not more than one year.

© 1992 by J., B. & L. Gould
Printed in the U.S.A.   EP

§474. False messages.

Every person who knowingly and willfully sends by telegraph or telephone to any person a false or forged message, purporting to be from a telegraph or telephone office, or from any other person, or who willfully delivers or causes to be delivered to any person any such message falsely purporting to have been received by telegraph or telephone, or who furnishes, or conspires to furnish, or causes to be furnished to any agent, operator, or employee, to be sent by telegraph or telephone, or to be delivered, any such message, knowing the same to be false or forged, with the intent to deceive, injure, or defraud another, is punishable by imprisonment in the state prison, or in the county jail not exceeding one year, or by fine not exceeding ten thousand dollars ($10,000), or by both such fine and imprisonment.

§475. Forged or unfinished bills or notes.

Every person who has in his or her possession, or receives from another person, any forged promissory note or bank bill, or bills, or any counterfeited trading stamp, or stamps, or lottery ticket or share purporting to be issued under the California State Lottery Act of 1984, or tickets or shares, for the payment of money or property, with the intention to pass the same, or to permit, cause, or procure the same to be uttered or passed, with the intention to defraud any person, knowing the same to be forged or counterfeited, or has or keeps in his or her possession any blank or unfinished note or bank bill made in the form or similitude of any promissory note or bill for payment of money or property, made to be issued by any incorporated bank or banking company, or any blank or unfinished check, money order, or traveler's check, made in the form or similitude of any check, money order, or traveler's check, whether the parties thereto are real or fictitious, with intention to fill up and complete the blank and unfinished note or bill, check, money order, or traveler's check, or to permit, or cause, or procure the same to be filled up and completed in order to utter or pass the same, or to permit, or cause, or procure the same to be uttered or passed, to defraud any person, is punishable by imprisonment in the state prison, or by imprisonment in the county jail for not more than one year. *(Amended by Stats 1986 ch 55 §26.)*

§475a. Fraudulent possession of money order, warrant or completed check.

Every person who has in his possession a completed check, money order, traveler's check, controller's warrant for the payment of money at the treasury, or county order or warrant, whether the parties thereto are real or fictitious, with intention to utter or pass the same, or to permit, cause, or procure the same to be uttered or passed, to defraud any person, is punishable by imprisonment in the state prison, or by imprisonment in the county jail for not more than one year.

§476. Possessing fictitious bill, note or check.

Every person who makes, passes, utters, or publishes, with intention to defraud any other person, or who, with the like intention, attempts to pass, utter, or publish, or who has in his possession, with like intent to utter, pass, or publish, any fictitious bill, note, or check, purporting to be the bill, note, or check, or other instrument in writing for the payment of money or property of some bank, corporation, copartnership, or individual, when, in fact, there is no such bank, corporation, copartnership, or individual in existence, knowing the bill, note, check, or instrument in writing to be fictitious, is punishable by imprisonment in the county jail for not more than one year, or in the state prison.

§476a. Delivering or making check with insufficient funds.

(a) Any person who for himself or as the agent or representative of another or as an officer of a corporation, willfully, with intent to defraud, makes or draws or utters or delivers any check, or draft or order upon any bank or depositary, or person, or firm, or corporation, for the payment of money, knowing at the time of such making, drawing, uttering or delivering that the maker or drawer or the corporation has not sufficient funds in, or credit with said bank or depositary, or person, or firm, or corporation, for the payment of such check, draft, or order and all other checks, drafts, or orders upon such funds then outstanding, in full upon its presentation, although no express representation is made with reference thereto, is punishable by imprisonment in the county jail for not more than one year, or in the state prison.

(b) However, if the total amount of all such checks, drafts, or orders that the defendant is charged with and convicted of making, drawing, or uttering does not exceed two hundred dollars ($200), the offense is punishable only by imprisonment in the county jail for not more than one year, except that this subdivision shall not be applicable if the defendant has previously been convicted of a violation of Section 470, 475, or 476, or of this section, or of the crime of petty theft in a case in which defendant's offense was a violation also of Section 470, 475, or 476 or of this section or if the defendant has previously been convicted of any offense under the laws of any other state or of the United States which, if committed in this state, would have been punishable as a violation of Section 470, 475 or 476 or of this section or if he has been so convicted of the crime of petty theft in a case in which, if defendant's offense had been committed in this state, it would have been a violation also of Section 470, 475, or 476, or of this section.

(c) Where such check, draft, or order is protested, on the ground of insufficiency of funds or credit, the notice of protest thereof shall be admissible as proof of presentation, nonpayment and protest and shall be presumptive evidence of knowledge of insufficiency of funds or credit with such bank or depositary, or person, or firm, or corporation.

(d) In any prosecution under this section involving two or more checks, drafts, or orders, it shall constitute prima facie evidence of the identity of the drawer of a check, draft, or order if:

(1) At the time of the acceptance of such check, draft or order from the drawer by the payee there is obtained from the drawer the following information: name and residence of the drawer, business or mailing address, either a valid driver's license number or Department of Motor Vehicles identification card number, and the drawer's home or work phone number or place of employment. Such information may be recorded on the check, draft, or order itself or may be retained on file by the payee and referred to on the check, draft, or order by identifying number or other similar means; and

(2) The person receiving the check, draft, or order witnesses the drawer's signature or endorsement, and, as evidence of that, initials the check, draft, or order at the time of receipt.

(e) The word "credit" as used herein shall be construed to mean an arrangement or understanding with the bank or depositary or person or firm or corporation for the payment of such check, draft or order.

(f) If any of the preceding paragraphs, or parts thereof, shall be found unconstitutional or invalid, the remainder of this section shall not thereby be invalidated, but shall remain in full force and effect.

§477. Counterfeiting coin, bullion, etc.

Every person who counterfeits any of the species of gold or silver coin current in this state, or any kind or species of gold dust, gold or silver bullion, or bars, lumps, pieces, or nuggets, or who sells, passes, or gives in payment such counterfeit coin, dust, bullion, bars, lumps, pieces, or nuggets, or permits, causes, or procures the same to be sold, uttered, or passed, with intention to defraud any person, knowing the same to be counterfeited, is guilty of counterfeiting.

§478. Punishment for counterfeiting.

Counterfeiting is punishable by imprisonment in the state prison for two, three or four years.

§479. Counterfeit gold or silver coins.

Every person who has in his possession, or receives for any other person, any counterfeit gold or silver coin of the species current in this state, or any counterfeit gold dust, gold or silver bullion or bars, lumps, pieces or nuggets, with the intention to sell, utter, put off or pass the same, or permits, causes or procures the same to be sold, uttered or passed, with intention to defraud any person, knowing the same to be counterfeit, is punishable by imprisonment in the state prison for two, three or four years.

§480. Possessing or making counterfeit dies or plates.

Every person who makes, or knowingly has in his possession any die, plate, or any apparatus, paper, metal, machine, or other thing whatever, made use of in counterfeiting coin current in this state, or in counterfeiting gold dust, gold or silver bars, bullion, lumps, pieces, or nuggets, or in counterfeiting bank notes or bills, is punishable by imprisonment in the state prison for two, three or four years; and all such dies, plates, apparatus, paper, metal, or machine, intended for the purpose aforesaid, must be destroyed.

§481. Alteration of tickets, etc.

Every person who counterfeits, forges, or alters any ticket, check, order, coupon, receipt for fare, or pass, issued by any railroad or steamship company, or by any lessee or manager thereof, designed to entitle the holder to ride in the cars or vessels of such company, or who utters, publishes, or puts into circulation, any such counterfeit or altered ticket, check, or order, coupon, receipt for fare, or pass, with intent to defraud any such railroad or steamship company, or any lessee thereof, or any other person, is punishable by imprisonment in the state prison, or in the county jail, not exceeding one year, or by fine not exceeding one thousand dollars, or by both such imprisonment and fine.

§481.1. Alteration of fare media.

(a) Every person who counterfeits, forges, or alters any fare media designed to entitle the holder to a ride on vehicles of a public transportation system, as defined by Section 99211 of the Public Utilities Code, or on vehicles operated by entities subsidized by the Department of Transportation is punishable by imprisonment in the county jail, not exceeding one year, or in the state prison.

(b) Every person who knowingly possesses any counterfeit, forged, or altered fare media designed to entitle the holder to a ride on vehicles of a public transportation system, as defined by Section 99211 of the Public Utilities Code, or on vehicles operated by entities subsidized by the Department of Transportation, or who utters, publishes, or puts into circulation any fare media with intent to defraud is punishable by imprisonment in the county jail not exceeding one year or by a fine not exceeding one thousand dollars ($1,000), or by both. *(Added by Stats 1987 ch 801 §5.)*

§482. Restoration of canceled ticket.

Every person who, for the purpose of restoring to its original appearance and nominal value in whole or in part, removes, conceals, fills up, or obliterates, the cuts, marks, punch-holes, or other evidence of cancellation, from any ticket, check, order, coupon, receipt for fare, or pass, issued by any railroad or steamship company, or any lessee or manager thereof, canceled in whole or in part, with intent to dispose of by sale or gift, or to circulate the same, or with intent to defraud the railroad or steamship company, or lessee thereof, or any other person, or who, with like intent to defraud, offers for sale, or in payment of fare on the railroad or vessel of the company, such ticket, check, order, coupon, or pass, knowing the same to have been so restored, in whole or in part, is punishable by imprisonment in the county jail not exceeding six months, or by a fine not exceeding one thousand dollars, or by both such imprisonment and fine.

§483. Sale of ticket to person not entitled to use it.

Except as otherwise provided in Section 26002.5 of the Government Code and Sections 40180.5 and 99151 of the Public Utilities Code, any person, firm, corporation, partnership, or association that shall sell to another any ticket, pass, scrip, mileage or commutation book, coupon, or other instrument for passage on a common carrier, for the use of any person not entitled to use the same according to the terms thereof, or of the book or portion thereof from which it was detached, shall be guilty of a misdemeanor.

CHAPTER 5

LARCENY

§484. Theft defined.

(a) Every person who shall feloniously steal, take, carry, lead, or drive away the personal property of another, or who shall fraudulently appropriate property which has been entrusted to him, or who shall knowingly and designedly, by any false or fraudulent representation or pretense, defraud any other person of money, labor or real or personal property, or who causes or procures others to report falsely of his wealth or mercantile character and by thus imposing upon any person, obtains credit and

© 1992 by J., B. & L. Gould
Printed in the U.S.A.   **EP**

thereby fraudulently gets or obtains possession of money, or property or obtains the labor or service of another, is guilty of theft. In determining the value of the property obtained, for the purposes of this section, the reasonable and fair market value shall be the test, and in determining the value of services received the contract price shall be the test. If there be no contract price, the reasonable and going wage for the service rendered shall govern. For the purposes of this section, any false or fraudulent representation or pretense made shall be treated as continuing, so as to cover any money, property or service received as a result thereof, and the complaint, information or indictment may charge that the crime was committed on any date during the particular period in question. The hiring of any additional employee or employees without advising each of them of every labor claim due and unpaid and every judgment that the employer has been unable to meet shall be prima facie evidence of intent to defraud.

(b) Except as provided in Section 10855 of the Vehicle Code, intent to commit theft by fraud is presumed if one who has leased or rented the personal property of another pursuant to a written contract fails to return the personal property to its owner within 20 days after the owner has made written demand by certified or registered mail following the expiration of the lease or rental agreement for return of the property so leased or rented.

(c) Notwithstanding the provisions of subdivision (b), if one presents with criminal intent identification which bears a false or fictitious name or address for the purpose of obtaining the lease or rental of the personal property of another, the presumption created herein shall apply upon the failure of the lessee to return the rental property at the expiration of the lease or rental agreement, and no written demand for the return of the leased or rented property shall be required.

(d) The presumptions created by subdivisions (b) and (c) are presumptions affecting the burden of producing evidence.

(e) Within 30 days after the lease or rental agreement has expired, the owner shall make written demand for return of the property so leased or rented. Notice addressed and mailed to the lessee or renter at the address given at the time of the making of the lease or rental agreement and to any other known address shall constitute proper demand. Where the owner fails to make such written demand the presumption created by subdivision (b) shall not apply.

§484b. Diversion of funds received.

Any person who receives money for the purpose of obtaining or paying for services, labor, materials or equipment and willfully fails to apply such money for such purpose by either willfully failing to complete the improvements for which funds were provided or willfully failing to pay for services, labor, materials or equipment provided incident to such construction, and wrongfully diverts the funds to a use other than that for which the funds were received, shall be guilty of a public offense and shall be punishable by a fine not exceeding ten thousand dollars ($10,000), or by imprisonment in the state prison, or in the county jail not exceeding one year, or by both such fine and such imprisonment if the amount diverted is in excess of one thousand dollars ($1,000). If the amount diverted is less than one thousand dollars ($1,000), the person shall be guilty of a misdemeanor.

§484c. Submission of false voucher to obtain construction loan.

Any person who submits a false voucher to obtain construction loan funds and does not use the funds for the purpose for which the claim was submitted is guilty of embezzlement.

§484d. Definitions.

As used in this section and Sections 484e to 484j, inclusive:

(1) "Cardholder" means any person to whom an access card is issued or any person who has agreed with the card issuer to pay obligations arising from the issuance of an access card to another person.

(2) "Access card" means any card, plate, code, account number, or other means of account access that can be used, alone or in conjunction with another access card, to obtain money, goods, services, or any other thing of value, or that can be used to initiate a transfer of funds, other than a transfer originated solely by a paper instrument.

(3) "Expired access card" means an access card which shows on its face it has elapsed.

(4) "Card issuer" means any person who issues an access card or the agent of that person with respect to that card.

(5) "Retailer" means every person who is authorized by an issuer to furnish money, goods, services, or anything else of value upon presentation of an access card by a cardholder.

(6) An access card is "incomplete" if part of the matter other than the signature of the cardholder which an issuer requires to appear on the access card before it can be used by a cardholder has not been stamped, embossed, imprinted, or written on it.

(7) "Revoked access card" means an access card which is no longer authorized for use by the issuer, that authorization having been suspended or terminated and written notice thereof having been given to the cardholder.

(8) "Counterfeit access card" means any access card that is counterfeit, fictitious, altered, or forged, or any false representation or depiction of an access card or a component thereof.

(9) "Traffic" means to transfer or otherwise dispose of property to another, or to obtain control of property with intent to transfer or dispose of it to another.

(10) "Card making equipment" means any equipment, machine, plate, mechanism, impression, or other device designed, used, or intended to be used to produce an access card. *(Amended by Stats 1986 ch 1436 §1.)*

§484e. Access card; theft.

(1) Every person who acquires an access card from another without the cardholder's or issuer's consent or who, with knowledge that it has been so acquired, acquires the access card, with intent to use it or to sell or transfer it to a person other than the issuer or the cardholder is guilty of petty theft.

(2) Every person who acquires an access card that he or she knows to have been lost, mislaid, or delivered under a mistake as to the identity or address of the cardholder, and who retains possession with intent to use it or to sell it or to transfer it to a person other than the issuer or the cardholder is guilty of petty theft.

(3) Every person who sells, transfers, conveys, or receives an access card with the intent to defraud, or who acquires an access card with the intent to use it fraudulently, is guilty of grand theft.

(4) Every person other than the issuer, who within any consecutive 12-month period, acquires access cards issued in the names of four or more persons which he or she has reason to know were taken or retained under circumstances which constitute a violation of subdivision (1), (2), or (3) is guilty of grand theft. *(Amended by Stats 1986 ch 1436 §2.)*

§484f. Access card; forgery.

(1) Every person who, with intent to defraud, designs, makes, alters, or embosses a counterfeit access card or utters or otherwise attempts to use a counterfeit access card is guilty of forgery.

(2) A person other than the cardholder or a person authorized by him or her who, with intent to defraud, signs the name of another or of a fictitious person to an access card, sales slip, sales draft, or instrument for the payment of money which evidences an access card transaction, is guilty of forgery. *(Amended by Stats 1986 ch 1436 §3.)*

§484g. Access card; fraudulent use.

Every person, who with intent to defraud, (a) uses for the purpose of obtaining money, goods, services or anything else of value an access card obtained or retained in violation of Section 484e or an access card which he or she knows is forged, expired, or revoked, or (b) obtains money, goods, services or anything else of value by representing without the consent of the cardholder that he or she is the holder of an access card or by representing that he or she is the holder of an access card and the card has not in fact been issued, is guilty of theft. If the value of all money, goods, services and other things of value obtained in violation of this section exceeds four hundred dollars ($400) in any consecutive six-month period, then the same shall constitute grand theft. *(Amended by Stats 1986 ch 1436 §4.)*

§484h. Access card offenses; retailer.

Every retailer or other person who, with intent to defraud:

(a) Furnishes money, goods, services or anything else of value upon presentation of an access card obtained or retained in violation of Section 484e or an access card which he or she knows is a counterfeit access card or is forged, expired, or revoked, and who receives any payment therefor, is guilty of theft. If the payment received by the retailer or other person for all money, goods, services, and other things of value furnished in violation of this section exceeds four hundred dollars ($400) in any consecutive six-month period, then the same shall constitute grand theft.

(b) Presents for payment a sales slip or other evidence of an access card transaction, and receives payment therefor, without furnishing in the transaction money, goods, services, or anything else of value that is equal in value to the amount of the sales slip or other evidence of an access card transaction, is guilty of theft. If the difference between the value of all money, goods, services, and anything else of value actually furnished and the payment or payments received by the retailer or other person therefor upon presentation of a sales slip or other evidence of an access card transaction exceeds four hundred dollars ($400) in any consecutive six-month period, then the same shall constitute grand theft. *(Amended by Stats 1986 ch 1436 §5.)*

§484i. Incomplete access card; possession.

(a) Every person who possesses an incomplete access card, with intent to complete it without the consent of the issuer is guilty of a misdemeanor.

(b) Every person who designs, makes, possesses, or traffics in card making equipment or incomplete access cards with the intent that the equipment or cards be used to make counterfeit access cards, is punishable by imprisonment in the county jail for not more than one year, or by imprisonment in the state prison. *(Amended by Stats 1986 ch 1436 §6.)*

§484j. Publication of access card number to avoid lawful charge.

Any person who publishes the number or code of an existing, canceled, revoked, expired or nonexistent access card, personal identification number, computer password, access code, debit card number, bank account number, or the numbering or coding which is employed in the issuance of access cards, with the intent that it be used or with knowledge or reason to believe that it will be used to avoid the payment of any lawful charge, or with intent to defraud or aid another in defrauding, is guilty of a misdemeanor. As used in this section, "publishes" means the communication of information to any one or more persons, either orally, in person or by telephone, radio or television, or on a computer network or computer bulletin board, or in a writing of any kind, including without limitation a letter or memorandum, circular or handbill, newspaper or magazine article, or book. *(Amended by Stats 1986 ch 1437 §2.)*

§484.1. Giving false information to pawnbrokers or secondhand dealers.

(a) Any person who knowingly gives false information or provides false verification as to the person's true identity or as to the person's ownership interest in property or the person's authority to sell property in order to receive money or other valuable consideration from a pawnbroker or secondhand dealer and who receives money or other valuable consideration from the pawnbroker or secondhand dealer is guilty of theft.

(b) Upon conviction of the offense described in subdivision (a), the court may require, in addition to any sentence or fine imposed, that the defendant make restitution to the pawnbroker or secondhand dealer in an amount not exceeding the actual losses sustained pursuant to the provisions of subdivision (c) of Section 13967 of the Government Code, if the defendant is denied probation, or Section 1203.04 of the Penal Code, if the defendant is granted probation. *(Added by Stats 1988 ch 896 §1, eff. 1/1/89.)*

§485. Appropriation of lost property.

One who finds lost property under circumstances which give him knowledge of or means of inquiry as to the true owner, and who appropriates such property to his own use, or to the use of another person not entitled thereto, without first making reasonable and just efforts to find the owner and to restore the property to him, is guilty of theft.

§486. Degrees of theft.

Theft is divided into two degrees, the first of which is termed grand theft; the second, petty theft.

© 1992 by J., B. & L. Gould
Printed in the U.S.A.   **EP**

§487. Grand theft defined.

Grand theft is theft committed in any of the following cases:

1. When the money, labor or real or personal property taken is of a value exceeding four hundred dollars ($400); provided, that when domestic fowls, avocados, olives, citrus or deciduous fruits, other fruits, vegetables, nuts, artichokes, or other farm crops are taken of a value exceeding one hundred dollars ($100); provided, further, that when fish, shellfish, molusks, crustaceans, kelp, algae, or other aquacultural products are taken from a commercial or research operation which is producing that product, of a value exceeding one hundred dollars ($100); provided, further, that where the money, labor, real or personal property is taken by a servant, agent or employee from his principal or employer and aggregates four hundred dollars ($400) or more in any 12 consecutive month period, then the same shall constitute grand theft.

For purposes of establishing that the value of avocados or citrus fruit under this subdivision exceeds one hundred dollars ($100), that value may be shown by the presentation of credible evidence which establishes that on the day of the theft avocados or citrus fruit of the same variety and weight exceeded one hundred dollars ($100) in wholesale value.

2. When the property is taken from the person of another.

3. When the property taken is a firearm, horse, mare, gelding, any bovine animal, any caprine animal, mule, jack, jenny, sheep, lamb, hog, sow, boar, gilt, barrow or pig.

This section shall remain in effect only until January 1, 1993, and as of that date is repealed, unless a later enacted statute, which is enacted before January 1, 1993, deletes or extends that date. *(Amended by Stats 1989 ch 930 §6, eff. 1/1/90 only until 1/1/93. See other section 487 below.)*

§487. Grand theft defined.

Grand theft is theft committed in any of the following cases:

1. When the money, labor or real or personal property taken is of a value exceeding four hundred dollars ($400); provided, that when domestic fowls, avocados, olives, citrus or deciduous fruits, other fruits, vegetables, nuts, artichokes, or other farm crops are taken of a value exceeding one hundred dollars ($100); provided, further, that when fish, shellfish, molusks, crustaceans, kelp, algae, or other aquacultural products are taken from a commercial or research operation which is producing that product, of a value exceeding one hundred dollars ($100); provided, further, that where the money, labor, real or personal property is taken by a servant, agent or employee from his principal or employer and aggregates four hundred dollars ($400) or more in any 12 consecutive month period, then the same shall constitute grand theft.

For purposes of establishing that the value of avocados or citrus fruit under this subdivision exceeds one hundred dollars ($100), that value may be shown by the presentation of credible evidence which establishes that on the day of the theft avocados or citrus fruit of the same variety and weight exceeded one hundred dollars ($100) in wholesale value.

2. When the property is taken from the person of another.

3. When the property taken is an automobile, firearm, horse, mare, gelding, any bovine animal, any caprine animal, mule, jack, jenny, sheep, lamb, hog, sow, boar, gilt, barrow or pig. *(Added by Stats 1989 ch 930 §6.1, eff. 1/1/90, oper. 1/1/93. See other section 487 above.)*

§487a. Stealing livestock carcass.

(a) Every person who shall feloniously steal, take, transport or carry the carcass of any bovine, caprine, equine, ovine, or suine animal or of any mule, jack or jenny, which is the personal property of another, or who shall fraudulently appropriate such property which has been entrusted to him, is guilty of grand theft.

(b) Every person who shall feloniously steal, take, transport, or carry any portion of the carcass of any bovine, caprine, equine, ovine, or suine animal or of any mule, jack, or jenny, which has been killed without the consent of the owner thereof, is guilty of grand theft.

§487b. Conversion of real into personal property; grand theft.

Every person who converts real estate of the value of one hundred dollars ($100) or more into personal property by severance from the realty of another, and with felonious intent to do so, steals, takes, and carries away such property is guilty of grand theft and is punishable by imprisonment in the state prison.

§487c. Conversion of real into personal property; petty theft.

Every person who converts real estate of the value of less than one hundred dollars ($100) into personal property by severance from the realty of another, and with felonious intent to do so steals, takes, and carries away such property is guilty of petit theft and is punishable by imprisonment in the county jail for not more than one year, or by a fine not exceeding one thousand dollars ($1,000), or by both such fine and imprisonment.

§487d. Theft of gold dust.

Every person who feloniously steals, takes, and carries away, or attempts to take, steal, and carry from any mining claim, tunnel, sluice, undercurrent, riffle box, or sulfurate machine, another's gold dust, amalgam, or quicksilver is guilty of grand theft and is punishable by imprisonment in the state prison.

§487e. Grand theft dog stealing.

Every person who feloniously steals, takes, or carries away a dog of another which is of a value exceeding four hundred dollars ($400) is guilty of grand theft.

§487f. Petty theft dog stealing.

Every person who feloniously steals, takes, or carries away a dog of another which is of a value not exceeding four hundred dollars ($400) is guilty of petty theft.

§487g. Dog stealing for sale, research, etc.

Every person who steals or maliciously takes or carries away any animal of another for purposes of sale, medical research, or other commercial uses, or who knowingly, by any false representation or pretense, defrauds another person of any animal for purposes of medical research or slaughter, is guilty of a public offense punishable by imprisonment in a county jail not exceeding one year or in the state prison. *(Amended by Stats 1991 ch 490 §2, eff. 1/1/92.)*

§487h. Stealing vehicle, trailer, or construction equipment; penalties.

(a) Every person who feloniously steals or takes any motor vehicle, as defined in Section 415 of the Vehicle Code, any trailer, as defined in Section 630 of the Vehicle Code, any special construction equipment, as defined in Section 565 of the Vehicle Code, or any vessel, as defined in Section 21 of the Harbors and Navigation Code, is guilty of grand theft, and upon conviction thereof, is punishable by imprisonment in the state prison for two, three, or four years or a fine of not more than ten thousand dollars ($10,000), or both, or by imprisonment in the county jail not to exceed one year or a fine of not more than one thousand dollars ($1,000), or both.

(b) Any person who, having been convicted of two previous misdemeanor violations of subdivision (a), former paragraph (3) of Section 487, involving an automobile, or Section 10851 of the Vehicle Code, or any combination of those offenses as misdemeanors, is subsequently convicted of a violation of subdivision (a) is punishable for the subsequent conviction by imprisonment in the state prison for two, three, or four years.

(c) Except in unusual cases where the interests of justice would best be served if the person is granted probation, probation shall not be granted to any person who is convicted of a felony violation of subdivision (a) or (b), and who has been previously convicted of two or more felony violations of the offense set forth in subdivision (a), the offense set forth in former paragraph (3) of Section 487, involving a vehicle, or the offense set forth in Section 10851 of the Vehicle Code, or who has been previously convicted of one felony violation of any of those offenses and at least two misdemeanor violations of those offenses.

(d) If the court grants probation under subdivision (c), it shall specify on the court record the reason or reasons for that order.

(e) This section shall remain in effect only until January 1, 1993, and as of that date is repealed, unless a later enacted statute, which is enacted before January 1, 1993, deletes or extends that date. *(Amended by Stats 1990 ch 1564 §1, eff. 9/30/90 only until 1/1/93.)*

§488. Petty theft defined.

Theft in other cases is petty theft.

§489. Punishment for grand theft.

Grand theft is punishable as follows:

(a) When the grand theft involves the theft of a firearm, by imprisonment in the state prison for 16 months, 2, or 3 years.

(b) In all other cases, by imprisonment in a county jail not exceeding one year or in the state prison. *(Amended by Stats 1989 ch 1167 §1.1, eff. 1/1/90.)*

§490. Punishment for petty theft.

Petty theft is punishable by fine not exceeding one thousand dollars ($1,000), or by imprisonment in the county jail not exceeding six months, or both.

§490a. Theft substituted for larceny, embezzlement or stealing.

Wherever any law or statute of this state refers to or mentions larceny, embezzlement, or stealing, said law or statute shall hereafter be read and interpreted as if the word "theft" were substituted therefor.

§490.1. Petty theft may be charged as as misdemeanor or infraction.

(a) Petty theft, where the value of the money, labor, real or personal property taken is of a value which does not exceed fifty dollars ($50), may be charged as a misdemeanor or an infraction, at the discretion of the prosecutor, provided that the person charged with the offense has no other theft or theft-related conviction.

(b) Any offense charged as an infraction under this section shall be subject to the provisions of subdivision (d) of Section 17 and Sections 19.6 and 19.7.

A violation which is an infraction under this section is punishable by a fine not exceeding two hundred fifty dollars ($250). *(Added by Stats 1991 ch 638 §2, eff. 1/1/92.)*

§490.5. Petty theft from merchant or library.

(a) Upon a first conviction for petty theft involving merchandise taken from a merchant's premises or a book or other library materials taken from a library facility, a person shall be punished by a mandatory fine of not less than fifty dollars ($50) and not more than one thousand dollars ($1,000) for each such violation; and may also be punished by imprisonment in the county jail, not exceeding six months, or both such fine and imprisonment.

(b) When an unemancipated minor's willful conduct would constitute petty theft involving merchandise taken from a merchant's premises or a book or other library materials taken from a library facility, any merchant or library facility who has been injured by that conduct may bring a civil action against the parent or legal guardian having control and custody of the minor. For the purposes of those actions the misconduct of the unemancipated minor shall be imputed to the parent or legal guardian having control and custody of the minor. The parent or legal guardian having control or custody of an unemancipated minor whose conduct violates this subdivision shall be jointly and severally liable with the minor to a merchant or to a library facility for damages of not less than fifty dollars ($50) nor more than five hundred dollars ($500), plus costs. In addition to the foregoing damages, the parent or legal guardian shall be jointly and severally liable with the minor to the merchant for the retail value of the merchandise if it is not recovered in a merchantable condition, or to a library facility for the fair market value of its book or other library materials. Recovery of such damages may be had in addition to, and is not limited by, any other provision of law which limits the liability of a parent or legal guardian for the tortious conduct of a minor. An action for recovery of damages, pursuant to this subdivision, may be brought in small claims court if the total damages do not exceed the jurisdictional limit of that court, or in any other appropriate court; however, total damages, including the value of the merchandise or book or other library materials, shall not exceed five hundred dollars ($500) for each action brought under this section.

The provisions of this subdivision are in addition to other civil remedies and do not limit merchants or other persons to elect to pursue other civil remedies, except that the provisions of Section 1714.1 of the Civil Code shall not apply herein.

(c) When an adult or emancipated minor has unlawfully taken merchandise from a merchant's premises, or a book or other library materials from a

© 1992 by J., B. & L. Gould
Printed in the U.S.A.   EP

library facility, the adult or emancipated minor shall be liable to the merchant or library facility for damages of not less than fifty dollars ($50) nor more than five hundred dollars ($500), plus costs. In addition to the foregoing damages, the adult or emancipated minor shall be liable to the merchant for the retail value of the merchandise if it is not recovered in merchantable condition, or to a library facility for the fair market value of its book or other library materials. An action for recovery of damages, pursuant to this subdivision, may be brought in small claims court if the total damages do not exceed the jurisdictional limit of such court, or in any other appropriate court. The provisions of this subdivision are in addition to other civil remedies and do not limit merchants or other persons to elect to pursue other civil remedies.

(d) In lieu of the fines prescribed by subdivision (a), any person may be required to perform public services designated by the court, provided that in no event shall any such person be required to perform less than the number of hours of such public service necessary to satisfy the fine assessed by the court as provided by subdivision (a) at the minimum wage prevailing in the state at the time of sentencing.

(e) All fines collected under this section shall be collected and distributed in accordance with Sections 1463 and 1463.1 of the Penal Code; provided, however, that a county may, by a majority vote of the members of its board of supervisors, allocate any amount up to, but not exceeding 50 percent of such fines to the county superintendent of schools for allocation to local school districts. The fines allocated shall be administered by the county superintendent of schools to finance public school programs, which provide counseling or other educational services designed to discourage shoplifting, theft, and burglary. Subject to rules and regulations as may be adopted by the Superintendent of Public Instruction, each county superintendent of schools shall allocate such funds to school districts within the county which submit project applications designed to further the educational purposes of this section. The costs of administration of this section by each county superintendent of schools shall be paid from the funds allocated to the county superintendent of schools.

(f) (1) A merchant may detain a person for a reasonable time for the purpose of conducting an investigation in a reasonable manner whenever the merchant has probable cause to believe the person to be detained is attempting to unlawfully take or has unlawfully taken merchandise from the merchant's premises.

A person employed by a library facility may detain a person for a reasonable time for the purpose of conducting an investigation in a reasonable manner whenever the person employed by a library facility has probable cause to believe the person to be detained is attempting to unlawfully remove or has unlawfully removed books or library materials from the premises of the library facility.

(2) In making the detention a merchant or a person employed by a library facility may use a reasonable amount of nondeadly force necessary to protect himself or herself and to prevent escape of the person detained or the loss of property.

(3) During the period of detention any items which a merchant or any items which a person employed by a library facility has probable cause to believe are unlawfully taken from the premises of the merchant or library facility and which are in plain view may be examined by the merchant or person employed by a library facility for the purposes of ascertaining the ownership thereof.

(4) A merchant, a person employed by a library facility, or an agent thereof, having probable cause to believe the person detained was attempting to unlawfully take or has taken any item from the premises, may request the person detained to voluntarily surrender the item. Should the person detained refuse to surrender the item of which there is probable cause to believe has been unlawfully taken from the premises, or attempted to be unlawfully taken from the premises, a limited and reasonable search may be conducted by those authorized to make the detention in order to recover the item. Only packages, shopping bags, handbags or other property in the immediate possession of the person detained, but not including any clothing worn by the person, may be searched pursuant to this subdivision. Upon surrender or discovery of the item, the person detained may also be requested, but may not be required, to provide adequate proof of his or her true identity.

(5) A peace officer who accepts custody of a person arrested for an offense contained in this section may, subsequent to the arrest, search the person arrested and his or her immediate possessions for any item or items alleged to have been taken.

(6) In any civil action brought by any person resulting from a detention or arrest by a merchant, it shall be a defense to such action that the merchant detaining or arresting such person had probable cause to believe that the person had stolen or attempted to steal merchandise and that the merchant acted reasonably under all the circumstances.

In any civil action brought by any person resulting from a detention or arrest by a person employed by a library facility, it shall be a defense to such action that the person employed by a library facility detaining or arresting such person had probable cause to believe that the person had stolen or attempted to steal books or library materials and that the person employed by a library facility acted reasonably under all the circumstances.

(g) As used in this section:

(1) "Merchandise" means any personal property, capable of manual delivery, displayed, held or offered for retail sale by a merchant.

(2) "Merchant" means an owner or operator, and the agent, consignee, employee, lessee, or officer of an owner or operator, of any premises used for the retail purchase or sale of any personal property capable of manual delivery.

(3) The terms "book or other library materials" include any book, plate, picture, photograph, engraving, painting, drawing, map, newspaper, magazine, pamphlet, broadside, manuscript, document, letter, public record, microform, sound recording, audiovisual material in any format, magnetic or other tape, electronic data-processing record, artifact, or other documentary, written or printed material regardless of physical form or characteristics, or any part thereof, belonging to, on loan to, or otherwise in the custody of a library facility.

(4) The term "library facility" includes any public library; any library of an educational, historical or eleemosynary institution, organization or society; any museum; any repository of public records.

(h) Any library facility shall post at its entrance and exit a conspicuous sign to read as follows:

"IN ORDER TO PREVENT THE THEFT OF BOOKS AND LIBRARY MATERIALS, STATE LAW AUTHORIZES THE DETENTION FOR A REASONABLE PERIOD OF ANY PERSON USING THESE FACILITIES SUSPECTED OF COMMITTING 'LIBRARY THEFT'" (PENAL CODE SECTION 490.5)." *(Amended by Stats 1988 ch 1036 §1, eff. 1/1/89.)*

§491. Dogs; value.

Dogs are personal property, and their value is to be ascertained in the same manner as the value of other property.

§492. Larceny of written instruments.

If the thing stolen consists of any evidence of debt, or other written instrument, the amount of money due thereupon, or secured to be paid thereby, and remaining unsatisfied, or which in any contingency might be collected thereon, or the value of the property the title to which is shown thereby, or the sum which might be recovered in the absence thereof, is the value of the thing stolen.

§493. Value of passage tickets.

If the thing stolen is any ticket or other paper or writing entitling or purporting to entitle the holder or proprietor thereof to a passage upon any railroad or vessel or other public conveyance, the price at which tickets entitling a person to a like passage are usually sold by the proprietors of such conveyance is the value of such ticket, paper, or writing.

§494. Written instruments completed but not delivered.

All the provisions of this chapter apply where the property taken is an instrument for the payment of money, evidence of debt, public security, or passage ticket, completed and ready to be issued or delivered, although the same has never been issued or delivered by the makers thereof to any person as a purchaser or owner.

§495. Severing and removing part of the realty declared larceny.

The provisions of this chapter apply where the thing taken is any fixture or part of the realty, and is severed at the time of the taking, in the same manner as if the thing had been severed by another person at some previous time.

§496. Concealing or receiving stolen property.

1. Every person who buys or receives any property which has been stolen or which has been obtained in any manner constituting theft or extortion, knowing the property to be so stolen or obtained, or who conceals, sells, withholds or aids in concealing, selling, or withholding any such property from the owner, knowing the property to be so stolen or obtained, is punishable by imprisonment in a state prison, or in a county jail for not more than one year; provided, that where the district attorney or the grand jury determines that such action would be in the interests of justice, the district attorney or the grand jury, as the case may be, may, if the value of the property does not exceed four hundred dollars ($400), specify in the accusatory pleading that the offense shall be a misdemeanor, punishable only by imprisonment in the county jail not exceeding one year.

2. Every swap meet vendor as defined in Section 21661 of the Business and Professions Code and every person whose principal business is dealing in or collecting used or secondhand merchandise or personal property, and every agent, employee or representative of such person, who buys or receives any property which has been stolen or obtained in any manner constituting theft or extortion, under such circumstances as should cause such person, agent, employee or representative to make reasonable inquiry to ascertain that the person from whom such property was bought or received had the legal right to sell or deliver it, without making such reasonable inquiry, shall be presumed to have bought or received such property knowing it to have been so stolen or obtained. This presumption may, however, be rebutted by proof.

3. When in a prosecution under this section it shall appear from the evidence that the defendant was a swap meet vendor or that the defendant's principal business was as set forth in the preceding paragraph, that the defendant bought, received, or otherwise obtained, or concealed, withheld or aided in concealing or withholding from the owner, any property which had been stolen or obtained in any manner constituting theft or extortion, and that the defendant bought, received, obtained, concealed or withheld such property under such circumstances as should have caused him or her to make reasonable inquiry to ascertain that the person from whom he bought, received, or obtained such property had the legal right to sell or deliver it to him or her, then the burden shall be upon the defendant to show that before so buying, receiving, or otherwise obtaining such property, he or she made such reasonable inquiry to ascertain that the person so selling or delivering the same to him or her had the legal right to so sell or deliver it.

4. Any person who has been injured by a violation of paragraph 1 of this section may bring an action for three times the amount of actual damages, if any, sustained by the plaintiff, costs of suit and reasonable attorney's fees.

5. Notwithstanding Section 664, any attempt to commit any act prohibited by this section, except an offense specified in the accusatory pleading as a misdemeanor, is punishable by imprisonment in a state prison, or in a county jail for not more than one year.

§496a. Purchasing metals used in transportation or utility service.

(a) Every person who, being a dealer in or collector of junk, metals or secondhand materials, or the agent, employee, or representative of such dealer or collector, buys or receives any wire, cable, copper, lead, solder, mercury, iron or brass which he knows or reasonably should know is ordinarily used by or ordinarily belongs to a railroad or other transportation, telephone, telegraph, gas, water or electric light company or county, city, city and county or other political subdivision of this state engaged in furnishing public utility service without using due diligence to ascertain that the person selling or delivering the same has a legal right to do so, is guilty of criminally receiving such property, and is punishable, by imprisonment in a state prison, or in a county jail for not more than one year, or by a fine of not more than two hundred fifty dollars ($250), or by both such fine and imprisonment.

© 1992 by J., B. & L. Gould
Printed in the U.S.A.   EP

(b) Any person buying or receiving material pursuant to subdivision (a) shall obtain evidence of his identity from the seller including, but not limited to, such person's full name, signature, address, driver's license number, vehicle license number, and the license number of the vehicle delivering the material.

The record of the transaction shall include an appropriate description of the material purchased and such record shall be maintained pursuant to Section 21607 of the Business and Professions Code.

§496b. Purchase of matter bearing library or school mark.

Every person who, being a dealer in or collector of second-hand books or other literary material, or the agent, employee or representative of such dealer, or collector, buys or receives any book, manuscript, map, chart, or other work of literature, belonging to, and bearing any mark or indicia of ownership by a public or incorporated library, college or university, without ascertaining by diligent inquiry that the person selling or delivering the same has a legal right to do so, is guilty of criminally receiving such property in the first degree if such property be of the value of more than fifty dollars, and is punishable by imprisonment in the county jail for not more than one year, or by a fine of not more than twice the value of the property received, or by both such fine and imprisonment; and is guilty of criminally receiving such property in the second degree if such property be of the value of fifty dollars or under, and is punishable by imprisonment in the county jail for not more than one month, or by a fine of not more than twice the value of the property received, or by both such fine and imprisonment.

§496c. Copying real estate title information without consent of owner.

Any person who shall copy, transcribe, photograph or otherwise make a record or memorandum of the contents of any private and unpublished paper, book, record, map or file, containing information relating to the title to real property or containing information used in the business of examining, certifying or insuring titles to real property and belonging to any person, firm or corporation engaged in the business of examining, certifying, or insuring titles to real property, without the consent of the owner of such paper, book, record, map or file, and with the intent to use the same or the contents thereof, or to dispose of the same or the contents thereof to others for use, in the business of examining, certifying, or insuring titles to real property, shall be guilty of theft, and any person who shall induce another to violate the provisions of this section by giving, offering, or promising to such another any gift, gratuity, or thing of value or by doing or promising to do any act beneficial to such another, shall be guilty of theft; and any person who shall receive or acquire from another any copy, transcription, photograph or other record or memorandum of the contents of any private and unpublished paper, book, record, map or file containing information relating to the title to real property or containing information used in the business of examining, certifying or insuring titles to real property, with the knowledge that the same or the contents thereof has or have been acquired, prepared or compiled in violation of this section shall be guilty of theft. The contents of any such private and unpublished paper, book, record, map or file is hereby defined to be personal property, and in determining

the value thereof for the purposes of this section the cost of acquiring and compiling the same shall be the test.

§497. Bringing embezzled or stolen property into state.

Every person who, in another state or country steals or embezzles the property of another, or receives such property knowing it to have been stolen or embezzled, and brings the same into this state, may be convicted and punished in the same manner as if such larceny, or embezzlement, or receiving, had been committed in this state.

§498. Evasion of payment for utility services.

(a) The following definitions govern the construction of this section:

(1) "Person" means any individual, or any partnership, firm, association, corporation, or other legal entity.

(2) "Utility" means any electrical, gas, or water corporation as those terms are defined in the Public Utilities Code, and electrical, gas, or water systems operated by any political subdivision.

(3) "Customer" means the person in whose name utility service is provided.

(4) "Utility service" means the provision of electricity, gas, water, or any other service provided by the utility for compensation.

(5) "Divert" means to change the intended course or path of electricity, gas, or water without the authorization or consent of the utility.

(6) "Tamper" means to rearrange, injure, alter, interfere with, or otherwise prevent from performing a normal or customary function.

(7) "Reconnection" means the reconnection of utility service by a customer or other person after service has been lawfully disconnected by the utility.

(b) Any person who, with intent to obtain for himself or herself utility services without paying the full lawful charge therefor, or with intent to enable another person to do so, or with intent to deprive any utility of any part of the full lawful charge for utility services it provides, commits, authorizes, solicits, aids, or abets any of the following shall be guilty of a misdemeanor:

(1) Diverts or causes to be diverted utility services, by any means whatsoever.

(2) Prevents any utility meter, or other device used in determining the charge for utility services, from accurately performing its measuring function by tampering or by any other means.

(3) Tampers with any property owned by or used by the utility to provide utility services.

(4) Makes or causes to be made any connection with or reconnection with property owned or used by the utility to provide utility services without the authorization or consent of the utility.

(5) Uses or receives the direct benefit of all or a portion of utility services with knowledge or reason to believe that the diversion, tampering, or unauthorized connection existed at the time of that use, or that the use or receipt was otherwise without the authorization or consent of the utility.

(c) In any prosecution under this section, the presence of any of the following objects, circumstances, or conditions on premises controlled by the customer or by the person using or receiving the direct benefit of all or a portion of utility services obtained in violation of this section shall permit an inference that the customer or person intended to and did violate this section:

(1) Any instrument, apparatus, or device primarily designed to be used to obtain utility services without paying the full lawful charge therefor.

(2) Any meter that has been altered, tampered with, or bypassed so as to cause no measurement or inaccurate measurement of utility services.

(d) If the value of all utility services obtained in violation of this section totals more than four hundred dollars ($400) or if the defendant has previously been convicted of an offense under this section or any former section which would be an offense under this section, or of an offense under the laws of another state or of the United States which would have been an offense under this section if committed in this state, then the violation is punishable by imprisonment in the county jail for not more than one year, or in the state prison.

(e) This section shall not be construed to preclude the applicability of any other provision of the criminal law of this state. *(Added by Stats 1985 ch 801 §1.)*

§§499, 499a. *Repealed by Stats 1985 ch 801.*

§499b. Taking vehicle for temporary use.

Any person who shall, without the permission of the owner thereof, take any automobile, bicycle, motorcycle, or other vehicle or motorboat or vessel, for the purpose of temporarily using or operating the same, shall be deemed guilty of a misdemeanor, and upon conviction thereof, shall be punished by a fine not exceeding four hundred dollars ($400), or by imprisonment not exceeding three months, or by both such fine and imprisonment.

§499b.1. Punishment for joyriding after prior conviction.

(a) Any person who, having been convicted of a previous violation of Section 10851 of the Vehicle Code, or of subdivision (3) of Section 487, involving a vehicle or vessel, and having served a term therefor in any penal institution or having been imprisoned therein as a condition of probation for such offense, is subsequently convicted of a violation of Section 499b, involving a vehicle or vessel, is punishable for such subsequent offense by imprisonment in the county jail not exceeding one year or the state prison for 16 months, two, or three years.

(b) Any person convicted of a violation of Section 499b, who has been previously convicted under charges separately brought and tried two or more times of a violation of Section 499b, all such violations involving a vehicle or vessel, and who has been imprisoned therefore as a condition of probation or otherwise at least once, is punishable by imprisonment in the county jail for not more than one year or in the state prison for 16 months, two, or three years.

(c) Any person convicted of a violation of Section 499b, who has been previously convicted under charges separately brought and tried three or more times of a violation of Section 499b, all the violations involving a vehicle or vessel, is punishable by imprisonment in the state prison for 16 months, two, or three years.

(d) Any person convicted of a violation of Section 499b, who has twice been previously convicted under charges separately brought and tried of a violation of Section 499b, all the violations involving a vehicle or

vessel, and who has been previously convicted of a violation of Section 487h, former paragraph (3) of Section 487, involving an automobile, or Section 10851 of the Vehicle Code, is punishable by imprisonment in the state prison for 16 months, two, or three years.

(e) This section shall remain in effect only until January 1, 1993, and as of that date is repealed, unless a later enacted statute, which is enacted before January 1, 1993, deletes or extends that date. *(Amended by Stats 1989 ch 930 §8, eff. 1/1/90 only until 1/1/93. See other section 499b.1 below.)*

§499b.1. Punishment for joyriding after prior conviction.

(a) Any person who, having been convicted of a previous violation of Section 10851 of the Vehicle Code, or of subdivision (3) of Section 487, involving a vehicle or vessel, and having served a term therefor in any penal institution or having been imprisoned therein as a condition of probation for such offense, is subsequently convicted of a violation of Section 499b, involving a vehicle or vessel, is punishable for such subsequent offense by imprisonment in the county jail not exceeding one year or the state prison for 16 months, two, or three years.

(b) Any person convicted of a violation of Section 499b, who has been previously convicted under charges separately brought and tried two or more times of a violation of Section 499b, all such violations involving a vehicle or vessel, and who has been imprisoned therefore as a condition of probation or otherwise at least once, is punishable by imprisonment in the county jail for not more than one year or in the state prison for 16 months, two, or three years. *(Added by Stats 1989 ch 930 §8.1, eff. 1/1/90, oper. 1/1/93. See other section 499b.1 above.)*

§499c. Trade secrets.

(a) As used in this section:

(1) "Access" means to approach, a way or means of approaching, nearing, admittance to, including to instruct, communicate with, store information in, or retrieve information from a computer system or computer network.

(2) "Article" means any object, material, device or substance or copy thereof, including any writing, record, recording, drawing, sample, specimen, prototype, model, photograph, micro-organism, blueprint, map, or tangible representation of computer program or information, including both human and computer readable information and information while in transit.

(3) "Benefit" means gain or advantage, or anything regarded by the beneficiary as gain or advantage, including benefit to any other person or entity in whose welfare he is interested.

(4) "Computer system" means a machine or collection of machines, one or more of which contain computer programs and information, that performs functions, including, but not limited to, logic, arithmetic, information storage and retrieval, communications, and control.

(5) "Computer network" means an interconnection of two or more computer systems.

(6) "Computer program" means an ordered set of instructions or statements, and related information that, when automatically executed in actual or modified form in a computer system, causes it to perform specified functions.

© 1992 by J., B. & L. Gould
Printed in the U.S.A.   EP

(7) "Copy" means any facsimile, replica, photograph or other reproduction of an article, and any note, drawing or sketch made of or from an article.

(8) "Representing" means describing, depicting, containing, constituting, reflecting or recording.

(9) "Trade secret" means the whole or any portion or phase of any scientific or technical information, design, process, procedure, formula, computer program or information stored in a computer, information in transit, or improvement which is secret and is not generally available to the public, and which gives one who uses it an advantage over competitors who do not know of or use the trade secret; and a trade secret shall be presumed to be secret when the owner thereof takes measures to prevent it from becoming available to persons other than those selected by the owner to have access thereto for limited purposes.

(b) Every person is guilty of theft who, with intent to deprive or withhold from the owner thereof the control of a trade secret, or with an intent to appropriate a trade secret to his or her own use or to the use of another, does any of the following:

(1) Steals, takes, carries away, or uses without authorization a trade secret.

(2) Fraudulently appropriates any article representing a trade secret entrusted to him.

(3) Having unlawfully obtained access to the article, without authority makes or causes to be made a copy of any article representing a trade secret.

(4) Having obtained access to the article through a relationship of trust and confidence, without authority and in breach of the obligations created by such relationship makes or causes to be made, directly from and in the presence of the article, a copy of any article representing a trade secret.

(c) Every person who promises or offers or gives, or conspires to promise or offer to give, to any present or former agent, employee or servant of another a benefit as an inducement, bribe or reward for conveying, delivering or otherwise making available an article representing a trade secret owned by his or her present or former principal, employer or master, to any person not authorized by such owner to receive or acquire the same and every person who being a present or former agent, employee, or servant, solicits, accepts, receives or takes a benefit as an inducement, bribe or reward for conveying, delivering or otherwise making available an article representing a trade secret owned by his or her present or former principal, employer or master, to any person not authorized by such owner to receive or acquire the same is punishable by imprisonment in the state prison, or in a county jail not exceeding one year, or by fine not exceeding five thousand dollars ($5,000), or by both such fine and such imprisonment.

(d) In a prosecution for a violation of this section it shall be no defense that the person so charged, returned or intended to return the article.

§499d. Taking aircraft without owner's consent.

Any person who operates or takes an aircraft not his own, without the consent of the owner thereof, and with intent to either permanently or temporarily deprive the owner thereof of his title to or possession of such vehicle, whether with or without intent to steal the same, or any person who is a party or accessory to or an accomplice in any operation or unauthorized taking or stealing is guilty of a felony, and upon conviction thereof shall be punished by imprisonment in the state prison, or in the county jail for not more than one year or by a fine of not more than ten thousand dollars ($10,000) or by both such fine and imprisonment.

§500. Fraudulently transmitting currency to foreign countries.

(a) Any person who receives money for the actual or purported purpose of transmitting the same or its equivalent to foreign countries as specified in Section 1800.5 of the Financial Code who fails to do at least one of the following acts unless otherwise instructed by the customer is guilty of a misdemeanor or felony as set forth in subdivision (b):

(1) Forward the money as represented to the customer within 10 days of receipt of the funds.

(2) Give instructions within 10 days of receipt of the customer's funds, committing equivalent funds to the person designated by the customer.

(3) Refund to the customer any money not forwarded as represented within 10 days of the customer's written request for a refund pursuant to subdivision (a) of Section 1810.5 of the Financial Code.

(b) (1) If the total value of the funds received from the customer is less than four hundred dollars ($400), the offense set forth in subdivision (a) is punishable by imprisonment in the county jail not exceeding one year or by a fine not exceeding one thousand dollars ($1,000), or by both imprisonment and fine.

(2) If the total value of the money received from the customer is four hundred dollars ($400) or more, or if the total value of all moneys received by the person from different customers is four hundred dollars ($400), or more and the receipts were part of a common scheme or plan, the offense set forth in subdivision (a) is punishable by imprisonment in the state prison for 16 months, 2, or 3 years, by a fine not exceeding ten thousand dollars ($10,000), or by both imprisonment and fine. (*Added by Stats 1989 ch 1196 §33, eff. 1/1/90.*)

§501. Trial for larceny or embezzlement of monies.

Upon a trial for larceny or embezzlement of money, bank notes, certificates of stock, or valuable securities, the allegation of the indictment or information, so far as regards the description of the property, is sustained, if the offender be proved to have embezzled or stolen any money, bank notes, certificates of stock, or valuable security, although the particular species of coin or other money, or the number, denomination, or kind of bank notes, certificates of stock, or valuable security, is not proved; and upon a trial for embezzlement, if the offender is proved to have embezzled any piece of coin or other money, any bank note, certificate of stock, or valuable security, although the piece of coin or other money, or bank note, certificate of stock, or valuable security, may have been delivered to him or her in order that some part of the value thereof should be returned to the party delivering the same, and such part shall have been returned accordingly. (*Added by Stats 1989 ch 897 §21, eff. 1/1/90.*)

§502. Computer crimes.

(a) It is the intent of the Legislature in enacting this section to expand the degree of protection afforded to individuals, businesses, and governmental agencies from tampering, interference, damage, and unauthorized access to lawfully created computer data and computer systems. The Legislature finds and declares that the proliferation of computer technology has resulted in a concomitant proliferation of computer crime and other forms of unauthorized access to computers, computer systems, and computer data.

The Legislature further finds and declares that protection of the integrity of all types and forms of lawfully created computers, computer systems, and computer data is vital to the protection of the privacy of individuals as well as to the well-being of financial institutions, business concerns, governmental agencies, and others within this state that lawfully utilize those computers, computer systems, and data.

(b) For the purposes of this section, the following terms have the following meanings:

(1) "Access" means to gain entry to, instruct, or communicate with the logical, arithmetical, or memory function resources of a computer, computer system, or computer network.

(2) "Computer network" means any system which provides communications between one or more computer systems and input/output devices including, but not limited to, display terminals and printers connected by telecommunication facilities.

(3) "Computer program or software" means a set of instructions or statements, and related data, that when executed in actual or modified form, cause a computer, computer system, or computer network to perform specified functions.

(4) "Computer services" includes, but is not limited to, computer time, data processing, or storage functions, or other uses of a computer, computer system, or computer network.

(5) "Computer system" means a device or collection of devices, including support devices and excluding calculators which are not programmable and capable of being used in conjunction with external files, one or more of which contain computer programs, electronic instructions, input data, and output data, that performs functions including, but not limited to, logic, arithmetic, data storage and retrieval, communication, and control.

(6) "Data" means a representation of information, knowledge, facts, concepts, computer software, computer programs or instructions. Data may be in any form, in storage media, or as stored in the memory of the computer or in transit or presented on a display device.

(7) "Supporting documentation" includes, but is not limited to, all information, in any form, pertaining to the design, construction, classification, implementation, use, or modification of a computer, computer system, computer network, computer program, or computer software, which information is not generally available to the public and is necessary for the operation of a computer, computer system, computer network, computer program, or computer software.

(8) "Injury" means any alteration, deletion, damage, or destruction of a computer system, computer network, computer program, or data caused by the access.

(9) "Victim expenditure" means any expenditure reasonably and necessarily incurred by the owner or lessee to verify that a computer system, computer network, computer program, or data was or was not altered, deleted, damaged, or destroyed by the access.

(10) "Computer contaminant" means any set of computer instructions that are designed to modify, damage, destroy, record, or transmit information within a computer, computer system, or computer network without the intent or permission of the owner of the information. They include, but are not limited to, a group of computer instructions commonly called viruses or worms, which are self-replicating or self-propagating and are designed to contaminate other computer programs or computer data, consume computer resources, modify, destroy, record, or transmit data, or in some fashion usurp the normal operation of the computer, computer system, or computer network.

(c) Except as provided in subdivision (h), any person who commits any of the following acts is guilty of a public offense:

(1) Knowingly accesses and without permission alters, damages, deletes, destroys, or otherwise uses any data, computer, computer system, or computer network in order to either (A) devise or execute any scheme or artifice to defraud, deceive, or extort, or (B) wrongfully control or obtain money, property, or data.

(2) Knowingly accesses and without permission takes, copies, or makes use of any data from a computer, computer system, or computer network, or takes or copies any supporting documentation, whether existing or residing internal or external to a computer, computer system, or computer network.

(3) Knowingly and without permission uses or causes to be used computer services.

(4) Knowingly accesses and without permission adds, alters, damages, deletes, or destroys any data, computer software, or computer programs which reside or exist internal or external to a computer, computer system, or computer network.

(5) Knowingly and without permission disrupts or causes the disruption of computer services or denies or causes the denial of computer services to an authorized user of a computer, computer system, or computer network.

(6) Knowingly and without permission provides or assists in providing a means of accessing a computer, computer system, or computer network in violation of this section.

(7) Knowingly and without permission accesses or causes to be accessed any computer, computer system, or computer network.

(8) Knowingly inntroduces any computer contaminant into any computer, computer system, or computer network.

(d) (1) Any person who violates any of the provisions of paragraph (1), (2), (4), or (5) of subdivision (c) is punishable by a fine not exceeding ten thousand dollars ($10,000), or by imprisonment in the state prison for 16 months, or two or three years, or by both that fine and imprisonment, or by a fine not exceeding five thousand dollars ($5,000), or by imprisonment in the county jail not exceeding one year, or by both that fine and imprisonment.

(2) Any person who violates paragraph (3) of subdivision (c) is punishable as follows:

(A) For the first violation which does not result in injury, and where the value of the computer services used does not exceed four hundred dollars ($400), by a fine not exceeding five thousand dollars ($5,000), or by imprisonment in the county jail not exceeding one year, or by both that fine and imprisonment.

(B) For any violation which results in a victim expenditure in an amount greater than five thousand dollars ($5,000) or in an injury, or if the value of the computer services used exceeds four hundred dollars

© 1992 by J., B. & L. Gould
Printed in the U.S.A.   EP

($400), or for any second or subsequent violation, by a fine not exceeding ten thousand dollars ($10,000), or by imprisonment in the state prison for 16 months, or two or three years, or by both that fine and imprisonment, or by a fine not exceeding five thousand dollars ($5,000), or by imprisonment in the county jail not exceeding one year, or by both that fine and imprisonment.

(3) Any person who violates paragraph (6), (7), or (8) of subdivision (c) is punishable as follows:

(A) For a first violation which does not result in injury, an infraction punishable by a fine not exceeding two hundred fifty dollars ($250).

(B) For any violation which results in a victim expenditure in an amount not greater than five thousand dollars ($5,000), or for a second or subsequent violation, by a fine not exceeding five thousand dollars ($5,000), or by imprisonment in the county jail not exceeding one year, or by both that fine and imprisonment.

(C) For any violation which results in a victim expenditure in an amount greater than five thousand dollars ($5,000), by a fine not exceeding ten thousand dollars ($10,000), or by imprisonment in the state prison for 16 months, or two or three years, or by both that fine and imprisonment, or by a fine not exceeding five thousand dollars ($5,000), or by imprisonment in the county jail not exceeding one year, or by both that fine and imprisonment.

(e) (1) In addition to any other civil remedy available, the owner or lessee of the computer, computer system, computer network, computer program, or data may bring a civil action against any person convicted under this section for compensatory damages, including any expenditure reasonably and necessarily incurred by the owner or lessee to verify that a computer system, computer network, computer program, or data was or was not altered, damaged, or deleted by the access. For the purposes of actions authorized by this subdivision, the conduct of an unemancipated minor shall be imputed to the parent or legal guardian having control or custody of the minor, pursuant to the provisions of Section 1714.1 of the Civil Code.

(2) In any action brought pursuant to this subdivision the court may award reasonable attorney's fees to a prevailing party.

(3) A community college, state university, or academic institution accredited in this state is required to include computer-related crimes as a specific violation of college or university student conduct policies and regulations that may subject a student to disciplinary sanctions up to and including dismissal from the academic institution. This paragraph shall not apply to the University of California unless the Board of Regents adopts a resolution to that effect.

(f) This section shall not be construed to preclude the applicability of any other provision of the criminal law of this state which applies or may apply to any transaction, nor shall it make illegal any employee labor relations activities that are within the scope and protection of state or federal labor laws.

(g) Any computer, computer system, computer network, or any software or data, owned by the defendant, which is used during the commission of any public offense described in subdivision (c) or any computer, owned by the defendant, which is used as a repository for the storage of software or data illegally obtained in violation of subdivision (c) shall be subject to forfeiture, as specified in Section 502.01.

(h) (1) Subdivision (c) does not apply to any person who accesses his or her employer's computer system, computer network, computer program, or data when acting within the scope of his or her lawful employment.

(2) Paragraph (3) of subdivision (c) does not apply to any employee who accesses or uses his or her employer's computer system, computer network, computer program, or data when acting outside the scope of his or her lawful employment, so long as the employee's activities do not cause an injury, as defined in paragraph (8) of subdivision (b), to the employer or another, or so long as the value of computer supplies and services, as defined in paragraph (4) of subdivision (b), which are used do not exceed accumulated total of one hundred dollars ($100).

(i) No activity exempted from prosecution under paragraph (2) of subdivision (h) which incidentally violates paragraph (2), (4), or (7) of subdivision (c) shall be prosecuted under those paragraphs.

(j) For purposes of bringing a civil or a criminal action under this section, a person who causes, by any means, the access of a computer, computer system, or computer network in one jurisdiction from another jurisdiction is deemed to have personally accessed the computer, computer system, or computer network in each jurisdiction.

(k) In determining the terms and conditions applicable to a person convicted of a violation of this section the court shall consider the following:

(1) The court shall consider prohibitions on access to and use of computers.

(2) Except as otherwise required by law, the court shall consider alternate sentencing, including community service, if the defendant shows remorse and recognition of the wrongdoing, and an inclination not to repeat the offense. (*Amended by Stats 1989 ch 1076, 1110, 1357 §1.3, eff 1/1/90.*)

§502.01. Computer crime penalty; forfeiture of property.

(a) As used in this section:

(1) "Property subject to forfeiture" means any property of the defendant that is a computer, computer system, or computer network, and any software or data residing thereon, if the computer, computer system, or computer network was used in committing a violation of subdivision (c) of Section 502 or a violation of Section 502.7 or was used as a repository for the storage of software or data obtained in violation of those provisions. If the defendant is a minor, it also includes property of the parent or guardian of the defendant.

(2) "Sentencing court" means the court sentencing a person found guilty of violating subdivision (c) of Section 502 or a violation of Section 502.7 or, in the case of a minor found to be a person described in Section 602 of the Welfare and Institutions Code because of a violation of those provisions, the juvenile court.

(3) "Interest" means any property interest in the property subject to forfeiture.

(4) "Security interest" means an interest that is a lien, mortgage, security interest, or interest under a conditional sales contract.

(b) The sentencing court shall, upon petition by the prosecuting attorney, at any time following sentencing, or by agreement of all parties, at the time of sentencing, conduct a hearing to determine whether any property or property interest is subject to forfeiture under this section. At the forfeiture hearing, the prosecuting attorney shall have the burden of establishing, by a preponderance of the evidence, that the property or property interests are subject to forfeiture. The prosecuting attorney may retain seized property that may be subject to forfeiture until the sentencing hearing.

(c) Prior to the commencement of a forfeiture proceeding, the law enforcement agency seizing the property subject to forfeiture shall make an investigation as to any person other than the defendant who may have an interest in it. At least 30 days before the hearing to determine whether the property should be forfeited, the prosecuting agency shall send notice of the hearing to any person who may have an interest in the property that arose before the seizure.

A person claiming an interest in the property shall file a motion for the redemption of that interest at least 10 days before the hearing on forfeiture, and a copy of the motion to the prosecuting agency and to the probation department.

If a motion to redeem an interest has been filed, the sentencing court shall hold a hearing to identify all persons who possess valid interests in the property. No person shall hold a valid interest in the property if, by a preponderance of the evidence, the prosecuting agency shows that the person knew or should have known that the property was being used in violation of subdivision (c) of Section 502 or Section 502.7, and that the person did not take reasonable steps to prevent that use, or if the interest is a security interest, the person knew or should have known at the time that the security interest was created that the property would be used for such a violation.

(d) If the sentencing court finds that a person holds a valid interest in the property, the following provisions shall apply:

(1) The court shall determine the value of the property.

(2) The court shall determine the value of each valid interest in the property.

(3) If the value of the property is greater than the value of the interest, the holder of the interest shall be entitled to ownership of the property upon paying the court the difference between the value of the property and the value of the valid interest.

If the holder of the interest declines to pay the amount determined under paragraph (2), the court may order the property sold and designate the prosecutor or any other agency to sell the property. The designated agency shall be entitled to seize the property and the holder of the interest shall forward any documentation underlying the interest, including any ownership certificates for that property, to the designated agency. The designated agency shall sell the property and pay the owner of the interest the proceeds, up to the value of that interest.

(4) If the value of the property is less than the value of the interest, the designated agency shall sell the property and pay the owner of the interest the proceeds, up to the value of that interest.

(e) If the defendant was a minor at the time of the offense, this subdivision shall apply to property subject to forfeiture that is the property of the parent or guardian of the minor.

(1) The prosecuting agency shall notify the parent or guardian of the forfeiture hearing at least 30 days before the date set for the hearing.

(2) The computer shall not be subject to forfeiture if the parent or guardian files a signed statement with the court at least 10 days before the date set for the hearing that the minor shall not have access to any computer owned by the parent or guardian for two years after the date on which the minor is sentenced.

(3) If the minor is convicted of a violation of subdivision (c) of Section 502 or Section 502.7 within two years after the date on which the minor is sentenced, and the violation involves a computer owned by the parent or guardian, the original property subject to forfeiture, and the property involved in the new offense, shall be subject to forfeiture notwithstanding paragraph (2).

(f) If the defendant is found to have the only valid interest in the property subject to forfeiture, it shall be distributed as follows:

(1) First, to the victim, if the victim elects to take the property as full or partial restitution for injury, victim expenditures, or compensatory damages, as defined in paragraph (1) of subdivision (e) of Section 502. If the victim elects to receive the property under this paragraph, the value of the property shall be determined by the court and that amount shall be credited against the restitution owed by the defendant. The victim shall not be penalized for electing not to accept the forfeited property in lieu of full or partial restitution.

(2) Second, at the discretion of the court, to one or more of the following agencies or entities:

(A) The prosecuting agency.

(B) The public entity of which the prosecuting agency is a part.

(C) The public entity whose officers or employees conducted the investigation resulting in forfeiture.

(D) Other state and local public entities, including school districts.

(E) Nonprofit charitable organizations.

(g) If the property is to be sold, the court may designate the prosecuting agency or any other agency to sell the property at auction. The proceeds of the sale shall be distributed by the court as follows:

(1) To the bona fide or innocent purchaser or encumbrancer, conditional sales vendor, or mortgagee of the property up to the amount of his or her interest in the property, if the court orders a distribution to that person.

(2) The balance, if any, to be retained by the court, subject to the provisions for distribution under subdivision (f). (*Amended by Stats 1990 ch 22 §1, eff. 1/1/91.*)

§502.1. *Repealed by Stats 1990 ch 22 §2, eff. 1/1/91.*

§502.5. Removal of mortgaged property.

Every person who, after mortgaging or encumbering by deed of trust any real property, and during the existence of such mortgage or deed of trust, or after such mortgaged or encumbered property shall have been sold under an order and decree of foreclosure or at trustee's sale, and with intent to defraud or injure the mortgagee or the beneficiary or trustee, under such deed of trust, his representatives, successors or assigns, or the purchaser of such mortgaged or encumbered premises at such foreclosure or trustee's sale, his representatives, successors or assigns, takes, removes or carries away from such mortgaged or encumbered premises, or otherwise disposes of or permits the taking, removal or carrying away or

© 1992 by J., B. & L. Gould
Printed in the U.S.A.   EP

otherwise disposing of any house, barn, windmill, water tank, pump, engine or other part of the freehold that is attached or affixed to such premises as an improvement thereon, without the written consent of the mortgagee or beneficiary, under deed of trust, his representatives, successors or assigns, or the purchaser at such foreclosure or trustee's sale, his representatives, successors or assigns, is guilty of larceny and shall be punished accordingly.

§502.7. Fraudulently obtaining telephone or telegraph service.

(a) Any person who, knowingly, willfully, and with intent to defraud a person providing telephone or telegraph service, avoids or attempts to avoid, or aids, abets or causes another to avoid the lawful charge, in whole or in part, for telephone or telegraph service by any of the following means is guilty of a misdemeanor or a felony, as provided in subdivision (f):

(1) By charging the service to an existing telephone number or credit card number without the authority of the subscriber thereto or the lawful holder thereof.

(2) By charging the service to a nonexistent telephone number or credit card number, or to a number associated with telephone service which is suspended or terminated, or to a revoked or canceled (as distinguished from expired) credit card number, notice of the suspension, termination, revocation, or cancellation of the telephone service or credit card having been given to the subscriber thereto or the holder thereof.

(3) By use of a code, prearranged scheme, or other similar stratagem or device whereby the person, in effect, sends or receives information.

(4) By rearranging, tampering with, or making connection with telephone or telegraph facilities or equipment, whether physically, electrically, acoustically, inductively, or otherwise, or by using telephone or telegraph service with knowledge or reason to believe that the rearrangement, tampering, or connection existed at the time of the use.

(5) By using any other deception, false pretense, trick, scheme, device, or means.

(b) Any person who (1) makes, possesses, sells, gives, or otherwise transfers to another, or offers or advertises any instrument, apparatus, or device with intent to use it or with knowledge or reason to believe it is intended to be used to avoid any lawful telephone or telegraph toll charge or to conceal the existence or place of origin or destination of any telephone or telegraph message; or (2) sells, gives, or otherwise transfers to another or offers, or advertises plans or instructions for making or assembling an instrument, apparatus, or device described in paragraph (1) of this subdivision with knowledge or reason to believe that they may be used to make or assemble the instrument, apparatus, or device is guilty of a misdemeanor or a felony, as provided in subdivision (f).

(c) Any person who publishes the number or code of an existing, canceled, revoked, expired, or nonexistent credit card, or the numbering or coding which is employed in the issuance of credit cards, with the intent that it be used or with knowledge or reason to believe that it will be used to avoid the payment of any lawful telephone or telegraph toll change is guilty of a misdemeanor. The provisions of subdivision (f) shall not apply to this subdivision. As used in this section, "publishes" means the communication of information to any one or more persons, either orally, in person or by telephone, radio, or television, or in a writing of any kind, including without limitation a letter or memorandum, circular or handbill, newspaper, or magazine article, or book.

(d) Subdivision (a) applies when the telephone or telegraph communication involved either originates or terminates, or both originates and terminates, in this state, or when the charges for service would have been billable, in normal course, by a person providing telephone or telegraph service in this state, but for the fact that the charge for service was avoided, or attempted to be avoided, by one or more of the means set forth in subdivision (a).

(e) Jurisdiction of an offense under this section is in the jurisdictional territory where the telephone call or telegram involved in the offense originates or where it terminates, or the jurisdictional territory to which the bill for the service is sent or would have been sent but for the fact that the service was obtained or attempted to be obtained by one or more of the means set forth in subdivision (a).

(f) If the total value of all telephone or telegraph services obtained in violation of this section aggregates over four hundred dollars ($400) within any period of twelve (12) consecutive months during the three years immediately prior to the time the indictment is found or the case is certified to the superior court, or prior to the time the information is filed, or if the defendant has previously been convicted of an offense in excess of four hundred dollars ($400) under this section or of an offense in excess of four hundred dollars ($400) under the laws of another state or of the United States which would have been an offense under this section if committed in this state, a person guilty of such offense is punishable by imprisonment in the county jail not exceeding one year, by a fine not exceeding one thousand dollars ($1,000), or both, or by imprisonment in the state prison, by a fine not exceeding ten thousand dollars ($10,000), or both.

(g) Any instrument, apparatus, device, plans, instructions, or written publication described in subdivision (b) or (c) may be seized under warrant or incident to a lawful arrest, and, upon the conviction of a person for a violation of subdivision (a), (b), or (c), the instrument, apparatus, device, plans, instructions, or written publication may be destroyed as contraband by the sheriff of the county in which the person was convicted or turned over to the person providing telephone or telegraph service in the territory in which it was seized.

(h) Any computer, computer system, computer network, or any software or data, owned by the defendant, which is used during the commission of any public offense described in this section or any computer, owned by the defendant, which is used as a repository for the storage of software or data illegally obtained in violation of this section shall be subject to forfeiture. *(Amended by Stats 1989 ch 1110 §6, eff. 1/1/90.)*

CHAPTER 6

EMBEZZLEMENT

§503. Embezzlement defined.

Embezzlement is the fraudulent appropriation of property by a person to whom it has been intrusted.

§504. Appropriation of state or private corporation property.

Every officer of this State, or of any county, city, city and county, or other municipal corporation or subdivision thereof, and every deputy, clerk, or servant of any such officer, and every officer, director, trustee, clerk, servant, or agent of any association, society, or corporation (public or private), who fraudulently appropriates to any use or purpose not in the due and lawful execution of his trust, any property which he has in his possession or under his control by virtue of his trust, or secretes it with a fraudulent intent to appropriate it to such use or purpose, is guilty of embezzlement.

§504a. Fraudulent removal, concealment or disposal of personal property.

Every person who shall fraudulently remove, conceal or dispose of any goods, chattels or effects, leased or let to him by any instrument in writing, or any personal property or effects of another in his possession, under a contract of purchase not yet fulfilled, and any person in possession of such goods, chattels or effects knowing them to be subject to such lease or contract of purchase who shall so remove, conceal or dispose of the same with intent to injure or defraud the lessor or owner thereof, is guilty of embezzlement.

§504b. Proceeds from sale of property.

Where under the terms of a security agreement, as defined in Section 9105 of the Commercial Code, the debtor has the right to sell the property covered thereby and is to account to the secured party for, and pay to the secured party the indebtedness secured by the security agreement from, the proceeds of the sale of any of the said property, and where such debtor, having sold the property covered by the security agreement and having received the proceeds of such sale, willfully and wrongfully, and with the intent to defraud, fails to pay to the secured party the amounts due under the security agreement, or the proceeds of such sale, whichever is the lesser amount, and appropriates such money to his own use, said debtor shall be guilty of embezzlement and shall be punishable as provided in Section 514.

§505. When carrier or other person having property for transportation, for hire, guilty of embezzlement.

Every carrier or other person having under his control personal property for the purpose of transportation for hire, who fraudulently appropriates it to any use or purpose inconsistent with the safe keeping of such property and its transportation according to his trust, is guilty of embezzlement, whether he has broken the package in which such property is contained, or has otherwise separated the items thereof, or not.

§506. Property held by trustee or fiduciary.

Every trustee, banker, merchant, broker, attorney, agent, assignee in trust, executor, administrator, or collector, or person otherwise entrusted with or having in his control property for the use of any other person, who fraudulently appropriates it to any use or purpose not in the due and lawful execution of his trust, or secretes it with a fraudulent intent to appropriate it to such use or purpose, and any contractor who appropriates money paid to him for any use or purpose, other than for that which he received it, is guilty of embezzlement, and the payment of laborers and materialmen for work performed or material furnished in the performance of any contract is hereby declared to be the use and purpose to which the contract price of such contract, or any part thereof, received by the contractor shall be applied.

§506a. Debt collector.

Any person who, acting as collector, or acting in any capacity in or about a business conducted for the collection of accounts or debts owing by another person, and who violates Section 506 of the Penal Code, shall be deemed to be an agent or person as defined in Section 506, and subject for a violation of Section 506, to be prosecuted, tried, and punished in accordance therewith and with law; and "collector" means every such person who collects, or who has in his or her possession or under his or her control property or money for the use of any other person, whether in his or her own name and mixed with his or her own property or money, or otherwise, or whether he or she has any interest, direct or indirect, in or to such property or money, or any portion thereof, and who fraudulently appropriates to his or her own use, or the use of any person other than the true owner, or person entitled thereto, or secretes that property or money, or any portion thereof, or interest therein not his or her own, with a fraudulent intent to appropriate it to any use or purpose not in the due and lawful execution of his or her trust. *(Amended by Stats 1987 ch 828 §30.)*

§506b. Real property sales contracts.

Any person who violates Section 2985.3 or 2985.4 of the Civil Code, relating to real property sales contracts, is guilty of a public offense punishable by a fine not exceeding ten thousand dollars ($10,000), or by imprisonment in the state prison, or in the county jail not exceeding one year, or by both such fine and imprisonment.

§507. Embezzlement; when bailee, tenant, or lodger guilty.

Every person intrusted with any property as bailee, tenant, or lodger, or with any power of attorney for the sale or transfer thereof, who fraudulently converts the same or the proceeds thereof to his own use, or secretes it or them with a fraudulent intent to convert to his own use, is guilty of embezzlement.

§508. Embezzlement; when clerk agent, or servant guilty.

Every clerk, agent, or servant of any person who fraudulently appropriates to his own use, or secretes with a fraudulent intent to appropriate to his own use, any property of another which has come into his control or care by virtue of his employment as such clerk, agent, or servant, is guilty of embezzlement.

§509. Distinct act of taking.

A distinct act of taking is not necessary to constitute embezzlement.

§510. Evidence of debt undelivered may be subject of embezzlement.

Any evidence of debt, negotiable by delivery only, and actually executed, is the subject of embezzlement, whether it has been delivered or issued as a valid instrument or not.

© 1992 by J., B. & L. Gould
Printed in the U.S.A.   EP

§511. Claim of title a ground of defense.

Upon any indictment for embezzlement, it is a sufficient defense that the property was appropriated openly and avowedly, and under a claim of title preferred in good faith, even though such claim is untenable. But this provision does not excuse the unlawful retention of the property of another to offset or pay demands held against him.

§512. Restoring property as defense.

The fact that the accused intended to restore the property embezzled, is no ground of defense or mitigation of punishment, if it has not been restored before an information has been laid before a magistrate, or an indictment found by a grand jury, charging the commission of the offense.

§513. Mitigation of punishment.

Whenever, prior to an information laid before a magistrate, or an indictment found by a grand jury, charging the commission of embezzlement, the person accused voluntarily and actually restores or tenders restoration of the property alleged to have been embezzled, or any part thereof, such fact is not a ground of defense, but it authorizes the court to mitigate punishment, in its discretion.

§514. Disqualification to hold office.

Every person guilty of embezzlement is punishable in the manner prescribed for theft of property of the value or kind embezzled; and where the property embezzled is an evidence of debt or right of action, the sum due upon it or secured to be paid by it must be taken as its value; if the embezzlement or defalcation is of the public funds of the United States, or of this state, or of any county or municipality within this state, the offense is a felony, and is punishable by imprisonment in the state prison; and the person so convicted is ineligible thereafter to any office of honor, trust, or profit in this state.

CHAPTER 7

EXTORTION

§518. Extortion defined.

Extortion is the obtaining of property from another, with his consent, or the obtaining of an official act of a public officer, induced by a wrongful use of force or fear, or under color of official right.

§519. Threats.

Fear, such as will constitute extortion, may be induced by a threat, either:

1. To do an unlawful injury to the person or property of the individual threatened or of a third person; or,

2. To accuse the individual threatened, or any relative of his, or member of his family, of any crime; or,

3. To expose, or to impute to him or them any deformity, disgrace or crime; or,

4. To expose any secret affecting him or them.

§520. Extortion of property; punishment.

Every person who extorts any money or other property from another, under circumstances not amounting to robbery, by means of force, or any threat, such as is mentioned in the preceding section, is punishable by imprisonment in the state prison for two, three or four years.

§521. Punishment of extortion committed under color of official right.

Every person who commits any extortion under color of official right, in cases for which a different punishment is not prescribed in this Code, is guilty of a misdemeanor.

§522. Obtaining signature by means of threats.

Every person who, by any extortionate means, obtains from another his signature to any paper or instrument, whereby, if such signature were freely given, any property would be transferred, or any debt, demand, charge, or right of action created, is punishable in the same manner as if the actual delivery of such debt, demand, charge, or right of action were obtained.

§523. Sending threatening letters with intent to extort money, etc.

Every person who, with intent to extort any money or other property from another, sends or delivers to any person any letter or other writing, whether subscribed or not, expressing or implying, or adapted to imply, any threat such as is specified in Section 519, is punishable in the same manner as if such money or property were actually obtained by means of such threat.

§524. Punishment for attempt.

Every person who attempts, by means of any threat, such as is specified in Section 519 of this code, to extort money or other property from another is punishable by imprisonment in the county jail not longer than one year or in the state prison or by fine not exceeding ten thousand dollars ($10,000), or by both such fine and imprisonment.

§526. Misleading use of documents resembling process of court.

Any person, who, with intent to obtain from another person any money, article of personal property or other thing of value, delivers or causes to be delivered to the other person any paper, document or written, typed or printed form purporting to be an order or other process of a court, or designed or calculated by its writing, typing or printing, or the arrangement thereof, to cause or lead the other person to believe it to be an order or other process of a court, when in fact such paper, document or written, typed or printed form is not an order or process of a court, is guilty of a misdemeanor, and each separate delivery of any paper, document or written, typed or printed form shall constitute a separate offense. (*Amended by Stats 1987 ch 828 §31.*)

§527. Selling and publishing fake court documents.

Any person who shall sell or offer for sale, print, publish, or distribute any paper, document or written, typed or printed form, designed or calculated by its writing, typing or printing, or the arrangement thereof, to cause or lead any person to believe it to be, or that it will be used as an order or other process of a court when in fact such paper, document or written, typed or printed form is not to be used as the order or process of a court, is guilty of a misdemeanor, and each separate publication, printing, distribution, sale or offer to sell any such paper, document or written, typed or printed form shall constitute a separate offense, and upon conviction thereof in addition to any other sentence imposed the court may order that all such papers or documents or written, typed or printed forms in the possession or under the control of the person found guilty of such misdemeanor shall be delivered to such court or the clerk thereof for destruction.

CHAPTER 8

FALSE PERSONATION AND CHEATS

§528. Marrying under false personation.

Every person who falsely personates another, and in such assumed character marries or pretends to marry, or to sustain the marriage relation towards another, with or without the connivance of such other, is guilty of a felony.

§529. False personation of another.

Every person who falsely personates another in either his private or official capacity, and in such assumed character either:

1. Becomes bail or surety for any party in any proceeding whatever, before any court or officer authorized to take such bail or surety;

2. Verifies, publishes, acknowledges, or proves, in the name of another person, any written instrument, with intent that the same may be recorded, delivered, or used as true; or,

3. Does any other act whereby, if done by the person falsely personated, he might, in any event, become liable to any suit or prosecution, or to pay any sum of money, or to incur any charge, forfeiture, or penalty, or whereby any benefit might accrue to the party personating, or to any other person;

Is punishable by a fine not exceeding ten thousand dollars ($10,000), or by imprisonment in the state prison, or in a county jail not exceeding one year, or by both such fine and imprisonment.

§529a. False or counterfeit birth record.

Every person who manufactures, produces, sells, offers, or transfers to another any document purporting to be either a certificate of birth or certificate of baptism, knowing such document to be false or counterfeit and with the intent to deceive, is guilty of a crime, and upon conviction therefor, shall be punished by imprisonment in the county jail not to exceed one year, or by imprisonment in the state prison. Every person who offers, displays, or has in his or her possession any false or counterfeit certificate of birth or certificate of baptism, or any genuine certificate of birth which describes a person then living or deceased, with intent to represent himself or herself as another or to conceal his or her true identity, is guilty of a crime, and upon conviction therefor, shall be punished by imprisonment in the county jail not to exceed one year. *(Amended by Stats 1987 ch 1477 §10.)*

§529.5. False identification cards and driver's licenses.

(a) Every person who manufactures, sells, offers for sale, or transfers any document, not amounting to counterfeit, purporting to be a government-issued identification card or driver's license, which by virtue of the wording or appearance thereon could reasonably deceive an ordinary person into believing that it is issued by a government agency, and who knows that the document is not a government-issued document, is guilty of a misdemeanor, punishable by imprisonment in a county jail not exceeding one year, or by a fine not exceeding one thousand dollars ($1,000), or by both the fine and imprisonment.

(b) Any person who, having been convicted of a violation of subdivision (a), is subsequently convicted of a violation of subdivision (a), is punishable for the subsequent conviction by imprisonment in a county jail not exceeding one year, or by a fine not exceeding five thousand dollars ($5,000), or by both the fine and imprisonment.

(c) Any person who possesses a document described in subdivision (a) and who knows that the document is not a government-issued document is guilty of a misdemeanor punishable by a fine of not less than one thousand dollars ($1,000) and not more than two thousand five hundred dollars ($2,500). The misdemeanor fine shall be imposed except in unusual cases where the interests of justice would be served. The court may allow an offender to work off the fine by doing community service. If community service work is not available, the misdemeanor shall be punishable by a fine of up to one thousand dollars ($1,000), based on the person's ability to pay.

(d) If an offense specified in this section is committed by a person when he or she is under 21 years of age, but is 13 years of age or older, the court also may suspend the person's driving privilege for one year, pursuant to Section 13202.5 of the Vehicle Code. *(Amended by Stats 1990 ch 960 §1, eff. 1/1/91.)*

§530. False personation for the purpose of obtaining money or property.

Every person who falsely personates another, in either his private or official capacity, and in such assumed character receives any money or property, knowing that it is intended to be delivered to the individual so personated, with intent to convert the same to his own use, or to that of another person, or to deprive the true owner thereof, is punishable in the same manner and to the same extent as for larceny of the money or property so received.

§531. Fraudulent conveyances.

Every person who is a party to any fraudulent conveyance of any lands, tenements, or hereditaments, goods or chattels, or any right or interest issuing out of the same, or to any bond, suit, judgment, or execution, contract or conveyance, had, made, or contrived with intent to deceive and defraud others, or to defeat, hinder, or delay creditors or others of their just debts, damages, or demands; or who, being a party as aforesaid, at any time wittingly and willingly puts in, uses, avows, maintains, justifies, or defends the same, or any of them, as true, and done, had, or made in good faith, or upon good consideration, or aliens, assigns, or sells any of the lands, tenements, hereditaments, goods, chattels, or other things before mentioned, to him or them conveyed as aforesaid, or any part thereof, is guilty of a misdemeanor.

§531a. Procuring conveyance by person without right.

Every person who, with intent to defraud, knowingly executes or procures another to execute any instru-

© 1992 by J., B. & L. Gould
Printed in the U.S.A.   EP

ment purporting to convey any real property, or any right or interest therein, knowing that such person so executing has no right to or interest in such property, or who files or procures the filing of any such instrument, knowing that the person executing the same had no right, title or interest in the property so purported to be conveyed, is guilty of a misdemeanor and is punishable by imprisonment for not more than one year or by fine of five thousand dollars or both.

§532. Obtaining money, labor, or property under false pretenses.

(a) Every person who knowingly and designedly, by any false or fraudulent representation or pretense, defrauds any other person of money, labor, or property, whether real or personal, or who causes or procures others to report falsely of his or her wealth or mercantile character, and by thus imposing upon any person obtains credit, and thereby fraudulently gets possession of money or property, or obtains the labor or service of another, is punishable in the same manner and to the same extent as for larceny of the money or property so obtained.

(b) Upon a trial for having, with an intent to cheat or defraud another designedly, by any false pretense, obtained the signature of any person to a written instrument, or having obtained from any person any labor, money, or property, whether real or personal, or valuable thing, the defendant cannot be convicted if the false pretense was expressed in language unaccompanied by a false token or writing, unless the pretense, or some note or memorandum thereof is in writing, subscribed by or in the handwriting of the defendant, or unless the pretense is proven by the testimony of two witnesses, or that of one witness and corroborating circumstances. This section does not apply to a prosecution for falsely representing or personating another, and, in that assumed character, marrying, or receiving any money or property. *(Amended by Stats 1989 ch 897 §22, eff. 1/1/90.)*

§532a. False financial statements.

(1) Any person who shall knowingly make or cause to be made, either directly or indirectly or through any agency whatsoever, any false statement in writing, with intent that it shall be relied upon, respecting the financial condition, or means or ability to pay, of himself, or any other person, firm or corporation, in whom he is interested, or for whom he is acting, for the purpose of procuring in any form whatsoever, either the delivery of personal property, the payment of cash, the making of a loan or credit, the extension of a credit, the execution of a contract of guaranty or suretyship, the discount of an account receivable, or the making, acceptance, discount, sale or indorsement of a bill of exchange, or promissory note, for the benefit of either himself or of such person, firm or corporation shall be guilty of a public offense.

(2) Any person who knowing that a false statement in writing has been made, respecting the financial condition or means or ability to pay, of himself, or a person, firm or corporation in which he is interested, or for whom he is acting, procures, upon the faith thereof, for the benefit either of himself, or of such person, firm or corporation, either or any of the things of benefit mentioned in the first subdivision of this section shall be guilty of a public offense.

(3) Any person who knowing that a statement in writing has been made, respecting the financial condition or means or ability to pay of himself or a person, firm or corporation, in which he is interested, or for whom he is acting, represents on a later day in writing that the statement theretofore made, if then again made on said day, would be then true, when in fact, said statement if then made would be false, and procures upon the faith thereof, for the benefit either of himself or of such person, firm or corporation either or any of the things of benefit mentioned in the first subdivision of this section shall be guilty of a public offense.

(4) Any person committing a public offense under subdivision (1), (2), or (3) shall be guilty of a misdemeanor, punishable by a fine of not more than one thousand dollars ($1,000), or by imprisonment in the county jail for not more than six months, or by both such fine and imprisonment. Any person who violates the provisions of subdivision (1), (2), or (3), by using a fictitious name, social security number, business name, or business address, or by falsely representing himself or herself to be another person or another business, is guilty of a felony and is punishable by a fine not exceeding five thousand dollars ($5,000) or by imprisonment in the state prison, or by both such fine and imprisonment, or by a fine not exceeding two thousand five hundred dollars ($2,500) or by imprisonment in the county jail not exceeding one year, or by both such fine and imprisonment.

(5) This section shall not be construed to preclude the applicability of any other provision of the criminal law of this state which applies or may apply to any transaction.

§532b. Impersonating veteran or ex-serviceman.

Any person who shall falsely represent himself as a veteran or ex-serviceman of any war in which the United States was engaged in connection with the soliciting of aid or the sale or attempted sale of any property shall be guilty of a misdemeanor.

§532c. Giving real estate at drawing of numbers or with admission tickets and charging for transfer thereof.

Any person, firm, corporation or copartnership who knowingly and designedly offers or gives with winning numbers at any drawing of numbers or with tickets of admission to places of public assemblage, any lot or parcel of real property and charges or collects fees in connection with the transfer thereof, is guilty of a misdemeanor.

§532d. False representations in solicitation of charitable contributions.

Any person who solicits or attempts to solicit or receives money or property of any kind for a charitable, religious or eleemosynary purpose and who, directly or indirectly, makes, utters, or delivers, either orally or in writing, an unqualified statement of fact concerning the purpose or organization for which the money or property is solicited or received, or concerning the cost and expense of solicitation or the manner in which the money or property or any part thereof is to be used, which statement is in fact false and was made, uttered, or delivered by that person either willfully and with knowledge of its falsity or negligently without due consideration of those facts which by the use of ordinary care he or she should have known, is guilty of a misdemeanor. An offense charged in violation of this section shall be proven by the testimony of one witness and corroborating circumstances. Nothing contained in this section shall be construed to limit the right of any city, county, or city and county to adopt regulations for charitable solicitations which are not in conflict with this section. *(Amended by Stats 1990 ch 253 §1, eff. 1/1/91.)*

§532e. Unlawful rebate.

Any person who receives money for the purpose of obtaining or paying for services, labor, materials or equipment incident to constructing improvements on real property and willfully rebates any part of the money to or on behalf of anyone contracting with such person, for provision of the services, labor, materials or equipment for which the money was given, shall be guilty of a misdemeanor; provided, however, that normal trade discount for prompt payment shall not be considered a violation of this section.

§533. Multiple sales of same parcel of real estate.

Every person who, after once selling, bartering, or disposing of any tract of land or town lot, or after executing any bond or agreement for the sale of any land or town lot, again willfully and with intent to defraud previous or subsequent purchasers, sells, barters, or disposes of the same tract of land or town lot, or any part thereof, or willfully and with intent to defraud previous or subsequent purchasers, executes any bond or agreement to sell, barter, or dispose of the same land or lot, or any part thereof, to any other person for a valuable consideration, is punishable by imprisonment in the state prison.

§534. Married person selling lands under false representations.

Every married person who falsely and fraudulently represents himself or herself as competent to sell or mortgage any real estate, to the validity of which sale or mortgage the assent or concurrence of his wife or her husband is necessary, and under such representations willfully conveys or mortgages the same, is guilty of felony.

§535. Mock auctions.

Every person who obtains any money or property from another, or obtains the signature of another to any written instrument, the false making of which would be forgery, by means of any false or fraudulent sale of property or pretended property, by auction, or by any of the practices known as mock auctions, is punishable by imprisonment in the state prison, or in the county jail not exceeding one year, or by fine not exceeding two thousand dollars ($2,000), or by both such fine and imprisonment; and, in addition thereto, forfeits any license he may hold as auctioneer, and is forever disqualified from receiving a license to act as auctioneer within this state.

§536. False statement of sales.

Every commission merchant, broker, agent, factor, or consignee, who shall willfully and corruptly make, or cause to be made, to the principal or consignor of such commission merchant, agent, broker, factor, or consignee, a false statement as to the price obtained for any property consigned or entrusted for sale, or as to the quality or quantity of any property so consigned or entrusted, or as to any expenditures made in connection therewith, shall be deemed guilty of a mis-

demeanor, and on conviction thereof, shall be punished by fine not exceeding one thousand dollars ($1,000) and not less than two hundred dollars ($200), or by imprisonment in the county jail not exceeding six months and not less than 10 days, or by both such fine and imprisonment.

§536a. Statement of sale by commission merchants, etc.

It is hereby made the duty of every commission merchant, broker, factor, or consignee, to whom any property is consigned or entrusted for sale, to make, when accounting therefor or subsequently, upon the written demand of his principal or consignor, a true written statement setting forth the name and address of the person or persons to whom a sale of the said property, or any portion thereof, was made, the quantity so sold to each purchaser, and the respective prices obtained therefor; provided, however, that unless separate written demand shall be made as to each consignment or shipment regarding which said statement is desired, prior to sale, it shall be sufficient to set forth in said statement only so many of said matters above enumerated as said commission merchant, broker, factor, or consignee may be able to obtain from the books of account kept by him; and that said statement shall not be required in case of cash sales where the amount of the transaction is less than fifty dollars. Any person violating the provisions of this section is guilty of a misdemeanor.

§537. Defrauding innkeepers.

(a) Any person who obtains any food, fuel, services, or accommodations at a hotel, inn, restaurant, boardinghouse, lodginghouse, apartment house, bungalow court, motel, marina, marine facility, autocamp, ski area, or public or private campground, without paying therefor, with intent to defraud the proprietor or manager thereof, or who obtains credit at an hotel, inn, restaurant, boarding-house, lodginghouse, apartment house, bungalow court, motel, marina, marine facility, autocamp, or public or private campground by the use of any false pretense, or who, after obtaining credit, food, fuel, services, or accommodations, at an hotel, inn, restaurant, boardinghouse, lodginghouse, apartment house, bungalow court, motel, marina, marine facility, autocamp, or public or private campground, absconds, or surreptitiously, or by force, menace, or threats, removes any part of his or her baggage therefrom with the intent not to pay for his or her food or accommodations is guilty of a public offense punishable as follows:

(1) If the value of the credit, food, fuel, services, or accommodations is four hundred dollars ($400) or less, by a fine not exceeding one thousand dollars ($1,000) or by imprisonment in the county jail for a term not exceeding six months, or both.

(2) If the value of the credit, food, fuel, services, or accommodations is greater than four hundred dollars ($400), by imprisonment in the county jail for a term of not more than one year, or in the state prison.

(b) Any person who uses or attempts to use ski area facilities for which payment is required without paying as required, or who resells a ski lift ticket to another when the resale is not authorized by the proprietor, is guilty of an infraction.

(c) Evidence that a person left the premises of such an hotel, inn, restaurant, boardinghouse, lodginghouse, apartment house, bungalow court, motel,

© 1992 by J., B. & L. Gould
Printed in the U.S.A.   EP

marina, marine facility, autocamp, ski area, or public or private campground, without paying or offering to pay for such food, fuel, services, use of facilities, or accommodation, or that the person, without authorization from the proprietor, resold his or her ski lift ticket to another person after making use of such facilities, shall be prima facie evidence of the following:

(1) That the person obtained such food, fuel, services, use of facilities or accommodations with intent to defraud the proprietor or manager.

(2) That, if, after obtaining the credit, food, fuel, services, or accommodations, the person absconded, or surreptitiously, or by force, menace, or threats, removed part of his or her baggage therefrom, the person did so with the intent not to pay for the credit, food, fuel, services, or accommodations. *(Amended by Stats 1985 ch 1329 §2.)*

§537b. Defrauding proprietors of livery stables.

Any person who obtains any livery hire or other accommodation at any livery or feed stable, kept for profit, in this state, without paying therefor, with intent to defraud the proprietor or manager thereof; or who obtains credit at any such livery or feed stable by the use of any false pretense; or who after obtaining a horse, vehicle, or other property at such livery or feed stable, willfully or maliciously abuses the same by beating, goading, overdriving or other willful or malicious conduct, or who after obtaining such horse, vehicle, or other property, shall, with intent to defraud the owner, manager or proprietor of such livery or feed stable, keep the same for a longer period, or take the same to a greater distance than contracted for; or allow a feed bill or other charges to accumulate against such property, without paying therefor; or abandon or leave the same, is guilty of a misdemeanor.

§537c. Unauthorized use of animals or equipment of stable.

Every owner, manager, proprietor, or other person, having the management, charge or control of any livery stable, feed or boarding stable, and every person pasturing stock, who shall receive and take into his possession, charge, care or control, any horse, mare, or other animal, or any buggy, or other vehicle, belonging to any other person, to be by him kept, fed, or cared for, and who, while said horse, mare or other animal or buggy or other vehicle, is thus in his possession, charge, care or under his control, as aforesaid, shall drive, ride or use, or knowingly permit or allow any person other than the owner or other person entitled so to do, to drive, ride, or otherwise use the same, without the consent or permission of the owner thereof, or other person charged with the care, control or possession of such property, shall be guilty of a misdemeanor.

§537e. Removal of serial numbers or identification marks.

(a) Any person who knowingly buys, sells, receives, disposes of, conceals, or has in his or her possession any personal property from which the manufacturer's serial number or any other distinguishing number or identification mark has been removed, defaced, covered, altered, or destroyed, is guilty of a public offense, punishable as follows:

(1) If the value of the property does not exceed four hundred dollars ($400), by imprisonment in the county jail not exceeding six months.

(2) If the value of the property exceeds four hundred dollars ($400), by imprisonment in the county jail not exceeding one year.

(3) If the property is an integrated computer chip or panel of a value of four hundred dollars ($400) or more, by imprisonment in the state prison for 16 months, or 2 or 3 years or by imprisonment in a county jail not exceeding one year.

For purposes of this subdivision, "personal property" includes, but is not limited to, the following:

(1) Any television, radio, recorder, phonograph, telephone, piano, or any other musical instrument or sound equipment.

(2) Any washing machine, sewing machine, vacuum cleaner, or other household appliance or furnishings.

(3) Any typewriter, adding machine, dictaphone, or any other office equipment or furnishings.

(4) Any computer, printed circuit, integrated chip or panel, or other part of a computer.

(5) Any tool or similar device, including any technical or scientific equipment.

(6) Any bicycle, exercise equipment, or any other entertainment or recreational equipment.

(7) Any electrical or mechanical equipment, contrivance, material, or piece of apparatus or equipment.

(8) Any clock, watch, watch case, or watch movement.

(9) Any vehicle or vessel, or any component part thereof.

(b) When property described in subdivision (a) comes into the custody of a peace officer it shall become subject to the provision of Chapter 12 (commencing with Section 1407), Title 10 of Part 2, relating to the disposal of stolen or embezzled property. Property subject to this section shall be considered stolen or embezzled property for the purposes of that chapter, and prior to being disposed of, shall have an identification mark imbedded or engraved in, or permanently affixed to it.

(c) This section does not apply to those cases or instances where any of the changes or alterations enumerated in subdivision (a) have been customarily made or done as an established practice in the ordinary and regular conduct of business, by the original manufacturer, or by his or her duly appointed direct representative, or under specific authorization from the original manufacturer. *(Amended by Stats 1990 ch 408 §1, eff. 1/1/91.)*

§537f. Regulation of sale of rebuilt storage batteries.

No storage battery composed in whole or in part of a used container, or used plate or plates and intended for use in the starting, lighting or ignition of automobiles, shall be sold or offered for sale in this State unless: the word "Rebuilt" together with the rebuilder's name and address is labeled on one side of the battery in letters not less than one-half inch in height with a one-eighth inch stroke.

Any person selling or offering for sale such a battery in violation of this section shall be guilty of a misdemeanor, punishable by a fine not exceeding two hundred fifty dollars, or by imprisonment in the county jail for not more than six months, or by both such fine and imprisonment.

© 1992 by J., B. & L. Gould
Printed in the U.S.A. EP

§537g. National crime information center owner identification number.

(a) Unless otherwise provided by law, any person who knowingly removes, defaces, covers, alters or destroys a National Crime Information Center owner identification number from the personal property of another without permission is guilty of a misdemeanor punishable by a fine not to exceed four hundred dollars ($400), imprisonment in the county jail not to exceed one year, or both.

(b) This section shall not apply to any action taken by an authorized person to dispose of property pursuant to Article 1 (commencing with Section 2080) of Chapter 4 of Title 6 of Part 4 of Division 3 of the Civil Code or pursuant to Chapter 12 (commencing with Section 1407) of Title 10 of Part 2 of this code.

§538. Mortgaged personal property.

Every person, who, after mortgaging any of the property, permitted to be mortgaged by the provisions of Sections 9102, 9105, and 9109 of the Commercial Code, excepting locomotives, engines, rolling stock of a railroad, steamboat machinery in actual use, and vessels, during the existence of the mortgage, with intent to defraud the mortgagee, his or her representative or assigns, takes, drives, carries away, or otherwise removes or permits the taking, driving, or carrying away, or other removal of the mortgaged property, or any part thereof, from the county where it was situated when mortgaged, without the written consent of the mortgagee, or who sells, transfers, slaughters, destroys, or in any manner further encumbers the mortgaged property, or any part thereof, or causes it to be sold, transferred, slaughtered, destroyed, or further encumbered, is guilty of theft, and is punishable accordingly. In the case of a sale, transfer, or further encumbrance at or before the time of making the sale, transfer, or encumbrance, the mortgagor informs the person to whom the sale, transfer, or encumbrance is made, of the existence of the prior mortgage, and also informs the prior mortgagee of the intended sale, transfer, or encumbrance, in writing, by giving the name and place of residence of the party to whom the sale, transfer, or encumbrance is to be made. *(Amended by Stats 1987 ch 828 §32.)*

§538.5. Falsely obtaining information from public utility.

Every person who transmits or causes to be transmitted by means of wire, radio or television communication any words, sounds, writings, signs, signals, or pictures for the purpose of furthering or executing a scheme or artifice to obtain, from a public utility, confidential, privileged, or proprietary information, trade secrets, trade lists, customer records, billing records, customer credit data, or accounting data by means of false or fraudulent pretenses, representations, personations, or promises is guilty of an offense punishable by imprisonment in the state prison, or by imprisonment in the county jail not exceeding one year.

§538a. Sending letter to newspaper with another's name.

Every person who signs any letter addressed to a newspaper with the name of a person other than himself and sends such letter to the newspaper, or causes it to be sent to such newspaper, with intent to lead the newspaper to believe that such letter was written by the person whose name is signed thereto, is guilty of a misdemeanor.

§538b. Unauthorized wearing of insignia.

Any person who wilfully wears the badge, lapel button, rosette, or any part of the garb, robe, habit, or any other recognized and established insignia or apparel of any secret society, or fraternal or religious order or organization, or of any sect, church or religious denomination, or uses the same to obtain aid or assistance within this State, with intent to deceive, unless entitled to wear and use the same under the constitution, by-laws or rules and regulations, or other laws or enactments of such society, order, organization, sect, church or religious denomination is guilty of a misdemeanor.

§538d. Impersonating an officer.

Any person other than one who by law is given the authority of a peace officer, who wilfully wears, exhibits, or uses the authorized badge, insigne, emblem, device, label, certificate, card, or writing, of a peace officer, with the intent of fraudulently personating a peace officer, or of fraudulently inducing the belief that he is a peace officer, is guilty of a misdemeanor.

Any person who wilfully wears, exhibits, or uses, or who wilfully makes, sells, loans, gives, or transfers to another, any badge, insigne, emblem, device, or any label, certificate, card, or writing, which falsely purports to be authorized for the use of one who by law is given the authority of a peace officer, or which so resembles the authorized badge, insigne, emblem, device, label, certificate, card, or writing of a peace officer as would deceive an ordinary reasonable person into believing that it is authorized for the use of one who by law is given the authority of a peace officer, is guilty of a misdemeanor.

§538e. Impersonating member of fire department.

Any person, other than an officer or member of a fire department, who willfully wears, exhibits, or uses the authorized badge, insigne, emblem, device, label, certificate, card, or writing of an officer or member of a fire department or a deputy state fire marshal, with the intent of fraudulently personating an officer or member of a fire department or the Office of the State Fire Marshal, or of fraudulently inducing the belief that he is an officer or member of a fire department or the Office of the State Fire Marshal, is guilty of a misdemeanor.

Any person who willfully wears, exhibits, or uses any badge, insigne, emblem, device, or any label, certificate, card, or writing, which falsely purports to be for the use of an officer or member of a fire department or deputy state fire marshal, or which so resembles the authorized badge, insigne, emblem, device, label, certificate, card, or writing of an officer or member of a fire department as would deceive an ordinary reasonable person into believing that it is authorized for use by an officer or member of a fire department or a deputy state fire marshal, is guilty of a misdemeanor.

Any person who, for the purpose of selling, leasing or otherwise disposing of merchandise, supplies or equipment used in fire prevention or suppression, falsely represents, in any manner whatsoever, to any other person that he is a fire marshal, fire inspector or member of a fire department, or that he has the

© 1992 by J., B. & L. Gould
Printed in the U.S.A.   **EP**

approval, endorsement or authorization of any fire marshal, fire inspector or fire department, or member thereof, is guilty of a misdemeanor.

CHAPTER 9

OFFENSES AGAINST RATIONING

§540. Counterfeiting, forging or stealing ration coupons.

Every person, who steals or, without authority to do so, alters, forges, or counterfeits any coupon, stamp, token, certificate, or other ration evidence or document issued by the United States government or any agency thereof in furtherance of its rationing program, or forges, or alters, without authority, any ration check shall be punishable by imprisonment in the state prison, or in the county jail not exceeding six months, or by fine not exceeding one thousand dollars ($1,000), or by both such fine and imprisonment.

§541. Transfer of altered, forged, or counterfeited ration coupons.

Every person who sells, gives, or otherwise transfers to another any altered, forged, or counterfeited coupon, stamp, token, certificate, ration check, or other ration evidence or document knowing the same to be altered, forged, or counterfeited shall be punishable by imprisonment in the state prison, or in the county jail not exceeding six months, or by fine not exceeding one thousand dollars ($1,000), or by both such fine and imprisonment.

§542. Unauthorized acquisition of altered, forged or counterfeited ration coupons.

Any person who buys, or otherwise knowingly and unlawfully acquires any altered, forged, or counterfeited coupon, stamp, token, certificate, ration check, or other ration evidence or document knowing the same to be altered, forged, or counterfeited shall be punishable by imprisonment in the state prison, or in the county jail not exceeding six months, or by fine not exceeding one thousand dollars ($1,000), or by both such fine and imprisonment.

§543. Unlawful acquisition or transfer of ration coupons.

Any person who knowingly either buys, or sells, or otherwise unlawfully acquires or transfers for a valuable consideration any coupon, stamp, token, certificate, ration check or other ration evidence or document issued by the United States government or any agency thereof or any altered, forged, or counterfeited coupon, stamp, token, certificate, ration check, or other ration evidence or document, shall be punishable by imprisonment in the state prison, or in the county jail not exceeding six months, or by fine not exceeding one thousand dollars ($1,000), or by both such fine and imprisonment.

CHAPTER 10

CRIMES AGAINST INSURED PROPERTY AND INSURERS

§548. Defrauding insurer.

(a) Every person who willfully injures, destroys, secretes, abandons, or disposes of any property which at the time is insured against loss or damage by theft, or embezzlement, or any casualty with intent to defraud or prejudice the insurer, whether the property is the property or in the possession of such person or any other person, is punishable by imprisonment in the state prison for two, three, or five years and by a fine not exceeding fifty thousand dollars ($50,000).

For purposes of this section, "casualty" does not include fire.

(b) Any person who violates subdivision (a) and who has a prior conviction of the offense set forth in that subdivision or in Section 556 of the Insurance Code, shall receive a two-year enhancement for each prior conviction in addition to the sentence provided under subdivision (a). The existence of any fact which would subject a person to a penalty enhancement shall be alleged in the information or indictment and either admitted by the defendant in open court, or found to be true by the jury trying the issue of guilt or by the court where guilt is established by plea of guilty or nolo contendere or by trial by the court sitting without a jury. *(Amended by Stats 1989 ch 730 §2, eff. 1/1/90.)*

§549. Fraudulent claims for Worker's compensation benefits.

Any firm, corporation, partnership, or association, or any person acting in his or her individual capacity, or in his or her capacity as a public or private employee, who solicits or refers any business to any individual or entity with the knowledge that, or with reckless disregard for whether, the individual or entity for whom the solicitation or referral is made, or the individual or entity who is solicited or referred, intends to violate Section 1871.1 or 1871.4 of the Insurance Code is guilty of a crime, punishable upon a first conviction by imprisonment in the county jail for not more than one year or by imprisonment in the state prison for 16 months 2 or 3 years, or by a fine not exceeding ten thousand dollars ($10,000), or by both that fine and imprisonment. A second or subsequent conviction is punishable by imprisonment in the state prison. *(Added by Stats 1991 ch 116 §35; amended by Stats 1991 ch 934 §18, eff. 1/1/92.)*

CHAPTER 11
(Renumbered Chapter 10 by Stats 1979 ch 373 §239.)

CHAPTER 12

UNLAWFUL INTERFERENCE WITH PROPERTY

ARTICLE 1

TRESPASSING OR LOITERING NEAR POSTED INDUSTRIAL PROPERTY

§552. Applicability of article.

This article does not apply to any entry in the course of duty of any peace or police officer or other duly authorized public officer, nor does it apply to the lawful use of an established and existing right of way for public road purposes.

§552.1. Exemptions for union activities.

This article does not prohibit:

(a) Any lawful activity for the purpose of engaging in any organizational effort on behalf of any labor union, agent, or member thereof, or of any employee group, or any member thereof, employed or formerly

© 1992 by J., B. & L. Gould
Printed in the U.S.A. **EP**

employed in any place of business or manufacturing establishment described in this article, or for the purpose of carrying on the lawful activities of labor unions, or members thereof.

(b) Any lawful activity for the purpose of investigation of the safety of working conditions on posted property by a representative of a labor union or other employee group who has upon his person written evidence of due authorization by his labor union or employee group to make such investigation.

§553. Definitions.

The following definitions apply to this article only:

(a) "Sign" means a sign not less than one (1) square foot in area and upon which in letters not less than two inches in height appear the words "trespassing-loitering forbidden by law," or words describing the use of the property followed by the words "no trespassing."

(b) "Posted property" means any property specified in Section 554 which is posted in a manner provided in Section 554.1.

(c) "Posted boundary" means a line running from sign to sign and such line need not conform to the legal boundary or legal description of any lot, parcel, or acreage of land, but only the area within the posted boundary shall constitute posted property, except as otherwise provided in subdivision (e) of Section 554.1. *(Amended by Stats 1988 ch 273 §1, eff. 1/1/89.)*

§554. Posted property.

Any property, except that portion of such property to which the general public is accorded access, may be posted against trespassing and loitering in the manner provided in Section 554.1, and thereby become posted property subject to the provisions of this article applicable to posted property, if such property consists of, or is used, or is designed to be used, for any one or more of the following:

(a) An oil well, oilfield, tank farm, refinery, compressor plant, absorption plant, bulk plant, marine terminal, pipeline, pipeline pumping station, or reservoir, or any other plant, structure, or works, used for the production, extraction, treatment, handling, storage, or transportation, of oil, gas, gasoline, petroleum, or any product or products thereof.

(b) A gas plant, gas storage station, gas meter, gas valve, or regulator station, gas odorant station, gas pipeline, or appurtenances, or any other property used in the transmission or distribution of gas.

(c) A reservoir, dam, generating plant, receiving station, distributing station, transformer, transmission line, or any appurtenances, used for the storage of water for the generation of hydroelectric power, or for the generation of electricity by water or steam or by any other apparatus or method suitable for the generation of electricity, or for the handling, transmission, reception, or distribution of electric energy.

(d) Plant, structures or facilities used for or in connection with the rendering of telephone or telegraph service or for radio or television broadcasting.

(e) A water well, dam, reservoir, pumping plant, aqueduct, canal, tunnel, siphon, conduit, or any other structure, facility, or conductor for producing, storing, diverting, conserving, treating, or conveying water.

(f) The production, storage, or manufacture of munitions, dynamite, black blasting powder, gunpowder, or other explosives.

(g) A railroad right-of-way, railroad bridge, railroad tunnel, railroad shop, railroad yard, or other railroad facility.

(h) A plant and facility for the collection, pumping, transmission, treatment, outfall, and disposal of sanitary sewerage or storm and waste water, including a water pollution or quality control facility.

(i) A quarry used for the purpose of extracting surface or subsurface material or where explosives are stored or used for that purpose.

§554.1. Manner of posting.

Any property described in Section 554 may be posted against trespassing and loitering in the following manner:

(a) If it is not enclosed within a fence and if it is of an area not exceeding one (1) acre and has no lineal dimension exceeding one (1) mile, by posting signs at each corner of the area and at each entrance.

(b) If it is not enclosed within a fence, and if it is of an area exceeding one (1) acre, or contains any lineal dimension exceeding one (1) mile, by posting signs along or near the exterior boundaries of the area at intervals of not more than 600 feet, and also at each corner, and, if such property has a definite entrance or entrances, at each such entrance.

(c) If it is enclosed within a fence and if it is of an area not exceeding one (1) acre, and has no lineal dimension exceeding one (1) mile, by posting signs at each corner of such fence and at each entrance.

(d) If it is enclosed within a fence and if it is of an area exceeding one (1) acre, or has any lineal dimension exceeding one (1) mile, by posting signs on, or along the line of, such fence at intervals of not more than 600 feet, and also at each corner and at each entrance.

(e) If it consists of poles or towers or appurtenant structures for the suspension of wires or other conductors for conveying electricity or telegraphic or telephonic messages or of towers or derricks for the production of oil or gas, by affixing a sign upon one or more sides of such poles, towers, or derricks, but such posting shall render only the pole, tower, derrick, or appurtenant structure posted property.

§555. Entry upon posted property.

It is unlawful to enter or remain upon any posted property without the written permission of the owner, tenant, or occupant in legal possession or control thereof. Every person who enters or remains upon posted property without such written permission is guilty of a separate offense for each day during any portion of which he enters or remains upon such posted property.

§555.1. Destruction of signs.

It is unlawful, without authority, to tear down, deface or destroy any sign posted pursuant to this article.

§555.2. Loitering; labor disputes.

It is unlawful to loiter in the immediate vicinity of any posted property. This section does not prohibit picketing in such immediate vicinity or any lawful activity by which the public is informed of the existence of an alleged labor dispute.

© 1992 by J., B. & L. Gould
Printed in the U.S.A.   EP

§555.3. Offense.
Violation of any of the provisions of this article is a misdemeanor.

§555.4. Territorial applicability.
The provisions of this article are applicable throughout the State in all counties and municipalities and no local authority shall enact or enforce any ordinance in conflict with such provisions.

§555.5. Severability.
If any provision of this article, or the application thereof to any person or circumstance, is held to be invalid, the remainder of the article, and the application of such provision to other persons or circumstances, shall not be affected thereby.

If any section, subsection, sentence, clause, or phrase of this article is for any reason held to be unconstitutional or invalid, such decision shall not affect the validity or constitutionality of the remaining portions of this article. The Legislature hereby declares that it would have passed this article and each section, subsection, sentence, clause, or phrase thereof, irrespective of the fact that one or more of the sections, subsections, sentences, clauses, or phrases thereof be declared unconstitutional or invalid.

ARTICLE 2

UNLAWFULLY PLACING SIGNS ON PUBLIC AND PRIVATE PROPERTY

§556. Advertisements on public property.
It is a misdemeanor for any person to place or maintain, or cause to be placed or maintained without lawful permission upon any property of the State, or of a city or of a county, any sign, picture, transparency, advertisement, or mechanical device which is used for the purpose of advertising or which advertises or brings to notice any person, article of merchandise, business or profession, or anything that is to be or has been sold, bartered, or given away.

§556.1. Advertisements on private property.
It is a misdemeanor for any person to place or maintain or cause to be placed or maintained upon any property in which he has no estate or right of possession any sign, picture, transparency, advertisement, or mechanical device which is used for the purpose of advertising, or which advertises or brings to notice any person, article of merchandise, business or profession, or anything that is to be or has been sold, bartered, or given away, without the consent of the owner, lessee, or person in lawful possession of such property before such sign, picture, transparency, advertisement, or mechanical device is placed upon the property.

§556.2. Legal notices.
Sections 556 and 556.1 do not prevent the posting of any notice required by law or order of any court, to be posted, nor the posting or placing of any notice, particularly pertaining to the grounds or premises upon which the notice is so posted or placed, nor the posting or placing of any notice, sign, or device used exclusively for giving public notice of the name, direction or condition of any highway, street, lane, road or alley.

§556.3. Public nuisance.
Any sign, picture, transparency, advertisement, or mechanical device placed on any property contrary to the provisions of Sections 556 and 556.1, is a public nuisance.

ARTICLE 3

TRESPASS ON PROPERTY BELONGING TO THE UNIVERSITY OF CALIFORNIA

§558. Entry upon certain lands forbidden.
Every person other than an officer, employee or student of the University of California, or licensee of the Regents of the University of California, is forbidden to enter upon those lands bordering on the Pacific Ocean in San Diego County, which were granted by Section 1 of Chapter 514 of the Statutes of 1929 to the Regents of the University of California for the uses and purposes of the University of California in connection with scientific research and investigation at the Scripps Institution of Oceanography, or upon state waters adjacent thereto, or to trespass upon the same, or to interfere with the exclusive possession, occupation, and use thereof by the Regents of the University of California.

Nothing herein contained shall be deemed or construed to affect in any manner the rights of navigation and fishery reserved to the people by the Constitution.

§558.1. Penalty for violation.
Every person who violates any of the provisions of Section 558 is guilty of a misdemeanor and upon conviction thereof shall be punished by a fine of not more than six hundred dollars ($600) or by imprisonment for not more than 30 days, or by both such fine and imprisonment.

CHAPTER 12.5

CRIMES INVOLVING BAILMENTS

§560. Documents of title.
Any bailee, as defined in Section 7102 of the Uniform Commercial Code, who issues or aids in issuing a document of title, or any person who secures the issue by a bailee of a document of title, or any person who negotiates or transfers for value a document of title knowing that the goods for which such document is issued have not been actually received by such bailee or are not under his control at the time of issuing such receipt shall be guilty of a crime and upon conviction shall be punished for each offense by imprisonment in the state prison or by a fine not exceeding ten thousand dollars ($10,000) or by both.

§560.1. Fraudulent issuance of receipt for goods.
Any bailee, as defined in Section 7102 of the Uniform Commercial Code, who fraudulently issues or aids in fraudulently issuing a receipt for goods knowing that it contains any false statement shall be guilty of a crime and upon conviction shall be punished for each offense by imprisonment not exceeding one year or by a fine not exceeding one thousand dollars ($1,000) or by both.

§560.2. Unlawful delivery of goods.

Any bailee, as defined in Section 7102 of the Uniform Commercial Code, who delivers goods out of the possession of such bailee knowing that a negotiable document of title the negotiation of which would transfer the right to the possession of such goods is outstanding and uncanceled without obtaining possession of such document at or before the time for such delivery shall, except for the cases in Sections 7210, 7308, 7601 and 7602 of the Uniform Commercial Code, be guilty of a crime and upon conviction shall be punished for each offense by imprisonment not exceeding one year or by a fine not exceeding one thousand dollars ($1,000) or by both.

§560.3. Unlawful negotiation of document of title with intent to deceive.

Any person who deposits goods with a bailee, as defined in Section 7102 of the Uniform Commercial Code, to which he has not title or upon which there is a security interest and who takes for such goods a negotiable document of title which he afterwards negotiates for value with intent to deceive and without disclosing his want of title or the existence of the security interest shall be guilty of a crime, and upon conviction shall be punished for such offense by imprisonment not exceeding one year or by a fine not exceeding one thousand dollars ($1,000) or by both.

§560.4. Unlawful issuance of negotiable document of title.

Any bailee, as defined in Section 7102 of the Uniform Commercial Code, who issues or aids in issuing a duplicate or additional negotiable document of title for goods knowing that a former negotiable document of title for the same goods or any part of them is outstanding and uncanceled without plainly placing upon the face thereof the word "duplicate," except in cases of bills in a set and documents issued as substitutes for lost, stolen or destroyed documents, shall be guilty of a crime and upon conviction shall be punished for each offense by imprisonment in the state prison or by a fine not exceeding ten thousand dollars ($10,000) or by both.

§560.5. Negotiable documents of title not showing ownership.

Where there are deposited with or held by a warehouseman goods of which he is owner either solely or jointly or in common with others such warehouseman or any of his officers, agents, or servants who knowing of this ownership issues or aids in issuing a negotiable document of title for such goods which does not state such ownership, shall be guilty of a crime and upon conviction shall be punished for each offense by imprisonment not exceeding one year or by a fine not exceeding one thousand dollars ($1,000) or by both.

§560.6. Warehouse receipts; violations.

(1) A corporation, firm, or person, and its or his agents or employees shall not issue, sell, pledge, assign, or transfer in this State any receipt, certificate, or other written instrument purporting to be a warehouse receipt, or in the similitude of a warehouse receipt, or designed to be understood as a warehouse receipt, for goods, wares, or merchandise stored or deposited, or claimed to be stored or deposited, in any warehouse, public or private, in any other state, unless such receipt, certificate, or other written instrument has been issued by the warehouseman operating such warehouse.

(2) A corporation, firm, or person, and its or his agents or employees shall not issue, sell, pledge, assign, or transfer in this State any receipt, certificate, or other written instrument for goods, wares, or merchandise claimed to be stored or deposited, in any warehouse, public or private, in any other state, knowing that there is no such warehouse located at the place named in such receipt, certificate, or other written instrument, or if there is a warehouse at such place knowing that there are no goods, wares, or merchandise stored or deposited therein as specified in such receipt, certificate, or other written instrument.

(3) A corporation, firm, or person, and its or his agents or employees shall not issue, sign, sell, pledge, assign, or transfer in this State any receipt, certificate, or other written instrument evidencing, or purporting to evidence, the creation of a security interest in, or sale, or bailment, of any goods, wares, or merchandise stored or deposited, or claimed to be stored or deposited, in any warehouse, public or private, in any other state, unless such receipt, certificate, or other written instrument plainly designates the number and location of such warehouse and contains a full, true, and complete copy of the receipt issued by the warehouseman operating the warehouse in which such goods, wares, or merchandise is stored or deposited, or is claimed to be stored or deposited. This section shall not apply to the issue, signing, sale, pledge, assignment, or transfer of bona fide warehouse receipts issued by the warehouseman operating public or bonded warehouses in other states according to the laws of the state in which such warehouses are located.

(4) Every corporation, firm, person, agent, or employee, who knowingly violates any of the provisions of this section is guilty of a misdemeanor, and shall be fined not less than fifty dollars ($50) nor more than one thousand dollars ($1,000), and may in addition be imprisoned in the county jail for not exceeding six months.

CHAPTER 12.6

CRIMES INVOLVING BRANDED CONTAINERS, CABINETS, OR OTHER DAIRY EQUIPMENT

§565. Misdemeanors.

It is a misdemeanor, punishable by a fine not exceeding one thousand dollars ($1,000), or by imprisonment in the county jail not exceeding six months, or both, for an unauthorized person to possess or use, or to obliterate or destroy the brand registration upon, containers (including milk cases), cabinets, or other dairy equipment, which have a value of four hundred dollars ($400) or less, when the containers, cabinets, or other dairy equipment are marked with a brand that is registered pursuant to Chapter 10 (commencing with Section 34501) of Part 1 of Division 15 of the Food and Agricultural Code. "Unauthorized person" shall have the meaning of that term as defined in Section 34564 of the Food and Agricultural Code.

§566. Felonies.

It is a felony, punishable by a fine not exceeding one thousand five hundred dollars ($1,500), or by imprisonment, or both, for an unauthorized person to

© 1992 by J., B. & L. Gould
Printed in the U.S.A.　　EP

possess or use, or to obliterate or destroy the brand registration upon, containers (including milk cases), cabinets, or other dairy equipment, which have a value in excess of four hundred dollars ($400), when the containers, cabinets, or other dairy equipment are marked with a brand that is registered pursuant to Chapter 10 (commencing with Section 34501) of Part 1 of Division 15 of the Food and Agricultural Code. "Unauthorized person" shall have the meaning of that term as defined in Section 34564 of the Food and Agricultural Code.

CHAPTER 12.7

UNLAWFUL SUBLEASING OF MOTOR VEHICLES

§570. Punishment for unlawful subleasing.

An act of unlawful subleasing of a motor vehicle, as defined in Section 571, shall be punishable by imprisonment in the state prison or in the county jail for not more than one year, or by a fine of not more than ten thousand dollars ($10,000), or by both that fine and imprisonment. *(Added by Stats 1987 ch 1072 §2.)*

§571. Requirements for unlawful subleasing.

(a) A person engages in an act of unlawful subleasing of a motor vehicle if all of the following conditions are met:

(1) The motor vehicle is subject to a lease contract, conditional sale contract, or security agreement the terms of which prohibit the transfer or assignment of any right or interest in the motor vehicle or under the lease contract, conditional sale contract, or security agreement.

(2) The person is not a party to the lease contract, conditional sale contract, or security agreement.

(3) The person transfers or assigns, or purports to transfer or assign, any right or interest in the motor vehicle or under the lease contract, conditional sale contract, or security agreement, to any person who is not a party to the lease contract, conditional sale contract, or security agreement.

(4) The person does not obtain, prior to the transfer or assignment described in paragraph (3), written consent to the transfer or assignment from the motor vehicle's lessor, seller, or secured party.

(5) The person receives compensation or some other consideration for the transfer or assignment described in paragraph (3).

(b) A person engages in an act of unlawful subleasing of a motor vehicle when the person is not a party to the lease contract, conditional sale contract, or security agreement, and assists, causes, or arranges an actual or purported transfer or assignment, as described in subdivision (a). *(Added by Stats 1987 ch 1072 §2.)*

§572. Transfers or assignments which are not unlawful subleases.

(a) The actual or purported transfer or assignment, or the assisting, causing, or arranging of an actual or purported transfer or assignment, of any right or interest in a motor vehicle or under a lease contract, conditional sale contract, or security agreement, by an individual who is a party to the lease contract, conditional sale contract, or security agreement is not an act of unlawful subleasing of a motor vehicle and is not subject to prosecution.

(b) This chapter shall not affect the enforceability of any provision of any lease contract, conditional sale contract, security agreement, or direct loan agreement by any party thereto. *(Added by Stats 1987 ch 1072 §2.)*

§573. Additional penalties and severability.

(a) The penalties under this chapter are in addition to any other remedies or penalties provided by law for the conduct proscribed by this chapter.

(b) If any provision of this chapter or the application thereof to any person or circumstance is held to be unconstitutional, the remainder of the chapter and the application of its provisions to other persons and circumstances shall not be affected thereby. *(Added by Stats 1987 ch 1072 §2.)*

§574. Definitions.

As used in this chapter, the following terms have the following meanings:

(a) "Buyer" has the meaning set forth in subdivision (c) of Section 2981 of the Civil Code.

(b) "Conditional sale contract" has the meaning set forth in subdivision (a) of Section 2981 of the Civil Code. Notwithstanding subdivision (k) of Section 2981 of the Civil Code, "conditional sale contract" includes any contract for the sale or bailment of a motor vehicle between a buyer and a seller primarily for business or commercial purposes.

(c) "Direct loan agreement" means an agreement between a lender and a purchaser whereby the lender has advanced funds pursuant to a loan secured by the motor vehicle which the purchaser has purchased.

(d) "Lease contract" means a lease contract between a lessor and lessee as this term and these parties are defined in Section 2985.7 of the Civil Code. Notwithstanding subdivision (d) of Section 2985.7 of the Civil Code, "lease contract" includes a lease for business or commercial purposes.

(e) "Motor vehicle" means any vehicle required to be registered under the Vehicle Code.

(f) "Person" means an individual, company, firm, association, partnership, trust, corporation, or other legal entity.

(g) "Purchaser" has the meaning set forth in subdivision (33) of Section 1201 of the Commercial Code.

(h) "Security agreement" and "secured party" have the meanings set forth, respectively, in paragraphs (*l*) and (m) of subdivision (1) of Section 9105 of the Commercial Code. "Security interest" has the meaning set forth in subdivision (37) of Section 1201 of the Commercial Code.

(i) "Seller" has the meaning set forth in subdivision (b) of Section 2981 of the Civil Code, and includes the present holder of the conditional sale contract. *(Added by Stats 1987 ch 1072 §2.)*

CHAPTER 13
(Repealed by Stats 1984 ch 144.)

CHAPTER 14

FRAUDULENT ISSUE OF DOCUMENTS OF TITLE TO MERCHANDISE

§577. Fictitious bills of lading, receipts, etc.

Every person, being the master, owner or agent of any vessel, or officer or agent of any railroad, express or transportation company, or otherwise being or representing any carrier, who delivers any bill of lading, receipt or other voucher, by which it appears that any merchandise of any description has been shipped on board any vessel, or delivered to any railroad, express or transportation company or other carrier, unless the same has been so shipped or delivered, and is at the time actually under the control of such carrier or the master, owner or agent of such vessel, or of some officer or agent of such company, to be forwarded as expressed in such bill of lading, receipt or voucher, is punishable by imprisonment in the state prison, or by a fine not exceeding one thousand dollars ($1,000), or both.

§578. Fictitious warehouse receipts.

Every person carrying on the business of a warehouseman, wharfinger, or other depository of property, who issues any receipt, bill of lading, or other voucher for any merchandise of any description, which has not been actually received upon the premises of such person, and is not under his actual control at the time of issuing such instrument, whether such instrument is issued to a person as being the owner of such merchandise or as security for any indebtedness, is punishable by imprisonment in the state prison, or by a fine not exceeding one thousand dollars ($1,000), or both.

§579. Good faith exceptions.

No person shall be convicted of an offense under Section 577 or 578 by reason that the contents of any barrel, box, case, cask, or other vessel or package mentioned in the bill of lading, receipt, or other voucher did not correspond with the description given in the instrument of the merchandise received, if the description corresponded substantially with the marks, labels, or brands upon the outside of the vessel or package, unless it appears that the accused knew that the marks, labels, or brands were untrue. *(Amended by Stats 1987 ch 828 §33.)*

§580. Issuance of second or duplicate receipt.

Every person mentioned in this chapter, who issues any second or duplicate receipt or voucher, of a kind specified therein, at a time while any former receipt or voucher for the merchandise specified in such second receipt is outstanding and uncanceled, without writing across the face of the same the word "Duplicate," in a plain and legible manner, is punishable by imprisonment in the state prison, or by a fine not exceeding one thousand dollars ($1,000), or both.

§581. Unauthorized sale or pledge of merchandise.

Every person mentioned in this chapter, who sells, hypothecates, or pledges any merchandise for which any bill of lading, receipt, or voucher has been issued by him, without the consent in writing thereto of the person holding such bill, receipt, or voucher, is punishable by imprisonment in the state prison, or by a fine not exceeding one thousand dollars ($1,000), or both.

§583. Property demanded by process of law.

Section 581 does not apply where property is demanded or sold by virtue of process of law. *(Amended by Stats 1987 ch 828 §34.)*

CHAPTER 15

MALICIOUS INJURIES TO RAILROAD BRIDGES, HIGHWAYS, BRIDGES AND TELEGRAPHS

§587. Railroads and railroad bridges.

Every person who maliciously, either:

1. Removes, displaces, injures, or destroys any part of any railroad, whether for steam or horse cars, or any track of any railroad, or any branch or branchway, switch, turnout, bridge, viaduct, culvert, embankment, station house, or other structure or fixture, or any part thereof, attached to or connected with any railroad; or,

2. Places any obstruction upon the rails or track of any railroad, or of any switch, branch, branchway, or turnout connected with any railroad;

Is punishable by imprisonment in the state prison, or in the county jail not exceeding one year.

§587a. Tampering with railroad apparatus.

Every person, who, without being thereunto duly authorized by the owner, lessee, or person or corporation engaged in the operation of any railroad, shall manipulate or in any wise tamper or interfere with any air brake or other device, appliance or apparatus in or upon any car or locomotive upon such railroad, and used or provided for use in the operation of such car or locomotive, or of any train upon such railroad, or with any switch, signal or other appliance or apparatus used or provided for use in the operation of such railroad, shall be deemed guilty of a misdemeanor.

§587b. Trespassing on trains.

Every person, who shall, without being thereunto authorized by the owner, lessee, person or corporation operating any railroad, enter into, climb upon, hold to, or in any manner attach himself to any locomotive, locomotive-engine tender, freight or passenger car upon such railroad, or any portion of any train thereon, shall be deemed guilty of a misdemeanor, and, upon conviction thereof shall be punished by a fine not exceeding fifty dollars ($50), or by imprisonment not exceeding 30 days, or by both such fine and imprisonment.

§587c. Evasion of railroad fare.

Every person who fraudulently evades, or attempts to evade the payment of his fare, while traveling upon any railroad, shall be deemed guilty of a misdemeanor, and upon conviction thereof, shall be punished by a fine of not more than five hundred dollars, or imprisonment not exceeding six months, or by both such fine and imprisonment.

§587.1. Maliciously moving train locomotive.

(a) Every person who maliciously moves or causes to be moved, without authorization, any locomotive, is guilty of a misdemeanor punishable by imprisonment in the county jail not exceeding one year.

(b) Every person who maliciously moves or causes to be moved, without authorization, any locomotive, when the moving creates a substantial likelihood of causing personal injury or death to another, is guilty of a public offense punishable by imprisonment in the state prison, or in the county jail not exceeding one year. *(Added by Stats 1988 ch 787 §1, eff. 1/1/89.)*

© 1992 by J., B. & L. Gould
Printed in the U.S.A.   EP

§588. Injuring or flooding public highway, bridge or private way.

Every person who negligently, willfully or maliciously digs up, removes, displaces, breaks down or otherwise injures or destroys any state or other public highway or bridge, or any private way, laid out by authority of law, or bridge upon any such highway or private way, or who negligently, willfully or maliciously sprinkles, drains, diverts or in any manner permits water from any sprinkler, ditch, canal, flume, or reservoir to flow upon or saturate by seepage any public highway, which act tends to damage such highway or tends to be a hazard to traffic thereon, shall be guilty of a misdemeanor. This section shall not apply to the natural flow of surface or flood waters that are not diverted, accelerated or concentrated by such person.

§588a. Throwing injurious substance on highway.

Any person who throws or deposits any oil, glass bottle, glass, nails, tacks, hoops, wire, cans, or any other substance likely to injure any person, animal or vehicle upon any public highway in the State of California shall be guilty of a misdemeanor; provided, however, that any person who willfully deposits any such substance upon any public highway in the State of California with the intent to cause great bodily injury to other persons using the highway shall be guilty of a felony.

§588b. Breaking down or removing authorized barrier, etc., on highway.

Any person who wilfully breaks down, removes, injures, or destroys any barrier or obstruction erected or placed in or upon any road or highway by the authorities in charge thereof, or by any authorized contractor engaged in the construction or maintenance thereof, or who tears down, defaces, removes, or destroys any warnings, notices, or directional signs erected, placed or posted in, upon, or adjacent to any road or highway, or who extinguishes, removes, injures, or destroys any warning light or lantern, or reflectorized warning or directional sign, erected, placed or maintained by any such authority in, upon or adjacent to any such road or highway, shall be guilty of a misdemeanor.

§590. Malicious treatment of highway mile or guide posts.

Every person who maliciously removes, destroys, injures, breaks or defaces any mile post, board or stone, or guide post erected on or near any highway, or any inscription thereon, is guilty of a misdemeanor.

§590a. Informer to receive half of fines.

One-half of all fines imposed and collected under Section 590 shall be paid to the informer who first causes a complaint to be filed charging the defendant with the violation of Section 590. *(Amended by Stats 1987 ch 828 §35.)*

§591. Lines conducting electricity.

A person who unlawfully and maliciously takes down, removes, injures, or obstructs any line of telegraph, telephone, or cable television, or any other line used to conduct electricity, or any part thereof, or appurtenances or apparatus connected therewith, or severs any wire thereof, or makes any unauthorized connection with any line, other than a telegraph, telephone, or cable television line, used to conduct electricity, or any part thereof, or appurtenances or apparatus connected therewith, is punishable by imprisonment in the state prison, or by a fine not exceeding five hundred dollars ($500), or imprisonment in the county jail not exceeding one year. *(Amended by Stats 1986 ch 756 §2.)*

§592. Taking water from canal, etc., without authority.

Every person who shall, without authority of the owner or managing agent, and with intent to defraud, take water from any canal, ditch, flume or reservoir used for the purpose of holding or conveying water for manufacturing, agricultural, mining, irrigating or generation of power, or domestic uses, or who shall without like authority, raise, lower or otherwise disturb any gate or other apparatus thereof, used for the control or measurement of water, or who shall empty or place, or cause to be emptied or placed, into any such canal, ditch, flume or reservoir, any rubbish, filth or obstruction to the free flow of the water, is guilty of a misdemeanor.

§593. Punishment for interfering with electric lines.

Every person who unlawfully and maliciously takes down, removes, injures, interferes with, or obstructs any line erected or maintained by proper authority for the purpose of transmitting electricity for light, heat, or power, or any part thereof, or any insulator or crossarm, appurtenance or apparatus connected therewith, or severs or in any way interferes with any wire, cable, or current thereof, is punishable by imprisonment in the state prison, or by fine not exceeding one thousand dollars ($1,000), or imprisonment in the county jail not exceeding one year.

§593a. Maliciously harming wood intended for manufacture of lumber.

(a) Every person who maliciously drives or places, in any tree, saw-log, shingle-bolt, or other wood, any iron, steel, ceramic, or other substance sufficiently hard to injure saws, knowing that the tree is intended to be harvested or that the saw-log, shingle-bolt, or other wood is intended to be manufactured into any kind of lumber or other wood product, is guilty of a felony.

(b) Any person who violates subdivision (a) and causes bodily injury to another person other than an accomplice shall, in addition and consecutive to the punishment prescribed for that felony, be punished by an additional prison term of three years. *(Amended by Stats 1987 ch 1132 §1.)*

§593b. Climbing electric poles or towers.

Every person who shall, without the written permission of the owner, lessee, or person or corporation operating any electrical transmission line, distributing line or system, climb upon any pole, tower or other structure which is a part of such line or system and is supporting or is designed to support a wire or wires, cable or cables, for the transmission or distribution of electric energy, shall be deemed guilty of a misdemeanor; provided, that nothing herein shall apply to employees of either privately or publicly owned public utilities engaged in the performance of their duties.

© 1992 by J., B. & L. Gould
Printed in the U.S.A. **EP**

§593c. Malicious interference with gas or hazardous liquid lines.

Every person who willfully and maliciously breaks, digs up, obstructs, interferes with, removes or injures any pipe or main or hazardous liquid pipeline erected, operated, or maintained for the purpose of transporting, conveying or distributing gas or other hazardous liquids for light, heat, power or any other purpose, or any part thereof, or any valve, meter, holder, compressor, machinery, appurtenance, equipment or apparatus connected with any such main or pipeline, or used in connection with or affecting the operation thereof or the conveying of gas or hazardous liquid therethrough, or shuts off, removes, obstructs, injures, or in any way interferes with any valve or fitting installed on, connected to, or operated in connection with any such main or pipeline, or controlling or affecting the flow of gas or hazardous liquid through any such main or pipeline, is guilty of a felony. *(Amended by Stats 1988 ch 844 §1, eff. 1/1/89.)*

§593d. Unauthorized connection to, and unauthorized devices for, television cable systems.

(a) Every person who knowingly and willfully makes or maintains an unauthorized connection or connections, whether physically, electrically, or inductively, or purchases, possesses, attaches or maintains the attachment of any unauthorized device or devices to any cable, wire or other component of a franchised or otherwise duly licensed cable television system or to a television cable or set, or makes or maintains any modification or alteration to any device installed with the authorization of a franchised or otherwise duly licensed cable television system, for the purpose of intercepting or receiving any program or other service carried by a franchised or otherwise duly licensed cable television system which such person is not authorized by that cable television system to receive, is guilty of a misdemeanor punishable by a fine not exceeding one thousand dollars ($1,000), or by imprisonment in the county jail not exceeding 90 days, or both. For the purposes of this section, each such purchase, possession, connection or attachment shall constitute a separate violation of this section.

(b) Every person who knowingly and willfully makes or maintains an unauthorized connection or connections with, whether physically, electrically or inductively, or attaches or maintains any attachment to, any cable, wire, or other component of a franchised or otherwise duly licensed cable television system, for the purpose of interfering with, altering or degrading any cable television service being transmitted to others, or for the purpose of transmitting or broadcasting any program or other service not intended to be transmitted or broadcast by the franchised or otherwise duly licensed cable television system, is guilty of a misdemeanor punishable by a fine not exceeding ten thousand dollars ($10,000), or by imprisonment in the county jail or both. For the purposes of this section, each such transmission or broadcast shall constitute a separate violation of this section.

(c) Every person who, without the express authorization of a franchised or other duly licensed cable television system, knowingly and willfully manufactures, imports into this state, distributes, sells, offers to sell, possesses for sale, or advertises for sale any device, or any plan or kit for a device or for a printed circuit, designed in whole or in part to decode, descramble or otherwise make intelligible any encoded, scrambled or other nonstandard signal carried by that cable television system, is guilty of a misdemeanor punishable by a fine not exceeding ten thousand dollars ($10,000) or by imprisonment in the county jail, or both. For the purpose this subdivision, "encoded, scrambled or other nonstandard signal" shall include, without limitation, any type of signal or transmission that is not intended to produce an intelligible program or service without the aid of a decoder, descrambler, filter, trap or some similar device. A second or subsequent conviction is punishable by a fine not exceeding twenty thousand dollars ($20,000) or by imprisonment in the county jail for up to one year, or both.

(d) Any person who violates this section shall be liable to the franchised or otherwise duly licensed cable television system for the greater of the following amounts:

(1) Five thousand dollars ($5,000).

(2) Three times the amount of actual damages, if any, sustained by the plaintiff, plus reasonable attorney's fees.

(e) Any franchised or otherwise duly licensed cable television system may, in accordance with the provisions of Chapter 3 (commencing with Section 525) of Title 7 of Part 2 of the Code of Civil Procedure, bring an action to enjoin and restrain any violation of this section, and may in the same action seek damages as provided in subdivision (d).

(f) It is not a necessary prerequisite to an action pursuant to this section that the plaintiff has suffered, or be threatened with, actual damages. *(Amended by Stats 1989 ch 964 §1, eff. 1/1/90.)*

§593e. Unauthorized cable television devices.

(a) Every person who knowingly and willfully makes or maintains an unauthorized connection or connections, whether physically, electrically, or inductively, or purchases, possesses, attaches, causes to be attached, assists others in or maintains the attachment of any unauthorized device or devices to a television set or to other equipment designed to receive a television broadcast or transmission, or makes or maintains any modification or alteration to any device installed with the authorization of a subscription television system, for the purpose of intercepting, receiving, or using any program or other service carried by the subscription television system which the person is not authorized by that subscription tele-vision system to receive or use, is guilty of a misdemeanor punishable by a fine not exceeding one thousand dollars ($1,000), or by imprisonment in the county jail not exceeding 90 days, or both. For the purposes of this section, each such purchase, possession, connection, attachment or modification shall constitute a separate violation of this section.

(b) Every person who, without the express authorization of a subscription television system, knowingly and willfully manufactures, imports into this state, assembles, distributes, sells, offers to sell, possesses, advertises for sale, or otherwise provides any device, any plan, or any kit for a device or for a printed circuit, designed in whole or in part to decode, descramble, intercept, or otherwise make intelligible any encoded, scrambled, or other non-standard signal carried by that subscription television system, is guilty of a misdemeanor punishable by a fine not exceeding ten thousand dollars ($10,000) or by imprisonment in the

© 1992 by J., B. & L. Gould
Printed in the U.S.A.   **EP**

county jail, or both. A second or subsequent conviction is punishable by a fine not exceeding twenty thousand dollars ($20,000) or by imprisonment in the county jail for up to one year, or both.

(c) Any person who violates the provisions of subdivision (a) shall be liable to the subscription television system for civil damages in the amount of the value of the connection and subscription fees service actually charged by the subscription television system for the period of unauthorized use according to proof.

Any person who violates the provisions of subdivision (b) shall be liable to the subscription television system at the election of the subscription television system for either of the following amounts:

(1) An award of statutory damages in an aggregate amount of not less than five hundred dollars ($500) or more than ten thousand dollars ($10,000), as the court deems just, for each device, plan, or kit for a device, or for a printed circuit manufactured, imported, assembled, sold, offered for sale, possessed, advertised for sale, or otherwise provided in violation of subdivision (b), to be awarded instead of actual damages and profits.

(2) Three times the amount of actual damages sustained by the plaintiff as a result of the violation or violations of this section and any revenues which have been obtained by the defendant as a result of the violation or violations, or an amount equal to three times the value of the services unlawfully obtained, or the sum of five hundred dollars ($500) for each unauthorized device manufactured, sold, used, or distributed, whichever is greater, and, when appropriate, punitive damages. For the purposes of this subdivision, revenues which have been obtained by the defendant as a result of a violation or violations of this section shall not be included in computing actual damages.

In a case where the court finds that any activity set forth in subdivision (b) was committed knowingly and willfully and for purposes of commercial advantage or private financial gain, the court in its discretion may increase the award of damages, whether actual or statutory, by an amount of not more than fifty thousand dollars ($50,000). It shall not constitute a use for "commercial advantage or private financial gain" for any person to receive a subscription television signal within a residential unit as defined herein.

(d) In any civil action filed pursuant to this section, the court shall allow the recovery of full costs plus an award of reasonable attorney's fees to the prevailing party.

(e) Any subscription television system may, in accordance with the provisions of Chapter 3 (commencing with Section 525) of Title 7 of Part 2 of the Code of Civil Procedure, bring an action to enjoin and restrain any violation of this section without having to make a showing of special or irreparable damage, and may in the same action seek damages as provided in subdivision (c). Upon the execution of a proper bond against damages for an injunction improvidently granted, a temporary restraining order or a preliminary injunction may be issued in any such action before a final determination on the merits.

(f) It is not necessary that the plaintiff have incurred actual damages, or be threatened with incurring actual damages, as a prerequisite to bringing an action pursuant to this section.

(g) For the purposes of this section, an encoded, scrambled, or other nonstandard signal shall include, without limitation, any type of distorted signal or transmission that is not intended to produce an intelligible program or service without the use of special devices or information provided by the sender for the receipt of such signal or transmission.

(h) (1) For the purposes of this section, a "subscription television system" means a television system which sends an encoded, scrambled, or other nonstandard signal over the air which is not intended to be received in an intelligible form without special equipment provided by or authorized by the sender.

(2) For purposes of this section, "residential unit" is defined as any single-family residence, mobile-home within a mobilehome park, condominium, unit or an apartment or multiple-housing unit leased or rented for residential purposes.

§593f. Selling unauthorized devices.

Every person who for profit knowingly and willfully manufactures, distributes, or sells any device or plan or kit for a device, or printed circuit containing circuitry for decoding or addressing with the purpose or intention of facilitating decoding or addressing of any over-the-air transmission by a Multi-point Distribution Service or Instructional Television Fixed Service made pursuant to authority granted by the Federal Communications Commission which is not authorized by the Multi-point Distribution Service or the Instructional Television Fixed Service is guilty of a misdemeanor punishable by a fine not exceeding two thousand five hundred dollars ($2,500) or by imprisonment in the county jail not exceeding 90 days, or both.

§593g. Possession of substance hard enough to injure lumber equipment.

Every person who, with the intent to use it in a violation of Section 593a, possesses any iron, steel, ceramic, or other substance sufficiently hard to injure saws or wood manufacturing or processing equipment, shall be punished by imprisonment in the county jail not to exceed one year. (Added by Stats 1987 ch 1414 §1.)

TITLE 14

MALICIOUS MISCHIEF

§594. Penalty for vandalism.

(a) Every person who maliciously (1) defaces with paint or any other liquid, (2) damages, or (3) destroys any real or personal property not his or her own, in cases otherwise than those specified by state law, is guilty of vandalism.

(b) (1) If the amount of defacement, damage, or destruction is fifty thousand dollars ($50,000) or more, vandalism is punishable by imprisonment in the state prison or in a county jail not exceeding one year, or by a fine of not more than fifty thousand dollars ($50,000), or by both that fine and imprisonment.

(2) If the amount of defacement, damage, or destruction is five thousand dollars ($5,000) or more but less than fifty thousand dollars ($50,000), vandalism is punishable by imprisonment in the state prison, or in a county jail not exceeding one year, or by a fine of not more than ten thousand dollars ($10,000), or by both that fine and imprisonment.

(3) If the amount of defacement, damage, or destruction is one thousand dollars ($1,000) or more but less than five thousand dollars ($5,000), vandalism is punishable by imprisonment in the county

jail not exceeding one year, or by a fine of five thousand dollars ($5,000), or by both that fine and imprisonment.

(4) If the amount of defacement, damage, or destruction is less than one thousand dollars ($1,000), vandalism is punishable by imprisonment in the county jail for not more than six months, or by a fine of not more than one thousand dollars ($1,000), or by both that fine and imprisonment.

(c) Upon conviction of any person under this section for acts of vandalism consisting of writing graffiti, the court may, in addition to any punishment imposed under subdivision (b), at the victim's option, order the defendant to either clean up and repair the damaged property himself or herself, or to pay for someone else to do so. (Amended by Stats 1989 ch 660 §2, eff. 1/1/90.)

§594.1. Possession, purchase or sale of aerosol paint container.

(a) It shall be unlawful for any person, firm, or corporation, except a parent or legal guardian, to sell or give or in any way furnish to another person, who is in fact under the age of 18 years, any aerosol container of paint that is capable of defacing property without first obtaining bona fide evidence of majority and identity.

For purposes of this subdivision, "bona fide evidence of majority and identity" is any document evidencing the age and identity of an individual which has been issued by a federal, state, or local governmental entity, and includes, but is not limited to, a motor vehicle operator's license, a registration certificate issued under the federal Selective Service Act, or an identification card issued to a member of the armed forces.

This subdivision shall not apply to the furnishing of six ounces or less of an aerosol container of paint to a minor for the minor's use or possession under the supervision of the minor's parent, guardian, instructor, or employer.

(b) It shall be unlawful for any person under the age of 18 years to purchase an aerosol container of paint that is capable of defacing property.

(c) Every retailer selling or offering for sale in this state aerosol containers of paint capable of defacing property shall post in a conspicuous place a sign in letters at least three-eighths of an inch high stating: "Any person who maliciously defaces real or personal property with paint is guilty of vandalism which is punishable by a fine, imprisonment, or both."

(d) It is unlawful for any person to carry on his or her person and in plain view to the public an aerosol container of paint while in any posted public facility, park, playground, swimming pool, beach or recreational area, other than a highway, street, alley or way, unless he or she has first received valid authorization from the governmental entity which has jurisdiction over the public area.

As used in this subdivision "posted" means a sign placed in a reasonable location or locations stating it is a misdemeanor to possess a spray can of paint in such public facility, park, playground, swimming pool, beach or recreational area without valid authorization.

(e) It is unlawful for any person under the age of 18 years to possess an aerosol container of paint for the purpose of defacing property while on any public highway, street, alley, or way, or other public place, regardless of whether that person is or is not in any automobile, vehicle, or other conveyance.

(f) Violation of any provision of this section is a misdemeanor. (Amended by Stats 1988 ch 925 §1, eff. 1/1/89.)

§594.3. Vandalizing place of worship.

(a) Any person who knowingly commits any act of vandalism to a church, synagogue, building owned and occupied by a religious educational institution, or other place primarily used as a place of worship where religious services are regularly conducted is guilty of a crime punishable by imprisonment in the state prison or by imprisonment in the county jail for not exceeding one year.

(b) Any person who knowingly commits any act of vandalism to a church, synagogue, building owned and occupied by a religious educational institution, or other place primarily used as a place of worship where religious services are regularly conducted, which is shown to have been committed by reason of the race, color, religion, or national origin of another individual or group of individuals and to have been committed for the purpose of intimidating and deterring persons from freely exercising their religious beliefs, is guilty of a felony punishable by imprisonment in the state prison.

§594.5. Local ordinance regulating aerosol containers.

Nothing in this code shall invalidate an ordinance of, nor be construed to prohibit the adoption of an ordinance by, a city, city and county, or county, if such ordinance regulates the sale of aerosol containers of paint or other liquid substances capable of defacing property.

§595. Specifications in following sections not restrictive of last section.

The specification of the Acts enumerated in the following sections of this Chapter is not intended to restrict or qualify the interpretation of the preceding section.

§596. Poisoning animals.

Every person who, without the consent of the owner, wilfully administers poison to any animal, the property of another, or exposes any poisonous substance, with the intent that the same shall be taken or swallowed by any such animal, is guilty of a misdemeanor.

However, the provisions of this section shall not apply in the case of a person who exposes poisonous substances upon premises or property owned or controlled by him for the purpose of controlling or destroying predatory animals or livestock-killing dogs and if, prior to or during the placing out of such poisonous substances, he shall have posted upon the property conspicuous signs located at intervals of distance not greater than one-third of a mile apart, and in any case not less than three such signs having words with letters at least one inch high reading "Warning—Poisoned bait placed out on these premises," which signs shall be kept in place until the poisonous substances have been removed. Whenever such signs have been conspicuously located upon the property or premises owned or controlled by him as hereinabove provided, such person shall not be charged with any civil liability to another party in the event that any domestic animal belonging to such party becomes injured or killed by trespassing or partaking of the poisonous substance or substances so placed.

© 1992 by J., B. & L. Gould
Printed in the U.S.A.   EP

§596.5. Cruelty towards elephants.

It shall be a misdemeanor for any owner or manager of an elephant to engage in abusive behavior towards the elephant, which behavior shall include the discipline of the elephant by any of the following methods:

(a) Deprivation of food, water, or rest.

(b) Use of electricity.

(c) Physical punishment resulting in damage, scarring, or breakage of skin.

(d) Insertion of any instrument into any bodily orifice.

(e) Use of martingales.

(f) Use of block and tackle. *(Added by Stats 1989 ch 1423 §1, eff. 1/1/90.)*

§597. Cruelty to animals.

(a) Except as provided in subdivision (c), of this section or Section 599c, every person who maliciously and intentionally maims, mutilates, tortures, or wounds a living animal, or maliciously and intentionally kills an animal, is guilty of an offense punishable by imprisonment in the state prison, or by a fine of not more than twenty thousand dollars ($20,000), or by both the fine and imprisonment, or, alternatively, by imprisonment in the county jail for not more than one year, or by a fine of not more than twenty thousand dollars ($20,000), or by both the fine and imprisonment.

(b) Except as otherwise provided in subdivision (a) or (c), every person who overdrives, overloads, drives when overloaded, overworks, tortures, torments, deprives of necessary sustenance, drink, or shelter, cruelly beats, mutilates, or cruelly kills any animal, or causes or procures any animal to be so overdriven, overloaded, driven when overloaded, overworked, tortured, tormented, deprived of necessary sustenance, drink, shelter, or to be cruelly beaten, mutilated, or cruelly killed; and whoever, having the charge or custody of any animal, either as owner or otherwise, subjects any animal to needless suffering, or inflicts unnecessary cruelty upon the animal, or in any manner abuses any animal, or fails to provide the animal with proper food, drink, or shelter or protection from the weather, or who drives, rides, or otherwise uses the animal when unfit for labor, is, for every such offense, guilty of a crime punishable as a misdemeanor or as a felony or alternatively punishable as a misdemeanor or a felony and by a fine of not more than twenty thousand dollars ($20,000).

(c) Every person who maliciously and intentionally maims, mutilates, or tortures any mammal, bird, reptile, amphibian, or fish as described in subdivision (d), is guilty of an offense punishable by imprisonment in the state prison, or by a fine of not more than twenty thousand dollars ($20,000), or by both the fine and imprisonment, or, alternatively, by imprisonment in the county jail for not more than one year, by a fine of not more than twenty thousand dollars ($20,000), or by both the fine and imprisonment.

(d) Subdivision (c) applies to any mammal, bird, reptile, amphibian, or fish which is a creature described as follows:

(1) Endangered species or threatened species as described in Chapter 1.5 (commencing with Section 2050) of Division 3 of the Fish and Game Code.

(2) Fully protected birds described in Section 3511 of the Fish and Game Code.

(3) Fully protected mammals described in Chapter 8 (commencing with Section 4700) of Part 3 of Division 4 of the Fish and Game Code.

(4) Fully protected reptiles and amphibians described in Chapter 2 (commencing with Section 5050) of Division 5 of the Fish and Game Code.

(5) Fully protected fish as described in Section 5515 of the Fish and Game Code.

This subdivision does not supersede or affect any provisions of law relating to taking of the described species, including, but not limited to, Section 12008 of the Fish and Game Code.

(e) For the purposes of subdivision (c) each act of malicious and intentional maiming, mutilating, or torturing a separate specimen of a creature described in subdivision (d) is a separate offense. If any person is charged with a violation of subdivision (c), the proceedings shall be subject to Section 12157 of the Fish and Game Code.

(f) Upon the conviction of a person charged with a violation of this section by causing or permitting an act of cruelty, as defined in Section 599b, all animals lawfully seized and impounded with respect to the violation by a peace officer, officer of a humane society, or officer of a pound or animal regulation department of a public agency shall be adjudged by the court to be forfeited and shall thereupon be awarded to the impounding officer for proper disposition. A person convicted of a violation of this section by causing or permitting an act of cruelty, as defined in Section 599b, shall be liable to the impounding officer for all costs of impoundment from the time of seizure to the time of proper disposition.

Mandatory seizure or impoundment shall not apply to animals in properly conducted scientific experiments or investigations performed under the authority of the faculty of a regularly incorporated medical college or university of this state. *(Amended by Stats 1988 chs 127 §2, 1522 §1, 1527 §1, 1556 §4, eff. 1/1/89.)*

§597a. Transporting animals in a cruel manner.

Whoever carries or causes to be carried in or upon any vehicle or otherwise any domestic animal in a cruel or inhuman manner, or knowingly and willfully authorizes or permits it to be subjected to unnecessary torture, suffering, or cruelty of any kind, is guilty of a misdemeanor; and whenever any such person is taken into custody therefor by any officer, such officer must take charge of such vehicle and its contents, together with the horse or team attached to such vehicle, and deposit the same in some place of custody; and any necessary expense incurred for taking care of and keeping the same, is a lien thereon, to be paid before the same can be lawfully recovered; and if such expense, or any part thereof, remains unpaid, it may be recovered, by the person incurring the same, of the owner of such domestic animal, in an action therefor.

§597b. Fighting animals or birds.

Any person who, for amusement or gain, causes any bull, bear, cock, or other animal, not including any dog, to fight with like kind of animal or creature, or causes any such animal, including any dog, to fight with a different kind of animal or creature, or with any human being; or who, for amusement or gain, worries or injures any such bull, bear, cock, dog or other animal, or causes any such bull, bear, cock, or other animal, not including any dog, to worry or injure each other; and any person who permits the same to be done on any premises under his charge or control; and any person who aids, abets, or is present at such fighting or worrying of such animal or creature, as a spectator, is guilty of a misdemeanor.

§597c. Possessing, training, or keeping of animals for fighting.

Whoever owns, possesses, keeps, or trains any bird or animal, with the intent that such bird or animal shall be engaged in an exhibition of fighting, or is present at any place, building, or tenement, where preparations are being made for an exhibition of the fighting of birds or animals, with the intent to be present at such exhibition, or is present at such exhibition, is guilty of a misdemeanor. This section shall not apply to an exhibition of fighting of a dog with another dog.

§597d. Arrests at animal fights authorized.

Any sheriff, constable, police, or peace officer, or officer qualified as provided in Section 607f of the Civil Code, may enter any place, building, or tenement, where there is an exhibition of the fighting of birds or animals, or where preparations are being made for such an exhibition, and, without a warrant, arrest all persons present. (Amended by Stats 1987 ch 828 §36.)

§597e. Liability for improper care of impounded domestic animals.

Any person who impounds, or causes to be impounded in any pound, any domestic animal, shall supply it during such confinement with a sufficient quantity of good and wholesome food and water, and in default thereof, is guilty of a misdemeanor. In case any domestic animal is at any time so impounded and continues to be without necessary food and water for more than 12 consecutive hours, it is lawful for any person, from time to time, as may be deemed necessary, to enter into and upon any pound in which the animal is confined, and supply it with necessary food and water so long as it remains so confined. Such person is not liable for the entry and may collect the reasonable cost of the food and water from the owner of the animal, and the animal is subject to enforcement of a money judgment for the reasonable cost of such food and water.

§597f. Abandoned or neglected animals.

(a) Every owner, driver, or possessor of any animal, who permits the animal to be in any building, enclosure, lane, street, square, or lot, of any city, city and county, or judicial district, without proper care and attention, shall, on conviction, be deemed guilty of a misdemeanor. And it shall be the duty of any peace officer, officer of the humane society, or officer of a pound or animal regulation department of a public agency, to take possession of the animal so abandoned or neglected and care for the animal until it is redeemed by the owner or claimant, and the cost of caring for the animal shall be a lien on the animal until the charges are paid. Every sick, disabled, infirm, or crippled animal, except a dog or cat, which shall be abandoned in any city, city and county, or judicial district, may, if after due search no owner can be found therefor, be killed by the officer; and it shall be the duty of all peace officers, an officer of such society, or officer of a pound or animal regulation department of a public agency to cause the animal to be killed on

information of such abandonment. The officer may likewise take charge of any animal, including a dog or cat, that by reason of lameness, sickness, feebleness, or neglect, is unfit for the labor it is performing, or that in any other manner is being cruelly treated; and, if the animal is not then in the custody of its owner, the officer shall give notice thereof to the owner, if known, and may provide suitable. care for the animal until it is deemed to be in a suitable condition to be delivered to the owner, and any necessary expenses which may be incurred for taking care of and keeping the animal shall be a lien thereon, to be paid before the animal can be lawfully recovered.

(b) It shall be the duty of all officers of pounds or humane societies, and animal regulation departments of public agencies to convey, and for police and sheriff departments, to cause to be conveyed all injured cats and dogs found without their owners in a public place directly to a veterinarian known by the officer or agency to be a veterinarian that ordinarily treats dogs and cats for a determination of whether the animal shall be immediately and humanely destroyed or shall be hospitalized under proper care and given emergency treatment.

If the owner does not redeem the animal within the locally prescribed waiting period, the veterinarian may personally perform euthanasia on the animal; or, if the animal is treated and recovers from its injuries, the veterinarian may keep the animal for purposes of adoption, provided the responsible animal control agency has first been contacted and has refused to take possession of the animal.

Whenever any animal is transferred pursuant to this subdivision to a veterinarian in a clinic, such as an emergency clinic which is not in continuous operation, the veterinarian may, in turn, transfer the animal to an appropriate facility.

If the veterinarian determines that the animal shall be hospitalized under proper care and given emergency treatment, the costs of any services which are provided pending the owner's inquiry to the agency, department, or society shall be paid from the dog license fees, fines, and fees for impounding dogs in the city, county, or city and county in which the animal was licensed or if the animal is unlicensed the jurisdiction in which the animal was found, subject to the provision that this cost be repaid by the animal's owner. No veterinarian shall be criminally or civilly liable for any decision which he or she makes or services which he or she provides pursuant to this section.

(c) An animal control agency which takes possession of an animal pursuant to subdivision (b), shall keep records of the whereabouts of the animal for a 72-hour period from the time of possession and those records shall be available to inspection by the public upon request.

(d) Notwithstanding any other provisions of this section, any officer of a pound or animal regulation department or humane society, or any officer of a police or sheriff's department may, with the approval of his or her immediate superior, humanely destroy any abandoned animal in the field in any case where the animal is too severely injured to move or where a veterinarian is not available and it would be more humane to dispose of the animal. (Amended by Stats 1989 ch 490 §1, eff. 1/1/90.)

© 1992 by J., B. & L. Gould
Printed in the U.S.A.   EP

§597g. Horse poling.

Poling a horse is a method of training horses to jump which consists of (1) forcing, persuading, or enticing a horse to jump in such manner that one or more of its legs will come in contact with an obstruction consisting of any kind of wire, or a pole, stick, rope or other object with brads, nails, tacks or other sharp points imbedded therein or attached thereto or (2) raising, throwing or moving a pole, stick, wire, rope or other object, against one or more of the legs of a horse while it is jumping an obstruction so that the horse, in either case, is induced to raise such leg or legs higher in order to clear the obstruction. The poling of any horse is unlawful and any person violating the provisions of this section is guilty of a misdemeanor.

§597h. Live animals; attaching to moving machine pursued by dogs.

It shall be unlawful for any person to tie or attach or fasten any live animal to any machine or device propelled by any power for the purpose of causing such animal to be pursued by a dog or dogs.

Any person violating any of the provisions of this section shall be guilty of a misdemeanor.

§597i. Cock fighting implements.

It shall be unlawful for anyone to manufacture, buy, sell, barter, exchange, or have in his possession any of the implements commonly known as gaffs or slashers, or any other sharp implement designed to be attached in place of the natural spur of a gamecock or other fighting bird. Anyone violating any of the provisions of this section shall be guilty of a misdemeanor and upon conviction thereof shall, in addition to any judgment or sentence imposed by the court, forfeit possession or ownership of such implements.

§597j. Cock owning or possessing for fighting.

Any person who owns, possesses or keeps any cock with the intent that such cock shall be used or engaged by himself or by his vendee or by any other person in any exhibition of fighting is guilty of a misdemeanor.

§597k. Use of bristle bur or tack bur on animals.

Anyone who, having care, custody or control of any horse or other animal, uses what is known as the bristle bur, tack bur, or other like device, by whatsoever name known or designated, on such horse or other animal for any purpose whatsoever, is guilty of a misdemeanor and is punishable by a fine of not less than fifty dollars ($50) nor more than five hundred dollars ($500), or by imprisonment in the county jail for not less than 10 days nor more than 175 days, or by both such fine and imprisonment.

§597l. Pet shops.

*It shall be unlawful for any person who operates a pet shop to fail to do all of the following:

(1) Maintain the facilities used for the keeping of pet animals in a sanitary condition.

(2) Provide proper heating and ventilation for the facilities used for the keeping of pet animals.

(3) Provide adequate nutrition for, and humane care and treatment of, all pet animals under his care and control.

(4) Take reasonable care to release for sale, trade, or adoption only those pet animals which are free of disease or injuries.

(5) Provide adequate space appropriate to the size, weight and specie of pet animals.

* So in original. Probably should be designated par. (a).

(b) As used in this section:

(1) "Pet animals" means dogs, cats, monkeys, and other primates, rabbits, birds, guinea pigs, hamsters, mice, snakes, iguanas, turtles, and any other species of animal sold or retained for the purpose of being kept as a household pet.

(2) "Pet shop" means every place or premises where pet animals are kept for the purpose of either wholesale or retail sale. "Pet shop" does not include any place or premises where pet animals are occasionally sold.

(c) Any person who violates any provision of this section is guilty of a misdemeanor and is punishable by a fine of not to exceed one thousand dollars ($1,000), or by imprisonment in the county jail for not more than 90 days, or by both such fine and imprisonment.

§597m. Prohibited bullfights.

It shall be unlawful for any person to promote, advertise, stage, hold, manage, conduct, participate in, engage in, or carry on any bullfight exhibition, any bloodless bullfight contest or exhibition, or any similar contest or exhibition, whether for amusement or gain or otherwise; provided, that nothing herein shall be construed to prohibit rodeos or to prohibit measures necessary to the safety of participants at rodeos.

This section shall not, however, be construed as prohibiting bloodless bullfights, contests, or exhibitions held in connection with religious celebrations or religious festivals.

Any person violating the provisions of this section is guilty of a misdemeanor.

§597n. Docked horses.

Any person who cuts the solid part of the tail of any horse in the operation known as "docking," or in any other operation performed for the purpose of shortening the tail of any horse, within the State of California, or procures the same to be done, or imports or brings into this state any docked horse, or horses, or drives, works, uses, races, or deals in any unregistered docked horse, or horses, within the State of California except as provided in Section 597r, is guilty of a misdemeanor. (Amended by Stats 1987 ch 828 §37.)

§597p. Registering docked horses.

Within 30 days after the passage of this act, every owner, or user of any docked-horse, within the State of California, shall register his or her docked horse, or horses by filing in the office of the county clerk of the county in which such docked horse, or horses, may then be kept, a certificate, which certificate shall contain the name, or names of the owner, together with his or her post office address, a full description of the color, age, size and the use made of such docked horse, or horses; which certificate shall be signed by the owner, or his, or her agent. The county clerk shall number such certificate consecutively and record the name in a book, or register to be kept for that purpose only; and shall receive as a fee for recording of such certificate, the sum of fifty cents ($0.50), and the clerk shall thereupon issue to such person so registering such horse or horses a certificate containing the facts recited in this section which upon demand shall be exhibited to any peace officer, and the same shall be conclusive evidence of a compliance with the provisions of Section 597n of this code.

§597q. Prima facie evidence of docked horses.

The driving, working, keeping, racing or using of any unregistered docked horse, or horses, after 60 days after the passage of this act, shall be deemed prima facie evidence of the fact that the party driving, working, keeping, racing or using such unregistered docked horse, or horses, docked the tail of such horse or horses.

§597r. Importing horses with docked tails.

Any person or persons violating any of the provisions of this act, shall be deemed guilty of a misdemeanor; provided, however, that the provisions of Sections 597n, 597p, and 597q, shall not be applied to persons owning or possessing any docked purebred stallions and mares imported from foreign countries for breeding or exhibition purposes only, as provided by an act of Congress entitled "An act regulating the importation of breeding animals" and approved March 3, 1903, and to docked native-bred stallions and mares brought into this State and used for breeding or exhibition purposes only; and provided further, that a description of each such animal so brought into the State, together with the date of importation and name and address of importer, be filed with the county clerk of the county where such animal is kept, within 30 days after the importation of such animal.

§597s. Dog or cat abandoned.

Every person who willfully abandons any domestic dog or cat is guilty of a misdemeanor.

§597t. Animals in confinement.

Every person who keeps an animal confined in an enclosed area shall provide it with an adequate exercise area. If the animal is restricted by a leash, rope, or chain, the leash, rope, or chain shall be affixed in such a manner that it will prevent the animal from becoming entangled or injured and permit the animal's access to adequate shelter, food, and water. Violation of this section constitutes a misdemeanor.

This section shall not apply to an animal which is in transit, in a vehicle, or in the immediate control of a person.

§597u. Killing animals by use of carbon monoxide.

No person, peace officer, officer of a humane society, or officer of a pound or animal regulation department of a public agency shall kill any dog or cat by the use of carbon monoxide gas unless all of the following are satisfied:

(a) The carbon monoxide gas chamber is equipped with internal lighting and viewport providing direct visual surveillance of the collapse and death of any dog or cat within the chamber.

(b) The gas generation process is adequate to achieve a carbon monoxide gas concentration throughout the chamber of at least 5 percent within 20 minutes after any dog or cat is placed in the chamber.

(c) If chemical generation through the use of sodium formate and sulfuric acid is used, the generated carbon monoxide gas has the irritating acid vapors filtered out by passing it through a 10 percent solution of sodium hydroxide prior to its entry into the carbon monoxide gas chamber.

(d) If carbon monoxide gas generation is by combustion of gasoline in an engine, all of the following shall be satisfied:

(1) The engine is maintained in good operating condition.

(2) The engine is operated only at idling speed with the richest fuel-air mixture the choke permits.

(3) Prior to entry into the chamber, the exhaust gas is cooled so that it does not exceed 125° Fahrenheit.

(4) The chamber is equipped with accurate temperature gauges monitored by attendants to assure that internal temperature of the chamber does not exceed 110° Fahrenheit.

(5) Prior to its entry into the lethal chamber the exhaust gas is first passed through an adequate water filtration process and subsequently through a cloth filtration process to remove irritants and carbon particles.

(6) The noise level from the engine shall not exceed 70 dBA when measured within the chamber.

(7) A flexible tubing or pipe at least 24 inches in length shall be placed between the chamber and the engine to minimize vibrations.

(e) Any dog or cat not covered by Section 597v is placed in an individual container or compartment of the carbon monoxide chamber, except dogs or cats from the same litter and their parents may be placed in the same container or compartment.

(f) The carbon monoxide gas chamber and its compartments shall be cleaned thoroughly after every cycle of operation.

§597v. Newborn dog or cat.

No person, peace officer, officer of a humane society, or officer of a pound or animal regulation department of a public agency shall kill any newborn dog or cat whose eyes have not yet opened by any other method than by the use of chloroform vapor or gas or by inoculation of barbiturates.

§597w. Killing cat or dog by use of high-altitude decompression chamber or nitrogen gas.

No person, peace officer, officer of a humane society, or officer of a pound or animal regulation department of a public agency shall kill any dog or cat by the use of any high-altitude decompression chamber or nitrogen gas.

§597y. Unlawful killing of dogs or cats.

Any violation of Section 597u, 597v, or 597w shall be a misdemeanor.

§597z. Entry into animal euthanasia facility for inspection.

A humane officer appointed under Section 607f of the Civil Code or the State Sealer may enter any facility utilizing a carbon monoxide gas chamber for the purpose of inspecting the operation of such facility to determine whether there is compliance with Section 597u.

§597.1. Care and disposition of neglected animals.

(a) Every owner, driver, or keeper of any animal who permits the animal to be in any building, enclosure, lane, street, square, or lot of any city, county, city and county, or judicial district without proper

© 1992 by J., B. & L. Gould
Printed in the U.S.A. **EP**

care and attention is guilty of a misdemeanor. Any peace officer, humane society officer, or animal control officer shall take possession of the stray or abandoned animal and shall provide care and treatment for the animal until the animal is deemed to be in suitable condition to be returned to the owner. When the officer has reasonable grounds to believe that very prompt action is required to protect the health or safety of the animal or the health or safety of others, the officer shall immediately seize the animal and comply with subdivision (f). In all other cases, the officer shall comply with the provisions of subdivision (g). The cost of caring for and treating any animal properly seized under this subdivision shall constitute a lien on the animal and the animal shall not be returned to its owner until the charges are paid, if the seizure is upheld pursuant to this section.

(b) Every sick, disabled, infirm, or crippled animal, except a dog or cat, which is abandoned in any city, county, city and county, or judicial district may be killed by the officer if, after a reasonable search, no owner of the animal can be found. It shall be the duty of all peace officers, humane society officers, and animal control officers to cause the animal to be killed or rehabilitated and placed in a suitable home on information that the animal is stray or abandoned. The officer may likewise take charge of any animal, including a dog or cat, that by reason of lameness, sickness, feebleness, or neglect, is unfit for the labor it is performing, or that in any other manner is being cruelly treated, and provide care and treatment for the animal until it is deemed to be in a suitable condition to be returned to the owner. When the officer has reasonable grounds to believe that very prompt action is required to protect the health or safety of an animal or the health or safety of others, the officer shall immediately seize the animal and comply with subdivision (f). In all other cases, the officer shall comply with subdivision (g). The cost of caring for and treating any animal properly seized under this subdivision shall constitute a lien on the animal and the animal shall not be returned to its owner until the charges are paid.

(c) Any peace officer, humane society officer, or animal control officer shall convey all injured cats and dogs found without their owners in a public place directly to a veterinarian known by the officer to be a veterinarian who ordinarily treats dogs and cats for a determination of whether the animal shall be immediately and humanely destroyed or shall be hospitalized under proper care and given emergency treatment.

If the owner does not redeem the animal within the locally prescribed waiting period, the veterinarian may personally perform euthanasia on the animal. If the animal is treated and recovers from its injuries, the veterinarian may keep the animal for purposes of adoption, provided the responsible animal control agency has first been contacted and has refused to take possession of the animal.

Whenever any animal is transferred to a veterinarian in a clinic, such as an emergency clinic which is not in continuous operation, the veterinarian may, in turn, transfer the animal to an appropriate facility.

If the veterinarian determines that the animal shall be hospitalized under proper care and given emergency treatment, the costs of any services which are provided pending the owner's inquiry to the responsible agency, department, or society shall be paid from the dog license fees, fines, and fees for impounding dogs in the city, county, or city and county in which the animal was licensed or, if the animal is unlicensed, shall be paid by the jurisdiction in which the animal was found, subject to the provision that this cost be repaid by the animal's owner. The cost of caring for and treating any animal seized under this subdivision shall constitute a lien on the animal and the animal shall not be returned to the owner until the charges are paid. No veterinarian shall be criminally or civilly liable for any decision which he or she makes or for services which he or she provides pursuant to this subdivision.

(d) An animal control agency which takes possession of an animal pursuant to subdivision (c) shall keep records of the whereabouts of the animal for a 72-hour period from the time of possession, and those records shall be available for inspection by the public upon request.

(e) Notwithstanding any other provision of this section, any peace officer, humane society officer, or any animal control officer may, with the approval of his or her immediate superior, humanely destroy any stray or abandoned animal in the field in any case where the animal is too severely injured to move or where a veterinarian is not available and it would be more humane to dispose of the animal.

(f) Whenever an officer authorized under this section seizes or impounds an animal based on a reasonable belief that prompt action is required to protect the health or safety of the animal or the health or safety of others, the officer shall, prior to the commencement of any criminal proceedings authorized by this section, provide the owner or keeper of the animal, if known or ascertainable after reasonable investigation, with the opportunity for a postseizure hearing to determine the validity of the seizure or impoundment, or both.

(1) The agency shall cause a notice to be affixed to a conspicuous place where the animal was situated or personally deliver a notice of the seizure or impoundment, or both, to the owner or keeper within 48 hours, excluding weekends and holidays. The notice shall include all of the following:

(A) The name, business address, and telephone number of the officer providing the notice.

(B) A description of the animal seized, including any identification upon the animal.

(C) The authority and purpose for the seizure, or impoundment, including the time, place, and circumstances under which the animal was seized.

(D) A statement that, in order to receive a postseizure hearing, the owner or person authorized to keep the animal, or his or her agent, shall request the hearing by signing and returning an enclosed declaration of ownership or right to keep the animal to the agency providing the notice within 10 days, including weekends and holidays, of the date of the notice. The declaration may be returned by personal delivery or mail.

(E) A statement that the cost of caring for and treating any animal properly seized under this section is a lien on the animal and that the animal shall not be returned to the owner until the charges are paid, and that failure to request or to attend a scheduled hearing shall result in liability for this cost.

(2) The postseizure hearing shall be conducted within 48 hours of the request, excluding weekends and holidays. The seizing agency may authorize its own officer or employee to conduct the hearing if the

hearing officer is not the same person who directed the seizure or impoundment of the animal and is not junior in rank to that person. The agency may utilize the services of a hearing officer from outside the agency for the purposes of complying with this section.

(3) Failure of the owner or keeper, or of his or her agent, to request or to attend a scheduled hearing shall result in a forfeiture of any right to a postseizure hearing or right to challenge his or her liability for costs incurred.

(4) The agency, department, or society employing the person who directed the seizure shall be responsible for the costs incurred for caring and treating the animal, if it is determined in the postseizure hearing that the seizing officer did not have reasonable grounds to believe very prompt action, including seizure of the animal, was required to protect the health or safety of the animal or the health or safety of others. If it is determined the seizure was justified, the owner or keeper shall be personally liable to the seizing agency for the cost of the seizure and care of the animal, the charges for the seizure and care of the animal shall be a lien on the animal, and the animal shall not be returned to its owner until the charges are paid and the seizing agency or hearing officer has determined that the animal is physically fit or the owner demonstrates to the seizing agency's or the hearing officer's satisfaction that the owner can and will provide the necessary care.

(g) Where the need for immediate seizure is not present and prior to the commencement of any criminal proceedings authorized by this section, the agency shall provide the owner or keeper of the animal, if known or ascertainable after reasonable investigation, with the opportunity for a hearing prior to any seizure or impoundment of the animal. The owner shall produce the animal at the time of the hearing unless, prior to the hearing, the owner has made arrangements with the agency to view the animal upon request of the agency, or unless the owner can provide verification that the animal was humanely destroyed. Any person who willfully fails to produce the animal or provide the verification is guilty of an infraction, punishable by a fine of not less than two hundred fifty dollars ($250) nor more than one thousand dollars ($1,000).

(1) The agency shall cause a notice to be affixed to a conspicuous place where the animal was situated or personally deliver a notice stating the grounds for believing the animal should be seized under subdivision (a) or (b). The notice shall include all of the following:

(A) The name, business address, and telephone number of the officer providing the notice.

(B) A description of the animal to be seized, including any identification upon the animal.

(C) The authority and purpose for the possible seizure or impoundment.

(D) A statement that, in order to receive a hearing prior to any seizure, the owner or person authorized to keep the animal, or his or her agent, shall request the hearing by signing and returning the enclosed declaration of ownership or right to keep the animal to the officer providing the notice within two days, excluding weekends and holidays, of the date of the notice.

(E) A statement that the cost of caring for and treating any animal properly seized under this section is a lien on the animal, that any animal seized shall

not be returned to the owner until the charges are paid, and that failure to request or to attend a scheduled hearing shall result in a conclusive determination that the animal may properly be seized and that the owner shall be liable for the charges.

(2) The preseizure hearing shall be conducted within 48 hours, excluding weekends and holidays, after receipt of the request. The seizing agency may authorize its own officer or employee to conduct the hearing if the hearing officer is not the same person who requests the seizure or impoundment of the animal and is not junior in rank to that person. The agency may utilize the services of a hearing officer from outside the agency for the purposes of complying with this section.

(3) Failure of the owner or keeper, or his or her agent, to request or to attend a scheduled hearing shall result in a forfeiture of any right to a preseizure hearing or right to challenge his or her liability for costs incurred pursuant to this section.

(4) The hearing officer, after the hearing, may affirm or deny the owner's or keeper's right to custody of the animal and, if reasonable grounds are established, may order the seizure or impoundment of the animal for care and treatment.

(h) If any animal is properly seized under this section, the owner or keeper shall be personally liable to the seizing agency for the cost of the seizure and care of the animal. Furthermore, if the charges for the seizure or impoundment and any other charges permitted under this section are not paid within 14 days of the seizure, or, if the owner, within 14 days of notice of availability of the animal to be returned, fails to pay charges permitted under this section and take possession of the animal, the animal shall be deemed to have been abandoned and may be disposed of by the impounding officer.

(i) If the animal requires veterinary care and the humane society or public agency is not assured, within 14 days of the seizure of the animal, that the owner will provide the necessary care, the animal shall not be returned to its owner and shall be deemed to have been abandoned and may be disposed of by the impounding officer. A veterinarian may humanely destroy an impounded animal without regard to the prescribed holding period when it has been determined that the animal has incurred severe injuries or is incurably crippled. A veterinarian also may immediately humanely destroy an impounded animal afflicted with a serious contagious disease unless the owner or his or her agent immediately authorizes treatment of the animal by a veterinarian at the expense of the owner or agent.

(j) No animal properly seized under this section shall be returned to its owner until, in the determination of the seizing agency or hearing officer, the animal is physically fit or the owner can demonstrate to the seizing agency's or hearing officer's satisfaction that the owner can and will provide the necessary care.

(k) Upon the conviction of a person charged with a violation of this section, all animals lawfully seized and impounded with respect to the violation shall be adjudged by the court to be forfeited and shall thereupon be transferred to the impounding officer for proper disposition. A person convicted of a violation of this section shall be personally liable to the seizing agency for all costs of impoundment from the time of seizure to the time of proper disposition. This section shall not prohibit the seizure or impoundment of

© 1992 by J., B. & L. Gould
Printed in the U.S.A.   EP

animals as evidence as provided for under any other provision of law.

(l) This section shall be operative in a public agency or a humane society under the jurisdiction of the public agency, or both, only if the governing body of that public agency, by ordinance or resolution, determines that this section shall be operative in the public agency or the humane society and that Section 597f shall not be operative. *(Added by Stats 1991 ch 4 §1, eff. 12/13/90, oper. 1/1/91.)*

§597.5. Dog fighting.

(a) Any person who does any of the following is guilty of a felony and is punishable by imprisonment in a state prison for 16 months, or two or three years, or by a fine not to exceed fifty thousand dollars ($50,000), or by both such fine and imprisonment:

(1) Owns, possesses, keeps, or trains any dog, with the intent that the dog shall be engaged in an exhibition of fighting with another dog.

(2) For amusement or gain, causes any dog to fight with another dog, or causes any dogs to injure each other.

(3) Permits any act in violation of paragraph (1) or (2) to be done on any premises under his or her charge or control, or aids or abets that act.

(b) Any person who is knowingly present, as a spectator, at any place, building, or tenement where preparations are being made for an exhibition of the fighting of dogs, with the intent to be present at those preparations, or is knowingly present at that exhibition or at any other fighting or injuring as described in paragraph (2) of subdivision (a), with the intent to be present at that exhibition, fighting, or injuring, is guilty of a misdemeanor.

(c) Nothing in this section shall prohibit any of the following:

(1) The use of dogs in the management of livestock, as defined by Section 14205 of the Food and Agricultural Code, by the owner of the livestock or his or her employees or agents or other persons in lawful custody thereof.

(2) The use of dogs in hunting as permitted by the Fish and Game Code, including, but not limited to, Sections 3286, 3509, 3510, 4002, and 4756, and by the rules and regulations of the Fish and Game Commission.

(3) The training of dogs or the use of equipment in the training of dogs for any purpose not prohibited by law. *(Amended by Stats 1987 ch 792 §1.)*

§598. Killing, etc., birds in cemeteries.

Every person who, within any public cemetery or burying-ground, kills, wounds, or traps any bird, or destroys any bird's nest other than swallows' nests, or removes any eggs or young birds from any nest, is guilty of a misdemeanor.

§598a. Killing dog or cat for its pelt.

(a) Every person is guilty of a misdemeanor who kills any dog or cat with the sole intent of selling or giving away the pelt of such animal.

(b) Every person is guilty of a misdemeanor who possesses, imports into this state, sells, buys, gives away or accepts any pelt of a dog or cat with the sole intent of selling or giving away the pelt of the dog or cat, or who possesses, imports into this state, sells, buys, gives away, or accepts any dog or cat, with the sole intent of killing or having killed such dog or cat

for the purpose of selling or giving away the pelt of such animal.

§598b. Illegal possession of animal carcasses.

(a) Every person is guilty of a misdemeanor who possesses, imports into this state, sells, buys, gives away, or accepts any carcass or part of any carcass of any animal traditionally or commonly kept as a pet or companion with the sole intent of using or having another person use any part of that carcass for food.

(b) Every person is guilty of a misdemeanor who possesses, imports into this state, sells, buys, gives away, or accepts any animal traditionally or commonly kept as a pet or companion with the sole intent of killing or having another person kill that animal for the purpose of using or having another person use any part of the animal for food.

(c) This section shall not be construed to interfere with the production, marketing, or disposal of any livestock, poultry, fish, shell fish, or any other agricultural commodity produced in this state. Nor shall this section be construed to interfere with the lawful killing of wildlife, or the lawful killing of any other animal under the laws of this state pertaining to game animals. *(Added by Stats 1989 ch 490 §2, eff. 1/1/90.)*

§599. Commercial use of poultry or rabbits.

Every person is guilty of a misdemeanor who:

(a) Sells or gives away, any live chicks, rabbits, ducklings, or other fowl as a prize for, or as an inducement to enter, any contest, game or other competition or as an inducement to enter a place of amusement or place of business; or

(b) Dyes or otherwise artificially colors any live chicks, rabbits, ducklings or other fowl, or sells, offers for sale, or gives away any live chicks, rabbits, ducklings, or other fowl which has been dyed or artificially colored; or

(c) Maintains or possesses any live chicks, rabbits, ducklings, or other fowl for the purpose of sale or display without adequate facilities for supplying food, water and temperature control needed to maintain the health of such fowl or rabbit; or

(d) Sells, offers for sale, barters, or for commercial purposes gives away, any live chicks, rabbits, ducklings, or other fowl on any street or highway. This section shall not be construed to prohibit established hatchery management procedures or the display, or sale of natural chicks, rabbits, ducklings, or other fowl in proper facilities by dealers, hatcheries, poultrymen, or stores regularly engaged in the business of selling the same.

§599a. Arrest warrants for violation of animal statutes.

When complaint is made, on oath, to any magistrate authorized to issue warrants in criminal cases, that the complainant believes that any provision of law relating to, or in any way affecting, dumb animals or birds, is being, or is about to be violated in any particular building or place, such magistrate must issue and deliver immediately a warrant directed to any sheriff, constable, police or peace officer or officer of any incorporated association qualified as provided by law, authorizing him to enter and search such building or place, and to arrest any person there present violating, or attempting to violate, any law relating to, or in any way affecting, dumb animals or birds, and to bring such person before some court or magistrate of competent jurisdiction, within the city, city and county, or judicial district within which such offense has been committed or attempted, to be dealt with according to law, and such attempt must be held to be a violation of Section 597.

§599aa. Seizure of fighting animals and birds.

Any authorized officer making an arrest under Section 597.5 shall, and any authorized officer making an arrest under Section 597b or 599a may, lawfully take possession of all birds or animals and all paraphernalia, implements or other property or things used or employed, or about to be employed, in the violation of any of the provisions of this code relating to the fighting of birds or animals. He shall state to the person in charge thereof at the time of such taking his name and residence. Such officer, after taking possession of such birds, animals, paraphernalia, implements or other property or things, shall file with the magistrate before whom the complaint is made against any person so arrested an affidavit stating therein the name of the person charged in such complaint, a description of the property so taken and the time and place of the taking thereof together with the name of the person for whom the same was taken and the name of the person who claims to own such property, if known, and that the affiant has reason to believe and does believe, stating the ground of such belief, that the property so taken was used or employed, or was about to be used or employed, in such violation of such provisions of this code. He shall thereupon deliver the property so taken to such magistrate, who shall, by order in writing, place the same in the custody of an officer or other proper person named and designated in such order, to be kept by him until the conviction or final discharge of such person complained against, and shall send a copy of such order without delay to the district attorney of the county. The officer or person so named and designated in such order shall immediately thereupon assume the custody of such property and shall retain the same, subject to the order of the court before which such person so complained against may be required to appear for trial. Upon the conviction of the person so charged, all property so seized shall be adjudged by the court to be forfeited and shall thereupon be destroyed or otherwise disposed of as the court may order. In the event of the acquittal or final discharge without conviction of the person so charged such court shall, on demand, direct the delivery of such property so held in custody to the owner thereof.

§599b. Definitions.

In this title the word "animal" includes every dumb creature; the words "torment," "torture," and "cruelty" include every act, omission, or neglect whereby unnecessary or unjustifiable physical pain or suffering is caused or permitted; and the words "owner" and "person" include corporations as well as individuals; and the knowledge and acts of any agent of, or person employed by, a corporation in regard to animals transported, owned, or employed by, or in the custody of, such corporation, must be held to be the act and knowledge of such corporation as well as such agent or employee.

§599c. Construction of title.

No part of this title shall be construed as interfering with any of the laws of this state known as the "game laws," or any laws for or against the destruction of certain birds, nor must this title be construed as interfering with the right to destroy any venomous reptile, or any animal known as dangerous to life, limb or property, or to interfere with the right to kill all animals used for food, or with properly conducted scientific experiments or investigations performed under the authority of the faculty of a regularly incorporated medical college or university of this state.

§599d. *Repealed by Stats 1987 ch 828.*

§599e. Killing unfit animals after notice by officer.

Every animal which is unfit, by reason of its physical condition, for the purpose for which such animals are usually employed, and when there is no reasonable probability of such animal ever becoming fit for the purpose for which it is usually employed, shall be by the owner or lawful possessor of the same, deprived of life within 12 hours after being notified by any peace officer, officer of said society, or employee of a pound or animal regulation department of a public agency who is a veterinarian, to kill the same, and such owner, possessor, or person omitting or refusing to comply with the provisions of this section shall, upon conviction, be deemed guilty of a misdemeanor, and after such conviction the court or magistrate having jurisdiction of such offense shall order any peace officer, officer of said society, or officer of a pound or animal regulation department of a public agency, to immediately kill such animal; provided, that this shall not apply to such owner keeping any old or diseased animal belonging to him on his own premises with proper care.

§600. Injuring horses or dogs used by peace officers.

(a) Any person who willfully and maliciously and with no legal justification strikes, beats, kicks, cuts, stabs, shoots with a firearm, administers any poison or other harmful or stupefying substance to, or throws, hurls, or projects at, or places any rock, object, or other substance which is used in such a manner as to be capable of producing injury and likely to produce injury, on or in the path of, any horse being used by, or any dog under the supervision of, any peace officer in the discharge or attempted discharge of his or her duties, is guilty of a public offense. If the injury inflicted is a serious injury, as defined in subdivision (c), the person shall be punished by imprisonment in the state prison for 16 months, two or three years, or in a county jail for not exceeding one year, or by a fine not exceeding two thousand dollars ($2,000), or by both a fine and imprisonment. If the injury inflicted is not a serious injury, the person shall be punished by imprisonment in the county jail for not exceeding one year, or by a fine not exceeding one thousand dollars ($1,000), or by both a fine and imprisonment.

(b) Any person who willfully and maliciously and with no legal justification interferes with or obstructs any horse or dog being used by any peace officer in the discharge or attempted discharge of his or her duties by frightening, teasing, agitating, harassing, or hindering the horse or dog shall be punished by imprisonment in a county jail for not exceeding one year, or by a fine not exceeding one thousand dollars ($1,000), or by both a fine and imprisonment.

© 1992 by J., B. & L. Gould
Printed in the U.S.A.   EP

(c) Any person who, in violation of this section, and with intent to inflict such injury or death, personally causes the death, destruction, or serious physical injury including bone fracture, loss or impairment of function of any bodily member, wounds requiring extensive suturing, or serious crippling, of any horse or dog, shall, upon conviction of a felony under this section, in addition and consecutive to the punishment prescribed for the felony, be punished by an additional term of imprisonment in the state prison for one year.

(d) Any person who, in violation of this section, and with the intent to inflict such injury, personally causes great bodily injury, as defined in Section 12022.7, to any person not an accomplice, shall, upon conviction of a felony under this section, in addition and consecutive to the punishment prescribed for the felony, be punished by an additional term of imprisonment in the state prison for two years unless the conduct described in this subdivision is an element of any other offense of which the person is convicted or receives an enhancement under Section 12002.7.

(e) In any case in which a defendant is convicted of a violation of this section, the defendant shall be ordered to make restitution to the agency owning the animal and employing the peace officer for any veterinary bills, replacement costs of the animal if it is disabled or killed, and the salary of the peace officer for the period of time his or her services are lost to the agency. *(Amended by Stats 1985 ch 765 §1.)*

§601. Trespass; credible threat to cause serious bodily injury.

(a) Any person is guilty of trespass who makes a credible threat to cause serious bodily injury, as defined in subdivision (a) of Section 417.6, to another person and who does any of the following:

(1) Within 14 days of the threat, unlawfully enters into the residence or real property contiguous to the residence of the person threatened without lawful purpose, and with the intent to execute the threat against the target of the threat.

(2) Within 14 days of the threat, knowing that the place is the threatened person's workplace, unlawfully enters into the workplace of the person threatened and carries out an act or acts to locate the threatened person within the workplace premises without lawful purpose, and with the intent to execute the threat against the target of the threat.

(b) Subdivision (a) is not applicable whenever the residence, the real property, or the workplace described in paragraph (1) or (2) of that subdivision that is entered is the residence, the real property, or the workplace of the person making the threat.

(c) This section shall not be applicable to persons engaged in labor union activities which are permitted to be carried out on the property by the California Agricultural Labor Relations Act, Part 3.5 (commencing with Section 1140) of Division 2 of the Labor Code, or by the National Labor Relations Act.

(d) A violation of subdivision (a) is punishable by imprisonment in the state prison, or in a county jail not exceeding one year, or by a fine not exceeding two thousand dollars ($2,000), or by both a fine and imprisonment. *(Added by Stats 1990 ch 1448 §1, eff. 1/1/91.)*

§602. Trespassing.

Notwithstanding Section 602.8, every person who willfully commits a trespass by any of the following acts is guilty of a misdemeanor:

(a) Cutting down, destroying, or injuring any kind of wood or timber standing or growing upon the lands of another.

(b) Carrying away any kind of wood or timber lying on those lands.

(c) Maliciously injuring or severing from the freehold of another anything attached to it, or its produce.

(d) Digging, taking, or carrying away from any lot situated within the limits of any incorporated city, without the license of the owner or legal occupant, any earth, soil, or stone.

(e) Digging, taking, or carrying away from land in any city or town laid down on the map or plan of the city, or otherwise recognized or established as a street, alley, avenue, or park, without the license of the proper authorities, any earth, soil, or stone.

(f) Maliciously tearing down, damaging, mutilating, or destroying any sign, signboard, or notice placed upon, or affixed to, any property belonging to the state, or to any city, county, city and county, town or village, or upon any property of any person, by the state or by an automobile association, which sign, signboard or notice is intended to indicate or designate a road, or a highway, or is intended to direct travelers from one point to another, or relates to fires, fire control, or any other matter involving the protection of the property, or putting up, affixing, fastening, printing, or painting upon any property belonging to the state, or to any city, county, town, or village, or dedicated to the public, or upon any property of any person, without license from the owner, any notice, advertisement, or designation of, or any name for any commodity, whether for sale or otherwise, or any picture, sign, or device intended to call attention to it.

(g) Entering upon any lands owned by any other person whereon oysters or other shellfish are planted or growing; or injuring, gathering, or carrying away any oysters or other shellfish planted, growing, or on any such lands, whether covered by water or not, without the license of the owner or legal occupant; or destroying or removing, or causing to be removed or destroyed, any stakes, marks, fences, or signs intended to designate the boundaries and limits of any such lands.

(h) Willfully opening, tearing down, or otherwise destroying any fence on the enclosed land of another, or opening any gate, bar, or fence of another and willfully leaving it open without the written permission of the owner, or maliciously tearing down, mutilating, or destroying any sign, signboard, or other notice forbidding shooting on private property.

(i) Building fires upon any lands owned by another where signs forbidding trespass are displayed at intervals not greater than one mile along the exterior boundaries and at all roads and trails entering the lands, without first having obtained written permission from the owner of the lands or the owner's agent, or the person in lawful possession.

(j) Entering any lands, whether unenclosed or enclosed by fence, for the purpose of injuring any property or property rights or with the intention of interfering with, obstructing, or injuring any lawful business or occupation carried on by the owner of the land, the owner's agent or by the person in lawful possession.

(k) Entering any lands under cultivation or enclosed by fence, belonging to, or occupied by, another, or entering upon uncultivated or unenclosed lands where signs forbidding trespass are displayed at intervals not less than three to the mile along all exterior boundaries and at all roads and trails entering the lands without the written permission of the owner of the land, the owner's agent or of the person in lawful possession, and

(1) Refusing or failing to leave the lands immediately upon being requested by the owner of the land, the owner's agent or by the person in lawful possession to leave the lands, or

(2) Tearing down, mutilating, or destroying any sign, signboard, or notice forbidding trespass or hunting on the lands, or

(3) Removing, injuring, unlocking, or tampering with any lock on any gate on or leading into the lands, or

(4) Discharging any firearm.

(l) Entering and occupying real property or structures of any kind without the consent of the owner, the owner's agent, or the person in lawful possession.

(m) Driving any vehicle, as defined in Section 670 of the Vehicle Code, upon real property belonging to or lawfully occupied by another and known not to be open to the general public, without the consent of the owner, the owner's agent, or the person in lawful possession.

(n) Refusing or failing to leave land, real property, or structures belonging to or lawfully occupied by another and not open to the general public, upon being requested to leave by (1) a peace officer at the request of the owner, the owner's agent, or the person in lawful possession, and upon being informed by the peace officer that he or she is acting at the request of the owner, the owner's agent, or the person in lawful possession, or (2) the owner, the owner's agent, or the person in lawful possession. The owner, the owner's agent, or the person in lawful possession shall make a separate request to the peace officer on each occasion when the peace officer's assistance in dealing with a trespass is requested. However, a single request for a peace officer's assistance may be made to cover a limited period of time not to exceed 30 days and identified by specific dates, during which there is a fire hazard or the owner, owner's agent or person in lawful possession is absent from the premises or property. In addition, a single request for a peace officer's assistance may be made for a period not to exceed six months when the premises or property is closed to the public and posted as being closed. However, this subdivision shall not be applicable to persons engaged in lawful labor union activities which are permitted to be carried out on the property by the California Agricultural Labor Relations Act, Part 3.5 (commencing with Section 1140) of Division 2 of the Labor Code, or by the National Labor Relations Act. For purposes of this section, land, real property, or structures owned or operated by any housing authority for tenants as defined under Section 34213.5 of the Health and Safety Code constitutes property not open to the general public; however, this subdivision shall not apply to persons on the premises who are engaging in activities protected by the California or United States Constitution, or to persons who are on the premises at the request of a resident or management and who are not loitering or otherwise suspected of violating or actually violating any law or ordinance.

(o) Entering upon any lands declared closed to entry as provided in Section 4256 of the Public Resources Code, if the closed areas shall have been posted with notices declaring the closure, at intervals not greater than one mile along the exterior boundaries or along roads and trails passing through the lands.

(p) Refusing or failing to leave a public building of a public agency during those hours of the day or night when the building is regularly closed to the public upon being requested to do so by a regularly employed guard, watchman, or custodian of the public agency owning or maintaining the building or property, if the surrounding circumstances are such as to indicate to a reasonable person that the person has no apparent lawful business to pursue.

(q) Knowingly skiing in an area or on a ski trail which is closed to the public and which has signs posted indicating the closure.

(r) Refusing or failing to leave a hotel or motel, where he or she has obtained accommodations and has refused to pay for those accommodations, upon request of the proprietor or manager, and the occupancy is exempt, pursuant to subdivision (b) of Section 1940 of the Civil Code, from Chapter 2 (commencing with Section 1940) of Title 5 of Part 4 of Division 3 of the Civil Code.

(s) Entering upon private property, including contiguous land, real property, or structures thereon belonging to the same owner, whether or not generally open to the public, after having been informed by a peace officer at the request of the owner, the owner's agent, or the person in lawful possession, and upon being informed by the peace officer that he or she is acting at the request of the owner, the owner's agent, or the person in lawful possession, that the property is not open to the particular person; or refusing or failing to leave the property upon being asked to leave the property in the manner provided in this subdivision.

This subdivision shall apply only to a person who has been convicted of a violent felony, as specified in subdivision (c) of Section 667.5, committed upon the particular private property. A single notification or request to the person as set forth above shall be valid and enforceable under this subdivision unless and until rescinded by the owner, the owner's agent, or the person in lawful possession of the property.

(t) (1) Knowingly entering, by an unauthorized person, upon any airport operations area if the area has been posted with notices restricting access to authorized personnel only and the postings occur not greater than every 150 feet along the exterior boundary.

(2) Any person convicted of a violation of paragraph (1) shall be punished as follows:

(A) By a fine not exceeding one hundred dollars ($100).

(B) By imprisonment in the county jail not exceeding six months, or by a fine not exceeding one thousand dollars ($1,000), or both, if the person refuses to leave the airport operations area after being requested to leave by a peace officer.

(C) By imprisonment in the county jail not exceeding six months, or by a fine not exceeding one thousand dollars ($1,000), or both, for a second or subsequent offense.

© 1992 by J., B. & L. Gould
Printed in the U.S.A.   EP

(3) As used in this subdivision the following definitions shall control:

(A) "Airport operations area" means that part of the airport used by aircraft for landing, taking off, surface maneuvering, loading and unloading, refueling, parking, or maintenance, where aircraft support vehicles and facilities exist, and which is not for public use or public vehicular traffic.

(B) "Authorized personnel" means any person who has a valid airport identification card issued by the airport operator or has a valid airline identification card recognized by the airport operator, or any person not in possession of an airport or airline identification card who is being escorted for legitimate purposes by a person with an airport or airline identification card.

(C) "Airport" means any facility whose function is to support commercial aviation. *(Amended by Stats 1990 ch 424 §1, eff. 1/1/91.)*

§602.1. Interfering with lawful business.

(a) Any person who intentionally interferes with any lawful business or occupation carried on by the owner or agent of a business establishment open to the public, by obstructing or intimidating those attempting to carry on business, or their customers, and who refuses to leave the premises of the business establishment after being requested to leave by the owner or the owner's agent, or by a peace officer acting at the request of the owner or owner's agent, is guilty of a misdemeanor, punishable by imprisonment in a county jail for up to 90 days, or by a fine of up to four hundred dollars ($400), or by both that imprisonment and fine.

(b) This section shall not apply to any of the following persons:

(1) Any person engaged in lawful labor union activities that are permitted to be carried out on the property by state or federal law.

(2) Any person on the premises who is engaging in activities protected by the California Constitution or the United States Constitution.

(c) Nothing in this section shall be deemed to supersede the application of any other law. *(Added by Stats 1991 ch 673 §1, eff. 1/1/92.)*

§602.2. Written permission to enter vacant or unimproved private land; application.

Any ordinance or resolution adopted by a county which requires written permission to enter vacant or unimproved private land from either the owner, the owner's agent, or the person in lawful possession of private land, shall not apply unless the land is immediately adjacent and contiguous to residential property, or enclosed by fence, or under cultivation, or posted with signs forbidding trespass, displayed at intervals of not less than three to a mile, along all exterior boundaries and at all roads and trails entering the private land. *(Added by Stats 1986 ch 34 §1.)*

§602.3. Lodgers; removal from owner-occupied dwelling units.

(a) A lodger who is subject to Section 1946.5 of the Civil Code and who remains on the premises of an owner-occupied dwelling unit after receipt of a notice terminating the hiring, and expiration of the notice period, provided in Section 1946.5 of the Civil Code is guilty of an infraction and may, pursuant to Section 837, be arrested for the offense by the owner, or in the event the owner is represented by a court-appointed conservator, executor, or administrator, by the owner's representative. Notwithstanding Section 853.5, the requirement of that section for release upon a written promise to appear shall not preclude an assisting peace officer from removing the person from the owner-occupied dwelling unit.

(b) The removal of a lodger from a dwelling unit by the owner pursuant to subdivision (a) is not a forcible entry under the provisions of Section 1159 of the Code of Civil Procedure and shall not be a basis for civil liability under that section.

(c) Chapter 5 (commencing with Section 1980) of Title 5 of Part 4 of Division 3 of the Civil Code applies to any personal property of the lodger which remains on the premises following the lodger's removal from the premises pursuant to this section.

(d) Nothing in this section shall be construed to limit the owner's right to have a lodger removed under other provisions of law.

(e) Except as provided in subdivision (b), nothing in this section shall be construed to limit or affect in any way any cause of action an owner or lodger may have for damages for any breach of the contract of the parties respecting the lodging.

(f) This section applies only to owner-occupied dwellings where a single lodger resides. Nothing in this section shall be construed to determine or affect in any way the rights of persons residing as lodgers in an owner-occupied dwelling where more than one lodger resides. *(Amended by Stats 1991 ch 930 §1, eff. 1/1/92.)*

§602.4. Peddling on airport property.

Every person who enters or remains on airport property owned by a city, county, or city and county but located in another county, and sells, peddles, or offers for sale any goods, merchandise, property, or services of any kind whatsoever, to members of the public, including transportation services, other than charter limousines licensed by the Public Utilities Commission, on or from the airport property, without the express written consent of the governing board of the airport property, or its duly authorized representative, is guilty of a misdemeanor.

Nothing in this section affects the power of a county, city, or city and county to regulate the sale, peddling or offering for sale of goods, merchandise, property, or services.

§602.5. Entering property without consent.

Every person other than a public officer or employee acting within the course and scope of his employment in performance of a duty imposed by law, who enters or remains in any noncommercial dwelling house, apartment, or other such place without consent of the owner, his agent, or the person in lawful possession thereof, is guilty of a misdemeanor.

§602.6. Trespassing at fairs.

Every person who enters or remains. in, or upon, any state, county, district, or citrus fruit fair buildings or grounds, when the buildings or grounds are not open to the general public, after having been ordered or directed by a peace officer or a fair manager to leave the building or grounds and when the order or direction to leave is issued after determination that the person has no apparent lawful business or other legitimate reason for remaining on the property, and fails to identify himself or herself and account for his or her presence, is guilty of a misdemeanor. *(Added by Stats 1990 ch 631 §1 eff. 1/1/91.)*

§602.7. Peddling on property, etc., of San Francisco Bay Area and Southern California Rapid Transit Districts.

Every person who enters or remains on any property, facility, or vehicle owned by the San Francisco Bay Area Rapid Transit District or the Southern California Rapid Transit District, and sells or peddles any goods, merchandise, property, or services of any kind whatsoever on the property, facilities, or vehicles, without the express written consent of the governing board of the San Francisco Bay Area Rapid Transit District or the governing board of the Southern California Rapid Transit District, or its duly authorized representatives, is guilty of an infraction.

Nothing in this section affects the power of a county, city, transit district, or city and county to regulate the sale or peddling of goods, merchandise, property, or services. *(Added by Stats 1986 ch 1232 §1.)*

§602.8. Trespass; penalty.

(a) Any person who without the written permission of the landowner, the owner's agent or of the person in lawful possession of the land, willfully enters any lands under cultivation or enclosed by fence, belonging to, or occupied by, another, or who willfully enters upon uncultivated or unenclosed lands where signs forbidding trespass are displayed at intervals not less than three to the mile along all exterior boundaries and at all roads and trails entering the lands, is guilty of an infraction or a misdemeanor.

(b) Any person convicted of a violation of subdivision (a) shall be punished as follows:

(1) For a first offense, punished as an infraction by a fine of ten dollars ($10).

(2) For a second offense on any contiguous land of the same owner, punished as an infraction by a fine of not less than one hundred dollars ($100) nor more than two hundred fifty dollars ($250).

(3) For a third or subsequent offense on any contiguous land of the same owner, by imprisonment in the county jail not exceeding six months, or by fine not exceeding one thousand dollars ($1,000), or both.

(c) Subdivision (a) shall not apply to any of the following:

(1) Any person engaged in lawful labor union activities which are permitted to be carried out on property by the California Agricultural Labor Relations Act, Part 3.5 (commencing with Section 1140) of Division 2 of the Labor Code, or by the National Labor Relations Act.

(2) Any person on the premises who is engaging in activities protected by the California or United States Constitution.

(3) Any person described in Section 22350 of the Business and Professions Code who is making a lawful service of process.

(d) For any infraction charged pursuant to this section, the defendant shall have the option to forfeit bail in lieu of making a court appearance. Notwithstanding subdivision (e) of Section 863.6, if the offender elects to forfeit bail pursuant to this subdivision, no further proceedings shall be had in the case. *(Added by Stats 1989 ch 870 §2, eff. 1/1/90.)*

§602.10. Obstruction of instruction at a college or university.

Every person who, by physical force and with the intent to prevent attendance or instruction, willfully obstructs or attempts to obstruct any student or teacher seeking to attend or instruct classes at any of the campuses or facilities owned, controlled, or administered by the Regents of the University of California, the Trustees of the California State University, or the governing board of a community college district shall be punished by a fine not exceeding five hundred dollars ($500), by imprisonment in a county jail for a period of not exceeding one year, or by both such fine and imprisonment.

As used in this section, "physical force" includes, but is not limited to, use of one's person, individually or in concert with others, to impede access to, or movement within, or otherwise to obstruct the students and teachers of the classes to which the premises are devoted.

§603. Unauthorized destruction of property.

Every person other than a peace officer engaged in the performance of his duties as such who forcibly and without the consent of the owner, representative of the owner, lessee or representative of the lessee thereof, enters a dwelling house, cabin, or other building occupied or constructed for occupation by humans, and who damages, injures or destroys any property of value in, around or appertaining to such dwelling house, cabin or other building, is guilty of a misdemeanor.

§604. Injuries to standing crops, etc.

Every person who maliciously injures or destroys any standing crops, grain, cultivated fruits or vegetables, the property of another, in any case for which a punishment is not otherwise prescribed by this code, is guilty of a misdemeanor.

§605. Removing, defacing or altering landmarks.

Every person who either:

1. Maliciously removes any monument erected for the purpose of designating any point in the boundary of any lot or tract of land, or a place where a subaqueous telegraph cable lies; or,

2. Maliciously defaces or alters the marks upon any such monument; or,

3. Maliciously cuts down or removes any tree upon which any such marks have been made for such purpose, with intent to destroy such marks;

—Is guilty of a misdemeanor.

§606. *Repealed by Stats 1987 ch 828.*

§607. Damage to water retaining structure.

Every person who wilfully and maliciously cuts, breaks, injures or destroys any bridge, dam, canal, flume, aqueduct, levee, embankment, reservoir, or other structure erected to create hydraulic power, or to drain or reclaim any swamp, overflow, tide or marsh land, or to store or conduct water for mining, manufacturing, reclamation, or agricultural purposes, or for the supply of the inhabitants of any city or town, or any embankment necessary to the same, or either of them or wilfully or maliciously makes, or causes to be made, any aperture or plows up the bottom or sides in such dam, canal, flume, aqueduct, reservoir, embank-

© 1992 by J., B. & L. Gould
Printed in the U.S.A.   EP

ment, levee, or structure, with intent to injure or destroy the same; or draws up, cuts or injures any piles fixed in the ground for the purpose of securing any sea bank, or sea wall, or any dock, quay or jetty, lock, or sea wall; or who, between the first day of October and the fifteenth day of April of each year, plows up or loosens the soil in the bed on the side of any natural water course, reclamation or drainage ditch, with an intent to destroy the same without removing such soil within 24 hours from such water course, reclamation or drainage ditch, or who, between the fifteenth day of April and the first day of October of each year, shall plow up or loosen the soil in the bed or on the sides of such natural water course, reclamation or drainage ditch, with an intent to destroy the same and shall not remove therefrom the soil so plowed up or loosened before the first day of October next thereafter, is guilty of a misdemeanor, and upon conviction, punishable by a fine of not exceeding one thousand dollars, or by imprisonment in a county jail not exceeding one year, or by both such fine and imprisonment; provided, that nothing in this section shall be construed so as to in any manner prohibit any person from digging or removing soil from any such water course, reclamation or drainage ditch, for the purpose of mining.

§610. Masking or removing signal lights.

Every person who unlawfully masks, alters, or removes any light or signal, or willfully exhibits any light or signal, with intent to bring any vessel into danger, is punishable by imprisonment in the state prison.

§615. Injuries to signals, monuments, etc., erected in United States Coast survey.

Every person who willfully injures, defaces, or removes any signal, monument, building, or appurtenance thereto, placed, erected, or used by persons engaged in the United States Coast survey, is guilty of a misdemeanor.

§616. Destroying or tearing down notices, etc., before expiration of time they were to remain set up.

Every person who intentionally defaces, obliterates, tears down, or destroys any copy or transcript, or extract from or of any law of the United States or of this State, or any proclamation, advertisement, or notification set up at any place in this State, by authority of any law of the United States or of this State, or by order of any Court, before the expiration of the time for which the same was to remain set up, is punishable by fine not less than twenty nor more than one hundred dollars, or by imprisonment in the County Jail not more than one month.

§617. Written instruments belonging to another.

Every person who maliciously mutilates, tears, defaces, obliterates, or destroys any written instrument, the property of another, the false making of which would be forgery, is punishable by imprisonment in the state prison.

§618. Opening or publishing sealed letters.

Every person who willfully opens or reads, or causes to be read, any sealed letter not addressed to himself, without being authorized so to do, either by the writer of such letter or by the person to whom it is addressed, and every person who, without the like authority, publishes any of the contents of such letter, knowing the same to have been unlawfully opened, is guilty of a misdemeanor.

§620. Altering telegraphic or telephonic messages.

Every person who willfully alters the purport, effect, or meaning of a telegraphic or telephonic message to the injury of another, is punishable by imprisonment in the state prison, or in the county jail not exceeding one year, or by fine not exceeding ten thousand dollars ($10,000), or by both such fine and imprisonment.

§622. Injuring works of art or improvements in any city, town, or village.

Every person, not the owner thereof, who willfully injures, disfigures, or destroys any monument, work of art, or useful or ornamental improvement within the limits of any village, town, or city, or any shade tree or ornamental plant growing therein, whether situated upon private ground or on any street, sidewalk, or public park or place, is guilty of a misdemeanor.

§622¹/₂. Archeological or historical objects.

Every person, not the owner thereof, who wilfully injures, disfigures, defaces, or destroys any object or thing of archeological or historical interest or value, whether situated on private lands or within any public park or place, is guilty of a misdemeanor.

§623. Cave damage.

(a) Except as otherwise provided in Section 599c, any person who, without the prior written permission of the owner of a cave, intentionally and knowingly does any of the following acts is guilty of a misdemeanor punishable by imprisonment in the county jail not exceeding one year, or by a fine not exceeding one thousand dollars ($1,000), or by both such fine and imprisonment:

(1) Breaks, breaks off, cracks, carves upon, paints, writes or otherwise marks upon or in any manner destroys, mutilates, injures, defaces, mars, or harms any natural material found in any cave.

(2) Disturbs or alters any archaeological evidence of prior occupation in any cave.

(3) Kills, harms, or removes any animal or plant life found in any cave.

(4) Burns any material which produces any smoke or gas which is harmful to any plant or animal found in any cave.

(5) Removes any material found in any cave.

(6) Breaks, forces, tampers with, removes or otherwise disturbs any lock, gate, door, or any other structure or obstruction designed to prevent entrance to any cave, whether or not entrance is gained.

(b) For purposes of this section:

(1) "Cave" means any natural geologically formed void or cavity beneath the surface of the earth, not including any mine, tunnel, aqueduct, or other man-made excavation, which is large enough to permit a person to enter.

(2) "Owner" means the person or private or public agency which has the right of possession to the cave.

(3) "Natural material" means any stalactite, stalagmite, helictite, anthodite, gypsum flower or needle, flowstone, drapery, column, tufa dam, clay or mud

© 1992 by J., B. & L. Gould
Printed in the U.S.A. **EP**

formation or concretion, crystalline mineral formation, and any wall, ceiling, or mineral protuberance therefrom, whether attached or broken, found in any cave.

(4) "Material" means all or any part of any archaeological, paleontological, biological, or historical item including, but not limited to, any petroglyph, pictograph, basketry, human remains, tool, beads, pottery, projectile point, remains of historical mining activity or any other occupation found in any cave.

(c) The entering or remaining in a cave by itself shall not constitute a violation of this section.

§624. Breaking water pipes.

Every person who willfully breaks, digs up, obstructs, or injures any pipe or main for conducting water, or any works erected for supplying buildings with water, or any appurtenances or appendages connected thereto, is guilty of a misdemeanor.

§625. Drawing water from works after they have been closed.

Every person who, with intent to defraud or injure, opens or causes to be opened, or draws water from any stopcock or faucet by which the flow of water is controlled, after having been notified that the same has been closed or shut for specific cause, by order of competent authority, is guilty of a misdemeanor.

§625b. Tampering with aircraft.

(a) Every person who willfully injures or tampers with any aircraft or the contents or parts thereof, or removes any part of or from an aircraft without the consent of the owner, and every person who, with intent to commit any malicious mischief, injury or other crime, climbs into or upon an aircraft or attempts to manipulate any of the controls, starting mechanism, brakes or other mechanism or device of an aircraft while it is at rest and unattended or who sets in motion any aircraft while it is at rest and unattended, is guilty of a misdemeanor and upon conviction shall be punished by imprisonment for not more than six months or by a fine of not more than one thousand dollars ($1,000), or by both such fine and imprisonment.

(b) Every person who willfully and maliciously damages, injures, or destroys any aircraft, or the contents or any part thereof, in such a manner as to render the aircraft unsafe for those flight operations for which it is designed and equipped is punishable by imprisonment in the state prison, or by imprisonment in a county jail not exceeding one year, or by a fine not exceeding ten thousand dollars ($10,000), or by both such fine and imprisonment.

§625c. Willfully injuring passenger transit vehicle.

Any person who, with the intent to cause great bodily injury to another person, willfully removes, tampers with, injures or destroys any passenger transit vehicle or the contents or parts thereof, or who willfully removes, tampers with or destroys, or places an obstruction upon any part of the transit system, including its right-of-way, structures, fixtures, tracks, switches or controls, or who willfully sets a vehicle in motion while it is at rest and unattended is guilty of a felony.

TITLE 15

MISCELLANEOUS CRIMES

CHAPTER 1

SCHOOLS

§626. Definitions.

(a) As used in this chapter:

(1) "University" means the University of California, and includes any affiliated institution thereof and any campus or facility owned, operated, or controlled by the Regents of the University of California.

(2) "State university" means any California state university, and includes any campus or facility owned, operated, or controlled by the Trustees of the California State University.

(3) "Community college" means any public community college established pursuant to the Education Code.

(4) "School" means any elementary school, junior high school, four-year high school, senior high school, adult school or any branch thereof, opportunity school, continuation high school, regional occupational center, evening high school, or technical school or any public right-of-way situated immediately adjacent to school property or any other place if a teacher and one or more students are required to be at that place in connection with assigned school activities.

(5) "Chief administrative officer" means:

(i) The president of the university or a state university, the Chancellor of the California State University, or the officer designated by the Regents of the University of California or pursuant to authority granted by the Regents of the University of California to administer and be the officer in charge of a campus or other facility owned, operated, or controlled by the Regents of the University of California, or the superintendent of a community college district.

(ii) For a school: the principal of the school; or a person who possesses a standard supervision credential or a standard administrative credential and who is designated by the principal; or a person who carries out the same functions as a person who possesses a credential and who is designated by the principal.

(b) For the purpose of determining the penalty to be imposed pursuant to this chapter, the court may consider a written report from the Department of Justice containing information from its records showing prior convictions; and the communication is prima facie evidence of the convictions, if the defendant admits them, regardless of whether or not the complaint commencing the proceedings has alleged prior convictions. (Amended by Stats 1988 ch 1113 §4, eff. 1/1/89.)

§626.1. Summary of laws; distribution, etc.

(a) It is the intent of the Legislature in enacting this section to ensure that students, parents, and all school officials and employees have access to a concise, easily understandable summary of California penal and civil law pertaining to crimes committed against persons or property on school grounds.

(b) On or before June 30, 1985, the Attorney General shall prepare and present to the Superintendent of Public Instruction, a handbook, written in easily understandable language, that contains a complete summary, with statutory citations, of California

© 1992 by J., B. & L. Gould
Printed in the U.S.A.　EP

penal and civil law pertaining to crimes (1) committed against persons or property on school grounds, and (2) identified on the forms prepared pursuant to Section 628.1 of the Penal Code. The handbook shall include, but shall not be limited to, all reporting requirements pertaining to these crimes, the sanctions for failure to report, an explanation as to what constitutes an act of violence or vandalism, an explanation of the procedure by which any person or the school may initiate the prosecution of offenders for these crimes or seek recovery for injury or damages for these crimes, an explanation of parental liability for injury or property damages resulting from the intentional acts of a minor, and an explanation of any right to benefits as a consequence of injury or damage resulting from these crimes. The Attorney General shall periodically, but no less than once every two years, update this handbook to reflect changes in the law.

(c) Upon receipt of the handbook pursuant to subdivision (b) from the Attorney General, the Superintendent of Public Instruction shall (1) provide for the expeditious duplication and distribution of this handbook to all superintendents of school districts, to county offices of education, and to principals or directors of county-operated programs, sites, and schools, and (2) request the superintendents to ensure that the principal or director of each county-operated program, site, or school notify parents and guardians of the contents and availability of the handbook at the school, program, or site in the next regular communication sent to each parent or guardian. *(Amended by Stats 1989 ch 1457 §1, eff. 1/1/90.)*

§626.2. Entry on campus after suspension or dismissal.

Every student or employee who, after a hearing, has been suspended or dismissed from a community college, a state university, the university, or a school for disrupting the orderly operation of the campus or facility of such institution, and as a condition of such suspension or dismissal has been denied access to the campus or facility, or both, of the institution for the period of the suspension or in the case of dismissal for a period not to exceed one year; who has been served by registered or certified mail, at the last address given by such person, with a written notice of such suspension or dismissal and condition; and who willfully and knowingly enters upon the campus or facility of the institution to which he or she has been denied access, without the express written permission of the chief administrative officer of the campus or facility, is guilty of a misdemeanor and shall be punished as follows:

(1) Upon a first conviction, by a fine of not exceeding five hundred dollars ($500), by imprisonment in the county jail for a period of not more than six months, or by both such fine and imprisonment.

(2) If the defendant has been previously convicted once of a violation of any offense defined in this chapter or Section 415.5, by imprisonment in the county jail for a period of not less than 10 days or more than six months, or by both such imprisonment and a fine of not exceeding five hundred dollars ($500), and shall not be released on probation, parole, or any other basis until he or she has served not less than 10 days.

(3) If the defendant has been previously convicted two or more times of a violation of any offense defined in this chapter or Section 415.5, by imprisonment in the county jail for a period of not less than 90 days or more

than six months, or by both such imprisonment and a fine of not exceeding five hundred dollars ($500), and shall not be released on probation, parole, or any other basis until he or she has served not less than 90 days.

Knowledge shall be presumed if notice has been given as prescribed in this section. The presumption established by this section is a presumption affecting the burden of proof.

§626.4. Notice of withdrawal of consent to remain on campus.

(a) The chief administrative officer of a campus or other facility of a community college, a state university, the university, or a school, or an officer or employee designated by the chief administrative officer to maintain order on such campus or facility, may notify a person that consent to remain on the campus or other facility under the control of the chief administrative officer has been withdrawn whenever there is reasonable cause to believe that such person has willfully disrupted the orderly operation of such campus or facility.

(b) Whenever consent is withdrawn by any authorized officer or employee, other than the chief administrative officer, such officer or employee shall as soon as is reasonably possible submit a written report to the chief administrative officer. The report shall contain all of the following:

(1) The description of the person from whom consent was withdrawn, including, if available, the person's name, address, and phone number.

(2) A statement of the facts giving rise to the withdrawal of consent.

If the chief administrative officer or, in the chief administrative officer's absence, a person designated by him or her for this purpose, upon reviewing the report, finds that there was reasonable cause to believe that such person has willfully disrupted the orderly operation of the campus or facility, he or she may enter written confirmation upon the report of the action taken by the officer or employee. If the chief administrative officer or, in the chief administrative officer's absence, the person designated by him or her, does not confirm the action of the officer or employee within 24 hours after the time that consent was withdrawn, the action of the officer or employee shall be deemed void and of no force or effect, except that any arrest made during such period shall not for this reason be deemed not to have been made for probable cause.

(c) Consent shall be reinstated by the chief administrative officer whenever he or she has reason to believe that the presence of the person from whom consent was withdrawn will not constitute a substantial and material threat to the orderly operation of the campus or facility. In no case shall consent be withdrawn for longer than 14 days from the date upon which consent was initially withdrawn. The person from whom consent has been withdrawn may submit a written request for a hearing on the withdrawal within the two-week period. The written request shall state the address to which notice of hearing is to be sent. The chief administrative officer shall grant such a hearing not later than seven days from the date of receipt of the request and shall immediately mail a written notice of the time, place, and date of such hearing to such person.

(d) Any person who has been notified by the chief administrative officer of a campus or other facility of a community college, a state university, the university, or a school, or by an officer or employee designated by the chief administrative officer to maintain order on such campus or facility, that consent to remain on the campus or facility has been withdrawn pursuant to subdivision (a); who has not had such consent reinstated; and who willfully and knowingly enters or remains upon such campus or facility during the period for which consent has been withdrawn is guilty of a misdemeanor. This subdivision does not apply to any person who enters or remains on such campus or facility for the sole purpose of applying to the chief administrative officer for the reinstatement of consent or for the sole purpose of attending a hearing on the withdrawal.

(e) This section shall not affect the power of the duly constituted authorities of a community college, a state university, the university, or a school, to suspend, dismiss, or expel any student or employee at the college, state university, university, or school.

(f) Any person convicted under this section shall be punished as follows:

(1) Upon a first conviction, by a fine of not exceeding five hundred dollars ($500), by imprisonment in the county jail for a period of not more than six months, or by both such fine and imprisonment.

(2) If the defendant has been previously convicted once of a violation of any offense defined in this chapter or Section 415.5, by imprisonment in the county jail for a period of not less than 10 days or more than six months, or by both such imprisonment and a fine of not exceeding five hundred dollars ($500), and shall not be released on probation, parole, or any other basis until he or she has served not less than 10 days.

(3) If the defendant has been previously convicted two or more times of a violation of any offense defined in this chapter or Section 415.5, by imprisonment in the county jail for a period of not less than 90 days or more than six months, or by both such imprisonment and a fine of not exceeding five hundred dollars ($500), and shall not be released on probation, parole, or any other basis until he or she has served not less than 90 days.

(g) This section shall not affect the rights of representatives of employee organizations to enter, or remain upon, school grounds while actually engaged in activities related to representation, as provided for in Chapter 10.7 (commencing with Section 3540) of Division 4 of Title 1 of the Government Code.

§626.6. Power to direct person to leave campus.

(a) In any case in which a person who is not a student or officer or employee of a community college, a state university, the university, or a school, and who is not required by his or her employment to be on the campus or any other facility owned, operated, or controlled by the governing board of any such community college, state university, university, or school, enters such campus or facility, and it reasonably appears to the chief administrative officer of the campus or facility or to an officer or employee designated by the chief administrative officer to maintain order on such campus or facility that such person is committing any act likely to interfere with the peaceful conduct of the activities of the campus or facility or has entered the campus or facility for the purpose of committing any such act, the chief administrative officer or officer or employee designated by him or her to maintain order on the campus or facility may direct the person to leave

the campus or facility, and if the person fails to do so or if the person willfully and knowingly reenters upon the campus or facility within 7 days after being directed to leave, he or she is guilty of a misdemeanor and shall be punished as follows:

(1) Upon a first conviction by a fine of not exceeding five hundred dollars ($500), by imprisonment in the county jail for a period of not more than six months, or by both such fine and imprisonment.

(2) If the defendant has been previously convicted once of a violation of any offense defined in this chapter or Section 415.5, by imprisonment in the county jail for a period of not less than 10 days or more than six months, or by both such imprisonment and a fine of not exceeding five hundred dollars ($500), and shall not be released on probation, parole, or any other basis until he or she has served not less than 10 days.

(3) If the defendant has been previously convicted two or more times of a violation of any offense defined in this chapter or Section 415.5, by imprisonment in the county jail for a period of not less than 90 days or more than six months, or by both such imprisonment and a fine of not exceeding five hundred dollars ($500), and shall not be released on probation, parole, or any other basis until he or she has served not less than 90 days.

For purposes of this section, a representative of a school employee organization engaged in activities related to representation, as provided for in Chapter 10.7 (commencing with Section 3540) of Division 4 of Title 1 of the Government Code, shall be deemed a person required by his or her employment to be in a school building or on the grounds of a school.

(b) The provisions of this section shall not be utilized to impinge upon the lawful exercise of constitutionally protected rights of freedom of speech or assembly.

(c) When a person is directed to leave pursuant to subdivision (a), the person directing him or her to leave shall inform the person that if he or she reenters the campus or facility within 7 days he or she will be guilty of a crime. (*Amended by Stats 1989 ch 1054 §1, eff. 1/1/90.*)

§626.8. Sex offender on school grounds.

(a) Any person who comes into any school building or upon any school ground, or street, sidewalk, or public way adjacent thereto, without lawful business thereon, and whose presence or acts interfere with the peaceful conduct of the activities of the school or disrupt the school or its pupils or school activities, or any specified sex offender who comes into any school building or upon any school ground, or street, sidewalk, or public way adjacent thereto, unless such person is a parent or guardian of a child attending that school, or is a student at the school or has prior written permission for the entry from the chief administrative officer of that school, is guilty of a misdemeanor if he or she:

(1) Remains there after being asked to leave by the chief administrative official of that school or his or her designated representative, or by a person employed as a member of a security or police department of a school district pursuant to Section 39670 of the Education Code, or a city police officer, or sheriff or deputy sheriff, or California Highway Patrol Officer; or

(2) Reenters or comes upon such place within 7 days of being asked to leave by a person specified in paragraph (1); or

© 1992 by J., B. & L. Gould
Printed in the U.S.A.   EP

(3) Has otherwise established a continued pattern of unauthorized entry.

The provisions of this section shall not be utilized to impinge upon the lawful exercise of constitutionally protected rights of freedom of speech or assembly.

(b) Punishment for violation of this section shall be as follows:

(1) Upon a first conviction by a fine of not exceeding five hundred dollars ($500), by imprisonment in the county jail for a period of not more than six months, or by both such fine and imprisonment.

(2) If the defendant has been previously convicted once of a violation of any offense defined in this chapter or Section 415.5, by imprisonment in the county jail for a period of not less than 10 days or more than six months, or by both such imprisonment and a fine of not exceeding five hundred dollars ($500), and shall not be released on probation, parole, or any other basis until he or she has served not less than 10 days.

(3) If the defendant has been previously convicted two or more times of a violation of any offense defined in this chapter or Section 415.5, by imprisonment in the county jail for a period of not less than 90 days or more than six months, or by both such imprisonment and a fine of not exceeding five hundred dollars ($500), and shall not be released on probation, parole, or any other basis until he or she has served not less than 90 days.

(c) As used in this section:

(1) "Specified sex offender" means any person required to register pursuant to Section 290, who has been convicted of a violation of Section 220, 261, 266, 267, 272, 288, or 289, or of subdivision (c), (d), or (f) of Section 286, or of subdivision (c), (d), or (f) of Section 288a, or of an attempt to commit any of these offenses.

(2) "Lawful business" means a reason for being present upon school property which is not otherwise prohibited by statute, by ordinance, or by any regulation adopted pursuant to statute or ordinance.

(3) "Continued pattern of unauthorized entry" means that on at least two prior occasions in the same school year the defendant came into any school building or upon any school ground, or street, sidewalk, or public way adjacent thereto, without lawful business thereon, and his or her presence or acts interfered with the peaceful conduct of the activities of such school or disrupted the school or its pupils or school activities, and the defendant was asked to leave by a person specified in paragraph (1) of subdivision (a).

(4) In the case of a specified sex offender, "continued pattern of unauthorized entry" means that on at least two prior occasions in the same school year the defendant came into any school building or upon any school ground, or street, sidewalk, or public way adjacent thereto, and the defendant was asked to leave by a person specified in paragraph (1) of subdivision (a).

(5) "School" means any preschool or school having any of grades kindergarten through 12.

(d) When a person is directed to leave pursuant to paragraph (1) of subdivision (a), the person directing him or her to leave shall inform the person that if he or she reenters the place within 7 days he or she will be guilty of a crime. (Amended by Stats 1989 ch 1054 §2, eff. 1/1/90.)

§626.9. Punishment for possession of firearms in public school or university.

(a) Any person who brings or possesses a loaded firearm upon the grounds of, or within, any public school, including the University of California, the California State University, the California Community Colleges, or any private school providing instruction in kindergarten or grades 1 to 12, inclusive, or any private university or college, unless it is with the written permission of the school district superintendent, his or her designee, or equivalent school authority, shall be punished by imprisonment in the state prison for two, three, or four years.

(b) Any person who brings or possesses a firearm upon the grounds of, or within, any public school, including the University of California, the California State University, the California Community Colleges, any private school providing instruction in kindergarten or grades 1 to 12, inclusive, or any private university or college, unless it is with the written permission of the school district superintendent, his or her designee, or equivalent school authority, shall be punished by imprisonment in the state prison for one, two, or three years.

(c) This section shall not apply to a duly appointed peace officer as defined in Chapter 4.5 (commencing with Section 830) of Title 3 of Part 2, a full-time paid peace officer of another state or the federal government who is carrying out official duties while in California, any person summoned by any of these officers to assist in making arrests or preserving the peace while he or she is actually engaged in assisting the officer, a member of the military forces of this state or of the United States who is engaged in the performance of his or her duties, a person holding a valid license to carry the firearm pursuant to Article 3 (commencing with Section 12050) of Chapter 1 of Title 2 of Part 4, or an armored vehicle guard, who is engaged in the performance of his or her duties, as defined in subdivision (e) of Section 7521 of the Business and Professions Code.

(d) For purposes of this section, a firearm shall be deemed to be loaded when there is an unexpended cartridge or shell, consisting of a case which holds a charge of powder and a bullet or shot, in, or attached in any manner to, the firearm, including, but not limited to, in the firing chamber, magazine, or clip thereof attached to the firearm. A muzzle-loader firearm shall be deemed to be loaded when it is capped or primed and has a powder charge and ball or shot in the barrel or cylinder. (Amended by Stats 1991 ch 1202 §4, eff. 1/1/92.)

§626.10. Bringing or possessing weapons on school grounds.

(a) Any person, except a duly appointed peace officer as defined in Chapter 4.5 (commencing with Section 830) of Title 3 of Part 2, a full-time paid peace officer of another state or the federal government who is carrying out official duties while in this state, a person summoned by any such officer to assist in making arrests or preserving the peace while the person is actually engaged in assisting any officer, or a member of the military forces of this state or the United States who is engaged in the performance of his or her duties, who brings or possesses any dirk, dagger, knife having a blade longer than 3½ inches, folding knife with a blade that locks into place, a razor with an unguarded blade, a taser, or a stun gun, as defined in subdivision (a) of Section 244.5, upon the grounds of, or within, any public school providing instruction in kindergarten or any of grades 1 through 12, inclusive, is guilty of a public offense punishable by imprisonment in the county jail not exceeding one year, or by imprisonment in the state prison.

(b) Any person, except a duly appointed peace officer as defined in Chapter 4.5 (commencing with Section 830) of Title 3 of Part 2, a full-time paid peace officer of another state or the federal government who is carrying out official duties while in this state, a person summoned by any such officer to assist in making arrests or preserving the peace while the person is actually engaged in assisting any such officer, or a member of the military forces of this state or the United States who is engaged in the performance of his or her duties, who brings or possesses any dirk, dagger, or knife having a fixed blade longer than 3½ inches upon the grounds of, or within, any university, the University of California, the California State University or the California community colleges is guilty of a public offense punishable by imprisonment in the county jail not exceeding one year or by imprisonment in the state prison.

(c) Subdivisions (a) and (b) shall not apply to any person who brings or possesses a knife having a blade longer than 3½ inches or a razor with an unguarded blade upon the grounds of, or within, a public school providing instruction in kindergarten or any of grades 1 through 12 or any university, state university, or community college at the direction of a faculty member of the university or state university, or a certificated or classified employee of the school for use in a university, state university, or a school-sponsored activity or class.

(d) Subdivisions (a) and (b) do not apply to any person who brings or possesses a knife having a blade longer than 3½ inches or a razor with an unguarded blade upon the grounds of, or within, a public school providing instruction in kindergarten or any of grades 1 through 12, inclusive, or any university, state university, or community college for a lawful purpose within the scope of the person's employment.

(e) Subdivision (b) shall not apply to any person who brings or possesses a knife having a fixed blade longer than 3½ inches upon the grounds of, or within, any university, state university, or community college, for lawful use in or around a residence or residential facility located upon those grounds or for lawful use in food preparation or consumption.

(f) Any certificated or classified employee or school peace officer of a public school providing instruction in kindergarten or any of grades 1 through 12, inclusive, may seize any of the weapons described in subdivision (a), and any certificated or classified employee or school peace officer of any university, state university, or community college may seize any of the weapons described in subdivision (b) from the possession of any person upon the grounds of, or within, the school if he knows or has reasonable cause to know the person is prohibited from bringing or possessing the weapon upon the grounds of, or within, the school. (*Amended by Stats 1988 ch 854 §2; ch 1113 §5.5, eff. 1/1/89.*)

§626.11. Evidence seized by teacher, etc., inadmissible.

(a) Any evidence seized by a teacher, official, employee, or governing board member of any university, state university, or community college, or by any person acting under his or her direction or with his or her consent in violation of standards relating to rights under the Fourth Amendment to the United States Constitution or under Section 13 of Article 1 of the State Constitution to be free from unreasonable searches and seizures, or in violation of state or federal constitutional rights to privacy, or any of them, is inadmissible in administrative disciplinary proceedings.

(b) Any provision in an agreement between a student and an educational institution specified in subdivision (a) relating to the leasing, renting, or use of a room of any student dormitory owned or operated by the institution by which the student waives a constitutional right under the Fourth Amendment to the United States Constitution or under Section 13 of Article 1 of the State Constitution, or under state or federal constitutional provision guaranteeing a right to privacy, or any of them, is contrary to public policy and void.

(c) Any evidence seized by a person specified in subdivision (a) after a nonconsensual entry not in violation of subdivision (a) into a dormitory room, which evidence is not directly related to the purpose for which the entry was initially made, is not admissible in administrative disciplinary proceedings.

CHAPTER 1.1

ACCESS TO SCHOOL PREMISES

§627. Legislative findings.

(a) The Legislature finds the following:

(1) Violent crimes perpetrated on public school grounds interfere with the education of students and threaten the health and safety of teachers, other employees, and students.

(2) Many serious crimes of violence are committed on school grounds by persons who are neither students nor school employees and who are not otherwise authorized to be present on school grounds.

(3) School officials and law enforcement officers, in seeking to control these persons, have been hindered by the lack of effective legislation restricting the access of unauthorized persons to school grounds and providing appropriate criminal sanctions for unauthorized entry.

(b) The Legislature declares that the purpose of this chapter is to safeguard the teachers, other employees, students, and property of public schools. The Legislature recognizes the right to visit school grounds for legitimate nonviolent purposes and does not intend by this enactment to interfere with the exercise of that right.

(c) The Legislature finds and declares that a disproportionate share of crimes committed on school campuses are committed by persons who are neither students, school officials, or staff, and who have no lawful business on the school grounds.

It is the intent of the Legislature in enacting this chapter to promote the safety and security of the public schools by restricting and conditioning the access of unauthorized persons to school campuses and to thereby implement the provisions of Section 28 of Article 1 of the California Constitution which guarantee all students and staff the inalienable constitutional right to attend safe, secure, and peaceful public schools. It is also the intent of the Legislature that the provisions of this chapter shall not be construed to infringe upon the legitimate exercise of constitutionally protected rights of freedom of speech and expression which may be expressed through rallies, demonstrations, and other forms of expression which may be appropriately engaged in by students and nonstudents in a campus setting.

© 1992 by J., B. & L. Gould
Printed in the U.S.A.   EP

§627.1. Definitions.

As used in this chapter, with regard to a public school:

(a) An "outsider" is any person other than:

(1) A student of the school; except that a student who is currently suspended from the school shall be deemed an outsider for purposes of this chapter.

(2) A parent or guardian of a student of the school.

(3) An officer or employee of the school district that maintains the school.

(4) A public employee whose employment requires him or her to be on school grounds, or any person who is on school grounds at the request of the school.

(5) A representative of a school employee organization who is engaged in activities related to the representation of school employees.

(6) An elected public official.

(7) A person who comes within the provisions of Section 1070 of the Evidence Code by virtue of his or her current employment or occupation.

(b) "School grounds" are the buildings and grounds of the public school.

(c) "School hours" extend from one hour before classes begin until one hour after classes end.

(d) "Principal" is the chief administrative officer of the public school.

(e) "Designee" is a person whom the principal has authorized to register outsiders pursuant to this chapter.

(f) "Superintendent" is the superintendent of the school district that maintains the school or a person (other than the principal or someone employed under the principal's supervision) who the superintendent has authorized to conduct hearings pursuant to Section 627.5.

§627.2. Registration.

No outsider shall enter or remain on school grounds during school hours without having registered with the principal or designee, except to proceed expeditiously to the office of the principal or designee for the purpose of registering. If signs posted in accordance with Section 627.6 restrict the entrance or route that outsiders may use to reach the office of the principal or designee, an outsider shall comply with such signs.

§627.3. Information to be provided by outsider.

In order to register, an outsider shall upon request furnish the principal or designee with the following:

(1) His or her name, address, and occupation.

(2) His or her age, if less than 21.

(3) His or her purpose in entering school grounds.

(4) Proof of identity.

(5) Other information consistent with the purposes of this chapter and with other provisions of law.

No person who furnishes the information and the proof of identity required by this section shall be refused registration except as provided by Section 627.4.

§627.4. Revocation or denial of registration.

(a) The principal or his or her designee may refuse to register an outsider if he or she has a reasonable basis for concluding that the outsider's presence or acts would disrupt the school, its students, its teachers, or its other employees; would result in damage to property; or would result in the distribution or use of unlawful or controlled substances.

(b) The principal, his or her designee, or school security officer may revoke an outsider's registration if he or she has a reasonable basis for concluding that the outsider's presence on school grounds would interfere or is interfering with the peaceful conduct of the activities of the school, or would disrupt or is disrupting the school, its students, its teachers, or its other employees.

§627.5. Hearing on propriety of denial or revocation.

Any person who is denied registration or whose registration is revoked may request a hearing before the principal or superintendent on the propriety of the denial or revocation. The request shall be in writing, shall state why the denial or revocation was improper, shall give the address to which notice of hearing is to be sent, and shall be delivered to either the principal or the superintendent within five days after the denial or revocation. The principal or superintendent shall promptly mail a written notice of the date, time, and place of the hearing to the person who requested the hearing. A hearing before the principal shall be held within seven days after the principal receives the request. A hearing before the superintendent shall be held within seven days after the superintendent receives the request.

§627.6. Posting signs.

At each entrance to the school grounds of every public school at which this chapter is in force, signs shall be posted specifying the hours during which registration is required pursuant to Section 627.2, stating where the office of the principal or designee is located and what route to take to that office, and setting forth the applicable requirements of Section 627.2 and the penalties for violation of this chapter.

§627.7. Violation of chapter.

(a) It is a misdemeanor punishable by imprisonment in the county jail not to exceed six months, or by a fine not to exceed five hundred dollars ($500), or by both, for an outsider to fail or refuse to leave the school grounds promptly after the principal, designee, or school security officer has requested the outsider to leave or to fail to remain off the school grounds for 7 days after being requested to leave, if the outsider does any of the following:

(1) Enters or remains on school grounds without having registered as required by Section 627.2.

(2) Enters or remains on school grounds after having been denied registration pursuant to subdivision (a) of Section 627.4.

(3) Enters or remains on school grounds after having registration revoked pursuant to subdivision (b) of Section 627.4.

(b) The provisions of this section shall not be utilized to impinge upon the lawful exercise of constitutionally protected rights of freedom of speech or assembly.

(c) When a person is directed to leave pursuant to subdivision (a), the person directing him or her to leave shall inform the person that if he or she reenters the place within 7 days he or she will be guilty of a crime. *(Amended by Stats 1989 ch 1054 §3, eff. 1/1/90.)*

§627.8. Subsequent violations.

Every outsider who willfully and knowingly violates this chapter after having been previously convicted of a violation of this chapter committed within seven years of the date of two or more prior violations that resulted in conviction, shall be punished by imprisonment in the county jail for not less than 10 days nor more than six months, or by both such imprisonment and a fine not exceeding five hundred dollars ($500).

§627.8a. Purpose of penalties.

The penalties imposed by the provisions of this chapter shall be utilized to prevent, deter, and punish those committing crimes on school campuses. The penalties imposed by the provisions of this chapter shall not be utilized to infringe upon the legitimate exercise of constitutionally protected rights of free speech or assembly.

§627.9. Powers of school board.

The governing board of any school district may:

(a) Exempt the district or any school or class of schools in the district from the operation of this chapter.

(b) Make exceptions to Section 627.2 for particular classes of outsiders.

(c) Authorize principals to exempt individual outsiders from the operation of Section 627.2; but any such exemption shall be in a writing which is signed and dated by the principal and which specifies the person or persons exempted and the date on which the exemption will expire.

(d) Exempt, or authorize principals to exempt, designated portions of school grounds from the operation of this chapter during some or all school hours.

§627.10. Violation of any other provision of law.

A person whose presence or conduct on school grounds violates another provision of law may be punished for that violation, regardless of whether he or she was registered pursuant to this chapter at the time of the violation; but no punishment shall be imposed contrary to Section 654.

CHAPTER 1. 2

REPORTING OF SCHOOL CRIME

§628. Legislative intent in enacting section.

It is the intent of the Legislature in enacting this section to ensure that schools, school districts, local government, and the Legislature have sufficient data and information about the type and frequency of crime occurring on school campuses to permit development of effective programs and techniques to combat crime on school campuses.

§628.1. Standard school crime reporting form.

By June 30, 1985, the State Department of Education, in consultation with the Department of Justice and a representative selection of school districts which currently compile school crime statistics, shall develop a standard school crime reporting form for use by all school districts throughout the state. No individual shall be identified by name or in any other manner on this reporting form. The form shall define what constitutes the criminal activity required to be reported and shall include, but not be limited to, all of the following:

(a) Description of the crime.

(b) Victim characteristics.

(c) Offender characteristics, if known.

(d) Total students enrolled at the school reporting the crime on November 15 for the first reporting period and April 15 for the second reporting period.

§628.2. Reports; compilation, and distribution.

On forms prepared and supplied by the State Department of Education, each principal of a school in a school district and each principal or director of a county-operated program, site, or school under the jurisdiction of the county superintendent of schools shall forward a completed report of crimes committed thereon at the end of each reporting period to the district superintendent or county superintendent of schools.

The district superintendent or, as appropriate, the county superintendent of schools, shall compile the school data and submit the aggregated data to the State Department of Education not later than February 1 for the reporting period of July 1 through December 31, and not later than August 1 for the reporting period January 1 through June 30.

The superintendent of any school district that maintains a police department pursuant to Section 39670 may direct the chief of police or other administrator of that department to prepare the completed report of crimes for one or more schools in the district, to compile the school data for the district, and to submit the aggregated data to the State Department of Education in accordance with this section. If the chief of police or other designated administrator completes the report of crimes, the chief of police or designated administrator shall provide information to each school principal about the school crime reporting program, the crime descriptions included in the reporting program, and validation criteria identified by the State Department of Education for each crime description.

The State Department of Education shall distribute, upon request, to each office of the county superintendent of schools and each county probation department, a summary of that county's district reports, county reports, and the summary of statewide aggregated data. This information shall be supplied not later than March 1 of each year for the previous school year. The department shall also submit to the Legislature a summary of the statewide aggregated data not later than March 1 of each year for the previous school year. In addition, commencing with the second annual report, the department shall also identify trends in school crime by comparing the numbers and rates of crimes and the resulting economic losses for each year against those of the previous year and the baseline reporting year.

All school district, county, and statewide reports prepared under this chapter shall be deemed public documents and shall be made available to the public at a price not to exceed the actual cost of duplication and distribution. (Amended by Stats 1989 ch 1457 §2, eff. 1/1/90.)

§628.4. Annual school crime report.

By June 30, 1991, the State Department of Education shall publish and distribute to all school districts and county offices of education an annual school crime reporting update that describes typical errors in school crime reporting procedures, describes effective and efficient methods of monitoring and recording school crime data, and identifies trends in school crime

© 1992 by J., B. & L. Gould
Printed in the U.S.A. EP

drawn from the annual school crime report submitted to the Legislature. *(Added by Stats 1989 ch 1457 §3, eff. 1/1/90.)*

§628.5. Implementation of school safety program.

The Legislature hereby recognizes that all pupils enrolled in California public schools have the inalienable right to attend classes on campuses that are safe, secure, and peaceful. The Legislature also recognizes the importance of accurate school crime data in developing and implementing school safety strategies and programs.

By June 30, 1990, the State Department of Education, in consultation with school districts and county offices of education, shall identify criteria for validating the reported incidence of each crime description contained on the standard school crime reporting forms prepared pursuant to Sections 628.1 and 628.2. Validation criteria shall be established for each crime description, that include, but shall not limited to, all of the following: assault, battery, assault with a deadly weapon, unlawful fighting, homicide, sex offenses, robbery, extortion, chemical substance offenses, possession of weapons, destructive devices, arson, burglary, theft, and vandalism. By January 1, 1991, the State Department of Education shall pilot test the validation criteria in a representative sampling of school districts and county offices of education. *(Added by Stats 1989 ch 1457 §4, eff. 1/1/90.)*

§628.6. Validation of school crime reports.

Beginning July 1, 1991, the State Department of Education shall use tested validation criteria in a representative sample of school districts and county offices of education to assess the accuracy of school crime data submitted to it by those agencies.

The State Department of Education shall inform school districts and county offices of education of the validation criteria for the crime descriptions included on the standard school crime reporting forms specified in Section 628.1. Each district and county office of education shall in turn notify their respective schools, programs, and sites of the validation criteria. *(Added by Stats 1989 ch 1457 §5, eff. 1/1/90.)*

CHAPTER 1.3

INTERCEPTION OF WIRE COMMUNICATIONS
(Added by Stats 1988 ch 111 §2; amended by Stats 1988 ch 1373 §2, eff. 1/1/89 only until 1/1/94.)

§629. Application for wiretapping order.

Each application for an order authorizing the interception of a wire communication shall be made in writing upon the personal oath or affirmation of the Attorney General or Chief Assistant Attorney General, Criminal Law Division, or of a district attorney, to the presiding judge of the superior court or one other judge designated by the presiding judge. Each application shall include all of the following information:

(a) The identity of the investigative or law enforcement officer making the application, and the officer authorizing the application.

(b) The identity of the law enforcement agency that is to execute the order.

(c) A statement attesting to a review of the application and the circumstances in support thereof by the chief executive officer, or his or her designee, of the law enforcement agency making the application. This statement shall name the chief executive officer or the designee who effected this review.

(d) A full and complete statement of the facts and circumstances relied upon by the applicant to justify his or her belief that an order should be issued, including (1) details as to the particular offense that has been, is being, or is about to be committed, (2) the fact that conventional investigative techniques had been tried and were unsuccessful, or why they reasonably appear to be unlikely to succeed or to be too dangerous, (3) a particular description of the nature and location of the facilities from which or the place where the communication is to be intercepted, (4) a particular description of the type of communication sought to be intercepted, and (5) the identity, if known, of the person committing the offense and whose communications are to be intercepted, or if that person's identity is not known, then the information relating to the person's identity that is known to the applicant.

(e) A statement of the period of time for which the interception is required to be maintained, and if the nature of the investigation is such that the authorization for interception should not automatically terminate when the described type of communication has been first obtained, a particular description of the facts establishing probable cause to believe that additional communications of the same type will occur thereafter.

(f) A full and complete statement of the facts concerning all previous applications known, to the individual authorizing and to the individual making the application, to have been made to any judge of a state or federal court for authorization to intercept wire communications involving any of the same persons, facilities, or places specified in the application, and the action taken by the judge on each of those applications.

(g) If the application is for the extension of an order, a statement setting forth the number of communications intercepted pursuant to the original order, and the results thus far obtained from the interception, or a reasonable explanation of the failure to obtain results.

The judge may require the applicant to furnish additional testimony or documentary evidence in support of the application. *(Added by Stats 1988 ch 111 §2; amended by Stats 1988 ch 1373 §2, eff. 1/1/89 only until 1/1/94.)*

§629.02. Wiretap order for specified drug offenses.

Upon application made under Section 629, the judge may enter an ex parte order, as requested or modified, authorizing interception of wire communications within the territorial jurisdiction of the court in which the judge is sitting, if the judge determines, on the basis of the facts submitted by the applicant, all of the following:

(a) There is probable cause to believe that an individual is committing, has committed, or is about to commit, one of the following offenses:

(1) Importation, possession for sale, transportation, manufacture, or sale of controlled substances in violation of Section 11351, 11351.5, 11352, 11378, 11378.5, 11379, 11379.5, or 11379.6 of the Health and Safety Code with respect to a substance containing heroin, cocaine, PCP, methamphetamine, or their analogs where the substance exceeds 10 gallons by

liquid volume or three pounds of solid substance by weight.

(2) Conspiracy to commit any of the above-mentioned crimes.

(b) There is probable cause to believe that particular communications concerning the illegal activities will be obtained through that interception.

(c) There is probable cause to believe that the facilities from which, or the place where, the wire communications are to be intercepted are being used, or are about to be used, in connection with the commission of the offense, or are leased to, listed in the name of, or commonly used by the person whose communications are to be intercepted.

(d) Normal investigative procedures have been tried and have failed or reasonably appear either to be unlikely to succeed if tried or to be too dangerous. *(Amended by Stats 1989 ch 1360 §110, eff. 1/1/90.)*

§629.04. Contents of wiretap order.

Each order authorizing the interception of any wire communication shall specify:

(a) The identity, if known, of the person whose communications are to be intercepted, or if the identity is not known, then that information relating to the person's identity known to the applicant.

(b) The nature and location of the communication facilities as to which, or the place where, authority to intercept is granted.

(c) A particular description of the type of communication sought to be intercepted, and a statement of the illegal activities to which it relates.

(d) The identity of the agency authorized to intercept the communications and of the person making the application.

(e) The period of time during which the interception is authorized including a statement as to whether or not the interception shall automatically terminate when the described communication has been first obtained. *(Added by Stats 1988 ch 111 §2; amended by Stats 1988 ch 1373 §2, eff. 1/1/89 only until 1/1/94.)*

§629.06. Oral approval of wiretap without order.

(a) Upon informal application by the Attorney General, the Chief Assistant Attorney General, Criminal Law Division, or a district attorney, the presiding judge of the superior court or one other judge designated by the presiding judge may grant oral approval for an interception, without an order, if he or she determines all of the following:

(1) There are grounds upon which an order could be issued under this chapter.

(2) There is probable cause to believe that an emergency situation exists with respect to the investigation of an offense enumerated in this chapter.

(3) There is probable cause to believe that a substantial danger to life or limb exists justifying the authorization for immediate interception of a private wire communication before an application for an order could with due diligence be submitted and acted upon.

(b) Approval for an interception under this section shall be conditioned upon filing with the judge, within 48 hours of the oral approval, a written application for an order which, if granted consistent with this chapter, shall also recite the oral approval under this subdivision and be retroactive to the time of the oral approval. *(Added by Stats 1988 ch 111 §2; amended by Stats 1988 ch 1373 §2, eff. 1/1/89 only until 1/1/94.)*

§629.08. Period of time of wiretap order.

No order entered under this chapter shall authorize the interception of any wire communication for any period longer than is necessary to achieve the objective of the authorization, nor in any event longer than 30 days. Extensions of an order may be granted, but only upon application for an extension made in accordance with Section 629 and upon the court making findings required by Section 629.02. The period of extension shall be no longer than the authorizing judge deems necessary to achieve the purposes for which it was granted and in no event any longer than 30 days. Every order and extension thereof shall contain a provision that the authorization to intercept shall be executed as soon as practicable, shall be conducted in such a way as to minimize the interception of communications not otherwise subject to interception under this chapter, and shall terminate upon attainment of the authorized objective, or in any event at the time expiration of the term designated in the order or any extensions. *(Added by Stats 1988 ch 111 §2; amended by Stats 1988 ch 1373 §2, eff. 1/1/89 only until 1/1/94.)*

§629.10. Reports to judge issuing wiretap order.

Whenever an order authorizing an interception is entered, the order shall require reports in writing or otherwise to be made to the judge who issued the order showing what progress has been made toward achievement of the authorized objective, or a satisfactory explanation for its lack, and the need for continued interception. If the judge finds that such progress has not been made, that the explanation for its lack is not satisfactory, or that no need exists for continued interception, he or she shall order that the interception immediately terminate. The reports shall be made at the intervals that the judge may require, but not less than one for each period of 72 hours. *(Added by Stats 1988 ch 111 §2; amended by Stats 1988 ch 1373 §2, eff. 1/1/89 only until 1/1/94.)*

§629.12. Annual wiretap reports by Attorney General.

(a) The Attorney General shall prepare and submit an annual report to the Legislature, the Judicial Council, and the Director of the Administrative Office of the United States Court on interceptions conducted under the authority of this chapter during the preceding year. Information for this report shall be provided to the Attorney General by any prosecutorial agency seeking an order pursuant to this chapter.

(b) The report shall include all of the following data:

(1) The number of orders or extensions applied for.

(2) The kinds of orders or extensions applied for.

(3) The fact that the order or extension was granted as applied for, was modified, or was denied.

(4) The period of interceptions authorized by the order, and the number and duration of any extensions of the order.

(5) The offense specified in the order or application, or extension of an order.

(6) The identity of the applying law enforcement officer and agency making the application and the person authorizing the application.

(7) The nature of the facilities from which or the place where communications were to be intercepted.

(8) A general description of the interceptions made under the order or extension, including (A) the ap-

© 1992 by J., B. & L. Gould
Printed in the U.S.A. **EP**

proximate nature and frequency of incriminating communications intercepted, (B) the approximate nature and frequency of other communications intercepted, (C) the approximate number of persons whose communications were intercepted, and (D) the approximate nature, amount, and cost of the manpower and other resources used in the interceptions.

(9) The number of arrests resulting from interceptions made under the order or extension, and the offenses for which arrests were made.

(10) The number of trials resulting from the interceptions.

(11) The number of motions to suppress made with respect to the interceptions, and the number granted or denied.

(12) The number of convictions resulting from the interceptions and the offenses for which the convictions were obtained and a general assessment of the importance of the interceptions.

(13) Except with regard to the initial report required by this section, the information required by paragraphs (8) to (12), inclusive, with respect to orders or extensions obtained in a preceding calendar year.

(14) Other data that the Legislature, the Judicial Council or the Director of the Administrative Office shall require.

(c) The annual report shall be filed no later than April of each year, and shall also include a summary analysis of the data reported pursuant to subdivision (b). The Attorney General may issue regulations prescribing the content and form of the reports required to be filed pursuant to this section by any prosecutorial agency seeking an order to intercept wire communications. *(Added by Stats 1988 ch 111 §2; amended by Stats 1988 ch 1373 §2, eff. 1/1/89 only until 1/1/94.)*

§629.14. Recording of contents of wire communications.

The contents of any wire communication intercepted by any means authorized by this chapter shall, if possible, be recorded on tape or other comparable device. The recording of the contents of any wire communication pursuant to this chapter shall be done in a way that will protect the recording from editing or other alterations and ensure that the audio tape recording can be immediately verified as to its authenticity and originality and that any alterations can be immediately detected. In addition, the monitoring or recording device shall be of a type and shall be installed to preclude any interruption or monitoring of the interception by any unauthorized means. Immediately upon the expiration of the period of the order, or extensions thereof, the recordings shall be made available to the judge issuing the order and sealed under his or her directions. Custody of the recordings shall be where the judge orders. They shall not be destroyed except upon an order of the issuing or denying judge and in any event shall be kept for 10 years. Duplicate recordings may be made for use or disclosure pursuant to the provisions of Sections 629.24 and 629.26 for investigations. The presence of the seal provided for by this section, or a satisfactory explanation for the absence thereof, shall be a prerequisite for the use or disclosure of the contents of any wire communication or evidence derived therefrom under Section 629.28. *(Added by Stats 1988 ch 111 §2; amended by Stats 1988 ch 1373 §2, eff. 1/1/89 only until 1/1/94.)*

§629.16. Sealing wiretap orders.

Applications made and orders granted pursuant to this chapter shall be sealed by the judge. Custody of the applications and orders shall be where the judge orders. The applications and orders shall be disclosed only upon a showing of good cause before a judge and shall not be destroyed except on order of the issuing or denying judge, and in any event shall be kept for 10 years. *(Added by Stats 1988 ch 111 §2; amended by Stats 1988 ch 1373 §2, eff. 1/1/89 only until 1/1/94.)*

§629.18. Notice of wiretap order to affected parties.

Within a reasonable time, but no later than 90 days, after the termination of the period of an order or extensions thereof, or after the filing of an application for an order of approval under Section 629.06 which has been denied, the issuing judge shall cause to be served upon persons named in the order or the application, and other known parties to intercepted communications, an inventory which shall include notice of all of the following:

(a) The fact of the entry of the order.

(b) The date of the entry and the period of authorized interception.

(c) The fact that during the period wire communications were or were not intercepted.

The judge, upon filing of a motion, may, in his or her discretion, make available to the person or his or her counsel for inspection the portions of the intercepted communications, applications, and orders that the judge determines to be in the interest of justice. On an ex parte showing of good cause to a judge, the serving of the inventory required by this section may be postponed. The period of postponement shall be no longer than the authorizing judge deems necessary to achieve the purposes for which it was granted. *(Added by Stats 1988 ch 111 §2; amended by Stats 1988 ch 1373 §2, eff. 1/1/89 only until 1/1/94.)*

§629.20. Transcript of wiretap.

The contents of any intercepted wire communication or evidence derived from it shall not be received in evidence or otherwise disclosed in any trial, hearing, or other proceeding, except a grand jury proceeding, unless each party, not less than 10 days before the trial, hearing, or proceeding, has been furnished with a transcript of the contents of the interception and with a copy of the court order and accompanying application under which the interception was authorized. This 10-day period may be waived by the judge if he or she finds that it was not possible to furnish the party with the above information 10 days before the trial, hearing, or proceeding, and that the party will not be prejudiced by the delay in receiving that information. *(Added by Stats 1988 ch 111 §2; amended by Stats 1988 ch 1373 §2, eff. 1/1/89 only until 1/1/94.)*

§629.22. Motion to suppress wiretap evidence.

Any person in any trial, hearing, or proceeding, may move to suppress some or all of the contents of any intercepted wire communications, or evidence derived therefrom, only on the basis that the contents or evidence were obtained in violation of the Fourth Amendment of the United States Constitution or of this chapter. The motion shall be made, determined, and be subject to review in accordance with the procedures set forth in Section 1538.5. *(Added by Stats 1988 ch 111 §2; amended by Stats 1988 ch 1373 §2, eff. 1/1/89 only until 1/1/94.)*

§629.24. Disclosure of wiretap order.

The Attorney General, any Deputy Attorney General, district attorney, or deputy district attorney, or any peace officer who, by any means authorized by this chapter, has obtained knowledge of the contents of any wire communication, or evidence derived therefrom, may disclose the contents to one of the individuals referred to in this section and to any investigative or law enforcement officer as defined in subdivision (7) of Section 2510 of Title 18 of the United States Code to the extent that the disclosure is permitted pursuant to Section 629.32 and is appropriate to the proper performance of the official duties of the individual making or receiving the disclosure. No other disclosure, except to a grand jury, of intercepted information is permitted prior to a public court hearing by any person regardless of how the person may have come into possession thereof. *(Added by Stats 1988 ch 111 §2; amended by Stats 1988 ch 1373 §2, eff. 1/1/89 only until 1/1/94.)*

§629.26. Use of wiretap information.

The Attorney General, any Deputy Attorney General, district attorney, or deputy district attorney, or any peace officer who, by any means authorized by this chapter, has obtained knowledge of the contents of any wire communication or evidence derived therefrom may use the contents or evidence to the extent the use is appropriate to the proper performance or his or her official duties and is permitted pursuant to Section 629.32. *(Added by Stats 1988 ch 111 §2; amended by Stats 1988 ch 1373 §2, eff. 1/1/89 only until 1/1/94.)*

§629.28. Disclosing wiretap information at judicial hearing.

Any person who has received, by any means authorized by this chapter, any information concerning a wire communication, or evidence derived therefrom, intercepted in accordance with the provisions of this chapter, may, pursuant to Section 629.32, disclose the contents of that communication or derivative evidence while giving testimony under oath or affirmation in any criminal court proceeding or in any grand jury proceeding. *(Added by Stats 1988 ch 111 §2; amended by Stats 1988 ch 1373 §2, eff. 1/1/89 only until 1/1/94.)*

§629.30. Privileged wire communications.

No otherwise privileged wire communication intercepted in accordance with, or in violation of, the provisions of this chapter shall lose its privileged character. When a peace officer, while engaged in intercepting wire communications in the manner authorized by this chapter, intercepts wire communications that are of a privileged nature he or she shall immediately cease the interception for at least two minutes. After a period of at least two minutes, interception may be resumed for up to 30 seconds during which time the officer shall determine if the nature of the communications is still privileged. If still of a privileged nature, the officer shall again cease interception for at least two minutes, after which the officer may again resume interception for up to 30 seconds to redetermine the nature of the communication. The officer shall continue to go on-line and off-line in this manner until such time as the communication is no longer privileged or the communication ends. The recording device shall be metered in such a way as to

authenticate upon review that interruptions occurred as set forth in this chapter. *(Added by Stats 1988 ch 111 §2; amended by Stats 1988 ch 1373 §2, eff. 1/1/89 only until 1/1/94.)*

§629.32. Interception of wire communications relating to other crimes.

(a) If a peace officer, while engaged in intercepting wire communications in the manner authorized by this chapter, intercepts wire communications relating to crimes other than those specified in the order of authorization, but which are enumerated in subdivision (a) of Section 629.02, (1) the contents thereof, and evidence derived therefrom, may be disclosed or used as provided in Sections 629.24 and 629.26 and (2) the contents and any evidence derived therefrom may be used under Section 629.28 when authorized by a judge if the judge finds upon subsequent application, that the contents were otherwise intercepted in accordance with the provisions of this chapter. The application shall be made as soon as practicable.

(b) If a peace officer, while engaged in intercepting wire communications in the manner authorized by this chapter, intercepts wire communication relating to crimes other than those specified in the order of authorization or enumerated in subdivision (a) of Section 629.02, the contents thereof, and evidence derived therefrom, may not be disclosed or used as provided in Sections 629.24 and 629.26, except to prevent the commission of a public offense. The contents and any evidence derived therefrom may not be used under Section 629.28, except where the evidence was obtained through an independent source or inevitably would have been discovered, and the use is authorized by a judge who finds that the contents were intercepted in accordance with this chapter.

(c) The use of the contents of an intercepted wire communication relating to crimes other than that specified in the order of authorization to obtain a search or arrest warrant entitles the person named in the warrant to notice of the intercepted wire communication and a copy of the contents thereof which were used to obtain the warrant. *(Added by Stats 1988 ch 111 §2; amended by Stats 1988 ch 1373 §2, eff. 1/1/89 only until 1/1/94.)*

§629.34. Punishment.

Any violation of this chapter is punishable by a fine not exceeding two thousand five hundred dollars ($2,500), or by imprisonment in the county jail not exceeding one year, or by imprisonment in the state prison, or by both such fine and imprisonment in the county jail or in the state prison. *(Added by Stats 1988 ch 111 §2; amended by Stats 1988 ch 1373 §2, eff. 1/1/89 only until 1/1/94.)*

§629.36. Remedies for illegal interception of wire communications.

Any person whose wire communication is intercepted, disclosed, or used in violation of this chapter shall have the following remedies:

(a) Have a civil cause of action against any person who intercepts, discloses, or uses, or procures any other person to intercept, disclose, or use the communications.

(b) Be entitled to recover, in that action, all of the following:

(1) Actual damages but not less than liquidated damages computed at the rate of one hundred dollars

© 1992 by J., B. & L. Gould
Printed in the U.S.A.   **EP**

($100) a day for each day of violation or one thousand dollars ($1,000), whichever is greater.

(2) Punitive damages.

(3) Reasonable attorney's fee and other litigation costs reasonable incurred.

A good faith reliance on a court order is a complete defense to any civil or criminal action brought under this chapter, or under Chapter 1.5 (commencing with Section 630) or any other law. *(Added by Stats 1988 ch 111 §2; amended by Stats 1988 ch 1373 §2, eff. 1/1/89 only until 1/1/94.)*

§629.38. Interception of wire communications in accordance with valid authorizing orders.

Nothing in Section 631 shall be construed as prohibiting any peace officer from intercepting any wire communication pursuant to an order issued in accordance with the provisions of this chapter. Nothing in Section 631 shall be construed as rendering inadmissible in any criminal proceeding in any court or before any grand jury any evidence obtained by means of an order issued in accordance with the provisions of this chapter. Nothing in Section 637 shall be construed as prohibiting the disclosure of the contents of any wire communication obtained by any means authorized by this chapter, if the disclosure is authorized by this chapter. Nothing in this chapter shall apply to any conduct authorized by Section 633. *(Added by Stats 1988 ch 111 §2; amended by Stats 1988 ch 1373 §2, eff. 1/1/89 only until 1/1/94.)*

§629.39. Covert entry into residential premises.

No order issued pursuant to this chapter shall either directly or indirectly authorize covert entry into or upon the premises of a residential dwelling, hotel room, or motel room for installation or removal of any interception device or for any other purpose. Notwithstanding that such entry is otherwise prohibited by any other section or code, this chapter expressly prohibits covert entry of a residential dwelling, hotel room, or motel room to facilitate an order to intercept wire communications. *(Added by Stats 1988 ch 111 §2; amended by Stats 1988 ch 1373 §2, eff. 1/1/89 only until 1/1/94.)*

§629.40. Assistance with the interception of wire communications.

An order authorizing the interception of a wire communication shall direct, upon request of the applicant, that a public utility engaged in the business of providing communications services and facilities, a landlord, custodian, or any other person furnish the applicant forthwith all information, facilities, and technical assistance necessary to accomplish the interception unobtrusively and with a minimum of interference with the services which the public utility, landlord, custodian, or other person is providing the person whose communications are to be intercepted. Any such public utility, landlord, custodian, or other person furnishing facilities or technical assistance shall be fully compensated by the applicant for the reasonable costs of furnishing the facilities and technical assistance. *(Added by Stats 1988 ch 111 §2; amended by Stats 1988 ch 1373 §2, eff. 1/1/89 only until 1/1/94.)*

§629.41. Good faith reliance upon court order.

A good faith reliance on a court order issued in accordance with this chapter by any public utility, landlord, custodian, or any other person furnishing information, facilities, and technical assistance as directed by the order is a complete defense to any civil or criminal action brought under this chapter, Chapter 1.5 (commencing with Section 630), or any other law. *(Added by Stats 1988 ch 111 §2; amended by Stats 1988 ch 1373 §2, eff. 1/1/89 only until 1/1/94.)*

§629.42. Constitutional validity.

Notwithstanding any other provision of law, any court to which an application is made in accordance with this chapter may take any evidence, make any finding, or issue any order required to conform the proceedings or the issuance of any order of authorization or approval to the provisions of the Constitution of the United States, any law of the United States, or this chapter. *(Added by Stats 1988 ch 111 §2; amended by Stats 1988 ch 1373 §2, eff. 1/1/89 only until 1/1/94.)*

§629.44. Training course on the interception of private wire communications.

(a) The Commission on Peace Officer Standards and Training, in consultation with the Attorney General, shall establish a course of training in the legal, practical, and technical aspects of the interception of private wire communications and related investigative techniques.

(b) The Attorney General shall set minimum standards for certification and periodic recertification of investigative or law enforcement officers as eligible to apply for orders authorizing the interception of private wire communications, to conduct the interceptions, and to use the communications or evidence derived from them in official proceedings.

(c) The Commission on Peace Officer Standards and Training may charge a reasonable enrollment fee for those students who are employed by an agency not eligible for reimbursement by the commission to offset the costs of the training. The Attorney General may charge a reasonable fee to offset the cost of certification. *(Added by Stats 1988 ch 111 §2; amended by Stats 1988 ch 1373 §2, eff. 1/1/89 only until 1/1/94.)*

§629.46. Severability.

If any provision of this chapter, or the application thereof to any person or circumstances, is held invalid, the remainder of the chapter, and the application of its provisions to other persons or circumstances, shall not be affected thereby. *(Added by Stats 1988 ch 111 §2; amended by Stats 1988 ch 1373 §2, eff. 1/1/89 only until 1/1/94.)*

§629.48. Effective dates.

This chapter shall remain in effect only until January 1, 1994, and as of that date is repealed. *(Added by Stats 1988 ch 111 §2; amended by Stats 1988 ch 1373 §2, eff. 1/1/89 only until 1/1/94.)*

CHAPTER 1.5

INVASION OF PRIVACY

§630. Legislative declaration of policy.

The Legislature hereby declares that advances in science and technology have led to the development of new devices and techniques for the purpose of eavesdropping upon private communications and that the invasion of privacy resulting from the continual and increasing use of such devices and techniques has created a serious threat to the free exercise of personal liberties and cannot be tolerated in a free and civilized society.

The Legislature by this chapter intends to protect the right of privacy of the people of this state.

The Legislature recognizes that law enforcement agencies have a legitimate need to employ modern listening devices and techniques in the investigation of criminal conduct and the apprehension of lawbreakers. Therefore, it is not the intent of the Legislature to place greater restraints on the use of listening devices and techniques by law enforcement agencies than existed prior to the effective date of this chapter.

§631. Punishment for unauthorized wiretaps.

(a) Any person who, by means of any machine, instrument, or contrivance, or in any other manner, intentionally taps, or makes any unauthorized connection, whether physically, electrically, acoustically, inductively, or otherwise, with any telegraph or telephone wire, line, cable, or instrument, including the wire, line, cable, or instrument of any internal telephonic communication system, or who willfully and without the consent of all parties to the communication, or in any unauthorized manner, reads, or attempts to read, or to learn the contents or meaning of any message, report, or communication while the same is in transit or passing over any such wire, line, or cable, or is being sent from, or received at any place within this state; or who uses, or attempts to use, in any manner, or for any purpose, or to communicate in any way, any information so obtained, or who aids, agrees with, employs, or conspires with any person or persons to unlawfully do, or permit, or cause to be done any of the acts or things mentioned above in this section, is punishable by a fine not exceeding two thousand five hundred dollars ($2,500), or by imprisonment in the county jail not exceeding one year, or by imprisonment in the state prison, or by both a fine and imprisonment in the county jail or in the state prison. If such person has previously been convicted of a violation of this section or Section 632 or 636, he or she is punishable by a fine not exceeding ten thousand dollars ($10,000), or by imprisonment in the county jail not exceeding one year, or by imprisonment in the state prison, or by both a fine and imprisonment in the county jail or in the state prison.

(b) This section shall not apply (1) to any public utility engaged in the business of providing communications services and facilities, or to the officers, employees or agents thereof, where the acts otherwise prohibited herein are for the purpose of construction, maintenance, conduct or operation of the services and facilities of the public utility, or where the public utility is acting in good faith reliance on a court order issued under Chapter 1.3 (commencing with Section 629), or (2) to the use of any instrument, equipment, facility, or service furnished and used pursuant to the tariffs of such a public utility, or (3) to any telephonic communication system used for communication exclusively within a state, county, city and county, or city correctional facility.

(c) Except as proof in an action or prosecution for violation of this section, no evidence obtained in violation of this section shall be admissible in any judicial, administrative, legislative or other proceeding.

(d) This section shall remain in effect only until January 1, 1994, and as of that date is repealed. *(Amended by Stats 1988 ch 111 §3; amended by Stats*

1988 ch 1373 §§3, 5, eff. 1/1/89 only until 1/1/94. See other section 631 below.)

§631. Punishment for unauthorized wiretaps.

(a) Any person who, by means of any machine, instrument, or contrivance, or in any other manner, intentionally taps, or makes any unauthorized connection, whether physically, electrically, acoustically, inductively, or otherwise, with any telegraph or telephone wire, line, cable, or instrument, including the wire, line, cable, or instrument of any internal telephonic communication system, or who willfully and without the consent of all parties to the communication, or in any unauthorized manner, reads, or attempts to read, or to learn the contents or meaning of any message, report, or communication while the same is in transit or passing over any such wire, line, or cable, or is being sent from, or received at any place within this state; or who uses, or attempts to use, in any manner, or for any purpose, or to communicate in any way, any information so obtained, or who aids, agrees with, employs, or conspires with any person or persons to unlawfully do, or permit, or cause to be done any of the acts or things mentioned above in this section, is punishable by a fine not exceeding two thousand five hundred dollars ($2,500), or by imprisonment in the county jail not exceeding one year, or by imprisonment in the state prison, or by both a fine and imprisonment in the county jail or in the state prison. If the person has previously been convicted of a violation of this section or Section 632 or 636, he or she is punishable by a fine not exceeding ten thousand dollars ($10,000), or by imprisonment in the county jail not exceeding one year, or by imprisonment in the state prison, or by both a fine and imprisonment in the county jail or in the state prison.

(b) This section shall not apply (1) to any public utility engaged in the business of providing communications services and facilities, or to the officers, employees or agents thereof, where the acts otherwise prohibited herein are for the purpose of construction, maintenance, conduct or operation of the services and facilities of such public utility, or (2) to the use of any instrument, equipment, facility, or service furnished and used pursuant to the tariffs of such a public utility, or (3) to any telephonic communication system used for communication exclusively within a state, county, city and county, or city correctional facility.

(c) Except as proof in an action or prosecution for violation of this section, no evidence obtained in violation of this section shall be admissible in any judicial, administrative, legislative or other proceeding.

(d) This section shall become operative on January 1, 1994. *(Added by Stats 1988 ch 111 §4; amended by Stats 1988 ch 1373 §4, eff. 1/1/89, oper. 1/1/94. See other section 631 above.)*

§632. Recording or eavesdropping on confidential communications.

(a) Every person who, intentionally and without the consent of all parties to a confidential communication, by means of any electronic amplifying or recording device, eavesdrops upon or records the confidential communication, whether the communication is carried on among the parties in the presence of one another or by means of a telegraph, telephone, or other device, except a radio, shall be punished by a fine not exceeding two thousand five hundred dollars ($2,500),

© 1992 by J., B. & L. Gould
Printed in the U.S.A.   EP

or imprisonment in the county jail not exceeding one year, or in the state prison, or by both that fine and imprisonment. If the person has previously been convicted of a violation of this section or Section 631, 632.5, 632.6, or 636, the person shall be punished by a fine not exceeding ten thousand dollars ($10,000), by imprisonment in the county jail not exceeding one year, or in the state prison, or by both that fine and imprisonment.

(b) The term "person" includes an individual, business association, partnership, corporation, or other legal entity, and an individual acting or purporting to act for or on behalf of any government or subdivision thereof, whether federal, state, or local, but excludes an individual known by all parties to a confidential communication to be overhearing or recording the communication.

(c) The term "confidential communication" includes any communication carried on in circumstances as may reasonably indicate that any party to the communication desires it to be confined to the parties thereto, but excludes a communication made in a public gathering or in any legislative, judicial, executive or administrative proceeding open to the public, or in any other circumstance in which the parties to the communication may reasonably expect that the communication may be overheard or recorded.

(d) Except as proof in an action or prosecution for violation of this section, no evidence obtained as a result of eavesdropping upon or recording a confidential communication in violation of this section shall be admissible in any judicial, administrative, legislative, or other proceeding.

(e) This section does not apply (1) to any public utility engaged in the business of providing communications services and facilities, or to the officers, employees or agents thereof, where the acts otherwise prohibited by this section are for the purpose of construction, maintenance, conduct or operation of the services and facilities of the public utility, or (2) to the use of any instrument, equipment, facility, or service furnished and used pursuant to the tariffs of such a public utility, or (3) to any telephonic communication system used for communication exclusively within a state, county, city and county, or city correctional facility.

(f) This section does not apply to the use of hearing aids and similar devices, by persons afflicted with impaired hearing, for the purpose of overcoming the impairment to permit the hearing of sounds ordinarily audible to the human ear. (Amended by Stats 1990 ch 696 §3, eff. 1/1/91.)

§632.2. Disclosure of victim's communications.

(a) Any person who, without the consent of the victim, willfully obtains or, except as provided in Section 1035.4 or Section 1037.2 of the Evidence Code, knowingly discloses any privileged information obtained from a confidential communication specified in Section 1035.4 or 1037.2 of the Evidence Code, is guilty of a misdemeanor.

(b) Notwithstanding subdivision (a), sexual assault victim counselors, as defined in Section 1035.2 of the Evidence Code, domestic violence counselors, as defined in Section 1037.1 of the Evidence Code, and victim-witness counselors employed by organizations providing programs specified in Section 13835.2, may confer among themselves, as necessary, in order to receive and disclose information, including records, relevant to their assigned cases.

(c) This section shall remain in effect only until January 1, 1994, and as of that date is repealed, unless a later enacted statute, which is enacted before January 1, 1994, deletes or extends that date. (Added by Stats 1990 ch 1342 §3, eff. 1/1/91 only until 1/1/94.)

§632.5. Intercepting cellular radio telephone communications.

(a) Every person who, maliciously and without the consent of all parties to the communication, intercepts, receives, or assists in intercepting or receiving a communication transmitted between cellular radio telephones or between any cellular radio telephone and a landline telephone shall be punished by a fine not exceeding two thousand five hundred dollars ($2,500), by imprisonment in the county jail not exceeding one year or in the state prison, or by both that fine and imprisonment. If the person has been previously convicted of a violation of this section or Section 631, 632, or 636, the person shall be punished by a fine not exceeding ten thousand dollars ($10,000), by imprisonment in the county jail not exceeding one year or in the state prison, or by both that fine and imprisonment.

(b) In the following instances, this section shall not apply:

(1) To any public utility engaged in the business of providing communications services and facilities, or to the officers, employees, or agents thereof, where the acts otherwise prohibited are for the purpose of construction, maintenance, conduct, or operation of the services and facilities of the public utility.

(2) To the use of any instrument, equipment, facility, or service furnished and used pursuant to the tariffs of the public utility.

(3) To any telephonic communication system used for communication exclusively within a state, county, city and county, or city correctional facility.

(c) As used in this section and Section 635, "cellular radio telephone" means a wireless telephone authorized by the Federal Communications Commission to operate in the frequency bandwidth reserved for cellular radio telephones. (Added by Stats 1985 ch 909 §3.)

§632.6. Intercepting cordless telephone communications.

(a) Every person who, maliciously and without the consent of all parties to the communication, intercepts, receives, or assists in intercepting or receiving a communication transmitted between cordless telephones as defined in subdivision (c), between any cordless telephone and a landline telephone, or between a cordless telephone and a cellular telephone shall be punished by a fine not exceeding two thousand five hundred dollars ($2,500), by imprisonment in the county jail not exceeding one year, or in the state prison, or by both that fine and imprisonment. If the person has been convicted previously of a violation of Section 631, 632, or 636, the person shall be punished by a fine not exceeding ten thousand dollars ($10,000), or by imprisonment in the county jail not exceeding one year, or in the state prison, or by both that fine and imprisonment.

(b) This section shall not apply in any of the following instances:

(1) To any public utility engaged in the business of providing communications services and facilities, or to the officers, employees, or agents thereof, where the acts otherwise prohibited are for the purpose of construction, maintenance, conduct, or operation of the services and facilities of the public utility.

(2) To the use of any instrument, equipment, facility, or service furnished and used pursuant to the tariffs of the public utility.

(3) To any telephonic communications system used for communication exclusively within a state, county, city and county, or city correctional facility.

(c) As used in this section and in Section 635, "cordless telephone" means a two-way low power communication system consisting of two parts—a "base" unit which connects to the public switched telephone network and a handset or "remote" unit—which are connected by a radio link and authorized by the Federal Communications Commission to operate in the frequency bandwidths reserved for cordless telephones. *(Added by Stats 1990 ch 696 §4, eff. 1/1/91.)*

§633. Law enforcement officers.

Nothing in Section 631, 632, 632.5, or 632.6 prohibits the Attorney General, any district attorney, or any assistant, deputy, or investigator of the Attorney General or any district attorney, any officer of the California Highway Patrol, any chief of police, assistant chief of police, or police officer of a city or city and county, any sheriff, undersheriff, or deputy sheriff regularly employed and paid as such of a county, or any person acting pursuant to the direction of one of these law enforcement officers acting within the scope of his or her authority, from overhearing or recording any communication which they could lawfully overhear or record prior to the effective date of this chapter.

Nothing in Section 631, 632, 632.5, or 632.6 renders inadmissible any evidence obtained by the above-named persons by means of overhearing or recording any communication which they could lawfully overhear or record prior to the effective date of this chapter. *(Amended by Stats 1990 ch 696 §5, eff. 1/1/91.)*

§633.1. Recording communication by airport law enforcement officer.

(a) Nothing in Section 631, 632, or 632.5 prohibits any person regularly employed as an airport law enforcement officer, as described in subdivision (k) of Section 830.4, acting within the scope of his or her authority, from recording any communication which is received on an incoming telephone line, for which the person initiating the call utilized a telephone number known to the public to be a means of contacting airport law enforcement officers. In order for a telephone call to be recorded under the subdivision, a series of electronic tones shall be used, placing the caller on notice that his or her telephone call is being recorded.

(b) Nothing in Section 631, 632, or 632.5 renders inadmissible any evidence obtained by an officer described in subdivision (a) if the evidence was received by means of recording any communication which is received on an incoming public telephone line, for which the person initiating the call utilized a telephone number known to the public to be a means of contacting airport law enforcement officers.

(c) This section shall only apply to airport law enforcement officers who are employed at an airport which maintains regularly scheduled international airport service and which maintains permanent facilities of the United States Customs Service. *(Added by Stats 1987 ch 467 §1.)*

§633.5. Recording confidential communications.

Nothing in Section 631, 633, 632.5, or 632.6 prohibits one party to a confidential communication from recording the communication for the purpose of obtaining evidence reasonably believed to relate to the commission by another party to the communication of the crime of extortion, kidnapping, bribery, any felony involving violence against the person, or a violation of Section 653m. Nothing in Section 631, 632, 632.5, or 632.6 renders any evidence so obtained inadmissible in a prosecution for extortion, kidnapping, bribery, any felony involving violence against the person, a violation of Section 653m, or any crime in connection therewith. *(Amended by Stats 1990 ch 696 §6, eff. 1/1/91.)*

§634. Invading privacy; trespassing.

Any person who trespasses on property for the purpose of committing any act, or attempting to commit any act, in violation of Section 631, 632, 632.5, 632.6, or 636 shall be punished by a fine not exceeding two thousand five hundred dollars ($2,500), by imprisonment in the county jail not exceeding one year or in the state prison, or by both that fine and imprisonment. If the person has previously been convicted of a violation of this section or Section 631, 632, 632.5, 632.6, or 636, the person shall he punished by a fine not exceeding ten thousand dollars ($10,000), by imprisonment in the county jail not exceeding one year or in the state prison, or by both that fine and imprisonment. *(Amended by Stats 1990 ch 696 §7, eff. 1/1/91.)*

§635. Eavesdropping devices; sale, punishment.

(a) Every person who manufactures, assembles, sells, offers for sale, advertises for sale, possesses, transports, imports, or furnishes to another any device which is primarily or exclusively designed or intended for eavesdropping upon the communication of another, or any device which is primarily or exclusively designed or intended for the unauthorized interception or reception of communications between cellular radio telephones or between a cellular radio telephone and a landline telephone in violation of Section 632.5, or communications between cordless telephones or between a cordless telephone and a landline telephone in violation of Section 632.6, shall be punished by a fine not exceeding two thousand five hundred dollars ($2,500), by imprisonment in the county jail not exceeding one year, or in the state prison, or by both that fine and imprisonment. If the person has previously been convicted of a violation of this section, the person shall be punished by a fine not exceeding ten thousand dollars ($10,000), by imprisonment in the county jail not exceeding one year, or in the state prison, or by both that fine and imprisonment.

(b) This section does not apply to either of the following:

(1) An act otherwise prohibited by this section when performed by any of the following:

(A) A communication utility or an officer, employee or agent thereof for the purpose of construction, maintenance, conduct, or operation of, or other-

© 1992 by J., B. & L. Gould
Printed in the U.S.A.   EP

wise incident to the use of, the services or facilities of the utility.

(B) A state, county, or municipal law enforcement agency or an agency of the federal government.

(C) A person engaged in selling devices specified in subdivision (a) for use by, or resale to, agencies of a foreign government under terms approved by the federal government, communication utilities, state, county, or municipal law enforcement agencies, or agencies of the federal government.

(2) Possession by a subscriber to communication utility service of a device specified in subdivision (a) furnished by the utility pursuant to its tariffs. *(Amended by Stats 1990 ch 696 §8, eff. 1/1/91.)*

§636. Eavesdropping on conversation of prisoner.

Every person, who, without permission from all parties to the conversation, eavesdrops on or records by means of an electronic or other device, a conversation, or any portion thereof, between a person who is in the physical custody of a law enforcement officer or other public officer, or who is on the property of a law enforcement agency or other public agency, and such person's attorney, religious advisor, or licensed physician, is guilty of a felony; provided, however, the provisions of this section shall not apply to any employee of a public utility engaged in the business of providing service and facilities for telephone or telegraph communications while engaged in the construction, maintenance, conduct or operation of the service or facilities of such public utility who listens in to such conversations for the limited purpose of testing or servicing such equipment.

§636.5. Police radio communication and interception.

Any person not authorized by the sender, who intercepts any police radio service communication, by use of a scanner or any other means, for the purpose of using that communication to assist in the commission of a criminal offense or to avoid or escape arrest, trial, conviction, or punishment or who divulges to any person he or she knows to be a suspect in the commission of any criminal offense, the existence, contents, substance, purport, effect or meaning of that communication concerning the offense with the intent that the suspect may avoid or escape from arrest, trial, conviction, or punishment is guilty of a misdemeanor.

Nothing in this section shall preclude prosecution of any person under Section 31 or 32.

As used in this section "police radio service communication" means a communication authorized by the Federal Communications Commission to be transmitted by a station in the police radio service. *(Amended by Stats 1991 ch 515 §1, eff. 1/1/92.)*

§637. Disclosing wire communication information.

Every person not a party to a telegraphic or telephonic communication who willfully discloses the contents of a telegraphic or telephonic message, or any part thereof, addressed to another person, without the permission of such person, unless directed so to do by the lawful order of a court, is punishable by imprisonment in the state prison, or in the county jail not exceeding one year, or by fine not exceeding five thousand dollars ($5,000), or by both fine and imprisonment.

§637.1. Opening wire communications.

Every person not connected with any telegraph or telephone office who, without the authority or consent of the person to whom the same may be directed, willfully opens any sealed envelope enclosing a telegraphic or telephonic message, addressed to another person, with the purpose of learning the contents of such message, or who fraudulently represents another person and thereby procures to be delivered to himself any telegraphic or telephonic message addressed to such other person, with the intent to use, destroy, or detain the same from the person entitled to receive such message, is punishable as provided in Section 637.

§637.2. Injunctive relief; damages.

(a) Any person who has been injured by a violation of this chapter may bring an action against the person who committed the violation for the greater of the following amounts:

(1) Three thousand dollars ($3,000).

(2) Three times the amount of actual damages, if any, sustained by the plaintiff.

(b) Any person may, in accordance with the provisions of Chapter 3 (commencing with Section 525) of Title 7 of Part 2 of the Code of Civil Procedure, bring an action to enjoin and restrain any violation of this chapter, and may in the same action seek damages as provided by subdivision (a).

(c) It is not a necessary prerequisite to an action pursuant to this section that the plaintiff has suffered, or be threatened with, actual damages.

§637.3. Voice prints, voice stress analyzers.

(a) No person or entity in this state shall use any system which examines or records in any manner voice prints or other voice stress patterns of another person to determine the truth or falsity of statements made by such other person without his or her express written consent given in advance of the examination or recordation.

(b) This section shall not apply to any peace officer, as defined in Section 830, while he is carrying out his official duties.

(c) Any person who has been injured by a violator of this section may bring an action against the violator for his actual damages or one thousand dollars ($1,000), whichever is greater.

§637.4. Polygraph examination.

(a) No state or local governmental agency involved in the investigation or prosecution of crimes, or any employee thereof, shall require or request any complaining witness, in a case involving the use of force, violence, duress, menace, or threat of great bodily harm in the commission of any sex offense, to submit to a polygraph examination as a prerequisite to filing an accusatory pleading.

(b) Any person who has been injured by a violator of this section may bring an action against the violator for his actual damages or one thousand dollars ($1,000), whichever is greater.

§637.5. Cable television corporations; prohibited acts; punishments.

(a) No person who owns, controls, operates, or manages a cable television corporation, or who leases channels on a cable system shall:

(1) Use any electronic device to record, transmit, or observe any events or listen to, record, or monitor

© 1992 by J., B. & L. Gould
Printed in the U.S.A.   EP

any conversations which take place inside a subscriber's residence, workplace, or place of business, without obtaining the express written consent of the subscriber. A cable television corporation may conduct electronic sweeps of subscriber households to monitor for signal quality.

(2) Provide any person with any individually identifiable information regarding any of its subscribers, including, but not limited to, the subscriber's television viewing habits, shopping choices, interests, opinions, energy uses, medical information, banking data or information, or any other personal or private information, without the subscriber's express written consent.

(b) Individual subscriber viewing responses or other individually identifiable information derived from subscribers may be retained and used by a cable television corporation only to the extent reasonably necessary for billing purposes and internal business practices, and to monitor for unauthorized reception of services. A cable television corporation may compile, maintain, and distribute a list containing the names and addresses of its subscribers if the list contains no other individually identifiable information and if subscribers are afforded the right to elect not to be included on such lists. However, a cable television corporation shall maintain adequate safeguards to ensure the physical security and confidentiality of any such subscriber information.

(c) A cable television corporation shall not make individual subscriber information available to government agencies in the absence of legal compulsion, including, but not limited to, a court order or subpoena. If requests for such information are made, a cable television corporation shall promptly notify the subscriber of the nature of the request and what government agency has requested the information prior to responding unless otherwise prohibited from doing so by law.

Nothing in this section shall be construed to prevent local franchising authorities from obtaining information necessary to monitor franchise compliance pursuant to franchise or license agreements. This information shall be provided so as to omit individually identifiable subscriber information whenever possible. Information obtained by local franchising authorities shall be used solely for monitoring franchise compliance and shall not be subject to the California Public Records Act (Chapter 3.5 (commencing with Section 6250), Division 7, Title 1, Government Code).

(d) Any individually identifiable subscriber information gathered by a cable television corporation shall be made available for subscriber examination within 30 days of receiving a request by a subscriber to examine such information on the premises of the corporation. Upon a reasonable showing by the subscriber that the information is inaccurate, a cable television corporation shall correct such information. Subscribers shall bear all costs of copying any records or information gathered by the cable television corporation and supplied to the subscriber.

(e) Upon a subscriber's application for cable television service, including, but not limited to, interactive service, a cable television corporation shall provide the applicant with a separate notice in an appropriate form explaining the subscriber's right to privacy protection afforded by this section.

(f) As used in this section:

(1) "Cable television corporation" shall have the same meaning as that term is given by Section 215.5 of the Public Utilities Code.

(2) "Individually identifiable information" means any information identifying an individual or his or her use of any service provided by a cable system other than the mere fact that such individual is a cable television subscriber.

(3) "Person" includes an individual, business association, partnership, corporation, or other legal entity, and an individual acting or purporting to act for or on behalf of any government, or subdivision thereof, whether federal, state, or local.

(4) "Interactive service" means any service offered by a cable television corporation involving the collection, reception, aggregation, storage, or use of electronic information transmitted from a subscriber to any other receiving point under the control of the cable television corporation, or vice versa.

(g) Nothing in this section shall be construed to limit the ability of a cable television corporation to market cable television or ancillary services to its subscribers.

(h) Any person receiving subscriber information from a cable television corporation shall be subject to the provisions of this section.

(i) Any aggrieved person may commence a civil action for damages for invasion of privacy against any cable television corporation, service provider, or person that leases a channel or channels on a cable television system that violates the provisions of this section.

(j) Any person who violates the provisions of this section is guilty of a misdemeanor punishable by a fine not exceeding three thousand dollars ($3,000), or by imprisonment in the county jail not exceeding one year, or by both such fine and imprisonment.

(k) The penalties and remedies provided by subdivisions (i) and (j) are cumulative, and shall not be construed as restricting any penalty or remedy, provisional or otherwise, provided by law for the benefit of any person, and no judgment under this section shall preclude any person from obtaining additional relief based upon the same facts.

(l) The provisions of this section are intended to set forth minimum state standards for protecting the privacy of subscribers to cable television services and are not intended to preempt more restrictive local standards.

§637.6. Disclosure of personal information by a business.

(a) No person who, in the course of business, acquires or has access to personal information concerning an individual, including, but not limited to, the individual's residence address, employment address, or hours of employment, for the purpose of assisting private entities in the establishment or implementation of carpooling or ridesharing programs, shall disclose that information to any other person or use that information for any other purpose without the prior written consent of the individual.

(b) As used in this section, "carpooling or ridesharing programs" include, but shall not be limited to, the formation of carpools, vanpools, buspools, the provision of transit routes, rideshare research, and the development of other demand management strategies such as variable working hours and telecommuting.

© 1992 by J., B. & L. Gould
Printed in the U.S.A.   EP

(c) Any person who violates this section is guilty of a misdemeanor, punishable by imprisonment in the county jail for not exceeding one year, or by a fine of not exceeding one thousand dollars ($1,000), or by both that imprisonment and fine. *(Added by Stats 1990 ch 304 §1, eff. 1/1/91.)*

CHAPTER 2

OF OTHER AND MISCELLANEOUS OFFENSES

§638. *Repealed by Stats 1989 ch 897 §23, eff. 1/1/90.*

§638a. *Repealed by Stats 1989 ch 897 §24, eff. 1/1/90.*

§639. Bribery to procure loan or extension of credit.

Every person who gives, offers, or agrees to give to any director, officer, or employee of a financial institution any emolument, gratuity, or reward, or any money, property, or thing of value for his own personal benefit or of personal advantage, for procuring or endeavoring to procure for any person a loan or extension of credit from such financial institution is guilty of a felony.

As used in this section and Section 639a, "financial institution" means any person or persons engaged in the business of making loans or extending credit or procuring the making of loans or extension of credit, including, but not limited to state and federal banks, savings and loan associations, trust companies, industrial loan companies, personal property brokers, consumer finance lenders, commercial finance lenders, credit unions, escrow companies, title insurance companies, insurance companies, small business investment companies, pawnbrokers, and retirement funds.

As used in this section and Section 639a the word "person" includes any person, firm, partnership, association, corporation, company, syndicate, estate, trust, business trust, or organization of any kind.

§639a. Acceptance of bribe.

Any officer, director or employee of a financial institution who asks, receives, consents, or agrees to receive any commission, emolument, gratuity, or reward or any money, property, or thing of value for his own personal benefit or of personal advantage for procuring or endeavoring to procure for any person a loan from such financial institution is guilty of a felony.

§640. Acts committed on facilities or vehicles of public transportation system.

Any of the following acts committed on or in the facilities or vehicles of a public transportation system as defined by Section 99211 of the Public Utilities Code, on or in the facilities of, or vehicles operated by entities subsidized by, the Department of Transportation, or on or in any leased or rented facilities or vehicles for which any of the above entities incur costs of cleanup, repair, or replacement as a result of any of those acts, is an infraction punishable by a fine not to exceed two hundred fifty dollars ($250) and by community service for a total time not to exceed 48 hours over a period not to exceed 30 days, during a time other than during his or her hours of school attendance or employment:

(a) Evasion of the payment of the fares of the system.

(b) Misuse of transfers, passes, tickets, or tokens with the intent to evade the payment of fares.

(c) Playing sound equipment on or in system facilities or vehicles.

(d) Smoking, eating, or drinking in or on system facilities or vehicles in those areas where those activities are prohibited by that system.

(e) Expectorating upon system facilities or vehicles.

(f) Willfully disturbing others on or in system facilities or vehicles by engaging in boisterous or unruly behavior. *(Amended by Stats 1990 ch 261 §1, eff. 1/1/91.)*

§640a. Vending and slot machines; unauthorized use.

1. Any person who shall knowingly and wilfully operate, or cause to be operated, or who shall attempt to operate, or attempt to cause to be operated, any automatic vending machine, slot machine or other receptacle designed to receive lawful coin of the United States of America in connection with the sale, use or enjoyment of property or service, by means of a slug or any false, counterfeited, mutilated, sweated or foreign coin, or by any means, method, trick or device whatsoever not lawfully authorized by the owner, lessee or licensee of such machine or receptacle, or who shall take, obtain or receive from or in connection with any automatic vending machine, slot machine or other receptacle designed to receive lawful coin of the United States of America in connection with the sale, use or enjoyment of property or service, any goods, wares, merchandise, gas, electric current, article of value, or the use or enjoyment of any musical instrument, phonograph or other property, without depositing in and surrendering to such machine or receptacle lawful coin of the United States of America to the amount required therefor by the owner, lessee or licensee of such machine or receptacle shall be guilty of a misdemeanor.

2. Any person who, with intent to cheat or defraud the owner, lessee, licensee or other person entitled to the contents of any automatic vending machine, slot machine or other receptacle, depository or contrivance designed to receive lawful coin of the United States of America in connection with the sale, use or enjoyment of property or service, or who, knowing or having cause to believe that the same is intended for unlawful use, shall manufacture for sale, or sell or give away any slug, device or substance whatsoever intended or calculated to be placed or deposited in any such automatic vending machine, slot machine or other such receptacle, depository or contrivance, shall be guilty of a misdemeanor.

§640b. Coin-box telephones.

1. Any person who knowingly, wilfully and with intent to defraud the owner, lessee or licensee of any coin-box telephone, shall operate or cause to be operated, attempt to operate, or attempt to cause to be operated, any coin-box telephone by means of any slug or any false, counterfeited, mutilated, sweated or foreign coin, or by any means, method, trick or device whatsoever not lawfully authorized by such owner, lessee or licensee, or any person who, knowingly, wilfully and with intent to defraud the owner, lessee or licensee of any coin-box telephone, shall take, obtain

or receive from or in connection with any such coin-box telephone, the use or enjoyment of any telephone or telegraph facilities or service, without depositing in or surrendering to such coin-box telephone lawful coin of the United States of America to the amount required therefor by such owner, lessee or licensee, shall be guilty of a misdemeanor.

2. Any person who, with the intent to cheat or defraud the owner, lessee or licensee or other person entitled to the contents of any coin-box telephone, or who, knowing or having cause to believe that the same is intended for unlawful use, shall manufacture for sale, or sell or give away any slug, device or substance whatsoever intended or calculated to be placed or deposited in any such coin-box telephone, shall be guilty of a misdemeanor.

§640.5. Affixing graffiti to governmental facilities or vehicles.

(a) Any person who writes, sprays, scratches, or otherwise affixes graffiti on or in the facilities or vehicles of a governmental entity, as defined by Section 811.2 of the Government Code, or on or in the facilities or vehicles of a public transportation system as defined by Section 99211 of the Public Utilities Code, or on or in the facilities of or vehicles operated by entities subsidized by, the Department of Transportation, or on or in any leased or rented facilities or vehicles for which any of the above entities incur costs of less than two hundred fifty dollars ($250) for cleanup, repair, or replacement is guilty of an infraction punishable by a fine not to exceed two hundred fifty dollars ($250) and by community service for a total time not to exceed 48 hours over a period not to exceed 30 days, during a time other than during his or her hours of school attendance or employment. This subdivision does not preclude application of Section 594.

(b) (1) Upon conviction of any person under subdivision (a), the court may, in addition to any punishment imposed pursuant to subdivision (a), at the victim's option, order the defendant to perform the necessary labor to clean up, repair, or replace the property damaged by that person, but shall not order the person to pay for any related costs incurred by the cleanup, repair, or replacement of the property.

(2) If a minor is personally unable to pay any fine levied for violating subdivision (a), the parent or legal guardian of the minor shall be liable for payment of the fine. A court may waive payment of the fine by the parent or legal guardian upon a finding of good cause.

(c) Any fine levied for a violation of subdivision (a) shall be credited by the county treasurer pursuant to Section 1463.29 to the governmental entity having jurisdiction over, or responsibility for, the facility or vehicle involved, to be used for removal of the graffiti. Before crediting these fines to the appropriate governmental entity, the county may determine the administrative costs it has incurred pursuant to this section, and retain an amount equal to those costs.

Any community service which is required pursuant to subdivision (a) of a person under the age of 18 years may be performed in the presence, and under the direct supervision, of the person's parent or legal guardian.

(d) As used in this section, graffiti means any form of unauthorized painting, writing, or inscription regardless of the content or nature of the material used in the commission of the act. (Amended by Stats 1991 ch 556 §1, eff. 1/1/92.)

§640.6. Affixing graffiti on real or personal property.

(a) Except as provided in Section 640.5, any person who writes, sprays, scratches, or otherwise affixes graffiti on any real or personal property not his or her own is guilty of an infraction punishable by a fine not to exceed two hundred fifty dollars ($250) if the amount of the defacement, damage, or destruction is less than two hundred fifty dollars ($250). This subdivision does not preclude application of Section 594.

(b) (1) Upon conviction of any person under subdivision (a), the court may, in addition to any punishment imposed pursuant to subdivision (a), order the defendant to complete community service not to exceed 48 hours for the first conviction. Upon the second and subsequent conviction, the court may order the defendant to complete community service not to exceed 96 hours. A defendant shall be ordered to complete community service during a time other than during his or her hours of school attendance or employment.

(2) Upon conviction of any person under subdivision (a), the court may, in addition to any punishment imposed pursuant to subdivision (a), at the victim's option, order the defendant to perform the necessary labor to clean up, repair, or replace the property damaged by that person, but shall not order the person to pay for any related costs incurred by the cleanup, repair, or replacement of the property.

(3) If a minor is personally unable to pay any fine levied for violating subdivision (a), the parent or legal guardian of the minor shall be liable for payment of the fine. A court may waive payment of the fine by the parent or legal guardian upon a finding of good cause.

Any community service which is required pursuant to subdivision (b) of a person under the age of 18 years may be performed in the presence, and under the direct supervision, of the person's parent or legal guardian.

(4) As used in this section, graffiti means any form of unauthorized painting, writing, or inscription regardless of the content or nature of the material used in the commission of the act. (Added by Stats 1991 ch 556 §2, eff. 1/1/92.)

§641. Bribery of telegraph or telephone employee.

Every person who, by the payment or promise of any bribe, inducement, or reward, procures or attempts to procure any telegraph or telephone agent, operator, or employee to disclose any private message, or the contents, purport, substance, or meaning thereof, or offers to any agent, operator, or employee any bribe, compensation, or reward for the disclosure of any private information received by him or her by reason of his or her trust as agent, operator, or employee, or uses or attempts to use any information so obtained, is punishable as provided in Section 639. (Amended by Stats 1987 ch 828 §40.)

§641.3. Commercial bribery.

(a) Any employee who solicits, accepts, or agrees to accept money or any thing of value from a person other than his or her employer, other than in trust for the employer, corruptly and without the knowledge or consent of the employer, in return for using or agreeing to use his or her position for the benefit of that other person, and any person who offers or gives an employee money or any thing of value under those circumstances, is guilty of commercial bribery.

© 1992 by J., B. & L. Gould
Printed in the U.S.A.   EP

(b) This section does not apply where the amount of money or monetary worth of the thing of value is one hundred dollars ($100) or less.

(c) Commercial bribery is punishable by imprisonment in the county jail for not more than one year if the amount of the bribe is one thousand dollars ($1,000) or less, or by imprisonment in the county jail, or in the state prison for 16 months, or two or three years if the amount of the bribe exceeds one thousand dollars ($1,000).

(d) For purposes of this section:

(1) "Employee" means an officer, director, agent, trustee, partner, or employee.

(2) "Employer" means a corporation, association, organization, trust, partnership, or sole proprietorship.

(3) "Corruptly" means that the person specifically intends to injure or defraud (A) his or her employer, (B) the employer of the person to whom he or she offers, gives, or agrees to give the money or a thing of value, (C) the employer of the person from whom he or she requests, receives, or agrees to receive the money or a thing of value, or (D) a competitor of any such employer. *(Added by Stats 1989 ch 308 §1, eff. 1/1/90.)*

§641.5. Use of solvents in clothes cleaning establishments.

(a) In any clothes cleaning establishment in which more than one gallon of a volatile, commercially moisture-free solvent of the chlorinated hydrocarbon type is used for dry cleaning, the performance of all the dry cleaning, drying, and deodorizing processes shall be completed entirely within fluid-tight machines or apparatus vented to the open air at a point not less than eight feet from any window or other opening and so used and operated as to prevent the escape of fumes, gases, or vapors into workrooms or workplaces.

(b) Except when operations are performed as provided in subdivision (a), no person shall operate a clothes cleaning establishment in which more than one gallon of a volatile, commercially moisture-free solvent of the chlorinated hydrocarbon type is used for dry cleaning except under either of the following conditions:

(1) All of the dry cleaning, drying, and deodorizing processes are performed in a single room or compartment designed and ventilated in such a manner that dangerous toxic concentrations of vapors will not accumulate in working areas.

(2) The dry cleaning processes are performed in fluid-tight machines or apparatus designed, installed, and operated in a manner that will prevent the escape of dangerous toxic concentrations of vapors to the working areas.

(c) "Volatile, commercially moisture-free solvent" means either of the following:

(1) Any commercially moisture-free liquid, volatile product or substance having the capacity to evaporate and, during evaporation, to generate and emit a gas or vapor.

(2) Any solvent commonly known to the clothes cleaning industry as a "chlorinated hydrocarbon solvent."

(d) Any violation of this section is a misdemeanor. *(Added by Stats 1986 ch 478 §3.)*

§641.6. Use of carbon tetrachloride or trichlorethylene.

Notwithstanding any other provision of law, no person engaged in the business of dry cleaning shall use carbon tetrachloride or trichlorethylene as a cleaning agent when engaged in onsite dry cleaning. For purposes of this section, "onsite dry cleaning" means dry cleaning which is performed in a residence or any commercial or public building other than a clothes cleaning establishment or plant. A violation of this section is a misdemeanor. *(Added by Stats 1986 ch 486 §3.)*

§642. Theft of articles from dead body.

Every person who wilfully and maliciously removes and keeps possession of and appropriates for his own use articles of value from a dead human body, the theft of which articles would be petty theft is guilty of a misdemeanor, or if the theft of the articles would be grand theft, a felony. This section shall not apply to articles removed at the request or direction of one of the persons enumerated in section 711 of the Health and Safety Code.

§643. Definition and disposal of fetal remains.

No person knowingly shall dispose of fetal remains in a public or private dump, refuse, or disposal site or place open to public view. For the purposes of this section, "fetal remains" means the lifeless product of conception regardless of the duration of the pregnancy.

Any violation of this section is a misdemeanor.

§645. Punishment for conviction for carnal abuse.

Whenever any person shall be adjudged guilty of carnal abuse of a female person under the age of ten years, the court may, in addition to such other punishment or confinement as may be imposed, direct an operation to be performed upon such person, for the prevention of procreation.

§646. Solicitation of personal injury claims.

It is unlawful for any person with the intent, or for the purpose of instituting a suit thereon outside of this state, to seek or solicit the business of collecting any claim for damages for personal injury sustained within this state, or for death resulting therefrom, with the intention of instituting suit thereon outside of this state, in cases where such right of action rests in a resident of this state, or his legal representative, and is against a person, copartnership, or corporation subject to personal service within this state.

Any person violating any of the provisions of this section is guilty of a misdemeanor, and is punishable by a fine of not less than one hundred dollars ($100) nor more than one thousand dollars ($1,000), by imprisonment in the county jail not less than 30 days nor more than six months, or by both fine and imprisonment at the discretion of the court but within said limits.

§646.5. Solicitation of employment from injured person.

No person shall knowingly and directly solicit employment from any injured person or from any other person to obtain authorization on behalf of the injured person, as an investigator to investigate the accident or act which resulted in injury or death to such person or damage to the property of such person. Nothing in this section shall prohibit the soliciting of employment as an investigator from such injured person's attorney.

Any person violating any provision of this section is guilty of a misdemeanor.

This section shall not apply to any business agent or attorney employed by a labor organization.

§646.6. Sale or use of photographs relating to accident.

No person shall knowingly and directly solicit any injured person, or anyone acting on behalf of any injured person, for the sale or use of photographs relating to the accident which resulted in the injury or death of such injured person.

Any person violating any provision of this section is guilty of a misdemeanor. Nothing in this section shall prohibit a person, other than a public employee acting within the scope of his or her employment, from soliciting the injured person's attorney for the sale or use of such photographs.

§646.9. Threatening violence.

(a) Any person who willfully, maliciously, and repeatedly follows or harasses another person and who makes a credible threat with the intent to place that person in reasonable fear of death or great bodily injury is guilty of the crime of stalking, punishable by imprisonment in a county jail for not more than one year or by a fine of not more than one thousand dollars ($1,000), or by both that fine and imprisonment.

(b) Any person who violates subdivision (a) when there is a temporary restraining order or an injunction, or both, in effect prohibiting the behavior described in subdivision (a) against the same party, is punishable by imprisonment in a county jail for not more than one year or by a fine of not more than one thousand dollars ($1,000), or by both that fine and imprisonment, or by imprisonment in the state prison.

(c) A second or subsequent conviction occurring within seven years of a prior conviction under subdivision (a) against the same victim, and involving an act of violence or "a credible threat" of violence, as defined in subdivision (e), is punishable by imprisonment in a county jail for not more than one year, or by a fine of not more than one thousand dollars ($1,000), or by both that fine and imprisonment, or by imprisonment in the state prison.

(d) For the purposes of this section, "harasses" means a knowing and willful course of conduct directed at a specific person which seriously alarms, annoys, or harasses the person, and which serves no legitimate purpose. The course of conduct must be such as would cause a reasonable person to suffer substantial emotional distress, and must actually cause substantial emotional distress to the person. "Course of conduct" means a pattern of conduct composed of a series of acts over a period of time, however short, evidencing a continuity of purpose. Constitutionally protected activity is not included within the meaning of "course of conduct."

(e) For the purposes of this section, "a credible threat" means a threat made with the intent and the apparent ability to carry out the threat so as to cause the person who is the target of the threat to reasonably fear for his or her safety. The threat must be against the life of, or a threat to cause great bodily injury to, a person as defined in Section 12022.7.

This section shall not apply to conduct which occurs during labor picketing. (Added by Stats 1990 ch 1527 §1, eff. 1/1/91.)

§647. Disorderly conduct, a misdemeanor.

Every person who commits any of the following acts is guilty of disorderly conduct, a misdemeanor:

(a) Who solicits anyone to engage in or who engages in lewd or dissolute conduct in any public place or in any place open to the public or exposed to public view.

(b) Who solicits or who agrees to engage in or who engages in any act of prostitution. A person agrees to engage in an act of prostitution when, with specific intent to so engage, he or she manifests an acceptance of an offer or solicitation to so engage, regardless of whether the offer or solicitation was made by a person who also possessed the specific intent to engage in prostitution. No agreement to engage in an act of prostitution shall constitute a violation of this subdivision unless some act, beside the agreement, be done within this state in furtherance of the commission of an act of prostitution by the person agreeing to engage in that act. As used in this subdivision, "prostitution" includes any lewd act between persons for money or other consideration.

(c) Who accosts other persons in any public place or in any place open to the public for the purpose of begging or soliciting alms.

(d) Who loiters in or about any toilet open to the public for the purpose of engaging in or soliciting any lewd or lascivious or any unlawful act.

(e) Who loiters or wanders upon the streets or from place to place without apparent reason or business and who refuses to identify himself or herself and to account for his or her presence when requested by any peace officer so to do, if the surrounding circumstances are such as to indicate to a reasonable person that the public safety demands such identification.

(f) Who is found in any public place under the influence of intoxicating liquor, any drug, controlled substance, toluene, or any combination of any intoxicating liquor, drug, controlled substance, or toluene, in such a condition that he or she is unable to exercise care for his or her own safety or the safety of others, or by reason of his or her being under the influence of intoxicating liquor, any drug, controlled substance, toluene, or any combination of any intoxicating liquor, drug, or toluene, interferes with or obstructs or prevents the free use of any street, sidewalk, or other public way.

(ff) When a person has violated subdivision (f) of this section, a peace officer, if he or she is reasonably able to do so, shall place the person, or cause him or her to be placed, in civil protective custody. Such person shall be taken to a facility, designated pursuant to Section 5170 of the Welfare and Institutions Code, for the 72-hour treatment and evaluation of inebriates. A peace officer may place a person in civil protective custody with that kind and degree of force which would be lawful were he or she effecting an arrest for a misdemeanor without a warrant. No person who has been placed in civil protective custody shall thereafter be subject to any criminal prosecution or juvenile court proceeding based on the facts giving rise to such placement. This subdivision shall not apply to the following persons:

(1) Any person who is under the influence of any drug, or under the combined influence of intoxicating liquor and any drug.

(2) Any person who a peace officer has probable cause to believe has committed any felony, or who has committed any misdemeanor in addition to subdivision (f) of this section.

(3) Any person who a peace officer in good faith believes will attempt escape or will be unreasonably difficult for medical personnel to control.

© 1992 by J., B. & L. Gould
Printed in the U.S.A.   EP

(g) Who loiters, prowls, or wanders upon the private property of another, at any time, without visible or lawful business with the owner or occupant thereof. As used in this subdivision, "loiter" means to delay or linger without a lawful purpose for being on the property and for the purpose of committing a crime as opportunity may be discovered.

(h) Who, while loitering, prowling, or wandering upon the private property of another, at any time, peeks in the door or window of any inhabited building or structure located thereon, without visible or lawful business with the owner or occupant thereof.

(i) Who lodges in any building, structure, vehicle, or place, whether public or private, without the permission of the owner or person entitled to the possession or in control thereof.

In any accusatory pleading charging a violation of subdivision (b) of this section, if the defendant has been once previously convicted of a violation of that subdivision, the previous conviction shall be charged in the accusatory pleading; and, if the previous conviction is found to be true by the jury, upon a jury trial, or by the court, upon a court trial, or is admitted by the defendant, the defendant shall be imprisoned in the county jail for a period of not less than 45 days and shall not be eligible for release upon completion of sentence, on probation, on parole, on work furlough or work release, or on any other basis until he or she has served a period of not less than 45 days in the county jail. In all cases in which probation is granted the court shall require as a condition thereof that such person be confined in the county jail for at least 45 days. In no event does the court have the power to absolve a person who violates this subdivision from the obligation of spending at least 45 days in confinement in the county jail.

In any accusatory pleading charging a violation of subdivision (b) of this section, if the defendant has been previously convicted two or more times of a violation of that subdivision, each such previous conviction shall be charged in the accusatory pleading; and, if two or more of such previous convictions are found to be true by the jury, upon a jury trial, or by the court, upon a court trial, or are admitted by the defendant, the defendant shall be imprisoned in the county jail for a period of not less than 90 days and shall not be eligible for release upon completion of sentence, on probation, on parole, on work furlough or work release, or on any other basis until he or she has served a period of not less than 90 days in the county jail. In all cases in which probation is granted the court shall require as a condition thereof that such person be confined in the confined in the county jail for at least 90 days. In no event does the court have the power to absolve a person who violates this subdivision from the obligation of spending at least 90 days in confinement in the county jail. *(Amended by Stats 1988 ch 524 §1, eff. 1/1/89.)*

§647a. *Amended and renumbered §647.6 by Stats 1987 ch 1418 §4.3.*

§647b. Molesting pupils attending adult school.

Every person who loiters about any school in which adults are in attendance at courses established pursuant to Chapter 10 (commencing with Section 52500) of Part 28 of the Education Code, and who annoys or molests any person in attendance therein shall be punished by a fine of not exceeding one thousand dollars ($1,000) or by imprisonment in the county jail for not exceeding six months, or by both such fine and imprisonment. *(Amended by Stats 1987 ch 828 §42.)*

§647c. Obstruction of street, sidewalk or other public places.

Every person who willfully and maliciously obstructs the free movement of any person on any street, sidewalk, or other public place or on or in any place open to the public is guilty of a misdemeanor.

Nothing in this section affects the power of a county or a city to regulate conduct upon a street, sidewalk, or other public place or on or in a place open to the public.

§647d. Alcohol treatment and recovery program.

(a) Notwithstanding any other provision of law, subdivision (b) shall become operative in a county only if the board of supervisors adopts the provisions of subdivision (b) by ordinance after a finding that sufficient alcohol treatment and recovery facilities exist or will exist to accommodate the persons described in that subdivision.

(b) In any accusatory pleading charging a violation of subdivision (f) of Section 647, if the defendant has been previously convicted two or more times of a violation of subdivision (f) of Section 647 within the previous 12 months, each such previous conviction shall be charged in the accusatory pleading. If two or more of the previous convictions are found to be true by the jury, upon a jury trial, or by the court, upon a court trial, or are admitted by the defendant, the defendant shall be imprisoned in the county jail for a period of not less than 90 days. The trial court may grant probation or suspend the execution of sentence imposed upon the defendant if the court, as a condition of the probation or suspension, orders the defendant to spend 60 days in an alcohol treatment and recovery program in a facility which, as a minimum, meets the standards described in the guidelines for alcoholic recovery home programs issued by the Division of Alcohol Programs of the Department of Alcohol and Drug Abuse.

(c) The provisions of Section 4019 shall apply to the conditional attendance of an alcohol treatment and recovery program described in subdivision (b).

§647e. Open alcoholic beverage containers.

(a) A city, county, or city and county may by local ordinance provide that no person who has in his or her possession any bottle, can or other receptacle containing any alcoholic beverage which has been opened, or a seal broken, or the contents of which have been partially removed, shall enter, be, or remain on the posted premises of, including the posted parking lot immediately adjacent to, any retail package off-sale alcoholic beverage licensee licensed pursuant to Division 9 (commencing with Section 23000) of the Business and Professions Code, or on any public sidewalk immediately adjacent to the licensed and posted premises. Any person violating any provision of such an ordinance shall be guilty of an infraction.

(b) As used in subdivision (a), "posted premises" means those premises which are subject to licensure under any retail package off-sale alcoholic beverage license, the parking lot immediately adjacent to the licensed premises and any public sidewalk immediately adjacent to the licensed premises on which clearly visible notices indicate to the patrons of the licensee and parking lot and to persons on the public sidewalk, that the provisions of subdivision (a) are applicable. Any local ordinance adopted pursuant to this section shall require posting of the premises.

(c) The provisions of this section shall not apply to a private residential parking lot which is immediately adjacent to the posted premises.

Nothing in this section shall affect the power of a county or a city, or city and county, to regulate the possession of an opened alcoholic beverage in any public place or in a place open to the public.

§647f. Prostitution; blood test positive for AIDS.

In any accusatory pleading charging a violation of subdivision (b) of Section 647, if the defendant has been previously convicted one or more times of a violation of that subdivision or of any other offense listed in subdivision (d) of Section 1202.1, and in connection with one or more of those convictions a blood test was administered pursuant to Section 1202.1 or 1202.6 with positive test results, of which the defendant was informed, the previous conviction and positive blood test results, of which the defendant was informed, shall be charged in the accusatory pleading. If the previous conviction and informed test results are found to be true by the trier of fact or are admitted by the defendant, the defendant is guilty of a felony. *(Amended by Stats 1989 ch 765 §1, eff. 1/1/90.)*

§647.1. Additional penalty for prostitution or lewd conduct involving controlled substances.

In addition to any fine assessed under Section 647, the judge may assess a fine not to exceed seventy dollars ($70) against any person who violates subdivision (a) or (b) of Section 647, or, if the offense involves intravenous use of a controlled substance, subdivision (f) of Section 647, with the proceeds of this fine to be used in accordance with Section 1463.23.

The court shall, however, take into consideration the defendant's ability to pay and no defendant shall be denied probation because of his or her inability to pay the fine permitted under this section. *(Added by Stats 1988 ch 1243 §8, eff. 1/1/89.)*

§647.6. Annoying or molesting children.

Every person who annoys or molests any child under the age of 18 is punishable by a fine not exceeding one thousand dollars ($1,000) or by imprisonment in the county jail for not exceeding one year or by both the fine and imprisonment. Every person who violates this section after having entered, without consent, an inhabited dwelling house, or trailer coach as defined in Section 635 of the Vehicle Code, or the inhabited portion of any other building, is punishable by imprisonment in the state prison, or in the county jail not exceeding one year. Every person who violates this section is punishable upon the second and each subsequent conviction by imprisonment in the state prison. Every person who violates this section after a previous felony conviction under this section, conviction under Section 288, or felony conviction under Section 311.4 involving a minor under the age of 14 years is punishable by imprisonment in the state prison for two, four, or six years. In any case in which a person is convicted of violating this section and probation is granted, the court shall require counseling as a condition of probation, unless the court makes

a written statement in the court record, that counseling would be inappropriate or ineffective. *(Amended by Stats 1987 ch 1418 §4.3.)*

§648. Issuing or circulating paper money.

Every person who makes, issues, or puts in circulation any bill, check, ticket, certificate, promissory note, or the paper of any bank, to circulate as money, except as authorized by the laws of the United States, for the first offense, is guilty of a misdemeanor, and for each and every subsequent offense is guilty of a felony.

§648a. Slugs or tokens resembling coins of United States.

Every person who has in his possession for any illegal purpose or who makes, sells, issues, or puts in circulation any slug or token of the size and shape, or of a size and shape such that the radius, the diameter and the thickness thereof are each within six one-hundredths of an inch of that of any coin of the United States of America is guilty of a misdemeanor. The term "slug" and the term "token," as used herein, mean any piece of metal or other material not a coin of the United States or a foreign country. However, tokens sold by and accepted as fares by electric railways and lettered checks having a returnable trade value shall not be subject to the provisions of this act.

§649. Misdirection of hotel guests by taxicab operators.

Any person engaged in the transportation of persons by taxicab or other means of conveyance who knowingly misdirects a prospective guest of any hotel, inn, boardinghouse or lodginghouse or knowingly takes such a prospective guest to a hotel, inn, boarding-house or lodginghouse different from that of his instructions from such prospective guest is guilty of a misdemeanor.

§649a. Inducing misdirection of hotel guests.

Any person engaged in the operation of any hotel, inn, boardinghouse or lodginghouse who pays another any compensation for inducing or attempting to induce, by false statement or misrepresentation, prospective guests of a given hotel, inn, boardinghouse or lodginghouse to enter, lodge at or become a guest of any other hotel, inn, boarding-house or lodginghouse is guilty of a misdemeanor.

§650. *Repealed by Stats 1991 ch 186 §3, eff. 1/1/92.*

§650.5. *Repealed by Stats 1991 ch 186 §4, eff. 1/1/92.*

§651. Misuse of federal order stamps; punishment.

It is a misdemeanor for any person to buy, receive, sell, give away, dispose of, exchange or barter any Federal order stamps except for the foods or cotton goods for which they are issued.

This section does not apply to any person buying, receiving, selling, giving away, disposing of, exchanging or bartering any Federal order stamps subsequent to the redemption of such stamps in the manner provided by State or Federal law for the foods or cotton goods for which they are issued.

As used in this section, Federal order stamps refers to stamps issued by the United States Department of Agriculture or its duly authorized agent for food and surplus food or cotton and surplus cotton.

© 1992 by J., B. & L. Gould
Printed in the U.S.A.   EP

§652. Unlawful to reward capture of "dead" or "dead or alive" person.

It is unlawful to offer a reward which has, either as its sole object or as one of its objects, the apprehension or capture of a person either "dead," or, in the alternative, "dead or alive." Any person who violates this section is guilty of a misdemeanor.

§653. Tattooing person under the age of 18.

Every person who tattoos or offers to tattoo a person under the age of 18 years is guilty of a misdemeanor.

As used in this section, to "tattoo" means to insert pigment under the surface of the skin of a human being, by pricking with a needle or otherwise, so as to produce an indelible mark or figure visible through the skin.

This section is not intended to apply to any act of a licensed practitioner of the healing arts performed in the course of his practice.

§653d. Sale of mining machinery without giving bill of sale or keeping record.

Every person who sells machinery used or to be used for mining purposes who fails to give to the buyer, at the time of sale, a bill of sale for the machinery, or who fails to keep a written record of the sale, giving the date thereof, describing the machinery, and showing the name and address of the buyer, and every buyer of such machinery, if in this State, who fails to keep a record of his purchase of such machinery, giving the name and address of the seller, describing the machinery, and showing the date of the purchase, is guilty of a misdemeanor.

§653f. Soliciting commission of certain offenses.

(a) Every person who, with the intent that the crime be committed, solicits another to offer or accept or join in the offer or acceptance of a bribe, or to commit or join in the commission of robbery, burglary, grand theft, receiving stolen property, extortion, perjury, subornation of perjury, forgery, kidnapping, arson or assault with a deadly weapon or instrument or by means of force likely to produce great bodily injury, or, by the use of force or a threat of force, to prevent or dissuade any person who is or may become a witness from attending upon, or testifying at, any trial, proceeding, or inquiry authorized by law, is punishable by imprisonment in the county jail not more than one year or in the state prison, or by fine of not more than ten thousand dollars ($10,000), or the amount which could have been assessed for commission of the offense itself, whichever is greater, or by both such fine and imprisonment.

(b) Every person who, with the intent that the crime be committed, solicits another to commit or join in the commission of murder is punishable by imprisonment in the state prison for three, six, or nine years.

(c) Every person who, with the intent that the crime be committed, solicits another to commit rape by force or violence, sodomy by force or violence, oral copulation by force or violence, or any violation of Section 264.1, 288, or 289, is punishable by imprisonment in a state prison for two, three or four years.

(d) Every person who, with the intent that the crime be committed, solicits another to commit an offense specified in Section 11352, 11379, 11379.5, 11379.6, or 11391 of the Health and Safety Code shall be punished by imprisonment in the county jail for a period not exceeding six months. Every person, who, having been convicted of soliciting another to commit an offense specified in this subdivision, is subsequently convicted of the proscribed solicitation, then the person convicted of the subsequent offense is punishable by imprisonment in the county jail not exceeding one year, or in the state prison.

This subdivision does not apply where the term of imprisonment imposed under other provisions of law would result in a longer term of imprisonment.

(e) An offense charged in violation of subdivision (a), (b), or (c) shall be proven by the testimony of two witnesses, or of one witness and corroborating circumstances. An offense charged in violation of subdivision (d) shall be proven by the testimony of one witness and corroborating circumstances. *(Amended by Stats 1989 ch 897 §25, eff. 1/1/90.)*

§653g. Loitering about schools or public places attended by children.

Every person who loiters about any school or public place at or near which children attend or normally congregate and who remains at any school or public place at or near which children attend or normally congregate, or who reenters or comes upon such school or place within 72 hours, after being asked to leave by the chief administrative official of that school or, in the absence of the chief administrative official, the person acting as the chief administrative official, or by a member of the security patrol of the school district who has been given authorization, in writing, by the chief administrative official of that school to act as his agent in performing this duty, or a city police officer, or sheriff or deputy sheriff, or California Highway Patrol officer, is a vagrant, and is punishable by a fine of not exceeding one thousand dollars ($1,000) or by imprisonment in the county jail for not exceeding six months, or by both such fine and imprisonment.

As used in this section, "loiter" means to delay, to linger, or to idle about any such school or public place without lawful business for being present.

§653h. Transfer of recorded sounds for unlawful use.

(a) Every person is guilty of a public offense punishable as provided in subdivisions (b) and (c), who:

(1) Knowingly and willfully transfers or causes to be transferred any sounds that have been recorded on a phonograph record, disc, wire, tape, film or other article on which sounds are recorded, with intent to sell or cause to be sold, or to use or cause to be used for commercial advantage or private financial gain through public performance, the article on which the sounds are so transferred, without the consent of the owner.

(2) Transports for monetary or like consideration within this state or causes to be transported within this state any such article with the knowledge that the sounds thereon have been so transferred without the consent of the owner.

(b) Any person who has been convicted of a violation of subdivision (a), shall be punished by imprisonment in the county jail not to exceed one year, by imprisonment in the state prison for two, three, or five years, or by a fine not to exceed two hundred fifty thousand dollars ($250,000), or by both, if the offense involves the transfer or transportation, or conduct causing that transfer or transportation, of not less than 1,000 of the articles described in subdivision (a).

(c) Any person who has been convicted of any other violation of subdivision (a) not described in subdivision (b), shall be punished by imprisonment in the county jail not to exceed one year, or by a fine of not more than twenty-five thousand dollars ($25,000), or by both. A second or subsequent conviction under subdivision (a) not described in subdivision (b) shall be punished by imprisonment in the state prison or by a fine not to exceed one hundred thousand dollars ($100,000), or by both.

(d) Every person who offers for sale or resale, or sells or resells, or causes the sale or resale, or rents, or possesses for these purposes, any article described in subdivision (a) with knowledge that the sounds thereon have been so transferred without the consent of the owner is guilty of a public offense.

(1) A violation of subdivision (d) involving not less than 100 of those articles shall be punishable by imprisonment in a county jail not to exceed one year or by a fine not to exceed ten thousand dollars ($10,000), or by both. A second or subsequent conviction for the conduct described in this paragraph shall be punishable by imprisonment in the county jail not to exceed one year or in the state prison, or by a fine not to exceed twenty-five thousand dollars ($25,000), or by both.

(2) A person who has been convicted of any violation of this subdivision not described in paragraph (1) shall be punished by imprisonment in the county jail not to exceed six months or by a fine not to exceed five thousand dollars ($5,000), or by both. A second conviction for the conduct described in this paragraph shall be punishable by imprisonment in the county jail not to exceed one year or by a fine not to exceed ten thousand dollars ($10,000), or by both. A third or subsequent conviction for the conduct described in this paragraph shall be punishable by imprisonment in the county jail not to exceed one year or in the state prison, or by a fine not to exceed twenty-five thousand dollars ($25,000), or by both.

(e) As used in this section, "person" means any individual, partnership, partnership's member or employee, corporation, association or corporation or association employee, officer or director; "owner" means the person who owns the original master recording embodied in the master phonograph record, master disc, master tape, master film or other article used for reproducing recorded sounds on phonograph records, discs, tapes, films or other articles on which sound is or can be recorded, and from which the transferred recorded sounds are directly or indirectly derived; and "master recording" means the original fixation of sounds upon a recording from which copies can be made.

(f) This section shall neither enlarge nor diminish the right of parties in private litigation.

(g) This section does not apply to any person engaged in radio or television broadcasting who transfers, or causes to be transferred, any such sounds (other than from the sound track of a motion picture) intended for, or in connection with broadcast transmission or related uses, or for archival purposes.

(h) This section does not apply to any not-for-profit educational institution or any federal or state governmental entity, if the institution or entity has as a primary purpose the advancement of the public's knowledge and the dissemination of information regarding America's musical cultural heritage, provided that this purpose is clearly set forth in the institution's or entity's charter, bylaws, certificate of incorporation, or similar document, and the institution or entity has, prior to the transfer, made a good faith effort to identify and locate the owner or owners of the sound recordings to be transferred and, provided that the owner or owners could not be and have not been located. Nothing in this section shall be construed to relieve an institution or entity of its contractual or other obligation to compensate the owners of sound recordings to be transferred. In order to continue the exemption permitted by this subdivision, the institution or entity shall make continuing efforts to locate such owners and shall make an annual public notice of the fact of the transfers in newspapers of general circulation serving the jurisdictions where the owners were incorporated or doing business at the time of initial affixations. The institution or entity shall keep on file a record of the efforts made to locate such owners for inspection by appropriate governmental agencies.

(i) This section applies only to such articles that were initially mastered prior to February 15, 1972. *(Amended by Stats 1988 ch 1257 §1, eff 1/1/89.)*

§653i. Leaving scene of a skiing accident.

Any person who is involved in a skiing accident and who leaves the scene of the accident knowing or having reason to believe that any other person involved in the accident is in need of medical and other assistance, except to notify the proper authorities or to obtain assistance, shall be guilty of an infraction punishable by fine not exceeding one thousand dollars ($1,000).

§653j. Encouraging minor to commit felony.

(a) Every person 18 years of age or older who, in any voluntary manner, solicits, induces, encourages, or intimidates any minor with the intent that the minor shall commit a felony in violation of paragraph (1) of subdivision (c) of Section 136.1 or Section 187, 211, 245, 246, 451, 459, or 520 of the Penal Code, or Section 10851 of the Vehicle Code; shall be punished by imprisonment in the state prison for a period of three, five, or seven years. If the minor is 16 years of age or older at the time of the offense, this section shall only apply when the adult is at least five years older than the minor at the time the offense is committed.

(b) In no case shall the court impose a sentence pursuant to subdivision (a) which exceeds the maximum penalty prescribed for the felony offense for which the minor was solicited, induced, encouraged, or intimidated to commit.

(c) Whenever a sentence is imposed under subdivision (a), the court shall consider the severity of the underlying crime as one of the circumstances in aggravation. *(Amended and renumbered by Stats 1989 ch 897 §26, eff. 1/1/90.)*

§653k. Switchblade knife; possession or transfer.

Every person who possesses in the passenger's or driver's area of any motor vehicle in any public place or place open to the public, carries upon his or her person, and every person who sells, offers for sale, exposes for sale, loans, transfers, or gives to any other person a switchblade knife having a blade over two inches in length is guilty of a misdemeanor.

© 1992 by J., B. & L. Gould
Printed in the U.S.A.   EP

For the purposes of this section a "switchblade knife" is a knife having the appearance of a pocketknife, and shall include a spring-blade knife, snap-blade knife, gravity knife or any other similar type knife, the blade or blades of which are two or more inches long and which can be released automatically by a flick of a button, pressure on the handle, flip of the wrist or other mechanical device, or is released by the weight of the blade or by any type of mechanism whatsoever.

For purposes of this section "passenger's or driver's area" means that part of a motor vehicle which is designed to carry the driver and passengers, including any interior compartment or space therein. (*Amended by Stats 1986 ch 1422 §1.*)

§653l. *Renumbered to §653j by Stats 1989 ch 897 §26, eff. 1/1/90.*

§653m. Obscene telephone calls.

(a) Every person who with intent to annoy telephones another and addresses to or about the other person any obscene language or addresses to the other person any threat to inflict injury to the person or property of the person addressed or any member of his or her family, is guilty of a misdemeanor.

(b) Every person who makes repeated telephone calls with intent to annoy another person at his or her residence, is, whether or not conversation ensues from making the telephone call, guilty of a misdemeanor. Nothing in this subdivision shall apply to telephone calls made in good faith.

(c) Any offense committed by use of a telephone as herein set out may be deemed to have been committed at either the place at which the telephone call or calls were made or at the place where the telephone call or calls were received.

(d) Subdivision (a) or (b) is violated when the person acting with intent to annoy makes a telephone call requesting a return call and performs the acts prohibited under subdivision (a) or (b) upon receiving the return call. (*Amended by Stats 1990 ch 383 §1, eff. 1/1/91.*)

§653n. Two-way mirrors; installation or maintenance.

Any person who installs or who maintains after April 1, 1970, any two-way mirror permitting observation of any restroom, toilet, bathroom, washroom, shower, locker room, fitting room, motel room, or hotel room, is guilty of a misdemeanor.

This section does not apply to such areas (a) in state or local public penal, correctional, custodial, or medical institutions which are used by, or for the treatment of, persons who are committed or voluntarily confined to such institutions or voluntarily receive treatment therein; (b) in private custodial or medical institutions, which are used by, or for the treatment of, persons who are committed or voluntarily confined to such institutions or voluntarily receive treatment therein; (c) in public or private treatment facilities which are used by, or for the treatment of, persons who are committed or voluntarily confined to such facilities or voluntarily receive treatment therein; (d) in buildings operated by state or local law enforcement agencies; or (e) in public or private educational institutions.

"Two-way mirror" as used in this section means a mirror or other surface which permits any person on one side thereof to see through it under certain conditions of lighting, while any person on the other side thereof or other surface at that time can see only the usual mirror or other surface reflection.

§653o. Endangered species.

(a) It is unlawful to import into this state for commercial purposes, to possess with intent to sell, or to sell within the state, the dead body, or any part or product thereof, of any alligator, crocodile, polar bear, leopard, ocelot, tiger, cheetah, jaguar, sable antelope, wolf (Canis lupus), zebra, whale, cobra, python, sea turtle, colobus monkey, kangaroo, vicuna, sea otter, free-roaming feral horse, dolphin or porpoise (Delphinidae), Spanish lynx, or elephant.

Any person who violates any provision of this section is guilty of a misdemeanor and shall be subject to a fine of not less than one thousand dollars ($1,000) and not to exceed five thousand dollars ($5,000) or imprisonment in the county jail for not to exceed six months, or both such fine and imprisonment, for each violation.

(b) The prohibitions against importation for commercial purposes, possession with intent to sell, and sale of the species listed in this section are severable. A finding of the invalidity of any one or more prohibitions shall not affect the validity of any remaining prohibitions.

§653p. Intent to sell endangered species.

It is unlawful to possess with the intent to sell, or to sell, within the state, the dead body, or any part or product thereof, of any species or subspecies of any fish, bird, mammal, amphibian, reptile, mollusk, invertebrate, or plant, the importation of which is illegal under the Federal Endangered Species Act of 1973 (Title 16, United States Code Sec. 1531 et seq.) and subsequent amendments, or under the Marine Mammal Protection Act of 1972 (Title 16, United States Code Sec. 1361 et seq.), or which is listed in the Federal Register by the Secretary of the Interior pursuant to the above acts. The violation of any federal regulations adopted pursuant to the above acts shall also be deemed a violation of this section and shall be prosecuted by the appropriate state or local officials.

§653q. Sale of dead seal.

It is unlawful to import into this state for commercial purposes, to possess with intent to sell, or to sell within the state, the dead body, or any part or product thereof, of any seal.

Any person who violates any provision of this section is guilty of a misdemeanor and shall be subject to a fine of not less than one thousand dollars ($1,000) and not to exceed five thousand dollars ($5,000) or imprisonment in the county jail for not to exceed six months, or both such fine and imprisonment, for each violation.

§653r. Sale of particular endangered species; misdemeanor.

Notwithstanding the provisions of Section 3 of Chapter 1557 of the Statutes of 1970, it shall be unlawful to possess with intent to sell, or to sell, within this state, after June 1, 1972, the dead body, or any part or product thereof, of any fish, bird, amphibian, reptile, or mammal specified in Section 653o or 653p.

Violation of this section constitutes a misdemeanor.

§653s. Sale of sounds of live performances.

(a) Any person who transports or causes to be transported for monetary or other consideration within this state, any article containing sounds of a live performance with the knowledge that the sounds thereon have been recorded or mastered without the consent of the owner of the sounds of the live performance is guilty of a public offense punishable as provided in subdivision (g) or (h).

(b) As used in this section and Section 653u:

(1) "Live performance" means the recitation, rendering, or playing of a series of musical, spoken, or other sounds in any audible sequence thereof.

(2) "Article" means the original disc, wire, tape, film, phonograph record, or other recording device used to record or master the sounds of the live performance and any copy or reproduction thereof which duplicates, in whole or in part, the original.

(3) "Person" means any individual, partnership, partnership member or employee, corporation, association, or corporation or association employee, officer, or director.

(c) In the absence of a written agreement or operation of law to the contrary, the performer or performers of the sounds of a live performance shall be presumed to own the right to record or master those sounds.

(d) For purposes of this section, a person who is authorized to maintain custody and control over business records reflecting the consent of the owner to the recordation or master recording of a live performance shall be a proper witness in any proceeding regarding the issue of consent.

Any witness called pursuant to this section shall be subject to all rules of evidence relating to the competency of a witness to testify and the relevance and admissibility of the testimony offered.

(e) This section shall neither enlarge nor diminish the rights and remedies of parties to a recording or master recording which they might otherwise possess by law.

(f) This section shall not apply to persons engaged in radio or television broadcasting or cablecasting who record or fix the sounds of a live performance for, or in connection with, broadcast or cable transmission and related uses in educational television or radio programs, for archival purposes, or for news programs or purposes if the recordation or master recording is not commercially distributed independent of the broadcast or cablecast by or through the broadcasting or cablecasting entity to subscribers or the general public.

(g) Any person who has been convicted of a violation of subdivision (a), shall be punished by imprisonment in the county jail not to exceed one year, or by imprisonment in the state prison for two, three, or five years, or by a fine not to exceed two hundred fifty thousand dollars ($250,000), or by both, if the offense involves the transportation or causing to be transported of not less than 1,000 articles described in subdivision (a).

(h) Any person who has been convicted of any other violation of subdivision (a) not described in subdivision (g) shall be punished by imprisonment in the county jail not to exceed one year, or by a fine not to exceed twenty-five thousand dollars ($25,000), or both. A second or subsequent conviction under subdivision (a) not described in subdivision (g) shall be punished by imprisonment in the county jail not to exceed one year or in the state prison, or by a fine not

to exceed one hundred thousand dollars ($100,000), or by both.

(i) Every person who offers for sale or resale, or sells or resells, or causes the sale or resale, or rents, or possesses for these purposes, any article described in subdivision (a) with knowledge that the sounds thereon have been so recorded or mastered without the consent of the owner of the sounds of a live performance is guilty of a public offense.

(1) A violation of subdivision (i) involving not less than 100 of those articles shall be punishable by imprisonment in a county jail not to exceed one year or by a fine not to exceed ten thousand dollars ($10,000), or by both. A second or subsequent conviction for the conduct described in this paragraph shall be punishable by imprisonment in the county jail not to exceed one year or in the state prison, or by a fine not to exceed twenty-five thousand dollars ($25,000), or by both.

(2) A person who has been convicted of any violation of this subdivision not described in paragraph (1) shall be punished by imprisonment in the county jail not to exceed six months or by a fine not to exceed five thousand dollars ($5,000), or by both. A second conviction for the conduct described in this paragraph shall be punishable by imprisonment in the county jail not to exceed one year or by a fine not to exceed ten thousand dollars ($10,000), or by both. A third or subsequent conviction for the conduct described in this paragraph shall be punishable by imprisonment in the county jail not to exceed one year or in the state prison, or by a fine not to exceed twenty-five thousand dollars ($25,000), or by both. *(Amended by Stats 1988 ch 1257 §2, eff. 1/1/89.)*

§653t. Malicious interruption of emergency radio transmission.

(a) A person commits a public offense if the person knowingly and maliciously interrupts, disrupts, impedes, or otherwise interferes with the transmission of a communication over a citizen's band radio channel, the purpose of which communication is to inform or inquire about an emergency.

(b) In this section, "emergency" means a condition or circumstance in which an individual is or is reasonably believed by the person transmitting the communication to be in imminent danger of serious bodily injury, in which property is or is reasonably believed by the person transmitting the communication to be in imminent danger of extensive damage or destruction, or in which that injury or destruction has occurred and the person transmitting is attempting to summon assistance.

(c) A violation of this section is a misdemeanor punishable by a fine not to exceed one thousand dollars ($1,000) or by imprisonment in a county jail not to exceed six months, or both, unless, as a result of the commission of the offense, serious bodily injury or property loss in excess of ten thousand dollars ($10,000) occurs, in which event the offense is a felony.

§653u. Recording live performances with intent to sell.

(a) Any person who records or masters or causes to be recorded or mastered on any article with the intent to sell for commercial advantage or private financial gain, the sounds of a live performance with the knowledge that the sounds thereon have been recorded or mastered without the consent of the owner

© 1992 by J., B. & L. Gould
Printed in the U.S.A.   **EP**

of the sounds of the live performance is guilty of a public offense punishable as provided in subdivisions (d) and (e).

(b) In the absence of a written agreement or operation of law to the contrary, the performer or performers of the sounds of a live performance shall be presumed to own the right to record or master those sounds.

(c) For purposes of this section, a person who is authorized to maintain custody and control over business records reflecting the consent of the owner to the recordation or master recording of a live performance shall be a proper witness in any proceeding regarding the issue of consent.

Any witness called pursuant to this section shall be subject to all rules of evidence relating to the competency of a witness to testify and the relevance and admissibility of the testimony offered.

(d) Any person who has been convicted of a violation of subdivision (a) shall be punished by imprisonment in the county jail not to exceed one year, or by imprisonment in the state prison for two, three, or five years, or by a fine not to exceed two hundred fifty thousand dollars ($250,000), or by both, if the offense involves the recording, mastering, or causing to be recorded or mastered at least 1,000 articles described in subdivision (a).

(e) Any person who has been convicted of any other violation of subdivision (a) not described in subdivision (d), shall be punished by imprisonment in the county jail not to exceed one year, or by a fine not to exceed twenty-five thousand dollars ($25,000), or by both. A second or subsequent conviction under subdivision (a) not described in subdivision (d) shall be punished by imprisonment in the county jail not to exceed one year or in the state prison or by a fine not to exceed one hundred thousand dollars ($100,000), or by both. *(Amended by Stats 1988 ch 1257 §3, eff. 1/1/89.)*

§653v. Forfeiture and destruction of illegal recordings.

Whenever any person is convicted of any violation of Section 653h, 653s, 653u, or 653w the court, in its judgment of conviction, shall, in addition to the penalty therein prescribed, order the forfeiture and destruction or other disposition of all articles, including, but not limited to, phonograph records, discs, wires, tapes, films, or any other article upon which sounds or images can be recorded or stored, and any and all electronic, mechanical, or other devices for manufacturing, reproducing or assembling these articles, which were used in connection with, or which were part of, any violation of Section 653h, 653s, 653u, or 653w. *(Amended by Stats 1985 ch 364 §2.)*

§653w. Failure to disclose origin of recording.

(a) A person is guilty of failure to disclose the origin of a recording or audiovisual work when, for commercial advantage or private financial gain, he or she knowingly advertises or offers for sale or resale, or sells or resells, or causes the rental, sale or resale, or rents, or manufactures, or possesses for these purposes, any recording or audiovisual work, the outside cover box or jacket of which does not clearly and conspicuously disclose the actual true name and address of the manufacturer thereof and the name of the actual author, artist, performer, producer, programmer, or group. This section does not require the original manufacturer or authorized licensees of software producers to disclose the contributing authors or programmers.

As used in this section, "recording" means any tangible medium upon which information or sounds are recorded or otherwise stored, including any phonograph record, disc, tape, audio cassette, wire, film, or other medium on which information or sounds are recorded or otherwise stored, but does not include sounds accompanying a motion picture or other audiovisual work.

As used in this section, "audiovisual works" are the physical embodiment of works that consist of related images which are intrinsically intended to be shown by the use of machines or devices such as projectors, viewers, or electronic equipment, together with accompanying sounds, if any, regardless of the nature of the material objects such as films or tapes on which the works are embodied.

(b) Any person who has been convicted of a violation of subdivision (a) shall be punished as follows:

(1) If the offense involves the advertising, offer for sale or resale, selling, rental, manufacturing, or possession for these purposes, of at least 1,000 articles of an audio recording or 100 articles of an audiovisual work described in subdivision (a), shall be punished by imprisonment in the county jail not to exceed one year, or by imprisonment in the state prison for two, three, or five years, or by a fine not to exceed two hundred fifty thousand dollars ($250,000), or by both.

(2) Any other violation of subdivision (a) not described in paragraph (1), shall, upon a first offense, be punished by imprisonment in the county jail not to exceed one year, or by a fine not to exceed twenty-five thousand dollars ($25,000), or by both.

(3) A second or subsequent conviction under subdivision (a) not described in paragraph (1), shall be punished by imprisonment in the county jail not to exceed one year or in the state prison or by a fine not to exceed one hundred thousand dollars ($100,000), or by both. *(Amended by Stats 1990 ch 942 §1, eff. 1/1/91.)*

§653.1. Hot air balloons; prohibitions.

(a) No person shall sell or distribute any balloon which is constructed of electrically conductive material, and filled with a gas lighter than air without:

(1) Affixing an object of sufficient weight to the balloon or its appurtenance to counter the lift capability of the balloon.

(2) Affixing a statement on the balloon, or ensuring that a statement is so affixed, that warns the consumer about the risk if the balloon comes in contact with electrical power lines.

(3) A printed identification of the manufacturer of the balloon.

(b) No person shall sell or distribute any balloon filled with a gas lighter than air, which is attached to an electrically conductive string, tether, streamer, or other electrically conductive appurtenance.

(c) No person shall sell or distribute any balloon which is constructed of electrically conductive material and filled with a gas lighter than air, which, is attached to another balloon constructed of electrically conductive material and filled with a gas lighter than air.

(d) No person or group shall release, outdoors, balloons made of electrically conductive material and filled with a gas lighter than air, as part of a public or civic event, promotional activity, or product advertisement.

(e) Any person who violates subdivision (a), (b), (c), or (d) shall be guilty of an infraction punishable by a fine not exceeding one hundred dollars ($100). Any person who violates subdivision (a), (b), (c), or (d) who has been previously convicted twice of violating subdivision (a), (b), (c), or (d) shall be guilty of a misdemeanor.

(f) This section shall not apply to manned hot air balloons, or to balloons used in governmental or scientific research projects.

(g) Electrical corporations shall report to the Public Utilities Commission every other month, from January 1, 1991, until June 30, 1993, on electrical service disruptions caused by balloons constructed of electrically conductive material, including, but not limited to, the location of the service disruption, the composition of the balloon, and the extent of the disruption. The commission shall provide a copy of each electrical corporation's bimonthly report to a representative designated by the metallic balloon manufacturers and shall report the following by December 31, 1993, to the Legislature:

(1) The number of outages reported by each electrical corporation on a monthly basis.

(2) A comparison of the monthly outages reported pursuant to Chapter 1122 of the Statutes of 1988, with the monthly outages reported by each electrical corporation pursuant to this act, reflecting the numerical trend of the outages. *(Added by Stats 1990 ch 1559 §1, eff. 1/1/91.)*

§653.5 *Repealed by Stats 1988 ch 1199 §24, eff. 1/1/89.*

CHAPTER 3

IMMIGRATION MATTERS

§653.55. False information of immigration matter.

It is a misdemeanor for any person for compensation to knowingly make a false or misleading material statement or assertion of fact in the preparation of an immigration matter which statement or assertion is detrimentally relied upon by another. Such a misdemeanor is punishable by imprisonment in the county jail not exceeding six months, or by a fine not exceeding two thousand five hundred dollars ($2,500), or by both.

§653.56. Definitions.

For purposes of this chapter:

(a) "Compensation" means money, property, or anything else of value.

(b) "Immigration matter" means any proceeding, filing, or action affecting the immigration or citizenship status of any person which arises under immigration and naturalization law, executive order or presidential proclamation, or action of the United States Immigration and Naturalization Service, the United States Department of State or the United States Department of Labor.

(c) "Person" means any individual, firm, partnership, corporation, association, other organization, or any employee or agent thereof.

(d) "Preparation" means giving advice on an immigration matter and includes drafting an application, brief, document, petition or other paper, or completing a form provided by a federal or state agency in an immigration matter.

§653.57. Violations of chapter.

Any person violating the provisions of this chapter may be enjoined by any superior court of competent jurisdiction upon an action for injunction, brought by the Attorney General, or any district attorney, county counsel, city attorney, or city prosecutor in this state, and the superior court shall, after proof of violation, issue an injunction or other appropriate order restraining such conduct.

§653.58. Penalty for violation of injunction.

Any person who intentionally violates any injunction issued pursuant to Section 653.57 shall be liable for a civil penalty not to exceed two thousand five hundred dollars ($2,500) for each violation. Where the conduct constituting a violation is of a continuing nature, each day of such conduct is a separate and distinct violation.

§653.59. Violations; penalty.

Any person who violates any provision of this chapter shall be liable for a civil penalty not to exceed two thousand five hundred dollars ($2,500) for each violation, which shall be assessed and recovered in a civil action brought in the name of the people of the State of California by the Attorney General, or any district attorney, county counsel, city attorney, or city prosecutor in this state in any court of competent jurisdiction. If the civil action was brought by the Attorney General, one-half of the penalty collected shall be paid to the treasurer of the county in which the judgment was entered, and one-half to the State General Fund. If the civil action was brought by a district attorney or county counsel, the entire amount of the penalty collected shall be paid to the treasurer of the county in which the judgment was entered. If the civil action was brought by a city attorney or city prosecutor, one-half of the penalty shall be paid to the treasurer of the county in which the judgment was entered and one-half to the city.

The action may be brought upon the complaint of any person acting for the interests of itself, or members, or the general public.

§653.60. Damages for injury.

Any person injured by violation of this chapter may recover: (a) his actual damages or five hundred dollars ($500), whichever is greater; and (b) the costs of the suit, including reasonable attorney's fees.

§653.61. Cumulative remedies or penalties.

The remedies or penalties provided by this chapter are cumulative to each other and to the remedies or penalties available under all other laws of this state.

CHAPTER 4

CRIMES COMMITTED WHILE IN CUSTODY IN CORRECTIONAL FACILITIES

§653.75. Public offense crime committed while in local detention facility.

Any person who commits any public offense while in custody in any local detention facility, as defined in Section 6031.4, or any state prison, as defined in

© 1992 by J., B. & L. Gould
Printed in the U.S.A.   EP

Section 4504, is guilty of a crime. That crime shall be punished as provided in the section prescribing the punishment for that public offense. *(Added by Stats 1987 ch 1005 §1.)*

TITLE 16

GENERAL PROVISIONS

§654. Offenses punishable by different provisions.

An act or omission which is made punishable in different ways by different provisions of this code may be punished under either of such provisions, but in no case can it be punished under more than one; an acquittal or conviction and sentence under either one bars a prosecution for the same act or omission under any other.

§654.1. Uncertified highway carriers.

It shall be unlawful for any person, acting individually or as an officer or employee of a corporation, or as a member of a copartnership or as a commission agent or employee of another person, firm or corporation, to sell or offer for sale or, to negotiate, provide or arrange for, or to advertise or hold himself out as one who sells or offers for sale or negotiates, provides or arranges for transportation of a person or persons on an individual fare basis over the public highways of the State of California unless such transportation is to be furnished or provided solely by, and such sale is authorized by, a carrier having a valid and existing certificate of convenience and necessity, or other valid and existing permit from the Public Utilities Commission of the State of California, or from the Interstate Commerce Commission of the United States, authorizing the holder of such certificate or permit to provide such transportation.

§654.2. Uncertified highway carriers; exceptions.

The provisions of Section 654.1 of the Penal Code shall not apply to the selling, furnishing, or providing of transportation of any person or persons in any of the following circumstances:

(a) When no compensation is paid or to be paid, either directly or indirectly, for the transportation.

(b) For the furnishing or providing of transportation to or from work of employees engaged in farmwork on any farm of the State of California.

(c) For the furnishing or providing of transportation to and from work of employees of any nonprofit cooperative association, organized pursuant to any law of the State of California.

(d) For the transportation of persons wholly or substantially within the limits of a single municipality or of contiguous municipalities.

(e) For transportation of persons over a route wholly or partly within a national park or state park where the transportation is sold in conjunction with, or as part of, a rail trip or trip over a regularly operated motorbus transportation system or line.

(f) For the transportation of persons between home and work locations or of persons having a common work-related trip purpose in a vehicle having a seating capacity of 15 passengers or less, including the driver, which is used for the purpose of ridesharing, as defined in Section 522 of the Vehicle Code, when the ridesharing is incidental to another purpose of the driver. This exemption does not apply if the primary purpose for the transportation of those persons is to make a profit. "Profit," as used in this subdivision, does not include the recovery of the actual costs incurred in owning and operating a vanpool vehicle, as defined in Section 668 of the Vehicle Code.

§654.3. Unlawful sale of transportation, punishment.

Violation of Section 654.1 shall be a misdemeanor, and upon first conviction the punishment shall be a fine of not over five hundred dollars ($500), or imprisonment in jail for not over 90 days, or both such fine and imprisonment. Upon second conviction the punishment shall be imprisonment in jail for not less than 30 days and not more than 180 days. Upon a third or subsequent conviction the punishment shall be confinement in jail for not less than 90 days and not more than one year, and a person suffering three or more convictions shall not be eligible to probation, the provisions of any law to the contrary notwithstanding.

§655. Acts punishable under foreign law.

An act or omission declared punishable by this Code is not less so because it is also punishable under the laws of another State, Government, or country, unless the contrary is expressly declared.

§656. Foreign conviction or aquittal.

Whenever on the trial of an accused person it appears that upon a criminal prosecution under the laws of another State, Government, or country, founded upon the act or omission in respect to which he is on trial, he has been acquitted or convicted, it is a sufficient defense.

§657. Contempts, how punishable.

A criminal act is not the less punishable as a crime because it is also declared to be punishable as a contempt.

§658. Mitigation of punishment in certain cases.

When it appears, at the time of passing sentence upon a person convicted upon indictment, that such person has already paid a fine or suffered an imprisonment for the act of which he stands convicted, under an order adjudging it a contempt, the Court authorized to pass sentence may mitigate the punishment to be imposed, in its discretion.

§659. Aiding in misdemeanor.

Whenever an act is declared a misdemeanor, and no punishment for counseling or aiding in the commission of such act is expressly prescribed by law, every person who counsels or aids another in the commission of such act is guilty of a misdemeanor.

§660. Sending letters, when deemed complete.

In the various cases in which the sending of a letter is made criminal by this Code, the offense is deemed complete from the time when such letter is deposited in any Post Office or any other place, or delivered to any person, with intent that it shall be forwarded.

§661. Removal from office for violation or neglect of official duty by public officers.

In addition to the penalty affixed by express terms, to every neglect or violation of official duty on the part of public officers, State, county, city, or township, where it is not so expressly provided, they may, in the discretion of the Court, be removed from office.

§662. Omission to perform duty, when punishable.

No person is punishable for an omission to perform an act, where such act has been performed by another person acting in his behalf and competent by law to perform it.

§663. Attempts to commit crimes, when punishable.

Any person may be convicted of an attempt to commit a crime, although it appears on the trial that the crime intended or attempted was perpetrated by such person in pursuance of such attempt, unless the Court, in its discretion, discharges the jury and directs such person to be tried for such crime.

§664. Unsuccessful attempt to commit crime; punishment.

Every person who attempts to commit any crime, but fails, or is prevented or intercepted in the perpetration thereof, is punishable, where no provision is made by law for the punishment of such attempts, as follows:

1. If the offense so attempted is punishable by imprisonment in the state prison, the person guilty of such attempt is punishable by imprisonment in the state prison for one-half the term of imprisonment prescribed upon a conviction of the offense so attempted; provided, however, that if the crime attempted is willful, deliberate, and premeditated murder, as defined in Section 189, the person guilty of that attempt shall be punishable by imprisonment in the state prison for life with the possibility of parole; provided, further, that if the crime attempted is any other one in which the maximum sentence is life imprisonment or death the person guilty of the attempt shall be punishable by imprisonment in the state prison for a term of five, seven, or nine years. The additional term provided in this section for attempted willful, deliberate, and premeditated murder shall not be imposed unless the fact that the attempted murder was willful, deliberate, and premeditated is charged in the accusatory pleading and admitted or found to be true by the trier of fact.

2. If the offense so attempted is punishable by imprisonment in a county jail, the person guilty of such attempt is punishable by imprisonment in a county jail for a term not exceeding one-half the term of imprisonment prescribed upon a conviction of the offense so attempted.

3. If the offense so attempted is punishable by a fine, the offender convicted of that attempt is punishable by a fine not exceeding one-half the largest fine which may be imposed upon a conviction of the offense so attempted.

4. If a crime is divided into degrees, an attempt to commit the crime may be of any such degree, and the punishment for the attempt shall be determined as provided by this section. *(Amended by Stats 1986 ch 519 §2.)*

§665. Restrictions upon the preceding sections.

Sections 663 and 664 do not protect a person who, in attempting unsuccessfully to commit a crime, accomplishes the commission of another and different crime, whether greater or less in guilt, from suffering the punishment prescribed by law for the crime committed. *(Amended by Stats 1987 ch 828 §45.)*

§666. Petit theft; punishment.

Every person who, having been convicted of petit theft, grand theft, auto theft under Section 10851 of the Vehicle Code, burglary, robbery, or a felony violation of Section 496 and having served a term therefor in any penal institution or having been imprisoned therein as a condition of probation for such offense, is subsequently convicted of petit theft, then the person convicted of that subsequent offense is punishable by imprisonment in the county jail not exceeding one year, or in the state prison. *(Amended by Stats 1988 ch 831 §1, eff. 1/1/89.)*

§666.5. Punishment for second conviction.

(a) Every person who, having been previously convicted of felony vehicle theft under Section 10851 of the Vehicle Code, or felony grand theft involving an automobile in violation of subdivision (3) of Section 487 or of Section 487h, regardless of whether or not the person actually served a prior prison term for those offenses, is subsequently convicted of any of these offenses shall be punishable by imprisonment in the state prison for three, four, or five years, or a fine of ten thousand dollars ($10,000), or both the fine and the imprisonment.

(b) The existence of any fact which would bring a person under subdivision (a) shall be alleged in the information or indictment and either admitted by the defendant in open court, or found to be true by the jury trying the issue of guilt or by the court where guilt is established by plea of guilty or nolo contendere or by trial by the court sitting without a jury.

(c) This section shall remain in effect only until January 1, 1993, and as of that date is repealed, unless a later enacted statute, which is enacted before January 1, 1993, deletes or extends that date. *(Amended by Stats 1989 ch 930 §9, eff. 1/1/90 only until 1/1/93. See other section 666.5 below.)*

§666.5. Punishment for second conviction.

(a) Every person who, having been previously convicted of felony vehicle theft under Section 10851 of the Vehicle Code, or felony grand theft involving an automobile in violation of subdivision (3) of Section 487, regardless of whether or not the person actually served a prior prison term for those offenses, is subsequently convicted of any of these offenses shall be punishable by imprisonment in the state prison for two, three, or four years, or a fine of ten thousand dollars ($10,000), or both the fine and the imprisonment.

(b) The existence of any fact which would bring a person under subdivision (a) shall be alleged in the information or indictment and either admitted by the defendant in open court, or found to be true by the jury trying the issue of guilt or by the court where guilt is established by plea of guilty or nolo contendere or by trial by the court sitting without a jury. *(Added by Stats 1989 ch 930 §9.1, eff. 1/1/93. See other section 666.5 above.)*

§666.7. Prior conviction of receiving stolen property; penalty.

(a) Every person who, having been twice previously convicted of receiving stolen property in violation of subdivision (1) of Section 496, involving any

© 1992 by J., B. & L. Gould
Printed in the U.S.A.   **EP**

vehicle, trailer, or vessel, regardless of whether or not the person actually served a prior prison term for those offenses, is subsequently convicted of that offense involving any vehicle, trailer, or vessel, shall be punishable by imprisonment in the state prison for two, three, or four years, or a fine of ten thousand dollars ($10,000), or both the fine and imprisonment.

(b) The existence of any fact which would bring a person under subdivision (a) shall be alleged in the information or indictment and either admitted by the defendant in open court, or found to be true by the jury trying the issue of guilt or by the court where guilt is established by plea of guilty or nolo contendere or by trial by the court sitting without a jury.

(c) This section shall remain in effect only until January 1, 1993, and as of that date is repealed, unless a later enacted statute, which is enacted before January 1, 1993, deletes or extends that date. *(Added by Stats 1989 ch 930 §10, eff. 1/1/90 only until 1/1/93.)*

§667. Habitual criminals.

(a) In compliance with subdivision (b) of Section 1385, any person convicted of a serious felony who previously has been convicted of a serious felony in this state or of any offense committed in another jurisdiction which includes all of the elements of any serious felony, shall receive, in addition to the sentence imposed by the court for the present offense, a five-year enhancement for each such prior conviction on charges brought and tried separately. The terms of the present offense and each enhancement shall run consecutively.

(b) This section shall not be applied when the punishment imposed under other provisions of law would result in a longer term of imprisonment. There is no requirement of prior incarceration or commitment for this section to apply.

(c) The Legislature may increase the length of the enhancement of sentence provided in this section by a statute passed by majority vote of each house thereof.

(d) As used in this section "serious felony" means a serious felony listed in subdivision (c) of Section 1192.7.

(e) Subdivision (a) shall not apply to a person convicted of selling, furnishing, administering, or giving, or offering to sell, furnish, administer, or give to a minor any methamphetamine-related drug or any precursors of methamphetamine unless the prior conviction was for a serious felony described in subparagraph (24) of subdivision (c) of Section 1192.7.

(f) The provisions of this section shall not be amended by the Legislature except by statute passed in each house by rollcall vote entered in the journal, two-thirds of the membership concurring, or by a statute that becomes effective only when approved by the electors. *(Amended by Stats 1989 ch 1043 §1, eff. 1/1/90.)*

§667.5. Enhancement of prison terms for new offenses because of prior prison terms.

Enhancement of prison terms for new offenses because of prior prison terms shall be imposed as follows:

(a) Where one of the new offenses is one of the violent felonies specified in subdivision (c), in addition and consecutive to any other prison terms therefor, the court shall impose a three-year term for each prior separate prison term served by the defendant where the prior was one of the violent felonies specified in

subdivision (c). However, no additional term shall be imposed under this subdivision for any prison term served prior to a period of 10 years in which the defendant remained free of both prison custody and the commission of an offense which results in a felony conviction.

(b) Except where subdivision (a) applies, where the new offense is any felony for which a prison sentence is imposed, in addition and consecutive to any other prison terms therefor, the court shall impose a one-year term for each prior separate prison term served for any felony; provided that no additional term shall be imposed under this subdivision for any prison term served prior to a period of five years in which the defendant remained free of both prison custody and the commission of an offense which results in a felony conviction.

(c) For the purpose of this section, "violent felony" shall mean any of the following:

(1) Murder or voluntary manslaughter.

(2) Mayhem.

(3) Rape as defined in subdivision (2) of Section 261.

(4) Sodomy by force, violence, duress, menace, or fear of immediate and unlawful bodily injury on the victim or another person.

(5) Oral copulation by force, violence, duress, menace, or fear of immediate and unlawful bodily injury on the victim or another person.

(6) Lewd acts on a child under the age of 14 years as defined in Section 288.

(7) Any felony punishable by death or imprisonment in the state prison for life.

(8) Any felony in which the defendant inflicts great bodily injury on any person other than an accomplice which has been charged and proved as provided for in Section 12022.7 or 12022.9 on or after July 1, 1977, or as specified prior to July 1, 1977, in Sections 213, 264, and 461, or any felony in which the defendant uses a firearm which use has been charged and proved as provided in Section 12022.5 or 12022.55.

(9) Any robbery perpetrated in an inhabited dwelling house, vessel, as defined in Section 21 of the Harbors and Navigation Code, which is inhabited and designed for habitation, inhabited trailer coach, as defined in the Vehicle Code, or in the inhabited portion of any other building, wherein it is charged and proved that the defendant personally used a deadly or dangerous weapon, as provided in subdivision (b) of Section 12022, in the commission of that robbery.

(10) Arson, in violation of subdivision (a) of Section 451.

(11) The offense defined in subdivision (a) of Section 289 where the act is accomplished against the victim's will by force, violence, duress, menace, or fear of immediate and unlawful bodily injury on the victim or another person.

(12) Attempted murder.

(13) A violation of Section 12308.

(14) Kidnapping, in violation of subdivision (b) of Section 207.

(15) Continuous sexual abuse of a child, in violation of Section 288.5.

The Legislature finds and declares that these specified crimes merit special consideration when imposing a sentence to display society's condemnation for such extraordinary crimes of violence against the person.

(d) For the purposes of this section the defendant shall be deemed to remain in prison custody for an offense until the official discharge from custody or until release on parole whichever first occurs including any time during which the defendant remains subject to reimprisonment for escape from custody or is reimprisoned on revocation of parole. The additional penalties provided for prior prison terms shall not be imposed unless they are charged and admitted or found true in the action for the new offense.

(e) The additional penalties provided for prior prison terms shall not be imposed for any felony for which the defendant did not serve a prior separate term in state prison.

(f) A prior conviction of a felony shall include a conviction in another jurisdiction for an offense which if committed in California is punishable by imprisonment in state prison if the defendant served one year or more in prison for the offense in the other jurisdiction. A prior conviction of a particular felony shall include a conviction in another jurisdiction for an offense which includes all of the elements of the particular felony as defined under California law if the defendant served one year or more in prison for the offense in the other jurisdiction.

(g) A prior separate prison term for the purposes of this section shall mean a continuous completed period of prison incarceration imposed for the particular offense alone or in combination with concurrent or consecutive sentences for other crimes, including any reimprisonment on revocation of parole which is not accompanied by a new commitment to prison, and including any reimprisonment after an escape from incarceration.

(h) Serving a prison term includes any confinement time in any state prison or federal penal institution as punishment for commission of an offense, including confinement in a hospital or other institution or facility credited as service of prison time in the jurisdiction of the confinement.

(i) For the purposes of this section, a commitment to the State Department of Health as a mentally disordered sex offender following a conviction of a felony, which commitment exceeds one year in duration, shall be deemed a prior prison term.

(j) For the purposes of this section, when a person subject to the custody, control, and discipline of the Director of Corrections is incarcerated at a facility operated by the Youth Authority, that incarceration shall be deemed to be a term served in state prison.

(k) Notwithstanding subdivisions (d) and (g) or any other provision of law, where one of the new offenses is committed while the defendant is temporarily removed from prison pursuant to Section 2690 or while the defendant is transferred to a community facility pursuant to Section 3416, 6253, or 6263, or while the defendant is on furlough pursuant to Section 6254, the defendant shall be subject to the full enhancements provided for in this section.

This subdivision shall not apply when a full, separate, and consecutive term is imposed pursuant to any other provision of law. *(Amended by Stats 1991 ch 451 §1, eff. 1/1/92.)*

§667.51. Enhancement of sentence for prior conviction for lewd act with child.

(a) Any person who is found guilty of violating Section 288 shall receive a five-year enhancement for a prior conviction of an offense listed in subdivision (b)

provided that no additional term shall be imposed under this subdivision for any prison term served prior to a period of 10 years in which the defendant remained free of both prison custody and the commission of an offense which results in a felony conviction.

(b) Section 261, 264.1, 285, 286, 288, 288a, 288.5, or 289.

(c) Section 261, 264.1, 286, 288, 288a, 288.5, or 289.

(d) A violation of Section 288 by a person who has been previously convicted two or more times of an offense listed in subdivision (c) is punishable as a felony by imprisonment in the state prison for 15 years to life. However, if the two or more prior convictions were for violations of Section 288, this subdivision is applicable only if the current violation or at least one of the prior convictions is for an offense other than a violation of subdivision (a) of Section 288. For purposes of this subdivision, a prior conviction is required to have been for charges brought and tried separately. The provisions of Article 2.5 (commencing with Section 2930) of Chapter 7 of Title 1 of Part 3 shall apply to reduce any minimum term in a state prison imposed pursuant to this section, but such person shall not otherwise be released on parole prior to such time. *(Amended by Stats 1989 ch 1402 §6, eff. 1/1/90.)*

§667.6. Enhancement of prison term for prior conviction for sex offenses.

(a) Any person who is found guilty of violating subdivision (2) or (3) of Section 261, Section 264.1, subdivision (b) of Section 288, Section 288.5, Section 289, or of committing sodomy or oral copulation in violation of Section 286 or 288a by force, violence, duress, menace, or fear of immediate and unlawful bodily injury on the victim or another person who has been convicted previously of any of those offenses shall receive a five-year enhancement for each of those prior convictions provided that no enhancement shall be imposed under this subdivision for any conviction occurring prior to a period of 10 years in which the person remained free of both prison custody and the commission of an offense which results in a felony conviction. In addition to the five-year enhancement imposed under this subdivision, the court may also impose a fine not to exceed twenty thousand dollars ($20,000) for anyone sentenced under these provisions. The fine imposed and collected pursuant to this subdivision shall be deposited in the Victim-Witness Assistance Fund to be available for appropriation to fund child sexual exploitation and child sexual abuse victim counseling centers and prevention programs established pursuant to Section 13837.

(b) Any person convicted of an offense specified in subdivision (a) who has served two or more prior prison terms as defined in Section 667.5 for any offense specified in subdivision (a), shall receive a 10-year enhancement for each of those prior terms provided that no additional enhancement shall be imposed under this subdivision for any prison term served prior to a period of 10 years in which the person remained free of both prison custody and the commission of an offense which results in a felony conviction. In addition to the 10-year enhancement imposed under this subdivision, the court may also impose a fine not to exceed twenty thousand dollars ($20,000) for any person sentenced under this subdivision. The fine imposed and collected pursuant to this subdivision shall be deposited in the Victim-Witness As-

© 1992 by J., B. & L. Gould
Printed in the U.S.A.   EP

sistance Fund to be available for appropriation to fund child sexual exploitation and child sexual abuse victim counseling centers and prevention programs established pursuant to Section 13837.

(c) In lieu of the term provided in Section 1170.1, a full, separate, and consecutive term may be imposed for each violation of Section 220, other than an assault with intent to commit mayhem, provided the person has been convicted previously of violating Section 220 for an offense other than an assault with intent to commit mayhem, subdivision (2) or (3) of Section 261, Section 264.1, subdivision (b) of Section 288, Section 288.5, Section 289, or of committing sodomy or oral copulation in violation of Section 286 or 288a by force, violence, duress, menace, or fear of immediate and unlawful bodily injury on the victim or another person whether or not the crimes were committed during a single transaction. If the term is imposed consecutively pursuant to this subdivision, it shall be served consecutively to any other term of imprisonment, and shall commence from the time the person would otherwise have been released from imprisonment. The term shall not be included in any determination pursuant to Section 1170.1. Any other term imposed subsequent to that term shall not be merged therein but shall commence at the time the person would otherwise have been released from prison.

(d) A full, separate, and consecutive term shall be served for each violation of Section 220, other than an assault with intent to commit mayhem, provided the person has been convicted previously of violating Section 220 for an offense other than an assault with intent to commit mayhem, subdivision (2) or (3) of Section 261, Section 264.1, subdivision (b) of Section 288, Section 289, or of committing sodomy or oral copulation in violation of Section 286 or 288a by force, violence, duress, menace, or fear of immediate and unlawful bodily injury on the victim or another person if the crimes involve separate victims or involve the same victim on separate occasions.

In determining whether crimes against a single victim were committed on separate occasions under this subdivision, the court shall consider whether, between the commission of one sex crime and another, the defendant had a reasonable opportunity to reflect upon his or her actions and nevertheless resumed sexually assaultive behavior. Neither the duration of time between crimes, nor whether or not the defendant lost or abandoned his or her opportunity to attack, shall be, in and of itself, determinative on the issue of whether the crimes in question occurred on separate occasions.

The term shall be served consecutively to any other term of imprisonment, and shall commence from the time the person would otherwise have been released from imprisonment. The term shall not be included in any determination pursuant to Section 1170.1. Any other term imposed subsequent to that term shall not be merged therein but shall commence at the time the person would otherwise have been released from prison.

(e) If the court orders a fine to be imposed pursuant to subdivision (a) or (b), the actual administrative cost of collecting that fine, not to exceed 2 percent of the total amount paid, may be paid into the general fund of the county treasury for the use and benefit of the county. (*Amended by Stats 1989 ch 1402 §7, eff. 1/1/90.*)

§667.7. Habitual offender.

(a) Any person convicted of a felony in which the person inflicted great bodily injury as provided in Section 12022.7, or personally used force which was likely to produce great bodily injury, who has served two or more separate prison terms as defined in Section 667.5 for the crime of murder; attempted murder; voluntary manslaughter; mayhem; rape by force, violence, or fear of immediate and unlawful bodily injury on the victim or another person; oral copulation by force, violence, duress, menace or fear of immediate and unlawful bodily injury on the victim or another person; sodomy by force, violence, duress, menace or fear of immediate and unlawful bodily injury on the victim or another person; lewd acts on a child under the age of 14 years by use of force, violence, duress, menace or fear of immediate and unlawful bodily injury on the victim or another person; a violation of subdivision (a) of Section 289 where the act is accomplished against the victim's will by means of force, violence, duress, menace, or fear of immediate and unlawful bodily injury on the victim or another person; kidnapping for ransom, extortion, or robbery; robbery involving the use of force or a deadly weapon; assault with intent to commit murder; assault with a deadly weapon; assault with a force likely to produce great bodily injury; assault with intent to commit rape, sodomy, oral copulation, penetration of a vaginal or anal opening in violation of Section 289, or lewd and lascivious acts on a child; arson of a structure; escape or attempted escape by an inmate with force or violence in violation of subdivision (a) of Section 4530, or of Section 4532; exploding a device with intent to murder in violation of Section 12308; exploding a destructive device which causes bodily injury in violation of Section 12309, or mayhem or great bodily injury in violation of Section 12310; exploding a destructive device with intent to injure, intimidate, or terrify, in violation of Section 12303.3; any felony in which the person inflicted great bodily injury as provided in Section 12022.7; or any felony punishable by death or life imprisonment with or without the possibility of parole is a habitual offender and shall be punished as follows:

(1) A person who served two prior separate prison terms shall be punished by imprisonment in the state prison for life and shall not be eligible for release on parole for 20 years, or the term determined by the court pursuant to Section 1170 for the underlying conviction, including any enhancement applicable under Chapter 4.5 (commencing with Section 1170) of Title 7 of Part 2, or any period prescribed by Section 190 or 3046, whichever is greatest. The provisions of Article 2.5 (commencing with Section 2930) of Chapter 7 of Title 1 of Part 3 shall apply to reduce any minimum term in a state prison imposed pursuant to this section, but the person shall not otherwise be released on parole prior to that time.

(2) Any person convicted of such a felony who has served three or more prior separate prison terms, as defined in Section 667.5, for the crimes specified in subdivision (a) of this section shall be punished by imprisonment in the state prison for life without the possibility of parole.

(b) This section shall not prevent the imposition of the punishment of death or imprisonment for life without the possibility of parole. No prior prison term shall be used for this determination which was served prior to a period of 10 years in which the person remained free of both prison custody and the commission of an offense which results in a felony conviction. As used in this section, a commitment to the Department of the Youth Authority after conviction for a felony shall constitute a prior prison term. The term imposed under this section shall be imposed only if the prior prison terms are alleged under this section in the accusatory pleading, and either admitted by the defendant in open court, or found to be true by the jury trying the issue of guilt or by the court where guilt is established by a plea of guilty or nolo contendere or by a trial by the court sitting without a jury. *(Amended by Stats 1987 ch 56 §123.)*

§667.75. Punishment for drug offenses involving minors.

Any person convicted of a violation of Section 11353, 11353.5, 11361, 11380, or 11380.5 of the Health and Safety Code who has previously served two or more prior separate prison terms, as defined in Section 667.5, for a violation of Section 11353, 11353.5, 11361, 11380, or 11380.5 of the Health and Safety Code, may be punished by imprisonment in the state prison for life and shall not be eligible for release on parole for 17 years, or the term determined by the court pursuant to Section 1170 for the underlying conviction, including any enhancement applicable under Chapter 4.5 (commencing with Section 1170) of Title 7 of Part 2, whichever is greatest. The provisions of Article 2.5 (commencing with Section 2930) of Chapter 7 of Title 1 of Part 3 shall apply to reduce any minimum term in a state prison imposed pursuant to this section, but the person shall not otherwise be released on parole prior to that time. No prior prison term shall be used for this determination which was served prior to a period of 10 years in which the person remained free of both prison custody and the commission of an offense which results in a felony conviction. As used in this section, a commitment to the Department of the Youth Authority after conviction for a felony shall constitute a prior prison term. The term imposed under this section shall be imposed only if the prior prison terms are alleged under this section in the accusatory pleading, and either admitted by the defendant in open court, or found to be true by the jury trying the issue of guilt or by the court where guilt is established by a plea of guilty or nolo contendere or by a trial by the court sitting without a jury. *(Added by Stats 1987 ch 729 §1.)*

§667.8. Enhancement of prison term for kidnapping victims to commit felony sexual offenses.

(a) Except as provided in subdivision (b), any person convicted of a felony violation of Section 261, 264.1, 286, 288a, or 289 who, for the purpose of committing that sexual offense, kidnapped the victim in violation of Section 207, shall be punished by an additional term of three years.

(b) Any person convicted of a felony violation of subdivision (c) of Section 286, Section 288, or subdivision (c) of Section 288a who, for the purpose of committing that sexual offense, kidnapped the victim, who was under the age of 14 years at the time of the offense, in violation of Section 207, shall be punished by an additional term of nine years. This subdivision is not applicable to conduct proscribed by Section 277, 278, or 278.5. *(Amended by Stats 1986 ch 249 §8.)*

§667.85. Prison term for kidnapping child under age of 14 years.

Any person convicted of a violation of Section 207, who kidnapped or carried away any child under the age of 14 years with the intent to permanently deprive the parent or legal guardian custody of that child, shall be punished by an additional term of five years. *(Added by Stats 1985 ch 1384 §1.)*

§667.9. Crimes against elderly, disabled persons, or infants.

(a) Any person who has a prior conviction for any of the offenses listed in subdivision (b), and who commits one or more of the crimes listed in subdivision (b) against a person who is 65 years of age or older, or against a person who is blind, a paraplegic, or a quadriplegic, or against a person who is under the age of 14 years, and that disability or condition is known or reasonably should be known to the person committing the crime, shall receive a two-year enhancement for each violation in addition to the sentence provided under Section 667.

(b) Subdivision (a) applies to the following crimes:

(1) Robbery, in violation of Section 211.

(2) Kidnapping, in violation of Section 207.

(3) Kidnapping for ransom, extortion, or robbery, in violation of Section 209.

(4) Rape by force, violence, or fear of immediate and unlawful bodily injury on the victim or another person in violation of subdivision (2) of Section 261.

(5) Sodomy or oral copulation by force, violence, duress, menace, or fear of immediate and unlawful bodily injury on the victim or another person in violation of Section 286 or 288a.

(6) Mayhem, as defined in Section 203.

(7) Burglary of the first degree, as defined in Section 460.

(c) The existence of any fact which would bring a person under subdivision (a) shall be alleged in the information or indictment and either admitted by the defendant in open court, or found to be true by the jury trying the issue of guilt or by the court where guilt is established by plea of guilty or nolo contendere or by trial by the court sitting without a jury. *(Amended by Stats 1987 ch 1462 §1.)*

§667.10. Enhancement of prison sentence for prior convictions for crimes against elderly, disabled or infants.

(a) Any person who has a prior conviction of the offense set forth in Section 289 and who commits that crime against a person who is 65 years of age or older, or against a person who is blind, a paraplegic, or a quadriplegic, or against a person who is under the age of 14 years, and that disability or condition is known or reasonably should be known to the person committing the crime, shall receive a two-year enhancement for each violation in addition to the sentence provided under Section 289.

(b) The existence of any fact which would bring a person under subdivision (a) shall be alleged in the information or indictment and either admitted by the defendant in open court, or found to be true by the jury trying the issue of guilt or by the court where guilt is established by plea of guilty or nolo contendere or by trial by the court sitting without a jury. *(Added by Stats 1985 ch 1086 §3.)*

© 1992 by J., B. & L. Gould
Printed in the U.S.A.   **EP**

§668. Prior conviction in another jurisdiction.

Every person who has been convicted in any other state, government, country, or jurisdiction of an offense for which, if committed within this state, such person could have been punished under the laws of this state by imprisonment in a state prison, is punishable for any subsequent crime committed within this state in the manner prescribed by law and to the same extent as if such prior conviction had taken place in a court of this state.

§669. Conviction of multiple offenses.

When any person is convicted of two or more crimes, whether in the same proceeding or court or in different proceedings or courts, and whether by judgment rendered by the same judge or by different judges, the second or other subsequent judgment upon which sentence is ordered to be executed shall direct whether the terms of imprisonment or any of them to which he is sentenced shall run concurrently or consecutively; life sentences, whether with or without the possibility of parole, may be imposed to run consecutively with one another or with any other term of imprisonment for a felony conviction. Whenever a person is committed to prison on a life sentence which is ordered to run consecutive to any determinate term of imprisonment imposed pursuant to Sections 1170, 1170.1, 667, 667.5, 12022, 12022.2, 12022.4, 12022.5, 12022.55, 12022.6, 12022.7, 12022.75, and 12022.9, the determinate term of imprisonment shall be served first and no part thereof shall be credited toward the person's eligibility for parole as calculated pursuant to Section 3046 or pursuant to any other section of law that establishes a minimum period of confinement under the life sentence before eligibility for parole.

In the event that the court at the time of pronouncing the second or other judgment upon such person had no knowledge of a prior existing judgment or judgments, or having knowledge, fails to determine how the terms of imprisonment shall run in relation to each other, then, upon such failure so to determine, or upon such prior judgment or judgments being brought to the attention of the court at any time prior to the expiration of 60 days from and after the actual commencement of imprisonment upon the second or other subsequent judgments, the court shall, in the absence of the defendant and within 60 days of such notice, determine how the term of imprisonment upon said second or other subsequent judgment shall run with reference to the prior incompleted term or terms of imprisonment. Upon the failure of the court so to determine how the terms of imprisonment on the second or subsequent judgment shall run, the term of imprisonment on the second or subsequent judgment shall run concurrently.

The Department of Corrections shall advise the court pronouncing the second or other subsequent judgment of the existence of all prior judgments against the defendant, the terms of imprisonment upon which have not been completely served. *(Amended by Stats 1988 ch 1484 §2, eff. 1/1/89.)*

§670. Natural disaster repair fraud; penalties.

(a) Any person who violates Section 7158 or 7159 of, or subdivision (b), (c), (d), or (e) of Section 7161 of, the Business and Professions Code or Section 470, 484, 487, or 532 of this code as part of a plan or scheme to defraud an owner or lessee of a residential or non-residential structure in connection with the offer or performance of repairs to the structure for damage caused by a natural disaster specified in subdivision (b), shall be subject to the penalties and enhancements specified in subdivision (c) and (d). The existence of any fact which would bring a person under this section shall be alleged in the information or indictment and either admitted by the defendant in open court, or found to be true by the jury trying the issue of guilt or by the court where guilt is established by a plead of guilty or nolo contendere or by trial by the court sitting without a jury.

(b) This section applies to natural disasters for which a state of emergency is proclaimed by the Governor pursuant to Section 8625 of the Government Code or for which an emergency or major disaster is declared by the President of the United States.

(c) The maximum or prescribed amounts of fines for offenses subject to this section shall be doubled. If the person has been previously convicted of a felony offense specified in subdivision (a), the person shall receive a one-year enhancement in addition to, and to run consecutively to, the term of imprisonment for any felony otherwise prescribed by this subdivision.

(d) Additionally, the court shall order any person sentenced pursuant to this section to make full restitution to the victim or to make restitution to the victim based on the person's ability to pay, as defined in subdivision (b) of Section 1203.1b. The payment of the restitution ordered by the court pursuant to this subdivision shall be made a condition of any probation granted by the court for an offense punishable under this section. Notwithstanding any other provision of law, the period of probation shall be at least five years or until full restitution is made to the victim, whichever first occurs.

*(f) Notwithstanding any other provision of law, the prosecuting agency shall be entitled to recover its costs of investigation and prosecution form any fines imposed for a conviction under this section. *(Added by Stats 1990 1st extra. ch 36 §4, eff. 9/24/90.)*
So in original. No subd. (e) enacted.

§672. Crime for which no fine prescribed.

Upon a conviction for any crime punishable by imprisonment in any jail or prison, in relation to which no fine is herein prescribed, the court may impose a fine on the offender not exceeding one thousand dollars ($1,000) in cases of misdemeanors or ten thousand dollars ($10,000) in cases of felonies, in addition to the imprisonment prescribed.

§673. Cruel or unusual punishments.

It shall be unlawful to use in the reformatories, institutions, jails, state hospitals or any other state, county, or city institution any cruel, corporal or unusual punishment or to inflict any treatment or allow any lack of care whatever which would injure or impair the health of the prisoner, inmate, or person confined; and punishment by the use of the strait jacket, gag, thumbscrew, shower bath or the tricing up of a prisoner, inmate or person confined is hereby prohibited. Any person who violates the provisions of this section or who aids, abets, or attempts in any way to contribute to the violation of this section shall be guilty of a misdemeanor.

© 1992 by J., B. & L. Gould
Printed in the U.S.A. **EP**

§674. Additional penalties for day care facility providers.

Any person who is a primary care provider in a day care facility and who is convicted of a felony violation of Section 261, 285, 286, 288, 288a, or 289, where the victim of the crime was a minor entrusted to his or her care by the minor's parent or guardian, a court, any public agency charged with the provision of social services, or a probation department, may be punished by an additional term of two years. If the crime was committed while voluntarily acting in concert with another, the person so convicted may be punished by an additional term of three years. The enhancements authorized by this section may be imposed in addition to any other required or authorized enhancement. *(Added by Stats 1985 ch 1010 §1.)*

§678. Valuation of property for grade of crime.

Whenever in this code the character or grade of an offense, or its punishment, is made to depend upon the value of property, such value shall be estimated exclusively in lawful money of the United States.

TITLE 17

RIGHTS OF VICTIMS AND WITNESSES OF CRIME
(Added by Stats 1986 ch 1427 §1.)

§679. Legislative intent.

In recognition of the civil and moral duty of victims and witnesses of crime to fully and voluntarily cooperate with law enforcement and prosecutorial agencies, and in further recognition of the continuing importance of this citizen cooperation to state and local law enforcement efforts and the general effectiveness and well-being of the criminal justice system of this state, the Legislature declares its intent, in the enactment of this title, to ensure that all victims and witnesses of crime are treated with dignity, respect, courtesy, and sensitivity. It is the further intent that the rights enumerated in Section 679.02 relating to victims and witnesses of crime are honored and protected by law enforcement agencies, prosecutors, and judges in a manner no less vigorous than the protections afforded criminal defendants. It is the intent of the Legislature to add to Section 679.02 references to new rights as or as soon after they are created. The failure to enumerate in that section a right which is enumerated elsewhere in the law shall not be deemed to diminish the importance or enforceability of that right. *(Added by Stats 1986 ch 1427 §1.)*

§679.01. Definitions.

As used in this title, the following definitions shall control:

(a) "Crime" means an act committed in this state which, if committed by a competent adult, would constitute a misdemeanor or felony.

(b) "Victim" means a person against whom a crime has been committed.

(c) "Witness" means any person who has been or is expected to testify for the prosecution, or who, by reason of having relevant information, is subject to call or likely to be called as a witness for the prosecution, whether or not any action or proceeding has yet been commenced. *(Added by Stats 1986 ch 1427 §1.)*

§679.02. Statutory rights of victims and witnesses.

(a) The following are hereby established as the statutory rights of victims and witnesses of crimes:

(1) To be notified as soon as feasible that a court proceeding to which he or she has been subpoenaed as a witness will not proceed as scheduled, provided the prosecuting attorney determines that the witness' attendance is not required.

(2) Upon request of the victim or a witness, to be informed by the prosecuting attorney of the final disposition of the case, as provided by Section 11116.10.

(3) For the victim, the victim's parents or guardian if the victim is a minor, or the next of kin of the victim if the victim has died, to be notified of all sentencing proceedings, and of the right to appear, to reasonably express his or her views, and to have the court consider his or her statements, as provided by Section 1191.1.

(4) For the victim, the victim's parents or guardian if the victim is a minor, or the next of kin of the victim if the victim has died, to be notified of all juvenile disposition hearings in which the alleged act would have been a felony if committed by an adult, and of the right to attend and to express his or her views, as provided by Section 656.2 of the Welfare and Institutions Code.

(5) Upon request by the victim or the next of kin of the victim if the victim has died, to be notified of any parole eligibility hearing and of the right to appear, to reasonably express his or her views, and to have his or her statements considered, as provided by Section 3043 of this code and by Section 1767 of the Welfare and Institutions Code.

(6) Upon request by the victim or the next of kin of the victim if the crime was a homicide, to be notified of an inmate's placement in a reentry or work furlough program, or notified of the inmate's escape as provided by Section 11155.

(7) To be notified that he or she may be entitled to witness fees and mileage, as provided by Section 1329.1.

(8) For the victim, to be provided with information concerning the victim's right to civil recovery and the opportunity to be compensated from the Restitution Fund pursuant to Chapter 5 (commencing with Section 13959) of Part 4 of Division 3 of Title 2 of the Government Code and Section 1191.2 of this code.

(9) To the expeditious return of his or her property which has allegedly been stolen or embezzled, when it is no longer needed as evidence, as provided by Chapter 12 (commencing with Section 1407) and Chapter 13 (commencing with Section 1417) of Title 10 of Part 2.

(10) To an expeditious disposition of the criminal action.

(11) To be notified, if applicable, in accordance with Sections 679.03 and 3058.8 if the defendant is to be placed on parole.

Nothing in this paragraph is intended to affect the right of the people and the defendant to an expeditious disposition as provided in Section 1050.

(b) The rights set forth in subdivision (a) shall be set forth in the information and educational materials prepared pursuant to Section 13897.1. The information and educational materials shall be distributed to local law enforcement agencies and local victims' programs by the Victims' Legal Resource Center established pursuant to Chapter 11 (commencing with Section 13897) of Title 6 of Part 4.

© 1992 by J., B. & L. Gould
Printed in the U.S.A.   EP

(c) Local law enforcement agencies shall make available copies of the materials described in subdivision (b) to victims and witnesses.

(d) Nothing in this section is intended to affect the rights and services provided to victims and witnesses by the local assistance centers for victims and witnesses. *(Amended by Stats 1988 ch 33 §1; ch 137 §1, eff. 1/1/89.)*

§679.03. Violent offense crimes; notice to witnesses and victims.

With respect to the conviction of a defendant involving a violent offense, as defined in subdivision (b) of Section 12021.1, the county district attorney, probation department, and victim-witness coordinator shall confer and establish an annual policy within existing resources to decide which one of their agencies shall inform each witness involved in the conviction who was threatened by the defendant following the defendant's arrest and each victim or next of kin of the victim of that offense of the right to request and receive a notice pursuant to Section 3058.8. If no agreement is reached, the presiding judge shall designate the appropriate county agency or department to provide this notification. *(Amended by Stats 1989 ch 624 §1, eff. 1/1/90.)*

PART 2

OF CRIMINAL PROCEDURE

PRELIMINARY PROVISIONS

§681. No person punishable but on legal conviction.

No person can be punished for a public offense, except upon a legal conviction in a Court having jurisdiction thereof.

§682. Prosecution by indictment or information.

Every public offense must be prosecuted by indictment or information, except:

1. Where proceedings are had for the removal of civil officers of the State;

2. Offenses arising in the militia when in actual service, and in the land and naval forces in the time of war, or which the State may keep, with the consent of Congress, in time of peace;

3. Offenses tried in municipal and justice courts;

4. All misdemeanors of which jurisdiction has been conferred upon superior courts sitting as juvenile courts;

5. A felony to which the defendant has pleaded guilty to the complaint before a magistrate, where permitted by law.

§683. Criminal action defined.

The proceeding by which a party charged with a public offense is accused and brought to trial and punishment, is known as a criminal action.

§684. Parties to a criminal action.

A criminal action is prosecuted in the name of the people of the State of California, as a party, against the person charged with the offense.

§685. The party prosecuted known as defendant.

The party prosecuted in a criminal action is designated in this Code as the defendant.

§686. Defendants' rights.

In a criminal action the defendant is entitled:

1. To a speedy and public trial.

2. To be allowed counsel as in civil actions, or to appear and defend in person and with counsel, except that in a capital case he shall be represented in court by counsel at all stages of the preliminary and trial proceedings.

3. To produce witnesses on his behalf and to be confronted with the witnesses against him, in the presence of the court, except that:

(a) Hearsay evidence may be admitted to the extent that it is otherwise admissible in a criminal action under the law of this state.

(b) The deposition of a witness taken in the action may be read to the extent that it is otherwise admissible under the law of this state.

§686.1. Capital cases.

Notwithstanding any other provision of law, the defendant in a capital case shall be represented in court by counsel at all stages of the preliminary and trial proceedings.

§686.2. Removal of spectator.

(a) The court may, after holding a hearing and making the findings set forth in subdivision (b), order the removal of any spectator who is intimidating a witness.

(b) The court may order the removal of a spectator only if it finds all of the following by clear and convincing evidence:

(1) The spectator to be removed is actually engaging in intimidation of the witness.

(2) The witness will not be able to give full, free, and complete testimony unless the spectator is removed.

(3) Removal of the spectator is the only reasonable means of ensuring that the witness may give full, free, and complete testimony.

(c) Subdivision (a) shall not be used as a means of excluding the press or a defendant from attendance at any portion of a criminal proceeding. *(Added by Stats 1990 ch 785 §1, eff. 1/1/91.)*

§686.5. Release or acquittal of person arrested.

In any case in which a person is arrested and released without trial or in which a person is arrested, tried, and acquitted, if such person is indigent and is released or acquitted at a place to which he has been transported by the arresting agency and which is more than 25 airline miles from the place of his arrest, the arresting agency shall, at his request, return or provide for return of such person to the place of his arrest.

§687. Second prosecution for the same offense prohibited.

No person can be subjected to a second prosecution for a public offense for which he has once been prosecuted and convicted or acquitted.

§688. Unlawful restraint.

No person charged with a public offense may be subjected, before conviction, to any more restraint than is necessary for his detention to answer the charge.

§689. Requisites for conviction.

No person can be convicted of a public offense unless by verdict of a jury, accepted and recorded by the court, by a finding of the court in a case where a jury has been waived, or by a plea of guilty.

§690. Applicability of part.

The provisions of Part 2 (commencing with Section 681) shall apply to all criminal actions and proceedings in all courts, except where jurisdictional limitations or the nature of specific provisions prevent, or special provision is made for particular courts or proceedings. *(Amended by Stats 1987 ch 828 §46.)*

§691. Definitions.

The following words have in Part 2 (commencing with Section 681) the signification attached to them in this section, unless it is otherwise apparent from the context:

(a) The words "inferior court" or "inferior courts" include municipal courts and justices' courts.

(b) The words "competent court" when used with reference to the jurisdiction over any public offense, mean any court the subject matter jurisdiction of which includes the offense so mentioned.

(c) The words "jurisdictional territory" when used with reference to a court, mean the city and county, county, city, township, or other limited territory over which the criminal jurisdiction of the court extends, as provided by law, and in case of a superior court mean the county in which the court sits.

(d) The words "accusatory pleading" include an indictment, an information, an accusation, a complaint filed with a magistrate charging a public offense of which the superior court has original trial jurisdiction, and a complaint filed with an inferior court charging a public offense of which the inferior court has original trial jurisdiction.

(e) The words "prosecuting attorney" include any attorney, whether designated as district attorney, city attorney, city prosecutor, prosecuting attorney, or by any other title, having by law the right or duty to prosecute, in behalf of the people, any charge of a public offense.

(f) The word "county" includes county, city and county, and city. *(Amended by Stats 1987 ch 828 §47.)*

TITLE 1

OF THE PREVENTION OF PUBLIC OFFENSES

CHAPTER 1

OF LAWFUL RESISTANCE

§692. Lawful resistance, by whom made.

Lawful resistance to the commission of a public offense may be made:

1. By the party about to be injured;
2. By other parties.

§693. By the party, in what cases and to what extent.

Resistance sufficient to prevent the offense may be made by the party about to be injured:

1. To prevent an offense against his person, or his family, or some member thereof.
2. To prevent an illegal attempt by force to take or injure property in his lawful possession.

§694. By other parties, in what cases.

Any other person, in aid or defense of the person about to be injured, may make resistance sufficient to prevent the offense.

CHAPTER 2

OF THE INTERVENTION OF THE OFFICERS OF JUSTICE

§697. Intervention of officers, in what cases.

Public offenses may be prevented by the intervention of the officers of justice:

1. By requiring security to keep the peace;
2. By forming a police in cities and towns, and by requiring their attendance in exposed places;
3. By suppressing riots.

§698. Persons acting in their aid justified.

When the officers of justice are authorized to act in the prevention of public offenses, other persons, who, by their command, act in their aid, are justified in so doing.

CHAPTER 3

SECURITY TO KEEP THE PEACE

§701. Information of threatened offense.

An information may be laid before any of the magistrates mentioned in Section eight hundred and eight, that a person has threatened to commit an offense against the person or property of another.

§702. Examination of complainant and witnesses.

When the information is laid before such magistrate he must examine on oath the informer, and any witness he may produce, and must take their depositions in writing, and cause them to be subscribed by the parties making them.

§703. Warrant of arrest.

If it appears from the depositions that there is just reason to fear the commission of the offense threatened, by the person so informed against, the magistrate must issue a warrant, directed generally to the Sheriff of the county, or any Constable, Marshal, or Policeman in the State, reciting the substance of the information, and commanding the officer forthwith to arrest the person informed of and bring him before the magistrate.

§704. Hearing before magistrate.

When the person informed against is brought before the magistrate, if the charge be controverted, the magistrate shall take testimony in relation thereto. The evidence shall be reduced to writing and subscribed by the witnesses. The magistrate may, in his or her discretion, order the testimony and proceedings to be taken down in shorthand, and for that purpose he or she may appoint a shorthand reporter. The deposition or testimony of the witnesses shall be

© 1992 by J., B. & L. Gould
Printed in the U.S.A.   **EP**

authenticated in the form prescribed in Section 869. *(Amended by Stats 1987 ch 828 §48.)*

§705. Person complained of, when to be discharged.

If it appears that there is no just reason to fear the commission of the offense alleged to have been threatened, the person complained of must be discharged.

§706. Duration and amount of security.

If, however, there is just reason to fear the commission of the offense, the person complained of may be required to enter into an undertaking in such sum, not exceeding five thousand dollars, as the magistrate may direct, to keep the peace towards the people of this state, and particularly towards the informer. The undertaking is valid and binding for six months, and may, upon the renewal of the information, be extended for a longer period, or a new undertaking may be required.

§707. Effect of giving or refusing to give security.

If the undertaking required by the last section is given, the party informed of must be discharged. If he does not give it, the magistrate must commit him to prison, specifying in the warrant the requirement to give security, the amount thereof, and the omission to give the same.

§708. Person committed for not giving security, how discharged.

If the person complained of is committed for not giving the undertaking required, he may be discharged by any magistrate upon giving the same.

§709. Undertaking to be filed in clerk's office.

The undertaking must be filed by the magistrate in the office of the Clerk of the county.

§710. Security, when required for assault committed in the presence of a court or magistrate.

A person who, in the presence of a Court or magistrate, assaults or threatens to assault another, or to commit an offense against his person or property or who contends with another with angry words, may be ordered by the Court or magistrate to give security, as in this Chapter provided, and if he refuses to do so, may be committed as provided in Section 707.

§711. Undertaking, when broken.

Upon the conviction of the person informed against of a breach of the peace, the undertaking is broken.

§712. Prosecution of undertaking.

Upon the District Attorney's producing evidence of such conviction to the Superior Court of the county, the Court must order the undertaking to be prosecuted, and the District Attorney must thereupon commence an action upon it in the name of the people of this State.

§713. Evidence of breach.

In the action the offense stated in the record of conviction must be alleged as a breach of the undertaking, and such record is conclusive evidence of the breach.

§714. Security for the peace not required, except in accordance with this Chapter.

Security to keep the peace, or be of good behavior, cannot be required except as prescribed in this Chapter.

CHAPTER 4

POLICE IN CITIES AND TOWNS, AND THEIR ATTENDANCE AT EXPOSED PLACES
(Repealed by Stats 1939 ch 60.)

CHAPTER 5

SUPPRESSION OF RIOTS

§723. Resistance to process.

When a sheriff or other public officer authorized to execute process finds, or has reason to apprehend that resistance will be made to the execution of the process, the officer may command as many able-bodied inhabitants of the officer's county as he or she may think proper to assist in overcoming the resistance and, if necessary, in seizing, arresting, and confining the persons resisting, and their aiders and abettors. *(Amended by Stats 1988 ch 160 §128, eff. 1/1/89.)*

§724. The officer to certify to Court the name of the resisters.

The officer must certify to the Court from which the process issued the names of the persons resisting, and their aiders and abettors, to the end that they may be proceeded against for their contempt of Court.

§726. Unlawful or riotous assemblies.

Where any number of persons, whether armed or not, are unlawfully or riotously assembled, the sheriff of the county and his deputies, the officials governing the town or city, or the judges of the justice courts and constables thereof, or any of them, must go among the persons assembled, or as near to them as possible, and command them, in the name of the people of the State, immediately to disperse.

§727. To arrest rioters if they do not disperse.

If the persons assembled do not immediately disperse, such magistrates and officers must arrest them, and to that end may command the aid of all persons present or within the county.

TITLE 2

MODE OF PROSECUTION

§737. Public offenses triable in superior court.

All public offenses triable in the superior court shall be prosecuted therein by indictment or information, except as provided in the Government Code, the Juvenile Court Law under Chapter 2 (commencing with Section 200) of Division 2 of the Welfare and Institutions Code, and Section 859a. *(Amended by Stats 1987 ch 828 §49.)*

§738. Preliminary examination.

Before an information is filed there must be a preliminary examination of the case against the defendant and an order holding him to answer made under Section 872. The proceeding for a preliminary examination must be commenced by written complaint, as provided elsewhere in this code.

§739. Filing of information, permissible charges.

When a defendant has been examined and committed, as provided in Section 872, it shall be the duty of the district attorney of the county in which the offense is triable to file in the superior court of that county within 15 days after the commitment, an information against the defendant which may charge the defendant with either the offense or offenses named in the order of commitment or any offense or offenses shown by the evidence taken before the magistrate to have been committed. The information shall be in the name of the people of the State of California and subscribed by the district attorney.

§740. Offenses triable in inferior courts.

Except as otherwise provided by law, all public offenses triable in the inferior courts must be prosecuted by written complaint under oath and subscribed by the complainant. Such complaint may be verified on information and belief.

TITLE 3

ADDITIONAL PROVISIONS REGARDING CRIMINAL PROCEDURE

CHAPTER 1

OF THE LOCAL JURISDICTION OF PUBLIC OFFENSES

§777. Offenses committed within the State.

Every person is liable to punishment by the laws of this State, for a public offense committed by him therein, except where it is by law cognizable exclusively in the courts of the United States; and except as otherwise provided by law the jurisdiction of every public offense is in any competent court within the jurisdictional territory of which it is committed.

§777a. Neglect of child.

If a parent violates the provisions of Section 270 of this code, the jurisdiction of such offense is in any competent court of either the jurisdictional territory in which the minor child is cared for or in which such parent is apprehended.

§777b. Perjury committed outside of State.

Perjury, in violation of Section 118, committed outside of the State of California is punishable in a competent court in the jurisdictional territory in this state in which occurs the act, transaction, matter, action, or proceeding, in relation to which the testimony, declaration, deposition, or certification was given or made.

§778. Offenses commenced without but consummated within State.

When the commission of a public offense, commenced without the State, is consummated within its boundaries by a defendant, himself outside the State, through the intervention of an innocent or guilty agent or any other means proceeding directly from said defendant, he is liable to punishment therefor in this State in any competent court within the jurisdictional territory of which the offense is consummated.

§778a. Offenses commenced within but consummated without state.

(a) Whenever a person, with intent to commit a crime, does any act within this state in execution or part execution of that intent, which culminates in the commission of a crime, either within or without this state, the person is punishable for that crime in this state in the same manner as if the the* crime had been committed entirely within this state.

*So in original. One "the" probably should be omitted.

(b) Whenever a person who, within this state, kidnaps another person within the meaning of Sections 207 and 209, and thereafter carries the person into another state or country and commits any crime of violence or theft against that person in the other state or country, the person is punishable for that crime of violence or theft in this state in the same manner as if the crime had been committed within this state. (Amended by Stats 1991 ch 635 §1, eff. 1/1/92.)

§778b. Offense without state punishable within.

Every person who, being out of this state, causes, aids, advises, or encourages any person to commit a crime within this state, and is afterwards found within this state, is punishable in the same manner as if he had been within this state when he caused, aided, advised, or encouraged the commission of such crime.

§779. When an inhabitant of this State is concerned in a duel out of the same, and a party wounded dies therein.

When an inhabitant or resident of this State, by previous appointment or engagement, fights a duel or is concerned as second therein, out of the jurisdiction of this State, and in the duel a wound is inflicted upon a person, whereof he dies in this State, the jurisdiction of the offense is in the county where the death happens.

§780. When an inhabitant leaves the State to evade the statute against dueling or challenges to fight.

When an inhabitant of this State leaves the same for the purpose of evading the operation of the provisions of the Code relating to dueling and challenges to fight, with the intent or for the purpose of doing any of the acts prohibited therein, the jurisdiction is in the county of which the offender was an inhabitant when the offense was committed.

§781. Offenses committed in multiple jurisdictional territories.

When a public offense is committed in part in one jurisdictional territory and in part in another, or the acts or effects thereof constituting or requisite to the consummation of the offense occur in two or more jurisdictional territories, the jurisdiction of such offense is in any competent court within either jurisdictional territory.

§782. Offenses on or near boundary of multiple jurisdictional territories.

When a public offense is committed on the boundary of two or more jurisdictional territories, or within 500 yards thereof, the jurisdiction of such offense is in any competent court within either jurisdictional territory.

© 1992 by J., B. & L. Gould
Printed in the U.S.A.   EP

§783. Offenses on vessel, train, motor vehicle, etc.

When a public offense is committed in this State, on board a vessel navigating a river, bay, slough, lake, or canal, or lying therein, in the prosecution of its voyage, or on a railroad train or car, motor vehicle, common carrier transporting passengers or on an aircraft prosecuting its trip, the jurisdiction is in any competent court, through, on, or over the jurisdictional territory of which the vessel, train, car, motor vehicle, common carrier or aircraft passes in the course of its voyage or trip, or in the jurisdictional territory of which the voyage or trip terminates.

§783.5. Offenses in park situated in more than one county.

When a public offense is committed in a park situated in more than one county, the jurisdiction over such an offense is in any competent court in any county in which any part of the park is situated. "Park," as used in this section means any area of land, or water, or both, which has been designated as a park or recreation area by any public agency or political subdivision of this state.

§784. Jurisdiction of a criminal action for kidnapping; false imprisonment; seizure for slavery; abduction.

The jurisdiction of a criminal action:

(a) For forcibly and without lawful authority seizing and confining another, or inveigling or kidnapping another, with intent, against his or her will, to cause him or her to be secretly confined or imprisoned in this state, or to be sent out of the state, or from one county to another, or to be sold as a slave, or in any way held to service;

(b) For inveigling, enticing, or taking away any person for the purpose of concubinage or prostitution, as defined in subdivision (b) of Section 647;

Is in any competent court within the jurisdictional territory in which the offense was committed, or in the jurisdictional territory out of which the person upon whom the offense was committed was taken or within the jurisdictional territory in which an act was done by the defendant in instigating, procuring, promoting, or aiding in the commission of the offense, or in abetting the parties concerned therein.

§784a. *Repealed by Stats 1991 ch 186 §5, eff. 1/1/92.*

§784.5. Child abduction.

The jurisdiction of a criminal action for a violation of Section 277, 278, or 278.5 shall be in any one of the following jurisdictional territories:

(a) Any jurisdictional territory in which the victimized person resides, or where the agency deprived of custody is located, at the time of the taking or deprivation.

(b) The jurisdictional territory in which the minor child was taken, detained, or concealed.

(c) The jurisdictional territory in which the minor child is found.

When the jurisdiction lies in more than one jurisdictional territory, the district attorneys concerned may agree which of them will prosecute the case.

§785. Jurisdiction for incest or bigamy.

When the offense of incest is committed in the jurisdictional territory of one competent court and the defendant is apprehended in the jurisdictional territory of another competent court the jurisdiction is in either court.

When the offense of bigamy is committed, the jurisdiction is in any competent court within the jurisdictional territory of which the marriage took place, or cohabitation occurred or the defendant was apprehended.

§786. Burglary, robbery, theft; etc.; jurisdiction.

When property taken in one jurisdictional territory by burglary, robbery, theft, or embezzlement has been brought into another, or when property is received in one jurisdictional territory with the knowledge that it has been stolen or embezzled and the property was stolen or embezzled in another jurisdictional territory, the jurisdiction of the offense is in any competent court within either jurisdictional territory, or any contiguous jurisdictional territory if the arrest is made within the contiguous territory, the prosecution secures on the record the defendant's knowing, voluntary, and intelligent waiver of the right of vicinage, and the defendant is charged with one or more property crimes in the arresting territory. *(Amended by Stats 1990 ch 156 §1, eff. 1/1/91.)*

§788. Treason.

The jurisdiction of a criminal action for treason, when the overt act is committed out of the State, is in any county of the State.

§789. Theft or receipt of stolen goods.

The jurisdiction of a criminal action for stealing or embezzling, in any other state, the property of another, or receiving it knowing it to have been stolen or embezzled, and bringing the same into this State, is in any competent court into or through the jurisdictional territory of which such stolen or embezzled property has been brought.

§790. Jurisdiction for murder or manslaughter.

The jurisdiction of a criminal action for murder or manslaughter is in the county where the fatal injury was inflicted or in the county in which the party injured died or in the county in which his body was found; provided, that if the defendant is indicted in the county in which the fatal injury was inflicted, at any time before his trial in another county, the sheriff of such other county must, if the defendant be in custody, deliver him upon demand to the sheriff of the county in which the fatal injury was inflicted. When the fatal injury is inflicted and the injured person died or his body was found within five hundred yards of the boundary of two or more counties, jurisdiction is in either county.

§791. Accessory in commission of offense.

In the case of an accessory, as defined in Section 32, in the commission of a public offense, the jurisdiction is in any competent court within the jurisdictional territory of which the offense of the accessory was committed, notwithstanding the principal offense was committed in another jurisdictional territory.

§792. Jurisdiction against principal not present at commission of offense.

The jurisdiction of a criminal action against a principal in the commission of a public offense, when such principal is not present at the commission of the offense is in the same court it would be under this code if he were so present and aiding and abetting therein.

§793. Conviction or acquittal in another State a bar, where the jurisdiction is concurrent.

When an act charged as a public offense is within the jurisdiction of another State or country, as well as of this State, a conviction or acquittal thereof in the former is a bar to the prosecution or indictment therefor in this State.

§794. Double jeopardy.

Where an offense is within the jurisdiction of two or more courts, a conviction or acquittal thereof in one court is a bar to a prosecution therefor in another.

§795. Prize-fighting.

The jurisdiction of a violation of Sections 412, 413, or 414, or a conspiracy to violate any of said sections, is in any competent court within the jurisdictional territory of which:

First. Any act is done towards the commission of the offense; or,

Second. The offender passed, whether into, out of, or through it, to commit the offense; or,

Third. The offender is arrested.

CHAPTER 2

TIME OF COMMENCING CRIMINAL ACTIONS

§799. Death; life imprisonment.

Prosecution for an offense punishable by death or by imprisonment in the state prison for life or for life without possibility of parole, or for the embezzlement of public money, may be commenced at any time.

§800. Imprisonment for eight years or more.

Except as provided in Section 799, prosecution for an offense punishable by imprisonment in the state prison for eight years or more shall be commenced within six years after commission of the offense.

§801. Imprisonment in state prison.

Except as provided in Sections 799 and 800, prosecution for an offense punishable by imprisonment in the state prison shall be commenced within three years after commission of the offense.

§801.5. Motor vehicle insurance fraud.

Notwithstanding Section 801 or any other provision of law, prosecution for a violation of Section 1871.1 of the Insurance Code shall be commenced within three years after discovery of the commission of the offense. (Amended by Stats 1990 ch 587 §1, eff. 1/1/91.)

§802. Offense not punishable by death or imprisonment.

(a) Except as provided in subdivision (b), prosecution for an offense not punishable by death or imprisonment in the state prison shall be commenced within one year after commission of the offense.

(b) Prosecution for a misdemeanor violation of section 647.6 or former Section 647a, committed with or upon a minor under the age of 14 years shall be commenced within two years after commission of the offense. (Amended by Stats 1991 ch 129 §1, eff. 1/1/92.)

§803. Time limitations on criminal prosecutions.

(a) Except as provided in this section, a limitation of time prescribed in this chapter is not tolled or extended for any reason.

(b) No time during which prosecution of the same person for the same conduct is pending in a court of this state is a part of a limitation of time prescribed in this chapter.

(c) A limitation of time prescribed in this chapter does not commence to run until discovery of an offense described in this subdivision. This subdivision applies to an offense punishable by imprisonment in the state prison, a material element of which is fraud or breach of a fiduciary obligation or the basis of which is misconduct in office by a public officer, employee, or appointee, including, but not limited to, the following offenses:

(1) Grand theft of any type, forgery, falsification of public records, or acceptance of a bribe by a public official or a public employee.

(2) A violation of Section 72, 118, 118a, 132, or 134.

(3) A violation of Section 25540, of any type, or Section 25541 of the Corporations Code.

(4) A violation of Section 1090 or 27443 of the Government Code.

(5) Felony welfare fraud or Medi-Cal fraud in violation of Section 11483 or 14107 of the Welfare and Institutions Code.

(6) Felony insurance fraud in violation of Section 548 of this code or Section 1871.1 of the Insurance Code.

(7) A violation of Section 580, 581, 582, 583, or 584 of the Business and Professions Code.

(8) A violation of Section 22430 of the Business and Professions Code.

(9) A violation of Section 10690 of the Health and Safety Code.

(10) A violation of Section 529a.

(d) If the defendant is out of the state when or after the offense is committed, the prosecution may be commenced as provided in Section 804 within the limitations of time prescribed by this chapter, and no time up to a maximum of three years during which the defendant is not within the state shall be a part of those limitations.

(e) A limitation of time prescribed in this chapter does not commence to run until the offense has been discovered, or could have reasonably been discovered, with regard to offenses under Division 7 (commencing with Section 13000) of the Water Code, under Chapter 6.5 (commencing with Section 25100), Chapter 6.7 (commencing with Section 25280), or Chapter 6.8 (commencing with Section 25300) of Division 20 of, or Part 4 (commencing with Section 41500) of Division 26 of the Health and Safety Code, or under Section 386.

(f) Notwithstanding any other limitation of time described in this section, a criminal complaint may be filed within one year of the date of a report to a responsible adult or agency by a child under 17 years of age that the child is a victim of a crime described in Section 261, 286, 288, 288a, or 289.

For purposes of this subdivision, a "responsible adult" or "agency" means a person or agency required to report pursuant to Section 11166. This subdivision shall only apply if:

(1) The limitation period specified in Section 800 or 801 has expired, and

© 1992 by J., B. & L. Gould
Printed in the U.S.A.　　EP

(2) The defendant has committed at least one violation of Section 261, 286, 288, 288a, or 289, against the same victim within the limitation period specified for that crime in either Section 800 or 801. *(Amended by Stats 1990 ch 587 §2, eff. 1/1/91.)*

§804. Commencement of prosecution.

For the purpose of this chapter, prosecution for an offense is commenced when any of the following occurs:

(a) An indictment or information is filed.

(b) A complaint is filed with an inferior court charging a public offense of which the inferior court has original trial jurisdiction.

(c) A case is certified to the superior court.

(d) An arrest warrant or bench warrant is issued, provided the warrant names or describes the defendant with the same degree of particularity required for an indictment, information, or complaint.

§805. Applicable time limitations.

For the purpose of determining the applicable limitation of time pursuant to this chapter:

(a) An offense is deemed punishable by the maximum punishment prescribed by statute for the offense, regardless of the punishment actually sought or imposed. Any enhancement of punishment prescribed by statute shall be disregarded in determining the maximum punishment prescribed by statute for an offense.

(b) The limitation of time applicable to an offense that is necessarily included within a greater offense is the limitation of time applicable to the lesser included offense, regardless of the limitation of time applicable to the greater offense.

§805.5. Operative date.

(a) As used in this section, "operative date" means January 1, 1985.

(b) Except as provided in subdivision (c), this chapter applies to an offense that was committed before, on, or after the operative date.

(c) This chapter does not apply, and the law applicable before the operative date does apply, to an offense that was committed before the operative date, if:

(1) Prosecution for the offense would be barred on the operative date by the limitation of time applicable before the operative date.

(2) Prosecution for the offense was commenced before the operative date. *(Amended and renumbered from section 806 by Stats 1986 ch 248 §161.)*

CHAPTER 3

COMPLAINTS BEFORE MAGISTRATES

§806. Proceeding for examination before magistrate.

A proceeding for the examination before a magistrate of a person on a charge of an offense originally triable in a superior court must be commenced by written complaint under oath subscribed by the complainant and filed with the magistrate. Such complaint may be verified on information and belief. When the complaint is used as a pleading to which the defendant pleads guilty under Section 859a of this code, the complaint shall contain the same allegations, including the charge of prior conviction or convictions

of crime, as are required for indictments and informations and, wherever applicable, shall be construed and shall have substantially the same effect as provided in this code for indictments and informations.

§807. Magistrate defined.

A magistrate is an officer having power to issue a warrant for the arrest of a person charged with a public offense.

§808. Designation of magistrates.

The following persons are magistrates:

1. The judges of the Supreme Court.
2. The judges of the courts of appeal.
3. The judges of the superior courts.
4. The judges of the municipal courts.
5. The judges of the justice courts.

§810. On-call magistrates.

(a) The presiding judge of the superior court, the presiding judge of each municipal court in a county, and the judge of each justice court in a county, shall, as often as is necessary, meet and designate on a schedule not less than one judge of the superior court, municipal court or justice court to be reasonably available on call as a magistrate for the setting of orders for discharge from actual custody upon bail, the issuance of search warrants, and for such other matters as may by the magistrate be deemed appropriate, at all times when a court is not in session in the county.

(b) The officer in charge of a jail, or a person he designates, in which an arrested person is held in custody shall assist the arrested person or his attorney in contacting the magistrate on call as soon as possible for the purpose of obtaining release on bail.

(c) Any telephone call made pursuant to this section by an arrested person while in custody or by such person's attorney shall not count or be considered as a telephone call for purposes of Section 851.5 of the Penal Code.

CHAPTER 4

THE WARRANT OF ARREST

§813. Arrest warrant; issuance.

(a) When a complaint is filed with a magistrate charging a public offense originally triable in the superior court of the county in which he or she sits, if the magistrate is satisfied from the complaint that the offense complained of has been committed and that there is reasonable ground to believe that the defendant has committed it, the magistrate shall issue a warrant for the arrest of the defendant, except that, upon the request of the prosecutor, a summons instead of an arrest warrant shall be issued; provided, that a judge of the justice court who is not a member of the State Bar may issue such a warrant or summons only upon the concurrence of the district attorney of the county in which he or she sits or the Attorney General.

(b) A summons issued pursuant to this section shall be in substantially the same form as an arrest warrant and shall contain all of the following:

(1) The name of the defendant.

(2) The date and time the summons was issued.

(3) The city or county where the summons was issued.

(4) The signature of the magistrate, judge, justice, or other issuing authority who is issuing the summons

with the title of his or her office and the name of the court or other issuing agency.

(5) The offense or offenses with which the defendant is charged.

(6) The time and place at which the defendant is to appear.

(7) Notification that the defendant is to complete the booking process on or before his or her first court appearance, as well as instructions for the defendant on completing the booking process.

(8) A provision for certification by the booking agency that the defendant has completed the booking process which shall be presented to the court by the defendant as proof of booking.

(c) If a defendant has been properly served with a summons and thereafter fails to appear at the designated time and place, a bench warrant for arrest shall issue. In absence of proof of actual receipt of the summons by the defendant, a failure to appear shall not be used in any future proceeding.

(d) A defendant who responds to a summons issued pursuant to this section and who has not been booked as provided in subdivision (b) shall be ordered by the court to complete the booking process.

(e) The prosecutor shall not request the issuance of a summons in lieu of an arrest warrant as provided in this section under any of the following circumstances:

(1) The offense charged involves violence.

(2) The offense charged involves a firearm.

(3) The offense charged involves resisting arrest.

(4) There are one or more outstanding arrest warrants for the person.

(5) The prosecution of the offense or offenses with which the person is charged, or the prosecution of any other offense or offenses would be jeopardized.

(6) There is reasonable likelihood that the offense or offenses would continue or resume, or that the safety of persons or property would be imminently endangered.

(7) There is reason to believe that the person would not appear at the time and place specified in the summons. *(Amended by Stats 1988 ch 664 §1, eff. 1/1/89.)*

§814. Arrest warrant form.

A warrant of arrest issued under Section 813 may be in substantially the following form:

County of _____

The people of the State of California to any peace officer of said State:

Complaint on oath having this day been laid before me that the crime of _____ (designating it generally) has been committed and accusing ___ (naming defendant) thereof, you are therefore commanded forthwith to arrest the above named defendant and bring him before me at ____ (naming the place), or in case of my

absence or inability to act, before the nearest or most accessible magistrate in this county.

Dated at ___ (place) this ___ day of ___ , 19 ___ .

_____
(Signature and full official title of magistrate.)

§815. Contents of an arrest warrant.

A warrant of arrest shall specify the name of the defendant or, if it is unknown to the magistrate, judge, justice, or other issuing authority, the defendant may be designated therein by any name. It shall also state

the time of issuing it, and the city or county where it is issued, and shall be signed by the magistrate, judge, justice, or other issuing authority issuing it with the title of his office and the name of the court or other issuing agency.

§815a. Amount of bail.

At the time of issuing a warrant of arrest, the magistrate shall fix the amount of bail which in his judgment in accordance with the provisions of Section 1275 will be reasonable and sufficient for the appearance of the defendant following his arrest, if the offense is bailable, and said magistrate shall endorse upon said warrant a statement signed by him, with the name of his office, dated at the county, city or town where it is made to the following effect "The defendant is to be admitted to bail in the sum of __ dollars" (stating the amount).

§816. Warrant directed to peace officer; execution.

A warrant of arrest shall be directed generally to any peace officer, or to any public officer or employee authorized to serve process where the warrant is for a violation of a statute or ordinance which such person has the duty to enforce, in the state, and may be executed by any of those officers to whom it may be delivered.

When a warrant of arrest has been delivered to a peace officer and the person named in the warrant is otherwise lawfully in the custody of the peace officer, the warrant may be executed by the peace officer or by any clerk of a city or county jail authorized to act and acting under the peace officer's direction.

§816a. Summons.

A summons issued pursuant to Section 813 shall be served by any peace officer, or any public officer or employee authorized to serve process when the summons is for a violation of a statute or ordinance which that person has the duty to enforce, within the state. Upon service of the summons, the officer or employee shall deliver one copy of the summons to the defendant and shall file a duplicate copy with the magistrate before whom the defendant is to appear. *(Added by Stats 1988 ch 664 §2, eff. 1/1/89.)*

§818. Citation in lieu of physical arrest; notice to appear.

In any case in which a peace officer serves upon a person a warrant of arrest for a misdemeanor offense under the Vehicle Code or under any local ordinance relating to stopping, standing, parking, or operation of a motor vehicle and where no written promise to appear has been filed and the warrant states on its face that a citation may be used in lieu of physical arrest, the peace officer may, instead of taking the person before a magistrate, prepare a notice to appear and release the person on his promise to appear, as prescribed by Sections 853.6 through 853.8 of the Penal Code. Issuance of a notice to appear and securing of a promise to appear shall be deemed a compliance with the directions of the warrant, and the peace officer issuing such notice to appear and obtaining such promise to appear shall endorse on the warrant "Section 818, Penal Code, complied with" and return the warrant to the magistrate who issued it.

© 1992 by J., B. & L. Gould
Printed in the U.S.A.   **EP**

§821. Felony offense; arrest procedure.

If the offense charged is a felony, and the arrest occurs in the county in which the warrant was issued, the officer making the arrest must take the defendant before the magistrate who issued the warrant or some other magistrate of the same county.

If the defendant is arrested in another county, the officer must, without unnecessary delay, inform the defendant in writing of his right to be taken before a magistrate in that county, note on the warrant that he has so informed defendant, and, upon being required by defendant, take him before a magistrate in that county, who must admit him to bail in the amount specified in the endorsement referred to in Section 815a, and direct the defendant to appear before the court or magistrate by whom the warrant was issued on or before a day certain which shall in no case be more than 25 days after such admittance to bail. If bail be forthwith given, the magistrate shall take the same and endorse thereon a memorandum of the aforesaid order for the appearance of the defendant, or, if the defendant so requires, he may be released on bail set on the warrant by the issuing court, as provided in Section 1269b of this code, without an appearance before a magistrate.

If the warrant on which the defendant is arrested in another county does not have bail set thereon, or if the defendant arrested in another county does not require the arresting officer to take him before a magistrate in that county for the purpose of being admitted to bail, or if such defendant, after being admitted to bail, does not forthwith give bail, the arresting officer shall immediately notify the law enforcement agency requesting the arrest in the county in which the warrant was issued that such defendant is in custody, and thereafter such law enforcement agency shall take custody of the defendant within five days, or five court days if the law enforcement agency requesting the arrest is more than 400 miles from the county in which the defendant is held in custody, in the county in which he was arrested and shall take such defendant before the magistrate who issued the warrant, or before some other magistrate of the same county.

§822. Procedure following arrest for misdemeanor offense.

If the offense charged is a misdemeanor, and the defendant is arrested in another county, the officer must, without unnecessary delay, inform the defendant in writing of his right to be taken before a magistrate in that county, note on the warrant that he has so informed defendant, and, upon being required by defendant, take him before a magistrate in that county, who must admit him to bail in the amount specified in the indorsement referred to in Section 815a, or if no bail is specified, the magistrate may set bail; if the defendant is admitted to bail the magistrate shall direct the defendant to appear before the court or magistrate by whom the warrant was issued on or before a day certain which shall in no case be more than 25 days after such admittance to bail. If bail be forthwith given, the magistrate shall take the same and indorse thereon a memorandum of the aforesaid order for the appearance of the defendant.

If the defendant arrested in another county on a misdemeanor charge does not require the arresting officer to take him before a magistrate in that county for the purpose of being admitted to bail, or if such

defendant, after being admitted to bail, does not forthwith give bail, the arresting officer shall immediately notify the law enforcement agency requesting the arrest in the county in which the warrant was issued that such defendant is in custody, and thereafter such law enforcement agency shall take custody of such defendant within five days in the county in which he was arrested and shall take such defendant before the magistrate who issued the warrant, or before some other magistrate of the same county.

If a defendant is arrested in another county on a warrant charging the commission of a misdemeanor, upon which warrant the amount of bail is indorsed as provided in Section 815a, and defendant is held in jail in the county of arrest pending appearance before a magistrate, the officer in charge of the jail shall, to the same extent as provided by Section 1269b, have authority to approve and accept bail from defendant in the amount indorsed on the warrant, to issue and sign an order for the release of the defendant, and, on posting of such bail, shall discharge defendant from custody.

§823. Admission to bail.

On taking the bail, the magistrate must certify that fact on the warrant, and deliver the warrant to the officer having charge of the defendant. The magistrate shall issue to defendant a receipt for the undertaking of bail. The officer must then discharge the defendant from arrest, and must, without delay, deliver the warrant to the clerk of the court at which the defendant is required to appear. If the undertaking of bail is in the form of a bond, the magistrate shall forward the bond to the court at which defendant is required to appear. If the undertaking is in the form of cash, the magistrate shall deposit the cash in the county treasury, notifying the county auditor thereof, and the county auditor shall, by warrant, transmit the amount of the undertaking to the court at which the defendant is required to appear. If authorized by the county auditor, the magistrate may deposit the money in a bank account pursuant to Section 68084 of the Government Code, and by check drawn on such bank account transmit the amount of the undertaking to the court at which the defendant is required to appear.

§824. Adult willfully misrepresenting himself as minor.

When an adult willfully misrepresents himself or herself to be a minor under 18 years of age when taken into custody and this misrepresentation effects a material delay in investigation which prevents the filing of a criminal complaint against him or her in a court of competent jurisdiction within 48 hours, the complaint shall be filed within 48 hours from the time the true age is determined, excluding nonjudicial days.

§825. Appearance before magistrate; extension of time.

(a) (1) Except as provided in paragraph (2), the defendant must in all cases be taken before the magistrate without unnecessary delay, and, in any event, within two days after his or her arrest, excluding Sundays and holidays; provided, however, that when the two days prescribed herein expire at a time when the court in which the magistrate is sitting is not in session, such time shall be extended to include the

© 1992 by J., B. & L. Gould
Printed in the U.S.A. **EP**

duration of the next regular court session on the judicial day immediately following.

(2) Commencing on January 1, 1990, and continuing through January 1, 1992, whenever the defendant is incarcerated in the California State Prison at Folsom, the applicable time limitation under paragraph (1) shall be seven days.

(b) After the arrest, any attorney at law entitled to practice in the courts of record of California, may, at the request of the prisoner or any relative of the prisoner, visit the person so arrested. Any officer having charge of the prisoner so arrested who willfully refuses or neglects to allow that attorney to visit a prisoner is guilty of a misdemeanor. Any officer having a prisoner in charge, who refuses to allow the attorney to visit the prisoner when proper application is made therefor, shall forfeit and pay to the party aggrieved the sum of five hundred dollars ($500), to be recovered by action in any court of competent jurisdiction. *(Amended by Stats 1989 ch 546 §1, eff. 1/1/90.)*

§825.5. Physician's right to visit prisoner.

Any physician and surgeon, including a psychiatrist, licensed to practice in this state, or any psychologist licensed to practice in this state who holds a doctoral degree and has at least two years of experience in the diagnosis and treatment of emotional and mental disorders, who is employed by the prisoner or his or her attorney to assist in the preparation of the defense, shall be permitted to visit the prisoner while he or she is in custody.

§826. Bring before magistrate not issuing warrant.

If on a warrant issued under Section 813 the defendant is brought before a magistrate other than the one who issued the warrant, the complaint on which the warrant was issued must be sent to that magistrate, or if it cannot be procured, a new complaint may be filed before that magistrate.

§827. Complaint of offenses triable in another county.

When a complaint is filed with a magistrate of the commission of a public offense originally triable in the superior court of another county of the State than that in which he sits, but showing that the defendant is in the county where the complaint is filed, the same proceedings must be had as prescribed in this chapter, except that the warrant must require the defendant to be taken before the nearest or most accessible magistrate of the county in which the offense is triable, and the complaint must be delivered by the magistrate to the officer to whom the warrant is delivered.

§827.1. Warrant of arrest for misdemeanor offense.

A person who is specified or designated in a warrant of arrest for a misdemeanor offense may be released upon the issuance of a citation, in lieu of physical arrest, unless one of the following conditions exists:

(a) The misdemeanor cited in the warrant involves violence.

(b) The misdemeanor cited in the warrant involves a firearm.

(c) The misdemeanor cited in the warrant involves resisting arrest.

(d) The misdemeanor cited in the warrant involves giving false information to a peace officer.

(e) The person arrested is a danger to himself or herself or others due to intoxication or being under the influence of drugs or narcotics.

(f) The person requires medical examination or medical care or was otherwise unable to care for his or her own safety.

(g) The person has other ineligible charges pending against him or her.

(h) There is reasonable likelihood that the offense or offenses would continue or resume, or that the safety of persons or property would be immediately endangered by the release of the person.

(i) The person refuses to sign the notice to appear.

(j) The person cannot provide satisfactory evidence of personal identification.

(k) The warrant of arrest indicates that the person is not eligible to be released on a citation.

The issuance of a citation under this section shall be undertaken in the manner set forth in Sections 853.6 to 853.8, inclusive. *(Amended by Stats 1988 ch 403 §1, eff. 1/1/89.)*

§828. Officer executing warrant; duties.

The officer who executes the warrant must take the defendant before the nearest or most accessible magistrate of the county in which the offense is triable, and must deliver to him the complaint and the warrant, with his return endorsed thereon, and the magistrate must then proceed in the same manner as upon a warrant issued by himself.

§829. Offense triable in inferior court of another county.

When a complaint is filed with a magistrate of the commission of a public offense triable in an inferior court of another county of the State than that in which he sits, but showing that the defendant is in the county where the complaint is filed, the officer must, upon being required by the defendant, take him before a magistrate of the county in which the warrant was issued, who must admit the defendant to bail in the amount specified in the endorsement referred to in Section 815a, and immediately transmit the warrant, complaint, and undertaking, to the clerk of the court in which the defendant is required to appear.

CHAPTER 4.5

PEACE OFFICERS

§830. Peace officers; definition; retirement.

Any person who comes within the provisions of this chapter and who otherwise meets all standards imposed by law on a peace officer is a peace officer, and notwithstanding any other provision of law, no person other than those designated in this chapter is a peace officer. The restriction of peace officer functions of any public officer or employee shall not affect his or her status for purposes of retirement. *(Amended by Stats 1989 ch 1165 §19, eff. 1/1/90.)*

§830.1. Justice personnel.

(a) Any sheriff, undersheriff, or deputy sheriff, employed in that capacity, of a county, any police officer, employed in that capacity and appointed by the chief of police or the chief executive of the agency, of a city, any police officer of a district (including police

© 1992 by J., B. & L. Gould
Printed in the U.S.A.   EP

officers of the San Diego Unified Port District Harbor Police) authorized by statute to maintain a police department, any marshal or deputy marshal of a municipal court, any constable or deputy constable, employed in that capacity, of a judicial district, any port warden or special officer of the Harbor Department of the City of Los Angeles, or any inspector or investigator employed in that capacity in the office of a district attorney, is a peace officer. The authority of these peace officers extends to any place in the state, as follows:

(1) As to any public offense committed or which there is probable cause to believe has been committed within the political subdivision which employs the peace officer.

(2) Where the peace officer has the prior consent of the chief of police, or person authorized by him or her to give consent, if the place is within a city or of the sheriff, or person authorized by him or her to give consent, if the place is within a county.

(3) As to any public offense committed or which there is probable cause to believe has been committed in the peace officer's presence, and with respect to which there is immediate danger to person or property, or of the escape of the perpetrator of the offense.

(b) The Deputy Director, assistant directors, chiefs, assistant chiefs, special agents, and narcotics agents of the Department of Justice, and those investigators who are designated by the Attorney General are peace officers. The authority of these peace officers extends to any place in the state as to a public offense committed or which there is probable cause to believe has been committed within state. *(Amended by Stats 1990 ch 1695 §9, eff. 1/1/91.)*

§830.2. State justice personnel and law enforcement officers.

The following persons are peace officers whose authority extends to any place in the state:

(a) Any member of the California Highway Patrol, provided that the primary duty of the peace officer shall be the enforcement of the provisions of the Vehicle Code or of any other law relating to the use or operation of vehicles upon the highways, as that duty is set forth in the Vehicle Code.

(b) Any member of the California State Police Division, provided that the primary duty of the peace officer shall be to provide police services for the protection of state officers, and the protection of state properties and occupants thereof, as set forth in the Government Code.

(c) A member of the University of California Police Department appointed pursuant to Section 92600 of the Education Code, provided that the primary duty of the peace officer shall be the enforcement of the law within the area specified in Section 92600 of the Education Code.

(d) A member of the California State University and College Police Departments appointed pursuant to Section 89560 of the Education Code, provided that the primary duty of the peace officer shall be the enforcement of the law within the area specified in Section 89560 of the Education Code.

(e) Any member of the Law Enforcement Liaison Unit of the Department of Corrections, provided that the primary duty of the peace officer shall be the investigation or apprehension of parolees, parole violators, or escapees from state institutions, the transportation of those persons, and the coordination of those activities with other criminal justice agencies.

(f) Members of the Wildlife Protection Branch of the Department of Fish and Game, provided that the primary duty of those deputies shall be the enforcement of the law as set forth in Section 856 of the Fish and Game Code.

(g) Employees of the Department of Parks and Recreation designated by the director pursuant to Section 5008 of the Public Resources Code, provided that the primary duty of the peace officer shall be the enforcement of the law as set forth in Section 5008 of the Public Resources Code.

(h) The Director of Forestry and employees or classes of employees of the Department of Forestry designated by the director pursuant to Section 4156 of the Public Resources Code, provided that the primary duty of the peace officer shall be the enforcement of the law as that duty is set forth in Section 4156 of the Public Resources Code.

(i) Persons employed by the Department of Alcoholic Beverage Control for the enforcement of Division 9 (commencing with Section 23000) of the Business and Professions Code and designated by the Director of Alcoholic Beverage Control, provided that the primary duty of any of these peace officers shall be the enforcement of the laws relating to alcoholic beverages, as that duty is set forth in Section 25755 of the Business and Professions Code.

(j) Marshals and police appointed by the Board of Directors of the California Exposition and State Fair pursuant to Section 3332 of the Food and Agricultural Code, provided that the primary duty of the peace officers shall be the enforcement of the law as prescribed in that section. *(Amended by Stats 1990 ch 82 §7, eff. 5/3/90.)*

§830.3. Local peace officers.

The following persons are peace officers whose authority extends to any place in the state for the purpose of performing their primary duty or when making an arrest pursuant to Section 836 of the Penal Code as to any public offense with respect to which there is immediate danger to person or property, or of the escape of the perpetrator of that offense, or pursuant to Section 8597 or 8598 of the Government Code. These peace officers may carry firearms only if authorized and under those terms and conditions as specified by their employing agencies:

(a) Persons employed by the Division of Investigation of the Department of Consumer Affairs and investigators of the Medical Board of California and the Board of Dental Examiners, who are designated by the Director of Consumer Affairs, provided that the primary duty of these peace officers shall be the enforcement of the law as that duty is set forth in Section 160 of the Business and Professions Code.

(b) Voluntary fire wardens designated by the Director of Forestry and Fire Protection pursuant to Section 4156 of the Public Resources Code, provided that the primary duty of these peace officers shall be the enforcement of the law as that duty is set forth in Section 4156 of that code.

(c) Employees of the Department of Motor Vehicles designated in Section 1655 of the Vehicle Code, provided that the primary duty of these peace officers shall be the enforcement of the law as that duty is set forth in Section 1655 of that code.

(d) Investigators of the California Horse Racing Board designated by the board, provided that the primary duty of these peace officers shall be the enforcement of Chapter 4 (commencing with Section 19400) of Division 8 of the Business and Professions Code and Chapter 10 (commencing with Section 330) of Title 9 of Part 1 of this code.

(e) The State Fire Marshal and assistant or deputy state fire marshals appointed pursuant to Section 13103 of the Health and Safety Code, provided that the primary duty of these peace officers shall be the enforcement of the law as that duty is set forth in Section 13104 of that code.

(f) Inspectors of the food and drug section designated by the chief pursuant to subdivision (a) of Section 216 of the Health and Safety Code, provided that the primary duty of these peace officers shall be the enforcement of the law as that duty is set forth in Section 216 of that code.

(g) All investigators of the Division of Labor Standards Enforcement designated by the Labor Commissioner, provided that the primary duty of these peace officers shall be enforcement of the law as prescribed in Section 95 of the Labor Code.

(h) All investigators of the State Departments of Health Services, Social Services, Mental Health, Developmental Services, Alcohol and Drug Programs and the Office of Statewide Health Planning and Development, and the Public Employees' Retirement System, provided that the primary duty of these peace officers shall be the enforcement of the law relating to the duties of his or her department, or office. Notwithstanding any other provision of law, investigators of the Public Employees' Retirement System shall not carry firearms.

(i) The Chief of the Bureau of Fraudulent Claims of the Department of Insurance and those investigators designated by the chief, provided that the primary duty of those investigators shall be enforcement of Section 1871.1 of the Insurance Code.

(j) Employees of the Department of Housing and Community Development designated under Section 18023 of the Health and Safety Code, provided that the primary duty of these peace officers shall be the enforcement of the law as that duty is set forth in Section 18023 of that code.

(k) Investigators of the office of the Controller, provided that the primary duty of these investigators shall be the enforcement of the law relating to the duties of that office. Notwithstanding any other law, except as authorized by the Controller, the peace officers designated pursuant to this subdivision shall not carry firearms.

(l) Investigators of the Department of Corporations designated by the Commissioner of Corporations, provided that the primary duty of these investigators shall be enforcement of the provisions of law administered by the Department of Corporations. Notwithstanding any other provision of law, the peace officers designated pursuant to this subdivision shall not carry firearms.

(m) Persons employed by the Contractors' State License Board designated by the Director of Consumer Affairs pursuant to Section 7011.5 of the Business and Professions Code, provided that the primary duty of these persons shall be the enforcement of the law as that duty is set forth in Section 7011.5, and in Chapter 9 (commencing with Section 7000) of Division 3, of that code. The Director of Consumer Affairs may designate

as peace officers not more than three persons who shall at the time of their designation be assigned to the special investigations unit of the board. Notwithstanding any other provision of law, the persons designated pursuant to this subdivision shall not carry firearms.

(n) The chief and coordinators of the Law Enforcement Division of the Office of Emergency Services.

(o) Investigators of the Office of the Secretary of State designated by the Secretary of State, provided that the primary duty of these peace officers shall be the enforcement of the law as prescribed in Chapter 3 (commencing with Section 8200) of Division I of Title 2 of, and Section 12172.5 of, the Government Code. Notwithstanding any other provision of law, the peace officers designated pursuant to this subdivision shall not carry firearms.

(p) The Deputy Director for Security designated by Section 8880.38 of the Government Code, and all lottery security personnel assigned to the California State Lottery and designated by the director, provided that the primary duty of any of those peace officers shall be the enforcement of the laws related to assuring the integrity, honesty, and fairness of the operation and administration of the California State Lottery.

(q) Investigators employed by the Investigation Division of the Employment Development Department designated by the director of the department, provided that the primary duty of those peace officers shall be the enforcement of the law as that duty is set forth in Section 317 of the Unemployment Insurance Code.

Notwithstanding any other provision of law, the peace officers designated pursuant to this subdivision shall carry firearms.

(r) The chief and assistant chief of museum security and safety of the California Museum of Science and Industry, as designated by the executive director pursuant to Section 4108 of the Food and Agricultural Code, provided that the primary duty of those peace officers shall be the enforcement of the law as that duty is set forth in Section 4108 of the Food and Agricultural Code.

(s) Notwithstanding any other provision of this section, a peace officer authorized by this section shall not be authorized to carry firearms by his or her employing agency until that agency has adopted a policy on the use of deadly force by those peace officers, and until those peace officers have been instructed in the employing agency's policy on the use of deadly force.

Every peace officer authorized pursuant to this section to carry firearms by his or her employing agency shall qualify in the use of the firearms at least every six months. (Amended by Stats 1991 ch 877 §2, 910 §5, eff. 1/1/92.)

§830.31. Special peace officers.

The following persons are peace officers whose authority extends to any place in the state for the purpose of performing their primary duty or when making an arrest pursuant to Section 836 as to any public offense with respect to which there is immediate danger to person or property, or of the escape of the perpetrator of that offense, or pursuant to Section 8597 or 8598 of the Government Code. Those peace officers may carry firearms only if authorized and under terms and conditions specified by their employing agency.

© 1992 by J., B. & L. Gould
Printed in the U.S.A.   EP

(a) Safety police officers of the County of Los Angeles, if the primary duty of the peace officer is the enforcement of the law in or about the properties owned, operated, or administered by the employing agency or when performing necessary duties with respect to patrons, employees, and properties of the employing agency.

(b) Persons designated by a local agency as park rangers, and regularly employed and paid as such, if the primary duty of the peace officer is the protection of park and other property of the agency and the preservation of the peace therein.

(c) Security officers of the Department of General Services of the City of Los Angeles designated by the general manager of the department, if the primary duty of the peace officer is the enforcement of the law in or about properties owned, operated, or administered by the employing agency or when performing necessary duties with respect to patrons, employees, and properties of the employing agency. Notwithstandiing any other provision of law, the peace officers designated by this subdivision shall not be authorized to carry firearms, if the primary duty of the peace officer is the enforcement of the law in or about properties owned, operated, or adminsitered by the employing agency or when performing necessary duties with respect to patrons, employees, and properties of the employing agency.

(d) Housing authority patrol officers employed by the housing authority of a city, district, county, or city and county or employed by the police department of a city and county, if the primary duty of the peace officer is the enforcement of the law in or about properties owned, operated, or administered by the employing agency or when performinng necessary duties with respect to patrons, employees, and properties of the employing agency. *(Added by Stats 1989 ch 1165 §24, eff. 1/1/90. Former §830.31, as amended by Stats 1989 ch 950 §2, was repealed by Stats 1989 ch 1165 §23, eff. 1/1/90.)*

§830.32. Peace officers appointed by Education Code; authority.

The following persons are peace officers whose authority extends to any place in the state for the purpose of performing their primary duty or when making an arrest pursuant to Section 836 as to any public offense with respect to which there is immediate danger to person or property, or of the escape of the perpetrator of that offense, or pursuant to Section 8597 or 8598 of the Government Code. Those peace officers may carry firearms only if authorized and under terms and conditions specified by their employing agency.

(a) Members of a community college police department appointed pursuant to Section 72330 of the Education Code, if the primary duty of the peace officer is the enforcement of the law as prescribed in Section 72330 of the Education Code.

(b) Persons employed as members of a police department of a school district pursuant to Section 39670 of the Education Code, if the primary duty of the peace officer is the enforcement of the law as prescribed in Section 39670 of the Education Code. *(Added by Stats 1989 ch 1165 §25, eff. 1/1/90.)*

§830.33. Municipality employees.

The following persons are peace officers whose authority extends to any place in the state for the purpose of performing their primary duty or when making an arrest pursuant to Section 836 as to any public offense with respect to which there is immediate danger to person or property, or of the escape of the perpetrator of that offense, or pursuant to Section 8597 or 8598 of the Government Code. Those peace officers may carry firearms only if authorized and under terms and conditions specified by their employing agency.

(a) A member of the San Francisco Bay Area Rapid Transit District Police Department appointed pursuant to Section 28767.5 of the Public Utilities Code, if the primary duty of the peace officer is the enforcement of the law in or about properties owned, operated, or administered by the district or when performing necessary duties with respect to patrons, employees, and properties of the district.

(b) Harbor or port police regularly employed and paid as such by a county, city, or district other than peace officers authorized under Section 830.1, if the primary duty of the peace officer is the enforcement of the law in or about the properties owned, operated, or administered by the harbor or port or when performing necessary duties with respect to patrons, employees, and properties of the harbor or port.

(c) Transit police officers of a county, city, or district, if the primary duty of the peace officer is the enforcement of the law in or about properties owned, operated, or administered by the employing agency or when performing necessary duties with respect to patrons, employees, and properties of the employing agency.

(d) Any person regularly employed as an airport law enforcement officer by a city, county, or district operating the airport or by a joint powers agency, created pursuant to Article 1 (commencing with Section 6500) of Chapter 5 of Division 7 of Title 1 of the Government Code, operating the airport, if the primary duty of the peace officer is the enforcement of the law in or about properties owned, operated, and administered by the employing agency or when performing necessary duties with respect to patrons, employees, and properties of the employing agency.

(e) Any railroad policeman commissioned by the Governor pursuant to Section 8226 of the Public Utilities Code, if the primary duty of the peace officer is the enforcement of the law in or about properties owned, operated, or administered by the employing agency or when performing necessary duties with respect to patrons, employees, and properties of the employing agency. *(Amended by Stats 1990 ch 82 §9, eff. 5/3/90.)*

§830.34. Security officers.

The following persons are peace officers whose authority extends to any place in the state for the purpose of performing their primary duty or when making an arrest pursuant to Section 836 as to any public offense with respect to which there is immediate danger to person or property, or of the escape of the perpetrator of that offense, or pursuant to Section 8597 or 8598 of the Government Code. Those peace officers may carry firearms only if authorized and under terms and conditions specified by their employing agency.

(a) Persons designated as a security officer by a municipal utility district pursuant to Section 12580 of the Public Utilities Code, if the primary duty of the officer is the protection of the properties of the utility district and the protection of the persons thereon.

(b) Persons designated as a security officer by a county water district pursuant to Section 30547 of the

Water Code, if the primary duty of the officer is the protection of the properties of the county water district and the protection of the persons thereon.

(c) The security director of the public utilities commission of a city and county, if the primary duty of the security director is the protection of the properties of the commission and the protection of the persons thereon. *(Added by Stats 1989 ch 1165 §27, eff. 1/1/90.)*

§830.35. Coroners and welfare investigators.

The following persons are peace officers whose authority extends to any place in the state for the purpose of performing their primary duty or when making an arrest pursuant to Section 836 as to any public offense with respect to which there is immediate danger to person or property, or of the escape of the perpetrator of that offense, or pursuant to Section 8597 or 8598 of the Government Code. Those peace officers may carry firearms only if authorized and under terms and conditions specified by their employing agency.

(a) A welfare fraud investigator or inspector, regularly empoyed and paid in that capacity by a county, if the primary duty of the peace officer is the enforcement of the provisions of the Welfare and Institutions Code.

(b) A child support investigator or inspector, regularly employed and paid in that capacity by a district attorney's office, if the primary duty of the peace officer is the enforcement of the provisions of the Welfare and Institutions Code and Section 270.

(c) The coroner and deputy coroners, regularly employed and paid in that capacity, of a county, if the primary duty of the peace officer are those duties set forth in Sections 27469 and 27491 to 27491.4, inclusive, of the Government Code. *(Added by Stats 1989 ch 1165 §28, eff. 1/1/90.)*

§830.36. Court officers.

The following persons are peace officers whose authority extends to any place in the state for the purpose of performing their primary duty or when making an arrest pursuant to Section 836 as to any public offense with respect to which there is immediate danger to person or property, or of the escape of the perpetrator of that offense, or pursuant to Section 8597 or 8598 of the Government Code. Those peace officers may carry firearms only if authorized and under terms and conditions specified by their employing agency.

(a) The Sergeant-at-Arms of each house of the Legislature, if the primary duty of the peace officer is the enforcement of the law in or about properties owned, operated, or administered by the employing agency or when performing necessary duties with respect to patrons, employees, and properties of the employing agency.

(b) Bailiffs of the Supreme Court and of the courts of appeal, and coordinators of security for the judicial branch, if the primary duty of the peace officer is the enforcement of the law in or about properties owned, operated, or administered by the employing agency or when performing necessary duties with respect to patrons, employees, and properties of the employing agency.

(c) Court service officer in a county of the second class and third class, if the primary duty of the peace officer is the enforcement of the law in or about properties owned, operated, or administered by the employing agency or when performing necessary duties with

respect to patrons, employees, and properties of the employing agency. *(Amended by Stats 1990 ch 82 §10, eff. 5/3/90; ch 187 §11, eff. 6/29/90, oper. 7/1/90; ch 1399 §3, eff. 1/1/91.)*

§830.37. Authority as peace officer; arson units.

The following persons are peace officers whose authority extends to any place in the state for the purpose of performing their primary duty or when making an arrest pursuant to Section 836 as to any public offense with respect to which there is immediate danger to person or property, or of the escape of the perpetrator of that offense, or pursuant to Section 8597 or 8598 of the Government Code. Those peace officers may carry firearms only if authorized and under terms and conditions specified by their employing agency.

(a) Members of an arson-investigating unit, regularly paid and employed in that capacity, of a fire department or fire protection agency of a county, city, city and county, district, or the state, if the primary duty of these peace officers is the detection and apprehension of persons who have violated any fire law or committed insurance fraud.

(b) Members other than members of an arson investigating unit, regularly paid and employed in that capacity, of a fire department or fire protection agency of a county, city, city and county, district, or the state, if the primary duty of these peace officers, when acting in that capacity, is the enforcement of laws relating to fire prevention or fire suppression.

(c) Voluntary fire wardens as are designated by the Director of Forestry pursuant to Section 4156 of the Public Resources Code, provided that the primary duty of these peace officers shall be the enforcement of the law as that duty is set forth in Section 4156 of that code.

(d) Firefighter/security guards by the Military Department, if the primary duty of the peace officer is the enforcement of the law in or about properties owned, operated, or administered by the employing agency or when performing necessary duties with respect to patrons, employees, and properties of the employing agency. *(Added by Stats 1989 ch 1165 §30, eff. 1/1/90.)*

§830.38. Mental institution officers.

The officers of a state hospital under the jurisdiction of the State Department of Mental Health or the State Department of Developmental Services appointed pursuant to Section 4313 or 4493 of the Welfare and Institutions Code, are peace officers whose authority extends to any place in the state for the purpose of performing their primary duty or when making an arrest pursuant to Section 836 as to any public offense with respect to which there is immediate danger to person or property, or of the escape of the perpetrator of that offense, or pursuant to Section 8597 or 8598 of the Government Code provided that the primary duty of the peace officers shall be the enforcement of the law as set forth in Sections 4311, 4313, 4491, and 4493 of the Welfare and Institutions Code. Those peace officers may carry firearms only if authorized and under terms and conditions specified by their employing agency. *(Added by Stats 1989 ch 1165 §30.5, eff. 1/1/90.)*

§830.39. Foreign state officers.

(a) Any regularly employed law enforcement officer of the Oregon State Police, the Nevada Depart-

© 1992 by J., B. & L. Gould
Printed in the U.S.A.   EP

ment of Motor Vehicles and Public Safety, or the Arizona Department of Public Safety is a peace officer in this state if all of the following conditions are met:

(1) The officer is providing, or attempting to provide, law enforcement services within this state on the state or county highways and areas immediately adjacent thereto, within a distance of up to 50 statute miles of the contiguous border of this state and the state employing the officer.

(2) The officer is providing, or attempting to provide, law enforcement services pursuant to either of the following:

(A) In response to a request for services initiated by a member of the California Highway Patrol.

(B) In response to a reasonable belief that emergency law enforcement services are necessary for the preservation of life, and a request for services by a member of the Department of the California Highway Patrol is impractical to obtain under the circumstances. In those situations, the officer shall obtain authorization as soon as practical.

(3) The officer is providing, or attempting to provide, law enforcement services for the purpose of assisting a member of the California Highway Patrol to provide emergency service in response to misdemeanor or felony criminal activity, pursuant to the authority of a peace officer as provided in subdivision (a) of Section 830.2, or, in the event of highway-related traffic accidents, emergency incidents or other similar public safety problems, whether or not a member of the California Highway Patrol is present at the scene of the event. Nothing in this section shall be construed to confer upon the officer the authority to enforce traffic or motor vehicle infractions.

(4) An agreement pursuant to Section 2403.5 of the Vehicle Code is in effect between the Department of the California Highway Patrol and the agency of the adjoining state employing the officer, the officer acts in accordance with that agreement, and the agreement specifies that the officer and employing agency of the adjoining state shall be subject to the same civil immunities and liabilities as a peace officer and his or her employing agency in this state.

(5) The officer receives no separate compensation from this state for providing law enforcement services within this state.

(6) The adjoining state employing the officer confers similar rights and authority upon a member of the California Highway Patrol who renders assistance within that state.

(b) Notwithstanding any other provision of law, any person who is acting as a peace officer in this state in the manner described in this section shall be deemed to have met the requirements of Section 1031 of the Government Code and the selection and training standards of the Commission on Peace Officer Standards and Training if the officer has completed the basic training required for peace officers in his or her state.

(c) In no case shall a peace officer of an adjoining state be authorized to provide services within a California jurisdiction during any period in which the regular law enforcement agency of the jurisdiction is involved in a labor dispute.
(Added by Stats 1989 ch 594 §6, eff. 1/1/90; amended and renumbered by Stats 1989 ch 1165 §25.5, eff. 1/1/90.)

§830.4. Security personnel; state and local.

The following persons are peace officers whose authority extends to any place in the state for the purpose of performing their duties under the conditions as specified by statute. Those peace officers may carry firearms only if authorized and under terms and conditions specified by their employing agency.

(a) Members of the California National Guard have the powers of peace officers when they are involved in any or all of the following:

(1) Called or ordered into active state service by the Governor pursuant to the provisions of Section 143 or 146 of the Military and Veterans Code.

(2) Serving within the area wherein military assistance is required.

(3) Directly assisting civil authorities in any of the situations specified in Section 143 or 146.

The authority of the peace officer under this subdivision extends to the area wherein military assistance is required as to a public offense committed or which there is reasonable cause to believe has been committed within that area. The requirements of Section 1031 of the Government Code are not applicable under those circumstances.

(b) Guards and messengers of the Treasurer's office when performing assigned duties as a guard or messenger.

(c) Security officers of the Department of Justice when performing assigned duties as security officers.

(d) Security officers of the California State Police Division. Notwithstanding any other provision of law, the act which designated the persons described in this subdivision as peace officers shall serve only to define those persons as peace officers, the extent of their jurisdiction, and the nature and scope of their authority, powers, and duties, and there shall be no change in the status of those persons for purposes of retirement, workers' compensation or similar injury or death benefits, or other employee benefits.

(e) Security officers of Hastings College of the Law.

These officers shall have authority of peace officers only within the City and County of San Francisco. Notwithstanding any other provisions of law, the peace officers designated by this subdivision shall not be authorized by this subdivision to carry firearms either on or off duty. Notwithstanding any other provision of law, the act which designated the persons described in this subdivision as peace officers shall serve only to define those persons as peace officers, the extent of their jurisdiction, and the nature and scope of their authority, powers, and duties, and there shall be no change in the status of those persons for purposes of retirement, workers' compensation or similar injury or death benefits, or other employee benefits.
(Added by Stats 1989 ch 1165 §32, eff. 1/1/90.)

§830.5. Parole, probation, or correctional officers.

The following persons are peace officers whose authority extends to any place in the state while engaged in the performance of the duties of their respective employment and for the purpose of carrying out the primary faction of their employment or as required under Sections 8597, 8598, and 8617 of the Government Code. Except as specified in this section, these peace officers may carry firearms only if authorized and under those terms and conditions specified by their employing agency:

(a) A parole officer of the Department of Corrections or the Department of the Youth Authority, probation officer, or deputy probation officer, or a board coordinating parole agent employed by the Youthful Offender Parole Board. Except as otherwise provided in this subdivision, the authority of these parole or probation officers shall extend only as follows:

(1) To conditions of parole or of probation by any person in this state on parole or probation.

(2) To the escape of any inmate or ward from a state or local institution.

(3) To the transportation of such persons.

(4) To violations of any penal provisions of law which are discovered in the course of and arise in connection with his or her employment.

Any parole officer of the Department of Corrections, the Department of the Youth Authority, or the Youthful Offender Parole Board is authorized to carry firearms but only as determined by the director on a case-by-case or unit-by-unit basis and only under those terms and conditions specified by the director or chairperson.

(b) A correctional officer employed by the Department of Corrections or any employee of the Department of the Youth Authority having custody of wards or any employee of the Department of Corrections designated by the Director of Corrections or any medical technical assistant series employee designated by the Director of Corrections or designated by the Director of Corrections and employed by the State Department of Mental Health to work in the California Medical Facility or employee of the Board of Prison Terms designated by the Secretary of the Youth and Adult Correctional Agency or employee of the Department of the Youth Authority designated by the Director of the Youth Authority or any superintendent, supervisor, or employee having custodial responsibilities in an institution operated by a probation department, or any transportation officer of a probation department.

(c) The following persons may carry a firearm while not on duty: a parole officer of the Department of Corrections or the Department of the Youth Authority, a correctional officer employed by the Department of Corrections or any employee of the Department of the Youth Authority having custody of wards or any employee of the Department of Corrections designated by the Director of Corrections. A parole officer of the Youthful Offender Parole Board may carry a firearm while not on duty only when so authorized by the chairperson of the board and only under the terms and conditions specified by the chairperson. Nothing in this section shall be interpreted to require licensure pursuant to Section 12025. The director or chairperson may deny, suspend, or revoke for good cause a person's right to carry a firearm under this subdivision. That person shall, upon request, receive a hearing, as provided for in the negotiated grievance procedure between the exclusive employee representative and the Department of Corrections, the Department of the Youth Authority, or the Youthful Offender Parole Board, to review the director's or the chairperson's decision.

(d) Persons permitted to carry firearms pursuant to this section, either on or off duty, shall meet the training requirements of Section 832 and shall qualify with the firearm at least quarterly. It is the responsibility of the individual officer or designee to maintain his or her eligibility to carry concealable firearms off duty. Failure to maintain quarterly qualifications by an officer or designee with any concealable firearms carried off duty shall constitute good cause to suspend or revoke that person's right to carry firearms off duty.

(e) The Department of Corrections shall allow reasonable access to its ranges for officers and designees of either department to qualify to carry concealable firearms off duty. The time spent on the range for purposes of meeting the qualification requirements shall be the person's own time during the person's off-duty hours.

(f) The Director of Corrections shall promulgate regulations consistent with this section. *(Amended by Stats 1990 ch 1194 §1, eff. 1/1/91.)*

§830.55. Duties of correctional officers.

(a) As used in this section, a correctional officer is a peace officer, employed by a city, county, or city and county which operates a facility described in Section 2910.5 of this code or Section 1753.3 of the Welfare and Institutions Code or facilities operated by counties pursuant to Section 6241 or 6242 of this code under contract with the Department of Corrections or the Department of the Youth Authority, who has the authority and responsibility for maintaining custody of specified state prison inmates or wards, and who performs tasks related to the operation of a detention facility used for the detention of persons who have violated parole or are awaiting parole back into the community or, upon court order, either for their own safekeeping or for the specific purpose of serving a sentence therein.

(b) A correctional officer shall have no right to carry or possess firearms in the performance of his or her prescribed duties, except, under the direction of the superintendent of the facility, while engaged in transporting prisoners, guarding hospitalized prisoners, or suppressing riots, lynchings, escapes, or rescues in or about a detention facility established pursuant to Section 2910.5 of this code or Section 1753.3 of the Welfare and Institutions Code.

(c) Each person described in this section as a correctional officer, within 90 days following the date of the initial assignment to that position, shall satisfactorily complete the training course specified in Section 832. In addition, each person designated as a correctional officer, within one year following the date of the initial assignment as an officer, shall have satisfactorily met the minimum selection and training standards prescribed by the Board of Corrections pursuant to Section 6035. Persons designated as correctional officers, before the expiration of the 90-day and one-year periods described in this subdivision, who have not yet completed the required training, may perform the duties of a correctional officer only while under the direct supervision of a correctional officer who has completed the training required in this section, and shall not carry or possess firearms in the performance of their prescribed duties.

(d) This section shall not be construed to confer any authority upon a correctional officer except while on duty.

(e) A correctional officer may use reasonable force in establishing and maintaining custody of persons delivered to him or her by a law enforcement officer, may make arrests for misdemeanors and felonies within the local detention facility pursuant to a duly issued warrant, and may make warrantless arrests

© 1992 by J. B. & L. Gould
Printed in the U.S.A.   EP

pursuant to Section 836.5 only during the duration of his or her job. *(Amended by Stats 1991 ch 1100 §1, eff. 1/1/92.)*

§830.6. Reserve or auxiliary personnel.

(a) (1) Whenever any qualified person is deputized or appointed by the proper authority as a reserve or auxiliary sheriff or city police officer, a reserve deputy sheriff, a reserve police officer of a regional park district or of a transit district, a reserve deputy of the Department of Fish and Game, a reserve special agent of the Department of Justice, a reserve officer of a community service district which is authorized under subdivision (h) of Section 61600 of the Government Code to maintain a police department or other police protection, or a reserve officer of a police protection district formed under Part 1 (commencing with Section 20000) of Division 14 of the Health and Safety Code, and is assigned specific police functions by that authority, the person is a peace officer; provided, the person qualifies as set forth in Section 832.6, and provided further, that the authority of the person as a peace officer shall extend only for the duration of the person's specific assignment. A transit district reserve officer may carry firearms only if authorized by, and under those terms and conditions as are specified by, his or her employing agency.

(2) Whenever any qualified person is deputized or appointed by the proper authority as a reserve or auxiliary sheriff or city police officer, a reserve deputy sheriff, or a reserve police officer of a regional park district or of a transit district, and is so designated by local ordinance or, if the local agency is not authorized to act by ordinance, by resolution, either individually or by class, and is assigned to the prevention and detection of crime and the general enforcement of the laws of this state by that authority, the person is a peace officer; provided the person qualifies as set forth in paragraph (1) of subdivision (a) of Section 832.6, and provided further, that the authority of the person shall include the full powers and duties of a peace officer as provided by Section 830.1, or in the case of a transit district reserve police officer, the powers and duties which are authorized in Section 830.33.

(b) Whenever any person is summoned to the aid of any uniformed peace officer, the summoned person shall be vested with the powers of a peace officer as are expressly delegated to him or her by the summoning officer or as are otherwise reasonably necessary to properly assist the officer. *(Amended by Stats 1991 ch 509 §1, eff. 1/1/92.)*

§830.65. Peace officer status for local officers appointed to Campaign Against Marijuana Planting.

(a) Any person who is a regularly employed police officer of a city or a regularly employed deputy sheriff of a county, or a reserve peace officer of a city or county and is appointed in the manner described in paragraph (1) or (2) of subdivision (a) of Section 832.6, may be appointed as a Campaign Against Marijuana Planting emergency appointee by the Attorney General pursuant to Section 5 of Chapter 1563 of the Statutes of 1985 to assist with a specific investigation, tactical operation, or search and rescue operation. When so appointed, the person shall be a peace officer of the Department of Justice, provided that the person's authority shall extend only for the duration of the specific assignment.

(b) Notwithstanding any other provision of law, any person who is appointed as a peace officer in the manner described in this section shall be deemed to have met the requirements of Section 1031 of the Government Code and the selection and training standards of the Commission on Peace Officer Standards and Training. *(Added by Stats 1988 ch 1482, §4 eff. 1/1/89.)*

§830.7. Private citizens with powers of arrest.

The following persons are not peace officers but may exercise the powers of arrest of a peace officer as specified in Section 836 during the course and within the scope of their employment, if they successfully complete a course in the exercise of those powers pursuant to Section 832:

(a) Persons designated by a cemetery authority pursuant to Section 8325 of the Health and Safety Code.

(b) Persons regularly employed as security officers for institutions of higher education, recognized under subdivision (a) of Section 94310.1 of the Education Code, if the institution has concluded a memorandum of understanding, permitting the exercise of that authority, with the sheriff or chief of police within whose jurisdiction the institution lies.

(c) Persons regularly employed as security officers for health facilities, as defined in Section 1250 of the Health and Safety Code, which are owned and operated by cities, counties, and cities and counties, if the facility has concluded a memorandum of understanding, permitting the exercise of that authority, with the sheriff or chief of police within whose jurisdictions the facility lies.

(d) Employees of the California Department of Forestry and Fire Protection designated by the Director of Forestry and approved by the Secretary of the Resources Agency.

(e) Employees of the Public Utilities Commission assigned to the Transportation Division, designated by the division director and approved by the commission, to the extent necessary to enforce the provisions of the Public Utilities Code. These employees may exercise the power to serve warrants as specified in Sections 1523 and 1530 during the course and within the scope of their employment, if they receive a course in the exercise of those powers pursuant to Section 832.

(f) Persons regularly employed as inspectors, supervisors, or security officers for transit districts, as defined in Section 99213 of the Public Utilities Code, if the district has concluded a memorandum of understanding permitting the exercise of that authority, with, as applicable, the sheriff, chief of police, or California Highway Patrol within whose jurisdiction the district lies. For purposes of this subdivision, the exercise of peace officer authority may include the authority to remove a vehicle from a railroad right-of-way as set forth in Section 22656 of the Vehicle Code. *(Amended by Stats 1991 ch 229 §1, 910 §6, eff. 1/1/92.)*

§830.8. Federal employees; criminal investigators.

(a) Federal criminal investigators and law enforcement officers are not California peace officers but may exercise the powers of arrest of a peace officer as specified in Section 836 and the powers of a peace officer specified in Section 5150 of the Welfare and Institutions Code for violations of state or local laws provided that these investigators and law enforcement officers are engaged in the enforcement of federal criminal laws and exercise the arrest powers only incidental to the performance of their federal duties. These investigators and law enforcement officers, prior to the exercise of these arrest powers, shall have been certified by their agency heads as having satisfied the training requirements of Section 832.

(b) Duly authorized federal employees who comply with the training requirements set forth in Section 832 are peace officers when they are engaged in enforcing applicable state or local laws on property owned or possessed by the United States government, or on any street, sidewalk, or property adjacent thereto, and with the written consent of the sheriff or the chief of police, respectively, in whose jurisdiction the property is situated.

(c) National park rangers are not California peace officers but may exercise the powers of arrest of a peace officer as specified in Section 836 and the powers of a peace officer specified in Section 5150 of the Welfare and Institutions Code for violations of state or local laws provided these rangers are exercising the arrest powers incidental to the performance of their federal duties or providing or attempting to provide law enforcement services in response to a request initiated by California state park rangers to assist in preserving the peace and protecting state parks and other property for which California state park rangers are responsible. National park rangers, prior to the exercise of these arrest powers, shall have been certified by their agency heads as having satisfactorily completed the training requirements of Section 832.3, or the equivalent thereof. *(Amended by Stats 1990 ch 82 §12, eff. 5/3/90; ch 900 §1, eff. 1/1/91; ch 1695 §10.3, eff. 1/1/91.)*

§830.9. Animal control officers exercise powers of arrest and powers to serve warrant.

Animal control officers are not peace officers but may exercise the powers of arrest of a peace officer as specified in Section 836 and the power to serve warrants as specified in Sections 1523 and 1530 during the course and within the scope of their employment, if those officers successfully complete a course in the exercise of those powers pursuant to Section 832. That part of the training course specified in Section 832 pertaining to the carrying and use of firearms shall not be required for any animal control officer whose employing agency prohibits the use of firearms.

For the purposes of this section, "firearms" includes capture guns, blowguns, carbon dioxide operated rifles and pistols, air guns, handguns, rifles, and shotguns. *(Amended by Stats 1990 ch 82 §13, eff. 5/3/90.)*

§830.10. Identification badge.

Any uniformed peace officer shall wear a badge, nameplate, or other device which bears clearly on its face the identification number or name of the officer. *(Amended by Stats 1989 ch 1165 §38, eff. 1/1/90.)*

§830.11. Persons not peace officers.

(a) The following persons are not peace officers but may exercise the powers of arrest of a peace officer as specified in Section 836 and the power to serve warrants as specified in Sections 1523 and 1530 during the course and within the scope of their employment, if they receive a course in the exercise of those powers pursuant to Section 832. The authority and powers of

the persons designated under this section shall extend to any place in the state:

(1) Persons employed by the State Banking Department designated by the Superintendent of Banks, provided that the primary duty of those persons shall be the enforcement of, and investigations relating to, the provisions of law administered by the State Banking Department.

(2) Persons employed by the Department of Savings and Loan designated by the Commissioner of Savings and Loan, provided that the primary duty of those persons shall be the enforcement of, and investigations relating to, the provisions of law administered by the Department of Savings and Loan.

(3) Persons employed by the Department of Real Estate designated by the Real Estate Commissioner, provided that the primary duty of these persons shall be the enforcement of the laws set forth in Part 1 (commencing with Section 10000) and Part 2 (commencing with Section 11000) of Division 4 of the Business and Professions Code. The Real Estate Commissioner may designate persons under this section, who at the time of their designation, are assigned to the Special Investigations Unit, internally known as the Crisis Response Team.

(4) Persons employed by the State Lands Commission designated by the executive officer, provided that the primary duty of those persons shall be the enforcement of the law relating to the duties of the State Lands Commission.

(b) Notwithstanding any other provision of law, persons designated pursuant to this section shall not carry firearms.

(c) Persons designated pursuant to this section shall be included as "peace officers of the state" under paragraph (2) of subdivision (c) of Section 11105 for the purpose of receiving state summary criminal history information and shall be furnished that information on the same basis as peace officers of the state designated in paragraph (2) of subdivision (c) of Section 11105. *(Amended by Stats 1989 ch 640 §§7, 8; 699 §§1, 2, eff. 9/21/89.)*

§830.12. Persons not peace officers may issue citations.

Notwithstanding any other provision of law, persons designated by a local agency as litter control officers, vehicle abatement officers, registered sanitarians, and solid waste specialists, are not peace officers, may not exercise the powers of arrest of a peace officer, as specified in Section 836, and shall not be authorized to carry or use firearms within the scope and course of their employment. These persons may, however, be authorized by the governing board of the particular local agency to issue citations involving violations of laws relating to abandoned vehicles and littering. *(Added by Stats 1988 ch 726 §1, eff. 1/1/89.)*

§831. Custodial officers, not peace officers.

(a) A custodial officer is a public officer, not a peace officer, employed by a law enforcement agency of a city or county who has the authority and responsibility for maintaining custody of prisoners and performs tasks related to the operation of a local detention facility used for the detention of persons usually pending arraignment or upon court order either for their own safekeeping or for the specific purpose of serving a sentence therein.

© 1992 by J., B. & L. Gould
Printed in the U.S.A.   EP

(b) A custodial officer shall have no right to carry or possess firearms in the performance of his or her prescribed duties.

(c) Each person described in this section as a custodial officer shall, within 90 days following the date of the initial assignment to the position, satisfactorily complete the training course specified in Section 832. In addition, each person designated as a custodial officer shall, within one year following the date of the initial assignment as a custodial officer, have satisfactorily met the minimum selection and training standards prescribed by the Board of Corrections pursuant to Section 6035. Persons designated as custodial officers, before the expiration of the 90-day and one-year periods described in this subdivision, who have not yet completed the required training, may perform the duties of a custodial officer only while under the direct supervision of a peace officer as described in Section 830.1, who has completed the training prescribed by the Commission on Peace Officer Standards and Training, or a custodial officer who has completed the training required in this section.

(d) At any time 20 or more custodial officers are on duty, there shall be at least one peace officer, as described in Section 830.1, on duty at the same time to supervise the performance of the custodial officers.

(e) This section shall not be construed to confer any authority upon any custodial officer except while on duty.

(f) A custodial officer may use reasonable force in establishing and maintaining custody of persons delivered to him or her by a law enforcement officer; may make arrests for misdemeanors and felonies within the local detention facility pursuant to a duly issued warrant; may release without further criminal process persons arrested for intoxication; and may release misdemeanants on citation to appear in lieu of or after booking. (*Amended by Stats 1991 ch 1100 §2, eff. 1/1/92.*)

§831.5. Custodial officers.

(a) As used in this section, a custodial officer is a public officer, not a peace officer, employed by a law enforcement agency of San Diego County, Fresno County, or a county having a population of 425,000 or less who has the authority and responsibility for maintaining custody of prisoners and performs tasks related to the operation of a local detention facility used for the detention of persons usually pending arraignment or upon court order either for their own safekeeping or for the specific purpose of serving a sentence therein. A custodial officer includes a person designated as a correctional officer, jailer, or other similar title. The duties of custodial officer may include the serving of warrants, court orders, writs and subpoenas in the detention facility or under circumstances arising directly out of maintaining custody of prisoners and related tasks.

(b) A custodial officer shall have no right to carry or possess firearms in the performance of his or her prescribed duties, except, under the direction of the sheriff or chief of police, while engaged in transporting prisoners; guarding hospitalized prisoners; or suppressing jail riots, lynchings, escapes, or rescues in or about a detention facility falling under the care and custody of the sheriff or chief of police.

(c) Each person described in this section as a custodial officer shall, within 90 days following the date of the initial assignment to that position, satisfactorily complete the training course specified in Section 832. In addition, each person designated as a custodial officer shall, within one year following the date of the initial assignment as a custodial officer, have satisfactorily met the minimum selection and training standards prescribed by the Board of Corrections pursuant to Section 6035. Persons designated as custodial officers, before the expiration of the 90-day and one-year periods described in this subdivision, who have not yet completed the required training, shall not carry or possess firearms in the performance of their prescribed duties, but may perform the duties of a custodial officer only while under the direct supervision of a peace officer as described in Section 830.1, who has completed the training prescribed by the Commission on Peace Officer Standards and Training, or a custodial officer who has completed the training required in this section.

(d) At any time 20 or more custodial officers are on duty, there shall be at least one peace officer, as described in Section 830.1, on duty at the same time to supervise the performance of the custodial officers.

(e) This section shall not be construed to confer any authority upon any custodial officer except while on duty.

(f) A custodial officer may use reasonable force in establishing and maintaining custody of persons delivered to him or her by a law enforcement officer; may make arrests for misdemeanors and felonies within the local detention facility pursuant to a duly issued warrant; may make warrantless arrests pursuant to Section 836.5 only during the duration of his or her job; may release without further criminal process persons arrested for intoxication; and may release misdemeanants on citation to appear in lieu of or after booking. (*Amended by Stats 1991 ch 265 §1, 1100 §3, eff. 1/1/92.*)

§831.6. Transportation officers.

(a) A transportation officer is a public officer, not a peace officer, appointed on a contract basis by a peace officer to transport a prisoner or prisoners.

(b) A transportation officer shall have the authority of a public officer, and shall have the right to carry or possess firearms, only while engaged in the transportation of a prisoner or prisoners for the duration of the contract.

(c) Each person described in this section as a transportation officer shall, prior to the transportation of any prisoner, have satisfactorily completed the training course specified in Section 832.

(d) A transportation officer may use reasonable force in establishing and maintaining custody of persons delivered to him or her by a peace officer.

§832. Training course required.

(a) Every person described in this chapter as a peace officer shall satisfactorily complete an introductory course of training prescribed by the Commission on Peace Officer Standards and Training. On or after July 1, 1989, satisfactory completion of the course shall be demonstrated by passage of an appropriate examination developed or approved by the commission. Training in the carrying and use of firearms shall not be required of any peace officer whose employing agency prohibits the use of firearms.

(b) (1) Every peace officer described in this chapter, prior to the exercise of the powers of a peace officer, shall have satisfactorily completed the course of training described in subdivision (a).

(2) Every peace officer described in Section 13510 or in subdivision (a) of Section 830.2 may satisfactorily complete the training required by this section as part of the training prescribed pursuant to Section 13510.

(c) Persons described in this chapter as peace officers who have not satisfactorily completed the course described in subdivision (a), as specified in subdivision (b), shall not have the powers of a peace officer until they satisfactorily complete the course.

(d) Any peace officer who, on March 4, 1972, possesses or is qualified to possess the basic certificate as awarded by the Commission on Peace Officer Standards and Training shall be exempted from this section.

(e) (1) Any person completing the training described in subdivision (a) who does not become employed as a peace officer within three years from the date of passing the examination described in subdivision (a), or who has a three-year or longer break in service as a peace officer, shall pass the examination described in subdivision (a) prior to the exercise of the powers of a peace officer, except for any person described in paragraph (2).

(2) The requirement in paragraph (1) does not apply to any person who meets any of the following requirements:

(A) Is returning to a management position that is at the second level of supervision or higher.

(B) Has successfully requalified for a basic course through the Commission on Peace Officer Standards and Training.

(C) Has maintained proficiency through teaching the course described in subdivision (a).

(D) During the break in California service, was continuously employed as a peace officer in another state or at the federal level.

(f) The commission may charge appropriate fees for the examination required by subdivision (e), not to exceed actual costs. *(Amended by Stats 1991 ch 509 §2, eff. 1/1/92.)*

§832.1. Required training for airport security officers.

Any airport security officer, airport policeman, or airport special officer, regularly employed and paid by a city, county, city and county, or district who is a peace officer shall have completed a course of training relative to airport security approved by the Commission on Peace Officers Standards and Training. Any such airport officer so employed on the effective date of this section shall have completed the course of instruction required by this section by September 1, 1973. Any airport officer so employed after such effective date shall have completed the course of instruction within 90 days after such employment.

Any officer who has not satisfactorily completed such course within such prescribed time shall not continue to have the powers of a peace officer until they have satisfactorily completed such course.

§832.2. Required training for school peace officers.

(a) It is the intent of the Legislature to ensure the safety of students, staff, and the public on or about California's public schools, by providing school peace officers with training that will enable them to deal with the increasingly diverse and dangerous situations they encounter.

(b) Every school peace officer, as described in Sections 39670 and 72331 of the Education Code, shall complete a course of training approved by the Commission on Peace Officer Standards and Training relating directly to the role of school peace officers. Any person employed as a school peace officer prior to the date that the Commission on Peace Officer Standards and Training approves the course of training shall complete the course of instruction within three years from the date that the Commission on Peace Officer Standards and Training approves the course of training. Any person who is not employed as a school peace officer until on or after the date that the Commission on Peace Officer Standards and Training approves the course of training shall complete the course of instruction within one year from the date his or her employment commences.

The school peace officer training course shall address guidelines and procedures for reporting offenses to other law enforcement agencies that deal with violence on campus and other school related matters, as determined by the Commission on Peace Officer Standards and Training. The Commission on Peace Officer Standards and Training shall develop and approve the course of training no later than January 1, 1991, and shall consult with school peace officers regarding the content and hourly requirement for this course.

(c) This section does not apply to any school peace officer whose employer requires its school peace officers to possess the basic certificate that is awarded by the Commission on Peace Officer Standards and Training or any school peace officer who possess the basic certificate that is awarded by the Commission on Peace Officers Standards and Training. *(Added by Stats 1989 ch 1078 §1, eff. 1/1/90.)*

§832.3. Completion of training course required after January 1, 1975.

(a) Except as provided in subdivision (b), any sheriff, undersheriff, or deputy sheriff of a county, any police officer of a city, and any police officer of a district authorized by statute to maintain a police department, who is first employed after January 1, 1975, shall successfully complete a course of training prescribed by the Commission on Peace Officer Standards and Training before exercising the powers of a peace officer, except while participating as a trainee in a supervised field training program approved by the Commission on Peace Officer Standards and Training. The training course for an undersheriff and deputy sheriff of a county and a police officer of a city shall be the same.

(b) For the purpose of standardizing the training required in subdivision (a), the commission shall develop a training proficiency testing program, including a standardized examination which enables (1) comparisons between presenters of such training and (2) development of a data base for subsequent training programs. Presenters approved by the commission to provide the training required in subdivision (a) shall administer the standardized examination to all graduates. Nothing in this subdivision shall make the completion of such examination a condition of successful completion of the training required in subdivision (a).

(c) Notwithstanding subdivision (c) of Section 84500 of the Education Code and any regulations adopted pursuant thereto, community colleges may

© 1992 by J., B. & L. Gould
Printed in the U.S.A.   **EP**

give preference in enrollment to employed law enforcement trainees who shall complete training as prescribed by this section. At least 15 percent of each presentation shall consist of nonlaw enforcement trainees if they are available. Preference should only be given when the trainee could not complete the course within the time required by statute, and only when no other training program is reasonably available. Average daily attendance for such courses shall be reported for state aid.

(d) Prior to July 1, 1987, the commission shall make a report to the Legislature on academy proficiency testing scores. This report shall include an evaluation of the correlation between academy proficiency test scores and performance as a peace officer. *(Amended by Stats 1987 ch 1433 §2.)*

§832.4. Certificate issued to peace officers.

(a) Any undersheriff or deputy sheriff of a county, any policeman of a city, and any policeman of a district authorized by statute to maintain a police department, who is first employed after January 1, 1974, and is responsible for the prevention and detection of crime and the general enforcement of the criminal laws of this state, shall obtain the basic certificate issued by the Commission on Peace Officer Standards and Training within 18 months of his employment in order to continue to exercise the powers of a peace officer after the expiration of such 18-month period.

(b) Every peace officer listed in subdivision (a) of Section 830.1, except a sheriff, elected constable, or elected marshal, who is employed after January 1, 1988, shall obtain the basic certificate issued by the Commission on Peace Officer Standards and Training upon completion of probation, but in no case later than 24 months after his or her employment, in order to continue to exercise the powers of a peace officer after the expiration of the 24-month period.

In those cases where the probationary period established by the employing agency is 24 months, the peace officers described in this subdivision may continue to exercise the powers of a peace officer for an additional three-month period to allow for the processing of the certification application. *(Amended by Stats 1987 ch 843 §1.)*

§832.5. Investigation of citizens' complaints against personnel.

(a) Each department or agency in this state which employs peace officers shall establish a procedure to investigate citizens' complaints against the personnel of such departments or agencies, and shall make a written description of the procedure available to the public.

(b) Complaints and any reports or findings relating thereto shall be retained for a period of at least five years.

§832.6. Persons deputized; training and duties.

(a) Every person deputized or appointed, as described in subdivision (a) of Section 830.6, shall have the powers of a peace officer only when the person is any of the following:

(1) Deputized or appointed pursuant to paragraph (1) of subdivision (a) of Section 830.6 and is assigned to the prevention and detection of crime and the general enforcement of the laws of this state, whether or not working alone, and the person has completed the basic training prescribed by the Commission on Peace Officer Standards and Training.

A person deputized or appointed pursuant to paragraph (2) of subdivision (a) of Section 830.6 shall have the powers of a peace officer when assigned to the prevention and detection of crime and the general enforcement of the laws of this state, whether or not working alone, and the person has completed the basic training course for deputy sheriffs and police officers prescribed by the Commission on Peace Officer Standards and Training.

(2) Assigned to the prevention and detection of crime and the general enforcement of the laws of this state while under the immediate supervision of a peace officer possessing a basic certificate issued by the Commission on Peace Officer Standards and Training, the person is engaged in a field training program approved by the Commission on Peace Officer Standards and Training, and the person has completed the course required by Section 832 and any other training prescribed by the commission.

(3) Deployed and authorized only to carry out limited duties not requiring general law enforcement powers in their routine performance. Those persons shall be permitted to perform these duties only under the direct supervision of a peace officer possessing a basic certificate issued by the commission, and shall have completed the training required under Section 832 and any other training prescribed by the commission for those persons. Notwithstanding the provisions of this paragraph, a level III reserve officer may perform search and rescue, personnel administration support, community public information services, communications technician services, and scientific services, which do not involve direct law enforcement without supervision.

(4) Assigned to the prevention and detection of a particular crime or crimes or to the detection or apprehension of a particular individual or individuals while working under the supervision of a California peace officer in a county adjacent to the state border who possesses a basic certificate issued by the Commission on Peace Officer Standards and Training, and the person is a law enforcement officer who is regularly employed by a local or state law enforcement agency in an adjoining state and has completed the basic training required for peace officers in his or her state.

This training shall fully satisfy any other training requirements required by law, including those specified in Section 832.

In no case shall a peace officer of an adjoining state provide services within a California jurisdiction during any period in which the regular law enforcement agency of the jurisdiction is involved in a labor dispute.

(b) Notwithstanding subdivision (a), a person who is issued a level I reserve officer certificate before January 1, 1981, shall have the full powers and duties of a peace officer as provided by Section 830.1 if so designated by local ordinance or, if the local agency is not authorized to act by ordinance, by resolution, either individually or by class, if the appointing authority determines the person is qualified to perform general law enforcement duties by reason of the person's training and experience. persons who were qualified to be issued the level I reserve officer certificate before January 1, 1981, and who state in writing under penalty of perjury that they applied for but were not issued the certificate before January 1, 1981, may be issued the certificate before July 1, 1984. For purposes of this section, certificates so issued shall be deemed to have the full force and effect of any level I reserve officer certificate issued prior to January 1, 1981.

(c) In carrying out this section, the commission:

(1) May use proficiency testing to satisfy reserve training standards.

(2) Shall provide for convenient training to remote areas in the state.

(3) Shall establish a professional certificate for reserve officers as defined in paragraph (1) of subdivision (a) and may establish a professional certificate for reserve officers as defined in paragraphs (2) and (3) of subdivision (a).

(d) In carrying out paragraphs (1) and (3) of subdivision (c), the commission may establish and levy appropriate fees, provided the fees do not exceed the cost for administering the respective services. These fees shall be deposited in the Peace Officers' Training Fund established by Section 13520.

(e) The commission shall include an amount in its annual budget request to carry out this section. *(Amended by Stats 1989 ch 594 §7, eff. 1/1/90.)*

§832.7. Confidentiality of peace officer personnel records.

(a) Peace officer personnel records and records maintained by any state or local agency pursuant to Section 832.5, or information obtained from these records, are confidential and shall not be disclosed in any criminal or civil proceeding except by discovery pursuant to Sections 1043 and 1046 of the Evidence Code. This section shall not apply to investigations or proceedings concerning the conduct of police officers or a police agency conducted by a grand jury, a district attorney's office, or the Attorney General's office.

(b) Notwithstanding subdivision (a), a department or agency which employs peace officers may disseminate data regarding the number, type, or disposition of complaints (sustained, not sustained, exonerated, or unfounded, made against its officers if that information is in a form which does not identify the individuals involved.

(c) Nothing in this section shall prohibit a department or agency from notifying the complaining party of the disposition of his or her complaint.

The notification described in this subdivision shall not be conclusive or binding or admissible as evidence in any separate or subsequent action or proceeding brought before an arbitrator, court, or judge of this state or the United States.

(d) Nothing in this section shall affect the discovery or disclosure of information contained in a peace officer's personnel file pursuant to Section 1043 of the Evidence Code. *(Amended by Stats 1989 ch 615 §1, eff. 1/1/90.)*

§832.8. Personnel records.

As used in Section 832.7, "personnel records" means any file maintained under that individual's name by his or her employing agency and containing records relating to any of the following:

(a) Personal data, including marital status, family members, educational and employment history, home addresses, or similar information.

(b) Medical history.

(c) Election of employee benefits.

(d) Employee advancement, appraisal, or discipline.

(e) Complaints, or investigations of complaints, concerning an event or transaction in which he or she participated, or which he or she perceived, and pertaining to the manner in which he or she performed his or her duties.

(f) Any other information the disclosure of which would constitute an unwarranted invasion of personal privacy. *(Amended by Stats 1990 ch 264 §1, eff. 1/1/91.)*

CHAPTER 5

ARREST, BY WHOM AND HOW MADE

§833. Searching persons for dangerous weapons.

A peace officer may search for dangerous weapons any person whom he has legal cause to arrest, whenever he has reasonable cause to believe that the person possesses a dangerous weapon. If the officer finds a dangerous weapon, he may take and keep it until the completion of the questioning, when he shall either return it or arrest the person. The arrest may be for the illegal possession of the weapon.

§833.5. Detention for determination of probable offense.

(a) In addition to any other detention permitted by law, if a peace officer has reasonable cause to believe that a person has a firearm or other deadly weapon with him or her in violation of any provision of law relating to firearms or deadly weapons the peace officer may detain that person to determine whether a crime relating to firearms or deadly weapons has been committed.

For purposes of this section "reasonable cause to detain" requires that the circumstances known or apparent to the officer must include specific and articulable facts causing him or her to suspect that some offense relating to firearms or deadly weapons has taken place or is occurring or is about to occur and that the person he or she intends to detain is involved in that offense. The circumstances must be such as would cause any reasonable peace officer in like position, drawing when appropriate on his or her training and experience, to suspect the same offense and the same involvement by the person in question.

(b) Incident to any detention permitted pursuant to subdivision (a), a peace officer may conduct a limited search of the person for firearms or weapons if the peace officer reasonably concludes that the person detained may be armed and presently dangerous to the peace officer or others. Any firearm or weapon seized pursuant to a valid detention or search pursuant to this section shall be admissible in evidence in any proceeding for any purpose permitted by law.

(c) This section shall not be construed to otherwise limit the authority of a peace officer to detain any person or to make an arrest based on reasonable cause.

(d) This section shall not be construed to permit a peace officer to conduct a detention or search of any person at the person's residence or place of business absent a search warrant or other reasonable cause to detain or search.

(e) If a firearm or weapon is seized pursuant to this section and the person from whom it was seized owned the firearm or weapon and is convicted of a violation

© 1992 by J., B. & L. Gould
Printed in the U.S.A.   EP

of any offense relating to the possession of such firearm or weapon, the court shall order the firearm or weapon to be deemed a nuisance and disposed of in the manner provided by Section 12028.

§834. Arrest defined. By whom defined.

An arrest is taking a person into custody, in a case and in the manner authorized by law. An arrest may be made by a peace officer or by a private person.

§834a. Resisting arrest; duty to refrain.

If a person has knowledge, or by the exercise of reasonable care, should have knowledge, that he is being arrested by a peace officer, it is the duty of such person to refrain from using force or any weapon to resist such arrest.

§835. Method of arrest.

An arrest is made by an actual restraint of the person, or by submission to the custody of an officer. The person arrested may be subjected to such restraint as is reasonable for his arrest and detention.

§835a. Effecting arrest; resistance.

Any peace officer who has reasonable cause to believe that the person to be arrested has committed a public offense may use reasonable force to effect the arrest, to prevent escape or to overcome resistance.

A peace officer who makes or attempts to make an arrest need not retreat or desist from his efforts by reason of the resistance or threatened resistance of the person being arrested; nor shall such officer be deemed an aggressor or lose his right to self-defense by the use of reasonable force to effect the arrest or to prevent escape or to overcome resistance.

§836. Arrests with or without warrants.

A peace officer may make an arrest in obedience to a warrant, or may, pursuant to the authority granted him by the provisions of Chapter 4.5 (commencing with Section 830) of Title 3 of Part 2, without a warrant, arrest a person:

1. Whenever he has reasonable cause to believe that the person to be arrested has committed a public offense in his presence.

2. When a person arrested has committed a felony, although not in his presence.

3. Whenever he has reasonable cause to believe that the person to be arrested has committed a felony, whether or not a felony has in fact been committed.

§836.3. Arrest of convicted escapee.

A peace officer may make an arrest in obedience to a warrant delivered to him, or may, without a warrant, arrest a person who, while charged with or convicted of a misdemeanor, has escaped from any county or city jail, prison, industrial farm or industrial road camp or from the custody of the officer or person in charge of him while engaged on any county road or other county work or going to or returning from such county road or other county work or from the custody of any officer or person in whose lawful custody he is when such escape is not by force or violence.

§836.5. Arrest by public officer or employee without warrant.

(a) A public officer or employee, when authorized by ordinance, may arrest a person without a warrant whenever he has reasonable cause to believe that the person to be arrested has committed a misdemeanor in his presence which is a violation of a statute or ordinance which the officer or employee has the duty to enforce.

(b) There shall be no civil liability on the part of, and no cause of action shall arise against, any public officer or employee acting pursuant to subdivision (a) and within the scope of his authority for false arrest or false imprisonment arising out of any arrest which is lawful or which the public officer or employee, at the time of the arrest, had reasonable cause to believe was lawful. No such officer or employee shall be deemed an aggressor or lose his right to self-defense by the use of reasonable force to effect the arrest, prevent escape, or overcome resistance.

(c) In any case in which a person is arrested pursuant to subdivision (a) and the person arrested does not demand to be taken before a magistrate, the public officer or employee making the arrest shall prepare a written notice to appear and release the person on his promise to appear, as prescribed by Chapter 5C (commencing with Section 853.6). The provisions of that chapter shall thereafter apply with reference to any proceeding based upon the issuance of a written notice to appear pursuant to this authority.

(d) The governing body of a local agency, by ordinance, may authorize its officers and employees who have the duty to enforce a statute or ordinance to arrest persons for violations of such statute or ordinance as provided in subdivision (a).

(e) For the purpose of this section, "ordinance" includes an order, rule, or regulation of any air pollution control district.

(f) For purposes of this section, a "public officer or employee" includes an officer or employee of a nonprofit transit corporation wholly owned by a local agency and formed to carry out the purposes of the local agency.

§836.6. Escape from custody.

(a) It is unlawful for any person who is remanded by a magistrate or judge of any court in this state to the custody of a sheriff, marshal, or other police agency, to thereafter escape or attempt to escape from that custody.

(b) It is unlawful for any person who has been lawfully arrested by any peace officer and who knows, or by the exercise of reasonable care should have known, that he or she has been so arrested, to thereafter escape or attempt to escape from that peace officer.

(c) Any person who violates subdivision (a) or (b) is guilty of a misdemeanor, punishable by imprisonment in a county jail not to exceed one year. However, if the escape or attempted escape is by force or violence, and the person proximately causes a peace officer serious bodily injury, the person shall be punished by imprisonment in the state prison for two, three, or four years, or by imprisonment in a county jail not to exceed one year. *(Added by Stats 1991 ch 171 §1, eff. 1/1/92.)*

§837. Arrests by private persons.

A private person may arrest another:

1. For a public offense committed or attempted in his presence.

2. When the person arrested has committed a felony, although not in his presence.

3. When a felony has been in fact committed, and he has reasonable cause for believing the person arrested to have committed it.

§838. Magistrates may order arrest.

A magistrate may orally order a peace officer or private person to arrest anyone committing or attempting to commit a public offense in the presence of such magistrate.

§839. Persons making arrest may summon assistance.

Any person making an arrest may orally summon as many persons as he deems necessary to aid him therein.

§840. When arrest can be made.

An arrest for the commission of a felony may be made on any day and at any time of the day or night. An arrest for the commission of a misdemeanor or an infraction cannot be made between the hours of 10 o'clock p.m. of any day and 6 o'clock a. m. of the succeeding day, unless:

(1) The arrest is made without a warrant pursuant to Section 836 or 837.

(2) The arrest is made in a public place.

(3) The arrest is made when the person is in custody pursuant to another lawful arrest.

(4) The arrest is made pursuant to a warrant which, for good cause shown, directs that it may be served at any time of the day or night.

§841. Informing person arrested of intention, cause, and authority.

The person making the arrest must inform the person to be arrested of the intention to arrest him, of the cause of the arrest, and the authority to make it, except when the person making the arrest has reasonable cause to believe that the person to be arrested is actually engaged in the commission of or an attempt to commit an offense, or the person to be arrested is pursued immediately after its commission, or after an escape.

The person making the arrest must, on request of the person he is arresting, inform the latter of the offense for which he is being arrested.

§842. Showing of warrant; arrest without possession of warrant.

An arrest by a peace officer acting under a warrant is lawful even though the officer does not have the warrant in his possession at the time of the arrest, but if the person arrested so requests it, the warrant shall be shown to him as soon as practicable.

§843. What force may be used.

When the arrest is being made by an officer under the authority of a warrant, after information of the intention to make the arrest, if the person to be arrested either flees or forcibly resists, the officer may use all necessary means to effect the arrest.

§844. Forcible entry.

To make an arrest, a private person, if the offense is a felony, and in all cases a peace officer, may break open the door or window of the house in which the person to be arrested is, or in which they have reasonable grounds for believing the person to be, after having demanded admittance and explained the pur-

pose for which admittance is desired. *(Amended by Stats 1989 ch 1360 §112, eff. 1/1/90.)*

§845. Doors and windows may be broken, when.

Any person who has lawfully entered a house for the purpose of making an arrest, may break open the door or window thereof if detained therein, when necessary for the purpose of liberating himself, and an officer may do the same, when necessary for the purpose of liberating a person who, acting in his aid, lawfully entered for the purpose of making an arrest, and is detained therein.

§846. Weapons may be taken from persons arrested.

Any person making an arrest may take from the person arrested all offensive weapons which he may have about his person, and must deliver them to the magistrate before whom he is taken.

§847. Delivery of prisoner after arrest.

A private person who has arrested another for the commission of a public offense must, without unnecessary delay, take the person arrested before a magistrate, or deliver him to a peace officer. There shall be no civil liability on the part of and no cause of action shall arise against any peace officer, acting within the scope of his authority, for false arrest or false imprisonment arising out of any arrest when:

(a) Such arrest was lawful or when such peace officer, at the time of such arrest had reasonable cause to believe such arrest was lawful; or

(b) When such arrest was made pursuant to a charge made, upon reasonable cause, of the commission of a felony by the person to be arrested; or

(c) When such arrest was made pursuant to the requirements of Penal Code Sections 142, 838 or 839.

§847.5. Return of fugitive after escape from bail.

If a person has been admitted to bail in another state, escapes bail, and is present in this State, the bail bondsman or other person who is bail for such fugitive, may file with a magistrate in the county where the fugitive is present an affidavit stating the name and whereabouts of the fugitive, the offense with which the alleged fugitive was charged or of which he was convicted, the time and place of same, and the particulars in which the fugitive has violated the terms of his bail, and may request the issuance of a warrant for arrest of the fugitive, and the issuance, after hearing, of an order authorizing the affiant to return the fugitive to the jurisdiction from which he escaped bail. The magistrate may require such additional evidence under oath as he deems necessary to decide the issue. If he concludes that there is probable cause for believing that the person alleged to be a fugitive is such, he may issue a warrant for his arrest. The magistrate shall notify the district attorney of such action and shall direct him to investigate the case and determine the facts of the matter. When the fugitive is brought before him pursuant to the warrant, the magistrate shall set a time and place for hearing, and shall advise the fugitive of his right to counsel and to produce evidence at the hearing. He may admit the fugitive to bail pending the hearing. The district attorney shall appear at the hearing. If, after hearing, the magistrate is satisfied from the evidence that the person is a fugitive he may issue an order authorizing affiant to return the fugitive to the jurisdiction from which he escaped bail.

© 1992 by J., B. & L. Gould
Printed in the U.S.A.   EP

A bondsman or other person who is bail for a fugitive admitted to bail in another state who takes the fugitive into custody, except pursuant to an order issued under this section, is guilty of a misdemeanor.

§848. Duty of officer arresting with warrant.

An officer making an arrest, in obedience to a warrant, must proceed with the person arrested as commanded by the warrant, or as provided by law.

§849. Taking arrestee before magistrate or releasing from custody.

(a) When an arrest is made without a warrant by a peace officer or private person, the person arrested, if not otherwise released, shall, without unnecessary delay, be taken before the nearest or most accessible magistrate in the county in which the offense is triable, and a complaint stating the charge against the arrested person shall be laid before such magistrate.

(b) Any peace officer may release from custody, instead of taking such person before a magistrate, any person arrested without a warrant whenever:

(1) He or she is satisfied that there are insufficient grounds for making a criminal complaint against the person arrested.

(2) The person arrested was arrested for intoxication only, and no further proceedings are desirable.

(3) The person was arrested only for being under the influence of a controlled substance or drug and such person is delivered to a facility or hospital for treatment and no further proceedings are desirable.

(c) Any record of arrest of a person released pursuant to paragraphs (1) and (3) of subdivision (b) shall include a record of release. Thereafter, such arrest shall not be deemed an arrest, but a detention only.

§849.5. Record of release; arrest deemed detention only.

In any case in which a person is arrested and released and no accusatory pleading is filed charging him with an offense, any record of arrest of the person shall include a record of release. Thereafter, the arrest shall not be deemed an arrest, but a detention only.

§850. Transmission of telegraphic copy.

(a) A telegraphic copy of a warrant or an abstract of a warrant may be sent by telegraph, teletype, or any other electronic devices, to one or more peace officers, and such copy or abstract is as effectual in the hands of any officer, and he shall proceed in the same manner under it, as though he held the original warrant issued by a magistrate or the issuing authority or agency.

(b) Except as otherwise provided in Section 1549.2 relating to Governor's warrants of extradition, an abstract of the warrant as herein referred to shall contain the following information: the warrant number, the charge, the court or agency of issuance, the subject's name, address and description, the bail, the name of the issuing magistrate or authority, and if the offense charged is a misdemeanor, whether the warrant has been certified for night service.

(c) When the subject of a written or telegraphic warrant or abstract of warrant is in custody on another charge, the custodial officer shall, immediately upon receipt of information as to the existence of any such warrant or abstract, obtain and deliver a written copy of the warrant or abstract to the subject and shall inform him of his rights under Section 1381, where applicable, to request a speedy trial and under Section 858.7 relating to Vehicle Code violations.

§851. Telegraphic warrants.

Every officer causing telegraphic copies or abstracts of warrants to be sent, must certify as correct, and file in the telegraphic office from which such copies are sent, a copy of the warrant, and must return the original with a statement of his action thereunder.

§851.5. Telephone call right of arrested person.

(a) Immediately upon being booked, and, except where physically impossible, no later than three hours after arrest, an arrested person has the right to make at least three completed telephone calls, as described in subdivision (b).

The arrested person shall be entitled to make at least three such calls at no expense if the calls are completed to telephone numbers within the local calling area.

(b) At any police facility or place where an arrestee is detained, a sign containing the following information in bold block type shall be posted in a conspicuous place:

That the arrestee has the right to free telephone calls within the local dialing area, or at his own expense if outside the local area, to three of the following:

(1) An attorney of his choice or, if he has no funds, the public defender or other attorney assigned by the court to assist indigents, whose telephone number shall be posted. This phone call shall not be monitored, eavesdropped upon, or recorded.

(2) A bail bondsman.

(3) A relative or other person.

(c) These telephone calls shall be given immediately upon request, or as soon as practicable.

(d) This provision shall not abrogate a law enforcement officer's duty to advise a suspect of his right to counsel or of any other right.

(e) Any public officer or employee who willfully deprives an arrested person of any right granted by this section is guilty of a misdemeanor.

§851.6. Certificate describing arrest.

(a) In any case in which a person is arrested and released pursuant to paragraph (1) or (3) of subdivision (b) of Section 849, the person shall be issued a certificate, signed by the releasing officer or his superior officer, describing the action as a detention.

(b) In any case in which a person is arrested and released and no accusatory pleading is filed charging him with an offense, the person shall be issued a certificate by the law enforcement agency which arrested him describing the action as a detention.

(c) The Attorney General shall prescribe the form and content of such certificate.

(d) Any reference to the action as an arrest shall be deleted from the arrest records of the arresting agency and of the Bureau of Criminal Identification and Investigation of the Department of Justice. Thereafter, any such record of the action shall refer to it as a detention.

§851.7. Petition to seal court records: conditions for relief.

(a) Any person who has been arrested for a misdemeanor, with or without a warrant, while a minor, may, during or after minority, petition the court in which the proceedings occurred or, if there were no court proceedings, the court in whose jurisdiction the arrest occurred, for an order sealing the records in the case, including any records of arrest and detention, if any of the following occurred:

(1) He was released pursuant to paragraph (1) of subdivision (b) of Section 849.

(2) Proceedings against him were dismissed, or he was discharged, without a conviction.

(3) He was acquitted.

(b) If the court finds that the petitioner is eligible for relief under subdivision (a), it shall issue its order granting the relief prayed for. Thereafter, the arrest, detention, and any further proceedings in the case shall be deemed not to have occurred, and the petitioner may answer accordingly any question relating to their occurrence.

(c) This section applies to arrests and any further proceedings that occurred before, as well as those that occur after, the effective date of this section.

(d) This section does not apply to any person taken into custody pursuant to Section 625 of the Welfare and Institutions Code, or to any case within the scope of Section 781 of the Welfare and Institutions Code, unless, after a finding of unfitness for the juvenile court or otherwise, there were criminal proceedings in the case, not culminating in conviction. If there were criminal proceedings not culminating in conviction, this section shall be applicable to such criminal proceedings if such proceedings are otherwise within the scope of this section.

(e) This section does not apply to arrests for, and any further proceedings relating to, any of the following:

(1) Offenses for which registration is required under Section 290.

(2) Offenses under Division 10 (commencing with Section 11000) of the Health and Safety Code.

(3) Offenses under the Vehicle Code or any local ordinance relating to the operation, stopping, standing, or parking of a vehicle.

(f) In any action or proceeding based upon defamation, a court, upon a showing of good cause, may order any records sealed under this section to be opened and admitted in evidence. The records shall be confidential and shall be available for inspection only by the court, jury, parties, counsel for the parties, and any other person who is authorized by the court to inspect them. Upon the judgment in the action or proceeding becoming final, the court shall order the records sealed.

(g) This section shall apply in any case in which a person was under the age of 21 at the time of the commission of an offense as to which this section is made applicable if such offense was committed prior to March 7, 1973.

§851.8. Sealing and destruction of arrest records.

(a) In any case where a person has been arrested and no accusatory pleading has been filed, the person arrested may petition the law enforcement agency having jurisdiction over the offense to destroy its records of the arrest. A copy of such petition shall be served upon the district attorney of the county having jurisdiction over the offense. The law enforcement agency having jurisdiction over the offense, upon a determination that the person arrested is factually innocent, shall, with the concurrence of the district attorney, seal its arrest records, and the petition for relief under this section for three years from the date of the arrest and thereafter destroy its arrest records and the petition. The law enforcement agency having jurisdiction over the offense shall notify the Depart-

ment of Justice, and any law enforcement agency which arrested the petitioner or participated in the arrest of the petitioner for an offense for which the petitioner has been found factually innocent under this subdivision, of the sealing of the arrest records and the reason therefor. The Department of Justice and any law enforcement agency so notified shall forthwith seal their records of the arrest and the notice of sealing for three years from the date of the arrest, and thereafter destroy their records of the arrest and the notice of sealing. The law enforcement agency having jurisdiction over the offense and the Department of Justice shall request the destruction of any records of the arrest which they have given to any local, state, or federal agency or to any other person or entity. Each such agency, person, or entity within the State of California receiving such a request shall destroy its records of the arrest and such request, unless otherwise provided in this section.

(b) If, after receipt by both the law enforcement agency and the district attorney of a petition for relief under subdivision (a), the law enforcement agency and district attorney do not respond to the petition by accepting or denying such petition within 60 days after the running of the relevant statute of limitations or within 60 days after receipt of the petition in cases where the statute of limitations has previously lapsed, then the petition shall be deemed to be denied. In any case where the petition of an arrestee to the law enforcement agency to have an arrest record destroyed is denied, petition may be made to the municipal or justice court which would have had territorial jurisdiction over the matter. A copy of such petition shall be served on the district attorney of the county having jurisdiction over the offense at least 10 days prior to the hearing thereon. The district attorney may present evidence to the court at such hearing. Notwithstanding Section 1538.5 or 1539, any judicial determination of factual innocence made pursuant to this section may be heard and determined upon declarations, affidavits, police reports, or any other evidence submitted by the parties which is material, relevant and reliable. A finding of factual innocence and an order for the sealing and destruction of records pursuant to this section shall not be made unless the court finds that no reasonable cause exists to believe that the arrestee committed the offense for which the arrest was made. In any court hearing to determine the factual innocence of a party, the initial burden of proof shall rest with the petitioner to show that no reasonable cause exists to believe that the arrestee committed the offense for which the arrest was made. If the court finds that this showing of no reasonable cause has been made by the petitioner, then the burden of proof shall shift to the respondent to show that a reasonable cause exists to believe that the petitioner committed the offense for which the arrest was made. If the court finds the arrestee to be factually innocent of the charges for which the arrest was made, then the court shall order the law enforcement agency having jurisdiction over the offense, the Department of Justice, and any law enforcement agency which arrested the petitioner or participated in the arrest of the petitioner for an offense for which the petitioner has been found factually innocent under this section to seal their records of the arrest and the court order to seal and destroy such records, for three years from the date of the arrest and thereafter to destroy their records of the arrest and the court order to seal and

© 1992 by J., B. & L. Gould
Printed in the U.S.A.   EP

destroy such records. The court shall also order the law enforcement agency having jurisdiction over the offense and the Department of Justice to request the destruction of any records of the arrest which they have given to any local, state, or federal agency, person or entity. Each state or local agency, person or entity within the State of California receiving such a request shall destroy its records of the arrest and the request to destroy such records, unless otherwise provided in this section. The court shall give to the petitioner a copy of any court order concerning the destruction of the arrest records.

(c) In any case where a person has been arrested, and an accusatory pleading has been filed, but where no conviction has occurred, the defendant may, at any time after dismissal of the action, petition the court which dismissed the action for a finding that the defendant is factually innocent of the charges for which the arrest was made. A copy of such petition shall be served on the district attorney of the county in which the accusatory pleading was filed at least 10 days prior to the hearing on the petitioner's factual innocence. The district attorney may present evidence to the court at such hearing. Such hearing shall be conducted as provided in subdivision (b). If the court finds the petitioner to be factually innocent of the charges for which the arrest was made, then the court shall grant the relief as provided in subdivision (b).

(d) In any case where a person has been arrested and an accusatory pleading has been filed, but where no conviction has occurred, the court may, with the concurrence of the district attorney, grant the relief provided in subdivision (b) at the time of the dismissal of the accusatory pleading.

(e) Whenever any person is acquitted of a charge and it appears to the judge presiding at the trial wherein such acquittal occurred that the defendant was factually innocent of such charge, the judge may grant the relief provided in subdivision (b).

(f) In any case where a person who has been arrested is granted relief pursuant to subdivision (a) or (b), the law enforcement agency having jurisdiction over the offense or court shall issue a written declaration to the arrestee stating that it is the determination of the law enforcement agency having jurisdiction over the offense or court that the arrestee is factually innocent of the charges for which he was arrested and that the arrestee is thereby exonerated. Thereafter, the arrest shall be deemed not to have occurred and the person may answer accordingly any question relating to its occurrence.

(g) The Department of Justice shall furnish forms to be utilized by persons applying for the destruction of their arrest records and for the written declaration that one person was found factually innocent under subdivisions (a) and (b).

(h) Documentation of arrest records destroyed pursuant to subdivision (a), (b), (c), (d), or (e) which are contained in investigative police reports shall bear the notation "Exonerated" whenever reference is made to the arrestee. The arrestee shall be notified in writing by the law enforcement agency having jurisdiction over the offense of the sealing and destruction of the arrest records pursuant to this section.

(i) Any finding that an arrestee is factually innocent pursuant to subdivision (a), (b), (c), (d), or (e) shall not be admissible as evidence in any action.

(j) Destruction of records of arrest pursuant to subdivision (a), (b), (c), (d), or (e) shall be accomplished by permanent obliteration of all entries or notations upon such records pertaining to the arrest, and the record shall be prepared again so that it appears that the arrest never occurred. However, where (1) the only entries on the record pertain to the arrest and (2) the record can be destroyed without necessarily effecting the destruction of other records, then the document constituting the record shall be physically destroyed.

(k) No records shall be destroyed pursuant to subdivision (a), (b), (c), (d), or (e) if the arrestee or a codefendant has filed a civil action against the peace officers or law enforcement jurisdiction which made the arrest or instituted the prosecution and if the agency which is the custodian of such records has received a certified copy of the complaint in such civil action, until the civil action has been resolved. Any records sealed pursuant to this section by the court in the civil actions, upon a showing of good cause, may be opened and submitted into evidence. The records shall be confidential and shall be available for inspection only by the court, jury, parties, counsel for the parties and any other person authorized by the court. Immediately following the final resolution of the civil action, records subject to subdivision (a), (b), (c), (d), or (e) shall be sealed and destroyed pursuant to subdivision (a), (b), (c), (d), or (e).

(l) For arrests occurring on or after January 1, 1981, and for accusatory pleading filed on or after January 1, 1981, petitions for relief under this section may be filed up to two years from the date of the arrest or filing of the accusatory pleading, whichever is later. Until January 1, 1983, petitioners can file for relief under this section for arrests which occurred or accusatory pleadings which were filed up to five years prior to the effective date of the statute. Any time restrictions on filing for relief under this section may be waived upon a showing of good cause by the petitioner and in the absence of prejudice.

(m) Any relief which is available to a petitioner under this section for an arrest shall also be available for an arrest which has been deemed to be or described as a detention under Section 849.5 or 851.6.

(n) The provisions of this section shall not apply to any offense which is classified as an infraction.

(o) (1) The provisions of this section shall be repealed on the effective date of a final judgment based on a claim under the California or United States Constitution holding that evidence which is relevant, reliable, and material may not be considered for purposes of a judicial determination of factual innocence under this section. For purposes of this subdivision, a judgment by the appellate department of a superior court is a final judgment if it is published and if it is not reviewed on appeal by a district court of appeal. A judgment of a district court of appeal is a final judgment if it is published and if it is not reviewed by the California Supreme Court.

(2) Any such decision referred to in this subdivision shall be stayed pending appeal.

(3) If not otherwise appealed by a party to the action, any such decision referred to in this subdivision which is a judgment by the appellate department of the superior court, shall be appealed by the Attorney General.

§851.85. Record sealing by trial judge.

Whenever a person is acquitted of a charge and it appears to the judge presiding at the trial wherein such acquittal occurred that the defendant was factually innocent of the charge, the judge may order that the records in the case be sealed, including any record of arrest or detention, upon the written or oral motion of any party in the case or the court, and with notice to all parties to the case. If such an order is made, the court shall give to the defendant a copy of such order and inform the defendant that he may thereafter state that he was not arrested for such charge and that he was found innocent of such charge by the court.

CHAPTER 5a

UNIFORM ACT ON FRESH PURSUIT

§852. Short title.
This chapter may be cited as the Uniform Act on Fresh Pursuit.

§852.1. Definitions.
As used in this chapter:

(a) "State" means any State of the United States and the District of Columbia.

(b) "Peace officer" means any peace officer or member of any duly organized State, county, or municipal peace unit or police force of another State.

(c) "Fresh Pursuit" includes close pursuit and hot pursuit.

§852.2. Authority of officer from other State to make arrest.
Any peace officer of another State, who enters this State in fresh pursuit, and continues within this State in fresh pursuit, of a person in order to arrest him on the ground that he has committed a felony in the other State, has the same authority to arrest and hold the person in custody, as peace officers of this State have to arrest and hold a person in custody on the ground that he has committed a felony in this State.

§852.3. Procedure.
If an arrest is made in this State by a peace officer of another State in accordance with the provisions of section 852.2 of this Code, he shall without unnecessary delay take the person arrested before a magistrate of the county in which the arrest was made, who shall conduct a hearing for the purpose of determining the lawfulness of the arrest. If the magistrate determines that the arrest was lawful, he shall commit the person arrested to await a reasonable time for the issuance of an extradition warrant by the Governor of this State or admit him to bail for such purpose. If the magistrate determines that the arrest was unlawful, he shall discharge the person arrested.

§852.4. Construction.
Section 852.2 of this Code shall not be construed so as to make unlawful any arrest in this State which would otherwise be lawful.

CHAPTER 5b

COLORADO RIVER CRIME ENFORCEMENT COMPACT
(Added by Stats 1985 ch 754 §1.)

§853.1. Colorado River Crime Enforcement Compact.
(a) Pursuant to the authority vested in this state by Section 112 of Title 4 of the United States Code, the Legislature of the State of California hereby ratifies the Colorado River Crime Enforcement Compact as set forth in Section 853.2.

(b) The purpose of this compact is to promote the interests of justice with regard to crimes committed on the Colorado River by avoiding jurisdictional issues as to whether a criminal act sought to be prosecuted was committed on one side or the other of the exact boundary of the channel, and thus avoiding the risk that an offender may go free on technical grounds because neither state is able to establish that the offense was committed within its boundaries.

(c) This compact shall become operative when ratified by law in the State of Arizona; and shall remain in full force and effect so long as the provisions of this compact, as ratified by the State of Arizona, remain substantively the same as the provisions of this compact, as ratified by this section. This compact may be amended in the same manner as is required for it to be ratified to become operative. *(Added by Stats 1985 ch 754 §1.)*

§853.2. Jurisdiction of Colorado River Crime Enforcement Compact.
(a) All courts and officers now or hereafter having and exercising jurisdiction in any county which is now or may hereafter be formed in any part of this state bordering upon the Colorado River, or any lake formed by, or which is a part of, the Colorado River, shall have and exercise jurisdiction in all criminal cases upon those waters concurrently with the courts of and officers of the State of Arizona, so far and to the extent that any of these bodies of water form a common boundary between this state and the State of Arizona.

(b) This section applies only to those crimes which are established in common between the States of Arizona and California; and an acquittal or conviction and sentence by one state shall bar a prosecution for the same act or omission by the other.

(c) This compact shall not be construed to bar the enforcement of the penal laws of either state not established in common with the other, provided that the act or omission proscribed occurs on that state's side of the river channel boundary.

(d) This compact does not apply to Division 3.5 (commencing with Section 9840) of the Vehicle Code, relating to registration of vessels, or to Section 658.7 of the Harbors and Navigation Code, relating to the display of a ski flag. *(Amended by Stats 1990 ch 751 §2, eff. 1/1/91.)*

CHAPTER 5c

CITATIONS FOR MISDEMEANORS

§853.5. Infractions; release procedures.
Except as otherwise provided by law, in any case in which a person is arrested for an offense declared to be an infraction, the person may be released according to the procedures set forth by this chapter for the release of persons arrested for an offense declared to be a misdemeanor. In all cases, except as specified in Sections 40302, 40303, 40305, and 40305.5 of the Vehicle Code, in which a person is arrested for an infraction, a peace officer shall only require the arrestee to present his driver's license or other satisfactory evidence of his identity for examination and to sign a written promise to appear. Only if the arrestee refuses to present such identification or, refuses to sign such

© 1992 by J., B. & L. Gould
Printed in the U.S.A.   EP

a written promise may the arrestee be taken into custody.

§853.6. Notice to appear.

(a) In any case in which a person is arrested for an offense declared to be a misdemeanor, including a violation of any city or county ordinance, and does not demand to be taken before a magistrate, that person shall, instead of being taken before a magistrate, be released according to the procedures set forth by this chapter. If the person is released, the officer or superior shall prepare in duplicate a written notice to appear in court, containing the name and address of the person, the offense charged, and the time when, and place where, the person shall appear in court. If, pursuant to subdivision (i), the person is not released prior to being booked and the officer in charge of the booking or his or her superior determines that the person should be released, the officer or superior shall prepare a written notice to appear in a court.

In any case in which a person is arrested for a misdemeanor violation of a protective court order involving domestic violence, as defined in subdivision (b) of Section 13700, the person shall be taken before a magistrate instead of being released according to the procedures set forth in this chapter, unless the arresting officer determines that there is not a reasonable likelihood that the offense will continue or resume or that the safety of persons or property would be imminently endangered by release of the person arrested.

Nothing in this subdivision shall be construed to affect a defendant's ability to be released on bail or on his or her own recognizance.

(b) Unless waived by the person, the time specified in the notice to appear shall be at least 10 days after arrest if the duplicate notice is to be filed by the officer with the magistrate.

(c) The place specified in the notice shall be the court of the magistrate before whom the person would be taken if the requirement of taking an arrested person before a magistrate were complied with, or shall be an officer authorized by that court to receive a deposit of bail.

(d) The officer shall deliver one copy of the notice to appear to the arrested person, and the arrested person, in order to secure release, shall give his or her written promise to appear in court as specified in the notice by signing the duplicate notice which shall be retained by the officer. Upon the signing of the duplicate notice, the arresting officer shall immediately release the person arrested from custody.

(e) The officer shall, as soon as practicable, file the duplicate notice, as follows:

(1) It shall be filed with the magistrate if the offense charged is an infraction.

(2) It shall be filed with the magistrate if the prosecuting attorney has previously directed the officer to do so.

(3) The duplicate notice and underlying police reports in support of the charge or charges shall be filed with the prosecuting attorney in cases other than those specified in paragraphs (1) and (2).

If the duplicate notice is filed with the prosecuting attorney, he or she, within his or her discretion, may initiate prosecution by filing the notice or a formal complaint with the magistrate specified in the duplicate notice within 25 days from the time of arrest. If the prosecution is not to be initiated, the prosecutor shall send notice to the person arrested at the address on the notice to appear. The failure by the prosecutor to file the notice or formal complaint within 25 days of the time of the arrest shall not bar further prosecution of the misdemeanor charged in the notice to appear. However, any further prosecution shall be preceded by a new and separate citation or an arrest warrant.

Upon the filing of the notice with the magistrate by the officer, or the filing of the notice or formal complaint by the prosecutor, the magistrate may fix the amount of bail which in his or her judgment, in accordance with Section 1275, is reasonable and sufficient for the appearance of the defendant and shall indorse upon the notice a statement signed by him or her in the form set forth in Section 815a. The defendant may, prior to the date upon which he or she promised to appear in court, deposit with the magistrate the amount of bail set by the magistrate. At the time the case is called for arraignment before the magistrate, if the defendant does not appear, either in person or by counsel, the magistrate may declare the bail forfeited, and may, in his or her discretion, order that no further proceedings shall be had in the case, unless the defendant has been charged with violation of Section 374.3 or 374.7 of this code or of Section 11357, 11360, or 13002 of the Health and Safety Code, or a violation punishable under Section 5008.7 of the Public Resources Code, and he or she has previously been convicted of a violation of that section or a violation which is punishable under that section, except in cases where the magistrate finds that undue hardship will be imposed upon the defendant by requiring him or her to appear, the magistrate may declare the bail forfeited and order that no further proceedings be had in the case.

Upon the making of the order that no further proceedings be had, all sums deposited as bail shall immediately be paid into the county treasury for distribution pursuant to Section 1463.

(f) No warrant shall be issued for the arrest of a person who has given a written promise to appear in court, unless and until he or she has violated that promise or has failed to deposit bail, to appear for arraignment, trial, or judgment or to comply with the terms and provisions of the judgment, as required by law.

(g) The officer may either book the arrested person prior to release or indicate on the citation that the arrested person shall be booked. If it is indicated on the citation that the arrested person is to be booked, the magistrate shall, before the proceedings are finally concluded, order the defendant to be booked by the arresting agency.

(h) A peace officer shall use the written notice to appear procedure set forth in this section for any misdemeanor offense in which the officer has arrested a person without a warrant pursuant to Section 836 or in which he or she has taken custody of a person pursuant to Section 847.

(i) Whenever any person is arrested by a peace officer for a misdemeanor, that person shall be released according to the procedures set forth by this chapter unless one of the following is a reason for nonrelease, in which case the arresting officer may release the person, or the arresting officer shall indicate, on a form to be established by his or her employing law enforcement agency, which of the following was a reason for the nonrelease:

(1) The person arrested was so intoxicated that he or she could have been a danger to himself or herself or to others.

(2) The person arrested required medical examination or medical care or was otherwise unable to care for his or her own safety.

(3) The person was arrested under one or more of the circumstances listed in Sections 40302 and 40303 of the Vehicle Code.

(4) There were one or more outstanding arrest warrants for the person.

(5) The person could not provide satisfactory evidence of personal identification.

(6) The prosecution of the offense or offenses for which the person was arrested, or the prosecution of any other offense or offenses, would be jeopardized by immediate release of the person arrested.

(7) There was a reasonable likelihood that the offense or offenses would continue or resume, or that the safety of persons or property would be imminently endangered by release of the person arrested.

(8) The person arrested demanded to be taken before a magistrate or refused to sign the notice to appear.

(9) There is reason to believe that the person would not appear at the time and place specified in the notice. The basis for this determination shall be specifically stated.

The form shall be filed with the arresting agency as soon as practicable and shall be made available to any party having custody of the arrested person, subsequent to the arresting officer, and to any person authorized by law to release him or her for custody before trial.

(j) Once the arresting officer has prepared the written notice to appear and has delivered a copy to the person arrested, the officer shall deliver the remaining original and all copies as provided by subdivision (e).

Any person, including the arresting officer and any member of the officer's department or agency, or any peace officer, who alters, conceals, modifies, nullifies, or destroys, or causes to be altered, concealed, modified, nullified, or destroyed, the face side of the remaining original or any copy of a citation that was retained by the officer, for any reason, before it is filed with the magistrate or with a person authorized by the magistrate to receive deposit of bail, is guilty of a misdemeanor.

If, after an arrested person has signed and received a copy of a notice to appear, the arresting officer determines that, in the interest of justice, the citation or notice should be dismissed, the arresting agency may recommend, in writing, to the magistrate that the charges be dismissed. The recommendation shall cite the reasons for the recommendation and shall be filed with the court.

If the magistrate makes a finding that there are grounds for dismissal, the finding shall be entered in the record and the charges dismissed.

Under no circumstances shall a personal relationship with any officer, public official, or law enforcement agency be grounds for dismissal. (Amended by Stats 1991 ch 453 §1, eff. 1/1/92.)

§853.6a. Minor referred to juvenile court, etc.

If the person arrested appears to be under the age of 18 years, and the arrest is for a violation listed in Section 256 of the Welfare and Institutions Code, the notice under Section 853.6 shall instead provide that the person shall appear before the juvenile court, a juvenile court referee, or a juvenile traffic hearing officer within the county in which the offense charged is alleged to have been committed, and the officer shall instead, as soon as practicable, file the duplicate notice with the prosecuting attorney unless the prosecuting attorney directs the officer to file the duplicate notice with the clerk of the juvenile court, the juvenile court referee, or the juvenile traffic hearing officer. If the notice is filed with the prosecuting attorney, within 48 hours before the date specified on the notice to appear, the prosecutor, within his or her discretion, may initiate proceedings by filing the notice or a formal petition with the clerk of the juvenile court, or the juvenile court referee or juvenile traffic hearing officer, before whom the person is required to appear by the notice. (Amended by Stats 1991 ch 1202 §5, eff. 1/1/92.)

§853.7. Willfully violating written promise to appear.

Any person who willfully violates his or her written promise to appear or a lawfully granted continuance of his or her promise to appear in court is guilty of a misdemeanor, regardless of the disposition of the charge upon which he or she was originally arrested. (Amended by Stats 1988, ch 403 §2, eff. 1/1/89.)

§853.7a. Courts; penalty assessments.

(a) In addition to the fees authorized or required by any other provision of law, a county may, by resolution of the board of supervisors, authorize the courts of that county to impose an assessment of seven dollars ($7) upon every person convicted under Section 853.7, whether or not a fine is imposed.

(b) The clerk of the court shall deposit the amounts collected under this section in the county treasury. All money so deposited shall be used exclusively for the development and operation of an automated county warrant system. (Added by Stats 1986 ch 151 §1.)

§853.8. Failure to appear; issuance of arrest warrant.

When a person signs a written promise to appear at the time and place specified in the written promise to appear and has not posted bail as provided in Section 853.6, the magistrate shall issue and have delivered for execution a warrant for his or her arrest within 20 days after his or her failure to appear as promised or within 20 days after his or her failure to appear after a lawfully granted continuance of his or her promise to appear. (Amended by Stats 1988, ch 403 §3, eff. 1/1/89.)

CHAPTER 5d

FILING COMPLAINT AFTER CITATION

§853.9. Written notice which constitutes complaint.

(a) Whenever written notice to appear has been prepared, delivered, and filed by an officer or the prosecuting attorney with the court pursuant to the provisions of Section 853.6 of this code, an exact and legible duplicate copy of the notice when filed with the magistrate, in lieu of a verified complaint, shall constitute a complaint to which the defendant may plead "guilty" or "nolo contendere."

© 1992 by J., B. & L. Gould
Printed in the U.S.A.   EP

If, however, the defendant violates his or her promise to appear in court, or does not deposit lawful bail, or pleads other than "guilty" or "nolo contendere" to the offense charged, a complaint shall be filed which shall conform to the provisions of this code and which shall be deemed to be an original complaint; and thereafter proceedings shall be had as provided by law, except that a defendant may, by an agreement in writing, subscribed by him or her and filed with the court, waive the filing of a verified complaint and elect that the prosecution may proceed upon a written notice to appear.

(b) Notwithstanding the provisions of subdivision (a) of this section, whenever the written notice to appear has been prepared on a form approved by the Judicial Council, an exact and legible duplicate copy of the notice when filed with the magistrate shall constitute a complaint to which the defendant may enter a plea and, if the notice to appear is verified, upon which a warrant may be issued. If the notice to appear is not verified, the defendant may, at the time of arraignment, request that a verified complaint be filed.

CHAPTER 6

RETAKING AFTER AN ESCAPE OR RESCUE

§854. May be at any time or in any place in the state.

If a person arrested escape or is rescued, the person from whose custody he escaped or was rescued, may immediately pursue and retake him at any time and in any place within the state.

§855. May break open door or window if admittance refused.

To retake the person escaping or rescued, the person pursuing may break open an outer or inner door or window of a dwelling-house, if, after notice of his intention, he is refused admittance.

CHAPTER 7

EXAMINATION OF THE CASE, AND DISCHARGE OF THE DEFENDANT, OR HOLDING HIM TO ANSWER

§858. Informing defendant of charge and right to counsel.

When the defendant is brought before the magistrate upon an arrest, either with or without warrant, on a charge of having committed a public offense, the magistrate must immediately inform him of the charge against him, and of his right to the aid of counsel in every stage of the proceedings. If it appears that the defendant may be a minor, the magistrate shall ascertain whether such is the case, and if the magistrate concludes that it is probable that the defendant is a minor, and unless the defendant is a member of the armed forces of the United States and the offense charged is a misdemeanor, he shall immediately either notify the parent or guardian of the minor, by telephone, telegram, or messenger, of the arrest, or appoint counsel to represent the minor.

§858.5. Vehicle Code violation; procedure.

(a) In any case in which a defendant is, on his demand, brought before a magistrate pursuant to Section 822 after arrest for a misdemeanor Vehicle Code violation, the magistrate shall give such instructions to the defendant as required by law and inform the defendant of his rights under this section, and, if the defendant desires to plead guilty or nolo contendere to the charge in the complaint, he may so advise the magistrate. If the magistrate determines that such plea would be in the interest of justice, he shall direct the defendant to appear before a specified appropriate court in the county in which defendant has been arrested at a designated certain time, which in no case shall be more than 10 calendar days from the date of arrest, for plea and sentencing. The magistrate shall request the court in which the complaint has been filed to transmit a certified copy of the complaint and any citation and any factual report which may have been prepared by the law enforcement agency that investigated the case to the court in which defendant is to appear for plea and sentencing. If the court of which the request is made deems such action to be in the interest of justice, and the district attorney of the county in which that court sits, after notice from the court of the request it has received, does not object to such action, the court shall immediately transmit a certified copy of the complaint and the report of the law enforcement agency that investigated the case, and, if not, shall advise the requesting magistrate of its decision not to take such action.

When defendant appears for plea and sentencing, and if a copy of the complaint has been transmitted, the court shall read the copy of the complaint to him, and the defendant may plead guilty or nolo contendere. Such court shall have jurisdiction to accept the plea and impose a sentence. Such court shall notify the court in which the complaint was originally filed of the disposition of the case. If defendant does not plead guilty or nolo contendere, or if transmittal of a copy of the complaint has been refused or if a copy of the complaint has not been received, the court shall terminate the proceedings under this section and shall direct the defendant to appear before the court or magistrate by whom the warrant was issued on or before a certain day which in no case shall be more than five days after the date such direction is made.

(b) Any fines imposed by a court which is given authority to sentence pursuant to this section shall be remitted to the court in which the complaint was originally filed for disposition as required by law. The county of the sentencing court shall bear all costs incurred incident to acceptance of the plea and sentencing, and no part of such costs shall be deducted from the fine remitted to the court in which the complaint was filed.

§858.7. Defendant's rights; appearance, plea.

(a) In any case in which the defendant has been convicted of a misdemeanor and is serving a sentence as a result of such conviction and there has been filed and is pending in another county a complaint charging him with a misdemeanor Vehicle Code violation, the defendant may appear before the court that sentenced him, and a magistrate of that court shall give such instructions to the defendant as required by law and inform the defendant of his rights under this section, and, if the defendant desires to plead guilty or nolo contendere to the charge in the complaint, he may so advise the magistrate. If the magistrate determines that such plea would be in the interest of justice, he shall direct the defendant to appear before a specified appropriate court in the county in which defendant is serving his sentence at a designated certain time for plea and sentencing. The magistrate shall request the court in which the complaint has been filed to transmit a certified copy of the complaint and any citation and any factual report which may have been prepared by the law enforcement agency that investigated the case to the court in which defendant is to appear for plea and sentencing. If the court of which the request is made deems such action to be in the interest of justice, and the district attorney of the county in which that court sits, after notice from the court of the request it has received, does not object to such action, the court shall immediately transmit a certified copy of the complaint and any report of the law enforcement agency that investigated the case, and, if not, shall advise the requesting magistrate of its decision not to take such action.

When defendant appears for plea and sentencing, and if a copy of the complaint has been transmitted, the court shall read the copy of the complaint to him, and the defendant may plead guilty or nolo contendere. Such court shall have jurisdiction to accept the plea and impose a sentence. Such court shall notify the court in which the complaint was originally filed of the disposition of the case. If defendant does not plead guilty or nolo contendere, or if transmittal of a copy of the complaint has been refused or if a copy of the complaint has not been received, the court shall terminate the proceedings under this section and shall direct the defendant to appear before the court in which the complaint was filed and is pending on or before a certain day.

(b) (1) Any fines imposed by a court which is given authority to sentence pursuant to this section shall be remitted to the court in which the complaint was originally filed for disposition as required by law. Except as otherwise provided in paragraph (2) of this subdivision, the county of the sentencing court shall bear all costs incurred incident to acceptance of the plea and sentencing, and no part of such costs shall be deducted from the fine remitted to the court in which the complaint was filed.

(2) In any case in which a defendant is sentenced to imprisonment pursuant to this section, and as a result of such sentence he is required to be imprisoned for a time in addition to, and not concurrent with, the time he is imprisoned as a result of the sentence he is otherwise serving, the county in which the complaint was originally filed shall bear the cost of such additional time of imprisonment that the defendant is required to serve. Such cost may be deducted from any fine required to be remitted pursuant to paragraph (1) of this subdivision to the court in which the complaint was originally filed.

(c) As used in this section, "complaint" includes, but is not limited to, a notice to appear which is within the provisions of Section 40513 of the Vehicle Code.

§859. Superior court procedure.
When the defendant is charged with the commission of a public offense over which the superior court has original jurisdiction, by a written complaint subscribed under oath and on file in a court within the county in which the public offense is triable, he or she shall, without unnecessary delay, be taken before a magistrate of the court in which the complaint is on file. The magistrate shall immediately deliver to the defendant a copy of the complaint, inform the defend-

ant that he or she has the right to have the assistance of counsel, ask the defendant if he or she desires the assistance of counsel, and allow the defendant reasonable time to send for counsel. However, in a capital case, the court shall inform the defendant that the defendant must be represented in court by counsel at all stages of the preliminary and trial proceedings and that the representation will be at the defendant's expense if the defendant is able to employ counsel or at public expense if he or she is unable to employ counsel, inquire of him or her whether he or she is able to employ counsel and, if so, whether the defendant desires to employ counsel of the defendant's choice or to have counsel assigned for him or her, and allow the defendant a reasonable time to send for his or her chosen or assigned counsel. The magistrate must, upon the request of the defendant, require a peace officer to take a message to any counsel whom the defendant may name, in the judicial district in which the court is situated. The officer shall, without delay and without a fee, perform that duty. If the defendant desires and is unable to employ counsel, the court shall assign counsel to defend him or her; in a capital case, if the defendant is able to employ counsel and either refuses to employ counsel or appears without counsel after having had a reasonable time to employ counsel, the court shall assign counsel to defend him or her. If it appears that the defendant may be a minor, the magistrate shall ascertain whether that is the case, and if the magistrate concludes that it is probable that the defendant is a minor, he or she shall immediately either notify the parent or guardian of the minor, by telephone or messenger, of the arrest, or appoint counsel to represent the minor. (Amended by Initiative Measure, Prop 115 §15, approved 6/5/90.)

§859a. Pleas.
(a) If the public offense charged is a felony not punishable with death, the magistrate shall immediately upon the appearance of counsel for the defendant read the complaint to the defendant and ask him or her whether he or she pleads guilty or not guilty to the offense charged therein and to a previous conviction or convictions of crime if charged. While the charge remains pending before the magistrate and when the defendant's counsel is present, the defendant may plead guilty to the offense charged, or, with the consent of the magistrate and the district attorney or other counsel for the people, plead nolo contendere to the offense charged or plead guilty or nolo contendere to any other offense the commission of which is necessarily included in that with which he or she is charged, or to an attempt to commit the offense charged and to the previous conviction or convictions of crime if charged upon a plea of guilty or nolo contendere. The magistrate may then fix a reasonable bail as provided by this code, and upon failure to deposit the bail or surety, shall immediately commit the defendant to the sheriff and certify the case, including a copy of all proceedings therein and any testimony that in his or her discretion he or she may require to be taken, to the superior court, and thereupon the proceedings shall be had as if the defendant had pleaded guilty in that court. This subdivision shall not be construed to authorize the receiving of a plea of guilty or nolo contendere from any defendant not represented by counsel. If the defendant subsequently files a written motion to withdraw the plea under Section 1018, the

© 1992 by J., B. & L. Gould
Printed in the U.S.A.   EP

motion shall be heard and determined by the court before which the plea was entered.

(b) Notwithstanding Section 1191 or 1203, the magistrate shall, upon the receipt of a plea of guilty or nolo contendere and upon the performance of the other duties of the magistrate under this section, immediately appoint a time for pronouncing judgment in the superior court, municipal court, or justice court and refer the case to the probation officer if eligible for probation, as prescribed in Section 1191. (*Amended by Stats 1991 ch 613 §6, eff. 1/1/92.*)

§859b. Examination when defendant pleads not guilty to felony.

At the time the defendant appears before the magistrate for arraignment, if the public offense is a felony to which the defendant has not pleaded guilty in accordance with Section 859a, the magistrate, immediately upon the appearance of counsel, or if none appears, after waiting a reasonable time therefor as provided in Section 859, shall set a time for the examination of the case and shall allow not less than two days, excluding Sundays and holidays, for the district attorney and the defendant to prepare for the examination. The magistrate shall also issue subpoenas, duly subscribed, for witnesses within the state, required either by the prosecution or the defense.

Both the defendant and the people have the right to a preliminary examination at the earliest possible time, and unless both waive that right or good cause for a continuance is found as provided for in Section 1050, the preliminary examination shall be held within 10 court days of the date the defendant is arraigned or pleads, whichever occurs later.

Whenever the defendant is in custody, the magistrate shall dismiss the complaint if the preliminary examination is set or continued beyond 10 court days from the time of the arraignment or plea and the defendant has remained in custody for 10 or more court days solely on that complaint, unless either of the following occur:

(a) The defendant personally waives his or her right to preliminary examination within the 10 court days.

(b) The prosecution establishes good cause for a continuance beyond the 10-court-day period.

For purposes of this subdivision, "good cause" includes, but is not limited to, those cases involving allegations that a violation of one or more of the sections specified in subdivision (a) of Section 11165.1 or in Section 11165.6 has occurred and the prosecuting attorney assigned to the case has another trial, preliminary hearing, or motion to suppress in progress in that court or another court. Any continuance under this paragraph shall be limited to a maximum of three additional court days.

If the preliminary examination is set or continued beyond the 10-court-day period, the defendant shall be released pursuant to Section 1318 unless:

(1) The defendant requests the setting of continuance of the preliminary examination beyond the 10-court-day period.

(2) The defendant is charged with a capital offense in a cause where the proof is evident and the presumption great.

(3) A witness necessary for the preliminary examination is unavailable due to the actions of the defendant.

(4) The illness of counsel.

(5) The unexpected engagement of counsel in a jury trial.

(6) Unforeseen conflicts of interest which require appointment of new counsel.

The magistrate shall dismiss the complaint if the preliminary examination is set or continued more than 60 days from the date of the arraignment or plea, unless the defendant personally waives his or her right to a preliminary examination within the 60 days. (*Amended by Stats 1989 ch 897 §26.5, eff. 1/1/90.*)

§859.1. Minor under sixteen years: criminal proceedings.

(a) In any criminal proceeding in which the defendant is charged with any offense specified in Section 868.8 on a minor under the age of 16 years, the court shall, upon motion of the prosecuting attorney, conduct a hearing to determine whether the testimony of, and testimony relating to, a minor shall be closed to the public in order to protect the minor's reputation.

(b) In making this determination, the court shall consider all of the following:

(1) The nature and seriousness of the offense.

(2) The age of the minor.

(3) The extent to which the size of the community would preclude the anonymity of the victim.

(4) The likelihood of public opprobrium due to the status of the victim.

(5) Whether there is an overriding public interest in having an open hearing.

(6) Whether the prosecution has demonstrated a substantial probability that the identity of the witness would otherwise be disclosed to the public during that proceeding, and demonstrated a substantial probability that the disclosure of his or her identity would cause serious harm to the minor witness.

(7) Whether the witness has disclosed information concerning the case to the public through press conferences, public meetings, or other means.

(8) Other factors the court may deem necessary to protect the interests of justice. (*Added by Stats 1990 ch 1276 §1, eff. 1/1/91.*)

§860. Examination procedure.

At the time set for the examination of the case, if the public offense is

1. Not a felony, but within the jurisdiction of the superior court, or is

2. A felony punishable with death, or is

3. A felony to which the defendant has not pleaded guilty in accordance with Section 859a of this code, then, if the defendant requires the aid of counsel, the magistrate must allow the defendant a reasonable time to send for counsel, and may postpone the examination for not less than two nor more than five days for that purpose. The magistrate must, immediately after the appearance of counsel, or if, after waiting a reasonable time therefor none appears, proceed to examine the case; provided, however, that a defendant represented by counsel may when brought before the magistrate as provided in Section 858 or at any time subsequent thereto, waive his right to an examination before such magistrate, and thereupon it shall be the duty of the magistrate to make an order holding the defendant to answer, and it shall be the duty of the district attorney within 15 days thereafter, to file in the superior court of the county in which the offense is triable the information; provided, further, however, that nothing contained herein shall prevent

© 1992 by J., B. & L. Gould
Printed in the U.S.A. **EP**

the district attorney nor the magistrate from requiring that an examination be held as provided in this chapter. Nothing contained in this section shall affect the jurisdiction or procedure of the superior court sitting as a juvenile court.

§861. Examination; postponement, duration.

The preliminary examination shall be completed at one session or the complaint shall be dismissed, unless the magistrate, for good cause shown by affidavit, postpones it. The postponement shall not be for more than 10 court days, unless either of the following occur:

(a) The defendant personally waives his or her right to a continuous preliminary examination.

(b) The prosecution establishes good cause for a postponement beyond the 10-court day period. If the magistrate postpones the preliminary examination beyond the 10-court day period, and the defendant is in custody, the defendant shall be released pursuant to subdivision (b) of Section 859b.

The preliminary examination shall not be postponed beyond 60 days from the date the motion to postpone the examination is granted, unless by consent or on motion of the defendant.

Nothing in this section shall preclude the magistrate from interrupting the preliminary examination to conduct brief court matters so long as a substantial majority of the court's time is devoted to the preliminary examination. *(Amended by Stats 1988, ch 277 §1, eff. 1/1/89.)*

§861.5. Postponement of preliminary examination for one court day.

Notwithstanding subdivision (a) of Section 861, the magistrate may postpone the preliminary examination for one court day in order to accommodate the special physical, mental, or emotional needs of a child witness who is 10 years of age or younger.

The magistrate shall admonish both the prosecution and defense against coaching the child witness prior to the witness' next appearance in the preliminary examination. *(Added by Stats 1985 ch 308 §1.)*

§862. On postponement, defendant to be committed or discharged on bail.

If a postponement is had, the magistrate must commit the defendant for examination, admit him to bail or discharge him from custody upon the deposit of money as provided in this Code, as security for his appearance at the time to which the examination is postponed.

§863. Form of commitment.

The commitment for examination is made by an indorsement, signed by the magistrate on the warrant of arrest, to the following effect: "The within-named A. B. having been brought before me under this warrant, is committed for examination to the Sheriff of ___ ." If the Sheriff is not present, the defendant may be committed to the custody of a peace-officer.

§864. Witnesses' depositions; reading.

At the examination, the magistrate must first read to the defendant the depositions of the witnesses examined on taking the information.

§865. Examination of witnesses to be in presence of defendant, etc.

The witnesses must be examined in the presence of the defendant, and may be cross-examined in his behalf.

§866. Examination of defendant's witnesses.

(a) When the examination of witnesses on the part of the people is closed, any witness the defendant shall produce shall be sworn and examined.

Upon the request of the prosecuting attorney, the magistrate shall require an offer of proof from the defense as to the testimony expected from the witness. The magistrate shall not permit the testimony of any defense witness unless the offer of proof discloses to the satisfaction of the magistrate, in his or her sound discretion, that the testimony of that witness, if believed, would be reasonably likely to establish an affirmative defense, negate an element of a crime charged, or impeach the testimony of a prosecution witness or the statement of a declarant testified to by a prosecution witness.

(b) It is the purpose of a preliminary examination to establish whether there exists probable cause to believe that the defendant has committed a felony. The examination shall not be used for purposes of discovery.

(c) This section shall not be construed to compel or authorize the taking of depositions of witnesses. *(Amended by Initiative Measure, Prop 115 §16, approved 6/5/90.)*

§866.5. Defendant's examination.

The defendant may not be examined at the examination, unless he is represented by counsel, or unless he waives his right to counsel after being advised at such examination of his right to aid of counsel.

§867. Exclusion of witnesses.

While a witness is under examination, the magistrate shall, upon motion of either party, exclude all potential and actual witnesses who have not been examined.

The magistrate shall also order the witnesses not to converse with each other until they are all examined. The magistrate may also order, where feasible, that the witnesses be kept separated from each other until they are all examined.

This section does not apply to the investigating officer or the investigator for the defendant, nor does it apply to officers having custody of persons brought before the magistrate.

Either party may challenge the exclusion of any person under this section. Upon motion of either party, the magistrate shall hold a hearing, on the record, to determine if the person sought to be excluded is, in fact, a person excludable under this section. *(Amended by Stats 1986 ch 868 §1.)*

§868. Exclusion of public; defendant's request.

The examination shall be open and public. However, upon the request of the defendant and a finding by the magistrate that exclusion of the public is necessary in order to protect the defendant's right to a fair and impartial trial, the magistrate shall exclude from the examination every person except the clerk, court reporter and bailiff, the prosecutor and his or her counsel, the Attorney General, the district attorney of the county, the investigating officer, the officer having

© 1992 by J., B. & L. Gould
Printed in the U.S.A. **EP**

custody of a prisoner witness while the prisoner is testifying, the defendant and his or her counsel, the officer having the defendant in custody, and a person chosen by the prosecuting witness who is not himself or herself a witness but who is present to provide the prosecuting witness moral support, provided that the person so chosen shall not discuss prior to or during the preliminary examination the testimony of the prosecuting witness with any person, other than the prosecuting witness, who is a witness in the examination. Upon motion of the prosecution, members of the alleged victim's family shall be entitled to be present and seated during the examination. The court shall grant the motion unless the magistrate finds that the exclusion is necessary to protect the defendant's right to a fair and impartial trial, or unless information provided by the defendant or noticed by the court establishes that there is a reasonable likelihood that the attendance of members of the alleged victim's family poses a risk of affecting the content of the testimony of the victim or any other witness. The court shall admonish members of the alleged victim's family who are present and seated during the examination not to discuss any testimony with family members, witnesses, or the public. Nothing in this section shall affect the exclusion of witnesses as provided in Section 867 of the Penal Code.

For purposes of this section and Section 867, members of the alleged victim's family shall include the alleged victim's spouse, parents, legal guardian, children, or siblings. *(Amended by Stats 1988, ch 277 §2, eff. 1/1/89.)*

§868.5. Child witness in sexual assault case; support.

(a) Notwithstanding any other provision of law, a prosecuting witness in a case involving a violation of Section 187, 203, 205, 207, 211, 220, 240, 242, 243.4, 245, 261, 262, 273a, 273d, 273.5, 273.6, 277, 285, 286, 288, 288a, 288.5, 289, 647.6, or former Section 647a, or a violation of subdivision (1) of Section 314, shall be entitled, for support, to the attendance of up to two persons of his or her own choosing, one of whom may be a witness, at the preliminary hearing and at the trial, or at a juvenile court proceeding, during the testimony of the prosecuting witness. Only one of those support persons may accompany the witness to the witness stand, although the other may remain in the courtroom during the witness' testimony. The person or persons so chosen shall not be a person described in Section 1070 of the Evidence Code unless the person or persons are related to the prosecuting witness as a parent, guardian, or sibling and do not make notes during the hearing or proceeding.

(b) If the person or persons so chosen are also prosecuting witnesses, the prosecution shall present evidence that the person's attendance is both desired by the prosecuting witness for support and will be helpful to the prosecuting witness. Upon that showing, the court shall grant the request unless information presented by the defendant or noticed by the court establishes that the support person's attendance during the testimony of the prosecuting witness would pose a substantial risk of influencing or affecting the content of that testimony. In the case of a juvenile court proceeding, the judge shall inform the support person or persons that juvenile court proceedings are confidential and may not be discussed with anyone not in attendance at the proceedings. In all cases, the judge shall admonish the support person or persons to not prompt, sway, or influence the witness in any way. Nothing in this section shall preclude a court from exercising its discretion to remove a person from the courtroom whom it believes is prompting, swaying, or influencing the witness.

(c) The testimony of the person or persons so chosen who are also prosecuting witnesses shall be presented before the testimony of the prosecuting witness. The prosecuting witness shall be excluded from the courtroom during that testimony. Whenever the evidence given by that person or those persons would be subject to exclusion because it has been given before the corpus delicti has been established, the evidence shall be admitted subject to the court's or the defendant's motion to strike that evidence from the record if the corpus delicti is not later established by the testimony of the prosecuting witness. *(Amended by Stats 1991 ch 336 §1, eff. 1/1/92.)*

§868.6. Special rooms for child witnesses.

(a) It is the purpose of this section to provide a nonthreatening environment for minors involved in the judicial system in order to better enable them to speak freely and accurately of the experiences that are the subject of judicial inquiry.

(b) Each county is encouraged to provide a room, located within, or within a reasonable distance from, the courthouse, for the use of minors under the age of 16. Should any such room reach full occupancy, preference shall be given to minors under the age of 16 whose appearance has been subpoenaed by the court. The room may be multipurpose in character. The county may seek the assistance of civic groups in the furnishing of the room and the provision of volunteers to aid in its operation and maintenance. If a county newly constructs, substantially remodels or refurbishes any courthouse or facility used as a courthouse on or after January 1, 1988, that courthouse or facility shall contain the room described in this subdivision. *(Added by Stats 1986 ch 976 §1.)*

§868.7. Closing examination on motion of prosecutors.

(a) Notwithstanding any other provision of law, the magistrate may, upon motion of the prosecutor, close the examination in the manner described in Section 868 during the testimony of a witness:

(1) Who is a minor and is the complaining victim of a sex offense, where testimony before the general public would be likely to cause serious psychological harm to the witness and where no alternative procedures, including, but not limited to, video taped deposition or contemporaneous examination in another place communicated to the courtroom by means of closed-circuit television, are available to avoid the perceived harm.

(2) Whose life would be subject to a substantial risk in appearing before the general public, and where no alternative security measures, including, but not limited to, efforts to conceal his or her features or physical description, searches of members of the public attending the examination, or the temporary exclusion of other actual or potential witnesses, would be adequate to minimize the perceived threat.

(b) In any case where public access to the courtroom is restricted during the examination of a witness pursuant to this section, a transcript of the testimony of such witness shall be made available to the public as soon as is practicable.

This section shall become operative on January 1, 1987.

§868.8. Special precautions to protect a minor.

Notwithstanding any other provision of law, in any criminal proceeding in which the defendant is charged with a violation of Section 243.4, 261, 273a, 273d, 285, 286, 288, 288a, 288.5, or 289, subdivision (1) of Section 314, Section 647.6, or former Section 647a, committed with or upon a minor under the age of 11, the court shall take special precautions to provide for the comfort and support of the minor and to protect the minor from coercion, intimidation, or undue influence as a witness, including, but not limited to, any of the following:

(a) In the court's discretion, the witness may be allowed reasonable periods of relief from examination and cross-examination during which he or she may retire from the courtroom. The judge may also allow other witnesses in the proceeding to be examined when the child witness retires from the courtroom.

(b) Notwithstanding Section 68110 of the Government Code, in his or her discretion, the judge may remove his or her robe if the judge believes that this formal attire intimidates the minor.

(c) In the court's discretion the judge, parties, witnesses, support persons, and court personnel may be relocated within the courtroom to facilitate a more comfortable and personal environment for the child witness.

(d) In the court's discretion, the taking of the child's testimony may be limited to the hours during which the child is normally in school, if there is no good cause to take the child's testimony during other hours. *(Amended by Stats 1989 ch 1402 §9, eff. 1/1/90.)*

§869. Deposition testimony in homicide cases.

The testimony of each witness in cases of homicide shall be reduced to writing, as a deposition, by the magistrate, or under his or her direction, and in other cases upon the demand of the prosecuting attorney, or the defendant, or his or her counsel. The magistrate before whom the examination is had may, in his or her discretion, order the testimony and proceedings to be taken down in shorthand in all examinations herein mentioned, and for that purpose he or she may appoint a shorthand reporter. The deposition or testimony of the witness shall be authenticated in the following form:

(a) It shall state the name of the witness, his or her place of residence, and his or her business or profession; except that if the witness is a peace officer, it shall state his or her name, and the address given in his or her testimony at the hearing.

(b) It shall contain the questions put to the witness and his or her answers thereto, each answer being distinctly read to him or her as it is taken down, and being corrected or added to until it conforms to what he or she declares is the truth, except in cases where the testimony is taken down in short-hand, the answer or answers of the witness need not be read to him or her.

(c) If a question put be objected to on either side and overruled, or the witness declines answering it, that fact, with the ground on which the question was overruled or the answer declined, shall be stated.

(d) The deposition shall be signed by the witness, or if he or she refuses to sign it, his or her reason for refusing shall be stated in writing, as he or she gives it, except in cases where the deposition is taken down in shorthand, it need not be signed by the witness.

(e) The reporter shall, within 10 days after the close of the examination, if the defendant be held to answer the charge in superior court, or in any other case if either the defendant or the prosecution orders the transcript, transcribe his or her shorthand notes, making an original and one copy and as many additional copies thereof as there are defendants (other than fictitious defendants), regardless of the number of charges or fictitious defendants included in the same examination, and certify and deliver the original and all copies to the county clerk of the county in which the defendant was examined. The reporter shall, before receiving any compensation as a reporter, file with the auditor of the county his or her affidavit setting forth that the transcript has been delivered to the county clerk within the time herein provided for. The compensation of the reporter for any services rendered by him or her as the reporter in any court of this state shall be reduced one-half if the provisions of this section as to the time of filing said transcript have not been complied with by him or her.

(f) In every case in which a transcript is delivered as provided in this section, the county clerk shall file the original of the transcript with the papers in the case, and shall deliver a copy of the transcript to the district attorney immediately upon his or her receipt thereof and shall deliver a copy of said transcript to each defendant (other than a fictitious defendant) at least five days before trial or upon earlier demand by him or her without cost to him or her; provided, that if any defendant be held to answer to two or more charges upon the same examination and thereafter the district attorney shall file separate informations upon said several charges, the delivery to each such defendant of one copy of the transcript of the examination shall be a compliance with this section as to all of those informations.

(g) If the transcript is delivered by the reporter within the time hereinbefore provided for, the reporter shall be entitled to receive the compensation fixed and allowed by law to reporters in the superior courts of this state. *(Amended by Stats 1987 ch 828 §51.)*

§870. Examination and copying of depositions.

The magistrate or his or her clerk shall keep the depositions taken on the information or the examination, until they are returned to the proper court; and shall not permit them to be examined or copied by any person except a judge of a court having jurisdiction of the offense, or authorized to issue writs of habeas corpus, the Attorney General, district attorney, or other prosecuting attorney, and the defendant and his or her counsel; provided however, upon demand by the defendant or his or her attorney the magistrate shall order a transcript of the depositions taken on the information, or on the examination, to be immediately furnished the defendant or his or her attorney, after the commitment of the defendant as provided by Sections 876 and 877, and the reporter furnishing the depositions, shall receive compensation and be paid by the county for the same as provided by subdivision (f) of Section 869. *(Amended by Stats 1987 ch 828 §52.)*

© 1992 by J., B. & L. Gould
Printed in the U.S.A.   EP

§871. Discharge of defendant.

If, after hearing the proofs, it appears either that no public offense has been committed or that there is not sufficient cause to believe the defendant guilty of a public offense, the magistrate shall order the complaint dismissed and the defendant to be discharged, by an indorsement on the depositions and statement, signed by the magistrate, to the following effect: "There being no sufficient cause to believe the within named A. B. guilty of the offense within mentioned, I order that the complaint be dismissed and that he or she shall be discharged."

§871.5. Complaint, reinstatement.

(a) When an action is dismissed by a magistrate pursuant to Section 859b, 861, 871, 1008, 1381, 1381.5, 1385, 1387, or 1389, or a portion thereof is dismissed pursuant to those same sections which may not be charged by information under the provisions of Section 739, the prosecutor may make a motion in the superior court within 15 days to compel the magistrate to reinstate the complaint or a portion thereof and to reinstate the custodial status of the defendant under the same terms and conditions as when the defendant last appeared before the magistrate.

(b) Notice of the motion shall be made to the defendant and the magistrate. The only ground for the motion shall be that, as a matter of law, the magistrate erroneously dismissed the action or a portion thereof.

(c) The superior court shall hear and determine the motion on the basis of the record of the proceedings before the magistrate. If the motion is litigated to decision by the prosecutor, the prosecution is prohibited from refiling the dismissed action, or portion thereof.

(d) Within 10 days after the magistrate has dismissed the action or a portion thereof, the prosecuting attorney may file a written request for a transcript of the proceedings with the clerk of the magistrate. The reporter shall immediately transcribe his or her shorthand notes pursuant to Section 869 and file with the clerk of the superior court an original plus one copy, and as many copies as there are defendants (other than a fictitious defendant). The reporter shall be entitled to compensation in accordance with the provisions of Section 869. The clerk of the superior court shall deliver a copy of the transcript to the prosecuting attorney immediately upon its receipt and shall deliver a copy of the transcript to each defendant (other than a fictitious defendant) upon his or her demand without cost.

(e) When a court has ordered the resumption of proceedings before the magistrate, the magistrate shall resume the proceedings and when so ordered, issue an order of commitment for the reinstated offense or offenses within 10 days after the superior court has entered an order to that effect or within 10 days after the remittitur is filed in the superior court. Upon receipt of the remittitur, the superior court shall forward a copy to the magistrate.

(f) Pursuant to paragraph (9) of subdivision (a) of Section 1238 the people may take an appeal from the denial of the motion by the superior court to reinstate the complaint or a portion thereof. If the motion to reinstate the complaint is granted, the defendant may seek review thereof only pursuant to Sections 995 and 999a. Such review may only be sought in the event the defendant is held to answer pursuant to Section 872.

(g) Nothing contained herein shall preclude a magistrate, upon the resumption of proceedings, from considering a motion made pursuant to Section 1318.

If the superior court grants the motion for reinstatement and orders the magistrate to issue an order of commitment, the defendant, in lieu of resumed proceedings before the magistrate, may elect to waive his or her right to be committed by a magistrate, and consent to the filing of an amended or initial information containing the reinstated charge or charges. After arraignment thereon, he or she may adopt as a motion pursuant to Section 995, the record and proceedings of the motion taken pursuant to this section and the order issued pursuant thereto, and may seek review of the order in the manner prescribed in Section 999a.

§871.6. Petition for immediate appellate review.

If in a felony case the magistrate sets the preliminary examination beyond the time specified in Section 859b, in violation of Section 859b, or continues the preliminary hearing without good cause and good cause is required by law for such a continuance, the people or the defendant may file a petition for writ of mandate or prohibition in the superior court seeking immediate appellate review of the ruling setting the hearing or granting the continuance. Such a petition shall have precedence over all other cases in the court to which the petition is assigned. If the superior court grants a peremptory writ, it shall issue the writ and a remittitur three court days after its decision becomes final as to the court if this action is necessary to prevent mootness or to prevent frustration of the relief granted, notwithstanding the rights of the parties to seek review in a court of appeal. When the superior court issues the writ and remittitur as provided in this section, the writ shall command the magistrate to proceed with the preliminary hearing without further delay, other than that reasonably necessary for the parties to obtain the attendance of their witnesses.

The court of appeal may stay or recall the issuance of the writ and remittitur. The failure of the court of appeal to stay or recall the issuance of the writ and remittitur shall not deprive the parties of any right they would otherwise have to appellate review or extraordinary relief. (Added by Initiative Measure, Prop 115, §17, approved 6/5/90.)

§872. Indorsement on complaint; sufficient cause.

(a) If, however, it appears from the examination that a public offense has been committed, and there is sufficient cause to believe that the defendant is guilty, the magistrate shall make or indorse on the complaint an order, signed by him or her, to the following effect: "It appearing to me that the offense in the within complaint mentioned (or any offense, according to the fact, stating generally the nature thereof), has been committed, and that there is sufficient cause to believe that the within named A.B. is guilty, I order that he or she be held to answer to the same."

(b) Notwithstanding Section 1200 of the Evidence Code, the finding of probable cause may be based in whole or in part upon the sworn testimony of a law enforcement officer relating the statements of declarants made out of court offered for the truth of the matter asserted. Any law enforcement officer testifying as to hearsay statements shall either have five years of law enforcement experience or have completed a training course certified by the Commission of Peace Officer Standards and Training which includes training in the investigation and reporting of cases and testifying at preliminary hearings. *(Amended by Initiative Measure, Prop 115 §18, approved 6/5/90.)*

§872.5. Evidence rule.

The best evidence rule shall not apply to preliminary examinations. *(Added by Stats 1986 ch 992 §1.)*

§873. Order for commitment.

If the offense is not bailable, the following words must be added to the indorsement: "And he is hereby committed to the Sheriff of the County of _____."

§875. Order for commitment for offense which is bailable.

If the offense is bailable, and the defendant is admitted to bail, the following words must be added to the order, "and that he be admitted to bail in the sum of ____ dollars, and is committed to the sheriff of the county of _____ until he gives such bail."

§876. Commitment, how made and to whom delivered.

If the magistrate order the defendant to be committed, he must make out a commitment, signed by him, with his name of office, and deliver it, with the defendant, to the officer to whom he is committed, or if that officer is not present, to a peace-officer, who must deliver the defendant into the proper custody together with the commitment.

§877. Form of commitment.

The commitment must be to the following effect except when it is made under the provisions of section 859a of this code.

County of _____ (as the case may be).

The people of the State of California to the sheriff of the county of _____.

An order having been this day made by me, that A. B. be held to answer upon a charge of (stating briefly the nature of the offense, and giving as near as may be the time when and the place where the same was committed), you are commanded to receive him into your custody and detain him until he is legally discharged.

Dated this ____ day of ____ nineteen ____.

§877a. Form of commitment under §859a.

When the commitment is made under the provisions of section 859a of this code, it must be made to the following effect:

County of _____ (as the case may be).

The people of the State of California to the sheriff of the county of _____.

A. B. having pleaded guilty to the offense of (stating briefly the nature of the offense, and giving as near as may be the time when and the place where the same was committed), you are commanded to receive him into your custody and detain him until he is legally discharged.

Dated this ____ day of ____ nineteen ____.

§878. Written undertaking by witness.

On holding the defendant to answer or on a plea of guilty where permitted by law, the magistrate may take from each of the material witnesses examined before him on the part of the people a written undertaking, to the effect that he will appear and testify at the court to which the depositions and statements or case are to be sent, or that he will forfeit the sum of five hundred dollars.

§879. Security for the appearance of witnesses, when and how required.

When the magistrate or a judge of the court in which the action is pending is satisfied, by proof on oath, that there is reason to believe that any such witness will not appear and testify unless security is required, he may order the witness to enter into a written undertaking, with sureties, in such sum as he may deem proper, for his appearance as specified in the preceding section.

§880. Infants required to give security.

Infants who are material witnesses against the defendant may be required to procure sureties for their appearance, as provided in the last section.

§881. Material witnesses; commitment.

(a) If a witness, required to enter into an undertaking to appear and testify, either with or without sureties, refuses compliance with the order for that purpose, the magistrate shall commit him or her to prison until he or she complies or is legally discharged.

(b) If a witness fails to appear at the preliminary hearing in response to a subpoena, the court may hear evidence, including testimony or an affidavit from the arresting or interviewing officer, and if the court determines on the basis of the evidence that the witness is a material witness, the court shall issue a bench warrant for the arrest of the witness, and upon the appearance of the witness, may commit him or her into custody until the conclusion of the preliminary hearing, or until the defendant enters a plea of nolo contendere, or the witness is otherwise legally discharged.

The court may order the witness to enter into a written undertaking to the effect that he or she will appear and testify at the time and place ordered by the court or that he or she will forfeit an amount that the court deems proper.

(c) Once the material witness has been taken into custody on the bench warrant he or she shall be brought before the magistrate issuing the warrant, if available, within two court days for a hearing to determine if the witness should be released on security of appearance or maintained in custody.

(d) A material witness shall remain in custody under this section for no longer than 10 days.

(e) If a material witness is being held in custody under this section the prosecution is entitled to have the preliminary hearing proceed, as to this witness only, within 10 days of the arraignment of the defendant. Once this material witness has completed his or her testimony the defendant shall be entitled to a reasonable continuance. *(Amended by Stats 1987 ch 828 §53.)*

§882. Conditional examination of witness.

When, however, it satisfactorily appears by examination, on oath of the witness, or any other person, that the witness is unable to procure sureties, he or she may be forthwith conditionally examined on behalf of the people. The examination shall be by question and answer, in the presence of the defendant, or after notice to him or her, if on bail, and conducted in

© 1992 by J., B. & L. Gould
Printed in the U.S.A.   **EP**

the same manner as the examination before a committing magistrate is required by this code to be conducted, and the witness thereupon discharged; and the deposition may be used upon the trial of the defendant, except in cases of homicide, under the same conditions as mentioned in Section 1345; but this section does not apply to an accomplice in the commission of the offense charged. (*Amended by Stats 1987 ch 828 §54.*)

§883. Magistrate to return depositions, etc., to the Court.

When a magistrate has discharged a defendant, or has held him to answer, he must return, without delay, to the Clerk of the Court at which the defendant is required to appear, the warrant, if any, the depositions, and all undertakings of bail, or for the appearance of witnesses taken by him.

TITLE 4

GRAND JURY PROCEEDINGS

CHAPTER 1

GENERAL PROVISIONS

§888. Grand jury defined.

A grand jury is a body of the required number of persons returned from the citizens of the county before a court of competent jurisdiction, and sworn to inquire of public offenses committed or triable within the county.

Each grand jury or, if more than one has been duly impaneled pursuant to Sections 904.5 to 904.9, inclusive, one grand jury in each county, shall be charged and sworn to investigate or inquire into county matters of civil concern, such as the needs of county officers, including the abolition or creation of offices for, the purchase, lease, or sale of equipment for, or changes in the method or system of, performing the duties of the agencies subject to investigation pursuant to Section 914.1. (*Amended by Stats 1988 ch 1297 §1, eff. 1/1/89.*)

§888.2. Required number defined.

As used in this title as applied to a grand jury, "required number" means 23 in a county having a population exceeding four million and 19 in other counties.

§889. Indictment defined.

An indictment is an accusation in writing, presented by the grand jury to a competent court, charging a person with a public offense.

§890. Fees for jurors.

Unless a higher fee or rate of mileage is otherwise provided by statute or county or city and county ordinance, the fees for grand jurors are ten dollars ($10) a day for each day's attendance as a grand juror, and fifteen cents ($0.15) a mile, in going only, for each mile actually traveled in attending court as a grand juror.

§890.1. How paid.

The per diem and mileage of grand jurors where allowed by law shall be paid by the treasurer of the county out of the general fund of the county upon warrants drawn by the county auditor upon the written order of the judge of the superior court of the county.

§891. Recording, listening to grand jury proceedings.

Every person who, by any means whatsoever, wilfully and knowingly, and without knowledge and consent of the grand jury, records, or attempts to record, all or part of the proceedings of any grand jury while it is deliberating or voting, or listens to or observes, or attempts to listen to or observe, the proceedings of any grand jury of which he is not a member while such jury is deliberating or voting is guilty of a misdemeanor.

This section is not intended to prohibit the taking of notes by a grand juror in connection with and solely for the purpose of assisting him in the performance of his duties as such juror.

§892. Proceeding against corporation.

The grand jury may proceed against a corporation.

CHAPTER 2

FORMATION OF GRAND JURY

ARTICLE 1

QUALIFICATIONS OF GRAND JURORS

§893. Competency.

(a) A person is competent to act as a grand juror only if he possesses each of the following qualifications:

(1) He is a citizen of the United States of the age of 18 years or older who shall have been a resident of the state and of the county or city and county for one year immediately before being selected and returned.

(2) He is in possession of his natural faculties, of ordinary intelligence, of sound judgment, and of fair character.

(3) He is possessed of sufficient knowledge of the English language.

(b) A person is not competent to act as a grand juror if any of the following apply:

(1) The person is serving as a trial juror in any court of this state.

(2) The person has been discharged as a grand juror in any court of this state within one year.

(3) The person has been convicted of malfeasance in office or any felony or other high crime.

(4) The person is serving as an elected public officer.

§894. Jury duty; exemption.

Sections 204, 218, and 219 of the Code of Civil Procedure specify the exemptions and the excuses which relieve a person from liability to serve as a grand juror. (*Amended by Stats 1989 ch 1416 §37, eff. 1/1/90.*)

ARTICLE 2

LISTING AND SELECTION OF GRAND JURORS

§895. Number of jurors required.

During the month preceding the beginning of the fiscal year of the county, the superior court of each county shall make an order designating the estimated number of grand jurors that will, in the opinion of the court, be required for the transaction of the business of the court during the ensuing fiscal year as provided in Section 905.5.

§896. Interview, selection and list of jurors.

(a) Immediately after such order is made, the court shall select the grand jurors required by personal interview for the purpose of ascertaining whether they possess the qualifications prescribed by subdivision (a) of Section 893. If a person so interviewed, in the opinion of the court, possesses such qualifications, in order for his name to be listed he shall sign a statement declaring that he will be available for jury service for the number of hours usually required of a member of the grand jury in that county.

(b) The selections shall be made of men and women who are not exempt from serving and who are suitable and competent to serve as grand jurors pursuant to Sections 893, 898, and 899. The court shall list the persons so selected and required by the order to serve as grand jurors during the ensuing fiscal year of the county, or until a new list of grand jurors is provided, and shall at once place this list in the possession of the county clerk.

§898. Jury lists for Los Angeles County.

The list of grand jurors made in a county having a population in excess of four million shall contain the number of persons which has been designated by the court in its order.

§899. Selection procedure.

The names for the grand jury list shall be selected from the different wards, judicial districts, or supervisorial districts of the respective counties in proportion to the number of inhabitants therein, as nearly as the same can be estimated by the persons making the lists. The grand jury list shall be kept separate and distinct from the trial jury list. In a county of the first class, the names for such list may be selected from the county at large.

§900. County clerk's duties.

On receiving the list of persons selected by the court, the county clerk shall file it in his office and have such list, which shall include the name of the judge who selected each person on the list, published one time in a newspaper of general circulation, as defined in Section 6000 of the Government Code, in the county. The county clerk shall thereupon do either of the following:

(a) Write down the names on the list onto separate pieces of paper of the same size and appearance, fold each piece so as to conceal the name thereon, and deposit the pieces in a box to be called the "grand jury box."

(b) Assign a number to each name on the list and place, in a box to be called the "grand jury box," markers of the same size, shape, and color, each containing a number which corresponds with a number on the list.

§901. Regular jurors.

(a) The persons whose names are so returned shall be known as regular jurors, and shall serve for one year and until other persons are selected and returned.

(b) If the superior court so decides, the presiding judge may name up to 10 regular jurors not previously so named, who served on the previous grand jury and who so consent, to serve for a second year.

(c) The court may also decide to select grand jurors pursuant to Section 908.2. *(Amended by Stats 1988 ch 886 §1, eff. 1/1/89.)*

§902. Drawing of grand jurors.

The names of persons drawn for grand jurors shall be drawn from the grand jury box by withdrawing either the pieces of paper placed therein pursuant to subdivision (a) of Section 900 or the markers placed therein pursuant to subdivision (b) of Section 900. If, at the end of the fiscal year of the county, there are the names of persons in the grand jury box who have not been drawn during the fiscal year to serve and have not served as grand jurors, the names of such persons may be placed on the list of grand jurors drawn for the succeeding fiscal year.

ARTICLE 3

JURY COMMISSIONERS

§903. Applicability.

This article applies in each county in which a jury commissioner is appointed pursuant to Section 195 of the Code of Civil Procedure and in each county in which the secretary of the judges of the superior court performs the duties of jury commissioner pursuant to Section 69893 of the Government Code. *(Amended by Stats 1989 ch 1416 §38, eff. 1/1/90.)*

§903.1. List of qualified jurors.

Pursuant to written rules or instructions adopted by a majority of the judges of the superior court of the county, the jury commissioner shall furnish the judges of the court annually a list of persons qualified to serve as grand jurors during the ensuing (fiscal) year (of the county), or until a new list of jurors is required. From time to time, a majority of the judges of the superior court may adopt such rules or instructions as may be necessary for the guidance of the jury commissioner, who shall at all times be under the supervision and control of the judges of the court. Any list of jurors prepared pursuant to this article must, however, meet the requirements of Section 899.

§903.2. Powers and duties of jury commissioner.

The jury commissioner shall diligently inquire and inform himself in respect to the qualifications of persons resident in his county who may be liable to be summoned for grand jury duty. He may require any person to answer, under oath to be administered by him, all such questions as he may address to such person, touching his name, age, residence, occupation, and qualifications as a grand juror, and also all questions as to similar matters concerning other persons of whose qualifications for grand jury duty he has knowledge.

The commissioner and his assistants, referred to in Sections 69895 and 69896 of the Government Code, shall have power to administer oaths and shall be allowed actual traveling expenses incurred in the performance of their duties. Such traveling expenses shall be audited, allowed, and paid out of the general fund of the county.

© 1992 by J., B. & L. Gould
Printed in the U.S.A.   EP

§903.3. Selection of jurors.

Pursuant to the rules or instructions adopted by a majority of the judges of the superior court, the jury commissioner shall return to the judges the list of persons recommended by him for grand jury duty. The judges of the superior court shall examine the jury list so returned and from such list a majority of the judges may select, to serve as grand jurors in the superior court of the county during the ensuing year or until a new list of jurors is required, such persons as, in their opinion, should be selected for grand jury duty. The persons so selected shall, in the opinion of the judges selecting them, be persons suitable and competent to serve as jurors, as required by law.

§903.4. Disregarding list of jurors.

The judges are not required to select any names from the list returned by the jury commissioner, but may, if in their judgment the due administration of justice requires, make all or any selections from among the body of persons in the county suitable and competent to serve as grand jurors regardless of the list returned by the jury commissioner.

ARTICLE 4

IMPANELING OF GRAND JURY

§904. Drawing grand jurors.

Every superior court, whenever in its opinion the public interest so requires, shall make and file with the county clerk an order directing a grand jury to be drawn. Such order shall designate the number of grand jurors to be drawn, which shall not be less than 29 nor more than 40 in counties having a population exceeding four million and not less than 25 nor more than 30 in other counties.

§904.4. Additional grand juries, counties with population between 370,000 and 400,000.

(a) In any county having a population of more than 370,000 but less than 400,000 as established by Section 28020 of the Government Code, the presiding judge of the superior court, upon application by the district attorney, may order and direct the drawing and impanelment at any time of one additional grand jury.

(b) The presiding judge may select persons, at random, from the list of trial jurors in civil and criminal cases and shall examine them to determine if they are competent to serve as grand jurors. When a sufficient number of competent persons have been selected, they shall constitute the additional grand jury.

(c) Any additional grand jury which is impaneled pursuant to this section may serve for a period of one year from the date of impanelment, but may be discharged at any time within the one-year period by order of the presiding judge. In no event shall more than one additional grand jury be impaneled pursuant to this section at the same time.

(d) Whenever an additional grand jury is impaneled pursuant to this section, it may inquire into any matters that are subject to grand jury inquiry and shall have the sole and exclusive jurisdiction to return indictments, except for any matters that the regular grand jury is inquiring into at the time of its impanelment.

(e) If an additional grand jury is also authorized by another section, the county may impanel the additional grand jury authorized by this section, or by the other section, but not both. *(Added by Stats 1991 ch 1109 §1, eff. 1/1/92.)*

§904.5. *Repealed by Stats 1991 ch 464 §1, eff. 10/2/91.*

§904.6. Additional grand juries in cities and counties.

(a) In any county or city and county, the presiding judge of the superior court may order and direct the impanelment, at any time, of one additional grand jury pursuant to this section.

(b) The presiding judge shall select persons, at random, from the list of trial jurors in civil and criminal cases and shall examine them to determine if they are competent to serve as grand jurors. When a sufficient number of competent persons have been selected, they shall constitute the additional grand jury.

(c) Any additional grand jury which is impaneled pursuant to this section may serve for a period of one year from the date of impanelment, but may be discharged at any time within the one-year period by order of the presiding judge. In no event shall more than one additional grand jury be impaneled pursuant to this section at the same time.

(d) Whenever an additional grand jury is impaneled pursuant to this section, it may inquire into any matters which are subject to grand jury inquiry and shall have the sole and exclusive jurisdiction to return indictments, except for any matters which the regular grand jury is inquiring into at the time of its impanelment.

(e) It is the intent of the Legislature that all persons qualified for jury service shall have an equal opportunity to be considered for service as criminal grand jurors in the county in which they reside, and that they have an obligation to serve, when summoned for that purpose. All persons selected for the additional criminal grand jury shall be selected at random from a source or sources reasonably representative of a cross section of the population which is eligible for jury service in the county. *(Amended by Stats 1991 ch 464 §2, eff. 10/2/91.)*

§904.7. *Repealed by Stats 1991 ch 464 §3, eff. 10/2/91.*

§904.8. *Repealed by Stats 1991 ch 464 §4, eff. 10/2/91.*

§904.9. *Repealed by Stats 1991 ch 464 §5, eff. 10/2/91.*

§905. Minimum impanelment.

In all counties there shall be at least one grand jury drawn and impaneled in each year.

§905.5. Service in fiscal or calendar year.

(a) Except as otherwise provided in subdivision (b), the grand jury shall be impaneled and serve during the fiscal year of the county in the manner provided in this chapter.

(b) The board of supervisors of a county may provide that the grand jury shall be impaneled and serve during the calendar year. The board of supervisors shall provide for an appropriate transition from fiscal year term to calendar year term or from calendar year term to fiscal year term for the grand jury. The provisions of subdivisions (a) and (b) of Section 901 shall not be deemed a limitation on any appropriate transition provisions as determined by resolution or ordinance; and, except as otherwise provided in this chapter, no transition grand jury shall serve more than 18 months.

§906. Drawing of names of grand jurors.

The order shall designate the time at which the drawing will take place. The names of the grand jurors shall be drawn, and the list of names certified and summoned, as is provided for drawing and summoning trial jurors. The names of any persons drawn, who are not impaneled upon the grand jury, may be again placed in the grand jury box.

§907. Failure to attend.

Any grand juror summoned, who wilfully and without reasonable excuse fails to attend, may be attached and compelled to attend and the court may also impose a fine not exceeding fifty dollars ($50), upon which execution may issue. If the grand juror was not personally served, the fine shall not be imposed until upon an order to show cause an opportunity has been offered the grand juror to be heard.

§908. Reducing or adding to grand jury.

If the required number of the persons summoned as grand jurors are present and not excused, such required number shall constitute the grand jury. If more than the required number of such persons are present, the clerk shall write their names on separate ballots, which he shall fold so that the names cannot be seen, place them in a box, and draw out the required number of them. The persons whose names are on the ballots so drawn shall constitute the grand jury. If less than the required number of such persons are present, the panel may be filled as provided in Section 226 of the Code of Civil Procedure. If more of the persons summoned to complete a grand jury attend than are required, the requisite number shall be obtained by writing the names of those summoned and not excused on ballots, depositing them in a box, and drawing as above provided.

§908.1. Vacancies in grand jury.

When, after the grand jury consisting of the required number of persons has been impaneled pursuant to law, the membership is reduced for any reason, such vacancies within an existing grand jury may be filled, so as to maintain the full membership at the required number of persons, by the clerk of the superior court, in the presence of the court, drawing out sufficient names to fill the vacancies from the grand jury box, pursuant to law, or from a special venire as provided in Section 226 of the Code of Civil Procedure. No person selected as a grand juror to fill a vacancy pursuant to this section shall vote as a grand juror on any matter upon which evidence has been taken by the grand jury prior to the time of his selection.

§908.2. Balloting for grand jurors.

(a) Upon the decision of the superior court pursuant to Section 901 to adopt this method of selecting grand jurors, when the required number of persons have been impaneled as the grand jury pursuant to law, the clerk shall write the names of each such person on separate ballots. The clerk shall fold the ballots so that the names cannot be seen, place them in a box, and draw out half of such ballots, or in a county where the number of grand jurors is uneven, one more than half. The persons whose names are on the ballots so drawn shall serve for 12 months until July 1 of the following year. The persons whose names are not on the ballots so drawn shall serve for six months until January 1 of the following year.

(b) Each subsequent year, on January 2 and July 2, a sufficient number of grand jurors shall be impaneled to replace those whose service concluded the previous day. Those persons impaneled on January 2, shall serve until January 1 of the following year. Those persons impaneled on July 2, shall serve until July 1 of the following year. No person shall serve on the grand jury for more than one year.

(c) The provisions of subdivisions (a) and (b) shall not be applicable to the selection of grand jurors for an additional grand jury authorized pursuant to Sections 904.5, 904.6, 904.7, 904.8, and 904.9.

§909. Accepting or excusing grand jurors.

Before accepting a person drawn as a grand juror, the court shall be satisfied that such person is duly qualified to act as such juror. When a person is drawn and found qualified he shall be accepted unless the court, on the application of the juror and before he is sworn, excuses him from such service for any of the reasons prescribed in this title or in Chapter 1 (commencing with Section 190), Title 3, Part 1 of the Code of Civil Procedure.

§910. Challenges to the panel.

No challenge shall be made or allowed to the panel from which the grand jury is drawn, nor to an individual grand juror, except when made by the court for want of qualification, as prescribed in Section 909.

§911. Grand jury oath.

The following oath shall be taken by each member of the grand jury: "I do solemnly swear (affirm) that I will support the Constitution of the United States and of the State of California, and all laws made pursuant to and in conformity therewith, will diligently inquire into, and true presentment make, of all public offenses against the people of this state, committed or triable within this county, of which the grand jury shall have or can obtain legal evidence. Further, I will not disclose any evidence brought before the grand jury, nor anything which I or any other grand juror may say, nor the manner in which I or any other grand juror may have voted on any matter before the grand jury. I will keep the charge that will be given to me by the court."

§912. Foreman.

From the persons summoned to serve as grand jurors and appearing, the court shall appoint a foreman. The court shall also appoint a foreman when the person already appointed is excused or discharged before the grand jury is dismissed.

§913. Attorney General demanding grand jury.

If a grand jury is not in existence, the Attorney General may demand the impaneling of a grand jury by those charged with the duty to do so, and upon such demand by him, it shall be their duty to do so.

© 1992 by J., B. & L. Gould
Printed in the U.S.A.   **EP**

CHAPTER 3

POWERS AND DUTIES OF GRAND JURY

ARTICLE 1

GENERAL PROVISIONS

§914. Court; charges.

When the grand jury is impaneled and sworn, it shall be charged by the court. In doing so, the court shall give the grand jurors such information as it deems proper, or as is required by law, as to their duties, and as to any charges for public offenses returned to the court or likely to come before the grand jury.

§914.1. Additional instructions.

When a grand jury is impaneled, for purposes which include the investigation of, or inquiry into, county matters of civil concern, the judge of the superior court of the county, in addition to other matters requiring action, shall call its attention to the provisions of Chapter 1 (commencing with Section 23000) of Division 1 of Title 3, and Sections 24054 and 26525 of the Government Code, and instruct it to ascertain by a careful and diligent investigation whether such provisions have been complied with, and to note the result of such investigation in its report. At such time the judge shall also inform and charge the grand jury especially as to its powers, duties, and responsibilities under Article 1 (commencing with Section 888) of Chapter 2, and Article 2 (commencing with Section 925), Article 3 (commencing with Section 934) of this chapter, Article 3 (commencing with Section 3060) of Chapter 7 of Division 4 of Title 1 of the Government Code, and Section 17006 of the Welfare and Institutions Code. (*Amended by Stats 1988 ch 1297 §2, eff. 1/1/89.*)

§914.5. Limitation on expenditures.

The grand jury shall not spend money or incur obligations in excess of the amount budgeted for its investigative activities pursuant to this chapter by the county board of supervisors unless the proposed expenditure is approved in advance by the presiding judge of the superior court after the board of supervisors has been advised of the request.

§915. Retiring for deliberation.

When the grand jury has been impaneled, sworn, and charged, it shall retire to a private room, except when operating under a finding pursuant to Section 939.1 and inquire into the offenses and matters of civil concern cognizable by it. On the completion of the business before the grand jury or expiration of the term of prescribed service of one or more grand jurors, the court shall discharge it or the affected individual jurors. (*Amended by Stats 1988 ch 1297 §3, eff. 1/1/89.*)

§916. Choosing officers.

Each grand jury shall choose its officers, except the foreman, and shall determine its rules of proceeding. Adoption of its rules of procedure and all public actions of the grand jury, whether concerning criminal or civil matters unless otherwise prescribed in law, including adoption of final reports, shall be only with the concurrence of that number of grand jurors necessary to find an indictment pursuant to Section 940. Rules of procedure shall include guidelines for that grand jury to ensure that all findings included in its final reports are supported by documented evidence, including reports of contract auditors or consultants, official records, or interviews attended by no fewer than two grand jurors and that all problems identified in a final report are accompanied by suggested means for their resolution, including financial, when applicable. (*Amended by Stats 1988 ch 1297 §4, eff. 1/1/89.*)

§916.1. Foreman; in absence.

If the foreman of a grand jury is absent from any meeting or if he is disqualified to act, the grand jury may select a member of that body to act as foreman pro tempore, who shall perform the duties, and have all the powers, of the regularly appointed foreman in his absence or disqualification.

§917. Public offenses; inquiries.

The grand jury may inquire into all public offenses committed or triable within the county and present them to the court by indictment.

§918. Juror's knowledge of public offenses.

If a member of a grand jury knows, or has reason to believe, that a public offense, triable within the county has been committed, he may declare it to his fellow jurors, who may thereupon investigate it.

§919. Inquiry into case of non-indicted prisoner.

(a) The grand jury may inquire into the case of every person imprisoned in the jail of the county on a criminal charge and not indicted.

(b) The grand jury shall inquire into the condition and management of the public prisons within the county.

(c) The grand jury shall inquire into the willful or corrupt misconduct in office of public officers of every description within the county.

§920. Inquiry into sales and transfers of lands.

The grand jury may investigate and inquire into all sales and transfers of land, and into the ownership of land, which, under the state laws, might or should escheat to the State of California. For this purpose, the grand jury may summon witnesses before it and examine them and the records. The grand jury shall direct that proper escheat proceedings be commenced when, in the opinion of the grand jury, the evidence justifies such proceedings.

§921. Free access; public prisons and public records.

The grand jury is entitled to free access, at all reasonable times, to the public prisons, and to the examination, without charge, of all public records within the county.

§922. Removal of local public officers.

The powers and duties of the grand jury in connection with proceedings for the removal of district, county, or city officers are prescribed in Article 3 (commencing with Section 3060), Chapter 7, Division 4, Title 1, of the Government Code.

§923. Investigating matters.

Whenever the Attorney General considers the public interest requires, he may, with or without the concurrence of the district attorney, direct the grand jury to convene for the investigation and consideration of such matters of a criminal nature as he desires to submit to it. He may take full charge of the presentation of such matters to the grand jury, issue subpoenas, prepare indictments, and do all other things incident thereto to the same extent as the district attorney may do.

§924. Disclosure of information or indictment information.

Every grand juror who willfully discloses the fact of an information or indictment having been made for a felony, until the defendant has been arrested, is guilty of a misdemeanor.

§924.1. Willfully disclosing evidence.

(a) Every grand juror who, except when required by a court, willfully discloses any evidence adduced before the grand jury, or anything which he himself or any other member of the grand jury has said, or in what manner he or she or any other grand juror has voted on a matter before them, is guilty of a misdemeanor.

(b) Every interpreter for the disabled appointed to assist a member of the grand jury pursuant to Section 939.11 who, except when required by a court, willfully discloses any evidence adduced before the grand jury, or anything which he or she or any member of the grand jury has said, or in what manner any grand juror has voted on a matter before them, is guilty of a misdemeanor. *(Amended by Stats 1986 ch 357 §1.)*

§924.2. Secrecy of voting; disclosure of testimony.

Each grand juror shall keep secret whatever he himself or any other grand juror has said, or in what manner he or any other grand juror has voted on a matter before them. Any court may require a grand juror to disclose the testimony of a witness examined before the grand jury, for the purpose of ascertaining whether it is consistent with that given by the witness before the court, or to disclose the testimony given before the grand jury by any person, upon a charge against such person for perjury in giving his testimony or upon trial therefor.

§924.3. Questioning juror.

A grand juror cannot be questioned for anything he may say or any vote he may give in the grand jury relative to a matter legally pending before the jury, except for a perjury of which he may have been guilty in making an accusation or giving testimony to his fellow jurors.

§924.4. Information and evidences for succeeding grand jury.

Notwithstanding the provisions of Sections 924.1 and 924.2, any grand jury or, if the grand jury is no longer empaneled, the presiding or sole judge of the superior court, may provide the succeeding grand jury with any information or evidence acquired by the grand jury during the course of any investigation conducted by it during its term of service, except any information or evidence which relates to a criminal investigation or which could form part or all of the basis for issuance of an indictment. Transcripts of testimony reported during any session of the grand jury shall be made available to the succeeding grand jury upon its request.

§924.6. Disclosure of testimony when no indictment is returned.

If no indictment is returned, the court that impaneled the grand jury shall, upon application of either party, order disclosure of all or part of the testimony of a witness before the grand jury to a defendant and the prosecutor in connection with any pending or subsequent criminal proceeding before any court if the court finds following an in camera hearing, which shall include the court's review of the grand jury's testimony, that the testimony is relevant, and appears to be admissible.

ARTICLE 2

INVESTIGATION OF COUNTY, CITY, AND DISTRICT AFFAIRS

§925. Examinations of county operations, etc.

The grand jury shall investigate and report on the operations, accounts, and records of the officers, departments, or functions of the county including those operations, accounts, and records of any special legislative district or other district in the county created pursuant to state law for which the officers of the county are serving in their ex officio capacity as officers of the districts. The investigations may be conducted on some selective basis each year, but the grand jury shall not duplicate any examination of financial statements which has been performed by or for the board of supervisors pursuant to Section 25250 of the Government Code; this provision shall not be construed to limit the power of the grand jury to investigate and report on the operations, accounts, and records of the officers, departments, or functions of the county. The grand jury may enter into a joint contract with the board of supervisors to employ the services of an expert as provided for in Section 926.

§925a. Examination of books and records of incorporated city or joint powers agency.

The grand jury may at any time examine the books and records of any incorporated city or joint powers agency located in the county. In addition to any other investigatory powers granted by this chapter, the grand jury may investigate and report upon the operations, accounts, and records of the officers, departments, functions, and the method or system of performing the duties of any such city or joint powers agency and make such recommendations as it may deem proper and fit.

The grand jury may investigate and report upon the needs of all joint powers agencies in the county, including the abolition or creation of agencies and the equipment for, or the method or system of performing the duties of, the several agencies. It shall cause a copy of any such report to be transmitted to the governing body of any affected agency.

As used in this section, "joint powers agency" means an agency described in Section 6506 of the Government Code whose jurisdiction encompasses all or part of a county.

§926. Employment of experts or assistants.

(a) If, in the judgment of the grand jury, the services of one or more experts are necessary for the

© 1992 by J., B. & L. Gould
Printed in the U.S.A. **EP**

purposes of Sections 925, 925a, 928, 933.1, and 933.5 or any of them, the grand jury may employ one or more experts, at an agreed compensation, to be first approved by the court. If, in the judgment of the grand jury, the services of assistants to such experts are required, the grand jury may employ such assistants, at a compensation to be agreed upon and approved by the court. Expenditures for the services of experts and assistants for the purposes of Section 933.5 shall not exceed the sum of thirty thousand dollars ($30,000) annually, unless such expenditures shall also be approved by the board of supervisors.

(b) When making an examination of the books, records, accounts, and documents maintained and processed by the county assessor, the grand jury, with the consent of the board of supervisors, may employ expert auditors or appraisers to assist in the examination. Auditors and appraisers, while performing pursuant to the directive of the grand jury, shall have access to all records and documents that may be inspected by the grand jury subject to the same limitations on public disclosure as apply to the grand jury.

(c) Any contract entered into by a grand jury pursuant to this section may include services to be performed after the discharge of the jury, but in no event may a jury contract for services to be performed later than six months after the end of the fiscal year during which the jury was impaneled.

(d) Any contract entered into by a grand jury pursuant to this section shall stipulate that the product of that contract shall be delivered on or before a time certain to the then-current grand jury of that county for such use as that jury finds appropriate to its adopted objectives. *(Amended by Stats 1988 ch 1297 §4.5, eff. 1/1/89.)*

§927. Investigating and reporting upon salaries of county-elected officials.

A grand jury may, and when requested by the board of supervisors shall, investigate and report upon the needs for increase or decrease in salaries of the county-elected officials. A copy of such report shall be transmitted to the board of supervisors.

§928. Investigating and reporting upon needs of county officers.

Every grand jury may investigate and report upon the needs of all county officers in the county, including the abolition or creation of offices and the equipment for, or the method or system of performing the duties of, the several offices. Such investigation and report shall be conducted selectively each year. The grand jury shall cause a copy of such report to be transmitted to each member of the board of supervisors of the county.

§930. Comments not deemed privileged.

If any grand jury shall, in the report above mentioned, comment upon any person or official who has not been indicted by such grand jury such comments shall not be deemed to be privileged.

§931. Expenses of grand jurors; payment.

All expenses of the grand jurors incurred under this article shall be paid by the treasurer of the county out of the general fund of the county upon warrants drawn by the county auditor upon the written order of the judge of the superior court of the county.

§932. Suit to recover money due county.

After investigating the books and accounts of the various officials of the county, as provided in the foregoing sections of this article, the grand jury may order the district attorney of the county to institute suit to recover any money that, in the judgment of the grand jury, may from any cause be due the county. The order of the grand jury, certified by the foreman of the grand jury and filed with the county clerk of the county, shall be full authority for the district attorney to institute and maintain any such suit.

§933. Report of findings and recommendations.

(a) No later than the end of each fiscal or calendar year of a county, each grand jury impaneled during that fiscal or calendar year shall submit to the presiding judge of the superior court a final report of its findings and recommendations that pertain to county government matters other than fiscal matters during the fiscal or calendar year. Final reports on any appropriate subject may be submitted to the presiding judge of the superior court at any time during the term of service of a grand jury. A final report may be submitted for comment to responsible officers, agencies, or departments, including the county board of supervisors, when applicable, upon finding of the presiding judge that the report is in compliance with this title. One copy of each report found to be in compliance with this title shall be placed on file with the county clerk and remain on file in the office of the county clerk.

(b) No later than the end of each fiscal or calendar year, each grand jury impaneled during that fiscal or calendar year shall submit to the presiding judge of the superior court a final report of its findings and recommendations that pertain to fiscal matters of county government during the fiscal or calendar year of the county.

(c) No later than 90 days after the grand jury submits a final report on the operations of any public agency subject to its reviewing authority, the governing body of the public agency shall comment to the presiding judge of the superior court on the findings and recommendations pertaining to matters under the control of the governing body, and every elective county officer or agency head for which the grand jury has responsibility pursuant to Section 914.1 shall comment within 60 days to the presiding judge of the superior court, with an information copy sent to the board of supervisors, on the findings and recommendations pertaining to matters under the control of that county officer or agency head and any agency or agencies which that officer or agency head supervises or controls. In any city and county, the mayor shall also comment on the findings and recommendations. All such comments and reports shall forthwith be submitted to the presiding judge of the superior court who impaneled the grand jury. A copy of all responses to grand jury reports shall be placed on file with the clerk of the public agency and the office of the county clerk, or the mayor when applicable, and shall remain on file in those offices. One copy shall be placed on file with the applicable grand jury final report by, and in the control of the currently impaneled grand jury, where it shall be maintained for a minimum of five years. *(Amended by Stats 1988 ch 1297 §5, eff. 1/1/89.)*

§933.1. Examining books and records of redevelopment agency.

A grand jury may at any time examine the books and records of a redevelopment agency, a housing authority, created pursuant to Division 24 (commencing with Section 33000) of the Health and Safety Code, or a joint powers agency created pursuant to Chapter 5 (commencing with Section 6500) of Division 7 of Title 1 of the Government Code, and, in addition to any other investigatory powers granted by this chapter, may investigate and report upon the method or system of performing the duties of such agency or authority. *(Amended by Stats 1986 ch 279 §1.)*

§933.5. Examining books and records of special agencies.

A grand jury may at any time examine the books and records of any special-purpose assessing or taxing district located wholly or partly in the county or the local agency formation commission in the county, and, in addition to any other investigatory powers granted by this chapter, may investigate and report upon the method or system of performing the duties of such district or commission.

§933.6. Examining books and records of non-profit corporations.

A grand jury may at any time examine the books and records of any nonprofit corporation established by or operated on behalf of a public entity the books and records of which it is authorized by law to examine, and, in addition to any other investigatory powers granted by this chapter, may investigate and report upon the method or system of performing the duties of such nonprofit corporation. *(Added by Stats 1986 ch 279 §2.)*

ARTICLE 3

LEGAL AND OTHER ASSISTANTS FOR GRAND JURIES

§934. Right to ask advice.

The grand jury may, at all times, ask the advice of the court, or the judge thereof, or of the district attorney, or of the county counsel. Unless such advice is asked, the judge of the court, or county counsel as to civil matters, shall not be present during the sessions of the grand jury.

§935. District Attorney's duty to give information; interrogation rights.

The district attorney of the county may at all times appear before the grand jury for the purpose of giving information or advice relative to any matter cognizable by the grand jury, and may interrogate witnesses before the grand jury whenever he thinks it necessary. When a charge against or involving the district attorney, or assistant district attorney, or deputy district attorney, or anyone employed by or connected with the office of the district attorney, is being investigated by the grand jury, such district attorney, or assistant district attorney, or deputy district attorney, or all or anyone or more of them, shall not be allowed to be present before such grand jury when such charge is being investigated, in an official capacity but only as a witness, and he shall only be present while a witness and after his appearance as such witness shall leave the place where the grand jury is holding its session.

§936. Special counsel and special investigators.

When requested so to do by the grand jury of any county, the Attorney General may employ special counsel and special investigators, whose duty it shall be to investigate and present the evidence in such investigation to such grand jury.

The services of such special counsel and special investigators shall be a county charge of such county.

§936.5. Employment by presiding judge.

(a) When requested to do so by the grand jury of any county, the presiding judge of the superior court may employ special counsel and special investigators, whose duty it shall be to investigate and present the evidence of the investigation to the grand jury.

(b) Prior to the appointment, the presiding judge shall conduct an evidentiary hearing and find that a conflict exists that would prevent the local district attorney, the county counsel, and the Attorney General from performing such investigation. Notice of the hearing shall be given to each of them unless he or she is a subject of the investigation. The finding of the presiding judge may be appealed by the district attorney, the county counsel, or the Attorney General. The order shall be stayed pending the appeal made under this section.

(c) The authority to appoint is contingent upon the certification by the auditor-comptroller of the county, that the grand jury has funds appropriated to it sufficient to compensate the special counsel and investigator for services rendered pursuant to the court order. In the absence of a certification the court has no authority to appoint. In the event the county board of supervisors or a member thereof is under investigation, the county has an obligation to appropriate the necessary funds.

§936.7. Special counsel; contract; public and confidential record.

(a) In a county of the eighth class, as defined by Sections 28020 and 28029 of the Government Code, upon a request by the grand jury, the presiding judge of the superior court may retain, in the name of the county, a special counsel to the grand jury. The request shall be presented to the presiding judge in camera, by an affidavit, executed by the foreperson of the grand jury, which specifies the reason for the request and the nature of the services sought, and which certifies that the appointment of the special counsel is reasonably necessary to aid the work of the grand jury. The affidavit shall be confidential and its contents may not be made public except by order of the presiding judge upon a showing of good cause. The special counsel shall be selected by the presiding judge following submission of the name of the nominee to the board of supervisors for comment.

The special counsel shall be retained under a contract executed by the presiding judge in the name of the county. The contract shall contain the following terms:

(1) The types of legal services to be rendered to the grand jury; provided, (i) that the special counsel's duties shall not include any legal advisory, investigative, or prosecutorial service which by statute is vested within the powers of the district attorney and (ii) that the special counsel may not perform any investigative

© 1992 by J., B. & L. Gould
Printed in the U.S.A.   **EP**

or prosecutorial service whatsoever except upon advance written approval by the presiding judge which specifies the number of hours of these services, the hourly rate therefor, and the subject matter of the inquiry.

(2) The hourly rate of compensation of the special counsel for legal advisory services delivered, together with a maximum contract amount payable for all services rendered under the contract during the term thereof, and all service authorizations issued pursuant thereto.

(3) That the contract may be canceled in advance of the expiration of its term by the presiding judge pursuant to service upon the special counsel of 10 days' advance written notice.

(b) The maximum contract amount shall be determined by the board of supervisors and included in the grand jury's annual operational budget. The maximum amount shall be subject to increase by the presiding judge through contract amendment during the term thereof, subject to and in compliance with the procedure prescribed by Section 914.5.

(c) The contract shall constitute a public record and shall be subject to public inspection and copying pursuant to the provisions of the California Public Records Act (Chapter 3.5 (commencing with Section 6250) of Division 7 of Title 1 of the Government Code). However, at the sole discretion of the board of supervisors, any or all of the following steps may be taken:

(1) The nomination by the presiding judge, and any or all actions by the board of supervisors in commenting upon the nominee and the comments, may be made confidential.

(2) The deliberations and actions may be undertaken in meetings from which the public is excluded, and the communication containing comments may constitute a confidential record which is not subject to public inspection or copying except at the sole discretion of the board of supervisors. Moreover, any written authorization by the presiding judge pursuant to paragraph (1) of subdivision (a) shall constitute a confidential record which is not subject to public inspection or copying except in connection with a dispute concerning compensation for services rendered. *(Added by Stats 1988 ch 886 §2, eff. 1/1/89.)*

§937. Interpreter.

The grand jury or district attorney may require by subpoena the attendance of any person before the grand jury as interpreter. While his services are necessary, such interpreter may be present at the examination of witnesses before the grand jury. The compensation for services of such interpreter constitutes a charge against the county, and shall be fixed by the grand jury.

§938. Appointment and duties of stenographic reporter.

(a) Whenever criminal causes are being investigated before the grand jury, it shall appoint a competent stenographic reporter. He shall be sworn and shall report in shorthand the testimony given in such causes and shall transcribe the shorthand in all cases where an indictment is returned or accusation presented.

(b) At the request of the grand jury, the reporter shall also prepare transcripts of any testimony reported during any session of the immediately preceding grand jury.

§938.1. Stenographic records.

(a) If an indictment has been found or accusation presented against a defendant, such stenographic reporter shall certify and deliver to the county clerk an original transcription of his shorthand notes and a copy thereof and as many additional copies as there are defendants, other than fictitious defendants, regardless of the number of charges or fictitious defendants included in the same investigation. The reporter shall complete such certification and delivery within 10 days after the indictment has been found or the accusation presented unless the court for good cause makes an order extending the time. The time shall not be extended more than 20 days. The county clerk shall file the original of the transcript, deliver a copy of the transcript to the district attorney immediately upon his receipt thereof and deliver a copy of such transcript to each such defendant or his attorney. If the copy of the testimony is not served as provided in this section the court shall on motion of the defendant continue the trial to such time as may be necessary to secure to the defendant receipt of a copy of such testimony 10 days before such trial. If several criminal charges are investigated against a defendant on one investigation and thereafter separate indictments are returned or accusations presented upon said several charges, the delivery to such defendant or his attorney of one copy of the transcript of such investigation shall be a compliance with this section as to all of such indictments or accusations.

(b) The transcript shall not be open to the public until 10 days after its delivery to the defendant or his attorney. Thereafter the transcript shall be open to the public unless the court orders otherwise on its own motion or on motion of a party pending a determination as to whether all or part of the transcript should be sealed. If the court determines that there is a reasonable likelihood that making all or any part of the transcript public may prejudice a defendant's right to a fair and impartial trial, that part of the transcript shall be sealed until the defendant's trial has been completed.

§938.2. Requirements before stenographer compensated.

(a) For preparing any transcript in any case pursuant to subdivision (a) of Section 938.1, the stenographic reporter shall draw no salary or fees from the county for preparing such transcript in any case until all such transcripts of testimony in such case so taken by him are written up and delivered. Before making the order for payment to the reporter, the judge of the superior court shall require the reporter to show by affidavit or otherwise that he has written up and delivered all testimony taken by him, in accordance with subdivision (a) of Section 938 and Section 938.1.

(b) Before making the order for payment to a reporter who has prepared transcripts pursuant to subdivision (b) of Section 938, the judge of the superior court shall require the reporter to show by affidavit or otherwise that he has written up and delivered all testimony requested of him in accordance with that subdivision.

§938.3. Rate of compensation.

The services of the stenographic reporter shall constitute a charge against the county, and the stenographic reporter shall be compensated for reporting and transcribing at the same rates as prescribed in Sections 69947 to 69954, inclusive, of the Government Code, to be paid out of the county treasury on a warrant of the county auditor when ordered by the judge of the superior court. *(Amended by Stats 1987 ch 828 §56.)*

ARTICLE 4

CONDUCT OF INVESTIGATIONS

§939. Persons who may be present during private sessions.

No person other than those specified in Article 3 (commencing with Section 934), and in Sections 939.1 and 939.11, and the officer having custody of a prisoner witness while the prisoner is testifying, is permitted to be present during the criminal sessions of the grand jury except the members and witnesses actually under examination. Members of the grand jury who have been excused pursuant to Section 939.5 shall not be present during any part of these proceedings. No persons other than grand jurors shall be permitted to be present during the expression of the opinions of the grand jurors, or the giving of their votes, on any criminal or civil matter before them. *(Amended by Stats 1988 ch 415 §1; ch 1297 §7, eff. 1/1/89.)*

§939.1. Public sessions.

The grand jury acting through its foreman and the attorney general or the district attorney may make a joint written request for public sessions of the grand jury. The request shall be filed with the superior court. If the court, or the judge thereof, finds that the subject matter of the investigation affects the general public welfare, involving the alleged corruption, misfeasance, or malfeasance in office or dereliction of duty of public officials or employees or of any person allegedly acting in conjunction or conspiracy with such officials or employees in such alleged acts, the court or judge may make an order directing the grand jury to conduct its investigation in a session or sessions open to the public. The order shall state the finding of the court. The grand jury shall comply with the order.

The conduct of such investigation and the examination of witnesses shall be by the members of the grand jury and the district attorney.

The deliberation of the grand jury and its voting upon such investigation shall be in private session. The grand jury may find indictments based wholly or partially upon the evidence introduced at such public session.

§939.11. Grand juries; interpreters.

Any member of the grand jury who has a hearing, sight, or speech disability may request an interpreter when his or her services are necessary to assist the juror to carry out his or her duties. The request shall be filed with the superior court. If the court, or the judge thereof, finds that an interpreter is necessary, the court shall make an order to that effect and may require by subpoena the attendance of any person before the grand jury as interpreter. If the services of an interpreter are necessary, the court shall instruct the grand jury and the interpreter that the interpreter is not to participate in the jury's deliberations in any manner except to facilitate communication between the disabled juror and the other jurors. The court shall place the interpreter under oath not to disclose any grand jury matters, including the testimony of any witness, statements of any grand juror, or the vote of any grand juror, except in the due course of judicial proceedings. *(Added by Stats 1986 ch 357 §3.)*

§939.2. Requiring attendance of witnesses.

A subpoena requiring the attendance of a witness before the grand jury may be signed and issued by the district attorney, his investigator or, upon request of the grand jury, by any judge of the superior court, for witnesses in the state, in support of the prosecution, for those witnesses whose testimony, in his opinion is material in an investigation before the grand jury, and for such other witnesses as the grand jury, upon an investigation pending before them, may direct.

§939.3. Self-incrimination.

In any investigation or proceeding before a grand jury for any felony offense when a person refuses to answer a question or produce evidence of any other kind on the ground that he may be incriminated thereby, proceedings may be had under Section 1324.

§939.4. Oath.

The foreman may administer an oath to any witness appearing before the grand jury.

§939.5. Foreman's statement.

Before considering a charge against any person, the foreman of the grand jury shall state to those present the matter to be considered and the person to be charged with an offense in connection therewith. He shall direct any member of the grand jury who has a state of mind in reference to the case or to either party which will prevent him from acting impartially and without prejudice to the substantial rights of the party to retire. Any violation of this section by the foreman or any member of the grand jury is punishable by the court as a contempt.

§939.6. Reception of evidence.

(a) Subject to subdivision (b), in the investigation of a charge, the grand jury shall receive no other evidence than such as is:

(1) Given by witnesses produced and sworn before the grand jury;

(2) Furnished by writings, material objects, or other things presented to the senses; or

(3) Contained in a deposition that is admissible under subdivision 3 of Section 686.

(b) The grand jury shall receive none but evidence that would be admissible over objection at the trial of a criminal action, but the fact that evidence which would have been excluded at trial was received by the grand jury does not render the indictment void where sufficient competent evidence to support the indictment was received by the grand jury.

§939.7. Evidence required and weighed.

The grand jury is not required to hear evidence for the defendant, but it shall weigh all the evidence submitted to it, and when it has reason to believe that other evidence within its reach will explain away the charge, it shall order the evidence to be produced, and for that purpose may require the district attorney to issue process for the witnesses.

© 1992 by J., B. & L. Gould
Printed in the U.S.A.   EP

§939.8. Indictment after hearing evidence.

The grand jury shall find an indictment when all the evidence before it, taken together, if unexplained or uncontradicted, would, in its judgment, warrant a conviction by a trial jury.

§939.9. Jury's actions based on its own investigation.

A grand jury shall make no report, declaration, or recommendation on any matter except on the basis of its own investigation of the matter made by such grand jury. A grand jury shall not adopt as its own the recommendation of another grand jury unless the grand jury adopting such recommendation does so after its own investigation of the matter as to which the recommendation is made, as required by this section.

§939.91. Reports on investigations.

(a) A grand jury which investigates a charge against a person, and as a result thereof cannot find an indictment against such person, shall, at the request of such person and upon the approval of the court which impaneled the grand jury, report or declare that a charge against such person was investigated and that the grand jury could not as a result of the evidence presented find an indictment. The report or declaration shall be issued upon completion of the investigation of the suspected criminal conduct, or series of related suspected criminal conduct, and in no event beyond the end of the grand jury's term.

(b) A grand jury shall, at the request of the person called and upon the approval of the court which impaneled the grand jury, report or declare that any person called before the grand jury for a purpose, other than to investigate a charge against such person, was called only as a witness to an investigation which did not involve a charge against such person. The report or declaration shall be issued upon completion of the investigation of the suspected criminal conduct, or series of related suspected criminal conduct, and in no event beyond the end of the grand jury's term.

TITLE 5

THE PLEADINGS

CHAPTER 1

FINDING AND PRESENTMENT OF THE INDICTMENT

§940. Minimum number of grand jurors to find indictment.

An indictment cannot be found without concurrence of at least 14 grand jurors in a county in which the required number of members of the grand jury prescribed by Section 888.2 is 23, and at least 12 grand jurors in other counties. When so found it must be endorsed, "A true bill," and the endorsement must be signed by the foreman of the grand jury.

§943. Names of witnesses inserted at foot of indictment.

When an indictment is found, the names of the witnesses examined before the Grand Jury, or whose depositions may have been read before them, must be inserted at the foot of the indictment, or indorsed thereon, before it is presented to the Court.

§944. Indictment presented and filed.

An indictment, when found by the grand jury, must be presented by their foreman, in their presence, to the court, and must be filed with the clerk. No recommendation as to the dollar amount of bail to be fixed shall be made to any court by any grand jury.

§945. Proceedings when defendant is not in custody.

When an indictment is found against a defendant not in custody, the same proceedings must be had as are prescribed in Sections nine hundred and seventy-nine to nine hundred and eighty-four, inclusive, against a defendant who fails to appear for arraignment.

CHAPTER 2

RULES OF PLEADING

§948. Form of and rules of pleading.

All the forms of pleading in criminal actions, and the rules by which the sufficiency of pleadings is to be determined, are those prescribed by this Code.

§949. First pleading on the part of the people.

The first pleading on the part of the people in the superior court is the indictment, information, accusation, or the complaint in any case certified to the superior court under Section 859a or the complaint filed in accordance with the provisions of Section 272. The first pleading on the part of the people in all inferior courts is the complaint except as otherwise provided by law. *(Amended by Stats 1987 ch 828 §57.)*

§950. Accusatory pleading.

The accusatory pleading must contain:

1. The title of the action, specifying the name of the court to which the same is presented, and the names of the parties;

2. A statement of the public offense or offenses charged therein.

§951. Indictment or information form.

An indictment or information may be in substantially the following form: The people of the State of California against A. B. In the superior court of the State of California, in and for the county of _____. The grand jury (or the district attorney) of the county of _____ hereby accuses A. B. of a felony (or misdemeanor), to wit: (giving the name of the crime, as murder, burglary, etc.), in that on or about the ___ day of ___, 19 _, in the county of ____, State of California, he (here insert statement of act or omission, as for example, "murdered C.D.").

§952. Charging an offense.

In charging an offense, each count shall contain, and shall be sufficient if it contains in substance, a statement that the accused has committed some public offense therein specified. Such statement may be made in ordinary and concise language without any technical averments or any allegations of matter not essential to be proved. It may be in the words of the enactment describing the offense or declaring the matter to be a public offense, or in any words sufficient to give the accused notice of the offense of which he is accused. In charging theft it shall be sufficient to allege that the defendant unlawfully took the labor or property of another.

§953. Fictitious or erroneous name.

When a defendant is charged by a fictitious or erroneous name, and in any stage of the proceedings his true name is discovered, it must be inserted in the subsequent proceedings, referring to the fact of his being charged by the name mentioned in the accusatory pleading.

§954. Charging more than one count or offense.

An accusatory pleading may charge two or more different offenses connected together in their commission, or different statements of the same offense or two or more different offenses of the same class of crimes or offenses, under separate counts, and if two or more accusatory pleadings are filed in such cases in the same court, the court may order them to be consolidated. The prosecution is not required to elect between the different offenses or counts set forth in the accusatory pleading, but the defendant may be convicted of any number of the offenses charged, and each offense of which the defendant is convicted must be stated in the verdict or the finding of the court; provided, that the court in which a case is triable, in the interests of justice and for good cause shown, may in its discretion order that the different offenses or counts set forth in the accusatory pleading be tried separately or divided into two or more groups and each of said groups tried separately. An acquittal of one or more counts shall not be deemed an acquittal of any other count.

§954.1. Admissibility of evidence for multiple offenses.

In cases in which two or more different offenses of the same class of crimes or offenses have been charged together in the same accusatory pleading, or where two or more accusatory pleadings charging offenses of the same class of crimes or offenses have been consolidated, evidence concerning one offense or offenses need not be admissible as to the other offense or offenses before the jointly charged offenses may be tried together before the same trier of fact. *(Added by Initiative Measure, Prop 115 §19, approved 6/5/90.)*

§955. Time offense committed.

The precise time at which the offense was committed need not be stated in the accusatory pleading, but it may be alleged to have been committed at any time before the finding or filing thereof, except where the time is a material ingredient in the offense.

§956. Person injured; place offense committed.

When an offense involves the commission of, or an attempt to commit a private injury, and is described with sufficient certainty in other respects to identify the act, an erroneous allegation as to the person injured, or intended to be injured, or of the place where the offense was committed, or of the property involved in its commission, is not material.

§957. Words used in accusatory pleading; construction.

The words used in an accusatory pleading are construed in their usual acceptance in common language, except such words and phrases as are defined by law, which are construed according to their legal meaning.

§958. Words used in statutes.

Words used in a statute to define a public offense need not be strictly pursued in the accusatory pleading, but other words conveying the same meaning may be used.

§959. Accusatory pleading; when sufficient.

The accusatory pleading is sufficient if it can be understood therefrom:

1. That it is filed in a court having authority to receive it, though the name of the court be not stated.

2. If an indictment, that it was found by a grand jury of the county in which the court was held, or if an information, that it was subscribed and presented to the court by the district attorney of the county in which the court was held.

3. If a complaint, that it is made and subscribed by some natural person and sworn to before some officer entitled to administer oaths.

4. That the defendant is named, or if his name is unknown, that he is described by a fictitious name, with a statement that his true name is to the grand jury, district attorney, or complainant, as the case may be, unknown.

5. That the offense charged therein is triable in the court in which it is filed, except in case of a complaint filed with a magistrate for the purposes of a preliminary examination.

6. That the offense was committed at some time prior to the filing of the accusatory pleading.

§959.1. Accusatory pleading in electronic form.

(a) Notwithstanding Sections 740, 806, 949, and 959 or any other provision of the law to the contrary, a criminal prosecution may be commenced by filing an accusatory pleading in electronic form with the magistrate or in a court having authority to receive it.

(b) As used in this section, accusatory pleadings include, but are not limited to, the complaint, the information, the indictment, and any citation or notice to appear issued on a form approved by the Judicial Council.

(c) A magistrate or court is authorized to receive and file an accusatory pleading in electronic form if all of the following conditions are met:

(1) The accusatory pleading is issued in the name of, and transmitted by, a public prosecutor or law enforcement agency filing pursuant to Chapter 5c (commencing with Section 853.5) or Chapter 5d (commencing with Section 853.9), or by a clerk of the court with respect to complaints issued for the offenses of failure to appear, pay a fine, or comply with an order of the court.

(2) The magistrate or court has the facility to electronically store the accusatory pleading for the statutory period of record retention.

(3) The magistrate or court has the ability to reproduce the accusatory pleading in physical form upon demand and payment of any costs involved.

An accusatory pleading shall be deemed to have been filed when it has been received by the magistrate or court.

When transmitted in electronic form, the accusatory pleading shall be exempt from any requirement that it be subscribed by a natural person. It is sufficient to satisfy any requirement that an accusatory pleading, or any part of it, be sworn to before an officer entitled to administer oaths, if the pleading, or any part of it, was in fact sworn to and the electronic

© 1992 by J., B. & L. Gould
Printed in the U.S.A.   EP

form indicates which parts of the pleading were sworn to and the name of the officer who administered the oath.

(4) Notwithstanding any other provision of law, a notice of parking violation or a notice to appear may be received and filed by court in electronic form, if the following conditions are met:

(A) The notice of parking violation is issued and transmitted by a law enforcement agency prosecuting pursuant to Article 3 (commencing with Section 40200) of Chapter 1 of Division 17 of the Vehicle Code.

(B) The court has the facility to electronically store the data elements of the notice of parking violation for the statutory period of record retention and to produce those data elements in printed form upon demand and payment of any costs involved.

(C) The issuing agency has the ability to reproduce the notice of parking violation in physical form upon demand and payment of any costs involved, as provided in Section 40206.5 of the Vehicle Code. *(Amended by Stats 1990 ch 289 §1, eff. 1/1/91.)*

§960. Defects or imperfections.

No accusatory pleading is insufficient, nor can the trial, judgment, or other proceeding thereon be affected by reason of any defect or imperfection in matter of form which does not prejudice a substantial right of the defendant upon the merits.

§961. Presumptions of law and matters.

Neither presumptions of law, nor matters of which judicial notice is authorized or required to be taken, need be stated in an accusatory pleading.

§962. Judgments, etc., how pleaded.

In pleading a judgment or other determination of, or proceeding before, a Court or officer of special jurisdiction, it is not necessary to state the facts constituting jurisdiction; but the judgment or determination may be stated as given or made, or the proceedings had. The facts constituting jurisdiction, however, must be established on the trial.

§963. Private statutes or ordinances, how pleaded.

In pleading a private statute, or an ordinance of a county or a municipal corporation, or a right derived therefrom, it is sufficient to refer to the statute or ordinance by its title and the day of its passage, and the court must thereupon take judicial notice thereof in the same manner that it takes judicial notice of matters listed in Section 452 of the Evidence Code.

§964. *Repealed by Stats 1991 ch 186 §6, eff. 1/1/92.*

§965. Forged instrument.

When an instrument which is the subject of an indictment or information for forgery has been destroyed or withheld by the act or the procurement of the defendant, and the fact of such destruction or withholding is alleged in the indictment, or information, and established on the trial, the misdescription of the instrument is immaterial.

§966. Pleading for perjury or subornation of perjury.

In an accusatory pleading for perjury, or subornation of perjury, it is sufficient to set forth the substance of the controversy or matter in respect to which the offense was committed, and in what court and before whom the oath alleged to be false was taken, and that the court, or the person before whom it was taken, had authority to administer it, with proper allegations of the falsity of the matter on which the perjury is assigned; but the accusatory pleading need not set forth the pleadings, records, or proceedings with which the oath is connected, nor the commission or authority of the court or person before whom the perjury was committed.

§967. Pleading of theft or conspiracy to cheat or defraud.

In an accusatory pleading charging the theft of money, bank notes, certificates of stock or valuable securities, or a conspiracy to cheat or defraud a person of any such property, it is sufficient to allege the theft, or the conspiracy to cheat or defraud, to be of money, bank notes, certificates of stock or valuable securities without specifying the coin, number, denomination, or kind thereof.

§968. Selling, etc., of obscene material.

An accusatory pleading charging exhibiting, publishing, passing, selling, or offering to sell, or having in possession, with such intent, any lewd or obscene book, pamphlet, picture, print, card, paper, or writing, need not set forth any portion of the language used or figures shown upon such book, pamphlet, picture, print, card, paper, or writing; but it is sufficient to state generally the fact of the lewdness or obscenity thereof.

§969. Prior felony conviction or attempt to commit felony.

In charging the fact of a previous conviction of felony, or of an attempt to commit an offense which, if perpetrated, would have been a felony, or of theft, it is sufficient to state, "That the defendant, before the commission of the offense charged herein, was in (giving the title of the court in which the conviction was had) convicted of a felony (or attempt, etc., or of theft)." If more than one previous conviction is charged, the date of the judgment upon each conviction may be stated, and all known previous convictions, whether in this State or elsewhere, must be charged.

§969a. Amendment of indictment or information to include all prior felonies.

Whenever it shall be discovered that a pending indictment or information does not charge all prior felonies of which the defendant has been convicted either in this State or elsewhere, said indictment or information may be forthwith amended to charge such prior conviction or convictions, and if such amendment is made it shall be made upon order of the court, and no action of the grand jury (in the case of an indictment) shall be necessary. Defendant shall promptly be rearraigned on such information or indictment as amended and be required to plead thereto.

§969b. Establishing prima facie evidence.

For the purpose of establishing prima facie evidence of the fact that a person being tried for a crime or public offense under the laws of this State has been convicted of an act punishable by imprisonment in a state prison, county jail or city jail of this State, and has served a term therefor in any penal institution, or has been convicted of an act in any other state, which would be punishable as a crime in this State, and has served a term therefor in any state penitentiary, reformatory, county jail or city jail, or has been convicted of an act declared to be a crime by any act or law of the United States, and has served a term therefor in any penal institution, the records or copies of records of any state penitentiary, reformatory, county jail, city jail, or federal penitentiary in which such person has been imprisoned, when such records or copies thereof have been certified by the official custodian of such records, may be introduced as such evidence.

§969c. Charging defendant with use of weapon or firearm.

Whenever a defendant uses a weapon or was armed with a firearm under such circumstances as to bring such defendant within the operation of Section 12022 the fact that the defendant so used a weapon or was armed with a firearm may be charged in the accusatory pleading. This charge, if made, shall be added to and be a part of the count or each of the counts of the accusatory pleading which charge the offense at the time of the commission of which the defendant used a weapon or was armed with a firearm. That portion of any count which charges that the defendant used a weapon or was armed with a firearm shall be sufficient if it can be understood therefrom that at the time of his commission of the offense set forth in the count, the defendant used a weapon or was armed with a firearm. The nature of the weapon or firearm must be set forth. One such charge may name more than one weapon or firearm. If the defendant pleads not guilty of the offense charged in any count which alleges that the defendant used a weapon or was armed with a firearm, the question whether or not he used a weapon or was armed with a firearm as alleged must be tried by the court or jury which tries the issue upon the plea of not guilty. If the defendant pleads guilty of the offense charged the question whether or not he used a weapon or was armed with a firearm as alleged must be determined by the court before pronouncing judgment.

§969d. Charging defendant with armed robbery, etc.

Whenever a defendant used a firearm as recited in Section 12022.5, the fact that the defendant used a firearm may be charged in the accusatory pleading. This charge, if made, shall be added to and be a part of the count or each of the counts of the accusatory pleading which charged the offense. That portion of any count which charges that the defendant used a firearm shall be sufficient if it can be understood therefrom that at the time of his commission of the offense set forth in the count the defendant used a firearm. The nature of the firearm must be set forth. One such charge may name more than one firearm. If the defendant pleads not guilty to the offense charged in any count which alleges that the defendant used a firearm, the question whether or not he used a firearm as alleged must be tried by the court or jury which tries the issue upon the plea of not guilty. If the defendant pleads guilty of the offense charged the question whether or not he used a firearm as alleged must be determined by the court before pronouncing judgment.

§969e. Previous conviction.

In charging the fact of a previous conviction for a violation of Section 5652 of the Fish and Game Code, or of Section 13001 or 13002 of the Health and Safety Code or of Section 374b or 374d of the Penal Code or of Section 23111, 23112, or 23113 of the Vehicle Code, it is sufficient to state, "That the defendant, before the commission of the offense charged herein, was in (giving the title of the court in which the conviction was had) convicted of a violation of (specifying the section violated)."

§969f. Serious felony.

(a) Whenever a defendant has committed a serious felony as defined in subdivision (c) of Section 1192.7, the facts that make the crime constitute a serious felony may be charged in the accusatory pleading. However, the crime shall not be referred to as a serious felony nor shall the jury be informed that the crime is defined as a serious felony. This charge, if made, shall be added to and be a part of the count or each of the counts of the accusatory pleading which charged the offense. If the defendant pleads not guilty to the offense charged in any count which alleges that defendant committed a serious felony, the question whether or not the defendant committed a serious felony as alleged shall be tried by the court or jury which tries the issue upon the plea of not guilty. If the defendant pleads guilty of the offense charged, the question whether or not the defendant committed a serious felony as alleged shall be separately admitted or denied by the defendant.

(b) In charging an act or acts that bring the defendant within the operation of paragraph (8) or (23) of subdivision (c) of Section 1192.7, it is sufficient for purposes of subdivision (a) if the pleading states the following:

"It is further alleged that in the commission and attempted commission of the foregoing offense, the defendant _____, personally [inflicted great bodily injury on another person, other than an accomplice] [used a firearm, to wit: _____,] [used a dangerous and deadly weapon, to wit: _____,] within the meaning of Sections 667 and 1192.7 of the Penal Code." *(Added by Stats 1991 ch 249 §1, eff. 1/1/92.)*

§969½. Amendments of complaint to include prior convictions.

Whenever it shall be discovered that a pending complaint to which a plea of guilty has been made under section 859a of this code does not charge all prior felonies of which the defendant has been convicted either in this state or elsewhere, said complaint may be forthwith amended to charge such prior conviction or convictions and such amendments may and shall be made upon order of the court. The defendant shall thereupon be arraigned before the court to which the complaint has been certified and must be asked whether he has suffered such previous conviction. If he answers that he has, his answer must be entered by the clerk in the minutes of the court, and must, unless withdrawn by consent of the court, be conclusive of the fact of his having suffered such previous conviction in all subsequent proceedings. If he answers that he has not, his answer must be entered by the clerk in the minutes of the court, and the question whether or not he has suffered such previous conviction must be tried by a jury impanelled for that

© 1992 by J., B. & L. Gould
Printed in the U.S.A.   **EP**

purpose, unless a jury is waived, in which case it may be tried by the court. The refusal of the defendant to answer is equivalent to a denial that he has suffered such previous conviction.

§970. Naming of several defendants.
When several defendants are named in one accusatory pleading, any one or more may be convicted or acquitted.

§971. Distinction between accessory before the fact and principals, abrogated.
The distinction between an accessory before the fact and a principal, and between principals in the first and second degree is abrogated; and all persons concerned in the commission of a crime, who by the operation of other provisions of this code are principals therein, shall hereafter be prosecuted, tried and punished as principals and no other facts need be alleged in any accusatory pleading against any such person than are required in an accusatory pleading against a principal.

§972. Accessory; trial, prosecution.
An accessory to the commission of a felony may be prosecuted, tried, and punished, though the principal may be neither prosecuted nor tried, and though the principal may have been acquitted.

§973. Accusatory pleading; lost or destroyed.
If the accusatory pleading in any criminal action has heretofore been lost or destroyed or shall hereafter be lost or destroyed, the court must, upon the application of the prosecuting attorney or of the defendant, order a copy of such pleading to be filed and substituted for the original and when filed and substituted, as provided in this section, the copy shall have the same force and effect as if it were the original pleading.

TITLE 6

PLEADINGS AND PROCEEDINGS BEFORE TRIAL

CHAPTER 1

ARRAIGNMENT OF THE DEFENDANT

§976. Court.
(a) When the accusatory pleading is filed, the defendant shall be arraigned thereon before the court in which it is filed, unless the action is transferred to some other court for trial. However, within any county, if the defendant is in custody, upon the approval of both the presiding judge of the court in which the accusatory pleading is filed and the presiding judge of the court nearest to the place in which he or she is held in custody the arraignment may be before the court nearest to that place of custody.

(b) A defendant arrested in another county shall have the right to be taken before a magistrate in the arresting county for the purpose of being admitted to bail, as provided in Section 821 or 822. The defendant shall be informed of this right.

(c) Prior to being taken from the place where he or she is in custody to the place where he or she is to be arraigned, the defendant shall be allowed to make three completed telephone calls, at no expense to the defendant, in addition to any other telephone calls which the defendant is entitled to make pursuant to law.

§976.5. Accusatory pleading in Sierra County; arraignment in Nevada County.
(a) Notwithstanding any other provision of law, when an accusatory pleading is filed in Sierra County and the defendant is in the custody of Nevada County, he or she may be arraigned before a court in Nevada County.

(b) This section shall not interfere with the right of a defendant to demur to an accusatory pleading, as specified in Chapter 3 (commencing with Section 1002) of Title 6.

(c) This section shall remain in effect only until January 1, 1996, and as of that date is repealed, unless a later enacted statute, which is enacted before January 1, 1996, deletes or extends that date. *(Added by Stats 1990 ch 259 §1, eff. 1/1/91 only until 1/1/96.)*

§977. Defendant's presence at arraignment.
(a) In all cases in which the accused is charged with a misdemeanor only, he may appear by counsel only.

(b) In all cases in which a felony is charged, the accused must be present at the arraignment, at the time of plea, during the preliminary hearing, during those portions of the trial when evidence is taken before the trier of fact, and at the time of the imposition of sentence. The accused shall be personally present at all other proceedings unless he shall, with leave of court, execute in open court, a written waiver of his right to be personally present, approved by his counsel, which waiver must then be filed with the court; provided, however, that the court may specifically direct that defendant be personally present at any particular proceeding or portion thereof. The waiver shall be substantially in the following form:

WAIVER OF DEFENDANT'S PERSONAL PRESENCE

The undersigned defendant, having been advised of his right to be present at all stages of the proceedings, including but not limited to presentation of and arguments on questions of law, and to be confronted by and cross-examine all witnesses, hereby waives the right to be present at the hearing of any motion or other proceeding in this cause, including when the case is set for trial, when a continuance is ordered, when a motion to set aside the indictment or information pursuant to the provisions of the Penal Code, Section 995 and following is heard, when a motion for reduction of bail or for a personal recognizance release is heard, when a motion to reduce sentence is heard, and when questions of law are presented to or considered by the court. The undersigned defendant hereby requests the court to proceed during every absence of his which the court may permit pursuant to this waiver, and hereby agrees that his interest will be deemed represented at all times by the presence of his attorney the same as if the defendant himself were personally present in court, and further agrees that notice to his attorney that his presence in court on a particular day at a particular time is required will be deemed notice to him of the requirement of his appearance at said time and place.

Dated: _____

_____
Defendant

_____
Address

Approved:

Dated: _____

_____

Attorney for Defendant.

§977.1. Mentally incompetent or disabled defendant.

The resolution of questions of fact or issues of law by trial or hearing which can be made without the assistance or participation of the defendant is not prohibited by the existence of any pending proceeding to determine whether the defendant is or remains mentally incompetent or gravely disabled pursuant to the provisions of either this code or the Welfare and Institutions Code.

§977.2. Pilot project; use of audio-visual communication.

(a) Notwithstanding Section 977, the board of supervisors of any California county may establish a pilot project. The board shall establish the project with the approval of the presiding judge, the district attorney, and the public defender. The project shall be developed in close consultation between the presiding judge, the district attorney, the public defender, and the sheriff, and shall not exceed six years in duration.

(b) The project shall permit the initial arraignment in municipal or superior court, in all counties, of defendants held in any state, county, or local penal facility within the county on felony or misdemeanor charges, except for those defendants who were indicted by a grand jury, to be conducted by two-way electronic audio-video communication between the defendant and the courtroom in lieu of the physical presence of the defendant in the courtroom. If the defendant is represented by counsel, the attorney shall be present with the defendant, and may enter a plea, during the arraignment. The defendant shall have the right to make his or her plea while physically present in the courtroom if he or she so requests. If the defendant decides not to exercise the right to be physically present in the courtroom, he or she shall execute a written waiver of that right.

(c) Each county conducting a pilot project pursuant to this section shall submit reports to the Legislative Analyst no later than September 30 of each year. The report shall include the following data:

(1) The number of add-on pleas, and the number of cases disposed of, through the use of audiovideo arraignment.

(2) The number of defendants who refuse to sign the waiver of personal appearance and are transported to the courtroom to be physically present for the arraignment proceedings.

(3) The number and impact of add-on defendants arraigned.

(4) Initial costs and maintenance costs of the project.

(5) Cost savings, including transportation costs, over the previous method of arraignment.

(6) The impact of audiovideo arraignment on all participants in the procedures used under this section, including, but not limited to, security personnel, attorneys, judges, defendants, and court employees.

(7) Any other benefits or problems incurred.

(8) Any future plans for the project.

Other specific data for inclusion in the report may be specified by the Judicial Council.

(d) The Legislative Analyst shall review and summarize all data submitted by the counties and shall submit a final report on the fiscal effects of this section along with any recommendations to the Legislature no later than December 1, 1991. The Judicial Council shall submit a final report on the nonfiscal, policy consequences of this section along with any recommendations to the Legislature no later than December 1, 1991.

(e) Notwithstanding any other provision of this section, a judge may order a defendant's personal appearance in court for arraignment. A judge may, pursuant to this section, accept a plea of guilty or no contest from a defendant who is not physically in the courtroom.

(f) This section shall remain in effect only until January 1, 1993, and as of that date is repealed, unless a later enacted statute, which is enacted on or before January 1, 1993, deletes or extends that date. *(Amended by Stats 1991 ch 179 §1, eff. 1/1/92 only until 1/1/93.)*

§977.3. *Repealed by Stats 1990 ch 427 §2, eff. 7/26/90.*

§978. If in custody, to be brought before Court.

When his personal appearance is necessary, if he is in custody, the Court may direct and the officer in whose custody he is must bring him before it to be arraigned.

§978.5. Issuance of bench warrant of arrest.

(a) A bench warrant of arrest may be issued whenever a defendant fails to appear in court as required by law including, but not limited to, the following situations:

(1) If the defendant is ordered by a judge or magistrate to personally appear in court at a specific time and place.

(2) If the defendant is released from custody on bail and is ordered by a judge or magistrate, or other person authorized to accept bail, to personally appear in court at a specific time and place.

(3) If the defendant is released from custody on his own recognizance and promises to personally appear in court at a specific time and place.

(4) If the defendant is released from custody or arrest upon citation by a peace officer or other person authorized to issue citations and the defendant has signed a promise to personally appear in court at a specific time and place.

(5) If a defendant is authorized to appear by counsel and the court or magistrate orders that the defendant personally appear in court at a specific time and place.

(6) If an information or indictment has been filed in the superior court and the court has fixed the date and place for the defendant personally to appear for arraignment.

(b) The bench warrant may be served in any county in the same manner as a warrant of arrest.

§979. Bench warrant for non-appearance at arraignment.

If the defendant has been discharged on bail or has deposited money or other property instead thereof, and does not appear to be arraigned when his personal

© 1992 by J., B. & L. Gould
Printed in the U.S.A. **EP**

presence is necessary, the court, in addition to the forfeiture of the undertaking of bail or of the money or other property deposited, may order the issuance of a bench warrant for his arrest.

§980. Who may issue bench warrant.

At any time after the order for a bench warrant is made, whether the court is sitting or not, the clerk may, on application of the prosecuting attorney, issue a bench warrant to one or more counties. *(Amended by Stats 1989 ch 1417 §20.8, eff. 1/1/90.)*

§981. Form for bench warrant in felony prosecution.

The bench warrant upon the indictment or information must, if the offense is a felony, be substantially in the following form: County of _____ . The People of the State of California to any Sheriff, Constable, Marshal, or Policeman in this State: An indictment having been found (or information filed) on the __ day of ____ , A.D. eighteen _____ , in the Superior Court of the County of ____ , charging C. D. with the crime of _____ (designating it generally); you are, therefore, commanded forthwith to arrest the above named C. D., and bring him before that Court (or if the indictment and information has been sent to another Court, then before that Court, naming if), to answer said indictment (or information), or if the Court be not in session, that you deliver him into the custody of the Sheriff of the County of _____ .

Given under my hand, with the seal of said Court affixed, this __ day of ____ , A.D. ___ .

By order of said Court.

[SEAL]

E.F., Clerk.

§982. Bailable and nonbailable offenses; holding of defendant.

The defendant, when arrested under a warrant for an offense not bailable, must be held in custody by the Sheriff of the county in which the indictment is found or information filed, unless admitted to bail after an examination upon a writ of habeas corpus; but if the offense is bailable, there must be added to the body of the bench-warrant a direction to the following effect: "Or, if he requires it, that you take him before any magistrate in that county, or in the county in which you arrest him, that he may give bail to answer to the indictment (or information)"; and the Court, upon directing it to issue, must fix the amount of bail, and an indorsement must be made thereon and signed by the Clerk, to the following effect: "The defendant is to be admitted to bail in the sum of ____ dollars."

§983. Service.

The bench warrant may be served in any county in the same manner as a warrant of arrest.

§984. Giving bail in another county.

If the defendant is brought before a magistrate of another county for the purpose of giving bail, the magistrate must proceed in respect thereto in the same manner as if the defendant had been brought before him upon a warrant of arrest, and the same proceedings must be had thereon.

§985. Ordering defendant into custody or giving increased bail.

When the information or indictment is for a felony, and the defendant, before the filing thereof, has given bail for his appearance to answer the charge, the Court to which the indictment or information is presented, or in which it is pending, may order the defendant to be committed to actual custody, unless he gives bail in an increased amount, to be specified in the order.

§986. Defendant, if present when order made, to be committed; if not, bench warrant to issue.

If the defendant is present when the order is made, he must be forthwith committed. If he is not present, a bench-warrant must be issued and proceeded upon in the manner provided in this Chapter.

§987. Right to counsel; capital and non-capital cases.

(a) In a noncapital case, if the defendant appears for arraignment without counsel, he shall be informed by the court that it is his right to have counsel before being arraigned, and shall be asked if he desires the assistance of counsel. If he desires and is unable to employ counsel the court shall assign counsel to defend him.

(b) In a capital case, if the defendant appears for arraignment without counsel, the court shall inform him that he must be represented by counsel at all stages of the preliminary and trial proceedings and that such representation will be at his expense if he is able to employ counsel or at public expense if he is unable to employ counsel, inquire of him whether he is able to employ counsel and, if so, whether he desires to employ counsel of his choice or to have counsel assigned to him, and allow him a reasonable time to send for his chosen or assigned counsel. If the defendant is unable to employ counsel, the court shall assign counsel to defend him. If the defendant is able to employ counsel and either refuses to employ counsel or appears without counsel after having had a reasonable time to employ counsel, the court shall assign counsel to him.

The court shall at the first opportunity inform the defendant's trial counsel, whether retained by the defendant or court-appointed, of the additional duties imposed upon trial counsel in any capital case as set forth in paragraph (1) of subdivision (b) of Section 1240.1.

(c) In order to assist the court in determining whether a defendant is able to employ counsel in any case, the court may require a defendant to file a financial statement under penalty of perjury. The financial statement shall be confidential and privileged and shall not be admissible in evidence in any criminal proceeding except the prosecution of an alleged offense of perjury based upon false material contained in the financial statement. The financial statement shall be made available to the prosecution only for purposes of investigation of an alleged offense of perjury based upon false material contained in the financial statement at the conclusion of the proceedings for which such financial statement was required to be submitted. The financial statement shall not be confidential and privileged in a proceeding under Section 987.8.

(d) In a capital case, the court may appoint an additional attorney as a cocounsel upon a written request of the first attorney appointed. The request shall be supported by an affidavit of the first attorney setting forth in detail the reasons why a second attorney should be appointed. Any such affidavit filed with the court shall be confidential and privileged. The court shall appoint a second attorney when it is convinced by the reasons stated in the affidavit that the appointment is necessary to provide the defendant with effective representation. If the request is denied, the court shall state on the record its reasons for denial of the request.

§987.05. Assigning defense counsel in felony cases.

In assigning defense counsel in felony cases, whether it is the public defender or private counsel, the court shall only assign counsel who represents, on the record, that he or she will be ready to proceed with the preliminary hearing or trial, as the case may be, within the time provisions prescribed in this code for preliminiary hearings and trials, except in those unusual cases where the court finds that, due to the nature of the case, counsel cannot reasonably be expected to be ready within the prescribed period if he or she were to begin preparing the case forthwith and continue to make diligent and constant efforts to be ready. In the case where the time of preparation for preliminary hearing or trial is deemed greater than the statutory time, the court shall set a reasonable time period for preparation. In making this determination, the court shall not consider counsel's convenience, counsel's calendar conflicts, or counsel's other business. The court may allow counsel a reasonable time to become familiar with the case in order to determine whether he or she can be ready. In cases where counsel, after making representations that he or she will be ready for preliminary examination or trial, and without good cause is not ready on the date set, the court may relieve counsel from the case and may impose sanctions upon counsel, including, but not limited to, finding the assigned counsel in contempt of court, imposing a fine, or denying any public funds as compensation for counsel's services. Both the prosecuting attorney and defense counsel shall have a right to present evidence and argument as to a reasonable length of time for preparation and on any reasons why counsel could not be prepared in the set time. *(Added by Initiative Measure, Prop 115 §20, approved 6/5/90.)*

§987.1. Continuance of representation.

Counsel at the preliminary examination shall continue to represent a defendant who has been ordered to stand trial until the date set for his arraignment in superior count unless relieved by the court upon the substitution of other counsel or for cause.

§987.2. Assigned counsel's compensation.

(a) In any case in which a person, including a person who is a minor, desires but is unable to employ counsel, and in which counsel is assigned in the superior court, municipal court, or justice court to represent the person in a criminal trial, proceeding or appeal, the following assigned counsel shall receive a reasonable sum for compensation and for necessary expenses, the amount of which shall be determined by the court, to be paid out of the general fund of the county:

(1) In a county or city and county in which there is no public defender.

(2) In a county of the first or second class where there is no contract for criminal defense services between the county and one or more responsible attorneys.

(3) In a case in which the court finds that, because of a conflict of interest or other reasons, the public defender has properly refused.

(4) In a county of the first or second class where attorneys contracted by the county are unable to represent the person accused.

(b) The sum provided for in subdivision (a) may be determined by contract between the court and one or more responsible attorneys after consultation with the board of supervisors as to the total amount of compensation and expenses to be paid, which shall be within the amount of funds allocated by the board of supervisors for the cost of assigned counsel in those cases.

(c) In counties that utilize an assigned private counsel system as either the primary method of public defense or as the method of appointing counsel in cases where the public defender is unavailable, the county, the courts, or the local county bar association working with the courts are encouraged to do all of the following:

(1) Establish panels that shall be open to members of the State Bar of California.

(2) Categorize attorneys for panel placement on the basis of experience.

(3) Refer cases to panel members on a rotational basis within the level of experience of each panel, except that a judge may exclude an individual attorney from appointment to an individual case for good cause.

(4) Seek to educate those panel members through an approved training program.

(5) Establish a cost-efficient plan to insure maximum recovery of costs pursuant to Section 987.8.

(d) In a county of the first or second class, the court shall first utilize the services of the public defender to provide criminal defense services for indigent defendants. In the event that the public defender is unavailable and the county and the courts have contracted with one or more responsible attorneys or with a panel of attorneys to provide criminal defense services for indigent defendants, the court shall utilize the services of the county-contracted attorneys prior to assigning any other private counsel. Nothing in this subdivision shall be construed to require the appointment of counsel in any case in which the counsel has a conflict of interest. In the interest of justice, a court may depart from that portion of the procedure requiring appointment of a county-contracted attorney after making a finding of good cause and stating the reasons therefor on the record.

(e) Notwithstanding any other provision of this section, where an indigent defendant is first charged in one county and establishes an attorney-client relationship with the public defender, defense services contract attorney, or private attorney, and where the defendant is then charged with an offense in a second or subsequent county, the court in the second or subsequent county may appoint the same counsel as was appointed in the first county to represent the defendant when all of the following conditions are met:

(1) The offense charged in the second or subsequent county would be joinable for trial with that charged in the first if it took place in the same county, or involves evidence which would be cross-admissible.

© 1992 by J., B. & L. Gould
Printed in the U.S.A.   EP

(2) The court finds that the interests of justice and economy will be best served by unitary representation.

(3) Counsel appointed in the first county consents to the appointment.

(f) The county may recover costs of public defender services under Chapter 6 (commencing with Section 4750) of Title 5 of Part 3 for any case subject to Section 4750.

(g) Counsel shall be appointed to represent, in the municipal or justice court, a person who desires but is unable to employ counsel, when it appears that the appointment is necessary to provide an adequate and effective defense for the defendant.

(h) As used in this section, "county of the first or second class" means the county of the first class and county of the second class as provided by Sections 28020, 28022, and 28023 of the Government Code. *(Amended by Stats 1990 ch 632 §1, eff. 1/1/91.)*

§987.3. Reasonable compensation; factors.

Whenever in this code a court-appointed attorney is entitled to reasonable compensation and necessary expenses, the judge of the court shall consider the following factors, no one of which alone shall be controlling:

(a) Customary fee in the community for similar services rendered by privately retained counsel to a nonindigent client.

(b) The time and labor required to be spent by the attorney.

(c) The difficulty of the defense.

(d) The novelty or uncertainty of the law upon which the decision depended.

(e) The degree of professional ability, skill, and experience called for and exercised in the performance of the services.

(f) The professional character, qualification, and standing of the attorney.

§987.4. Minor's parents liable for expenses of assigned counsel.

When the public defender or an assigned counsel represents a person who is a minor in a criminal proceeding, at the expense of a county, the court may order the parent or guardian of such minor to reimburse the county for all or any part of such expense, if it determines that the parent or guardian has the ability to pay such expense.

§987.6. State reimbursement.

(a) From any state moneys made available to it for such purpose, the Department of Finance shall, pursuant to this section, pay to the counties an amount not to exceed 10 percent of the amounts actually expended by the counties in providing counsel in accordance with the law whether by public defender, assigned counsel, or both, for persons charged with violations of state criminal law or involuntarily detained under the Lanterman-Petris-Short Act, Division 5 (commencing with Section 5000) of the Welfare and Institutions Code, who desire, but are unable to afford, counsel.

(b) Application for payment shall be made in such manner and at such times as prescribed by the Department of Finance and the department may adopt rules necessary or appropriate to carry out the purposes of this section.

§987.8. Defendant's ability to pay costs of assigned counsel; determination.

(a) Upon a finding by the court that a defendant is entitled to counsel but is unable to employ counsel, the court may hold a hearing or, in its discretion, order the defendant to appear before a county officer designated by the court, to determine whether the defendant owns or has an interest in any real property or other assets subject to attachment and not otherwise exempt by law. The court may impose a lien on any real property owned by the defendant, or in which the defendant has an interest to the extent permitted by law. The lien shall contain a legal description of the property, shall be recorded with the recorder in the county or counties in which the property is located, and shall have priority over subsequently recorded liens or encumbrances. The county shall have the right to enforce its lien for the payment of providing legal assistance to an indigent defendant in the same manner as other lienholders by way of attachment, except that a county shall not enforce its lien on a defendant's principal place of residence pursuant to a writ of execution. No lien shall be effective as against a bona fide purchaser without notice of the lien.

(b) In any case in which a defendant is provided legal assistance, either through the public defender or private counsel appointed by the court, upon conclusion of the criminal proceedings in the trial court, or upon the withdrawal of the public defender or appointed private counsel, the court may, after notice and a hearing, make a determination of the present ability of the defendant to pay all or a portion of the cost thereof. The court may, in its discretion, hold one such additional hearing within six months of the conclusion of the criminal proceedings. The court may, in its discretion, order the defendant to appear before a county officer designated by the court to make an inquiry into the ability of the defendant to pay all or a portion of the legal assistance provided.

(c) In any case in which the defendant hires counsel replacing a publicly provided attorney; in which the public defender or appointed counsel was required by the court to proceed with the case after a determination by the public defender that the defendant is not indigent; or, in which the defendant, at the conclusion of the case, appears to have sufficient assets to repay, without undue hardship, all or a portion of the cost of the legal assistance provided to him or her, by monthly installments or otherwise; the court shall make a determination of the defendant's ability to pay as provided in subdivision (b), and may, in its discretion, make other orders as provided in that subdivision.

This subdivision shall be operative in a county only upon the adoption of a resolution by the board of supervisors to that effect.

(d) If the defendant, after having been ordered to appear before a county officer, has been given proper notice and fails to appear before a county officer within 20 working days, the county officer shall recommend to the court that the full cost of the legal assistance shall be ordered to be paid by the defendant. The notice to the defendant shall contain all of the following:

(1) A statement of the cost of the legal assistance provided to the defendant as determined by the court.

(2) The defendant's procedural rights under this section.

(3) The time limit within which the defendant's response is required.

(4) A warning that if the defendant fails to appear before the designated officer, the officer will recommend that the court order the defendant to pay the full cost of the legal assistance provided to him or her.

(e) At a hearing, the defendant shall be entitled to, but shall not be limited to, all of the following rights:

(1) The right to be heard in person.

(2) The right to present witnesses and other documentary evidence.

(3) The right to confront and cross-examine adverse witnesses.

(4) The right to have the evidence against him or her disclosed to him or her.

(5) The right to a written statement of the findings of the court.

If the court determines that the defendant has the present ability to pay all or a part of the cost, the court shall set the amount to be reimbursed and order the defendant to pay the sum to the county in the manner in which the court believes reasonable and compatible with the defendant's financial ability. Failure of a defendant who is not in custody to appear after due notice is a sufficient basis for an order directing the defendant to pay the full cost of the legal assistance determined by the court. The order to pay all or a part of the costs may be enforced in the manner provided for enforcement of money judgments generally but may not be enforced by contempt.

Any order entered under this subdivision is subject to relief under Section 473 of the Code of Civil Procedure.

(f) Prior to the furnishing of counsel or legal assistance by the court, the court shall give notice to the defendant that the court may, after a hearing, make a determination of the present ability of the defendant to pay all or a portion of the cost of counsel. The court shall also give notice that, if the court determines that the defendant has the present ability, the court shall order him or her to pay all or a part of the cost. The notice shall inform the defendant that the order shall have the same force and effect as a judgment in a civil action and shall be subject to enforcement against the property of the defendant in the same manner as any other money judgment.

(g) As used in this section:

(1) "Legal assistance" means legal counsel and supportive services including, but not limited to, medical and psychiatric examinations, investigative services, expert testimony, or any other form of services provided to assist the defendant in the preparation and presentation of the defendant's case.

(2) "Ability to pay" means the overall capability of the defendant to reimburse the costs, or a portion of the costs, of the legal assistance provided to him or her, and shall include, but not be limited to, all of the following:

(A) The defendant's present financial position.

(B) The defendant's reasonably discernible future financial position. In no event shall the court consider a period of more than six months from the date of the hearing for purposes of determining the defendant's reasonably discernible future financial position. Unless the court finds unusual circumstances, a defendant sentenced to state prison shall be determined not to have a reasonably discernible future financial ability to reimburse the costs of his or her defense.

(C) The likelihood that the defendant shall be able to obtain employment within a six-month period from the date of the hearing.

(D) Any other factor or factors which may bear upon the defendant's financial capability to reimburse the county for the costs of the legal assistance provided to the defendant.

(h) At any time during the pendency of the judgment rendered according to the terms of this section, a defendant against whom a judgment has been rendered may petition the rendering court to modify or vacate its previous judgment on the grounds of a change in circumstances with regard to the defendant's ability to pay the judgment. The court shall advise the defendant of this right at the time it renders the judgment.

(i) This section shall apply to all proceedings, including contempt proceedings, in which the party is represented by a public defender or appointed counsel. *(Amended by Stats 1989 ch 1217(4), eff. 1/1/90.)*

§987.81. Legal assistance.

(a) In any case in which a defendant is provided legal assistance, either through the public defender or private counsel appointed by the court, upon conclusion of the criminal proceedings in the trial court, or upon the withdrawal of the public defender or appointed private counsel, the court shall consider the available information concerning the defendant's ability to pay the costs of legal assistance and may, after notice, as provided in subdivision (b), hold a hearing to make a determination of the present ability of the defendant to pay all or a portion of the cost thereof. Notwithstanding the above, in any case where the court has ordered the probation officer to investigate and report to the court pursuant to subdivision (b) of Section 1203, the court may hold such a hearing. The court may, in its discretion, hold one such additional hearing within six months of the conclusion of the criminal proceedings.

(b) Concurrent with the furnishing of counsel or legal assistance by the court, the court shall order the defendant to appear before a county officer designated by the court to make an inquiry into the ability of the defendant to pay all or a portion of the legal assistance provided. Prior to the furnishing of counsel or legal assistance by the court, the court shall give notice to the defendant that the court shall, after a hearing, make a determination of the present ability of the defendant to pay all or a portion of the cost of counsel. The court shall also give notice that, if the court determines that the defendant has the present ability, the court shall order him or her to pay all or a part of the cost. The notice shall inform the defendant that the order shall have the same force and effect as a judgment in a civil action and shall be subject to enforcement against the property of the defendant in the same manner as any other money judgment.

(c) The provisions of this section shall apply only in a county in which the board of supervisors adopts a resolution which elects to proceed under this section. *(Added by Stats 1985 ch 1188 §1.)*

§987.9. Funds for indigent defendant.

In the trial of a capital case or a case under subdivision (a) of Section 190.05 the indigent defendant, through the defendant's counsel, may request the court for funds for the specific payment of investigators, experts, and others for the preparation or presentation of the defense. The application for funds shall be by affidavit and shall specify that the funds are reasonably necessary for the preparation or

© 1992 by J., B. & L. Gould
Printed in the U.S.A.   **EP**

presentation of the defense. The fact that an application has been made shall be confidential and the contents of the application shall be confidential. Upon receipt of an application, a judge of the court, other than the trial judge presiding over the case in question, shall rule on the reasonableness of the request and shall disburse an appropriate amount of money to the defendant's attorney. The ruling on the reasonableness of the request shall be made at an in camera hearing. In making the ruling, the court shall be guided by the need to provide a complete and full defense for the defendant.

The Controller shall not reimburse any county for costs that exceed Board of Control standards for travel and per diem expenses. The Controller may reimburse extraordinary costs in unusual cases if the county provides sufficient documentation of the need for those expenditures.

At the termination of the proceedings, the attorney shall furnish to the court a complete accounting of all moneys received and disbursed pursuant to this section.

The Controller shall adopt regulations pursuant to Chapter 3.5 (commencing with Section 11340) of Part 1 of Division 3 of Title 2 of the Government Code, controlling reimbursements under this section. The regulations shall consider compensation for investigators, expert witnesses, and other expenses that may or may not be reimbursable pursuant to this section. Notwithstanding the provisions of Chapter 3.5 (commencing with Section 11340) of Part 1 of Division 3 of Title 2 of the Government Code, the Controller shall follow any regulations adopted until final approval by the Office of Administrative Law. *(Amended by Stats 1985 ch 1510 §3.)*

§988. Arraignment; procedure.

The arraignment must be made by the court, or by the clerk or prosecuting attorney under its direction, and consists in reading the accusatory pleading to the defendant and delivering to him a true copy thereof, and of the endorsements thereon, if any, including the list of witnesses, and asking him whether he pleads guilty or not guilty to the accusatory pleading; provided, that where the accusatory pleading is a complaint charging a misdemeanor triable in an inferior court, a copy of the same need not be delivered to any defendant unless requested by him.

§989. Defendant's true name.

When the defendant is arraigned, he must be informed that if the name by which he is prosecuted is not his true name, he must then declare his true name, or be proceeded against by the name in the accusatory pleading. If he gives no other name, the court may proceed accordingly; but if he alleges that another name is his true name, the court must direct an entry thereof in the minutes of the arraignment, and the subsequent proceedings on the accusatory pleading may be had against him by that name, referring also to the name by which he was first charged therein.

§990. Answer time.

If on the arraignment, the defendant requires it, he must be allowed a reasonable time to answer, which shall be not less than one day for an offense originally triable in the superior court and not more than seven days for an offense originally triable in an inferior court.

§991. Probable cause in misdemeanor cases; determination.

(a) If the defendant is in custody at the time he appears before the magistrate for arraignment and, if the public offense is a misdemeanor to which the defendant has pleaded not guilty, the magistrate, on motion of counsel for the defendant or the defendant, shall determine whether there is probable cause to believe that a public offense has been committed and that the defendant is guilty thereof.

(b) The determination of probable cause shall be made immediately unless the court grants a continuance for good cause not to exceed three court days.

(c) In determining the existence of probable cause, the magistrate shall consider any warrant of arrest with supporting affidavits, and the sworn complaint together with any documents or reports incorporated by reference thereto, which, if based on information and belief, state the basis for such information, or any other documents of similar reliability.

(d) If, after examining these documents, the court determines that there exists probable cause to believe that the defendant has committed the offense charged in the complaint, it shall set the matter for trial.

If the court determines that no such probable cause exists, it shall dismiss the complaint and discharge the defendant.

(e) Within 15 days of the dismissal of a complaint pursuant to this section the prosecution may refile the complaint.

A second dismissal pursuant to this section is a bar to any other prosecution for the same offense.

CHAPTER 2

SETTING ASIDE THE INDICTMENT OR INFORMATION

§995. Factors.

(a) Subject to subdivision (b) of Section 995a, the indictment or information shall be set aside by the court in which the defendant is arraigned, upon his or her motion, in either of the following cases:

(1) If it is an indictment:

(A) Where it is not found, endorsed, and presented as prescribed in this code.

(B) That the defendant has been indicted without reasonable or probable cause.

(2) If it is an information:

(A) That before the filing thereof the defendant had not been legally committed by a magistrate.

(B) That the defendant had been committed without reasonable or probable cause.

(b) In cases in which the procedure set out in subdivision (b) of Section 995a is utilized, the court shall reserve a final ruling on the motion until those procedures have been completed.

§995a. Amendment of technical errors.

(a) If the names of the witnesses examined before the grand jury are not inserted at the foot of the indictment or indorsed thereon, the court shall order them to be so inserted or indorsed; and if the information be not subscribed by the district attorney, the court may order it to be so subscribed.

(b) (1) Without setting aside the information, the court may, upon motion of the prosecuting attorney, order further proceedings to correct errors alleged by the defendant if the court finds that such errors are minor errors of omission, ambiguity, or technical defect which can be expeditiously cured or corrected without a rehearing of a substantial portion of the evidence. The court may remand the cause to the committing magistrate for further proceedings, or if the parties and the court agree, the court may itself sit as a magistrate and conduct further proceedings. When remanding the cause to the committing magistrate, the court shall state in its remand order which minor errors it finds could be expeditiously cured or corrected.

(2) Any further proceedings conducted pursuant to this subdivision may include the taking of testimony and shall be deemed to be a part of the preliminary examination.

(3) The procedure specified in this subdivision may be utilized only once for each information filed. Any further proceedings conducted pursuant to this subdivision shall not be deemed to extend the time within which a defendant must be brought to trial under Section 1382.

§996. Waiver of defects.

If the motion to set aside the indictment or information is not made, the defendant is precluded from afterwards taking the objections mentioned in Section 995.

§997. Motion.

The motion must be heard at the time it is made, unless for cause the court postpones the hearing to another time. The court may entertain such motion prior to trial whether or not a plea has been entered and such plea need not be set aside in order to consider the motion. If the motion is denied, and the accused has not previously answered the indictment or information, either by demurring or pleading thereto, he shall immediately do so. If the motion is granted, the court must order that the defendant, if in custody, be discharged therefrom; or, if admitted to bail, that his bail be exonerated; or, if he has deposited money, or if money has been deposited by another or others instead of bail for his appearance, that the same be refunded to him or to the person or persons found by the court to have deposited said money on behalf of said defendant, unless it directs that the case be resubmitted to the same or another grand jury, or that an information be filed by the district attorney; provided, that after such order of resubmission the defendant may be examined before a magistrate, and discharged or committed by him, as in other cases, if before indictment or information filed he has not been examined and committed by a magistrate.

§998. Resubmission.

If the court directs the case to be resubmitted, or an information to be filed, the defendant, if already in custody, shall remain, unless he or she is admitted to bail; or, if already admitted to bail, or money has been deposited instead thereof, the bail or money is answerable for the appearance of the defendant to answer a new indictment or information; and, unless a new indictment is found or information filed before the next grand jury of the county is discharged, the court shall, on the discharge of such grand jury, make the order prescribed by Section 997. (Amended by Stats 1987 ch 828 §58.)

§999. No bar to future prosecution.

An order to set aside an indictment or information, as provided in this chapter, is no bar to a future prosecution for the same offense.

§999a. Petition for writ of prohibition.

A petition for a writ of prohibition, predicated upon the ground that the indictment was found without reasonable or probable cause or that the defendant had been committed on an information without reasonable or probable cause, or that the court abused its discretion in utilizing the procedure set out in subdivision (b) of Section 995a, must be filed in the appellate court within 15 days after a motion made under Section 995 to set aside the indictment on the ground that the defendant has been indicted without reasonable or probable cause or that the defendant had been committed on an information without reasonable or probable cause, has been denied by the trial court. A copy of such petition shall be served upon the district attorney of the county in which the indictment is returned or the information is filed. The alternative writ shall not issue until five days after the service of notice upon the district attorney and until he has had an opportunity to appear before the appellate court and to indicate to the court the particulars in which the evidence is sufficient to sustain the indictment or commitment.

CHAPTER 2.2

CAREER CRIMINALS
(Amended and renumbered from Chapter 2.3 by Stats 1987 ch 56 §125.)

§999b. Legslative findings.

The Legislature hereby finds a substantial and disproportionate amount of serious crime is committed against the people of California by a relatively small number of multiple and repeat felony offenders, commonly known as career criminals. In enacting this chapter, the Legislature intends to support increased efforts by district attorneys' offices to prosecute career criminals through organizational and operational techniques that have been proven effective in selected counties in this and other states.

§999c. California Career Criminal Prosecution Program.

(a) There is hereby established in the Office of Criminal Justice Planning a program of financial and technical assistance for district attorneys' offices, designated the California Career Criminal Prosecution Program. All funds appropriated to the Office of Criminal Justice Planning for the purposes of this chapter shall be administered and disbursed by the executive director of such office in consultation with the California Council on Criminal Justice, and shall to the greatest extent feasible be coordinated or consolidated with federal funds that may be made available for these purposes.

(b) The executive director is authorized to allocate and award funds to counties in which career criminal prosecution units are established in substantial compliance with the policies and criteria set forth below in Sections 999d, 999e, 999f, and 999g.

(c) Such allocation and award of funds shall be made upon application executed by the county's district attorney and approved by its board of supervisors.

© 1992 by J., B. & L. Gould
Printed in the U.S.A.   EP

Funds disbursed under this chapter shall not supplant local funds that would, in the absence of the California Career Criminal Prosecution Program, be made available to support the prosecution of felony cases. Funds available under this program shall not be subject to review as specified in Section 14780 of the Government Code.

(d) Annually, commencing April 1, 1982, the executive director shall, in cooperation with public defender representatives, prepare a report to the Legislature describing the operation and results of the statewide program and assessing any and all fiscal and workload burdens imposed by the statewide program upon local court public defender offices and assigned counsel with recommendations where appropriate.

§999d. Units receiving enhanced prosecution efforts and resources.

Career criminal prosecution units receiving funds under this chapter shall concentrate enhanced prosecution efforts and resources upon individuals identified under selection criteria set forth in Section 999e. Enhanced prosecution efforts and resources shall include, but not be limited to:

(a) "Vertical" prosecutorial representation, whereby the prosecutor who makes the initial filing or appearance in a career criminal case will perform all subsequent court appearances on that particular case through its conclusion, including the sentencing phase;

(b) Assignment of highly qualified investigators and prosecutors to career criminal cases; and

(c) Significant reduction of caseloads for investigators and prosecutors assigned to career criminal cases.

§999e. Criteria for persons subject to career criminal prosecution.

(a) An individual shall be the subject of career criminal prosecution efforts who is under arrest for the commission or attempted commission of one or more of the following felonies: robbery, burglary, arson, any unlawful act relating to controlled substances in violation of Section 11351, 11351.5, or 11352 of the Health and Safety Code, receiving stolen property, grand theft and grand theft auto, and lewd or lascivious conduct upon a child; and who is either being prosecuted for three or more separate offenses not arising out of the same transaction involving one or more of such felonies, or has suffered at least one conviction during the preceding 10 years for any felony listed in paragraph (1) of this subdivision, or at least two convictions during the preceding 10 years for any felony listed in paragraph (2) of this subdivision:

(1) Robbery of the first degree, burglary of the first degree, arson as defined in Section 451, unlawfully causing a fire as defined in Section 452, forcible rape, sodomy or oral copulation committed with force, lewd or lascivious conduct committed upon a child, kidnapping as defined in Section 209, or murder.

(2) Grand theft, grand theft auto, receiving stolen property, robbery of the second degree, burglary of the second degree, kidnapping as defined in Section 207, assault with a deadly weapon or instrument, or any unlawful act relating to controlled substances in violation of Section 11351 or 11352 of the Health and Safety Code.

For purposes of this chapter, the 10-year periods specified in this section shall be exclusive of any time which the arrested person has served in state prison.

(b) In applying the career criminal selection criteria set forth above, a district attorney may elect to limit career criminal prosecution efforts to persons arrested for any one or more of the felonies listed in subdivision (a) of this section if crime statistics demonstrate that the incidence of such one or more felonies presents a particularly serious problem in the county.

(c) In exercising the prosecutorial discretion granted by Section 999g, the district attorney shall consider the following: (1) the character, background, and prior criminal background of the defendant; and (2) the number and the seriousness of the offenses currently charged against the defendant. *(Amended by Stats 1987 ch 223 §1.)*

§999f. Policies for career criminal cases.

(a) Each district attorney's office establishing a career criminal prosecution unit and receiving state support under this chapter shall adopt and pursue the following policies for career criminal cases:

(1) A plea of guilty or a trial conviction will be sought on all the offenses charged in the accusatory pleading against an individual meeting career criminal selection criteria.

(2) All reasonable prosecutorial efforts will be made to resist the pretrial release of a charged defendant meeting career criminal selection criteria.

(3) All reasonable prosecutorial efforts will be made to persuade the court to impose the most severe authorized sentence upon a person convicted after prosecution as a career criminal.

(4) All reasonable prosecutorial efforts will be made to reduce the time between arrest and disposition of charge against an individual meeting career criminal selection criteria.

(b) The prosecution shall not negotiate a plea agreement with a defendant in a career criminal prosecution; and Sections 1192.1 to 1192.5, inclusive, shall not apply, nor shall any plea of guilty or nolo contendere authorized by any such section, or any plea of guilty or nolo contendere as a result of any plea agreement be approved by the court in a career criminal prosecution.

(c) For purposes of this section a "plea agreement" means an agreement by the defendant to plead guilty or nolo contendere in exchange for any or all of the following: a dismissal of charges, a reduction in the degree of a charge, a change of a charge to a lesser or different crime, a specific manner or extent of punishment.

(d) This section does not prohibit the reduction of the offense charged or dismissal of counts in the interest of justice when a written declaration by the prosecuting attorney stating the specific factual and legal basis for such reduction or dismissal is presented to the court and the court, in writing, acknowledges acceptance of such declaration. A copy of such declaration and acceptance shall be retained in the case file. The only basis upon which charges may be reduced or counts dismissed by the court shall be in cases where the prosecuting attorney decides that there is insufficient evidence to prove the people's case, the testimony of a material witness cannot be obtained, or a reduction or dismissal would not result in a substantial change in sentence.

In any case in which the court or magistrate grants the prosecuting attorney's motion for a reduction of charges or dismissal of counts because there would be no substantial change in sentence, the court or magistrate shall require the prosecuting attorney to put on the record in open court the following:

(1) The charges filed in the complaint or information and the maximum statutory penalty that could be given if the defendant were convicted of all such charges.

(2) The charges which would be filed against the defendant if the court or magistrate grants the prosecuting attorney's motion and the maximum statutory penalty which can be given for these charges.

(e) This section does not prohibit a plea agreement when there are codefendants, and the prosecuting attorney determines that the information or testimony of the defendant making the agreement is necessary for the conviction of one or more of the other codefendants. The court shall condition its acceptance of the plea agreement on the defendant giving the information or testimony.

Before the court can accept the plea agreement, the prosecuting attorney shall present a written declaration to the court, specifying the legal and factual reasons for the agreement, and the court shall acknowledge in writing its acceptance of that declaration. A copy of the declaration and acceptance shall be retained in the case file.

§999g. Selection; extraordinary circumstances.

The selection criteria set forth in Section 999e shall be adhered to for each career criminal case unless, in the reasonable exercise of prosecutor's discretion, extraordinary circumstances require the departure from such policies in order to promote the general purposes and intent of this chapter.

§999h. Characterization.

The characterization of a defendant as a "career criminal" as defined by this chapter may not be communicated to the trier of fact.

CHAPTER 2.3

REPEAT SEXUAL OFFENDERS
(Renumbered from Chapter 2.4 by Stats 1987 ch 56 §126.)

§999i. Legislative findings.

The Legislature hereby finds that repeat sexual offenders present a clear and present danger to the mental and physical well-being of the citizens of the State of California, especially of its children. The Legislature further finds that the concept of vertical prosecution, in which one deputy district attorney is assigned to a case from its filing to its completion, is a proven way of demonstrably increasing the likelihood of convicting repeat sex offenders and ensuring appropriate sentences for such offenders. In enacting this chapter, the Legislature intends to support increased efforts by district attorneys' offices to prosecute repeat sexual offenders through organizational and operational techniques that have already proven their effectiveness in selected counties in this and other states, as demonstrated by the California Career Criminal Prosecution Program and the California Gang Violence Suppression Program, as well as sexual assault prosecution units in several counties.

§999j. Repeat Sexual Offender Prosecution Program.

(a) There is hereby established in the Office of Criminal Justice Planning a program of financial and technical assistance for district attorneys' offices, designated the Repeat Sexual Offender Prosecution Program. All funds appropriated to the Office of Criminal Justice Planning for the purposes of this chapter shall be administered and disbursed by the executive director of such office, and shall to the greatest extent feasible, be coordinated or consolidated with any federal or local funds that may be made available for these purposes.

The Office of Criminal Justice Planning shall establish guidelines for the provision of grant awards to proposed and existing programs prior to the allocation of funds under this chapter. These guidelines shall contain the criteria for the selection of agencies to receive funding, as developed in consultation with an advisory group to be known as the Repeat Sexual Offender Prosecution Program Steering Committee. The membership of the Steering Committee shall be designated by the Executive Director of the Office of Criminal Justice Planning.

A draft of the guidelines shall be developed and submitted to the Chairpersons of the Assembly Criminal Law and Public Safety Committee and the Senate Judiciary Committee within 60 days of the effective date of this chapter and issued within 90 days of the same effective date. These guidelines shall set forth the terms and conditions upon which the Office of Criminal Justice Planning is prepared to offer grants pursuant to statutory authority. The guidelines shall not constitute rules, regulations, orders, or standards of general application.

(b) The executive director is authorized to allocate and award funds to counties in which repeat sexual offender prosecution units are established or are proposed to be established in substantial compliance with the policies and criteria set forth below in Sections 999k, 999l, and 999m.

(c) Such allocation and award of funds shall be made upon application executed by the county's district attorney and approved by its board of supervisors. Funds disbursed under this chapter shall not supplant local funds that would, in the absence of the California Repeat Sexual Offender prosecution program, be made available to support the prosecution of repeat sexual offender felony cases. Local grant awards made under this program shall not be subject to review as specified in Section 14780 of the Government Code.

(d) Annually, commencing January 1985, or after one year of program operation, the executive director shall, in cooperation with local district attorneys whose offices are selected for funding, prepare a report to the Legislature describing the operation and results of the statewide program.

§999k. Prosecution efforts and resources enhanced.

Repeat sexual offender prosecution units receiving funds under this chapter shall concentrate enhanced prosecution efforts and resources upon individuals identified under selection criteria set forth in Section 999l. Enhanced prosecution efforts and resources shall include, but not be limited to:

© 1992 by J., B. & L. Gould
Printed in the U.S.A.   EP

(a) Vertical prosecutorial representation, whereby the prosecutor who makes the initial filing or appearance in a repeat sexual offender case will perform all subsequent court appearances on that particular case through its conclusion, including the sentencing phase.

(b) The assignment of highly qualified investigators and prosecutors to repeat sexual offender cases. "Highly qualified" for the purposes of this chapter shall be defined as: (1) individuals with one year of experience in the investigation and prosecution of felonies or specifically the felonies listed in subdivision (a) of Section 999*l*; or (2) individuals whom the district attorney has selected to receive training as set forth in Section 13836; or (3) individuals who have attended a program providing equivalent training as approved by the Office of Criminal Justice Planning.

(c) A significant reduction of caseloads for investigators and prosecutors assigned to repeat sexual offender cases.

(d) Coordination with local rape victim counseling centers, child abuse services programs, and victim witness assistance programs. Such coordination shall include, but not be limited to: referrals of individuals to receive client services; participation in local training programs; membership and participation in local task forces established to improve communication between criminal justice system agencies and community service agencies; and cooperating with individuals serving as liaison representatives of local rape victim counseling centers and victim witness assistance programs.

§999*l*. Selection criteria.

(a) An individual shall be the subject of a repeat sexual offender prosecution effort who is under arrest for the commission or attempted commission of one or more of the following offenses: assault with intent to commit rape, sodomy, oral copulation or any violation of Section 264.1, Section 288, or Section 289; rape, in violation of Section 261; sexual battery, in violation of Section 243.4; sodomy, in violation of Section 286; lewd acts on a child under 14, in violation of Section 288; oral copulation, in violation of Section 288a; penetration of genital or anal openings by a foreign object, in violation of Section 289; and (1) who is being prosecuted for offenses involving two or more separate victims, or (2) who is being prosecuted for the commission or attempted commission of three or more separate offenses not arising out of the same transaction involving one or more of the above-listed offenses, or (3) who has suffered at least one conviction during the preceding 10 years for any of the above-listed offenses. For purposes of this chapter, the 10-year periods specified in this section shall be exclusive of any time which the arrested person has served in state prison or in a state hospital pursuant to a commitment as a mentally disordered sex offender.

(b) In applying the repeat sexual offender selection criteria set forth above: (1) a district attorney may elect to limit repeat sexual offender prosecution efforts to persons arrested for any one or more of the offenses listed in subdivision (a) if crime statistics demonstrate that the incidence of such one or more offenses presents a particularly serious problem in the county; (2) a district attorney shall not reject cases for filing exclusively on the basis that there is a family or personal relationship between the victim and the alleged offender.

(c) In exercising the prosecutorial discretion granted by Section 999n, the district attorney shall consider the following: (1) the character, the background, and prior criminal background of the defendant, and (2) the number and seriousness of the offenses currently charged against the defendant.

§999m. Program policies.

Each district attorney's office establishing a repeat sexual offender prosecution unit and receiving state support under this chapter shall adopt and pursue the following policies for repeat sexual offender cases:

(a) All reasonable prosecutorial efforts will be made to resist the pretrial release of a charged defendant meeting repeat sexual offender selection criteria.

(b) All reasonable prosecutorial efforts will be made to persuade the court to impose the most severe authorized sentence upon a person convicted after prosecution as a repeat sexual offender. In the prosecution of an intrafamily sexual abuse case, discretion may be exercised as to the type and nature of sentence recommended to the court.

(c) All reasonable prosecutorial efforts will be made to reduce the time between arrest and disposition of charge against an individual meeting repeat sexual offender criteria.

§999n. Adherence to selection criteria.

(a) The selection criteria set forth in Section 999*l* shall be adhered to for each repeat sexual offender case unless, in the reasonable exercise of prosecutor's discretion, extraordinary circumstances require departure from such policies in order to promote the general purposes and intent of this chapter.

(b) Each district attorney's office establishing a repeat sexual offender prosecution unit and receiving state support under this chapter shall submit the following information, on a quarterly basis, to the Office of Criminal Justice Planning:

(1) The number of sexual assault cases referred to the district attorney's office for possible filing.

(2) The number of sexual assault cases filed for felony prosecution.

(3) The number of sexual assault cases taken to trial.

(4) The percentage of sexual assault cases tried which resulted in conviction.

§999o. Characterization.

The characterization of a defendant as a "repeat sexual offender" as defined by this chapter shall not be communicated to the trier of fact.

§999p. Use of federal funds.

The Office of Criminal Justice Planning is encouraged to utilize any federal funds which may become available in order to implement the provisions of this chapter.

CHAPTER 2.4

CHILD ABUSERS
(Added by Stats 1985 ch 1097 §1.)

§999q. Legislative intent.

The Legislature hereby finds that child abusers present a clear and present danger to the mental health and physical well-being of the citizens of the State of California, especially of its children. The

Legislature further finds that the concept of vertical prosecution, in which a specially trained deputy district attorney or prosecution unit is assigned to a case from its filing to its completion, is a proven way of demonstrably increasing the likelihood of convicting child abusers and ensuring appropriate sentences for such offenders. In enacting this chapter, the Legislature intends to support increased efforts by district attorneys' offices to prosecute child abusers through organizational and operational techniques that have already proven their effectiveness in selected counties in this and other states, as demonstrated by the California Career Criminal Prosecution Program, the California Gang Violence Suppression Program, and the Repeat Sexual Offender Prosecution Program. *(Added by Stats 1985 ch 1097 §1.)*

§999r. Financial and technical assistance.

(a) There is hereby established in the Office of Criminal Justice Planning a program of financial and technical assistance for district attorneys' offices, designated the Child Abuser Prosecution Program. All funds appropriated to the Office of Criminal Justice Planning for the purposes of this chapter shall be administered and disbursed by the executive director of such office, and shall to the greatest extent feasible, be coordinated or consolidated with any federal or local funds that may be made available for these purposes.

The Office of Criminal Justice Planning shall establish guidelines for the provision of grant awards to proposed and existing programs prior to the allocation of funds under this chapter. These guidelines shall contain the criteria for the selection of agencies to receive funding and the terms and conditions upon which the Office of Criminal Justice Planning is prepared to offer grants pursuant to statutory authority. The guidelines shall not constitute rules, regulations, orders, or standards of general application. The guidelines shall be submitted to the appropriate policy committees of the Legislature prior to their adoption.

(b) The executive director is authorized to allocate and award funds to counties in which child abuser offender prosecution units are established or are proposed to be established in substantial compliance with the policies and criteria set forth below in Sections 999s, 999t, and 999u.

(c) The allocation and award of funds shall be made upon application executed by the county's district attorney and approved by its board of supervisors. Funds disbursed under this chapter shall not supplant local funds that would, in the absence of the California Child Abuser Prosecution Program, be made available to support the prosecution of child abuser felony cases. Local grant awards made under this program shall not be subject to review as specified in Section 14780 of the Government Code. *(Added by Stats 1985 ch 1097 §1.)*

§999s. Child abuser prosecution units.

Child abuser prosecution units receiving funds under this chapter shall concentrate enhanced prosecution efforts and resources upon individuals identified under selection criteria set forth in Section 999t. Enhanced prosecution efforts and resources shall include, but not be limited to:

(a) Vertical prosecutorial representation, whereby the prosecutor who, or prosecution unit which, makes the initial filing or appearance in a case performs all subsequent court appearances on that particular case through its conclusion, including the sentencing phase.

(b) The assignment of highly qualified investigators and prosecutors to child abuser cases. "Highly qualified" for the purposes of this chapter means: (1) individuals with one year of experience in the investigation and prosecution of felonies or specifically the felonies listed in subdivision (a) of Section 999*l* or 999t; or (2) individuals whom the district attorney has selected to receive training as set forth in Section 13836; or (3) individuals who have attended a program providing equivalent training as approved by the Office of Criminal Justice Planning.

(c) A significant reduction of caseloads for investigators and prosecutors assigned to child abuser cases.

(d) Coordination with local rape victim counseling centers, child abuse services programs, and victim witness assistance programs. That coordination shall include, but not be limited to: referrals of individuals to receive client services; participation in local training programs; membership and participation in local task forces established to improve communication between criminal justice system agencies and community service agencies; and cooperating with individuals serving as liaison representatives of child abuse and child sexual abuse programs, local rape victim counseling centers and victim witness assistance programs. *(Added by Stats 1985 ch 1097 §1.)*

§999t. Selection for prosecution.

(a) An individual may be the subject of a child abuser prosecution effort who is under arrest for the sexual assault of a child as defined in subdivision (b) of Section 11165.

(b) In applying the child abuser selection criteria set forth above: (1) a district attorney may elect to limit child abuser prosecution efforts to persons arrested for any one or more of the offenses described in subdivision (a) if crime statistics demonstrate that the incidence of such one or more offenses presents a particularly serious problem in the county; (2) a district attorney shall not reject cases for filing exclusively on the basis that there is a family or personal relationship between the victim and the alleged offender.

(c) In exercising the prosecutorial discretion granted by Section 999v, the district attorney shall consider the character, the background, and the prior criminal background of the defendant. *(Added by Stats 1985 ch 1097 §1.)*

§999u. Policies for district attorney's office.

Each district attorney's office establishing a child abuser prosecution unit and receiving state support under this chapter shall adopt and pursue the following policies for child abuser cases:

(a) Except as provided in subdivision (b), all reasonable prosecutorial efforts will be made to resist the pretrial release of a charged defendant meeting child abuser selection criteria.

(b) Nothing in this chapter shall be construed to limit the application of diversion programs authorized by law. All reasonable efforts shall be made to utilize diversion alternatives in appropriate cases.

(c) All reasonable prosecutorial efforts will be made to reduce the time between arrest and disposi-

© 1992 by J., B. & L. Gould
Printed in the U.S.A.   EP

tion of charge against an individual meeting child abuser criteria. *(Added by Stats 1985 ch 1097 §1.)*

§999v. Information submitted by prosecution.

(a) The selection criteria set forth in Section 999t shall be adhered to for each child abuser case unless, in the reasonable exercise of prosecutor's discretion, extraordinary circumstances require departure from such policies in order to promote the general purposes and intent of this chapter.

(b) Each district attorney's office establishing a child abuser prosecution unit and receiving state support under this chapter shall submit the following information, on a quarterly basis, to the Office of Criminal Justice Planning:

(1) The number of child abuser cases referred to the district attorney's office for possible filing.

(2) The number of child abuser cases filed for felony prosecution.

(3) The number of sexual assault cases taken to trial.

(4) The number of child abuser cases tried which resulted in conviction. *(Added by Stats 1985 ch 1097 §1.)*

§999w. Non-disclosure to jury.

The characterization of a defendant as a "child abuser" as defined by this chapter shall not be communicated to the trier of fact. *(Added by Stats 1985 ch 1097 §1.)*

§999x. Implementation of provisions with federal funds.

The Office of Criminal Justice Planning is encouraged to utilize any federal funds which may become available in order to implement the provisions of this chapter. *(Added by Stats 1985 ch 1097 §1.)*

§999y. Report to Legislature.

The Office of Criminal Justice Planning shall report annually to the Legislature concerning the program established by this chapter. *(Added by Stats 1985 ch 1097 §1.)*

CHAPTER 2.5

SPECIAL PROCEEDINGS IN NARCOTICS AND DRUG ABUSE CASES

§1000. Applicability of chapter.

(a) This chapter shall apply whenever a case is before any court upon an accusatory pleading for a violation of Section 11350, 11357, 11364, 11365, 11377, or 11550 of the Health and Safety Code, or Section 11358 of the Health and Safety Code if the marijuana planted, cultivated, harvested, dried, or processed is for personal use, or Section 11368 of the Health and Safety Code if the narcotic drug was secured by a fictitious prescription and is for the personal use of the defendant and was not sold or furnished to another, or Section 11370.1 of the Health and Safety Code if the amount possessed is one-half gram or less of a substance containing cocaine base, one gram or less of a substance containing cocaine, one gram or less of a substance containing heroin, one gram or less of a substance containing methamphetamine, one-eighth gram or less of a crystalline substance containing phencyclidine, one milliliter or less of a liquid substance containing phencyclidine, one-half gram or less of plant material containing phencyclidine, or one hand-rolled cigarette treated with phencyclidine, or subdivision (d) of Section 653f if the solicitation was for acts directed to personal use only, or Section 381 or subdivision (f) of Section 647 of the Penal Code, if for being under the influence of a controlled substance, or Section 4230 of the Business and Professions Code, and it appears to the district attorney that, except as provided in subdivision (b) of Section 11357 of the Health and Safety Code, all of the following apply to the defendant:

(1) The defendant has no conviction for any offense involving controlled substances prior to the alleged commission of the charged divertible offense.

(2) The offense charged did not involve a crime of violence or threatened violence.

(3) There is no evidence of a violation relating to narcotics or restricted dangerous drugs other than a violation of the sections listed in this subdivision.

(4) The defendant's record does not indicate that probation or parole has ever been revoked without thereafter being completed.

(5) The defendant's record does not indicate that he or she has been diverted pursuant to this chapter within five years prior to the alleged commission of the charged divertible offense.

(6) The defendant has no prior felony conviction within five years prior to the alleged commission of the charged divertible offense.

(b) The district attorney shall review his or her file to determine whether or not paragraphs (1) to (6), inclusive, of subdivision (a) are applicable to the defendant. Upon the agreement of the district attorney, law enforcement, the public defender, the presiding judge of the criminal division of the municipal court or a judge designated by the presiding judge, and the probation department of each county, this procedure shall be completed as soon as possible after the initial filing of the charges. If the defendant is found eligible, the district attorney shall file with the court a declaration in writing or state for the record the grounds upon which the determination is based, and shall make this information available to the defendant and his or her attorney. This procedure is intended to allow the court to set the diversion hearing at the arraignment. If the defendant is found ineligible, the district attorney shall file with the court a declaration in writing or state for the record the grounds upon which the determination is based, and shall make this information available to the defendant and his or her attorney. Nothing in this subdivision shall be construed to affect the obligation of a probation department to conduct an investigation and make a report to the court, pursuant to subdivision (b) of Section 1000.1 and Section 1000.2.

(c) Successful completion of diversion for a violation of Section 11368 of the Health and Safety Code shall not prohibit any administrative agency from taking disciplinary action against a licensee or from denying a license. Nothing in this subdivision shall be construed to expand or restrict the provisions of Section 1000.5. *(Amended by Stats 1991 ch 469 §2, eff. 1/1/92.)*

§1000.1. Notice to defendant of applicability of chapter.

(a) If the district attorney determines that this chapter may be applicable to the defendant, he shall advise the defendant and his attorney in writing of such determination. This notification shall include:

(1) A full description of the procedures of diversionary investigation.

(2) A general explanation of the roles and authorities of the probation department, the district attorney, the community program, and the court in the diversion process.

(3) A clear statement that the court may decide in a hearing not to divert the defendant and that he may have to stand trial for the alleged offense.

(4) A clear statement that should the defendant fail in meeting the terms of his diversion, or should he be convicted of a misdemeanor which reflects the divertee's propensity for violence, or should the divertee be convicted of any felony, he may be required, after a court hearing, to stand trial for the original alleged offense.

(5) An explanation of criminal record retention and disposition resulting from participation in the diversion and the divertee's rights relative to answering questions about his arrest and diversion following successful completion of the diversion program.

(b) If the defendant consents and waives his right to a speedy trial, the district attorney shall refer the case to the probation department. The probation department shall make an investigation and take into consideration the defendant's age, employment and service records, educational background, community and family ties, prior controlled substance use, treatment history, if any, demonstrable motivation, and other mitigating factors in determining whether the defendant is a person who would be benefited by education, treatment, or rehabilitation. The probation department shall also determine which community programs or programs of the probation department the defendant would benefit from and which of those programs would accept the defendant. The probation department shall report its findings and recommendation to the court. The court shall make the final determination regarding education, treatment, or rehabilitation for the defendant.

(c) No statement, or any information procured therefrom, made by the defendant to any probation officer or drug treatment worker, which is made during the course of any investigation conducted by the probation department or drug treatment program pursuant to subdivision (b), and prior to the reporting of the probation department's findings and recommendations to the court, shall be admissible in any action or proceeding brought subsequent to the investigation.

No statement, or any information procured therefrom, with respect to the specific offense with which the defendant is charged, which is made to any probation officer or drug program worker subsequent to the granting of diversion, shall be admissible in any action or proceeding.

In the event that diversion is either denied, or is subsequently revoked once it has been granted, neither the probation investigation nor statements or information divulged during that investigation shall be used in any sentencing procedures.

§1000.2. Court hearing.

The court shall hold a hearing and, after consideration of the probation department's report and any other information considered by the court to be relevant to its decision, shall determine if the defendant consents to further proceedings under this chapter

and waives his right to a speedy trial and if the defendant should be diverted and referred for education, treatment, or rehabilitation. If the court does not deem the defendant a person who would be benefited by diversion, or if the defendant does not consent to participate, the proceedings shall continue as in any other case.

At such time that a defendant's case is diverted, any bail bond or undertaking, or deposit in lieu thereof, on file by or on behalf of the defendant shall be exonerated, and the court shall enter an order so directing.

The period during which the further criminal proceedings against the defendant may be diverted shall be for no less than six months nor longer than two years. Progress reports shall be filed by the probation department with the court not less than every six months.

§1000.3. Reinstitution of criminal proceedings; determination.

If it appears to the probation department that the divertee is performing unsatisfactorily in the assigned program, or that the divertee is not benefiting from education, treatment, or rehabilitation, or that the divertee is convicted of a misdemeanor which reflects the divertee's propensity for violence, or if the divertee is convicted of a felony, after notice to the divertee, the court shall hold a hearing to determine whether the criminal proceedings should be reinstituted. If the court finds that the divertee is not performing satisfactorily in the assigned program, or that the divertee is not benefiting from diversion, or the court finds that the divertee has been convicted of a crime as indicated above, the criminal case shall be referred back to the court for resumption of the criminal proceedings. If the divertee has performed satisfactorily during the period of diversion, at the end of the period of diversion, the criminal charges shall be dismissed.

§1000.5. Records filed with Department of Justice.

Any record filed with the Department of Justice shall indicate the disposition in those cases diverted pursuant to this chapter. Upon successful completion of a diversion program the arrest upon which the diversion was based shall be deemed to have never occurred. The divertee may indicate in response to any question concerning his prior criminal record that he was not arrested or diverted for such offense. A record pertaining to an arrest resulting in successful completion of a diversion program shall not, without the divertee's consent, be used in any way which could result in the denial of any employment, benefit, license, or certificate.

CHAPTER 2.6

SPECIAL PROCEEDINGS IN CASES INVOLVING DOMESTIC VIOLENCE

§1000.6. Applicability of chapter.

(a) Upon the determination of the judge presiding, this chapter shall apply whenever a case is before the court upon an accusatory pleading for an act of domestic violence which is charged as, or reduced to, a misdemeanor and all of the following apply to the defendant:

© 1992 by J., B. & L. Gould
Printed in the U.S.A.   EP

(1) The defendant has no conviction for any offense involving violence within seven years prior to the alleged commission of the charged divertible offense.

(2) The defendant's record does not indicate that probation or parole has ever been revoked without thereafter being completed.

(3) The defendant has not been diverted pursuant to this chapter within five years prior to the charged divertible offense.

Notwithstanding the foregoing, the provisions of this chapter are not applicable to a person who is charged with a violation of subdivision (a) of Section 245, Section 273.5, as added by Chapter 912 of the Statutes of 1977.

(b) The prosecuting attorney shall, and the defense attorney may, review his or her file to determine whether or not paragraphs (1) to (3), inclusive, of subdivision (a) are applicable to the defendant. If the defendant is found eligible, the prosecuting attorney shall notify the court, the defendant, and the defense attorney, and the defense attorney may move that the defendant be diverted pursuant to this chapter. If the defendant is found by the prosecuting attorney to be ineligible for diversion, the prosecuting attorney shall file with the court a declaration in writing or state for the record the grounds upon which the determination is based, and shall make this information available to the defendant and his or her attorney.

(c) No admission of guilt shall be required of a defendant in order for this chapter to be applicable.

(d) As used in this chapter "domestic violence" means intentionally or recklessly causing or attempting to cause bodily injury to a family or household member or placing a family or household member in reasonable apprehension of imminent serious bodily injury to himself or herself or another.

(e) As used in this chapter "family or household member" means a spouse, former spouse, parent, any other person related by consanguinity, or any person who regularly resides or who within the previous six months regularly resided in the household. "Family or household member" does not include a child.

§1000.7. Notice to defendant of applicability of chapter.

(a) If the prosecuting attorney determines that this chapter may be applicable to the defendant, he or she shall advise the defendant and his or her attorney in writing of such determination. This notification shall include:

(1) A full description of the procedures of diversionary investigation.

(2) A general explanation of the roles and authorities of the court, the prosecuting attorney, the probation department, and the community program in the diversion process.

(3) A clear statement that the court may decide in a hearing not to divert such person and that he or she may have to stand trial for the alleged offense.

(4) A clear statement that, for the period of diversion, the divertee may be enjoined from contacting, and shall be enjoined from annoying, molesting, attacking, striking, threatening, harassing, sexually assaulting, battering, or disturbing the peace of, the victim.

(5) A clear statement that should such person fail in meeting the terms of his or her diversion, or should he or she be convicted of any offense involving violence, he or she may be required, after a court hearing, to stand trial for the original alleged offense.

(6) An explanation of criminal record retention and disposition resulting from participation in the diversion and the divertee's rights relative to answering questions about his or her arrest and diversion following successful completion of the diversion program.

(b) If the defendant consents and waives his or her right to a speedy trial the court shall refer the case to the probation department. The probation department shall make an investigation and take into consideration the defendant's age, employment and service records, educational background, community and family ties, prior incidents of violence, treatment history, if any, demonstrable motivation, and other mitigating factors in determining whether the defendant is a person who would be benefited by education, treatment, or rehabilitation. The probation department shall also determine which community programs the defendant would benefit from and which of those programs would accept the defendant. The probation department shall report its findings and recommendation to the court.

§1000.8. Post-hearing determinations; diverse programs.

(a) The court shall hold a hearing and, after consideration of the probation department's report and any other information considered by the court to be relevant to its decision, shall determine if the defendant consents to further proceedings under this chapter and waives his or her right to a speedy trial and if the defendant should be diverted and referred for batterer's treatment counseling directed specifically to the violent conduct of the defendant. The court, in determining the defendant's eligibility for diversion, shall consider the nature and extent of the injury inflicted upon the victim, any prior incidents of domestic violence by the defendant, and any factors which would adversely influence the likelihood of successful completion of the diversion program. If the court does not deem the defendant a person who would be benefited by diversion, or if the defendant does not consent to participate, the proceedings shall continue as in any other case. If the court orders a defendant to be diverted, the court shall make inquiry into the financial condition of the defendant and upon a finding that the defendant is able in whole or part to pay the expense of such counseling the court may order him or her to pay for all or part of such expense.

Nothing in this subdivision shall prohibit the placement of a defendant in another appropriate counseling program if the court determines that there is no available batterer's treatment counseling program.

(b) At such time that the defendant's case is diverted, any bail bond or undertaking, or deposit in lieu thereof, on file by or on behalf of him or her shall be exonerated, and the court shall enter an order so directing.

(c) The period during which further criminal proceedings against a person may be diverted pursuant to this chapter shall be for no less than six months nor longer than two years.

The court shall set forth in writing or state on the record its reason for granting or denying diversion. The court's decision in such matter shall be final and shall not constitute an appealable order. *(Amended by Stats 1988 ch 193 §2, eff. 6/16/88.)*

§1000.9. Reinstitution of criminal proceedings; determination.

If it appears to the prosecuting attorney, the court, or the probation department that the divertee is performing unsatisfactorily in the assigned program, or that the divertee is not benefiting from counseling, or that he or she is convicted of any offense involving violence, after notice to the divertee, and upon request of the probation officer or on its own motion, the court shall hold a hearing to determine whether the criminal proceedings should be reinstituted. If the court finds that the divertee is not performing satisfactorily in the assigned program, or that the divertee is not benefiting from diversion, or the court finds that the divertee has been convicted of a crime as indicated above, the criminal case shall be referred back to the court for resumption of the criminal proceedings. If the divertee has performed satisfactorily during the period of diversion, at the end of the period of diversion, the criminal charges shall be dismissed.

§1000.10. Deletion of arrest record.

Any records filed with the Department of Justice shall indicate the disposition in those cases diverted pursuant to this chapter. Upon successful completion of a diversion program the arrest upon which the diversion was based shall be deemed to have never occurred. The divertee may indicate in response to any question concerning his or her prior criminal record that he or she was not arrested or diverted for such offense. A record pertaining to an arrest resulting in successful completion of a diversion program shall not, without the divertee's consent, be used in any way which could result in the denial of any employment, benefit, license, or certificate.

§1000.11. Inadmissibility of certain statements or information.

No statement, or any information procured therefrom, with respect to the specific offense with which the defendant is charged, which is made to any probation officer or community program worker during the process of determining the defendant's eligibility for diversion or subsequent to the granting of diversion, shall be admissible in any action or proceeding.

CHAPTER 2.65

CHILD ABUSE AND NEGLECT COUNSELING

§1000.12. Legislative intent.

(a) It is the intent of the Legislature that nothing in this chapter is intended to deprive a prosecuting attorney of the ability to prosecute persons suspected of committing any crime in which a minor is a victim of an act of abuse or neglect to the fullest extent of the law, if the prosecuting attorney so chooses.

(b) In lieu of prosecuting a person suspected of committing any crime in which a minor is a victim of an act of abuse or neglect, the prosecuting attorney may refer that person to the county department in charge of public social services or the probation department for counseling or psychological treatment and such other services as the department deems necessary. The prosecuting attorney shall seek the advice of the county department in charge of public social services or the probation department in determining whether or not to make the referral. (*Amended by Stats 1985 ch 1262 §1.*)

§1000.13. Referral for counseling; conditions.

(a) Notwithstanding Section 1000.12 no person suspected of violating any section of this code in which a minor is a victim of sexual abuse shall be referred for counseling in lieu of prosecution except upon written agreement between the prosecuting attorney and the suspected person and unless all of the following apply to the suspected person:

(1) The person is a family member of the victim. For the purposes of this chapter "family member" means a parent, stepparent, sibling, aunt, uncle, cousin, grandparent, or a member of the victim's household who has developed a family relationship with the victim.

(2) The person's criminal record does not indicate that diversion has been terminated, or probation or parole has been revoked, without thereafter being completed within the previous 10 years.

(3) The person has not been referred for counseling or other services pursuant to this chapter prior to the commission of the present alleged offense.

(4) The person has no prior conviction for any felony sexual offense or any offense in which a minor is a victim of sexual abuse and has no conviction for any felony offense involving violence against another person during the previous 10 years in which the suspected person remained free of prison custody.

(b) The prosecuting attorney may impose additional relevant criteria for determining whether to refer the suspected person under this chapter.

§1000.14. Progress reports.

If the person suspected of sexually abusing a child is referred to a counseling program, pursuant to Section 1000.13 the county department responsible for public social services or the probation department shall monitor the progress of the referred person in the counseling program and shall report to the prosecuting attorney regarding that progress at agreed upon intervals. If the person successfully completes the counseling program, the department shall report that fact in writing to both the prosecuting attorney and the person.

§1000.15. Failure to complete counseling program.

If the person suspected of sexually abusing a child fails to participate in or fails to successfully complete the counseling program as directed, or is subsequently charged with any offense involving violence against another person, or offense involving abuse or neglect of a child, the county department responsible for public social services or the probation department shall report that failure or subsequently charged offense to the prosecuting attorney who shall determine whether or not to institute prosecution of the suspected person for the violation giving rise to the referral.

§1000.16. Inadmissibility of certain statements.

No statement or information prepared therefrom, with respect to the specific offense of which the person is suspected, which is made to any social or community program worker or the probation department during any counseling program assigned pursuant to this chapter shall be admissible in any future criminal action or proceeding.

© 1992 by J., B. & L. Gould
Printed in the U.S.A.   EP

§1000.17. Cost to be paid by suspected abuser.

If the person is referred pursuant to this chapter he or she shall be responsible for paying the administrative cost of the referral and the expense of such counseling as determined by the county department responsible for public social services or the probation department. The administrative cost of the referral shall not exceed one hundred dollars ($100) for any person referred pursuant to this chapter for an offense punishable as a felony and shall not exceed fifty dollars ($50) for any person referred pursuant to the chapter for an offense punishable as a misdemeanor. The department shall take into consideration the ability of the referred party to pay and no such person shall be denied counseling services because of his or her inability to pay.

§1000.18. Maximum time for counseling program.

The counseling program shall not exceed five years from the time the person suspected of abusing or neglecting the child is referred pursuant to this chapter. If the suspected person successfully completes the counseling program under this chapter he or she shall not be prosecuted for the alleged offense.

CHAPTER 2.67

COUNSELING FOR CHILD ABUSE OR SEXUAL MOLESTATION
(Added by Stats 1985 ch 82 §1.)

§1000.30. Two year pilot project program for treatment to child sex abusers.

The Office of Criminal Justice Planning shall, pursuant to Chapter 1660 of the Statutes of 1984, establish a pilot project for a period of two years in not more than three counties. The pilot projects shall test a program to provide treatment to child sexual abuse perpetrators, including intrafamilial and pedophiliac abusers, and including abusers who are incarcerated, as well as those who are not. The office shall designate the pilot project counties from among those counties that wish to participate. The office shall give priority to selection of at least two of the three pilot projects in counties where an existing project provides services to child sexual abuse perpetrators and where the proposed pilot project is an expansion of, and integrated with, existing services.

These counties shall provide all of the following information to the Office of Criminal Justice Planning:

(a) Identification of sexual abuse perpetrator treatment and victim services as a need in the county's child abuse services plan developed pursuant to Section 18962 of the Welfare and Institutions Code.

(b) Evidence in the application to provide service under this chapter that county mental health, welfare department, district attorney, juvenile court, superior court, municipal court, probation department, and private child welfare service agencies are participating in and coordinating case referral, case management, and service delivery to the target population.

(c) Evidence as to how incest offender treatment will be integrated with victim treatment.

Nothing in this section prohibits the use by district attorneys of counseling and other treatment programs as a diversion from prosecution. In pilot counties, diversion services shall be integrated with the services provided under this chapter. *(Added by Stats 1985 ch 82 §1.)*

§1000.31. Applicable designated counties.

The provisions of this chapter shall be applicable in the designated counties for the duration of the pilot project. *(Added by Stats 1985 ch 82 §1.)*

§1000.32. Exceptions provided in pilot project counties.

(a) Except as provided in subdivision (b), in any case in which the defendant has been convicted in a pilot project county of violating Section 261, 264.1, 285, 286, 288, 288a, or 289, and the victim is a person who was under 18 years of age at the time the offense was committed, the court shall, in addition to any other punishment or confinement that may be imposed, require counseling of the convicted person pursuant to Section 1000.33, when the person is confined or placed on probation within the county.

(b) Notwithstanding subdivision (a), a court may exclude from counseling and other treatment programs any convicted person described in subdivision (a) who is confined within the county, if the person is found by the court not to be amenable to counseling or other treatment services on either of the following bases:

(1) The person is a repeat offender who has previously been ordered by a court to receive counseling and who has been found by either the court or a counselor to be nonresponsive or not amenable to counseling services.

(2) The person has professed to the court that he or she continues to sexually abuse children and has refused counseling services. *(Added by Stats 1985 ch 82 §1.)*

§1000.33. Action by the county mental health department.

In a pilot project county, the county mental health department shall do both of the following:

(a) Assign a counselor to the convicted person described in Section 1000.32. The counselor shall be qualified, as determined by the county mental health department, in carnal abuse or sexual molestation counseling, as appropriate.

(b) Determine and collect from the convicted person a fee for the counseling, according to ability to pay, but not exceeding actual cost. *(Added by Stats 1985 ch 82 §1.)*

§1000.34. Reimbursement for costs incurred while conducting the pilot project.

The state shall reimburse each pilot project county less any fees received pursuant to subdivision (b) of Section 1000.33 for any costs it incurs in conducting the pilot project under this chapter. *(Added by Stats 1985 ch 82 §1.)*

§1000.35. Cost and potential benefits of counseling programs.

In order that the Legislature may determine the cost and potential benefits of the counseling programs authorized by this chapter, the Office of Criminal Justice Planning shall submit a written report to the Legislature within six months of completion of all of the pilot projects authorized by this chapter. The reports shall detail all of the following information:

(a) The number of defendants who participated in the counseling programs during the pilot project.

(b) The cost of the pilot project, including data concerning the amount of the cost recovered from participants in the counseling programs.

(c) The nature of the treatment provided to participants in the counseling programs.

(d) The results of the treatment provided to participants in the counseling programs, including data concerning recidivism by participants, other criminal offenses committed by participants, and failures to participate in the counseling programs.

(e) The results of combining counseling services to intrafamilial and pedophiliac child sexual abusers. *(Added by Stats 1985 ch 82 §1.)*

§1000.36. Funds appropriated in the 1985-86 Budget Act.

To the extent that funds are appropriated for that purpose, the Office of Criminal Justice Planning shall award project funds to three counties which meet the criteria set forth in Section 1000.30. Pilot counties shall utilize each of the following:

(a) Third-party payments, where appropriate.

(b) Defendant fees, where ordered by the court.

(c) Existing counseling treatment and education services, where appropriate.

(d) Project funds to provide case management for each defendant and to purchase appropriate services where subdivisions (a), (b), and (c) are not applicable. *(Amended by Stats 1985 ch 1257 §3.)*

CHAPTER 2.7

MISDEMEANOR DIVERSION

§1001. Intent of Legislature.

It is the intent of the Legislature that neither this chapter, Chapter 2.5 (commencing with Section 1000) of this title, nor any other provision of law be construed to preempt other current or future pretrial or precomplaint diversion programs. It is also the intent of the Legislature that current or future posttrial diversion programs not be preempted, except as provided in Section 13201 or 13352.5 of the Vehicle Code. Sections 1001.2 to 1001.11, inclusive, of this chapter shall apply only to pretrial diversion programs as defined in Section 1001.1. *(Amended by Stats 1985 ch 1257 §3.)*

§1001.1. Pretrial diversion defined.

As used in Sections 1001.2 to 1001.11, inclusive, of this chapter, pretrial diversion refers to the procedure of postponing prosecution of an offense filed as a misdemeanor either temporarily or permanently at any point in the judicial process from the point at which the accused is charged until adjudication.

§1001.2. Inapplicability of chapter to problem drinking programs.

(a) This chapter shall not apply to any pretrial diversion or posttrial programs for the treatment of problem drinking or alcoholism utilized for persons convicted of one or more offenses under Section 23152 or 23153 or former Section 23102 of the Vehicle Code or to pretrial diversion programs established pursuant to Chapter 2.5 (commencing with Section 1000) of this title nor shall this chapter be deemed to authorize any pretrial diversion or posttrial programs for persons

alleged to have committed violation of Section 23152 or 23153 of the Vehicle Code.

(b) The district attorney of each county shall review annually any diversion program established pursuant to this chapter, and no program shall continue without the approval of the district attorney. No person shall be diverted under a program unless it has been approved by the district attorney. Nothing in this subdivision shall authorize the prosecutor to determine whether a particular defendant shall be diverted.

§1001.3. Admission of guilt not prerequisite for placement in program.

At no time shall a defendant be required to make an admission of guilt as a prerequisite for placement in a pretrial diversion program.

§1001.4. Right to hearing.

A divertee is entitled to a hearing, as set forth by law, before his or her pretrial diversion can be terminated for cause.

§1001.5. Inadmissibility of certain statements.

No statement, or information procured therefrom, made by the defendant in connection with the determination of his or her eligibility for diversion, and no statement, or information procured therefrom, made by the defendant, subsequent to the granting of diversion or while participating in such program, and no information contained in any report made with respect thereto, and no statement or other information concerning the defendant's participation in such program shall be admissible in any action or proceeding. However, if a divertee is recommended for termination for cause, information regarding his or her participation in such program may be used for purposes of the termination proceedings.

§1001.6. Exoneration of bail bond.

At such time that a defendant's case is diverted, any bail bond or undertaking, or deposit in lieu thereof, on file by or on behalf of the defendant shall be exonerated, and the court shall enter an order so directing.

§1001.7. Criminal charges dismissed.

If the divertee has performed satisfactorily during the period of diversion, the criminal charges shall be dismissed at the end of the period of diversion.

§1001.8. Filed records.

Any record filed with the Department of Justice shall indicate the disposition of those cases diverted pursuant to this chapter.

§1001.9. Deletion of arrest on record.

Upon successful completion of a diversion program, the arrest upon which the diversion was based shall be deemed to have never occurred. The divertee may indicate in response to any question concerning his or her prior criminal record that he or she was not arrested or diverted for such offense. A record pertaining to an arrest resulting in successful completion of a diversion program shall not, without the divertee's consent, be used in any way which could result in the denial of any employment, benefit, license, or certificate.

© 1992 by J., B. & L. Gould
Printed in the U.S.A.   **EP**

CHAPTER 2.71

AIDS PREVENTION PROGRAM IN DRUG ABUSE AND PROSTITUTION CASES
(Added by Stats 1988 ch 1243 §9, eff. 1/1/89.)

§1001.10. AIDS education program.

(a) The judge shall require any person described in subdivision (b), as a condition of either placing the person on probation or of permitting the person to participate in a drug diversion program to agree to participate in an AIDS education program. Testing for AIDS antibodies shall be offered but no person described in subdivision (b) shall be required to be tested.

(b) This section shall apply to any person who has either been placed on probation or granted diversion for, any of the following:

(1) A violation of subdivision (a) of Section 11350 of the Health and Safety Code, subdivision (a) of Section 11377 of the Health and Safety Code, Section 11550 of the Health and Safety Code, Section 4143 or 4149 of the Business and Professions Code, or of subdivision (f) of Section 647 if the offense involves intravenous use of a controlled substance.

(2) A violation of subdivision (a) or (b) of Section 647. *(Amended by Stats 1989 ch 534 §2, eff. 1/1/90.)*

§1001.11. Agency responsible; contents of AIDS program.

(a) The health department in each county shall select an agency, or agencies, in the county that shall provide AIDS prevention education to those persons sentenced to probation or a drug diversion program in accordance with Section 1001.10. The health department shall endeavor to select an agency, or agencies, that currently provide AIDS prevention education programs to substance abusers or prostitutes. If no agency is currently providing this education, the county agency responsible for substance abuse shall develop an AIDS prevention education program either within the agency or under contract with a community-based, nonprofit organization in the county. The health department shall forward to the courts a list of agencies selected for purposes of referral in accordance with Section 1001.10. Reimbursement for the costs of implementing this section shall be made out of moneys deposited with the county treasurer in accordance with Section 1463.23.

(b) An AIDS prevention education program providing services pursuant to subdivision (a) shall, at a minimum, include details about the transmission of human immunodeficiency virus (HIV), the etiologic agent for AIDS, symptoms of AIDS or AIDS-related conditions, prevention through avoidance or cleaning of needles, sexual practices which constitute high risk, low risk, and no risk (including abstinence), and resources for assistance if the person decides to take a test for the etiologic agent for AIDS and receives a positive test result. The program shall also include other relevant medical and prevention information as it becomes available.

(c) A person sentenced to a drug diversion program pursuant to Section 1001.10 shall not be required to participate in an AIDS prevention education program, provided that the drug diversion program includes an AIDS prevention education component that meets the requirements of subdivision (b). *(Added by Stats 1988 ch 1243 §9, eff. 1/1/89.)*

CHAPTER 2.75

DIVERSION FEES

§1001.15. Administrative fee; expenses covered.

(a) In addition to the fees authorized or required by other provisions of law, a judge may require the payment of an administrative fee, as part of an enrollment fee in a diversion program, by a defendant accused of a felony to cover the cost of any criminalistics laboratory analysis and the cost of processing a request or application for diversion pursuant to Chapter 2.5 (commencing with Section 1000), not to exceed one hundred fifty dollars ($150). The fee shall be payable at the time of enrollment in the diversion program. The court shall take into consideration the defendant's ability to pay, and no defendant shall be denied diversion because of his or her inability to pay. One-third of the fee collected shall be deposited in the criminalistics laboratories fund in the county treasury, and two-thirds of the fee collected shall be used to cover the administrative cost of processing the request or application. The portion deposited in the criminalistics laboratories fund shall be expended as provided in Section 11372.5 of the Health and Safety Code.

(b) As used in this section, "criminalistics laboratory" means a laboratory operated by, or under contract with, a city, county, or other public agency, including a criminalistics laboratory of the Department of Justice, which has not less than one regularly employed forensic scientist engaged in the analysis of solid dose material and body fluids for controlled substances, and which is registered as an analytical laboratory with the Drug Enforcement Administration of the United States Department of Justice for the processing of all scheduled controlled substances.

(c) In addition to the fees authorized or required by other provisions of law, a judge may require the payment of an administrative fee, as part of an enrollment fee in a diversion program, by a defendant accused of a felony to cover the cost of processing a request or application for diversion pursuant to Chapter 2.6 (commencing with Section 1000.6), not to exceed one hundred dollars ($100). The fee shall be payable at the time of enrollment in the diversion program. The court shall take into consideration the defendant's ability to pay, and no defendant shall be denied diversion because of his or her inability to pay. *(Amended by Stats 1987 ch 375 §1.)*

§1001.16. Administrative fee paid by accused misdemeanant.

(a) In addition to the fees authorized or required by other provisions of law, a judge may require the payment of an administrative fee, as part of an enrollment fee in a diversion program, by a defendant accused of a misdemeanor to cover the cost of any criminalistics laboratory analysis in a case involving a violation of the California Uniform Controlled Substances Act under Division 10 (commencing with Section 11000) of the Health and Safety Code and the cost of processing a request or application for diversion, not to exceed one hundred dollars ($100). The fee shall be payable at the time of enrollment in the diversion program. The court shall take into consideration the defendant's ability to pay, and no defendant shall be denied diversion because of his or her inability to pay.

One-half of the fee collected shall be deposited in the criminalistic laboratories fund in the county treasury, and one-half of the fee collected shall be used to cover the administrative cost of processing the request or application. The portion deposited in the criminalistic laboratories fund shall be expended as provided in Section 11372.5 of the Health and Safety Code.

(b) As used in this section, "criminalistics laboratory" means a laboratory operated by, or under contract with, a city, county, or other public agency, including a criminalistics laboratory of the Department of Justice, which has not less than one regularly employed forensic scientist engaged in the analysis of solid dose material and body fluids for controlled substances and which is registered as an analytical laboratory with the Drug Enforcement Administration of the United States Department of Justice for the processing of all scheduled controlled substances.

(c) This section shall apply to all misdemeanor pretrial diversion programs established pursuant to this title. *(Amended by Stats 1988 ch 160 §130, eff. 1/1/89.)*

§1001.17. Disposition of funds.

Funds collected pursuant to this chapter shall be deposited in the general fund of the county in which they are collected.

CHAPTER 2.8

DIVERSION OF MENTALLY RETARDED DEFENDANTS

§1001.20. Terms defined.

As used in this chapter:

(a) "Mentally retarded" means the condition of significantly subaverage general intellectual functioning existing concurrently with deficits in adaptive behavior and manifested during the developmental period.

(b) "Diversion-related treatment and habilitation" means, but is not limited to, specialized services or special adaptations of generic services, directed towards the alleviation of mental retardation or towards social, personal, physical, or economic habilitation or rehabilitation of an individual with such a disability, and includes, but is not limited to, diagnosis, evaluation, treatment, personal care, day care, domiciliary care, special living arrangements, physical, occupational, and speech therapy, training, education, sheltered employment, mental health services, recreation, counseling of the individual with such disability and of his family, protective and other social and socio-legal services, information and referral services, follow-along services, and transportation services necessary to assure delivery of services to mentally retarded persons.

(c) "Regional center" means a regional center for the developmentally disabled established under the Lanterman Developmental Disabilities Services Act which is organized as a private nonprofit community agency to plan, purchase, and coordinate the delivery of services which cannot be provided by state agencies to developmentally disabled persons residing in a particular geographic catchment area, and which is licensed and funded by the State Department of Developmental Services.

(d) "Director of a regional center" means the executive director of a regional center for the developmentally disabled or his or her designee.

(e) "Agency" means the prosecutor, the probation department, and the regional center involved in a particular defendant's case.

(f) "Dual agency diversion" means a treatment and habilitation program developed with court approval by the regional center, administered jointly by the regional center and by the probation department, which is individually tailored to the needs of the defendant as derived from the defendant's individual program plan pursuant to Section 4646 of the Welfare and Institutions Code, and which includes, but is not limited to, treatment specifically addressed to the criminal offense charged, for a specified period of time as prescribed in Section 1001.28.

(g) "Single agency diversion" means a treatment and habilitation program developed with court approval by the regional center, administered solely by the regional center without involvement by the probation department, which is individually tailored to the needs of the defendant as derived from the defendant's individual program plan pursuant to Section 4646 of the Welfare and Institutions Code, and which includes, but is not limited to, treatment specifically addressed to the criminal offense charged, for a specified period of time as prescribed in Section 1001.28.

§1001.21. Applicability of chapter in criminal proceedings.

(a) This chapter shall apply whenever a case is before any court upon an accusatory pleading at any stage of the criminal proceedings, for any person who has been evaluated by a regional center for the developmentally disabled and who is determined to be developmentally disabled by such regional center, and who therefore is eligible for its services.

(b) This chapter applies to any offense which is charged as or reduced to a misdemeanor, except that diversion shall not be ordered when the defendant previously has been diverted under this chapter within two years prior to the present criminal proceedings.

§1001.22. Determinations; reports.

The court shall consult with the prosecutor, the defense counsel, the probation department, and the appropriate regional center in order to determine whether a defendant may be diverted pursuant to this chapter. If the defendant is not represented by counsel, the court shall appoint counsel to represent the defendant. When the court suspects that a defendant may be mentally retarded, as defined in subdivision (a) of Section 1001.20, and the defendant consents to the diversion process and to his or her case being evaluated for eligibility for regional center services, and waives his or her right to a speedy trial, the court shall order the prosecutor, the probation department, and the regional center to prepare reports on specified aspects of the defendant's case. Each report shall be prepared concurrently.

(a) The regional center shall submit a report to the probation department within 25 judicial days of the court's order. The regional center's report shall include a determination as to whether the defendant is mentally retarded and eligible for regional center diversion-related treatment and habilitation services, and the regional center shall also submit to the court a proposed diversion program, individually tailored to the needs of the defendant as derived from the defend-

© 1992 by J., B. & L. Gould
Printed in the U.S.A.   EP

ant's individual program plan pursuant to Section 4646 of the Welfare and Institutions Code, which shall include, but not be limited to, treatment addressed to the criminal offense charged for a period of time as prescribed in Section 1001.28. The regional center's report shall also contain a statement whether such a proposed program is available for the defendant through the treatment and habilitation services of the regional centers pursuant to Section 4648 of the Welfare and Institutions Code.

(b) The prosecutor shall submit a report on specified aspects of the defendant's case, within 30 judicial days of the court's order, to the court, to each of the other agencies involved in the case, and to the defendant. The prosecutor's report shall include all of the following:

(1) A statement of whether the defendant's record indicates the defendant's diversion pursuant to this chapter within two years prior to the alleged commission of the charged divertible offense.

(2) If the prosecutor recommends that this chapter may be applicable to the defendant, he or she shall recommend either a dual or single agency diversion program and shall advise the court, the probation department, the regional center, and the defendant, in writing, of such determination within 20 judicial days of the court's order to prepare the report.

(3) If the prosecutor recommends against diversion, the prosecutor's report shall include a declaration in writing to state for the record the grounds upon which such recommendation was made, and the court shall determine, pursuant to Section 1001.23, whether the defendant shall be diverted.

(4) If dual agency diversion is recommended by the prosecutor, a copy of the prosecutor's report shall also be provided by the prosecutor to the probation department, the regional center, and the defendant within the above prescribed time period. This notification shall include all of the following:

(i) A full description of the proceedings for diversion and the prosecutor's investigation procedures.

(ii) A general explanation of the role and authority of the probation department, the prosecutor, the regional center, and the court in the diversion program process.

(iii) A clear statement that the court may decide in a hearing not to divert the defendant and that he or she may have to stand trial for the alleged offense.

(iv) A clear statement that should the defendant fail in meeting the terms of his or her diversion, or if, during the period of diversion the defendant is subsequently charged with a felony, the defendant may be required, after a hearing, to stand trial for the original diverted offense.

(c) The probation department shall submit a report on specified aspects of the defendant's case within 30 judicial days of the court's order, to the court, to each of the other agencies involved in the case, and to the defendant. The probation department's report to the court shall be based upon an investigation by the probation department and consideration of the defendant's age, mental retardation, employment record, educational background, ties to community agencies and family, treatment history, criminal record if any, and demonstrable motivation and other mitigating factors in determining whether the defendant is a person who would benefit from a diversion-related treatment and habilitation program. The

regional center's report in full shall be appended to the probation department's report to the court.

§1001.23. Proceedings after determinations.

(a) Upon the court's receipt of the reports from the prosecutor, the probation department, and the regional center, and a determination by the regional center that the defendant is not mentally retarded, the criminal proceedings for the offense charged shall proceed. If the defendant is found to be mentally retarded and eligible for regional center services, and the court determines from the various reports submitted to it that the proposed diversion program is acceptable to the court, the prosecutor, the probation department, and the regional center, and if the defendant consents to diversion and waives his or her right to a speedy trial, the court may order, without a hearing, that the diversion program be implemented for a period of time as prescribed in Section 1001.28.

(b) After consideration of the probation department's report, the report of the regional center, and the report of the prosecutor relating to his or her recommendation for or against diversion, and any other relevant information, the court shall determine if the defendant shall be diverted under either dual or single agency supervision, and referred for habilitation or rehabilitation diversion pursuant to this chapter. If the court does not deem the defendant a person who would benefit by diversion at the time of the hearing, the suspended criminal proceedings may be reinstituted, or such other disposition as authorized by law may be made, and diversion may be ordered at a later date.

(c) Where a dual agency diversion program is ordered by the court, the regional center shall submit a report to the probation department on the defendant's progress in the diversion program not less than every six months. Within five judicial days after receiving the regional center's report, the probation department shall submit its report on the defendant's progress in the diversion program, with the full report of the regional center appended, to the court and to the prosecutor. Where single agency diversion is ordered by the court, the regional center alone shall report the defendant's progress to the court and to the prosecutor not less than every six months.

§1001.24. Inadmissibility of certain statements made by defendant.

No statement, or information procured therefrom, made by the defendant to any probation officer, the prosecutor, or any regional center designee during the course of the investigation conducted by either the regional center or the probation department pursuant to this chapter, and prior to the reporting to the probation department of the regional center's findings of eligibility and recommendations to the court, shall be admissible in any action or proceeding brought subsequent to this investigation.

§1001.25. Inadmissibility of certain statements.

No statement, or information procured therefrom, with respect to the specific offense with which the defendant is charged, which is made to a probation officer, a prosecutor, or a regional center designee subsequent to the granting of diversion shall be admissible in any action or proceeding brought subsequent to the investigation.

© 1992 by J., B. & L. Gould
Printed in the U.S.A. **EP**

§1001.26. Inadmissibility of information in sentencing procedures.

In the event that diversion is either denied or is subsequently revoked once it has been granted, neither the probation investigation nor the statements or other information divulged by the defendant during the investigation by the probation department or the regional center shall be used in any sentencing procedures.

§1001.27. Bail exonerated.

At such time as the defendant's case is diverted, any bail, bond, or undertaking, or deposit in lieu thereof, on file or on behalf of the defendant shall be exonerated, and the court shall enter an order so directing.

§1001.28. Time limitations for criminal proceedings.

The period during which criminal proceedings against the defendant may be diverted shall be no longer than two years. The responsible agency or agencies shall file reports on the defendant's progress in the diversion program with the court and with the prosecutor not less than every six months.

(a) Where dual agency diversion has been ordered, the probation department shall be responsible for the progress reports. The probation department shall append to its own report a copy of the regional center's assessment of the defendant's progress.

(b) Where single agency diversion has been ordered, the regional center alone shall be responsible for the progress reports.

§1001.29. Diversion program modified.

If it appears that the divertee is not meeting the terms and conditions of his or her diversion program, the court may hold a hearing and amend such program to provide for greater supervision by the responsible regional center alone, by the probation department alone, or by both the regional center and the probation department. However, notwithstanding any such modification of a diversion order, the court may hold a hearing to determine whether the diverted criminal proceedings should be reinstituted if it appears that the divertee's performance in the diversion program is unsatisfactory, or if the divertee is subsequently charged with a felony during the period of diversion.

(a) In cases of dual agency diversion, a hearing to reinstitute the diverted criminal proceedings may be initiated by either the court, the prosecutor, the regional center, or the probation department.

(b) In cases of single agency diversion, a hearing to reinstitute the diverted criminal proceedings may be initiated only by the court, the prosecutor, or the regional center.

(c) No hearing for either of these purposes shall be held unless the moving agency or the court has given the divertee prior notice of the hearing.

(d) Where the cause of the hearing is a subsequent charge of a felony against the divertee subsequent to the diversion order, any hearing to reinstitute the diverted criminal proceedings shall be delayed until such time as probable cause has been established in court to bind the defendant over for trial on the subsequently charged felony.

§1001.30. Defendant's withdrawal of consent.

At any time during which the defendant is participating in a diversion program, he or she may withdraw consent to further participate in the diver-sion program, and at such time as such consent is withdrawn, the suspended criminal proceedings may resume or such other disposition may be made as is authorized by law.

§1001.31. Criminal charges dismissed.

If the divertee has performed satisfactorily during the period of diversion, the criminal charges shall be dismissed at the end of the diversion period.

§1001.32. Records must indicate disposition of cases.

Any record filed with the State Department of Justice shall indicate the disposition of those cases diverted pursuant to this chapter.

§1001.33. Deletion of arrest on record.

Upon successful completion of a diversion program, the arrest upon which the diversion was based shall be deemed to have never occurred. The divertee may indicate in response to any question concerning his or her prior criminal record that he or she was not arrested or diverted for such offense. A record pertaining to an arrest resulting in successful completion of a diversion program shall not, without the divertee's consent, be used in any way which may result in the denial of any employment, benefit, license, or certificate.

§1001.34. Program implementation.

Notwithstanding any other provision of law, the diversion-related individual program plan shall be fully implemented by the regional centers upon court order and approval of the diversion-related treatment and habilitation plan.

§1001.35. *Repealed by Stats 1986 ch 166.*

CHAPTER 2.81

PRETRIAL DIVERSION OF TRAFFIC VIOLATORS
(Added by Stats 1990 ch 1303 §1, eff. 1/1/91.)

§1001.40. Pretrial diversion.

Notwithstanding any other provision of law, a county acting on behalf of one or more individual courts may by ordinance establish a program that provides for pretrial diversion by the court of any person issued a notice to appear for a traffic violation to attend any traffic violator school licensed pursuant to Chapter 1.5 (commencing with Section 11200) of Division 5 of the Vehicle Code. *(Added by Stats 1990 ch 1303 §1, eff. 1/1/91.)*

CHAPTER 2.9

DIVERSION OF MISDEMEANOR OFFENDERS

§1001.50. Operation; review.

(a) Notwithstanding any other provision of law, this chapter shall become operative in a county only if the board of supervisors adopts the provisions of this chapter by ordinance.

(b) The district attorney of each county shall review annually any diversion program established pursuant to this chapter, and no program shall continue without the approval of the district attorney. No person shall be diverted under a program unless it has

© 1992 by J., B. & L. Gould
Printed in the U.S.A.   **EP**

been approved by the district attorney. Nothing in this subdivision shall authorize the prosecutor to determine whether a particular defendant shall be diverted.

(c) As used in this chapter, "pretrial diversion" means the procedure of postponing prosecution either temporarily or permanently at any point in the judicial process from the point at which the accused is charged until adjudication.

§1001.51. Applicability of chapter.

(a) This chapter shall apply whenever a case is before any court upon an accusatory pleading concerning the commission of a misdemeanor, except a misdemeanor specified in subdivision (b), and it appears to the court that all of the following apply to the defendant:

(1) The defendant's record does not indicate that probation or parole has ever been revoked without thereafter being completed.

(2) The defendant's record does not indicate that he has been diverted pursuant to this chapter within five years prior to the filing of the accusatory pleading which charges the divertible offense.

(3) The defendant has never been convicted of a felony, and has not been convicted of a misdemeanor within five years prior to the filing of the accusatory pleading which charges the divertible offense.

(b) This chapter shall not apply to any pretrial diversion or posttrial program otherwise established by this code, nor shall this chapter be deemed to authorize any pretrial diversion or posttrial program for any person alleged to have committed a violation of Section 23152 or 23153 of the Vehicle Code.

(c) This chapter shall not apply whenever the accusatory pleading charges the commission of a misdemeanor:

(1) For which incarceration would be mandatory upon conviction of the defendant.

(2) For which registration would be required pursuant to Section 290 upon conviction of the defendant.

(3) Which the magistrate determines shall be prosecuted as a misdemeanor pursuant to paragraph (5) of subdivision (b) of Section 17.

(4) Which involves the use of force or violence against a person, unless the charge is of a violation of Section 241 or 243.

(5) For which the granting of probation is prohibited.

(6) Which is a driving offense punishable as a misdemeanor pursuant to the Vehicle Code.

§1001.52. Preliminary investigation.

(a) If the defendant consents and waives his right to a speedy trial, the case shall be referred to the probation department. The probation department shall conduct such investigation as is necessary to determine whether the defendant qualifies for diversion under subdivision (a) of Section 1001.51, and whether he or she is a person who would be benefited by education, treatment or rehabilitation. The probation department shall also determine which educational, treatment or rehabilitative plan would benefit the defendant. The probation department shall report its findings and recommendation to the court. If the recommendation includes referral to a community program, the report shall contain a statement regarding the program's willingness to accept the defendant and the manner in which the services they offer can assist the defendant in completing the diversion program successfully.

(b) No statement, or any information procured therefrom, made by the defendant to any probation officer, which is made during the course of any investigation conducted by the probation department pursuant to subdivision (b), and prior to the reporting of the probation department's findings and recommendations to the court, shall be admissible in any action or proceeding brought subsequent to the investigation.

No statement, or any information procured therefrom, with respect to the specific offense with which the defendant is charged, which is made to any probation officer subsequent to the granting of diversion, shall be admissible in any action or proceeding.

In the event that diversion is either denied, or is subsequently revoked once it has been granted, neither the probation investigation nor statements or information divulged during that investigation shall be used in any pretrial sentencing procedures.

§1001.53. Hearing and determination.

The court shall hold a hearing and, after consideration of the probation department's report, and any other relevant information, shall determine if the defendant consents to further proceedings under this chapter and waives his or her right to a speedy trial. If the court orders a defendant to be diverted, the court may make inquiry into the financial condition of the defendant, and upon a finding that the defendant is able in whole or in part, to pay the reasonable cost of diversion, the court may order him or her to pay all or part of such expense. The reasonable cost of diversion shall not exceed the amount determined to be the actual average cost of diversion services.

If the court does not deem the defendant to be a person who would be benefited by diversion, or if the defendant does not consent to participate, the proceedings shall continue as in any other case.

At such time that a defendant's case is diverted, any bail bond or undertaking, or deposit in lieu thereof, on file by or on behalf of the defendant shall be exonerated, and the court shall enter an order so directing.

The period during which the further criminal proceedings against the defendant may be diverted shall be for the length of time required to complete and verify the diversion program but in no case shall it exceed two years.

§1001.54. Reinstituting criminal proceedings.

If it appears to the probation department that the divertee is performing unsatisfactorily in the assigned program, or that the divertee is not benefiting from education, treatment or rehabilitation, or that the divertee is convicted of a misdemeanor in which force or violence is used, or if the divertee is convicted of a felony, after notice to the divertee, the court shall hold a hearing to determine whether the criminal proceedings should be reinstituted. If the court finds that the divertee is not performing satisfactorily in the assigned program, or that the divertee is not benefiting from diversion, or the court finds that the divertee has been convicted of a crime as indicated above, the criminal case shall be referred back to the court for resumption of the criminal proceedings. If the divertee has performed satisfactorily during the period of diversion, at the end of the period of diversion, the criminal charges shall be dismissed.

§1001.55. Records.

Any record filed with the Department of Justice shall indicate the disposition in those cases diverted pursuant to this chapter. Upon successful completion of a diversion program, the arrest upon which the diversion was based shall be deemed to have never occurred. The divertee may indicate in response to any question concerning his prior criminal record that he was not arrested or diverted for such offense. A record pertaining to an arrest resulting in successful completion of a diversion program shall not, without the divertee's consent, be used in any way which could result in the denial of any employment, benefit, license, or certificate.

CHAPTER 2.9A

BAD CHECK DIVERSION
(Added by Stats 1985 ch 1059 §1.)

§1001.60. General provisions.

Upon the adoption of a resolution by the board of supervisors declaring that there are sufficient funds available to fund the program, the district attorney may create within his office a diversion program pursuant to this chapter for persons who write bad checks. For purposes of this chapter, "writing a bad check" means making, drawing, uttering, or delivering any check or draft upon any bank or depository for the payment of money where there is probable cause to believe there has been a violation of Section 476a. The program may be conducted by the district attorney or by a private entity under contract with the district attorney. *(Added by Stats 1985 ch 1059 §1.)*

§1001.61. Referral of bad check case.

The district attorney may refer a bad check case to the diversion program. Except as provided in Section 1001.64, this chapter does not limit the power of the district attorney to prosecute bad check complaints. *(Added by Stats 1985 ch 1059 §1.)*

§1001.62. Determining bad check case.

On receipt of a bad check case, the district attorney shall determine if the case is one which is appropriate to be referred to the bad check diversion program. In determining whether to refer a case to the bad check diversion program, the district attorney shall consider, but is not limited to, all of the following:

(a) The amount of the bad check.

(b) If the person has a prior criminal record or has previously been diverted.

(c) The number of bad check grievances against the person previously received by the district attorney.

(d) Whether there are other bad check grievances currently pending against the person.

(e) The strength of the evidence, if any, of intent to defraud the victim. *(Added by Stats 1985 ch 1059 §1.)*

§1001.63. Notice of referral.

On referral of a bad check case to the diversion program, a notice shall be forwarded by mail to the person alleged to have written the bad check which contains all of the following:

(a) The date and amount of the bad check.

(b) The name of the payee.

(c) The date before which the person must contact the person designated by the district attorney concerning the bad check.

(d) A statement of the penalty for issuance of a bad check. *(Added by Stats 1985 ch 1059 §1.)*

§1001.64. Written agreement.

The district attorney may enter into a written agreement with the person to forego prosecution on the bad check for a period to be determined by the district attorney, not to exceed six months, pending all of the following:

(a) Completion of a class or classes conducted by the district attorney or private entity under contract with the district attorney.

(b) Full restitution being made to the victim of the bad check.

(c) Full payment of the collection fee, if any, specified in Section 1001.65. *(Added by Stats 1985 ch 1059 §1.)*

§1001.65. Fees.

(a) A district attorney may collect a fee if his or her office collects and processes a bad check. The amount of the fee shall not exceed twenty-five dollars ($25) for each bad check.

(b) Notwithstanding subdivision (a), if a bad check case is not referred to a diversion program pursuant to this chapter, the court may impose a bad check collection fee for the collection and processing of a bad check by the district attorney of not more than twenty-five dollars ($25) for each bad check, not to exceed one thousand dollars ($1000) in the aggregate. The court may also, as a condition of probation, require a defendant to participate in and successfully complete a check writing education class. If so required, the court shall make inquiry into the financial condition of the defendant, and upon a finding that the defendant is able in whole or part to pay the expense of the education class, the court may order him or her to pay for all or part of that expense. *(Amended by Stats 1988 ch 1036 §2, eff. 1/1/89.)*

§1001.66. Admission of guilt.

At no time shall a defendant be required to make an admission of guilt as a prerequisite for placement in a precomplaint diversion program. *(Added by Stats 1985 ch 1059 §1.)*

§1001.67. Statements by defendant not admissible.

No statement, or information procured therefrom, made by the defendant in connection with the determination of his or her eligibility for diversion, and no statement, or information procured therefrom, made by the defendant, subsequent to the granting of diversion or while participating in the program, and no information contained in any report made with respect thereto, and no statement or other information concerning the defendant's participation in the program shall be admissible in any action or proceeding. *(Added by Stats 1985 ch 1059 §1.)*

§1001.68. *Repealed by Stats 1985 ch 1059.*

CHAPTER 2.9B

PARENTAL DIVERSION
(Added by Stats 1988 ch 1256 §3, eff. 9/23/88.)

§1001.70. Division program; review and approval.

(a) Every local prosecutor with jurisdiction to prosecute violations of Section 272 shall review annually any diversion program established pursuant to

© 1992 by J., B. & L. Gould
Printed in the U.S.A.   EP

this chapter, and no program shall commence or continue without the approval of the local prosecutor. No person shall be diverted under a program unless it has been approved by the local prosecutor. Nothing in this subdivision shall authorize the prosecutor to determine whether a particular defendant shall be diverted.

(b) As used in this chapter, "pretrial diversion" means the procedure of postponing prosecution either temporarily or permanently at any point in the judicial process from the point at which the accused is charged until adjudication. (*Added by Stats 1988 ch 1256 §3, eff. 9/23/88.*)

§1001.71. Chapter application.

This chapter shall apply whenever a case is before any court upon an accusatory pleading alleging a parent or legal guardian to have violated Section 272 with respect to his or her minor child, and all of the following apply to the defendant:

(a) The defendant's record does not indicate that probation or parole has ever been revoked without thereafter being completed.

(b) The defendant's record does not indicate that he or she has previously been diverted pursuant to this chapter. (*Added by Stats 1989 ch 144 §2, eff. 1/1/90.*)

§1001.72. Probation department's investigation and recommendation of diversion.

(a) If the defendant consents and waives his or her right to a speedy trial, the case shall be referred to the probation department. The probation department shall conduct an investigation as is necessary to determine whether the defendant qualifies for diversion under this chapter, and whether he or she is a person who would be benefited by education, treatment, or rehabilitation. The probation department shall also determine which education, treatment, or rehabilitative plan would benefit the defendant. The probation department shall report its findings and recommendations to the court. If the recommendation includes referral to a community program, the report shall contain a statement regarding the program's willingness to accept the defendant and the manner in which the services they offer can assist the defendant in completing the diversion program successfully.

(b) No statement, or any information procured therefrom, made by the defendant to any probation officer, which is made during the course of any investigation conducted by the probation department pursuant to subdivision (a), prior to the reporting of the probation department's findings and recommendations to the court, shall be admissible in any action or proceeding brought subsequent to the investigation.

No statement, or any information procured therefrom, with respect to the specific offense with which the defendant is charged which is made to any probation officer subsequent to the granting of diversion, shall be admissible in any action or proceeding.

In the event that diversion is either denied or is subsequently revoked once it has been granted, neither the probation investigation nor statements or information divulged during that investigation shall be used in any pretrial sentencing procedures. (*Added by Stats 1988 ch 1256 §3, eff. 9/23/88.*)

§1001.73. Diversion recommendation hearing.

The court shall hold a hearing and, after consideration of the probation department's report, and any

other relevant information, shall determine if the defendant consents to further proceedings under this chapter and waives his or her right to a speedy trial. If the court orders a defendant to be diverted, the court may make inquiry into the financial condition of the defendant, and upon a finding that the defendant is able, in whole or in part, to pay the reasonable cost of diversion, the court may order him or her to pay all or part of the expense. The reasonable cost of diversion shall not exceed the amount determined to be the actual average cost of diversion services.

If the court does not deem the defendant to be a person who would be benefited by diversion or if the defendant does not consent to participate, the proceedings shall continue as in any other case.

At the time that a defendant's case is diverted, any bail bond or undertaking, or deposit in lieu thereof, on file by or on behalf of the defendant shall be exonerated, and the court shall enter an order so directing.

The period during which the further criminal proceedings against the defendant may be diverted shall be for the length of time required to complete and verify the diversion program but in no case shall it exceed two years. (*Added by Stats 1988 ch 1256 §3, eff. 9/23/88.*)

§1001.74. Criminal proceedings; reinstitution.

If it appears to the probation department that the divertee is performing unsatisfactorily in the assigned program, or that the divertee is not benefiting from education, treatment, or rehabilitation, or that the divertee is convicted of a misdemeanor in which force or violence was used, or if the divertee is convicted of a felony, after notice to the divertee, the court shall hold a hearing to determine whether the criminal proceedings should be reinstituted. If the court finds that the divertee is not performing satisfactorily in the assigned program, or that the divertee has been convicted of a crime as indicated above, the criminal case shall be referred back to the court for resumption of the criminal proceedings. If the divertee has performed satisfactorily during the period of diversion, the criminal charges shall be dismissed. (*Added by Stats 1988 ch 1256 §3, eff. 9/23/88.*)

§1001.75. Diversion program's successful completion.

Any record filed with the Department of Justice shall indicate the disposition in those cases diverted pursuant to this chapter. Upon successful completion of a diversion program, the arrest upon which the diversion was based shall be deemed to have never occurred. The divertee may indicate in response to any question concerning his or her prior criminal record that he or she was not arrested or diverted for that offense. A record pertaining to an arrest resulting in successful completion of a diversion program shall not, without the divertee's consent, be used in any way which would result in the denial of any employment, benefit, license, or certificate. (*Added by Stats 1988 ch 1256 §3, eff. 9/23/88.*)

CHAPTER 3

DEMURRER AND AMENDMENT

§1002. Pleading on part of defendant.
The only pleading on the part of the defendant is either a demurrer or a plea.

§1003. Demurrer or plea, when put in.
Both the demurrer and plea must be put in, in open court, either at the time of the arraignment or at such other time as may be allowed to the defendant for that purpose.

§1004. Grounds.
The defendant may demur to the accusatory pleading at any time prior to the entry of a plea, when it appears upon the face thereof either:

1. If an indictment, that the grand jury by which it was found had no legal authority to inquire into the offense charged, or, if an information or complaint that the court has no jurisdiction of the offense charged therein;

2. That it does not substantially conform to the provisions of Sections 950 and 952, and also Section 951 in case of an indictment or information;

3. That more than one offense is charged, except as provided in Section 954;

4. That the facts stated do not constitute a public offense;

5. That it contains matter which, if true, would constitute a legal justification or excuse of the offense charged, or other legal bar to the prosecution.

§1005. Form.
The demurrer must be in writing, signed either by the defendant or his counsel, and filed. It must distinctly specify the grounds of objection to the accusatory pleading or it must be disregarded.

§1006. Hearing of argument.
Upon the demurrer being filed, the argument upon the objections presented thereby must be heard immediately, unless for exceptional cause shown, the court shall grant a continuance. Such continuance shall be for no longer time than the ends of justice require, and the court shall enter in its minutes the facts requiring it.

§1007. Order.
Upon considering the demurrer, the court must make an order either overruling or sustaining it. If the demurrer is overruled, the court must permit the defendant, at his election, to plead, which he must do forthwith, unless the court extends the time. If the demurrer is sustained, by a superior court, the court must, if the defect can be remedied by amendment, permit the indictment or information to be amended, either forthwith or within such time, not exceeding 10 days, as it may fix, or, if the defect or insufficiency therein cannot be remedied by amendment, the court may direct the filing of a new information or the submission of the case to the same or another grand jury. If the demurrer is sustained by an inferior court, the court must, if the defect can be remedied, permit the filing of an amended complaint within such time not exceeding 10 days as it may fix. The orders made under this section shall be entered in the docket or minutes of the court.

§1008. Dismissing action.
If the demurrer is sustained, and no amendment of the accusatory pleading is permitted, or, in case an amendment is permitted, no amendment is made or amended pleading is filed within the time fixed therefor, the action shall be dismissed, and, except as provided in Section 1010, the court must order, if the defendant is in custody, that he be discharged or if he has been admitted to bail, that his bail be exonerated, or, if money or other property has been deposited instead of bail for his appearance, that such money or other property be refunded to him or to the person or persons found by the court to have deposited such money or other property on his behalf.

§1009. Amending accusatory instrument.
An indictment, accusation or information may be amended by the district attorney, and an amended complaint may be filed by the prosecuting attorney in any inferior court, without leave of court at any time before the defendant pleads or a demurrer to the original pleading is sustained. The court in which an action is pending may order or permit an amendment of an indictment, accusation or information, or the filing of an amended complaint, for any defect or insufficiency, at any stage of the proceedings, or if the defect in an indictment or information be one that cannot be remedied by amendment, may order the case submitted to the same or another grand jury, or a new information to be filed. The defendant shall be required to plead to such amendment or amended pleading forthwith, or, at the time fixed for pleading, if he has not yet pleaded and the trial or other proceeding shall continue as if the pleading had been originally filed as amended, unless the substantial rights of the defendant would be prejudiced thereby, in which event a reasonable postponement, not longer than the ends of justice require, may be granted. An indictment or accusation cannot be amended so as to change the offense charged, nor an information so as to charge an offense not shown by the evidence taken at the preliminary examination. A complaint cannot be amended to charge an offense not attempted to be charged by the original complaint, except that separate counts may be added which might properly have been joined in the original complaint. The amended complaint must be verified but may be verified by some person other than the one who made oath to the original complaint.

§1010. Resubmission.
When a criminal action in the superior court is dismissed after the sustaining of a demurrer, or at any other stage of the proceedings because of any defect or insufficiency of the indictment or information, if the court directs that the case be resubmitted to the same or another grand jury or that a new information be filed, the defendant shall not be discharged from custody, nor his bail exonerated nor money or other property deposited instead of bail on his behalf refunded, but the same proceedings must be had on such direction as are prescribed in Sections 997 and 998.

§1012. Failure to take by demurrer; waiver.
When any of the objections mentioned in Section 1004 appears on the face of the accusatory pleading, it can be taken only by demurrer, and failure so to take it shall be deemed a waiver thereof, except that the objection to the jurisdiction of the court and the objection that the facts stated do not constitute a public offense may be taken by motion in arrest of judgment.

274

CHAPTER 4

PLEA

§1016. Kinds of pleas.

There are six kinds of pleas to an indictment or an information, or to a complaint charging an offense triable in any inferior court:

1. Guilty.
2. Not guilty.
3. Nolo contendere, subject to the approval of the court. The court shall ascertain whether the defendant completely understands that a plea of nolo contendere shall be considered the same as a plea of guilty and that, upon a plea of nolo contendere, the court shall find the defendant guilty. The legal effect of such a plea, to a crime punishable as a felony, shall be the same as that of a plea of guilty for all purposes. In cases other than those punishable as felonies, the plea and any admissions required by the court during any inquiry it makes as to the voluntariness of, and factual basis for, the plea may not be used against the defendant as an admission in any civil suit based upon or growing out of the act upon which the criminal prosecution is based.
4. A former judgment of conviction or acquittal of the offense charged.
5. Once in jeopardy.
6. Not guilty by reason of insanity.

A defendant who does not plead guilty may enter one or more of the other pleas. A defendant who does not plead not guilty by reason of insanity shall be conclusively presumed to have been sane at the time of the commission of the offense charged; provided, that the court may for good cause shown allow a change of plea at any time before the commencement of the trial. A defendant who pleads not guilty by reason of insanity, without also pleading not guilty, thereby admits the commission of the offense charged.

§1016.5. Advisement on record.

(a) Prior to acceptance of a plea of guilty or nolo contendere to any offense punishable as a crime under state law, except offenses designated as infractions under state law, the court shall administer the following advisement on the record to the defendant:

If you are not a citizen, you are hereby advised that conviction of the offense for which you have been charged may have the consequences of deportation, exclusion from admission to the United States, or denial of naturalization pursuant to the laws of the United States.

(b) Upon request, the court shall allow the defendant additional time to consider the appropriateness of the plea in light of the advisement as described in this section. If, after January 1, 1978, the court fails to advise the defendant as required by this section and the defendant shows that conviction of the offense to which defendant pleaded guilty or nolo contendere may have the consequences for the defendant of deportation, exclusion from admission to the United States, or denial of naturalization pursuant to the laws of the United States, the court, on defendant's motion, shall vacate the judgment and permit the defendant to withdraw the plea of guilty or nolo contendere, and enter a plea of not guilty. Absent a record that the court provided the advisement required by this section, the defendant shall be presumed not to have received the required advisement.

(c) With respect to pleas accepted prior to January 1, 1978, it is not the intent of the Legislature that a court's failure to provide the advisement required by subdivision (a) of Section 1016.5 should require the vacation of judgment and withdrawal of the plea or constitute grounds for finding a prior conviction invalid. Nothing in this section, however, shall be deemed to inhibit a court, in the sound exercise of its discretion, from vacating a judgment and permitting a defendant to withdraw a plea.

(d) The Legislature finds and declares that in many instances involving an individual who is not a citizen of the United States charged with an offense punishable as a crime under state law, a plea of guilty or nolo contendere is entered without the defendant knowing that a conviction of such offense is grounds for deportation, exclusion from admission to the United States, or denial of naturalization pursuant to the laws of the United States. Therefore, it is the intent of the Legislature in enacting this section to promote fairness to such accused individuals by requiring in such cases that acceptance of a guilty plea or plea of nolo contendere be preceded by an appropriate warning of the special consequences for such a defendant which may result from the plea. It is also the intent of the Legislature that the court in such cases shall grant the defendant a reasonable amount of time to negotiate with the prosecuting agency in the event the defendant or the defendant's counsel was unaware of the possibility of deportation, exclusion from admission to the United States, or denial of naturalization as a result of conviction. It is further the intent of the Legislature that at the time of the plea no defendant shall be required to disclose his or her legal status to the court.

§1017. Making and entering.

Every plea must be made in open court and, may be oral or in writing, shall be entered upon the minutes of the court, and shall be taken down in shorthand by the official reporter if one is present. All pleas of guilty or nolo contendere to misdemeanors or felonies shall be oral or in writing. The plea, whether oral or in writing, shall be in substantially the following form:

1. If the defendant plead guilty: "The defendant pleads that he or she is guilty of the offense charged."
2. If he or she plead not guilty: "The defendant pleads that he or she is not guilty of the offense charged."
3. If he or she plead a former conviction or acquittal: "The defendant pleads that he or she has already been convicted (or acquitted) of the offense charged, by the judgment of the court of _____ (naming it), rendered at _____ (naming the place), on the _____ day of _____."
4. If he or she plead once in jeopardy: "The defendant pleads that he or she has been once in jeopardy for the offense charged (specifying the time, place, and court)."
5. If he or she plead not guilty by reason of insanity: "The defendant pleads that he or she is not guilty of the offense charged because he or she was insane at the time that he or she is alleged to have committed the unlawful act." *(Amended by Stats 1990 ch 632 §2, eff. 1/1/91.)*

§1018. Required appearance of defendant.

Unless otherwise provided by law, every plea shall be entered or withdrawn by the defendant himself or herself in open court. No plea of guilty of a felony for which the maximum punishment is death, or life imprisonment without the possibility of parole, shall be received from a defendant who does not appear with counsel, nor shall that plea be received without the consent of the defendant's counsel. No plea of guilty of a felony for which the maximum punishment is not death or life imprisonment without the possibility of parole shall be accepted from any defendant who does not appear with counsel unless the court shall first fully inform him or her of the right to counsel and unless the court shall find that the defendant understands the right to counsel and freely waives it, and then only if the defendant has expressly stated in open court, to the court, that he or she does not wish to be represented by counsel. On application of the defendant at any time before judgment or within six months after an order granting probation is made if entry of judgment is suspended, the court may, and in case of a defendant who appeared without counsel at the time of the plea the court shall, for a good cause shown, permit the plea of guilty to be withdrawn and a plea of not guilty substituted. Upon indictment or information against a corporation a plea of guilty may be put in by counsel. This section shall be liberally construed to effect these objects and to promote justice. *(Amended by Stats 1991 ch 421 §1, eff. 1/1/92.)*

§1019. Not guilty plea; allegations put in issue.

The plea of not guilty puts in issue every material allegation of the accusatory pleading, except those allegations regarding previous convictions of the defendant to which an answer is required by Section 1025.

§1020. Defenses may be given under plea of not guilty.

All matters of fact tending to establish a defense other than one specified in the fourth, fifth, and sixth subdivisions of Section 1016, may be given in evidence under the plea of not guilty.

§1021. Former acquittal.

If the defendant was formerly acquitted on the ground of variance between the accusatory pleading and the proof or the accusatory pleading was dismissed upon an objection to its form or substance, or in order to hold the defendant for a higher offense, without a judgment of acquittal, it is not an acquittal of the same offense.

§1022. Acquittal on merits.

Whenever the defendant is acquitted on the merits, he is acquitted of the same offense, notwithstanding any defect in form or substance in the accusatory pleading on which the trial was had.

§1023. Double jeopardy.

When the defendant is convicted or acquitted or has been once placed in jeopardy upon an accusatory pleading, the conviction, acquittal, or jeopardy is a bar to another prosecution for the offense charged in such accusatory pleading, or for an attempt to commit the same, or for an offense necessarily included therein, of which he might have been convicted under that accusatory pleading.

§1024. Refusal to answer accusatory pleading.

If the defendant refuses to answer the accusatory pleading, by demurrer or plea, a plea of not guilty must be entered.

§1025. Effect of previous conviction.

When a defendant who is charged in the accusatory pleading with having suffered a previous conviction pleads either guilty or not guilty of the offense charged against him, he must be asked whether he has suffered such previous conviction. If he answers that he has, his answer must be entered in the minutes of the court, and must, unless withdrawn by consent of the court, be conclusive of the fact of his having suffered such previous conviction in all subsequent proceedings. If he answers that he has not, his answer must be entered in the minutes of the court, and the question whether or not he has suffered such previous conviction must be tried by the jury which tries the issue upon the plea of not guilty, or in case of a plea of guilty, by a jury impaneled for that purpose, or by the court if a jury is waived. The refusal of the defendant to answer is equivalent to a denial that he has suffered such previous conviction. In case the defendant pleads not guilty, and answers that he has suffered the previous conviction, the charge of the previous conviction must not be read to the jury, nor alluded to on the trial.

§1026. Not guilty by reason of insanity plea.

(a) When a defendant pleads not guilty by reason of insanity, and also joins with it another plea or pleas, the defendant shall first be tried as if only such other plea or pleas had been entered, and in that trial the defendant shall be conclusively presumed to have been sane at the time the offense is alleged to have been committed. If the jury shall find the defendant guilty, or if the defendant pleads only not guilty by reason of insanity, then the question whether the defendant was sane or insane at the time the offense was committed shall be promptly tried, either before the same jury or before a new jury in the discretion of the court. In that trial, the jury shall return a verdict either that the defendant was sane at the time the offense was committed or was insane at the time the offense was committed. If the verdict or finding is that the defendant was sane at the time the offense was committed, the court shall sentence the defendant as provided by law. If the verdict or finding be that the defendant was insane at the time the offense was committed, the court, unless it shall appear to the court that the sanity of the defendant has been recovered fully, shall direct that the defendant be confined in a state hospital for the care and treatment of the mentally disordered or any other appropriate public or private treatment facility approved by the community program director, or the court may order the defendant placed on outpatient status pursuant to Title 15 (commencing with Section 1600) of Part 2.

(b) Prior to making the order directing that the defendant be confined in a state hospital or other treatment facility or placed on outpatient status, the court shall order the community program director or a designee to evaluate the defendant and to submit to the court within 15 judicial days of the order a written recommendation as to whether the defendant should be placed on outpatient status or confined in a state hospital or other treatment facility. No person shall be admitted to a state hospital or other treatment facility or placed on outpatient status under this section without having been evaluated by the community program director or a designee. If, however, it appears to the court that the sanity of the defendant has been recovered fully, the defendant shall be remanded to the custody of the sheriff until the issue of sanity shall

© 1992 by J., B. & L. Gould
Printed in the U.S.A.   EP

have been finally determined in the manner prescribed by law. A defendant committed to a state hospital or other treatment facility or placed on outpatient status pursuant to Title 15 (commencing with Section 1600) of Part 2 shall not be released from confinement, parole, or outpatient status unless and until the court which committed the person shall, after notice and hearing, find and determine that the person's sanity has been restored. Nothing in this section shall prevent the transfer of the patient from one state hospital to any other state hospital by proper authority. Nothing in this section shall prevent the transfer of the patient to a hospital in another state in the manner provided in Section 4119 of the Welfare and Institutions Code.

(c) If the defendant is committed or transferred to a state hospital pursuant to this section, the court may, upon receiving the written recommendation of the medical director of the state hospital and the community program director that the defendant be transferred to a public or private treatment facility approved by the community program director, order the defendant transferred to that facility. If the defendant is committed or transferred to a public or private treatment facility approved by the community program director, the court may, upon receiving the written recommendation of the community program director, order the defendant transferred to a state hospital or to another public or private treatment facility approved by the community program director. Where either the defendant or the prosecuting attorney chooses to contest either kind of order of transfer, a petition may be filed in the court requesting a hearing which shall be held if the court determines that sufficient grounds exist. At that hearing, the prosecuting attorney or the defendant may present evidence bearing on the order of transfer. The court shall use the same procedures and standards of proof as used in conducting probation revocation hearings pursuant to Section 1203.2.

(d) Prior to making an order for transfer under this section, the court shall notify the defendant, the attorney of record for the defendant, the prosecuting attorney, and the community program director or a designee.

(e) When the court, after considering the placement recommendation of the community program director required in subdivision (b), orders that the defendant be confined in a state hospital or other public or private treatment facility, the court shall provide copies of the following documents which shall be taken with the defendant to the state hospital or other treatment facility where the defendant is to be confined:

(1) The commitment order, including a specification of the charges.

(2) A computation or statement setting forth the maximum term of commitment in accordance with Section 1026.5.

(3) A computation or statement setting forth the amount of credit for time served, if any, to be deducted from the maximum term of commitment.

(4) State Summary Criminal History information.

(5) Any arrest reports prepared by the police department or other law enforcement agency.

(6) Any court-ordered psychiatric examination or evaluation reports.

(7) The community program director's placement recommendation report.

(f) If the defendant is confined in a state hospital or other treatment facility as an inpatient, the medical director of the facility shall, at six-month intervals, submit a report in writing to the court and the community program director of the county of commitment, or a designee, setting forth the status and progress of the defendant. The court shall transmit copies of these reports to the prosecutor and defense counsel.

(g) When directing that the defendant be confined in a state hospital pursuant to subdivision (a), the court shall select the state hospital in accordance with the policies established by the State Department of Mental Health.

(h) For purposes of this section and Sections 1026.1 to 1026.6, inclusive, "community program director" means the person, agency, or entity designated by the State Department of Mental Health pursuant to Section 1605 of this code and Section 5709.8 of the Welfare and Institutions Code. *(Amended by Stats 1989 ch 625 §1, eff. 1/1/90.)*

§1026.1. Release from state hospital or other facility.

A person committed to a state hospital or other treatment facility under the provisions of Section 1026 shall be released from the state hospital or other treatment facility only under one or more of the following circumstances:

(a) Pursuant to the provisions of Section 1026.2.

(b) Upon expiration of the maximum term of commitment as provided in subdivision (a) of Section 1026.5, except as such term may be extended under the provisions of subdivision (b) of Section 1026.5.

(c) As otherwise expressly provided in Title 15 (commencing with Section 1600) of Part 2.

§1026.2. Application for release; hearing.

(a) An application for the release of a person who has been committed to a state hospital or other treatment facility, as provided in Section 1026, upon the ground that sanity has been restored, may be made to the superior court of the county from which the commitment was made, either by the person, or by the medical director of the state hospital or other treatment facility to which the person is committed or by the community program director where the person is on outpatient status under Title 15 (commencing with Section 1600). The court shall give notice of the hearing date to the prosecuting attorney, the community program director or a designee, and the medical director or person in charge of the facility providing treatment to the committed person at least 15 judicial days in advance of the hearing date.

(b) Pending the hearing, the medical director or person in charge of the facility in which the person is confined shall prepare a summary of the person's programs of treatment and shall forward the summary to the community program director or a designee and to the court. The community program director or a designee shall review the summary and shall designate a facility within a reasonable distance from the court in which the person may be detained pending the hearing on the application for release. The facility so designated shall continue the program of treatment, shall provide adequate security, and shall, to the greatest extent possible, minimize interference with the person's program of treatment.

(c) A designated facility need not be approved for 72-hour treatment and evaluation pursuant to the provisions of the Lanterman-Petris-Short Act (Part 1 (commencing with Section 5000) of Division 5 of the Welfare and Institutions Code). However, a county jail may not be designated unless the services specified in subdivision (b) are provided and accommodations are provided which ensure both the safety of the person and the safety of the general population of the jail. If there is evidence that the treatment program is not being complied with or accommodations have not been provided which ensure both the safety of the committed person and the safety of the general population of the jail, the court shall order the person transferred to an appropriate facility or make any other appropriate order, including continuance of the proceedings.

(d) No hearing upon the application shall be allowed until the person committed has been confined or placed on outpatient status for a period of not less than 180 days from the date of the order of commitment.

(e) The court shall hold a hearing to determine if the person applying for restoration of sanity would no longer be a danger to the health and safety of others, including himself or herself, if under supervision and treatment in the community. If the court at the hearing determines the applicant will not be a danger to the health and safety of others, including himself or herself, while under supervision and treatment in the community, the court shall order the applicant placed with an appropriate forensic conditional release program for one year. All or a substantial portion of the program shall include outpatient supervision and treatment. The court shall retain jurisdiction. The court at the end of the one year, shall have a trial to determine if sanity has been restored, which means the applicant is no longer a danger to the health and safety of others, including himself or herself. The court shall not determine whether the applicant has been restored to sanity until the applicant has completed the one year in the appropriate forensic conditional release program. The court shall notify the persons required to be notified in subdivision (a) of the hearing date.

(f) If the applicant is on parole or outpatient status and has been on it for one year or longer, then it is deemed that the applicant has completed the required one year in an appropriate forensic conditional release program and the court shall, if all other applicable provisions of law have been met, hold the trial on restoration of sanity as provided for in this section.

(g) Before placing an applicant in an appropriate forensic conditional release program, the community program director shall submit to the court a written recommendation as to what forensic conditional release program is the most appropriate for supervising and treating the applicant. If the court does not accept the community program director's recommendation, the court shall specify the reason or reasons for its order on the court record. Sections 1605 to 1610, inclusive, shall be applicable to the person placed in the forensic conditional release program unless otherwise ordered by the court.

(h) If the court determines that the person should be transferred to an appropriate forensic conditional release program, the community program director or a designee shall make the necessary placement arrangements, and, within 21 days after receiving notice of the court finding, the person shall be placed in the community in accordance with the treatment and supervision plan, unless good cause for not doing so is made known to the court.

(i) If at the trial for restoration of sanity the court rules adversely to the applicant, the court may place the applicant on outpatient status, pursuant to Title 15 (commencing with Section 1600) of Part 2, unless the applicant does not meet all of the requirements of Section 1603.

(j) If the court denies the application to place the person in an appropriate forensic conditional release program or if restoration of sanity is denied, no new application may be filed by the person until one year has elapsed from the date of the denial.

(k) In any hearing authorized by this section, the applicant shall have the burden of proof by a preponderance of the evidence.

(l) If the application for the release is not made by the medical director of the state hospital or other treatment facility to which the person is committed or by the community program director where the person is on outpatient status under Title 15 (commencing with Section 1600), no action on the application shall be taken by the court without first obtaining the written recommendation of the medical director of the state hospital or other treatment facility or of the community program director where the person is on outpatient status under Title 15 (commencing with Section 1600).

(m) This section shall remain in effect only until January 1, 1994, and as of that date is repealed, unless a later enacted statute, which is enacted before January 1, 1994, deletes or extends that date. *(Amended by Stats 1991 ch 183 §1, eff. 1/1/92 only until 1/1/94. See other section 1026.2 below.)*

§1026.2. Application for release; hearing.

(a) An application for the release of a person who has been committed to a state hospital or other treatment facility, as provided in Section 1026, upon the ground that sanity has been restored, may be made to the superior court of the county from which the commitment was made, either by the person, or by the medical director of the state hospital or other treatment facility to which the person is committed or by the community program director where the person is on outpatient status under Title 15 (commencing with Section 1600) of Part 2. The court shall give notice of the hearing date to the prosecuting attorney, the community program director or a designee, and the medical director or person in charge of the facility providing treatment to the committed person at least 15 judicial days in advance of the hearing date.

(b) Pending the hearing, the medical director or person in charge of the facility in which the person is confined shall prepare a summary of the person's programs of treatment and shall forward the summary to the community program director or a designee and to the court. The community program director or a designee shall review the summary and shall designate a facility within a reasonable distance from the court in which the person may be detained pending the hearing on the application for release. The facility so designated shall continue the program of treatment, shall provide adequate security, and shall, to the greatest extent possible, minimize interference with the person's program of treatment.

(c) A designated facility need not be approved for 72-hour treatment and evaluation pursuant to the provisions of the Lanterman-Petris-Short Act (Part 1

© 1992 by J., B. & L. Gould
Printed in the U.S.A.   **EP**

(commencing with Section 5000) of Division 5 of the Welfare and Institutions Code); however, a county jail may not be designated unless the services specified above are provided, and accommodations are provided which ensure both the safety of the person and the safety of the general population of the jail. If there is evidence that the treatment program is not being complied with, or accommodations have not been provided which ensure both the safety of the committed person and the safety of the general population of the jail, the court shall order the person transferred to an appropriate facility or make any other appropriate order, including continuance of the proceedings.

(d) No hearing upon the application for release shall be allowed until the person committed shall have been confined or placed on outpatient status or on parole under Section 1611 for a period of not less than 90 days from the date of the order of commitment. If the finding of the court is adverse to releasing the person on the ground that sanity has not been restored, no application shall be filed by the person until one year has elapsed from the date of hearing upon the last preceding application. In any hearing authorized by this section, the burden of proving that sanity has been restored shall be upon the applicant. The court shall notify the community program director or a designee and the medical director or person in charge of the facility providing treatment to the committed person whether or not the defendant was found by the court to have recovered sanity.

(e) If the application for the release is not made by the medical director of the state hospital or other treatment facility to which the person is committed or by the community program director where the person is on outpatient status under Title 15 (commencing with Section 1600), no action on the application shall be taken by the court without first obtaining the written recommendation of the medical director of the state hospital or other treatment facility or by the community program director where the person is on outpatient status under Title 15 (commencing with Section 1600).

(f) This section shall become operative on January 1, 1994. *(Amended by Stats 1987 ch 1343 §2, eff. 1/1/94. See other section 1206.2 above.)*

§1026.3. Placement on outpatient status.

A person committed to a state hospital or other treatment facility under Section 1026, and a person placed pursuant to subdivision (e) of Section 1026.2 as amended by Section 3.5 of Chapter 1488 of the Statutes of 1984, may be placed on outpatient status from the commitment as provided in Title 15 (commencing with Section 1600) of Part 2. *(Amended by Stats 1985 ch 260 §2.)*

§1026.4. Escape from state hospital or other mental health facility.

(a) Every person committed to a state hospital or other public or private mental health facility pursuant to the provisions of Section 1026, who escapes from or who escapes while being conveyed to or from the state hospital or facility, is punishable by imprisonment in the county jail not to exceed one year or in a state prison for a determinate term of one year and one day. The term of imprisonment imposed pursuant to this section shall be served consecutively to any other sentence or commitment.

(b) The medical director or person in charge of a state hospital or other public or private mental health facility to which a person has been committed pursuant to the provisions of Section 1026 shall promptly notify the chief of police of the city in which the hospital or facility is located, or the sheriff of the county if the hospital or facility is located in an unincorporated area, of the escape of the person, and shall request the assistance of the chief of police or sheriff in apprehending the person, and shall within 48 hours of the escape of the person orally notify the court that made the commitment, the prosecutor in the case, and the Department of Justice of the escape. *(Amended by Stats 1989 ch 568 §1, eff. 1/1/90.)*

§1026.5. Determining the maximum term of commitment.

(a) (1) In the case of any person committed to a state hospital or other treatment facility pursuant to Section 1026 or placed on outpatient status pursuant to Section 1604, who committed a felony on or after July 1, 1977, the court shall state in the commitment order the maximum term of commitment, and the person may not be kept in actual custody longer than the maximum term of commitment, except as provided in this section. For the purposes of this section, "maximum term of commitment" shall mean the longest term of imprisonment which could have been imposed for the offense or offenses of which the person was convicted, including the upper term of the base offense and any additional terms for enhancements and consecutive sentences which could have been imposed less any applicable credits as defined by Section 2900.5, and disregarding any credits which could have been earned pursuant to Article 2.5 (commencing with Section 2930) of Chapter 7 of Title 1 of Part 3.

(2) In the case of a person confined in a state hospital or other treatment facility pursuant to Section 1026 or placed on outpatient status pursuant to Section 1604, who committed a felony prior to July 1, 1977, and who could have been sentenced under Section 1168 or 1170 if the offense was committed after July 1, 1977, the Board of Prison Terms shall determine the maximum term of commitment which could have been imposed under paragraph (1), and the person may not be kept in actual custody longer than the maximum term of commitment, except as provided in subdivision (b). The time limits of this section are not jurisdictional.

In fixing a term under this section, the board shall utilize the upper term of imprisonment which could have been imposed for the offense or offenses of which the person was convicted, increased by any additional terms which could have been imposed based on matters which were found to be true in the committing court. However, if at least two of the members of the board after reviewing the person's file determine that a longer term should be imposed for the reasons specified in Section 1170.2, a longer term may be imposed following the procedures and guidelines set forth in Section 1170.2, except that any hearings deemed necessary by the board shall be held within 90 days of September 28, 1979. Within 90 days of the date the person is received by the state hospital or other treatment facility, or of September 28, 1979, whichever is later, the Board of Prison Terms shall provide each person with the determination of the person's maximum term of commitment or shall notify the person that a hearing will be scheduled to determine the term.

Within 20 days following the determination of the maximum term of commitment the board shall provide the person, the prosecuting attorney, the committing court, and the state hospital or other treatment facility with a written statement setting forth the maximum term of commitment, the calculations, and any materials considered in determining the maximum term.

(3) In the case of a person committed to a state hospital or other treatment facility pursuant to Section 1026 or placed on outpatient status pursuant to Section 1604 who committed a misdemeanor, the maximum term of commitment shall be the longest term of county jail confinement which could have been imposed for the offense or offenses which the person was found to have committed, and the person may not be kept in actual custody longer than this maximum term.

(4) Nothing in this subdivision limits the power of any state hospital or other treatment facility or of the committing court to release the person, conditionally or otherwise, for any period of time allowed by any other provision of law.

(b) (1) A person may be committed beyond the term prescribed by subdivision (a) only under the procedure set forth in this subdivision and only if the person has been committed under Section 1026 for a felony and by reason of a mental disease, defect, or disorder represents a substantial danger of physical harm to others.

(2) Not later than 180 days prior to the termination of the maximum term of commitment prescribed in subdivision (a), the medical director of a state hospital in which the person is being treated, or the medical director of the person's treatment facility or the local program director, if the person is being treated outside a state hospital setting, shall submit to the prosecuting attorney his or her opinion as to whether or not the patient is a person described in paragraph (1). If requested by the prosecuting attorney, the opinion shall be accompanied by supporting evaluations and relevant hospital records. The prosecuting attorney may then file a petition for extended commitment in the superior court which issued the original commitment. The petition shall be filed no later than 90 days before the expiration of the original commitment unless good cause is shown. The petition shall state the reasons for the extended commitment, with accompanying affidavits specifying the factual basis for believing that the person meets each of the requirements set forth in paragraph (1).

(3) When the petition is filed, the court shall advise the person named in the petition of the right to be represented by an attorney and of the right to a jury trial. The rules of discovery in criminal cases shall apply. If the person is being treated in a state hospital when the petition is filed, the court shall notify the community program director of the petition and the hearing date.

(4) The court shall conduct a hearing on the petition for extended commitment. The trial shall be by jury unless waived by both the person and the prosecuting attorney. The trial shall commence no later than 30 calendar days prior to the time the person would otherwise have been released, unless that time is waived by the person or unless good cause is shown.

(5) Pending the hearing, the medical director or person in charge of the facility in which the person is confined shall prepare a summary of the person's programs of treatment and shall forward the summary to the community program director or a designee, and to the court. The community program director or a designee shall review the summary and shall designate a facility within a reasonable distance from the court in which the person may be detained pending the hearing on the petition for extended commitment. The facility so designated shall continue the program of treatment, shall provide adequate security, and shall, to the greatest extent possible, minimize interference with the person's program of treatment.

(6) A designated facility need not be approved for 72-hour treatment and evaluation pursuant to the provisions of the Lanterman-Petris-Short Act (Part 1 (commencing with Section 5000) of Division 5 of the Welfare and Institutions Code). However, a county jail may not be designated unless the services specified in paragraph (5) are provided and accommodations are provided which ensure both the safety of the person and the safety of the general population of the jail. If there is evidence that the treatment program is not being complied with or accommodations have not been provided which ensure both the safety of the committed person and the safety of the general population of the jail, the court shall order the person transferred to an appropriate facility or make any other appropriate order, including continuance of the proceedings.

(7) The person shall be entitled to the rights guaranteed under the federal and State Constitutions for criminal proceedings. All proceedings shall be in accordance with applicable constitutional guarantees. The state shall be represented by the district attorney who shall notify the Attorney General in writing that a case has been referred under this section. If the person is indigent, the county public defender or State Public Defender shall be appointed. The State Public Defender may provide for representation of the person in any manner authorized by Section 15402 of the Government Code. Appointment of necessary psychologists or psychiatrists shall be made in accordance with this article and Penal Code and Evidence Code provisions applicable to criminal defendants who have entered pleas of not guilty by reason of insanity.

(8) If the court or jury finds that the patient is a person described in paragraph (1), the court shall order the patient recommitted to the facility in which the patient was confined at the time the petition was filed. This commitment shall be for an additional period of two years from the date of termination of the previous commitment.

(9) A person committed under this subdivision shall be eligible for release to outpatient status pursuant to the provisions of Title 15 (commencing with Section 1600) of Part 2.

(10) Prior to termination of a commitment under this subdivision, a petition for recommitment may be filed to determine whether the patient remains a person described in paragraph (1). The recommitment proceeding shall be conducted in accordance with the provisions of this subdivision.

(11) Any commitment under this subdivision places an affirmative obligation on the treatment facility to provide treatment for the underlying causes of the person's mental disorder. *(Amended by Stats 1991 ch 183 §2, eff. 1/1/92.)*

© 1992 by J., B. & L. Gould
Printed in the U.S.A.   **EP**

§1026.6. Notification upon release.

Whenever any person who has been committed to a state hospital pursuant to Section 1026 is released for any reason, including placement on outpatient status, the director of the hospital shall notify the community program director of the county, and the chief law enforcement officer of the jurisdiction, in which the person will reside upon release, if that information is available. *(Amended by Stats 1986 ch 64 §1.)*

§1027. Examination by psychiatrists and licensed psychologists.

(a) When a defendant pleads not guilty by reason of insanity the court must select and appoint two, and may select and appoint three, psychiatrists, or licensed psychologists who have a doctoral degree in psychology and at least five years of postgraduate experience in the diagnosis and treatment of emotional and mental disorders, to examine the defendant and investigate his mental status. It is the duty of the psychiatrists or psychologists so selected and appointed to make the examination and investigation, and to testify, whenever summoned, in any proceeding in which the sanity of the defendant is in question. The psychiatrists or psychologists so appointed by the court shall be allowed, in addition to their actual traveling expenses, such fees as in the discretion of the court seems just and reasonable, having regard to the services rendered by the witnesses. The fees allowed shall be paid by the county where the indictment was found or in which the defendant was held for trial.

(b) Any report on the examination and investigation made pursuant to subdivision (a) shall include, but not be limited to, the psychological history of the defendant, the facts surrounding the commission of the acts forming the basis for the present charge used by the psychiatrist or psychologist in making his examination of the defendant, and the present psychological or psychiatric symptoms of the defendant, if any.

(c) This section does not presume that a psychiatrist or psychologist can determine whether a defendant was sane or insane at the time of the alleged offense. This section does not limit a court's discretion to admit or exclude, pursuant to the Evidence Code, psychiatric or psychological evidence about the defendant's state of mind or mental or emotional condition at the time of the alleged offense.

(d) Nothing contained in this section shall be deemed or construed to prevent any party to any criminal action from producing any other expert evidence with respect to the mental status of the defendant; where expert witnesses are called by the district attorney in such action, they shall only be entitled to such witness fees as may be allowed by the court.

(e) Any psychiatrist or psychologist so appointed by the court may be called by either party to the action or by the court itself and when so called shall be subject to all legal objections as to competency and bias and as to qualifications as an expert. When called by the court, or by either party, to the action, the court may examine the psychiatrist, or psychologist as deemed necessary, but either party shall have the same right to object to the questions asked by the court and the evidence adduced as though the psychiatrist or psychologist were a witness for the adverse party. When the psychiatrist or psychologist is called and examined by the court the parties may cross-examine him in the order directed by the court. When called by either party to the action the adverse party may examine him the same as in the case of any other witness called by such party.

CHAPTER 5

TRANSMISSION OF CERTAIN INDICTMENTS AND INFORMATIONS

§1029. Transmission of certificates; assignment of judge.

When an indictment is found or an information filed in the superior court against a judge thereof, a certificate of that fact must be transmitted by the clerk to the chairman of the Judicial Council, who shall thereupon designate and assign a judge of the superior court of another county to preside at the trial of such indictment or information, and hear and determine all pleas and motions affecting the defendant thereunder before and after judgment.

CHAPTER 6

CHANGE OF VENUE

§1033. Reasons for change of venue in superior court.

In a criminal action pending in the superior court, the court shall order a change of venue:

(a) On motion of the defendant, to another county when it appears that there is a reasonable likelihood that a fair and impartial trial cannot be had in the county. When a change of venue is ordered by the superior court, it shall be for the trial itself. All proceedings before trial shall occur in the county of original venue, except when it is evident that a particular proceeding must be heard by the judge who is to preside over the trial.

(b) On its own motion or on motion of any party, to an adjoining county when it appears as a result of the exhaustion of all of the jury panels called that it will be impossible to secure a jury to try the cause in the county.

§1034. Reasons for change of venue in municipal or justice court.

In a criminal action pending in a municipal or justice court, the court shall order a change of venue:

(1) On motion of the defendant, to another judicial district when it appears that there is a reasonable likelihood that a fair and impartial trial cannot be had in the judicial district. When a change of venue is ordered by a municipal or justice court, it shall be for the trial itself. All proceedings before trial shall occur in the judicial district of original venue, except when it is evident that a particular proceeding must be heard by the judge who is to preside over the trial.

(2) On its own motion or on motion of any party, to an adjoining judicial district in the same county when it appears as a result of the exhaustion of all of the jury panels called that it will be impossible to secure a jury to try the cause in the judicial district or, when for the same reason it appears that it will be impossible to try the cause in any judicial district in the county, to a judicial district in an adjoining county.

§1035. Convenience of parties.

(a) In a criminal action pending in a municipal or justice court, the court shall order a change of venue to another judicial district in the same county on motion of the prosecution if it appears that the change will be for the convenience of all parties to the action and the defendant and his attorney, if any, consent in writing to the change.

(b) A defendant arrested, held, or present in a county other than that in which an indictment, information, felony complaint, or felony probation violation is pending against the defendant, may state in writing his or her agreement to plead guilty or nolo contendere to some or all of the pending charges, to waive trial or hearing in the county in which the pleading is pending, and to consent to disposition of the case in the county in which that defendant was arrested, held, or present, subject to the approval of the district attorney for each county. Upon receipt of the defendant's statement and of the written approval of the district attorneys, the clerk of the court in which the pleading is pending shall transmit the papers in the proceeding or certified copies thereof to the clerk of the court for the county in which the defendant is arrested, held, or present, and the prosecution shall continue in that county. However, the proceedings shall be limited solely to the purposes of plea and sentencing and not for trial. If, after the proceeding has been transferred pursuant to this section, the defendant pleads not guilty, the clerk shall return the papers to the court in which the prosecution was commenced and the proceeding shall be restored to the docket of that court. The defendant's statement that the defendant wishes to plead guilty or nolo contendere shall not be used against the defendant. *(Amended by Stats 1990 ch 632 §4, eff. 1/1/91.)*

§1036. Sheriff to deliver defendant to custody of sheriff of other county.

(a) Unless the court reserves jurisdiction to hear other pretrial motions, if a defendant is incarcerated and the court orders a change of venue to another county, the court shall direct the sheriff to deliver the defendant to the custody of the sheriff of the other county for the purpose of trial.

(b) If the defendant is incarcerated and the court orders that the jury be selected from the county to which the venue would otherwise have been transferred pursuant to Section 1036.7, the court shall direct the sheriff to deliver the defendant to the custody of the sheriff of that county for the purpose of jury selection. *(Amended by Stats 1987 ch 780 §1.)*

§1036.5. Court motion to set aside order.

Following the resolution of pre-trial motions, and prior to the issuance of an order under Section 1036 or the transmittal of the case file for the purpose of trial to the court to which venue has been ordered transferred, the court may, upon its own motion or the motion of any party and on appropriate notice to the court to which venue has been transferred, set aside its order to change venue on the ground that the conditions which originally required the order to change venue, as set forth in Section 1033 or 1034, no longer apply.

§1036.7. Change of venue ordered.

When a change of venue is ordered and the court, upon motion to transfer a jury or on its own motion and upon unanimous consent of all defendants, deter-

mines that it would be in the interests of the administration of justice to move the jury rather than to move the pending action, a change of venue may be accomplished by the selection of a jury in the county or judicial district to which the venue would otherwise have been transferred, and the selected jury shall be moved to the court in which the criminal action is pending. *(Added by Stats 1987 ch 780 §2.)*

§1037. Charging costs incurred by county.

(a) When a court orders a change of venue to another county all costs incurred by that county, which are not payable pursuant to Section 4750, for the transfer, preparation and trial of the action, the guarding, keeping and transportation of the prisoner, any appeal or other proceeding relating to the action and execution of the sentence shall be a charge against the county in which the action originated.

(b) Claim for the costs described in subdivision (a) shall be forwarded to the treasurer and auditor of the county in which the action originated and the treasurer shall pay the amount of such costs out of the general funds of the county.

(c) The term "all costs" means all reasonable and necessary costs incurred by the county as a result of the change of venue which would not have been incurred but for the change, and does not include normal salaries, overhead, and other expenses which would have been incurred by the county in any event.

(d) The trial court may, in its sound discretion, approve any cost as reasonable and necessary under this section. Prior to the trial court's issuing any order approving such a cost, the clerk shall give 10 days' written notice of the court's intention to issue an order to the auditor of the county in which the action originated. The auditor may appear for the limited purpose of opposing the issuance of the order. If he or she fails to appear, the county of origin may not in any other proceeding contest the imposition of these costs. *(Amended by Stats 1988 ch 235 §1, eff. 1/1/89.)*

§1038. Rules of practice and procedure.

The Judicial Council shall adopt rules of practice and procedure for the change of venue in criminal actions.

CHAPTER 7

THE MODE OF TRIAL

§1041. Arising of issues of fact.

An issue of fact arises:

1. Upon a plea of not guilty.

2. Upon a plea of a former conviction or acquittal of the same offense.

3. Upon a plea of once in jeopardy.

4. Upon a plea of not guilty by reason of insanity.

§1042. Provision.

Issues of fact shall be tried in the manner provided in Article 1, section 7 of the Constitution of this State.

§1042.5. Trial of infraction and public offense.

Trial of an infraction shall be by the court, but when a defendant has been charged with an infraction and with a public offense for which there is a right to jury trial and a jury trial is not waived, the court may order that the offenses be tried together by jury or that they be tried separately with the infraction being tried by

© 1992 by J., B. & L. Gould
Printed in the U.S.A.   **EP**

the court either in the same proceeding or a separate proceeding as may be appropriate.

§1043. Personal presence of defendant; exceptions.

(a) Except as otherwise provided in this section, the defendant in a felony case shall be personally present at the trial.

(b) The absence of the defendant in a felony case after the trial has commenced in his presence shall not prevent continuing the trial to, and including, the return of the verdict in any of the following cases:

(1) Any case in which the defendant, after he has been warned by the judge that he will be removed if he continues his disruptive behavior, nevertheless insists on conducting himself in a manner so disorderly, disruptive, and disrespectful of the court that the trial cannot be carried on with him in the courtroom.

(2) Any prosecution for an offense which is not punishable by death in which the defendant is voluntarily absent.

(c) Any defendant who is absent from a trial pursuant to paragraph (1) of subdivision (b) may reclaim his right to be present at the trial as soon as he is willing to conduct himself consistently with the decorum and respect inherent in the concept of courts and judicial proceedings.

(d) Subdivisions (a) and (b) shall not limit the right of a defendant to waive his right to be present in accordance with Section 977.

(e) If the defendant in a misdemeanor case fails to appear in person at the time set for trial or during the course of trial, the court shall proceed with the trial, unless good cause for a continuance exists, if the defendant has authorized his counsel to proceed in his absence pursuant to subdivision (a) of Section 977.

If there is no authorization pursuant to subdivision (a) of Section 977 and if the defendant fails to appear in person at the time set for trial or during the course of trial, the court, in its discretion, may do one or more of the following, as it deems appropriate:

(1) Continue the matter.

(2) Order bail forfeited or revoke release on the defendant's own recognizance.

(3) Issue a bench warrant.

(4) Proceed with the trial if the court finds the defendant has absented himself voluntarily with full knowledge that the trial is to be held or is being held.

Nothing herein shall limit the right of the court to order the defendant to be personally present at the trial for purposes of identification unless counsel stipulate to the issue of identity.

§1043.5. Personal presence of defendant at preliminary hearing; exceptions.

(a) Except as otherwise provided in this section, the defendant in a preliminary hearing shall be personally present.

(b) The absence of the defendant in a preliminary hearing after the hearing has commenced in his presence shall not prevent continuing the hearing to, and including, holding to answer, filing an information, or discharging the defendant in any of the following cases:

(1) Any case in which the defendant, after he has been warned by the judge that he will be removed if he continued his disruptive behavior, nevertheless insists on conducting himself in a manner so disorderly, disruptive, and disrespectful of the court that the

hearing cannot be carried on with him in the courtroom.

(2) Any prosecution for an offense which is not punishable by death in which the defendant is voluntarily absent.

(c) Any defendant who is absent from a preliminary hearing pursuant to paragraph (1) of subdivision (b) may reclaim his right to be present at the hearing as soon as he is willing to conduct himself consistently with the decorum and respect inherent in the concept of courts and judicial proceedings.

(d) Subdivisions (a) and (b) shall not limit the right of a defendant to waive his right to be present in accordance with Section 977.

§1044. Judges' duties.

It shall be the duty of the judge to control all proceedings during the trial, and to limit the introduction of evidence and the argument of counsel to relevant and material matters, with a view to the expeditious and effective ascertainment of the truth regarding the matters involved.

§1045. Verbatim record requested.

In any misdemeanor or infraction matter, where a verbatim record of the proceedings is not required to be made and where the right of a party to request a verbatim record is not provided for pursuant to any other provision of law or rule of court, if any party makes a request at least five days in advance and deposits the required fees, the court shall order that a verbatim record be made of all proceedings. Except as otherwise provided by law or rule the party requesting any reporting, recording, or transcript pursuant to this section shall pay the cost of such reporting, recording, or transcript.

This section shall cease to be operative upon a final decision of an appellate court holding that there is a constitutional right or other requirement that a verbatim record or transcript be provided at public expense for indigent or any other defendants in cases subject to the provisions of this section.

CHAPTER 8

FORMATION OF THE TRIAL JURY AND THE CALENDAR OF ISSUES FOR TRIAL

§1046. Formation of trial jury.

Trial juries for criminal actions are formed in the same manner as trial juries in civil actions.

§§1046a, 1046.5. *Repealed by Stats 1988 ch 1245 §§15, 16, eff. 1/1/89.*

§1047. *Repealed by Stats 1989 ch 897 §27, eff. 1/1/90.*

§1048. Order of disposing of issues.

(a) The issues on the calendar shall be disposed of in the following order, unless for good cause the court directs an action to be tried out of its order:

(1) Prosecutions for felony, when the defendant is in custody.

(2) Prosecutions for misdemeanor, when the defendant is in custody.

(3) Prosecutions for felony, when the defendant is on bail.

(4) Prosecutions for misdemeanor, when the defendant is on bail.

(b) Notwithstanding subdivision (a), all criminal actions in which (1) a minor is detained as a material witness or is the victim of the alleged offense, (2) a person who was 70 years of age or older at the time of the alleged offense or is a dependent adult, as defined in subdivision (d) of Section 368, was a witness to, or is the victim of, the alleged offense or (3) any person is a victim of an alleged violation of Section 261, 264.1, 273a, 273d, 285, 286, 288, 288a, or 289, committed by the use of force, violence, or the threat thereof, shall be given precedence over all other criminal actions in the order of trial. In those actions, continuations shall be granted by the court only after a hearing and determination of the necessity thereof, and in any event, the trial shall be commenced within 30 days after arraignment, unless for good cause the court shall direct the action to be continued, after a hearing and determination of the necessity of the continuance, and states the findings for a determination of good cause on the record.

(c) Nothing in this section shall be deemed to provide a statutory right to a trial within 30 days. *(Amended by Stats 1986 ch 588 §1.)*

§1048.01. Pilot project in Alameda County.

(a) Notwithstanding Section 1048, there is hereby created in Alameda County a pilot project whereby the issues on the calendar shall be disposed of in the following order, unless for good cause the court directs an action to be tried out of its order:

(1) Prosecutions for felony, when the defendant is in custody.

(2) Prosecutions for misdemeanor, when the defendant is in custody.

(3) Prosecution of a defendant who is an alleged serious drug offender.

(4) Prosecutions for felony, when the defendant is on bail.

(5) Prosecutions for misdemeanor, when the defendant is on bail.

(b) Notwithstanding subdivision (a), all criminal actions in which (1) minor is detained as a material witness or is the victim of the alleged offense, (2) a person who was 70 years of age or older at the time of the alleged offense or is a dependent adult, as defined in subdivision (d) of Section 368, was a witness to, or is the victim of, the alleged offense or (3) any person is a victim of an alleged violation of Section 261, 264.1, 273a, 273d, 285, 286, 288, 288a, or 289, committed by the use of force, violence, or the threat thereof, shall be given precedence over all other criminal actions in the order of trial. In those actions, continuations shall be granted by the court only after a hearing and determination of the necessity thereof, and in any event, the trial shall be commenced within 30 days after arraignment, unless for good cause the court shall direct the action to be continued, after a hearing and determination of the necessity of the continuance, and states the findings for a determination of good cause on the record.

(c) For purposes of this section only, "an alleged serious drug offender" means any of the following:

(1) A defendant who is charged with a violation of Section 11353, 11353.5, 11361, 11379.6, 11380, 11380.5, or 11383 of the Health and Safety Code.

(2) A defendant who is charged with an enhancement that is set forth in Section 11370.4 or 11379.8 of the Health and Safety Code.

(3) A defendant who is charged with an offense that is set forth in Section 11351, 11351.5, 11352, 11378, 11378.5, 11379, 11379.5, 11379.6, or 11383 of the Health and Safety Code and has two or more prior convictions for any of these offenses.

(4) A defendant who has been released from custody on bail or on his or her own recognizance for an offense set forth in paragraph (3) and prior to judgment becoming final is charged with another offense set forth in paragraph (3).

(d) Nothing in this section shall be deemed to provide a statutory right to trial within 30 days.

(e) This section shall remain in effect only until January 1, 1994, and as of that date is repealed unless a later enacted statute, which is enacted before January 1, 1994, deletes or extends that date. *(Added by Stats 1988 ch 1246 §1, eff. 1/1/89 only until 1/1/94.)*

§1048.1. Scheduling a trial date in superior court for sexual assault offense.

In scheduling a trial date at an arraignment in superior court involving an alleged sexual assault offense, as described in paragraph (1) of subdivision (b) of Section 11165, or an alleged child abuse offense, as described in subdivision (g) of Section 11165, reasonable efforts shall be made to avoid setting that trial, as assigned to a particular prosecuting attorney, on the same day that another trial is set involving the same prosecuting attorney. *(Added by Stats 1987 ch 461 §2.)*

§1049. Time allowed to prepare for trial.

After his plea, the defendant is entitled to at least five days to prepare for trial.

§1049.5. Scheduling felony cases.

In felony cases, the court shall set a date for trial which is within 60 days of the defendant's arraignment in the superior court unless, upon a showing of good cause as prescribed in Section 1050, the court lengthens the time. If the court, after a hearing as prescribed in Section 1050, finds that there is good cause to set the date for trial beyond the 60 days, it shall state on the record the facts proved that justify its finding. A statement of facts proved shall be entered in the minutes. *(Added by Initiative Measure, Prop 115 §21, approved 6/5/90.)*

§1050. Criminal cases' precedence.

(a) The welfare of the people of the State of California requires that all proceedings in criminal cases shall be set for trial and heard and determined at the earliest possible time. To this end the Legislature finds that the criminal courts are becoming increasingly congested with resulting adverse consequences to the welfare of the people and the defendant. Excessive continuances contribute substantially to this congestion and cause substantial hardship to victims and other witnesses. Continuances also lead to longer periods of presentence confinement for those defendants in custody and the concomitant overcrowding and increased expenses of local jails. It is therefore recognized that the people, the defendant, and the victims and other witnesses have the right to an expeditious disposition, and to that end it shall be the duty of all

© 1992 by J., B. & L. Gould
Printed in the U.S.A.   **EP**

courts and judicial officers and of all counsel, both for the prosecution and the defense, to expedite these proceedings to the greatest degree that is consistent with the ends of justice. In accordance with this policy, criminal cases shall be given precedence over, and set for trial and heard without regard to the pendency of, any civil matters or proceedings.

(b) To continue any hearing in a criminal proceeding, including the trial, (1) a written notice shall be filed and served on all parties to the proceeding at least two court days before the hearing sought to be continued, together with affidavits or declarations detailing specific facts showing that a continuance is necessary; and (2), within two court days of learning that he or she has a conflict in the scheduling of any court hearing, including a trial, an attorney shall notify the calendar clerk of each court involved, in writing, indicating which hearing was set first. A party shall not be deemed to have been served within the meaning of this section until that party actually has received a copy of the documents to be served, unless the party, after receiving actual notice of the request for continuance, waives the right to have the documents served in a timely manner. Regardless of the proponent of the motion, the prosecuting attorney shall notify people's witnesses and the defense attorney shall notify defense's witnesses of the notice of motion, the date of the hearing, and the witnesses' right to be heard by the court. The superior and municipal courts of a county may adopt rules, which shall be consistent, regarding the method of giving the notice or waiver of service required by this subdivision, where a continuance is sought because of a conflict between scheduled appearances in the courts of that county.

(c) Notwithstanding subdivision (b), a party may make a motion for a continuance without complying with the requirements of that subdivision. However, unless the moving party shows good cause for the failure to comply with those requirements, the court may impose sanctions as provided in Section 1050.5.

(d) When a party makes a motion for a continuance without complying with the requirements of subdivision (b), the court shall hold a hearing on whether there is good cause for the failure to comply with those requirements. At the conclusion of the hearing the court shall make a finding whether good cause has been shown and if it finds that there is good cause, shall state on the record the facts proved that justify its finding. A statement of the finding and a statement of facts proved shall be entered in the minutes. If the moving party is unable to show good cause for the failure to give notice, the motion for continuance shall not be granted.

(e) Continuances shall be granted only upon a showing of good cause. Neither the convenience of the parties nor a stipulation of the parties is in and of itself good cause.

(f) At the conclusion of the motion for continuance, the court shall make a finding whether good cause has been shown and, if it finds that there is good cause, shall state on the record the facts proved that justify its finding. A statement of facts proved shall be entered in the minutes.

(g) When deciding whether or not good cause for a continuance has been shown, the court shall consider the general convenience and prior commitments of all witnesses, including peace officers. Both the general convenience and prior commitments of each witness also shall be considered in selecting a continuance date if the motion is granted. The facts as to inconvenience or prior commitments may be offered by the witness or by a party to the case.

For purposes of this section, "good cause" includes, but is not limited to, those cases involving allegations that a violation of one or more of the sections specified in subdivision (a) of Section 11165.1 or Section 11165.6 has occurred and the prosecuting attorney assigned to the case has another trial, preliminary hearing, or motion to suppress in progress in that court or another court. A continuance under this paragraph shall be limited to a maximum of 10 additional court days.

(h) Upon a showing that the attorney of record at the time of the defendant's first appearance in the superior court is a Member of the Legislature of this state and that the Legislature is in session or that a legislative interim committee of which the attorney is a duly appointed member is meeting or is to meet within the next seven days, the defendant shall be entitled to a reasonable continuance not to exceed 30 days.

(i) A continuance shall be granted only for that period of time shown to be necessary by the evidence considered at the hearing on the motion. Whenever any continuance is granted, the court shall state on the record the facts proved that justify the length of the continuance, and those facts shall be entered in the minutes.

(j) Whenever it shall appear that any court may be required, because of the condition of its calendar, to dismiss an action pursuant to Section 1382, the court must immediately notify the Chairman of the Judicial Council.

(k) This section shall not apply when the preliminary examination is set on a date less than 10 court days from the date of the defendant's arraignment on the complaint, and the prosecution or the defendant moves to continue the preliminary examination to a date not more than 10 court days from the date of the defendant's arraignment on the complaint. (Amended by Stats 1989 ch 897 §27.5, eff. 1/1/90.)

§1050.1. Jointly charged defendants.

In any case in which two or more defendants are jointly charged in the same complaint, indictment, or information, and the court or magistrate, for good cause shown, continues the arraignment, preliminary hearing, or trial of one or more defendants, the continuance shall, upon motion of the prosecuting attorney, constitute good cause to continue the remaining defendants' cases so as to maintain joinder. The court or magistrate shall not cause jointly charged cases to be severed due to the unavailability or unpreparedness of one or more defendants unless it appears to the court or magistrate that it will be impossible for all defendants to be available and prepared within a reasonable period of time. (Added by Initiative Measure, Prop 115 §22, approved 6/5/90.)

§1050.5. Continuance based upon inability of material witness or defendant to attend.

(a) When, pursuant to subdivision (c) of Section 1050, the court imposes sanctions for failure to comply with the provisions of subdivision (b) of Section 1050, the court may impose one or both of the following sanctions when the moving party is the prosecuting or defense attorney:

(1) A fine not exceeding one thousand dollars ($1,000) upon counsel for the moving party.

(2) The filing of a report with an appropriate disciplinary committee.

(b) The authority to impose sanctions provided for by this section shall be in addition to any other authority or power available to the court. *(Added by Stats 1985 ch 949 §3.)*

§1051. Continuance after defense witness testifies.

Upon a trial for any offense, if a defense witness testifies, there shall be good cause for a reasonable continuance unless the court finds that the prosecutor was or should, with due diligence, have been aware of such evidence. If the continuance is granted because of the defendant's testimony, it shall not exceed one day.

CHAPTER 9

POSTPONEMENT OF THE TRIAL

§1053. Substitution of judges.

If after the commencement of the trial of a criminal action or proceeding in any court the judge or justice presiding at such trial shall die, become ill, or for any other reason be unable to proceed with the trial, any other judge or justice of the court in which the trial is proceeding may proceed with and finish the trial; or if there be no other judge or justice of that court available, then the clerk, sheriff, marshal or constable shall adjourn the court and notify the Chairman of the Judicial Council of the facts, and shall continue the case from day to day until such time as said chairman shall designate and assign a judge or justice of some other court, and such judge or justice shall arrive, to proceed with and complete the trial, or until such time as by stipulation in writing between the prosecuting attorney and the attorney for the defendant, filed with the court, a judge or justice shall be agreed upon by them, and such judge or justice shall arrive to complete said trial. The judge or justice authorized by the provision of this section to proceed with and complete the trial shall have the same power, authority and jurisdiction as if the trial had been commenced before such judge or justice.

CHAPTER 10

DISCOVERY
(Added by Initiative Measure, Prop 115 §23, approved 6/5/90.)

§1054. Purpose of chapter.

This chapter shall be interpreted to give effect to all of the following purposes:

(a) To promote the ascertainment of truth in trials by requiring timely pretrial discovery.

(b) To save court time by requiring that discovery be conducted informally between and among the parties before judicial enforcement is requested.

(c) To save court time in trial and avoid the necessity for frequent interruptions and postponements.

(d) To protect victims and witnesses from danger, harrassment, and undue delay of the proceedings.

(e) To provide that no discovery shall occur in criminal cases except as provided by this chapter, other express statutory provisions, or as mandated by the Constitution of the United States. *(Added by Initiative Measure, Prop 115 §23, approved 6/5/90.)*

§1054.1. Disclosure of information from prosecuting attorney.

The prosecuting attorney shall disclose to the defendant or his or her attorney all of the following materials and information, if it is in the possession of the prosecuting attorney or if the prosecuting attorney knows it to be in the possession of the investigating agencies:

(a) The names and addresses of persons the prosecutor intends to call as witnesses at trial.

(b) Statements of all defendants.

(c) All relevant real evidence seized or obtained as a part of the investigation of the offenses charged.

(d) The existence of a felony conviction of any material witness whose credibility is likely to be critical to the outcome of the trial.

(e) Any exculpatory evidence.

(f) Relevant written or recorded statements of witnesses or reports of the statements of witnesses whom the prosecutor intends to call at the trial, including any reports or statements of experts made in conjunction with the case, including the results of physical or mental examinations, scientific tests, experiments, or comparisons which the prosecutor intends to offer in evidence at the trial. *(Added by Initiative Measure, Prop 115 §23, approved 6/5/90.)*

§1054.2. Nondisclosure of telephone numbers.

No attorney may disclose or permit to be disclosed to a defendant the address or telephone number of a victim or witness whose name is disclosed to the attorney pursuant to subdivision (a) of Section 1054.1 unless specifically permitted to do so by the court after a hearing and a showing of good cause. *(Added by Initiative Measure, Prop 115 §23, approved 6/5/90.)*

§1054.3. Disclosure of information from defendant.

The defendant and his or her attorney shall disclose to the prosecuting attorney:

(a) The names and address of persons, other than the defendant, he or she intends to call as witnesses at trial, together with any relevant written or recorded statements of those persons, or reports of the statements of those persons, including any reports or statements of experts made in connection with the case, and including the results of physical or mental examinations, scientific tests, experiments, or comparisons which the defendant intends to offer in evidence at the trial.

(b) Any real evidence which the defendant intends to offer in evidence at the trial. *(Added by Initiative Measure, Prop 115 §23, approved 6/5/90.)*

§1054.4. Nontestimonial information.

Nothing in this chapter shall be construed as limiting any law enforcement or prosecuting agency from obtaining nontestimonial evidence to the extent permitted by law on the effective date of this section. *(Added by Initiative Measure, Prop 115 §23, approved 6/5/90.)*

§1054.5. Obtaining discovery information as specified this chapter.

(a) No order requiring discovery shall be made in criminal cases except as provided in this chapter. This

© 1992 by J., B. & L. Gould
Printed in the U.S.A.　　EP

chapter shall be the only means by which the defendant may compel the disclosure or production of information from prosecuting attorneys, law enforcement agencies which investigated or prepared the case against the defendant, or any other persons or agencies which the prosecuting attorney or investigating agency may have employed to assist them in performing their duties.

(b) Before a party may seek court enforcement of any of the disclosures required by this chapter, the party shall make an informal request of opposing counsel for the desired materials and information. If within 15 days the opposing counsel fails to provide the materials and information requested, the party may seek a court order. Upon a showing that a party has not complied with Section 1054.1 or 1054.3 and upon a showing that the moving party complied with the informal discovery procedure provided in this subdivision, a court may make any order necessary to enforce the provisions of this chapter, including, but not limited to, immediate disclosure, contempt proceedings, delaying or prohibiting the testimony of a witness or the presentation of real evidence, continuance of the matter, or any other lawful order. Further, the court may advise the jury of any failure or refusal to disclose and of any untimely disclosure.

(c) The court may prohibit the testimony of a witness pursuant to subdivision (b) only if all other sanctions have been exhausted. The court shall not dismiss a charge pursuant to subdivision (b) unless required to do so by the Constitution of the United States. *(Added by Initiative Measure, Prop 115 §23, approved 6/5/90.)*

§1054.6. Nondisclosure of attorney work product.

Neither the defendant nor the prosecuting attorney is required to disclose any materials or information which are work product as defined in subdivision (c) of Section 2018 of the Code of Civil Procedure, or which are privileged pursuant to an express statutory provision, or are privileged as provided by the Constitution of the United States. *(Added by Initiative Measure, Prop 115 §23, approved 6/5/90.)*

§1054.7. "Good cause" and disclosure regulation.

The disclosures required under this chapter shall be made at least 30 days prior to the trial, unless good cause is shown why a disclosure should be denied, restricted, or deferred. If the material and information becomes known to, or comes into the possession of, a party within 30 days of trial, disclosure shall be made immediately, unless good cause is shown why a disclosure should be denied, restricted, or deferred. "Good cause" is limited to threats or possible danger to the safety of a victim or witness, possible loss or destruction of evidence, or possible compromise of other investigations by law enforcement.

Upon the request of any party, the court may permit a showing of good cause for the denial or regulation of disclosures, or any portion of that showing, to be made in camera. A verbatim record shall be made of any such proceeding. If the court enters an order granting relief following a showing in camera, the entire record of the showing shall be sealed and preserved in the records of the court, and shall be made available to an appellate court in the event of an appeal or writ. In its discretion, the trial court may after trial and conviction, unseal any previously sealed matter. *(Added by Initiative Measure, Prop 115 §23, approved 6/5/90.)*

TITLE 7

OF PROCEEDINGS AFTER THE COMMENCEMENT OF THE TRIAL AND BEFORE JUDGMENT

CHAPTER 1

CHALLENGING THE JURY

§1055. *Repealed by Stats 1988 ch 1245 §17, eff. 1/1/89.*

§§1057 to 1064. *Repealed by Stats 1988 ch 1245 §§18 to 25, eff. 1/1/89.*

§1065. Discharge of jury.

If, either upon an exception to the challenge or a denial of the facts, the challenge is allowed, the Court must discharge the jury so far as the trial in question is concerned. If it is disallowed, the Court must direct the jury to be impaneled.

§§1066 to 1071. *Repealed by Stats 1988 ch 1245 §§26 to 32, eff. 1/1/89.*

§§1073, 1074. *Repealed by Stats 1988 ch 1245 §§33, 34, eff. 1/1/89.*

§1076. *Repealed by Stats 1988 ch 1245 §35, eff. 1/1/89.*

§1078. *Repealed by Stats 1988 ch 1245 §36, eff. 1/1/89.*

§§1081, 1082. *Repealed by Stats 1988 ch 1245 §§37, 38, eff. 1/1/89.*

§1083. Decision on challenge.

The Court must allow or disallow the challenge, and its decision must be entered in the minutes of the Court.

§§1086 to 1088. *Repealed by Stats 1988 ch 1245 §§39 to 41, eff. 1/1/89.*

§1089. Alternate jurors.

Whenever, in the opinion of a judge of a superior or of a municipal court about to try a defendant against whom has been filed any indictment or information or complaint, the trial is likely to be a protracted one, the court may cause an entry to that effect to be made in the minutes of the court, and thereupon, immediately after the jury is impaneled and sworn, the court may direct the calling of one or more additional jurors, in its discretion, to be known as "alternate jurors."

Such alternate jurors must be drawn from the same source, and in the same manner, and have the same qualifications as the jurors already sworn, and be subject to the same examination and challenges; provided, that the prosecution and the defendant shall each be entitled to as many peremptory challenges to such alternate jurors as there are alternate jurors called. When two or more defendants are tried jointly each defendant shall be entitled to as many peremptory challenges to such alternate jurors as there are alternate jurors called. The prosecution shall be entitled to additional peremptory challenges equal to the number of all the additional separate challenges allowed the defendant or defendants to such alternate jurors.

Such alternate jurors shall be seated so as to have equal power and facilities for seeing and hearing the proceedings in the case, and shall take the same oath as the jurors already selected, and must attend at all times upon the trial of the cause in company with the other jurors; and for a failure so to do are liable to be punished for contempt.

They shall obey the orders of and be bound by the admonition of the court, upon each adjournment of the court; but if the regular jurors are ordered to be kept in the custody of the sheriff or marshal during the trial of the cause, such alternate jurors shall also be kept in confinement with the other jurors; and upon final submission of the case to the jury such alternate jurors shall be kept in the custody of the sheriff or marshal and shall not be discharged until the original jurors are discharged, except as hereinafter provided.

If at any time, whether before or after the final submission of the case to the jury, a juror dies or becomes ill, or upon other good cause shown to the court is found to be unable to perform his duty, or if a juror requests a discharge and good cause appears therefor, the court may order him to be discharged and draw the name of an alternate, who shall then take his place in the jury box, and be subject to the same rules and regulations as though he had been selected as one of the original jurors.

CHAPTER 2

THE TRIAL

§1093. Required order of procedure.

The jury having been impaneled and sworn, unless waived, the trial shall proceed in the following order, unless otherwise directed by the court:

(a) If the accusatory pleading be for a felony, the clerk shall read it, and state the plea of the defendant to the jury, and in cases where it charges a previous conviction, and the defendant has confessed the same, the clerk in reading it shall omit therefrom all that relates to such previous conviction. In all other cases this formality may be dispensed with.

(b) The district attorney, or other counsel for the people, may make an opening statement in support of the charge. Whether or not the district attorney, or other counsel for the people, makes an opening statement, the defendant or his or her counsel may then make an opening statement, or may reserve the making of an opening statement until after introduction of the evidence in support of the charge.

(c) The district attorney, or other counsel for the people shall then offer the evidence in support of the charge. The defendant or his or her counsel may then offer his or her evidence in support of the defense.

(d) The parties may then respectively offer rebutting testimony only, unless the court, for good reason, in furtherance of justice, permit them to offer evidence upon their original case.

(e) When the evidence is concluded, unless the case is submitted on either side, or on both sides, without argument, the district attorney, or other counsel for the people, and counsel for the defendant, may argue the case to the court and jury; the district attorney, or other counsel for the people, opening the argument and having the right to close.

(f) The judge may then charge the jury, and shall do so on any points of law pertinent to the issue, if requested by either party; and the judge may state the testimony, and he or she may make such comment on the evidence and the testimony and credibility of any witness as in his or her opinion is necessary for the proper determination of the case and he or she may declare the law. At the beginning of the trial or from time to time during the trial, and without any request from either party, the trial judge may give the jury such instructions on the law applicable to the case as the judge may deem necessary for their guidance on hearing the case. Upon the jury retiring for deliberation, the court shall advise the jury of the availability of a written copy of the jury instructions. The court may, at its discretion, provide the jury with a copy of the written instructions given. However, if the jury requests the court to supply a copy of the written instructions, the court shall supply the jury with a copy. *(Amended by Stats 1986 ch 1045 §2.)*

§1093.5. Instructions; when given.

In any criminal case which is being tried before the court with a jury, all requests for instructions on points of law must be made to the court and all proposed instructions must be delivered to the court before commencement of argument. Before the commencement of the argument, the court, on request of counsel, must: (1) decide whether to give, refuse, or modify the proposed instructions; (2) decide which instructions shall be given in addition to those proposed, if any; and (3) advise counsel of all instructions to be given. However, if, during the argument, issues are raised which have not been covered by instructions given or refused, the court may, on request of counsel, give additional instructions on the subject matter thereof.

§1094. When order of trial may be departed from.

When the state of the pleadings requires it, or in any other case, for good reasons, and in the sound discretion of the Court, the order prescribed in the last section may be departed from.

§1095. Number of counsel to argue cause.

If the offense charged is punishable with death, two counsel on each side may argue the cause. In any other case the court may, in its discretion, restrict the argument to one counsel on each side.

§1096. Presumed innocence; reasonable doubt.

A defendant in a criminal action is presumed to be innocent until the contrary is proved, and in case of a reasonable doubt whether his guilt is satisfactorily shown, he is entitled to an acquittal, but the effect of this presumption is only to place upon the state the burden of proving him guilty beyond a reasonable doubt. Reasonable doubt is defined as follows: "It is not a mere possible doubt; because everything relating to human affairs, and depending on moral evidence, is open to some possible or imaginary doubt. It is that state of the case, which, after the entire comparison and consideration of all the evidence, leaves the minds of jurors in that condition that they can not say they feel an abiding conviction, to a moral certainty, of the truth of the charge."

© 1992 by J., B. & L. Gould
Printed in the U.S.A.   EP

§1096a. Instructions; read §1096.

In charging a jury, the court may read to the jury section 1096 of this code, and no further instruction on the subject of the presumption of innocence or defining reasonable doubt need be given.

§1097. Reasonable doubt re degree of offense.

When it appears that the defendant has committed a public offense, or attempted to commit a public offense, and there is reasonable ground of doubt in which of two or more degrees of the crime or attempted crime he is guilty, he can be convicted of the lowest of such degrees only.

§1098. Joint or separate trials for jointly charged defendants.

When two or more defendants are jointly charged with any public offense, whether felony or misdemeanor, they must be tried jointly, unless the court order separate trials. In ordering separate trials, the court in its discretion may order a separate trial as to one or more defendants, and a joint trial as to the others, or may order any number of the defendants to be tried at one trial, and any number of the others at different trials, or may order a separate trial for each defendant; provided, that where two or more persons can be jointly tried, the fact that separate accusatory pleadings were filed shall not prevent their joint trial.

§1099. Discharge to be witness for people.

When two or more defendants are included in the same accusatory pleading, the court may, at any time before the defendants have gone into their defense, on the application of the prosecuting attorney, direct any defendant to be discharged, that he may be a witness for the people.

§1100. Discharge to be witness for codefendant.

When two or more defendants are included in the same accusatory pleading, and the court is of opinion that in regard to a particular defendant there is not sufficient evidence to put him on his defense, it must order him to be discharged before the evidence is closed, that he may be a witness for his codefendant.

§1101. Effect of such discharge.

The order mentioned in Sections 1099 and 1100 is an acquittal of the defendant discharged, and is a bar to another prosecution for the same offense. *(Amended by Stats 1987 ch 828 §64.)*

§1102. Rules of evidence in civil applicable to criminal cases, except, etc.

The rules of evidence in civil actions are applicable also to criminal actions, except as otherwise provided in this Code.

§1102.5. *Repealed by Initiative Measure, Prop 115 §24, approved 6/5/90.*

§1102.6. Criminal procedure; victim's rights.

(a) The victim shall be entitled to be present and seated at the trial. If the court finds that the presence of the victim would pose a substantial risk of influencing or affecting the content of any testimony, the court shall exclude the victim from the trial entirely or in part so as to effect the purposes of this section.

(b) Upon the court's granting of the victim's request, the defendant may object to the order of the victim's testimony, in which case the victim shall testify first, subject to exclusion if the foundation or corpus delicti is not later established by the testimony of other prosecuting witnesses.

(c) Upon the request of either party or upon the court's own motion, the victim shall be excluded from any hearing on a motion pursuant to this section.

(d) The court, on its own motion or on the motion of either party, may remove a victim from the trial or any portion of it for the same causes and in the same manner as is provided for the exclusion or removal of the defendant, pursuant to paragraph (1) of subdivision (b) of Section 1043 and paragraph (1) of subdivision (b) of Section 1043.5. The prosecution may request the removal of the victim at any time and, upon that request, the court shall require the removal of the victim.

(e) As used in this section, "victim" means (1) the alleged victim of the offense and one member of the victim's immediate family and (2) in the event that the victim is unable to attend the trial, up to two members of the victim's immediate family who are actual or potential witnesses.

(f) The failure of a victim to exercise any right granted under this section is not a cause or ground for an appeal by the defendant of a conviction or for any court to set aside, reverse, or remand the criminal conviction. *(Added by Stats 1986 ch 1273 §2.)*

§1102.7. *Repealed by Initiative Measure, Prop 115 §25, approved 6/5/90.*

§1103. *Repealed by Stats 1989 ch 897 §28, eff. 1/1/90.*

§1103a. *Repealed by Stats 1989 ch 897 §29, eff. 1/1/90.*

§1104. *Repealed by Stats 1989 ch 897 §30, eff. 1/1/90.*

§1105. *Repealed by Stats 1989 ch 897 §31, eff. 1/1/90.*

§1106. *Repealed by Stats 1989 ch 897 §32, eff. 1/1/90.*

§1107. *Repealed by Stats 1989 ch 897 §33, eff. 1/1/90.*

§1108. Abortion; seducing.

Upon a trial for procuring or attempting to procure an abortion, or aiding or assisting therein, or for inveigling, enticing, or taking away an unmarried female of previous chaste character, under the age of eighteen years, for the purpose of prostitution, or aiding or assisting therein, the defendant cannot be convicted upon the testimony of the woman upon or with whom the offense was committed, unless she is corroborated by other evidence.

§1109. *Repealed by Stats 1989 ch 897 §34, eff. 1/1/90.*

§1110. *Repealed by Stats 1989 ch 897 §35, eff. 1/1/90.*

§1111. Testimony of accomplice.

A conviction cannot be had upon the testimony of an accomplice unless it be corroborated by such other evidence as shall tend to connect the defendant with the commission of the offense; and the corroboration is not sufficient if it merely shows the commission of the offense or the circumstances thereof. An accomplice is hereby defined as one who is liable to prosecution for the identical offense charged against the defendant on trial in the cause in which the testimony of the accomplice is given.

§1112. Witnesses in sexual assault prosecutions.

Notwithstanding the provisions of subdivision (d) of Section 28 of Article I of the California Constitution, the trial court shall not order any prosecuting witness, complaining witness, or any other witness, or victim in any sexual assault prosecution to submit to a psychiatric or psychological examination for the purpose of assessing his or her credibility.

§1113. Discharge of jury; no jurisdiction or facts.

The Court may direct the jury to be discharged where it appears that it has not jurisdiction of the offense, or that the facts charged do not constitute an offense punishable by law.

§1114. Discharge of jury; discharge of defendant.

If the jury be discharged because the Court has not jurisdiction of the offense charged, and it appear that it was committed out of the jurisdiction of this State, the defendant must be discharged.

§1115. Discharge of jury; offense committed in another county.

If the offense was committed within the exclusive jurisdiction of another county of this State, the Court must direct the defendant to be committed for such time as it deems reasonable, to await a warrant from the proper county for his arrest; or if the offense is a misdemeanor only, it may admit him to bail in an undertaking, with sufficient sureties, that he will, within such time as the Court may appoint, render himself amenable to a warrant for his arrest from the proper county; and, if not sooner arrested thereon, will attend at the office of the sheriff of the county where the trial was had, at a certain time particularly specified in the undertaking, to surrender himself upon the warrant, if issued, or that his bail will forfeit such sum as the Court may fix, to be mentioned in the undertaking; and the Clerk must forthwith transmit a certified copy of the indictment or information, and of all the papers filed in the action, to the District Attorney of the proper county, the expense of which transmission is chargeable to that county.

§1116. Discharge of jury; defendant not arrested on warrant from proper county.

If the defendant is not arrested on a warrant from the proper county, as provided in section 1115, he must be discharged from custody, or his bail in the action is exonerated, or money deposited instead of bail must be refunded to him or to the person or persons found by the court to have deposited said money on behalf of said defendant, as the case may be, and the sureties in the undertaking, as mentioned in that section, must be discharged. If he is arrested, the same proceedings must be had thereon as upon the arrest of a defendant in another county on a warrant of arrest issued by a magistrate.

§1117. Discharge of jury; facts not constituting an offense.

If the jury is discharged because the facts as charged do not constitute an offense punishable by law, the court must order that the defendant, if in custody, be discharged; or if admitted to bail, that his bail be exonerated; or, if he has deposited money or if money has been deposited by another or others instead of bail for his appearance, that the money be refunded to him or to the person or persons found by the court to have deposited said money on behalf of said defendant, unless in its opinion a new indictment or information can be framed upon which the defendant can be legally convicted, in which case it may direct the district attorney to file a new information, or (if the defendant has not been committed by a magistrate) direct that the case be submitted to the same or another grand jury; and the same proceedings must be had thereon as are prescribed in section 998; provided, that after such order or submission the defendant may be examined before a magistrate, and discharged or committed by him as in other cases.

§1118. Court trial without jury.

In a case tried by the court without a jury, a jury having been waived, the court on motion of the defendant or on its own motion shall order the entry of a judgment of acquittal of one or more of the offenses charged in the accusatory pleading after the evidence of the prosecution has been closed if the court, upon weighing the evidence then before it, finds the defendant not guilty of such offense or offenses. If such a motion for judgment of acquittal at the close of the evidence offered by the prosecution is not granted, the defendant may offer evidence without first having reserved that right.

§1118.1. Trial by jury; insufficient evidence.

In a case tried before a jury, the court on motion of the defendant or on its own motion, at the close of the evidence on either side and before the case is submitted to the jury for decision, shall order the entry of a judgment of acquittal of one or more of the offenses charged in the accusatory pleading if the evidence then before the court is insufficient to sustain a conviction of such offense or offenses on appeal. If such a motion for judgment of acquittal at the close of the evidence offered by the prosecution is not granted, the defendant may offer evidence without first having reserved that right.

§1118.2. Judgment of acquittal; nonappealable.

A judgment of acquittal entered pursuant to the provisions of Section 1118 or 1118.1 shall not be appealable and is a bar to any other prosecution for the same offense.

§1119. View of premises, by jury.

When, in the opinion of the court, it is proper that the jury should view the place in which the offense is charged to have been committed, or in which any other material fact occurred, or any personal property which has been referred to in the evidence and cannot conveniently be brought into the courtroom, it may order the jury to be conducted in a body, in the custody of the sheriff, marshal or constable, as the case may be, to the place, or to such property, which must be shown to them by a person appointed by the court for that purpose; and the officer must be sworn to suffer no person to speak or communicate with the jury, nor to do so himself, on any subject connected with the trial, and to return them into court without unnecessary delay, or at a specified time.

© 1992 by J., B. & L. Gould
Printed in the U.S.A.   EP

§1120. Personal knowledge of juror.

If a juror has any personal knowledge respecting a fact in controversy in a cause, he must declare the same in open court during the trial. If, during the retirement of the jury, a juror declare a fact which could be evidence in the cause, as of his own knowledge, the jury must return into court. In either of these cases, the juror making the statement must be sworn as a witness and examined in the presence of the parties in order that the court may determine whether good cause exists for his discharge as a juror.

§1121. Separation or custody of jury.

The jurors sworn to try an action may, in the discretion of the court, be permitted to separate or be kept in charge of a proper officer. Where the jurors are permitted to separate, the court shall properly admonish them. Where the jurors are kept in charge of a proper officer, the officer must be sworn to keep the jurors together until the next meeting of the court, to suffer no person to speak to them or communicate with them, nor to do so himself, on any subject connected with the trial, and to return them into court at the next meeting thereof.

§1122. Jury must be admonished.

The jury must also, at each adjournment of the court before the submission of the cause to the jury, whether permitted to separate or kept in charge of officers, be admonished by the court that it is their duty not to converse among themselves or with anyone else on any subject connected with the trial, or to form or express any opinion thereon until the cause is finally submitted to them.

§1123. *Repealed by Stats 1988 ch 1245 §42, eff. 1/1/89.*

§1124. Court to decide questions of law arising during trial.

The Court must decide all questions of law which arise in the course of a trial.

§1125. *Repealed by Stats 1991 ch 186 §7, eff. 1/1/92.*

§1126. Questions of law and fact; who decides.

In a trial for any offense, questions of law are to be decided by the court, and questions of fact by the jury. Although the jury has the power to find a general verdict, which includes questions of law as well as of fact, they are bound, nevertheless, to receive as law what is laid down as such by the court. *(Amended by Stats 1991 ch 186 §8, eff. 1/1/92.)*

§1127. Instructions; generally.

All instructions given shall be in writing, unless there is a phonographic reporter present and he takes them down, in which case they may be given orally; provided however, that in all misdemeanor cases oral instructions may be given pursuant to stipulation of the prosecuting attorney and counsel for the defendant. In charging the jury the court may instruct the jury regarding the law applicable to the facts of the case, and may make such comment on the evidence and the testimony and credibility of any witness as in its opinion is necessary for the proper determination of the case and in any criminal case, whether the defendant testifies or not, his failure to explain or to deny by his testimony any evidence or facts in the case against him may be commented upon by the court. The court shall inform the jury in all cases that the jurors are the exclusive judges of all questions of fact submitted to them and of the credibility of the witnesses. Either party may present to the court any written charge on the law, but not with respect to matters of fact, and request that it be given. If the court thinks it correct and pertinent, it must be given; if not, it must be refused. Upon each charge presented and given or refused, the court must endorse and sign its decision and a statement showing which party requested it. If part be given and part refused, the court must distinguish, showing by the endorsement what part of the charge was given and what part refused.

§1127a. In-custody informant.

(a) As used in this section, an "in-custody informant" means a person, other than a codefendant, percipient witness, accomplice, or coconspirator whose testimony is based upon statements made by the defendant while both the defendant and the informant are held within a correctional institution.

(b) In any criminal trial or proceeding in which an in-custody informant testifies as a witness, upon the request of a party, the court shall instruct the jury as follows:

"The testimony of an in-custody informant should be viewed with caution and close scrutiny. In evaluating such testimony, you should consider the extent to which it may have been influenced by the receipt of, or expectation of, any benefits from the party calling that witness. This does not mean that you may arbitrarily disregard such testimony, but you should give it the weight to which you find it to be entitled in the light of all the evidence in the case."

(c) When the prosecution calls an in-custody informant as a witness in any criminal trial, contemporaneous with the calling of that witness, the prosecution shall file with the court a written statement setting out any and all consideration promised to, or received by, the in-custody informant.

The statement filed with the court shall not expand or limit the defendant's right to discover information that is otherwise provided by law. The statement shall be provided to the defendant or the defendant's attorney prior to trial and the information contained in the statement shall be subject to rules of evidence.

(d) For purposes of subdivision (c), "consideration" means any plea bargain, bail consideration, reduction or modification of sentence, or any other leniency, benefit, immunity, financial assistance, reward, or amelioration of current or future conditions of incarceration in return for, or in connection with, the informant's testimony in the criminal proceeding in which the prosecutor intends to call him or her as a witness. *(Added by Stats 1989 ch 901 §1, eff. 1/1/90.)*

§1127b. Expert testimony.

When, in any criminal trial or proceeding, the opinion of any expert witness is received in evidence, the court shall instruct the jury substantially as follows:

Duly qualified experts may give their opinions on questions in controversy at a trial. To assist the jury in deciding such questions, the jury may consider the opinion with the reasons stated therefor, if any, by the expert who gives the opinion. The jury is not bound to accept the opinion of any expert as conclusive, but should give to it the weight to which they shall find it to be entitled. The jury may, however, disregard any such opinion if it shall be found by them to be unreasonable.

No further instruction on the subject of opinion evidence need be given.

§1127c. Evidence of flight.

In any criminal trial or proceeding where evidence of flight of a defendant is relied upon as tending to show guilt, the court shall instruct the jury substantially as follows:

The flight of a person immediately after the commission of a crime, or after he is accused of a crime that has been committed, is not sufficient in itself to establish his guilt, but is a fact which, if proved, the jury may consider in deciding his guilt or innocence. The weight to which such circumstance is entitled is a matter for the jury to determine.

No further instruction on the subject of flight need be given.

§1127d. Sexual conduct.

(a) In any criminal prosecution for the crime of rape, or for violation of Section 261.5, or for an attempt to commit, or assault with intent to commit, any such crime, the jury shall not be instructed that it may be inferred that a person who has previously consented to sexual intercourse with persons other than the defendant or with the defendant would be therefore more likely to consent to sexual intercourse again. However, if evidence was received that the victim consented to and did engage in sexual intercourse with the defendant on one or more occasions prior to that charged against the defendant in this case, the jury shall be instructed that this evidence may be considered only as it relates to the question of whether the victim consented to the act of intercourse charged against the defendant in the case, or whether the defendant had a good faith reasonable belief that the victim consented to the act of sexual intercourse. The jury shall be instructed that it shall not consider this evidence for any other purpose.

(b) A jury shall not be instructed that the prior sexual conduct in and of itself of the complaining witness may be considered in determining the credibility of the witness pursuant to Chapter 6 (commencing with Section 780) of Division 6 of the Evidence Code. *(Amended by Stats 1990 ch 269 §1, eff. 1/1/91.)*

§1127e. Term unchaste character.

The term "unchaste character" shall not be used by any court in any criminal case in which the defendant is charged with a violation of Section 261 or 261.5 of the Penal Code, or attempt to commit or assault with intent to commit any crime defined in any such section, in any instruction to the jury.

§1127f. Testimony of a child.

In any criminal trial or proceeding in which a child 10 years of age or younger testifies as a witness, upon the request of a party, the court shall instruct the jury, as follows:

In evaluating the testimony of a child you should consider all of the factors surrounding the child's testimony, including the age of the child and any evidence regarding the child's level of cognitive development. Although, because of age and level of cognitive development, a child may perform different-

ly as a witness from an adult, that does not mean that a child is any more or less credible a witness than an adult. You should not discount or distrust the testimony of a child solely because he or she is a child. *(Added by Stats 1986 ch 1051 §3.)*

§1128. Decision in court or retirement for deliberation.

After hearing the charge, the jury may either decide in court or may retire for deliberation. If they do not agree without retiring for deliberation, an officer must be sworn to keep them together for deliberation in some private and convenient place, and, during such deliberation, not to permit any person to speak to or communicate with them, nor to do so himself, unless by order of the court, or to ask them whether they have agreed upon a verdict, and to return them into court when they have so agreed, or when ordered by the court. The court shall fix the time and place for deliberation. The jurors shall not deliberate on the case except under such circumstances. If the jurors are permitted by the court to separate, the court shall properly admonish them. When the jury is composed of both men and women and the jurors are not permitted by the court to separate, in the event that it shall become necessary to retire for the night, the women must be kept in a room or rooms separate and apart from the men.

§1129. When defendant on bail appears for trial he may be committed.

When a defendant who has given bail appears for trial, the Court may, in its discretion, at any time after his appearance for trial, order him to be committed to the custody of the proper officer of the county, to abide the judgment or further order of the Court, and he must be committed and held in custody accordingly.

§1130. Failure of prosecuting attorney to attend.

If the prosecuting attorney fails to attend at the trial in the superior court, the court must appoint some attorney at law to perform the duties of the prosecuting attorney on such trial.

§1131. *Repealed by Stats 1989 ch 897 §36, eff. 1/1/90.*

CHAPTER 3

CONDUCT OF THE JURY AFTER THE CAUSE IS SUBMITTED TO THEM

§1135. *Repealed by Stats 1989 ch 897 §37, eff. 1/1/90.*

§1136. *Repealed by Stats 1988 ch 1245 §43, eff. 1/1/89.*

§1137. What papers the jury may take with them.

Upon retiring for deliberation, the jury may take with them all papers (except depositions) which have been received as evidence in the cause, or copies of such public records or private documents given in evidence as ought not, in the opinion of the court, to be taken from the person having them in possession. They may also take with them the written instructions given, and notes of the testimony or other proceedings on the trial, taken by themselves or any of them, but

© 1992 by J., B. & L. Gould
Printed in the U.S.A. EP

none taken by any other person. The court shall provide for the custody and safekeeping of such items.

§1138. Further information.

After the jury have retired for deliberation, if there be any disagreement between them as to the testimony, or if they desire to be informed on any point of law arising in the case, they must require the officer to conduct them into court. Upon being brought into court, the information required must be given in the presence of, or after notice to, the prosecuting attorney, and the defendant or his counsel, or after they have been called.

§1138.5. Previous testimony.

Except for good cause shown, the judge in his of* her discretion need not be present in the court while testimony previously received in evidence is read to the jury. *(Added by Stats 1987 ch 88 §2.)*
*So in original. Probably should be "or".

§1140. Discharge prohibited after cause submitted.

Except as provided by law, the jury cannot be discharged after the cause is submitted to them until they have agreed upon their verdict and rendered it in open court, unless by consent of both parties, entered upon the minutes, or unless, at the expiration of such time as the court may deem proper, it satisfactorily appears that there is no reasonable probability that the jury can agree.

§1141. Retrial of cause after discharge of jury.

In all cases where a jury is discharged or prevented from giving a verdict by reason of an accident or other cause, except where the defendant is discharged during the progress of the trial, or after the cause is submitted to them, the cause may be again tried.

§1142. Court may adjourn during absence of jury, but deemed open for all purposes connected with cause.

While the jury are absent the Court may adjourn from time to time, as to other business, but it must nevertheless be open for every purpose connected with the cause submitted to the jury until a verdict is rendered or the jury discharged.

§1143. *Repealed by Stats 1988 ch 1245 §44, eff. 1/1/89.*

CHAPTER 4

THE VERDICT OR FINDING

§1147. Non-appearance of juror after deliberation; retrial.

When the jury have agreed upon their verdict, they must be conducted into court by the officer having them in charge. Their names must then be called, and if all do not appear, the rest must be discharged without giving a verdict. In that case the action may be again tried.

§1148. Personal appearance of defendant on return of verdict.

If charged with a felony the defendant must, before the verdict is received, appear in person, unless, after the exercise of reasonable diligence to procure the presence of the defendant, the court shall find that it will be in the interest of justice that the verdict be received in his absence. If for a misdemeanor, the verdict may be rendered in his absence.

§1149. Manner of taking verdict.

When the jury appear they must be asked by the Court, or Clerk, whether they have agreed upon their verdict, and if the foreman answers in the affirmative, they must, on being required, declare the same.

§1150. General or special verdict.

The jury must render a general verdict, except that in a superior court, when they are in doubt as to the legal effect of the facts proved, they may, except upon a trial for libel, find a special verdict.

§1151. Form of general verdict.

A general verdict upon a plea of not guilty is either "guilty" or "not guilty," which imports a conviction or acquittal of the offense charged in the accusatory pleading. Upon a plea of a former conviction or acquittal of the offense charged, or upon a plea of once in jeopardy, the general verdict is either "for the people" or "for the defendant." When the defendant is acquitted on the ground of a variance between the accusatory pleading and the proof, the verdict is "not guilty by reason of variance between charge and proof."

§1152. Special verdict.

A special verdict is that by which the jury find the facts only, leaving the judgment to the Court. It must present the conclusions of fact as established by the evidence, and not the evidence to prove them, and these conclusions of fact must be so presented as that nothing remains to the Court but to draw conclusions of law upon them.

§1153. Special verdict, how rendered.

The special verdict must be reduced to writing by the jury, or in their presence entered upon the minutes of the Court, read to the jury and agreed to by them, before they are discharged.

§1154. Form of special verdict.

The special verdict need not be in any particular form, but is sufficient if it presents intelligibly the facts found by the jury. *(Amended by Stats 1987 ch 828 §65.)*

§1155. Judgment given on special verdict.

The court must give judgment upon the special verdict as follows:

1. If the plea is not guilty, and the facts prove the defendant guilty of the offense charged in the indictment or information, or of any other offense of which he could be convicted under that indictment or information, judgment must be given accordingly. But if otherwise, judgment of acquittal must be given.

2. If the plea is a former conviction or acquittal or once in jeopardy of the same offense, the court must give judgment of acquittal or conviction, as the facts prove or fail to prove the former conviction or acquittal or jeopardy.

§1156. Defect or insufficiency in special verdict.

If the jury do not, in a special verdict, pronounce affirmatively or negatively on the facts necessary to enable the court to give judgment, or if they find the evidence of facts merely, and not the conclusions of fact, from the evidence, as established to their satisfaction, the court shall direct the jury to retire and return another special verdict. The court may explain to the jury the defect or insufficiency in the special verdict returned, and the form which the special verdict to be returned must take.

§1157. Jury or court must find degree of crime.

Whenever a defendant is convicted of a crime or attempt to commit a crime which is distinguished into degrees, the jury, or the court if a jury trial is waived, must find the degree of the crime or attempted crime of which he is guilty. Upon the failure of the jury or the court to so determine, the degree of the crime or attempted crime of which the defendant is guilty, shall be deemed to be of the lesser degree.

§1158. Finding upon charge of being armed with weapon.

Whenever the fact of a previous conviction of another offense is charged in an accusatory pleading, and the defendant is found guilty of the offense with which he is charged, the jury, or the judge if a jury trial is waived, must unless the answer of the defendant admits such previous conviction, find whether or not he has suffered such previous conviction. The verdict or finding upon the charge of previous conviction may be: "We (or I) find the charge of previous conviction true" or "We (or I) find the charge of previous conviction not true," according as the jury or the judge find that the defendant has or has not suffered such conviction. If more than one previous conviction is charged a separate finding must be made as to each.

§1158a. Finding upon charge of being armed with weapon.

(a) Whenever the fact that a defendant was armed with a weapon either at the time of his commission of the offense or at the time of his arrest, or both, is charged in accordance with section 969c of this code, in any count of the indictment or information to which the defendant has entered a plea of not guilty, the jury, if they find a verdict of guilty of the offense with which the defendant is charged, or of any offense included therein, must also find whether or not the defendant was armed as charged in the count to which the plea of not guilty was entered. The verdict of the jury upon a charge of being armed may be: "We find the charge of being armed contained in the _____ count true," or "We find the charge of being armed contained in the _____ count not true," as they find that the defendant was or was not armed as charged in any particular count of the indictment or information. A separate verdict upon the charge of being armed must be returned for each count which alleges that the defendant was armed.

(b) Whenever the fact that a defendant used a firearm is charged in accordance with Section 969d in any count of the indictment or information to which the defendant has entered a plea of not guilty, the jury if they find a verdict of guilty of the offense with which the defendant is charged must also find whether or not the defendant used a firearm as charged in the count to which the plea of not guilty was entered. A verdict of the jury upon a charge of using a firearm may be: "We find the charge of using a firearm contained in the ___ count true," or "We find the charge of using a firearm contained in the ___ count not true," as they find that the defendant used or did not use a firearm as charged in any particular count of the indictment or information. A separate verdict upon the charge of using a firearm shall be returned for each count which alleges that defendant used a firearm.

§1159. Lesser included offense or attempt.

The jury, or the judge if a jury trial is waived, may find the defendant guilty of any offense, the commission of which is necessarily included in that with which he is charged, or of an attempt to commit the offense.

§1160. Verdict as to some of several joint defendants or offenses.

On a charge against two or more defendants jointly, if the jury cannot agree upon a verdict as to all, they may render a verdict as to the defendant or defendants in regard to whom they do agree, on which a judgment must be entered accordingly, and the case as to the other may be tried again.

Where two or more offenses are charged in any accusatory pleading, if the jury cannot agree upon a verdict as to all of them, they may render a verdict as to the charge or charges upon which they do agree, and the charges on which they do not agree may be tried again.

§1161. In what cases court may direct a reconsideration of the verdict.

When there is a verdict of conviction, in which it appears to the Court that the jury have mistaken the law, the Court may explain the reason for that opinion and direct the jury to reconsider their verdict, and if, after the reconsideration, they return the same verdict, it must be entered; but when there is a verdict of acquittal, the Court cannot require the jury to reconsider it. If the jury render a verdict which is neither general nor special, the Court may direct them to reconsider it, and it cannot be recorded until it is rendered in some form from which it can be clearly understood that the intent of the jury is either to render a general verdict or to find the facts specially and to leave the judgment to the Court.

§1162. When judgment may be given on informal verdict.

If the jury persist in finding an informal verdict, from which, however, it can be clearly understood that their intention is to find in favor of the defendant upon the issue, it must be entered in the terms in which it is found, and the Court must give judgment of acquittal. But no judgment of conviction can be given unless the jury expressly finds against the defendant upon the issue, or judgment is given against him on a special verdict.

§1163. Polling the jury.

When a verdict is rendered, and before it is recorded, the jury may be polled, at the request of either party, in which case they must be severally asked whether it is their verdict, and if any one answer in the negative, the jury must be sent out for further deliberation.

§1164. Recording the verdict.

(a) When the verdict given is receivable by the court, the clerk shall record it in full upon the minutes,

© 1992 by J., B. & L. Gould
Printed in the U.S.A.   EP

and if requested by any party shall read it to the jury, and inquire of them whether it is their verdict. If any juror disagrees, the fact shall be entered upon the minutes and the jury again sent out; but if no disagreement is expressed, the verdict is complete, and the jury shall, subject to subdivision (b), be discharged from the case.

(b) No jury shall be discharged until the court has verified on the record that the jury has either reached a verdict or has formally declared its inability to reach a verdict on all issues before it, including, but not limited to, the degree of the crime or crimes charged, and the truth of any alleged prior conviction whether in the same proceeding or in a bifurcated proceeding. *(Amended by Stats 1990 ch 800 §1, eff. 1/1/91.)*

§1165. Judgment of acquittal.

Where a general verdict is rendered or a finding by the court is made in favor of the defendant, except on a plea of not guilty by reason of insanity, a judgment of acquittal must be forthwith given. If such judgment is given, or a judgment imposing a fine only, without imprisonment for nonpayment is given, and the defendant is not detained for any other legal cause, he must be discharged, if in custody, as soon as the judgment is given, except that where the acquittal is because of a variance between the pleading and the proof which may be obviated by a new accusatory pleading, the court may order his detention, to the end that a new accusatory pleading may be preferred, in the same manner and with like effect as provided in Section 1117.

§1166. Commitment of defendant upon general verdict of conviction.

If a general verdict is rendered against the defendant, or a special verdict is given, he must be remanded, if in custody, or if on bail he may be committed to the proper officer of the county to await the judgment of the court upon the verdict. When committed his bail is exonerated, or if money is deposited instead of bail it must be refunded to the defendant or to the person or persons found by the court to have deposited said money on behalf of said defendant.

§1167. Verdict by judge, nonjury trial.

When a jury trial is waived, the judge or justice before whom the trial is had shall, at the conclusion thereof, announce his findings upon the issues of fact, which shall be in substantially the form prescribed for the general verdict of a jury and shall be entered upon the minutes.

§1168. Sentence to state prison.

(a) Every person who commits a public offense, for which any specification of three time periods of imprisonment in any state prison is now prescribed by law or for which only a single term of imprisonment in state prison is specified shall, unless such convicted person be placed on probation, a new trial granted, or the imposing of sentence suspended, be sentenced pursuant to Chapter 4.5 (commencing with Section 1170) of Title 7 of Part 2.

(b) For any person not sentenced under such provision, but who is sentenced to be imprisoned in the state prison, including imprisonment not exceeding one year and one day, the court imposing the sentence shall not fix the term or duration of the period of imprisonment.

CHAPTER 4.5

TRIAL COURT SENTENCING

ARTICLE 1

INITIAL SENTENCING

§1170. Findings and declarations.

(a) (1) The Legislature finds and declares that the purpose of imprisonment for crime is punishment. This purpose is best served by terms proportionate to the seriousness of the offense with provision for uniformity in the sentences of offenders committing the same offense under similar circumstances. The Legislature further finds and declares that the elimination of disparity and the provision of uniformity of sentences can best be achieved by determinate sentences fixed by statute in proportion to the seriousness of the offense as determined by the Legislature to be imposed by the court with specified discretion.

(2) In any case in which the punishment prescribed by statute for a person convicted of a public offense is a term of imprisonment in the state prison of 16 months, two or three years; two, three, or four years; two, three, or five years; three, four, or five years; two, four, or six years; three, four, or six years; three, five, or seven years; three, six, or eight years; five, seven, or nine years; five, seven, or 11 years, or any other specification of three time periods, the court shall sentence the defendant to one of the terms of imprisonment specified unless such convicted person is given any other disposition provided by law, including a fine, jail, probation, or the suspension of imposition or execution of sentence or is sentenced pursuant to subdivision (b) of Section 1168 because he or she had committed his or her crime prior to July 1, 1977. In sentencing the convicted person, the court shall apply the sentencing rules of the Judicial Council. The court, unless it determines that there are circumstances in mitigation of the punishment prescribed, shall also impose any other term which it is required by law to impose as an additional term. Nothing in this article shall affect any provision of law which imposes the death penalty, which authorizes or restricts the granting of probation or suspending the execution or imposition of sentence, or expressly provides for imprisonment in the state prison for life. In any case in which the amount of preimprisonment credit under Section 2900.5 or any other provision of law is equal to or exceeds any sentence imposed pursuant to this chapter, the entire sentence, including any period of parole under Section 3000, shall be deemed to have been served and the defendant shall not be actually delivered to the custody of the Director of Corrections. However, any such sentence shall be deemed a separate prior prison term under Section 667.5, and a copy of the judgment and other necessary documentation shall be forwarded to the Director of Corrections.

(b) When a judgment of imprisonment is to be imposed and the statute specifies three possible terms, the court shall order imposition of the middle term, unless there are circumstances in aggravation or mitigation of the crime. At least four days prior to the time set for imposition of judgment, either party or the victim, or the family of the victim if the victim is deceased, may submit a statement in aggravation or mitigation to dispute facts in the record or the probation officer's report, or to present additional facts. In determining whether there are circumstances that justify imposition of the upper or lower term, the court may consider the record in the case, the probation officer's report, other reports including reports received pursuant to Section 1203.03 and statements in aggravation or mitigation submitted by the prosecution, the defendant, or the victim, or the family of the victim if the victim is deceased, and any further evidence introduced at the sentencing hearing. The court shall set forth on the record the facts and reasons for imposing the upper or lower term. The court may not impose an upper term by using the fact of any enhancement upon which sentence is imposed under Section 667.5, 1170.1, 12022, 12022.4, 12022.5, 12022.6, or 12022.7 or under any other section of law. A term of imprisonment shall not be specified if imposition of sentence is suspended.

(c) The court shall state the reasons for its sentence choice on the record at the time of sentencing. The court shall also inform the defendant that as part of the sentence after expiration of the term he or she may be on parole for a period as provided in Section 3000.

(d) When a defendant subject to this section or subdivision (b) of Section 1168 has been sentenced to be imprisoned in the state prison and has been committed to the custody of the Director of Corrections, the court may, within 120 days of the date of commitment on its own motion, or at any time upon the recommendation of the Director of Corrections or the Board of Prison Terms, recall the sentence and commitment previously ordered and resentence the defendant in the same manner as if he or she had not previously been sentenced, provided the new sentence, if any, is no greater than the initial sentence. The resentence under this subdivision shall apply the sentencing rules of the Judicial Council so as to eliminate disparity of sentences and to promote uniformity of sentencing. Credit shall be given for time served.

(e) Any sentence imposed under this article shall be subject to the provisions of Sections 3000 and 3057 and any other applicable provisions of law.

(f) (1) Within one year after the commencement of the term of imprisonment, the Board of Prison Terms shall review the sentence to determine whether the sentence is disparate in comparison with the sentences imposed in similar cases. If the Board of Prison Terms determines that the sentence is disparate, the board shall notify the judge, the district attorney, the defense attorney, the defendant, and the Judicial Council. The notification shall include a statement of the reasons for finding the sentence disparate.

Within 120 days of receipt of this information, the sentencing court shall schedule a hearing and may recall the sentence and commitment previously ordered and resentence the defendant in the same manner as if the defendant had not been sentenced previously, provided the new sentence is no greater than the initial sentence. In resentencing under this subdivision the court shall apply the sentencing rules of the Judicial Council and shall consider the information provided by the Board of Prison Terms.

(2) The review under this section shall concern the decision to deny probation and the sentencing decisions enumerated in paragraphs (2), (3), and (4), of subdivision (a) of Section 1170.3 and apply the sentencing rules of the Judicial Council and the information regarding the sentences in this state of other persons convicted of similar crimes so as to eliminate

disparity of sentences and to promote uniformity of sentencing.

(g) Prior to sentencing pursuant to this chapter, the court may request information from the Board of Prison Terms concerning the sentences in this state of other persons convicted of similar crimes under similar circumstances.

(h) A sentence to state prison for a determinate term for which only one term is specified, is a sentence to state prison under this section. *(Amended by Stats 1988 ch 635 §1, eff. 1/1/89.)*

§1170.1. Aggregate and consecutive terms of imprisonment.

(a) Except as provided in subdivision (c) and subject to Section 654, when any person is convicted of two or more felonies, whether in the same proceeding or court or in different proceedings or courts, and whether by judgment rendered by the same or by a different court, and a consecutive term of imprisonment is imposed under Sections 669 and 1170, the aggregate term of imprisonment for all these convictions shall be the sum of the principal term, subordinate term, and any additional term imposed pursuant to Section 667, 667.5, 667.6, or 12022.1, and pursuant to Section 11370.2 of the Health and Safety Code. The principal term shall consist of the greatest term of imprisonment imposed by the court for any of the crimes, including any enhancements imposed pursuant to Section 667.8, 667.85, 12022, 12022.2, 12022.3, 12022.4, 12022.5, 12022.55, 12022.6, 12022.7, 12022.75, 12022.8, or 12022.9 and an enhancement imposed pursuant to Section 11370.4 or 11379.8 of the Health and Safety Code. The subordinate term for each consecutive offense which is not a "violent felony" as defined in subdivision (c) of Section 667.5 shall consist of one-third of the middle term of imprisonment prescribed for each other such felony conviction for which a consecutive term of imprisonment is imposed, and shall exclude any enhancements. In no case shall the total of subordinate terms for such consecutive offenses which are not "violent felonies" as defined in subdivision (c) of Section 667.5 exceed five years. The subordinate term for each consecutive offense which is a "violent felony" as defined in subdivision (c) of Section 667.5, including those offenses described in paragraph (8) or (9) of subdivision (c) of Section 667.5, shall consist of one-third of the middle term of imprisonment prescribed for each other such felony conviction for which a consecutive term of imprisonment is imposed, and shall include one-third of any enhancements imposed pursuant to Section 667.8, 667.85, 12022, 12022.2, 12022.4, 12022.5, 12022.55, 12022.7, 12022.75, or 12022.9.

(b) When a consecutive term of imprisonment is imposed under Sections 669 and 1170 for two or more convictions for kidnapping, as defined in Section 207, involving both separate victims and separate occasions, the aggregate term shall be calculated as provided in subdivision (a), except that the subordinate term for each subsequent kidnapping conviction shall consist of the middle term for each kidnapping conviction for which a consecutive term of imprisonment is imposed and shall include one-third of any enhancements imposed pursuant to Section 667.8, 667.85, 12022, 12022.2, 12022.4, 12022.5, 12022.55, 12022.7, 12022.75, or 12022.9. The five-year limitation on the total of subordinate terms provided

© 1992 by J., B. & L. Gould
Printed in the U.S.A.　EP

in subdivision (a) shall not apply to subordinate terms for second and subsequent convictions of kidnapping, as defined in Section 207, involving separate victims and separate occasions.

(c) In the case of any person convicted of one or more felonies committed while the person is confined in a state prison, or is subject to reimprisonment for escape from such custody and the law either requires the terms to be served consecutively or the court imposes consecutive terms, the term of imprisonment for all the convictions which the person is required to serve consecutively shall commence from the time the person would otherwise have been released from prison. If the new offenses are consecutive with each other, the principal and subordinate terms shall be calculated as provided in subdivision (a), except that the total of subordinate terms may exceed five years. This subdivision shall be applicable in cases of convictions of more than one offense in different proceedings, and convictions of more than one offense in the same or different proceedings.

(d) When the court imposes a prison sentence for a felony pursuant to Section 1170 the court shall also impose the additional terms provided in Sections 667, 667.5, 667.8, 667.85, 12022, 12022.2, 12022.4, 12022.5, 12022.55, 12022.6, 12022.7, 12022.75, and 12022.9, and the additional terms provided in Section 11370.2, 11370.4, or 11379.8 of the Health and Safety Code, unless the additional punishment therefor is stricken pursuant to subdivision (h). The court shall also impose any other additional term which the court determines in its discretion or as required by law shall run consecutive to the term imposed under Section 1170. In considering the imposition of such additional term, the court shall apply the sentencing rules of the Judicial Council.

(e) When two or more enhancements under Sections 12022, 12022.4, 12022.5, 12022.55, 12022.7, and 12022.9 may be imposed for any single offense, only the greatest enhancement shall apply; however, in cases of lewd or lascivious acts upon or with a child under the age of 14 years accomplished by means of force or fear, as described in Section 288, kidnapping as defined in Section 207, penetration of a genital or anal opening by a foreign object, as defined in Section 289, oral copulation, sodomy, robbery, rape or burglary, or attempted lewd or lascivious acts upon or with a child under the age of 14 years accomplished by means of force or fear, kidnapping, penetration of a genital or anal opening by a foreign object, oral copulation, sodomy, robbery, rape, murder, or burglary the court may impose both (1) one enhancement for weapons as provided in either Section 12022, 12022.4, or subdivision (a) of, or paragraph (2) of subdivision (b) of, Section 12022.5 and (2) one enhancement for great bodily injury as provided in either Section 12022.7 or 12022.9.

(f) The enhancements provided in Sections 667, 667.5, 667.6, 667.8, 667.85, 12022, 12022.1, 12022.2, 12022.3, 12022.4, 12022.5, 12022.55, 12022.6, 12022.7, 12022.75, 12022.8, and 12022.9, and in Section 11370.2, 11370.4, or 11379.8 of the Health and Safety Code, shall be pleaded and proven as provided by law.

(g) The term of imprisonment shall not exceed twice the number of years imposed by the trial court as the base term pursuant to subdivision (b) of Section 1170 unless the defendant stands convicted of a "violent felony" as defined in subdivision (c) of Section 667.5, or a consecutive sentence is being imposed pursuant to subdivision (b) or (c) of this section, or an enhancement is imposed pursuant to Section 667, 667.5, 667.8, 667.85, 12022, 12022.2, 12022.4, 12022.5, 12022.55, 12022.6, 12022.7, 12022.75, or 12022.9, or an enhancement is being imposed pursuant to Section 11370.2, 11370.4, or 11379.8 of the Health and Safety Code, or the defendant stands convicted of felony escape from an institution in which he or she is lawfully confined.

(h) Notwithstanding any other provision of law, the court may strike the additional punishment for the enhancements provided in Sections 667.5, 667.8, 667.85, 12022, 12022.2, 12022.4, 12022.6, 12022.7, 12022.75, and 12022.9, or the enhancements provided in Section 11370.2, 11370.4, or 11379.8 of the Health and Safety Code, if it determines that there are circumstances in mitigation of the additional punishment and states on the record its reasons for striking the additional punishment.

(i) For any violation of subdivision (2) or (3) of Section 261, Section 264.1, subdivision (b) of Section 288, subdivision (a) of Section 289, or sodomy or oral copulation by force, violence, duress, menace or fear of immediate and unlawful bodily injury on the victim or another person as provided in Section 286 or 288a, the number of enhancements which may be imposed shall not be limited, regardless of whether such enhancements are pursuant to this or some other section of law. Each of such enhancements shall be a full and separately served enhancement and shall not be merged with any term or with any other enhancement. *(Amended by Stats 1990 ch 41 §2; ch 835 §1, eff. 1/1/91.)*

§1170.13. Punishment for consecutive offenses.

(a) Notwithstanding the provisions of subdivision (a) of Section 1170.1 which provide for the imposition of a subordinate term for a consecutive offense of one-third of the middle term of imprisonment, if a person is convicted pursuant to subdivision (b) of Section 139, the subordinate term for each consecutive offense shall consist of 100 percent of the middle term. The total term of imprisonment imposed pursuant to this subdivision may exceed five years, but shall not exceed 15 years.

(b) Notwithstanding the provisions of subdivision (c) of Section 1170.1, whenever a person is convicted pursuant to subdivision (b) of Section 139 while the person is confined in a state prison, or is subject to reimprisonment for escape from such custody, the term of imprisonment for all those convictions which the person is required to serve consecutively shall commence from the time the person would otherwise have been released from prison. Punishment for the new offenses shall be calculated as provided in subdivision (a) of this section, except that the total term of imprisonment imposed may exceed 15 years. *(Added by Stats 1989 ch 1378 §4, eff. 1/1/90.)*

§1170.15. Enhancement for crime against witness.

Notwithstanding the provisions of subdivision (a) of Section 1170.1 which provide for the imposition of a subordinate term for a consecutive offense of one-third of the middle term of imprisonment, if a person is convicted of a felony, and of an additional felony which is a violation of Section 136.1 or 137 and which was committed against the victim of, or a witness or potential witness with respect to, or a person who was about to give material information pertaining to, the first felony, or of a felony violation of Section 653f which was committed to dissuade a witness or potential witness to the first felony, the subordinate term for each consecutive offense which is a felony described in this section shall consist of 100 percent of the middle term of imprisonment for the felony for which a consecutive term of imprisonment is imposed, and shall include 100 percent of any enhancements imposed pursuant to Section 12022, 12022.5, or 12022.7. A term of imprisonment imposed pursuant to this section may exceed twice the number of years imposed by the trial court as a base term pursuant to subdivision (b) of Section 1170.

§1170.2. Inmates who committed felonies before July 1, 1977.

(a) In the case of any inmate who committed a felony prior to July 1, 1977, who would have been sentenced under Section 1170 if he or she had committed it after July 1, 1977, the Board of Prison Terms shall determine what the length of time of imprisonment would have been under Section 1170 without consideration of good-time credit and utilizing the middle term of the offense bearing the longest term of imprisonment of which the prisoner was convicted increased by any enhancements justified by matters found to be true and which were imposed by the court at the time of sentencing for such felony. These matters include: being armed with a deadly or dangerous weapon as specified in Section 211a, 460, 3024, or 12022 prior to July 1, 1977, which may result in a one-year enhancement pursuant to the provisions of Section 12022; using a firearm as specified in Section 12022.5 prior to July 1, 1977, which may result in a two-year enhancement pursuant to the provisions of Section 12022.5; infliction of great bodily injury as specified in Section 213, 264, or 461 prior to July 1, 1977, which may result in a three-year enhancement pursuant to the provisions of Section 12022.7; any prior felony conviction as specified in any statute prior to July 1, 1977, which prior felony conviction is the equivalent of a prior prison term as defined in Section 657.5, which may result in the appropriate enhancement pursuant to the provisions of Section 667.5; and any consecutive sentence.

(b) If the calculation required under subdivision (a) is less than the time to be served prior to a release date set prior to July 1, 1977, or if a release date had not been set, the Board of Prison Terms shall establish the prisoner's parole date, subject to subdivision (d), on the date calculated under subdivision (a) unless at least two of the commissioners of the Board of Prison Terms after reviewing the prisoner's file, determine that due to the number of crimes of which the prisoner was convicted, or due to the number of prior convictions suffered by the prisoner, or due to the fact that the prisoner was armed with a deadly weapon when the crime was committed, or used a deadly weapon during the commission of the crime, or inflicted or attempted to inflict great bodily injury on the victim of the crime, the prisoner should serve a term longer than that calculated in subdivision (a), in which event the prisoner shall be entitled to a hearing before a panel consisting of at least two commissioners of the Board of Prison Terms as provided for in Section 3041.5. The Board of Prison Terms shall notify each prisoner who is scheduled for such a hearing within

90 days of July 1, 1977, or within 90 days of the date the prisoner is received by or returned to the custody of the Department of Corrections, whichever is later. The hearing shall be held before October 1, 1978, or within 120 days of receipt of the prisoner, whichever is later. It is the intent of the Legislature that the hearings provided for in this subdivision shall be accomplished in the most expeditious manner possible. At the hearing the prisoner shall be entitled to be represented by legal counsel, a release date shall be set, and the prisoner shall be informed in writing of the extraordinary factors specifically considered determinative and on what basis the release date has been calculated. In fixing a term under this section the board shall be guided by, but not limited to, the term which reasonably could be imposed on a person who committed a similar offense under similar circumstances on or after July 1, 1977, and further, the board shall be guided by the following finding and declaration hereby made by the Legislature: that the necessity to protect the public from repetition of extraordinary crimes of violence against the person is the paramount consideration.

(c) Nothing in this section shall be deemed to keep an inmate in the custody of the Department of Corrections for a period of time longer than he would have been kept in its custody under the provisions of law applicable to him prior to July 1, 1977. Nothing in this section shall be deemed to require the release of an inmate sentenced to consecutive sentences under the provisions of law applicable to him prior to July 1, 1977, earlier than if he had been sentenced to concurrent sentences.

(d) In the case of any prisoner who committed a felony prior to July 1, 1977, who would have been sentenced under Section 1170 if the felony was committed on or after July 1, 1977, the good behavior and participation provisions of Article 2.5 (commencing with Section 2930) of Chapter 7 of Title 1 of Part 3 shall apply from July 1, 1977, and thereafter.

(e) In the case of any inmate who committed a felony prior to July 1, 1977, who would have been sentenced under Section 1168 if the felony was committed on or after July 1, 1977, the Board of Prison Terms shall provide for release from prison as provided for by this code.

(f) In the case of any inmate who committed a felony prior to July 1, 1977, the length, conditions, revocation, and other incidents of parole shall be the same as if the prisoner had been sentenced for an offense committed on or after July 1, 1977.

(g) Nothing in this chapter shall affect the eligibility for parole under Article 3 (commencing with Section 3040) of Chapter 8 of Title 1 of Part 3 of an inmate sentenced pursuant to Section 1168 as operative prior to July 1, 1977, for a period of parole as specified in subdivision (b) of Section 3000.

(h) In fixing a term under this section, the Board of Prison Terms shall utilize the terms of imprisonment as provided in Chapter 1139 of the Statutes of 1976 and Chapter 165 of the Statutes of 1977. *(Amended by Stats 1989 ch 568 §1.5, eff. 1/1/90.)*

§1170.3. Adoption of rules to promote uniformity in sentencing.

The Judicial Council shall seek to promote uniformity in sentencing under Section 1170, by:

© 1992 by J., B. & L. Gould
Printed in the U.S.A.   EP

(a) The adoption of rules providing criteria for the consideration of the trial judge at the time of sentencing regarding the court's decision to:

(1) Grant or deny probation.

(2) Impose the lower or upper prison term.

(3) Impose concurrent or consecutive sentences.

(4) Determine whether or not to impose an enhancement where that determination is permitted by law.

(b) The adoption of rules standardizing the minimum content and the sequential presentation of material in probation officer reports submitted to the court. *(Amended by Stats 1988 ch 635 §2, eff. 1/1/89.)*

§1170.4. Information re sentencing practices.

The Judicial Council shall collect, analyze, and quarterly distribute and publish relevant information to trial judges and other interested persons relating to sentencing practices in this state and other jurisdictions. Such information shall be taken into consideration by the Judicial Council in the adoption of rules pursuant to Section 1170.3.

§1170.5. Sentencing institutes for trial court judges.

The Judicial Council shall conduct annual sentencing institutes for trial court judges pursuant to Section 68551 of the Government Code, toward the end of assisting the judge in the imposition of appropriate sentences.

§1170.6. Study and review of sentences and penalties.

The Judicial Council shall continually study and review the statutory sentences and the operation of existing criminal penalties and shall report to the Governor and to the appropriate policy committees of the Legislature its analysis regarding this subject matter and as to all proposed legislation affecting felony sentences. The review and analysis shall take into consideration all of the following:

(a) The nature of the offense with the degree of danger the offense presents to society.

(b) The penalty of the offense as compared to penalties for offenses that are in their nature more serious.

(c) The penalty of the offense as compared to penalties for the same offense in other jurisdictions.

(d) The penalty of the offense as compared to recommendations for sentencing suggested by national commissions and other learned bodies.

§1170.7. Obtaining controlled substance; aggravating circumstance in robbery.

Robbery or attempted robbery for the purpose of obtaining any controlled substance, as defined in Division 10 (commencing with Section 11000) of the Health and Safety Code, when committed against a pharmacist, pharmacy employee, or other person lawfully possessing controlled substances, shall be considered a circumstance in aggravation of the crime in imposing a term under subdivision (b) of Section 1170. *(Amended by Stats 1987 ch 828 §67.)*

§1170.71. Harmful matter; sentencing.

The fact that a person who commits a violation of Section 288 has used obscene or harmful matter to induce, persuade, or encourage the minor to engage in a lewd or lascivious act shall be considered a circum-

stance in aggravation of the crime in imposing a term under subdivision (b) of Section 1170. *(Added by Stats 1985 ch 165 §1.)*

§1170.73. Quantity of controlled substance; sentencing.

Upon conviction of a felony violation of Section 11377, 11378, or 11378.5 of the Health and Safety Code, the court shall consider the quantity of controlled substance involved in determining whether to impose an aggravated term under subdivision (b) of Section 1170. *(Added by Stats 1990 ch 777 §1, eff. 1/1/91.)*

§1170.74. Crystalline form of methamphetamine; sentencing.

Upon conviction of a felony violation of Section 11377, 11378, 11379, or 11379.6 of the Health and Safety Code, for an offense involving methamphetamine, the fact that the controlled substance is the crystalline form of methamphetamine shall be considered a circumstance in aggravation of the crime in imposing a term under subdivision (b) of Section 1170. *(Added by Stats 1990 ch 952 §1, eff. 1/1/91.)*

§1170.75. Felony committed or attempted because of victim's race, color; aggravating circumstances.

Except where the court imposes additional punishment under Section 422.75 or in a case in which the person has been convicted of an offense subject to Section 1170.8, the fact that a person committed a felony or attempted to commit a felony because of the victim's race, color, religion, nationality, country of origin, ancestry, disability, gender, or sexual orientation, shall be considered a circumstance in aggravation of the crime in imposing a term under subdivision (b) of Section 1170. *(Amended by Stats 1991 ch 607 §9, 1184 §3.5, eff. 1/1/92.)*

§1170.78. Committing arson in retaliation against owner of occupant.

Upon a conviction of a violation of Section 451, the fact that the person committed the offense in retaliation against the owner or occupant of the property or structure burned, or against one believed by the person to be the owner or occupant of the property or structure burned, for any eviction or other legal action taken by the owner or occupant, or believed owner or occupant, shall be a circumstance in aggravation of the crime in imposing a term under subdivision (b) of Section 1170. *(Added by Stats 1991 ch 602 §7, eff. 1/1/92.)*

§1170.8. Crime against church or person in church; aggravating circumstances.

(a) The fact that a robbery or an assault with a deadly weapon or instrument or by means of any force likely to produce great bodily injury was committed against a person while that person was in a church, synagogue, or building owned and occupied by a religious educational institution, or any other place primarily used as a place of worship where religious services are regularly conducted, shall be considered a circumstance in aggravation of the crime in imposing a term under subdivision (b) of Section 1170.

(b) Upon conviction of any person for a violation of Section 451 or 453, he fact that the person intentionally burned, or intended to burn, a church, synagogue,

© 1992 by J., B. & L. Gould
Printed in the U.S.A.   **EP**

or building owned and occupied by a religious educational institution, or any other place primarily used as a place of worship where religious services are regularly conducted, shall be considered a circumstance in aggravation of the crime in imposing a term under subdivision (b) of Section 1170.

§1170.81. Attempted murder of peace officer; sentencing.

The fact that the intended victim of an attempted life term crime was a peace officer, as described in subdivisions (a) and (b) of Section 830.1, or Section 830.2, 830.5 or 830.6, while the peace officer was engaged in the performance of his or her duties, and the defendant knew or reasonably should have known that the victim was a peace officer engaged in the performance of his or her duties, shall be considered a circumstance in aggravation of the crime in imposing a term under subdivision (b) of Section 1170. (*Added by Stats 1990 ch 1031 §1, eff. 1/1/91.*)

§1170.84. Tying, binding or confining; aggravation.

Upon conviction of any serious felony, listed in subdivision (c) of Section 1192.7, it shall be considered a circumstance in aggravation of the crime in imposing a term under subdivision (b) of Section 1170 if, during the course of the serious felony, the person engaged in the tying, binding, or confining of any victim. (*Added by Stats 1990 ch 1216 §1, eff. 1/1/91.*)

§1170.85. Felony assault or battery; aggravation.

(a) Upon conviction of any felony assault or battery offense, it shall be considered a circumstance in aggravation of the crime in imposing a term under subdivision (b) of Section 1170 if the offense was committed to prevent or dissuade a person who is or may become a witness from attending upon or testifying at any trial, proceeding, or inquiry authorized by law, or if the offense was committed because the person provided assistance or information to a law enforcement officer, or to a public prosecutor in a criminal or juvenile court proceeding.

(b) Upon conviction of any felony it shall be considered a circumstance in aggravation in imposing a term under subdivision (b) of Section 1170 if the victim of an offense is particularly vulnerable, or unable to defend himself or herself, due to age or significant disability. (*Amended by Stats 1985 ch 1108 §3.*)

§1170.9. Vietnam vet may be committed to federal officials.

In the case of any person convicted of a felony who would otherwise be sentenced to state prison the court shall consider whether the defendant was a member of the military forces of the United States who served in combat in Vietnam and who suffers from substance abuse or psychological problems resulting from that service. If the court concludes that the defendant is such a person, the court may order the defendant committed to the custody of federal correctional officials for incarceration for a term equivalent to that which the defendant would have served in state prison. The court may make such a commitment only if the defendant agrees to such a commitment, the court has determined that appropriate federal programs exist, and federal law authorizes the receipt of the defendant under such conditions.

§1170.95. Residential burglaries; subordinate terms.

(a) Notwithstanding Section 1170.1 relating to the maximum total of subordinate terms for consecutive offenses which are not "violent felonies," the total of the subordinate terms for consecutive offenses which are all residential burglaries may exceed five years but shall not exceed 10 years.

(b) Notwithstanding Section 1170.1, the term of imprisonment may exceed twice the number of years imposed by the trial court as the base term pursuant to subdivision (b) of Section 1170 if the defendant stands convicted of at least two residential burglaries.

(c) Notwithstanding Section 1170.1, relating to the maximum total of subordinate terms for consecutive offenses that are not "violent felonies," the total of the subordinate terms for consecutive offenses that are all residential robberies may exceed five years but shall not exceed 10 years.

(d) Notwithstanding Section 1170.1, the term of imprisonment may exceed twice the number of years imposed by the trial court as the base term pursuant to subdivision (b) of Section 1170 if the defendant stands convicted of at least two residential robberies.

(e) Notwithstanding Section 1170.1 relating to the maximum total of subordinate terms for consecutive offenses that are not "violent felonies," the total of the subordinate terms for consecutive offenses that are all residential arsons may exceed five years but shall not exceed 10 years.

(f) Notwithstanding Section 1170.1, the term of imprisonment may exceed twice the number of years imposed by the trial court as the base term pursuant to subdivision (b) of Section 1170 if the defendant stands convicted of at least two residential arsons.

(g) When a consecutive term of imprisonment is imposed pursuant to Sections 669 and 1170 which involves two or more convictions for robbery where it is charged and found that in each of those robberies that the defendant personally used a deadly or dangerous weapon in the commission of that robbery, as provided in subdivision (b) of Section 12022, and each of those robberies is not a violent felony, as defined in subdivision (c) of Section 667.5, the aggregate term shall be calculated as provided in subdivision (a) of Section 1170.1, except that the subordinate term for each subsequent robbery conviction shall consist of one-third of the middle term of imprisonment and one-third of the enhancement provided in subdivision (b) of Section 12022. Notwithstanding Section 1170.1, the total number of subordinate terms imposed under this subdivision may exceed five years but shall not exceed 10 years.

(h) As used in this section, "residential burglary" means burglary of an inhabited dwelling house or trailer coach, as defined in Section 635 of the Vehicle Code, or the inhabited portion of any other building.

(i) As used in this section, "residential robbery" means a robbery that is perpetrated in an inhabited dwelling house or trailer coach, as defined in Section 635 of the Vehicle Code, or the inhabited portion of any other building.

(j) As used in this section, "residential arson" means arson committed in violation of subdivision (b) of Section 451 where it is charged and proved that the defendant intentionally set fire to or burned or caused the burning of a distinct inhabited structure or a distinct inhabited property in the commission of that offense. (*Amended by Stats 1988 ch 244 §1; ch 811 §2, eff. 1/1/89.*)

© 1992 by J., B. & L. Gould
Printed in the U.S.A.   EP

CHAPTER 5

BILLS OF EXCEPTION

§1176. Written instructions.

When written instructions have been presented, and given, modified, or refused, or when the charge of the court has been taken down by the reporter, the questions presented in such instructions or charge need not be excepted to; but the judge must make and sign an indorsement upon such instructions, showing the action of the court thereon.

CHAPTER 6

NEW TRIALS

§1179. New trial defined.

A new trial is a reexamination of the issue in the same Court, before another jury, after a verdict has been given.

§1180. Granting; effect.

The granting of a new trial places the parties in the same position as if no trial had been had. All the testimony must be produced anew, and the former verdict or finding cannot be used or referred to, either in evidence or in argument, or be pleaded in bar of any conviction which might have been had under the accusatory pleading.

§1181. Grounds.

When a verdict has been rendered or a finding made against the defendant, the court may, upon his application, grant a new trial, in the following cases only:

1. When the trial has been had in his absence except in cases where the trial may lawfully proceed in his absence;

2. When the jury has received any evidence out of court, other than that resulting from a view of the premises, or of personal property;

3. When the jury has separated without leave of the court after retiring to deliberate upon their verdict, or been guilty of any misconduct by which a fair and due consideration of the case has been prevented;

4. When the verdict has been decided by lot, or by any means other than a fair expression of opinion on the part of all the jurors;

5. When the court has misdirected the jury in a matter of law, or has erred in the decision of any question of law arising during the course of the trial, and when the district attorney or other counsel prosecuting the case has been guilty of prejudicial misconduct during the trial thereof before a jury;

6. When the verdict or finding is contrary to law or evidence, but if the evidence shows the defendant to be not guilty of the degree of the crime of which he was convicted, but guilty of a lesser degree thereof, or of a lesser crime included therein, the court may modify the verdict, finding or judgment accordingly without granting or ordering a new trial, and this power shall extend to any court to which the cause may be appealed;

7. When the verdict or finding is contrary to law or evidence, but in any case wherein authority is vested by statute in the trial court or jury to recommend or determine as a part of its verdict or finding the punishment to be imposed, the court may modify such verdict or finding by imposing the lesser punishment without granting or ordering a new trial, and this power shall extend to any court to which the case may be appealed;

8. When new evidence is discovered material to the defendant, and which he could not, with reasonable diligence, have discovered and produced at trial. When a motion for a new trial is made upon the ground of newly discovered evidence, the defendant must produce at the hearing, in support thereof, the affidavits of the witnesses by whom such evidence is expected to be given, and if time is required by the defendant to procure such affidavits, the court may postpone the hearing of the motion for such length of time as, under all circumstances of the case, may seem reasonable.

9. When the right to a phonographic report has not been waived, and when it is not possible to have a phonographic report of the trial transcribed by a stenographic reporter as provided by law or by rule because of the death or disability of a reporter who participated as a stenographic reporter at the trial or because of the loss or destruction, in whole or in substantial part, of the notes of such reporter, the trial court or a judge, thereof, or the reviewing court shall have power to set aside and vacate the judgment, order or decree from which an appeal has been taken or is to be taken and to order a new trial of the action or proceeding.

§1182. Application.

The application for a new trial must be made and determined before judgment, the making of an order granting probation, the commitment of a defendant for observation as a mentally disordered sex offender, or the commitment of a defendant for narcotics addiction or insanity, whichever first occurs, and the order granting or denying the application shall be immediately entered by the clerk in the minutes.

CHAPTER 7

ARREST OF JUDGMENT

§1185. Motion; defined, grounds.

A motion in arrest of judgment is an application on the part of the defendant that no judgment be rendered on a plea, finding, or verdict of guilty, or on a finding or verdict against the defendant, on a plea of a former conviction, former acquittal or once in jeopardy. It may be founded on any of the defects in the accusatory pleading mentioned in Section 1004, unless the objection has been waived by a failure to demur, and must be made and determined before the judgment is pronounced. When determined, the order must be immediately entered in the minutes.

§1186. Court's own motion.

The court may, on its own motion, at any time before judgment is pronounced, arrest the judgment for any of the defects in the accusatory pleading upon which a motion in arrest of judgment may be founded as provided in Section 1185, by order for that purpose entered upon its minutes.

§1187. Effect of an order.

The effect of an order arresting judgment, in a superior court, is to place the defendant in the same situation in which he was immediately before the indictment was found or information filed. In any

© 1992 by J., B. & L. Gould
Printed in the U.S.A. **EP**

other court the effect is to place the defendant in the situation in which he was before the trial was had.

§1188. Recommitment or readmitting to bail.

If, from the evidence on the trial, there is reason to believe the defendant guilty, and a new indictment or information can be framed upon which he may be convicted, the court may order him to be recommitted to the officer of the proper county, or admitted to bail anew, to answer the new indictment or information. If the evidence shows him guilty of another offense, he must be committed or held thereon, and in neither case shall the verdict be a bar to another prosecution. But if no evidence appears sufficient to charge him with any offense, he must, if in custody, be discharged; or if admitted to bail, his bail is exonerated; or if money has been deposited instead of bail, it must be refunded to the defendant or to the person or persons found by the court to have deposited said money on behalf of said defendant; and the arrest of judgment shall operate as an acquittal of the charge upon which the indictment or information was founded.

TITLE 8

OF JUDGMENT AND EXECUTION

CHAPTER 1

THE JUDGMENT

§1191. Time for pronouncing.

In the superior court, after a plea, finding, or verdict of guilty, or after a finding or verdict against the defendant on a plea of a former conviction or acquittal, or once in jeopardy, the court shall appoint a time for pronouncing judgment, which shall be within 20 judicial days after the verdict, finding, or plea of guilty, during which time the court shall refer the case to the probation officer for a report if eligible for probation and pursuant to Section 1203. However, the court may extend the time not more than 10 days for the purpose of hearing or determining any motion for a new trial, or in arrest of judgment, and may further extend the time until the probation officer's report is received and until any proceedings for granting or denying probation have been disposed of. If, in the opinion of the court, there is a reasonable ground for believing a defendant insane, the court may extend the time for pronouncing sentence until the question of insanity has been heard and determined, as provided in this code. If the court orders defendant placed in a diagnostic facility pursuant to Section 1203.03, the time otherwise allowed by this section for pronouncing judgment is extended by a period equal to (1) the number of days which elapse between the date of the order and the date on which notice is received from the Director of Corrections advising whether or not the Department of Corrections will receive defendant in the facility, and (2) if the director notifies the court that it will receive the defendant, the time which elapses until his or her return to the court from the facility. *(Amended by Stats 1990 ch 570 §1, eff. 1/1/91.)*

§1191.1. Victims' statements.

The victim of any crime, or his or her parent or guardian if the victim is a minor, or the next of kin of the victim if the victim has died, has the right to attend all sentencing proceedings under this chapter and shall be given adequate notice by the probation officer of all sentencing proceedings concerning the person who committed the crime.

The victim, or his or her parent or guardian if the victim is a minor, or next of kin has the right to appear, personally or by counsel, at the sentencing proceeding and to reasonably express his or her views concerning the crime, the person responsible, and the need for restitution. The court in imposing sentence shall consider the statements of victims, parents, or guardians, and next of kin made pursuant to this section and shall state on the record its conclusion concerning whether the person would pose a threat to public safety if granted probation.

The provisions of this section shall not be amended by the Legislature except by statute passed in each house by rollcall vote entered in the journal, two-thirds of the membership concurring, or by a statute that becomes effective only when approved by the electors.

§1191.15. Victim's statement; written, audio, video.

(a) The court may permit the victim of any crime, or his or her parent or guardian if the victim is a minor, or the next of kin of the victim if the victim has died, to file with the court a written, audiotaped, or videotaped statement expressing his or her views concerning the crime, the person responsible, and the need for restitution, in lieu of or in addition to such person personally appearing at the time of judgment and sentence. The court shall consider any such statement filed with the court prior to imposing judgment and sentence.

Whenever an audio or video statement is filed with the court, a written transcript of the tape shall also be provided by the person filing the statement, and shall be made available as a public record of the court after the judgment and sentence have been imposed.

(b) Whenever such a written, audio, or video statement is filed with the court, it shall remain sealed until the time set for imposition of judgment and sentence except that the court, the probation officer, and counsel for the parties may view and listen to such statements not more than two court days prior to the date set for imposition of judgment and sentence.

(c) No person may, and no court shall, permit any person to duplicate, copy, or reproduce by any audio or visual means any audiotaped or videotaped statement submitted to the court under the provisions of this section.

(d) Nothing in this section shall be construed to prohibit the prosecutor from representing to the court the views of the victim or his or her parent or guardian or the next of kin.

(e) In the event the court permits an audio or video statement to be filed, the court shall not be responsible for providing any equipment or resources needed to assist the victim in preparing the statement. *(Added by Stats 1988 ch 935 §1, eff. 1/1/89.)*

§1191.2. Victim's right to civil recovery and compensation from fund.

In providing notice to the victim pursuant to Section 1191.1, the probation officer shall also provide the victim with information concerning the victim's right to civil recovery against the defendant and the victim's opportunity to be compensated from the Restitution Fund. This information shall be in the form of written

© 1992 by J., B. & L. Gould
Printed in the U.S.A.   EP

material prepared by the Judicial Council and shall be provided to each victim for whom the probation officer has a current mailing address.

§1191.25. Notification of victim.

The prosecution shall make a good faith attempt to notify any victim of a crime which was committed by, or is alleged to have been committed by, an in-custody informant, as defined in subdivision (a) of Section 1127a, within a reasonable time before the in-custody informant is called to testify. The notice shall include information concerning the prosecution's intention to offer the in-custody informant a modification or reduction in sentence or dismissal of the case or early parole in exchange for the in-custody informant's testimony in another case. The notification or attempt to notify the victim shall be made prior to the commencement of the trial in which the in-custody informant is to testify where the intention to call him or her is known at that time, but in no case shall the notice be made later than the time the in-custody informant is called to the stand.

Nothing contained in this section is intended to affect the right of the people and the defendant to an expeditious disposition of a criminal proceeding, as provided in Section 1050. The victim of any case alleged to have been committed by the in-custody informant may exercise his or her right to appear at the sentencing of the in-custody informant pursuant to Section 1191.1, but the victim shall not have a right to intervene in the trial in which the in-custody informant is called to testify. (*Added by Stats 1989 ch 901 §2, eff. 1/1/90.*)

§1191.3. Conduct and worktime credits.

(a) At the time of sentencing or pronouncement of judgment in which sentencing is imposed, the court shall make an oral statement that statutory law permits the award of conduct and worktime credits up to one-third or one-half of the sentence that is imposed by the court, that the award and calculation of credits is determined by the sheriff in cases involving imprisonment in county jails and by the Department of Corrections in cases involving imprisonment in the state prison, and that credit for presentence incarceration served by the defendant is calculated by the probation department under current state law.

As used in this section, "victim" means the victim of the offense, the victim's parent or guardian if the victim is a minor, or the victim's next of kin.

(b) The probation officer shall provide a general estimate of the credits to which the defendant may be entitled for previous time served, and conduct or worktime credits authorized under Sections 2931, 2933, or 4019, and shall inform the victim pursuant to Section 1191.1. The probation officer shall file this estimate with the court and it shall become a part of the court record.

(c) This section applies to all felony convictions. (*Added by Stats 1987 ch 1247 §3.*)

§1192. Court to determine degree of offense.

Upon a plea of guilty, or upon conviction by the court without a jury, of a crime or attempted crime distinguished or divided into degrees, the court must, before passing sentence, determine the degree. Upon the failure of the court to so determine, the degree of the crime or attempted crime of which the defendant is guilty, shall be deemed to be of the lesser degree.

§1192.1. Plea of guilty specifying degree of crime.

Upon a plea of guilty to an information or indictment accusing the defendant of a crime or attempted crime divided into degrees when consented to by the prosecuting attorney in open court and approved by the court, such plea may specify the degree thereof and in such event the defendant cannot be punished for a higher degree of the crime or attempted crime than the degree specified.

§1192.2. Plea of guilty before committing magistrate.

Upon a plea of guilty before a committing magistrate as provided in Section 859a, to a crime or attempted crime divided into degrees, when consented to by the prosecuting attorney in open court and approved by such magistrate, such plea may specify the degree thereof and in such event, the defendant cannot be punished for a higher degree of the crime or attempted crime than the degree specified.

§1192.3. Payment of restitution when charges dismissed.

(a) A plea of guilty or nolo contendere to an accusatory pleading charging a public offense, other than a felony specified in Section 1192.5 or 1192.7, which public offense did not result in damage for which restitution may be ordered, made on the condition that charges be dismissed for one or more public offenses arising from the same or related course of conduct by the defendant which did result in damage for which restitution may be ordered, may specify the payment of restitution by the defendant as a condition of the plea or any probation granted pursuant thereto, so long as the plea is freely and voluntarily made, there is factual basis for the plea, and the plea and all conditions are approved by the court.

(b) If restitution is imposed which is attributable to a count dismissed pursuant to a plea bargain, as described in this section, the court shall obtain a waiver pursuant to People v. Harvey (1979) 25 Cal. 3d 754 from the defendant as to the dismissed count. (*Added by Stats 1988 ch 287 §1, eff. 1/1/89.*)

§1192.4. Withdrawal of guilty plea.

If the defendant's plea of guilty pursuant to Section 1192.1 or 1192.2 is not accepted by the prosecuting attorney and approved by the court, the plea shall be deemed withdrawn and the defendant may then enter such plea or pleas as would otherwise have been available. The plea so withdrawn may not be received in evidence in any criminal, civil, or special action or proceeding of any nature, including proceedings before agencies, commissions, boards, and tribunals.

§1192.5. Plea of guilty or nolo contendere specifying punishment.

Upon a plea of guilty or nolo contendere to an accusatory pleading charging a felony, other than a violation of subdivision (2) or (3) of Section 261, Section 264.1, Section 286 by force, violence, duress, menace or threat of great bodily harm, subdivision (b) of Section 288, Section 288a by force, violence, duress, menace or threat of great bodily harm, or Section 289, the plea may specify the punishment to the same extent as it may be specified by the jury on a plea of not guilty or fixed by the court on a plea of guilty, nolo contendere, or not guilty, and may specify the exercise

© 1992 by J., B. & L. Gould
Printed in the U.S.A. **EP**

by the court thereafter of other powers legally available to it.

Where such plea is accepted by the prosecuting attorney in open court and is approved by the court, the defendant, except as otherwise provided in this section, cannot be sentenced on such plea to a punishment more severe than that specified in the plea and the court may not proceed as to such plea other than as specified in the plea.

If the court approves of the plea, it shall inform the defendant prior to the making of the plea that (1) its approval is not binding, (2) it may, at the time set for the hearing on the application for probation or pronouncement of judgment, withdraw its approval in the light of further consideration of the matter, and (3) in such case, the defendant shall be permitted to withdraw his plea if he desires to do so. The court shall also cause an inquiry to be made of the defendant to satisfy itself that the plea is freely and voluntarily made, and that there is a factual basis for such plea.

If such plea is not accepted by the prosecuting attorney and approved by the court, the plea shall be deemed withdrawn and the defendant may then enter such plea or pleas as would otherwise have been available.

If such plea is withdrawn or deemed withdrawn, it may not be received in evidence in any criminal, civil, or special action or proceeding of any nature, including proceedings before agencies, commissions, boards, and tribunals.

§1192.6. Statement explaining dismissal or recommending punishment.

(a) In each felony case in which the charges contained in the original accusatory pleading are amended or dismissed, the record shall contain a statement explaining the reason for the amendment or dismissal.

(b) In each felony case in which the prosecuting attorney seeks a dismissal of a charge in the complaint, indictment, or information, he or she shall state the specific reasons for the dismissal in open court, on the record.

(c) When, upon a plea of guilty or nolo contendere to an accusatory pleading charging a felony, whether or not that plea is entered pursuant to Section 1192.5, the prosecuting attorney recommends what punishment the court should impose or how it should exercise any of the powers legally available to it, the prosecuting attorney shall state the specific reasons for the recommendation in open court, on the record. The reasons for the recommendation shall be transcribed and made part of the court file.

§1192.7. Plea bargaining.

(a) Plea bargaining in any case in which the indictment or information charges any serious felony, any felony in which it is alleged that a firearm was personally used by the defendant, or any offense of driving while under the influence of alcohol, drugs, narcotics, or any other intoxicating substance, or any combination thereof, is prohibited, unless there is insufficient evidence to prove the people's case, or testimony of a material witness cannot be obtained, or a reduction or dismissal would not result in a substantial change in sentence.

(b) As used in this section "plea bargaining" means any bargaining, negotiation, or discussion between a criminal defendant, or his or her counsel, and a prosecuting attorney or judge, whereby the defendant agrees to plead guilty or nolo contendere, in exchange for any promises, commitments, concessions, assurances, or consideration by the prosecuting attorney or judge relating to any charge against the defendant or to the sentencing of the defendant.

(c) As used in this section, "serious felony" means any of the following:

(1) Murder or voluntary manslaughter; (2) mayhem; (3) rape; (4) sodomy by force, violence, duress, menace, threat of great bodily injury, or fear of immediate and unlawful bodily injury on the victim or another person; (5) oral copulation by force, violence, duress, menace, threat of great bodily injury, or fear of immediate and unlawful bodily injury on the victim or another person; (6) lewd or lascivious act on a child under the age of 14 years; (7) any felony punishable by death or imprisonment in the state prison for life; (8) any other felony in which the defendant personally inflicts great bodily injury on any person, other than an accomplice, or any felony in which the defendant personally uses a firearm; (9) attempted murder; (10) assault with intent to commit rape or robbery; (11) assault with a deadly, weapon or instrument on a peace officer; (12) assault by a life prisoner on a noninmate; (13) assault with a deadly weapon by an inmate; (14) arson; (15) exploding a destructive device or any explosive with intent to injure; (16) exploding a destructive device or any explosive causing great bodily injury or mayhem; (17) exploding a destructive device or any explosive with intent to murder; (18) burglary of an inhabited dwelling house, or trailer coach as defined by the Vehicle Code, or inhabited portion of any other building; (19) robbery or bank robbery; (20) kidnapping; (21) holding of a hostage by a person confined in a state prison; (22) attempt to commit a felony punishable by death or imprisonment in the state prison for life; (23) any felony in which the defendant personally used a dangerous or deadly weapon; (24) selling, furnishing, administering, giving, or offering to sell, furnish, administer, or give to a minor any heroin, cocaine, phencyclidine (PCP), or any methamphetamine-related drug, as described in paragraph (2) of subdivision (d) of Section 11055 of the Health and Safety Code, or any of the precursors of methamphetamines, as described in subparagraph (A) of paragraph (1) of subdivision (f) of Section 11055 or subdivision (a) of Section 11100 of the Health and Safety Code; (25) any violation of subdivision (a) of Section 289 where the act is accomplished against the victim's will by force, violence, duress, menace, or fear of immediate and unlawful bodily injury on the victim or another person; (26) grand theft involving a firearm; (27) any attempt to commit a crime listed in this subdivision other than assault.

(d) As used in this section, "bank robbery" take or attempt to take, by force or violence, or by intimidation from the person or presence of another any property or money or any other thing of value belonging to, or in the care, custody, control, management, or possession of, any bank, credit union, or any savings and loan association.

As used in this subdivision, the following terms have the following meanings:

(1) "Bank" means any member bank of the Federal Reserve System, and any bank, banking association, trust company, savings bank, or other banking institution organized or operating under the laws of the

© 1992 by J., B. & L. Gould
Printed in the U.S.A.   EP

United States, and any bank the deposits of which are insured by the Federal Deposit Insurance Corporation.

(2) "Savings and loan association" means any federal savings and loan association and any "insured institution" as defined in Section 401 of the National Housing Act, as amended, and any federal credit union as defined in Section 2 of the Federal Credit Union Act.

(3) "Credit union" means any federal credit union and any state-chartered credit union the accounts of which are insured by the Administrator of the National Credit Union Administration.

(e) The provisions of this section shall not be amended by the Legislature except by statute passed in each house by rollcall vote entered in the journal, two-thirds of the membership concurring, or by a statute that becomes effective only when approved by the electors. (Amended by Stats 1989 ch 1043, 1044 §2.5, eff. 1/1/90.)

§1192.8. Serious felony; defined.

For purposes of subdivision (c) of Section 1192.7, "serious felony" also means any violation of Section 288.5. (Added by Stats 1989 ch 1402 §10, eff. 1/1/90.)

§1193. Pronouncing judgment.

Judgment upon persons convicted of commission of crime shall be pronounced as follows:

(a) If the conviction is for a felony, the defendant shall be personally present when judgment is pronounced against him or her unless the defendant, in open court and on the record, or in a notarized writing, requests that judgment be pronounced against him or her in his or her absence, and that he or she be represented by an attorney when judgment is pronounced, and the court approves his or her absence during the pronouncement of judgment, or unless, after the exercise of reasonable diligence to procure the presence of the defendant, the court shall find that it will be in the interest of justice that judgment be pronounced in his or her absence; provided, that when any judgment imposing the death penalty has been affirmed by the appellate court, sentence may be reimposed upon the defendant in his or her absence by the court from which the appeal was taken, and in the following manner: upon receipt by the superior court from which the appeal is taken of the certificate of the appellate court affirming the judgment, the judge of the superior court shall forthwith make and cause to be entered an order pronouncing sentence against the defendant, and a warrant signed by the judge, and attested by the clerk under the seal of the court, shall be drawn, and it shall state the conviction and judgment and appoint a day upon which the judgment shall be executed, which shall not be less than 60 days nor more than 90 days from the time of making the order; and that, within five days thereafter, a certified copy of the order, attested by the clerk under the seal of the court, and attached to the warrant, shall, for the purpose of execution, be transmitted by registered mail to the warden of the state prison having the custody of the defendant and certified copies thereof shall be transmitted by registered mail to the Governor; and provided further, that when any judgment imposing the death penalty has been affirmed and sentence has been reimposed as above provided there shall be no appeal from the order fixing the time for and directing the execution of the judgment as herein provided. If a pro se defendant requests that judgment

in a noncapital case be pronounced against him or her in his or her absence, the court shall appoint an attorney to represent the defendant in the in absentia sentencing.

(b) If the conviction be of a misdemeanor, judgment may be pronounced against the defendant in his absence. (Amended by Stats 1986 ch 1222 §1.)

§1194. When defendant in custody, how brought before the court for judgment.

When the defendant is in custody, the Court may direct the officer in whose custody he is to bring him before it for judgment, and the officer must do so.

§1195. Effect of appearance or nonappearance of defendant on bail.

If the defendant has been released on bail, or has deposited money or property instead thereof, and does not appear for judgment when his personal appearance is necessary, the court, in addition to the forfeiture of the undertaking of bail, or of the money or property deposited, must, on application of the prosecuting attorney, direct the issuance of a bench warrant for the arrest of the defendant.

If the defendant, who is on bail, does appear for judgment and judgment is pronounced upon him or probation is granted to him, then the bail shall be exonerated or, if money or property has been deposited instead of bail, it must be returned to the defendant or to the person or persons found by the court to have deposited said money or property on behalf of said defendant.

§1196. Issuance of bench warrant.

The clerk, or the judge or justice, if there is no clerk, on application of the prosecuting attorney, must at any time after the order issue a bench warrant into one or more counties.

§1197. Bench warrant's form.

The bench warrant must be substantially in the following form:

County of _____

The people of the State of California to any peace officer in this State: ___ (name of defendant) having been on the ___ day of ____ , 19 ___ , duly convicted in the ___ court of ___ (naming the court) of the crime of ___ (designating it generally), you are therefore commanded forthwith to arrest the above named defendant and bring him before that court for judgment.

Given under my hand with the seal of said court affixed, this _ day of ____ , 19 _.

By order of said court.

_____
Clerk (or Judge, or Justice)

(SEAL)

§1198. Service.

The bench warrant may be served in any county in the same manner as a warrant of arrest.

§1199. Officer to arrest defendant.

Whether the bench warrant is served in the county in which it was issued or in another county, the officer must arrest the defendant and bring him before the court, or deliver him to any peace officer of the county from which the warrant issued, who must bring him before said court according to the command thereof.

§1200. Arraignment of defendant for judgment.

When the defendant appears for judgment he must be informed by the court, or by the clerk, under its direction, of the nature of the charge against him and of his plea, and the verdict, if any thereon, and must be asked whether he has any legal cause to show why judgment should not be pronounced against him.

§1201. Causes shown against pronouncement of judgment.

He or she may show, for cause against the judgment:

(a) That he or she is insane; and if, in the opinion of the court, there is reasonable ground for believing him or her insane, the question of insanity shall be tried as provided in Chapter 6 (commencing with Section 1367) of Title 10 of Part 2. If, upon the trial of that question, the jury finds that he or she is sane, judgment shall be pronounced, but if they find him or her insane, he or she shall be committed to the state hospital for the care and treatment of the insane, until he or she becomes sane; and when notice is given of that fact, as provided in Section 1372, he or she shall be brought before the court for judgment.

(b) That he or she has good cause to offer, either in arrest of judgment or for a new trial; in which case the court may, in its discretion, order the judgment to be deferred, and proceed to decide upon the motion in arrest of judgment or for a new trial. *(Amended by Stats 1987 ch 828 §68.)*

§1201.5. Motions subsequent to judgment.

Any motions made subsequent to judgment must be made only upon written notice served upon the prosecution at least three days prior to the date of hearing thereon. No affidavit or other writing shall be presented or considered in support thereof unless a copy of the same has been duly served upon the prosecution at least three days prior to a hearing thereon. Any appeal from an order entered upon a motion made other than as herein provided, must be dismissed by the court.

§1202. Pronouncing judgment.

If no sufficient cause is alleged or appears to the court at the time fixed for pronouncing judgment, as provided in Section 1191, why judgment should not be pronounced, it shall thereupon be rendered; and if not rendered or pronounced within the time so fixed or to which it is continued under the provisions of Section 1191, then the defendant shall be entitled to a new trial. If the court shall refuse to hear a defendant's motion for a new trial or when made shall neglect to determine such motion before pronouncing judgment or the making of an order granting probation, then the defendant shall be entitled to a new trial. *(Amended by Stats 1987 ch 828 §69.)*

§1202a. Delivery of defendant.

If the judgment is for imprisonment in the state prison the judgment shall direct that the defendant be delivered into the custody of the Director of Corrections at the state prison or institution designated by the Director of Corrections as the place for the reception of persons convicted of felonies, except where the judgment is for death in which case the defendant shall be taken to the warden of the California State Prison at San Quentin.

Unless a different place or places are so designated by the Director of Corrections, the judgment shall direct that the defendant be delivered into the custody of the Director of Corrections at the California State Prison at San Quentin. The Director of Corrections shall designate a place or places for the reception of persons convicted of felonies by order, which order or orders shall be served by registered mail, return receipt requested, upon each judge of each superior court in the state. The Director of Corrections may change the place or places of commitment by the issuance of a new order. Nothing contained in this section affects any provision of Section 3400. *(Amended by Stats 1987 ch 828 §70.)*

1202.1. Sexual offenders tested for AIDS.

(a) Notwithstanding Sections 199.20 and 199.22 of the Health and Safety Code, the court shall order every person convicted of a violation of a sexual offense listed in subdivision (d), whether or not a sentence or fine is imposed or probation is granted, to submit to a blood test for evidence of antibodies to the probable causative agent of acquired immune deficiency syndrome (AIDS). Each person tested under this section shall be informed of the results of the blood test.

(b) Notwithstanding Section 199.21 of the Health and Safety Code, the results of the blood test to detect antibodies to the probable causative agent of AIDS shall be transmitted by the clerk of the court to the Department of Justice.

(c) Notwithstanding Section 199.21 of the Health and Safety Code, the Department of Justice shall provide the results of a test or tests as to persons under investigation or being prosecuted under Section 647f or 12022.85, if the results are on file with the department, to the defense attorney upon request; and the results also shall be avaliable to the prosecuting attorney upon request for the sole purpose of preparing counts for a subsequent offense under Section 647f or sentence enhancement under Section 12022.85.

(d) For purposes of this section, sexual offenses include any of the following:

(1) Rape in violation of Section 261.

(2) Unlawful intercourse with a female under age 18 in violation of Section 261.5.

(3) Rape of a spouse in violation of Section 262.

(4) Sodomy in violation of Section 286.

(5) Oral copulation in violation of Section 288a. *(Added by Stats 1988 ch 1597 §2, eff. 1/1/90 contingent upon funding provided in the Budget Act of 1989.)*

§1202.4. Restitution fine.

(a) In any case in which a defendant is convicted of a felony, the court shall order the defendant to pay a restitution fine as provided in subdivision (a) of Section 13967 of the Government Code. Such restitution fine shall be in addition to any other penalty or fine imposed and shall be ordered regardless of the defendant's present ability to pay. However, if the court finds that there are compelling and extraordinary reasons, the court may waive imposition of the fine. When such a waiver is granted, the court shall state on the record all reasons supporting the waiver.

(b) In any case in which the defendant is ordered to pay restitution as a condition of probation, the order to pay the restitution fine, or portion thereof, may be stayed pending the successful completion of probation, and thereafter the stay shall become permanent.

© 1992 by J., B. & L. Gould
Printed in the U.S.A.   EP

(c) If the restitution fine has been stayed pending successful completion of probation, upon revocation of probation and imposition of sentence the stay shall be lifted. The amount of restitution fine shall be offset by any restitution payments actually made as a condition of probation. Nothing in this section authorizes the stay of an order of restitution to the victim. *(Amended by Stats 1990 ch 45 §4, eff. 1/1/91.)*

§1202.5. Crimes; fines.

(a) In any case in which a defendant is convicted of any of the offenses enumerated in Section 211, 459, 487, or 488, the court may order the defendant to pay a fine of ten dollars ($10) in addition to any other penalty or fine imposed. If the court determines that the defendant has the ability to pay all or part of the fine, the court may set the amount to be reimbursed and order the defendant to pay that sum to the county in the manner in which the court believes reasonable and compatible with the defendant's financial ability. In making a determination of whether a defendant has the ability to pay, the court shall take into account the amount of any other fine imposed upon the defendant and any amount the defendant has been ordered to pay in restitution.

(b) All fines collected pursuant to this section shall be transferred to the local law enforcement agency in the jurisdiction where the offense took place. All moneys collected shall be used exclusively to implement, support, and continue local crime prevention programs.

(c) As used in this section "law enforcement agency" includes, but is not limited to, police departments, sheriffs departments, and probation departments. *(Added by Stats 1985 ch 1321 §1.)*

§1202.6. AIDS education and testing.

(a) Notwithstanding Sections 199.20, 199.21, and 199.22 of the Health and Safety Code, upon the first conviction of any person for a violation of subdivision (b) of Section 647, the court shall, before sentencing or as a condition of probation, order the defendant to complete instruction in the causes and consequences of acquired immune deficiency syndrome (AIDS) pursuant to subdivision (d) and shall order the defendant to submit to testing for AIDS in accordance with subdivision (e). In addition, the court shall refer a defendant, where appropriate, to a program under Article 3.2 (commencing with Section 11320) of Chapter 2 of Part 3 of Division 9 of the Welfare and Institutions Code or to any drug diversion program, or both.

(b) Upon a second or subsequent conviction of a violation of subdivision (b) of Section 647, the court shall, before sentencing, order the defendant to submit to testing for AIDS in accordance with subdivision (e).

(c) At the sentencing hearing of a defendant ordered to submit to testing for AIDS pursuant to subdivision (a) or (b), the court shall furnish the defendant with a copy of the report submitted pursuant to subdivision (e) and shall direct the clerk to note the receipt of the report by the defendant in the records of the case.

If the results of the test described in the report are positive, the court shall make certain that the defendant understands the nature and meaning of the contents of the report and shall further advise the defendant of the penalty established in Section 647f for a subsequent violation of subdivision (b) of Section 647.

(d) The county health officer in each county shall select an agency, or agencies, in the county that shall provide AIDS prevention education. The county health officer shall endeavor to select an agency, or agencies, that currently provide AIDS prevention education programs to substance abusers or prostitutes. If no agency is currently providing this education, the county agency responsible for substance abuse shall develop an AIDS prevention education program either within the agency or under contract with a community-based, nonprofit organization in the county. The county health officer shall forward to the courts a list of agencies selected for purposes of referral.

An AIDS prevention education program providing services, at a minimum, shall include details about the transmission of human immunodeficiency virus (HIV), the etiologic agent for AIDS, symptoms of AIDS or AIDS-related conditions, prevention through avoidance or cleaning of needles, sexual practices which constitute high risk, low risk, and no risk (including abstinence), and resources for assistance if the person decides to take a test for the etiologic agent for AIDS and receives a positive test result. The program also shall include other relevant medical and prevention information as it becomes available.

(e) The court shall order testing of every defendant as ordered pursuant to subdivision (a) or (b) for evidence of antibodies to the probable causative agent of acquired immune deficiency syndrome. Notwithstanding Section 199.21 of the Health and Safety Code, written copies of the report on the test shall be furnished to both of the following:

(1) The court in which the defendant is to be sentenced.

(2) The State Department of Health Services.

(f) Except as provided in subdivisions (c) and (g), the reports required by subdivision (e) shall be confidential.

(g) The State Department of Health Services shall maintain the confidentiality of the reports received pursuant to subdivision (e), except that the department shall furnish copies of any such report to a district attorney upon request. *(Amended by Stats 1989 ch 765 §2, eff. 1/1/90.)*

§1202.7. Legislative finding and declaration of probation.

The Legislature finds and declares that the provision of probation services is an essential element in the administration of criminal justice. The safety of the public, which shall be a primary goal through the enforcement of court-ordered conditions of probation; the nature of the offense; the interests of justice, including punishment, reintegration of the offender into the community, and enforcement of conditions of probation; the loss to the victim; and the needs of the defendant shall be the primary considerations in the granting of probation. *(Amended by Stats 1986 ch 47 §1.)*

§1202.8. Probation supervision.

Persons placed on probation by a court shall be under the supervision of the county probation officer who shall determine both the level and type of supervision consistent with the court-ordered conditions of probation. *(Amended by Stats 1986 ch 47 §2.)*

§1203. Probation; conditional sentence.

(a) As used in this code, "probation" shall mean the suspension of the imposition or execution of a sentence and the order of conditional and revocable release in the community under the supervision of the probation officer. As used in this code, "conditional sentence" shall mean the suspension of the imposition or execution of a sentence and the order of revocable release in the community subject to the conditions established by the court without the supervision of the probation officer. It is the intent of the Legislature that both conditional sentence and probation are authorized whenever probation is authorized in any code as a sentencing option for infractions or misdemeanors.

(b) Except as provided in subdivision (j), in every case in which a person is convicted of a felony and is eligible for probation, before judgment is pronounced, the court shall immediately refer the matter to the probation officer to investigate and report to the court, at a specified time, upon the circumstances surrounding the crime and the prior history and record of the person, which may be considered either in aggravation or mitigation of the punishment. The probation officer shall immediately investigate and make a written report to the court of his or her findings and recommendations, including his or her recommendations as to the granting or denying of probation and the conditions of probation, if granted. Pursuant to Section 828 of the Welfare and Institutions Code, the probation officer shall include in his or her report any information gathered by a law enforcement agency relating to the taking of the defendant into custody as a minor, which shall be considered for purposes of determining whether adjudications of commissions of crimes as a juvenile warrant a finding that there are circumstances in aggravation pursuant to Section 1170 or to deny probation. The probation officer shall also include in the report his or her recommendation of the amount the defendant should be required to pay as a restitution fine pursuant to Section 13967 of the Government Code. The probation officer shall also include in his or her report a recommendation as to whether the court shall require, as a condition of probation, restitution to the victim or to the Restitution Fund. The report shall be made available to the court and the prosecuting and defense attorneys at least five days, or upon request of the defendant or prosecuting attorney, nine days prior to the time fixed by the court for the hearing and determination of the report, and shall be filed with the clerk of the court as a record in the case at the time of the hearing. The time within which the report shall be made available and filed may be waived by written stipulation of the prosecuting and defense attorneys which is filed with the court or an oral stipulation in open court which is made and entered upon the minutes of the court. At a time fixed by the court, the court shall hear and determine the application, if one has been made, or, in any case, the suitability of probation in the particular case. At the hearing, the court shall consider any report of the probation officer and shall make a statement that it has considered such report which shall be filed with the clerk of the court as a record in the case. If the court determines that there are circumstances in mitigation of the punishment prescribed by law or that the ends of justice would be served by granting probation to the person, it may place the person on probation. If probation is denied, the clerk of the court shall immediately send a copy of the report

to the Department of Corrections at the prison or other institution to which the person is delivered.

(c) If a defendant is not represented by an attorney, the court shall order the probation officer who makes the probation report to discuss its contents with the defendant.

(d) In every case in which a person is convicted of a misdemeanor, the court may either refer the matter to the probation officer for an investigation and a report or summarily pronounce a conditional sentence. If such a case is not referred to the probation officer, in sentencing the person, the court may consider any information concerning the person which could have been included in a probation report. The court shall inform the person of the information to be considered and permit him or her to answer or controvert such information. For this purpose, upon the request of the person, the court shall grant a continuance before the judgment is pronounced.

(e) Except in unusual cases where the interests of justice would best be served if the person is granted probation, probation shall not be granted to any of the following persons:

(1) Unless the person had a lawful right to carry a deadly weapon, other than a firearm, at the time of the perpetration of the crime or his or her arrest, any person who has been convicted of arson, robbery, burglary, burglary with explosives, rape with force or violence, murder, attempt to commit murder, trainwrecking, kidnapping, escape from the state prison, or a conspiracy to commit one or more of those crimes and was armed with such a weapon at either of those times.

(2) Any person who used or attempted to use a deadly weapon upon a human being in connection with the perpetration of the crime of which he or she has been convicted.

(3) Any person who willfully inflicted great bodily injury or torture in the perpetration of the crime of which he or she has been convicted.

(4) Any person who has been previously convicted twice in this state of a felony or in any other place of a public offense which, if committed in this state, would have been punishable as a felony.

(5) Unless the person has never been previously convicted once in this state of a felony or in any other place of a public offense which, if committed in this state, would have been punishable as a felony, any person who has been convicted of burglary with explosives, rape with force or violence, murder, attempt to commit murder, trainwrecking, extortion, kidnapping, escape from the state prison, a violation of Section 286, 288, or 288a, 288.5, or a conspiracy to commit one or more of those crimes.

(6) Any person who has been previously convicted once in this state of a felony or in any other place of a public offense which, if committed in this state, would have been punishable as a felony, if he or she committed any of the following acts:

(A) Unless the person had a lawful right to carry a deadly weapon at the time of the perpetration of the previous crime or his or her arrest for the previous crime, he or she was armed with a weapon at either of those times.

(B) The person used or attempted to use a deadly weapon upon a human being in connection with the perpetration of the previous crime.

© 1992 by J., B. & L. Gould
Printed in the U.S.A.   **EP**

(C) The person willfully inflicted great bodily injury or torture in the perpetration of the previous crime.

(7) Any public official or peace officer of this state or any city, county, or other political subdivision who, in the discharge of the duties of his or her public office or employment, accepted or gave or offered to accept or give any bribe, embezzled public money, or was guilty of extortion.

(8) Any person who knowingly furnishes or gives away phencyclidine.

(9) Any person who intentionally inflicted great bodily injury in the commission of arson under subdivision (a) of Section 451 or who intentionally set fire to, burned, or caused the burning of, an inhabited structure or inhabited property in violation of subdivision (b) of Section 451.

(10) Any person who, in the commission of a felony, inflicts great bodily injury or causes the death of a human being by the discharge of a firearm from or at an occupied motor vehicle proceeding on a public street or highway.

(11) Any person who possess a short-barreled rifle or a short-barreled shotgun under Section 12020, a machinegun under Section 12220, or a silencer under Section 12520.

(f) When probation is granted in a case which comes within the provisions of subdivision (e), the court shall specify on the record and shall enter on the minutes the circumstances indicating that the interests of justice would best be served by such a disposition.

(g) If a person is not eligible for probation, the judge shall refer the matter to the probation officer for an investigation of the facts relevant to determination of the amount of a restitution fine pursuant to Section 13967 of the Government Code in all cases where the determination is applicable. The judge, in his or her discretion, may direct the probation officer to investigate all facts relevant to the sentencing of the person. Upon such referral, the probation officer shall immediately investigate the circumstances surrounding the crime and the prior record and history of the person and make a written report to the court of his or her findings. The findings shall include a recommendation of the amount of the restitution fine as provided in Section 13967 of the Government Code.

(h) In any case in which a defendant is convicted of a felony and a probation report is prepared pursuant to subdivision (b) or (g), the probation officer shall obtain and include in the report a statement of the comments of the victim concerning the offense. The court may direct the probation officer not to obtain such a statement in any case where the victim has in fact testified at any of the court proceedings concerning the offense.

(i) No probationer shall be released to enter another state unless his or her case has been referred to the Administrator, Interstate Probation and Parole Compacts, pursuant to the Uniform Act for Out-of-State Probationer or Parolee Supervision (Article 3 (commencing with Section 11175) of Chapter 2 of Title 1 of Part 4).

(j) In any court where a county financial evaluation officer is available, in addition to referring the matter to the probation officer, the court may order the defendant to appear before such county financial evaluation officer for a financial evaluation of the defendant's ability to pay restitution, in which case the county financial evaluation officer shall report his or her findings regarding restitution and other court-related costs to the probation officer on the question of the defendant's ability to pay such costs.

Any order made pursuant to this subdivision may be enforced as a violation of the terms and conditions of probation upon willful failure to pay and at the discretion of the court and as stated in the order, may be enforced in the same manner as a judgment in a civil action, if any balance remains unpaid at the end of the defendant's probationary period. *(Amended by Stats 1989 ch 936 §1.5; ch 1402 §11.5, eff. 1/1/90.)*

§1203a. Terms of probation.

In all counties and cities and counties the courts therein, having jurisdiction to impose punishment in misdemeanor cases, shall have the power to refer cases, demand reports and to do and require all things necessary to carry out the purposes of Section 1203 of this code insofar as they are in their nature applicable to misdemeanors. Any such court shall have power to suspend the imposing or the execution of the sentence, and to make and enforce the terms of probation for a period not to exceed three years; provided, that when the maximum sentence provided by law exceeds three years imprisonment, the period during which sentence may be suspended and terms of probation enforced may be for a longer period than three years, but in such instance, not to exceed the maximum time for which sentence of imprisonment might be pronounced.

§1203b. Suspension of sentence; conditional sentence.

All courts shall have power to suspend the imposition or execution of a sentence and grant a conditional sentence in misdemeanor and infraction cases without referring such cases to the probation officer. Unless otherwise ordered by the court, persons granted a conditional sentence in the community shall report only to the court and the probation officer shall not be responsible in any way for supervising or accounting for such persons.

§1203c. Reports to Department of Corrections.

Notwithstanding any other provisions of law, wherever a person is committed to an institution under the jurisdiction of the Department of Corrections, whether probation has been applied for or not, or granted and revoked, it shall be the duty of the probation officer of the county from which the person is committed to send to the Department of Corrections a report upon the circumstances surrounding the offense and the prior record and history of the defendant as may be required by the Administrator of the Youth and Adult Corrections Agency. These reports shall accompany the commitment papers. The reports shall be prepared in the form prescribed by the administrator following consultation with the Board of Corrections, except that in a case in which defendant is ineligible for probation, a report upon the circumstances surrounding the offense and the prior record and history of defendant, prepared by the probation officer on request of the court and filed with the court before sentence, shall be deemed to meet any such requirements of form. In order to allow the probation officer opportunity to interview, for the purpose of preparation of these reports, the prisoner shall be held in the county jail for 48 hours, excluding Saturdays, Sundays and holidays, subsequent to imposition of sentence and prior to delivery to the custody of the Director of Corrections, unless the probation officer shall have indicated need for a lesser period of time.

§1203d. Availability of probation report.

No court shall pronounce judgment upon any defendant, as to whom the court has requested a probation report pursuant to Section 1203.10, unless a copy of the probation report has been made available to the court, the prosecuting attorney, and the defendant or his or her attorney, at least two days or, upon the request of the defendant, five days prior to the time fixed by the court for consideration of the report with respect to pronouncement of judgment. The report shall be filed with the clerk of the court as a record in the case at the time the court considers the report.

If the defendant is not represented by an attorney, the court, upon ordering the probation report, shall also order the probation officer who prepares the report to discuss its contents with the defendant.

The sentence recommendations of the report shall also be made available to the victim of the crime, or the victim's next of kin if the victim has died, through the district attorney's office. The victim or the victim's next of kin shall be informed of the availability of this information through the notice provided pursuant to Section 1191.1. *(Amended by Stats 1985 ch 984 §1.)*

§1203h. Psychological evaluation to determine counseling of person convicted of child abuse or neglect.

If the court initiates an investigation pursuant to subdivision (a) or (d) of Section 1203 and the convicted person was convicted of violating any section of this code in which a minor is a victim of an act of abuse or neglect, then the investigation may include a psychological evaluation to determine the extent of counseling necessary for successful rehabilitation and which may be mandated by the court during the term of probation. Such evaluation may be performed by psychiatrists, psychologists, or licensed clinical social workers. The results of the examination shall be included in the probation officer's report to the court.

§1203m. Educational programs in Sacramento County.

(a) In each of the 1990, 1991, and 1992 calendar years, up to 200 criminal defendants between the ages of 18 and 30 years, inclusive, who are sentenced in the Superior Court of Sacramento County, and up to 200 criminal defendants of that age who are sentenced in the Municipal Court of Sacramento County may be required, as a condition of probation, to enroll, and to maintain reasonable progress, in public or private literacy or other educational programs designated by the court. The programs designated for this purpose may be operated in any school district, community college district, or private school, and shall be designed and operated to assist in the improvement of reading, writing, speaking, and calculating skills, to increase the number and quality of employment opportunities, and to reduce the likelihood of criminal behavior, so as to reduce the public and private costs, both direct and indirect, of criminal misconduct. Each probationer may be required, pursuant to this requirement, to complete up to 200 hours of instruction over a period of one year.

(b) Any school district or community college district in which any probationer enrolls pursuant to this section shall be entitled, as a result, to state funding calculated in accordance with average daily attendance computations as set forth in the Education Code. Any probationer who enrolls in a private school pursuant to this section shall pay the enrollment costs for that program.

(c) For purposes of this section, the first calendar year shall commence on January 1, 1990. Thereafter, each subsequent calendar year shall commence one year from the first day of the prior calendar year.

(d) This section shall remain in effect only until January 1, 1994, and as of that date is repealed, unless a later enacted statute, which is chaptered before January 1, 1994, deletes or extends that date. *(Amended by Stats 1991 ch 124 §2, eff. 1/1/92 only until 1/1/94.)*

§1203.01. Statement of views on convicted person.

Immediately after judgment has been pronounced, the judge and the district attorney, respectively, may cause to be filed with the clerk of the court a brief statement of their views respecting the person convicted or sentenced and the crime committed, together with such reports as the probation officer may have filed relative to the prisoner. The judge and district attorney shall cause such statements to be filed if no probation officer's report has been filed. The attorney for the defendant and the law enforcement agency that investigated the case may likewise file with the clerk of the court statements of their views respecting the defendant and the crime of which he or she was convicted. Immediately after the filing of those statements and reports, the clerk of the court shall mail a copy thereof, certified by those clerk, with postage prepaid, addressed to the Department of Corrections at the prison or other institution to which the person convicted is delivered. Within 60 days after judgment has been pronounced, the clerk shall mail a copy of the charging documents, the transcript of the proceedings at the time of the defendant's guilty plea, if the defendant pleaded guilty, and the transcript of the proceedings at the time of sentencing, with postage prepaid, to the prison or other institution to which the person convicted is delivered. The clerk shall also mail a copy of any statement submitted by the court, district attorney, or law enforcement agency, pursuant to this section, with postage prepaid, addressed to the attorney for the defendant, if any, and to the defendant in care of the Department of Corrections, and a copy of any statement submitted by the attorney for the defendant, with postage prepaid, shall be mailed to the district attorney. *(Amended by Stats 1989 ch 702 §1, eff. 1/1/90.)*

§1203.015. *Repealed by its own terms, eff. 1/1/90.*

§1203.016. Home detention program.

(a) Notwithstanding any other provision of the law, the board of supervisors of any county may authorize the correctional administrator, as defined in subdivision (h), to offer a program under which minimum security inmates and low-risk offenders committed to a county jail or other county correctional facility or inmates participating in a work furlough program may voluntary participate in a home detention program during their sentence in lieu of confinement in the county jail or other county correctional facility.

© 1992 by J., B. & L. Gould
Printed in the U.S.A.   EP

(b) The board of supervisors may prescribe reasonable rules and regulations under which a home detention program may operate. As a condition of participation in the home detention program, the inmate shall give his or her consent in writing to participate in the home detention program and shall in writing agree to comply with the rules and regulations of the program, including, but not limited to, the following rules:

(1) The participant shall remain within the interior premises of his or her residence during the hours designated by the correctional administrator.

(2) The participant shall admit any person or agent designated by the correctional administrator into his or her residence at any time for purposes of verifying the participant's compliance with the conditions of his or her detention.

(3) The participant shall agree to the use of electronic monitoring or supervising devices for the purpose of helping to verify his or her compliance with the rules and regulations of the home detention program. The devices shall not be used to eavesdrop or record any conversation, except a conversation between the participant and the person supervising the participant which is to be used solely for the purposes of voice identification.

(4) The participant shall agree that the correctional administrator in charge of the county correctional facility from which the participant was released may, without further order of the court, immediately retake the person into custody to serve the balance of his or her sentence if the electronic monitoring or supervising devices are unable for any reason to properly perform their function at the designated place of home detention or if the person fails to remain within the place of home detention as stipulated in the agreement or for any other reason no longer meets the established criteria for release under this section. A copy of the agreement shall be delivered to the participant and a copy retained by the correctional administrator.

(c) Whenever the peace officer supervising a participant has reasonable cause to believe that the participant is not complying with the rules or conditions of the program, or that the electronic monitoring devices are unable to function properly in the designated place of confinement, the peace officer may, under general or specific authorization of the correctional administrator, and without a warrant of arrest, retake the person into custody to complete the remainder of the original sentence.

(d) Nothing in this section shall be construed to require the correctional administrator to allow a person to participate in this program if it appears from the record that the person has not satisfactorily complied with reasonable rules and regulations while in custody. A person shall be eligible for participation in a home detention program only if the correctional administrator concludes that the person meets the criteria for release established under this section.

(e) The correctional administrator may permit home detention program participants to seek and retain employment in the community, attend psychological counseling sessions or educational or vocational training classes, or seek medical and dental assistance.

(f) At the time of sentencing or at any time that the court deems it necessary, the court may restrict or deny the defendant's participation in a home detention program.

(g) The board of supervisors may prescribe a program administrative fee, not to exceed the pro rata cost of the electronic monitoring or supervising device and the cost of administration of the program, to be paid by each home detention participant according to his or her ability to pay. Inability to pay shall not preclude participation in the program.

(h) As used in this section, the following words used in this section have the following meanings:

(1) "Correctional administrator" means the sheriff, probation officer, or other official in charge of a county correctional facility or work furlough program.

(2) "Minimum security inmate" means an inmate who, by established local classification criteria, would be eligible for placement in a Type IV local detention facility, as described in Title 15 of the California Code of Regulations, or for placement into the community for work or school activities, or who is determined to be a minimum security risk under a classification plan developed pursuant to Section 1050 of Title 15 of the California Code of Regulations.

(3) "Low-risk offender" means a probationer, as defined by the National Institute of Corrections model probation system.

(i) The Board of Corrections shall monitor home detention programs operated pursuant to this section and shall report to the Legislature on or before January 1, 1992, regarding their effectiveness. The report shall include an evaluation of the costs of the programs, the impact upon jail overcrowding, and the effect upon the safety of the public.

(j) This section shall remain operative only until January 1, 1993, and as of that date is repealed. *(Added by Stats 1988 ch 1603 §3, eff. 1/1/89 only until 1/1/93.)*

§1203.02. Intoxication inquiry.

The court, or judge thereof, in granting probation to a defendant convicted of any of the offenses enumerated in Section 290 of this code shall inquire into the question whether the defendant at the time the offense was committed was intoxicated or addicted to the excessive use of alcoholic liquor or beverages at that time or immediately prior thereto, and if the court, or judge thereof, believes that the defendant was so intoxicated, or so addicted, such court, or judge thereof, shall require as a condition of such probation that the defendant totally abstain from the use of alcoholic liquor or beverages.

§1203.03. Placement in diagnostic facility.

(a) In any case in which a defendant is convicted of an offense punishable by imprisonment in the state prison, the court, if it concludes that a just disposition of the case requires such diagnosis and treatment services as can be provided at a diagnostic facility of the Department of Corrections, may order that defendant be placed temporarily in such facility for a period not to exceed 90 days, with the further provision in such order that the Director of the Department of Corrections report to the court his diagnosis and recommendations concerning the defendant within the 90-day period.

(b) The Director of the Department of Corrections shall, within the 90 days, cause defendant to be observed and examined and shall forward to the court his diagnosis and recommendation concerning the disposition of defendant's case. Such diagnosis and recommendation shall be embodied in a written report and copies of the report shall be served only upon the defendant or his counsel, the probation officer, and the prosecuting attorney by the court receiving such report. After delivery of the copies of the report, the information contained therein shall not be disclosed to anyone else without the consent of the defendant. After disposition of the case, all copies of the report, except the one delivered to the defendant or his counsel, shall be filed in a sealed file and shall be available thereafter only to the defendant or his counsel, the prosecuting attorney, the court, the probation officer, or the Department of Corrections.

(c) Notwithstanding subdivision (b), the probation officer may retain a copy of the report for the purpose of supervision of the defendant if the defendant is placed on probation by the court. The report and information contained therein shall be confidential and shall not be disclosed to anyone else without the written consent of the defendant. Upon the completion or termination of probation, the copy of the report shall be returned by the probation officer to the sealed file prescribed in subdivision (b).

(d) The Department of Corrections shall designate the place to which a person referred to it under the provisions of this section shall be transported. After the receipt of any such person, the department may return the person to the referring court if the director of the department, in his discretion, determines that the staff and facilities of the department are inadequate to provide such services.

(e) The sheriff of the county in which an order is made placing a defendant in a diagnostic facility pursuant to this section, or any other peace officer designated by the court, shall execute the order placing such defendant in the center or returning him therefrom to the court. The expense of such sheriff or other peace officer incurred in executing such order is a charge upon the county in which the court is situated.

(f) It is the intention of the Legislature that the diagnostic facilities made available to the counties by this section shall only be used for the purposes designated and not in lieu of sentences to local facilities.

(g) Time spent by a defendant in confinement in a diagnostic facility of the Department of Corrections pursuant to this section or as an inpatient of the California Rehabilitation Center shall be credited on the term of imprisonment in state prison, if any, to which defendant is sentenced in the case.

(h) In any case in which a defendant has been placed in a diagnostic facility pursuant to this section and, in the course of his confinement, he is determined to be suffering from a remediable condition relevant to his criminal conduct, the department may, with the permission of defendant, administer treatment for such condition. If such treatment will require a longer period of confinement than the period for which defendant was placed in the diagnostic facility, the Director of Corrections may file with the court which placed defendant in the facility a petition for extension of the period of confinement, to which shall be attached a writing signed by defendant giving his consent to the extension. If the court finds the petition and consent in order, it may order the extension, and transmit a copy of the order to the Director of Corrections.

§1203.04. Restitution or community service as condition of probation.

(a) In every case where a person is convicted of a crime and is granted probation, the court shall require, as a condition of probation, that the person make restitution as follows:

(1) To the victim, if the crime involved a victim. For purposes of this section, "victim" shall include the immediate surviving family of the actual victim in homicide cases. Payments shall be made to the Restitution Fund to the extent the victim has received assistance pursuant to Article 1 (commencing with Section 13959) of Chapter 5 of Part 4 of Division 3 of Title 2 of the Government Code.

(2) To the Restitution Fund, if the crime did not involve a victim.

(b) If the court finds, and states its reasons for the finding on the record, that there are compelling and extraordinary reasons why restitution should not be required as provided in subdivision (a), the court shall require, as a condition of probation, that the person perform specified community service.

(c) The court may avoid imposing the requirement of community service as a condition of probation only if it finds, and states its reasons for the finding on the record, that there are compelling and extraordinary reasons not to require community service in addition to its finding as to why restitution pursuant to subdivision (a) should not be required.

(d) For purposes of paragraph (1) of subdivision (a), "restitution" means full or partial payment for the value of stolen or damaged property, medical expenses, and wages or profits lost due to injury or to time spent as a witness or in assisting the police or prosecution, which losses were caused by the defendant as a result of committing the crime for which he or she was convicted. The value of stolen or damaged property shall be the replacement cost of like property, or the actual cost of repairing the property when repair is possible.

Restitution collected pursuant to this section shall be credited to any other judgments obtained by the victim against the defendant arising out of the crime for which the defendant was convicted.

(e) For purposes of paragraph (2) of subdivision (a), the amount of restitution to be paid to the Restitution Fund shall be set at the discretion of the court and commensurate with the seriousness of the offense; but shall not exceed ten thousand dollars ($ 10,000) if the person is convicted of a felony; and shall not exceed one thousand dollars ($1,000) if the person is convicted of a misdemeanor.

(f) Nothing in this section shall be construed to limit the authority of the court to grant or deny probation or provide conditions of probation.

(g) As used in this section, probation includes a "conditional sentence" as that term is defined in subdivision (a) of Section 1203.

(h) When the court orders the defendant to pay restitution pursuant to this section, the court shall, if applicable, also order an income deduction pursuant to Section 13967.2 of the Government Code. (*Amended by Stats 1990 ch 45 §5, eff. 1/1/91.*)

§1203.045. Probation prohibited after certain theft convictions.

(a) Except in unusual cases where the interests of justice would best be served if the person is granted probation, probation shall not be granted to any per-

© 1992 by J., B. & L. Gould
Printed in the U.S.A.   EP

son convicted of a crime of theft of an amount exceeding one hundred thousand dollars ($100,000).

(b) The fact that the theft was of an amount exceeding one hundred thousand dollars ($100,000) shall be alleged in the accusatory pleading, and either admitted by the defendant in open court, or found to be true by the jury trying the issue of guilt or by the court where guilt is established by plea of guilty or nolo contendere or by trial by the court sitting without a jury.

(c) When probation is granted, the court shall specify on the record and shall enter on the minutes the circumstances indicating that the interests of justice would best be served by such a disposition.

§1203.046. Prohibition of probation; corruption of minor.

(a) Except in unusual cases where the interests of justice would best be served if the person is granted probation, probation shall not be granted to any person who is convicted of violating Section 653j by using, soliciting, inducing, encouraging, or intimidating a minor to commit a felony in violation of that section.

(b) When probation is granted pursuant to subdivision (a), the court shall specify on the record and shall enter into the minutes the circumstances indicating that the interests of justice would best be served by that disposition. *(Amended by Stats 1989 ch 897 §37.5, eff. 1/1/90.)*

§1203.047. Computer crimes, probation.

A person convicted of a violation of paragraph (1), (2), (4), or (5) of subdivision (c) of Section 502, or of a felony violation of paragraph (3), (6), (7), or (8) of subdivision (c) of Section 502, or a violation of subdivision (b) of Section 502.7 may be granted probation, but, except in unusual cases where the ends of justice would be better served by a shorter period, the period of probation shall not be less than three years and the following terms shall be imposed. During the period of probation, that person shall not accept employment where that person would use a computer connected by any means to any other computer, except upon approval of the court and notice to and opportunity to be heard by the prosecuting attorney, probation department, prospective employer, and the convicted person. Court approval shall not be given unless the court finds that the proposed employment would not pose a risk to the public. *(Added by Stats 1989 ch 1357 §3, eff. 1/1/90.)*

§1203.048. Granting of probation.

(a) Except in unusual cases where the interests of justice would best be served if the person is granted probation, probation shall not be granted to any person convicted of a violation of Section 502 or subdivision (b) of Section 502.7 involving the taking of or damage to property with a value exceeding one hundred thousand dollars ($100,000).

(b) The fact that the value of the property taken or damaged was an amount exceeding one hundred thousand dollars ($100,000) shall be alleged in the accusatory pleading, and either admitted by the defendant in open court, or found to be true by the jury trying the issue of guilt or by the court where guilt is established by plea of guilt or nolo contendere or by trial by the court sitting without a jury.

(c) When probation is granted, the court shall specify on the record and shall enter on the minutes

the circumstances indicating that the interests of justice would best be served by such a disposition. *(Added by Stats 1989 ch 1357 §4, eff. 1/1/90.)*

§1203.05. Probation report; inspection or copying.

Any report of the probation officer filed with the court, including any report arising out of a previous arrest of the person who is the subject of the report, may be inspected or copied only as follows:

(a) By any person, from the date judgment is pronounced or probation granted or, in the case of a report arising out of a previous arrest, from the date the subsequent accusatory pleading is filed, to and including 60 days from the date judgment is pronounced or probation is granted, whichever is earlier.

(b) By any person, at any time, by order of the court, upon filing a petition therefor by such person.

(c) By the general public, if the court upon its own motion orders that a report or reports shall be open or that the contents of the report or reports shall be disclosed.

(d) By any person authorized or required by law to inspect or receive copies of the report.

§1203.055. Confinement of persons convicted of crimes committed on or at public transit vehicle.

(a) Notwithstanding any other provision of law, in sentencing a person convicted of committing or of attempting to commit one or more of the offenses listed in subdivision (b) against a person who is a passenger, operator, driver, or other occupant of any public transit vehicle whether the offense or attempt is committed within the vehicle or directed at the vehicle, the court shall require that the person serve some period of confinement. If probation is granted, it shall be a condition of probation that the person shall be confined in the county jail for some period of time. If the time spent in jail prior to arraignment is less than 24 hours, it shall not be considered to satisfy the requirement that some period of confinement be imposed.

As used in this subdivision, "public transit vehicle" means any motor vehicle, streetcar, trackless trolley, bus, shuttle, light rail system, rapid transit system, subway, train, taxi cab, or jitney, which transports members of the public for hire.

(b) Subdivision (a) applies to the following crimes:

(1) Murder.

(2) A violation of Section 241, 241.3, 241.4, 244, 245, 245.2, or 246.

(3) Robbery, in violation of Section 211.

(4) Kidnapping, in violation of Section 207.

(5) Kidnapping for ransom, extortion, or robbery, in violation of Section 209.

(6) Battery, in violation of Section 243, 243.1, or 243.3.

(7) Rape, in violation of Section 261, 262, 264, or 264.1.

(8) Assault with intent to commit rape or sodomy, in violation of Section 220.

(9) Any other offense in which the defendant inflicts great bodily injury on any person other than an accomplice. As used in this paragraph, "great bodily injury" means "great bodily injury" as defined in Section 12022.7.

(10) Grand theft, in violation of subdivision (1) of Section 487.

(11) Throwing of a hard substance or shooting a missile at the transit vehicle, in violation of Section 219.2.

(12) Unlawfully causing a fire, in violation of Section 452.

(13) Drawing, exhibiting, or using a firearm or deadly weapon, in violation of Section 417.

(14) A violation of Section 214.

(c) Probation shall not be granted to, nor shall the execution or imposition of sentence be suspended for, any person convicted of a felony offense falling within this section if the person has been previously convicted and sentenced pursuant to this section.

(d) (1) The existence of any fact which would make a person ineligible for probation under subdivisions (a) and (c) shall be alleged in the accusatory pleading, and either admitted by the defendant in open court, or found to be true by the jury trying the issue of guilt or by the court where guilt is established by a plea of guilty or nolo contendere or by a trial by the court sitting without a jury.

A finding bringing the defendant within this section shall not be stricken pursuant to Section 1385 or any provision of law.

(2) This subdivision does not prohibit the adjournment of criminal proceedings pursuant to Division 3 (commencing with Section 3000) or Division 6 (commencing with Section 6000) of the Welfare and Institutions Code.

(e) The court shall require, as a condition of probation for any person convicted of committing a crime which took place on a public transit vehicle, except in any case in which the court makes a finding and states on the record clear and compelling reasons why the condition would be inappropriate, that the person make restitution to the victim. If restitution is found to be inappropriate, the court shall require as a condition of probation, except in any case in which the court makes a finding and states on the record its reasons that the condition would be inappropriate, that the defendant perform specified community service. Nothing in this subdivision shall be construed to limit the authority of a court to provide additional conditions of probation.

(f) In any case in which a person is convicted of committing a crime which took place on a public transit vehicle, the probation officer shall immediately investigate and report to the court at a specified time whether, as a result of the crime, property damage or loss or personal injury was caused by the defendant, the amount of the damage, loss, or injury, and the feasibility of requiring restitution to be made by the defendant. When a probation report is required pursuant to Section 1203 the information required by this subdivision shall be added to that probation report. *(Amended by Stats 1990 ch 45 §6, eff. 1/1/91.)*

§1203.06. Ineligibility for probation after committing violent crimes.

Notwithstanding the provisions of Section 1203:

(a) Probation shall not be granted to, nor shall the execution or imposition of sentence be suspended for, any of the following persons:

(1) Any person who personally used a firearm during the commission or attempted commission of any of the following crimes:

(i) Murder.

(ii) Robbery, in violation of Section 211.

(iii) Kidnapping, in violation of Section 207.

(iv) Kidnapping for ransom, extortion, or robbery, in violation of Section 209.

(v) Burglary of the first degree, as defined in Section 460.

(vi) Except as provided in Section 1203.065, rape in violation of subdivision (2) of Section 261.

(vii) Assault with intent to commit rape or sodomy, in violation of Section 220.

(viii) Escape, in violation of Section 4530 or 4532.

(ix) A felony violation of Section 136.1 or 137.

(2) Any person previously convicted of a felony specified in subparagraphs (i) through (viii) of paragraph (1), or assault with intent to commit murder under former Section 217, who is convicted of a subsequent felony and who was personally armed with a firearm at any time during its commission or attempted commission or was unlawfully armed with a firearm at the time of his or her arrest for the subsequent felony.

(b) (1) The existence of any fact which would make a person ineligible for probation under subdivision (a) shall be alleged in the accusatory pleading, and either admitted by the defendant in open court, or found to be true by the jury trying the issue of guilt or by the court where guilt is established by plea of guilty or nolo contendere or by trial by the court sitting without a jury.

(2) This subdivision does not prohibit the adjournment of criminal proceedings pursuant to Division 6 (commencing with Section 6000) of the Welfare and Institutions Code.

(3) As used in subdivision (a) "used a firearm" means to display a firearm in a menacing manner, to intentionally fire it, or to intentionally strike or hit a human being with it.

(4) As used in subdivision (a) "armed with a firearm" means to knowingly carry a firearm as a means of offense or defense. *(Amended by Stats 1987 ch 828 §73.)*

§1203.065. Ineligibility for probation after certain sex crimes.

(a) Notwithstanding any other provision of law, probation shall not be granted to, nor shall the execution or imposition of sentence be suspended for, any person convicted of violating subdivision (2) of Section 261, or Section 264.1, or Section 266h, or Section 266i, or Section 266j, or subdivision (a) of Section 289, or of committing sodomy or oral copulation in violation of Section 286 or 288a by force, violence, duress, menace, or fear of immediate and unlawful bodily injury on the victim or another person or subdivision (c) of Section 311.4.

(b) Except in unusual cases where the interests of justice would best be served if the person is granted probation, probation shall not be granted to any person convicted of a violation of Section 220 for assault with intent to commit any of the following: rape, sodomy, oral copulation, any violation of Section 264.1, any violation of subdivision (b) of Section 288, or any violation of Section 289.

When probation is granted, the court shall specify on the record and shall enter on the minutes the circumstances indicating that the interests of justice would best be served by such a disposition.

(c) This section does not prohibit the adjournment of criminal proceedings pursuant to Division 3 (commencing with Section 3000) or Division 6 (commencing

© 1992 by J., B. & L. Gould
Printed in the U.S.A.   **EP**

with Section 6000) of the Welfare and Institutions Code. *(Amended by Stats 1989 ch 897 §38, eff. 1/1/90.)*

§1203.066. Ineligibility for probation after committing lewd act with child.

(a) Notwithstanding Section 1203, probation shall not be granted to, nor shall the execution or imposition of sentence be suspended for, nor shall a finding bringing the defendant within the provisions of this section be stricken pursuant to Section 1385 for, any of the following persons:

(1) A person convicted of violating Section 288 when the act is committed by the use of force, violence, duress, menace, or fear of immediate and unlawful bodily injury on the victim or another person.

(2) A person who caused bodily injury on the child victim in committing a violation of Section 288.

(3) A person convicted of a violation of Section 288 and who was a stranger to the child victim or made friends with the child victim for the purpose of committing an act in violation of Section 288, unless the defendant honestly and reasonably believed the victim was 14 years old or older.

(4) A person who used a weapon during the commission of a violation of Section 288.

(5) A person convicted of committing a violation of Section 288 and who has had a prior conviction of Section 261, 264.1, 267, 285, 288, or 289, of committing sodomy or oral copulation in violation of Section 286 or 288a by force, violence, duress, menace, or fear of immediate and unlawful bodily injury on the victim or another person, of assaulting another with intent to commit a crime specified in this paragraph in violation of Section 220, or a violation of Section 266.

(6) A person convicted of kidnapping the child victim in violation of either Section 207 or 209 and who kidnapped the victim for the purpose of committing a violation of Section 288.

(7) A person who is convicted of committing a violation of Section 288 on more than one victim at the same time or in the same course of conduct.

(8) A person who in violating Section 288 or 288.5 has substantial sexual conduct with a victim under the age of 11 years.

(9) A person who occupies a position of special trust and commits an act of substantial sexual conduct. "Position of special trust" means that position occupied by a person in a position of authority who by reason of that position is able to exercise undue influence over the victim. Position of authority includes, but is not limited to, the position occupied by a natural parent, adoptive parent, stepparent, foster parent, relative, household member, adult youth leader, recreational director who is an adult, adult athletic manager, adult coach, teacher, counselor, religious leader, doctor, or employer.

(10) A person who, in committing a violation of Section 288, used obscene matter, as defined in Section 311, or matter (as defined in Section 311) depicting sexual conduct, as defined in Section 311.3.

(b) "Substantial sexual conduct" means penetration of the vagina or rectum by the penis of the offender or by any foreign object, oral copulation, or masturbation of either the victim or the offender.

(c) Paragraphs (7), (8), (9), and (10) of subdivision (a) shall not apply when the court makes all of the following findings:

(1) The defendant is the victim's natural parent, adoptive parent, stepparent, relative, or is a member of the victim's household who has lived in the household.

(2) Imprisonment of the defendant is not in the best interest of the child.

(3) Rehabilitation of the defendant is feasible in a recognized treatment program designed to deal with child molestation, and if the defendant is to remain in the household, a program that is specifically designed to deal with molestation within the family.

(4) There is no threat of physical harm to the child victim if there is no imprisonment. The court upon making its findings pursuant to this subdivision is not precluded from sentencing the defendant to jail or prison, but retains the discretion not to. The court shall state its reasons on the record for whatever sentence it imposes on the defendant.

The court shall order the psychiatrist or psychologist appointed pursuant to Section 288.1 to include a consideration of the factors specified in paragraphs (2), (3), and (4) in making his or her report to the court.

(d) The existence of any fact which would make a person ineligible for probation under subdivision (a) shall be alleged in the accusatory pleading, and either admitted by the defendant in open court, or found to be true by te jury trying the issue of guilt or by the court where guilt is established by plea of guilty or nolo contendere or by trial by the court sitting without a jury. *(Amended by Stats 1989 ch 1402 §12, eff. 1/1/90.)*

§1203.07. Ineligibility for probation for persons committing controlled substances violations.

(a) Notwithstanding Section 1203, probation shall not be granted to, nor shall the execution or imposition of sentence be suspended for, any of the following persons:

(1) Any person who is convicted of violating Section 11351 of the Health and Safety Code by possessing for sale 14.25 grams or more of a substance containing heroin.

(2) Any person who is convicted of violating Section 11352 of the Health and Safety Code by selling or offering to sell 14.25 grams or more of a substance containing heroin.

(3) Any person convicted of violating Section 11351 of the Health and Safety Code by possessing heroin for sale or convicted of violating Section 11352 of the Health and Safety Code by selling or offering to sell heroin, and who has one or more prior convictions for violating Section 11351 or Section 11352 of the Health and Safety Code.

(4) Any person who is convicted of violating Section 11378.5 of the Health and Safety Code by possessing for sale 14.25 grams or more of any salt or solution of phencyclidine or any of its analogs as specified in paragraph (21), (22), or (23) of subdivision (d) of Section 11054 or in paragraph (3) of subdivision (e) of Section 11055 of the Health and Safety Code, or any of the precursors of phencyclidine as specified in paragraph (2) of subdivision (f) of Section 11055 of the Health and Safety Code.

(5) Any person who is convicted of violating Section 11379.5 of the Health and Safety Code by transporting for sale, importing for sale, or administering, or offering to transport for sale, import for sale, or administer, or by attempting to import for sale or transport for sale, phencyclidine or any of its analogs or precursors.

(6) Any person who is convicted of violating Section 11379.5 of the Heath and Safety Code by selling or offering to sell phencyclidine or any of its analogs or precursors.

(7) Any person who is convicted of violating Section 11379.6 of the Health and Safety Code by manufacturing or offering to perform an act involving the manufacture of phencyclidine or any of its analogs or precursors.

As used in this section "manufacture" refers to the act of any person who manufactures, compounds, converts, produces, derives, processes, or prepares, either directly or indirectly by chemical extraction or independently by means of chemical synthesis.

(8) Any person who is convicted of violating Section 11380 of the Health and Safety Code by using, soliciting, inducing, encouraging, or intimidating a minor to act as an agent to manufacture, compound, or sell any controlled substance specified in subdivision (d) of Section 11054 of the Health and Safety Code, except paragraphs (13), (14), (15), (20), (21), (22), and (23) of subdivision (d), or specified in subdivision (d), (e), or (f) of Section 11055 of the Health and Safety Code, except paragraph (3) of subdivision (e) and subparagraphs (A) and (B) of paragraph (2) of subdivision (f).

(9) Any person who is convicted of violating Section 11380.5 of the Health and Safety Code by the use of a minor as an agent or who solicits, induces, encourages, or intimidates a minor with the intent that the minor shall violate the provisions of Section 11378.5, 11379.5, or 11379.6 of the Health and Safety Code insofar as the violation relates to phencyclidine or any of its analogs or precursors.

(10) Any person who is convicted of violating subdivision (b) of Section 11383 of the Health and Safety Code by possessing piperidine, pyrrolidine, or morpholine, and cyclohexanone, with intent to manufacture phencyclidine or any of its analogs.

(11) Any person convicted of violating Section 11351, 11351.5, or 11378 of the Health and Safety Code by possessing for sale cocaine base, cocaine, or methamphetamine, or convicted of violating Section 11352 or 11379 of the Health and Safety Code, by selling or offering to sell cocaine base, cocaine, or methamphetamine and who has one or more convictions for violating Section 11351, 11351.5, 11352, 11378, 11378.5, 11379, or 11379.5 of the Health and Safety Code. For purposes of prior convictions under Sections 11352, 11379, and 11379.5 of the Health and Safety Code, this subdivision shall not apply to the transportation, offering to transport, or attempting to transport a controlled substance.

(b) The existence of any fact which would make a person ineligible for probation under subdivision (a) shall be alleged in the information or indictment, and either admitted by the defendant in open court, or found to be true by the jury trying the issue of guilt or by the court where guilt is established by plea of guilty or nolo contendere or by trial by the court sitting without a jury. *(Amended by Stats 1989 ch 1135 §2, eff. 1/1/90.)*

§1203.073. Probation after conviction for possession of controlled substances.

(a) A person convicted of a felony specified in subdivision (b) may be granted probation only in an unusual case where the interests of justice would best be served. When probation is granted in such a case, the court shall specify on the record and shall enter in the minutes the circumstances indicating that the interests of justice would best be served by such a disposition.

(b) Except as provided in subdivision (a), probation shall not be granted to, nor shall the execution or imposition of sentence be suspended for, any of the following persons:

(1) Any person who is convicted of violating Section 11351 of the Health and Safety Code by possessing for sale, or Section 11352 of the Health and Safety Code by selling, a substance containing 28.5 grams or more of cocaine as specified in paragraph (6) of subdivision (b) of Section 11055 of the Health and Safety Code, or 57 grams or more of a substance containing cocaine as specified in paragraph (6) of subdivision (b) of Section 11055 of the Health and Safety Code.

(2) Any person who is convicted of violating Section 11378 of the Health and Safety Code by possessing for sale, or Section 11379 of the Health and Safety Code by selling a substance containing 28.5 grams or more of methamphetamine or 57 grams or more of a substance containing methamphetamine.

(3) Any person who is convicted of violating subdivision (a) of Section 11379.6 of the Health and Safety Code, except those who manufacture phencyclidine, or who is convicted of an act which is punishable under subdivision (b) of Section 11379.6 of the Health and Safety Code, except those who offer to perform an act which aids in the manufacture of phencyclidine.

(4) Except as otherwise provided in Section 1203.07, any person who is convicted of violating Section 11353 or 11380 of the Health and Safety Code by using, soliciting, inducing, encouraging, or intimidating a minor to manufacture, compound, or sell heroin, cocaine base as specified in paragraph (1) of subdivision (f) of Section 11054 of the Health and Safety Code, cocaine as specified in paragraph (6) of subdivision (b) of Section 11055 of the Health and Safety Code, or methamphetamine.

(5) Any person who is convicted of violating Section 11351.5 of the Health and Safety Code by possessing for sale a substance containing 14.25 grams or more of cocaine base as specified in paragraph (1) of subdivision (f) of Section 11054 of the Health and Safety Code or 57 grams or more of a substance containing at least five grams of cocaine base as specified in paragraph (1) of subdivision (f) of Section 11054 of the Health and Safety Code.

(6) Any person who is convicted of violating Section 11352 of the Health and Safety Code by transporting for sale, importing for sale, or administering, or by offering to transport for sale, import for sale, or administer, or by attempting to import for sale or transport for sale, cocaine base as specified in paragraph (1) of subdivision (f) of Section 11054 of the Health and Safety Code.

(7) Any person who is convicted of violating Section 11352 of the Health and Safety Code by selling or offering to sell cocaine base as specified in paragraph (1) of subdivision (f) of Section 11054 of the Health and Safety Code.

(8) Any person convicted of violating Section 11379.6, 11382, or 11383 of the Health and Safety Code with respect to methamphetamine, if he or she has one or more prior convictions for a violation of Section 11378, 11379, 11379.6, 11380, 11382, or 11383 with respect to methamphetamine.

© 1992 by J., B. & L. Gould
Printed in the U.S.A.   EP

(c) As used in this section, the term "manufacture" refers to the act of any person who manufactures, compounds, converts, produces, derives, processes, or prepares, either directly or indirectly by chemical extraction or independently by means of chemical synthesis.

(d) The existence of any previous conviction or fact which would make a person ineligible for probation under this section shall be alleged in the information or indictment, and either admitted by the defendant in open court, or found to be true by the jury trying the issue of guilt or by the court where guilt is established by a plea of guilty or nolo contendere or by trial by the court sitting without a jury. *(Amended by Stats 1991 ch 224 §1, eff. 1/1/92.)*

§1203.074. Granting of probation in unusual cases.

(a) A person convicted of a felony specified in subdivision (b) may be granted probation only in an unusual case where the interests of justice would best be served; when probation is granted in such a case, the court shall specify on the record and shall enter in the minutes the circumstances indicating that the interests of justice would best be served by such a disposition.

(b) Except as provided in subdivision (a), probation shall not be granted to, nor shall the execution or imposition of sentence be suspended for, any person who is convicted of violating Section 11366.6 of the Health and Safety Code. *(Added by Stats 1985 ch 1533 §3.)*

§1203.075. Ineligibility of probation for person who inflicts great bodily injury on another.

Notwithstanding the provisions of Section 1203:

(a) Probation shall not be granted to, nor shall the execution or imposition of sentence be suspended for, nor shall a finding bringing the defendant within the provisions of this section be stricken pursuant to Section 1385 for, any person who, with the intent to inflict such injury, personally inflicts great bodily injury on the person of another in the commission or attempted commission of any of the following crimes:

(1) Murder.

(2) Robbery, in violation of Section 211.

(3) Kidnapping, in violation of Section 207.

(4) Kidnapping for ransom, extortion, or robbery, in violation of Section 209.

(5) Burglary of the first degree, as defined in Section 460.

(6) Rape, in violation of subdivision (2) of Section 261.

(7) Assault with intent to commit rape or sodomy, in violation of Section 220.

(8) Escape, in violation of Section 4530 or 4532.

(9) A violation of subdivision (a) of Section 289.

(10) Sodomy, in violation of Section 286.

(11) Oral copulation, in violation of Section 288a.

(b) (1) The existence of any fact which would make a person ineligible for probation under subdivision (a) shall be alleged in the accusatory pleading, and either admitted by the defendant in open court, or found to be true by the jury trying the issue of guilt or by the court where guilt is established by a plea of guilty or nolo contendere or by a trial by the court sitting without a jury.

(2) This subdivision does not prohibit the adjournment of criminal proceedings pursuant to Division 3 (commencing with Section 3000) or Division 6 (commencing with Section 6000) of the Welfare and Institutions Code.

(3) As used in subdivision (a), "great bodily injury" means "great bodily injury" as defined in Section 12022.7. *(Amended by Stats 1987 ch 828 §74.)*

§1203.076. Probation; minimum sentence for conviction for controlled substance violations.

Any person convicted of violating Section 11352 of the Health and Safety Code relating to the sale of cocaine, cocaine hydrochloride, or heroin, or Section 11379.5 of the Health and Safety Code, who is eligible for probation and who is granted probation shall, as a condition thereof, be confined in the county jail for at least 180 days. The imposition of the minimum 180-day sentence shall be imposed in every case where probation has been granted, except that the court may, in an unusual case where the interests of justice would best be served, absolve a person from spending the 180-day sentence in the county jail if the court specifies on the record and enters into the minutes, the circumstances indicating that the interests of justice would best be served by that disposition. *(Added by Stats 1988 ch 1244 §1, eff. 1/1/89.)*

§1203.08. Ineligibility for probation after prior convictions.

(a) Notwithstanding any other provision of law, probation shall not be granted to, nor shall the execution or imposition of sentence be suspended for, any adult person convicted of a designated felony who has been previously convicted as an adult under charges separately brought and tried two or more times of any designated felony or in any other place of a public offense which, if committed in this state, would have been punishable as a designated felony, if all the convictions occurred within a 10-year period. Such 10-year period shall be calculated exclusive of any period of time during which the person has been confined in a state or federal prison.

(b) (1) The existence of any fact which would make a person ineligible for probation under subdivision (a) shall be alleged in the information or indictment, and either admitted by the defendant in open court, or found to be true by the jury trying the issue of guilt or by the court where guilt is established by plea of guilty or nolo contendere or by trial by the court sitting without a jury.

(2) Except where the existence of such fact was not admitted or found to be true pursuant to paragraph (1), or the court finds that a prior conviction was invalid, the court shall not strike or dismiss any prior convictions alleged in the information or indictment.

(3) This subdivision does not prohibit the adjournment of criminal proceedings pursuant to Division 3 (commencing with Section 3000) or Division 6 (commencing with Section 6000) of the Welfare and Institutions Code.

(c) As used in this section, "designated felony" means any felony specified in Section 187, 192, 207, 209, 211, 217, 245, 288, or subdivision (2), (3), or (4) of Section 261, subdivision 1 of Section 460, or when great bodily injury occurs in perpetration of an assault to commit robbery, mayhem, or rape, as defined in Section 220.

§1203.085. Ineligibility for probation if parolee commits violent felony.

(a) Any person convicted of an offense punishable by imprisonment in a state prison but without an alternate sentence to the county jail shall not, in any case, be granted probation or have the execution or imposition of sentence suspended, if such offense was committed while the person was on state prison parole, pursuant to Section 3000, following a term of imprisonment imposed for a "violent felony" as defined in subdivision (c) of Section 667.5.

(b) Any person convicted of a "violent felony" as defined in subdivision (c) of Section 667.5, shall not, in any case, be granted probation or have the execution or imposition of sentence suspended, if such offense was committed while the person was on state prison parole, pursuant to Section 3000.

(c) The existence of any fact which would make a person ineligible for probation under subdivision (a) or (b) shall be alleged in the information or indictment, and either admitted by the defendant in open court, or found to be true by the jury trying the issue of guilt or by the court where guilt is established by plea of guilty or nolo contendere or by trial by the court sitting without a jury.

§1203.09. Ineligibility of probation for person committing offense against aged or handicapped.

(a) Notwithstanding any other provision of law, probation shall not be granted to, nor shall the execution or imposition of sentence be suspended for, any person who commits or attempts to commit one or more of the crimes listed in subdivision (b) against a person who is 60 years of age or older; or against a person who is blind, a paraplegic, a quadriplegic, or a person confined to a wheelchair and such disability is known or reasonably should be known to the person committing the crime; and who during the course of the offense inflicts great bodily injury upon such person.

(b) Subdivision (a) applies to the following crimes:
(i) Murder.
(ii) Robbery, in violation of Section 211.
(iii) Kidnapping, in violation of Section 207.
(iv) Kidnapping for ransom, extortion, or robbery, in violation of Section 209.
(v) Burglary of the first degree, as defined in Section 460.
(vi) Rape by force or violence, in violation of subdivision (2) of Section 261.
(vii) Assault with intent to commit rape or sodomy, in violation of Section 220.

(c) The existence of any fact which would make a person ineligible for probation under either subdivision (a) or (f) shall be alleged in the information or indictment, and either admitted by the defendant in open court, or found to be true by the jury trying the issue of guilt or by the court where guilt is established by plea of guilty or nolo contendere or by trial by the court sitting without a jury.

(d) As used in this section "great bodily injury" means "great bodily injury" as defined in Section 12022.7.

(e) This section shall apply in all cases, including those cases where the infliction of great bodily injury is an element of the offense.

(f) Except in unusual cases where the interests of justice would best be served if the person is granted probation, probation shall not be granted to, nor shall the execution or imposition of sentence be suspended for, any person convicted of having committed one or more of the following crimes against a person who is 60 years of age or older: assault with a deadly weapon or instrument, battery which results in physical injury which requires professional medical treatment, robbery, or mayhem. *(Amended by Stats 1990 ch 68 §1, eff. 1/1/91.)*

§1203.095. Mandatory imprisonment in cases of specified firearm offenses.

(a) Except as provided in subdivision (b), but notwithstanding any other provision of law, if any person convicted of a violation of paragraph (2) of subdivision (a) of Section 245, of a violation of subdivision (b) of Section 245 involving an assault with a firearm, of a violation of Section 246, or a violation of subdivision (b) of Section 417, is granted probation or the execution or imposition of sentence is suspended, it shall be a condition thereof that he or she be imprisoned for at least six months, and if any person convicted of a violation of paragraph (2) of subdivision (a) of Section 417 is granted probation or the execution or imposition of sentence is suspended, it shall be a condition thereof that he or she be imprisoned for at least three months.

(b) The provisions of subdivision (a) shall apply except in unusual cases where the interests of justice would best be served by granting probation or suspending the imposition or execution of sentence without the imprisonment required by subdivision (a), or by granting probation or suspending the imposition or execution of sentence with conditions other than those set forth in subdivision (a), in which case the court shall specify on the record and shall enter on the minutes the circumstances indicating that the interests of justice would best be served by such a disposition.

(c) This section does not prohibit the adjournment of criminal proceedings pursuant to Division 3 (commencing with Section 3000) or Division 6 (commencing with Section 6000) of the Welfare and Institutions Code.

§1203.096. Substance abuse counseling or education recommended by court.

(a) Upon conviction of any felony in which the defendant is sentenced to state prison and in which the court makes the findings set forth in subdivision (b), a court shall, in addition to any other terms of imprisonment, fine, and conditions, recommend in writing that the defendant participate in a counseling or education program having a substance abuse component while imprisoned.

(b) The court shall make the recommendation specified in subdivision (a) if it finds that any of the following are true:
(1) That the defendant at the time of the commission of the offense was under the influence of any alcoholic beverages.
(2) That the defendant at the time of the commission of the offense was under the influence of any controlled substance.
(3) That the defendant has a demonstrated history of substance abuse.
(4) That the offense or offenses for which the defendant was convicted are drug related. *(Added by Stats 1991 ch 552 §1, eff. 1/1/92.)*

© 1992 by J., B. & L. Gould
Printed in the U.S.A.   EP

§1203.1. Order granting probation.

The court or judge thereof, in the order granting probation, may suspend the imposing, or the execution, of the sentence and may direct that the suspension may continue for a period of time not exceeding the maximum possible term of the sentence, except as hereinafter set forth, and upon those terms and conditions as it shall determine. The court, or judge thereof, in the order granting probation and as a condition thereof may imprison the defendant in the county jail for a period not exceeding the maximum time fixed by law in the case; however, where the maximum possible term of the sentence is five years or less, then the period of suspension of imposition or execution of sentence may, in the discretion of the court, continue for not over five years; may fine the defendant in a sum not to exceed the maximum fine provided by law in the case; or may in connection with granting probation, impose either imprisonment in county jail, or fine, or both, or neither; shall provide for restitution in proper cases; and may require bonds for the faithful observance and performance of any or all of the conditions of probation.

The court shall consider whether the defendant as a condition of probation shall make restitution to the victim or the Restitution Fund. Any restitution payment received by a probation department in the form of cash or money order shall be forwarded to the victim within 30 days from the date the payment is received by the department. Any restitution payment received by a probation department in the form of a check or draft shall be forwarded to the victim within 45 days from the date the payment is received by the department, provided, that payment need not be forwarded to a victim until 180 days from the date the first such payment is received, if the restitution payments for that victim received by the probation department total less than fifty dollars ($50). In cases where the court has ordered the defendant to pay restitution to multiple victims and where the administrative cost of disbursing restitution payments to multiple victims involves a significant cost, any restitution payment received by a probation department shall be forwarded to multiple victims when it is cost effective to do so, but in no event shall restitution disbursements be delayed beyond 180 days from the date the payment is received by the probation department. In counties or cities or counties where road camps, farms or other public work is available the court may place the probationer in such a road camp, farm, or other public work instead of jail; Section 25359 of the Government Code shall apply to probation and the court shall have the same power to require adult probationers to work, as prisoners confined in the county jail are required to work, at public work. Each county board of supervisors may fix the scale of compensation of the adult probationers in that county. In all cases of probation the court may require as a condition of probation that the probationer go to work and earn money for the support of his or her dependents or to pay a fine imposed or reparation condition, to keep an account of his or her earnings to report them to the probation officer and apply those earnings as directed by the court.

The court shall also consider whether the defendant as a condition of probation shall make restitution to a public agency for the costs of an emergency response pursuant to Article 8 (commencing with Section 53150) of Chapter 1 of Part 1 of Division 2 of the Government Code.

In all such cases if as a condition of probation a judge of the superior court sitting by authority of law elsewhere than at the county seat requires a convicted person to serve his or her sentence at intermittent periods the sentence may be served on the order of the judge at the city jail nearest to the place at which the court is sitting, and the cost of his or her maintenance shall be a county charge.

Upon conviction of any offense involving child abuse or neglect, the court may require, in addition to any or all of the above-mentioned terms of imprisonment, fine, and other reasonable conditions, that the defendant shall participate in counseling or education programs, or both, including, but not limited to, parent education or parenting programs operated by community colleges, school districts, other public agencies, or private agencies.

The court may impose and require any or all of the above-mentioned terms of imprisonment, fine, and conditions, and other reasonable conditions, as it may determine are fitting and proper to the end that justice may be done, that amends may be made to society for the breach of the law, for any injury done to any person resulting from that breach, and generally and specifically for the reformation and rehabilitation of the probationer, and that should the probationer violate any of the terms or conditions imposed by the court in the matter, it shall have authority to modify and change any and all such terms and conditions and to reimprison the probationer in the county jail within the limitations of the penalty of the public offense involved. Upon the defendant being released from the county jail under the terms of probation as originally granted or any modification subsequently made, and in all cases where confinement in a county jail has not been a condition of the grant of probation, the court shall place the defendant or probationer in and under the charge of the probation officer of the court, for the period or term fixed for probation. However, upon the payment of any fine imposed and the fulfillment of all conditions of probation, probation shall cease at the end of the term of probation, or sooner, in the event of modification. In counties and cities and counties in which there are facilities for taking fingerprints, those of each probationer shall be taken and a record of them kept and preserved.

Notwithstanding any other provisions of law to the contrary, except as provided in Sections 13967 and 13967.5 of the Government Code and Sections 1202.4, 1203.04, 1463.16, paragraph (1) of subdivision (a) of Section 1463.18, and Section 1464, all fines collected by a county probation officer in any of the courts of this state, as a condition of the granting of probation or as a part of the terms of probation, shall be paid into the county treasury and placed in the general fund for the use and benefit of the county.

If the court orders restitution to be made to the victim, the board of supervisors may add a fee to cover the actual administrative cost of collecting restitution but not to exceed 10 percent of the total amount ordered to be paid. The fees shall be paid into the general fund of the county treasury for the use and benefit of the county. *(Amended by Stats 1988 ch 975 §2, eff. 1/1/89. Another §1203.1 was repealed by Stats 1988 ch 975 §3, eff. 1/1/89.)*

§1203.1a. Probation officer's power to authorize temporary removal or release.

The probation officer of the county may authorize the temporary removal under custody or temporary release without custody of any inmate of the county jail, honor farm, or other detention facility, who is confined or committed as a condition of probation, after suspension of imposition of sentence or suspension of execution of sentence, for purposes preparatory to his return to the community, within 30 days prior to his release date, if he concludes that such an inmate is a fit subject therefor. Any such temporary removal shall not be for a period of more than three days. When an inmate is released for purposes preparatory to his return to the community, the probation officer may require the inmate to reimburse the county, in whole or in part, for expenses incurred by the county in connection therewith.

§1203.1ab. Prohibition of controlled substance use.

Upon conviction of any offense involving the unlawful possession, use, sale, or other furnishing of any controlled substance, as defined in Chapter 2 (commencing with Section 11053) of Division 10 of the Health and Safety Code, in addition to any or all of the terms of imprisonment, fine, and other reasonable conditions specified in or permitted by Section 1203.1, unless it makes a finding that this condition would not serve the interests of justice, the court, when recommended by the probation officer, shall require as a condition of probation that the defendant shall not use or be under the influence of any controlled substance and shall submit to drug and substance abuse testing as directed by the probation officer. If the defendant is required to submit to testing and has the financial ability to pay all or part of the costs associated with that testing, the court shall order the defendant to pay a reasonable fee, which shall not exceed the actual cost of the testing. *(Added by Stats 1987 ch 879 §1.)*

§1203.1b. Payment of probation costs.

(a) In any case in which a defendant is convicted of an offense and granted probation, the court, taking into account any amount which the defendant is ordered to pay in fines, assessments, and restitution, shall make a determination of the ability of the defendant to pay all or a portion of the reasonable cost of probation; and of conducting the presentence investigation and preparing the presentence report made pursuant to Section 1203. The reasonable cost of these services and of probation shall not exceed the amount determined to be the actual average cost thereof. The court shall order the defendant to appear before a county officer designated by the court to make an inquiry into the ability of the defendant to pay all or a portion of such costs. At a hearing, the defendant shall be entitled to have, but shall not be limited to, the opportunity to be heard in person, to present witnesses and other documentary evidence, and to confront and cross-examine adverse witnesses, and to disclosure of the evidence against the defendant, and a written statement of the findings of the court or the county officer. If the court determines that the defendant has the ability to pay all or part of the costs, the court shall set the amount to be reimbursed and order the defendant to pay that sum to the county in the manner in which the court believes reasonable and compatible with the defendant's financial ability; or

with the consent of the defendant, the court shall order the probation officer to set the amount of payment, which shall not exceed the maximum amount set by the court, and the manner in which the payment shall be made to the county. In making a determination of whether a defendant has the ability to pay, the court shall take into account the amount of any fine imposed upon the defendant and any amount the defendant has been ordered to pay in restitution. The court may hold additional hearings during the probationary period.

If practicable, the court or the probation officer shall order payments to be made on a monthly basis. Execution may be issued on the order in the same manner as a judgment in a civil action. The order to pay all or part of the costs shall not be enforced by contempt. A payment schedule for reimbursement of the costs of presentence investigation based on income shall be developed by the probation department of each county and approved by the presiding judges of the municipal and superior courts.

(b) The term "ability to pay" means the overall capability of the defendant to reimburse the costs, or a portion of the costs, of conducting the presentence investigation, preparing the presentence report, and probation, and shall include, but shall not be limited to, the defendant's:

(1) Present financial position.

(2) Reasonably discernible future financial position. In no event shall the court consider a period of more than six months from the date of the hearing for purposes of determining reasonably discernible future financial position.

(3) Likelihood that the defendant shall be able to obtain employment within the six-month period from the date of the hearing.

(4) Any other factor or factors which may bear upon the defendant's financial capability to reimburse the county for the costs.

(c) At any time during the pendency of the judgment rendered according to the terms of this section, a defendant against whom a judgment has been rendered may petition the rendering court to modify or vacate its previous judgment on the grounds of a charge of circumstances with regard to the defendant's ability to pay the judgment. The court shall advise the defendant of this right at the time of rendering of the judgment.

(d) All sums paid by a defendant pursuant to this section shall be allocated for the operating expenses of the county probation department.

(e) The provisions of this section shall be operative in a county upon the adoption of an ordinance to that effect by the board of supervisors. *(Amended by Stats 1989 ch 1059 §1, eff. 1/1/90.)*

§1203.1bb. Payment of cost of ignition interlock device.

(a)* The reasonable cost of probation determined under subdivision (a) of Section 1203.1b shall include the cost of purchasing and installing an ignition interlock device pursuant to Section 23235 of the Vehicle Code. Any defendant subject to this section shall pay the manufacturer of the ignition interlock device directly for the cost of its purchase and installation, in accordance with the payment schedule ordered by the court. If practicable, the court shall order payment to be made to the manufacturer of the ignition interlock device within a six-month period.

© 1992 by J., B. & L. Gould
Printed in the U.S.A.   EP

This subdivision does not require any county to pay the costs of purchasing and installing any ignition interlock devices ordered pursuant to Section 23235 of the Vehicle Code. The Office of Traffic Safety shall consult with the presiding judge or his or her designee in each county to determine an appropriate means, if any, to provide for installation of ignition interlock devices in cases in which the defendant has no ability to pay. (*Added by Stats 1990 ch 1403 §4, eff. 9/28/90.*) *So in original. No par. (b) designated.*

§1203.1c. Payment of costs of incarceration in local detention facility.

(a) In any case in which a defendant is convicted of an offense and is ordered to serve a period of confinement in a county jail, city jail, or other local detention facility as a term of probation or a conditional sentence, the court may, after a hearing, make a determination of the ability of the defendant to pay all or a portion of the reasonable costs of such incarceration, including incarceration pending disposition of the case. The reasonable cost of such incarceration shall not exceed the amount determined by the board of supervisors, with respect to the county jail, and by the city council, with respect to the city jail, to be the actual average cost thereof on a per-day basis. The court may, in its discretion, hold additional hearings during the probationary period. The court may, in its discretion before such hearing, order the defendant to file a statement setting forth his or her assets, liability and income, under penalty of perjury, and may order the defendant to appear before a county officer designated by the board of supervisors to make an inquiry into the ability of the defendant to pay all or a portion of such costs. At the hearing, the defendant shall be entitled to have the opportunity to be heard in person or to be represented by counsel, to present witnesses and other evidence, and to confront and cross-examine adverse witnesses. A defendant represented by counsel appointed by the court in the criminal proceedings shall be entitled to such representation at any hearing held pursuant to this section. If the court determines that the defendant has the ability to pay all or a part of the costs, the court may set the amount to be reimbursed and order the defendant to pay that sum to the county, or to the city with respect to incarceration in the city jail, in the manner in which the court believes reasonable and compatible with the defendant's financial ability. Execution may be issued on the order in the same manner as on a judgment in a civil action. The order to pay all or part of the costs shall not be enforced by contempt.

If practicable, the court shall order payments to be made on a monthly basis and the payments shall be made payable to the county officer designated by the board of supervisors, or to a city officer designated by the city council with respect to incarceration in the city jail.

A payment schedule for reimbursement of the costs of incarceration pursuant to this section based upon income shall be developed by the county officer designated by the board of supervisors, or by the city council with respect to incarceration in the city jail, and approved by the presiding judges of the municipal and superior courts.

(b) "Ability to pay" means the overall capability of the defendant to reimburse the costs, or a portion of the costs, of incarceration and includes, but is not limited to, the defendant's:

(1) Present financial obligations, including family support obligations, and fines, penalties and other obligations to the court.

(2) Reasonably discernible future financial position. In no event shall the court consider a period of more than one year from the date of the hearing for purposes of determining reasonable discernible future position.

(3) Likelihood that the defendant shall be able to obtain employment within the one year period from the date of the hearing.

(4) Any other factor or factors which may bear upon the defendant's financial ability to reimburse the county or city for the costs.

(c) All sums paid by a defendant pursuant to this section shall be deposited in the general fund of the county or city.

(d) This section shall be operative in a county upon the adoption of an ordinance to that effect by the board of supervisors, and shall be operative in a city upon the adoption of an ordinance to that effect by the city council. Such ordinance shall include a designation of the officer responsible for collection of moneys ordered pursuant to this section and shall include a determination, to be reviewed annually, of the average per-day costs of incarceration in the county jail, city jail, or other local detention facility. (*Amended by Stats 1985 ch 1485 §4.5.*)

§1203.1d. Determination of costs, reimbursement, penalty assessments.

In determining the amount and manner of disbursement under an order made pursuant to this code requiring a defendant to make reparation or restitution to a victim of a crime, to pay any money as reimbursement for legal assistance provided by the court, to pay any cost of probation or probation investigation, or to pay any cost of jail or other confinement, or to pay any other reimbursable costs, the court, after determining the amount of any fine and penalty assessments, and a county financial evaluation officer when making a financial evaluation, shall first determine the amount of restitution to be ordered paid to any victim, and shall then determine the amount of the other reimbursable costs.

If payment is made in full, the payment shall be apportioned and disbursed in the amounts ordered by the court.

If reasonable and compatible with the defendant's financial ability, the court may order payments to be made in installments.

With respect to installment payments, the board of supervisors may establish the priorities of payment, first between fines, penalty assessments, and reparation or restitution, and then between other reimbursable costs. The board of supervisors may also establish priorities of payment between orders or parts of orders in cases where defendants have been ordered to pay more than one court order.

Documentary evidence, such as bills, receipts, repair estimates, insurance payment statements, payroll stubs, business records, and similar documents relevant to the value of the stolen or damaged property, medical expenses, and wages and profits lost shall not be excluded as hearsay evidence. (*Amended by Stats 1986 ch 634 §1.*)

§1203.1e. Ability to pay parole supervision costs.

(a) In any case in which a defendant is ordered to serve a period of confinement in a county jail or other local detention facility, and the defendant is eligible to be released on parole by the county board of parole commissioners, the court shall, after a hearing, make a determination of the ability of the person to pay all or a portion of the reasonable cost of providing parole supervision. The reasonable cost of those services shall not exceed the amount determined to be the actual average cost of providing parole supervision.

(b) If the court determines that the person has the ability to pay all or part of the costs, the court may set the amount to be reimbursed and order the person to pay that sum to the county in the manner in which the court believes reasonable and compatible with the person's financial ability. In making a determination of whether a person has the ability to pay, the court shall take into account the amount of any fine imposed upon the person and any amount the person has been ordered to pay in restitution.

If practicable, the court shall order payments to be made on a monthly basis as directed by the court. Execution may be issued on the order in the same manner as a judgment in a civil action. The order to pay all or part of the costs shall not be enforced by contempt.

(c) For the purposes of this section, "ability to pay" means the overall capability of the person to reimburse the costs, or a portion of the costs, of providing parole supervision and shall include, but shall not be limited to, consideration of all of the following factors:

(1) Present financial position.

(2) Reasonably discernible future financial position. In no event shall the board consider a period of more than six months from the date of the hearing for purposes of determining reasonably discernible future financial position.

(3) Likelihood that the person shall be able to obtain employment within the six-month period from the date of the hearing.

(4) Any other factor or factors which may bear upon the person's financial capability to reimburse the county for the costs.

(d) At any time during the pendency of the order made under this section, a person against whom an order has been made may petition the court to modify or vacate its previous order on the grounds of a change of circumstances with regard to the person's ability to pay. The court shall advise the person of this right at the time of making the order.

(e) All sums paid by any person pursuant to this section shall be deposited in the general fund of the county.

(f) The parole of any person shall not be denied or revoked in whole or in part based upon the inability or failure to pay under this section.

(g) The county board of parole commissioners shall not have access to offender financial data prior to the rendering of any parole decision.

(h) This section shall become operative on January 1, 1995. *(Added by Stats 1991 ch 437 §2, eff. 9/19/91, oper. 1/1/95. Former section 1203.1e repealed by Stats 1991 ch 437 §1, eff. 9/19/91.)*

§1203.1f. Ability to pay determination hearings.

If practicable, the court shall consolidate the ability to pay determination hearings authorized pursuant to Sections 987.8, 1203.1b, and 1203.1c into one proceeding, and the determination of ability to pay made at the consolidated hearing may be used for all purposes relating to these listed sections.

This section shall remain operative until January 1, 1995, and as of that date is repealed. *(Amended by Stats 1991 ch 437 §3, eff. 9/19/91 only until 1/1/95. See other section 1203.1f below.)*

§1203.1f. Ability to pay determination hearings.

If practicable, the court shall consolidate the ability to pay determination hearings authorized pursuant to Sections 987.8, 1203.1b, 1203.1c, and 1203.1e into one proceeding, and the determination of ability to pay made at the consolidated hearing may be used for all purposes relating to these listed sections.

This section shall become operative on January 1, 1995. *(Added by Stats 1991 ch 437 §4, eff. 9/19/91, oper. 1/1/95. See other section 1203.1f above.)*

§1203.1g. Conviction of sexual assault on minor.

In any case in which a defendant is convicted of sexual assault on a minor, and the defendant is eligible for probation, the court as a condition of probation, shall order him or her to make restitution for the costs of medical or psychological treatment incurred by the victim as a result of the assault and that he or she seek and maintain employment and apply that portion of his or her earnings specified by the court toward those costs.

As used in this section, "sexual assault" has the meaning specified in Section 11165. The defendant is entitled to a hearing concerning any modification of the amount of restitution based on the costs of medical and psychological treatment incurred by the victim subsequent to the issuance of the order of probation. *(Amended by Stats 1990 ch 45 §7, eff. 1/1/91.)*

§1203.1h. Child abuse; medical costs.

(a) In addition to any other costs which a court is authorized to require a defendant to pay, upon conviction of any offense involving child abuse or neglect, the court may require that the defendant pay to a law enforcement agency incurring the cost, the cost of any medical examinations conducted on the victim in order to determine the nature or extent of the abuse or neglect. If the court determines that the defendant has the ability to pay all or part of the medical examination costs, the court may set the amount to be reimbursed and order the defendant to pay that sum to the law enforcement agency in the manner in which the court believes reasonable and compatible with the defendant's financial ability. In making a determination of whether a defendant has the ability to pay, the court shall take into account the amount of any fine imposed upon the defendant and any amount the defendant has been ordered to pay in restitution.

(b) In addition to any other costs which a court is authorized to require a defendant to pay, upon conviction of any offense involving sexual assault or attempted sexual assault, including child molestation, the court may require that the defendant pay, to the law enforcement agency, county, or local governmental agency incurring the cost, the cost of any medical examinations conducted on the victim for the collection and preservation of evidence. If the court determines that the defendant has the ability to pay all or part of the cost of the medical examination, the court may set the amount to be reimbursed and order the

© 1992 by J., B. & L. Gould
Printed in the U.S.A.   **EP**

defendant to pay that sum to the law enforcement agency, county, or local governmental agency, in the manner in which the court believes reasonable and compatible with the defendant's financial ability. In making the determination of whether a defendant has the ability to pay, the court shall take into account the amount of any fine imposed upon the defendant and any amount the defendant has been ordered to pay in restitution. In no event shall a court penalize an indigent defendant by imposing an additional period of imprisonment in lieu of payment. *(Amended by Stats 1991 ch 377 §1, eff. 1/1/92.)*

§1203.1i. House confinement.

(a) In any case in which a defendant is convicted of a violation of any building standards adopted by a local entity by ordinance or resolution, including, but not limited to, local health, fire, building, or safety ordinances or resolutions, or any other ordinance or resolution relating to the health and safety of occupants of buildings, by maintaining a substandard building, as specified in Section 17920.3 of the Health and Safety Code, the court, or judge thereof, in making an order granting probation, in addition to any other orders, may order the defendant placed under house confinement, or may order the defendant to serve both a term of imprisonment in the county jail and to be placed under house confinement.

This section only applies to violations involving a dwelling unit occupied by persons specified in subdivision (a) of Section 1940 of the Civil Code who are not excluded by subdivision (b) of that section.

(b) If the court orders a defendant to serve all or part of his or her sentence under house confinement, pursuant to subdivision (a), he or she may also be ordered to pay the cost of having a police officer or guard stand guard outside the area in which the defendant has been confined under house confinement if it has been determined that the defendant is able to pay these costs.

(c) As used in this section, "house confinement" means confinement to a residence or location designated by the court and specified in the probation order. *(Added by Stats 1987 ch 1063 §1.)*

§1203.1j. Elderly victim; restitution.

In any case in which the defendant is convicted of assault, battery, or assault with a deadly weapon on a victim 65 years of age or older, and the defendant knew or reasonably should have known the elderly status of the victim, the court, as a condition of probation, shall order the defendant to make restitution for the costs of medical or psychological treatment incurred by the victim as a result of the crime, and that the defendant seek and maintain legitimate employment and apply that portion of his or her earnings specified by the court toward those costs.

The defendant shall be entitled to a hearing, concerning any modification of the amount of restitution, based on the costs of medical and psychological treatment incurred by the victim subsequent to the issuance of the order of probation. *(Amended by Stats 1990 ch 45 §8, eff. 1/1/91.)*

§1203.1k. Restitution based on determination of probation officer.

For any order of restitution made under Section 1203.1, the court may order the specific amount of restitution and the manner in which restitution shall

be made to a victim based on the probation officer's report or it may, with the consent of the defendant, order the probation officer to set the amount of restitution and the manner in which restitution shall be made to a victim. The defendant shall have the right to a hearing before the judge to dispute the determinations made by the probation officer in regard to the amount or manner in which restitution is to be made to the victim. If the court orders restitution to be made to the Restitution Fund, the court, and not the probation officer, shall determine the amount and the manner in which restitution is to be made to the Restitution Fund. *(Added by Stats 1987 ch 890 §1.)*

§1203.1l. Restitution to public agency.

In any case in which, pursuant to Section 1203.1, the court orders the defendant, as a condition of probation, to make restitution to a public agency for the costs of an emergency response, all of the following shall apply:

(a) The probation department shall obtain the actual costs for an emergency response from a public agency, and shall include the public agency's documents supporting the actual costs for the emergency response in the probation department's sentencing report to the court.

(b) At the sentencing hearing, the defendant has the right to confront witnesses and present evidence in opposition to the amount claimed to be due to the public agency for its actual costs for the emergency response.

(c) The collection of the emergency response costs is the responsibility of the public agency seeking the reimbursement. If a defendant fails to make restitution payment when a payment is due, the public agency shall by verified declaration notify the probation department of the delinquency. The probation department shall make an investigation of the delinquency and shall make a report to the court of the delinquency. The report shall contain any recommendation that the probation officer finds to be relevant regarding the delinquency and future payments. The court, after a hearing on the delinquency, may make modifications to the existing order in the furtherance of justice.

(d) The defendant has the right to petition the court for a modification of the emergency response reimbursement order whenever he or she has sustained a substantial change in economic circumstances. The defendant has a right to a hearing on the proposed modification, and the court may make any modification to the existing order in the furtherance of justice. *(Amended and renumbered by Stats 1989 ch 1360 §114, eff. 1/1/90.)*

§1203.2. Revocation of probation upon rearrest.

(a) At any time during the probationary period of a person released on probation under the care of a probation officer pursuant to this chapter, or of a person released on conditional sentence or summary probation not under the care of a probation officer, if any probation officer or peace officer has probable cause to believe that the probationer is violating any term or condition of his or her probation or conditional sentence, the officer may, without warrant or other process and at any time until the final disposition of the case, rearrest the person and bring him or her before the court or the court may, in its discretion, issue a warrant for his or her rearrest. Upon such rearrest, or upon the issuance of a warrant for rearrest the court may revoke and terminate such probation if the interests of justice so require and the court, in its judgment, has reason to believe from the report of the probation officer or otherwise that the person has violated any of the conditions of his or her probation, has become abandoned to improper associates or a vicious life, or has subsequently committed other offenses, regardless whether he or she has been prosecuted for such offenses. However, probation shall not be revoked for failure of a person to make restitution pursuant to Section 1203.04 as a condition of probation unless the court determines that the defendant has willfully failed to pay and has the ability to pay. Restitution shall be consistent with a person's ability to pay. The revocation, summary or otherwise, shall serve to toll the running of the probationary period.

(b) Upon its own motion or upon the petition of the probationer, probation officer or the district attorney of the county in which the probationer is supervised, the court may modify, revoke, or terminate the probation of the probationer pursuant to this subdivision. The court shall give notice of its motion, and the probation officer or the district attorney shall give notice of his or her petition to the probationer, his or her attorney of record, and the district attorney or the probation officer, as the case may be. The probationer shall give notice of his or her petition to the probation officer and notice of any motion or petition shall be given to the district attorney in all cases. The court shall refer its motion or the petition to the probation officer. After the receipt of a written report from the probation officer, the court shall read and consider the report and either its motion or the petition and may modify, revoke, or terminate the probation of the probationer upon the grounds set forth in subdivision (a) if the interests of justice so require.

The notice required by this subdivision may be given to the probationer upon his or her first court appearance in the proceeding. Upon the agreement by the probationer in writing to the specific terms of a modification or termination of a specific term of probation, any requirement that the probationer make a personal appearance in court for the purpose of a modification or termination shall be waived. Prior to the modification or termination and waiver of appearance, the probationer shall be informed of his or her right to consult with counsel, and if indigent the right to secure court appointed counsel. If the probationer waives his or her right to counsel a written waiver shall be required. If probationer consults with counsel and thereafter agrees to a modification or termination of the term of probation and waiver of personal appearance, the agreement shall be signed by counsel showing approval for the modification or termination and waiver.

(c) Upon any revocation and termination of probation the court may, if the sentence has been suspended, pronounce judgment for any time within the longest period for which the person might have been sentenced. However, if the judgment has been pronounced and the execution thereof has been suspended, the court may revoke the suspension and order that the judgment shall be in full force and effect. In either case, the person shall be delivered over to the proper officer to serve his or her sentence, less any credits herein provided for.

(d) In any case of revocation and termination of probation, including, but not limited to, cases in which the judgment has been pronounced and the execution thereof has been suspended, upon the revocation and termination, the court may, in lieu of any other sentence, commit the person to the Department of the Youth Authority if he or she is otherwise eligible for such commitment.

(e) If probation has been revoked before the judgment has been pronounced, the order revoking probation may be set aside for good cause upon motion made before pronouncement of judgment. If probation has been revoked after the judgment has been pronounced, the judgment and the order which revoked the probation may be set aside for good cause within 30 days after the court has notice that the execution of the sentence has commenced. If an order setting aside the judgment, the revocation of probation, or both is made after the expiration of the probationary period, the court may again place the person on probation for that period and with those terms and conditions as it could have done immediately following conviction. *(Amended by Stats 1989 ch 1319 §1, eff. 1/1/90.)*

§1203.2a. Sentencing probationer who is committed for other offense.

If any defendant who has been released on probation is committed to a prison in this state or another state for another offense, the court which released him or her on probation shall have jurisdiction to impose sentence, if no sentence has previously been imposed for the offense for which he or she was granted probation, in the absence of the defendant, on the request of the defendant made through his or her counsel, or by himself or herself in writing, if such writing is signed in the presence of the warden of the prison in which he or she is confined or the duly authorized representative of the warden, and the warden or his or her representative attests both that the defendant has made and signed such request and that he or she states that he or she wishes the court to impose sentence in the case in which he or she was released on probation, in his or her absence and without him or her being represented by counsel.

The probation officer may, upon learning of the defendant's imprisonment, and must within 30 days after being notified in writing by the defendant or his or her counsel, or the warden or duly authorized representative of the prison in which the defendant is confined, report such commitment to the court which released him or her on probation.

Upon being informed by the probation officer of the defendant's confinement, or upon receipt from the warden or duly authorized representative of any prison in this state or another state of a certificate showing that the defendant is confined in prison, the court shall issue its commitment if sentence has previously been imposed. If sentence has not been previously imposed and if the defendant has requested the court through counsel or in writing in the manner herein provided to impose sentence in the case in which he or she was released on probation in his or her absence and without the presence of counsel to represent him or her, the court shall impose sentence and issue its commitment, or shall make other final order terminating its jurisdiction over the defendant in the case in which the order of probation was made. If the case is one in which sentence has previously been imposed, the court shall be deprived of jurisdiction

© 1992 by J., B. & L. Gould
Printed in the U.S.A.   EP

over defendant if it does not issue its commitment or make other final order terminating its jurisdiction over defendant in the case within 60 days after being notified of the confinement. If the case is one in which sentence has not previously been imposed, the court is deprived of jurisdiction over defendant if it does not impose sentence and issue its commitment or make other final order terminating its jurisdiction over defendant in the case within 30 days after defendant has, in the manner prescribed by this section, requested imposition of sentence.

Upon imposition of sentence hereunder the commitment shall be dated as of the date upon which probation was granted. If the defendant is then in a state prison for an offense committed subsequent to the one upon which he or she has been on probation, the term of imprisonment of such defendant under a commitment issued hereunder shall commence upon the date upon which defendant was delivered to prison under commitment for his or her subsequent offense. Any terms ordered to be served consecutively shall be served as otherwise provided by law.

In the event the probation officer fails to report such commitment to the court or the court fails to impose sentence as herein provided, the court shall be deprived thereafter of all jurisdiction it may have retained in the granting of probation in said case. (Amended by Stats 1989 ch 897 §39, 1420 §2, eff. 1/1/90.)

§1203.3. Revoke, modify, or terminate term of probation.

(a) The court shall have authority at any time during the term of probation to revoke, modify, or change its order of suspension of imposition or execution of sentence. The court may at any time when the ends of justice will be subserved thereby, and when the good conduct and reform of the person so held on probation shall warrant it, terminate the period of probation, and discharge the person so held.

(b) The exercise of the court's authority in subdivision (a) to revoke, modify, change, or terminate probation is subject to the following:

(1) Before any sentence or term or condition of probation is modified, a hearing shall be held in open court before the judge. The prosecuting attorney shall be given a two-day written notice and an opportunity to be heard on the matter.

(A) If the sentence or term or condition of probation is modified pursuant to this section, the judge shall state the reasons for that modification on the record.

(B) As used in this section, modification of sentence shall include reducing a felony to a misdemeanor.

(2) No order shall be made without written notice first given by the court or the clerk thereof to the proper probation officer of the intention to revoke, modify, or change its order.

(3) In all cases, if the court has not seen fit to revoke the order of probation and impose sentence or pronounce judgment, the defendant shall at the end of the term of probation or any extension thereof, be by the court discharged subject to the provisions of these sections.

(c) If a probationer is ordered to serve time in jail, and the probationer escapes while serving that time, the probation is revoked as a matter of law on the day of the escape.

(d) If probation is revoked pursuant to subdivision (c), upon taking the probationer into custody, the probationer shall be accorded a hearing or hearings consistent with the holding in the case of People v. Vickers, 8 Cal. 3d 451. The purpose of that hearing or hearings is not to revoke probation, as the revocation has occurred as a matter of law in accordance with subdivision (c), but rather to afford the defendant an opportunity to require the prosecution to establish that the alleged violation did in fact occur and to justify the revocation.

(e) This section does not apply to cases covered by Section 1203.2. (Amended by Stats 1991 ch 655 §2, eff. 1/1/92.)

§1203.4. Change of plea or setting aside verdict of guilty after probation.

(a) In any case in, which a defendant has fulfilled the conditions of probation for the entire period of probation, or has been discharged prior to the termination of the period of probation, or in any other case in which a court, in its discretion and the interests of justice, determines that a defendant should be granted the relief available under this section, the defendant shall, at any time after the termination of the period of probation, if he or she is not then serving a sentence for any offense, on probation for any offense, or charged with the commission of any offense, be permitted by the court to withdraw his or her plea of guilty or plea of nolo contendere and enter a plea of not guilty; or, if he or she has been convicted after a plea of not guilty, the court shall set aside the verdict of guilty; and, in either case, the court shall thereupon dismiss the accusations or information against the defendant and except as noted below, he or she shall thereafter be released from all penalties and disabilities resulting from the offense of which he or she has been convicted, except as provided in Section 13555 of the Vehicle Code. The probationer shall be informed, in his or her probation papers, of this right and privilege and his or her right, if any, to petiton for a certificate of rehabilitation and pardon. The probationer may make the application and change of plea in person or by attorney, or by the probation officer authorized in writing; however, in any subsequent prosecution of the defendant for any other offense, the prior conviction may be pleaded and proved and shall have the same effect as if probation had not been granted or the accusation or information dismissed. The order shall state, and the probationer shall be informed, that the order does not relieve him or her of the obligation to disclose the conviction in response to any direct question contained in any questionnaire or application for public office, for licensure by any state or local agency, or for contracting with the California State Lottery.

Dismissal of an accusation or information pursuant to this section does not permit a person to own, possess, or have in his or her custody or control any firearm capable of being concealed upon the person or prevent his or her conviction under Section 12021.

This subdivision shall apply to all application for relief under this section which are filed on or after November 23, 1970.

(b) Subdivision (a) of this section does not apply to any misdemeanor which is within the provisions of subdivision (b) of Section 42001 of the Vehicle Code, or to any infraction.

(c) A person who petitions for a change of plea or setting aside a verdict under this section may be required to reimburse the county for the cost of services rendered at a rate to be determined by the county board of supervisors not to exceed sixty dollars ($60), and to reimburse any city for the cost of services rendered at a rate to be determined by the city council not to exceed sixty dollars ($60). Ability to make this reimbursement shall be determined by the court using the standards set forth in paragraph (2) of subdivision (f) of Section 987.8 and shall not be a prerequisite to a person's eligibility under this section. The court may order reimbursement in any case in which the petitioner appears to have the ability to pay, without undue hardship, all or any portion of the cost for services established pursuant to this subdivision.

(d) No relief shall be granted under this section unless the prosecuting attorney has given 15 days' notice of the petition for relief. The probation officer shall notify the prosecuting attorney when a petition is filed, pursuant to this section.

It shall be presumed that the prosecuting attorney has received notice if proof of service is filed with the court.

(e) If, after receiving notice pursuant to subdivision (d), the prosecuting attorney fails to appear and object to petition for dismissal, the prosecuting attorney may not move to set aside or otherwise appeal the grant of that petiton. (*Amended by Stats 1989 ch 917 §11, eff. 1/1/90.*)

§1203.4a. Change of plea; dismissal of charge after serving sentence.

(a) Every defendant convicted of a misdemeanor and not granted probation shall, at any time after the lapse of one year from the date of pronouncement of judgment, if he or she has fully complied with and performed the sentence of the court, is not then serving a sentence for any offense and is not under charge of commission of any crime and has, since the pronouncement of judgment, lived an honest and upright life and has conformed to and obeyed the laws of the land, be permitted by the court to withdraw his or her plea of guilty or nolo contendere and enter a plea of not guilty; or if he or she has been convicted after a plea of not guilty, the court shall set aside the verdict of guilty; and in either case the court shall thereupon dismiss the accusatory pleading against such defendant, who shall thereafter be released from all penalties and disabilities resulting from the offense of which he has been convicted, except as provided in Section 12021.1 of this code or Section 13555 of the Vehicle Code. The defendant shall be informed of the provisions of this section, either orally or in writing, at the time he or she is sentenced. The defendant may make such application and change of plea in person or by attorney, or by the probation officer authorized in writing; provided, that in any subsequent prosecution of such defendant for any other offense, the prior conviction may be pleaded and proved and shall have the same effect as if relief had not been granted pursuant to this section.

This subdivision applies to convictions which occurred before as well as those occurring after, the effective date of this section.

(b) Subdivision (a) does not apply to any misdemeanor falling within the provisions of subdivision (b) of Section 42001 of the Vehicle Code, or to any infraction.

(c) A person who petitions for a dismissal of a charge under this section may be required to reimburse the county for the cost of services rendered at a rate to be determined by the county board of supervisors not to exceed sixty dollars ($60), and to reimburse any city for the cost of services rendered at a rate to be determined by the city council not to exceed sixty dollars ($60). Ability to make this reimbursement shall be determined by the court using the standards set forth in paragraph (2) of subdivision (f) of Section 987.8 and shall not be a prerequisite to a person's eligibility under this section. The court may order reimbursement in any case in which the petitioner appears to have the ability to pay, without undue hardship, all or any portion of the cost for services established pursuant to this subdivision. (*Amended by Stats 1988 ch 1394 §1, eff. 1/1/89.*)

§1203.45. Petition to seal minor's misdemeanor record.

(a) In any case in which a person was under the age of 18 years at the time of commission of a misdemeanor and is eligible for, or has previously received, the relief provided by Section 1203.4 or 1203.4a, that person, in a proceeding under Section 1203.4 or 1203.4a, or a separate proceeding, may petition the court for an order sealing the record of conviction and other official records in the case, including records of arrests resulting in the criminal proceeding and records relating to other offenses charged in the accusatory pleading, whether defendant was acquitted or charges were dismissed. If the court finds that the person was under the age of 18 at the time of the commission of the misdemeanor, and is eligible for relief under Section 1203.4 or 1203.4a or has previously received such relief, it may issue its order granting the relief prayed for. Thereafter the conviction, arrest, or other proceeding shall be deemed not to have occurred, and the petitioner may answer accordingly any question relating to their occurrence.

(b) This section applies to convictions which occurred before, as well as those which occur after, the effective date of this section.

(c) This section shall not apply to offenses for which registration is required under Section 290, to violations of Division 10 (commencing with Section 11000) of the Health and Safety Code, or to misdemeanor violations of the Vehicle Code relating to operation of a vehicle or of any local ordinance relating to operation, standing, stopping, or parking of a motor vehicle.

(d) This section does not apply to a person convicted of more than one offense, whether the second or additional convictions occurred in the same action in which the conviction as to which relief is sought occurred or in another action, except in the following cases:

(1) One of the offenses includes the other or others.

(2) The other conviction or convictions were for the following:

(i) Misdemeanor violations of Chapters 1 (commencing with Section 21000) to 9 (commencing with Section 22500), inclusive, or Chapters 12 (commencing with Section 23100) to 14 (commencing with Section 23340), inclusive, of Division 11 of the Vehicle Code, other than Section 23103, 23104, 23152, 23153, or 23220.

© 1992 by J., B. & L. Gould
Printed in the U.S.A.   EP

(ii) Violation of any local ordinance relating to the operation, stopping, standing, or parking of a motor vehicle.

(3) The other conviction or convictions consisted of any combination of paragraphs (1) and (2).

(e) This section shall apply in any case in which a person was under the age of 21 at the time of the commission of an offense as to which this section is made applicable if that offense was committed prior to March 7, 1973.

(f) In any action or proceeding based upon defamation, a court, upon a showing of good cause, may order any records sealed under this section to be opened and admitted into evidence. The records shall be confidential and shall be available for inspection only by the court, jury, parties, counsel for the parties, and any other person who is authorized by the court to inspect them. Upon the judgment in the action or proceeding becoming final, the court shall order the records sealed.

(g) A person who petitions for an order sealing a record under this section may be required to reimburse the county for the cost of services rendered at a rate to be determined by the county board of supervisors not to exceed sixty dollars ($60), and to reimburse any city for the cost of services rendered at a rate to be determined by the city council not to exceed sixty dollars ($60). Ability to make this reimbursement shall be determined by the court using the standards set forth in paragraph (2) of subdivision (f) of Section 987.8 and shall not be a prerequisite to a person's eligibility under this section. The court may order reimbursement in any case in which the petitioner appears to have the ability to pay, without undue hardship, all or any portion of the cost for services established pursuant to this subdivision.

§1203.5. Adult probation officers; assistant and deputy.

The offices of adult probation officer, assistant adult probation officer, and deputy adult probation officer are hereby created. The probation officers, assistant probation officers, and deputy probation officers appointed in accordance with Chapter 2 (commencing with Section 200 of Division 2 of Part 1 of the Welfare and Institutions Code shall be ex officio adult probation officers, assistant adult probation officers, and deputy adult probation officers except in any county or city and county whose charter provides for the separate office of adult probation officer. When the separate office of adult probation officer has been established he or she shall perform all the duties of probation officers except for matters under the jurisdiction of the juvenile court. Any adult probation officer may accept appointment as member of the Board of Corrections and serve in that capacity in addition to his or her duties as adult probation officer and may receive the per diem allowance authorized in Section 6025.1. *(Amended by Stats 1987 ch 828 §77.)*

§1203.6. Appointment, removal and compensation.

The adult probation officer shall be appointed and may be removed for good cause by the judge of the superior court or, in a county with two superior court judges, by the judge who is senior in point of service. In the case of a superior court of more than two judges, a majority of the judges shall make the appointment, and may effect removal.

The salary of the probation officer shall be established by the board of supervisors.

The adult probation officer shall appoint and may remove all assistants, deputies and other persons employed in his department, and their compensation shall be established, according to the merit system or civil service system provisions of the county. If no merit system or civil service system exists in the county, the board of supervisors shall provide for appointment, removal, and compensation of such personnel.

This section is applicable in a charter county whose charter establishes the office of adult probation officer and provides that such officer shall be appointed in accordance with general law subject to the merit system provisions of the charter.

§1203.9. Transfer of probation cases.

(a) Whenever any person is released upon probation, the case may be transferred to any court of the same rank in any other county in which the person resides permanently, meaning the stated intention to remain for the duration of probation; provided that the court of the receiving county shall first be given an opportunity to determine whether the person does reside in and has stated the intention to remain in that county for the duration of probation. If the court finds that the person does not reside in or has not stated an intention to remain in that county for the duration of probation, it may refuse to accept the transfer. The court and the probation department shall give the matter of investigating those transfers precedence over all actions or proceedings therein, except actions or proceedings to which special precedence is given by law, to the end that all those transfers shall be completed expeditiously.

(b) If the court of the receiving county finds that the person does permanently reside in or has permanently moved to such county, it may, in its discretion, either accept the entire jurisdiction over the case, or assume supervision of the probationer on a courtesy basis.

(c) The order of transfer shall contain an order committing the probationer to the care and custody of the probation officer of the receiving county. A copy of the orders and probation reports shall be transmitted to the court and probation officer of the receiving county within two weeks of the finding by that county that the person does permanently reside in or has permanently moved to that county, and thereafter the receiving court shall have entire jurisdiction over the case, with the like power to again request transfer of the case whenever it seems proper. *(Amended by Stats 1991 ch 1202 §6, eff. 1/1/92.)*

§1203.10. Investigations and reports by probation officers.

At the time of the plea or verdict of guilty of any person over eighteen years of age, the probation officer of the county of the jurisdiction of said criminal shall, when so directed by the court, inquire into the antecedents, character, history, family environment, and offense of such person, and must report the same to the court and file his report in writing in the records of such court. When directed, his report shall contain his recommendation for or against the release for such person on probation. If any such person shall be released on probation and committed to the care of the probation officer, such officer shall keep a complete and accurate record in suitable books or other form in writing of the history of the case in court, and of the name of the probation officer, and his act in connection with said case; also the age, sex, nativity, residence, education, habit of temperance, whether married or single, and the conduct, employment and occupation, and parents' occupation, and condition of such person committed to his care during the term of such probation and the result of such probation. Such record of such probation officer shall be and constitute a part of the records of the court, and shall at all times be open to the inspection of the court or of any person appointed by the court for that purpose, as well as of all magistrates, and the chief of police, or other heads of the police, unless otherwise ordered by the court. Said books of records shall be furnished for the use of said probation officer of said county, and shall be paid for out of the county treasury.

Five years after termination of probation in any case subject to this section, the probation officer may destroy any records and papers in his possession relating to such case.

§1203.11. Probation or parole officer may serve restraining orders.

A probation or parole officer or parole agent of the Department of Corrections may serve any process regarding the issuance of a temporary restraining order or other protective order against a person committed to the care of the probation or parole officer or parole agent when the person appears for an appointment with the probation or parole officer or parole agent at their office. *(Added by Stats 1991 ch 866 §5, eff. 1/1/92.)*

§1203.12. Statement of terms of probation.

The probation officer shall furnish to each person who has been released on probation, and committed to his care, a written statement of the terms and conditions of his probation unless such a statement has been furnished by the court, and shall report to the court, or judge, releasing such person on probation, any violation or breach of the terms and conditions imposed by such court on the person placed in his care.

§1203.13. Establishment of crime prevention councils.

The probation officer of any county may establish, or assist in the establishment of, any public council or committee having as its object the prevention of crime, and may cooperate with or participate in the work of any such councils or committees for the purpose of preventing or decreasing crime, including the improving of recreational, health, and other conditions in the community.

§1203.14. Activities to prevent adult delinquency.

Notwithstanding any other provision of law, probation departments may engage in activities designed to prevent adult delinquency. These activities include rendering direct and indirect services to persons in the community. Probation departments shall not be limited to providing services only to those persons on probation being supervised under Section 1203.10, but may provide services to any adults in the community.

§1204. Evidence in aggravation or mitigation of punishment.

The circumstances shall be presented by the testimony of witnesses examined in open court, except that when a witness is so sick or infirm as to be unable to attend, his deposition may be taken by a magistrate of the county, out of court, upon such notice to the adverse party as the court may direct. No affidavit or testimony, or representation of any kind, verbal or written, can be offered to or received by the court, or a judge thereof, in aggravation or mitigation of the punishment, except as provided in this and the preceding section. This section shall not be construed to prohibit the filing of a written report by a defendant or defendant's counsel on behalf of a defendant if such a report presents a study of his background and personality and suggests a rehabilitation program. If such a report is submitted, the prosecution or probation officer shall be permitted to reply to or to evaluate the program.

§1204.5. Judge not to read or consider report of officer or witness before plea entered.

In any criminal action, after the filing of any complaint or other accusatory pleading and before a plea, finding, or verdict of guilty, no judge of any court shall read or consider any written report of any law enforcement officer or witness to any offense, or any information reflecting the arrest or conviction record of a defendant, or any affidavit or representation of any kind, verbal or written, except as provided in the rules of evidence applicable at the trial, or with the consent of the accused given in open court, or affidavits in connection with the issuance of a warrant or the hearing of any law and motion matter, or any application for an order fixing or changing bail, or a petition for a writ.

§1205. Judgment imposing fine; imprisonment pending satisfaction.

(a) A judgment that the defendant pay a fine, with or without other punishment, may also direct that he or she be imprisoned until the fine is satisfied and may further direct that the imprisonment begin at and continue after the expiration of any imprisonment imposed as a part of the punishment or of any other imprisonment to which he or she may theretofore have been sentenced. Each of these judgments shall specify the extent of the imprisonment for nonpayment of the fine, which shall not be more than one day for each thirty dollars ($30) of the fine, nor exceed in any case the term for which the defendant might be sentenced to imprisonment for the offense of which he or she has been convicted. A defendant held in custody for nonpayment of a fine shall be entitled to credit on the fine for each day he or she is so held in custody, at the rate specified in the judgment. When the defendant has been convicted of a misdemeanor, a judgment that the defendant pay a fine may also direct that he or she pay the fine within a limited time or in installments on specified dates and that in default of payment as therein stipulated he or she be imprisoned in the discretion of the court either until the defaulted installment is satisfied or until the fine is satisfied in full; but unless the direction is given in the judgment, the fine shall be payable forthwith.

(b) Except as otherwise provided in case of fines imposed as conditions of probation, the defendant shall pay the fine to the clerk of the court, or to the

© 1992 by J., B. & L. Gould
Printed in the U.S.A.   **EP**

judge thereof if there is no clerk, unless the defendant is taken into custody for nonpayment of the fine, in which event payments made while he or she is in custody shall be made to the officer who holds him or her in custody and all amounts so paid shall be forthwith paid over by the officer to the court which rendered the judgment. The clerk shall report to the court every default in payment of a fine or any part thereof, or if there is no clerk, the court shall take notice of the default. If time has been given for payment of a fine or it has been made payable in installments, the court shall, upon any default in payment, immediately order the arrest of the defendant and order him or her to show cause why he or she should not be imprisoned until the fine or installment thereof, as the case may be, is satisfied in full. If the fine, or installment, is payable forthwith and it is not so paid, the court shall without further proceedings, immediately commit the defendant to the custody of the proper officer to be held in custody until the fine or installment thereof, as the case may be, is satisfied in full.

(c) This section applies to any violation of any of the codes or statutes of this state punishable by a fine or by a fine and imprisonment.

Nothing in this section shall be construed to prohibit the clerk of the court, or the judge thereof if there is no clerk, from turning these accounts over to another county department or a collecting agency for processing and collection.

(d) The defendant shall pay to the clerk of the court or the collecting agency a fee for the processing of installment accounts. This fee shall equal the administrative and clerical costs, as determined by the board of supervisors, except that the fee shall not exceed thirty dollars ($30). The Legislature hereby authorizes the establishment of the following program described in this section, to be implemented in any county, upon the adoption of a resolution by the board of supervisors authorizing it. The board of supervisors in any county may establish a fee for the processing of accounts receivable that are not to be paid in installments. The defendant shall pay to the clerk of the court or the collecting agency the fee established for the processing of the accounts. The fee shall equal the administrative and clerical costs, as determined by the board of supervisors, except that the fee shall not exceed thirty dollars ($30). *(Amended by Stats 1989 ch 49 §3, eff. 1/1/90.)*

§1205.1. *Added by Stats 1991 ch 90 §24, eff. 6/30/91; amended by Stats 1991 ch 189 §15, eff. 7/29/91; repealed by Stats 1991 ch 1168 §4.7, eff. 10/14/91.*

§1205.3. Order specifying amount of fine or number of hours of community service work.

In any case in which a defendant is convicted of an offense and granted probation, and the court orders the defendant either to pay a fine or to perform specified community service work as a condition of probation, the court shall specify in its order the amount of the fine and the number of hours of community service work that shall be performed as an alternative to payment of the fine.

§1205.5. Inapplicability of §1205 to restitution fines.

The provisions of Section 1205 shall not apply to restitution fines ordered in felony cases.

§1207. Entry and filing of judgment.

When judgment upon a conviction is rendered, the clerk, or if there is no clerk, the judge, must enter the same in the minutes, stating briefly the offense for which the conviction was had, and the fact of a prior conviction, if any. A copy of the judgment of conviction shall be filed with the papers in the case.

§1208. Work furlough for county jail prisoners.

(a) The provisions of this section, insofar as they relate to employment, shall be operative in any county in which the board of supervisors by ordinance finds, on the basis of employment conditions, the state of the county jail facilities, and other pertinent circumstances, that the operation of this section, insofar as it relates to employment, in that county is feasible. The provisions of this section, insofar as they relate to job training, shall be operative in any county in which the board of supervisors by ordinance finds, on the basis of job training conditions, the state of the county jail facilities, and other pertinent circumstances, that the operation of this section, insofar as it relates to job training, in that county is feasible. The provisions of this section, insofar as they relate to education, shall be operative in any county in which the board of supervisors by ordinance finds, on the basis of education conditions, the state of the county jail facilities, and other pertinent circumstances, that the operation of this section, insofar as it relates to education, in that county is feasible. In any ordinance the board shall prescribe whether the sheriff, the probation officer, the director of the county department of corrections, or the superintendent of a county industrial farm or industrial road camp in the county shall perform the functions of the work furlough administrator. The board may, in that ordinance, provide for the performance of any or all functions of the work furlough administrator by any one or more of those persons, acting separately or jointly as to any of the functions; and may, by a subsequent ordinance, revise the provisions within the authorization of this section. The board of supervisors may also terminate the operation of this section, either with respect to employment, job training, or education in the county if it finds by ordinance that because of changed circumstances, the operation of this section, either with respect to employment, job training, or education in that county is no longer feasible.

Notwithstanding any other provision of law, the board of supervisors may by ordinance designate a facility for confinement of prisoners classified for the work furlough program and designate the work furlough administrator as the custodian of the facility. The work furlough administrator may, with the approval of the board of supervisors, enter into contracts with appropriate public or nonprofit private agencies or private entities to provide a facility and services for the housing, sustenance, counseling, supervision, and related services for inmates eligible for work furlough. No agency or private entity entering into a contract may itself employ any person who is in the work furlough program. The sheriff or director of the county department of corrections, as the case may be, is authorized to transfer custody of prisoners to the work furlough administrator to be confined in a facility for the period during which they are in the work furlough program.

All privately operated work furlough facilities and programs used for the detention of persons sentenced into the custody of the sheriff, the director of a county department of corrections, or the chief probation officer, shall be under the jurisdiction of, and subject to the terms of a contract entered into with, the work furlough administrator. Each contract shall include, but not be limited to, a provision whereby the private agency or entity agrees to operate in compliance with all appropriate state and local building, zoning, health, safety, and fire statutes, ordinances, and regulations and the minimum jail standards for Type IV facilities as established by regulations adopted by the Board of Corrections. The private agency or entity shall select and train its personnel in accordance with selection and training requirements adopted by the Board of Corrections as set forth in Subchapter 1 (commencing with Section 100) of Chapter 1 of Division 1 of Title 15 of the California Code of Regulations. Failure to comply with the appropriate health, safety, and fire laws or minimum jail standards adopted by the board may be cause for termination of the contract. Upon discovery of a failure to comply with these requirements, the work furlough administrator shall notify the privately operated program director that the contract may be canceled if the specified deficiencies are not corrected within 60 days.

All private work furlough facilities and programs shall be inspected biennially by the Board of Corrections unless the work furlough administrator requests an earlier inspection pursuant to Section 6031.1. Each private agency or entity shall pay a fee to the Board of Corrections commensurate with the cost of those inspections and a fee commensurate with the cost of the initial review of the facility.

(b) When a person is convicted of a misdemeanor and sentenced to the county jail, or is imprisoned in the county jail for nonpayment of a fine, for contempt, or as a condition of probation for any criminal offense, the work furlough administrator may, if he or she concludes that the person is a fit subject to continue in his or her regular employment, direct that the person be permitted to continue in that employment, if that is compatible with the requirements of subdivision (d), or may authorize the person to secure employment for himself or herself, unless the court at the time of sentencing or committing has ordered that the person not be granted work furloughs. The work furlough administrator may, if he or she concludes that the person is a fit subject to continue in his or her job training program, direct that the person be permitted to continue in that job training program, if that is compatible with the requirements of subdivision (d), or may authorize the person to secure local job training for himself or herself, unless the court at the time of sentencing has ordered that person not be granted work furloughs. The work furlough administrator may, if he or she concludes that the person is a fit subject to continue in his or her regular educational program, direct that the person be permitted to continue in that educational program, if that is compatible with the requirements of subdivision (d), or may authorize the person to secure education for himself or herself, unless the court at the time of sentencing has ordered that person not be granted work furloughs.

(c) If the work furlough administrator so directs that the prisoner be permitted to continue in his or her regular employment, job training, or educational program, the administrator shall arrange for a continuation of that employment or for that job training or

education, so far as possible without interruption. If the prisoner does not have regular employment or a regular job training or educational program, and the administrator has authorized the prisoner to secure employment, job training, or education for himself or herself, the prisoner may do so, and the administrator may assist the prisoner in doing so. Any employment, job training, or education so secured shall be suitable for the prisoner. The employment, and the job training or educational program if it includes earnings by the prisoner, shall be at a wage at least as high as the prevailing wage for similar work in the area where the work is performed and in accordance with the prevailing working conditions in that area. In no event may any employment, job training, or educational program involving earnings by the prisoner be permitted where there is a labor dispute in the establishment in which the prisoner is, or is to be, employed, trained, or educated.

(d) Whenever the prisoner is not employed or being trained or educated and between the hours or periods of employment, training, or education, the prisoner shall be confined in the facility designated by the board of supervisors for work furlough confinement unless the work furlough administrator directs otherwise. If the prisoner is injured during a period of employment, job training, or education, the work furlough administrator shall have the authority to release him or her from the facility for continued medical treatment by private physicians or at medical facilities at the expense of the employer, workers' compensation insurer, or the prisoner. The release shall not be construed as assumption of liability by the county or work furlough administrator for medical treatment obtained.

The work furlough administrator may release any prisoner classified for the work furlough program for a period not to exceed 72 hours for medical, dental, or psychiatric care, or for family emergencies or pressing business which would result in severe hardship if the release were not granted, or to attend those activities as the administrator deems may effectively promote the prisoner's successful return to the community, including, but not limited to, an attempt to secure housing, employment, entry into educational programs, or participation in community programs.

(e) The earnings of the prisoner may be collected by the work furlough administrator, and it shall be the duty of the prisoner's employer to transmit the wages to the administrator at the latter's request. Earnings levied upon pursuant to writ of execution or in other lawful manner shall not be transmitted to the administrator. If the administrator has requested transmittal of earnings prior to levy, that request shall have priority. In a case in which the functions of the administrator are performed by a sheriff, and the sheriff receives a writ of execution for the earnings of a prisoner subject to this section but has not yet requested transmittal of the prisoner's earnings pursuant to this section, the sheriff shall first levy on the earnings pursuant to the writ. When an employer or educator transmits earnings to the administrator pursuant to this subdivision, the sheriff shall have no liability to the prisoner for those earnings. From the earnings the administrator shall pay the prisoner's board and personal expenses, both inside and outside the jail, and shall deduct so much of the costs of administration of this section as is allocable to the prisoner or if the prisoner is unable to pay that sum,

© 1992 by J., B. & L. Gould
Printed in the U.S.A.   EP

a lesser sum as is reasonable, and, in an amount determined by the administrator, shall pay the support of the prisoner's dependents, if any. If sufficient funds are available after making the foregoing payments, the administrator may, with the consent of the prisoner, pay, in whole or in part, the preexisting debts of the prisoner. Any balance shall be retained until the prisoner's discharge. Upon discharge the balance shall be paid to the prisoner.

(f) The prisoner shall be eligible for time credits pursuant to Sections 4018 and 4019.

(g) In the event the prisoner violates the conditions laid down for his or her conduct, custody, job training, education, or employment, the work furlough administrator may order the balance of the prisoner's sentence to be spent in actual confinement.

(h) Willful failure of the prisoner to return to the place of confinement not later than the expiration of any period during which he or she is authorized to be away from the place of confinement pursuant to this section is punishable as provided in Section 4532.

(i) As used in this section, the following definitions apply:

(1) "Education" includes vocational and educational training and counseling, and psychological, drug abuse, alcoholic, and other rehabilitative counseling.

(2) "Educator" includes a person or institution providing that training or counseling.

(3) "Employment" includes care of children, including the daytime care of children of the prisoner.

(4) "Job training" may include, but shall not be limited to, job training assistance as provided through the Job Training Partnership Act (Public Law 97-300; 29 U.S.C.A. Sec. 1501 et seq.).

(j) This section shall be known and may be cited as the "Cobey Work Furlough Law." *(Amended by Stats 1989 ch 48 §1, eff. 1/1/90.)*

§1208.2. Work furlough and electronic home detention programs; fees.

(a) (1) This section shall apply to individuals authorized to participate in a work furlough program pursuant to Section 1208, or to individuals authorized to participate in an electronic home detention program pursuant to Section 1208.1, or to individuals authorized to participate in a county parole program pursuant to Article 3.5 (commencing with Section 3074) of Chapter 8 of Title 1 of Part 3.

(2) As used in this section, as appropriate, "administrator" means the work furlough administrator, county corrections administrator, county electronic home detention administrator, county board of parole commissioners, or county parole administrator.

(b) A board of supervisors which implements programs identified in paragraph (1) of subdivision (a), may prescribe a program administrative fee and an application fee, that together do not exceed the pro rata cost of the program to which the prisoner is accepted, including both equipment and supervision costs.

(c) The administrator, or his or her designee, shall not consider a prisoner's ability or inability to pay all or a portion of the program fee for the purposes of granting or denying participation in any of the programs, and shall not have access to the prisoner's financial data prior to rendering a decision.

(d) For purposes of this section, "ability to pay" means the overall capability of the person to reimburse the costs, or a portion of the costs, of providing supervision and shall include, but shall not be limited to, consideration of all of the following factors:

(1) Present financial position.

(2) Reasonably discernible future financial position. In no event shall the administrator, or his or her designee, consider a period of more than six months from the date of acceptance into the program for purposes of determining reasonably discernible future financial position.

(3) Likelihood that the prisoner shall be able to obtain employment within the six-month period from the date of acceptance into the program.

(4) Any other factor that may bear upon the prisoner's financial capability to reimburse the county for the fees fixed pursuant to subdivision (b).

(e) The administrator, or his or her designee, may charge a prisoner the fee set by the board of supervisors or any portion of the fee, based on the prisoner's ability to pay, and may determine the method and frequency of payment. The administrator, or his or her designee, shall have the option to waive the fees for program supervision when deemed necessary, justified, or in the interests of justice. The fees charged for program supervision may be modified or waived at any time based on the changing financial position of the prisoner. All fees paid by prisoners for program supervision shall be deposited into the general fund of the county.

(f) No prisoner shall be denied consideration for, or be removed from, participation in any of the programs to which this section applies because of an inability to pay all or a portion of the program supervision fees. At any time during a prisoner's sentence, the prisoner may request that the administrator, or his or her designee, modify or suspend the payment of fees on the grounds of a change in circumstances with regard to the prisoner's ability to pay.

(g) If the prisoner and the administrator, or his or her designee, are unable to come to an agreement regarding the prisoner's ability to pay, or the amount which is to be paid, or the method and frequency with which payment is to be made, the administrator, or his or her designee, shall advise the appropriate court of the fact that the prisoner and administrator, or his or her designee, have not been able to reach agreement and the court shall then resolve the disagreement by determining the prisoner's ability to pay, the amount which is to be paid, and the method and frequency with which payment is to be made.

(h) At the time a prisoner is approved for any of the programs to which this section applies, the administrator, or his or her designee, shall furnish the prisoner a written statement of the prisoner's rights in regard to the program for which the prisoner has been approved, including, but not limited to, both of the following:

(1) The fact that the prisoner cannot be denied consideration for or removed from participation in the program because of an inability to pay.

(2) The fact that if the prisoner is unable to reach agreement with the administrator, or his or her designee, regarding the prisoner's ability to pay, the amount which is to be paid, or the manner and frequency with which payment is to be made, that the matter shall be referred to the court to resolve the differences.

(i) This section shall remain operative until January 1, 1995, and as of that date is repealed. *(Added by Stats 1991 ch 437 §5, eff. 9/19/91 only until 1/1/95.)*

§1208.3. Protection of prisoner's employment rights; verification.

The administrator is not prohibited by subdivision (c) of Section 1208.2 from verifying any of the following:

(a) That the prisoner is receiving wages at a rate of pay not less than the prevailing minimum wage requirement as provided for in subdivision (c) of Section 1208.

(b) That the prisoner is working a specified minimum number of required hours.

(c) That the prisoner is covered under an appropriate or suitable workers' compensation insurance plan as may otherwise be required by law.

The purpose of the verification shall be solely to insure that the prisoner's employment rights are being protected, that the prisoner is not being taken advantage of, that the job is suitable for the prisoner, and that the prisoner is making every reasonable effort to make a productive contribution to the community.

(d) This section shall remain operative until January 1, 1995, and as of that date is repealed. *(Added by Stats 1991 ch 437 §6, eff. 9/19/91 only until 1/1/95.)*

§1208.5. Work furlough agreements between counties.

The boards of supervisors of two or more counties having work furlough programs established pursuant to Section 1208, home detention programs established pursuant to Section 1208.1, or county parole programs established pursuant to Article 3.5 (commencing with Section 3074) of Chapter 8 of Title 1 of Part 3, may enter into agreements whereby a person sentenced to, or imprisoned in, the jail of one county, but regularly residing in another county or regularly employed in another county, may be transferred from the custody of the sheriff, administrator, as defined in paragraph (2) of subdivision (a) of Section 1208.2, or their designees, of the county in which he or she is confined, to the custody of the appropriate administrator of the county in which he or she resides or is employed, in order that he or she may be enabled to continue in his or her regular employment or education in the other county through that county's work furlough program, home detention program, or county parole program. These agreements may make provision for the support of transferred persons by the county from which they are transferred. The board of supervisors of any county may, by ordinance, delegate the authority to enter into these agreements to the work furlough administrator, corrections administrator, county home detention program administrator, county board of parole commissioners, county parole administrator, or their designees.

This section shall remain operative until January 1, 1995, and as of that date is repealed. *(Amended by Stats 1991 ch 437 §7, eff. 9/19/91 only until 1/1/95. See other section 1208.5 below.)*

§1208.5. Work furlough agreements between counties.

The boards of supervisors of two or more counties having work furlough programs may enter into agreements whereby a person sentenced to, or imprisoned in, the jail of one county, but regularly residing in another county or regularly employed in another county, may be transferred by the sheriff of the county in which he or she is confined to the jail of the county in which he or she resides or is employed, in order that he or she may be enabled to continue in his or her regular employment or education in such other county through such county's work furlough program. Such agreement may make provision for the support of transferred persons by the county from which they are transferred. The board of supervisors of any county may, by ordinance, delegate the authority to enter into such agreements to the work furlough administrator.

This section shall become operative on January 1, 1995. *(Added by Stats 1991 ch 437 §8, eff. 9/19/91, oper. 1/1/95. See other section 1208.5 above.)*

§1209. Administrative costs.

Upon conviction of any criminal offense for which the court orders the confinement of a person in the county jail, or other suitable place of confinement, either as the final sentence or as a condition of any grant of probation, and allows the person so sentenced to continue in his or her regular employment by serving the sentence on weekends or similar periods during the week other than their regular workdays and by virtue of this schedule of serving the sentence the prisoner is ineligible for work furlough under Section 1208, the county may collect from the defendant according to the defendant's ability to pay so much of the costs of administration of this section as are allocable to such defendant. The amount of this fee shall not exceed the actual costs of such confinement and may be collected prior to completion of each weekly or monthly period of confinement until the entire sentence has been served, and the funds shall be deposited in the county treasury pursuant to county ordinance.

The court, upon allowing sentences to be served on weekends or other nonemployment days, shall conduct a hearing to determine if the defendant has the ability to pay all or a part of the costs of administration without resulting in unnecessary economic hardship to the defendant and his or her dependents. At the hearing, the defendant shall be entitled to have, but shall not be limited to, the opportunity to be heard in person, to present witnesses and other documentary evidence, and to confront and cross-examine adverse witnesses, and to disclosure of the evidence against the defendant, and a written statement of the findings of the court. If the court determines that the defendant has the ability to pay all or part of the costs of administration without resulting in unnecessary economic hardship to the defendant and his or her dependents, the court shall advise the defendant of the provisions of this section and order him or her to pay all or part of the fee as required by the sheriff, probation officer, or Director of the County Department of Corrections, whichever the case may be. In making a determination of whether a defendant has the ability to pay, the court shall take into account the amount of any fine imposed upon the defendant and any amount the defendant has been ordered to pay in restitution.

As used in this section, the term "ability to pay" means the overall capability of the defendant to reimburse the costs, or a portion of the costs, and shall include, but shall not be limited to, the following:

(a) The defendant's present financial position.

(b) The defendant's reasonably discernible future financial position. In no event shall the court consider a period of more than six months from the date of the hearing for purposes of determining reasonably discernible future financial position.

© 1992 by J., B. & L. Gould
Printed in the U.S.A.   EP

(c) Likelihood that the defendant shall be able to obtain employment within the six-month period from the date of the hearing.

(d) Any other factor or factors which may bear upon the defendant's financial capability to reimburse the county for the costs.

Execution may be issued on the order in the same manner as a judgment in a civil action.

The order to pay all or part shall not be enforced by contempt. At any time during the pendency of the judgment, a defendant against whom a judgment has been rendered may petition the rendering court to modify or vacate its previous judgment on the grounds of a change of circumstances with regard to the defendant's ability to pay the judgment. The court shall advise the defendant of this right at the time of making the judgment.

CHAPTER 2

THE EXECUTION

§1213. Copies of probationary orders or entry of judgment.

When a probationary order or a judgment, other than of death, has been pronounced, a copy of the entry of that portion of the probationary order ordering the defendant confined in a city or county jail as a condition of probation, or a copy of the entry of the judgment, or, if the judgment is for imprisonment in a state prison, either a copy of the minute order or an abstract of the judgment as provided in Section 1213.5, certified by the clerk of the court, or by the judge if there is no clerk, shall be forthwith furnished to the officer whose duty it is to execute the probationary order or judgment, and no other warrant or authority is necessary to justify or require its execution.

If a copy of the minute order is used as the commitment document, the first page or pages shall be identical in form and content to that prescribed by the Judicial Council for an abstract of judgment, and such other matters as appropriate may be added thereafter.

§1213.5. Abstract of judgment by Council.

The abstract of judgment provided for in Section 1213 shall be prescribed by the Judicial Council. (*Amended by Stats 1986 ch 248 §164.*)

§1214. Enforcement of judgment for fine.

(a) If the judgment is for a fine, including a restitution fine ordered pursuant to Section 13967 of the Government Code, with or without imprisonment, the judgment may be enforced in the manner provided for the enforcement of money judgments generally.

(b) In any case in which a defendant is ordered to pay restitution as a condition of probation or of a conditional sentence, including where restitution is required by Section 1203.04, the order to pay restitution is deemed a money judgment if the defendant was informed of his or her right to have a judicial determination of the amount and was provided with a hearing, waived a hearing, or stipulated to the amount of the restitution ordered, and shall constitute a civil judgment enforceable in the same manner as is provided for the enforcement of any other money judgment. Upon the victim's request, the court shall provide the victim in whose favor the order of restitution is entered with a certified copy of that order.

(c) Chapter 3 (commencing with Section 683.010) of Division 1 of Title 9 of Part 2 of the Code of Civil Procedure shall not apply to a judgment for any fine ordered pursuant to Section 13967 of the Government Code. (*Amended by Stats 1988 ch 566 §1; ch 662 §2, eff. 1/1/89.*)

§1214.1. Civil assessment against defendant for failure to appear.

(a) In addition to any other penalty in criminal cases, the court may impose a civil assessment of up to two hundred fifty dollars ($250) against any defendant who fails, after notice, and without good cause to appear in court for any proceeding authorized by law.

(b) The assessment shall not become effective until at least 10 calendar days after the court mails a warning notice to the defendant by first-class mail to the address shown on the notice to appear or to the defendant's last known address. If the defendant appears within the time specified in the notice and shows good cause for the failure to appear, the court shall vacate the assessment.

(c) If an assessment is imposed under this section, no bench warrant or warrant of arrest shall be issued with respect to the failure to appear at the proceeding for which the assessment is imposed.

(d) The assessment imposed under subdivision (a) shall be subject to the due process requirements governing defense and collection of civil money judgments generally. (*Added by Stats 1985 ch 979 §1.*)

§1214.2. Enforcement of order to pay fine.

(a) Except as provided in subdivision (c), if a defendant is ordered to pay a fine as a condition of probation, the order to pay a fine may be enforced during the term of probation in the same manner as is provided for the enforcement of money judgments.

(b) Except as provided in subdivision (c), an order to pay a fine as a condition of probation may also be enforced as follows:

(1) With respect to a willful failure to pay during the term of probation, in the same manner as a violation of the terms and conditions of probation.

(2) If any balance remains unpaid at the end of the term of probation, in the same manner as a judgment in a civil action.

(c) If an order to pay a fine as a condition of probation is stayed, a writ of execution shall not issue until the stay is lifted. (*Added by Stats 1987 ch 454 §1.*)

§1214.3. Establishment of "Misdemeanor and Traffic Violation Pilot Project".

(a) Any county, by resolution of its board of supervisors, may establish a "Misdemeanor and Traffic Violation Pilot Project" within any judicial district within the county pursuant to this section.

(b) Notwithstanding any other provision of law, whenever a person is issued a citation for any violation of this code or of the Vehicle Code not declared to be a felony, or for any violation of an ordinance of a city, county, or a city and county relating to a traffic offense, and fails to appear, the person shall be advised in writing by the court of the nature of the violation and of the procedures relative to additional civil assessments described in this section.

(c) The defendant shall do one of the following within 30 days of receipt of the mailed notice:

(1) Pay the fine or post bail.

(2) Return the completed financial statement to the court.

(3) Return the promise to appear for trial.

(d) The notice shall include a return envelope from the court and a statement that failure to proceed pursuant to subdivision (c) will result in the issuance of a judgment in the amount of five hundred dollars ($500), in addition to liability for the amount of the fine.

(e) Where appropriate, all written advisements or notices given or sent pursuant to this section shall be in both English and Spanish.

(f) If the defendant does not respond within 30 days of receipt of the notice, the court shall send the defendant a notice of intent to issue judgment which shall advise the defendant that if he or she does not appear within 10 days, the five hundred dollars ($500) will become collectible as civil damages.

(g) If the defendant does not respond within 10 days of the issuance of the intent to issue judgment, the court shall issue a writ of execution and the five hundred dollars ($500) shall be collectible as civil damages.

(h) If a writ of execution is issued for collection of a civil assessment, the same writ also shall include an attachment for the amount of the fine or forfeiture for the underlying offense.

(i) The costs of levying, storing, or safekeeping all personal and real property seized by a levying officer in effectuating any process issued pursuant to this section shall be the responsibility of the owner of the property.

(j) After the writ of execution has been issued, the defendant may appear and, upon a showing of good cause, the civil fine shall be set aside, but subject to an administrative fee equal to 14 percent of the fine or forfeiture imposed, not to exceed five hundred dollars ($500). Thereafter, the defendant may address the underlying offense de novo. The clerk of the court shall transfer the amounts collected under this subdivision to the county treasurer for deposit in the county treasury. All moneys so deposited shall be transferred as follows: 50 percent of the money to the agency levying or collecting the judgment to be used exclusively for that agency, and 50 percent of that money to a fund in the county treasury and used exclusively to develop, maintain, and operate an automated county warrant system. The assessment imposed shall be subject to the due process requirements governing defense and collection of civil money judgments generally.

(k) Except in cases in which it is determined that the defendant has insufficient attachable assets, in which case the court may issue a bench warrant, no bench warrant or warrant of arrest shall be issued with respect to the failure to appear at the proceeding for which the judgment is imposed.

(l) For counties opting to participate in the pilot project, notwithstanding Section 1463, out of the moneys deposited with the county treasurer pursuant to Section 1463, there shall be transferred once a month an amount equal to the specified percentage of civil assessments collected during the preceding month upon a judgment made pursuant to Section 1214.1, in accordance with the following schedule:

(1) Twenty percent to be transferred to the law enforcement agency that issued the underlying citation, for use of that agency.

(2) Twenty-five percent to be transferred to the agency levying or collecting the judgment, for use of that agency.

(3) Five percent to be transferred to a county fund and used exclusively to develop, maintain, and operate an automated warrant system.

(4) Twenty-five percent to be deposited in the general fund of the county.

(5) Twenty-five percent to be transferred to the judicial district issuing the writ of execution.

(m) If the judgment is for a fine, with or without imprisonment, the judgment may be enforced in the manner provided for the enforcement of money judgments generally.

(n) This section shall remain in effect only until January 1, 1993, and as of that date is repealed, unless a later enacted statute, which is enacted before January 1, 1993, deletes or extends that date. *(Amended by Stats 1991 ch 1103 §1, eff. 1/1/92 only until 1/1/93.)*

§1214.5. Interest in cases involving more than $50 in restitution.

(a) In any case in which the defendant is ordered to pay more than fifty dollars ($50) in restitution as a condition of probation, the court may, as an additional condition of probation since the court determines that the defendant has the ability to pay, as defined in Section 1203.1b (b), order the defendant to pay interest at the rate of 10 percent per annum on the principal amount remaining unsatisfied.

(b) (1) Except as provided in paragraph (2), interest commences to accrue on the date of entry of the judgment or order.

(2) Unless the judgment or order otherwise provides, if restitution is payable in installments, interest commences to accrue as to each installment on the date the installment becomes due. *(Added by Stats 1985 ch 412 §2.)*

§1215. Commitment until compliance with judgment.

If the judgment is for imprisonment, or a fine and imprisonment until it be paid, the defendant must forthwith be committed to the custody of the proper officer and by him or her detained until the judgment is complied with. Where, however, the court has suspended sentence, or where, after imposing sentence, the court has suspended the execution thereof and placed the defendant on probation, as provided in Section 1203, the defendant, if over the age of 16 years, shall be placed under the care and supervision of the probation officer of the court committing him or her, until the expiration of the period of probation and the compliance with the terms and conditions of the sentence, or of the suspension thereof. Where, however, the probation has been terminated as provided in Section 1203, and the suspension of the sentence, or of the execution revoked, and the judgment pronounced, the defendant shall be committed to the custody of the proper officer and be detained until the judgment be complied with. *(Amended by Stats 1987 ch 828 §80.)*

§1216. Sheriff's duty on receiving abstract of judgment.

If the judgment is for imprisonment in the state prison, the sheriff of the county shall, upon receipt of a certified abstract or minute order thereof, take and

© 1992 by J., B. & L. Gould
Printed in the U.S.A.   EP

deliver the defendant to the warden of the state prison. He shall also deliver to the warden the certified abstract of the judgment or minute order, and take from the warden a receipt for the defendant.

§1217. Sheriff's duty on judgment of death.

When judgment of death is rendered, a commitment signed by the judge, and attested by the clerk under the seal of the court must be drawn and delivered to the sheriff. It must state the conviction and judgment, and must direct the sheriff to deliver the defendant, within 10 days from the time of judgment, to the warden of the State prison of this State designated by the State Board of Prison Directors for the execution of the death penalty, to be held pending the decision upon his appeal.

§1218. Statement of conviction and judgment to be sent to Governor.

The judge of the court at which a judgment of death is had, must, immediately after the judgment, transmit to the Governor, by mail or otherwise, a statement of the conviction and judgment, and a complete transcript of all the testimony given at the trial including any arguments made by respective counsel and a copy of the clerk's transcript.

§1219. Governor may require opinion of Justices of Supreme Court, etc., thereon.

The Governor may thereupon require the opinion of the Justices of the Supreme Court and of the Attorney General, or any of them, upon the statement so furnished.

§1227. Unexecuted judgment of death; proceedings.

If for any reason other than the pendency of an appeal pursuant to subdivision (b) of Section 1239 of this code a judgment of death has not been executed, and it remains in force, the court in which the conviction was had shall, on application of the district attorney, or may upon its own motion, make and cause to be entered an order appointing a day upon which the judgment shall be executed, which must not be less than 30 days nor more than 60 days from the time of making such order; and immediately thereafter, a certified copy of such order, attested by the clerk, under the seal of the court, shall, for the purpose of execution, be transmitted by registered mail to the warden of the state prison having the custody of the defendant; provided, that if the defendant be at large, a warrant for his apprehension may be issued, and upon being apprehended, he shall be brought before the court, whereupon the court shall make an order directing the warden of the state prison to whom the sheriff is instructed to deliver the defendant to execute the judgment at a specified time, which shall not be less than 30 days nor more than 60 days from the time of making such order.

From an order fixing the time for and directing the execution of such judgment as herein provided, there shall be no appeal.

§1227.5. Carrying out execution after stay or reprieve by Governor.

Notwithstanding Section 1227, where a judgment of death has not been executed by reason of a stay or reprieve granted by the Governor, the execution shall be carried out on the day immediately after the period of the stay or reprieve without further judicial proceedings.

TITLE 9

APPEALS FROM SUPERIOR COURTS

CHAPTER 1

APPEALS, WHEN ALLOWED AND HOW TAKEN, AND THE EFFECT THEREOF

§1235. Appeals, questions of law.

Either party to a criminal action within the original trial jurisdiction of a superior court may appeal from that court on questions of law alone, as prescribed in this title and in rules adopted by the Judicial Council. The provisions of this title apply only to such appeals.

§1236. Parties; how designated on appeal.

The party appealing is known as the appellant, and the adverse party as the respondent, but the title of the action is not changed in consequence of the appeal.

§1237. Appealable cases.

An appeal may be taken by the defendant:

(a) From a final judgment of conviction except as provided in Section 1237.5. A sentence, an order granting probation, or the commitment of a defendant for insanity, the indeterminate commitment of a defendant as a mentally disordered sex offender, or the commitment of a defendant for controlled substance addiction shall be deemed to be a final judgment within the meaning of this section. Upon appeal from a final judgment the court may review any order denying a motion for a new trial.

(b) From any order made after judgment, affecting the substantial rights of the party.

§1237.5. Appeal prerequisites.

No appeal shall be taken by a defendant from a judgment of conviction upon a plea of guilty or nolo contendere, or a revocation of probation following an admission of violation, except where the defendant has filed as part of the notice of appeal a written statement, executed under oath or penalty of perjury showing reasonable constitutional, jurisdictional, or other grounds going to the legality of the proceedings.

This section shall remain in effect only until January 1, 1992, and as of that date is repealed, unless a later enacted statute, which is enacted before January 1, 1992, deletes or extends that date. *(Amended by Stats 1988 ch 851 §1, eff. 1/1/89 only until 1/1/92. See other section 1237.5 below.)*

§1237.5. Appeal prerequisites.

No appeal shall be taken by the defendant from a judgment of conviction upon a plea of guilty or nolo contendere, or a revocation of probation following an admission of violation, except where both of the following are met:

(a) The defendant has filed with the trial court a written statement, executed under oath or penalty of perjury showing reasonable constitutional, jurisdictional, or other grounds going to the legality of the proceedings.

(b) The trial court has executed and filed a certificate of probable cause for such appeal with the county clerk.

This section shall become operative on January 1, 1992. *(Added by Stats 1988 ch 851 §2, eff. 1/1/89, oper. 1/1/92. See other section 1237.5 above.)*

§1238. Appeals by prosecution.

(a) An appeal may be taken by the people from any of the following:

(1) An order setting aside the indictment, information, or complaint.

(2) A judgment for the defendant on a demurrer to the indictment, accusation, or information.

(3) An order granting a new trial.

(4) An order arresting judgment.

(5) An order made after judgment, affecting the substantial rights of the people.

(6) An order modifying the verdict or finding by reducing the degree of the offense or the punishment imposed or modifying the offense to a lesser offense.

(7) An order dismissing a case prior to trial made upon motion of the court pursuant to Section 1385 whenever such order is based upon an order granting defendant's motion to return or suppress property or evidence made at a special hearing as provided in this code.

(8) An order or judgment dismissing or otherwise terminating the action before the defendant has been placed in jeopardy or where the defendant has waived jeopardy.

(9) An order denying the motion of the people to reinstate the complaint or a portion thereof pursuant to Section 871.5.

(10) The imposition of an unlawful sentence, whether or not the court suspends the execution of the sentence, except that portion of a sentence imposing a prison term which is based upon a court's choice that a term of imprisonment (A) be the upper, middle, or lower term, unless the term selected is not set forth in an applicable statute, or (B) be consecutive or concurrent to another term of imprisonment, unless an applicable statute requires that the term be consecutive. As used in this paragraph, "unlawful sentence" means the imposition of a sentence not authorized by law or the imposition of a sentence based upon an unlawful order of the court which strikes or otherwise modifies the effect of an enhancement or prior conviction.

(b) If, pursuant to paragraph (8) of subdivision (a), the people prosecute an appeal to decision, or any review of such decision, it shall be binding upon them and they shall be prohibited from refiling the case which was appealed.

(c) When an appeal is taken pursuant to paragraph (7) of subdivision (a), the court may review the order granting defendant's motion to return or suppress property or evidence made at a special hearing as provided in this code.

(d) Nothing contained in this section shall be construed to authorize an appeal from an order granting probation. Instead, the people may seek appellate review of any grant of probation, whether or not the court imposes sentence, by means of a petition for a writ of mandate or prohibition which is filed within 60 days after probation is granted. The review of any grant of probation shall include review of any order underlying the grant of probation. *(Amended by Stats 1988 ch 527 §1; ch 528 §1, eff. 1/1/89.)*

§1238.5. Defendant's right of appeal.

Upon appeal by the prosecution pursuant to Section 1238, where the notice of appeal is filed after the expiration of the time available to defendant to seek review of an otherwise reviewable order or ruling and the appeal by the prosecution relates to a matter decided during the time available to the defendant to seek review of the otherwise reviewable order or ruling, the time for defendant to seek such review is reinstated to run from the date the notice of appeal was filed with proof of service upon defendant or his counsel.

The Judicial Council shall provide by rule for the consolidation of such petition for review with the prosecution appeal.

§1239. Taking appeal; appeal from death judgment.

(a) Where an appeal lies on behalf of the defendant or the people, it may be taken by the defendant or his or her counsel, or by counsel for the people, in the manner provided in rules adopted by the Judicial Council.

(b) When upon any plea a judgment of death is rendered, an appeal is automatically taken by the defendant without any action by him or his counsel. The defendant's trial counsel, whether retained by the defendant or court appointed, shall continue to represent the defendant until completing the additional duties set forth in paragraph (1) of subdivision (e) of section 1240.1. *(Amended by Stats 1988 ch 551 §1, eff. 1/1/89.)*

§1240. State Public Defender.

(a) When in a proceeding falling within the provisions of Section 15421 of the Government Code a person is not represented by a public defender acting pursuant to Section 27706 of the Government Code or other counsel and he is unable to afford the services of counsel, the court shall appoint the State Public Defender to represent the person except as follows:

(1) The court shall appoint counsel other than the State Public Defender when the State Public Defender has refused to represent the person because of conflict of interest or other reason.

(2) The court may, in its discretion, appoint either the State Public Defender or the attorney who represented the person at his trial when the person requests the latter to represent him on appeal and the attorney consents to the appointment. In unusual cases, where good cause exists, the court may appoint any other attorney.

(3) A court may appoint a county public defender, private attorney, or nonprofit corporation with which the State Public Defender has contracted to furnish defense services pursuant to Government Code Section 15402.

(4) When a judgment of death has been rendered the Supreme Court may, in its discretion, appoint counsel other than the State Public Defender or the attorney who represented the person at trial.

(b) If counsel other than the State Public Defender is appointed pursuant to this section, he may exercise the same authority as the State Public Defender pursuant to Chapter 2 (commencing with Section 15420) of Part 7 of Division 3 of Title 2 of the Government Code.

§1240.1. Indigent appeals.

(a) In any noncapital criminal, juvenile court, or civil commitment case wherein the defendant would be entitled to the appointment of counsel on appeal if

© 1992 by J., B. & L. Gould
Printed in the U.S.A.   **EP**

indigent, it shall be the duty of the attorney who represented the person at trial to provide counsel and advice as to whether arguably meritorious grounds exist for reversal or modification of the judgment on appeal. The attorney shall admonish the defendant that he or she is not able to provide advice concerning his or her own competency, and that the State Public Defender or other counsel should be consulted for advice as to whether an issue regarding the competency of counsel should be raised on appeal. The trial court may require trial counsel to certify that he or she has counseled the defendant as to whether arguably meritorious grounds for appeal exist at the time a notice of appeal is filed. Nothing in this section shall be construed to prevent any person having a right to appeal from doing so.

(b) It shall be the duty of every attorney representing an indigent defendant in any criminal, juvenile court, or civil commitment case to execute and file on his or her client's behalf a timely notice of appeal when the attorney is of the opinion that arguably meritorious grounds exist for a reversal or modification of the judgment or orders to be appealed from, and where, in the attorney's judgment, it is in the defendant's interest to pursue such relief as may be available to him or her on appeal; or when directed to do so by a defendant having a right to appeal.

With the notice of appeal the attorney shall file a brief statement of the points to be raised on appeal and a designation of any document, paper, pleading, or transcript of oral proceedings necessary to properly present those points on appeal when the document, paper, pleading or transcript of oral proceedings would not be included in the normal record on appeal according to the applicable provisions of the California Rules of Court. The executing of the notice of appeal by the defendant's attorney shall not constitute an undertaking to represent the defendant on appeal unless the undertaking is expressly stated in the notice of appeal.

If the defendant was represented by appointed counsel on the trial level, or if it appears that the defendant will request the appointment of counsel on appeal by reason of indigency, the trial attorney shall also assist the defendant in preparing and submitting a motion for the appointment of counsel and any supporting declaration or affidavit as to the defendant's financial condition. These documents shall be filed with the trial court at the time of filing a notice of appeal, and shall be transmitted by the clerk of the trial court to the clerk of the appellate court within three judicial days of their receipt. The appellate court shall act upon that motion without unnecessary delay. An attorney's failure to file a motion for the appointment of counsel with the notice of appeal shall not foreclose the defendant from filing a motion at any time it becomes known to him or her that the attorney has failed to do so, or at any time he or she shall become indigent if he or she was not previously indigent.

(c) The State Public Defender shall, at the request of any attorney representing a prospective indigent appellant or at the request of the prospective indigent appellant himself or herself, provide counsel and advice to the prospective indigent appellant or attorney as to whether arguably meritorious grounds exist on which the judgment or order to be appealed from would be reversed or modified on appeal.

(d) The failure of a trial attorney to perform any duty prescribed in this section, assign any particular point or error in the notice of appeal, or designate any particular thing for inclusion in the record on appeal shall not foreclose any defendant from filing a notice of appeal on his or her own behalf or from raising any point or argument on appeal; nor shall it foreclose the defendant or his or her own counsel on appeal from requesting the augmentation or correction of the record on appeal in the reviewing court.

(e) (1) In order to expedite certification of the entire record on appeal in all capital cases, defendant's trial counsel, whether retained by the defendant or court-appointed, shall continue to represent the defendant until the entire record on the automatic appeal is certified. In any capital case, trial counsel shall check that the entire record on appeal has been prepared, and shall check for errors or omissions in that record and request any corrections thereto within the time provided by rules adopted by the Judicial Council.

(2) The duties imposed on trial counsel in paragraph (1) shall not foreclose the defendant's appellate counsel from requesting additions or corrections to the entire record on appeal in either the trial court or the Supreme Court. *(Amended by Stats 1988 ch 551 §2, eff. 1/1/89.)*

§1241. Appeal counsel's fees.

In any case in which counsel other than a public defender has been appointed by the Supreme Court or by a court of appeal to represent a party to any appeal or proceeding, such counsel shall receive a reasonable sum for compensation and necessary expenses, the amount of which shall be determined by the court and paid from any funds appropriated to the Judicial Council for that purpose. Claim for the payment of such compensation and expenses shall be made on a form prescribed by the Judicial Council and presented by counsel to the clerk of the appointing court. After the court has made its order fixing the amount to be paid the clerk shall transmit a copy of the order to the State Controller who shall draw his warrant in payment thereof and transmit it to the payee.

§1242. Effect of an appeal by the people.

An appeal taken by the people in no case stays or affects the operation of a judgment in favor of the defendant, until judgment is reversed.

§1243. Stay of execution pending appeal.

An appeal to the Supreme Court or to a court of appeal from a judgment of conviction stays the execution of the judgment in all cases where sentence of death has been imposed, but does not stay the execution of the judgment or order granting probation in any other case unless the trial or appellate court shall so order. The granting or refusal of such order shall rest in the discretion of the court. If such order is made, the clerk of the court shall issue a certificate stating that such order has been made.

§1244. Effect of an appeal by the defendant.

If the certificate provided for in the preceding section is filed, the Sheriff must, if the defendant be in his custody, upon being served with a copy thereof, keep the defendant in his custody without executing the judgment, and detain him to abide the judgment on appeal.

§1245. Further execution suspended.

If before the granting of the certificate, the execution of the judgment has commenced, the further

© 1992 by J., B. & L. Gould
Printed in the U.S.A. **EP**

execution thereof is suspended, and upon service of a copy of such certificate the defendant must be restored, by the officer in whose custody he is, to his original custody.

§1246. Rules of record on appeal.

The record on appeal shall be made up and filed in such time and manner as shall be prescribed in rules adopted by the Judicial Council.

CHAPTER 1a

JUDICIAL COUNCIL RULES

§1247k. Rules on appeal in criminal cases.

The Judicial Council shall have the power to prescribe by rules for the practice and procedure on appeal, and for the time and manner in which the records on such appeals shall be made up and filed, in all criminal cases in all courts of this State.

The Judicial Council shall report the rules prescribed by it to the Legislature on or before March 31, 1943.

The rules reported as aforesaid shall take effect on July 1, 1943, and thereafter all laws in conflict therewith shall be of no further force or effect.

CHAPTER 2

DISMISSING AN APPEAL FOR IRREGULARITY

§1248. Dismissal of appeal.

If the appeal is irregular in any substantial particular, but not otherwise, the appellate court may order it to be dismissed.

CHAPTER 3

ARGUMENT OF THE APPEAL

§1252. Continuance.

On an appeal in a criminal case, no continuance shall be granted upon stipulation of counsel, and no continuance shall be granted for any longer period than the ends of justice shall require. On an appeal by a defendant, the appellate court shall, in addition to the issues raised by the defendant, consider and pass upon all rulings of the trial court adverse to the State which it may be requested to pass upon by the Attorney General.

§1253. Judgment may be affirmed, but cannot be reversed without argument.

The judgment may be affirmed if the appellant fail to appear, but can be reversed only after argument, though the respondent fail to appear.

§1254. Number of counsel to be heard.

Upon the argument of the appeal, if the offense is punishable with death, two counsel must be heard on each side, if they require it. In any other case the Court may, in its discretion, restrict the argument to one counsel on each side.

§1255. Defendant need not be present.

The defendant need not personally appear in the Appellate Court.

§1256. Duty of district attorney to cooperate with attorney general.

It shall be the duty of the district attorney to cooperate with and assist the attorney general in presenting all criminal matters on appeal.

CHAPTER 4

JUDGMENT UPON APPEAL

§1258. Court to give judgment without regard to technical errors.

After hearing the appeal, the court must give judgment without regard to technical errors or defects, or to exceptions, which do not affect the substantial rights of the parties.

§1259. Questions of law reviewable upon appeal by defendant.

Upon an appeal taken by the defendant, the appellate court may, without exception having been taken in the trial court, review any question of law involved in any ruling, order, instruction, or thing whatsoever said or done at the trial or prior to or after judgment, which thing was said or done after objection made in and considered by the lower court, and which affected the substantial rights of the defendant. The appellate court may also review any instruction given, refused or modified, even though no objection was made thereto in the lower court, if the substantial rights of the defendant were affected thereby.

§1260. Appellate court rulings.

The court may reverse, affirm, or modify a judgment or order appealed from, or reduce the degree of the offense or attempted offense or the punishment imposed, and may set aside, affirm, or modify any or all of the proceedings subsequent to, or dependent upon, such judgment or order, and may, if proper, order a new trial and may, if proper, remand the cause to the trial court for such further proceedings as may be just under the circumstances.

§1261. New trial, where to be had.

When a new trial is ordered it must be directed to be had in the Court of the county from which the appeal was taken.

§1262. Reversal as order for new trial.

If a judgment against the defendant is reversed, such reversal shall be deemed an order for a new trial, unless the appellate court shall otherwise direct. If the appellate court directs a final disposition of the action in the defendant's favor, the court must, if he is in custody, direct him to be discharged therefrom; or if on bail that his bail may be exonerated; or if money or other property was deposited instead of bail, that it be refunded to the defendant or to the person or persons found by the court to have deposited said money or other property on behalf of said defendant. If a judgment against the defendant is reversed and the case is dismissed, or if the appellate court directs a final disposition of the action in defendant's favor, and defendant has theretofore paid a fine in the case, such act shall also be deemed an order of the court that the fine, assessment thereon, be returned to defendant.

© 1992 by J., B. & L. Gould
Printed in the U.S.A.   **EP**

§1263. Judgment to be executed on affirmance.

If a judgment against the defendant is affirmed, the original judgment must be enforced.

§1265. Reversal as order for new trial.

After the certificate of the judgment has been remitted to the court below, the appellate court has no further jurisdiction of the appeal or of the proceedings thereon, and all orders necessary to carry the judgment into effect must be made by the court to which the certificate is remitted; provided, however, that if a judgment has been affirmed on appeal no motion shall be made or proceeding in the nature of a petition for a writ of error coram nobis shall be brought to procure the vacation of said judgment, except in the court which affirmed the judgment on appeal. When a judgment is affirmed by a court of appeal and a hearing is not granted by the Supreme Court, the application for the writ shall be made to the court of appeal.

TITLE 10

MISCELLANEOUS PROCEEDINGS

CHAPTER 1

BAIL

ARTICLE 1

IN WHAT CASES THE DEFENDANT MAY BE ADMITTED TO BAIL

§1268. Admission to bail defined.

Admission to bail is the order of a competent Court or magistrate that the defendant be discharged from actual custody upon bail.

§1269. Taking of bail defined.

The taking of bail consists in the acceptance, by a competent court or magistrate, of the undertaking of sufficient bail for the appearance of the defendant, according to the terms of the undertaking, or that the bail will pay to the people of this State a specified sum. Upon filing, the clerk shall enter in the register of actions the date and amounts of such bond and the name or names of the surety or sureties thereon. In the event of the loss or destruction of such bond, such entries so made shall be prima facie evidence of the due execution of such bond as required by law.

Whenever any bail bond has been deposited in any criminal action or proceeding in a justice, municipal, or superior court or in any proceeding in habeas corpus in a superior court, either before or after the effective date of this amendment to this section, and it is made to appear to the satisfaction of the court by affidavit or by testimony in open court that more than three years have elapsed since the exoneration or release of said bail, the court must direct that such bond be destroyed.

§1269a. Orders admitting defendant to bail.

Except as otherwise provided by law, no defendant charged in a warrant of arrest with any public offense shall be discharged from custody upon bail except upon a written order of a competent court or magistrate admitting the defendant to bail in the amount specified in the indorsement referred to in Section 815a, and where an undertaking is furnished, upon a written order of such court or magistrate approving the undertaking. All such orders must be signed by such court or magistrate and delivered to the officer having custody of the defendant before the defendant is released. Any officer releasing any defendant upon bail otherwise than as herein provided shall be guilty of a misdemeanor.

§1269b. Authority to approve and accept bail.

(a) The officer in charge of a jail where an arrested person is held in custody, an officer of a sheriff's department or police department of a city who is in charge of a jail or employed at a fixed police or sheriff's facility and is acting under an agreement with the agency which keeps the jail wherein an arrested person is held in custody, an employee of a sheriff's department or police department of a city who is assigned by such department to collect bail, the clerk of the justice or municipal court of the judicial district in which the offense was alleged to have been committed, and the clerk of the superior court in which the case against the defendant is pending may approve and accept bail in the amount fixed by the warrant of arrest, schedule of bail, or order admitting to bail in cash or surety bond executed by a certified, admitted surety insurer as provided in the Insurance Code, to issue and sign an order for the release of the arrested person, and to set a time and place for the appearance of the arrested person before the appropriate court and give notice thereof.

(b) If a defendant has appeared before a judge of the court on the charge contained in the complaint, indictment, or information, the bail shall be in the amount fixed by the judge at the time of the appearance; if that appearance has not been made, the bail shall be in the amount fixed in the warrant of arrest or, if no warrant of arrest has been issued, the amount of bail shall be pursuant to the uniform countywide schedule of bail for the county in which the defendant is required to appear, previously fixed and approved as provided in subdivisions (c) and (d).

(c) It is the duty of the superior, municipal and justice court judges in each county to prepare, adopt, and to annually revise, by a majority vote, at a meeting called by the presiding judge of the superior court of the county, a uniform countywide schedule of bail for all bailable felony offenses.

In adopting a uniform countywide schedule of bail for all bailable offenses the judges shall consider the seriousness of the offense charged. In considering the seriousness of the offense charged the judges shall assign an additional amount of required bail for each aggravating or enhancing factor chargeable in the complaint, including, but not limited to, additional bail for charges alleging facts which would bring a person within any of the following sections: Section 667.5, 667.51, 667.6, 667.8, 667.85, 667.9, 667.10, 12022, 12022.1, 12022.2, 12022.3, 12022.4, 12022.5, 12022.6, 12022.7, 12022.8, or 12022.9 of the Penal Code, or Section 11356.5, 11370.2, or 11370.4 of the Health and Safety Code.

In considering offenses wherein a violation of Chapter 6 (commencing with Section 11350) of Division 10 of the Health and Safety Code is alleged, the judge shall assign an additional amount of required bail for offenses involving large quantities of controlled substances.

(d) The municipal and justice court judges in each county shall prepare, adopt, and annually revise, sub-

© 1992 by J., B. & L. Gould
Printed in the U.S.A. **EP**

ject to Section 40310 of the Vehicle Code, by a majority vote, at a meeting called by the presiding judge of the municipal court or the senior judge of the justice court at each county seat, a uniform, countywide schedule of bail for all misdemeanor and infraction offenses. For nonparking Vehicle Code offenses where a personal appearance is not required, the bail for each offense shall be no more than 20 percent above or below the amount set forth by the Uniform Traffic Bail Schedule approved by the Judicial Council. The Judicial Council shall revise the Uniform Traffic Bail Schedule by January 1, 1989. The revision shall include the assignment of increased bail amounts for repeat offenders.

(e) Each countywide bail schedule shall contain a list of the offenses and the amounts of bail applicable thereto as the judges determine to be appropriate. If the schedules do not list all offenses specifically, they shall contain a general clause for designated amounts of bail as the judges of the county determine to be appropriate for all the offenses not specifically listed in the schedules. A copy of the countywide bail schedule shall be sent to the officer in charge of the county jail, to the officer in charge of each city jail within the county, to each superior, municipal and justice court judge and commissioner in the county, and to the Judicial Council.

(f) Upon posting such bail the defendant or arrested person shall be discharged from custody as to the offense on which the bail is posted.

All money and surety bonds so deposited with an officer authorized to receive bail shall be transmitted immediately to the judge or clerk of the court by which the order was made or warrant issued or bail schedule fixed. If, in the case of felonies, an indictment is filed, the judge or clerk of the court shall transmit all of the money and surety bonds to the county clerk.

(g) If a defendant or arrested person so released fails to appear at the time and in the court so ordered upon his or her release from custody, Sections 1305 and 1306 apply. *(Amended by Stats 1988 ch 988 §1, eff. 1/1/89.)*

§1269c. Orders for higher or lower bail.

In any case in which a defendant is arrested without a warrant for a bailable felony offense and a peace officer has reasonable cause to believe that the amount of bail set forth in the schedule of bail for that offense is insufficient to assure defendant's appearance, the peace officer shall prepare a declaration under penalty of perjury setting forth the facts and circumstances in support of his belief and file it with a magistrate, as defined in Section 808, in the county in which the offense is alleged to have been committed or having jurisdiction of the person of the defendant, or a commissioner of such magistrate, requesting an order setting a higher bail. The defendant, either personally or through his attorney, friend, or member of family, also may make application to such magistrate for release on bail lower than that provided in the schedule of bail or on his own recognizance. The magistrate or commissioner to whom such application is made is authorized to set bail in such amount as he deems sufficient to assure the defendant's appearance, and to set such bail on such terms and conditions as he, in his discretion, deems appropriate, or he may authorize the defendant's release on his own recognizance. If, after such an application is made, no order changing the amount of bail is issued within eight hours after booking, the defendant shall be entitled to

be released on posting the amount of bail set forth in the applicable bail schedule.

§1270. Recognizance release.

(a) Any person, who has been arrested for, or charged with, an offense other than a capital offense may be released on his or her own recognizance by a court or magistrate who could release a defendant from custody upon the defendant giving bail, including a defendant arrested upon an out-of-county warrant, provided that a defendant who is in custody and is arraigned on a complaint alleging an offense which is a misdemeanor, and a defendant who appears before a court or magistrate upon an out-of-county warrant arising out of a case involving only misdemeanors, shall be entitled to an own recognizance release unless the court makes a finding upon the record that an own recognizance release will not reasonably assure the appearance of the defendant as required. In this event the court shall then set bail and specify the conditions, if any, whereunder the defendant shall be released. If the complaint or the out-of-county warrant arises out of a case alleging a misdemeanor offense in which the commission, attempted commission, or conspiracy to commit the offense involves the possession or use of a firearm, or in which there is a violation of Chapter 9 (commencing with Section 240) of Title 8 of Part 1, willful disobedience of any process or order lawfully issued by any court in violation of Section 166, or Section 186.22, 262, 273a, 273d, 273.5, 273.6, 368, 417, 422, 422.6, 646.9, 647.6, 653k, or 653m, Section 1275 shall apply in considering whether to grant or deny a release under this section.

(b) Article 9 (commencing with Section 1318) shall apply to any person who is released pursuant to this section. *(Amended by Stats 1990 ch 1527 §2, eff. 1/1/91.)*

§1270.1. Hearing to set bail for violent felony.

Before any person arrested for a violent felony is released on bail, which bail is set in an amount which is either more or less than the amount contained in the schedule of bail for that felony, a hearing shall be held in open court before the magistrate or judge. The prosecuting attorney shall be given a two court-day written notice and an opportunity to be heard on the matter. The hearing required by this section shall be held within the time period prescribed in Section 825.

If the judge or magistrate sets the bail in an amount which is either more or less than the amount contained in the schedule of bail for that violent felony, the judge or magistrate shall state the reasons for that decision and shall address the issue of threats made against the victim or witness, if they were made, in the record. This statement shall be included in the record.

As used in this section, the term "violent felony" means any crime specified in subdivision (c) of Section 667.5. *(Added by Stats 1988 ch 492 §1, eff. 1/1/89.)*

§1270.2. Review of order fixing the amount of bail.

When a person is detained in custody on a criminal charge prior to conviction for want of bail, that person is entitled to an automatic review of the order fixing the amount of the bail by the judge or magistrate having jurisdiction of the offense. That review shall be held not later than five days from the time of the original order fixing the amount of bail on the original

© 1992 by J., B. & L. Gould
Printed in the U.S.A.   **EP**

accusatory pleading. The defendant may waive this review. *(Added by Stats 1986 ch 658 §1.)*

§1270.5. Nonbailable capital offenses.

A defendant charged with an offense punishable with death cannot be admitted to bail, when the proof of his or her guilt is evident or the presumption thereof great. The finding of an indictment does not add to the strength of the proof or the presumptions to be drawn therefrom. *(Amended and renumbered by Stats 1986 ch 248 §165.)*

§1271. In what cases defendant may be admitted to bail before conviction.

If the charge is for any other offense, he may be admitted to bail before conviction, as a matter of right.

§1272. Admitting to bail after application for probation or on appeal.

After conviction of an offense not punishable with death, a defendant who has made application for probation or who has appealed may be admitted to bail:

1. As a matter of right, before judgment is pronounced pending application for probation in cases of misdemeanors, or when the appeal is from a judgment imposing a fine only.

2. As a matter of right, before judgment is pronounced pending application for probation in cases of misdemeanors, or when the appeal is from a judgment imposing imprisonment in cases of misdemeanors.

3. As a matter of discretion in all other cases, except that a person convicted of an offense subject to this subdivision, who makes a motion for release on bail subsequent to a sentencing hearing, shall provide notice of the hearing on the bail motion to the prosecuting attorney at least five court days prior to the hearing.

§1272.1. Criteria for release on bail pending appeal.

Release on bail pending appeal under subdivision (3) of Section 1272 shall be ordered by the court if the defendant demonstrates all the following:

(a) By clear and convincing evidence, the defendant is not likely to flee. Under this subdivision the court shall consider the following criteria:

(1) The ties of the defendant to the community, including his or her employment, the duration of his or her residence, the defendant's family attachments and his or her property holdings.

(2) The defendant's record of appearance at past court hearings or of flight to avoid prosecution.

(3) The severity of the sentence the defendant faces.

(b) By clear and convincing evidence, the defendant does not pose a danger to the safety of any other person or to the community.

Under this subdivision the court shall consider, among other factors, whether the crime for which the defendant was convicted is a violent felony, as defined in subdivision (c) of Section 667.5.

(c) The appeal is not for the purpose of delay and, based upon the record in the case, raises a substantial legal question which, if decided in favor of the defendant, is likely to result in reversal.

For purposes of this subdivision, a "substantial legal question" means a close question, one of more substance than would be necessary to a finding that it was not frivolous. In assessing whether a substantial legal question has been raised on appeal by the defendant, the court shall not be required to determine whether it committed error.

In making its decision on whether to grant defendants' motions for bail under subdivision (3) of Section 1272, the court shall include a brief statement of reasons in support of an order granting or denying a motion for bail on appeal. The statement need only include the basis for the order with sufficient specificity to permit meaningful review. *(Amended by Stats 1989 ch 150 §1, eff. 1/1/90.)*

§1273. Types of bail.

If the offense is bailable, the defendant may be admitted to bail before conviction:

First. For his appearance before the magistrate, on the examination of the charge, before being held to answer.

Second. To appear at the court to which the magistrate is required to return the depositions and statement, upon the defendant being held to answer after examination.

Third. After indictment, either before the bench warrant is issued for his arrest, or upon any order of the court committing him, or enlarging the amount of bail, or upon his being surrendered by his bail to answer the indictment in the Court in which it is found, or to which it may be transferred for trial.

And after conviction, and upon an appeal:

First. If the appeal is from a judgment imposing a fine only, on the undertaking of bail that he will pay the same, or such part of it as the appellate court may direct, if the judgment is affirmed or modified, or the appeal is dismissed.

Second. If judgment of imprisonment has been given, that he will surrender himself in execution of the judgment, upon its being affirmed or modified, or upon the appeal being dismissed, or that in case the judgment be reversed, and that the cause be remanded for a new trial, that he will appear in the Court to which said cause may be remanded, and submit himself to the orders and process thereof.

§1274. When bail is matter of discretion, notice of application must be given to district attorney.

When the admission to bail is a matter of discretion, the Court or officer to whom the application is made must require reasonable notice thereof to be given to the District Attorney of the county.

§1275. Considerations in fixing amount of bail.

In setting, reducing, or denying bail, the judge or magistrate shall take into consideration the protection of the public, the seriousness of the offense charged, the previous criminal record of the defendant, and the probability of his or her appearing at trial or hearing of the case. The public safety shall be the primary consideration. No bail shall be accepted unless the judge or magistrate be convinced that no portion of the consideration, pledge, security, deposit, or indemnification paid, given, made, or promised for its execution was feloniously obtained.

In considering the seriousness of the offense charged, the judge or magistrate shall include consideration of the alleged injury to the victim, and alleged threats to the victim or a witness to the crime charged, the alleged use of a firearm or other deadly weapon in the commission of the crime charged, and the alleged use or possession of controlled substances by the defendant.

In considering offenses wherein a violation of Chapter 6 (commencing with Section 11350) of Division 10 of the Health and Safety Code is alleged, the judge or magistrate shall consider the following: (1) the alleged amounts of controlled substances involved in the commission of the offense, and (2) whether the defendant is currently released on bail for an alleged violation of Chapter 6 (commencing with Section 11350) of Division 10 of the Health and Safety Code.

In any case wherein a person is arrested for a violation of Section 11351, 11351.5, 11352, 11378, 11378.5, 11379, 11379.5, or 11379.6 of the Health and Safety Code and the person is on probation for a violation of one of those sections or where an allegation pursuant to Section 11370.4 or 11379.8 of the Health and Safety Code may be pleaded and proven, and a peace officer has reasonable cause to believe that the consideration, pledge, security, deposit, or indemnification paid, given, made, or promised for bail was feloniously obtained, the peace officer shall prepare a declaration under penalty of perjury setting forth the facts and circumstances in support of his or her belief and file it with a magistrate, as defined in Section 808, in the county in which the offense is alleged to have been committed or having jurisdiction of the person of the defendant, or a commissioner of the magistrate, requesting an order denying bail. The defendant either personally, or through his or her attorney, friend, or member of his or her family, may also make application to the magistrate for release on bail. The magistrate or commissioner to whom the application is made may deny release on bail pending the hearing described in Section 825. If, after the application is made, no order granting or denying bail is issued within eight hours after booking, the defendant shall be entitled to release on posting the amount of bail set forth in the applicable bail schedule.

The preceding paragraph shall only apply for the period described in Section 825 in which an arrestee shall be taken to a magistrate.

The bail of any defendant found to have willfully mislead the court regarding the source of bail may be increased as a result of the misrepresentation. The misrepresentation may be a factor considered in any subsequent bail hearing. *(Amended by Stats 1990 ch 117 §1, eff. 1/1/91.)*

§1276. Acceptance of bond or undertaking.

(a) A bail bond or undertaking of bail of an admitted surety insurer shall be accepted or approved by a court or magistrate without further acknowledgment if executed by a licensed bail agent of the insurer under penalty of perjury and issued in the name of the insurer by a person authorized to do so by an unrevoked power of attorney on file in the office of the clerk of the county in which the court or magistrate is located.

(b) One person may both execute and issue the bail bond or undertaking of bail if qualified as provided in this section.

§1276.5. Disclosure statement for bail bond secured by lien against real property.

(a) At the time of an initial application to a bail bond licensee for a bail bond which is to be secured by a lien against real property, the bail bond licensee shall provide the property owner with a written disclosure statement in the following form:
"DISCLOSURE OF LIEN AGAINST REAL PROPERTY DO NOT SIGN THIS DOCUMENT UNTIL YOU READ AND UNDERSTAND IT!
THIS BAIL BOND WILL BE SECURED BY REAL PROPERTY YOU OWN OR IN WHICH YOU HAVE AN INTEREST. THE FAILURE TO PAY THE BAIL BOND PREMIUMS WHEN DUE OR THE FAILURE OF THE DEFENDANT TO COMPLY WITH THE CONDITIONS OF BAIL COULD RESULT IN THE LOSS OF YOUR PROPERTY!"

(b) The disclosure required in subdivision (a) shall be made in 14-point bold type by either of the following means:

(1) A separate and specific document attached to or accompanying the application.

(2) A clear and conspicuous statement on the face of the application.

(c) The property owner shall be given a completed copy of the disclosure statement and of the note and deed of trust or other instrument creating the lien against real property prior to the execution of any instrument creating a lien against real property. The failure to fully comply with subdivision (a) or (b), or this subdivision, shall render the deed of trust or other instrument creating the lien against real property voidable.

(d) Within 30 days after notice is given by any individual, agency, or entity to the surety or bail bond licensee of the expiration of the time for appeal of the order exonerating the bail bond, or within 30 days after the payment in full of all moneys owed on the bail bond obligation secured by any lien against real property, whichever is later in time, the bail bond licensee shall deliver to the property owner a fully executed and notarized reconveyance of title, a certificate of discharge, or a full release of any lien against real property to secure performance of the conditions of the bail bond. If a timely notice of appeal of the order exonerating the bail bond is filed with the court, that 30-day period shall begin on the date the determination of the appellate court affirming the order exonerating the bail bond becomes final. Upon the reconveyance, the licensee shall deliver to the property owner the original note and deed of trust, security agreement, or other instrument which secures the bail bond obligation. If the licensee fails to comply with this subdivision, the property owner may petition the superior court to issue an order directing the clerk of the superior court to execute a full reconveyance of title, a certificate of discharge, or a full release of any lien against real property created to secure performance of the conditions of the bail bond. The petition shall be verified and shall allege facts showing that the licensee has failed to comply with this subdivision.

(e) The violation of this section shall make the violator liable to the person affected by the violation for all damages which that person may sustain by reason of the violation plus statutory damages in the sum of three hundred dollars ($300). The property owner shall be entitled, if he or she prevails, to recover court costs and reasonable attorney's fees as determined by the court in any action brought to enforce this section. *(Added by Stats 1991 ch 838 §1, eff. 1/1/92.)*

© 1992 by J., B. & L. Gould
Printed in the U.S.A. **EP**

ARTICLE 2

BAIL UPON BEING HELD TO ANSWER BEFORE INDICTMENT

§1277. What magistrates may admit to bail.

When the defendant has been held to answer upon an examination for a public offense, the admission to bail may be by the magistrate by whom he is so held, or by any magistrate who has power to issue the writ of habeas corpus.

§1278. Written undertaking for bail.

Bail is put in by a written undertaking, executed by two sufficient sureties (with or without the defendant, in the discretion of the magistrate), and acknowledged before the court or magistrate, in substantially the following form:

An order having been made on the ____ day of ____, 19__, by ____, a judge of the Justice Court of ____ County (or as the case may be), that ____ be held to answer upon a charge of (stating briefly the nature of the offense), upon which he or she has been admitted to bail in the sum of ____ dollars ($ ____); we, ____ and ____, of ____ (stating their place of residence and occupation), hereby undertake that the above-named ____ will appear and answer any charge in any accusatory pleading based upon the acts supporting the charge above mentioned, in whatever court it may be prosecuted, and will at all times hold himself or herself amenable to the orders and process of the court, and if convicted, will appear for pronouncement of judgment or grant of probation, or if he or she fails to perform either of these conditions, that we will pay to the people of the State of California the sum of ____ dollars ($ ____) (inserting the sum in which the defendant is admitted to bail). If the forfeiture of this bond be ordered by the court, judgment may be summarily made and entered forthwith against the said (naming the sureties), and the defendant if he or she be a party to the bond, for the amount of their respective undertakings herein, as provided by Sections 1305 and 1306. *(Amended by Stats 1987 ch 828 §81.)*

§1279. Qualifications considered for bail.

The qualifications of bail are as follows:

1. Each of them must be a resident, householder, or freeholder within the state; but the court or magistrate may refuse to accept any person as bail who is not a resident of the county where bail is offered;

2. They must each be worth the amount specified in the undertaking, exclusive of property exempt from execution, except that if any of the sureties is not worth the amount specified in the undertaking, exclusive of property exempt from execution, but owns any equity in real property, a hearing must be held before the magistrate to determine the value of such equity. Witnesses may be called and examined at such hearing and if the magistrate is satisfied that the value of the equity is equal to twice the amount of the bond such surety is justified. In any case, the court or magistrate, on taking bail, may allow more than two sureties to justify severally in amounts less than that expressed in the undertaking, if the whole justification be equivalent to that of sufficient bail.

§1280. Bail, how to justify.

The bail must in all cases justify by affidavit taken before the magistrate, that they each possess the qualifications provided in the preceding section. The magistrate may further examine the bail upon oath concerning their sufficiency, in such manner as he may deem proper.

§1280a. Contents of affidavits.

All affidavits for the justification of bail shall set forth the amount of the bail undertaking, a notice that the affidavit shall constitute a lien upon the real property described in the affidavit immediately upon the recordation of the affidavit with the county recorder pursuant to Section 1280b, and the legal description and assessor's parcel numbers of the real estate owned by the bail, which is scheduled as showing that they each possess the qualifications provided in the preceding sections, the affidavit shall also show all encumbrances upon the real estate known to affiants and shall show the number of bonds, if any, on which each bail has qualified, within one year before the date of the affidavit, together with the amount of each such bond, the date on which, the county in which, and the name of the principal for whom each bond was executed.

The affidavit shall also state the amount of each bail's liability on bonds executed in previous years and not exonerated at the date of the execution of the affidavit and be signed and acknowledged by the owner of the real property. *(Amended by Stats 1987 ch 828 §82.)*

§1280b. Filing of affidavits for justification of bail.

It shall be the duty of the judge or magistrate to file with the clerk of the court, within 24 hours after presentation to him or her, all affidavits for the justification of bail, by delivering or mailing them to the clerk of the court. Certified copies of the affidavits for justification of bail involving equity in real property may upon the written order of the judge or magistrate be recorded with the county recorder. *(Amended by Stats 1988 ch 676 §1, eff. 1/1/89.)*

§1280.1. Attachment lien.

(a)* From the time of recording an affidavit for the justification of bail, the affidavit shall constitute an attachment lien governed by Sections 488.500, 488.510 and 489.310 of the Code of Civil Procedure in the amount of the bail undertaking, until exonerated, released, or otherwise discharged. Any release of the undertaking shall be effected by an order of the court, filed with the clerk of the court, with a certified copy of the order recorded in the office of the county recorder.

So in original. No par. (b) has been enacted.

If the bail is forfeited and summary judgment is entered, pursuant to Sections 1305 and 1306, the lien shall have the force and effect of a judgment lien, by recordation of an abstract of judgment, which may be enforced and satisfied pursuant to Section 1306 as well as through the applicable execution process set forth in Title 9 (commencing with Section 680.010) of Part 2 of the Code of Civil Procedure. *(Amended by Stats 1988 ch 676 §2, eff. 1/1/89.)*

§1281. Order for discharge of defendant.

Upon the allowance of bail and the execution and approval of the undertaking, the magistrate must, if the defendant is in custody, make and sign an order for his discharge, upon the delivery of which to the proper officer the defendant must be discharged.

§1281a. Justification and approval of bail for accused felon.

A judge of any municipal or justice court within the county, wherein a cause is pending against any person charged with a felony, may justify and approve bail in the said cause, and may execute an order for the release of the defendant which shall authorize the discharge of the defendant by any officer having said defendant in custody.

ARTICLE 3

BAIL UPON AN INDICTMENT BEFORE CONVICTION

§1284. Procedure on noncapital offense.

When the offense charged is not punishable with death, the officer serving the bench warrant must, if required, take the defendant before a magistrate in the county in which it is issued, or in which he is arrested, for the purpose of giving bail. If the defendant appears before such magistrate without the bench warrant having been served upon him, the magistrate shall deliver him into the custody of the sheriff for the purpose of immediate booking and the recording of identification data, whereupon the sheriff shall deliver the defendant back before the magistrate for the purpose of giving bail.

§1285. Delivery into custody.

If the offense charged is punishable with death, the officer arresting the defendant must deliver him into custody, according to the command of the bench warrant.

§1286. Bail on habeas corpus.

When the defendant is so delivered into custody he must be held by the sheriff, unless admitted to bail on examination upon a writ of habeas corpus.

§1287. Writ undertaking for bail.

The bail shall be put in by a written undertaking, executed by two sufficient sureties (with or without the defendant, in the discretion of the court or magistrate), and acknowledged before the court or magistrate, in substantially the following form:

An indictment having been found on the ____ day of ____ , 19 ____ , in the Superior Court of the County of _____ , charging _____ with the crime of _____ (designating it generally) and he or she having been admitted to bail in the sum of ____ dollars ($ ____), we, _____ and ____ , of ____ (stating their place of residence and occupation), hereby undertake that the above-named _____ will appear and answer any charge in any accusatory pleading based upon the acts supporting the indictment above mentioned, in whatever court it may be prosecuted, and will at all times render himself or herself amenable to the orders and process of the court, and, if convicted, will appear for pronouncement of judgment or grant of probation; or, if he or she fails to perform either of these conditions, that we will pay to the people of the State of California the sum of ____ dollars ($ ____) (inserting the sum in which the defendant is admitted to bail). If the forfeiture of this bond be ordered by the court, judgment may be summarily made and entered forthwith against the said (naming the sureties, and the defendant if he or she be a party to the bond), for the amount of their respective undertakings herein, as provided by Sections 1305 and 1306. *(Amended by Stats 1987 ch 828 §83.)*

§1288. Applicability of certain sections.

The provisions contained in sections 1279, 1280, 1280a and 1281, in relation to bail before indictment, apply to bail after indictment.

§1289. Cause to increase or reduce amount of bail.

After a defendant has been admitted to bail upon an indictment or information, the Court in which the charge is pending may, upon good cause shown, either increase or reduce the amount of bail. If the amount be increased, the Court may order the defendant to be committed to actual custody, unless he give bail in such increased amount. If application be made by the defendant for a reduction of the amount, notice of the application must be served upon the District Attorney.

ARTICLE 4

BAIL ON APPEAL

§1291. Magistrates power to admit to bail.

In the cases in which defendant may be admitted to bail upon an appeal, the order admitting him to bail may be made by any Magistrate having the power to issue a writ of habeas corpus, or by the Magistrate before whom the trial was had.

§1292. Qualifications of bail and how put in, and condition of undertaking.

The bail must possess the qualifications, and must be put in, in all respects, as provided in Article 2 of this Chapter 1, except that the undertaking must be conditioned as prescribed in Section 1273, for undertakings of bail on appeal.

ARTICLE 5

DEPOSIT INSTEAD OF BAIL

§1295. Defendant's right to make deposit in lieu of bail.

The defendant, or any other person, at any time after an order admitting defendant to bail or after the arrest and booking of a defendant for having committed a misdemeanor, instead of giving bail may deposit with the clerk of the court in which the defendant is held to answer or notified to appear for arraignment, the sum mentioned in the order, or if no order, in the schedule of bail previously fixed by the judges of said court, and upon delivering to the officer in whose custody defendant is a certificate of the deposit, defendant must be discharged from custody.

Where more than one such deposit is made with respect to any charge in any accusatory pleading based upon the acts supporting the original charge as a result of which an earlier deposit was made, the defendant shall receive credit in the amount of any such earlier deposit.

© 1992 by J., B. & L. Gould
Printed in the U.S.A.   EP

§1296. Deposit after bail is given and before forfeiture.

If the defendant has given bail, he may, at any time before the forfeiture of the undertaking, in like manner deposit the sum mentioned in the recognizance, and upon the deposit being made the bail is exonerated.

§1297. Receipt issued for deposit of money.

When money has been deposited, a receipt shall be issued in the name of the depositor. If the money remains on deposit at the time of a judgment for the payment of a fine, the clerk must, under the direction of the court, if the defendant be the depositor, apply the money in satisfaction thereof, and after satisfying the fine and costs, must refund the surplus, if any, to the defendant. If the person to whom the receipt for the deposit was issued was not the defendant, the deposit after judgment shall be returned to him within 10 days after he claims it by submitting the receipt, and, if a claim is not made within 10 days of the exoneration of bail, the clerk shall immediately notify the depositor of the exoneration of bail.

§1298. Deposit of bonds or equity in lieu of money for bail.

In lieu of a deposit of money, the defendant or any other person may deposit bonds of the United States or of the State of California of the face value of the cash deposit required, and these bonds shall be treated in the same manner as a deposit of money or the defendant or any other person may give as security any equity in real property which he or she owns, provided, that no charge is made to the defendant for the giving as security of any equity in real property. A hearing, at which witnesses may be called or examined, shall be held before the magistrate to determine the value of such equity and if the magistrate finds that the value of the equity is equal to twice the amount of the cash deposit required he shall allow such bail. The clerk shall, under order of the court, when occasion arises therefor, sell the bonds or the equity and apply the proceeds of the sale in the manner that a deposit of cash may be required to be applied.

The county treasurer shall, upon request of the judge, keep the deposit and return it to the clerk on order of the judge.

ARTICLE 6

EXONERATION

§1300. Methods and authorization to surrender defendant in their exoneration.

(a) At any time before the forfeiture of their undertaking, or deposit by a third person, the bail or the depositor may surrender the defendant in their exoneration, or he may surrender himself, to the officer to whose custody he was committed at the time of giving bail, in the following manner:

(1) A certified copy of the undertaking of the bail, or a certified copy of the certificate of deposit where a deposit is made, must be delivered to the officer who must detain the defendant in his custody thereon as upon a commitment, and by a certificate in writing acknowledge the surrender.

(2) The bail or depositor, upon surrendering the defendant, shall make reasonable effort to give notice to the defendant's last attorney of record, if any, of such surrender.

(3) The officer to whom the defendant is surrendered shall, within 48 hours of the surrender, bring the defendant before the court in which the defendant is next to appear on the case for which he has been surrendered. The court shall advise the defendant of his right to move the court for an order permitting the withdrawal of any previous waiver of time and shall advise him of the authority of the court, as provided in subdivision (b), to order return of the premium paid by the defendant or other person, or any part of it.

(4) Upon the undertaking, or certificate of deposit, and the certificate of the officer, the court in which the action or appeal is pending may, upon notice of five days to the district attorney of the county, with a copy of the undertaking, or certificate of deposit, and the certificate of the officer, order that the bail or deposit be exonerated. However, if the defendant is released on his own recognizance or on another bond before the issuance of such an order, the court shall order that the bail or deposit be exonerated without prejudice to the court's authority under subdivision (b). On filing the order and papers used on the application, they are exonerated accordingly.

(b) Notwithstanding subdivision (a), if the court determines that good cause does not exist for the surrender of a defendant who has not failed to appear or has not violated any order of the court, it may, in its discretion, order the bail or the depositor to return to the defendant or other person who has paid the premium or any part of it, all of the money so paid or any part of it.

§1301. Arrest of defendant by bail.

For the purpose of surrendering the defendant, the bail or any person who has deposited money or bonds to secure the release of the defendant, at any time before such bail or other person is finally discharged, and at any place within the state, may himself arrest defendant, or by written authority indorsed on a certified copy of the undertaking or a certified copy of the certificate of deposit, may empower any person of suitable age to do so.

Any bail or other person who so arrests a defendant in this state shall, without unnecessary delay, and, in any event, within 48 hours of the arrest, deliver the defendant to the court or magistrate before whom the defendant is required to appear or to the custody of the sheriff or police for confinement in the appropriate jail in the county or city in which defendant is required to appear. Any bail or other person who arrests a defendant outside this state shall, without unnecessary delay after the time defendant is brought into this state, and, in any event, within 48 hours after defendant is brought into this state, deliver the defendant to the custody of the court or magistrate before whom defendant is required to appear or to the custody of the sheriff or police for confinement in the appropriate jail in the county or city in which defendant is required to appear.

Any bail or other person who willfully fails to deliver a defendant to the court, magistrate, sheriff, or police as required by this section is guilty of a misdemeanor.

The provisions of this section relating to the time of delivery of a defendant are for his benefit and, with the consent of the bail, may be waived by him. To be valid, such waiver shall be in writing, signed by the defendant, and delivered to such bail or other person within 48 hours after the defendant's arrest or entry into this state, as the case may be. The defendant, at any time and in the same manner, may revoke said waiver. Whereupon, he shall be delivered as provided herein without unnecessary delay and, in any event within 48 hours from the time of such revocation.

If any 48-hour period specified in this section terminates on a Saturday, Sunday, or holiday, delivery of a defendant by a bail or other person to the court or magistrate or to the custody of the sheriff or police may, without violating this section, take place before noon on the next day following which is not a Saturday, Sunday, or holiday.

§1302. Return of money deposit on surrender.

If money has been deposited instead of bail, and the defendant, at any time before the forfeiture thereof, surrenders himself or herself to the officer to whom the commitment was directed, in the manner provided in Sections 1300 and 1301, the court shall order a return of the deposit to the defendant or to the person or persons found by the court to have deposited said money on behalf of the defendant, upon the production of the certificate of the officer showing the surrender, and upon a notice of five days to the district attorney, with a copy of the certificate. *(Amended by Stats 1987 ch 828 §84.)*

§1303. Exoneration of bail application to public offense.

If an action or proceeding against a defendant who has been admitted to bail is dismissed, the bail shall not be exonerated until a period of 15 days has elapsed since the entry of the order of dismissal. If, within such period, the defendant is arrested and charged with a public offense arising out of the same act or omission upon which the action or proceeding was based, the bail shall be applied to the public offense. If an undertaking of bail is on file, the clerk of the court shall promptly mail notice to the surety on the bond and the bail agent who posted the bond whenever the bail is applied to a public offense pursuant to this section.

§1304. Exoneration of bail; time limit.

Any bail, or moneys or bonds deposited in lieu of bail, or any equity in real property as security in lieu of bail, or any agreement whereby the defendant is released on his or her own recognizance shall be exonerated two years from the effective date of the initial bond, provided that the court is informed in writing at least 60 days prior to 2 years after the initial bond of the fact that the bond is to be exonerated, or unless the court determines otherwise and informs the party executing the bail of the reasons that the bail is not exonerated.

ARTICLE 7

FORFEITURE OF THE UNDERTAKING OF BAIL OR OF THE DEPOSIT OF MONEY

§1305. Forfeiture of bail for non-appearance.

(a) If, without sufficient excuse, the defendant neglects to appear for arraignment or for trial or judgment, or upon any other occasion when his or her presence in court is lawfully required, or to surrender himself or herself in execution of the judgment, the court shall direct the fact to be entered upon its

minutes, and, unless within 15 court days from arraignment no complaint has been filed or the charges have been dismissed, the undertaking of bail or the money deposited instead of bail, as the case may be, shall thereupon be declared forfeited, and, if the amount of the forfeiture exceeds three hundred dollars ($300), the clerk of the court shall promptly, upon entering the fact of the failure to appear in the minutes, mail notice of the forfeiture to the surety on the bond or depositor of money instead of bond, and shall execute a certificate of the mailing and place it in the court's file in the case. If the surety is an authorized corporate surety insurer, and if the bond has plainly printed or stamped thereon the address of its principal office, the notice shall be mailed to the surety at that address, and mailing to the bail agent or solicitor who posted the bond shall not constitute compliance with this section. The clerk shall, at the same time, send a copy of the notice to the bail agent or solicitor who posted the bond. If the clerk fails to mail the notice within 30 days after the entry, the surety or depositor shall be released from all obligations under the bond.

But, if at any time within 180 days after the entry in the minutes or, if mailing of notice of forfeiture is required, within 180 days after mailing the notice of forfeiture, the defendant appears and satisfactorily excuses the defendant's neglect or shows to the satisfaction of the court that the absence of the defendant was not with the connivance of the bail, the court shall, under terms as may be just and that are equal with respect to all forms of pretrial release, direct the forfeiture of the undertaking or the deposit to be set aside and the bail or the money deposited instead of bail exonerated immediately. The court may order the bail reinstated and the defendant released again on the same bond after notice to the bail, provided that the bail has not surrendered the defendant. If, at any time within 180 days after the entry in the minutes or mailing, as the case may be, the bail should surrender the defendant to the court or to custody, the court shall, under terms as may be just, direct the forfeiture of the undertaking or the deposit to be set aside and the bail or the money deposited instead of bail exonerated immediately.

If, within 180 days after the entry in the minutes or mailing, as the case may be, it is made to appear to the satisfaction of the court that the defendant is dead or is otherwise permanently unable to appear in court due to illness, insanity, or detention by civil or military authorities, and that the absence of the defendant was not with the connivance of the bail, the court shall, under terms as may be just and that are equal with respect to all forms of pretrial release, direct the forfeiture of the undertaking or the deposit to be set aside and the bail or the money deposited instead of bail exonerated immediately. If, within 180 days after the entry in the minutes or mailing, as the case may be, it is made to appear to the satisfaction of the court that the defendant is temporarily disabled by reason of illness, insanity, or detention by civil or military authorities and is, therefore, unable to appear in court at any time during the remainder of the 180 days and that the absence of the defendant has not been with the connivance of the bail, then the period of time during which the disability continues shall not be deemed part of the 180 days. Upon a finding by the court that a reasonable period of time is necessary in order to return the defendant to court upon the ter-

© 1992 by J., B. & L. Gould
Printed in the U.S.A.   **EP**

mination of the disability, then the period of time, as fixed by the court, shall not be deemed part of the 180 days.

Unless waived by the district attorney, other prosecuting attorney, or county counsel, as the case may be, no order discharging the forfeiture of the undertaking or deposit shall be made without notice by the bail to the district attorney, prosecuting attorney, or county counsel, as specified by the board of supervisors after consultation with the county counsel and the district attorney, who may request a hearing within 10 days after receipt of the notice. The notice may be given by the surety insurer, its bail agent, the surety, or the depositor of money, any of whom may give the notice and appear either in person or by an attorney. The court shall then set the date, time, and place of hearing and give notice to the district attorney, prosecuting attorney, and county counsel and to the bail. The district attorney, prosecuting attorney, or county counsel, as the case may be, shall recover the costs incurred in successfully opposing a motion to discharge the forfeiture of the undertaking or deposit prior to the division of the forfeited bail money between the cities and the county in accordance with Section 1463. The costs shall be recovered from the forfeited bail money.

(b) If, without sufficient excuse, the defendant neglects to appear for arraignment, trial, judgment, or upon any other occasion when his or her presence in court is lawfully required, or to surrender himself or herself in execution of the judgment, but the court has reason to believe that sufficient excuse may exist for his or her neglect to appear or surrender himself or herself, the court may continue the case for a period as it deems reasonable to enable the defendant to appear without ordering a forfeiture of bail or issuing a bench warrant. *(Amended by Stats 1990 ch 1073 §2, eff. 1/1/91.)*

§1305.2. Notice of assessment made a condition of discharge of forfeiture.

If an assessment is made a condition of the order to set aside the forfeiture of an undertaking, deposit, or bail under Section 1305, the clerk of the court shall within 30 days mail notice thereof to the surety or depositor at the address of its principal office and shall execute a certificate of mailing and place it in the court's file in the case. The time limit for payment shall in no event be less than 30 days after the date of mailing of the notice.

If the assessment has not been paid by the date specified, the court shall determine if a certificate of mailing has been executed, and if none has, the court shall cause a notice to be mailed to the surety or depositor, and the surety or depositor shall be allowed an additional 30 days to pay the assessment. *(Added by Stats 1988 ch 1294 §1, eff. 1/1/89.)*

§1306. Summary judgment against bondsman.

(a) When any bond is forfeited and the period of time specified in Section 1305 has elapsed without the forfeiture having been set aside, the court which has declared the forfeiture, regardless of the amount of the bail, shall enter a summary judgment against each bondsman named in the bond in the amount for which the bondsman is bound. The judgment shall be the amount of the bond plus costs, and notwithstanding any other law, no penalty assessments shall be levied or added to the judgment.

(b) If a court grants relief from bail forfeiture, it shall impose a monetary payment as a condition of relief to compensate the people for the costs of returning a defendant to custody pursuant to Section 1305, except for cases where the court determines that in the best interest of justice no costs should be imposed. The amount imposed shall reflect the actual costs of returning the defendant to custody.

(c) If, because of the failure of any court to promptly perform the duties enjoined upon it pursuant to this section, summary judgment is not entered within 90 days after the date upon which it may first be entered, the right to do so expires and the bail is exonerated.

(d) A dismissal of the complaint, indictment, or information after the default of the defendant shall not release or affect the obligation of the bail bond or undertaking.

(e) The district attorney or county counsel shall:

(1) Demand immediate payment of the judgment within 30 days after the summary judgment becomes final.

(2) If the judgment remains unpaid for a period of 20 days after demand has been made, shall forthwith enforce the judgment in the manner provided for enforcement of money judgments generally. If the judgment is appealed by the surety or bondsman, the undertaking required to be given in these cases shall be provided by a surety other than the one filing the appeal. The undertaking shall comply with the enforcement requirements of Section 917.1 of the Code of Civil Procedure.

(f) The right to enforce a summary judgment entered against a bondsman pursuant to this section shall expire two years after the entry of the judgment. *(Amended by Stats 1991 ch 90 §25, eff. 6/30/91; ch 613 §7, eff. 1/1/92.)*

§1306.1. Payment of bail deposits pursuant to Vehicle Code.

The provisions of Sections 1305 and 1306 shall not affect the payment of bail deposits into the city or county treasury, as the case may be, pursuant to Section 40512 of the Vehicle Code in those cases arising under Section 40500 of the Vehicle Code.

§1307. Disposition of forfeited deposit.

If, by reason of the neglect of the defendant to appear, money deposited instead of bail is forfeited, and the forfeiture is not discharged or remitted, the clerk with whom it is deposited must, at the end of 180 days, unless the court has before that time discharged the forfeiture, pay over the money deposited to the county treasurer.

§1308. Unpaid summary judgment.

No court or magistrate shall accept any person or corporation as surety on bail if any summary judgment against any that person or corporation entered pursuant to Section 1306 remains unpaid after the expiration of 20 days after service of notice of the entry of the summary judgment provided, that, if during the 20 days on an action or proceeding available at law is initiated to determine the validity of the order of forfeiture or summary judgment rendered thereon, this section shall be rendered inoperative until that action or proceeding has finally been determined, provided that an appeal bond is posted in compliance with Section 917.1 of the Code of Civil Procedure. The clerk of the court in which the judgment is rendered shall serve notice of the entry of judgment upon the judgment debtor within five days after the date of the entry of the summary judgment. *(Amended by Stats 1987 ch 173.)*

§1309. Disposition of unclaimed monies.

Whenever any money has been or is deposited as bail in any criminal action or proceeding, including but not limited to any proceeding in habeas corpus, in a superior court either before or after the effective date of this code section and it is made to appear to the satisfaction of the court or judge by affidavit or by testimony in open court that more than three years have elapsed since the exoneration or release of said bail and that said money cannot be paid out because the owner thereof cannot be found, the court or judge must direct that such money shall be deposited in the general fund of the county.

ARTICLE 8

RECOMMITMENT OF THE DEFENDANT, AFTER HAVING GIVEN BAIL OR DEPOSITED MONEY INSTEAD OF BAIL

§1310. Forfeiture or insufficiency of bail.

The court to which the committing magistrate returns the depositions, or in which an indictment, information, or appeal is pending, or to which a judgment on appeal is remitted to be carried into effect, may, by an order entered upon its minutes, direct the arrest of the defendant and his or her commitment to the officer to whose custody he or she was committed at the time of giving bail, and his or her detention until legally discharged, in the following cases:

(a) When, by reason of his or her failure to appear, he or she has incurred a forfeiture of his or her bail, or of money deposited instead thereof.

(b) When it satisfactorily appears to the court that his or her bail, or either of them, are dead or insufficient, or have removed from the state.

(c) Upon an indictment being found or information filed in the cases provided in Section 985. *(Amended by Stats 1987 ch 828 §85.)*

§1311. Contents of order.

The order for the recommitment of the defendant must recite generally the facts upon which it is founded, and direct that the defendant be arrested by any Sheriff, Constable, Marshal, or Policeman in this State, and committed to the officer in whose custody he was at the time he was admitted to bail, to be detained until legally discharged.

§1312. Defendant may be arrested in any county.

The defendant may be arrested pursuant to the order, upon a certified copy thereof, in any county, in the same manner as upon a warrant of arrest, except that when arrested in another county the order need not be indorsed by a magistrate of that county.

§1313. If for failure to appear for judgment, defendant must be committed.

If the order recites, as the ground upon which it is made, the failure of the defendant to appear for judgment upon conviction, the defendant must be committed according to the requirement of the order.

§1314. If for other cause, be admitted to bail.

If the order be made for any other cause, and the offense is bailable, the Court may fix the amount of bail, and may cause a direction to be inserted in the order that the defendant be admitted to bail in the sum fixed, which must be specified in the order.

§1315. Bail in such case, by whom taken.

When the defendant is admitted to bail, the bail may be taken by any magistrate in the county, having authority in a similar case to admit to bail, upon the holding of the defendant to answer before an indictment, or by any other magistrate designated by the Court.

§1316. Form of the undertaking.

When bail is taken upon the recommitment of the defendant, the undertaking must be in substantially the following form:

An order having been made on the _____ day of _, A.D. eighteen _____ , by the Court (naming it), that A. B. be admitted to bail in the sum of ____ dollars, in an action pending in that Court against him in behalf of the people of the State of California, upon an (information, presentment, indictment, or appeal, as the case may be), we, C. D. and E. F., of (stating their places of residence and occupation), hereby undertake that the above-named A. B. will appear in that or any other Court in which his appearance may be lawfully required upon that (information, presentment, indictment, or appeal, as the case may be), and will at all times render himself amenable to its orders and process, and appear for judgment and surrender himself in execution thereof; or if he fails to perform either of these conditions, that we will pay to the people of the State of California the sum of _____ dollars (insert the sum in which the defendant is admitted to bail).

§1317. Bail must possess what qualifications, and how put in.

The bail must possess the qualifications, and must be put in, in all respects, in the manner prescribed in Article 2 of this Chapter 1.

ARTICLE 9

PROCEDURE RELATING TO RELEASE ON OWN RECOGNIZANCE

§1318. Signed release agreement.

(a) The defendant shall not be released from custody under an own recognizance until the defendant files with the clerk of the court or other person authorized to accept bail a signed release agreement which includes:

(1) The defendant's promise to appear at all times and places, as ordered by the court or magistrate and as ordered by any court in which, or any magistrate before whom the charge is subsequently pending.

(2) The defendant's promise to obey all reasonable conditions imposed by the court or magistrate.

(3) The defendant's promise not to depart this state without leave of the court.

(4) Agreement by the defendant to waive extradition if the defendant fails to appear as required and is apprehended outside of the State of California.

(5) The acknowledgment of the defendant that he or she has been informed of the consequences and penalties applicable to violation of the conditions of

© 1992 by J., B. & L. Gould
Printed in the U.S.A.   EP

release. *(Amended by Stats 1988 ch 403 §4, eff. 1/1/89.)*

§1318.1. Court's investigative staff.

A court may, with the concurrence of the board of supervisors, employ an investigative staff for the purpose of recommending whether a defendant should be released on his or her own recognizance.

The salaries of such staff are a proper charge against the county. *(Amended by Stats 1985 ch 1432 §2.)*

§1319. Release after violent felony arrest.

Before any person arrested for a violent felony is released on his or her own recognizance, a hearing shall be held in open court before the magistrate or judge, and the prosecuting attorney shall be given notice and a reasonable opportunity to be heard on the matter. A defendant charged with a violent felony shall not be released on his or her own recognizance where it appears by clear and convincing evidence that he or she previously has been charged with a felony offense and has willfully and without excuse from the court failed to appear in court as required while that charge was pending.

The judge or magistrate who, pursuant to this section, grants or denies release on a person's own recognizance shall, within the time period prescribed in Section 825, state the reasons for that decision in the record. This statement shall be included in the court's minutes.

As used in this section, the term "violent felony" means any crime defined in Section 667.5. *(Added by Stats 1986 ch 543 §1.)*

§1320. Willful failure to appear as required.

(a) Every person who is charged with the commission of a misdemeanor who is released from custody on his or her own recognizance and who in order to evade the process of the court willfully fails to appear as required, is guilty of a misdemeanor. It shall be presumed that a defendant who willfully fails to appear within 14 days of the date assigned for his or her appearance intended to evade the process of the court.

(b) Every person who is charged with the commission of a felony who is released from custody on his or her own recognizance and who in order to evade the process of the court willfully fails to appear as required, is guilty of a felony, and upon conviction shall be punished by a fine not exceeding five thousand dollars ($5,000) or by imprisonment in the state prison, or in the county jail for not more than one year, or by both such fine and imprisonment. It shall be presumed that a defendant who willfully fails to appear within 14 days of the date assigned for his or her appearance intended to evade the process of the court. *(Amended by Stats 1985 ch 1432 §3.)*

§1320.5. Willful failure to appear on felony charge.

Every person who is charged with the commission of a felony, who is released from custody on bail, and who in order to evade the process of the court willfully fails to appear as required, is guilty of a felony. Upon a conviction under this section, the person shall be punished by a fine not exceeding ten thousand dollars ($10,000) or by imprisonment in the state prison, or in the county jail for not more than one year, or by both the fine and imprisonment. Willful failure to appear

within 14 days of the date assigned for appearance may be found to have been for the purpose of evading the process of the court. *(Amended by Stats 1985 ch 780 §1.)*

CHAPTER 2

WHO MAY BE WITNESSES IN CRIMINAL ACTIONS

§1321. Who are competent witnesses.

The rules for determining the competency of witnesses in civil actions are applicable also to criminal actions and proceedings, except as otherwise provided in this code.

§1324. Self-incrimination, felony proceedings.

In any felony proceeding or in any investigation or proceeding before a grand jury for any felony offense if a person refuses to answer a question or produce evidence of any other kind on the ground that he may be incriminated thereby, and if the district attorney of the county in writing requests the superior court in and for that county to order that person to answer the question or produce the evidence, a judge of the superior court shall set a time for hearing and order the person to appear before the court and show cause, if any, why the question should not be answered or the evidence produced, and the court shall order the question answered or the evidence produced unless it finds that to do so would be clearly contrary to the public interest, or could subject the witness to a criminal prosecution in another jurisdiction, and that person shall comply with the order. After complying, and if, but for this section, he would have been privileged to withhold the answer given or the evidence produced by him, that person shall not be prosecuted or subjected to penalty or forfeiture for or on account of any fact or act concerning which, in accordance with the order, he was required to answer or produce evidence. But he may nevertheless be prosecuted or subjected to penalty or forfeiture for any perjury, false swearing or contempt committed in answering, or failing to answer, or in producing, or failing to produce, evidence in accordance with the order.

§1324.1. Self-incrimination, misdemeanor proceedings.

In any misdemeanor proceeding in any court, if a person refuses to answer a question or produce evidence of any other kind on the ground that he may be incriminated thereby, the person may agree in writing with the district attorney of the county, or the prosecuting attorney of a city, as the case may be, to testify voluntarily pursuant to this section. Upon written request of such district attorney, or prosecuting attorney, the court having jurisdiction of the proceeding shall approve such written agreement, unless the court finds that to do so would be clearly contrary to the public interest. If, after court approval of such agreement, and if, but for this section, the person would have been privileged to withhold the answer given or the evidence produced by him, that person shall not be prosecuted or subjected to penalty or forfeiture for or on account of any fact or act concerning which, in accordance with such agreement, he answered or produced evidence, but he may, nevertheless, be prosecuted or subjected to penalty or forfeiture for any perjury, false swearing or contempt committed in answering or in producing evidence in accordance with such agreement. If such person fails to give any answer or to produce any evidence in accordance with such agreement, that person shall be prosecuted or subjected to penalty or forfeiture in the same manner and to the same extent as he would be prosecuted or subjected to penalty or forfeiture but for this section.

CHAPTER 3

COMPELLING THE ATTENDANCE OF WITNESSES

§1326. Issuance of subpoena.

The process by which the attendance of a witness before a court or magistrate is required is a subpoena. It may be signed and issued by any of the following:

(1) A magistrate before whom a complaint is laid or his clerk, the district attorney or his investigator, or the public defender or his investigator, for witnesses in the state.

(2) The district attorney, his investigator, or, upon request of the grand jury, any judge of the superior court, for witnesses in the state, in support of an indictment or information, to appear before the court in which it is to be tried.

(3) The district attorney or his investigator, the public defender or his investigator, the clerk of the court in which a criminal action is to be tried, or, if there is no clerk, the judge of the court. The clerk or judge shall, at any time, upon application of the defendant, and without charge, issue as many blank subpoenas, subscribed by him, for witnesses in the state, as the defendant may require.

(4) The attorney of record for the defendant.

§1327. Form of subpoena.

A subpoena authorized by Section 1326 shall be substantially in the following form:

The people of the State of California to A. B.:

You are commanded to appear before C. D., a judge of the Justice Court of _____ Judicial District, in _____ County (or as the case may be), at (naming the place), on (stating the day and hour), as a witness in a criminal action prosecuted by the people of the State of California against E. F.

Given under my hand this _____ day of _____, A.D. 19 _____. G.H., Judge of the Justice Court (or "J. K., District Attorney," or "J. K., District Attorney Investigator," or "D. E., Public Defender," or "D. E., Public Defender Investigator," or "F. G., Defense Counsel," or "By order of the court, L. M., Clerk," or as the case may be). If books, papers, or documents are required, a direction to the following effect must be contained in the subpoena: "And you are required, also, to bring with you the following" (describing intelligibly the books, papers, or documents required).

§1328. Service of subpoena.

(a) A subpoena may be served by any person, except that the defendant may not serve a subpoena in the criminal action to which he or she is a party, but a peace officer shall serve in his or her county any subpoena delivered to him or her for service, either on the part of the people or of the defendant, and shall, without delay, make a written return of the service, subscribed by him or her, stating the time and place of service. The service is made by delivering a copy of the subpoena to the witness personally.

(b) When service is to be made on a minor, service shall be made on the minor's parent, guardian, conservator, or similar fiduciary, or if one of them cannot be located with reasonable diligence, then service shall be made on any person having the care or control of the minor or with whom the minor resides or by whom the minor is employed, unless the parent, guardian, conservator, or fiduciary or other specified person is the defendant, and on the minor if the minor is 12 years of age or older. The person so served shall have the obligation of producing the minor at the time and place designated in the subpoena. A willful failure to produce the minor is punishable as a contempt pursuant to Section 1218 of the Code of Civil Procedure. The person so served shall be allowed the fees and expenses that are provided for subpoenaed witnesses.

(c) Whenever any peace officer designated in Section 830 is required as a witness before any court or magistrate in any action or proceeding in connection with a matter regarding an event or transaction which he or she has perceived or investigated in the course of his or her duties, a subpoena requiring his or her attendance may be served either by delivering a copy to the peace officer personally or by delivering two copies to his or her immediate superior or agent designated by his or her immediate superior to receive the service. If service is made upon the immediate superior or agent designated by the immediate superior, the immediate superior or the agent shall deliver a copy of the subpoena to the peace officer as soon as possible and in no event later than a time which will enable the peace officer to comply with the subpoena.

(d) If the immediate superior or his or her designated agent upon whom service is attempted to be made knows he or she will be unable to deliver a copy of the subpoena to the peace officer within a time which will allow the peace officer to comply with the subpoena, the immediate superior or agent may refuse to accept service of process and is excused from any duty, liability, or penalty arising in connection with the service, upon notifying the server of that fact.

(e) If the immediate superior or his or her agent is tendered service of a subpoena less than five working days prior to the date of hearing, and he or she is not reasonably certain he or she can complete the service, he or she may refuse acceptance.

(f) If the immediate superior or agent upon whom service has been made, subsequently determines that he or she will be unable to deliver a copy of the subpoena to the peace officer within a time which will allow the peace officer to comply with the subpoena, the immediate superior or agent shall notify the server or his or her office or agent not less than 48 hours prior to the hearing date indicated on the subpoena, and is thereby excused from any duty, liability, or penalty arising because of his or her failure to deliver a copy of the subpoena to the peace officer. The server, so notified, is therewith responsible for preparing the written return of service and for notifying the originator of the subpoena if required.

(g) Notwithstanding subdivision (c), in the case of peace officers employed by the California Highway Patrol, if service is made upon the immediate superior or upon an agent designated by the immediate superior of the peace officer, the immediate superior or the agent shall deliver a copy of the subpoena to the peace officer on the officer's first workday following acceptance of service of process. In this case, failure of the immediate superior or the designated agent to deliver

© 1992 by J., B. & L. Gould
Printed in the U.S.A.   EP

the subpoena shall not constitute a defect in service. *(Amended by Stats 1991 ch 315 §1, eff. 1/1/92.)*

§1328a. Telegraphic copy of subpoena for witness.

A telegraphic copy of a subpoena for a witness in a criminal proceeding may be sent by telegraph or teletype to one or more peace officers, and such copy is as effectual in the hands of any officer, and he must proceed in the same manner under it, as though he held the original subpoena issued.

§1328b. Certification and filing of copy.

Every officer causing telegraphic copies of subpoenas to be sent, must certify as correct, and file in the telegraph office from which such copies are sent, a copy of the subpoena, and must return the original with a statement of his action thereunder.

§1328c. Service and return of copy.

A peace officer must serve in his county or city any subpoena delivered to him by telegraph or teletype for service and must without delay make a return of the service by telegraph or teletype. Any officer making a return of service of a subpoena by telegraph or teletype must certify as to his actions in making the service and file in the telegraph office from which the return is sent a written statement with his signature in the same form as the return on an original subpoena. The service of a teletype subpoena is made by showing the original teletype to the witness personally and informing him of its contents and delivering to him a copy of the teletype.

§1328d. Delivery by mail or messenger.

Notwithstanding Section 1328, a subpoena may be delivered by mail or messenger. Service shall be effected when the witness acknowledges receipt of the subpoena to the sender, by telephone, by mail, or in person, and identifies himself or herself by reference to his or her date of birth and his or her driver's license number or Department of Motor Vehicles identification card number. The sender shall make a written notation of the identifying information obtained during any acknowledgment by telephone or in person. A subpoena issued and acknowledged pursuant to this section shall have the same force and effect as a subpoena personally served. Failure to comply with a subpoena issued and acknowledged pursuant to this section may be punished as a contempt and the subpoena may so state; provided, that a warrant of arrest or a body attachment may not be issued based upon a failure to appear after being subpoenaed pursuant to this section.

A party requesting a continuance based upon the failure of a witness to appear in court at the time and place required for his or her appearance or testimony pursuant to a subpoena, shall prove to the court that the party has complied with the provisions of this section. Such a continuance shall only be granted for a period of time which would allow personal service of the subpoena and in no event longer than that allowed by law, including the requirements of Sections 861 and 1382. *(Amended by Stats 1986 ch 992 §2.)*

§1328.5. Peace officer's residence address not required.

Whenever any peace officer is a witness before any court or magistrate in any criminal action or proceed-

ing in connection with a matter regarding an event or transaction which he has perceived or investigated in the course of his duties, where his testimony would become a matter of public record, and where he is required to state the place of his residence, he need not state the place of his residence, but in lieu thereof, he may state his business address.

§1328.6. Specialist's residence address not required.

Whenever any criminalist, questioned document examiner, latent print analyst, polygraph examiner employed by the Department of Justice, a police department, a sheriff's office, or a district attorney's office, an intelligence specialist or other technical specialist employed by the Department of Justice, a custodial officer employed in a local detention facility, or an employee of the county welfare department or the department which administers the county public social services program, is a witness before any court or magistrate in any criminal action or proceeding in connection with a matter regarding an event or transaction which he or she has perceived or investigated in the course of his or her official duties, where his or her testimony would become a matter of public record, and where he or she is required to state the place of his or her residence, he or she need not state the place of his or her residence, but in lieu thereof, he or she may state his or her business address, unless the court finds, after an in camera hearing, that the probative value of the witness's residential address outweighs the creation of substantial danger to the witness.

Nothing in this section shall abridge or limit a defendant's right to discover or investigate this information. This section is not intended to apply to confidential informants.

§1329. Fees and expenses of witnesses.

(a) When a person attends before a magistrate, grand jury, or court, as a witness in a criminal case, whether upon a subpoena or in pursuance of an undertaking, or voluntarily, the court, at its discretion, if the attendance of the witness be upon a trial may by an order upon its minutes, or in any criminal proceeding, by a written order, direct the county auditor to draw his warrant upon the county treasurer in favor of such witness for witness' fees at the rate of twelve dollars ($12) for each day's actual attendance and for a reasonable sum to be specified in the order for the necessary expenses of such witness. The court, in its discretion, may make an allowance under this section, or under any appropriate section in Chapter 1 (commencing with Section 68070), Title 8, of the Government Code, other than Section 68093. The allowances are county charges.

(b) The court, in its discretion, may authorize payment to such a witness, if he is employed and if his salary is not paid by his employer during the time he is absent from his employment because of being such a witness, of a sum equal to his gross salary for such time, but such sum shall not exceed eighteen dollars ($18) per day. The sum is a county charge.

A person compensated under the provisions of this subdivision may not receive the payment of witness' fees as provided for in subdivision (a).

§1329.1. Notice of entitlement.

Any witness who is subpoenaed in any criminal action or proceeding shall be given written notice on the subpoena that the witness may be entitled to receive fees and mileage. Such notice shall indicate generally the manner in which a request or claim for fees and mileage should be made.

§1330. Obligations to attend as witness.

No person is obliged to attend as a witness before a court or magistrate out of the county where the witness resides, or is served with the subpoena, unless the distance be less than 150 miles from his or her place of residence to the place of trial, or unless the judge of the court in which the offense is triable, or a justice of the Supreme Court, or a judge of a superior court, or, in the case of a minor concerning whom a petition has been filed pursuant to Article 16 (commencing with Section 650) of Chapter 2 of Part 1 of Division 2 of the Welfare and Institutions Code, by the judge of the juvenile court hearing the petition, upon an affidavit of the district attorney or prosecutor, or of the defendant, or his or her counsel, or in the case involving a minor in whose behalf a petition has been filed in the juvenile court, of the probation officer approving the filing of the petition or of any party to the action, or his or her counsel, stating that he or she believes the evidence of the witness is material, and his or her attendance at the examination, trial, or hearing is material and necessary, shall endorse on the subpoena an order for the attendance of the witness.

When a subpoena duces tecum is duly issued according to any other provision of law and is served upon a custodian of records or other qualified witness as provided in Article 4 (commencing with Section 1560) of Chapter 2 of Division 11 of the Evidence Code, and his or her personal attendance is not required by the terms of the subpoena, the limitations of this section shall not apply. *(Amended by Stats 1987 ch 828 §86.)*

§1331. Disobedience to subpoena, etc.

Disobedience to a subpoena, or a refusal to be sworn or to testify as a witness, may be punished by the Court or magistrate as a contempt. A witness disobeying a subpoena issued on the part of the defendant, unless he show good cause for his nonattendance, is liable to the defendant in the sum of one hundred dollars, which may be recovered in a civil action.

§1331.5. Agreement to appear.

Any person who is subpoenaed to appear at a session of court, or at the trial of an issue therein, may, in lieu of appearance at the time specified in the subpoena, agree with the party at whose request the subpoena was issued, to appear at another time or upon such notice as may be agreed upon. Any failure to appear pursuant to such agreement may be punished as a contempt, and a subpoena shall so state. The facts establishing such agreement and the failure to appear may be shown by the affidavit of any person having personal knowledge of the facts and the court may grant such continuance as may be appropriate.

§1332. Written undertaking by material witness.

(a) Notwithstanding the provisions of Sections 878 to 883, inclusive, when the court is satisfied, by proof on oath, that there is good cause to believe that any material witness for the prosecution or defense, whether the witness is an adult or a minor, will not appear and testify unless security is required, at any proceeding in connection with any criminal prosecution or in connection with a wardship petition pursuant to Section 602 of the Welfare and Institutions Code, the court may order the witness to enter into a written undertaking to the effect that he or she will appear and testify at the time and place ordered by the court or that he or she will forfeit an amount the court deems proper.

(b) If the witness required to enter into an undertaking to appear and testify, either with or without sureties, refuses compliance with the order for that purpose, the court may commit the witness, if an adult, to the custody of the sheriff, and if a minor, to the custody of the probation officer or other appropriate agency, until the witness complies or is legally discharged.

(c) When a person is committed pursuant to this section, he or she is entitled to an automatic review of the order requiring a written undertaking and the order committing the person, by a judge or magistrate having jurisdiction over the offense other than the one who issued the order. This review shall be held not later than two days from the time of the original order of commitment.

(d) If it is determined that the witness must remain in custody, the witness is entitled to a review of that order after 10 days.

(e) When a witness has entered into an undertaking to appear, upon his or her failure to do so the undertaking is forfeited in the same manner as undertakings of bail. *(Amended by Stats 1987 ch 828 §87.)*

CHAPTER 3a

ATTENDANCE OF WITNESSES OUTSIDE THE STATE

§1334. Short title.

This chapter may be cited as the Uniform Act to Secure the Attendance of Witnesses from without the State in Criminal Cases.

§1334.1. Terms defined.

As used in this chapter:

(a) "Witness" includes any person whose testimony is desired in any proceeding or investigation by a grand jury or in any criminal action, prosecution, or proceeding.

(b) "State" means any State or Territory of the United States and the District of Columbia.

(c) "Grand jury investigation" means any grand jury investigation which has commenced or is about to commence.

(d) "Per diem" means a sum of money the purpose of which is to provide for personal expenses, including, but not limited to, food and lodging. *(Amended by Stats 1987 ch 322 §1.)*

§1334.2. Witness required in foreign court; fees.

If a judge of a court of record in any state, which by its laws provides for commanding persons within that state to attend and testify in this state, issues a certificate under the seal of the court that there is a criminal prosecution pending in the court, or that there is a grand jury investigation, that a person within this state is a material witness in that prosecution or grand jury investigation, and that his or her

© 1992 by J., B. & L. Gould
Printed in the U.S.A.   EP

presence will be required for a specified number of days, then, upon presentation of the certificate to a judge of a court of record in the county in which the person is, a time and place for a hearing shall be fixed by the judge and he or she shall make an order directing the witness to appear at the hearing.

If, at the hearing, the judge determines that the witness is material and necessary, that it will not cause undue hardship to the witness to be compelled to attend and testify in the prosecution or grand jury investigation in the other state, and that the laws of the state in which the prosecution is pending or in which there is a grand jury investigation will give to the witness protection from arrest and service of civil and criminal process and will furnish in advance to the witness the sum of ten cents ($0.10) for each mile necessarily traveled if the witness elects surface travel or the minimum round trip scheduled airline fare plus twenty cents ($0.20) a mile for necessary surface travel at either end of the flight if the witness elects air travel, and, except as provided in subdivision (b) of Section 1334.3, a per diem of twenty dollars ($20) for each day that he or she is required to travel and attend as a witness and that the judge of the court in which the witness is ordered to appear will order the payment of witness fees authorized by law for each day the witness is required to attend the court plus reimbursement for any additional expenses of the witness which the judge of the court in which the witness is ordered to appear shall find reasonable and necessary, he or she shall issue a subpoena, with a copy of the certificate attached, directing the witness to attend and testify in the court where the prosecution is pending, or where the grand jury investigation is, at a time and place specified in the subpoena. In any of these hearings the certificate shall be prima facie evidence of all the facts stated therein.

If the certificate recommends that the witness be taken into immediate custody and delivered to an officer of the requesting state to assure his or her attendance therein, the judge may, in lieu of notification of the hearing, direct that the witness be forthwith brought before him or her for the hearing.

If the judge at the hearing is satisfied of the desirability of the custody and delivery, for which determination the certificate shall be prima facie proof of this desirability, he or she may, in lieu of issuing a subpoena, order that the witness be forthwith taken into custody and delivered to an officer of the requesting state.

If the witness, who is subpoenaed as provided in this section, after being paid or tendered by some properly authorized person the sum or fare, and per diem set forth in this section, fails without good cause to attend and testify as directed in the subpoena, he or she shall be punished in the manner provided for the punishment of any witness who disobeys a subpoena issued from a court of record in this state. *(Amended by Stats 1988 ch 160 §133, eff. 1/1/89.)*

§1334.3. Witness from another state; fees.

(a) If a person in any state, which by its laws has made provision for commanding persons within its borders to attend and testify in criminal prosecutions or grand jury investigations in this state, is a material witness in a prosecution pending in a court of record in this state, or in a grand jury investigation, a judge of such court may issue a certificate under the seal of the court stating these facts and specifying the num-

ber of days the witness will be required. This certificate shall be presented to a judge of a court of record in the county of such other state in which the witness is found.

If the certificate recommends that the witness be taken into immediate custody and delivered to an officer of this state to assure his or her attendance in this state, the judge may direct that the witness be forthwith brought before him or her. If the judge is satisfied of the desirability of the custody and delivery, for which determination the certificate shall be prima facie proof, he or she may order that the witness be forthwith taken into custody and delivered to an officer of this state. This order shall be sufficient authority to the officer to take the witness into custody and hold him or her unless and until he or she may be released by bail, recognizance, or order of the judge issuing the certificate.

If the witness is subpoenaed to attend and testify in this state, he or she shall be tendered the sum of ten cents ($0.10) for each mile necessarily traveled if the witness elects surface travel or the minimum round trip scheduled airlines fare plus twenty cents ($0.20) a mile for necessary surface travel at either end of the flight if the witness elects air travel, and except as provided in subdivision (b), a per diem of twenty dollars ($20) for each day that he or she is required to travel and attend as a witness. The judge of the court in which the witness is ordered to appear shall order the payment of witness fees authorized by law for each day the witness is required to attend the court plus reimbursement for any additional expenses of the witness which the judge of the court shall find reasonable and necessary. A witness who has appeared in accordance with the provisions of the subpoena shall not be required to remain within this state a longer period of time than the period mentioned in the certificate, unless otherwise ordered by the court. If the witness fails without good cause to attend and testify as directed in the subpoena, he or she shall be punished in the manner provided for the punishment of any witness who disobeys a subpoena issued from a court of record in this state.

(b) If the witness subpoenaed to attend and testify in this state is at the time he or she is required to appear and testify an inmate of a state prison, county jail, or other penal facility, the witness shall, while attending in this state as a witness, be furnished food and lodging in the jail or other appropriate penal facility in the county in which the witness is attending court, and food and lodging of that penal facility shall be rendered in lieu of the per diem specified in subdivision (a). *(Amended by Stats 1987 ch 322 §3.)*

§1334.4. Exemption from arrest, etc.

If a person comes into this State in obedience to a subpoena directing him to attend and testify in this State, he shall not, while in this State pursuant to the subpoena or order, be subject to arrest or the service of process, civil or criminal, in connection with matters which arose before his entrance into this State under the subpoena.

§1334.5. Exemption from arrest while passing through state.

If a person passes through this State while going to another State in obedience to a subpoena or order to attend and testify in that State or while returning therefrom, he shall not while so passing through this

State be subject to arrest or the service of process, civil or criminal, in connection with matters which arose before his entrance into this State under the subpoena or order.

§1334.6. Interpretation of chapter.

This chapter shall be so interpreted and construed as to effectuate its general purpose to make uniform the law of the States which enact similar legislation.

CHAPTER 4

EXAMINATION OF WITNESSES CONDITIONALLY

§1335. Public offense cases where conditional examination allowed.

(a) When a defendant has been charged with a public offense triable in any court, he or she in all cases, and the people in cases other than those for which the punishment may be death, may, if the defendant has been fully informed of his or her right to counsel as provided by law, have witnesses examined conditionally in his or her or their behalf, as prescribed in this chapter.

(b) When a defendant has been charged with a serious felony, the people may, if the defendant has been fully informed of his or her right to counsel as provided by law, have a witness examined conditionally as prescribed in this chapter if the people have evidence that the life of the witness is in jeopardy.

(c) As used in this section, "serious felony" means any of the felonies listed in subdivision (c) of Section 1192.7 or any violation of Section 11351, 11352, 11378, or 11379 of the Health and Safety Code. *(Amended by Stats 1985 ch 783 §2.)*

§1336. Reasons for application.

(a) When a material witness for the defendant, or for the people, is about to leave the state, or is so sick or infirm as to afford reasonable grounds for apprehension that he or she will be unable to attend the trial, the defendant or the people may apply for an order that the witness be examined conditionally.

(b) When the people have evidence that the life of a prosecution witness is in jeopardy, the people may apply for an order that the witness be examined conditionally. *(Amended by Stats 1985 ch 783 §3.)*

§1337. Affidavit of application.

The application shall be made upon affidavit stating all of the following:

(1) The nature of the offense charged.

(2) The state of the proceedings in the action.

(3) The name and residence of the witness, and that his or her testimony is material to the defense or the prosecution of the action.

(4) That the witness is about to leave the state, or is so sick or infirm as to afford reasonable grounds for apprehending that he or she will not be able to attend the trial, or that the life of the witness is in jeopardy. *(Amended by Stats 1985 ch 783 §4.)*

§1338. Application to court; notice.

The application may be made to the court or a judge thereof, and must be made upon three days' notice to the opposite party.

§1339. Order by court.

If the court or judge is satisfied that the examination of the witness is necessary, an order must be made that the witness be examined conditionally, at a specified time and place, and before a magistrate designated therein.

§1340. Defendant's right to be present.

The defendant has the right to be present in person and with counsel at such examination, and if the defendant is in custody, the officer in whose custody he is, must be informed of the time and place of such examination, and must take the defendant thereto, and keep him in the presence and hearing of the witness during the examination.

§1341. When examination cannot take place.

If, at the time and place so designated, it is shown to the satisfaction of the magistrate that the witness is not about to leave the state, or is not sick or infirm, or that the life of the witness is not in jeopardy, or that the application was made to avoid the examination of the witness on the trial, the examination cannot take place. *(Amended by Stats 1985 ch 783 §5.)*

§1342. Attendance of witness, how enforced.

The attendance of the witness may be enforced by a subpoena, issued by the magistrate before whom the examination is to be taken.

§1343. Testimony, how taken and authenticated.

The testimony given by the witness must be reduced to writing, and authenticated in the same manner as the testimony of a witness taken in support of an information.

§1344. Deposition to be transmitted to Clerk.

The deposition taken must, by the magistrate, be sealed up and transmitted to the Clerk of the Court in which the action is pending or may come for trial.

§1345. Deposition or copy read in evidence.

The deposition, or a certified copy thereof, may be read in evidence by either party on the trial if the court finds that the witness is unavailable as a witness within the meaning of Section 240 of the Evidence Code. The same objections may be taken to a question or answer contained in the deposition as if the witness had been examined orally in court.

CHAPTER 4.5

EXAMINATION OF VICTIMS OF SEXUAL CRIMES

§1346. Videotape of victim's preliminary hearing testimony.

(a) When a defendant has been charged with a violation of Section 243.4, 261, 261.5, 264.1, 273a, 273d, 285, 286, 288, 288a, 288.5, or 289, where the victim either is a person 15 years of age or less or is developmentally disabled as a result of mental retardation, as specified in subdivision (a) of Section 4512 of the Welfare and Institutions Code, the people may apply for an order that the victim's testimony at the preliminary hearing, in addition to being stenographically recorded, be recorded and preserved on video tape.

© 1992 by J., B. & L. Gould
Printed in the U.S.A.   EP

(b) The application for the order shall be in writing and made three days prior to the preliminary hearing.

(c) Upon timely receipt of the application, the magistrate shall order that the testimony of the victim given at the preliminary hearing be taken and preserved on video tape. The video tape shall be transmitted to the clerk of the court in which the action is pending.

(d) If at the time of trial the court finds that further testimony would cause the victim emotional trauma so that the victim is medically unavailable or otherwise unavailable within the meaning of Section 240 of the Evidence Code, the court may admit the video tape of the victim's testimony at the preliminary hearing as former testimony under Section 1291 of the Evidence Code.

(e) Any video tape which is taken pursuant to this section is subject to a protective order of the court for the purpose of protecting the privacy of the victim. This subdivision does not affect the provisions of subdivision (b) of Section 868.7.

(f) Any video tape made pursuant to this section shall be made available to the prosecuting attorney, the defendant, and his or her attorney for viewing during ordinary business hours. Any video tape which is made available pursuant to this section is subject to a protective order of the court for the purpose of protecting the privacy of the victim.

(g) The tape shall be destroyed after five years have elapsed from the date of entry of judgment; provided, however, that if an appeal is filed, the tape shall not be destroyed until a final judgment on appeal has been rendered. *(Amended by Stats 1989 ch 1402 §13, eff. 1/1/90.)*

§1347. Use of closed-circuit television in cases involving minors.

(a) It is the intent of the Legislature in enacting this section to provide the court with discretion to employ unusual court procedures to protect the rights of a child witness, the rights of the defendant, and the integrity of the judicial process. In exercising its discretion, the court necessarily will be required to balance the rights of the defendant against the need to protect a child witness and to preserve the integrity of the court's truthfinding function. This discretion is intended to be used selectively when the facts and circumstances in the individual case present compelling evidence of the need to use these unusual procedures.

(b) Notwithstanding any other law, the court in any criminal proceeding, upon written notice of the prosecutor made at least three days prior to the date of the preliminary hearing or trial date on which the testimony of the minor is scheduled, or during the course of the proceeding on the court's own motion, may order that the testimony of a minor 10 years of age or younger at the time of the motion be taken by contemporaneous examination and cross-examination in another place and out of the presence of the judge, jury, defendant, and attorneys, and communicated to the courtroom by means of closed-circuit television, if the court makes all of the following findings:

(1) The minor's testimony will involve a recitation of the facts of an alleged sexual offense committed on or with the minor.

(2) The impact on the minor of one or more of the factors enumerated in subparagraphs (A) to (D), inclusive, is shown by clear and convincing evidence to be so substantial as to make the minor unavailable as a witness unless closed-circuit television is used.

(A) Threats of serious bodily injury to be inflicted on the minor or a family member, of incarceration or deportation of the minor or a family member, or of removal of the minor from the family or dissolution of the family, in order to prevent or dissuade the minor from attending or giving testimony at any trial or court proceeding or to prevent the minor from reporting the alleged sexual offense or from assisting in criminal prosecution.

(B) Use of a firearm or any other deadly weapon during the commission of the crime.

(C) Infliction of great bodily injury upon the victim during the commission of the crime.

(D) Conduct on the part of the defendant or defense counsel during the hearing or trial which causes the minor to be unable to continue his or her testimony.

In making the determination required by this section, the court shall consider the age of the minor, the relationship between the minor and the defendant or defendants, any handicap or disability of the minor, and the nature of the acts charged. The minor's refusal to testify shall not alone constitute sufficient evidence that the special procedure described in this section is necessary in order to obtain the minor's testimony.

(3) The equipment available for use of closed-circuit television would accurately communicate the image and demeanor of the minor to the judge, jury, defendant or defendants, and attorneys.

(c) If the court orders the use of closed-circuit television, two-way closed-circuit television shall be used, except that if the impact on the minor of one or more of the factors enumerated in subparagraphs (A) to (D), inclusive, of paragraph (2) of subdivision (b), is shown by clear and convincing evidence to be so substantial as to make the minor unavailable as a witness even if two-way closed-circuit television is used, one-way closed-circuit television may be used. The prosecution shall give the defendant at least 30 days written notice of the prosecution's intent to seek the use of one-way closed-circuit television, unless good cause is shown to the court why this 30-day notice requirement should not apply.

(d) (1) The hearing on a motion brought pursuant to this section shall be conducted out of the presence of the jury.

(2) Notwithstanding Section 804 of the Evidence Code or any other law, the court, in determining the merits of the motion, shall not compel the minor to testify at the hearing; nor shall the court deny the motion on the ground that the minor has not testified.

(3) In determining whether the impact on an individual child of one or more of the four factors enumerated in paragraph (2) of subdivision (b) is so substantial that the minor is unavailable as a witness unless two-way or one-way closed-circuit television is used, the court may question the minor in chambers, or at some other comfortable place other than the courtroom, on the record for a reasonable period of time with the support person, the prosecutor, and defense counsel present. The defendant or defendants shall not be present. The court shall conduct the questioning of the minor and shall not permit the prosecutor or defense counsel to examine the minor. The prosecutor and defense counsel shall be permitted to submit proposed questions to the court prior to the session in chambers. Defense counsel shall be afforded a reasonable opportunity to consult with the defend-

ant or defendants prior to the conclusion of the session in chambers.

(e) When the court orders the testimony of a minor to be taken in another place outside of the courtroom, the court shall do all of the following:

(1) Make a brief statement on the record, outside of the presence of the jury, of the reasons in support of its order. While the statement need not include traditional findings of fact, the reasons shall be set forth with sufficient specificity to permit meaningful review and to demonstrate that discretion was exercised in a careful, reasonable, and equitable manner.

(2) Instruct the members of the jury that they are to draw no inferences from the use of closed-circuit television as a means of facilitating the testimony of the minor.

(3) Instruct respective counsel, outside of the presence of the jury, that they are to make no comment during the course of the trial on the use of closed-circuit television procedures.

(4) Instruct the support witness, outside of the presence of the jury, that he or she is not to coach, cue, or in any way influence or attempt to influence the testimony of the minor.

(5) Order that a complete record of the examination of the minor, including the images and voices of all persons who in any way participate in the examination, be made and preserved on videotape in addition to being stenographically recorded. The videotape shall be transmitted to the clerk of the court in which the action is pending and shall be made available for viewing to the prosecuting attorney, the defendant, and his or her attorney during ordinary business hours. The videotape shall be destroyed after five years have elapsed from the date of entry of judgment. If an appeal is filed, the tape shall not be destroyed until a final judgment on appeal has been ordered. Any videotape which is taken pursuant to this section is subject to a protective order of the court for the purpose of protecting the privacy of the witness. This subdivision does not affect the provisions of subdivision (b) of Section 868.7.

(f) When the court orders the testimony of a minor to be taken in another place outside the courtroom, only the minor, a support person designated pursuant to Section 868.5, a nonuniformed bailiff, and, after consultation with the prosecution and the defense, a representative appointed by the court, shall be physically present for the testimony. A videotape shall record the image of the minor and his or her testimony, and a separate videotape shall record the image of the support person.

(g) When the court orders the testimony of a minor to be taken in another place outside the courtroom, the minor shall be brought into the judge's chambers prior to the taking of his or her testimony to meet for a reasonable period of time with the judge, the prosecutor, and defense counsel. A support person for the minor shall also be present. This meeting shall be for the purpose of explaining the court process to the child and to allow the attorneys an opportunity to establish rapport with the child to facilitate later questioning by closed-circuit television. No participant shall discuss the defendant or any of the facts of the case with the minor during this meeting.

(h) When the court orders the testimony of a minor to be taken in another place outside the courtroom, nothing in this section shall prohibit the court from ordering the minor to be brought into the courtroom

for a limited purpose including the identification of the defendant or defendants as the court deems necessary.

(i) The examination shall be under oath, and the defendant shall be able to see and hear the minor witness and if two-way closed-circuit television is used, the defendant's image shall be transmitted live to the witness.

(j) Nothing in this section shall affect the disqualification of witnesses pursuant to Section 701 of the Evidence Code.

(k) The cost of examination by contemporaneous closed-circuit television ordered pursuant to this section shall be borne by the court out of its existing budget. *(Amended by Stats 1991 ch 948 §1, eff. 1/1/92.)*

§1348.5. Three-year pilot program.

(a) On or before July 1, 1987, upon adoption of a resolution of the board of supervisors, a county may establish a three-year pilot project, whereby the court, in any criminal action in which an act of child abuse or molestation is alleged against a member of the child's immediate family, may appoint a children's representative to represent the interests of the minor who was a victim of, or a witness to, the alleged act of abuse or molestation, provided that the victim or witness is under the age of 14. Counties participating in the program shall report to the Legislature before December 31, 1988, on the interim results of the program, and shall submit a final report to the Legislature on or before September 30, 1990, on the results of this program.

(b) The program shall be considered to be successful if the participation of child witnesses in criminal matters has increased 10 percent after the first year and increased 20 percent after the third year of the program. The amount of the increase shall be determined by comparing the 1986 participation rate with the participation rate data for 1987 and 1989, respectively.

(c) The court shall consider all of the following guidelines in appointing the children's representative.

(1) The person's willingness and ability to undertake working with and accompanying the child witness through all proceedings, including criminal proceedings, dependency proceedings, and civil proceedings.

(2) The person's willingness and availability to communicate with the child witness.

(3) The person's willingness and availability to express the child's concerns to those authorized to come in contact with the child as a result of the proceedings.

(d) After considering the guidelines stated in subdivision (b), the court, in its discretion, may appoint a trained volunteer as a children's representative, including a person who has received training from a program formed and operated under the guidelines established by the National Court Appointed Special Advocate Association.

(e) In cases involving more than one child victim under the age of 14, the court may, if it finds it appropriate, appoint a children's representative for each of the victims.

(f) In consideration of the special ethical responsibilities of attorneys and the attendant problems that might be raised by an attorney serving as a children's representative, the court shall not appoint attorneys as children's representatives under this section.

© 1992 by J., B. & L. Gould
Printed in the U.S.A.   **EP**

(g) In order to be appointed as a children's representative, the volunteer shall meet all of the following requirements:

(1) Possess adequate training in the court process, the dynamics of child abuse and neglect, child abuse laws, the social service system, and how to avoid becoming a witness in a case. Volunteers shall receive this training from persons who are involved in the judicial process (prosecutors, defense attorneys, county counsel, social services, child protective services, judges, and advisory board). Each county shall establish such a training program.

(2) Be screened for a criminal record pursuant to Section 11105.3, including, but not limited to, a fingerprint check. A criminal conviction, other than a conviction of a sexually related crime or a conviction of child abuse, shall not bar a person from acting as a children's representative.

(3) Meet other requirements as deemed necessary by the court.

(4) Not have any interest in the case, nor any connection to either the prosecution or defense.

(h) The requirements of this section are the minimum requirements for the appointment of a volunteer as a children's representative. Each county participating in the program shall appoint a volunteer special children's representative advisory board, which shall develop additional criteria requiring additional initial training, continuing in-service training, a system to screen volunteer applicants on an individual basis, and guidelines for supervising and monitoring the volunteers.

The board shall be appointed by the board of supervisors and shall be composed as specified by the board as nominated by the local child abuse council.

(i) The court shall admonish the children's representative that he or she shall not discuss the facts and circumstances of the case with the child witness.

(j) The court shall appoint an administrator whose duties shall be to enforce the guidelines established by this section and the guidelines set up by the volunteer advisory board. The administrator's duties shall also include monitoring the training program and supervising the volunteers.

(k) The children's representative shall do all of the following:

(1) Accompany the child witness through all proceedings, including criminal proceedings, dependency proceedings, and civil proceedings.

(2) Explain to the child witness in terms he or she will understand, based upon his or her age and maturity, the nature and progress of the proceedings and what the child will be called upon to do, including, but not limited to, telling the child that he or she is expected to tell the truth. These explanations shall be made prior to the child's courtroom appearance.

(3) Be available to observe the minor in all aspects of the case, in order to consult with the court as to any special needs of the minor. These consultations shall take place prior to the testimony of the child. For purposes of this paragraph, the court, during a recess, may recognize the children's representative when the representative indicates a need to address the court. The representative shall indicate such a need through the court clerk or bailiff. If a jury is present in the courtroom when the court decides to meet with the representative, the judge shall excuse the jury or convene an in-chambers session with the representative, the defense attorney, and the prosecuting attorney. The session shall be on the record.

(*l*) It is the intent of the Legislature that the court shall consider the goal of continuity between the children's representative and a child victim or witness in the various court proceedings. The Legislature thereby declares that it is desirable for a children's representative appointed to represent the interests of the minor in a dependency proceeding to continue to represent the minor's interest in any ensuing criminal and civil proceedings.

(m) The children's representative shall not be required to testify with respect to the contents of a dependency proceeding in any other proceeding.

(n) The judge may appoint a children's representative at the initial proceeding or any proceeding thereafter. The minor or a person representing the minor may request the appointment of a representative.

(o) The children's representative is not immune from prosecution for dissuading a witness or from interfering with any judicial proceeding.

(p) The children's representative shall not discuss the facts and circumstances of the case with the child witness.

(q) Nothing in this act shall be construed to confer or create a privilege between the child and the children's representative.

(r) The inability of the children's representative to attend any proceeding is not cause for a continuance.

(s) The children's representative shall not be involved in any investigatory interviewing with the child. (*Added by Stats 1986 ch 976 §2.*)

CHAPTER 5

EXAMINATION OF WITNESSES ON COMMISSION

§1349. Nonresident witness' examination.

When an issue of fact is joined upon an indictment or information, the defendant may have any material witness, residing out of the state, examined in his behalf, as prescribed in this chapter, and not otherwise.

§1350. When defendant may apply for an order to examine, etc.

When a material witness for the defendant resides out of the state, the defendant may apply for an order that the witness be examined on a commission.

§1351. Commission defined.

A commission is a process issued under the seal of the court and the signature of the Clerk, directed to some person designated as commissioner, authorizing him to examine the witness upon oath on interrogatories annexed thereto, to take and certify the deposition of the witness, and to return it according to the directions given with the commission.

§1352. Application made on affidavit.

The application must be made upon affidavit, stating:

1. The nature of the offense charged;

2. The state of the proceedings in the action, and that an issue of fact has been joined therein;

3. The name of the witness, and that his testimony is material to the defense of the action;

4. That the witness resides out of the State.

§1353. Notice.

The application may be made to the court, or a Judge thereof, and must be upon three days' notice to the district attorney.

§1354. Order of commission.

If the court to whom the application is made is satisfied of the truth of the facts stated, and that the examination of the witness is necessary to the attainment of justice, an order must be made that a commission be issued to take his testimony; and the Court may insert in the order a direction that the trial be stayed for a specified time, reasonably sufficient for the execution and return of the commission.

§1355. Interrogations, how settled and allowed.

When the commission is ordered, the defendant must serve upon the district attorney, without delay, a copy of the interrogatories to be annexed thereto, with two days' notice of the time at which they will be presented to the court or judge. The district attorney may in like manner serve upon the defendant or his counsel cross-interrogatories, to be annexed to the commission, with the like notice. In the interrogatories either party may insert any questions pertinent to the issue. When the interrogatories and cross-interrogatories are presented to the Court or Judge, according to the notice given, the Court or Judge must modify the questions so as to conform them to the rules of evidence, and must indorse upon them his allowance and annex them to the commission.

§1356. Direction as to the return of the commission.

Unless the parties otherwise consent, by an indorsement upon the commission, the court or judge must indorse thereon a direction as to the manner in which it must be returned, and may, in his discretion, direct that it be returned by mail or otherwise, addressed to the clerk of the court in which the action is pending, designating his name and the place where his office is kept.

§1357. Execution of commission.

The commissioner, unless otherwise specially directed, may execute the commission in the following order:

(a) He or she shall publicly administer an oath to the witness that his or her answers given to the interrogatories shall be the truth, the whole truth, and nothing but the truth.

(b) He or she shall cause the examination of the witness to be reduced to writing and subscribed by the witness.

(c) He or she shall write the answers of the witness as near as possible in the language in which he or she gives them, and read to the witness each answer as it is taken down, and correct or add to it until it conforms to what he or she declares is the truth.

(d) If the witness declines to answer a question, that fact, with the reason assigned by him or her for declining, shall be stated.

(e) If any papers or documents are produced before him or her and proved by the witness, they, or copies of them, shall be annexed to the deposition subscribed by the witness and certified by the commissioner.

(f) The commissioner shall subscribe his or her name to each sheet of the deposition, and annex the deposition, with the papers and documents proved by the witness, or copies thereof, to the commission, and shall close it up under seal, and address it as directed by the indorsement thereon.

(g) If there is a direction on the commission to return it by mail, the commissioner shall immediately deposit it in the nearest post office. If any other direction is made by the written consent of the parties, or by the court or judge, on the commission, as to its return, the commissioner shall comply with the direction.

A copy of this section shall be annexed to the commission. *(Amended by Stats 1989 ch 1360 §115, eff. 1/1/90.)*

§1358. Delivery of commission by agent.

If the commission and return be delivered by the commissioner to an agent, he must deliver the same to the Clerk to whom it is directed, or to the Judge of the Court in which the action is pending, by whom it may be received and opened, upon the agent making affidavit that he received it from the hands of the Commissioner, and that it has not been opened or altered since he received it.

§1359. Commission, how returned, when delivered to an agent for that purpose.

If the agent is dead, or from sickness or other casualty unable personally to deliver the commission and return, as prescribed in the last section, it may be received by the clerk or judge from any other person, upon his making an affidavit that he received it from the agent; that the agent is dead, or from sickness or other casualty unable to deliver it; that it has not been opened or altered since the person making the affidavit received it; and that he believes it has not been opened or altered since it came from the hands of the commissioner.

§1360. When and how filed.

The clerk or judge receiving and opening the commission and return shall immediately file it, with the affidavit mentioned in Sections 1358 and 1359, in the office of the clerk of the court in which the indictment is pending. If the commission and return is transmitted by mail, the clerk to whom it is addressed shall receive it from the post office, and open and file it in his or her office, where it must remain, unless otherwise directed by the court or judge. *(Amended by Stats 1987 ch 828 §89.)*

§1361. Commission and return to open for inspection, copies, etc.

The commission and return must at all times be open to the inspection of the parties, who must be furnished by the Clerk with copies of the same or of any part thereof, on payment of his fees.

§1362. Depositions read in evidence.

The depositions taken under the commission may be read in evidence by either party on the trial if the court finds that the witness is unavailable as a witness within the meaning of Section 240 of the Evidence Code. The same objections may be taken to a question in the interrogatories or to an answer in the deposition as if the witness had been examined orally in court.

© 1992 by J., B. & L. Gould
Printed in the U.S.A.

EP

CHAPTER 5.5

SEX OFFENDERS

§1364. Voluntary, experimental treatment program.

The State Department of Mental Health shall develop a voluntary experimental treatment program that can be evaluated, limited to no more than 50 beds, for persons convicted of sex offenses against a person under the age of 14 years or of a sex offense accomplished against the victim's will by means of force, violence, duress, menace, or fear of immediate and unlawful bodily injury to the victim. The screening of inmates for the program shall be performed jointly by the State Department of Mental Health and the Department of Corrections, based upon program criteria, procedures, and guidelines developed by the State Department of Mental Health in consultation with the Department of Corrections.

The treatment shall only be done during the last two years of incarceration, and only persons who voluntarily consent shall be included in the program. The Department of Corrections shall inform such convicted persons of the state hospital program established pursuant to this section.

The Director of Corrections shall, if he or she receives a recommendation for such treatment, and with the consent of the convicted person, transfer, unless he or she is a security risk, the person to an appropriate state hospital designated by the State Director of Mental Health for treatment. No such transfer may occur without the approval of the medical director of the state hospital. In no event shall the person be placed on outpatient status pursuant to such treatment. In no event shall the person be released prior to his or her determinate sentence date, nor shall treatment pursuant to this section exceed the term of imprisonment imposed. The medical director of the state hospital shall make a recommendation prior to the person's release date whether the person should receive outpatient treatment as a condition of parole. If outpatient treatment is provided it shall be funded as provided in Section 5709.8 of the Welfare and Institutions Code.

If the person refuses to cooperate in his or her treatment while in the state hospital, or is found unamenable to treatment, or if the person requests a return to the Department of Corrections, the medical director of the state hospital shall cause the person to be returned to the Department of Corrections.

Physical transfer of the inmate from the Department of Corrections to the state hospital and return shall be the responsibility of the Department of Corrections. Upon request of the medical director of the state hospital for return of the person to prison, the Director of Corrections shall immediately send for, take, and receive the person back into prison.

All days of confinement in a state hospital for testing and treatment shall be credited to the person's term of imprisonment and the provisions of Section 2931 shall apply. (Amended by Stats 1987 ch 828 §90.)

§1365. Program's design; evaluation reports.

The program described in Section 1364 shall be established according to a valid experimental design in order that the most effective, newest, and promising methods of treatment of sex offenders may be rigorously tested. The State Department of Mental Health shall submit an evaluation report to the Legislature by July 1, 1985. Subsequent evaluation reports shall include treatment outcome measures and shall be submitted every two years thereafter until the termination of the program. The program established pursuant to Section 1364 shall terminate June 30, 1995. (Amended by Stats 1990 ch 57 §12, eff. 4/20/90.)

CHAPTER 6

INQUIRY INTO THE COMPETENCE OF THE DEFENDANT BEFORE TRIAL OR AFTER CONVICTION

§1367. Effect of mental incompetence.

A person cannot be tried or adjudged to punishment while such person is mentally incompetent. A defendant is mentally incompetent for purposes of this chapter if, as a result of mental disorder or developmental disability, the defendant is unable to understand the nature of the criminal proceedings or to assist counsel in the conduct of a defense in a rational manner.

Section 1370 shall apply to a person who is incompetent as a result of a mental disorder. Section 1370.1 shall apply to a person who is incompetent as a result of a developmental disability and shall apply to a person who is incompetent as a result of a mental disorder, but is also developmentally disabled.

§1368. Inquiry into defendant's mental competence.

(a) If, during the pendency of an action and prior to judgment, a doubt arises in the mind of the judge as to the mental competence of the defendant, he shall state that doubt in the record and inquire of the attorney for the defendant whether, in the opinion of the attorney, the defendant is mentally competent. If the defendant is not represented by counsel, the court shall appoint counsel. At the request of the defendant or his counsel or upon its own motion, the court shall recess the proceedings for as long as may be reasonably necessary to permit counsel to confer with defendant and to form an opinion as to the mental competence of the defendant at that point in time.

(b) If counsel informs the court that he believes the defendant is or may be mentally incompetent, the court shall order that the question of the defendant's mental competence is to be determined in a hearing which is held pursuant to Sections 1368.1 and 1369. If counsel informs the court that he believes the defendant is mentally competent, the court may nevertheless order a hearing. Any hearing shall be held in the superior court.

(c) Except as provided in Section 1368.1, when an order for a hearing into the present mental competence of the defendant has been issued, all proceedings in the criminal prosecution shall be suspended until the question of the present mental competence of the defendant has been determined.

If a jury has been impaneled and sworn to try the defendant, the jury shall be discharged only if it appears to the court that undue hardship to the jurors would result if the jury is retained on call.

If the defendant is declared mentally incompetent, the jury shall be discharged.

§1368.1. Demurrer or motion to dismiss.

(a) If the action is on a complaint charging a felony, proceedings to determine mental competence shall be held prior to the filing of an information unless the counsel for the defendant requests a preliminary examination under the provisions of Section 859b. At such preliminary examination, counsel for the defendant may (1) demur, (2) move to dismiss the complaint on the ground that there is not reasonable cause to believe that a felony has been committed and that the defendant is guilty thereof, or (3) make a motion under Section 1538.5.

(b) If the action is on a complaint charging a misdemeanor, counsel for the defendant may (1) demur, (2) move to dismiss the complaint on the ground that there is not reasonable cause to believe that a public offense has been committed and that the defendant is guilty thereof, or (3) make a motion under Section 1538.5.

(c) In ruling upon any demurrer or motion described in subdivision (a) or (b), the court may hear any matter which is capable of fair determination without the personal participation of the defendant.

(d) In any case originating in a municipal or justice court, any demurrer or motion described in subdivision (a) or (b) shall be made in the court having jurisdiction over the complaint. The defendant shall not be certified to the superior court by the municipal or justice court until the demurrer or motion has been decided.

§1369. Trial of question of mental competence.

A trial by court or jury of the question of mental competence shall proceed in the following order:

(a) The court shall appoint a psychiatrist or licensed psychologist, and any other expert the court may deem appropriate, to examine the defendant. In any case where the defendant or the defendant's counsel informs the court that the defendant is not seeking a finding of mental incompetence, the court shall appoint two psychiatrists, licensed psychologists, or a combination thereof. One of the psychiatrists or licensed psychologists may be named by the defense and one may be named by the prosecution. If it is suspected the defendant is developmentally disabled, the court shall appoint the director of the regional center for the developmentally disabled established under Division 4.5 (commencing with Section 4500) of the Welfare and Institutions Code, or the designee of the director, to examine the defendant. The court may order the developmentally disabled defendant to be confined for examination in a residential facility or state hospital.

The regional center director shall recommend to the court a suitable residential facility or state hospital. Prior to issuing an order pursuant to this section, the court shall consider the recommendation of the regional center director. While the person is confined pursuant to order of the court under this section, he or she shall be provided with necessary care and treatment.

(b) (1) The counsel for the defendant shall offer evidence in support of the allegation of mental incompetence.

(2) If the defense declines to offer any evidence in support of the allegation of mental incompetence, the prosecution may do so.

(c) The prosecution shall present its case regarding the issue of defendant's present mental competence.

(d) Each party may offer rebutting testimony, unless the court, for good reason in furtherance of justice,

also permits other evidence in support of the original contention.

(e) When the evidence is concluded, unless the case is submitted without final argument, the prosecution shall make its final argument and the defense shall conclude with its final argument to the court or jury.

(f) In a jury trial, the court shall charge the jury, instructing them on all matters of law necessary for the rendering of a verdict. It shall be presumed that the defendant is mentally competent unless it is proved by a preponderance of the evidence that the defendant is mentally incompetent. The verdict of the jury shall be unanimous.

§1370. Proceedings after finding mentally incompetent.

(a) (1) If the defendant is found mentally competent, the criminal process shall resume, the trial on the offense charged shall proceed, and judgment may be pronounced. If the defendant is found mentally incompetent, the trial or judgment shall be suspended until the person becomes mentally competent, and the court shall order that (i) in the meantime, the defendant be delivered by the sheriff to a state hospital for the care and treatment of the mentally disordered or to any other available public or private treatment facility approved by the community program director which will promote the defendant's speedy restoration to mental competence, or placed on outpatient status as specified in Section 1600, and (ii) upon the filing of a certificate of restoration to competence, the defendant be returned to court in accordance with the provisions of Section 1372. The court shall transmit a copy of its order to the community program director or a designee.

(2) Prior to making the order directing that the defendant be confined in a state hospital or other treatment facility or placed on outpatient status, the court shall order the community program director or a designee to evaluate the defendant and to submit to the court within 15 judicial days of such order a written recommendation as to whether the defendant should be required to undergo outpatient treatment, or committed to a state hospital or to any other treatment facility. No person shall be admitted to a state hospital or other treatment facility or placed on outpatient status under this section without having been evaluated by the community program director or a designee.

(3) When the court, after considering the placement recommendation of the community program director that is required in paragraph (2), orders that the defendant be confined in a state hospital or other public or private treatment facility, the court shall provide copies of the following documents which shall be taken with the defendant to the state hospital or other treatment facility where the defendant is to be confined:

(A) The commitment order, including a specification of the charges.

(B) A computation or statement setting forth the maximum term of commitment in accordance with subdivision (c).

(C) A computation or statement setting forth the amount of credit for time served, if any, to be deducted from the maximum term of commitment.

(D) State Summary Criminal History information.

(E) Any arrest reports prepared by the police department or other law enforcement agency.

© 1992 by J., B. & L. Gould
Printed in the U.S.A.   EP

(F) Any court-ordered psychiatric examination or evaluation reports.

(G) The community program director's placement recommendation report.

(4) When directing that the defendant be confined in a state hospital pursuant to this subdivision, the court shall select the hospital in accordance with the policies established by the State Department of Mental Health.

(5) If the defendant is committed or transferred to a state hospital pursuant to this section, the court may, upon receiving the written recommendation of the medical director of the state hospital and the community program director that the defendant be transferred to a public or private treatment facility approved by the community program director, order the defendant transferred to that facility. If the defendant is committed or transferred to a public or private treatment facility approved by the community program director, the court may, upon receiving the written recommendation of the community program director, transfer the defendant to a state hospital or to another public or private treatment facility approved by the community program director. In the event of dismissal of the criminal charges before the defendant recovers competence, the person shall be subject to the applicable provisions of the Lanterman-Petris-Short Act (Part 1 (commencing with Section 5000) of Division 5 of the Welfare and Institutions Code). Where either the defendant or the prosecutor chooses to contest either kind of order of transfer, a petition may be filed in the court for a hearing, which shall be held if the court determines that sufficient grounds exist. At the hearing, the prosecuting attorney or the defendant may present evidence bearing on the order of transfer. The court shall use the same standards as are used in conducting probation revocation hearings pursuant to Section 1203.2.

Prior to making an order for transfer under this section, the court shall notify the defendant, the attorney of record for the defendant, the prosecuting attorney, and the community program director or a designee.

(b) (1) Within 90 days of a commitment made pursuant to subdivision (a), the medical director of the state hospital or other treatment facility to which the defendant is confined shall make a written report to the court and the community program director for the county or region of commitment, or a designee, concerning the defendant's progress toward recovery of mental competence. Where the defendant is on outpatient status, the outpatient treatment staff shall make a written report to the community program director concerning the defendant's progress toward recovery of mental competence. Within 90 days of placement on outpatient status, the community program director shall report to the court on this matter. If the defendant has not recovered mental competence, but the report discloses a substantial likelihood that the defendant will regain mental competence in the foreseeable future, the defendant shall remain in the state hospital or other treatment facility or on outpatient status. Thereafter, at six-month intervals or until the defendant becomes mentally competent, where the defendant is confined in a treatment facility, the medical director of the hospital or person in charge of the facility shall report in writing to the court and the community program director or a designee regarding the defendant's progress toward recovery of mental competence. Where the defendant

is on outpatient status, after the initial 90-day report, the outpatient treatment staff shall report to the community program director on the defendant's progress toward recovery, and the community program director shall report to the court on this matter at six-month intervals. A copy of these reports shall be provided to the prosecutor and defense counsel by the court. If the report indicates that there is no substantial likelihood that the defendant will regain mental competence in the foreseeable future, the committing court shall order the defendant to be returned to the court for proceedings pursuant to paragraph (2) of subdivision (c). The court shall transmit a copy of its order to the community program director or a designee.

(2) Any defendant who has been committed or has been on outpatient status for 18 months and is still hospitalized or on outpatient status shall be returned to the committing court where a hearing shall be held pursuant to the procedures set forth in Section 1369. The court shall transmit a copy of its order to the community program director or a designee.

(3) If it is determined by the court that no treatment for the defendant's mental impairment is being conducted, the defendant shall be returned to the committing court. The court shall transmit a copy of its order to the community program director or a designee.

(c) (1) If, at the end of three years from the date of commitment or a period of commitment equal to the maximum term of imprisonment provided by law for the most serious offense charged in the information, indictment, or misdemeanor complaint, whichever is shorter, the defendant has not recovered mental competence, the defendant shall be returned to the committing court. The court shall notify the community program director or a designee of such return and of any resulting court orders.

(2) Whenever any defendant is returned to the court pursuant to paragraph (1) or (2) of subdivision (b) or paragraph (1) of this subdivision and it appears to the court that the defendant is gravely disabled, as defined in paragraph (2) of subdivision (h) of Section 5008 of the Welfare and Institutions Code, the court shall order the conservatorship investigator of the county of commitment of the defendant to initiate conservatorship proceedings for the defendant pursuant to Chapter 3 (commencing with Section 5350) of Part 1 of Division 5 of the Welfare and Institutions Code. Any hearings required in the conservatorship proceedings shall be held in the superior court in the county which ordered the commitment. The court shall transmit a copy of the order directing initiation of conservatorship proceedings to the community program director or a designee and shall notify the community program director or a designee of the outcome of the proceedings.

(d) The criminal action remains subject to dismissal pursuant to Section 1385. If the criminal action is dismissed, the court shall transmit a copy of the order of dismissal to the community program director or a designee.

(e) If the criminal charge against the defendant is dismissed, the defendant shall he released from any commitment ordered under this section, but without prejudice to the initiation of any proceedings which may be appropriate under the Lanterman-Petris-Short Act, Part 1 (commencing with Section 5000) of Division 5 of the Welfare and Institutions Code.

(f) As used in this chapter, "community program director" means the person, agency, or entity designated by the State Department of Mental Health pursuant to Section 1605 of this code and Section 5709.8 of the Welfare and Institutions Code. *(Amended by Stats 1989 ch 625 §2, eff. 1/1/90.)*

§1370.1. Proceeding after finding of developmentally disabled.

(a) (1) If the defendant is found mentally competent, the criminal process shall resume, the trial on the offense charged shall proceed, and judgment may be pronounced. If the defendant is found mentally incompetent and is developmentally disabled, the trial or judgment shall be suspended until the defendant becomes mentally competent, and the court shall consider a recommendation for placement, which recommendation shall be made to the court by the director of a regional center or designee, and that (A) in the meantime, the defendant be delivered by the sheriff or other person designated by the court to a state hospital for the care and treatment of the developmentally disabled or any other available residential facility approved by the director of a regional center for the developmentally disabled established under Division 4.5 (commencing with Section 4500) of the Welfare and Institutions Code as will promote the defendant's speedy attainment of mental competence, or be placed on outpatient status pursuant to the provisions of Section 1370.4 and Title 15 (commencing with Section 1600) of Part 2, and (B) upon becoming competent, the defendant be returned to the committing court pursuant to the procedures set forth in paragraph (2) of subdivision (a) of Section 1372 or by another person designated by the court. The court shall transmit a copy of its order to the regional center director or designee and to the Director of Developmental Services.

As used in this section, "developmental disability" means a disability which originates before an individual attains age 18, continues, or can be expected to continue, indefinitely and constitutes a substantial handicap for such individual, and shall not include other handicapping conditions that are solely physical in nature. As defined by the Director of Developmental Services, in consultation with the Superintendent of Public Instruction, this term shall include mental retardation, cerebral palsy, epilepsy, and autism. This term shall also include handicapping conditions found to be closely related to mental retardation or to require treatment similar to that required for mentally retarded individuals, but shall not include other handicapping conditions that are solely physical in nature.

(2) Prior to making such order directing the defendant be confined in a state hospital or other residential facility or be placed on outpatient status, the court shall order the regional center director or designee to evaluate the defendant and to submit to the court within 15 judicial days of such order a written recommendation as to whether the defendant should be committed to a state hospital or to any other available residential facility approved by the regional center director. No person shall be admitted to a state hospital or other residential facility or accepted for outpatient status under Section 1370.4 without having been evaluated by the regional center director or designee.

If the defendant is committed or transferred to a state hospital pursuant to this section, the court may, upon receiving the written recommendation of the medical director of the state hospital and the regional

center director that the defendant be transferred to a residential facility approved by the regional center director, order the defendant transferred to such facility. If the defendant is committed or transferred to a residential facility approved by the regional center director, the court may, upon receiving the written recommendation of the regional center director, transfer the defendant to a state hospital or to another residential facility approved by the regional center director.

In the event of dismissal of the criminal charges before the defendant recovers competence, the person shall be subject to the applicable provisions of the Lanterman-Petris-Short Act (Part 1 (commencing with Section 5000) of Division 5 of the Welfare and Institutions Code) or to commitment or detention pursuant to a petition filed pursuant to Section 6502 of the Welfare and Institutions Code.

The defendant or prosecuting attorney may contest either kind of order of transfer by filing a petition with the court for a hearing, which shall be held if the court determines that sufficient grounds exist. At such hearing the prosecuting attorney or the defendant may present evidence bearing on the order of transfer. The court shall use the same standards as used in conducting probation revocation hearings pursuant to Section 1203.2.

Prior to making an order for transfer under this section, the court shall notify the defendant, the attorney of record for the defendant, the prosecuting attorney, and the regional center director or designee.

(b) (1) Within 90 days of a commitment made pursuant to subdivision (a), the medical director of the state hospital or other facility to which the defendant is committed or the outpatient supervisor where the defendant is placed on outpatient status shall make a written report to the regional center director or a designee concerning the defendant's progress toward becoming mentally competent. If the defendant has not become mentally competent, but the report discloses a substantial likelihood the defendant will become mentally competent in the foreseeable future, the defendant shall remain in the state hospital or other facility or on outpatient status. Thereafter, at six-month intervals or until the defendant becomes mentally competent, the medical director of the hospital or person in charge of the facility or the outpatient supervisor shall report to the regional center director or his designee regarding the defendant's progress toward becoming mentally competent. The regional center director shall transmit that report immediately to the court as part of the defendant's progress report. The court shall provide to the prosecutor and defense counsel copies of all reports under this section. If the report indicates that there is no substantial likelihood that the defendant will become mentally competent in the foreseeable future, the committing court shall order the defendant to be returned to the court for proceedings pursuant to paragraph (2) of subdivision (c). The court shall transmit a copy of its order to the regional center director or designee and to the Director of Developmental Services.

(2) Any defendant who has been committed or has been on outpatient status for 18 months, and is still hospitalized or on outpatient status shall be returned to the committing court where a hearing shall be held pursuant to the procedures set forth in Section 1369. The court shall transmit a copy of its order to the regional center director or designee and the Director of Developmental Services.

© 1992 by J., B. & L. Gould
Printed in the U.S.A.   EP

(3) If it is determined by the court that no treatment for the defendant's mental impairment is being conducted, the defendant shall be returned to the committing court. A copy of this order shall be sent to the regional center director or designee and to the Director of Developmental Services.

(c) (1) At the end of three years from the date of commitment or a period of commitment equal to the maximum term of imprisonment provided by law for the most serious offense charged in the information, indictment, or misdemeanor complaint, whichever is shorter, any defendant who has not become mentally competent shall be returned to the committing court. The court shall notify the regional center director or designee and the Director of Developmental Services of such return and of any resulting court orders.

(2) In the event of dismissal of the criminal charges before the defendant becomes mentally competent, the defendant shall be subject to the applicable provisions of the Lanterman-Petris-Short Act (Part 1 (commencing with Section 5000) of Division 5 of the Welfare and Institutions Code), or to commitment and detention pursuant to a petition filed pursuant to Section 6502 of the Welfare and Institutions Code. If it is found that the person is not subject to commitment or detention pursuant to the applicable provision of the Lanterman-Petris-Short Act (Part 1 (commencing with Section 5000) of Division 5 of the Welfare and Institutions Code or to commitment or detention pursuant to a petition filed pursuant to Section 6502 of the Welfare and Institutions Code, the individual shall not be subject to further confinement pursuant to this article and the criminal action remains subject to dismissal pursuant to Section 1385. The court shall notify the regional center director and the Director of Developmental Services of any such dismissal.

(d) Notwithstanding any other provision of this section, the criminal action remains subject to dismissal pursuant to Section 1385. If at any time prior to the maximum period of time allowed for proceedings under this article, the regional center director concludes that the behavior of the defendant related to the defendant's criminal offense has been eliminated during time spent in court-ordered programs, the court may, upon recommendation of the regional center director, dismiss the criminal charges. The court shall transmit a copy of any order of dismissal to the regional center director and to the Director of Developmental Services.

§1370.2. Dismissal of misdemeanor charge against mentally incompetent person.

If a person is adjudged mentally incompetent pursuant to the provisions of this chapter, the superior court may dismiss any misdemeanor charge pending against the mentally incompetent person. Ten days notice shall be given to the district attorney of any motion to dismiss pursuant to this section. The court shall transmit a copy of any order dismissing a misdemeanor charge pursuant to this section to either the community program director or the regional center director and the Director of Developmental Services, as appropriate. (Amended by Stats 1985 ch 1232 §6.)

§1370.3. Outpatient status of committed person.

A person committed to a state hospital or other treatment facility under the provisions of this chapter may be placed on outpatient status from such commitment as provided in Title 15 (commencing with Section 1600) of Part 2.

§1370.4. Provisions for outpatient status.

If, in the evaluation ordered by the court under Section 1370.1, the regional center director, or a designee, is of the opinion that the defendant is not a danger to the health and safety of others while on outpatient treatment and will benefit from such treatment, and has obtained the agreement of the person in charge of a residential facility and of the defendant that the defendant will receive and submit to outpatient treatment and that the person in charge of the facility will designate a person to be the outpatient supervisor of the defendant, the court may order the defendant to undergo outpatient treatment. All of the provisions of Title 15 (commencing with Section 1600) of Part 2 shall apply where a defendant is placed on outpatient status under this section, except that the regional center director shall be substituted for the community program director, the Director of Developmental Services for the Director of Mental Health, and a residential facility for a treatment facility for the purposes of this section. (Amended by Stats 1985 ch 1232 §7.)

§1370.5. Escape from state hospital or mental health facility.

(a) Every person committed to a state hospital or other public or private mental health facility pursuant to the provisions of Section 1370 or 1370.1, who escapes from or who escapes while being conveyed to or from a state hospital or facility, is punishable by imprisonment in the county jail not to exceed one year or in the state prison for a determinate term of one year and one day. The term of imprisonment imposed pursuant to this section shall be served consecutively to any other sentence or commitment.

(b) The medical director or person in charge of a state hospital or other public or private mental health facility to which a person has been committed pursuant to the provisions of Section 1370 or 1370.1 shall promptly notify the chief of police of the city in which the hospital or facility is located, or the sheriff of the county if the hospital or facility is located in an unincorporated area, of the escape of the person, and shall request the assistance of the chief of police or sheriff in apprehending the person, and shall within 48 hours of the escape of the person orally notify the court that made the commitment, the prosecutor in the case, and the Department of Justice of the escape. (Amended by Stats 1989 ch 568 §2, eff. 1/1/90.)

§1371. Exoneration of bail.

The commitment of the defendant, as mentioned in section 1370 of this code, exonerates his bail, or entitles a person, authorized to receive the property of the defendant, to a return of any money he may have deposited instead of bail, or gives, to the person or persons found by the court to have deposited any money instead of bail on behalf of said defendant, a right to the return of such money.

§1372. Certification of restoration to competence.

(a) (1) If the medical director of the state hospital or other facility to which the defendant is committed, or the community program director or regional center director providing outpatient services under Title 15 (commencing with Section 1600) of Part 2 or Section 1370.4, determines that the defendant has regained mental competence, such director shall immediately certify that fact to the court.

(2) Upon the filing of a certificate of restoration, the defendant shall be returned to the committing court in the following manner: A patient who remains confined in a state hospital or other treatment facility shall be redelivered to the sheriff of the county from which the patient was committed. The sheriff shall immediately return the person to the court for further proceedings. The patient who is on outpatient status shall be returned to court through arrangements made by the outpatient treatment supervisor.

(b) If the defendant becomes mentally competent after a conservatorship has been established pursuant to the applicable provisions of the Lanterman-Petris-Short Act, Part 1 (commencing with Section 5000) of Division 5 of the Welfare and Institutions Code, and Section 1370, the conservator shall certify that fact to the sheriff and district attorney of the county in which defendant's case is pending, defendant's attorney of record, and the committing court.

(c) When a defendant is returned to court with a certification that competence has been regained, the court shall notify either the community program director or the regional center director and the Director of Developmental Services, as appropriate, of the date of any hearing on the defendant's competence and whether or not the defendant was found by the court to have recovered competence.

(d) Where the committing court approves the certificate of restoration to competence as to a person in custody, the court shall hold a hearing to determine whether the person is entitled to be admitted to bail or released on own recognizance status pending conclusion of the proceedings. Where the superior court approves the certificate of restoration to competence regarding a person on outpatient status, unless it appears that the person has refused to come to court, that person shall remain released either on own recognizance status, or, in the case of a developmentally disabled person, either on the defendant's promise or on the promise of a responsible adult to secure the person's appearance in court for further proceedings. Where the person has refused to come to court, the court shall set bail and may place the person in custody until bail is posted.

(e) A defendant subject to either subdivision (a) or (b) who is not admitted to bail or released under subdivision (d) may, at the discretion of the court, upon recommendation of the director of the facility where the defendant is receiving treatment, be returned to the hospital or facility of his or her original commitment or other appropriate secure facility approved by either the community program director or the regional center director. The recommendation submitted to the court shall be based on the opinion that the person will need continued treatment in a hospital or treatment facility in order to maintain competence to stand trial or that placing the person in a jail environment would create a substantial risk that the person would again become incompetent to stand trial before criminal proceedings could be resumed. *(Amended by Stats 1985 ch 1232 §8.)*

§1373. Expenses of sending to state hospital or other facility.

The expense of sending the defendant to the state hospital or other facility, and of bringing him back, are chargeable to the county in which the indictment was found or information filed; but the county may recover them from the estate of the defendant, if he has any, or from a relative, bound to provide for and maintain him.

§1373.5. Interest on recovery of rejected claim.

In every case where a claim is presented to the county for money due under the provisions of section 1373 of this code, interest shall be allowed from the date of rejection, if rejected and recovery is finally had thereon.

§1374. Opinion of outpatient treatment staff.

When a defendant who has been found incompetent is on outpatient status under Title 15 (commencing with Section 1600) of Part 2 and the outpatient treatment staff is of the opinion that the defendant has recovered competence, the supervisor shall communicate such opinion to the community program director. If the community program director concurs, that opinion shall be certified by such director to the committing court. The court shall calendar the case for further proceeding pursuant to Section 1372. *(Amended by Stats 1985 ch 1232 §9.)*

§1375. Claims by state.

Claims by the state for all amounts due from any county by reason of the provisions of Section 1373 of this code shall be processed and paid by the county pursuant to the provisions of Chapter 4 (commencing with Section 29700) of Division 3 of Title 3 of the Government Code.

§1375.5. Commitment time credited on prison term.

Time spent by a defendant in a hospital or other facility as a result of a commitment therein as a mentally incompetent pursuant to this chapter shall be credited on the term of any imprisonment, if any, for which the defendant is sentenced in the criminal case which was suspended pursuant to Section 1370 or 1370.1.

As used in this section, "time spent in a hospital or other facility" includes days a defendant is treated as an outpatient pursuant to Title 15 (commencing with Section 1600) of Part 2.

CHAPTER 7

COMPROMISING CERTAIN PUBLIC OFFENSES BY LEAVE OF THE COURT

§1377. Exceptions.

When the person injured by an act constituting a misdemeanor has a remedy by a civil action, the offense may be compromised as provided in the next section, except when it is committed:

1. By or upon an officer of justice, while in the execution of the duties of his office;

2. Riotously;

3. With an intent to commit a felony;

4. In violation of any court order as described in Section 273.6, unless the offense charged is the first such offense committed by the defendant against the family or household member under Section 273.6.

§1378. Stay of proceedings on payment of satisfaction for injury.

If the person injured appears before the court in which the action is pending at any time before trial, and acknowledges that he has received satisfaction for

© 1992 by J., B. & L. Gould
Printed in the U.S.A.   EP

the injury, the court may, in its discretion, on payment of the costs incurred, order all proceedings to be stayed upon the prosecution, and the defendant to be discharged therefrom; but in such case the reasons for the order must be set forth therein, and entered on the minutes. The order is a bar to another prosecution for the same offense.

§1379. No public offense to be compromised except as herein provided.

No public offense can be compromised, nor can any proceeding or prosecution for the punishment thereof upon a compromise be stayed, except as provided in this chapter.

CHAPTER 8

DISMISSAL OF THE ACTION FOR WANT OF PROSECUTION OR OTHERWISE

§1381. Right of prisoner to speedy trial.

Whenever a defendant has been convicted, in any court of this state, of the commission of a felony or misdemeanor and has been sentenced to and has entered upon a term of imprisonment in a state prison or has been sentenced to and has entered upon a term of imprisonment in a county jail for a period of more than 90 days or has been committed to and placed in a county jail for more than 90 days as a condition of probation or has been committed to and placed in an institution subject to the jurisdiction of the Department of the Youth Authority or whenever any person has been committed to the custody of the Director of Corrections pursuant to Chapter 1 (commencing with Section 3000) of Division 3 of the Welfare and Institutions Code and has entered upon his or her term of commitment, and at the time of the entry upon the term of imprisonment or commitment there is pending, in any court of this state, any other indictment, information, complaint, or any criminal proceeding wherein the defendant remains to be sentenced, the district attorney of the county in which the matters are pending shall bring the defendant to trial or for sentencing within 90 days after the person shall have delivered to said district attorney written notice of the place of his or her imprisonment or commitment and his or her desire to be brought to trial or for sentencing unless a continuance beyond the 90 days is requested or consented to by the person, in open court, and the request or consent entered upon the minutes of the court in which event the 90-day period shall commence to run anew from the date to which the consent or request continued the trial or sentencing. In the event that the defendant is not brought to trial or for sentencing within the 90 days the court in which the charge or sentencing is pending shall, on motion or suggestion of the district attorney, or of the defendant or person confined in the county jail or committed to the custody of the Director of Corrections or his or her counsel, or of the Department of Corrections, or of the Department of the Youth Authority, or on its own motion, dismiss the action. If a charge is filed against a person during the time the person is serving a sentence in any state prison or county jail of this state or while detained by the Director of Corrections pursuant to Chapter 1 (commencing with Section 3000) of Division 3 of the Welfare and Institutions Code or while detained in any institution subject to the jurisdiction of the Department of the Youth Authority it is hereby made mandatory upon the district attorney of the county in which the charge is filed to bring it to trial within 90 days after the person shall have delivered to said district attorney written notice of the place of his or her imprisonment or commitment and his or her desire to be brought to trial upon the charge, unless a continuance is requested or consented to by the person, in open court, and the request or consent entered upon the minutes of the court, in which event the 90-day period shall commence to run anew from the date to which the request or consent continued the trial. In the event the action is not brought to trial within the 90 days the court in which the action is pending shall, on motion or suggestion of the district attorney, or of the defendant or person committed to the custody of the Director of Corrections or to a county jail or his or her counsel, or of the Department of Corrections, or of the Department of the Youth Authority, or on its own motion, dismiss the charge. The sheriff, custodian, or jailer shall endorse upon the written notice of the defendant's desire to be brought to trial or for sentencing the cause of commitment, the date of commitment, and the date of release. *(Amended by Stats 1987 ch 828 §91.)*

§1381.5. Right of federal prisoner to speedy trial.

Whenever a defendant has been convicted of a crime and has entered upon a term of imprisonment therefor in a federal correctional institution located in this state, and at the time of entry upon such term of imprisonment or at any time during such term of imprisonment there is pending in any court of this state any criminal indictment, information, complaint, or any criminal proceeding wherein the defendant remains to be sentenced the district attorney of the county in which such matters are pending, upon receiving from such defendant a request that he be brought to trial or for sentencing, shall promptly inquire of the warden or other head of the federal correctional institution in which such defendant is confined whether and when such defendant can be released for trial or for sentencing. If an assent from authorized federal authorities for release of the defendant for trial or sentencing is received by the district attorney he shall bring him to trial or sentencing within 90 days after receipt of such assent, unless the federal authorities specify a date of release after 90 days, in which event the district attorney shall bring the prisoner to trial or sentencing at such specified time, or unless the defendant requests, in open court, and receives, or, in open court, consents to, a continuance, in which event he may be brought to trial or sentencing within 90 days from such request or consent.

If a defendant is not brought to trial or for sentencing as provided by this section, the court in which the action is pending shall, on motion or suggestion of the district attorney, or representative of the United States, or the defendant or his counsel, dismiss the action.

§1382. Dismissal for lack of speedy trial.

(a) The court, unless good cause to the contrary is shown, shall order the action to be dismissed in the following cases:

(1) When a person has been held to answer for a public offense and an information is not filed against that person within 15 days thereafter.

(2) When a defendant is not brought to trial in a superior court within 60 days after the finding of the indictment or filing of the information or, in case the cause is to be tried again following a mistrial, an order granting a new trial from which an appeal is not taken, or an appeal from the superior court, within 60 days after the mistrial has been declared, after entry of the order granting the new trial, or after the filing of the remittitur in the trial court, or after the issuance of a writ or order which in effect grants a new trial, within 60 days after notice of the writ or order is filed in the trial court and served upon the prosecuting attorney, or within 90 days after notice of the writ or order is filed in the trial court and served upon the prosecuting attorney in any case where the district attorney chooses to resubmit the case for a preliminary examination after an appeal or the issuance of a writ reversing a judgment of conviction upon a plea of guilty prior to a preliminary hearing in a municipal or justice court. However, an action shall not be dismissed under this paragraph if either of the following circumstances exist:

(A) The defendant enters a general waiver of the 60-day trial requirement. A general waiver of the 60-day trial requirement entitles the superior court to set or continue a trial date without the sanction of dismissal should the case fail to proceed on the date set for trial. If the defendant, after proper notice to all parties, later withdraws his or her waiver in the superior court, the defendant shall be brought to trial within 60 days of the date of that withdrawal. If a general time waiver is not expressly entered, the provisions of subparagraph (B) shall apply.

(B) The defendant requests or consents to the setting of a trial date beyond the 60-day period. Whenever a case is set for trial beyond the 60-day period by request or consent, expressed or implied, of the defendant without a general waiver, the defendant shall be brought to trial on the date set for trial or within 10 days thereafter.

Whenever a case is not set for trial after a defendant enters either a general waiver as to the 60-day trial requirement or requests or consents, expressed or implied, to the setting of a trial date beyond the 60-day period pursuant to this paragraph, the court may not grant a motion of the defendant to vacate the date set for trial and to set an earlier trial date unless all parties are properly noticed and the court finds good cause for granting that motion.

(3) Regardless of when the complaint is filed, when a defendant in a misdemeanor case in an inferior court is not brought to trial within 30 days after he or she is arraigned or enters his or her plea, whichever occurs later, if the defendant is in custody at the time of arraignment or plea, or in all other cases, within 45 days after the defendant's arraignment or entry of the plea, whichever occurs later, or in case the cause is to be tried again following a mistrial, an order granting a new trial from which an appeal is not taken, or an appeal from the inferior court, within 30 days after the mistrial has been declared, after entry of the order granting the new trial, or after the remittitur is filed in the trial court or, if the new trial is to be held in the superior court, within 30 days after the judgment on appeal becomes final. However, an action shall not be dismissed under this subdivision if either of the following circumstances exist:

(A) It is set for trial on a date beyond the prescribed period at the request of the defendant or with the defendant's consent, express or implied, and the defendant is brought to trial on the date so set for trial or within 10 days thereafter.

(B) It is not tried on the date set for trial because of the defendant's neglect or failure to appear, in which case the defendant shall be deemed to have been arraigned within the meaning of this subdivision on the date of his or her subsequent arraignment on a bench warrant or his or her submission to the court.

(b) Whenever a defendant has been ordered to appear in superior court on a case set for trial or set for a hearing prior to trial, if the defendant fails to appear on that date and a bench warrant is issued, the defendant shall be brought to trial within 60 days after the defendant next appears in the superior court unless a trial date had previously been set which is beyond that 60-day period.

(c) If the defendant is not represented by counsel, the defendant shall not be deemed under this section to have consented to the date for the defendant's trial unless the court has explained to the defendant his or her rights under this section and the effect of his or her consent. *(Amended by Stats 1991 ch 655 §3, eff. 1/1/92.)*

§1383. Continuance of action.

If the defendant is not charged or tried, as provided in Section 1382, and sufficient reason therefor is shown, the court may order the action to be continued from time to time, and in the meantime may discharge the defendant from custody on his or her own undertaking of bail for his or her appearance to answer the charge at the time to which the action is continued. *(Amended by Stats 1987 ch 828 §92.)*

§1384. Discharge of defendant if action dismissed.

If the judge or magistrate directs the action to be dismissed, the defendant must, if in custody, be discharged therefrom; or if admitted to bail, his bail is exonerated, or money deposited instead of bail must be refunded to him or to the person or persons found by the court to have deposited said money on behalf of said defendant.

§1385. Order of dismissal.

(a) The judge or magistrate may, either of his or her own motion or upon the application of the prosecuting attorney, and in furtherance of justice, order an action to be dismissed. The reasons for the dismissal must be set forth in an order entered upon the minutes. No dismissal shall be made for any cause which would be ground of demurrer to the accusatory pleading.

(b) This section does not authorize a judge to strike any prior conviction of a serious felony for purposes of enhancement of a sentence under Section 667. *(Amended by Stats 1986 ch 85 §2.)*

§1385.1. Special circumstances pleas.

Notwithstanding Section 1385 or any other provision of law, a judge shall not strike or dismiss any special circumstance which is admitted by a plea of guilty or nolo contendere or is found by a jury or court as provided in Sections 190.1 to 190.5, inclusive. *(Added by Initiative Measure, Prop 115 §26, approved 6/5/90.)*

© 1992 by J., B. & L. Gould
Printed in the U.S.A.   **EP**

§1386. Abolition of nolle prosequi.

The entry of a nolle prosequi is abolished, and neither the Attorney General nor the district attorney can discontinue or abandon a prosecution for a public offense, except as provided in Section 1385. *(Amended by Stats 1987 ch 828 §93.)*

§1387. Order of dismissal to bar other action.

(a) An order terminating an action pursuant to this chapter, or Section 859b, 861, 871, or 995, is a bar to any other prosecution for the same offense if it is a felony or if it is a misdemeanor charged together with a felony and the action has been previously terminated pursuant to this chapter, or Section 859b, 861, 871, or 995, or if it is a misdemeanor not charged together with a felony, except in those felony cases, or those cases where a misdemeanor is charged with a felony, where subsequent to the dismissal of the felony or misdemeanor the judge or magistrate finds any of the following:

(1) That substantial new evidence has been discovered by the prosecution which would not have been known through the exercise of due diligence at, or prior to, the time of termination of the action.

(2) That the termination of the action was the result of the direct intimidation of a material witness, as shown by a preponderance of the evidence.

(3) That the termination of the action was the result of the failure to appear by the complaining witness, who had been personally subpoenaed in a prosecution arising under subdivision (e) of Section 243 or Section 262, 273.5, or 273.6. This paragraph shall apply only within six months of the original dismissal of the action, and may be invoked only once in each action. Nothing in this section shall preclude a defendant from being eligible for diversion.

(b) An order terminating an action is not a bar to prosecution if a complaint is dismissed before the commencement of a preliminary hearing in favor of an indictment filed pursuant to Section 944 and the indictment is based upon the same subject matter as charged in the dismissed complaint, information, or indictment.

However, if the previous termination was pursuant to Section 859b, 861, 871, or 995, the subsequent order terminating an action is not a bar to prosecution if:

(1) Good cause is shown why the preliminary examination was not held within 60 days from the date of arraignment or plea.

(2) The motion pursuant to Section 995 was granted because of any of the following reasons:

(A) Present insanity of the defendant.

(B) A lack of counsel after the defendant elected to represent himself or herself rather than being represented by appointed counsel.

(C) Ineffective assistance of counsel.

(D) Conflict of interest of defense counsel.

(E) Violation of time deadlines based upon unavailability of defense counsel.

(F) Defendant's motion to withdraw a waiver of the preliminary examination.

(3) The motion pursuant to Section 995 was granted after dismissal by the magistrate of the action pursuant to Section 871 and was recharged pursuant to Section 739. *(Amended by Stats 1991 ch 400 §2, eff. 1/1/92.)*

§1387.1. *Repealed by Stats 1989 ch 1360 §116, eff. 1/1/90.*

§1388. Refiling of case; rearraignment.

(a) In any case where an order for the dismissal of a felony action is made, as provided in this chapter, and where the defendant had been released on his own recognizance for that action, if the prosecutor files another accusatory pleading against the same defendant for the same offense, unless the defendant is present in court at the time of refiling, the district attorney shall send a letter to the defendant at his last known place of residence, and shall send a copy to the attorney of record, stating that the case has been refiled, and setting forth the date, time and place for rearraignment.

(b) If the defendant fails to appear for arraignment as stated, or at such time, date, and place as has been subsequently agreed to by defendant's counsel and the district attorney, then the court shall issue and have delivered for execution a warrant for his arrest within 20 days after his failure to appear.

(c) If the defendant was released on his own recognizance on the original charge, he shall, if he appears as provided in subdivisions (a) and (b), be released on his own recognizance on the refiled charge unless it is shown that changed conditions require a different disposition, in which case bail shall be set at the discretion of the judge.

CHAPTER 8.5

AGREEMENT ON DETAINERS

§1389. Agreement on detainers.

The agreement on detainers is hereby enacted into law and entered into by this State with all other jurisdictions legally joining therein in the form substantially as follows:

The Agreement on Detainers

The contracting states solemnly agree that:

Article 1

The party states find that charges outstanding against a prisoner, detainers based on untried indictments, informations or complaints, and difficulties in securing speedy trial of persons already incarcerated in other jurisdictions, produce uncertainties which obstruct programs of prisoner treatment and rehabilitation. Accordingly, it is the policy of the party states and the purpose of this agreement to encourage the expeditious and orderly disposition of such charges and determination of the proper status of any and all detainers based on untried indictments, informations or complaints. The party states also find that proceedings with reference to such charges and detainers, when emanating from another jurisdiction, cannot properly be had in the absence of cooperative procedures. It is the further purpose of this agreement to provide such cooperative procedures.

Article II

As used in this agreement:

(a) "State" shall mean a state of the United States; the United States of America; a territory or possession of the United States; the District of Columbia; the Commonwealth of Puerto Rico.

(b) "Sending state" shall mean a state in which a prisoner is incarcerated at the time that he initiates a request for final disposition pursuant to Article III hereof or at the time that a request for custody or availability is initiated pursuant to Article IV hereof.

(c) "Receiving state" shall mean the state in which trial is to be had on an indictment, information or complaint pursuant to Article III or Article IV hereof.

Article III

(a) Whenever a person has entered upon a term of imprisonment in a penal or correctional institution of a party state, and whenever during the continuance of the term of imprisonment there is pending in any other party state any untried indictment, information or complaint on the basis of which a detainer has been lodged against the prisoner, he shall be brought to trial within one hundred eighty days after he shall have cause to be delivered to the prosecuting officer and the appropriate court of the prosecuting officer's jurisdiction written notice of the place of his imprisonment and his request for a final disposition to be made of the indictment, information or complaint: provided that for good cause shown in open court, the prisoner or his counsel being present, the court having jurisdiction of the matter may grant any necessary or reasonable continuance. The request of the prisoner shall be accompanied by a certificate of the appropriate official having custody of the prisoner, stating the term of commitment under which the prisoner is being held, the time already served, the time remaining to be served on the sentence, the amount of good time earned, the time of parole eligibility of the prisoner, and any decisions of the state parole agency relating to the prisoner.

(b) The written notice and request for final disposition referred to in paragraph (a) hereof shall be given or sent by the prisoner to the warden, commissioner of corrections or other official having custody of him, who shall promptly forward it together with the certificate to the appropriate prosecuting official and court by registered or certified mail, return receipt requested.

(c) The warden, commissioner of corrections or other official having custody of the prisoner shall promptly inform him of the source and contents of any detainer lodged against him and shall also inform him of his right to make a request for final disposition of the indictment, information or complaint on which the detainer is based.

(d) Any request for final disposition made by a prisoner pursuant to paragraph (a) hereof shall operate as a request for final disposition of all untried indictments, informations or complaints on the basis of which detainers have been lodged against the prisoner from the state to whose prosecuting official the request for final disposition is specifically directed. The warden, commissioner of corrections or other official having custody of the prisoner shall forthwith notify all appropriate prosecuting officers and courts in the several jurisdictions within the state to which the prisoner's request for final disposition is being sent of the proceeding being initiated by the prisoner. Any notification sent pursuant to this paragraph shall be accompanied by copies of the prisoner's written notice, request, and the certificate. If trial is not had on any indictment, information or complaint contemplated hereby prior to the return of the prisoner to the original place of imprisonment, such indictment, information or complaint shall not be of any further force or effect, and the court shall enter an order dismissing the same with prejudice.

(e) Any request for final disposition made by a prisoner pursuant to paragraph (a) hereof shall also be deemed to be a waiver of extradition with respect to any charge or proceeding contemplated thereby or included therein by reason of paragraph (d) hereof, and a waiver of extradition to the receiving state to serve any sentence there imposed upon him, after completion of his term of imprisonment in the sending state. The request for final disposition shall also constitute a consent by the prisoner to the production of his body in any court where his presence may be required in order to effectuate the purposes of this agreement and a further consent voluntarily to be returned to the original place of imprisonment in accordance with the provisions of this agreement. Nothing in this paragraph shall prevent the imposition of a concurrent sentence if otherwise permitted by law.

(f) Escape from custody by the prisoner subsequent to his execution of the request for final disposition referred to in paragraph (a) hereof shall void the request.

Article IV

(a) The appropriate officer of the jurisdiction in which an untried indictment, information or complaint is pending shall be entitled to have a prisoner against whom he has lodged a detainer and who is serving a term of imprisonment in any party state made available in accordance with Article V(a) hereof upon presentation of a written request for temporary custody or availability to the appropriate authorities of the state in which the prisoner is incarcerated: provided that the court having jurisdiction of such indictment, information or complaint shall have duly approved, recorded and transmitted the request: and provided further that there shall be a period of thirty days after receipt by the appropriate authorities before the request be honored, within which period the governor of the sending state may disapprove the request for temporary custody or availability, either upon his own motion or upon motion of the prisoner.

(b) Upon receipt of the officer's written request as provided in paragraph (a) hereof, the appropriate authorities having the prisoner in custody shall furnish the officer with a certificate stating the term of commitment under which the prisoner is being held, the time already served, the time remaining to be served on the sentence, the amount of good time earned, the time of parole eligibility of the prisoner, and any decisions of the state parole agency relating to the prisoner. Said authorities simultaneously shall furnish all other officers and appropriate courts in the receiving state who have lodged detainers against the prisoner with similar certificates and with notices informing them of the request for custody or availability and of the reasons therefor.

(c) In respect of any proceeding made possible by this Article, trial shall be commenced within one hundred twenty days of the arrival of the prisoner in the receiving state, but for good cause shown in open court, the prisoner or his counsel being present, the court having jurisdiction of the matter may grant any necessary or reasonable continuance.

(d) Nothing contained in this Article shall be construed to deprive any prisoner of any right which he may have to contest the legality of his delivery as provided in paragraph (a) hereof, but such delivery may not be opposed or denied on the ground that the

© 1992 by J., B. & L. Gould
Printed in the U.S.A.   EP

executive authority of the sending state has not affirmatively consented to or ordered such delivery.

(e) If trial is not had on any indictment, information or complaint contemplated hereby prior to the prisoner's being returned to the original place of imprisonment pursuant to Article V(e) hereof, such indictment, information or complaint shall not be of any further force or effect, and the court shall enter an order dismissing the same with prejudice.

Article V

(a) In response to a request made under Article III or Article IV hereof, the appropriate authority in a sending state shall offer to deliver temporary custody of such prisoner to the appropriate authority in the state where such indictment, information or complaint is pending against such person in order that speedy and efficient prosecution may be had. If the request for final disposition is made by the prisoner, the offer of temporary custody shall accompany the written notice provided for in Article III of this agreement. In the case of a federal prisoner, the appropriate authority in the receiving state shall be entitled to temporary custody as provided by this agreement or to the prisoner's presence in federal custody at the place for trial, whichever custodial arrangement may be approved by the custodian.

(b) The officer or other representative of a state accepting an offer of temporary custody shall present the following upon demand:

(1) Proper identification and evidence of his authority to act for the state into whose temporary custody the prisoner is to be given.

(2) A duly certified copy of the indictment, information or complaint on the basis of which the detainer has been lodged and on the basis of which the request for temporary custody of the prisoner has been made.

(c) If the appropriate authority shall refuse or fail to accept temporary custody of said person, or in the event that an action on the indictment, information or complaint on the basis of which the detainer has been lodged is not brought to trial within the period provided in Article III or Article IV hereof, the appropriate court of the jurisdiction where the indictment, information or complaint has been pending shall enter an order dismissing the same with prejudice, and any detainer based thereon shall cease to be of any force or effect.

(d) The temporary custody referred to in this agreement shall be only for the purpose of permitting prosecution on the charge or charges contained in one or more untried indictments, informations or complaints which form the basis of the detainer or detainers or for prosecution on any other charge or charges arising out of the same transaction. Except for his attendance at court and while being transported to or from any place at which his presence may be required, the prisoner shall be held in a suitable jail or other facility regularly used for persons awaiting prosecution.

(e) At the earliest practicable time consonant with the purposes of this agreement, the prisoner shall be returned to the sending state.

(f) During the continuance of temporary custody or while the prisoner is otherwise being made available for trial as required by this agreement, time being served on the sentence shall continue to run but good time shall be earned by the prisoner only if, and to the extent that, the law and practice of the jurisdiction which imposed the sentence may allow.

(g) For all purposes other than that for which temporary custody as provided in this agreement is exercised, the prisoner shall be deemed to remain in the custody of and subject to the jurisdiction of the sending state and any escape from temporary custody may be dealt with in the same manner as an escape from the original place of imprisonment or in any other manner permitted by law.

(h) From the time that a party state receives custody of a prisoner pursuant to this agreement until such prisoner is returned to the territory and custody of the sending state, the state in which the one or more untried indictments, informations or complaints are pending or in which trial is being had shall be responsible for the prisoner and shall also pay all costs of transporting, caring for, keeping and returning the prisoner. The provisions of this paragraph shall govern unless the states concerned shall have entered into a supplementary agreement providing for a different allocation of costs and responsibilities as between or among themselves. Nothing herein contained shall be construed to alter or affect any internal relationship among the departments, agencies and officers of and in the government of a party state, or between a party state and its subdivisions, as to the payment of costs, or responsibilities therefor.

Article VI

(a) In determining the duration and expiration dates of the time periods provided in Articles III and IV of this agreement, the running of said time periods shall be tolled whenever and for as long as the prisoner is unable to stand trial, as determined by the court having jurisdiction of the matter.

(b) No provision of this agreement, and no remedy made available by this agreement, shall apply to any person who is adjudged to be mentally ill.

Article VII

Each state party to this agreement shall designate an officer who, acting jointly with like officers of other party states, shall promulgate rules and regulations to carry out more effectively the terms and provisions of this agreement, and who shall provide, within and without the state, information necessary to the effective operation of this agreement.

Article VIII

This agreement shall enter into full force and effect as to a party state when such state has enacted the same into law. A state party to this agreement may withdraw herefrom by enacting a statute repealing the same. However, the withdrawal of any state shall not affect the status of any proceedings already initiated by inmates or by state officers at the time such withdrawal takes effect, nor shall it affect their rights in respect thereof.

Article IX

This agreement shall be liberally construed so as to effectuate its purposes. The provisions of this agreement shall be severable and if any phrase, clause, sentence or provision of this agreement is declared to be contrary to the constitution of any party state or of the United States or the applicability thereof to any government, agency, person or circumstance is held invalid, the validity of the remainder of this agreement and the applicability thereof to any government, agency, person or circumstance shall not be affected

© 1992 by J., B. & L. Gould
Printed in the U.S.A. **EP**

thereby. If this agreement shall be held contrary to the constitution of any state party hereto, the agreement shall remain in full force and effect as to the remaining states and in full force and effect as to the state affected as to all severable matters.

§1389.1. Appropriate court defined.

The phrase "appropriate court" as used in the agreement on detainers shall, with reference to the courts of this State, mean the court in which the indictment, information, or complaint is filed.

§1389.2. Enforcement.

All courts, departments, agencies, officers, and employees of this State and its political subdivisions are hereby directed to enforce the agreement on detainer and to co-operate with one another and with other states in enforcing the agreement and effectuating its purpose.

§1389.4. Violation of §4530.

Every person who has been imprisoned in a prison or institution in this State and who escapes while in the custody of an officer of this or another state in another state pursuant to the agreement on detainers is deemed to have violated Section 4530 and is punishable as provided therein.

§1389.5. Duty of warden.

It shall be lawful and mandatory upon the warden or other official in charge of a penal or correctional institution in this State to give over the person of any inmate thereof whenever so required by the operation of the agreement on detainer. Such official shall inform such inmate of his rights provided in paragraph (a) of Article IV of the Agreement on Detainers in Section 1389 of this code.

§1389.6. Who administers.

The Administrator, Interstate Probation and Parole Compacts, shall administer this agreement.

§1389.7. Cooperation on term-fixing and parole.

When, pursuant to the agreement on detainers or other provision of law, a person in actual confinement under sentence of another jurisdiction is brought before a California court and sentenced by the judge to serve a California sentence concurrently with the sentence of the other jurisdiction or has been transferred to another jurisdiction for concurrent service of previously imposed sentences, the Board of Prison Terms, and the panels and members thereof, may meet in such other jurisdiction, or enter into cooperative arrangements with corresponding agencies in the other jurisdiction, as necessary to carry out the term-fixing and parole functions.

§1389.8. Return of prisoner to sending state.

It shall be the responsibility of the agent of the receiving state to return the prisoner to the sending state upon completion of the proceedings.

CHAPTER 9

PROCEEDINGS AGAINST CORPORATIONS

§1390. Summons issuance upon accusatory pleading.

Upon the filing of an accusatory pleading against a corporation, the court shall issue a summons, signed by the judge with his name of office, requiring the corporation to appear before him, at a specified time and place, to answer the charge, the time to be not less than 10 days after the issuing of the summons.

§1391. Form of summons.

The summons shall be substantially in the following form:

County of (as the case may be).

The people of the State of California to the (naming the corporation):

You are hereby summoned to appear before me at (naming the place), on (specifying the day and hour), to answer an accusatory pleading, for (designating the offense generally).

Dated this _____ day of _____ , 19 _

G. H., Judge, (name of the court).

§1392. Service of summons.

The summons must be served at least five days before the day of appearance fixed therein, by delivering a copy thereof and showing the original to the president or other head of the corporation, or to the secretary, cashier, managing agent, or an agent of the corporation designated for service of civil process.

§1393. Proceedings; time and manner.

At the appointed time in the summons, the magistrate shall proceed with the charge in the same manner as in other cases.

§1396. Appearance by counsel.

If an accusatory pleading is filed, the corporation may appear by counsel to answer the same, except that in the case of misdemeanors arising from operation of motor vehicles, or of infractions arising from operation of motor vehicles, a corporation may appear by its president, vice president, secretary or managing agent for the purpose of entering a plea of guilty. If it does not thus appear, a plea of not guilty shall be entered, and the same proceedings had thereon as in other cases.

§1397. Fine on conviction, how collected.

When a fine is imposed upon a corporation on conviction, it may be collected by virtue of the order imposing it in the manner provided for enforcement of money judgments generally.

CHAPTER 10

ENTITLING AFFIDAVITS

§1401. Necessity.

It is not necessary to entitle an affidavit or deposition in the action, whether taken before or after indictment or information, or upon an appeal; but if made without a title, or with an erroneous title, it is as valid and effectual for every purpose as if it were duly entitled, if it intelligibly refer to the proceeding, indictment, information, or appeal in which it is made.

CHAPTER 11

ERRORS AND MISTAKES IN PLEADINGS AND OTHER PROCEEDINGS

§1404. When not material.

Neither a departure from the form or mode prescribed by this Code in respect to any pleading or

© 1992 by J., B. & L. Gould
Printed in the U.S.A.   EP

proceeding, nor an error or mistake therein, renders it invalid, unless it has actually prejudiced the defendant, or tended to his prejudice, in respect to a substantial right.

CHAPTER 12

DISPOSAL OF PROPERTY STOLEN OR EMBEZZLED

§1407. Holding in custody by peace officer.

When property, alleged to have been stolen or embezzled, comes into the custody of a peace officer, he shall hold it subject to the provisions of this chapter relating to the disposal thereof.

§1408. Return to owner; demand and receipt.

On the application of the owner and on satisfactory proof of his ownership of the property, after reasonable notice and opportunity to be heard has been given to the person from whom custody of the property was taken and any other person as required by the magistrate, the magistrate before whom the complaint is laid, or who examines the charge against the person accused of stealing or embezzling it, shall order it to be delivered, without prejudice to the state, to the owner, on his paying the necessary expenses incurred in its preservation, to be certified by the magistrate. The order entitles the owner to demand and receive the property.

§1409. Return to owner if in custody of magistrate.

If property stolen or embezzled comes into the custody of the magistrate, it shall be delivered, without prejudice to the state, to the owner upon his application to the court and on satisfactory proof of his title, after reasonable notice and opportunity to be heard has been given to the person from whom custody of the property was taken and any other person as required by the magistrate, and on his paying the necessary expenses incurred in its preservation, to be certified by the magistrate.

§1410. Return to owner by court.

If the property stolen or embezzled has not been delivered to the owner, the court before which a trial is had for stealing or embezzling it, upon the application of the owner to the court and on proof of his title, after reasonable notice and opportunity to be heard has been given to the person from whom custody of the property was taken and any other person as required by the court, may order it to be restored to the owner without prejudice to the state.

§1411. Unclaimed stolen property disposition.

If the ownership of the property stolen or embezzled and the address of the owner, and the address of the owner of a security interest therein, can be reasonably ascertained, the peace officer who took custody of the property shall notify the owner, and a person having a security interest therein, by letter of the location of the property and the method by which the owner may obtain it. This notice shall be given upon the conviction of a person for an offense involving the theft, embezzlement, or possession of the property, or if a conviction was not obtained, upon the making of a decision by the district attorney not to file the case or upon the termination of the proceedings in the case. Except as provided in Section 217 of the Welfare and Institutions Code, if the property stolen or embezzled is not claimed by the owner before the expiration of three months after the giving of this notice, or, in any case in which such a notice is not given, before the expiration of six months from the conviction of a person for an offense involving the theft, embezzlement, or possession of the property, or if a conviction was not obtained, then from the time the property came into the possession of the peace officer or the case involving the person from whom it was obtained is disposed of, whichever is later, the magistrate or other officer having it in custody may, on the payment of the necessary expenses incurred in its preservation, deliver it to the county treasurer or other proper county officer, by whom it shall be sold and the proceeds paid into the county treasury. However, notwithstanding any other provision of law, if the person from whom custody of the property was taken is a secondhand dealer or licensed pawnbroker and reasonable but unsuccessful efforts have been made to notify the owner of the property and the property is no longer needed for the criminal proceeding, the property shall be returned to the secondhand dealer or pawnbroker who had custody of the property and be treated as regularly acquired property. If the property is transferred to the county purchasing agent it may be sold in the manner provided by Article 7 (commencing with Section 25500) of Chapter 5 of Part 2 of Division 2 of Title 3 of the Government Code for the sale of surplus personal property. If the county officer determines that any of the property transferred to him or her for sale is needed for a public use, the property may be retained by the county and need not be sold. The magistrate or other officer having the property in custody may, however, provide for the sale of the property in the manner provided for the sale of unclaimed property which has been held for at least three months pursuant to Section 2080.4 of the Civil Code. *(Amended by Stats 1987 ch 828 §94.)*

§1412. Receipt by officers for money, etc., taken from a person arrested for a public offense.

When money or other property is taken from a defendant, arrested upon a charge of a public offense, the officer taking it must at the time give duplicate receipts therefor, specifying particularly the amount of money or the kind of property taken; one of which receipts he must deliver to the defendant and the other of which he must forthwith file with the Clerk of the Court to which the depositions and statement are to be sent. When such property is taken by a police officer of any incorporated city or town, he must deliver one of the receipts to the defendant, and one, with the property, at once to the Clerk or other person in charge of the police-office in such city or town.

§1413. Police property clerk's duties.

(a) The clerk or person having charge of the property section for any police department in any incorporated city or town, or for any sheriff's department in any county, shall enter in a suitable book a description of every article of property alleged to be stolen or embezzled, and brought into the office or taken from the person of a prisoner, and shall attach a number to each article, and make a corresponding entry thereof. He may engrave or imbed an identification number in property described in Section 537e for the purposes thereof.

(b) The clerk or person in charge of the property section may, upon satisfactory proof of the ownership of property held pursuant to Section 1407, and upon presentation of proper personal identification, deliver it to the owner. Such delivery shall be without prejudice to the state or to the person from whom custody of the property was taken or to any other person who may have a claim against the property. Prior to such delivery such clerk or person in charge of the property section shall make and retain a complete photographic record of such property. The person to whom property is delivered shall sign, under penalty of perjury, a declaration of ownership, which shall be retained by the clerk or person in charge of the property section. This subdivision shall not apply to any property subject to forfeiture under any provision of law. This subdivision shall not apply unless the clerk or person in charge of the property section has served upon the person from whom custody of the property was taken a notice of a claim of ownership and a copy of the satisfactory proof of ownership tendered and has allowed such person reasonable opportunity to be heard as to why the property should not be delivered to the person claiming ownership.

If the person upon whom a notice of claim and proof of ownership has been served does not respond asserting a claim to the property within 15 days from the date of receipt of the service, the property may be disposed of in a manner not inconsistent with the provisions of this section.

(c) The magistrate before whom the complaint is laid, or who examines the charge against the person accused of stealing or embezzling the property, or the court before which a trial is had for stealing or embezzling it, shall upon application by the person from whom custody of the property was taken, review the determination of the clerk or person in charge of the property section, and may order the property taken into the custody of the court upon a finding that the person to whom the property was delivered is not entitled thereto. Such court shall make its determination in the same manner as a determination is made when the matter is before the court pursuant to Sections 1408 to 1410, inclusive.

(d) The clerk or person in charge of the property section is not liable in damages for any official action performed hereunder in good faith.

CHAPTER 13

DISPOSITION OF EVIDENCE IN CRIMINAL CASES
(Added by Stats 1985 ch 875 §3.)

§1417. Procedure.

All exhibits which have been introduced or filed in any criminal action or proceeding shall be retained by the clerk of the court who shall establish a procedure to account for the exhibits properly, subject to Sections 1417.2 and 1417.3 until final determination of the action or proceedings and the exhibits shall thereafter be distributed or disposed of as provided in this chapter. *(Amended by Stats 1990 ch 382 §3, eff. 1/1/91.)*

§1417.1. No order for destruction of exhibit until final determination of action or proceeding.

No order shall be made for the destruction of an exhibit prior to the final determination of the action or proceeding. For the purposes of this chapter, the date when a criminal action or proceeding becomes final is as follows:

(a) When no notice of appeal is filed, 30 days after the last day for filing that notice.

(b) When a notice of appeal is filed, 30 days after the date the clerk of the court receives the remittitur affirming the judgment.

(c) When an order for a rehearing, a new trial, or other proceeding is granted and the ordered proceedings have not been commenced within one year thereafter, one year after the date of that order.

(d) In cases where the death penalty is imposed, 30 days after the date of execution of sentence. *(Added by Stats 1985 ch 875 §3.)*

§1417.2. Delivery of exhibit prior to the final determination of action or proceeding.

Notwithstanding Section 1417.5, the court may, on application of the party entitled thereto or an agent designated in writing by the owner, order an exhibit delivered to that party at any time prior to the final determination of the action or proceeding, upon stipulation of the parties or upon notice and motion if both of the following requirements are met:

(a) No prejudice will be suffered by either party.

(b) A full and complete photographic record is made of the exhibits so released.

The party to whom the exhibit is being returned shall provide the photographic record. This section shall not apply to any material, the release of which is prohibited by Section 1417.6. *(Added by Stats 1985 ch 875 §3.)*

§1417.3. Return of exhibit to state.

(a) At any time prior to the final determination of the action or proceeding, exhibits offered by the state or defendant shall be returned to the party offering them by order of the court when an exhibit poses a security, storage, or safety problem, as recommended by the clerk of the court. If an exhibit by its nature is severable the court shall order the clerk to retain a portion of the exhibit not exceeding three pounds by weight or one cubic foot by volume and shall order the return of the balance of the exhibit to the district attorney. The clerk, upon court order, shall substitute a full and complete photographic record of any exhibit or part of any exhibit returned to the state under this section. The party to whom the exhibit is being returned shall provide the photographic record.

(b) Exhibits toxic by their nature that pose a health hazard to humans shall be introduced to the court in the form of a photographic record and a written chemical analysis certified by competent authority. Where the court finds that good cause exists to depart from this procedure, toxic exhibits may be brought into the courtroom and introduced. However, following introduction of the exhibit, the person or persons previously in possession of the exhibit shall take responsibility for it and the court shall not be required to store the exhibit. *(Amended by Stats 1990 ch 382 §4, eff. 1/1/91.)*

§1417.5. Disposal of all exhibits.

Except as provided in Section 1417.6, 60 days after the final determination of a criminal action or proceeding, the clerk of the court shall dispose of all exhibits introduced or filed in the case and remaining in the clerk's possession, as follows:

372

© 1992 by J., B. & L. Gould
Printed in the U.S.A.　**EP**

(a) The court shall, on application of the owner or any person entitled to possession of the exhibits or an agent designated in writing by the owner, order the release of any exhibits that will not prejudice the state.

(b) If the party entitled to an exhibit fails to apply for the return of the exhibit prior to the date for disposition under this section, the following procedures shall apply:

(1) Exhibits of stolen or embezzled property, other than money shall be disposed of pursuant to court order as provided in Section 1417.6.

(2) Exhibits of property other than property which is stolen or embezzled or property which consists of money or currency shall, except as otherwise provided in this paragraph and in paragraph (3), be transferred to the appropriate county agency for sale to the public in the same manner provided by Article 7 (commencing with Section 25500) of Chapter 5 of Part 2 of Division 2 of Title 3 of the Government Code for the sale of surplus personal property. If the county determines that any property is needed for a public use, the property may be retained by the county and need not be sold.

(3) Exhibits of property, other than money, currency, or stolen or embezzled property, that are determined by the court to have no value at public sale shall be destroyed or otherwise disposed of pursuant to court order.

(4) Exhibits of money or currency shall be disposed of pursuant to Section 1420. *(Amended by Stats 1986 ch 734 §2.)*

§1417.6. Instruments used in the commission of crime.

The provisions of Section 1417.5 shall not apply to any dangerous or deadly weapons, narcotic or poisonous drugs, explosives, or any property of any kind or character whatsoever the possession of which is prohibited by law and which was used by a defendant in the commission of the crime of which the defendant was convicted, or with which the defendant was armed or which the defendant had upon his or her person at the time of the defendant's arrest.

Any of this property introduced or filed as an exhibit shall be, by order of the trial court, destroyed or otherwise disposed of under the conditions provided in the order no sooner than 60 days following the final determination of the criminal action or proceeding. *(Added by Stats 1985 ch 875 §3.)*

§1417.7. Proposed disposition of an exhibit.

Not less than 15 days before any proposed disposition of an exhibit pursuant to Section 1417.3, 1417.5, or 1417.6, the court shall notify the district attorney (or other prosecuting attorney), the attorney of record for each party, and each party who is not represented by counsel of the proposed disposition. Before the disposition, any party, at his or her own expense, may cause to be prepared a photographic record of all or part of the exhibit by a person who is not a party or attorney of a party. The clerk of the court shall observe the taking of the photographic record and, upon receipt of a declaration of the person making the photographic record that the copy and negative of the photograph delivered to the clerk is a true, unaltered, and unretouched print of the photographic record taken in the presence of the clerk and the clerk shall certify the photographic record as such without charge and retain it unaltered for a period of 60 days following

the final determination of the criminal action or proceeding. A certified photographic record of exhibits shall be deemed a certified copy of a writing in official custody pursuant to Section 1507 of the Evidence Code. *(Added by Stats 1985 ch 875 §3.)*

§§1418 to 1419. *Repealed by Stats 1985 ch 875.*

CHAPTER 14

DISPOSITION OF UNCLAIMED MONEY HELD BY DISTRICT ATTORNEY OR COURT CLERK

(Heading amended by Stats 1985 ch 875 §4.)

§1420. Deposit with county treasurer; notice.

All money received by a district attorney or clerk of the court in any criminal action or proceeding, the owner or owners of which are unknown, and which remains unclaimed in the possession of the district attorney or clerk of the court after final judgment in the criminal action or proceeding, shall be deposited with the county treasurer. Upon the expiration of two years after the deposit, the county treasurer shall cause a notice pursuant to Section 1421 to be published in the county once a week for two successive weeks in a newspaper of general circulation published in the county. *(Amended by Stats 1985 ch 875 §5.)*

§1421. Notice contents.

The notice shall state the amount of money, the criminal action or proceeding in which the money was received by the district attorney or clerk of the court, the fund in which it is held and that it is proposed that the money will become the property of the county on a designated date not less than 45 days nor more than 60 days after the first publication of the notice. *(Amended by Stats 1985 ch 875 §6.)*

§1422. Transfer to general fund.

Unless some person files a verified complaint seeking to recover all, or a designated part, of the money in a court of competent jurisdiction within the county in which the notice is published, and serves a copy of the complaint and the summons issued thereon upon the county treasurer before the date designated in the notice, upon that date the money becomes the property of the county and shall be transferred by the treasurer to the general fund.

CHAPTER 15

DISQUALIFICATION OF PROSECUTING ATTORNEYS

§1424. Notice of motion; hearing.

Notice of any motion to disqualify a district attorney from performing any authorized duty shall be served on the district attorney and the Attorney General at least 10 days before the motion is heard. The notice of motion must set forth a statement of the facts relevant to the claimed disqualification and the legal authorities relied upon by the moving party. The Attorney General may appear at the hearing on the motion and may file with the court hearing the motion a written opinion on the disqualification issue. The motion shall not be granted unless it is shown by the evidence that a conflict of interest exists such as would render it unlikely that the defendant would receive a fair trial. An order recusing the district attorney from any proceeding may be appealed by the district attorney or the Attorney General. The order recusing the district attorney shall be stayed pending any appeal authorized by this section.

An appeal from an order of recusal from a superior court or from a case involving any charges punishable as a felony shall be made pursuant to Chapter 1 (commencing with Section 1235) of Title 9, regardless of the court in which the order is made. An appeal from an order of recusal in a misdemeanor case shall be made pursuant to Chapter 2 (commencing with Section 1466) of Title 11. *(Amended by Stats 1988 ch 527 §2, eff. 1/1/89.)*

TITLE 11

PROCEEDINGS IN INFERIOR COURTS AND APPEALS FROM SUCH COURTS

CHAPTER 1

PROCEEDINGS IN INFERIOR COURTS

§1427. Issuance of arrest warrant; form.

(a) When a complaint is presented to a judge of an inferior court of the commission of a public offense appearing to be triable in his court, he must, if satisfied therefrom that the offense complained of has been committed and that there is reasonable ground to believe that the defendant has committed it, issue a warrant, for the arrest of the defendant.

(b) Such warrant of arrest and proceedings upon it shall be in conformity to the provisions of this code regarding warrants of arrest, and it may be in the following form:
County of ____
The people of the State of California, to any peace officer in this state:
Complaint upon oath having been this day made before me that the offense of ____ (designating it generally) has been committed and accusing ____ (name of defendant) thereof you are therefore commanded forthwith to arrest the above-named defendant and bring him forthwith before the ____ court of ____ (stating full title of court) at ____ (naming place).
Witness my hand and the seal of said court this ____ day of ____ , 19 ___.

(Signed)

_____
Judge of said court

If it appears that the offense complained of has been committed by a corporation, no warrant of arrest shall issue, but the judge must issue a summons substantially in the form prescribed in Section 1391. Such summons must be served at the time and in the manner designated in Section 1392 except that if the offense complained of is a violation of the Vehicle Code or a local ordinance adopted pursuant to the Vehicle Code, such summons may be served by deposit by the clerk of the court in the United States mail of an envelope enclosing the summons, which envelope shall be addressed to a person authorized to accept service of legal process on behalf of the defendant, and which envelope shall be mailed by registered mail or certified mail with a return receipt requested. Promptly upon such mailing, the clerk of the court shall execute a certificate of such mailing and place it in the file of the court for that case. At the time stated in the summons the corporation may appear by counsel and answer the complaint, except that in the case of misdemeanors arising from operation of motor vehicles, or of infractions arising from operation of motor vehicles, a corporation may appear by its president, vice president, secretary or managing agent for the purpose of entering a plea of guilty. If it does not appear, a plea of not guilty shall be entered, and the same proceedings had therein as in other cases.

§1428. Docket entries.

A docket must be kept by the judge or clerk of each justice court and by the clerk of each municipal court having jurisdiction of criminal actions or proceedings, in which must be entered the title of each criminal action or proceeding and under each title all the orders and proceedings in such action or proceeding. Wherever by any other section of this code made applicable to such courts an entry of any judgment, order or other proceeding in the minutes is required, an entry thereof in the docket shall be made and shall be deemed a sufficient entry in the minutes for all purposes.

§1429. Procedure on guilty plea; misdemeanor cases.

In the case of a misdemeanor triable in any inferior court the plea of the defendant may be made by said defendant or by his counsel. If such defendant pleads guilty, the court may, before entering such plea or pronouncing judgment, examine witnesses to ascertain the gravity of the offense committed; and if it appear to the court that a higher offense has been committed than the offense charged in the complaint, the court may order the defendant to be committed or admitted to bail, to answer any indictment which may be found against him by the grand jury, or any complaint which may be filed charging him with such higher offense.

§1429.5. Procedure on plea of not guilty by reason of insanity; misdemeanor cases.

When a defendant pleads not guilty by reason of insanity to a misdemeanor charge, and also joins with it another plea or pleas, he shall first be tried as if he had entered such other plea or pleas only, and in such trial he shall be conclusively presumed to have been sane at the time the offense is alleged to have been committed. If the defendant shall be found guilty, or if the defendant pleads only not guilty by reason of insanity, then the defendant shall be certified to the superior court of the county for prompt trial to determine the question whether the defendant was sane or insane at the time the offense was committed. The superior court shall proceed as provided in Sections 1026 and 1027. If the verdict or finding be that the defendant was sane at the time the offense was committed the superior court shall remand the defendant to the court from which he was certified which court shall sentence the defendant as provided by law. If the verdict or finding be that the defendant was insane at the time the offense was committed the superior court shall proceed as provided in Section 1026.

§1430. *Repealed by Initiative Measure, Prop 115 §27, approved 6/5/90.*

§1445. Rendering judgment.

When the defendant pleads guilty, or is convicted, either by the court, or by a jury, the court shall render

© 1992 by J., B. & L. Gould
Printed in the U.S.A.   EP

judgment thereon of fine or imprisonment, or both, as the case may be. (*Amended by Stats 1989 ch 1360 §117, eff. 1/1/90.*)

§1447. Malicious prosecution; costs.

When the defendant is acquitted in an inferior court, if the court certify in the minutes that the prosecution was malicious and without probable cause, the court may order the complainant to pay the costs of the action, or to give an undertaking to pay the costs within 30 days after the trial.

§1448. Judgment against complainant for costs.

If the complainant does not pay the costs, or give an undertaking therefor, the court may enter judgment against the complainant for the amount of the costs, which may be enforced in the manner provided for enforcement of money judgments generally.

§1449. Pronouncing judgments; extensions.

In inferior courts, after a plea, finding or verdict of guilty, or after a finding or verdict against the defendant on a plea of former conviction or acquittal, or once in jeopardy, the court must appoint a time for pronouncing judgment which must not be less than six hours, nor more than five days, after the verdict or plea of guilty, unless the defendant waives the postponement; provided, however, that the court may extend the time not more than 10 days for the purpose of hearing or determining any motion for a new trial, or in arrest of judgment; and provided further, that the court may extend the time not more than 21 days in any case where the question of probation is considered; provided, however, that upon request of the defendant or the probation officer such time may be further extended not more than 90 days additional. In case of postponement, the court may hold the defendant to bail to appear for judgment. If in the opinion of the court there is a reasonable ground for believing a defendant insane, the court may extend the time of pronouncing judgment and may commit the defendant to custody until the question of insanity has been heard and determined.

In the event that the defendant is a veteran who was discharged from service for mental disability, upon his request his case shall be referred to the probation officer, who shall secure a military medical history of such defendant and present it to the court together with his recommendation for or against probation.

§1457. Defendant discharged upon payment of fine.

Upon payment of the fine, the officer must discharge the defendant, if he is not detained for any other legal cause, and pay over the fine to the court which rendered the judgment.

§1458. Undertaking of bail; form.

The provisions of this code relative to bail are applicable to bail in cases triable in inferior courts. The defendant, at any time after his arrest and before conviction, may be admitted to bail. The undertaking of bail in such a case shall be in substantially the following form:

A complaint having been filed on the __ day of ___, 19____, in the _____ Court of _____ County of _____ (stating title and location of court) charging _____ (naming defendant) as defendant with the crime of _____ (designating it generally) and he having been admitted to bail in the sum of ___ dollars ($___) (stating amount);

We, ____ and ___, of ___ (stating their places of residence and occupation), hereby undertake that the above-named defendant will appear and answer any charge in any accusatory pleading based upon the acts supporting the complaint above mentioned and all duly authorized amendments thereof, in whatever court it may be prosecuted, and will at all times hold himself amenable to the orders and process of the court, and, if convicted, will appear for pronouncement of judgment or grant of probation or if he fails to perform either of these conditions, that we will pay to the people of the State of California the sum of ____ dollars ($__) (inserting the sum in which the defendant is admitted to bail). If the forfeiture of this bond is ordered by the court, judgment may be summarily made and entered forthwith against the said ____ (naming the sureties and the defendant if he is a party to the bond) for the amount of their respective undertakings herein, as provided by Sections 1305 and 1306 of the California Penal Code.

§1459. Undertakings of bail by admitted surety insurers; form.

Undertakings of bail filed in inferior courts by admitted surety insurers shall meet all other requirements of law and the obligation of the insurer shall be in the following form:

_____ (stating the title and the location of the court).

Defendant ___ (stating the name of the defendant) having been admitted to bail in the sum of ___ dollars ($__) (stating the amount of bail fixed) and ordered to appear in the above-entitled court on ___, 19__ (stating the date for appearance in court), on _____ (stating only the word "misdemeanor" or the word "felony") charge/s;

Now, the ____ (stating the name of admitted surety insurer and state of incorporation) hereby undertakes that the above-named defendant will appear in the above-named court on the date above set forth to answer any charge in any accusatory pleading based upon the acts supporting the complaint filed against him/her and all duly authorized amendments thereof, in whatever court it may be prosecuted, and will at all times hold him/herself amenable to the orders and process of the court and, if convicted, will appear for pronouncement of judgment or grant of probation or if he/she fails to perform either of these conditions, that the ___ (stating the name of admitted surety insurer and state of incorporation) will pay to the people of the State of California the sum of __ dollars ($__) (stating the amount of the undertaking of the admitted surety insurer).

If the forfeiture of this bond be ordered by the court, judgment may be summarily made and entered forthwith against the said ____ (stating the name of admitted surety insurer and state of incorporation) for the amount of its undertaking herein, as provided by Sections 1305 and 1306 of the California Penal Code.

Stating the name of admitted surety insurer and state of incorporation),
(Signature)
By _____
Attorney in fact
(Corporate seal)

© 1992 by J., B. & L. Gould
Printed in the U.S.A. **EP**

(Jurat of notary public or other officer authorized to administer oaths.)

§1462. Criminal case jurisdiction.

(a) Each municipal and justice court shall have jurisdiction in all criminal cases amounting to misdemeanor, where the offense charged was committed within the county in which the municipal or justice court is established except those of which the juvenile court is given jurisdiction and those of which other courts are given exclusive jurisdiction. Each municipal and justice court shall have exclusive jurisdiction in all cases involving the violation of ordinances of cities or towns situated within the district in which the court is established.

(b) Each municipal and justice court shall have jurisdiction in all noncapital criminal cases to receive a plea of guilty or nolo contendere, appoint a time for pronouncing judgment under Section 859a, pronounce judgment, and refer the case to the probation officer if eligible for probation.

(c) The superior courts shall have jurisdiction in all misdemeanor criminal cases to receive a plea of guilty or nolo contendere, appoint a time for pronouncing judgment, and pronounce judgment. *(Amended by Stats 1991 ch 613 §8, eff. 1/1/92.)*

§1462.1. Same and concurrent jurisdiction.

The jurisdiction of the municipal and justice courts is the same and concurrent.

§1462.2. Proper court for trial of misdemeanor criminal cases.

Except as otherwise provided in the Vehicle Code, the proper court for the trial of criminal cases amounting to misdemeanor shall be determined as follows: Any municipal or justice court, having jurisdiction of the subject matter of the case, established in the county within which the offense charged was committed, is the proper court for the trial of the case; otherwise, the court having jurisdiction of the subject matter, nearest to the place where the offense was committed, is the proper court for the trial of the case.

If an action or proceeding is commenced in a court having jurisdiction of the subject matter thereof other than the court herein designated as the proper court for the trial, the action may, notwithstanding, be tried in the court where commenced, unless the defendant, at the time he pleads, requests an order transferring the action or proceeding to the proper court. If after such request it appears that the action or proceeding was not commenced in the proper court, the court shall order the action or proceeding transferred to the proper court. The judge must, at the time of arraignment, inform the defendant of his right to be tried in the district wherein the offense was committed.

§1462.3. Disposition of fines.

Notwithstanding any other provision of law, a municipal or justice court shall authorize the following entities upon request to receive, deposit, accept forfeiture, and otherwise process the posting of bail for state and local parking violations issued by an employee or agent of the California State University, the University of California, the California Department of Parks and Recreation, the California State Police, the California Exposition and State Fair, the Department of Forestry and Fire Protection or any jurisdiction that provides fire protection for the department by contract, a community college district, a regional park district, a park and recreation district, a municipal utility district, a police protection district, a community service district, a transit district, a school district, a port district, a harbor district, a metropolitan development board, a fire protection district, a bridge and highway district, or a housing authority. Any entity which maintains an administrative appeals process for the review of all contested violations it has issued shall transfer, once a month, an amount equal to 5 percent of the amounts deposited directly with the entity, to the general fund of the county. Any entity which does not maintain an administrative appeals process for the review of all contested violations it has issued shall transfer, once a month, an amount equal to 15 percent of the amounts deposited directly with the entity, to the general fund of the county.

Where such an entity and a municipal or justice court have, prior to June 1, 1991, entered into an agreement governing the distribution of revenue from parking penalties, those agreements shall remain in full force and effect until changed by mutual agreement.

If the authorization is sought by the California State University or any campus thereof to receive, deposit, accept forfeiture, and otherwise process the posting of bail for state and local parking violations issued by their employee or agent, all parking fines and forfeitures collected pursuant to this section by or on behalf of the California State University or any campus thereof shall be deposited, once a month, to the State Treasury to the credit of the State University Parking Revenue Fund.

If authorization is not sought by an entity whose employees issue written notices of state and local parking violations, out of the moneys deposited with the county treasurer from the court's receipt, deposit, acceptance of forfeiture, and other processing of bail, 25 percent shall be transferred, once a month, to the General Fund of the state, with respect to state agencies, or to the general fund of the local entity with respect to a local entity issuing the written notice, or to the State Treasury to the credit of the State University Parking Revenue Fund with respect to the California State University, and the remainder shall be transferred to the county general fund. A municipal or justice court and an entity listed above may adjust the percentage herein by mutual agreement. *(Added by Stats 1991 ch 189 §16, eff. 7/29/91; amended by Stats 1991 ch 1168 §5, eff. 10/14/91.)*

§1462.5. Proration of installment or partial payment of fines.

Each installment or partial payment of a fine, penalty, forfeiture or fee shall be prorated among the state and local shares according to the uniform accounting system established by the State Controller pursuant to Section 71380 of the Government Code. In cases subject to Section 1463.18 of the Penal Code, proration shall not occur until the minimum amounts have been transferred to the Restitution Fund as provided in that section.

§1463. Disposition of fines and forfeitures.

All fines and forfeitures imposed and collected for crimes other than parking offenses shall be dis-

© 1992 by J., B. & L. Gould
Printed in the U.S.A.　**EP**

tributed in accordance with Section 1463.001. Fines and forfeitures imposed and collected for parking offenses shall be distributed as provided in Section 1463.009.

The following definitions shall apply to terms used in this chapter:

(a) "Arrest" means any law enforcement action, including issuance of a notice to appear or notice of violation, which results in a criminal charge.

(b) "City" includes any city, city and county, district, authority or other local agency (other than a county) which employs persons authorized to make arrests or to issue notices to appear, or notices of violation which may be filed in court.

(c) "City arrest" means an arrest by an employee of a city, or by a California Highway Patrol officer within the limits of a city.

(d) "County" means the county in which the arrest took place.

(e) "County arrest" means an arrest by a California Highway Patrol officer outside the limits of a city, or any arrest by a county officer or by any other state officer.

(f) "Court" means the superior, municipal, or justice court or a juvenile forum established under Section 257 of the Welfare and Institutions Code, in which the case arising from the arrest is filed.

(g) "Division of moneys" means an allocation of base fine proceeds between agencies as required by statute including, but not limited to, Sections 1463.003, 1463.9, 1463.23, 1463.26, and Sections 13001, 13002, and 13003 of the Fish and Game Code, and Section 11502 of the Health and Safety Code.

(h) "Offense" means any infraction, misdemeanor, or felony, and any act by a juvenile leading to an order to pay a financial sanction by reason of the act being defined as an infraction, misdemeanor, or felony, whether defined in this or any other code, except any parking offense as defined in subdivision (i).

(i) "Parking offense" means any offense charged pursuant to Article 3 (commencing with Section 40200) of Chapter 1 of Division 17 of the Vehicle Code, including registration and equipment offenses included on a notice of parking violation.

(j) "Penalty allocation" means the deposit of a specified part of moneys to offset designated processing costs, as provided by Section 1463.16 and by Section 68090.8 of the Government Code.

(k) "Total parking penalty" means the total sum to be collected for a parking offense, whether as fine, forfeiture of bail, or payment of penalty to the Department of Motor Vehicles. It may include the following components:

(1) The base parking penalty as established pursuant to Section 40203.5 of the Vehicle Code.

(2) The Department of Motor Vehicles (DMV) fees added upon the placement of a hold pursuant to Section 40220 of the Vehicle Code.

(3) The surcharges required by Section 76000 of the Government Code.

(4) The notice penalty added to the base parking penalty when a notice of delinquent parking violations is given.

(*l*) "Total fine or forfeiture" means the total sum to be collected upon a conviction, or the total amount of bail forfeited or deposited as cash bail subject to forfeiture. It may include, but is not limited to, the following components as specified for the particular offense:

(1) The "base fine" upon which the state penalty and additional county penalty is calculated.

(2) The "county penalty" required by Section 76000 of the Government Code.

(3) The "service charge" permitted by Section 853.7 of the Penal Code and Sections 40508.5 and 41103.5 of the Vehicle Code.

(4) The "special penalty" dedicated for blood alcohol analysis, alcohol program services, traumatic brain injury research, and similar purposes.

(5) The "state penalty" required by Section 1464. *(Added by Stats 1991 ch 189 §18, eff. 7/29/91. Former section 1463 amended by Stats 1991 ch 90 §26, eff. 6/30/91; repealed by Stats 1991 ch 189 §17, eff. 7/29/91.)*

§1463.001. Disposition of fines and forfeitures.

All fines and forfeitures imposed and collected for crimes other than parking offenses resulting from a filing in a court shall, as soon as practicable after receipt thereof, be deposited with the county treasurer, and each month the total fines and forfeitures which have accumulated within the past month shall be distributed, as follows:

(a) The state penalties, county penalties, special penalties, service charges, and penalty allocations shall be transferred to the proper funds as required by law.

(b) The base fines shall be distributed, as follows:

(1) Any base fines which are subject to specific distribution under any other section shall first be distributed to the specified funds of the state or local agency. Any amount due to the county, including amounts collected pursuant to Section 1203.1, but excluding fees to cover the actual cost of formal probation, shall be divided between the state and county, with 75 percent transferred to the General Fund and 25 percent transferred to the proper funds of the county, subject to the limitations established by Section 1463.003. Any amount due to cities shall be divided between each city and the state, with 50 percent deposited to the General Fund, and 50 percent deposited to the treasury of the appropriate city, subject to the limitations established by Section 1463.003.

(2) Of base fines resulting from county arrest not included in paragraph (1), 25 percent shall be transferred into the proper funds of the county, subject to the limitations established by Section 1463.003, and 75 percent shall be transferred to the General Fund.

(3) Of base fines resulting from city arrests not included in paragraph (1), an amount equal to the applicable county percentages set forth in Section 1463.002, as modified by Section 1463.28, shall be divided between the state and county, with 75 percent transferred to the General Fund and 25 percent transferred into the proper funds of the county, subject to the limitations established by Section 1463.003. The remainder of base fines resulting from city arrests shall be divided between each city and the state, with 50 percent deposited to the General Fund, and 50 percent deposited to the treasury of the appropriate city, subject to the limitations established by Section 1463.003.

(c) The distribution specified in subdivision (b) applies to all funds subject thereto distributed on or after July 1, 1991, regardless of whether the court has elected to allocate and distribute funds pursuant to Section 1464.8. *(Added by Stats 1991 ch 189 §19, eff. 7/29/91; amended by Stats 1991 ch 1168 §6, eff. 10/14/91.)*

§1463.002. Distribution of fines and forfeitures.

The base fine amounts from city arrests shall be subject to distribution according to the following schedule:

County and city	Percentage
Alameda	
Alameda	18
Albany	29
Berkeley	19
Emeryville	13
Hayward	10
Livermore	7
Oakland	22
Piedmont	44
Pleasanton	17
San Leandro	9
County percentage	21
Amador	
Amador	25
Ione	25
Jackson	25
Plymouth	25
Sutter Creek	25
County percentage	29
Butte	
Biggs	75
Chico	22
Gridley	49
Oroville	9
County percentage	20
Calaveras	
Angels	62
County percentage	62
Colusa	
Colusa	13
Williams	17
County percentage	16
Contra Costa	
Antioch	11
Brentwood	24
Concord	18
El Cerrito	19
Hercules	14
Martinez	22
Pinole	22
Pittsburg	5
Richmond	14
San Pablo	12
Walnut Creek	24
County percentage	14
Del Norte	
Crescent City	19
County percentage	19
El Dorado	
Placerville	14
County percentage	14
Fresno	
Clovis	23
Coalinga	21
Firebaugh	16
Fowler	34

County and city	Percentage
Fresno	26
Huron	24
Kerman	14
Kingsburg	34
Mendota	11
Orange Cove	24
Parlier	21
Reedley	30
Sanger	29
San Joaquin	15
Selma	14
County percentage	24
Glenn	
Orland	27
Willows	36
County percentage	32
Humboldt	
Arcata	9
Blue Lake	26
Eureka	11
Ferndale	30
Fortuna	17
Trinidad	11
County percentage	11
Imperial	
Brawley	8
Calexico	10
Calipatria	30
El Centro	5
Holtville	16
Imperial	6
Westmorland	12
County percentage	8
Inyo	
Bishop	25
County percentage	25
Kern	
Bakersfield	10
Delano	13
Maricopa	36
Shafter	15
Taft	19
Tehachapi	12
Wasco	28
County percentage	12
Kings	
Corcoran	31
Hanford	21
Lemoore	25
County percentage	25
Lake	
Lakeport	33
County percentage	33
Lassen	
Susanville	21
County percentage	21
Los Angeles	
Alhambra	13
Arcadia	11
Avalon	54

© 1992 by J., B. & L. Gould
Printed in the U.S.A.   **EP**

Azusa	11	Merced	
Bell	11	Atwater	23
Beverly Hills	14	Dos Palos	21
Burbank	14	Gustine	23
Claremont	5	Livingston	14
Compton	16	Los Banos	13
Covina	11	Merced	18
Culver City	10	County percentage	18
El Monte	11		
El Segundo	11	Modoc	
Gardena	22	Alturas	42
Glendale	16	County percentage	42
Glendora	12		
Hawthorne	7	Monterey	
Hermosa Beach	14	Carmel	17
Huntington Park	12	Gonzales	10
Inglewood	16	Greenfield	13
La Verne	14	King City	36
Long Beach	14	Monterey	13
Los Angeles	8	Pacific Grove	22
Lynwood	9	Salinas	36
Manhattan Beach	13	Soledad	16
Maywood	15	County percentage	23
Monrovia	11		
Montebello	11	Napa	
Monterey Park	11	Calistoga	37
Palos Verdes Estates	10	Napa	11
Pasadena	9	St. Helena	12
Pomona	12	County percentage	14
Redondo Beach	15		
San Fernando	17	Nevada	
San Gabriel	16	Grass Valley	7
San Marino	5	Nevada City	17
Santa Monica	11	County percentage	9
Sierra Madre	11		
Signal Hill	24	Orange	
South Gate	13	County percentage	15
South Pasadena	9		
Torrance	16	Placer	
Vernon	25	Auburn	18
West Covina	11	Colfax	8
Whittier	11	Lincoln	26
County percentage	11	Rocklin	16
		Roseville	10
Madera		County percentage	14
Chowchilla	17		
Madera	16	Plumas	
County percentage	17	Portola	19
		County percentage	19
Marin			
Belvedere	16	Riverside	
Corte Madera	12	Banning	35
Fairfax	30	Beaumont	15
Larkspur	30	Blythe	9
Mill Valley	13	Coachella	12
Ross	18	Corona	12
San Anselmo	11	Elsinore	10
San Rafael	13	Hemet	35
Sausalito	21	Indio	16
County percentage	16	Palm Springs	35
		Perris	14
Mendocino		Riverside	16
Fort Bragg	19	San Jacinto	41
Point Arena	40	County percentage	35
Ukiah	10		
Willits	24	Sacramento	
County percentage	17	Folsom	31
		Galt	25
		Isleton	13
		North Sacramento	10

© 1992 by J., B. & L. Gould
Printed in the U.S.A. **EP**

Sacramento	21
County percentage	26
San Benito	
Hollister	9
San Juan Bautista	28
County percentage	11
San Bernardino	
Barstow	23
Chino	14
Colton	21
Fontana	15
Needles	33
Ontario	20
Redlands	28
Rialto	15
San Bernardino	20
Upland	14
County percentage	20
San Diego	
Carlsbad	8
Chula Vista	23
Coronado	25
Del Mar	8
El Cajon	17
Escondido	16
Imperial Beach	8
La Mesa	23
Lemon Grove	8
National City	14
Oceanside	15
San Marcos	8
Vista	8
San Diego	6
County percentage	25
San Joaquin	
Lodi	18
Manteca	8
Ripon	11
Stockton	14
Tracy	15
County percentage	14
San Luis Obispo	
Arroyo Grande	9
Paso Robles	26
Pismo Beach	8
San Luis Obispo	21
County percentage	16
San Mateo	
Atherton	27
Belmont	7
Burlingame	38
Colma	40
Daly City	24
Hillsborough	75
Menlo Park	12
Millbrae	16
Redwood City	27
San Bruno	13
San Carlos	8
San Mateo	42
South San Francisco	12
County percentage	21

Santa Barbara	
Guadalupe	28
Lompoc	16
Santa Barbara	11
Santa Maria	12
County percentage	13
Santa Clara	
Alviso	75
Campbell	16
Gilroy	28
Los Altos	16
Los Gatos	30
Morgan Hill	11
Mountain View	13
Palo Alto	21
San Jose	13
Santa Clara	16
Sunnyvale	26
County percentage	16
Santa Cruz	
Capitola	21
Santa Cruz	23
Watsonville	21
County percentage	22
Shasta	
Redding	22
County percentage	22
Sierra	
Loyalton	75
County percentage	75
Siskiyou	
Dorris	18
Dunsmuir	29
Etna	18
Fort Jones	46
Montague	75
Mount Shasta	37
Tulelake	33
Yreka	30
County percentage	29
Solano	
Benicia	17
Dixon	18
Fairfield	18
Rio Vista	19
Suisun	7
Vacaville	15
Vallejo	18
County percentage	19
Sonoma	
Cloverdale	40
Cotati	40
Healdsburg	40
Petaluma	24
Rohnert Park	40
Santa Rosa	40
Sebastopol	40
Sonoma	40
County percentage	40
Stanislaus	
Ceres	14

© 1992 by J., B. & L. Gould
Printed in the U.S.A.   **EP**

Modesto	15
Newman	10
Oakdale	15
Patterson	20
Riverbank	18
Turlock	19
County percentage	15

Sutter

Live Oak	17
Yuba City	17
County percentage	17

Tehama

Corning	26
Red Bluff	39
Tehama	10
County percentage	31

Tulare

Dinuba	21
Exeter	23
Lindsay	24
Porterville	26
Tulare	20
Visalia	17
Woodlake	15
County percentage	21

Tuolumne

Sonora	23
County percentage	23

Ventura

Fillmore	16
Ojai	16
Oxnard	16
Port Hueneme	16
Santa Paula	16
Ventura	16
County percentage	16

Yolo

Davis	22
Winters	19
Woodland	20
County percentage	20

Yuba

Marysville	15
Wheatland	38
County percentage	15

With respect to any city arrest from a city which is not set forth in the above schedule, the county percentage shall apply. A county and city therein may, by mutual agreement, adjust these percentages. Where a county and a city have, prior to June 1, 1991, entered into an agreement to adjust the percentage specified in this section, or where a county and a city have entered into an agreement governing the distribution of revenue from parking penalties, those agreements shall remain in full force and effect until changed by mutual agreement. (*Added by Stats 1991 ch 189 §20, eff. 7/29/91.*)

§1463.003. Transfers to general fund.

The maximum amount of the fines and forfeitures which may be retained in the 1991-92 fiscal year by a county under this chapter shall be calculated by com-

puting the amount of fines and forfeitures retained by the county in the 1990-91 fiscal year, plus an amount equal to 5 percent. All moneys in excess of 25 percent of that total amount shall be transferred on a monthly basis to the General Fund.

With respect to any city in existence on July 1, 1990, the maximum amount of the fines and forfeitures which may be retained in the 1991-92 fiscal year by a city under this chapter shall be calculated by computing the amount of nonparking fines and forfeitures retained by the city in the 1990-91 fiscal year plus an amount equal to 5 percent. All moneys in excess of 50 percent of that total amount shall be transferred on a monthly basis to the General Fund. (*Added by Stats 1991 ch 189 §21, eff. 7/29/91; amended by Stats 1991 ch 1168 §7, eff. 10/14/91.*)

§1463.004. Alternative distribution of fines and forfeitures.

(a) If a sentencing judge specifies only the total fine or forfeiture, or if an automated case-processing system requires it, percentage calculations may be employed to establish the components of total fines or forfeitures, provided that the aggregate monthly distributions resulting from the calculations are the same as would be produced by strict observance of the statutory distributions.

(b) If a fund would receive less than one hundred dollars ($100) in monthly distributions of total fines and forfeitures by a particular court for at least 11 months of each year, the court may omit that fund from the system for calculating distributions, and shall instead apply the distribution provided for by Section 1463.001. (*Added by Stats 1991 ch 189 §22, eff. 7/29/91.*)

§1463.005. Distribution of fines and forfeitures from certain arrests.

Notwithstanding Section 1463.001, in a county subject to Section 77202.5 of the Government Code, of base fines resulting from arrests not subject to allocation under paragraph (1) of subdivision (b) of Section 1463.001, by a California Highway Patrol Officer on state highways constructed as freeways within the city whereon city police officers enforced the provisions of the Vehicle Code on April 1, 1965, 25 percent shall be deposited in the treasury of the appropriate city, 12.5 percent shall be deposited in the proper funds of the county, and the remainder shall be deposited in the General Fund. (*Added by Stats 1991 ch 1168 §7.5, eff. 10/14/91.*)

§1463.006. Disposition of moneys to person or agency.

Any money deposited with the court or with the clerk thereof which, by order of the court or for any other reason, should be returned, in whole or in part, to any person, or which is by law payable to the state or to any other public agency, shall be paid to that person or to the state or to the other public agency by warrant of the county auditor, which shall be drawn upon the requisition of the clerk of the court.

All money deposited as bail which has not been claimed within one year after the final disposition of the case in which the money was deposited, or within one year after an order made by the court for the return or delivery of the money to any person, shall be apportioned between the city and the county and paid or transferred in the manner provided by statute for the apportionment and payment of fines and forfeitures. This paragraph controls over any conflicting provisions of law. *(Added by Stats 1991 ch 189 §23, eff. 7/29/91.)*

§1463.009. Distribution of parking penalties.

(a) All parking penalties resulting from a filing in a court shall as soon as practicable after receipt thereof, be deposited with the county treasurer, and each month the total parking penalties which have accumulated within the past month shall be distributed, as follows:

(1) The surcharges and DMV fees shall be transferred to the proper funds as required by law.

(2) The remaining base parking penalties shall be distributed as follows:

(A) Any base parking penalties which are subject to specific distribution under any other section shall first be distributed to the specified funds.

(B) Base parking penalties resulting from notices of parking violation issued by the county, shall be transferred into the proper funds of the county.

(C) From base parking penalties resulting from notices of parking violation issued by a city, an amount equal to the applicable county percentage set forth in Section 1463.002, as modified by Section 1463.28, shall be transferred into the proper funds of the county. The remainder of base fines resulting from city arrests shall be deposited to the treasury of the appropriate city.

(b) Except as otherwise provided by agreement between the city and the court, after forwarding all surcharges and DMV fees to the proper account, a city shall retain the base parking penalties resulting from notices which it has processed with the consent of the court. Where a county and a city have, prior to June 1, 1991, entered into an agreement to adjust the percentage specified in Section 1463.002, or where a county and a city have entered into an agreement governing the distribution of revenue from parking penalties, those agreements shall remain in full force and effect until changed by mutual agreement.

(c) This section does not require any county or municipal or justice court to process a parking penalty under Article 3 (commencing with Section 40200) of Chapter 1 of Division 17 of the Vehicle Code for a city, district, or any other issuing agency prior to the filing of a complaint. *(Added by Stats 1991 ch 189 §24, eff. 7/29/91.)*

§1463.01. Distribution of fines from reckless driving and DUI offenses.

In any case in which a person is convicted of a violation of Section 23103, 23104, 23152, or 23153 of the Vehicle Code, the distribution of funds required pursuant to Section 1463, and the distribution of penalties and assessments, including, but not limited to, those imposed and collected under Sections 1463.14, 1463.16, 1463.18, and 1464, Section 11372.5 of the Health and Safety Code, Chapter 12 (commencing with Section 76000) of Title 8 of the Government Code, and Sections 23199, 23249.55, and 42006 of the Vehicle Code, may, upon approval of the Controller, be determined and made monthly upon the basis of probability sampling.

The sampling shall be procedural in nature and shall not substantively modify the distributions otherwise required by law. The procedure for the sampling shall be prescribed by the county auditor.

The accuracy of the distribution shall be verified during an annual audit to be performed consistent

with Section 71383 of the Government Code and the distribution shall be adjusted in the subsequent fiscal year as may be necessary to compensate for any departure from the distributions otherwise required by law. *(Added by Stats 1990 ch 1303 §1.5, eff. 1/1/91.)*

§1463.02. *Repealed by Stats 1991 ch 90 §27, eff. 6/30/91.*

§1463.03. *Repealed by Stats 1991 ch 90 §28, eff. 6/30/91.*

§1463.04. Transfer of funds into State Treasury to the credit of Winter Recreation Fund.

Notwithstanding Section 1463, out of the moneys deposited with the county treasurer pursuant to Section 1463, there shall be transferred once a month into the State Treasury to the credit of the Winter Recreation Fund an amount equal to 50 percent of all fines and forfeitures collected during the preceding month upon conviction or upon the forfeiture of bail from any person of any violation of Section 5091.15 of the Public Resources Code, and an amount equal to the remaining 50 percent shall be transferred to the county general fund and deposited in a special account which shall be used exclusively to pay for the cost of furthering the purposes of the California SNO-PARK Permit Program, including, but not limited to, the snow removal, maintenance, and development of designated parking areas. *(Added by Stats 1991 ch 189 §25, eff. 7/29/91. Former section 1463.04 repealed by Stats 1991 ch 90 §29, eff. 6/30/91.)*

§1463.05. *Repealed by Stats 1991 ch 90 §30, eff. 6/30/91.*

§1463.06. *Repealed by Stats 1991 ch 90 §31, eff. 6/30/91.*

§1463.1. Bail funds, deposit in bank.

Notwithstanding the provisions of Section 1463, any municipal court or justice court may elect, with prior approval of the county auditor, to deposit in a bank account pursuant to Section 53679 of the Government Code, all moneys deposited as bail with such court, or with the clerk thereof.

All moneys received and disbursed through such bank account shall be properly and uniformly accounted for under such procedures as the State Controller may deem necessary.

§1463.2. *Repealed by Stats 1991 ch 90 §32, eff. 6/30/91.*

§1463.3. *Repealed by Stats 1991 ch 90 §33, eff. 6/30/91.*

§1463.4. *Repealed by Stats 1991 ch 90 §34, eff. 6/30/91.*

§1463.5. Distribution of funds upon the basis of probability sampling.

The distribution of funds required pursuant to Section 1463, and the distribution of assessments imposed and collected under Section 1464 and Section 42006 of the Vehicle Code, may be determined and made upon the basis of probability sampling. The sampling shall be procedural in nature and shall not substantively modify the distributions required pur-

© 1992 by J., B. & L. Gould
Printed in the U.S.A.   **EP**

suant to Sections 1463 and 1464 and Section 42006 of the Vehicle Code. The procedure for the sampling shall be prescribed by the county auditor and the procedure and its implementation shall be approved by the board of supervisors and a majority of the cities within a county. The reasonableness of the distribution shall be verified during the audit performed pursuant to Section 71383 of the Government Code. *(Amended by Stats 1989 ch 897 §40, eff. 1/1/90.)*

§1463.5a. *Repealed by Stats 1991 ch 90 §35, eff. 6/30/91.*

§1463.6. *Repealed by Stats 1991 ch 90 §36, eff. 6/30/91.*

§1463.7. Funds transferred to State College Parking Revenue Fund and to Regents of University of California.

Funds transferred to the Regents of the University of California pursuant to Section 1462.3 may not be utilized to purchase land or to construct any parking facility. These funds shall be utilized for the development, enhancement, and operation of alternate methods of transportation of students and employees of the University of California and for the mitigation of the impact of off-campus student and employee parking in university communities. *(Added by Stats 1991 ch 189 §26, eff. 7/29/91. Former section 1463.7 repealed by Stats 1991 ch 90 §37, eff. 6/30/91.)*

§1463.8. *Repealed by Stats 1991 ch 90 §38, eff. 6/30/91.*

§1463.9. Deposit of fines and forfeitures for littering highway.

Notwithstanding the provisions of Section 1463, 50 percent of all fines and forfeitures collected upon conviction, or upon forfeiture of bail, for violations of Section 13002 of the Health and Safety Code, Sections 23111 and 23112, and subdivision (a) of Section 23113 of the Vehicle Code, and Section 374.3 of this code shall be kept separate and apart from any other fines and forfeitures. These fines and forfeitures shall, as soon as practicable after their receipt, be deposited with the county treasurer of the county in which the court is situated and shall be distributed as prescribed in Section 1463, except that the money distributed to any county or city shall be expended only for litter cleanup activities within that city or county. *(Added by Stats 1991 ch 189 §27, eff. 7/29/91. Former section 1463.9 repealed by Stats 1991 ch 90 §39, eff. 6/30/91.)*

§1463.10. *Repealed by Stats 1991 ch 90 §40, eff. 6/30/91.*

§1463.11. *Repealed by Stats 1991 ch 90 §41, eff. 6/30/91.*

§1463.12. *Repealed by Stats 1991 ch 90 §42, eff. 6/30/91.*

§1463.13. *Repealed by Stats 1991 ch 90 §43, eff. 6/30/91.*

§1463.14. Special account to cover costs of blood alcohol and other tests.

(a) Notwithstanding the provisions of Section 1463, of the moneys deposited with the county treasurer pursuant to Section 1463, fifty dollars ($50) for each conviction of a violation of Section 23103, 23104, 23152, or 23153 of the Vehicle Code shall be deposited in a special account which shall be used exclusively to pay for the cost of performing for the county, or a city or special district within the county, analysis of blood, breath or urine for alcohol content or for the presence of drugs, or for services related to that testing. The sum shall not exceed the reasonable cost of providing the services for which the sum is intended.

On November 1 of each year, the treasurer of each county shall determine those moneys in the special account which were not expended during the preceding fiscal year, and shall transfer those moneys into the general fund of the county. The county may retain an amount of that money equal to its administrative cost incurred pursuant to this section, and shall distribute the remainder pursuant to Section 1463.

(b) The Board of Supervisors of Contra Costa County may, by resolution, authorize the imposition of a fifty dollar ($50) assessment by the court upon each defendant convicted of a violation of Section 23152 or 23153 of the Vehicle Code for deposit in the account from which the fifty dollar ($50) distribution specified in subdivision (a) is deducted.

(c) The board of supervisors of a county other than Contra Costa County may, by resolution, authorize an additional penalty upon each defendant convicted of a violation of Section 23152 or 23153 of the Vehicle Code, of an amount equal to the cost of testing for alcohol content, less the fifty dollars ($50) deposited as provided in subdivision (a). The additional penalty authorized by this subdivision shall be imposed only in those instances where the defendant has the ability to pay, but in no case shall the defendant be ordered to pay a penalty in excess of fifty dollars ($50). The penalty authorized shall be deposited directly with the county, or city or special district within the county, which performed the test, in the special account described in subdivision (a), and shall not be the basis for any additional assessment pursuant to Section 1464 or 1465, or Chapter 12 (commencing with Section 76010) of Title 8 of the Government Code.

For purposes of this subdivision, "ability to pay" means the overall capability of the defendant to pay the additional penalty authorized by this subdivision, taking into consideration all of the following:

(A) Present financial obligations, including family support obligations, and fines, penalties, and other obligations to the court.

(B) Reasonably discernible future financial position over the next 12 months.

(C) Any other factor or factors which may bear upon the defendant's financial ability to pay the additional penalty.

(D) The Department of Justice shall promulgate rules and regulations to implement the provisions of this section. *(Added by Stats 1991 ch 189 §28, eff. 7/29/91. Former section 1463.14 repealed by Stats 1991 ch 90 §44, eff. 6/30/91.)*

§1463.15. *Repealed by Stats 1991 ch 90 §45, eff. 6/30/91.*

§1463.16. Vehicle Code fines allocated to alcoholism program.

(a) Notwithstanding Section 1203.1 or 1463, fifty dollars ($50) of each fine for each conviction of a violation of Section 23103, 23104, 23152, or 23153 of the Vehicle Code shall be deposited with the county treasurer in a special account for exclusive allocation by the county for the county's alcoholism program, with approval of the board of supervisors, for alcohol programs and services for the general population. These funds shall be allocated through the local planning process pursuant to specific provision in the county alcohol program plan which is submitted to the State Department of Alcohol and Drug Programs. Programs shall be certified by the Department of Alcohol and Drug Programs or have made application for certification to be eligible for funding under this section. The county shall implement the intent and procedures of subdivision (b) of Section 11812 of the Health and Safety Code while distributing funds under this section.

(b) In a county of the 1st, 2nd, 3rd, or 15th class, notwithstanding Section 1463, of the moneys deposited with the county treasurer pursuant to Section 1463, fifty dollars ($50) for each conviction of a violation of Section 23103, 23104, 23152, or 23153 of the Vehicle Code shall be deposited in a special account for exclusive allocation by the administrator of the county's alcoholism program, with approval of the board of supervisors, for alcohol programs and services for the general population. These funds shall be allocated through the local planning process pursuant to a specific provision in the county plan which is submitted to the State Department of Alcohol and Drug Programs. For those services for which standards have been developed and certification is available, programs shall be certified by the State Department of Alcohol and Drug Programs or shall apply for certification to be eligible for funding under this section. The county alcohol administrator shall implement the intent and procedures of subdivision (b) of Section 11812 of the Health and Safety Code while distributing funds under this section.

(c) The Board of Supervisors of Contra Costa County may, by resolution, authorize the imposition of a fifty dollar ($50) assessment by the court upon each defendant convicted of a violation of Section 23152 or 23153 of the Vehicle Code for deposit in the account from which the fifty dollar ($50) distribution specified in subdivision (a) is deducted.

(d) It is the specific intent of the Legislature that funds expended under this part shall be used for ongoing alcoholism program services as well as for contracts with private nonprofit organizations to upgrade facilities to meet state certification and state licensing standards and federal nondiscrimination regulations relating to accessibility for handicapped persons.

(e) Counties may retain up to 5 percent of the funds collected to offset administrative costs of collection and disbursement. (Added by Stats 1991 ch 189 §29, eff. 7/29/91. Former section 1463.16 repealed by Stats 1991 ch 90 §46, eff. 6/30/91.)

§1463.17. *Repealed by Stats 1991 ch 90 §47, eff. 6/30/91.*

§1463.18. Disposition of moneys from driving-under-the-influence convictions.

(a) Notwithstanding the provisions of Section 1463, moneys which are collected for a conviction of a violation of Section 23152 or 23153 of the Vehicle Code and which are required to be deposited with the county

treasurer pursuant to Section 1463 shall be allocated as follows:

(1) The first twenty dollars ($20) of any amount collected for a conviction shall be transferred to the Restitution Fund. This amount shall be aggregated by the county treasurer and transferred to the State Treasury once per month for deposit in the Restitution Fund.

(2) The balance of the amount collected, if any, shall be deposited by the county treasurer pursuant to Section 1463.

(b) The amount transferred to the Restitution Fund pursuant to this section shall be in addition to any amount of any additional fine or assessment imposed pursuant to Section 13967 of the Government Code. The amount deposited to the Restitution Fund pursuant to this section shall be used for the purpose of indemnification of victims pursuant to Section 13965 of the Government Code, with priority given to victims of alcohol-related traffic offenses. *(Added by Stats 1991 ch 189 §30, eff. 7/29/91. Former section 1463.18 repealed by Stats 1991 ch 90 §48, eff. 6/30/91)*

§1463.19. *Repealed by Stats 1991 ch 90 §49, eff. 6/30/91.*

§1463.20. *Repealed by Stats 1991 ch 90 §50, eff. 6/30/91.*

§1463.21. *Repealed by Stats 1991 ch 90 §51, eff. 6/30/91.*

§1463.22. Defraying costs of municipal and justice courts.

(a) Notwithstanding Section 1463, of the moneys deposited with the county treasurer pursuant to Section 1463, seventeen dollars and fifty cents ($17.50) for each alleged violation of Section 16028 of the Vehicle Code shall be deposited by the county treasurer in a special account and allocated to defray costs of municipal and justice courts incurred in administering Sections 16028, 16030, and 16031 of the Vehicle Code. The amount required to be deposited in a special account pursuant to this subdivision shall be deposited regardless of whether the charge is dismissed pursuant to subdivision (e) of Section 16028 of the Vehicle Code or otherwise. Any moneys in the special account in excess of the amount required to defray those costs shall be redeposited and distributed by the county treasurer pursuant to Section 1463.

(b) Notwithstanding Section 1463, of the moneys deposited with the county treasurer pursuant to Section 1463, three dollars ($3) for each conviction for a violation of Section 16028 of the Vehicle Code shall be initially deposited by the county treasurer in a special account, and shall be transmitted once per month to the Controller for deposit in the Motor Vehicle Account in the State Transportation Fund. These moneys shall be available, when appropriated, to defray the administrative costs incurred by the Department of Motor Vehicles pursuant to Sections 16031, 16032, 16034, and 16035 of the Vehicle Code. It is the intent of this subdivision to provide sufficient revenues to pay for all of the department's costs in administering those sections of the Vehicle Code.

(c) Notwithstanding Section 1463, of the moneys deposited with the county treasurer pursuant to Section 1463, ten dollars ($10) upon the conviction of, or upon the forfeiture of bail from, any person arrested

© 1992 by J., B. & L. Gould
Printed in the U.S.A.   EP

or notified for a violation of Section 16028 of the Vehicle Code shall be deposited by the county treasurer in a special account and shall be transmitted monthly to the Controller for deposit in the General Fund. *(Added by Stats 1991 ch 189 §31, eff. 7/29/91. Former section 1463.22 repealed by Stats 1991 ch 90 §52, eff. 6/30/91.)*

§1463.23. AIDS education program by county health department.

Notwithstanding Section 1463, out of the moneys deposited with the county treasurer pursuant to Section 1463, fifty dollars ($50) of each fine imposed pursuant to Section 4383 of the Business and Professions Code, subdivision (c) of Section 11350, subdivision (c) of Section 11377, or subdivision (b) of Section 11550 of the Health and Safety Code or subdivision (b) of Section 264, subdivision (m) of Section 286, subdivision (m) of Section 288a or Section 647.1, shall be deposited in a special account in the county treasury which shall be used exclusively to pay for the reasonable costs of establishing and providing for the county, or any city within the county, an AIDS (acquired immune deficiency syndrome) education program under the direction of the county health department, in accordance with Chapter 2.71 (commencing with Section 1001.10) of Title 6, and for the costs of collecting and administering funds received for purposes of this section. *(Added by Stats 1991 ch 189 §32, eff. 7/29/91. Former section 1463.23 repealed by Stats 1991 ch 90 §53, eff. 6/30/91.)*

§1463.24. *Repealed by Stats 1991 ch 90 §54, eff. 6/30/91.*

§1463.25. Deposit of funds from alcohol abuse education and penalty assessments.

Notwithstanding Section 1203.1 or 1463, and in addition to any allocation under Section 1463.16, the moneys from alcohol abuse education and prevention penalty assessments collected pursuant to Section 23196 of the Vehicle Code shall be initially deposited by the county treasurer in a special county alcohol abuse and prevention fund for exclusive allocation by the county alcohol program administrator, subject to the approval of the board of supervisors, for the county's alcohol abuse education and prevention program pursuant to Section 11802 of the Health and Safety Code.

A county shall not use more than 5 percent of the funds deposited in the special account for administrative costs. *(Added by Stats 1991 ch 189 §33, eff. 7/29/91. Former section 1463.25 repealed by Stats 1991 ch 90 §55, eff. 6/30/91.)*

§1463.26. Transfer of fines and forfeitures to traffic funds and county general funds.

Notwithstanding Section 1463, out of moneys deposited with the county treasurer pursuant to Section 1463, there shall be transferred, once a month, to the traffic fund of the city, an amount equal to one-third of all fines and forfeitures collected during the preceding month upon the conviction of, or upon the forfeiture of bail by, any person charged with a violation of Section 21655.5 or 21655.8 of the Vehicle Code within that city, and an amount equal to one-third of those fines and forfeitures shall be transferred into the general fund of the county, and an amount equal to one-third of those fines and forfeitures shall be trans-

ferred to the agency whose approval is required for high-occupancy vehicle lanes on state highways pursuant to Section 21655.6 of the Vehicle Code. If the arrest for a violation of either Section 21655.5 or 21655.8 of the Vehicle Code was not within a city, then 50 percent of the fines and forfeitures shall be transferred to the general fund of the county and 50 percent shall be transferred to the agency having authority to approve high-occupancy vehicle lanes pursuant to Section 21655.6 of the Vehicle Code. Money received by the agency having the authority to approve high-occupancy vehicle lanes pursuant to Section 21655.6 of the Vehicle Code shall be used by that agency for the purposes of improving traffic flow and traffic operations upon the state highway system within the jurisdiction of that agency. In counties where there exists a county transportation commission created pursuant to Division 12 (commencing with Section 130000) of the Public Utilities Code, that commission is the agency for purposes of this section. *(Added by Stats 1991 ch 189 §34, eff. 7/29/91. Former section 1463.26 repealed by Stats 1991 ch 90 §56, eff. 6/30/91.)*

1463.27. *Repealed by Stats 1991 ch 90 §57, eff. 6/30/91.*

§1463.28. Disposition of fines and forfeitures resulting from increases in bail amount.

(a) Notwithstanding any other provision of law, for each option county, as defined by Section 77004 of the Government Code, which has adopted the resolution specified in subdivision (b), that portion of fines and forfeitures, whether collected by the courts or by other processing agencies, which are attributable to an increase in the bail amounts adopted subsequent to the resolution pursuant to subdivision (c) or (d) of Section 1269b which would otherwise be divided between the county and cities within the county shall be deposited into the county general fund up to the annual limit listed in subdivision (b) for that county. Fine and forfeiture increments which exceed the specified annual limit shall be divided between the county and the cities within the county as otherwise provided by law. The scheduled bail amounts in such a county may exceed any limit established pursuant to subdivision (d) of Section 1269b.

(b) The counties which may adopt a resolution directing that future increments in fines and forfeitures as specified in subdivision (a) be deposited in the county general fund and the annual limit applicable to those counties is as follows:

County	Annual Limit
Alpine	$ 300,000
Amador	200,000
Butte	900,000
Calaveras	300,000
Contra Costa	100,000
Del Norte	200,000
Fresno	700,000
Humboldt	200,000
Kings	300,000
Lake	400,000
Lassen	200,000
Los Angeles	15,000,000
Madera	600,000
Mariposa	200,000
Mendocino	600,000
Modoc	200,000
Mono	200,000

Plumas 200,000
San Benito 300,000
San Diego 5,200,000
San Joaquin 1,000,000
Santa Clara 3,200,000
Sierra 300,000
Stanislaus 1,900,000
Sutter 800,000
Trinity 200,000
Tulare 2,000,000
Tuolumne 400,000
Yolo 700,000
Yuba 900,000

(Amended by Stats 1991 ch 90 §58, eff. 6/30/91.)

§1463.29. *Amended by Stats 1991 ch 38 §1, eff. 1/1/92; repealed by Stats 1991 ch 90 §59, eff. 6/30/91.*

§1464. Penalty assessment.

(a) Subject to Chapter 12 (commencing with Section 76000) of Title 8 of the Government Code there shall be levied a state penalty in an amount equal to ten dollars ($10) for every ten dollars ($10) or fraction thereof, upon every fine, penalty, or forfeiture imposed and collected by the courts for criminal offenses, including all offenses involving a violation of a section of the Vehicle Code or any local ordinance adopted pursuant to the Vehicle Code, except offenses relating to parking. Any bail schedule adopted pursuant to Section 1269b may include the necessary amount to pay the state penalties established by this section and Chapter 12 (commencing with Section 76000) of Title 8 of the Government Code for all matters where a personal appearance is not mandatory and the bail is posted primarily to guarantee payment of the fine.

(b) Where multiple offenses are involved, the state penalty shall be based upon the total fine or bail for each case. When a fine is suspended, in whole or in part, the state penalty shall be reduced in proportion to the suspension.

(c) When any deposited bail is made for an offense to which this section applies, and for which a court appearance is not mandatory, the person making the deposit shall also deposit a sufficient amount to include the state penalty prescribed by this section for forfeited bail. If bail is returned, the state penalty made thereon pursuant to this section shall also be returned.

(d) In any case where a person convicted of any offense, to which this section applies, is in prison until the fine is satisfied, the judge may waive all or any part of the state penalty, the payment of which would work a hardship on the person convicted or his or her immediate family.

(e) After a determination by the court of the amount due, the clerk of the court shall collect the same and transmit it to the county treasury. The portion thereof attributable to Chapter 12 (commencing with Section 76000) of Title 8 of the Government Code shall be deposited in the appropriate county fund and the balance shall then be transmitted to the State Treasury with 70 percent to be deposited in the State Penalty Fund, which is hereby created and 30 percent to remain on deposit in the General Fund. The transmission to the State Treasury shall be carried out in the same manner as fines collected for the state by a county.

(f) The moneys so deposited in the State Penalty Fund shall be distributed as follows:

(1) Once a month there shall be transferred into the Fish and Game Preservation Fund an amount equal to 0.33 percent of the state penalty funds deposited in the State Penalty Fund during the preceding month, but in no event shall the total amount be less than the state penalty levied on fines or forfeitures for violation of state laws relating to the protection or propagation of fish and game. These moneys are to be used for the education or training of department employees which fulfills a need consistent with the objectives of the Department of Fish and Game.

(2) Once a month there shall be transferred into the Restitution Fund an amount equal to 32.02 percent of the state penalty funds deposited in the State Penalty Fund during the preceding month. Those funds shall be made available in accordance with subdivision (b) of Section 13967 of the Government Code.

(3) Once a month there shall be transferred into the Peace Officers' Training Fund an amount equal to 23.99 percent of the state penalty funds deposited in the State Penalty Fund during the preceding month.

(4) Once a month there shall be transferred into the Driver Training Penalty Assessment Fund an amount equal to 25.70 percent of the state penalty funds deposited in the State Penalty Fund during the preceding month.

(5) Once a month there shall be transferred into the Corrections Training Fund an amount equal to 7.88 percent of the state penalty funds deposited in the State Penalty Fund during the preceding month. Money in the Corrections Training Fund is not continuously appropriated and shall be appropriated in the Budget Act.

(6) Once a month there shall be transferred into the Local Public Prosecutors and Public Defenders Training Fund established pursuant to Section 11503 an amount equal to 0.78 percent of the state penalty funds deposited in the State Penalty Fund during the preceding month. The amount so transferred shall not exceed the sum of eight hundred fifty thousand dollars ($850,000) in any fiscal year. The remainder in excess of eight hundred fifty thousand dollars ($850,000) shall be transferred to the Restitution Fund.

(7) Once a month there shall be transferred into the Victim-Witness Assistance Fund an amount equal to 8.64 percent of the state penalty funds deposited in the State Penalty Fund during the preceding month.

(8) (A) Once a month there shall be transferred into the Traumatic Brain Injury Fund, created pursuant to Section 4358 of the Welfare and Institutions Code, an amount equal to 0.66 percent of the state penalty funds deposited into the State Penalty Fund during the preceding month, until the amount deposited in the Traumatic Brain Injury Fund, as determined by the Department of Finance, for any fiscal year equals five hundred thousand dollars ($500,000). All moneys in excess of that amount shall be distributed pro rata pursuant to paragraphs (1) to (7), inclusive, and utilized in accordance with this subdivision.

(B) Any moneys deposited in the State Penalty Fund attributable to the assessments made pursuant to subdivision (i) of Section 27315 of the Vehicle Code on or after the date that Chapter 6.6 (commencing with Section 5564) of Part 1 of Division 5 of the Welfare and Institutions Code is repealed shall be utilized in accordance with paragraphs (1) to (8), inclusive, of this subdivision. *(Amended by Stats 1991 ch 90 §60, eff. 6/30/91; ch 189 §35, eff. 7/29/91; ch 613 §9, eff. 1/1/92.)*

© 1992 by J., B. & L. Gould
Printed in the U.S.A.   **EP**

§1464.05. Assessment defined.

Wherever the word "assessment" appears in any reference to Section 1464 in any law or regulation with regard to a fine, penalty, or bail forfeiture, it shall be deemed to refer to the penalty, state penalty, or additional penalty required by Section 1464. *(Added by Stats 1990 ch 1293 §3, eff. 1/1/91.)*

§1464.5. *Repealed by Stats 1991 ch 189 §36, eff. 7/29/91.*

§1464.8. Allocation of fines and forfeitures.

Notwithstanding any other provision of law, when an allocation and distribution of any fine, forfeiture, penalty, fee, or assessment collected in any criminal case is made, including, but not limited to, moneys collected pursuant to this chapter, Section 13003 of the Fish and Game Code, Chapter 12 (commencing with Section 76000) of Title 8 of the Government Code, and Sections 11372.5 and 11502 of the Health and Safety Code, the allocation and distribution of any payment may be based upon the law in effect during the accounting period when the payment is made. *(Added by Stats 1991 ch 90 §61, eff. 6/30/91; amended by Stats 1991 ch 189 §37, eff. 7/29/91.)*

§1465. *Repealed by Stats 1991 ch 189 §38, eff. 7/29/91.*

§1465.5. Additional assessment: parking disabled or veteran's parking spaces.

An assessment of two dollars ($2) for every ten dollars ($10) or fraction thereof, for every fine, forfeiture, or parking penalty imposed and collected pursuant to Section 42001.5 of the Vehicle Code for violation of Section 22507.8 of the Vehicle Code, may be imposed by each county upon the adoption of a resolution by the board of supervisors. An assessment imposed by this section shall be collected and disbursed as provided in Section 9394.5 of the Welfare and Institutions Code.

(b)* This section shall remain in effect only until January 1, 1995, and as of that date is repealed, unless a later enacted statute, which is enacted before January 1, 1995, deletes or extends that date. *(Amended by Stats 1991 ch 430 §1, eff. 9/19/91 only until 1/1/95.)*
*So in original. No subd. (a) designated.

CHAPTER 2

APPEALS FROM INFERIOR COURTS

§1466. Who may appeal; appealable decisions.

An appeal may be taken from a judgment or order of an inferior court, in a criminal case, to the superior court of the county in which the inferior court is located, in the following cases.

(a) By the people:

(1) From an order recusing the district attorney pursuant to Section 1424.

(2) From an order or judgment dismissing or otherwise terminating the action before the defendant has been placed in jeopardy or where the defendant has waived jeopardy.

(3) From a judgment for the defendant upon the sustaining of a demurrer.

(4) From an order granting a new trial.

(5) From an order arresting judgment.

(6) From any order made after judgment affecting the substantial rights of the people.

(b) By the defendant:

(1) From a final judgment of conviction. A sentence, an order granting probation, a conviction in a case in which before final judgment the defendant is committed for insanity or is given an indeterminate commitment as a mentally disordered sex offender, or the conviction of a defendant committed for controlled substance addiction shall be deemed to be a final judgment within the meaning of this section. Upon appeal from a final judgment or an order granting probation the court may review any order denying a motion for a new trial.

(2) From any order made after judgment affecting his or her substantial rights. *(Amended by Stats 1988 ch 527 §3, eff. 1/1/89.)*

§1467. Granting or refusal of stay of execution.

An appeal from a judgment of conviction does not stay the execution of the judgment in any case unless the trial or reviewing court shall so order. The granting or refusal of such order shall rest in the discretion of the court.

§1468. Procedure on appeal.

Appeals to the superior courts shall be taken, heard and determined, the decisions thereon shall be remitted to the inferior courts, and the records on such appeals shall be made up and filed in such time and manner as shall be prescribed in rules adopted by the Judicial Council.

§1469. Reviewing questions of law.

Upon appeal by the people the reviewing court may review any question of law involved in any ruling affecting the judgment or order appealed from, without exception having been taken in the trial court. Upon an appeal by a defendant the court may, without exception having been taken in the trial court, review any question of law involved in any ruling, order, instruction, or thing whatsoever said or done at the trial or prior to or after judgment, which thing was said or done after objection made in and considered by the trial court and which affected the substantial rights of the defendant. The court may also review any instruction given, refused or modified, even though no objection was made thereto in the trial court if the substantial rights of the defendant were affected thereby. The reviewing court may reverse, affirm or modify the judgment or order appealed from, and may set aside, affirm or modify any or all of the proceedings subsequent to, or dependent upon, such judgment or order, and may, if proper, order a new trial. If a new trial is ordered upon appeal, it must be had in the court from which the appeal is taken.

CHAPTER 3

TRANSFER OF MUNICIPAL AND JUSTICE COURT APPEALS

§1471. Order for hearing and decision.

A court of appeal may order any case on appeal within the original jurisdiction of the municipal and justice courts in its district transferred to it for hearing and decision as provided by rules of the Judicial Council when the superior court certifies, or the court of appeal determines, that such transfer appears necessary to secure uniformity of decision or to settle important questions of law.

No case in which there is a right on appeal to a trial anew in the superior court shall be transferred pursuant to this section before a decision in such case becomes final therein.

A court to which any such case is transferred shall have similar power to review any matter and make orders and judgments as the superior court by statute would have in such case, except as otherwise expressly provided and except that if the case was tried anew in the superior court, the reviewing court shall have similar power to review any matter and make orders and judgments as it has by statute in a case within the original jurisdiction of the superior court.

TITLE 12

SPECIAL PROCEEDINGS OF A CRIMINAL NATURE

CHAPTER 1

OF THE WRIT OF HABEAS CORPUS

§1473. Who may prosecute.

(a) Every person unlawfully imprisoned or restrained of his liberty, under any pretense whatever, may prosecute a writ of habeas corpus, to inquire into the cause of such imprisonment or restraint.

(b) A writ of habeas corpus may be prosecuted for, but not limited to, the following reasons:

(1) False evidence that is substantially material or probative on the issue of guilt or punishment was introduced against a person at any hearing or trial relating to his incarceration; or

(2) False physical evidence, believed by a person to be factual, probative, or material on the issue of guilt, which was known by the person at the time of entering a plea of guilty, which was a material factor directly related to the plea of guilty by the person.

(c) Any allegation that the prosecution knew or should have known of the false nature of the evidence referred to in subdivision (b) is immaterial to the prosecution of a writ of habeas corpus brought pursuant to subdivision (b).

(d) Nothing in this section shall be construed as limiting the grounds for which a writ of habeas corpus may be prosecuted or as precluding the use of any other remedies.

§1474. Application for, how made.

Application for the writ is made by petition, signed either by the party for whose relief it is intended, or by some person in his behalf, and must specify:

1. That the person in whose behalf the writ is applied for is imprisoned or restrained of his liberty, the officer or person by whom he is so confined or restrained, and the place where, naming all the parties, if they are known, or describing them, if they are not known;

2. If the imprisonment is alleged to be illegal, the petition must also state in what the alleged illegality consists;

3. The petition must be verified by the oath or affirmation of the party making the application.

§1475. Successive applications.

The writ of habeas corpus may be granted in the manner provided by law. If the writ has been granted by any court or a judge thereof and after the hearing thereof the prisoner has been remanded, he shall not be discharged from custody by the same or any other court of like general jurisdiction, or by a judge of the same or any other court of like general jurisdiction, unless upon some ground not existing in fact at the issuing of the prior writ. Should the prisoner desire to urge some point of law not raised in the petition for or at the hearing upon the return of the prior writ, then, in case such prior writ had been returned or returnable before a superior court or a judge thereof, no writ can be issued upon a second or other application except by the appropriate court of appeal or some judge thereof, or by the Supreme Court or some judge thereof, and in such an event such writ must not be made returnable before any superior court or any judge thereof. In the event, however, that the prior writ was returned or made returnable before a court of appeal or any judge thereof, no writ can be issued upon a second or other application except by the Supreme Court or some judge thereof, and such writ must be made returnable before said Supreme Court or some judge thereof.

Every application for a writ of habeas corpus must be verified, and shall state whether any prior application or applications have been made for a writ in regard to the same detention or restraint complained of in the application, and if any such prior application or applications have been made the later application must contain a brief statement of all proceedings had therein, or in any of them, to and including the final order or orders made therein, or in any of them, on appeal or otherwise.

Whenever the person applying for a writ of habeas corpus is held in custody or restraint by any officer of any court of this state or any political subdivision thereof, or by any peace officer of this state, or any political subdivision thereof, a copy of the application for such writ must in all cases be served upon the district attorney of the county wherein such person is held in custody or restraint at least 24 hours before the time at which said writ is made returnable and no application for such writ can be heard without proof of such service in cases where such service is required.

If such person is in custody for violation of an ordinance of a city which has a city attorney, a copy of the application for the writ must also be served on the city attorney of the city whose ordinance is the basis for the charge at least 24 hours before the time at which the writ is made returnable, provided that failure to serve such city attorney shall not deprive the court of jurisdiction to hear the application.

§1476. Endorsement of petition.

Any court or judge authorized to grant the writ, to whom a petition therefor is presented, must endorse upon the petition the hour and date of its presentation and the hour and date of the granting or denial of the writ, and must, if it appear that the writ ought to issue, grant the same without delay; and if the person by or upon whose behalf the application for the writ is made be detained upon a criminal charge, may admit him to bail, if the offense is bailable, pending the determination of the proceeding.

© 1992 by J., B. & L. Gould
Printed in the U.S.A.   EP

§1477. Writ, what to contain.

The writ must be directed to the person having custody of or restraining the person on whose behalf the application is made, and must command him to have the body of such person before the court or judge before whom the writ is returnable, at a time and place therein specified.

§1478. Service of writ by clerk.

If the writ is directed to the sheriff or other ministerial officer of the court out of which it issues, it must be delivered by the clerk to such officer without delay, as other writs are delivered for service. If it is directed to any other person, it must be delivered to the sheriff or a marshal, and be by him served upon such person by delivering the copy to him without delay, and make his return on the original to the court of issuance. If the person to whom the writ is directed cannot be found, or refuses admittance to the officer or person serving or delivering such writ, it may be served or delivered by leaving it at the residence of the person to whom it is directed, or by affixing it to some conspicuous place on the outside either of his dwelling house or of the place where the party is confined or under restraint.

§1479. Proceedings upon disobedience to the writ.

If the person to whom the writ is directed refuses, after service, to obey the same, the Court or Judge, upon affidavit, must issue an attachment against such person, directed to the Sheriff or Coroner, commanding him forthwith to apprehend such person and bring him immediately before such Court or Judge; and upon being so brought, he must be committed to the jail of the county until he makes due return to such writ, or is otherwise legally discharged.

§1480. Return, what to contain.

The person upon whom the writ is served must state in his return, plainly and unequivocally:

1. Whether he has or has not the party in his custody, or under his power or restraint;

2. If he has the party in his custody or power, or under his restraint, he must state the authority and causes of such imprisonment or restraint;

3. If the party is detained by virtue of any writ, warrant, or other written authority, a copy thereof must be annexed to the return, and the original produced and exhibited to the court or judge on the hearing of such return;

4. If the person upon whom the writ is served had the party in his power or custody, or under his restraint, at any time prior or subsequent to the date of the writ of habeas corpus, but has transferred such custody or restraint to another, the return must state particularly to whom, at what time and place, for what cause, and by what authority such transfer took place;

5. The return must be signed by the person making the same, and, except when such person is a sworn public officer, and makes such return in his official capacity, it must be verified by his oath.

§1481. Body must be produced, when.

The person to whom the writ is directed, if it is served, must bring the body of the party in his custody or under his restraint, according to the command of the writ, except in the cases specified in the next section.

§1482. When hearing may proceed without production of the body.

When, from sickness or infirmity of the person directed to be produced, he cannot, without danger, be brought before the Court or Judge, the person in whose custody or power he is may state that fact in his return to the writ, verifying the same by affidavit. If the Court or Judge is satisfied of the truth of such return, and the return to the writ is otherwise sufficient, the Court or Judge may proceed to decide on such return, and to dispose of the matter as if such party had been produced on the writ, or the hearing thereof may be adjourned until such party can be produced.

§1483. Hearing on return.

The Court or Judge before whom the writ is returned must, immediately after the return, proceed to hear and examine the return, and such other matters as may be properly submitted to their hearing and consideration.

§1484. Proceedings on the hearing.

The party brought before the Court or Judge, on the return of the writ, may deny or controvert any of the material facts or matters set forth in the return, or except to the sufficiency thereof, or allege any fact to show either that his imprisonment or detention is unlawful, or that he is entitled to his discharge. The Court or Judge must thereupon proceed in a summary way to hear such proof as may be produced against such imprisonment or detention, or in favor of the same, and to dispose of such party as the justice of the case may require, and have full power and authority to require and compel the attendance of witnesses, by process or subpoena and attachment, and to do and perform all other acts and things necessary to a full and fair hearing and determination of the case.

§1485. When Court may discharge the party.

If no legal cause is shown for such imprisonment or restraint, or for the continuation thereof, such Court or Judge must discharge such party from the custody or restraint under which he is held.

§1486. When to remand party.

The Court or Judge, if the time during which such party may be legally detained in custody has not expired, must remand such party, if it appears that he is detained in custody:

1. By virtue of process issued by any Court or Judge of the United States, in a case where such Court or Judge has exclusive jurisdiction; or,

2. By virtue of the final judgment or decree of any competent Court of criminal jurisdiction, or of any process issued upon such judgment or decree.

§1487. Grounds of discharge in certain cases.

If it appears on the return of the writ that the prisoner is in custody by virtue of process from any Court of this state, or Judge or officer thereof, such prisoner may be discharged in any of the following cases, subject to the restrictions of the last section:

1. When the jurisdiction of such Court or officer has been exceeded;

2. When the imprisonment was at first lawful, yet by some act, omission, or event which has taken place afterwards, the party has become entitled to a discharge;

3. When the process is defective in some matter of substance required by law, rendering such process void;

© 1992 by J., B. & L. Gould
Printed in the U.S.A. **EP**

4. When the process, though proper in form, has been issued in a case not allowed by law;

5. When the person having the custody of the prisoner is not the person allowed by law to detain him;

6. Where the process is not authorized by any order, judgment, or decree of any Court, nor by any provision of law;

7. Where a party has been committed on a criminal charge without reasonable or probable cause.

§1488. No discharge for defect in form of warrant.

If any person is committed to prison, or is in custody of any officer on any criminal charge, by virtue of any warrant of commitment of a magistrate, such person must not be discharged on the ground of any mere defect of form in the warrant of commitment.

§1489. Court may examine witnesses and discharge, hold to bail, or recommit.

If it appears to the Court or Judge, by affidavit or otherwise, or upon the inspection of the process or warrant of commitment, and such other papers in the proceedings as may be shown to the Court or Judge, that the party is guilty of a criminal offense, or ought not to be discharged, such Court or Judge, although the charge is defective or unsubstantially set forth in such process or warrant of commitment, must cause the complainant or other necessary witnesses to be subpoenaed to attend at such time as ordered, to testify before the Court or Judge; and upon the examination he may discharge such prisoner, let him to bail, if the offense be bailable, or recommit him to custody, as may be just and legal.

§1490. Writ for purpose of bail.

When a person is imprisoned or detained in custody on any criminal charge, for want of bail, such person is entitled to a writ of habeas corpus for the purpose of giving bail, upon averring that fact in his petition, without alleging that he is illegally confined.

§1491. Non-violent offenses; when bail must be set immediately.

Any judge before whom a person who has been committed upon a criminal charge may be brought on a writ of habeas corpus, if the same is bailable, may take an undertaking of bail from such person as in other cases, and file the same in the proper court. Whenever a writ of habeas corpus is returned to a court for hearing and the petitioner is charged with an offense other than a crime of violence or committed with a deadly weapon or involving the forcible taking or destruction of the property of another, but the prisoner does not stand convicted of any offense, the amount of the bail must be set immediately if no bail has theretofore been fixed.

§1492. Judge, when to remand.

If a party brought before the court or judge on the return of the writ is not entitled to his discharge, and is not bailed, where such bail is allowable, the court or judge must remand him to custody or place him under the restraint from which he was taken, if the person under whose custody or restraint he was is legally entitled thereto.

§1493. Person in illegal custody may be committed to legal custody.

In cases where any party is held under illegal restraint or custody, or any other person is entitled to the restraint or custody of such party, the Judge or Court may order such party to be committed to the restraint or custody of such person as is by law entitled thereto.

§1494. Disposition of party, pending proceedings on return.

Until judgment is given on the return, the Court or Judge before whom any party may be brought on such writ may commit him to the custody of the Sheriff of the county, or place him in such care or under such custody as his age or circumstances may require.

§1495. Defect of form in the writ immaterial, when.

No writ of habeas corpus can be disobeyed for defect of form, if it sufficiently appear therefrom in whose custody or under whose restraint the party imprisoned or restrained is, the officer or person detaining him, and the Court or Judge before whom he is to be brought.

§1496. Imprisonment after discharge, in what cases permitted.

No person who has been discharged by the order of the court or judge upon habeas corpus can be again imprisoned, restrained, or kept in custody for the same cause, except in the following cases:

1. If he has been discharged from custody on a criminal charge, and is afterwards committed for the same offense, by legal order or process;

2. If, after a discharge for defect of proof, or for any defect of the process, warrant, or commitment in a criminal case, the prisoner is again arrested on sufficient proof and committed by legal process for the same offense.

§1497. Warrant may issue instead of writ, in certain cases.

When it appears to any court, or judge, authorized by law to issue the writ of habeas corpus, that any one is illegally held in custody, confinement, or restraint, and that there is reason to believe that the person will be carried out of the jurisdiction of the court or judge before whom the application is made, or will suffer some irreparable injury before compliance with the writ of habeas corpus can be enforced, the court or judge may cause a warrant to be issued, reciting the facts, and directed to any peace officer, commanding the peace officer to take the person held in custody, confinement, or restraint, and immediately bring him or her before the court or judge, to be dealt with according to law.

§1498. Warrant may include person charged with illegal detention.

The Court or Judge may also insert in such warrant a command for the apprehension of the person charged with such illegal detention and restraint.

§1499. Warrant, how executed.

The officer to whom such warrant is delivered must execute it by bringing the person therein named before the Court or Judge who directed the issuing of such warrant.

© 1992 by J., B. & L. Gould
Printed in the U.S.A.　　EP

§1500. Return and hearing on.

The person alleged to have such party under illegal confinement or restraint may make return to such warrant as in case of a writ of habeas corpus, and the same may be denied, and like allegations, proofs, and trial may thereupon be had as upon a return to a writ of habeas corpus.

§1501. Party may be discharged or remanded.

If such party is held under illegal restraint or custody, he must be discharged; and if not, he must be restored to the care or custody of the person entitled thereto.

§1502. Writ and process may issue and be served at any time.

Any writ or process authorized by this chapter may be issued and served on any day or at any time.

§1503. By whom issued and when returnable.

All writs, warrants, process, and subpoenas authorized by the provisions of this chapter must be issued by the clerk of the court, and, except subpoenas, must be sealed with the seal of such court, and served and returned forthwith, unless the court or judge shall specify a particular time for any such return.

§1504. Return made at county seat.

All such writs and process, when made returnable before a judge, must be returned before him at the county seat, and there heard and determined.

§1505. Refusal to comply with writ.

If the officer or person to whom a writ of habeas corpus is directed, refuses obedience to the command thereof, he shall forfeit and pay to the person aggrieved a sum not exceeding ten thousand dollars ($10,000), to be recovered by action in any court of competent jurisdiction.

§1506. Appeals.

An appeal may be taken to the court of appeal by the people from a final order of a superior court made upon the return of a writ of habeas corpus discharging a defendant or otherwise granting all or any part of the relief sought, in all criminal cases, excepting criminal cases where judgment of death has been rendered, and in such cases to the Supreme Court; and in all criminal cases where an application for a writ of habeas corpus has been heard and determined in a court of appeal, either the defendant or the people may apply for a hearing in the Supreme Court. Such appeal shall be taken and such application for hearing in the Supreme Court shall be made in accordance with rules to be laid down by the Judicial Council. If the people appeal from an order granting the discharge or release of the defendant, or petition for hearing in either the court of appeal or the Supreme Court, the defendant shall be admitted to bail or released on his own recognizance or any other conditions which the court deems just and reasonable, subject to the same limitations, terms, and conditions which are applicable to, or may be imposed upon, a defendant who is awaiting trial. If the order grants relief other than a discharge or release from custody, the trial court or the court in which the appeal or petition for hearing is pending may, upon application by the people, in its discretion, and upon such conditions as it deems just stay the execution of the order pending final determination of the matter.

§1507. Noncriminal cases; appeals.

Where an application for a writ of habeas corpus has been made by or on behalf of any person other than a defendant in a criminal case, an appeal may be taken to the court of appeal from a final order of a superior court granting all or any part of the relief sought; and where such application has been heard and determined in a court of appeal, either on an application filed in that court or on appeal from a superior court, and all or any part of the relief sought has been granted, an application may be made for a hearing in the Supreme Court. Such appeal shall be taken and such application for hearing in the Supreme Court shall be made in accordance with rules to be laid down by the Judicial Council. The court which made the order granting relief or the court in which the appeal or petition for hearing is pending may, in its discretion, and upon such conditions as it deems just stay the execution of the order pending final determination of the matter.

§1508. Returns when isssued by certain courts.

(a) A writ of habeas corpus issued by the Supreme Court or a judge thereof may be made returnable before the issuing judge or his court, before any court of appeal or judge thereof, or before any superior court or judge thereof.

(b) A writ of habeas corpus issued by a court of appeal or a judge thereof may be made returnable before the issuing judge or his court or before any superior court or judge thereof located in that appellate district.

(c) A writ of habeas corpus issued by a superior court or a judge thereof may be made returnable before the issuing judge or his court.

CHAPTER 2

PRETRIAL REVIEW

§1510. Time limits.

The denial of a motion made pursuant to Section 995 or 1538.5 may be reviewed prior to trial only if the motion was made by the defendant in the trial court not later than 45 days following defendant's arraignment on the complaint if a misdemeanor, or 60 days following defendant's arraignment on the information or indictment if a felony, unless within these time limits the defendant was unaware of the issue or had no opportunity to raise the issue.

§1511. Legislative intent.

(a) In addition to petitions for a writ of mandate, prohibition, or review which the people are authorized to file pursuant to any other statute or pursuant to any court decision, the people may also seek review of an order granting a defendant's motion for severance or discovery by a petition for a writ of mandate or prohibition.

(b) In construing the legislative intent of subdivision (a), no inference shall be drawn from the amendment to Assembly Bill 1052 of the 1989-90 Regular Session of the Legislature which deleted reference to the case of People v. Superior Court, 69 Cal. 2d 491. (*Added by Stats 1989 ch 560 §1, eff. 1/1/90. See other section 1511 below.*)

§1511. Issuance of writ of mandate and remittitur.

If in a felony case the superior court sets the trial beyond the period of time specified in Section 1049.5, in violation of Section 1049.5, or continues the hearing of any matter without good cause, and good cause is required by law for such a continuance, either party may file a petition for writ of mandate or prohibition in the court of appeal seeking immediate appellate review of the ruling setting the trial or granting the continuance. Such a petition shall have precedence over all other cases in the court to which the petition is assigned, including, but not limited to, cases that originated in the juvenile court. If the court of appeal grants a peremptory writ, it shall issue the writ and a remittitur three court days afer its decision becomes final as to that court if such action is necessay to prevent mootness or to prevent frustration of the relief granted, notwithstanding the right of the parties to file a petiton for review in the Supreme Court. When the court of appeal issues the writ and remittitur as provided herein, the writ shall command the superior court to proceed with the criminal case without further delay, other than that reasonably necessary for the parties to obtain the attendance of their witnesss.

The Supreme Court may stay or recall the issuance of the writ and remittitur. The Supreme Court's failure to stay or recall the issuance of the writ and remittitur shall not deprive the respondent or the real party in interest of its right to file a petition for review in the Supreme Court. *(Added by Initiative Measure, Prop 115 §28, approved 6/5/90. See other section 1511 above.)*

CHAPTER 3

OF SEARCH WARRANTS

§1523. Search warrant defined.

A search warrant is an order in writing, in the name of the people, signed by a magistrate, directed to a peace-officer, commanding him to search for personal property, and bring it before the magistrate.

§1524. Grounds.

(a) A search warrant may be issued upon any of the following grounds:

(1) When the property was stolen or embezzled.

(2) When the property or things were used as the means of committing a felony.

(3) When the property or things are in the possession of any person with the intent to use it as a means of committing a public offense, or in the possession of another to whom he or she may have delivered it for the purpose of concealing it or preventing its being discovered.

(4) When the property or things to be seized consist of any item or constitutes any evidence which tends to show a felony has been committed, or tends to show that a particular person has committed a felony.

(5) When the property or things to be seized consist of evidence which tends to show that sexual exploitation of a child, in violation of Section 311.3, has occurred or is occurring.

(b) The property or things described in subdivision (a) may be taken on the warrant from any place, or from any person in whose possession it may be.

(c) Notwithstanding subdivision (a) or (b), no search warrant shall issue for any documentary evidence in the possession or under the control of any person, who is a lawyer as defined in Section 950 of the Evidence Code, a physician as defined in Section 990 of the Evidence Code, a psychotherapist as defined in Section 1010 of the Evidence Code, or a clergyman as defined in Section 1030 of the Evidence Code, and who is not reasonably suspected of engaging or having engaged in criminal activity related to the documentary evidence for which a warrant is requested unless the following procedure has been complied with:

(1) At the time of the issuance of the warrant the court shall appoint a special master in accordance with subdivision (d) to accompany the person who will serve the warrant. Upon service of the warrant, the special master shall inform the party served of the specific items being sought and that the party shall have the opportunity to provide the items requested. If the party, in the judgment of the special master, fails to provide the items requested, the special master shall conduct a search for the items in the areas indicated in the search warrant.

(2) If the party who has been served states that an item or items should not be disclosed, they shall be sealed by the special master and taken to court for a hearing.

At the hearing the party searched shall be entitled to raise any issues which may be raised pursuant to Section 1538.5 as well as a claim that the item or items are privileged, as provided by law. Any such hearing shall be held in the superior court. The court shall provide sufficient time for the parties to obtain counsel and make any motions or present any evidence. The hearing shall be held within three days of the service of the warrant unless the court makes a finding that the expedited hearing is impracticable. In that case the matter shall be heard at the earliest possible time.

(3) Any such warrant must, whenever practicable, be served during normal business hours. In addition, any such warrant must be served upon a party who appears to have possession or control of the items sought. If after reasonable efforts, the party serving the warrant is unable to locate any such person, the special master shall seal and return to the court for determination by the court any item which appears to be privileged as provided by law.

(d) As used in this section, a "special master" is an attorney who is a member in good standing of the California State Bar and who has been selected from a list of qualified attorneys which is maintained by the State Bar particularly for the purposes of conducting the searches described in this section. These attorneys shall serve without compensation. A special master shall be considered a public employee, and the governmental entity which caused the search warrant to be issued shall be considered the employer of the special master and the applicable public entity, for purposes of Division 3.6 (commencing with Section 810) of Title 1 of the Government Code, relating to claims and actions against public entities and public employees. In selecting the special master the court shall make every reasonable effort to insure that the person selected has no relationship with any of the parties involved in the pending matter. Any information obtained by the special master shall be confidential and shall not be divulged except in direct response to inquiry by the court.

In any case in which the magistrate determines that, after reasonable efforts have been made to obtain a special master, a special master is not available and would not be available within a reasonable period of

© 1992 by J., B. & L. Gould
Printed in the U.S.A. **EP**

time, the magistrate may direct the party seeking the order to conduct the search in the manner described in this section in lieu of the special master.

(e) Any search conducted pursuant to this section by a special master may be conducted in such a manner as to permit the party serving the warrant or his or her designee to accompany the special master as he or she conducts his search. However, that party or his or her designee shall not participate in the search nor shall he or she examine any of the items being searched by the special master except upon agreement of the party upon whom the warrant has been served.

(f) As used in this section "documentary evidence" includes, but is not limited to, writings, documents, blueprints, drawings, photographs, computer printouts, microfilms, X-rays, files, diagrams, ledgers, books, tapes, audio and video recordings, films or papers of any type or description.

(g) No warrant shall issue for any item or items described in Section 1070 of the Evidence Code.

§1524.1. AIDS testing for defendants.

(a) The primary purpose of the testing and disclosure provided in this section is to benefit the victim of a crime by informing the victim whether the defendant is infected with the AIDS virus. It is also the intent of the Legislature in enacting this section to protect the health of both victims of crime and those accused of committing a crime. Nothing in this section shall be construed to authorize mandatory testing or disclosure of test results for the purpose of a charging decision by a prosecutor, nor, except as specified in subdivisions (g) and (i), shall this section be construed to authorize breach of the confidentiality provisions contained in Chapter 1.11 (commencing with Section 199.20) of Part 1 of Division 1 of the Health and Safety Code.

(b) (1) Notwithstanding the provisions of Chapter 1.11 (commencing with Section 199.20) of Part 1 of Division 1 of the Health and Safety Code, when a defendant has been charged by complaint, information, or indictment with a crime, or a minor is the subject of a petition filed in juvenile court alleging commission of a crime, the court, at the request of the victim, may issue a search warrant for the purpose of testing the accused's blood with any HIV test, as defined in Section 26 of the Health and Safety Code only under the following circumstances: When the court finds, upon the conclusion of the hearing described in paragraph (2), or in those cases in which a preliminary hearing is not required to be held, the court also finds that there is probable cause to believe that the accused committed the offense, and that there is probable cause to believe that blood, semen, or any other body fluid identified by the State Department of Health Services in appropriate regulations as capable of transmitting the human immunodeficiency virus has been transferred from the accused to the victim.

(2) Prior to the issuance of a search warrant pursuant to paragraph (1), the court, where applicable and at the conclusion of the preliminary examination if the defendant is ordered to answer pursuant to Section 872, shall conduct a hearing at which both the victim and the defendant have the right to be present. During the hearing only affidavits, counter affidavits, and medical reports regarding the facts which support or rebut the issuance of a search warrant under paragraph (1) shall be admissible.

(c) (1) In all cases in which the person has been charged by complaint, information, or indictment with a crime, or is the subject of a petition filed in a juvenile court alleging the commission of a crime, the prosecutor shall advise the victim of his or her right to make this request. To assist the victim of the crime to determine whether he or she should make this request, the prosecutor shall refer the victim to the local health officer for prerequest counseling to help that person understand the extent to which the particular circumstances of the crime may or may not have put the victim at risk of transmission of HIV from the accused, to ensure that the victim understands both the benefits and limitations of the current tests for HIV, to help the victim decide whether he or she wants to request that the accused be tested, and to help the victim decide whether he or she wants to be tested.

(2) The Department of Justice, in cooperation with the California District Attorneys Association, shall prepare a form to be used in providing victims with the notice required by paragraph (1).

(d) If the victim decides to request HIV testing of the accused, the victim shall request the issuance of a search warrant, as described in subdivision (b).

Neither the failure of a prosecutor to refer or advise the victim as provided in this subdivision, nor the failure or refusal by the victim to seek or obtain counseling, shall be considered by the court in ruling on the victim's request.

(e) The local health officer shall make provision for administering all HIV tests ordered pursuant to subdivision (b).

(f) Any blood tested pursuant to subdivision (b) shall be subjected to appropriate confirmatory tests to ensure accuracy of the first test results, and under no circumstances shall test results be transmitted to the victim or the accused unless any initially reactive test result has been confirmed by appropriate confirmatory tests for positive reactors.

(g) The local health officer shall have the responsibility for disclosing test results to the victim who requested the test and to the accused who was tested. However, no positive test results shall be disclosed to the victim or to the accused without also providing or offering professional counseling appropriate to the circumstances.

(h) The local health officer and victim shall comply with all laws and policies relating to medical confidentiality subject to the disclosure authorized by subdivisions (g) and (i).

(i) Any victim who receives information from the health officer pursuant to subdivision (g) may disclose the test results as the victim deems necessary to protect his or her health and safety or the health and safety of his or her family or sexual partner.

(j) Any person transmitting test results or disclosing information pursuant to this section shall be immune from civil liability for any actions taken in compliance with this section.

(k) The results of any blood tested pursuant to subdivision (b) shall not be used in any criminal proceeding as evidence of either guilt or innocence. *(Amended by Stats 1989 ch 1360 §118, eff. 1/1/90.)*

§1525. Probable cause.

A search warrant cannot be issued but upon probable cause, supported by affidavit, naming or describing the person, and particularly describing the property and the place to be searched.

The application shall specify when applicable, that the place to be searched is in the possession or under the control of an attorney, physician, psychotherapist or clergyman.

§1526. Examination of person seeking warrant.

(a) The magistrate may, before issuing the warrant, examine on oath the person seeking the warrant and any witnesses he may produce, and must take his affidavit or their affidavits in writing, and cause same to be subscribed by the party or parties making same.

(b) In lieu of the written affidavit required in subdivision (a), the magistrate may take an oral statement under oath which shall be recorded and transcribed. The transcribed statement shall be deemed to be an affidavit for the purposes of this chapter. In such cases, the recording of the sworn oral statement and the transcribed statement shall be certified by the magistrate receiving it and shall be filed with the clerk of the court. In the alternative in such cases, the sworn oral statement shall be recorded by a certified court reporter and the transcript of the statement shall be certified by the reporter, after which the magistrate receiving it shall certify the transcript which shall be filed with the clerk of the court.

§1527. Affidavits.

The affidavit or affidavits must set forth the facts tending to establish the grounds of the application, or probable cause for believing that they exist.

§1528. Issuance; authorization to sign duplicate.

(a) If the magistrate is thereupon satisfied of the existence of the grounds of the application, or that there is probable cause to believe their existence, he must issue a search warrant, signed by him with his name of office, to a peace officer in his county, commanding him forthwith to search the person or place named, for the property or things specified, and to retain such property or things in his custody subject to order of the court as provided by Section 1536.

(b) The magistrate may orally authorize a peace officer to sign the magistrate's name on a duplicate original warrant. A duplicate original warrant shall be deemed to be a search warrant for the purposes of this chapter, and it shall be returned to the magistrate as provided for in Section 1537. In such cases, the magistrate shall enter on the face of the original warrant the exact time of the issuance of the warrant and shall sign and file the original warrant and the duplicate original warrant with the clerk of the court as provided for in Section 1541.

§1529. Warrant form.

The warrant shall be in substantially the following form:

County of _____

The people of the State of California to any sheriff, constable, marshal, or policeman in the County of __ :

Proof, by affidavit, having been this day made before me by (naming every person whose affidavit has been taken), that (stating the grounds of the application, according to Section 1524, or, if the affidavit be not positive, that there is probable cause for believing that ____ stating the ground of the application in the same manner), you are therefore commanded, in the daytime (or at any time of the day or night, as the case may be, according to Section 1533), to make search on the person of C. D. (or in the house situated ____ , describing it or any other place to be searched, with reasonable particularity, as the case may be) for the following property: (describing it with reasonable particularity); and if you find the same or any part thereof, to bring it forthwith before me (or this court) at (stating the place).

Given under my hand, and dated this __ day of ___, A.D. 19.

E. F., Judge of the Justice Court (or as the case may be).

§1530. By whom served.

A search warrant may in all cases be served by any of the officers mentioned in its directions, but by no other person, except in aid of the officer on his requiring it, he being present and acting in its execution.

§1531. Officer may break open door, etc., to execute warrant.

The officer may break open any outer or inner door or window of a house, or any part of a house, or anything therein, to execute the warrant, if, after notice of his authority and purpose, he is refused admittance.

§1532. May break open door, etc., to liberate person acting in his aid.

He may break open any outer or inner door or window of a house, for the purpose of liberating a person who, having entered to aid him in the execution of the warrant, is detained therein, or when necessary for his own liberation.

§1533. Direction to serve warrant in daytime or night.

Upon a showing of good cause, the magistrate may, in his or her discretion, insert a direction in a search warrant that it may be served at any time of the day or night. In the absence of such a direction, the warrant shall be served only between the hours of 7 a.m. and 10 p.m.

When establishing "good cause" under this section, the magistrate shall consider the safety of the peace officers serving the warrant and the safety of the public as a valid basis for nighttime endorsements. *(Amended by Stats 1986 ch 257 §1.)*

§1534. Time limit of execution.

(a) A search warrant shall be executed and returned within 10 days after date of issuance. A warrant executed within the 10-day period shall be deemed to have been timely executed and no further showing of timeliness need be made. After the expiration of 10 days, the warrant, unless executed, is void. The documents and records of the court relating to the warrant need not be open to the public until the execution and return of the warrant or the expiration of the 10-day period after issuance. Thereafter, if the warrant has been executed, the documents and records shall be open to the public as a judicial record.

(b) If a duplicate original search warrant has been executed, the peace officer who executed the warrant shall enter the exact time of its execution on its face.

(c) A search warrant may be made returnable before the issuing magistrate or his court.

§1535. Officer to give receipt for property taken.

When the officer takes property under the warrant, he must give a receipt for the property taken (specifying it in detail) to the person from whom it was taken by him, or in whose possession it was found; or, in the

© 1992 by J., B. & L. Gould
Printed in the U.S.A.   EP

absence of any person, he must leave it in the place where he found the property.

§1536. Retention of property by officer.

All property or things taken on a warrant must be retained by the officer in his custody, subject to the order of the court to which he is required to return the proceedings before him, or of any other court in which the offense in respect to which the property or things taken is triable.

§1537. Return of warrant and delivery of inventory of property taken.

The officer must forthwith return the warrant to the magistrate, and deliver to him a written inventory of the property taken, made publicly or in the presence of the person from whose possession it was taken, and of the applicant for the warrant, if they are present, verified by the affidavit of the officer at the foot of the inventory, and taken before the magistrate at the time, to the following effect: "I, R. S., the officer by whom this warrant was executed, do swear that the above inventory contains a true and detailed account of all the property taken by me on the warrant."

§1538. Copy of inventory, to whom delivered.

The magistrate must thereupon, if required, deliver a copy of the inventory to the person from whose possession the property was taken, and to the applicant for the warrant.

§1538.5. Motions by defendant in proceedings.

(a) A defendant may move for the return of property or to suppress as evidence any tangible or intangible thing obtained as a result of a search or seizure on either of the following grounds:

(1) The search or seizure without a warrant was unreasonable.

(2) The search or seizure with a warrant was unreasonable because (i) the warrant is insufficient on its face; (ii) the property or evidence obtained is not that described in the warrant; (iii) there was not probable cause for the issuance of the warrant; (iv) the method of execution of the warrant violated federal or state constitutional standards; (v) there was any other violation of federal or state constitutional standards.

(b) When consistent with the procedures set forth in this section and subject to the provisions of Section 170 through 170.6 of the Code of Civil Procedure, the motion should first be heard by the magistrate who issued the search warrant if there is a warrant.

(c) Whenever a search or seizure motion is made in the municipal, justice, or superior court as provided in this section, the judge or magistrate shall receive evidence on any issue of fact necessary to determine the motion.

(d) If a search or seizure motion is granted pursuant to the proceedings authorized by this section, the property or evidence shall not be admissible against the movant at any trial or other hearing unless further proceedings authorized by this section, Section 871.5, Section 1238, or Section 1466 are utilized by the people.

(e) If a search or seizure motion is granted at a trial, the property shall be returned upon order of the court unless it is otherwise subject to lawful detention. If the motion is granted at a special hearing, the property shall be returned upon order of the court only if, after the conclusion of any further proceedings authorized by this section or Section 1238 or Section 1466, the property is not subject to lawful detention or

if the time for initiating such proceedings has expired, whichever occurs last. If the motion is granted at a preliminary hearing, the property shall be returned upon order of court after 10 days unless the property is otherwise subject to lawful detention or unless, within that time, further proceedings authorized by this section, Section 871.5, or Section 1238 are utilized; if they are utilized, the property shall be returned only if, after the conclusion of such proceedings, the property is no longer subject to lawful detention.

(f) If the property or evidence relates to a felony offense initiated by a complaint, the motion shall be made in the superior court only upon filing of an information, except that the defendant may make the motion at the preliminary hearing in the municipal or justice court but the motion in the municipal or justice court shall be restricted to evidence sought to be introduced by the people at the preliminary hearing.

(g) If the property or evidence relates to a misdemeanor complaint, the motion shall be made in the municipal or justice court before trial and heard prior to trial at a special hearing relating to the validity of the search or seizure. If the property or evidence relates to a misdemeanor filed together with a felony, the procedure provided for a felony in this section and Sections 1238 and 1539 shall be applicable.

(h) If, prior to the trial of a felony or misdemeanor, opportunity for this motion did not exist or the defendant was not aware of the grounds for the motion, the defendant shall have the right to make this motion during the course of trial in the municipal, justice, or superior court.

(i) If the property or evidence obtained relates to a felony offense initiated by complaint and the defendant was held to answer at the preliminary hearing, or if the property or evidence relates to a felony offense initiated by indictment, the defendant shall have the right to renew or make the motion in the superior court at a special hearing relating to the validity of the search or seizure which shall be heard prior to trial and at least 10 days after notice to the people unless the people are willing to waive a portion of this time. If the offense was initiated by indictment or if the offense was initiated by complaint and no motion was made at the preliminary hearing, the defendant shall have the right to fully litigate the validity of a search or seizure on the basis of the evidence presented at a special hearing. If the motion was made at the preliminary hearing, unless otherwise agreed to by all parties, evidence presented at the special hearing shall be limited to the transcript of the preliminary hearing and to evidence which could not reasonably have been presented at the preliminary hearing, except that the people may recall witnesses who testified at the preliminary hearing. If the people object to the presentation of evidence at the special hearing on the grounds that the evidence could reasonably have been presented at the preliminary hearing, the defendant shall be entitled to an in camera hearing to determine that issue. The superior court shall base its ruling on all evidence presented at the special hearing and on the transcript of the preliminary hearing, and the findings of the magistrate shall be binding on the superior court as to evidence or property not affected by evidence presented at the special hearing. After the special hearing is held in the superior court, any review thereafter desired by the defendant prior to trial shall be by means of an extraordinary writ of mandate or prohibition filed within 30 days after the denial of his or her motion at the special hearing.

(j) If the property or evidence relates to a felony offense initiated by complaint and the defendant's motion for the return of the property or suppression of the evidence at the preliminary hearing is granted, and if the defendant is not held to answer at the preliminary hearing, the people may file a new complaint or seek an indictment after the preliminary hearing, and the ruling at the prior hearing shall not be binding in any subsequent proceeding. In the alternative, the people may move to reinstate the complaint, or those parts of the complaint for which the defendant was not held to answer, pursuant to Section 871.5. If the property or evidence relates to a felony offense initiated by complaint and the defendant's motion for the return or suppression of the property or evidence at the preliminary hearing is granted, and if the defendant is held to answer at the preliminary hearing, the ruling at the preliminary hearing shall be binding upon the people unless, upon notice to the defendant and the court in which the preliminary hearing was held and upon the filing of an information, the people within 15 days after the preliminary hearing request in the superior court a special hearing, in which case the validity of the search or seizure shall be relitigated de novo on the basis of the evidence presented at the special hearing, and the defendant shall be entitled, as a matter of right, to a continuance of the special hearing for a period of time up to 30 days. If defendant's motion is granted at a special hearing in the superior court, the people, if they have additional evidence relating to the motion and not presented at the special hearing, shall have the right to show good cause at the trial why such evidence was not presented at the special hearing and why the prior ruling at the special hearing should not be binding, or the people may seek appellate review as provided in subdivision (o), unless the court prior to the time such review is sought has dismissed the case pursuant to Section 1385. If the property or evidence seized relates solely to a misdemeanor complaint, and the defendant made a motion for the return of property or the suppression of evidence in the municipal court or justice court prior to trial, both the people and defendant shall have the right to appeal any decision of that court relating to that motion to the superior court of the county in which such inferior court is located, in accordance with the California Rules of Court provisions governing appeals from municipal and justice courts in criminal cases. If the people prosecute review by appeal or writ to decision, or any review thereof, in a felony or misdemeanor case, it shall be binding upon them.

(k) If the defendant's motion to return property or suppress evidence is granted and the case is dismissed pursuant to Section 1385, or the people appeal in a misdemeanor case pursuant to subdivision (j), the defendant shall be released pursuant to Section 1318 if he or she is in custody and not returned to custody unless the proceedings are resumed in the trial court and he or she is lawfully ordered by the court to be returned to custody.

If the defendant's motion to return property or suppress evidence is granted and the people file a petition for writ of mandate or prohibition pursuant to subdivision (o) or a notice of intention to file such a petition, the defendant shall be released pursuant to Section 1318 unless (1) he or she is charged with a capital offense in a case where the proof is evident and the presumption great, or (2) he or she is charged with a noncapital offense defined in Chapter 1 (commenc-

ing with Section 187) of Title 8 of Part 1 and the court orders that the defendant be discharged from actual custody upon bail.

(l) If the defendant's motion to return property or suppress evidence is granted, the trial of a criminal case shall be stayed to a specified date pending the termination in the appellate courts of this state of the proceedings provided for in this section, Section 871.5, Section 1238, or Section 1466 and, except upon stipulation of the parties, pending the time for the initiation of such proceedings. Upon the termination of such proceedings, the defendant shall be brought to trial as provided by Section 1382, and subject to the provisions of Section 1382, whenever the people have sought and been denied appellate review pursuant to subdivision (o), the defendant shall be entitled to have the action dismissed if he or she is not brought to trial within 30 days of the date of the order which is the last denial of the petition. Nothing contained in this subdivision shall prohibit a court, at the same time as it rules upon the search and seizure motion, from dismissing a case pursuant to Section 1385 when such dismissal is upon the court's own motion and is based upon an order at the special hearing granting the defendant's motion to return property or suppress evidence. In a misdemeanor case, the defendant shall be entitled to a continuance of up to 30 days if he or she intends to file a motion to return property or suppress evidence and needs this time to prepare for the special hearing on the motion. In case of an appeal by the defendant in a misdemeanor case from the denial of such motion, he or she shall be entitled to bail as a matter of right, and, in the discretion of the trial or appellate court, may be released on his or her own recognizance pursuant to Section 1318.

(m) The proceedings provided for in this section, Section 871.5, Section 995, Section 1238, and Section 1466 shall constitute the sole and exclusive remedies prior to conviction to test the unreasonableness of a search or seizure where the person making the motion for the return of property or the suppression of evidence is a defendant in a criminal case and the property or thing has been offered or will be offered as evidence against him or her. A defendant may seek further review of the validity of a search or seizure on appeal from a conviction in a criminal case notwithstanding the fact that such judgment of conviction is predicated upon a plea of guilty. Such review on appeal may be obtained by the defendant providing that at some stage of the proceedings prior to conviction he or she has moved for the return of property or the suppression of the evidence.

(n) Nothing contained in this section shall prohibit a person from making a motion, otherwise permitted by law, to return property, brought on the ground that the property obtained is protected by the free speech and press provisions of the Federal and State Constitutions. Nothing in this section shall be construed as altering (i) the law of standing to raise the issue of an unreasonable search or seizure; (ii) the law relating to the status of the person conducting the search or seizure; (iii) the law relating to the burden of proof regarding the search or seizure; (iv) the law relating to the reasonableness of a search or seizure regardless of any warrant which may have been utilized; or (v) the procedure and law relating to a motion made pursuant to Section 871.5 or 995 or the procedures which may be initiated after the granting or denial of such a motion.

© 1992 by J., B. & L. Gould
Printed in the U.S.A.　　EP

(o) Within 30 days after a defendant's motion is granted at a special hearing in the superior court, the people may file a petition for writ of mandate or prohibition, seeking appellate review of the ruling regarding the search or seizure motion. If the trial of a criminal case is set for a date which is less than 30 days from the granting of a defendant's motion at a special hearing in the superior court, the people, if they have not filed such a petition and wish to preserve their right to file such a petition, shall file in the superior court on or before the trial date or within 10 days after the special hearing, whichever occurs last, a notice of intention to file such a petition and shall serve a copy of the notice upon the defendant. *(Amended by Stats 1987 ch 828 §99.)*

§1539. Taking of testimony.

(a) If a special hearing be held in the superior court pursuant to Section 1538.5, or if the grounds on which the warrant was issued be controverted and a motion to return property be made (i) by a defendant on grounds not covered by Section 1538.5; (ii) by a defendant whose property has not been offered or will not be offered as evidence against him; or (iii) by a person who is not a defendant in a criminal action at the time the hearing is held, the judge or magistrate must proceed to take testimony in relation thereto, and the testimony of each witness must be reduced to writing and authenticated by a shorthand reporter in the manner prescribed in Section 869.

(b) The reporter shall forthwith transcribe his shorthand notes pursuant to this section if any party to a special hearing in the superior court files a written request for its preparation with the clerk of the court in which the hearing was held. The reporter shall forthwith file in the superior court an original and as many copies thereof as there are defendants (other than a fictitious defendant) or persons aggrieved. The reporter shall be entitled to compensation in accordance with the provisions of Section 869. In every case in which a transcript is filed as provided in this section, the county clerk shall deliver the original of such transcript so filed with him to the district attorney immediately upon receipt thereof and shall deliver a copy of such transcript to each defendant (other than a fictitious defendant) upon demand by him without cost to him.

(c) Upon a motion by a defendant pursuant to this chapter, the defendant shall be entitled to discover any previous application for a search warrant in the case which was refused by a magistrate for lack of probable cause. *(Amended by Stats 1985 ch 866 §1.)*

§1540. Property, when to be restored to person from whom it was taken.

If it appears that the property taken is not the same as that described in the warrant, or that there is no probable cause for believing the existence of the grounds on which the warrant was issued, the magistrate must cause it to be restored to the person from whom it was taken.

§1541. Annexing, filing and return of affidavits, warrants and inventory.

The magistrate must annex the affidavit, or affidavits, the search warrant and return, and the inventory, and if he has not power to inquire into the offense in respect to which the warrant was issued, he must at once file such warrant and return and such affidavit, or affidavits, and inventory with the clerk of the court having power to so inquire.

§1542. When magistrate may direct defendant to be searched in his presence.

When a person charged with a felony is supposed by the magistrate before whom he is brought to have on his person a dangerous weapon, or anything which may be used as evidence of the commission of the offense, the magistrate may direct him to be searched in his presence, and the weapon or other thing to be retained, subject to his order, or to the order of the Court in which the defendant may be tried.

CHAPTER 3.5

DISCLOSURE OF MEDICAL RECORDS TO LAW ENFORCEMENT AGENCIES

§1543. Provisions.

(a) Records of the identity, diagnosis, prognosis, or treatment of any patient maintained by a health care facility which are not privileged records required to be secured by the special master procedure in Section 1524, or records required by law to be confidential, shall only be disclosed to law enforcement agencies pursuant to this section:

(1) In accordance with the prior written consent of the patient; or

(2) If authorized by an appropriate order of a court of competent jurisdiction in the county where the records are located, granted after application showing good cause therefor. In assessing good cause, the court:

(A) Shall weigh the public interest and the need for disclosure against the injury to the patient, to the physician-patient relationship, and to the treatment services;

(B) Shall determine that there is a reasonable likelihood that the records in question will disclose material information or evidence of substantial value in connection with the investigation or prosecution; or

(3) By a search warrant obtained pursuant to Section 1524.

(b) The prohibitions of this section continue to apply to records concerning any individual who has been a patient, irrespective of whether or when he ceases to be a patient.

(c) Except where an extraordinary order under Section 1544 is granted or a search warrant is obtained pursuant to Section 1524, any health care facility whose records are sought under this chapter shall be notified of the application and afforded an opportunity to appear and be heard thereon.

(d) Both disclosure and dissemination of any information from the records shall be limited under the terms of the order to assure that no information will be unnecessarily disclosed and that dissemination will be no wider than necessary.

This chapter shall not apply to investigations of fraud in the provision or receipt of Medi-Cal benefits, investigations of insurance fraud performed by the Department of Insurance or the California Highway Patrol and investigations and research regarding occupational health and safety performed by or under agreement with the Department of Industrial Relations. Access to medical records in such investigations shall be governed by all laws in effect at the time access is sought.

(e) Nothing in this chapter shall prohibit disclosure by a medical facility or medical provider of information contained in medical records where disclosure to specific agencies is mandated by statutes or regulations.

(f) This chapter shall not be construed to authorize disclosure of privileged records to law enforcement agencies by the procedure set forth in this chapter, where such privileged records are required to be secured by the special master procedure set forth in subdivision (c) of Section 1524 or required by law to be confidential.

§1544. Petition for extraordinary order.

A law enforcement agency applying for disclosure of patient records under Section 1543 may petition the court for an extraordinary order delaying the notice of the application to the health care facility required by subdivision (f) of Section 1543 for a period of 30 days, upon a showing of good cause to believe that notice would seriously impede the investigation.

§1545. Terms defined.

For the purposes of this chapter:

(a) "Health care facility" means any clinic, health dispensary, or health facility, licensed pursuant to Division 2 (commencing with Section 1200) of the Health and Safety Code, or any mental hospital, drug abuse clinic, or detoxification center.

(b) "Law enforcement agency" means the Attorney General of the State of California, every district attorney, and every agency of the State of California expressly authorized by statute to investigate or prosecute law violators.

CHAPTER 4

PROCEEDINGS AGAINST FUGITIVES FROM JUSTICE

§1547. Reward for information leading to arrest and conviction of escaped convict and other criminals.

(a) The Governor may offer a reward of not more than fifty thousand dollars ($50,000), payable out of the General Fund, for information leading to the arrest and conviction of any of the following:

(1) Any convict who has escaped from a state prison, prison camp, prison farm, or the custody of any prison officer or employee or as provided in Section 3059 or 4530.

(2) Any person who has committed, or is charged with the commission of, an offense punishable by death.

(3) Any person engaged in the robbery or hijacking of, or any attempt to rob or hijack, any person upon or in charge of, in whole or in part, any public conveyance engaged at the time in carrying passengers within this state.

(4) Any person who kills, assaults with a deadly weapon, or inflicts serious bodily harm upon a police officer who is acting in the line of duty.

(5) Any person who has committed a crime involving the burning or bombing of public property, including any public hospital housed in a privately owned facility.

(6) Any person who has committed a crime involving the burning or bombing of any private hospital. A reward may be offered by the Governor in conjunction with such a crime only if a reward in conjunction with the same crime is offered by the hospital, or any other public or private donor on its behalf. The amount of the reward offered by the Governor shall not exceed the aggregate amount offered privately, or fifty thousand dollars ($50,000), whichever is less. Nothing in this paragraph shall preclude a private hospital, or any public or private donor on its behalf, from offering a reward in an amount exceeding fifty thousand dollars ($50,000). If a person providing information for a reward under this paragraph so requests, his or her name and address shall remain confidential. This confidentiality, however, shall not preclude or obstruct the investigations of law enforcement authorities.

(7) Any person who commits a violation of Section 11413.

(8) Any person who commits a violation of Section 207.

(9) Any person who has committed a crime involving the burning or bombing of any bookstore or public or private library not subject to Section 11413. A reward may be offered by the Governor in conjunction with such a crime only if a reward in conjunction with the same crime is offered by the bookstore or library, or any other public or private donor on its behalf. The amount of the reward offered by the Governor shall not exceed the aggregate amount offered privately, or fifty thousand dollars ($50,000), whichever is less. Nothing in this paragraph shall preclude a bookstore or public or private library, or any public or private donor on its behalf from offering a reward in an amount exceeding fifty thousand dollars ($50,000). If a person providing information for a reward under this paragraph so requests, his or her name and address shall remain confidential. This confidentiality, however, shall not preclude or obstruct the investigations of law enforcement authorities.

(b) The reward shall be paid to the person giving the information, immediately upon the conviction of the person so arrested.

(c) As used in this section, "hijacking" means an unauthorized person causing, or attempting to cause, by violence or threat of violence, a public conveyance to go to an unauthorized destination. *(Amended by Stats 1989 chs 20 §1, 1162 §1, eff. 1/1/90.)*

§1548. Terms defined.

As used in this chapter:

(a) "Governor" means any person performing the functions of Governor by authority of the law of this state.

(b) "Executive authority" means the Governor or any person performing the functions of Governor in a State other than this State.

(c) "State," referring to a State other than the State of California, means any other State or Territory, organized or unorganized, of the United States of America.

(d) "Laws of the United States" means: (1) those laws of the United States passed by Congress pursuant to authority given to Congress by the Constitution of the United States where the laws of the United States are controlling, and (2) those laws of the United States not controlling the several States of the United States but which are not in conflict with the provisions of this chapter.

§1548.1. Duty of Governor to arrest and deliver up fugitive.

Subject to the provisions of this chapter, the Constitution of the United States, and the laws of the

© 1992 by J., B. & L. Gould
Printed in the U.S.A.   **EP**

United States, it is the duty of the Governor of this State to have arrested and delivered up to the executive authority of any other State any person charged in that State with treason, felony, or other crime, who has fled from justice and is found in this State.

§1548.2. Demand.

No demand for the extradition of a person charged with crime in another State shall be recognized by the Governor unless it is in writing alleging that the accused was present in the demanding State at the time of the commission of the alleged crime, and that thereafter he fled from that State. Such demand shall be accompanied by a copy of an indictment found or by information or by a copy of an affidavit made before a magistrate in the demanding State together with a copy of any warrant which was issued thereon; or such demand shall be accompanied by a copy of a judgment of conviction or of a sentence imposed in execution thereof, together with a statement by the executive authority of the demanding State that the person claimed has escaped from confinement or has violated the terms of his bail, probation or parole. The indictment, information, or affidavit made before the magistrate must substantially charge the person demanded with having committed a crime under the law of that State; and the copy of indictment, information, affidavit, judgment of conviction or sentence must be certified as authentic by the executive authority making the demand.

§1548.3. Investigation and report.

When a demand is made upon the Governor of this State by the executive authority of another State for the surrender of a person so charged with crime, the Governor may call upon the Attorney General or any district attorney in this State to investigate or assist in investigating the demand, and to report to him the situation and circumstances of the person so demanded, and whether he ought to be surrendered according to the provision of this chapter.

§1549. Agreement for extradition.

When it is desired to have returned to this state a person charged in this state with a crime, and the person is imprisoned or is held under criminal proceedings then pending against him or her in another state, the Governor of this state may agree with the executive authority of the other state for the extradition of the person before the conclusion of the proceedings or his or her term of sentence in the other state, upon the condition that the person be returned to the other state at the expense of this state as soon as the prosecution in this state is terminated.

The Governor of this state may also surrender on demand of the executive authority of any other state any person in this state who is charged in the manner provided in Section 1548.2 with having violated the laws of the demanding state even though such person left the demanding state involuntarily. *(Amended by Stats 1987 ch 828 §101.)*

§1549.1. Surrender of person not in other state when committing act resulting in crime therein.

The Governor of this state may also surrender, on demand of the executive authority of any other state, any person in this state charged in the other state in the manner provided in Section 1548.2 with commit-

ting an act in this state, or in a third state, intentionally resulting in a crime in the state whose executive authority is making the demand. The provisions of this chapter, not otherwise inconsistent, shall apply to those cases, even though the accused was not in the demanding state at the time of the commission of the crime, and has not fled therefrom. Neither the demand, the oath, nor any proceedings under this chapter pursuant to this section need state or show that the accused has fled from justice from, or at the time of the commission of the crime was in, the demanding or other state. *(Amended by Stats 1987 ch 828 §102.)*

§1549.2. Contents, direction, and execution of warrant.

If a demand conforms to the provisions of this chapter, the Governor or agent authorized in writing by the Governor whose authorization has been filed with the Secretary of State shall sign a warrant of arrest, which shall be sealed with the State Seal, and shall be directed to any peace officer or other person whom he may entrust with the execution thereof. The warrant must substantially recite the facts necessary to the validity of its issuance. The provisions of Section 850 shall be applicable to such warrant, except that it shall not be necessary to include a warrant number, address, or description of the subject, provided that a complaint under Section 1551 is then pending against the subject.

§1549.3. Authority conferred.

Such warrant shall authorize the peace officer or other person to whom it is directed:

(a) To arrest the accused at any time and any place where he may be found within the State;

(b) To command the aid of all peace officers or other persons in the execution of the warrant; and

(c) To deliver the accused, subject to the provisions of this chapter, to the duly authorized agent of the demanding State.

§1550. Authority to command assistance.

Every peace officer or other person empowered to make the arrest hereunder shall have the same authority, in arresting the accused, to command assistance therefor as the persons designated in Section 150. Failure or refusal to render that assistance is a violation of Section 150. *(Amended by Stats 1987 ch 828 §103.)*

§1550.1. Taking prisoner before magistrate; proceedings.

No person arrested upon such warrant shall be delivered over to the agent of the executive authority demanding him unless he is first taken forthwith before a magistrate, who shall inform him of the demand made for his surrender, and of the crime with which he is charged, and that he has the right to demand and procure counsel. If the accused or his counsel desires to test the legality of the arrest, the magistrate shall remand the accused to custody, and fix a reasonable time to be allowed him within which to apply for a writ of habeas corpus. If the writ is denied, and probable cause appears for an application for a writ of habeas corpus to another court, or justice or judge thereof, the order denying the writ shall remand the accused to custody, and fix a reasonable time within which the accused may again apply for a writ of habeas corpus. When an application is made for a writ of habeas corpus as contemplated by this section, a copy of the application shall be served as provided in Section 1475, upon the district attorney of the county in which the accused is in custody, and upon the agent of the demanding state. A warrant issued in accordance with the provisions of Section 1549.2 shall be presumed to be valid, and unless a court finds that the person in custody is not the same person named in the warrant, or that the person is not a fugitive from justice, or otherwise subject to extradition under Section 1549.1, or that there is no criminal charge or criminal proceeding pending against the person in the demanding state, or that the documents are not on their face in order, the person named in the warrant shall be held in custody at all times, and shall not be eligible for release on bail.

§1550.2. Delivery in disobedience to preceding section.

Any officer or other person entrusted with a Governor's warrant who delivers to the agent of the demanding State a person in his custody under such Governor's warrant, in wilful disobedience to the preceding section, is guilty of a misdemeanor and, on conviction thereof, shall be fined not more than $1,000 or be imprisoned not more than six months, or both.

§1550.3. Confinement of prisoner.

The officer or persons executing the Governor's warrant of arrest, or the agent of the demanding State to whom the prisoner has been delivered may confine the prisoner in the jail of any county or city through which he may pass. The keeper of such jail must receive and safely keep the prisoner until the officer or person having charge of him is ready to proceed on his route. Such officer or person shall be charged with the expense of keeping the prisoner.

The officer or agent of a demanding State to whom a prisoner has been delivered following extradition proceedings in another State, or to whom a prisoner has been delivered after waiving the extradition in such other State, and who is passing through this State with such a prisoner for the purpose of immediately returning such prisoner to the demanding State may confine the prisoner in the jail of any county or city through which he may pass. The keeper of such jail must receive and safely keep the prisoner until the officer or agent having charge of him is ready to proceed on his route. Such officer or agent shall be charged with the expense of keeping the prisoner. Such officer or agent shall produce and show to the keeper of such jail satisfactory written evidence of the fact that he is actually transporting such prisoner to the demanding State after a requisition by the executive authority thereof. Such prisoner shall not be entitled to demand a new requisition while in this State.

§1551. Issuance of warrant by magistrate.

(a) Whenever any person within this State is charged by a verified complaint before any magistrate of this State with the commission of any crime in any other State, or, with having been convicted of a crime in that State and having escaped from confinement, or having violated the terms of his bail, probation or parole; or (b) whenever complaint is made before any magistrate in this State setting forth on the affidavit of any credible person in another State that a crime

has been committed in such other State and that the accused has been charged in such State with the commission of the crime, or that the accused has been convicted of a crime in that State and has escaped from bail, probation or parole and is believed to be in this State; then the magistrate shall issue a warrant directed to any peace officer commanding him to apprehend the person named therein, wherever he may be found in this State, and to bring him before the same or any other magistrate who is available in or convenient of access to the place where the arrest is made. A certified copy of the sworn charge or complaint and affidavit upon which the warrant is issued shall be attached to the warrant.

§1551.05. Extradition proceedings against outpatients.

(a) Any person on outpatient status pursuant to Title 15 (commencing with Section 1600) of Part 2 or pursuant to subdivision (d) of Section 2972 who leaves this state without complying with Section 1611, or who fails to return to this state on the date specified by the committing court, shall be subject to extradition in accordance with this section.

(b) When the return to this state is required by a person who is subject to extradition pursuant to subdivision (a), the Director of Mental Health shall present to the Governor a written application for requisition for the return of that person. In the requisition application there shall be stated the name of the person, the type of judicial commitment the person is under, the nature of the underlying criminal act which was the basis for the judicial commitment, the circumstances of the noncompliance with Section 1611, and the state in which the person is believed to be, including the specific location of the person, if known.

(c) The application shall be verified, shall be executed in duplicate, and shall be accompanied by two certified copies of the court order of judicial commitment and of the court order authorizing outpatient status. The director may also attach any affidavits or other documents in duplicate as are deemed proper to be submitted with the application. One copy of the application, with the action of the Governor indicated by endorsement thereon, and one copy of the court orders shall be filed in the office of the Secretary of State. The other copies of all papers shall be forwarded with the Governor's requisition.

(d) Upon receipt of an application under this section, the Governor or agent authorized in writing by the Governor whose authorization has been filed with the Secretary of State, may sign a requisition for the return of the person. *(Added by Stats 1988 ch 74 §1, eff. 1/1/89.)*

§1551.1. Arrest without warrant.

The arrest of a person may also be lawfully made by any peace officer, without a warrant, upon reasonable information that the accused stands charged in the courts of any other state with a crime punishable by death or imprisonment for a term exceeding one year, or that the person has been convicted of a crime punishable in the state of conviction by imprisonment for a term exceeding one year and thereafter escaped from confinement or violated the terms of his or her bail, probation or parole. When so arrested the accused shall be taken before a magistrate with all practicable speed and complaint shall be made against him or her under oath setting forth the ground for the arrest as in Section 1551. *(Amended by Stats 1987 ch 828 §104.)*

© 1992 by J., B. & L. Gould
Printed in the U.S.A.   **EP**

§1551.2. Hearing.

At the initial appearance of a person arrested under Section 1551 or 1551.1, he shall be informed of the reason for his arrest and of his right to demand and procure counsel. If the person denies that he is the same person charged with or convicted of a crime in the other state, a hearing shall be held within 10 days to determine whether there is probable cause to believe that he is the same person and whether he is charged with or convicted of a crime in the other state. At the hearing, the magistrate shall accept a certified copy of an indictment found, an information, a verified complaint, a judgment or sentence, or other judicial proceedings against that person in the state in which the crime is charged or the conviction occurred, and such copy shall constitute conclusive proof of its contents. Witnesses from the other state shall not be required to be present at the hearing.

§1551.3. Notices of arrest by magistrate and district attorney.

Immediately upon the arrest of the person charged, the magistrate must give notice thereof to the district attorney. The district attorney must immediately thereafter give notice to the executive authority of the State, or to the prosecuting attorney or presiding judge of the court of the city or county within the State having jurisdiction of the offense, to the end that a demand may be made for the arrest and surrender of the person charged.

§1552. Commitment time limit.

If at the hearing before the magistrate, it appears that the accused is the person charged with having committed the crime alleged, the magistrate must, by a warrant reciting the accusation, commit him to the county jail for such a time, not exceeding thirty days and specified in the warrant, as will enable the arrest of the accused to be made under a warrant of the Governor on a requisition of the executive authority of the State having jurisdiction of the offense, unless the accused give bail as provided in section 1552.1, or until he shall be legally discharged.

§1552.1. Admission to bail.

Unless the offense with which the prisoner is charged, is shown to be an offense punishable by death or life imprisonment under the laws of the state in which it was committed, or it is shown that the prisoner is alleged to have escaped or violated the terms of his parole following conviction of a crime punishable in the state of conviction by imprisonment for a term exceeding one year, the magistrate may admit the person arrested to bail by bond or undertaking, with sufficient sureties, and in such sum as he deems proper, conditioned upon the appearance of such person before him at a time specified in such bond or undertaking, and for his surrender upon the warrant of the Governor of this state. Nothing in this section or in Section 1553 shall be deemed to prevent the immediate service of a Governor's warrant issued under Section 1549.2.

§1552.2. Discharge or recommitment.

If the accused is not arrested under warrant of the Governor by the expiration of the time specified in the warrant, bond, or undertaking, a magistrate may discharge him or may recommit him for a further period of 60 days. In the latter event a justice of the Supreme Court or court of appeal or a judge of the superior court may again take bail for his appearance and surrender, as provided in Section 1552.1 but within a period not to exceed 60 days after the date of such new bond or undertaking.

§1553. Forfeiture of bail; order for arrest.

If the prisoner is admitted to bail, and fails to appear and surrender himself according to the conditions of his bond, the magistrate, by proper order, shall declare the bond forfeited and order his immediate arrest without warrant if he be within this State. Recovery may be had on such bond in the name of the people of the State as in the case of other bonds or undertakings given by a defendant in criminal proceedings.

§1553.1. Surrender to other state or holding in this state.

(a) If a criminal prosecution has been instituted against a person charged under Section 1551 under the laws of this state and is still pending, the Governor, with the consent of the Attorney General, may surrender the person on demand of the executive authority of another state or hold him or her until he or she has been tried and discharged or convicted and served his or her sentence in this state.

(b) If a criminal prosecution has been instituted under the laws of this state against a person charged under Section 1551, the restrictions on the length of commitment contained in Sections 1552 and 1552.2 shall not be applicable during the period that the criminal prosecution is pending in this state.

§1553.2. Inquiry as to guilt or innocence.

The guilt or innocence of the accused as to the crime with which he is charged may not be inquired into by the Governor or in any proceeding after the demand for extradition accompanied by a charge of crime in legal form as above provided has been presented to the Governor, except as such inquiry may be involved in identifying the person held as the person charged with the crime.

§1554. Recall warrant.

The Governor may recall his warrant of arrest or may issue another warrant whenever he deems it proper.

§1554.1. Warrant for return of person from foreign state or country.

Whenever the Governor of this State shall demand the return of a person charged with crime in this State or with escaping from confinement or violating the terms of his bail, probation or parole in this State, from the executive authority of any other State or of any foreign government or the chief justice or an associate justice of the Supreme Court of the District of Columbia authorized to receive such demand, he shall issue a warrant under the seal of this State to an agent, commanding him to receive the person so demanded and to convey him to the proper officer in the county in this State in which the offense was committed.

§1554.2. Application for requisition for return from other state.

(a) When the return to this state of a person charged with crime in this state is required, the district attorney shall present to the Governor his written application for a requisition for the return of the person charged. In such application there shall be stated the name of the person so charged, the crime charged against him, the approximate time, place and circumstances of its commission, and the state in which he is believed to be, including the location of the accused therein at the time the application is made. Such application shall certify that, in the opinion of the district attorney, the ends of justice require the arrest and return of the accused to this state for trial and that the proceeding is not instituted to enforce a private claim.

(b) When the return to this state is required of a person who has been convicted of a crime in this state and who has escaped from confinement or has violated the terms of his bail, probation or parole, the district attorney of the county in which the offense was committed, the Board of Prison Terms, the Director of Corrections, the California Institution for Women, the Youth Authority, or the sheriff of the county from which escape from confinement was made, shall present to the Governor a written application for a requisition for the return of such person. In such application there shall be stated the name of the person, the crime of which he was convicted, the circumstances of his escape or of the violation of the terms of his bail, probation or parole, and the state in which he is believed to be, including the location of such person therein at the time application is made.

(c) The application shall be verified, shall be executed in duplicate, and shall be accompanied by two certified copies of the indictment, the information, or the verified complaint made to the magistrate stating the offense with which the accused is charged, or the judgment of conviction or the sentence. The officer or board requesting the requisition may also attach such affidavits and other documents in duplicate as are deemed proper to be submitted with such application. One copy of the application, with the action of the Governor indicated by endorsement thereon, and one of the certified copies of the indictment, verified complaint, information, or judgment of conviction or sentence shall be filed in the office of the Secretary of State. The other copies of all papers shall be forwarded with the Governor's requisition.

(d) Upon receipt of an application under this section, the Governor or agent authorized in writing by the Governor whose authorization has been filed with the Secretary of State, may sign a requisition for the return of the person charged and any other document incidental to that requisition or to the return of the person charged.

§1555. Exemption from civil process.

A person brought into this State on, or after waiver of extradition based on a criminal charge shall not be subject to service of process in civil actions arising out of the same facts as the criminal proceedings for which he is returned, until he has been convicted in the criminal proceeding, or, if acquitted, until he has had reasonable opportunity to return to the State from which he was extradited.

§1555.1. Waiver of extradition proceedings.

Any person arrested in this state charged with having committed any crime in another state or alleged to have escaped from confinement, or broken the terms of his or her bail, probation or parole may waive the issuance and service of the Governor's warrant provided for in this chapter and all other procedure

incidental to extradition proceedings, by subscribing in the presence of a magistrate within this state a writing which states that he or she consents to return to the demanding state; provided, however, that before such waiver shall be subscribed by such person, the magistrate shall inform him or her of his or her rights to require the issuance and service of a warrant of extradition as provided in this chapter.

If such waiver is executed, it shall forthwith be forwarded to the office of the Governor of this state, and filed therein. The magistrate shall remand the person to custody without bail, unless otherwise stipulated by the district attorney with the concurrence of the other state, and shall direct the officer having such person in custody to deliver such person forthwith to the duly authorized agent of the demanding state, and shall deliver to such agent a copy of such waiver.

Nothing in this section shall be deemed to limit the rights of the accused person to return voluntarily and without formality to the demanding state, provided that state consents, nor shall this procedure of waiver be deemed to be an exclusive procedure or to limit the powers, rights or duties of the officers of the demanding state or of this state.

§1555.2. Refusal to sign waiver of extradition.

(a) If the arrested person refuses to sign a waiver of extradition under Section 1555.1, a hearing shall be held, upon application of the district attorney, to determine whether the person is alleged to have violated the terms of his release within the past five years on bail or own recognizance while charged with a crime punishable in the charging state by imprisonment for a term exceeding one year, or on probation or parole following conviction of a crime punishable in the state of conviction by imprisonment for a term exceeding one year, and whether, as a condition of that release, the person was required to waive extradition.

(b) At the hearing, the district attorney shall present a certified copy of the order from the other state conditionally releasing the person, including the condition that he was required to waive extradition together with a certified copy of the order from the other state directing the return of the person for violating the terms of his conditional release. The magistrate shall accept these certified copies as conclusive proof of their contents and shall presume the validity of the extradition waiver condition.

(c) If the magistrate finds that there is probable cause to believe that the arrested person is the same person named in the conditional release order and the order commanding his return, the magistrate shall forthwith issue an order remanding the person to custody without bail and directing the delivery of the person to duly accredited agents of the other state.

(d) Notwithstanding the provisions of subdivision (c), the district attorney may stipulate, with the concurrence of the other state, that the arrested person may be released on bail or own recognizance pending the arrival of duly accredited agents from the other state.

(e) If the arrested person or his counsel desires to test the legality of the order issued under subdivision (c), the magistrate shall fix a reasonable time to be allowed him within which to apply for a writ of habeas corpus. If the writ is denied and probable cause appears for an application for a writ of habeas corpus to another court, or justice or judge thereof, the order denying the writ shall fix a reasonable time within

© 1992 by J., B. & L. Gould
Printed in the U.S.A.   EP

which the accused may again apply for a writ of habeas corpus. Unless otherwise stipulated pursuant to subdivision (d), the arrested person shall remain in custody without bail.

§1555.3. Rights not waived by state.

Nothing in this chapter shall be deemed to constitute a waiver by this state of its right, power or privilege to try any demanded person for crime committed within this state, or of its right, power or privilege to regain custody of such person by extradition proceedings or otherwise for the purpose of trial, sentence or punishment for any crime committed within this state; nor shall any proceedings had under this chapter which result in, or fail to result in, extradition be deemed a waiver by this state of any of its rights, privileges or jurisdiction in any manner whatsoever.

§1556. Trial of extradited person for further crimes.

After a person has been brought back to this State by extradition proceedings, he may be tried in this State for other crimes which he may be charged with having committed in this State as well as for the crime or crimes specified in the requisition for his extradition.

§1556.1. Interpretation and construction of chapter.

The provisions of this chapter shall be so interpreted and construed as to effectuate its general purposes to make uniform the law of those states which enact legislation based upon the Uniform Criminal Extradition Act.

§1556.2. Title.

This chapter may be cited as the Uniform Criminal Extradition Act.

§1557. Employing person to return fugitive from justice.

(a) This section shall apply when this state, or a city, county, or city and county employs a person to travel to a foreign jurisdiction outside this state for the express purpose of returning a fugitive from justice to this state when the Governor of this state, in the exercise of the authority conferred by Section 2, Article IV, of the Constitution of the United States, or by the laws of this state, has demanded the surrender of such fugitive from the executive authority of any state of the United States, or of any foreign government.

(b) Upon the approval of the Governor, the State Controller shall audit and pay out of the State Treasury as provided in subdivision (c) or (d) the accounts of the person employed to bring back such fugitive, including any money paid by such person for all of the following:

(1) Money paid to the authorities of a sister state for statutory fees in connection with the detention and surrender of such fugitive.

(2) Money paid to the authorities of the sister state for the subsistence of the fugitive while detained by such sister state without payment of which, the authorities of such state refuse to surrender such fugitive.

(3) Where it is necessary to present witnesses or evidence in the sister state, without which the sister state would not surrender the fugitive, the cost of producing such witnesses or evidence in the sister state.

(4) Where the appearance of witnesses has been authorized in advance by the Governor, who may authorize such appearance in unusual cases where the interests of justice would be served, the cost of producing witnesses to appear in the sister state on behalf of the fugitive in opposition to his extradition.

(c) No amount shall be paid out of the State Treasury to a city, county, or city and county except as specified herein.

(1) When a warrant has been issued by any magistrate after the filing of a complaint or the finding of an indictment and its presentation to the court and filing by the clerk, and the person named therein as defendant is a fugitive from justice, who has been found and arrested in any state of the United States or in any foreign government, the county auditor shall draw his warrant and the county treasurer shall pay to the person designated to return the fugitive, the amount of expenses estimated by the district attorney to be incurred in the return of such fugitive.

(2) If the person designated to return the fugitive is a city officer, the city officer authorized to draw warrants on the city treasury shall draw his warrant and the city treasurer shall pay to such person the amount of expenses estimated by the district attorney to be incurred in the return of such fugitive.

(3) The person designated to return the fugitive shall make no disbursements from any such fund so advanced without a receipt being obtained therefor showing the amount, the purpose for which the sum is expended, place, date, and to whom paid.

(4) Such receipts must be filed by such person with the county auditor or appropriate city officer or State Controller, as the case may be, together with an affidavit by such person that the expenditures represented by the receipts were necessarily made in the performance of duty, and when such advance has been made by the county or city treasurer to the person designated to return the fugitive, and has thereafter been audited by the State Controller, the payment thereof shall be made by the State Treasurer to the county or city treasurer, which has advanced the funds.

(5) In every case where the expenses of such person so employed to bring back such fugitive as herein provided, are less than the amount advanced on the recommendation of the district attorney, such persons so employed to bring back such fugitive shall return to the county or city treasurer, as appropriate, the difference in amount between the aggregate amount of receipts so filed by him, as herein employed, and the amount advanced to such person upon the recommendation of the district attorney.

(6) When no advance has been made to the person designated to return the fugitive, the sums expended by him, when audited by the State Controller, shall be paid by the State Treasurer to the person so designated.

(7) Any payments made out of the State Treasury pursuant to the provisions of this section shall be made from appropriations for the fiscal year in which such payments are made.

(d) Payments to state agencies will be made in accord with the rules of the Board of Control.

§1558. Payment to public officer prohibited.

No compensation, fee, profit, or reward of any kind can be paid to or received by a public officer of this state, a corporation or firm, or other person, for a service rendered in procuring from the Governor the demand mentioned in Section 1557, or the surrender of the fugitive, or for conveying him or her to this state, or detaining him or her therein, except as provided for in that section. Every person who violates any of the provisions of this section is guilty of a misdemeanor. *(Amended by Stats 1990 ch 222 §1, eff. 1/1/91.)*

CHAPTER 5

MISCELLANEOUS PROVISIONS RESPECTING SPECIAL PROCEEDINGS OF A CRIMINAL NATURE

§1562. Parties to special proceedings, how designated.

The party prosecuting a special proceeding of a criminal nature is designated in this Code as the complainant, and the adverse party as the defendant.

§1563. Entitling affidavits.

The provisions of Section 1401, in respect to entitling affidavits, are applicable to such proceedings.

§1564. Subpoenas.

The Courts and magistrates before whom such proceedings are prosecuted may issue subpoenas for witnesses, and punish their disobedience in the same manner as in a criminal action.

TITLE 13

PROCEEDINGS FOR BRINGING PERSONS IMPRISONED IN THE STATE PRISON, OR THE JAIL OF ANOTHER COUNTY, BEFORE A COURT

§1567. Bringing prisoners before court.

When it is necessary to have a person imprisoned in the state prison brought before any court, or a person imprisoned in a county jail brought before a court sitting in another county, an order for that purpose may be made by the court and executed by the sheriff of the county where it is made. The order shall be signed by the judge or magistrate and sealed with the seal of the court, if any.   ⬧

The order shall be to the following effect:

County of _____ (as the case may be).

The people of the State of California to the warden of ____ (or sheriff of _____, as the case may be):

An order having been made this day by me, that A. B. be produced in this court as witness in the case of _____, you are commanded to deliver him or her into the custody of _____ .

Dated this ____ day of _____, 19__ .

TITLE 14

DISPOSITION OF FINES AND FORFEITURES
(Repealed by Stats 1979 ch 373.)

TITLE 15

OUTPATIENT STATUS FOR MENTALLY DISORDERED AND DEVELOPMENTALLY DISABLED OFFENDERS

§1600. Applicability of this title.

Any person committed to a state hospital or other treatment facility under the provisions of Section 1026, or Chapter 6 (commencing with Section 1367) of Title 10 of this code, or Section 6316 or 6321 of the Welfare and Institutions Code may be placed on outpatient status from such commitment subject to the procedures and provisions of this title, except that a developmentally disabled person may be placed on outpatient status from such commitment under the provisions of this title as modified by Section 1370.4.

§1600.5. Mentally disordered criminal offenders.

For a person committed as a mentally disordered sex offender or committed pursuant to Section 1026 or 1026.5, who is placed on outpatient status under the provisions of this title, time spent on outpatient status, except when placed in a locked facility, shall not count as actual custody and shall not be credited toward the person's maximum term of commitment. Time spent in any locked facility shall count as actual custody and shall be credited toward the person's maximum term of commitment. *(Added by Stats 1985 ch 1416 §2.)*

§1601. Violent persons.

(a) In the case of any person charged with and found incompetent on a charge of, convicted of, or found not guilty by reason of insanity of murder, mayhem, aggravated mayhem, a violation of Section 207 or 209 in which the victim suffers intentionally inflicted great bodily injury, robbery with a deadly or dangerous weapon or in which the victim suffers great bodily injury, a violation of subdivision (a) or (b) of Section 451, a violation of subdivision 2 or 3 of Section 261, a violation of Section 459 in the first degree, a violation of Section 220 in which the victim suffers great bodily injury, a violation of Section 288, a violation of Section 12303.1, 12303.2, 12303.3, 12308, 12309, or 12310, or any felony involving death, great bodily injury, or an act which poses a serious threat of bodily harm to another person, outpatient status under this title shall not be available until that person has actually been confined in a state hospital or other facility for 180 days or more after having been committed under the provisions of law specified in Section 1600.

(b) In the case of any person charged with, and found incompetent on a charge of, or convicted of, any misdemeanor or any felony other than those described in subdivision (a), or found not guilty of any misdemeanor by reason of insanity, outpatient status under this title may be granted by the court prior to actual confinement in a state hospital or other treatment facility under the provisions of law specified in Section 1600. *(Amended by Stats 1989 ch 897 §42, eff. 1/1/90.)*

§1602. Conditions required.

(a) Any person subject to the provisions of subdivision (b) of Section 1601 may be placed on outpatient status, if all of the following conditions are satisfied:

(1) In the case of a person who is an inpatient, the director of the state hospital or other treatment facility to which the person has been committed advises the court that the defendant will not be a danger to the health and safety of others while on outpatient status, and will benefit from such outpatient status.

(2) In all cases, the community program director or a designee advises the court that the defendant will not be a danger to the health and safety of others while on outpatient status, will benefit from such status, and

© 1992 by J., B. & L. Gould
Printed in the U.S.A.   EP

identifies an appropriate program of supervision and treatment.

(3) After actual notice to the prosecutor and defense counsel, and after a hearing in court, the court specifically approves the recommendation and plan for outpatient status.

(b) The community program director or a designee shall prepare and submit the evaluation and the treatment plan specified in paragraph (2) of subdivision (a) to the court within 15 calendar days after notification by the court to do so, except that in the case of a person who is an inpatient, the evaluation and treatment plan shall be submitted within 30 calendar days after notification by the court to do so.

(c) Any evaluations and recommendations pursuant to paragraphs (1) and (2) of subdivision (a) shall include review and consideration of complete, available information regarding the circumstances of the criminal offense and the person's prior criminal history. *(Amended by Stats 1985 ch 1232 §10.)*

§1603. Additional conditions.

(a) Any person subject to subdivision (a) of Section 1601 may be placed on outpatient status if all of the following conditions are satisfied:

(1) The director of the state hospital or other treatment facility to which the person has been committed advises the committing court that the defendant would no longer be a danger to the health and safety of others, including himself or herself, while under supervision and treatment in the community, and will benefit from such status.

(2) The community program director advises the court that the defendant will benefit from that status, and identifies an appropriate program of supervision and treatment.

(3) After actual notice to the prosecutor and defense counsel, and to the victim or next of kin of the victim of the offense for which the person was committed where a request for the notice has been filed with the court, and after a hearing in court, the court specifically approves the recommendation and plan for outpatient status pursuant to Section 1604. The burden shall be on the victim or next of kin to the victim to keep the court apprised of the party's current mailing address.

In any case in which the victim or next of kin to the victim has filed a request for notice with the director of the state hospital or other treatment facility, he or she shall be notified by the director at the inception of any program in which the committed person would be allowed any type of day release unattended by the staff of the facility.

(b) The community program director shall prepare and submit the evaluation and the treatment plan specified in paragraph (2) of subdivision (a) to the court within 30 calendar days after notification by the court to do so.

(c) Any evaluations and recommendations pursuant to paragraphs (1) and (2) of subdivision (a) shall include review and consideration of complete, available information regarding the circumstances of the criminal offense and the person's prior criminal history.

(d) This section shall remain in effect only until January 1, 1994, and as of that date is repealed, unless a later enacted statute, which is enacted before January 1, 1994, deletes or extends that date. *(Amended by Stats 1987 ch 1343 §3, eff. only until 1/1/94. See other section 1603 below.)*

§1603. Additional conditions.

(a) Any person subject to subdivision (a) of Section 1601 may be placed on outpatient status if all of the following conditions are satisfied:

(1) The director of the state hospital or other treatment facility to which the person has been committed advises the committing court that the defendant is no longer likely to be a danger to the health and safety of others while on outpatient status, and will benefit from that status.

(2) The community program director advises the court that the defendant will benefit from that status, and identifies an appropriate program of supervision and treatment.

(3) After actual notice to the prosecutor and defense counsel, and after a hearing in court, the court specifically approves the recommendation and plan for outpatient status pursuant to Section 1604.

(b) The community program director shall prepare and submit the evaluation and the treatment plan specified in paragraph (2) of subdivision (a) to the court within 30 calendar days after notification by the court to do so.

(c) Any evaluations and recommendations pursuant to paragraphs (1) and (2) of subdivision (a) shall include review and consideration of complete, available information regarding the circumstances of the criminal offense and the person's prior criminal history.

(d) This section shall become operative January 1, 1994. *(Amended by Stats 1987 ch 1343 §5, eff. 1/1/94. See other section 1603 above.)*

§1604. Eligibility recommendation.

(a) Upon receipt by the committing court of the recommendation of the director of the state hospital or other treatment facility to which the person has been committed that the person may be eligible for outpatient status as set forth in subdivision (a)(1) of Section 1602 or 1603, the court shall immediately forward such recommendation to the community program director, prosecutor, and defense counsel. The court shall provide copies of the arrest reports and the state summary criminal history information to the community program director.

(b) Within 30 calendar days the community program director or a designee shall submit to the court and, when appropriate, to the director of the state hospital or other treatment facility, a recommendation regarding the defendant's eligibility for outpatient status, as set forth in subdivision (a)(2) of Section 1602 or 1603 and the recommended plan for outpatient supervision and treatment. The plan shall set forth specific terms and conditions to be followed during outpatient status. The court shall provide copies of this report to the prosecutor and the defense counsel.

(c) The court shall calendar the matter for hearing within 15 judicial days of the receipt of the community program director's report and shall give notice of the hearing date to the prosecutor, defense counsel, the community program director, and, when appropriate, to the director of the state hospital or other facility. In any hearing conducted pursuant to this section, the court shall consider the circumstances and nature of the criminal offense leading to commitment and shall consider the person's prior criminal history.

(d) The court shall, after a hearing in court, either approve or disapprove the recommendation for outpatient status. If the approval of the court is given, the defendant shall be placed on outpatient status subject to the terms and conditions specified in the supervision and treatment plan. If the outpatient treatment occurs in a county other than the county of commitment, the court shall transmit a copy of the case record to the superior court in the county where outpatient treatment occurs, so that the record will be available if revocation proceedings are initiated pursuant to Section 1608 or 1609. *(Amended by Stats 1985 ch 1232 §14.)*

§1605. Supervisor.

(a) In accordance with Section 1615 of this code and Section 5709.8 of the Welfare and Institutions Code, the State Department of Mental Health shall be responsible for the supervision of persons placed on outpatient status under this title. The State Department of Mental Health shall designate, for each county or region comprised of two or more counties, a community program director who shall be responsible for administering the community treatment programs for persons committed from that county or region under the provisions specified in Section 1600.

(b) The State Department of Mental Health shall notify in writing the superior court, the district attorney, the county public defender or public defense agency, and the county mental health director of each county as to the person designated to be the community program director for that county, and timely written notice shall be given whenever a new community program director is to be designated.

(c) The community program director shall be the outpatient treatment supervisor of persons placed on outpatient status under this title. The community program director may delegate the outpatient treatment supervision responsibility to a designee.

(d) The outpatient treatment supervisor shall, at 90-day intervals following the beginning of outpatient treatment, submit to the court, the prosecutor and defense counsel, and to the community program director, where appropriate, a report setting forth the status and progress of the defendant. *(Amended by Stats 1991 ch 435 §1, eff. 1/1/92.)*

§1606. Status termination; hearing.

Outpatient status shall be for a period not to exceed one year. At the end of the period of outpatient status approved by the court, the court shall, after actual notice to the prosecutor, the defense counsel, and the community program director, and after a hearing in court, either discharge the person from commitment under appropriate provisions of the law, order the person confined to a treatment facility, or renew its approval of outpatient status. Prior to such hearing, the community program director shall furnish a report and recommendation to the medical director of the state hospital, where appropriate, and to the court, which the court shall make available to the prosecutor and defense counsel. The person shall remain on outpatient status until the court renders its decision unless hospitalized under other provision of the law. The hearing pursuant to the provisions of this section shall be held no later than 30 days after the end of the one-year period of outpatient status unless good cause exists. The court shall transmit a copy of its order to the community program director or a designee. *(Amended by Stats 1985 ch 1232 §16.)*

§1607. Supervisor's opinion on regained competence.

If the outpatient supervisor is of the opinion that the person has regained competence to stand trial, or is no longer insane, or is no longer a mentally disordered sex offender, the community program director shall submit such opinion to the medical director of the state hospital, where appropriate, and to the court which shall calendar the case for further proceedings under the provisions of Section 1372 or 1026.2 of this code or Section 6325 of the Welfare and Institutions Code. *(Amended by Stats 1985 ch 1232 §17.)*

§1608. Status revoked.

If at any time during the outpatient period, the outpatient treatment supervisor is of the opinion that the person requires extended inpatient treatment or refuses to accept further outpatient treatment and supervision, the community program director shall notify the superior court in either the county which approved outpatient status or in the county where outpatient treatment is being provided of such opinion by means of a written request for revocation of outpatient status. The community program director shall furnish a copy of this request to the defense counsel and to the prosecutor in both counties if the request is made in the county of treatment rather than the county of commitment.

Within 15 judicial days, the court where the request was filed shall hold a hearing and shall either approve or disapprove the request for revocation of outpatient status. If the court approves the request for revocation, the court shall order that the person be confined in a state hospital or other treatment facility approved by the community program director. The court shall transmit a copy of its order to the community program director or a designee. Where the county of treatment and the county of commitment differ and revocation occurs in the county of treatment, the court shall enter the name of the committing county and its case number on the order of revocation and shall send a copy of the order to the committing court and the prosecutor and defense counsel in the county of commitment. *(Amended by Stats 1985 ch 1232 §18.)*

§1609. Confining person found dangerous during outpatient period.

If at any time during the outpatient period or placement with a local mental health program pursuant to subdivision (b) of Section 1026.2 the prosecutor is of the opinion that the person is a danger to the health and safety of others while on that status, the prosecutor may petition the court for a hearing to determine whether the person shall be continued on that status. Upon receipt of the petition, the court shall calendar the case for further proceedings within 15 judicial days and the clerk shall notify the person, the community program director, and the attorney of record for the person of the hearing date. Upon failure of the person to appear as noticed, if a proper affidavit of service and advisement has been filed with the court, the court may issue a body attachment for such person. If, after a hearing in court conducted using the same standards used in conducting probation revocation hearings pursuant to Section 1203.2, the judge determines that the person is a danger to the health and safety of others, the court shall order that the person be confined in a state hospital or other treatment facility which has been approved by the community program director. *(Amended by Stats 1985 ch 1232 §19.)*

§1610. Confinement pending hearing.

(a) Upon the filing of a request for revocation under Section 1608 or 1609 and pending the court's

© 1992 by J., B. & L. Gould
Printed in the U.S.A.   EP

decision on revocation, the person subject to revocation may be confined in a facility designated by the community program director when it is the opinion of that director that the person will now be a danger to self or to another while on outpatient status and that to delay confinement until the revocation hearing would pose an imminent risk of harm to the person or to another. The facility so designated shall continue the patient's program of treatment, shall provide adequate security so as to ensure both the safety of the person and the safety of others in the facility, and shall, to the extent possible, minimize interference with the person's program of treatment. Upon the request of the community program director or a designee, a peace officer shall take, or cause to be taken, the person into custody and transport the person to a facility designated by the community program director for confinement under this section. Within one judicial day after the person is confined in a jail under this section, the community program director shall apply in writing to the court for authorization to confine the person pending the hearing under Section 1608 or Section 1609 or subdivision (c). The application shall be in the form of a declaration, and shall specify the behavior or other reason justifying the confinement of the person in a jail. Upon receipt of the application for confinement, the court shall consider and rule upon it, and if the court authorizes detention in a jail, the court shall actually serve copies of all orders and all documents filed by the community program director upon the prosecuting and defense counsel. The community program director shall notify the court in writing of the confinement of the person and of the factual basis for the opinion that the immediate confinement in a jail was necessary. The court shall supply a copy of these documents to the prosecutor and defense counsel.

(b) The facility designated by the community program director may be a state hospital, a local treatment facility, a county jail, or any other appropriate facility, so long as the facility can continue the person's program of treatment, provide adequate security, and minimize interference with the person's program of treatment. If the facility designated by the community program director is a county jail, the patient shall be separated from the general population of the jail. The designated facility need not be approved for 72-hour treatment and evaluation pursuant to the provisions of the Lanterman-Petris-Short Act (Part 1 (commencing with Section 5000) of Division 5 of the Welfare and Institutions Code); however, a county jail may not be designated unless the services specified above are provided, and accommodations are provided which ensure both the safety of the person and the safety of the general population of the jail. Within three judicial days of the patient's confinement in a jail, the community program director shall report to the court regarding what type of treatment the patient is receiving in the facility. If there is evidence that the treatment program is not being complied with, or accommodations have not been provided which ensure both the safety of the committed person and the safety of the general population of the jail, the court shall order the person transferred to an appropriate facility, including an appropriate state hospital. Nothing in this subdivision shall be construed as authorizing jail facilities to operate as health facilities, as defined in Section 1250 of the Health and Safety Code, without complying with applicable requirements of law.

(c) A person confined under this section shall have the right to judicial review of his or her confinement in a jail under this section in a manner similar to that which is prescribed in Article 5 (commencing with Section 5275) of Chapter 2 of Part 1 of Division 5 of the Welfare and Institutions Code and to an explanation of rights in the manner prescribed in Section 5325 of the Welfare and Institutions Code.

Nothing in this section shall prevent hospitalization pursuant to the provisions of Section 5150, 5250, 5350, or 5353 of the Welfare and Institutions Code.

(d) A person whose confinement in a treatment facility under Section 1608 or 1609 is approved by the court shall not be released again to outpatient status unless court approval is obtained under Section 1602 or 1603. *(Amended by Stats 1988 ch 996 §1, eff. 9/20/88.)*

§1611. Outpatient must obtain permission to leave state.

(a) No person who is on outpatient status pursuant to this title or Section 2972 shall leave this state without first obtaining prior written approval to do so from the committing court. The prior written approval of the court for the person to leave this state shall specify when the person may leave, when the person is required to return, and may specify other conditions or limitations at the discretion of the court. The written approval for the person to leave this state may be in a form and format chosen by the committing court.

In no event shall the court give written approval for the person to leave this state without providing notice to the prosecutor, the defense counsel, and the community program director. The court may conduct a hearing on the question of whether the person should be allowed to leave this state and what conditions or limitations, if any, should be imposed.

(b) Any person who violates subdivision (a) is guilty of a misdemeanor. *(Added by Stats 1988 ch 74 §2, eff. 1/1/89.)*

§1612. Release from treatment facility.

Any person committed to a state hospital or other treatment facility under the provisions of Section 1026, or Chapter 6 (commencing with Section 1367) of Title 10 of this code, or former Section 6316 or 6321 of the Welfare and Institutions Code shall not be released therefrom except as expressly provided in this title or Section 1026.2.

§1613. *Repealed by Stats 1987 ch 828.*

§1614. Prior law.

Persons ordered to undergo outpatient treatment under former Sections 1026.1 and 1374 of the Penal Code and subdivision (a) of Section 6325.1 of the Welfare and Institutions Code shall, on January 1, 1981, be considered as being on outpatient status under this title and this title shall apply to such persons.

§1615. Judicially committed patients; responsibility for treatment and supervision.

Pursuant to Section 5709.8 of the Welfare and Institutions Code, the State Department of Mental Health shall be responsible for the community treatment and supervision of judicially committed patients. These services shall be available on a county or regional basis. The department may provide these services directly or through contract with private providers or counties. The program or programs through which these services are provided shall be known as the Forensic Conditional Release Program.

The department shall contact all county mental health programs by January 1, 1986, to determine their interest in providing an appropriate level of supervision and treatment of judicially committed patients at reasonable cost. County mental health agencies may agree or refuse to operate such a program.

The State Department of Mental Health shall ensure consistent data gathering and program standards for use statewide by the Forensic Conditional Release Program. *(Amended by Stats 1988 ch 37 §1, eff. 1/1/89.)*

§1616. Mental disorder among the state prison inmates and parolees.

The state shall contract with a research agency which shall determine the prevalence of severe mental disorder among the state prison inmates and parolees, including persons admitted to prison, the resident population, and those discharged to parole. An evaluation of the array of services shall be performed, including the correctional, state hospital, and local inpatient programs; residential-level care and partial day care within the institutions as well as in the community; and the individual and group treatment which may be provided within the correctional setting and in the community upon release. The review shall include the interrelationship between the security and clinical staff, as well as the architectural design which aids meeting the treatment needs of these mentally ill offenders while maintaining a secure setting. Administration of these programs within the institutions and in the community shall be reviewed by the contracting agency. The ability of treatment programs to prevent reoffenses by inmates with severe mental disorders shall also be addressed. The process for evaluating inmates and parolees to determine their need for treatment and the ability to differentiate those who will benefit from treatment and those who will not shall be reviewed.

The State Department of Mental Health, the Department of Corrections, and the Department of Justice shall cooperate with the research agency conducting this study.

The research agency conducting this study shall consult with the State Department of Mental Health, the Department of Corrections, the Department of Justice, and the Forensic Mental Health Association of California in the design of the study. *(Added by Stats 1985 ch 1416 §4.)*

§1617. Conditional release program.

The State Department of Mental Health shall research the demographic profiles and other related information pertaining to persons receiving supervision and treatment in the Forensic Conditional Release Program. An evaluation of the program shall determine its effectiveness in successfully reintegrating these persons into society after release from state institutions. This evaluation of program effectiveness shall include, but not be limited to, a determination of the rates of reoffense while these persons are served by the program and after their discharge. This evaluation shall also address the effectiveness of the various treatment components of the program and their intensity.

The State Department of Mental Health may contract with an independent research agency to perform this research and evaluation project. Any independent research agency conducting this research shall consult with the Forensic Mental Health Association concerning the development of the research and evaluation design. *(Amended by Stats 1988 ch 37 §2, eff. 1/1/89.)*

§1618. Application of waiver of liability.

The administrators and the supervision and treatment staff of the Forensic Conditional Release Program shall not be held criminally or civilly liable for any criminal acts committed by the persons on parole or judicial commitment status who receive supervision or treatment. This waiver of liability shall apply to employees of the State Department of Mental Health and the agencies or persons under contract to this department to provide supervision or treatment to mentally ill parolees or persons under judicial commitment. *(Amended by Stats 1988 ch 37 §3, eff. 1/1/89.)*

§1619. Criminal history of persons treated in the Conditional Release Program.

The Department of Justice shall automate the criminal histories of all persons treated in the Forensic Conditional Release Program, as well as all persons committed as not guilty by reason of insanity pursuant to Section 1026, incompetent to stand trial pursuant to Section 1370 or 1370.2, any person currently under commitment as a mentally disordered sex offender, and persons treated pursuant to Section 1364 or 2684 or Article 4 (commencing with Section 2960) of Chapter 7 of Title 1 of Part 3. *(Amended by Stats 1988 ch 37 §4, eff. 1/1/89.)*

§1620. Mental Health Agencies providing treatment to patients.

The Department of Justice shall provide mental health agencies providing treatment to patients pursuant to Sections 1600 to 1610, inclusive, or pursuant to Article 4 (commencing with Section 2960) of Chapter 7 of Title 1 of Part 3, with access to criminal histories of those mentally ill offenders who are receiving treatment and supervision. Treatment and supervision staff who have access to these criminal histories shall maintain the confidentiality of the information and shall sign a statement to be developed by the Department of Justice which informs them of this obligation. *(Amended by Stats 1987 ch 687 §6.)*

PART 3

OF IMPRISONMENT AND THE DEATH PENALTY

TITLE 1

IMPRISONMENT OF MALE PRISONERS IN STATE PRISONS

CHAPTER 1

ESTABLISHMENT OF STATE PRISONS

ARTICLE 1

CALIFORNIA INSTITUTION FOR MEN

§2000. State prison.

There is and shall continue to be a State prison to be known as the California Institution for Men.

© 1992 by J., B. & L. Gould
Printed in the U.S.A.   EP

§2001. Location of state prison.
The California Institution for Men shall be located at Chino, San Bernardino County, California.

§2002. Purpose of prison.
The primary purpose of the California Institution for Men shall be for the imprisonment of male offenders who, in the opinion of the department, seem capable of moral rehabilitation and restoration to good citizenship.

ARTICLE 2

CALIFORNIA STATE PRISON AT SAN QUENTIN

§2020. State prison.
There is and shall continue to be a State prison to be known as the California State Prison at San Quentin.

§2021. Location of state prison.
The California State Prison at San Quentin shall be located at San Quentin, in Marin County, California.

§2022. Purpose of prison.
The primary purpose of the California State Prison at San Quentin shall be to provide confinement, industrial and other training, treatment, and care to persons confined therein.

ARTICLE 3

CALIFORNIA STATE PRISON AT FOLSOM

§2030. State prison.
There is and shall continue to be a State prison to be known as the California State Prison at Folsom.

§2031. Location of state prison.
The California State Prison at Folsom shall be located at Folsom, in Sacramento County, California.

§2032. Purpose of prison.
The primary purpose of the California State Prison at Folsom shall be to provide confinement, industrial and other training, treatment, and care to persons confined therein.

ARTICLE 4

THE DEUEL VOCATIONAL INSTITUTION

§2035. Establishment of institution.
There is hereby established an institution for the confinement of males under the custody of the Director of Corrections and the Youth Authority to be known as the Deuel Vocational Institution.

§2036. Purpose of institution.
The Deuel Vocational Institution shall be an intermediate security-type institution. Its primary purpose shall be to provide custody, care, industrial, vocational and other training, guidance and reformatory help for young men, too mature to be benefited by the programs of institutions under the jurisdiction of the Youth Authority and too immature in crime for confinement in prisons.

§2037. Persons confined.
There may be transferred to and confined in the Deuel Vocational Institution any male, subject to the custody, control and discipline of the Director of Corrections, or any male, subject to the custody, control and discipline of the Youth Authority who has been committed to the Youth Authority under the provisions of Section 1731.5 of the Welfare and Institutions Code, who the Director of Corrections or Youth Authority, as the case may be, believes will be benefited by confinement in such an institution. *(Amended by Stats 1987 ch 828 §107.)*

§2038. Rules and regulations, government and management.
The Director of Corrections shall make rules and regulations for the government of the Deuel Vocational Institution and the management of its affairs.

§2039. Superintendent, officers, employees; appointment and compensation.
The Governor, upon recommendation of the Director of Corrections and in accordance with Section 6050, shall appoint a warden for the Deuel Vocational Institution. The director shall appoint, subject to civil service, those officers and employees as may be necessary. *(Amended by Stats 1989 ch 1420 §3, eff. 1/1/90.)*

§2040. Construction, equipment of buildings.
The Director of Corrections shall construct and equip, in accordance with law, suitable buildings, structures, and facilities for the Deuel Vocational Institution.

§2041. Applicability of Part 3.
Part 3 (commencing with Section 2000) shall apply to the Deuel Vocational Institution and to the persons confined therein so far as those provisions may be applicable. Whenever the name California Vocational Institution appears in any statute, it shall be deemed for all purposes to refer to the Deuel Vocational Institution. *(Amended by Stats 1987 ch 828 §108.)*

§2042. Escape.
Every minor person confined in the Deuel Vocational Institute who escapes or attempts to escape therefrom is guilty of a crime and shall be imprisoned in a state prison, or in the county jail for not exceeding one year.

ARTICLE 4.5

CALIFORNIA CORRECTIONAL CENTER

§2043. Establishment of state prison.
The Director of Corrections is authorized to establish a state prison for the confinement of males under the custody of the Director of Corrections to be known as the California Correctional Center at Susanville.

§2043.1. Primary purpose.
The primary purpose of the state prison authorized to be established by Section 2043 shall be to provide custody and care, and industrial, vocational, and other training to persons confined therein.

§2043.2. Transfer.
Any person under the custody of the Director of Corrections may be transferred to the California Correctional Center at Susanville in accordance with law.

§2043.3. Government and management.

The Director of Corrections shall make rules and regulations for the government of the California Correctional Center at Susanville and the management of its affairs.

§2043.4. Superintendent, other officials and employees; appointment.

The warden of the California Correctional Center at Susanville shall be appointed pursuant to Section 6050 and the Director of Corrections shall appoint, subject to civil service, those other officials and employees as may be necessary. *(Amended by Stats 1989 ch 1420 §4, eff. 1/1/90.)*

§2043.5. Applicability of Part 3.

Part 3 (commencing with Section 2000) shall apply to the California Correctional Center at Susanville and to the persons confined therein, insofar as those provisions may be applicable. *(Amended by Stats 1987 ch 828 §109.)*

ARTICLE 5

CORRECTIONAL TRAINING FACILITY

§2045. Establishment of facility.

The Director of Corrections with the approval of the Board of Corrections, is authorized to establish a State prison for the confinement of males under the custody of the Director of Corrections.

§2045.1. Purpose of facility.

The prison authorized to be established by Section 2045 shall be a medium security type institution. Its primary purpose shall be to provide custody, care, industrial, vocational, and other training to persons confined therein. However, the Director of Corrections may designate a portion of all of the prison to serve the same purposes and to have the same security standards as the institution provided for by Article 4 (commencing at Section 2035) of Chapter 1 of Title 1 of Part 3. *(Amended by Stats 1987 ch 828 §110.)*

§2045.3. Rules and regulations; government and management.

The Director of Corrections shall make rules and regulations for the government of said institution and the management of its affairs.

§2045.4. Warden, other officials and employees; appointment.

The Governor, upon recommendation of the Director of Corrections and in accordance with Section 6050, shall appoint a warden for the California Training Facility. The director shall appoint, subject to civil service, those officers and employees as may be necessary. *(Amended by Stats 1989 ch 1420 §5, eff. 1/1/90.)*

§2045.5. Construction and equipment; buildings.

The Director of Corrections shall construct and equip in accordance with law, suitable buildings, structures and facilities for said institution.

§2045.6. Applicability of Part 3.

The provisions of Part 3 (commencing with Section 2000) apply to the institution and to the persons confined therein insofar as those provisions may be applicable. *(Amended by Stats 1987 ch 828 §111.)*

ARTICLE 6

CALIFORNIA MEN'S COLONY

§2046. Establishment of colony.

The Director of Corrections is authorized to establish a state prison for the confinement of males under the custody of the Director of Corrections. It shall be a medium security institution and shall be known as the California Men's Colony.

§2046.1. Type; purpose.

The prison authorized to be established by Section 2046 shall be a medium security type institution. Its primary purpose shall be to provide custody, care, industrial, vocational, and other training to persons confined therein. *(Amended by Stats 1987 ch 828 §112.)*

§2046.2. Transfers.

Any person under the custody of the Director of Corrections may be transferred to the said prison in accordance with law.

§2046.3. Rules and regulations; government and management.

The Director of Corrections shall make rules and regulations for the government of the said prison and the management of its affairs.

§2046.4. Warden, officials and employees; appointment and compensation.

A warden for the said prison shall be appointed pursuant to Section 6050, and the Director of Corrections shall appoint, subject to civil service, such other officials and employees as may be necessary therefor, and shall fix their compensation.

§2046.5. Construction and equipment; buildings.

The Director of Corrections shall construct and equip in accordance with law, suitable buildings, structures, and facilities for the said prison.

§2046.6. Applicability of Part 3.

The provisions of this part shall apply to the prison and to the persons confined therein insofar as those provisions may be applicable. *(Amended by Stats 1988 ch 160 §135, eff. 1/1/89.)*

§2046.7. *Repealed by Stats 1987 ch 1435.*

ARTICLE 7

CALIFORNIA CORRECTIONAL INSTITUTION AT TEHACHAPI

§2048. Establishment.

The Director of Corrections is authorized to establish a state prison for the confinement of males under the custody of the Director of Corrections, to be known as the California Correctional Institution at Tehachapi. The California Correctional Institution at Tehachapi shall be situated on such state land as is, as of the effective date of this article, the site of the Tehachapi Branch, California Institution for Men.

© 1992 by J., B. & L. Gould
Printed in the U.S.A.   EP

§2048.1. Purpose of prison.

The primary purpose of the prison authorized to be established by Section 2048 shall be to provide custody and care, and industrial, vocational, and other training to persons confined therein.

§2048.2. Transfers.

Any person under the custody of the Director of Corrections may be transferred to the California Correctional Institution at Tehachapi in accordance with law.

§2048.3. Rules and regulations; government and management.

The Director of Corrections shall make rules and regulations for the government of the California Correctional Institution at Tehachapi and the management of its affairs.

§2048.4. Superintendent, officials and employees; appointment.

The warden of the California Correctional Institution at Tehachapi shall be appointed pursuant to Section 6050, and the Director of Corrections shall appoint, subject to civil service, those other officials and employees as may be necessary. (*Amended by Stats 1989 ch 1420 §6, eff. 1/1/90.*)

§2048.5. Construction and equipment; buildings.

The Director of Corrections shall construct and equip, in accordance with law, suitable buildings, structures, and facilities for the California Correctional Institution at Tehachapi.

§2048.6. Applicability of Part 3.

The provisions of Part 3 (commencing with Section 2000) apply to the California Correctional Institution of Tehachapi and to the persons confined therein insofar as those provisions may be applicable. (*Amended by Stats 1987 ch 828 §114.*)

§2048.7. Director's authority.

Notwithstanding other provisions of the law, the Director of Corrections shall have the authority to modify the percentage of the inmate population of the Southern Maximum Security Complex to be employed by the Prison Industry Authority, or to participate in vocational training commensurate with security requirements in relation to the type of inmates housed therein, provided that the percentage of the inmate population to be employed by the Prison Industry Authority or to participate in vocational training shall be no less than 60 percent of the inmates in the general population. Authority is also vested in the director to utilize up to 100 percent of the cells of the facility to house special cases. The director may also choose to double occupy each cell if systemwide overcrowding demands that measure.

The Director of Corrections may implement the provisions of this section only if the encumbrance of those funds is authorized by the Department of Finance, not sooner than 30 days after notification in writing of the necessity therefor, to the chairman of the committee in each house which considers appropriations and the Chairman of the Joint Legislative Budget Committee. (*Amended by Stats 1987 ch 1056 §4.*)

ARTICLE 8

SPECIAL SECURITY FACILITY

§2049 to 2049.6. *Repealed by Stats 1988 ch 610 §2, eff. 1/1/89.*

CHAPTER 2

ADMINISTRATION OF STATE PRISONS

ARTICLE 1

MISCELLANEOUS POWERS AND DUTIES OF DEPARTMENT AND DIRECTOR OF CORRECTIONS

§2050. *Repealed by Stats 1988 ch 610 §3, eff. 1/1/89.*

§2051. Contracts for prison supplies; bids.

The department is hereby authorized to contract for provisions, clothing, medicines, forage, fuel, and all other staple supplies needed for the support of the prisons for any period of time, not exceeding one year, and such contracts shall be limited to bona fide dealers in the several classes of articles contracted for. Contracts for such articles as the department may desire to contract for, shall be given to the lowest bidder at a public letting thereof, if the price bid is a fair and reasonable one, and not greater than the usual value and prices.

Each bid shall be accompanied by such security as the department may require, conditional upon the bidder entering into a contract upon the terms of his bid, on notice of the acceptance thereof, and furnishing a penal bond with good and sufficient sureties in such sum as the department may require, and to its satisfaction that he will faithfully perform his contract.

If the proper officer of the prison reject any article, as not complying with the contract, or if a bidder fail to furnish the articles awarded to him when required, the proper officer of the prison may buy other articles of the kind rejected or called for, in the open market, and deduct the price thereof, over the contract price, from the amount due to the bidder, or charge the same up against him.

Notice of the time, place, and conditions of the letting of contracts shall be given for at least two consecutive weeks in two newspapers printed and published in the City and County of San Francisco, and in one newspaper printed and published in the County of Sacramento, and in the county where the prison to be supplied is situated.

If all the bids made at such letting are deemed unreasonably high, the department may, in its discretion, decline to contract and may again advertise for such time and in such papers as it sees proper for proposals, and may so continue to renew the advertisement until satisfactory contracts are made; and in the meantime the department may contract with anyone whose offer is regarded as just and equitable, or may purchase in the open market.

No bids shall be accepted, nor a contract entered into in pursuance thereof, when such bid is higher than any other bid at the same letting for the same class or schedule of articles, quality considered, and when a contract can be had at such lower bid.

When two or more bids for the same article or articles are equal in amount, the department may select the one which, all things considered, may by it be thought best for the interest of the State, or it may divide the contract between the bidders as in its judgment may seem proper and right.

The department shall have power to let a contract in the aggregate or they may segregate the items, and enter into a contract with the bidder or bidders who may bid lowest on the several articles.

The department shall have the power to reject the bid of any person who had a prior contract and who had not, in the opinion of the department, faithfully complied therewith.

§2052. Contracting for utilities; erection of buildings.

(a) The department shall have power to contract for the supply of electricity, gas and water for said prisons, upon such terms as the department shall deem to be for the best interests of the state, or to manufacture gas or electricity, or furnish water itself, at its option. It shall also have power to erect and construct or cause to be erected and constructed, electrical apparatus or other illuminating works in its discretion with or without contracting therefor, on such terms as it may deem just. The department shall have full power to erect any building or structure deemed necessary by it, or to alter or improve the same, and to pay for the same from the fund appropriated for the use or support of the prisons, or from the earnings thereof, without advertising or contracting therefor.

(b) With respect to any facility under the jurisdiction of the Prison Industry Authority, the Prison Industry Authority shall have the same powers which are vested in the department pursuant to subdivision (a).

§2053. Prisoner literacy.

(a) The Legislature finds and declares that there is a correlation between prisoners who are functionally literate and those who successfully reintegrate into society upon release. It is therefore the intent of the Legislature, in enacting "The Prisoner Literacy Act," to raise the percentage of prisoners who are functionally literate, in order to provide for a corresponding reduction in the recidivism rate.

(b) The Department of Corrections shall determine the reading level of each prisoner upon commitment. The department shall report to the Legislature on or before July 1, 1988, regarding the reading levels of prisoners, the number of prisoners who are enrolled in reading programs, the recidivism rates of prisoners based upon their reading levels, the department's estimate of the amount of time it would take an average inmate to achieve a 9th grade reading level, the costs involved in implementing reading programs on a systemwide basis, the department's estimate on the amount of time necessary to establish a systemwide reading program, and any barriers which currently exist to the implementation of a systemwide reading program. (Added by Stats 1987 ch 575 §2.)

§2053.1. Literacy programs for inmates.

The Director of the Department of Corrections shall implement in every state prison literacy programs that are designed to ensure that upon parole inmates are able to achieve a ninth-grade reading level. The department shall prepare an implementation plan for this program, and shall request the necessary funds to implement this program as follows:

(a) To make the program available to at least 25 percent of eligible inmates in the state prison system by July 1, 1991.

(b) To make the program available to at least 60 percent of eligible inmates in the state prison system by January 1, 1996.

In complying with the requirements of this section, the department shall give strong consideration to computer assisted training and other innovations which have proven to be effective in reducing illiteracy of disadvantaged adults. (Added by Stats 1989 ch 989 §1, eff. 1/1/90.)

§2054. Classes for inmates.

The Director of Corrections may establish and maintain classes for inmates by utilizing personnel of the Department of Corrections, or by entering into an agreement with the governing board of a school district or private school or the governing boards of school districts under which the district shall maintain classes for such inmates. The governing board of a school district or private school may enter into such an agreement regardless of whether the institution or facility at which the classes are to be established and maintained is within or without the boundaries of the school district.

Any agreement entered into between the Director of Corrections and a school district or private school pursuant to this section may require the Department of Corrections to reimburse the school district or private school for the cost to the district or private school of maintaining such classes. "Cost" as used herein includes contributions required of any school district to the State Teachers' Retirement System, but such cost shall not include an amount in excess of the amount expended by the district for salaries of the teachers for such classes, increased by one-fifth. Salaries of such teachers for the purposes of this section shall not exceed the salaries as set by the governing board for teachers in other classes for adults maintained by the district, or private schools.

Attendance or average daily attendance in classes established pursuant to this section or in classes in trade and industrial education or vocational training for adult inmates of institutions or facilities under the jurisdiction of the Department of Corrections shall not be reported to the State Department of Education for apportionment and no apportionment from the State School Fund shall be made on account of average daily attendance in such classes.

No school district or private school shall provide for the academic education of adult inmates of state institutions or facilities under the jurisdiction of the Department of Corrections except in accordance with this section.

The Legislature hereby declares that for each fiscal year funds for the support of the academic education program for inmates of the institutions or facilities under the jurisdiction of the Department of Corrections shall be provided, upon appropriation by the Legislature, to the Department of Corrections at the rate of forty dollars ($40) multiplied by the total number of inmates which the Department of Corrections estimates will be in such institutions or facilities on December 31st of the fiscal year, except as provided in Section 2054.1.

© 1992 by J., B. & L. Gould
Printed in the U.S.A.   EP

§2054.1. Rate increase or decrease.

The rate specified in Section 2054 shall be further increased or decreased in the same proportion as the median salaries for full-time high school teachers in the public schools of this State have increased or decreased since the 1956-57 Fiscal Year.

"Median salaries" as used herein is the amount which the Superintendent of Public Instruction reports will be paid to full-time high school teachers in the public schools of this State during the fiscal year. Such reports shall be based upon information compiled by the Department of Education on salaries of certificated employees in the public schools of this State.

This section applies only to the program of academic education for inmates.

§2055. Insuring products.

The Director of Corrections may, in his discretion, from time to time insure any or all products produced at any prison or institution under the jurisdiction of the Director of Corrections, whether the products are finished or unfinished, the materials from which such products are made or to be made, and the equipment necessary for the production thereof, against any or all risks of loss, wherever such products, materials, or equipment are located, while in the possession of the Department of Corrections and while in transit thereto or therefrom or in storage, in such amounts as the director deems proper. The cost of such insurance shall be paid from the Correctional Industries Revolving Fund.

§2056. Rebuilding shops.

If any of the shops or buildings in which convicts are employed require rebuilding or repair for any reason, they may be rebuilt or repaired immediately, under the direction of the Prison Industry Authority.

§2057. Report to Governor.

The department shall, on or before the first day of December of each even-numbered year, report to the Governor on the condition of the prisons, together with a detailed statement of receipts and expenditures, and such suggestions concerning the prisoners as may appear to be necessary and expedient.

§2058. Printing of report.

There shall be printed for the use of the prisons at least 500 copies of the biennial report of the department, and the clerk shall transmit to each of the state prisons in the United States one copy of such report.

§2059. Compensation of officers and employees.

The department shall fix the compensation of its officers and employees, other than those of wardens and clerks, at a gross rate which shall include a cash allowance for board and lodging, but in no case shall the money compensation, exclusive of the cash allowance for board and lodging, be less than one hundred ten dollars ($110) per month. There shall be deducted from the gross salaries of the officers and employees of the prison the value of any board, lodging, services or supplies rendered or sold to each such officer or employee. The deduction for board and lodging shall not exceed the cash allowance therefor.

§2060. Traveling expenses.

For the purposes of Sections 11009 and 11030 of the Government Code, the following constitute, among other proper purposes, state business for officers and employees of the department for which such officers and employees shall be allowed actual and necessary traveling expenses when the state travel and expense have been approved by the Governor and the Director of Finance as provided in that section.

Attending meetings of any national association or organization, having as its principal purpose the study of matters relating to penology, including prison management and paroles, or to a particular field thereof, conferring with officers or employees of the United States relative to problems relating to penology, including prison management and paroles, in California, conferring with officers or employees of other states engaged in the performance of similar duties, and obtaining information useful to the department in the conduct of its work. (Amended by Stats 1987 ch 828 §116.)

ARTICLE 2

WARDENS

§2078. Prosecution of suits.

It shall be the duty of the department to prosecute all suits, at law or in equity, that may be necessary to protect the rights of the State in matters of property connected with the prisons and their management, such suits to be prosecuted in the name of the department.

§2079. Supervision of prisons.

Subject to the orders and the policies established by the department, it shall be the duty of the wardens to supervise the government, discipline and policy of the prisons, and to enforce all orders and regulations.

§2080. Copy of rules and regulations furnished to prisoner.

A copy of the rules and regulations prescribing the duties and obligations of prisoners shall be furnished to each prisoner in a state prison or other facility under the jurisdiction of the Department of Corrections.

§2081. Register of institution violations.

The director shall cause to be kept at each institution a register of institution violations and what kind of punishments, if any, are administered to prisoners or inmates; the offense committed; the rule or rules violated; the nature of punishment administered; the authority ordering such punishment; the duration of time during which the offender was subjected to punishment; and the condition of the prisoner's health.

§2081.5. Case records of prisoners.

The Director of Corrections shall keep complete case records of all prisoners under custody of the department, which records shall be made available to the Board of Prison Terms at such times and in such form as the board may prescribe.

Case records shall include all information received by the Director of Corrections from the courts, probation officers, sheriffs, police departments, district attorneys, State Department of Justice, Federal Bureau of Investigation, and other interested agencies and persons. Case records shall also include a record of diagnostic findings, considerations, actions and dispositions with respect to classification, treatment, employment, training, and discipline as related to the institutional correctional program followed for each prisoner.

The director shall appoint, after consultation with the Board of Prison Terms, such employees of the various institutions under his control as may be necessary for the proper performance of the duties of the Board of Prison Terms, and when requested shall also have in attendance at hearings of the Board of Prison Terms, psychiatric or medical personnel. The director shall furnish, after consultation with the Board of Prison Terms and the Director of General Services, such hearing rooms and other physical facilities at such institutions as may be necessary for the proper performance of the duties of the Board of Prison Terms.

§2082. Reports on prisoners.

The Director of Corrections shall within 30 days after receiving persons convicted of crime and sentenced to serve terms in the respective prisons under the jurisdiction of the Director of Corrections, except those cases under juvenile court commitment, furnish to the Department of Justice two copies of a report containing the fingerprints and descriptions, including complete details of marks, scars, deformities, or other peculiarities, and a statement of the nature of the offense for which the person is committed. One copy shall be transmitted by the Department of Justice to the Federal Bureau of Investigation. The director shall notify the Department of Justice whenever any of the prisoners dies, escapes, is discharged, released on parole, transferred to or returned from a state hospital, taken out to court or returned therefrom, or whose custody is terminated in any other manner. The Director of Corrections may furnish to the Department of Justice such other fingerprints and information as may be useful for law enforcement purposes. Any expenditures incurred in carrying out the provisions of this section shall be paid for out of the appropriation made for the support of state's prisons or the Department of Corrections.

§2084. Prisoners' beds, blankets, food.

The department shall provide each prisoner with a bed, sufficient covering of blankets, and with garments of substantial material and of distinctive manufacture, and with sufficient plain and wholesome food of such variety as may be most conducive to good health. (Amended by Stats 1987 ch 828 §117.)

§2085. Prisoners' money and valuables.

The department shall keep a correct account of all money and valuables upon the prisoner when delivered at the prison, and shall pay the amount, or the proceeds thereof, or return the same to the prisoner when discharged.

§2085.5. Prisoners' payment of restitution.

In any case in which a prisoner owes a restitution fine imposed pursuant to subdivision (a) of Section 13967 of the Government Code, the Director of Corrections may deduct a reasonable amount not to exceed 20 percent from the wages of a prisoner and shall transfer such amount, exclusive of the costs of ad-

ministering the provisions of this section, which shall be retained by the director, to the State Board of Control for deposit in the Restitution Fund in the State Treasury. Any amount so deducted shall be credited against the amount owing on such fine. The sentencing court shall be provided a record of any such payments.

§2086. Temporary rules and regulations, in case of emergency.

The wardens may make temporary rules and regulations, in case of emergency to remain in force until the department otherwise provides.

§2087. Duties prescribed by department.

The wardens shall perform such other duties as may be prescribed by the department.

§2090. Federal prisoners.

The department is hereby authorized to receive from the Federal Government any federal prisoner and to charge and receive from the United States, for the use of the State, an amount sufficient for the support of each such federal prisoner, the cost of all clothing that may be furnished, and one dollar ($1) per month for the use of the prisoner. No other or further charges shall be made by any officer for or on account of such prisoners.

§2091. *Repealed by Stats 1989 ch 1420 §7, eff. 1/1/90.*

ARTICLE 3

PAROLE AND COMMUNITY SERVICES DIVISION

§2400. Division of Parole and Community Services.

There is in the Department of Corrections, a division known as the Parole and Community Services Division.

§2401. Officers and employees; selection, appointment, status.

All officers and employees of the division shall be selected and appointed by the department pursuant to the State Civil Service Act. The status, positions, and rights of the officers and employees of the division who, prior to the effective date of this section, were included in the state civil service system shall not be affected by the enactment of Section 2399 or this section at the 1957 Regular Session, and their status, positions, and rights shall continue to be retained by them pursuant to the State Civil Service Act.

§2401.5. Division; appointment of head.

The head of the Parole and Community Services Division shall be appointed by the director pursuant to the State Civil Service Act.

§2402. Organization of division.

The director shall organize the division.

§2403. Divisions of functions and duties.

The division shall perform such functions and duties as specified from time to time by the director.

© 1992 by J., B. & L. Gould
Printed in the U.S.A.   **EP**

ARTICLE 6

PROHIBITION UPON WARDENS, CLERKS, OFFICERS AND EMPLOYEES

§2540. Prohibition of unauthorized compensation.

No officer or employee of the department shall receive directly, or indirectly, any compensation for his services other than that prescribed or authorized by law or the director; nor shall he receive any compensation whatever, directly or indirectly, for any act or service which he may do or perform for or on behalf of any contractor, or agent, or employee of a contractor. For any violation of the provisions of this section the officer or employee shall be discharged from his office or service; and every contractor, or employee, or agent of a contractor engaged therein, shall be expelled from the prison grounds, and not again permitted within the same as a contractor, agent, or employee.

§2541. Unauthorized dealings with prisoners.

No officer or employee of the department, or contractor, or employee of a contractor, shall, without permission of the director, make any gift or present to a prisoner, or receive any from a prisoner, or have any barter or dealings with a prisoner. For every violation of the provisions of this section, the party engaged therein shall incur the same penalty as prescribed in the preceding section. No officer or employee of the prison shall be interested, directly or indirectly, in any contract or purchase made or authorized to be made by anyone for or on behalf of the prisons.

§2541.1. *Repealed by its own terms.*

CHAPTER 3

CIVIL RIGHTS OF PRISONERS

ARTICLE 1

CIVIL RIGHTS

§2600. Loss of rights.

A person sentenced to imprisonment in a state prison may, during any such period of confinement, be deprived of such rights, and only such rights, as is necessary in order to provide for the reasonable security of the institution in which he is confined and for the reasonable protection of the public.

§2601. Civil rights retained.

Notwithstanding any other provision of law, each person described in Section 2600 shall have the following civil rights:

(a) To inherit, own, sell, or convey real or personal property, including all written and artistic material produced or created by such person during the period of imprisonment; provided that, to the extent authorized in Section 2600, the Department of Corrections may restrict or prohibit sales or conveyances that are made for business purposes.

(b) To correspond, confidentially, with any member of the State Bar or holder of public office, provided that the prison authorities may open and inspect incoming mail to search for contraband.

(c) To purchase, receive, read, and permit other inmates to read any and all legal materials, news-papers, periodicals, and books accepted for distribution by the United States Post Office, except those which describe the making of any weapon, explosive, poison, or destructive device, or which in the judgment of the Director of Corrections, in the director's sole discretion, depicts, portrays, or describes a sexual assault upon a correctional employee. Nothing in this section shall be construed as limiting the right of prison authorities (1) to open and inspect any and all packages received by an inmate and (2) to establish reasonable restrictions as to the number of newspapers, magazines, and books that the inmate may have in his or her cell or elsewhere in the prison at one time.

(d) To have personal visits; provided that the department may provide such restrictions as are necessary for the reasonable security of the institution.

(e) To initiate civil actions.

(f) To marry.

(g) To create a power of appointment.

(h) To make a will.

(i) To receive all benefits provided for in Sections 3370 and 3371 of the Labor Code and in Section 5069. *(Amended by Stats 1987 ch 828 §118.)*

ARTICLE 2

PRISONERS AS WITNESSES

§2620. Superior court proceedings.

When it is necessary to have a person imprisoned in the state prison brought before any court to be tried for an offense triable in the superior court, or for an examination before a grand jury or magistrate preliminary to such trial, or for the purpose of hearing a motion or other proceeding, to vacate a judgment, an order for his temporary removal from said prison, and for his production before such court, grand jury or magistrate, must be made by the superior court of the county in which said action, motion, or examination is pending or by a judge thereof; such order shall be made only upon the affidavit of the district attorney or defense attorney, stating the purpose for which said person is to be brought before the court, grand jury or magistrate or upon the court's own motion. The order shall be executed by the sheriff of the county in which it shall be made, whose duty it shall be to bring the prisoner before the proper court, grand jury or magistrate, to safely keep him, and when his presence is no longer required to return him to the prison from whence he was taken; the expense of executing such order shall be a proper charge against and shall be paid by, the county in which the order shall be made.

Such order shall recite the purposes for which said person is to be brought before the court, grand jury or magistrate, and shall be signed by the judge making the order and sealed with the seal of the court. The order must be to the following effect:

County of _____ (as the case may be).

The people of the State of California to the warden of _____:

An order having been made this day by me, that A.B. be produced in the __ court (or before the grand jury, as the case may be) to be prosecuted or examined for the crime of ____, an offense triable in the superior court (or to have said motion heard), you are commanded to deliver him into the custody of ____ for the purpose of (recite purposes).

Dated this ____ day of ____, 19__.

When a prisoner is removed from a state prison under this section he shall remain in the constructive custody of the warden thereof. During the prisoner's absence from the prison, he may be ordered to appear in other felony proceedings as a defendant or witness in the courts of the county from which the original order directing removal issued. A copy of the written order directing the prisoner to appear before any such court shall be forwarded by the district attorney to the warden of the prison having protective custody of the prisoner.

§2621. Criminal actions.

When the testimony of a material witness is required in a criminal action, before any court in this state, or in an examination before a grand jury or magistrate for an offense triable in the superior court and such witness is a prisoner in a state prison, an order for his temporary removal from such prison, and for his production before such court, grand jury or magistrate, may be made by the superior court of the county in which such action or examination is pending or by a judge thereof; but in case the prison is out of the county in which the application is made, such order shall be made only upon the affidavit of the district attorney or of the defendant or his counsel, showing that the testimony is material and necessary; and even then the granting of the order shall be in the discretion of said superior court or a judge thereof. The order shall be executed by the sheriff of the county in which it is made, whose duty it shall be to bring the prisoner before the proper court, grand jury or magistrate, to safely keep him, and when he is no longer required as a witness, to return him to the prison whence he was taken; the expense of executing such order shall be a proper charge against, and shall be paid by, the county in which the order shall be made. Such orders shall recite the purposes for which said person is to be brought before the court, grand jury or magistrate, and shall be signed by the magistrate or judge making the order, and sealed with the seal of the court, if any.

Such order must be to the following effect:

County of ___ (as the case may be).

The people of the State of California to the warden of _____ :

An order having been made this day by me, that A.B. be produced in this court as witness in the case of ___ , you are commanded to deliver him into the custody of ___ for the purpose of (recite purposes).

Dated this ___ day of ___ , 19__.

When a prisoner is removed from a state prison under this section he shall remain in the constructive custody of the warden thereof. During the prisoner's absence from the prison, he may be ordered to appear in other felony proceedings as a defendant or witness in the courts of the county from which the original order directing removal issued. A copy of the written order directing the prisoner to appear before any such court shall be forwarded by the district attorney to the warden of the prison having protective custody of the prisoner.

§2621.5. Applicability of Section 4750.

The provisions of Sections 2620 and 2621 which impose a charge upon the counties shall not apply to cases coming within the provisions of Section 4750. *(Amended by Stats 1986 ch 1310 §4.)*

§2622. Use of depositions of prisoners.

When the order for personal appearance is not made pursuant to Section 2620 or Section 2621 the deposition of the prisoner may be taken in the manner provided for in the case of a witness who is sick, and Chapter 4 (commencing with Section 1335) of Title 10 of Part 2 shall, so far as applicable, govern in the application for and in the taking and use of that deposition. The deposition may be taken before any magistrate or notary public of the county in which the prison is situated; or in case the defendant is unable to pay for taking the deposition, before an officer of the prison designated by the board, whose duty it shall be to act without compensation. Every officer before whom testimony shall be taken under this section, shall have authority to administer, and shall administer, an oath to the witness that his or her testimony shall be the truth, the whole truth, and nothing but the truth. *(Amended by Stats 1987 ch 828 §119.)*

§2623. Depositions in a civil action or special proceeding.

If in a civil action or special proceeding a witness be a prisoner, confined in a state prison within this State, an order for his examination in the prison by deposition may be made.

1. By the court itself in which the action or special proceeding is pending, unless it be a justice court or small claims court.

2. By a judge of the superior court of the county where the action or proceeding is pending, if pending before a justice or small claims court or before a judge or other person out of court.

Such order can only be made on the motion of a party, upon affidavit showing the nature of the action or proceeding, the testimony expected from the witness, and its materiality. The deposition, when ordered, shall be taken in accordance with Section 2622.

§2625. Termination of prisoner's parental or marital rights.

In any action brought under Section 232 of the Civil Code, and Section 366.26 of the Welfare and Institutions Code, where the action seeks to terminate the parental rights of any prisoner or any action brought under Section 300 of the Welfare and Institutions Code, where the action seeks to adjudicate the child of a prisoner a dependent child of the court, the superior court of the county in which the action is pending, or a judge thereof, shall order notice of any court proceeding regarding the action transmitted to the prisoner.

For the purposes of this section only, the term "prisoner" includes any individual in custody in a state prison, in the California Rehabilitation Center, or a county jail, or who is a ward of the Department of the Youth Authority or who, upon a verdict or finding that the individual was insane at the time of committing an offense, or mentally incompetent to be tried or adjudged to punishment, is confined in a state hospital for the care and treatment of the mentally disordered or in any other public or private treatment facility.

Service of notice shall be made pursuant to Section 235 of the Civil Code or Section 337 or 366.23 of the Welfare and Institutions Code, as appropriate.

Upon receipt by the court of a statement from the prisoner or his or her attorney indicating the prisoner's desire to be present during the court's proceedings, the court shall issue an order for the temporary removal of the prisoner from the institution, and for the prisoner's production before the court. No proceeding may be held under Section 232 of the Civil Code or Section 366.26 of the Welfare and Institutions

© 1992 by J., B. & L. Gould
Printed in the U.S.A.   **EP**

Code and no petition to adjudge the child of a prisoner a dependent child of the court pursuant to subdivision (a), (b), (c), (d), (e), (f), (i), or (j) of Section 300 of the Welfare and Institutions Code may be adjudicated without the physical presence of the prisoner or the prisoner's attorney, unless the court has before it a knowing waiver of the right of physical presence signed by the prisoner or an affidavit signed by the warden, superintendent or other person in charge of the institution, or his or her designated representative stating that the prisoner has, by express statement or action, indicated an intent not to appear at the proceeding.

In any other action in which a prisoner's parental or marital rights are subject to adjudication, an order for the prisoner's temporary removal from the institution and for the prisoner's production before the court may be made by the superior court of the county in which the action is pending, or by a judge thereof. A copy of the order shall be transmitted to the warden, superintendent, or other person in charge of the institution not less than 48 hours before the order is to be executed. The order shall be executed by the sheriff of the county in which it shall be made, whose duty it shall be to bring the prisoner before the proper court, to keep the prisoner safely, and when the prisoner's presence is no longer required, to return the prisoner to the institution from which he or she was taken; the expense of executing the order shall be a proper charge against and shall be paid by, the county in which the order shall be made.

The order shall be to the following effect:

County of _____ (as the case may be).

The people of the State of California to the warden of _____:

An order having been made this day by me, that A. B. be produced in this court as a party in the case of _____, you are commanded to deliver A. B. into the custody of _____ for the purpose of (recite purposes).

Dated this _____ day of _____, 19___.

When a prisoner is removed from the institution pursuant to this section, the prisoner shall remain in the constructive custody of the warden, superintendent, or other person in charge of the institution. *(Amended by Stats 1991 ch 820 §1, eff. 1/1/92.)*

CHAPTER 4

TREATMENT OF PRISONERS

ARTICLE 1

MISTREATMENT OF PRISONERS

§2650. Injury to person.

The person of a prisoner sentenced to imprisonment in the State prison is under the protection of the law, and any injury to his person, not authorized by law, is punishable in the same manner as if he were not convicted or sentenced.

§2651. Punishment limitation.

No punishment, except as may be authorized by the Director of Corrections, shall be inflicted and then only by the order and under the direction of the wardens. Nothing in this section shall be construed as a limitation or impairment of the authority of the Board of Prison Terms in exercising its functions.

§2652. Unlawful punishments.

It shall be unlawful to use in the prisons, any cruel, corporal or unusual punishment or to inflict any treatment or allow any lack of care whatever which would injure or impair the health of the prisoner, inmate or person confined; and punishment by the use of the strait jacket, gag, thumb-screw, shower-bath or the tricing up of prisoners, inmates or persons confined is hereby prohibited. Any person who violates the provisions of this section or who aids, abets, or attempts in any way to contribute to the violation of this section shall be guilty of a misdemeanor.

§2652.5. Neck chains, restraints.

No person employed by the Department of Corrections, the Department of the Youth Authority, or any city or county jail facility shall place any chain or other mechanical restraint around the neck of any prisoner for any purpose. Any violation of this section shall be a misdemeanor.

§§2653 to 2655. *Repealed by Stats 1987 ch 828.*

§2656. Orthopedic or prosthetic devices.

(a) A person sentenced to incarceration or who is being held pursuant to a pending criminal matter in a county or city jail, or other county or city custodial correctional facility shall not be deprived of the possession or use of any orthopedic or prosthetic appliance, if such appliance has been prescribed or recommended and fitted by a physician.

(b) If, however, the person in charge of the county or city custodial or correctional facility has probable cause to believe possession of such orthopedic or prosthetic appliance constitutes an immediate risk of bodily harm to any person in the facility or threatens the security of the facility, such appliance may be removed.

If such appliance is removed, the prisoner shall be deprived of such appliance only during such time as the facts which constitute probable cause for its removal continue to exist; if such facts cease to exist, then the person in charge of the facility shall return such appliance to the prisoner.

When such appliance is removed, the prisoner shall be examined by a physician within 24 hours after such removal.

If the examining physician determines that removal is or will be injurious to the health or safety of the prisoner, he shall so inform the prisoner and the person in charge of the facility. Upon receipt of the physician's opinion, the person in charge of the facility shall either return the appliance to the prisoner or refuse to return such appliance to the prisoner, informing the physician and the prisoner of the reasons for such refusal and promptly providing the prisoner with a form, as specified in subdivision (c) of this section, by which the prisoner may petition the superior court of the county in which the facility is located for return of the appliance.

Upon petition by the prisoner, the court shall either order the appliance returned to the petitioner or within two judicial days after the petition is filed receive evidence relevant to the granting or denial of the petition. When evidence is received, the court shall consider the opinion of the physician who examined the prisoner and the opinion of the person in charge of the facility and all other evidence, it deems relevant. A decision shall be promptly made and shall be based upon a weighing of the risk of immediate harm to persons within the facility and the threat to the security of the facility created by the appliance's presence in the facility as against the risk to the health and safety of the petitioner by its removal.

(c) The form for a request for return of an orthopedic or prosthetic appliance as required in subdivision (b) of this section shall be substantially as follows:

(Name of the facility) ___ day of ___ 19__ .

I, ____ (person in charge of the facility), have today received a request for the return of an orthopedic or prosthetic appliance, namely, ____ (description of appliance or device) from the undersigned prisoner.

_____

Signature or mark of prisoner making request for return of appliance or device

When the prisoner has signed or made his mark upon such form, the person in charge of the facility shall promptly file the completed form with the superior court.

(d) No person incarcerated in any facility of the Department of Corrections shall be deprived of the use or possession of any orthopedic or prosthetic appliance unless both the inmate's personal physician and a department physician concur in the professional opinion that such appliance is no longer needed.

§2657. Disciplinary action of prisoners.

(a) No person confined in a state prison, as defined in Section 4504, shall be subject to any institutional disciplinary action subsequent to an acquittal in a court of law upon criminal charges brought and tried for the act or omission which is the sole basis of the institutional disciplinary action.

(b) Where the act or omission resulting in acquittal is in any way referred to in any Department of Corrections file pertaining to the prisoner, the fact of acquittal by a court of law shall be clearly inscribed near each such reference.

ARTICLE 2

ORGANIC THERAPY

§2670. Fundamental rights.

It is hereby recognized and declared that all persons, including all persons involuntarily confined, have a fundamental right against enforced interference with their thought processes, states of mind, and patterns of mentation through the use of organic therapies; that this fundamental right requires that no person with the capacity for informed consent who refuses organic therapy shall be compelled to undergo such therapy; and that in order to justify the use of organic therapy upon a person who lacks the capacity for informed consent, other than psychosurgery as referred to in subdivision (c) of Section 2670.5 which is not to be administered to such persons, the state shall establish that the organic therapy would be beneficial to the person, that there is a compelling interest in administering such therapy, and that there are no less onerous alternatives to such therapy.

§2670.5. Administering to prisoners.

(a) No person confined or detained under Title 1 (commencing with Section 2000) and Title 2 (commencing with Section 3200) shall be administered or subjected to any organic therapy as defined in subdivision (c) without his or her informed consent, provided that:

(1) If the person gives his or her informed consent to organic therapy, it shall be administered only if there has been compliance with Sections 2675 to 2680, inclusive.

(2) If the person lacks the capacity for informed consent to organic therapy other than psychosurgery as referred to in subdivision (c), in order to proceed with the therapy, the warden shall secure an order from the superior court to authorize the administration of the therapy in accordance with Sections 2675 to 2680, inclusive.

(b) No person confined or detained under Title 1 (commencing with Section 2000) or Title 2 (commencing with Section 3200) who lacks the capacity for informed consent shall be administered or subjected to psychosurgery as referred to in subdivision (c).

(c) The term organic therapy refers to:

(1) Psychosurgery, including lobotomy, stereotactic surgery, electronic, chemical or other destruction of brain tissues, or implantation of electrodes into brain tissue.

(2) Shock therapy, including, but not limited to, any convulsive therapy and insulin shock treatments.

(3) The use of any drugs, electric shocks, electronic stimulation of the brain, or infliction of physical pain when used as an aversive or reinforcing stimulus in a program of aversive, classical, or operant conditioning.

(d) A person does not waive his or her right to refuse any organic therapy by having previously given his or her informed consent to the therapy, and the person may withdraw his or her consent at any time.

If required by sound medical-psychiatric practice, the attending physician shall, after the person withdraws his or her previously given informed consent, gradually phase the person out of the therapy if sudden cessation would create a serious risk of mental or physical harm to the person.

(e) Nothing in this article shall be construed to prevent the attending physician from administering nonorganic therapies such as psychotherapy, psychoanalysis, group therapy, milieu therapy, or other therapies or programs involving communication or interaction among physicians, patients, and others, with or without the use of drugs when used for purposes other than described in paragraph (3) of subdivision (c).

(f) Nothing in this article shall be construed to prevent the administration of drugs not connected with a program of conditioning and intended to cause negative physical reactions to ingestion of alcohol or drugs. *(Amended by Stats 1989 ch 1420 §8, eff. 1/1/90.)*

§2671. Shock treatments and therapy.

(a) Notwithstanding Section 2670.5, if a confined person has inflicted or attempted to inflict substantial physical harm upon the person of another or himself, or presents, as a result of mental disorder, an imminent threat of substantial harm to others or himself, the attending physician may in such emergency employ or authorize for no longer than seven days in any three month period the immediate use of shock treatments in order to alleviate such danger.

(b) Notwithstanding Section 2670.5, if a confined person gives his informed consent to a program of

© 1992 by J., B. & L. Gould
Printed in the U.S.A.   **EP**

shock therapy for a period not to exceed three months, the attending physician may administer such therapy for a period not to exceed three months in any one-year period without prior judicial authorization.

§2672. Informed consent to organic therapy.

(a) For purposes of this article, "informed consent" means that a person must knowingly and intelligently, without duress or coercion, and clearly and explicitly manifest his consent to the proposed organic therapy to the attending physician.

(b) A person confined shall not be deemed incapable of informed consent solely by virtue of being diagnosed as a mentally ill, disordered, abnormal or mentally defective person.

(c) A person confined shall be deemed incapable of informed consent if such person cannot understand, or knowingly and intelligently act upon, the information specified in Section 2673.

(d) A person confined shall be deemed incapable of informed consent if for any reason he cannot manifest his consent to the attending physician.

§2673. Duty of attending physician to provide required information.

(a)* For purposes of this article, "informed consent" requires that the attending physician directly communicate with the person and clearly and explicitly provide all the following information prior to the person's decision:

(1) The nature and seriousness of the person's illness, disorder or defect.

(2) The nature of the proposed organic therapy and its intended duration.

(3) The likelihood of improvement or deterioration, temporary or permanent, without the administration of the proposed organic therapy.

(4) The likelihood and degree of improvement, remission, control, or cure resulting from the administration of such organic therapy, and the likelihood, nature, and extent of changes in and intrusions upon the person's personality and patterns of behavior and thought or mentation and the degree to which these changes may be irreversible. This information shall indicate the probable duration and intensity of such therapy and whether such therapy may have to be continued indefinitely for optimum therapeutic benefit.

(5) The likelihood, nature, extent, and duration of side effects of the proposed organic therapy, and how and to what extent they may be controlled, if at all.

(6) The uncertainty of the benefits and hazards of the proposed organic therapy because of the lack of sufficient data available to the medical profession, or any other reason for such uncertainty.

(7) The reasonable alternative organic therapy or psychotherapeutic modality of therapy, or nonorganic behavior modification programs, and why the organic therapy recommended is the therapy of choice. These alternatives shall be described and explained to the person in the manner specified in this section.

(8) Whether the proposed therapy is generally regarded as sound by the medical profession, or is considered experimental.

*So in original. No subd. (b) has been enacted.

§2674. Written manifestation of informed consent.

A written manifestation of informed consent shall be obtained in all cases by the attending physician and

shall be preserved and available to the person, his attorney, his guardian, or his conservator.

§2675. Petition for order authorizing organic therapy.

(a) If the proposed organic therapy is not prohibited by subdivision (a) or (b) of Section 2670.5, then in order to administer such therapy the warden or superintendent of the institution in which the person is confined shall petition the superior court of the county in which the person is confined for an order authorizing such organic therapy.

(b) The petition shall summarize the facts which the attending physician is required to communicate to the person pursuant to Section 2673, and shall state whether the person has the capacity for informed consent, and, if so, whether the person has given his or her informed consent to the proposed therapy. The petition shall clearly specify what organic therapy the institution proposes to administer to the person. The petition shall specify what mental illness, disorder, abnormality, or defect justifies the administration of such therapy. Copies of the petition shall be personally served upon the person and served upon his attorney, guardian or conservator on the same day as it is filed with the clerk of the superior court.

(c) The person confined, or his attorney, guardian, or conservator may file a response to such petition for organic therapy. Said response shall be filed no later than 10 days after service of the said petition unless the court grants a continuance not to exceed 10 additional days, and shall be served on the warden or superintendent on the same day it is filed. *(Amended by Stats 1989 ch 1420 §9, eff. 1/1/90.)*

§2676. Petition for order prohibiting organic therapy.

(a) Any person, or his or her attorney, guardian, or conservator may file a petition with the superior court of the county in which he or she is confined for an order to prohibit the administration upon him or her of an organic therapy. The filing of such a petition shall constitute a refusal of consent or withdrawal of any prior consent to an organic therapy. The clerk of the court shall serve a copy of the petition, on the same day it is filed, upon the warden.

(b) The warden shall file a response to the petition to prohibit the enforced administration of any organic therapy. The response shall be filed no later than 10 days after the filing of the petition, unless the court grants a continuance not to exceed 10 additional days, and shall be personally served upon the person and served upon his or her attorney, guardian, or conservator on the same day as it is filed with the clerk of the superior court. The response shall not constitute a petition for an order to proceed with any organic therapy pursuant to Section 2675, which shall be the exclusive procedure for authorization to administer any organic therapy. *(Amended by Stats 1989 ch 1420 §10, eff. 1/1/90.)*

§2677. Court appointment of public defender, other attorney and independent medical expert.

At the time of filing of a petition pursuant to Section 2676 by the person, or pursuant to Section 2675 by the warden, the court shall appoint the public defender or other attorney to represent the person unless the person is financially able to provide his or her own attorney. The attorney shall advise the person of his or her rights in relation to the proceeding in question and shall represent him or her before the court.

The court shall also appoint an independent medical expert on the person's behalf to examine the person's medical, mental, or emotional condition and to testify thereon, unless the person is financially able to obtain the expert testimony. However, if the person has given his or her informed consent to the proposed organic therapy, other than psychosurgery as referred to in subdivision (c) of Section 2670.5, and his or her attorney concurs in the proposed administration of the organic therapy, the court may waive the requirement that the an independent medical expert be appointed. *(Amended by Stats 1989 ch 1420 §11, eff. 1/1/90.)*

§2678. Proceedings.

The court shall conduct the proceedings within 10 judicial days from the filing of the petition described in Section 2675 or 2676, whichever is filed earlier, unless the warden's attorney or the person's attorney requests a continuance, which may be for a maximum of 10 additional judicial days. The court shall conduct the proceedings in accordance with constitutional guarantees of due process of law and the procedures under Section 13 of Article I of the California Constitution. *(Amended by Stats 1989 ch 1420 §12, eff. 1/1/90.)*

§2679. Determination of court.

(a) The court shall determine whether the state has proven, by clear and convincing evidence, that the confined person has the capacity for informed consent and has manifested his informed consent.

(b) If the court has determined that the person lacks the capacity for informed consent, the court shall determine by clear and convincing evidence that such therapy, other than psychosurgery as referred to in subdivision (c) of Section 2670.5, would be beneficial; that there is a compelling interest justifying the use of the organic therapy upon the person; that there are no less onerous alternatives to such organic therapy; and that such organic therapy is in accordance with sound medical-psychiatric practice. If the court so determines, then the court shall authorize the administration of the organic therapy for a period not to exceed six months.

(c) If the court has determined that the person has the capacity for informed consent and has manifested his informed consent to organic therapy, the court shall determine by clear and convincing evidence that such therapy would be beneficial; that there is a compelling interest justifying the use of the organic therapy upon the person; that there are no less onerous alternatives to such organic therapy; and that such organic therapy is in accordance with sound medical-psychiatric practice. If the court so determines then the court shall authorize the administration of the organic therapy for a period not to exceed six months.

§2680. Confined person's rights.

(a) If it is determined by the attending physician that a confined person should be administered organic therapy, the person shall be advised and informed of his or her rights under this article, and he or she shall be provided a copy of this article.

(b) This article shall apply to prisoners confined under this part in public or private hospitals, sanitariums, and similar facilities, and to the personnel of the facilities.

(c) A person shall be entitled to communicate in writing and by visiting with his or her parents, guardian, or conservator regarding any proposed administration of any organic therapy. The communication shall not be censored. The person shall be entitled to communicate in writing with his or her attorney pursuant to Section 2600.

(d) This article shall not prohibit the attending physician from terminating organic therapy prior to the period authorized for that therapy by the court, pursuant to Section 2679. *(Amended by Stats 1988 ch 160 §136, eff. 1/1/89.)*

ARTICLE 3

DISPOSITION OF INSANE PRISONERS

§2684. Transfer to state hospital for treatment.

If, in the opinion of the Director of Corrections, the rehabilitation of any mentally ill, mentally deficient, or insane person confined in a state prison may be expedited by treatment at any one of the state hospitals under the jurisdiction of the State Department of Mental Health or the State Department of Developmental Services, the Director of Corrections, with the approval of the Board of Prison Terms for persons sentenced pursuant to subdivision (b) of Section 1168, shall certify that fact to the director of the appropriate department who shall evaluate the prisoner to determine if he would benefit from care and treatment in a state hospital. If the director of the appropriate department so determines, the superintendent of the hospital shall receive the prisoner and keep him until in the opinion of the superintendent such person has been treated to such an extent that he will not benefit from further care and treatment in the state hospital.

§2685. Reception and treatment of prisoner.

Upon the receipt of a prisoner, as herein provided, the superintendent of the state hospital shall notify the Director of Corrections of that fact, giving his name, the date, the prison from which he was received, and from whose hands he was received. When in the opinion of the superintendent the mentally ill, mentally deficient or insane prisoner has been treated to such an extent that such person will not benefit by further care and treatment in the state hospital, the superintendent shall immediately notify the Director of Corrections of that fact. The Director of Corrections shall immediately send for, take and receive the prisoner back into prison. The time passed at the state hospital shall count as part of the prisoner's sentence.

ARTICLE 4

TEMPORARY REMOVAL OF PRISONERS

§2690. Authorization.

The Director of Corrections may authorize the temporary removal from prison or any other institution for the detention of adults under the jurisdiction of the Department of Corrections of any inmate, including removal for the purpose of attending college classes. The director may require that such temporary removal be under custody. Unless the inmate is removed for medical treatment, the removal shall not be for a period longer than three days. The director may require the inmate to reimburse the state, in whole or in part, for expenses incurred by the state in

© 1992 by J., B. & L. Gould
Printed in the U.S.A.   EP

connection with such temporary removal other than for medical treatment.

§2691. Ineligibility.

No person imprisoned for a felony listed in Section 667.6 shall be removed or released under Section 2690 from the detention institution where he or she is confined for the purpose of attending college classes in any city or county nor shall that person be placed in a community correctional center pursuant to Chapter 9.5 (commencing with Section 6250) of Title 7 of Part 3. No person under the jurisdiction of the adult court and confined under the jurisdiction of the Department of the Youth Authority for conviction of a felony listed in Section 667.6 shall be removed or released from the place of confinement for attendance at any educational institution in any city or county. *(Amended by Stats 1987 ch 828 §124.)*

§2692. Treatment of AIDS afflicted inmates.

The Director of Corrections may enter into contracts with public or private agencies located either within or outside of the state for the housing, care, and treatment of inmates afflicted with acquired immune deficiency syndrome (AIDS) or AIDS-related complex (ARC). *(Added by Stats 1986 ch 921 §1.)*

CHAPTER 5

EMPLOYMENT OF PRISONERS

ARTICLE 1

EMPLOYMENT OF PRISONERS GENERALLY

§2700. Labor required; compensation.

The Department of Corrections shall require of every able-bodied prisoner imprisoned in any state prison as many hours of faithful labor in each day and every day during his or her term of imprisonment as shall be prescribed by the rules and regulations of the Director of Corrections.

Whenever by any statute a price is required to be fixed for any services to be performed in connection with the work program of the Department of Corrections, the compensation paid to prisoners shall be included as an item of cost in fixing the final statutory price.

Prisoners not engaged on work programs under the jurisdiction of the Prison Industry Authority, but who are engaged in productive labor outside of such programs may be compensated in like manner. The compensation of such prisoners shall be paid either out of funds appropriated by the Legislature for that purpose or out of such other funds available to the Department of Corrections for expenditure, as the Director of Finance may direct.

When any prisoner escapes, the director shall determine what portion of his or her earnings shall be forfeited and such forfeiture shall be deposited in the State Treasury in a fund known as the Inmate Welfare Fund of the Department of Corrections.

§2701. Needed services.

The Department of Corrections is hereby authorized and empowered to cause the prisoners in the state prisons of this state to be employed in the rendering of such services as are now, or may hereafter be, needed by the state, or any political subdivision thereof, or that may be needed for any state, county, district, municipal, school, or other public use, or that may be needed by any public institution of the state or of any political subdivision thereof, or that may be needed for use by the federal government, or any department, agency, or corporation thereof, or that may be needed for use by the government of any other state, or any department, agency, or corporation thereof, except for services provided by enterprises under the jurisdiction of the Prison Industry Authority. The Department of Corrections may enter into contracts for the purposes of this article.

§2702. Access to computer systems after committing computer crime.

No person imprisoned after conviction of a violation of Section 502 or of subdivision (b) of Section 502.7 shall be permitted to work on or have access to any computer system of the department. *(Added by Stats 1989 ch 1357 §5, eff. 1/1/90.)*

§2706. Supervision of work.

All prisoners shall be employed under supervision of the wardens respectively, and such skilled foremen as they may deem necessary in the performance of work for the state.

§2707. Machinery and tools.

The director is further authorized and empowered to purchase, install, and equip, such machinery, tools, supplies, materials, and equipment as may be necessary to carry out the provisions of this article.

§2708. Limitation.

No inmate of any State prison shall be employed in the manufacture or production, of any article, intended for the private and personal use of any State officer, or officer, or employee, of any State institution; provided, that this act shall not prevent repairing of any kind nor the employment of such inmates in household or domestic work connected with such prison.

§2713. Inmates' earnings paid upon release.

Whenever an inmate is paid for his labor, performed under the supervision of the Department of Corrections or any other public agency, and is discharged, all sums due him shall be paid upon release. If an inmate is released on parole all sums due him shall be paid to the inmate as prescribed by the director.

§2713.1. Extra payment upon release.

In addition to any other payment to which he is entitled by law, each prisoner upon his release shall be paid the sum of two hundred dollars ($200), from such appropriations that may be made available for the purposes of this section.

The department may prescribe rules and regulations (a) to limit or eliminate any payments provided for in this section to prisoners who have not served for at least six consecutive months prior to their release in instances where the department determines that such a payment is not necessary for rehabilitation of the prisoner, (b) to establish procedures for the payment of the sum of two hundred dollars ($200) within the first 60 days of a prisoner's release, and (c) to eliminate any payment provided for in this section to a parolee who upon release has not been paid the entire amount prescribed by this section and who willfully absconds after release on parole, but before any remaining balance of the two hundred dollar ($200) release funds has been paid.

The provisions of this section shall not be applicable if a prisoner is released to the custody of another state or to the custody of the federal government.

§2715. Transfer of state lands for establishing prison farms.

Land belonging to the State of California may, with the approval of the Department of Finance, be transferred to the jurisdiction of the director for the purpose of establishing thereon a prison farm and prisoners in the state prisons may be transferred to such farm. Products from said farm shall first be used for supplying the state prisons, prison camps, or the prison farm and any surplus may be sold to any other state institution.

§2716. Vocational training.

(a) The Director of Corrections may enter into agreements with other state agencies for the use of inmates confined in the state prisons to perform work necessary and proper to be done by them in facilities of such state agencies for the purpose of vocational training and the improvement of job skills preparatory to release.

(b) The director shall determine which prisoners shall be eligible for such assignment and training.

(c) Suitable facilities for the housing, care, and feeding of the inmates may be provided by the agency for whom the work is performed at the location of such agency.

(d) The director shall have full jurisdiction over the discipline and control of the inmates assigned.

(e) The provisions of Title 5 (commencing with Section 4500) of Part 3 shall apply to all persons on such assignment.

§2717. *Repealed by Stats 1985 ch 1031.*

ARTICLE 1.5

JOINT VENTURE PROGRAM
(Added by Initiative Measure, Prop 139 §5, approved 6/5/90.)

§2717.1. Definitions.

(a) For the purposes of this section, joint venture program means a contract entered into between the Director of Corrections and any public entity, nonprofit or for profit entity, organization, or business for the purpose of employing inmate labor.

(b) Joint venture employer means any public entity, nonprofit or for profit entity, organization, or business which contracts with the Director of Corrections for the purpose of employing inmate labor. *(Added by Initiative Measure, Prop 139 §5, approved 6/5/90.)*

§2717.2. Establishing joint venture programs.

The Director of Corrections shall establish joint venture programs within state prison facilities to allow joint venture employers to employ inmates confined in the state prison system for the purpose of producing goods or services. While recognizing the constraints of operating within the prison system, such programs will be patterned after operations outside of prison so as to provide inmates with the skills and work habits necessary to become productive members of society upon their release form state prison. *(Added by Initiative Measure, Prop 139 §5, approved 6/5/90.)*

§2717.3. Provisions governing joint venture.

The Director of Corrections shall prescribe by rules and regulations provisions governing the operation and implementation of joint venture programs, which shall be in furtherance of the findings and declarations in the Prison Inmate Labor Initiative of 1990. *(Added by Initiative Measure, Prop 139 §5, approved 6/5/90.)*

§2717.4. Joint Venture Policy Advisory Board.

There is hereby established within the Department of Corrections the Joint Venture Policy Advisory Board. The Joint Venture Policy Advisory Board shall consist of the Director of Corrections, who shall serve as chair, the Director of the Employment Development Department, and five members, to be appointed by the Governor, three of whom shall be public members, one of whom shall represent organized labor and one of whom shall represent industry. Five members shall constitute a quorum and a vote of the majority of the members in office shall be necessary for the transaction of the business of the board. Appointed members of the board shall be compensated at the rate of two hundred dollars ($200) for each day while on official business of the board and shall be reimbursed for necessary expenses. The initial terms of the members appointed by the Governor shall be for one year (one member), two years (two members), three years (one member), and four years (one member), as determined by the Governor. After the initial term, all members shall serve for four years.

(b)* The board shall advise the Director of Corrections of policies that further the purposes of the Prison Inmate Labor Initiative of 1990 to be considered in the implementation of joint venture programs. *(Added by Initiative Measure, Prop 139 §5, approved 6/5/90.)*
*So in original. No subd. (a) designated.

§2717.5. Establishing joint venture contracts.

In establishing joint venture contracts the Director of Corrections shall consider the impact on the working people of California and give priority consideration to inmate employment which will retain or reclaim jobs in California, support emerging California industries, or create jobs for a deficient labor market. *(Added by Initiative Measure, Prop 139 §5, approved 6/5/90.)*

§2717.6. Regulations regarding employment.

(a) No contract shall be executed with a joint venture employer that will initiate employment by inmates in the same job classification as non-inmate employees of the same employer who are on strike, as defined in Section 1132.6 of the Labor Code, as it reads on January 1, 1990, or who are subject to lockout, as defined in Section 1132.8 of the Labor Code, as it reads on January 1, 1990.

(b) Total daily hours worked by inmates employed in the same job classification as non-inmate employees of the same joint venture employer who are on strike, as defined in Section 1132.6 of the Labor Code, as it reads on January 1, 1990, or who are subject to lockout, as defined in Section 1132.8 of the Labor Code, as it reads on January 1, 1990, shall not exceed, for the duration of the strike, the average daily hours worked for the preceding six months, or if the program has been in operation for less than six months, the average for the period of operation.

© 1992 by J., B. & L. Gould
Printed in the U.S.A.   **EP**

(c) The determination that a condition described in paragraph (b) above shall be made by the Director after notification by the union representing the workers on strike or subject to lockout. The limitation on work hours shall take effect 48 hours after receipt by the Director of written notice of the condition by the union. *(Added by Initiative Measure, Prop 139 §5, approved 6/5/90.)*

§2717.7. Sale of inmate provided goods and services.

Notwithstanding Section 2812 of the Penal Code or any other provision of law which restricts the sale of inmate-provided services or inmate-manufactured goods, services performed and articles manufactured by joint venture programs may by sold to the public. *(Added by Initiative Measure, Prop 139 §5, approved 6/5/90.)*

§2717.8. Compensation to prisoners.

The compensation of prisoners engaged in programs pursuant to contract between the Department of Corrections and joint venture employers for the purpose of conducting programs which use inmate labor shall be comparable to wages paid by the joint venture employer to non-inmate employees performing similar work for that employer. If the joint venture employer does not employ such non-inmate employees in similar work, compensation shall be comparable to wages paid for work of a similar nature in the locality in which the work is to be performed. Such wages shall be subject to deductions, as determined by the Director of Corrections, which shall not, in the aggregate, exceed 80 percent of gross wages and shall be limited to the following:

(1) Federal, state, and local taxes.

(2) Reasonable charges for room and board, which shall be remitted to the Director of Corrections.

(3) Any lawful restitution fine or contributions to any fund established by law to compensate the victims of crime of not more than 20 percent, but not less than 5 percent, of gross wages, which shall be remitted to the Director of Corrections for disbursement.

(4) Allocations for support of family pursuant to state statute, court order, or agreement by the prisoner. *(Added by Initiative Measure, Prop 139 §5, approved 6/5/90.)*

ARTICLE 4

EMPLOYMENT AT ROAD CAMPS

§2760. Employment authority.

The Department of Transportation of the State of California may employ or cause to be employed, prisoners confined in the state prisons in the improvement and maintenance of any state highway.

§2760.1. Department defined.

"Department", as used in this article, means the Department of Transportation.

§2761. Determination of eligibility for employment.

The Director of Corrections shall determine which prisoners shall be eligible for employment by the Department of Transportation in the improvement and maintenance of state highways, and shall establish lists of prisoners eligible for such employment.

Upon the requisition of said department, the Director of Corrections shall send to the place and at the time designated the number of prisoners requisitioned or such number thereof as have been determined to be eligible for such employment and are available.

The director may return to prison any prisoner transferred to camp pursuant to this section, when the need for such prisoner's labor has ceased or when the prisoner is guilty of any violation of the rules and regulations of the prison or camp.

§2762. Rate of compensation.

The Director of Corrections shall fix a daily rate to be expended for convict labor, and when so fixed, the Department of Transportation shall monthly set aside funds to the director to pay for this labor from funds appropriated in the Budget Act for this purpose, and where no funds are available to the Department of Transportation the director may set aside the department's own funds to pay for this labor from funds appropriated in the Budget Act for this purpose. The Department of Corrections shall set up an account for each convict which shall be credited monthly with an amount computed by multiplying the daily rate by the number of days such convict actually performed labor during the month. Such account shall be debited monthly with the convict's proportionate share of expenses of camp maintenance, including the expenses for food, medicine, medical attendance, clerical and accounting personnel, and the expenses necessary to maintain care and welfare facilities such as camp hospital for first aid, barbershop and cobbler shop, and the convict's personal expenses covering his drawings from the commissary for clothing, toilet articles, tobacco, candy, and other personal items. The charge for camp maintenance may be made at a standard rate determined by the department maintaining the camps to be adequate to cover expenses and shall be adjusted periodically at the discretion of the department as needs of the camp require. No charge shall be made against such account for the costs of transporting prisoners to and from prison and camp or for the expense of guarding prisoners, which items shall be paid by the Department of Corrections from appropriations made for the support of the department. The director, by regulation, may fix the maximum amount, over and above all deductions, that a convict may receive. The Department of Corrections, in computing the debits to be made to the convict's accounts, may add not to exceed 10 percent on all items.

§2765. Forfeiture of prisoner's earnings.

When any prisoner shall wilfully violate the terms of his employment or the rules and regulations of the Department of Corrections, the Director of Corrections may in his discretion determine what portion of all moneys earned by the prisoner shall be forfeited by the said prisoner and such forfeiture shall be deposited in the State Treasury in a fund known as the Inmate Welfare Fund of the Department of Corrections.

§2766. Intent.

This article is not intended to restore, in whole or in part, the civil rights of any prisoner used hereunder, and such article shall not be so construed.

§2767. Driving motor vehicles.

No prisoner while engaged in such construction, maintenance and improvement of a state highway shall drive a motor truck or other vehicle or wagon outside of the limits established for the camp or construction work.

§2768. Building bridges.

Said prisoners when employed under the provisions of this article shall not be used for the purpose of building any bridge or structure of like character which requires the employment of skilled labor.

§2770. Supervision of work.

The Department of Transportation shall designate and supervise all road work done under the provisions of this article. It shall provide, supervise and maintain necessary camps and commissariat, except that where no funds are available to the Department of Transportation, the director may provide, erect, and maintain the necessary camps.

§2771. Discipline and control.

The Director of Corrections shall have full jurisdiction at all times over the discipline and control of the prisoners employed on said roads.

§2772. Interference with prisoners; other misconduct.

Any person who, without authority, interferes with or in any way interrupts the work of any prisoners employed pursuant to this article, and any person not authorized by law, who gives or attempts to give to any prisoner so employed any controlled substances or any intoxicating liquors of any kind whatever, or firearms, weapons or explosives of any kind, is guilty of a felony and upon conviction thereof shall be punished by imprisonment in the state prison and shall be disqualified from holding any state office or position in the employ of this state. Any person who interferes with the discipline or good conduct of any prisoner employed pursuant to this article, while such prisoner is in the confines or limits of the state prison road camp is guilty of a misdemeanor and upon conviction thereof shall be punished by imprisonment in the county jail for a term not more than six months, or by a fine of not more than two hundred dollars ($200), or by both such fine and imprisonment. Any peace officer or any officer or guard of any state prison or any superintendent of such road work, having in charge the prisoners employed upon such highways or state roads, may arrest without a warrant any person violating any provisions of this article.

ARTICLE 5

EMPLOYMENT IN PUBLIC PARKS, FORESTS, ETC.

§2780. Employment authority.

Any department, division, bureau, commission or other agency of the State of California or the Federal Government may use or cause to be used convicts confined in the state prisons to perform work necessary and proper to be done by them at permanent, temporary, and mobile camps to be established under this article. The director may enter into contracts for the purposes of this article.

§2780.1. Payment and crediting of money.

Money received from the rendering of services under the prison camp work program shall be paid to the Treasurer monthly and shall be credited to the support appropriation of the prison rendering such services, in augmentation thereof. The appropriation to be credited shall be the appropriation current at the time of rendering the services. Nothing in this section shall apply to prison road camps established under Article 4 (commencing with Section 2760) of this chapter, except that, by mutual agreement between the Department of Transportation and the Department of Corrections, subject to the approval of the Department of Finance, such prison road camps may be administered, instead, under the provisions of this article.

§2780.5. Use of prisoners during fire emergencies.

The Director of Corrections may, during declared fire emergencies, allow the Director of the Department of Forestry and Fire Protection to use prisoners for fire suppression efforts outside of the boundaries of California, not to exceed a distance in excess of 25 miles from the California border, along the borders of Oregon, Nevada, or Arizona. *(Added by Stats 1989 ch 419 §1, eff. 1/1/90.)*

§2781. Determination of eligibility.

The Director of Corrections shall determine which prisoners shall be eligible for employment under Section 2780, and shall establish and modify lists of prisoners eligible for such employment. Upon the requisition of an agency mentioned in Section 2780, the Director of Corrections may send to the place and at the time designated the number of prisoners requisitioned or such number thereof as have been determined to be eligible for such employment and are available.

The director may return to prison any prisoner transferred to camp pursuant to this section, when the need for such prisoner's labor has ceased or when the prisoner is guilty of any violation of the rules and regulations of the prison or camp.

§2782. Rate of compensation.

The director may fix a daily rate to be expended for such convict labor, and when so fixed, the agency shall monthly set aside funds to the director to pay for such labor, and where no funds are available from the agency the director may set aside the department's own funds to pay for such labor. The director, by regulation, may authorize any or all deductions to be made from the pay due convicts as provided for convicts at road camps under Section 2762. The director, by regulation, may also fix the maximum amount, over and above all deductions, that a convict may receive.

§2785. Forfeiture of earnings.

Whenever prisoners are paid for their labor under this article and a prisoner wilfully violates the terms of his employment or the rules of the camp or the Department of Corrections the Director of Corrections may in his discretion determine what portion of all moneys earned by the prisoner shall be forfeited by the prisoner and such forfeiture shall be deposited in the State Treasury in the fund known as the Inmate Welfare Fund of the Department of Corrections.

§2786. Appropriation of prisoners' employment fund.

All money in said fund is hereby appropriated for educational and recreational purposes at the various

© 1992 by J., B. & L. Gould
Printed in the U.S.A. EP

prison camps established under this article and shall be expended by the director upon warrants drawn upon the State Treasury by the State Controller after approval of the claims by the State Board of Control.

§2787. Supervision of work by agency.

The agency providing work for convicts under this article shall designate and supervise all work done under the provisions of this article. The agency shall provide, erect and maintain the necessary camps, except that where no funds are available to the agency, the director may provide, erect and maintain the necessary camps. The director shall supervise and manage the necessary camps and commissariat.

§2788. Discipline and control.

The director shall have full jurisdiction at all times over the discipline and control of the convicts performing work under this article.

§2790. Interference with convicts.

Any person, who, without authority, interferes with or in any way interrupts the work of any convict used pursuant to this article and any person not authorized by law, who gives or attempts to give to any state prison convict so employed any controlled substances, or any intoxicating liquors of any kind whatever, or firearms, weapons or explosives of any kind is guilty of a felony and upon conviction thereof shall be punished by imprisonment in the state prison and shall be disqualified from holding any state office or position in the employ of this state. Any person who interferes with the discipline or good conduct of any convict used pursuant to this article, while such convict is in such camps is guilty of a misdemeanor and upon conviction thereof shall be punished by imprisonment in the county jail for a term not more than six months, or by a fine of not more than four hundred dollars ($400), or by both such fine and imprisonment. Any peace officer or any officer or guard of any state prison or any superintendent of such work, having in charge the convicts used in such camps, may arrest without a warrant any person violating any provisions of this article.

§2791. Construction of article.

This article is not intended to restore, in whole or in part, the civil rights of any convict used hereunder, and such article shall not be so construed.

§2792. Camps for employment of parolees.

Camps may be established under this article for the employment of paroled prisoners.

CHAPTER 6

SALE OF PRISON-MADE GOODS

ARTICLE 1

PRISON INDUSTRY AUTHORITY

§2800. Establishment of Prison Industry Authority.

There is hereby established the Prison Industry Authority. As used in this article "authority" means the Prison Industry Authority.

§2801. Purposes of authority.

The purposes of the authority are:

(a) To develop and operate industrial, agricultural, and service enterprises employing prisoners in institutions under the jurisdiction of the Department of Corrections, which enterprises may be located either within those institutions or elsewhere, all as may be determined by the authority.

(b) To create and maintain working conditions within the enterprises as much like those which prevail in private industry as possible, to assure prisoners employed therein the opportunity to work productively, to earn funds, and to acquire or improve effective work habits and occupational skills.

(c) To operate a work program for prisoners which will ultimately be self-supporting by generating sufficient funds from the sale of products and services to pay all the expenses of the program, and one which will provide goods and services which are or will be used by the Department of Corrections, thereby reducing the cost of its operation.

§2802. Board of directors.

The authority shall be under the policy direction of a board of directors, to be known as the Prison Industry Board, and to be referred to hereafter as the board. The board shall consist of eleven members:

(a) The Director of Corrections shall be a member.

(b) The Director of the Department of General Services, or his or her designee, shall be a member.

(c) The Director of Commerce, or his or her designee, shall be a member.

(d) The Speaker of the Assembly shall appoint two members to represent the general public.

(e) The Senate Rules Committee shall appoint two members to represent the general public.

(f) The Governor shall appoint four members. Of these, two shall be representatives of organized labor, and two shall be representatives of industry. The initial term of one of the members appointed by the Speaker of the Assembly shall be two years, and the initial term of the other shall be three years. The initial term of one of the members appointed by the Senate Rules Committee shall be two years, and the initial term of the other shall be three years. The initial terms of the four members appointed by the Governor shall be four years. All subsequent terms of all members shall be for four years. Each member's term shall continue until the appointment and qualification of his successor.

§2803. Duties of chairman; meetings.

The Director of Corrections shall be the chairman of the board. The chairman shall be the administrative head of the board and shall exercise all duties and functions necessary to insure that the responsibilities of the board are successfully discharged. The board shall meet regularly at least four times during each fiscal year, and shall hold extra meetings on the call of the chairman or a majority of the board. Six members of the board, including the chairman, shall constitute a quorum. The vote of a majority of the members in office is necessary for the transaction of the business of the board.

§2804. Per diem rate; travel expenses.

The appointed members of the board shall receive a per diem to be determined by the chairman, but not less than the usual per diem rate allowed to the Department of Corrections employees during travel out of state. All members, including the chairman, shall also receive their actual and necessary expenses of travel incurred in attending meetings of the commission and in making investigations, either as a board or individually as members of the board at the request of the chairman. All the expenses shall be paid from the Prison Industries Revolving Fund.

§2805. Jurisdiction of authority over operations.

The authority shall assume jurisdiction over the operation of all industrial, agricultural, and service operations formerly under the jurisdiction of the Correctional Industries Commission. In addition, the authority shall have the power to establish new industrial, agricultural and service enterprises which it deems appropriate, to initiate and develop new vocational training programs, and to assume jurisdiction over existing vocational training programs. The authority shall have control over and the power to buy and sell all equipment, supplies and materials used in the operations over which it assumes control and jurisdiction.

§2806. Prison Industries Revolving Fund.

There is hereby constituted a permanent revolving fund in the sum of not less than seven hundred thirty thousand dollars ($730,000), to be known as the Prison Industries Revolving Fund, and to be used to meet the expenses necessary in the purchasing of materials and equipment, salaries, construction and cost of administration of the prison industries program. The fund may also be used to refund deposits either erroneously made or made in cases where delivery of products cannot be consummated. The fund shall at all times contain the amount of at least seven hundred thirty thousand dollars ($730,000), either in cash or in receivables, consisting of raw materials, finished or unfinished products, inventory at cost, equipment, or any combination of the above. Money received from the rendering of services or the sale of products in the prisons and institutions under the jurisdiction of the board shall be paid to the State Treasurer monthly and shall be credited to the fund. At any time that the authority and the Director of Finance jointly determine that the balance in said revolving fund is greater than is necessary to carry out the purposes of the authority, they shall so inform the Controller and request a transfer of the unneeded balance from the revolving fund to the General Fund of the State of California. The Controller is authorized to transfer balances upon request. Funds deposited in the revolving fund are not subject to annual appropriation by the Legislature and may be used without a time limit by the authority.

The Prison Industries Revolving Fund is not subject to the provisions of Articles 2 (commencing with Section 13320) and 3 (commencing with Section 13335) of Chapter 3 of Part 3 of Division 3 of Title 2 of the Government Code.

The revolving fund created by Section 2714 known as the Correctional Industries Revolving Fund is abolished, and the Controller shall transfer the balance in that revolving fund to the Prison Industries Revolving Fund. Any major capital outlay project undertaken by the authority shall be subject to review by the Public Works Board pursuant to the provisions of Part 10.5 (commencing with Section 15752) of Division 3 of Title 2 of the Government Code.

§2807. Operation of industrial, agricultural and service enterprises.

(a) The authority is hereby authorized and empowered to operate industrial, agricultural, and service enterprises which will provide products and services needed by the state, or any political subdivision thereof, or by the federal government, or any department, agency, or corporation thereof, or for any other public use. Products may be purchased by state agencies to be offered for sale to inmates of the department and to any other person under the care of the state who resides in state-operated institutional facilities.

(b) All things authorized to be produced under subdivision (a) shall be purchased by the state, or any agency thereof, and may be purchased by any county, city, district, or political subdivision, or any agency thereof, or by any state agency to offer for sale to persons residing in state-operated institutions, at the prices fixed by the board. State agencies shall make maximum utilization of these products, and shall consult with the staff of the authority to develop new products and adapt existing products to meet their needs.

(c) The following state agencies and officers shall report by January 1 of each year to the Director of General Services and to the Chairperson of the joint Legislative Budget Committee on their use in the prior fiscal year of goods and services provided by the authority, and shall include comments on planned future use of these goods and services:

(1) The State and Consumer Services Agency.
(2) The Business, Transportation and Housing Agency.
(3) The Health and Welfare Agency.
(4) The Resources Agency.
(5) The Youth and Adult Correctional Agency.
(6) The Environmental Affairs Agency.
(7) Department of Food and Agriculture.
(8) The Attorney General.
(9) The Secretary of State.
(10) The Treasurer.
(11) The Controller.
(12) The Superintendent of Public Instruction.

Reports submitted under this subdivision shall be specific as to department and unit under each agency's or office's jurisdiction. (Amended by Stats 1989 ch 369 §1, eff. 1/1/90.)

§2808. Powers and duties of Prison Industry Board.

The board shall, in the exercise of its duties, have all the powers and do all the things which the board of directors of a private corporation would do, except as specifically limited in this article, including, but not limited to, the following:

(a) To enter into contracts and leases, execute leases, pledge the equipment, inventory and supplies under the control of the authority and the anticipated future receipts of any enterprise under the jurisdiction of the authority as collateral for loans, and execute other necessary instruments and documents.

(b) To assure that all funds received by the authority are kept in commercial accounts according to standard accounting practices.

(c) To arrange for an independent annual audit.

(d) To review and approve the annual budget for the authority, in order to assure that the solvency of the Prison Industries Revolving Fund is maintained.

© 1992 by J., B. & L. Gould
Printed in the U.S.A.   EP

(e) To contract to employ a general manager to serve as the chief administrative officer of the authority. The person so appointed shall serve at the pleasure of the chairman. The general manager shall have wide and successful experience with a productive enterprise and have a demonstrated appreciation of the problems associated with prison management.

(f) To apply for and administer grants and contracts of all kinds.

(g) To establish, notwithstanding any other provision of law, procedures governing the purchase of raw materials, component parts, and any other goods and services which may be needed by the authority or in the operation of any enterprise under its jurisdiction. Such procedures shall contain provisions for appeal to the board from any action taken in connection with them.

(h) To establish, expand, diminish, or discontinue industrial, agricultural and service enterprises under its jurisdiction to enable the authority to operate as a self-supporting organization, to provide as much employment for inmates as is feasible, and to provide diversified work activities to minimize the impact on existing private industry in the state.

(i) To hold public hearings pursuant to paragraph (h) above to provide an opportunity for persons or organizations who may be affected to appear and present testimony concerning the plans and activities of the authority. The authority shall assure adequate public notice of such hearings. No new industrial, agricultural, or service enterprise which involves a gross annual production of more than fifty thousand dollars ($50,000) shall be established unless and until a hearing concerning the enterprise has been held by a committee of persons designated by the board including at least two board members. The board shall take into consideration the effect of a proposed enterprise on California industry and shall not approve the establishment of the enterprise if the board determines it would have a comprehensive and substantial adverse impact on California industry which cannot be mitigated.

(j) To periodically determine the prices at which activities, supplies, and services shall be sold.

(k) To report to the Legislature in writing, on or before February 1 of each year, regarding:

(1) The financial activity and condition of each enterprise under its jurisdiction.

(2) The plans of the board regarding any significant changes in existing operations.

(3) The plans of the board regarding the development of new enterprises.

(4) A breakdown, by institution, of the number of prisoners at each institution, working in enterprises under the jurisdiction of the authority, said number to indicate the number of prisoners which are not working full time. *(Amended by Stats 1985 ch 1413 §1.)*

§2809. Employment of civilians.

Notwithstanding any other provision of law, the authority may recruit and employ such civilian staff as may be necessary to carry out the purposes of this article, and shall establish recruiting, testing, hiring, promotion, disciplinary, and dismissal procedures and practices which will meet the unique personnel needs of the authority. The practices may include incentives based on productivity, profit-sharing plans, or other criteria which will encourage civilian employee involvement in the productivity goals of the authority.

The procedures and practices shall apply to all employees working in enterprises under the jurisdiction of the authority. The Director of Corrections shall be the appointing authority for all personnel of the authority other than the general manager.

§2810. Borrowing money.

The board may authorize the borrowing of money by the authority for purposes of:

(a) Operating the business affairs of the authority.

(b) Purchasing new equipment, materials and supplies.

(c) Constructing new facilities, or repairing, remodeling, or demolishing old facilities. Funds may be borrowed from private sources, upon such terms as the board deems appropriate, including but not limited to, the use of equipment under the jurisdiction of the authority, and of the future income of an enterprise under the jurisdiction of the authority, as collateral to secure any loan. *(Amended by Stats 1985 ch 966 §1.)*

§2810.5. Loan from Pooled Money Investment Board.

Notwithstanding any other provision of law, the Pooled Money Investment Board may grant loans to the authority when money is appropriated for that purpose by the Legislature, upon application by the Prison Industry Board, in order to finance the establishment of a new industrial, agricultural, or service enterprise. All loans shall bear the same interest rate as the pooled money market investment rate and shall have a maximum repayment period of 20 years from the date of approval of the loan.

Prior to making its decision to grant a loan, the Pooled Money Investment Board shall require the authority to demonstrate all of the following:

(a) The proposed industry project cannot be feasibly financed from private sources under Section 2810. The authority shall present proposed loan conditions from at least two private sources.

(b) The proposed industry project cannot feasibly be financed from proceeds from other Prison Industry Authority enterprises.

(c) The proceeds from the proposed project provide for a reasonable payback schedule to the General Fund. *(Amended by Stats 1985 ch 966 §2.)*

§2811. Compensation schedule for prisoner employees.

The board shall adopt and maintain a compensation schedule for prisoner employees. Such compensation schedule shall be based on quantity and quality of work performed and shall be required for its performance, but in no event shall such compensation exceed one-half the minimum wage provided in Section 1182 of the Labor Code, except as otherwise provided in this code. This compensation shall be credited to the account of the prisoner.

Such compensation shall be paid from the Prison Industries Revolving Fund.

§2812. Unlawful sale of articles manufactured by convict labor.

It is unlawful for any person to sell, expose for sale, or offer for sale within this state, any article or articles manufactured wholly or in part by convict or other prison labor, except articles the sale of which is specifically sanctioned by law.

© 1992 by J., B. & L. Gould
Printed in the U.S.A. **EP**

Every person selling, exposing for sale, or offering for sale any article manufactured in this state wholly or in part by convict or other prison labor, the sale of which is not specifically sanctioned by law, is guilty of a misdemeanor.

§2813. Manufacture of articles of handiwork.

The director may provide for the manufacture of small articles of handiwork by the prisoners out of raw materials purchased by the prisoners with their own funds or funds borrowed from the Inmates' Welfare Fund, or from raw materials furnished by the director without compensation therefor as provided in this section which articles may be sold to the public at the state prisons, in public buildings, at fairs, or on property operated by nonprofit associations. State-owned property shall not be given to prisoners for use under this section, unless all proceeds from the sale thereof shall be deposited in the Inmates' Welfare Fund. The director may provide that all or a part of the sale price of all other articles manufactured and sold under this section be deposited to the account of the prisoner manufacturing the article.

§2813.5. Sale of vehicles restored by inmates.

Notwithstanding any other provision of this chapter except subdivision (i) of Section 2808, and notwithstanding subdivision (l) of Section 22851.3 of the Vehicle Code, the Director of Corrections may provide for the inmates in trade and industrial education or vocational training classes established under Section 2054 to restore and rebuild donated salvageable and abandoned vehicles. If these vehicles comply with Section 24007.5 of the Vehicle Code, they may be sold at public auction to private persons. This activity shall be subject to the public hearing requirements of subdivision (i) of Section 2808 at any time this activity involves a gross annual production of more than fifty thousand dollars ($50,000).

The proceeds of the sale after deduction of the cost of materials shall be deposited in the Restitution Fund in the State Treasury and, upon appropriation by the Legislature, may be used for indemnification of victims of crimes. (*Amended by Stats 1991 ch 1157 §1, eff. 1/1/92.*)

§2814. Sale of agricultural and animal products.

Notwithstanding any provision of this chapter, products and byproducts of agricultural and animal husbandry enterprises, except nursery stock, may be sold to private persons, at public or private sale, under rules prescribed by the board.

§2815. Sale of products from industrial enterprises to foreign governments.

The authority may, under rules prescribed by the board, dispose of products developed from the operations of industrial enterprises in prisons and institutions under the jurisdiction of the authority by sale to foreign governments, corporations for distribution in foreign countries, and private persons or their agents in markets outside the United States and in countries which permit the importation of prison-made goods. All sales made pursuant to this section shall be reported to the Legislature in the board's annual report pursuant to Section 2808.

§2816. Transfers or deposits of money into Prison Industries Revolving Fund.

With the approval of the Department of Finance, there shall be transferred to, or deposited in, the Prison Industries Revolving Fund for purposes authorized by this section, money appropriated from any source including sources other than state appropriations.

Notwithstanding subdivision (i) of Section 2808, the chairman, in consultation with the board, may order any authorized public works project involving construction, renovation, or repair of prison facilities to be performed by inmate labor when the total expenditure does not exceed two hundred thousand dollars ($200,000). Projects entailing expenditure of greater than two hundred thousand dollars ($200,000) shall be reviewed and approved by the board.

Money so transferred or deposited shall be available for expenditure by the department for the purposes for which appropriated, contributed or made available, without regard to fiscal years and irrespective of the provisions of Sections 13340 and 16304 of the Government Code. Money transferred or deposited pursuant to this section shall be used only for purposes authorized in this section.

§2817. Creation and purpose of Inmate Construction Revolving Account.

The Inmate Construction Revolving Account is hereby created in the Prison Industries Revolving Fund, established in Section 2806, to receive funds transferred or deposited for the purposes described in Section 2816.

§2818. Creation of New Industries Revolving Account.

The New Industries Revolving Account is hereby created in the Prison Industries Revolving Fund to receive General Fund or other public money transferred or deposited for the purpose of financing new enterprises or the expansion of existing enterprises. Money in the fund may be disbursed by the board subject to the conditions prescribed in Section 2810.5. (*Added by Stats 1985 ch 966 §3.*)

ARTICLE 2

SALE OF PRISON GOODS MADE OUTSIDE CALIFORNIA

§2880. Subjection to state law.

To the extent and insofar as the same may be permitted under the provisions of the Constitution of the United States and the acts of Congress, all goods, wares, and merchandise manufactured, produced, or mined wholly or in part by prisoners (except prisoners on parole or probation) or manufactured, produced, or mined wholly or in part in any state prison, transported into the State of California and remaining herein for use, consumption, sale, or storage, shall upon arrival and delivery in this state be subject to the operation and effect of the laws of this state to the same extent and in the same manner as though those commodities had been manufactured, produced, or mined in this state by prisoners or in any state prison, and shall not be exempt therefrom by reason of being introduced in the original package or otherwise. (*Amended by Stats 1987 ch 828 §125.*)

© 1992 by J., B. & L. Gould
Printed in the U.S.A.　　EP

§2881. Labeling of goods.

No person, firm, partnership, association or corporation within this State shall sell or offer, trade, consign, keep, expose or display for sale any goods, wares or merchandise manufactured, assembled, produced or mined in whole or in part by prisoners in any penitentiary, prison, reformatory or other establishment in which prison labor is employed, unless such prison-made goods, wares, or merchandise are plainly, legibly, conspicuously and indelibly branded, molded, embossed, stenciled or labeled with the words "Convict-made" in plain, bold letters followed by the name of such penitentiary, prison, reformatory or other establishment in which the goods, wares or merchandise were made.

§2882. Size and wording of label.

It is hereby specifically provided that any article of prison-made goods, wares or merchandise, as described in the preceding section, may be labeled by the attachment of a label not smaller than four inches long and two inches wide, upon which is printed the words "Convict-made" in plain, bold letters followed by the name of such penitentiary, prison, reformatory, or other establishment in which the goods, wares or merchandise were made; provided, that in the judgment of officials charged with the enforcement of this article such prison-made goods, wares or merchandise can not be legibly, conspicuously and indelibly branded, molded, embossed, stenciled or labeled as provided in said preceding section.

§2883. Consistency of label.

The size and type of such stenciling or label must be consistent with the size and character of the merchandise to which such stenciling or label applies. The size, type and character of such stenciling or label will be subject to the approval of the officials of the State of California responsible for the enforcement of this article.

§2884. Disinfection or sterilization of prison-made goods.

No person, firm, partnership, association or corporation within this state shall sell or offer, trade, consign, keep, expose, or display for sale any goods, wares or merchandise manufactured, assembled, produced, or mined in whole or in part by prisoners in any penitentiary, prison, reformatory, or other establishment in which prison labor is employed, unless those prison-made goods, wares, or merchandise have first been disinfected or sterilized in a plant located in California and licensed by the State Department of Health Services in accordance with any regulations of the State Department of Health Services now in force or which later may be made effective.

It is hereby further provided that certificate of that disinfection or sterilization must accompany, be stamped on or attached to those goods, wares, or merchandise in a manner or form prescribed by the officials of the State of California responsible for the enforcement of this article. *(Amended by Stats 1987 ch 828 §126.)*

§2885. Display of sign.

No person, firm, partnership, association, or corporation within this State shall sell or offer, trade, consign, keep, expose or display for sale any goods, wares or merchandise manufactured, assembled, produced or mined in whole or in part by the prisoners in any penitentiary, prison, reformatory or other establishment in which prison labor is employed, unless such person, firm, partnership, association or corporation shall keep permanently and conspicuously displayed within the same inclosure and within 10 feet of the place where said prison-made goods, wares or merchandise are kept, exposed, displayed or offered for sale a suitable sign, at least 36 inches wide and 10 inches high, on which appear in legible letters not less than two inches high the following words: "Convict-made products on sale here."

§2886. Advertising in periodicals or publications.

Any person, firm, partnership, association or corporation within this State, when advertising in any periodical or publication any goods, wares or merchandise made in whole or in part by prisoners in any penitentiary, prison, reformatory or other establishment in which prison labor is employed, must insert the words "Convict-made," in such advertisement in type or other letters conforming in size or shape to those used in the text of said periodical or publication.

§2887. Punishment of fine and/or imprisonment for violations.

Any person, firm, partnership, association or corporation violating the provisions of this article shall be guilty of a misdemeanor and upon conviction thereof shall be punished by a fine of not less than fifty dollars ($50) or more than five hundred dollars ($500) for each offense, or by imprisonment in the county jail for not less than 30 days or more than six months or by both such fine and imprisonment.

§2888. Inspection of records.

The State Superintendent of Weights and Measures or any deputy or inspector authorized by him, shall have access to any premises or any records held by any person, firm, partnership, association or corporation containing any information pertaining to the prison-made goods, wares or merchandise referred to herein.

§2889. Supervised enforcement.

The enforcement of the provisions of this article shall be under the supervision of the State Superintendent of Weights and Measures.

§2890. Application of article.

The provisions of this article shall not apply to any goods, wares or merchandise manufactured in any penitentiary or prison of this State.

§2891. Sale of unsanctioned goods.

No person or corporation may sell, expose for sale or offer for sale any goods, wares or merchandise manufactured, produced or mined wholly or in part by prisoners (except prisoners on parole or probation) or manufactured, produced or mined wholly or in part in any State prison the sale of which is not specifically sanctioned by law; and any person or corporation violating any provision of this section is guilty of a misdemeanor.

© 1992 by J., B. & L. Gould
Printed in the U.S.A. **EP**

CHAPTER 7

EXECUTION OF SENTENCES OF IMPRISONMENT

ARTICLE 1

COMMENCEMENT OF TERM

§2900. Delivery and reception of prisoner.

(a) The term of imprisonment fixed by the judgment in a criminal action commences to run only upon the actual delivery of the defendant into the custody of the Director of Corrections at the place designated by the Director of Corrections as a place for the reception of persons convicted of felonies.

(b) Except as otherwise provided in this section, the place of reception shall be an institution under the jurisdiction of the Director of Corrections.

(1) As an emergency measure, the Director of Corrections may direct that persons convicted of felonies may be received and detained in jails or other facilities and that the judgment will commence to run upon the actual delivery of the defendant into such place and that any persons previously received and confined for conviction of a felony may be, as an emergency, temporarily housed at such place and the time during which such person is there shall be computed as a part of the term of judgment.

(2) In any case in which, pursuant to the agreement on detainers or other provision of law, a prisoner of another jurisdiction is, before completion of actual confinement in a penal or correctional institution of a jurisdiction other than the State of California, sentenced by a California court to a term of imprisonment for a violation of California law, and the judge of the California court orders that the California sentence shall run concurrently with the sentence which such person is already serving, the Director of Corrections shall designate the institution of the other jurisdiction as the place for reception of such person within the meaning of the preceding provisions of this section. He may also designate the place in California for reception of such person in the event that actual confinement under the prior sentence ends before the period of actual confinement required under the California sentence.

(3) In any case in which a person committed to the Director of Corrections is subsequently committed to a penal or correctional institution of another jurisdiction, the subsequent commitment is ordered to be served concurrently with the California commitment, the prisoner is placed in a penal or correctional institution of other jurisdiction, and the prisoner is not received by the Director of Corrections pursuant to subdivision (a), the Director of Corrections shall designate the institution of the other jurisdiction as the place for reception and service of the California term.

(c) Except as provided in this section, all time served in an institution designated by the Director of Corrections shall be credited as service of the term of imprisonment.

(1) If a person is ordered released by a court from the custody and jurisdiction of the Director of Corrections pursuant to Section 1272 or 1506 or any other provision of law permitting the legal release of prisoners, time during which the person was released shall not be credited as service of the prison term.

(2) If a prisoner escapes from the custody and jurisdiction of the Director of Corrections, the prisoner shall be deemed an escapee and fugitive from justice, until the prisoner is available to return to the custody of the Director of Corrections or the State of California. Time during which the prisoner is an escapee shall not be credited as service of the prison term.

(d) The Department of Corrections may contract for the use of any facility of the state or political subdivision thereof to care for persons received in accordance with this section. *(Amended by Stats 1987 ch 828 §127.)*

§2900.1. Credit for service under invalid judgment.

Where a defendant has served any portion of his sentence under a commitment based upon a judgment which judgment is subsequently declared invalid or which is modified during the term of imprisonment, such time shall be credited upon any subsequent sentence he may receive upon a new commitment for the same criminal act or acts.

§2900.5. Time in custody credited to term of imprisonment.

(a) In all felony and misdemeanor convictions, either by plea or by verdict, when the defendant has been in custody, including, but not limited to, any time spent in a jail, camp, work furlough facility, halfway house, rehabilitation facility, hospital, prison, juvenile detention facility, similar residential institution, or home detention program, all days of custody of the defendant, including days served as a condition of probation in compliance with a court order, and including days credited to the period of confinement pursuant to Section 4019, shall be credited upon his or her term of imprisonment, or credited to any fine which may be imposed, at the rate of not less than thirty dollars ($30) per day, or more, in the discretion of the court imposing the sentence. If the total number of days in custody exceeds the number of days of the term of imprisonment to be imposed, the entire term of imprisonment shall be deemed to have been served. In any case where the court has imposed both a prison or jail term of imprisonment and a fine, any days to be credited to the defendant shall first be applied to the term of imprisonment imposed, and thereafter the remaining days, if any, shall be applied to the fine.

(b) For the purposes of this section, credit shall be given only where the custody to be credited is attributable to proceedings related to the same conduct for which the defendant has been convicted. Credit shall be given only once for a single period of custody attributable to multiple offenses for which a consecutive sentence is imposed.

(c) For the purposes of this section, "term of imprisonment" includes any period of imprisonment imposed as a condition of probation or otherwise ordered by a court in imposing or suspending the imposition of any sentence, and also includes any term of imprisonment, including any period of imprisonment prior to release on parole and any period of imprisonment prior to discharge, whether established or fixed by statute, by any court, or by any duly authorized administrative agency.

(d) It shall be the duty of the court imposing the sentence to determine the date or dates of any admission to and release from custody prior to sentencing, and the total number of days to be credited pursuant

© 1992 by J., B. & L. Gould
Printed in the U.S.A.   **EP**

to this section. The total number of days to be credited shall be contained in the abstract of judgment provided for in Section 1213.

(e) It shall be the duty of any agency to which a person is committed to apply the credit provided for in this section for the period between the date of sentencing and the date the person is delivered to the agency.

(f) If a defendant serves time in a camp, work furlough facility, halfway house, rehabilitation facility, hospital, juvenile detention facility, similar residential facility, or home detention program in lieu of imprisonment in county jail, and the statute under which the defendant is sentenced requires a mandatory minimum period of time in jail, the time spent in these facilities or programs shall qualify as mandatory time in jail.

(g) This section shall remain operative until January 1, 1995, and as of that date is repealed. *(Amended by Stats 1991 ch 437 §9, eff. 9/19/91 only until 1/1/95. See other section 2900.5 below.)*

§2900.5. Time in custody credited to term of imprisonment.

(a) In all felony and misdemeanor convictions, either by plea or by verdict, when the defendant has been in custody, including but not limited to any time spent in a jail, camp, work furlough facility, halfway house, rehabilitation facility, hospital, prison, juvenile detention facility, or similar residential institution, all days of custody of the defendant, including days served as a condition of probation in compliance with a court order, and including days credited to the period of confinement pursuant to Section 4019, shall be credited upon his or her term of imprisonment, or credited to any fine which may be imposed, at the rate of not less than thirty dollars ($30) per day, or more, in the discretion of the court imposing the sentence. If the total number of days in custody exceeds the number of days of the term of imprisonment to be imposed, the entire term of imprisonment shall be deemed to have been served. In any case where the court has imposed both a prison or jail term of imprisonment and a fine, any days to be credited to the defendant shall first be applied to the term of imprisonment imposed, and thereafter the remaining days, if any, shall be applied to the fine.

(b) For the purposes of this section, credit shall be given only where the custody to be credited is attributable to proceedings related to the same conduct for which the defendant has been convicted. Credit shall be given only once for a single period of custody attributable to multiple offenses for which a consecutive sentence is imposed.

(c) For the purposes of this section, "term of imprisonment" includes any period of imprisonment imposed as a condition of probation or otherwise ordered by a court in imposing or suspending the imposition of any sentence, and also includes any term of imprisonment, including any period of imprisonment prior to release on parole and any period of imprisonment and parole, prior to discharge, whether established or fixed by statute, by any court, or by any duly authorized administrative agency.

(d) It shall be the duty of the court imposing the sentence to determine the date or dates of any admission to, and release from, custody prior to sentencing and the total number of days to be credited pursuant to this section. The total number of days to be credited shall be contained in the abstract of judgment provided for in Section 1213.

(e) It shall be the duty of any agency to which a person is committed to apply the credit provided for in this section for the period between the date of sentencing and the date the person is delivered to the agency.

(f) This section shall become operative on January 1, 1995. *(Added by Stats 1991 ch 437 §10, eff. 9/19/91, oper. 1/1/95. See other section 2900.5 above.)*

§2901. Wardens' duty.

It is hereby made the duty of the wardens of the State prisons to receive persons sentenced to imprisonment in a State prison, and such persons shall be imprisoned until duly released according to law.

§2902. Federal prisoners.

All criminals sentenced to prison by the authority of the United States or of any state or territory of the United States, may be received by the Director of Corrections and imprisoned in California state prisons in accordance with the sentence of the court by which they were tried. The prisoners so confined shall be subject in all respects to discipline and treatment as though committed under the laws of this State and the Director of Corrections is authorized to enter into contracts with the proper agencies of the United States and of other states and territories of the United States with regard to the per diem rate such agencies shall pay to the State of California for the keep of each prisoner.

§2903. Women offenders.

(a) In any case in which a woman offender can be sentenced to imprisonment in the county jail, or be required to serve a term of imprisonment therein as a condition of probation, or has already been so sentenced or imprisoned, the court which tried the offender may, with the consent of the offender and on application of the sheriff or on its own motion, with the consent of the offender, commit the offender to the sheriff with directions for placement in the California Institution for Women in lieu of placement in the county jail if the court finds that the local detention facilities are inadequate for the rehabilitation of the offenders and if the court concludes that the offender will benefit from that treatment and care as is available at that institution and the county has entered into a contract with the state under subdivision (b). The offenders may be received by the Director of Corrections and imprisoned in the California Institution for Women in accordance with the commitment of the court by which tried. The prisoners so confined shall be subject in all respects to discipline, diagnosis, and treatment as though committed under the laws of this state concerning felony prisoners.

(b) The Director of Corrections may enter into contracts, with the approval of the Director of General Services, with any county in this state, upon request of the board of supervisors thereof, wherein the Department of Corrections agrees to furnish diagnosis and treatment services and detention for selected women county prisoners. The county shall reimburse the state for the cost of the services, the cost to be determined by the Director of Finance. In any contract entered into pursuant to this subdivision, the county shall agree to pay that amount which is reasonably necessary for payment of an allowance to each released or paroled prisoner for transportation to the prisoner's county of residence or county where employment is available, and may agree to provide suitable clothing and a cash gratuity to the prisoners in the

© 1992 by J., B. & L. Gould
Printed in the U.S.A. **EP**

event that they are discharged from that institution because of parole or completion of the term for which they were sentenced. Each county auditor shall include in his state settlement report rendered to the Controller in the months of January and June the amounts due under any contract authorized by this section, and the county treasurer, at the time of settlement with the state in those months, shall pay to the State Treasurer upon order of the Controller, the amounts found to be due.

(c) The Department of Corrections shall accept the women county prisoners if it believes that they can be materially benefited by the confinement, care, treatment and employment and if adequate facilities to provide the care are available. None of those persons shall be transported to any facility under the jurisdiction of the Department of Corrections until the director has notified the referring court that the person may be transported to the California Institution for Women and the time at which she can be received.

(d) The sheriff of the county in which an order is made placing a woman county prisoner pursuant to this section, or any other peace officer designated by the court, shall execute the order placing the person in the institution or returning her therefrom to the court. The expenses of the peace officer incurred in executing the order is a charge upon the county in which the court is situated.

(e) The Director of Corrections may return to the committing authority any woman prisoner transferred pursuant to this section when that person is guilty of any violation of rules and regulations of the California Institution for Women or the Department of Corrections.

(f) No woman prisoner placed in the California Institution for Women pursuant to this section shall thereafter be deemed to have been guilty of a felony solely by virtue of such placement, and she shall have the same rights to parole and to time off for good behavior as she would have had if she had been confined in the county jail.

ARTICLE 1.5

TRANSFER OF PRISONERS

§2910. Director of Corrections' agreement with city, county; transfer of prisoners.

(a) The Director of Corrections may enter into an agreement with a city, county, or city and county, to permit transfer of prisoners in the custody of the Director of Corrections to a jail or other adult correctional facility of the city, county, or city and county, if the sheriff or corresponding official having jurisdiction over the facility has consented thereto. The agreement shall provide for contributions to the city, county, or city and county toward payment of costs incurred with reference to such transferred prisoners.

(b) When an agreement entered into pursuant to subdivision (a) is in effect with respect to a particular local facility, the Director of Corrections may transfer prisoners whose terms of imprisonment have been fixed and parole violators to the facility.

(c) Prisoners so transferred to a local facility may, with approval of the Director of Corrections, participate in programs of the facility, including work furlough rehabilitation programs.

(d) Prisoners transferred to such facilities are subject to the rules and regulations of the facility in which

they are confined, but remain under the legal custody of the Department of Corrections and shall be subject at any time, pursuant to the rules and regulations of the Director of Corrections, to be detained in the county jail upon the exercise of a state parole or correctional officer's peace officer powers as specified in Section 830.5, with the consent of the sheriff or corresponding official having jurisdiction over the facility.

(e) The Director of Corrections, to the extent possible, shall select city, county, or city and county facilities in areas where medical, food, and other support services are available from nearby existing prison facilities.

(f) The Director of Corrections, with the approval of the Department of General Services, may enter into an agreement to lease state property for a period not in excess of 20 years to be used as the site for a facility operated by a city, county, or city and county authorized by this section.

(g) No agreement may be entered into under this section unless the cost per inmate in the facility is no greater than the average costs of keeping an inmate in a comparable facility of the department, as determined by the director. (Amended by Stats 1987 ch 1450 §1.5.)

§2910.5. Long-term agreements with city and county.

(a) Pursuant to Section 2910, the Director of Corrections may enter into a long-term agreement not to exceed 20 years with a city, county, or city and county to place parole violators and other state inmates in a facility which is specially designed and built for the incarceration of parole violators and specified state prison inmates.

(b) The agreement shall provide that persons providing security at the facilities shall be peace officers as defined in Sections 830.1 and 830.55 who have satisfactorily met the minimum selection and training standards prescribed by the Board of Corrections for local correctional personnel established under Section 6035.

(c) A parole violator or other inmate may be confined in a facility established under this section.

(1) If convicted within the last 10 years of a violent felony, as defined in subdivision (c) of Section 667.5, or convicted of a crime, as defined in Sections 207, 210.5, 214, 217.1, or 220, or if that person has a history of escape or attempted escape, the Department of Corrections, prior to placing the parole violator or inmate in the facility, shall review each individual case to make certain that this placement is in keeping with the need to protect society.

(2) No inmate or parole violator who has received a sentence of life imprisonment within the past 20 years shall be eligible.

(3) The superintendent of the facility also shall review each individual case where the inmate or parolee has been convicted within the last 10 years of a crime specified in this subdivision and shall ascertain whether this is an appropriate placement. The superintendent shall reject those whom he or she determines are inappropriate due to their propensity for violence or escape and shall submit written findings for the rejection to the Department of Corrections.

(4) No parole violator who receives a revocation sentence greater than 12 months shall be confined in a facility established under this section.

© 1992 by J., B. & L. Gould
Printed in the U.S.A.   EP

(5) The Department of Corrections shall establish additional guidelines as to inmates eligible for the facilities.

(d) In determining the reimbursement rate pursuant to an agreement entered into pursuant to subdivision (a), the director shall take into consideration the costs incurred by the city, county, or city and county for services and facilities provided and any other factors that are necessary and appropriate to fix the obligations, responsibilities, and rights of the respective parties.

(e) Facilities operated by the county shall be under the supervision of the sheriff. Facilities operated by the city shall be under the supervision of a chief of police or a facility superintendent who shall have at least five years similar experience.

(f) Cities or counties contracting with the Department of Corrections for a facility pursuant to this section shall be responsible for managing and maintaining the security of the facility pursuant to the regulations and direction of the Director of Corrections. No city or county may contract with any private provider to manage, operate, or maintain the security of the facility. *(Amended by Stats 1991 ch 1100 §4, eff. 1/1/92.)*

§2910.6. Agreement to construct and operate correctional programs.

The Director of Corrections may enter into an agreement consistent with applicable law for a city, county, or city and county to construct and operate community corrections programs, restitution centers, halfway houses, work furlough programs, or other correctional programs authorized by state law. *(Added by Stats 1987 ch 1450 §2.5.)*

§2911. Contracts for confinement and care of convicts.

(a) The Director of Corrections may enter into contracts, with the approval of the Director of General Services, with appropriate officials or agencies of the United States for the confinement, care, education, treatment and employment of such persons convicted of criminal offenses in the courts of this state and committed to state prisons as the director believes can benefit by such confinement, care, education, treatment, and employment.

(b) Any contract entered into pursuant to subdivision (a) shall provide for (1) reimbursement to the United States government for the cost of such services, including any costs incurred by such government in transporting such prisoners, and (2) such other matters as may be necessary and appropriate to fix the obligations, responsibilities and rights of the respective parties to the contract.

(c) No inmate may be transferred from an institution within this state to a federal facility pursuant to such a contract unless he has executed, in the presence of the warden or other head of the institution in this state in which he is confined, a written consent to the transfer. The inmate shall have the right to a private consultation with an attorney of his choice, concerning his rights and obligations under this section, prior to his appearance before the warden or other head of the institution for the purpose of executing the written consent.

(d) Whenever a contract has been made pursuant to this section the director may direct the transfer of an inmate to the facility designated and shall thereafter deliver the inmate to the custody of the appropriate federal officials for transportation to such facility. An inmate so transferred shall at all times be subject to the jurisdiction of this state and may at any time be removed from the facility in which he is confined for return to this state, for transfer to another facility in which this state may have a contractual or other right to confine inmates, for release on probation or parole, for discharge, or for any other purpose permitted by the laws of this state; in all other respects, an inmate transferred to a federal facility shall be subject to all provisions of the law or regulations applicable to persons committed for violations of laws of the United States not inconsistent with the sentence imposed on such inmate.

(e) The Board of Prison Terms, and the panels and members thereof, may meet at the federal facility where an inmate is confined pursuant to this section or enter into cooperative arrangements with corresponding federal agencies or officials, as necessary to carry out the term-fixing and parole functions. Nothing in this subdivision shall be deemed to waive an inmate's right to personally appear before the Board of Prison Terms.

(f) Any inmate confined pursuant to a contract entered into pursuant to this section shall be released within the territory of this state unless the inmate, this state and the federal government shall agree upon release in some other place. This state shall bear the cost of return of the inmate to its territory.

§2913. Notice of contract.

A city shall give notice to, and consult with, the county prior to contracting with the state pursuant to Section 2910 of this code or Section 1753.3 of the Welfare and Institutions Code. *(Added by Stats 1987 ch 1450 §2.6.)*

ARTICLE 2.5

CREDIT ON TERM OF IMPRISONMENT

§2930. Programs available.

(a) The Department of Corrections shall inform every prisoner sentenced under Section 1170, for a crime committed prior to January 1, 1983, not later than 14 days after reception in prison, of all applicable prison rules and regulations including the possibility of receiving a one-third reduction of the sentence for good behavior and participation. Within 14 days of the prisoner's arrival at the institution to which the prisoner is ultimately assigned by the Department of Corrections, the prisoner shall be informed of the range of programs offered by that institution and their availability at that institution. The prisoner's central file shall reflect compliance with the provisions of this section not later than 90 days after reception in prison.

(b) The department shall, within 90 days after July 1, 1977, inform every prisoner who committed a felony before July 1, 1977, and who would have been sentenced under Section 1170 if the felony had been committed after July 1, 1977, of all applicable prison rules and regulations, which have not previously been provided, of the range of programs offered and their availability, and the possibility of receiving a reduction for good behavior and participation of one-third of the prisoner's remaining sentence after July 1, 1977. The prisoner's central file shall reflect compliance with the provisions of this section.

§2931. Reduction of prison term for good behavior.

(a) In any case in which a prisoner was sentenced to the state prison pursuant to Section 1170, or if he committed a felony before July 1, 1977, and he would have been sentenced under Section 1170 if the felony had been committed after July 1, 1977, the Department of Corrections shall have the authority to reduce the term prescribed under such section by one-third for good behavior and participation consistent with subdivision (d) of Section 1170.2. A document shall be signed by a prison official and given to the prisoner, at the time of compliance with Section 2930, outlining the conditions which the prisoner shall meet to receive the credit. The conditions specified in such document may be modified upon any of the following:

(1) Mutual consent of the prisoner and the Department of Corrections.

(2) The transfer of the prisoner from one institution to another.

(3) The department's determination of the prisoner's lack of adaptability or success in a specific program or assignment. In such case the prisoner shall be entitled to a hearing regarding the department's decision.

(4) A change in custodial status.

(b) Total possible good behavior and participation credit shall result in a four-month reduction for each eight months served in prison or in a reduction based on this ratio for any lesser period of time. Three months of this four-month reduction, or a reduction based on this ratio for any lesser period, shall be based upon forbearance from any act for which the prisoner could be prosecuted in a court of law, either as a misdemeanor or a felony, or any act of misconduct described as a serious disciplinary infraction by the Department of Corrections.

(c) One month of this four-month reduction, or a reduction based on this ratio for a lesser period, shall be based solely upon participation in work, educational, vocational, therapeutic or other prison activities. Failure to succeed after demonstrating a reasonable effort in the specified activity shall not result in loss of participation credit. Failure to participate in the specified activities can result in a maximum loss of credit of 30 days for each failure to participate. However, those confined for other than behavior problems shall be given specified activities commensurate with the custodial status.

(d) This section shall not apply to any person whose crime was committed on or after January 1, 1983.

§2932. Denial of time credits for misbehavior.

(a) (1) For any time credit accumulated pursuant to Section 2931 or to Section 2933, not more than 360 days of credit may be denied or lost for a single act of murder, attempted murder, solicitation of murder, manslaughter, rape, sodomy, or oral copulation accomplished against the victim's will, attempted rape, attempted sodomy, or attempted oral copulation accomplished against the victim's will, assault or battery causing serious bodily injury, assault with a deadly weapon or caustic substance, taking of a hostage, escape with force or violence, or possession or manufacture of a deadly weapon or explosive device, whether or not prosecution is undertaken for purposes of this paragraph. Solicitation of murder shall be proved by the testimony of two witnesses, or of one witness and corroborating circumstances.

(2) Not more than 180 days of credit may be denied or lost for a single act of misconduct, except as specified in paragraph (1), which could be prosecuted as a felony whether or not prosecution is undertaken.

(3) Not more than 90 days of credit may be denied or lost for a single act of misconduct which could be prosecuted as a misdemeanor, whether or not prosecution is undertaken.

(4) Not more than 30 days of credit may be denied or lost for a single act of misconduct defined by regulation as a serious disciplinary offense by the Department of Corrections. Any person confined due to a change in custodial classification following the commission of any serious disciplinary infraction shall, in addition to any loss of time credits, be ineligible to receive participation or worktime credit for a period not to exceed the number of days of credit which have been lost for the act of misconduct or 180 days, whichever is less. Any person confined in a secure housing unit for having committed any misconduct specified in paragraph (1) in which great bodily injury is inflicted upon a nonprisoner shall, in addition to any loss of time credits, be ineligible to receive participation or worktime credit for a period not to exceed the number of days of credit which have been lost for that act of misconduct, or for the period that the prisoner is confined in a secure housing unit, whichever is less. In unusual cases, an inmate may be denied the opportunity to participate in a credit qualifying assignment for up to six months beyond the period specified in this subdivision if the Director of Corrections finds, after a hearing, that no credit qualifying program may be assigned to the inmate without creating a substantial risk of physical harm to staff or other inmates. At the end of the six-month period and of successive six-month periods, the denial of the opportunity to participate in a credit qualifying assignment may be renewed upon a hearing and finding by the director.

The prisoner may appeal the decision through the department's review procedure, which shall include a review by an individual independent of the institution who has supervisorial authority over the institution.

(b) For any credit accumulated pursuant to Section 2931, not more than 30 days of participation credit may be denied or lost for a single failure or refusal to participate. Any act of misconduct described by the Department of Corrections as a serious disciplinary infraction if committed while participating in work, educational, vocational, therapeutic, or other prison activity shall be deemed a failure to participate.

(c) Any procedure not provided for by this section, but necessary to carry out the purposes of this section, shall be those procedures provided for by the Department of Corrections for serious disciplinary infractions if those procedures are not in conflict with this section.

(1) (A) The Department of Corrections shall, using reasonable diligence to investigate, provide written notice to the prisoner. The written notice shall be given within 15 days after the discovery of information leading to charges that may result in a possible denial of credit, except that if the prisoner has escaped, the notice shall be given within 15 days of the prisoner's return to the custody of the Director of Corrections. The written notice shall include the specific charge, the date, the time, the place that the alleged misbehavior took place, the evidence relied upon, a written explanation of the procedures that will be employed at the proceedings and the prisoner's rights

© 1992 by J., B. & L. Gould
Printed in the U.S.A.   EP

at the hearing. The hearing shall be conducted by an individual who shall be independent of the case and shall take place within 30 days of the written notice.

(B) The Department of Corrections may delay written notice beyond 15 days when all of the following factors are true:

(i) An act of misconduct is involved which could be prosecuted as murder, attempted murder, or assault on a prison employee, whether or not prosecution is undertaken.

(ii) Further investigation is being undertaken for the purpose of identifying other prisoners involved in the misconduct.

(iii) Within 15 days after the discovery of information leading to charges that may result in a possible denial of credit, the investigating officer makes a written request to delay notifying that prisoner and states the reasons for the delay.

(iv) The warden of the institution approves of the delay in writing.

The period of delay under this paragraph shall not exceed 30 days. The prisoner's hearing shall take place within 30 days of the written notice.

(2) The prisoner may elect to be assigned an employee to assist in the investigation, preparation, or presentation of a defense at the disciplinary hearing if it is determined by the department that: (i) the prisoner is illiterate; or (ii) the complexity of the issues or the prisoner's confinement status makes it unlikely that the prisoner can collect and present the evidence necessary for an adequate comprehension of the case.

(3) The prisoner may request witnesses to attend the hearing and they shall be called unless the person conducting the hearing has specific reasons to deny this request. The specific reasons shall be set forth in writing and a copy of the document shall be presented to the prisoner.

(4) The prisoner has the right, under the direction of the person conducting the hearing, to question all witnesses.

(5) At the conclusion of the hearing the charge shall be dismissed if the facts do not support the charge, or the prisoner may be found guilty on the basis of a preponderance of the evidence.

(d) If found guilty the prisoner shall be advised in writing of the guilty finding and the specific evidence relied upon to reach this conclusion and the amount of time-credit loss. The prisoner may appeal the decision through the Department of Corrections' review procedure, and may, upon final notification of appeal denial, within 15 days of the notification demand review of the department's denial of credit to the Board of Prison Terms, and the board may affirm, reverse, or modify the department's decision or grant a hearing before the board at which hearing the prisoner shall have the rights specified in Section 3041.5.

(e) Each prisoner subject to Section 2931 shall be notified of the total amount of good behavior and participation credit which may be credited pursuant to Section 2931, and his or her anticipated time-credit release date. The prisoner shall be notified of any change in the anticipated release date due to denial or loss of credits, award of worktime credit, under Section 2933, or the restoration of any credits previously forfeited.

(f) If the conduct the prisoner is charged with also constitutes a crime, the Department of Corrections may refer the case to criminal authorities for possible prosecution. The department shall notify the prisoner, who may request postponement of the disciplinary proceedings pending the referral.

The prisoner may revoke his or her request for postponement of the disciplinary proceedings up until the filing of the accusatory pleading. In the event of the revocation of the request for postponement of the proceeding, the department shall hold the hearing within 30 days of the revocation.

Notwithstanding the notification requirements in this paragraph and subparagraphs (A) and (B) of paragraph (1) of subdivision (c), in the event the case is referred to criminal authorities for prosecution and the authority requests that the prisoner not be notified so as to protect the confidentiality of its investigation, no notice to the prisoner shall be required until an accusatory pleading is filed with the court, or the authority notifies the warden, in writing, that it will not prosecute or it authorizes the notification of the prisoner. The notice exceptions provided for in this paragraph shall only apply if the criminal authority requests of the warden, in writing, and within the 15 days provided in subparagraph (A) of paragraph (1) of subdivision (c), that the prisoner not be notified. Any period of delay of notice to the prisoner shall not exceed 30 days beyond the 15 days referred to in subdivision (c). In the event that no prosecution is undertaken, the procedures in subdivision (c) shall apply, and the time periods set forth in that subdivision shall commence to run from the date the warden is notified in writing of the decision not to prosecute. In the event the authority either cancels its requests that the prisoner not be notified before it makes a decision on prosecution or files an accusatory pleading, the provisions of this paragraph shall apply as if no request had been received, beginning from the date of the cancellation or filing.

In the case where the prisoner is prosecuted by the district attorney, the Department of Corrections shall not deny time credit where the prisoner is found not guilty and may deny credit if the prisoner is found guilty, in which case the procedures in subdivision (c) shall not apply.

(g) If time credit denial proceedings or criminal prosecution prohibit the release of a prisoner who would have otherwise been released, and the prisoner is found not guilty of the alleged misconduct, the amount of time spent incarcerated, in excess of what the period of incarceration would have been absent the alleged misbehavior, shall be deducted from the prisoner's parole period.

(h) Nothing in the amendments to this section made at the 1981-82 Regular Session of the Legislature shall affect the granting or revocation of credits attributable to that portion of the prisoner's sentence served prior to January 1, 1983. *(Amended by Stats 1989 ch 1420 §13, eff. 1/1/90.)*

§2933. Worktime credit.

(a) It is the intent of the Legislature that persons convicted of a crime and sentenced to state prison, under Section 1170, serve the entire sentence imposed by the court, except for a reduction in the time served in the custody of the Director of Corrections for performance in work, training or education programs established by the Director of Corrections. Worktime credits shall apply for performance in work assignments and performance in elementary, high school, or vocational education programs. Enrollment in a two-

or four-year college program leading to a degree shall result in the application of time credits equal to that provided in Section 2931. For every six months of full-time performance in a credit qualifying program, as designated by the director, a prisoner shall be awarded worktime credit reductions from his or her term of confinement of six months. A lesser amount of credit based on this ratio shall be awarded for any lesser period of continuous performance. Less than maximum credit should be awarded pursuant to regulations adopted by the director for prisoners not assigned to a full-time credit qualifying program. Every prisoner who refuses to accept a full-time credit qualifying assignment or who is denied the opportunity to earn worktime credits pursuant to subdivision (a) of Section 2932 shall be awarded no worktime credit reduction. Every prisoner who voluntarily accepts a half-time credit qualifying assignment in lieu of a full-time assignment shall be awarded worktime credit reductions from his or her term of confinement of three months for each six-month period of continued performance. Except as provided in subdivision (a) of Section 2932, every prisoner willing to participate in a full-time credit qualifying assignment but who is either not assigned to a full-time assignment or is assigned to a program for less than full time, shall receive no less credit than is provided under Section 2931. Under no circumstances shall any prisoner receive more than six months' credit reduction for any six-month period under this section.

(b) Worktime credit is a privilege, not a right. Worktime credit must be earned and may be forfeited pursuant to the provisions of Section 2932. Except as provided in subdivision (a) of Section 2932, every prisoner shall have a reasonable opportunity to participate in a full-time credit qualifying assignment in a manner consistent with institutional security and available resources.

(c) Under regulations adopted by the Department of Corrections, which shall require a period of not more than one year free of disciplinary infractions, worktime credit which has been previously forfeited may be restored by the director. The regulations shall provide for separate classifications of serious disciplinary infractions as they relate to restoration of credits; the time period required before forfeited credits or a portion thereof may be restored; and the percentage of forfeited credits that may be restored for such time periods. For credits forfeited for commission of a felony specified in paragraph (1) of subdivision (a) of Section 2932, the Department of Corrections may provide that up to 180 days of lost credit shall not be restored and up to 90 days of credit shall not be restored for a forfeiture resulting from conspiracy or attempts to commit one of those acts; provided that no credits may be restored if they were forfeited for a serious disciplinary infraction in which the victim died or was permanently disabled. Upon application of the prisoner and following completion of the required time period free of disciplinary offenses, forfeited credits eligible for restoration under the regulations shall be restored unless, at a hearing, it is found that the prisoner refused to accept or failed to perform in a credit qualifying assignment or extraordinary circumstances are present that require that credits not be restored. "Extraordinary circumstances" shall be defined in the regulations adopted by the director.

The prisoner may appeal the finding through the Department of Corrections review procedure, which shall include a review by an individual independent of the institution who has supervisorial authority over the institution.

(d) The provisions of subdivision (c) shall also apply in cases of credit forfeited under Section 2931 for offenses and serious disciplinary infractions occurring on or after January 1, 1983.

(e) Any person sentenced to a term in the state prison under subdivision (a) of Section 190 shall be eligible only for credit pursuant to subdivisions (a), (b), and (c) of Section 2931. *(Amended by Stats 1988 ch 121 §1, eff. 6/7/88.)*

§2933.5. Worktime credits; ineligibility.

(a) Notwithstanding any other provision of law, the following persons shall be ineligible to earn credit on their terms of imprisonment pursuant to this chapter.

(1) Every person convicted of any felony offense listed in paragraph (2), and who has been previously convicted two or more times, on charges separately brought and tried, and who previously has served two or more separate prior prison terms, as defined in subdivision (g) of Section 667.5, of any offense or offenses listed in paragraph (2).

(2) As used in this subdivision, "felony offense" includes any of the following:

(A) Murder, as defined in Sections 187 and 189.

(B) Voluntary manslaughter, as defined in subdivision (a) of Section 192.

(C) Mayhem as defined in Section 203.

(D) Aggravated mayhem, as defined in Section 205.

(E) Kidnapping for the purpose of committing child molestation, as described in subdivision (b) of Section 207, in which great bodily injury was personally inflicted as provided in Section 12022.7.

(F) Assault with vitriol, corrosive acid, or caustic chemical of any nature, as described in Section 244.

(G) Rape, as defined in subdivision (2) of Section 261.

(H) Sodomy by means of force, violence, duress, menace or fear of immediate and unlawful bodily injury on the victim or another person, as described in subdivision (c) of Section 286.

(I) Sodomy while voluntarily acting in concert, as described in subdivision (d) of Section 286.

(J) Lewd or lascivious acts on a child under the age of 14 years, as described in subdivision (b) of Section 288.

(K) Oral copulation by means of force, violence, duress, menace, or fear of immediate and unlawful bodily injury on the victim or another person, as described in subdivision (c) of Section 288a.

(L) Continuous sexual abuse of a child, as described in Section 288.5.

(M) Penetration by foreign object, as described in subdivision (a) of Section 289.

(N) Exploding a destructive device or explosive with intent to injure, as described in Section 12303.3, with intent to murder, as described in Section 12308, or resulting in great bodily injury or mayhem, as described in Section 12309.

(O) Any felony in which the defendant personally inflicted great bodily injury as provided in Section 12022.7.

(b) A prior conviction of an offense listed in subdivision (a) shall include a conviction in another jurisdiction for an offense which includes all of the

© 1992 by J., B. & L. Gould
Printed in the U.S.A.   **EP**

elements of the particular felony as defined under California law.

(c) This section shall apply whenever the present felony is committed on or after the effective date of this section, regardless of the date of commission of the prior offense or offenses resulting in credit-earning ineligibility.

(d) This section shall be in addition to, and shall not preclude the imposition of, any applicable sentence enhancement terms, or probation ineligibility and habitual offender provisions authorized under any other section. *(Added by Stats 1990 ch 1700 §3, eff. 1/1/91.)*

§2934. Waiver of right to receive good credits.

Under rules prescribed by the Director of Corrections, a prisoner subject to the provisions of Section 2931 may waive the right to receive time credits as provided in Section 2931 and be subject to the provisions of Section 2933. In order to exercise a waiver under this section, a prisoner must apply in writing to the Department of Corrections. A prisoner exercising a waiver under this section shall retain only that portion of good behavior and participation credits, which have not been forfeited pursuant to Section 2932, attributable to the portion of the sentence served by the prisoner prior to the effective date of the waiver. A waiver under this section shall, if accepted by the department, become effective at a time to be determined by the Director of the Department of Corrections.

§2935. Additional reduction of sentence.

Under the guidelines prescribed by the rules and regulations of the director, the Director of Corrections may grant up to 12 additional months of reduction of the sentence to a prisoner who has performed a heroic act in a life-threatening situation, or who has provided exceptional assistance in maintaining the safety and security of a prison.

ARTICLE 3

BLACKLIST OR EXTORTION OF DISCHARGED PRISONER

§2947. Extortion of an ex-felon.

Any person who knowingly and willfully communicates to another, either orally or in writing, any statement concerning any person then or theretofore convicted of a felony, and then finally discharged, and which communication is made with the purpose and intent to deprive such person so convicted of employment, or to prevent him from procuring the same, or with the purpose and intent to extort from him any money or article of value; and any person who threatens to make any such communication with the purpose and intent to extort money or any article of value from such person so convicted of a felony is guilty of a misdemeanor.

ARTICLE 4

DISPOSITION OF MENTALLY DISORDERED PRISONERS UPON DISCHARGE

§2960. Inpatient treatment in state hospital.

The Legislature finds that there are prisoners who have a treatable, severe mental disorder that was one of the causes of, or was an aggravating factor in the commission of the crime for which they were incarcerated. Secondly, the Legislature finds that if the severe mental disorders of those prisoners are not in remission or cannot be kept in remission at the time of their parole or upon termination of parole, there is a danger to society, and the state has a compelling interest in protecting the public. Thirdly, the Legislature finds that in order to protect the public from those persons it is necessary to provide mental health treatment until the severe mental disorder which was one of the causes of or was an aggravating factor in the person's prior criminal behavior is in remission and can be kept in remission.

The Legislature further finds and declares the Department of Corrections should evaluate each prisoner for severe mental disorders during the first year of the prisoner's sentence, and that severely mentally disordered prisoners should be provided with an appropriate level of mental health treatment while in prison and when returned to the community. *(Amended by Stats 1986 ch 858 §1.)*

§2962. Required treatment as parole condition; prisoner's criteria.

As a condition of parole, a prisoner who meets the following criteria shall be required to be treated by the State Department of Mental Health, and the State Department of Mental Health shall provide the necessary treatment:

(a) The prisoner has a severe mental disorder that is not in remission or cannot be kept in remission without treatment.

The term "severe mental disorder" means an illness or disease or condition that substantially impairs the person's thought, perception of reality, emotional process, or judgment; or which grossly impairs behavior; or that demonstrates evidence of an acute brain syndrome for which prompt remission, in the absence of treatment, is unlikely. The term "severe mental disorder" as used in this section does not include a personality or adjustment disorder, epilepsy, mental retardation or other developmental disabilities, or addiction to or abuse of intoxicating substances.

The term "remission" means a finding that the overt signs and symptoms of the severe mental disorder are controlled either by psychotropic medication or psychosocial support. A person "cannot be kept in remission without treatment" if during the year prior to the question being before the Board of Prison Terms or a trial court, he or she has been in remission and he or she has been physically violent, except in self-defense, or he or she has made a serious threat of substantial physical harm upon the person of another so as to cause the target of the threat to reasonably fear for his or her safety or the safety of his or her immediate family, or he or she has intentionally caused property damage, or he or she has not voluntarily followed the treatment plan. In determining if a person has voluntarily followed the treatment plan, the standard shall be whether the person has acted as a reasonable person would in following the treatment plan.

(b) The severe mental disorder was one of the causes of or was an aggravating factor in the commission of a crime for which the prisoner was sentenced to prison.

(c) The prisoner has been in treatment for the severe mental disorder for 90 days or more within the year prior to the prisoner's parole or release.

(d) (1) Prior to release on parole, the person in charge of treating the prisoner and a practicing psychiatrist or psychologist from the State Department of Mental Health have evaluated the prisoner at a facility of the Department of Corrections, and a chief psychiatrist of the Department of Corrections has certified to the Board of Prison Terms that the prisoner has a severe mental disorder, that the disorder is not in remission, or cannot be kept in remission without treatment, that the severe mental disorder was one of the causes or was an aggravating factor in the prisoner's criminal behavior, that the prisoner has been in treatment for the severe mental disorder for 90 days or more within the year prior to his or her parole release day, that the prisoner used force or violence or caused serious bodily injury in committing the crime referred to in subdivision (b), and that by reason of his or her severe mental disorder the prisoner represents a substantial danger of physical harm to others. For prisoners being treated by the State Department of Mental Health pursuant to Section 2684, the certification shall be by a chief psychiatrist of the Department of Corrections, and the evaluation shall be done at a state hospital by the person at the state hospital in charge of treating the prisoner and a practicing psychiatrist or psychologist from the Department of Corrections.

(2) If the professionals doing the evaluation pursuant to paragraph (1) do not concur that (1) the prisoner has a severe mental disorder, or (2) that the disorder is not in remission or cannot be kept in remission without treatment, or (3) that the severe mental disorder was a cause of, or aggravated, the prisoner's criminal behavior, and a chief psychiatrist has certified the prisoner to the Board of Prison Terms pursuant to this paragraph, then the Board of Prison Terms shall order a further examination by two independent professionals, as provided for in Section 2978.

(3) Only if both independent professionals who evaluate the prisoner pursuant to paragraph (2) concur with the chief psychiatrist's certification of the issues described in paragraph (2), shall this subdivision be applicable to the prisoner. The professionals appointed pursuant to Section 2978 shall inform the prisoner that the purpose of their examination is not treatment but to determine if the prisoner meets certain criteria to be involuntarily treated as a mentally disordered offender. It is not required that the prisoner appreciate or understand that information.

(e) The crime referred to in subdivision (b) was a crime in which the prisoner used force or violence, or caused serious bodily injury as defined in paragraph (5) of subdivision (f) of Section 243.

(f) As used in this chapter, "substantial danger of physical harm" does not require proof of a recent overt act. *(Amended by Stats 1991 ch 435 §2, eff. 1/1/92.)*

§2964. Inpatient or outpatient treatment program.

(a) The treatment required by Section 2962 shall be inpatient unless the State Department of Mental Health certifies to the Board of Prison Terms that there is reasonable cause to believe the parolee can be safely and effectively treated on an outpatient basis, in which case the Board of Prison Terms shall permit the State Department of Mental Health to place the parolee in an outpatient treatment program specified by the State Department of Mental Health. Any

prisoner who is to be required to accept treatment pursuant to Section 2962 shall be informed in writing of his or her right to request a hearing pursuant to Section 2966. Prior to placing a parolee in a local outpatient program, the State Department of Mental Health shall consult with the local outpatient program as to the appropriate treatment plan. Notwithstanding any other law, a parolee ordered to have outpatient treatment pursuant to this section may be placed in an outpatient treatment program used to provide outpatient treatment under Title 15 (commencing with Section 1600) of Part 2, but the procedural provisions of Title 15 shall not apply. The community program director or a designee of an outpatient program used to provide treatment under Title 15 in which a parolee is placed, may place the parolee, or cause the parolee to be placed, in a secure mental health facility if the parolee can no longer be safely or effectively treated in the outpatient program, and until the parolee can be safely and effectively treated in the program. Upon the request of the community program director or a designee, a peace officer shall take the parolee into custody and transport the parolee, or cause the parolee to be taken into custody and transported, to a facility designated by the community program director, or a designee, for confinement under this section. Within 15 days after placement in a secure facility the State Department of Mental Health shall conduct a hearing on whether the parolee can be safely and effectively treated in the program unless the patient or the patient's attorney agrees to a continuance, or unless good cause exists that prevents the State Department of Mental Health from conducting the hearing within that period of time. If good cause exists, the hearing shall be held within 21 days after placement in a secure facility. For purposes of this section, "good cause" means the inability to secure counsel, an interpreter, or witnesses for the hearing within the 15-day time period. Before deciding to seek revocation of the parole of a parolee receiving mental health treatment pursuant to Section 2962, and return him or her to prison, the parole officer shall consult with the director of the parolee's outpatient program. Nothing in this section shall prevent hospitalization pursuant to Section 5150, 5250, or 5353 of the Welfare and Institutions Code.

(b) If the State Department of Mental Health has not placed a parolee on outpatient treatment within 60 days after receiving custody of the parolee or after parole is continued pursuant to Section 3001, the parolee may request a hearing before the Board of Prison Terms, and the board shall conduct a hearing to determine whether the prisoner shall be treated as an inpatient or an outpatient. At the hearing, the burden shall be on the State Department of Mental Health to establish that the prisoner requires inpatient treatment as described in this subdivision. If the prisoner or any person appearing on his or her behalf at the hearing requests it, the board shall appoint two independent professionals as provided for in Section 2978. *(Amended by Stats 1991 ch 435 §3, eff. 1/1/92.)*

§2966. Hearing re Section 2962 criteria.

(a) A prisoner may request a hearing before the Board of Prison Terms, and the board shall conduct a hearing if so requested, for the purpose of proving that the prisoner meets the criteria in Section 2962. At the hearing, the burden of proof shall be on the person or

© 1992 by J., B. & L. Gould
Printed in the U.S.A.   EP

agency who certified the prisoner under subdivision (d) of Section 2962. If the prisoner or any person appearing on his or her behalf at the hearing requests it, the board shall appoint two independent professionals as provided for in Section 2978. The prisoner shall be informed at the hearing of his or her right to request a trial pursuant to subdivision (b). The Board of Prison Terms shall provide a prisoner who requests a trial, a petition form and instructions for filing the petition.

(b) A prisoner who disagrees with the determination of the Board of Prison Terms that he or she meets the criteria of Section 2962, may file in the superior court of the county in which he or she is incarcerated or is being treated a petition for a hearing on whether he or she, as of the date of the Board of Prison Terms hearing, met the criteria of Section 2962. The court shall conduct a hearing on the petition within 60 calendar days after the petition is filed, unless either time is waived by the petitioner or his or her counsel, or good cause is shown. The order of the Board of Prison Terms shall be in effect until the completion of the court proceedings. The court shall advise the petitioner of his or her right to be represented by an attorney and of the right to a jury trial. The attorney for the petitioner shall be given a copy of the petition, and any supporting documents. The hearing shall be a civil hearing; however, in order to reduce costs, the rules of criminal discovery, as well as civil discovery, shall be applicable. The standard of proof shall be beyond a reasonable doubt, and if the trial is by jury, the jury shall be unanimous in its verdict. The trial shall be by jury unless waived by both the person and the district attorney.

(c) If the Board of Prison Terms continues a parolee's mental health treatment under Section 2962 when it continues the parolee's parole under Section 3001, the procedures of this section shall only be applicable for the purpose of determining if the parolee has a severe mental disorder, whether the parolee's severe mental disorder is not in remission or cannot be kept in remission without treatment, and whether by reason of his or her severe mental disorder, the parolee represents a substantial danger of physical harm to others. *(Amended by Stats 1989 ch 228 §2, eff. 7/27/89.)*

§2968. Discontinuation of treatment upon remission.

If the prisoner's severe mental disorder is put into remission during the parole period, and can be kept in remission, the Director of Mental Health shall notify the Board of Prison Terms and the State Department of Mental Health shall discontinue treating the parolee. *(Added by Stats 1986 ch 858 §5.)*

§2970. Evaluation on remission; continued treatment.

Not later than 180 days prior to the termination of parole, or release from prison if the prisoner refused to agree to treatment as a condition of parole as required by Section 2962, unless good cause is shown for the reduction of that 180-day period, if the prisoner's severe mental disorder is not in remission or cannot be kept in remission without treatment, the medical director of the state hospital which is treating the parolee, or the community program director in charge of the parolee's outpatient program, or the Director of Corrections, shall submit to the district attorney of the county in which the parolee is receiving outpatient treatment, or for those in prison or in a state mental hospital, the district attorney of the county of commitment, his or her written evaluation on remission. If requested by the district attorney, the written evaluation shall be accompanied by supporting affidavits.

The district attorney may then file a petition with the superior court for continued involuntary treatment for one year. The petition shall be accompanied by affidavits specifying that treatment, while the prisoner was released from prison on parole, has been continuously provided by the State Department of Mental Health either in a state hospital or in an outpatient program. The petition shall also specify that the prisoner has a severe mental disorder, that the severe mental disorder is not in remission or cannot be kept in remission if the person's treatment is not continued, and that, by reason of his or her severe mental disorder, the prisoner represents a substantial danger of physical harm to others. *(Amended by Stats 1991 ch 435 §4, eff. 1/1/92.)*

§2972. Hearing on continued treatment petition.

(a) The court shall conduct a hearing on the petition under Section 2970 for continued treatment. The court shall advise the person of his or her right to be represented by an attorney and of the right to a jury trial. The attorney for the person shall be given a copy of the petition, and any supporting documents. The hearing shall be a civil hearing, however, in order to reduce costs the rules of criminal discovery, as well as civil discovery, shall be applicable.

The standard of proof under this section shall be proof beyond a reasonable doubt, and if the trial is by jury, the jury shall be unanimous in its verdict. The trial shall be by jury unless waived by both the person and the district attorney. The trial shall commence no later than 30 calendar days prior to the time the person would otherwise have been released, unless the time is waived by the person or unless good cause is shown.

(b) The people shall be represented by the district attorney. If the person is indigent, the county public defender shall be appointed.

(c) If the court or jury finds that the patient has a severe mental disorder, that the patient's severe mental disorder is not in remission or cannot be kept in remission without treatment, and that by reason of his or her severe mental disorder, the patient represents a substantial danger of physical harm to others, the court shall order the patient recommitted to the facility in which the patient was confined at the time the petition was filed, or recommitted to the outpatient program in which he or she was being treated at the time the petition was filed, or committed to the State Department of Mental Health if the person was in prison. The commitment shall be for a period of one year from the date of termination of parole or a previous commitment or the scheduled date of release from prison as specified in Section 2970.

(d) A person shall be released on outpatient status if the committing court finds that there is reasonable cause to believe that the committed person can be safely and effectively treated on an outpatient basis. Except as provided in this subdivision, the provisions of Title 15 (commencing with Section 1600) of Part 2, shall apply to persons placed on outpatient status pursuant to this paragraph. The standard for revocation under Section 1609 shall be that the person cannot be safely and effectively treated on an outpatient basis.

(e) Prior to the termination of a commitment under this section, a petition for recommitment may be filed to determine whether the patient's severe mental disorder is not in remission or cannot be kept in remission without treatment, and whether by reason of his or her severe mental disorder, the patient represents a substantial danger of physical harm to others. The recommitment proceeding shall be conducted in accordance with the provisions of this section.

(f) Any commitment under this article places an affirmative obligation on the treatment facility to provide treatment for the underlying causes of the person's mental disorder.

(g) Except as provided in this subdivision, the person committed shall be considered to be an involuntary mental health patient and he or she shall be entitled to those rights set forth in Article 7 (commencing with Section 5325) of Chapter 2 of Part 1 of Division 5 of the Welfare and Institutions Code. Commencing January 1, 1986, the State Department of Mental Health may adopt regulations to modify those rights as is necessary in order to provide for the reasonable security of the inpatient facility in which the patient is being held. This subdivision and the regulations adopted pursuant thereto shall become operative on January 1, 1987, except that regulations may be adopted prior to that date. *(Amended by Stats 1989 ch 228 §4, eff. 7/27/89.)*

§2974. Placement in state hospital before release.

Before releasing any inmate or terminating supervision of any parolee who is a danger to self or others, or gravely disabled as a result of mental disorder, and who does not come within the provisions of Section 2962, the Director of Corrections may, upon probable cause, place, or cause to be placed, the person in a state hospital pursuant to the Lanterman-Petris-Short Act, Part 1 (commencing with Section 5000) of Division 5 of the Welfare and Institutions Code. *(Added by Stats 1986 ch 858 §8.)*

§2976. Cost of inpatient or outpatient treatment.

(a) The cost of inpatient or outpatient treatment under Section 2962 or 2972 shall be a state expense while the person is under the jurisdiction of the Department of Corrections or the State Department of Mental Health.

(b) Any person placed outside of a facility of the Department of Corrections for the purposes of inpatient treatment under this article shall not be deemed to be released from imprisonment or from the custody of the Department of Corrections prior to the expiration of the maximum term of imprisonment of the person. *(Amended by Stats 1991 ch 435 §5, eff. 1/1/92.)*

§2978. Independent professionals; requirements.

(a) Any independent professionals appointed by the Board of Prison Terms for purposes of this article shall not be state government employees; shall have at least five years of experience in the diagnosis and treatment of mental disorders; and shall include

psychiatrists, and licensed psychologists who have a doctoral degree in psychology.

(b) On July 1 of each year the Department of Corrections and the State Department of Mental Health shall submit to the Board of Prison Terms a list of 20 or more independent professionals on which both departments concur. The professionals shall not be state government employees and shall have at least five years of experience in the diagnosis and treatment of mental disorders and shall include psychiatrists and licensed psychologists who have a doctoral degree in psychology. For purposes of this article, when the Board of Prison Terms receives the list, they shall only appoint independent professionals from the list. The list shall not be binding on the Board of Prison Terms until they have received it, and shall not be binding after June 30 following receipt of the list. *(Amended by Stats 1987 ch 687 §10.)*

§2980. Applicability of article.

This article applies to persons who committed their crimes on and after January 1, 1986. *(Amended by Stats 1989 ch 228 §5, eff. 7/27/89.)*

§2981. Proof of treatment for 90 days.

For the purpose of proving the fact that a prisoner has received 90 days or more of treatment within the year prior to the prisoner's parole or release, the records or copies of records of any state penitentiary, county jail, federal penitentiary, or state hospital in which that person has been confined, when the records or copies thereof have been certified by the official custodian of those records, may be admitted as evidence. *(Added by Stats 1987 ch 687 §11.)*

CHAPTER 8

LENGTH OF TERM OF IMPRISONMENT AND PAROLES

ARTICLE 1

GENERAL PROVISIONS

§3000. Length of parole.

The Legislature finds and declares that the period immediately following incarceration is critical to successful reintegration of the offender into society and to positive citizenship. It is in the interest of public safety for the state to provide for the supervision of and surveillance of parolees and to provide educational, vocational, family and personal counseling necessary to assist parolees in the transition between imprisonment and discharge. A sentence pursuant to Section 1168 or 1170 shall include a period of parole, unless waived, as provided in this section. Notwithstanding any provision to the contrary in Article 3 (commencing with Section 3040) of this chapter:

(a) At the expiration of a term of imprisonment of one year and one day, or a term of imprisonment imposed pursuant to Section 1170, or at the expiration of such term as reduced pursuant to Section 2931, if applicable, the inmate shall be released on parole for a period not exceeding three years, unless the board for good cause waives parole and discharges the inmate from custody of the department.

(b) In the case of any inmate sentenced under Section 1168, the period of parole shall not exceed five years in the case of an inmate imprisoned for any

© 1992 by J., B. & L. Gould
Printed in the U.S.A.   **EP**

offense other than first or second degree murder for which the inmate has received a life sentence, and shall not exceed three years in the case of any other inmate, unless in either case the board for good cause waives parole and discharges the inmate from custody of the department. This subdivision shall be also applicable to inmates who committed crimes prior to July 1, 1977, to the extent specified in Section 1170.2.

(c) The board shall consider the request of any inmate regarding the length of his parole and the conditions thereof.

(d) Upon successful completion of parole, or at the end of the maximum statutory period of parole specified for the inmate under subdivision (a) or (b), as the case may be, whichever is earlier, the inmate shall be discharged from custody. The date of the maximum statutory period of parole under this subdivision and subdivisions (a) and (b) shall be computed from the date of initial parole, or July 1, 1977, whichever is later, and shall be a period chronologically determined. Time during which parole is suspended because the prisoner has absconded or has been returned to custody as a parole violator shall not be credited toward such period of parole unless the prisoner is found not guilty of the parole violation. However, in no case, except as provided in Section 3064, may a prisoner subject to three years on parole be retained under parole supervision or in custody for a period longer than four years from the date of his initial parole, and, except as provided in Section 3064, in no case may a prisoner subject to five years on parole be retained under parole supervision or in custody for a period longer than seven years from the date of his initial parole.

(e) It is not the intent of this section to diminish resources presently allocated to the Department of Corrections for parole functions.

(f) The Department of Corrections shall meet with each inmate at least 30 days prior to his good time release date, unless such release date is within 30 days of July 1, 1977, and shall provide, under guidelines specified by the Board of Prison Terms, the conditions of parole and the length of parole up to the maximum period of time provided by law. The inmate has the right to reconsideration of the length of parole and conditions thereof by the Board of Prison Terms.

§3000.1. Discharge or retention from parole; consideration hearings.

(a) In the case of any inmate sentenced under Section 1168 for any offense of first or second degree murder with a maximum term of life imprisonment, the period of parole, if parole is granted, shall be the remainder of the inmate's life.

(b) Notwithstanding any other provision of law, when any person referred to in subdivision (a) has been released on parole from the state prison, and has been on parole continuously for seven years in the case of any person imprisoned for first degree murder, and five years in the case of any person imprisoned for second degree murder, since release from confinement, the board shall, within 30 days, discharge such person from parole, unless the board, for good cause, determines that such person will be retained on parole. The board shall make a written record of its determination and transmit a copy thereof to the parolee.

(c) In the event of a retention on parole, the parolee shall be entitled to a review by the board each year thereafter.

(d) There shall be a hearing as provided in Sections 3041.5 and 3041.7 within 12 months of the date of any revocation of parole to consider the release of the inmate on parole, and notwithstanding the provisions of paragraph (2) of subdivision (b) of Section 3041.5, there shall be annual parole consideration hearings thereafter, unless the person is released or otherwise ineligible for parole release. The panel or board shall release the person within one year of the date of the revocation unless it determines that the circumstances and gravity of the parole violation are such that consideration of the public safety requires a more lengthy period of incarceration or unless there is a new prison commitment following a conviction.

(e) The provisions of Section 3042 shall not apply to any hearing held pursuant to this section.

§3001. Release after continuous parole; determination of board.

(a) Notwithstanding any other provision of law, when any person referred to in subdivision (a) of Section 3000 who was not imprisoned for committing a violent felony, as defined in subdivision (c) of Section 667.5, has been released on parole from the state prison, and has been on parole continuously for one year since release from confinement, within 30 days, that person shall be discharged from parole, unless the Department of Corrections recommends to the Board of Prison Terms that the person be retained on parole and the Board of Prison Terms acts by determining, for good cause, that the person will be retained on parole. Notwithstanding any other provision of law, when any person referred to in subdivision (a) of Section 3000 who was imprisoned for committing a violent felony, as defined in subdivision (c) of Section 667.5, has been released on parole from the state prison, and has been on parole continuously for two years since release from confinement, the board shall, within 30 days, discharge that person from parole, unless the board for good cause, determines that the person will be retained on parole. The board shall make a written record of its determination and transmit a copy thereof to the parolee.

(b) Notwithstanding any other provision of law, when any person referred to in subdivision (b) of Section 3000 has been released on parole from the state prison, and has been on parole continuously for three years since release from confinement, the board shall, within 30 days, discharge such person from parole, unless the board, for good cause, determines that such person will be retained on parole. The board shall make a written record of its determination and transmit a copy thereof to the parolee.

(c) In the event of a retention on parole, the parolee shall be entitled to a review by the board each year thereafter until the maximum statutory period of parole has expired.

(d) The amendments to this section made during the 1987-88 Regular Session of the Legislature shall only be applied prospectively and shall not extend the parole period for any person whose eligibility for discharge from parole was fixed as of the effective date of those amendments. (*Amended by Stats 1988 ch 1357 §1, eff. 9/25/88.*)

§3002. Psychological evaluation of child abusers.

In considering the imposition of conditions of parole upon a prisoner convicted of violating any section of this code in which a minor is a victim of an act of abuse or neglect, the Department of Corrections shall provide for a psychological evaluation to be performed on the prisoner to determine the extent of counseling which may be mandated as a condition of parole. Such examination may be performed by psychiatrists, psychologists, or licensed clinical social workers.

§3003. Return to county of commitment after release on parole.

(a) Except as provided in subdivision (d), an inmate who is released on parole shall be returned to the county from which he or she was committed.

For purposes of this subdivision, "county from which he or she was committed" means the county where the crime for which the inmate was convicted occurred.

(b) Notwithstanding subdivision (a), an inmate may be returned to another county in a case where that would be in the best interests of the public and of the parolee. If the Board of Prison Terms setting the conditions of parole for inmates sentenced pursuant to subdivision (b) of Section 1168 or the Department of Corrections setting the conditions of parole for inmates sentenced pursuant to Section 1170 decides on a return to another county, it shall place its reasons in writing in the parolee's permanent record. In making its decision, the authority may consider, among others, the following factors:

(1) The need to protect the life or safety of a victim, the parolee, a witness or any other person.

(2) Public concern that would reduce the chance that the inmate's parole would be successfully completed.

(3) The verified existence of a work offer, or an educational or vocational training program.

(4) The last legal residence of the inmate having been in another county.

(5) The existence of family in another county with whom the inmate has maintained strong ties and whose support would increase the chance that the inmate's parole would be successfully completed.

(6) The lack of necessary outpatient treatment programs for parolees receiving treatment pursuant to Section 2960.

(c) Notwithstanding any other provision of law, an inmate who is released on parole shall not be returned to within 35 miles of the actual residence of a victim of, or a witness to, a violent felony as defined in paragraphs (1) to (7), inclusive, of subdivision (c) of Section 667.5 and any felony in which the defendant inflicts great bodily injury on any person other than an accomplice which has been charged and proved as provided for in Section 12022.7 or 12022.9, if the victim or witness has requested additional distance in the placement of the inmate on parole, and if the Board of Prison Terms or the Department of Corrections finds that there is a need to protect the life, safety, or well-being of a victim or witness.

(d) An inmate may be paroled to another state pursuant to any other provision of law. *(Amended by Stats 1990 ch 148 §1; ch 1692 §1, eff. 1/1/91.)*

§3004. Electronic monitoring devices.

Notwithstanding any other law, the Department of Corrections and the Board of Prison Terms may require, as a condition of release on parole or reinstatement on parole, or as an intermediate sanction in lieu of return to prison, that an inmate or parolee agree in writing to the use of electronic monitoring or supervising devices for the purpose of helping to verify his or her compliance with all other conditions of parole. The devices shall not be used to eavesdrop or record any conversation, except a conversation between the parolee and the agent supervising the parolee which is to be used solely for the purposes of voice identification. *(Added by Stats 1991 ch 215 §1, eff. 1/1/92.)*

ARTICLE 3

PAROLES

§3040. Authority of Board.

The Board of Prison Terms shall have the power to allow prisoners imprisoned in the state prisons pursuant to subdivision (b) of Section 1168 to go upon parole outside the prison walls and enclosures. The board may parole prisoners in the state prisons to camps for paroled prisoners established under Section 2792.

§3041. Review and recommendations.

(a) In the case of any prisoner sentenced pursuant to any provision of law, other than Chapter 4.5 (commencing with Section 1170) of Title 7 of Part 2, the Board of Prison Terms shall meet with each such inmate during the third year of incarceration for the purposes of reviewing the inmate's file, making recommendations, and documenting activities and conduct pertinent to granting or withholding post-conviction credit. One year prior to the inmate's minimum eligible parole release date a panel consisting of at least two commissioners of the Board of Prison Terms shall again meet with the inmate and shall normally set a parole release date as provided in Section 3041.5. The release date shall be set in a manner that will provide uniform terms for offenses of similar gravity and magnitude in respect to their threat to the public, and that will comply with the sentencing rules that the Judicial Council may issue and any sentencing information relevant to the setting of parole release dates. The board shall establish criteria for the setting of parole release dates and in doing so shall consider the number of victims of the crime for which the prisoner was sentenced and other factors in mitigation or aggravation of the crime. At least one commissioner of the panel shall have been present at the last preceding meeting, unless it is not feasible to do so or where the last preceding meeting was the initial meeting. Any person on the hearing panel may request review of any decision regarding parole to the full board for an en banc hearing. In case of such a review, a majority vote of the full Board of Prison Terms in favor of parole is required to grant parole to any prisoner.

(b) The panel or board shall set a release date unless it determines that the gravity of the current convicted offense or offenses, or the timing and gravity of current or past convicted offense or offenses, is such that consideration of the public safety requires a more lengthy period of incarceration for this individual, and that a parole date, therefore, cannot be fixed at this meeting.

(c) For the purpose of reviewing the suitability for parole of those prisoners eligible for parole under prior law at a date earlier than that calculated under Section 1170.2, the board shall appoint panels of at least two persons to meet annually with each such prisoner until such time as the person is released pursuant to

© 1992 by J., B. & L. Gould
Printed in the U.S.A.   EP

such proceedings or reaches the expiration of his term as calculated under Section 1170.2. *(Amended by Stats 1986 ch 1446 §3.)*

§3041.1. Request for review of parole decisions.

Up to 90 days prior to a scheduled parole release date, the Governor shall have the power to request review of any decision concerning the grant or denial of parole to any prisoner in a state prison. The Governor shall state the reason or reasons for the request, and whether the request is based on a public safety concern, a concern that the gravity of current or past convicted offenses may have been given inadequate consideration, or on other factors. When a request has been made, the full board, sitting en banc, shall review the parole decision. In case of a review, a vote in favor of parole by a majority of the current board members shall be required to grant parole to any prisoner. In carrying out any review, the board shall comply with the provisions of this chapter.

§3041.2. Boatwright-Eaves Parole Review Act of 1988.

(a) During the 30 days following the granting, denial, revocation, or suspension by a parole authority of the parole of a person sentenced to an indeterminate prison term based upon a conviction of murder, the Governor, when reviewing the authority's decision pursuant to subdivision (b) of Section 8 of Article V of the Constitution, shall review materials provided by the parole authority.

(b) If the Governor decides to reverse or modify a parole decision of a parole authority pursuant to subdivision (b) of Section 8 of Article V of the Constitution, he or she shall send a written statement to the inmate specifying the reasons for his or her decision. *(Added by Stats 1988 ch 1626 §2, eff. 1/1/89.)*

§3041.5. Hearings to review parole suitability.

(a) At all hearings for the purpose of reviewing a prisoner's parole suitability, or the setting, postponing, or rescinding of parole dates, the following shall apply:

(1) At least 10 days prior to any hearing by the Board of Prison Terms, the prisoner shall be permitted to review his or her file which will be examined by the board and shall have the opportunity to enter a written response to any material contained in the file.

(2) The prisoner shall be permitted to be present, to ask and answer questions, and to speak on his or her own behalf.

(3) Unless legal counsel is required by some other provision of law, a person designated by the Department of Corrections shall be present to insure that all facts relevant to the decision be presented, including, if necessary, contradictory assertions as to matters of fact that have not been resolved by departmental or other procedures.

(4) The prisoner shall be permitted to request and receive a stenographic record of all proceedings.

(5) If the hearing is for the purpose of postponing or rescinding of parole dates, the prisoner shall have rights set forth in paragraphs (3) and (4) of subdivision (c) of Section 2932.

(b) (1) Within 10 days following any meeting where a parole date has been set, the board shall send the prisoner a written statement setting forth his or her parole date, the conditions he or she must meet in order to be released on the date set, and the consequences of failure to meet those conditions.

(2) Within 20 days following any meeting where a parole date has not been set for the reasons stated in subdivision (b) of Section 3041, the board shall send the prisoner a written statement setting forth the reason or reasons for refusal to set a parole date, and suggest activities in which he or she might participate that will benefit him or her while he or she is incarcerated.

The board shall hear each case annually thereafter, except the board may schedule the next hearing no later than the following:

(A) Two years after any hearing at which parole is denied if the board finds that it is not reasonable to expect that parole would be granted at a hearing during the following year and states the bases for the finding.

(B) Three years after any hearing at which parole is denied if the prisoner has been convicted, in the same or different proceedings, of more than one offense which involves the taking of a life, and the board finds that it is not reasonable to expect that parole would be granted at a hearing during the following years and states the bases for the finding.

(C) Five years after any hearing at which parole is denied if the prisoner has been convicted, in the same or different proceedings, of more than two murders, and the board finds that it is not reasonable to expect that parole would be granted at a hearing during the following years and states the bases for the finding in writing. If the board defers a hearing five years, the prisoner's central file shall be reviewed by a deputy commissioner within three years at which time the deputy commissioner may direct that a hearing be held within one year. The prisoner shall be notified in writing of the deputy commissioner's decision.

(3) Within 10 days of any board action resulting in the postponement of a previously set parole date, the board shall send the prisoner a written statement setting forth a new date and the reason or reasons for that action and shall offer the prisoner an opportunity for review of that action.

(4) Within 10 days of any board action resulting in the rescinding of a previously set parole date, the board shall send the prisoner a written statement setting forth the reason or reasons for that action, and shall schedule the prisoner's next hearing within 12 months and in accordance with paragraph (2). *(Amended by Stats 1990 ch 1053 §1, eff. 1/1/91.)*

§3041.7. Life prisoner's right to counsel.

At any hearing for the purpose of setting, postponing, or rescinding a parole release date of a prisoner under a life sentence, such prisoner shall be entitled to be represented by counsel and the provisions of Section 3041.5 shall apply. The Board of Prison Terms shall provide by rule for the invitation of the prosecutor of the county from which the prisoner was committed, or his representative, to represent the interests of the people at any such hearing. The Board of Prison Terms shall notify the prosecutor and the Attorney General at least 30 days prior to the date of the hearing.

Notwithstanding Section 12550 of the Government Code, the prosecutor of the county from which the prisoner was committed, or his representative, who shall not be the Attorney General, shall be the sole representative of the interests of the people.

§3042. Notice of hearings for parole.

(a) At least 30 days before the Board of Prison Terms meets to review or consider the parole

© 1992 by J., B. & L. Gould
Printed in the U.S.A. **EP**

suitability or the setting of a parole date for any prisoner sentenced to a life sentence, the board shall send written notice thereof to each of the following persons: the judge of the superior court before whom the prisoner was tried and convicted, the attorney who represented the defendant at trial, the district attorney of the county in which the offense was committed, the law enforcement agency that investigated the case, and where the prisoner was convicted of the murder of a peace officer, the law enforcement agency which had employed that peace officer at the time of the murder.

(b) The Board of Prison Terms shall record all such hearings and transcribe recordings of those hearings within 30 days of any hearing. Those transcripts, including the transcripts of all prior hearings, shall be filed and maintained in the office of the Board of Prison Terms and shall be made available to the public no later than 30 days from the date of the hearing. No prisoner shall actually be released on parole prior to 60 days from the date of the hearing.

(c) At any hearing, the presiding hearing officer shall state his or her findings and supporting reasons on the record.

(d) Any statements, recommendations, or other materials considered shall be incorporated into the transcript of the hearing, unless the material is confidential in order to preserve institutional security and the security of others who might be endangered by disclosure.

(e) This section shall not apply to any hearing held to consider advancing a prisoner's parole date due to his or her conduct since his or her last hearing. *(Amended by Stats 1991 ch 1017 §1, eff. 1/1/92.)*

§3043. Victim's statements.

Upon request, notice of any hearing to review or consider the parole suitability or the setting of a parole date for any prisoner in a state prison shall be sent by the Board of Prison Terms at least 30 days before the hearing to any victim of a crime committed by the prisoner, or to the next of kin of the victim if the victim has died. The requesting party shall keep the board apprised of his or her current mailing address.

The victim, next of kin, or two members of the victim's immediate family have the right to appear, personally or by counsel, at the hearing and to adequately and reasonably express his or her views concerning the crime and the person responsible. The board, in deciding whether to release the person on parole, shall consider the statements of victims, next of kin, and immediate family members of the victim made pursuant to this section and shall include in its report a statement of whether the person would pose a threat to public safety if released on parole.

In those cases where there are more than two immediate family members of the victim who wish to attend any hearing covered in this section, the board may, in its discretion, allow attendance of additional immediate family members or limit attendance to the following order of preference: spouse, children, parents, siblings, grandchildren, and grandparents.

The provisions of this section shall not be amended by the Legislature except by statute passed in each house by rollcall vote entered in the journal, two-thirds of the membership concurring, or by a statute that becomes effective only when approved by the electors. *(Amended by Stats 1990 ch 278 §1, eff. 1/1/91.)*

§3043.1. Support during victim's statements.

Notwithstanding any other provision of law, a victim, his or her next of kin, or any immediate family member of the victim who appears at any hearing to review or consider the parole suitability or the setting of a parole date for any prisoner pursuant to Section 3043 shall be entitled to the attendance of one person of his or her own choosing at the hearing for support. The person so chosen shall not participate in the hearing nor make comments while in attendance. *(Added by Stats 1990 ch 278 §2, eff. 1/1/91.)*

§3043.2. Victim's written or taped statements.

(a) In lieu of personal appearance at any hearing to review the parole suitability or the setting of a parole date, the Board of Prison Terms may permit the victim, his or her next of kin, or immediate family members to file with the board a written, audiotaped, or videotaped statement expressing his or her views concerning the crime and the person responsible. The board shall consider any statement filed prior to reaching a decision, and shall include in its report a statement of whether the person would pose a threat to public safety if released on parole.

(b) Whenever an audio or video statement is filed with the board, a written transcript of the tape shall also be provided by the person filing the statement.

(c) Nothing in this section shall be construed to prohibit the prosecutor from representing to the board the views of the victim, his or her immediate family members, or next of kin.

(d) In the event the board permits an audio or video statement to be filed, the board shall not be responsible for providing any equipment or resources needed to assist the victim in preparing the statement. *(Added by Stats 1990 ch 278 §3, eff. 1/1/91.)*

§3043.3. Immediate family defined.

As used in Sections 3043, 3043.1, and 3043.2, the term "immediate family" shall include the victim's spouse, parent, grandparent, brother, sister, and children or grandchildren who are related by blood, marriage, or adoption. *(Added by Stats 1990 ch 278 §4, eff. 1/1/91.)*

§3043.5. Condit-Nolan Public Participation in Parole Act of 1984.

(a) This section shall be known as the "Condit-Nolan Public Participation in Parole Act of 1984."

(b) Any person interested in the grant or denial of parole to any prisoner in a state prison shall have the right to submit a statement of views in support of or in opposition to the granting of parole. The board, in deciding whether to release the person on parole, shall review all information received from the public to insure that the gravity and timing of all current or past convicted offenses have been given adequate consideration and to insure that the safety of the public has been adequately considered. Upon completion of its review, the board shall include in its report a statement that it has reviewed all information received from the public and its conclusion as to whether the person would pose a threat to the public safety if released on parole.

§3045. Pardon on ground of not guilty.

Any sentence based on conviction of crime of which the person was previously pardoned on the express ground that he was not guilty shall not be counted as a previous conviction.

© 1992 by J., B. & L. Gould
Printed in the U.S.A.   EP

§3046. Life prisoner's minimum time before parole.

No prisoner imprisoned under a life sentence may be paroled until he or she has served at least seven calendar years or has served a term as established pursuant to any other section of law that establishes a minimum period of confinement under a life sentence before eligibility for parole, whichever is greater. Where two or more life sentences are ordered to run consecutively to each other pursuant to Section 669, no prisoner so imprisoned may be paroled until he or she has served at least seven calendar years, or has served a term as established pursuant to any other section of law that establishes a minimum period of confinement under a life sentence before eligibility for parole, on each of the life sentences which are ordered to run consecutively, whichever is greater. The Board of Prison Terms shall, in considering a parole for a prisoner, consider all statements and recommendations which may have been submitted by the judge, district attorney, and sheriff, pursuant to Section 1203.01, or in response to notices given under Section 3042, and recommendations of other persons interested in the granting or denying of the parole. The board shall enter on its order granting or denying parole to these prisoners, the fact that the statements and recommendations have been considered by it. *(Amended by Stats 1988 ch 214 §1, eff. 1/1/89.)*

§3049. Minimum imprisonment in other cases.

In all other cases not heretofore provided for, no prisoner sentenced prior to July 1, 1977 may be paroled until he has served the minimum term of imprisonment provided by law for the offense of which he was convicted, except that in cases where the prisoner was serving a sentence on December 31, 1947, and in which the minimum term of imprisonment is more than one year, he may be paroled at any time after the expiration of one-half of the minimum term, with benefit of credits, but in no case shall he be paroled until he has served one calendar year; provided, that any prisoner, received on or after January 1, 1948, at any state prison or institution under the jurisdiction of the Director of Corrections, whose minimum term of imprisonment is more than one year, may be paroled at any time after the expiration of one-third of the minimum term. In all other cases he may be paroled at any time after he has served the minimum term prescribed by law.

§3049.5. Parole after participation in research programs.

Notwithstanding the provisions of Section 3049, any prisoner selected for inclusion in a specific research program approved by the Board of Corrections may be paroled upon completion of the diagnostic study provided for in Section 5079. The number of prisoners released in any year under this provision shall not exceed 5 percent of the total number of all prisoners released in the preceding year.

This section shall not apply to a prisoner who, while committing the offense for which he has been imprisoned, physically attacked any person by any means. A threat of attack is not a physical attack for the purposes of this section unless such threat was accompanied by an attempt to inflict physical harm upon some person.

The Board of Corrections shall report to the Legislature on the fifth Legislative day of the 1974 Regular Session of the Legislature regarding any research program completed or in progress authorized under this section, and thereafter it shall report annually.

§3051. *Repealed by Stats 1987 ch 828.*

§3052. Establish and enforce rules and regulations.

The Board of Prison Terms shall have the power to establish and enforce rules and regulations under which prisoners committed to state prisons may be allowed to go upon parole outside the prison buildings and enclosures when eligible for parole.

§3053. Impose conditions on parole.

The Board of Prison Terms upon granting any parole to any prisoner may also impose on the parole such conditions as it may deem proper.

§3053.5. Intoxication inquiry.

Upon granting parole to any prisoner convicted of any of the offenses enumerated in Section 290, the Board of Prison Terms shall inquire into the question whether the defendant at the time the offense was committed was intoxicated or addicted to the excessive use of alcoholic liquor or beverages at that time or immediately prior thereto, and if it is found that the person was so intoxicated or so addicted, it shall impose as a condition of parole that such prisoner shall totally abstain from the use of alcoholic liquor or beverages.

§3056. Legal custody of parolees.

Prisoners on parole shall remain under the legal custody of the department and shall be subject at any time to be taken back within the inclosure of the prison.

§3057. Confinement after parole revocation.

(a) Confinement pursuant to a revocation of parole in the absence of a new conviction and commitment to prison under other provisions of law, shall not exceed 12 months, except as provided in subdivision (c).

(b) Upon completion of confinement pursuant to parole revocation without a new commitment to prison, the inmate shall be released on parole for a period which shall not extend beyond that portion of the maximum statutory period of parole specified by Section 3000 which was unexpired at the time of each revocation.

(c) Notwithstanding the limitations in subdivision (a) and in Section 3060.5 upon confinement pursuant to a parole revocation, the board may extend the confinement pursuant to a parole revocation, the board may extend the confinement pursuant to parole revocation for a maximum of an additional 12 months for subsequent acts of misconduct committed by the parolee while confined pursuant to that parole revocation. Upon a finding of good cause to believe that a parolee has committed a subsequent act of misconduct and utilizing procedures governing parole revocation proceedings, the board may extend the period of confinement pursuant to parole revocation as follows: (1) not more than 180 days for an act punishable as a felony whether or not prosecution is undertaken, (2) not more than 90 days for an act punishable as a misdemeanor, whether or not prosecution is undertaken, and (3) not more than 30 days for an act defined as a serious disciplinary offense pursuant to subdivision (a) of Section 2932.

(d)(1) Except for parolees specified in paragraph (2), any revocation period imposed under subdivision (a) may be reduced in the same manner and to the same extent as a term of imprisonment may be reduced by worktime credits under Section 2933. Worktime credit must be earned and may be forfeited pursuant to the provisions of Section 2932.

Worktime credit forfeited shall not be restored.

(2) The following parolees shall not be eligible for credit under this subdivision:

(A) Parolees who are sentenced under Section 1168 with a maximum term of life imprisonment.

(B) Parolees who violated a condition of parole relating to association with specified persons, entering prohibited areas, attendance at parole outpatient clinic, or psychiatric attention.

(C) Parolees who were revoked for conduct described in, or that could be prosecuted under any of the following sections, whether or not prosecution is undertaken: Section 189, Section 191.5, subdivision (a) or paragraph (3) of subdivision (c) of Section 192, Section 203, 207, 211, 217.1, or 220, subdivision (b) of Section 241, Section 244, paragraph (1) or (2) of subdivision (a) of Section 245, subdivision (2) of Section 261, Section 264.1, subdivision (c) or (d) of Section 286, Section 288, subdivision (c) or (d) of Section 288a, Section 289, 347, or 404, subdivision (a) of Section 451, Section 12020, 12021, 12022, 12022.5, 12022.7, 12022.8, 12025, or 12560, or Section 664 for any attempt to engage in conduct described in or that could be prosecuted under any of the above-mentioned sections.

(D) Parolees who were revoked for any reason if they had been granted parole after conviction of any of the offenses specified in subparagraph (C).

(E) Parolees who the Board of Prison Terms finds at a revocation hearing to be unsuitable for reduction of the period of confinement because of the circumstances and gravity of the parole violation, or because of prior criminal history. *(Amended by Stats 1988 ch 1608 §4, eff. 1/1/89.)*

§3058. Extortion of ex-felon.

Any person who knowingly and wilfully communicates to another, either orally or in writing, any statement concerning any person then or theretofore convicted of a felony, and then on parole, and which communication is made with the purpose and intent to deprive said person so convicted of employment, or to prevent him from procuring the same, or with the purpose and intent to extort from him any money or article of value; and any person who threatens to make any said communication with the purpose and intent to extort money or any article of value from said person so convicted of a felony, is guilty of a misdemeanor.

§3058.5. Information furnished to local authorities.

The Department of Corrections shall provide within 10 days, upon request, to the chief of police of a city or the sheriff of a county, information available to the department, including actual, glossy photographs, no smaller than 3⅛ x 3⅛ inches in size, and, in conjunction with the Department of Justice, fingerprints, concerning persons then on parole who are or may be residing or temporarily domiciled in that city or county. *(Amended by Stats 1986 ch 600 §1.)*

§3058.6. Release of prisoners.

(a) Whenever any person confined to state prison is serving a term for the conviction of a violent felony listed in subdivision (c) of Section 667.5, the Board of Prison Terms, with respect to inmates sentenced pursuant to subdivision (b) of Section 1168 or the Department of Corrections, with respect to inmates sentenced pursuant to Section 1170, shall notify the sheriff or chief of police, or both and the district attorney, having jurisdiction over the community in which the person is scheduled to be released on parole or rereleased following a period of confinement pursuant to a parole revocation without a new commitment. Except as provided in subdivision (b), the notification shall be made at least 15 days prior to the scheduled release date and, in all cases, shall include the name of the person who is scheduled to be released, whether or not the parolee is required to register with law enforcement, and the community in which the person will reside.

(b) When an inmate serving a term for the conviction of a violent felony listed in subdivision (c) of Section 667.5 is scheduled to be released pursuant to subdivision (b) of Section 3003 to a county other than the county from which he or she was committed, the board or department shall provide written notice of that release to the sheriff or police chief, or both, and to the district attorney, having jurisdiction over the community in which the inmate is scheduled to be released. The notification shall be made at least 45 days prior to the scheduled release date and, in all cases, shall include the name of the person who is scheduled to be released, whether or not the person is required to register with local law enforcement, and the community in which the person will reside.

Those agencies receiving the notice referred to in this subdivision shall have 15 days from receipt of the notice to provide written comment to the board or department regarding the impending release. Those comments shall be considered by the board or department which may, based on those comments, modify its decision regarding the community in which the person is scheduled to be released.

(c) In the event that the court orders the immediate release of an inmate, the department shall notify the sheriff or chief of police, or both, and the district attorney, having jurisdiction over the community in which the person is scheduled to be released on parole at the time of release.

(d) The notification required by this section shall be made whether or not a request has been made under Section 3058.5.

(e) The time limits imposed by this section are not applicable where the release date of an inmate has been advanced by restoration of behavior credits, presentence credits, or other process or procedure that could not have reasonably been anticipated by the Department of Corrections and where, as the result of the time adjustments, there is less than 30 days remaining on the sentence before the inmate's release on parole, but notice shall be given as soon as practicable. In no case shall notice required by this section to the appropriate agency be later than the day of release on parole. If, after the 45-day notice to law enforcement and to the district attorney relating to an out-of-county placement, there is change of county placement, notice to the ultimate county of placement shall be made upon the determination of the county of

© 1992 by J., B. & L. Gould
Printed in the U.S.A.   EP

placement. *(Amended by Stats 1988 ch 137 §3, eff. 1/1/89.)*

§3058.8. Notification of release date of prisoner.

At the time a notification is sent pursuant to subdivision (a) of Section 3058.6, the Board of Prison Terms or the Department of Corrections, as the case may be, shall also send a notice to persons described in Section 679.03 who have requested a notice informing those persons of the fact that the person who committed the violent offense is scheduled to be released and specifying the proposed date of release. Notice of the community in which the person is scheduled to reside shall also be given only if it is (1) in the county of residence of a witness, victim, or family member of a victim who has requested notification; or (2) within 25 miles of the actual residence of a witness, victim, or family member of a victim who has requested notification. If, after providing the witness, victim, or next of kin with the notice, there is any change in the release date or the community in which the person is to reside, the board or the department shall provide the witness, victim, or next of kin with the revised information.

In order to be entitled to receive the notice set forth in this section, the requesting party shall keep the department or board informed of his or her current mailing address. *(Added by Stats 1988 ch 137 §4, eff. 1/1/89.)*

§3059. Escaped prisoner.

If any paroled prisoner shall leave the state without permission of the Board of Prison Terms, he shall be held as an escaped prisoner and arrested as such.

§3060. Suspension or revocation of parole.

The Board of Prison Terms shall have full power to suspend or revoke any parole, and to order returned to prison any prisoner upon parole. The written order of any member of the Board of Prison Terms shall be a sufficient warrant for any peace or prison officer to return to actual custody any conditionally released or paroled prisoner.

§3060.5. Revocation of parole upon refusal to sign parole agreement.

Notwithstanding any other provision of law, the Board of Prison Terms shall revoke the parole of any prisoner who refuses to sign a parole agreement setting forth the general and any special conditions applicable to the parole, and shall order the prisoner returned to prison. Confinement pursuant to any single revocation of parole under this section shall not, absent a new conviction and commitment to prison under other provisions of law, exceed six months, except as provided in subdivision (c) of Section 3057.

§3061. Execute order for return.

It is hereby made the duty of all peace officers to execute any such order in like manner as ordinary criminal process.

§3062. Power of Governor to revoke paroles.

The Governor of the state shall have like power to revoke the parole of any prisoner. The written authority of the Governor shall likewise be sufficient to authorize any peace officer to retake and return said prisoner to the state prison. His written order revoking the parole shall have the same force and effect and be executed in like manner as the order of the Board of Prison Terms.

§3063. Cause for suspension or revocation.

No parole shall be suspended or revoked without cause, which cause must be stated in the order suspending or revoking the parole.

§3063.5. Parole revocation proceedings.

In parole revocation proceedings, a parolee or his or her attorney shall receive a copy of any police, arrest, and crime reports, and child abuse reports made pursuant to Sections 11166 and 11166.2 pertaining to such proceedings. Portions of those reports containing confidential information need not be disclosed if the parolee or his or her attorney has been notified that confidential information has not been disclosed. Portions of child abuse reports made pursuant to Sections 11166 and 11166.2 containing identifying information relating to the reporter shall not be disclosed. However, the parolee or his or her attorney shall be notified that information relating to the identity of the reporter has not been disclosed. *(Amended by Stats 1989 ch 1169 §1, eff. 1/1/90.)*

§3063.6. Parole revocation panel.

Parole revocation proceedings may be conducted by a panel of not less than two persons.

§3064. Prisoner designated as escapee and fugitive.

From and after the suspension or revocation of the parole of any prisoner and until his return to custody he is an escapee and fugitive from justice and no part of the time during which he is an escapee and fugitive from justice shall be part of his term.

§3065. Application of provisions of article.

Except as otherwise provided in Section 1170.2 and Article 1 (commencing with Section 3000) of this chapter, the provisions of this article are to apply to all prisoners serving sentence in the state prisons on July 1, 1977, to the end that at all times the same provisions relating to sentence, imprisonments and paroles of prisoners shall apply to all the inmates thereof.

ARTICLE 3.5

COUNTY BOARDS OF PAROLE COMMISSIONERS

§3074. Legislative findings and declaration re successful reintegration of offenders.

The Legislature finds and declares that the period immediately following incarceration is critical to successful reintegration of the offender into society and to positive citizenship. It is in the interest of public safety for a county to provide for the supervision of parolees, and to provide educational, vocational, family and personal counseling necessary to assist parolees in the transition between imprisonment and discharge.

§3075. County boards; membership.

There is in each county a board of parole commissioners, consisting of the following: (1) the sheriff or, in a county with a department of corrections, the director of such department, (2) the probation officer, and (3) a member not a public official to be selected from the public by the presiding judge, if any, or, if none, by the senior judge in point of service, of the superior court. The public member of the county board of parole commissioners shall be entitled to his actual traveling and other necessary expenses incurred in the discharge of his duties. In addition the public member shall be entitled to per diem at such rate as may be provided by the board of supervisors. The public member shall hold office for a term of one year and in no event for a period exceeding three consecutive years. The term shall commence on the date of appointment.

§3075.3. Contra Costa county parole board.

There is in Contra Costa County a board of parole commissioners, consisting of the following: (1) the sheriff or, in a county with a department of corrections, the director of that department, (2) the probation officer, and (3) a member not a public official to be selected from the public by the presiding judge, if any, or, if none, by the senior judge in point of service, of the superior court. The public member of the county board of parole commissioners or his or her alternate shall be entitled to actual traveling and other necessary expenses incurred in the discharge of their duties. In addition the public member or his or her alternate shall be entitled to per diem at such rate as may be provided by the board of supervisors. The public member or his or her alternate shall hold office for a term of one year and in no event for a period exceeding three consecutive years. The term shall commence on the date of appointment. *(Added by Stats 1989 ch 624 §3, eff. 1/1/90.)*

§3076. Rules and regulations established and enforced by board.

(a) The board may make, establish and enforce rules and regulations adopted under this article.

(b) The board shall act at regularly called meetings at which two-thirds of the members are present, and shall make and establish rules and regulations in writing stating the reasons therefor under which any prisoner who is confined in or committed to any county jail, work furlough facility, industrial farm, or industrial road camp, or in any city jail, work furlough facility, industrial farm, or industrial road camp under a judgment of imprisonment or as a condition of probation for any criminal offense, unless the court at the time of committing has ordered that such prisoner confined as a condition of probation upon conviction of a felony not be granted parole, may be allowed to go upon parole outside of such jail, work furlough facility, industrial farm, or industrial road camp, but to remain, while on parole, in the legal custody and under the control of the board establishing the rules and regulations for his parole, and subject at any time to be taken back within the enclosure of any such jail, work furlough facility, industrial farm, or industrial road camp.

(c) The board shall provide a complete copy of its written rules and regulations and reasons therefor and any amendments thereto to each of the judges of the county's justice, municipal and superior courts.

The board shall provide to the persons in charge of the county's correctional facilities a copy of the sections of its written rules and regulations and any amendments thereto which govern eligibility for parole, and the name and telephone number of the person or agency to contact for additional information.

Such rules and regulations governing eligibility either shall be conspicuously posted and maintained within each county correctional facility so that all prisoners have access to a copy, or shall be given to each prisoner.

§3077. County with jurisdiction to grant parole.

Whenever a prisoner is sentenced in one county and incarcerated in another county, only the county in which he was sentenced shall have jurisdiction to grant parole.

§3078. Application for parole; recommendation of judge.

(a) The board shall notify the sentencing judge of an inmate's application for parole.

(b) The sentencing judge may make a recommendation regarding such application, and the board shall give careful consideration to such recommendation.

§3079. Granting or denial of parole.

(a) No application for parole shall be granted or denied except by a vote of the board at a meeting at which a quorum of its members are present. This paragraph shall not be applied to the denial of applicants who are ineligible by order of the superior court, or to the granting of parole in emergency situations.

(b) An applicant shall be permitted to appear and speak on his behalf at the meeting at which his application is considered by the board.

§3080. Parolee leaving county without permission defined as escaped prisoner.

If any paroled prisoner leaves the county in which he is imprisoned without permission from the board granting his parole, he shall be arrested as an escaped prisoner and held as such.

§3081. Term of parole; violation of parole conditions.

(a) Each county board may retake and imprison any prisoner upon parole granted under the provisions of this article.

(b) Each county board may release any prisoner on parole for a term not to exceed two years upon such conditions and under such rules and regulations as may seem fit and proper for his rehabilitation, and should the prisoner so paroled violate any of the conditions of his parole or any of the rules and regulations governing his parole, he shall, upon order of the parole commission, be returned to the jail from which he was paroled and be confined therein for the unserved portion of his sentence.

(c) The written order of each county board shall be a sufficient warrant for all officers named therein to authorize them, or any of them, to return to actual custody any conditionally released or paroled prisoner. All chiefs of police, marshals of cities, sheriffs, constables, and all other police and peace officers of this state shall execute any such order in like manner as ordinary criminal process.

(d) In computing the unserved sentence of a person returned to jail because of the revocation of his parole no credit shall be granted for the time between his release from jail on parole and his return to jail because of the revocation of his parole.

© 1992 by J., B. & L. Gould
Printed in the U.S.A.

EP

§3082. Release of alien prisoners.

Each county board may make and establish written rules and regulations for the unconditional release of and may unconditionally release any prisoner who is an alien and who voluntarily consents to return or to be returned to his native land and who actually returns or is returned thereto. The necessary expenses of the transportation of such alien prisoner and officers or attendants in charge of such prisoner, may be paid by the county, upon order of the board of supervisors authorizing or ratifying the return of the prisoner at the expense of the county.

§3083. Temporary commissioners.

Whenever the board designates deputies to serve as temporary commissioners in considering applications for parole of prisoners, such temporary commissioners or deputies may also exercise all the powers granted by this article relative to the unconditional release of alien prisoners.

§3084. Return to state institution.

Each county board may release to the State Department of Corrections for return to a state prison or correctional institution any county or city jail inmate who is a state parole violator, when notified by the Board of Prison Terms.

§3085. Deputies as temporary commissioners.

The members of the board may for the purpose of considering applications for parole of prisoners from city or county jails, or industrial farms, or work furlough facilities, or industrial road camps, designate deputies of their respective offices to serve for them as temporary commissioners when they are unable to serve.

§3085.1. Appointment of alternate by presiding judge in Contra Costa county.

The presiding judge, if any, or, if none, the senior judge in point of service, of the superior court in Contra Costa County may appoint an alternate for the public member who shall serve in the absence of the public member. *(Added by Stats 1989 ch 624 §3.3, eff. 1/1/90.)*

§3086. Admission of guilt not required when setting terms or discharge dates.

Each county board shall not require, when setting terms or discharge dates, an admission of guilt to any crime for which an inmate was committed.

§3087. Supervision of parolee.

No prisoner shall be paroled without supervision.

§3088. Parole officer's supervision.

A prisoner who is released on parole pursuant to this article shall be supervised by a county parole officer of the county board of parole commissioners. *(Amended by Stats 1991 ch 229 §2, eff. 1/1/92.)*

§3089. County parole officer.

(a) A county parole officer who is not a peace officer, as defined in Chapter 4.5 (commencing with Section 830) of Title 3 of Part 2, is a public officer who works at the direction of the County Board of Parole Commissioners, as provided for in Section 3075, and is responsible for supervising prisoners released on parole by the board.

(b) A county parole officer who is a public officer, as defined in subdivision (a), shall have no right to carry or possess firearms in the performance of his or her prescribed duties.

(c) A county parole officer, as defined in subdivision (a), shall comply with the standards for selection and training established by the Board of Corrections pursuant to Section 6035. *(Added by Stats 1991 ch 229 §3, eff. 1/1/92.)*

TITLE 2

IMPRISONMENT OF FEMALE PRISONERS IN STATE INSTITUTIONS

CHAPTER 1

ESTABLISHMENT OF INSTITUTION FOR WOMEN

§3200. Continuation and designation of institute.

There is and shall continue to be within the State an institution for the punishment, treatment, supervision, custody and care of females convicted of felonies to be known as "The California Institution for Women."

§3201. Purpose of institution.

The purpose of said institution shall be to provide custody, care, protection, industrial, vocational, and other training, and reformatory help, for women confined therein.

§3202. Included with "State prison" or "prison."

As used in the sections of this Part 3 of the Penal Code providing for penal offenses and punishments therefor, the term "State prison" or "prison" shall refer to and include the California Institution for Women.

CHAPTER 2

ADMINISTRATION OF INSTITUTION

ARTICLE 1

ADMINISTRATION OF INSTITUTION FOR WOMEN

§3320. Superintendent and other officers.

The warden of the California Institution for Women shall be a woman, who shall have immediate charge and management of the institution, subject to the control of the department. The department may employ other assistants, officers, and employees for the institution. *(Amended by Stats 1989 ch 1420 §14, eff. 1/1/90.)*

§3322. Employee's sex.

All regularly employed assistants, officers and employees whose duties bring them in contact with the inmates of the institution shall be women as far as practicable.

§3325. Authority over female convicts.

The warden described in this chapter shall, subject to the control of the director, have those powers, perform those duties and exercise those functions, respecting females convicted of felonies, as the wardens now exercise over male prisoners. *(Amended by Stats 1989 ch 1420 §15, eff. 1/1/90.)*

§3326. Operation of commissary.

The department is authorized to provide the necessary facilities, equipment, and personnel to operate a commissary at said institution for the sale of toilet articles, candy, tobacco products, gum, notions, and other sundries.

CHAPTER 3

PRISONERS

§3400. Transfer of woman to institution.

Upon the commitment or transfer of any woman to the institution it shall be the duty of the officer having custody of her or required to take custody of her, to deliver her to said institution, receiving therefor the fees payable for the transportation of prisoners to the state prisons. Such officer shall at the same time deliver to said institution a certified abstract of the judgment of conviction and of the order of commitment or order of transfer. Every woman so committed or transferred under this act shall be accompanied by a woman attendant from the place of commitment or transfer until delivered to said institution.

§3402. Institution to maintain records of inmates.

There shall be kept at said institution a record of the history and progress of every woman confined therein during the period of her confinement, and so far as practically possible, prior and subsequent thereto, and all judges, courts, officials and employees, district attorneys, sheriffs, chiefs of police and peace officers, shall furnish said institution with all data in their possession or knowledge relative to any inmate that said institution may request. If upon the arrest of any woman it be discovered that she was theretofore an inmate of said institution, the institution shall be promptly notified of her arrest.

§3403. Mental and physical examination upon commitment.

Every woman upon being committed to said institution shall be examined mentally and physically, and shall be given the care, treatment and training adapted to her particular condition. Such care, treatment and training shall be along the lines best suited to develop her mentality, character and industrial capacity; provided, however, no inmate shall be confined longer than the term of her commitment.

§3404. Safekeeping of prisoner likely to be removed.

When there is any reasonable grounds to believe that a prisoner may be forcibly removed from the California Institution for Women, the warden shall report the fact to the Governor, who may order the removal of the prisoner to any California State prison for safekeeping, and it is hereby made the duty of the warden of the prison to accept and detain the prisoner for the further execution of her sentence. The Governor may thereafter order the prisoner returned to the California Institution for Women for the further execution of her sentence according to law.

The necessary costs and expenses incurred in carrying out the provisions of this section shall be a proper charge against any fund hereafter appropriated as an emergency fund, or similar appropriation for contingencies, notwithstanding any limitations or restrictions that may be imposed upon the expenditure of any appropriation. *(Amended by Stats 1989 ch 1420 §16, eff. 1/1/90.)*

§3405. Permitting abortion of pregnant prisoner.

No condition or restriction upon the obtaining of an abortion by a prisoner, pursuant to the Therapeutic Abortion Act (Chapter 11 (commencing with Section 25950), Division 20 of the Health and Safety Code), other than those contained in that act, shall be imposed. Prisoners found to be pregnant and desiring abortions, shall be permitted to determine their eligibility for an abortion pursuant to law, and if determined to be eligible, shall be permitted to obtain an abortion.

The rights provided for females by this section shall be posted in at least one conspicuous place to which all female prisoners have access. *(Amended by Stats 1987 ch 828 §129.)*

§3406. Pregnant prisoner's medical services.

Any female prisoner shall have the right to summon and receive the services of any physician and surgeon of her choice in order to determine whether she is pregnant. The warden may adopt reasonable rules and regulations with regard to the conduct of examinations to effectuate this determination.

If the prisoner is found to be pregnant, she is entitled to a determination of the extent of the medical services needed by her and to the receipt of these services from the physician and surgeon of her choice. Any expenses occasioned by the services of a physician and surgeon whose services are not provided by the institution shall be borne by the prisoner.

Any physician providing services pursuant to this section shall possess a current, valid, and unrevoked certificate to engage in the practice of medicine issued pursuant to Chapter 5 (commencing with Section 2000) of Division 2 of the Business and Professions Code.

The rights provided for prisoners by this section shall be posted in at least one conspicuous place to which all female prisoners have access. *(Amended by Stats 1989 ch 1420 §17, eff. 1/1/90.)*

§3409. Personal hygiene, birth control, and family planning services.

(a) Any woman inmate shall upon her request be allowed to continue to use materials necessary for (1) personal hygiene with regard to her menstrual cycle and reproductive system and (2) birth control measures as prescribed by her physician.

(b) Each and every woman inmate shall be furnished by the department with information and education regarding the availability of family planning services.

(c) Family planning services shall be offered to each and every woman inmate at least 60 days prior to a scheduled release date. Upon request any woman inmate shall be furnished by the department with the services of a licensed physician or she shall be furnished by the department or by any other agency which contracts with the department with services necessary to meet her family planning needs at the time of her release.

© 1992 by J., B. & L. Gould
Printed in the U.S.A.   **EP**

CHAPTER 4

COMMUNITY TREATMENT PROGRAMS

§3410. Community defined.

The term "community" shall, for the purposes of this chapter, mean an environment away from the prison setting which is in an urban or suburban area.

§3411. Establishment.

The Department of Corrections shall on or before January 1, 1980, establish and implement a community treatment program under which women inmates sentenced to state prison pursuant to Section 1168 or 1170 who have one or more children under the age of six years, whether born prior to or after January 1, 1976, shall be eligible to participate within the provisions of this section. The community treatment program shall provide for the release of the mother and child or children to a public or private facility in the community suitable to the needs of the mother and child or children, and which will provide the best possible care for the mother and child. In establishing and operating such program, the department shall have as a prime concern the establishment of a safe and wholesome environment for the participating children. *(Amended by Stats 1988 ch 1044 §1, eff. 9/20/88.)*

§3412. Pediatric care; needs.

The Department of Corrections shall provide pediatric care consistent with medical standards and, to the extent feasible, shall be guided by the need to provide the following:

(a) A stable, care giving, stimulating environment for the children as developed and supervised by professional guidance in the area of child development.

(b) Programs geared to assure the stability of the parent-child relationship during and after participation in the program, to be developed and supervised by appropriate professional guidance. These programs shall, at a minimum, be geared to accomplish the following:

(1) The mother's mental stability.

(2) The mother's familiarity with good parenting and housekeeping skills.

(3) The mother's ability to function in the community, upon parole or release, as a viable member.

(4) The securing of adequate housing arrangements after participation in the program.

(5) The securing of adequate child care arrangements after participation in the program.

(c) Utilization of the least restrictive alternative to incarceration and restraint possible to achieve the objectives of correction and of this chapter consistent with public safety and justice.

§3413. Implementation of chapter.

In determining how to implement this chapter, the Department of Corrections shall be guided by the need to utilize the most cost-efficient methods possible. Therefore, the Director of Corrections may enter into contracts, with the approval of the Director of General Services, with appropriate public or private agencies, to provide housing, sustenance, services as provided in subdivision (a) and (b) of Section 3412, and supervision for such inmates as are eligible for placement in community treatment programs. Prisoners in the care of such agencies shall be subject to all provisions of law applicable to them.

§3414. Rules and regulations established.

The department shall establish reasonable rules and regulations concerning the operation of the program.

§3415. Desire of woman prisoner to be in program; notice.

(a) The probation department shall, no later than the day that any woman is sentenced to the state prison, notify such woman of the provisions of this chapter, if the term of the state imprisonment does not exceed six years on the basis of either the probable release or parole date computed as if the maximum amount of good time credit would be granted. The probation department shall determine such term of state imprisonment at such time for the purposes of this section.

(b) The woman may, upon the receipt of such notice and upon sentencing to a term in state prison, give notice of her desire to be admitted to a program under this chapter. The probation department or the defendant shall transmit such notice to the Department of Corrections, and to the appropriate local social services agency that conducts investigations for child neglect and dependency hearings.

§3416. Admission and retention of mother and child in program.

(a) If any woman received by or committed to the Department of Corrections has a child under six years of age, or gives birth to a child while an inmate under the jurisdiction of the Department of Corrections, the child and his or her mother shall, upon her request, be admitted to and retained in a community treatment program established by the Department of Corrections, subject to the provisions of this chapter.

(b) Women transferred to community treatment programs remain under the legal custody of the department and shall be subject at any time, pursuant to the rules and regulations of the Director of Corrections, to be detained in the county jail upon the exercise of a state parole or correctional officer's peace officer powers as specified in Section 830.5, with the consent of the sheriff or corresponding official having jurisdiction over the facility.

§3417. Admission requirements.

(a) Subject to reasonable rules and regulations adopted pursuant to Section 3414, the Department of Corrections shall admit to the program any applicant whose child was born prior to the receipt of the inmate by the department, if all of the following requirements are met:

(1) The applicant has a probable release or parole date with a maximum time to be served of six years, calculated after deduction of any possible good time credit.

(2) The applicant was the primary caretaker of the infant prior to incarceration. "Primary caretaker" as used in this chapter means a parent who has consistently assumed responsibility for the housing, health, and safety of the child prior to incarceration. A parent who, in the best interests of the child, has arranged for temporary care for the child in the home of a relative or other responsible adult shall not for that reason be excluded from the category, "primary caretaker."

(3) The applicant had not been found to be an unfit parent in any court proceeding. An inmate applicant

whose child has been declared a dependent of the juvenile court pursuant to Section 300 of the Welfare and Institutions Code shall be admitted to the program only after the court has found that participation in the program is in the child's best interest and that it meets the needs of the parent and child pursuant to paragraph (3) of subdivision (e) of Section 361.5 of the Welfare and Institutions Code. The fact that an inmate applicant's child has been found to come within Section 300 of the Welfare and Institutions Code shall not, in and of itself, be grounds for denying the applicant the opportunity to participate in the program.

(b) The Department of Corrections shall deny placement in the community treatment program if it determines that an inmate would pose an unreasonable risk to the public, or if any one of the following factors exist, except in unusual circumstances or if mitigating circumstances exist, including, but not limited to, the remoteness in time of the commission of the offense:

(1) The inmate has been convicted of any of the following:

(A) A sex offense listed in Section 667.6.

(B) A sex offense requiring registration pursuant to Section 290.

(C) A violent offense listed in subdivision (c) of Section 667.5.

(D) Arson as defined in Sections 450 to 455, inclusive.

(E) The unlawful sale or possession for sale, manufacture, or transportation of controlled substances as defined in Chapter 6 (commencing with Section 11350) of Division 10 of the Health and Safety Code, if large scale for profit as defined by the department.

(2) There is probability the inmate may abscond from the program as evidenced by any of the following:

(A) A conviction of escape, of aiding another person to escape, or of an attempt to escape from a jail or prison.

(B) The presence of an active detainer from a law enforcement agency, unless the detainer is based solely upon warrants issued for failure to appear on misdemeanor Vehicle Code violations.

(3) It is probable the inmate's conduct in a community facility will be adverse to herself or other participants in the program, as determined by the Director of Corrections or as evidenced by any of the following:

(A) The inmate's removal from a community program which resulted from violation of state laws, rules, or regulations governing Department of Corrections' inmates.

(B) A finding of the inmate's guilt of a serious rule violation, as defined by the Director of Corrections, which resulted in a credit loss on one occasion of 91 or more days or in a credit loss on more than one occasion of 31 days or more and the credit has not been restored.

(C) A current written opinion of a staff physician or psychiatrist that the inmate's medical or psychiatric condition is likely to cause an adverse effect upon the inmate or upon other persons if the inmate is placed in the program.

(c) Nothing in this section shall be interpreted to limit the discretion of the Director of Corrections to deny or approve placement when subdivision (b) does not apply.

(d) The Department of Corrections shall determine if the applicant meets the requirements of this section within 30 days of the parent's application to the program. The department shall establish an ap-

peal procedure for the applicant to appeal an adverse decision by the department.

(e) The department may, in its discretion, admit a pregnant inmate to the program prior to the birth of the child if it determines that the admission would otherwise comply with this chapter, and there is space available. *(Amended by Stats 1991 ch 820 §2, eff. 1/1/92.)*

§3418. Notification of program to inmates giving birth after sentencing.

In the case of any inmate who gave birth to a child after the date of sentencing, and in the case of any inmate who gave birth to a child prior to such date and meets the requirements of Section 3417 but has not yet made application for admission to a program, the department shall, at the earliest possible date, but in no case later than the birth of the child, or the receipt of the inmate to the custody of the Department of Corrections, as the case may be, notify the inmate of the provisions of this chapter.

§3419. Inmate giving birth after receipt; eligibility to program.

In the case of any inmate who gives birth after her receipt by the Department of Corrections, the department shall, subject to reasonable rules and regulations promulgated pursuant to Section 3414, upon her request, declare the inmate eligible to participate in a program pursuant to this chapter if all of the requirements of Section 3417 are met.

§3420. Notice of application for admission to child's caretaker or guardian; fitness proceedings.

(a) Within five days after the receipt of an inmate by the Department of Corrections who has already applied for admission to a program, or of her application for admission to a program, whichever is later, the department shall give notice of her application to the child's current caretaker or guardian, if any, and if it has not already been notified pursuant to Section 3415, the appropriate local social services agency that conducts investigations for child neglect and dependency hearings.

(b) The department and the individuals and agencies notified shall have five days from the date of such notice to decide whether or not to challenge the appropriateness of the applicant's entry into the program. Lack of a petition filed by that time shall result in a presumption that the individuals and agencies notified do not challenge the appropriateness of the applicant's entry into the program.

(c) The local agency which has been notified pursuant to Section 3415 shall not initiate the process of considering whether or not to file until after the sentencing court has sentenced the applicant.

(d) The appropriate local agency that conducts investigations for child neglect and dependency hearings, the Department of Corrections, and the current guardian or caretaker of the child, shall have the authority to file for a fitness proceeding against the mother after the mother has applied in writing to participate in the program.

(e) The determination of whether or not to file shall be based in part on the likelihood of the mother being a fit parent for the child in question both during the program and afterwards. Program content shall be taken into account in this determination. There shall

© 1992 by J., B. & L. Gould
Printed in the U.S.A.   **EP**

be a presumption affecting the burden of producing evidence in favor of filing for a fitness proceeding under the following circumstances:

(1) The applicant was convicted of one or more of the following violent felonies:

(i) Murder.

(ii) Mayhem.

(iii) Aggravated mayhem.

(iv) Kidnapping as defined in Section 207 or 209.

(v) Lewd acts on a child under 14 as defined in Section 288.

(vi) Any felony in which the defendant inflicts great bodily injury on a person other than accomplices which has been alleged and proven.

(vii) Forcible rape in violation of subdivision (2), (3), or (4) of Section 261.

(viii) Sodomy by force, violence, duress, menace, or threat of great bodily injury.

(ix) Oral copulation by force, violence, duress, menace, or threat of great bodily injury.

(2) The applicant was convicted of child abuse in the current or any proceeding.

(f) Fitness petitions shall be resolved in the court of first instance as soon as possible for purposes of this section. Given the need to place the child as soon as possible, the first determination by the court as to the applicant's fitness as a mother shall determine her eligibility for the program for the current application. Outcomes of appeals shall not affect eligibility. *(Amended by Stats 1989 ch 897 §43, eff. 1/1/90.)*

§3421. Age limit of children in program.

Children of women inmates may only participate in the program until they reach the age of six years, at which time the Board of Prison Terms may arrange for their care elsewhere under any procedure authorized by statute and transfer the mother to another placement under the jurisdiction of the Department of Corrections if necessary; and provided further, that at its discretion in exceptional cases, including, but not limited to cases where the mother's period of incarceration is extended, the board may retain such child and mother for a longer period of time.

§3422. Funds for payment of costs for care of mother and child.

The costs for care of any mother and child placed in a community treatment program pursuant to this section shall be paid for out of funds allocated to the department in the normal budgetary process. The department shall make diligent efforts to procure other funding sources for the program.

§3423. Removal to hospital for childbirth; payment of costs.

Any woman inmate who would give birth to a child during her term of imprisonment may be temporarily taken to a hospital outside the prison for the purposes of childbirth, and the charge for hospital and medical care shall be charged against the funds allocated to the institution. The board shall provide for the care of any children so born and shall pay for their care until suitably placed, including, but not limited to, placement in a community treatment program.

§3424. Evaluation of cost efficiency; report and recommendations.

On or before March 30, 1983, the Department of Corrections shall evaluate the cost efficiency and ef-

fect of this chapter and shall report back to the Legislature on efforts to procure outside funding sources together with the department's recommendations as to whether or not this chapter should be altered or repealed and if so, why.

TITLE 2.1

BIOMEDICAL AND BEHAVIORAL RESEARCH

CHAPTER 1

DEFINITIONS

§3500. Terms defined.

For purposes of this title:

(a) "Behavioral research" means studies involving, but not limited to, the investigation of human behavior, emotion, adaptation, conditioning, and response in a program designed to test certain hypotheses through the collection of objective data. Behavioral research does not include the accumulation of statistical data in the assessment of the effectiveness of programs to which inmates are routinely assigned, such as, but not limited to, education, vocational training, productive work, counseling, recognized therapies, and programs which are not experimental in nature.

(b) "Biomedical research" means research relating to or involving biological, medical, or physical science.

(c) "Psychotropic drug" means any drug that has the capability of changing or controlling mental functioning or behavior through direct pharmacological action. Such drugs include, but are not limited to, antipsychotic, antianxiety, sedative, antidepressant, and stimulant drugs. Psychotropic drugs also include mind-altering and behavior-altering drugs which, in specified dosages, are used to alleviate certain physical disorders, and drugs which are ordinarily used to alleviate certain physical disorders but may, in specified dosages, have mind-altering or behavior-altering effects.

(d) "Research" means a class of activities designed to develop or contribute to generalizable knowledge such as theories, principles, or relationships, or the accumulation of data on which they may be based, that can be corroborated by accepted scientific observation and inferences.

(e) "Research protocol" means a formal document setting forth the explicit objectives of a research project and the procedures of investigation designed to reach those objectives.

(f) "Phase I drug" means any drug which is designated as a phase I drug for testing purposes under the federal Food and Drug Administration criteria in Section 312.1 of Title 21 of the Code of Federal Regulations. *(Amended by Stats 1985 ch 1553 §1.)*

CHAPTER 2

GENERAL PROVISIONS AND PROHIBITIONS

§3501. Right to participate.

The Legislature affirms the fundamental right of competent adults to make decisions about their participation in behavioral research. *(Amended by Stats 1985 ch 1553 §1.5.)*

© 1992 by J., B. & L. Gould
Printed in the U.S.A. **EP**

§3502. Research conducted on prisoner.

Except as provided in Section 1706 of the Welfare and Institutions Code, no biomedical research shall be conducted on any prisoner in this state. *(Amended by Stats 1989 ch 1367 §1, eff. 10/2/89.)*

§3502.5. Medical treatment to prisoners.

(a) Notwithstanding Section 3502, any physician who provides medical care to prisoners is not prohibited from providing, a patient who is a prisoner with a drug or treatment available only through a treatment protocol or treatment IND (investigational new drug), as defined in Section 312 of Title 21 of the Code of Federal Regulations, if the physician determines that access to that drug is in the best medical interest of the patient, and the patient has given informed consent under Section 3521.

(b) Notwithstanding any other provision of law, neither a public entity nor a public employee shall be liable for any injury caused by the administration of a drug pursuant to subdivision (a), where the administration is made in accordance with a treatment IND or a treatment protocol as defined in Section 312 of Title 21 of the Code of Federal Regulations.

(c) This section shall remain in effect only until January 2, 1996, and as of that date is repealed unless a later enacted statute, which is enacted before January 2, 1996, deletes or extends that date. *(Added by Stats 1989 ch 979 §2, eff. 9/29/89 only until 1/2/96.)*

§§3503, 3503.1. *Repealed by Stats 1985 ch 1553.*

§3504. Prompt treatment of prisoner's injuries.

Any physical or mental injury of a prisoner resulting from the participation in behavioral research, irrespective of causation of such injury, shall be treated promptly and on a continuing basis until the injury is cured. *(Amended by Stats 1985 ch 1553 §5.)*

§3505. Limitations.

Behavioral research shall be limited to studies of the possible causes, effects and processes of incarceration and studies of prisons as institutional structures or of prisoners as incarcerated persons which present minimal or no risk and no more than mere inconvenience to the subjects of the research. Informed consent shall not be required for participation in behavioral research when the department determines that it would be unnecessary or significantly inhibit the conduct of such research. In the absence of such determination, informed consent shall be required for participation in behavioral research. *(Amended by Stats 1985 ch 1553 §6.)*

§§3506, 3507. *Repealed by Stats 1985 ch 1553.*

§3508. Limitations on use of behavioral modification techniques.

Behavioral modification techniques shall be used only if such techniques are medically and socially acceptable means by which to modify behavior and if such techniques do not inflict permanent physical or psychological injury.

§3509. *Repealed by Stats 1985 ch 1553.*

§3509.5. Enforcement of rules.

Nothing in this title is intended to diminish the authority of any official or agency to adopt and enforce rules pertaining to prisoners, so long as such rules are not inconsistent with this title.

CHAPTER 3

ADMINISTRATION

§§3510 to 3514. *Repealed by Stats 1985 ch 1553.*

§3515. Duties of the department.

The duties of the department are to determine:

(a) That the risks to the prisoners consenting to research are outweighed by the sum of benefits to the prisoners and the importance of the knowledge to be gained.

(b) That the rights and welfare of the prisoners are adequately protected, including the security of any confidential personal information.

(c) That the procedures for selection of prisoners are equitable and that subjects are not unjustly deprived of the opportunity to participate.

(d) That adequate provisions have been made for compensating research related injury.

(e) That the rate of remuneration is comparable to that received by nonprisoner volunteers in similar research.

(f) That the conduct of the activity will be reviewed at timely intervals.

(g) That legally effective informed consent will be obtained by adequate and appropriate methods. *(Amended by Stats 1985 ch 1553 §15.)*

§3516. Determination as to conduct of research.

No behavioral research shall be conducted on any prisoner in this state in the absence of a determination by the department consistent with this title. *(Amended by Stats 1985 ch 1553 §16.)*

§3517. Promulgation of rules and regulations for administration.

The department shall promulgate rules and regulations reasonably necessary for the effective administration of the provisions of this title. Action on proposals submitted shall be taken within 60 days. The regulations shall be submitted to the Joint Legislative Prison Committee for review and shall not become operative until 60 days after submission. *(Amended by Stats 1985 ch 1553 §17.)*

§3518. Promulgation of rules and regulations prescribing procedures.

The department shall promulgate rules and regulations prescribing procedures to be followed by any person who has a grievance concerning the operation of any particular research program conducted pursuant to this title. *(Amended by Stats 1985 ch 1553 §18.)*

§3519. Evaluation of impact of research.

The department shall evaluate the impact of research on human subjects approved and conducted pursuant to this title, including any adverse reactions. *(Amended by Stats 1985 ch 1553 §19.)*

§3520. Biannual review report.

The department shall make a biannual report containing a review of each research program which has been approved and conducted. The report shall be transmitted to the Legislature and shall be made available to the public. *(Amended by Stats 1985 ch 1553 §20.)*

© 1992 by J., B. & L. Gould
Printed in the U.S.A.　　EP

CHAPTER 4

PRISONERS' RIGHTS AS RESEARCH SUBJECTS

§3521. Informed consent; required conditions.

For the purposes of this title, a prisoner shall be deemed to have given his informed consent only if each of the following conditions are satisfied:

(a) Consent is given without duress, coercion, fraud, or undue influence.

(b) The prisoner is informed in writing of the potential risks or benefits, or both, of the proposed research.

(c) The prisoner is informed orally and in writing in the language in which the subject is fluent of each of the following:

(1) An explanation of the biomedical or behavioral research procedures to be followed and their purposes, including identification of any procedures which are experimental.

(2) A description of all known attendant discomfort and risks reasonably to be expected.

(3) A disclosure of any appropriate alternative biomedical or behavioral research procedures that might be advantageous for the subject.

(4) The nature of the information sought to be gained by the experiment.

(5) The expected recovery time of the subject after completion of the experiment.

(6) An offer to answer any inquiries concerning the applicable biomedical or behavioral research procedures.

(7) An instruction that the person is free to withdraw his consent and to discontinue participation in the research at any time without prejudice to the subject.

§3522. Information on remuneration and treatment for research-related injuries.

At the time of furnishing a prisoner the writing required by subdivision (b) of Section 3521, the prisoner shall also be given information as to (a) the amount of remuneration the prisoner will receive for the research and (b) the manner in which the prisoner may obtain prompt treatment for any research-related injuries. Such information shall be provided in writing on a form to be retained by the prisoner.

§3523. Amount of remuneration

The amount of such remuneration shall be comparable to that which is paid to nonprisoner volunteers in similar research.

CHAPTER 5

REMEDIES

§3524. Action for injury.

(a) A prisoner may maintain an action for injury to such prisoner, including physical or mental injury, or both, caused by the wrongful or negligent act of a person during the course of the prisoner's participation in biomedical or behavioral research conducted pursuant to this title.

(b) In any action pursuant to this section, such damages may be awarded as under all of the circumstances of the case may be just.

(c) When the death of a prisoner is caused by the wrongful act or neglect of another, his or her heirs or personal representatives on their behalf may maintain an action for damages against the person causing the death, or if dead, such person's personal representatives.

(d) If an action arising out of the same wrongful act or neglect may be maintained pursuant to subdivision (c) for wrongful death to any such prisoner, the action authorized by subdivision (a) shall be consolidated therewith for trial on motion of any interested party.

(e) For the purposes of this section, heirs mean only the following:

(1) Those persons who would be entitled to succeed to the property of the decedent according to the provisions of Part 2 (commencing with Section 6400) of Division 6 of the Probate Code, and

(2) Whether or not qualified under paragraph (1), if they were dependent on the decedent, the putative spouse, children of the putative spouse, stepchildren, and parents. As used in this paragraph, "putative spouse" means the surviving spouse of a void or voidable marriage who is found by the court to have believed in good faith that the marriage to the decedent was valid.

TITLE 3

EXECUTION OF DEATH PENALTY

CHAPTER 1

EXECUTING DEATH PENALTY

§3600. Male prisoner's detention pending execution.

Every male person, upon whom has been imposed the judgment of death, shall be delivered to the warden of the California state prison designated by the department for the execution of the death penalty, there to be kept until the execution of the judgment.

§3601. Female prisoner's detention after judgment of death.

Every female person, upon whom has been imposed the judgment of death, shall be delivered to the warden of the Central California Women's Facility, there to be held pending decision upon appeal. (Amended by Stats 1991 ch 1016 §1, eff. 1/1/92.)

§3602. Female prisoner's detention on affirmance of appeal.

Upon the affirmance of her appeal, the female person sentenced to death shall thereafter be delivered to the warden of the California state prison designated by the department for the execution of the death penalty, not earlier than three days before the day upon which judgment is to be executed; provided, however, that in the event of a commutation of sentence said female prisoner shall be returned to the California Institution for Women, there to be confined pursuant to such commutation.

§3603. Where executed.

The judgment of death shall be executed within the walls of one of the State prisons designated by the court by which judgment is rendered.

© 1992 by J., B. & L. Gould
Printed in the U.S.A. **EP**

§3604. Lethal gas.

The punishment of death shall be inflicted by the administration of a lethal gas.

§3605. Who must be present.

The warden of the State prison where the execution is to take place shall be present at the execution and must invite the presence of two physicians, the Attorney General of the State, and at least 12 reputable citizens, to be selected by him; and he or she shall at the request of the defendant, permit those ministers of the Gospel, not exceeding two, as the defendant may name, and any persons, relatives or friends, not to exceed five, to be present at the execution, together with such peace officers as he may think expedient, to witness the execution. But no other persons than those mentioned in this section can be present at the execution, nor can any person under 18 years of age be allowed to witness the execution. *(Amended by Stats 1986 ch 248 §167.)*

§3607. Return on death warrant; information.

After the execution, the warden must make a return upon the death warrant to the county clerk of the court by which the judgment was rendered, showing the time, mode, and manner in which it was executed.

CHAPTER 2

SUSPENSION OF EXECUTION OF DEATH PENALTY; INSANITY; PREGNANCY

§3700. Authority.

No judge, court, or officer, other than the Governor, can suspend the execution of a judgment of death, except the warden of the State prison to whom he is delivered for execution, as provided in the six succeeding sections, unless an appeal is taken.

§3700.5. Sanity examination before execution.

Whenever a court makes and causes to be entered an order appointing a day upon which a judgment of death shall be executed upon a defendant, the warden of the state prison to whom such defendant has been delivered for execution or, if the defendant is a female, the warden of the California Institution for Women, shall notify the Director of Corrections who shall thereupon select and appoint three alienists, all of whom must be from the medical staffs of the Department of Corrections, to examine the defendant, under the judgment of death, and investigate his or her sanity. It is the duty of the alienists so selected and appointed to examine such defendant and investigate his or her sanity, and to report their opinions and conclusions thereon, in writing, to the Governor, to the warden of the prison at which the execution is to take place at least 20 days prior to the day appointed for the execution of the judgment of death upon the defendant. The warden shall furnish a copy of the report to counsel for the defendant upon his or her request. *(Amended by Stats 1989 ch 1420 §19, eff. 1/1/90.)*

§3701. Insane defendant; hearing.

If, after his delivery to the warden for execution, there is good reason to believe that a defendant, under judgment of death, has become insane, the warden must call such fact to the attention of the district attorney of the county in which the prison is situated, whose duty it is to immediately file in the superior court of such county a petition, stating the conviction and judgment, and the fact that the defendant is believed to be insane, and asking that the question of his sanity be inquired into. Thereupon the court must at once cause to be summoned and impaneled, from the regular jury list of the county, a jury of 12 persons to hear such inquiry.

§3702. Witnesses at hearing.

The district attorney must attend the hearing, and may produce witnesses before the jury, for which purpose he may issue process in the same manner as for witnesses to attend before the grand jury, and disobedience thereto may be punished in like manner as disobedience to process issued by the court.

§3703. Verdict; orders if defendant insane.

The verdict of the jury must be entered upon the minutes, and thereupon the court must make and cause to be entered an order reciting the fact of such inquiry and the result thereof, and when it is found that the defendant is insane, the order must direct that he be taken to a medical facility of the Department of Corrections, and there kept in safe confinement until his reason is restored.

§3704. Execution of judgment if defendant sane or after regaining sanity.

If it is found that the defendant is sane, the warden must proceed to execute the judgment as specified in the warrant; if it is found that the defendant is insane, the warden must suspend the execution and transmit a certified copy of the order mentioned in the last section to the Governor, and deliver the defendant, together with a certified copy of such order, to the superintendent of the medical facility named in such order. When the defendant recovers his sanity, the superintendent of such medical facility must certify that fact to the judge of the superior court from which the defendant was committed as insane, who must thereupon fix a date upon which, after 10 days' written notice to the defendant and the district attorney of the county from which the defendant was originally sentenced and the district attorney of the county from which he was committed to the medical facility, a hearing shall be had before said judge sitting without a jury to determine whether or not the defendant has in fact recovered his sanity. If the defendant appears without counsel, the court shall appoint counsel to represent him at said hearing. If the judge should determine that the defendant has recovered his sanity he must certify that fact to the Governor, who must thereupon issue to the warden his warrant appointing a day for the execution of the judgment, and the warden shall thereupon return the defendant to the state prison pending the execution of the judgment. If, however, the judge should determine that the defendant has not recovered his sanity he shall direct the return of the defendant to a medical facility of the Department of Corrections, to be there kept in safe confinement until his sanity is restored.

§3704.5. Transfer of defendant to medical facility of department.

Any defendant who, on March 4, 1972, is in a state hospital under court order pursuant to Section 3703, as that section read on March 3, 1972, shall be transferred to a medical facility of the Department of Cor-

© 1992 by J., B. & L. Gould
Printed in the U.S.A.   EP

rections, designated by the Director of Corrections, and there kept in safe confinement until his or her reason is restored. Section 3704 shall apply when the defendant recovers his or her sanity. (*Amended by Stats 1988 ch 160 §137, eff. 1/1/89.*)

§3705. Pregnancy investigation of female sentenced to death.

If there is good reason to believe that a female against whom a judgment of death is rendered is pregnant, such proceedings must be had as are provided in Section 3701, except that instead of a jury, as therein provided, the court may summon three disinterested physicians, of good standing in their profession, to inquire into the supposed pregnancy, who shall, in the presence of the court, but with closed doors, if requested by the defendant, examine the defendant and hear any evidence that may be produced, and make a written finding and certificate of their conclusion, to be approved by the court and spread upon the minutes. The provisions of Section 3702 apply to the proceedings upon such inquiry.

§3706. Suspension of judgment for pregnancy; reissuance after pregnancy.

If it is found that the female is not pregnant, the warden must execute the judgment; if it is found that she is pregnant the warden must suspend the execution of the judgment, and transmit a certified copy of the finding and certificate to the Governor. When the Governor receives from the warden a certificate that the defendant is no longer pregnant, he must issue to the warden his warrant appointing a day for the execution of the judgment.

TITLE 4

COUNTY JAILS, FARMS AND CAMPS

CHAPTER 1

COUNTY JAILS

§4000. Sheriffs as keepers of jails.

The common jails in the several counties of this State are kept by the sheriffs of the counties in which they are respectively situated, and are used as follows:

1. For the detention of persons committed in order to secure their attendance as witnesses in criminal cases;

2. For the detention of persons charged with crime and committed for trial;

3. For the confinement of persons committed for contempt, or upon civil process, or by other authority of law;

4. For the confinement of persons sentenced to imprisonment therein upon a conviction for crime.

§4000.5. Transfer of county prisoners to work site.

Notwithstanding any other provision of law, the sheriff of any county may transfer prisoners committed to any jail of the county to any industrial road camp maintained by the county. (*Added by Stats 1989 ch 897 §44, eff. 1/1/90.*)

§4001. Separate accommodation of different classes of prisoners.

Each county jail must contain a sufficient number of rooms to allow all persons belonging to either one of the following classes to be confined separately and distinctly from persons belonging to either of the other classes:

1. Persons committed on criminal process and detained for trial;

2. Persons already convicted of crime and held under sentence;

3. Persons detained as witnesses or held under civil process, or under an order imposing punishment for a contempt.

§4001.1. Payment for informant's testimony.

(a) No law enforcement or correctional official shall give, offer, or promise to give any monetary payment in excess of fifty dollars ($50) in return for an in-custody informant's testimony in any criminal proceeding. Nothing contained herein shall prohibit payments incidental to the informant's testimony such as expenses incurred for witness or immediate family relocation, lodging, housing, meals, phone calls, travel, or witness fees authorized by law, provided those payments are supported by appropriate documentation demonstrating that the money was used for the purposes for which it was given.

(b) No law enforcement agency and no in-custody informant acting as an agent for the agency, may take some action, beyond merely listening to statements of a defendant, that is deliberately designed to elicit incriminating remarks.

(c) As used in this section, an "in-custody informant" means a person described in subdivision (a) of Section 1127a. (*Added by Stats 1989 ch 901 §3, eff. 1/1/90.*)

§4002. Placing different classes in same room.

Persons committed on criminal process and detained for trial, persons convicted and under sentence, and persons committed upon civil process, shall not be kept or put in the same room, nor shall male and female prisoners, except husband and wife, sleep, dress or undress, bathe, or perform eliminatory functions in the same room. However, persons committed on criminal process and detained for trial may be kept or put in the same room with persons convicted and under sentence for the purpose of participating in supervised activities and for the purpose of housing, provided, that the housing occurs as a result of a classification procedure which is based upon consideration of criminal sophistication, seriousness of crime charged, presence or absence of assaultive behavior, age, and other criteria that will provide for the safety of the prisoners and staff. Nothing in this section shall be construed to impose any requirement upon a county to confine male and female prisoners in the same or an adjoining facility or impose any duty upon a county to establish or maintain programs which involve the joint participation of male and female prisoners.

§4003. Receipts for personal property.

Whenever any weapon or other personal property is taken from an arrested person, it shall be the duty of the desk clerk or other proper officer of any city, county or city and county jail, to which such person is committed for detention, to give a receipt to such person without delay for the property taken.

§4004. Actual confinement.

A prisoner committed to the county jail for examination, or upon conviction for a public offense, must be actually confined in the jail until he is legally discharged; and if he is permitted to go at large out of the jail, except by virtue of a legal order or process, it is an escape; provided, however, that during the pendency of a criminal proceeding, the superior court or an inferior court, as the case may be, before which said proceeding is pending may make a legal order, good cause appearing therefor, for the removal of the prisoner from the county jail in custody of the sheriff. In judicial districts where there is a marshal, the marshal shall maintain custody of such prisoner while he is in the municipal court facility pursuant to such court order. The superior court of the county may make a legal order, good cause appearing therefor, for the removal of prisoners confined in the county jail, after conviction, in the custody of the sheriff.

If facilities are no longer available in the county jail due to crowded conditions, a sheriff may transfer a person committed to the county jail upon conviction for a public offense to facilities which are available in the city jail, as provided for in Section 4004.5.

§4004.5. Facilities used for holding prisoners held for examination or during trial.

(a) A city may furnish facilities to be used for holding prisoners held for examination or during trial without cost to the county or upon such terms as may be agreed upon by the governing body of such city and the board of supervisors, and the marshal or constable may keep such prisoners in their custody in such city jail.

(b) A city may furnish facilities to be used for holding persons convicted of a public offense who have been transferred from the county jail by the sheriff due to crowded conditions upon such terms as may be agreed upon by the governing body of such city and the board of supervisors. The agreed terms may indicate that the facilities are to be provided free of charge to the county.

§4005. Sheriff's duties.

(a) Except as provided in subdivision (b), the sheriff shall receive, and keep in the county jail, any prisoner committed thereto by process or order issued under the authority of the United States, until he or she is discharged according to law, as if he or she had been committed under process issued under the authority of this state; provision being made by the United States for the support of the prisoner.

(b) The sheriff shall receive, and keep in the county jail, any prisoner committed thereto by process or order issued under the authority of the United States, until he or she is discharged according to law, as if he or she had been committed under process issued under the authority of this state, but only if the sheriff determines that adequate space in appropriate detention areas currently exists for this purpose. Provision shall be made by the United States for the support of the prisoner. This subdivision shall apply only in counties where a facility operated by the United States Bureau of Prisons exists within 200 miles of the county seat. *(Amended by Stats 1986 ch 523 §1.)*

§4006. Sheriff answerable for safekeeping.

A sheriff, to whose custody a prisoner is committed as provided in the last section, is answerable for his safekeeping in the courts of the United States, according to the laws thereof.

§4007. Commitment to jail or another county.

When there is no jail in the county, or when the jail becomes unfit or unsafe for the confinement of prisoners, the judge of the superior court may, by a written order filed with the county clerk, designate the jail of a contiguous county for the confinement of any prisoner of his or her county, and may at any time modify or vacate the order.

When there are reasonable grounds to believe that a prisoner may be forcibly removed from a county jail, the sheriff may remove the prisoner to any California state prison for safekeeping and it is the duty of the warden of the prison to accept and detain the prisoner in his or her custody until his or her removal is ordered by the superior court of the county from which he or she was delivered. Immediately upon receiving the prisoner the warden shall advise the Director of Corrections of that fact in writing.

When a county prisoner requires medical treatment necessitating hospitalization which cannot be provided at the county jail or county hospital because of lack of adequate detention facilities, and when the prisoner also presents a serious custodial problem because of his or her past or present behavior, the judge of the superior court may, on the request of the county sheriff and with the consent of the Director of Corrections, designate by written order the nearest state prison or correctional facility which would be able to provide the necessary medical treatment and secure confinement of the prisoner. The written order of the judge shall be filed with the county clerk. The court shall immediately calendar the matter for a hearing to determine whether the order shall continue or be rescinded. The hearing shall be held within 48 hours of the initial order or the next judicial day, whichever occurs later. The prisoner shall not be transferred to the state prison or correctional facility prior to the hearing, except upon a determination by the physician responsible for the prisoner's health care that a medical emergency exists which requires the transfer of the prisoner to the state prison or correctional facility prior to the hearing. The prisoner shall be entitled to be present at the hearing and to be represented by counsel. The prisoner may waive his or her right to this hearing in writing at any time. If the prisoner waives his or her right to the hearing, the county sheriff shall notify the prisoner's attorney of the transfer within 48 hours, or the next business day, whichever is later. The court may modify or vacate the order at any time.

The rate of compensation for the prisoner's medical treatment and confinement within a California state prison or correctional facility shall be established by the Department of Corrections, and shall be charged against the county making the request.

When there are reasonable grounds to believe that there is a prisoner in a county jail who is likely to be a threat to other persons in the facility or who is likely to cause substantial damage to the facility, the judge of the superior court may, on the request of the county sheriff and with the consent of the Director of Corrections, designate by written order the nearest state prison or correctional facility which would be able to secure confinement of the prisoner, subject to space available. The written order of the judge must be filed with the county clerk. The court shall immediately

© 1992 by J., B. & L. Gould
Printed in the U.S.A. **EP**

calendar the matter for a hearing to determine whether the order shall continue or be rescinded. The hearing shall be held within 48 hours of the initial order or the next judicial day, whichever occurs later. The prisoner shall be entitled to be present at the hearing and to be represented by counsel. The court may modify or vacate that order at any time. The rate of compensation for the prisoner's confinement within a California state prison or correctional facility shall be established by the Department of Corrections and shall be charged against the county making the request. *(Amended by Stats 1990 ch 1353 §1, eff. 1/1/91.)*

§4008. Service of copy of appointment transferring prisoner to other county.

A copy of the appointment, certified by the county clerk, must be served on the sheriff or keeper of the jail designated, who must receive into his jail all prisoners authorized to be confined therein, pursuant to the last section, and who is responsible for the safekeeping of the persons so committed, in the same manner and to the same extent as if he were sheriff of the county for whose use his jail is designated, and with respect to the persons so committed he is deemed the sheriff of the county from which they were removed.

§4009. Commitment to jail of other county revoked.

When a jail is erected in a county for the use of which the designation was made, or its jail is rendered fit and safe for the confinement of prisoners, the judge of the superior court of that county must, by a written revocation, filed with the county clerk thereof, declare that the necessity for the designation has ceased, and that it is revoked.

§4010. Service of copy of revocation of commitment.

The county clerk must immediately serve a copy of the revocation upon the sheriff of the county, who must thereupon remove the prisoners to the jail of the county from which the removal was had.

§4011. Hospitalization of prisoners.

(a) When it is made to appear to any judge by affidavit of the sheriff or other official in charge of county correctional facilities or district attorney and oral testimony that a prisoner confined in any city or county jail within the jurisdiction of the court requires medical or surgical treatment necessitating hospitalization, which treatment cannot be furnished or supplied at such city or county jail, the court in its discretion may order the removal of such person or persons from such city or county jail to the county hospital in such county; provided, if there is no county hospital in such county, then to any hospital designated by such court; and it shall be the duty of the sheriff or other official in charge of county correctional facilities to maintain the necessary guards, who may be private security guards, for the safekeeping of such prisoner, the expense of which shall be a charge against the county.

(b) The cost of such medical services and such hospital care and treatment shall be charged against the county subject to subdivisions (c) and (d), in the case of a prisoner in or taken from the county jail, or against the city in the case of a prisoner in or taken from the city jail, and the city or county may recover the same by appropriate action from the person so served or cared for, or any person or agency responsible for his care and maintenance. If the prisoner is in the county jail under contract with a city or under some other arrangement with the city to keep the city prisoner in the county jail, then the city shall be charged, subject to subdivisions (c) and (d), for the prisoner's care and maintenance with the same right of recovery against any responsible person or any other agency.

(c) When such prisoner is poor and indigent the cost of such medical services and such hospital care and treatment shall, in the case of persons removed from the city jail be paid out of the general fund of such city, and in the case of persons removed from the county jail to a hospital other than a county hospital, such cost shall be paid out of the general fund of such county or city and county. In the case of city jail prisoners removed to the county hospital, the cost of such hospital care and treatment to be paid by the city to the county, shall be the rate per day fixed by the board of supervisors of such county. Such board of supervisors may, but need not, fix different rates for different classes of patients, or for different wards, and any and all such rates may be changed by such board of supervisors at any time, but shall at all times approximate as nearly as may be, the average actual cost to the county of such hospital care and treatment either in such wards or for such classes of patients or otherwise.

(d) In the event such prisoner is financially able to pay for his care, support and maintenance, the medical superintendent of such hospital other than a county hospital may, with the approval of such judge, enter into a special agreement with such person, or with his relatives or friends, for his care, support, maintenance, and other hospital expenses.

Any prisoner may decline such care or treatment and provide other care and treatment for himself at his own expense.

§4011.1. Recovery of treatment under Medi-Cal Act.

(a) Notwithstanding Section 29602 of the Government Code and any other provisions of this chapter, a county, city or the Department of the Youth Authority is authorized to make claim for and recovery of the costs of necessary hospital, medical, surgical, dental, or optometric care rendered to any prisoner confined in a county or city jail or any juvenile confined in a detention facility, who would otherwise be entitled to that care under the Medi-Cal Act (Chapter 7 (commencing with Section 14000) part 3, Division 9, Welfare and Institutions Code), and who is eligible for that care on the first day of confinement or detention, to the extent that federal financial participation is available, or under the provisions of any private program or policy for that care, and the county, city or the Department of the Youth Authority shall be liable only for the costs of that care as cannot be recovered pursuant to this section. No person who is eligible for Medi-Cal shall be eligible for benefits under the provisions of this section, and no county or city or the Department of the Youth Authority is authorized to make a claim for any recovery of costs for services for that person, unless federal financial participation is available for all or part of the costs of providing services to that person under the Medi-Cal Act.

Notwithstanding any other provision of law, any county or city making a claim pursuant to this section and under the Medi-Cal Act shall reimburse the Health Care Deposit Fund for the state costs of paying those medical claims. Funds allocated to the county from the County Health Services Fund pursuant to Part. 4.5 (commencing with Section 16700) of Division 9 of the Welfare and Institutions Code may be utilized by the county or city to make that reimbursement.

(b) Notwithstanding Section 29602 of the Government Code and any other provisions of this chapter, to the extent that recovery of costs of necessary hospital, medical, surgical, dental, or optometric care are not accomplished under subdivision (a), a county, city, or the Department of the Youth Authority is authorized to make claim for and recover from a prisoner or a person legally responsible for a prisoner's care and maintenance the costs of necessary hospital, medical, surgical, dental, or optometric care rendered to any prisoner confined in a county or city jail, or any juvenile confined in a detention facility, where the prisoner or the person legally responsible for the prisoner's care and maintenance is financially able to pay for the prisoner's care, support, and maintenance. Nothing in this subdivision shall be construed to authorize a city, a county, or the Department of the Youth Authority to make a claim against a spouse of a prisoner.

(c) Necessary hospital, medical, dental, or optometric care, as used in this section, does not include care rendered with respect to an injury occurring during confinement in a county or city jail or juvenile detention facility, nor does it include any care or testing mandated by law.

(d) Subdivisions (b) and (c) shall apply only where there has been a determination of the present ability of the prisoner or responsible third party to pay all or a portion of the cost of necessary hospital, medical, surgical, dental, or optometric care. The person legally responsible for the prisoner's care shall provide a financial disclosure statement, executed under penalty of perjury, based on his or her past year's income tax return, to the Department of the Youth Authority. The city, county, or Department of the Youth Authority may request that the prisoner appear before a designated hearing officer for an inquiry into the ability of the prisoner or responsible third party to pay all or part of the cost of the care provided.

(e) Notice of this request shall be provided to the prisoner or responsible third party, which shall contain the following:

(1) A statement of the cost of the care provided to the prisoner.

(2) The prisoner's or responsible third party's procedural rights under this section.

(3) The time limit within which the prisoner or responsible third party may respond.

(4) A warning that if the prisoner or responsible third party fails to appear before, or respond to, the designated officer, the officer may petition the court for an order requiring him or her to make payment of the full cost of the care provided to the prisoner.

(f) At the hearing, the prisoner or responsible third party shall be entitled to, but shall not be limited to, all of the following rights:

(1) The right to be heard in person.

(2) The right to present witnesses and documentary evidence.

(3) The right to confront and cross-examine adverse witnesses.

(4) The right to have adverse evidence disclosed to him or her.

(5) The right to a written statement of the findings of the designated hearing officer.

(g) If the hearing officer determines that the prisoner or responsible third party has the present ability to pay all or a part of the cost, the officer shall set the amount to be reimbursed, and shall petition the court to order the prisoner or responsible third party to pay the sum to the city, county, or state, in the manner in which it finds reasonable and compatible to the prisoner's or responsible third party's financial ability. The courts order shall be enforceable in the manner provided for money judgments in a civil action under the Code of Civil Procedure.

(h) At any time prior to satisfaction of the judgment rendered according to the terms of this section, a prisoner or responsible third party against whom a judgment has been rendered, may petition the rendering court for a modification of the previous judgment on the grounds of a change of circumstance with regard to his or her ability to pay the judgment. The prisoner or responsible third party shall be advised of this right at the time the original judgment is rendered.

(i) As used in this section, "Ability to pay" means the overall capacity of the prisoner or responsible third party to reimburse the costs, or a portion of the costs, of the care provided to the prisoner, and shall include, but not be limited to, all of the following:

(1) The prisoner's or responsible third party's present financial position.

(2) The prisoner's or responsible third party's discernible future financial position.

(3) The likelihood that the prisoner or responsible third party will be able to obtain employment in the future.

(4) Any other factor or factors which may bear upon the prisoner's or responsible third party's financial position. (*Amended by Stats 1989 ch 282 §1, eff. 1/1/90.*)

§4011.5. Hospitalization authority of jailer or sheriff.

Whenever it appears to a sheriff or jailer that a prisoner in a county jail or a city jail under his charge is in need of immediate medical or hospital care, and that the health and welfare of the prisoner will be injuriously affected unless he is forthwith removed to a hospital, the sheriff or jailer may authorize the immediate removal of the prisoner under guard to a hospital, without first obtaining a court order as provided in Section 4011. In any such case, however, if the condition of the prisoner prevents his return to the jail within 48 hours from the time of his removal, the sheriff or jailer shall apply to a judge of the superior court for an order authorizing the continued absence of the prisoner from the jail in the manner provided in Section 4011. The provisions of Section 4011 governing the cost of medical and hospital care of prisoners and the liability therefor, shall apply to the cost of, and the liability for, medical or hospital care of prisoners removed from jail pursuant to this section.

§4011.6. Transfer of mentally disordered prisoners.

In any case in which it appears to the person in charge of a county jail, city jail, or juvenile detention facility, or to any judge of a court in the county in which the jail or juvenile detention facility is located, that a

© 1992 by J., B. & L. Gould
Printed in the U.S.A.　　EP

person in custody in that jail or juvenile detention facility may be mentally disordered, he or she may cause the prisoner to be taken to a facility for 72-hour treatment and evaluation pursuant to Section 5150 of the Welfare and Institutions Code and he or she shall inform the facility in writing, which shall be confidential, of the reasons that the person is being taken to the facility. The local mental health director or his or her designee may examine the prisoner prior to transfer to a facility for treatment and evaluation. Upon transfer to a facility, Article 1 (commencing with Section 5150), Article 4 (commencing with Section 5250), Article 4.5 (commencing with Section 5260), Article 5 (commencing with Section 5275), Article 6 (commencing with Section 5300), and Article 7 (commencing with Section 5325) of Chapter 2 and Chapter 3 (commencing with Section 5350) of Part 1 of Division 5 of the Welfare and Institutions Code shall apply to the prisoner.

Where the court causes the prisoner to be transferred to a 72-hour facility, the court shall forthwith notify the local mental health director or his or her designee, the prosecuting attorney, and counsel for the prisoner in the criminal or juvenile proceedings about that transfer. Where the person in charge of the jail or juvenile detention facility causes the transfer of the prisoner to a 72-hour facility the person shall immediately notify the local mental health director or his or her designee and each court within the county where the prisoner has a pending proceeding about the transfer. Upon notification by the person in charge of the jail or juvenile detention facility the court shall forthwith notify counsel for the prisoner and the prosecuting attorney in the criminal or juvenile proceedings about that transfer.

If a prisoner is detained in, or remanded to, a facility pursuant to those articles of the Welfare and Institutions Code, the facility shall transmit a report, which shall be confidential, to the person in charge of the jail or juvenile detention facility or judge of the court who caused the prisoner to be taken to the facility and to the local mental health director or his or her designee, concerning the condition of the prisoner. A new report shall be transmitted at the end of each period of confinement provided for in those articles, upon conversion to voluntary status, and upon filing of temporary letter of conservatorship.

A prisoner who has been transferred to an inpatient facility pursuant to this section may convert to voluntary inpatient status without obtaining the consent of the court, the person in charge of the jail or juvenile detention facility, or the local mental health director. At the beginning of that conversion to voluntary status, the person in charge of the facility shall transmit a report to the person in charge of the jail or juvenile detention facility or judge of the court who caused the prisoner to be taken to the facility, counsel for the prisoner, prosecuting attorney, and local mental health director or his or her designee.

If the prisoner is detained in, or remanded to, a facility pursuant to those articles of the Welfare and Institutions Code, the time passed in the facility shall count as part of the prisoner's sentence. When the prisoner is detained in, or remanded to, the facility, the person in charge of the jail or juvenile detention facility shall advise the professional person in charge of the facility of the expiration date of the prisoner's sentence. If the prisoner is to be released from the facility before the expiration date, the professional person in charge shall notify the local mental health

director or his or her designee, counsel for the prisoner, the prosecuting attorney, and the person in charge of the jail or juvenile detention facility, who shall send for, take, and receive the prisoner back into the jail or juvenile detention facility.

A defendant, either charged with or convicted of a criminal offense, or a minor alleged to be within the jurisdiction of the juvenile court, may be concurrently subject to the provisions of the Lanterman-Petris-Short Act (Part 1 (commencing with Section 5000) of Division 5 of the Welfare and Institutions Code).

If a prisoner is detained in a facility pursuant to those articles of the Welfare and Institutions Code and if the person in charge of the facility determines that arraignment or trial would be detrimental to the well-being of the prisoner, the time spent in the facility shall not be computed in any statutory time requirements for arraignment or trial in any pending criminal or juvenile proceedings. Otherwise, this section shall not affect any statutory time requirements for arraignment or trial in any pending criminal or juvenile proceedings.

For purposes of this section, the term "juvenile detention facility" includes any state, county, or private home or institution in which wards or dependent children of the juvenile court or persons awaiting a hearing before the juvenile court are detained. (Amended by Stats 1988 ch 160 §138, eff. 1/1/89.)

§4011.7. Misdemeanant's medical care.

Notwithstanding the provisions of Sections 4011 and 4011.5, when it appears that the prisoner in need of medical or surgical treatment necessitating hospitalization or in need of medical or hospital care was arrested for, charged with, or convicted of an offense constituting a misdemeanor, the court in proceedings under Section 4011 or the sheriff or jailer in action taken under Section 4011.5 may direct that the guard be removed from the prisoner while he is in the hospital. If such direction is given, any such prisoner who knowingly escapes or attempts to escape from such hospital shall upon conviction thereof be guilty of a misdemeanor and punishable by imprisonment for not to exceed one year in the county jail if such escape or attempt to escape was not by force or violence. However, if such escape is by force or violence such prisoner shall be guilty of a felony and punishable by imprisonment in the state prison, or in the county jail for not exceeding one year; provided, that when such second term of imprisonment is to be served in the county jail it shall commence from the time such prisoner would otherwise be discharged from such jail.

§4011.8. Voluntary treatment, mental health service.

A person in custody who has been charged with or convicted of a criminal offense may make voluntary application for inpatient or outpatient mental health services in accordance with Section 5003 of the Welfare and Institutions Code. If such services require absence from the jail premises, consent from the person in charge of the jail or from any judge of a court in the county in which the jail is located, and from the director of the county mental health program in which services are to be rendered, shall be obtained. The local mental health director or his designee may examine the prisoner prior to transfer from the jail.

Where the court approves voluntary treatment for a jail inmate for whom criminal proceedings are pending, the court shall forthwith notify counsel for the prisoner and the prosecuting attorney about such approval. Where the person in charge of the jail approves voluntary treatment for a prisoner for whom criminal proceedings are pending, the person in charge of the jail shall immediately notify each court within the county where the prisoner has a pending proceeding about such approval; upon notification by the jailer the court shall forthwith notify the prosecuting attorney and counsel for the prisoner in the criminal proceedings about such transfer.

If the prisoner voluntarily obtains treatment in a facility or is placed on outpatient treatment pursuant to Section 5003 of the Welfare and Institutions Code, the time passed therein shall count as part of the prisoner's sentence. When the prisoner is permitted absence from the jail for voluntary treatment, the person in charge of the jail shall advise the professional person in charge of the facility of the expiration date of the prisoner's sentence. If the prisoner is to be released from the facility before such expiration date, the professional person in charge shall notify the local mental health director or his designee, counsel for the prisoner, the prosecuting attorney, and the person in charge of the jail, who shall send for, take, and receive the prisoner back into the jail.

A denial of an application for voluntary mental health services shall be reviewable only by mandamus.

§4011.9. Removal of hospital guard; certain situations.

Notwithstanding the provisions of Sections 4011 and 4011.5, when it appears that the prisoner in need of medical or surgical treatment necessitating hospitalization or in need of medical or hospital care was arrested for, charged with, or convicted of an offense constituting a felony, the court in proceedings under Section 4011 or the sheriff or jailer in action taken under Section 4011.5 may direct that the guard be removed from the prisoner while he is in the hospital, if it reasonably appears that the prisoner is physically unable to effectuate an escape or the prisoner does not constitute a danger to life or property.

§4012. Transfer of prisoners; outbreak of disease.

When a pestilence or contagious disease breaks out in or near a jail, and the physician thereof certifies that it is liable to endanger the health of the prisoners, the county judge may, by a written appointment, designate a safe and convenient place in the county, or the jail in a contiguous county, as the place of their confinement. The appointment must be filed in the office of the county clerk, and authorize the sheriff to remove the prisoners to the place or jail designated, and there confine them until they can be safely returned to the jail from which they were taken.

§4013. Delivery of judicial proceedings papers.

A sheriff or jailer upon whom a paper in a judicial proceeding, directed to a prisoner in his custody, is served, must forthwith deliver it to the prisoner, with a note thereon of the time of its service. For a neglect to do so he is liable to the prisoner for all damages occasioned thereby.

§4014. Temporary guards' employment.

The sheriff, when necessary, may, with the assent in writing of the county judge, or in a city, of the mayor

thereof, employ a temporary guard for the protection of the county jail, or for the safekeeping of prisoners, the expenses of which are a county charge.

§4015. Sheriff must receive duly committed prisoners' necessities.

The sheriff shall receive all persons committed to jail by competent authority. The board of supervisors shall provide the sheriff with necessary food, clothing, and bedding, for those prisoners, which shall be of a quality and quantity at least equal to the minimum standards and requirements prescribed by the Board of Corrections for the feeding, clothing, and care of prisoners in all county, city and other local jails and detention facilities. Except as provided in Section 4016, the expenses thereof shall be paid out of the county treasury. *(Amended by Stats 1987 ch 828 §133.)*

§4016. Persons committed on civil process.

Whenever a person is committed upon process in a civil action or proceeding, except when the people of this State are a party thereto, the sheriff is not bound to receive such person, unless security is given on the part of the party at whose instance the process is issued, by a deposit of money, to meet the expenses for him of necessary food, clothing, and bedding, or to detain such person any longer than these expenses are provided for. This section does not apply to cases where a party is committed as a punishment for disobedience to the mandates, process, writs, or orders of court.

§4016.5. Alleged parole violator; reimbursement for costs of detention.

A city or county shall be reimbursed by the Department of Corrections for costs incurred resulting from the detention of state prisoners or parolees and from parole revocation proceedings when the detention meets any of the following conditions:

(a) The detention relates to a violation of the conditions of parole or the rules and regulations of the Director of Corrections and does not relate to a new criminal charge.

(b) The detention is pursuant to (1) an order of the Board of Prison Terms under the authority granted by Section 3060, or (2) an order of the Governor under the authority granted by Section 3062 or (3) an exercise of a state parole or correctional officer's peace officer powers as specified in Section 830.5.

(c) Security services and facilities are provided for hearings which are conducted by the Board of Prison Terms to revoke parole.

Such reimbursement shall be expended for maintenance, upkeep, and improvement of jail conditions, facilities, and services. Before the county is reimbursed by the department, the total amount of all charges against that county authorized by law for services rendered by the department shall be first deducted from the gross amount of reimbursement authorized by this section. The net reimbursement shall be calculated and paid monthly by the department. The department shall withhold all or part of the net reimbursement to a county whose jail facility or facilities do not conform to minimum standards for local detention facilities as authorized by Section 6030 only if the county is failing to make reasonable efforts to correct differences, with consideration given to the resources available for those purposes.

"Costs incurred resulting from the detention," as used in this section, shall include the same cost factors

© 1992 by J., B. & L. Gould
Printed in the U.S.A.   EP

as are utilized by the Department of Corrections in determining the cost of prisoner care in state correctional facilities.

§4017. Prisoners required to perform labor or engage in fire prevention or suppression.

All persons confined in the county jail, industrial farm, road camp, or city jail under a final judgment of imprisonment rendered in a criminal action or proceeding and all persons confined in the county jail, industrial farm, road camp, or city jail as a condition of probation after suspension of imposition of a sentence or suspension of execution of sentence may be required by an order of the board of supervisors or city council to perform labor on the public works or ways in the county or city, respectively, and to engage in the prevention and suppression of forest, brush and grass fires upon lands within the county or city, respectively, or upon lands in adjacent counties where the suppression of fires would afford fire protection to lands within the county.

Whenever any such person so in custody shall suffer injuries or death while working in the prevention or suppression of forest, brush or grass fires he shall be considered to be an employee of the county or city, respectively, for the purposes of compensation under the provisions of the Labor Code regarding workmen's compensation and such work shall be performed under the direct supervision of a local, state or federal employee whose duties include fire prevention and suppression work. A regularly employed member of an organized fire department shall not be required to directly supervise more than 20 such persons so in custody.

As used in this section, "labor on the public works" includes clerical and menial labor in the county jail, industrial farm, camps maintained for the labor of such persons upon the ways in the county, or city jail.

§4017.5. Labor by persons confined for contempt.

In any case in which a person is confined to a city or county jail for a definite period of time for contempt pursuant to an action or proceeding other than a criminal action or proceeding, all of the provisions of law authorizing, requiring, or otherwise relating to, the performance of labor or work by persons sentenced to such facilities for like periods of time under a judgment of imprisonment, or a fine and imprisonment until the fine is paid or as a condition of probation after suspension of imposition of a sentence or suspension of execution of sentence, in a criminal action or proceeding, shall apply.

Nothing in this section shall be construed to authorize the confinement of any prisoner contrary to the provisions of Section 4001.

§4018. Rules and regulations.

The board of supervisors making such order may prescribe and enforce the rules and regulations under which such labor is to be performed; and provide clothing of such a distinctive character for said prisoners as such board, in its discretion, may deem proper.

§4018.1. Information about AIDS for inmates.

Subject to the availability of adequate state funding for these purposes, the sheriff of each county shall provide inmates who have been sentenced for drug-related offenses with information about behavior that places a person at high risk for contracting the human immunodeficiency virus (HIV), and about the prevention of the transmission of acquired immune deficiency syndrome (AIDS). Each county sheriff or the chief county probation officer shall provide all inmates who have been sentenced for drug-related offenses, who are within one month of release, or who have been placed on probation, with information about behavior that places a person at high risk for contracting HIV, about the prevention of the transmission of AIDS, and about agencies and facilities that provide testing, counseling, medical, and support services for AIDS victims. Information about AIDS prevention shall be solicited by each county sheriff or chief county probation officer from the State Department of Health Services, the county health officer, or local agencies providing services to persons with AIDS. The Director of Health Services, or his or her designee, shall approve protocols pertaining to the information to be disseminated under this section. *(Added by Stats 1988 ch 1301 §1, eff. 1/1/89.)*

§4018.5. Vocational training, rehabilitation of prisoners.

The sheriff or other official in charge of county correctional facilities may, subject to the approval of the board of supervisors, provide for the vocational training and rehabilitation of prisoners confined in the county jail, or any county industrial farm or county or joint county road camp. The sheriff or other official in charge of county correctional facilities may, subject to such approval, enter into an agreement with the governing board of any school district maintaining secondary schools, for the maintenance, by the district, for such prisoners, of adult education classes conducted pursuant to the Education Code.

§4018.6. Temporary removal or release.

The sheriff of the county may authorize the temporary removal under custody or temporary release without custody of any inmate of the county jail, honor farm, or other detention facility for family emergencies or for purposes preparatory to his return to the community, if the sheriff concludes that such inmate is a fit subject therefor. Any such temporary removal shall not be for a period of more than three days. When an inmate is released for purposes preparatory to his return to the community, the sheriff may require the inmate to reimburse the county, in whole or in part, for expenses incurred by the county in connection therewith.

§4019. Deductions; confinement period.

(a) The provisions of this section shall apply in all of the following cases:

(1) When a prisoner is confined in or committed to a county jail, industrial farm, or road camp, or any city jail, industrial farm, or road camp, including all days of custody from the date of arrest to the date on which the serving of the sentence commences, under a judgment of imprisonment, or a fine and imprisonment until the fine is paid in a criminal action or proceeding.

(2) When a prisoner is confined in or committed to the county jail, industrial farm, or road camp or any city jail, industrial farm, or road camp as a condition of probation after suspension of imposition of a sentence or suspension of execution of sentence, in a criminal action or proceeding.

(3) When a prisoner is confined in or committed to the county jail, industrial farm, or road camp or any

city jail, industrial farm, or road camp for a definite period of time for contempt pursuant to a proceeding, other than a criminal action or proceeding.

(4) When a prisoner is confined in a county jail, industrial farm, or road camp, or a city jail, industrial farm, or road camp following arrest and prior to the imposition of sentence for a felony conviction.

(b) Subject to the provisions of subdivision (d), for each six-day period in which a prisoner is confined in or committed to a facility as specified in this section, one day shall be deducted from his or her period of confinement unless it appears by the record that the prisoner has refused to satisfactorily perform labor as assigned by the sheriff, chief of police, or superintendent of an industrial farm or road camp.

(c) For each six-day period in which a prisoner is confined in or committed to a facility as specified in this section, one day shall be deducted from his or her period of confinement unless it appears by the record that the prisoner has not satisfactorily complied with the reasonable rules and regulations established by the sheriff, chief of police, or superintendent of an industrial farm or road camp.

(d) Nothing in this section shall be construed to require the sheriff, chief of police, or superintendent of an industrial farm or road camp to assign labor to a prisoner if it appears from the record that the prisoner has refused to satisfactorily perform labor as assigned or that the prisoner has not satisfactorily complied with the reasonable rules and regulations of the sheriff, chief of police, or superintendent of any industrial farm or road camp.

(e) No deduction may be made under this section unless the person is committed for a period of six days or longer.

(f) It is the intent of the Legislature that if all days are earned under this section, a term of six days will be deemed to have been served for every four days spent in actual custody.

§4019.3. Money credit for work.

The board of supervisors may provide that each prisoner confined in or committed to a county jail shall be credited with a sum not to exceed two dollars ($2) for each eight hours of work done by him in such county jail.

§4019.5. Kangaroo court and sanitary committee.

(a) "Kangaroo court" as used in this section means a mock court conducted by any prisoner or group of prisoners for the purpose of inflicting punishment upon any fellow prisoner in any prison, jail, jail camp, or other place of detention.

(b) "Sanitary committee" means a committee of prisoners formed ostensibly for the purpose of enforcing institutional sanitation but actually used for the purpose of inflicting punishment on any fellow prisoner, or group of prisoners in any prison, jail, jail camp, or other place of detention.

(c) It is unlawful for any sheriff, deputy sheriff, constable, police officer, warden or keeper of a jail to delegate to any prisoner or group of prisoners, authority to exercise the right of punishment over any other prisoner or group of prisoners in any county or city prison, jail, jail camp, or other place of detention at which any person charged with or convicted of crime is detained.

(d) It is unlawful for any such sheriff, deputy sheriff, constable, police officer, warden or keeper of a jail to knowingly permit any prisoner or group of prisoners to assume authority over any other prisoner or group of prisoners by the operation of "kangaroo courts" or "sanitary committees."

(e) Every public official in charge of a prison, jail or other place of detention shall keep a record of all disciplinary infractions and punishment administered therefor.

(f) This section shall not prevent the use of skilled inmates, under adequate and proper supervision and guidance of jailers or other employed personnel, as instructors of other inmates in the performance of assigned work, if such relationship does not include the exercise of disciplinary authority.

§4020. Cutting prisoners' hair.

Whenever the board of health of any city or county, or the board of supervisors of any county, or the county physician of any county of this State, presents, or causes to be presented to the sheriff, or other officer having charge of any county jail or prison in any county or city, in this State, a certificate, or order, in writing, to the effect that it is by them, or him, considered necessary for the purpose of protecting the public health, or to prevent the introduction or spreading of disease, or to protect or improve the health of criminals under sentence, that the hair of any criminal or criminals be cut, such sheriff, or other officer, must cut, or cause to be cut, the hair of any such person or persons in his charge convicted of a misdemeanor and sentenced to a longer term of imprisonment than 15 days, to a uniform length of one and one-half inches from the scalp of such person or persons so imprisoned.

§4020.4. Female deputy sheriff; appointment.

In every county having a population of more than 275,000, there shall be a female deputy sheriff in charge of female prisoners.

The sheriff of the county shall appoint the female deputy sheriff in charge of female prisoners.

§4020.7. Powers and duties.

The duties and powers of the female deputy sheriff or other suitable woman assigned to jail duty shall be as follows:

(a) She shall have free access at all reasonable times to the immediate presence of all female prisoners in the county jail to which she is assigned, including the right of personal visitation and conversation with them, and in all cases of searching the persons of female prisoners in such jail, the female deputy sheriff shall make such search;

(b) The female deputy sheriff or other suitable woman shall by example, advice, and admonition employ her best abilities to secure and promote the health, welfare, and reformation of all such prisoners.

§4020.8. Access to female prisoners.

No officer, deputy, jailer, keeper, guard, or person having charge or control of any such county jail shall refuse the duly appointed and qualified female deputy sheriff thereof, or other suitable woman having the care of female prisoners, free access at all reasonable times to the immediate presence of all female prisoners therein, including the right of visitation and conversation with them, or in such jail allow the searching of the person of a female prisoner to be made

© 1992 by J., B. & L. Gould
Printed in the U.S.A.   EP

except by the female deputy sheriff of such jail or other suitable woman, or obstruct the performance by the female deputy sheriff, or other suitable woman, of her official duties.

§4021. Acting female deputy sheriff; searches of prisoners of opposite sex.

(a) Whenever any female prisoner or prisoners are confined in any local detention facility in the state there shall be an appropriately trained female custodial person assigned, available, and accessible for the supervision of the female prisoners.

(b) It shall be unlawful for any officer, station officer, jailer, or custodial personnel to search the person of any prisoner of the opposite sex, or to enter into the room or cell occupied by any prisoner of the opposite sex, except in the company of an employee of the same sex as the prisoner. Except as provided herein, the provisions of this subdivision shall not be applied to discriminate against any employee by prohibiting appointment or work assignment on the basis of the sex of the employee.

As used in this subdivision "station officer" means an unarmed civilian employee who assists a peace officer in the processing of persons who have been arrested and who performs duties including, but not limited to, booking and fingerprinting and maintaining custody and control of persons who have been arrested.

As used in this subdivision, "employee" means a deputy sheriff, correctional officer, custodial officer, medical staff person or designated civilian employee whose duties may include, but are not limited to, maintaining custody and control of persons who have been arrested or sentenced, or both.

§4022. Construction of terms county jail and city jail.

Whenever by the terms of this code, or of any other law of the State, it is provided that a prisoner shall be confined in any county jail, such provision shall be construed to authorize any prisoner convicted in a municipal or justice court to be confined, with the consent of the city, in any city jail in the judicial district in which the offense was committed, and as to such prisoner so confined in such city jail, the designations, county jail and city jail shall be interchangeable, and in such case the obligations to which the county is liable in case of confinement in a county jail, shall become liabilities of the city where such prisoner is confined in a city jail.

§4023. Full-time physician.

Whenever the daily average of more than 100 persons are confined in any county or city jail there shall be available at all times a duly licensed and practicing physician for the care and treatment of all persons confined therein. Such daily average shall be determined by the number of persons confined in such jails during the last fiscal year. For county jails, such physician shall be designated by the sheriff. The salary of such physician shall be fixed by the supervisors of the county and shall be paid out of the same fund of the county as other claims against the county for salaries are paid. For city jails, such physician shall be designated and his salary fixed by the council of the city and shall be paid out of the general fund of such city. Any prisoner may decline such care or treatment

and provide other care or treatment for himself at his own expense.

In the event a prisoner elects to decline treatment by the county or city jail physician and to provide medical treatment at his own expense, the sheriff or chief of police may have him removed from the county or city jail to a privately owned and operated medical facility or hospital located in the county approved by a judge of the superior court for such treatment. The prisoner shall be liable for the costs incurred by the county or city in providing the necessary custody and security of the prisoner only to the extent that such costs exceed the costs which would have been incurred by the county or city in providing such custody and security if it had provided treatment for him. The prisoner shall at all times remain in the location specified by the court and at no time be permitted to be housed or detained at any facility other than that designated.

§4023.5. Personal hygiene, birth control and family planning services.

(a) Any female confined in any local detention facility shall upon her request be allowed to continue to use materials necessary for (1) personal hygiene with regard to her menstrual cycle and reproductive system and (2) birth control measures as prescribed by her physician.

(b) Each and every female confined in any local detention facility shall be furnished by the county with information and education regarding the availability of family planning services.

(c) Family planning services shall be offered to each and every woman inmate at least 60 days prior to a scheduled release date. Upon request any woman inmate shall be furnished by the county with the services of a licensed physician or she shall be furnished by the county or by any other agency which contracts with the county with services necessary to meet her family planning needs at the time of her release.

(d) For the purposes of this section, "local detention facility" means any city, county, or regional facility used for the confinement of any female prisoner for more than 24 hours.

§4023.6. Female prisoners' pregnancy services.

Any female prisoner in any local detention facility shall have the right to summon and receive the services of any physician and surgeon of her choice in order to determine whether she is pregnant. The superintendent of such facility may adopt reasonable rules and regulations with regard to the conduct of examinations to effectuate such determination.

If the prisoner is found to be pregnant, she is entitled to a determination of the extent of the medical services needed by her and to the receipt of such services from the physician and surgeon of her choice. Any expenses occasioned by the services of a physician and surgeon whose services are not provided by the facility shall be borne by the prisoner.

For the purposes of this section, "local detention facility" means any city, county, or regional facility used for the confinement of any female prisoner for more than 24 hours.

Any physician providing services pursuant to this section shall possess a current, valid, and unrevoked certificate to engage in the practice of medicine issued pursuant to Chapter 5 (commencing with Section

2000) of Division 2 of the Business and Professions Code.

The rights provided for prisoners by this section shall be posted in at least one conspicuous place to which all female prisoners have access.

§4024. Time of day of discharge from jail.

The sheriff may discharge any prisoner from the county jail at such time on the last day such prisoner may be confined as the sheriff shall consider to be in the best interests of the prisoner.

§4024.1. Accelerated release.

(a) The sheriff, chief of police, or any other person responsible for a county or city jail may apply to the presiding judge of the justice, municipal, or superior court to receive general authorization for a period of 30 days to release inmates pursuant to the provisions of this section.

(b) Whenever, after being authorized by a court pursuant to subdivision (a), the actual inmate count exceeds the actual bed capacity of a county or city jail, the sheriff, chief of police, or other person responsible for such county or city jail may accelerate the release, discharge, or expiration of sentence date of sentenced inmates up to a maximum of five days.

(c) The total number of inmates released pursuant to this section shall not exceed a number necessary to balance the inmate count and actual bed capacity.

(d) Inmates closest to their normal release, discharge, or expiration of sentence date shall be given accelerated release priority.

(e) The number of days that release, discharge, or expiration of sentence is accelerated shall in no case exceed 10 percent of the particular inmate's original sentence, prior to the application thereto of any other credits or benefits authorized by law.

§4024.2. Labor on public works and ways.

(a) Notwithstanding any other provision of law, the board of supervisors of any county may authorize the sheriff or other official in charge of county correctional facilities to offer a voluntary program under which any person committed to the facility may participate in a work release program pursuant to criteria described in subdivision (b), in which one day of participation will be in lieu of one day of confinement.

(b) The criteria for a work release program are the following:

(1) The work release program shall consist of manual labor to improve or maintain levees or public facilities, including, but not limited to, streets, parks, and schools.

(2) In addition, the sheriff or other official may permit a prisoner participating in a work release program to receive work release credit for participation in education, vocational training, or substance abuse programs in lieu of performing labor in a work release program on an hour-for-hour basis. However, credit for that participation may not exceed one-half of the hours established for the work release program, and the remaining hours shall consist of manual labor described in paragraph (1).

(3) The work release program shall be under the direction of a responsible person appointed by the sheriff or other official in charge.

(4) The hours of labor to be performed pursuant to this section shall be uniform for all persons committed to a facility in a county and may be determined by the sheriff or other official in charge of county correctional facilities, and each day shall be a minimum of 8 and a maximum of 10 hours, in accordance with the normal working hours of county employees assigned to supervise the programs. However, reasonable accommodation may be made for participation in a program under paragraph (2).

As used in this section, "labor on levees or on the public works and ways" means manual labor to improve or maintain levees or public facilities, including, but not limited to, streets, parks, and schools.

(c) The board of supervisors may prescribe reasonable rules and regulations under which a work release program is operated and may provide that such persons wear clothing of a distinctive character while performing such work. As a condition of participating in a work release program, a person shall give his or her promise to appear for work or assigned activity by signing a notice to appear before the sheriff or at the education, vocational, or substance abuse program at a time and place specified in the notice and shall sign an agreement that the sheriff may immediately retake such person into custody to serve the balance of his or her sentence if such person fails to appear for the program at the time and place agreed to, does not perform the work or activity assigned, or for any other reason is no longer a fit subject for release under this section. A copy of the notice shall be delivered to the person and a copy shall be retained by the sheriff. Any person who willfully violates his or her written promise to appear at the time and place specified in the notice is guilty of a misdemeanor.

Whenever a peace officer has reasonable cause to believe the person has failed to appear at the time and place specified in the notice or fails to appear or work at the time and place agreed to or has failed to perform the work assigned, the peace officer may, without a warrant, retake the person into custody, or the court may issue an arrest warrant for the retaking of the person into custody, to complete the remainder of the original sentence. A peace officer may not retake a person into custody under this subdivision, without a warrant for arrest, unless the officer has a written order to do so, signed by the sheriff or other person in charge of the program, which describes with particularity the person to be retaken.

(d) Nothing in this section shall be construed to require the sheriff or other such official to assign a person to a program pursuant to this section if it appears from the record that the person has refused to satisfactorily perform as assigned or has not satisfactorily complied with the reasonable rules and regulations governing such assignment or any other order of the court.

A person shall be eligible for work release under this section only if the sheriff or other official in charge concludes that the person is a fit subject therefor.

(e) The board of supervisors may prescribe a program administrative fee, not to exceed the pro rata cost of administration, to be paid by each person according to his or her ability to pay. (*Amended by Stats 1990 ch 146 §1, eff. 6/19/90.*)

§4025. Establishment of jail store.

(a) The sheriff of each county may establish, maintain and operate a store in connection with the county jail and for this purpose may purchase confectionery, tobacco and tobacco users' supplies, postage and writing materials, and toilet articles and supplies and to

© 1992 by J., B. & L. Gould
Printed in the U.S.A.   EP

sell these goods, articles, and supplies for cash to inmates in the jail.

(b) The sale prices of the articles offered for sale at the store shall be fixed by the sheriff. Any profit shall be deposited in an inmate welfare fund to be kept in the treasury of the county.

(c) There shall also be deposited in the inmate welfare fund 10 percent of all gross sales of inmate hobbycraft.

(d) There shall be deposited in the inmate welfare fund any money, refund, rebate, or commission received from a telephone company or pay telephone provider when the money, refund, rebate, or commission is attributable to the use of pay telephones which are primarily used by inmates while incarcerated.

(e) The money and property deposited in the inmate welfare fund shall be expended by the sheriff solely for the benefit, education, and welfare of the inmates confined within the jail. An itemized report of these expenditures shall be submitted annually to the board of supervisors.

(f) The operation of a store within any other county adult detention facility which is not under the jurisdiction of the sheriff shall be governed by the provisions of this section, except that the board of supervisors shall designate the proper county official to exercise the duties otherwise allocated in this section to the sheriff.

(g) The operation of a store within any city adult detention facility shall be governed by the provisions of this section, except that city officials shall assume the respective duties otherwise outlined in this section for county officials.

(h) The treasurer may, pursuant to Article 1 (commencing with Section 53600), or Article 2 (commencing with Section 53630), of Chapter 4 of Part 1 of Division 2 of Title 5 of the Government Code, deposit, invest, or reinvest any part of the inmate welfare fund, in excess of that which the treasurer deems necessary for immediate use. The interest or increment accruing on these funds shall be deposited in the inmate welfare fund.

(i) The sheriff may expend money from the inmate welfare fund to provide indigent inmates, prior to release from the county jail or any other adult detention facility under the jurisdiction of the sheriff, with essential clothing and transportation expenses within the county or, at the discretion of the sheriff, transportation to the inmate's county of residence, if the county is within the state or 500 miles from the county of incarceration. This subdivision does not authorize expenditure of money from the inmate welfare fund for the transfer of any inmate to the custody of any other law enforcement official or jurisdiction. *(Amended by Stats 1989, ch 127 §1 eff. 1/1/90.)*

§4026. Manufacture and sale of convict-made goods.

The sheriff or other officer in charge of a county or city jail may provide for the manufacture of small articles of handiwork by prisoners out of raw materials purchased by the prisoners with their own funds or funds borrowed from the inmate welfare fund, which articles may be sold to the public at the county or city jails, in public buildings, at fairs, or on property operated by nonprofit associations. County-or city-owned property shall not be sold or given to prisoners for use under this section, except as expressly permitted by this section. The sheriff or other officer in

charge shall comply with subdivision (c) of Section 4025 and provide that the balance of the sale price of the articles be deposited to the account of the prisoner manufacturing the article after repaying the inmate welfare fund any amount borrowed.

§4027. Exercise of religious freedom.

It is the intention of the Legislature that all prisoners confined in local detention facilities shall be afforded reasonable opportunities to exercise religious freedom.

As used in this section "local detention facility" means any city, county, or regional facility used for the confinement of prisoners for more than 24 hours.

§4028. Permitting abortion for pregnant prisoner.

No condition or restriction upon the obtaining of an abortion by a female detained in any local detention facility, pursuant to the Therapeutic Abortion Act (Chapter 11 (commencing with Section 25950), Division 20 of the Health and Safety Code), other than those contained in that act, shall be imposed. Females found to be pregnant and desiring abortions shall be permitted to determine their eligibility for an abortion pursuant to law, and if determined to be eligible, shall be permitted to obtain an abortion.

For the purposes of this section, "local detention facility" means any city, county, or regional facility used for the confinement of any female person for more than 24 hours.

The rights provided for females by this section shall be posted in at least one conspicuous place to which all female prisoners have access. *(Amended by Stats 1987 ch 828 §134.)*

§4029. Equal facilities and programs for prisoners of both sexes.

(a) Whenever within any county adult detention facility or part of any county detention facility used for the confinement of adults, not including any city jail, any facility, including but not limited to any room or cell, vocational training facility, recreation area, rest area, dining room, store, or facility for the exercise of religious freedom, is provided for use by any prisoner for any purpose, a separate facility of equal quality, or separate use of the same facility, or joint use of the same facility where appropriate, shall be provided for prisoners of the opposite sex for such purpose.

(b) Whenever within any county adult detention facility or part of any county detention facility used for the confinement of adults, not including any city jail, any program, service or privilege, including but not limited to any general or vocational education, physical education or recreation, work furlough program, psychological counseling, work within the institution, visiting privileges, or medical treatment, is provided for any prisoner, such a program, service or privilege of equal quality shall be provided for prisoners of the opposite sex, except when the proportion of prisoners of one sex is so small that the cost of providing any program, service or privilege described in this subdivision, other than medical treatment or health maintenance, for such prisoners would not be justified in relation to the reduction in the level of any other program, service or privilege that would result from the diversion of funds for such purpose.

(c) Nothing in this section shall require the establishment of any facility for the use of, or the making available of any program, service or privilege to, any prisoner. Nothing in this section shall require any facility, program, service or privilege established or available prior or subsequent to January 1, 1975, to be made available to any particular male or female prisoner or number of such prisoners, except that any type of facility, program, service or privilege which is made accessible or available to all male or female prisoners in any class defined by subdivisions 1, 2, and 3 of Section 4001 shall be made accessible or available to all prisoners of the opposite sex in such class as provided in subdivisions (a) and (b), and any criterion other than the sex of the prisoner which is used for the selection of a particular prisoner or group of prisoners to have, or to have access to, any facility, program, service or privilege shall be equally applied to the selection of all prisoners, regardless of sex.

(d) Every county shall comply with subdivisions (a), (b), and (c) by January 1, 1979. Such compliance shall not be required unless the Legislature provides funds to assist in the accomplishment of such compliance. Every county shall report to the Legislature by January 1, 1976, as to whether such compliance can be accomplished, and stating the reasons why it cannot be accomplished if that be the case.

(e) Whenever within any county adult detention facility or part of any county detention facility used for the confinement of adults, not including any city jail, an inpatient psychiatric facility designated by the county mental health director to treat patients under Division 5 (commencing with Section 5000) and Division 6 (commencing with Section 6000) of the Welfare and Institutions Code, is provided for prisoners of one sex who may not depart from the detention facility for treatment elsewhere, and where the proportion of prisoners of the opposite sex requiring the same type of treatment is so small that the cost of providing a separate program of equal quality would not be justified in relation to the reduction in the level of another program, service, or privilege that would result from the diversion of funds for such purpose, the above designated mental health treatment program may treat prisoners of both sexes if each of the following conditions is met:

(1) The program is one that would be considered suitable for the treatment of patients of both sexes if it were located in a psychiatric treatment facility devoted to evaluation and treatment under Division 5 (commencing with Section 5000) and Division 6 (commencing with Section 6000) of the Welfare and Institutions Code for patients who are not prisoners.

(2) A female deputy sheriff or other suitable woman assigned to jail duty is assigned to the treatment program in accordance with Sections 4020.4, 4020.7, 4020.8, and 4021 of this code. Notwithstanding the provisions of Section 4020.4 of this code, in a county of any size, the sheriff may designate a female member of the mental health treatment staff for this assignment.

§4030. Strip and body cavity searches.

(a) The Legislature finds and declares that law enforcement policies and practices for conducting strip or body cavity searches of detained persons vary widely throughout California. Consequently, some people have been arbitrarily subjected to unnecessary strip and body cavity searches after arrests for minor misdemeanor and infraction offenses. Some present search practices violate state and federal constitution-

al rights to privacy and freedom from unreasonable searches and seizures.

It is the intent of the Legislature in enacting this section to protect the state and federal constitutional rights of the people of California by establishing a statewide policy strictly limiting strip and body cavity searches.

(b) The provisions of this section shall apply only to prearraignment detainees arrested for infraction or misdemeanor offenses and to any minor detained prior to a detention hearing on the grounds that he or she is a person described in Section 300, 601, or 602 of the Welfare and Institutions Code alleged to have committed a misdemeanor or infraction offense. The provisions of this section shall not apply to any person in the custody of the Director of the Department of Corrections or the Director of the Youth Authority.

(c) As used in this section, "strip search" means a search which requires a person to remove or arrange some or all of his or her clothing so as to permit a visual inspection of the underclothing, breasts, buttocks, or genitalia of such person.

(d) As used in this section:

(1) "Body cavity" only means the stomach or rectal cavity of a person, and vagina of a female person.

(2) "Visual body cavity search" means visual inspection of a body cavity.

(3) "Physical body cavity search" means physical intrusion into a body cavity for the purpose of discovering any object concealed in the body cavity.

(e) Notwithstanding any other provision of law, including Section 40304.5 of the Vehicle Code, when a person is arrested and taken into custody, that person may be subjected to patdown searches, metal detector searches, and thorough clothing searches in order to discover and retrieve concealed weapons and contraband substances prior to being placed in a booking cell.

(f) No person arrested and held in custody on a misdemeanor or infraction offense, except those involving weapons, controlled substances or violence nor any minor detained prior to a detention hearing on the grounds that he or she is a person described in Section 300, 601 or 602 of the Welfare and Institutions Code, except for those minors alleged to have committed felonies or offenses involving weapons, controlled substances or violence, shall be subjected to a strip search or visual body cavity search prior to placement in the general jail population, unless a peace officer has determined there is reasonable suspicion based on specific and articulable facts to believe such person is concealing a weapon or contraband, and a strip search will result in the discovery of the weapon or contraband. No strip search or visual body cavity search or both may be conducted without the prior written authorization of the supervising officer on duty. The authorization shall include the specific and articulable facts and circumstances upon which the reasonable suspicion determination was made by the supervisor.

(g)(1) Except pursuant to the provisions of paragraph (2), no person arrested and held in custody on a misdemeanor or infraction offense not involving weapons, controlled substances or violence, shall be confined in the general jail population unless all of the following are true:

(i) The person is not cited and released.

(ii) The person is not released on his or her own recognizance pursuant to Article 9 (commencing with Section 1318) of Chapter 1 of Title 10 of Part 2.

© 1992 by J., B. & L. Gould
Printed in the U.S.A.   EP

(iii) The person is not able to post bail within a reasonable time not less than three hours.

(2) No person may be housed in the general jail population prior to release pursuant to the provisions of paragraph (1) unless a documented emergency exists and there is no reasonable alternative to such placement. Such person shall be placed in the general population only upon prior written authorization documenting the specific facts and circumstances of the emergency. The written authorization shall be signed by the uniformed supervisor of the facility or by a uniformed watch commander. Any person confined in the general jail population pursuant to paragraph (1) shall retain all rights to release on citation, his or her own recognizance, or bail which were preempted as a consequence of the emergency.

(h) No person arrested on a misdemeanor or infraction offense, nor any minor described in subdivision (b), shall be subjected to a physical body cavity search except under the authority of a search warrant issued by a magistrate specifically authorizing the physical body cavity search.

(i) A copy of the prior written authorization required by subdivisions (f) and (g) and the search warrant required by subdivision (h) shall be placed in the agency's records and made available, on request, to the person searched or his or her authorized representative. With regard to any strip, visual or body search, the time, date and place of the search, the name and sex of the person conducting the search and a statement of the results of the search, including a list of any items removed from the person searched, shall be recorded in the agency's records and made available, upon request, to the person searched or his or her authorized representative.

(j) Persons conducting a strip search or a visual body cavity search shall not touch the breasts, buttocks, or genitalia of the person being searched.

(k) A physical body cavity search shall be conducted under sanitary conditions, and only by a physician, nurse practitioner, registered nurse, licensed vocational nurse or emergency medical technician Level II licensed to practice in this state. Any physician engaged in providing health care to detainees and inmates of the facility may conduct physical body cavity searches.

(l) All persons conducting or otherwise present during a strip search or visual or physical body cavity search shall be of the same sex as the person being searched, except for physicians or licensed medical personnel.

(m) All strip, visual and physical body cavity searches shall be conducted in an area of privacy so that the search cannot be observed by persons not participating in the search. Persons are considered to be participating in the search if their official duties relative to search procedure require them to be present at the time the search is conducted.

(n) A person who knowingly and willfully authorizes or conducts a strip, visual or physical body cavity search in violation of this section is guilty of a misdemeanor.

(o) Nothing in this section shall be construed as limiting any common law or statutory rights of any person regarding any action for damages or injunctive relief, or as precluding the prosecution under another provision of law of any peace officer or other person who has violated this section.

(p) Any person who suffers damage or harm as a result of a violation of this section may bring a civil action to recover actual damages, or one thousand dollars ($1,000), whichever is greater. In addition, the court may, in its discretion, award punitive damages, equitable relief as it deems necessary and proper, and costs, including reasonable attorney's fees.

CHAPTER 1.5

JOINT COUNTY JAILS

§4050. Title.

This chapter may be cited as the Joint County Jail Act.

§4051. Formation of district.

Any two or more counties may form a district for the purpose of establishing and operating a joint county jail to serve such counties.

§4052. Powers of jail districts.

Any district organized under this chapter shall have and exercise the powers expressly granted in this chapter, together with such other powers as are reasonably implied therefrom and necessary and proper to carry out the objects and purposes of this chapter.

§4053. Initiation of proceedings to create joint district.

The board of supervisors of any county may initiate proceedings proposing the creation of a joint district for the purpose of maintaining a joint county jail under the provisions of this chapter to be composed of two or more counties by the adoption of a resolution reciting the following:

(1) That it will be beneficial to the public interest to create a joint district for the establishment or operation, or both, of a joint county jail to which persons from any of the counties proposed to be included in the proposed district may be committed.

(2) The names of the counties proposed to be included in the proposed district which will be benefited by the formation thereof.

(3) That it is proposed to create a joint district for the establishment or operation, or both, of a joint county jail under the provisions of this chapter for the counties so named.

§4054. Adoption of resolution.

When adopted, certified copies of the resolution provided for in Section 4053, shall be transmitted to the several clerks of the boards of supervisors in each of the counties named in the resolution other than that in which the proceedings are initiated.

Upon the adoption of the resolution provided for in Section 4053, the board of supervisors of the county adopting the same shall name and appoint two members of the board to represent the county upon the board of directors of the joint district proposed to be organized.

§4055. Considerations by supervisors.

Upon receipt of the resolution adopted under Section 4053, the boards of supervisors of the counties affected and to whom the same may be directed shall consider the advisability of creating and organizing a joint district as proposed in said resolution and, upon determining the facts involved therein, shall severally adopt resolutions either rejecting or approving the proposal to create such joint district. Each resolution of approval shall, in addition to the matters otherwise required herein, also name and appoint the members of the board of supervisors of the county adopting the resolution qualified to represent such county upon the board of directors of the proposed joint district. A certified copy of the resolution of approval shall be forthwith transmitted to the clerk of the board of supervisors initiating the proceedings.

§4056. Adoption of resolution declaring creation and organization of district.

The board of supervisors of any county initiating proceedings for the creation of a joint district under this chapter shall, after the receipt of a copy of the resolution approving the proposal to form such district as provided in Section 4055 from the board of supervisors of each county proposed to be included within any such joint district, adopt a resolution declaring the creation and organization of said joint district and setting forth the names of the counties composing said district. A certified copy of the resolution shall be transmitted to and filed with the Secretary of State, whereupon the joint district shall be deemed created and organized and shall exercise all the powers granted in this chapter and shall bear the name and designation of "Joint County Jail District No. ____ of the State of California."

§4057. District numbers.

All districts organized under this chapter shall be numbered in the order of their creation, the number to be assigned to said district forthwith upon the organization thereof by the Secretary of State, and the Secretary of State shall keep and maintain in his office a list and register showing the joint county jail districts organized under this chapter.

§4058. Certificate of organization; board of directors.

The Secretary of State shall furnish and transmit to the clerk of the board of supervisors of the county adopting the initial resolution for the organization of any district under this chapter a certificate of the organization of the same. Upon receipt of the certificate the clerk shall within 10 days send a certified copy of the certificate to each of the clerks of the several boards of supervisors of the counties constituting the district, and shall also within the time specified in this section notify each supervisor appointed as a member of the board of directors of the district of such fact and of the time and place of the first meeting of the board of directors of the district. The time and place of the meeting shall be fixed and determined by the clerk of the board adopting the initial resolution, but said time of meeting shall be within 30 days after the date of mailing notices thereof. The necessary expense incurred by supervisors in attending and in going to and coming from any meeting of the board of directors of the district shall constitute a county charge of their respective counties.

§4059. Designation as board of directors.

The body formed under Section 4058 shall be called the board of directors of such district.

§4060. Binding agreements.

The members of the board of directors may enter into an agreement for and on behalf of the counties appointing them binding said counties to the joint

enterprise provided for in this chapter and apportioning the cost of establishing and maintaining a joint county jail.

§4061. Charges against counties; collection.

All sums found due from any county according to the provisions of this chapter are a charge against said county, and may be collected in the manner provided by law by the board of directors of a district formed under this chapter, or, in its behalf by the board of supervisors of any county in the district by an action instituted and tried in any county in the district in which the same may be filed.

§4062. Joint county jail.

The board of directors may establish the joint county jail provided for in this chapter and shall provide for the feeding, care, and treatment of prisoners therein, and must conform to such standards for construction, feeding, clothing, bedding and programming as are imposed pursuant to law on county jails.

§4063. Cash revolving fund.

Each county in a district formed under this chapter shall pay from its general fund its proportionate share to the board of directors of such amount as the board may designate to constitute a cash revolving fund to carry on the work and expense of maintaining such joint county jail. Each month a statement of the expense of the joint county jail shall be sent to the board of supervisors of each county in the district, together with a claim for its proportionate share of expenses. Amounts when received shall be paid into the cash revolving fund.

§4064. Commitment to joint county jail.

Convicted persons may be committed to a joint county jail from a county comprising the district the same as if the commitment were to a jail maintained by that county alone.

§4065. Applicability of Chapter 1.

The provisions of Chapter 1 (commencing at Section 4000) of this title shall, so far as appropriate, be applicable to a joint county jail established pursuant to this chapter, and the person appointed by the board of directors to superintend a joint county jail has such powers and duties as has a sheriff, with respect to county jails, under Chapter 1.

§4066. Rules and regulations.

The board of directors may make rules and regulations for the government of a joint county jail not inconsistent with law.

§4067. Dissolution of joint county jail district.

A joint county jail district formed under this chapter may be dissolved in the following manner:

(a) The board or boards of supervisors of a county or counties containing more than fifty percent (50%) of the population of the entire district shall by a unanimous vote adopt a resolution stating that the existence of a joint county jail is no longer desirable for the public welfare and announcing the intention to withdraw therefrom and to dissolve said district.

(b) The resolution or resolutions so adopted shall be communicated to the clerks of the boards of supervisors of all the counties comprising the district and also to the Secretary of State.

© 1992 by J., B. & L. Gould
Printed in the U.S.A. EP

(c) If it appears that the resolution was unanimously adopted by the board or boards of supervisors in the counties desiring to withdraw, and that such county or counties contain more than fifty percent (50%) of the entire population in the district, the Secretary of State shall thereupon certify to the clerks of the boards of supervisors of the counties composing the district that the district is dissolved.

(d) Thereupon the board of directors of the district shall within 90 days:

(1) Abolish the joint county jail;

(2) Return all prisoners therein to the custody of the sheriffs of their respective counties;

(3) Dispose of all equipment belonging to said joint county jail and the district;

(4) Render an accounting to the clerks of the boards of supervisors of the counties composing such district of all sums of money received and paid out since their last previous accounting, including the balance of revolving fund on hand at said last previous accounting;

(5) Apportion and repay to said counties all sums of money then remaining in their hands, and they shall thereupon be relieved of further responsibility in said matter.

CHAPTER 2

COUNTY INDUSTRIAL FARMS AND ROAD CAMPS

ARTICLE 1

COUNTY INDUSTRIAL FARMS

§4100. Article's purpose.

It is the purpose of this article to make possible the substitution of constructive labor for profitless prison confinement in order that those who are charged with or convicted of public offenses and deprived of their liberty may become better citizens because of their disciplinary experience.

§4101. Establishment authority.

In each county an industrial farm or industrial road camp may be established under the provisions of this article.

§4102. Resolution of intention to establish.

Before establishing an industrial farm or industrial road camp in any county the board of supervisors thereof shall adopt a resolution of its intention so to do. The resolution shall state an amount per person per day for which persons from incorporated cities will be maintained on an industrial farm. Certified copies of the resolution shall be forwarded by the clerk of the board of supervisors to the clerks of all incorporated cities within the county.

§4103. Matters set forth in resolution.

Upon receipt of the resolution as provided in Section 4102, the legislative body of any incorporated city wishing to avail itself of the use of a proposed industrial farm shall adopt a resolution setting forth the following matters:

1. The number of persons sentenced to imprisonment in the jail of such city during the fiscal year last preceding the adoption of the resolution of intention by the board of supervisors;

2. The total number of days for which all such persons were imprisoned in the jail of the city during such fiscal year;

3. A declaration of the desire of the city adopting the resolution to have the prisoners of the city cared for by the county on the industrial farm or industrial road camp and of the agreement of the city to pay the county quarterly for the care of the prisoners of the city at the rate set forth in the resolution of intention.

A certified copy of the resolution provided for in this section shall be forwarded to the clerk of the board of supervisors.

§4104. Facts in board of supervisor's minutes.

Any board of supervisors having adopted a resolution of intention to establish an industrial farm or industrial road camp shall ascertain and enter in its minutes the following facts:

(a) The number of persons sentenced to imprisonment in the county jail during the fiscal year last preceding the adoption of the resolution of intention.

(b) The total number of days for which all persons were imprisoned in the county jail during that fiscal year.

(c) The number of persons sentenced from the superior court of the county to any state prison upon conviction of a violation of Section 270 or Section 270a during that fiscal year.

(d) The total number of days for which all persons so sentenced to state prisons were therein imprisoned during that fiscal year. (Amended by Stats 1987 ch 828 §135.)

§4105. Establishment upon ascertaining facts.

Upon ascertaining the facts provided for in Sections 4102 to 4104, inclusive, the board of supervisors may proceed to establish an industrial farm or industrial road camp.

§4106. Land acquisition.

For the purpose of establishing an industrial farm the board of supervisors may acquire by condemnation, purchase, lease or donation as many acres of land suitable for agriculture as may be necessary for the purposes of the farm. Such land may be situate within or without the county and may consist of separate parcels. If the land is without the county no industrial farm may be established thereon without the consent of the board of supervisors of the county in which the land is located. The board of supervisors shall erect on such land such buildings and structures and make such improvements and institute such industries as are necessary or convenient to carry out the purposes of this article.

§4107. Personal property acquisition.

The board of supervisors shall secure by purchase or otherwise personal property convenient or necessary to carry out the purposes of this article. Stock, machinery, or any other property belonging to the county and in use on the county farm or elsewhere may be used on an industrial farm.

§4108. Superintendent and other employees.

The board of supervisors shall employ a superintendent of an industrial farm or camp and such other subordinate persons as may be necessary for the proper administration thereof and the keeping of the prisoners imprisoned thereon. As part of the compensation to be agreed upon for such superintendent and other persons board and lodging may be furnished.

§4109. Rules of discipline.

The board shall also adopt rules governing the administration of a farm or camp formed under the provisions of this article and discipline thereon in furtherance of the purposes of this article, which rules shall be enforced by the superintendent and those subordinate to him.

§4110. Women prisoners.

If women are to be sentenced to an industrial farm, the board of supervisors establishing it shall provide thereon separate quarters for women prisoners, or may establish a separate industrial farm for women prisoners. Nothing in the section shall be construed to impose any requirement upon a county to confine male and female prisoners in the same or an adjoining facility or impose any duty upon a county to establish or maintain programs which involve the joint participation of male and female prisoners.

§4111. Separate farm for women prisoners.

If a separate farm for women prisoners is established it shall be considered as a part of the industrial farm of the county within the meaning of all provisions of this article, except that none but women prisoners shall be admitted to it. A woman assistant to the superintendent of an industrial farm shall be in immediate charge of any farm established for women prisoners only.

§4112. Resolution of establishment of farm or camp.

When land has been acquired and such buildings and structures erected and improvements made as may be immediately necessary for the carrying out of the purposes of this article or arrangements have been made for an industrial road camp or camps, the board of supervisors shall adopt a resolution proclaiming that an industrial farm or road camp has been established in the county and designating a day on and after which persons will be admitted to such farm or camp. Certified copies of the resolution shall be forwarded by the clerk of the board of supervisors to each municipal court judge and each justice court judge in the county.

§4114. County classification committee.

Each county which establishes an industrial farm or camp shall provide a county classification committee, which shall function as follows:

(1) The sheriff shall appoint the members of this committee, which may include members of his staff and qualified citizens of the county. If there is a county jail physician, he shall be an ex officio member of this committee. All committee members shall serve without remuneration.

(2) The committee shall meet at least once weekly for the purpose of assigning each person who has been sentenced to the county jail to the proper degree of custody and treatment within one of the available adult detention facilities operated by the county. Any person assigned to medical treatment may decline such treatment and provide other care or treatment for himself at his own expense.

(3) Each county prisoner serving a jail sentence of over 30 days shall appear before the committee during the first third of his sentence.

(4) City prisoners who have been recommended to the committee by the chief of police may be transferred to the county industrial farm or camp at the option of the committee.

§4115. Initial place of detention.

The county jail shall serve as the initial place of detention for all adult persons committed to the custody of the sheriff, except city prisoners who are transferred to a farm or camp by the county classification committee.

§4115.5. Transfer of prisoners because of inadequate facilities.

The board of supervisors of a county where adequate facilities are not available for prisoners who would otherwise be confined in its county adult detention facilities may enter into an agreement with the board or boards of supervisors of one or more nearby counties whose county adult detention facilities are adequate and are readily accessible from the first county, permitting commitment of misdemeanants, and any persons required to serve a term of imprisonment in county adult detention facilities as a condition of probation, to a jail in a county having adequate facilities that is a party to the agreement. Such agreement must make provision for support of a person so committed or transferred by the county from which he is committed. When such an agreement is in effect commitments may be made by the court and support of any such person shall be a charge upon the county from which he is committed.

§4116. Direct commitment to industrial farm or camp.

No person shall be committed directly by any court to a county industrial farm or camp except as provided in the Welfare and Institutions Code. All other commitments shall be made to the sheriff for placement in such county adult detention facility as the county classification committee may designate.

§4117. Transfer to industrial camp or farm.

No person shall be transferred to an industrial farm or camp unless he has appeared before the county classification committee and has been assigned to that facility.

§4118. Caring for city prisoners.

The legislative body of any incorporated city located in a county which has established an industrial farm or industrial road camp may adopt and forward to the board of supervisors a certified copy of a resolution stating that the city desires to have its prisoners cared for on the industrial farm or camp and agrees to pay therefor quarterly at a rate per prisoner per day, which rate shall be set forth in the resolution.

§4119. Resolution on care of city prisoners.

At its option the board of supervisors may adopt a resolution stating that the county will care for the prisoners of the city on its industrial farm or camp at the rate set forth in the city's resolution specified in Section 4118. A certified copy of the resolution provided for in this section shall be forwarded to the clerk of the city named therein, who shall immediately notify the chief of police of the city.

Thereafter, the chief of police of the city, or his representative, shall meet regularly with the county

© 1992 by J., B. & L. Gould
Printed in the U.S.A.   EP

classification committee for the purpose of determining the eligibility of certain city prisoners for transfer to a county industrial farm or camp. The committee shall consider for transfer only those city prisoners who have been selected and recommended for transfer by the chief of police. In each case, the committee may transfer or reject such prisoners as it sees fit.

§4120. Prisoners' discharge.

Upon the expiration of the sentence of any person imprisoned in any industrial farm or camp, he shall be discharged, and either furnished with transportation to the place where he was convicted or given a sum of money sufficient to pay his fare to such place.

§4121. Costs.

The cost of establishing and maintaining an industrial farm or industrial road camp formed under this article shall be paid out of the county general fund. Any revenue derived from such farm or camp, including that received from any city for the care of its prisoners on said farm, shall be paid into the county general fund.

§4122. Transporting city prisoners; cost.

The cost of transporting city prisoners to an industrial farm or camp shall be borne by the city from whose courts they were committed. All other transportation charges shall be borne by the county and paid out of the general fund.

§4123. County expense for transferred prisoners.

Any person transferred from an industrial farm or camp to the county jail shall be maintained at the jail at the expense of the county as are other prisoners in such jail.

§4124. Rate for care of city prisoners; based on average cost.

Each county board of supervisors may specify a rate to be charged for the care of city prisoners, which rate shall not exceed the average cost to the county of caring for one prisoner per day. In calculating this average cost, the value of the farm products used in other county institutions and in supplying the needs of paupers, incompetents, poor and indigent persons and persons incapacitated by age, disease or accident shall be deducted from the cost of maintenance, and the cost of the original investment in establishing an industrial farm shall not be included. The reasonable value of services rendered by city prisoners to the extent that such services inure to the benefit of the county shall be deducted from the average cost of caring for city prisoners. Cities may, under terms and conditions suitable to the board of supervisors, be assigned prisoners for the purposes authorized by Section 36904 of the Government Code. By mutual agreement between cities and the county, the rate may be changed from time to time.

§4125. Money credit for work.

Each person in custody on any industrial farm or industrial road camp who is found to have any person or persons dependent on him for support, as provided in Section 4127, shall be credited with a sum not to exceed two dollars ($2) for each day of eight hours work done by him on such farm or camp. Every other person in custody on an industrial farm or camp shall be credited with a sum not to exceed one dollar ($1) for each day of eight hours work done by him on such firm or camp.

§4125.1. Contracts for prison labor.

The board of supervisors may contract with the United States or the State of California, or any department or agency thereof, for the performance of work and labor by any person in custody on any county industrial farm or industrial road camp or confined in the county jail or branch thereof under a final judgment of imprisonment rendered in a criminal action or proceeding or as a condition of probation in the suppression of fires within and upon the national forests, state parks, or other lands of the United States or the State of California, or within and upon such other lands, of whatever ownership, contiguous to, or adjacent to said state or federal lands, the suppression of fires upon which other lands affords fire protection to said state or federal lands. Such payments as may be so contracted for and to be paid by the United States or by the State of California for the work and labor so performed by any person so in custody may, by order of the board of supervisors, be credited in full or in part, and upon such terms and conditions as the board shall determine, to any such person so in custody and performing such work and labor, and all in addition to those credits hereinbefore provided in Section 4125 of this code.

Whenever any such person so in custody shall perform the services herein specified he shall be subject to workmen's compensation benefits to the same extent as a county employee, and the board of supervisors shall provide and cover any such person so in custody, while performing such services, with accident, death and compensation insurance as is otherwise regularly provided for employees of the county.

The term "suppression of fires" as herein used shall include the construction of firebreaks and other works of improvement for the prevention and suppression of fire whether or not constructed in the actual course of suppression of existing fires.

§4126. Maximum money credit per day.

The maximum amount per day to be credited to a person in custody on an industrial farm or camp shall be fixed from time to time by the board of supervisors and shall be as large as is justified by the production on the farm or camp but shall not exceed the sums mentioned in this article.

The superintendent of an industrial farm may by order cause an amount less than the maximum per day to be credited to any person because of lack of effort on the part of the person, the amount credited to be in proportion to the effort.

The sum to the credit of each person employed upon an industrial farm upon his discharge shall be paid him in addition to any transportation charge otherwise paid under this article. Any person may, by written order, direct the payment of any sums credited to him under this article to any person dependent upon him or to whom he is indebted.

§4127. Payment of money credits.

The court by whom any person was sentenced may at any time by written order direct payment of all or any part of the sums to be credited to any such person under this article to any person or persons dependent for support on the prisoner. At the time of sentencing the court shall by making inquiry or taking evidence find whether or not any person or persons are dependent upon the defendant for support. A copy of the finding of the court shall be transmitted to the county classification committee.

§4128. Payments to persons other than prisoners.

Payments authorized under this article to be made to any person other than the prisoner may be made weekly on any day designated by the superintendent of the farm or camp.

§4129. Superintendent's revolving fund.

For the purpose of making the payments designated in this article the board of supervisors shall by order provide the superintendent with a revolving fund. Upon order of the board of supervisors the county auditor shall draw a warrant in favor of the superintendent of an industrial farm or camp and the county treasurer shall cash it. Thereafter the superintendent shall receive from the county general fund upon demands supported by receipts all sums paid out by him under the provisions of this section and shall return all sums so received to the revolving fund.

The provisions of Section 29323 of the Government Code are applicable to a revolving fund established pursuant to this section.

§4130. Use of industrial farm products.

So far as practicable those in custody on an industrial farm shall be employed in productive labor. The products of an industrial farm shall be used: first, to maintain the prisoners and employees on such farm; second, to supply other county institutions having need of the same with the farm's products; third, to supply the needs of paupers, incompetents, poor and indigent persons and those incapacitated by age, disease or accident with whose relief and support the county is charged.

§4131. Maintenance of discipline.

Subject to regulations adopted by the board of supervisors the superintendent shall maintain discipline on an industrial farm. Whenever the superintendent reports to the county classification committee which assigned any prisoner to an industrial farm or camp that the prisoner refuses to abide by the rules of the farm or camp or refuses to work thereon, the committee may make an order transferring the prisoner to the county jail or city jail for the unexpired term of his sentence, and all sums credited to the prisoner shall be forfeited by him unless they have been ordered paid to some person dependent upon him. Thereafter the committee may reassign the person to the industrial farm or industrial road camp upon recommendation of the superintendent of the farm or camp.

§4131.5. Battery upon non-inmate.

Every person confined in, sentenced to, or serving a sentence in, a city or county jail, industrial farm, or industrial road camp in this state, who commits a battery upon the person of any individual who is not himself a person confined or sentenced therein, is guilty of a public offense and is punishable by imprisonment in a state prison, or in a county jail for not more than one year.

§4133. Attempts to escape from industrial farm; punishment for.

The boundary of every industrial farm established under the provisions of this article shall be marked by a fence, hedge or by some other visible line. Every person confined on any industrial farm who escapes therefrom or attempts to escape therefrom shall upon conviction thereof be imprisoned in a state prison, or in the county jail or industrial farm for not to exceed one year. Any such imprisonment shall begin at the expiration of the imprisonment in effect at the time of the escape.

§4134. Advisory board; members.

Any board of supervisors which has established or desires to establish an industrial farm or industrial road camp may at any time appoint an advisory board to consist of not less than three nor more than five persons, one member of which shall be a penologist and one member a physician.

§4135. Duties of board.

The advisory board shall acquaint itself with the conduct of the jails in the county, keep itself informed about the administration of the industrial farm or industrial road camp, and report its recommendations and suggestions to the board of supervisors. It may visit any jail within the county, examine the records thereof, and ascertain whether or not there are any other persons illegally committed to or detained at any jail.

The advisory board shall encourage recreational and educational activities on the industrial farm.

§4136. Applicability of §§4011, 4011.5, 4011.6 and 4011.7.

Sections 4011, 4011.5, 4011.6 and 4011.7 are applicable to county industrial firms, county industrial road camps, and joint county road camps established pursuant to this chapter.

§4137. Authority to remove prisoners for medical care, funerals and educational services.

The board of supervisors of any county in which a county industrial farm, industrial road camp, or honor camp has been established may, by ordinance, authorize the sheriff or any such person responsible to the board for the care, treatment, and custody of prisoners assigned to him as sentenced misdemeanants or felons, serving time as a condition of probation, to remove such prisoners from the facility to which they have been assigned under custody, without court order, for purposes such as: private medical, vision, or dental care, psychological care, vocational services, educational services, and funerals.

ARTICLE 2

JOINT COUNTY ROAD CAMP ACT

§4200. Title.

This article shall be known and may be cited as the Joint County Road Camp Act.

§4201. District; purpose of forming.

Any two or more counties may form a district for the purpose of requiring all persons confined in the county jails of such counties, under a final judgment of imprisonment rendered in a criminal action or proceeding, to perform labor on the public works or

© 1992 by J., B. & L. Gould
Printed in the U.S.A.   EP

public highways in all or any of such counties, and to maintain for that purpose one or more joint county road camps in which such jail prisoners of any or all of said counties may work together.

§4202. Powers of district granted.

Any district organized under this article shall have and exercise the powers expressly granted in this article, together with such other powers as are reasonably implied therefrom and necessary and proper to carry out the objects and purposes of this article.

§4203. Resolution for forming joint district.

The board of supervisors of any county may initiate proceedings proposing the creation of a joint district for the purpose of maintaining a joint county road camp or camps under the provisions of this article to be composed of two or more counties having a combined population of not less than 50,000 persons, according to the official census next preceding the formation of such district, by the adoption of a resolution reciting the following:

(1) That it will be beneficial to the public interest to create a joint district wherein persons confined in any county jail within such district under a final judgment of imprisonment rendered in a criminal action or proceeding may be required to perform labor on the public works or ways within said district, and that a joint county road camp or camps be established and maintained for that purpose.

(2) The names of the counties proposed to be included in the proposed district which will be benefited by the formation thereof.

(3) That it is proposed to create a joint district for the establishment and maintenance of a joint county road camp under the provisions of this article composed of the counties so named.

§4204. Adoption of resolution.

When adopted certified copies of the resolution provided for in Section 4203, shall be transmitted to the several clerks of the boards of supervisors in each of the counties named in the resolution other than that in which the proceedings are initiated.

Upon the adoption of the resolution provided for in Section 4203, the board of supervisors of the county adopting the same shall name and appoint a member of the board to represent the county upon the board of directors of the joint district proposed to be organized.

§4205. Consideration of resolution.

Upon receipt of the resolution adopted under Section 4203, the boards of supervisors of the counties affected and to whom the same may be directed shall consider the advisability of creating and organizing a joint district as proposed in said resolution and, upon determining the facts involved therein, shall severally adopt resolutions either rejecting or approving the proposal to create such joint district. Each resolution of approval shall, in addition to the matter otherwise required therein, also name and appoint the member of the board of supervisors of the county adopting the resolution qualified to represent such county upon the board of directors of the proposed joint district. A certified copy of the resolution of approval shall be forthwith transmitted to the clerk of the board of supervisors initiating the proceedings.

§4206. Declaration of creation and organization name.

The board of supervisors of any county initiating proceedings for the creation of a joint district under this article shall, after the receipt of a copy of the resolution approving the proposal to form such district as provided in Section 4205 from the board of supervisors of each county proposed to be included within any such joint district, adopt a resolution declaring the creation and organization of said joint district and setting forth the names of the counties composing said district. A certified copy of the resolution shall be transmitted to and filed with the Secretary of State, whereupon the joint district shall be deemed created and organized and shall exercise all the powers granted in this article and shall bear the name and designation of "Joint County Road Camp District No. __ of the State of California."

§4207. District numbers.

All districts organized under this article shall be numbered in the order of their creation, the number to be assigned to said district forthwith upon the organization thereof by the Secretary of State, and the Secretary of State shall keep and maintain in his office a list and register showing the joint county road camp districts organized under this article.

§4208. Certificate of organization of district.

The Secretary of State shall furnish and transmit to the clerk of the board of supervisors of the county adopting the initial resolution for the organization of any district under this article a certificate of the organization of the same. Upon receipt of the certificate the clerk shall within 10 days send a certified copy of the certificate to each of the clerks of the several boards of supervisors of the counties constituting the district, and shall also within the time specified in this section notify each supervisor appointed as a member of the board of directors of the district of such fact and of the time and place of the first meeting of the board of directors of the district. The time and place of the meeting shall be fixed and determined by the clerk of the board adopting the initial resolution, but said time of meeting shall be within 30 days after the date of mailing notices thereof. The necessary expense incurred by supervisors in attending and in going to and coming from any meeting of the board of directors of the district shall constitute a county charge of their respective counties.

§4209. Designation of board of directors.

The body formed under Section 4208 shall be called the board of directors of such district.

§4210. Binding agreement.

The delegates from each county may enter into an agreement with the other counties for and on behalf of the county appointing them, binding said counties to the joint enterprise provided for in this article and apportioning the cost of establishing and maintaining a road camp or camps, such cost to be apportioned on the basis of the population of the respective counties as determined by the official declaration of the State Legislature determining the population of counties next preceding such apportionment.

§4211. Collection of expenses from counties.

All sums found due from any county according to the provisions of this article are a debt against said

© 1992 by J., B. & L. Gould
Printed in the U.S.A. **EP**

county, and may be collected in the manner provided by law by the said board of directors of a district formed under this article, or, in its behalf, by the board of supervisors of any county in the district by an action instituted and tried in any county in the district in which the same may be first filed.

§4212. Maintenance and furnishing of road camps.

The board of directors may establish the road camp or camps provided for in this article, and may furnish such camp or camps with the necessary personnel and equipment to transport, feed, clothe, shelter and lodge the prisoners who shall work therein and with the necessary hand tools and appliances for their work, and may employ one or more persons to supervise the camp and the work of the prisoners.

§4213. Revolving fund.

Each county in a district formed under this article shall pay from its general fund its proportionate share to the board of directors of such amount as the board may designate to constitute a cash revolving fund to carry on the work and expense of maintaining such camp or camps. Each month a statement of the expense of the camp shall be sent to the board of supervisors of each county in the district, together with a claim for its proportionate share of expenses. Amounts when received shall be paid into the cash revolving fund.

§4214. Parole to work in camp.

Within 15 days after any person is confined in the county jail of any county within a district under a final judgment of imprisonment rendered in a criminal action or proceeding, the county parole commissioners of such county shall meet and determine whether he should be paroled to work in the joint county road camps established under this article. If it appears to the commissioners that a prisoner is a fit subject for parole to a camp formed under this article, they shall forthwith parole him with the requirement that he perform labor in such joint county road camp wherever it may then be situated, or may thereafter be moved to during his term of imprisonment, and he shall forthwith be transferred by the sheriff of the county in which he is confined to said road camp at the expense of the county in which he was sentenced to imprisonment.

§4215. Prisoners employed in state highway work.

The boards of directors of joint county road camp districts may contract with the State Department of Public Works for the employment of jail prisoners in the construction, improvement, or maintenance of any portion of any state highway now existing, to be constructed, or under construction within said district and may also contract with any board of supervisors or with any supervisor of any road district, within said district, for the employment of jail prisoners on any county road or county public work within any county or road district lying within any district created under this article.

§4216. Maintenance expenses.

When the prisoners of a road camp are engaged in the construction or maintenance of any portion of the state highway the expense of maintaining them together with the compensation of such prisoners fixed

by the board of directors as provided in this article, and the expense of supervision and maintenance of the road camp and the prisoners thereof, shall be paid for by the district and the State Department of Public Works upon such terms and in such proportions as may be agreed upon by the Department of Public Works and the district.

§4217. Funds.

Any money expended by the Department of Public Works under the provisions of this article shall be taken from any funds available for the construction or maintenance of the highway upon which the prisoners of the district labor.

§4218. Contracts between State Department of Public Works and joint districts.

The State Department of Public Works may contract with the boards of directors of the joint districts created under this article for all the purposes stated in this article.

§4219. Work on county roads; expenses.

When a joint road camp, and the prisoners thereof, are employed in the construction or maintenance of any county way, road or public work, the total expense of maintenance, operation and supervision, of said camp, and the compensation of the prisoners thereof shall be paid for from any funds which may be available for the construction or maintenance of such road, highway or other public works on which said prisoners are employed, or from the county general fund upon a four-fifths vote of the board of supervisors of said county.

§4220. Payment by warrant.

All payments provided for in Section 4219 shall be made by warrants drawn on the proper fund in favor of "Joint County Road Camp District No. __" (inserting the number assigned by the Secretary of State), and shall become a portion of the revolving fund provided for in this article.

§4221. Disposition of revolving fund surplus.

Whenever the revolving fund provided for in this article after payment of all bills due against a district exceeds twenty thousand dollars ($20,000) or exceeds such lesser sum as the board of directors shall determine to be a sufficient working fund for the purposes of this article, the board shall apportion such surplus to be repaid to the counties forming the district, in the same proportion in which they are required to contribute to the revolving fund in the first instance, the payments to go into the county general funds of such counties.

§4222. Reasonable compensation for prisoners.

The board of directors may make such rules as it deems proper for the government of camps and the conduct of prisoners therein and may fix a reasonable compensation, not to exceed seventy-five cents ($0.75) per day, for each prisoner performing labor in a camp.

§4223. Charges.

Each prisoner shall be charged with the cost of all tools and appliances for the performance of labor which are furnished to him, and upon his release or discharge from a camp, he shall deliver to the superintendent thereof all tools and appliances for which he

© 1992 by J., B. & L. Gould
Printed in the U.S.A.   EP

is charged and shall thereupon be entitled to full credit for the cost of the tools and appliances so returned. The cost of any appliances and tools not returned as provided in this section shall be deducted from the compensation due the prisoner.

§4224. When prisoner may be paid.

All sums earned by any prisoner may be retained until he has completed his sentence, or until he is released or discharged, and shall thereupon be paid to him. If any prisoner has dependents, his compensation shall be paid to such dependents monthly as earned.

§4225. Establishment of camp by single county.

The board of supervisors of any county not included within any joint county road camp district, and having a population of 150,000 or more persons, may establish and maintain a county road camp as provided in this article, and may provide a board of directors thereof, by passing the resolution and receiving the certificate of organization provided for in this article.

§4226. Single-county board; powers and duties.

The board of supervisors of any county covered by Section 4225 shall nominate three of its members to serve as directors of the district formed thereunder, and such directors shall have and exercise all the powers and perform all the duties granted to and imposed by this article upon boards of directors of joint county road camp districts, and such county shall constitute, and be recognized and dealt with in all respects as a joint county road camp district within the meaning of this article.

§4227. Manner of dissolving joint district.

A joint county road camp district formed under this article may be dissolved in the following manner:

1. The board or boards of supervisors of a county or counties containing more than fifty percent (50%) of the population of the entire district shall by a unanimous vote adopt a resolution stating that the existence of a county road camp is no longer desirable for the public welfare and announcing the intention to withdraw therefrom and to dissolve said district.

2. The resolution or resolutions so adopted shall be communicated to the clerks of the boards of supervisors of all the counties comprising the district and also to the Secretary of State.

3. If it appears that the resolution was unanimously adopted by the board or boards of supervisors in the counties desiring to withdraw, and that such county or counties contain more than fifty percent (50%) of the entire population in the district, the Secretary of State shall thereupon certify to the clerks of the boards of supervisors of the counties composing the district that the district is dissolved.

4. Thereupon the board of directors of the district shall within 90 days:

(a) Abolish the road camp or camps;

(b) Return all prisoners therein to their respective county jails;

(c) Dispose of all equipment belonging to said camp or camps and the district;

(d) Render an accounting to the clerks of the boards of supervisors of the counties composing such district of all sums of money received and paid out since their last previous accounting, including the balance of revolving fund on hand at said last previous accounting;

(e) Apportion and repay to said counties all sums of money then remaining in their hands, and they shall thereupon be relieved of further responsibility in said matter.

ARTICLE 3

ADVISORY COMMITTEES FOR ADULT DETENTION FACILITIES

§4300. Establishment.

The board of supervisors may establish in each county a county advisory committee on adult detention.

§4301. Members' appointment.

There shall be 6, 9, or 12 members of the committee. One-third shall be appointed by the board of supervisors; one-third by the sheriff, and one-third by the presiding or senior judge of the superior court. Of the members appointed by the judge of the superior court, one shall be a member of the State Bar. *(Amended by Stats 1989 ch 1389 §9, eff. 1/1/90.)*

§4302. Members' terms.

The members of the committee shall hold office for four years, and until their successors are appointed and qualify. Of those first appointed by the sheriff, superior court judge, and the board of supervisors, one shall hold office for two years, and one for four years; and the respective terms of the members first appointed shall be determined by lot as soon as possible after their appointment. When a vacancy occurs in the committee by expiration of the term of office of any member thereof, his successors shall be appointed to hold office for a term of four years. When a vacancy occurs for any other reason, the appointee shall hold office for the unexpired term of his predecessor.

§4303. Members' expenses paid.

Members of the committee shall serve without compensation, but shall be allowed their reasonable expenses as approved by the presiding or senior judge of the superior court. Such expenses shall be a charge upon the county in which the court has jurisdiction, and shall be paid out of the county treasury upon a written order of the judge of the superior court directing the county auditor to draw his warrant upon the county treasurer for the specified amount of such expenses. All orders by the superior court judge upon the county treasurer shall be filed in duplicate with the county board of supervisors and sheriff.

§4304. Annual report.

The committee shall file a report within 90 days after the thirty-first day of December of the calendar year for which such report is made, copies of which shall be filed with the county board of supervisors, the presiding or senior judge, the sheriff, the Board of Corrections, and the Attorney General.

§4305. Annual inspection.

The committee shall annually inspect the city and county adult detention facilities. Such inspection shall be concerned with the conditions of inmate employment, detention, care, custody, training, and treatment on the basis of, but not limited to, the minimum standards established by the Board of Corrections. A report of such visitations together with pertinent recommendations shall be annually filed in accordance with the provisions of Section 4304 of this code.

CHAPTER 2.5

PILOT JAIL INDUSTRY PROGRAMS

§4325. Establishment of Jail Industry Commission.

The board of supervisors of a county of the ninth class or the 19th class, as described in Sections 28030 and 28040, respectively, of the Government Code, or both county boards, with the concurrence of the sheriff of the county, may establish by ordinance or resolution, a Jail Industry Commission for that county, which commission shall have the same purposes, powers, and duties with respect to the county jail as the Prison Industry Authority has under Article 1 (commencing with Section 2800) of Chapter 6 of Title 1 with respect to institutions under the jurisdiction of the Department of Corrections. As used in this chapter, "commission" means a Jail Industry Commission. *(Added by Stats 1987 ch 1303 §3.)*

§4326. Composition of commission.

The commission shall be composed of nine members, four of whom shall be appointed by, and serve at the pleasure of, the board of supervisors, and three of whom shall be appointed by, and serve at the pleasure of, the sheriff. The chairperson of the board of supervisors or his or her designee shall also be a member. The sheriff shall be ex officio chairperson of the commission.

The board of supervisors shall provide for the compensation of members of the commission, and shall provide for the meetings, support staff, and general operations of the commission. *(Added by Stats 1987 ch 1303 §3.)*

§4327. Jail Industries Fund.

Upon the establishment of the commission, the board of supervisors shall establish a Jail Industries Fund, which may be a revolving fund, for funding the operations of the commission. All jail industry income shall be deposited in, and any prisoner compensation shall be paid to the account of the prisoner from, the Jail Industries Fund. *(Added by Stats 1987 ch 1303 §3.)*

§4328. Funds; use of.

Funds in a Jail Industries Fund may only be used for the operation or expansion of the jail industry program or to cover operating and construction costs of county detention facilities, and may not be transferred to the county general fund. *(Added by Stats 1987 ch 1303 §3.)*

§4329. Commission term.

No commission established pursuant to Section 4325 or any county jail industry program conducted under the authority of a commission, shall remain in existence for more than four years from the date of its establishment. *(Amended by Stats 1990 ch 976 §2, eff. 9/18/90.)*

CHAPTER 3

BLOOD DONATIONS

§4350. Applications of chapter.

This chapter applies to prisoners confined in city, county, or city and county jails, or industrial farms or road camps established pursuant to this title, who are under a sentence of 30 days or more.

§4351. Voluntary donation; prior examination.

Any prisoner, to whom this chapter applies, may voluntarily donate blood to a blood bank duly licensed by the State Department of Public Health. Prior to blood donation the prisoner shall be given an examination with all clothes removed by a physician and surgeon of the blood bank to whom blood is to be donated, and donations shall be refused unless such physician shall find the prisoner to be a suitable person for blood donation. No more than one such donation shall be permitted during any 72-day period.

TITLE 4.5

COUNTY JAIL CAPITAL EXPENDITURE BOND ACT OF 1981

CHAPTER 1

FINDINGS AND DECLARATIONS

§4400. Title.

This title shall be known and may be cited as the County Jail Capital Expenditure Bond Act of 1981.

§4401. Findings and declarations.

It is found and declared that:

(a) Numerous county jails throughout California are dilapidated and overcrowded.

(b) Capital improvements are necessary to protect life and safety of the persons confined or employed in jail facilities and to upgrade the health and sanitary conditions of such facilities.

(c) County jails are threatened with closure or the imposition of court supervision if health and safety deficiencies are not corrected immediately.

(d) Due to fiscal constraints associated with the loss of local property tax revenues, counties are unable to finance the construction of adequate jail facilities.

(e) A 1980 survey authorized by the State Board of Corrections concluded that more than two hundred million dollars ($200,000,000) would be necessary merely to bring county and city jails up to the standards in effect when they were built. Subsequent hearings by the Senate Judiciary Committee's Subcommittee on Corrections concluded that at least five hundred million dollars ($500,000,000) would be necessary to bring such facilities up to present standards, without allowing for inflationary increases in construction costs in ensuing years.

(f) Imposition of limits on taxing powers of local agencies, imposed by Proposition 13 and other measures, has severely limited ability of local jurisdictions to raise funds for jail construction or renovation, though the need for such facilities is increasing.

CHAPTER 2

FISCAL PROVISIONS

§4410. State General Obligation Bond Law.

The State General Obligation Bond Law is adopted for the purpose of the issuance, sale, and repayment of, and otherwise providing with respect to, the bonds authorized to be issued pursuant to this title, and the provisions of that law are included in this title as

© 1992 by J., B. & L. Gould
Printed in the U.S.A.　　EP

though set out in full in this chapter except that, notwithstanding anything in the State General Obligation Bond Law, the maximum maturity of the bonds shall not exceed 20 years from the date of each respective series. The maturity of each respective series shall be calculated from the date of such series.

§4411. Terms defined.

As used in this title, and for the purpose of this title, the following words shall have the following meanings:

(a) "Committee" means the County Jail Capital Expenditure Finance Committee created by Section 4413.

(b) "Fund" means the County Jail Expenditure Fund.

§4412. Creation of County Jail Capital Expenditure Fund.

There is in the State Treasury the County Jail Capital Expenditure Fund, which fund is hereby created.

§4413. Creation of County Jail Capital Expenditure Finance Committee.

For the purpose of authorizing the issuance and sale, pursuant to the State General Obligation Bond Law, of the bonds authorized by this title, the County Jail Capital Expenditure Finance Committee is hereby created. The committee consists of the Governor or his designated representative, the Controller, the Treasurer, and the Director of Finance. The County Jail Capital Expenditure Committee shall be the "committee" as that term is used in the State General Obligation Bond Law, and the Treasurer shall serve as chairman of the committee. The Board of Corrections is hereby designated as "the board" for purposes of this title and for the purposes of the State General Obligation Bond Law.

§4414. Authority and power to create debts or liabilities.

The committee is hereby authorized and empowered to create a debt or debts, liability or liabilities, of the State of California, in the aggregate amount of two hundred eighty million dollars ($280,000,000), in the manner provided in this title. Such debt or debts, liability or liabilities, shall be created for the purpose of providing the funds to be used for the object and work specified in Section 4415 and for administrative costs incurred in connection therewith.

§4415. Expenditures; limitations.

Moneys in the fund shall be available for expenditure in accordance with this title by the Board of Corrections. Prior to the disbursement of any money in the fund the board, the Subcommittee on Corrections of the Senate Judiciary Committee and the Subcommittee on County Jails of the Assembly Criminal Justice Committee shall reexamine the factors specified in subdivisions (a) and (b) to determine whether they are still suitable and applicable to the distribution of the proceeds of the bonds authorized by this title. Moneys in the fund shall be available for expenditure for the following purposes:

(a) For the construction, reconstruction, remodeling, and replacement of county jail facilities, and the performance of deferred maintenance activities on such facilities pursuant to rules and regulations adopted by the Board of Corrections, in accordance with the provisions of Section 6029.1. No expenditure shall be made unless county matching funds of 25 percent are provided.

(b) In performing the duties set forth in subdivision (a), the Board of Corrections shall consider all of the following:

(1) The extent to which the county requesting aid has exhausted all other available means of raising the requested funds for the capital improvements and the extent to which the funds from the County Jail Capital Expenditure Fund will be utilized to attract other sources of capital financing for county jail facilities.

(2) The extent to which the capital improvements are necessary to the life or safety of the persons confined or employed in the facility or the health and sanitary conditions of the facility.

(3) The extent to which the county has utilized reasonable alternatives to pre-conviction and post-conviction incarceration, including, but not limited to, programs to facilitate release upon one's own recognizance where appropriate to individual's pending trial, sentencing alternatives to custody, and civil commitment or diversion programs consistent with public safety for those with drug or alcohol-related problems or mental or developmental disabilities.

§4416. Bonds as legally binding general obligations.

(a) When sold, the bonds authorized by this title shall constitute valid and legally binding general obligations of the State of California, and the full faith and credit of the State of California is hereby pledged for the punctual payment of both principal and interest thereon.

(b) There shall be collected annually in the same manner and at the same time as other state revenue is collected such a sum, in addition to the ordinary revenues of the state, as shall be required to pay the interest and principal on the bonds maturing each year, and it is hereby made the duty of all officers charged by law with any duty in regard to the collection of the revenue to do and perform each and every act which shall be necessary to collect that additional sum.

(c) All money deposited in the fund which has been derived from premium and accrued interest on bonds sold shall be available for transfer to the General Fund as a credit to expenditures for bond interest.

§4417. Transfer of money to general fund.

All money deposited in the fund pursuant to any provision of law requiring repayments to the state for assistance financed by the proceeds of the bonds authorized by this title shall be available for transfer to the General Fund. When transferred to the General Fund such money shall be applied as a reimbursement to the General Fund on account of principal and interest on the bonds which has been paid from the General Fund.

§4418. Appropriations.

There is hereby appropriated from the General Fund in the State Treasury for the purpose of this title, such an amount as will equal the following:

(a) That sum annually as will be necessary to pay the principal of and the interest on the bonds issued and sold pursuant to the provisions of this title, as principal and interest become due and payable.

(b) That sum as is necessary to carry out the provisions of Section 4419, which sum is appropriated without regard to fiscal years.

§4419. Authorization of withdrawals from General Fund.

For the purpose of carrying out the provisions of this title, the Director of Finance may by executive order authorize the withdrawal from the General Fund of an amount or amounts not to exceed the amount of the unsold bonds which the committee has by resolution authorized to be sold for the purpose of carrying out this title. Any amounts withdrawn shall be deposited in the fund and shall be dispersed by the board in accordance with this title. Any money made available under this section to the board shall be returned by the board to the General Fund from moneys received from the sale of bonds sold for the purpose of carrying out this title. Such withdrawals from the General Fund shall be returned to the General Fund with interest at the rate which would have otherwise been earned by such sums in the Pooled Money Investment Fund.

§4419.5. Tax-exempt bonds.

Notwithstanding any other provision of this bond act, or of the State General Obligation Bond Law (Chapter 4 (commencing with Section 16720) of Part 3 of Division 4 of Title 2 of the Government Code), if the Treasurer sells bonds pursuant to this bond act that include a bond counsel opinion to the effect that the interest on the bonds is excluded from gross income for federal tax purposes under designated conditions, the Treasurer may maintain separate accounts for the bond proceeds invested and the investment earnings on those proceeds, and may use or direct the use of those proceeds or earnings to pay any rebate, penalty, or other payment required under federal law, or take any other action with respect to the investment and use of those bond proceeds, as may be required or desirable under federal law in order to maintain the tax-exempt status of those bonds and to obtain any other advantage under federal law on behalf of the funds of this state. *(Added by Stats 1991 ch 652 §16, eff. 1/1/92.)*

§4420. Authorizing the sale of bonds.

The committee may authorize the State Treasurer to sell all or any part of the bonds herein authorized at such time or times as may be fixed by the Treasurer.

§4421. Proceeds from bonds sale.

All proceeds from the sale of bonds, except those derived from premiums and accrued interest, shall be available for the purpose provided in Section 4415 but shall not be available for transfer to the General Fund to pay principal and interest on bonds. The money in the fund may be expended only as herein provided.

§4422. Budget Act limitations.

All proposed appropriations for the projects specified in this title, shall be included in a section in the Budget Bill for the 1982-83 and each succeeding fiscal year, for consideration by the Legislature. All appropriations shall be subject to all limitations enacted in the Budget Act and to all fiscal procedures prescribed by law with respect to the expenditures of state funds, unless expressly exempted from such laws by a statute enacted by the Legislature. No funds

derived from the bonds authorized by this title may be expended pursuant to an appropriation not contained in such section of the Budget Act.

TITLE 4.6

COUNTY JAIL CAPITAL EXPENDITURE BOND ACT OF 1984

CHAPTER 1

FINDINGS AND DECLARATIONS

§4450. Short title.

This title shall be known and may be cited as the County Jail Capital Expenditure Bond Act of 1984.

§4451. Findings and declarations.

It is found and declared that:

(a) While the County Jail Capital Expenditure Bond Act of 1981 has helped eliminate many of the critically overcrowded conditions found in the 164 county jail facilities in the state, many problems remain.

(b) Numerous county jails throughout California are dilapidated and overcrowded.

(c) Capital improvements are necessary to protect life and safety of the persons confined or employed in jail facilities and to upgrade the health and sanitary conditions of those facilities.

(d) County jails are threatened with closure or the imposition of court supervision if health and safety deficiencies are not corrected immediately.

(e) Due to fiscal constraints associated with the loss of local property tax revenues, counties are unable to finance the construction of adequate jail facilities.

(f) Imposition of limits on taxing powers of local agencies, imposed by Proposition 13 and other measures, has severely limited the ability of local jurisdictions to raise funds for jail construction or renovation, though the need for such facilities is increasing.

CHAPTER 2

FISCAL PROVISIONS

§4460. State General Obligation Bond Law.

The State General Obligation Bond Law is adopted for the purpose of the issuance, sale, and repayment of, and otherwise providing with respect to, the bonds authorized to be issued pursuant to this title, and the provisions of that law are included in this title as though set out in full in this chapter except that, notwithstanding anything in the State General Obligation Bond Law, the maximum maturity of the bonds shall not exceed 20 years from the date of each respective series. The maturity of each respective series shall be calculated from the date of these series.

§4461. Terms defined.

As used in this title, and for the purpose of this title, the following words shall have the following meanings:

(a) "Committee" means the County Jail Capital Expenditure Finance Committee created by Section 4463.

(b) "Fund" means the County Jail Expenditure Fund.

© 1992 by J., B. & L. Gould
Printed in the U.S.A.   **EP**

§4462. County Jail Capital Expenditure Fund.

There is in the State Treasury the County Jail Capital Expenditure Fund, which fund is hereby created.

§4463. County Jail Capital Expenditure Finance Committee.

For the purpose of authorizing the issuance and sale, pursuant to the State General Obligation Bond Law, of the bonds authorized by this title, the County Jail Capital Expenditure Finance Committee is hereby created. The committee consists of the Governor or his or her designated representative, the Controller, the Treasurer, and the Director of Finance. The County Jail Capital Expenditure Committee shall be the "committee" as that term is used in the State General Obligation Bond Law, and the Treasurer shall serve as chairman of the committee. The Board of Corrections is hereby designated as "the board" for purposes of this title and for the purposes of the State General Obligation Bond Law.

§4464. Creation of debts or liabilities.

The committee is hereby authorized and empowered to create a debt or debts, liability or liabilities, of the State of California, in the aggregate amount of two hundred fifty million dollars ($250,000,000), in the manner provided in this title. Such debt or debts, liability or liabilities, shall be created for the purpose of providing the funds to be used for the object and work specified in Section 4465 and for administrative costs incurred in connection therewith.

§4465. Purpose of fund.

Moneys in the fund shall be available for the construction, reconstruction, remodeling, and replacement of county jail facilities, and the performance of deferred maintenance on county jail facilities pursuant to criteria adopted by the Legislature.

§4465.3. Allocations.

Money in the fund shall be allocated in accordance with the provisions of Chapter 444 of the Statutes of 1984. *(Amended by Stats 1987 ch 828 §136.)*

§4465.5. Areas to accommodate misdemeanants.

During the design and planning stage for county jail facilities whose construction, reconstruction, or remodeling is financed by the fund, consideration shall be given to proper design to allow for areas where persons arrested for misdemeanors who are attempting to obtain release on bail can be safely accommodated without the necessity of unclothed body searches.

§4466. Sale of bonds; payment of interest and principal.

(a) When sold, the bonds authorized by this title shall constitute valid and legally binding general obligations of the State of California, and the full faith and credit of the State of California is hereby pledged for the punctual payment of both principal and interest thereon.

(b) There shall be collected annually in the same manner and at the same time as other state revenue is collected such a sum, in addition to the ordinary revenues of the state, as shall be required to pay the interest and principal on the bonds maturing each year, and it is hereby made the duty of all officers charged by law with any duty in regard to the collection of the revenue to do and perform each and every act which shall be necessary to collect that additional sum.

(c) All money deposited in the fund which has been derived from premium and accrued interest on bonds sold shall be available for transfer to the General Fund as a credit to expenditures for bond interest.

§4467. Transfer of money to General Fund.

All money deposited in the fund pursuant to any provision of law requiring repayments to the state for assistance financed by the proceeds of the bonds authorized by this title shall be available for transfer to the General Fund. When transferred to the General Fund, this money shall be applied as a reimbursement to the General Fund on account of principal and interest on the bonds which have been paid from the General Fund.

§4468. Appropriations.

There is hereby appropriated from the General Fund in the State Treasury for the purpose of this title, such an amount as will equal the following:

(a) That sum annually as will be necessary to pay the principal of and the interest on the bonds issued and sold pursuant to the provisions of this title, as principal and interest become due and payable.

(b) That sum as is necessary to carry out the provisions of Section 4469, which sum is appropriated without regard to fiscal years.

§4469. Authorizing withdrawals from General Fund.

For the purpose of carrying out the provisions of this title, the Director of Finance may by executive order authorize the withdrawal from the General Fund of an amount or amounts not to exceed the amount of the unsold bonds which the committee has by resolution authorized to be sold for the purpose of carrying out this title. Any amounts withdrawn shall be deposited in the fund and shall be disbursed by the board in accordance with this title. Any money made available under this section to the board shall be returned by the board to the General Fund from moneys received from the sale of bonds sold for the purpose of carrying out this title. These withdrawals from the General Fund shall be returned to the General Fund with interest at the rate which would have otherwise been earned by these sums in the Pooled Money Investment Fund.

§4470. Authorization of Treasurer to sell bonds.

The committee may authorize the Treasurer to sell all or any part of the bonds herein authorized at such time or times as may be fixed by the Treasurer.

§4471. Proceeds from sale; purposes.

All proceeds from the sale of bonds, except those derived from premiums and accrued interest, shall be available for the purpose provided in Section 4465 but shall not be available for transfer to the General Fund to pay principal and interest on bonds. The money in the fund may be expended only as herein provided.

© 1992 by J., B. & L. Gould
Printed in the U.S.A. **EP**

TITLE 4.7

COUNTY CORRECTIONAL FACILITY
CAPITAL EXPENDITURE BOND ACT OF 1986
(Added by Stats 1986 ch 12 §1.)

CHAPTER 1

FINDINGS AND DECLARATIONS

§4475. Title.
This title shall be known and may be cited as the
County Correctional Facility Capital Expenditure
Bond Act of 1986. *(Added by Stats 1986 ch 12 §1.)*

§4476. Problems unsolved by Bond Acts.
It is found and declared that:
(a) While the County Jail Capital Expenditure Bond
Act of 1981 and the County Jail Capital Expenditure
Bond Act of 1984 have helped eliminate many of the
critically overcrowded conditions found in the 164
county jail facilities in the state, many problems remain.
(b) Numerous county jails and juvenile facilities
throughout California are dilapidated and overcrowded.
(c) Capital improvements are necessary to protect
life and safety of the persons confined or employed in
jail facilities and to upgrade the health and sanitary
conditions of those facilities.
(d) County jails are threatened with closure or the
imposition of court supervision if health and safety
deficiencies are not corrected immediately.
(e) Due to fiscal constraints associated with the
loss of local property tax revenues, counties are unable
to finance the construction of adequate jail and
juvenile facilities.
(f) Local facilities for adults and juveniles are
operating over capacity and the population of these
facilities is still increasing. It is essential to the public
safety that construction of new facilities proceed as
expeditiously as possible to relieve overcrowding and
to maintain public safety and security. *(Added by Stats
1986 ch 12 §1.)*

CHAPTER 2

FISCAL PROVISIONS

§4480. State General Obligation Bond Law.
The State General Obligation Bond Law is adopted
for the purpose of the issuance, sale, and repayment
of, and otherwise providing with respect to, the bonds
authorized to be issued pursuant to this title, and the
provisions of that law are included in this title as
though set out in full in this chapter except that,
notwithstanding anything in the State General
Obligation Bond Law, the maximum maturity of the
bonds shall not exceed 20 years from the date of each
respective series. The maturity of each respective
series shall be calculated from the date of these series.
(Added by Stats 1986 ch 12 §1.)

§4481. Terms defined.
As used in this title, and for the purpose of this title,
the following words shall have the following meanings:
(a) "Committee" means the 1986 County Correctional Facility Capital Expenditure Finance Committee created by Section 4483.

(b) "Fund" means the 1986 County Correctional
Facility Expenditure Fund.
(c) "County juvenile facilities" means county
juvenile halls, juvenile homes, ranches, or camps, and
other juvenile detention facilities. *(Added by Stats
1986 ch 12 §1.)*

§4482. Creation of Expenditure Fund.
There is in the State Treasury the 1986 County Correctional Facility Capital Expenditure Fund, which
fund is hereby created. *(Added by Stats 1986 ch 12 §1.)*

§4483. Creation of Finance Committee.
For the purpose of authorizing the issuance and
sale, pursuant to the State General Obligation Bond
Law, of the bonds authorized by this title, the 1986
County Correctional Facility Capital Expenditure
Finance Committee is hereby created. The committee
consists of the Governor or his or her designated
representative, the Controller, the Treasurer, and the
Director of Finance. The County Correctional Facility
Capital Expenditure Committee shall be the "committee" as that term is used in the State General Obligation Bond Law, and the Treasurer shall serve as
chairman of the Committee. The Board of Corrections
is hereby designated as "the board" for purposes of this
title and for the purposes of the State General Obligation Bond Law. *(Added by Stats 1986 ch 12 §1.)*

§4484. Powers of committee.
The committee is hereby authorized and empowered to create a debt or debts, liability or liabilities, of the State of California, in the aggregate amount
of four hundred ninety-five million dollars
($495,000,000), in the manner provided in this title.
That debt or debts, liability or liabilities, shall be
created for the purpose of providing the funds to be
used for the object and work specified in Section 4485
and for administrative costs incurred in connection
therewith. *(Added by Stats 1986 ch 12 §1.)*

§4485. Use of fund moneys.
Moneys in the fund may be available for the construction, reconstruction, remodeling, and replacement of county jail facilities, including, but not limited
to, separate facilities for care of mentally ill inmates
and persons arrested because of intoxication, and the
performance of deferred maintenance on county jail
facilities except that up to twenty million dollars
($20,000,000) of the money in the fund shall be avail-
able for the construction, reconstruction, remodeling,
and replacement of county juvenile facilities, and the
performance of deferred maintenance on county
juvenile facilities. However, deferred maintenance for
jails and juvenile facilities shall only include items
with a useful life of at least 10 years.
Expenditure shall be made only if county matching
funds of 25 percent are provided as determined by the
Legislature, except that this requirement may be
modified or waived by the Legislature where it determines that it is necessary to facilitate the expeditious
and equitable construction of state and local correctional facilities. *(Added by Stats 1986 ch 12 §1.)*

§4485.5. Accommodation for person arrested for
misdemeanors.
During the design and planning stage for county
jail facilities whose construction, reconstruction, or
remodeling is financed by the fund, consideration

© 1992 by J., B. & L. Gould
Printed in the U.S.A.   EP

shall be given to proper design to allow for areas where persons arrested for misdemeanors who are attempting to obtain release on bail can be safely accommodated without the necessity of unclothed body searches. *(Added by Stats 1986 ch 12 §1.)*

§4485.6. Eligibility for funds.

In order to be eligible to receive funds derived from the issuance of General Obligation Bonds under this title, a county shall do all of the following:

(a) Adopt a plan to prohibit the detention of all juveniles in county jails unless otherwise authorized by law.

(b) Demonstrate that it has adequate facilities for mentally ill inmates or detainees and for those persons arrested because of inebriation, or demonstrate that it has a plan for the provision of services to these persons.

(c) Demonstrate that it has utilized, to the greatest practicable extent, alternatives to jail incarceration such as sheriff's work release under Section 4024.2, own recognizance release, and weekend work programs. *(Added by Stats 1986 ch 12 §1.)*

§4485.7. Moneys available for joint use correctional facilities.

Moneys in the fund may be available for construction of joint-use correctional facilities housing county and state or federal prisoners or any combination thereof in proportion to the county's benefit. *(Added by Stats 1986 ch 12 §1.)*

§4486. Obligation of the State.

(a) When sold, the bonds authorized by this title shall constitute valid and legally binding general obligations of the State of California, and the full faith and credit of the State of California is hereby pledged for the punctual payment of both principal and interest thereon.

(b) There shall be collected annually in the same manner and at the same time as other state revenue is collected such a sum, in addition to the ordinary revenues of the state, as shall be required to pay the interest and principal on the bonds maturing each year, and it is hereby made the duty of all officers charged by law with any duty in regard to the collection of the revenue to do and perform each and every act which shall be necessary to collect that additional sum.

(c) All money deposited in the fund which has been derived from premium and accrued interest on bonds sold shall be available for transfer to the General Fund as a credit to expenditures for bond interest. *(Added by Stats 1986 ch 12 §1.)*

§4487. Transfer of money to General Fund.

All money deposited in the fund pursuant to any provision of law requiring repayments to the state for assistance financed by the proceeds of the bonds authorized by this title shall be available for transfer to the General Fund. When transferred to the General Fund, this money shall be applied as a reimbursement to the General Fund on account of principal and interest on the bonds which have been paid from the General Fund. *(Added by Stats 1986 ch 12 §1.)*

§4488. Appropriation of sum equal to annual principal and interest.

There is hereby appropriated from the General Fund in the State Treasury for the purpose of this title such an amount as well equal the following:

(a) That sum annually as will be necessary to pay the principal of and the interest on the bonds issued and sold pursuant to the provisions of this title, as principal and interest become due and payable.

(b) That sum as is necessary to carry out the provisions of Section 4489, which sum is appropriated without regard to fiscal years. *(Added by Stats 1986 ch 12 §1.)*

§4489. Powers of Director of Finance.

For the purpose of carrying out the provisions of this title, the Director of Finance may by executive order authorize the withdrawal from the General Fund of an amount or amounts not to exceed the amount of the unsold bonds which the committee has by resolution authorized to be sold for the purpose of carrying out this title. Any amounts withdrawn shall be deposited in the fund and shall be disbursed by the board in accordance with this title. Any money made available under this section to the board shall be returned by the board to the General Fund from moneys received from the sale of bonds sold for the purpose of carrying out this title. These withdrawals from the General Fund shall be returned to the General Fund with interest at the rate which would have otherwise been earned by these sums in the Pooled Money Investment Fund. *(Added by Stats 1986 ch 12 §1.)*

§4489.5. Tax-exempt bonds.

Notwithstanding any other provision of this bond act, or of the State General Obligation Bond Law (Chapter 4 (commencing with Section 16720) of Part 3 of Division 4 of Title 2 of the Government Code), if the Treasurer sells bonds pursuant to this bond act that include a bond counsel opinion to the effect that the interest on the bonds is excluded from gross income for federal tax purposes under designated conditions, the Treasurer may maintain separate accounts for the bond proceeds invested and the investment earnings on those proceeds, and may use or direct the use of those proceeds or earnings to pay any rebate, penalty, or other payment required under federal law, or take any other action with respect to the investment and use of those bond proceeds, as may be required or desirable under federal law in order to maintain the tax-exempt status of those bonds and to obtain any other advantage under federal law on behalf of the funds of this state. *(Added by Stats 1991 ch 652 §17, eff. 1/1/92.)*

§4490. Sale of bonds.

The committee may authorize the Treasurer to sell all or any part of the bonds herein authorized at such time or times as may be fixed by the Treasurer. *(Added by Stats 1986 ch 12 §1.)*

§4491. Use of proceeds from sales.

All proceeds from the sale of bonds, except those derived from premiums and accrued interest, shall be available for the purpose provided in Section 4485 but shall not be available for transfer to the General Fund to pay principal and interest on bonds. The money in the fund may be expended only as herein provided. *(Added by Stats 1986 ch 12 §1.)*

§4492. Interest credited to fund.

Notwithstanding Section 16305.7 of the Government Code, all interest or other increment resulting from the investment of moneys deposited in the fund shall be credited to the fund. *(Added by Stats 1986 ch 12 §1.)*

§4493. Expenditure of moneys.

Money in the fund may only be expended for projects specified in this title as allocated in appropriations made by the Legislature. *(Added by Stats 1986 ch 12 §1.)*

§4494. Intent of bond act.

(a) It is the intent of the people in enacting this bond act that jail authorization and construction proceed as quickly as possible. Due to the severe shortage of jail facilities and the need to begin construction of jail facilities as soon as possible, all decisions of the board regarding construction, reconstruction, remodeling, or replacement of jail facilities financed by this title shall be final.

(b) No court shall have jurisdiction over these decisions of the board absent a showing, beyond a reasonable doubt, of a gross abuse of discretion by the board.

(c) Should an action be commenced alleging gross abuse of discretion by the board, no court shall have jurisdiction to delay, prohibit, or interfere with the construction, reconstruction, remodeling, or replacement of the subject jail facilities. The sole remedy available to the court is a mandate that steps be taken to mitigate the abuse of discretion.

(d) Nothing in this title is intended in any way to delay, prohibit, or interfere with the construction of jail facilities. *(Added by Stats 1986 ch 12 §1.)*

§4495. Affects of invalidity.

If any provision of this title, or the application thereof, is held to be invalid, that invalidity shall not affect the other provisions or applications of the title which can be given effect without the invalid provision or application, and to this end the provisions of this title are severable. *(Added by Stats 1986 ch 12 §1.)*

TITLE 4.8

COUNTY CORRECTIONAL FACILITY CAPITAL EXPENDITURE AND YOUTH FACILITY BOND ACT OF 1988
(Added by Stats 1988 ch 264 §1, eff. 11/8/88.)

CHAPTER 1

GENERAL PROVISIONS

§4496. Title.

This title shall be known and may be cited as the County Correctional Facility Capital Expenditure and Youth Facility Bond Act of 1988. *(Added by Stats 1988 ch 264 §1, eff. 11/8/88.)*

§4496.02. Findings and declarations.

The Legislature finds and declares all of the following:

(a) While the County Jail Capital Expenditure Bond Act of 1981, the County Jail Capital Expenditure Bond Act of 1984, and the County Correctional Facility Capital Expenditure Bond Act of 1986 have helped eliminate many of the critically overcrowded conditions found in county correctional facilities in the state, many problems remain.

(b) Numerous county jails and juvenile facilities throughout California are dilapidated and over-crowded.

(c) Capital improvements are necessary to protect life and safety of the persons confined or employed in jail facilities and to upgrade the health and sanitary conditions of those facilities.

(d) County jails are threatened with closure or the imposition of court supervision if health and safety deficiencies are not corrected immediately.

(e) Due to fiscal constraints associated with the loss of local property tax revenues, counties are unable to finance the construction of adequate jail and juvenile facilities.

(f) Local facilities for adults and juveniles are operating over capacity and the population of these facilities is still increasing. It is essential to the public safety that construction of new facilities proceed as expeditiously as possible to relieve overcrowding and to maintain public safety and security. *(Added by Stats 1988 ch 264 §1, eff. 11/8/88.)*

§4496.04. Terms defined.

As used in this title, the following terms have the following meanings:

(a) "Committee" means the 1988 County Correctional Facility Capital Expenditure and Youth Facility Finance Committee created pursuant to Section 4496.34.

(b) "Fund" means the 1988 County Correctional Facility Capital Expenditure and Youth Facility Bond Fund created pursuant to Section 4496.10.

(c) "County correctional facilities" means county jail facilities, including separate facilities for the care of mentally ill inmates and persons arrested because of intoxication, but does not include county juvenile facilities.

(d) "County juvenile facilities" means county juvenile halls, juvenile homes, ranches, or camps, and other juvenile detention facilities.

(e) "Youth center" means a facility where children, ages 6 to 17, inclusive, come together for programs and activities, including, but not limited to, recreation, health and fitness, delinquency prevention such as antigang programs and programs fostering resistance to peer group pressures, counseling for problems such as drug and alcohol abuse and suicide, citizenship and leadership development, and youth employment.

(f) "Youth shelter" means a facility that provides a variety of services to homeless minors living on the street or abused and neglected children to assist them with their immediate survival needs and to help reunite them with their parents or, as a last alternative, to find a suitable home. *(Added by Stats 1988 ch 264 §1, eff. 11/8/88.)*

CHAPTER 2

PROGRAM

§4496.10. 1988 County Correctional Facility Capital Expenditure and Youth Facility Bond Fund.

The proceeds of bonds issued and sold pursuant to this chapter shall be deposited in the 1988 County Correctional Facility Capital Expenditure and Youth Facility Bond Fund, which is hereby created. *(Added by Stats 1988 ch 264 §1, eff. 11/8/88.)*

© 1992 by J., B. & L. Gould
Printed in the U.S.A.   **EP**

§4496.12. Moneys in fund; availability.

(a)(1) Moneys in the fund, up to a limit of four hundred ten million dollars ($410,000,000), may be available for the construction, reconstruction, remodeling, and replacement of county correctional facilities, and the performance of deferred maintenance on county correctional facilities. However, deferred maintenance for facilities shall only include items with a useful life of at least 10 years.

(2) Moneys in the fund, up to a limit of sixty-five million dollars ($65,000,000), may be available for the construction, reconstruction, remodeling, and replacement of county juvenile facilities, and the performance of deferred maintenance on county juvenile facilities, but may only be used for the purpose of reducing overcrowding and eliminating health, fire, and life safety hazards.

(3) Expenditure shall be made only if county matching funds of 25 percent are provided as determined by the Legislature, except that this requirement may be modified or waived by the Legislature where it determines that it is necessary to facilitate the expeditious and equitable construction of state and local correctional facilities.

(b) Moneys in the fund, up to a limit of twenty-five million dollars ($25,000,000), may be available for the purpose of making awards to public or private nonprofit agencies or joint ventures, or a combination of those entities, for purpose of purchasing equipment and for acquiring, renovating, or constructing youth centers or youth shelters, as may be provided by statute. Fifteen million dollars ($15,000,000) shall be available for youth centers and ten million dollars ($10,000,000) shall be available for youth shelters and shall be distributed by the Department of the Youth Authority. However, any remaining money that has not been awarded under this subdivision within two years of the effective date of this title shall be available for both youth centers and youth shelters. *(Added by Stats 1988 ch 264 §1, eff. 11/8/88.)*

§4496.16. Conditions of eligibility for funds.

In order to be eligible to receive funds for the purposes specified in subdivision (a) of Section 4496.12 derived from the issuance of bonds under this title, a county shall do all of the following:

(a) Adopt a plan to prohibit the detention of all juveniles in county jails unless otherwise authorized by law.

(b) Demonstrate that it has adequate facilities for mentally ill inmates or detainees and for those persons arrested because of inebriation, or demonstrate that it has a plan for the provision of services to these persons.

(c) Demonstrate that it has utilized, to the greatest practicable extent, alternatives to jail incarceration. *(Added by Stats 1988 ch 264 §1, eff. 11/8/88.)*

§4496.17 Administration of funds for juvenile facilities.

The Department of the Youth Authority shall administer funds appropriated for juvenile facilities as specified in paragraph (2) of subdivision (a) of Section 4496.12. *(Added by Stats 1989 ch 1130 §1, eff. 9/29/89.)*

§4496.19. Limitations on expenditures.

Money in the fund may only be expended for projects specified in this chapter as allocated in appropriations made by the Legislature. *(Added by Stats 1988 ch 264 §1, eff. 11/8/88.)*

CHAPTER 3

FISCAL PROVISIONS

§4496.30. Issuance of bonds.

Bonds in the total amount of five hundred million dollars ($500,000,000), exclusive of refunding bonds, or so much thereof as is necessary, may be issued and sold to provide a fund to be used for carrying out the purposes expressed in this title and to be used to reimburse the General Obligation Bond Expense Revolving Fund pursuant to Section 16724.5 of the Government Code. The bonds shall, when sold, be and constitute a valid and binding obligation of the State of California, and the full faith and credit of the State of California is hereby pledged for the punctual payment of both principal of, and interest on, the bonds as the principal and interest become due and payable. *(Added by Stats 1988 ch 264 §1, eff. 11/8/88.)*

§4496.32. Application of General Obligation Bond Law.

The bonds authorized by this title shall be prepared, executed, issued, sold, paid, and redeemed as provided in the State General Obligation Bond Law (Chapter 4 (commencing with Section 16720) of Part 3 of Division 4 of Title 2 of the Government Code), and all of the provisions of that law apply to the bonds and to this chapter and are hereby incorporated in this chapter as though set forth in full in this title. *(Added by Stats 1988 ch 264 §1, eff. 11/8/88.)*

§4496.34. 1988 County Correctional Facility Capital Expenditure and Youth Facility Finance Committee.

(a) Solely for the purpose of authorizing the issuance and sale, pursuant to the State General Obligation Bond Law, of the bonds authorized by this title, the 1988 County Correctional Facility Capital Expenditure and Youth Facility Finance Committee is hereby created. For purposes of this title, the finance committee is "the committee" as that term is used in the State General Obligation Bond Law. The committee consists of the Governor, the Controller, the Treasurer, the Director of Finance, or their designated representatives. A majority of the committee may act for the committee.

(b) For purposes of the State General Obligation Bond Law, the Board of Corrections is designated as the "board." *(Added by Stats 1988 ch 264 §1, eff. 11/8/88.)*

§4496.36. Determination whether to issue bonds.

The committee shall determine whether or not it is necessary or desirable to issue bonds authorized pursuant to this chapter in order to carry out the actions specified in Section 4496.12 and, if so, the amount of bonds to be issued and sold. Successive issues of bonds may be authorized and sold to carry out those actions progressively, and it is not necessary that all of the bonds authorized to be issued be sold at any one time. *(Added by Stats 1988 ch 264 §1, eff. 11/8/88.)*

§4496.38. Collection of revenue.

There shall be collected each year and in the same manner and at the same time as other state revenue is collected, in addition to the ordinary revenues of the state, a sum in an amount required to pay the prin-

© 1992 by J., B. & L. Gould
Printed in the U.S.A. EP

cipal of, and interest on, the bonds each year, and it is the duty of all officers charged by law with any duty in regard to the collection of the revenue to do and perform each and every act which is necessary to collect that additional sum. *(Added by Stats 1988 ch 264 §1, eff. 11/8/88.)*

§4496.40. Appropriation of moneys from General Fund.

Notwithstanding Section 13340 of the Government Code, there is hereby appropriated from the General Fund in the State Treasury, for the purposes of this chapter, an amount that will equal the total of the following:

(a) The sum annually necessary to pay the principal of, and interest on, bonds issued and sold pursuant to this chapter, as the principal and interest become due and payable.

(b) The sum which is necessary to carry out the provisions of Section 4496.42, appropriated without regard to fiscal years. *(Added by Stats 1988 ch 264 §1, eff. 11/8/88.)*

§4496.42. Withdrawal of moneys from General Fund.

For the purposes of carrying out this title, the Director of Finance may authorize the withdrawal from the General Fund of an amount or amounts not to exceed the amount of the unsold bonds which have been authorized by the committee to be sold for the purpose of carrying out this chapter. Any amounts withdrawn shall be deposited in the fund. Any money made available under this section, plus any interest that the amounts would have earned in the Pooled Money Investment Account, shall be returned to the General Fund from money received from the sale of bonds for the purpose of carrying out this title. *(Added by Stats 1988 ch 264 §1, eff. 11/8/88.)*

§4496.43. Tax-exempt bonds.

Notwithstanding any other provision of this bond act, or of the State General Obligation Bond Law (Chapter 4 (commencing with Section 16720) of Part 3 of Division 4 of Title 2 of the Government Code), if the Treasurer sells bonds pursuant to this bond act that include a bond counsel opinion to the effect that the interest on the bonds is excluded from gross income for federal tax purposes under designated conditions, the Treasurer may maintain separate accounts for the bond proceeds invested and the investment earnings on those proceeds, and may use or direct the use of those proceeds or earnings to pay any rebate, penalty, or other payment required under federal law, or take any other action with respect to the investment and use of those bond proceeds, as may be required or desirable under federal law in order to maintain the tax-exempt status of those bonds and to obtain any other advantage under federal law on behalf of the funds of this state. *(Added by Stats 1991 ch 652 §18, eff. 1/1/92.)*

§4496.44. Availability for transfer.

All money deposited in the fund which is derived from premium and accrued interest on bonds sold shall be reserved in the fund and shall be available for transfer to the General Fund as a credit to expenditures for bond interest. *(Added by Stats 1988 ch 264 §1, eff. 11/8/88.)*

§4496.46. Refunding bonds.

The bonds may be refunded in accordance with Article 6 (commencing with Section 16780) of Chapter 4 of Part 3 of Division 4 of Title 2 of the Government Code. *(Added by Stats 1988 ch 264 §1, eff. 11/8/88.)*

§4496.47. Request of loan from Pooled Money Investment Account.

The board may request the Pooled Money Investment Board to make a loan from the Pooled Money Investment Account, in accordance with Section 16312 of the Government Code, for the purposes of carrying out the provisions of this chapter. The amount of the request shall not exceed the amount of the unsold bonds which the committee has by resolution authorized to be sold for the purpose of carrying out this chapter. The board shall execute such documents as required by the Pooled Money Investment Board to obtain and repay the loan. Any amounts loaned shall be deposited in the fund to be allocated by the board in accordance with this chapter. *(Added by Stats 1988 ch 264 §1, eff. 11/8/88.)*

§4496.48. Limitations on disbursement of proceeds.

The Legislature hereby finds and declares that, inasmuch as the proceeds from the sale of bonds authorized by this title are not "proceeds of taxes" as that term is used in Article XIII B of the California Constitution, the disbursement of these proceeds is not subject to the limitations imposed by that article. *(Added by Stats 1988 ch 264 §1, eff. 11/8/88.)*

TITLE 4.85

COUNTY CORRECTIONAL FACILITIES CAPITAL EXPENDITURE AND YOUTH FACILITY BOND ACT OF 1988 ALLOCATIONS
(Added by Stats 1989 ch 1327 §5, eff. 10/2/89.)

CHAPTER 1

GENERAL

§4497. Legislative intent.

(a) The Legislature finds and declares that approval by the electors of the County Correctional Facilities Capital Expenditure and Youth Facility Bond Act of 1988 has made new funds available for the construction and renovation of county jails and county juvenile facilities. The Legislature hereby directs the Board of Corrections to allocate and administer the moneys intended in the County Correctional Facilities Capital Expenditure and Youth Facility Bond Act of 1988 for county jails, and the Department of the Youth Authority to allocate and administer the moneys intended in the County Correctional Facilities Capital Expenditure and Youth Facility Bond Act of 1988 for juvenile facilities, in accordance with the provisions of this title.

(b) Money appropriated for allocation under this title may be used for the renovation, replacement, reconstruction, or construction of county jail facilities, county medical facilities designated to house persons charged with or convicted of a crime and who are mentally ill, and county juvenile facilities. Money appropriated by this title may also be used for construction of separate local detention facility space for detoxification of persons arrested because of intoxication.

© 1992 by J., B. & L. Gould
Printed in the U.S.A.   **EP**

(c) It is the Legislature's intention to make the money appropriated for allocation under this title available to counties with established and documented needs for capital projects for jail and juvenile facilities. However, that money shall not be used to build facilities that the counties cannot afford to operate fully and safely. *(Added by Stats 1989 ch 1327 §5, eff. 10/2/89.)*

CHAPTER 2

COUNTY JAILS

§4497.02. Definitions.
(a) For the purpose of this chapter:
(1) "Board" means the Board of Corrections.
(2) "Fund" means the 1988 County Correctional Facilities Capital Expenditure and Youth Facility Fund.
(b) The Board of Corrections shall not itself be deemed a responsible agency, as defined by Section 21069 of the Public Resources Code, or otherwise be subject to the California Environmental Quality Act for any activities under this title, the County Jail Capital Expenditure Bond Acts of 1981 or 1984, or the County Facility Capital Expenditure Bond Act of 1986. This subdivision does not exempt any local agency from the requirements of the California Environmental Quality Act. *(Added by Stats 1989 ch 1327 §5, eff. 10/2/89.)*

§4497.04. Moneys allocated.
Money appropriated to the board for allocation pursuant to this chapter shall be allocated as follows:
(a) Funding shall be provided for those projects entitled to be funded under subdivision (c) of Section 3 of Chapter 444, Statutes of 1984, as amended, and Section 5 of Chapter 1519, Statutes of 1986, to the extent that those projects have not received full funding.
(b) The following additional amounts shall be allocated to the counties for the construction, reconstruction, replacement, or renovation of county jail facilities. These funds shall not be used to supplant local funds directed to previously approved state projects. Nor shall these funds be used to reimburse counties whose match on previously approved projects exceeded the required 25 percent. These funds may be used for allocations specified in subdivisions (c) and (d) of Chapter 444, Statutes of 1984, as amended, and Section 5, subdivision (b) of Chapter 1519, Statutes of 1986.

County	Allocation
Alameda	$ 6,441,198
Alpine	62,541
Amador	0
Butte	1,900,266
Calaveras	0
Colusa	0
Contra Costa	1,420,488
Del Norte	1,317,106
El Dorado	0
Fresno	4,326,606
Glenn	732,094
Humboldt	2,116,523
Imperial	0
Inyo	1,214,025
Kern	9,650,404
Kings	891,687
Lake	1,699,291
Lassen	727,717
Los Angeles	172,682,741
Madera	0
Marin	2,166,458
Mariposa	117,478
Mendocino	1,214,270
Merced	2,446,318
Modoc	181,761
Mono	120,421
Monterey	7,429,146
Napa	358,819
Nevada	1,179,930
Orange	21,723,387
Placer	2,022,123
Plumas	166,775
Riverside	10,476,076
Sacramento	6,299,898
San Benito	1,270,642
San Bernardino	10,874,718
San Diego	32,675,959
San Francisco	17,015,321
San Joaquin	12,377,292
San Luis Obispo	2,033,185
San Mateo	2,452,925
Santa Barbara	2,438,604
Santa Clara	11,780,710
Santa Cruz	2,889,829
Shasta	0
Sierra	119,234
Siskiyou	0
Solano	1,125,732
Sonoma	3,877,521
Stanislaus	3,649,178
Sutter	964,137
Tehama	532,947
Trinity	225,380
Tulare	2,513,889
Tuolumne	677,876
Ventura	14,733,637
Yolo	686,721
Yuba	1,844,691
TOTAL	$387,845,675

(c) If any county declares that it is unable to use the funds allocated to it under this section, or if any county is unable to satisfy the prerequisites for funding listed in Section 4494.10, the amount allocated to the county in this section shall revert to the state, to be reallocated by the board.
(d) If funds beyond those needed for the itemized amounts become available for reallocation, the board shall reallocate those funds under subdivision (e).
(e) Reverted funds under this chapter or subdivision (c) of Chapter 1519 of the Statutes of 1986 shall be reallocated to counties pursuant to the development and adoption of a new allocation plan as determined by an allocation advisory committee appointed by the board. The allocation advisory committee shall convene upon notification by the board that funds have been reverted. Reallocated funds shall be distributed three times. The first distribution shall occur on December 31, 1990; the second distribution shall occur on December 31, 1992, and the final distribution shall occur on December 31, 1993. If any county seeking funds has not completed architectural drawings at the time reallocation funds become available, the county shall be removed from reallocation consideration until it has completed architectural drawings.
(f) Any county that receives funds pursuant to this chapter or pursuant to Chapter 444 of the Statutes of

1984, as amended, or Chapter 1519 of the Statutes of 1986, that, in the aggregate, total ten million dollars ($10,000,000) or less may pool or combine those funds for the purpose of financing a jail construction project, subject to approval of the project pursuant to this chapter. However, under no circumstances shall the pooling of successive bond allocations relieve or exempt the county from its obligation to meet the 25 percent local match requirement.

This subdivision shall not be interpreted as an authorization to utilize allocated funds to reimburse counties whose match on previously approved and completed projects exceeded the required 25 percent. *(Added by Stats 1989 ch 1327 §5, eff. 10/2/89.)*

§4497.05. Joint funding of projects.

Money in the 1986 County Correctional Facility Capital Expenditure Fund and money in the 1988 County Correctional Facility Capital Expenditure and Youth Facility Bond Fund may be used on the same project so long as the project is consistent with the purposes set forth in Sections 4485 and 4496.12 and is subject to the restrictions and requirements set forth in subdivision (f) of Section 4497.04. The deadlines applicable under this title shall be applicable to the joint use of funds under this section. *(Added by Stats 1990 ch 619 §1, eff. 1/1/91.)*

§4497.06. Administration of funds.

(a) The board shall administer the funds allocated in this chapter to adult jail facilities, according to existing County Correctional Facilities Capital Expenditure Fund regulations, except as those regulations may be amended to comply with the provisions of this chapter.

(b) The board shall apply its regulations in the approval or disapproval of county jail projects, except that the board may approve a project if the board finds, after conducting a public hearing, that although the county cannot possibly meet the regulations, the county will nonetheless comply with Section 4485.6. *(Added by Stats 1989 ch 1327 §5, eff. 10/2/89.)*

§4497.08. Encumbrance of funds.

No state moneys shall be encumbered in contracts with a county, nor released to a county, for construction or renovation of a local jail facility pursuant to this chapter until the conditions of this chapter have been fulfilled by the county. *(Added by Stats 1989 ch 1327 §5, eff. 10/2/89.)*

§4497.10. County funding eligibility requirements.

To be eligible for funding consideration, a county shall, to the satisfaction of the board, do all of the following:

(a) Certify that juveniles are not housed in the county's adult detention facilities, except where authorized by law; and document the existence of, or plans for, separate housing for juveniles.

(b) Document the existence of, or plans for, separate housing for persons detained or arrested because of intoxication, which will prevent mixing of this category of prisoner with other prisoners. If the county has no existing provisions for detoxification housing, it shall make provisions for that housing as part of its proposed project.

(c) Document the existence of, or plans for, separate housing for mentally disordered defendants or convicted prisoners which will prevent mixing of this category of prisoner with other prisoners until the time that the responsible health authority or his or her designee clears specific prisoners for nonseparate housing, based on clinical judgment. If the county has no existing provisions for separate housing of mentally disordered prisoners, it shall make provisions for that housing as part of its proposed project.

(d) Submit a formal project proposal to the board on or before September 30, 1990. The project proposal shall describe the construction or renovation project to be undertaken and shall include an estimated budget for the project. The proposal shall also identify how county funding obligations, both for construction and operation of the facility, will be met. The project proposal shall be consistent with the needs and priorities identified in the needs assessment by the county.

Failure to submit a project proposal shall be deemed a declaration by the county that it does not intend to request its allocation under subdivisions (a) and (b) of Section 4497.04, and the amounts allocated in those subdivisions to the county shall be available for reallocation by the board. The board may waive this requirement for submission of a proposal within one year if it determines there are unavoidable delays in the county's preparation of a project proposal.

(e) Submit architectural drawings which shall be approved by the board for compliance with minimum jail standards and by the State Fire Marshal for compliance with fire safety requirements. If the board concludes that a county's proposed construction or renovation contains serious design deficiencies that, while they would not require a refusal to enter into the contract, would seriously impair the facility's functioning, it shall notify the sheriff and the board of supervisors of that county of the deficiencies and shall delay entering into a contract with the county for at least 30 days after mailing the letter. This letter shall be a public record.

(f) The county shall certify that it owns, or has long-term possession of, the construction site.

(g) The county shall have filed a final notice of determination on its environmental impact report with the board.

(h) The county has formally adopted a plan to finance the construction of the proposed facility.

(i) The county shall have submitted a preliminary staffing plan for the proposed facility, along with an analysis of other operating costs anticipated for the facility, to the board for review and comment. Prior to submission of the staffing plan and operating costs analysis of the board, the county board of supervisors shall have reviewed and approved the submittal in or following public hearings. The sheriff shall also have reviewed and commented on the preliminary staffing plan and the operating cost analysis. The board shall comment in writing to the sheriff and board of supervisors. This letter shall be a public record.

(j) The county shall submit either a major or minor needs assessment documenting the need for and purpose of the proposed project. The needs assessment shall meet all requirements listed in the applicable County Correctional Facility Capital Expenditure Fund regulations. The board may exempt a county from performing a new needs assessment if any of the following conditions exist:

(1) The board determines that a prior needs assessment is in substantial compliance and it justifies the project being funded in Section 4497.04.

© 1992 by J., B. & L. Gould
Printed in the U.S.A.   EP

(2) A county receives funds from this bond act in an amount of three hundred thousand dollars ($300,000) or less.

If exempted from performing a needs assessment, counties shall provide an analysis of specific jail deficiencies, including levels of security, program, including, but not limited to, medical and mental health care, housing, and administration. This analysis shall also include specific plans for correcting the deficiencies.

(k) Demonstrate to the board unless the county's sole project is a remodel of an existing adult detention facility which will not result in the addition of any beds, that it is using, to the greatest extent feasible, alternatives to incarceration based on the following measures: an incarceration rate of no more than one standard deviation above the mean for all counties and, either a pretrial misdemeanor incarceration rate of no more than one standard deviation above the mean for all counties or a sentenced prisoner alternatives percentage or 5 percent or more as related to total sentenced prisoner admissions.

(1) The data to be used in establishing the incarceration rate will be the 1989 calendar year average daily population as reported by each county to the board and the Department of Finance Report on Population by County.

(2) The pretrial misdemeanor incarceration rate will be based on an average of the daily pretrial misdemeanor jail population, developed from a four-day sample period in 1989 specified by the board.

(3) The sentenced prisoner alternatives percentage will be based on enrollment in three programs: Section 4024.2 of the Penal Code (work-in-lieu of jail), county parole, and home detention if the placement is made after some jail time is served.

(4) Counties failing to demonstrate adequate use of alternatives to incarcerations by the above measure by March 30, 1990, shall be reevaluated annually by the board. If any county is unable to satisfy the requirements of this section by September 30, 1993, the amount allocated to the county shall revert to the state, to be reallocated by the board pursuant to subdivision (c) of Section 4497.04.

(l) Begin construction or renovation work within four years of the effective date of this title. If a county fails to meet this requirement, any allocations to the county under this chapter shall be deemed void and moneys allocated to the county shall revert to the board for reallocation. The board may waive this requirement if it determines that there are unavoidable delays in the initial construction activities.

(m) Counties shall provide for the construction of appropriate courtroom facilities and hearing room facilities within any jail construction plan submitted to the board. Those courtroom facilities and hearing room facilities shall be utilized for purposes of holding appropriate arraignments and bail hearings and for the conduct of parole revocation hearings. The board may waive this requirement where county specific circumstances dictate. (Added by Stats 1989 ch 1327 §5, eff. 10/2/89.)

§4497.12. Matching funds by county.

(a) County match on projects funded under this chapter shall be a minimum of 25 percent of the total project costs.

(b) The county match requirement imposed upon counties pursuant to the receipt of state moneys shall not be required to be made on a pro rata basis where the requirement would impede the expeditious and equitable construction of county correctional facilities. However, under no circumstances shall the county match for any county project be less than 25 percent.

(c) Costs eligible for state funding and as county match shall be those defined in applicable existing sections of the County Correctional Facilities Capital Expenditure Fund regulations, which regulations may be amended. (Amended by Stats 1990 ch 1056 §1; ch 1057 §1, eff. 1/1/91.)

§4497.14. Requirement for funding prior to construction.

(a) The board shall not approve the expenditures of funds allocated under this act for the construction of county detention facilities until a master site plan for county detention facilities has been prepared and adopted by the board of supervisors of the county proposing to construct the facility. The board of supervisors shall determine the location of any detention facilities pursuant to a master plan, which determination shall not be subject to any initiative or ordinance adopted by initiative. In developing the plan, the board of supervisors shall consider alternatives to additional detention facilities and the specific concerns of incorporated cities and other community representatives, and shall give special consideration to existing federal, state, and local detention facilities in order to avoid over-concentration of inmates in one geographic area of the county. If the board of supervisors decides to locate new or expanded detention facilities near existing detention facilities, it shall publicly state its reasons for that decision.

The board shall only approve expenditure of funds allocated under this chapter for the construction of detention facilities in accordance with the plan adopted pursuant to this section. The board may exempt a county from this requirement if the master site plan remains unchanged from that approved under the provisions of the County Correctional Facilities Capital Expenditure Bond Act of 1986.

(b) The board shall establish construction costs controls and shall set forth in regulation procedures for setting maximum state funding levels for appropriate construction unit costs, including cost per cell for specified categories of facilities. These cost controls shall be based on average costs in recently constructed facilities in California that are comparable in size, use, location, and other relevant factors.

Allocations listed in Section 4497.04 notwithstanding, the state contribution shall be up to 75 percent of total project costs or up to 75 percent of the applicable construction cost norms, whichever is lower. Nothing in this section is intended, however, to prescribe maximum limits on county funding levels for the projects.

Prior to releasing any funds to a county, the board shall review construction cost levels in the funded projects for compliance with cost control regulations.

(c) Prior to entering into a contract with a county, the board shall review or approve or both review and approve the county submissions required by this chapter regarding the facility or facilities proposed for funding.

(d) The board shall collect annually from all counties information on county incarceration rates, average daily jail populations as a proportion of the total county population or total arrests or both; pretrial misdemeanant ratios, the percentage which unsentenced prisoners charged only with misdemeanors constitute the total average daily unsentenced jail population; and sentenced alternatives ratios, for example, average daily populations in work-in-lieu of jail programs and county parole as a percentage of the total average daily sentenced misdemeanant prisoner population. All counties that have received or will receive state funds for jail construction shall supply the board the information necessary to comply with this section. *(Added by Stats 1989 ch 1327 §5, eff. 10/2/89.)*

§4497.16. Failure to comply.

If after a hearing, the board makes a finding that a county has failed to comply with a condition or plan approved by the board relating to the requirements of Section 4485.6, the board may require the county to pay an amount equal to the pro rata portion of the principal and interest, paid by the state on bonds the proceeds of which were allocated pursuant to this chapter to the county for the period of noncompliance. The repayment provisions shall not be applicable if the noncompliance with the condition or plan is the result of circumstances beyond the control of the county, or the board finds the county cannot reasonably comply under the circumstances. *(Added by Stats 1989 ch 1327 §5, eff. 10/2/89.)*

§4497.18. Annual report to Legislature.

(a) As part of its annual report to the Legislature, the board shall provide to the Legislature a report on the status of funds expended, interest being earned, actions implementing the prerequisites for funding listed in Section 4497.04, and any reallocations of funds pursuant to Section 4497.04. The report shall contain a complete listing of funds allocated to each county. The board shall also submit appropriate recommendations, if any, on needed changes in the program and on other matters pertinent to jail funding on which the board wishes to inform the Legislature. The report shall be submitted to the Legislature on or before July 1 of each year.

(b) In order to provide information pertinent to the performance of this funding program and to any additional funding needs, counties receiving funds under this chapter shall, as a condition of the funding contract, report to the board, at intervals and in a manner to be determined by the board. The sheriff or other official in charge of operating the adult detention system in a county receiving funds under this act shall maintain an inmate accounting system. Data to be maintained on an annual basis includes the following:

(1) Average daily population of sentenced and unsentenced prisoners by categories of male, female, and juvenile.

(2) Jail admissions of sentenced and unsentenced prisoners by categories of male, female, booking charge, date and time of booking, date and time of release, and operating expenses.

(3) Detention system capital and operating expenses. *(Added by Stats 1989 ch 1327 §5, eff. 10/2/89.)*

CHAPTER 3

JUVENILE FACILITIES

§4497.20. Department of Youth to administer funds.

(a) The Department of the Youth Authority is hereby directed to administer the moneys intended for juvenile facilities in the County Correctional Facility Capital Expenditure and Youth Facility Bond Act of 1988, in accordance with the provisions of this chapter.

(b) It is the intention of the Legislature to make the money appropriated for allocation under this chapter available to counties with established and documented needs for capital projects for juvenile facilities.

(c) Counties that apply for funds to alleviate overcrowding shall submit a preliminary staffing plan for the proposed facility, along with an analysis of other operating costs anticipated for the facility, to the Department of the Youth Authority for review and comment. Prior to submission of the staffing plan and operating cost analysis to the department, the board of supervisors shall have reviewed and approved the submittal in or following public hearings. The chief probation officer shall also have reviewed and commented on the preliminary staffing plan and operating cost analysis. The department shall comment in writing to the chief probation officer and board of supervisors. This response shall be a public record.

(d) The Department of the Youth Authority shall conduct an assessment of the needs of counties for juvenile facilities in California which shall be submitted to the Legislature by June 30, 1990. *(Added by Stats 1989 ch 1327 §5, eff. 10/2/89.)*

§4497.22. Allocation of funds.

Funds appropriated to the Department of the Youth Authority for allocation under this chapter shall be allocated as provided by this chapter. *(Added by Stats 1989 ch 1327 §5, eff. 10/2/89.)*

§4497.24. Funds to establish juvenile facilities.

Two million dollars ($2,000,000) shall be set aside initially for the counties that did not have juvenile facilities on January 1, 1987. These funds shall be used to construct county juvenile facilities and are hereby allocated as follows:

Amador	$ 33,000
Calaveras	80,000
Colusa	75,000
Inyo	846,000
Lassen	350,000
Mariposa	50,000
Modoc	126,000
Mono	18,000
Plumas	45,000
San Benito	243,000
Sierra	10,000
Trinity	30,000
Tuolumne	94,000

(Added by Stats 1989 ch 1327 §5, eff. 10/2/89.)

§4497.26. Funds to improve facilities.

Ten million dollars ($10,00,000) shall be set aside initially for counties that do not have efficient and adequate facilities for youth with special problems. Two or more counties may apply jointly to construct those facilities regionally. No more than three million three hundred thousand dollars ($3,300,000) shall be awarded for the construction of each regional facility. *(Added by Stats 1989 ch 1327 §5, eff. 10/2/89.)*

§4497.28. Funds to alleviate overcrowding.

Forty-eight million seven hundred fifty thousand dollars ($48,750,000) shall be set aside initially for counties to alleviate overcrowding and eliminate health, fire, and life safety deficiencies in juvenile

© 1992 by J., B. & L. Gould
Printed in the U.S.A.   EP

facilities or provide efficient and adequate facility for youth with special problems. These funds are hereby allocated on a per capita share basis to all counties except those listed in Section 4497.24, as follows:

Alameda	$ 2,161,656
Butte	303,787
Contra Costa	1,329,808
Del Norte	34,798
El Dorado	210,354
Fresno	1,064,299
Humboldt	201,133
Imperial	196,087
Kern	901,792
Kings	163,725
Lake	89,431
Los Angeles	14,970,647
Madera	143,542
Marin	400,004
Mendocino	132,407
Merced	297,871
Monterey	605,660
Napa	184,952
Nevada	134,321
Orange	3,934,095
Placer	272,121
Riverside	1,700,581
Sacramento	1,696,928
San Bernardino	2,235,602
San Diego	4,123,745
San Francisco	1,275,871
San Joaquin	794,440
San Luis Obispo	360,682
San Mateo	1,093,529
Santa Barbara	596,961
Santa Clara	2,488,758
Santa Cruz	393,914
Shasta	242,890
Siskiyou	75,338
Solano	544,764
Sonoma	636,457
Stanislaus	591,915
Sutter	107,352
Tehama	81,253
Tulare	517,621
Ventura	1,125,195
Yolo	234,887
Yuba	98,827

(Added by Stats 1989 ch 1327 §5, eff. 10/2/89.)

§4497.30. Initial bond interest costs.

Three million twenty-five thousand dollars ($3,025,000) shall be set aside initially for bond interest costs and two hundred fifty thousand dollars ($250,000) shall be set aside to conduct a statewide assessment of the counties' needs for juvenile facilities. *(Added by Stats 1989 ch 1327 §5, eff. 10/2/89.)*

§4497.32. Excess funds.

(a) Funds which were set aside initially as provided by Sections 4497.24 to 4497.30, inclusive, that are not used and funds that were allocated under the provisions of the County Correctional Facility Capital Expenditure Bond Act of 1986 that are not used shall be allocated by the Department of the Youth Authority to those counties that received an allocation under Section 4497.28 which was not sufficient to fund the remaining portion of the total cost of the approved projects. The amount of each of those county's alloca-

tion shall be that county's per capita share of the total funds available for all counties with partially funded projects, or the amount needed to complete funding of that county's approved projects, whichever is less. At no time shall the allocation exceed 75 percent of the total eligible costs.

(b) The allocation procedure described in subdivision (a) shall be repeated until all of the available funds are awarded.

(c) Funds awarded by the Department of the Youth Authority under this section shall be used for the construction, reconstruction, remodeling, or replacement of county juvenile facilities, and for the performance of deferred maintenance on juvenile facilities, but may only be used for the purpose of reducing current overcrowding and eliminating health, fire, and life safety hazards. *(Added by Stats 1989 ch 1327 §5, eff. 10/2/89.)*

§4497.34. Funding to overcrowded facilities.

(a) Counties with overcrowded juvenile facilities shall not be eligible to receive funds to construct, reconstruct, remodel, or replace juvenile facilities unless they have adopted a plan to correct overcrowded conditions within their facilities which includes the use of alternatives to detention. The corrective action plan shall provide for the use of five or more methods or procedures to minimize the number of minors detained and shall be approved by the board of supervisors during or subsequent to a public hearing.

(b) To be eligible for funding under this chapter, the county shall enter into a contract with the Department of the Youth Authority and begin construction or renovation work within four years of the operative date of the regulations that implement this chapter. If a county fails to meet this requirement, any allocations or awards to that county under this chapter shall be deemed void and any moneys allocated or awarded to that county shall revert to the Department of the Youth Authority for reallocation to another county as provided by Section 4497.32. The department may waive this requirement if it determines that there are unavoidable delays in starting construction.

(c) To be eligible for funding for juvenile facilities under the County Correctional Facility Capital Expenditure Bond Act of 1986, the county shall enter into a contract with the Department of the Youth Authority and begin construction or renovation work by July 31, 1991. If a county fails to meet this requirement, all allocations or awards that have been made to that county under that act shall be deemed void and any moneys allocated or awarded to that county shall revert to the Department of the Youth Authority and are reappropriated for reallocation as provided by Section 4497.32. The department may waive this requirement if it determines that there are unavoidable delays in starting construction. *(Added by Stats 1989 ch 1327 §5, eff. 10/2/89.)*

§4497.36. Application for funding.

An application for funds shall be in the manner and form prescribed by the Department of the Youth Authority. *(Added by Stats 1989 ch 1327 §5, eff. 10/2/89.)*

§4497.38. Matching funding.

Awards shall be made only if county matching funds of 25 percent are provided. *(Added by Stats 1989 ch 1327 §5, eff. 10/2/89.)*

§4497.40. Reports to Legislature.

The Department of the Youth Authority shall report to the Legislature by July 1, 1991, on the status of funds expended and provide a complete list of funds allocated to each county. *(Added by Stats 1989 ch 1327 §5, eff. 10/2/89.)*

CHAPTER 4

PURCHASE OF CORRECTIONAL INDUSTRY PRODUCTS FOR CORRECTIONAL, JUVENILE, AND YOUTH FACILITIES

§4497.50. Requirements for funding.

In order to be eligible to receive funds derived from the issuance of General Obligation Bonds under the County Correctional Facility Capital Expenditure and Youth Facility Bond Act of 1988, a county or city and county shall do all the following:

(a) In the design and planning of facilities whose construction, reconstruction, or remodeling is financed under the County Correctional Facility Capital Expenditure and Youth Facility Bond Act of 1988, products for construction, renovation, equipment, and furnishings produced and sold by the Prison Industry Authority or local jail industry programs shall be utilized in the plans and specifications unless the county or city and county demonstrates either of the following to the satisfaction of the Board of Corrections or the Department of the Youth Authority:

(1) The products cannot be produced and delivered without causing delay to the construction of the property.

(2) The products are not suitable for the facility or competitively priced and cannot otherwise be reasonably adapted.

(b) Counties and cities and counties shall consult with the staff of the Prison Industry Authority or local jail industry program to develop new products and adapt existing products to their needs.

(c) The Board of Corrections or the Department of the Youth Authority shall not enter into any contract with any county or city and county until that county's or city and county's plan for purchase from and consultation with the Prison Industry Authority or local jail industry program is reviewed and approved by the Board of Corrections or the Department of the Youth Authority. *(Added by Stats 1989 ch 1327 §5, eff. 10/2/89.)*

§4497.52. Contracts for purchase of prison products.

Notwithstanding any other provision of law, a county or city and county may contract for the purchase of products as specified in Section 4497.50 with the Prison Industry Authority or local jail industry program without the formality of obtaining bids or otherwise complying with provisions of the Public Contract Code. *(Added by Stats 1989 ch 1327 §5, eff. 10/2/89.)*

§4497.54. Designation of liaison.

The Prison Industry Authority shall designate an individual as County Jail and Juvenile Facility Liaison who shall work with counties to maximize the utilization of Prison Industry Authority products for construction, renovation, equipment, and furnishing, to ensure that manufactured products meet the contract specifications and delivery dates, and to assure consultation with counties for development of new products and adaption of existing products to meet their needs. *(Added by Stats 1989 ch 1327 §5, eff. 10/2/89.)*

§4497.56. Maximization of prison products.

It is the intent of the Legislature to maximize the utilization of Prison Industry Authority products for jail construction, renovation, equipment, and furnishings to ensure that prisoners work productively and contribute to reducing the cost to the taxpayers of their incarceration. *(Added by Stats 1989 ch 1327 §5, eff. 10/2/89.)*

TITLE 5

OFFENSES RELATING TO PRISONS AND PRISONERS

CHAPTER 1

OFFENSES BY PRISONERS

§4500. Aggravated assault by life prisoner.

Every person while undergoing a life sentence, who is sentenced to state prison within this state, and who, with malice aforethought, commits an assault upon the person of another with a deadly weapon or instrument, or by any means of force likely to produce great bodily injury is punishable with death or life imprisonment without possibility of parole. The penalty shall be determined pursuant to the provisions of Sections 190.3 and 190.4; however, in cases in which the person subjected to such assault does not die within a year and a day after such assault as a proximate result thereof, the punishment shall be imprisonment in the state prison for life without the possibility of parole for nine years.

For the purpose of computing the days elapsed between the commission of the assault and the death of the person assaulted, the whole of the day on which the assault was committed shall be counted as the first day.

Nothing in this section shall be construed to prohibit the application of this section when the assault was committed outside the walls of any prison if the person committing the assault was undergoing a life sentence and was serving a sentence to a state prison at the time of the commission of the assault and was not on parole, on probation, or released on bail pending an appeal. *(Amended by Stats 1986 ch 1445 §1.)*

§4501. Aggravated assault by other prisoners.

Every person confined in a state prison of this state except one undergoing a life sentence who commits an assault upon the person of another with a deadly weapon or instrument, or by any means of force likely to produce great bodily injury, shall be guilty of a felony and shall be imprisoned in the state prison for two, four, or six years to be served consecutively.

§4501.5. Battery on non-prisoner by prisoner.

Every person confined in a state prison of this state who commits a battery upon the person of any individual who is not himself a person confined therein shall be guilty of a felony and shall be imprisoned in the state prison for two, three, or four years, to be served consecutively.

© 1992 by J., B. & L. Gould
Printed in the U.S.A.   EP

§4502. Possession of weapon by prisoner.

Every person confined in a state prison or who, while being conveyed to or from any state prison or while at any prison road camp, prison forestry camp, or other prison camps or prison farms or while being conveyed to or from any such place or while under the custody of prison officials, officers or employees, possesses or carries upon his person or has under his custody or control any instrument or weapon of the kind commonly known as a blackjack, slungshot, billy, sandclub, sandbag, or metal knuckles, any explosive substance, or fixed ammunition, any dirk or dagger or sharp instrument, any pistol, revolver or other firearm, or any tear gas or tear gas weapon, is guilty of a felony and shall be punishable by imprisonment in a state prison for two, three, or four years to be served consecutively. *(Amended by Stats 1988 ch 124 §1, eff. 1/1/89.)*

§4503. Prisoner holding hostages.

Any person confined therein who holds as hostage any person within any prison or facility under the jurisdiction of the Director of Corrections, or who by force or threat of force holds any person or persons against their will in defiance of official orders within any such prison or facility, shall be guilty of a felony and shall be imprisoned in the state prison for three, five, or seven years to be served consecutively.

§4504. Confined in "state prison" and "confined in" explained.

For purposes of this chapter:

(a) A person is deemed confined in a "state prison" if he is confined in any of the prisons and institutions specified in Section 5003 by order made pursuant to law, including, but not limited to, commitments to the Department of Corrections or the Department of the Youth Authority, regardless of the purpose of such confinement and regardless of the validity of the order directing such confinement, until a judgment of a competent court setting aside such order becomes final.

(b) A person is deemed "confined in" a prison although, at the time of the offense, he is temporarily outside its walls or bounds for the purpose of serving on a work detail or for the purpose of confinement in a local correctional institution pending trial or for any other purpose for which a prisoner may be allowed temporarily outside the walls or bounds of the prison, but a prisoner who has been released on parole is not deemed "confined in" a prison for purposes of this chapter.

CHAPTER 2

ESCAPES AND RESCUES

ARTICLE 1

ESCAPES

§4530. Escape from state prison, road camp.

(a) Every prisoner confined in a state prison who, by force or violence, escapes or attempts to escape therefrom and every prisoner committed to a state prison who, by force or violence, escapes or attempts to escape while being conveyed to or from such prison or any other state prison, or any prison road camp, prison forestry camp, or other prison camp or prison

farm or any other place while under the custody of prison officials, officers or employees; or who, by force, or violence, escapes or attempts to escape from any prison road camp, prison forestry camp or other prison camp or prison farm or other place while under the custody of prison officials, officers or employees; or who, by force or violence, escapes or attempts to escape while at work outside or away from prison under custody of prison officials, officers, or employees, is punishable by imprisonment in a state prison for a term of two, four, or six years. The second term of imprisonment of a person convicted under this subdivision shall commence from the time he would otherwise be discharged from prison. No additional probation report shall be required with respect to such offense.

(b) Every prisoner who commits an escape or attempts an escape as described in subdivision (a), without force or violence, is punishable by imprisonment in the state prison for 16 months, or two or three years to be served consecutively. No additional probation report shall be required with respect to such offense.

(c) The willful failure of a prisoner who is employed or continuing his education, or who is authorized to secure employment or education, or who is temporarily released pursuant to Section 2690, 2910, or 6254, or Section 3306 of the Welfare and Institutions Code, to return to the place of confinement not later than the expiration of a period during which he or she is authorized to be away from the place of confinement, is an escape from the place of confinement punishable as provided in this section. A conviction of a violation of this subdivision, not involving force or violence, shall not be charged as a prior felony conviction in any subsequent prosecution for a public offense. *(Amended by Stats 1987 ch 828 §137.)*

§4530.5. Deuel Vocational Institute deemed state prison.

For the purposes of punishing escapes or attempts to escape under Section 4530, a person is deemed confined in a "state prison" if he is an adult prisoner confined in the Deuel Vocational Institution.

§4532. Escape from prison, jail, farm or work furlough.

(a) Every prisoner arrested and booked for, charged with, or convicted of a misdemeanor, and every person committed under the terms of Section 5654, 5656, or 5677 of the Welfare and Institutions Code as an inebriate, who is confined in any county or city jail or prison or industrial farm or industrial road camp or who is engaged on any county road or other county work or who is in the lawful custody of any officer or person, or who is employed or continuing in his or her regular educational program or authorized to secure employment or education away from the place of confinement, pursuant to the Cobey Work Furlough Law (Section 1208), or who is authorized for temporary release for family emergencies or for purposes preparatory to his or her return to the community pursuant to Section 4018.6, and who thereafter escapes or attempts to escape from the county or city jail, prison, industrial farm or industrial road camp or from the custody of the officer or person in charge of him or her while engaged in or going to or returning from the county work or from the custody of any officer or person in whose lawful custody he or she is, is guilty of a felony and, if the escape or attempt to escape was not by force or violence, is punishable by imprisonment in the state prison for a determinate term of one year and one day, or in the county jail not exceeding one year. However, if the escape or attempt to escape is by force or violence, the person is guilty of a felony and is punishable by imprisonment in the state prison for two, four, or six years to be served consecutively, or in the county jail not exceeding one year. When the second term of imprisonment is to be served in the county jail, it shall commence from the time the prisoner would otherwise have been discharged from jail.

The willful failure of a prisoner, whether convicted of a felony or a misdemeanor, employed or continuing in his or her regular educational program or authorized to secure employment or education pursuant to the Cobey Work Furlough Law (Section 1208) or authorized for temporary release for family emergencies or for purposes preparatory to his or her return to the community pursuant to Section 4018.6, to return to the place of confinement not later than the expiration of a period during which, pursuant to that law, he or she is authorized to be away from that place of confinement, is an escape from the place of confinement punishable as provided in this subdivision.

A conviction of violation of this subdivision, not by force or violence, shall not be charged as a prior felony conviction in any subsequent prosecution for a public offense.

(b) Every prisoner arrested and booked for, charged with, or convicted of a felony, and every person committed by order of the juvenile court, who is confined in any county or city jail or prison or industrial farm or industrial road camp or who is engaged on any county road or other county work or who is in the lawful custody of any officer or person, or who is confined pursuant to Section 4011.9, who escapes or attempts to escape from the county or city jail, prison, industrial farm or industrial road camp or from the custody of the officer or person in charge of him or her while engaged in or going to or returning from the county work or from the custody of any officer or person in whose lawful custody he or she is, or from confinement pursuant to Section 4011.9, is guilty of a felony and, if the escape or attempt to escape was not by force or violence, is punishable by imprisonment in the state prison for 16 months, or two or three years to be served consecutively, or in the county jail not exceeding one year. If the escape or attempt to escape is by force or violence, the person is guilty of a felony and is punishable by imprisonment in the state prison for a full term of two, four, or six years to be consecutive to any other term of imprisonment, commencing from the time the person would otherwise have been released from imprisonment and the term shall not be subject to reduction pursuant to subdivision (a) of Section 1170.1, or in the county jail for a consecutive term not to exceed one year, that term to commence from the time the prisoner would otherwise have been discharged from the jail.

(c) Except in unusual cases where the interests of justice would best be served if the person is granted probation, probation shall not be granted to any person who is convicted of a felony offense under this section in that he or she escaped or attempted to escape from a secure main jail facility, from a court building or while being transported between the court building and the jail facility. In any case in which a person is convicted of such an offense designated as a misdemeanor, he or she shall be confined in the county jail for not less than 90 days nor more than one year except in unusual cases where the interests of justice would best be served by the granting of probation. For the purposes of this subdivision, "main jail facility" means the facility used for the detention of persons pending arraignment, after arraignment, during trial, and upon sentence or commitment. The facility shall not include an industrial farm, industrial road camp, work furlough facility, or any other nonsecure facility used primarily for sentenced prisoners. As used in this subdivision, "secure" means that the facility contains an outer perimeter characterized by the use of physically restricting construction, hardware, and procedures designed to eliminate ingress and egress from the facility except through a closely supervised gate or doorway.

If the court grants probation under this subdivision, it shall specify the reason or reasons for that order on the court record.

Any sentence imposed under this subdivision shall be served consecutive to any other sentence in effect or pending. *(Amended by Stats 1991 ch 1162 §1, eff. 1/1/92.)*

§4533. Prison keepers.

Every keeper of a prison, sheriff, deputy sheriff, constable, or jailor, or person employed as a guard, who fraudulently contrives, procures, aids, connives at, or voluntarily permits the escape of any prisoner in custody, is punishable by imprisonment in the state prison, and fine not exceeding ten thousand dollars ($10,000).

§4534. Other persons aiding escape.

Any person who wilfully assists any paroled prisoner whose parole has been revoked, any escapee, any prisoner confined in any prison or jail, or any person in the lawful custody of any officer or person, to escape, or in an attempt to escape from such prison or jail, or custody, is punishable as provided in Section 4533.

§4535. Sending, etc., escape implements into prison.

Every person who carries or sends into a prison or jail anything useful to aid a prisoner or inmate in making his escape, with intent thereby to facilitate the escape of any prisoner or inmate confined therein, is guilty of a felony.

§4536. Escape from state hospital or mental health facility.

(a) Every person committed to a state hospital or other public or private mental health facility as a mentally disordered sex offender, who escapes from or who escapes while being conveyed to or from such state hospital or other public or private mental health facility, is punishable by imprisonment in the state prison or in the county jail not to exceed one year. The term imposed pursuant to this section shall be served consecutively to any other sentence or commitment.

(b) The medical director or person in charge of a state hospital or other public or private mental health facility to which a person has been committed as a mentally disordered sex offender shall promptly notify the chief of police of the city in which the hospital or facility is located, or the sheriff of the county if the

© 1992 by J., B. & L. Gould
Printed in the U.S.A.   EP

hospital or facility is located in an unincorporated area, of the escape of the person, and shall request the assistance of the chief of police or sheriff in apprehending the person, and shall, within 48 hours of the escape of the person, orally notify the court that made the commitment, the prosecutor in the case, and the Department of Justice of the escape.

§4537. Escape from secure detention facility; release of information about escaped minor.

(a) The person in charge of any secure detention facility, including, but not limited to, a prison, a juvenile hall, a county jail, or any institution under the jurisdiction of the California Youth Authority, shall promptly notify the chief of police of the city in which the facility is located, or the sheriff of the county if the facility is located in an unincorporated area, of an escape by a person in its custody.

(b) The person in charge of any secure detention facility under the jurisdiction of the Department of Corrections or the Department of the Youth Authority shall release the name of, and any descriptive information about, any person who has escaped from custody to other law enforcement agencies, or to other persons if the release of the information would be necessary to assist in recapturing the person or to protect the public from substantial physical harm.

(c) In addition to the requirements of subdivisions (a) and (b), in cases of escape by persons in the custody of the Department of Corrections who have been convicted of a felony listed in subdivision (c) of Section 667.5 or who have effected the escape by force or violence as proscribed by subdivision (a) of Section 4530, prompt notification shall be given to the newspapers of general circulation within the county in which the escape occurred, and to television stations regularly broadcasting news into and within the county, accompanied by a photograph and description of the escapee. (*Amended by Stats 1990 ch 819 §1, eff. 1/1/91.*)

ARTICLE 2

RESCUES

§4550. Punishments for aiding escapes.

Every person who rescues or attempts to rescue, or aids another person in rescuing or attempting to rescue any prisoner from any prison, or prison road camp or any jail or county road camp, or from any officer or person having him in lawful custody, is punishable as follows:

1. If such prisoner was in custody upon a conviction of a felony punishable with death: by imprisonment in the state prison for two, three or four years;

2. If such prisoner was in custody otherwise than as specified in subsection 1 hereof: by imprisonment in the state prison, or by imprisonment in the county jail not to exceed one year.

CHAPTER 3

UNAUTHORIZED COMMUNICATIONS WITH PRISONS AND PRISONERS

§4570. Communication with prisoners; furnishing reading matter.

Every person who, without the permission of the warden or other officer in charge of any State prison, or prison road camp, or prison forestry camp, or other prison camp or prison farm or any other place where prisoners of the State prison are located under the custody of prison officials, officers or employees, or any jail, or any county road camp in this State, communicates with any prisoner or person detained therein, or brings therein or takes therefrom any letter, writing, literature, or reading matter to or from any prisoner or person confined therein, is guilty of a misdemeanor.

§4570.1. Unauthorized communication during transportation of prisoners.

Every person who, without permission of the peace officer or corrections officer in charge of any vehicle, bus, van or automobile used for the transportation of prisoners, delivers a written communication to any prisoner or person detained therein, or being escorted to or from that vehicle, or takes from or gives to the prisoner any item, is guilty of a misdemeanor.

§4570.5. False identification to secure admission to prison, etc.

Every person who falsely identifies himself either verbally or by presenting any fraudulent written instrument to prison officials, officers, or employees of any state prison, prison road camp, or prison forestry camp, or other prison camp or prison farm, or any jail, or any county industrial farm, or any county road camp, for the purpose of securing admission to the premises or grounds of any such prison, camp, farm, or jail, and such person would not otherwise qualify for admission, is guilty of a misdemeanor.

§4571. Trespassing upon prison or adjacent lands.

Every person who, having been previously convicted of a felony and confined in any State prison in this State, without the consent of the warden or other officer in charge of any State prison or prison road camp, or prison forestry camp, or other prison camp or prison farm or any other place where prisoners of the State prison are located under the custody of prison officials, officers or employees, or any jail or any county road camp in this State, comes upon the grounds of any such institution, or lands belonging or adjacent thereto, is guilty of a felony.

§4572. *Repealed by Stats 1991 ch 186 §9, eff. 1/1/92.*

§4573. Bringing narcotics or alcoholic beverages into prison.

Except when otherwise authorized by law, or when authorized by the person in charge of the prison or other institution referred to in this section or by an officer of the institution empowered by the person in charge of the institution to give the authorization, any person, who knowingly brings or sends into, or knowingly assists in bringing into, or sending into, any state prison, prison road camp, prison forestry camp, or other prison camp or prison farm or any other place where prisoners of the state are located under the custody of prison officials, officers or employees, or into any county, city and county, or city jail, road camp, farm or other place where prisoners or inmates are located under custody of any sheriff, chief of police, peace officer, probation officer or employees, or within the grounds belonging to the institution, any controlled substance, the possession of which is prohibited by Division 10 (commencing with Section

11000) of the Health and Safety Code, any device, contrivance, instrument, or paraphernalia intended to be used for unlawfully injecting or consuming a controlled substance, is guilty of a felony punishable by imprisonment in the state prison for two, three, or four years.

The prohibitions and sanctions addressed in this section shall be clearly and prominently posted outside of, and at the entrance to, the grounds of all detention facilities under the jurisdiction of, or operated by, the state or any city, county, or city and county. *(Amended by Stats 1990 ch 1580 §2, eff. 1/1/91.)*

§4573.5. Drugs other than narcotics.

Any person who knowingly brings into any state prison or other institution under the jurisdiction of the Department of Corrections, or into any prison camp, prison farm, or any other place where prisoners or inmates of these institutions are located under the custody of prison or institution officials, officers, or employees, or into any county, city and county, or city jail, road camp, farm or any other institution or place where prisoners or inmates are being held under the custody of any sheriff, chief of police, peace officer, probation officer, or employees, or within the grounds belonging to any institution or place, any alcoholic beverage, any drugs, other than controlled substances, in any manner, shape, form, dispenser, or container, or any device, contrivance, instrument, or paraphernalia intended to be used for unlawfully injecting or consuming any drug other than controlled substances, without having authority so to do by the rules of the Department of Corrections, the rules of the prison, institution, camp, farm, place, or jail, or by the specific authorization of the warden, superintendent, jailer, or other person in charge of the prison, jail, institution, camp, farm, or place, is guilty of a felony.

The prohibitions and sanctions addressed in this section shall be clearly and prominently posted outside of, and at the entrance to, the grounds of all detention facilities under the jurisdiction of, or operated by, the state or any city, county, or city and county. *(Amended by Stats 1990 ch 1580 §3, eff. 1/1/91.)*

§4573.6. Possession of controlled substances or alcoholic beverages in prison.

Any person who knowingly has in his or her possession in any state prison, prison road camp, prison forestry camp, or other prison camp or prison farm or any place where prisoners of the state are located under the custody of prison officials, officers, or employees, or in any county, city and county, or city jail, road camp, farm, or any place or institution, where prisoners or inmates are being held under the custody of any sheriff, chief of police, peace officer, probation officer, or employees, or within the grounds belonging to any jail, road camp, farm, place or institution, any controlled substances, the possession of which is prohibited by Division 10 (commencing with Section 11000) of the Health and Safety Code, any device, contrivance, instrument, or paraphernalia intended to be used for unlawfully injecting or consuming controlled substances, without being authorized to so possess the same by the rules of the Department of Corrections, rules of the prison or jail, institution, camp, farm or place, or by the specific authorization of the warden, superintendent, jailer, or other person

in charge of the prison, jail, institution, camp, farm or place, is guilty of a felony punishable by imprisonment in the state prison for two, three, or four years.

The prohibitions and sanctions addressed in this section shall be clearly and prominently posted outside of, and at the entrance to, the grounds of all detention facilities under the jurisdiction of, or operated by, the state or any city, county, or city and county. *(Amended by Stats 1990 ch 1580 §4, eff. 1/1/91.)*

§4573.8. Possession of drugs or alcoholic beverages in prison.

Any person who knowingly has in his or her possession in any state prison, prison road camp, prison forestry camp, or other prison camp or prison farm or any place where prisoners of the state are located under the custody of prison officials, officers, or employees, or in any county, city and county, or city jail, road camp, farm, or any place or institution, where prisoners or inmates are being held under the custody of any sheriff, chief of police, peace officer, probation officer, or employees, or within the grounds belonging to any jail, road camp, farm, place, or institution, drugs in any manner, shape, form, dispenser, or container, any device, contrivance, instrument, or paraphernalia intended to be used for unlawfully injecting or consuming drugs, or alcoholic beverages, without being authorized to possess the same by rules of the Department of Corrections, rules of the prison or jail, institution, camp, farm, or place, or by the specific authorization of the warden, superintendent, jailer, or other person in charge of the prison, jail, institution, camp, farm, or place, is guilty of a felony.

The prohibitions and sanctions addressed in this section shall be clearly and prominently posted outside of, and at the entrance to, the grounds of all detention facilities under the jurisdiction of, or operated by, the state or any city, county, or city and county. *(Added by Stats 1990 ch 1580 §5, eff. 1/1/91.)*

§4573.9. Selling, furnishing, administering, or giving away of contolled substances to inmates.

Notwithstanding any other provision of law, any person, other than a person held in custody, who sells, furnishes, administers, or gives away, or offers to sell, furnish, administer, or give away to any person held in custody in any state prison or other institution under the jurisdiction of the Department of Corrections, or in any prison camp, prison farm, or any other place where prisoners or inmates of these institutions are located under the custody of prison institution officials, officers, or employees, or in any county, city and county, or city jail, road camp, farm, or any other institution or place where prisoners or inmates are being held under the custody of any sheriff, chief of police, peace officer, probation officer, or employees, or within the grounds belonging to any institution or place, any controlled substance, the possession of which is prohibited by Division 10 (commencing with Section 11000) of the Health and Safety Code, if the recipient is not authorized to possess the same by the rules of the Department of Corrections, rules of the prison or jail, institution, camp, farm, or place, or by the specific authorization of the warden, superintendent, jailer, or other person in charge of the prison, jail, institution, camp, farm, or place, is guilty of a

© 1992 by J., B. & L. Gould
Printed in the U.S.A.   EP

felony punishable by imprisonment in the state prison for two, four, or six years.

The prohibitions and sanctions addressed in this section shall be clearly and prominently posted outside of, and at the entrance to, the grounds of all detention facilities under the jurisdiction of, or operatd* by, the state or any city, county, or city and county. (Added by Stats 1990 ch 1580 §6, eff. 1/1/91.) *So in original. Probably should be "operated".

§4574. Bringing or sending firearm, deadly weapon, explosive, or tear gas into prison.

(a) Except when otherwise authorized by law, or when authorized by the person in charge of the prison or other institution referred to in this section or by an officer of the institution empowered by the person in charge of the institution to give such authorization, any person, who knowingly brings or sends into, or knowingly assists in bringing into, or sending into, any state prison or prison road camp or prison forestry camp, or other prison camp or prison farm or any other place where prisoners of the state prison are located under the custody of prison officials, officers or employees, or any jail or any county road camp in this state, or within the grounds belonging or adjacent to any such institution, any firearms, deadly weapons, or explosives, and any person who, while lawfully confined in a jail or county road camp possesses therein any firearm, deadly weapon, explosive, tear gas or tear gas weapon, is guilty of a felony and punishable by imprisonment in the state prison for two, three, or four years.

(b) Except as provided in subdivision (a), any person who knowingly brings or sends into such places any tear gas or tear gas weapons which results in the release of such tear gas or use of such weapon is guilty of a felony and punishable by imprisonment in the state prison for two, three, or four years.

(c) Except as provided in subdivision (a), any person who knowingly brings or sends into such places any tear gas or tear gas weapons is guilty of a misdemeanor and punishable by imprisonment in the county jail not exceeding six months, or by fine not exceeding one thousand dollars ($1,000), or by both such fine and imprisonment.

CHAPTER 4

DEMOLISHING PRISONS AND JAILS

§4600. Punishment for demolishing or damaging jail property.

Every person who willfully and intentionally breaks down, pulls down, or otherwise destroys or injures any jail, prison, or any public property in any jail or prison, is punishable by a fine not exceeding ten thousand dollars ($10,000), and by imprisonment in the state prison, except that where the damage or injury to any city, city and county or county jail property or prison property is determined to be four hundred dollars ($400) or less, such person is guilty of a misdemeanor.

CHAPTER 5

TRIALS OF PRISONERS

§4700. Repealed by Stats 1986 ch 1310.

§4700.1. Transportation of prisoners.

For any trial or hearing referred to in Section 4750, the sheriff of the county where such trial or hearing is had and the person in charge of the prison may agree that the county shall transport prisoners in a state prison to and from such prison. Upon such agreement, the county, and not the Department of Corrections, shall perform the transportation referred to in this section. (Amended by Stats 1986 ch 1310 §6.)

§4700.2. Repealed by Stats 1987 ch 1303.

§4700.5. Repealed by Stats 1986 ch 1310.

§4701. Escape jurisdiction.

The jurisdiction of a criminal action for escaping from any State prison is in any county of the State.

§4702. Venue of escape offense.

Whenever any prisoner confined in a jail established and maintained by the sheriff in another county, is tried for any offense committed in such jail or for escaping or attempting to escape therefrom, the venue shall be in the county establishing and maintaining such jail and the costs shall be charged against that county.

§4703. Responsibility for prosecution of prisoners' crimes.

With the concurrence of the Attorney General, the district attorney may transfer the responsibility for the prosecution of any crime committed by prisoners in physical custody in the state prisons in the district attorney's county. As used in this section, crimes committed while in physical custody shall include escapes and attempted escapes but shall not include any crimes committed while a prisoner has been conditionally released from state prison on work furlough, parole, or upon any other conditional release where the inmate is in constructive but not actual physical custody.

CHAPTER 6

LOCAL EXPENSES

§4750. Reimbursement for costs.

A city or county shall be entitled to reimbursement for reasonable and necessary costs connected with state prisons or prisoners in connection with any of the following:

(a) Any crime committed at a state prison, whether by a prisoner, employee, or other person.

With respect to a prisoner, "crime committed at a state prison" as used in this subdivision, includes, but is not limited to, crimes committed by the prisoner while detained in local facilities as a result of a transfer pursuant to Section 2910 or 6253, or in conjunction with any hearing, proceeding, or other activity for which reimbursement is otherwise provided by this section.

(b) Any crime committed by a prisoner in furtherance of an escape. Any crime committed by an escaped prisoner within 10 days after the escape and within 100 miles of the facility from which the escape occurred shall be presumed to have been a crime committed in furtherance of an escape.

(c) Any hearing on any return of a writ of habeas corpus prosecuted by or on behalf of a prisoner.

(d) Any trial or hearing on the question of the sanity of a prisoner.

(e) Any costs not otherwise reimbursable under Section 1557 or any other related provision in connection with any extradition proceeding for any prisoner released to hold.

(f) Any costs incurred by a coroner in connection with the death of a prisoner.

(g) Any costs incurred in transporting a prisoner within the host county or as requested by the prison facility or incurred for increased security while a prisoner is outside a state prison. (*Amended by Stats 1987 ch 1303 §5.*)

§4751. Incurred costs.

Costs incurred include all of the following:

(a) Costs of law enforcement agencies in connection with any matter set forth in Section 4750, including the investigation or evaluation of any of those matters regardless of whether a crime has in fact occurred, a hearing held, or an offense prosecuted.

(b) Costs of any trial or hearing of any matter set forth in Section 4750, including costs for the preparation of the trial, pretrial hearing, actual trial or hearing, expert witness fees, the costs of guarding or keeping the prisoner, the transportation of the prisoner, the costs of appeal, and the execution of the sentence. The cost of detention in a city or county correctional facility shall include the same cost factors as are utilized by the Department of Corrections in determining the cost of prisoner care in state correctional facilities.

(c) The costs of the prosecuting attorney in investigating, evaluating, or prosecuting cases related to any matter set forth in Section 4750, whether or not the prosecuting attorney decides to commence legal action.

(d) Costs incurred by the public defender or court appointed attorney with respect to any matter set forth in Section 4750.

(e) Any other costs reasonably incurred by a county in connection with any matter set forth in Section 4750. (*Added by Stats 1986 ch 1310 §8.*)

§4752. Determination of reasonable and necessary costs.

As used in this chapter, reasonable and necessary costs shall be based upon all operating costs, including the cost of elected officials while serving in line functions and including all administrative costs associated with providing the necessary services and securing reimbursement therefor. Administrative costs include a proportional allowance for overhead determined in accordance with current accounting practices. (*Added by Stats 1986 ch 1310 §8.*)

§4753. Statement of costs.

A city or county shall designate an officer or agency to prepare a statement of costs that shall be reimbursed under this chapter.

The statement shall be sent to the Controller for approval. The Controller shall reimburse the city or county within 60 days after receipt of the statement or provide a written statement as to the reason for not making reimbursement at that time. If sufficient funds are not available, the Controller shall request the Director of Finance to include any amounts necessary to satisfy the claims in a request for a deficiency appropriation. (*Amended by Stats 1987 ch 1303 §6.*)

§4754. Prisoner defined.

As used in this chapter, "prisoner" means any person committed to a state prison, including a person who has been transferred to any other facility, has escaped, or is otherwise absent, but does not include a person while on parole. (*Added by Stats 1986 ch 1310 §8.*)

§4755. Detainer.

Whenever a person has entered upon a term of imprisonment in a penal or correctional institution, and whenever during the continuance of the term of imprisonment there is a detainer lodged against the prisoner by a law enforcement or prosecutorial agency of the state or its subdivisions, the Department of Corrections may do either of the following:

(a) Release the inmate to the agency lodging the detainer, within five days, or five court days if the law enforcement agency lodging the detainer is more than 400 miles from the county in which the institution is located, prior to the scheduled release date provided the inmate is kept in custody until the scheduled release date.

(b) Retain the inmate in custody up to five days, or five court days if the law enforcement agency lodging the detainer is more than 400 miles from the county in which the institution is located, after the scheduled release date to facilitate pickup by the agency lodging the detainer.

If a person has been retained in custody under this subdivision in response to the issuance of a warrant of arrest charging a particular offense and the defendant is released from custody following the retention period without pickup by the agency lodging the detainer, a subsequent court order shall be issued before the arrest of that person for the same offense which was charged in the prior warrant.

As used in this section "detainer" means a warrant of arrest. (*Amended by Stats 1987 ch 1303 §7.*)

TITLE 6

REPRIEVES, PARDONS AND COMMUTATIONS

CHAPTER 1

POWERS AND DUTIES OF GOVERNOR

§4800. General authority to grant pardons, reprieves, commutations.

The general authority to grant reprieves, pardons and commutations of sentence is conferred upon the Governor by Section 8 of Article V of the Constitution of the State of California.

§4801. Submission of names of eligible prisoners.

The Board of Prison Terms may report to the Governor from time to time the names of any and all persons imprisoned in any state prison who, in its judgment, ought to have a commutation of sentence or be pardoned and set at liberty on account of good conduct, or unusual term of sentence, or any other cause which, in their opinion, should entitle the prisoner to a pardon or commutation of sentence.

© 1992 by J., B. & L. Gould
Printed in the U.S.A.   EP

§4802. Person twice convicted of a felony.

In the case of a person twice convicted of felony, the application for pardon or commutation of sentence shall be made directly to the Governor, who shall transmit all papers and documents relied upon in support of and in opposition to the application to the Board of Prison Terms.

§4803. Facts and recommendations for consideration.

When an application is made to the Governor for pardon or commutation of sentence, or when an application has been referred to the Board of Prison Terms, he or it may require the judge of the court before which the conviction was had, or the district attorney by whom the action was prosecuted, to furnish him or it, without delay, with a summarized statement of the facts proved on the trial, and of any other facts having reference to the propriety of granting or refusing said application, together with his recommendation for or against the granting of the same and his reason for such recommendation.

§4804. Written notice of intent to apply.

At least 10 days before the Governor acts upon an application for a pardon, written notice of the intention to apply therefor, signed by the person applying, must be served upon the district attorney of the county where the conviction was had, and proof, by affidavit, of the service must be presented to the Governor.

§4806. Inapplicability of §4804.

The provisions of Section 4804 are not applicable:
1. When there is imminent danger of the death of the person convicted or imprisoned;
2. When the term of imprisonment of the applicant is within 10 days of its expiration.

§4807. Governor's report to Legislature.

The Governor must, at the beginning of every session, communicate to the Legislature in addition to each case of reprieve, or pardon, as provided in Article V, Section 8, of the Constitution of California, each commutation, stating the name of the person convicted, the crime of which he was convicted, the sentence and its date, the date of the commutation and the reason for granting the same.

§4807.2. Statement of compensation for procuring pardon or commutation.

Every application for pardon or commutation of sentence shall be accompanied by a full statement of any compensation being paid to any person for procuring or assisting in procuring the pardon or commutation or the pardon or commutation shall be denied.

§4807.3. Statement of receipt of compensation for procuring pardon or commutation.

Every person who receives or agrees to receive any compensation or who receives any gift for procuring or assisting in procuring a pardon or commutation of sentence for any applicant must file with the Governor a full statement of the amount and character of such compensation or gift within 10 days of the receipt thereof. Any failure to file a full statement as required by this section is a misdemeanor.

§4810. Board of Prison Terms; powers and duties.

(a) The Board of Prison Terms shall succeed to and shall exercise and perform all powers and duties granted to and imposed upon the Advisory Pardon Board by law.

(b) The Advisory Pardon Board is abolished.

(c) The report required of the Board of Prison Terms by Section 4814 may be included in the report of the department.

§4812. Board's investigations, reports and recommendations.

Upon request of the Governor the Board of Prison Terms shall investigate and report on all applications for reprieves, pardons and commutation of sentence and shall make such recommendations to the Governor with reference thereto as to it may seem advisable. To that end the board shall examine and consider all applications so referred and all transcripts of judicial proceedings and all affidavits or other documents submitted in connection therewith, and shall have power to employ assistants and take testimony and to examine witnesses under oath and to do any and all things necessary to make a full and complete investigation of and concerning all applications referred to it. Members of the board and its administrative officer are, and each of them is, hereby authorized to administer oaths.

§4813. Board's recommendation on twice convicted felon.

In the case of applications of persons twice convicted of a felony, the Board of Prison Terms, after investigation, shall transmit its written recommendation upon such application to the Governor, together with all papers filed in connection with the application.

§4814. Biennial report to Governor.

The Board of Prison Terms shall, on or before the first day of December of each even-numbered year, report to the Governor upon the status and history of matters under its consideration, together with an account of expenditures and such suggestions pertinent to its duties as may appear to be necessary and expedient.

CHAPTER 2
(No Chapter 2 has been enacted.)

CHAPTER 3

DUTIES OF SUPREME COURT

§4850. Forwarding applications to Supreme Court clerk.

No application which has not received a recommendation from the Board of Prison Terms favorable to the applicant shall be forwarded to the Clerk of the Supreme Court, unless the Governor, notwithstanding the fact that the board has failed to make a recommendation favorable to the applicant, especially refers an application to the justices for their recommendation.

§4851. Other papers to be forwarded to clerk.

In all cases where the Board of Prison Terms has made a recommendation favorable to the applicant

© 1992 by J., B. & L. Gould
Printed in the U.S.A.   EP

and in those cases referred by the Governor, notwithstanding an adverse recommendation, the application, together with all papers and documents relied upon in support of and in opposition to the application, including prison records and recommendation of the Board of Prison Terms, shall be forwarded to the Clerk of the Supreme Court for consideration of the justices. *(Amended by Stats 1987 ch 828 §139.)*

§4852. Transmission to Governor.

If a majority of the justices recommend that clemency be granted, the clerk of the Supreme Court shall transmit the application, together with all papers and documents filed in the case, to the Governor; otherwise the documents shall remain in the files of the court.

CHAPTER 3.5

PROCEDURE FOR RESTORATION OF RIGHTS AND APPLICATION FOR PARDON

§4852.01. Petition for certificate of rehabilitation and pardon.

(a) Any person convicted of a felony who has been released from a state prison or other state penal institution or agency in California, whether discharged on completion of the term for which he was sentenced or released on parole prior to May 13, 1943, who has not been incarcerated in a state prison or other state penal institution or agency since his release and who presents satisfactory evidence of a three-year residence in this state immediately prior to the filing of the petition for a certificate of rehabilitation and pardon provided for by this chapter, may file such petition pursuant to the provisions of this chapter.

(b) Any person convicted of a felony who, on May 13, 1943, was confined in a state prison or other institution or agency to which he was committed and any person convicted of a felony after that date who is committed to a state prison or other institution or agency may file a petition for a certificate of rehabilitation and pardon pursuant to the provisions of this chapter.

(c) Any person convicted of a felony the accusatory pleading of which has been dismissed pursuant to Section 1203.4 may file a petition for certificate of rehabilitation and pardon pursuant to the provisions of this chapter; provided the petitioner has not been incarcerated in any prison, jail, detention facility or other penal institution or agency since the dismissal of the accusatory pleading and is not on probation for the commission of any other felony, and petitioner presents satisfactory evidence of three years residence in this state prior to the filing of the petition.

(d) This chapter shall not apply to persons convicted of misdemeanors; to persons serving a mandatory life parole; to persons committed under death sentences; or to persons in the military service.

§4852.03. Rehabilitation periods.

(a) The period of rehabilitation shall begin to run upon the discharge of the petitioner from custody due to his or her completion of the term to which he or she was sentenced or upon his or her release on parole or probation, whichever is sooner. For purposes of this chapter, the period of rehabilitation shall constitute three years' residence in this state, plus a period of time determined by the following rules:

(1) To the three years there shall be added four years in the case of any person convicted of violating Section 187, 209, 219, 4500 or 12310, or subdivision (a) of Section 1672 of the Military and Veterans Code, or of committing any other offense which carries a life sentence.

(2) To the three years there shall be added two years in the case of any person convicted of committing any offense which is not listed in paragraph (1) and which does not carry a life sentence.

(3) The trial court hearing the application for the certificate of rehabilitation may, if the defendant was ordered to serve consecutive sentences, order that his or her statutory period of rehabilitation be extended for an additional period of time which when combined with the time already served will not exceed the period prescribed by statute for the sum of the maximum penalties for all the crimes.

(4) Any person who was discharged after completion of his or her term or was released on parole before May 13, 1943, is not subject to the periods of rehabilitation set forth in these rules.

(b) Unless and until the period of rehabilitation, as stipulated in this section, has passed, the petitioner shall be ineligible to file his or her petition for a certificate of rehabilitation with the court. Any certificate of rehabilitation which is issued and under which the petitioner has not fulfilled the requirements of this chapter shall be void.

(c) A change of residence within this state does not interrupt the period of rehabilitation prescribed by this section. *(Amended by Stats 1988 ch 160 §139, eff. 1/1/89.)*

§4852.04. Counsel and assistance.

Each person who may initiate the proceedings provided for in this chapter shall be entitled to receive counsel and assistance from all rehabilitative agencies, including the adult probation officer of the county and all state parole officers, and, in the case of persons under the age of 30 years, from the Youth Authority.

§4852.05. Conduct during rehabilitation period.

During the period of rehabilitation the person shall live an honest and upright life, shall conduct himself with sobriety and industry, shall exhibit a good moral character, and shall conform to and obey the laws of the land.

§4852.06. Petition for ascertainment and declaration of rehabilitation and certificate.

Except as provided in subdivision (a) of Section 4852.01, after the expiration of the minimum period of rehabilitation applicable to him (and, in the case of persons released upon parole or probation, after the termination of parole or probation), each person who has complied with the requirements of Section 4852.05 may file in the superior court of the county in which he then resides a petition for ascertainment and declaration of the fact of his rehabilitation and of matters incident thereto, and for a certificate of rehabilitation under this chapter. No such petition shall be filed until and unless the petitioner has continuously resided in this state, after leaving prison, for a period of not less than three years immediately preceding the date of filing the petition.

© 1992 by J., B. & L. Gould
Printed in the U.S.A.　　**EP**

§4852.07. Notices of filing of petition and time of hearing.

The petitioner shall give notice of the filing of the petition to the district attorney of the county in which the petition is filed, to the district attorney of each county in which the petitioner was convicted of a felony or of a crime the accusatory pleading of which was dismissed pursuant to Section 1203.4, and to the office of the Governor, together with notice of the time of the hearing of the petition, at least 30 days prior to the date set for such hearing.

§4852.08. Petitioner's representation by counsel.

During the proceedings upon the petition, the petitioner may be represented by counsel of his own selection; if he has no such counsel he shall be represented by the public defender, if there is one in the county, and if there is none, by the adult probation officer of the county or if in the opinion of the court the petitioner needs counsel, the court shall assign counsel to represent him.

§4852.09. Court fees not required.

No filing fee nor court fees of any kind shall be required of a petitioner in proceedings under this chapter.

§4852.1. Testimony.

The court in which the petition is filed may require such testimony as it deems necessary, and the production, for the use of the court and without expense of any kind to the petitioner, of all records and reports relating to the petitioner and the crime of which he was convicted, including the record of the trial, the report of the probation officer, if any, the records of the prison, jail, detention facility or other penal institution from which the petitioner has been released showing his conduct during the time he was there, the records of the penal institution or agency doctor and psychiatrist, the records of the parole officer concerning him if he was released on parole, the records of the Youth Authority concerning him if he has been committed to the authority, and written reports or records of any other law enforcement agency concerning the conduct of the petitioner since his release on probation or parole or discharge from custody. All persons having custody of any such records shall make them available for the use of the court in the proceeding.

§4852.11. Reports by peace officers and violations of law.

Any peace officer shall report to the court, upon receiving a request as provided in Section 4852.1, all violations of law committed by said petitioner which may come to his knowledge. Upon receiving satisfactory proof of such violation the court may deny the petition and determine a new period of rehabilitation not to exceed the original period of rehabilitation for the same crime. In that event, before granting the petition, the court may thereafter require the petitioner to fulfill all the requirements provided to be fulfilled before the granting of the certificate under the original petition.

§4852.12. Investigations and reports on petitioner.

(a) In any proceeding for the ascertainment and declaration of the fact of rehabilitation under this chapter, the court, upon the filing of the application for petition of rehabilitation, may request from the district attorney an investigation of the residence of the petitioner, the criminal record of the petitioner as shown by the records of the Department of Justice, any representation made to the court by the applicant, the conduct of the petitioner during his period of rehabilitation, including all matters mentioned in Section 4852.11, and any other information the court may deem necessary in making its determination. If so requested, the district attorney shall provide the court with a full and complete report of such investigations.

(b) In any proceeding for the ascertainment and declaration of the fact of rehabilitation under this chapter of a person convicted of a crime the accusatory pleading of which has been dismissed pursuant to Section 1203.4, the district attorney, upon request of the court, shall deliver to the court the criminal record of petitioner as shown by the records of the Department of Justice. The district attorney may investigate any representation made to the court by petitioner and may file with the court a report of the investigation including all matters known to the district attorney relating to the conduct and place and duration of residence of the petitioner during the period of rehabilitation and all known violations of law committed by petitioner.

§4852.13. Order declaring rehabilitation and recommendation of full pardon.

If, after hearing, the court finds that the petitioner has demonstrated by his course of conduct his rehabilitation and his fitness to exercise all of the civil and political rights of citizenship, the court shall make an order declaring that the petitioner has been rehabilitated, and recommending that the Governor grant a full pardon to the petitioner. Such order shall be filed with the clerk of the court, and shall be known as a certificate of rehabilitation.

§4852.14. Certified copies of certificate.

The clerk of the court shall immediately transmit certified copies of the certificate of rehabilitation to the Governor, to the Board of Prison Terms and the Department of Justice, and, in the case of persons twice convicted of a felony, to the Supreme Court.

§4852.15. Chapter construed.

Nothing in this chapter shall be construed to abridge or impair the power or authority conferred by law on any officer, board, or tribunal to revoke or suspend any right, privilege, or franchise for any act or omission not involved in his or her conviction, or to require the reinstatement of the right or privilege to practice or carry on any profession or occupation the practice or conduct of which requires the possession or obtaining of a license, permit, or certificate. Nothing in this chapter shall affect any provision of Chapter 5 (commencing with Section 2000) of Division 2 of the Business and Professions Code or the power or authority conferred by law on the Board of Medical Examiners therein, or the power or authority conferred by law upon any board that issues a certificate permitting any person to practice or apply his or her art or profession on the person of another. Nothing in this chapter shall affect any provision of Chapter 4 (commencing with Section 6000) of Division 3 of the Business and Professions Code or the power or authority in relation to attorneys at law and the practice of the law in the State of California conferred by law upon or otherwise possessed by the courts, or the power or authority conferred by law upon the State Bar of California or any board or committee thereof. *(Amended by Stats 1987 ch 828 §141.)*

§4852.16. Certificate of rehabilitation as application for full pardon.

The certified copy of a certificate of rehabilitation transmitted to the Governor shall constitute an application for a full pardon upon receipt of which the Governor may, without any further investigation, issue a pardon to the person named therein, except that, pursuant to Section 8 of Article V of the Constitution, the Governor shall not grant a pardon to any person twice convicted of felony, except upon the written recommendation of a majority of the judges of the Supreme Court.

§4852.17. Reports of certificate of rehabilitation or pardon; rights granted.

Whenever a person is issued a certificate of rehabilitation or granted a pardon from the Governor under this chapter, the fact shall be immediately reported to the Department of Justice by the court, Governor, officer, or governmental agency by whose official action the certificate is issued or the pardon granted. The Department of Justice shall immediately record the facts so reported on the former criminal record of the person, and transmit those facts to the Federal Bureau of Investigation at Washington, D.C. When the criminal record is thereafter reported by the department, it shall also report the fact that the person has received a certificate of rehabilitation, or pardon, or both.

Whenever a person is granted a full and unconditional pardon by the Governor, based upon a certificate of rehabilitation, the pardon shall entitle the person to exercise thereafter all civil and political rights of citizenship, including but not limited to: (1) the right to vote; (2) the right to own, possess, and keep any type of firearm that may lawfully be owned and possessed by other citizens; except that this right shall not be restored, and Sections 12001 and 12021 shall apply, if the person was ever convicted of a felony involving the use of a dangerous weapon. *(Amended by Stats 1987 ch 828 §142.)*

§4852.18. Sample forms for petition.

The Board of Prison Terms shall furnish to the county clerk of each county a set of sample forms for a petition for certificate of rehabilitation and pardon, a notice of filing of petition for certificate of rehabilitation and pardon, and a certificate of rehabilitation. The county clerk shall have a sufficient number of these forms printed to meet the needs of the people of his county, and he shall make these forms available at no charge to persons requesting them.

§4852.19. Construction of chapter.

This chapter shall be construed as providing an additional, but not an exclusive, procedure for the restoration of rights and application for pardon. Nothing in this chapter shall be construed as repealing any other provision of law providing for restoration of rights or application for pardon.

§4852.2. Acceptance of fee for representing petitioner.

Every person, other than an individual who is licensed to practice law in the State of California, pursuant to Article 4 (commencing with Section 6060) of Chapter 4 of Division 3 of the Business and Professions Code and who is acting in that capacity, who solicits or accepts any fee, money, or anything of value for his or her services, or his or her purported services, in representing a petitioner in any proceeding under this chapter, or in any application to the Governor for a pardon under this chapter, is guilty of a misdemeanor. *(Amended by Stats 1990 ch 632 §5, eff. 1/1/91.)*

§4852.21. Written information of procedure relating to certificate of rehabilitation and pardon.

(a) Any person to whom this chapter applies shall, prior to his discharge or release on parole from a state prison or other state penal institution or agency, be informed in writing by the official in charge of the place of confinement of his right to petition for, and of the procedure for filing the petition for, and obtaining, a certificate of rehabilitation and pardon pursuant to this chapter.

(b) Prior to dismissal of the accusatory pleading pursuant to Section 1203.4, the defendant shall be informed in writing by the clerk of the court dismissing the accusatory pleading of the defendant's right, if any, to petition for, and of the procedure for filing a petition for, and obtaining, a certificate of rehabilitation and pardon pursuant to this chapter.

CHAPTER 4

EFFECT OF FULL PARDON

§4853. Restoration of rights and privileges.

In all cases in which a full pardon has been granted by the Governor of this state or will hereafter be granted by the Governor to a person convicted of an offense to which the pardon applies, it shall operate to restore to the convicted person, all the rights, privileges, and franchises of which he or she has been deprived in consequence of that conviction or by reason of any matter involved therein; provided, that nothing herein contained shall abridge or impair the power or authority conferred by law on any board or tribunal to revoke or suspend any right, privilege or franchise for any act or omission not involved in the conviction; provided further, that nothing in this article shall affect any of the provisions of the Medical Practice Act (Chapter 5 (commencing with Section 2000) of Division 2 of the Business and Professions Code) or the power or authority conferred by law on the Board of Medical Examiners therein, or the power or authority conferred by law upon any board that issues a certificate which permits any person or persons to apply his or her or their art or profession on the person of another. *(Amended by Stats 1987 ch 828 §143.)*

§4854. Restoration of right to own, possess, and keep firearm.

In the granting of a pardon to a person, the Governor may provide that the person is entitled to exercise the right to own, possess and keep any type of firearm that may lawfully be owned and possessed by other

© 1992 by J., B. & L. Gould
Printed in the U.S.A.   EP

citizens; except that this right shall not be restored, and Sections 12001 and 12021 shall apply, if the person was ever convicted of a felony involving the use of a dangerous weapon. *(Amended by Stats 1987 ch 828 §144.)*

CHAPTER 5

INDEMNITY FOR PERSONS ERRONEOUSLY CONVICTED AND PARDONED

§4900. Reasons warranting pardon; claim for pecuniary injury.

Any person who, having been convicted of any crime against the State of California amounting to a felony, and having been imprisoned therefor in a State prison of this State shall hereafter be granted a pardon by the Governor of this State for the reason that the crime with which he was charged was either not committed at all or, if committed, was not committed by him, or who, being innocent of the crime with which he was charged for either of the foregoing reasons, shall have served the term or any part thereof for which he was imprisoned, may, under the conditions hereinafter provided, present a claim against the State to the State Board of Control for the pecuniary injury sustained by him through such erroneous conviction and imprisonment.

§4901. Claim presentation time.

Such claim, accompanied by a statement of the facts constituting the claim, verified in the manner provided for the verification of complaints in civil actions, must be presented by the claimant to the Board of Control within a period of six months after judgment of acquittal or discharge given, or after pardon granted, or after release from imprisonment, and at least four months prior to the next meeting of the Legislature of this State; and no claim not so presented shall be considered by the Board of Control.

§4902. Time and place of hearing; notice.

Upon presentation of any such claim, the Board of Control shall fix a time and place for the hearing of the claim, and shall mail notice thereof to the claimant and to the Attorney General of this State at least 15 days prior to the time fixed for such hearing.

§4903. Proceedings at hearing.

On such hearing the claimant shall introduce evidence in support of the claim, and the Attorney General may introduce evidence in opposition thereto. The claimant must prove the facts set forth in the statement constituting the claim, including the fact that the crime with which he was charged was either not committed at all, or, if committed, was not committed by him, the fact that he did not, by any act or omission on his part, either intentionally or negligently, contribute to the bringing about of his arrest or conviction for the crime with which he was charged, and the pecuniary injury sustained by him through his erroneous conviction and imprisonment.

§4904. Limitation on indemnification.

If the evidence shows that the crime with which the claimant was charged was either not committed at all, or, if committed, was not committed by the claimant, and that the claimant did not, by any act or omission either intentionally or negligently, contribute to the bringing about of his arrest or conviction, and that the claimant has sustained pecuniary injury through his erroneous conviction and imprisonment, the Board of Control shall report the facts of the case and its conclusions to the next Legislature of this state, with a recommendation that an appropriation be made by the Legislature for the purpose of indemnifying the claimant for such pecuniary injury; but the amount of the appropriation so recommended shall not exceed in any case, the sum of ten thousand dollars ($10,000).

§4905. Recommendations for appropriations.

The Board of Control shall make up its report and recommendation and shall give to the Controller of this State a statement showing its recommendations for appropriations under the provisions of this chapter, as provided by law in cases of other claimants against this State for which no appropriations have been made.

§4906. Rules and regulations.

The Board of Control is hereby authorized to make all needful rules and regulations consistent with the law for the purpose of carrying into effect the provisions of this chapter.

TITLE 7

ADMINISTRATION OF THE STATE CORRECTIONAL SYSTEM

CHAPTER 1

THE DEPARTMENT OF CORRECTIONS

§5000. Existence.

There is in the Youth and Adult Correctional Agency the Department of Corrections.

§5001. Composition of department.

The department is composed of the Director of Corrections and the Prison Industry Authority. *(Amended by Stats 1985 ch 1413 §2.)*

§5002. Powers and duties.

(a) The department shall succeed to and is hereby vested with all of the powers and duties exercised and performed by the following departments, boards, bureaus, commissions, and officers when such powers and duties are not otherwise vested by law:

(1) The Department of Penology.

(2) The State Board of Prison Directors.

(3) The Bureau of Paroles.

(4) The warden and the clerk of the California State Prison at San Quentin.

(5) The warden and the clerk of the California State Prison at Folsom.

(6) The warden of and the clerk of the California Institution for Men.

(7) The California Crime Commission.

(b) Whenever any designation of any of the departments, boards, bureaus, commissions, or officers mentioned in subdivision (a) is contained in any provision of law and this designation is expressly made to refer to the Department of Corrections, the Board of Corrections or the Board of Prison Terms, then the Department of Corrections, the Board of Corrections or the Board of Prison Terms, to whichever one the designation is made to refer, shall exercise the power or perform the duty heretofore exercised or performed by the particular departments, boards, bureaus, or officers mentioned in subdivision (a).

(c) The powers and duties of the State Board of Prison Directors and of the clerks of the state prisons and the California Institution for Men are transferred to and shall be exercised and performed by the Department of Corrections, except as may be otherwise expressly provided by law.

(d) The powers and duties of wardens of the state prisons and the California Institution for Men, presently or hereafter, expressly vested by law in them shall be exercised by them but such exercise shall be subject to the supervision and control of the Director of Corrections. All powers and duties not expressly vested in the wardens are transferred to and shall be exercised and performed by the Department of Corrections. When the designation of warden is expressly made to refer to the Department of Corrections, the department shall exercise the power and perform the duty heretofore exercised or performed by the warden.

(e) The Board of Prison Terms shall succeed to and is hereby vested with all of the powers and duties exercised and performed by the following boards when such powers and duties are not otherwise vested by law:

(1) The Board of Prison Terms and Paroles.
(2) The Advisory Pardon Board.
(3) The Adult Authority.
(4) The Women's Board of Terms and Paroles.
(5) The Community Release Board. *(Amended by Stats 1989 ch 1420 §20, eff. 1/1/90.)*

§5003. Jurisdiction of department.

The department has jurisdiction over the following prisons and institutions:

(a) The California State Prison at San Quentin.
(b) The California State Prison at Folsom.
(c) The California Institution for Men.
(d) The California Institution for Women.
(e) The Deuel Vocational Institution.
(f) The California Medical Facility.
(g) The Correctional Training Facility.
(h) The California Men's Colony.
(i) The California Correctional Institution at Tehachapi.
(j) The California Rehabilitation Center.
(k) The California Correctional Center at Susanville.
(l) The Sierra Correctional Center.
(m) The Richard J. Donovan Correctional Facility at Rock Mountain.
(n) Mule Creek State Prison.
(o) Northern California Women's Facility.
(p) Pelican Bay State Prison.
(q) Avenal State Prison.
(r) California State Prison—King's County at Corcoran.
(s) Chuckawalla Valley State Prison.
(t) Those other institutions and prison facilities as the Department of Corrections or the Director of Corrections may be authorized by law to establish, including, but not limited to, prisons in Madera, Kern, Imperial, and Los Angeles Counties. *(Amended by Stats 1990 ch 981 §11, eff. 9/18/90; ch 980 §3, eff. 1/1/91.)*

§5003.5. Advisory powers; establishment of policies.

The Board of Prison Terms is empowered to advise and recommend to the Director of Corrections on general and specific policies and procedures relating to the duties and functions of the director. The director is empowered to advise and recommend to the Board of Prison Terms on matters of general and specific policies and procedures, relating to the duties and functions of the board. The director and the board shall meet for purposes of exchange of information and advice.

It is the intention of the Legislature that the Board of Prison Terms and the Director of Corrections shall cooperate with each other in the establishment of the classification, transfer, and discipline policies of the Department of Corrections, to the end that the objectives of the State Correctional System can best be attained. The director and the Board of Prison Terms shall, not less than four times each calendar year, meet for the purpose of discussion of classification, transfer, and discipline policies and problems and it is the intent of the Legislature that whenever possible there shall be agreement on these subjects. But for the purpose of maintaining responsibility for the secure and orderly administration of the prison system, the Director of Corrections shall have the final right to determine the policies on classification, transfer and discipline.

In the event there is no agreement the Board of Prison Terms shall file in writing with the Board of Corrections a statement of its proposals or recommendations to the director, and the director shall answer such statement in writing to the Board of Prison Terms, and a copy of both documents shall be transmitted to the Governor and to the Board of Corrections.

§5004. Mutual police aid.

The Director of Corrections and the legislative body of any county or city may enter into agreements for mutual police aid. Pursuant to such agreements the director may authorize employees of state prisons and institutions to cooperate, anywhere within the State, with county and city peace officers in connection with any existing emergency. While so employed the employees shall have all the benefits of workmen's compensation laws, retirement laws, and all other similar laws and for such purposes shall be deemed to be performing services in the course of their regular official duties.

§5004.5. Mutual Aid Escape Pursuit Plan and Agreement.

The director shall require each state prison under the department's jurisdiction to develop a Mutual Aid Escape Pursuit Plan and Agreement with local law enforcement agencies. The plan, together with any supporting information, shall be submitted for annual review to the city council of the city containing or nearest to the institution and to the county board of supervisors of the county containing the prison.

Nothing in this section shall require the department to disclose any information which may threaten the security of an institution or the safety of the surrounding community.

© 1992 by J., B. & L. Gould
Printed in the U.S.A.   EP

§5005. Maintenance of canteen.

The department may maintain a canteen at any prison or institution under its jurisdiction for the sale to persons confined therein of toilet articles, candy, tobacco products, notions, and other sundries, and may provide the necessary facilities, equipment, personnel, and merchandise for the canteen. The director shall specify what commodities shall be sold in the canteen. The sale prices of the articles offered for sale shall be fixed by the director at the amounts that will, as far as possible, render each canteen self-supporting. The department may undertake to insure against damage or loss of canteen and handicraft materials, supplies and equipment owned by the Inmate Welfare Fund of the Department of Corrections as provided in Section 5006.

The canteen operations at any prison or institution referred to in this section shall be audited biennially by the Department of Finance, and at the end of each intervening fiscal year, each prison or institution shall prepare a statement of operations. At least one copy of any audit report or statement of operations shall be posted at the canteen and at least one copy shall be available to inmates at the library of each prison or institution. *(Amended by Stats 1988 ch 160 §140, eff. 1/1/89.)*

§5006. Inmate Welfare Fund.

All moneys now held for the benefit of prisoners including that known as the Inmate Canteen Fund of the California Institution for Men, and the Inmate Welfare Fund of the California Institution for Women, and the Trust Contingent Fund of the State Prison at Folsom, and the S.P.L. Commissary, Canteen Account, Hobby Association, Camp Account, Library Fund, News Agency of the State Prison at San Quentin, the Prisoners' Fund, and the Prisoners' Employment Fund, shall be deposited in the inmate Welfare Fund of the Department of Corrections, in the State Treasury, which fund is hereby created. The money in the fund shall be used for the benefit, education, and welfare of inmates of prisons and institutions under the jurisdiction of the Department of Corrections, including but not limited to the establishment, maintenance, employment of personnel for, and purchase of items for sale to inmates at canteens maintained at the state institutions, and for the establishment, maintenance, employment of personnel and necessary expenses in connection with the operation of the hobby shops at institutions under the jurisdiction of the Department of Corrections.

There shall be deposited in the Inmate Welfare Fund all net proceeds from the operation of canteens and hobby shops and any moneys which may be assigned to the state prison by prisoners for deposit in the fund. The moneys in the fund shall constitute a trust held by the Director of Corrections for the benefit and welfare as herein defined of all of the inmates of institutions and prisons under the jurisdiction of the Department of Corrections.

The Department of Finance shall conduct a biennial audit of the Inmate Welfare Fund to include an audit report which shall summarize expenditures from the fund by major categories. At the end of each intervening fiscal year, a statement of operations shall be prepared which shall contain the same information as would be provided in the biennial audit. At least one copy of any statement of operations or audit report shall be placed in each library maintained by the Department of Corrections and shall be available there to any inmate.

§5006.1. Prohibition on expenditures.

Notwithstanding any provision in Section 5006, money in the Inmate Welfare Fund shall not be expended to pay charges for any or all of the following purposes:

(a) Overtime for staff coverage of special events.

(b) Television repair and recordings.

(c) Athletic and recreation supplies.

(d) Athletic uniforms.

(e) Original complement of television sets and replacement of television equipment.

The department shall pay such charges out of any money appropriated for such purposes.

§5007. Investment of money in Fund; disposition of interest earned.

The Director of Corrections may invest any money in the Inmate Welfare Fund that in his opinion is not necessary for immediate use, with the approval of the Department of Finance, and interest earned and other increment derived from investments made pursuant to this section shall be paid into the Inmate Welfare Fund of the Department of Corrections.

§5008. Deposit or investment of inmates' funds.

The Director of Corrections shall deposit any funds of inmates in his possession in trust with the Treasurer pursuant to Section 16305.3 of the Government Code, except that the Director of Corrections, when specifically authorized on a separate written form by the inmate and subject to the approval of the Department of Finance, may deposit such funds in interest-bearing bank accounts or invest or reinvest such funds in any of the securities which are described in Article 1 (commencing with Section 16430) of Chapter 3 of Part 2 of Division 4 of Title 2 of the Government Code and for the purposes of deposit or investment only may mingle the funds of any inmate with the funds of other inmates. The director shall deposit the interest or increment accruing on such funds in the Inmate Welfare Fund. Any interest or increment accruing on the funds of a parolee shall be deposited in his or her account.

§5008.1. Information about AIDS.

Subject to the availability of adequate state funding for these purposes, the Director of Corrections shall provide all inmates at each penal institution and prison facility under the jurisdiction of the department with information about behavior that places a person at high risk for contracting the human immunodeficiency virus (HIV), and about the prevention of transmission of acquired immune deficiency syndrome (AIDS). The director shall provide all inmates, who are within one month of release or being placed on parole, with information about agencies and facilities that provide testing, counseling, medical, and support services for AIDS victims. Information about AIDS prevention shall be solicited by the director from the State Department of Health Services, the county health officer, or local agencies providing services to persons with AIDS. The Director of Health Services, or his or her designee, shall approve protocols pertaining to the information to be disseminated under this section. *(Added by Stats 1988 ch 1301 §2, eff. 1/1/89.)*

§5009. Religious freedom of prisoners.

It is the intention of the Legislature that all prisoners shall be afforded reasonable opportunities to exercise religious freedom.

§5011. Admission of guilt not required.

(a) The Department of Corrections shall not require, as a condition for any form of treatment or custody that the department offers, an admission of guilt to any crime for which an inmate was committed to the custody of the department.

(b) The Board of Prison Terms shall not require, when setting parole dates, an admission of guilt to any crime for which an inmate was committed.

§5020. Department of Corrections and the California Youth Authority; proposed inmate computer project.

(a) The Department of Corrections and the California Youth Authority shall conduct a two-year pilot project in juvenile halls, the Youth Authority, and the state prison system if and when the necessary computer hardware, software, and technical assistance is donated to the departments to implement innovative individualized education programs in these institutions.

(b) The Department of the Youth Authority and the Department of Corrections shall, within budgetary limitations, provide staff to be trained and participate in educating and testing the inmates. At the end of the project period, the departments shall evaluate the effectiveness of the training techniques employed and report to the Legislature on their findings.

§5021. Report of deaths.

(a) Any death that occurs in any facility operated by the Department of Corrections, the Department of the Youth Authority, the State Department of Mental Health, a city, county, or city and county, including county juvenile facilities, or any facility which is under contract with any of these entities for the incarceration, rehabilitation, holding, or treatment of persons accused or convicted of crimes, shall be reported within a reasonable time, not to exceed two hours, of its discovery by authorities in the facility to the county sheriff, or his or her designated representative, and to the coroner's office, of the county in which the facility is located, as provided in Section 27491 of the Government Code. These deaths shall also be reported to the district attorney, or his or her designated representative, of the county in which the facility is located as soon as a representative of the district attorney's office is on duty. If the facility is located within the city limits of an incorporated city, the report shall also be made to the chief of police in that city, or to his or her designated representative, within a reasonable time, not to exceed two hours, of its discovery.

Any death of a person in a facility operated by the Department of Corrections or by the Department of the Youth Authority shall also be reported to the Chief of Medical Services in the Central Office of the Department of Corrections, or his or her designated representative, or to the Chief of Medical Services in the Central Office of the Department of the Youth Authority, or his or her designated representative, whichever applies, as soon as a representative of that office is on duty.

(b) The initial report of the death of a person required in subdivision (a) may be transmitted by telephone, direct contact, or by written notification, and shall outline all pertinent facts known at the time the report is made and all persons to contact, in addition to any other information the reporting person or officer deems pertinent.

(c) The initial report of the death of a person as required in subdivision (a) shall be supplemented by a written report, which shall be submitted to the entities listed in subdivision (a) within eight hours of the discovery of the death. This written report shall include all circumstances and details of the death that were known at the time the report was prepared, and shall include the names of all persons involved in the death, and all persons with knowledge of the circumstances surrounding the death. *(Added by Stats 1990 ch 1580 §1, eff. 1/1/91.)*

CHAPTER 2

THE DIRECTOR OF CORRECTIONS

§5050. Office of Director of Corrections.

The Office of Director of Corrections is hereby created.

§5051. Appointment and removal of director.

The director shall be appointed by the Governor with the advice and consent of the Senate. He or she shall hold office at the pleasure of the Governor, but before the director may be removed, charges against him or her, which charges may be preferred by any person, shall be heard by the Board of Corrections. The Board of Corrections shall make detailed findings with respect to the charges and submit the findings to the Governor. The Governor may, but need not, abide by the findings of the Board of Corrections, and may retain or remove the director. If the Governor removes the director his or her action shall be final. He or she shall receive an annual salary provided for by Chapter 6 (commencing with Section 11550) of Part 1 of Division 3 of Title 2 of the Government Code, and shall devote his or her entire time to the duties of his or her office. *(Amended by Stats 1987 ch 828 §146.)*

§5051.2. Administrative experience.

The Director of Corrections shall have wide and successful administrative experience in adult or youth correctional programs embodying rehabilitative concepts.

§5051.5. Selecting candidates for appointment; compilation of list.

The Governor may request the State Personnel Board to use extensive recruitment and merit selection techniques and procedures to provide a list of persons qualified for appointment as Director of Corrections. The Governor may appoint any person from such list of qualified persons or may reject all names and appoint another person who meets the requirements of this chapter.

§5052. Powers of Director.

The Director of Corrections and any other officer or employee of the Department of Corrections designated in writing by the director, shall have the power of a head of a department pursuant to Article 2 (commencing at Section 11180) of Chapter 2, Part 1, Division 3, Title 2, of the Government Code.

© 1992 by J., B. & L. Gould
Printed in the U.S.A.   **EP**

§5053. Chief administrative officer of Department of Corrections.

The Director of Corrections is the chief administrative officer of the Department of Corrections.

§5054. Supervision and control over State prisons.

The supervision, management and control of the State prisons, and the responsibility for the care, custody, treatment, training, discipline and employment of persons confined therein are vested in the director.

§5054.1. Order of Director of Corrections.

The Director of Corrections has full power to order returned to custody any person under the director's jurisdiction. The written order of the Director of Corrections shall be sufficient warrant for any peace officer to return to actual custody any escaped state prisoner. It is hereby made the duty of all peace officers to execute the order in like manner as ordinary criminal process. *(Added by Stats 1986 ch 585 §1.)*

§5055. Exercise of powers and duties.

All powers and duties granted to and imposed upon the Department of Corrections shall be exercised by the Director of Corrections, except where such powers and duties are expressly vested by law in the Board of Prison Terms.

Whenever a power is granted to the Director of Corrections or a duty is imposed upon the director, the power may be exercised or the duty performed by a deputy of the director or by a person authorized pursuant to law by the director.

§5056. Citizens' Advisory Committee.

(a) Each state prison under the jurisdiction of the department shall have a citizens' advisory committee. Each committee shall consist of nine members appointed by the institution's warden from a list of nominations submitted to him or her as follows:

(1) Two persons from nominations submitted by the Assembly member in whose district the prison is located.

(2) Two persons from nominations submitted by the Senator in whose district the prison is located.

(3) Two persons from nominations submitted by the city council of the city containing or nearest to the institution.

(4) Two persons from nominations submitted by the county board of supervisors of the county containing the institution.

(5) One person from nominations submitted by the chief of police of the city containing or nearest to the institution and the county sheriff of the county containing the institution.

(b) Each committee shall select its own chairperson by a majority vote of its members. The term of office of all members shall be two years. In the event of a vacancy due to resignation, death, or absence from three consecutive meetings, the appointing power shall fill the vacancy following receipt of written notification that a vacancy has occurred.

(c) Each committee shall meet at least once every two months or as often, on the call of the chairperson, as necessary to carry out the purposes and duties of the committee. Meetings of the committee shall be open to the public. The warden of the institution shall meet with the committee at least four times a year.

The advisory committees of the several institutions shall have the power of visitation of prison facilities and personnel in furtherance of the goals of this section.

(d) Nothing in this section shall be construed to require the disclosure by the department of information which may threaten the security of an institution or the safety of the surrounding community. Nor shall the power of visitation specified in subdivision (c) extend to situations where institutional security would be jeopardized. *(Amended by Stats 1989 ch 1420 §21, eff. 1/1/90.)*

§5057. Accounting and auditing system of the department.

Subject to the powers of the Department of Finance under Section 13300 of the Government Code, the director must establish an accounting and auditing system for all of the agencies and institutions including the prisons which comprise the department, except the Youth Authority, in such form as will best facilitate their operation, and may modify the system from time to time.

The accounting and auditing system must include such accounts and records as are found necessary to properly account for all money and property of the prisoners and the inmates.

Except where other disposition is provided by law, all money belonging to the state received by the department, shall be reported to the Controller and deposited in the State Treasury monthly.

§5057.5. Acceptance of gift or donation of goods.

(a) Notwithstanding Section 11005 of the Government Code, the Director of Corrections may accept a gift or donation of goods or services to the state following a review and determination by the director that the gift or donation is not subject to illegal or discriminatory conditions, that it does not involve the expenditure of state funds, and that the acceptance of the gift is in the best interests of the state.

(b) Notwithstanding subdivision (a), the acceptance of a gift or donation that would involve any expenditure of state funds shall be subject to Section 11005 of the Government Code.

(c) It is the intent of the Legislature in enacting this section to recognize the significant contribution that private donors of goods and services can make in supporting the corrections system, and the development of effective vocational education and correctional industries in our prison system. With that objective in mind, the Director of Corrections is encouraged to further develop the current system of gifts and donations through the design of a prompt and efficient review procedure that will encourage donors and protect the interests of the state.

§5058. Rules and regulations.

(a) The director may prescribe and amend rules and regulations for the administration of the prisons. The rules and regulations shall be promulgated and filed pursuant to Chapter 3.5 (commencing with Section 11340) of Part 1 of Division 3 of Title 2 of the Government Code, and shall, to the extent practical, be stated in language that is easily understood by the general public.

(b) The director shall maintain, publish and make available to the general public, a compendium of the rules and regulations promulgated by the director pursuant to this section.

(c) The following exceptions to the procedures specified in this section shall apply to the Department of Corrections:

(1) The director may specify an effective date that is any time more than 30 days after the rule or regulation is filed with the Secretary of State; provided that no less than 20 days prior to that effective date, copies of the rule or regulation shall be posted in conspicuous places throughout each institution and shall be mailed to all persons or organizations who request them.

(2) The director may rely upon a summary of the information compiled by a hearing officer if the summary and the testimony taken regarding the proposed action shall be retained as part of the public record for at least one year after the adoption, amendment, or repeal. *(Amended by Stats 1987 ch 828 §147.)*

§5058.5. Additional medically or psychologically necessary services provided.

In addition to the services rendered by physicians and surgeons, including psychiatrists, or by psychologists, pursuant to Sections 5068 and 5079, physicians and surgeons, including psychiatrists and psychologists, employed by, or under contract to provide mental health services to, the Department of Corrections may also provide the following medically or psychologically necessary services: prescreening of mental disorders; determination of the mental competency of inmates to participate in classification hearings; evaluation of parolees during temporary detention; determining whether mental health treatment should be a condition of parole; and such other services as may be required which are consistent with their licensure.

§5059. Title's affect on Department of Transportation.

This title shall not affect the powers or jurisdiction of the Department of Transportation as to road camps pursuant to Article 4 (commencing with Section 2760) of Chapter 5 of Title 1 of Part 3. *(Amended by Stats 1987 ch 828 §148.)*

§5060. Employment assistance for released prisoners.

The Director of Corrections may assist persons discharged, paroled, or otherwise released from confinement in an institution of the department and may secure employment for them, and for such purposes he may employ necessary officers and employees, may purchase tools, and give any other assistance that, in his judgment, he deems proper for the purpose of carrying out the objects and spirit of this section. Repayment of cash assistance received under this section from the current or any prior appropriation, shall be credited to the appropriation current at time of such repayment.

§5061. Disposition of funds of deceased prisoner.

Whenever any person confined in any state institution subject to the jurisdiction of the Director of Corrections dies, and any personal funds or property of that person remains in the hands of the Director of Corrections, the funds may be applied in an amount not exceeding three hundred dollars ($300) to the payment of his or her burial expenses and charges related thereto. If no demand is made upon the direc-

tor by the owner of the funds or property or his or her legally appointed representative, the director shall hold and dispose of those funds or property as follows:

(a) If the decedent leaves a will, the director shall, within 30 days after the date of death of the decedent, deliver the will to the clerk of the superior court having jurisdiction of the estate. If an executor is named in the will, the director shall furnish him or her written notice of the delivery of the will as provided in this section.

(b) All money or other personal property of the decedent remaining in the custody or possession of the director shall be held by him or her for a period of one year from the date of death of the decedent, for the benefit of the heirs, legatees or successors in interest of that decedent.

(c) Upon the expiration of the one-year period, any money remaining unclaimed in the custody or possession of the director shall be delivered by him or her to the Treasurer for deposit in the Unclaimed Property Fund under Article 1 (commencing with Section 1440) of Chapter 6 of Title 10 of Part 3 of the Code of Civil Procedure.

(d) Upon the expiration of the one-year period, all personal property and documents of the decedent, other than cash, remaining unclaimed in the custody or possession of the director, shall be disposed of as follows:

(1) All deeds, contracts or assignments shall be filed by the director with the public administrator of the county of commitment of the decedent.

(2) All other personal property shall be sold by the director at public auction, or upon a sealed-bid basis, and the proceeds of the sale delivered by him or her to the Treasurer in the same manner as is provided in this section with respect to unclaimed money of the decedent. If he or she deems it expedient to do so, the director may accumulate the property of several decedents and sell the property in such lots as he or she may determine, provided that he or she makes a determination as to each decedent's share of the proceeds.

(3) If any personal property of the decedent is not salable at public auction, or upon a sealed-bid basis, or if it has no intrinsic value, or if its value is not sufficient to justify the deposit of the property in the State Treasury, the director may order it destroyed.

(4) All other unclaimed personal property of the decedent not disposed of as provided in paragraphs (1), (2), or (3), shall be delivered by the director to the Controller for deposit in the State Treasury under Article 1 (commencing with Section 1440) of Chapter 6 of Title 10 of Part 3 of the Code of Civil Procedure. *(Amended by Stats 1988 ch 160 §141, eff. 1/1/89.)*

§5062. Unclaimed funds or property of prisoners.

Whenever any person confined in any state institution subject to the jurisdiction of the Director of Corrections escapes, or is discharged or paroled from such institution, and any personal funds or property of that person remains in the hands of the Director of Corrections, and no demand is made upon the director by the owner of the funds or property or his or her legally appointed representative, all money and other intangible personal property of the person, other than deeds, contracts, or assignments, remaining in the custody or possession of the director shall be held by him or her for a period of seven years from the date of

© 1992 by J., B. & L. Gould
Printed in the U.S.A.   EP

that escape, discharge, or parole, for the benefit of that person or his or her successors in interest.

Upon the expiration of the seven-year period, any money and other intangible personal property, other than deeds, contracts, or assignments, remaining unclaimed in the custody or possession of the director shall be subject to Article 1 (commencing with Section 1500) of Chapter 7 of Title 10 of Part 3 of the Code of Civil Procedure.

Upon the expiration of one year from the date of that escape, discharge, or parole:

(a) All deeds, contracts, or assignments shall be filed by the director with the public administrator of the county of commitment of that person.

(b) All tangible personal property other than money, remaining unclaimed in his or her custody or possession, shall be sold by the director at public auction, or upon a sealed-bid basis, and the proceeds of the sale shall be held by him or her subject to Section 5008 and subject to Article 1 (commencing with Section 1500) of Chapter 7 of Title 10 of Part 3 of the Code of Civil Procedure. If he or she deems it expedient to do so, the director may accumulate the property of several inmates and may sell the property in such lots as he or she may determine, provided that he or she makes a determination as to each inmate's share of the proceeds.

If any tangible personal property covered by this section is not salable at public auction or upon a sealed-bid basis, or if it has no intrinsic value, or if its value is not sufficient to justify its retention by the director to be offered for sale at public auction or upon a sealed-bid basis at a later date, the director may order it destroyed. *(Amended by Stats 1987 ch 828 §150.)*

§5063. Notice of intended disposition.

Before any money or other personal property or documents are delivered to the State Treasurer, State Controller, or public administrator, or sold at auction or upon a sealed-bid basis, or destroyed, under the provisions of Section 5061, and before any personal property or documents are delivered to the public administrator, or sold at auction or upon a sealed-bid basis, or destroyed, under the provisions of Section 5062, of this code, notice of said intended disposition shall be posted at least 30 days prior to the disposition, in a public place at the institution where the disposition is to be made, and a copy of such notice shall be mailed to the last known address of the owner or deceased owner, at least 30 days prior to such disposition. The notice prescribed by this section need not specifically describe each item of property to be disposed of.

§5064. Schedule of money and property delivered to State.

At the time of delivering any money or other personal property to the Treasurer or Controller under Section 5061 or of Article 1 (commencing with Section 1500) of Chapter 7 of Title 10 of Part 3 of the Code of Civil Procedure, the director shall deliver to the Controller a schedule setting forth a statement and description of all money and other personal property delivered, and the name and last known address of the owner or deceased owner. *(Amended by Stats 1987 ch 828 §151.)*

§5065. No suit may be maintained after destruction of property.

When any personal property has been destroyed as provided in Section 5061 or 5062, no suit shall thereafter be maintained by any person against the State or any officer thereof for or on account of such property.

§5066. *Repealed by Stats 1987 ch 828.*

§5067. Correctional Conservation Camp Services Division.

There is, in the Department of Corrections, a Correctional Conservation Camp Services Division, which shall be headed by a Deputy Director of Corrections, appointed by the Governor, on the recommendation of the Director of Corrections to serve at the pleasure of the Governor. The division shall operate the conservation centers, branches thereof, and permanent, temporary and mobile camps operating therefrom, and shall have charge, subject to the general direction of the Director of Corrections, of all other institutions in the department and activities of persons in the custody of the director relating to conservation work. The director shall appoint such personnel as are necessary to enable the division to carry out its functions.

§5068. Examination and study of all committed persons.

The Director of Corrections shall cause each person who is newly committed to a state prison to be examined and studied. This includes the investigation of all pertinent circumstances of the person's life such as the existence of any strong community and family ties, the maintenance of which may aid in the person's rehabilitation, and the antecedents of the violation of law because of which he or she has been committed to prison. Any person may be reexamined to determine whether existing orders and dispositions should be modified or continued in force.

Upon the basis of the examination and study, the Director of Corrections shall classify prisoners; and when reasonable, the director shall assign a prisoner to the institution of the appropriate security level and gender population nearest the prisoner's home, unless other classification factors make such a placement unreasonable.

As used in this section, "reasonable" includes consideration of the safety of the prisoner and the institution, the length of term, and the availability of institutional programs and housing.

As used in this section, "prisoner's home" means a place where the prisoner's spouse, parents, or children reside at the time of commitment.

When the diagnostic study of any inmate committed under subdivision (b) of Section 1168 so indicates, the director shall cause a psychiatric or psychological report to be prepared for the Community Release Board prior to the release of the inmate. The report shall be prepared by a psychiatrist or psychologist licensed to practice in this state.

Before the release of any inmate committed under subdivision (b) of Section 1168, the director shall provide the Community Release Board with a written evaluation of the prisoner. *(Amended by Stats 1989 ch 1061 §2, eff. 1/1/90.)*

§5068.5. Requirements for providing mental health services; exemptions.

(a) Notwithstanding any other provision of law, except as provided in subdivision (b), any person employed or under contract to provide diagnostic, treatment, or other mental health services in the state or to supervise or provide consultation on these services in the state correctional system shall be a physician and surgeon, a psychologist, or other health professional, licensed to practice in this state.

(b) Notwithstanding Section 5068 or Section 704 of the Welfare and Institutions Code, the following persons are exempt from the requirements of subdivision (a), so long as they continue in employment in the same class and in the same department:

(1) Persons employed on January 1, 1985, as psychologists to provide diagnostic or treatment services including those persons on authorized leave but not including intermittent personnel.

(2) Persons employed on January 1, 1989, to supervise or provide consultation on the diagnostic or treatment services including persons on authorized leave but not including intermittent personnel.

(c) Additionally, the requirements of subdivision (a) may be waived in order for a person to gain qualifying experience for licensure as a psychologist in this state. However, the waiver shall not exceed two years from the date of the commencement of employment. The requirements of subdivision (a) may be waived for a person recruited for employment from outside this state and who possesses experience sufficient to qualify for admission to a licensing examination on the date of his or her employment for a period of one year from the date of his or her employment. *(Amended by Stats 1989 ch 1360 §120, eff. 1/1/90.)*

§5069. Rehabilitation services for injured inmates.

(a) The administrative director of the Division of Industrial Accidents shall formulate procedures for the selection and orderly referral of injured inmates of state penal or correctional institutions who may be benefited by rehabilitation services and retrained for other positions upon release from incarceration. The State Department of Rehabilitation shall cooperate in both designing and monitoring results of rehabilitation programs for the disabled inmates. The primary purpose of this section is to rehabilitate injured inmates in order that they might engage in suitable and gainful employment upon their release.

(b) The director shall notify the injured inmate of the availability of rehabilitation services in those cases where there is continuing disability of 28 days and beyond. A copy of such notification shall be forwarded to the State Department of Rehabilitation.

(c) The initiation of a rehabilitation plan shall be the responsibility of the director.

(d) Upon establishment of a rehabilitation plan, the injured inmate shall cooperate in carrying it out.

(e) The injured inmate shall receive such medical and vocational rehabilitative services as may be reasonably necessary to restore him to suitable employment.

(f) The injured inmate's rehabilitation benefit is an additional benefit and shall not be converted to or replace any workmen's compensation benefit available to him.

§5070. Sex discrimination prohibited in academic and vocational training programs.

Notwithstanding any other provision of law, the sex of a prison inmate shall not prevent the Director of Corrections from assigning any prison inmate to academic or vocational training programs situated in correctional institutions established for the incarceration of offenders of the opposite sex.

CHAPTER 3

THE BOARD OF PRISON TERMS

§5075. Board of Prison Terms.

The Board of Prison Terms shall be composed of nine commissioners, each of whom shall be appointed by the Governor, with the advice and consent of the Senate, for a term of four years and until the appointment and qualification of his successor. Commissioners shall be eligible for reappointment.

The chairman of the board shall be designated by the Governor from time to time. The chairman shall be the administrative head of the board and shall exercise all duties and functions necessary to insure that the responsibilities of the board are successfully discharged. He shall be the appointing authority for all civil service positions of employment in the board.

The terms of the commissioners shall expire as follows: two on March 15, 1978, two on March 15, 1979, two on March 15, 1980, and three on March 15, 1981. Successor commissioners shall hold office for terms of four years, each term to commence on the expiration date of the term of the predecessor. The Governor shall fill every vacancy for the balance of the unexpired term. The selection of persons and their appointment by the Governor and confirmation by the Senate shall reflect as nearly as possible a cross-section of the racial, sexual, economic, and geographic features of the population of the state.

It is the further intent of this section that the board shall adopt such policies and practices as will permit continuing operations and improvements without any further increase in the number of its commissioners. *(Amended by Stats 1986 ch 1446 §4.)*

§5076. Time to be devoted; salary.

Each commissioner of the board shall devote his entire time to the duties of his office and shall receive an annual salary provided for by Chapter 6 (commencing with Section 11550) of Part 1 of Division 3 of Title 2 of the Government Code. *(Amended by Stats 1986 ch 1446 §5.)*

§5076.1. Times and places of meetings; business.

The board shall meet at each of the state prisons at such times as may be necessary for a full and complete study of the cases of all prisoners whose applications for parole come before it. Other times and places of meeting may also be fixed by the board. Each commissioner of the board shall receive his actual necessary traveling expenses incurred in the performance of his official duties. Where the board performs its functions by meeting en banc in either public or executive sessions to decide matters of general policy, at least five members shall be present, and no such action shall be valid unless it is concurred in by a majority vote of those present.

© 1992 by J., B. & L. Gould
Printed in the U.S.A.   EP

The board may meet and transact business in panels. Each panel shall consist of at least three persons. No action shall be valid unless concurred in by a majority vote of the persons present.

Consideration of parole release for persons sentenced to life imprisonment pursuant to subdivision (b) of Section 1168 shall be heard by a panel, a majority of whose commissioners are commissioners of the Board of Prison Terms. A recommendation for recall of a sentence under subdivisions (d) and (f) of Section 1170 shall be made by a panel, a majority of whose commissioners are commissioners of the Board of Prison Terms.

The board may employ deputy commissioners to whom it may assign appropriate duties, including that of hearing cases and making decisions. Such decisions shall be made in accordance with policies approved by a majority of the total membership of the board. *(Amended by Stats 1986 ch 1446 §6.)*

§5076.2. Rules and regulations.

(a) Any rules and regulations, including any resolutions and policy statements, promulgated by the Board of Prison Terms, shall be promulgated and filed pursuant to Chapter 3.5 (commencing with Section 11340) of Part 1 of Division 3 of Title 2 of the Government Code, and shall, to the extent practical, be stated in language that is easily understood by the general public.

(b) The Board of Prison Terms shall maintain, publish and make available to the general public, a compendium of its rules and regulations, including any resolutions and policy statements, promulgated pursuant to this section.

(c) The exception specified in this subdivision to the procedures specified in this section shall apply to the Board of Prison Terms. The chairperson may specify an effective date that is any time more than 30 days after the rule or regulation is filed with the Secretary of State. However, no less than 20 days prior to that effective date, copies of the rule or regulation shall be posted in conspicuous places throughout each institution and shall be mailed to all persons or organizations who request them. *(Amended by Stats 1988 ch 160 §142, eff. 1/1/89.)*

§5076.3. Subpoenas; issuance.

The Chairman of the Board of Prison Terms shall have the authority of a head of a department set forth in subdivision (e) of Section 11181 of the Government Code to issue subpoenas as provided in Article 2 (commencing with Section 11180) of Chapter 2 of Division 3 of Title 2 of the Government Code. The board shall adopt regulations on the policies and guidelines for the issuance of subpoenas.

§5077. Review of decisions for good-time credit and parole.

The Board of Prison Terms shall review all prisoners' requests for reconsideration of denial of good-time credit, and setting of parole length or conditions, and shall have the authority to modify the previously made decisions of the Department of Corrections as to these matters. The revocation of parole shall be determined by the Board of Prison Terms.

§5078. Powers and duties.

(a) The Board of Prison Terms shall succeed to and shall exercise and perform all powers and duties granted to, exercised by, and imposed upon the Adult Authority, the California Women's Board of Terms and Paroles, and the Community Release Board.

(b) The Adult Authority and California Women's Board of Terms and Paroles are abolished.

§5079. Psychiatric and diagnostic clinics.

The Director of Corrections shall provide facilities and licensed professional personnel for a psychiatric and diagnostic clinic and such branches thereof as may be required at one or more of the state prisons or institutions under the jurisdiction of the Department of Corrections. The director shall have full administrative authority and responsibility for operation of the clinics. All required mental health treatment or diagnostic services shall be provided under the supervision of a psychiatrist licensed to practice in this state, or a psychologist licensed to practice in this state and who holds a doctoral degree and has at least two years of experience in the diagnosis and treatment of emotional and mental disorders. All such clinics shall be under the direction of such a psychiatrist or psychologist. A psychiatrist shall be available to assume responsibility for all acts of diagnosis or treatment which may only be performed by a licensed physician and surgeon.

The work of the clinic shall include a scientific study of each prisoner, his or her career and life history, the cause of his or her criminal acts and recommendations for his or her care, training, and employment with a view to his or her reformation and to the protection of society. The recommendation shall be submitted to the Director of Corrections and shall not be effective until approved by the director. The Director of Corrections may modify or reject the recommendations as he or she sees fit.

§5080. Requests for transfers of prisoners; compliance.

The Director of Corrections may transfer persons confined in one state prison institution or facility of the Department of Corrections to another. The Board of Prison Terms may request the Director of Corrections to transfer an inmate who is under its parole-granting jurisdiction if, after review of the case history in the course of routine procedures, such transfer is deemed advisable for the further diagnosis, and treatment of the inmate. The director shall as soon as practicable comply with such request, provided that, if facilities are not available he shall report that fact to the Board of Prison Terms and shall make the transfer as soon as facilities become available; provided further, that if in the opinion of the Director of Corrections such transfer would endanger security he may report that fact to the Board of Prison Terms and refuse to make such transfer.

When transferring an inmate from one state prison institution, or facility of the Department of Corrections to another, the director may, as necessary or convenient, authorize transportation via a route that lies partly outside this state.

§5081. Removal of members for misconduct, incompetency or neglect.

The Governor may remove any member of the Board of Prison Terms for misconduct, incompetency or neglect of duty after a full hearing by the Board of Corrections.

© 1992 by J., B. & L. Gould
Printed in the U.S.A. **EP**

§5082. Employees; selection, appointment.

(a) Any number of employees of the Board of Prison Terms as are needed to carry out its functions shall be selected and appointed pursuant to the State Civil Service Act. Nothing shall prohibit the Board of Prison Terms from employing any person employed formerly by the Adult Authority or Women's Board of Terms and Paroles.

(b) The provisions of Chapter 6 (commencing with Section 6050) of Title 7 of Part 3, relating to the employment of personnel by the department, do not apply to the employees of the Board of Prison Terms. *(Amended by Stats 1987 ch 828 §155.)*

CHAPTER 3.5

THE ROBERT PRESLEY INSTITUTE OF CORRECTIONS RESEARCH AND TRAINING
(Heading amended by Stats 1987 ch 1450 §3.)

§5085. Purpose.

(a) There is hereby created in state government the Robert Presley Institute of Corrections Research and Training, hereafter referred to as "the institute" for the purposes of supporting research as provided by Section 5091, and enhancing education and training for corrections personnel within the youth and adult corrections system in California.

(b) The Legislature declares that the institute shall research and recommend short-term and long-term approaches to address the following:

(1) Evaluate the assumptions of our penal system including the prevention of violence, protection of public safety, safe, secure, and cost-effective incarceration, and the reintegration of offenders into society.

(2) Identify the methods and practices necessary for the most beneficial operation of the state's correctional institutions.

(3) Reduce prison, jail, and youth facility violence and recidivism rates.

(4) Ensure that California remains the nationwide leader in modern, humane, secure, and efficient correctional systems.

(5) Review current educational and training practices for correctional staff and recommend new curricula and training regimens intended to enhance the professionalism, expertise, and effectiveness of these personnel. *(Amended by Stats 1987 ch 1450 §4.)*

§5085.5. Areas in need of improved methods and research.

The Legislature further finds and declares the following:

(a) That the Department of Corrections and the Department of the Youth Authority require assistance in improving methods for the training and education of adult and youth corrections line employees, supervisors, managers, and directors.

(b) That there is a need for theoretical and applied research in the subjects of the following:

(1) Correctional facility management, planning, design, and construction.

(2) Inmate diagnosis, classification, and treatment.

(3) Staff security and inmate discipline.

(4) Ward and inmate vocational training, and development of job skills for their permanent civilian employment.

(5) Correctional facility overcrowding.

(6) Prison, jail, and street gang activity.

(7) Safe, secure, and cost-effective incarceration in California's correctional institutions.

(8) New approaches to inmate and ward rehabilitation during and after incarceration.

(9) New methods to reduce recidivism and the consequent victimization of California citizens. *(Amended by Stats 1987 ch 56 §133.)*

§5086. Board of trustees.

The institute shall be governed by a 17-member board of trustees, hereafter referred to as "the board," which shall consult with the governing body of the University of California, and the governing bodies of the California State University and the California community colleges. The institute shall also consult with the Governor and the Legislature on matters related to corrections research, education, and training. *(Amended by Stats 1987 ch 1450 §4.5.)*

§5087. Voting members.

The board shall be composed of 17 voting members. The members shall be selected from persons with experience or education in the fields of corrections, correctional training, criminal justice, criminal law, sociology, public health, architecture, urban planning, mental health, public protection, political science, psychology, or psychiatry. The Director of Corrections and the Director of the Youth Authority shall serve as ex officio voting members of the board. The Chairperson of the Board of the National Institute of Corrections or his or her designee, shall serve as an ex officio voting member of the board. The chancellor of the campus affiliated with the institute is authorized to serve either as an ex officio voting member of the board, or as a gubernatorial appointee of the board, as specified in Section 5088. *(Amended by Stats 1990 ch 548 §1, eff. 8/27/90.)*

§5088. Appointment of members of board.

The Governor shall appoint six members of the board. The Governor may, in addition, appoint as a member of the board the chancellor of the campus affiliated with the institute, rather than that chancellor serving as an ex officio voting member of the board as provided in Section 5087. One of these appointees shall be designated by the Governor as chairperson. The Speaker of the Assembly and the Senate Rules Committee shall each appoint two members of the board. The Chancellors of the California State University and the California Community Colleges shall each appoint one member of the board. The President of the University of California is authorized to appoint one member of the board. *(Amended by Stats 1990 ch 548 §2, eff. 8/27/90.)*

§5088.5. Length of service.

The three members first appointed by the Governor shall serve for a period of three years and the other three members for a period of two years. The one member first appointed by the Speaker of the Assembly and the Senate Rules Committee shall serve for a period of three years and the other member for a period of two years. The members first appointed by the governing bodies of the University of California, the California State University, and the California community colleges shall serve for a period of three years. Thereafter, all appointments shall be for a period of four years. *(Added by Stats 1986 ch 1288 §1.)*

© 1992 by J., B. & L. Gould
Printed in the U.S.A.　　**EP**

§5089. Vacancies; meeting times.

(a) In the event of a vacancy due to resignation, death, removal by the appointing authority pursuant to subdivision (b), or expiration of term of a appointed office, the appointing authority shall fill the vacancy following receipt of written notification from the board that a vacancy has occurred.

(b) Vacancies shall be filled by appointment for the unexpired term. The appointing authority may remove any member of the board disqualified by reason of neglect of any duty required by law, or for incompetency, or dishonorable conduct.

(c) The board shall meet regularly at least four times during each year with at least one meeting each year to be held in a geographic location readily available to a large segment of the population of California. The board shall hold extra meetings as necessary on the call of the chairperson or a majority of the voting members of the board. Nine voting members of the board constitute a quorum. The vote of a majority of the voting members of the board is necessary for the transaction of the business of the board. *(Amended by Stats 1987 ch 1450 §6.5.)*

§5090. Authority to appoint and hire.

(a) The board shall have the authority to appoint such technical and other advisory committees as it deems necessary to achieve the mandate of the institute as intended by the Legislature. The appointed members of the technical and other advisory committees appointed by the board shall be reimbursed for travel and other expenses at the rates allowed to state employees but shall otherwise serve without compensation.

(b) The board shall have the authority to hire an executive director, obtain services of legal counsel, and employ such other staff as necessary to carry out the purposes of the institute. The board shall fix the compensation of all employed staff members in accordance with law. The executive director shall serve at the pleasure of the board and is exempt from civil service. *(Added by Stats 1986 ch 1288 §1.)*

§5091. Legislative intent.

It is the intent of the Legislature that beginning January 1, 1987, the institute shall do all of the following:

(a) Finance research on issues of interest to state and local correctional agencies, universities, colleges, and other academic or corrections research institutions. The board shall receive and assign priority to research requests from correctional agencies, the Legislature and others. With respect to assigning priority to research requests, the board shall give preference to research tasks beyond the ordinary capability of in-house agency research divisions.

(b) Establish a clearinghouse for correctional information and research and disseminate material of interest, including the results of institute-financed research, to correctional practitioners, the Legislature, universities, colleges, courts, and the public.

(c) Sponsor seminars in which experts and theoreticians from various fields relevant to correctional practice may interact for the purpose of assisting the conduct of California corrections. *(Amended by Stats 1987 ch 1450 §7.)*

§5092. Program development.

On or before March 1, 1988, the institute shall develop a detailed and specific program for implementation by the Legislature, the Department of Corrections, and the Department of the Youth Authority that establishes a career path, which is integrated with an educational and training regimen for all youth and adult state corrections personnel in California. This program shall recommend specific actions to improve the job and career competence of state youth and adult corrections personnel and to encourage and foster the attainment of postsecondary educational degrees by correctional officers. Any minimum training and education standards recommended shall include standards for entry, basic, intermediate, advanced, supervisory, management, and specialized corrections personnel. *(Added by Stats 1986 ch 1288, §1.)*

§5093. Permanent home for institute near Riverside campus.

It is the intent of the Legislature that a permanent home for the institute be established on or in the immediate vicinity of the Riverside campus of the University of California. *(Added by Stats 1986 ch 1288 §1.)*

§5094. Funding.

(a) It is the intent of the Legislature that funding for the institute's training, education, and research projects should be appropriated by the Legislature. The board is encouraged to seek additional funds from the state college and university systems, private colleges and universities, foundations, the federal government, and other sources deemed appropriate by the board.

(b) The executive director shall, subject to review and approval of the board, negotiate the terms, services, and costs of contracts and research projects consistent with funds available. The board shall approve contracts negotiated by the executive director and shall retain legal counsel for purposes of contract review.

(c) Consistent with the funds available, the executive director shall obtain all necessary office space, equipment, supplies, and services he or she deems necessary for the institute to perform its mandated duties. *(Amended by Stats 1987 ch 1450 §8.)*

§5095. Expenses; reimbursement.

The board members shall receive per diem, travel, and other expenses while employed by the state to carry out the function of the institute. Per diem shall be one hundred dollars ($100) for each day engaged in the performance of the duties of the institute pursuant to this chapter. Travel and other expenses shall be reimbursed at rates allowed to state employees. *(Added by Stats 1986 ch 1288, §1.)*

§5096. Appropriated fund.

The sum of one hundred fifty thousand dollars ($150,000) is hereby appropriated from the General Fund to the institute for the purposes of this act. *(Added by Stats 1986 ch 1288, §1.)*

CHAPTER 4

THE YOUTH AUTHORITY

§6001. Establishment, organization of youth authority.

The establishment, organization, jurisdiction, powers, duties, responsibilities, and functions of the

Youth Authority are continued as provided in the Youth Authority Act (Chapter 1 (commencing with Section 1700) of Division 2.5 of the Welfare and Institutions Code). *(Amended by Stats 1987 ch 828 §156.)*

§6003. Powers and duties.

The Youth Authority and the Director of Corrections may, pursuant to Section 11253 and Sections 11256 to 11259, inclusive, of the Government Code, provide for the performance of any of the duties or the exercise of any of the powers of the Youth Authority by the Department of Corrections, subject to the direction and control of the Youth Authority, except that the power of classification and segregation of persons committed to the authority shall be exercised by the authority, and shall not be exercised by any other agency. *(Amended by Stats 1987 ch 828 §157.)*

§6004. Exercise of powers and duties; operation of facilities.

Whenever the Director of Corrections or the Department of Corrections exercises any power or performs any duty of the Youth Authority pursuant to the authorization in Section 6003:

(a) The exercise of the power or the performance of the duty by the Director of Corrections or the Department of Corrections shall constitute an exercise of the power or a performance of the duty by the Youth Authority for the purposes of the Youth Authority Act (Chapter 1 (commencing with Section 1700) of Division 2.5 of the Welfare and Institutions Code).

(b) The operation of any service, place, institution, hospital, agency, or facility by the Department of Corrections under the authorization in Section 6003 shall be deemed operation by the Youth Authority.

(c) All public officers and other persons under a duty to make any reports or provide any information, access, or assistance to the Youth Authority in respect to the power or duty so exercised shall make the reports, or provide the information, access, or assistance to the Director of Corrections or the Department of Corrections. *(Amended by Stats 1987 ch 828 §158.)*

§6005. Trial costs of prisoners.

Whenever a person confined to a correctional institution under the supervision of the Department of the Youth Authority is charged with a public offense committed within the confines of such institution and is tried for such public offense, the county clerk of a county or the city finance officer of a city incurring any costs in connection with such matter must make out a statement of all the costs incurred by the county or city for the investigation, and the preparation of the trial, and the actual trial of such case, and of all guarding and keeping of such person, and of the execution of the sentence of such person, properly certified to by a judge of the superior court of such county. The statement shall be sent to the department for its approval. After such approval the department must cause the amount of such costs to be paid out of the money appropriated for the support of the department to the county treasurer of the county or the city finance officer of the city incurring such costs.

CHAPTER 5

THE BOARD OF CORRECTIONS

ARTICLE 1

GENERAL PROVISIONS

§6024. Board of Corrections.

There is in the Youth and Adult Correctional Agency a Board of Corrections.

§6025. Members; chairman, terms.

(a) The Board of Corrections shall be composed of 11 members, one of whom shall be the Secretary of the Youth and Adult Correctional Agency who shall be designated as the chairperson, one of whom shall be the Director of Corrections, one of whom shall be the Director of the Youth Authority, and eight of whom shall be appointed by the Governor after consultation with, and with the advice of, the Secretary of the Youth and Adult Correctional Agency, and with the advice and consent of the Senate. The gubernatorial appointments shall include:

(1) A county sheriff in charge of a local detention facility which has a Board of Corrections rated capacity of 200 or less inmates.

(2) A county sheriff in charge of a local detention facility which has a Board of Corrections rated capacity of over 200 inmates.

(3) A county supervisor or county administrative officer.

(4) A chief probation officer.

(5) A manager or administrator of a county local detention facility.

(6) An administrator of a local community-based correctional program.

(7) Two public members.

(b) Of the members first appointed by the Governor, two shall be appointed for a term of two years, three for a term of three years, and three for a term of four years. The length of the original term to be served by each such member first appointed shall be determined by lot. Their successors shall serve for a term of three years and until appointment and qualification of their successors, each term to commence on the expiration date of the term of the predecessor.

(c) The board shall select a vice chairperson from among its members. Six members of the board shall constitute a quorum.

(d) When the Board of Corrections is hearing charges against any member, the individual concerned shall not sit as a member of the board for the period of hearing of charges and the determination of recommendations to the Governor.

(e) If any appointed member is not in attendance for three consecutive meetings the board shall recommend to the Governor that the member be removed and the Governor shall make a new appointment, with the advice and consent of the Senate, for the remainder of the term. *(Amended by Stats 1989 ch 1327 §6, eff. 10/2/89.)*

§6025.1. Travel.

Members of the board shall receive no compensation, but shall be reimbursed for their actual and necessary travel expenses incurred in the performance of their duties. For purposes of compensation, attendance at meetings of the board shall be deemed

© 1992 by J., B. & L. Gould
Printed in the U.S.A.   **EP**

performance by a member of the duties of his state or local governmental employment.

§6025.5. Filing rules and regulations with board.

The Director of Corrections, Board of Prison Terms, the Youthful Offender Parole Board, and the Director of the Youth Authority shall file with the Board of Corrections for information of the board or for review and advice to the respective agency as the board may determine, all rules, regulations and manuals relating to or in implementation of policies, procedures, or enabling laws.

§6025.6. Board of Corrections; delegation of authority and duties.

The Board of Corrections may delegate any ministerial authority or duty conferred or imposed upon the board to a subordinate officer subject to those conditions as it may choose to impose. *(Added by Stats 1991 ch 1017 §2, eff. 1/1/92.)*

§6026. Correlating programs for adults and youths.

The Board of Corrections shall be the means whereby the Department of Corrections and the Department of the Youth Authority may correlate their individual programs for the adults and youths under the jurisdiction of each.

§6027. Study of crime; report.

It shall be the duty of the Board of Corrections to make a study of the entire subject of crime, with particular reference to conditions in the State of California, including causes of crime, possible methods of prevention of crime, methods of detection of crime and apprehension of criminals, methods of prosecution of persons accused of crime, and the entire subject of penology, including standards and training for correctional personnel, and to report its findings, its conclusions and recommendations to the Governor and the Legislature at such times as they may require.

§6028. Special commissions.

Upon request of the Board of Corrections or upon his own initiative, the Governor from time to time may create by executive order one or more special commissions to assist the Board of Corrections in the study of crime pursuant to Section 6027. Each such special commission shall consist of not less than three nor more than five members, who shall be appointed by the Governor. The members of any such special commission shall serve without compensation, except that they shall receive their actual and necessary expenses incurred in the discharge of their duties.

The executive order creating each special commission shall specify the subjects and scope of the study to be made by the commission, and shall fix a time within which the commission shall make its final report. Each commission shall cease to exist when it makes its final report.

§6028.1. Special commission's powers and limitations.

Each such special commission may investigate any and all matters relating to the subjects specified in the order creating it. In the exercise of its powers the commission shall be subject to the following conditions and limitations:

(a) A witness at any hearing shall have the right to have present at such hearing counsel of his own choice, for the purpose of advising him concerning his constitutional rights.

(b) No hearing shall be televised or broadcast by radio, nor shall any mechanical, photographic or electronic record of the proceedings at any hearing be televised or broadcast by radio.

§6028.2. Furnishing commission with facilities, supplies, and personnel.

The Secretary of the Youth and Adult Correctional Agency may furnish for the use of any such commission such facilities, supplies, and personnel as may be available therefor.

§6028.3. Reports and recommendations by special commissions.

All such special commissions shall make all their reports and recommendations to the Board of Corrections. The Board of Corrections shall consider such reports and recommendations, and shall transmit them to the Governor and the Legislature, together with its own comments and recommendations on the subject matter thereof, within the first 30 days of the next succeeding general or budget session of the Legislature. The Board of Corrections shall also file copies of such reports with the Attorney General, the State Library and such other state departments as may appear to have an official interest in the subject matter of the report or reports in question.

§6028.4. Report of appointees and expenses.

The Governor shall report to each regular session of the Legislature the names of any persons appointed under Section 6028 together with a statement of expenses incurred.

§6029. Recommendation on remodeling of prisons.

(a) The plans and specifications of every jail, prison, or other place of detention of persons charged with or convicted of crime or of persons detained pursuant to the Juvenile Court Law (Chapter 2 (commencing with Section 200) of Division 2 of the Welfare and Institutions Code) or the Youth Authority Act (Chapter 1 (commencing with Section 1700) of Division 2.5 of the Welfare and Institutions Code), if those plans and specifications involve construction, reconstruction, remodeling, or repairs of an aggregate cost in excess of fifteen thousand dollars ($15,000), shall be submitted to the board for its recommendations. Upon request of any city, city and county, or county, the board shall consider the entire program or group of detention facilities currently planned or under consideration by the city, city and county, or county, and make a study of the entire needs of the city, city and county, or county therefor, and make recommendations thereon. No state department or agency other than the board shall have authority to make recommendations in respect to plans and specifications for the construction of county jails or other county detention facilities or for alterations thereto, except such recommendations as the board may request from any such state department or agency.

(b) As used in this section, "place of detention" includes, but is not limited to, a correctional treatment center, as defind in subdivision (k) of Section 1250 of the Health and Safety Code, which is operated by a city, city and county, or county. *(Amended by Stats 1989 ch 1327 §7, eff. 10/2/89.)*

§6029.1. County Jail Capital Expenditure Fund.

(a) There is hereby created the County Jail Capital Expenditure Fund. Moneys in the County Jail Capital Expenditure Fund shall be expended by the Board of Corrections as specified in this section to assist counties to finance jail construction. Moneys in the County Jail Capital Expenditure Fund shall be available for encumbrance without regard to fiscal years, and notwithstanding any other provision of law, shall not revert to the General Fund or be transferred to any other fund or account in the State Treasury except for purposes of investment as provided in Article 4 (commencing with Section 16470) of Chapter 3 of Part 2 of Division 4 of Title 2 of the Government Code. All interest or other increment resulting from such investment shall be deposited in the County Jail Capital Expenditure Fund, notwithstanding Section 16305.7 of the Government Code.

(b) As used in this section, "construction" shall include, but not be limited to, reconstruction, remodeling, replacement of facilities, and the performance of deferred maintenance activities on facilities pursuant to rules and regulations regarding such activities as shall be adopted by the Board of Corrections.

(c) The Board of Corrections shall provide financial assistance to counties from the County Jail Capital Expenditure Fund according to policies, criteria, and procedures adopted by the board pursuant to recommendations made by the Subcommittee on Corrections of the Senate Judiciary Committee and an appropriate subcommittee of the Assembly Criminal Justice Committee and after consulting with a representative sample of county boards of supervisors and sheriffs.

(d) In performing the duties set forth in this section, the Board of Corrections and the policy committees of the Legislature shall consider the following:

(1) The extent to which the county requesting aid has exhausted all other available means of raising the requested funds for the capital improvements and the extent to which the funds from the County Jail Capital Expenditure Fund will be utilized to attract other sources of capital financing for county jail facilities;

(2) The extent to which a substantial county match shall be required and any circumstances under which the county match may be reduced or waived;

(3) The extent to which the county's match shall be based on the county's previous compliance with Board of Corrections standards;

(4) The extent to which the capital improvements are necessary to the life or safety of the persons confined or employed in the facility or the health and sanitary conditions of the facility;

(5) The extent to which the county has utilized reasonable alternatives to pre- and post-conviction incarceration, including, but not limited to, programs to facilitate release upon one's own recognizance where appropriate to individuals pending trial, sentencing alternatives to custody, and civil commitment or diversion programs consistent with public safety for those with drug or alcohol related problems or mental or developmental disabilities.

§6029.5. Money for joint use correctional facilities.

The Board of Corrections is authorized to expend money from the County Jail Capital Expenditure Fund, created pursuant to Sections 4412 and 6029.1, on joint use correctional facilities housing county and state or federal prisoners or any combination thereof in proportion to the county benefit.

§6030. Minimum standards for local detention facilities.

(a) The Board of Corrections shall establish minimum standards for local detention facilities by July 1, 1972. The Board of Corrections shall review such standards biennially and make any appropriate revisions.

(b) The standards shall include, but not be limited to, the following: health and sanitary conditions, fire and life safety, security, rehabilitation programs, recreation, treatment of persons confined in local detention facilities, and personnel training.

(c) Such standards shall require that at least one person on duty at the facility is knowledgeable in the area of fire and life safety procedures.

(d) The standards shall also include requirements relating to the acquisition, storage, labeling, packaging, and dispensing of drugs.

(e) In establishing minimum standards, the Board of Corrections shall seek the advice of the following:

(1) For health and sanitary conditions:

The State Department of Health Services, physicians, psychiatrists, local public health officials, and other interested persons.

(2) For fire and life safety:

The State Fire Marshal, local fire officials, and other interested persons.

(3) For security, rehabilitation programs, recreation, and treatment of persons confined in local detention facilities:

The Department of Corrections, the Department of the Youth Authority, local juvenile justice commissions, local correctional officials, experts in criminology and penology, and other interested persons.

(4) For personnel training:

The Commission on Peace Officer Standards and Training, psychiatrists, experts in criminology and penology, the Department of Corrections, the Department of the Youth Authority, local correctional officials, and other interested persons. *(Amended by Stats 1986 ch 376 §1.)*

§6030.1. *Repealed by Stats 1986 ch 376, eff. 1/1/89.*

§6031. Inspection of local detention facilities.

The Board of Corrections shall inspect each local detention facility in the state by January 1, 1974, and shall inspect each such facility biennially thereafter.

§6031.1. Biennial inspections of facilities.

Inspections of local detention facilities shall be made biennially. Inspections of privately operated work furlough facilities and programs shall be made biennially unless the work furlough administrator requests an earlier inspection. Inspections shall include, but not be limited to, the following:

(a) Health and safety inspections conducted pursuant to Section 459 of the Health and Safety Code.

(b) Fire suppression preplanning inspections by the local fire department.

(c) Security, rehabilitation programs, recreation, treatment of persons confined in the facilities, and personnel training by the staff of the Board of Corrections.

Reports of each facility's inspection shall be furnished to the official in charge of the local detention

© 1992 by J., B. & L. Gould
Printed in the U.S.A.   EP

facility or, in the case of a privately operated facility, the work furlough administrator, the local governing body, the grand jury, and the presiding or sole judge of the superior court in the county where the facility is located. These reports shall set forth the areas wherein the facility has complied and has failed to comply with the minimum standards established pursuant to Section 6030. *(Amended by Stats 1987 ch 1054 §2.)*

§6031.2. Reports of sub-standard local detention facilities.

The Board of Corrections shall file with the Legislature by March 31, 1974, and on June 30, in each even-numbered year thereafter, reports of the inspection of those local detention facilities that have not complied with the minimum standards established pursuant to Section 6030. The reports shall specify those areas in which the facility has failed to comply and the estimated cost to the facility necessary to accomplish compliance with the minimum standards.

The reports shall also include an evaluation of standards required of, and training provided for, correctional personnel. The reports shall specify those areas in which standards and training are, in the board's estimation, inadequate. *(Amended by Stats 1991 ch 1017 §3, eff. 1/1/92.)*

§6031.3. Board's application for available funds.

The Board of Corrections is authorized to apply for any funds that may be available from the federal government to further the purposes of Sections 6030 to 6031.2, inclusive.

§6031.4. Local detention facility defined.

(a) For the purpose of this title, "local detention facility" means any city, county, city and county, or regional facility used for the confinement for more than 24 hours of adults, or of both adults and minors, but does not include that portion of a facility for the confinement of both adults and minors which is devoted only to the confinement of minors.

(b) In addition to those provided for in subdivision (a), for the purposes of this title, "local detention facility" also includes any city, county, city and county, or regional facility, constructed on or after January 1, 1978, used for the confinement, regardless of the length of confinement, of adults or of both adults and minors, but does not include that portion of a facility for the confinement of both adults and minors which is devoted only to the confinement of minors.

(c) "Local detention facility" also includes any adult detention facility that holds local prisoners under contract on behalf of cities, counties, or cities and counties. Nothing in this subdivision shall be construed as affecting the establishment of private detention facilities.

(d) For purposes of this title, a local detention facility does not include those rooms that are used for holding persons for interviews, interrogations, or investigations, and are either separate from a jail or located in the administrative area of a law enforcement facility. *(Amended by Stats 1988 ch 386 §2, eff. 8/6/88.)*

§6031.5. Correctional personnel defined.

For the purposes of this chapter, the term "correctional personnel" means either of the following:

(1) Any person described by subdivision (a) or (b) of Section 830.5, 830.55, 831, or 831.5.

(2) Any class of persons who perform supervision, custody, care, or treatment functions and are employed by the Department of Corrections, the Department of the Youth Authority, any correctional or detention facility, probation department, community-based correctional program, or other state or local public facility or program responsible for the custody, supervision, treatment, or rehabilitation of persons accused of, or adjudged responsible for, criminal or delinquent conduct. *(Amended by Stats 1991 ch 1100 §5, eff. 1/1/92.)*

ARTICLE 2

STANDARDS AND TRAINING OF LOCAL CORRECTIONS AND PROBATION OFFICERS

§6035. Minimum standards for selection and training.

(a) For the purpose of raising the level of competence of local corrections and probation officers and other correctional personnel, the board shall adopt, and may from time to time amend, rules establishing minimum standards for the selection and training of these personnel employed by any city, county, or city and county who provide for the custody, supervision, treatment, or rehabilitation of persons accused of, or adjudged responsible for, criminal or delinquent conduct who are currently under local jurisdiction. All of these rules shall be adopted and amended pursuant to Chapter 3.5 (commencing with Section 11340) of Part 1 of Division 3 of Title 2 of the Government Code.

(b) Any city, county, or city and county receiving state aid pursuant to Article 3 (commencing with Section 6040) shall adhere to the standards for selection and training established by the board. The board may defer the promulgation of selection standards until necessary research for job relatedness is completed. In such case, and until selection standards are adopted, a city, county, or city and county may receive state aid upon certification of willingness to adhere to the training standards pursuant to Section 6041.

(c) Minimum training standards may include, but are not limited to, basic, entry, continuation, supervisory, management, and specialized assignments.

(d) Selection and training standards shall apply to all local corrections and probation officers and other correctional personnel employed by jurisdictions receiving funds under Article 3 (commencing with Section 6040). Exemptions from this requirement for personnel hired prior to July 1, 1980, shall be determined by the board. For the purpose of the exemptions, the board may develop written or oral equivalency examinations, a certification process which recognizes standards equivalency through a combination of professional experience and training, or a combination of examination and certification. *(Amended by Stats 1991 ch 1100 §6, eff. 1/1/92.)*

§6036. Powers of the board.

For purposes of implementing this article, the board shall have the following powers:

(a) Approve or certify, or both, training and education courses at institutions approved by the board.

(b) Make such inquiries as may be necessary to determine whether every city, county, and city and county receiving state aid pursuant to this chapter is adhering to the standards for selection and training established pursuant to this chapter.

(c) Develop and operate a professional certificate program which provides recognition of achievement for local corrections and probation officers whose agencies participate in the program.

(d) Adopt such regulations as are necessary to carry out the purposes of this chapter.

(e) Develop and present training courses for local corrections and probation officers.

(f) Perform such other activities and studies as would carry out the intent of this article.

§6037. Minimizing costs.

In exercising its functions, the board shall endeavor to minimize costs of administration so that a maximum of funds will be expended for the purpose of providing training and other services to eligible corrections and probation departments.

ARTICLE 3

CORRECTIONS TRAINING FUND

§6040. Creation.

There is hereby created in the State Treasury a Corrections Training Fund, which is hereby appropriated, without regard to fiscal years, exclusively for the costs of administration, the development of appropriate standards, the development of training, program evaluation, and grants to local government pursuant to this article.

§6041. Application for state aid.

Any city, county, or city and county which desires to receive state aid pursuant to this article shall make application to the board for such aid. The initial application shall be accompanied by a certified copy of an ordinance adopted by the governing body providing that, while receiving any state aid pursuant to this article, the city, county, or city and county, will adhere to the standards for selection and training established by the board. The application shall contain such information as the board may request.

§6042. Annual allocation of aid.

The board shall annually allocate and the State Treasurer shall periodically pay from the Corrections Training Fund, at intervals specified by the board, to each city, county, or city and county which has applied and qualified for aid pursuant to this article an amount determined by the board pursuant to standards set forth in its regulations. In no event shall any allocation be made to any city, county, or city and county which is not adhering to the selection and training standards established by the board as applicable to such city, county, or city and county.

§6043. Eligibility for funds.

Peace officer personnel, whose jurisdictions are eligible for training subvention pursuant to Chapter 1 (commencing with Section 13500) of Title 4 of Part 4 shall not be eligible to receive funds under this article, except that peace officers assigned full time to correctional duties may undergo training in correctional subjects and their jurisdictions may receive funds under this article for such training.

§6044. Board's annual report.

In order for the Legislature to determine the need to continue or modify the standards and training

program for local corrections personnel, the board shall on June 30, 1981, and annually thereafter, submit a report to the Legislature regarding the progress and effectiveness of the program.

CHAPTER 6

APPOINTMENT OF PERSONNEL

§6050. Proceedings for appointment; removal.

The Governor, upon recommendation of the director, and with the advice and consent of the Senate, shall appoint the wardens of the various state prisons. Each warden shall be subject to removal by the director. If the director removes the warden, his or her action shall be final. The wardens shall be exempt from civil service.

The Department of Personnel Administration shall fix the compensation of the wardens and superintendents of the state prisons. *(Amended by Stats 1989 ch 1420 §22, eff. 1/1/90.)*

§6052. *Repealed by Stats 1987 ch 828.*

§6053. Transfer of civil service people to department; maximum age.

(a) All persons other than temporary appointees heretofore serving in the state civil service and engaged in the performance of a function transferred to the department or engaged in the administration of a law the administration of which is transferred to the department shall remain in the state civil service and are hereby transferred to the department on the effective date of this section; and their status, positions and rights shall not be affected by their transfer and shall continue to be retained by them pursuant to the State Civil Service Act. The director, pursuant to the State Civil Service Act, shall be the appointing authority for the department for all civil service positions except those civil service positions in the Youth Authority. Positions not heretofore established which are exclusively for the California Institution for Women or exclusively for the Youth Authority shall be filled pursuant to the State Civil Service Act.

(b) Any open examination for the position of correctional officer, correctional program supervisor, and other custodial positions which normally afford entry into the Department of Corrections service shall require a demonstration of the physical ability to effectively carry out the duties and responsibilities of the position in a manner which would not inordinately endanger the health or safety of a custodial person or the health and safety of others.

§6054. Annuity contracts for department's employees.

The director may purchase annuity contracts for permanent employees of the department if all of the following conditions are met:

(a) The annuity contract is under an annuity plan which meets the requirements of subdivision (b) of Section 403 of the Internal Revenue Code of 1954 of the United States.

(b) The purchase of the annuities meets the requirements of the Insurance Code and the Government Code applicable to the purchase.

(c) The salary of an employee for whom the contract is purchased is reduced by the amount of the cost of the contract.

© 1992 by J., B. & L. Gould
Printed in the U.S.A.   EP

(d) The employee makes an application to the director for the purchase and reduction of salary. *(Amended by Stats 1987 ch 828 §162.)*

§6055. Time off with pay for mental health treatment courses.

The Department of Corrections and the Department of the Youth Authority may provide time off with pay to security and treatment personnel who take courses approved by the departments on mental health treatment related to their jobs. The departments may also provide financial compensation to pay for the cost of such courses.

CHAPTER 7

DEFINITIONS

§6080. Department and director defined.

As used in this part, the following terms have the meanings described below:

(a) "Department" refers to the Department of Corrections.

(b) "Director" refers to the Director of Corrections.

§6081. Inclusion of California Institute for Women.

As used in this code, "prison" and "state prison" include the California Institution for Women.

§6082. Inclusion of all facilities, camps, hospitals and institutions.

References in this title and in Title 5 (commencing with Section 4500) to prisons refer to all facilities, camps, hospitals and institutions for the confinement, treatment, employment, training and discipline of persons in the legal custody of the Department of Corrections. *(Amended by Stats 1987 ch 828 §163.)*

CHAPTER 8

THE MEDICAL FACILITY

§6100. Establishment of Medical Facility.

There is hereby established an institution under the jurisdiction of the Department of Corrections to be known as the Medical Facility.

§6101. Location of facility.

The Medical Facility shall be located in the northern part of the State.

§6102. Primary purpose.

The primary purpose of the medical facility shall be the receiving, segregation, confinement, treatment and care of males under the custody of the Department of Corrections or any agency thereof who are any of the following:

(a) Mentally disordered.

(b) Developmentally disabled.

(c) Addicted to the use of controlled substances.

(d) Suffering from any other chronic disease or condition. *(Amended by Stats 1986 ch 120 §1.)*

§6103. Construction of suitable buildings and facilities.

The Director of Corrections shall construct and equip, in accordance with law, suitable buildings, structures, and facilities for the Medical Facility.

§6104. Rules and regulations.

The Director of Corrections shall make rules and regulations for the government of the Medical Facility and the management of its affairs.

§6105. Appointment of superintendent.

The Governor, upon recommendation of the Director of Corrections and in accordance with Section 6050, shall appoint a warden for the medical facility. The director shall appoint, subject to civil service, other officers and employees as may be necessary. *(Amended by Stats 1989 ch 1420 §23, eff. 1/1/90.)*

§6106. Responsibilities of director of corrections.

The supervision, management, and control of the Medical Facility and the responsibility for the care, custody, treatment, training, discipline and employment of persons confined therein are vested in the Director of Corrections. The provisions of Part 3 (commencing with Section 2000) apply to the institution as a prison under the jurisdiction of the Department of Corrections and to the persons confined therein insofar as those provisions may be applicable. *(Amended by Stats 1987 ch 828 §164.)*

CHAPTER 9

CONSERVATION CENTERS

§6200. Establishment of conservation centers.

There are hereby established, under the jurisdiction of the Director of Corrections, the Sierra Conservation Center, the North Coast Conservation Center and the Southern Conservation Center, hereafter referred to collectively as the "conservation centers."

§6201. Primary purpose.

The primary purpose of the conservation centers shall be the receiving, employment, care, custody and education of inmates in the custody of the Director of Corrections assigned thereto.

§6202. Work of inmates.

Work of inmates assigned to the conservation centers may be performed at the conservation centers or branches thereof or in or from permanent, temporary, and mobile camps established pursuant to this chapter or pursuant to Article 5 (commencing with Section 2780) of Chapter 5 of Title 1 of Part 3. The provisions of Sections 2780.1 to 2786, inclusive, and Sections 2788 to 2791, inclusive, are applicable to camps established pursuant to this article as well as those established pursuant to that Article 5. The Director of Corrections may, at such times as the director deems proper and on such terms as the director deems wise, enter into contracts or cooperative agreements with any public agency, local, state, or federal, for the performance of other conservation projects which are appropriate for the public agencies under policies which shall be established by the Prison Industry Authority.

Inmates and wards may be assigned to perform public conservation projects, including, but not limited to, forest fire prevention and control, forest and watershed management, recreational area development, fish and game management, soil conservation, and forest watershed revegetation.

No productive industrial enterprise subject to the jurisdiction of the Prison Industry Authority shall be

© 1992 by J., B. & L. Gould
Printed in the U.S.A. **EP**

established at any center or branch thereof or camp established pursuant to this chapter except in compliance with Chapter 3.5 (commencing with Section 5085) of Title 7 of Part 3.

§6203. Construction of suitable buildings and facilities.

The Director of Corrections shall, in accordance with law, construct and provide equipment for suitable buildings, structures, and facilities for the conservation centers, branches thereof, and permanent, temporary, and mobile camps operated therefrom. The director may, as necessary, lease equipment needed for the operation of mobile camps. The Sierra Conservation Center shall be located in the Tuolumne area of California. The North Coast Conservation Center shall be located in the North Coast area of California. The Southern Conservation Center shall be located on the grounds of the California Institution for Men at Chino. The director may establish such branches of the conservation centers as may be necessary.

§6204. Rules and regulations of conservation centers.

The Director of Corrections shall make rules and regulations for the government of the conservation centers in the management of their affairs.

§6205. Superintendent, officers and employees.

Each conservation center shall be headed by a warden, appointed pursuant to Section 6050, and the Director of Corrections shall appoint, subject to civil service, other officers and employees as may be necessary. *(Amended by Stats 1989 ch 1420 §24, eff. 1/1/90.)*

§6206. Responsibilities of Director of Corrections.

The supervision, management, and control of the conservation centers and the responsibility for the care, custody, treatment, training, discipline, and employment of persons confined therein or in branches thereof or in permanent, temporary, and mobile camps operating therefrom are vested in the Director of Corrections.

§6207. Applicability of Part 3 to conservation centers.

The provisions of Part 3 (commencing with Section 2000), insofar as applicable, apply to the conservation centers and branches thereof and any permanent, temporary, and mobile camps operating therefrom and to the persons confined therein. *(Amended by Stats 1987 ch 828 §165.)*

§6208. Transfers to conservation centers.

Any persons under the custody of the Director of Corrections may be transferred to the conservation centers in accordance with law.

CHAPTER 9.2

RESTITUTION CENTERS

§6220. Restitution centers.

The Director of Corrections may establish and operate facilities to be known as restitution centers.

§6221. Purpose of restitution centers.

The purpose of restitution centers is to provide a means for those sentenced to prison to be able to pay their victims financial restitution as ordered by the sentencing court, or as agreed upon by the defendant and his or her victims.

§6222. Location of centers.

The location for a restitution center or centers shall be determined by the Director of Corrections with approval from the county board of supervisors or city council in whose jurisdiction the center will be located.

§6223. Locations maximizing employment opportunities.

Restitution centers shall be located in areas which will maximize the employment opportunities of persons sentenced to the centers.

§6224. Responsibility for supervision, management, control.

The supervision, management, and control of the restitution centers and the responsibility for the care, custody, discipline, and employment of persons confined therein are vested in the Director of Corrections.

§6225. Supervision of inmates.

Supervision of inmates in the restitution centers shall be by peace officer personnel of the Department of Corrections on a 24-hour basis.

§6226. Reimbursement for additional law enforcement costs.

The Director of Corrections in establishing a restitution center shall enter into an agreement with the county, city, or city and county in which the facility is located to reimburse the county, city, or city and county for any additional direct law enforcement costs that will occur as a result of the restitution center.

§6227. Placement into restitution center.

The court may order the Department of Corrections to place an eligible defendant in a restitution center if the court makes a restitution order, or if a restitution agreement is entered into by the victims and the defendant. The Department of Corrections may send a defendant to a reception center for classification prior to placing the defendant in the restitution center.

§6228. Placement eligibility.

A defendant is eligible for placement in a restitution center if he or she has not served a prison term within the 10 years prior to the present conviction, the defendant does not have a criminal history of an arrest or conviction for the sale or use of drugs or for a crime involving violence or sex, the defendant did not receive a sentence of more than 36 months, the defendant presents no unacceptable risk to the community, and the defendant is employable. The provisions of Article 2.5 (commencing with Section 2930) of Chapter 7 of Title 1 of Part 3, shall be applicable to prisoners in restitution centers.

§6229. Restitution center community advisory board.

In each county, city, or city and county, in which a restitution center is established, there shall be a restitution center community advisory board to assist the Director of Corrections in establishing and promoting

© 1992 by J., B. & L. Gould
Printed in the U.S.A.   EP

the restitution program of the center. The board shall include the sheriff or chief of police of the local jurisdiction, the district attorney, a superior court judge selected by the presiding superior court judge, the chief probation officer, a member of the city council or the board of supervisors of the local jurisdiction, selected by the council or board, and two public members chosen by the city council or board of supervisors. The public member shall serve for two years. All members shall receive only actual expenses approved by the Director of Corrections. The expenses shall be paid by the Department of Corrections.

§6230. Maintenance of restitution center; compensation.

(a) Offenders shall perform all the labor necessary to maintain the restitution center and meet the offenders' needs unless the director finds that a particular task can be better performed by other persons.

(b) The director may employ and pay compensation to offenders to perform work at a center.

§6231. Distribution of wages.

(a) Wages earned by an offender, less any deductions for taxes, shall be paid directly to the Department of Corrections.

(b) Wage moneys received by the department shall be used to reimburse the offender for costs directly associated with continued employment, including transportation, special tools or clothing, meals away from the center, union dues, and other employee-mandated costs. The remaining wages shall be distributed as follows:

(1) One-third shall be transferred to the Department of Corrections to pay the costs of operating and maintaining the restitution center.

(2) One-third shall be used to pay restitution pursuant to the agreement or court order. After the restitution is paid these moneys shall be paid to the jurisdiction which prosecuted the offender to defray the court costs and attorney fees incurred in the offender's prosecution. If all restitution, court costs and attorney fees are paid, these moneys shall be paid to the local jurisdiction for crime prevention.

(3) One-third shall be placed in a savings account for the offender, to provide support for the offender's immediate family, to purchase items necessary for the offender's employment or to give to the offender to purchase personal accessories. Any moneys in the savings account or not expended pursuant to this paragraph at the time the offender is released from the restitution center shall be paid to the offender.

§6233. Conditions for leaving restitution center; punishment.

(a) An offender shall not leave a restitution center except to go to work or when specifically authorized and shall return to the restitution center immediately after work or when required by the person in charge of the restitution center.

(b) An offender who violates this section is guilty of escape, and notwithstanding any other provision of law shall be punishable as provided in Section 4530.

§6234. Employment.

(a) The offender shall not be allowed to take employment if the rate of pay or other conditions of employment are less than those paid or provided for work of a similar nature in the locality in which the work is performed.

(b) To help in administering the restitution center programs, the director may use volunteer help.

(c) If an offender does not secure employment within three months after being sent to a restitution center, the director may, at any time thereafter, transfer the offender to another Department of Corrections facility if employment has not been obtained.

(d) If the offender violates any of the rules and regulations governing the restitution center, the director may transfer the offender to another Department of Corrections facility.

§6235. Regulations.

The Department of Corrections shall, pursuant to Chapter 3.5 (commencing with Section 11340) of Part 1 of Division 3 of Title 2 of the Government Code, adopt regulations for administering restitution centers. To the extent practical, the rules and regulations shall be stated in language that is easily understood by the general public.

§6236. Short title.

This chapter shall be known as "Restitution Centers."

CHAPTER 9.4

SUBSTANCE ABUSE COMMUNITY CORRECTIONAL DETENTION CENTERS
(Added by Stats 1990 ch 1594 §1, eff. 1/1/91.)

§6240. Legislative findings and intent.

The Legislature finds and declares the following:

(a) The number of people in state prisons whose primary commitment offense was for drug law violations represents approximately 24 percent of the inmate population. Based on a representative sample study of new felon admissions during 1988, it is estimated that approximately 76 percent of the new commitment admissions to prison have a known history of drug abuse.

The number of parole violators returned to prison for drug violations increased 2200 percent from 1980 to 1988. In fiscal year 1988–89, drug charges were a known contributing factor in over 64 percent of parolees returned to prison for parole violations.

(b) The relationship between public safety, recidivism, and substance abuse is undeniable and significant.

(c) As pointed out by the California Blue Ribbon Commission on Inmate Population Management in its January 1990 report, both state and local correction systems are presently lacking sufficient programs and strategies to intervene with substance abuse and other behaviors that contribute to criminality. Judges and parole authorities lack the options of community correctional facilities and programs with substance abuse intervention and treatment when managing parole violators, probationers, parolees, and nonviolent offenders with a history of substance abuse.

(d) There presently does not exist a model for a state and local center to house substance abusers, increase employability skills, provide counseling and support, and make treatment programs available to intervene and treat substance abuse, to reduce the crime problem and the social costs which these offenders bring upon society, themselves, and their families.

It is, therefore, the intent of the Legislature to provide for the establishment of substance abuse community correctional centers and programs to be operated locally in order to implement state-of-the-art rehabilitation programs commensurate with public safety considerations.

It is further the intent of the Legislature to focus these efforts in local communities in order to blend state and local efforts to achieve a higher success rate and lower recidivism, and to reduce the number of substance abusers and offenders who are currently being sent to state prison.

It is also the intent of the Legislature that these programs and housing facilities be built and operated in a manner providing maximum safety to the public commensurate with the purpose of the programming, and that the facilities be kept drug-free by whatever legal means are required.

The facilities and the programs shall be designed and operated in joint efforts by the state and counties, with primary funding from the state for construction of the facilities.

It is the intent of the Legislature that funds disbursed pursuant to this chapter be used to construct the maximum possible number of community beds for this purpose commensurate with public safety requirements. *(Added by Stats 1990 ch 1594 §1, eff. 1/1/91.)*

§6240.5. Name of act.

This act shall be known, and may be cited, as the Substance Abuse Community Correctional Treatment Act. *(Added by Stats 1990 ch 1594 §1, eff. 1/1/91.)*

§6240.6. Definitions.

For purposes of this chapter, the following definitions shall apply:

(a) "Board" means the Board of Corrections.

(b) "Department" means the Department of Corrections.

(c) "Center" means a substance abuse community correctional detention center.

(d) "Construction" means new construction, reconstruction, remodeling, renovation, or replacement of facilities, or a combination thereof.

(e) "Facility" means the physical buildings, rooms, areas, and equipment used for the purpose of a substance abuse community correctional detention center. *(Added by Stats 1990 ch 1594 §1, eff. 1/1/91.)*

§6241. Funding.

(a) The Substance Abuse Community Correctional Detention Centers Fund is hereby created within the State Treasury. The Board of Corrections is authorized to provide funds, as appropriated by the Legislature, for the purpose of establishing substance abuse community correctional detention centers. These facilities shall be operated locally in order to manage parole violators, those select individuals sentenced to state prison for short periods of time, and other sentenced local offenders with a known history of substance abuse, and as further defined by this chapter.

(b) The facilities constructed with funds disbursed pursuant to this chapter in a county shall contain no less than 50 percent of total beds for use by the Department of Corrections.

(1) Upon agreement, the county and the department may negotiate any other mix of state and local bed space, providing the state's proportionate share

shall not be less than 50 percent in the portion of the facilities financed through state funding.

(2) Nothing in this chapter shall prohibit the county from using county funds or nonrestricted jail bond funds to build and operate additional facilities in conjunction with the centers provided for in this chapter.

(c) Thirty million dollars ($30,000,000) in funds shall be provided from the 1990 Prison Construction Fund and the 1990–B Prison Construction Fund, with fifteen million dollars ($15,000,000) each from the June 1990 bond issue and the November 1990 bond issue, for construction purposes set forth in this chapter, provided that funding is appropriated in the state budget from the June and November 1990, prison bond issues for purposes of this chapter.

(d) Funds shall be awarded to counties based upon the following policies and criteria:

(1) Priority shall be given to urban counties with populations of 450,000 or more, as determined by Department of Finance figures. The board may allocate up to 10 percent of the funding to smaller counties or combinations of counties as pilot projects, if it concludes that proposals meet the requirements of this chapter, commensurate with the facilities and programming that a smaller county can provide.

(2) Upon application and submission of proposals by eligible counties, representatives of the board shall evaluate proposals and select recipients.

To help ensure that state-of-the-art drug rehabilitation and related programs are designed, implemented, and updated under this chapter, the board shall consult with not less than three authorities recognized nationwide with experience or expertise in the design or operation of successful programs in order to assist the board in all of the following:

(A) Drawing up criteria on which requests for proposals will be sought.

(B) Selecting proposals to be funded.

(C) Assisting the board in evaluation and operational problems of the programs, if those services are approved by the board.

Funding also shall be sought by the board from the federal government and private foundation sources in order to defray the costs of the board's responsibilities under this chapter.

(3) Preference shall be given to counties that can demonstrate a financial ability and commitment to operate the programs it is proposing for a period of at least three years and to make improvements as proposed by the department and the board.

(4) Applicants receiving awards under this chapter shall be selected from among those deemed appropriate for funding according to the criteria, policies, and procedures established by the board. Criteria shall include success records of the types of programs proposed based on nationwide standards for successful programs, if available, expertise and hands-on experience of persons who will be in charge of proposed programs, cost effectiveness, including cost per bed, speed of construction, a demonstrated ability to construct the maximum number of beds which shall result in an overall net increase in the number of beds in the county for state and local offenders, comprehensiveness of services, location, participation by private or community-based organizations, and demonstrated ability to seek and obtain supplemental funding as required in support of the overall administration of this facility from sources such as the Department of

© 1992 by J., B. & L. Gould
Printed in the U.S.A.   **EP**

Alcohol and Drug Programs, the Office of Criminal Justice Planning, the National Institute of Corrections, the Department of Justice, and other state and federal sources.

(5) Funds disbursed under subdivision (c) shall be used for construction of substance abuse community correctional centers, with a level of security in each facility commensurate with public safety for the types of offenders being housed in or utilizing the facilities.

(6) Funds disbursed under this chapter shall not be used for the purchase of the site. Sites shall be provided by the county. However, a participating county may negotiate with the state for use of state land at nearby corrections facilities or other state facilities, provided that the locations fit in with the aims of the programs established by this chapter.

The county shall be responsible for ensuring the siting, acquisition, design, and construction of the center consistent with the California Environmental Quality Act pursuant to Division 13 (commencing with Section 21000) of the Public Resources Code.

(7) Staff of the department and the board, as well as persons selected by the board, shall be available to counties for consultation and technical services in preparation and implementation of proposals accepted by the board.

(8) The board also shall seek advice from the Department of Alcohol and Drug Programs in exercising its responsibilities under this chapter.

(9) Funds shall be made available to the county and county agency which is selected to administer the program by the board of supervisors of that county.

(10) Area of greatest need can be a factor considered in awarding contracts to counties.

(11) Particular consideration shall be given to counties that can demonstrate an ability to provide continuing counseling and programming for offenders in programs established under this chapter, once the offenders have completed the programs and have returned to the community.

(12) A county may propose a variety of types and sizes of facilities to meet the needs of its plan and to provide the services for varying types of offenders to be served under this chapter. Funds granted to a county may be utilized for construction of more than one facility.

Any county wishing to use existing county-owned sites or facilities may negotiate those arrangements with the Department of Corrections and the Board of Corrections to meet the needs of its plan. *(Added by Stats 1990 ch 1594 §1, eff. 1/1/91.)*

§6241.5. Use of state-owned lands.

Because of the difficulties of finding locations for programs described in this chapter, the state shall assist in making state-owned lands available to counties for purposes of this chapter, so long as those efforts do not impede an agency's operations or planned expansions and are commensurate with public safety requirements. *(Added by Stats 1990 ch 1594 §1, eff. 1/1/91.)*

§6242. Administration and operation.

(a) The county shall assume full responsibility to administer and operate the center and program consistent with the criteria set forth within this chapter and those established by the board. This shall include maintenance and compliance with all codes, regulations, and health standards.

(b) The county shall select a local governmental department to operate the facility in accordance with the standards and oversight provided for in this chapter.

The facility shall be owned by the department for the duration of the payment of the bond used to finance construction of the facility. Upon completion of bond repayment, ownership of the facility shall be vested in the county. Ownership of a county facility renovated with funds awarded pursuant to this chapter shall be by the department for the period of bond repayment, after which ownership shall revert to the county. The department shall retain the option to lease from the county no less than 50 percent of inmate beds after completion of bond repayment.

If a county willfully terminates its participation in this act prior to completion of bond repayment or if its grant is terminated by the board for noncompliance with program regulations, ownership of the facility shall remain vested in the department. The department shall retain the option to lease as provided in this subdivision.

(c) Counties or the department shall operate all services and programs in secure facilities pursuant to this chapter with only county or state merit system employees, except that private nonprofit providers or individual professionals with demonstrated expertise and community experience may also be utilized to provide substance abuse treatment programs. Treatment programs outside secure facilities pursuant to this chapter may be provided only by county or state staff, by private nonprofit providers, or by individual professionals with demonstrated expertise and experience in providing services to this population of the community.

(d) Custody in secure facilities shall be provided by peace officers, as defined in Sections 830.1 and 830.55, or custodial officers, as defined in Section 831 and 831.5, who have satisfactorily met the minimum selection and training standards prescribed by the Board of Corrections for local corrections and probation officers and other correctional personnel established under Section 6035.

(e) Parolees, parole violators, and state prisoners shall remain under overall supervision of state parole officers.

(f) The department shall contract to reimburse the county for allotted bed space and programming for state offenders based on actual cost plus a reasonable fee, but in no instance shall that amount exceed the average cost of housing an inmate in a state prison facility, as determined annually by the director.

(g) A county may bill the state for services provided to state parolees pursuant to this chapter on a pro rata basis of the cost of providing the programs and services, if requested by the department.

(h) The department and the board, as well as participating counties, shall seek funding from the federal government and from private foundation sources to help meet the costs of the programs outlined in this chapter.

(i) It shall be the responsibility of the board, the department, and the design and implementation panel to keep abreast of improvements in programs of the types established by this chapter, and to attempt to revise and update programs as state-of-the-art advances develop.

(j) Requests for proposals shall be ready for submission to eligible counties within nine months after

© 1992 by J., B. & L. Gould
Printed in the U.S.A. **EP**

the effective date of this chapter. Eligible counties shall submit proposals within six months after the request for proposals is submitted.

(k) An amount totaling no more than 1½ percent of the total amount of funds to be disbursed under this chapter is hereby appropriated from the 1990 Prison Construction Fund and the 1990-B Prison Construction Fund to the board to be used for administrative costs.

(*l*) Following formal acceptance of proposals submitted by counties, the board shall have authority to modify, expand, or revise county programs, if requested by counties, or if the board concludes that changes should be made to improve, expand, or reduce the scope or approach of programs. This shall be done after formal notice to a county of proposed changes and opportunity for a county to submit evidence. The board also shall be able to recommend additional or reduced funding for a program, if funding becomes available upon appropriation by the Legislature. (*Amended by Stats 1991 ch 1100 §7, eff. 1/1/92.*)

§6242.5. Construction of facilities.

(a) The board shall establish minimum standards, including security requirements, for the construction of facilities pursuant to this chapter.

(b) The board shall develop an architectural program describing the functions which the facility will be expected to serve, but which deemphasizes the correctional and detention nature of the exterior of the facilities in order to ease the difficulty in finding acceptable sites.

(c) Counties may substitute renovation of an existing structure for new construction, but renovation costs per bed shall not exceed the cost of new construction based on initial cost and useful life of the facility, and shall meet the program design standards established by the board. However, participation by a county or use of existing facilities for programs under this chapter shall not be utilized by a county to avoid meeting its needs for jail-bed construction and housing of jail inmates.

(d) Per-bed cost of secure facilities proposed by a county shall not exceed the cost of current similar construction by the department.

(e) The county shall lease the site on which the facility is located to the state for a term of not less than the period of bond repayment. The department shall pay to the county as lease the sum of one dollar ($1) per year beginning the first month after the first payment for the repayment of the bond to continue through the duration of the bond used to finance construction of the facility. (*Added by Stats 1990 ch 1594 §1, eff. 1/1/91.*)

§6242.6. Progress reports.

(a) The board shall provide evaluation of the progress, activities, and performance of each center and participating county's progress established pursuant to this chapter and shall report the findings thereon to the Legislature two years after the operational onset of each facility.

(b) The board also shall provide to the Joint Legislative Committee on Prison Construction and Operations and to the Joint Legislative Budget Committee, on January 1 of each year beginning 1992, a report on the progress of contracting with counties for centers as provided in this chapter.

(c) The board shall select an outside monitoring firm in cooperation with the Auditor General's office,

to critique and evaluate the programs and their rates of success based on recidivism rates, drug use, and other factors it deems appropriate. Two years after the programs have begun operations, the report shall be provided to the Joint Legislative Prisons Committee, participating counties, the department, the Department of Alcohol and Drug Programs, the State Department of Health Services, and other sources the board deems of value. Notwithstanding subdivision (k) of Section 6242, one hundred fifty thousand dollars ($150,000) is hereby appropriated from the funds disbursed under this chapter from the 1990 Prison Construction Fund to the Board of Corrections to be used for program evaluation under this subdivision.

(d) The department shall be responsible for the ongoing monitoring of contract compliance for state offenders placed in each center. (*Amended by Stats 1991 ch 1017 §4, eff. 1/1/92.*)

§6243. Eligibility to participate in program.

Primary offender groups to be dealt with in the programs established by this chapter shall be probation or parole violators who would otherwise be returned to jail or prison.

The following standards for selection shall apply:

(a) The Director of Corrections, or his or her designee, together with local parole officials, shall select offenders committed to state prison for placement in not less than 50 percent of the program beds established by this chapter. Eligible offenders shall be parole violators and felons committed to state prison who, after credit deduction for presentence incarceration and pursuant to Section 2933, would otherwise have served an actual term of six months or less in state prison. Offenders selected shall have a demonstrated history of alcohol or controlled substances abuse, or both, but shall not include any of the following:

(1) Offenders convicted at anytime of a violent felony, as defined in subdivision (c) of Section 667.5 whether in California or any other jurisdiction for an offense with the same elements.

(2) Offenders who have lost work credits while currently in prison for an offense listed in paragraph (1) of subdivision (a) of Section 2932, except for assault with a deadly weapon or a caustic substance.

(3) Offenders currently convicted of burglary of an inhabited dwelling.

(4) Offenders convicted on two or more separate occasions of violations of Section 11351, 11351.5, 11352, 11353, 11370.1, 11370.6, 11378.5, 11379, 11379.5, or 11379.6 of the Health and Safety Code for selling or transporting for sale, manufacturing for sale, processing for sale, importing for sale, or administering any controlled substance listed in these sections, or for attempting to commit any of these offenses for those purposes and who has served at least one term in prison for violating one of these sections.

(b) The maximum period of participation in a center program shall not exceed the maximum period for which the offender could have been incarcerated in county jail or state prison. Upon release from a center, a state offender shall be subject to the parole provisions of Section 3000. Local offenders shall be subject to all conditions of probation, if probation was imposed at the time of sentencing.

(c) The parole of an offender placed in a center following revocation of parole shall remain revoked during the period of participation in a center.

© 1992 by J., B. & L. Gould
Printed in the U.S.A.   **EP**

(d) Individuals eligible for this program who are deemed unfit for participation by either custodial or program staff at any time shall be transferred to a state prison or county facility to which they would otherwise have been committed and shall serve their remaining sentence minus the time served at the center.

(e) Except upon agreement between the county and the department, placement of state offenders in a center is limited to parolees on parole in that county and new commitments sentenced from that county.

(f) The county shall select local offenders for placement in up to 50 percent of the program beds established by this chapter. These offenders shall be persons convicted and sentenced to county jail, whether or not as a condition of probation, and who have a demonstrated history of abuse of alcohol or controlled substances, or both.

(g) State prisoners participating in these programs shall be eligible for work credit time reductions under provisions applicable to state prisoners committed to state prison.

(h) Primary emphasis in this program shall be toward parole violators and persons sentenced to prison or jail for short terms and for whom rehabilitation efforts should be provided.

(i) The department shall regularly notify the sheriff's department and the probation department of a participating county of offenders placed into the program or released from the program established by this chapter. The county shall likewise regularly notify local parole officials of persons placed into or released from its programs set up by this chapter.

The sheriff's department, probation and parole officials, and the Board of Prison Terms shall be permitted to recommend for or against placement of persons into these programs, as shall the judiciary of the county.

(j) Facilities may not serve as housing or parole or probation offices for offenders not a part of programs set up by this chapter. *(Added by Stats 1990 ch 1594 §1, eff. 1/1/91.)*

§6245. Plan proposal.

(a)* In submitting a proposal, a county's plan shall (1) include at least all of the following elements that meet standards established by the board in its request for proposal, and (2) demonstrate that its program will have strong links to the community organizations involved in providing those elements, and that those community organizations have helped in designing the proposal:

(1) A rigorous program of substance abuse testing.
(2) A drug-free environment.
(3) Substance abuse treatment.
(4) Employment services.
(5) Basic education services.
(6) Mental health services and family counseling.
(7) A strong linkage to probation and parole.
(Added by Stats 1990 ch 1594 §1, eff. 1/1/91.)
So in original. No subd. (b) enacted.

§6246. Oversight committee.

Each recipient county shall set up a program oversight committee, under rules and guidelines the Board of Corrections formulates, which shall include representatives from the following groups:

(a) Parole officials.
(b) Probation officials.
(c) Sheriff's department officials.
(d) County alcohol and drug abuse officials.
(e) Program contractors.
(f) Local judiciary personnel.
(g) Social welfare agency personnel.
(h) Local labor and employment representatives.

Responsibilities of the program oversight committee shall include, but not be limited to, regular reviews of program operations and criteria for offenders being placed into it, discussion and resolution of problems that may arise, costs, and other duties that may be assigned it by the Board of Corrections. *(Added by Stats 1990 ch 1594 §1, eff. 1/1/91.)*

CHAPTER 9.5

COMMUNITY CORRECTIONAL CENTERS

§6250. Establishment and operation.

(a) The Director of Corrections may establish and operate facilities to be known as community correctional centers.

(b) No later than 30 days after the department has designated a site as a potential site, the director shall notify the county board of supervisors or city council in whose jurisdiction the center may be located. The notification shall set forth the specifics of the site location, design, and operational characteristics for the facility. The department shall not contract for the facility until it has received and reviewed the comments of every local agency notified under this section or the expiration of 60 days after having given notice to the local agency, whichever occurs first.

Upon receipt of the notice, the city, county, or city and county may hold a public hearing concerning the impact of the facility on the community. At the conclusion of the public hearing, the city, county, or city and county may make a recommendation to the department as to the appropriateness of the proposed site, specific design and operational features to help make the facility more compatible with the community, and alternative locations, if appropriate.

Upon receipt of comments and recommendations, the department shall determine whether to proceed with the facility, to modify the proposal, or to select an alternative site. If the department selects a site recommended by the local agency after a hearing conducted pursuant to this section, no further review or hearings are required by this subdivision.

(c) The notice referred to in subdivision (b) may be delivered by hand or sent by any form of mail requiring a return receipt. Failure to provide the notice shall be grounds for extinguishing the contract upon motion of the board of supervisors or city council.

(d) The Director of Corrections shall not change the use of or significantly increase the capacity of a community correctional center established pursuant to subdivision (a) unless the director has first notified the county board of supervisors or city council in whose jurisdiction the center is located at least 30 days prior to the change of use or capacity. Failure to provide the notice shall be grounds for enjoining the change in use or capacity. *(Amended by Stats 1988 ch 849 §1, eff. 1/1/89.)*

§6251. Primary purpose of facilities.

The primary purpose of such facilities is to provide housing, supervision, counseling, and other correctional programs for persons committed to the Department of Corrections.

§6252. Rules and regulations.

The Director of Corrections shall make rules and regulations for the government of the community correctional centers in the management of their affairs.

§6253. Placement of parolees; fees.

(a) The Director of Corrections may transfer inmates whose terms of imprisonment have been fixed from the state prisons and facilities of the Department of Corrections to community correctional centers, and place parolees in the community correctional centers. The director may charge the resident reasonable fees, based on ability to pay, for room, board and so much of the costs of administration as are allocable to such resident. Fees may not exceed actual, demonstrable costs to the department. No fees shall be collected from an inmate or parolee after his or her residency in the center has terminated.

Notwithstanding any other provision of law, no inmate or parolee shall be denied placement in a community correctional center on the basis of inability to pay fees authorized by this section.

(b) Inmates transferred to community correctional centers remain under the legal custody of the department and shall be subject at any time, pursuant to the rules and regulations of the Director of Corrections, to be detained in the county jail upon the exercise of a state parole or correctional officer's peace officer powers as specified in Section 830.5, with the consent of the sheriff or corresponding official having jurisdiction over the facility.

§6254. Furloughs granted.

The Director of Corrections may grant furloughs to residents of community correctional centers for the purpose of employment, education, including vocational training, or arranging a suitable employment and residence program.

§6255. Applicability of statutory provisions.

The provisions of Title 5 (commencing with Section 4500) of Part 3 shall apply to all persons placed in a community correctional center by the Director of Corrections except that those persons who are on active parole shall be subject to the provisions of Article 3 (commencing with Section 3040) of Chapter 8, Title 1, Part 3.

§6256. Contracts for housing.

The Director of Corrections may enter into contracts, with the approval of the Director of General Services, with appropriate public or private agencies, to provide housing, sustenance, and supervision for such inmates as are eligible for placement in community correctional centers. Prisoners in the care of such agencies shall be subject to all provisions of law applicable to them.

The Department of Corrections shall reimburse such agencies for their services from such funds as may be appropriated for the support of state prisoners.

§6257. Repealed by Stats 1983 ch 956 §5, eff. 1/1/90.

§6258. Establishment of community correctional reentry centers.

(a) The Director of Corrections may contract for the establishment and operation of separate community correctional reentry centers for men and women, provided that the per-inmate cost for operat-ing these facilities under contract will be less than the per-inmate cost of maintaining custody of the inmates by the department.

(b) The purpose of the community correctional reentry center is to provide an enhancement program to increase the likelihood of a successful parole. The objective of the program is to make the inmates aware of their responsibility to society, and to assist the inmates with educational and employment training to ensure employability once on parole.

(c) A community correctional reentry center shall prepare the inmate for reintegration into society. These centers shall provide counseling in the areas of drug and alcohol abuse, stress, employment skills, victim awareness, and shall, in general, prepare the inmate for return to society. The program shall also emphasize literacy training and utilize computer-supported training so that the inmate can read and write at least at a ninth grade level.

(d) In awarding contracts pursuant to this section, the director may entertain proposals for the establishment and operation of community correctional reentry centers from public and private entities and shall give preference to community correctional reentry centers located near large population centers. *(Added by Stats 1989 ch 879 §1, eff. 1/1/90.)*

§6258.1 Transfer of inmate to community correctional reentry facility.

No inmate shall be transferred to a community correctional reentry facility unless all of the following conditions are met:

(a) The inmate applies for a transfer to a community correctional reentry facility.

(b) The inmate is not currently serving a sentence for conviction of any offense described in subdivision (c) of Section 667.5.

(c) The inmate has less than 120 days left to serve in a correctional facility.

(d) The inmate has not been convicted previously of an escape pursuant to Section 4532 of the penal Code.

(e) The department determines that the inmate would benefit from the transfer. *(Added by Stats 1989 ch 879 §2, eff. 1/1/90.)*

CHAPTER 9.6

WORK FURLOUGH PROGRAMS

§6260. Findings and declarations.

The Legislature finds and declares the following: that overcrowding in correctional institutions is not a desirable method of housing state inmates; that other methods of housing should be developed for appropriate state inmates, particularly if they can be less costly; that reentry programs for inmates who are nearing the completion of their term of incarceration provides a more normal environment and an opportunity to begin reintegrating into society; and that work furlough programs are appropriate only for specified types of inmates for a limited period of time prior to release back into society; and that existing law already recognizes the appropriateness of placing inmates in community facilities.

§6261. Contracts for reentry work furlough programs.

(a) To the extent that public and private nonprofit and profit corporations have available beds and satisfy

© 1992 by J., B. & L. Gould
Printed in the U.S.A.   **EP**

the criteria specified in this chapter, the Department of Corrections shall contract with them to provide reentry work furlough programs for all inmates 120 days prior to scheduled release and who are not excluded under this chapter.

(b) The Department of Corrections shall contract with private nonprofit and profit corporations for at least ⅓ of all reentry work furlough beds, unless the department determines these beds are not available or do not comply with this chapter. The department shall report annually in writing to the fiscal and appropriate policy committees of the Legislature of the actions performed to locate those beds or reasons for noncompliance. This provision shall not be interpreted to impair existing contracts. *(Amended by Stats 1988 ch 1608 §5, eff. 1/1/89.)*

§6262. Contracting corporations' qualifications.

The Department of Corrections may contract with a public or private nonprofit or profit corporation meeting all the following conditions:

(a) Availability of a work furlough facility in compliance with standards established by the Department of Corrections.

(b) Location of a facility in proximity to geographical areas providing employment opportunities and public transportation services.

(c) Cost proposals equal to or less than the per capita amount for housing in a correctional institution, including administrative costs.

(d) Criteria for placement that does not differ significantly from the policies of the Department of Corrections.

(e) Submission by the agency of operational guidelines that are approved by the Department of Corrections pursuant to its classification manual.

(f) Compliance with other requirements deemed appropriate by the Department of Corrections, including, but not limited to, visiting procedures, 24-hour security, and recreation.

(g) Efficient fiscal management and financially solvent.

§6263. Denial of placement.

(a) The Department of Corrections shall deny placement in a reentry work furlough program if it determines that an inmate would pose an unreasonable risk to the public, or if any one of the following factors exist, except in unusual circumstances, including, but not limited to, the remoteness in time of the commission of the offense:

(1) Conviction of a crime involving sex or arson.

(2) History of forced escape, or of drug use, sales, or addiction.

(3) Parole program or employment outside the area served by the facility.

(4) History of serious institutional misconduct.

(5) Prior placement in a protective housing unit within a correctional institution, except a person placed there while assisting a public entity in a civil or criminal matter.

(6) More than one conviction of a crime of violence.

(b) Nothing in this section shall be interpreted to limit the discretion of the Department of Corrections to deny placement when the provisions of subdivision (a) do not apply.

(c) Inmates transferred to reentry work furlough remain under the legal custody of the department and shall be subject at any time, pursuant to the rules and regulations of the Director of Corrections, to be detained in the county jail upon the exercise of a state parole or correctional officer's peace officer powers as specified in Section 830.5, with the consent of the sheriff or corresponding official having jurisdiction over the facility.

§6264. Review of work furlough consideration.

The Department of Corrections shall review each inmate for work furlough consideration at least 120 days prior to his or her scheduled parole date.

§6265. Inmate violating conditions; discipline.

Any inmate violating the conditions of the work furlough prescribed by the Department of Corrections shall be subject to the disciplinary procedures identified in its classification manual.

§6266. Reasonable fees.

The director may charge the inmate in a work furlough program reasonable fees, based on ability to pay for room, board, and so much of the costs of administration as are allocable to the inmate. Fees may not exceed the actual, demonstrable costs to the department. No fees shall be collected from an inmate after his or her tenure in a work furlough program is terminated.

Notwithstanding any other provision of law, no inmate shall be denied placement in a work furlough program on the basis of inability to pay fees authorized by this section.

CHAPTER 10

REGIONAL JAIL CAMPS

§6300. Establishment.

The Department of Corrections is authorized to establish and operate regional jail camps.

§6301. Purpose.

The primary purpose of the camps shall be the confinement, treatment, and care of persons sentenced to long jail terms, including persons so imprisoned as a condition of probation. *(Amended by Stats 1987 ch 828 §166.)*

§6302. Rules and regulations.

The Director of Corrections shall make rules and regulations governing eligibility for commitment or transfer to such camps and rules and regulations for the government of such camps. Subject to the rules and regulations of the Director of Corrections, and if there is in effect for the county a contract entered into pursuant to Section 6303, a county prisoner may be committed to a regional jail camp in lieu of commitment to a county jail or other county detention facility.

§6303. County prisoners' acceptance, costs.

(a) The director may enter into a contract, with the approval of the Director of General Services, with any county of the state, upon the request of the board of supervisors thereof, wherein the Director of Corrections agrees to furnish confinement, care, treatment, and employment of county prisoners. The county shall reimburse the state for the cost of such services, such cost to be determined by the Director of Finance. Each county auditor shall include in his state settlement report rendered to the Controller in the months of January and June the amounts due under any contract authorized by this section, and the county treasurer, at the time of settlement with the state in such months, shall pay to the State Treasurer upon order of the Controller, the amounts found to be due.

(b) The Department of Corrections shall accept such county prisoner if it believes that the prisoner can be materially benefited by such confinement, care, treatment, and employment, and if adequate facilities to provide such care are available. No such person shall be transported to any facility under the jurisdiction of the Department of Corrections until the director has notified the referring court of the place to which said person is to be transmitted and the time at which he can be received.

(c) The sheriff of the county in which such an order is made placing a misdemeanant in a jail camp pursuant to this chapter, or any other peace officer designated by the court, shall execute an order placing such county prisoner in the jail camp or returning him therefrom to the court. The expense of such sheriff or peace officer incurred in executing such order is a charge upon the county in which the court is situated.

§6304. Return of prisoner.
The Director of Corrections may return to the committing authority any person committed transferred to a regional jail camp pursuant to this chapter when there is no suitable employment or when such person is guilty of any violation of rules and regulations of the regional jail camp.

CHAPTER 10.5

PRISON VISITOR SERVICES

§6350. Findings and declaration.
The Legislature finds and declares the following:

(a) Maintaining an inmate's family and community relationships is an effective correctional technique which reduces recidivism.

(b) Enhancing visitor services increases the frequency and quality of visits, thereby discouraging violent prisoner activity.

(c) The location of prisons and lack of services to assist visitors impedes visiting.

§6351. Contracts with private nonprofit agencies.
The Department of Corrections shall contract with a private nonprofit agency or agencies to establish and operate a visitor center outside each state adult prison in California which has a population of more than 300 inmates.

§6352. Minimum services to be provided.
Each visitor center shall provide, at a minimum, each of the following services to prison visitors:

(a) Assistance to visitors with transportation between public transit terminals and prisons.

(b) Child care for visitors' children.

(c) Emergency clothing.

(d) Information on visiting regulations and processes.

(e) Referral to other agencies and services.

(f) A sheltered area, which is outside of the security perimeter, for visitors who are waiting before or after visits.

In addition, each center shall maintain working relations with the local community and institution. *(Amended by Stats 1988 ch 160 §143, eff. 1/1/89.)*

§6353. Annual reports.
Each nonprofit agency which the department contracts with pursuant to Section 6351 shall submit to the department and to the Legislature an annual report which includes, but is not limited to, the following information:

(a) A description of the barriers to visiting.

(b) A quantitative and narrative description of the services which it rendered.

(c) A description of the impact of the centers which it provided on visiting.

(d) A description of areas for improvement of services or coordination with other public or private agencies.

(e) A description of the community resources which it utilized.

§6354. Criteria for selecting agencies.
The Department of Corrections shall employ all the following criteria in selecting the agency or agencies with which it contracts pursuant to Section 6351:

(a) The number and quality of services proposed in comparison to direct program costs.

(b) Prior experience in establishing and operating prison visitor service centers in California.

(c) Prior experience in working cooperatively with the department, other correctional agencies, community programs, inmates, visitors, and the general public.

(d) The ability to use volunteers and other community resources to maximize the cost effectiveness of this program.

(e) The identified needs of visitors.

§6355. Additional programs not limited.
Nothing in this chapter is intended to limit the department in developing additional programs or making all reasonable efforts to promote visits to prisoners.

§6356. Cooperation with the Department of Transportation.
The department shall cooperate with the Department of Transportation in the development of public transportation services to prisons, pursuant to Section 14035.9 of the Government Code and Section 99317.9 of the Public Utilities Code. *(Amended by Stats 1987 ch 603 §2.)*

CHAPTER 11

MASTER PLAN CONSTRUCTION

§7000. Master plan; inclusions and definition.
(a) The Department of Corrections shall prepare plans for, and construct facilities and renovations included within, its master plan for, which funds have been appropriated by the Legislature.

(b) "Master plan" means the department's "Facility Requirements Plan," dated April 7, 1980, and any subsequent revisions.

§7001. Power conferred upon department.
Any power, function, or jurisdiction for planning or construction of facilities or renovations pursuant to

© 1992 by J., B. & L. Gould
Printed in the U.S.A.   **EP**

the master plan which is conferred by statute upon the Department of General Services shall be deemed to be conferred upon the department.

§7002. Responsibility transferred.

The department may transfer the responsibility for undertaking any aspect of the master plan to the Department of General Services or the Office of the State Architect which, upon such transfer, shall perform those functions with all deliberate speed.

§7003. Preliminary plans and proposals; review and approval.

(a) For each facility included within its master plan, at least 30 days prior to submission pursuant to subdivision (b), the department shall submit the site plans and project planning guide which is to include preliminary staffing ratios, to the Joint Legislative Committee on Prison Construction and Operation for review.

The chairman may request a longer period of review if necessary for the committee and if feasible for compliance by the department.

(b) The department shall submit completed preliminary plans, proposed staffing patterns and proposed inmate work programs for all facilities included within its master plan, as defined in subdivision (b) of Section 7000, as soon as is practicable, but no later than 30 days prior to submission to the Public Works Board, to the Joint Legislative Committee on Prison Construction and Operation and the fiscal committees of the Senate and Assembly for review and approval. The department shall submit proposed staffing patterns at the time preliminary plans for inmate housing facilities are submitted. The department shall submit proposed inmate work-training programs at the time preliminary plans for the industrial vocational education buildings are submitted.

If each committee does not, by majority vote of the committee membership, approve the submittal, the Public Works Board shall not act upon the affected plans. If a committee fails to take any action with respect to the submitted plans within 45 days after submittal, this inaction shall be deemed to be approval for purposes of this section. (*Amended by Stats 1986 ch 1314 §1.*)

§7003.5. Reports on sites for proposed prison facilities.

(a) The department shall provide the Joint Legislative Committee on Prison Construction and Operations with periodic reports on the progress of site selection for new prison facilities.

(b) On January 1 and July 1 of each year, the department shall report to the Joint Legislative Committee on Prison Construction and Operation on areas being considered for proposed prison facilities, the size of the facilities planned, financing, and how each facility fits into the department's master plan insofar as this information is available to the department at the time the report is presented to the committee. The report shall also include the status of each proposed prison, and sites being planned for priliminary studies if known at that time.

(c) The committee may take appropriate advisory action concerning any submittals required by this section.

(d) This section applies to regular prison facilities, major enlargements of existing facilities, prison hospital construction and expansion, and return to custody facilities, whether or not built or operated exclusively by the department. (*Added by Stats 1988 ch 1044 §3, eff. 9/20/88.*)

§7004. Plan for soliciting and receiving local public comment regarding placement of correctional facility.

The plans required pursuant to Section 7000 shall contain the department's plan for soliciting and receiving local public comment regarding the placement of a correctional facility in any particular community. The plan shall include provision for notice to a community, including the city, county, or city and county, under consideration for construction of a facility within 30 days after the department has identified a possible site for the proposed facility, public hearings on the proposed facility, and dissemination of the response of the department to comments of the community on the proposed facility.

The plan developed by the department concerning public comment on placement of correctional facilities shall be submitted to the Legislature and the Governor within 60 days of the effective date of this section. The plan shall be implemented as of the date of submission to the Governor and Legislature with respect to all prospective placements of correctional facilities. The Legislature and the Governor shall also be sent any subsequent changes or revisions of the plan by the department.

§7006. Transfer title of property of Preston School of Industry at Ione.

(a) The Department of the Youth Authority is authorized to transfer to the Department of Corrections title to any property of the Preston School of Industry at Ione not currently being used by the Department of the Youth Authority.

(b) The Department of the Youth Authority is authorized to transfer to the Department of Corrections title to any property of the Northern California Youth Center near Stockton not currently being used by the Department of the Youth Authority.

§7007. *Repealed by Stats 1989 ch 1360 §121, eff. 1/1/90.*

§7008. Bed capacity.

(a) Division 13 (commencing with Section 21000) of the Public Resources Code shall not apply to the addition of 150 Level I and Level II beds authorized by Section 5 of this act at San Gabriel Canyon, provided that the department has made the following finding with respect to that facility:

(1) The increase in bed capacity, if any, shall not exceed, 5 percent of the total capacity of the facility prior to the increase.

(2) Any modifications made to existing structures are internal only. No external additions to existing structures or construction of new structures shall be done. Modular structures used exclusively for prisoner program activity shall be exempt from this requirement.

(3) Any modifications to a facility shall not result in a significant depletion in water, sewage, or other environmental resources. The department shall present substantial evidence that this requirement has been met in the findings described in subdivision (b).

(b) The department shall make findings that the requirements of subdivision (a) have been met, and shall make the findings available to the public. *(Amended by Stats 1985 ch 953 §2.)*

§7009. Lease or lease-purchase arrangements; investigation and findings.

(a) The Director of Corrections and the Legislative Analyst shall investigate the advisability of using lease or lease-purchase arrangements to finance the acquisition, construction, and the underwriting of prison facilities authorized by the Legislature. For purposes of this section, the director may solicit bids for any lease or lease-purchase in a newspaper of general circulation in the county in which the authorized project is located.

(b) The director and the Legislative Analyst shall report their findings and recommendations relative to lease or lease-purchase arrangements to the Legislature no later than January 1, 1984.

§7010. Bids for lease for establishing prison site in Los Angeles County.

(a) The Director of Corrections may solicit bids for any lease or lease-purchase for the establishment of a prison facility for a site in Los Angeles County.

(b) The director may not accept any lease or lease-purchase bid or execute any lease or lease-purchase agreement unless and until the bid or agreement is submitted for review and approval under the procedure described in Section 7003.

(c) Any lease or lease-purchase agreement executed pursuant to this section shall contain, as a condition of the agreement, stipulations requiring compliance with the provisions of Chapter 1 (commencing with Section 1720) of Part 7 of the Labor Code in the construction of any facility within the scope of the agreement.

§7011. Submission to certain counties and authorities.

(a) The Department of Corrections shall submit to the Joint Legislative Prison Committee, the Kings County Board of Supervisors, the Corcoran City Council, and the State Public Works Board, at least 30 days prior to the acquisition of real property for a prison facility to be located in the vicinity of Corcoran in Kings County, an environmental assessment study, which shall include a discussion of impacts and mitigation measures, if necessary, for the following areas:

(1) Geology.
(2) Hydrology — groundwater.
(3) Water quality — surface waters.
(4) Plant and animal life — endangered and rare species.
(5) Air quality.
(6) Noise.
(7) Light and glare.
(8) Transportation and circulation.
(9) Utilities — gas, electricity, telephone, solid waste, sewage disposal, and drinking water.
(10) Archaeology.
(11) Energy.

(b) The factors set forth in subdivision (a) shall be assessed only as they relate to the direct impacts caused off the site as a result of the construction, operation, and maintenance of the prison facility upon completion and occupancy.

(c) Notwithstanding any other provisions of law, other than Section 7003 and those provisions of the Government Code that require the approval of the State Public Works Board, the Department of Finance, or the Director of Finance for capital outlay projects, the approval of the study by the State Public Works Board is the only approval required for the acquisition of real property, planning, design, and construction of the prison facility and the operation and maintenance of the facility. The State Public Works Board shall not act on the study until it receives a recommendation from the Joint Legislative Prison Committee. Approval of the study by the State Public Works Board shall be final and binding on all parties.

(d) If the committee does not, by a majority vote of the committee membership, take any action on the study within 30 days after submittal, that inaction shall be deemed to be a recommendation of concurrence for the purposes of this section.

(e) Prior to providing a recommendation to the State Public Works Board, but within the 30-day period specified in subdivision (d), the committee shall hold a public hearing in Corcoran. Notice of the hearing shall be published in a newspaper of general circulation in, or adjacent to, Corcoran. The notice shall be at least one-quarter page in size. The Corcoran City Council and the Kings County Board of Supervisors shall be invited to participate in the hearing. *(Amended by Stats 1985 ch 931 §2.)*

§7012. Property location for prison facilities, submission to certain authorities.

(a) The Department of Corrections shall submit to the Joint Legislative Prison Committee, the State Public Works Board, the appropriate county board of supervisors, and the local city council at least 30 days prior to the acquisition of real property for prison facilities to be located in Riverside and Del Norte Counties, an environmental assessment study, which shall include a discussion of impacts and mitigation measures, if necessary, for the following areas:

(1) Geology.
(2) Hydrology — groundwater.
(3) Water quality — surface waters.
(4) Plant and animal life — endangered and rare species.
(5) Air quality.
(6) Noise.
(7) Light and glare.
(8) Utilities — gas, electricity, telephone, solid waste, sewage disposal, and drinking water.
(9) Archaeology.
(10) Energy.

(b) The factors set forth in subdivision (a) shall be assessed only as they relate to the direct impacts caused off the site as a result of the construction, operation, and maintenance of the prison facility upon completion and occupancy.

(c) Notwithstanding any other provision of law, other than Section 7003, the approval of the study by the State Public Works Board is the only approval required for compliance with any applicable environmental requirements. The Public State Works Board shall not act on the study until it receives a recommendation from the Joint Legislative Prison Committee. Approval of the study by the State Public Works Board shall be final and binding on all parties.

(d) If the committee does not, by a majority vote of the committee membership, take any action on the study within 30 days after submittal, that inaction shall be deemed to be a recommendation of concurrence for the purposes of this section.

© 1992 by J., B. & L. Gould
Printed in the U.S.A.   **EP**

(e) Prior to providing a recommendation to the State Public Works Board, but within the 30-day period specified in subdivision (d), the committee shall hold a public hearing in the community in the vicinity of the proposed site. Notice of the hearing shall be published in a newspaper of general circulation in, or adjacent to, that community. The notice shall be at least one-quarter page in size. The city council and the county board of supervisors shall be invited to participate in the hearing. *(Added by Stats 1985 ch 933 §2.3.)*

§7013. Water supply contract with the Department of Water Resources.

The Department of Corrections shall contract, or make a good-faith effort to contract, with the Department of Water Resources or the Bureau of Reclamation, or both, to secure a water supply for the prison at Avenal. *(Added by Stats 1985 ch 931 §2.5.)*

§7014. Joint Legislative Prison Committee; reimbursement.

The Joint Legislative Prison Committee shall be reimbursed, from funds appropriated to the Department of Corrections for support, for costs, as agreed to by the Department of Corrections, incurred by the committee in reviewing environmental assessment studies pursuant to this chapter. The chairperson of the committee shall certify the costs to the Controller who shall, upon receipt of the certification, transfer funds from the unencumbered balance of funds appropriated to the Department of Corrections for support. The funds shall be transferred to the contingent fund of the Legislature which was used to pay the costs incurred in reviewing the environmental studies. *(Added by Stats 1986 ch 1393 §5.)*

§7015. Construction of courthouse in Folsom.

(a) Except as provided in subdivision (b), the Department of Corrections may contract with the City of Folsom for the construction of a courthouse and related facilities, not to exceed one million nine hundred thousand dollars ($1,900,000) in costs. Under this contract, the Department of Corrections is authorized to make payments to the City of Folsom in consideration for the construction of the courthouse, provided that the sums paid to the city are realized from savings to the department by the location of the courthouse in the immediate proximity of Folsom Prison.

Under this contract, the Department of Corrections is authorized to make annual payments to the City of Folsom in an amount not to exceed the approximate savings realized in each fiscal year. These funds shall come from the operating budget of the department.

In negotiating this contract, the Department of Corrections shall note the extent to which the courthouse will serve the interests of the County of Sacramento independent of matters pertaining to individuals in state custody and shall seek appropriate participation in the funding of the courthouse from the county.

(b) The Department of Corrections may not contract with the City of Folsom for a court facility unless a majority of the members of the Sacramento County Board of Supervisors, the presiding judge of the Sacramento County Municipal Court, and the presiding judge of the Sacramento County Superior Court all agree, in writing, to operate a court facility in the City of Folsom as provided by subdivision (a). *(Added by Stats 1988 ch 1393 §2, eff. 1/1/89.)*

§7016. Construction of courthouse in County of Kern.

The Department of Corrections may contract with the County of Kern for the construction and financing of a courthouse and related facilities. Under this contract, the Department of Corrections is authorized to make payments to the County of Kern in consideration for the construction and financing of the courthouse and related facilities, provided that the sums paid to the county are realized from savings to the department by the location of the courthouse in the proximity of the California Correctional Facility in Tehachapi.

In accordance with the contract, the Department of Corrections is authorized to make annual payments to the County of Kern from the approximate savings realized in each fiscal year. These funds shall come from the operating budget of the department. In negotiating this contract, the Department of Corrections shall note the extent to which the courthouse will serve the interest of the County of Kern independent of matters pertaining to individuals in state custody, and seek appropriate county participation in funding. *(Added by Stats 1988 ch 1400 §2, eff. 1/1/89.)*

CHAPTER 12

NEW PRISON CONSTRUCTION BOND ACT OF 1981

§7100. Short title.

This chapter shall be known and may be cited as the New Prison Construction Bond Act of 1981.

§7101. General Obligation Bond Law.

The State General Obligation Bond Law is adopted for the purpose of the issuance, sale and repayment of, and otherwise providing with respect to, the bonds authorized to be issued by this chapter, and the provisions of that law are included in this chapter as though set out in full in this chapter except that, notwithstanding anything in the State General Obligation Bond Law, the maximum maturity of the bonds shall not exceed 20 years from the date of each respective series. The maturity of each respective series shall be calculated from the date of such series.

§7102. New Prison Construction Fund.

There is in the State Treasury the New Prison Construction Fund, which fund is hereby created.

§7103. New Prison Construction Committee.

The New Prison Construction Committee is hereby created. The committee shall consist of the Controller, the State Treasurer, and the Director of Finance. Such committee shall be the "committee," as that term is used in the State General Obligation Bond Law.

§7104. Creation of debts or liabilities.

The committee is hereby authorized and empowered to create a debt or debts, liability or liabilities, of the State of California, in the aggregate of four hundred ninety-five million dollars ($495,000,000), in the manner provided in this chapter. Such debt or debts, liability or liabilities, shall be created for the purpose of providing the fund to be used for the object and work specified in Section 7106.

§7105. Issuing and sale of bonds.

The committee may determine whether or not it is necessary or desirable to issue any bonds authorized under this chapter, and if so, the amount of bonds then to be issued and sold. The committee may authorize the State Treasurer to sell all or any part of the bonds herein authorized at such time or times as may be fixed by the State Treasurer.

§7106. Use of moneys.

The moneys in the fund shall be used for the construction, renovation, remodeling, and deferred maintenance of state correctional facilities.

§7106.5. Joint use correctional facilities; construction.

The moneys in the fund may be used for construction of joint use correctional facilities housing county and state or federal prisoners or any combination thereof in proportion to the state benefit.

§7107. Payment of bonds.

All bonds herein authorized, which shall have been duly sold and delivered as herein provided, shall constitute valid and legally binding general obligations of the State of California, and the full faith and credit of the State of California is hereby pledged for the punctual payment of both principal and interest thereon.

There shall be collected annually in the same manner and at the same time as other state revenue is collected such a sum, in addition to the ordinary revenues of the state, as shall be required to pay the principal and interest on such bonds as herein provided, and it is hereby made the duty of all officers charged by law with any duty in regard to the collection of such revenue to do and perform each and every act which shall be necessary to collect such additional sum.

All money deposited in the fund which has been derived from premium and accrued interest on bonds sold shall be available for transfer to the General Fund as a credit to expenditures for bond interest.

All money deposited in the fund pursuant to any provision of law requiring repayments to the state which are financed by the proceeds of the bonds authorized by this chapter shall be available for transfer to the General Fund. When transferred to the General Fund such money shall be applied as a reimbursement to the General Fund on account of principal and interest on the bonds which has been paid from the General Fund.

§7108. Amounts appropriated from General Fund.

There is hereby appropriated from the General Fund in the State Treasury for the purpose of this chapter such an amount as will equal the following:

(a) Such sum annually as will be necessary to pay the principal of and the interest on the bonds issued and sold pursuant to the provisions of this chapter.

(b) Such sum as is necessary to carry out the provisions of Section 7109, which sum is appropriated without regard to fiscal years.

§7109. Amounts withdrawn from General Fund.

For the purpose of carrying out the provisions of this chapter, the Director of Finance may by executive order authorize the withdrawal from the General Fund of an amount or amounts not to exceed the amount of the unsold bonds which the committee has by resolution authorized to be sold for the purpose of carrying out this chapter. Any amounts withdrawn shall be deposited in the fund and shall be disbursed by the committee in accordance with this chapter. Any money made available under this section to the board shall be returned by the board to the General Fund from moneys received from the sale of bonds sold for the purpose of carrying out this chapter. Such withdrawals from the General Fund shall be returned to the General Fund with interest at the rate which would otherwise have been earned by those sums in the Pooled Money Investment Fund.

§7110. Proceeds from sale of bonds.

All proceeds from the sale of bonds, except those derived from premiums and accrued interest, shall be available for the purpose provided in Section 7106 but shall not be available for transfer to the General Fund to pay principal and interest on bonds. The money in the fund may be expended only as herein provided.

§7111. Limits on expenditure.

Money in the fund may only be expended for projects specified in this chapter pursuant to appropriations by the Legislature.

CHAPTER 13

NEW PRISON CONSTRUCTION BOND ACT OF 1984

§7200. Title.

This chapter shall be known and may be cited as the New Prison Construction Bond Act of 1984.

§7201. State General Obligation Bond Law.

The State General Obligation Bond Law is adopted for the purpose of the issuance, sale and repayment of, and otherwise providing with respect to, the bonds authorized to be issued by this chapter, and the provisions of that law are included in this chapter as though set out in full in this chapter except that, notwithstanding anything in the State General Obligation Bond Law, the maximum maturity of the bonds shall not exceed 20 years from the date of each respective series. The maturity of each respective series shall be calculated from the date of such series.

§7202. 1984 Prison Construction Fund.

There is in the State Treasury the 1984 Prison Construction Fund, which fund is hereby created.

§7203. 1984 Prison Construction Committee.

The 1984 Prison Construction Committee is hereby created. The committee shall consist of the Controller, the State Treasurer, and the Director of Finance. That committee shall be the "committee," as that term is used in the State General Obligation Bond Law.

§7204. Creation of debts or liabilities.

The committee is hereby authorized and empowered to create a debt or debts, liability or liabilities, of the State of California, in the aggregate of three hundred million dollars ($300,000,000), in the manner provided in this chapter. That debt or debts, liability or liabilities, shall be created for the purpose of provid-

© 1992 by J., B. & L. Gould
Printed in the U.S.A.   EP

ing the fund to be used for the object and work specified in Section 7206.

§7205. Determination of necessity to issue bonds.

The committee may determine whether or not it is necessary or desirable to issue any bonds authorized under this chapter, and if so, the amount of bonds then to be issued and sold. The committee may authorize the Treasurer to sell all or any part of the bonds herein authorized at such time or times as may be fixed by the Treasurer.

§7206. Moneys in fund; use.

The moneys in the fund shall be used for the construction, renovation, remodeling, and deferred maintenance of state correctional facilities.

§7207. Sale of bonds; payment of principal and interest.

All bonds herein authorized, which shall have been duly sold and delivered as herein provided, shall constitute valid and legally binding general obligations of the State of California and the full faith and credit of the State of California is hereby pledged for the punctual payment of both principal and interest thereon.

There shall be collected annually in the same manner and at the same time as other state revenue is collected such a sum, in addition to the ordinary revenues of the state, as shall be required to pay the principal and interest on such bonds as herein provided, and it is hereby made the duty of all officers charged by law with any duty in regard to the collection of such revenue to do and perform each and every act which shall be necessary to collect such additional sum.

All money deposited in the fund which has been derived from premium and accrued interest on bonds sold shall be available for transfer to the General Fund as a credit to expenditures for bond interest.

All money deposited in the fund pursuant to any provision of law requiring repayments to the state which are financed by the proceeds of the bonds authorized by this chapter shall be available for transfer to the General Fund. When transferred to the General Fund such money shall be applied as a reimbursement to the General Fund on account of principal and interest on the bonds which has been paid from the General Fund.

§7208. Appropriations from the General Fund.

There is hereby appropriated from the General Fund in the State Treasury for the purpose of this chapter such an amount as will equal the following:

(a) Such sum annually as will be necessary to pay the principal of and the interest on the bonds issued and sold pursuant to the provisions of this chapter.

(b) Such sum as is necessary to carry out the provisions of Section 7209, which sum is appropriated without regard to fiscal years.

§7209. General Fund withdrawals.

For the purpose of carrying out the provisions of this chapter, the Director of Finance may by executive order authorize the withdrawal from the General Fund of an amount or amounts not to exceed the amount of the unsold bonds which the committee has by resolution authorized to be sold for the purpose of carrying out this chapter. Any amounts withdrawn shall be deposited in the fund and shall be disbursed by the committee in accordance with this chapter. Any money made available under this section to the board shall be returned by the board to the General Fund from moneys received from the sale of bonds sold for the purpose of carrying out this chapter. Such withdrawals from the General Fund shall be returned to the General Fund with interest at the rate which would otherwise have been earned by those sums in the Pooled Money Investment Fund.

§7210. Proceeds from sale of bonds; availability.

All proceeds from the sale of bonds, except those derived from premiums and accrued interest, shall be available for the purpose provided in Section 7206 but shall not be available for transfer to the General Fund to pay principal and interest on bonds. The money in the fund may be expended only as herein provided.

§7211. Authorized expenditures.

Money in the fund may only be expended for projects specified in this chapter pursuant to appropriations by the Legislature.

CHAPTER 14

NEW PRISON CONSTRUCTION BOND ACT OF 1986

§7300. Chapter title.

This chapter shall be known and may be cited as the New Prison Construction Bond Act of 1986. *(Added by Stats 1986 ch 409 §1.)*

§7301. State General Obligation Bond Law.

The State General Obligation Bond Law is adopted for the purpose of the issuance, sale and repayment of, and otherwise providing with respect to, the bonds authorized to be issued by this chapter, and the provisions of that law are included in this chapter as though set out in full in this chapter except that, notwithstanding anything in the State General Obligation Bond Law, the maximum maturity of the bonds shall not exceed 20 years from the date of each respective series. The maturity of each respective series shall be calculated from the date of such series. *(Added by Stats 1986 ch 409 §1.)*

§7302. 1986 Prison Construction Fund.

There is in the State Treasury the 1986 Prison Construction Fund, which fund is hereby created. The proceeds of the sale of bonds authorized by this act shall be deposited in this fund and may be transferred upon request of the Department of Corrections and upon approval of the Director of Finance, to the 1984 Prison Construction Fund established by Section 7202. If the moneys are so transferred, "fund" means the 1984 Prison Construction Fund. *(Added by Stats 1986 ch 409 §1.)*

§7303. 1986 Prison Construction Committee.

The 1986 Prison Construction Committee is hereby created. The committee shall consist of the Controller, the State Treasurer, and the Director of Finance. That committee shall be the "committee," as that term is used in the State General Obligation Bond Law.

The Department of Corrections is the "board" for the purpose of the State General Obligation Bond Law and this chapter. *(Added by Stats 1986 ch 409 §7.)*

§7304. Committee powers debts and liabilities.

The committee is hereby authorized and empowered to create a debt or debts, liability or liabilities, of the State of California, in the aggregate of five hundred million dollars ($500,000,000), in the manner provided in this chapter. That debt or debts, liability or liabilities, shall be created for the purpose of providing the fund to be used for the object and work specified in Section 7306. *(Added by Stats 1986 ch 409 §1.)*

§7305. Committee powers: issuance of bonds.

The committee may determine whether or not it is necessary or desirable to issue any bonds authorized under this chapter, and if so, the amount of bonds then to be issued and sold. The committee may authorize the Treasurer to sell all or any part of the bonds herein authorized at such time or times as may be fixed by the Treasurer. *(Added by Stats 1986 ch 409 §1.)*

§7306. Purpose of fund.

The moneys in the fund shall be used for the acquisition, construction, renovation, remodeling, and deferred maintenance of state youth and adult corrections facilities. *(Added by Stats 1986 ch 409 §1.)*

§7307. Provisions of bonds.

(a) All bonds herein authorized, which shall have been duly sold and delivered as herein provided, shall constitute valid and legally binding general obligations of the State of California, and the full faith and credit of the State of California is hereby pledged for the punctual payment of both principal and interest thereon.

(b) There shall be collected annually in the same manner and at the same time as other state revenue is collected such a sum, in addition to the ordinary revenues of the state, as shall be required to pay the principal and interest on those bonds, and it is hereby made the duty of all officers charged by law with any duty in regard to the collection of that revenue to do and perform each and every act which shall be necessary to collect that additional sum.

(c) All money deposited in the fund which has been derived from premium and accrued interest on bonds sold shall be available for transfer to the General Fund as a credit to expenditures for bond interest.

(d) All money deposited in the fund pursuant to any provision of law requiring repayments to the state which are financed by the proceeds of the bonds authorized by this chapter shall be available for transfer to the General Fund. When transferred to the General Fund that money shall be applied as a reimbursement to the General Fund on account of principal and interest on the bonds which has been paid from the General Fund. *(Added by Stats 1986 ch 409 §1.)*

§7308. Appropriation from General Fund.

There is hereby appropriated from the General Fund in the State Treasury for the purpose of this chapter such an amount as will equal the following:

(a) That sum annually as will be necessary to pay the principal of and the interest on the bonds issued and sold pursuant to the provisions of this chapter.

(b) That sum as is necessary to carry out the provisions of Section 7309, which sum is appropriated without regard to fiscal years. *(Added by Stats 1986 ch 409 §1.)*

§7309. Withdrawal from General Fund.

For the purpose of carrying out the provisions of this chapter, the Director of Finance may by executive order authorize the withdrawal from the General Fund of an amount or amounts not to exceed the amount of the unsold bonds which the committee has by resolution authorized to be sold for the purpose of carrying out this chapter. Any amounts withdrawn shall be deposited in the fund and shall be disbursed by the committee in accordance with this chapter. Any money made available under this section to the board shall be returned by the board to the General Fund from moneys received from the sale of bonds sold for the purpose of carrying out this chapter. Those withdrawals from the General Fund shall be returned to the General Fund with interest at the rate which would otherwise have been earned by those sums in the Pooled Money Investment Fund. *(Added by Stats 1986 ch 409 §1.)*

§7309.5. Tax-exempt bonds.

Notwithstanding any other provision of this bond act, or of the State General Obligation Bond Law (Chapter 4 (commencing with Section 16720) of Part 3 of Division 4 of Title 2 of the Government Code), if the Treasurer sells bonds pursuant to this bond act that include a bond counsel opinion to the effect that the interest on the bonds is excluded from gross income for federal tax purposes under designated conditions, the Treasurer may maintain separate accounts for the bond proceeds invested and the investment earnings on those proceeds, and may use or direct the use of those proceeds or earnings to pay any rebate, penalty, or other payment required under federal law, or take any other action with respect to the investment and use of those bond proceeds, as may be required or desirable under federal law in order to maintain the tax-exempt status of those bonds and to obtain any other advantage under federal law on behalf of the funds of this state. *(Added by Stats 1991 ch 652 §19, eff. 1/1/92.)*

§7310. Restrictions on transfer.

All proceeds from the sale of bonds, except those derived from premiums and accrued interest, shall be available for the purpose provided in Section 7306 but shall not be available for transfer to the General Fund to pay principal and interest on bonds. The money in the fund may be expended only as herein provided. *(Added by Stats 1986 ch 409 §1.)*

§7311. Legislative appropriation required.

Money in the fund may only be expended pursuant to appropriations by the Legislature. *(Added by Stats 1986 ch 409 §1.)*

CHAPTER 15

NEW PRISON CONSTRUCTION BOND ACT OF 1988
(Added by Stats 1988 ch 43 §2, eff. 11/8/88.)

§7400. Identification of chapter.

This chapter shall be known and may be cited as the New Prison Construction Bond Act of 1988. *(Added by Stats 1988 ch 43 §2, eff. 11/8/88.)*

© 1992 by J., B. & L. Gould
Printed in the U.S.A.   **EP**

§7401. General Obligation Bond Law.

The State General Obligation Bond Law is adopted for the purpose of the issuance, sale and repayment of, and otherwise providing with respect to, the bonds authorized to be issued by this chapter, and the provisions of that law are included in this chapter as though set out in full in this chapter except that, notwithstanding anything in the State General Obligation Bond Law, the maximum maturity of the bonds shall not exceed 20 years from the date of each respective series. The maturity of each respective series shall be calculated from the date of that series. *(Added by Stats 1988 ch 43 §2, eff. 11/8/88.)*

§7402. Prison Construction Fund of 1988.

There is in the State Treasury the 1988 Prison Construction Fund, which fund is hereby created. The proceeds of the sale of bonds authorized by this act shall be deposited in the fund, and may be transferred upon request of the Department of Corrections and upon approval of the Director of Finance, to the New Prison Construction Fund established by Section 7102, the 1984 Prison Construction Fund established by Section 7202, or the 1986 Prison Construction Fund established by Section 7302, or any combination thereof. If the moneys are so transferred, "fund" means the New Prison Construction Fund, 1984 Prison Construction Fund, or 1986 Prison Construction Fund, or any combination thereof, as is appropriate. At least 30 days prior to requesting a transfer as authorized by this section, the Department of Corrections shall notify the chairpersons of the fiscal committees in each house of the Legislature, and the Chairperson and the Vice Chairperson of the Joint Legislative Budget Committee. *(Added by Stats 1988 ch 43 §2; amended by Stats 1988 ch 386 §3, eff. 11/8/88.)*

§7403. 1988 Prison Construction Committee membership.

The 1988 Prison Construction Committee is hereby created. The committee shall consist of the Controller, the Treasurer, and the Director of Finance. That committee shall be the "committee," as that term is used in the State General Obligation Bond Law.

The Department of Corrections is the "board" for the purpose of the State General Obligation Bond Law and this chapter. *(Added by Stats 1988 ch 43 §2, eff. 11/8/88.)*

§7404. Debts and liabilities.

The committee is hereby authorized and empowered to create a debt or debts, liability or liabilities, of the State of California, in the aggregate principal amount of eight hundred seventeen million dollars ($817,000,000), exclusive of refunding bonds, in the manner provided in this chapter. That debt or debts, liability or liabilities, shall be created for the purpose of providing the fund to be used for the object and work specified in Section 7406. *(Added by Stats 1988 ch 43 §2, eff. 11/8/88.)*

§7405. Issuance of bonds.

The committee may determine whether or not it is necessary or desirable to issue any bonds authorized under this chapter, and if so, the amount of bonds then to be issued and sold. The committee may authorize the Treasurer to sell all or any part of the bonds herein authorized at such time or times as may be fixed by the Treasurer. *(Added by Stats 1988 ch 43 §2, eff. 11/8/88.)*

§7406. Uses and appropriations of moneys in fund.

(a) Except as provided in subdivision (b), the moneys in the fund shall be used for the acquisition, construction, renovation, remodeling, and deferred maintenance of state youth and adult correctional facilities.

(b) Of the moneys in the fund, forty million dollars ($40,000,000) is hereby appropriated to the Board of Corrections to fund those projects entitled to be funded under subdivision (c) of Section 3 of Chapter 444 of the Statutes of 1984, as amended, to the extent that those projects have not received full funding and for any costs associated with the sale of bonds and any administrative costs incurred by the Board of Corrections in the administration of the County Jail Capital Expenditure Bond Acts of 1981 and 1984 and the County Correctional Facility Capital Expenditure Bond Act of 1986.

(c) Notwithstanding subdivision (b) of Section 11 of Chapter 1519 of the Statutes of 1986 or any other provision of law to the contrary, and subject to the annual Budget Act appropriations by the Legislature, administrative costs shall not exceed 1½ percent of the amount allocated for any costs incurred by the Board of Corrections in the administration of the County Jail Capital Expenditure Bond Acts of 1981 and 1984 and the County Correctional Facility Capital Expenditure Bond Act of 1986. *(Added by Stats 1988 ch 43 §2, eff. 11/8/88.)*

§7407. Responsibility for and availability of moneys in fund.

(a) All bonds herein authorized, which shall have been duly sold and delivered as herein provided, shall constitute valid and legally binding general obligations of the State of California, and the full faith and credit of the State of California is hereby pledged for the punctual payment of both the principal thereof and interest thereon.

(b) There shall be collected annually in the same manner and at the same time as other state revenue is collected such a sum, in addition to the ordinary revenues of the state, as shall be required to pay the principal of and interest on those bonds, and it is hereby made the duty of all officers charged by law with any duty in regard to the collection of that revenue to do and perform each and every act which shall be necessary to collect that additional sum.

(c) All money deposited in the fund which has been derived from premiums or accrued interest on bonds sold shall be available for transfer to the General Fund as a credit to expenditures for bond interest.

(d) All money deposited in the fund pursuant to any provision of law requiring repayments to the state which are financed by the proceeds of the bonds authorized by this chapter shall be available for transfer to the General Fund. When transferred to the General Fund that money shall be applied as a reimbursement to the General Fund on account of the principal of and interest on the bonds which has been paid from the General Fund. *(Added by Stats 1988 ch 43 §2, eff. 11/8/88.)*

§7408. Appropriation of moneys from General Fund.

Notwithstanding Section 13340 of the Government Code, there is hereby appropriated from the General Fund in the State Treasury for the purpose of this chapter such an amount as will equal the following:

(a) That sum annually as will be necessary to pay the principal of and the interest on the bonds issued and sold pursuant to this chapter.

(b) That sum as is necessary to carry out the provisions of Section 7409, which sum is appropriated without regard to fiscal years. *(Added by Stats 1988 ch 43 §2, eff. 11/8/88.)*

§7409. Withdrawal and return of moneys in General Fund.

For the purpose of carrying out this chapter, the Director of Finance may by executive order authorize the withdrawal from the General Fund of an amount or amounts not to exceed the amount of the unsold bonds which the committee has by resolution authorized to be sold for the purpose of carrying out this chapter. Any amounts withdrawn shall be deposited in the fund and shall be disbursed by the committee in accordance with this chapter. Any money made available under this section to the board shall be returned by the board to the General Fund from moneys received from the sale of bonds sold for the purpose of carrying out this chapter. Those withdrawals from the General Fund shall be returned to the General Fund with interest at the rate which would otherwise have been earned by those sums in the Pooled Money Investment Account. *(Added by Stats 1988 ch 43 §2, eff. 11/8/88.)*

§7409.5. Tax-exempt bonds.

Notwithstanding any other provision of this bond act, or of the State General Obligation Bond Law (Chapter 4 (commencing with Section 16720) of Part 3 of Division 4 of Title 2 of the Government Code), if the Treasurer sells bonds pursuant to this bond act that include a bond counsel opinion to the effect that the interest on the bonds is excluded from gross income for federal tax purposes under designated conditions, the Treasurer may maintain separate accounts for the bond proceeds invested and the investment earnings on those proceeds, and may use or direct the use of those proceeds or earnings to pay any rebate, penalty, or other payment required under federal law, or take any other action with respect to the investment and use of those bond proceeds, as may be required or desirable under federal law in order to maintain the tax-exempt status of those bonds and to obtain any other advantage under federal law on behalf of the funds of this state. *(Added by Stats 1991 ch 652 §20, eff. 1/1/92.)*

§7410. Request for loan from Pooled Money Investment Account loan.

The board may request the Pooled Money Investment Board to make a loan from the Pooled Money Investment Account, in accordance with Section 16312 of the Government Code, for the purposes of carrying out the provisions of this chapter. The amount of the request shall not exceed the amount of the unsold bonds which the committee has by resolution authorized to be sold for the purpose of carrying out this chapter. The board shall execute any documents required by the Pooled Money Investment Board to obtain and repay the loan. Any amounts loaned shall be deposited in the fund to be allocated by the board in accordance with this chapter. *(Added by Stats 1988 ch 43 §2, eff. 11/8/88.)*

§7411. Refunding of bonds.

Any bonds issued and sold pursuant to this chapter may be refunded by the issuance of refunding bonds in accordance with Article 6 (commencing with Section 16780) of Chapter 4 of Part 3 of Division 2 of Title 2 of the Government Code. Approval by the electors of the state for the issuance of bonds shall include the approval of the issuance of any bonds issued to refund any bonds originally issued or any previously issued refunding bonds. *(Added by Stats 1988 ch 43 §2, eff. 11/8/88.)*

§7412. Proceeds from bond sales.

All proceeds from the sale of bonds, except those derived from premiums and accrued interest, shall be available for the purpose provided in Section 7406 but shall not be available for transfer to the General Fund to pay the principal of and interest on bonds. The money in the fund may be expended only as herein provided. *(Added by Stats 1988 ch 43 §2, eff. 11/8/88.)*

§7413. Expenditures.

Money in the fund may only be expended pursuant to appropriations by the Legislature. *(Added by Stats 1988 ch 43 §2, eff. 11/8/88.)*

§7414. Constitutional limitations.

The Legislature hereby finds and declares that, inasmuch as the proceeds from the sale of bonds authorized by this chapter are not "proceeds of taxes" as that term is used in Article XIII B of the California Constitution, the disbursement of these proceeds is not subject to the limitations imposed by that article. *(Added by Stats 1988 ch 43 §2, eff. 11/8/88.)*

CHAPTER 16

NEW PRISON CONSTRUCTION BOND ACT OF 1990

(Added by Stats 1990 ch 5 §1; Initiative Measure, Prop 120 §1, approved 6/5/90.)

§7420. Chapter title.

This chapter shall be known and may be cited as the New Prison Construction Bond Act of 1990. *(Added by Stats 1990 ch 5 §1; Initiative Measure, Prop 120 §1, approved 6/5/90.)*

§7421. State General Obligation Bond Law.

The State General Obligation Bond Law is adopted for the purpose of the issuance, sale and repayment of, and otherwise providing with respect to, the bonds authorized to be issued by this chapter, and the provisions of that law are included in this chapter as though set out in full in this chapter except that, notwithstanding anything in the State General Obligation Bond Law, the maximum maturity of the bonds shall not exceed 20 years from the date of each respective series. The maturity of each respective series shall be calculated from the date of that series. *(Added by Stats 1990 ch 5 §1; Initiative Measure, Prop 120 §1, approved 6/5/90.)*

§7422. 1990 Prison Construction Fund.

There is in the State Treasury the 1990 Prison Construction Fund, which fund is hereby created. The proceeds of the sale of bonds authorized by this chapter shall be deposited in the fund. Upon request of the Department of Corrections and upon approval of the

© 1992 by J., B. & L. Gould
Printed in the U.S.A.   EP

Director of Finance, appropriations or augmentations to appropriations made from the 1984 Prison Construction Fund established by Section 7202, the 1986 Prison Construction Fund established by Section 7302, or the 1988 Prison Construction Fund established by Section 7402, or any combination thereof, may be funded from the 1990 Prison Construction Fund. If the moneys are so funded, "fund" means the 1984 Prison Construction Fund, the 1986 Prison Construction Fund, or the 1988 Prison Construction Fund, or any combination thereof, as is appropriate. At least 30 days prior to requesting funding for appropriations or augmentations to appropriations for other bond acts as authorized by this section, the Department of Corrections shall notify the chairpersons of the fiscal committees in each house of the Legislature, and the chairperson and the vice chairperson of the joint Legislative Budget Committee. *(Added by Stats 1990 ch 5 §1; Initiative Measure, Prop 120 §1, approved 6/5/90.)*

§7423. 1990 Prison Construction Committee.

The 1990 Prison Construction Committee is hereby created. The committee shall consist of the Controller, the Treasurer, and the Director of Finance, or their designated representatives. A majority may act for the committee. The Treasurer shall chair the committee. That committee shall be the "committee," as that term is used in the State General Obligation Bond Law.

When funds are appropriated to the Department of Corrections, the Department of Corrections is the "board" for the purpose of the State General Obligation Bond Law and this chapter. When funds are appropriated to the Department of Youth Authority, the Department of Youth Authority is the "board" for the purpose of the State General Obligation Bond Law and this chapter. *(Added by Stats 1990 ch 5 §1; Initiative Measure, Prop 120 §1, approved 6/5/90.)*

§7424. Debts and liabilities.

The committee is hereby authorized and empowered to create a debt or debts, liability or liabilities, of the State of California, in the aggregate principal amount of four hundred fifty million dollars ($450,000,000), exclusive of refunding bonds, in the manner provided in this chapter. That debt or debts, liability or liabilities, shall be created for the purpose of providing the fund to be used for the object and work specified in Section 7426. *(Added by Stats 1990 ch 5 §1; Initiative Measure, Prop 120 §1, approved 6/5/90.)*

§7425. Issuance of bonds.

The committee may determine whether or not it is necessary or desirable to issue any bonds authorized under this chapter, and if so, the amount of bonds then to be issued and sold. The committee may authorize the Treasurer to sell all or any part of the bonds herein authorized at such time or times as may be fixed by the Treasurer. *(Added by Stats 1990 ch 5 §1; Initiative Measure, Prop 120 §1, approved 6/5/90.)*

§7426. Purpose of fund.

The moneys in the fund shall be used for the acquisition, construction, renovation, remodeling, and deferred maintenance of state youth and adult correctional facilities. *(Added by Stats 1990 ch 5 §1; Initiative Measure, Prop 120 §1, approved 6/5/90.)*

§7426.5. Refinancing of interim debt.

Moneys deposited in the fund may also be used for the refinancing of interim debt incurred for any of the purposes specified in Section 7426. *(Added by Stats 1990 ch 5 §1; Initiative Measure, Prop 120 §1, approved 6/5/90.)*

§7427. Provisions of bonds.

(a) All bonds herein authorized, which shall have been duly sold and delivered as herein provided, shall constitute valid and legally binding general obligations of the State of California, and the full faith and credit of the State of California is hereby pledged for the punctual payment of both the principal thereof and interest thereon.

(b) There shall be collected annually in the same manner and at the same time as other state revenue is collected that sum, in addition to the ordinary revenues of the state, that is required to pay the principal of and interest on those bonds, and it is hereby made the duty of all officers charged by law with any duty in regard to the collection of that revenue to do and perform each and every act which shall be necessary to collect that additional sum.

(c) All money deposited in the fund that has been derived from premiums or accrued interest on bonds sold shall be available for transfer to the General Fund as a credit to expenditures for bond interest.

(d) All money deposited in the fund pursuant to any provision of law requiring repayments to the state that is financed by the proceeds of the bonds authorized by this chapter shall be available for transfer to the General Fund. When transferred to the General Fund that money shall be applied as a reimbursement to the General Fund on account of the principal of and interest on the bonds which have been paid from the General Fund. *(Added by Stats 1990 ch 5 §1; Initiative Measure, Prop 120 §1, approved 6/5/90.)*

§7428. Appropriation from General Fund.

Notwithstanding Section 13340 of the Government Code, there is hereby appropriated from the General Fund in the State Treasury for the purpose of this chapter such an amount as will equal the following:

(a) That sum annually as will be necessary to pay the principal of and the interest on the bonds issued and sold pursuant to this chapter.

(b) That sum as is necessary to carry out the provisions of Section 7429, which sum is appropriated without regard to fiscal years. *(Added by Stats 1990 ch 5 §1; Initiative Measure, Prop 120 §1, approved 6/5/90.)*

§7429. Withdrawal from General Fund.

For the purpose of carrying out this chapter, the Director of Finance may by executive order authorize the withdrawal from the General Fund of an amount or amounts not to exceed the amount of the unsold bonds which the committee has by resolution authorized to be sold for the purpose of carrying out this chapter. Any amounts withdrawn shall be deposited in the fund and shall be disbursed by the committee in accordance with this chapter. Any money made available under this section to the board shall be returned by the board to the General Fund from moneys received from the sale of bonds sold for the purpose of carrying out this chapter. Those withdrawals from the General Fund shall be returned to the General Fund with interest at the rate which would otherwise have been earned by those sums in the Pooled Money Investment Account. *(Added by Stats 1990 ch 5 §1; Initiative Measure, Prop 120 §1, approved 6/5/90.)*

§7430. Loans from Pooled Money Investment Account.

The board may request the Pooled Money Investment Board to make a loan from the Pooled Money Investment Account, in accordance with Section 16312 of the Government Code, for the purposes of carrying out the provisions of this chapter. The amount of the request shall not exceed the amount of the unsold bonds which the committee has by resolution authorized to be sold for the purpose of carrying out this chapter. The board shall execute any documents required by the Pooled Money Investment Board to obtain and repay the loan. Any amounts loaned shall be deposited in the fund to be allocated by the board in accordance with this chapter. *(Added by Stats 1990 ch 5 §1; Initiative Measure, Prop 120 §1, approved 6/5/90.)*

§7431. Refunds of bonds.

Any bonds issued and sold pursuant to this chapter may be refunded by the issuance of refunding bonds in accordance with Article 6 (commencing with Section 16780) of Chapter 4 of Part 3 of Division 2 of Title 2 of the Government Code. Approval by the electors of the state for the issuance of bonds shall include the approval of the issuance of any bonds issued to refund any bonds originally issued or any previously issued refunding bonds. *(Added by Stats 1990 ch 5 §1; Initiative Measure, Prop 120 §1, approved 6/5/90.)*

§7432. Restrictions on transfers.

All proceeds from the sale of bonds, except those derived from premiums and accrued interest, shall be available for the purpose provided in Section 7426 but shall not be available for transfer to the General Fund to pay the principal of and interest on bonds. The money in the fund may be expended only as herein provided.

Notwithstanding any provision of this chapter or the State General Obligation Bond Law set forth in Chapter 4 (commencing with Section 16720) of Part 3 of Division 4 of Title 2 of the Government Code, if the Treasurer sells bonds pursuant to this chapter the interest on which is intended to be excluded from gross income from federal tax purposes, the Treasurer is authorized to maintain separate accounts for the investment of bond proceeds and the investment earnings on the proceeds, and the Treasurer is authorized to use or direct the use of the proceeds or earnings to pay any rebate, penalty, or other payment required under federal law, or to take any other action with respect to the investment and use of bond proceeds required or desirable under federal law so as to maintain the tax-exempt status of those bonds and to obtain any other advantage under federal law on behalf of the funds of this state. *(Added by Stats 1990 ch 5 §1; Initiative Measure, Prop 120 §1, approved 6/5/90.)*

§7433. Legislative appropriation required.

Money in the fund may only be expended pursuant to appropriations by the Legislature. The Department of Corrections and the Department of the Youth Authority, annually on or before January 10, shall submit their respective five-year facility master plans to the Legislature. Each plan shall include a program of proposed expenditures from the 1990 Prison Construction Fund. *(Added by Stats 1990 ch 5 §1; Initiative Measure, Prop 120 §1, approved 6/5/90.)*

§7434. Constitutional limitations.

The Legislature hereby finds and declares that, inasmuch as the proceeds from the sale of bonds authorized by this chapter are not "proceeds of taxes" as that term is used in Article XIII B of the California Constitution, the disbursement of these proceeds is not subject to the limitations imposed by that article. *(Added by Stats 1990 ch 5 §1; Initiative Measure, Prop 120 §1, approved 6/5/90.)*

TITLE 8

MEDICAL TESTING OF PRISONERS

(Added by Stats 1988 ch 1579 §2; amended by Stats 1991 ch 768 §1, eff. 10/10/91 only until 1/1/95, oper. only until 7/1/94.)

CHAPTER 1

GENERAL PROVISIONS

§7500. Findings and declarations.

The Legislature finds and declares all of the following:

(a) The public peace, health, and safety is endangered by the spread of acquired immune deficiency syndrome (AIDS) within state and local correctional institutions.

(b) The spread of AIDS within prison and jail populations presents a grave danger to inmates within those populations, law enforcement personnel, and other persons in contact with a prisoner infected with the AIDS virus, both during and after the prisoner's confinement. Law enforcement personnel and prisoners are particularly vulnerable to this danger, due to the high number of assaults and other violent acts which occur within correctional institutions.

(c) AIDS has the frightening potential of spreading more rapidly within the closed society of correctional institutions than outside these institutions. The major public health problem is compounded by the further potential of rapid spread of communicable disease outside correctional institutions, through contacts of an infected prisoner who is not treated and monitored upon his or her release.

(d) New diseases of epidemic proportions, such as AIDS may suddenly and tragically infect large numbers of people. This title primarily addresses a current problem of this nature, the spread of AIDS among those in correctional institutions and among the people of California.

(e) AIDS and AIDS-related conditions pose a major threat to the public health and safety of those governmental employees and others whose responsibilities bring them into most direct contact with persons afflicted with those illnesses, and the protection of the health and safety of these personnel is of equal importance to the people of the State of California as is the protection of the health of those afflicted with the diseases who are held in custodial situations.

(f) Testing described in this title of individuals housed within state and local correctional facilities for evidence of infection by the human immunodeficiency virus (HIV), AIDS, or AIDS-related complex would

© 1992 by J., B. & L. Gould
Printed in the U.S.A.   EP

help provide a level of information necessary for effective disease control within these institutions and would help preserve the health of public employees, inmates, and persons in custody, as well as that of the public at large. This testing is not intended to be, and shall not be construed as, a prototypical method of disease control for the public at large. *(Added by Stats 1988 ch 1579 §2; amended by Stats 1991 ch 768 §1, eff. 10/10/91 only until 1/1/95, oper. only until 7/1/94.)*

§7501. Intent of Legislature.

In order to address the public health crisis described in Section 7500, it is the intent of the Legislature to do all of the following:

(a) Establish a procedure through which custodial and law enforcement personnel are required to report certain situations and may request and be granted a confidential HIV test of an inmate convicted of a crime, or a person arrested or taken into custody, if the custodial or law enforcement officer has reason to believe he or she has come into contact with the blood or semen of an inmate or in any other manner has come into contact with the inmate in a way that could result in HIV infection, based on the latest determinations and conclusions by the federal Centers for Disease Control and the State Department of Health Services on means for the transmission of AIDS, and if appropriate medical authorities, as provided for in this title, reasonably believe there is good medical reason for the test.

(b) Permit inmates to file similar requests stemming from contacts with other inmates.

(c) Require that probation and parole officers be notified when an inmate being released from incarceration is infected with AIDS, and permit these officers to notify certain persons who will come into contact with the parolee or probationer, if authorized by law.

(d) Authorize prison medical staff authorities to request tests of a jail or prison inmate under certain circumstances, if they reasonably believe, based upon the existence of supporting evidence, that the inmate may be suffering from AIDS or AIDS-related diseases and is a danger to other inmates or staff.

(e) Require supervisory and medical personnel of correctional institutions to which this title applies to notify staff if they are coming into close and direct contact with persons in custody who have tested positive or who have AIDS, and provide appropriate counseling and safety equipment. *(Added by Stats 1988 ch 1579 §2; amended by Stats 1991 ch 768 §1, eff. 10/10/91 only until 1/1/95, oper. only until 7/1/94.)*

§7502. Terms defined.

As used in this title, the following terms shall have the following meanings:

(a) "Correctional institution" means any state prison, county jail, city jail, California Youth Authority facility, county or city-operated juvenile facility, including juvenile halls, camps, or schools, or any other state or local correctional institution.

(b) "Counseling" means counseling by a licensed physician and surgeon, registered nurse, or other health professional who meets guidelines which shall be established by the State Department of Health Services for purposes of providing counseling on AIDS to inmates, persons in custody, and other persons pursuant to this title.

(c) "Law enforcement employee" means correctional officers, peace officers, and other staff of a correctional institution, California Highway Patrol officers, county sheriff's deputies, city police officers, parole officers, probation officers, and city, county, or state employees including but not limited to, judges, bailiffs, court personnel, and public defenders, who, as part of the judicial process involving an inmate of a correctional institution, or a person charged with a crime, including a minor charged with an offense for which he or she may be made a ward of the court under Section 602 of the Welfare and Institutions Code, are engaged in the custody, transportation, or care of these persons.

(d) "AIDS" means acquired immune deficiency syndrome.

(e) "Human immunodeficiency virus" or "HIV" means the etiologic virus of AIDS.

(f) "HIV test" or "HIV testing" means any clinical laboratory test approved by the federal Food and Drug Administration for HIV, component of HIV, or antibodies to HIV.

(g) "Inmate" means any of the following:

(1) A person in a state prison, or city and county jail, who has been either convicted of a crime or arrested or taken into custody, whether or not he or she has been charged with a crime.

(2) Any person in a California Youth Authority facility, or County- or city-operated juvenile facility, who has committed an act, or been charged with committing an act specified in Section 602 of the Welfare and Institutions Code.

(h) "Bodily fluids" means blood, semen, or any other bodily fluid identified by either the federal Centers for Disease Control or State Department of Health Services in appropriate regulations as capable of transmitting HIV.

(i) "Minor" means a person under 15 years of age. *(Added by Stats 1988 ch 1579 §2; amended by Stats 1991 ch 768 §1, eff. 10/10/91 only until 1/1/95, oper. only until 7/1/94.)*

§7503. Delegation of responsibilities of chief medical officer.

The State Department of Health Services shall adopt guidelines permitting a chief medical officer to delegate his or her medical responsibilities under this title to other qualified physicians and surgeons, and his or her nonmedical responsibilities to other qualified persons, as appropriate. The chief medical officer shall not, however, delegate the duty to determine whether mandatory testing is required as provided for in Chapter 2 (commencing with Section 7510). *(Added by Stats 1988 ch 1579 §2; amended by Stats 1991 ch 768 §1, eff. 10/10/91 only until 1/1/95, oper. only until 7/1/94.)*

§7504. Provisions for testing of prisoners.

Actions taken pursuant to this title shall not be subject to subdivisions (a) to (c), inclusive, of Section 199.21 of the Health and Safety Code. In addition, the requirements of subdivision (a) of Section 199.22 of the Health and Safety Code, shall not apply to testing performed pursuant to this title. *(Added by Stats 1988 ch 1579 §2; amended by Stats 1991 ch 768 §1, eff. 10/10/91 only until 1/1/95, oper. only until 7/1/94.)*

CHAPTER 2

PROCEDURES FOR REQUIRING HIV
TESTING

§7510. Reporting incident of possible contamination.

(a) A law enforcement employee who believes that he or she came into contact with bodily fluids of either an inmate of a correctional institution, a person not in a correctional institution who has been arrested or taken into custody whether or not the person has been charged with a crime, including a person detained for or charged with an offense for which he or she may be made a ward of the court under Section 602 of the Welfare and Institutions Code, or a person on probation or parole due to conviction of a crime, shall report the incident through the completion of a form provided by the State Department of Health Services. The form shall be directed to the chief medical officer, as defined in subdivision (c), who serves the applicable law enforcement agency. Utilizing this form the law enforcement employee may request an HIV test of the person who is the subject of the report. The forms may be combined with regular incident reports or other forms used by the correctional institution or law enforcement agency.

(b) The report required by subdivision (a) shall be submitted by the end of the law enforcement employee's shift during which the incident occurred, or if not practicable, as soon as possible, but no longer than two days after the incident, except that the chief medical officer may waive this filing period requirement if he or she finds that good cause exists. The report shall include names of witnesses to the incident, names of persons involved in the incident, and if feasible, any written statements from these parties. The law enforcement employee shall assist in the investigation of the incident, as requested by the chief medical officer.

(c) For purposes of this section and Section 7511, "chief medical officer" means:

(1) In the case of a report filed by a staff member of a state prison, the chief medical officer of that facility.

(2) In the case of a parole officer filing a report, the chief medical officer of the nearest state prison.

(3) In the case of a report filed by an employee of the California Youth Authority, the chief medical officer of the facility.

(4) In the case of a report filed against a subject who is an inmate of a city or county jail or a county- or city-operated juvenile facility, or who has been arrested or taken into custody whether or not the person has been charged with a crime, but who is not in a correctional facility, including a person detained for or charged with an offense for which he or she may be made a ward of the court under Section 602 of the Welfare and Institutions Code, the county health officer of the county in which the individual is jailed or charged with the crime.

(5) In the case of a report filed by a probation officer, the county health officer of the county in which the probation officer is employed.

(6) In any instance where the chief medical officer, as determined pursuant to this subdivision, is not a physician or surgeon, the chief medical officer shall designate a physician or surgeon to perform his or her duties under this title. *(Amended by Stats 1989 ch*

1360 §122; Stats 1991 ch 768 §1, eff. 10/10/91 only until 1/1/95, oper. only until 7/1/94.)

§7511. Ordering HIV testing.

(a) The chief medical officer shall, regardless of whether a report filed pursuant to Section 7510 contains a request for HIV testing, decide whether or not to require HIV testing of the inmate or other person who is the subject of the report filed pursuant to Section 7510, within five calendar days of receipt of the report. If the chief medical officer decides to require HIV testing, he or she shall specify in his or her decision the circumstances, if any, under which followup testing will also be required.

(b) The chief medical officer shall order an HIV test only if he or she finds that, considering all of the facts and circumstances, there is a significant risk that HIV was transmitted. In making this decision, the chief medical officer shall take the following factors into consideration:

(1) Whether an exchange of bodily fluids occurred which could have resulted in a significant risk of AIDS infection, based on the latest written guidelines and standards established by the federal Centers for Disease Control and the State Department of Health Services.

(2) Whether the person exhibits medical conditions or clinical findings categorizing him or her as a possible AIDS victim.

(3) Whether the health of the institution staff or inmates may have been endangered as to AIDS infection resulting from the reported incident.

(c) Prior to reaching a decision, the chief medical officer shall receive written or oral testimony from the law enforcement employee filing the report, from the subject of the report, and from witnesses to the incident, as he or she deems necessary for a complete investigation. The decision shall be in writing and shall state the reasons for the decision. A copy shall be provided by the chief medical officer to the law enforcement employee who filed the report and to the subject of the report, and where the subject is a minor, to the parents or guardian of the minor, unless the parent or guardian of the minor cannot be located. *(Added by Stats 1988 ch 1579 §2; amended by Stats 1991 ch 768 §§1, 2, eff. 10/10/91 only until 1/1/95, oper. only until 7/1/94.)*

§7512. Request for testing by an inmate.

(a) An inmate of a correctional institution may request HIV testing of another inmate of that institution if he or she has reason to believe that he or she has come into contact with the bodily fluids of that inmate, in situations, which may include, but are not limited to, rape or sexual contact with a potentially infected inmate, tattoo or drug needle sharing, an incident involving injury in which bodily fluids are exchanged, or confinement with a cellmate under circumstances involving possible mingling of bodily fluids. A request may be filed under this section only within two calendar days of the date when the incident causing the request occurred, except that the chief medical officer may waive this filing period requirement when he or she finds that good cause exists.

(b) An inmate in a California Youth Authority facility or any county- or city-operated juvenile facility who is 15 years of age or older, may file a request for a test of another inmate in that facility, in the same manner as an inmate in a state prison, and is subject

© 1992 by J., B. & L. Gould
Printed in the U.S.A.   EP

to the same procedures and rights. An inmate in a California Youth Authority facility or a county- or city-operated juvenile facility who is a minor may file such a request through a staff member of the facility in which he or she is confined. A staff member may file this request on behalf of a minor on his or her own volition if he or she believes that a situation meeting the criteria specified in subdivision (a) has occurred warranting the request. The filing of a request by staff on behalf of an inmate of a California Youth Authority facility or a local juvenile facility shall be within two calendar days of its discovery by staff, except that the chief medical officer may waive this filing period requirement if he or she finds that good cause exists.

When a request is filed on behalf of a minor, the facility shall notify the parent or guardian of the minor of the request and seek permission from the parent or guardian for the test request to proceed. If the parent or guardian refuses to grant permission for the test, the Director of the Youth Authority may request the juvenile court in the county in which the facility is located, to rule on whether the test request procedure set forth in this title shall continue. The juvenile court shall make a ruling within five days of the case being brought before the court.

If the parent or guardian cannot be located, the superintendent of the facility shall approve or disapprove the request for a test.

(c) Upon receipt of a request for testing as provided in this section, a law enforcement employee shall submit the request to the chief medical officer, the identity of which shall be determined as if the request had been made by an employee of the facility. The chief medical officer shall follow the procedures set forth in Section 7511 with respect to investigating the request and reaching a decision as to mandatory testing of the inmate who is the subject of the request. The inmate submitting the request shall provide names or testimony of witnesses within the limits of his or her ability to do so. The chief medical officer shall make his or her decision based on the criteria set forth in Section 7511. A copy of the chief medical officer's decision shall be provided to the person submitting the request for HIV testing, to the subject of the request, and to the superintendent of the correctional institution. In the case of a minor, a copy of the decision shall be provided to the parents or guardian of the minor, unless the parent or guardian of the minor cannot be located. *(Added by Stats 1988 ch 1579 §2; amended by Stats 1991 ch 768 §1, eff. 10/10/91 only until 1/1/95, oper. only until 7/1/94.)*

§7512.5. Testing inmate without a report.

In the absence of the filing of a report pursuant to Section 7510 or a request pursuant to Section 7512, the chief medical officer, may order a test of an inmate if he or she concludes there are clinical symptoms of AIDS or AIDS-related complex, as recognized by the Centers for Disease Control.

A copy of the decision shall be provided to the inmate, and where the inmate is a minor, to the parents or guardian of the minor, unless the parent or guardian of the minor cannot be located. Any decision made pursuant to this section shall not be appealable to a three-member panel provided for under Section 7515. *(Added by Stats 1988 ch 1579 §2; amended by Stats 1991 ch 768 §1, eff. 10/10/91 only until 1/1/95, oper. only until 7/1/94.)*

§7513. Right to appeal.

A description of the right to appeal a chief medical officer's decision shall accompany the copies of the decision required to be provided by Sections 7511, 7512, and 7512.5. *(Added by Stats 1988 ch 1579 §2; amended by Stats 1991 ch 768 §1, eff. 10/10/91 only until 1/1/95, oper. only until 7/1/94.)*

§7514. Voluntary testing and counseling.

(a) It shall be the chief medical officer's responsibility to see that personal counseling is provided to a law enforcement employee filing a report pursuant to Section 7510, an inmate filing a request pursuant to Section 7512, and any potential test subject, at the time the initial report or request for tests is made, at the time when tests are ordered, and at the time when test results are provided to the employee, inmate, or test subject.

The chief medical officer may provide additional counseling to any of these individuals, upon his or her request, or whenever the chief medical officer deems advisable, and may arrange for the counseling to be provided in other jurisdictions. The chief medical officer shall encourage the subject of the report or request, the law enforcement employee who filed the report, the person who filed the request pursuant to Section 7512, or in the case of a minor, the minor on whose behalf the request was filed, to undergo voluntary HIV testing if the chief medical officer deems it medically advisable. All testing required by this title or any voluntary testing resulting from the provisions of this title, shall be at the expense of the appropriate correctional institution.

(b) On or before January 15, 1993, 1994, and 1995, the Department of Corrections, the Department of the California Youth Authority, and each law enforcement agency in which a request for a test has been filed during the previous calendar year, shall report data to the Joint Legislative Committee on Prison Construction and Operation on all requests made during that period, plus specifics of the disposition of each request, the counseling provided, and its extent for each case. This data shall be provided by the committee to the Legislative Analyst, who shall compile a report to the Legislature on or before January 30, 1995, on whether the program is meeting the objectives of this title. The report shall include a recommendation on whether the program should be continued, terminated, or changed.

The Legislative Analyst shall consult with the Office of Aids, within the State Department of Health Services, in preparing its evaluation.

Names of persons seeking tests or the subject of a request for a test shall not be included in any document made public as a result of this section.

Notwithstanding the repeal of this section in accordance with Section 7555, the duties imposed by this subdivision shall continue in effect until they have been complied with. *(Added by Stats 1988 ch 1579 §2; amended by Stats 1991 ch 768 §§1, 3, eff. 10/10/91 only until 1/1/95, oper. only until 7/1/94.)*

§7515. Appeal of chief medical officer's decision.

(a) A decision of the chief medical officer made pursuant to Section 7511, 7512, or 7516 may be appealed, within three calendar days of receipt of the decision, to a three-person panel, either by the person required to be tested, or his or her parent or guardian when the subject is a minor, the law enforcement employee filing a report pursuant to either Section 7510 or 7516, or the person requesting testing pursuant to Section 7512, whichever is applicable, or the chief medical officer, upon his or her own motion. If no request for appeal is filed under this subdivision, the chief medical officer's decision shall be final.

(b) A panel required pursuant to subdivision (a) shall consist of three members, as follows:

(1) The chief medical officer making the original decision.

(2) When the decision arises out of a report filed pursuant to Section 7510, a supervisory representative from the law enforcement agency employing the person who filed the report. When a decision arises out of a chief medical officer's decision made pursuant to Section 7512.5, a supervisory representative of the correctional institution appointed by the institution's superintendent. When the decision arises out of a request filed pursuant to Section 7512, a supervisory representative of the law enforcement agency with jurisdiction over the facility.

(3) A physician and surgeon not on the staff of, or under contract with, a state, county, or city correctional institution or with an employer of a law enforcement employee as defined in subdivision (b) of Section 7502, and who has knowledge of the diagnosis and treatment of AIDS. The physician and surgeon appointed pursuant to this paragraph shall be selected by the State Department of Health Services from among a list of persons to be compiled by that department. The State Department of Health Services shall adopt standards for selecting persons for the list required by this paragraph, as well as for their reimbursement, and shall, to the extent possible, utilize its normal process for selecting consultants in compiling this list. The physician and surgeon appointed pursuant to this paragraph shall preside at the hearing and serve as chairperson.

A correctional institution or a county may create an ongoing panel or panels to hear appeals under this section, except that one member each shall meet the requirements of paragraphs (1), (2), and (3).

No panel shall be created under this paragraph by a state correctional institution except with the prior approval of the State Department of Health Services, and no panel shall be created pursuant to this paragraph by a county or city correctional institution except with the prior approval of the county health officer.

(c) A hearing conducted pursuant to this section shall be closed, except that each of the following persons shall have the right to attend the hearing, speak on the issues presented at the hearing, and call witnesses to testify at the hearing:

(1) The chief medical officer, who may also bring staff essential to the hearing, as well as the other two members of the panel.

(2) The subject of the chief medical officer's decision, except that a subject who is a minor may attend only with the consent of his or her parent or guardian, and if the subject is a minor, his or her parent or guardian.

(3) The law enforcement employee filing the report pursuant to Section 7510, or the person requesting HIV testing pursuant to Section 7512, whichever is applicable, and if the person is a minor, his or her parent or guardian.

(d) The subject of the test, or the person requesting the test pursuant to Section 7512, or who filed the report pursuant to Section 7510, whichever is applicable, may appoint a representative to attend the hearing in order to assist him or her.

(e) When a hearing is sought pursuant to this section, the decision shall be rendered within 10 days of the date upon which the appeal is filed pursuant to subdivision (a). A unanimous vote of all the panel shall be necessary in order to require that the subject of the hearing undergo HIV testing.

The criteria specified in Section 7511 for use by the chief medical officer shall also be utilized by the panel in making its decision.

The decision shall be in writing, stating reasons for the decision, and shall be signed by the members. A copy shall be provided by the chief medical officer to the person requesting the test, or filing the report, whichever is applicable, to the subject of the test, and, when the subject is in a correctional institution, to the superintendent of the institution, except that when the subject of the test or the person upon whose behalf the request for the test was made is a minor, copies shall also be provided to the parent or guardian of the person, unless the parent or guardian cannot be located. *(Added by Stats 1988 ch 1579 §2; amended by Stats 1991 ch 768 §1, eff. 10/10/91 only until 1/1/95, oper. only until 7/1/94.)*

§7516. Report of activities placing inmates at risk of AIDS.

(a) When a custodial officer or staff person of a correctional institution, observes or is informed of activity in a correctional institution that is classified as causing, or known to cause, the transmission of the AIDS virus, as described in subdivision (b), he or she may file a written report with the facility's chief medical officer which, in the case of city or county jails, shall be the county health officer.

(b) Reportable activities within a correctional institution for which a report may be filed pursuant to subdivision (a) include, but are not limited to, all of the following activities, if they could result in the transmission of AIDS, according to the standards provided for in this chapter:

(1) Sexual activity resulting in exchange of bodily fluids.

(2) IV drug use.

(3) Incidents involving injury to inmates or staff in which bodily fluids are exchanged.

(4) Tampering with medical and food supplies or medical or food equipment.

(5) Tattooing among inmates.

(c) The medical officer may investigate the report, conduct interviews, and determine whether the situation reported caused the probable exchange of body fluids in a manner that could result in the transmission of HIV, utilizing the criteria set forth in Section 7511, and pose a danger to the health and safety of the institution's staff and inmate population.

If the chief medical officer concludes this may have occurred, he or she shall require HIV testing of any inmate which he or she deems necessary pursuant to the investigation. Whenever an inmate is required to undergo an HIV test pursuant to this subdivision, he or she may appeal that decision as provided for in Section 7515.

(d) Testing under this section may only be required by a unanimous vote of all three members of the panel. The rights guaranteed inmates under Section 7515 shall apply.

© 1992 by J., B. & L. Gould
Printed in the U.S.A.　**EP**

When a hearing is convened pursuant to this section, the hearing shall be closed, except that both the person filing the original report and the chief medical officer as well as other panel members may also call witnesses to testify at the hearing.

When a hearing is sought pursuant to this section, the decision shall be rendered within 20 days of the date the hearing is sought by the medical officer.

(e) This section shall apply to situations involving individual inmates or group situations but shall not be utilized to require testing of all inmates in a correctional institution.

(f) The findings of the panel shall be set forth in writing, including reasons for the panel's decision, and shall be signed by the members of the panel. A copy of the decision shall be provided to the superintendent of the correctional institution, the subjects of the report and to any inmates or officers whom the panel concludes may have been exposed to HIV infection as established by provisions of this title. *(Added by Stats 1988 ch 1579 §2; amended by Stats 1991 ch 768 §1, eff. 10/10/91 only until 1/1/95, oper. only until 7/1/94.)*

§7516.5. Appeals to superior court.

Any decision by a panel pursuant to Section 7515 or 7516 may be appealed to the superior court, either by a law enforcement employee filing a report pursuant to Section 7510, a person requesting an HIV test pursuant to Section 7512, a medical officer convening a panel pursuant to Section 7516, or any person required to be tested pursuant to a panel's decision. A person required to be tested pursuant to Section 7512.5 may also appeal the decision to the superior court.

The court shall schedule a hearing as expeditiously as possible to review the decision of the panel or a decision made pursuant to Section 7512.5. The court shall uphold the decision being appealed if that decision is based upon substantial evidence. *(Added by Stats 1988 ch 1579 §2; amended by Stats 1991 ch 768 §1, eff. 10/10/91 only until 1/1/95, oper. only until 7/1/94.)*

§7516.8. Distribution of copies of decision.

It shall be the responsibility of the chief medical officer to see that copies of the hearing decision are distributed in accordance with requirements of this chapter. *(Added by Stats 1988 ch 1579 §2; amended by Stats 1991 ch 768 §1, eff. 10/10/91 only until 1/1/95, oper. only until 7/1/94.)*

§7517. All records confidential.

Except as otherwise permitted by this title or any provision of law, any records, including decisions of a chief medical officer or an appeals panel, compiled pursuant to this chapter shall be confidential. *(Added by Stats 1988 ch 1579 §2; amended by Stats 1991 ch 768 §1, eff. 10/10/91 only until 1/1/95, oper. only until 7/1/94.)*

§7518. Guidelines of Department of Health Services.

(a) The State Department of Health Services shall, in consultation with local and state law enforcement agencies, county health officers, and federal health authorities, adopt guidelines for the making of decisions pursuant to this chapter.

(b) Oversight responsibility for implementation of Section 7515 in state prisons shall be vested with the Chief of Medical Services in the Department of Corrections. Oversight responsibility for implementation of Section 7515 in California Youth Authority facilities shall be vested with the Chief of Medical Services in the Department of the Youth Authority. Oversight responsibility for implementation of Section 7515 with respect to reports involving parole or probation officers shall be vested with the Chief of Parole and Community Services Division in the Department of Corrections.

Oversight responsibility at the county level shall rest with the county health officer. *(Added by Stats 1988 ch 1579 §2; amended by Stats 1991 ch 768 §1, eff. 10/10/91 only until 1/1/95, oper. only until 7/1/94.)*

§7519. Refusal to submit to testing.

(a) When an individual, including a minor charged with an offense for which he or she may be made a ward of the court under Section 602 of the Welfare and Institutions Code, has either been charged with a crime, but is not being held in a correctional institution due to his or her release, either through the granting of bail, a release on the individual's own recognizance, or for any other reason, or been convicted of a crime, but not held in a correctional institution due to the imposition of probation, a fine, or any other alternative sentence, and the individual is required to undergo initial or followup testing pursuant to this title, the failure of the individual to submit to the test may be grounds for revocation of the individual's release or probation or other sentence, whichever is applicable.

(b) Any refusal by a parolee or probationer to submit to testing required pursuant to this title may be ruled as a violation of the person's parole or probation. *(Added by Stats 1988 ch 1579 §2; amended by Stats 1991 ch 768 §1, eff. 10/10/91 only until 1/1/95, oper. only until 7/1/94.)*

CHAPTER 3

NOTIFICATION REQUIREMENT

§7520. Notification of test results to parole or probation officer.

Upon the release of an inmate from a correctional institution, a medical representative of the institution shall notify the inmate's parole or probation officer, where it is the case, that the inmate has tested positive for infection with HIV, or has been diagnosed as having AIDS or AIDS-related conditions. The representative of the correctional institution shall obtain the latest available medical information concerning any precautions which should be taken under the circumstances, and shall convey that information to the parole or probation officer.

When a parole or probation officer learns from responsible medical authorities that a parolee or probationer under his or her jurisdiction has AIDS, or AIDS-related conditions, or has tested positive for HIV infection, the parole or probation officer shall be responsible for ensuring that the parolee or probationer contacts the county health department in order to be, or through his or her own physician and surgeon is, made aware of counseling and treatment for AIDS commensurate with that available to the general population of that county. *(Added by Stats 1988 ch 1579 §2; amended by Stats 1991 ch 768 §1, eff. 10/10/91 only until 1/1/95, oper. only until 7/1/94.)*

§7521. Informing spouse and arresting officers.

(a) When a parole or probation officer learns from responsible medical authorities that a parolee or probationer in his or her custody has any of the conditions listed in Section 7520, but that the parolee or probationer has not properly informed his or her spouse, the officer may ensure that this information is relayed to the spouse only through either the chief medical officer of the institution from which the person was released or the physician and surgeon treating the spouse or the parolee or probationer. The parole or probation officer shall seek to ensure that proper counseling accompanies release of this information to the spouse, through the person providing the information to the inmate's spouse.

(b) If a parole or probation officer has received information from appropriate medical authorities that one of his or her parolees or probationers has AIDS or AIDS-related conditions, and the parolee or probationer has a record of assault on a peace officer, and the officer seeks the aid of local law enforcement officers to apprehend or take into custody the parolee or probationer, he or she shall inform the officers assisting him or her in apprehending or taking into custody the parolee or probationer, of the person's condition, to aid them in protecting themselves from contracting AIDS.

(c) Local law enforcement officers receiving information pursuant to this subdivision shall maintain confidentiality of information received pursuant to subdivision (b). Willful use or disclosure of this information is a misdemeanor. Parole or probation officers who willfully or negligently disclose information about AIDS infection, other than as prescribed under this title or any other provision of law, shall also be guilty of a misdemeanor. *(Added by Stats 1988 ch 1579 §2; amended by Stats 1991 ch 768 §1, eff. 10/10/91 only until 1/1/95, oper. only until 7/1/94.)*

§7522. Notification by supervisory and medical personnel.

(a) Supervisory and medical personnel in correctional institutions shall notify all law enforcement employees when those employees have had direct contact with the bodily fluids of, inmates or persons charged or in custody who either have tested positive for infection with HIV, or been diagnosed as having AIDS or AIDS-related conditions.

(b) Supervisory and medical personnel at correctional institutions shall provide to employees covered by this section the latest medical information regarding precautions to be taken under the circumstances, and shall furnish proper protective clothing and other necessary protective devices or equipment, and instruct staff on the applicability of this title. *(Added by Stats 1988 ch 1579 §2; amended by Stats 1991 ch 768 §1, eff. 10/10/91 only until 1/1/95, oper. only until 7/1/94.)*

§7523. Disclosure of information.

Information obtained by a law enforcement employee pursuant to this chapter shall be confidential, and shall not be disclosed except as specifically authorized by this chapter. Information obtained by a member of a panel pursuant to Section 7515 or 7516 shall not be disclosed except as authorized by this title. *(Added by Stats 1988 ch 1579 §2; amended by Stats 1991 ch 768 §1, eff. 10/10/91 only until 1/1/95, oper. only until 7/1/94.)*

CHAPTER 4

TESTING PROCEDURES

§7530. Procedures for HIV testing.

The following procedures shall apply to testing conducted under this title:

(a) The withdrawal of blood shall be performed in a medically approved manner. Only a physician, registered nurse, licensed vocational nurse, licensed medical technician, or licensed phlebotomist may withdraw blood specimens for the purposes of this title.

(b) The chief medical officer, as specified in Chapter 2 (commencing with Section 7510), shall order that the blood specimens be transmitted to a licensed medical laboratory which has been approved by the State Department of Health Services for the conducting of HIV testing, and that tests including all readily available confirmatory tests, be conducted thereon for medically accepted indications of exposure to or infection with HIV. The State Department of Health Services shall adopt standards for the approval of medical laboratories for the conducting of HIV testing under this title. The State Department of Health Services shall adopt standards for the conducting of tests under Section 7530.

(c) Copies of the test results shall be sent by the laboratory to the chief medical officer who made the decision under either Section 7511 or 7512 or who convened the panel under Section 7515 or 7516. The laboratory shall be responsible for protecting the confidentiality of these test results. Willful or negligent breach of this responsibility shall be grounds for a violation of the contract.

(d) The test results shall be sent by the chief medical officer to the designated recipients with the following disclaimer:

"The tests were conducted in a medically approved manner but tests cannot determine exposure to or infection by AIDS or other communicable diseases with absolute accuracy. Persons receiving this test result should continue to monitor their own health and should consult a physician as appropriate."

(e) If the person subject to the test is a minor, copies of the test result shall also be sent to the minor's parents or guardian.

(f) All persons, other than the test subject, who receive test results shall maintain the confidentiality of personal identifying data relating to the test results, except for disclosure which may be necessary to obtain medical or psychological care or advice, or to comply with this title.

(g) The specimens and the results of the tests shall not be admissible evidence in any criminal or disciplinary proceeding.

(h) Any person performing testing, transmitting test results, or disclosing information in accordance with this title shall be immune from civil liability for any action undertaken in accordance with this title. *(Added by Stats 1988 ch 1579 §2; amended by Stats 1991 ch 768 §1, eff. 10/10/91 only until 1/1/95, oper. only until 7/1/94.)*

§7531. Positive test results.

Notwithstanding any other provision of law, no positive test results obtained pursuant to this title shall be disclosed to any person unless the initial positive test result has been confirmed by appropriate confirmatory tests for positive reactors. *(Added by*

© 1992 by J., B. & L. Gould
Printed in the U.S.A.   EP

Stats 1988 ch 1579 §2; amended by Stats 1991 ch 768 §1, eff. 10/10/91 only until 1/1/95, oper. only until 7/1/94.)

CHAPTER 5

PENALTIES

§7540. Acts which are misdemeanors.

A person committing any of the following acts shall be guilty of a misdemeanor:

(a) Willful false reporting in conjunction with a report or a request for testing under this title.

(b) Willful use or disclosure of test results or confidential information in violation of any of the provisions of this title. *(Added by Stats 1988 ch 1579 §2; amended by Stats 1991 ch 768 §1, eff. 10/10/91 only until 1/1/95, oper. only until 7/1/94.)*

CHAPTER 6

MISCELLANEOUS PROVISIONS

§7550. Standardized forms.

The State Department of Health Services shall prepare standardized forms for the reports, notices, and findings required by this title, and distribute these forms to the Department of Corrections, the Department of the Youth Authority, and to each county health officer within three months of the effective date of this title. *(Added by Stats 1988 ch 1579 §2; amended by Stats 1991 ch 768 §1, eff. 10/10/91 only until 1/1/95, oper. only until 7/1/94.)*

§7551. Responsibilities of agency.

A correctional, custodial, or law enforcement agency to which this title applies shall be responsible for informing staff of the provisions of this title, and assisting in its implementation as it applies to the respective agency. *(Added by Stats 1988 ch 1579 §2; amended by Stats 1991 ch 768 §1, eff. 10/10/91 only until 1/1/95, oper. only until 7/1/94.)*

§7552. AIDS and HIV prevention programs.

(a) It is recommended that every city or county correctional, custodial, and law enforcement agency to which this title applies have a comprehensive AIDS and HIV prevention and education program in operation, by March 31, 1989. Recommended goals for the programs include all of the following:

(1) Education. Implementation of an educational plan which includes education and training for officers, support staff, and inmates on the prevention and transmission of HIV, with regular updates, at least every three months, with all persons held in custody for at least 12 hours in a correctional institution being provided at least with a pamphlet approved by the county health officer, with more detailed education for persons kept beyond three days.

(2) Body fluid precautions. Because all bodily fluids are considered as potentially infectious, supplying all employees of correctional institutions with the necessary equipment and supplies to follow accepted universal bodily fluids precautions, including gloves and devices to administer cardiopulmonary resuscitation, when dealing with infected persons or those in high-risk groups for HIV infection.

(3) Separate housing for infected individuals. Making available adequate separate housing facilities for housing inmates who have tested positive for HIV infection and who continue to engage in activities which transmit HIV, with facilities comparable to those of other inmates with access to recreational and educational facilities, commensurate with the facilities available in the correctional institution.

(4) Adequate AIDS medical services. The provision of medical services appropriate for the diagnosis and treatment of HIV infection.

(5) These guidelines are advisory only and do not constitute a state mandate.

(b) The program shall require confidentiality of information in accordance with this title and other provisions of the law.

(c) The Board of Corrections and the State Department of Health Services shall assist in developing the programs. *(Added by Stats 1988 ch 1579 §2; amended by Stats 1991 ch 768 §1, eff. 10/10/91 only until 1/1/95, oper. only until 7/1/94.)*

§7553. Surveys of inmates.

With the approval of the county health officer, the State Department of Health Services, as it deems necessary for HIV detection and prevention, may conduct periodic anonymous unlinked serologic surveys of all or portions of the inmate population or persons under custody within a city or county. *(Added by Stats 1988 ch 1579 §2; amended by Stats 1991 ch 768 §1, eff. 10/10/91 only until 1/1/95, oper. only until 7/1/94.)*

§7554. Peace officers' occupational exposure to HIV.

(a) The purpose of this section is to establish the extent of peace officers' occupational exposure for HIV infection.

(b) The correctional, custodial, or law enforcement agency to which this title applies or the chief medical officer of a correctional, custodial, or law enforcement agency to which this title applies shall report each reportable incident involving a law enforcement employee under this title together with the disposition of each case to the State Department of Health Services.

The report shall include all of the following: the assignment of the law enforcement employee; the type of incident; the type of injury sustained; the treatment rendered to the injured employee; citations to criminal laws which were allegedly violated; and the identity of the employing agency. Under no circumstances shall the identity of the law enforcement employee or the source person be transmitted by the local law enforcement agency or the chief medical officer of the local agency to the State Department of Health Services.

(c) The State Department of Health Services shall release the data, upon written request, to any law enforcement agency or to any bona fide, nonprofit law enforcement research body primarily concerned with peace officer health issues, provided that the identity of any law enforcement employee, any person who is the subject of a report, or any tested person under this title shall remain anonymous. Any unauthorized release of information leading to the identity of a person whose identity is protected under this section shall constitute a misdemeanor.

(d) The State Department of Health Services shall report to the Legislature on or before July 1 of each year regarding the number, type, and disposition of each report described in subdivision (b), with an evaluation of that data, provided that the reported information does not disclose the identity of any individual law enforcement employee.

(e) For purposes of this section, a "reportable incident" means an incident described in subdivision (a) of Section 7510. A "source person" means a person whose bodily fluids are believed to have contacted the bodily fluids of a law enforcement employee as described in subdivision (a) of Section 7510. *(Added by Stats 1990 ch 1138 §1; amended by Stats 1991 ch 768 §4, eff. 10/10/91 only until 1/1/95, oper. only until 7/1/94.)*

§7555. Repeal date of title.

This title shall remain operative only until July 1, 1994, and as of January 1, 1995, is repealed, unless a later enacted statute, which is enacted before January 1, 1995, deletes or extends the dates upon which this title becomes inoperative and is repealed.

Notwithstanding this section, whenever, prior to July 1, 1994, a law enforcement agency employee has filed a report pursuant to Section 7510, or a request for a human immunodeficiency virus (HIV) test has been filed pursuant to Section 7512, or any other procedure for requiring a test has been commenced pursuant to this title, the proceedings shall be permitted to continue on or after July 1, 1994, until they have been concluded. *(Added by Stats 1991 ch 768 §5, eff. 10/10/91 only until 1/1/95, oper. only until 7/1/94.)*

TITLE 9

LIVE-IN ALTERNATIVE TO INCARCERATION REHABILITATION PROGRAMS WITH SPECIAL FOCUS ON SUBSTANCE ABUSERS
(Added by Stats 1990 ch 398 §1, eff. 1/1/91.)

§8000. Legislative findings.

The Legislature finds and declares that the existence of live-in alternative to incarceration rehabilitation programs with special focus on substance abusers provide a useful alternative to incarceration and promotes the resumption of useful lives by persons with impairments caused by drug or alcohol abuse, or persons with criminal records who, because of these impairments, cannot be absorbed into the competitive labor market, or who otherwise have little or no chance of rehabilitation. *(Added by Stats 1990 ch 398 §1, eff. 1/1/91.)*

§8001. Live-in alternative to incarceration rehabilitation program with special focus on substances abusers.

For purposes of this title, a live-in alternative to incarceration rehabilitation program with special focus on substance abusers means any long-term (two-year minimum) private, nonprofit program that has operated and complied with the following conditions for at least five years prior to the effective date of this section:

(a) Participants live full time at the program site and receive room and board, and all necessary support at no cost to the participant.

(b) All necessary support shall include reasonable medical, dental, psychological, and legal services, counseling, entertainment, clothing, academic, life-skills, and interpersonal education, vocational training, rehabilitation, transportation, and recreation activities.

(c) Neither the directors nor the officers of the program shall be compensated in any manner other than the manner in which the participants of the program are compensated.

(d) The program shall not be operated with any public funds. *(Added by Stats 1990 ch 398 §1, eff. 1/1/91.)*

§8002. Provisions exempt from Labor Code.

Notwithstanding any other provision of law, the participants, director, and staff of a live-in alternative to incarceration rehabilitation program with special focus on substance abusers, when participating in operations owned and operated by the program, are exempt from the wage and hour provisions and Section 1025 of the Labor Code, so long as all revenues generated by the operation are used for the support of the program. All providers who bid on public work shall include in their bid the prevailing wage rate as required by the request. *(Added by Stats 1990 ch 398 §1, eff. 1/1/91.)*

TITLE 10

GENERAL PROVISIONS

§10000. Provisions of Part 3 construed as restatements.

The provisions of Part 3 (commencing with Section 2000), insofar as they are substantially the same as existing provisions relating to the same subject matter, shall be construed as restatements and continuations thereof and not as new enactments. *(Amended by Stats 1987 ch 828 §167.)*

§10001. Tenure of persons holding office.

All persons who, at the time this act goes into effect, hold office under any of the acts repealed by this act, which offices are continued by this act, continue to hold the same according to the former tenure thereof.

§10002. Effect of act on pending actions.

No action or proceeding commenced before this act takes effect, and no right accrued, is affected by the provisions of this act, but all procedure thereafter taken therein shall conform to the provisions of this act so far as possible.

§10003. Severability.

If any portion of Part 3 (commencing with Section 2000) is held unconstitutional, that decision shall not affect the validity of any other portion of Part 3 (commencing with Section 2000). *(Amended by Stats 1987 ch 828 §168.)*

§10004. Headings.

Division, chapter, article, and section headings contained herein shall not be deemed to govern, limit, modify or in any manner affect the scope, meaning or intent of the provisions of any division, chapter, article or section hereof.

§10005. Exercise of powers and duties by deputies, officers or other authorized persons.

Whenever, by the provisions of this act, a power is granted to a public officer or a duty imposed upon such an officer, the power may be exercised or the duty performed by a deputy of the officer or by a person authorized pursuant to law by the officer.

© 1992 by J., B. & L. Gould
Printed in the U.S.A. **EP**

PART 4

OF PREVENTION OF CRIMES AND APPREHENSION OF CRIMINALS

TITLE 1

INVESTIGATION AND CONTROL OF CRIMES AND CRIMINALS

CHAPTER 1

INVESTIGATION, IDENTIFICATION, AND INFORMATION RESPONSIBILITIES OF THE DEPARTMENT OF JUSTICE

ARTICLE 1

ADMINISTRATION

§11006. Appointment of investigators, employees.

The Attorney General shall appoint such agents and other employees as he deems necessary to carry out the provisions of this chapter.

All persons employed after July 1, 1973, within the Department of Justice designated as peace officers and performing investigative duties shall be required by the department to obtain a certificate from the Commission on Peace Officer Standards and Training.

§11008. Training schools for peace officers.

The Attorney General shall from time to time arrange for and organize schools at convenient centers in the State to train peace officers in their powers and duties and in the use of approved equipment and methods for detection, identification and apprehension of criminals.

ARTICLE 2

CRIMINAL INVESTIGATION

§11050. Investigators in statewide crimes.

In any crime of statewide importance, the Attorney General may, upon the request of any district attorney, sheriff or chief of police, assign to such officer so requesting, an investigator or investigators for the investigation or detection of crimes, and the apprehension or prosecution of criminals.

§11050.5. Laboratory facilities, technical experts, criminalists; availability.

(a) The Attorney General may, upon the request of any district attorney, sheriff, chief of police, or other local, state or federal law enforcement official, make available to such official so requesting, the department's laboratory facilities and personnel and the department's technical experts, including but not limited to such personnel as fingerprint examiners, criminalists, document examiners and intelligence specialists for the purpose of assisting in the investigation of criminal matters, the detection of crimes and the apprehension or prosecution of criminals.

(b) The Attorney General may, upon the request of any public defender or private defense counsel appointed by the court, make available to such public defender or such private appointed counsel, the department's laboratory facilities and personnel and the department's technical experts, including but not limited to such personnel as fingerprint examiners, criminalists, document examiners and intelligence specialists for the purpose of assisting in the representation by such public defender or private appointed counsel of persons in criminal proceedings. The Attorney General may contract with each county whose public defender or such private appointed counsel makes requests pursuant to this subdivision for the payment of the reasonable costs of time and material in making available information, services or facilities pursuant to this subdivision. No information, services or facilities shall be made available to such public defender or private appointed counsel unless the county so contracts with the Attorney General.

(c) A copy of any information, including the results of any analysis, furnished by the Attorney General to a public defender, or private defense counsel appointed by the court, pursuant to subdivision (b) shall be sent to the district attorney of the county in which the public defender is located. If this subdivision or its application to any person or circumstance is invalid, subdivision (b) shall not be operative.

(d) The Department of Justice may charge a fee for the laboratory services it performs.

§11051. Department of Justice; duties.

The Department of Justice shall perform such other duties in the investigation, detection, apprehension, prosecution or suppression of crimes as may be assigned by the Attorney General in the performance of his duties under Article V, Section 21 of the Constitution.

§11052. Investigators' powers.

For the purpose of carrying out the provisions of this chapter, the investigators shall have all the powers conferred by law upon any peace officer of this State.

§11053. Additional special investigators during emergency or war.

After the effective date of this chapter, and thereafter until the Governor finds and proclaims that an emergency no longer exists in preparing for the national defense, or whenever the United States is engaged in war, or whenever a war emergency has been declared to exist by the President of the United States, the Attorney General may appoint for the duration of the war or emergency, as the case may be, such additional special criminal investigators not to exceed nine in number as he deems necessary to carry out the provisions of this chapter. There shall not be more than 15 such investigators employed at any one time. The employment of such investigators shall terminate not later than 90 days after the conclusion of peace or the official termination of the emergency by the President or the Governor.

§11054. Authorization of Attorney General to investigate state agencies or officials.

No investigation of the acts or conduct of any state agency or state official shall be initiated or made through or by the bureau or any employee thereof, without the authorization of the Attorney General particularly specifying the office, department or person to be investigated and the scope and purposes of the investigation.

ARTICLE 2.3

CALIFORNIA CRIMINALISTICS INSTITUTE
(Added by Stats 1986 ch 1040 §1.)

§11060. Purposes.

There is hereby established in the Bureau of Forensic Services of the Department of Justice the California Criminalistics Institute.

The purposes of the institute shall include, but need not be limited to, the facilitation of a comprehensive and coordinated approach to meet the high technology forensic science needs of crime laboratories operated by the department and local law enforcement agencies, the provision of a statewide upgrading of advanced laboratory services incorporating new and developing technologies, the provision of training and methodology development for all law enforcement agencies, and the handling of advanced casework laboratory referral services.

The California Criminalistics Institute is intended for use by state and local forensic scientists and law enforcement personnel. Priorities regarding training and methodology development shall be established and monitored by a users' advisory board to be chaired by the Chief of the Bureau of Forensic Services of the Department of Justice and shall be comprised of representatives from the California Association of Criminalistics (CAC), the California Association of Crime Laboratory Directors (CACLD), the California Association of Toxicologists (CAT), the California Division of the International Association of Identification (IAI), the Drug Enforcement Administration (DEA), the Federal Bureau of Investigation (FBI), and the Peace Officers Standards and Training (POST). Members of the users' advisory board shall be selected by member organizations. *(Added by Stats 1986 ch 1040 §1.)*

ARTICLE 2.5

CRIMINAL RECORD DISSEMINATION

§11075. Criminal offender record information defined.

(a) As used in this article, "criminal offender record information" means records and data compiled by criminal justice agencies for purposes of identifying criminal offenders and of maintaining as to each such offender a summary of arrests, pretrial proceedings, the nature and disposition of criminal charges, sentencing, incarceration, rehabilitation, and release.

(b) Such information shall be restricted to that which is recorded as the result of an arrest, detention, or other initiation of criminal proceedings or of any consequent proceedings related thereto.

§11076. Agencies to which criminal offender information disseminated.

Criminal offender record information shall be disseminated, whether directly or through any intermediary, only to such agencies as are, or may subsequently be, authorized access to such records by statute.

§11077. Responsibilities of Attorney General.

The Attorney General is responsible for the security of criminal offender record information. To this end, he shall:

(a) Establish regulations to assure the security of criminal offender record information from unauthorized disclosures at all levels of operation in this state.

(b) Establish regulations to assure that such information shall be disseminated only in situations in which it is demonstrably required for the performance of an agency's or official's functions.

(c) Coordinate such activities with those of any interstate systems for the exchange of criminal offender record information.

(d) Cause to be initiated for employees of all agencies that maintain, receive, or are eligible to maintain or receive, criminal offender record information a continuing educational program in the proper use and control of criminal offender record information.

(e) Establish such regulations as he finds appropriate to carry out his functions under this article.

§11078. Listing of agencies holding criminal offender record information.

Each agency holding or receiving criminal offender record information in a computerized system shall maintain, for such period as is found by the Attorney General to be appropriate, a listing of the agencies to which it has released or communicated such information.

§11079. Inquiries and investigations by Attorney General.

The Attorney General may conduct such inquiries and investigations as he finds appropriate to carry out functions under this article. He may for this purpose direct any agency that maintains, or has received, or that is eligible to maintain or receive criminal offender records to produce for inspection statistical data, reports, and other information concerning the storage and dissemination of criminal offender record information. Each such agency is authorized and directed to provide such data, reports, and other information.

§11080. Right of access to information.

Nothing in this article shall be construed to affect the right of access of any person or public agency to individual criminal offender record information that is authorized by any other provision of law.

§11080.5. Authorization to receive information concerning parolees.

A chief of police of a city or the sheriff of a county shall be authorized to request and receive relevant information concerning persons when on parole who are or may be residing or temporarily domiciled in that city or county and who have been convicted of a federal crime which could have been prosecuted as a felony under the penal provisions of this state.

§11081. Authorized access.

Nothing in this article shall be construed to authorize access of any person or public agency to individual criminal offender record information unless such access is otherwise authorized by law.

ARTICLE 3

CRIMINAL IDENTIFICATION AND STATISTICS

§11100. File cards of criminal methods of operation.

The Attorney General shall provide for the installation of a proper system and file in the office of the bureau, cards containing an outline of the method of

© 1992 by J., B. & L. Gould
Printed in the U.S.A. **EP**

operation employed by criminals in the commission of crime.

§11101. Filing information regarding felons, violators of military law.

The Attorney General shall procure from any available source, and file for record and report in the office of the bureau, all descriptions, information, and measurements of all persons convicted of a felony, or imprisoned for violating any of the military, naval, or criminal laws of the United States, and of all well-known and habitual criminals.

§11102. Identification systems.

The department may use the following systems of identification: the Bertillon, the fingerprint system, and any system of measurement that may be adopted by law in the various penal institutions of the state.

§11103. Files of all persons confined in penal institutions.

The Attorney General shall keep on file in the office of the bureau a record consisting of duplicates of all measurements, processes, operations, signaletic cards, measurements, and descriptions of all persons confined in penal institutions of the state as far as possible, in accordance with whatever system or systems may be commonly used in the state.

§11104. Systematic record and index.

The Attorney General shall file all measurements, information and descriptions received and shall make a complete and systematic record and index, providing a method of convenience, consultation, and comparison.

§11105. State summary criminal history information; master record.

(a) (1) The Department of Justice shall maintain state summary criminal history information.

(2) As used in this section:

(i) "State summary criminal history information" means the master record of information compiled by the Attorney General pertaining to the identification and criminal history of any person, such as name, date of birth, physical description, fingerprints, date of arrests, arresting agencies and booking numbers, charges, dispositions, and similar data about such person.

(ii) "State summary criminal history information" does not refer to records and data compiled by criminal justice agencies other than the Attorney General, nor does it refer to records of complaints to or investigations conducted by, or records of intelligence information or security procedures of, the office of the Attorney General and the Department of Justice.

(b) The Attorney General shall furnish state summary criminal history information to any of the following, when needed in the course of their duties, provided that when information is furnished to assist an agency, officer, or official of state or local government, a public utility, or any entity, in fulfilling employment, certification, or licensing duties, the provisions of Chapter 1321 of the Statutes of 1974 and of Section 432.7 of the Labor Code shall apply:

(1) The courts of the state.

(2) Peace officers of the state as defined in Section 830.1, subdivisions (a), (b), and (f) of Section 830.2, subdivision (a) of Section 830.3, subdivisions (a) and (b) of Section 830.5, and subdivision (a) of Section 830.31.

(3) District attorneys of the state.

(4) Prosecuting city attorneys of any city within the state.

(5) Probation officers of the state.

(6) Parole officers of the state.

(7) A public defender or attorney of record when representing a person in proceedings upon a petition for a certificate of rehabilitation and pardon pursuant to Section 4852.08 of the Penal Code.

(8) A public defender or attorney of record when representing a person in a criminal case and when authorized access by statutory or decisional law.

(9) Any agency, officer, or official of the state when such criminal history information is required to implement a statute or regulation that expressly refers to specific criminal conduct applicable to the subject person of the state summary criminal history information, and contains requirements or exclusions, or both, expressly based upon such specified criminal conduct.

(10) Any city or county, or city and county, or district, or any officer, or official thereof when access is needed in order to assist such agency, officer, or official in fulfilling employment, certification, or licensing duties, and when such access is specifically authorized by the city council, board of supervisors or governing board of the city, county, or district when such criminal history information is required to implement a statute, ordinance, or regulation that expressly refers to specific criminal conduct applicable to the subject person of the state summary criminal history information, and contains requirements or exclusions, or both, expressly based upon such specified criminal conduct.

(11) The subject of the state summary criminal history information under procedures established under Article 5 (commencing with Section 11120), Chapter 1, Title 1 of Part 4 of the Penal Code.

(12) Any person or entity when access is expressly authorized by statute when such criminal history information is required to implement a statute or regulation that expressly refers to specific criminal conduct applicable to the subject person of the state summary criminal history information, and contains requirements or exclusions, or both, expressly based upon such specified criminal conduct.

(13) Health officers of a city, county, or city and county, or district, when in the performance of their official duties enforcing Section 3110 of the Health and Safety Code.

(14) Any managing or supervising correctional officer of a county jail or other county correctional facility.

(c) The Attorney General may furnish state summary criminal history information upon a showing of a compelling need to any of the following, provided that when information is furnished to assist an agency, officer, or official of state or local government, a public utility, or any entity, in fulfilling employment, certification, or licensing duties, the provisions of Chapter 1321 of the Statutes of 1974 and of Section 432.7 of the Labor Code shall apply:

(1) Any public utility as defined in Section 216 of the Public Utilities Code which operates a nuclear energy facility when access is needed in order to assist in employing persons to work at such facility, provided that, if the Attorney General supplies such data, he

© 1992 by J., B. & L. Gould
Printed in the U.S.A. **EP**

shall furnish a copy of such data to the person to whom the data relates.

(2) To a peace officer of the state other than those included in subdivision (b).

(3) To a peace officer of another country.

(4) To public officers (other than peace officers) of the United States, other states, or possessions or territories of the United States, provided that access to records similar to state summary criminal history information is expressly authorized by a statute of the United States, other states, or possessions or territories of the United States when such information is needed for the performance of their official duties.

(5) To any person when disclosure is requested by a probation, parole, or peace officer with the consent of the subject of the state summary criminal history information and for purposes of furthering the rehabilitation of the subject.

(6) The courts of the United States, other states or territories or possessions of the United States.

(7) Peace officers of the United States, other states, or territories or possessions of the United States.

(8) To any individual who is the subject of the record requested when needed in conjunction with an application to enter the United States or any foreign nation.

(9) Any public utility as defined in Section 216 of the Public Utilities Code, when access is needed in order to assist in employing current or prospective employees who in the course of their employment may be seeking entrance to private residences. The information provided shall be limited to the record of convictions and any arrest for which the person is released on bail or on his or her own recognizance pending trial.

If the Attorney General supplies the data pursuant to this paragraph, the Attorney General shall furnish a copy of the data to the current or prospective employee to whom the data relates.

Any information obtained from the state summary criminal history is confidential and the receiving public utility shall not disclose its contents, other than for the purpose for which it was acquired. The state summary criminal history information in the possession of the public utility and all copies made from it shall be destroyed not more than 30 days after employment or promotion or transfer is denied or granted, except for those cases where a current or prospective employee is out on bail or on his or her own recognizance pending trial, in which case the state summary criminal history information and all copies shall be destroyed not more than 30 days after the case is resolved.

A violation of any of the provisions of this paragraph is a misdemeanor, and shall give the current or prospective employee who is injured by the violation a cause of action against the public utility to recover damages proximately caused by the violations. Any public utility's request for state summary criminal history information for purposes of employing current or prospective employees who may be seeking entrance to private residences in the course of their employment shall be deemed a "compelling need" as required to be shown in this subdivision.

Nothing in this section shall be construed as imposing any duty upon public utilities to request state summary criminal history information on any current or prospective employees.

(10) To any campus of the California State University and Colleges or the University of California, or any four-year college or university accredited by a regional accreditation organization approved by the United States Department of Education, when needed in conjunction with an application for admission by a convicted felon to any special education program for convicted felons, including, but not limited to, university alternatives and halfway houses. Only conviction information shall be furnished. The college or university may require the convicted felon to be fingerprinted, and any inquiry to the department under this section shall include the convicted felon's fingerprints and any other information specified by the department.

(d) Whenever an authorized request for state summary criminal history information pertains to a person whose fingerprints are on file with the Department of Justice and the department has no criminal history of that person, and the information is to be used for employment, licensing, or certification purposes, the fingerprint card accompanying such request for information, if any, may be stamped "no criminal record" and returned to the person or entity making the request.

(e) Whenever state summary criminal history information is furnished as the result of an application and is to be used for employment, licensing or certification purposes, the Department of Justice may charge the person or entity making the request a fee which it determines to be sufficient to reimburse the department for the cost of furnishing such information. In addition, the Department of Justice may add a surcharge to the fee to fund maintenance and improvements to the systems from which the information is obtained. Notwithstanding any other provisions of law, any person or entity required to pay a fee to the department for information received under this section may charge the applicant a fee sufficient to reimburse the person or entity for such expense. All moneys received by the department pursuant to this section, Sections 11105.3 and 12054 of the Penal Code, and Section 13588 of the Education Code shall be deposited in a special account in the General Fund to be available for expenditure by the department to offset costs incurred pursuant to such sections and for maintenance and improvements to the systems from which the information is obtained when appropriated by the Legislature therefor.

(f) Whenever there is a conflict, the processing of criminal fingerprints and fingerprints of applicants for security guard or alarm agent registrations or firearms qualification permits submitted pursuant to Section 7514 of the Business and Professions Code shall take priority over the processing of applicant fingerprints.

(g) It is not a violation of this section to disseminate statistical or research information obtained from a record, provided that the identity of the subject of the record is not disclosed.

(h) It is not a violation of this section to include information obtained from a record in (1) a transcript or record of a judicial or administrative proceeding or (2) any other public record when the inclusion of the information in the public record is authorized by a court, statute, or decisional law.

(i) Notwithstanding any other provision of law, the Department of Justice or any state or local law enforcement agency may require the submission of

© 1992 by J., B. & L. Gould
Printed in the U.S.A.   **EP**

fingerprints for the purpose of conducting summary criminal history information checks which are authorized by law. *(Amended by Stats 1990 ch 1570 §2, eff. 1/1/91.)*

§11105.01. State summary criminal history information; additional recipients.

In addition to furnishing state summary criminal history information to the persons and entities set forth in Section 11105 and subject to the requirements and conditions set forth in that section, the Attorney General shall furnish state summary criminal history information to the Director, the Deputy Director for Security, and lottery security officers of the California State Lottery. *(Added by Stats 1986 ch 55 §27.)*

§11105.05. Information regarding Olympic Game personnel; destruction.

Any information generated pursuant to the provisions of paragraph (11) of subdivision (c) of Section 11105 shall be destroyed at the end of the limitation period for the filing of a civil action arising out of the screening or accreditation of persons as current or prospective employees, concessionaires and contractors and their subcontractors, agents and employees for Olympic Games purposes. The knowing and willful failure to (1) notify the recipient as required by Section 11105, or (2) to destroy any information as required by this section, is a misdemeanor punishable in a county jail not exceeding one year or by a fine not exceeding one thousand dollars ($1,000) or both.

§11105.1. Persons furnished with state summary criminal history information.

(a) The following persons shall be furnished with state summary criminal history information when needed in the course of their duties:

(1) The director of a state hospital or other treatment facility to which a person is committed for treatment under Sections 1026 and 1370 of the Penal Code, or Section 5250, if committed for being dangerous to others, or Section 5300, or former Section 6316 or 6321, of the Welfare and Institutions Code.

(2) The community program director or the director's designee under any of the following conditions:

(A) When ordered to evaluate a defendant for the court under paragraph (2) of subdivision (a) of Section 1370 and subdivision (b) of Section 1026 of the Penal Code, or paragraph (2) of subdivision (a) of former Section 6316 of the Welfare and Institutions Code.

(B) When ordered to provide outpatient treatment and supervision services under Title 15 (commencing with Section 1600) of Part 2 of the Penal Code.

(C) When a patient is committed for being dangerous to others under Section 5250 of the Welfare and Institutions Code.

(D) When the director or the director's designee provides evaluation, supervision, or treatment for a person under Section 2964 or 2972.

(3) The officer providing conservatorship investigation under Section 5354 of the Welfare and Institutions Code in cases where referral for conservatorship is made while the proposed conservatee is being treated under Section 1026 or 1370 of the Penal Code or Section 5250, if committed for being dangerous to others, or Section 5300, or former Section 6316 or 6321, of the Welfare and Institutions Code.

(b) In all instances pursuant to subdivision (a), the criminal history record shall be transmitted by the court with the request for evaluation or during the conservatorship investigation or with the order committing the person to a treatment facility or approving outpatient status, except that the director of a state hospital, the county mental health director, and the officer providing conservatorship investigation may receive the state summary criminal history information from the law enforcement agency that referred the person for evaluation and treatment under Section 5150 of the Welfare and Institutions Code if the person has been subsequently committed for being dangerous to others under Section 5250 of the Welfare and Institutions Code. Information obtained under this subdivision shall not be included in any document which will become part of a public record. *(Amended by Stats 1988 ch 657 §3, eff. 1/1/89.)*

§11105.2. Subsequent arrest notification.

(a) The Department of Justice may provide subsequent arrest notification to any agency authorized by Section 11105 to receive state summary criminal history information to assist in fulfilling employment, licensing, or certification duties upon the arrest of any person whose fingerprints are maintained on file at the Department of Justice as the result of an application for licensing, employment, or certification. The notification shall consist of a current copy of the person's state summary criminal history transcript.

(b) Any agency, other than a law enforcement agency employing peace officers as defined in Section 830.1, subdivisions (a), (b), and (f) of Section 830.2, subdivision (a) of Section 830.3, subdivisions (a) and (b) of Section 830.5, and subdivision (a) of Section 830.31, shall enter into a contract with the Department of Justice in order to receive notification of subsequent arrests for licensing, employment, or certification purposes.

(c) Any agency which submits the fingerprints of applicants for licensing, employment, or certification to the Department of Justice for the purpose of establishing a record of the applicant to receive notification of subsequent arrests shall immediately notify the department when the employment of the applicant is terminated, when the applicant's license or certificate is revoked, or when the applicant may no longer renew or reinstate the license or certificate. The Department of Justice shall terminate subsequent arrest notification on any applicant upon the request of the licensing, employment, or certifying authority.

(d) Any agency receiving a notification of subsequent arrest for a person unknown to the agency, or for a person no longer employed by the agency, or no longer eligible to renew the certificate or license for which subsequent arrest notification service was established shall immediately return the subsequent arrest notification to the Department of Justice, informing the department that the agency is no longer interested in the applicant. The agency shall not record or otherwise retain any information received as a result of the subsequent arrest notice.

(e) Any agency which submits the fingerprints of an applicant for employment, licensing, or certification to the Department of Justice for the purpose of establishing a record at the department to receive notification of subsequent arrest shall immediately notify the department if the applicant is not subsequently employed, or if the applicant is denied licensing or certification.

(f) An agency which fails to provide the Department of Justice with notification as set forth in subdivisions (c), (d), and (e) may be denied further subsequent arrest notification service.

(g) Notwithstanding subdivisions (c), (d), and (f), subsequent arrest notification by the Department of Justice and retention by the employing agency shall continue as to retired peace officers listed in subdivision (c) of Section 830.5. (Amended by Stats 1987 ch 56 §138.)

§11105.3. Sex offender's records, where employment involves minors.

(a) Notwithstanding any other provision of law, a human resource agency or an employer may request from the Department of Justice records of all convictions or any arrest for which the person is released on bail or on his or her own recognizance pending trial, involving any sex crimes, drug crimes, or crimes of violence of a person who applies for a license, employment, or volunteer position, in which he or she would have supervisory or disciplinary power over a minor or any person under their care. The department shall furnish the information to the requesting employer and shall also send a copy of the information to the applicant.

(b) Any request for records under subdivision (a) shall include the applicant's fingerprints, which may be taken by the requester, and any other data specified by the department. The request shall be on a form approved by the department, and the department may charge a fee to be paid by the requester for the actual cost of processing the request. However, no fee shall be charged a nonprofit organization or any agency responsible for the licensing of facilities pursuant to Article 1 (commencing with Section 1500) of Chapter 3, Chapter 3.2 (commencing with Section 1569), and Chapter 3.4 (commencing with Section 1596.70) of Division 2 of the Health and Safety Code for processing the request. The department shall destroy an application within six months after the requested information is sent to the employer and applicant.

(c) A human resource agency may request from the Department of Justice full criminal history records, to the extent those records are otherwise available under Section 226.55 of the Civil Code, or Section 1522 of the Health and Safety Code, for persons who apply to the agency to adopt a child or to be a foster parent. Requests for criminal history information obtained pursuant to this subdivision shall be used only for the purposes stated in and in compliance with any requirements or conditions provided in those sections.

(d) The department shall adopt regulations to implement the provisions of this section.

(e) As used in this section, "employer" means any nonprofit corporation or other organizations specified by the Attorney General which employs or uses the services of volunteers in positions in which the volunteer or employee has supervisory or disciplinary power over a child or children.

(f) As used in this section, "human resource agency" means a public or private entity, excluding any agency responsible for licensing of facilities pursuant to the California Community Care Facilities Act (Chapter 3 (commencing with Section 1500)), the California Residential Care Facilities for the Elderly Act (Chapter 3.2 (commencing with Section 1569)), Chapter 3.01 (commencing with Section 1568.01), and the California Child Day Care Facilities Act (Chapter 3.4 (commencing with Section 1596.70)) of Division 2 of the Health and Safety Code, responsible for determining the character and fitness of a person who is (1) applying for a license, employment, or as a volunteer within the human services field that involves the care and security of children, the elderly, the handicapped, or the mentally impaired, or (2) applying to adopt a child or to be a foster parent.

(g) As used in this section, "sex crime" means a conviction for a violation or attempted violation of Section 220, 261, 261.5, 264.1, 267, 272, 273a, 273d, 285, 286, 288, 288a, 289, 314, 647.6, or former Section 647a, or subdivision (d) of Section 647, or commitment as a mentally disordered sex offender under former Article 1 (commencing with Section 6300) of Chapter 2 of Part 2 of Division 6 of the Welfare and Institutions Code.

(h) As used in this section, "drug crime" means any crime described in the California Uniform Controlled Substances Act (Division 10 (commencing with Section 11000) of the Health and Safety Code), provided that, except as otherwise provided in subdivision (c), no record of a misdemeanor conviction shall be transmitted to the requester unless the subject of the request has a total of three or more misdemeanor or felony convictions defined in this subdivision or subdivision (g) within the immediately preceding 10-year period.

(i) As used in this section, "crime of violence" means any felony or misdemeanor conviction within 10 years of the date of the employer's request under subdivision (a), for any of the offenses specified in subdivision (c) of Section 667.5 or a violation or attempted violation of Chapter 3 (commencing with Section 207), Chapter 8 (commencing with Section 236), or Chapter 9 (commencing with Section 240) of Title 8 of Part 1, provided that, except as otherwise provided in subdivision (c), no record of a misdemeanor conviction shall be transmitted to the requester unless the subject of the request has a total of three or more misdemeanor or felony convictions defined in this subdivision or subdivision (g) within the immediately preceding 10-year period.

(j) Conviction for a violation or attempted violation of an offense committed outside the State of California is a sex crime, drug crime, or crime of violence if the offense would have been a crime as defined in this section if committed in California.

(k) Any criminal history information obtained pursuant to this section is confidential and no recipient shall disclose its contents other than for the purpose for which it was acquired. (Amended by Stats 1991 ch 937 §5, eff. 1/1/92.)

§11105.4. Access of private security organizations to criminal history information.

(a) Notwithstanding any other provision of law, a contract or proprietary security organization may request the following criminal history information concerning its prospective employees:

(1) Any criminal history information that a human resource agency may request pursuant to Section 11105.3, except criminal history information described in subdivision (c) of that section.

(2) Any criminal history information that a bank may request pursuant to Section 777.5 of the Financial Code.

(b) The Department of Justice shall promulgate regulations to assure that criminal record information

© 1992 by J., B. & L. Gould
Printed in the U.S.A. **EP**

is not released to persons or entities not authorized to receive the information under this section.

(c) Any criminal history information obtained pursuant to this section shall be subject to the same requirements and conditions that the information is subject to when obtained by a human resource agency or a bank.

(d) The Legislature finds that contract security organizations and private security organizations often provide security service for financial institutions and human resource agencies, and, consequently, they have the same need for criminal history information as do those entities. Therefore, the Legislature intends to provide authority for contract security organizations and proprietary security organizations to obtain criminal history information to the extent that financial institutions and human resource agencies have that authority concerning their own employees.

(e) As used in this section, "contract security organization" means a person, business, or organization licensed to provide services as a private patrol operator, as defined in subdivision (b) of Section 7521 of the Business and Professions Code.

As used in this section, "proprietary security organization" means an organization within a business entity that has the primary responsibility of protecting the employees and property of its employer, and which allocates a substantial part of its annual budget to providing security and protective services for its employer, including providing qualifying and in-service training to members of the organization.

(f) Any criminal history information obtained pursuant to this section is confidential and no recipient shall disclose its contents other than for the purpose for which it was acquired. (*Added by Stats 1990 ch 1570 §4, eff. 1/1/91.*)

§11105.5. Notice of sealed record.

When the Department of Justice receives a report that the record of a person has been sealed under Section 851.7, 851.8, or 1203.45, it shall send notice of that fact to all officers and agencies that it had previously notified of the arrest or other proceedings against the person. (*Amended by Stats 1985 ch 106 §109.*)

§11106. Attorney General's records.

(a) In order to assist in the investigation of crime, the arrest and prosecution of criminals, and the recovery of lost, stolen, or found property, the Attorney General shall keep and properly file a complete record of all copies of fingerprints, copies of applications for licenses to carry concealed weapons, dealers' records of sales of firearms, reports provided pursuant to subdivision (a) of Section 12078, forms provided pursuant to Section 12084, and reports of stolen, lost, found, pledged, or pawned property in any city or county of this state, and shall, upon proper application therefor, furnish to the officers mentioned in Section 11105, hard copy printouts of those records as photographic, photostatic, and nonerasable optically stored reproductions.

(b) Notwithstanding subdivision (a), the Attorney General shall not retain or compile any information from reports filed pursuant to subdivision (a) of Section 12078 for firearms that are not pistols, revolvers, or other firearms capable of being concealed upon the person, from forms submitted pursuant to Section 12084 for firearms that are not pistols, revolvers, or

other firearms capable of being concealed upon the person, or from dealers' records of sales for firearms that are not pistols, revolvers, or other firearms capable of being concealed upon the person. All copies of the forms submitted pursuant to Section 12084 for firearms that are not pistols, revolvers, or other firearms capable of being concealed upon the person, or of the dealers' records of sales for firearms that are not pistols, revolvers, or other firearms capable of being concealed upon the person shall be destroyed within five days of the clearance by the Attorney General, unless the purchaser or transferor is ineligible to take possession of the firearm. All copies of the reports filed pursuant to subdivision (a) of Section 12078 for firearms that are not pistols, revolvers, or other firearms capable of being concealed upon the person shall be destroyed within five days of the receipt by the Attorney General, unless retention is necessary for use in a criminal prosecution.

A violation of this subdivision is a misdemeanor. (*Amended by Stats 1991 ch 5 §1; ch 951 §1, eff. 1/1/92.*)

§11106.1. Reproduction of original instruments.

Any system of microphotography, optical disk, or reproduction by other techniques which do not permit additions, deletions, or changes to the original document, may be used by the Department of Justice as a photographic reproduction process to record some or all instruments, papers, and notices that are required or permitted by law to be recorded or filed. All storage medium shall comply with minimum standards of quality approved by the National Institute of Standards and Technology. (*Added by Stats 1989 ch 257 §3, eff. 1/1/90.*)

§11106.2. Use of reproductions as originals.

Any criminal justice agency may cause any or all files or records in its official custody to be microphotographed or otherwise reproduced pursuant to Section 11106.1, as in the case of original filings or recordings, or both. Every reproduction shall be deemed and considered an original, and as a transcript, exemplification or certified copy, as the case may be, of the original. (*Added by Stats 1989 ch 257 §4, eff. 1/1/90.*)

§11107. Daily reports of misdemeanors, felonies and sexual exploitation of children.

Each sheriff or police chief executive shall furnish all of the following information to the Department of Justice on standard forms approved by the department:

Daily reports of those misdemeanors and felonies that are required to be reported by the Attorney General including, but not limited to, forgery, fraudbunco, bombings, receiving or selling stolen property, safe and commercial burglary, grand theft, child abuse, homicide, threats, and offenses involving lost, stolen, found, pledged, or pawned property.

The reports required by this section shall describe the nature and character of each such crime and note all particular circumstances thereof and include all additional or supplemental data. The Attorney General may also require that the report shall indicate whether or not the submitting agency considers the information to be confidential because it was compiled for the purpose of a criminal investigation of suspected criminal activities. The term "criminal investigation" includes the gathering and maintenance of information pertaining to suspected criminal activity.

§11107.5. Required reporting by Attorney General to the Legislature concerning child abuse.

The Attorney General shall report annually to the Legislature concerning the information pertaining to the sexual abuse of children reported to the Department of Justice pursuant to Sections 11107 and 11169. No confidential information shall be released in the reports submitted to the Legislature.

§11108. Descriptions of stolen serialized property; reports of stolen nonserialized property.

Each sheriff or police chief executive shall submit descriptions of serialized property which has been reported stolen, lost, found, recovered or under observation, directly into the appropriate Department of Justice automated property system for firearms, stolen bicycles, stolen vehicles, or other property, as the case may be.

Reports of stolen nonserialized property which has unique characteristics or inscriptions permitting accurate identification shall be sent by each sheriff or police chief executive directly to the Special Services Section of the department by letter or teletype.

§11111. Records of stolen and lost bicycles.

The Department of Justice shall maintain records relative to stolen and lost bicycles in the Criminal Justice Information System. Such records shall be accessible to authorized law enforcement agencies through the California Law Enforcement Telecommunications System.

§11112. Fingerprinting for employment purposes.

The Department of Justice, in providing fingerprint clearances for employment purposes, shall facilitate the processing of fingerprint cards of employees of, and applicants for employment with, community care facilities, as defined in Section 1502 of the Health and Safety Code, which provide services to children, and child day care facilities, as defined in Section 1596.750 of the Health and Safety Code. *(Added by Stats 1986 ch 927 §6.)*

§§11112.1 to 11112.7. *See Article 3.5, infra.*

§11113. Fingerprint of deceased persons whose deaths require coroner's inquiry.

Each coroner shall furnish the Department of Justice promptly with copies of fingerprints on standardized eight-inch by eight-inch cards, and descriptions and other identifying data, including date and place of death, of all deceased persons whose deaths are in classifications requiring inquiry by the coroner where the coroner is not satisfied with the decedent's identification. When it is not physically possible to furnish prints of the 10 fingers, prints or partial prints of any fingers, with other identifying data, shall be forwarded by the coroner to the department.

In all cases where there is a criminal record on file in the department for the decedent, the department shall notify the Federal Bureau of Investigation and each California sheriff and chief of police, in whose jurisdiction the decedent has been arrested, of the date and place of death of the decedent.

§11114. *Repealed by Stats 1988 ch 1456 §1, eff. 1/1/89.*

§11114.1. *Repealed by Stats 1988 ch 1456 §2, eff. 1/1/89.*

§11114.2. *Repealed by Stats 1988 ch 1456 §3, eff. 1/1/89.*

§11114.3. *Repealed by Stats 1988 ch 1456 §4, eff. 1/1/89.*

ARTICLE 3.5

FINGERPRINTS

§11112.1. Terms defined.

As used in this article:

(a) "California Identification System" or "Cal-ID" means the automated system maintained by the Department of Justice for retaining fingerprint files and identifying latent fingerprints.

(b) "Remote Access Network" or "RAN" means a uniform statewide network of equipment and procedures allowing local law enforcement agencies direct access to the California Identification System.

(c) "Department" means the Department of Justice.

(d) "Cal-ID Telecommunications System" means a statewide telecommunications network dedicated to the transmission of fingerprint identification data in conjunction with Cal-ID for use by law enforcement agencies.

§11112.2. Master plan for RAN.

The department shall develop a master plan recommending the type, number, and location of equipment necessary to implement RAN. The department shall also develop policy guidelines and administrative procedures to facilitate the implementation and use of RAN. The RAN master plan shall include reasonable interface specifications to access Cal-ID and shall be provided to any supplier of automated fingerprint identification systems interested in bidding on RAN by May 15, 1986.

The master plan shall provide for the use of facsimile and direct image "live read" fingerprint equipment under RAN, including point-of-booking terminals.

The department shall amend the master plan to include additional processing, matching, and communications equipment at the Department of Justice, and to recommend the type, number, and location of equipment necessary to implement facsimile and direct image "live read" fingerprint equipment as part of RAN, including point-of-booking terminals. Funding shall be on a shared basis between the state and a region pursuant to Section 11112.5. *(Amended by Stats 1988 ch 1263 §1, eff. 1/1/89.)*

§11112.3. RAN Advisory Committee.

(a) The Attorney General shall appoint a RAN Advisory Committee to review the master plan, policy guidelines, and administrative procedures prepared by the department and advise the Attorney General of any modifications the committee deems necessary. Final approval and acceptance of the RAN Advisory Committee proposals shall be made by the Attorney General.

© 1992 by J., B. & L. Gould
Printed in the U.S.A.   EP

(b) The RAN Advisory Committee shall be composed of one representative from each of the following: The League of California Cities, California Peace Officers' Association, California District Attorneys' Association, California Police Chiefs' Association, California State Sheriffs' Association, County Supervisors' Association of California, Department of General Services, Office of Information Technology, and the Department of Justice. The members of the committee shall select a chairperson. The members shall serve without compensation, but reasonable and necessary travel and per diem expenses incurred by committee members shall be reimbursed by the department. The RAN Advisory Committee shall terminate January 1, 1989, unless extended by legislation enacted prior thereto. *(Added by Stats 1985 ch 1234 §3.)*

§11112.4. Local RAN boards.

(a) Within each county or group of counties eligible to receive funding under the department's master plan for equipment, which elects to participate in the remote access network, a local RAN board shall be established. Where a single county is eligible to receive funding, that county's RAN board shall be the local RAN board. Where a group of counties is eligible for funding, the local RAN board shall consist of a regional board. The RAN board shall determine the placement of RAN equipment within the county or counties, and coordinate acceptance, delivery, and installation of RAN equipment. The board shall also develop any procedures necessary regulate the ongoing use and maintenance of that equipment, adhering to the policy guidelines and procedures adopted by the department. The local board shall consider placement of equipment on the basis of the following criteria:

(1) The crime rate of the jurisdiction or jurisdictions served by the agency.

(2) The number of criminal offenses reported by the agency or agencies to the department.

(3) The potential number of fingerprint cards and latent fingerprints processed.

(4) The number of sworn personnel of the agency or agencies.

(b) Except as provided in subdivision (c), each RAN board shall be composed of seven members, as follows: a member of the board of supervisors, the sheriff, the district attorney, the chief of police of the department having the largest number of sworn personnel within the county, a second chief selected by all other police chiefs within the county, a mayor elected by the city selection committee established pursuant to Section 50270 of the Government Code, and a member-at-large chosen by the other members. In any county lacking two chiefs of police, a substitute member shall be selected by the other members on the board. Groups of counties forming a region shall establish a seven-member board with each county having equal representation on the board and at least one member-at-large. If the number of participating counties precludes equal representation on a seven-member board, the size of the board shall be expanded so that each county has at least two representatives and there is a single member-at-large.

(c) In any county with a population of 5,000,000 or more, each local board shall be composed of seven members, as follows: a member of the board of supervisors, the sheriff, the district attorney, the chief of police of the department having the largest number of sworn personnel within the county, a second chief

selected by all other police chiefs within the county, the mayor of the city with the greatest population within the county, and a member-at-large chosen by the other members. In any county lacking two chiefs of police, a substitute member shall be selected by the other members of the board.

(d) A county which is a part of a regional board may form a local RAN advisory board. The purpose of the local RAN advisory board shall be to provide advice and recommendations to the county's representatives on the regional RAN board. The local RAN advisory board may appoint alternate members to the regional RAN board from the local RAN advisory board to serve and work in the place of a regional RAN board member who is absent or who disqualifies himself or herself from participation in a meeting of the regional RAN board.

If a vacancy occurs in the office of a regional RAN board in a county which has established a local RAN advisory board, an alternate member selected by the local RAN advisory board may serve and vote in place of the former regional RAN board member until the appointment of a regional RAN board member is made to fill the vacancy. *(Amended by Stats 1987 ch 174 §1.)*

§11112.5. Costs.

(a) Costs for equipment purchases based upon the master plan approved by the Attorney General, including state sales tax, freight, insurance, and installation, shall be prorated between the state and local governmental entity. The state's share shall be 70 percent. The local government's share shall be 30 percent, paid in legal tender. Purchases may be made under the existing Cal-ID contract through the Department of General Services.

(b) Alternatively, at the discretion of the local board, an independent competitive procurement may be initiated under the following conditions:

(1) Prior to submitting a bid in an independent procurement, any prospective bidder must demonstrate the ability to meet or exceed performance levels established in the existing Cal-ID contract and demonstrate the ability to interface with Cal-ID and meet or exceed performance levels established in the existing Cal-ID contract without degrading the performance of the Cal-ID system.

(2) Both qualifying benchmarks will be at the prospective bidder's expense and will be conducted by the Department of Justice.

(3) In the event that no vendor other than the existing contract vendor qualifies to bid, purchases shall be made by the Department of General Services on behalf of local agencies pursuant to the existing Cal-ID contract.

(c) Competitive local procurements must adhere to the following guidelines:

(1) Administrative requirements contained within Section 5200 of the State Administrative Manual shall be met.

(2) Local procurements shall not increase the costs the state would otherwise be obligated to pay.

(3) Final bids submitted in an independent procurement shall contain a signed contract that represents an irrevocable offer that does not materially deviate from the terms and conditions of the existing Cal-ID contract.

(4) The selected vendor shall post a performance bond in an amount equal to 25 percent of the local equipment costs. The bond shall remain in effect until

the local acceptance test has been successfully completed.

(5) Requests for tender, including contract language, shall be approved by the Department of General Services prior to release. The Department of General Services and the Department of Justice shall be represented on the evaluation and selection team.

(d) The local government agency shall be responsible for all costs related to conducting a local bid, site preparation, equipment maintenance, ongoing operational costs, file conversion over and above those records that are available on magnetic media from the Department of Justice, and equipment enhancements or systems design which exceed the basic design specifications of the Department of Justice. The state shall provide sufficient circuitry from Sacramento to each county, or group of counties to handle all fingerprint data traffic. The state shall provide for annual maintenance of that line. *(Added by Stats 1985 ch 1234 §3.)*

§11112.6. Uses and maintenance of the system.

(a) The Cal-ID Telecommunications System shall be under the direction of the Attorney General and shall be used exclusively for the official business of the state, and the official business of any city, county, city and county, or other public agency.

(b) The Cal-ID Telecommunications System shall provide telecommunication lines to one location in every participating county.

(c) The Cal-ID Telecommunications System shall be maintained at all times by the department with equipment and facilities adequate to meet the needs of law enforcement. The system shall be designed to accommodate present and future data transmission equipment. *(Added by Stats 1985 ch 1234 §3.)*

§11112.7. Attorney General's report to Legislature.

The Attorney General shall provide an annual status report to the Legislature beginning January 1, 1987, with the final report due January 1, 1990. The report shall include the status of the project to date, funds expended, and need, if any, for revision to the master plan. *(Amended by Stats 1988 ch 1263 §3, eff. 1/1/89.)*

§§11113 to 11114.3. *See Article 3, supra.*

ARTICLE 4

CRIMINAL RECORDS

§11115. Disposition reports.

In any case in which a sheriff, police department or other law enforcement agency makes an arrest and transmits a report of the arrest to the Department of Justice or to the Federal Bureau of Investigation, it shall be the duty of such law enforcement agency to furnish a disposition report to such agencies whenever the arrested person is transferred to the custody of another agency or is released without having a complaint or accusation filed with a court. The disposition report in such cases shall be furnished to the appropriate agencies within 30 days of release or transfer to another agency.

If either of the following dispositions is made, the disposition report shall so state:

(a) "Arrested for intoxication and released," when the arrested party is released pursuant to paragraph (2) of subdivision (b) of Section 849.

(b) "Detention only," when the detained party is released pursuant to paragraph (1) of subdivision (b) of Section 849 or issued a certificate pursuant to subdivision (b) of Section 851.6. In such cases the report shall state the specific reason for such release, indicating that there was no ground for making a criminal complaint because (1) further investigation exonerated the arrested party, (2) the complainant withdrew the complaint, (3) further investigation appeared necessary before prosecution could be initiated, (4) the ascertainable evidence was insufficient to proceed further, (5) the admissible or adducible evidence was insufficient to proceed further, or (6) other appropriate explanation for release.

§11116.5. Answer to question regarding arrest.

Any dismissal and reason therefor provided by Section 11115 or 13151.1 may be used by the person subject to the disposition as an answer to any question regarding his arrest or detention history or any question regarding the outcome of a criminal proceeding against him.

§11116.6. Entry of disposition.

The dispositions provided by Sections 11115 and 13151.1 must be entered on all appropriate records of the party arrested, detained, or against whom criminal proceedings are brought.

§11116.7. Certificate of disposition.

Whenever an accusatory pleading is filed in any court of this state alleging a public offense for which a defendant may be punished by incarceration, for a period in excess of 90 days, the court shall furnish upon request of the defendant named therein a certificate of disposition which describes the disposition of the accusatory pleading in that court when such disposition is one described in Section 13151.1. The certificate of disposition shall be signed by the judge, shall substantially conform with the requirements of Section 11116.8, and the seal of the court shall be affixed thereto.

In the event that the initial disposition of the accusatory pleading is changed, a new disposition certificate showing the changed disposition shall be issued by the court changing the same upon request of the defendant or his counsel of record.

§11116.8. Certificate of disposition; contents.

The certificate of disposition provided by Section 11116.7 shall describe the charge or charges set forth in the original and any amended accusatory pleading, together with the disposition of each charge in the original and any amended accusatory pleading.

§11116.9. Additional certified copies of disposition certificate.

The clerk of the court in which the disposition is made shall provide the defendant or his counsel of record with additional certified copies of the disposition certificate upon the payment of the fees provided by law for certified copies of court records.

§11116.10. Notice to victim of final disposition of case.

(a) Upon the request of a victim or a witness of a crime, the prosecuting attorney shall, within 60 days of the final disposition of the case, inform the victim or witness by letter of such final disposition. Such

© 1992 by J., B. & L. Gould
Printed in the U.S.A.   **EP**

notice shall state the information described in Section 13151.1.

(b) As used in this section, "victim" means any person alleged or found, upon the record, to have sustained physical or financial injury to person or property as a direct result of the crime charged.

(c) As used in this section, "witness" means any person who has been or is expected to testify for the prosecution, or who, by reason of having relevant information, is subject to call or likely to be called as a witness for the prosecution, whether or not any action or proceeding has yet been commenced.

(d) As used in this section, "final disposition," means an ultimate termination of the case at the trial level including, but not limited to, dismissal, acquittal, or imposition of sentence by the court, or a decision by the prosecuting attorney, for whatever reason, not to file the case.

(e) Subdivision (a) does not apply in any case where the offender or alleged offender is a minor unless the minor has been declared not a fit and proper subject to be dealt with under the juvenile court law.

(f) This section shall not apply to any case in which a disposition was made prior to the effective date of this section. *(Amended by Stats 1986 ch 1427 §2.)*

§11117. Procedures and forms for disposition.

The Department of Justice shall prescribe and furnish the procedures and forms to be used for the disposition and other reports required in this article and in Sections 13151 and 13152. The department shall add the reports received to all appropriate criminal records.

Neither the reports required in this article nor those required in Sections 13151 and 13152 shall be admissible in evidence in any civil action.

ARTICLE 5

EXAMINATION OF RECORDS

§11120. Record defined.

As used in this article, "record" with respect to any person means the state summary criminal history information as defined in subdivision (a) of Section 11105, maintained under such person's name by the Department of Justice.

§11121. Intent of article.

It is the function and intent of this article to afford persons concerning whom a record is maintained in the files of the bureau an opportunity to obtain a copy of the record compiled from such files, and to refute any erroneous or inaccurate information contained therein.

§11122. Application for copy of record.

Any person desiring a copy of the record relating to himself shall obtain an application form furnished by the department which shall require his fingerprints in addition to such other information as the department shall specify. Applications may be obtained from police departments, sheriff departments, or the Department of Justice. The fingerprinting agency may fix a reasonable fee for affixing the applicant's fingerprints to the form, and shall retain such fee.

§11123. Fees.

The applicant shall submit the completed application directly to the department. The application shall be accompanied by a fee not to exceed twenty-five dollars ($25) that the department determines equals the costs of processing the application and providing a copy of the record to the applicant. All fees received by the department under this section are hereby appropriated without regard to fiscal years for the support of the Department of Justice in addition to such other funds as may be appropriated therefor by the Legislature. Any request for waiver of fee shall accompany the original request for the record and shall include a claim and proof of indigency.

§11124. Procedure after receipt of application.

When an application is received by the department, the department shall determine whether a record pertaining to the applicant is maintained. If such record is maintained, the department shall furnish a copy of the record to the applicant or to an individual designated by the applicant. If no such record is maintained, the department shall so notify the applicant or an individual designated by the applicant. Delivery of the copy of the record, or notice of no record, may be by mail or other appropriate means agreed to by the applicant and the department.

§11125. Requiring another to obtain record.

No person or agency shall require another person to obtain a copy of a record or notification that a record exists or does not exist, as provided in Section 11124, unless specifically authorized by law. A violation of this section is a misdemeanor.

§11126. Written request for and correction of record.

(a) If the applicant desires to question the accuracy or completeness of any material matter contained in the record, he may submit a written request to the department in a form established by it. The request shall include a statement of the alleged inaccuracy or incompleteness in the record, and its materiality, and shall specify any proof or corroboration available. Upon receipt of such request, the department shall forward it to the person or agency which furnished the questioned information. Such person or agency shall, within 30 days of receipt of such written request for clarification, review its information and forward to the department the results of such review.

(b) If such agency concurs in the allegations of inaccurateness or incompleteness in the record, and finds that the error is material, it shall correct its record and shall so inform the department, which shall correct the record accordingly. The department shall inform the applicant of its correction of the record under this subdivision within 30 days. The department and the agency shall notify all persons and agencies to which they have disseminated the incorrect record in the past 90 days of the correction of the record, and the applicant shall be informed that such notification has been given. The department and the agency shall also notify those persons or agencies to which the incorrect record has been disseminated which have been specifically requested by the applicant to receive notification of the correction of the record, and the applicant shall be informed that such notification has been given.

(c) If such agency denies the allegations of inaccurateness or incompleteness in the record, the matter shall be referred for administrative adjudication in accordance with Chapter 5 (commencing with Section

11500) of Part 1, Division 3, Title 2 of the Government Code for a determination of whether inaccuracy or incompleteness exists in the record. The agency from which the questioned information originated shall be the respondent in the hearing. If a material inaccuracy or incompleteness is found in any record, the agency in charge of that record shall be directed to correct it accordingly, and to inform the department, which shall correct its record accordingly. The department and the agency shall notify all persons and agencies to which they have disseminated the incorrect record in the past 90 days of the correction of the record, and the applicant shall be informed that such notification has been given. The department and the agency shall also notify those persons or agencies to which the incorrect record has been disseminated which have been specifically requested by the applicant to receive notification of the correction of the record, and the applicant shall be informed that such notification has been given. Judicial review of the decision shall be governed by Section 11523 of the Government Code. The applicant shall be informed of the decision within 30 days of its issuance in accordance with Section 1 1518 of the Government Code.

§11127. Necessary regulations.
The department shall adopt all regulations necessary to carry out the provisions of this article.

ARTICLE 6

UNLAWFUL FURNISHING OF STATE SUMMARY CRIMINAL HISTORY INFORMATION

§11140. Terms defined.
As used in this article:

(a) "Record" means the state summary criminal history information as defined in subdivision (a) of Section 11105, or a copy thereof, maintained under a person's name by the Department of Justice.

(b) "A person authorized by law to receive a record" means any person or public agency authorized by a court, statute, or decisional law to receive a record.

§11141. Employee furnishing information.
Any employee of the Department of Justice who knowingly furnishes a record or information obtained from a record to a person who is not authorized by law to receive the record or information is guilty of a misdemeanor.

§11142. Authorized person furnishing information.
Any person authorized by law to receive a record or information obtained from a record who knowingly furnishes the record or information to a person who is not authorized by law to receive the record or information is guilty of a misdemeanor.

§11143. Buying, receiving, of information.
Any person, except those specifically referred to in Section 1070 of the Evidence Code, who, knowing he is not authorized by law to receive a record or information obtained from a record, knowingly buys, receives, or possesses the record or information is guilty of a misdemeanor.

§11144. When information may be disseminated.
(a) It is not a violation of this article to disseminate statistical or research information obtained from a record, provided that the identity of the subject of the record is not disclosed.

(b) It is not a violation of this article to disseminate information obtained from a record for the purpose of assisting in the apprehension of a person wanted in connection with the commission of a crime.

(c) It is not a violation of this article to include information obtained from a record in (1) a transcript or record of a judicial or administrative proceeding or (2) any other public record when the inclusion of the information in the public record is authorized by a court, statute, or decisional law.

CHAPTER 1.5

NATIONAL SEARCH OF CRIMINAL RECORDS

§11145. Contracts with independent vendors.
In lieu of a national check of fingerprint records conducted by the Federal Bureau of Investigation through the California Department of Justice, state agencies shall contract with an independent vendor to conduct a national search of the individuals' criminal records, as provided in this chapter.

§11146. Applicability of chapter.
This chapter applies to:

(a) The California Commission for Teacher Preparation and Licensing, in licensing of all teaching and services credential applicants, pursuant to Section 44341 of the Education Code.

(b) The State Department of Social Services in licensing those community care facility operators providing services to children as mandated in Section 1522 of the Health and Safety Code.

§11147. Information required of applicants.
In order that a thorough search may be conducted, the agencies listed in Section 11146 shall require applicants, as a condition of employment or licensing, to provide (a) their social security and drivers' license numbers, (b) educational history, (c) three personal references, (d) five-year employment and residence history, and, (e) if appropriate, any other names they may have been known under. This information shall be provided under penalty of perjury.

§11148. Qualifications of vendor.
The agencies listed in Section 11146 may contract with any vendor demonstrating the capability to conduct such background searches in a timely manner and with the assurance of complete confidentiality. Any such vendor shall (a) be a licensed private investigator as defined in Section 7521 of the Business and Professions Code; (b) have been in business for at least five years; (c) be able to furnish bank references; (d) provide a minimum of one million dollars ($1,000,000) in liability insurance, with the contracting agency being named as an additional insured; and (e) be able to provide services, via subcontracts if necessary, in all areas of the state.

No contract shall be let unless it provides therein that the cost per applicant for a search, including administrative costs, shall not exceed forty dollars

© 1992 by J., B. & L. Gould
Printed in the U.S.A.   EP

($40). The state shall not be liable for any amount in excess of forty dollars ($40) per applicant.

§11149. Applications to include results of fingerprint checks.

In order to expedite the work of the vendor, all applications submitted to the vendor shall include the results of the fingerprint checks conducted by the California Department of Justice.

§11149.1. Exemption from Chapter 1 provisions.

Vendors are exempted from any provisions of Chapter 1 (commencing with Section 1798) of Title 1.8 of Part 4 of Division 3 of the Civil Code which prevent the vendor from conducting the national search of individual criminal records required by this chapter.

§11149.2. Charge to applicant for actual cost.

Notwithstanding any other provision of law, applicants may be charged for the actual cost of the national search required by this statute, including administrative costs, not to exceed forty dollars ($40).

§11149.3. Furnishing information to unauthorized persons.

Any vendor or employee of a vendor who knowingly furnishes a record or information obtained from a record to a person who is not authorized by law to receive the record or information shall be guilty of a misdemeanor and fined not more than five thousand dollars ($5,000), or imprisoned in a county jail for not more than one year, or both.

§11149.4. Invasion of privacy; civil action.

Any vendor or employee of a vendor who intentionally discloses information, not otherwise public, which that person knows or should reasonably know was obtained from confidential information, shall be subject to a civil action for invasion of privacy by the individual to whom the information pertains.

In any successful action brought under this section, the complainant, in addition to any special or general damages awarded, shall be awarded a minimum of two thousand five hundred dollars ($2,500) in exemplary damages as well as attorney's fees and other litigation costs reasonably incurred in the suit.

The right, remedy, and cause of action set forth in this section shall be nonexclusive and is in addition to all other rights, remedies, and causes of action for invasion of privacy, inherent in Section 1, Article I of the California Constitution.

CHAPTER 2

CONTROL OF CRIMES AND CRIMINALS

ARTICLE 1

RELEASE OF PERSONS CONVICTED OF ARSON

§11150. Notification to police departments.

Prior to the release of a person convicted of arson from an institution under the jurisdiction of the Department of Corrections, the Director of Corrections shall notify in writing the State Fire Marshal and all police departments and the sheriff in the county in which the person was convicted and, if known, in the county in which he is to reside. The notice shall state the name of the person to be released, the county in which he was convicted and, if known, the county in which he will reside.

§11151. Release of person convicted of arson; notification by Department of Mental Hygiene.

Within five days after release of a person convicted of arson from an institution under the jurisdiction of the Department of Mental Hygiene, the Director of Mental Hygiene shall send the notice provided in Section 11150.

§11152. Notification of local fire departments.

Upon receipt of a notice as provided in Section 11150 or 11151, the State Fire Marshal shall notify all regularly organized fire departments in the county in which the person was convicted and, if known, in the county in which he is to reside.

ARTICLE 1.5

REPORTS OF DISPOSITION OF INMATES

§11155. Notification of placement in reentry or work furlough program; and of escape.

(a) As soon as placement of an inmate in any reentry or work furlough program is planned, but in no case less than 60 days prior to that placement, the Department of Corrections shall send written notice, if notice has been requested, to all of the following: (1) the chief of police of the city, if any, in which the inmate will reside, if known, or in which placement will be made, (2) the sheriff of the county in which the inmate will reside, if known, or in which placement will be made, and (3) the victim, if any, of the crime for which the inmate was convicted or the next of kin of the victim if the crime was a homicide, if the victim or the next of kin has submitted a request for notice with the department. Information regarding victims or next of kin requesting the notice, and the notice, shall be confidential and not available to the inmate.

(b) In the event of an escape of an inmate from any facility under the jurisdiction of the Department of Corrections, the department shall immediately notify, by the most reasonable and expedient means available, the chief of police of the city, and the sheriff of the county, in which the inmate resided immediately prior to the inmate's arrest and conviction, and, if previously requested, to the victim, if any, of the crime for which the inmate was convicted, or to the next of kin of the victim if the crime was a homicide. If the inmate is recaptured, the department shall send written notice thereof to the persons designated in this subdivision within 30 days after regaining custody of the inmate.

(c) Except as provided in subdivision (d), the Department of Corrections shall send the notices required by this section to the last address provided to the department by the requesting party. It is the responsibility of the requesting party to provide the department with a current address.

(d) Whenever the department sends the notice required by this section to a victim, it shall do so by return-receipt mail. In the event the victim does not reside at the last address provided to the department, the department shall make a diligent, good faith effort to learn the whereabouts of the victim in order to comply with these notification requirements. *(Amended by Stats 1990 ch 1692 §2, eff. 1/1/91.)*

§11156. Notification contents.

The notice sent to the chief of police and county sheriff pursuant to Section 11155 shall include an actual glossy photograph no smaller than 3⅛ x 3⅛ inches in size, in conjunction with the Department of Justice, fingerprints of each inmate in the reentry or work furlough program. *(Amended by Stats 1986 ch 600 §5.)*

§11157. Notice to victims to receive notices provided by article.

The victims may be notified of the opportunity to receive the notices provided by this article by means of adding a paragraph to the information contained on subpoena forms which are used in subpoenaing victims as material witnesses to any court proceedings resulting from the perpetration of the crime in which the victim was involved.

§11158. Victim defined.

As used in this article, "victim" means any person alleged or found, upon the record, to have sustained physical or financial injury to person or property as a direct result of the crime charged.

ARTICLE 2

REPORTS OF INJURIES BY HOSPITALS

§11160. Wound or injuries; report to police.

Every person, firm or corporation conducting any hospital or pharmacy in the state, or the managing agent thereof, or the person managing or in charge of such hospital or pharmacy, or in charge of any ward or part of such hospital to which any person suffering from any wound or other injury inflicted by his own act or by the act of another by means of a knife, gun, pistol or other deadly weapon, or in cases where injuries have been inflicted upon any person in violation of any penal law of this state shall come or be brought, shall report the same immediately, both by telephone and in writing, to the chief of police, city marshal, town marshal or other head of the police department of any city, city and county, town or municipal corporation of this state, or to the sheriff, if such hospital or pharmacy is located outside the incorporated limits of a city, town or other municipal corporation. The report shall state the name of the injured person, if known, his whereabouts and the character and extent of his injuries.

For the purposes of this section "injury" shall not include any psychological or physical condition brought about solely through the voluntary administration of a narcotic or restricted dangerous drug.

§11161. Report of wound or injuries; by physician or surgeon.

Every physician or surgeon who has under his charge or care any person suffering from any wound or injury inflicted in the manner specified in Section 11160 shall make a report of the kind specified in this article to the appropriate officers named in Section 11160.

§11161.8. Report of neglect or abuse of patient transferred from health facility.

Every person, firm, or corporation conducting any hospital in the state, or the managing agent thereof, or the person managing or in charge of such hospital, or in charge of any ward or part of such hospital, who receives a patient transferred from a health facility, as defined in Section 1250 of the Health and Safety Code or from a community care facility, as defined in Section 1502 of the Health and Safety Code, who exhibits a physical injury or condition which, in the opinion of the admitting physician, reasonably appears to be the result of neglect or abuse, shall report such fact by telephone and in writing, within 36 hours, to both the local police authority having jurisdiction and the county health department.

Any registered nurse, licensed vocational nurse, or licensed clinical social worker employed at such hospital may also make a report under this section, if, in the opinion of such person, a patient exhibits a physical injury or condition which reasonably appears to be the result of neglect or abuse.

Every physician and surgeon who has under his charge or care any such patient who exhibits a physical injury or condition which reasonably appears to be the result of neglect or abuse shall make such report.

The report shall state the character and extent of the physical injury or condition.

No employee shall be discharged, suspended, disciplined, or harassed for making a report pursuant to this section.

No person shall incur any civil or criminal liability as a result of making any report authorized by this section.

§11162. Punishment for violation of this article.

Any person, firm or corporation violating any provision of this article is guilty of a misdemeanor and is punishable by imprisonment in the county jail not exceeding six months or by a fine not exceeding five hundred dollars ($500), or by both.

ARTICLE 2.4

CHILD ABUSE AND NEGLECT REPORTING ACT

§11164. Intent and purpose of article.

(a) This article shall be known and may be cited as the Child Abuse and Neglect Reporting Act.

(b) The intent and purpose of this article is to protect children from abuse. In any investigation of suspected child abuse, all persons participating in the investigation of the case shall consider the needs of the child victim and shall do whatever is necessary to prevent psychological harm to the child victim. *(Added by Stats 1987 ch 1444 §1.5.)*

§11165. Child defined.

As used in this article "child" means a person under the age of 18 years. *(Added by Stats 1987 ch 1459 §2.)*

§11165.1. Sexual abuse defined.

As used in this article, "sexual abuse" means sexual assault or sexual exploitation as defined by the following:

(a) "Sexual assault" means conduct in violation of one or more of the following sections: Section 261 (rape), 264.1 (rape in concert), 285 (incest), 286 (sodomy), subdivision (a) or (b) of Section 288 (lewd or lascivious acts upon a child under 14 years of age), 288a (oral copulation), 289 (penetration of a genital or anal opening by a foreign object), or 647a (child molestation).

© 1992 by J., B. & L. Gould
Printed in the U.S.A.   EP

(b) Conduct described as "sexual assault" includes, but is not limited to, all of the following:

(1) Any penetration, however slight, of the vagina or anal opening of one person by the penis of another person, whether or not there is the emission of semen.

(2) Any sexual contact between the genitals or anal opening of one person and the mouth or tongue of another person.

(3) Any intrusion by one person into the genitals or anal opening of another person, including the use of any object for this purpose, except that, it does not include acts performed for a valid medical purpose.

(4) The intentional touching of the genitals or intimate parts (including the breasts, genital area, groin, inner thighs, and buttocks) or the clothing covering them, of a child, or of the perpetrator by a child, for purposes of sexual arousal or gratification, except that, it does not include acts which may reasonably be construed to be normal caretaker responsibilities; interactions with, or demonstrations of affection for, the child; or acts performed for a valid medical purpose.

(5) The intentional masturbation of the perpetrator's genitals in the presence of a child.

(c) "Sexual exploitation" refers to any of the following:

(1) Conduct involving matter depicting a minor engaged in obscene acts in violation of Section 311.2 (preparing, selling, or distributing obscene matter) or subdivision (a) of Section 311.4 (employment of minor to perform obscene acts).

(2) Any person who knowingly promotes, aids, or assists, employs, uses, persuades, induces, or coerces a child, or any person responsible for a child's welfare, who knowingly permits or encourages a child to engage in, or assist others to engage in, prostitution or a live performance involving obscene sexual conduct, or to either pose or model alone or with others for purposes of preparing a film, photograph, negative, slide, drawing, painting, or other pictorial depiction, involving obscene sexual conduct. For the purpose of this section, "person responsible for a child's welfare" means a parent, guardian, foster parent, or a licensed administrator or employee of a public or private residential home, residential school, or other residential institution.

(3) Any person who depicts a child in, or who knowingly develops, duplicates, prints, or exchanges, any film, photograph, video tape, negative, or slide in which a child is engaged in an act of obscene sexual conduct, except for those activities by law enforcement and prosecution agencies and other persons described in subdivisions (c) and (e) of Section 311.3. *(Added by Stats 1987 ch 1459 §5.)*

§11165.2. Neglect defined.

As used in this article, "neglect" means the negligent treatment or the maltreatment of a child by a person responsible for the child's welfare under circumstances indicating harm or threatened harm to the child's health or welfare. The term includes both acts and omissions on the part of the responsible person.

(a) "Severe neglect" means the negligent failure of a person having the care or custody of a child to protect the child from severe malnutrition or medically diagnosed nonorganic failure to thrive. "Severe neglect" also means those situations of neglect where any person having the care or custody of a child willfully causes or permits the person or health of the child to be placed in a situation such that his or her person or health is endangered, as proscribed by Section 11165.3, including the intentional failure to provide adequate food, clothing, shelter, or medical care.

(b) "General neglect" means the negligent failure of a person having the care or custody of a child to provide adequate food, clothing, shelter, medical care, or supervision where no physical injury to the child has occurred.

For the purposes of this chapter, a child receiving treatment by spiritual means as provided in Section 16509.1 of the Welfare and Institutions Code or not receiving specified medical treatment for religious reasons, shall not for that reason alone be considered a neglected child. An informed and appropriate medical decision made by parent or guardian after consultation with a physician or physicians who have examined the minor does not constitute neglect. *(Added by Stats 1987 ch 1459 §7.)*

§11165.3. Cruelty to a child.

As used in this article, "willful cruelty or unjustifiable punishment of a child" means a situation where any person willfully causes or permits any child to suffer, or inflicts thereon, unjustifiable physical pain or mental suffering, or having the care or custody of any child, willfully causes or permits the person or health of the child to be placed in a situation such that his or her person or health is endangered. *(Added by Stats 1987 ch 1459 §9.)*

§11165.4. Corporal punishment; injury.

As used in this article, "unlawful corporal punishment or injury" means a situation where any person willfully inflicts upon any child any cruel or inhuman corporal punishment or injury resulting in a traumatic condition. It does not include an amount of force that is reasonable and necessary for a person employed by or engaged in a public school to quell a disturbance threatening physical injury to person or damage to property, for purposes of self-defense, or to obtain possession of weapons or other dangerous objects within the control of the pupil, as authorized by Section 49001 of the Education Code. It also does not include the exercise of the degree of physical control authorized by Section 44807 of the Education Code. It also does not include an amount of force that is reasonable and necessary for a peace officer to quell a disturbance threatening physical injury to person or damage to property to prevent physical injury to person or damage to property, for purposes of self-defense, to obtain possession of weapons or other dangerous objects within the control of the child, or to apprehend an escapee. *(Amended by Stats 1988 ch 39 §1, eff. 1/1/89.)*

§11165.5. Abuse in out-of-home care defined.

As used in this article, "abuse in out-of-home care" means a situation of physical injury on a child which is inflicted by other than accidental means, or of sexual abuse or neglect, or unlawful corporal punishment or injury, or the willful cruelty or unjustifiable punishment of a child, as defined in this article, where the person responsible for the child's welfare is a licensee, administrator, or employee of any facility licensed to care for children, or an administrator or employee of a public or private school or other institution or agency. "Abuse in out-of-home care" does not include an injury caused by reasonable and necessary force used by a peace officer to quell a disturbance threatening physical injury to person or damage to property, to prevent physical injury to person or damage to property, for purposes of self-defense, to obtain possession of weapons or other dangerous objects within the control of a child, or to apprehend an escapee. *(Amended by Stats 1988 ch 39 §2, eff. 1/1/89.)*

§11165.6. Child abuse defined.

As used in this article, "child abuse" means a physical injury which is inflicted by other than accidental means on a child by another person. "Child abuse" also means the sexual abuse of a child or any act or omission proscribed by Section 273a (willful cruelty or unjustifiable punishment of a child) or 273d (unlawful corporal punishment or injury). "Child abuse" also means the neglect of a child or abuse in out-of-home care, as defined in this article. "Child abuse" does not mean a mutual affray between minors. "Child abuse" does not include an injury caused by reasonable and necessary force used by a peace officer to quell a disturbance threatening physical injury to person or damage to property, to prevent physical injury to person or damage to property, for purposes of self-defense, to obtain possession of weapons or other dangerous objects within the control of a child, or to apprehend an escapee. *(Amended by Stats 1988 ch 39 §3, eff. 1/1/89.)*

§11165.7. Child care custodian defined.

(a) As used in this article, "child care custodian" means a teacher; an instructional aide, a teacher's aide, or a teacher's assistant employed by any public or private school, who has been trained in the duties imposed by this article, if the school district has so warranted to the State Department of Education; a classified employee of any public school who has been trained in the duties imposed by this article, if the school has so warranted to the State Department of Education; an administrative officer, supervisor of child welfare and attendance, or certificated pupil personnel employee of any public or private school; an administrator of a public or private day camp; an administrator or employee of a public or private youth center, youth recreation program, or youth organization; an administrator or employee of a public or private organization whose duties require direct contact and supervision of children; a licensee, an administrator, or an employee of a licensed community care or child day care facility; a headstart teacher; a licensing worker or licensing evaluator; a public assistance worker; an employee of a child care institution including, but not limited to, foster parents, group home personnel, and personnel of residential care facilities; a social worker, probation officer, or parole officer; an employee of a school district police or security department; or any person who is an administrator or presenter of, or a counselor in, a child abuse prevention program in any public or private school.

(b) Training in the duties imposed by this article shall include training in child abuse identification and training in child abuse reporting. As part of that training, school districts shall provide to all employees being trained a written copy of the reporting requirements and a written disclosure of the employees' confidentiality rights.

(c) School districts which do not train the employees specified in subdivision (a) in the duties of child care custodians under the child abuse reporting laws shall report to the State Department of Education the reasons why this training is not provided.

(d) Volunteers of public or private organizations whose duties require direct contact and supervision of children are encouraged to obtain training in the identification and reporting of child abuse. *(Amended by Stats 1991 ch 132 §1, eff. 1/1/92.)*

§11165.8. Health practitioner defined.

As used in this article, "health practitioner" means a physician and surgeon, psychiatrist, psychologist, dentist, resident, intern, podiatrist, chiropractor, licensed nurse, dental hygienist, optometrist, or any other person who is currently licensed under Division 2 (commencing with Section 500) of the Business and Professions Code; a marriage, family and child counselor; any emergency medical technician I or II, paramedic, or other person certified pursuant to Division 2.5 (commencing with Section 1797) of the Health and Safety Code; a psychological assistant registered pursuant to Section 2913 of the Business and Professions Code; a marriage, family and child counselor trainee, as defined in subdivision (c) of Section 4980.03 of the Business and Professions Code; an unlicensed marriage, family and child counselor intern registered under Section 4980.44 of the Business and Professions Code; a state or county public health employee who treats a minor for venereal disease or any other condition; a coroner; a medical examiner or any other person who performs autopsies; or a religious practitioner who diagnoses, examines, or treats children. *(Amended by Stats 1988 ch 1580 §1, eff. 1/1/89.)*

§11165.9. Child protective agency defined.

As used in this article, "child protective agency" means a police or sheriff's department, a county probation department, or a county welfare department. It does not include a school district police or security department. *(Added by Stats 1987 ch 1459 §16.)*

§11165.10. Commercial film and photographic print processor defined.

As used in this article, "commercial film and photographic print processor" means any person who develops exposed photographic film into negatives, slides, or prints, or who makes prints from negatives or slides, for compensation. The term includes any employee of such a person; it does not include a person who develops film or makes prints for a public agency. *(Added by Stats 1987 ch 1459 §17.)*

§11165.11. Licensing agency defined.

As used in this article, "licensing agency" means the State Department of Social Services office responsible for the licensing and enforcement of the California Community Care Facilities Act (Chapter 3 (commencing with Section 1500) of Division 2 of the Health and Safety Code), the California Child Day Care Act (Chapter 3.4 (commencing with Section 1596.70) of Division 2 of the Health and Safety Code), and Chapter 3.5 (commencing with Section 1596.90) of Division 2 of the Health and Safety Code), or the county licensing agency which has contracted with the state for performance of those duties. *(Added by Stats 1987 ch 1459 §18.)*

© 1992 by J., B. & L. Gould
Printed in the U.S.A.   EP

§11165.12. Reports: definitions.

As used in this article, the following definitions shall control:

(a) "Unfounded report" means a report which is determined by a child protective agency investigator to be false, to be inherently improbable, to involve an accidental injury, or not to constitute child abuse, as defined in Section 11165.6.

(b) "Substantiated report" means a report which is determined by a child protective agency investigator, based upon some credible evidence, to constitute child abuse or neglect, as defined in Section 11165.6.

(c) "Unsubstantiated report" means a report which is determined by a child protective agency investigator not to be unfounded, but in which the findings are inconclusive and there is insufficient evidence to determine whether child abuse or neglect, as defined in Section 11165.6, has occurred. *(Amended by Stats 1990 ch 1330 §1, eff. 1/1/91.)*

§11165.13. Substance exposed newborn not basis for child abuse report.

For purposes of this article, a positive toxicology screen at the time of the delivery of an infant is not in and of itself a sufficient basis for reporting child abuse or neglect. However, any indication of maternal substance abuse shall lead to an assessment of the needs of the mother and child pursuant to Section 10901 of the Health and Safety Code. If other factors are present that indicate risk to a child, then a report shall be made. However, a report based on risk to a child which relates solely to the inability of the parent to provide the child with regular care due to the parent's substance abuse shall be made only to county welfare departments and not to law enforcement agencies. *(Added by Stats 1990 ch 1603 §2, eff. 1/1/91, oper. 7/1/91.)*

§11165.14. Abuse occuring on school grounds or by school employee.

The local child protective agency shall investigate a child abuse complaint filed by a parent or guardian of a pupil with a school or a local child protective agency against a school employee or other person that commits an act of child abuse, as defined in this article, against a pupil at a schoolsite and shall transmit a substantiated report, as defined in Section 11165.12, of that investigation to the governing board of the appropriate school district or county office of education. A substantiated report received by a governing board of a school district or county office of education shall be subject to the provisions of Section 44031 of the Education Code. *(Added by Stats 1991 ch 1102 §5, eff. 1/1/92.)*

§11166. Child abuse; duties to report.

(a) Except as provided in subdivision (b), any child care custodian, health practitioner, or employee of a child protective agency who has knowledge of or observes a child in his or her professional capacity or within the scope of his or her employment whom he or she knows or reasonably suspects has been the victim of child abuse shall report the known or suspected instance of child abuse to a child protective agency immediately or as soon as practically possible by telephone and shall prepare and send a written report thereof within 36 hours of receiving the information concerning the incident. A child protective agency shall be notified and a report shall be prepared and sent even if the child has expired, regardless of whether or not the possible abuse was a factor contributing to the death, and even if suspected child abuse was discovered during an autopsy. For the purposes of this article, "reasonable suspicion" means that it is objectively reasonable for a person to entertain such a suspicion, based upon facts that could cause a reasonable person in a like position, drawing when appropriate on his or her training and experience, to suspect child abuse. For the purpose of this article, the pregnancy of a minor does not, in and of itself, constitute the basis of reasonable suspicion of sexual abuse.

(b) Any child care custodian, health practitioner, or employee of a child protective agency who has knowledge of or who reasonably suspects that mental suffering has been inflicted on a child or his or her emotional well-being is endangered in any other way, may report such known or suspected instance of child abuse to a child protective agency.

(c) Any commercial film and photographic print processor who has knowledge of or observes, within the scope of his or her professional capacity or employment, any film, photograph, videotape, negative or slide depicting a child under the age of 14 years engaged in an act of sexual conduct, shall report such instance of suspected child abuse to the law enforcement agency having jurisdiction over the case immediately or as soon as practically possible by telephone and shall prepare and send a written report of it with a copy of the film, photograph, videotape, negative or slide attached within 36 hours of receiving the information concerning the incident. As used in this subdivision, "sexual conduct" means any of the following:

(1) Sexual intercourse, including genital-genital, oral-genital, anal-genital, or oral-anal, whether between persons of the same or opposite sex or between humans and animals.

(2) Penetration of the vagina or rectum by any object.

(3) Masturbation, for the purpose of sexual stimulation of the viewer.

(4) Sadomasochistic abuse for the purpose of sexual stimulation of the viewer.

(5) Exhibition of the genitals, pubic or rectal areas of any person for the purpose of sexual stimulation of the viewer.

(d) Any other person who has knowledge of or observes a child whom he or she knows or reasonably suspects has been a victim of child abuse may report the known or suspected instance of child abuse to a child protective agency.

(e) When two or more persons who are required to report are present and jointly have knowledge of a known or suspected instance of child abuse, and when there is agreement among them, the telephone report may be made by a member of the team selected by mutual agreement and a single report may be made and signed by such selected member of the reporting team. Any member who has knowledge that the member designated to report has failed to do so, shall thereafter make the report.

(f) The reporting duties under this section are individual, and no supervisor or administrator may impede or inhibit the reporting duties and no person making such a report shall be subject to any sanction for making the report. However, internal procedures to facilitate reporting and apprise supervisors and administrators of reports may be established provided that they are not inconsistent with the provisions of this article.

The internal procedures shall not require any employee required to make reports by this article to disclose his or her identity to the employer.

(g) A county probation or welfare department shall immediately or as soon as practically possible report by telephone to the law enforcement agency having jurisdiction over the case, to the agency given the responsibility for investigation of cases under Section 300 of the Welfare and Institutions Code, and to the district attorney's office every known or suspected instance of child abuse as defined in Section 11165.6, except acts or omissions coming within subdivision (b) of Section 11165.2, or reports made pursuant to Section 11165.13 based on risk to a child which relate solely to the inability of the parent to provide the child with regular care due to the parent's substance abuse, which shall only be reported to the county welfare department. A county probation or welfare department shall also send a written report thereof within 36 hours of receiving the information concerning the incident to any agency to which it is required to make a telephone report under this subdivision.

A law enforcement agency shall immediately or as soon as practically possible report by telephone to the agency given responsibility for investigation of cases under Section 300 of the Welfare and Institutions Code and to the district attorney's office every known or suspected instance of child abuse reported to it, except acts or omissions coming within subdivision (b) of Section 11165.2, which shall only be reported to the county welfare department. A law enforcement agency shall report to the county welfare department every known or suspected instance of child abuse reported to it which is alleged to have occurred as a result of the action of a person responsible for the child's welfare, or as the result of the failure of a person responsible for the child's welfare to adequately protect the minor from abuse when the person responsible for the child's welfare knew or reasonably should have known that the minor was in danger of abuse. A law enforcement agency shall also send a written report thereof within 36 hours of receiving the information concerning the incident to any agency to which it is required to make a telephone report under this subdivision. *(Amended by Stats 1990 ch 1603 §3, eff. 1/1/91, oper. 7/1/91.)*

§11166.1. Report of abuse in State Department of Social Services facility.

When a child protective agency receives a report of abuse alleged to have occurred in facilities licensed to care for children by the State Department of Social Services, it shall, within 24 hours, notify the licensing office with jurisdiction over the facility. The child protective agency shall send the licensing agency a copy of its investigation and any other pertinent materials. *(Amended and renumbered by Stats 1987 ch 56 §141. Former section 11166.1·repealed by Stats 1988 ch 269 §2, eff. 1/1/89.)*

§11166.2. Additional reports required by a child protective agency.

In addition to the reports required under Section 11166, a child protective agency shall immediately or as soon as practically possible report by telephone to the appropriate licensing agency every known or suspected instance of child abuse when the instance of abuse occurs while the child is being cared for in a child day care facility, involves a child day care licensed staff person, or occurs while the child is under the supervision of a community care facility or involves a community care facility licensee or staff person. A child protective agency shall also send a written report thereof within 36 hours of receiving the information concerning the incident to any agency to which it is required to make a telephone report under this subdivision. A child protective agency shall send the licensing agency a copy of its investigation report and any other pertinent materials. *(Amended by Stats 1990 ch 650 §1, eff. 1/1/91.)*

§11166.3. Investigation and reporting of suspected child abuse cases.

(a) The Legislature intends that in each county the law enforcement agencies and the county welfare or social services department shall develop and implement cooperative arrangements in order to coordinate existing duties in connection with the investigation of suspected child abuse cases. The local law enforcement agency having jurisdiction over a case reported under Section 11166 shall report to the county welfare department that it is investigating the case within 36 hours after starting its investigation. The county welfare department or social services department shall, in cases where a minor is a victim of actions specified in Section 288 of this code and a petition has been filed pursuant to Section 300 of the Welfare and Institutions Code with regard to the minor, in accordance with the requirements of subdivision (c) of Section 288, evaluate what action or actions would be in the best interest of the child victim. Notwithstanding any other provision of law, the county welfare department or social services department shall submit in writing its findings and the reasons therefor to the district attorney on or before the completion of the investigation. The written findings and the reasons therefor shall be delivered or made accessible to the defendant or his or her counsel in the manner specified in Sections 859 and 1430. The child protective agency shall send a copy of its investigative report and any other pertinent materials to the licensing agency upon the request of the licensing agency.

(b) The local law enforcement agency having jurisdiction over a case reported under Section 11166 shall report to the district office of the State Department of Social Services any case reported under this section if the case involves a facility specified in paragraph (5) or (6) of Section 1502 or in Section 1596.750 or 1596.76 of the Health and Safety Code and the licensing of the facility has not been delegated to a county agency. The law enforcement agency shall send a copy of its investigation report and any other pertinent materials to the licensing agency upon the request of the licensing agency. *(Amended by Stats 1988 ch 898 §1, eff. 1/1/89. Former section 11166.3 repealed by Stats 1988 ch 898 §2, eff. 1/1/89.)*

§11166.4. *Section 11166.4 subordinated to Stats 1987 ch 531 §4 amendment to section 11166.1.*

§11166.5. Employment as child care custodian.

(a) Any person who enters into employment on and after January 1, 1985, as a child care custodian, health practitioner, or with a child protective agency, prior to

© 1992 by J., B. & L. Gould
Printed in the U.S.A. EP

commencing his or her employment, and as a prerequisite to that employment, shall sign a statement on a form provided to him or her by his or her employer to the effect that he or she has knowledge of the provisions of Section 11166 and will comply with its provisions.

The statement shall include the following provisions:

Section 11166 of the Penal Code requires any child care custodian, health practitioner, or employee of a child protective agency who has knowledge of or observes a child in his or her professional capacity or within the scope of his or her employment whom he or she knows or reasonably suspects has been the victim of child abuse to report the known or suspected instance of child abuse to a child protective agency immediately or as soon as practically possible by telephone and to prepare and send a written report thereof within 36 hours of receiving the information concerning the incident.

"Child care custodian" includes teachers; an instructional aide, a teacher's aide, or a teacher's assistant employed by any public or private school, who has been trained in the duties imposed by this article, if the school district has so warranted to the State Department of Education; a classified employee of any public school who has been trained in the duties imposed by this article, if the school has so warranted to the State Department of Education; administrative officers, supervisors of child welfare and attendance, or certificated pupil personnel employees of any public or private school; administrators of a public or private day camp; administrators and employees of public or private youth centers, youth recreation programs, or youth organizations; administrators and employees of public or private organizations whose duties require direct contact and supervision of children and who have been trained in the duties imposed by this article; licensees, administrators, and employees of licensed community care or child day care facilities; headstart teachers; licensing workers or licensing evaluators; public assistance workers; employees of a child care institution including, but not limited to, foster parents, group home personnel, and personnel of residential care facilities; social workers, probation officers, or parole officers; employees of a school district police or security department; or any person who is an administrator or a presenter of, or a counselor in, a child abuse prevention program in any public or private school.

"Health practitioner" includes physicians and surgeons, psychiatrists, psychologists, dentists, residents, interns, podiatrists, chiropractors, licensed nurses, dental hygienists, optometrists, or any other person who is licensed under Division 2 (commencing with Section 500) of the Business and Professions Code; marriage, family, and child counselors; emergency medical technicians I or II, paramedics, or other persons certified pursuant to Division 2.5 (commencing with Section 1797) of the Health and Safety Code; psychological assistants registered pursuant to Section 2913 of the Business and Professions Code; marriage, family, and child counselor trainees as defined in subdivision (c) of Section 4980.03 of the Business and Professions Code; unlicensed marriage, family, and child counselor interns registered under Section 4980.44 of the Business and Professions Code; state or county public health employees who treat minors for venereal disease or any other condition; coroners;

paramedics; and religious practitioners who diagnose, examine, or treat children.

The signed statements shall be retained by the employer. The cost of printing, distribution, and filing of these statements shall be borne by the employer.

This subdivision is not applicable to persons employed by child protective agencies, public or private youth centers, youth recreation programs, and youth organizations as members of the support staff or maintenance staff and who do not work with, observe, or have knowledge of children as part of their official duties.

(b) On and after January 1, 1986, when a person is issued a state license or certificate to engage in a profession or occupation, the members of which are required to make a report pursuant to Section 11166, the state agency issuing the license or certificate shall send a statement substantially similar to the one contained in subdivision (a) to the person at the same time as it transmits the document indicating licensure or certification to the person. In addition to the requirements contained in subdivision (a), the statement shall also indicate that failure to comply with the requirements of Section 11166 is a misdemeanor, punishable by up to six months in jail or by a fine of one thousand dollars ($1,000) or by both.

(c) As an alternative to the procedure required by subdivision (b), a state agency may cause the required statement to be printed on all application forms for a license or certificate printed on or after January 1, 1986. *(Amended by Stats 1991 ch 132 §2, eff. 1/1/92.)*

§11166.7. Child death teams; autopsies.

(a) Each county may establish an interagency child death team to assist local agencies in identifying and reviewing suspicious child deaths and facilitating communication among persons who perform autopsies and the various persons and agencies involved in child abuse cases. Interagency child death teams have been used successfully to ensure that incidents of child abuse are recognized and other siblings and nonoffending family members receive the appropriate services in cases where a child has expired.

(b) Each county may develop a protocol that may be used as a guideline by persons performing autopsies on children to assist coroners and other persons who perform autopsies in the identification of child abuse, in the determination of whether child abuse contributed to death or whether child abuse had occurred prior to but was not the actual cause of death, and in the proper written reporting procedures for child abuse, including the designation of the cause and mode of death.

(c) In developing an interagency child death team and an autopsy protocol, each county, working in consultation with local members of the California State Coroner's Association and county child abuse prevention coordinating councils, may solicit suggestions and final comments from persons, including but not limited to, the following:

(1) Experts in the field of forensic pathology.

(2) Pediatricians with expertise in child abuse.

(3) Coroners and medical examiners.

(4) Criminologists.

(5) District attorneys.

(6) Child protective services staff.

(7) Law enforcement personnel.

(8) Representatives of local agencies which are involved with child abuse reporting.

(9) County health department staff who deals with children's health issues.

(10) Local professional associations of persons described in paragraphs (1) to (9), inclusive. *(Added by Stats 1988 ch 1580 §3, eff. 1/1/89.)*

§11166.8. Development and implementation of child death teams.

Subject to available funding, the Attorney General, working with the California Consortium of Child Abuse Councils, shall develop a protocol for the development and implementation of interagency child death teams for use by counties, which shall include relevant procedures for both urban and rural counties. The protocol shall be designed to facilitate communication among persons who perform autopsies and the various persons and agencies involved in child abuse cases so that incidents of child abuse are recognized and other siblings and nonoffending family members receive the appropriate services in cases where a child has expired. The protocol shall be completed on or before January 1, 1991. *(Added by Stats 1988 ch 1580 §4, eff. 1/1/89.)*

§11167. Reporters' identities confidential; required information.

(a) A telephone report of a known or suspected instance of child abuse shall include the name of the person making the report, the name of the child, the present location of the child, the nature and extent of the injury, and any other information, including information that led that person to suspect child abuse, requested by the child protective agency.

(b) Information relevant to the incident of child abuse may also be given to an investigator from a child protective agency who is investigating the known or suspected case of child abuse.

(c) Information relevant to the incident of child abuse may be given to the licensing agency when it is investigating a known or suspected case of child abuse, including the investigation report, and other pertinent materials.

(d) The identity of all persons who report under this article shall be confidential and disclosed only between child protective agencies, or to counsel representing a child protective agency, or to the district attorney in a criminal prosecution or in an action initiated under Section 602 of the Welfare and Institutions Code arising from alleged child abuse, or to counsel appointed pursuant to Section 318 of the Welfare and Institutions Code, or to the county counsel or district attorney in an action initiated under Section 232 of the Civil Code or Section 300 of the Welfare and Institutions Code, or to a licensing agency when abuse in out-of-home care is reasonably suspected, or when those persons waive confidentiality, or by court order.

No agency or person listed in this subdivision shall disclose the identity of any person who reports under this article to that person's employer, except with the employee's consent or by court order.

(e) Persons who may report pursuant to subdivision (d) of Section 11166 are not required to include their names. *(Amended by Stats 1987 ch 531 §6.)*

§11167.5. Reports; confidentiality and disclosure.

(a) The reports required by Sections 11166 and 11166.2 shall be confidential and may be disclosed only as provided in subdivision (b). Any violation of the confidentiality provided by this article shall be a misdemeanor punishable by up to six months in jail or by a fine of five hundred dollars ($500) or by both.

(b) Reports of suspected child abuse and information contained therein may be disclosed only to the following:

(1) Persons or agencies to whom disclosure of the identity of the reporting party is permitted under Section 11167.

(2) Persons or agencies to whom disclosure of information is permitted under subdivision (b) of Section 11170.

(3) Persons or agencies with whom investigations of child abuse are coordinated under the regulations promulgated under Section 11174.

(4) Multidisciplinary personnel teams as defined in subdivision (d) of Section 18951 of the Welfare and Institutions Code.

(5) Persons or agencies responsible for the licensing of facilities which care for children, as specified in Section 11165.7.

(6) The State Department of Social Services or any county licensing agency which has contracted with the state, as specified in paragraph (3) of subdivision (b) of Section 11170, when an individual has applied for a community care license or child day care license, or for employment in an out-of-home care facility, or when a complaint alleges child abuse by an operator or employee of an out-of-home care facility.

(7) Hospital scan teams. As used in this paragraph, "hospital scan team" means a team of three or more persons established by a hospital, or two or more hospitals in the same county, consisting of health care professionals and representatives of law enforcement and child protective services, the members of which are engaged in the identification of child abuse. The disclosure authorized by this section includes disclosure among hospital scan teams located in the same county.

(8) Coroners and medical examiners when conducting a postmortem examination of a child.

(9) The Board of Prison Terms may subpoena reports that (A) are not unfounded, pursuant to Section 11165.12, and (B) concern only the current incidents upon which the parole revocation proceedings are pending against a parolee charged with child abuse. The reports and information shall be confidential pursuant to subdivision (d) of Section 11167.

(c) Nothing in this section shall be interpreted to require the Department of Justice to disclose information contained in records maintained under Section 11169 or under the regulations promulgated pursuant to Section 11174, except as otherwise provided in this article.

(d) This section shall not be interpreted to allow disclosure of any reports or records relevant to the reports of child abuse if the disclosure would be prohibited by any other provisions of state or federal law applicable to the reports or records relevant to the reports of child abuse. *(Amended by Stats 1989 ch 153, §2, 1169 §2, eff. 1/1/90.)*

§11168. Forms for reports.

The written reports required by Section 11166 shall be submitted on forms adopted by the Department of Justice after consultation with representatives of the various professional medical associations and hospital associations and county probation or welfare departments. Such forms shall be distributed by the child protective agencies.

© 1992 by J., B. & L. Gould
Printed in the U.S.A.   EP

§11169. Child protective agency; duty to furnish reports.

A child protective agency shall forward to the Department of Justice a report in writing of every case it investigates of known or suspected child abuse which is determined not to be unfounded, other than cases coming within subdivision (b) of Section 11165.2. A child protective agency shall not forward a report to the Department of Justice unless it has conducted an active investigation and determined that the report is not unfounded, as defined in Section 11165.12. If a report has previously been filed which subsequently proves to be unfounded, the Department of Justice shall be notified in writing of that fact and shall not retain the report. The report required by this section shall be in a form approved by the Department of Justice. A child protective agency receiving a written report from another child protective agency shall not send such report to the Department of Justice.

The immunity provisions of Section 11172 shall not apply to the submission of a report by a child protective agency pursuant to this section. However, nothing in this section shall be construed to alter or diminish any other immunity provisions of state or federal law. *(Amended by Stats 1988 ch 269 §4; ch 1497 §1, eff. 1/1/89.)*

§11170. Index of child abuse reports by Department of Justice.

(a) The Department of Justice shall maintain an index of all reports of child abuse submitted pursuant to Section 11169. The index shall be continually updated by the department and shall not contain any reports that are determined to be unfounded. The department may adopt rules governing recordkeeping and reporting pursuant to this article.

(b)(1) The Department of Justice shall immediately notify a child protective agency which submits a report pursuant to Section 11169, or a district attorney who requests notification, of any information maintained pursuant to subdivision (a) which is relevant to the known or suspected instance of child abuse reported by the agency. A child protective agency shall make that information available to the reporting medical practitioner, child custodian, guardian ad litem appointed under Section 326, or counsel appointed under Section 317 or 318 of the Welfare and Institutions Code, or the appropriate licensing agency, if he or she is treating or investigating a case of known or suspected child abuse.

(2) When a report is made pursuant to subdivision (a) of Section 11166, the investigating agency shall, upon completion of the investigation or after there has been a final disposition in the matter, inform the person required to report of the results of the investigation and of any action the agency is taking with regard to the child or family.

(3) The department shall make available to the State Department of Social Services or to any county licensing agency which has contracted with the state for the performance of licensing duties any information received subsequent to January 1, 1981, pursuant to this section concerning any person who is an applicant for licensure or any adult who resides or is employed in the home of an applicant for licensure or who is an applicant for employment in a position having supervisorial or disciplinary power over a child or children, or who will provide 24-hour care for a child or children in a residential home or facility, pursuant

to Section 1522.1 or 1596.877 of the Health and Safety Code, or Section 226 of the Civil Code. If the department has information which has been received subsequent to January 1, 1981, concerning such a person, it shall also make available to the State Department of Social Services or the county licensing agency any other information maintained pursuant to subdivision (a).

(4) Persons or agencies, as specified in subdivision (b), if investigating a case of known or suspected child abuse, or the State Department of Social Services or any county licensing agency pursuant to paragraph (3), to whom disclosure of any information maintained pursuant to subdivision (a) is authorized, are responsible for obtaining the original investigative report from the reporting agency, and for drawing independent conclusions regarding the quality of the evidence disclosed, and its sufficiency for making decisions regarding investigation, prosecution, or licensing. *(Amended by Stats 1990 ch 1330 §2, eff. 1/1/91, oper. only until 7/1/91. See other section 11170 below.)*

§11170. Index of child abuse reports by Department of Justice.

(a) The Department of Justice shall maintain an index of all reports of child abuse submitted pursuant to Section 11169. The index shall be continually updated by the department and shall not contain any reports that are determined to be unfounded. The department may adopt rules governing recordkeeping and reporting pursuant to this article.

(b)(1) The Department of Justice shall immediately notify a child protective agency which submits a report pursuant to Section 11169, or a district attorney who requests notification, of any information maintained pursuant to subdivision (a) which is relevant to the known or suspected instance of child abuse reported by the agency. A child protective agency shall make that information available to the reporting medical practitioner, child custodian, guardian ad litem appointed under Section 326, or counsel appointed under Section 317 or 318 of the Welfare and Institutions Code, or the appropriate licensing agency, if he or she is treating or investigating a case of known or suspected child abuse.

(2) When a report is made pursuant to subdivision (a) of Section 11166, the investigating agency shall, upon completion of the investigation or after there has been a final disposition in the matter, inform the person required to report of the results of the investigation and of any action the agency is taking with regard to the child or family.

(3) The department shall make available to the State Department of Social Services or to any county licensing agency which has contracted with the state for the performance of licensing duties any information received subsequent to January 1, 1981, pursuant to this section concerning any person who is an applicant for licensure or any adult who resides or is employed in the home of an applicant for licensure or who is an applicant for employment in a position having supervisorial or disciplinary power over a child or children, or who will provide 24-hour care for a child or children in a residential home or facility, pursuant to Section 1522.1 or 1596.877 of the Health and Safety Code, or Section 222.70, 224.30, 226.52, or 227.10 of the Civil Code. If the department has information which has been received subsequent to January 1,

1981, concerning such a person, it shall also make available to the State Department of Social Services or the county licensing agency any other information maintained pursuant to subdivision (a).

(4) Persons or agencies, as specified in subdivision (b), if investigating a case of known or suspected child abuse, or the State Department of Social Services or any county licensing agency pursuant to paragraph (3), to whom disclosure of any information maintained pursuant to subdivision (a) is authorized, are responsible for obtaining the original investigative report from the reporting agency, and for drawing independent conclusions regarding the quality of the evidence disclosed, and its sufficiency for making decisions regarding investigation, prosecution, or licensing. *(Amended by Stats 1990 ch 1363 §15.7, eff. 1/1/91, oper. 7/1/91. See other section 11170 above.)*

§11171. X-rays by physician; no consent needed.

(a) A physician and surgeon or dentist or their agents and by their direction may take skeletal X-rays of the child without the consent of the child's parent or guardian, but only for purposes of diagnosing the case as one of possible child abuse and determining the extent of such child abuse.

(b) Neither the physician-patient privilege nor the psychotherapist-patient privilege applies to information reported pursuant to this article in any court proceeding or administrative hearing.

§11171.5. Order for X-ray without parental consent.

(a) If a peace officer, in the course of an investigation of child abuse, has reasonable cause to believe that the child has been the victim of physical abuse, the officer may apply to a magistrate for an order directing that the victim be X-rayed without parental consent.

Any X-ray taken pursuant to this subdivision shall be administered by a physician and surgeon or dentist or their agents.

(b) With respect to the cost of an X-ray taken by the county coroner or at the request of the county coroner in suspected child abuse cases, the county may charge the parent or legal guardian of the child-victim the costs incurred by the county for the X-ray.

(c) No person who administers an X-ray pursuant to this section shall be entitled to reimbursement from the county for any administrative cost that exceeds 5 percent of the cost of the X-ray. *(Added by Stats 1985 ch 317 §1.)*

§11172. Liabilities of persons required to make report.

(a) No child care custodian, health practitioner, employee of a child protective agency, or commercial film and photographic print processor who reports a known or suspected instance of child abuse shall be civilly or criminally liable for any report required or authorized by this article. Any other person reporting a known or suspected instance of child abuse shall not incur civil or criminal liability as a result of any report authorized by this article unless it can be proven that a false report was made and the person knew that the report was false or was made with reckless disregard of the truth or falsity of the report, and any such person who makes a report of child abuse known to be false or with reckless disregard of the truth or falsity of the report is liable for any damages caused. No person required to make a report pursuant to this

article, nor any person taking photographs at his or her direction, shall incur any civil or criminal liability for taking photographs of a suspected victim of child abuse, or causing photographs to be taken of a suspected victim of child abuse, without parental consent, or for disseminating the photographs with the reports required by this article. However, the provisions of this section shall not be construed to grant immunity from this liability with respect to any other use of the photographs.

(b) Any child care custodian, health practitioner, or employee of a child protective agency who, pursuant to a request from a child protective agency, provides the requesting agency with access to the victim of a known or suspected instance of child abuse shall not incur civil or criminal liability as a result of providing that access.

(c) The Legislature finds that even though it has provided immunity from liability to persons required to report child abuse, that immunity does not eliminate the possibility that actions may be brought against those persons based upon required reports of child abuse. In order to further limit the financial hardship that those persons may incur as a result of fulfilling their legal responsibilities, it is necessary that they not be unfairly burdened by legal fees incurred in defending those actions. Therefore, a child care custodian, health practitioner, an employee of a child protective agency, or commercial film and photographic print processor may present a claim to the State Board of Control for reasonable attorneys' fees incurred in any action against that person on the basis of making a report required or authorized by this article if the court has dismissed the action upon a demurrer or motion for summary judgment made by that person, or if he or she prevails in the action. The State Board of Control shall allow that claim if the requirements of this subdivision are met, and the claim shall be paid from an appropriation to be made for that purpose. Attorneys' fees awarded pursuant to this section shall not exceed an hourly rate greater than the rate charged by the Attorney General of the State of California at the time the award is made and shall not exceed an hourly rate greater than the rate charged by the Attorney General of the State of California at the time the award is made and shall not exceed an aggregate amount of fifty thousand dollars ($50,000).

This subdivision shall not apply if a public entity has provided for the defense of the action pursuant to Section 995 of the Government Code.

(d) A court may award attorney's fees to a commercial film and photographic print processor when a suit is brought against the processor because of a disclosure mandated by this article and the court finds this suit to be frivolous.

(e) Any person who fails to report an instance of child abuse which he or she knows to exist or reasonably should know to exist, as required by this article, is guilty of a misdemeanor and is punishable by confinement in the county jail for a term not to exceed six months or by a fine of not more than one thousand dollars ($1,000) or by both. *(Amended by Stats 1987 ch 1459 §23.)*

§11174. Investigation guidelines.

The Department of Justice, in cooperation with the State Department of Social Services, shall prescribe by regulation guidelines for the investigation of abuse

© 1992 by J., B. & L. Gould
Printed in the U.S.A.   **EP**

in out-of-home care, as defined in Section 11165.5, and shall ensure that the investigation is conducted in accordance with the regulations and guidelines. *(Amended by Stats 1988 ch 269 §5, eff. 1/1/89.)*

§11174.1. Child abuse; child care facilities.

(a) The Department of Justice, in cooperation with the State Department of Social Services, shall prescribe by regulation guidelines for the investigation of child abuse, as defined in Section 11165.6, in facilities licensed to care for children, and shall ensure that the investigation is conducted in accordance with the regulations and guidelines.

(b) For community treatment facilities, day treatment facilities, group homes, and foster family agencies, the State Department of Social Services shall prescribe the following regulations:

(1) Regulations designed to assure that all licensees and employees of community treatment facilities, day treatment facilities, group homes, and foster family agencies licensed to care for children have had appropriate training, as determined by the State Department of Social Services, in consultation with representatives of licensees, on the provisions of this article.

(2) Regulations designed to assure the community treatment facilities, day treatment facilities, group homes, and foster family agencies licensed to care for children maintain a written protocol for the investigation and reporting of child abuse, as defined in Section 11165.6, alleged to have occurred involving a child placed in the facility.

(c) The State Department of Social Services shall provide such orientation and training as it deems necessary to assure that its officers, employees, or agents who conduct inspections of facilities licensed to care for children are knowledgeable about the reporting requirements of this article and have adequate training to identify conditions leading to, and the signs of, child abuse, as defined in Section 11165.6. *(Amended by Stats 1989 ch 1053 §2, eff. 9/29/89.)*

§11174.3. Interviewing of suspected victim of child abuse.

(a) Whenever a representative of a child protective agency deems it necessary, a suspected victim of child abuse may be interviewed during school hours, on school premises, concerning a report of suspected child abuse that occurred within the child's home. The child shall be afforded the option of being interviewed in private or selecting any adult who is a member of the staff of the school, including any certificated or classified employee or volunteer aide, to be present at the interview. A representative of the child protective agency shall inform the child of that right prior to the interview. The purpose of the staff person's presence at the interview is to lend support to the child and enable him or her to be as comfortable as possible; however, the member of the staff so elected shall not participate in the interview. The member of the staff so present shall not discuss the facts or circumstances of the case with the child. The member of the staff so present, including, but not limited to, a volunteer aide, is subject to the confidentiality requirements of this article, a violation of which is punishable as specified in Section 11167.5. A representative of the school shall inform a member of the staff so selected by a child of the requirements of this section prior to the interview. A staff member selected by a child may decline the

request to be present at the interview. If the staff person selected agrees to be present, the interview shall be held at a time during school hours when it does not involve an expense to the school. Failure to comply with the requirements of this section does not affect the admissibility of evidence in a criminal or civil proceeding.

(b) The Superintendent of Public Instruction shall notify each school district, and each child protective agency shall notify each of its employees who participate in the investigation of reports of child abuse, of the requirements of this section. *(Added by Stats 1987 ch 640 §2.)*

§1174.5. *Repealed by Stats 1987 ch 1444.*

ARTICLE 3

UNIFORM ACT FOR OUT-OF-STATE PAROLEE SUPERVISION

§11175. Title of article.

This article may be cited as the Uniform Act for Out-of-State Probationer or Parolee Supervision.

§11176. Interstate compacts.

Pursuant to the authority vested in this State by that certain act of Congress, approved June 6, 1934, and entitled "An act granting the consent of Congress to any two or more states to enter into agreements or compacts for cooperative effort and mutual assistance in the prevention of crime, and for other purposes," the Governor is hereby authorized and directed to enter into a compact or compacts on behalf of this State with any of the United States legally joining therein.

§11177. Compact form.

The compact or compacts authorized by Section 11176 shall be in substantially the following form:

A compact entered into by and among the contracting states, signatories hereto, with the consent of the Congress of the United States of America, granted by an act entitled "An act granting the consent of Congress to any two or more states to enter into agreements or compacts for cooperative effort and mutual assistance in the prevention of crime and for other purposes."

The contracting states solemnly agree:

(1) That it shall be competent for the duly constituted judicial and administrative authorities of a state party to this compact (herein called "sending state"), to permit any person convicted of an offense within such state and placed on probation or released on parole to reside in any other state party to this compact (herein called "receiving state") while on probation or parole, if

(a) Such person is in fact a resident of or has his family residing within the receiving state and can obtain employment there;

(b) Though not a resident of the receiving state and not having his family residing there, the receiving state consents to such person being sent there.

Before granting such permission, opportunity shall be granted to the receiving state to investigate the home and prospective employment of such person.

A resident of the receiving state, within the meaning of this section, is one who has been an actual inhabitant of such state continuously for more than one year prior to his coming to the sending state and has not resided within the sending state more than six continuous months immediately preceding the commission of the offense for which he has been convicted.

(2) That each receiving state will assume the duties of visitation of and supervision over probationers or parolees of any sending state and in the exercise of those duties will be governed by the same standards that prevail for its own probationers and parolees.

(3) That duly accredited officers of a sending state may at all times enter a receiving state and there apprehend and retake any person on probation or parole. For that purpose no formalities will be required other than establishing the authority of the officer and the identity of the person to be retaken. All legal requirements to obtain extradition of fugitives from justice are hereby expressly waived on the part of states party hereto, as to such persons. The decision of the sending state to retake a person on probation or parole shall be conclusive upon and not reviewable within the receiving state. If at the time when a state seeks to retake a probationer or parolee there should be pending against him within the receiving state any criminal charge, or he should be suspected of having committed within such state a criminal offense, he shall not be retaken without the consent of the receiving state until discharged from prosecution or from imprisonment for such offense.

(4) That the duly accredited officers of the sending state will be permitted to transport prisoners being retaken through any and all states parties to this compact, without interference.

(5) That the governor of each state may designate an officer who, acting jointly with like officers of other contracting states, if and when appointed, shall promulgate such rules and regulations as may be deemed necessary to more effectively carry out the terms of this compact.

(6) That this compact shall become operative immediately upon its ratification by any state as between it and any other state or states so ratifying. When ratified it shall have the full force and effect of law within such state, the form of ratification to be in accordance with the laws of the ratifying state.

(7) That this compact shall continue in force and remain binding upon each ratifying state until renounced by it. The duties and obligations hereunder of a renouncing state shall continue as to parolees or probationers residing therein at the time of withdrawal until retaken or finally discharged by the sending state. Renunciation of this compact shall be by the same authority which ratified it, by sending six months' notice in writing of its intention to withdraw from the compact to the other states party hereto.

§11177.1. Probationer or parolee; hearing prior to returning to sending state; habeas corpus availability.

(a) Before a probationer or parolee may be returned to the sending state under this compact, he shall have a right to counsel and to a hearing before a magistrate to determine whether he is in fact a probationer or parolee who was allowed to reside in this or any other state pursuant to this compact, whether his return to the sending state has been ordered, and whether there is probable cause to believe he is the same person whose return is sought. At the hearing, the magistrate shall accept certified copies of probation or parole documents showing that this compact has been invoked and that the

probationer or parolee has been ordered returned to the sending state, and these documents shall constitute conclusive proof of their contents. If the magistrate concludes that the probationer or parolee is subject to the terms of this compact, an order shall be issued forthwith directing the delivery to the sending state of the probationer or parolee.

(b) If the probationer or parolee or his counsel desires to test the legality of the order issued under subdivision (a), the magistrate shall fix a reasonable time to be allowed him within which to apply for a writ of habeas corpus. If the writ is denied and probable cause appears for an application for a writ of habeas corpus to another court, or justice or judge thereof, the order denying the writ shall fix a reasonable time within which the accused may again apply for a writ of habeas corpus.

§11177.5. Deputization of agent of another state.

The officer designated by the Governor pursuant to subdivision 5 of Section 11177 of this code may deputize any person regularly employed by another state to act as an officer and agent of this State in effecting the return of any person who has violated the terms and conditions of parole or probation as granted by this State. In any matter relating to the return of such a person, any agent so deputized shall have all the powers of a police officer of this State.

Any deputization pursuant to this section shall be in writing and any person authorized to act as an agent of this State pursuant hereto shall carry formal evidence of his deputization and shall produce the same upon demand.

§11177.6. Sharing cost of effecting return of violator.

The officer designated by the Governor pursuant to subdivision 5 of Section 11177 of this code may, subject to the approval of the Department of General Services, enter into contracts with similar officials of any other state or states for the purpose of sharing an equitable portion of the cost of effecting the return of any person who has violated the terms and conditions of parole or probation as granted by this state.

§11178. Invalidity and affectuation.

If any portion of this article is held unconstitutional, such decision shall not affect the validity of any other portions of this act.

§11179. Article construction.

This article and compacts made pursuant thereto shall be construed as separate and distinct from any act or acts of this State relating to the extradition of fugitives from justice.

ARTICLE 4

INTERSTATE CORRECTIONS COMPACTS

§11189. Provisions and adoption of compact.

The Interstate Corrections Compact as set forth in this section is hereby adopted and entered into with all other jurisdictions joining therein. The provisions of the interstate compact are as follows:

INTERSTATE CORRECTIONS COMPACT

This section may be cited as the Interstate Corrections Compact.

© 1992 by J., B. & L. Gould
Printed in the U.S.A.   EP

The Interstate Corrections Compact is hereby enacted into law and entered into by this state with any other states legally joining therein in the form substantially as follows:

INTERSTATE CORRECTIONS COMPACT

ARTICLE I

Purpose and Policy

The party states, desiring by common action to fully utilize and improve their institutional facilities and provide adequate programs for the confinement, treatment and rehabilitation of various types of offenders, declare that it is the policy of each of the party states to provide such facilities and programs on a basis of cooperation with one another, thereby serving the best interests of such offenders and of society and effecting economies in capital expenditures and operational costs. The purpose of this compact is to provide for the mutual development and execution of such programs of cooperation for the confinement, treatment and rehabilitation of offenders with the most economical use of human and material resources.

ARTICLE II

Definitions

As used in this compact, unless the context clearly requires otherwise:

(a) "State" means a state of the United States; the United States of America; a territory or possession of the United States; the District of Columbia; the Commonwealth of Puerto Rico.

(b) "Sending state" means a state party to this compact in which conviction or court commitment was had.

(c) "Receiving state" means a state party to this compact to which an inmate is sent for confinement other than a state in which conviction or court commitment was had.

(d) "Inmate" means a male or female offender who is committed, under sentence to or confined in a penal or correctional institution.

(e) "Institution" means any penal or correctional facility, including but not limited to a facility for the mentally ill or mentally defective, in which inmates as defined in (d) above may lawfully be confined.

ARTICLE III

Contracts

(a) Each party state may make one or more contracts with any one or more of the other party states for the confinement of inmates on behalf of a sending state in institutions situated within receiving states. Any such contract shall provide for:

1. Its duration.

2. Payments to be made to the receiving state by the sending state for inmate maintenance, extraordinary medical and dental expenses, and any participation in or receipt by inmates of rehabilitative or correctional services, facilities, programs or treatment not reasonably included as part of normal maintenance.

3. Participation in programs of inmate employment, if any; the disposition or crediting of any payments received by inmates on account thereof; and the crediting of proceeds from or disposal of any products resulting therefrom.

4. Delivery and retaking of inmates.

5. Such other matters as may be necessary and appropriate to fix the obligations, responsibilities and rights of the sending and receiving states.

(b) The terms and provisions of this compact shall be a part of any contract entered into by the authority of or pursuant thereto, and nothing in any such contract shall be inconsistent therewith.

ARTICLE IV

Procedures and Rights

(a) Whenever the duly constituted authorities in a state party to this compact, and which has entered into a contract pursuant to Article III, shall decide that confinement in, or transfer of an inmate to, an institution within the territory of another party state is necessary or desirable in order to provide adequate quarters and care or an appropriate program of rehabilitation or treatment, said officials may direct that the confinement be within an institution within the territory of said other party state, the receiving state to act in that regard solely as agent for the sending state.

(b) The appropriate officials of any state party to this compact shall have access, at all reasonable times, to any institution in which it has a contractual right to confine inmates for the purpose of inspecting the facilities thereof and visiting such of its inmates as may be confined in the institution.

(c) Inmates confined in an institution pursuant to the terms of this compact shall at all times be subject to the jurisdiction of the sending state and may at any time be removed therefrom for transfer to a prison or other institution within the sending state, for transfer to another institution in which the sending state may have a contractual or other right to confine inmates, for release on probation or parole, for discharge, or for any other purpose permitted by the laws of the sending state; provided that the sending state shall continue to be obligated to such payments as may be required pursuant to the terms of any contract entered into under the terms of Article III.

(d) Each receiving state shall provide regular reports to each sending state on the inmates of that sending state in institutions pursuant to this compact including a conduct record of each inmate and certify said record to the official designated by the sending state, in order that each inmate may have official review of his or her record in determining and altering the disposition of said inmate in accordance with the law which may obtain in the sending state and in order that the same may be a source of information for the sending state.

(e) All inmates who may be confined in an institution pursuant to the provisions of this compact shall be treated in a reasonable and humane manner and shall be treated equally with such similar inmates of the receiving state as may be confined in the same institution. The fact of confinement in a receiving state shall not deprive any inmate so confined of any legal rights which said inmate would have had if confined in an appropriate institution of the sending state.

(f) Any hearing or hearings to which an inmate confined pursuant to this compact may be entitled by the laws of the sending state may be had before the appropriate authorities of the sending state, or of the receiving state if authorized by the sending state. The receiving state shall provide adequate facilities for such hearings as may be conducted by the appropriate officials of a sending state. In the event such hearing or hearings are had before officials of the receiving state, the governing law shall be that of the sending state and a record of the hearing or hearings as prescribed by the sending state shall be made. Said record together with any recommendations of the hearing officials shall be transmitted forthwith to the official or officials before whom the hearing would have been had if it had taken place in the sending state. In any and all proceedings had pursuant to the provisions of this subdivision, the officials of the receiving state shall act solely as agents of the sending state and no final determination shall be made in any matter except by the appropriate officials of the sending state.

(g) Any inmate confined pursuant to this compact shall be released within the territory of the sending state unless the inmate, and the sending and receiving states, shall agree upon release in some other place. The sending state shall bear the cost of such return to its territory.

(h) Any inmate confined pursuant to the terms of this compact shall have any and all rights to participate in and derive any benefits or incur or be relieved of any obligations or have such obligations modified or his status changed on account of any action or proceeding in which he could have participated if confined in any appropriate institution of the sending state located within such state.

(i) The parent, guardian, trustee, or other person or persons entitled under the laws of the sending state to act for, advise, or otherwise function with respect to any inmate shall not be deprived of or restricted in his exercise of any power in respect of any inmate confined pursuant to the terms of this compact.

ARTICLE V

Acts Not Reviewable in Receiving State: Extradition

(a) Any decision of the sending state in respect of any matter over which it retains jurisdiction pursuant to this compact shall be conclusive upon and not reviewable within the receiving state, but if at the time the sending state seeks to remove an inmate from an institution in the receiving state there is pending against the inmate within such state any criminal charge or if the inmate is formally accused of having committed within such state a criminal offense, the inmate shall not be returned without the consent of the receiving state until discharged from prosecution or other form of proceeding, imprisonment or detention for such offense. The duly accredited officers of the sending state shall be permitted to transport inmates pursuant to this compact through any and all states party to this compact without interference.

(b) An inmate who escapes from an institution in which he is confined pursuant to this compact shall be deemed a fugitive from the sending state and from the state in which the institution is situated. In the case of an escape to a jurisdiction other than the sending or receiving state, the responsibility for institution of extradition or rendition proceedings shall be that of the sending state, but nothing contained herein shall be construed to prevent or affect the activities of officers and agencies of any jurisdiction directed toward the apprehension and return of an escapee.

ARTICLE VI

Federal Aid

Any state party to this compact may accept federal aid for use in connection with any institution or program, the use of which is or may be affected by this compact or any contract pursuant hereto and any inmate in a receiving state pursuant to this compact may participate in any such federally aided program or activity for which the sending and receiving states have made contractual provision, provided that if such program or activity is not part of the customary correctional regimen, the express consent of the appropriate official of the sending state shall be required therefor.

ARTICLE VII

Entry Into Force

This compact shall enter into force and become effective and binding upon the states so acting when it has been enacted into law by any two states. Thereafter, this compact shall enter into force and become effective and binding as to any other of said states upon similar action by such state.

ARTICLE VIII

Withdrawal and Termination

This compact shall continue in force and remain binding upon a party state until it shall have enacted a statute repealing the same and providing for the sending of formal written notice of withdrawal from the compact to the appropriate officials of all other party states. An actual withdrawal shall not take effect until one year after the notices provided in said statute have been sent. Such withdrawal shall not relieve the withdrawing state from its obligations assumed hereunder prior to the effective date of withdrawal. Before the effective date of withdrawal, a withdrawing state shall remove to its territory, at its own expense, such inmates as it may have confined pursuant to the provisions of this compact.

ARTICLE IX

Other Arrangements Unaffected

Nothing contained in this compact shall be construed to abrogate or impair any agreement or other arrangement which a party state may have with a nonparty state for the confinement, rehabilitation or treatment of inmates nor to repeal any other laws of a party state authorizing the making of cooperative institutional arrangements.

ARTICLE X

Construction and Severability

The provisions of this compact shall be liberally construed and shall be severable. If any phrase, clause, sentence or provision of this compact is declared to be contrary to the constitution of any participating state or of the United States or the applicability thereof to any government, agency, person or circumstance is held invalid, the validity of the remainder of this compact and the applicability thereof to any government, agency, person or circumstance shall not be affected thereby. If this compact shall be held contrary

© 1992 by J., B. & L. Gould
Printed in the U.S.A.   EP

to the constitution of any state participating therein, the compact shall remain in full force and effect as to the remaining states and in full force and effect as to the state affected as to all severable matters.

§11190. Enactments into law: form and contents.

The Western Interstate Corrections Compact as contained herein is hereby enacted into law and entered into on behalf of this State with any and all other states legally joining therein in a form substantially as follows:

WESTERN INTERSTATE CORRECTIONS COMPACT

ARTICLE I

Purpose and Policy

The party states, desiring by common action to improve their institutional facilities and provide programs of sufficiently high quality for the confinement, treatment and rehabilitation of various types of offenders, declare that it is the policy of each of the party states to provide such facilities and programs on a basis of co-operation with one another, thereby serving the best interests of such offenders and of society. The purpose of this compact is to provide for the development and execution of such programs of co-operation for the confinement, treatment and rehabilitation of offenders.

ARTICLE II

Definitions

As used in this compact, unless the context clearly requires otherwise:

(a) "State" means a state of the United States, or, subject to the limitation contained in Article VII, Guam.

(b) "Sending state" means a state party to this compact in which conviction was had.

(c) "Receiving state" means a state party to this compact to which an inmate is sent for confinement other than a state in which conviction was had.

(d) "Inmate" means a male or female offender who is under sentence to or confined in a prison or other correctional institution.

(e) "Institution" means any prison, reformatory or other correctional facility (including but not limited to a facility for the mentally ill or mentally defective) in which inmates may lawfully be confined.

ARTICLE III

Contracts

(a) Each party state may make one or more contracts with any one or more of the other party states for the confinement of inmates on behalf of a sending state in institutions situated within receiving states. Any such contract shall provide for:

1. Its duration.
2. Payments to be made to the receiving state by the sending state for inmate maintenance, extraordinary medical and dental expenses, and any participation in or receipt by inmates of rehabilitative or correctional services, facilities, programs or treatment not reasonably included as part of normal maintenance.

3. Participation in programs of inmate employment, if any; the disposition or crediting of any payments received by inmates on accounts thereof; and the crediting of proceeds from or disposal of any products resulting therefrom.

4. Delivery and retaking of inmates.

5. Such other matters as may be necessary and appropriate to fix the obligations, responsibilities and rights of the sending and receiving states.

(b) Prior to the construction or completion of construction of any institution or addition thereto by a party state, any other party state or states may contract therewith for the enlargement of the planned capacity of the institution or addition thereto, or for the inclusion therein of particular equipment or structures, and for the reservation of a specific per centum of the capacity of the institution to be kept available for use by inmates of the sending state or states so contracting. Any sending state so contracting may, to the extent that moneys are legally available therefor, pay to the receiving state, a reasonable sum as consideration for such enlargement of capacity, or provision of equipment or structures, and reservation of capacity. Such payment may be in a lump sum or in installments as provided in the contract.

(c) The terms and provisions of this compact shall be a part of any contract entered into by the authority of or pursuant thereto, and nothing in any such contract shall be inconsistent therewith.

ARTICLE IV

Procedures and Rights

(a) Whenever the duly constituted judicial or administrative authorities in a state party to this compact, and which has entered into a contract pursuant to Article III, shall decide that confinement in, or transfer of an inmate to, an institution within the territory of another party state is necessary in order to provide adequate quarters and care or desirable in order to provide an appropriate program of rehabilitation or treatment, said officials may direct that the confinement be within an institution within the territory of said other party state, the receiving state to act in that regard solely as agent for the sending state.

(b) The appropriate officials of any state party to this compact shall have access, at all reasonable times, to any institution in which it has a contractual right to confine inmates for the purpose of inspecting the facilities thereof and visiting such of its inmates as may be confined in the institution.

(c) Inmates confined in an institution pursuant to the terms of this compact shall at all times be subject to the jurisdiction of the sending state and may at any time be removed therefrom for transfer to a prison or other institution within the sending state, for transfer to another institution in which the sending state may have a contractual or other right to confine inmates, for release on probation or parole, for discharge, or for any other purpose permitted by the laws of the sending state; provided that the sending state shall continue to be obligated to such payments as may be required pursuant to the terms of any contract entered into under the terms of Article III.

(d) Each receiving state shall provide regular reports to each sending state on the inmates of that sending state in institutions pursuant to this compact including a conduct record of each inmate and certify said record to the official designated by the sending

© 1992 by J., B. & L. Gould
Printed in the U.S.A. **EP**

state, in order that each inmate may have the benefit of his or her record in determining and altering the disposition of said inmate in accordance with the law which may obtain in the sending state and in order that the same may be a source of information for the sending state.

(e) All inmates who may be confined in an institution pursuant to the provisions of this compact shall be treated in a reasonable and humane manner and shall be cared for and treated equally with such similar inmates of the receiving state as may be confined in the same institution. The fact of confinement in a receiving state shall not deprive any inmate so confined of any legal rights which said inmate would have had if confined in an appropriate institution of the sending state.

(f) Any hearing or hearings to which an inmate confined pursuant to this compact may be entitled by the laws of the sending state may be had before the appropriate authorities of the sending state or of the receiving state if authorized by the sending state. The receiving state shall provide adequate facilities for such hearings as may be conducted by the appropriate officials of a sending state. In the event such hearing or hearings are had before officials of the receiving state, the governing law shall be that of the sending state and a record of the hearing or hearings as prescribed by the sending state shall be made. Said record together with any recommendations of the hearing officials shall be transmitted forthwith to the official or officials before whom the hearing would have been had if it had taken place in the sending state. In any and all proceedings had pursuant to the provisions of this subdivision, the officials of the receiving state shall act solely as agents of the sending state and no final determination shall be made in any matter except by the appropriate officials of the sending state. Costs of records made pursuant to this subdivision shall be borne by the sending state.

(g) Any inmate confined pursuant to this compact shall be released within the territory of the sending state unless the inmate, and the sending and receiving states, shall agree upon release in some other place. The sending state shall bear the cost of such return to its territory.

(h) Any inmate confined pursuant to the terms of this compact shall have any and all rights to participate in and derive any benefits or incur or be relieved of any obligations or have such obligations modified or his status changed on account of any action or proceeding in which he could have participated if confined in any appropriate institution of the sending state located within such state.

(i) The parent, guardian, trustee, or other person or persons entitled under the laws of the sending state to act for, advise, or otherwise function with respect to any inmate shall not be deprived of or restricted in his exercise of any power in respect of any inmate confined pursuant to the terms of this compact.

ARTICLE V

Acts Not Reviewable in Receiving State; Extradition

(a) Any decision of the sending state in respect of any matter over which it retains jurisdiction pursuant to this compact shall be conclusive upon and not reviewable within the receiving state, but if at the time the sending state seeks to remove an inmate from an institution in the receiving state there is pending against the inmate within such state any criminal charge or if the inmate is suspected of having committed within such state a criminal offense, the inmate shall not be returned without the consent of the receiving state until discharged from prosecution or other form of proceeding, imprisonment or detention for such offense. The duly accredited officers of the sending state shall be permitted to transport inmates pursuant to this compact through any and all states party to this compact without interference.

(b) An inmate who escapes from an institution in which he is confined pursuant to this compact shall be deemed a fugitive from the sending state and from the state in which the institution is situated. In the case of an escape to a jurisdiction other than the sending or receiving state, the responsibility for institution of extradition proceedings shall be that of the sending state, but nothing contained herein shall be construed to prevent or affect the activities of officers and agencies of any jurisdiction directed toward the apprehension and return of an escapee.

ARTICLE VI

Federal Aid

Any state party to this compact may accept federal aid for use in connection with any institution or program, the use of which is or may be affected by this compact or any contract pursuant hereto and any inmate in a receiving state pursuant to this compact may participate in any such federally aided program or activity for which the sending and receiving states have made contractual provision provided that if such program or activity is not part of the customary correctional regimen the express consent of the appropriate official of the sending state shall be required therefor.

ARTICLE VII

Entry Into Force

This compact shall enter into force and become effective and binding upon the states so acting when it has been enacted into law by any two contiguous states from among the States of Alaska, Arizona, California, Colorado, Hawaii, Idaho, Montana, Nebraska, Nevada, New Mexico, Oregon, Utah, Washington and Wyoming. For the purpose of this article, Alaska and Hawaii shall be deemed contiguous to each other; to any and all of the States of California, Oregon and Washington; and to Guam. Thereafter, this compact shall enter into force and become effective and binding as to any other of said states, or any other state contiguous to at least one party state upon similar action by such state. Guam may become party to this compact by taking action similar to that provided for joinder by any other eligible party state and upon the consent of Congress to such joinder. For the purposes of this article, Guam shall be deemed contiguous to Alaska, Hawaii, California, Oregon and Washington.

ARTICLE VIII

Withdrawal and Termination

This compact shall continue in force and remain binding upon a party state until it shall have enacted a statute repealing the same and providing for the sending of formal written notice of withdrawal from

© 1992 by J., B. & L. Gould
Printed in the U.S.A.   **EP**

the compact to the appropriate officials of all other party states. An actual withdrawal shall not take effect until two years after the notices provided in said statute have been sent. Such withdrawal shall not relieve the withdrawing state from its obligations assumed hereunder prior to the effective date of withdrawal. Before the effective date of withdrawal, a withdrawing state shall remove to its territory, at its own expense, such inmates as it may have confined pursuant to the provisions of this compact.

ARTICLE IX

Other Arrangements Unaffected

Nothing contained in this compact shall be construed to abrogate or impair any agreement or other arrangement which a party state may have with a nonparty state for the confinement, rehabilitation or treatment of inmates nor to repeal any other laws of a party state authorizing the making of co-operative institutional arrangements.

ARTICLE X

Construction and Severability

The provisions of this compact shall be liberally construed and shall be severable. If any phrase, clause, sentence or provision of this compact is declared to be contrary to the constitution of any participating state or of the United States or the applicability thereof to any government, agency, person or circumstance is held invalid, the validity of the remainder of this compact and the applicability thereof to any government, agency, person or circumstance shall not be affected thereby. If this compact shall be held contrary to the constitution of any state participating therein, the compact shall remain in full force and effect as to the remaining states and in full force and effect as to the state affected as to all severable matters.

§11191. Transfer or commitment of inmate by consent, through corrections compact.

Any court or other agency or officer of this state having power to commit or transfer an inmate (as defined in Article 11(d) of the Interstate Corrections Compact or of the Western Interstate Corrections Compact) to any institution for confinement may commit or transfer such inmate to any institution within or without this state if this state has entered into a contract or contracts for the confinement of inmates in said institution pursuant to Article III of the Interstate Corrections Compact or of the Western Interstate Corrections Compact, but no inmate sentenced under California law may be committed or transferred to an institution outside of this state, unless he has executed a written consent to the transfer. The inmate shall have the right to a private consultation with an attorney of his choice, or with a public defender if the inmate cannot afford counsel, concerning his rights and obligations under this section, and shall be informed of such right prior to executing the written consent. At any time more than five years after the transfer, the inmate shall be entitled to revoke his consent and to transfer to an institution in this state. In such cases, the transfer shall occur within the next 30 days.

§11192. Compact enforcement.

The courts, departments, agencies and officers of this State and its subdivisions shall enforce this compact and shall do all things appropriate to the effectuation of its purposes and intent which may be within their respective jurisdictions including but not limited to the making and submission of such reports as are required by the compact.

§11193. Hearings; right of inmates in another state.

Any inmate sentenced under California law who is imprisoned in another state, pursuant to a compact, shall be entitled to all hearings, within 120 days of the time and under the same standards, which are normally accorded to persons similarly sentenced who are confined in institutions in this state. If the inmate consents in writing, such hearings may be conducted by the corresponding agencies or officials of such other jurisdiction. The Board of Prison Terms or its duly authorized representative is hereby authorized and directed to hold such hearings as may be requested by such other jurisdiction or the inmate pursuant to this section or to Article IV(f) of the Interstate Corrections Compact or of the Western Interstate Corrections Compact.

§11194. State's participation in corrections compact.

The Director of Corrections is hereby empowered to enter into such contracts on behalf of this state as may be appropriate to implement the participation of this state in the Interstate Corrections Compact and the Western Interstate Corrections Compact pursuant to Article III thereof. No such contract shall be of any force or effect until approved by the Director of General Services. Such contracts may authorize confinement of inmates in, or transfer of inmates from, only such institutions in this state as are under the jurisdiction of the Department of Corrections, and no such contract may provide for transfer out of this state of any person committed to the custody of the Director of the Youth Authority. No such contract may authorize the confinement of an inmate, who is in the custody of the Director of Corrections, in an institution of a state other than a state that is a party to the Interstate Corrections Compact or to the Western Interstate Corrections Compact. The Director of Corrections, subject to the approval of the Board of Prison Terms, must first determine, on the basis of an inspection made by his direction, that such institution of another state is a suitable place for confinement of prisoners committed to his custody before entering into a contract permitting such confinement, and shall, at least annually, redetermine the suitability of such confinement. In determining the suitability of such institution of another state, the director shall assure himself that such institution maintains standards of care and discipline not incompatible with those of the State of California and that all inmates therein are treated equitably, regardless of race, religion, color, creed or national origin.

§11194.5. Confinement of county prisoners in adjacent states.

(a) At the request of the board of supervisors of any county that is adjacent to another state, the county sheriff shall negotiate with the appropriate officials of the adjacent state to contract pursuant to the authority of Article III of a compact executed under Section 11189 or 11190 for the confinement of county jail prisoners in corresponding facilities located in the adjacent state. The sheriff shall determine that the corresponding facilities are a suitable place of confinement of prisoners submitted to his or her custody and shall at least annually redetermine the suitability as a precondition to any contract under this section. In determining the suitability of the facilities of the other states, the sheriff shall assure himself or herself that it maintains standards of care and discipline not incompatible with those of this state and that all inmates therein are treated equally, regardless of race, religion, color, creed, or national origin.

(b) With the approval of the board of supervisors including agreement as to terms for payments to be made for prisoner maintenance and expenses, the county sheriff may enter into a contract negotiated under subdivision (a).

(c) No prisoner may be transferred to an institution outside of this state under this section unless he or she has executed a written consent to the transfer.

(d) Any person who was sent to another state from a county under the authority of this section shall be released within the territory of the county unless the person, the sheriff of the sending county, and the corresponding official or agency of the other state shall agree upon release in another place. The county shall bear the cost of transporting the person to the place of release. *(Added by Stats 1986 ch 860 §1.)*

§11195. Transferred prisoners on release from prison outside this state.

Every prisoner released from a prison without this state to which he has been committed or transferred from this state pursuant to this article shall be entitled to the same benefits, including, but not limited to money and tools, as are allowed to a prisoner released from a prison in this state. Any person who has been sent to another state for confinement pursuant to this article shall be released within the territory of this state unless the person, the Director of Corrections of California, and the corresponding agency or official of the other state shall agree upon release in some other place. This state shall bear the cost of transporting the person to the place of release.

§11196. Construction; severability.

The provisions of this article shall be severable and if any phrase, clause, sentence, or provision of this article is declared to be unconstitutional or the applicability thereof to any state, agency, person or circumstance is held invalid, the constitutionality of this article and the applicability thereof to any other state, agency, person or circumstance shall, with respect to all severable matters, not be affected thereby. It is the legislative intent that the provisions of this article be reasonably and liberally construed.

§11197. Notice to defense counsel of witness sentenced under California law and committed in another state to testify for prosecution.

No person sentenced under California law who is committed or transferred to an institution outside of this state shall be competent to testify for the prosecution in any criminal proceeding in this state unless counsel for each defendant in such proceeding is notified that the prosecution may call the person as a witness and is given an opportunity to interview the person no less than 10 days before the commencement of the proceeding or, in the event the prosecution is not at that time considering the possibility of using such

testimony, the notice and opportunity for interview shall be given at the earliest possible time. Nothing in this section shall be construed to compel the prisoner to submit to such an interview.

CHAPTER 3

PREVENTION AND ABATEMENT OF UNLAWFUL ACTIVITIES

ARTICLE 1

UNLAWFUL LIQUOR SALE ABATEMENT LAW

§11200. Liquor unlawfully sold, as nuisance.

Every building or place used for the purpose of unlawfully selling, serving or giving away any spirituous, vinous, malt or other alcoholic liquor, and every building or place in or upon which such liquors are unlawfully sold, served or given away, is a nuisance which shall be enjoined, abated and prevented, whether it is a public or private nuisance.

§11201. Abatement as remedy for nuisance.

Whenever there is reason to believe that a nuisance as defined in this article is kept, maintained or exists in any county, the district attorney, in the name of the people of the State of California, shall, or the city attorney of an incorporated city, or any citizen of the state resident within the county, in his or her own name may, maintain an action in equity to abate and prevent the nuisance and to perpetually enjoin the person or persons conducting or maintaining it, and the owner, lessee or agent of the building, or place, in or upon which the nuisance exists, from directly or indirectly maintaining or permitting it.

The complaint in the action shall be verified unless filed by the district attorney. *(Amended by Stats 1987 ch 1076 §5.)*

§11202. Procedure for abatement; writ of injunction.

Whenever the existence of a nuisance is shown in an action brought under this article to the satisfaction of the court or judge thereof, either by verified complaint or affidavit, and the court or judge is satisfied that the owner of the property has received written notice of the existence of the nuisance, signed by the complainant or the district attorney at least two weeks prior to the filing of the complaint, the court or judge shall allow a temporary writ of injunction to abate and prevent the continuance or recurrence of the nuisance. On granting such writ the court or judge shall require an undertaking on the part of the applicant to the effect that the applicant will pay to the party enjoined such damages, not exceeding an amount to be specified, as the opposing party may sustain by reason of the injunction, if the court finally decides that the applicant was not entitled to the injunction.

§11203. Actions having precedence; costs.

Actions brought under this article shall have precedence over all other actions, excepting criminal proceedings, election contests and hearings on injunctions. If a complaint is filed under this article by a citizen, it shall not be dismissed by the plaintiff or for want of prosecution except upon a sworn statement made by the complainant and his attorney, setting forth the reasons why the action should be dismissed,

© 1992 by J., B. & L. Gould
Printed in the U.S.A.   EP

and the dismissal ordered by the court. In case of failure to prosecute any such action with reasonable diligence, or at the request of the plaintiff, the court, in its discretion, may substitute any other citizen consenting thereto for the plaintiff. If the action is brought by a citizen and the court finds there was no reasonable ground or cause therefor, the costs shall be taxed against such citizen.

§11204. Lien upon building for plaintiff's costs.

If the existence of a nuisance is established in an action as provided in this article, an order of abatement shall be entered as part of the judgment in the case, and plaintiff's costs in such action are a lien upon the building and place, enforceable and collectible by execution issued by order of the court.

§11205. Violation of injunction; contempt.

Any violation or disobedience of an injunction or order expressly provided for in this article is punishable as a contempt of court by a fine of not less than two hundred dollars ($200) nor more than one thousand dollars ($1,000), or by imprisonment in the county jail for not less than one nor more than six months, or by both.

§11206. Fine is a lien upon building.

Whenever the owner of a building or place upon which an act or acts constituting a contempt as defined in this article has been committed is guilty of a contempt of court, and is fined therefor in any proceedings under this article, the fine is a lien upon such building and place to the extent of the interest of such person therein, enforceable and collectible by execution issued by order of the court.

§11207. Person defined.

"Person," as used in this article, means individuals, corporations, associations, partnerships, trustees, lessees, agents and assignees.

ARTICLE 2

RED LIGHT ABATEMENT LAW

§11225. Place of illegal gambling or prostitution a nuisance.

(a) Every building or place used for the purpose of illegal gambling as defined by state law or local ordinance, lewdness, assignation, or prostitution, and every building or place in or upon which acts of illegal gambling as defined by state law or local ordinance, lewdness, assignation, or prostitution, are held or occur, is a nuisance which shall be enjoined, abated and prevented, and for which damages may be recovered, whether it is a public or private nuisance.

Nothing in this subdivision shall be construed to apply the definition of a nuisance to a private residence where illegal gambling is conducted on an intermittent basis and without the purpose of producing profit for the owner or occupier of the premises.

(b) Every building or place used as a bathhouse which as a primary activity encourages or permits conduct that according to the guidelines of the federal Centers for Disease Control can transmit AIDS, including, but not limited to, anal intercourse, oral copulation, or vaginal intercourse, is a nuisance which shall be enjoined, abated, and prevented, and for which damages may be recovered, whether it is a public or private nuisance.

For purposes of this subdivision, a "bathhouse" means a business which, as its primary purpose, provides facilities for a spa, whirlpool, communal bath, sauna, steam bath, mineral bath, mud bath, or facilities for swimming. *(Amended by Stats 1988 ch 917 §1, eff. 1/1/89.)*

§11226. Action to abate.

Whenever there is reason to believe that a nuisance as defined in this article is kept, maintained or is in existence in any county, the district attorney, in the name of the people of the State of California, shall, or the city attorney of an incorporated city, or any citizen of the state resident within the county, in his or her own name may, maintain an action in equity to abate and prevent the nuisance and to perpetually enjoin the person conducting or maintaining it, and the owner, lessee or agent of the building, or place, in or upon which the nuisance exists, from directly or indirectly maintaining or permitting it.

The complaint in the action shall be verified unless filed by the district attorney or the city attorney. *(Amended by Stats 1987 ch 1076 §6.)*

§11227. Temporary writ of injunction against nuisance.

Whenever the existence of a nuisance is shown in an action brought under this article to the satisfaction of the court or judge thereof, either by verified complaint or affidavit, the court or judge shall allow a temporary writ of injunction to abate and prevent the continuance or recurrence of such nuisance.

§11228. Actions to have precedence.

Actions brought under this article have precedence over all actions, excepting criminal proceedings, election contests and hearings on injunctions, and in such actions evidence of the general reputation of a place is admissible for the purpose of proving the existence of a nuisance. If the complaint is filed by a citizen, it shall not be dismissed by the plaintiff or for want of prosecution except upon a sworn statement made by the complainant and his attorney, setting forth the reasons why the action should be dismissed, and the dismissal ordered by the court. In case of failure to prosecute any such action with reasonable diligence, or at the request of the plaintiff, the court, in its discretion, may substitute any other citizen consenting thereto for the plaintiff. If the action is brought by a citizen and the court finds there was no reasonable ground or cause therefor, the costs shall be taxed against such citizen.

§11229. Violation of injunction or order.

Any violation or disobedience of an injunction or order expressly provided for by this article is punishable as a contempt of court by a fine of not less than two hundred dollars ($200) nor more than one thousand dollars ($1,000), by imprisonment in the county jail for not less than one nor more than six months, or by both.

§11230. Order of abatement; payment of damages.

If the existence of a nuisance is established in an action as provided in this article, an order of abatement shall be entered as a part of the judgment in the case, directing the removal from the building or place of all fixtures, musical instruments and movable property used in conducting, maintaining, aiding or abetting the nuisance, and directing the sale thereof in the manner provided for the sale of chattels under execution, and the effectual closing of the building or place against its use for any purpose, and that it be kept closed for a period of one year, unless sooner released. While such order remains in effect as to closing, such building or place is and shall remain in the custody of the court. For removing and selling the movable property, the officer is entitled to charge and receive the same fees as he would for levying upon and selling like property on execution. For closing the premises and keeping them closed, a reasonable sum shall be allowed by the court.

In lieu of ordering the building or place closed, the court may order the person who is responsible for the existence of the nuisance to pay damages in an amount not to exceed the fair market rental value of the building or place for one year. The actual amount of rent being received for the rental of the building or place, or the existence of any vacancy therein, may be considered, but shall not be the sole determinant of the fair market rental value. Expert testimony may be used to determine the fair market rental value.

Damages collected pursuant to this section shall be deposited in the Restitution Fund in the State Treasury, the proceeds of which shall be available for appropriation by the Legislature to indemnify persons filing claims pursuant to Article 1 (commencing with Section 13959) of Chapter 5 of Part 4 of Division 3 of Title 2 of the Government Code.

§11231. Application of proceeds of sale.

The proceeds of the sale of the property, as provided in Section 11230, shall be applied as follows:

1. To the fees and costs of removal and sale;
2. To the allowances and costs of closing and keeping closed the building or place;
3. To the payment of plaintiff's costs in the action;
4. The balance, if any, shall be paid to the owner of the property so sold.

If the proceeds of the sale do not fully discharge all such costs, fees and allowances, the building and place shall also be sold under execution issued upon the order of the court or judge and the proceeds of such sale applied in like manner.

§11232. Cancellation of abatement order.

If the owner of the building or place is not guilty of any contempt of court in the proceedings, and appears and pays all costs, fees and allowances which are a lien on the building or place and files a bond in the full value of the property, to be ascertained by the court, conditioned that the owner will immediately abate any nuisance that may exist at the building or place and prevent the nuisance from being established or kept thereat within a period of one year thereafter, the court, or judge thereof, may, if satisfied of the owner's good faith, order the premises closed under the order of abatement, to be delivered to the owner, and the order of abatement canceled so far as the order relates to the property. The release of the property under the provisions of this section does not release it from any judgment, lien, penalty or liability to which it may be subject by law.

§11233. Fine as lien on building.

Whenever the owner of a building or place upon which an act or acts constituting a contempt as defined

in this article has been committed, is guilty of a contempt of court and fined therefor under this article, the fine shall be a lien upon the building and place to the extent of the interest of such person therein, enforceable and collectible by execution issued by the order of the court.

§11234. Person defined.

"Person" as used in this article means individuals, corporations, associations, partnerships, trustees, lessees, agents and assignees.

§11235. Building defined.

"Building" as used in this article means so much of any building or structure of any kind as is or may be entered through the same outside entrance.

ARTICLE 3

CONTROL OF GAMBLING SHIPS

§11300. Soliciting visitation.

It is unlawful for any person, within this State, to solicit, entice, induce, persuade or procure, or to aid in soliciting, enticing, inducing, persuading or procuring any person to visit any gambling ship, whether such gambling ship be within or without the jurisdiction of the State.

§11301. Craft defined.

As used in this article "craft" includes every boat, ship, vessel, craft, barge, hulk, float or other thing capable of floating.

§11302. Soliciting entry on auxiliary craft.

It is unlawful for any person, within this State, to solicit, entice, induce, persuade or procure, or to aid in soliciting, enticing, inducing, persuading or procuring any person to visit any craft, whether such craft is within or without the jurisdiction of the State, from which craft any person is transported, conveyed or carried to any gambling ship, whether such gambling ship is within or without the jurisdiction of the State.

§11303. Conveying of persons to gambling ship.

It is unlawful for any person, firm, association or corporation to transport, convey or carry, or to aid in transporting, conveying or carrying any person to any gambling ship, whether such gambling ship is within or without the jurisdiction of the State.

§11304. Conveying of persons to auxiliary vessel.

It is unlawful for any person, firm, association or corporation to transport, convey or carry, or to aid in transporting, conveying or carrying any person to any craft, whether such craft is within or without the jurisdiction of the State, from which craft any person is transported, conveyed, or carried to any gambling ship, whether such gambling ship is within or without the jurisdiction of the State.

§11305. Means of conveyance.

Any boat, ship, vessel, watercraft, barge, airplane, seaplane or aircraft, hereinafter called "means of conveyance," used for the purpose of transporting, conveying or carrying persons in violation of this article is a public nuisance which shall be enjoined, abated and prevented.

© 1992 by J., B. & L. Gould
Printed in the U.S.A. EP

§11306. District attorney to maintain action to prevent and abate nuisance.

Whenever there is reason to believe that a nuisance as defined in this article is kept, maintained or exists in any county, the district attorney, in the name of the people, shall, or any citizen of the State resident in the county, in his own name, may, maintain an action to abate and prevent the nuisance and perpetually to enjoin the person or persons conducting or maintaining it, whether as principal, agent, servant, employee or otherwise, from directly or indirectly maintaining or permitting the nuisance.

Unless filed by the district attorney, the complaint in the action shall be verified.

In any such action the plaintiff, at the time of issuing the summons, or at any time afterward, may have the means of conveyance, with its tackle, apparel and furniture, seized and kept as security for the satisfaction of any judgment that may be entered in the action.

§11307. Bond.

When any means of conveyance is seized pursuant to Section 11306, the owner thereof or any other person otherwise entitled to possession thereof may apply to the court in which the action is pending for leave to file bond and regain possession of the means of conveyance during the pendency of the proceedings. The bond shall be in an amount determined by the judge to be the actual value of the means of conveyance at the time of its release. Upon giving said bond conditioned upon compliance with the terms of any temporary writ of injunction entered in the action and upon the return of the means of conveyance to the custody of the court in the event the same is ordered forfeited, the person on whose behalf such bond is given shall be put in possession of said means of conveyance and may use it until it is finally ordered delivered up and forfeited, if such be the judgment of the court.

§11308. Temporary injunction against nuisance.

If the existence of a nuisance as defined in this article is shown in any action brought under this article to the satisfaction of the court or judge, either by verified complaint or affidavit, the court or judge shall allow a temporary writ of injunction to abate and prevent the continuance or recurrence of the nuisance. On granting the temporary writ the court or judge shall require an undertaking on the part of the applicant to the effect that the applicant will pay to the defendant enjoined such damages, not exceeding an amount to be specified, as the defendant sustains by reason of the injunction if the court finally decides that the applicant was not entitled to it.

§11309. Actions; precedence, dismissal, substitution for plaintiff.

Actions brought under this article shall have precedence over all other actions, except criminal proceedings, election contests and hearings on injunctions.

If the complaint is filed by a citizen it shall not be dismissed by him or for want of prosecution except upon a sworn statement made by him and his attorney, setting forth the reasons why the action should be dismissed, and by dismissal ordered by the court.

In case of failure to prosecute the action with reasonable diligence, or at the request of the plaintiff, the court, in its discretion, may substitute any other citizen consenting thereto for the plaintiff.

If the action is brought by a citizen and the court finds there was no reasonable ground or cause therefor, the costs shall be taxed against him.

§11310. Nuisance; costs in action as lien.

If the existence of a nuisance as defined in this article is established in an action brought thereunder, an order of abatement shall be entered as part of the judgment in the case, and plaintiff's costs in the action are a lien upon the means of conveyance, and upon its tackle, apparel and furniture. The lien is enforceable and collectible by execution issued by order of the court.

§11311. Violation of injunction or order of abatement.

A violation or disobedience of an injunction or order for abatement provided for in this article is punishable as a contempt of court by a fine of not less than two hundred dollars ($200) or more than one thousand dollars ($1,000), or by imprisonment in the county jail for not less than one nor more than six months, or by both.

§11312. Contents of abatement order.

If the existence of a nuisance as defined in this article is established in an action brought thereunder, an order of abatement shall be entered as a part of the judgment, which order shall direct the seizure and forfeiture of the means of conveyance with its tackle, apparel and furniture, and the sale thereof in the manner provided for the sale of like chattels under execution.

While the order of abatement remains in effect, the means of conveyance is in the custody of the court.

For seizing and selling the means of conveyance, the officer is entitled to charge and receive the same fees as he would for levying upon and selling like property on execution.

§11313. Order of application of proceeds of sale.

The proceeds of the sale of the means of conveyance shall be applied as follows:

First—To the fees and costs of the seizure and sale.

Second—To the payment of the plaintiff's costs in the action.

Third—The balance, if any, shall be paid into the State Treasury to the credit of the General Fund.

§11314. Cancellation of abatement.

If the owner of the means of conveyance has not been guilty of any contempt of court in a proceeding brought under this article, and appears and pays all costs, fees, and allowances that are a lien on the means of conveyance and files a bond in the full value of the means of conveyance, to be ascertained by the court, conditioned that the owner will immediately abate the nuisance and prevent it from being established or resumed within a period of one year thereafter, the court or judge may, if satisfied of the owner's good faith, order the means of conveyance to be delivered to the owner, and the order of abatement canceled so far as it may relate thereto. The release of such means of conveyance under the provisions of this section does not release it from any judgment, lien, penalty, or liability to which it may be subject.

§11315. Fine for contempt of court as lien upon property.

Whenever the owner of the means of conveyance, or the owner of any interest therein, has been guilty of a contempt of court, and fined in any proceeding under this article, the fine is a lien upon the property to the extent of his interest in it. The lien is enforceable and collectible by execution issued by order of the court.

§11316. Violation of provisions of article.

Any person, firm, association or corporation, either as principal, agent, servant, employee or otherwise, who violates any of the provisions of this article is guilty of a misdemeanor.

§11317. Gambling ship defined.

The term "gambling ship" as used in this article means any boat, ship, vessel, watercraft or barge kept, operated or maintained for the purpose of gambling, whether within or without the jurisdiction of the State, and whether it is anchored, lying to, or navigating.

§11318. Severability.

If any section, subsection, paragraph, sentence or clause of this article is for any reason held to be invalid, the Legislature hereby declares that had it known of the invalidity of that portion at the time of this enactment, it would have passed the remainder of the article without the invalid portion and that it is the intention of the Legislature that the remainder of the article operate in the event of the invalidity of any portion thereof.

ARTICLE 4

CRIMINAL SYNDICALISM
(Repealed by Stats 1991 ch 186 §10, eff. 1/1/92.)

§§11400 to 11402. *Repealed by Stats 1991 ch 186 §10, eff. 1/1/92.*

ARTICLE 4.5

TERRORIZING

§11410. Legislative finding.

The Legislature finds and declares that it is the right of every person regardless of race, color, creed, religion or national origin, to be secure and protected from fear, intimidation, and physical harm caused by the activities of violent groups and individuals. It is not the intent of this chapter to interfere with the exercise of rights protected by the Constitution of the United States. The Legislature recognizes the constitutional right of every citizen to harbor and express beliefs on any subject whatsoever and to associate with others who share similar beliefs. The Legislature further finds however, that the advocacy of unlawful violent acts by groups against other persons or groups under circumstances where death or great bodily injury is likely to result is not constitutionally protected, poses a threat to public order and safety and should be subject to criminal and civil sanctions.

§11411. Terrorizing: use of crosses, etc.

(a) Any person who places or displays a sign, mark, symbol, emblem, or other physical impression, including, but not limited to, a Nazi swastika on the private property of another, without authorization, for the purpose of terrorizing the owner or occupant of that private property or in reckless disregard of the risk of terrorizing the owner or occupant of that private property shall be punished by imprisonment in the county jail not to exceed one year, by a fine not to exceed five thousand dollars ($5,000), or by both the fine and imprisonment for the first conviction and by imprisonment in the county jail not to exceed one year, by a fine not to exceed fifteen thousand dollars ($15,000), or by both the fine and imprisonment for any subsequent conviction.

(b) Any person who engages in a pattern of conduct for the purpose of terrorizing the owner or occupant of private property or in reckless disregard of terrorizing the owner or occupant of that private property, by placing or displaying a sign, mark, symbol, emblem, or other physical impression, including, but not limited to, a Nazi swastika, on the private property of another on two or more occasions, shall be punished by imprisonment in the state prison for 16 months or 2 or 3 years, by a fine not to exceed ten thousand dollars ($10,000), or by both the fine and imprisonment, or by imprisonment in a county jail not to exceed one year, by a fine not to exceed five thousand dollars ($5,000), or by both the fine and imprisonment. A violation of this subdivision shall not constitute felonious conduct for purposes of Section 186.22.

(c) Any person who burns or desecrates a cross or other religious symbol, knowing it to be a religious symbol, on the private property of another without authorization for the purpose of terrorizing the owner or occupant of that private property or in reckless disregard of the risk of terrorizing the owner or occupant of that private property shall be punished by imprisonment in the state prison for 16 months or 2 or 3 years, by a fine of not more than ten thousand dollars ($10,000), or by both the fine and imprisonment, or by imprisonment in a county jail not to exceed one year, by a fine not to exceed five thousand dollars ($5,000), or by both the fine and imprisonment for the first conviction and by imprisonment in the state prison for 16 months or 2 or 3 years, by a fine of not more than ten thousand dollars ($10,000), or by both the fine and imprisonment, or by imprisonment in a county jail not to exceed one year, by a fine not to exceed fifteen thousand dollars ($15,000), or by both the fine and imprisonment for any subsequent conviction.

(d) As used in this section, "terrorize" means to cause a person of ordinary emotions and sensibilities to fear for personal safety. *(Amended by Stats 1991 ch 605 §1, eff. 1/1/92.)*

§11412. Causing another person to refrain from exercising religion by means of threat.

Any person who, with intent to cause, attempts to cause or causes another to refrain from exercising his or her religion or from engaging in a religious service by means of a threat, directly communicated to such person, to inflict an unlawful injury upon any person or property, and it reasonably appears to the recipient of the threat that such threat could be carried out is guilty of a felony.

§11413. Terrorizing.

(a) Any person who explodes, ignites, or attempts to explode or ignite any destructive device or any explosive, or who commits arson, in or about any of the

© 1992 by J., B. & L. Gould
Printed in the U.S.A.   **EP**

places listed in subdivision (b), for the purpose of terrorizing another or in reckless disregard of terrorizing another is guilty of a felony, and shall be punished by imprisonment in the state prison for three, five, or seven years, and a fine not exceeding ten thousand dollars ($10,000).

(b) Subdivision (a) applies to the following places:

(1) Any health facility licensed under Chapter 2 (commencing with Section 1250) of Division 2 of the Health and Safety Code, or any place where medical care is provided by a licensed health care professional.

(2) Any church, temple, synagogue, or other place of worship.

(3) The buildings, offices, and meeting sites of organizations that counsel for or against abortion or among whose major activities are lobbying, publicizing, or organizing with respect to public or private issues relating to abortion.

(4) Any place at which a lecture, film-showing, or other private meeting or presentation that educates or propagates with respect to abortion practices or policies, whether on private property or at a meeting site authorized for specific use by a private group on public property, is taking place.

(5) Any bookstore or public or private library.

(6) Any building or facility designated as a courthouse.

(7) The home or office of a judicial officer.

(c) As used in this section, "judicial officer" means a magistrate, judge, justice, commissioner, referee, or any person appointed by a court to serve in one of these capacities, of any state or federal court located in this state.

(d) As used in this section, "terrorizing" means to cause a person of ordinary emotions and sensibilities to fear for personal safety. *(Amended by Stats 1990 ch 643 §1, eff. 1/1/91.)*

ARTICLE 5

MARATHON DANCES AND EXHIBITIONS
(Repealed by Stats 1990 ch 569 §2, eff. 1/1/91.)

§§11450 to 11454. *Repealed by Stats 1990 ch 569 §2, eff. 1/1/91.*

ARTICLE 6

PARAMILITARY ORGANIZATIONS

§11460. Assembling, teaching, etc.

(a) Any two or more persons who assemble as a paramilitary organization for the purpose of practicing with weapons shall be punished by imprisonment in the county jail for not more than one year or by a fine of not more than one thousand dollars ($1,000), or by both.

As used in this subdivision, "paramilitary organization" means an organization which is not an agency of the United States government or of the State of California, or which is not a private school meeting the requirements set forth in Section 12154 of the Education Code, but which engages in instruction or training in guerilla warfare or sabotage, or which, as an organization, engages in rioting or the violent disruption of, or the violent interference with, school activities.

(b) (1) Any person who teaches or demonstrates to any other person the use, application, or making of any firearm, explosive, or destructive device, or technique capable of causing injury or death to persons, knowing

or having reason to know or intending that such objects or techniques will be unlawfully employed for use in, or in the furtherance of a civil disorder, or any person who assembles with one or more other persons for the purpose of training with, practicing with, or being instructed in the use of any firearm, explosive, or destructive device, or technique capable of causing injury or death to persons, with the intent to cause or further a civil disorder, shall be punished by imprisonment in the county jail for not more than one year or by a fine of not more than one thousand dollars ($1,000), or by both.

Nothing in this subdivision shall make unlawful any act of any peace officer or a member of the military forces of this state or of the United States, performed in the lawful course of his official duties.

(2) As used in this section:

(A) "Civil disorder" means any disturbance involving acts of violence which cause an immediate danger of or results in damage or injury to the property or person of any other individual.

(B) "Destructive device" has the same meaning as in Section 12301.

(C) "Explosive" has the same meaning as in Section 12000 of the Health and Safety Code.

(D) "Firearm" means any device designed to be used as a weapon, or which may readily be converted to a weapon, from which is expelled a projectile by the force of any explosion or other form of combustion, or the frame or receiver of any such weapon.

(E) "Peace officer" means any peace officer or other officer having the powers of arrest of a peace officer, specified in Chapter 4.5 (commencing with Section 830) of Title 3 of Part 2.

TITLE 1.5

STATEWIDE PROGRAMS OF EDUCATION, TRAINING, AND RESEARCH FOR LOCAL PUBLIC PROSECUTORS AND PUBLIC DEFENDERS

§11500. Purpose of title.

The purpose of this title is to improve the administration of criminal justice by providing funding for statewide programs of education, training, and research for local public prosecutors and public defenders.

§11501. Financial assistance program.

(a) There is hereby established in the Office of Criminal Justice Planning, a program of financial assistance to provide for statewide programs of education, training, and research for local public prosecutors and public defenders. All funds made available to the Office of Criminal Justice Planning for the purposes of this chapter shall be administered and distributed by the executive director of the office.

(b) The Executive Director of the Office of Criminal Justice Planning is authorized to allocate and award funds to public agencies or private nonprofit organizations for purposes of establishing statewide programs of education, training, and research for public prosecutors and public defenders, which programs meet criteria established pursuant to Section 11502.

(c) Annually, the executive director shall submit a report to the Legislature describing the operation and accomplishments of the statewide programs authorized by this title. *(Amended by Stats 1985 ch 510 §1.)*

§11502. Selection of programs.

(a) Criteria for selection of education, training, and research programs for local public prosecutors and public defenders shall be developed by the Office of Criminal Justice Planning in consultation with an advisory group entitled the Prosecutors and Public Defenders Education and Training Advisory Committee.

(b) The Prosecutors and Public Defenders Education and Training Advisory Committee shall be composed of six local public prosecutors and six local public defender representatives, all of whom are appointed by the Executive Director of the Office of Criminal Justice Planning, who shall provide staff services to the advisory committee. In appointing the members of the committee, the executive director shall invite the Attorney General, the State Public Defender, the Speaker of the Assembly, and the Senate President pro Tempore to participate as ex officio members of the committee.

(c) The Office of Criminal Justice Planning, in consultation with the advisory committee, shall develop specific guidelines including criteria for selection of organizations to provide education, training, and research services.

(d) In determining the equitable allocation of funds between prosecution and defense functions, the Office of Criminal Justice Planning and the advisory committee shall give consideration to the amount of local government expenditures on a statewide basis for the support of those functions.

(e) The administration of the overall program shall be performed by the Office of Criminal Justice Planning. The office may, out of any appropriation for this program, expend an amount not to exceed 7.5 percent for any fiscal year for such purposes.

(f) No funds appropriated pursuant to this title shall be used to support a legislative advocate.

(g) To the extent necessary to meet the requirements of the State Bar of California relating to certification of training for legal specialists, the executive director shall insure that, where appropriate, all programs funded under this title are open to all members of the State Bar of California. The program guidelines established pursuant to subdivision (c) shall provide for the reimbursement of costs for all participants deemed eligible by the Office of Criminal Justice Planning, in conjunction with the Legal Training Advisory Committee, by means of course attendance. *(Amended by Stats 1985 ch 510 §2.)*

§11503. Local Public Prosecutors and Public Defenders Training Fund created.

There is hereby created in the State Treasury the Local Public Prosecutors and Public Defenders Training Fund for the support of the Prosecutors and Public Defenders Education and Training Program, established pursuant to this title. *(Added by Stats 1986 ch 40 §1.)*

§11504. Allocation of funds.

To the extent funds are appropriated from the Assessment Fund to the Local Public Prosecutors and Public Defenders Training Fund established pursuant to Section 11503, the Office of Criminal Justice Planning shall allocate financial resources for statewide programs of education, training, and research for local public prosecutors and public defenders. *(Added by Stats 1985 ch 510 §3.)*

TITLE 2

CONTROL OF DEADLY WEAPONS

CHAPTER 1

FIREARMS
(Amended by Stats 1990 ch 1090 §1, eff. 1/1/91.)

ARTICLE 1

GENERAL PROVISIONS

§12000. Title.

This chapter shall be known and may be cited as "The Dangerous Weapons' Control Law."

§12001. Terms defined.

(a) As used in this title, the terms "pistol," "revolver," and "firearm capable of being concealed upon the person" shall apply to and include any device designed to be used as a weapon, from which is expelled a projectile by the force of any explosion, or other form of combustion, and which has a barrel less than 16 inches in length. These terms also include any device which has a barrel 16 inches or more in length which is designed to be interchanged with a barrel less than 16 inches in length.

(b) As used in this title, "firearm" means any device, designed to be used as a weapon, from which is expelled through a barrel a projectile by the force of any explosion or other form of combustion.

(c) As used in Sections 12021, 12021.1, 12070, 12071, 12072, and 12073 of this code, and Sections 8100 and 8103 of the Welfare and Institutions Code, the term "firearm" includes the frame or receiver of any such weapon.

(d) For the purpose of Sections 12025 and 12031, the term "firearm" also shall include any rocket, rocket propelled projectile launcher, or similar device containing any explosive or incendiary material whether or not the device is designed for emergency or distress signaling purposes.

(e) (1) For purposes of Sections 12070, 12071, and subdivisions (b), (c), and (d) of Section 12072, the term "firearm" does not include an unloaded firearm which is defined as an "antique firearm" in Section 921 (a) (16) of Title 18 of the United States Code.

(2) For purposes of Sections 12070, 12071, and subdivisions (b), (c), and (d) of Section 12072, the term "firearm" does not include an unloaded firearm that meets both of the following:

(A) It is not a pistol, revolver, or other firearm capable of being concealed upon the person.

(B) It is a curio or relic, as defined in Section 178.11 of Title 27 of the Code of Federal Regulations.

(f) Nothing shall prevent a device defined as a "pistol," "revolver," or "firearm capable of being concealed upon the person" from also being found to be a short-barreled shotgun or a short-barreled rifle, as defined in Section 12020.

(g) For purposes of Section 12551, the term "firearm" also shall include any instrument which expels a metallic projectile, such as a BB or a pellet, through the force of air pressure, CO_2 pressure, or spring action, or any spot marker gun. *(Amended by Stats 1991 ch 950 §2, 955 §1.1, eff. 1/1/92.)*

© 1992 by J., B. & L. Gould
Printed in the U.S.A.   **EP**

§12001.1. *Repealed by Stats 1991 ch 950 §4, eff. 1/1/92.*

§12001.5. Construction of short-barreled guns.

Except as expressly provided in Section 12020, and solely in accordance with Section 12020, no person may manufacture, import into this state, keep for sale, offer for sale, give, lend, or possess any short-barreled shotgun or short-barreled rifle, as defined in Section 12020, and nothing else in this chapter shall be construed as authorizing the manufacture, importation into the state, keeping for sale, offering for sale, or giving, lending, or possession of any short-barreled shotgun or short-barreled rifle, as defined in Section 12020. *(Amended by Stats 1988 ch 1269 §1.1, eff. 1/1/89.)*

§12001.6. Offenses which involve the violent use of firearm.

As used in this chapter, an offense which involves the violent use of a firearm includes any of the following:

(a) A violation of paragraph (2) or (3) of subdivision (a) of Section 245 or a violation of subdivision (c) of Section 245.

(b) A violation of Section 246.

(c) A violation of paragraph (2) of subdivision (a) of Section 417.

(d) A violation of subdivision (b) of Section 417. *(Amended by Stats 1989 ch 19 §1.1, eff. 1/1/90.)*

§12002. Exemptions; law enforcement and security officers.

(a) Nothing in this chapter prohibits police officers, special police officers, peace officers or law enforcement officers from carrying any wooden club, baton, or any equipment authorized for the enforcement of law or ordinance in any city or county.

(b) Nothing in this chapter prohibits a uniformed security guard, regularly employed and compensated as such by a person engaged in any lawful business, while actually employed and engaged in protecting and preserving property or life within the scope of his or her employment, from carrying any wooden club or baton if the uniformed security guard has satisfactorily completed a course of instruction certified by the Department of Consumer Affairs in the carrying and use of the club or baton. The training institution certified by the Department of Consumer Affairs to present this course, whether public or private, is authorized to charge a fee covering the cost of the training.

(c) The Department of Consumer Affairs, in cooperation with the Commission on Peace Officer Standards and Training, shall develop standards for a course in the carrying and use of the club or baton.

(d) Any uniformed security guard who successfully completes a course of instruction under this section is entitled to receive a permit to carry and use a club or baton within the scope of his or her employment, issued by the Department of Consumer Affairs. The department may authorize certified training institutions to issue permits to carry and use a club or baton. A fee in the amount provided by law shall be charged by the Department of Consumer Affairs to offset the costs incurred by the department in course certification, quality control activities associated with the course and issuance of the permit.

(e) Any person who has received a permit or certificate which indicates satisfactory completion of a club or baton training course approved by the Commission on Peace Officer Standards and Training prior to January 1, 1983, shall not be required to obtain a baton or club permit or complete a course certified by the Department of Consumer Affairs.

§12003. Severability.

If any section, subsection, sentence, clause or phrase of this chpater is for any reason held to be unconstitutional such decision shall not affect the validity of the remaining portions of this chapter. The Legislature hereby declares that it would have passed this act and each section, subsection, sentence, clause and phrase thereof, irrespective of the fact that any one or more other sections, subsections, sentences, clauses or phrases be declared unconstitutional.

ARTICLE 2

UNLAWFUL CARRYING AND POSSESSION OF CONCEALED WEAPONS

§12020. Manufacture, sale, possession, import, of certain dangerous weapons.

(a) Any person in this state who manufactures or causes to be manufactured, imports into the state, keeps for sale, or offers or exposes for sale, or who gives, lends, or possesses any cane gun or wallet gun, any plastic firearm, any firearm which is not immediately recognizable as a firearm, any camouflaging firearm container, any ammunition which contains or consists of any fléchette dart, any bullet containing or carrying an explosive agent, any ballistic knife, any multiburst trigger activator, any nunchaku, any short-barreled shotgun, any short-barreled rifle, any metal knuckles, any belt buckle knife, any leaded cane, any zip gun, any shuriken, any unconventional pistol, any lipstick case knife, any cane sword, any shobi-zue, any air gauge knife, any writing pen knife, or any instrument or weapon of the kind commonly known as a blackjack, slungshot, billy, sandclub, sap, or sandbag, or who carries concealed upon his or her person any explosive substance, other than fixed ammunition or who carries concealed upon his or her person any dirk or dagger, is guilty of a felony, and upon conviction shall be punishable by imprisonment in a county jail not exceeding one year or in the state prison. A bullet containing or carrying an explosive agent is not a destructive device as that term is used in Section 12301.

(b) Subdivision (a) does not apply to any of the following:

(1) The sale to, purchase by, or possession of short-barreled shotguns or short-barreled rifles by police departments, sheriffs' offices, marshals' offices, the California Highway Patrol, the Department of Justice, or the military or naval forces of this state or of the United States for use in the discharge of their official duties or the possession of short-barreled shotguns and short-barreled rifles by regular, salaried, full-time members of a police department, sheriff's office, marshal's office, the California Highway Patrol, or the Department of Justice when on duty and the use is authorized by the agency and is within the course and scope of their duties.

(2) The manufacture, possession, transportation or sale of short-barreled shotguns or short-barreled rifles when authorized by the Department of Justice pursuant to Article 6 (commencing with Section

12095) of this chapter and not in violation of federal law.

(3) The possession of a nunchaku on the premises of a school which holds a regulatory or business license and teaches the arts of self-defense.

(4) The manufacture of a nunchaku for sale to, or the sale of a nunchaku to, a school which holds a regulatory or business license and teaches the arts of self-defense.

(5) Any antique firearm. For purposes of this section, "antique firearm" means any firearm not designed or redesigned for using rimfire or conventional center fire ignition with fixed ammunition and manufactured in or before 1898 (including any matchlock, flintlock, percussion cap, or similar type of ignition system or replica thereof, whether actually manufactured before or after the year 1898) and also any firearm using fixed ammunition manufactured in or before 1898, for which ammunition is no longer manufactured in the United States and is not readily available in the ordinary channels of commercial trade.

(6) Tracer ammunition manufactured for use in shotguns.

(7) Any firearm or ammunition which is a curio or relic as defined in Section 178.11 of Title 27 of the Code of Federal Regulations and which is in the possession of a person permitted to possess such items pursuant to Chapter 44 (commencing with Section 921) of Title 18 of the United States Code and the regulations issued pursuant thereto. Any person prohibited by Section 12021, 12021.1, or 12101 of this code or Section 8100 or 8103 of the Welfare and Institutions Code from possessing firearms or ammunition who obtains title to these items by bequest or intestate succession may retain title for not more than one year, but actual possession of these items at any time shall be punishable pursuant to Section 12021, 12021.1, or 12101 of this code or Section 8100 or 8103 of the Welfare and Institutions Code. Within the year the person shall transfer title to the firearms or ammunition by sale, gift, or other disposition. Any person who violates this paragraph is in violation of subdivision (a).

(8) Any other weapon as defined in subsection (e) of Section 5845 of Title 26 of the United States Code and which is in the possession of a person permitted to possess the weapons pursuant to the federal Gun Control Act of 1968 (Public Law 90-618), as amended, and the regulations issued pursuant thereto. Any person prohibited by Section 12021, 12021.1, or 12101 of this code or Section 8100 or 8103 of the Welfare and Institutions Code from possessing these weapons who obtains title to these weapons by bequest or intestate succession may retain title for not more than one year, but actual possession of these weapons at any time is punishable pursuant to Section 12021, 12021.1, or 12101 of this code or Section 8100 or 8103 of the Welfare and Institutions Code. Within that year the person shall transfer title to the weapons by sale, gift, or other disposition. Any person who violates this paragraph is in violation of subdivision (a). The exemption provided in this subdivision does not apply to pen guns.

(9) Instruments or devices that are possessed by federal, state, and local historical societies, museums, and institutional collections which are open to the public, provided that these instruments or devices are properly housed, secured from unauthorized handling, and, if the instrument or device is a firearm, unloaded.

(10) Instruments or devices, other than short-barreled shotguns or short-barreled rifles, that are possessed or utilized during the course of a motion picture, television, or video production or entertainment event by an authorized participant therein in the course of making that production or event or by an authorized employee or agent of the entity producing that production or event.

(11) Instruments or devices, other than short-barreled shotguns or short-barreled rifles, that are sold by, manufactured by, exposed or kept for sale by, possessed by, imported by, or lent by persons who are in the business of selling instruments or devices listed in subdivision (a) solely to the entities referred in paragraphs (9) and (10) when engaging in transactions with those entities.

(12) The sale to, possession of, or purchase of any weapon, device, or ammunition, other than a short-barreled rifle or short-barreled shotgun, by any federal, state, county, city and county, or city agency that is charged with the enforcement of any law for use in the discharge of their official duties, or the possession of any weapon, device, or ammunition, other than short-barreled rifles and shotguns, when on duty and the use is authorized by the agency and is within the course and scope of their duties.

(13) Weapons, devices, and ammunition, other than short-barreled rifles and short-barreled shotguns, that are sold by, manufactured by, exposed, or kept for sale by, possessed by, imported by, or lent by, persons who are in the business of selling weapons, devices, and ammunition listed in subdivision (a) solely to the entities referred to in paragraph (12) when engaging in transactions with those entities.

(14) The manufacture for, sale to, exposing or keeping for sale to, importation of, or lending of wooden clubs or batons to special police officers or uniformed security guards authorized to carry any wooden club or baton pursuant to Section 12002 by entities that are in the business of selling wooden batons or clubs to special police officers and uniformed security guards when engaging in transactions with those persons.

(15) Prior to January 1, 1992, the possession of a multiburst trigger activator by a person who is not prohibited by Section 12021, 12021.1, or 12101 of this code or Section 8100 or 8103 of the Welfare and Institutions Code from possessing firearms.

(c) (1) As used in this section, a "short-barreled shotgun" means any of the following:

(A) A firearm which is designed or redesigned to fire a fixed shotgun shell and having a barrel or barrels of less than 18 inches in length.

(B) A firearm which has an overall length of less than 26 inches and which is designed or redesigned to fire a fixed shotgun shell.

(C) Any weapon made from a shotgun (whether by alteration, modification, or otherwise) if that weapon, as modified, has an overall length of less than 26 inches or a barrel or barrels of less than 18 inches in length.

(D) Any device which may be readily restored to fire a fixed shotgun shell which, when so restored, is a device defined in subparagraphs (A) to (C), inclusive.

(E) Any part, or combination of parts, designed and intended to convert a device into a device defined in subparagraphs (A) to (C), inclusive, or any combination of parts from which a device defined in subparagraphs (A) to (C), inclusive, can be readily

584

© 1992 by J., B. & L. Gould
Printed in the U.S.A.   **EP**

assembled if those parts are in the possession or under the control of the same person.

(2) As used in this section, a "short-barreled rifle" means any of the following:

(A) A rifle having a barrel or barrels of less than 16 inches in length.

(B) A rifle with an overall length of less than 26 inches.

(C) Any weapon made from a rifle (whether by alteration, modification, or otherwise) if that weapon as modified has an overall length of less than 26 inches or a barrel or barrels of less than 16 inches in length.

(D) Any device which may be readily restored to fire a fixed cartridge which, when so restored, is a device defined in subparagraphs (A) to (C), inclusive.

(E) Any part, or combination of parts, designed and intended to convert a device into a device defined in subparagraphs (A) to (C), inclusive, or any combination of parts from which a device defined in subparagraphs (A) to (C), inclusive, may be readily assembled if those parts are in the possession or under the control of the same person.

(3) As used in this section, a "nunchaku" means an instrument consisting of two or more sticks, clubs, bars or rods to be used as handles, connected by a rope, cord, wire, or chain, in the design of a weapon used in connection with the practice of a system of self-defense such as karate.

(4) As used in this section, a "wallet gun" means any firearm mounted or enclosed in a case, resembling a wallet, designed to be or capable of being carried in a pocket or purse, if such firearm may be fired while mounted or enclosed in such case.

(5) As used in this section, a "cane gun" means any firearm mounted or enclosed in a stick, staff, rod, crutch, or similar device, designed to be, or capable of being used as, an aid in walking, if such firearm may be fired while mounted or enclosed therein.

(6) As used in this section, a "fléchette dart" means a dart, capable a being fired from a firearm, which measures approximately one inch in length, with tail fins which take up five-sixteenths of an inch of the body.

(7) As used in this section, "metal knuckles" means any device or instrument made wholly or partially of metal which is worn for purposes of offense or defense in or on the hand and which either protects the wearer's hand while striking a blow or increases the force of impact from the blow or injury to the individual receiving the blow. The metal contained in the device may help support the hand or fist, provide a shield to protect it, or consist of projections or studs which would contact the individual receiving a blow.

(8) As used in this section, a "ballistic knife" means a device that propels a knifelike blade as a projectile by means of a coil spring, elastic material, or compressed gas. Ballistic knife does not include any device which propels an arrow or a bolt by means of any common bow, compound bow, crossbow, or underwater spear gun.

(9) As used in this section, a "camouflaging firearm container" means a container which meets all of the following:

(A) It is designed and intended to enclose a firearm.

(B) It is designed and intended to allow the firing of the enclosed firearm by external controls while the firearm is in the container.

(C) It is not readily recognizable as containing a firearm.

"Camouflaging firearm container" does not include any camouflaging covering used while engaged in lawful hunting or while going to or returning from a lawn hunting expedition.

(10) As used in this section, a "zip gun" means any weapon or device which meets all of the following criteria:

(A) It was not imported as a firearm by an importer licensed pursuant to Chapter 44 (commencing with Section 921) of Title 18 of the United States Code and the regulations issued pursuant thereto.

(B) It was not originally designed to be a firearm by a manufacturer licensed pursuant to Chapter 44 (commencing with Section 921) of Title 18 of the United States Code and the regulations issued pursuant thereto.

(C) No tax was paid on the weapon or device nor was an exemption from paying tax on that weapon or device granted under Section 4181 and subchapters F (commencing with Section 4216) and G (commencing with Section 4221) of Chapter 32 of Title 26 of the United States Code, as amended, and the regulations issued pursuant thereto.

(D) It is made or altered to expel a projectile by the force of an explosion or other form of combustion.

(E) It has a barrel or barrels less than 18 inches in length or an overall length of less than 26 inches.

(11) As used in this section, a "shuriken" means any instrument, without handles, consisting of a metal plate having three or more radiating points with one or more sharp edges and designed in the shape of a polygon, trefoil, cross, star, diamond, or other geometric shape for use as a weapon for throwing.

(12) As used in this section, an "unconventional pistol" means a pistol or revolver that does not have a rifled bore and has a barrel or barrels of less than 18 inches in length or has an overall length of less than 26 inches.

(13) As used in this section, a "belt buckle knife" is a knife which is made an integral part of a belt buckle and consists of a blade with a length of at least 2½ inches.

(14) As used in this section, a "lipstick case knife" means a knife enclosed within and made an integral part of a lipstick case.

(15) As used in this section, a "cane sword" means a cane, swagger stick, stick, staff, rod, pole, umbrella, or similar device, having concealed within it a blade that may be used as a sword or stiletto.

(16) As used in this section, a "shobi-zue" means a staff, crutch, stick, rod, or pole concealing a knife or blade within it which may be exposed by a flip of the wrist or by a mechanical action.

(17) As used in this section, a "leaded cane" means a staff, crutch, stick, rod, pole, or similar device, unnaturally weighted with lead.

(18) As used in this section, an "air gauge knife" means a device that appears to be an air gauge but has concealed within it a pointed, metallic shaft that is designed to be a stabbing instrument which is exposed by mechanical action or gravity which locks into place when extended.

(19) As used in this section, a "writing pen knife" means a device that appears to be a writing pen but has concealed within it a pointed, metallic shaft that is designed to be a stabbing instrument which is exposed by mechanical action or gravity which locks into place when extended or the pointed, metallic shaft is exposed by the removal of the cap or cover on the device.

© 1992 by J., B. & L. Gould
Printed in the U.S.A. **EP**

(20) As used in this section, a "rifle" means a weapon designed or redesigned, made or remade, and intended to be fired from the shoulder and designed or redesigned and made or remade to use the energy of the explosive in a fixed cartridge to fire only a single projectile through a rifled bore for each single pull of the trigger.

(21) As used in this section, a "shotgun" means a weapon designed or redesigned, made or remade, and intended to be fired from the shoulder and designed or redesigned and made or remade to use the energy of the explosive in a fixed shotgun shell to fire through a smooth bore either a number of projectiles (ball shot) or a single projectile for each pull of the trigger.

(22) As used in this section, a "plastic firearm" means any weapon which meets one of the following requirements:

(A) When, after removal of grips, stocks, and magazines, it is not as detectable as the Security Exemplar, by walk-through metal detectors calibrated and operated to detect the Security Exemplar.

(B) When any major component of which, when subjected to inspection by the types of X-ray machines commonly used at airports, does not generate an image that accurately depicts the shape of the component. Barium sulfate or other compounds may be used in the fabrication of the component.

(C) For purposes of this paragraph, the terms "firearm," "major component," and "Security Exemplar" have the same meanings as those terms are defined in Section 922 of Title 18 of the United States Code.

All firearm detection equipment newly installed in nonfederal public buildings in this state shall be of a type identified by either the United States Attorney General, the Secretary of Transportation, or the Secretary of the Treasury, as appropriate, as available state-of-the-art equipment capable of detecting a plastic firearm, as defined, while distinguishing innocuous metal objects likely to be carried on one's person sufficient for reasonable passage of the public.

(23) As used in this section, a "multiburst trigger activator" means a device designed or redesigned to be attached to a semiautomatic firearm which allows the firearm to discharge two or more shots in a burst by activating the device.

(d) Knives carried in sheaths which are worn openly suspended from the waist of the wearer are not concealed within the meaning of this section. *(Amended by Stats 1990 ch 350 §17; ch 1690 §1, eff. 1/1/91.)*

§12020.5. Advertisement of unlawful weapons.

It shall be unlawful for any person, as defined in Section 12277, in any newspaper, magazine, circular, form letter, or open publication, published, distributed, or circulated in this state, or on any billboard, card, label, or other advertising medium, or by means of any other advertising device, to advertise the sale of any weapon or device whose possession is prohibited by Section 12020, 12220, or 12280. *(Amended by Stats 1990 ch 81 §1, eff. 1/1/91.)*

§12021. Possession of concealable firearms by felons and narcotic addicts.

(a) Any person who has been convicted of a felony under the laws of the United States, of the State of California, or any other state, government, or country, or of an offense enumerated in Section 12001.6, or who is addicted to the use of any narcotic drug, who owns or has in his or her possession or under his or her custody or control any firearm is guilty of a felony.

(b) Notwithstanding subdivision (a), any person who has been convicted of a felony or of an offense enumerated in Section 12001.6, when that conviction results from certification by the juvenile court for prosecution as an adult in an adult court under Section 707 of the Welfare and Institutions Code, who owns or has in his or her possession or under his or her custody or control any firearm is guilty of a felony.

(c) (1) Except as provided in subdivision (a) or paragraph (2) of this subdivision, any person who has been convicted of a misdemeanor violation of Section 136.5, 140, 171b, 171c, 171d, 241, 243, 244.5, 245, 245.5, 246.3, 247, 417, 417.2, 626.9, subdivision (b) or (d) of Section 12034, subdivision (a) of Section 12100, 12320, or 12590 and who, within 10 years of the conviction, owns, or has in his or her possession or under his or her custody or control, any firearm is guilty of a public offense, which shall be punishable by imprisonment in the state prison or in a county jail not exceeding one year, by a fine not exceeding one thousand dollars ($1,000), or by both that imprisonment and fine. The court, on forms prescribed by the Department of Justice, shall notify the department of persons subject to this subdivision. However, the prohibition in this paragraph may be reduced, eliminated, or conditioned as provided in paragraph (2).

(2) Any person, whose continued employment or livelihood is dependent on the ability to legally possess a firearm, who is subject to the prohibition imposed by this subdivision because of a conviction prior to the effective date of the amendments which added this paragraph to this section, at any time until January 1, 1993, may petition the court for relief from this prohibition. The court may reduce or eliminate the prohibition, impose conditions on reduction or elimination of the prohibition, or otherwise grant relief from the prohibition as the court deems appropriate. In making its decision, the court may consider the petitioner's continued employment, the interest of justice, any relevant evidence, and the totality of the circumstances. It is the intent of the Legislature that courts exercise broad discretion in fashioning appropriate relief under this paragraph in cases in which relief is warranted. However, nothing in this paragraph shall be construed to require courts to grant relief to any particular petitioner. It is the intent of the Legislature in enacting this paragraph to permit persons who were convicted of an offense specified in this subdivision prior to the effective date of the amendments which added this paragraph to this section to seek relief from the prohibition imposed by this subdivision.

(d) Any person who, as an express condition of probation, is prohibited or restricted from owning, possessing, controlling, receiving, or purchasing a firearm and who owns, or has in his or her possession or under his or her custody or control, any firearm but who is not subject to subdivision (a) or (c) is guilty of a public offense, which shall be punishable by imprisonment in the state prison or in a county jail not exceeding one year, by a fine not exceeding one thousand dollars ($1,000), or by both that imprisonment and fine. The court, on forms provided by the Department of Justice, shall notify the department of persons subject to this subdivision. The notice shall include a copy of the order of probation and a copy of

© 1992 by J., B. & L. Gould
Printed in the U.S.A.   EP

any minute order or abstract reflecting the order and conditions of probation.

(e) Any person who (1) is alleged to have committed an offense listed in subdivision (b) of Section 707 of the Welfare and Institutions Code, (2) is found to be a fit and proper subject to be dealt with under the juvenile court law, and (3) is subsequently adjudged a ward of the juvenile court within the meaning of Section 602 of the Welfare and Institutions Code because the person committed an offense listed in subdivision (b) of Section 707 of the Welfare and Institutions Code shall not own, or have in his or her possession or under his or her custody or control, any firearm until the age of 30 years. A violation of this subdivision shall be punishable by imprisonment in the state prison or in a county jail not exceeding one year, by a fine not exceeding one thousand dollars ($1,000), or by both that imprisonment and fine. The juvenile court, on forms prescribed by the Department of Justice, shall notify the department of persons subject to this subdivision. Notwithstanding any other law, the forms required to be submitted to the department pursuant to this subdivision may be used to determine eligibility to acquire a firearm.

(f) Subdivision (a) shall not apply to a person who has been convicted of a felony under the laws of the United States unless either of the following criteria is satisfied:

(1) Conviction of a like offense under California law can only result in imposition of felony punishment.

(2) The defendant was sentenced to a federal correctional facility for more than 30 days, or received a fine of more than one thousand dollars ($1,000), or received both punishments.

(g) Every person who purchases or receives, or attempts to purchase or receive, a firearm knowing that he or she is subject to a restraining order issued pursuant to subdivision (a) of Section 546 of the Code of Civil Procedure, or paragraph (2) of subdivision (a) of Section 547 of the Code of Civil Procedure, and predicated on paragraph (2), (3), or (6) of subdivision (a) of Section 4359 of the Civil Code, is guilty of a public offense, which shall be punishable by imprisonment in the state prison or in a county jail not exceeding one year, by a fine not exceeding one thousand dollars ($1,000), or both that imprisonment and fine. This subdivision does not apply unless the copy of the restraining order personally served on the person against whom the restraining order is issued contains a notice in bold print stating (1) that the person is prohibited from purchasing or receiving or attempting to purchase or receive a firearm and (2) specifying the penalties for violating this subdivision, or a court has provided actual verbal notice of the firearm prohibition and penalty as provided in subdivision (f) of Section 550 of the Code of Civil Procedure. However, this subdivision does not apply if the firearm is received as part of the disposition of community property pursuant to Section 4800 of the Civil Code. *(Amended by Stats 1991 ch 953 §4, eff. 10/14/91, oper. only until 1/1/92; ch 955 §3, eff. 1/1/92.)*

§12021.1. Possession of firearms by persons previously convicted of certain violent crimes.

(a) Notwithstanding the provisions of subdivision (a) of Section 12021, any person who has been previously convicted of any of the offenses listed in subdivision (b) and who owns or has in his or her possession or under his or her custody or control any firearm is guilty of a felony. A dismissal of an accusatory pleading pursuant to Section 1203.4a involving an offense set forth in subdivision (b) does not affect the finding of a previous conviction. If probation is granted, or if the imposition or execution of sentence is suspended, it shall be a condition of the probation or suspension that the defendant serve at least six months in a county jail.

(b) As used in this section, a violent offense includes any of the following:

(1) Murder or voluntary manslaughter.

(2) Mayhem.

(3) Rape.

(4) Sodomy by force, violence, duress, menace, or threat of great bodily harm.

(5) Oral copulation by force, violence, duress, menace, or threat of great bodily harm.

(6) Lewd acts on a child under the age of 14 years.

(7) Any felony punishable by death or imprisonment in the state prison for life.

(8) Any other felony in which the defendant inflicts great bodily injury on any person, other than an accomplice, which has been charged and proven, or any felony in which the defendant uses a firearm which use has been charged and proven.

(9) Attempted murder.

(10) Assault with intent to commit rape or robbery.

(11) Assault with a deadly weapon or instrument on a peace officer.

(12) Assault by a life prisoner on a noninmate.

(13) Assault with a deadly weapon by an inmate.

(14) Arson.

(15) Exploding a destructive device or any explosive with intent to injure.

(16) Exploding a destructive device or any explosive causing great bodily injury.

(17) Exploding a destructive device or any explosive with intent to murder.

(18) Robbery.

(19) Kidnapping.

(20) Taking of a hostage by an inmate of a state prison.

(21) Attempt to commit a felony punishable by death or imprisonment in the state prison for life.

(22) Any felony in which the defendant personally used a dangerous or deadly weapon.

(23) Escape from a state prison by use of force or violence.

(24) Assault with a deadly weapon or force likely to produce great bodily injury.

(25) Any attempt to commit a crime listed in this subdivision other than an assault.

(26) Any offense enumerated in Section 12001.6.

(c) Any person previously convicted of any of the offenses listed in subdivision (b) which conviction results from certification by the juvenile court for prosecution as an adult in adult court under the provisions of Section 707 of the Welfare and Institutions Code, who owns or has in his or her possession or under his or her custody or control any firearm is guilty of a felony. If probation is granted, or if the imposition or execution of sentence is suspended, it shall be a condition of the probation or suspension that the defendant shall serve at least six months in a county jail.

(d) The court shall apply the minimum sentence as specified in subdivisions (a) and (c) except in unusual cases where the interests of justice would best be served by granting probation or suspending the imposition or execution of sentence without the imprisonment required by subdivisions (a) and (c), or by granting probation or suspending the imposition or execution of sentence with conditions other than those set forth in subdivisions (a) and (c), in which case the court shall specify on the record and shall enter on the minutes the circumstances indicating that the interests of justice would best be served by such a disposition. *(Amended by Stats 1989 ch 254 §2, 1044 §4, eff. 1/1/90.)*

§12021.5. Possession of firearm during street gang crime.

Every person who carries a loaded or unloaded firearm on his or her person, or in a vehicle, during the commission or attempted commission of any street gang crimes described in subdivision (a) or (b) of Section 186.22, shall, upon the conviction of any such felony or attempted felony of which he or she is convicted, be punished by an additional term of imprisonment in the state prison for one, two, or three years in the court's discretion. The court shall impose the middle term unless there are circumstances in aggravation or mitigation. The court shall state the reasons for its enhancement choice on the record at the time of sentence. *(Added by Stats 1989 ch 841 §1, eff. 1/1/90.)*

§12022. Possession or use of firearm or weapon while committing felony.

(a) (1) Except as provided in subdivisions (c) and (d), any person who is armed with a firearm in the commission or attempted commission of a felony shall, upon conviction of such felony or attempted felony, in addition and consecutive to the punishment prescribed for the felony or attempted felony of which he or she has been convicted, be punished by an additional term of one year, unless such arming is an element of the offense of which he or she was convicted. This additional term shall apply to any person who is a principal in the commission or attempted commission of a felony if one or more of the principals is armed with a firearm, whether or not such person is personally armed with a firearm.

(2) Except as provided in subdivision (c), and notwithstanding subdivision (d), if the firearm is an assault weapon, as defined in Section 12276, or a machinegun, as defined in Section 12200, the additional term described in this subdivision shall be three years whether or not the arming is an element of the offense of which he or she was convicted. The additional term provided in this paragraph shall apply to any person who is a principal in the commission or attempted commission of a felony if one or more of the principals is armed with an assault weapon or machinegun whether or not the person is personally armed with an assault weapon or machinegun.

(b) Any person who personally uses a deadly or dangerous weapon in the commission or attempted commission of a felony shall, upon conviction of such felony or attempted felony, in addition and consecutive to the punishment prescribed for the felony or attempted felony of which he or she has been convicted, be punished by an additional term of one year, unless use of a deadly or dangerous weapon is an element of the offense of which he or she was convicted.

When a person is found to have personally used a deadly or dangerous weapon in the commission or attempted commission of a felony as provided in this subdivision; and the weapon is owned by that person, the court shall order that the weapon be deemed a nuisance and disposed of in the manner provided in Section 12025.

(c) Notwithstanding the enhancement set forth in subdivision (a), any person who is personally armed with a firearm in the commission or attempted commission of a violation of Section 11351, 11351.5, 11352, 11366.5, 11366.6, 11378, 11378.5, 11379, 11379.5, or 11379.6 of the Health and Safety Code, shall, upon conviction of that offense and in addition and consecutive to the punishment prescribed for the offense of which he or she has been convicted, be punished by an additional term of imprisonment in the state prison for three, four, or five years in the court's discretion. The court shall order the middle term unless there are circumstances in aggravation or mitigation. The court shall state the reasons for its enhancement choice on the record at the time of the sentence.

(d) Notwithstanding the enhancement set forth in subdivision (a), any person not personally armed with a firearm who, knowing that another principal is personally armed with a firearm, is a principal in the commission or attempted commission of an offense specified in subdivision (c), shall, upon conviction of that offense, be punished by an additional term of one, two, or three years in the court's discretion. The court shall order the imposition of the middle term unless there are circumstances in aggravation or mitigation. The court shall state the reasons for its enhancement choice on the record at the time of sentencing.

(e) For purposes of imposing an enhancement under Section 1170.1, the enhancements under this section shall count as one, single enhancement.

(f) Notwithstanding any other provision of law, the court may strike the additional punishment for the enhancements provided in subdivision (c) or (d) in an unusual case where the interests of justice would best be served, if the court specifies on the record and enters into the minutes the circumstances indicating that the interests of justice would best be served by that disposition. *(Amended by Stats 1989 chs 18 §2, 19 §1.6, 1167 §1.2, 1284 §1, eff. 10/1/89, 1284 §2, eff. 1/1/90.)*

§12022.1. Penalty enhancement.

(a) For the purposes of this section only:

(1) "Primary offense" means a felony offense for which a person has been released from custody on bail or on his or her own recognizance prior to the judgment becoming final, including the disposition of any appeal, or for which release on bail or his or her own recognizance has been revoked.

(2) "Secondary offense" means a felony offense alleged to have been committed while the person is released from custody for a primary offense.

(b) Any person arrested for a secondary offense which was alleged to have been committed while that person was released from custody on a primary offense shall be subject to a penalty enhancement of an additional two years in state prison which shall be served consecutive to any other term imposed by the court.

(c) The enhancement allegation provided in subdivision (b) shall be pleaded in the information or indictment which alleges the secondary offense and shall be proved as provided by law. The enhancement allegation may be pleaded in a complaint but need not be proved at the preliminary hearing for the secondary offense.

© 1992 by J., B. & L. Gould
Printed in the U.S.A.   **EP**

(d) Whenever there is a conviction for the secondary offense and the enhancement is proved, and the person is sentenced on the secondary offense prior to the conviction of the primary offense, the imposition of the enhancement shall be stayed pending imposition of the sentence for the primary offense. The stay shall be lifted by the court hearing the primary offense at the time of sentencing for that offense and shall be recorded in the abstract of judgment. If the person is acquitted of the primary offense the stay shall be permanent.

(e) If the person is convicted of a felony for the primary offense, is sentenced to state prison for the primary offense, and is convicted of a felony for the secondary offense, any state prison sentence for the secondary offense shall be consecutive to the primary sentence.

(f) If the person is convicted of a felony for the primary offense, is granted probation for the primary offense, and is convicted of a felony for the secondary offense, any state prison sentence for the secondary offense shall be enhanced as provided in subdivision (b).

(g) If the primary offense conviction is reversed on appeal, the enhancement shall be suspended pending retrial of that felony. Upon retrial and reconviction, the enhancement shall be reimposed. If the person is no longer in custody for the secondary offense upon reconviction of the primary offense, the court may, at its discretion, reimpose the enhancement and order him or her recommitted to custody. *(Amended by Stats 1985 ch 533 §1.)*

§12022.2. Additional term; possession of armor penetrating ammunition.

(a) Any person who, while armed with a firearm in the commission or attempted commission of any felony, has in his or her immediate possession ammunition for the firearm designed primarily to penetrate metal or armor, shall upon conviction of that felony or attempted felony, in addition and consecutive to the punishment prescribed for the felony or attempted felony, be punished by an additional term of three, four, or five years. The court shall order the middle term unless there are circumstances in aggravation or mitigation. The court shall state the reasons for its enhancement choice on the record at the time of the sentence.

(b) Any person who wears a body vest in the commission or attempted commission of a violent offense, as defined in subdivision (b) of Section 12021.1, shall, upon conviction of that felony or attempted felony, in addition and consecutive to the punishment prescribed for the felony or attempted felony, be punished by an additional term of one, two, or three years. The court shall order the middle term unless there are circumstances in aggravation or mitigation. The court shall state the reasons for its enhancement choice on the record at the time of the sentence.

(c) As used in this section, "body vest" means any bullet-resistant material intended to provide ballistic and trauma protection for the wearer. *(Amended by Stats 1991 ch 584 §1, eff. 1/1/92.)*

§12022.3. Enhancement for violating certain sections.

For each violation of Section 261, 262, 264.1, 286, 288, 288a, or 289, and in addition to the sentence provided, any person shall receive the following:

(a) A three-, four-, or five-year enhancement if the person uses a firearm or any other deadly weapon in the commission of the violation.

(b) A one-, two-, or three-year enhancement if the person is armed with a firearm or any other deadly weapon. The court shall order the middle term unless there are circumstances in aggravation or mitigation. The court shall state the reasons for its enhancement choice on the record at the time of the sentence. *(Amended by Stats 1991 ch 512 §1, eff. 1/1/92.)*

§12022.4. Additional term for furnishing firearms to another.

Any person who, during the commission or attempted commission of a felony, furnishes or offers to furnish a firearm to another for the purpose of aiding, abetting, or enabling that person or any other person to commit a felony shall, in addition and consecutive to the punishment prescribed by the felony or attempted felony of which the person has been convicted, be punished by an additional term of one, two, or three years in the state prison. The court shall order the middle term unless there are circumstances in aggravation or mitigation. The court shall state the reasons for its enhancement choice on the record at the time of the sentence. The additional term provided in this section shall not be imposed unless the fact of the furnishing is charged in the accusatory pleading and admitted or found to be true by the trier of fact. *(Amended by Stats 1989 ch 1167 §4, eff. 1/1/90.)*

§12022.5. Additional term of imprisonment for use of firearm.

(a) Except as provided in subdivisions (b) and (c), any person who personally uses a firearm in the commission or attempted commission of a felony shall, upon conviction of such felony or attempted felony, in addition and consecutive to the punishment prescribed for the felony or attempted felony of which he or she has been convicted, be punished by an additional term of imprisonment in the state prison for three, four, or five years, unless use of a firearm is an element of the offense of which he or she was convicted. The court shall order imposition of the middle term unless there are circumstances in aggravation or mitigation. The court shall state its reasons for its enhancement choice on the record at the time of sentencing.

(b) (1) Notwithstanding subdivision (a), any person who is convicted of a felony or an attempt to commit a felony, including murder or attempted murder, in which that person discharged a firearm at an occupied motor vehicle which caused great bodily injury or death to the person of another, shall, upon conviction of that felony or attempted felony, in addition and consecutive to the sentence prescribed for the felony or attempted felony, be punished by an additional term of imprisonment in the state prison for five years.

(2) Notwithstanding subdivision (a), any person who personally uses an assault weapon, as specified in Section 12276, or a machinegun, as defined in Section 12200, in the commission or attempted commission of a felony, shall, upon conviction of that felony or attempted felony, in addition and consecutive to the sentence prescribed for the felony or attempted felony, be punished by an additional term of imprisonment in the state prison for five years.

(c) Notwithstanding the enhancement set forth in subdivision (a), any person who personally uses a firearm in the commission or attempted commission of a violation of Section 11351, 11351.5, 11352, 11366.5, 11366.6, 11378, 11378.5, 11379, 11379.5, or 11379.6 of the Health and Safety Code, shall, upon conviction of that offense and in addition and consecutive to the punishment prescribed for the offense of which he or she has been convicted, be punished by an additional term of imprisonment in the state prison for three, four, or five years in the court's discretion. The court shall order the imposition of middle term unless there are circumstances in aggravation or mitigation. The court shall state the reasons for its enhancement choice on the record.

(d) The additional term provided by this section may be imposed in cases of assault with a firearm under paragraph (2) of subdivision (a) of Section 245, or assault with a deadly weapon which is a firearm under Section 245.

(e) When a person is found to have personally used a firearm, an assault weapon, or a machinegun in the commission or attempted commission of a felony as provided in this section and the firearm, assault weapon, or machinegun is owned by that person, the court shall order that the firearm be deemed a nuisance and disposed of in the manner provided in Section 12028.

(f) For purposes of imposing an enhancement under Section 1170.1, the enhancements under this section shall count as one, single enhancement. *(Amended by Stats 1990 ch 41 §3, eff. 1/1/91.)*

§12022.55. Additional term for discharge of firearm from motor vehicle.

Notwithstanding Section 12022.5, any person who, with the intent to inflict great bodily injury or death, inflicts great bodily injury, as defined in Section 12022.7, or causes the death of a person, other than an occupant of a motor vehicle, as a result of discharging a firearm from a motor vehicle in the commission of a felony or attempted felony, shall, upon conviction of the felony or attempted felony, in addition and consecutive to the punishment prescribed for the felony or attempted felony of which he or she has been convicted, be punished by an additional term of imprisonment in the state prison for five years. *(Added by Stats 1987 ch 1147 §2.)*

§12022.6. Additional term for damaging or destruction of property.

When any person takes, damages, or destroys any property in the commission or attempted commission of a felony, with the intent to cause that taking, damage, or destruction, the court shall impose an additional term as follows:

(a) If the loss exceeds twenty-five thousand dollars ($25,000), the court shall in addition and consecutive to the punishment prescribed for the felony or attempted felony of which the defendant has been convicted impose an additional term of one year.

(b) If the loss exceeds one hundred thousand dollars ($100,000), the court shall in addition and consecutive to the punishment prescribed for the felony or attempted felony of which the defendant has been convicted impose an additional term of two years.

In any accusatory pleading involving multiple charges of taking, damage, or destruction, the additional terms provided in this section may be imposed if the aggregate losses to the victims from all felonies exceed the amounts specified in this section. All plead-

ings under this section remain subject to the rules of joinder and severance stated in Section 954.

The additional terms provided in this section shall not be imposed unless the facts of the taking, damage, or destruction in excess of the amounts provided in this section are charged in the accusatory pleading and admitted or found to be true by the trier of fact.

This section applies to, but is not limited to, property taken, damaged, or destroyed in violation of Section 502 or subdivision (b) of Section 502.7.

(c) This section shall remain in effect only until July 1, 1992, and as of that date is repealed unless a later enacted statute, which is enacted before July 1, 1992, deletes or extends that date. *(Amended by Stats 1990 ch 1571 §1, eff. 1/1/91 only until 7/1/92. See other section 12022.6 below.)*

§12022.6. Additional term for damaging or destruction of property.

Any person who takes, damages or destroys any property in the commission of a felony, with the intent to cause such taking, damage or destruction, and the loss exceeds:

(a) Twenty-five thousand dollars ($25,000), the court shall in addition and consecutive to the punishment prescribed for the felony or attempted felony of which the defendant has been convicted impose an additional term of one year.

(b) One hundred thousand dollars ($100,000) the court shall, in addition and consecutive to the punishment prescribed for the felony or attempted felony of which the defendant has been convicted, impose an additional term of two years.

The additional terms provided in this section shall not be imposed unless the facts of the taking, damage, or destruction in excess of amounts provided in this section are charged in the accusatory pleading and admitted or found to be true by the trier of fact.

This section applies to, but is not limited to, property or subdivision (b) of Section 502.7.

This section shall become operative on July 1, 1992. *(Added by Stats 1990 ch 1571 §2, eff. 1/1/91, oper. 7/1/92. See other section 12022.6 above.)*

§12022.7. Additional term for bodily harm inflicted during commission of felony.

Any person who, with the intent to inflict such injury, personally inflicts great bodily injury on any person other than an accomplice in the commission or attempted commission of a felony shall, in addition and consecutive to the punishment prescribed for the felony or attempted felony of which he has been convicted, be punished by an additional term of three years, unless infliction of great bodily injury is an element of the offense of which he is convicted.

As used in this section, great bodily injury means a significant or substantial physical injury.

This section shall not apply to murder or manslaughter or a violation of Section 451 or 452. The additional term provided in this section shall not be imposed unless the fact of great bodily injury is charged in the accusatory pleading and admitted or found to be true by the trier of fact.

§12022.75. Additional term for administration of controlled substance against victim's will.

Any person who, for the purpose of committing a felony, administers by injection, inhalation, ingestion, or any other means, any controlled substance listed in

© 1992 by J., B. & L. Gould
Printed in the U.S.A.   **EP**

Section 11054, 11055, 11056, 11057, or 11058 of the Health and Safety Code, against the victim's will by means of force, violence, or fear of immediate and unlawful bodily injury to the victim or another person, shall, in addition and consecutive to the penalty provided for the felony or attempted felony of which he or she has been convicted, be punished by an additional term of three years. *(Added by Stats 1987 ch 706 §5.)*

§12022.8. Enhancement for great bodily injury or certain sex offenses.

Any person who inflicts great bodily injury, as defined in Section 12022.7, on any victim in a violation of subdivision (2) or (3) of Section 261, Section 264.1, subdivision (b) of Section 288, Section 289, or sodomy or oral copulation by force, violence, duress, menace, or fear of immediate and unlawful bodily injury on the victim or another person as provided in Section 286 or 288a shall receive a five-year enhancement for each such violation in addition to the sentence provided for the felony conviction. *(Amended by Stats 1986 ch 1299 §15.)*

§12022.85. Enhancement for violation of sexual offense with knowledge of having AIDS or carrying AIDS virus.

(a) Any person who violates one or more of the offenses listed in subdivision (b) with knowledge that he or she has acquired immune deficiency syndrome (AIDS) or with the knowledge that he or she carries antibodies of the human immunodeficiency virus at the time of the commission of those offenses, shall receive a three-year enhancement for each such violation in addition to the sentence provided under those sections.

(b) Subdivision (a) applies to the following crimes:

(1) Rape in violation of Section 261.

(2) Unlawful intercourse with a female under age 18 in violation of Section 261.5.

(3) Rape of a spouse in violation of Section 262.

(4) Sodomy in violation of Section 286.

(5) Oral copulation in violation of Section 288a.

(c) For purposes of proving the knowledge requirement of this section, the prosecuting attorney may use test results received under subdivision (c) of Section 1202.1 or subdivision (g) of Section 1202.6. *(Added by Stats 1988 ch 1597 §4, eff. 1/1/90, contingent upon funding provided in the Budget Act of 1989.)*

§12022.9. Enhancement for inflicting injury upon pregnant woman causing termination of pregnancy.

Any person who, during the commission or attempted commission of a felony, who knows or reasonably should know that the victim is pregnant, with intent to inflict injury, and without the consent of the woman, personally inflicts injury upon a pregnant woman which results in the termination of the pregnancy shall, in addition and consecutive to the punishment prescribed by the felony or attempted felony of which the person has been convicted, be punished by an additional term of five years in the state prison. The additional term provided in this section shall not be imposed unless the fact of such injury is charged in the accusatory pleading and admitted or found to be true by the trier of fact.

Nothing in this section shall be construed as affecting the applicability of subdivision (a) of Section 187 of the Penal Code. *(Added by Stats 1985 ch 1375 §1.)*

§12023. Evidence of intent when committing offense while armed.

In the trial of a person charged with committing or attempting to commit a felony against the person of another while armed with any of the weapons mentioned in Section 12020, or while armed with any pistol, revolver, or other firearm capable of being concealed upon the person, without having a license or permit to carry such firearm as provided by this chapter, the fact that he was so armed shall be prima facie evidence of his intent to commit the felony if such weapon was used in the commission of the offense.

§12025. Carrying concealable firearms without license.

(a) Except as otherwise provided in this chapter, any person who carries concealed within any vehicle which is under his or her control or direction any pistol, revolver, or other firearm capable of being concealed upon the person without having a license to carry such firearm as provided in this chapter is guilty of a misdemeanor. Any person convicted under this subdivision who has previously been convicted of any felony, or of any crime made punishable by this chapter, is guilty of a felony, and if probation is granted, or if the execution or imposition of sentence is suspended, it shall be a condition thereof that he or she be imprisoned in the county jail for not less than three months.

(b) Any person who carries concealed upon his or her person any pistol, revolver, or other firearm capable of being concealed upon the person without having a license to carry such firearm as provided in this chapter is guilty of a misdemeanor punishable by imprisonment in the county jail not to exceed one year, or by a fine not to exceed one thousand dollars ($1,000), or by both such fine and imprisonment, except any person, having been convicted of a crime against the person, property or a narcotics or dangerous drug violation, who carries concealed upon his or her person any pistol, revolver, or other firearm capable of being concealed upon the person without having a license to carry such firearm as provided in this chapter is guilty of a public offense and is punishable by imprisonment in a state prison, or by imprisonment in a county jail not to exceed one year, or by a fine not to exceed one thousand dollars ($1,000), or by both such fine and imprisonment. Any person convicted under this subdivision who has previously been convicted of any felony or of any crime made punishable by this chapter, is guilty of a felony, and if probation is granted, or if the execution or imposition of sentence is suspended, it shall be a condition thereof that he or she be imprisoned in the county jail for not less than three months.

(c) Firearms carried openly in belt holsters are not concealed within the meaning of this section, nor are knives which are carried openly in sheaths suspended from the waist of the wearer.

(d) Every person convicted under this section who has previously been convicted of a misdemeanor offense enumerated in Section 12001.6 shall be punished by imprisonment in the county jail for at least three months and not exceeding six months, or, if granted probation, or if the execution or imposition of sentence is suspended, it shall be a condition thereof that he or she be imprisoned in the county jail for at least three months.

(e) The court shall apply the three-month minimum sentence as specified in subdivisions (a), (b), and (d) except in unusual cases where the interests of justice would best be served by granting probation or suspending the imposition or execution of sentence without the minimum imprisonment required in subdivisions (a), (b), and (d) or by granting probation or suspending the imposition or execution of sentence with conditions other than those set forth in subdivisions (a), (b), and (d), in which case, the court shall specify on the record and shall enter on the minutes the circumstances indicating that the interests of justice would best be served by such a disposition.

§12025.5. Carrying concealed firearms; justification.

A violation of Section 12025 is justifiable when a person who possesses a firearm reasonably believes that he or she is in grave danger because of circumstances forming the basis of a current restraining order issued by a court against another person or persons who has or have been found to pose a threat to his or her life or safety. This section may not apply when the circumstances involve a reciprocal restraining order issued pursuant to Section 4359 of the Civil Code absent a factual finding of a specific threat to the person's life or safety. It is not the intent of the Legislature to limit, restrict, or narrow the application of current statutory or judicial authority to apply this or other justifications to defendants charged with violating Section 12025 or of committing other similar offenses.

Upon trial for violating Section 12025, the trier of fact shall determine whether the defendant was acting out of a reasonable belief that he or she was in grave danger. *(Added by Stats 1990 ch 1249 §1, eff. 1/1/91.)*

§12026. Exception; possession of concealable firearms in residence or place of business.

(a) Notwithstanding Section 12025, any citizen of the United States or legal resident over the age of 18 years who resides or is temporarily within this state, and who is not within the excepted classes prescribed by Section 12021, shall not be prohibited from owning, possessing, keeping, or carrying, either openly or concealed, anywhere within the citizen's or legal resident's place of residence, place of business, or on private property owned or lawfully possessed by the citizen or legal resident any pistol, revolver, or other firearm capable of being concealed upon the person, and no permit or license to purchase, own, possess, keep, or carry, either openly or concealed, any such firearm within the citizen's or legal resident's place of residence, place of business, or on private property owned or lawfully possessed by the citizen or legal resident, shall be required of the citizen or legal resident.

(b) Nothing in this section shall be construed as affecting the application of Section 12031. *(Amended by Stats 1989 ch 958 §1, eff. 1/1/90.)*

§12026.1. Transporting or carrying a firearm.

(a) Section 12025 shall not be construed to prohibit any citizen of the United States over the age of 18 years who resides or is temporarily within this state, and who is not within the excepted class-es prescribed by Section 12021, from transporting or carrying any pistol, revolver, or other firearm capable of being concealed upon the person, provided that the following applies to the firearm:

(1) The firearm is within a motor vehicle and it is locked in the vehicle's trunk or in a locked container in the vehicle other than the utility or glove compartment.

(2) The firearm is carried by the person directly to or from any motor vehicle for any lawful purpose and, while carrying the firearm, the firearm is contained within a locked container.

(b) The provisions of this section do not prohibit or limit the otherwise lawful carrying or transportation of any pistol, revolver, or other firearm capable of being concealed upon the person in accordance with this chapter.

(c) As used in this section, "locked container" means a secure container which is fully enclosed and locked by a padlock, key lock, combination lock, or similar locking device. *(Added by Stats 1986 ch 998 §1, eff. 1/1/89.)*

§12026.2. Keene-Hauser Safe Transport Law.

(a) Section 12025 does not apply to or affect any of the following:

(1) The possession of a firearm by an authorized participant in a motion picture, television, or video production or entertainment event when the participant lawfully uses the firearm as part of that production or event or while going directly to or directly from that production or event.

(2) The possession of a firearm in a locked container by a member of any club or organization, organized for the purpose of lawfully collecting and lawfully displaying pistols, revolvers, or other firearms, while the member is at meetings of the clubs or organizations or while going directly to and coming directly from those meetings.

(3) The transportation of a firearm by a participant when going directly to or coming directly from a recognized safety or hunter safety class, or a recognized sporting event involving that firearm.

(4) The transportation of a firearm by a person mentioned in Section 12026, directly between any of the places mentioned in Section 12026.

(5) The transportation of a firearm by a person when going directly to or coming directly from a fixed place of business or private residential property for the purpose of the lawful repair or the lawful transfer of that firearm.

(6) The transportation of a firearm by a person listed in Section 12026 when going directly from the place where that person lawfully received that firearm to that person's place of residence or place of business or to private property owned or lawfully possessed by that person.

(7) The transportation of a firearm by a person when going directly to or coming directly from a gun show, swap meet, or similar event to which the public is invited, for the purposes of displaying that firearm in a lawful manner.

(8) The transportation of a firearm by an authorized employee or agent of a supplier of firearms when going directly to or coming directly from a motion picture, television, or video production or entertainment event for the purpose of providing that firearm to an authorized participant to lawfully use as a part of that production or event.

(9) The transportation of a firearm by a person when going directly to or coming directly from a target range, which holds a regulatory or business license, for the purposes of practicing shooting at targets with that firearm at that target range.

© 1992 by J., B. & L. Gould
Printed in the U.S.A.   EP

(10) The transportation of a firearm by a person when going directly to or coming directly from a place designated by a person authorized to issue licenses pursuant to Section 12050 when done at the request of the issuing agency so that the issuing agency can determine whether or not a license should be issued to that person to carry that firearm.

(11) The transportation of a firearm by a person when going directly to or coming directly from a law enforcement agency for the purpose of a lawful transfer of that firearm pursuant to Section 12084.

(12) The transportation of a firearm by a person when going directly to or coming directly from lawful camping activity for purposes of having that firearm available for lawful personal protection while at the lawful campsite. This paragraph shall not be construed to override the statutory authority granted to the Department of Parks and Recreation or any other state or local governmental agencies to promulgate rules and regulations governing the administration of parks and campgrounds.

(b) In order for a firearm to be exempted under subdivision (a), while being transported to or from a place, the firearm shall be unloaded, kept in a locked container, as defined in subdivision (d), and the course of travel shall include only those deviations between authorized locations as are reasonably necessary under the circumstances.

(c) This section does not prohibit or limit the otherwise lawful carrying or transportation of any pistol, revolver, or other firearm capable of being concealed upon the person in accordance with this chapter.

(d) As used in this section, "locked container" means a secure container which is fully enclosed and locked by a padlock, key lock, combination lock, or similar locking device. The term "locked container" does not include the utility or glove compartment of a motor vehicle. *(Amended by Stats 1991 ch 5 §2; ch 951 §2, eff. 1/1/92.)*

§12027. Exceptions; peace officers, military personnel.

Section 12025 does not apply to, or affect, any of the following:

(a) (1) (A) Any peace officer, listed in Section 830.1 or 830.2, whether active or honorably retired, other duly appointed peace officers, honorably retired peace officers listed in subdivision (c) of Section 830.5, full-time paid peace officers of other states and the federal government who are carrying out official duties while in California, or any person summoned by any of these officers to assist in making arrests or preserving the peace while he or she is actually engaged in assisting that officer. Any peace officer described in this paragraph who has been honorably retired shall be issued an identification certificate by the agency from which the officer has retired. The issuing agency may charge a fee necessary to cover any reasonable expenses incurred by the agency in issuing certificates pursuant to this subdivision.

(B) Any officer retired after January 1, 1981, shall have an endorsement on the identification stating that the issuing agency approves the officer's carrying of a concealed firearm.

(C) No endorsement or renewal endorsement issued pursuant to paragraph (2) shall be effective unless it is in the format set forth in subparagraph (D), except that any peace officer listed in subdivision (f) of Section 830.2 or in subdivision (c) of Section 830.5,

who is retired between January 2, 1981, and on or before December 31, 1988, and who is authorized to carry a concealed firearm pursuant to this section, shall not be required to have an endorsement in the format set forth in subparagraph (D) until the time of the issuance, on or after January 1, 1989, of a renewal endorsement pursuant to paragraph (2).

(D) A certificate issued pursuant to this paragraph for persons retiring after January 1, 1981, shall be in the following format: it shall be on a 2x3 inch card, bear the photograph of the retiree, the retiree's name, address, date of birth, the date that the retiree retired, name and address of the agency from which the retiree retired, have stamped on it the endorsement "CCW Approved" and the date the endorsement is to be renewed.

(E) For purposes of this section and Section 12031, "CCW" means "carry concealed weapons."

(2) A retired peace officer who retired after January 1, 1981, shall petition the issuing agency for the renewal of his or her privilege to carry a concealed firearm every five years. An honorably retired peace officer, described in paragraph (1), retired prior to January 1, 1981, shall not be required to obtain an endorsement from the issuing agency to carry a concealed firearm. The agency from which a peace officer is honorably retired may, upon initial retirement of that peace officer, or at any time subsequent thereto, deny or revoke, for good cause the retired officer's privilege to carry a concealed firearm.

(3) An honorably retired peace officer listed in subdivision (c) of Section 830.5 authorized to carry concealed firearms by this subdivision shall meet the training requirements of Section 832 and shall qualify with the firearm at least annually. The individual retired peace officer shall be responsible for maintaining his or her eligibility to carry a concealed firearm. The Department of Justice shall provide subsequent arrest notification pursuant to Section 11105.2 regarding honorably retired peace officers listed in subdivision (c) of Section 830.5 to the agency from which the officer has retired.

(b) The possession or transportation of unloaded firearms as merchandise by a person engaged in the business of manufacturing, repairing, or dealing in firearms who is licensed to engage in that business or the authorized representative or authorized agent of that person while engaged in the lawful course of the business.

(c) Members of the Army, Navy, or Marine Corps of the United States, or the National Guard, when on duty, or organizations which are by law authorized to purchase or receive those weapons from the United States or this state.

(d) Duly authorized military or civil organizations while parading, or the members thereof when going to and from the places of meeting of their respective organizations.

(e) Guards or messengers of common carriers, banks, and other financial institutions while actually employed in and about the shipment, transportation, or delivery of any money, treasure, bullion, bonds, or other thing of value within this state.

(f) Members of any club or organization organized for the purpose of practicing shooting at targets upon established target ranges, whether public or private, while the members are using pistols, revolvers, or other firearms capable of being concealed upon the person upon the target ranges, or while going to and from the ranges.

(g) Licensed hunters or fishermen while engaged in hunting or fishing, or while going to or returning from the hunting or fishing expedition.

(h) Transportation of unloaded firearms by a person operating a licensed common carrier or an authorized agent or employee thereof when transported in conformance with applicable federal law.

(i) Upon approval of the sheriff of the county in which they reside, honorably retired federal officers or agents of federal law enforcement agencies including, but not limited to, the Federal Bureau of Investigation, the Secret Service, the United States Customs Service, the Federal Bureau of Alcohol, Tobacco, and Firearms, the Federal Bureau of Narcotics, the Drug Enforcement Administration, the United States Border Patrol, and officers or agents of the Internal Revenue Service who were authorized to carry weapons while on duty, who were assigned to duty within the state for a period of not less than one year, or who retired from active service in the state.

Retired federal officers or agents shall provide the sheriff with certification from the agency from which they retired certifying their service in the state, the nature of their retirement, and indicating the agency's concurrence that the retired federal officer or agent should be accorded the privilege of carrying a concealed firearm.

Upon that approval, the sheriff shall issue a permit to the retired federal officer or agent indicating that he or she may carry a concealed firearm in accordance with this subdivision. The permit shall be valid for a period not exceeding five years, shall be carried by the retiree while carrying a concealed firearm, and may be revoked for good cause.

The sheriff of the county in which the retired federal officer or agent resides may require recertification prior to a permit renewal, and may suspend the privilege for cause. The sheriff may charge a fee necessary to cover any reasonable expenses incurred by the county. *(Amended by Stats 1991 ch 952 §1, eff. 1/1/92.)*

§12027.1. Notice of hearing; revocation of retired officer's right to carry concealed weapon.

(a) (1) As specified in subdivision (a) of Section 12027, any peace officer employed by a local agency and listed in Section 830.1 of the Penal Code, retired after January 1, 1981, shall have an endorsement on the identification certificate stating that the issuing agency approves the officer's carrying of a concealed firearm.

(2) A retired peace officer may have his or her privilege to carry a concealed firearm revoked or denied by violating any departmental rule, or state or federal law that, if violated by an officer on active duty, would result in that officer's arrest, suspension, or removal from the agency.

(b) (1) An endorsement may be revoked or denied by the issuing agency only upon a showing of good cause. Good cause shall be determined at a hearing, as specified in subdivision (d).

(2) An endorsement may be revoked only after a hearing, as specified in subdivision (d). Any retired peace officer whose endorsement is to be revoked shall have 15 days to respond to a notice of that hearing, pursuant to this paragraph, as specified in subdivision

(d). A retired peace officer who fails to respond to the notice of the hearing, pursuant to this paragraph, shall forfeit his or her right to respond.

(3) An endorsement may be denied prior to the hearing, as specified in subdivision (d). If a hearing is not conducted prior to the denial of an endorsement, a retired peace officer, within 15 days of the denial, shall have the right to request a hearing. A retired peace officer who fails to request a hearing pursuant to this paragraph shall forfeit his or her right to the hearing.

(c) A retired peace officer, when notified of the revocation of his or her privilege to carry a concealed firearm, after the hearing, or upon forfeiting his or her right to a hearing, shall immediately surrender to the issuing agency his or her identification certificate. The issuing agency shall reissue a new identification without an endorsement.

(d) Any hearing conducted under this section shall be held before a three-member hearing board. One member of the board shall be selected by the local agency and one member shall be selected by the retired peace officer or his or her employee organization. The third member shall be selected jointly by the local agency and the retired peace officer or his or her employee organization.

Any decision by the board shall be binding on the local agency and the retired peace officer.

(e) No peace officer who is retired after January 1, 1989, because of a psychological disability shall be issued an endorsement to carry a concealed firearm pursuant to this section. *(Amended by Stats 1991 ch 952 §2, eff. 1/1/92.)*

§12028. Nuisances; surrender, destruction of weapons.

(a) The unlawful concealed carrying upon the person or within the vehicle of the carrier of any explosive substance, other than fixed ammunition, dirk, or dagger, as provided in Section 12020, the unlawful concealed carrying upon the person or within the vehicle of the carrier of any weapons in violation of Section 12025, and the unlawful possession or carrying of any item in violation of Section 653k is a nuisance.

(b) A firearm of any nature owned or possessed in violation of Section 12021, 12021.1, or 12101 or used in the commission of any misdemeanor as provided in this code, any felony, or an attempt to commit any misdemeanor as provided in this code or any felony, is, upon a conviction of the defendant or upon a juvenile court finding that an offense which would be a misdemeanor or felony if committed by an adult was committed or attempted by the juvenile with the use of a firearm, a nuisance. A finding that the defendant was guilty of the offense but was insane at the time the offense was committed is a conviction for the purposes of this section.

(c) Any weapon described in subdivision (a), or, upon conviction of the defendant or upon a juvenile court finding that an offense which would be a misdemeanor or felony if committed by an adult was committed or attempted by the juvenile with the use of a firearm, any weapon described in subdivision (b) shall be surrendered to the sheriff of a county or the chief of police or other head of a municipal police department of any city or city and county or the Commissioner of the California Highway Patrol. For purposes of this subdivision, the Commissioner of the California Highway Patrol shall receive only weapons

© 1992 by J., B. & L. Gould
Printed in the U.S.A.   **EP**

that were confiscated by a member of the California Highway Patrol. The officers to whom the weapons are surrendered, except upon the certificate of a judge of a court of record, or of the district attorney of the county, that the retention thereof is necessary or proper to the ends of justice, may annually, between the 1st and 10th days of July, in each year, offer the weapons, which the officers in charge of them consider to have value with respect to sporting, recreational, or collection purposes, for sale at public auction to persons licensed pursuant to Section 12071 to engage in businesses involving any weapon purchased. If any weapon has been stolen and is thereafter recovered from the thief or his or her transferee, or is used in such a manner as to constitute a nuisance pursuant to subdivision (a) or (b) without the prior knowledge of its lawful owner that it would be so used, it shall not be so offered for sale but shall be restored to the lawful owner, as soon as its use as evidence has been served, upon his or her identification of the weapon and proof of ownership.

(d) If, under this section, a weapon is not of the type that can be sold to the public, generally, or is not sold pursuant to subdivision (c), the weapon, in the month of July, next succeeding, or sooner, if necessary to conserve local resources including space and utilization of personnel who maintain files and security of those weapons, shall be destroyed so that it can no longer be used as such a weapon except upon the certificate of a judge of a court of record, or of the district attorney of the county, that the retention of it is necessary or proper to the ends of justice.

(e) This section does not apply to any firearm in the possession of the Department of Fish and Game or which was used in the violation of any provision of the Fish and Game Code or any regulation adopted pursuant thereto, or which is forfeited pursuant to Section 5008.6 of the Public Resources Code.

(f) No stolen weapon shall be sold or destroyed pursuant to subdivision (c) or (d) unless reasonable notice is given to its lawful owner, if his or her identity and address can be reasonably ascertained. *(Amended by Stats 1991 ch 5 §3; ch 961 §3, eff. 1/1/92.)*

§12028.5. Taking temporary custody of firearm at scene of domestic violence.

(a) As used in this section, the following definitions shall apply:

(1) "Abuse" means intentionally or recklessly causing or attempting to cause bodily injury, or placing another person in reasonable apprehension of imminent serious bodily injury to himself, herself, or another.

(2) "Domestic violence" is abuse perpetrated against any of the following:

(A) A spouse, former spouse, cohabitant, former cohabitant, any other adult person related by consanguinity or affinity within the second degree, or a person with whom the respondent has had a dating or engagement relationship.

(B) A person who is the parent of a child and the presumption applies that the male parent is the father of any child of the female pursuant to the Uniform Parentage Act (Part 7 (commencing with Section 7000) of Division 4 of the Civil Code).

(3) "Deadly weapon" means any weapon, the possession or concealed carrying of which is prohibited by Section 12020.

(b) A sheriff, undersheriff, deputy sheriff, marshal, deputy marshal, or police officer of a city, as defined in subdivision (a) of Section 830.1, a member of the University of California Police Department, as defined in subdivision (c) of Section 830.2, an officer listed in Section 830.6 while acting in the course and scope of his or her employment as a peace officer, a member of a California State University Police Department, as defined in subdivision (d) of Section 830.2, and a peace officer of the Department of Parks and Recreation, as defined in subdivision (g) of Section 830.2, who is at the scene of a domestic violence incident involving a threat to human life or a physical assault, may take temporary custody of any firearm or other deadly weapon in plain sight or discovered pursuant to a consensual search as necessary for the protection of the peace officer or other persons present. Upon taking custody of a firearm or other deadly weapon, the officer shall give the owner or person who possessed the firearm a receipt. The receipt shall describe the firearm or other deadly weapon and list any identification or serial number on the firearm. The receipt shall indicate where the firearm or other deadly weapon can be recovered and the date after which the owner or possessor can recover the firearm or other deadly weapon. No firearm or other deadly weapon shall be held less than 48 hours. Except as provided in subdivision (e), if a firearm or other deadly weapon is not retained for use as evidence related to criminal charges brought as a result of the domestic violence incident or is not retained because it was illegally possessed, the firearm or other deadly weapon shall be made available to the owner or person who was in lawful possession 48 hours after the seizure or as soon thereafter as possible, but no later than 72 hours after the seizure. In any civil action or proceeding for the return of firearms or ammunition or other deadly weapon seized by any state or local law enforcement agency and not returned within 72 hours following the initial seizure, except as provided in subdivision (c), the court shall allow reasonable attorney's fees to the prevailing party.

(c) Any firearm or other deadly weapon which has been taken into custody which has been stolen shall be restored to the lawful owner, as soon as its use for evidence has been served, upon his or her identification of the firearm or other deadly weapon and proof of ownership.

(d) Any firearm or other deadly weapon taken into custody and held by a police, university police, or sheriff's department or by a marshal's office, or by a peace officer of the Department of Parks and Recreation, as defined in subdivision (g) of Section 830.2, for longer than 12 months and not recovered by the owner or person who has lawful possession at the time it was taken into custody, shall be considered a nuisance and sold or destroyed as provided in subdivision (c) of Section 12028. Firearms or other deadly weapons not recovered within 12 months due to an extended hearing process as provided in subdivision (i), are not subject to destruction until the court issues a decision, and then only if the court does not order the return of the firearm or other deadly weapon to the owner.

(e) In those cases where a law enforcement agency has reasonable cause to believe that the return of a firearm or other deadly weapon would be likely to result in endangering the victim or the person reporting the assault or threat, the agency shall advise the owner of the firearm or other deadly weapon, and within 10 days of the seizure, initiate a petition in

© 1992 by J., B. & L. Gould
Printed in the U.S.A. **EP**

superior court to determine if the firearm or other deadly weapon should be returned.

(f) The law enforcement agency shall inform the owner or person who had lawful possession of the firearm or other deadly weapon, at that person's last known address by registered mail, return receipt requested, that he or she has 30 days from the date of receipt of the notice to respond to the court clerk to confirm his or her desire for a hearing, and that the failure to respond shall result in a default order forfeiting the confiscated firearm or other deadly weapon. For the purposes of this subdivision, the person's last known address shall be presumed to be the address provided to the law enforcement officer by that person at the time of the domestic violence incident. In the event the person whose firearm or other deadly weapon was seized does not reside at the last address provided to the agency, the agency shall make a diligent, good faith effort to learn the whereabouts of the person and to comply with these notification requirements.

(g) If the person requests a hearing, the court clerk shall set a hearing no later than 30 days from receipt of that request. The court clerk shall notify the person, the law enforcement agency involved, and the district attorney of the date, time, and place of the hearing. Unless it is shown by clear and convincing evidence that the return of the firearm or other deadly weapon would result in endangering the victim or the person reporting the assault or threat, the court shall order the return of the firearm or other deadly weapon and shall award reasonable attorney's fees to the prevailing party.

(h) If the person does not request a hearing or does not otherwise respond within 30 days of the receipt of the notice, the law enforcement agency may file a petition for an order of default and may dispose of the firearm or other deadly weapon as provided in Section 12028.

(i) If, at the hearing, the court does not order the return of the firearm or other deadly weapon to the owner or person who had lawful possession, that person may petition the court for a second hearing within 12 months from the date of the initial hearing. If the owner or person who had lawful possession does not petition the court within this 12-month period for a second hearing or is unsuccessful at the second hearing in gaining return of the firearm or other deadly weapon, the firearm or other deadly weapon may be disposed of as provided in Section 12028.

(j) The law enforcement agency, or the individual law enforcement officer, shall not be liable for any act in the good faith exercise of this section. *(Amended by Stats 1991 ch 866 §6, eff. 1/1/92.)*

§12029. Unlawful weapons as nuisances.

Except as provided in Section 12020, blackjacks, slungshots, billies, nunchakus, sandclubs, sandbags, shurikens, metal knuckles, short-barreled shotguns or short-barreled rifles as defined in Section 12020, and any other item which is listed in subdivision (a) of Section 12020 and is not listed in subdivision (a) of Section 12028 are nuisances, and the Attorney General, district attorney, or city attorney may bring an action to enjoin the manufacture of, importation of, keeping for sale of, offering or exposing for sale, giving, lending, or possession of, any of the foregoing items. These weapons shall be subject to confiscation and summary destruction whenever found within the state. These weapons shall be destroyed in the same manner as other weapons described in Section 12028, except that upon the certification of a judge or of the district attorney that the ends of justice will be subserved thereby, the weapon shall be preserved until the necessity for its use ceases. *(Amended by Stats 1988 ch 512 §3; ch 1269 §3, eff. 1/1/89.)*

§12030. Official use of surrendered firearms.

(a) The officer having custody of any firearms which may be useful to the California National Guard, the Coast Guard Auxiliary, or to any military or naval agency of the federal or state government, including but not limited to, the California National Guard military museum and resource center, may, upon the authority of the legislative body of the city, city and county, or county by which he or she is employed and the approval of the Adjutant General, deliver the firearms to the commanding officer of a unit of the California National Guard, the Coast Guard Auxiliary, or any other military agency of the state or federal government in lieu of destruction as required by this chapter. The officer delivering the firearms shall take a receipt for them containing a complete description thereof and shall keep the receipt on file in his or her office as a public record.

(b) Any law enforcement agency which has custody of any firearms, or any parts of any firearms, which are subject to destruction as required by this chapter may, in lieu of destroying the weapons, retain and use any of them as may be useful in carrying out the official duties of the agency, or upon approval of a court, may release them to any other law enforcement agency for use in carrying out the official duties of that agency, or may turn over to the criminalistics laboratory of the Department of Justice or the criminalistics laboratory of a police department, sheriff's office, or district attorney's office any weapons which may be useful in carrying out the official duties of their respective agencies.

(c) Any firearm, or part of any firearm, which, rather than being destroyed, is used for official purposes pursuant to this section shall be destroyed by the agency using the weapon when it is no longer needed by the agency for use in carrying out its official duties. In the case of firearms or weaponry donated to the California National Guard military museum and resource center, they may be disposed of pursuant to Section 179 of the Military and Veterans Code.

(d) Any law enforcement agency which has custody of any firearms, or any parts of any firearms, which are subject to destruction as required by this chapter may, in lieu of destroying the firearms, obtain an order from the superior court directing the release of the firearms to the sheriff. The sheriff shall enter such weapons into the Automated Firearms System (AFS) with a complete description of each weapon, including the make, type, category, caliber, and serial number of the firearms, and the name of the academy receiving the weapon entered into the AFS miscellaneous field. The sheriff shall then release the firearms to the basic training academy certified by the Commission on Peace Officer Standards and Training, so that the firearms may be used for instructional purposes in the certified courses. As used in this section, the term "firearms" shall not include destructive devices, as defined in Section 12301. All firearms released to an academy shall be under the care, custody, and control of the particular academy.

© 1992 by J., B. & L. Gould
Printed in the U.S.A.   **EP**

Any firearms, or part of any firearms, which is not destroyed, and is used for the purposes authorized by this section, shall be returned to the law enforcement agency which had original custody of the firearms when it is no longer needed by the basic training academy, or when the basic training academy is no longer certified by the commission.

(e) Any law enforcement agency that retains custody of any firearm pursuant to this section or that destroys a firearm pursuant to Section 12028 shall notify the Department of Justice of the retention or destruction. This notification shall consist of a complete description of each firearm, including the name of the manufacturer or brand name, model, caliber, and serial number. *(Amended by Stats 1986 ch 768 §1.)*

§12031. Loaded firearm in public place or street.

(a) (1) Except as provided in subdivision (b), (c), or (d), every person who carries a loaded firearm on his or her person or in a vehicle while in any public place or on any public street in an incorporated city or in any public place or on any public street in a prohibited area of unincorporated territory is guilty of a misdemeanor.

(2) Notwithstanding subdivisions 2 and 3 of Section 836, a peace officer may make an arrest without a warrant:

(A) When the person arrested has violated this section, although not in the officer's presence.

(B) Whenever the officer has reasonable cause to believe that the person to be arrested has violated this section, whether or not this section has, in fact, been violated.

(3) (A) Every person convicted under this section who has previously been convicted of an offense enumerated in Section 12001.6, or of any crime made punishable under this chapter, shall serve a term of at least three months in a county jail, or, if granted probation, or if the execution or imposition of sentence is suspended, it shall be a condition thereof that he or she be imprisoned for a period of at least three months.

(B) The court shall apply the three-month minimum sentence except in unusual cases where the interests of justice would best be served by granting probation or suspending the imposition or execution of sentence without the minimum imprisonment required in this subdivision or by granting probation or suspending the imposition or execution of sentence with conditions other than those set forth in this subdivision, in which case, the court shall specify on the record and shall enter on the minutes the circumstances indicating that the interests of justice would best be served by such a disposition.

(b) Subdivision (a) shall not apply to any of the following:

(1) Peace officers listed in Section 830.1 or 830.2, whether active or honorably retired, other duly appointed peace officers, honorably retired peace officers listed in subdivision (c) of Section 830.5, full-time paid peace officers of other states and the federal government who are carrying out official duties while in California, or any person summoned by any of those officers to assist in making arrests or preserving the peace while the person is actually engaged in assisting that officer. Any peace officer described in this paragraph who has been honorably retired shall be issued an identification certificate by the agency from which the officer has retired. The issuing agency may charge a fee necessary to cover any reasonable expenses incurred by the agency in issuing certificates pursuant to this paragraph and paragraph (3).

Any officer retired after January 1, 1981, shall have an endorsement on the identification certificate stating that the issuing agency approves the officer's carrying of a loaded firearm.

No endorsement or renewal endorsement issued pursuant to paragraph (2) shall be effective unless it is in the format set forth in subparagraph (D) of paragraph (1) of subdivision (a) of Section 12027, except that any peace officer listed in subdivision (f) of Section 830.2 or in subdivision (c) of Section 830.5, who is retired between January 2, 1981, and on or before December 31, 1988, and who is authorized to carry a loaded firearm pursuant to this section, shall not be required to have an endorsement in the format set forth in subparagraph (D) of paragraph (1) of subdivision (a) of Section 12027 until the time of the issuance, on or after January 1, 1989, of a renewal endorsement pursuant to paragraph (2).

(2) A retired peace officer who retired after January 1, 1981, shall petition the issuing agency for renewal of his or her privilege to carry a loaded firearm every five years. An honorably retired peace officer, described in paragraph (1), retired prior to January 1, 1981, shall not be required to obtain an endorsement from the issuing agency to carry a firearm. The agency from which a peace officer is honorably retired may, upon initial retirement of the peace officer, or at any time subsequent thereto, deny or revoke, for good cause, the retired officer's privilege to carry a firearm.

(3) An honorably retired peace officer listed in subdivision (c) of Section 830.5 authorized to carry loaded firearms by this subdivision shall meet the training requirements of Section 832 and shall qualify with the firearm at least annually. The individual retired peace officer shall be responsible for maintaining his or her eligibility to carry a loaded firearm. The Department of Justice shall provide subsequent arrest notification pursuant to Section 11105.2 regarding honorably retired peace officers listed in subdivision (c) of Section 830.5 to the agency from which the officer has retired.

(4) Members of the military forces of this state or of the United States engaged in the performance of their duties.

(5) Persons who are using target ranges for the purpose of practice shooting with a firearm or who are members of shooting clubs while hunting on the premises of those clubs.

(6) The carrying of pistols, revolvers, or other firearms capable of being concealed upon the person by persons who are authorized to carry those weapons pursuant to Article 3 (commencing with Section 12050) of Chapter 1 of Title 2 of Part 4.

(7) Armored vehicle guards, as defined in Section 7521 of the Business and Professions Code, (A) if hired prior to January 1, 1977; or (B) if hired on or after that date, if they have received a firearms qualification card from the Department of Consumer Affairs, in each case while acting within the course and scope of their employment.

(8) Upon approval of the sheriff of the county in which they reside, honorably retired federal officers or agents of federal law enforcement agencies including, but not limited to, the Federal Bureau of Investigation, the Secret Service, the United States Customs Service, the Federal Bureau of Alcohol, Tobacco, and Firearms, the Federal Bureau of Narcotics, the Drug

Enforcement Administration, the United States Border Patrol, and officers or agents of the Internal Revenue Service who were authorized to carry weapons while on duty, who were assigned to duty within the state for a period of not less than one year, or who retired from active service in the state.

Retired federal officers or agents shall provide the sheriff with certification from the agency from which they retired certifying their service in the state, the nature of their retirement, and indicating the agency's concurrence that the retired federal officer or agent should be accorded the privilege of carrying a loaded firearm.

Upon approval, the sheriff shall issue a permit to the retired federal officer or agent indicating that he or she may carry a loaded firearm in accordance with this paragraph. The permit shall be valid for a period not exceeding five years, shall be carried by the retiree while carrying a loaded firearm, and may be revoked for good cause.

The sheriff of the county in which the retired federal officer or agent resides may require recertification prior to a permit renewal, and may suspend the privilege for cause. The sheriff may charge a fee necessary to cover any reasonable expenses incurred by the county.

(c) Subdivision (a) shall not apply to any of the following who have completed a regular course in firearms training approved by the Commission on Peace Officer Standards and Training:

(1) Patrol special police officers appointed by the police commission of any city, county, or city and county under the express terms of its charter who also, under the express terms of the charter, (A) are subject to suspension or dismissal after a hearing on charges duly filed with the commission after a fair and impartial trial, (B) are not less than 18 years of age nor more than 40 years of age, (C) possess physical qualifications prescribed by the commission, and (D) are designated by the police commission as the owners of a certain beat or territory as may be fixed from time to time by the police commission.

(2) The carrying of weapons by animal control officers or zookeepers, regularly compensated as such by a governmental agency when acting in the course and scope of their employment and when designated by a local ordinance or, if the governmental agency is not authorized to act by ordinance, by a resolution, either individually or by class, to carry the weapons, or by persons who are authorized to carry the weapons pursuant to Section 607f of the Civil Code, while actually engaged in the performance of their duties pursuant to that section.

(3) Harbor police officers designated pursuant to Section 663.5 of the Harbors and Navigation Code.

(d) Subdivision (a) shall not apply to any of the following who have been issued a certificate pursuant to Section 12033. The certificate shall not be required of any person who is a peace officer, who has completed all training required by law for the exercise of his or her power as a peace officer, and who is employed while not on duty as a peace officer.

(1) Guards or messengers of common carriers, banks, and other financial institutions while actually employed in and about the shipment, transportation, or delivery of any money, treasure, bullion, bonds, or other thing of value within this state.

(2) Guards of contract carriers operating armored vehicles pursuant to California Highway Patrol and Public Utilities Commission authority (A) if hired prior to January 1, 1977; or (B) if hired on or after January 1, 1977, if they have completed a course in the carrying and use of firearms which meets the standards prescribed by the Department of Consumer Affairs.

(3) Private investigators and private patrol operators who are licensed pursuant to Chapter 11.5 (commencing with Section 7512) of, and alarm company operators who are licensed pursuant to Chapter 11.6 (commencing with Section 7590) of, Division 3 of the Business and Professions Code, while acting within the course and scope of their employment.

(4) Uniformed security guards or night watch persons employed by any public agency, while acting within the scope and in the course of their employment.

(5) Uniformed security guards, regularly employed and compensated in that capacity by persons engaged in any lawful business, and uniformed alarm agents employed by an alarm company operator, while actually engaged in protecting and preserving the property of their employers or on duty or en route to or from their residences or their places of employment, and security guards and alarm agents en route to or from their residences or employer-required range training. Nothing in this paragraph shall be construed to prohibit cities and counties from enacting ordinances requiring alarm agents to register their names.

(6) Uniformed employees of private patrol operators and private investigators licensed pursuant to Chapter 11.5 (commencing with Section 7512) of Division 3 of the Business and Professions Code while acting within the course and scope of their employment.

(e) In order to determine whether or not a firearm is loaded for the purpose of enforcing this section, peace officers are authorized to examine any firearm carried by anyone on his or her person or in a vehicle while in any public place or on any public street in an incorporated city or prohibited area of an unincorporated territory. Refusal to allow a peace officer to inspect a firearm pursuant to this section constitutes probable cause for arrest for violation of this section.

(f) As used in this section, "prohibited area" means any place where it is unlawful to discharge a weapon.

(g) A firearm shall be deemed to be loaded for the purposes of this section when there is an unexpended cartridge or shell, consisting of a case which holds a charge of powder and a bullet or shot, in, or attached in any manner to, the firearm, including, but not limited to, in the firing chamber, magazine, or clip thereof attached to the firearm; except that a muzzle-loader firearm shall be deemed to be loaded when it is capped or primed and has a powder charge and ball or shot in the barrel or cylinder.

(h) Nothing in this section shall prevent any person engaged in any lawful business, including a nonprofit organization, or any officer, employee, or agent authorized by that person for lawful purposes connected with that business, from having a loaded firearm within the person's place of business, or any person in lawful possession of private property from having a loaded firearm on that property.

(i) Nothing in this section shall prevent any person from carrying a loaded firearm in an area within an incorporated city while engaged in hunting, provided that the hunting at that place and time is not prohibited by the city council.

© 1992 by J., B. & L. Gould
Printed in the U.S.A.   EP

(j) (1) Nothing in this section is intended to preclude the carrying of any loaded firearm, under circumstances where it would otherwise be lawful, by a person who reasonably believes that the person or property of himself or herself or of another is in immediate, grave danger and that the carrying of the weapon is necessary for the preservation of that person or property. As used in this subdivision, "immediate" means the brief interval before and after the local law enforcement agency, when reasonably possible, has been notified of the danger and before the arrival of its assistance.

(2) A violation of this section is justifiable when a person who possesses a firearm reasonably believes that he or she is in grave danger because of circumstances forming the basis of a current restraining order issued by a court against another person or persons who has or have been found to pose a threat to his or her life or safety. This paragraph may not apply when the circumstances involve a reciprocal restraining order issued pursuant to Section 4359 of the Civil Code absent a factual finding of a specific threat to the person's life or safety. It is not the intent of the Legislature to limit, restrict, or narrow the application of current statutory or judicial authority to apply this or other justifications to defendants charged with violating Section 12025 or of committing other similar offenses.

Upon trial for violating this section, the trier of fact shall determine whether the defendant was acting out of a reasonable belief that he or she was in grave danger.

(k) Nothing in this section is intended to preclude the carrying of a loaded firearm by any person while engaged in the act of making or attempting to make a lawful arrest.

(l) Nothing in this section shall prevent any person from having a loaded weapon, if it is otherwise lawful, at his or her place of residence, including any temporary residence or campsite. *(Amended by Stats 1991 ch 952 §3, 1022 §1.1, eff. 1/1/92.)*

§12031.1. Emergency or distress signaling devices.

Nothing in Section 12031 shall prevent any person from storing aboard any vessel or aircraft any loaded or unloaded rocket, rocket propelled projectile launcher, or similar device designed primarily for emergency or distress signaling purposes, or from possessing such a device while in a permitted hunting area or traveling to or from such area and carrying a valid California permit or license to hunt.

§12031.5. Carrying a loaded firearm.

(a) Except as provided in subdivision (b), every person who has been convicted previously of violating Section 12031 and who carries a loaded firearm on his or her person or in a vehicle while in any public place or on any public street in an incorporated city or in a prohibited area of unincorporated territory is guilty of a public offense, punishable by imprisonment in the state prison, or in a county jail not exceeding one year.

(b) Notwithstanding subdivision (a), any person who has been convicted previously of violating Section 12031 and who violates subdivision (a) of this section and who is actively engaged in, or going to or from, a recreational, sport, including, but not limited to, competitive shooting or hunting activity which may require the use of a firearm is guilty of a misdemeanor.

As used in this subdivision, "going to or from" includes a reasonable diversion from the direct route of travel.

(c) A violation of this section which is punished by imprisonment in a county jail not exceeding one year shall not constitute a conviction of a crime punishable by imprisonment for a term exceeding one year for the purposes of determining federal firearms eligibility under Section 922(g)(1) of Title 18 of the United States Code. *(Added by Stats 1991 ch 1022 §2, eff. 1/1/92.)*

§12032. Destruction and disposition of firearms in custody of officer.

Notwithstanding any provision of law or of any local ordinance to the contrary, when any firearm is in the possession of any officer of the state, or of a county, city and county or city, and such firearm is an exhibit filed in any criminal action or proceeding which is no longer needed or is unclaimed or abandoned property, which has been in the possession of the officer for at least 180 days, the firearm shall be sold, or destroyed, as provided for in Section 12028.

This section shall not apply to any firearm in the possession of the Department of Fish and Game or which was used in the violation of any provision of law, or regulation thereunder, in the Fish and Game Code.

§12033. Firearms use and powers of arrest training course.

The Department of Consumer Affairs may issue a certificate to any person referred to in subdivision (d) of Section 12031, upon notification by the school where the course was completed, that the person has successfully completed a course in the carrying and use of firearms and a course of training in the exercise of the powers of arrest which meet the standards prescribed by the department pursuant to Section 7545 of the Business and Professions Code.

§12034. Driver or owner of motor vehicle permitting other person to carry or discharge firearm in vehicle.

(a) It is a misdemeanor for a driver of any motor vehicle or the owner of any motor vehicle, whether or not the owner of the vehicle is occupying the vehicle, knowingly to permit any other person to carry into or bring into the vehicle a firearm in violation of Section 12031 of this code or Section 2006 of the Fish and Game Code.

(b) Any driver or owner of any vehicle, whether or not the owner of the vehicle is occupying the vehicle, who knowingly permits any other person to discharge any firearm from the vehicle is punishable by imprisonment in the county jail for not more than one year or in state prison for 16 months or two or three years.

(c) Any person who willfully and maliciously discharges a firearm from a motor vehicle at another person other than an occupant of a motor vehicle is guilty of a felony punishable by imprisonment in state prison for three, five, or seven years.

(d) Except as provided in Section 3002 of the Fish and Game Code, any person who willfully and maliciously discharges a firearm from a motor vehicle is guilty of a public offense punishable by imprisonment in the county jail for not more than one year or in the state prison. *(Amended by Stats 1987 ch 1147 §3.)*

§12035. Criminal storage of firearms; firearms accessible to children.

(a) As used in this section, the following definitions shall apply:

(1) "Locking device" means a device which temporarily prevents the firearm from functioning.

(2) "Loaded firearm" has the same meaning as set forth in subdivision (g) of Section 12031.

(3) "Child" means a person under 14 years of age.

(4) "Great bodily injury" has the same meaning as set forth in Section 12022.7.

(5) "Locked container" has the same meaning as set forth in subdivision (d) of Section 12026.2.

(b) (1) Except as provided in subdivision (c), a person commits the crime of "criminal storage of a firearm of the first degree" if he or she keeps any loaded firearm within any premise which is under his or her custody or control and he or she knows or reasonably should know that a child is likely to gain access to the firearm without the permission of the child's parent or legal guardian and the child obtains access to the firearm and thereby causes death or great bodily injury to himself, herself, or any other person.

(2) Except as provided in subdivision (c), a person commits the crime of "criminal storage of a firearm of the second degree" if he or she keeps any loaded firearm within any premise which is under his or her custody or control and he or she knows or reasonably should know that a child is likely to gain access to the firearm without the permission of the child's parent or legal guardian and the child obtains access to the firearm and thereby causes injury, other than great bodily injury, to himself, herself, or any other person, or exhibits the firearm either in a public place or in violation of Section 417.

(c) Subdivision (b) shall not apply whenever any of the following occurs:

(1) The child obtains the firearm as a result of an illegal entry to any premises by any person.

(2) The firearm is kept in a locked container or in a location which a reasonable person would believe to be secure.

(3) The firearm is carried on the person or within such a close proximity thereto so that the individual can readily retrieve and use the firearm as if carried on the person.

(4) The firearm is equipped with a locking device.

(5) The person is a peace officer or a member of the armed forces or national guard and the child obtains the firearm during, or incidental to, the performance of the person's duties.

(6) The child obtains, or obtains and discharges, the firearm in a lawful act of self-defense or defense of another person, or persons.

(7) The person who keeps a loaded firearm on any premise which is under his or her custody or control has no reasonable expectation, based on objective facts and circumstances, that a child is likely to be present on the premise.

(d) Criminal storage of a firearm is punishable as follows:

(1) Criminal storage of a firearm in the first degree, by imprisonment in the state prison for 16 months, or 2 or 3 years, by a fine not exceeding ten thousand dollars ($10,000), or by both that imprisonment and fine; or by imprisonment in a county jail not exceeding one year, by a fine not exceeding one thousand dollars ($1,000), or by both that imprisonment and fine.

(2) Criminal storage of a firearm in the second degree, by imprisonment in a county jail not exceeding one year, by a fine not exceeding one thousand dollars ($1,000), or by both that imprisonment and fine.

(e) If the person who allegedly violated this section is the parent or guardian of a child who is injured or who dies as the result of an accidental shooting, the district attorney shall consider, among other factors, the impact of the injury or death on the person alleged to have violated this section when deciding whether to prosecute an alleged violation. It is the Legislature's intent that a parent or guardian of a child who is injured or who dies as the result of an accidental shooting shall be prosecuted only in those instances in which the parent or guardian behaved in a grossly negligent manner or where similarly egregious circumstances exist. This subdivision shall not otherwise restrict, in any manner, the factors that a district attorney may consider when deciding whether to prosecute alleged violations of this section.

(f) If the person who allegedly violated this section is the parent or guardian of a child who is injured or who dies as the result of an accidental shooting, no arrest of the person for the alleged violation of this section shall occur until at least seven days after the date upon which the accidental shooting occurred.

In addition to the limitation contained in this subdivision, a law enforcement officer shall consider the health status of a child who suffers great bodily injury as the result of an accidental shooting prior to arresting a person for a violation of this section, if the person to be arrested is the parent or guardian of the injured child. The intent of this subdivision is to encourage law enforcement officials to delay the arrest of a parent or guardian of a seriously injured child while the child remains on life-support equipment or is in a similarly critical medical condition.

(g) (1) The fact that the person who allegedly violated this section attended a firearm safety training course prior to the purchase of the firearm that is obtained by a child in violation of this section shall be considered a mitigating factor by a district attorney when he or she is deciding whether to prosecute the alleged violation.

(2) In any action or trial commenced under this section, the fact that the person who allegedly violated this section attended a firearm safety training course prior to the purchase of the firearm that is obtained by a child in violation of this section, shall be admissible. *(Added by Stats 1991 ch 956 §2, eff. 1/1/92.)*

ARTICLE 3

LICENSES TO CARRY CONCEALED WEAPONS

§12050. Issuance; criteria, restrictions.

(a) The sheriff of a county or the chief or other head of a municipal police department of any city or city and county, upon proof that the person applying is of good moral character, that good cause exists for the issuance, and that the person applying is a resident of the county, may issue to such person a license to carry concealed a pistol, revolver, or other firearm for any period of time not to exceed one year from the date of the license, or in the case of a peace officer appointed pursuant to Section 830.6, three years from the date of the license.

© 1992 by J., B. & L. Gould
Printed in the U.S.A.   EP

Of Prevention of Crimes

§12070

(b) A license may include any reasonable restrictions or conditions which the issuing authority deems warranted, including restrictions as to the time, place, and circumstances under which the person may carry a concealed firearm.

(c) Any restrictions imposed pursuant to subdivision (b) shall be indicated on any license issued on or after the effective date of the amendments to this section enacted at the 1970 Regular Session of the Legislature.

§12051. License applications; violation for making false statements.

(a) Applications for licenses shall be filed in writing, signed by the applicant, and shall state the name, occupation, residence and business address of the applicant, his or her age, height, weight, color of eyes and hair, and reason for desiring a license to carry the weapon. Any license issued upon such application shall set forth the foregoing data and shall, in addition, contain a description of the weapon or weapons authorized to be carried, giving the name of the manufacturer, the serial number and the caliber.

Applications and licenses shall be uniform throughout the state, upon forms to be prescribed by the Attorney General. Such forms shall contain a provision whereby the applicant attests to the truth of statements contained in the application.

(b) Any person who files an application required by subdivision (a) knowing that statements contained therein are false is guilty of a misdemeanor. Any person knowingly making a false statement on the application regarding the denial or revocation of a concealed weapons license, a criminal conviction, a finding of not guilty by reason of insanity, the use of a controlled substance, a dishonorable discharge from military service, a commitment to a mental institution, or a renunciation of United States citizenship is guilty of a felony.

§12052. Fingerprints of applicants.

The fingerprints of each applicant shall be taken and two copies on forms prescribed by the Department of Justice shall be forwarded to the department. Upon receipt of the fingerprints and the fee as prescribed in Section 12054, the department shall promptly furnish the forwarding licensing authority a report of all data and information pertaining to any applicant of which there is a record in its office. No license shall be issued by any licensing authority until after receipt of such report from the department.

Provided, however, that if the license applicant has previously applied to the same licensing authority for a license to carry concealed firearms and the applicant's fingerprints and fee have been previously forwarded to the Department of Justice, as herein provided, the licensing authority shall note such previous identification numbers and other data which would provide positive identification in the files of the Department of Justice on the copy of any subsequent license submitted to the department in conformance with Section 12053 and no additional application form or fingerprints shall be required.

§12053. Maintenance of records.

When any such license is issued a record thereof shall be maintained in the office of the licensing authority. Copies of each license issued shall be filed immediately by the issuing officer or authority with the Department of Justice.

§12054. Fee.

Each applicant for a new license or for the renewal of a license shall pay at the time of filing his application a fee determined by the Department of Justice not to exceed the application processing costs of the Department of Justice for the direct costs of furnishing the report required by Section 12052. After the department establishes fees sufficient to reimburse the department for processing costs, fees charged shall increase at a rate not to exceed the legislatively approved annual cost-of-living adjustments for the department's budget. The officer receiving the application and the fee shall transmit the fee, with the fingerprints if required, to the Department of Justice. The licensing authority of any city or county may charge an additional fee, not to exceed three dollars ($3), for processing any such application, and shall transmit such additional fee, if any, to the city or county treasury.

ARTICLE 4

LICENSES TO SELL FIREARMS
(Article heading amended by Stats 1990 ch 9 §3, eff. 1/1/91.)

§12070. Unlicensed sale; penalty.

(a) No person shall engage in the business of selling, leasing, or transferring firearms unless he or she has been issued a license pursuant to Section 12071. Any person violating this section is guilty of a misdemeanor.

(b) As used in this article, engaging in the business of selling, leasing, or transferring of firearms does not include any of the following:

(1) The sale, lease, or transfer of any firearm by a person acting pursuant to a court order or pursuant to the Enforcement of Judgments Law (Title 9 (commencing with Section 680.010) of Part 2 of the Code of Civil Procedure), or by a person who liquidates a personal firearm collection to satisfy a court judgment.

(2) The sale, lease, or transfer of firearms by a person acting pursuant to subdivision (c) of Section 12028.

(3) The sale, lease, or transfer of a firearm by a person who obtains title to the firearm by intestate succession or by bequest, provided the person disposes of the firearm within 60 days of receipt of the firearm.

(4) The infrequent sale, lease, or transfer of firearms.

(5) The sale, lease, or transfer of used firearms other than pistols, revolvers, or other firearms capable of being concealed upon the person, at gun shows or events, as specified in subparagraph (B) of paragraph (1) of subdivision (b) of Section 12071, by a person other than a licensee or dealer, provided the person has a valid federal firearms license and a certificate of eligibility issued by the Department of Justice, as specified in Section 12071, and provided all the sales, leases, or transfers fully comply with subdivision (d) of Section 12072. However, the person shall not engage in the sale, lease, or transfer of used firearms other than pistols, revolvers, or other firearms capable of being concealed upon the person at more than 12 gun shows or events in any calendar year and shall not sell, lease, or transfer more than 15 used firearms

other than pistols, revolvers, or other firearms capable of being concealed upon the person at any single gun show or event. In no event shall the person sell more than 75 used firearms other than pistols, revolvers, or other firearms capable of being concealed upon the person in any calendar year.

A person described in this paragraph shall be known as a "Gun Show Trader."

The Department of Justice shall adopt regulations to administer this program and shall recover the full costs of administration from fees assessed applicants.

As used in this paragraph, the term "used firearm" means a firearm that has been sold previously at retail and is more than three years old.

(6) The activities of a law enforcement agency pursuant to Section 12084.

(c) As used in this section, "infrequent" means:

(1) For pistols, revolvers, and other firearms capable of being concealed upon the person, less than six transactions per calendar year. For this purpose, "transaction" means a single sale, lease, or transfer of any number of pistols, revolvers, or other firearms capable of being concealed upon the person.

(2) For firearms other than pistols, revolvers, or other firearms capable of being concealed upon the person, occasional and without regularity. (*Amended by Stats 1991 ch 5 §4; ch 951 §3, 955 §4.1, eff. 1/1/92.*)

§12071. Authorization for retail license; regulations.

(a)(1) The duly constituted licensing authorities of any city, county, or city and county shall accept applications for, and may grant, licenses permitting the licensee to sell at retail within the city, county, or city and county, any firearms. If a license is granted, it shall be either in the form of a regulatory or business license or in the form prescribed by the Attorney General. The license shall be valid for not more than one year from the date of issue.

(2) The Department of Justice shall issue a statewide gun show license to all persons licensed pursuant to paragraph (1) upon demonstration by the person that he or she currently is licensed under paragraph (1). The department shall adopt regulations to implement this license program. The full costs incurred by the department in administering this program shall be recovered by fees assessed on persons who apply for a statewide gun show license.

(b) A license is subject to forfeiture for a breach of any of the following prohibitions and requirements:

(1)(A) Except as provided in subparagraph (B), the business shall be carried on only in the building designated in the license.

(B) A person licensed pursuant to subdivision (a) may, for purposes of complying with Section 12082, take possession of the firearm and commence preparation of the register for the sale, delivery, or transfer of firearms at a gun show or event, as defined in paragraph (b) of Section 178.100 of Title 27 of the Code of Federal Regulations, or its successor, if the gun show or event is not conducted from any motorized or towed vehicle and the licensee has obtained a statewide gun show license from the Department of Justice.

(2) The license or a copy thereof, certified by the issuing authority, shall be displayed on the premises where it can easily be seen.

(3) No firearm shall be delivered:

(A) Prior to January 1, 1996, within 15 days of the application for the purchase, or, after notice by the department pursuant to subdivision (c) of Section 12076, within 15 days of the submission to the department of corrected copies of the register, or within 15 days of the submission to the department of any fee required pursuant to subdivision (d) of Section 12076, whichever is later. On or after January 1, 1996, within 15 days of the application for the purchase of a pistol, revolver, or other firearm capable of being concealed upon the person, or, after notice by the department pursuant to subdivision (c) of Section 12076, within 15 days of the submission to the department of corrected copies of the register, or within 15 days of the submission to the department of any fee required pursuant to subdivision (d) of Section 12076, whichever is later. On or after January 1, 1996, within 10 days of the application for the purchase of any other firearm, or, after notice by the department pursuant to subdivision (c) of Section 12076, within 10 days of the submission to the department of corrected copies of the register, or within 10 days of the submission to the department of any fee required pursuant to subdivision (d) of Section 12076, whichever is later.

(B) Unless unloaded and securely wrapped or unloaded and in a locked container.

(C) Unless the purchaser or transferee either is personally known to the dealer or presents clear evidence of his or her identity and age to the dealer.

(D) Whenever the dealer is notified by the Department of Justice that the person is in a prohibited class described in Section 12021 or 12021.1 of this code or Section 8100 or 8103 of the Welfare and Institutions Code.

(4) No pistol, revolver, or other firearm capable of being concealed upon the person or imitation thereof, or placard advertising the sale or other transfer thereof, shall be displayed in any part of the premises where it can readily be seen from the outside.

(5) The licensee shall agree to and shall act properly and promptly in processing transfers of firearms pursuant to Section 12082.

(6) The licensee shall comply with Sections 12073 and 12077 and subdivisions (a) and (b) of Section 12072.

(7) The licensee shall post conspicuously within the licensed premises the following warning in block letters not less than three inches in height:

"IF YOU LEAVE A LOADED FIREARM WITHIN THE REACH OR EASY ACCESS OF A CHILD, YOU MAY BE FINED OR IMPRISONED, OR BOTH, IF THE CHILD GAINS ACCESS TO, AND IMPROPERLY USES, THE FIREARM."

(8) All persons who receive a statewide gun show license shall publicly display the license at any gun show at which the licensee conducts activities as authorized pursuant to subparagraph (B) of paragraph (1).

(c) As used in this article, "clear evidence of his or her identity and age" includes, but is not limited to, a motor vehicle operator's license, a state identification card, an armed forces identification card, an employment identification card which contains the bearer's signature and photograph, or any similar documentation which provides the seller reasonable assurance of the identity and age of the purchaser. (*Amended by Stats 1991 ch 5 §5; ch 950 §5, 955 §5, 956 §3, eff. 1/1/92.*)

© 1992 by J., B. & L. Gould
Printed in the U.S.A.   **EP**

§12071.1. Certificate of eligibility required for gun shows.

(a) No person shall produce, promote, sponsor, operate, or otherwise organize a gun show or event, as specified in subparagraph (B) of paragraph (1) of subdivision (b) of Section 12071, unless that person possesses a valid certificate of eligibility from the Department of Justice. A certificate of eligibility shall be issued by the department to an applicant unless the department's records indicate that the applicant is a person prohibited from possessing firearms.

(b) The Department of Justice shall adopt regulations to administer the certificate of eligibility program under this section and shall recover the full costs of administering the program by fees assessed applicants who apply for certificates.

(c) A knowing violation of this section shall be a misdemeanor and make the person ineligible for a certificate of eligibility for one year from the date of the violation or conviction, whichever is later.

(d) No later than 24 hours prior to the commencement of a gun show or event, the producer or promoter thereof shall, upon request, make available within 24 hours, or a later specified time, to the local law enforcement agency a complete and accurate list of all persons, entities, and organizations that have leased or rented, or are known to the producer to intend to lease or rent, any table, display space, or area at the gun show or event for the purpose of selling, leasing, or transferring firearms.

The producer shall thereafter, upon request, for every day the gun show or event operates, make available within 24 hours, or a later specified time, to the local law enforcement agency, an accurate, complete, and current list of the persons, entities, and organizations that have leased or rented, or are known to the producer to intend to lease or rent, any table, display space, or area at the gun show or event for the purpose of selling, leasing, or transferring firearms.

This subdivision applies to persons, entities, and organizations whether or not they participate in the entire gun show or event, or only a portion thereof.

(e) It is the intent of the Legislature that the certificate of eligibility program established pursuant to this section be incorporated into the certificate of eligibility program established pursuant to Section 12071 to the maximum extent practicable. *(Added by Stats 1991 ch 955 §6, eff. 1/1/92.)*

§12072. Restrictions.

(a) (1) Any person, corporation, or firm who shall knowingly supply, sell, or give possession or control of any firearm to any person within any of the classes prohibited by Section 12021 or 12021.1 shall be punished by imprisonment in the state prison, or in a county jail for a period not exceeding one year, or by a fine of not exceeding one thousand dollars ($1,000), or by both the fine and imprisonment.

(2) No person, corporation, or dealer shall sell, deliver, or otherwise transfer any firearm to any person whom he or she has cause to believe to be within any of the classes prohibited by Section 12021 or 12021.1 of this code or Section 8100 or 8103 of the Welfare and Institutions Code.

(b) No person licensed under Section 12071 shall sell, deliver, or transfer any pistol, revolver, or firearm capable of being concealed upon the person to any person under the age of 21 years or any other firearm to a person under the age of 18 years.

(c) No dealer licensed pursuant to Section 12071, whether or not acting pursuant to Section 12082, shall deliver a firearm to a purchaser or transferee, as follows:

(1) Prior to January 1, 1996, within 15 days of the application for the purchase, or, after notice by the department pursuant to subdivision (c) of Section 12076, within 15 days of the submission to the department of corrected copies of the register, or within 15 days of the submission to the department of any fee required pursuant to subdivision (d) of Section 12076, whichever is later. On or after January 1, 1996, within 15 days of the application for the purchase of a pistol, revolver, or other firearm capable of being concealed upon the person, or, after notice by the department pursuant to subdivision (c) of Section 12076, within 15 days of the submission to the department of corrected copies of the register, or within 15 days of the submission of any fee required pursuant to subdivision (d) of Section 12076, whichever is later. On or after January 1, 1996, within 10 days of the application for the purchase of any other firearm, or, after notice by the department pursuant to subdivision (c) of Section 12076, within 10 days of the submission to the department of corrected copies of the register, or within 10 days of the submission to the department of any fee required pursuant to subdivision (d) of Section 12076, whichever is later.

(2) Unless unloaded and securely wrapped or unloaded and in a locked container.

(3) Unless the purchaser or transferee presents clear evidence of his or her identity and age, as defined in Section 12071, to the dealer or is personally known to the dealer.

(4) Whenever the dealer is notified by the Department of Justice that the person is in a prohibited class described in Section 12021 or 12021.1 of this code or Section 8100 or 8103 of the Welfare and Institutions Code.

(5) Commencing July 1, 1993, no pistol, revolver, or other firearm capable of being concealed upon the person shall be delivered unless the purchaser or transferee presents to the dealer a basic firearm safety certificate.

(d) Where neither party to the transaction holds a dealer's license issued pursuant to Section 12071, in order for a person to sell or otherwise transfer a firearm, the parties to the transaction shall complete the transaction through either of the following:

(1) A licensed dealer pursuant to Section 12082.

(2) A law enforcement agency pursuant to Section 12084.

(e) No person may commit an act of collusion relating to Article 8 (commencing with Section 12800) of Chapter 6. For purposes of this section and Section 12071, collusion may be proven by any one of the following factors:

(1) Answering a test applicant's questions during an objective test relating to basic firearms safety.

(2) Knowingly misgrading the examination.

(3) Providing an advance copy of the test to an applicant.

(4) Taking or allowing another person to take the basic firearms safety course for one who is the applicant for the basic firearms safety certificate.

(5) Allowing another to take the objective test for the applicant, purchaser, or transferee.

(6) Allowing others to give unauthorized assistance during the examination.

(7) Reference to materials during the examination and cheating by the applicant.

(8) Providing originals or photocopies of the objective test, or any version thereof, to any person other than as specified in subdivision (f) of Section 12805.

(f) Except as provided in paragraph (1) of subdivision (a), a violation of this section is a misdemeanor. A second or subsequent violation of this section shall be punished in accordance with the penalty and probation provisions of subdivision (c) of Section 12100 concerning subsequent convictions and probation. *(Amended by Stats 1991 ch 950 §13, 951 §4.1, eff. 1/1/92.)*

§12073. Maintain register of sales.

(a) Every person engaged in the business of selling, leasing, or otherwise transferring a firearm, whether the seller, lessor, or transferor is a retail dealer, pawnbroker, or otherwise, except as provided by this chapter, shall keep a register in which shall be entered the information prescribed in Section 12077.

(b) This section shall not apply to wholesale dealers in their business intercourse with retail dealers, nor to wholesale or retail dealers in the regular or ordinary transport of unloaded firearms as merchandise to other wholesale or retail dealers by mail, express or other mode of shipment, to points outside of the city or county wherein they are situated. *(Amended by Stats 1991 ch 951 §5, eff. 1/1/92.)*

§12074. Preparation of register and copies.

The register shall be prepared by and obtained from the State Printer and shall be furnished by the State Printer to the dealers on application at a cost to be determined by the Department of General Services for each 100 leaves in quadruplicate, one original and three duplicates for the making of carbon copies. The original and duplicate copies shall differ in color, and shall be in the form provided by this article.

§12075. Forwarding names and addresses of dealers.

The State Printer upon issuing a register shall forward to the Department of Justice the name and business address of the dealer together with the series and sheet numbers of the register. The register shall not be transferable. If the dealer moves his business to a different location he shall notify the department of such fact in writing within 48 hours.

§12076. Contents of register; disposition of copies.

(a) The purchaser or transferee of any firearm shall be required to present clear evidence of his or her identity and age, as defined in Section 12071, to the dealer, and the dealer shall require him or her to sign his or her current legal name and affix his or her residence address and date of birth to the register in quadruplicate. The salesperson shall affix his or her signature to the register in quadruplicate as a witness to the signature and identification of the purchaser or transferee. Any person furnishing a fictitious name or address or knowingly furnishing any incorrect information or knowingly omitting any information required to be provided for the register and any person violating any provision of this section is guilty of a misdemeanor.

(b) Two copies of the original sheet of the register, on the date of sale or transfer, shall be placed in the mail, postage prepaid, and properly addressed to the Department of Justice in Sacramento. The third copy of the original shall be mailed, postage prepaid, to the chief of police, or other head of the police department, of the city or county wherein the sale or transfer is made. Where the sale or transfer is made in a district where there is no municipal police department, the third copy of the original sheet shall be mailed to the sheriff of the county wherein the sale or transfer is made.

The third copy for firearms, other than pistols, revolvers, or other firearms capable of being concealed upon the person shall be destroyed within five days of receipt and no information shall be compiled therefrom.

(c) The department shall examine its records, as well as those records that it is authorized to request from the State Department of Mental Health pursuant to Section 8104 of the Welfare and Institutions Code, in order to determine if the purchaser or transferee is a person described in Section 12021 or 12021.1 of this code or Section 8100 or 8103 of the Welfare and Institutions Code.

If the department determines that the purchaser or transferee is a person described in Section 12021 or 12021.1 of this code or Section 8100 or 8103 of the Welfare and Institutions Code, it shall immediately notify the dealer and the chief of the police department of the city or county in which the sale or transfer was made, or if the sale or transfer was made in a district in which there is no municipal police department, the sheriff of the county in which the sale or transfer was made, of that fact.

If the department determines that the copies of the register submitted to it pursuant to subdivision (b) contain any blank spaces or inaccurate, illegible, or incomplete information, preventing identification of the purchaser or transferee or the pistol, revolver, or other firearm to be purchased or transferred, or if any fee required pursuant to subdivision (d) is not submitted by the dealer in conjunction with submission of copies of the register, the department may notify the dealer of that fact. Upon notification by the department, the dealer shall submit corrected copies of the register to the department, or shall submit any fee required pursuant to subdivision (d), or both, as appropriate and, if notification by the department is received by the dealer at any time prior to delivery of the firearm to be purchased or transferred, the dealer shall withhold delivery until the conclusion of the waiting period described in Sections 12071 and 12072.

(d) The Department of Justice may charge the dealer a fee sufficient to reimburse all of the following:

(1) (A) The department for the cost of furnishing this information. All money received by the department pursuant to this section shall be deposited in the Dealers' Record of Sale Special Account of the General Fund, which is hereby created, to be available, upon appropriation by the Legislature, for expenditure by the department to offset the costs incurred pursuant to this section and Section 12289.

(B) The department for the cost of meeting its obligations under paragraph (2) of subdivision (b) of Section 8100 of the Welfare and Institutions Code.

(2) Local mental health facilities for state-mandated local costs resulting from the reporting requirements imposed by the amendments to Section 8103 of the Welfare and Institutions Code, made by the act which also added this paragraph.

© 1992 by J., B. & L. Gould
Printed in the U.S.A.   **EP**

(3) The State Department of Mental Health for the costs resulting from the requirements imposed by the amendments to Section 8104 of the Welfare and Institutions Code made by the act which also added this paragraph.

(4) Local mental hospitals, sanitariums, and institutions for state-mandated local costs resulting from the reporting requirements imposed by Section 8105 of the Welfare and Institutions Code.

(5) Local law enforcement agencies for state-mandated local costs resulting from the notification requirements set forth in subdivision (b) of Section 550 of the Code of Civil Procedure created by the act which also added this paragraph.

(6) Local law enforcement agencies for state-mandated local costs resulting from the notification requirements set forth in subdivision (c) of Section 8105 of the Welfare and Institutions Code.

The fee established pursuant to this subdivision shall not exceed the sum of the actual processing costs of the department, the estimated reasonable costs of the local mental health facilities for complying with the reporting requirements imposed by the act which added paragraph (2) to this subdivision, the costs of the State Department of Mental Health for complying with the requirements imposed by the act which added paragraph (3) to this subdivision, the estimated reasonable costs of local mental hospitals, sanitariums, and institutions for complying with the reporting requirements imposed by the act which added paragraph (4) to this subdivision, the estimated reasonable costs of local law enforcement agencies for complying with the notification requirements set forth in subdivision (b) of Section 550 of the Code of Civil Procedure created by the act which added paragraph (5) to this subdivision, and the estimated reasonable costs of local law enforcement agencies for complying with the notification requirements set forth in subdivision (c) of Section 8105 of the Welfare and Institutions Code created by the act which added paragraph (6) to this subdivision.

(e) Whenever the Department of Justice acts pursuant to this section as it pertains to firearms other than pistols, revolvers, or other firearms capable of being concealed upon the person, its acts or omissions shall be deemed to be discretionary within the meaning of the California Tort Claims Act pursuant to Division 3.6 (commencing with Section 810) of Title 1 of the Government Code. *(Amended by Stats 1991 ch 951 §6, eff. 1/1/92; ch 953 §5, eff. 10/14/91, oper. only until 1/1/92; ch 954 §1.7, eff. 1/1/92.)*

§12076.1. *Repealed by Stats 1991 ch 953 §6, eff. 10/14/91.*

§12077. Form of the register of sales.

(a) (1) The Department of Justice shall prescribe the form of the register described in Section 12074. There shall be two forms of the register with the format set forth in paragraph (2) of this subdivision for pistols, revolvers, and other firearms capable of being concealed upon the person and the format set forth in paragraph (3) of this subdivision for all firearms other than pistols, revolvers, or other firearms capable of being concealed upon the person.

(2) For pistols, revolvers, and other firearms capable of being concealed upon the person, information contained in the register shall be the date and time of sale, make of firearm, peace officer exemption status pursuant to subdivision (a) of Section 12078 and the agency name, manufacturer's name if stamped on the firearm, model name or number, if stamped on the firearm, if applicable, serial number, other number (if more than one serial number is stamped on the firearm), caliber, type of firearm, if the firearm is new or used, barrel length, color of the firearm, full name of purchaser, purchaser's complete date of birth, purchaser's local address, if current address is temporary, complete permanent address of purchaser, identification of purchaser, purchaser's place of birth (state or country), purchaser's complete telephone number, purchaser's occupation, purchaser's sex, purchaser's physical description, all legal names and aliases ever used by the purchaser, yes or no answer to questions that prohibit purchase including, but not limited to, conviction of a felony as described in Section 12021 or an offense described in Section 12021.1, the purchaser's status as a person described in Section 8100 of the Welfare and Institutions Code, whether the purchaser is a person who has been adjudicated by a court to be a danger to others or found not guilty by reason of insanity, whether the purchaser is a person who has been found incompetent to stand trial or placed under conservatorship by a court pursuant to Section 8103 of the Welfare and Institutions Code, signature of purchaser, signature of salesperson (as a witness to the purchaser's signature), name and complete address of the dealer or firm selling the firearm as shown on the dealer's license, the establishment number, if assigned, the dealer's complete business telephone number, and a statement that any person signing a fictitious name or address or knowingly furnishing any incorrect information or knowingly omitting any information required to be provided for the register is guilty of a misdemeanor.

(3) For firearms other than pistols, revolvers, or other firearms capable of being concealed upon the person, information contained in the register shall be the date and time of sale, peace officer exemption status pursuant to subdivision (a) of Section 12078 and the agency name, auction or event waiting period exemption pursuant to subdivision (g) of Section 12078, full name of purchaser, purchaser's complete date of birth, purchaser's local address, if current address is temporary, complete permanent address of purchaser, identification of purchaser, purchaser's place of birth (state or country), purchaser's complete telephone number, purchaser's occupation, purchaser's sex, purchaser's physical description, all legal names and aliases ever used by the purchaser, yes or no answer to questions that prohibit purchase, including, but not limited to, conviction of a felony as described in Section 12021 or an offense described in Section 12021.1, the purchaser's status as a person described in Section 8100 of the Welfare and Institutions Code, whether the purchaser is a person who has been adjudicated by a court to be a danger to others or found not guilty by reason of insanity, whether the purchaser is a person who has been found incompetent to stand trial or placed under conservatorship by a court pursuant to Section 8103 of the Welfare and Institutions Code, signature of purchaser, signature of salesperson (as a witness to the purchaser's signature), name and complete address of the dealer or firm selling the firearm as shown on the dealer's license, the establishment number, if assigned, the dealer's complete business telephone number, and a statement that any person signing a fictitious name or address

or knowingly furnishing any incorrect information or knowingly omitting any information required to be provided for the register is guilty of a misdemeanor.

(b) (1) The original of each dealer's record of sale of a firearm document shall be retained by the dealer in consecutive order. Each book of 50 originals shall become the permanent register of transactions that shall be retained for not less than three years from the date of last transaction and shall be provided for the inspection of any peace officer, Department of Justice employee designated by the Attorney General or agents of the federal Bureau of Alcohol, Tobacco, and Firearms upon the presentation of proper identification.

(2) Dealers shall use ink to complete each document.

(3) The dealer or salesperson making a sale shall ensure that all information is provided legibly. The dealer and salespersons shall be informed that incomplete or illegible information will delay sales.

(4) Each original shall contain instructions regarding the procedure for completion of the form and routing of the form. Dealers shall comply with these instructions which shall include the information set forth in this subdivision.

(5) One firearm transaction shall be reported on each record of sale document.

(c) As used in this section, the following definitions shall control:

(1) "Purchaser" means the purchaser or transferee of a firearm.

(2) "Purchase" means the purchase or transfer of a firearm. *(Amended by Stats 1991 ch 951 §6.5, 955 §7.1, eff. 1/1/92.)*

§12078. Sales to authorized peace officers.

(a) The preceding provisions of this article do not apply to deliveries, transfers, or sales of firearms made to persons properly identified as full-time paid peace officers as defined in Chapter 4.5 (commencing with Section 830) of Title 3 of Part 2, provided that the peace officers are authorized by their employer to carry firearms while in the performance of their duties, nor to deliveries, transfers, or sales of firearms made to authorized representatives of cities, cities and counties, counties, state or federal governments for use by those governmental agencies. Proper identification is defined as verifiable written certification from the head of the agency by which the purchaser or transferee is employed, identifying the purchaser or transferee as a peace officer who is authorized to carry firearms while in the performance of his or her duties, and authorizing the purchase or transfer. The certification shall be delivered to the seller or transferor at the time of purchase and transfer and the purchaser or transferee shall identify himself or herself as the person authorized in the certification. On the day the sale, delivery, or transfer is made, where a peace officer is receiving the firearm, and either a dealer is not the seller or transferor, or is not otherwise the person responsible for the delivery of the firearm, or the transfer or sale is not conducted through a law enforcement agency pursuant to Section 12084, the peace officer shall forward by prepaid mail to the Department of Justice a report of the same and the type of information concerning the seller or transferor, the buyer or transferee, and the firearm as is indicated in Section 12077. On the day the sale, delivery, or transfer is made, where a dealer is the seller, trans-

feror, or otherwise responsible for delivery of the firearm, the dealer shall forward by prepaid mail to the Department of Justice a report of the same and the type of information concerning the buyer or transferee and the firearm as is indicated in Section 12077. On the day the sale, delivery, or transfer is made, where the transfer is conducted pursuant to Section 12084, the law enforcement agency shall forward by prepaid mail to the Department of Justice a report of the same and the type of information concerning the buyer or transferee and the firearm as is indicated in Section 12084. The reports which peace officers shall complete shall be provided to them by the department at cost. All receipts from the sale of these forms shall be deposited into the Dealer's Record of Sale Special Account of the General Fund. No report need be submitted to the Department of Justice where a peace officer receiving the firearm received it from his or her employer in accordance with the applicable rules, regulations, or procedures of the employer.

(b) Section 12070 and subdivisions (c) and (d) of Section 12072 shall not apply to deliveries, sales, or transfers of firearms between or to importers and manufacturers of firearms licensed to engage in such business pursuant to Chapter 44 (commencing with Section 921) of Title 18 of the United States Code and the regulations issued pursuant thereto.

(c) Subdivision (d) of Section 12072 shall not apply to the infrequent transfers of firearms by gift, bequest, intestate succession, or other means by one individual to another where both individuals are members of the same immediate family.

As used in this subdivision, immediate family member includes the third lineal degree of consanguinity.

(d) Subdivision (d) of Section 12072 shall not apply to the infrequent loan of firearms between persons who are personally known to each other for any lawful purpose, if the loan does not exceed 30 days in duration.

(e) Section 12071 and subdivisions (c) and (d) of Section 12072 shall not apply to the delivery of a firearm to a gunsmith for service or repair.

(f) Section 12070 shall not apply to the sale, delivery, or transfer of firearms by manufacturers or importers licensed pursuant to Chapter 44 (commencing with Section 921) of Chapter 18 of the United States Code and the regulations issued pursuant thereto to dealers licensed pursuant to Section 12071.

(g) (1) Subdivision (d) of Section 12072 shall not apply to the infrequent sale or transfer of a firearm, other than a pistol, revolver, or other firearm capable of being concealed upon the person, at auctions or similar events conducted by nonprofit mutual or public benefit corporations organized pursuant to the Corporations Code.

As used in this paragraph, the term "infrequent" shall not be construed to prohibit different local chapters of the same nonprofit corporation from conducting auctions or similar events, provided the individual local chapter conducts the auctions or similar events infrequently. It is the intent of the Legislature that different local chapters, representing different localities, be entitled to invoke the exemption created by this paragraph, notwithstanding the frequency with which other chapters of the same nonprofit corporation may conduct auctions of similar events.

(2) Subdivision (d) of Section 12072 shall not apply to the transfer of a firearm other than a pistol, revolv-

© 1992 by J., B. & L. Gould
Printed in the U.S.A.   EP

er, or other firearm capable of being concealed upon the person, if the firearm is donated for an auction or similar event described in paragraph (1) and the firearm is delivered to the nonprofit corporation immediately preceding, or contemporaneous with, the auction or similar event.

(3) The waiting period described in Sections 12071 and 12072 shall not apply to a dealer who delivers a firearm other than a pistol, revolver, or other firearm capable of being concealed upon the person, at an auction or similar event described in paragraph (1), as authorized by subparagraph (C) of paragraph (1) of subdivision (b) of Section 12071. Within 48 hours of the sale, delivery, or transfer, the dealer shall forward by prepaid mail to the Department of Justice a report of the same as is indicated in paragraph (3) of subdivision (a) of Section 12077.

(h) Section 12070 and subdivision (d) of Section 12072 shall not apply to the loan of a firearm for the purposes of shooting at targets if the loan occurs on the premises of a target facility which holds a business or regulatory license or on the premises of any club or organization organized for the purposes of practicing shooting at targets upon established ranges, whether public or private, if the firearm is at all times kept within the premises of the target range or on the premises of the club or organization. *(Amended by Stats 1991 ch 5 §7; ch 951 §7, 955 §8.1, eff. 1/1/92.)*

§12079. *Repealed by Stats 1988 ch 1394 §6, eff. 1/1/89.*

§12080. Pamphlet on state firearms laws.
(a) The Department of Justice shall prepare a pamphlet which summarizes California firearms laws as they pertain to persons other than law enforcement officers or members of the armed services.

(b) The pamphlet shall include the following matters:
(1) Lawful possession.
(2) Licensing procedures.
(3) Transportation and use of firearms.
(4) Acquisition of hunting licenses.
(5) The safe handling and use of firearms.
(6) Various methods of safe storage and child proofing of firearms.
(7) The availability of firearms safety programs and devices.
(8) The responsibilities of firearms ownership.
(9) The operation of various types of firearms.
(10) The lawful use of deadly force.

(c) The department shall offer copies of the pamphlet at actual cost to firearms dealers licensed pursuant to Section 12071 who shall have copies of the most current version available for sale to retail purchasers or transferees of firearms. The cost of the pamphlet, if any, may be added to the sale price of the firearm. Other interested parties may purchase copies directly from the Department of General Services. The pamphlet shall declare that it is merely intended to provide a general summary of laws applicable to firearms and is not designed to provide individual guidance for specific areas. Individuals having specific questions shall be directed to contact their local law enforcement agency or private counsel.

(d) The Department of Justice or any other public entity shall be immune from any liability arising from the drafting, publication, or dissemination of the pamphlet or any reliance upon it. All receipts from the sale of these pamphlets shall be deposited as reimbursements to the support appropriation for the Department of Justice. *(Amended by Stats 1991 ch 950 §17, eff. 1/1/92.)*

§12081. No waiting period to transfer to licensed person.
(a) A party may sell, deliver, or otherwise transfer a firearm to a person licensed under Section 12071 without waiting to deliver the firearm until the conclusion of the waiting period described in Section 12071 or 12072.

(b) A basic firearms safety certificate shall not be required for any of the following transactions:
(1) The sale, transfer, or delivery of a pistol, revolver, or other firearm capable of being concealed upon the person to a dealer licensed pursuant to Section 12071.

(2) The sale, transfer, or delivery of a pistol, revolver, or other firearm capable of being concealed upon the person between or to importers and manufacturers of firearms licensed to engage in that business pursuant to Chapter 44 (commencing with Section 921) of Title 18 of the United States Code and the regulations issued pursuant thereto.

(3) The sale, transfer, or delivery of a pistol, revolver, or other firearm capable of being concealed upon the person to an active member of the United States Armed Forces, the National Guard, the Air National Guard, and the active reserve components of the United States, who is properly identified. For purposes of this paragraph, proper identification includes the Armed Forces Identification Card, or other written documents certifying that the person is an active member of the United States Armed Forces, the National Guard, the Air National Guard, or the active reserve components of the United States.

(4) The sale, transfer, or delivery of a pistol, revolver, or other firearm capable of being concealed upon the person to any person honorably discharged from the United States Armed Forces, the National Guard, the Air National Guard, or active reserve components of the United States who is properly identified. For purposes of this paragraph, proper identification includes a Retired Armed Forces Identification Card, or other written document certifying the person as being honorably discharged.

(5) The sale, transfer, or delivery of a pistol, revolver, or other firearm capable of being concealed upon the person to any of the following persons who are properly identified:
(A) Any California or federal peace officer who is authorized to carry a firearm while on duty.
(B) Any honorably retired peace officer, as defined in Section 830.1, 830.2, or subdivision (c) of Section 830.5.
(C) Any honorably retired federal officers or agents who were authorized to, and did, carry firearms in the course and scope of their duties and are authorized to carry firearms pursuant to subdivision (i) of Section 12027.
(D) Any persons who have permits to carry concealed weapons pursuant to Article 3 (commencing with Section 12050) of Chapter 1.
(E) Any persons who have a certificate of competency or a certificate of completion in hunter safety as provided in Article 2.5 (commencing with Section 3049) of Chapter 1 of Part 1 of Division 4 of the Fish

© 1992 by J., B. & L. Gould
Printed in the U.S.A. **EP**

and Game Code, which bears a hunter safety instruction validation stamp affixed thereto.

(F) Any person who holds a valid hunting license issued by the State of California.

(G) Any person who is authorized to carry loaded firearms pursuant to subdivision (c) or (d) of Section 12031.

(H) Any person who has been issued a certificate pursuant to Section 12033.

(I) Any basic firearms safety instructor certified by the department pursuant to Section 12805.

(J) Persons who are properly identified as authorized participants in shooting matches approved by the Director of Civilian Marksmanship pursuant to the applicable provisions of Title 10 of the United States Code.

(K) Persons who have successfully completed the course of training specified in Section 832. *(Amended by Stats 1991 ch 950 §18, eff. 1/1/92.)*

§12082. Sale or transfer of firearm through a dealer; regulations.

A person shall complete any sale or other transfer of a firearm through a dealer licensed pursuant to Section 12071 in accordance with this section in order to comply with subdivision (d) of Section 12072. The Attorney General shall adopt regulations under this section to allow the seller or transferor and the purchaser or transferee to complete a sale or other transfer through a dealer, and to allow those persons and the dealer to comply with the requirements of this section and of Sections 12071, 12072, 12076, and 12077 and to preserve the confidentiality of records. The register shall state the name and address of the seller or transferor of the firearm in addition to any other information required by Section 12077. The seller or transferor shall deliver the firearm to the dealer who shall retain possession of that firearm. The dealer shall then deliver the firearm to the purchaser or transferee, if it is not prohibited, in accordance with the provisions of subdivision (c) of Section 12072. If the dealer cannot legally transfer the firearm to the purchaser or transferee, the dealer shall forthwith, without waiting for the conclusion of the waiting period described in Sections 12071 and 12072, return the firearm to the transferor or seller. The dealer shall not return the firearm to the seller or transferor when to do so would constitute a violation of subdivision (a) of Section 12072. If the dealer cannot legally return the firearm to the transferor or seller, then the dealer shall forthwith deliver the firearm to the sheriff of the county or the chief of police or other head of a municipal police department of any city or city and county who shall then dispose of the firearm in the manner provided by Sections 12028 and 12032. The purchaser or transferee may be required by the dealer to pay a fee not to exceed ten dollars ($10), plus the fee which the Department of Justice may charge pursuant to subdivision (d) of Section 12076. Nothing in these provisions shall prevent a dealer from charging a smaller fee. The fee that the department may charge is the fee that would be applicable pursuant to subdivision (d) of Section 12076, if the dealer was selling, transferring, or delivering a firearm to a purchaser or transferee without any other parties being involved in the transaction.

A violation of this section by a dealer is a misdemeanor. *(Amended by Stats 1991 ch 5 §8; ch 955 §9, eff. 1/1/92.)*

§12083. Feasibility study of background check systems.

(a) The Department of Justice shall undertake a feasibility study concerning proposed changes in firearm statutes, particularly as they relate to this article, which would accomplish the following:

(1) Introduce a system whereby licensed firearm dealers may utilize an 800 hotline telephone number or a 976 telephone number in order to contact the Department of Justice to determine the eligibility of a person to purchase and possess a firearm.

(2) Reduce the current 15-day waiting period to a lesser waiting period as the result of the introduction of automation, computerization, or other devices or means which have increased efficiency in screening the eligibility of persons to purchase and possess firearms.

(3) Establish a licensing procedure allowing individuals who possess particular kinds of identification and have certain personal historical background, including, for example, completion of a hunter safety course, to obtain a firearm without being subject to a background check for eligibility.

(4) If the federal government develops a system for immediate and accurate identification of felons, as described in Section 6213 of Public Law 100-690, establish a means for the Department of Justice to utilize that system.

(5) Implement a system whereby a firearm purchaser utilizes a record check similar to those checks utilized by private credit reporting agencies.

(6) Incorporate private entities into the background check process by the use of bonding requirements, employing private credit reporting procedures, and by adopting similar methods and procedures.

(7) Revise existing statutory licensing requirements in order that local licensing authorities implement essentially uniform licensing procedures under Section 12071.

(8) Revise the intrafamilial firearms exemption as created by subdivision (c) of Section 12078 to determine whether the exemption needs to be clarified.

(b) The Department of Justice shall provide the results of this feasibility study to the Legislature on or before July 1, 1991.

(c) The intent of this section is to encourage the rapid development and deployment of an alternative background check system by which it may be determined if prospective purchasers of all firearms are ineligible to purchase or possess a firearm. The full deployment of an alternative background check system is highly desirable and may greatly reduce, if not eliminate, the need for California to administer the existing background check system, as authorized by this article. *(Added by Stats 1990 ch 9 §12, eff. 1/1/91; amended by Stats 1991 ch 5 §9, eff. 12/13/90, oper. 1/1/91.)*

§12084. Law Enforcement Firearms Transfer Form (LEFT).

(a) As used in this section, the following definitions shall control:

(1) "Agency" means a sheriff's department in a county of less than 200,000 persons, according to the most recent federal decennial census which elects to process purchases, sales, or transfers of firearms.

(2) "Seller" means the seller or transferor of a firearm.

© 1992 by J., B. & L. Gould
Printed in the U.S.A.   EP

(3) "Purchaser" means the purchaser or transferee of a firearm.

(4) "Purchase" means the purchase, sale, or transfer of a firearm.

(5) "Department" means the Department of Justice.

(6) "LEFT" means the Law Enforcement Firearms Transfer Form consisting of the transfer form utilized to purchase a firearm in accordance with this section.

(b) As an alternative to completing the sale or transfer of a firearm through a licensed dealer pursuant to Section 12082 in order to comply with the provisions of subdivision (d) of Section 12072, the parties to the purchase of a firearm may complete the transaction through an agency in accordance with this section in order to comply with the provisions of subdivision (d) of Section 12072.

(c) (1) LEFTs shall be prepared by the State Printer and shall be furnished to agencies on application at a cost to be determined by the Department of General Services for each 100 leaves in quintuplicate, one original and four duplicates for the making of carbon copies. The original and duplicate copies shall differ in color, and shall be in the form provided by this section. The State Printer, upon issuing the LEFT, shall forward to the department the name and address of the agency together with the series and sheet numbers on the LEFT. The LEFT shall not be transferable.

(2) The department shall prescribe the form of the LEFT. It shall be in the same exact format set forth in Sections 12077 and 12082, with the same distinct formats for firearms that are pistols, revolvers, and other firearms capable of being concealed upon the person and for firearms that are not pistols, revolvers, and other firearms capable of being concealed upon the person, except that instead of the listing of information concerning a dealer, the LEFT shall contain the name, telephone number, and address of the law enforcement agency.

(3) The original of each LEFT shall be retained in consecutive order. Each book of 50 originals shall become the permanent record of transactions that shall be retained not less than three years from the date of the last transaction and shall be provided for the inspection of any peace officer, department employee designated by the Attorney General, or agents of the federal Bureau of Alcohol, Tobacco and Firearms upon the presentation of proper identification.

(4) Ink shall be used to complete each LEFT. The agency shall ensure that all information is provided legibly. The purchaser and seller shall be informed that incomplete or illegible information delays purchases.

(5) Each original LEFT shall contain instructions regarding the procedure for completion of the form and the routing of the form. The agency shall comply with these instructions which shall include the information set forth in this subdivision.

(6) One firearm transaction shall be reported on each LEFT.

(d) The following procedures shall be followed in processing the purchase:

(1) Without waiting for the conclusion of any waiting period to elapse, the seller shall immediately deliver the firearm to the agency solely to complete the LEFT. Upon completion of the LEFT, the firearm shall be immediately returned by the agency to the seller without waiting for the waiting period to elapse.

(2) The purchaser shall be required to present clear evidence of his or her identity and age, as defined

in Section 12071, to the agency. The agency shall require the purchaser to complete the original and one copy of the LEFT. An employee of the agency shall then affix his or her signature as a witness to the signature and identification of the purchaser.

(3) Two copies of the LEFT shall, on that date of purchase, be placed in the mail, postage prepaid to the department at Sacramento. The third copy shall be provided to the purchaser and the fourth copy to the seller.

(4) The department shall examine its records, as well as those records that it is authorized to request from the State Department of Mental Health pursuant to Section 8104 of the Welfare and Institutions Code, in order to determine if the purchaser is a person described in Section 12021 or 12021.1 of this code or Section 8100 or 8103 of the Welfare and Institutions Code.

(5) If the department determines that the copies of the LEFT submitted to it pursuant to paragraph (3) contain any blank spaces or inaccurate, illegible, or incomplete information, preventing identification of the purchaser or the firearm to be purchased, or if any fee required pursuant to paragraph (6) is not submitted by the agency in conjunction with submission of the copies of the LEFT, or if the department determines that the person is a person described in Section 12021 or 12021.1 of this code or Section 8100 or 8103 of the Welfare and Institutions Code, it shall immediately notify the agency of that fact. Upon notification by the department, the purchaser shall submit any fee required pursuant to paragraph (6), as appropriate, and if notification by the department is received by the agency at any time prior to delivery of the firearm, the delivery of the firearm shall be withheld until the conclusion of the waiting period described in paragraph (7).

(6) The department and the agency may both charge a fee not to exceed the actual cost of processing the purchaser sufficient to reimburse both of the following:

(A) The agency for processing the transfer.

(B) The department for providing the information. The department shall charge the same fee as it would charge a dealer pursuant to Section 12082. All sums received by the department pursuant to this section shall be deposited in the Dealers' Record of Sale Special Account of the General Fund.

(7) The firearm shall not be delivered to the purchaser as follows:

(A) Prior to January 1, 1996, within 15 days of application for the purchase or, after notice by the department pursuant to paragraph (5), within 15 days of the submission to the department of any fees required pursuant to this subdivision, or within 15 days of a corrected LEFT, whichever is later. On or after January 1, 1996, within 15 days of the application for the purchase of a pistol, revolver, or other firearm capable of being concealed upon the person, or after notice by the department pursuant to paragraph (5), within 15 days of the submission to the department of any fees required pursuant to this subdivision, or within 15 days of the submission to the department of corrected copies of the LEFT, whichever is later. On or after January 1, 1996, within 10 days of the application for purchase of a firearm other than a pistol, revolver, or other firearm capable of being concealed upon the person, or after notice by the department pursuant to paragraph (5), or within 10 days of submission to the department of any fees required pursuant to this subdivision, or within 10 days of the submission to the department of corrected copies of the LEFT, whichever is later.

(B) Unless unloaded.

(C) In the case of a pistol, revolver, or other firearm capable of being concealed upon the person, unless securely wrapped or in a locked container.

(D) Unless the purchaser presents clear evidence of his or her identity and age to the agency.

(E) Whenever the agency is notified by the department that the person is in a prohibited class described in Section 12021 or 12021.1 or Section 8100 or 8103 of the Welfare and Institutions Code.

(F) Unless done at the agency's premises.

(G) In the case of a pistol, revolver, or other firearm capable of being concealed upon the person, commencing October 1, 1993, unless the purchaser presents to the seller a basic firearm safety certificate.

(e) The action of a law enforcement agency acting pursuant to Section 12084 shall be deemed to be a discretionary act within the meaning of the California Tort Claims Act pursuant to Division 3.6 (commencing with Section 810) of Title 1 of the Government Code.

(f) Whenever the Department of Justice acts pursuant to this section as it pertains to firearms other than pistols, revolvers, or other firearms capable of being concealed upon the person, its acts or omissions shall be deemed to be discretionary within the meaning of the California Tort Claims Act pursuant to Division 3.6 (commencing with Section 810) of Title 1 of the Government Code.

(g) Any person furnishing a fictitious name or address or knowingly furnishing any incorrect information or knowingly omitting any information required to be provided for the LEFT is guilty of a misdemeanor. *(Added by Stats 1991 ch 951, §8.1, eff. 1/1/92; amended by Stats 1991 ch 950 §19, eff. 1/1/92.)*

ARTICLE 5

OBLITERATION OF IDENTIFICATION MARKS

§12090. Penalty for unauthorized alteration of firearm.

Any person who changes, alters, removes or obliterates the name of the maker, model, manufacturer's number, or other mark of identification, including any distinguishing number or mark assigned by the Department of Justice on any pistol, revolver, or any other firearm, without first having secured written permission from the department to make such change, alteration or removal shall be punished by imprisonment in the state prison.

§12091. Possession of firearm; presumptive evidence.

Possession of any pistol or revolver upon which the name of the maker, model, manufacturer's number or other mark of identification has been changed, altered, removed, or obliterated, shall be presumptive evidence that the possessor has changed, altered, removed, or obliterated the same.

§12092. Assigning new I.D. mark.

The Department of Justice upon request may assign a distinguishing number or mark of identification to any pistol or revolver whenever it is without a manufacturer's number, or other mark of identification or whenever the manufacturer's number or other mark of identification or the distinguishing number or mark assigned by the department has been destroyed or obliterated.

§12093. Placing mark on new pistol or revolver.

Any person may place or stamp on any pistol, revolver, or other firearm any number or identifying indicium, provided the number or identifying indicium does not change, alter, remove, or obliterate the manufacturer's name, number, model, or other mark of identification. This section does not prohibit restoration by the owner of the name of the maker, model, or of the original manufacturer's number or other mark of identification when such restoration is authorized by the department, nor prevent any manufacturer from placing in the ordinary course of business the name of the maker, model, manufacturer's number, or other mark of identification upon a new firearm.

§12094. Purchase, sale of firearm without mark.

Any person with knowledge of any change, alteration, removal, or obliteration described herein, who buys, receives, disposes of, sells, offers for sale, or has in his possession any pistol, revolver, or other firearm which has had the name of the maker, model, or the manufacturer's number or other mark of identification including any distinguishing number or mark assigned by the Department of Justice changed, altered, removed, or obliterated is guilty of a misdemeanor.

ARTICLE 6

PERMITS

§12095. Short-barreled shotguns, rifles, used as props for motion pictures.

(a) If it finds that it does not endanger the public safety, the Department of Justice may issue permits initially valid for a period of one year, and renewable annually thereafter, for the manufacture, possession, transportation, or sale of short-barreled shotguns or short-barreled rifles upon a showing that good cause exists for the issuance thereof to the applicant for the permit. No permit shall be issued to a person who is under 18 years of age.

(b) Good cause, for the purposes of this section, shall be limited to only the following:

(1) The permit is sought for the manufacture, possession, or use with blank cartridges, of a short-barreled rifle or short-barreled shotgun, solely as props for a motion picture, television, or video production or entertainment event.

(2) The permit is sought for the manufacture of, exposing for sale, keeping for sale, sale of, importation or lending of short-barreled rifles or short-barreled shotguns to the entities listed in paragraph (1) of subdivision (b) of Section 12020 by persons who are licensed as dealers or manufacturers under the provisions of Chapter 53 (commencing with Section 5801) of Title 26 of the United States Code, as amended, and the regulations issued pursuant thereto. *(Added by Stats 1988 ch 1269 §5, eff. 1/1/89. Former section 12095 repealed by Stats 1988 ch 1269 §4, eff. 1/1/89.)*

© 1992 by J., B. & L. Gould
Printed in the U.S.A.   EP

§12096. Permit applications.

Applications for permits shall be filed in writing, signed by the applicant if an individual, or by a member or officer qualified to sign if the applicant is a firm or corporation, and shall state the name, business in which engaged, business address, and a full description of the use to which the short-barreled shotguns or short-barreled rifles are to be put.

Applications and permits shall be uniform throughout the state on forms prescribed by the Department of Justice.

Each applicant for a permit shall pay at the time of filing his or her application a fee determined by the Department of Justice not to exceed the application processing costs of the Department of Justice. A permit granted pursuant to this article may be renewed one year from the date of issuance, and annually thereafter, upon the filing of a renewal application and the payment of a permit renewal fee not to exceed the application processing costs of the Department of Justice. After the department establishes fees sufficient to reimburse the department for processing costs, fees charged shall increase at a rate not to exceed the legislatively approved annual cost-of-living adjustments for the department's budget. *(Added by Stats 1988 ch 1269 §5, eff. 1/1/89. Former section 12096 repealed by Stats 1988 ch 1269 §4, eff. 1/1/89.)*

§12097. Possession of permit; identification number of weapon.

(a) Every person, firm, or corporation to whom a permit is issued shall keep it on his or her person or at the place where the short-barreled shotguns or short-barreled rifles are kept. The permit shall be open to inspection by any peace officer or any other person designated by the authority issuing the permit.

(b) Every short-barreled shotgun or short-barreled rifle possessed pursuant to the provisions of this article shall bear a unique identifying number. If a weapon does not bear a unique identifying number, the Department of Justice shall assign a number which shall be placed or stamped on that weapon. *(Added by Stats 1988 ch 1269 §5 eff. 1/1/89. Former section 12097 repealed by Stats 1988 ch 1269 §4, eff. 1/1/89.)*

§12098. Revocation of permits.

Permits issued in accordance with this article may be revoked by the issuing authority at any time when it appears that the need for the short-barreled shotguns or short-barreled rifles has ceased or that the holder of the permit has used the short-barreled shotguns or short-barreled rifles for purposes other than those allowed by the permit or that the holder of the permit has not exercised great care in retaining custody of any weapons possessed under the permit. *(Added by Stats 1988 ch 1269 §5 eff. 1/1/89. Former section 12098 repealed by Stats 1988 ch 1269 §4, eff. 1/1/89.)*

ARTICLE 7

JUVENILES

§12100. Penalty for selling or transferring firearm to minor.

(a) No person or corporation shall sell any pistol, revolver, or other firearm capable of being concealed upon the person to any minor.

(b) No person or corporation shall furnish, give, or otherwise transfer possession of any pistol, revolver, or other firearm capable of being concealed upon the person to any minor without the prior written consent or implied permission of a parent or legal guardian. The written consent shall be presented to the person or corporation at the time of the furnishing, giving, or other transfer of legal possession.

(c) (1) Every person who violates this section is guilty of a misdemeanor.

(2) A person is punishable by imprisonment in the state prison, or in a county jail not exceeding one year, if one of the following applies:

(A) He or she violates this section or Section 12072 and has been convicted previously of violating this section or Section 12072.

(B) He or she violates this section or Section 12072 and has been convicted previously of violating Section 8101 of the Welfare and Institutions Code or of a crime set forth in subdivision (b) of Section 12021.1 or in Section 12020, 12220, 12520, or 12560.

(C) He or she violates this section or Section 12072 and is in a prohibited class described in Section 12021 or 12021.1 of this code or in Section 8100 or 8103 of the Welfare and Institutions Code.

(3) A person convicted of a second or subsequent violation of this section, Section 12072 of this code, or Section 8101 of the Welfare and Institutions Code may be granted probation only in an unusual case where the interests of justice would best be served. When probation is granted, the court shall specify on the record and shall enter in the minutes the circumstances indicating that the interests of justice would best be served by that disposition. Except as provided in this paragraph, probation shall not be granted, nor shall the execution or imposition of sentence be suspended for any person who has been convicted previously of this section, Section 12072 of this code, or Section 8101 of the Welfare and Institutions Code. *(Amended by Stats 1991 ch 165 §1, eff. 1/1/92.)*

§12101. Possession of firearm or live ammunition by minor; violation.

(a) A minor may not possess a pistol, revolver, or other firearm capable of being concealed upon the person unless he or she has the written consent of his or her parent or legal guardian or unless he or she is accompanied by his or her parent or legal guardian, while he or she has such firearm in his or her possession.

(b) A minor may not possess live ammunition unless he or she has the written consent of his or her parent or legal guardian or is accompanied by his or her parent or legal guardian, except while going to or from an organized lawful recreational or competitive shooting activity or lawful hunting activity.

(c) Every minor who violates this section is guilty of a misdemeanor. Every minor who violates this section is punishable upon the second and each subsequent conviction by imprisonment in a state prison or in a county jail not exceeding one year. Every minor who violates this section, upon a second or subsequent conviction, and every minor who violates this section and who has been convicted previously of a crime set forth in subdivision (b) of Section 12021.1 or in Section 12020, 12220, 12520, or 12560, is punishable by imprisonment in a state prison or in a county jail not exceeding one year. *(Added by Stats 1988 ch 1386 §3, eff. 1/1/89.)*

CHAPTER 2

MACHINE GUNS

ARTICLE 1

GENERAL PROVISIONS

§12200. Machinegun defined.

The term "machinegun" as used in this chapter means any weapon which shoots, or is designed to shoot, automatically, more than one shot, without manual reloading, by a single function of the trigger, and includes any frame or receiver which can only be used with that weapon. The term also includes any part or combination of parts designed and intended for use in converting a weapon into a machinegun. The term also includes any weapon deemed by the federal Bureau of Alcohol, Tobacco, and Firearms as readily convertible to a machinegun under Chapter 53 (commencing with Section 5801) of Title 26 of the United States Code. *(Amended by Stats 1986 ch 1423 §1.)*

§12201. Exceptions for police departments.

Nothing in this chapter shall prohibit the sale to, purchase by, or possession of machineguns by police departments, sheriffs' offices, city marshal's offices, the California Highway Patrol, the Department of Justice, or the military or naval forces of this state or of the United States for use in the discharge of their official duties; nor shall anything in this chapter prohibit the possession of machineguns by regular, salaried, full-time peace officer members of a police department, sheriff's office, city marshal's office, the California Highway Patrol, or the Department of Justice when on duty and their use is within the scope of their duties. *(Amended by Stats 1987 ch 1360 §2.)*

ARTICLE 2

UNLAWFUL POSSESSION OF MACHINE GUNS

§12220. Penalty for unauthorized sale, possession or transportation of machine gun.

(a) Any person, firm, or corporation, who within this state possesses or knowingly transports a machinegun, except as authorized by this chapter, is guilty of a public offense and upon conviction thereof shall be punished by imprisonment in the state prison, or by a fine not to exceed ten thousand dollars ($10,000), or by both such fine and imprisonment.

(b) Any person, firm, or corporation who within this state intentionally converts a firearm into a machinegun, or who sells, or offers for sale, or knowingly manufactures a machinegun, except as authorized by this chapter, is punishable by imprisonment in the state prison for four, six, or eight years. *(Amended by Stats 1990 ch 81 §2, eff. 1/1/91.)*

ARTICLE 3

PERMITS

§12230. Permit for possession and transportation of machine guns.

The Department of Justice may issue permits for the possession, manufacture, and transportation or possession, manufacture, or transportation of machineguns, upon a satisfactory showing that good cause exists for the issuance thereof to the applicant for the permit, but no permit shall be issued to a person who is under 18 years of age. *(Amended by Stats 1990 ch 81 §3, eff. 1/1/91.)*

§12231. Permit applications.

Applications for permits shall be filed in writing, signed by the applicant if an individual, or by a member or officer qualified to sign if the applicant is a firm or corporation, and shall state the name, business in which engaged, business address and a full description of the use to which the firearms are to be put.

Applications and permits shall be uniform throughout the state on forms prescribed by the Department of Justice.

Each applicant for a permit shall pay at the time of filing his or her application a fee determined by the Department of Justice not to exceed the application processing costs of the Department of Justice. A permit granted pursuant to this article may be renewed one year from the date of issuance, and annually thereafter, upon the filing of a renewal application and the payment of a permit renewal fee not to exceed the application processing costs of the Department of Justice. After the department establishes fees sufficient to reimburse the department for processing costs, fees charged shall increase at a rate not to exceed the legislatively approved annual cost-of-living adjustments for the department's budget.

§12232. Possession and inspection of permit.

Every person, firm or corporation to whom a permit is issued shall keep it on his person or at the place where the firearms are kept. The permit shall be open to inspection by any peace officer or any other person designated by the authority issuing the permit.

§12233. Permit revocation.

Permits issued in accordance with this chapter may be revoked by the issuing authority at any time when it appears that the need for the firearms has ceased or that the holder of the permit has used the firearms for purposes other than those allowed by the permit or that the holder of the permit has not exercised great care in retaining custody of any weapons possessed under the permit.

ARTICLE 4

LICENSES TO SELL MACHINE GUNS

§12250. Issuances; conditions.

(a) The Department of Justice may grant licenses in a form to be prescribed by it effective for not more than one year from the date of issuance, to permit the sale at the place specified in the license of machineguns subject to all of the following conditions, upon breach of any of which the license shall be revoked:

1. The business shall be carried on only in the place designated in the license.

2. The license or a certified copy thereof must be displayed on the premises in a place where it may easily be read.

3. No machinegun shall be delivered to any person not authorized to receive the same under the provisions of this chapter.

© 1992 by J., B. & L. Gould
Printed in the U.S.A.   EP

4. A complete record must be kept of sales made under the authority of the license, showing the name and address of the purchaser, the descriptions and serial numbers of the weapons purchased, the number and date of issue of the purchaser's permit, if any, and the signature of the purchaser or purchasing agent. This record shall be open to the inspection of any peace officer or other person designated by the Attorney General.

(b) Applications for licenses shall be filed in writing, signed by the applicant if an individual or by a member or officer qualified to sign if the applicant is a firm or corporation, and shall state the name, business in which engaged, business address and a full description of the use to which the firearms are to be put.

Applications and licenses shall be uniform throughout the state on forms prescribed by the Department of Justice.

Each applicant for a license shall pay at the time of filing his or her application a fee determined by the Department of Justice not to exceed the application processing costs of the Department of Justice. A license granted pursuant to this article may be renewed one year from the date of issuance, and annually thereafter, upon the filing of a renewal application and the payment of a license renewal fee not to exceed the application processing costs of the Department of Justice. After the department establishes fees sufficient to reimburse the department for processing costs, fees charged shall increase at a rate not to exceed the legislatively approved annual cost-of-living adjustments for the department's budget.

§12251. Possession as nuisance; surrender and destruction.

It shall be a public nuisance to possess any machinegun in violation of this chapter, and the Attorney General, any district attorney or any city attorney may bring an action before the superior court to enjoin the possession of any such machinegun.

Any such machinegun found to be in violation of this chapter shall be surrendered to the Department of Justice, and the department shall destroy such machinegun so as to render it unusable and unrepairable as a machinegun, except upon the filing of a certificate with the department by a judge or district attorney stating that the preservation of such machinegun is necessary to serve the ends of justice.

CHAPTER 2.3

ROBERTI-ROOS ASSAULT WEAPONS CONTROL ACT OF 1989

(Added by Stats 1989 ch 19 §3, eff. 1/1/90. Chapter 2.3, as added by Stats 1989 ch 18 §4, eff. 1/1/90, repealed by Stats 1989 ch 19 §2.5, eff. 1/1/90.)

ARTICLE 1

GENERAL PROVISIONS

§12275. Title.

This chapter shall be known as the Roberti-Roos Assault Weapons Control Act of 1989. *(Added by Stats 1989 ch 19 §3, eff. 1/1/90. Section 12275, as added by Stats 1989 ch 18 §4, eff. 1/1/90, repealed by Stats 1989 ch 19 §2.5, eff. 1/1/90.)*

§12275.5. Restrictions on assault weapons.

The Legislature hereby finds and declares that the proliferation and use of assault weapons poses a threat to the health, safety, and security of all citizens of this state. The Legislature has restricted the assault weapons specified in Section 12276 based upon finding that each firearm has such a high rate of fire and capacity for firepower that its function as a legitimate sports or recreational firearm is substantially outweighed by the danger that it can be used to kill and injure human beings. It is the intent of the Legislature in enacting this chapter to place restrictions on the use of assault weapons and to establish a registration and permit procedure for their lawful sale and possession. It is not, however, the intent of the Legislature by this chapter to place restrictions on the use of those weapons which are primarily designed and intended for hunting, target practice, or other legitimate sports or recreational activities. *(Added by Stats 1989 ch 19 §3, eff. 1/1/90. Section 12275.5, as added by Stats 1989 ch 18 §4, eff. 1/1/90, repealed by Stats 1989 ch 19 §2.5, eff. 1/1/90.)*

§12276. Assault weapon defined.

As used in this chapter, "assault weapon" shall mean the following designated semiautomatic firearms:

(a) All of the following specified rifles:

(1) All AK series including, but not limited to, the models identified as follows:

(A) Made in China AK, AKM, AKS, AK47, AK47S, 56, 56S, 84S, and 86S.

(B) Norinco 56, 56S, 84S, and 86S.

(C) Poly Technologies AKS and AK47.

(D) MAADI AK47 and ARM.

(2) UZI and Galil.

(3) Baretta AR-70.

(4) CETME Sporter.

(5) Colt AR-15 series.

(6) Daewoo K-1, K-2, Max 1, Max 2, AR 100, and AR110C.

(7) Fabrique Nationale FAL, LAR, FNC, 308 Match, and Sporter.

(8) MAS 223.

(9) HK-91, HK-93, HK-94, HK-PSG-1.

(10) The following MAC types:

(A) RPB Industries Inc. sM10 and sM11.

(B) SWD Incorporated M11.

(11) SKS with detachable magazine.

(12) SIG AMT, PE-57, SG 550, SG 551.

(13) Springfield Armory BM59 AND SAR-48.

(14) Sterling MK-6.

(15) Steyer AUG.

(16) Valmet M62S, M71S, and M78S.

(17) Armalite AR-180.

(18) Bushmaster Assault Rifle.

(19) Calico M-900.

(20) J&R ENG M-68.

(21) Weaver Arms Nighthawk.

(b) All of the following specified pistols:

(1) UZI.

(2) Encom MP-9 and MP-45.

(3) The following MAC types:

(A) RPB Industries Inc. sM10 and sM11.

(B) SWD Incorporated M-11.

(C) Advance Armament Inc. M-11.

(D) Military Armament Corp. Ingram M-11.

(4) Intratec TEC-9.

(5) Sites Spectre.

(6) Sterling MK-7.

(7) Calico M-950.

(8) Bushmaster Pistol.

(c) All of the following specified shotguns:

(1) Franchi SPAS 12 and LAW 12.

(2) Striker 12.

(3) The Streetsweeper type S/S Inc. SS/12.

(d) Any firearm declared by the court pursuant to Section 12276.5 to be an assault weapon that is specified as an assault weapon in a list promulgated pursuant to Section 12276.5.

(e) The term "series" includes all other models that are only variations, with minor differences, of those models listed in subdivision (a), regardless of the manufacturer.

(f) This section is declaratory of existing law, as amended, and a clarification of the law and the Legislature's intent which bans the weapons enumerated in this section, the weapons included in the list promulgated by the Attorney General pursuant to Section 12276.5, and any other models which are only variations of those weapons with minor differences, regardless of the manufacturer. The Legislature has defined assault weapons as the types, series, and models listed in this section because it was the most effective way to identify and restrict a specific class of semiautomatic weapons. *(Amended by Stats 1991 ch 954 §2, eff. 1/1/92.)*

§12276.5. Declaration of temporary suspension.

(a) Upon request by the Attorney General filed in a verified petition in a superior court of a county with a population of more than 1,000,000, the superior court shall issue a declaration of temporary suspension of the manufacture, sale, distribution, transportation, or importation into the state, or the giving or lending of a firearm alleged to be an assault weapon within the meaning of Section 12276 because the firearm is either of the following:

(1) Another model by the same manufacturer or a copy by another manufacturer of an assault weapon listed in subdivision (a), (b), or (c) of Section 12276 which is identical to one of the assault weapons listed in those subdivisions except for slight modifications or enhancements including, but not limited to: a folding or retractable stock; adjustable sight; case deflector for left-handed shooters; shorter barrel; wooden, plastic or metal stock; larger magazine size; different caliber provided that the caliber exceeds .22 rimfire; or bayonet mount. The court shall strictly construe this paragraph so that a firearm which is merely similar in appearance but not a prototype or copy cannot be found to be within the meaning of this paragraph.

(2) A firearm first manufactured or sold to the general public in California after June 1, 1989, which has been redesigned, renamed, or renumbered from one of the firearms listed in subdivision (a), (b), or (c) of Section 12276, or which is manufactured or sold by another company under a licensing agreement to manufacture or sell one of the firearms listed in subdivision (a), (b), or (c) of Section 12276, regardless of the company of production or distribution, or the country of origin.

(b) Upon the issuance of a declaration of temporary suspension by the superior court and after the Attorney General has completed the notice requirements of subdivisions (c) and (d), the provisions of subdivision (a) of Section 12280 shall apply with respect to those weapons.

(c) Upon declaration of temporary suspension, the Attorney General shall immediately notify all police, sheriffs, district attorneys, and those requesting notice pursuant to subdivision (d), shall notify industry and association publications for those who manufacture, sell, or use firearms, and shall publish notice in not less than 10 newspapers of general circulation in geographically diverse sections of the state of the fact that the declaration has been issued.

(d) The Attorney General shall maintain a list of any persons who request to receive notice of any declaration of temporary suspension and shall furnish notice under subdivision (c) to all these persons immediately upon a superior court declaration. Notice shall also be furnished by the Attorney General by certified mail, return receipt requested (or substantial equivalent if the person who is to receive the notice resides outside the United States), to any known manufacturer and California distributor of the weapon which is the subject of the temporary suspension order or their California statutory agent for service. The notice shall be deemed effective upon mailing.

(e) After issuing a declaration of temporary suspension under this section, the superior court shall set a date for hearing on a permanent declaration that the weapon is an assault weapon. The hearing shall be set no later than 30 days from the date of issuance of the declaration of temporary suspension. The hearing may be continued for good cause thereafter. Any manufacturer or California distributor of the weapon which is the subject of the temporary suspension order has the right, within 20 days of notification of the issuance of the order, to intervene in the action. Any manufacturer or California distributor who fails to timely exercise its right of intervention, or any other person who manufactures, sells, or owns the assault weapon may, in the court's discretion, thereafter join the action as amicus curiae.

(f) At the hearing, the burden of proof is upon the Attorney General to show by a preponderance of evidence that the weapon which is the subject of the declaration of temporary suspension is an assault weapon. If the court finds the weapon to be an assault weapon, it shall issue a declaration that it is an assault weapon under Section 12276. Any party to the matter may appeal the court's decision. A declaration that the weapon is an assault weapon shall remain in effect during the pendency of the appeal unless ordered otherwise by the appellate court.

(g) The Attorney General shall prepare a description for identification purposes, including a picture or diagram, of each assault weapon listed in Section 12276, and any firearm declared to be an assault weapon pursuant to this section, and shall distribute the description to all law enforcement agencies responsible for enforcement of this chapter. Those law enforcement agencies shall make the description available to all agency personnel.

(h) The Attorney General shall promulgate a list that specifies all firearms designated as assault weapons in Section 12276 or declared to be assault weapons pursuant to this section. The Attorney General shall file that list with the Secretary of State for publication in the California Code of Regulations. Any declaration that a specified firearm is an assault weapon shall be implemented by the Attorney General who, within 90 days, shall promulgate an amended list which shall include the specified firearm declared to be an assault weapon. The Attorney General shall file

© 1992 by J., B. & L. Gould
Printed in the U.S.A.   EP

the amended list with the Secretary of State for publication in the California Code of Regulations.

Chapter 3.5 (commencing with Section 11340) of Division 3 of Title 2 of the Government Code, pertaining to the adoption of rules and regulations, shall not apply to any list of assault weapons promulgated pursuant to this section.

(i) The Attorney General shall adopt those rules and regulations that may be necessary or proper to carry out the purposes and intent of this chapter. *(Amended by Stats 1991 ch 954 §3, eff. 1/1/92.)*

§12277. Person defined.

As used in this chapter, "person" means an individual, partnership, corporation, association, or any other group or entity, regardless of how it was created. *(Added by Stats 1989 ch 19 §3, eff. 1/1/90. Section 12277, as added by Stats 1989 ch 18 §4, eff. 1/1/90, repealed by Stats 1989 ch 19 §2.5, eff. 1/1/90.)*

ARTICLE 2

UNLAWFUL ACTIVITIES

§12280. Punishment for possession or manufacture of assault weapons.

(a) (1) Any person who, within this state, manufactures or causes to be manufactured, distributes, transports, or imports into the state, keeps for sale, or offers or exposes for sale, or who gives or lends any assault weapon, except as provided by this chapter, is guilty of a felony, and upon conviction shall be punished by imprisonment in the state prison for four, six, or eight years.

(2) In addition and consecutive to the punishment imposed under paragraph (1), any person who transfers, lends, sells, or gives any assault weapon to a minor in violation of paragraph (1) shall receive an enhancement of one year.

(b) Except as provided in Section 12288, any person who, within this state, possesses any assault weapon, except as provided in this chapter, is guilty of a public offense and upon conviction shall be punished by imprisonment in the state prison, or in a county jail, not exceeding one year. However, if the person presents proof that he or she lawfully possessed the assault weapon prior to June 1, 1989, or prior to the date it was specified as an assault weapon, and has since either registered the firearm and any other lawfully obtained firearm subject to this chapter pursuant to Section 12285 or relinquished them pursuant to Section 12288, a first-time violation of this subdivision shall be an infraction punishable by a fine of up to five hundred dollars ($500), but not less than three hundred fifty dollars ($350), if the person has otherwise possessed the firearm in compliance with subdivision (c) of Section 12285. In these cases, the firearm shall be returned unless the court finds in the interest of public safety, after notice and hearing, that the assault weapon should be destroyed pursuant to Section 12028.

(c) Notwithstanding Section 654 or any other provision of law, any person who commits another crime while violating this section may receive an additional, consecutive punishment of one year for violating this section in addition and consecutive to the punishment, including enhancements, which is prescribed for the other crime.

(d) Subdivisions (a) and (b) shall not apply to the sale to, purchase by, or possession of assault weapons by the Department of Justice, police departments, sheriffs' offices, marshals' offices, the Department of Corrections, the California Highway Patrol, the California State Police, district attorneys' offices, or the military or naval forces of this state or of the United States for use in the discharge of their official duties; nor shall anything in this chapter prohibit the possession or use of assault weapons by sworn members of these agencies when on duty and the use is within the scope of their duties.

(e) Subdivision (b) shall not apply to the possession of an assault weapon by any person during the 1990 calendar year, or during the 90-day period immediately after the date it was specified as an assault weapon, if all of the following are applicable:

(1) The person is eligible under this chapter to register the particular assault weapon by January 1, 1991.

(2) The person lawfully possessed the particular assault weapon described in paragraph (1) prior to June 1, 1989, or prior to the date it was specified as an assault weapon.

(3) The person is otherwise in compliance with this chapter.

(f) Subdivisions (a) and (b) shall not apply to the manufacture by persons who are issued permits pursuant to Section 12287 of assault weapons for sale to the following:

(1) Exempt entities listed in subdivision (d).

(2) Entities and persons who have been issued permits pursuant to Section 12286.

(3) Entities outside the state who have, in effect, a federal firearms dealer's license solely for the purpose of distribution to an entity listed in paragraphs (4) to (6), inclusive.

(4) Federal military and law enforcement agencies.

(5) Law enforcement and military agencies of other states.

(6) Foreign governments and agencies approved by the United States State Department.

(g) Subdivision (a) shall not apply to a person who is the executor or administrator of an estate that includes an assault weapon registered under Section 12285 which is disposed of as authorized by the probate court, if the disposition is otherwise permitted by this chapter.

(h) Subdivision (b) shall not apply to a person who is the executor or administrator of an estate that includes an assault weapon registered under Section 12285, if the assault weapon is possessed at a place set forth in paragraph (1) of subdivision (c) of Section 12285 or as authorized by the probate court.

(i) Subdivision (a) shall not apply to:

(1) A person who lawfully possesses and has registered an assault weapon pursuant to this chapter who lends that assault weapon to another if all the following apply:

(A) The person to whom the assault weapon is lent is 18 years of age or over and is not in a class of persons prohibited from possessing firearms by virtue of Section 12021 or 12021.1 of this code or Section 8100 or 8103 of the Welfare and Institutions Code.

(B) The person to whom the assault weapon is lent remains in the presence of the registered possessor of the assault weapon.

(C) The assault weapon is possessed at any of the following locations:

(i) While on a target range which holds a regulatory or business license for the purpose of practicing shooting at that target range.

(ii) While on the premises of a target range of a public or private club or organization organized for the purpose of practicing shooting at targets.

(iii) While attending any exhibition, display, or educational project which is about firearms and which is sponsored by, conducted under the auspices of, or approved by a law enforcement agency or a nationally or state recognized entity that fosters proficiency in, or promotes education about, firearms.

(2) The return of an assault weapon to the registered possessor which is lent by the same pursuant to paragraph (1).

(j) Subdivision (b) shall not apply to the possession of an assault weapon by a person to whom an assault weapon is lent pursuant to subdivision (i).

(k) As used in this chapter, the date a firearm is "specified as an assault weapon" is the earliest of the following:

(1) The effective date of an amendment to Section 12276 which adds the designation of the specified firearm.

(2) The effective date of the list promulgated pursuant to Section 12276.5 which adds or changes the designation of the specified firearm. *(Amended by Stats 1991 ch 952 §4, 954 §4.5, eff. 1/1/92.)*

ARTICLE 3

REGISTRATION AND PERMITS

§12285. Registration and possession of assault weapons.

(a) Any person who lawfully possesses an assault weapon, as defined in Section 12276, prior to June 1, 1989, shall register the firearm by January 1, 1991, and any person who lawfully possessed an assault weapon prior to the date it was specified as an assault weapon pursuant to Section 12276.5 shall register the firearm within 90 days, with the Department of Justice pursuant to those procedures which the department may establish. The registration shall contain a description of the firearm that identifies it uniquely, including all identification marks, the full name, address, date of birth, and thumbprint of the owner, and any other information as the department may deem appropriate. The department may charge a fee for registration of up to twenty dollars ($20) per person but not to exceed the actual processing costs of the department. After the department establishes fees sufficient to reimburse the department for processing costs, fees charged shall increase at a rate not to exceed the legislatively approved annual cost-of-living adjustment for the department's budget or as otherwise increased through the Budget Act.

(b) No assault weapon possessed pursuant to this section may be sold or transferred on or after January 1, 1990, to anyone within this state other than to a licensed gun dealer, as defined in subdivision (c) of Section 12290, or as provided in Section 12288. Any person who (1) obtains title to an assault weapon registered under this section by bequest or intestate succession, (2) moves into the state in lawful possession of an assault weapon, or (3) lawfully possessed a firearm subsequently declared to be an assault

weapon pursuant to Section 12276.5 shall, within 90 days, either render the weapon permanently inoperable, sell the weapon to a licensed gun dealer, obtain a permit from the Department of Justice in the same manner as specified in Article 3 (commencing with Section 12230) of Chapter 2, or remove the weapon from this state. A person who lawfully possessed a firearm which was subsequently declared to be an assault weapon pursuant to Section 12276.5 may alternatively register the firearm within 90 days of the declaration issued pursuant to subdivision (f) of Section 12276.5.

(c) A person who has registered an assault weapon under this section may possess it only under the following conditions unless a permit allowing additional uses is first obtained under Section 12286:

(1) At that person's residence, place of business, or other property owned by that person, or on property owned by another with the owner's express permission.

(2) While on the premises of a target range of a public or private club or organization organized for the purpose of practicing shooting at targets.

(3) While on a target range which holds a regulatory or business license for the purpose of practicing shooting at that target range.

(4) While on the premises of a shooting club which is licensed pursuant to the Fish and Game Code.

(5) While attending any exhibition, display, or educational project which is about firearms and which is sponsored by, conducted under the auspices of, or approved by a law enforcement agency or a nationally or state recognized entity that fosters proficiency in, or promotes education about, firearms.

(6) While transporting the assault weapon between any of the places mentioned in this subdivision, or to any licensed gun dealer, as defined in subdivision (c) of Section 12290, for servicing or repair pursuant to subdivision (b) of Section 12290, if the assault weapon is transported as required by Section 12026.1.

(d) No person who is under the age of 18 years, no person who is prohibited from possessing a firearm by Section 12021 or 12021.1 of this code, and no person described in Section 8100 or 8103 of the Welfare and Institutions Code may register or possess an assault weapon.

(e) The department's registration procedures shall provide the option of joint registration for assault weapons owned by family members residing in the same household.

(f) For 90 days following the effective date of Senate Bill 263 of the 1991-92 Regular Session, a forgiveness period shall exist to allow persons specified in subdivision (b) of Section 12280 to register with the Department of Justice assault weapons which they lawfully possessed prior to June 1, 1989.

(g) Any person who registers his or her assault weapon during the 90-day forgiveness period described in subdivision (f), and any person whose registration form was received by the Department of Justice after January 1, 1991, and who was issued a temporary registration prior to the end of the forgiveness period, shall not be charged with a violation of subdivision (b) of Section 12280, if law enforcement becomes aware of that violation only as a result of the registration of the assault weapon. This subdivision shall have no effect upon persons charged with a violation of subdivision (b) of Section 12280 of the Penal Code prior to the effective date of this bill,

© 1992 by J., B. & L. Gould
Printed in the U.S.A.   **EP**

provided that law enforcement was aware of the violation before the weapon was registered. *(Amended by Stats 1991 ch 954 §5, eff. 1/1/92.)*

§12286. Obtaining a permit to possess an assault weapon.

Any person who lawfully acquired an assault weapon before June 1, 1989, and wishes to use it in a manner different than specified in subdivision (c) of Section 12285, any person who lawfully acquired an assault weapon between June 1, 1989, and January 1, 1990, and wishes to keep it after January 1, 1990, or any person who wishes to acquire an assault weapon after January 1, 1990, shall first obtain a permit from the Department of Justice in the same manner as specified in Article 3 (commencing with Section 12230) of Chapter 2. *(Amended by Stats 1990 ch 216 §90, eff. 1/1/91.)*

§12287. Eligibility for permit to manufacture assault weapons.

(a) The Department of Justice may, upon a finding of good cause, issue permits for the manufacture of assault weapons to federally licensed manufacturers of firearms for the sale to, purchase by, or possession of assault weapons by, any of the following:

(1) The agencies listed in subdivision (d) of Section 12280.

(2) Entities and persons who have been issued permits pursuant to Section 12286.

(3) Entities outside the state who have, in effect, a federal firearms dealer's license solely for the purpose of distribution to an entity listed in paragraphs (4) to (6), inclusive.

(4) Federal law enforcement and military agencies.

(5) Law enforcement and military agencies of other states.

(6) Foreign governments and agencies approved by the United States State Department.

(b) Application for the permits, the keeping and inspection thereof, and the revocation of permits shall be undertaken in the same manner as specified in Article 3 (commencing with Section 12230) of Chapter 2. *(Added by Stats 1990 ch 653 §3, eff. 1/1/91.)*

§12288. Relinquishing an assault weapon.

Any individual may arrange in advance to relinquish an assault weapon to a police or sheriff's department. The assault weapon shall be transported in accordance* Section 12026.1. *(Added by Stats 1989 ch 19 §3, eff. 1/1/90.)*
*So in original. Probably "with" should be inserted.

§12289. Registration of assault weapons; public education and notification program.

The Department of Justice shall conduct a public education and notification program regarding the registration of assault weapons, including outreach to local law enforcement agencies and utilization of public service announcements in a variety of media approaches, to ensure maximum publicity of the limited forgiveness period of the registration requirement specified in subdivision (f) of Section 12285 and the consequences of nonregistration. The department shall develop posters describing gunowners' responsibilities under this chapter which shall be posted in a conspicuous place in every licensed gun store in the state during the forgiveness period.

Any costs incurred by the Department of Justice to implement this section which cannot be absorbed by the department shall be funded from the Dealers' Record of Sale Special Account, as set forth in subdivision (d) of Section 12076, upon appropriation by the Legislature. *(Added by Stats 1991 ch 954 §6, eff. 1/1/92.)*

ARTICLE 4

LICENSED GUN DEALERS

§12290. Licensed gun dealer defined.

(a) Any licensed gun dealer, as defined in subdivision (c), who lawfully possesses an assault weapon pursuant to Section 12285, in addition to the uses allowed in Section 12285, may transport the weapon between dealers or out of the state, display it at any gun show licensed by a state or local governmental entity, sell it to a resident outside the state, or sell it to a person who has been issued a permit pursuant to Section 12286. Any transporting allowed by this section must be done as required by Section 12026.1.

(b) (1) Any licensed gun dealer, as defined in subdivision (c), may take possession of any assault weapon for the purposes of servicing or repair from any person to whom it is legally registered or who has been issued a permit to possess it pursuant to this chapter.

(2) Any licensed gun dealer may transfer possession of any assault weapon received pursuant to paragraph (1), to a gunsmith for purposes of accomplishing service or repair of the same. Transfers are permissible only to the following persons:

(A) A gunsmith who is in the dealer's employ.

(B) A gunsmith with whom the dealer has contracted for gunsmithing services. In order for this subparagraph to apply, the gunsmith receiving the assault weapon must hold all of the following:

(i) A dealer's license issued pursuant to Chapter 44 (commencing with Section 921) of Title 18 of the United States Code and the regulations issued pursuant thereto.

(ii) Any business license required by a state or local governmental entity.

(c) The term "licensed gun dealer," as used in this article, means a person who has a federal firearms license, any business license required by a state or local governmental entity, and a seller's permit issued by the State Board of Equalization. *(Amended by Stats 1990 ch 177 §7, eff. 6/27/90; ch 1257 §1, eff. 1/1/91.)*

CHAPTER 2.5

DESTRUCTIVE DEVICES

§12301. Destructive device defined.

(a) The term "destructive device," as used in this chapter, shall include any of the following weapons:

(1) Any projectile containing any explosive or incendiary material or any other chemical substance, including, but not limited to, that which is commonly known as tracer or incendiary ammunition, except tracer ammunition manufactured for use in shotguns.

(2) Any bomb, grenade, explosive missile, or similar device or any launching device therefor.

(3) Any weapon of a caliber greater than .60 caliber which fires fixed ammunition, or any ammunition therefor, other than a shotgun, shotgun ammunition,

or an antique cannon. For purposes of this section, the term "antique cannon" means any cannon manufactured before January 1, 1899, which has been rendered incapable of firing or for which ammunition is no longer manufactured in the United States and is not readily available in the ordinary channels of commercial trade.

(4) Any rocket, rocket-propelled projectile, or similar device of a diameter greater than 0.60 inch, or any launching device therefor, and any rocket, rocket-propelled projectile, or similar device containing any explosive or incendiary material or any other chemical substance, other than the propellant for such device, except such devices as are designed primarily for emergency or distress signaling purposes.

(5) Any breakable container which contains a flammable liquid with a flashpoint of 150 degrees Fahrenheit or less and has a wick or similar device capable of being ignited, other than a device which is commercially manufactured primarily for the purpose of illumination.

(b) The term "explosive," as used in this chapter, shall mean any explosive defined in Section 12000 of the Health and Safety Code. (*Amended by Stats 1986 ch 262 §1.*)

§12302. Sale allowed to peace officers, military, or firefighters.

Nothing in this chapter shall prohibit the sale to, purchase by, possession of, or use of destructive devices by:

(a) Any peace officer listed in Section 830.1 or 830.2 or any peace officer in the Department of Justice authorized by the Attorney General, while on duty and acting within the scope and course of his employment.

(b) Any member of the Army, Navy, Air Force, or Marine Corps of the United States, or the National Guard, while on duty and acting within the scope and course of his employment.

Nothing in this chapter shall prohibit the sale to, purchase by, possession by, or use by any person who is a regularly employed and paid officer, employee or member of a fire department or fire protection or firefighting agency of the federal government, the State of California, a city, county, city and county, district, or other public or municipal corporation or political subdivision of this state, while on duty and acting within the scope and course of his employment, of any equipment used by such department or agency in the course of fire suppression.

§12303. Punishment for possession of destructive device.

Any person, firm, or corporation who, within this state, possesses any destructive device, other than fixed ammunition of a caliber greater than .60 caliber, except as provided by this chapter, is guilty of a public offense and upon conviction thereof shall be punished by imprisonment in the county jail for a term not to exceed one year, or in state prison, or by a fine not to exceed ten thousand dollars ($10,000) or by both such fine and imprisonment.

§12303.1. Punishment for carrying or placing destructive device in vehicle carrying passengers or common carrier.

Every person who willfully does any of the following is guilty of a felony and is punishable by imprisonment in the state prison for two, four, or six years:

(a) Carries any explosive or destructive device on any vessel, aircraft, car, or other vehicle that transports passengers for hire.

(b) Places or carries any explosive or destructive device, while on board any such vessel, aircraft, car or other vehicle, in any hand baggage, roll, or other container.

(c) Places any explosive or destructive device in any baggage which is later checked with any common carrier.

§12303.2. Possession of destructive devices in public place.

Every person who recklessly or maliciously has in his possession any destructive device or any explosive on a public street or highway, in or near any theater, hall, school, college, church, hotel, other public building, or private habitation, in, on, or near any aircraft, railway passenger train, car, cable road or cable car, vessel engaged in carrying passengers for hire, or other public place ordinarily passed by human beings is guilty of a felony, and shall be punishable by imprisonment in the state prison for a period of two, four, or six years.

§12303.3. Exploding or igniting; to injure or intimidate.

Every person who possesses, explodes, ignites, or attempts to explode or ignite any destructive device or any explosive with intent to wrongfully injure or destroy any property, is guilty of a felony, and shall be punished by imprisonment in the state prison for a period of three, five, or seven years.

§12303.6. Selling or transporting.

Any person, firm, or corporation who, within this state, sells, offers for sale, or knowingly transports any destructive device, other than fixed ammunition of a caliber greater than .60 caliber, except as provided by this chapter, is guilty of a felony and is punishable by imprisonment in the state prison for two, three or four years.

§12304. Selling, possessing or transporting fixed ammunition of certain caliber.

Any person, firm or corporation who, within this state, sells, offers for sale, possesses or knowingly transports any fixed ammunition of a caliber greater than .60 caliber, except as provided in this chapter, is guilty of a public offense and upon conviction thereof shall be punished by imprisonment in the county jail for a term not to exceed six months or by a fine not to exceed one thousand dollars ($1,000), or by both such fine and imprisonment.

A second or subsequent conviction shall be punished by imprisonment in the county jail for a term not to exceed one year, or by imprisonment in the state prison, or by a fine not to exceed three thousand dollars ($3,000), or by both such fine and imprisonment.

§12305. Required permit for use of destructive device by dealers.

(a) Every dealer, manufacturer, importer, and exporter of any destructive device, or any motion picture or television studio using destructive devices in the conduct of its business, shall obtain a permit for the conduct of that business from the Department of Justice.

© 1992 by J., B. & L. Gould
Printed in the U.S.A.　　**EP**

(b) Any person, firearm, or corporation not mentioned in subdivision (a) shall obtain a permit from the Department of Justice in order to possess or transport any destructive device.

(c) Applications for permits shall be filed in writing, signed by the applicant if an individual, or by a member or officer qualified to sign if the applicant is a firm or corporation, and shall state the name, business in which engaged, business address and a full description of the use to which the destructive devices are to be put.

(d) Applications and permits shall be uniform throughout the state on forms prescribed by the Department of Justice.

(e) Each applicant for a permit shall pay at the time of filing his or her application a fee not to exceed the application processing costs of the Department of Justice. A permit granted pursuant to this article may be renewed one year from the date of issuance, and annually thereafter, upon the filing of a renewal application and the payment of a permit renewal fee not to exceed the application processing costs of the Department of Justice. After the department establishes fees sufficient in amount to cover processing costs, the amount of the fees shall only increase at a rate not to exceed the legislatively approved cost-of-living adjustment for the department. *(Amended by Stats 1988 ch 1394 §8, eff. 1/1/89.)*

§12306. *Repealed by Stats 1988 ch 1394 §9, eff. 1/1/89.*

§12307. Possession as nuisance; surrender and destruction.

The possession of any destructive device in violation of this chapter shall be deemed to be a public nuisance and the Attorney General or district attorney of any city, county, or city and county may bring an action before the superior court to enjoin the possession of any such destructive device.

Any such destructive device found to be in violation of this chapter shall be surrendered to the Department of Justice, and the department shall destroy such destructive device so as to render it unusable and unrepairable as a destructive device, except upon the filing of a certificate with the department by a judge or district attorney stating that the preservation of such destructive device is necessary to serve the ends of justice.

§12308. Exploding, igniting destructive device with intent to murder.

Every person who explodes, ignites, or attempts to explode or ignite any destructive device or any explosive with intent to commit murder is guilty of a felony, and shall be punished by imprisonment in the state prison for a period of five, seven, or nine years.

§12309. Willfully causing bodily injury.

Every person who willfully and maliciously explodes or ignites any destructive device or any explosive which causes bodily injury to any person is guilty of a felony, and shall be punished by imprisonment in the state prison for a period of five, seven, or nine years.

§12310. Willfully causing death or mayhem.

(a) Every person who willfully and maliciously explodes or ignites any destructive device or any explosive which causes the death of any person is guilty of a felony, and shall be punished by imprisonment in the state prison for life without the possibility of parole.

(b) Every person who willfully and maliciously explodes or ignites any destructive device or any explosive which causes mayhem or great bodily injury to any person is guilty of a felony, and shall be punished by imprisonment in the state prison for life.

§12311. Probation prohibited.

No person convicted of a violation of this chapter shall be granted probation, and the execution of the sentence imposed upon such person shall not be suspended by the court.

§12312. Possessing materials with intent to make destructive device.

Every person who possesses any substance, material, or any combination of substances or materials, with the intent to make any destructive device or any explosive without first obtaining a valid permit to make such destructive device or explosive, is guilty of a felony, and is punishable by imprisonment in the state prison for two, three, or four years.

*CHAPTER 2.6

AMMUNITION DESIGNED PRIMARILY TO PENETRATE METAL OR ARMOR

(Two chapters 2.6 were added by Stats 1982 ch 949 §3 and Stats 1982 ch 950 §3. Chapter 2.6 as added by Stats 1982 ch 949 §3 was repealed by Stats 1990 ch 216 §91, eff. 1/1/91.)

§12320. Punishment for possession of ammunition.

Any person, firm, or corporation who, within this state knowingly possesses any handgun ammunition designed primarily to penetrate metal or armor is guilty of a public offense and upon conviction thereof shall be punished by imprisonment in the state prison, or in the county jail for a term not to exceed one year, or by a fine not to exceed five thousand dollars ($5,000), or by both such fine and imprisonment. *(Added by Stats 1982 ch 950 §3.)*

§12321. Penalty for manufacture, sale, or transport of ammunition.

Any person, firm, or corporation who, within this state, manufactures, imports, sells, offers to sell, or knowingly transports any handgun ammunition designed primarily to penetrate metal or armor is guilty of a felony and upon conviction thereof shall be punished by imprisonment in state prison, or by a fine not to exceed five thousand dollars ($5,000), or by both such fine and imprisonment. *(Added by Stats 1982 ch 950 §3.)*

§12322. Exemptions for military personnel.

Nothing in this chapter shall prohibit the sale to, purchase by, possession of, or use of any ammunition by any member of the Army, Navy, Air Force, or Marine Corps of the United States, or the National Guard, while on duty and acting within the scope and course of his or her employment, or any police agency or forensic laboratory or any person who is the holder of a valid permit issued pursuant to Section 12305. *(Amended by Stats 1990 ch 216 §92; ch 350 §18, eff. 1/1/91.)*

§12323. Handgun ammunition defined.

As used in this chapter, "handgun ammunition" means ammunition principally for use in pistols and revolvers, as defined in Section 12001, notwithstanding that the ammunition may also be used in some rifles. *(Added by Stats 1982 ch 950 §3.)*

§12324. Sales, possession of deactivated ammunition.

Nothing in this chapter shall prohibit the possession, importation, sale, attempted sale, or transport of ammunition from which the propellant has been removed and the primer has been permanently deactivated. *(Added by Stats 1982 ch 950 §3.)*

§12325. Government approved manufacturing contracts.

Nothing in this chapter shall prohibit the manufacture of ammunition under contracts approved by agencies of the state or federal government. *(Added by Stats 1982 ch 950 §3.)*

CHAPTER 3

PISTOLS

(Repealed by Stats 1990 ch 9 §13, eff. 1/1/91.)

§§12350, 12351. *Repealed by Stats 1990 ch 9 §13, eff. 1/1/91.*

CHAPTER 3.2

BOOBYTRAPS

§12355. Boobytrap devices; punishment.

(a) Except as provided in Chapter 2.5 (commencing with Section 12301), any person who assembles, maintains, places, or causes to be placed a boobytrap device as described in subdivision (c) is guilty of a felony punishable by imprisonment in the state prison for two, three, or five years.

(b) Possession of any device with the intent to use the device as a boobytrap is punishable by imprisonment in state prison, or in a county jail not exceeding one year, or by a fine not exceeding five thousand dollars ($5,000), or by both that fine and imprisonment.

(c) For purposes of this section, "boobytrap" means any concealed or camouflaged device designed to cause great bodily injury when triggered by an action of any unsuspecting person coming across the device. Boobytraps may include, but are not limited to, guns, ammunition, or explosive devices attached to trip wires or other triggering mechanisms, sharpened stakes, and lines or wire with hooks attached.

CHAPTER 3.5

BODY ARMOR CERTIFICATION

§12360. Acquisition by commissioner; certification.

No body armor shall be acquired by the commissioner pursuant to Section 2259.5 of the Vehicle Code unless, pursuant to subdivision (a) of Section 12361, the Department of Justice has certified such body armor.

§12361. Ballistic performance standards.

(a) Before a body armor may be purchased for use by state peace officers the Department of Justice, after consultation with the Department of the California Highway Patrol and the California State Police Division, shall establish minimum ballistic performance standards, and shall determine that such armor satisfies such standards.

(b) Only body armor that meets state requirements under subdivision (a) for acquisition or purchase shall be eligible for testing for certification under the ballistic performance standards established by the Department of Justice; and only body armor that is certified as acceptable by the department shall be purchased for use by state peace officers.

§12362. Applying for certification.

Any person engaged in the manufacture or sale of body armor may apply to the Department of Justice for certification that a particular type of body armor manufactured or sold by that person is acceptable. The applicant shall reimburse the state for any actual expenses incurred by the state in testing and certifying a particular type of body armor.

§12363. Application requirements.

Any application submitted pursuant to Section 12362 shall contain all of the following:

(a) Full written reports of any investigation conducted for the purpose of determining whether such body armor is acceptable.

(b) A full written statement of the design of such body armor.

(c) A full written statement of the methods used in, and the facilities and controls used for, the manufacture of such body armor.

(d) Such samples of body armor and its components as the department may require.

(e) Specimens of the instructions and advertisements used or proposed to be used for such body armor.

§12364. Ballistic testing.

The Department of Justice, in cooperation with the Office of Procurement of the Department of General Services, shall establish a schedule for ballistic testing for certification pursuant to subdivision (b) of Section 12361.

§12365. Grounds for refusal.

The department shall issue an order refusing to certify a body armor as acceptable if, after due notice to the applicant, the department finds any of the following:

(a) That the body armor does not satisfy the ballistic performance standards established by the department pursuant to subdivision (b) of Section 12361.

(b) That the application contains any misrepresentation of a material fact.

(c) That the application is materially incomplete.

(d) That the applicant has failed to reimburse the state as required by Section 12362.

§12366. Grounds for revocation.

The department shall issue an order revoking certification if, after due notice to the applicant, the department finds any of the following:

(a) That the experience or additional testing show that the body armor does not comply with the department's ballistic performance standards.

© 1992 by J., B. & L. Gould
Printed in the U.S.A.   EP

(b) That the application contains any misrepresentation of a material fact.

(c) The body armor must be retested for certification under new department standards.

§12367. Department regulations.

The department shall adopt and promulgate regulations for the fair and efficient enforcement of this chapter.

§12368. Purchase of armor by Department of General Services.

(a) All purchases of certified body armor under the provisions of this chapter shall be made by the Department of General Services on behalf of an authorized state agency or department. Purchases of such body armor shall be based upon written requests submitted by an authorized state agency or department to the Department of General Services.

(b) The Department of General Services shall make certified body armor available to peace officer members of the California State Police Division as defined by Section 830.2 of the Penal Code, and to peace officers of the Department of Justice as defined by Section 830.3 of the Penal Code, while engaged in enforcement activities.

§12369. Duties of Department.

The Department of General Services shall, pursuant to departmental regulation, after consultation with the Department of the California Highway Patrol and the California State Police Division, define the term "enforcement activities" for purposes of this chapter, and develop standards regarding what constitutes sufficient wear on body armor to necessitate replacement thereof.

CHAPTER 4

TEAR GAS WEAPONS

ARTICLE 1

GENERAL PROVISIONS

§12401. Tear gas defined.

"Tear gas" as used in this chapter shall apply to and include all liquid, gaseous, or solid substances intended to produce temporary physical discomfort or permanent injury through being vaporized or otherwise dispersed in the air, but does not apply to, and shall not include, any substance registered as an economic poison as provided in Chapter 2 (commencing with Section 12751) of Division 7 of the Agricultural Code provided that such substance is not intended to be used to produce discomfort or injury to human beings.

§12402. Tear gas weapon defined.

The term "tear gas weapon" as used in this chapter shall apply to and include:

(a) Any shell, cartridge, or bomb capable of being discharged or exploded, when the discharge or explosion will cause or permit the release or emission of tear gases.

(b) Any revolvers, pistols, fountain pen guns, billies, or other form of device, portable or fixed, intended for the projection or release of tear gas except those regularly manufactured and sold for use with firearm ammunition.

§12403. Exceptions for peace officers.

Nothing in this chapter shall prohibit any person who is a peace officer, as defined in Chapter 4.5 (commencing with Section 830) of Title 3 of Part 2, from purchasing, possessing, transporting, or using any tear gas weapon, if the weapon has been certified as acceptable under Article 5 (commencing with Section 12450) of this chapter and if the person has satisfactorily completed a course of instruction approved by the Commission on Peace Officer Standards and Training in the use of tear gas. *(Amended by Stats 1990 ch 350 §19, eff. 1/1/91.)*

§12403.1. Exceptions for military personnel.

Nothing in this chapter shall prohibit any member of the military and naval forces of this state or of the United States or any federal law enforcement officer from purchasing, possessing, or transporting any tear gas or tear gas weapon for official use in the discharge of his duties.

§12403.5. Exceptions for private investigators, private patrol operators.

Notwithstanding any other provision of law, a person holding a license as a private investigator or private patrol operator issued pursuant to Chapter 11 (commencing with Section 7500), Division 3 of the Business and Professions Code, or uniformed patrolmen employees of a private patrol operator, may purchase, possess, or transport any tear gas weapon, if it is used solely for defensive purposes in the course of the activity for which the license was issued and if such person has satisfactorily completed a course of instruction approved by the Commission on Peace Officer Standards and Training in the use of tear gas.

§12403.6. Official activities excepted.

Provisions within this chapter shall not be construed to prohibit any Department of Justice or Department of Health employee, while acting within the scope of his duties, from possessing any tear gas or tear gas weapon for the purposes of examination, testing, or court appearance or any other official activity undertaken pursuant to the provisions of this chapter.

§12403.7. Use or possession for self-defense; limitations.

(a) Notwithstanding any other provision of law, any person may purchase, possess or use tear gas and tear gas weapons for the projection or release of tear gas if such tear gas and tear gas weapons are approved by the Department of Justice and are used solely for self-defense purposes, subject to the following requirements:

(1) No person convicted of a felony or any crime involving an assault under the laws of the United States, of the State of California, or any other state, government, or country or convicted of misuse of tear gas under paragraph (8) shall purchase, possess, or use tear gas or tear gas weapons.

(2) No person who is addicted to any narcotic drug shall purchase, possess, or use tear gas or tear gas weapons.

(3) No person shall sell or furnish any tear gas or tear gas weapon to a minor.

(4) No person who is a minor shall purchase, possess, or use tear gas or tear gas weapons.

(5) (A) No person shall purchase, possess or use any tear gas weapon which expels a projectile, or which expels the tear gas by any method other than an aerosol spray, or which is of a type, or size of container, other than authorized by regulation of the Department of Justice.

(B) The department, with the cooperation of the State Department of Health Services, shall develop standards and promulgate regulations regarding the type of tear gas and tear gas weapons which may lawfully be purchased, possessed, and used pursuant to this section.

(C) The regulations of the department shall include a requirement that every tear gas container and tear gas weapon which may be lawfully purchased, possessed, and used pursuant to this section have a label which states: "WARNING: The use of this substance or device for any purpose other than self-defense is a felony under the law. The contents are dangerous—use with care."

(D) The regulations of the department shall include a requirement that after January 1, 1984, every tear gas container and tear gas weapon which may be lawfully purchased, possessed, and used pursuant to this section have a label which discloses the date on which the useful life of the tear gas weapon expires.

(6) (A) No person shall purchase, possess, or use any tear gas or any tear gas weapon who has not completed a course certified by the Department of Justice in the use of tear gas and tear gas weapons pursuant to which a card is issued identifying the person who has completed such a course. Such a course shall be taken under the auspices of any institution approved by the Department of Justice to offer tear gas training. Such a training institution is authorized to charge a fee covering the actual cost of such training. The requirements of this paragraph shall not apply to a person who is a retired peace officer, as peace officer is defined in Chapter 4.5 (commencing with Section 830) of Title 3 of Part 2, if the person prior to retirement had satisfactorily completed a course of instruction approved by the Commission on Peace Officer Standards and Training in the use of tear gas and tear gas weapons.

(B) The Department of Justice, in cooperation with the Commission on Peace Officer Standards and Training, shall develop standards for a course in the use of tear gas and tear gas weapons.

(7) If the purchase of tear gas or any tear gas weapon is denied, the vendor denying such purchase shall inform the person in writing of the reason for such denial. The valid identification card specified in paragraph (6) shall be carried on the person when carrying tear gas or tear gas weapons and shall be presented for examination to the vendor from whom any tear gas or tear gas weapons are purchased. The sale of tear gas or tear gas weapons by a vendor to a person who fails to present a valid identification card specified in paragraph (6) is a violation of Section 12420.

(8) Any person who uses tear gas or tear gas weapons except in self-defense or as authorized for training purposes by the department is guilty of a public offense and is punishable by imprisonment in a state prison for 16 months, or two or three years or in a county jail not to exceed one year or by fine not to exceed one thousand dollars ($1,000) or by both such fine and imprisonment, except that if such use is against a peace officer, as defined in Chapter 4.5 (commencing with Section 830) of Title 3 of Part 2, engaged in the performance of his or her official duties and the person committing the offense knows or reasonably should know that the victim is a peace officer, the offense is punishable by imprisonment in a state prison for 16 months or two or three years or by fine of one thousand dollars ($1,000) or by both such fine and imprisonment.

(b) Such identification card as specified in paragraph (6) of subdivision (a) shall be valid so long as the person meets the requirements in subdivision (a), and shall be nontransferable.

All forms, cards, and other documentation necessary to administer the provisions of this section shall be uniform throughout the state as prescribed by the Department of Justice.

The Department of Justice may adopt and promulgate such regulations concerning the purchase and disposal of self-defense tear gas weapons, the standards for tear gas training courses, and the approval of facilities at which such training shall occur as are necessary to insure the safe use and possession of such tear gas weapons.

(c) Any person who successfully completes training under this section for which the course and training facility must be approved by the Department of Justice is entitled to receive a certificate of completion issued by the Department of Justice. A fee shall be charged by the Department of Justice for the certificate. The fee shall be no more than is necessary to reimburse the Department of Justice for the costs of approving the courses, the facilities, maintaining control of the quality of the courses, and issuing the certificate of completion. The Department of Justice may provide by regulation the manner in which the fee is collected and paid.

§12403.8. Purchase, possession and use of tear gas by a minor.

(a) Notwithstanding the provisions of paragraph (4) of subdivision (a) of Section 12403.7, a minor who has attained the age of 16 may purchase, possess, and use tear gas or tear gas weapons pursuant to the provisions of this chapter if he or she has completed a course of instruction certified by the Department of Justice and has obtained the written consent of his or her parent or guardian.

(b) Notwithstanding the provisions of paragraph (3) of subdivision (a) of Section 12403.7, a person may sell or furnish tear gas or a tear gas weapon to a minor who has attained the age of 16 and who presents a valid identification card containing a statement of consent to the purchase signed by the minor's parent or guardian and indicating that the minor has completed a course certified by the Department of Justice in the use of tear gas and tear gas weapons.

(c) The Department of Justice shall prescribe the form of the identification card required by subdivision (b). The card shall be issued as provided in Section 12403.7.

§12404. Authorization to possess.

Nothing in this chapter authorizes the possession of tear gas or tear gas weapons in any institution described in Section 4574, or within the grounds belonging or adjacent to any such institution, except where authorized by the person in charge of such institution.

© 1992 by J., B. & L. Gould
Printed in the U.S.A.   **EP**

ARTICLE 2

UNLAWFUL POSSESSION AND SALE

§12420. Unauthorized sale, possession or transportation of tear gas.

Any person, firm, or corporation who within this state knowingly sells or offers for sale, possesses, or transports any tear gas or tear gas weapon, except as permitted under the provisions of this chapter, is guilty of a public offense and upon conviction thereof shall be punishable by imprisonment in the county jail for not exceeding one year or by a fine not to exceed two thousand dollars ($2,000), or by both.

§12421. I.D. name and number.

Each tear gas weapon sold, transported or possessed under the authority of this chapter shall bear the name of the manufacturer and a serial number applied by him.

§12422. Altering, removing, I.D. marks.

Any person who changes, alters, removes or obliterates the name of the manufacturer, the serial number or any other mark of identification on any tear gas weapon is guilty of a public offense and, upon conviction, shall be punished by imprisonment in the state prison or by a fine of not more than two thousand dollars ($2,000) or by both.

Possession of any such weapon upon which the same shall have been changed, altered, removed, or obliterated, shall be presumptive evidence that such possessor has changed, altered, removed, or obliterated the same.

ARTICLE 3

PERMITS

§12423. Permit for possession and transportation.

The Department of Justice may issue a permit for the possession and transportation of tear gas or tear gas weapons upon proof that good cause exists for the issuance thereof to the applicant for such permit. The permit may also allow the applicant to install, maintain, and operate a protective system involving the use of tear gas or tear gas weapons in any place which is accurately and completely described in the application for the permit.

§12424. Applications for permits.

Applications for permits shall be filed in writing, signed by the applicant if an individual, or by a member or officer qualified to sign if the applicant is a firm or corporation, and shall state the name, business in which engaged, business address and a full description of the place or vehicle in which the tear gas or tear gas weapons are to be transported, kept, installed, or maintained.

If the tear gas or tear gas weapons are to be used in connection with, or to constitute, a protective system, the application shall also contain the name of the person who is to install the protective system.

Applications and permits shall be uniform throughout the state upon forms prescribed by the Department of Justice.

Each applicant for a permit shall pay at the time of filing his or her application a fee determined by the Department of Justice not to exceed the application processing costs of the Department of Justice. A permit granted pursuant to this article may be renewed one year from the date of issuance, and annually thereafter, upon the filing of a renewal application and the payment of a permit renewal fee not to exceed the application processing costs of the Department of Justice. After the department establishes fees sufficient to reimburse the department for processing costs, fees charged shall increase at a rate not to exceed the legislatively approved annual cost-of-living adjustments for the department's budget.

§12424.5. Requirements for an annual permit.

Notwithstanding Section 12423, a bank, a savings and loan association, a credit union, or an industrial loan company which maintains more than one office or branch may make a single annual application for a permit. In addition to the requirements set forth in this article, that application shall separately state the business address and a full description of each office or branch in which the tear gas or tear gas weapons are to be kept, installed, or maintained. Any location additions or deletions as to offices or branches shall be reported to the department within 60 days of the change.

A single permit issued under this section shall allow for the possession, operation, and maintenance of tear gas at each office or branch named in the application, including location changes. *(Added by Stats 1986 ch 617 §1.)*

§12425. Inspection.

Every person, firm or corporation to whom a permit is issued shall either carry the permit upon his person or keep it in the place described in the permit. The permit shall be open to inspection by any peace officer or other person designated by the authority issuing the permit.

§12426. Revocation or suspension of permits.

Permits issued in accordance with this article may be revoked or suspended by the issuing authority at any time when it appears that the need for the possession or transportation of the tear gas or tear gas weapons or protective system involving the use thereof, has ceased, or that the holder of the permit has engaged in an unlawful business or occupation or has wrongfully made use of the tear gas or tear gas weapons or the permit issued or that the holder of the permit was in the possession of tear gas or tear gas weapons not authorized under the provisions of this chapter.

ARTICLE 4

LICENSES TO SELL

§12435. Issuance.

The Department of Justice may grant licenses in a form to be prescribed by it effective for not more than one year from the date of issuance, to permit the sale at retail of tear gas or tear gas weapons, and to permit the installation and maintenance of protective systems involving the use of tear gas or tear gas weapons subject to all of the following conditions upon breach of any of which the license shall be subject to forfeiture:

(a) Under a sales license for the sale of tear gas or tear gas weapons issued by the department, the business shall be carried on only in the building designated in the license, except that self-defense products may be sold at the place of instruction.

(b) The license or certified copy thereof shall be displayed at each sales premises in a place where it may easily be read.

(c) No tear gas or tear gas weapon shall be delivered to any person not authorized to possess or transport the same under the provisions of this chapter. No protective system involving the use of tear gas or tear gas weapons shall be installed, nor shall supplies be sold for the maintenance of such system, unless the licensee has personal knowledge of the existence of a valid permit for the operation and maintenance of the system.

(d) A permanent complete sales register shall be kept of self-defense tear gas and tear gas weapons sales made under the authority of the license, showing all of the following:

(1) The purchaser's name, date of birth, and address; the purchaser's identification card number and date of issue; the purchaser's response to questions pertaining to his or her eligibility to purchase tear gas or tear gas weapons pursuant to the requirements of subdivision (a) of Section 12403.7.

(2) The quantity and description, including serial numbers of articles purchased.

(3) The business name, address, and telephone number; the business retail tear gas sales license number; and the name and signature of the person making the sales.

(4) The date and time of sale.

(e) This sales register shall be open to the inspection of any peace officer or other person designated by the Attorney General.

(f) The original copy of the sales register shall be retained as part of the vendor's permanent record of sales. The duplicate copy of the sales register of each transaction shall, on the date of sale, be placed in the mail, postage prepaid, and properly addressed to the chief of police or sheriff who has jurisdiction over the purchaser's place of residence.

(g) The sales register requirements of this section shall not apply to wholesale or retail dealers in their normal business intercourse with other wholesale or retail dealers.

(h) The sales register required for each tear gas weapon sale shall be prepared by and obtained from the Department of General Services and shall be furnished by the Department of General Services to the licensed vendor on application at a cost to be determined by the Department of General Services for each 100 leaves in duplicate, one original and one duplicate for the making of one carbon copy. The original and duplicate copy shall differ in color, and shall be in a form prescribed by the Department of Justice.

The Department of General Services upon issuing a register shall forward to the Department of Justice the name and business address of the vendor together with the series and sheet numbers of the register. The register shall not be transferable. If the vendor moves his business to a different location he shall notify the Department of Justice of such fact in writing within 48 hours.

(i) Each applicant for the tear gas sales license described in this section shall pay at the time of filing his or her application a fee determined by the Department of Justice not to exceed the application processing costs of the Department of Justice. A license

granted pursuant to this article may be renewed one year from the date of issuance, and annually thereafter, upon the filing of a renewal application and the payment of a license renewal fee not to exceed the application processing costs of the Department of Justice. After the department establishes fees sufficient to reimburse the department for processing costs, fees charged shall increase at a rate not to exceed the legislatively approved annual cost-of-living adjustments for the department's budget.

ARTICLE 5

CERTIFICATION OF ACCEPTABILITY

§12450. Requirement.

No tear gas or tear gas weapon shall be possessed, sold or transported in this state after January 1, 1971, unless, pursuant to the provisions of this article, the Department of Justice has certified that particular type and brand of tear gas or tear gas weapon to be acceptable.

§12451. Definition of acceptable.

The term "acceptable" as used in this article when referring to tear gas or a tear gas weapon, means that such tear gas or tear gas weapon is reasonably free from any undue hazard when used by, or upon a human being taking into consideration such factors as the following:

(a) The reasonable safety, availability, and effectiveness of other devices, including other tear gas or tear gas weapons, capable of being used under the same circumstances and for the same purposes, including such factors as anticipated effective storage life for the particular product.

(b) The amount of hazard inherent in the use of the tear gas or tear gas weapon when weighed against the amount of hazard inherent in the kinds of conduct the tear gas or tear gas weapon is designed to control.

(c) The manner in which the tear gas or tear gas weapon can be expected to be used as well as the manner in which the manufacturer or seller thereof has recommended that it be used.

§12452. Application for certification; definition of manufacturer.

(a) Any manufacturer of tear gas or tear gas weapons may apply to the Department of Justice, hereinafter referred to as the "department" in this article, for certification that a particular type and brand of tear gas or tear gas weapon manufactured or assembled by that person is acceptable.

(b) The term "manufacturer" as used in this article means any person, firm, or corporation which makes tear gas or tear gas weapons, or which assembles raw materials or components to create tear gas or tear gas weapons.

(c) No device submitted for certification by a party other than the actual manufacturer prior to January 1, 1985, shall be sold after January 1, 1986, unless the device has been recertified pursuant to the provisions of this section as amended during the 1984 portion of the 1983-84 Regular Session of the Legislature.

§12453. Application contents.

Any application submitted pursuant to Section 12452 shall contain all of the following:

© 1992 by J., B. & L. Gould
Printed in the U.S.A.　**EP**

(a) Full reports of any investigation conducted by any public or private agency for the purpose of determining whether such tear gas or tear gas weapon is acceptable.

(b) A full statement of the composition of each component of such tear gas or tear gas weapon.

(c) A full statement of the methods used in, and the facilities and controls used for, the manufacture, processing and packing of such tear gas or tear gas weapon.

(d) Such samples of such tear gas or tear gas weapon and its components as the bureau may require.

(e) Specimens of the labeling, instructions, and advertisements used or proposed to be used for such tear gas or tear gas weapon.

§12454. Hearing to grant or deny certification.

Within 180 days after the filing of an application as provided for in Section 12452, or such additional period as may be agreed upon by the department and the applicant, the department shall either:

(a) Issue an order certifying such tear gas or tear gas weapon as acceptable.

(b) Give the applicant notice for an opportunity for a hearing before the department on the question whether such tear gas or tear gas weapon is acceptable. If the applicant elects to accept the opportunity for hearing by written request within 30 days after such notice, such hearing shall commence not more than 60 days after receiving such request unless the department and the applicant otherwise agree. Such hearing shall be heard on an expedited basis and the department shall issue an order granting or denying certification within 90 days after the date fixed by the department for filing final briefs.

§12455. Certification denied.

The department shall issue an order refusing to certify or recertify or terminating a previously granted certification of any tear gas or tear gas weapon as acceptable if after due notice to the applicant the department finds any of the following:

(a) That the tear gas or tear gas weapon is not acceptable, for any reason, including the following:

(1) That the tear gas or tear gas weapon creates a risk of unreasonable danger to the life or health of human beings which outweighs the social utility of the use of such tear gas or tear gas weapon.

(2) That upon evaluation or reevaluation the tear gas or tear gas weapon is found not to meet the current criteria of the rules and regulations promulgated by the department.

(3) That the effective life of the tear gas or tear gas weapon is found not to meet the criteria of the department.

(4) That the tear gas or tear gas weapon is found to be nonfunctioning or is otherwise found to be ineffective as provided in the rules and regulations promulgated by the department.

(b) That the application contains any misrepresentation of a material fact.

(c) That the application is materially incomplete.

§12456. Revocation.

The department shall issue an order revoking certification if, after due notice to the applicant, the department finds any of the following:

(a) That experience or additional testing show that the tear gas or tear gas weapon is not acceptable as defined in Section 12451.

(b) That the application contains any misrepresentation of a material fact.

§12457. Regulations for enforcement.

The department may adopt and promulgate all regulations necessary for the fair and efficient enforcement of the provisions of this chapter.

§12457.1. Department's powers.

The department shall have and exercise the powers expressly granted in this chapter, together with such other powers as are reasonably implied therefrom and necessary and proper to carry out the objects and purposes of this chapter.

Such powers include but are not limited to the authority to do the following:

(a) Periodically make tests of and review the certification of each type of tear gas or tear gas weapon as provided in the rules and regulations promulgated by the department pursuant to this chapter.

(b) Require the manufacturer of any tear gas or tear gas weapon to submit to the department complete written laboratory reports detailing the specifications of such tear gas or tear gas weapon for the purposes of testing, inspection, evaluation or reevaluation in accordance with the rules and regulations promulgated by the department.

(c) Cause any tear gas or tear gas weapon to be submitted by a manufacturer to the department for certification to be submitted to any laboratory of the department's choice.

(d) Consider the reports or other materials submitted by the manufacturer or by any other laboratory, private or public, in accordance with the rules and regulations promulgated by the department.

(e) Certify or refuse to certify any such tear gas or tear gas weapon pursuant to this chapter.

(f) Require reimbursement by the manufacturer to the department for any actual expenses incurred in conducting such testing, evaluation, and inspection of any such tear gas or tear gas weapon, or in reviewing and considering any report the manufacturer has caused to be submitted to the department pursuant to this chapter.

(g) Caused every type or brand of tear gas or tear gas weapon certified prior to January 1, 1976 to be reevaluated pursuant to the provisions of this article by January 1, 1978.

(h) Define acceptability of testing, evaluating and inspecting procedures and standards of proficiency in the rules and regulations promulgated by the department.

§12458. Reports by Department of Health.

Prior to certification of any tear gas or tear gas weapon, the department shall request from the State Department of Health a report on each type and brand of tear gas or the contents of each type and brand of tear gas weapon submitted to it by the department. At the Attorney General's discretion, the State Department of Health shall prepare and transmit such report to the department, and shall also submit supplemental reports whenever the facts warrant such action. All the reports shall be for the purpose of aiding the department in determining whether the type and brand of tear gas or the contents of the dispensed material of the particular type and brand of tear gas weapon are harmful, toxic, or present any health hazards to human beings, and shall be based on any one or more of the following:

(a) Investigations conducted by the facilities of the State Department of Health.

(b) Investigations conducted by independent laboratories.

(c) Any other investigations approved by the State Department of Health.

The applicant shall reimburse the State Department of Health and the Department of Justice for any actual expenses incurred by such departments in connection with such reports.

CHAPTER 5

FIREARM DEVICES

ARTICLE 1

GENERAL PROVISIONS

§12500. Silencer defined.

The term "silencer" as used in this chapter means any device or attachment of any kind designed, used, or intended for use in silencing, diminishing, or muffling the report of a firearm. The term "silencer" also includes any combination of parts, designed or redesigned, and intended for use in assembling a silencer or fabricating a silencer and any part intended only for use in such assembly or fabrication. *(Amended by Stats 1988 ch 124 §3, eff. 1/1/89.)*

§12501. Possession of silencers.

Section 12520 shall not apply to, or affect, any of the following:

(a) The sale to, purchase by, or possession of silencers by agencies listed in Section 830.1, or the military or naval forces of this state or of the United States for use in the discharge of their official duties.

(b) The possession of silencers by regular, salaried, full-time peace officers who are employed by an agency listed in Section 830.1, or by the military or naval forces of this state or of the United States when on duty and when the use of silencers is authorized by the agency and is within the course and scope of their duties.

(c) The manufacture, possession, transportation, or sale or other transfer of silencers to an entity described in subdivision (a) by dealers or manufacturers registered under Chapter 53 (commencing with Section 5801) of Title 26 of the United States Code, and the regulations issued pursuant thereto. *(Repealed and added by Stats 1990 ch 81 §§4, 5 eff. 1/1/91.)*

ARTICLE 2

UNLAWFUL POSSESSION OF FIREARM SILENCERS

§12520. Penalty for possession of silencer.

Any person, firm, or corporation who within this state possesses a silencer is guilty of a felony and upon conviction thereof shall be punished by imprisonment in the state prison or by a fine not to exceed ten thousand dollars ($10,000) or by both. *(Amended by Stats 1990 ch 81 §6, eff. 1/1/91.)*

CHAPTER 6

MISCELLANEOUS

ARTICLE 1

MINORS

§12550. *Repealed by Stats 1988 ch 1605 §4, eff. 1/1/89.*

§12551. Sale of firearm to minor.

Every person who sells to a minor any firearm is guilty of a misdemeanor. *(Amended by Stats 1988 ch 1605 §5, eff. 1/1/89.)*

§12552. Furnishing firearms to minors.

Every person who furnishes any firearm, air gun, or gas-operated gun, designed to fire a bullet, pellet or metal projectile, to any minor, without the express or implied permission of the parent or legal guardian of the minor, is guilty of a misdemeanor.

§12553. Definition of firearm.

As used in this article, "firearm" means any firearm except any pistol, revolver, or other firearm capable of being concealed upon the person. *(Added by Stats 1988 ch 1386 §4, eff. 1/1/89.)*

ARTICLE 2

FELONS

(Repealed by Stats 1990 ch 9 §14, eff. 1/1/91.)

§12560. *Repealed by Stats 1990 ch 9 §14, eff. 1/1/91.*

ARTICLE 3

RIFLES AND SHOTGUNS

(Repealed by Stats 1988 ch 40 §1, eff. 1/1/89.)

§12570. *Repealed by Stats 1988 ch 40 §1, eff. 1/1/89.*

ARTICLE 4

BLOWGUNS

§12580. Definition of blowgun.

"Blowgun," as used in this article, means a hollow tube designed and intended to be used as a tube through which a dart is propelled by the force of the breath of the user.

§12581. Definition of blowgun ammunition.

"Blowgun ammunition," as used in this article, means a dart designed and intended for use in a blowgun.

§12582. Sale, possession, etc.

Any person who knowingly manufactures, sells, offers for sale, possesses, or uses a blowgun or blowgun ammunition in this state is guilty of a misdemeanor.

§12583. Use and possession of blowguns.

Nothing in this article shall prohibit the sale to, purchase by, possession of, or use of blowguns or blowgun ammunition by zookeepers, animal control officers, Department of Fish and Game personnel, humane officers whose names are maintained in the

© 1992 by J., B. & L. Gould
Printed in the U.S.A.   EP

county record of humane officers pursuant to Section 607f of the Civil Code, or veterinarians in the course and scope of their business in order to administer medicine to animals. *(Added by Stats 1990 ch 81 §7, eff. 1/1/91.)*

ARTICLE 5

PICKETING

§12590. Unlawful acts.

(a) Any person who does any of the following acts while engaged in picketing, or other informational activities in a public place relating to a concerted refusal to work, is guilty of a misdemeanor:

(1) Carries concealed upon his person or within any vehicle which is under his or her control or direction any pistol, revolver, or other firearm capable of being concealed upon the person.

(2) Carries a loaded firearm upon his or her person or within any vehicle which is under his or her control or direction.

(3) Carries a deadly weapon.

(4) Wears the uniform of a peace officer, whether or not the person is a peace officer.

(b) This section shall not be construed to authorize or ratify any picketing or other informational activities not otherwise authorized by law.

(c) Section 12027 shall not be construed to authorize any conduct described in paragraph (1) of subdivision (a), nor shall subdivision (b) of Section 12031 be construed to authorize any conduct described in paragraph (2) of subdivision (a).

ARTICLE 6

LESS LETHAL WEAPONS

§12600. Purchase, possession by peace officer.

A person who is a peace officer as defined in Chapter 4.5 (commencing with Section 830) of Title 3 of Part 2 may if authorized by and under such terms and conditions as are specified by his or her employing agency purchase, possess, or transport any less lethal weapon or ammunition therefor, for official use in the discharge of his or her duties.

§12601. Definition of less lethal weapon and less lethal ammunition.

(a) "Less lethal weapon" shall apply to and include any device which is designed to or which has been converted to expel or propel less lethal ammunition by any action, mechanism, or process for the purpose of incapacitating, immobilizing, or stunning a human being through the infliction of any less than lethal impairment of physical condition, function, or senses, including physical pain or discomfort. It is not necessary that a weapon leave any lasting or permanent incapacitation, discomfort, pain, or other injury or disability in order to qualify as a less lethal weapon.

(b) Less lethal weapon includes the frame or receiver of any weapon described in subdivision (a), but shall not include any of the following unless such part or weapon has been converted as described in subdivision (a):

(1) Pistol, revolver, or firearm defined in Section 12001.

(2) Machine gun defined in Section 12200.

(3) Rifle or shotgun using fixed ammunition consisting of standard primer and powder and not capable of being concealed upon the person.

(4) Pistols, rifles, and shotguns which are firearms having a barrel less than 0.18 inches in diameter and which are designed to expel a projectile by any mechanical means or by compressed air or gas.

(5) When used as designed or intended by the manufacturer, any weapon commonly regarded as a toy gun, and which as such is incapable of inflicting any impairment of physical condition, function, or senses.

(6) A destructive device defined in Section 12301.

(7) A tear gas weapon defined in Section 12402.

(8) A bow or crossbow designed to shoot arrows.

(9) A device commonly known as a slingshot.

(10) A device designed for the firing of stud cartridges, explosive rivets, or similar industrial ammunition.

(11) A device designed for signaling, illumination, or safety.

(c) "Less lethal ammunition" means any ammunition which (1) is designed to be used in any less lethal weapon or any other kind of weapon (including, but not limited to, firearms, pistols, revolvers, shotguns, rifles, and spring, compressed air, and compressed gas weapons) and (2) when used in such less lethal weapon or other weapon is designed to immobilize or incapacitate or stun a human being through the infliction of any less than lethal impairment of physical condition, function, or senses, including physical pain or discomfort.

ARTICLE 7

STUN GUNS

§12650. Stun gun defined.

"Stun gun" as used in this chapter shall include any item, except a taser, used or intended to be used as either an offensive or defensive weapon capable of temporarily immobilizing a person by the infliction of an electrical charge. *(Added by Stats 1985 ch 1227 §3.)*

§12651. Exceptions for purchase of weapon.

Notwithstanding any other provision of law, any person may purchase, possess, or use a stun gun, subject to the following requirements:

(a) No person convicted of a felony or any crime involving an assault under the laws of the United States, of the State of California, or any other state, government, or country or convicted of misuse of a stun gun under Section 244.5, shall purchase, possess, or use stun guns.

(b) No person who is addicted to any narcotic drug shall purchase, possess, or use a stun gun.

(c) No person shall sell or furnish any stun gun to a minor unless the minor is at least 16 years of age and has the written consent of his or her parent or legal guardian.

Violation of this subdivision shall be a public offense punishable by a fifty dollar ($50) fine for the first offense. Any subsequent violation of this subdivision is a misdemeanor.

(d) No minor shall possess any stun gun unless the minor is at least 16 years of age and has the written consent of his or her parent or legal guardian. *(Added by Stats 1985 ch 1227 §3.)*

§12652. Sale of weapon; requirements.

Each stun gun sold shall contain both of the following:

(a) The name of the manufacturer stamped on the stun gun.

(b) The serial number applied by the manufacturer. *(Added by Stats 1985 ch 1227 §3.)*

§12653. Violation of article a misdemeanor.

Unless otherwise specified, any violation of this article is a misdemeanor. *(Added by Stats 1985 ch 1227 §3.)*

§12654. Instruction booklet for weapon.

Each stun gun sold in this state shall be accompanied by an instruction booklet.

Violation of this section shall be a public offense punishable by a fifty dollar ($50) fine for each weapon sold without the booklet. *(Added by Stats 1985 ch 1227 §3.)*

ARTICLE 8

BASIC FIREARM SAFETY INSTRUCTION AND CERTIFICATE
(Added by Stats 1991 ch 950 §20, eff. 1/1/92.)

§12800. Safe handling and storage of firearms; childproofing; owner responsibilities.

(a) The Legislature finds and declares as follows:

(1) Although California has a 15-day waiting period and background check for the acquisition and purchase of pistols, revolvers, and firearms capable of being concealed upon the person, a demonstrated knowledge of firearms safety is not required. Therefore, a person is able to obtain one of these firearms in California without having any idea of how to safely use, handle, or store it.

(2) In contrast, it is necessary for an individual to complete a firearms-related hunter safety course before a hunting license is issued. It has been documented that this program has saved lives, and has been beneficial to sportsmen and firearms owners.

(3) It is inconsistent for a person to have to go through a firearms-related hunter safety course before being able to use a firearm to hunt, yet not be required to have any basic knowledge about the safe handling and operation of pistols, revolvers, and other firearms capable of being concealed upon the person before acquiring them.

(b) The Legislature further finds and declares as follows:

(1) It has been documented that firearms accidents are one of the leading causes of accidental deaths for children ages 14 years and under. Almost all of the firearms involved in these accidents are pistols, revolvers, or other firearms capable of being concealed upon the person.

(2) On average, one child 18 years of age or under is accidentally killed, and 10 are injured, by a firearm every day across the United States.

(3) Firearm wounds to children who are 16 years of age and under have increased 300 percent in major urban areas since 1986.

(4) In 1987, the last year for which statistics are available, there were 44 accidental firearms deaths among California children 18 years of age and younger.

(5) Although statistics are not kept for injuries resulting from accidental shootings, it is estimated that for every firearms death, there are at least five nonfatal firearms injuries. Using this figure, it is estimated that approximately 220 California children were injured in nonfatal accidental shootings in 1987.

(6) Research has indicated that easy access in homes to loaded pistols, revolvers, and other firearms capable of being concealed upon the person is a chief contributing factor in unintentional shootings of children. Nearly 8,700,000 youngsters in the United States have access to pistols, revolvers, and other firearms capable of being concealed upon the person.

(7) Educating purchaser and transferees of pistols, revolvers, and other firearms capable of being concealed upon the person would make them more aware of their responsibilities as gun owners and help to eliminate the ignorance or neglect that lead to children playing with a loaded pistol, revolver, and other firearms capable of being concealed upon the person.

(c) It is, therefore, the intent of the Legislature, in enacting this article, to require in this state that purchasers and transferees of pistols, revolvers, and other firearms capable of being concealed upon the person obtain a basic familiarity with those firearms, including, but not limited to, the safe handling and storage of those firearms, methods for childproofing those firearms, and the responsibilities associated with ownership of those firearms.

(d) It is further the intent of the Legislature, in enacting this article, to establish a program that would help to eliminate the potential for accidental deaths and injuries, particularly those involving children, which are caused by the unsafe handling of pistols, revolvers, and other firearms capable of being concealed upon the person. *(Added by Stats 1991 ch 950 §20, eff. 1/1/92.)*

§12801. Basic firearms safety certificate; defined.

As used in this article, "basic firearms safety certificate" means the certificate issued to persons who have complied with this article. *(Added by Stats 1991 ch 950 §20, eff. 1/1/92.)*

§12802. Basic firearms safety certificate; issuance.

(a) No basic firearms safety certificate shall be issued to any person unless that person has complied with this article. Proof of compliance with this article shall be forwarded to the Department of Justice as frequently as the department may determine.

(b) It is the intent of the Legislature to require a basic firearms safety certificate for persons who anticipate the purchase or transfer of a pistol, revolver, or other firearm capable of being concealed upon the person. This requirement of a certificate is not intended to be a requirement for the mere possession of a firearm. *(Added by Stats 1991 ch 950 §20, eff. 1/1/92.)*

§12803. Basic firearms safety course.

(a) Beginning on January 1, 1993, and prior to July 1, 1993, the Department of Justice shall do all of the following:

(1) Develop the course content and instructional materials for a basic firearms safety course. The course shall consist of not less than two, nor more than four, hours of instruction, including, but not limited to, instruction in the following areas as they pertain

© 1992 by J., B. & L. Gould
Printed in the U.S.A.   EP

to pistols, revolvers, and other firearms capable of being concealed upon the person:

(A) The safe use, handling, and storage of those firearms.

(B) Methods for childproofing those firearms.

(C) The laws applicable to the carrying and handling of those firearms.

(D) The responsibilities of ownership of those firearms.

(2) Develop an instructional manual and, if the department deems necessary, audiovisual materials, to be issued to an instructor certified by the department. The department shall make the instructional manual available to firearms dealers licensed pursuant to Section 12071, who shall have it available to the general public. Essential portions of the manual may be included in the pamphlet described in Section 12080.

(3) Prescribe a minimum level of skill, knowledge, and competency to be required of all basic firearms safety instructors, and develop and provide the guidelines to be used to certify the instructors.

(4) Develop an objective test on the subject matter of the basic firearms safety course. The objective test shall be based on the instructional manual referred to in paragraph (2). There shall be no less than five distinct versions of the objective test. The purpose of the objective test shall be to ensure knowledge of basic firearms safety. The test shall consist of not less than 20, nor more than 30, questions. An applicant shall respond successfully to at least 75 percent of the total number of questions in order to pass the test.

(b) The department shall solicit input from any reputable association or organization which has, as one of its objectives, the promotion of firearms safety in the development of the basic firearms safety course.

(c) The department shall periodically update the curriculum of the basic firearms safety course, instructional materials, the basic firearms safety manual, the objective test, and guidelines for certifying basic firearms safety instructors, as needed.

(d) The department shall develop basic firearms safety certificates to be issued by the department, or an instructor certified by the department, to those persons who have complied with this article.

(e) The department shall ensure that the course shall be available to persons at convenient times and locations in a person's county of residency by January 1, 1993.

(f) The Department of Justice shall be immune from any liability arising from implementing this section. *(Added by Stats 1991 ch 950 §20, eff. 1/1/92.)*

§12804. Basic firearms safety course; records of issuance to be kept by department.

(a) The department shall maintain adequate records on who has successfully completed the basic firearms safety course or otherwise complied with this article.

(b) Proficiency in the use of any pistol, revolver, or other firearm capable of being concealed upon the person shall not be a prerequisite to acquiring the basic firearms safety certificate.

(c) No person shall be required to complete the course more than once, except that any person who has completed the course and is unable to produce the certificate shall be required to take the course again unless a duplicate certificate is issued pursuant to

Section 12807. *(Added by Stats 1991 ch 950 §20, eff. 1/1/92.)*

§12805. Designation of basic firearms safety instructor.

(a) The department shall designate as a basic firearms safety instructor any person certified by a nationally recognized organization that fosters safety in firearms or any person found by the department to be competent to give instruction in the basic firearms safety course established pursuant to this article, if the person is otherwise qualified pursuant to Section 12803.

(b) The department shall designate as a basic firearms safety instructor, dealers licensed pursuant to Section 12071 or their employees if they otherwise are qualified to act as instructors. Where the license is issued in the name of a corporation or partnership, then the managing officer or partner shall be designated as instructors if they are otherwise qualified pursuant to Section 12803.

(c) The department shall revoke the certification of any instructor when the department determines that it is in the best interests of the state to do so.

(d) Upon successful completion of the basic firearms safety course, which shall be conditioned solely upon the attendance of the course as specified in Section 12803, a person shall immediately be issued a basic firearms safety certificate by the instructor.

(e) The instructor may also administer the objective test referred to in Section 12809 at the site where the basic firearms safety course is given. Any person receiving a passing grade, as specified in Section 12803, on the test shall be immediately issued a basic firearms safety certificate by the instructor. Any person who fails to pass the test administered by the course instructor, shall be given additional instructional materials by the instructor and be told that they may not retake the test under any circumstance until 24 hours have elapsed.

(f) Instructors shall forward to the department the names of those persons who have received basic firearms safety certificates, the method by which the person obtained the basic firearms safety certificate, and assure that originals or photocopies of the objective test, or any version thereof, are not made available to applicants for the objective test, whether or not they pass the objective test.

(g) Instructors shall notify applicants for the basic firearms safety certificate that they may be issued a basic firearms safety certificate by attending the basic firearms safety course, by passing the objective test, or are exempt from this article by virtue of subdivision (b) of Section 12081. *(Added by Stats 1991 ch 950 §20, eff. 1/1/92.)*

§12806. Fees from instruction course shall be deposited in the Firearms Safety Training Fund Special Account.

(a) A fee to cover the costs of giving the basic firearms safety course instruction and issuance of the basic firearm safety certificate may be charged by the instructor to each person participating and receiving instruction in basic firearms safety. The department may impose a charge not to exceed ten dollars ($10) for each person participating and receiving instruction in the basic firearms safety course to cover the department's cost in carrying out this article as determined annually by the department. The instructor of the course shall collect and submit the charge to the department to be deposited into the Firearms Safety Training Fund Special Account as provided in subdivision (b).

(b) All money received by the department pursuant to this article shall be deposited in the Firearms Safety Training Fund Special Account, which is hereby created in the General Fund and continuously appropriated for expenditure by the department for the costs incurred pursuant to this article. *(Added by Stats 1991 ch 950 §20, eff. 1/1/92.)*

§12807. Duplicate certificate issued in case of loss or destruction.

(a) In case of loss or destruction of a basic firearms safety certificate, a duplicate certificate shall be issued by the department.

(b) A fee, not to exceed five dollars ($5), may be charged by the department to each person applying for a duplicate certificate. *(Added by Stats 1991 ch 950 §20, eff. 1/1/92.)*

§12808. Certifying existing firearms safety courses.

Upon application to the department, the department shall certify any existing firearms safety course or program which provides, as a minimum, as part of its curriculum, instruction in all of the subject matters in accordance with the basic firearms safety course established pursuant to this article, and shall authorize the course or program to issue basic firearms safety certificates to those who complete the course or program. *(Added by Stats 1991 ch 950 §20, eff. 1/1/92.)*

§12809. Objective test in place of basic firearms safety course.

(a) Any person who has reason to believe that he or she does not need to complete the basic firearms safety course may take an objective test on the subject matter of the basic firearms safety course from an instructor certified by the department. The objective test shall contain written notice to the applicant on the top of the first page that he or she may not take the test more than twice within a six-month period.

(b) Any person receiving a passing grade on the test shall be immediately issued a basic firearms safety certificate by the instructor. When the objective test is being administered, the certified instructor may only give administrative instructions. Any person who fails to pass the objective test upon the first attempt shall be given additional instructional materials by the instructor such as a videotape or booklet. The person may not retake the objective test under any circumstances until 24 hours have elapsed after the failure to pass the objective test upon the first attempt. The person failing the test on the first attempt shall take another version of the test upon the second attempt. All tests shall be taken from the same instructor except upon permission of the department, which shall be granted only for good cause shown. The instructor shall make himself or herself available to the applicant during regular business hours in order to retake the test. If the person fails the objective test upon a second attempt, then the person shall attend the basic firearms safety course pursuant to Section 12805 in order to be issued a basic firearms safety certificate.

(c) The Department of Justice shall set the fee for taking the objective test and issuance of the basic firearms safety certificate at an amount commensurate with the actual cost to the department, but not to exceed twenty dollars ($20), ten dollars ($10) of which shall be forwarded to the department to cover its costs. The fee paid shall entitle the applicant to take the objective test twice if necessary. Commencing with the 1993-93 fiscal year, the department may submit a budget change proposal to the Department of Finance if funds beyond those funds otherwise appropriated to the department are required for the startup costs of the programs specified in this article. The Department of Finance shall transfer funds from a nongeneral fund special account used by the Department of Justice to the Firearms Safety Training Fund Special Account as a loan of those funds. Any funds received by the department pursuant to the budget change proposal submitted pursuant to this section shall be immediately reimbursed from the Firearms Safety Training Fund Special Account as funds in that account are available back to the nongeneral fund special account from which the funds were borrowed.

(d) (1) If a dealer licensed pursuant to Section 12071 or his or her employee, or where the managing officer or partner is certified as an instructor pursuant to this article, he or she shall also comply with all of the following provisions:

(A) Designate a separate room or partitioned area for a person to take the objective test.

(B) Maintain adequate supervision to assure that no acts of collusion occur while the objective test is being administered.

(C) If the firearm is a pistol, revolver, or other firearm capable of being concealed upon the person, it shall not be delivered unless the dealer provides the purchaser or transferee instructions at the time of delivery on how to operate the firearm, including, but not limited to methods of loading and unloading the firearm, and the location of any safety on the firearm and how the safety operates.

(2) If the provisions specified in subparagraphs (A) and (B) of paragraph (1) cannot be complied with, the applicant shall be advised that he or she may take the objective test wherever the basic firearms safety course is being offered. *(Added by Stats 1991 ch 950 §20, eff. 1/1/92.)*

TITLE 3

CRIMINAL STATISTICS

CHAPTER 1

DEPARTMENT OF JUSTICE

ARTICLE 1

DUTIES OF THE DEPARTMENT
(Chapter 1, Article 1 headings amended by Stats 1986 ch 248 §§169, 170.)

§13010. Duties.

It shall be the duty of the department:

(a) To collect data necessary for the work of the department from all persons and agencies mentioned in Section 13020 and from any other appropriate source;

(b) To prepare and distribute to all such persons and agencies, cards or other forms used in reporting data to the department. Such cards or forms may, in addition to other items, include items of information

© 1992 by J., B. & L. Gould
Printed in the U.S.A.   EP

needed by federal bureaus or departments engaged in the development of national and uniform criminal statistics;

(c) To recommend the form and content of records which must be kept by such persons and agencies in order to insure the correct reporting of data to the department;

(d) To instruct such persons and agencies in the installation, maintenance, and use of such records and in the reporting of data therefrom to the department;

(e) To process, tabulate, analyze and interpret the data collected from such persons and agencies;

(f) To supply, at their request, to federal bureaus or departments engaged in the collection of national criminal statistics data they need from this state;

(g) To present to the Governor, on or before July 1st, a printed annual report containing the criminal statistics of the preceding calendar year and to present at such other times as the Attorney General may approve reports on special aspects of criminal statistics. A sufficient number of copies of all reports shall be printed or otherwise prepared to enable the Attorney General to send a copy to all public officials in the state dealing with criminals and to distribute them generally in channels where they will add to the public enlightenment; and

(h) To periodically review the requirements of units of government using criminal justice statistics, and to make recommendations for changes it deems necessary in the design of criminal justice statistics systems, including new techniques of collection and processing made possible by automation.

§13011. Serving as statistical and research agency.

The department may serve as statistical and research agency to the Department of Corrections, the Board of Prison Terms, the Board of Corrections, the Department of the Youth Authority, and the Youthful Offender Parole Board.

§13012. Annual report.

The annual report of the department provided for in Section 13010 shall contain statistics showing:

(a) The amount and the types of offenses known to the public authorities;

(b) The personal and social characteristics of criminals and delinquents; and

(c) The administrative actions taken by law enforcement, judicial, penal and correctional agencies or institutions in dealing with criminals or delinquents.

(d) The number of citizens complaints received by law enforcement agencies under Section 832.5. Such statistics shall indicate the total number of such complaints, the number alleging criminal conduct of either a felony or misdemeanor, and the number sustained in each category. The report shall not contain a reference to any individual agency but shall be by gross numbers only.

It shall be the duty of the department to give adequate interpretation of such statistics and so to present the information that it may be of value in guiding the policies of the Legislature and of those in charge of the apprehension, prosecution and treatment of the criminals and delinquents, or concerned with the prevention of crime and delinquency. The report shall include also statistics which are comparable with national uniform criminal statistics published by federal bureaus or departments heretofore mentioned.

§13013. Proposed systems to collect data on criminal activity after rehabilitation.

The department shall prepare a written proposal to be submitted to the Legislature on or before July 1, 1985, which outlines a proposed system or systems by which data could be collected which could determine subsequent criminal activity of persons exposed to rehabilitation treatment programs after having been found by the juvenile court to be within the provisions of Section 602 of the Welfare and Institutions Code. The proposal shall be prepared after consultation with interested parties, including juvenile court judges, probation officers, prosecutors, attorneys who represent minors in juvenile court proceedings, organizations which provide services to minors, and law enforcement officials who specialize in cases involving minors. The proposal shall preserve the confidentiality of records concerning minors wherever possible and shall include information concerning all of the following:

(a) An estimate of the cost of the proposed system or systems, including an estimate of the cost to the state and to city and county government.

(b) A summary of current law governing obtaining, transmitting, storing, accumulating, and utilizing fingerprints of minors, including a summary of current law in this area governing the department, other state officials, and city and county officials.

(c) A summary of the changes in current law which would be required in order to implement the proposed system or systems.

(d) A summary of the impact which the proposed system or systems would have on access to fingerprints of minors, including a summary of persons or agencies who would obtain increased or decreased access to fingerprints of minors as a result of the proposed system or systems.

ARTICLE 2

DUTIES OF PUBLIC AGENCIES AND OFFICERS
(Article 3 heading renumbered Article 2 by Stats 1986 ch 248 §171.)

§13020. Records and reports of statistical data.

It shall be the duty of every constable, city marshal, chief of police, railroad and steamship police, sheriff; coroner, district attorney, city attorney and city prosecutor having criminal jurisdiction, probation officer, county board of parole commissioners, work furlough administrator, the Department of Justice, Health and Welfare Agency, Department of Corrections, Department of Youth Authority, Youthful Offender Parole Board, Board of Prison Terms, State Department of Health, Department of Benefit Payments, State Fire Marshal, Liquor Control Administrator, constituent agencies of the State Department of Investment, and every other person or agency dealing with crimes or criminals or with delinquency or delinquents, when requested by the Attorney General:

(a) To install and maintain records needed for the correct reporting of statistical data required by him;

(b) To report statistical data to the department at such times and in such manner as the Attorney General prescribes; and

(c) To give to the Attorney General, or his accredited agent, access to statistical data for the purpose of carrying out the provisions of this title.

§13021. Reports re violations of Chapter 7.5.

Local law enforcement agencies shall report to the Department of Justice such information as the Attorney General may by regulation require relative to misdemeanor violations of Chapter 7.5 (commencing with Section 311) of Title 9 of Part 1 of this code.

§13022. Reports re justifiable homicides.

Each sheriff and chief of police shall annually furnish the Department of Justice, on a form prescribed by the Attorney General, a report of all justifiable homicides committed in his jurisdiction. In cases where both a sheriff and chief of police would be required to report a justifiable homicide under this section, only the chief of police shall report such homicide.

§13023. Reports to the Department of Justice.

Commencing July 1, 1990, subject to the availability of adequate funding, the Attorney General shall direct local law enforcement agencies to report to the Department of Justice, in a manner to be prescribed by the Attorney General, such information as may be required relative to any criminal acts or attempted criminal acts to cause physical injury, emotional suffering, or property damage where there is a reasonable cause to believe that the crime was motivated, in whole or in part, by the victim's race, ethnicity, religion, sexual orientation, or physical or mental disability. On or before July 1, 1992, and every July 1 thereafter, the Department of Justice shall submit a report to the Legislature analyzing the results of the information obtained from local law enforcement agencies pursuant to this section. *(Added by Stats 1989 ch 1172 §1, eff. 1/1/90.)*

CHAPTER 2

CRIMINAL OFFENDER RECORD INFORMATION

ARTICLE 1

LEGISLATIVE FINDINGS AND DEFINITIONS

§13100. General findings and declarations.

The Legislature finds and declares as follows:

(a) That the criminal justice agencies in this state require, for the performance of their official duties, accurate and reasonably complete criminal offender record information.

(b) That the Legislature and other governmental policymaking or policy-researching bodies, and criminal justice agency management units require greatly improved aggregate information for the performance of their duties.

(c) That policing agencies and courts require speedy access to information concerning all felony and selected misdemeanor arrests and final dispositions of such cases.

(d) That criminal justice agencies may require regular access to detailed criminal histories relating to any felony arrest that is followed by the filing of a complaint.

(e) That, in order to achieve the above improvements, the recording, reporting, storage, analysis, and dissemination of criminal offender record information in this state must be made more uniform and efficient, and better controlled and coordinated.

§13101. Definition of criminal justice agencies.

As used in this chapter, "criminal justice agencies" are those agencies at all levels of government which perform as their principal functions, activities which either:

(a) Relate to the apprehension, prosecution, adjudication, incarceration, or correction of criminal offenders; or

(b) Relate to the collection, storage, dissemination or usage of criminal offender record information.

§13102. Criminal offender record information defined.

As used in this chapter, "criminal offender record information" means records and data compiled by criminal justice agencies for purposes of identifying criminal offenders and of maintaining as to each such offender a summary of arrests, pretrial proceedings, the nature and disposition of criminal charges, sentencing, incarceration, rehabilitation, and release.

Such information shall be restricted to that which is recorded as the result of an arrest, detention, or other initiation of criminal proceedings or of any consequent proceedings related thereto. It shall be understood to include, where appropriate, such items for each person arrested as the following:

(a) Personal identification.

(b) The fact, date, and arrest charge; whether the individual was subsequently released and, if so, by what authority and upon what terms.

(c) The fact, date, and results of any pretrial proceedings.

(d) The fact, date, and results of any trial or proceeding, including any sentence or penalty.

(e) The fact, date, and results of any direct or collateral review of that trial or proceeding; the period and place of any confinement, including admission, release; and, where appropriate, readmission and rerelease dates.

(f) The fact, date, and results of any release proceedings.

(g) The fact, date, and authority of any act of pardon or clemency.

(h) The fact and date of any formal termination to the criminal justice process as to that charge or conviction.

(i) The fact, date, and results of any proceeding revoking probation or parole.

It shall not include intelligence, analytical, and investigative reports and files, nor statistical records and reports in which individuals are not identified and from which their identities are not ascertainable.

§13103. Nonerasable storage media; destroying originals.

Notwithstanding any other provisions of law relating to retention of public records, any criminal justice agency may cause the original records filed pursuant to this chapter to be destroyed if all of the following requirements are met:

(a) The records have been reproduced onto microfilm or optical disk, or by any other techniques which do not permit additions, deletions, or changes to the original document.

(b) If the records have been reproduced onto optical disk, at least one year has elapsed since the date of registration of the records.

(c) The nonerasable storage medium used meets the minimum standards recommended by the Nation-

© 1992 by J., B. & L. Gould
Printed in the U.S.A.   **EP**

al Institute of Standards and Technology for permanent record purposes.

(d) Adequate provisions are made to ensure that the nonerasable storage medium reflects additions or corrections to the records.

(e) A copy of the nonerasable storage medium is maintained in a manner which permits it to be used for all purposes served by the original record.

(f) A copy of the nonerasable storage medium has been stored at a separate physical location in a place and manner which will reasonably assure its preservation indefinitely against loss or destruction. *(Added by Stats 1989 ch 257 §5, eff. 1/1/90.)*

§13104. Reproduction as original.

Any certified reproduction of any record stored on a nonerasable storage medium under the provisions of this chapter shall be deemed to be a certification of the original record. *(Added by Stats 1989 ch 257 §6, eff. 1/1/90.)*

ARTICLE 2

RECORDING INFORMATION

§13125. Form.

All basic information stored in state or local criminal offender record information systems shall be recorded, when applicable and available, in the form of the following standard data elements:
The following personal identification data:
  Name—(full name)
    Aliases
    Monikers
    Race
    Sex
    Date of birth
    Place of birth (state or country)
    Height
    Weight
    Hair color
    Eye color
    CII number
    FBI number
    Social security number
    California operators license number
    Fingerprint classification number
      Henry
      NCIC
    Address
The following arrest data:
  Arresting agency
  Booking number
  Date of arrest
  Offenses charged
    Statute citations
    Literal descriptions
  Police disposition
    Released
    Cited and released
    Turned over to
    Complaint filed
The following lower court data:
  County and court name
  Date complaint filed
  Original offenses charged in complaint to
    superior court
    Held to answer
    Certified plea
  Disposition—lower court

    Not convicted
    Dismissed
    Acquitted
      Court trial
      Jury trial
    Convicted
    Plea
      Court trial
      Jury trial
    Date of disposition
    Convicted offenses
    Sentence
    Proceedings suspended
      Reason suspended
The following superior court data:
  County
  Date complaint filed
  Type of proceeding
    Indictment
    Information
    Certification
  Original offenses charged in indictment or
    information
  Disposition
    Not convicted
    Dismissed
    Acquitted
      Court trial
      Jury trial
      On transcript
    Convicted—felony, misdemeanor
    Plea
      Court trial
      Jury trial
      On transcript
    Date of disposition
    Convicted offenses
    Sentence
    Proceedings suspended
    Reason suspended
    Source of reopened cases
The following corrections data:
  Adult probation
    County
    Type of court
    Court number
    Offense
    Date on probation
    Date removed
    Reason for removal
  Jail (unsentenced prisoners only)
    Offenses charged
    Name of jail or institution
    Date received
    Date released
  Reason for release
    Bail on own recognizance
    Bail
    Other
  Committing agency
  County jail (sentenced prisoners only)
    Name of jail, camp, or other
    Convicted offense
    Sentence
    Date received
    Date released
    Reason for release
    Committing agency
  Youth Authority

County
Type of court
Court number
Youth Authority number
Date received
Convicted offense
Type of receipt
  Original commitment
  Parole violator
Date released
Type of release
  Custody
  Supervision
Date terminated
Department of Corrections
County
Type of court
Court number
Department of Corrections number
  Date received
  Convicted offense
  Type of receipt
  Original commitment
  Parole violator
  Date released
  Type of release
    Custody
    Supervision
  Date terminated
Mentally disordered sex offenders
County
Hospital number
Date received
Date discharged
Recommendation

§13127. Inclusion of fingerprint identification number.

Each recording agency shall insure that each portion of a criminal offender record that it originates shall include, for all felonies and reportable misdemeanors, the state or local unique and permanent fingerprint identification number, within 72 hours of origination of such records, excluding Saturday, Sunday, and holidays.

§13128. Records of offenders while in custody.

For purposes of the maintenance of criminal records pursuant to Chapter 4 (commencing with Section 653.75) of Title 15, whenever a person is arrested for a public offense committed while in custody in any local detention facility, as defined in Section 6031.4, or any state prison, as defined in Section 4504, the state summary criminal history record shall include the section number of the public offense violated and information related to the "in custody" status of that person. *(Added by Stats 1987 ch 1005 §2.)*

ARTICLE 3

REPORTING INFORMATION

§13150. Arrest data.

For each arrest made, the reporting agency shall report to the Department of Justice, concerning each arrest, the applicable identification and arrest data described in Section 13125 and fingerprints, except as otherwise provided by law or as prescribed by the Department of Justice.

§13151. Court dispositions of cases.

The superior, municipal, or justice court that disposes of a case for which an arrest was required to be reported to the Department of Justice pursuant to Section 13150 or for which fingerprints were taken and submitted to the Department of Justice by order of the court shall assure that a disposition report of such case containing the applicable data elements enumerated in Section 13125, or Section 13151.1 if such disposition is one of dismissal, is furnished to the Department of Justice within 30 days according to the procedures and on a format prescribed by the department. The court shall also furnish a copy of such disposition report to the law enforcement agency having primary jurisdiction to investigate the offense alleged in the complaint or accusation. Whenever a court shall order any action subsequent to the initial disposition of a case, the court shall similarly report such proceedings to the department.

§13151.1. Reasons for dismissal of charge in disposition report.

When a disposition described in Section 13151 is one of dismissal of the charge, the disposition report shall state one of the following reasons, as appropriate:

(a) Dismissal in furtherance of justice, pursuant to Section 1385 of the Penal Code. In addition to this dismissal label, the court shall set forth the particular reasons for dismissal.

(b) Case compromised; defendant discharged because restitution or other satisfaction was made to the injured person, pursuant to Sections 1377 and 1378.

(c) Court found insufficient cause to believe defendant guilty of a public offense; defendant discharged without trial pursuant to Section 871.

(d) Dismissal due to delay; action against defendant dismissed because the information was not filed or the action was not brought to trial within the time allowed by Section 1381, 1381.5, or 1382.

(e) Accusation set aside pursuant to Section 995. In addition to this dismissal label, the court shall set forth the particular reasons for the dismissal.

(f) Defective accusation; defendant discharged pursuant to Section 1008, when the action is dismissed pursuant to that section after demurrer is sustained, because no amendment of the accusatory pleading is permitted or amendment is not made or filed within the time allowed.

(g) Defendant became a witness for the people and was discharged pursuant to Section 1099.

(h) Defendant discharged at trial because of insufficient evidence, in order to become a witness for his codefendant pursuant to Section 1100.

(i) Judgment arrested; defendant discharged, when the court finds defects in the accusatory pleading pursuant to Sections 1185 to 1187, inclusive, and defendant is released pursuant to Section 1188.

(j) Judgment arrested; defendant recommitted, when the court finds defects in the accusatory pleading pursuant to Sections 1185 to 1187, inclusive, and defendant is recommitted to answer a new indictment or information pursuant to Section 1188.

(k) Mistrial; defendant discharged. In addition to this dismissal label, the court shall set forth the particular reasons for its declaration of a mistrial.

(*l*) Mistrial; defendant recommitted. In addition to this dismissal label, the court shall set forth the particular reasons for its declaration of a mistrial.

© 1992 by J., B. & L. Gould
Printed in the U.S.A.   **EP**

(m) Any other dismissal by which the case was terminated. In addition to the dismissal label, the court shall set forth the particular reasons for the disposition.

§13152. Report of admissions or releases.

Admissions or releases from detention facilities shall be reported by the detention agency to the Department of Justice within 30 days of such action.

§13153. Maintenance of information relating to arrests for public drunkeness; restriction.

Criminal offender record information relating to arrests for being found in any public place under the influence of intoxicating liquor under subdivision (f) of Section 647 shall not be reported or maintained by the Department of Justice without special individual justification.

§13154. Report of arrest.

Each reporting agency shall report to the Department of Justice each arrest for the commission of a public offense while in custody in any local detention facility, or any state prison, as provided in Chapter 4 (commencing with Section 653.75) of Title 15, for inclusion in that person's state summary criminal history record. The report shall include the public offense committed and a reference indicating that the offense occurred while the person was in custody in a local detention facility or state prison. *(Added by Stats 1987 ch 1005 §3.)*

ARTICLE 4

INFORMATION SERVICE

§13175. Furnishing data to fingerprint agency.

When a criminal justice agency supplies fingerprints, or a fingerprint identification number, or such other personal identifiers as the Department of Justice deems appropriate, to the Department of Justice, such agency shall, upon request, be provided with identification, arrest, and, where applicable, final disposition data relating to such person within 72 hours of receipt by the Department of Justice.

§13176. Providing criminal history of fingerprinted person.

When a criminal justice agency entitled to such information supplies fingerprints, or a fingerprint identification number, or such other personal identifiers as the Department of Justice deems appropriate, to the Department of Justice, such agency shall, upon request, be provided with the criminal history of such person, or the needed portion thereof, within 72 hours of receipt by the Department of Justice.

§13177. Requiring reports.

Nothing in this chapter shall be construed to prohibit the Department of Justice from requiring criminal justice agencies to report any information which is required by any other statute to be reported to the department.

ARTICLE 5

ACCESS TO INFORMATION

§13200. Rights of access not affected.

Nothing in this chapter shall be construed to affect the right of access of any person or public agency to individual criminal offender record information that is authorized by any other provision of law.

§13201. Rights of access not authorized.

Nothing in this chapter shall be construed to authorize access of any person or public agency to individual criminal offender record information unless such access is otherwise authorized by law.

§13202. Providing information to public agencies and research bodies.

Every public agency or bona fide research body immediately concerned with the prevention or control of crime, the quality of criminal justice, or the custody or correction of offenders may be provided with such criminal offender record information as is required for the performance of its duties, provided that any material identifying individuals is not transferred, revealed, or used for other than research or statistical activities and reports or publications derived therefrom do not identify specific individuals, and provided that such agency or body pays the cost of the processing of such data as determined by the Attorney General.

§13203. Providing information on arrest of peace officer to governmental employer.

Any criminal justice agency shall be authorized to release information concerning an arrest or detention of a peace officer which did not result in conviction, or information concerning a referral to, and participation in, any postarrest diversion program to a government agency employer of that peace officer. *(Added by Stats 1990 ch 769 §2, eff. 1/1/91.)*

ARTICLE 6

LOCAL SUMMARY CRIMINAL HISTORY INFORMATION

§13300. Local summary criminal history information.

(a) As used in this section:

(1) "Local summary criminal history information" means the master record of information compiled by any local criminal justice agency pursuant to Chapter 2 (commencing with Section 13100) of Title 3 of Part 4 of the Penal Code pertaining to the identification and criminal history of any person, such as name, date of birth, physical description, dates of arrests, arresting agencies and booking numbers, charges, dispositions, and similar data about the person.

(2) "Local summary criminal history information" does not refer to records and data compiled by criminal justice agencies other than that local agency, nor does it refer to records of complaints to or investigations conducted by, or records of intelligence information or security procedures of, the local agency.

(3) "Local agency" means a local criminal justice agency.

(b) A local agency shall furnish local summary criminal history information to any of the following, when needed in the course of their duties, provided that when information is furnished to assist an agency, officer, or official of state or local government, a public utility, or any entity, in fulfilling employment, certification, or licensing duties, Chapter 1321 of the Statutes of 1974 and of Section 432.7 of the Labor Code shall apply:

(1) The courts of the state.

(2) Peace officers of the state as defined in Section 830.1, subdivisions (a) and (b) of Section 830.2, subdivisions (a), (b), and (j) of Section 830.3, subdivisions (a), (b), and (c) of Section 830.5, and Section 830.5a.

(3) District attorneys of the state.

(4) Prosecuting city attorneys of any city within the state.

(5) Probation officers of the state.

(6) Parole officers of the state.

(7) A public defender or attorney of record when representing a person in proceedings upon a petition for a certificate of rehabilitation and pardon pursuant to Section 4852.08.

(8) A public defender or attorney of record when representing a person in a criminal case and when authorized access by statutory or decisional law.

(9) Any agency, officer, or official of the state when the criminal history information is required to implement a statute, a regulation, or an ordinance that expressly refers to specific criminal conduct applicable to the subject person of the local summary criminal history information, and contains requirements or exclusions, or both, expressly based upon the specified criminal conduct.

(10) Any city or county, or city and county, or district, or any officer, or official thereof when access is needed in order to assist the agency, officer, or official in fulfilling employment, certification, or licensing duties, and when the access is specifically authorized by the city council, board of supervisors or governing board of the city, county, or district when the criminal history information is required to implement a statute, a regulation, or an ordinance that expressly refers to specific criminal conduct applicable to the subject person of the local summary criminal history information, and contains requirements or exclusions, or both, expressly based upon the specified criminal conduct.

(11) The subject of the local summary criminal history information.

(12) Any person or entity when access is expressly authorized by statute when the criminal history information is required to implement a statute, a regulation, or an ordinance that expressly refers to specific criminal conduct applicable to the subject person of the local summary criminal history information, and contains requirements or exclusions, or both, expressly based upon the specified criminal conduct.

(13) Any managing or supervising correctional officer of a county jail or other county correctional facility.

(c) The local agency may furnish local summary criminal history information, upon a showing of a compelling need, to any of the following, provided that when information is furnished to assist an agency, officer, or official of state or local government, a public utility, or any entity, in fulfilling employment, certification, or licensing duties, Chapter 1321 of the Statutes of 1974 and of Section 432.7 of the Labor Code shall apply:

(1) Any public utility as defined in Section 216 of the Public Utilities Code which operates a nuclear energy facility when access is needed in order to assist in employing persons to work at the facility, provided that, if the local agency supplies the data, it shall furnish a copy of this data to the person to whom the data relates.

(2) To a peace officer of the state other than those included in subdivision (b).

(3) To a peace officer of another country.

(4) To public officers (other than peace officers) of the United States, other states, or possessions or territories of the United States, provided that access to records similar to local summary criminal history information is expressly authorized by a statute of the United States, other states, or possessions or territories of the United States when this information is needed for the performance of their official duties.

(5) To any person when disclosure is requested by a probation, parole, or peace officer with the consent of the subject of the local summary criminal history information and for purposes of furthering the rehabilitation of the subject.

(6) The courts of the United States, other states, or territories or possessions of the United States.

(7) Peace officers of the United States, other states, or territories or possessions of the United States.

(8) To any individual who is the subject of the record requested when needed in conjunction with an application to enter the United States or any foreign nation.

(9) Any public utility as defined in Section 216 of the Public Utilities Code, when access is needed in order to assist in employing persons who will be seeking entrance to private residences in the course of their employment. The information provided shall be limited to the record of convictions and any arrest for which the person is released on bail or on his or her own recognizance pending trial.

If the local agency supplies the data pursuant to this paragraph, it shall furnish a copy of the data to the person to whom the data relate.

Any information obtained from the local summary criminal history is confidential and the receiving public utility shall not disclose its contents, other than for the purpose for which it was acquired. The local summary criminal history information in the possession of the public utility and all copies made from it shall be destroyed 30 days after employment is denied or granted, including any appeal periods, except for those cases where an employee or applicant is out on bail or on his or her own recognizance pending trial, in which case the state summary criminal history information and all copies shall be destroyed 30 days after the case is resolved, including any appeal periods.

A violation of any of the provisions of this paragraph is a misdemeanor, and shall give the employee or applicant who is injured by the violation a cause of action against the public utility to recover damages proximately caused by the violation.

Nothing in this section shall be construed as imposing any duty upon public utilities to request local summary criminal history information on any current or prospective employee.

Seeking entrance to private residences in the course of employment shall be deemed a "compelling need" as required to be shown in this subdivision.

(d) Whenever an authorized request for local summary criminal history information pertains to a person whose fingerprints are on file with the local agency

© 1992 by J., B. & L. Gould
Printed in the U.S.A.   EP

and the local agency has no criminal history of that person, and the information is to be used for employment, licensing, or certification purposes, the fingerprint card accompanying the request for information, if any, may be stamped "no criminal record" and returned to the person or entity making the request.

(e) A local agency taking fingerprints of a person who is an applicant for licensing, employment, or certification may charge a fee not to exceed ten dollars ($10) in order to cover the cost of taking the fingerprints and processing the required documents.

(f) Whenever local summary criminal history information furnished pursuant to this section is to be used for employment, licensing, or certification purposes, the local agency shall charge the person or entity making the request a fee which it determines to be sufficient to reimburse the local agency for the cost of furnishing the information, provided that no fee shall be charged to any public law enforcement agency for local summary criminal history information furnished to assist it in employing, licensing, or certifying a person who is applying for employment with the agency as a peace officer, or criminal investigator. Any state agency required to pay a fee to the local agency for information received under this section may charge the applicant a fee sufficient to reimburse the agency for the expense.

(g) Whenever there is a conflict, the processing of criminal fingerprints shall take priority over the processing of applicant fingerprints.

(h) It is not a violation of this article to disseminate statistical or research information obtained from a record, provided that the identity of the subject of the record is not disclosed.

(i) It is not a violation of this article to include information obtained from a record in (1) a transcript or record of a judicial or administrative proceeding or (2) any other public record when the inclusion of the information in the public record is authorized by a court, statute, or decisional law.

(j) Notwithstanding any other provision of law, the Department of Justice or any state or local law enforcement agency may require the submission of fingerprints for the purpose of conducting summary criminal history information record checks which are authorized by law.

(k) Any local criminal justice agency shall be authorized to release information concerning an arrest or detention of a peace officer which did not result in conviction, or information concerning a referral to, and participation in, any postarrest diversion program to a government agency employer of that peace officer. *(Amended by Stats 1990 ch 769 §3, eff. 1/1/91.)*

§13300.1. Destruction of material regarding Olympic games personnel.

Any information generated pursuant to the provisions of paragraph (10) of subdivision (c) of Section 13300 shall be destroyed at the end of the limitation period for the filing of a civil action arising out of the screening or accreditation of persons as current or prospective employees, concessionaires and contractors and their subcontractors, agents and employees for Olympic Games purposes. The knowing and willful failure (1) to notify the recipient as required by Section 13300, or (2) to destroy any information as required by this section is a misdemeanor punishable in a county jail not exceeding one year or by a fine not exceeding one thousand dollars ($1,000) or both.

§13301. Definition of record; who may receive.

As used in this article:

(a) "Record" means the master local summary criminal history information as defined in subdivision (a) of Section 13300, or a copy thereof.

(b) "A person authorized by law to receive a record" means any person or public agency authorized by a court, statute, or decisional law to receive a record.

§13302. Employee furnishing information to unauthorized person.

Any employee of the local criminal justice agency who knowingly furnishes a record or information obtained from a record to a person who is not authorized by law to receive the record or information is guilty of a misdemeanor.

§13303. Authorized person furnishing information.

Any person authorized by law to receive a record or information obtained from a record who knowingly furnishes the record or information to a person who is not authorized by law to receive the record or information is guilty of a misdemeanor.

§13304. Unauthorized person who buys, receives, or possesses information.

Any person, except those specifically referred to in Section 1070 of the Evidence Code, who, knowing he is not authorized by law to receive a record or information obtained from a record, knowingly buys, receives, or possesses the record or information is guilty of a misdemeanor.

§13305. Conduct not violations.

(a) It is not a violation of this article to disseminate statistical or research information obtained from a record, provided that the identity of the subject of the record is not disclosed.

(b) It is not a violation of this article to disseminate information obtained from a record for the purpose of assisting in the apprehension of a person wanted in connection with the commission of a crime.

(c) It is not a violation of this article to include information obtained from a record in (1) a transcript or record of a judicial or administrative proceeding or (2) any other public record when the inclusion of the information in the public record is authorized by a court, statute, or decisional law.

ARTICLE 7

EXAMINATION OF LOCAL RECORDS

§13320. Definitions; intent.

(a) As used in this article, "record" with respect to any person means the local summary criminal history information as defined in subdivision (a) of Section 13300, maintained under such person's name by the local criminal justice agency.

(b) As used in this article, "agency" means any agency or consortium of agencies.

(c) It is the function and intent of this article to afford persons concerning whom a record is maintained in the files of the local criminal justice agency a reasonable opportunity to examine the record compiled from such files, and to refute any erroneous or inaccurate information contained therein.

§13321. Application for own records.

Any person desiring to examine a record relating to himself shall make application to the agency maintaining the record in the form prescribed by that agency which may require the submission of fingerprints.

§13322. Application fee.

The agency may require the application be accompanied by a fee not to exceed twenty-five dollars ($25) that the agency determines is equal to the cost of processing the application and making a record available for examination.

§13323. Maintenance of records.

When an application is received by the agency, the agency shall upon verification of the applicant's identity determine whether a record pertaining to the applicant is maintained. If such record is maintained, the agency shall at its discretion either inform the applicant by mail of the existence of the record and specify a time when the record may be examined at a suitable facility of the agency or shall mail the subject a copy of the record.

§13324. Written request for proof or corroboration.

(a) If the applicant desires to question the accuracy or completeness of any material matter contained in the record, he may submit a written request to the agency in the form established by it. The request shall include a statement of the alleged inaccuracy or incompleteness in the record, its materiality, and shall specify any proof or corroboration available. Upon receipt of such request, the agency shall, within 60 days of receipt of such written request for clarification, review its information and forward to the applicant the results of such review.

(b) If the agency concurs in the allegations of inaccuracy or incompleteness in the record and finds that the error is material, it shall correct its record, and the agency shall inform the applicant of its correction of any material error in the record under this subdivision within 60 days. The agency shall notify all criminal justice agencies to which it has disseminated the incorrect record from an automated system in the past two years of the correction of the record.

The agency shall furnish the applicant with a list of all the noncriminal justice agencies to which the incorrect record has been disseminated from an automated system in the past two years unless it interferes with the conduct of an authorized investigation.

(c) If the agency denies the allegations of inaccuracy or incompleteness in the record, the matter shall at the option of the applicant be referred for administrative adjudication in accordance with the rules of the local governing body.

§13325. Regulations adopted.

The agency shall adopt all regulations necessary to carry out the provisions of this article.

§13326. Employee not required to furnish record.

No person shall require an employee or prospective employee to obtain a copy of a record or notification

that a record exists as provided in Section 13323. A violation of this section is a misdemeanor.

TITLE 4

STANDARDS AND TRAINING OF LOCAL LAW ENFORCEMENT OFFICERS

CHAPTER 1

COMMISSION ON PEACE OFFICER STANDARDS AND TRAINING

ARTICLE 1

ADMINISTRATION

§13500. Establishment of Commission on Peace Officer Standards and Training.

There is in the Department of Justice a Commission on Peace Officer Standards and Training, hereafter referred to in this chapter as the commission. The commission consists of 11 members appointed by the Governor, after consultation with, and with the advice of, the Attorney General and with the advice and consent of the Senate.

The commission shall be composed of the following members:

(1) Two members shall be (i) sheriffs or chiefs of police or peace officers nominated by their respective sheriffs or chiefs of police, (ii) peace officers who are deputy sheriffs or city policemen, or (iii) any combination thereof.

(2) Three members shall be sheriffs or chiefs of police or peace officers nominated by their respective sheriffs or chiefs of police.

(3) One member shall be a peace officer of the rank of sergeant or below with a minimum of five years' experience as a deputy sheriff or city policeman.

(4) One member shall be elected officer or chief administrative officer of a county in this state.

(5) One member shall be elected officer or chief administrative officer of a city in this state.

(6) Two members shall be public members who shall not be peace officers.

(7) One member shall be an educator or trainer in the field of criminal justice.

The Attorney General shall be an ex officio member of the commission.

Of the members first appointed by the Governor, three shall be appointed for a term of one year, three for a term of two years, and three for a term of three years. Their successors shall serve for a term of three years and until appointment and qualification of their successors, each term to commence on the expiration date of the term of the predecessor.

The additional member provided for by the Legislature in its 1973-1974 Regular Session shall be appointed by the Governor on or before January 15, 1975, and shall serve for a term of three years.

The additional member provided for by the Legislature in its 1977-78 Regular Session shall be appointed by the Governor on or after July 1, 1978, and shall serve for a term of three years.

§13501. Chairman and vice chairman; selection.

The commission shall select a chairman and a vice chairman from among its members. A majority of the members of the commission shall constitute a quorum.

638

§13502. Expenses of members.

Members of the commission shall receive no compensation, but shall be reimbursed for their actual and necessary travel expenses incurred in the performance of their duties. For purposes of compensation, attendance at meetings of the commission shall be deemed performance by a member of the duties of his local governmental employment.

§13503. Commission's powers.

In carrying out its duties and responsibilities, the commission shall have all of the following powers:

(a) To meet at such times and places as it may deem proper;

(b) To employ an executive secretary and, pursuant to civil service, such clerical and technical assistants as may be necessary;

(c) To contract with such other agencies, public or private, or persons as it deems necessary, for the rendition and affording of such services, facilities, studies, and reports to the commission as will best assist it to carry out its duties and responsibilities;

(d) To cooperate with and to secure the cooperation of county, city, city and county, and other local law enforcement agencies in investigating any matter within the scope of its duties and responsibilities, and in performing its other functions;

(e) To develop and implement programs to increase the effectiveness of law enforcement and when such programs involve training and education courses to cooperate with and secure the cooperation of state-level officers, agencies, and bodies having jurisdiction over systems of public higher education in continuing the development of college-level training and education programs;

(f) To cooperate with and secure the cooperation of every department, agency, or instrumentality in the state government;

(g) To do any and all things necessary or convenient to enable it fully and adequately to perform its duties and to exercise the power granted to it.

§13504. Personnel in Department of Justice.

The Attorney General shall, so far as compatible with other demands upon the personnel in the Department of Justice, make available to the commission the services of such personnel to assist the commission in the execution of the duties imposed upon it by this chapter.

§13505. Funds for training services to local law enforcement agencies.

In exercising its functions, the commission shall endeavor to minimize costs of administration so that a maximum of funds will be expended for the purpose of providing training and other services to local law enforcement agencies. All expenses shall be a proper charge against the revenue accruing under Article 3 (commencing with Section 13520). *(Amended by Stats 1985 ch 106 §112.)*

§13506. Adoption of regulations.

The commission may adopt such regulations as are necessary to carry out the purposes of this chapter.

§13507. District defined.

As used in this chapter, "district" means any of the following:

(a) A regional park district.

(b) A district authorized by statute to maintain a police department.

(c) The University of California.

(d) The California State University and Colleges.

(e) A community college district.

(f) A school district.

(g) A transit district.

(h) A harbor district. *(Amended by Stats 1989 ch 950 §3, eff. 1/1/90.)*

§13508. Establishment of learning technology laboratory.

(a) The commission shall do each of the following:

(1) Establish a learning technology laboratory that would conduct pilot projects with regard to needed facilities and otherwise implement modern instructional technology to improve the effectiveness of law enforcement training.

(2) Develop an implementation plan for the acquisition of law enforcement facilities and technology. In developing this plan, the commission shall consult with appropriate law enforcement and training organizations. The implementation plan shall include each of the following items:

(A) An evaluation of pilot and demonstration projects.

(B) Recommendations for the establishment of regional skills training centers, training conference centers, and the use of modern instructional technology.

(C) A recommended financing structure.

(3) Report to the Legislature on or before January 1, 1995, as to the status and effectiveness of the pilot projects implemented under this section.

(b) The commission may enter into joint powers agreements with other governmental agencies for the purpose of developing and deploying needed technology and facilities.

(c) Any pilot project conducted pursuant to this section shall terminate on or before January 1, 1995 unless funding is provided for the project continuation. *(Added by Stats 1991 ch 1074 §2, eff. 1/1/92, oper. upon appropriation of funds by the Budget Act of 1992.)*

ARTICLE 2

FIELD SERVICES AND STANDARDS FOR RECRUITMENT AND TRAINING

§13510. Rules for minimum standards.

(a) For the purpose of raising the level of competence of local law enforcement officers, the commission shall adopt, and may from time to time amend, rules establishing minimum standards relating to physical, mental, and moral fitness which shall govern the recruitment of any city police officers, peace officer members of a county sheriffs office, marshals or deputy marshals of a municipal court, peace officer members of a county coroner's office notwithstanding Section 13526, reserve officers, as defined in subdivision (a) of Section 830.6, police officers of a district authorized by statute to maintain a police department, peace officer members of a police department operated by a joint powers agency established by Article 1 (commencing with Section 6500) of Chapter 5 of Division 7 of Title 1 of the Government Code, regularly employed and paid inspectors and investigators of a district attorney's office, as defined in

Section 830.1, who conduct criminal investigations, or peace officer members of a district, in any city, county, city and county, or district receiving state aid pursuant to this chapter, and shall adopt, and may from time to time amend, rules establishing minimum standards for training of city police officers, peace officer members of county sheriff's offices, marshals or deputy marshals of a municipal court, peace officer members of a county coroner's office notwithstanding Section 13526, reserve officers, as defined in subdivision (a) of Section 830.6, police officers of a district authorized by statute to maintain a police department, peace officer members of a police department operated by a joint powers agency established by Article 1 (commencing with Section 6500) of Chapter 5 of Division 7 of Title 1 of the Government Code, regularly employed and paid inspectors and investigators of a district attorney's office, as defined in Section 830.1, who conduct criminal investigations, and peace officer members of a district which shall apply to those cities, counties, cities and counties, and districts receiving state aid pursuant to this chapter. Those rules shall be adopted and amended pursuant to Chapter 3.5 (commencing with Section 11340) of Part 1 of Division 3 of Title 2 of the Government Code.

(b) The commission shall conduct research concerning job-related educational standards and job-related selection standards to include vision, hearing, physical ability, and emotional stability. Job-related standards which are supported by this research shall be adopted by the commission prior to January 1, 1985, and shall apply to those peace officer classes identified in subdivision (a). The commission shall consult with local entities during the conducting of related research into job-related selection standards.

(c) For the purpose of raising the level of competence of local public safety dispatchers, the commission shall adopt, and may from time to time amend, rules establishing minimum standards relating to the recruitment and training of local public safety dispatchers having a primary responsibility for providing dispatching services for local law enforcement agencies described in subdivision (a), which standards shall apply to those cities, counties, cities and counties, and districts receiving state aid pursuant to this chapter. These standards also shall apply to consolidated dispatch centers operated by an independent public joint powers agency established pursuant to Article 1 (commencing with Section 6500) of Chapter 5 of Division 7 of Title 1 of the Government Code when providing dispatch services to the law enforcement personnel listed in subdivision (a). Those rules shall be adopted and amended pursuant to Chapter 3.5 (commencing with Section 11340) of Part 1 of Division 3 of Title 2 of the Government Code. As used in this section, "primary responsibility" refers to the performance of law enforcement dispatching duties for a minimum of 50 percent of the time worked within a pay period.

(d) Nothing in this section shall prohibit a local agency from establishing selection and training standards which exceed the minimum standards established by the commission. *(Amended by Stats 1991 ch 910 §7, eff. 1/1/92.)*

§13510.1. Certification program.

(a) The commission shall establish a certification program for peace officers specified in Sections 13510 and 13522 and for the California Highway Patrol.

(b) Basic, intermediate, advanced, supervisory, management, and executive certificates shall be established for the purpose of fostering professionalization, education, and experience necessary to adequately accomplish the general police service duties performed by peace officer members of city police departments, county sheriffs' departments, districts, university and state university and college departments, or by the California Highway Patrol.

(c) Certificates shall be awarded on the basis of a combination of training, education, experience, and other prerequisites, as determined by the commission.

(d) Persons who are determined by the commission to be eligible peace officers may make application for such certificates, provided they are employed by an agency which participates in the Peace Officer Standards and Training (POST) program.

(e) Certificates remain the property of the commission and the commission shall have the power to cancel any certificate.

(f) The commission shall cancel certificates issued to persons who have been convicted of, or entered a plea of guilty or nolo contendere to, a crime classified by statute or the Constitution as a felony.

§13510.2. Illegal acts involving certificates.

Any person who knowingly commits any of the following acts is guilty of a misdemeanor, and for each offense is punishable by a fine of not more than one thousand dollars ($1,000) or imprisonment in the county jail not to exceed one year, or by both a fine and imprisonment:

(a) Presents or attempts to present as the person's own the certificate of another.

(b) Knowingly permits another to use his or her certificate.

(c) Knowingly gives false evidence of any material kind to the commission, or to any member thereof, including the staff, in obtaining a certificate.

(d) Uses, or attempts to use, a canceled certificate.

§13510.5. Rules for minimum standards for training.

For the purpose of maintaining the level of competence of state law enforcement officers, the commission shall adopt, and may, from time to time amend, rules establishing minimum standards for training of peace officers as defined in Chapter 4.5 (commencing with Section 830) of Title 3 of Part 2, who are employed by any railroad company, the California State Police Division, the University of California Police Department, a California State University police department, the Department of Alcoholic Beverage Control, the Division of Investigation of the Department of Consumer Affairs, the Wildlife Protection Branch of the Department of Fish and Game, the Department of Forestry, the Department of Motor Vehicles, the California Horse Racing Board, the State Fire Marshal, the Bureau of Food and Drug, the Division of Labor Law Enforcement, the Director of Parks and Recreation, the State Department of Health Services, the State Department of Social Services, the State Department of Mental Health, the State Department of Developmental Services, the State Department of Alcohol and Drug Programs, the Office of Statewide Health Planning and Development, and the Department of Justice. All rules shall be adopted and amended pursuant to Chapter 3.5 (commencing with

© 1992 by J., B. & L. Gould
Printed in the U.S.A.   **EP**

Section 11340) of Part 1 of Division 3 of Title 2 of the Government Code.

§13511. Test in lieu of course.

(a) In establishing standards for training, the commission shall, so far as consistent with the purposes of this chapter, permit required training to be obtained at institutions approved by the commission.

(b) In those instances where persons have acquired prior equivalent peace officer training, the commission shall, no later than July 1, 1981, and thereafter, provide the opportunity for testing in lieu of attendance at a basic training academy or accredited college. Tests shall be constructed to verify possession of minimum knowledge and skills required by the commission as outlined in its basic course. These tests shall be scheduled periodically in convenient locations, and an opportunity shall be provided for testing and retesting under procedural guidelines established by the commission. The retesting procedures shall be designed so that any portion which has been previously passed need not be retaken. The commission shall charge a fee to cover administrative costs which is sufficient to cover all the costs associated with the testing conducted under this subdivision. *(Amended by Stats 1986 ch 33 §1.)*

§13511.5. Criminal history.

Each applicant for admission to a basic course of training certified by the Commission on Peace Officer Standards and Training who is not sponsored by a local or other law enforcement agency, or is not a peace officer employed by a state or local agency, department, or district, shall be required to submit written certification from the Department of Justice pursuant to Sections 11122, 11123, and 11124 that the applicant has no criminal history background which would disqualify him or her, pursuant to Section 12021, from owning, possessing, or having under his or her control any pistol, revolver, or other firearm capable of being concealed on the person.

§13512. Inquiries by commission.

The commission shall make such inquiries as may be necessary to determine whether every city, county, city and county, and district receiving state aid pursuant to this chapter is adhering to the standards for recruitment and training established pursuant to this chapter.

§13513. Establishment of counseling service.

Upon the request of a local jurisdiction, the commission shall provide a counseling service to such local jurisdiction for the purpose of improving the administration, management or operations of a police agency and may aid such jurisdiction in implementing improved practices and techniques.

§13514. Tear gas training course.

The commission shall prepare a course of instruction for the training of peace officers in the use of tear gas. Such course of instruction may be given, upon approval by the commission, by any agency or institution engaged in the training or instruction of peace officers.

§13516. Sexual assault cases; procedures.

(a) The commission shall prepare guidelines establishing standard procedures which may be followed by police agencies in the investigation of sexual assault cases, and cases involving the sexual exploitation or sexual abuse of children, including, police response to, and treatment of, victims of these crimes.

(b) The course of training leading to the basic certificate issued by the commission shall, on and after July 1, 1977, include adequate instruction in the procedures described in subdivision (a). No reimbursement shall be made to local agencies based on attendance on or after that date at any course which does not comply with the requirements of this subdivision.

(c) The commission shall prepare and implement a course for the training of specialists in the investigation of sexual assault cases, child sexual exploitation cases, and child sexual abuse cases. Officers assigned to investigation duties which include the handling of cases involving the sexual exploitation or sexual abuse of children, shall successfully complete that training within six months of the date the assignment was made.

(d) It is the intent of the Legislature in the enactment of this section to encourage the establishment of sex crime investigation units in police agencies throughout the state, which units shall include, but not be limited to, investigating crimes involving the sexual exploitation and sexual abuse of children.

(e) It is the further intent of the Legislature in the enactment of this section to encourage the establishment of investigation guidelines that take into consideration the sensitive nature of the sexual exploitation and sexual abuse of children with respect to both the accused and the alleged victim. *(Amended by Stats 1986 ch 32 §3.)*

§13517. Guidelines for child abuse or neglect cases.

(a) The commission shall prepare guidelines establishing standard procedures which may be followed by police agencies in the detection, investigation, and response to cases in which a minor is a victim of an act of abuse or neglect prohibited by this code. The guidelines shall include procedures for determining whether or not a child should be taken into protective custody. The guidelines shall also include procedures for minimizing the number of times a child is interviewed by law enforcement personnel.

(b) The course of training leading to the basic certificate issued by the commission shall, not later than July 1, 1979, include adequate instruction in the procedures described in subdivision (a).

(c) The commission shall prepare and implement an optional course of training of specialists in the investigation of cases in which a minor is a victim of an act of abuse or neglect prohibited by this code.

(d) The commission shall consult with the State Office of Child Abuse Prevention in developing the guidelines and optional course of training. *(Amended by Stats 1985 ch 672 §1.)*

§13517.5. Guidelines.

The commission shall prepare guidelines establishing standard procedures which may be followed by police agencies and prosecutors in interviewing minor witnesses. *(Added by Stats 1987 ch 612 §1.)*

§13518. Training in first aid and CPR.

(a) Every city police officer, sheriff, deputy sheriff, marshal, deputy marshal, peace officer member of the

California State Police, peace officer member of the California Highway Patrol, and police officer of a district authorized by statute to maintain a police department, except those whose duties are primarily clerical or administrative, shall meet the training standards prescribed by the Emergency Medical Services Authority for the administration of first aid and cardiopulmonary resuscitation. This training shall include instruction in the use of a portable manual mask and airway assembly designed to prevent the spread of communicable diseases. In addition, satisfactory completion of periodic refresher training or appropriate testing in cardiopulmonary resuscitation and other first aid as prescribed by the Emergency Medical Services Authority shall also be required.

(b) The course of training leading to the basic certificate issued by the commission shall include adequate instruction in the procedures described in subdivision (a). No reimbursement shall be made to local agencies based on attendance at any such course which does not comply with the requirements of this subdivision.

(c) As used in this section, "primarily clerical or administrative" means the performance of clerical or administrative duties for a minimum of 90 percent of the time worked within a pay period. *(Amended by Stats 1987 ch 1334 §1.)*

§13518.1. Provision of masks.

In order to prevent the spread of communicable disease, every law enforcement agency employing peace officers described in subdivision (a) of Section 13518 shall provide to each of these peace officers an appropriate portable manual mask and airway assembly for use when applying cardiopulmonary resuscitation. *(Added by Stats 1987 ch 1334 §2.)*

§13519. Law enforcement officer training in domestic violence.

(a) The commission shall implement by January 1, 1986, a course or courses of instruction for the training of law enforcement officers in California in the handling of domestic violence complaints and also shall develop guidelines for law enforcement response to domestic violence. The course or courses of instruction and the guidelines shall stress enforcement of criminal laws in domestic violence situations, availability of civil remedies and community resources, and protection of the victim. Where appropriate, the training presenters shall include domestic violence experts with expertise in the delivery of direct services to victims of domestic violence, including utilizing the staff of shelters for battered women in the presentation of training.

As used in this section, "law enforcement officer" means any officer or employee of a local police department or sheriff's office, any peace officer of the Department of Parks and Recreation, as defined in subdivision (g) of Section 830.2, any peace officer of the University of California Police Department, as defined in subdivision (c) of Section 830.2, or any peace officer of the California State University Police Departments, as defined in subdivision (d) of Section 830.2.

(b) The course of basic training for law enforcement officers shall, no later than January 1, 1986, include adequate instruction in the procedures and techniques described below:

(1) The provisions set forth in Title 5 (commencing with Section 13700) relating to response, enforcement of court orders, and data collection.

(2) The legal duties imposed on police officers to make arrests and offer protection and assistance including guidelines for making felony and misdemeanor arrests.

(3) Techniques for handling incidents of domestic violence that minimize the likelihood of injury to the officer and that promote the safety of the victim.

(4) The nature and extent of domestic violence.

(5) The legal rights of, and remedies available to, victims of domestic violence.

(6) The use of an arrest by a private person in a domestic violence situation.

(7) Documentation, report writing, and evidence collection.

(8) Domestic violence diversion as provided in Chapter 2.6 (commencing with Section 1000.6) of Title 6 of Part 2.

(9) Tenancy issues and domestic violence.

(10) The impact on children of law enforcement intervention in domestic violence.

(11) The services and facilities available to victims and batterers.

(12) The use and applications of this code in domestic violence situations.

(13) Verification and enforcement of temporary restraining orders when (A) the suspect is present and (B) the suspect has fled.

(14) Verification and enforcement of stay-away orders.

(15) Cite and release policies.

(16) Emergency assistance to victims and how to assist victims in pursuing criminal justice options.

The guidelines developed by the commission shall also incorporate the foregoing factors.

(c) (1) All law enforcement officers who have received their basic training before January 1, 1986, shall participate in supplementary training on domestic violence subjects, as prescribed and certified by the commission.

(2) Except as provided in paragraph (3), the training specified in paragraph (1) shall be completed no later than January 1, 1989.

(3) The training for peace officers of the Department of Parks and Recreation, as defined in subdivision (g) of Section 830.2, shall be completed no later than January 1, 1992, and the training for peace officers of the University of California Police Department and the California State University Police Departments, as defined in Section 830.2, shall be completed no later than January 1, 1993.

Local law enforcement agencies are encouraged to include, as part of their advanced officer training program, periodic updates and training on domestic violence. The commission shall assist where possible.

(d) The course of instruction, the learning and performance objectives, the standards for the training, and the guidelines shall be developed by the commission in consultation with appropriate groups and individuals having an interest and expertise in the field of domestic violence. The groups and individuals shall include, but shall not be limited to, the following: one representative each from the California Peace Officers' Association, the Peace Officers' Research Association of California, the State Bar of California, the California Women Lawyers' Association, and the State Commission on the Status of Women; two rep-

© 1992 by J., B. & L. Gould
Printed in the U.S.A.   EP

resentatives from the commission; two representatives from the California Alliance Against Domestic Violence; two peace officers, recommended by the commission, who are experienced in the provision of domestic violence training; and two domestic violence experts, recommended by the California Alliance Against Domestic Violence, who are experienced in the provision of direct services to victims of domestic violence. At least one of the persons selected shall be a former victim of domestic violence.

The commission, in consultation with these groups and individuals, shall review existing training programs to determine in what ways domestic violence training might be included as a part of ongoing programs.

(e) Forty thousand dollars ($40,000) is appropriated from the Peace Officers Training Fund in augmentation of Item 8120-001-268 of the Budget Act of 1984, to support the travel, per diem, and associated costs for convening the necessary experts. *(Amended by Stats 1991 ch 912 §1, eff. 1/1/92.)*

§13519.1. Officer training; missing persons, runaways.

(a) The commission shall implement by July 1, 1988, a course or courses of instruction for the training of law enforcement officers and law enforcement dispatchers in the handling of missing person and runaway cases and shall also develop guidelines for law enforcement response to missing person and runaway cases. The course or courses of instruction and the guidelines shall include, but not be limited to, timeliness and priority of response, assisting persons who make missing person reports to contact the appropriate law enforcement agency in the jurisdiction of the residence address of the missing person or runaway and the appropriate law enforcement agency in the jurisdiction where the missing person or runaway was last seen, and coordinating law enforcement agencies for the purpose of efficiently and effectively taking and investigating missing person reports.

As used in this section, "law enforcement" includes any officers or employees of a local police or sheriff's office or of the California Highway Patrol.

(b) The course of basic training for law enforcement officers and law enforcement dispatchers shall, not later than January 1, 1989, include adequate instruction in the handling of missing person and runaway cases developed pursuant to subdivision (a).

(c) All law enforcement officers and law enforcement dispatchers who have received their basic training before January 1, 1989, shall participate in supplementary training on missing person and runaway cases, as prescribed and certified by the commission. The training required by this subdivision shall be completed not later than January 1, 1991. *(Added by Stats 1987 ch 705 §3.)*

§13519.2. Instruction on handling disabled persons.

(a) The commission shall, on or before July 1, 1990, include in the basic training course for law enforcement officers, adequate instruction in the handling of persons with developmental disabilities or mental illness, or both. Officers who complete the basic training prior to July 1, 1990, shall participate in supplementary training on this topic. This supplementary training shall be completed on or before July 1, 1992.

Further training courses to update this instruction shall be established, as deemed necessary by the commission.

(b) The course of instruction relating to the handling of developmentally disabled or mentally ill persons shall be developed by the commission in consultation with appropriate groups and individuals having an interest and expertise in this area. In addition to providing instruction on the handling of these persons, the course shall also include information on the cause and nature of developmental disabilities and mental illness, as well as the community resources available to serve these persons. *(Added by Stats 1988 ch 593 §1, eff. 1/1/89.)*

§13519.3. Peace officer training in infant death.

(a) Effective July 1, 1990, the commission shall establish, for those peace officers specified in subdivision (a) of Section 13510 who are assigned to patrol or investigations, a course on the nature of sudden infant death syndrome and the handling of cases involving the sudden deaths of infants. The course shall include information on the community resources available to assist families and child care providers who have lost a child to sudden infant death syndrome. Officers who are employed after January 1, 1990, shall complete a course in sudden infant death syndrome prior to the issuance of the Peace Officer Standards and Training basic certificate, and shall complete training on this topic on or before July 1, 1992.

(b) The commission, in consultation with experts in the field of sudden infant death syndrome, shall prepare guidelines establishing standard procedures which may be followed by law enforcement agencies in the investigation of cases involving sudden deaths of infants.

(c) The course relating to sudden infant death syndrome and the handling of cases of sudden infant deaths shall be developed by the commission in consultation with experts in the field of sudden infant death syndrome. The course shall include instruction in the standard procedures developed pursuant to subdivision (b). In addition, the course shall include information on the nature of sudden infant death syndrome which shall be taught by experts in the field of sudden infant death syndrome.

(d) The commission shall review and modify the basic course curriculum to include sudden infant death syndrome awareness as part of death investigation training.

(e) When the instruction and training are provided by a local agency, a fee shall be charged sufficient to defray the entire cost of instruction and training. *(Added by Stats 1989 ch 1111 §7, eff. 1/1/90.)*

§13519.4. Instruction in racial and cultural differences.

Effective July 1, 1991, the commission shall develop and disseminate guidelines and training for all law enforcement officers in California as described in subdivision (a) of Section 13510 and who adhere to the standards approved by the commission, on the racial and cultural differences among the residents of this state. The course or courses of instruction and the guidelines shall stress understanding and respect for racial and cultural differences, and development of effective, noncombative methods of carrying out law enforcement duties in a racially and culturally diverse environment. *(Added by Stats 1990 ch 480 §1, eff. 1/1/91.)*

§13519.5. Instruction in gang and drug law enforcement.

The commission shall, on or before July 1, 1991, implement a course or courses of instruction to provide ongoing training to the appropriate peace officers on methods of gang and drug law enforcement. *(Added by Stats 1990 ch 333 §2, eff. 1/1/91.)*

ARTICLE 3

PEACE OFFICERS' TRAINING FUND AND ALLOCATIONS THEREFROM

§13520. Peace Officers' Training Fund.

There is hereby created in the State Treasury a Peace Officers' Training Fund, which is hereby appropriated, without regard to fiscal years, exclusively for costs of administration and for grants to local governments and districts pursuant to this chapter.

§13522. Application for state aid.

Any city, county, city and county, or district which desires to receive state aid pursuant to this chapter shall make application to the commission for the aid. The initial application shall be accompanied by a certified copy of an ordinance, or in the case of the University of California, the California State University, and agencies not authorized to act by ordinance, by a resolution, adopted by its governing body providing that while receiving any state aid pursuant to this chapter, the city, county, city and county, or district will adhere to the standards for recruitment and training established by the commission. The application shall contain any information the commission may request. *(Amended by Stats 1990 ch 333 §3, eff. 1/1/91.)*

§13523. Allocations of state aid.

The commission shall annually allocate and the State Treasurer shall periodically pay from the Peace Officers' Training Fund, at intervals specified by the commission, to each city, county, and district which has applied and qualified for aid pursuant to this chapter an amount determined by the commission pursuant to standards set forth in its regulations. The commission shall grant aid only on a basis that is equally proportionate among cities, counties, and districts. State aid shall only be provided for training expenses of full-time regularly paid employees, as defined by the commission, of eligible agencies from cities, counties, or districts.

In no event shall any allocation be made to any city, county, or district which is not adhering to the standards established by the commission as applicable to such city, county, or district.

§13524. State aid for inspector and investigator training.

Any county wishing to receive state aid pursuant to this chapter for the training of regularly employed and paid inspectors and investigators of a district attorney's office, as defined in Section 830.1 who conduct criminal investigations, shall include such request for aid in its application to the commission pursuant to Sections 13522 and 13523.

§13525. State aid.

Any city, county, city and county, district, or joint powers agency which desires to receive state aid pursuant to this chapter for the training of regularly employed and paid local public safety dispatchers, as described in subdivision (c) of Section 13510, shall include that request for aid in its application to the commission pursuant to Sections 13522 and 13523. *(Amended by Stats 1990 ch 333 §4, eff. 1/1/91.)*

§13526. Nonallocation of funds.

In no event shall any allocation be made from the Peace Officers' Training Fund to a local government agency if the agency was not entitled to receive funding under any of the provisions of this article, as they read on December 31, 1989. *(Added by Stats 1989 ch 1165 §40, eff. 1/1/90.)*

§13526.1. Allocation to Harbor Department of Los Angeles.

(a) It is the intent of the Legislature in adding this section that effect be given to amendments made by Chapter 950 of the Statutes of 1989. The Legislature recognizes those amendments were intended to make port wardens and special officers of the Harbor Department of the City of Los Angeles entitled to allocations from the Peace Officers' Training Fund for state aid pursuant to this chapter, notwithstanding the amendments made by Chapter 1165 of the Statutes of 1989, which added Section 13526 to this code.

(b) Notwithstanding Section 13526, for the purposes of this chapter, the port wardens and special officers of the Harbor Department of the City of Los Angeles shall be entitled to receive funding from the Peace Officers' Training Fund. *(Added by Stats 1990 ch 1695 §12, eff. 1/1/91.)*

ARTICLE 4

PEACE OFFICERS
(Added by Stats 1989 ch 1165 §41, eff. 1/1/90.)

§13540. Request for redesignation of peace officer.

Any person or persons desiring peace officer status under Chapter 4.5 (commencing with Section 830) of Title 3 of Part 4* who, on January 1, 1990, were not entitled to be designated as peace officers under Chapter 4.5 shall request the Commission on Peace Officer Standards and Training to undertake a feasibility study regarding designating that person or persons as peace officers. The request and study shall be undertaken in accordance with regulations adopted by the commission. The commission may charge any person requesting a study, a fee, not to exceed the actual cost of undertaking the study. Nothing in this article shall apply to or otherwise affect the authority of the Director of Corrections, the Director of the Youth Authority, the Director of the Youthful Offender Parole Board, or the Secretary of the Youth and Adult Correctional Agency to designate peace officers as provided for in Section 830.5. *(Amended by Stats 1990 ch 82 §14, eff. 5/3/90.)*

*So in original. Probably should be "2".

© 1992 by J., B. & L. Gould
Printed in the U.S.A.   EP

§13541. Requirements for peace officer redesignation.

Any study undertaken under this article shall include, but shall not be limited to, the current and proposed duties and responsibilities of persons employed in the category seeking the designation change, their field law enforcement duties and responsibilities, their supervisory and management structure, and their proposed training methods and funding sources. *(Added by Stats 1989 ch 1165 §41, eff. 1/1/90.)*

§13542. Redesignation of peace officer.

In order for the commission to give a favorable recommendation as to a change in designation to peace officer status, the person or persons desiring the designation change shall be employed by an agency with a supervisory structure consisting of a chief law enforcement officer, the agency shall agree to comply with the training requirements set forth in Section 832, and shall be subject to the funding restriction set forth in Section 13526. The commission shall issue the study and its recommendations to the requesting person or agency within 18 months of the request if the request is made in accordance with the regulations of the commission. A copy of that study and recommendations shall also be submitted to the Legislature. *(Amended by Stats 1990 ch 82 §14.5, eff. 5/3/90.)*

TITLE 4.5

YOUTH AND ADULT CORRECTIONAL PEACE OFFICER STANDARDS AND TRAINING

§13600. Legislative findings and declaration.

(a) The Legislature finds and declares that peace officers of the state correctional system, including youth and adult correctional facilities, have a role in the criminal justice system that has previously been ignored in terms of creation and application of sound selection criteria for applicants and their training prior to assuming their duties. For the purposes of this section, correctional peace officers are peace officers as defined in Section 830.5 and employed by the Department of Corrections or the Department of the Youth Authority.

The Legislature further finds that sound applicant selection and training are essential to public safety and in carrying out the missions of the Youth and Correctional Agency in the custody and care of the state's offender population. The greater degree of professionalism which will result from sound screening criteria and a significant training curriculum will greatly aid the Youth and Adult Correctional Agency in maintaining smooth, efficient, and safe operations and effective programs in the Departments of Corrections and the Youth Authority.

(b) The Department of Corrections-Department of Youth Authority Joint Apprenticeship Committee, as referred to in the Memorandum of Understanding for Unit 6, in consultation with the Presley Institute, shall research, establish, and monitor standards for the selection and training of correctional peace officer apprentices. Any standard for selection established under this subdivision shall be subject to approval by the State Personnel Board. The Joint Apprenticeship Committee may disapprove any training courses created pursuant to the standards developed by the committee if it determines that the courses do not meet the prescribed standards. *(Amended by Stats 1987 ch 853 §1.)*

§13601. Advanced curricula.

The Joint Apprenticeship Committee, in consultation with the Presley Institute, shall develop standards for advanced correctional peace officer and supervisory curricula. Those standards shall be approved by both a majority of the management representatives and a majority of the Unit 6 representatives to the Joint Apprenticeship Committee. Upon approval, the standards shall be effective as soon as practicable after funding is made available through the state budget process. When a correctional peace officer is promoted, he or she shall be required to complete these secondary training experiences as a prerequisite to successful passage of probation.

The Joint Apprenticeship Committee shall develop standards for the training of correctional peace officers in the handling of stress associated with their duties. The Joint Apprenticeship Committee may disapprove any training courses created pursuant to the standards developed by the committee if it determines that the courses do not meet the prescribed standards. *(Amended by Stats 1987 ch 853 §2.)*

§13602. Joint use of training academy at Galt.

The departments shall jointly use the training academy at Galt. The academy shall be known as the Richard A. McGee Academy. The training divisions, in using the funds, shall endeavor to minimize costs of administration so that a maximum amount of the funds will be used for providing training and support to correctional peace officers while being trained by the departments.

TITLE 5

LAW ENFORCEMENT RESPONSE TO DOMESTIC VIOLENCE

CHAPTER 1

GENERAL PROVISIONS

§13700. Terms defined.

As used in this title:

(a) "Abuse" means intentionally or recklessly causing or attempting to cause bodily injury, or placing another person in reasonable apprehension of imminent serious bodily injury to himself, or another.

(b) "Domestic Violence" is abuse committed against an adult or fully emancipated minor who is a spouse, former spouse, cohabitant, former cohabitant, or a person with whom the suspect has had a child or has or has had a dating or engagement relationship.

(c) "Officer" means any law-enforcement officer employed by a local police department or sheriff's office, consistent with Section 830.1.

(d) "Victim" means a person who is a victim of domestic violence.

§13701. Policies; standards.

Every law enforcement agency in this state shall develop, adopt, and implement written policies and standards for officers' response to domestic violence calls by January 1, 1986. These policies shall reflect that domestic violence is alleged criminal conduct.

Further, they shall reflect existing policy that a request for assistance in a situation involving domestic violence is the same as any other request for assistance where violence has occurred. These existing local policies and those developed shall be in writing and shall be available to the public upon request and shall include specific standards for the following:

(a) Felony arrests.

(b) Misdemeanor arrests.

(c) Use of citizen arrests.

(d) Verification and enforcement of temporary restraining orders when (1) the suspect is present and (2) when the suspect has fled.

(e) Verification and enforcement of stay-away orders.

(f) Cite and release policies.

(g) Emergency assistance to victims, such as medical care, transportation to a shelter, and police standbys for removing personal property.

(h) Assisting victims in pursuing criminal options, such as giving the victim the report number and directing the victim to the proper investigation unit.

(i) Furnishing written notice to victims at the scene, including, but not limited to, all of the following information:

(1) (A) A statement informing the victim that despite official restraint of the person alleged to have committed domestic violence, the restrained person may be released at any time.

(B) A statement that, "For further information about a shelter you may contact _____."

(C) A statement that, "For information about other services in the community, where available, you may contact _____."

(2) A statement informing the victim of domestic violence that he or she can ask the district attorney to file a criminal complaint.

(3) A statement informing the victim of the right to go to the superior court and file a petition requesting any of the following orders for relief:

(A) An order restraining the attacker from abusing the victim and other family members.

(B) An order directing the attacker to leave the household.

(C) An order preventing the attacker from entering the residence, school, business, or place of employment of the victim.

(D) An order awarding the victim or the other parent custody of or visitation with a minor child or children.

(E) An order restraining the attacker from molesting or interfering with minor children in the custody of the victim.

(F) An order directing the party not granted custody to pay support of minor children, if that party has a legal obligation to do so.

(G) An order directing the defendant to make specified debit payments coming due while the order is in effect.

(H) An order directing that either or both parties participate in counseling.

(4) A statement informing the victim of the right to file a civil suit for losses suffered as a result of the abuse, including medical expenses, loss of earnings, and other expenses for injuries sustained and damage to property, and any other related expenses incurred by the victim or any agency that shelters the victim.

(5) In the case of an alleged violation of Section 261, 261.5, 262, 286, 288a, or 289, a "Victims of Domestic Violence" card which shall include, but is not limited to, the following information:

(A) The names and locations of rape victim counseling centers within the county, including those centers specified in Section 13837, and their 24-hour counseling service telephone numbers.

(B) A simple statement on the proper procedures for a victim to follow after a sexual assault.

(C) A statement that sexual assault by a person who is known to the victim, including sexual assault by a person who is the spouse of the victim, is a crime.

(j) Writing of reports.

In the development of these policies and standards, each local department is encouraged to consult with domestic violence experts, such as the staff of the local shelter for battered women and their children. Departments may utilize the response guidelines developed by the commission in developing local policies. *(Amended by Stats 1991 ch 999 §2, eff. 1/1/92.)*

§13702. Policies: dispatcher's response to calls.

Every law enforcement agency in this state shall develop, adopt, and implement written policies and standards for dispatchers' response to domestic violence calls by July 1, 1991. These policies shall reflect that calls reporting threatened, imminent, or ongoing domestic violence, and the violation of any protection order, including orders issued pursuant to Section 136.2, and restraining orders, shall be ranked among the highest priority calls. Dispatchers are not required to verify the validity of the protective order before responding to the request for assistance. *(Added by Stats 1990 ch 1692 §4, eff. 1/1/91.)*

CHAPTER 2

RESTRAINING ORDERS

§13710. Records of protection orders, restraining orders.

(a) Law enforcement agencies shall maintain a complete and systematic record of all protection orders with respect to domestic violence incidents, including orders which have not yet been served, issued pursuant to Section 136.2, restraining orders, and proofs of service in effect. This shall be used to inform law enforcement officers responding to domestic violence calls of the existence, terms, and effective dates of protection orders in effect.

(b) The terms and conditions of the protection order remain enforceable, notwithstanding the acts of the parties, and may be changed only by order of the court.

(c) Upon request, law enforcement agencies shall serve the party to be restrained at the scene of a domestic violence incident or at any time the party is in custody. *(Amended by Stats 1990 ch 1692 §5, eff. 1/1/91.)*

§13711. Court clerk's duty to distribute information pamphlet.

Whenever a protection order with respect to domestic violence incidents, including orders issued pursuant to Section 136.2 and restraining orders, is applied for or issued, it shall be the responsibility of the clerk of the superior court to distribute a pamphlet to the person who is to be protected by the order that includes the following:

© 1992 by J., B. & L. Gould
Printed in the U.S.A. **EP**

(a) Information as specified in subdivision (i) of Section 13701.

(b) Notice that it is the responsibility of the victim to request notification of an inmate's release.

(c) Notice that the terms and conditions of the protection order remain enforceable, notwithstanding any acts of the parties, and may be changed only by order of the court. *(Added by Stats 1990 ch 1692 §6, eff. 1/1/91.)*

CHAPTER 3

STAY-AWAY ORDERS
(Repealed by Stats 1985 ch 281.)

CHAPTER 4

DATA COLLECTION

§13730. Domestic violence related calls; recording.

(a) Each law enforcement agency shall develop a system, by January 1, 1986 for recording all domestic violence-related calls for assistance made to the department including whether weapons are involved. Monthly, the total number of domestic violence calls received and the numbers of such cases involving weapons shall be compiled by each law enforcement agency and submitted to the Attorney General.

(b) The Attorney General shall report annually to the Governor, the Legislature, and the public, the total number of domestic violence-related calls received by California law enforcement agencies, the number of cases involving weapons, and a breakdown of calls received by agency, city, and county.

(c) Each law enforcement agency shall develop an incident report form that includes a domestic violence identification code by January 1, 1986. In all incidents of domestic violence, a report shall be written and shall be thus identified on the face of the report as a domestic violence incident.

CHAPTER 5

TERMINATION
(Repealed by Stats 1989 ch 714 §1, eff. 1/1/90.)

§13731. *Repealed by Stats 1989 ch 714 §1, eff. 1/1/90.*

TITLE 6

CALIFORNIA COUNCIL ON CRIMINAL JUSTICE

CHAPTER 1

GENERAL PROVISIONS AND DEFINITIONS

§13800. Terms defined.

As used in this title:

(a) "Council" means the California Council on Criminal Justice.

(b) "Office" means the Office of Criminal Justice Planning.

(c) "Local boards" means local criminal justice planning boards.

(d) "Federal acts" means the Federal Omnibus Crime Control and Safe Streets Act of 1968, the Federal Juvenile Delinquency Prevention and Control Act of 1968, and any act or acts amendatory or supplemental thereto.

§13801. Construction.

Nothing in this title shall be construed as authorizing the council, the office, or the local boards to undertake direct operational criminal justice responsibilities.

CHAPTER 2

CALIFORNIA COUNCIL ON CRIMINAL JUSTICE

§13810. Creation and membership.

There is hereby created in the state government the California Council on Criminal Justice, which shall be composed of the following members: the Attorney General; the Administrative Director of the Courts; 19 members appointed by the Governor, including the Commissioner of the Department of the Highway Patrol, the Director of the Department of Corrections, the Director of the Department of the Youth Authority, and the State Public Defender; eight members appointed by the Senate Rules Committee; and eight members appointed by the Speaker of the Assembly.

The remaining appointees of the Governor shall include different persons from each of the following categories: a district attorney, a sheriff, a county public defender, a county probation officer, a member of a city council, a member of a county board of supervisors, a faculty member of a college or university qualified in the field of criminology, police science, or law, a person qualified in the field of criminal justice research and six private citizens, including a representative of a citizens, professional, or community organization. The Senate Committee on Rules shall include among its appointments different persons from each of the following categories: a member of the Senate Committee on Judiciary, a representative of the counties, a representative of the cities, a judge designated by the Judicial Council, and four private citizens, including a representative of a citizens, professional, or community organization. The Speaker of the Assembly shall include among his appointments different persons from each of the following categories: a representative of the counties, a representative of the cities, a member of the Assembly Committee on Criminal Justice, a chief of police, a peace officer, and three private citizens, including a representative of a citizens, professional, or community organization directly related to delinquency prevention.

The Governor shall select a chairman from among the members of the council.

§13811. Meetings; attendance.

The council shall meet no more than 12 times per year.

The council may create subcommittees of its own membership and each subcommittee shall meet as often as the subcommittee members find necessary. It is the intent of the Legislature that all council members shall actively participate in all council deliberations required by this chapter. Any member who misses three consecutive meetings or who attends less than 50 percent of the council's regularly called meetings in any calendar year for any cause except severe temporary illness or injury shall be automatically removed from the council.

§13812. Expenses reimbursed.

Members of the council shall receive no compensation for their services but shall be reimbursed for their expenses actually and necessarily incurred by them in the performance of their duties under this title. No compensation or expenses shall be received by the members of any continuing task forces, review committees or other auxiliary bodies created by the council who are not council members, except that persons requested to appear before the council with regard to specific topics on one or more occasions shall be reimbursed for the travel expenses necessarily incurred in fulfilling such requests.

The Advisory Committee on Juvenile Justice and Delinquency Prevention appointed by the Governor pursuant to federal law may be reimbursed by the Office of Criminal Justice Planning for expenses necessarily incurred by the members. Staff support for the committee will be provided by the Office of Criminal Justice Planning.

§13813. Duties.

The council shall act as the supervisory board of the state planning agency pursuant to federal acts. It shall annually review and approve, or review, revise and approve, the comprehensive state plan for the improvement of criminal justice and delinquency prevention activities throughout the state, shall establish priorities for the use of such funds as are available pursuant to federal acts, and shall approve the expenditure of all funds pursuant to such plans or federal acts; provided that the approval of such expenditures may be granted to single projects or to groups of projects.

CHAPTER 3

OFFICE OF CRIMINAL JUSTICE PLANNING

§13820. Creation.

There is hereby created in the state government the Office of Criminal Justice Planning. The office shall be administered by an executive director, who shall be appointed by, and be responsible to, the Governor, and hold office at the pleasure of the Governor. The executive director shall be in sole charge of the administration of the office.

§13821. Executive director's duties.

The executive director may appoint such deputies, assistants and other officers and employees and consultants as he may deem necessary and prescribe their powers and duties. The executive director shall establish policies and procedures for governing the internal operation of the office and coordination with local planning agencies, grant recipients and state and local officials.

§13822. Information from state.

The executive director may request and receive from any department or agency of the state or any political subdivision thereof such assistance, information and data as will enable him to carry out his functions and duties.

§13823. Powers.

(a) In cooperation with local boards, the office shall:

(1) Develop with the advice and approval of the council, the comprehensive statewide plan for the improvement of criminal justice and delinquency prevention activity throughout the state.

(2) Define, develop and correlate programs and projects for the state criminal justice agencies.

(3) Receive and disburse federal funds, perform all necessary and appropriate staff services required by the council, and otherwise assist the council in the performance of its duties as established by federal acts.

(4) Develop comprehensive, unified and orderly procedures to insure that all local plans and all state and local projects are in accord with the comprehensive state plan, and that all applications for grants are processed efficiently.

(5) Cooperate with and render technical assistance to the Legislature, state agencies, units of general local government, combinations of such units, or other public or private agencies, organizations or institutions in matters relating to criminal justice and delinquency prevention.

(6) Conduct evaluation studies of the programs and activities assisted by the federal acts.

(b) The office may:

(1) Collect, evaluate, publish, and disseminate statistics and other information on the condition and progress of criminal justice in the state.

(2) Perform other functions and duties as required by federal acts, rules, regulations or guidelines in acting as the administrative office of the state planning agency for distribution of federal grants.

§13823.2. Crimes against the elderly; Legislative findings.

(a) The Legislature hereby finds and declares all of the following:

(1) That violent and serious crimes are being committed against the elderly on an alarmingly regular basis.

(2) That in 1985, the United States Department of Justice reported that approximately 1 in every 10 elderly households in the nation would be touched by crime.

(3) That the California Department of Justice, based upon limited data received from local law enforcement agencies, reported that approximately 10,000 violent crimes were committed against elderly victims in 1985.

(4) That while the elderly may not be the most frequent targets of crime, when they are victimized the impact of each vicious attack has long-lasting effects. Injuries involving, for example, a broken hip may never heal properly and often leave the victim physically impaired. The loss of money used for food and other daily living expenses for these costs may be life-threatening for the older citizen on a fixed income. In addition, stolen or damaged property often cannot be replaced.

(5) Although the State of California currently funds programs to provide assistance to victims of crime and to provide general crime prevention information, there are limited specialized efforts to respond directly to the needs of elderly victims or to provide prevention services tailored for the senior population.

© 1992 by J., B. & L. Gould
Printed in the U.S.A.   EP

(b) It is the intent of the Legislature that victim services, crime prevention, and criminal justice training programs funded by the Office of Criminal Justice Planning shall include, consistent with available resources, specialized components that respond to the diverse needs of elderly citizens residing in the state. *(Added by Stats 1987 ch 1462 §3.)*

§13823.20. Foot patrols in drug crime areas; demonstration project.

(a) The Office of Criminal Justice Planning shall establish a demonstration project in the City of Los Angeles for the purpose of creating police foot patrols in high intensity drug-related crime areas. Funds for these demonstration projects shall be allocated to the City of Los Angeles no later than 30 days following enactment of this section.

(b) The office also shall issue a request for proposal to select at least three additional cities for police foot patrol demonstration projects. Funds for this request for proposal shall be awarded no later than 90 days following enactment of this section.

(c) The police department in each city shall identify targeted areas for foot patrols based on high incidence of crime related to drug trafficking and other drug crimes. At a minimum, the Los Angeles Police Department shall target areas in south Los Angeles, central Los Angeles, east Los Angeles, and the San Fernando Valley.

(d) The Office of Criminal Justice Planning shall conduct an evaluation of the foot patrol programs created by this section and shall submit a report to the Legislature no later than August 31, 1991.

(e) The evaluation shall examine the effectiveness of the program relative to the following objectives:

(1) Each city shall demonstrate empirically that areas targeted for foot patrols have a high incidence of drug-related crimes.

(2) Officers are deployed to the targeted areas at least 20 percent of the time of each week.

(3) Against a baseline period established by the city police department, the following reductions occur in the aggregate for the targeted areas during the pilot period:

(A) An 8 percent reduction in radio calls.

(B) A 6 percent reduction in repressible crime.

(C) A 12 percent reduction in violent crime.

(4) Each city shall demonstrate whether changes in the incidence of drug-related crimes in areas adjacent to the targeted areas are appreciable and the extent to which those changes may be caused by increased foot patrol activity in the targeted areas. *(Added by Stats 1990 ch 1320 §2, eff. 9/25/90.)*

§13823.3. Funds for local domestic violence programs.

The office may expend funds for local domestic violence programs, subject to the availability of funds therefor.

§13823.4. Family Violence Prevention Program.

(a) The Legislature finds the problem of family violence to be of serious and increasing magnitude. The Legislature also finds that acts of family violence often result in other crimes and social problems.

(b) There is in the Office of Criminal Justice Planning, a Family Violence Prevention Program. This program shall provide financial and technical assistance to local domestic and family violence centers in implementing family violence prevention programs.

The goals and functions of the program shall include all of the following:

(1) Promotion of community involvement through public education geared specifically toward reaching and educating the friends and neighbors of members of violent families.

(2) Development and dissemination of model protocols for the training of criminal justice system personnel in domestic violence intervention and prevention.

(3) Increasing citizen involvement in family violence prevention.

(4) Identification and testing of family violence prevention models.

(5) Replication of successful models, as appropriate, through the state.

(6) Identification and testing of domestic violence model protocols and intervention systems in major service delivery institutions.

(7) Development of informational materials and seminars to enable emulation or adaptation of the models by other communities.

(8) Provision of domestic violence prevention education and skills to students in schools.

(c) The executive director shall allocate funds to local centers meeting the criteria for funding that shall be established by the Office of Criminal Justice Planning in consultation with practitioners and experts in the field of family violence prevention. All centers receiving funds pursuant to this section shall have had an ongoing recognized program, supported by either public or private funds, dealing with an aspect of family violence, for at least two years prior to the date specified for submission of applications for funding pursuant to this section. All centers funded pursuant to this section shall utilize volunteers to the greatest extent possible.

The centers may seek, receive, and make use of any funds which may be available from all public and private sources to augment any state funds received pursuant to this section. Sixty percent of the state funds received pursuant to this section shall be used to develop and implement model program protocols and materials. Forty percent of the state funds received pursuant to this section shall be allocated to programs to disseminate model program protocols and materials. Dissemination shall include training for domestic violence agencies in California. Each of the programs funded under this section shall focus on no more than two targeted areas. These targeted model areas shall be determined by the Office of Criminal Justice Planning in consultation with practitioners and experts in the field of domestic violence, using the domestic violence model priorities survey of the California Alliance Against Domestic Violence.

Centers receiving funding shall provide matching funds of at least 10 percent of the funds received pursuant to this section.

(d) The Office of Criminal Justice Planning shall develop and disseminate throughout the state information and materials concerning family violence prevention, including, but not limited to, a procedures manual on prevention models. The office shall also establish a resource center for the collection, retention, and distribution of educational materials related to family violence and its prevention. *(Amended by Stats 1988 ch 1371 §3, eff. 1/1/89.)*

§13823.5. Collection of evidence from sexual assault victims.

(a) The Office of Criminal Justice Planning, with the assistance of the advisory committee established pursuant to Section 13836, shall establish a protocol for the examination and treatment of victims of sexual assault and attempted sexual assault, including child molestation, and the collection and preservation of evidence therefrom. The protocol shall contain recommended methods for meeting the standards specified in Section 13823.11.

(b) In addition to the protocol, the office shall develop informational guidelines, containing general reference information on evidence collection, examination of victims and psychological and medical treatment for victims of sexual assault and attempted sexual assault, including child molestation.

In developing the protocol and the informational guidelines, the office and the advisory committee shall seek the assistance and guidance of organizations assisting victims of sexual assault; qualified health care professionals, criminalists, and administrators who are familiar with emergency room procedures; victims of sexual assault; and law enforcement officials.

(c) The office, in cooperation with the State Department of Health Services and the Department of Justice, shall adopt a standard and a complete form or forms for the recording of medical and physical evidence data disclosed by a victim of sexual assault or attempted sexual assault, including child molestation.

Each qualified health care professional who conducts an examination for evidence of a sexual assault or an attempted sexual assault, including child molestation, shall use the standard form adopted pursuant to this section, and shall make such observations and perform such tests as may be required for recording of the data required by the form. The forms shall be subject to the same principles of confidentiality applicable to other medical records.

The office shall make copies of the standard form or forms available to every public or private general acute care hospital, as requested.

The standard form shall be used to satisfy the reporting requirements specified in Sections 11160 and 11161 in cases of sexual assault, and may be used in lieu of the form specified in Section 11168 for reports of child abuse.

(d) The office shall distribute copies of the protocol and the informational guidelines to every general acute care hospital, law enforcement agency, and prosecutor's office in the state.

(e) As used in this chapter, "qualified health care professional" means a physician and surgeon currently licensed pursuant to Chapter 5 (commencing with Section 2000) of Division 2 of the Business and Professions Code, or a nurse currently licensed pursuant to Chapter 6 (commencing with Section 2700) of Division 2 of the Business and Professions Code and working in consultation with a physician and surgeon who conducts examinations or provides treatment as described in Section 13823.9 in a general acute care hospital or in a physician and surgeon's office. *(Amended by Stats 1988 ch 1575 §3, eff. 1/1/89.)*

§13823.6. *Amended and renumbered §13826.25 by Stats 1988 ch 1575 §4, eff. 1/1/89.*

§13823.7. Examination and treatment of victims of sexual assault or attempted sexual assault.

The protocol adopted pursuant to Section 13823.5 for the examination and treatment of victims of sexual assault or attempted sexual assault, including child molestation, and the collection and preservation of evidence therefrom shall include provisions for all of the following:

(a) Notification of injuries and a report of suspected child sexual abuse to law enforcement authorities.

(b) Obtaining consent for the examination, for the treatment of injuries, for the collection of evidence, and for the photographing of injuries.

(c) Taking a patient history of sexual assault and other relevant medical history.

(d) Performance of the physical examination for evidence of sexual assault.

(e) Collection of physical evidence of assault.

(f) Collection of other medical specimens.

(g) Procedures for the preservation and disposition of physical evidence. *(Added by Stats 1985 ch 812 §6.)*

§13823.9. Hospital examination of victims of sexual assault or attempted sexual assault.

(a) Every public or private general acute care hospital that examines a victim of sexual assault or attempted sexual assault, including child molestation, shall comply with the standards specified in Section 13823.11 and the protocol and guidelines adopted pursuant to Section 13823.5.

(b) Each county with a population of more than 100,000 shall arrange that professional personnel trained in the examination of victims of sexual assault, including child molestation, shall be present or on call either in the county hospital which provides emergency medical services or in any general acute care hospital which has contracted with the county to provide emergency medical services. In counties with a population of 1,000,000 or more, the presence of these professional personnel shall be arranged at least one general acute care hospital for each 1,000,000 persons in the county.

(c) Each county shall designate at least one general acute care hospital to perform examinations on victims of sexual assault, including child molestation.

(d)(1) The protocol published by the Office of Criminal Justice Planning shall be used as a guide for the procedures to be used by every public or private general acute care hospital in the state for the examination and treatment of victims of sexual assault and attempted sexual assault, including child molestation, and the collection and preservation of evidence therefrom.

(2) The informational guide developed by the Office of Criminal Justice Planning shall be consulted where indicated in the protocol, as well as to gain knowledge about all aspects of examination and treatment of victims of sexual assault and child molestation. *(Added by Stats 1985 ch 812 §7.)*

§13823.95. Victim not to be charged for costs.

No costs incurred by a qualified health care professional, hospital, or other emergency medical facility for the examination of the victim of a sexual assault,

© 1992 by J., B. & L. Gould
Printed in the U.S.A.   EP

as described in the protocol developed pursuant to Section 13823.5, when the examination is performed, pursuant to Sections 13823.5 and 13823.7, for the purposes of gathering evidence for possible prosecution, shall be charged directly or indirectly to the victim of the assault. Those costs shall be treated as local costs and charged to the local governmental agency in whose jurisdiction the alleged offense was committed.

Bills for these costs shall be submitted to the law enforcement agency in the jurisdiction in which the alleged offense was committed which requests the examination.

The law enforcement agency in the jurisdiction in which the alleged offense was committed which requests the examination has the option of determining whether or not the examination will be performed in the office of a physician and surgeon. *(Amended by Stats 1991 ch 824 §1, eff. 1/1/92.)*

§13823.11. Standards for treatment of sexual assault victims.

The minimum standards for the examination and treatment of victims of sexual assault or attempted sexual assault, including child molestation and the collection and preservation of evidence therefrom include all of the following:

(a) Law enforcement authorities shall be notified.

(b) In conducting the physical examination, the outline indicated in the form adopted pursuant to subdivision (c) of Section 13823.5 shall be followed.

(c) Consent for a physical examination, treatment, and collection of evidence shall be obtained.

(1) Consent to an examination for evidence of sexual assault shall be obtained prior to the examination of a victim of sexual assault and shall include separate written documentation of consent to each of the following:

(A) Examination for the presence of injuries sustained as a result of the assault.

(B) Examination for evidence of sexual assault and collection of physical evidence.

(C) Photographs of injuries.

(2) Consent to treatment shall be obtained in accordance with usual hospital policy.

(3) A victim of sexual assault shall be informed that he or she may refuse to consent to an examination for evidence of sexual assault, including the collection of physical evidence, but that such a refusal is not a ground for denial of treatment of injuries and for possible pregnancy and venereal disease, if the person wishes to obtain treatment and consents thereto.

(4) Pursuant to Section 34.9 of the Civil Code, a minor may consent to hospital, medical, and surgical care related to a sexual assault without the consent of a parent or guardian.

(5) In cases of known or suspected child abuse, the consent of the parents or legal guardian is not required. In the case of suspected-child abuse and non-consenting parents, the consent of the local agency providing child protective services or the local law enforcement agency shall be obtained. Local procedures regarding obtaining consent for the examination and treatment of, and the collection of evidence from, children from child protective authorities shall be followed.

(d) A history of sexual assault shall be taken.

The history obtained in conjunction with the examination for evidence of sexual assault shall follow the outline of the form established pursuant to subdivision (c) of Section 13823.5 and shall include all of the following:

(1) A history of the circumstances of the assault.

(2) For a child, any previous history of child sexual abuse and an explanation of injuries, if different from that given by parent or person accompanying the child.

(3) Physical injuries reported.

(4) Sexual acts reported, whether or not ejaculation is suspected, and whether or not a condom or lubricant was used.

(5) Record of relevant medical history.

(e) Each adult and minor victim of sexual assault who consents to a medical examination for collection of evidentiary material shall have a physical examination which includes, but is not limited to, all of the following:

(1) Inspection of the clothing, body, and external genitalia for injuries and foreign materials.

(2) Examination of the mouth, vagina, cervix, penis, anus, and rectum, as indicated.

(3) Documentation of injuries and evidence collected.

Prepubital children shall not have internal vaginal or anal examinations unless absolutely necessary (this does not preclude careful collection of evidence using a swab).

(f) The collection of physical evidence shall conform to the following procedures:

(1) Each victim of sexual assault who consents to an examination for collection of evidence shall have the following items of evidence collected, except where he or she specifically objects:

(A) Clothing worn during assault.

(B) Foreign materials revealed by an examination of the clothing, body, external genitalia, and pubic hair combings.

(C) Swabs and slides from the mouth, vagina, rectum, and penis, as indicated, to determine the presence or absence of sperm and sperm motility, and for genetic marker typing.

(2) Each victim of sexual assault who consents to an examination for the collection of evidence shall have reference specimens taken, except when he or she specifically objects thereto. A reference specimen is a standard from which to obtain baseline information (for example pubic and head hair, blood, and saliva for genetic marker typing). These specimens shall be taken in accordance with the standards of the local criminalistics laboratory.

(3) A baseline gonorrhea culture, and syphilis serology, shall be taken, if indicated by the history of contact. Specimens for a pregnancy test shall be taken, if indicated by the history of contact.

(g) Preservation and disposition of physical evidence shall conform to the following procedures:

(1) All swabs and slides shall be air dried prior to packaging.

(2) All items of evidence including laboratory specimens shall be clearly labeled as to the identity of the source and the identity of the person collecting them.

(3) The evidence shall have a form attached which documents its chain of custody and shall be properly sealed.

(4) The evidence shall be turned over to the proper law enforcement agency. *(Added by Stats 1985 ch 812 §8.)*

§13823.12. Failure to comply.

Failure to comply fully with Section 13823.11 or with the protocol or guidelines, or to utilize the form established by the Office of Criminal Justice Planning pursuant to Section 13823.5, shall not constitute grounds to exclude evidence, nor shall the court instruct or comment to the trier of fact in any case that less weight may be given to the evidence based on the failure to comply. *(Added by Stats 1988 ch 1575 §5, eff. 1/1/89.)*

§13823.13. Treatment of sexual assault victims.

(a) The Office of Criminal Justice Planning shall develop a course of training for qualified health care professionals relating to the examination and treatment of victims of sexual assault. In developing the curriculum for the course, the Office of Criminal Justice Planning shall consult with health care professionals and appropriate law enforcement agencies. The Office of Criminal Justice Planning shall also obtain recommendations from the same health care professionals and appropriate law enforcement agencies on the best means to disseminate the course of training on a statewide basis.

(b) The training course developed pursuant to subdivision (a) shall be designed to train qualified health care professionals to do all of the following:

(1) Perform a health assessment of victims of sexual assault in accordance with any applicable minimum standards set forth in Section 13823.11.

(2) Collect and document physical and laboratory evidence in accordance with any applicable minimum standards set forth in Section 13823.11.

(3) Provide information and referrals to victims of sexual assault to enhance the continuity of care of victims.

(4) Present testimony in court.

(c) As used in this section, "qualified health care professional" means a physician and surgeon currently licensed pursuant to Chapter 5 (commencing with Section 2000) of Division 2 of the Business and Professions Code, or a nurse currently licensed pursuant to Chapter 6 (commencing with Section 2700) of Division 2 of the Business and Professions Code who works in consultation with a physician and surgeon or who conducts examinations described in Section 13823.9 in a general acute care hospital or in the office of a physician and surgeon.

(d) As used in this section, "appropriate law enforcement agencies" may include, but shall not be limited to, the Attorney General of the State of California, any district attorney, and any agency of the State of California expressly authorized by statute to investigate or prosecute law violators. *(Added by Stats 1989 ch 1210 §1, eff. 1/1/90.)*

§13823.15. Domestic violence.

(a) The Legislature finds the problem of domestic violence to be of serious and increasing magnitude. The Legislature also finds that existing domestic violence services are underfunded and that some areas of the state are unserved.

(b) There is in the Office of Criminal Justice Planning, a Comprehensive Statewide Domestic Violence Program. The goals of the program shall be to provide local assistance to existing service providers, to maintain and expand services based on a demonstrated need, and to establish a targeted or directed program for the development and establishment of domestic

violence services in currently unserved and underserved areas. The program shall provide financial and technical assistance to local domestic violence centers in implementing all of the following services:

(1) Twenty-four-hour crisis hotlines.

(2) Counseling.

(3) Business centers.

(4) Emergency "safe" homes or shelters for victims and families.

(5) Emergency food and clothing.

(6) Emergency response to calls from law enforcement.

(7) Hospital emergency room protocol and assistance.

(8) Emergency transportation.

(9) Supportive peer counseling.

(10) Counseling for children.

(11) Court and social service advocacy.

(12) Legal assistance with temporary restraining orders, devices, and custody disputes.

(13) Community resource and referral.

(14) Household establishment assistance.

Priority for financial and technical assistance shall be given to emergency shelter programs and "safe" homes for victims of domestic violence and their children.

(c) The Executive Director of the Office of Criminal Justice Planning shall allocate funds to local centers meeting the criteria for funding that shall be established by the office in consultation with practitioners and experts in the field of domestic violence. All organizations funded pursuant to this section shall utilize volunteers to the greatest extent possible.

The centers may seek, receive, and make use of any funds which may be available from all public and private sources to augment any state funds received pursuant to this section.

Centers receiving funding shall provide cash or an in-kind match of at least 10 percent of the funds received pursuant to this section.

(d) The Office of Criminal Justice Planning shall conduct statewide training workshops on domestic violence for local centers, law enforcement, and other service providers designed to enhance service programs. The workshops shall be planned in conjunction with practitioners and experts in the field of domestic violence prevention.

(e) The Office of Criminal Justice Planning shall develop and disseminate throughout the state information and materials concerning domestic violence. The office shall also establish a resource center for the collection, retention, and distribution of educational materials related to domestic violence. The office may utilize and contract with existing domestic violence technical assistance centers in this state in complying with the requirements of this subdivision.

(f) The Office of Criminal Justice Planning may hire the support staff and utilize all resources necessary to carry out the purposes of this section. The office shall not utilize more than 10 percent of any funds appropriated for the purpose of the program established by this section for the administration of that program. *(Added by Stats 1985 ch 705 §1.)*

§13824. Projects eligible for council funds; publication.

A brief description of all projects eligible for a commitment of council funds shall be made available to the public through a publication of the council

© 1992 by J., B. & L. Gould
Printed in the U.S.A.   EP

having statewide circulation at least 30 days in advance of the meeting at which funds for such project can be committed by vote of the council.

§13825. *Repealed by Stats 1988 ch 1247 §1, eff. 1/1/91.*

CHAPTER 3.5

GANG VIOLENCE SUPPRESSION

§13826. Legislative findings.

The Legislature finds and declares all of the following:

(a) That violent activity by gangs is a serious and growing problem in the State of California.

(b) There is an increasing percentage of school age pupils involved in gang activity.

(c) There are many schools that serve a disproportionate number of youth involved in gang activity which are unable to effectively implement programs designed to prevent youth from becoming involved in gang activity. There is no statewide funded educational program developed for this purpose.

(d) There is evidence that gang involvement among youth begins at an early age.

(e) There is evidence that the parents of gang members lack appropriate parenting skills.

(f) There is evidence that drug activity is increasing among youth involved in gang activity.

(g) There is evidence that gang members have no contact with positive role models.

(h) There is evidence that most gang members lack basic educational skills.

In enacting this chapter, the Legislature intends to support increased efforts by district attorneys' offices to prosecute the perpetrators of gang violence, support increased efforts by local law enforcement agencies to identify, investigate, and apprehend perpetrators of gang violence, support increased efforts by county probation departments to intensively supervise gang members who are on court-ordered probation, support gang violence prevention and intervention efforts by school districts and county offices of education, and support gang violence suppression efforts by community-based organizations. *(Added by Stats 1986 ch 929 §2.)*

§13826.1. Creation of Gang Violence Suppression Program.

(a) There is hereby established in the Office of Criminal Justice Planning, the Gang Violence Suppression Program, a program of financial and technical assistance for district attorneys' offices, local law enforcement agencies, county probation departments, school districts, county offices of education, or any consortium thereof, and community-based organizations which are primarily engaged in the suppression of gang violence. All funds appropriated to the Office of Criminal Justice Planning for the purposes of this chapter shall be administered and disbursed by the executive director of the office in consultation with the California Council on Criminal Justice, and shall to the greatest extent feasible be coordinated or consolidated with federal funds that may be made available for these purposes.

(b) The executive director is authorized to allocate and award funds to cities, counties, school districts, county offices of education, or any consortium thereof,

and community-based organizations in which gang violence suppression programs are established in substantial compliance with the policies and criteria set forth in this chapter.

(c) The allocation and award of funds shall be made on the application of the district attorney, chief law enforcement officer or chief probation officer of the applicant unit of government and approved by the legislative body, on the application of school districts, county offices of education, or any consortium thereof, or on the application of the chief executive of a community-based organization. All programs funded pursuant to this chapter shall work cooperatively to ensure the highest quality provision of services and to reduce unnecessary duplication. Funds disbursed under this chapter shall not supplant local funds that would, in the absence of the Gang Violence Suppression Program, be made available to support the activities set forth in this chapter. Funds awarded under this program as local assistance grants shall not be subject to review as specified in Section 14780 of the Government Code.

(d) The executive director shall prepare and issue written program and administrative guidelines and procedures for the Gang Violence Suppression Program, consistent with this chapter. These guidelines shall set forth the terms and conditions upon which the Office of Criminal Justice Planning is prepared to offer grants of funds pursuant to statutory authority. The guidelines do not constitute rules, regulations, orders, or standards of general application.

(e) Annually, commencing November 1, 1984, the executive director shall prepare a report to the Legislature describing in detail the operation of the statewide program and the results obtained by district attorneys' offices, local law enforcement agencies, county probation departments, school districts, county offices of education, or any consortium thereof, and community-based organizations receiving funds under this chapter and under comparable federally financed awards.

(f) Criteria for selection of district attorneys' offices, local law enforcement agencies, county probation departments, school districts, county offices of education, or any consortium thereof, and community-based organizations to receive gang violence suppression funding shall be developed in consultation with the Gang Violence Suppression Advisory Committee whose members shall be appointed by the Executive Director of the Office of Criminal Justice Planning, unless otherwise designated.

(g) The Gang Violence Suppression Advisory Committee shall be composed of five district attorneys; two chief probation officers; two representatives of community-based organizations; three attorneys primarily engaged in the practice of juvenile criminal defense; three law enforcement officials with expertise in gang-related investigations; one member from the California Youth Authority Gang Task Force nominated by the Director of the California Youth Authority; one member of the Department of Corrections Law Enforcement Liaison Unit nominated by the Director of the Department of Corrections; one member from the Department of Justice nominated by the Attorney General; one member from the Employment Development Department nominated by the Director of the Employment Development Department; one member from the State Department of Social Services nominated by the Director of the State Department of

Social Services; the Superintendent of Public Instruction, or his or her designee; one member of the California School Boards Association; and one representative of a school program specializing in the education of the target population identified in this chapter.

(1) The Gang Violence Suppression Advisory Committee shall assist in the coordination and review of gang prevention, intervention, and suppression programs on a state level. The executive director shall convene the Gang Violence Suppression Advisory Committee as deemed necessary by the committee to perform its duties and responsibilities under this section.

(2) The executive director shall prepare an annual report to the Legislature describing in detail the coordination of the programs described in paragraph (1) administered by state boards and departments and submit recommendations to the Legislature and the Governor regarding statutory strategies for the improvement of those programs. This report, with the recommendations, may be incorporated into the annual report specified in subdivision (e).

(h) This section shall remain operative only until January 1, 1994, and as of that date is repealed unless a later enacted statute, which is enacted before January 1, 1994, deletes or extends that date. *(Amended by Stats 1989 ch 1344 §1, eff. 1/1/90 only until 1/1/94. See other section 13826.1 below.)*

§13826.1. Creation of Gang Violence Suppression Program.

(a) There is hereby established in the Office of Criminal Justice Planning, the Gang Violence Suppression Program, a program of financial and technical assistance for district attorneys' offices, local law enforcement agencies, county probation departments, school districts, county offices of education, or any consortium thereof, and community-based organizations which are primarily engaged in the suppression of gang violence. All funds appropriated to the Office of Criminal Justice Planning for the purposes of this chapter shall be administered and disbursed by the executive director of the office in consultation with the California Council on Criminal Justice, and shall to the greatest extent feasible be coordinated or consolidated with federal funds that may be made available for these purposes.

(b) The executive director is authorized to allocate and award funds to cities, counties, school districts, county offices of education, or any consortium thereof, and community-based organizations in which gang violence suppression programs are established in substantial compliance with the policies and criteria set forth in this chapter.

(c) The allocation and award of funds shall be made on the application of the district attorney, chief law enforcement officer or chief probation officer of the applicant unit of government and approved by the legislative body, on the application of school districts, county offices of education, or any consortium thereof, or on the application of the chief executive of a community-based organization. All programs funded pursuant to this chapter shall work cooperatively to ensure the highest quality provision of services and to reduce unnecessary duplication. Funds disbursed under this chapter shall not supplant local funds that would, in the absence of the Gang Violence Suppression Program, be made available to support the activities set forth in this chapter. Funds awarded under

this program as local assistance grants shall not be subject to review as specified in Section 14780 of the Government Code.

(d) The executive director shall prepare and issue written program and administrative guidelines and procedures for the Gang Violence Suppression Program, consistent with this chapter. These guidelines shall set forth the terms and conditions upon which the Office of Criminal Justice Planning is prepared to offer grants of funds pursuant to statutory authority. The guidelines do not constitute rules, regulations, orders, or standards of general application.

(e) Annually, commencing November 1, 1984, the executive director shall prepare a report to the Legislature describing in detail the operation of the statewide program and the results obtained by district attorneys' offices, local law enforcement agencies, county probation departments, school districts, county offices of education, or any consortium thereof, and community-based organizations receiving funds under this chapter and under comparable federally financed awards.

(f) Criteria for selection of district attorneys' offices, local law enforcement agencies, county probation departments, school districts, county offices of education, or any consortium thereof, and community-based organizations to receive gang violence suppression funding shall be developed in consultation with the Gang Violence Suppression Advisory Committee whose members shall be appointed by the Executive Director of the Office of Criminal Justice Planning, unless otherwise designated.

(g) The Gang Violence Suppression Advisory Committee shall be composed of five district attorneys; two chief probation officers; two representatives of community-based organizations; three attorneys primarily engaged in the practice of juvenile criminal defense; three law enforcement officials with expertise in gang-related investigations; one member from the California Youth Authority Gang Task Force nominated by the Director of the California Youth Authority; one member of the Department of Corrections Law Enforcement Liaison Unit nominated by the Director of the Department of Corrections; one member from the Department of Justice nominated by the Attorney General; the Superintendent of Public Instruction, or his or her designee; one member of the California School Boards Association; and one representative of a school program specializing in the education of the target population identified in this chapter.

(h) This section shall be operative January 1, 1994. *(Added by Stats 1989 ch 1344 §1, oper. 1/1/94. See other section 13826.1 above.)*

§13826.11. Legislative findings: After School Alternative Program.

(a)* The Legislature hereby finds and declares the following:

(1) There is a greater threat to public safety resulting from gang- and drug-related activity in and near California's inner cities.

(2) Young people, especially at-risk youth, are more vulnerable to gang- and drug-related activity during the potentially unsupervised hours between the end of school and the time their parents or guardians return home from work.

(3) Without local prevention and treatment efforts, hard drugs will continue to threaten and destroy families and communities in and near the inner cities.

© 1992 by J., B. & L. Gould
Printed in the U.S.A.　EP

Drug-related violence may then escalate dramatically in every community, and thereby burden the criminal justice system to the point that it cannot function effectively.

(4) Los Angeles currently leads the nation in the number of gang members and gang sites, the consumption of drugs, the amount of drugs confiscated, drug-related violent crimes, and has the greatest number of young people between 6 and 18 years of age who are "at risk."

(5) It is the intent of the Legislature that a pilot program, the "After School Alternative Program" (ASAP), be established and implemented within a specified Los Angeles community. This community program would utilize the public schools, businesses, and community facilities to provide supportive programs and activities to young people during the time between the end of school and the return home of their parents or guardians (from approximately 3 p.m. to 7 p.m.). *(Added by Stats 1990 ch 1625 §1, eff. 1/1/91.)*
*So in original. No subd. (b) has been enacted.

§13826.12. After School Alternative Program.

(a) There is hereby created within the Office of Criminal Justice Planning, a pilot program known as "After School Alternative Program" (ASAP). The establishment of the pilot program pursuant to this section shall be contingent upon the availability and receipt of federal funding for this purpose. The goal of the pilot program shall be to reduce gang activity and drug-related crime in and near the targeted schools, businesses, and community sites. This shall be accomplished by coordinating the efforts of community-based organizations, public schools, law enforcement officials, parents, and business leaders in participating communities to prevent the illicit activities of current and potential gang members and drug users by making alternative activities available. These activities may be provided at school or community sites, and may include:

(1) Recreational, arts, crafts, or academic tutorial programs.

(2) Job counseling and training, with the participation of community business representatives.

(3) Presentations by law enforcement officials, and informal get-togethers.

(4) Group and individual (as needed) drug and/or gang counseling.

(5) Community awareness presentations.

(b) A Los Angeles community may elect to participate in the pilot project established pursuant to subdivision (a) by establishing and operating an ASAP program. The community may be any designated area that contains up to two public high schools and feeder schools, as well as having active business enterprises and a viable local community-based organization. The project shall operate for a two-year period commencing on July 1, 1991. The project shall implement a program model to be developed by the Office of Criminal Justice Planning, in cooperation with local community-based organizations, school districts, and law enforcement agencies.

(c) Each city, or city and county, that participates in the ASAP pilot project shall submit a report to the Legislature regarding the operation of its pilot program in the 1991-92 fiscal year no later than June 30, 1992, and in the 1992-93 fiscal year no later than June 30, 1993.

(d) This section shall remain operative only until June 30, 1993, and as of that date is repealed unless a later enacted statute, which is enacted before June 30, 1993, deletes or extends that date. *(Added by Stats 1990 ch 1625 §2, eff. 1/1/91 only until 6/30/93.)*

§13826.15. Gang Violence Suppression Program: priority of funding.

(a) The Legislature hereby finds and declares that the implementation of the Gang Violence Suppression Program, as provided in this chapter, has made a positive impact in the battle against crimes committed by gang members in California.

The Legislature further finds and declares that the program, when it was originally created in 1981, provided financial and technical assistance only for district attorneys' offices. Since that time, however, the provisions of the program have been amended by the Legislature to enable additional public entities and community-based organizations to participate in the program. In this respect, the Office of Criminal Justice Planning, pursuant to Section 13826.1, administers funding for the program by awarding grants to worthy applicants. Therefore, it is the intent of the Legislature in enacting this measure to assist the Office of Criminal Justice Planning in setting forth guidelines for this funding.

(b) The Office of Criminal Justice Planning may give priority to applicants for new grant awards, as follows:

(1) First priority may be given to applicants representing unfunded single components, as specified in Sections 13826.2, 13826.4, 13826.5, 13826.6, and 13826.65, in those counties that receive Gang Violence Suppression Program funding for some, but not all, of the program's components. The purpose of establishing this priority is to provide funding for a full complement of the five Gang Violence Suppression Program components in those counties that have less than all five components established.

(2) Second priority may be given to those applicants that propose a multiagency, or multijurisdictional single component project, whereby more than one agency would be funded as a joint project under the single components specified in Sections 13826.2, 13826.4, 13826.5, 13826.6, and 13826.65, and the funding would be provided through a single grant award.

(3) Third priority may be given to applicants that propose multijurisdictional multicomponent projects, whereby all five Gang Violence Suppression Program components, as specified in Sections 13826.2, 13826.4, 13826.5, 13826.6, and 13826.65, would be funded in a county that does not currently receive Gang Violence Suppression Program funds.

(4) Fourth priority may be given to those single agency single component applicants, in counties wherein the program component is not currently funded. *(Added by Stats 1990 ch 280 §1, eff. 1/1/91.)*

§13826.2. Enhanced prosecution efforts and resources.

Gang violence prosecution units receiving funds under this chapter shall concentrate enhanced prosecution efforts and resources upon cases identified under criteria set forth in Section 13826.3. Enhanced prosecution efforts shall include, but not be limited to:

(a) "Vertical" prosecutorial representation, whereby the prosecutor who makes the initial filing or appearance in a gang-related case will perform all subsequent court appearances on that particular case through its conclusion, including the sentencing phase.

(b) Assignment of highly qualified investigators and prosecutors to gang-related cases.

(c) Significant reduction of caseloads for investigators and prosecutors assigned to gang-related cases.

(d) Measures taken in coordination with law enforcement agencies to protect cooperating witnesses from intimidation or retribution at the hands of gang members or associates.

§13826.25. Training for prosecutors in gang-related subjects.

The Office of Criminal Justice Planning through its programs established under Title 1.5 (commencing with Section 11500) shall provide special training for prosecutors in the areas of gang violence, vertical prosecution, gang identification, and witness intimidation.

This section shall become inoperative on July 1, 1993, unless a later enacted statute which becomes effective on or before July 1, 1993, deletes or extends that date. This section shall remain in effect only until January 1, 1994, and on that date is repealed unless a later enacted statute which becomes effective on or before January 1, 1994, deletes or extends that date. *(Amended by Stats 1989 ch 1344 §3, eff. 1/1/90 only until 1/1/94.)*

§13826.3. Individuals who are subject to gang violence prosecution efforts.

(a) An individual shall be subject to gang violence prosecution efforts who is under arrest for the commission or the attempted commission of any gang-related violent crime where the individual is (1) a known member of a gang, and (2) has exhibited a prior criminal background.

(b) For purposes of this chapter, gang-related means that the suspect or victim of the crime is a known member of a gang.

(c) For purposes of this chapter, gang violence prosecution includes both criminal prosecutions and proceedings in Juvenile Court in which a petition is filed pursuant to Section 602 of the Welfare and Institutions Code.

§13826.4. Enhanced law enforcement efforts and resources.

Law enforcement agencies receiving funds under this chapter shall concentrate enhanced law enforcement efforts and resources upon cases identified under criteria set forth in Section 13826.3. Enhanced law enforcement criteria efforts shall include, but not be limited to:

(a) The formation of a specialized gang violence unit whose staff shall be composed of the most highly qualified and trained personnel.

(b) The efforts of the gang violence unit shall include, but not be limited to:

(1) Increased efforts to apprehend, prosecute, and convict violent "hard core" target gang members.

(2) Increasing the clearance rate of reported crimes which are targeted as gang related.

(3) Establishing more positive relations with, and encouraging the support of local citizens, community-based organizations, business representatives, and other criminal agencies.

(4) Aiding and assisting other criminal justice and governmental agencies in protecting cooperating witnesses from intimidation or retribution at the hands of gang members and their associates.

(c) Law enforcement agencies receiving funds under this program shall maintain a crime analysis capability which provides the following type of information:

(1) Identification of active gang members who have exhibited a prior criminal background.

(2) Identification of evolving or existing crime patterns that are gang related.

(3) Providing investigative leads.

(4) Maintaining statistical information pertaining to gang related criminal activity.

§13826.5. Implementing county probation department activities.

County probation departments receiving funding under this chapter shall strictly enforce court-ordered conditions of probation for gang members.

(a) County probation departments supported under the Gang Violence Suppression Program shall implement the following activities:

(1) A Gang Violence Intensive Supervision Unit dealing with gang members shall be established.

(2) Criteria used to determine which probationer shall be assigned to the Gang Violence Intensive Supervision Unit shall be approved by the district attorney having a Gang Violence Prosecution Unit described in Section 13826.2.

(3) Probationers whose cases are assigned to the intensive supervision unit shall be informed of what types of behavior are prescribed or forbidden. The notice shall be provided in both oral and written form.

(4) Probationers whose cases are assigned to the intensive supervision unit shall be informed, in writing, that all court-ordered conditions of probation will be strictly enforced.

(5) Deputy probation officers in the intensive supervision unit shall have reduced probationer caseloads and shall coordinate their supervision efforts with law enforcement and prosecution personnel. The coordination shall include informing law enforcement and prosecution personnel of the conditions set for probationers and of the strict enforcement procedures to be implemented.

(6) Deputy probation officers in the intensive supervision unit shall coordinate with the district attorney in ensuring that court-ordered conditions of probation are consistently enforced.

(7) Intensive supervision unit deputy probation officers shall coordinate, whenever feasible, with community-based organizations in seeking to ensure that probationers adhere to their court-ordered conditions.

(b) County probation departments may implement the California TEAM (Together Each Achieves More) Sports Camp Program, as described in Article 23.5 (commencing with Section 875) of Chapter 2 of Part 1 of Division 2 of the Welfare and Institutions Code. *(Amended by Stats 1989 ch 1360 §124, eff. 1/1/90.)*

§13826.6. Implementing community-based organizations activities.

For purposes of this chapter, a "community-based" organization is defined as a nonprofit operation established to serve gang members, their families, schools,

© 1992 by J., B. & L. Gould
Printed in the U.S.A.   EP

and the community with programs of community supervision and service which maintain community participation in the planning, operation and evaluation of their programs.

(a) Unless funded pursuant to subdivision (c), community-based organizations supported under the Gang Violence Suppression program shall implement the following activities:

(1) Providing information to law enforcement agencies concerning gang related activities in the community.

(2) Providing information to school administrators and staff concerning gang related activities in the community.

(3) Provide conflict resolution by means of intervention or mediation to prevent and limit gang crisis situations.

(4) Increase witness cooperation through coordination with local law enforcement and prosecutors and by education of the community about the roles of these government agencies and the availability of witness protection services.

(b) Community-based organizations funded pursuant to subdivision (a) shall also implement at least one of the following activities:

(1) Maintaining a 24-hour public telephone message center for the receipt of information and to assist individuals seeking services from the organization.

(2) Maintaining a "rumor control" public telephone service to provide accurate and reliable information to concerned citizens.

(3) Providing technical assistance and training concerning gang related activities to school staff members, law enforcement personnel, and community members including parental groups. This training and assistance shall include coverage of how to prevent and minimize intergang confrontations.

(4) Providing recreational activities for gang members or potential gang members.

(5) Providing job training and placement services for youth.

(6) Referring gang members, as needed, to appropriate agencies for the treatment of health, psychological, and drug-related problems.

(7) Administration of the Urban Corps Program pursuant to Section 13826.62.

(8) Mobilizing the community to share joint responsibility with local criminal justice personnel to prevent and suppress gang violence.

(c) Community-based organizations funded under the Gang Violence Suppression Program for specialized school prevention and intervention activities shall only be required to implement activities in the schools which are designed to discourage students from joining gangs and which offer or encourage students to participate in alternative programs. *(Amended by Stats 1990 ch 1625 §3, eff. 1/1/91.)*

§13826.62. Establishment of Urban Corps Program.

(a) There is hereby established in the Office of Criminal Justice Planning, the Urban Corps Program. The Urban Corps Program is established as an optional activity under Section 13826.6. Community-based organizations receiving grants to participate in the Urban Corps Program shall implement the following activities:

(1) Identification of publicly and privately administered programs in the county dealing with the suppression or prevention of criminal gang activities, or both.

(2) Maintenance of a listing of programs within the county identified as dealing with the suppression or prevention of criminal gang activities, or both.

(3) Surveying gang suppression and prevention organizations for the types of services and activities each is engaged in, and identifying needs among these organizations for resources to provide services and fulfill their activities.

(4) Recruitment of volunteers, identification of their skills, abilities and interests, and matching volunteers with the resources needs of gang prevention and suppression organizations.

(5) Establishment of an urban respite program for the purpose of preventing self-destructive activities and diverting (A) identified youth gang members, and (B) youths who are at risk of becoming gang members, for the purposes of reducing or eliminating incentives for those youths to participate in gang-related crime activities.

(b) The Urban Corps Program shall operate within the Office of Criminal Justice Planning for two years following the establishment of a contract with a community-based organization to administer the program.

(c) The Office of Criminal Justice Planning shall complete and submit a report on the Urban Corps Program to the Legislature within six months after the completion of the project. The report shall include all of the following:

(1) A master list of available community resources that are involved in the suppression or prevention of criminal gang activities, or both.

(2) A list of volunteers and private sector resources recruited.

(3) The number of volunteers trained.

(4) The number of volunteers matched with identified needs.

(5) The number of private sector resources matched with identified needs.

(6) The number of youth gang members and the number of youths who are at risk and who were referred to the urban respite program.

(7) The number of gang members and the number of youths who are at risk and who participated in the urban respite program.

(d) This section shall be implemented to the extent that funds are available to the Office of Criminal Justice Planning for this purpose. *(Added by Stats 1989 ch 791 §2, eff. 1/1/90.)*

§13826.65. Gang violence prevention curriculum.

School districts, county offices of education, or any consortium thereof, receiving funding under this chapter shall develop or adopt and implement a gang violence prevention curriculum, provide gang violence prevention and intervention services for school-aged children, and shall be encouraged to do all of the following:

(a) Establish a local steering committee comprised of representatives of each local program funded under this chapter, corporations, small businesses, and other appropriate local, county, and community organization knowledgeable in the area of youth gang violence.

(b) Develop and distribute information concerning parent education and parenting classes, including methods whereby parents may recognize youth gang involvement.

(c) Identify and utilize the resources of appropriate community-based organizations involved in the coordination of after school activities for school-aged youth.

(d) Establish contact between positive role models and youth involved in gang activity through adopt-a-youth programs and similar programs.

(e) Incorporate into gang prevention activities references to the relationship between drug abuse and gang violence.

(f) Develop partnerships between schools and businesses for the purpose of enhancing pupil achievement through such methods as tutorial services, field trips, role modeling, and other supportive services.

(g) Develop methods of assuring followup services for children receiving the initial gang violence prevention and intervention services. *(Added by Stats 1986 ch 929 §4.)*

§13826.7. Utilization of federal funds.

The Office of Criminal Justice Planning and the California Council on Criminal Justice are encouraged to utilize any federal funds that may become available for purposes of this act. This act becomes operative only if federal funds are made available for its implementation.

CHAPTER 3.7

JUVENILE SEX OFFENDERS
(Amended by Stats 1990 ch 1344 §8, eff. 9/26/90 only until 1/1/93. See other Chapter 3.7, infra.)

§13827. Juvenile Sex Offender Treatment Act.

This chapter shall he known and may be cited as the Juvenile Sex Offender Treatment Act. *(Amended by Stats 1990 ch 1344 §§1, 8, eff. 9/26/90 only until 1/1/93.)*

§13827.1. Program established.

From any funds appropriated therefor, the Office of Criminal Justice Planning shall establish a program to provide financial and technical assistance to county designated treatment programs for juvenile sex offenders declared to be wards of the juvenile court pursuant to Section 602 of the Welfare and Institutions Code, but who are not committed to the Department of the Youth Authority. The eligible counties shall be selected from among those counties submitting applications to the office requesting to be selected to participate in the program, based on a determination that the counties would be capable of establishing such a program. Capability may be demonstrated by current county efforts to provide treatment programs to juvenile sex offenders.

The programs shall terminate on July 1, 1992. *(Amended by Stats 1990 ch 1344 §§2, 8, eff. 9/26/90 only until 1/1/93.)*

§13827.2. Requirements for participation by counties.

A county that applies to participate in the program established by this chapter shall demonstrate the following in its application for participation:

(a) Identification of the need for a juvenile sex offender treatment program.

(b) Evidence that the county agency providing mental health services, the county agency providing public assistance, the district attorney, the juvenile court, the probation department, private entities, and local school districts are participating in and coordinating case referral, case management, and service delivery to the persons whom they serve. *(Amended by Stats 1990 ch 1344 §8, eff. 9/26/90 only until 1/1/93.)*

§13827.3. Required participation in treatment services.

Notwithstanding any other provision of law, in a county in which a program is established, on and after the date of the establishment of that program, any person who is adjudged to be a ward of the juvenile court pursuant to Section 602 of the Welfare and Institutions Code on the basis of the violation of Section 261, 264.1, 266, 285, 286, 288, 288a, or 289, and who is not committed to the Department of the Youth Authority, shall be ordered to participate in the treatment services provided by the program. *(Amended by Stats 1990 ch 1344 §§3, 8, eff. 9/26/90 only until 1/1/93.)*

§13827.4. Counselors assigned.

The county agency providing mental health services in a county participating in the program shall assign a counselor to any person described in Section 13827.3. Any counselor so assigned shall be qualified to treat juvenile sex offenders, as determined by the county in conjunction with the Office of Criminal Justice Planning. *(Amended by Stats 1990 ch 1344 §§4, 8, eff. 9/26/90 only until 1/1/93.)*

§13827.5. *Repealed by Stats 1990 ch 1344 §5, eff. 9/26/90.*

§13827.6. Required written report due on or before January 1, 1991.

On or before January 1, 1991, the Office of Criminal Justice Planning shall submit a written report to the Legislature containing all of the following information:

(a) The number of juveniles that participated in the program.

(b) The costs of the programs.

(c) The nature of the treatment provided to participants in the programs.

(d) The results of the treatment provided to participants in the programs, including data concerning recidivism by participants and any other nonsexually-related criminal offenses committed by participants.

(e) The results of combining intrafamily and pedophile treatment. *(Amended by Stats 1990 ch 1344 §§6, 8, eff. 9/26/90 only until 1/1/93.)*

§13827.7. Utilization of funds from public and private sources.

Counties selected to participate in the program shall utilize any funds available from public and private sources for the purposes of the program and existing treatment services prior to utilizing state funds allocated for the purposes of the program. *(Amended by Stats 1990 ch 1344 §§7, 8, eff. 9/26/90 only until 1/1/93.)*

© 1992 by J., B. & L. Gould
Printed in the U.S.A.   **EP**

CHAPTER 3.7

JUDICIAL TRAINING PROGRAMS FOR CHILD SEXUAL ABUSE CASES
(Added by Stats 1986 ch 792 §1. See other Chapter 3.7, supra.)

§13828. Victims of child sexual abuse.

The Legislature hereby finds and declares that there is a need to develop and provide training programs regarding the handling of judicial proceedings involving the victims of child sexual abuse. It is the intent of the Legislature in enacting this chapter to provide training programs which will ensure that children who are the victims of sexual abuse shall be treated with special consideration during all proceedings related to allegations of child sexual abuse, including all trials and administrative hearings. *(Added by Stats 1986 ch 792 §1.)*

§13828.1. Training program for judicial branch.

From funds appropriated for those purposes, the Judicial Council shall establish and maintain an ongoing program to provide training for the judicial branch of government relating to the handling of child sexual abuse cases. *(Added by Stats 1986 ch 792 §1.)*

§13828.2. Report on training programs.

On or before January 1, 1988, the Secretary of the Judicial Council shall submit a report to the Legislature regarding training programs on the handling of child sexual abuse cases funded and provided in the 1986-87 fiscal year in order to enable the Legislature to evaluate the costs and potential benefits of these programs. *(Added by Stats 1986 ch 792 §1.)*

CHAPTER 4

CRIMINAL JUSTICE PLANNING COMMITTEE FOR STATE JUDICIAL SYSTEM

ARTICLE 1

GENERAL PROVISIONS

§13830. Creation; Legislative findings.

There is hereby created in state government a Judicial Criminal Justice Planning Committee of seven members. The Judicial Council shall appoint the members of the committee who shall hold office at its pleasure. In this respect the Legislature finds as follows:

(a) The California court system has a constitutionally established independence under the judicial and separation of power clauses of the State Constitution.

(b) The California court system has a statewide structure created under the Constitution, state statutes and state court rules, and the Judicial Council of California is the constitutionally established state agency having responsibility for the operation of that structure.

(c) The California court system will be directly affected by the criminal justice planning that will be done under this title and by the federal grants that will be made to implement that planning.

(d) For effective planning and implementation of court projects it is essential that the executive Office of Criminal Justice Planning have the advice and assistance of a state judicial system planning committee.

§13831. Advice and assistance to Council of Criminal Justice.

The California Council on Criminal Justice may request the advice and assistance of the Judicial Criminal Justice Planning Committee in carrying out its functions under Chapter 2 of this title.

§13832. Federal funds.

The Office of Criminal Justice Planning shall consult with, and shall seek the advice of, the Judicial Criminal Justice Planning Committee in carrying out its functions under Chapter 3 of this title insofar as they affect the California court system.

In addition, any grant of federal funds made or approved by the office which is to be implemented in the California court system shall be submitted to the Judicial Criminal Justice Planning Committee for its review and recommendations before being presented to the California Council on Criminal Justice for its action.

§13833. Reimbursement for expenses of committee.

The expenses necessarily incurred by the members of the Judicial Criminal Justice Planning Committee in the performance of their duties under this title shall be paid by the Judicial Council, but it shall be reimbursed by the Office of Criminal Justice Planning to the extent that federal funds can be made available for that purpose. Staff support for the committee's activities shall be provided by the Judicial Council, but the cost of that staff support shall be reimbursed by the Office of Criminal Justice Planning to the extent that federal funds can be made available for that purpose.

§13834. Committee's report to Governor and Legislature.

The committee shall report annually, on or before December 31 of each year, to the Governor and to the Legislature on items affecting judicial system improvements.

ARTICLE 2

LOCAL ASSISTANCE CENTERS FOR VICTIMS AND WITNESSES

§13835. Legislative findings and declarations.

The Legislature finds and declares as follows:

(a) That there is a need to develop methods to reduce the trauma and insensitive treatment that victims and witnesses may experience in the wake of a crime, since all too often citizens who become involved with the criminal justice system, either as victims or witnesses to crime, are further victimized by that system.

(b) That when a crime is committed, the chief concern of criminal justice agencies has been apprehending and dealing with the criminal, and that after police leave the scene of the crime, the victim is frequently forgotten.

(c) That victims often become isolated and receive little practical advice or necessary care.

(d) That witnesses must make arrangements to appear in court regardless of their own schedules, child care responsibilities, or transportation problems, and that they often find long waits, crowded courthouse hallways, confusing circumstances and, after testifying, receive no information as to the disposition of the case.

(e) That a large number of victims and witnesses are unaware of both their rights and obligations.

(f) That although the State of California has a fund for needy victims of violent crimes, and compensation is available for medical expenses, lost income or wages, and rehabilitation costs, the application process may be difficult, complex, and time-consuming, and victims may not be aware that the compensation provisions exist.

It is, therefore, the intent of the Legislature to provide services to meet the needs of both victims and witnesses of crime through the funding of local comprehensive centers for victim and witness assistance.

§13835.2. Funding requirements.

(a) Funds appropriated from the Victim-Witness Assistance Fund shall be made available through the Office of Criminal Justice Planning to any public or private nonprofit agency for the assistance of victims and witnesses which meets all of the following requirements:

(1) It provides comprehensive services to victims and witnesses of all types of crime. It is the intent of the Legislature to make funds available only to programs which do not restrict services to victims and witnesses of a particular type of crime, and which do not restrict services to victims of crime where there is a suspect in the case.

(2) It is recognized by the board of supervisors as the major provider of comprehensive services to victims and witnesses in the county.

(3) It is selected by the board of supervisors as the agency to receive funds pursuant to this article.

(4) It assists victims of crime in the preparation, verification, and presentation of their claims to the State Board of Control for indemnification pursuant to Article 1 (commencing with Section 13959) of Part 4 of Division 3 of Title 2 of the Government Code.

(5) It cooperates with the State Board of Control in verifying the data required by Article 1 (commencing with Section 13959) of Part 4 of Division 3 of Title 2 of the Government Code.

(b) The Office of Criminal Justice Planning shall consider the following factors, together with any other circumstances it deems appropriate, in awarding funds to public or private nonprofit agencies designated as victim and witness assistance centers:

(1) The capability of the agency to provide comprehensive services as defined in this article.

(2) The stated goals and objectives of the center.

(3) The number of people to be served and the needs of the community.

(4) Evidence of community support.

(5) The organizational structure of the agency which will operate the center.

(6) The capability of the agency to provide confidentiality of records.

(c) The Office of Criminal Justice Planning shall conduct an evaluation of the activities and performance of the centers established pursuant to Chapter 1256 of the Statutes of 1977 to determine their ability to comply with the intent of this article, and shall report the findings thereon to the Legislature by January 1, 1985. *(Amended by Stats 1990 ch 1342 §4, eff. 1/1/91.)*

§13835.4. Activities.

In order to insure the effective delivery of comprehensive services to victims and witnesses, a center established by an agency receiving funds pursuant to this article shall carry out all of the following activities in connection with both primary and optional services:

(a) Translation services for non-English speaking victims and witnesses or the hearing-impaired.

(b) Follow-up contact to determine whether the client received the necessary assistance.

(c) Field visits to a client's home, place of business, or other location, whenever necessary to provide services.

(d) Service to victims and witnesses of all types of crime.

(e) Volunteer participation to encourage community involvement.

(f) Services for elderly victims of crime, appropriate to their special needs.

§13835.5. Primary services and optional services.

(a) Comprehensive services shall include all of the following primary services:

(1) Crisis intervention, providing timely and comprehensive responses to the individual needs of victims.

(2) Emergency assistance, directly or indirectly providing food, housing, clothing, and, when necessary, cash.

(3) Resource and referral counseling to agencies within the community which are appropriate to meet the victim's needs.

(4) Direct counseling of the victim on problems resulting from the crime.

(5) Assistance in the processing, filing, and verifying of claims filed by victims of crime pursuant to Article 1 (commencing with Section 13959) of Part 4 of Division 3 of Title 2 of the Government Code.

(6) Assistance in obtaining the return of a victim's property held as evidence by law enforcement agencies, if requested.

(7) Orientation to the criminal justice system.

(8) Court escort.

(9) Presentations to and training of criminal justice system agencies.

(10) Public presentations and publicity.

(11) Monitoring appropriate court cases to keep victims and witnesses apprised of the progress and outcome of their case.

(12) Notification to friends, relatives, and employers of the occurrence of the crime and the victim's condition, upon request of the victim.

(13) Notification to the employer of the victim or witness, if requested by the victim or witness, informing the employer that the employee was a victim of or witness to a crime and asking the employer to minimize any loss of pay or other benefits which may result because of the crime or the employee's participation in the criminal justice system.

(b) Comprehensive services may include the following optional services, if their provision does not preclude the efficient provision of primary services:

(1) Employer intervention.

(2) Creditor intervention.

(3) Child care.

© 1992 by J., B. & L. Gould
Printed in the U.S.A.   EP

(4) Assistance in obtaining restitution for the victim.

(5) Notification to witnesses of any change in the court calendar.

(6) Funeral arrangements.

(7) Crime prevention information.

(8) Witness protection, including arranging for law enforcement protection or relocating witnesses in new residences.

(9) Assistance in obtaining temporary restraining orders.

(10) Transportation.

(11) Provision of a waiting area during court proceedings separate from defendants and families and friends of defendants. *(Amended by Stats 1986 ch 1427 §3.)*

§13835.6. Standards defining activities and services.

(a) The Office of Criminal Justice Planning, in cooperation with representatives from local victim and witness assistance centers, shall develop standards defining the activities and services enumerated in this article.

(b) The Office of Criminal Justice Planning in cooperation with representatives from local victim and witness assistance centers, shall develop a method of evaluating the activities and performance of centers established pursuant to this article.

By January 1, 1985, the Office of Criminal Justice Planning shall prepare and submit to the Legislature a report summarizing the effectiveness of victim and witness assistance centers established pursuant to this article. That report shall include, but not be limited to, the effectiveness in achieving the functions and the services enumerated in the article.

§13835.7. Establishment of Victim-Witness Assistance Fund.

There is in the State Treasury the Victim-Witness Assistance Fund. Funds appropriated thereto shall be dispensed to the Office of Criminal Justice Planning exclusively for the purposes specified in this article and for the support of the centers specified in Section 13837. *(Amended by Stats 1987 ch 1232 §5.)*

§13835.10. Quality services for victims of crime.

(a) The Legislature finds and declares all of the following:

(1) That the provision of quality services for victims of crime is of high priority.

(2) That existing victim service programs do not have sufficient financial resources to consistently recruit and employ fully trained personnel.

(3) That there is no consistency in the training provided to the various agencies serving victims.

(4) That comprehensive training for victim service agencies is geographically limited or unavailable.

(5) That there is currently no statewide comprehensive training system in place for the state to insure that all service providers receive adequate training to provide quality services to victims of crime.

(6) It is the intention of the Legislature to establish a statewide training program within the Office of Criminal Justice Planning to provide comprehensive standardized training to victim service providers.

(b) The Office of Criminal Justice Planning shall establish a statewide victim-assistance training program, the purpose of which is to develop minimum training and selection standards, certify training courses, and provide funding to enable local victim service providers to acquire the required training.

(c) (1) For the purpose of raising the level of competence of local victim service providers, the office shall adopt guidelines establishing minimum standards of training for employees of victim-witness and sexual assault programs funded by the office to provide services to victims of crime. The office shall establish an advisory committee composed of recognized statewide victim service organizations, representatives of local victim service programs, and others selected at the discretion of the executive director to consult on the research and development of the training, selection, and equivalency standards.

(2) Any local unit of government, community-based organization, or any other public or private nonprofit entity funded by the office as a victim- witness or sexual assault program to provide services to victims of crime shall adhere to the training and selection standards established by the office. The standards for sexual assault victim service programs developed by the advisory committee established pursuant to Section 13836 shall be the standards for purposes of this section. With the exception of the sexual assault standards, the office shall conduct or contract with an appropriate firm or entity for research on validated standards pursuant to this section in consultation with the advisory committee established pursuant to paragraph (1). The office may defer the adoption of the selection standards until the necessary research is completed. Until the standards are adopted, affected victim service programs may receive state funding from the office upon certification of their willingness to adhere to the training standards adopted by the office.

(3) Minimum training and selection standards may include, but shall not be limited to, basic entry, continuation, supervisory, management, specialized curricula, and confidentiality.

(4) Training and selection standards shall apply to all victim service and management personnel of the victim-witness and sexual assault agencies funded by the office to provide services to victims of crime. Exemptions from this requirement may be made by the office. An agency which, despite good faith efforts, is unable to meet the standards established pursuant to this section, may apply to the office for an exemption. For the purpose of exemptions, the office may establish procedures that allow for partial adherence. The office may develop equivalency standards which recognize professional experience, education, training, or a combination of the above, for personnel hired before July 1, 1987.

(5) Nothing in this section shall prohibit an agency, funded by the office to provide services to victims of crime, from establishing training and selection standards which exceed the minimum standards established by the office pursuant to this section.

(d) For purposes of implementing this section, the office has all of the following powers:

(1) To approve or certify, or both, training courses selected by the office.

(2) To make those inquiries which may be necessary to determine whether every local unit of government, community-based organization, or any other public or private entity receiving state aid from the office as a victim-witness or sexual assault program for the provision of services to victims of crime, is

adhering to the standards for training and selection established pursuant to this section.

(3) To adopt those guidelines which are necessary to carry out the purposes of this section.

(4) To develop or present, or both, training courses for victim service providers, or to contract with coalitions, councils, or other designated entities, to develop or present, or both, those training courses.

(5) To perform other activities and studies necessary to carry out the intent of this section.

(e) In order for the Legislature to determine the need to continue or modify the standards and training programs for local victim service providers, the office shall report to the Legislature on October 1, 1990, and biannually thereafter, regarding the progress and effectiveness of the training program.

(f) (1) The office may utilize any funds that may become available from the Victim-Witness Assistance Fund to fund the cost of training staff of victim service agencies which are funded by the office from the fund. The office may utilize federal or other state funds that may become available to fund the cost of training staff of victim service agencies which are not eligible for funding from the Victim-Witness Assistance Fund.

(2) Peace officer personnel whose jurisdictions are eligible for training subvention pursuant to Chapter 1 (commencing with Section 13500) of Title 4 of this part and correctional or probation personnel whose jurisdictions are eligible for state aid pursuant to Article 2 (commencing with Section 6035) of Chapter 5 of Title 7 of Part 3 are not eligible to receive training reimbursements under this section unless the person receiving the training is assigned to provide victim services in accordance with a grant award agreement with the office and is attending training to meet the established standards. *(Amended by Stats 1990 ch 1342 §5, eff. 1/1/91.)*

ARTICLE 3

TRAINING OF SEXUAL ASSAULT INVESTIGATORS

§13836. Advisory committee.

The Office of Criminal Justice Planning shall establish an advisory committee which shall develop a course of training for district attorneys in the investigation and prosecution of sexual assault cases, child sexual exploitation cases, and child sexual abuse cases and shall approve grants awarded pursuant to Section 13837. The courses shall include training in the unique emotional trauma experienced by victims of these crimes.

It is the intent of the Legislature in the enactment of this chapter to encourage the establishment of sex crime prosecution units, which shall include, but not be limited to, child sexual exploitation and child sexual abuse cases, in district attorneys' offices throughout the state.

§13836.1. Committee members.

Such committee shall consist of 11 members. Five shall be appointed by the executive director of the Office of Criminal Justice Planning, and shall include three district attorneys or assistant or deputy district attorneys, one representative of a city police department or a sheriff or a representative of a sheriff's department, and one public defender or assistant or deputy public defender of a county. Six shall be public members appointed by the Commission on the Status of Women, and shall include one representative of a rape crisis center, and one medical professional experienced in dealing with sexual assault trauma victims. The committee members shall represent the points of view of diverse ethnic and language groups.

Members of the committee shall receive no compensation for their services but shall be reimbursed for their expenses actually and necessarily incurred by them in the performance of their duties. Staff support for the committee shall be provided by the Office of Criminal Justice Planning.

§13836.2. Reimbursement costs.

(a) The office shall reimburse each county for the costs of salaries and transportation to the extent necessary to permit up to 10 percent of the staff of the district attorney to complete the course of training established pursuant to this chapter. The office shall prescribe the manner in which the training shall be obtained. The training shall be offered at least twice each year in both northern and southern California.

(b) The office shall seek certification from the State Bar of the course as a course which may be taken to complete the Criminal Law Specialist Certificate. *(Amended by Stats 1985 ch 1262 §6.)*

ARTICLE 4

RAPE VICTIM COUNSELING CENTERS

§13837. Grants for counseling centers and prevention programs.

The Office of Criminal Justice Planning shall provide grants to proposed and existing local rape, child sexual exploitation, and child sexual abuse victim counseling centers and prevention programs. Grant recipients shall provide appropriate in-person counseling and referral services during normal business hours, and maintain other standards or services which shall be determined to be appropriate by the advisory committee established pursuant to Section 13836 as grant conditions. Rape victim counseling centers shall provide a 24-hour telephone counseling service for sex crime victims. The advisory committee shall identify the criteria to be utilized in awarding the grants provided by this chapter before any funds are allocated.

In order to be eligible for funding pursuant to this chapter, the centers shall demonstrate an ability to receive and make use of any funds available from governmental, voluntary, philanthropic, or other sources which may be used to augment any state funds appropriated for purposes of this chapter. Each center receiving funds pursuant to this chapter shall make every attempt to qualify for any available federal funding.

© 1992 by J., B. & L. Gould
Printed in the U.S.A.   EP

State funds provided to establish centers shall be utilized when possible, as determined by the advisory committee, to expand the program and shall not be expended to reduce fiscal support from other public or private sources. The centers shall maintain quarterly and final fiscal reports in a form to be prescribed by the administering agency. In granting funds, the advisory committee shall give priority to centers which are operated in close proximity to medical treatment facilities.

§13838. Peer counselor defined.

"Peer counselor" means a provider of mental health counseling services who has completed a specialized course in rape crisis counseling skills development, participates in continuing education in rape crisis counseling skills development, and provides rape crisis counseling in consultation with a mental health practitioner licensed within the State of California. *(Added by Stats 1987 ch 1357 §4.)*

CHAPTER 5

CALIFORNIA COMMUNITY CRIME RESISTANCE PROGRAM

§13840. Legislative intent.

The Legislature hereby finds the resistance to crime and juvenile delinquency requires the cooperation of both community and law enforcement officials; and that successful crime resistance programs involving the participation of citizen volunteers and community leaders shall be identified and given recognition. In enacting this chapter, the Legislature intends to recognize successful crime resistance and prevention programs, disseminate successful techniques and information and to encourage local agencies to involve citizen volunteers in efforts to combat crime and related problems.

§13841. Terms defined.

As used in this chapter:

(a) "Community" means city or county governments or portions or combinations thereof.

(b) "Elderly or senior citizen" means individuals 55 years of age or older.

(c) "Teenagers and young adults" means individuals between the ages of 15 and 24 years of age.

(d) "Community policing" means the coalescing of community organizations, residents, law enforcement, public social services, education, churches, and local governmental entities to unitedly combat illegal drug activity within a designated neighborhood, and create employment opportunity for neighborhood residents. In no case shall "community policing" include expenditures for the purchase of law enforcement equipment which would have been purchased from existing resources in the normal course of business. *(Amended by Stats 1990 ch 1419 §1, eff. 1/1/91.)*

§13842. California Crime Resistance Task Force established.

(a) There is hereby established in the Office of Criminal Justice Planning an advisory group entitled "The California Crime Resistance Task Force." All funds appropriated to the Office of Criminal Justice Planning for the purposes of this chapter shall be administered and disbursed by the executive director of such office and shall to the greatest extent feasible

be coordinated or consolidated with federal funds that may be made available for these purposes.

(b) The California Crime Resistance Task Force, to consist of not more than 16 members, shall be composed of two elected city officials, two elected county officials, six community members, and six law enforcement officials designated by the Governor in recognition of successful endeavors in the area of crime prevention and other forms of crime resistance. When this chapter takes effect the existing members of the California Crime Resistance Task Force shall continue as full members.

(c) Members of the task force shall assist the Governor and the Office of Criminal Justice Planning in furthering citizen involvement in local law enforcement and crime resistance efforts.

(d) The California Crime Resistance Task Force shall be chaired by the Governor or his designated representative.

(e) The Executive Director of the Office of Criminal Justice Planning shall serve as secretary of the task force. He shall accept and administer on behalf of the task force any funds made available to the California Community Crime Resistance Program.

(f) Funds awarded under this program as local assistance grants shall not be subject to review as specified in Section 14780 of the Government Code.

§13843. Application and allocation and award of funds.

(a) Allocation and award of funds made available under this chapter shall be made upon application to the Office of Criminal Justice Planning. All applications shall be reviewed and evaluated by the Office of Criminal Justice Planning.

(b) The Executive Director of the Office of Criminal Justice Planning may allocate and award funds to communities developing and providing ongoing citizen involvement and crime resistance programs in compliance with the established policies and criteria of the Office of Criminal Justice Planning. Applications receiving funding under this section shall be selected from among those deemed appropriate for funding according to the criteria, policy, and procedures established by the Office of Criminal Justice Planning.

(c) With the exception of funds awarded for programs authorized under paragraph (2) of subdivision (b) of Section 13844, no single award of funds under this chapter shall exceed a maximum of two hundred fifty thousand dollars ($250,000) for a 12-month grant period.

(d) Funds disbursed under this chapter shall not supplant local funds that would, in the absence of the California Community Crime Resistance Program, be made available to support crime resistance programs.

(e) Funds disbursed under this chapter shall be supplemented with local funds constituting, at a minimum, 10 percent of the total crime resistance program budget during the initial year and 20 percent in subsequent periods of funding.

(f) Annually, up to a maximum of 10 percent of the total funds appropriated to the Community Crime Resistance Program may be used by the Office of Criminal Justice Planning to support statewide technical assistance, training, and public awareness activities relating to crime prevention.

(g) Funds awarded under this program as local assistance grants shall not be subject to review as specified in Section 14780 of the Government Code.

(h) Guidelines shall set forth the terms and conditions upon which the Office of Criminal Justice Planning is prepared to offer grants of funds pursuant to statutory authority. The guidelines do not constitute rules, regulations, orders or standards of general application.

(i) Biannually, commencing November 1, 1990, the executive director shall prepare a report to the Legislature describing in detail the operation of the program and results obtained from the California Community Crime Resistance Program. The first report due shall reflect the implementation plan for the program expansion authorized pursuant to paragraph (2) of subdivision (b) of Section 13844, and shall include the results of a statewide survey conducted by the office to determine the types of community policing programs that already exist to combat illegal drug activity in targeted neighborhoods. *(Amended by Stats 1990 ch 1419 §2, eff. 1/1/91.)*

§13844. Activities required.

(a) Use of funds granted under the California Community Crime Resistance Program are restricted to the following activities:

(1) Further the goal of a statewide crime prevention network by supporting the initiation or expansion of local crime prevention efforts.

(2) Provide information and encourage the use of new and innovative refinements to the traditional crime prevention model in localities that currently maintain a well-established crime prevention program.

(3) Support the development of a coordinated service network, including information exchange and case referral between such programs as local victim- witness assistance programs, sexual assault programs, gang violence reduction programs, drug suppression programs, elderly care custodians, state and local elderly service programs, or any other established and recognizable local programs devoted to the lessening of crime and the promotion of the community's well-being.

(b) With respect to the initiation or expansion of local crime prevention efforts, projects supported under the California Community Crime Resistance Program shall do either of the following:

(1) Carry out as many of the following activities as deemed, in the judgment of the Office of Criminal Justice Planning, to be consistent with available resources:

(A) Crime prevention programs using tailored outreach techniques in order to provide effective and consistent services for the elderly in the following areas:

(i) Crime prevention information to elderly citizens regarding personal safety, fraud, theft, grand theft, burglary, and elderly abuse.

(ii) Services designed to respond to the specific and diverse crime prevention needs of elderly residential communities.

(iii) Specific services coordinated to assist in the installation of security devices or provision of escort services and victim assistance.

(B) Programs to provide training, information, and prevention literature to peace officers, elderly care custodians, health practitioners, and social service providers regarding physical abuse and neglect within residential health care facilities for the elderly.

(C) Programs to promote neighborhood involvement such as, but not limited to, block clubs and other community or resident-sponsored anti-crime programs.

(D) Personal safety programs.

(E) Domestic violence prevention programs.

(F) Crime prevention programs specifically geared to youth in schools and school district personnel.

(G) Programs which make available to residents and businesses information on locking devices, building security and related crime resistance approaches.

(H) In cooperation with the Commission on Peace Officer Standards and Training, support for the training of peace officers in crime prevention and its effects on the relationship between citizens and law enforcement.

(I) Efforts to address the crime prevention needs of communities with high proportions of teenagers and young adults, low-income families, and non- English-speaking residents, including juvenile delinquency diversion, social service referrals, and making available crime resistance literature in appropriate languages other than English.

(2) Implement a community policing program in targeted neighborhoods that are drug infested. The goal of this program shall be to empower the people against illegal drug activity. A program funded pursuant to this chapter shall be able to target one or more neighborhoods within the grant period. In order to be eligible for funding, the program shall have the commitment of the community, local law enforcement, school districts, and community service groups; and shall be supported by either the city council or the board of supervisors, whichever is applicable.

(c) With respect to the support of new and innovative techniques, communities taking part in the California Crime Resistance Program shall carry out those activities as determined by the Office of Criminal Justice Planning, that conform to local needs and are consistent with available expertise and resources. These techniques may include, but are not limited to, community policing programs or activities involving the following:

(1) Programs to reinforce the security of "latchkey" children, including neighborhood monitoring, special contact telephone numbers, emergency procedure training for the children, daily telephone checks for the children's well-being, and assistance in developing safe alternatives to unsupervised conditions for children.

(2) Programs dedicated to educating parents in procedures designed to do all of the following:

(A) Minimize or prevent the abduction of children.

(B) Assist children in understanding the risk of child abduction.

(C) Maximize the recovery of abducted children.

(3) Programs devoted to developing automated systems for monitoring and tracking crimes within organized neighborhoods.

(4) Programs devoted to developing timely "feedback mechanisms" whose goals would be to alert residents to new crime problems and to reinforce household participation in neighborhood security organizations.

(5) Programs devoted to creating and packaging special crime prevention approaches tailored to the special needs and characteristics of California's cultural and ethnic minorities.

© 1992 by J., B. & L. Gould
Printed in the U.S.A.   EP

(6) Research into the effectiveness of local crime prevention efforts including the relationships between crime prevention activities, participants' economic and demographic characteristics, project costs, local or regional crime rate, and law enforcement planning and staff deployment.

(7) Programs devoted to crime and delinquency prevention through the establishment of partnership initiatives utilizing elderly and juvenile volunteers.

(d) All approved programs shall utilize volunteers to assist in implementing and conducting community crime resistance programs. Programs providing elderly crime prevention programs shall recruit senior citizens to assist in providing services.

(e) Programs funded pursuant to this chapter shall demonstrate a commitment to support citizen involvement with local funds after the program has been developed and implemented with state moneys. *(Amended by Stats 1990 ch 1419 §3, eff. 1/1/91.)*

§13845. Criteria for funding.
Selection of communities to receive funding shall include consideration of, but need not be limited to, the following:

(1) Compliance with subdivisions (a), (b), and (c) of Section 13844.

(2) The rate of reported crime, by type, including, but not limited to, the seven major offenses, in the community making the application.

(3) The number of elderly citizens residing in the community compared to the degree of service to be offered by the program for the elderly population.

(4) The number and ratio of elderly crime victims compared to the total senior citizen population in that community.

(5) The number of teenagers and young adults residing in the community.

(6) The number and ratio of crimes committed by teenagers and young adults.

(7) The proportion of families with an income below the federally established poverty level in the community.

(8) The proportion of non-English-speaking citizens in the community.

(9) The display of efforts of cooperation between the community and their local law enforcement agency in dealing with the crime problem.

(10) Demonstrated effort on the part of the applicant to show how funds that may be awarded under this program may be coordinated or consolidated with other local, state or federal funds available for the activities set forth in Section 13844.

(11) Applicant must be a city or county government, or portion or combinations thereof. *(Amended by Stats 1987 ch 1462 §5.)*

§13845.5. Additional criteria for funding.
Notwithstanding Section 13845, the selection of communities to receive funding pursuant to paragraph (2) of subdivision (b) of Section 13844 shall include consideration of, but is not limited to, the following:

(a) The rate of reported drug crime within the community making the application.

(b) The degree to which the program proposes to empower the people within the targeted neighborhoods to combat drug crime.

(c) The display of efforts of cooperation between the community and its local law enforcement agency in dealing with the drug crime problem.

(d) The commitment of the targeted neighborhoods to fight the drug problem.

(e) The commitment of local governmental entities to join with law enforcement and the citizens to fight the drug problem. At a minimum, this commitment shall be demonstrated by the school districts, parks and recreation departments, public social services, and code enforcement agencies.

(f) The approval of the program by either the city council or the county board of supervisors.

(g) Demonstrated effort on the part of the applicant to show how funds that may be awarded under this program may be coordinated or consolidated with other local, state, or federal funds available for the activities set forth in Section 13844.

(h) Applicant shall be a city or county law enforcement agency, or portion, or combination thereof. *(Added by Stats 1990 ch 1419 §4, eff. 1/1/91.)*

§13846. Evaluating and monitoring grants.
(a) Evaluation and monitoring of all grants made under this section shall be the responsibility of the Office of Criminal Justice Planning. The Office of Criminal Justice Planning shall issue standard reporting forms for reporting the level of activities and number of crimes reported in participating communities. The information shall be used in the biannual report to the Legislature required in subdivision (i) of Section 13843. The biannual report shall include, but not be limited to:

(1) The level of volunteer participation.

(2) The level of home and business security inspections.

(3) The number of programs directed at senior citizens and teenagers.

(4) The report due November 1, 1992, as set forth in subdivision (i) of Section 13843, shall also include the plan for implementation of the program expansion authorized pursuant to this chapter and shall include the results of a survey conducted by the office to determine the types of community policing programs that already exist to combat illegal drug activity in targeted neighborhoods.

(b) Information on successful programs shall be made available and relayed to other California communities through the Office of Criminal Justice Planning technical assistance procedures. *(Amended by Stats 1990 ch 1419 §5, eff. 1/1/91.)*

CHAPTER 5.5

RURAL INDIAN CRIME PREVENTION PROGRAM
(Added by Stats 1990 ch 132 §1, eff. 6/11/90.)

§13847. Establishment of Rural Indian Crime Prevention Program.
(a) There is hereby established in the Office of Criminal Justice Planning a program of financial and technical assistance for local law enforcement, called the Rural Indian Crime Prevention Program. The program shall target the relationship between law enforcement and Native American communities to encourage and to strengthen cooperative efforts and to implement crime suppression and prevention programs.

(b) The Executive Director of the Office of Criminal Justice Planning may allocate and award funds to those local units of government, or combinations thereof, in which a special program is established in law enforcement agencies that meets the criteria set forth in Sections 13847.1 and 13847.2.

(c) The allocation and award of funds shall be made upon application executed by the chief law enforcement officer of the applicant unit of government and approved by the legislative body. Funds disbursed under this chapter shall not supplant local funds that would, in the absence of the Rural Indian Crime Prevention Program, be made available to support the suppression and prevention of crime on reservations and rancherias.

(d) The executive director shall prepare and issue administrative guidelines and procedures for the Rural Indian Crime Prevention Program consistent with this chapter.

(e) The guidelines shall set forth the terms and conditions upon which the Office of Criminal Justice Planning is prepared to offer grants of funds pursuant to statutory authority. The guidelines do not constitute rules, regulations, orders, or standards of general application.

(f) Every three years, commencing on and after January 1, 1991, the executive director shall prepare a report to the Legislature describing in detail the operation of the program and the results obtained from law enforcement rural Indian crime prevention programs receiving funds under this chapter. *(Added by Stats 1990 ch 132 §1, eff. 6/11/90.)*

§13847.1. Funding of Rural Indian Crime Prevention Program.

Law enforcement agencies receiving funds under this chapter shall meet the following criteria:

(a) Training of law enforcement personnel to be culturally sensitive in the delivery of services to the Native American communities. This training shall include, but shall not be limited to, all of the following:

(1) The creation of an Indian community officer position.

(2) The recruiting and training of Native American volunteers to assist in implementing and conducting reservation or rancheria crime prevention programs.

(b) Increasing community crime awareness by establishing community involvement programs, such as community or neighborhood watch programs, tailored for reservations and rancherias.

(c) Establishing drug traffic intervention programs on reservations through the increased use of law enforcement and special assignment officers.

(d) Developing a delinquency prevention or diversion program for Indian teenagers and young adults. *(Added by Stats 1990 ch 132 §1, eff. 6/11/90.)*

§13847.2. Rural Indian Crime Prevention Program Committee.

(a) The Rural Indian and Law Enforcement Local Advisory Committee shall be composed of a chief executive of a law enforcement agency, two tribal council members, two tribal elders, one Indian law enforcement officer, one Indian community officer, one representative of the Bureau of Indian Affairs, and any additional members that may prove to be crucial to the committee. All members of the advisory committee shall be designated by the executive director, who shall provide staff services to the advisory committee.

(b) The executive director, in consultation with the advisory committee, shall develop specific guidelines, and administrative procedures, for the selection of projects to be funded by the Rural Indian Crime Prevention Program which guidelines shall include the selection criteria described in this chapter.

(c) Administration of the overall program and the evaluation and monitoring of all grants made under this chapter shall be performed by the Office of Criminal Justice Planning, provided that funds expended for these functions shall not exceed 5 percent of the total annual amount made available for the purpose of this chapter. *(Added by Stats 1990 ch 132 §1, eff. 6/11/90.)*

CHAPTER 6

CALIFORNIA CAREER CRIMINAL APPREHENSION PROGRAM
(Amended by Stats 1985 ch 477 §1, eff. only until 1/1/96.)

§13850. Intent of Legislature.

The Legislature hereby finds that a substantial and disproportionate amount of serious crime is committed against the people of California by a relatively small number of multiple and repeat felony offenders, commonly known as career criminals. In enacting this chapter, the Legislature intends to support increased efforts by local law enforcement agencies to investigate and apprehend career criminals through management, organization and operational techniques that have been demonstrated to be effective in selected cities and counties in this and other states, and through advanced state-of-the-art techniques that focus law enforcement efforts and resources on identifying persons subject to career criminal apprehension efforts. *(Amended by Stats 1985 ch 477 §1, eff. only until 1/1/96.)*

§13851. Establishment; funds; guidelines and procedures.

(a) There is hereby established in the Office of Criminal Justice Planning a program of financial, training, and technical assistance for local law enforcement, called the California Career Criminal Apprehension Program. All funds made available to the Office of Criminal Justice Planning for the purposes of this chapter shall be administered and disbursed by the executive director of such office.

(b) The executive director is authorized to allocate and award funds to those local units of government or combinations thereof, in which a special program is established in law enforcement agencies that meets the criteria set forth in Sections 13852 and 13853.

(c) Such allocation and award of funds shall be made upon application executed by the chief law enforcement officer of the applicant unit of government and approved by the legislative body. Funds disbursed under this chapter shall not supplant local funds that would, in the absence of the California Career Criminal Apprehension Program, be made available to support the apprehension of multiple or repeat felony criminal offenders.

(d) The Executive Director of the Office of Criminal Justice Planning shall prepare and issue administrative guidelines and procedures for the California Career Criminal Apprehension Program consistent with this chapter.

© 1992 by J., B. & L. Gould
Printed in the U.S.A.   **EP**

(e) These guidelines shall set forth the terms and conditions upon which the Office of Criminal Justice Planning is prepared to offer grants of funds pursuant to statutory authority. The guidelines do not constitute rules, regulations, orders or standards of general application.

(f) Every three years, commencing on and after October 1, 1990, the executive director shall prepare a report to the Legislature describing in detail the operation of the program and the results obtained from law enforcement career criminal apprehension programs receiving funds under this chapter. *(Amended by Stats 1985 ch 477 §2, eff. only until 1/1/96.)*

§13852. Law enforcement agencies receiving funds.

Law enforcement agencies receiving funds under this chapter shall employ enhanced law enforcement management efforts and resources. Enhanced law enforcement efforts and resources shall include, but not be limited to:

(a) Crime analysis, which is the timely collection and study of local crime data to perform all of the following:

(1) Identify evolving or existing crime patterns, particularly those involving career felony criminals.

(2) Provide investigative leads.

(3) Identify geographical areas or population groups experiencing relatively severe crime victimization, in order to improve effectiveness of crime prevention efforts.

(4) Provide supporting data for improved allocation of overall law enforcement agency resources.

(b) Improved management of patrol and investigative operations involving use of information resulting from crime analysis, which may include participation in multijurisdictional investigative units and measures to increase continuity of investigative efforts from the initial patrol response through the arrest and prosecution of the offender. Such measures may include:

(1) Innovative personnel deployment techniques.

(2) Innovative techniques of case screening.

(3) Management of continuing investigations.

(4) Monitoring of investigation operations.

(c)(1) Each career criminal apprehension program, supported under this chapter, shall concentrate on the identification and arrest of career criminals and the support of their subsequent prosecution. The determination of which suspected felony offenders shall be the subject of career criminal apprehension efforts shall be in accordance with written criteria developed by the applicant law enforcement agency, consistent with Section 13853 and approved by the head district attorney. Highly qualified and experienced personnel shall be assigned to staff career criminal apprehension programs.

(2) Each career criminal apprehension program as one of its ongoing functions, shall maintain coordination with the prosecutor assigned to each case resulting from its efforts. This coordination should include, but not be limited to, case preparation, processing, and adjudication. *(Amended by Stats 1985 ch 477 §3, eff. only until 1/1/96.)*

§13853. Persons subject to apprehension efforts.

An individual may be the subject of career criminal apprehension efforts who is under investigation for the commission or attempted commission of one or more of the following felonies: homicide, rape or sexual assault, child molestation, robbery, burglary, arson, any unlawful act relating to controlled substances in violation of Section 11351 or 11352 of the Health and Safety Code, receiving stolen property, grand theft and grand theft auto; and who is determined to have committed three or more separate felony offenses not arising out of the same transaction, or has suffered at least one conviction during the preceding 10 years for the commission or attempted commission of any felony listed in subdivision (a), or at least two convictions during the preceding 10 years for the commission or attempted commission of any felony listed in subdivision (b):

(a) Robbery of the first degree, burglary of the first degree, arson as defined in Section 451 or 452, forcible rape, sodomy or oral copulation committed with force, lewd or lascivious conduct committed upon a child, kidnapping as defined in Section 209, or murder.

(b) Grand theft, grand theft auto, receiving stolen property, robbery of the second degree, burglary of the second degree, kidnapping as defined in Section 207, assault with a deadly weapon or instrument, or any unlawful act relating to controlled substances in violation of Section 11351 or 11352 of the Health and Safety Code.

For purposes of this chapter, the 10-year period specified in this section shall be exclusive of any time which the arrested person has served in state prison. *(Amended by Stats 1987 ch 223 §3, eff. only until 1/1/96.)*

§13854. Steering committee.

(a) Criteria for selection of law enforcement agencies to receive career criminal apprehension program funding shall be developed in consultation with an advisory group entitled "The Career Criminal Apprehension Program Steering Committee."

(b) The Career Criminal Apprehension Program Steering Committee shall be composed of four police chiefs, three sheriffs, two district attorneys, two attorneys primarily engaged in the practice of criminal defense, one city manager and one county administrative officer, all of whom are designated by the executive director of the Office of Criminal Justice Planning, who shall provide staff services to the steering committee.

(c) The Executive Director of the Office of Criminal Justice Planning, in consultation with the steering committee, shall develop specific guidelines, and administrative procedures, for the selection of the California Career Criminal Apprehension Program whose guidelines shall include the selected criteria described in the subdivisions above.

(d) Administration of the overall program and the evaluation and monitoring of all grants made under this chapter shall be performed by the Office of Criminal Justice Planning, provided that funds expended for such functions shall not exceed 7.5 percent of the total annual amount made available for the purpose of this chapter.

(e) Local assistance grants made pursuant to this chapter shall not be subject to review pursuant to Section 10290 of the Public Contract Code. *(Amended by Stats 1985 ch 477 §5, eff. only until 1/1/96.)*

CHAPTER 6.5

ARMED CAREER CRIMINALS
(Added by Stats 1990 ch 1554 §1, eff. 1/1/91 only until 1/1/96.)

§13855. Legislative findings and intent.

The Legislature hereby finds that a small number of repeat felony offenders, known as a* career criminals, commit a disproportionate number of crimes, often while armed with firearms. In enacting this chapter, the Legislature intends to assist law enforcement authorities in identifying, apprehending, prosecuting, and imprisoning armed career criminals. *(Added by Stats 1990 ch 1554 §1, eff. 1/1/91 only until 1/1/96.)*

*So in original. Probably "a" should be deleted.

§13855.1. Definitions.

As used in this chapter, "armed career criminal" means a person who has previously been convicted of three serious felonies in this state, or offenses committed in other jurisdictions which include all of the elements of a serious felony. As used in this section, "serious felony" means a serious felony listed in subdivision (c) of Section 1192.7. *(Added by Stats 1990 ch 1554 §1, eff. 1/1/91 only until 1/1/96.)*

§13855.2. Information from government files.

The Department of Justice may request the Department of Corrections, the Department of Motor Vehicles, and local law enforcement agencies to provide existing information from their files regarding persons identified as armed career criminals. The Department of Corrections, the Department of Motor Vehicles, and law enforcement agencies shall, when requested by the Department of Justice, provide copies of existing information maintained in their files regarding persons identified as armed career criminals and provide followup information as it becomes available. *(Added by Stats 1990 ch 1554 §1, eff. 1/1/91 only until 1/1/96.)*

§13855.4. Armed Career Criminal Pilot Project.

(a) The Armed Career Criminal Pilot Project is hereby created. The Department of Justice shall, subject to the availability of funds, implement the project to do all of the following:

(1) Evaluate the propensity of armed career criminals released from federal, state, and local penal institutions to commit further offenses.

(2) Utilize information from the Departments of Justice, Corrections, and Motor Vehicles, and appropriate federal agencies to provide law enforcement officials within the pilot project with comprehensive information on armed career criminals in their communities.

(3) Assist in identifying suspects based upon analysis and comparison of methods of operations.

(4) Provide information for sentencing purposes.

(5) Develop an automated data-processing system to store, search, and retrieve information collected on armed career criminals.

(b) The pilot program shall operate in all counties, except the following counties: Imperial, Los Angeles, Orange, Riverside, Santa Barbara, San Bernardino, San Diego, San Luis Obispo, and Ventura.

(c) The department shall provide reports to the Legislature on the Armed Career Criminal Project every March 1, beginning in 1992. The report shall include the number of files reviewed, the number of career criminals monitored, the number of crimes solved, and documentation showing how this program contributed to solving these crimes. The pilot program shall be considered successful if each year (1) 400,000 files are reviewed, (2) 1,000 career criminals are monitored, (3) documentation can be provided showing that at least 300 violent felony crimes were solved that would not have been solved without this pilot, and (4) there is at least an annual 10 percent increase in the number of crimes solved as a result of this pilot program. *(Added by Stats 1990 ch 1554 §1, eff. 1/1/91 only until 1/1/96.)*

§13855.5. Repeal of chapter.

This chapter shall remain in effect only until January 1, 1996, and as of that date is repealed, unless a later enacted statute, which is enacted before January 1, 1996, deletes or extends that date. *(Added by Stats 1990 ch 1554 §1, eff. 1/1/91 only until 1/1/96.)*

CHAPTER 7

SUPPRESSION OF DRUG ABUSE IN SCHOOLS

§13860. Legislative findings and declarations.

The Legislature finds and declares that a substantial drug abuse and drug trafficking problem exists among school-age children on and around school campuses in the State of California. By enacting this chapter, it is the intention of the Legislature to support increased efforts by local law enforcement agencies, working in conjunction with school districts and county drug offices to suppress trafficking and prevent drug abuse among school age children on and around school campuses through the development of innovative and model programs by local law enforcement agencies and schools and drug abuse agencies. As used in this chapter, drugs are defined as marijuana, inhalants, narcotics, dangerous drugs, pharmaceuticals, glue and alcohol. It is the further intention of the Legislature to establish a program of financial and technical assistance for local law enforcement and school districts.

§13861. Program; establishment funds.

There is hereby created in the Office of Criminal Justice Planning the Suppression of Drug Abuse in Schools Program. All funds made available to the Office of Criminal Justice Planning for the purposes of this chapter shall be administered and disbursed by the executive director of the office in consultation with the State Suppression of Drug Abuse in Schools Advisory Committee established pursuant to Section 13863.

(a) The executive director, in consultation with the State Suppression of Drug Abuse in Schools Advisory Committee, is authorized to allocate and award funds to local law enforcement agencies and public schools jointly working to develop drug abuse prevention and drug trafficking suppression programs in substantial compliance with the policies and criteria set forth in Sections 13862 and 13863.

(b) The allocation and award of funds shall be made upon the joint application by the chief law enforcement officer of the coapplicant law enforcement

© 1992 by J., B. & L. Gould
Printed in the U.S.A.   EP

agency and approved by the law enforcement agency's legislative body and the superintendent and board of the school district coapplicant. The joint application of the law enforcement agency and the school district shall be submitted for review to the Local Suppression on* Drug Abuse in Schools Advisory Committee established pursuant to paragraph (4) of subdivision (a) of Section 13862. After review, the application shall be submitted to the Office of Criminal Justice Planning. Funds disbursed under this chapter may enhance but shall not supplant local funds that would, in the absence of the Suppression of Drug Abuse in Schools Program, be made available to suppress and prevent drug abuse among school-age children and to curtail drug trafficking in and around school areas.

*So in original. Probably should be "of".

(c) The coapplicant local law enforcement agency and the coapplicant school district may enter into interagency agreements between themselves which will allow the management and fiscal tasks created pursuant to this chapter and assigned to both the law enforcement agency and the school district to be performed by only one of them.

(d) Within 90 days of the effective date of this chapter, the Executive Director of the Office of Criminal Justice Planning in consultation with the State Suppression of Drug Abuse in Schools Advisory Committee established pursuant to Section 13863 shall prepare and issue administrative guidelines and procedures for the Suppression of Drug Abuse in Schools Program consistent with this chapter. In addition to all other formal requirements that may apply to the enactment of such guidelines and procedures a complete and final draft shall be submitted within 60 days of the effective date of this chapter to the Chairpersons of the Committee on Criminal Law and Public Safety of the Assembly and the Judiciary Committee of the Senate of the California Legislature.

(e) By July 1, 1984, or after a full year of program operation, the executive director shall prepare and submit an annual report to the Legislature describing in detail the operation of the program and the results obtained from the Suppression of Drug Abuse in Schools Program receiving funds under this chapter. The report shall also list the full costs applicable both to the Office of Criminal Justice Planning for processing and reviewing applications, and to the state and local agencies for obtaining grants, from any source, to support the program. The purpose of the program evaluation shall be to identify successful methods of conducting Suppression of Drug Abuse in Schools Programs. Ongoing evaluation findings shall be used to replicate proven successful methods, identify, implement, and refine new methods.

§13862. Enhanced efforts and resources.

Law enforcement agencies and school districts receiving funds under this chapter shall concentrate enhanced apprehension, prevention and education efforts and resources on drug abuse and drug trafficking in and around school campuses.

(a) These enhanced apprehension, prevention, and education efforts shall include, but not be limited to:

(1) Drug traffic intervention programs.

(2) School and classroom-oriented programs, using tested drug abuse education curriculum that provides indepth and accurate information on drugs, which may include the participation of local law enforcement agencies and qualified drug abuse preven-

tion specialists and which are designed to increase teachers' and students' awareness of drugs and their effects.

(3) Family oriented programs aimed at preventing drug abuse which may include the participation of community-based organizations experienced in the successful operation of such programs.

(4) The establishment of a Local Suppression of Drug Abuse in Schools Advisory Committee. The committee shall be established and appointed by the board of supervisors of each county and city and county. However, if the agency receiving funds under this chapter is a city agency and the program does not involve any county agency, or if a county agency is involved and the county board of supervisors consents, the committee shall be established and appointed by the city council. The committee may be a newly created committee or an existing local drug abuse committee as designated by the board or city council. The committee shall be composed of, at a minimum, the following:

(A) Local law enforcement executives.

(B) School district executives.

(C) School site staff, which includes administrators, teachers, or other credentialed personnel.

(D) Parents.

(E) Students.

(F) School peace officers.

(G) County drug program administrators designated pursuant to Section 11962 of the Health and Safety Code.

(H) Drug prevention program executives.

(5) Development and distribution of appropriate written and audio-visual aids for training of school and law enforcement staff for handling drug-related problems and offenses. Appropriate existing aids may be utilized in lieu of development of new materials.

(6) Development of prevention and intervention programs for elementary school teachers and students, including utilization of existing prevention and intervention programs.

(7) Development of a coordinated intervention system that identifies students with chronic drug abuse problems and facilitates their referral to a drug abuse treatment program.

(b) Enhanced apprehension, prevention, and education efforts commenced under this section shall be a joint effort between local law enforcement and local school districts in cooperation with county drug program offices. These efforts shall include, but not be limited to, the concentration of apprehension efforts in "problem" areas identified by local school authorities.

(c) Funds appropriated pursuant to this chapter may be used in part to support state-level development and statewide distribution of appropriate written and audio-visual aids for public awareness and training of school and law enforcement staff for handling drug-related problems and offenses. When existing aids can be identified, these aids may be utilized in lieu of the development of new aids. (Amended by Stats 1988 ch 935 §2, eff. 1/1/89.)

§13863. Funding.

Criteria for the selection of law enforcement agencies and school districts to receive Suppression of Drug Abuse in Schools Program funding shall be developed by the State Suppression of Drug Abuse in Schools Advisory Committee.

(a) The State Suppression of Drug Abuse in Schools Advisory Committee shall be composed of two police chiefs, two sheriffs, two district attorneys, one attorney primarily engaged in criminal defense, one representative of parent groups, one representative of the Department of Alcohol and Drug Programs, one county drug program administrator designated pursuant to Section 11962 of the Health and Safety Code, a school peace officer, and a representative of community-based drug abuse programs, all of whom are appointed by the Governor. In addition, the Attorney General shall designate one member representing the Department of Justice and the Superintendent of Public Instruction shall designate four members, one representing the Department of Education, and three schoolsite personnel. Staff services to the committee shall be provided by the Executive Director of the Office of Criminal Justice Planning. Committee members shall be reimbursed for actual expenses involved in the conduct of committee business. The committee shall review applications for grant awards and shall recommend approval for those applications which are deemed appropriate and are consistent with the guidelines and administrative procedures established pursuant to this section and this chapter.

(b) Each committee member or his or her designee shall be personally present to cast a vote or be counted toward a quorum. An appointed member of the committee unable to attend any meeting may designate a representative to attend the meetings on his or her behalf. The representative shall be accorded full privilege to address the committee on any matter under consideration and shall have the right to vote on any motions entertained by the committee.

(c) The State Suppression of Drug Abuse in Schools Advisory Committee shall develop specific guidelines and administrative procedures for the Suppression of Drug Abuse in Schools Program.

(d) These guidelines and administrative procedures shall set forth the terms and conditions upon which the Office of Criminal Justice Planning is prepared to offer grants of funds pursuant to statutory authority. The guidelines and administrative procedures do not constitute rules, regulations, orders, or standards of general application.

(e) Administration of the overall program and the evaluation and monitoring of all grants made under this chapter shall be performed by the Office of Criminal Justice Planning.

(f) The Office of Criminal Justice Planning shall, to the extent possible, coordinate the administration of the Suppression of Drug Abuse in Schools Program with those of the Department of Alcohol and Drug Programs and the State Department of Education established pursuant to Article 2 (commencing with Section 11965) of Chapter 2 of Part 3 of Division 10.5 of the Health and Safety Code.

(g) Local assistance grants made pursuant to this chapter shall not be subject to review pursuant to Section 14780 of the Government Code.

(h) Funds disbursed under this chapter shall not be used for the acquisition of equipment.

(i) Funds disbursed under this chapter shall not be used to purchase information or drugs.

(j) In the interest of maximizing the use of funds for program support and implementation, local law enforcement agencies and school districts receiving funds under this chapter are expressly discouraged from using Suppression of Drug Abuse in Schools

Program funds for personnel costs. Where it can be demonstrated that personnel costs are essential to the success of the program and that sufficient law enforcement and school personnel are not available to carry out the program, exceptions to this section may be requested through the Executive Director of the Office of Criminal Justice Planning.

(k) No more than 5 percent of the total amount of funds disbursed under this chapter shall be used for administrative costs. *(Amended by Stats 1989 ch 63 §1, eff. 1/1/90.)*

§13864. Comprehensive Alcohol and Drug Prevention Education Program.

There is hereby created, in the Office of Criminal Justice Planning, the Comprehensive Alcohol and Drug Prevention Education component of the Suppression of Drug Abuse in Schools Program in public elementary schools in grades 4 to 6, inclusive. Notwithstanding Section 13861 or any other provision in this code, all Comprehensive Alcohol and Drug Prevention Education component funds made available to the Office of Criminal Justice Planning in accordance with the Classroom Instructional Improvement and Accountability Act shall be administered by and disbursed to county superintendents of schools in this state by the Executive Director of the Office of Criminal Justice Planning. All applications for that funding shall be reviewed and evaluated by the Office of Criminal Justice Planning, in consultation with the State Department of Alcohol and Drug Programs and the State Department of Education.

(a) The executive director is authorized to allocate and award funds to county department superintendents of schools for allocation to individual school districts or to a consortium of two or more school districts. Applications funded under this section shall comply with the criteria, policies, and procedures established under subdivision (b) of this section.

(b) As a condition of eligibility for the funding described in this section, the school district or consortium of school districts shall have entered into an agreement with a local law enforcement agency to jointly implement a comprehensive alcohol and drug abuse prevention, intervention, and suppression program developed by the Office of Criminal Justice Planning, in consultation with the State Department of Alcohol and Drug Programs and the State Department of Education, containing all of the following components:

(1) A standardized age-appropriate curriculum designed for pupils in grades 4 to 6, inclusive, specifically tailored and sensitive to the socioeconomic and ethnic characteristics of the target pupil population. Although new curricula shall not be required to be developed, existing curricula may be modified and adapted to meet local needs. The elements of the standardized comprehensive alcohol and drug prevention education program curriculum shall be defined and approved by the Governor's Policy Council on Drug and Alcohol Abuse, as established by Executive Order # D-70-80.

(2) A planning process that shall include both assessment of the school district's characteristics, resources and the extent of problems related to juvenile drug abuse, and input from local law enforcement agencies.

© 1992 by J., B. & L. Gould
Printed in the U.S.A.   **EP**

(3) A school district governing board policy that provides for a coordinated intervention system that, at a minimum, includes procedures for identification, intervention, and referral of at-risk alcohol- and drug-involved youth, and identifies the roles and responsibilities of law enforcement, school personnel, parents, and pupils.

(4) Early intervention activities that include, but are not limited to, the identification of pupils who are high risk or have chronic drug abuse problems, assessment, and referral for appropriate services, including ongoing support services.

(5) Parent education programs to initiate and maintain parental involvement, with an emphasis for parents of at-risk pupils.

(6) Staff and in-service training programs, including both indepth training for the core team involved in providing program services and general awareness training for all school faculty and administrative, credentialed, and noncredentialed school personnel.

(7) In-service training programs for local law enforcement officers.

(8) School, law enforcement, and community involvement to ensure coordination of program services. Pursuant to that coordination, the school district or districts and other local agencies are encouraged to use a single community advisory committee or task force for drug, alcohol, and tobacco abuse prevention programs, as an alternative to the creation of a separate group for that purpose under each state or federally funded program.

(c) The application of the county superintendent of schools shall be submitted to the Office of Criminal Justice Planning. Funds made available to the Office of Criminal Justice Planning for allocation under this section are intended to enhance, but shall not supplant, local funds that would, in the absence of the Comprehensive Alcohol and Drug Prevention Education component, be made available to prevent, intervene in, or suppress drug abuse among school age children. For districts that are already implementing a comprehensive drug abuse prevention program for pupils in grades 4 to 6, inclusive, the county superintendent shall propose the use of the funds for drug prevention activities in school grades other than 4 to 6, inclusive, compatible with the program components of this section. The expenditure of funds for that alternative purpose shall be approved by the executive director.

(1) Unless otherwise authorized by the Office of Criminal Justice Planning, each county superintendent of schools shall be the fiscal agent for any Comprehensive Alcohol and Drug Prevention Education component award, and shall be responsible for ensuring that each school district within that county receives the allocation prescribed by the Office of Criminal Justice Planning. Each county superintendent shall develop a countywide plan that complies with program guidelines and procedures established by the Office of Criminal Justice Planning pursuant to subdivision (d). A maximum of 5 percent of the county's allocation may be used for administrative costs associated with the project.

(2) Each county superintendent of schools shall establish and chair a local coordinating committee to assist the superintendent in developing and implementing a countywide implementation plan. This committee shall include the county drug administrator, law enforcement executives, school district governing board members and administrators, school faculty, parents, and drug prevention and intervention program executives selected by the superintendent and approved by the county board of supervisors.

(d) The Executive Director of the Office of Criminal Justice Planning, in consultation with the State Department of Alcohol and Drug Programs and the State Department of Education, shall prepare and issue guidelines and procedures for the Comprehensive Alcohol and Drug Prevention Education component consistent with this section.

(e) The Comprehensive Alcohol and Drug Prevention Education component guidelines shall set forth the terms and conditions upon which the Office of Criminal Justice Planning is prepared to award grants of funds pursuant to this section. The guidelines shall not constitute rules, regulations, orders, or standards of general application.

(f) Funds awarded under the Comprehensive Alcohol and Drug Prevention Education Program shall not be subject to Section 10318 of the Public Contracts Code.

(g) Commencing January 1, 1991, or six months after a full year of program operation, whichever occurs later, the executive director shall prepare and submit an annual report to the Legislature describing the operation of the program and the results obtained from the Comprehensive Alcohol and Drug Prevention Education component receiving funds under this section.

(h) Funds available pursuant to Item 8100-111-001 and Provision 1 of Item 8100-001-001 of the Budget Act of 1989, or the successor provision of the appropriate Budget Act, shall be allocated to implement this section.

(i) The Executive Director of the Office of Criminal Justice Planning shall collaborate, to the extent possible, with other state agencies that administer drug, alcohol, and tobacco abuse prevention education programs to streamline and simplify the process whereby local educational agencies apply for drug, alcohol, and tobacco education funding under this section and under other state and federal programs. The Office of Criminal Justice Planning, the State Department of Alcohol and Drug Programs, the State Department of Education, and other state agencies, to the extent possible, shall develop joint policies and collaborate planning in the administration of drug, alcohol, and tobacco abuse prevention education programs. *(Amended by Stats 1990 ch 923 §4, eff. 1/1/91.)*

CHAPTER 8

INFORMATION ON RACIAL, ETHNIC AND RELIGIOUS CRIMES

§13870. Establishing statewide information center.

The Legislature finds that racial, ethnic, and religious crimes occur throughout California and that no single agency now either provides assistance or monitors the full range of this crime in the state on a consistent basis. The Legislature further declares that exposure of the facts about racial, ethnic, and religious crimes will lead to greater public awareness of the problem of bigotry and prejudice and will provide a foundation for developing remedies to the problem.

In enacting this chapter, the Legislature intends to take the preliminary steps needed to establish a statewide information center to receive and evaluate information reflecting racial, ethnic, and religious crime. It is intended that this information will provide a precise picture of the geographic distribution of these crimes and trends over time.

§13871. Project to collect information about crimes; duties.

The Attorney General shall, on January 1, 1985, commence a one-year project to develop a program model to collect, compile, and analyze information about racial, ethnic, and religious crimes. The project shall include, but not be limited to, all of the following duties:

(a) Develop uniform guidelines for consistent identification of racial, ethnic, and religious crimes.

(b) Recommend an appropriate means for statewide collection of data on racial, ethnic, and religious crimes.

(c) Recommend an appropriate state agency to implement collection of this information.

(d) Submit to the Legislature a final report describing the findings of the study by January 1, 1986.

§13872. Crimes focused in this chapter.

The crimes that shall be the focus of this chapter shall include a wide variety of incidents, which reflect obvious racial, ethnic, or religious motivations, ranging from vandalizing a place of worship to assaults between members of gangs, including, but not limited to, incidents that occur on school grounds and between gang members and any other incidents that law enforcement officers on a case-by-case basis identify as having a racial, ethnic or religious motivation. They shall not include incidents of discrimination in employment.

CHAPTER 9

CALIFORNIA MAJOR NARCOTIC VENDORS PROSECUTION LAW

§13880. Prosecuting drug producers and sellers through effective organizational and operative techniques.

(a) The Legislature finds and declares that the production and sale of narcotics is an ever increasing problem because of the substantial illicit profits derived therefrom. The Legislature further finds and declares that a substantial and disproportionate amount of serious crime is associated with the cultivation, processing, manufacturing, and sale of narcotics.

(b) The Legislature finds and declares that the level of production, distribution, and sale of narcotics in small counties in this state threatens the well-being not only of citizens of those counties, but of the rest of the state as well. Since many of these counties have experienced less growth in their general purpose revenues than the rest of the state, and yet are required to bear the burden of funding disproportionate criminal justice costs associated with the production, distribution, and sale of narcotics, the Legislature recognizes the need to provide financial assistance for these counties.

(c) The Legislature intends to support intensified efforts by district attorneys' offices to prosecute drug producers and sellers through organizational and operational techniques that have been proven effective in selected jurisdictions in this and other states. *(Amended by Stats 1987 ch 306 §1.)*

§13881. Funds.

(a) There is hereby established in the Office of Criminal Justice Planning a program of financial and technical assistance for district attorneys' offices, designated the California Major Narcotic Vendors Prosecution Law. All funds appropriated to the Office of Criminal Justice Planning for the purposes of this chapter shall be administered and disbursed by the executive director of the office in consultation with the California Council on Criminal Justice, and shall to the greatest extent feasible be coordinated or consolidated with federal funds that may be made available for these purposes.

(b) The executive director is authorized to allocate and award funds to counties in which the California Major Narcotic Vendors Prosecution Law is implemented in substantial compliance with the policies and criteria set forth in this chapter.

(c) The allocation and award of funds shall be made upon application executed by the county's district attorney and approved by its board of supervisors. Funds disbursed under this chapter shall not supplant local funds that would, in the absence of the California Major Narcotic Vendors Prosecution Law, be made available to support the prosecution of felony drug cases. Funds available under this program shall not be subject to review, as specified in Section 14780 of the Government Code.

(d) The executive director shall prepare and issue written program and administrative guidelines and procedures for the California Major Narcotic Vendors Prosecution Program consistent with this chapter, which shall be submitted to the Chairpersons of the Assembly Public Safety Committee and the Senate Judiciary Committee. These guidelines shall permit the selection of a county for the allocation and award of funds only on a finding by the Office of Criminal Justice Planning that the county is experiencing a proportionately significant increase in major narcotic cases. Further, the guidelines shall provide for the allocation and award of funds to small county applicants, as designated by the executive director. The guidelines shall also provide that any funds received by a county under this chapter shall be used only for the prosecution of cases involving major narcotic dealers. For purposes of this subdivision, "small county" means a county having a population of 200,000 or less.

(e) Annually, commencing January 1, 1986, the executive director shall, in cooperation with public defender representatives, prepare a report to the Legislature describing the operation and results of the statewide program and assessing any and all fiscal and workload burdens imposed by the statewide program upon local public defender offices and assigned counsel, with recommendations where appropriate. The report shall include the impact of additional federal funds in this area. *(Amended by Stats 1987 ch 306 §2.)*

§13882. Prosecution.

California major narcotic vendors prosecution units receiving funds under this chapter shall concentrate enhanced prosecution efforts and resources upon individuals identified under selection criteria set forth in Section 13883. Enhanced prosecution efforts and resources shall include, but not be limited to, all of the following:

(a) "Vertical" prosecutorial representation, whereby the prosecutor who makes the initial filing or appearance in a drug case will perform all subsequent

© 1992 by J., B. & L. Gould
Printed in the U.S.A.   EP

court appearances on that particular case through its conclusion, including the sentencing phase.

(b) Assignment of highly qualified investigators and prosecutors to drug cases.

(c) Significant reduction of caseloads for investigators and prosecutors assigned to drug cases.

§13883. Drug prosecution efforts for felonies.

(a) An individual may be the subject of the California Major Narcotic Vendors Prosecution Law prosecution efforts who is under arrest for the commission or attempted commission of one or more felonies relating to controlled substances in violation of Section 11351, 11352, 11358, 11378, 11378.5, 11379, 11379.5, or 11383 of the Health and Safety Code.

(b) In applying the criteria set forth in subdivision (a), a district attorney may, consistent with the provisions of subdivision (d) of Section 13881, elect to limit drug prosecution efforts to persons arrested for any one or more of the felonies listed in subdivision (a) if crime statistics demonstrate that the incidence of that felony or felonies presents a particularly serious problem in the county.

(c) In exercising the prosecutorial discretion granted by this section, the district attorney shall consider (1) the character, background, and prior criminal background of the defendant, and (2) the number and the seriousness of the offenses currently charged against the defendant.

§13884. Policies.

(a) Each district attorney's office establishing a California major narcotic vendors prosecution unit and receiving state support under this chapter shall adopt and pursue the following policies for the California Major Narcotic Vendors Prosecution Law cases:

(1) All reasonable prosecutorial efforts shall be made to resist the pretrial release of a charged defendant selected for prosecution under the California Major Narcotic Vendors Prosecution Law.

(2) All reasonable prosecutorial efforts shall be made to persuade the court to impose the most severe authorized sentence upon a person convicted after prosecution under the California Major Narcotic Vendors Prosecution Law.

(3) All reasonable prosecutorial efforts shall be made to reduce the time between arrest and disposition of charge against an individual selected for prosecution under the California Major Narcotic Vendors Prosecution Law.

(b) The selection criteria set forth in Section 13883 shall be adhered to for each California Major Narcotic Vendors Prosecution Law case unless, in the reasonable exercise of prosecutor's discretion, extraordinary circumstances require the departure from those policies in order to promote the general purposes and intent of this chapter.

CHAPTER 10

SERIOUS HABITUAL OFFENDER PROGRAM
(Added by Stats 1988 ch 1134 §2, oper. 7/1/89 only until 7/1/94; eff. only until 1/1/95.)

§13890. Legislative findings and intent.

The Legislature hereby finds that a substantial and disproportionate amount of serious sex offenses are committed against the people of California by a relatively small number of multiple and repeat sex offenders. In enacting this chapter, the Legislature intends to support efforts of the criminal justice community through a focused effort by law enforcement and prosecuting agencies to identify, locate, apprehend, and prosecute serious habitual sex offenders. *(Added by Stats 1988 ch 1134 §2, oper. 7/1/89 only until 7/1/94; eff. only until 1/1/95.)*

§13891. Pilot project.

The Attorney General shall, subject to the availability of funds, establish in the Department of Justice a Serious Habitual Offender Program pilot project, which is hereby created, which shall evaluate the number of arrests and convictions for sex offenses and the length of sentences for repeat offenders. The pilot project shall operate for five years in the following counties: San Francisco, San Mateo, Santa Clara, Santa Cruz, Alameda, Contra Costa, Napa, Sonoma, Solano, and Marin. *(Added by Stats 1988 ch 1134 §2, oper. 7/1/89 only until 7/1/94; eff. only until 1/1/95.)*

§13891.1. Serious habitual sex offenders defined.

As used in this chapter, "serious habitual sex offenders" means those persons who have been either of the following: (a) convicted of two or more violent offenses against a person involving force or violence which include at least one sex offense and reside in the Serious Habitual Offender Program pilot project area; or (b) convicted of an offense listed in Section 290 of the Penal Code, reside in the Serious Habitual Offender Program pilot project area, and also meet one of the following criteria:

(1) Have three or more felony arrests for sex offenses prescribed in Section 290 on their criminal record.

(2) Have five or more felony arrests for any type of offense on their criminal record.

(3) Have 10 or more arrests (either felony or misdemeanor) for any type of offense on their criminal record.

(4) Have five or more arrests (either felony or misdemeanor) for any type of offense, including (A) at least one conviction for multiple sex offenses (a conviction arising from the commission of two or more offenses listed in subdivision (a) of Section 290 in one transaction), or including (B) at least two arrests for a single sex offense listed in subdivision (a) of Section 290 of the Penal Code. *(Added by Stats 1988 ch 1134 §2, oper. 7/1/89 only until 7/1/94; eff. only until 1/1/95.)*

§13891.2. Information file.

The Department of Justice shall establish and maintain a comprehensive file of existing information maintained by law enforcement agencies, the Department of Corrections, the Department of Motor Vehicles, and the Department of Justice. The Department of Justice may request the Department of Corrections, the Department of Motor Vehicles, and law enforcement agencies to provide existing information from their files regarding persons identified as serious habitual sex offenders. The Department of Corrections, the Department of Motor Vehicles, and law enforcement agencies shall, when requested by the Department of Justice, provide copies of existing information maintained in their files regarding persons identified by the Department of Justice as serious habitual sex offenders and provide followup information to the Department of Justice as it becomes available. This serious habitual sex offender file shall be maintained by the Department of Justice and shall contain a complete physical description and method of operation of the serious habitual sex offender, information describing his or her interaction with criminal justice agencies, and his or her prior criminal record. The Department of Justice shall also prepare a summary profile of each serious habitual sex offender for distribution to law enforcement agencies. *(Added by Stats 1988 ch 1134 §2, oper. 7/1/89 only until 7/1/94; eff. only until 1/1/95.)*

§13891.3. Providing offenders' profiles to law enforcement agencies.

The Department of Justice shall provide a summary profile of each serious habitual sex offender to each law enforcement agency in the pilot project area when the individual registers in the pilot project area or moves to the pilot project area.

Upon request, the department shall provide the complete file of information on a serious habitual sex offender to law enforcement agencies, district attorneys, and the courts in the pilot project area for the purpose of identifying, apprehending, prosecuting, and sentencing serious habitual sex offenders. *(Added by Stats 1988 ch 1134 §2, oper. 7/1/89 only until 7/1/94; eff. only until 1/1/95.)*

§13892. Establishment of advisory committee.

The Attorney General shall establish an advisory committee to assist in the implementation and operation of the Serious Habitual Offender Program. The committee shall provide recommendations to the Department of Justice related to the operating policies of the Serious Habitual Offender Program, training needs for local law enforcement agencies and prosecutors in implementing the program, and the possible expansion of the pilot project to a statewide program. Members on the committee shall serve at the pleasure of the Attorney General without compensation, except for travel and per diem expenses, in accordance with applicable law. The advisory committee shall be comprised of 12 members who shall be appointed by the Attorney General and who shall include the following persons:

(a) One member from the California Peace Officers' Association.

(b) One member from the California District Attorneys' Association.

(c) One member from the Department of Justice.

(d) One member from the Department of Corrections.

(e) One member from the Department of Motor Vehicles.

(f) One member from a district attorney's office in the pilot project area.

(g) Four members from law enforcement agencies in the pilot project area.

(h) One member from a professional organization involved in implementing the Serious Habitual Offender Program, including, but not limited to, the Juvenile Officers' Association, Bay Area Crime Analysts, and Sexual Assault Investigators' Association.

(i) One member from the California Public Defenders Association.

The Serious Habitual Offender Program shall provide staff assistance to the advisory committee. The chairperson of the advisory committee shall be selected by the members of the committee. *(Added by Stats 1988 ch 1134 §2, oper. 7/1/89 only until 7/1/94; eff. only until 1/1/95.)*

§13893. Attorney General's report to Legislature.

On or before July 1, 1994, the Attorney General shall submit a written report to the Legislature containing the following information:

(a) A summary of the pilot project operation, activities, and cost.

(b) A quantifiable evaluation of the success of the pilot project based on comparisons with counties not participating in the pilot project and considering the following factors:

(1) The number of arrests and convictions for sex offenses.

(2) The number of requests by law enforcement and prosecuting agencies for information or assistance from the Serious Habitual Offender Program.

(3) The number of serious habitual offenders identified as suspects in unsolved sexual assault cases.

(4) The number of cases in which assistance from the Serious Habitual Offender Program was instrumental in the arrest, conviction, or enhanced sentencing of persons identified as serious habitual offenders.

(c) The potential cost and impact of a statewide serious habitual sex offender program. *(Added by Stats 1988 ch 1134 §2, oper. 7/1/89 only until 7/1/94; eff. only until 1/1/95.)*

§13894. Date operative; date repealed.

This chapter shall become operative on July 1, 1989, shall become inoperative on July 1, 1994, and, as of January 1, 1995, is repealed, unless a later enacted statute, which becomes effective on or before January 1, 1995, deletes or extends the dates on which it becomes inoperative, and is repealed. *(Added by Stats 1988 ch 1134 §2, oper. 7/1/89 only until 7/1/94; eff. only until 1/1/95.)*

CHAPTER 10.3

COMPUTER FINGERPRINT PROGRAM
(Added by Stats 1990 ch 1243 §1, eff. 1/1/91.)

§13894.5. Legislative findings and intent.

The Legislature finds and declares all of the following:

(a) The people of California have a public safety interest in ensuring that individuals who are arrested and convicted of driving a motor vehicle while under the influence of an alcoholic beverage, any drugs, or any controlled substances receive the appropriate sentence or penalty based on that individual's complete driving history.

(b) An accurate record of the prior arrests and convictions of a person for driving under the influence may not be available to the judge at the time of sentencing because the person may have used an alias or some other form of false identification.

(c) There is a need for a reporting system that can identify, in a timely fashion, the prior arrest histories of those arrested for driving under the influence.

(d) The intent of this act is to require that a pilot project relating to the fingerprinting of those persons arrested for driving under the influence be implemented in a designated county. *(Added by Stats 1990 ch 1243 §1, eff. 1/1/91.)*

© 1992 by J., B. & L. Gould
Printed in the U.S.A.   **EP**

§13894.6. Selection of county for pilot project.

The Department of Justice shall designate an appropriate county or portion of a county, with the county's consent, for a pilot fingerprint project. The designated area should be as self-contained as possible to increase the likelihood that the arrestees' residences, places of work, and general driving patterns are within its boundaries. In consultation with the department, the sheriff of the designated county shall fingerprint persons who are arrested for a violation of Section 23152 or 23153 of the Vehicle Code using a livescan fingerprint computer system. The sheriff of the county designated by the Department of Justice shall cooperate with the department in the county's implementation of the pilot project. *(Added by Stats 1990 ch 1243 §1, eff. 1/1/91.)*

§13894.7. Data tracking of DUI offenders.

Under the pilot project, the sheriff of the designated county shall statistically track the persons arrested for driving under the influence for an 18-month period to determine whether the same individuals are arrested for subsequent driving offenses during the pilot period and whether the person's prior records in the pilot project fingerprint data base are successfully matched as a result of the fingerprint identification process. *(Added by Stats 1990 ch 1243 §1, eff. 1/1/91.)*

§13894.8. Fingerprinting of DUI offenders.

The sheriff of the portion of the county designated by the Department of Justice shall take the fingerprints of persons arrested for driving under the influence of alcohol or drugs, or both, with the livescan fingerprint computer system. *(Added by Stats 1990 ch 1243 §1, eff. 1/1/91.)*

§13894.9. Report on pilot project.

The Bureau of Crime Statistics, within the Department of Justice, shall advise on the study's design, review the findings, and assist the county in preparing a report to the Legislature which shall be submitted by the designated county to the Legislature on or before November 1, 1992. The report shall include all of the following:

(a) The basis for the selection of the county or the portion of a county designated for the implementation of the pilot project, including consideration of the number of persons arrested for driving under the influence in the jurisdiction chosen, the geography, and the population.

(b) The staffing and other support requirements of the designated county sheriff's department which assisted in the taking and processing of the fingerprints with regard to the implementation of the pilot project.

(c) Any recommendations by the sheriff or the department for legislation as a result of the pilot project. *(Added by Stats 1990 ch 1243 §1, eff. 1/1/91.)*

CHAPTER 11

VICTIMS' LEGAL RESOURCE CENTER
(Added by Stats 1985 ch 1443 §1.)

§13897. Victims of crime.

The Legislature finds and declares each of the following:

(a) The citizens of California have expressed great concern for the plight of crime victims.

(b) It is in the best interest, not only of the victims and their families, but also of all the citizens of California to ensure that crime victims receive comprehensive assistance in overcoming the effects of victimization.

(c) While many options and rights exist for the crime victim, including providing financial assistance pursuant to Chapter 5 (commencing with Section 13959) of Part 4 of Division 3 of Title 2 of the Government Code, participation in sentencing and parole eligibility hearings of criminal perpetrators, civil litigation against the perpetrator and third parties, assistance from victim-witness programs, and private support and counseling services, research indicates that many crime victims suffer needlessly because they are not aware of these options and rights, or are apprehensive or uncertain about where to go for assistance or how to exercise their rights.

(d) It is thus necessary to provide a resource center, statewide in scope, where victims of crime, their families, and providers of services to victims of crime can receive referral information, assistance, and legal guidance in order to deal effectively with the needs of victims of crime and minimize the continuing victimization process, which often results from a complex justice system. This resource center shall be independent, offer victims assistance in understanding and effectively exercising their legal rights, provide information about their rights and the workings of the criminal justice system, and direct them to appropriate local resources and agencies which can offer further assistance. The resource center shall provide, on a statewide basis, information assistance for all crime victims without charge and shall complement the efforts of various local programs, including victim-witness programs, rape crisis units, domestic violence projects, and child abuse centers. *(Amended by Stats 1988 ch 1640 §1, eff. 1/1/89.)*

§13897.1. Resource center for crime victims.

There shall be established a resource center which shall operate a statewide, toll-free information service, consisting of legal and other information, for crime victims and providers of services to crime victims. The center shall provide information and educational materials discussing victims' legal rights. The center shall distribute these materials to administrative agencies, law enforcement agencies, victim-service programs, local, regional, and statewide education systems, appropriate human service agencies, and political, social, civic, and religious leaders and organizations.

As used in this chapter, "provider of services to crime victims" means any hospital, doctor, attorney, local or statewide rape crisis center, domestic violence center, child abuse counseling center, or victims' witness center that seeks to assist crime victims in understanding and exercising their legal rights, including those under Chapter 5 (commencing with Section 13959) of Part 4 of Division 3 of Title 2 of the Government Code. *(Amended by Stats 1988 ch 1640 §2, eff. 1/1/89.)*

§13897.2. Granting of award for resource center.

(a) The Office of Criminal Justice Planning shall grant an award to an appropriate private, nonprofit organization, to provide a statewide resource center, as described in Section 13897.1.

(b) The center shall:

(1) Provide callers with information about victims' legal rights to compensation pursuant to Chapter 5

(commencing with Section 13959) of Part 4 of Division 3 of Title 2 of the Government Code and, where appropriate, provide victims with guidance in exercising these rights.

(2) Provide callers who provide services to victims of crime with legal information regarding the legal rights of victims of crime.

(3) Advise callers about any potential civil causes of action, and where appropriate, provide callers with references to local legal aid and lawyer referral services.

(4) Advise and assist callers in understanding and implementing their rights to participate in sentencing and parole eligibility hearings as provided by statute.

(5) Advise callers about victims' rights in the criminal justice system, assist them in overcoming problems, including the return of property, and inform them of any procedures protecting witnesses.

(6) Refer callers, as appropriate, to local programs, which include victim-witness programs, rape crisis units, domestic violence projects, and child sexual abuse centers.

(7) Refer callers to local resources for information about appropriate public and private benefits and the means of obtaining aid.

(8) Publicize the existence of the toll-free service through the print and electronic media, including public service announcements, brochures, press announcements, various other educational materials, and agreements for the provision of publicity, by private entities.

(9) Compile comprehensive referral lists of local resources that include the following: victims' assistance resources, including legal and medical services, financial assistance, personal counseling and support services, and victims' support groups.

(10) Produce promotional materials for distribution to law enforcement agencies, state and local agencies, print, radio, and television media outlets, and the general public. These materials shall include placards, video and audio training materials, written handbooks, and brochures for public distribution. Distribution of these materials shall be coordinated with the local victims' service programs.

(11) Research, compile, and maintain a library of legal information concerning crime victims and their rights.

(12) Provide a 20-percent minimum cash match for all funds appropriated pursuant to this chapter which match may include federal and private funds in order to supplement any funds appropriated by the Legislature.

(c) The resource center shall be located so as to assure convenient and regular access between the center and those state agencies most concerned with crime victims. The entity receiving the grant shall be a private, nonprofit organization, independent of law enforcement agencies, and have qualified staff knowledgeable in the legal rights of crime victims and the programs and services available to victims throughout the state. The subgrantee shall have an existing statewide, toll-free information service and have demonstrated substantial capacity and experience serving crime victims in areas required by this act.

(d) The services of the resource center shall not duplicate the victim service activities of the Office of Criminal Justice Planning or those activities of local victim programs funded through the office.

(e) The subgrantee shall be compensated at its federally approved indirect cost rate, if any. For the purposes of this section, "federally approved indirect cost rate" means that rate established by the federal Department of Health and Human Services or other federal agency for the subgrantee. Nothing in this section shall be construed as requiring the Office of Criminal Justice Planning to permit the use of federally approved indirect cost rates for other subgrantees of other grants administered by the office.

(f) All information and records retained by the center in the course of providing services under this chapter shall be confidential and privileged pursuant to Article 3 (commencing with Section 950) of Chapter 4 of Division 8 of the Evidence Code and Article 4 (commencing with Section 6068) of Chapter 4 of Division 3 of the Business and Professions Code. Nothing in this subdivision shall prohibit compilation and distribution of statistical data by the center. (Amended by Stats 1988 ch 1640 §3, eff. 1/1/89.)

§13897.3. Guidelines and standards for monitoring the effectiveness of the resource center program.

The Office of Criminal Justice Planning shall develop written guidelines for funding and performance standards for monitoring the effectiveness of the resource center program. The program shall be evaluated by a public or private nonprofit entity under a contract with the Office of Criminal Justice Planning. (Added by Stats 1985 ch 1443 §1.)

TITLE 6.5

LOCAL CRIMINAL JUSTICE PLANNING

§13900. Legislative intent.

The Legislature finds and declares:

(a) That crime is a local problem that must be dealt with by state and local governments if it is to be controlled effectively.

(b) That criminal justice needs and problems vary greatly among the different local jurisdictions of this state.

(c) That effective planning and coordination can be accomplished only through the direct, immediate and continuing cooperation of local officials charged with general governmental and criminal justice agency responsibilities.

(d) That planning for the efficient use of criminal justice resources requires a permanent coordinating effort on the part of local governments and local criminal justice and delinquency prevention agencies.

§13901. Districts.

(a) For the purposes of coordinating local criminal justice activities and planning for the use of state and federal action funds made available through any grant programs, criminal justice and delinquency prevention planning districts shall be established.

(b) On January 1, 1976, all planning district boundaries shall remain as they were immediately prior to that date. Thereafter, the number and boundaries of such planning districts may be altered from time to time by a two-thirds vote of the California Council on Criminal Justice pursuant to this section; provided that no county shall be divided into two or more districts, nor shall two or more counties which do not comprise a contiguous area form a single such district.

© 1992 by J., B. & L. Gould
Printed in the U.S.A.   EP

(c) Prior to taking any action to alter the boundaries of any planning district, the council shall adopt a resolution indicating its intention to take the action and, at least 90 days prior to the taking of the action, shall forward a copy of the resolution to all units of government directly affected by the proposed action together with notice of the time and place at which the action will be considered by the council.

(d) If any county or a majority of the cities directly affected by the proposed action objects thereto, and a copy of the resolution of each board of supervisors or city council stating its objection is delivered to the executive office of the Office of Criminal Justice Planning within 30 days following the giving of the notice of the proposed action, the council, or a duly constituted committee thereof, shall conduct a public meeting within the boundaries of the district as they are proposed to be determined. Notice of the time and place of the meeting shall be given to the public and to all units of local government directly affected by the proposed action, and reasonable opportunity shall be given to members of the public and representatives of such units to present their views on the proposed action.

§13902. Constituting districts.

Each county placed within a single county planning district may constitute a planning district upon execution of a joint powers agreement or arrangement acceptable to the county and to at least that one-half of the cities in the district which contain at least one-half of the population of the district. Counties placed within a multicounty planning district may constitute a planning district upon execution of a joint powers agreement or other arrangement acceptable to the participating counties and to at least that one-half of the cities in such district which contain at least one-half of the population of such district. If no combination of one-half of the cities of a district contains at least one-half of the population of the district, then agreement of any half of the cities in such district is sufficient to enable execution of joint powers agreements or other acceptable arrangements for constituting planning districts.

§13903. Funds.

Planning districts may be the recipients of criminal justice and delinquency prevention planning or coordinating funds made available to units of general local government or combinations of units of general local government by federal or state law. Such planning districts shall establish local criminal justice and delinquency prevention planning boards, but shall not be obligated to finance their activities in the event that federal or state support of such activities is lacking.

§13904. Membership of local boards.

(a) The membership of each local board shall be consistent with state and federal statutes and guidelines; shall be representative of a broad range of community interests and viewpoints; and shall be balanced in terms of racial, sexual, age, economic, and geographic factors. Each local board shall consist of not less than 21 and not more than 30 members, a majority of whom shall be locally elected officials.

(b) The California Council on Criminal Justice shall promulgate standards to ensure that the composition of each board complies with subdivision (a). The council shall annually review the composition of each board, and if it finds that the composition of a local board complies with the standards, it shall so certify. Cer-

tification shall be effective for one year; provided that if the membership of a board changes by more than 25 percent during a period of certification, the council may withdraw the certificate prior to its expiration.

(c) If the council determines that the composition of a local board does not comply with the standards, it shall direct the appropriate appointing authority to reappoint the local board and shall again review the composition pursuant to this section after such reappointments are made. The council may void decisions made by such board after such finding and due notice. The council may approve the allocation of planning or action funds only to those districts which have been certified pursuant to this section.

§13905. Representatives of public; appointment.

Except as otherwise provided in Section 13904, representatives of the public shall be appointed to local criminal justice and delinquency prevention planning boards, of a number not to exceed the number of representatives of government on that board. At least one-fifth of the membership of such boards shall be representatives of citizens, professional and community organizations, including organizations directly related to delinquency prevention.

§13906. Powers of board.

Planning boards may contract with other public or private entities for the performance of services, may appoint an executive officer and other employees, and may receive and expend funds in order to carry out planning and coordinating responsibility.

TITLE 6.7

HIGH-TECHNOLOGY CRIME PREVENTION
(Repealed by Stats 1986 ch 1435 §2, eff. 1/1/89.)

TITLE 6.8

TARGETED URBAN CRIME NARCOTICS TASK FORCE
(Repealed by Stats 1985 ch 423 §1, eff. 1/1/88.)

TITLE 7

CALIFORNIA CRIME TECHNOLOGICAL RESEARCH FOUNDATION
(Added by Stats 1967 ch 1661 §4; amended by Stats 1971 ch 1119 §§1—8; Stats 1974 ch 750 §1; repealed by Stats 1991 ch 1091 §120, eff. 1/1/92.)

TITLE 7

CALIFORNIA CHILD VICTIM WITNESS PILOT AND DEMONSTRATION PROGRAMS
(Added by Stats 1989 ch 1220 §1, eff. 1/1/90 only until 1/1/94.)

ARTICLE 1

GENERAL

§14000. California Child Victim Witness Pilot and Demonstration Programs.

This title shall be known and may be cited as the California Child Victim Witness Pilot and Demonstration Programs. *(Added by Stats 1989 ch 1220 §1, eff. 1/1/90 only until 1/1/94.)*

§14001. Legislative intent.

The Legislature finds and declares that there is a continuing need to improve the treatment of children in legal proceedings by developing methods to achieve all of the following:

(a) Eliminate unnecessary repetitive interviews and court appearances of child victim witnesses.

(b) Streamline and improve investigative and judicial practices and procedures involving child victim witnesses.

(c) Improve the truth-finding process in cases involving child victim witnesses.

(d) Protect the rights of the child victims, their families, and the accused.

(Added by Stats 1989 ch 1220 §1, eff. 1/1/90 only until 1/1/94.)

§14002. Pilot program guidelines.

(a) It is the intent of the Legislature to establish up to three pilot program and demonstration projects, specifically, three investigative, judicial, and child advocacy pilot and demonstration projects, in counties to improve the treatment of child victim witnesses in legal proceedings by funding those projects for three years.

(b) The investigative pilot and demonstration projects shall incorporate the essential elements for improving and streamlining the investigative process as it affects child victim witnesses, as those elements were identified by the California Child Victim Witness Judicial Advisory Committee, created under former Section 14152. Those elements shall include the following:

(1) Interviewing children in a child oriented setting.

(2) Using a child interview specialist to conduct comprehensive interviews with children.

(3) Developing interdisciplinary child interview protocols.

(4) Memorializing the comprehensive interview to eliminate or minimize the need for subsequent interviews.

(5) Conducting multidisciplinary team reviews to make recommendations on child abuse cases and the needs of child victim witnesses.

(6) Ensuring that initial medical evidentiary examinations of suspected child abuse victims are conducted by medical professionals with expertise in diagnosing child abuse.

(7) Assigning a child advocate.

(8) Providing appropriate mental health services.

(c) The judicial pilot and demonstration projects shall incorporate the California Child Victim Witness Judicial Advisory Committee's proposals for streamlining and improving California's judiciary as it affects child victim witnesses and their families, including all of the following:

(1) Restructuring the superior court to create a family relations division coequal with the civil and criminal divisions.

(2) Developing special relationships among different courts.

(3) Addressing the special problems relating to child victim witnesses in the courts.

(d) The child advocacy pilot and demonstration projects shall provide a full range of advocacy and support services to child victim witnesses throughout all investigative and judicial proceedings, including providing a knowledgeable, caring person who shall undertake each of the following:

(1) Overseeing the child's emotional well-being and best interests.

(2) Protecting the child's legal rights.

(3) Identifying other advocacy services for the child.

(Added by Stats 1989 ch 1220 §1, eff. 1/1/90 only until 1/1/94.)

ARTICLE 2

CALIFORNIA CHILD VICTIM WITNESS PILOT AND DEMONSTRATION PROGRAMS

§14005. Pilot program established.

There is hereby established a three-year pilot program in the office of the Attorney General, and a three-year pilot program in the Judicial Council, which programs shall be known as the California Child Victim Witness Pilot and Demonstration Programs. The program operated by the office of the Attorney General shall consist of an investigative pilot and demonstration program, and the program operated by the Judicial Council shall consist of judicial and child advocacy pilot and demonstration programs. Each program shall operate in up to three counties which have made application to and have been designated by the administering agency of the respective programs. *(Added by Stats 1989 ch 1220 §1, eff. 1/1/90 only until 1/1/94.)*

§14006. Pilot program locations.

The office of the Attorney General and the Judicial Council shall, after consultation and coordination with each other, determine the counties in which the respective projects will be operated. Each shall give preference for selection of the pilot projects to those counties willing to operate all three pilot and demonstration projects, or alternatively to counties which otherwise provided the most comprehensive proposals for the projects. *(Added by Stats 1989 ch 1220 §1, eff. 1/1/90 only until 1/1/94.)*

ARTICLE 3

INVESTIGATIVE PILOT AND DEMONSTRATION PROJECTS

§14008. Establishment of Investigative Pilot Program.

The office of the Attorney General shall establish and fund from moneys appropriated by the Legislature for purposes of this article up to three investigative pilot and demonstration projects for a three-year period in order to implement and evaluate the recommendations of the California Child Victim Witness Judicial Advisory Committee. Each county investigative pilot and demonstration project designated by the Attorney General should:

(a) Require the mandatory use of videotaping of the comprehensive child victim interview, with the understanding and agreement of the child. This videotaping shall be conducted only after initial interviews and contacts have been made, if necessary, by the district attorney, local law enforcement agencies, or social services agencies.

© 1992 by J., B. & L. Gould
Printed in the U.S.A.   **EP**

(b) Establish a child victim witness center or centers, or special interview settings.

(c) Develop interagency agreements and protocols for interviewing child victims, including procedures to limit the number of interviewers and minimize the number of interviews.

(d) Train child interview specialists selected by a team composed of representatives from the district attorney's office, local law enforcement agencies, and social services agencies.

(e) Require that comprehensive interviews be conducted by a child interview specialist.

(f) Establish procedures for maintaining the confidentiality of audio and video tape interviews of child victim witnesses.

(g) Establish multidisciplinary teams to review and make recommendations on child abuse cases and the needs of child victim witnesses.

(h) Adopt procedures to ensure that initial medical evidentiary examinations of suspected child abuse victims are conducted by a medical professional with expertise in diagnosing child abuse, and that the results of the examination are used in the judicial process, so long as the results are otherwise admissible under law, and in the development of medical treatment plans for the child.

(i) Develop procedures for providing mental health services for child victim witnesses. (*Added by Stats 1989 ch 1220 §1, eff. 1/1/90 only until 1/1/94.*)

ARTICLE 4

JUDICIAL PILOT AND DEMONSTRATION PROJECTS

§14010. Judicial Pilot Program established.

The Judicial Council shall establish and fund from moneys appropriated by the Legislature for purposes of this article up to three judicial demonstration projects for a three-year period in order to implement and evaluate the recommendations of the California Child Victim Witness Judicial Advisory Committee. Each county judicial pilot and demonstration project designated by the Judicial Council shall:

(a) Restructure the superior court to create a family relations division grouping civil, child, family, and human relations-oriented legal actions within that division. The family relations division shall be coequal with the civil and criminal divisions with a supervising judge. The administrative support, including staffing, of the family relations division shall be no less than the level of administrative support of the civil or criminal divisions. However, if the administrative support for the juvenile, probate, civil, and family court proceedings to be processed by the family relations division is, prior to the implementation of this act, at a level which is higher than the administrative support of the civil or criminal divisions, then the administrative support for the family relations division shall be no less than the above-specified level of administrative support for the juvenile, probate, civil, and family court which existed prior to the implementation of this act. Restructuring plans shall include the following elements:

(1) Policies which ensure that judges are assigned to the family relations division for substantial periods of time and that they are selected based upon interest and ability.

(2) Procedures to enable, to the maximum extent possible, one judge to hear all actions in the family relations division relating to a child victim witness, and to enable the judge to combine hearings whenever it is appropriate.

(3) A plan to educate family relations court judges in all of the legal proceedings which may be heard within the division and in family dynamics and child development.

(4) Protective orders to protect children who appear in any division of the family relations court and to protect against unauthorized disclosure of audio or video tape interviews or testimony of a child victim witness.

(b) Develop formal relationships among court systems, including the following:

(1) Developing efficient means for courts and court systems to communicate with each other regarding proceedings involving the same child or family, including effective methods for the immediate transmission of court orders.

(2) Developing effective methods for exchanging information among investigative and supervisory agencies serving the court to ensure that all relevant information concerning the child or family is before the court.

(3) Developing special procedures for coordination and cooperation in case management when a child is involved in criminal and dependency proceedings, domestic relations and dependency proceedings, dependency and delinquency proceedings, or related domestic violence proceedings.

(c) Address special problems relating to child victim witnesses, including the following:

(1) Developing guidelines for managing courtroom examinations of child witnesses for the purposes of reducing the child's stress and eliciting more accurate testimony.

(2) Developing procedures for appointing a child development expert, when appropriate, to advise the court in developing guidelines for courtroom examination of a child in all legal proceedings.

(3) Developing guidelines for controlling access to children who are victims or witnesses in legal proceedings.

(4) Modifying courts and courtrooms to accommodate the needs of children and families when possible. (*Added by Stats 1989 ch 1220 §1, eff. 1/1/90 only until 1/1/94.*)

ARTICLE 5

CHILD ADVOCACY PILOT AND DEMONSTRATION PROJECTS

§14012. Child Advocacy Program established.

The Judicial Council shall establish and fund from moneys appropriated by the Legislature for purposes of this article up to three child advocacy demonstration projects for a three-year period in order to implement and evaluate the recommendations of the California Child Victim Witness Judicial Advisory Committee. Each county child advocacy demonstration project shall:

(a) Establish a child advocacy program or office to provide a full range of advocacy and support services to child victim witnesses throughout investigative and judicial proceedings.

© 1992 by J., B. & L. Gould
Printed in the U.S.A. **EP**

(b) Provide to each child victim witness a knowledgeable, caring person whose primary responsibility is to guide the child through the difficult investigative and court processes, to look out for the child's emotional well-being and best interests, to protect the child's legal rights, and to identify other advocacy services for the child.

(c)(1) Make available to each child victim witness an attorney trained in the representation of the child's interests. This attorney shall not have standing to represent the child's interests before the court and jury in criminal cases. However, each county child advocacy demonstration project shall establish procedures to receive information and advice from the attorney where the attorney believes it is necessary to protect the rights and best interests of the child.

(2) Subject to the restrictions in paragraph (1) on the attorney's standing, the attorney shall have the same rights and limitations in representing the interests of the child as an attorney representing the interests of any nonparty in criminal proceedings.

(d) Require that attorneys for children in family relations actions continue, to the maximum extent possible, to represent children in related proceedings and in relations with other agencies such as schools, mental health agencies, regional centers, and community services agencies.

(e) Ensure that children receive all necessary mental health services and are not harmed by the system itself.

(f) Provide multiple support services for child victim witnesses. *(Added by Stats 1989 ch 1220 §1, eff. 1/1/90 only until 1/1/94.)*

ARTICLE 6

RESEARCH AND EVALUATION

§14013. Research and Evaluation committee.

Each administering agency shall establish a Research and Evaluation Advisory Panel consisting of at least five panel members, which panels shall coordinate the research design, operation, and evaluation of the pilot and demonstration projects. By June 30, 1990, the panels shall establish procedures for determining and describing current investigative, judicial, and child advocacy services and their costs, and for measuring the advantages, disadvantages, and associated cost savings, if any, of the changes in those services affected by the pilot and demonstration projects. The panels shall ensure uniformity of data collection in the various projects so that valid comparisons can be drawn, and ensure that the project evaluation is carried out in a manner that allows for valid and unambiguous conclusions. *(Added by Stats 1989 ch 1220 §1, eff. 1/1/90 only until 1/1/94.)*

§14014. Collection of program data.

(a) Each investigative pilot and demonstration project shall collect the following baseline data either for a period of six months before the commencement of the project or during the operation of the project so long as there is a randomly selected and statistically valid comparison group of those served and not served by the project:

(1) The number and identity of the interviewers, the number and length of interviews, and the optimal number of interviews for each child victim witness.

(2) The number and type of interview settings, and the optimal number of interview settings, for each child victim witness.

(3) The number of medical examinations of suspected child abuse victims and the type of medical tests and procedures conducted, including the number of initial medical evidentiary examinations conducted by medical professionals with an expertise in diagnosing child abuse and their qualifications.

(4) The number of interviews of child victim witnesses that are videotaped or audiotaped.

(5) The number and percentage of child abuse cases that receive multidisciplinary team reviews, the qualifications of the members of the teams, and the results of the interviews.

(6) A description of any established interagency procedures or protocols for interviewing child victim witnesses.

(7) A description of any established procedures for selecting and training child interviewers.

(8) A description of any established procedures for ensuring the confidentiality of audiotape and videotape interviews of child victim witnesses.

(9) A description of any established procedures for providing mental heath or other support services to child victim witnesses.

(10) Data on perceptions of the investigative process, including the number and quality of interviewers, interviews, interview settings, and medical examinations, and the availability of mental health or other support services.

(11) Any other information appropriate to collect.

(b) The panel appointed by the office of the Attorney General shall evaluate the investigative pilot and demonstration project in each county for the purpose of determining whether each project has been successful in meeting the following goals or objectives:

(1) Reducing the number of interviewers and the number of interviews after the initial interview for child victim witnesses by at least 25 percent.

(2) Reducing the number of interview settings for child victim witnesses by at least 50 percent.

(3) Reducing the number of medical examinations of suspected child abuse victims after the initial examination by at least 25 percent.

(4) Videotaping 100 percent of the interviews of child victim witnesses who agree to be videotaped.

(5) Conducting multidisciplinary team reviews in 100 percent of the child abuse cases.

(6) Developing interagency agreements and protocols for interviewing child victim witnesses, focusing on reducing the stress on the child caused by the investigation.

(7)(A) Providing 40 hours of training to child interview specialists selected by a team composed of representatives from the district attorney's office, local enforcement agencies, and social services agencies.

(B) Improving the qualifications, selection process, and training of interviewers.

(8) Establishing or improving procedures for maintaining the confidentiality of audiotape and videotape interviews of child victim witnesses.

(9) Developing procedures for providing mental health and other support services to child victim witnesses.

(10) Reducing the traumatic impact of the investigative process on the minor by 30 percent.

(c) The panel appointed by the office of the Attorney General shall collect data from each investigative

© 1992 by J., B. & L. Gould
Printed in the U.S.A.   **EP**

pilot and demonstration project for purposes of comparing the costs for child victim witnesses not served by the project. Savings will be measured by costs related to, but not limited to, the reduction in the number of interviewers, interview settings, and medical examinations, and other savings associated with coordination efforts. *(Added by Stats 1989 ch 1220 §1, eff. 1/1/90 only until 1/1/94.)*

§14015. Evaluation of program.

The panel appointed by the Judicial Council shall evaluate each judicial pilot and demonstration project to determine whether the goals and objectives specified in Section 14001 and subdivision (c) of Section 14002 have been met. The evaluation and goals shall include:

(a) The effect of court restructuring on tracking, coordination, and consolidating proceedings in the family relations division involving the same child or family, including whether court restructuring, coordinating, and consolidating of procedures and actions involving the same child or family in the family relations division produces a 20-percent decrease in the average number of court hearings involving a child who may be a minor as defined in Section 300 of the Welfare and Institutions Code, a decrease of 30 percent in the amount of time this minor spends awaiting and attending court hearings, a 20-percent reduction in the duplication or overlap of services for children, and a measurable increase in the level of satisfaction with the legal process, as reported by children, families, attorneys, judges, and other groups and individuals involved in the process.

(b) The effect of existing and newly established formal relationships between the court system on the management of cases involving child victim witnesses, including whether newly instituted case management strategies and techniques diminish by 30 percent the traumatic impact on minors of courtroom appearances, and increase by 30 percent the number of children permitted to testify in court.

(c) The effect of special child victim witness courtroom management strategies and techniques on the child's emotional state, including whether newly instituted rules controlling access to, and protecting the emotional and physical well-being of, minors reduce by 30 percent the number of contacts within the court setting, including court appearances and excluding the contacts with the child advocate appointed to protect the child.

(d) The cost of providing special services, techniques, and physical plants for the pilot and demonstration program, their benefit to the justice system, and their potential utilization in a cost-beneficial manner to other proceedings. *(Added by Stats 1989 ch 1220 §1, eff. 1/1/90 only until 1/1/94.)*

§14016. Evaluation of program results.

The panel appointed by the Judicial Council shall evaluate each child advocacy pilot and demonstration project to determine whether the goals and objectives specified in Section 14001 and subdivision (d) of Section 14002 have been met. The evaluation and goals shall include:

(a) Whether 100 percent of the minors, who are involved in at least two related court proceedings, are provided a capable and supportive child advocate, the number of other minors provided a child advocate, the types of services performed by each advocate, the cost of that service, and the benefit to each minor and the justice system. If an advocate was not provided, an explanation of why not shall be included.

(b) Whether an attorney was available throughout the proceeding to the child advocate or the minor, the nature and extent of services provided, the source of funds for services, cost of services, and the number of contacts.

(c) Whether each minor subject to the projects was provided all necessary mental heath services, the nature and extent of the mental health and other support services recommended for, and those actually provided to, the minor, the cost of services provided, the source of payments for those services, whether future mental health services will be likely to be necessary, and whether there exists a source for their payment.

(d) Whether the provision of the services to the minor minimize the traumatic impact of the court proceedings.

(e) Whether the project has increased the use of volunteers in providing support services to the courts by at least 40 percent and whether the volunteers have made contributions beyond their direct provision of services and what these contributions are, and whether the use of volunteers has created any problems of undesirable side effects and what those are, including the costs of arranging and providing those services.

(f) Any other information the Judicial Council or advisory panels determine is appropriate. *(Added by Stats 1989 ch 1220 §1, eff. 1/1/90 only until 1/1/94.)*

§14017. Program results.

Not later than July 1, 1994, the Attorney General and the Judicial Council shall report to the Legislature on the results of each of the pilot and demonstration projects. The reports shall include the evaluations of the Research and Evaluation Advisory Panels, recommendations as to whether the techniques utilized in the pilot and demonstration projects should be required or encouraged on a statewide basis, and how any expenses related to the changes should be financed. Recommended changes in the law shall be included in the reports. *(Added by Stats 1989 ch 1220 §1, eff. 1/1/90 only until 1/1/94.)*

§14020. Filing of complaint to declare minor a dependent child.

Nothing in this title shall alter or impair the existing statutory authority of a district attorney to determine whether a criminal complaint should be filed and prosecuted, or of a county welfare department or probation officer to determine whether a petition to declare a minor a dependent child of the count should be filed, or, except as expressly stated, of law enforcement agencies, probation officers, or county welfare departments to determine whether additional interviews should be conducted. *(Added by Stats 1989 ch 1220 §1, eff. 1/1/90 only until 1/1/94.)*

§14021. Repealer.

This title shall remain in effect only until January 1, 1994, and as of that date is repealed, unless a later enacted statute, which is enacted before January 1, 1994, deletes or extends that date. *(Added by Stats 1989 ch 1220 §1, eff. 1/1/90 only until 1/1/94.)*

TITLE 8

BUILDING SECURITY

§14050. *Repealed by Stats 1989 ch 756 §5, eff. 1/1/90.*

§14051. Consultation between law enforcement and fire officials.

The chief law enforcement and fire officials of every city shall consult with the chief officer of their city who is charged with the enforcement of laws or ordinances regulating the erection, construction, or alteration of buildings within their jurisdiction for the purpose of developing local security standards and regulations supplemental to those adopted as part of Title 24 of the California Administrative Code, relating to building standards. The chief law enforcement and fire officials of every county shall consult with the chief officer of their county who is charged with the enforcement of laws or ordinances regulating the erection, construction, or alteration of buildings within their jurisdiction for the purpose of developing local security standards and regulations supplemental to those adopted as part of Title 24 of the California Administrative Code, relating to building standards. No provision of this or any other code shall prevent a city or county from enacting building security standards stricter than those enacted by the state.

TITLE 9

BLUE RIBBON COMMISSION ON INMATE POPULATION MANAGEMENT
(Added by Stats 1987 ch 1225 §1, eff. only until 1/1/90.)

TITLE 10

COMMUNITY VIOLENCE PREVENTION AND CONFLICT RESOLUTION

§14110. Legislative findings.

The Legislature finds the following:

(a) The incidence of violence in our state continues to present an increasing and dominating societal problem that must be addressed at its root causes in order to reduce significantly its effects upon our society.

(b) As an initial step toward that goal, the Legislature passed Assembly Bill No. 23 of the 1979-80 Regular Session which created the California Commission on Crime Control and Violence Prevention which was charged with compiling the latest research on root causes of violence, in order to lay the foundation for a credible, effective violence eradication program.

(c) The commission produced a final report in 1982 entitled "Ounces of Prevention," which established that long-term prevention is a valuable and viable public policy and demonstrated that there are reachable root causes of violence in our society.

(d) The report contains comprehensive findings and recommendations in 10 broad categorical areas for the removal of individual, familial, and societal causal factors of crime and violence in California.

(e) The recommendations in the report are feasible and credible, propose an effective means of resolving conflict and removing the root causes of violence in our society, and should be implemented, so that their value may be provided to our citizenry.

§14111. Further legislative findings.

The Legislature further finds that:

(a) It is in the public interest to translate the findings of the California Commission on Crime Control and Violence Prevention into community-empowering, community-activated violence prevention efforts that would educate, inspire, and inform the citizens of California about, coordinate existing programs relating to, and provide direct services addressing the root causes of, violence in California.

(b) The recommendations in the report of the commission can serve as both the foundation and guidelines for short, intermediate, and long-term programs to address and alleviate violence in California.

(c) It is in the public interest to facilitate the highest degree of coordination between, cooperation among, and utilization of public, nonprofit, and private sector resources, programs, agencies, organizations, and institutions toward maximally successful violence prevention and crime control efforts.

(d) Prevention is a sound fiscal, as well as social, policy objective. Crime and violence prevention programs can and should yield substantially beneficial results with regard to the exorbitant costs of both violence and crime to the public and private sectors.

(e) The Office of Criminal Justice Planning is the appropriate state agency to contract for programs addressing the root causes of violence.

§14112. Legislative intent.

The Legislature therefore intends:

(a) To develop community violence prevention and conflict resolution programs, in the state, based upon the recommendations of the California Commission on Crime Control and Violence Prevention, that would present a balanced, comprehensive educational, intellectual, and experiential approach toward eradicating violence in our society.

(b) That these programs shall be regulated, and funded pursuant to contracts with the Office of Criminal Justice Planning.

§14113. Two-year community violence prevention and conflict resolution pilot programs.

(a) The Office of Criminal Justice Planning shall contract for four two-year community violence prevention and conflict resolution pilot programs throughout this state. They shall be commenced after July 1, 1985. Each of the four pilot programs may continue for a maximum of two years.

(b) Each program shall address the following subject areas as they interrelate with violence and to the extent they affect the geographic area served by the programs:

(1) Parenting, birthing, early childhood development, self-esteem, and family violence, to include child, spousal, and elderly abuse.

(2) Economic factors and institutional racism.

(3) Schools and educational factors.

(4) Alcohol, diet, drugs, and other biochemical and biological factors.

(5) Conflict resolution.

(6) The media.

© 1992 by J., B. & L. Gould
Printed in the U.S.A. **EP**

§14114. First priority programs.

First priority shall be given to programs which provide community education, outreach, coordination, and include creative and effective ways to translate the recommendations of the California Commission on Crime Control and Violence Prevention into practical use in one or more of the subject areas set forth in Section 14113. At least three of the programs shall do all of the following:

(a) Use the recommendations of the California Commission on Crime Control and Violence Prevention and incorporate as many of those recommendations as possible into its program.

(b) Develop an intensive community-level educational program directed toward violence prevention. This educational component shall incorporate the commission's works "Ounces of Prevention" and "Taking Root," and shall be designed appropriately to reach the educational, ethnic, and socioeconomic individuals, groups, agencies, and institutions in the community.

(c) Include the imparting of conflict resolution skills.

(d) Coordinate with existing community-based, public and private, programs, agencies, organizations, and institutions, local, regional, and statewide public educational systems, criminal and juvenile justice systems, mental and public health agencies, appropriate human service agencies, and churches and religious organizations.

(e) Seek to provide specific resource and referral services to individuals, programs, agencies, organizations, and institutions confronting problems with violence and crime if the service is not otherwise available to the public.

(f) Reach all local ethnic, cultural, linguistic, and socioeconomic groups in the service area to the maximum extent feasible.

§14114.5. Further functions of programs.

Other programs shall include subdivisions (a) and (f) of Section 14114 and may include public lectures or sponsoring of conferences, or both.

§14115. Direct services; first priority.

(a) First priority programs may additionally provide specific direct services or contract for those services in one or more of the program areas as necessary to carry out the recommendations of the commission when those services are not otherwise available in the community and existing agencies do not furnish them. Direct services may include, but are not limited to, any of the following:

(1) Training seminars for law enforcement and human service agencies and operatives.

(2) Crisis intervention training and counseling.

(3) Casework and program consultation with local human service providers.

(4) Drug and alcohol counseling and treatment referral.

(5) Conflict resolution training and services, including the principles and practices of conflict mediation, arbitration, and "citizen tribunal" programs.

(b) All direct services are subject to Section 5328 of the Welfare and Institutions Code.

§14116. Programs given second priority.

Second priority shall be given to programs that conform to the requirements of Section 14114, except that the educational component of subdivision (f) of that section shall not be mandatory in each subject area, but shall be provided in at least three of those areas, and the programs shall provide specific direct services or contract for services in one or more program areas.

§14117. Governing boards or inter-agency coordinating teams.

(a) Each program shall have a governing board or an interagency coordinating team, or both, of at least nine members representing a cross section of existing and recipient, community-based, public and private persons, programs, agencies, organizations, and institutions. Each team shall do all of the following:

(1) As closely as possible represent the socioeconomic, ethnic, linguistic, and cultural makeup of the community and shall evidence an interest in and commitment to the categorical areas of violence prevention and conflict resolution.

(2) Be responsible for the implementation, evaluation, and operation of the program and all its constituent elements, including such specific direct services as may be provided pursuant to Section 14115.

(3) Be accountable for the distribution of all funds.

(4) Designate and appoint a responsible administrative authority acceptable to the Office of Criminal Justice Planning prior to the receipt of a grant.

(5) Submit an annual report to the Office of Criminal Justice Planning which shall include information on all of the following:

(A) The number of learning events.

(B) The number of persons trained.

(C) An overview of the changing level of information regarding root causes of violence.

(D) An overview of the changing level of attitude regarding root causes of violence.

(E) The changing level of behavior regarding root causes of violence.

(F) The degree to which the program has been successful in satisfying the requirements set forth in subdivisions (e) and (f) of Section 14114.

(G) Other measures of program efficacy as specified by the Office of Criminal Justice Planning.

(b) Coordinating teams established under this section may adopt local policies, procedures, and bylaws consistent with this title.

§14118. Duties of Office of Criminal Justice Planning.

(a) During the first six months of calendar year 1985, the Office of Criminal Justice Planning shall prepare and issue written program, fiscal, and administrative guidelines for the contracted programs that are consistent with this title, including guidelines for identifying recipient programs, agencies, organizations, and institutions, and organizing the coordinating teams. The Office of Criminal Justice Planning shall then issue a request for proposals. The responses to the request for proposals shall be rated according to the priorities set forth in subdivision (b) and additional criteria established by the guidelines. The highest rated responses shall be selected. The Office of Criminal Justice Planning shall do all of the following:

(1) Subject the proposed program and administrative guidelines to a 30-day period of broad public evaluation with public hearings commencing in May

1985, prior to adoption, including specific solicitation of input from culturally, geographically, socioeconomically, educationally, and ethnically diverse persons, programs, agencies, organizations, and institutions.

(2) Provide adequate public notice of the public evaluation around the state in major metropolitan and rural newspapers and related media outlets, and to local public, private, and nonprofit human service executives and advisory boards, and other appropriate persons and organizations.

(3) Establish a mechanism for obtaining, evaluating, and incorporating when appropriate and feasible, public input regarding the written program and administrative guidelines prior to adoption.

(b) Applicants for contracts under this title may be existing community-based public and nonprofit programs, agencies, organizations, and institutions, newly developed nonprofit corporations, or joint proposals from combinations of either or both of the above.

§14119. Further duties of Office of Criminal Justice Planning.

(a) Commencing on or after July 1, 1985, the Office of Criminal Justice Planning shall contract for no more than four pilot programs as described in Section 14113.

(b) Commencing on or after July 1, 1985, the Office of Criminal Justice Planning shall promote, organize, and conduct a series of one-day crime and violence prevention training workshops around the state. The Office of Criminal Justice Planning shall seek participation in the workshops from ethnically, linguistically, culturally, educationally, and economically diverse persons, agencies, organizations, and institutions.

(c) The training workshops shall have all of the following goals:

(1) To identify phenomena which are thought to be root causes of crime and violence.

(2) To identify local manifestations of those root causes.

(3) To examine the findings and recommendations of the California Commission on Crime Control and Violence Prevention.

(4) To focus on team building and interagency cooperation and coordination toward addressing the local problems of crime and violence.

(5) To examine the merits and necessity of a local crime and violence prevention effort.

(d) There shall be at least three workshops.

§14120. Funding of programs.

(a) Programs shall be funded, depending upon the availability of funds, for a period of two years.

(b) The Office of Criminal Justice Planning shall provide 50 percent of the program costs, to a maximum amount of fifty thousand dollars ($50,000) per program per year. The recipient shall provide the remaining 50 percent with other resources which may include in-kind contributions and services. The administrative expenses for the pilot programs funded under Section 14120 shall not exceed 10 percent.

(c) Programs should be seeking private sector moneys and developing ways to become self-sufficient upon completion of pilot program funding.

(d) The recipient programs shall be responsible for a year end independent audit.

(e) The Office of Criminal Justice Planning shall do an interim evaluation of the programs, commencing in July 1986, and shall report to the Legislature and the people with the results of the evaluation prior to October 31, 1986. The evaluation shall include, but not be limited to, an assessment and inventory of all of the following:

(1) The number of learning events.

(2) The number of persons trained.

(3) The changing level of information regarding root causes of violence.

(4) The changing level of attitude regarding root causes of violence.

(5) The changing level of behavior regarding root causes of violence.

(6) The reduced level of violence in our society.

(7) The degree to which the program has succeeded in reaching and impacting positively upon local ethnic, cultural, and socioeconomic groups in the service area.

A final evaluation shall be made with a report prior to October 31, 1987, which shall also include specific recommendations to the Legislature and the people of this state regarding methods and means by which these violence prevention and crime control programmatic efforts can be enhanced and improved.

§14121. Support staff.

The Office of Criminal Justice Planning may hire support staff and utilize resources necessary to carry out the purposes of this title.

TITLE 11

CALIFORNIA CHILD VICTIM WITNESS PROTECTION ACT
(Repealed by Stats 1986 ch 1282, eff. 1/1/89.)

TITLE 11

RECORDS AND REPORTS OF MONETARY INSTRUMENT TRANSACTIONS
(Added by Stats 1986 ch 1039 §3, eff. only until 1/1/97.)

§14160. Reports of monetary instrument transactions.

(a) It is the purpose of this title to require certain reports or records of transactions involving monetary instruments as defined herein where those reports or records have a high degree of usefulness in criminal investigations or proceedings.

(b) The Attorney General shall adopt rules and regulations for the administration and enforcement of this title.

(c) It is the intent of the Legislature that the rules and regulations prescribed by the Attorney General for the administration and enforcement of this title shall be designed to minimize the cost and difficulty of compliance and shall, to the greatest extent possible, result in report and record-keeping forms consistent with those in use for compliance with Sections 5311 et seq. of Title 31 of the United States Code, Section 6050 I of Title 26 of the United States Code, and regulations adopted thereunder.

(d) Nothing in this title shall be construed to give rise to a private cause of action for relief or damages. *(Added by Stats 1986 ch 1039 §3, eff. only until 1/1/97.)*

©·1992 by J., B. & L. Gould
Printed in the U.S.A.   EP

§14161. Terms defined.

As used in this title:

(a) "Financial institution" means, when located or doing business in this state, any national bank or banking association, state bank or banking association, commercial bank or trust company organized under the laws of the United States or any state, any private bank, industrial savings bank, savings bank or thrift institution, savings and loan association, or building and loan association organized under the laws of the United States or any state, any insured institution as defined in Section 401 of the National Housing Act, any credit union organized under the laws of the United States or any state, any national banking association or corporation acting under Chapter 6 (commencing with Section 601) of Title 12 of the United States Code, any foreign bank, any currency dealer or exchange, any person or business engaged primarily in the cashing of checks, any person or business who regularly engages in the issuing, selling, or redeeming of travelers' checks, money orders, or similar instruments, any broker or dealer in securities registered or required to be registered with the Securities and Exchange Commission under the Securities Exchange Act of 1934 or with the Commissioner of Corporations under Part 3 (commencing with Section 25200) of Division 1 of Title 4 of the Corporations Code, any licensed transmitter of funds or other person or business regularly engaged in transmitting funds to a foreign nation for others, any investment banker or investment company, any insurer, any dealer in gold, silver, or platinum bullion or coins, diamonds, emeralds, rubies, or sapphires, any pawnbroker, any telegraph company, any personal property broker, any person or business acting as a real property securities dealer within the meaning of Section 10237 of the Business and Professions Code, whether licensed to do so or not, any person or business acting within the meaning and scope of subdivisions (d) and (e) of Section 10131 and Section 10131.1 of the Business and Professions Code, whether licensed to do so or not, and any person or business defined as a "bank," "financial agency," or "financial institution" by Section 5312 of Title 31 of the United States Code and Section 103.11 of Title 31 of the Code of Federal Regulations and any successor provisions thereto.

(b) "Transaction" includes the deposit, withdrawal, transfer, bailment, loan, or exchange of currency, or a monetary instrument, as defined by subdivision (d), by, through, or to, a financial institution, as defined by subdivision (a). "Transaction" does not include the purchase of gold, silver, or platinum bullion or coins, or diamonds, emeralds, rubies, or sapphires by a bona fide dealer therein, and does not include the sale of gold, silver, or platinum bullion or coins, or diamonds, emeralds, rubies, or sapphires by a bona fide dealer therein in exchange for other than a monetary instrument, and does not include the exchange of gold, silver, or platinum bullion or coins, or diamonds, emeralds, rubies, or sapphires by a bona fide dealer therein for gold, silver, or platinum bullion or coins, or diamonds, emeralds, rubies, or sapphires.

(c) "Monetary instrument" means United States currency and coin; the currency and coin of any foreign country; any bank check, cashier's check, traveler's check, money order, stock, investment security or negotiable instrument in bearer form or otherwise in such form that title thereto passes upon delivery; gold, silver, or platinum bullion or coins; and diamonds, emeralds, rubies, or sapphires. "Monetary instrument" does not include bank checks, cashier's checks, traveler's checks or money orders made payable to the order of a named party which have not been endorsed or which bear restrictive endorsements.

(d) "Department" means the Department of Justice.

(e) "Criminal justice agency" means the Department of Justice and any district attorney's office, sheriff's department, police department, or city attorney's office of this state. *(Added by Stats 1986 ch 1039 §3, eff. only until 1/1/97.)*

§14162. Records of transactions above $10,000.

(a) A financial institution shall make and keep a record of each transaction by, through, or to, the financial institution which involves currency of more than ten thousand dollars ($10,000) or which results in the exchange of a monetary instrument or instruments of a value in excess of ten thousand dollars ($10,000) for another monetary instrument or instruments. A financial institution shall file a report of such a transaction with the department in a form and at the time as the department, by regulation, shall require. The filing with the department within the time specified in its regulations of a duplicate copy of a report of the transaction required by Section 60501 of Title 26 of the United States Code, and any regulations adopted thereunder, shall satisfy the reporting requirements of this subdivision. This subdivision does not apply to a financial institution, as defined in Section 5312 of Title 31 of the United States Code and Section 103.11 of Title 31 of the Code of Federal Regulations and any successor provisions thereto.

(b) A financial institution, as defined in Section 5312 of Title 31 of the United States Code and Section 103.11 of Title 31 of the Code of Federal Regulations and any successor provisions, shall file with the department, at any time as the department by regulation shall require, a duplicate copy of each report required by Sections 5313 and 5314 of Title 31 of the United States Code and by Sections 103.22 and 103.23 of Title 31 of the Code of Federal Regulations, and any successor provisions thereto. The filing pursuant to this subdivision shall satisfy all reporting and recordkeeping requirements of this title. *(Added by Stats 1986 ch 1039 §3, eff. only until 1/1/97.)*

§14163. Monetary instrument transactions exempted.

Except as otherwise provided, a financial institution may exempt from the reporting requirements of Section 14162 monetary instrument transactions exempted from the reporting requirements of Section 5313 of Title 31 of the United States Code. However, the exemption shall be approved in writing and with the signature of two or more officers of the financial institution and subject to review and disapproval for reasonable cause by the department. An exemption disapproved by the department in writing shall be effective to require reporting pursuant to Section 14162 within five business days of the time the disapproval is communicated to the financial institution. The department may require, by regulation, the maintenance, and may provide for the inspection, of records of exemptions granted under this section. *(Added by Stats 1986 ch 1039 §3, eff. only until 1/1/97.)*

© 1992 by J., B. & L. Gould
Printed in the U.S.A. **EP**

§14164. Liability.

(a) A financial institution, or any officer, employee, or agent thereof, that keeps and files a record in reliance on Section 14162, shall not be liable to its customer, to a state or local agency, or to any person for any loss or damage caused in whole or in part by the making, filing, or governmental use of the report, or any information contained therein.

(b) This title does not preclude a financial institution, in its discretion, from instituting contact with, and thereafter communicating with and disclosing customer financial records to, appropriate federal, state, or local law enforcement agencies when the financial institution has reason to suspect that the records or information demonstrate that the customer has violated any provision of this title or Section 186.10. (*Added by Stats 1986 ch 1039 §3, eff. only until 1/1/97.*)

§14165. Violation reports.

(a) The department shall analyze the reports required by Section 14162 and shall report any possible violations indicated by this analysis to the appropriate criminal justice agency.

(b) The department, in the discretion of the Attorney General, may make a report or information contained in a report filed under Section 14162 available to a district attorney or a deputy district attorney in this state, upon request made by the district attorney or his or her designee. The report or information shall be available only for a purpose consistent with this title and subject to regulations prescribed by the Attorney General, which shall require the district attorney or his or her designee seeking the report or information contained in the report to specify in writing the specific reasons for believing that a provision of this title or Section 186.10 has been violated.

(c) The department shall destroy a report filed with it under Section 14162 at the end of the fifth calendar year after receipt of the report, unless either of the following is true:

(1) The report or information contained in the report is known by the department to be the subject of an existing criminal proceeding.

(2) The department has received subsequent reports concerning the person or persons involved in the reported transaction.

If a report is retained beyond five years pursuant to paragraph (2), the department shall destroy the report at the end of the 10th calendar year after receipt of the report, unless the report or information contained in the report is the subject of existing criminal proceedings. (*Added by Stats 1986 ch 1039 §3; amended by Stats 1991 ch 1049 §5, eff. 1/1/92 only until 1/1/97.*)

§14166. Punishment for violation.

Any person (a) who willfully violates any provision of this title or any regulation adopted to implement Section 14162, (b) who, knowingly and with the intent either (1) to disguise the fact that a monetary instrument was derived from criminal activity or (2) to promote, manage, establish, carry on, or facilitate the promotion, management, establishment, or carrying on of any criminal activity, furnishes or provides to a financial institution or any officer, employee, or agent thereof or to the department, any false, inaccurate, or incomplete information or conceals a material fact in connection with a transaction for which a report is required to be filed pursuant to Section 14162 or in connection with an exemption prescribed in Section 14163, or (c) who, knowingly and with the intent either (1) to disguise the fact that a monetary instrument was derived from criminal activity or (2) to promote, manage, establish, carry on, or facilitate the promotion, management, establishment, or carrying on of any criminal activity, conducts a monetary instrument transaction or series of transactions by or through one or more financial institutions as part of a scheme and with the intent to avoid the making or filing of a report required under Section 14162, shall be punished by imprisonment in the county jail for not more than one year or in the state prison, by a fine of not more than the greater of two hundred fifty thousand dollars ($250,000) or twice the monetary value of the financial transaction or transactions, or by both that imprisonment and fine.

Notwithstanding any other provision of law, any violation of this section as to each monetary instrument transaction or exemption constitutes a separate, punishable offense. (*Added by Stats 1986 ch 1039 §3, eff. only until 1/1/97.*)

§14167. Public record.

Any report, record, information, analysis, or request obtained by the department or any agency pursuant to this title is not a public record as defined in Section 6252 of the Government Code and is not subject to disclosure under Section 6253 of the Government Code.

This title shall remain in effect until January 1, 1997, and as of that date is repealed. (*Amended by Stats 1991 ch 1049 §6, eff. 1/1/92 only until 1/1/97.*)

TITLE 12

VIOLENT CRIME INFORMATION CENTER
(Added by Stats 1988 ch 1456 §5, oper. 7/1/89.)

§14200. Establishment of Violent Crime Information Center.

The Attorney General shall establish and maintain the Violent Crime Information Center to assist in the identification and the apprehension of persons responsible for specific violent crimes and for the disappearance and exploitation of persons, particularly children and dependent adults. The center shall establish and maintain programs which include, but are not limited to, all of the following: developing violent offender profiles; assisting local law enforcement agencies and county district attorneys by providing investigative information on persons responsible for specific violent crimes and missing person cases; providing physical description information and photographs, if available, of missing persons to county district attorneys, nonprofit missing persons organizations, and schools; and providing statistics on missing dependent adults and on missing children, including, as may be applicable, family abductions, nonfamily abductions, voluntary missing, and lost children or lost dependent adults.

This section shall become operative on July 1, 1989. (*Added by Stats 1988 ch 1456 §5, oper. 7/1/89.*)

© 1992 by J., B. & L. Gould
Printed in the U.S.A.   EP

§14201. Information center's computer system.

(a) The Attorney General shall establish within the center and shall maintain an online, automated computer system designed to effect an immediate law enforcement response to reports of missing persons. The Attorney General shall design the computer system, using any existing system, including the California Law Enforcement Telecommunications System, to include an active file of information concerning persons reported to it as missing and who have not been reported as found. The computer system shall also include a confidential historic data base. The Attorney General shall develop a system of cataloging missing person reports according to a variety of characteristics in order to facilitate locating particular categories of reports as needed.

(b) The Attorney General's active files described in subdivision (a) shall be made available to law enforcement agencies. The Attorney General shall provide to these agencies the name and personal description data of the missing person including, but not limited to, the person's date of birth, color of eyes and hair, sex, height, weight, and race, the time and date he or she was reported missing, the reporting agency, and any other data pertinent to the purpose of locating missing persons. However, the Attorney General shall not release the information if the reporting agency requests the Attorney General in writing not to release the information because it would impair a criminal investigation.

(c) The Attorney General shall distribute a missing children and dependent adults bulletin on a quarterly basis to local law enforcement agencies, district attorneys, and public schools. The Attorney General shall also make this information accessible to other parties involved in efforts to locate missing children and dependent adults and to those other persons as the Attorney General deems appropriate.

This section shall become operative on July 1, 1989. *(Added by Stats 1988 ch 1456 §5, oper. 7/1/89.)*

§14202. Investigative support unit.

(a) The Attorney General shall establish and maintain within the center an investigative support unit and an automated violent crime method of operation system to facilitate the identification and apprehension of persons responsible for murder, kidnap, including parental abduction, false imprisonment, or sexual assault. This unit shall be responsible for identifying perpetrators of violent felonies collected from the center and analyzing and comparing data on missing persons in order to determine possible leads which could assist local law enforcement agencies. This unit shall only release information about active investigations by police and sheriff's departments to local law enforcement agencies.

(b) The Attorney General shall make available to the investigative support unit files organized by category of offender or victim and shall seek information from other files as needed by the unit. This set of files may include, among others, the following:

(1) Missing or unidentified, deceased persons dental files filed pursuant to this title or Section 10254 of the Health and Safety Code.

(2) Child abuse reports filed pursuant to Section 11169.

(3) Sex offender registration files maintained pursuant to Section 290.

(4) State summary criminal history information maintained pursuant to Section 11105.

(5) Information obtained pursuant to the parent locator service maintained pursuant to Section 11478.5 of the Welfare and Institutions Code.

(6) Information furnished to the Department of Justice pursuant to Section 11107.

(7) Other Attorney General's office files as requested by the investigative support unit.

This section shall become operative on July 1, 1989. *(Added by Stats 1988 ch 1456 §5, oper. 7/1/89.)*

§14203. Information accepted and generated by registry.

(a) The online missing persons registry shall accept and generate complete information on a missing person.

(b) The information on a missing person shall be retrievable by any of the following:

(1) The person's name.

(2) The person's date of birth.

(3) The person's social security number.

(4) Whether a dental chart has been received, coded, and entered into the National Crime Information Center Missing Person System by the Attorney General.

(5) The person's physical description, including hair and eye color and body marks.

(6) The person's known associates.

(7) The person's last known location.

(8) The name or assumed name of the abductor, if applicable, other pertinent information relating to the abductor or the assumed abductor, or both.

(9) Any other information, as deemed appropriate by the Attorney General.

(c) The Attorney General, in consultation with local law enforcement agencies and other user groups, shall develop the form in which information shall be entered into the system.

(d) The Attorney General shall establish and maintain within the center a separate, confidential historic data base relating to missing children and dependent adults. The historic data base may be used only by the center for statistical and research purposes. The historic data base shall be set up to categorize cases relating to missing children and dependent adults by type. These types shall include the following: runaways, voluntary missing, lost, abduction involving movement of the victim in the commission of the crime or sexual exploitation of the victim, nonfamily abduction, family abduction, and any other categories as determined by the Attorney General. In addition, the data shall include the number of missing children and missing dependent adults in this state and the category of each case.

(e) The center may supply information about specific cases from the historic data base to a local police department, sheriff's department, or district attorney, only in connection with an investigation by the police department, sheriff's department, or district attorney of a missing person case or a sex crime as defined in subdivision (e) of Section 11105.3.

This section shall become operative on July 1, 1989. *(Added by Stats 1988 ch 1456 §5, oper. 7/1/89.)*

§14204. Training of personnel.

The Attorney General shall provide training on the services provided by the center to line personnel, supervisors, and investigators in the following fields: law enforcement, district attorneys' offices, California Youth Authority, the Department of Corrections, including the Parole and Community Services Unit, probation departments, court mediation services, and the judiciary. The Commission on Peace Officer Standards and Training shall provide for the presentation of training to peace officers which will enable them to more efficiently handle, on the local level, the tracing of missing persons and victims of violent crimes.

This section shall become operative on July 1, 1989. *(Added by Stats 1988 ch 1456 §5, oper. 7/1/89.)*

§14205. Missing person reports.

(a) All local police and sheriffs' departments shall accept any report, including any telephonic report, of a missing person, including runaways, without delay and shall give priority to the handling of these reports over the handling of reports relating to crimes involving property. In cases where the person making a report of a missing person or runaway, contacts, including by telephone, the California Highway Patrol, the California Highway Patrol may take the report, and shall immediately advise the person making the report of the name and telephone number of the police or sheriff's department having jurisdiction of the residence address of the missing person and of the name and telephone number of the police or sheriff's department having jurisdiction of the place where the person was last seen. In cases of reports involving missing persons, including, but not limited to, runaways, the local police or sheriff's department shall immediately take the report and make an assessment of reasonable steps to be taken to locate the person. If the missing person is under 12 years of age, or there is evidence that the person is at risk, the department shall broadcast a "Be On the Look-Out" bulletin, without delay, within its jurisdiction.

(b) If the person reported missing is under 12 years of age, or if there is evidence that the person is at risk, the local police, sheriff's department, or the California Highway Patrol shall submit the report to the Attorney General's office within four hours after accepting the report. After the California Law Enforcement Telecommunications System online missing person registry becomes operational, the reports shall be submitted, within four hours after accepting the report, to the Attorney General's office through the use of the California Telecommunications System.

(c) In cases where the report is taken by a department, other than that of the city or county of residence of the missing person or runaway, the department, or division of the California Highway Patrol taking the report shall, without delay, and, in the case of children under 12 years of age or where there was evidence that the missing person was at risk, within no more than 24 hours, notify, and forward a copy of the report to the police or sheriff's department or departments having jurisdiction of the residence address of the missing person or runaway and of the place where the person was last seen. The report shall also be submitted by the department or division of the California Highway Patrol which took the report to the center. *(Added by Stats 1988 ch 1456 §5, eff. 1/1/89.)*

§14206. Procedure of report.

(a)(1) When any person makes a report of a missing person to a police department, sheriff's department, district attorney's office, California Highway Patrol, or other law enforcement agency, the report shall be given in person or by mail in a format acceptable to the Attorney General. That form shall include a statement authorizing the release of the dental or skeletal X-rays, or both, of the person reported missing and authorizing the release of a recent photograph of a person reported missing who is under 18 years of age. Included with the form shall be instructions which state that if the person reported missing is still missing 30 days after the report is made, the release form signed by a member of the family or next of kin of the missing person shall be taken by the family member or next of kin to the dentist, physician and surgeon, or medical facility in order to obtain the release of the dental or skeletal X-rays, or both, of that person or may be taken by a peace officer, if others fail to take action, to secure those X-rays. Notwithstanding any other provision of law, dental or skeletal X-rays, or both, shall be released by the dentist, physician and surgeon, or medical facility to the person presenting the request and shall be submitted within 10 days by that person to the police or sheriff's department or other law enforcement agency having jurisdiction over the investigation. When the person reported missing has not been found within 30 days and no family or next of kin exists or can be located, the law enforcement agency may execute a written declaration, stating that an active investigation seeking the location of the missing person is being conducted, and that the dental or skeletal X-rays, or both, are necessary for the exclusive purpose of furthering the investigation. Notwithstanding any other provision of law, the written declaration, signed by a peace officer, is sufficient authority for the dentist, physician and surgeon, or medical facility to release the missing person's dental or skeletal X-rays, or both.

(2) The form provided under this subdivision shall also state that if the person reported missing is under 18 years of age, the completed form shall be taken to the dentist, physician and surgeon, or medical facility immediately when the law enforcement agency determines that the disappearance involves evidence that the person is at risk or when the law enforcement agency determines that the person missing is under 12 years of age and has been missing at least 14 days. The form shall further provide that the dental or skeletal X-rays, or both, and a recent photograph of the missing child shall be submitted immediately to the law enforcement agency. Whenever authorized under this subdivision to execute a written declaration to obtain the release of dental or skeletal X-rays, or both, is provided, the investigating law enforcement agency may obtain those X-rays when a person reported missing is under 18 years of age and the law enforcement agency determines that the disappearance involves evidence that the person is at risk. In each case, the law enforcement agency shall confer immediately with the coroner or medical examiner and shall submit its report including the dental or skeletal X-rays, or both, within 24 hours thereafter to the Attorney General. The Attorney General's office shall code and enter the dental or skeletal X-rays, or both, into the center.

(b) When a person reported missing has not been found within 45 days, the sheriff, chief of police, or other law enforcement agency conducting the investigation for the missing person shall confer with the coroner or medical examiner prior to the preparation of a missing person report. The coroner or medical examiner shall cooperate with the law enforcement

© 1992 by J., B. & L. Gould
Printed in the U.S.A. **EP**

agency. After conferring with the coroner or medical examiner, the sheriff, chief of police, or other law enforcement agency initiating and conducting the investigation for the missing person shall submit a missing person report and the dental or skeletal X-rays, or both, and photograph received pursuant to subdivision (a) to the Attorney General's office in a format acceptable to the Attorney General.

Nothing in this section prohibits a parent or guardian of a child, reported to a law enforcement agency as missing, from voluntarily submitting fingerprints, and other documents, to the law enforcement agency accepting the report for inclusion in the report which is submitted to the Attorney General. *(Added by Stats 1988 ch 1456 §5, eff. 1/1/89.)*

§14207. Procedure when missing person is located.

(a) When a person reported missing has been found, the sheriff, chief of police, coroner or medical examiner, or the law enforcement agency locating the missing person shall immediately report that information to the Attorney General's office.

(b) When a child under 12 years of age or a missing person, where there was evidence that the person was at risk, is found, the report indicating that the person is found shall be made not later than 24 hours after the person is found. A report shall also be made to the law enforcement agency that made the initial missing person report. The Attorney General's office shall then notify the National Crime Information Center that the missing person has been found.

(c) In the event that a missing person is found alive or dead in less than 24 hours and the local police or sheriff's department has reason to believe that the person had been abducted, the department shall submit a report to the center in a format established by the Attorney General. In the event that a missing person has been found before he or she has been reported missing to the center, the information related to the incident shall be submitted to the center. *(Added by Stats 1988 ch 1456 §5, eff. 1/1/89.)*

§14208. Missing children hotline; posters.

(a) The Department of Justice shall operate a statewide, toll-free telephone hotline 24 hours per day, seven days per week to receive information regarding missing children and dependent adults and relay this information to the appropriate law enforcement authorities.

(b) The Department of Justice shall select up to six children per month from the missing children registry maintained pursuant to former Section 11114 or pursuant to the system maintained pursuant to Sections 14201 and 14202 and shall produce posters with photographs and information regarding these children, including the missing children hotline telephone number and reward information. The department shall make these posters available to parties as prescribed and as the department deems appropriate. *(Added by Stats 1988 ch 1456 §5, eff. 1/1/89.)*

§14209. Photographs of missing children.

(a) The Department of Justice shall provide appropriate local reporting agencies with a list of persons still listed as missing who are under 18 years of age, with an appropriate waiver form in order to assist the reporting agency in obtaining a photograph of each of the missing children.

(b) Local reporting agencies shall attempt to obtain the most recent photograph available for persons still listed as missing and forward those photographs to the Department of Justice.

(c) The department shall include these photographs, as they become available, in the quarterly bulletins pursuant to subdivision (c) of Section 14201.

(d) State and local elected officials, agencies, departments, boards, and commissions may enclose in their mailings information regarding missing children or dependent adults obtainable from the Department of Justice or any organization that is recognized as a nonprofit, tax-exempt organization under state or federal law and that has an ongoing missing children program. Elected officials, agency secretaries, and directors of departments, boards, and commissions are urged to develop policies to enclose missing children or dependent adults information in mailings when it will not increase postage costs, and is otherwise deemed appropriate. *(Added by Stats 1988 ch 1456 §5, eff. 1/1/89.)*

§14210. Law enforcement agencies' assistance in making reports.

(a) The Legislature finds and declares that it is the duty of all law enforcement agencies to immediately assist any person who is attempting to make a report of a missing person or runaway.

(b) The Department of the California Highway Patrol shall continue to implement the written policy, required to be developed and adopted pursuant to former Section 11114.3, for the coordination of each of its divisions with the police and sheriffs' departments located within each division in taking, transmitting, and investigating reports of missing persons, including runaways.

(c) The Department of the California Highway Patrol shall report to the Legislature on or before June 30, 1989, regarding the experience under, and the effects of, subdivision (b). *(Added by Stats 1988 ch 1456 §5, eff. 1/1/89.)*

§14213. Missing person and other terms defined.

(a) As used in this title, "missing person" includes, but is not limited to, a child who has been taken, detained, concealed, enticed away, or retained by a parent in violation of Chapter 4 (commencing with Section 277) of Title 9 of Part 1. It also includes any child who is missing voluntarily or involuntarily, or under circumstances not conforming to his or her ordinary habits or behavior and who may be in need of assistance.

(b) As used in this title, "evidence that the person is at risk" includes, but is not limited to, evidence or indications of any of the following:

(1) The person missing is the victim of a crime or foul play.

(2) The person missing is in need of medical attention.

(3) The person missing has no pattern of running away or disappearing.

(4) The person missing may be the victim of parental abduction.

(5) The person missing is mentally impaired.

(c) As used in this title, "child" is any person under the age of 18.

(d) As used in this title, "center" means the Violent Crime Information Center.

(e) As used in this title, "dependent adult" is any person described in subdivision (e) of Section 368.

(f) As used in this title, "dental or medical records or X-rays" include all those records or X-rays which are in the possession of a dentist, physician and surgeon, or medical facility. *(Added by Stats 1988 ch 1456 §5, eff. 1/1/89.)*

PART 5

PEACE OFFICERS' MEMORIAL
(Added by Stats 1985 ch 1518 §1.)

§15000. *Repealed 1/1/90 by its own terms.*

§15001. Construction of Peace Officers' Memorial.

(a) The construction of a memorial to California peace officers on the grounds of the State Capitol is hereby authorized. For purposes of this part, the grounds of the State Capitol are that property in the City of Sacramento bounded by Ninth, Fifteenth, "L," and "N" Streets. The actual site for the memorial shall be selected by the commission after consultation with the Department of General Services and the State Office of Historic Preservation.

(b) Funds for the construction of the memorial shall be provided through private contributions for this purpose. *(Added by Stats 1985 ch 1518 §1.)*

§15002. *Repealed 1/1/90 by its own terms.*

§15003. Ceremonies.

Peace officer memorial ceremonies, including the dedication of the memorial and any subsequent ceremonies, shall be conducted by the Peace Officers Research Association of California. *(Added by Stats 1985 ch 1518 §1.)*

§15004. *Repealed 1/1/90 by its own terms.*

© 1992 by J., B. & L. Could
Printed in the U.S.A.   **EP**

BUSINESS AND PROFESSIONS CODE

DIVISION 1

DEPARTMENT OF CONSUMER AFFAIRS

CHAPTER 1

THE DEPARTMENT

§119. Misdemeanors regarding use of licenses.

Any person who does any of the following is guilty of a misdemeanor:

(a) Displays or causes or permits to be displayed or has in his or her possession either of the following:

(1) A canceled, revoked, suspended, or fraudulently altered license.

(2) A fictitious license or any document simulating a license or purporting to be or have been issued as a license.

(b) Lends his or her license to any other person or knowingly permits the use thereof by another.

(c) Displays or represents any license not issued to him or her as being his or her license.

(d) Fails or refuses to surrender to the issuing authority upon its lawful written demand any license, registration, permit, or certificate which has been suspended, revoked, or canceled.

(e) Permits any unlawful use of a license issued to him or her.

(f) Photographs, photostats, duplicates, or in any way reproduces any license or facsimile thereof in such a manner that it could be mistaken for a valid license, or displays or has in his or her possession any such photograph, photostat, duplicate, reproduction, or facsimile unless authorized by this code.

As used in this section, "license" includes "certificate," "permit," "authority," and "registration" or any other indicia giving authorization to engage in a business or profession regulated by this code or referred to in Sections 1000 and 3600. *(Amended by Stats 1990 ch 350 §1; ch 1207 §1, eff. 1/1/91.)*

§123. Subversion of license examinations.

It is a misdemeanor for any person to engage in any conduct which subverts or attempts to subvert any licensing examination or the administration of an examination, including, but not limited to:

(a) Conduct which violates the security of the examination materials; removing from the examination room any examination materials without authorization; the unauthorized reproduction by any means of any portion of the actual licensing examination; aiding by any means the unauthorized reproduction of any portion of the actual licensing examination; paying or using professional or paid examination-takers for the purpose of reconstructing any portion of the licensing examination; obtaining examination questions or other examination material, except by specific authorization either before, during, or after an examination; or using or purporting to use any examination questions or materials which were improperly removed or taken from any examination for the purpose of instructing or preparing any applicant for examination; or selling, distributing, buying, receiving, or having unauthorized possession of any portion of a future, current, or previously administered licensing examination.

(b) Communicating with any other examinee during the administration of a licensing examination; copying answers from another examinee or permitting one's answers to be copied by another examinee; having in one's possession during the administration of the licensing examination any books, equipment, notes, written or printed materials, or data of any kind, other than the examination materials distributed, or otherwise authorized to be in one's possession during the examination; or impersonating any examinee or having an impersonator take the licensing examination on one's behalf.

Nothing in this section shall preclude prosecution under the authority provided for in any other provision of law.

In addition to any other penalties, a person found guilty of violating this section, shall be liable for the actual damages sustained by the agency administering the examination not to exceed ten thousand dollars ($10,000) and the costs of litigation.

(c) If any provision of this section or the application thereof to any person or circumstances is held invalid, that invalidity shall not affect other provisions or applications of the section that can be given effect without the invalid provision or application, and to this end the provisions of this section are severable. *(Amended by Stats 1991 ch 647 §1, eff. 1/1/92.)*

§125. Offenses by licensees.

Any person, licensed under the provisions of Division 1, 2, or 3 of this code is guilty of a misdemeanor and subject to the disciplinary provisions of this code applicable to him, who conspires with a person not so licensed to violate any provision of this code or who, with intent to aid or assist such person in violating such provisions:

(a) Allows his license to be used by such person.

(b) Acts as his agent or partner.

§128. Vendee selling when in violation of license requirements.

Notwithstanding any other provision of law, it is a misdemeanor to sell equipment, supplies, or services to any person with knowledge that the equipment, supplies, or services are to be used in the performance of a service or contract in violation of the licensing requirements of this code.

The provisions of this section shall not be applicable to cash sales of less than one hundred dollars ($100).

For the purposes of this section, "person" includes, but is not limited to, a company, partnership, firm or corporation.

For the purposes of this section, "license" includes certificate or registration.

A violation of this section shall be punishable by a fine of not less than one thousand dollars ($1,000) and by imprisonment in the county jail not exceeding six months.

DIVISION 1.5

DENIAL, SUSPENSION AND REVOCATION OF LICENSES

CHAPTER 3

SUSPENSION AND REVOCATION OF LICENSES

§493. Record of conviction of crime as evidence.

Notwithstanding any other provision of law, in a proceeding conducted by a board within the department pursuant to law to deny an application for a license or to suspend or revoke a license or otherwise take disciplinary action against a person who holds a license, upon the ground that the applicant or the licensee has been convicted of a crime substantially related to the qualifications, functions, and duties of the licensee in question, the record of conviction of the crime shall be conclusive evidence of the fact that the conviction occurred, but only of that fact, and the board may inquire into the circumstances surrounding the commission of the crime in order to fix the degree of discipline or to determine if the conviction is substantially related to the qualifications, functions, and duties of the licensee in question.

As used in this section, "license" includes "certificate," "permit," "authority," and "registration." *(Amended and renumbered by Stats 1989 ch 1104 §1.3, eff. 1/1/90; formerly §117.)*

§496. Suspension or revocation of license.

A board may deny, suspend, revoke, or otherwise restrict a license on the ground that an applicant or licensee has violated Section 123 pertaining to subversion of licensing examinations. *(Added by Stats 1989 ch 1022 §3, eff. 1/1/90. Former §496 repealed by Stats 1989 ch 1022 §2, eff. 1/1/90.)*

DIVISION 2

HEALING ARTS

CHAPTER 1

GENERAL PROVISIONS

ARTICLE 4

FRAUDS OF MEDICAL RECORDS

§580. Sale of degree, etc.

No person, company or association shall sell or barter or offer to sell or barter any medical degree, podiatric degree, or osteopathic degree, or chiropractic degree, or any other degree which is required for licensure, certification, or registration under this division, or any degree, certificate, transcript, or any other writing, made or purporting to be made pursuant to any laws regulating the licensing and registration or issuing of a certificate to physicians and surgeons, podiatrists, osteopathic physicians, chiropractors, persons lawfully engaged in any other system or mode of treating the sick or afflicted, or to any other person licensed, certified, or registered under this division. *(Amended by Stats 1986 ch 220 §2.)*

§581. Unlawfully purchasing or altering diploma, etc.

No person, company, or association shall purchase or procure by barter or by any unlawful means or method, or have in possession any diploma, certificate, transcript, or any other writing with intent that it shall be used as evidence of the holder's qualifications to practice as a physician and surgeon, osteopathic physician, podiatrist, any other system or mode of treating the sick or afflicted, as provided in the Medical Practice Act, Chapter 5 (commencing with Section 2000), or to practice as any other licentiate under this division or in any fraud of the law regulating this practice or, shall with fraudulent intent, alter in a material regard, any such diploma, certificate, transcript, or any other writing. *(Amended by Stats 1986 ch 220 §3.)*

§582. Using illegally obtained, altered, or counterfeit diploma, etc.

No person, company, or association shall use or attempt to use any diploma, certificate, transcript, or any other writing which has been purchased, fraudulently issued, illegally obtained, counterfeited, or materially altered, either as a certificate or as to character or color of certificate, to practice as a physician and surgeon, podiatrist, osteopathic physician, or a chiropractor, or to practice any other system or mode of treating the sick or afflicted, as provided in the Medical Practice Act, Chapter 5 (commencing with Section 2000) or to practice as any other licentiate under this division. *(Amended by Stats 1986 ch 220 §4.)*

§583. False statements.

No person shall in any document or writing required of an applicant for examination, license, certificate, or registration under this division, the Osteopathic Initiative Act, or the Chiropractic Initiative Act, willfully make a false statement in a material regard. *(Amended by Stats 1986 ch 220 §5.)*

§584. Violating security or impersonating during examination.

No person shall violate the security of any examination, as defined in subdivision (a) of Section 123, or impersonate, attempt to impersonate, or solicit the impersonation of, another in any examination for a license, certificate, or registration to practice as provided in this division, the Osteopathic Initiative Act, or the Chiropractic Initiative Act, or under any other law providing for the regulation of any other system or method of treating the sick or afflicted in this state. *(Amended by Stats 1989 ch 1022 §5, eff. 1/1/90.)*

§585. Fine or imprisonment.

Any person, company, or association violating the provisions of this article is guilty of a felony and upon conviction thereof shall be punishable by a fine of not less than two thousand dollars ($2,000) nor more than six thousand dollars ($6,000), or by imprisonment in the state prison. The enforcement remedies provided under this article are not exclusive and shall not preclude the use of any other criminal, civil, or administrative remedy. *(Amended by Stats 1986 ch 220 §7.)*

CHAPTER 4

DENTISTRY

ARTICLE 2

ADMISSION AND PRACTICE

§1627. Licensed until expiration or forfeiture.

The license of any dentist, existing at the time of the passage of this chapter, shall continue in force until it expires or is forfeited in the manner provided by this chapter.

© 1992 by J., B. & L. Gould
Printed in the U.S.A.   EP

ARTICLE 5

OFFENSES AGAINST THIS CHAPTER

§1700. Punishment for certain misdemeanor offenses.

Any person, company, or association is guilty of a misdemeanor, and upon conviction thereof shall be punished by imprisonment in the county jail not less than 10 days nor more than one year, or by a fine of not less than one hundred dollars ($100) nor more than one thousand five hundred dollars ($1,500), or by both fine and imprisonment, who:

(a) Assumes the degree of "doctor of dental surgery," "doctor of dental science," or "doctor of medicine" or appends the letters "D.D.S.", or "D.D.Sc." or "D.M.D." to his or her name without having had the right to assume the title conferred upon him or her by diploma from a recognized dental college or school legally empowered to confer the same.

(b) Assumes any title, or appends any letters to his or her name, with the intent to represent falsely that he or she has received a dental degree or license.

(c) Engages in the practice of dentistry without causing to be displayed in a conspicuous place in his or her office the name of each and every person employed there in the practice of dentistry.

(d) Within 10 days after demand is made by the executive officer of the board, fails to furnish to the board the name and address of all persons practicing or assisting in the practice of dentistry in the office of the person, company, or association, at any time within 60 days prior to the demand, together with a sworn statement showing under and by what license or authority this person, company, or association and any employees are or have been practicing dentistry. This sworn statement shall not be used in any prosecution under this section.

§1701. Misdemeanor on first conviction and felony on second.

Any person is for the first offense guilty of a misdemeanor and shall be punishable by a fine of not less than two hundred dollars ($200) or more than three thousand dollars ($3,000), or by imprisonment in the county jail for not to exceed six months, or both, and for the second or a subsequent offense is guilty of a felony and upon conviction thereof shall be punished by a fine of not less than two thousand dollars ($2,000) nor more than six thousand dollars ($6,000), or by imprisonment in the state prison, or by both such fine and imprisonment, who:

(a) Sells or barters or offers to sell or barter any dental degree or any license or transcript made or purporting to be made pursuant to the laws regulating the license and registration of dentists.

(b) Purchases or procures by barter any such diploma, license, or transcript with intent that the same shall be used in evidence of the holder's qualification to practice dentistry, or in fraud of the laws regulating such practice.

(c) With fraudulent intent, makes or attempts to make, counterfeits or alters in a material regard any such diploma, certificate or transcript.

(d) Uses, attempts or causes to be used, any such diploma, certificate or transcript which has been purchased, fraudulently issued, counterfeited or materially altered, either as a license to practice dentistry, or in order to procure registration as a dentist.

(e) In an affidavit, required of an applicant for examination, license or registration under this chapter, willfully makes a false statement in a material regard.

(f) Practices dentistry or offers to practice dentistry as it is defined in this chapter, either without a license, or when his license has been revoked or suspended.

(g) Under any false, assumed or fictitious name, either as an individual, firm, corporation or otherwise, or any name other than the name under which he is licensed, practices, advertises or in any other manner indicates that he is practicing or will practice dentistry, except such name as is specified in a valid permit issued pursuant to Section 1701.5.

ARTICLE 7

DENTAL AUXILIARIES

§1764. Misrepresentation as licensed by board.

Any person other than one who has been issued a license by the board who holds himself out as a registered dental assistant, or a registered dental assistant in extended functions, or a registered dental hygienist, or a registered dental hygienist in extended functions, or uses any other term indicating or implying he is licensed by the board in the aforementioned categories, is guilty of a misdemeanor.

CHAPTER 5

MEDICINE

ARTICLE 3

LICENSE REQUIRED AND EXEMPTIONS

§2052. Misdemeanor for practicing without a valid certificate.

Any person who practices or attempts to practice, or who advertises or holds himself or herself out as practicing, any system or mode of treating the sick or afflicted in this state, or who diagnoses, treats, operates for, or prescribes for any ailment, blemish, deformity, disease, disfigurement, disorder, injury, or other physical or mental condition of any person, without having at the time of so doing a valid, unrevoked, or unsuspended certificate as provided in this chapter, or without being authorized to perform such act pursuant to a certificate obtained in accordance with some other provision of law, is guilty of a misdemeanor.

§2053. Risking bodily harm with unlicensed practice.

Any person who willfully, under circumstances or conditions which cause or create risk of great bodily harm, serious physical or mental illness, or death, practices or attempts to practice, or advertises or holds himself or herself out as practicing, any system or mode of treating the sick or afflicted in this state, or diagnoses, treats, operates for, or prescribes for any ailment, blemish, deformity, disease, disfigurement, disorder, injury, or other physical or mental condition of any person, without having at the time of so doing a valid, unrevoked and unsuspended certificate as provided in this chapter, or without being authorized to perform that act pursuant to a certificate obtained in accordance with some other provision of law, is punishable by imprisonment in the county jail for not exceeding one year or in the state prison.

The remedy provided in this section shall not preclude any other remedy provided by law.

§2054. Misdemeanor for misrepresentation as physician or surgeon.

Any person who uses in any sign, business card, or letterhead, or, in an advertisement, the words "doctor" or "physician," the letters or prefix "Dr.," the initials "M.D.," or any other terms or letters indicating or implying that he or she is a physician and surgeon, physician, surgeon, or practitioner under the terms of this or any other law, or that he or she is entitled to practice hereunder, or who represents or holds himself or herself out as a physician and surgeon, physician, surgeon, or practitioner under the terms of this or any other law, without having at the time of so doing a valid, unrevoked, and unsuspended certificate as a physician and surgeon under this chapter, is guilty of a misdemeanor.

ARTICLE 22

PODIATRIC MEDICINE

§2474. Practicing podiatric medicine without valid certificate.

Any person who uses in any sign or in any advertisement or otherwise, the word or words "podiatrist", "foot specialist", or any other term or terms or any letters indicating or implying that he or she is a podiatrist, or that he or she practices podiatric medicine, or holds himself out as practicing podiatric medicine or foot correction as defined in Section 2472, without having at the time of so doing a valid, unrevoked, and unsuspended certificate as provided for in this chapter, is guilty of a misdemeanor.

CHAPTER 5.5

REGISTERED DISPENSING OPTICIANS

ARTICLE 1

GENERAL PROVISIONS

§2556. Unlawful practices regarding dispensing opticians.

It is unlawful to do any of the following: to advertise the furnishing of, or to furnish, the services of a refractionist, an optometrist, or a physician and surgeon; to directly or indirectly employ or maintain on or near the premises used for optical dispensing, a refractionist, an optometrist, a physician and surgeon, or a practitioner of any other profession for the purpose of any examination or treatment of the eyes; or to duplicate or change lenses without a prescription or order from a person duly licensed to issue the same.

§2556.5. Valid certification of dispensing optician.

Any person who holds himself out as a "dispensing optician" or "registered dispensing optician" or who uses any other term or letters indicating or implying that he is registered and holds a certificate under the terms of this law without having at the time of so doing

a valid, unrevoked certificate, as provided in this chapter, is guilty of a misdemeanor.

CHAPTER 6

NURSING

ARTICLE 5

PENAL PROVISIONS

§2795. Unlawful practice of nursing without valid license.

Except as provided in this chapter, it is unlawful for any person to do any of the following:

(a) To practice or to offer to practice nursing in this state unless the person holds a license in an active status.

(b) To use any title, sign, card, or device to indicate that he or she is qualified to practice or is practicing nursing, unless the person has been duly licensed or certified under this chapter. (*Amended by Stats 1990 ch 350 §2, eff. 1/1/91.*)

§2796. Use of title "registered nurse."

It is unlawful for any person or persons not licensed or certified as provided in this chapter to use the title "registered nurse," the letters "R.N.," or the words "graduate nurse," "trained nurse," or "nurse anesthetist."

It is unlawful for any person or persons not licensed or certified as provided in this chapter to impersonate a professional nurse or pretend to be licensed to practice professional nursing as provided in this chapter.

§2799. Punishment for violations.

Any person who violates any of the provisions of this chapter is guilty of a misdemeanor and upon a conviction thereof shall be punished by imprisonment in the county jail for not less than 10 days nor more than one year, or by a fine of not less than twenty dollars ($20) nor more than one thousand dollars ($1,000), or by both such fine and imprisonment.

CHAPTER 6.5

VOCATIONAL NURSING

ARTICLE 5

PENAL PROVISIONS

§2885. Use of title "Licensed Vocational Nurse."

It is unlawful for any person or persons not licensed as provided in this chapter to impersonate in any manner or pretend to be a licensed vocational nurse, or to use the title "Licensed Vocational Nurse," the letters "L.V.N.," or any other name, word or symbol in connection with or following his name so as to lead another or others to believe that he is a licensed vocational nurse.

§2886. Unlawful impersonation of applicants.

It is unlawful for a person to wilfully make any false representation or to impersonate any other person or permit or aid any person in any manner to impersonate him in connection with any examination or application for a license, or request to be examined or licensed.

© 1992 by J., B. & L. Gould
Printed in the U.S.A.   EP

§2887. Penalties upon conviction.

Any person who violates any of the provisions of this chapter is guilty of a misdemeanor and upon a conviction thereof shall be punished by imprisonment in the county jail for not less than 10 days nor more than one year, or by a fine of not less than twenty dollars ($20) nor more than one thousand dollars ($1,000), or by both such fine and imprisonment.

CHAPTER 7

OPTOMETRY

ARTICLE 3

ADMISSION TO PRACTICE

§3040. Misrepresentation as optometrist without certification.

It is unlawful for any person to engage in the practice of optometry or to display a sign or in any other way to advertise or hold himself out as an optometrist without having first obtained a certificate of registration from the board under the provisions of this chapter or under the provisions of any former act relating to the practice of optometry.

In any prosecution for a violation of this section, the use of test cards, test lenses, or of trial frames is prima facie evidence of the practice of optometry.

ARTICLE 6

OFFENSES AGAINST THE CHAPTER

§3120. Penalty upon conviction.

Any person who violates any of the provisions of this chapter is guilty of a misdemeanor and, upon conviction thereof, shall be punished by imprisonment in the county jail not less than ten days nor more than one year, or by a fine of not less than one hundred dollars nor more than one thousand five hundred dollars, or by both such fine and imprisonment.

§3123. Altering certificate of registration.

It is unlawful to alter with fraudulent intent in any material regard a certificate of registration issued by the board.

§3124. Use of fraudulently issued or counterfeit certificates.

It is unlawful to use or attempt to use any certificate of registration issued by the board which has been purchased, fraudulently issued, counterfeited or materially altered, as a valid certificate of registration.

§3127. Practice without certificate of registration.

It is unlawful to practice optometry in this State without having at the time of so doing a valid, un-revoked, and unexpired certificate of registration as an optometrist.

§3128. Advertising without valid certificate.

It is unlawful to advertise by displaying a sign or otherwise or hold himself out to be an optometrist without having at the time of so doing a valid un-revoked certificate of registration from the board.

§3129. Advertisements.

It is unlawful to advertise as being free or without cost the examination or treatment of the eyes or the furnishing of optometrical services.

CHAPTER 9

PHARMACY

ARTICLE 3

APPLICATION OF CHAPTER

§4050. Unlawful practice of pharmacy without registration.

Except as otherwise provided in this chapter, it is unlawful for any person to manufacture, compound, sell or dispense any dangerous drug or devices, or to dispense or compound any prescription of a medical practitioner unless he or she is a registered pharmacist under the provisions of this chapter.

§4054. Duties of pharmacist-in-charge.

(a) Every store, dispensary, pharmacy, laboratory or office for the sale, dispensing or compounding of drugs or chemicals, or for the dispensing of prescriptions of medical practitioners, shall be in charge of a registered pharmacist.

(b) Every pharmacy shall designate a pharmacist-in-charge. The pharmacist-in-charge shall be responsible for a pharmacy's compliance with laws and regulations, both state and federal, pertaining to the practice of pharmacy.

(c) Any nonpharmacist owner who commits any act which would subvert or tends to subvert the efforts of the pharmacist-in-charge to comply with the laws governing the operation of the pharmacy is guilty of a misdemeanor.

ARTICLE 5.3

MEDICAL DEVICE RETAILERS
(Amended and renumbered by Stats 1989 ch 1360 §3, eff. 1/1/90; formerly Article 5.5.)

§4143. Sale of hypodermic needle or syringe.

Except as otherwise provided by this article, no hypodermic needle or syringe shall be sold at retail except upon the prescription of a physician and surgeon, dentist, veterinarian, or podiatrist. *(Added by Stats 1985 ch 613 §2.)*

§4148. Disposal of hypodermic needle or syringe.

Any hypodermic needle or syringe which is to be disposed of, shall be contained, treated, and disposed of, pursuant to Chapter 6.1 (commencing with Section 25015 of Division 20 of the Health and Safety Code. *(Amended by Stats 1990 ch 1614 §1, eff. 1/1/91.)*

§4149. Illicit possession of needle or syringe.

No person shall possess or have under his or her control any hypodermic needle or syringe except when acquired in accordance with the provisions of this article. *(Added by Stats 1985 ch 613 §2.)*

§4150. Possession by false or fraudulent representation.

Any person obtaining possession of a hypodermic needle or hypodermic syringe by a false or fraudulent representation or design or by a forged or fictitious name, or contrary to, or in violation of, any of the provisions of this chapter, is guilty of a misdemeanor. *(Added by Stats 1985 ch 613 §2.)*

§4151. Misusing hypodermic needle or syringe.

Any person who has obtained a hypodermic needle or hypodermic syringe from any person to whom a permit has been issued as provided in this article and who uses, or permits or causes, directly or indirectly, the hypodermic needle or hypodermic syringe to be used for any purpose other than that for which it was purchased is guilty of a misdemeanor and upon conviction thereof if punishable by a fine not exceeding one thousand dollars ($1,000), or by imprisonment in a county jail not exceeding one year, or both a fine and imprisonment. *(Added by Stats 1985 ch 613 §2.)*

ARTICLE 7

DANGEROUS DRUGS

§4211. Dangerous drug defined.

"Dangerous drug" means any drug unsafe for self-medication, except veterinary drugs which are labeled as such, and includes the following:

(a) Any drug which bears the legend: "Caution: federal law prohibits dispensing without prescription" or words of similar import.

(b) Any device which bears the statement: "Caution: federal law restricts this device to sale by or on the order of a _____ ," or words of similar import, the blank to be filled in with the designation of the practitioner licensed to use or order use of the device.

(c) Any other drug or device which by federal or state law can be lawfully dispensed only on prescription or furnished pursuant to Section 4240.

Neither this section, nor any other provision of law, prohibits the sale of devices to clinics which have been issued a clinic permit pursuant to Article 3.5 (commencing with Section 4063) of Chapter 9 or to skilled nursing facilities or intermediate care facilities licensed pursuant to Chapter 2 (commencing with Section 1250) of Division 2 of the Health and Safety Code.

§4211.5. DMSO defined.

(a) As used in this section, "DMSO" means dimethyl sulfoxide.

(b) A licensed physician and surgeon shall, prior to treating a patient with a DMSO preparation, inform the patient in writing if DMSO has not been approved as a treatment or cure by the Food and Drug Administration for the disorder for which it is being prescribed.

(c) If DMSO is prescribed for any purpose other than for those purposes approved pursuant to Section 26670 of the Health and Safety Code, informed consent shall first be obtained from the patient.

As used in this subdivision, "informed consent" means the authorization given by the patient for treatment with DMSO after each of the following conditions have been satisfied:

(1) The patient is informed verbally in nontechnical terms about all of the following:

(A) A description of treatment procedures to be used in administering the DMSO.

(B) A description of any attendant discomfort and risks to the patient that can be reasonably expected from treatment with DMSO.

(C) An explanation of any benefits to the patient that can be reasonably expected.

(D) An explanation of any appropriate alternative procedures, drugs, or devices that might be advantageous to the patient, and their relative risks and benefits.

(E) An offer to answer any inquiries concerning the treatment or the procedures involved.

(2) The patient signs and dates a written consent form acknowledging that disclosure has been given pursuant to paragraph (1), and acknowledging consent to treatment with DMSO pursuant to this section.

The patient shall be provided with a copy of the signed and dated consent form.

(d) An organized health care system may require that the administration of DMSO within the organized health care system be performed pursuant to standardized procedures developed by the organized health care system through collaboration among administrators and health professionals.

(e) The following notification shall be affixed to all quantities of DMSO prescribed by a licensed physician and surgeon, or dispensed by a pharmacy pursuant to the order of a licensed physician and surgeon in California: "Warning: DMSO may be hazardous to your health. Follow the directions of the physician who prescribed the DMSO for you."

(f) The label of any retail package of DMSO shall include appropriate precautionary measures for proper handling and first aid treatment and a warning statement to keep the product out of reach of children.

§4227. Furnish drug without prescription; exceptions.

(a) No person shall furnish any dangerous drug or device except upon the prescription of a physician, dentist, podiatrist, or veterinarian.

(b) This section shall not apply to the furnishing of any dangerous drug or device by a manufacturer or wholesaler or pharmacy to each other or to a physician, dentist, podiatrist, or veterinarian, or to a laboratory under sales and purchase records that correctly give the date, the names and addresses of the supplier and the buyer, the drug or device and its quantity.

(c) A registered pharmacist, or a person exempted pursuant to Section 4050.7, may distribute dangerous drugs and devices directly to hemodialysis patients pursuant to regulations promulgated by the board. The board shall promulgate such regulations as are necessary to ensure the safe distribution of such drugs and devices to hemodialysis patients without interruption of supply including, but not limited to, the following: vendor licensing, records and labeling, patient receipts, patient training, report records, specific product and quantity limitations, verification order forms, reports and supplies, adequate establishment facilities, and reports to the board. A person who violates a regulation promulgated pursuant to this subdivision shall be liable upon order of the board to surrender his or her personal license. These penalties shall be in addition to penalties which may be imposed pursuant to Sections 4389 and 4350.5. If the board finds any hemodialysis drugs or devices dis-

© 1992 by J., B. & L. Gould
Printed in the U.S.A.　EP

tributed pursuant to this subdivision to be ineffective or unsafe for the intended use, the board may institute immediate recall of any or all of such drugs or devices distributed to individual patients.

(d) Home hemodialysis patients who receive any drugs or devices pursuant to subdivision (c) shall have completed a full course of home training given by a renal dialysis center accredited by the State Department of Health Services. The physician and surgeon prescribing the hemodialysis products shall submit proof satisfactory to the manufacturer or wholesaler that the patient has completed such program.

(e) A registered pharmacist may furnish a dangerous drug authorized for use pursuant to Section 2620.3 to a physical therapist or may furnish a topical pharmaceutical agent authorized for use pursuant to subdivision (e) of Section 3041 to an optometrist. A record containing the date, name and address of the buyer, and name and quantity of the drug shall be maintained. This subdivision shall not be construed to authorize the furnishing of a controlled substance as defined in Division 10 (commencing with Section 11000) of the Health and Safety Code.

(f) A medical device retailer shall dispense, furnish, transfer, or sell a dangerous device only to another medical device retailer, a pharmacy, a licensed physician and surgeon, a licensed health care facility, or a patient or his or her personal representative.

(g) A registered pharmacist may furnish electroneuromyographic needle electrodes or hypodermic needles used for the purpose of placing wire electrodes for kinesiological electromyographic testing to physical therapists who are certified by the Physical Therapy Examining Committee of California to perform tissue penetration in accordance with Section 2620.5. *(Amended by Stats 1990 ch 1087 §24, eff. 1/1/91.)*

§4227.1. Furnish dangerous drugs without prescriptions in an emergency.

Notwithstanding the provisions of Section 4227 or any other provision of law, a registered pharmacist in good faith may furnish without prescription a dangerous drug or device in reasonable quantities during a state of war emergency, a state of emergency, a local emergency, disaster, earthquake, flood, mudslide, explosion, bombing, nuclear attack, or act of God, to further the health and safety of the public. A record containing the date, name and address of the person to whom the drug or device is furnished, and the name, strength and quantity of the drug or device furnished shall be maintained. The pharmacist shall communicate this information to the patient's attending physician as soon as possible. Notwithstanding the provisions of Section 4230 or any other provision of law, a person may possess a dangerous drug or device furnished without prescription pursuant to this section. *(Amended by Stats 1987 ch 1115 §18.)*

§4227.2. Prohibition of furnishing dangerous devices without prescription.

Except as otherwise provided in this chapter, no person shall furnish a dangerous device except upon prescription of a physician, dentist, podiatrist, or veterinarian. *(Added by Stats 1987 ch 1115 §19.)*

§4227.3. Distributing samples: requirement of written request.

No manufacturer's sales representative shall distribute any dangerous drug as a complimentary sample without the written request of a physician, dentist, podiatrist or veterinarian. Such requests shall contain the names and addresses of the supplier and the requester, the name and quantity of the specific dangerous drug desired, and shall be preserved by the supplier with the records required by Section 4227.

§4228. Labeling containers.

(a) Except as provided in subdivisions (b) and (c) of this section, no person shall dispense any dangerous drug upon prescription except in a container correctly labeled with the information required by Sections 4047.5 and 4048.

(b) Physicians, dentists, podiatrists, and veterinarians may personally furnish any dangerous drug prescribed by them to the patient for whom prescribed, provided that such drug is properly labeled to show all information required in Sections 4047.5 and 4048 except the prescription number.

(c) Devices which bear the legend "Caution: federal law restricts this device to sale by or on the order of a ____ ," or words of similar meaning, are exempt from the requirements of Sections 4047.5 and 4048, and Section 26662 of the Health and Safety Code, when provided to patients in skilled nursing facilities or intermediate care facilities licensed pursuant to Chapter 2 (commencing with Section 1250) of Division 2 of the Health and Safety Code. *(Amended by Stats 1986 ch 493 §9.)*

§4229. Refillable and nonrefillable prescriptions.

No prescription for any dangerous drug or device may be refilled except upon authorization of the prescriber which may be given orally or at the time of giving the original prescription. No prescription for any dangerous drug which is a controlled substance as defined in Division 10 (commencing with Section 11000) of the Health and Safety Code may be designated refillable as needed. *(Amended by Stats 1987 ch 1115 §20.)*

§4229.5. Refilling prescription without prescriber's authorization; exceptions.

A prescription for a dangerous drug or device may be refilled without the prescriber's authorization if the prescriber is unavailable to authorize the refill and if, in the pharmacist's professional judgment, failure to refill the prescription might present an immediate hazard to the patient's health and welfare or might result in intense suffering. The pharmacist shall refill only a reasonable amount sufficient to maintain the patient until the prescriber can be contacted. The pharmacist shall note on the reverse side of the prescription the date and quantity of the refill and that the prescriber was not available and the basis for his judgment to refill the prescription without the prescriber's authorization. The pharmacist shall inform the patient that the prescription was refilled without the prescriber's authorization, indicating that the prescriber was not available and that, in the pharmacist's professional judgment, failure to provide the drug or device might result in an immediate hazard to the patient's health and welfare or might result in intense suffering. The pharmacist shall inform the prescriber within a reasonable period of time. Prior to refilling a prescription pursuant to this section, the pharmacist shall make every reasonable effort to contact the prescriber.

The prescriber shall not incur any liability as the result of a refilling of a prescription pursuant to this section. *(Amended by Stats 1987 ch 1115 §21.)*

§4230. Possession of controlled substance without prescription.

No person shall have in possession any controlled substance, except that furnished to such person upon the prescription of a physician, dentist, podiatrist, or veterinarian. The provisions of this section do not apply to the possession of any controlled substance by a manufacturer or wholesaler or a pharmacy or physician or podiatrist or dentist or veterinarian, when in stock in containers correctly labeled with the name and address of the supplier or producer.

§4231. Inspection of stock of dangerous drugs or devices.

All stock of any dangerous drug or device of a manufacturer, wholesaler, pharmacy, medical device retailer, physician, dentist, podiatrist, veterinarian, or laboratory, shipments through a customs broker or carrier shall be at all times during business hours open to inspection by authorized officers of the law. *(Amended by Stats 1987 ch 1115 §22.)*

§4232. Records open to inspection; maintain current inventory.

All records of manufacture and of sale, purchase or disposition of dangerous drugs or devices shall be at all times, during business hours, open to inspection by authorized officers of the law, and shall be preserved for at least three years from the date of making. A current inventory shall be kept by every manufacturer, wholesaler, pharmacy, medical device retailer, physician, dentist, podiatrist, or veterarian, laboratory, clinic, hospital, institution, or establishment holding a currently valid and unrevoked certificate, license, permit, registration or exemption under Division 2 (commencing with Section 1200) of the Health and Safety Code or under Part 3 (commencing with Section 1620) of Division 2 of, Chapter 2 (commencing with Section 2300) of Division 3 of, or Part 2 (commencing with Section 5699) of Division 6 of, the Welfare and Institutions Code who maintains a stock of dangerous drugs or devices.

The owner, officer, and partner of any pharmacy or medical device retailer shall be jointly responsible, with the pharmacist-in-charge, for maintaining the records and inventory described in this section.

The pharmacist-in-charge shall not be criminally responsible for acts of the owner, officer, partner, or employee which violate this section and of which the pharmacist-in-charge had no knowledge, or in which he or she did not knowingly participate.

Any person who fails, neglects, or refuses to maintain such records or who, when called upon by an authorized officer or a member of the board, fails, neglects or refuses to produce such records within a reasonable time, or who willfully produces or furnishes records which are false, is guilty of a misdemeanor. *(Amended by Stats 1987 ch 1115 §23.)*

§4234. Penalty for use of minor as an agent.

Every person who knowingly or willfully violates any provision of this article with respect to dangerous drugs by use of a minor as an agent is guilty of a felony.

Nothing contained in this section shall apply to a registered pharmacist furnishing such drugs pursuant to a prescription.

§4236. Collection and distribution of fines.

All fines collected for violations of the provisions of this article shall be paid one-half into the State Treasury to the credit of the Contingent Fund of the Board of Pharmacy and one-half to the treasurer of the jurisdiction in which the misdemeanor is prosecuted, to be deposited in the same fund as fines for other misdemeanors occurring in that jurisdiction are deposited.

§4238. Punishment for conviction of violation.

A conviction of the violation of any of the provisions of this article shall constitute grounds for the suspension or revocation of any certificate, license, permit, registration or exemption issued to such person under any of the provisions of the Business and Professions Code of the State of California or under the provisions of this article. The proceedings for suspension or revocation shall be conducted in accordance with the Administrative Procedure Act, Chapter 5 of Part 1 of Division 3 of Title 2 of the Government Code.

§4238.5. Restricted dangerous drug violations; grounds for suspension or revocation of certificate, license, permit, registration or exemption.

A conviction of the violation of any provision of Chapter 2 (commencing with Section 11910) of Division 10.5 of the Health and Safety Code shall constitute grounds for the suspension or revocation of any certificate, license, permit, registration or exemption issued to such person under any of the provisions of the Business and Professions Code of the State of California or under the provisions of this article. The proceedings for suspension or revocation shall be conducted in accordance with the Administrative Procedure Act (Chapter 5 (commencing with Section 11500 (of Part 1 of Division 3 of Title 2 of the Government Code).

§4239. Administration and enforcement.

The board shall administer and enforce this article and the former Division 10.5 (commencing with Section 11900) and Division 10.9 (commencing with Section 11990) of the Health and Safety Code, repealed and incorporated in Division 10 (commencing with Section 11000) of the Health and Safety Code by Chapter 1407 of the Statutes of 1972.

§4240. Limiting or restricting retail sale of drug dangerous to public health.

The board, in accordance with the Administrative Procedure Act (Chapter 3.5 (commencing with Section 11340) of Part 1 of Division 3 of Title 2 of the Government Code), may adopt regulations consistent with this chapter and Section 26663 of the Health and Safety Code or regulations adopted thereunder, limiting or restricting the furnishing of a particular drug upon a finding that the otherwise unrestricted retail sale of the drug pursuant to Section 4052 is dangerous to the public health or safety. Any knowing or willful violation of any such regulation shall be subject to

© 1992 by J., B. & L. Gould
Printed in the U.S.A.   **EP**

punishment in the same manner as is provided in Sections 4234 and 4382.

§4241. Notice of adoption of further rules.
Notice of the adoption of any further rules by the board shall be given to interested parties and no person shall be subject to any prosecution for violating any such rules until the board had given due public notice of the adoption of such rules.

§4242. Copy of laws and regulations.
The board shall upon request furnish any person with a copy of the laws or regulations relating to dangerous drugs, the furnishing or possession of which is restricted by this article or by further rules of the board.

ARTICLE 10

PROHIBITIONS AND OFFENSES AGAINST THE CHAPTER, GENERALLY

§4382. Punishment when no other penalty provided.
(a) Any person who knowingly violates any of the provisions of this chapter, when no other penalty is provided, is guilty of a misdemeanor, and upon conviction thereof shall be liable to punishment by a fine of not less than one hundred dollars ($100), and not more than one thousand ($1,000), or by imprisonment of not less than 30 days or exceeding six months, or by both such fine and imprisonment.

(b) In all other instances, any person who violates any of the provisions of this chapter, when no other penalty is provided, is guilty of an infraction, and upon conviction thereof may be punishable by a fine not to exceed five hundred dollars ($500).

§4383. Advertisements regarding nonresident pharmacy.
It is unlawful for any nonresident pharmacy which is not registered pursuant to Section 4050.1 to advertise its services in this state, or for any person who is a resident of this state to advertise the pharmacy services of a nonresident pharmacy which has not registered with the board, with the knowledge that the advertisement will or is likely to induce members of the public in this state to use the pharmacy to fill prescriptions. *(Added by Stats 1988 ch 1424 §6, eff. 1/1/92.)*

§4383.4. Proceeds of fine for AIDS education program.
In addition to any fine assessed under Section 4382, the judge may assess a fine not to exceed seventy dollars ($70) against any person who violates Section 4143 or 4149, with the proceeds of this fine to be used in accordance with Section 1463.23 of the Penal Code. The court shall, however, take into consideration the defendant's ability to pay and no defendant shall be denied probation because of his or her inability to pay the fine permitted under this section. *(Amended and renumbered by Stats 1989 ch 1360 §4, eff. 1/1/90; formerly §4383.)*

§4384. False representation.
Any person who attempts to secure or secures registration for himself or any other person under this chapter by making or causing to be made any false representations, or who fraudulently represents himself to be registered, is guilty of a misdemeanor, and upon conviction thereof shall be liable to punishment by a fine not exceeding two hundred dollars ($200), or by punishment for a term not exceeding 50 days, or by both such fine and imprisonment.

§4385. Acts by other than registered pharmacist.
Except as otherwise provided in this chapter, any person who permits the compounding or dispensing of prescriptions, or the furnishing of dangerous drugs in his pharmacy, except by a registered pharmacist, is guilty of a misdemeanor.

§4387. Managing pharmacy.
Any person, not being a registered pharmacist, who takes charge of, or acts as manager of any pharmacy, or who, not being a registered pharmacist compounds or dispenses a prescription or furnishes dangerous drugs except as otherwise provided in this chapter is guilty of a misdemeanor.

§4388. Selling while under the influence of alcohol or drugs.
Any person, who, while on duty, sells, dispenses or compounds any drug while under the influence of intoxicating liquor or narcotic or hypnotic drug shall be guilty of a misdemeanor.

§4390. Forgery of prescription.
(a) Every person who signs the name of another, or of a fictitious person, or falsely makes, alters, forges, utters, publishes, passes, or attempts to pass, as genuine, any prescription for any drugs is guilty of a forgery and upon conviction thereof shall be punished by imprisonment in the state prison, or by imprisonment in the county jail for not more than one year.

(b) Every person who has in his or her possession any drugs secured by such forged prescription shall be punished by imprisonment in the state prison, or by imprisonment in the county jail for not more than one year. *(Amended by Stats 1990 ch 350 §3, eff. 1/1/91.)*

§4390.1. Authorization regarding prescription blanks.
No person other than a physician, dentist, podiatrist, veterinarian, pharmacist, or other person authorized by law to dispense, administer, or prescribe controlled substances, or the person's agent acting under authorization by the person to print prescription blanks, and acting in the regular practice of the person's profession, shall knowingly and willfully manufacture, copy, reproduce, or possess, or cause to be manufactured, copied, reproduced, or possessed, any prescription blank which purports to bear the name, address, and federal registry or other identifying information of a physician, dentist, podiatrist, veterinarian, or other person authorized by law to dispense, administer, or prescribe controlled substances.

Every person who violates the provisions of this section shall be guilty of a misdemeanor.

§4390.5. False representation over telephone communication.
Every person who, in order to obtain any drug, falsely represents himself or herself to be a physician or other person who can lawfully prescribe the drug,

or falsely represents that he or she is acting on behalf of a person who can lawfully prescribe the drug, in a telephone communication with a registered pharmacist, shall be punished by imprisonment in the county jail for not more than one year.

CHAPTER 11

VETERINARY MEDICINE

ARTICLE 2

PRACTICE PROVISIONS

§4825. Licensure requirement for veterinarians.

It is unlawful for any person to practice veterinary medicine or any branch thereof in this State unless at the time of so doing, such person holds a valid, unexpired, and unrevoked license as provided in this chapter.

§4830.5. Report of injury or death during staged animal fight.

Whenever any licensee under this chapter has reasonable cause to believe that a dog has been injured or killed through participation in a staged animal fight, as prescribed in Section 597b of the Penal Code, it shall be the duty of such licensee to promptly report the same to the appropriate law enforcement authorities of the county, city, or city and county in which the same occurred.

No licensee shall incur any civil liability as a result of making any report pursuant to this section.

§4831. Punishment for violations.

Any person, who violates or aids or abets in violating any of the provisions of this chapter, is guilty of a misdemeanor and upon conviction thereof shall be punished by a fine of not less than five hundred dollars ($500), nor more than two thousand dollars ($2,000), or by imprisonment in the county jail for not less than thirty days nor more than one year, or by both such fine and imprisonment.

CHAPTER 12

ACUPUNCTURE

ARTICLE 2

CERTIFICATION REQUIREMENTS

§4935. Practicing acupuncture without license.

Any person who practices acupuncture or holds himself or herself out as practicing or engaging in the practice of acupuncture, unless he or she possesses an acupuncturist's license, or is participating in a course or tutorial program in acupuncture, as provided for in this chapter, is guilty of a misdemeanor.

A person holds himself or herself out as engaging in the practice of acupuncture by the use of any title or description of services incorporating the words "acupuncture", "acupuncturist", "certified acupuncturist", "licensed acupuncturist", "C.A.", "Lic. Ac.", "oriental medicine", "oriental herbalist", "certified herbalist", or by representing that he or she is trained, experienced, or an expert in the field of acupuncture,

oriental medicine, or Chinese medicine. *(Amended by Stats 1988 ch 1353 §1, eff. 1/1/89.)*

CHAPTER 13

MARRIAGE, FAMILY AND CHILD COUNSELORS

ARTICLE 5

LICENSED EDUCATIONAL PSYCHOLOGISTS

§4986.50. Unlawfully practicing as educational psychologist without license.

It is unlawful for any person to use any title or letters which imply that he or she is a licensed educational psychologist unless at the time of so doing he or she holds a valid, unexpired and unrevoked license issued under this article. *(Added by Stats 1986 ch 1365 §4.)*

§4986.81. Violation as misdemeanor.

Any person who violates any of the provisions of this article is guilty of a misdemeanor. *(Added by Stats 1986 ch 1365 §4.)*

CHAPTER 14

SOCIAL WORKERS

ARTICLE 4

CLINICAL SOCIAL WORKERS

§4996. Use of title Licensed Clinical Social Worker.

Only individuals who have received a license under this article may style themselves as "Licensed Clinical Social Workers". Every individual who styles himself or herself or who holds himself or herself out to be a licensed clinical social worker, or who uses any words or symbols indicating or tending to indicate that he or she is a licensed clinical social worker, without holding his or her license in good standing under this article, is guilty of a misdemeanor.

It is unlawful for any person to engage in the practice of clinical social work unless at the time of so doing such person holds a valid, unexpired, and unrevoked license under this article. *(Added by Stats 1985 ch 820 §1.)*

§4996.12. Punishment for violations.

Any person who violates this chapter shall be guilty of a misdemeanor punishable by imprisonment in the county jail not exceeding a period of six months, or by a fine not exceeding one thousand dollars ($1,000), or by both. *(Added by Stats 1985 ch 820 §1.)*

© 1992 by J., B. & L. Gould
Printed in the U.S.A.   EP

DIVISION 9

ALCOHOLIC BEVERAGES

CHAPTER 7

SUSPENSION AND REVOCATION OF LICENSES

§24202. Notification of arrest.

(a) All state and local law enforcement agencies shall immediately notify the department of any arrests made by them for violations over which the department has jurisdiction which involve a licensee or licensed premises. Notice shall be given within 10 days of the arrest. The department shall promptly cause an investigation to be made as to whether grounds exist for suspension or revocation of the license or licenses of the licensee.

(b) The department may not open or add an entry to a file or initiate an investigation of a licensee or suspend or revoke a license (1) solely because the licensee or an agent acting on behalf of the licensee has reported to a state or local law enforcement agency that suspected controlled substance violations have taken place on the licensed premises or (2) solely based on activities constituting violations described in such a report, unless the violations reported occurred with the actual knowledge and willful consent of the licensee. (*Amended by Stats 1990 ch 695 §1, eff. 1/1/91.*)

CHAPTER 16

REGULATORY PROVISIONS

ARTICLE 3

WOMEN AND MINORS

§25658. Sale and consumption of alcohol by minor.

(a) Every person who sells, furnishes, gives, or causes to be sold, furnished, or given away, any alcoholic beverage to any person under the age of 21 years is guilty of a misdemeanor.

(b) Any person under the age of 21 years who purchases any alcoholic beverage, or any person under the age of 21 years who consumes any alcoholic beverage in any on-sale premises, is guilty of a misdemeanor.

(c) Any on-sale licensee who knowingly permits a person under the age of 21 years to consume any alcoholic beverage in the on-sale premises, whether or not the licensee has knowledge that the person is under the age of 21 years, is guilty of a misdemeanor.

(d) Any person who violates this section shall be punished by a fine of not less than two hundred fifty dollars ($250), no part of which shall be suspended, or the person shall be required to perform not less than 24 hours or more than 32 hours of community service during hours when the person is not employed and is not attending school, or a combination of fine and community service as determined by the court. (*Amended by Stats 1990 ch 695 §2, eff. 1/1/91.*)

§25658.4. Off-sale of alcoholic beverages; restrictions.

(a) On and after January 1, 1992, no clerk shall make an off-sale of alcoholic beverages unless the clerk executes under penalty of perjury on the first day he or she makes such a sale an application and acknowledgment. The application and acknowledgment shall be in a form understandable to the clerk.

(1) The department shall specify the form of the application and acknowledgment which shall include at a minimum a summary of this division pertaining to the following:

(A) The prohibitions contained in Sections 25658, 25658.2, and 25658.5 pertaining to the sale to, and purchase of, alcoholic beverages by persons under 21 years of age.

(B) Bona fide evidence of majority as provided in Section 25660.

(C) Hours of operation as provided in Article 2 (commencing with Section 25630) of Chapter 16.

(D) The prohibitions contained in subdivision (a) of Sections 25602 and 25602.1 pertaining to sales to intoxicated person.

(E) Sections 23393 and 23394 as they pertain to on-premises consumption of alcoholic beverages in an off-sale premises.

(2) The application and acknowledgment shall also include a statement that the clerk has read and understands the summary, a statement that the clerk has never been convicted of violating this division or, if convicted, an explanation of the circumstances of each conviction, and a statement that the application and acknowledgment is executed under penalty of perjury.

(3) The licensee shall keep the executed application and acknowledgment on the premises at all times and available for inspection by the department. An application and acknowledgment is valid only at the off-premises for which it is issued and at no other premises. A violation of this subdivision by a licensee constitutes grounds for discipline by the department.

(b) On and after January 1, 1992, the licensee shall post a notice which contains and describes, in concise terms, prohibited sales of alcoholic beverages, a statement that the off-sale seller will refuse to make a sale if the seller reasonably suspects that the Alcoholic Beverage Control Act may be violated, and a statement that a minor who purchases or attempts to purchase alcoholic beverages is subject to suspension or delay in the issuance of his or her driver's license pursuant to Section 13202.5 of the Vehicle Code. The notice shall be posted at an entrance or at a point of sale in the licensed premises or in any other location that is visible to purchasers of alcoholic beverages and to the off-sale seller.

(c) As used in this section:

(1) "Off-sale seller" means any person holding a license issued by the department for off-sale of alcoholic beverages and any person employed by that licensee who in the course of that employment sells alcoholic beverages.

(2) "Clerk" means an off-sale seller who is not a licensee. (*Added by Stats 1990 ch 695 §3, eff. 1/1/91. See other section 25658.4 below.*)

§25658.4. Off-sale of alcoholic beverages; restrictions.

(a) On and after January 1, 1992, no clerk shall make an off-sale of alcoholic beverages unless the clerk executes under penalty of perjury on the first day he or she makes such a sale an application and acknowledgment. The application and acknowledgment shall be in a form understandable to the clerk.

(1) The department shall specify the form of the application and acknowledgment which shall include at a minimum a summary of this division pertaining to the following:

(A) The prohibitions contained in Sections 25658 and 25658.5 pertaining to the sale to, and purchase of, alcoholic beverages by persons under 21 years of age.

(B) Bona fide evidence of majority as provided in Section 25660.

(C) Hours of operation as provided in Article 2 (commencing with Section 25630) of Chapter 16.

(D) The prohibitions contained in subdivision (a) of Sections 25602 and 25602.1 pertaining to sales to intoxicated person.

(E) Sections 23393 and 23394 as they pertain to on-premises consumption of alcoholic beverages in an off-sale premises.

(2) The application and acknowledgment shall also include a statement that the clerk has read and understands the summary, a statement that the clerk has never been convicted of violating this division or, if convicted, an explanation of the circumstances of each conviction, and a statement that the application and acknowledgment is executed under penalty of perjury.

(3) The licensee shall keep the executed application and acknowledgment on the premises at all times and available for inspection by the department. A licensee with more than one licensed off-sale premises in the state may comply with this subdivision by maintaining an executed application and acknowledgment at a designated licensed premises, regional office, or headquarters office in the state. An executed application and acknowledgment maintained at the designated locations shall be valid for all licensed off-sale premises owned by the licensee. Any licensee maintaining an application and acknowledgment at a designated site other than the individual licensed off-sale premises shall notify the department in advance and in writing of the site where the application and acknowledgment shall be maintained and available for inspection. A licensee electing to maintain application and acknowledgments at a designated site other than the licensed premises shall maintain at each licensed premises a notice of where the executed application and acknowledgments are located. Any licensee with more than one licensed off-sale premises who elects to maintain the application and acknowledgments at a designated site other than each licensed premises shall provide the department, upon written demand, a copy of any employee's executed application and acknowledgment within 10 business days. A violation of this subdivision by a licensee constitutes grounds for discipline by the department.

(b) On and after January 1, 1992, the licensee shall post a notice which contains and describes, in concise terms, prohibited sales of alcoholic beverages, a statement that the off-sale seller will refuse to make a sale if the seller reasonably suspects that the Alcoholic Beverage Control Act may be violated, and a statement that a minor who purchases or attempts to purchase alcoholic beverages is subject to suspension or delay in the issuance of his or her driver's license pursuant to Section 13202.5 of the Vehicle Code. The notice shall be posted at an entrance or at a point of sale in the licensed premises or in any other location that is visible to purchasers of alcoholic beverages and to the off-sale seller.

(c) As used in this section:

(1) "Off-sale seller" means any person holding a retail off-sale license issued by the department and any person employed by that licensee who in the course of that employment sells alcoholic beverages.

(2) "Clerk" means an off-sale seller who is not a licensee. *(Added by Stats 1991 ch 726 §4, eff. 1/1/92. See other section 25658.4 above.)*

§25661. False evidence of age, presenting or possessing.

Any person under the age of 21 years who presents or offers to any licensee, his or her agent or employee, any written, printed, or photostatic evidence of age and identity which is false, fraudulent or not actually his or her own for the purpose of ordering, purchasing, attempting to purchase or otherwise procuring or attempting to procure, the serving of any alcoholic beverage, or who has in his or her possession any false or fraudulent written, printed, or photostatic evidence of age and identity, is guilty of a misdemeanor and shall be punished by a fine of at least two hundred fifty dollars ($250), no part of which shall be suspended; or the person shall be required to perform not less than 24 hours nor more than 32 hours of community service during hours when the person is not employed and is not attending school, or a combination of fine and community service as determined by the court. *(Amended by Stats 1989 ch 110 §1.)*

§25662. Alcoholic beverage; possession by person under 21.

(a) Any person under the age of 21 years who has any alcoholic beverage in his or her possession on any street or highway or in any public place or in any place open to the public is guilty of a misdemeanor. This section does not apply to possession by a person under the age of 21 years making a delivery of an alcoholic beverage in pursuance of the order of his or her parent, responsible adult relative, or any other adult designated by the parent or legal guardian, or in pursuance of his or her employment. That person shall have a complete defense if he or she was following, in a timely manner, the reasonable instructions of his or her parent legal guardian, responsible adult relative, or adult designee relating to disposition of the alcoholic beverage.

(b) Unless otherwise provided by law, where a peace officer has lawfully entered the premises, the peace officer may seize any alcoholic beverage in plain view which is in the possession of, or provided to, a person under the age of 21 years at social gatherings, when those gatherings are open to the public, 10 or more persons under the age of 21 years are participating, persons under the age of 21 years are consuming alcoholic beverages, and there is no supervision of the social gathering by a parent or guardian of one or more of the participants.

Where a peace officer has seized alcoholic beverages pursuant to this subdivision, the officer may destroy any alcoholic beverage contained in an opened container and in the possession of, or provided to, a person under the age of 21 years, and, with respect to alcoholic beverages in unopened containers, the officer shall impound those beverages for a period not to exceed seven working days pending a request for the release of those beverages by a person 21 years of age or older who is the lawful owner or resident of the property upon which the alcoholic beverages were seized. If no one requests release of the seized alcoholic

© 1992 by J., B. & L. Gould
Printed in the U.S.A. **EP**

beverages within that period, those beverages may be destroyed. *(Amended by Stats 1990 ch 1697 §1, eff. 1/1/91.)*

CHAPTER 17

ADMINISTRATIVE PROVISIONS

§25755. Authority as peace officers; inspecting premises; narcotics enforcement training.

(a) The director and the persons employed by the department for the administration and enforcement of this division are peace officers in the enforcement of the penal provisions of this division, the rules of the department adopted under the provisions of this division, and any other penal provisions of law of this state prohibiting or regulating the sale, exposing for sale, use, possession, giving away, adulteration, dilution, misbranding, or mislabeling of alcoholic beverages or intoxicating liquors, and these persons are authorized, while acting as peace officers, to enforce any penal provisions of law while in the course of their employment.

(b) The director, the persons employed by the department for the administration and enforcement of this division, peace officers listed in Section 830.1 of the Penal Code, and those officers listed in Section 830.6 of the Penal Code while acting in the course and scope of their employment as peace officers may, in enforcing the provisions of this division, visit and inspect the premises of any licensee at any time during which the licensee is exercising the privileges authorized by his or her license on the premises.

(c) Members of the California State Police Division and peace officers of the Department of Parks and Recreation, as defined in subdivisions (b) and (g) of Section 830.2 of the Penal Code, may, in enforcing the provisions of this division, visit and inspect the premises of any licensee located on state property at any time during which the licensee is exercising the privileges authorized by his or her license on the premises.

(d) Any agents assigned to the Drug Enforcement Narcotics Team by the director shall have successfully completed a four-week course on narcotics enforcement approved by the Commission on Peace Officer Standards and Training. In addition, all other agents of the department shall successfully complete the four-week course on narcotics enforcement approved by the Commission on Peace Officer Standards and Training by June 1, 1993. *(Amended by Stats 1990 ch 1695 §1, eff. 1/1/91.)*

This page intentionally left blank.

© 1992 by J., B. & L. Gould
Printed in the U.S.A. **EP**

EVIDENCE CODE

DIVISION 1

PRELIMINARY PROVISIONS AND CONSTRUCTION

§1. Short title.

This code shall be known as the Evidence Code.

§2. Common law restrictions.

The rule of the common law, that statutes in derogation thereof are to be strictly construed, has no application to this code. This code establishes the law of this state respecting the subject to which it relates, and its provisions are to be liberally construed with a view to effecting its objects and promoting justice.

§3. Constitutionality.

If any provision or clause of this code or application thereof to any person or circumstances is held invalid, such invalidity shall not affect other provisions or applications of the code which can be given effect without the invalid provision or application, and to this end the provisions of this code are declared to be severable.

§4. Construction of code.

Unless the provision or context otherwise requires, these preliminary provisions and rules of construction shall govern the construction of this code.

§5. Headings.

Division, chapter, article and section headings do not in any manner affect the scope, meaning, or intent of the provisions of this code.

§6. Reference to statutes.

Whenever any reference is made to any portion of this code or of any other statute, such reference shall apply to all amendments and additions heretofore or hereafter made.

§7. Definitions.

Unless otherwise expressly stated:

(a) "Division" means a division of this code.

(b) "Chapter" means a chapter of the division in which that term occurs.

(c) "Article" means an article of the chapter in which that term occurs.

(d) "Section" means a section of this code.

(e) "Subdivision" means a subdivision of the section in which that term occurs.

(f) "Paragraph" means a paragraph of the subdivision in which that term occurs.

§8. Tenses.

The present tense includes the past and future tenses; and the future, the present.

§9. Gender.

The masculine gender includes the feminine and neuter.

§10. Singular and plural.

The singular number includes the plural; and the plural, the singular.

§11. Use of "shall" and "may".

"Shall" is mandatory and "may" is permissive.

§12. Operative date of Code; applicability.

(a) This code shall become operative on January 1, 1967, and shall govern proceedings in actions brought on or after that date and, except as provided in subdivision (b), further proceedings in actions pending on that date.

(b) Subject to subdivision (c), a trial commenced before January 1, 1967, shall not be governed by this code. For the purpose of this subdivision:

(1) A trial is commenced when the first witness is sworn or the first exhibit is admitted into evidence and is terminated when the issue upon which such evidence is received is submitted to the trier of fact. A new trial, or a separate trial of a different issue, commenced on or after January 1, 1967, shall be governed by this code.

(2) If an appeal is taken from a ruling made at a trial commenced before January 1, 1967, the appellate court shall apply the law applicable at the time of the commencement of the trial.

(c) The provisions of Division 8 (commencing with Section 900) relating to privileges shall govern any claim of privilege made after December 31, 1966.

DIVISION 2

WORDS AND PHRASES DEFINED

§100. Application of definitions.

Unless the provision or context otherwise requires, these definitions govern the construction of this code.

§105. "Action," defined.

"Action" includes a civil action and a criminal action.

§110. "Burden of producing evidence," defined.

"Burden of producing evidence" means the obligation of a party to introduce evidence sufficient to avoid a ruling against him on the issue.

§115. "Burden of proof," defined.

"Burden of proof" means the obligation of a party to establish by evidence a requisite degree of belief concerning a fact in the mind of the trier of fact or the court. The burden of proof may require a party to raise a reasonable doubt concerning the existence or nonexistence of a fact or that he establish the existence or nonexistence of a fact by a preponderance of the evidence, by clear and convincing proof, or by proof beyond a reasonable doubt.

Except as otherwise provided by law, the burden of proof requires proof by a preponderance of the evidence.

§120. "Civil action," defined.

"Civil action" includes civil proceedings.

§125. "Conduct," defined.

"Conduct" includes all active and passive behavior, both verbal and nonverbal.

§130. "Criminal action," defined.

"Criminal action" includes criminal proceedings.

§135. "Declarant," defined.

"Declarant" is a person who makes a statement.

§140. "Evidence," defined.

"Evidence" means testimony, writings, material objects, or other things presented to the senses that are offered to prove the existence or nonexistence of a fact.

§145. "The hearing," defined.

"The hearing" means the hearing at which a question under this code arises, and not some earlier or later hearing.

§150. "Hearsay evidence," defined.

"Hearsay evidence" is defined in Section 1200.

§160. "Law," defined.

"Law" includes constitutional, statutory, and decisional law.

§165. "Oath", defined.

"Oath" includes affirmation or declaration under penalty of perjury.

§170. "Perceive," defined.

"Perceive" means to acquire knowledge through one's senses.

§175. "Person," defined.

"Person" includes a natural person, firm, association, organization, partnership, business trust, corporation, or public entity.

§180. "Personal property," defined.

"Personal property" includes money, goods, chattels, things in action, and evidences of debt.

§185. "Property," defined.

"Property" includes both real and personal property.

§190. "Proof," defined.

"Proof" is the establishment by evidence of a requisite degree of belief concerning a fact in the mind of the trier of fact or the court.

§195. "Public employee," defined.

"Public employee" means an officer, agent, or employee of a public entity.

§200. "Public entity," defined.

"Public entity" includes a nation, state, county, city and county, city, district, public authority, public agency, or any other political subdivision or public corporation, whether foreign or domestic.

§205. "Real property," defined.

"Real property" includes lands, tenements, and hereditaments.

§210. "Relevant evidence," defined.

"Relevant evidence" means evidence, including evidence relevant to the credibility of a witness or hearsay declarant, having any tendency in reason to prove or disprove any disputed fact that is of consequence to the determination of the action.

§220. "State," defined.

"State" means the State of California, unless applied to the different parts of the United States. In the latter case, it includes any state, district, commonwealth, territory, or insular possession of the United States.

§225. "Statement," defined.

"Statement" means (a) oral or written verbal expression or (b) nonverbal conduct of a person intended by him as a substitute for oral or written verbal expression.

§230. "Statute," defined.

"Statute" includes a treaty and a constitutional provision.

§235. "Trier of fact," defined.

"Trier of fact" includes (a) the jury and (b) the court when the court is trying an issue of fact other than one relating to the admissibility of evidence.

§240. "Unavailable as a witness," defined.

(a) Except as otherwise provided in subdivision (b), "unavailable as a witness" means that the declarant is any of the following:

(1) Exempted or precluded on the ground of privilege from testifying concerning the matter to which his or her statement is relevant.

(2) Disqualified from testifying to the matter.

(3) Dead or unable to attend or to testify at the hearing because of then existing physical or mental illness or infirmity.

(4) Absent from the hearing and the court is unable to compel his or her attendance by its process.

(5) Absent from the hearing and the proponent of his or her statement has exercised reasonable diligence but has been unable to procure his or her attendance by the court's process.

(b) A declarant is not unavailable as a witness if the exemption, preclusion, disqualification, death, inability, or absence of the declarant was brought about by the procurement or wrongdoing of the proponent of his or her statement for the purpose of preventing the declarant from attending or testifying.

(c) Expert testimony which establishes that physical or mental trauma resulting from an alleged crime has caused harm to a witness of sufficient severity that the witness is physically unable to testify or is unable to testify without suffering substantial trauma may constitute a sufficient showing of unavailability pursuant to paragraph (3) of subdivision (a). As used in this section, the term "expert" means a physician and surgeon, including a psychiatrist, or any person described by subdivision (b), (c), or (e) of Section 1010.

The introduction of evidence to establish the unavailability of a witness under this subdivision shall not be deemed procurement of unavailability, in absence of proof to the contrary.

§250. "Writing," defined.

"Writing" means handwriting, typewriting, printing, photostating, photographing, and every other means of recording upon any tangible thing any form of communication or representation, including letters, words, pictures, sounds, or symbols, or combinations thereof.

© 1992 by J., B. & L. Gould
Printed in the U.S.A.   **EP**

§255. "Original," defined.

"Original" means the writing itself or any counterpart intended to have the same effect by a person executing or issuing it. An "original" of a photograph includes the negative or any print therefrom. If data are stored in a computer or similar device, any printout or other output readable by sight, shown to reflect the data accurately, is an "original."

§260. "Duplicate," defined.

A "duplicate" is a counterpart produced by the same impression as the original, or from the same matrix, or by means of photography, including enlargements and miniatures, or by mechanical or electronic rerecording, or by chemical reproduction, or by other equivalent technique which accurately reproduces the original.

DIVISION 3

GENERAL PROVISIONS

CHAPTER 1

APPLICABILITY OF CODE

§300. Applicability of code.

Except as otherwise provided by statute, this code applies in every action before the Supreme Court or a court of appeal, superior court, municipal court, or justice court, including proceedings in such actions conducted by a referee, court commissioner, or similar officer, but does not apply in grand jury proceedings.

CHAPTER 2

PROVINCE OF COURT AND JURY

§310. Questions of law.

(a) All questions of law (including but not limited to questions concerning the construction of statutes and other writings, the admissibility of evidence, and other rules of evidence) are to be decided by the court. Determination of issues of fact preliminary to the admission of evidence are to be decided by the court as provided in Article 2 (commencing with Section 400) of Chapter 4.

(b) Determination of the law of an organization of nations or of the law of a foreign nation or a public entity in a foreign nation is a question of law to be determined in the manner provided in Division 4 (commencing with Section 450).

§311. Procedure when law of foreign nations or sister states cannot be determined.

If the law of an organization of nations, a foreign nation or a state other than this state, or a public entity in a foreign nation or a state other than this state, is applicable and such law cannot be determined, the court may, as the ends of justice require, either:

(a) Apply the law of this state if the court can do so consistently with the Constitution of the United States and the Constitution of this state; or

(b) Dismiss the action without prejudice or, in the case of a reviewing court, remand the case to the trial court with directions to dismiss the action without prejudice.

§312. Jury as trier of fact.

Except as otherwise provided by law, where the trial is by jury:

(a) All questions of fact are to be decided by the jury.

(b) Subject to the control of the court, the jury is to determine the effect and value of the evidence addressed to it, including the credibility of witnesses and hearsay declarants.

CHAPTER 3

ORDER OF PROOF

§320. Court to regulate order of proof.

Except as otherwise provided by law, the court in its discretion shall regulate the order of proof.

CHAPTER 4

ADMITTING AND EXCLUDING EVIDENCE

ARTICLE 1

GENERAL PROVISIONS

§350. Relevant evidence.

No evidence is admissible except relevant evidence.

§351. Relevant evidence; admissibility.

Except as otherwise provided by statute, all relevant evidence is admissible.

§351.1. Polygraph examination results not admissible.

(a) Notwithstanding any other provision of law, the results of polygraph examination, the opinion of a polygraph examiner, or in reference to an offer to take, failure to take, or taking of a polygraph examination, shall not be admitted into evidence in any criminal proceeding, including pretrial and post conviction motions and hearings, or in any trial or hearing of a juvenile for a criminal offense, whether heard in juvenile or adult court, unless all parties stipulate to the admission of such results.

(b) Nothing in this section is intended to exclude from evidence statements made during a polygraph examination which are otherwise admissible.

§352. Exclusion of evidence.

The court in its discretion may exclude evidence if its probative value is substantially outweighed by the probability that its admission will (a) necessitate undue consumption of time or (b) create substantial danger of undue prejudice, of confusing the issues, or of misleading the jury.

§352.1. Exclusion from evidence of address and telephone number of victim of sexual offense.

In any criminal proceeding under Section 261, Section 264.1, subdivision (d) of Section 286, or subdivision (d) of Section 288a of the Penal Code, or in any criminal proceeding under subdivision (c) of Section 286 or subdivision (c) of Section 288a of the Penal Code in which the defendant is alleged to have compelled the participation of the victim by force, violence, duress, menace, or threat of great bodily harm, the district attorney may, upon written motion with notice to the defendant or the defendant's attorney, if he or

© 1992 by J., B. & L. Gould
Printed in the U.S.A. **EP**

she is represented by an attorney, within a reasonable time prior to any hearing, move to exclude from evidence the current address and telephone number of any victim at such hearing.

The court may order that evidence of the victim's current address and telephone number be excluded from any hearings conducted pursuant to such criminal proceeding if the court finds that the probative value of such evidence is outweighed by the creation of substantial danger to the victim.

Nothing in this section shall abridge or limit the defendant's right to discover or investigate such information.

§353. Erroneous admission of evidence.

A verdict or finding shall not be set aside, nor shall the judgment or decision based thereon be reversed, by reason of the erroneous admission of evidence unless:

(a) There appears of record an objection to or a motion to exclude or to strike the evidence that was timely made and so stated as to make clear the specific ground of the objection or motion; and

(b) The court which passes upon the effect of the error or errors is of the opinion that the admitted evidence should have been excluded on the ground stated and that the error or errors complained of resulted in a miscarriage of justice.

§354. Erroneous exclusion of evidence.

A verdict or finding shall not be set aside, nor shall the judgment or decision based thereon be reversed, by reason of the erroneous exclusion of evidence unless the court which passes upon the effect of the error or errors is of the opinion that the error or errors complained of resulted in a miscarriage of justice and it appears of record that:

(a) The substance, purpose, and relevance of the excluded evidence was made known to the court by the question asked, an offer of proof, or by any other means;

(b) The rulings of the court made compliance with subdivision (a) futile; or

(c) The evidence was sought by questions asked during cross-examination or recross-examination.

§355. Limited admissibility.

When evidence is admissible as to one party or for one purpose and is inadmissible as to another party or for another purpose, the court upon request shall restrict the evidence to its proper scope and instruct the jury accordingly.

§356. Whole act, declaration, conversation, or writing may be given in evidence to understand part offered.

Where part of an act, declaration, conversation, or writing is given in evidence by one party, the whole on the same subject may be inquired into by an adverse party; when a letter is read, the answer may be given; and when a detached act, declaration, conversation, or writing is given in evidence, any other act, declaration, conversation, or writing which is necessary to make it understood may also be given in evidence.

ARTICLE 2

PRELIMINARY DETERMINATIONS ON ADMISSIBILITY OF EVIDENCE

§400. "Preliminary fact,", defined.

As used in this article, "preliminary fact" means a fact upon the existence or nonexistence of which depends the admissibility or inadmissibility of evidence. The phrase "the admissibility or inadmissibility of evidence" includes the qualification or disqualification of person to be a witness and the existence or nonexistence of privilege.

§401. "Proffered evidence," defined.

As used in this article, "proffered evidence" means evidence, the admissibility or inadmissibility of which is dependent upon the existence or nonexistence of a preliminary fact.

§402. Preliminary questions of fact.

(a) When the existence of a preliminary fact is disputed, its existence or nonexistence shall be determined as provided in this article.

(b) The court may hear and determine the question of the admissibility of evidence out of the presence or hearing of the jury; but in a criminal action, the court shall hear and determine the question of the admissibility of a confession or admission of the defendant out of the presence and hearing of the jury if any party so requests.

(c) A ruling on the admissibility of evidence implies whatever finding of fact is prerequisite thereto; a separate or formal finding is unnecessary unless required by statute.

§403. Preliminary questions of fact; admissibility of proffered evidence.

(a) The proponent of the proffered evidence has the burden of producing evidence as to the existence of the preliminary fact, and the proffered evidence is inadmissible unless the court finds that there is evidence sufficient to sustain a finding of the existence of the preliminary fact, when:

(1) The relevance of the proffered evidence depends on the existence of the preliminary fact;

(2) The preliminary fact is the personal knowledge of a witness concerning the subject matter of his testimony;

(3) The preliminary fact is the authenticity of a writing; or

(4) The proffered evidence is of a statement or other conduct of a particular person and the preliminary fact is whether that person made the statement or so conducted himself

(b) Subject to Section 702, the court may admit conditionally the proffered evidence under this section, subject to evidence of the preliminary fact being supplied later in the course of the trial.

(c) If the court admits the proffered evidence under this section, the court:

(1) May, and on request shall, instruct the jury to determine whether the preliminary fact exists and to disregard the proffered evidence unless the jury finds that the preliminary fact does exist.

(2) Shall instruct the jury to disregard the proffered evidence if the court subsequently determines that a jury could not reasonably find that the preliminary fact exists.

© 1992 by J., B. & L. Gould
Printed in the U.S.A.   EP

§404. Proffered evidence; privilege against self- incrimination.

Whenever the proffered evidence is claimed to be privileged under Section 940, the person claiming the privilege has the burden of showing that the proffered evidence might tend to incriminate him; and the proffered evidence is inadmissible unless it clearly appears to the court that the proffered evidence cannot possibly have a tendency to incriminate the person claiming the privilege.

§405. Preliminary questions of fact in other cases

With respect to preliminary fact determinations not governed by Section 403 or 404:

(a) When the existence of a preliminary fact is disputed, the court shall indicate which party has the burden of producing evidence and the burden of proof on the issue as implied by the rule of law under which the question arises. The court shall determine the existence or nonexistence of the preliminary fact and shall admit or exclude the proffered evidence as required by the rule of law under which the question arises.

(b) If a preliminary fact is also a fact in issue in the action:

(1) The jury shall not be informed of the court's determination as to existence or nonexistence of the preliminary fact.

(2) If the proffered evidence is admitted, the jury shall not be instructed to disregard the evidence if its determination of the fact differs from the court's determination of the preliminary fact.

§406. Weight or credibility of evidence.

This article does not limit the right of a party to introduce before the trier of fact evidence relevant to weight or credibility.

CHAPTER 5

WEIGHT OF EVIDENCE GENERALLY

§410. "Direct evidence," defined.

As used in this chapter, "direct evidence" means evidence that directly proves a fact, without an inference or presumption, and which in itself, if true, conclusively establishes that fact.

§411. One witness sufficient for proof of fact.

Except where additional evidence is required by statute, the direct evidence of one witness who is entitled to full credit is sufficient for proof of any fact.

§412. Strength of evidence offered.

If weaker and less satisfactory evidence is offered when it was within the power of the party to produce stronger and more satisfactory evidence, the evidence offered should be viewed with distrust.

§413. Failure to explain or deny evidence

In determining what inferences to draw from the evidence or facts in the case against a party, the trier of fact may consider, among other things, the party's failure to explain or to deny by his testimony such evidence or facts in the case against him, or his willful suppression of evidence relating thereto, if such be the case.

DIVISION 4

JUDICIAL NOTICE

§450. Judicial notice, as authorized by law.

Judicial notice may not be taken of any matter unless authorized or required by law.

§451. Mandatory judicially notice.

Judicial notice shall be taken of the following:

(a) The decisional, constitutional, and public statutory law of this state and of the United States and the provisions of any charter described in Section 3, 4, or 5 of Article XI of the California Constitution.

(b) Any matter made a subject of judicial notice by Section 11343.6, 11344.6, or 18576 of the Government Code or by Section 1507 of Title 44 of the United States Code.

(c) Rules of professional conduct for members of the bar adopted pursuant to Section 6076 of the Business and Professions Code and rules of practice and procedure for the courts of this state adopted by the Judicial Council.

(d) Rules of pleading, practice, and procedure prescribed by the United States Supreme Court, such as the Rules of the United States Supreme Court, the Federal Rules of Civil Procedure, the Federal Rules of Criminal Procedure, the Admiralty Rules, the Rules of the Court of Claims, the Rules of the Customs Court, and the General Orders and Forms in Bankruptcy.

(e) The true signification of all English words and phrases and of all legal expressions.

(f) Facts and propositions of generalized knowledge that are so universally known that they cannot reasonably be the subject of dispute.

§452. Additional matters which may be judicially noticed.

Judicial notice may be taken of the following matters to the extent that they are not embraced within Section 451.

(a) The decisional, constitutional, and statutory law of any state of the United States and the resolutions and private acts of the Congress of the United States and of the Legislature of this state.

(b) Regulations and legislative enactments issued by or under the authority of the United States or any public entity in the United States.

(c) Official acts of the legislative, executive, and judicial departments of the United States and of any state of the United States.

(d) Records of (1) any court of this state or (2) any court of record of the United States or of any state of the United States.

(e) Rules of court of (1) any court of this state or (2) any court of record of the United States or of any state of the United States.

(f) The law of an organization of nations and of foreign nations and public entities in foreign nations.

(g) Facts and propositions that are of such common knowledge within the territorial jurisdiction of the court that they cannot reasonably be the subject of dispute.

(h) Facts and propositions that are not reasonably subject to dispute and are capable of immediate and accurate determination by resort to sources of reasonably indisputable accuracy.

§453. Judicial notice upon request.

The trial court shall take judicial notice of any matter specified in Section 452 if a party requests it and:

(a) Gives each adverse party sufficient notice of the requests, through the pleadings or otherwise, to enable such adverse party to prepare to meet the request; and

(b) Furnishes the court with sufficient information to enable it to take judicial notice of the matter.

§454. Information consulted or used in taking judicial notice.

(a) In determining the propriety of taking judicial notice of a matter, or the tenor thereof:

(1) Any source of pertinent information, including the advice of persons learned in the subject matter, may be consulted or used, whether or not furnished by a party.

(2) Exclusionary rules of evidence do not apply except for Section 352 and the rules of privilege.

(b) Where the subject of judicial notice is the law of an organization of nations, a foreign nation, or a public entity in a foreign nation and the court resorts to the advice of persons learned in the subject matter, such advice, if not received in open court, shall be in writing.

§455. Court to afford opportunity to present relevant information.

With respect to any matter specified in Section 452 or in subdivision (f) of Section 451 that is of substantial consequence to the determination of the action:

(a) If the trial court has been requested to take or has taken or proposes to take judicial notice of such matter, the court shall afford each party reasonable opportunity, before the jury is instructed or before the cause is submitted for decision by the court, to present to the court information relevant to (1) the propriety of taking judicial notice of the matter and (2) the tenor of the matter to be noticed.

(b) If the trial court resorts to any source of information not received in open court, including the advice of persons learned in the subject matter, such information and its source shall be made a part of the record in the action and the court shall afford each party reasonable opportunity to meet such information before judicial notice of the matter may be taken.

§456. Denial of request to take judicial notice; notice on record.

If the trial court denies a request to take judicial notice of any matter, the court shall at the earliest practicable time so advise the parties and indicate for the record that it has denied the request.

§457. Instructing jury as to fact judicially noticed

If a matter judicially noticed is a matter which would otherwise have been for determination by the jury, the trial court may, and upon request shall, instruct the jury to accept as a fact the matter so noticed.

§458. Judicial notice by trial court in subsequent proceedings.

The failure or refusal of the trial court to take judicial notice of a matter, or to instruct the jury with respect to the matter, does not preclude the trial court in subsequent proceedings in the action from taking judicial notice of the matter in accordance with the procedure specified in this division.

§459. Judicial notice by reviewing court

(a) The reviewing court shall take judicial notice of (1) each matter properly noticed by the trial court and (2) each matter that the trial court was required to notice under Section 451 or 453. The reviewing court may take judicial notice of any matter specified in Section 452.

The reviewing court may take judicial notice of a matter in a tenor different from that noticed by the trial court.

(b) In determining the propriety of taking judicial notice of a matter, or the tenor thereof, the reviewing court has the same power as the trial court under Section 454.

(c) When taking judicial notice under this section of a matter specified in Section 452 or in subdivision (f) of Section 451 that is of substantial consequence to the determination of the action, the reviewing court shall comply with the provisions of subdivision (a) of Section 455 if the matter was not theretofore judicially noticed in the action.

(d) In determining the propriety of taking judicial notice of a matter specified in Section 452 or in subdivision (f) of Section 451 that is of substantial consequence to the determination of the action, or the tenor thereof, if the reviewing court resorts to any source of information not received in open court or not included in the record of the action, including the advice of persons learned in the subject matter, the reviewing court shall afford each party reasonable opportunity to meet such information before judicial notice of the matter may be taken.

§460. Advice of experts; appointment by court

Where the advice of persons learned in the subject matter is required in order to enable the court to take judicial notice of a matter, the court on its own motion or on motion of any party may appoint one or more such persons to provide such advice. If the court determines to appoint such a person, he shall be appointed and compensated in the manner provided in Article 2 (commencing with Section 730) of Chapter 3 of Division 6.

DIVISION 5

BURDEN OF PROOF; BURDEN OF PRODUCING EVIDENCE; PRESUMPTIONS AND INFERENCES

CHAPTER 1

BURDEN OF PROOF

ARTICLE 1

GENERAL

§500. Burden of proof as to existence or nonexistence of fact.

Except as otherwise provided by law, a party has the burden of proof as to each fact the existence or nonexistence of which is essential to the claim for relief or defense that he is asserting.

© 1992 by J., B. & L. Gould
Printed in the U.S.A.   EP

§501. Burden of proof; criminal action.

Insofar as any statute, except Section 522, assigns the burden of proof in a criminal action, such statute is subject to Penal Code Section 1096.

§502. Burden of proof; instructions to jury.

The court on all proper occasions shall instruct the jury as to which party bears the burden of proof on each issue and as to whether that burden requires that a party raise a reasonable doubt concerning the existence or nonexistence of a fact or that he establish the existence or nonexistence of a fact by a preponderance of the evidence, by clear and convincing proof, or by proof beyond a reasonable doubt.

ARTICLE 2

BURDEN OF PROOF ON SPECIFIC ISSUES

§520. Burden of proof in criminal cases.

The party claiming that a person is guilty of crime or wrongdoing has the burden of proof on that issue.

§521. Burden of proof in negligence actions.

The party claiming that a person did not exercise a requisite degree of care has the burden of proof on that issue.

§522. Burden of proof as to insanity.

The party claiming that any person, including himself, is or was insane has the burden of proof on that issue.

CHAPTER 2

BURDEN OF PRODUCING EVIDENCE

§550. Party who has burden of producing evidence as to fact.

(a) The burden of producing evidence as to a particular fact is on the party against whom a finding on the fact would be required in the absence of further evidence.

(b) The burden of producing evidence as to a particular fact is initially on the party with the burden of proof as to that fact.

CHAPTER 3

PRESUMPTIONS AND INFERENCES

ARTICLE 1

GENERAL

§600. Presumption and inference, defined

(a) A presumption is an assumption of fact that the law requires to be made from another fact or group of facts found or otherwise established in the action. A presumption is not evidence.

(b) An inference is a deduction of fact that may logically and reasonably be drawn from another fact or group of facts found or otherwise established in the action.

§601. Presumptions; classification.

A presumption is either conclusive or rebuttable. Every rebuttable presumption is either (a) a presumption affecting the burden of producing evidence or (b) a presumption affecting the burden of proof.

§602. Rebuttable presumption; statutorily provided prima facie evidence.

A statute providing that a fact or group of facts is prima facie evidence of another fact establishes a rebuttable presumption.

§603. Presumption affecting the burden of producing evidence, defined.

A presumption affecting the burden of producing evidence is a presumption established to implement no public policy other than to facilitate the determination of the particular action in which the presumption is applied.

§604. Presumption affecting burden of producing evidence, effect of.

The effect of a presumption affecting the burden of producing evidence is to require the trier of fact to assume the existence of the presumed fact unless and until evidence is introduced which would support a finding of its nonexistence, in which case the trier of fact shall determine the existence or nonexistence of the presumed fact from the evidence and without regard to the presumption. Nothing in this section shall be construed to prevent the drawing of any inference that may be appropriate.

§605. Presumption affecting the burden of proof, defined

A presumption affecting the burden of proof is a presumption established to implement some public policy other than to facilitate the determination of the particular action in which the presumption is applied, such as the policy in favor of establishment of a parent and child relationship, the validity of marriage, the stability of titles to property, or the security of those who entrust themselves or their property to the administration of others.

§606. Presumption affecting burden of proof, effect of.

The effect of a presumption affecting the burden of proof is to impose upon the party against whom it operates the burden of proof as to the nonexistence of the presumed fact.

§607. Presumption in a criminal action; reasonable doubt.

When a presumption affecting the burden of proof operates in a criminal action to establish presumptively any fact that is essential to the defendant's guilt, the presumption operates only if the facts that give rise to the presumption have been found or otherwise established beyond a reasonable doubt, and, in such case, the defendant need only raise a reasonable doubt as to the existence of the presumed fact.

ARTICLE 2

CONCLUSIVE PRESUMPTIONS

§620. Conclusive presumptions.

The presumptions established by this article, and all other presumptions declared by law to be conclusive, are conclusive presumptions.

§621. Paternity; blood tests.

(a) Except as provided in subdivision (b), the issue of a wife cohabiting with her husband, who is not impotent or sterile, is conclusively presumed to be a child of the marriage.

(b) Notwithstanding subdivision (a), if the court finds that the conclusions of all the experts, as disclosed by the evidence based upon blood tests performed pursuant to Chapter 2 (commencing with Section 890) of Division 7, are that the husband is not the father of the child, the question of paternity of the husband shall be resolved accordingly.

(c) The notice of motion for blood tests under subdivision (b) may be filed not later than two years from the child's date of birth by the husband, or for purposes of establishing paternity by the presumed father or the child through or by the child's guardian ad litem.

(d) The notice of motion for blood tests under subdivision (b) may be filed by the mother of the child not later than two years from the child's date of birth if the child's biological father has filed an affidavit with the court acknowledging paternity of the child.

(e) Subdivision (b) shall not apply to any case coming within Section 7005 of the Civil Code, or to any case in which the wife, with the consent of the husband, conceived by means of a surgical procedure.

(f) The notice of motion for the blood tests pursuant to subdivision (b) shall be supported by a declaration under oath submitted by the moving party stating the factual basis for placing the issue of paternity before the court. This requirement shall not apply to any case pending before the court on September 30, 1980.

(g) Subdivision (b) shall not apply to any case which has reached final judgment of paternity on September 30, 1980.

(h) As used in this section "presumed father" has the meaning given in Section 7004 of the Civil Code.

§622. Facts in written instrument.

The facts recited in a written instrument are conclusively presumed to be true as between the parties thereto, or their successors in interest; but this rule does not apply to the recital of a consideration.

§623. Equitable estoppel.

Whenever a party has, by his own statement or conduct, intentionally and deliberately led another to believe a particular thing true and to act upon such belief, he is not, in any litigation arising out of such statement or conduct, permitted to contradict it.

§624. Estoppel of tenant to deny title of landlord.

A tenant is not permitted to deny the title of his landlord at the time of the commencement of the relation.

ARTICLE 3

PRESUMPTIONS AFFECTING THE BURDEN OF PRODUCING EVIDENCE

§630. Presumptions affecting the burden of producing evidence.

The presumptions established by this article, and all other rebuttable presumptions established by law that fall within the criteria of Section 603, are presumptions affecting the burden of producing evidence.

§631. Delivery of money by one to another.

Money delivered by one to another is presumed to have been due to the latter.

§632. Delivery of thing by one to another.

A thing delivered by one to another is presumed to have belonged to the latter.

§633. Delivery of obligation to debtor.

An obligation delivered up to the debtor is presumed to have been paid.

§634. Person in possession of order on himself.

A person in possession of an order on himself for the payment of money, or delivery of a thing, is presumed to have paid the money or delivered the thing accordingly.

§ 635. Obligation possessed by creditor.

An obligation possessed by the creditor is presumed not to have been paid.

§636. Receipt of later rent or installments.

The payment of earlier rent or installments is presumed from a receipt for later rent or installments.

§637. Possession of things presumes ownership.

The things which a person possesses are presumed to be owned by him.

§638. Acts of ownership over property.

A person who exercises acts of ownership over property is presumed to be the owner of it.

§639. Rights of parties set forth correctly in judgment.

A judgment, when not conclusive, is presumed to correctly determine or set forth the rights of the parties, but there is no presumption that the facts essential to the judgment have been correctly determined.

§ 640. Date of writing.

A writing is presumed to have been truly dated.

§641. Letter correctly addressed and properly mailed.

A letter correctly addressed and properly mailed is presumed to have been received in the ordinary course of mail.

§642. Conveyance of real property.

A trustee or other person, whose duty it was to convey real property to a particular person, is presumed to have actually conveyed to him when such presumption is necessary to perfect title of such person or his successor in interest.

§643. Ancient document; authenticity.

A deed or will or other writing purporting to create, terminate, or affect an interest in real or personal property is presumed to be authentic if it:

(a) Is at least 30 years old;

(b) Is in such condition as to create no suspicion concerning its authenticity;

(c) Was kept, or if found was found, in a place where such writing, if authentic, would be likely to be kept or found; and

© 1992 by J., B. & L. Gould
Printed in the U.S.A.   EP

(d) Has been generally acted upon as authentic by persons having an interest in the matter.

§644. Book published by public authority.

A book, purporting to be printed or published by public authority, is presumed to have been so printed or published.

§645. Book containing reports of cases.

A book, purporting to contain reports of cases adjudged in the tribunals of the state or nation where the book is published, is presumed to contain correct reports of such cases.

§645.1. Printed materials.

Printed materials, purporting to be a particular newspaper or periodical, are presumed to be that newspaper or periodical if regularly issued at average intervals not exceeding three months.

§646. Res ipsa loquitur; jury instructions.

(a) As used in this section, "defendant" includes any party against whom the res ipsa loquitur presumption operates.

(b) The judicial doctrine of res ipsa loquitur is a presumption affecting the burden of producing evidence.

(c) If the evidence, or facts otherwise established, would support a res ipsa loquitur presumption and the defendant has introduced evidence which would support a finding that he was not negligent or that any negligence on his part was not a proximate cause of the occurrence, the court may, and upon request shall, instruct the jury to the effect that:—

(1) If the facts which would give rise to a res ipsa loquitur presumption are found or otherwise established, the jury may draw the inference from such facts that a proximate cause of the occurrence was some negligent conduct on the part of the defendant; and

(2) The jury shall not find that a proximate cause of the occurrence was some negligent conduct on the part of the defendant unless the jury believes, after weighing all the evidence in the case and drawing such inferences therefrom as the jury believes are warranted, that it is more probable than not that the occurrence was caused by some negligent conduct on the part of the defendant.

§647. Return of registered process server.

The return of a process server registered pursuant to Chapter 16 (commencing with Section 22350) of Division 8 of the Business and Professions Code upon process or notice establishes a presumption, affecting the burden of producing evidence, of the facts stated in the return.

ARTICLE 4

PRESUMPTIONS AFFECTING THE BURDEN OF PROOF

§660. Presumptions affecting the burden of proof.

The presumptions established by this article, and all other rebuttable presumptions established by law that fall within the criteria of Section 605, are presumptions affecting the burden of proof.

§662. Owner of legal title to property.

The owner of the legal title to property is presumed to be the owner of the full beneficial title. This presumption may be rebutted only by clear and convincing proof.

§663. Validity of ceremonial marriage.

A ceremonial marriage is presumed to be valid.

§664. Regular performance of official duty.

It is presumed that official duty has been regularly performed. This presumption does not apply on an issue as to the lawfulness of an arrest if it is found or otherwise established that the arrest was made without a warrant.

§665. Intention of voluntary act.

A person is presumed to intend the ordinary consequences of his voluntary act. This presumption is inapplicable in a criminal action to establish the specific intent of the defendant where specific intent is an element of the crime charged.

§666. Judicial jurisdiction.

Any court of this state or the United States, or any court of general jurisdiction in any other state or nation, or any judge of such a court, acting as such, is presumed to have acted in the lawful exercise of its jurisdiction. This presumption applies only when the act of the court or judge is under collateral attack.

§667. Death of person.

A person not heard from in five years is presumed to be dead.

§668. Unlawful intent.

An unlawful intent is presumed from the doing of an unlawful act.

This presumption is inapplicable in a criminal action to establish the specific intent of the defendant where specific intent is an element of the crime charged.

§669. Negligence.

(a) The failure of a person to exercise due care is presumed if:

(1) He violated a statute, ordinance, or regulation of a public entity;

(2) The violation proximately caused death or injury to person or property;

(3) The death or injury resulted from an occurrence of the nature which the statute, ordinance, or regulation was designed to prevent; and

(4) The person suffering the death or the injury to his person or property was one of the class of persons for whose protection the statute, ordinance, or regulation was adopted.

(b) This presumption may be rebutted by proof that:

(1) The person violating the statute, ordinance, or regulation did what might reasonably be expected of a person of ordinary prudence, acting under similar circumstances, who desired to comply with the law; or

(2) The person violating the statute, ordinance, or regulation was a child and exercised the degree of care ordinarily exercised by persons of his maturity, intelligence, and capacity under similar circumstances, but the presumption may not be rebutted by such proof if the violation occurred in the course of an activity

normally engaged in only by adults and requiring adult qualifications.

§669.1. State or local rules or guidelines for standards of conduct for public employees

A rule, policy, manual, or guideline of state or local government setting forth standards of conduct or guidelines for its employees in the conduct of their public employment shall not be considered a statute, ordinance, or regulation of that public entity within the meaning of Section 669, unless the rule, manual, policy, or guideline has been formally adopted as a statute, as an ordinance of a local governmental entity in this state empowered to adopt ordinances, or as a regulation by an agency of the state pursuant to the Administrative Procedure Act (Chapter 3.5 (commencing with Section 11340) of Division 3 of Title 2 of the Government Code), or by an agency of the United States government pursuant to the federal Administrative Procedure Act (Chapter 5 (commencing with Section 5001) of Title 5 of the United States Code). This section affects only the presumption set forth in Section 669, and is not otherwise intended to affect the admissibility or inadmissibility of the rule, policy, manual, or guideline under other provisions of law.

§669.5. Ordinances; residential construction.

(a) Any ordinance enacted by the governing body of a city, county, or city and county which (1) directly limits, by number, the building permits that may be issued for residential construction or the buildable lots which may be developed for residential purposes, or (2) changes the standards of residential development on vacant land so that the governing body's zoning is rendered in violation of Section 65913.1 of the Government Code is presumed to have an impact on the supply of residential units available in an area which includes territory outside the jurisdiction of the city, county, or city and county.

(b) With respect to any action which challenges the validity of an ordinance specified in subdivision (a) the city, county, or city and county enacting the ordinance shall bear the burden of proof that the ordinance is necessary for the protection of the public health, safety, or welfare of the population of the city, county, or city and county.

(c) This section does not apply to state and federal building code requirements or local ordinances which (1) impose a moratorium, to protect the public health and safety, on residential construction for a specified period of time, if, under the terms of the ordinance, the moratorium will cease when the public health or safety is no longer jeopardized by the construction, (2) create agricultural preserves under Chapter 7 (commencing with Section 51200) of Part 1 of Division 1 of Title 5 of the Government Code, or (3) restrict the number of buildable parcels or designate lands within a zone for nonresidential uses in order to protect agricultural uses as defined in subdivision (b) of Section 51201 of the Government Code or open-space land as defined in subdivision (b) of Section 65560 of the Government Code.

(d) This section shall not apply to a voter approved ordinance adopted by referendum or initiative prior to the effective date of this section which (1) requires the city, county, or city and county to establish a population growth limit which represents its fair share of each year's statewide population growth, or (2) which sets a growth rate of no more than the average population growth rate experienced by the state as a whole. Paragraph (2) of subdivision (a) does not apply to a voter-approved ordinance adopted by referendum or initiative which exempts housing affordable to persons and families of low or moderate income, as defined in Section 50093 of the Health and Safety Code, or which otherwise provides low- and moderate-income housing sites equivalent to such an exemption.

DIVISION 6

WITNESSES

CHAPTER 1

COMPETENCY

§700. Qualification of every person.

Except as otherwise provided by statute, every person, irrespective of age, is qualified to be a witness and no person is disqualified to testify to any matter.

§701. Disqualification of witness.

(a) A person is disqualified to be a witness if he or she is:

(1) Incapable of expressing himself or herself concerning the matter so as to be understood, either directly or through interpretation by one who can understand him; or

(2) Incapable of understanding the duty of a witness to tell the truth.

(b) In any proceeding held outside the presence of a jury, the court may reserve challenges to the competency of a witness until the conclusion of the direct examination of that witness.

§702. Personal knowledge of witness.

(a) Subject to Section 801, the testimony of a witness concerning a particular matter is inadmissible unless he has personal knowledge of the matter. Against the objection of a party, such personal knowledge must be shown before the witness may testify concerning the matter.

(b) A witness' personal knowledge of a matter may be shown by any otherwise admissible evidence, including his own testimony.

§703. Judge as witness, in absence of objection; motion for mistrial.

(a) Before the judge presiding at the trial of an action may be called to testify in that trial as a witness, he shall, in proceedings held out of the presence and hearing of the jury, inform the parties of the information he has concerning any fact or matter about which he will be called to testify.

(b) Against the objection of a party, the judge presiding at the trial of an action may not testify in that trial as a witness. Upon such objection, the judge shall declare a mistrial and order the action assigned for trial before another judge.

(c) The calling of the judge presiding at a trial to testify in that trial as a witness shall be deemed a consent to the granting of a motion for mistrial, and an objection to such calling of a judge shall be deemed a motion for mistrial.

(d) In the absence of objection by a party, the judge presiding at the trial of an action may testify in that trial as a witness.

© 1992 by J., B. & L. Gould
Printed in the U.S.A.   EP

§703.5. Judge or arbitrator as witness at subsequent proceedings; limitations.

No person presiding at any judicial or quasi-judicial proceeding, and no arbitrator, shall be competent to testify, in any subsequent civil proceeding as to any statement, conduct, decision or ruling, occurring at or in conjunction with the prior proceeding, except as to a statement or conduct that could (a) give rise to civil or criminal contempt, (b) constitute a crime, (c) be the subject of investigation by the State Bar or Commission on Judicial Performance, or (d) give rise to disqualification proceedings under paragraph (1) or (6) of subdivision (a) of Section 170.1 of the Code of Civil Procedure.

§704. Juror as witness, in absence of objection; motion for mistrial.

(a) Before a juror sworn and impaneled in the trial of an action may be called to testify before the jury in that trial as a witness, he shall, in proceedings conducted by the court out of the presence and hearing of the remaining jurors, inform the parties of the information he has concerning any fact or matter about which he will be called to testify.

(b) Against the objection of a party, a juror sworn and impaneled in the trial of an action may not testify before the jury in that trial as a witness. Upon such objection, the court shall declare a mistrial and order the action assigned for trial before another jury.

(c) The calling of a juror to testify before the jury as a witness shall be deemed a consent to the granting of a motion for a mistrial, and an objection to such calling of a juror shall be deemed a motion for mistrial.

(d) In the absence of objection by a party, a juror sworn and impaneled in the trial of an action may be compelled to testify in that trial as a witness.

CHAPTER 2

OATH AND CONFRONTATION

§710. Oath or affirmation required; child under 10.

Every witness before testifying shall take an oath or make an affirmation or declaration in the form provided by law, except that a child under the age of 10, in the court's discretion, may be required only to promise to tell the truth.

§711. Right of confrontation.

At the trial of an action, a witness can be heard only in the presence and subject to the examination of all the parties to the action, if they choose to attend and examine.

§712. Blood sample technique affidavits

Notwithstanding Sections 711 and 1200, at the trial of a criminal action, evidence of the technique used in taking blood samples may be given by a registered nurse, licensed vocational nurse, or licensed clinical laboratory technologist or clinical laboratory bioanalyst, by means of an affidavit. The affidavit shall be admissible, provided the party offering the affidavit as evidence has served all other parties to the action, or their counsel, with a copy of the affidavit no less than 10 days prior to trial. Nothing in this section shall preclude any party or his counsel from objecting to the introduction of the affidavit at any time, and requiring the attendance of the affiant, or compelling attendance by subpoena.

CHAPTER 3

EXPERT WITNESSES

ARTICLE 1

EXPERT WITNESSES GENERALLY

§720. Expert witnesses; qualifications.

(a) A person is qualified to testify as an expert if he has special knowledge, skill, experience, training, or education sufficient to qualify him as an expert on the subject to which his testimony relates. Against the objection of a party, such special knowledge, skill, experience, training, or education must be shown before the witness may testify as an expert.

(b) A witness' special knowledge, skill, experience, training, or education may be shown by any otherwise admissible evidence, including his own testimony.

§721. Expert witnesses; cross-examination

(a) Subject to subdivision (b), a witness testifying as an expert may be cross-examined to the same extent as any other witness and, in addition, may be fully cross-examined as to (1) his qualifications, (2) the subject to which his expert testimony relates, and (3) the matter upon which his opinion is based and the reasons for his opinion.

(b) If a witness testifying as an expert testifies in the form of an opinion, he may not be cross-examined in regard to the content or tenor of any scientific, technical, or professional text, treatise, journal, or similar publication unless:

(1) The witness referred to, considered, or relied upon such publication in arriving at or forming his opinion; or

(2) Such publication has been admitted in evidence.

§722. Credibility of expert witness; appointment; compensation.

(a) The fact of the appointment of an expert witness by the court may be revealed to the trier of fact.

(b) The compensation and expenses paid or to be paid to an expert witness by the party calling him is a proper subject of inquiry by any adverse party as relevant to the credibility of the witness and the weight of his testimony.

§723. Number of expert witnesses called.

The court may, at any time before or during the trial of an action, limit the number of expert witnesses to be called by any party.

ARTICLE 2

APPOINTMENT OF EXPERT WITNESS BY COURT

§730. Appointment of expert witness by court; requirement of license.

When it appears to the court, at any time before or during the trial of an action, that expert evidence is or may be required by the court or by any party to the action, the court on its own motion or on motion of any party may appoint one or more experts to investigate, to render a report as may be ordered by the court, and to testify as an expert at the trial of the action relative to the fact or matter as to which the expert evidence is or may be required. The court may fix the compensation for these services, if any, rendered by any person appointed under this section, in addition to any service as a witness, at the amount as seems reasonable to the court.

Nothing in this section shall be construed to permit a person to perform any act for which a license is required unless the person holds the appropriate license to lawfully perform that act.

§731. Compensation of court-appointed expert

(a) In all criminal actions and juvenile court proceedings, the compensation fixed under Section 730 shall be a charge against the county in which such action or proceeding is pending and shall be paid out of the treasury of such county on order of the court.

(b) In any county in which the board of supervisors so provides, the compensation fixed under Section 730 for medical experts in civil actions in such county shall be a charge against and paid out of the treasury of such county on order of the court.

(c) Except as otherwise provided in this section, in all civil actions, the compensation fixed under Section 730 shall, in the first instance, be apportioned and charged to the several parties in such proportion as the court may determine and may thereafter be taxed and allowed in like manner as other costs.

§732. Court-appointed expert as witness; examination.

Any expert appointed by the court under Section 730 may be called and examined by the court or by any party to the action. When such witness is called and examined by the court, the parties have the same right as is expressed in Section 775 to cross-examine the witness and to object to the questions asked and the evidence adduced.

§733. Producing other expert evidence on same fact.

Nothing contained in this article shall be deemed or construed to prevent any party to any action from producing other expert evidence on the same fact or matter mentioned in Section 730; but, where other expert witnesses are called by a party to the action, their fees shall be paid by the party calling them and only ordinary witness fees shall be taxed as costs in the action.

CHAPTER 4

INTERPRETERS AND TRANSLATORS

§750. Interpreters and translators subject to rules of law relating to witnesses.

A person who serves as an interpreter or translator in any action is subject to all the rules of law relating to witnesses.

§751. Oath required of interpreters and translators; filed with court.

(a) An interpreter shall take an oath that he or she will make a true interpretation to the witness in a language that the witness understands and that he or she will make a true interpretation of the witness' answers to questions to counsel, court, or jury, in the English language, with his or her best skill and judgment.

(b) In any proceeding in which a deaf or hard-of-hearing person is testifying under oath, the interpreter certified pursuant to subdivision (f) of Section 754 shall advise the court whenever he or she is unable to comply with his or her oath taken pursuant to subdivision (a).

(c) A translator shall take an oath that he or she will make a true translation in the English language of any writing he or she is to decipher or translate.

(d) An interpreter or translator regularly employed by the court and certified in accordance with Article 4 (commencing with Section 68560) of Chapter 2 of Title 8 of the Government Code, may file an oath as prescribed by this section with the clerk of the court. The filed oath shall serve for all subsequent court proceedings until the appointment is revoked by the court.

§752. Sworn interpreters for witnesses.

(a) When a witness is incapable of understanding the English language or is incapable of expressing himself or herself in the English language so as to be understood directly by counsel, court, and jury, an interpreter whom he or she can understand and who can understand him or her shall be sworn to interpret for him or her.

(b) The record shall identify the interpreter who may be appointed and compensated as provided in Article 2 (commencing with Section 730) of Chapter 3.

§753. Sworn translators of writings.

(a) When the written characters in a writing offered in evidence are incapable of being deciphered or understood directly, a translator who can decipher the characters or understand the language shall be sworn to decipher or translate the writing.

(b) The record shall identify the translator who may be appointed and compensated as provided in Article 2 (commencing with Section 730) of Chapter 3.

§754. Interpreters for deaf in civil or criminal actions.

(a) As used in this section, "deaf or hard-of-hearing person" means a person with a hearing loss so great as to prevent his or her understanding language spoken in a normal tone, but does not include a hard-of-hearing person provided with, and able to fully participate in the proceedings through the use of, an assistive listening system or computer-aided transcription equipment provided pursuant to Section 54.8 of the Civil Code.

(b) In any civil or criminal action, including any action involving a traffic or other infraction or any juvenile court proceeding, or any proceeding to determine the mental competency of a person, or any administrative hearing, where a party or witness is a deaf or hard-of-hearing person and the deaf or hard-of-hearing person is present and participating, the proceedings shall be interpreted in a language that the deaf or hard-of- hearing person understands by a qualified interpreter appointed by the court, tribunal, hearing officer, or other appropriate authority, or as agreed upon by the parties.

(c) For purposes of this section, "appointing authority" means a court, department, board, commission, agency, licensing or legislative body, or other body for proceedings requiring a qualified interpreter.

© 1992 by J., B. & L. Gould
Printed in the U.S.A.   EP

(d) For the purposes of this section, "interpreter" includes, but is not limited to, an oral interpreter, a sign language interpreter, or a deaf-blind interpreter, depending upon the needs of the deaf or hard-of-hearing person.

(e) For purposes of this section, "intermediary interpreter" means a deaf, hard-of-hearing, or hearing person who is able to assist in providing an accurate interpretation between spoken English and sign language or between variants of sign language or between American Sign Language and other foreign languages by acting as an intermediary between the deaf person and the qualified interpreter.

(f) For purposes of this section, "qualified interpreter" means an interpreter who has been certified as competent to interpret court proceedings by a testing organization, agency, or educational institution approved by the Judicial Council as qualified to administer tests to court interpreters for the deaf or hard-of-hearing.

(g) In the event that the appointed interpreter is not familiar with the deaf or hard-of-hearing person's use of particular signs or his or her particular variant of sign language, the court or other appointing authority shall, in consultation with the deaf or hard-of-hearing person or his or her representative, appoint an intermediary interpreter.

(h) Prior to July 1, 1992, the Judicial Council shall conduct a study to establish the guidelines pursuant to which it shall determine which testing organizations, agencies, or educational institutions will be approved to administer tests for certification of court interpreters for the deaf and hard-of-hearing. It is the intent of the Legislature that the study obtain the widest possible input from the public, including, but not limited to, educational institutions, the judiciary, linguists, members of the State Bar, court interpreters, members of professional interpreting organizations, and members of the deaf and hard-of-hearing communities. After obtaining public comment and completing its study, the Judicial Council shall publish these guidelines and shall approve one or more entities to administer testing for court interpreters for the deaf and hard-of-hearing. Initial approval of testing entities by the Judicial Council shall occur prior to July 1, 1992.

Commencing July 1, 1992, court interpreters for the deaf or hard-of-hearing shall meet the qualifications specified in subdivision (f)

(i) Persons appointed to serve as interpreters under this section shall be paid, in addition to actual travel costs, the prevailing rate paid to persons employed by the court to provide other interpreter services unless such service is considered to be a part of the person's regular duties as an employee of the state, county, or other political subdivision of the state. Payment of the interpreter's fee shall be a charge against the county, or other political subdivision of the state, in which such action is pending. Payment of the interpreter's fee in administrative proceedings shall be a charge against the appointing board, agency, commission, or licensing authority.

(j) No statement, written or oral, made by a person who is deaf or hard-of-hearing in reply to a question of a peace officer, or any other person having a prosecutorial function in any criminal or quasi-criminal investigation or proceeding, may be used against that deaf or hard-of-hearing person unless the statement was made knowingly, voluntarily, and in-

telligently and was accurately interpreted, or the court makes a special finding that the statement was made knowingly, voluntarily, and intelligently.

(k) In obtaining services of an interpreter for the purpose of obtaining a statement subject to subdivision (j), priority shall be given to first obtaining a qualified interpreter.

(l) Nothing in subdivision (j) or (k) shall be deemed to supersede the requirement of subdivision (b) for use of a qualified interpreter for deaf or hard-of-hearing persons participating as parties or witnesses in a trial or hearing.

(m) In any action or proceeding in which a deaf or hard-of-hearing person is a participant, the court or administrative authority shall not commence proceedings until the appointed interpreter is in full view of and spatially situated to assure proper communication with the deaf or hard-of- hearing person or persons involved as participants.

(n) Each superior court shall maintain a current roster of qualified interpreters certified pursuant to subdivision (f). *(Amended by Stats 1991 ch 883 §1, eff. 1/1/92.)*

§754.5. Interpreters; privileged communications.

Whenever an otherwise valid privilege exists between a deaf or hard- of-hearing person and another person, that privilege is not waived merely because an interpreter was used to facilitate their communication.

§755. Interpreters; medical examinations; civil actions.

(a) In any proceeding in a civil action for which a record is being made, excluding any action prosecuted in small claims court, in which a party does not proficiently speak or understand the English language and that person is present, an interpreter shall be present to interpret the proceedings in a language that the person understands, and to assist communication between the person and his or her attorney. The interpreter shall be selected from the list of recommended interpreters published pursuant to Article 4 (commencing with Section 68560) of Chapter 2 of Title 8 of the Government Code, unless good cause is found by the judge for the appointment of an interpreter not on the recommended list.

(b) During any medical examination, requested by an insurer or by the defendant, of a person who is a party to a civil action and who does not proficiently speak or understand the English language, conducted for the purpose of determining damages in a civil action, an interpreter shall be present to interpret the examination in a language that the person understands. The interpreter shall be selected from the list of recommended interpreters published pursuant to Article 4 (commencing with Section 68560) of Chapter 2 of Title 8 of the Government Code.

(c) The fees of interpreters utilized under subdivision (a) shall be paid as provided in Section 68092 of the Government Code. The fees of interpreters utilized under subdivision (b) shall be paid by the insurer or defendant requesting the medical examination.

(d) (1) In any civil action in which an interpreter is required under subdivision (a), the court shall not commence proceedings until the appointed interpreter is present and situated near the party and his or her attorney.

(2) The record of, or testimony concerning, any medical examination conducted in violation of subdivision (b) shall be inadmissible in the civil action for which it was conducted or any other civil action.

(e) This section does not prohibit the presence of any other person to assist a party.

(f) This section shall remain in effect only until January 1, 1993, and as of that date is repealed, unless a later enacted statute, which is enacted before January 1, 1993, deletes or extends that date. *(Added by Stats 1991 ch 883 §2, eff. 1/1/92 only until 1/1/93.)*

CHAPTER 5

METHOD AND SCOPE OR EXAMINATION

ARTICLE 1

DEFINITIONS

§760. "Direct examination," defined.
"Direct examination" is the first examination of a witness upon a matter that is not within the scope of a previous examination of the witness.

§761. "Cross-examination," defined.
"Cross-examination" is the examination of a witness by a party other than the direct examiner upon a matter that is within the scope of the direct examination of the witness.

§762. "Redirect examination," defined.
"Redirect examination" is an examination of a witness by the direct examiner subsequent to the cross-examination of the witness.

§763. "Recross-examination," defined.
"Recross-examination" is an examination of a witness by a cross-examiner subsequent to a redirect examination of the witness.

§764. "Leading question," defined.
A "leading question" is a question that suggests to the witness the answer that the examining party desires.

ARTICLE 2

EXAMINATION OF WITNESSES

§765. Control of manner of interrogation of witnesses; witnesses under 14.
(a) The court shall exercise reasonable control over the mode of interrogation of a witness so as to make such interrogation as rapid, as distinct, and as effective for the ascertainment of the truth, as may be, and to protect the witness from undue harassment or embarrassment.

(b) With a witness under the age of 14, the court shall take special care to protect him or her from undue harassment or embarrassment, and to restrict the unnecessary repetition of questions. The court shall also take special care to insure that questions are stated in a form which is appropriate to the age of the witness. The court may in the interests of justice, on objection by a party, forbid the asking of a question

which is in a form that is not reasonably likely to be understood by a person of the age of the witness.

§766. Witnesses; responsive answers
A witness must give responsive answers to questions, and answers that are not responsive shall be stricken on motion of any party.

§767. Leading questions.
(a) Except under special circumstances where the interests of justice otherwise require:
(1) A leading question may not be asked of a witness on direct or redirect examination.
(2) A leading question may be asked of a witness on cross-examination or recross-examination.
(b) The court may in the interests of justice permit a leading question to be asked of a child under 10 years of age in a case involving a prosecution under Section 273a, 273d, or 285 of the Penal Code.

§768. Examination of witnesses; writings.
(a) In examining a witness concerning a writing, it is not necessary to show, read or disclose to him any part of the writing.
(b) If a writing is shown to a witness, all parties to the action must be given an opportunity to inspect it before any question concerning it may be asked of the witness.

§769. Inconsistent statement or conduct of witness.
In examining a witness concerning a statement or other conduct by him that is inconsistent with any part of his testimony at the hearing, it is not necessary to disclose to him any information concerning the statement or other conduct.

§770. Inconsistent statement of witness; extrinsic evidence.
Unless the interests of justice otherwise require, extrinsic evidence of a statement made by a witness that is inconsistent with any part of his testimony at the hearing shall be excluded unless:
(a) The witness was so examined while testifying as to give him an opportunity to explain or to deny the statement; or
(b) The witness has not been excused from giving further testimony in the action.

§771. Writing used by witness to refresh memory.
(a) Subject to subdivision (c), if a witness, either while testifying or prior thereto, uses a writing to refresh his memory with respect to any matter about which he testifies, such writing must be produced at the hearing at the request of an adverse party and, unless the writing is so produced, the testimony of the witness concerning such matter shall be stricken.
(b) If the writing is produced at the hearing, the adverse party may, if he chooses, inspect the writing, cross-examine the witness concerning it, and introduce in evidence such portion of it as may be pertinent to the testimony of the witness.
(c) Production of the writing is excused, and the testimony of the witness shall not be stricken, if the writing:
(1) Is not in the possession or control of the witness or the party who produced his testimony concerning the matter; and

© 1992 by J., B. & L. Gould
Printed in the U.S.A.　　**EP**

(2) Was not reasonably procurable by such party through the use of the court's process or other available means.

§772. Examination of witnesses; order.

(a) The examination of a witness shall proceed in the following phases: direct examination, cross-examination, redirect examination, recross- examination, and continuing thereafter by redirect and recross-examination.

(b) Unless for good cause the court otherwise directs, each phase of the examination of a witness must be concluded before the succeeding phase begins.

(c) Subject to subdivision (d), a party may, in the discretion of the court, interrupt his cross-examination, redirect examination, or recross- examination of a witness, in order to examine the witness upon a matter not within the scope of a previous examination of the witness.

(d) If the witness is the defendant in a criminal action, the witness may not, without his consent, be examined under direct examination by another party.

§773. Cross-examination of witness.

(a) A witness examined by one party may be cross-examined upon any matter within the scope of the direct examination by each other party to the action in such order as the court directs.

(b) The cross-examination of a witness by any party whose interest is not adverse to the party calling him is subject to the same rules that are applicable to the direct examination.

§774. Re-examination of witness.

A witness once examined cannot be reexamined as to the same matter without leave of the court, but he may be reexamined as to any new matter upon which he has been examined by another party to the action. Leave may be granted or withheld in the court's discretion.

§775. Court may call and examine witnesses.

The court, on its own motion or on the motion of any party, may call witnesses and interrogate them the same as if they had been produced by a party to the action, and the parties may object to the questions asked and the evidence adduced the same as if such witness were called and examined by an adverse party. Such witnesses may be cross-examined by all parties to the action in such order as the court directs.

§776. Adverse party or witness; examination.

(a) party* to the record of any civil action, or a person identified with such a party, may be called and examined as if under cross-examination by any adverse party at any time during the presentation of evidence by the party calling the witness.
*So in original. Probably should be "A party".

(b) A witness examined by a party under this section may be cross-examined by all other parties to the action in such order as the court directs; but, subject to subdivision (e), the witness may be examined only as if under redirect examination by:

(1) In the case of a witness who is a party, his own counsel and counsel for a party who is not adverse to the witness.

(2) In the case of a witness who is not a party, counsel for the party with whom the witness is iden-

tified and counsel for a party who is not adverse to the party with whom the witness is identified.

(c) For the purpose of this section, parties represented by the same counsel are deemed to be a single party.

(d) For the purpose of this section, a person is identified with a party if he is:

(1) A person for whose immediate benefit the action is prosecuted or defended by the party.

(2) A director, officer, superintendent, member, agent, employee, or managing agent of the party or of a person specified in paragraph (1), or any public employee of a public entity when such public entity is the party.

(3) A person who was in any of the relationships specified in paragraph (2) at the time of the act or omission giving rise to the cause of action.

(4) A person who was in any of the relationships specified in paragraph (2) at the time he obtained knowledge of the matter concerning which he is sought to be examined under this section.

(e) Paragraph (2) of subdivision (b) does not require counsel for the party with whom the witness is identified and counsel for a party who is not adverse to the party with whom the witness is identified to examine the witness as if under redirect examination if the party who called the witness for examination under this section:

(1) Is also a person identified with the same party with whom the witness is identified.

(2) Is the personal representative, heir, successor, or assignee of a person identified with the same party with whom the witness is identified.

§777. Witnesses; exclusion from courtroom.

(a) Subject to subdivisions (b) and (c), the court may exclude from the courtroom any witness not at the time under examination so that such witness cannot hear the testimony of other witnesses.

(b) A party to the action cannot be excluded under this section.

(c) If a person other than a natural person is a party to the action, an officer or employee designated by its attorney is entitled to be present.

§778. Recall of witness after being excused.

After a witness has been excused from giving further testimony in the action, he cannot be recalled without leave of the court. Leave may be granted or withheld in the court's discretion.

CHAPTER 6

CREDIBILITY OF WITNESSES

ARTICLE 1

CREDIBILITY GENERALLY

§780. Credibility, generally.

Except as otherwise provided by statute, the court or jury may consider in determining the credibility of a witness any matter that has any tendency in reason to prove or disprove the truthfulness of his testimony at the hearing, including but not limited to any of the following:

(a) His demeanor while testifying and the manner in which he testifies.

(b) The character of his testimony.

(c) The extent of his capacity to perceive, to recollect, or to communicate any matter about which he testifies.

(d) The extent of his opportunity to perceive any matter about which he testifies.

(e) His character for honesty or veracity or their opposites.

(f) The existence or nonexistence of a bias, interest, or other motive.

(g) A statement previously made by him that is consistent with his testimony at the hearing.

(h) A statement made by him that is inconsistent with any part of his testimony at the hearing.

(i) The existence or nonexistence of any fact testified to by him.

(j) His attitude toward the action in which he testifies or toward the giving of testimony.

(k) His admission of untruthfulness.

§782. Prior sexual conduct of victim.

(a) In any prosecution under Section 261, 264.1, 286, 288, 288a, 288.5, or 289 of the Penal Code, or for assault with intent to commit, attempt to commit, or conspiracy to commit any crime defined in any of those sections, except where the crime is alleged to have occurred in a local detention facility, as defined in Section 6031.4, or in a state prison, as defined in Section 4504, if evidence of sexual conduct of the complaining witness is offered to attack the credibility of the complaining witness under Section 780, the following procedure shall be followed:

(1) A written motion shall be made by the defendant to the court and prosecutor stating that the defense has an offer of proof of the relevancy of evidence of the sexual conduct of the complaining witness proposed to be presented and its relevancy in attacking the credibility of the complaining witness.

(2) The written motion shall be accompanied by an affidavit in which the offer of proof shall be stated.

(3) If the court finds that the offer of proof is sufficient, the court shall order a hearing out of the presence of the jury, if any, and at such hearing allow the questioning of the complaining witness regarding the offer of proof made by the defendant.

(4) At the conclusion of the hearing, if the court finds that evidence proposed to be offered by the defendant regarding the sexual conduct of the complaining witness is relevant pursuant to Section 780, and is not inadmissible pursuant to Section 352 of this code, the court may make an order stating what evidence may be introduced by the defendant, and the nature of the questions to be permitted. The defendant may then offer evidence pursuant to the order of the court.

(b) As used in this section, "complaining witness" means the alleged victim of the crime charged, the prosecution of which is subject to this section.

§783. Prior sexual conduct of plaintiff in civil action.

In any civil action alleging conduct which constitutes sexual harassment, sexual assault, or sexual battery, if evidence of sexual conduct of the plaintiff is offered to attack credibility of the plaintiff under Section 780, the following procedures shall be followed:

(a) A written motion shall be made by the defendant to the court and the plaintiff's attorney stating that the defense has an offer of proof of the relevancy of evidence of the sexual conduct of the plaintiff proposed to be presented.

(b) The written motion shall be accompanied by an affidavit in which the offer of proof shall be stated.

(c) If the court finds that the offer of proof is sufficient, the court shall order a hearing out of the presence of the jury, if any, and at the hearing allow the questioning of the plaintiff regarding the offer of proof made by the defendant.

(d) At the conclusion of the hearing, if the court finds that evidence proposed to be offered by the defendant regarding the sexual conduct of the plaintiff is relevant pursuant to Section 780, and is not inadmissible pursuant to Section 352, the court may make an order stating what evidence may be introduced by the defendant, and the nature of the questions to be permitted. The defendant may then offer evidence pursuant to the order of the court.

ARTICLE 2

ATTACKING OR SUPPORTING CREDIBILITY

§785. Credibility of witness may be attacked for supported.

The credibility of a witness may be attacked or supported by any party including the party calling him.

§786. Inadmissibility of character evidence, generally.

Evidence of traits of his character other than honesty or veracity, or their opposites, is inadmissible to attack or support the credibility of a witness.

§787. Inadmissibility of specific instances of conduct.

Subject to Section 788, evidence of specific instances of his conduct relevant only as tending to prove a trait of his character is inadmissible to attack or support the credibility of a witness.

§788. Prior felony conviction.

For the purpose of attacking the credibility of a witness, it may be shown by the examination of the witness or by the record of the judgment that he has been convicted of a felony unless:

(a) A pardon based on his innocence has been granted to the witness by the jurisdiction in which he was convicted.

(b) A certificate of rehabilitation and pardon has been granted to the witness under the provisions of Chapter 3.5 (commencing with Section 4852.01) of Title 6 of Part 3 of the Penal Code.

(c) The accusatory pleading against the witness has been dismissed under the provisions of Penal Code Section 1203.4, but this exception does not apply to any criminal trial where the witness is being prosecuted for a subsequent offense.

(d) The conviction was under the laws of another jurisdiction and the witness has been relieved of the penalties and disabilities arising from the conviction pursuant to a procedure substantially equivalent to that referred to in subdivision (b) or (c).

§789. Inadmissibility of religious belief.

Evidence of his religious belief or lack thereof is inadmissible to attack or support the credibility of a witness.

© 1992 by J., B. & L. Gould
Printed in the U.S.A.   EP

§790. Character evidence.

Evidence of the good character of a witness is inadmissible to support his credibility unless evidence of his bad character has been admitted for the purpose of attacking his credibility.

§791. Witness' prior consistent statements.

Evidence of a statement previously made by a witness that is consistent with his testimony at the hearing is inadmissible to support his credibility unless it is offered after:

(a) Evidence of a statement made by him that is inconsistent with any part of his testimony at the hearing has been admitted for the purpose of attacking his credibility, and the statement was made before the alleged inconsistent statement; or

(b) An express or implied charge has been made that his testimony at the hearing is recently fabricated or is influenced by bias or other improper motive, and the statement was made before the bias, motive for fabrication, or other improper motive is alleged to have arisen.

CHAPTER 7

HYPNOSIS OF WITNESSES

§795. Hypnosis; admissibility of testimony.

(a) The testimony of a witness is not inadmissible in a criminal proceeding by reason of the fact that the witness has previously undergone hypnosis for the purpose of recalling events which are the subject of the witness' testimony, if all of the following conditions are met:

(1) The testimony is limited to those matters which the witness recalled and related prior to the hypnosis.

(2) The substance of the prehypnotic memory was preserved in written, audiotape, or video tape form prior to the hypnosis.

(3) The hypnosis was conducted in accordance with all of the following procedures:

(A) A written record was made prior to hypnosis documenting the subject's description of the event, and information which was provided to the hypnotist concerning the subject matter of the hypnosis.

(B) The subject gave informed consent to the hypnosis.

(C) The hypnosis session, including the pre- and post-hypnosis interviews, was video tape recorded for subsequent review.

(D) The hypnosis was performed by a licensed medical doctor, psychologist, or licensed clinical social worker experienced in the use of hypnosis or a licensed marriage, family and child counselor certified in hypnosis by the Board of Behavioral Science Examiners and independent of and not in the presence of law enforcement, the prosecution, or the defense.

(4) Prior to admission of the testimony, the court holds a hearing pursuant to Section 402 of the Evidence Code at which the proponent of the evidence proves by clear and convincing evidence that the hypnosis did not so affect the witness as to render the witness' prehypnosis recollection unreliable or to substantially impair the ability to cross-examine the witness concerning the witness' prehypnosis recollection. At the hearing, each side shall have the right to present expert testimony and to cross-examine witnesses.

(b) Nothing in this section shall be construed to limit the ability of a party to attack the credibility of a witness who has undergone hypnosis, or to limit other legal grounds to admit or exclude the testimony of that witness.

DIVISION 7

OPINION TESTIMONY AND SCIENTIFIC EVIDENCE

CHAPTER 1

EXPERT AND OTHER OPINION TESTIMONY

ARTICLE 1

EXPERT AND OTHER OPINION TESTIMONY GENERALLY

§800. Opinion testimony; lay witness.

If a witness is not testifying as an expert, his testimony in the form of an opinion is limited to such an opinion as is permitted by law, including but not limited to an opinion that is:

(a) Rationally based on the perception of the witness; and

(b) Helpful to a clear understanding of his testimony.

§801. Opinion testimony; expert witness.

If a witness is testifying as an expert, his testimony in the form of an opinion is limited to such an opinion as is:

(a) Related to a subject that is sufficiently beyond common experience that the opinion of an expert would assist the trier of fact; and

(b) Based on matter (including his special knowledge, skill, experience, training, and education) perceived by or personally known to the witness or made known to him at or before the hearing, whether or not admissible, that is of a type that reasonably may be relied upon by an expert in forming an opinion upon the subject to which his testimony relates, unless an expert is precluded by law from using such matter as a basis for his opinion.

§802. Basis of opinion.

A witness testifying in the form of an opinion may state on direct examination the reasons for his opinion and the matter (including, in the case of an expert, his special knowledge, skill, experience, training, and education) upon which it is based, unless he is precluded by law from using such reasons or matter as a basis for his opinion. The court in its discretion may require that a witness before testifying in the form of an opinion be first examined concerning the matter upon which his opinion is based.

§803. Improper basis of opinion; exclusion of testimony.

The court may, and upon objection shall, exclude testimony in the form of an opinion that is based in whole or in significant part on matter that is not a proper basis for such an opinion. In such case, the witness may, if there remains a proper basis for his opinion, then state his opinion after excluding from consideration the matter determined to be improper.

§804. Opinion based on opinion or statement of another.

(a) If a witness testifying as an expert testifies that his opinion is based in whole or in part upon the opinion or statement of another person, such other person may be called and examined by any adverse party as if under cross-examination concerning the opinion or statement.

(b) This section is not applicable if the person upon whose opinion or statement the expert witness has relied is (1) a party, (2) a person identified with a party within the meaning of subdivision (d) of Section 776, or (3) a witness who has testified in the action concerning the subject matter of the opinion or statement upon which the expert witness has relied.

(c) Nothing in this section makes admissible an expert opinion that is inadmissible because it is based in whole or in part on the opinion or statement of another person.

(d) An expert opinion otherwise admissible is not made inadmissible by this section because it is based on the opinion or statement of a person who is unavailable for examination pursuant to this section.

§805. Opinion on ultimate issue of fact.

Testimony in the form of an opinion that is otherwise admissible is not objectionable because it embraces the ultimate issue to be decided by the trier of fact.

ARTICLE 2

EVIDENCE OF MARKET VALUE OF PROPERTY

§810. Scope of article.

(a) Except where another rule is provided by statute, this article provides special rules of evidence applicable to any action in which the value of property is to be ascertained.

(b) This article does not govern ad valorem property tax assessment or equalization proceedings.

§811. "Value of property," defined.

As used in this article, "value of property" means market value of any of the following:

(a) Real property or any interest therein.

(b) Real property or any interest therein and tangible personal property valued as a unit.

§812. Law interpreting "market value" not affected

This article is not intended to alter or change the existing substantive law, whether statutory or decisional, interpreting the meaning of "market value," whether denominated "fair market value" or otherwise.

§813. Opinion testimony; value of property.

(a) The value of property may be shown only by the opinions of any of the following:

(1) Witnesses qualified to express such opinions.

(2) The owner or the spouse of the owner of the property or property interest being valued.

(3) An officer, regular employee, or partner designated by a corporation, partnership, or unincorporated association that is the owner of the property or property interest being valued, if the designee is knowledgeable as to the value of the property or property interest.

(b) Nothing in this section prohibits a view of the property being valued or the admission of any other admissible evidence (including but not limited to evidence as to the nature and condition of the property and, in an eminent domain proceeding, the character of the improvement proposed to be constructed by the plaintiff) for the limited purpose of enabling the court, jury, or referee to understand and weigh the testimony given under subdivision (a); and such evidence, except evidence of the character of the improvement proposed to be constructed by the plaintiff in an eminent domain proceeding, is subject to impeachment and rebuttal.

(c) For the purposes of subdivision (a), "owner of the property or property interest being valued" includes, but is not limited to, the following persons:

(1) A person entitled to possession of the property.

(2) Either party in an action or proceeding to determine the ownership of the property between the parties if the court determines that it would not be in the interest of efficient administration of justice to determine the issue of ownership prior to the admission of the opinion of the party.

§814. Basis for opinion; value of property.

The opinion of a witness as to the value of property is limited to such an opinion as is based on matter perceived by or personally known to the witness or made known to the witness at or before the hearing, whether or not admissible, that is of a type that reasonably may be relied upon by an expert in forming an opinion as to the value of property, including but not limited to the matters listed in Sections 815 to 821, inclusive, unless a witness is precluded by law from using such matter as a basis for an opinion.

§815. Basis for opinion; price of sale of property or property interest.

When relevant to the determination of the value of property, a witness may take into account as a basis for an opinion the price and other terms and circumstances of any sale or contract to sell and purchase which included the property or property interest being valued or any part thereof if the sale or contract was freely made in good faith within a reasonable time before or after the date of valuation, except that in an eminent domain proceeding where the sale or contract to sell and purchase includes only the property or property interest being taken or a part thereof, such sale or contract to sell and purchase may not be taken into account if it occurs after the filing of the lis pendens.

§816. Basis for opinion; price of sale of comparable property.

When relevant to the determination of the value of property, a witness may take into account as a basis for his opinion the price and other terms and circumstances of any sale or contract to sell and purchase comparable property if the sale or contract was freely made in good faith within a reasonable time before or after the date of valuation. In order to be considered comparable, the sale or contract must have been made sufficiently near in time to the date of valuation, and the property sold must be located sufficiently near the property being valued, and must be sufficiently alike in respect to character, size, situation, useability, and improvements, to make it clear that the property sold

© 1992 by J., B. & L. Gould
Printed in the U.S.A.　EP

and the property being valued are comparable in value and that the price realized for the property sold may be fairly considered as shedding light on the value of the property being valued.

§817. Rental value of property.

(a) Subject to subdivision (b), when relevant to the determination of the value of property, a witness may take into account as a basis for an opinion the rent reserved and other terms and circumstances of any lease which included the property or property interest being valued or any part thereof which was in effect within a reasonable time before or after the date of valuation, except that in an eminent domain proceeding where the lease includes only the property or property interest being taken or a part thereof, such lease may not be taken into account in the determination of the value of property if it is entered into after the filing of the lis pendens.

(b) A witness may take into account a lease providing for a rental fixed by a percentage or other measurable portion of gross sales or gross income from a business conducted on the leased property only for the purpose of arriving at an opinion as to the reasonable net rental value attributable to the property or property interest being valued as provided in Section 819 or determining the value of a leasehold interest.

§818. Comparable rental values.

For the purpose of determining the capitalized value of the reasonable net rental value attributable to the property or property interest being valued as provided in Section 819 or determining the value of a leasehold interest, a witness may take into account as a basis for his opinion the rent reserved and other terms and circumstances of any lease of comparable property if the lease was freely made in good faith within a reasonable time before or after the date of valuation.

§819. Capitalized value of net rental value.

When relevant to the determination of the value of property, a witness may take into account as a basis for his opinion the capitalized value of the reasonable net rental value attributable to the land and existing improvements thereon (as distinguished from the capitalized value of the income or profits attributable to the business conducted thereon).

§820. Replacement costs of improvements.

When relevant to the determination of the value of property, a witness may take into account as a basis for his opinion the value of the property or property interest being valued as indicated by the value of the land together with the cost of replacing or reproducing the existing improvements thereon, if the improvements enhance the value of the property or property interest for its highest and best use, less whatever depreciation or obsolescence the improvements have suffered.

§821. Nature of improvements and character of general vicinity of property.

When relevant to the determination of the value of property, a witness may take into account as a basis for his opinion the nature of the improvements on properties in the general vicinity of the property or property interest being valued and the character of the existing uses being made of such properties.

§822. Inadmissible evidence.

(a) In an eminent domain or inverse condemnation proceeding, notwithstanding the provisions of Sections 814 to 821, inclusive, the following matter is inadmissible as evidence and shall not be taken into account as a basis for an opinion as to the value of property:

(1) The price or other terms and circumstances of an acquisition of property or a property interest if the acquisition was for a public use for which the property could have been taken by eminent domain, except that the price or other terms and circumstances of an acquisition of property appropriated to a public use or a property interest so appropriated shall not be excluded under this section if the acquisition was for the same public use for which the property could have been taken by eminent domain.

(2) The price at which an offer or option to purchase or lease the property or property interest being valued or any other property was made, or the price at which such property or interest was optioned, offered, or listed for sale or lease, except that an option, offer, or listing may be introduced by a party as an admission of another party to the proceeding; but nothing in this subdivision permits an admission to be used as direct evidence upon any matter that may be shown only by opinion evidence under Section 813.

(3) The value of any property or property interest as assessed for taxation purposes or the amount of taxes which may be due on the property, but nothing in this subdivision prohibits the consideration of actual or estimated taxes for the purpose of determining the reasonable net rental value attributable to the property or property interest being valued.

(4) An opinion as to the value of any property or property interest other than that being valued.

(5) The influence upon the value of the property or property interest being valued of any noncompensable items of value, damage, or injury.

(6) The capitalized value of the income or rental from any property or property interest other than that being valued.

(b) In an action other than an eminent domain or inverse condemnation proceeding, the matters listed in subdivision (a) are not admissible as evidence, and may not be taken into account as a basis for an opinion as to the value of property, except to the extent permitted under the rules of law otherwise applicable.

(c) The amendments made to this section during the 1987 portion of the 1987-88 Regular Session of the Legislature shall not apply to or affect any petition filed pursuant to this section before January 1, 1988.

§823. Determination of value of property with no relevant market.

Notwithstanding any other provision of this article, the value of property for which there is no relevant market may be determined by any method of valuation that is just and equitable.

ARTICLE 3

OPINION TESTIMONY ON PARTICULAR SUBJECTS

§870. Opinion as to sanity of person.

A witness may state his opinion as to the sanity of a person when:

(a) The witness is an intimate acquaintance of the person whose sanity is in question;

(b) The witness was a subscribing witness to a writing, the validity of which is in dispute, signed by the person whose sanity is in question and the opinion relates to the sanity of such person at the time the writing was signed; or

(c) The witness is qualified under Section 800 or 801 to testify in the form of an opinion.

CHAPTER 2

BLOOD TESTS TO DETERMINE PATERNITY

§890. Short title.

This chapter may be cited as the Uniform Act on Blood Tests to Determine Paternity.

§891. Interpretation of Act.

This act shall be so interpreted and construed as to effectuate its general purpose to make uniform the law of those states which enact it.

§892. Order for blood tests; refusal.

In a civil action in which paternity is a relevant fact, the court may upon its own initiative or upon suggestion made by or on behalf of any person whose blood is involved, and shall upon motion of any party to the action made at a time so as not to delay the proceedings unduly, order the mother, child, and alleged father to submit to blood tests. If any party refuses to submit to such tests, the court may resolve the question of paternity against such party or enforce its order if the rights of others and the interests of justice so require. Any party's refusal to submit to such tests shall be admissible in evidence in any proceeding to determine paternity.

§893. Blood tests made by court-appointed experts.

The tests shall be made by experts qualified as examiners of blood types who shall be appointed by the court. The experts shall be called by the court as witnesses to testify to their findings and shall be subject to cross-examination by the parties. Any party or person at whose suggestion the tests have been ordered may demand that other experts, qualified as examiners of blood types, perform independent tests under order of court, the results of which may be offered in evidence. The number and qualifications of such experts shall be determined by the court.

§894. Compensation of court-appointed experts.

The compensation of each expert witness appointed by the court shall be fixed at a reasonable amount. It shall be paid as the court shall order. The court may order that it be paid by the parties in such proportions and at such times as it shall prescribe, or that the proportion of any party be paid by the county, and that, after payment by the parties or the county or both, all or part or none of it be taxed as costs in the action.

§895. Determination of question of paternity.

If the court finds that the conclusions of all the experts, as disclosed by the evidence based upon the tests, are that the alleged father is not the father of the child, the question of paternity shall be resolved accordingly. If the experts disagree in their findings or conclusions, or if the tests show the probability of the alleged father's paternity, the question, subject to the provisions of Section 352, shall be submitted upon all the evidence, including evidence based upon the tests.

§895.5. "Paternity index"; genetic markers.

(a) There is a rebuttable presumption, affecting the burden of proof, of paternity, if the court finds that the paternity index, as calculated by the experts qualified as examiners of genetic markers, is 100 or greater. This presumption may only be rebutted by a preponderance of the evidence.

(b) As used in this section:

(1) "Genetic markers" mean separate identifiable genes or complexes of genes generally isolated as a result of blood typing, at least seven of which are normally tested in a paternity determination.

(2) "Paternity index" means the commonly accepted indicator used for denoting the existence of paternity. It represents the mathematically computed probability that the putative father is the true father of the children, as opposed to any other man of similar ethnic background. The paternity index, computed using results of various paternity tests following accepted statistical principles for the computation of probability, shall be in accordance with the method of expression accepted at the International Conference on Parentage Testing at Airlie House, Virginia, May 1982, sponsored by the American Association of Blood Banks.

§896. Limitations on application in criminal actions.

This chapter applies to criminal actions subject to the following limitations and provisions:

(a) An order for the tests shall be made only upon application of a party or on the court's initiative.

(b) The compensation of the experts shall be paid by the county under order of court.

(c) The court may direct a verdict of acquittal upon the conclusions of all the experts under the provisions of Section 895; otherwise, the case shall be submitted for determination upon all the evidence.

§897. Right to call other expert witnesses; fees.

Nothing contained in this chapter shall be deemed or construed to prevent any party to any action from producing other expert evidence on the matter covered by this chapter; but, where other expert witnesses are called by a party to the action, their fees shall be paid by the party calling them and only ordinary witness fees shall be taxed as costs in the action.

DIVISION 8

PRIVILEGES

CHAPTER 1

DEFINITIONS

§900. Scope of definitions.

Unless the provision or context otherwise requires, the definitions in this chapter govern the construction of this division. They do not govern the construction of any other division.

© 1992 by J., B. & L. Gould
Printed in the U.S.A.   **EP**

§901. "Proceeding," defined.

"Proceeding" means any action, hearing, investigation, inquest, or inquiry (whether conducted by a court, administrative agency, hearing officer, arbitrator, legislative body, or any other person authorized by law) in which, pursuant to law, testimony can be compelled to be given.

§902. "Civil proceeding," defined.

"Civil proceeding" means any proceeding except a criminal proceeding.

§903. "Criminal proceeding," defined.

"Criminal proceeding" means:

(a) A criminal action; and

(b) A proceeding pursuant to Article 3 (commencing with Section 3060) of Chapter 7 of Division 4 of Title 1 of the Government Code to determine whether a public officer should be removed from office for willful or corrupt misconduct in office.

§905. "Presiding officer," defined.

"Presiding officer" means the person authorized to rule on a claim of privilege in the proceeding in which the claim is made.

CHAPTER 2

APPLICABILITY OF DIVISION

§910. Applicability of division in all proceedings.

Except as otherwise provided by statute, the provisions of this division apply in all proceedings. The provisions of any statute making rules of evidence inapplicable in particular proceedings, or limiting, the applicability of rules of evidence in particular proceedings, do not make this division inapplicable to such proceedings.

CHAPTER 3

GENERAL PROVISIONS RELATING TO PRIVILEGES

§911. General rules as to privileges.

Except as otherwise provided by statute:

(a) No person has a privilege to refuse to be a witness.

(b) No person has a privilege to refuse to disclose any matter or to refuse to produce any writing, object, or other thing.

(c) No person has a privilege that another shall not be a witness or shall not disclose any matter or shall not produce any writing, object, or other thing.

§912. Waiver of privilege.

(a) Except as otherwise provided in this section, the right of any person to claim a privilege provided by Section 954 (lawyer-client privilege), 980 (privilege for confidential marital communications), 994 (physician-patient privilege), 1014 (psychotherapist-patient privilege), 1033 (privilege of penitent), 1034 (privilege of clergyman), or 1035.8 (sexual assault victim-counselor privilege) is waived with respect to a communication protected by such privilege if any holder of the privilege, without coercion, has disclosed a significant part of the communication or has consented to such disclosure made by anyone. Consent to

disclosure is manifested by any statement or other conduct of the holder of the privilege indicating consent to the disclosure, including failure to claim the privilege in any proceeding in which the holder has the legal standing and opportunity to claim the privilege.

(b) Where two or more persons are joint holders of a privilege provided by Section 954 (lawyer-client privilege), 994 (physician-patient privilege), 1014 (psychotherapist-patient privilege), or 1035.8 (sexual assault victim-counselor privilege), a waiver of the right of a particular joint holder of the privilege to claim the privilege does not affect the right of another joint holder to claim the privilege. In the case of the privilege provided by Section 980 (privilege for confidential marital communications), a waiver of the right of one spouse to claim the privilege does not affect the right of the other spouse to claim the privilege.

(c) A disclosure that is itself privileged is not a waiver of any privilege.

(d) A disclosure in confidence of a communication that is protected by a privilege provided by Section 954 (lawyer-client privilege), 994 (physician-patient privilege), 1014 (psychotherapist-patient privilege), or 1035.8 (sexual assault victim-counselor privilege), when such disclosure is reasonably necessary for the accomplishment of the purpose for which the lawyer, physician, psychotherapist, or sexual assault counselor was consulted, is not a waiver of the privilege.

§913. Exercise of privilege; no presumption nor inference from.

(a) If in the instant proceeding or on a prior occasion a privilege is or was exercised not to testify with respect to any matter, or to refuse to disclose or to prevent another from disclosing any matter, neither the presiding officer nor counsel may comment thereon, no presumption shall arise because of the exercise of the privilege, and the trier of fact may not draw any inference therefrom as to the credibility of the witness or as to any matter at issue in the proceeding.

(b) The court, at the request of a party who may be adversely affected because an unfavorable inference may be drawn by the jury because a privilege has been exercised, shall instruct the jury that no presumption arises because of the exercise of the privilege and that the jury may not draw any inference therefrom as to the credibility of the witness or as to any matter at issue in the proceeding.

§914. Determination of claim of privilege; contempt.

(a) The presiding officer shall determine a claim of privilege in any proceeding in the same manner as a court determines such a claim under Article 2 (commencing with Section 400) of Chapter 4 of Division 3.

(b) No person may be held in contempt for failure to disclose information claimed to be privileged unless he has failed to comply with an order of a court that he disclose such information. This subdivision does not apply to any governmental agency that has constitutional contempt power, nor does it apply to hearings and investigations of the Industrial Accident Commission, nor does it impliedly repeal Chapter 4 (commencing with Section 9400) of Part 1 of Division 2 of Title 2 of the Government Code. If no other statutory procedure is applicable, the procedure prescribed by Section 1991 of the Code of Civil Procedure shall be followed in seeking an order of a court that the person disclose the information claimed to be privileged.

§915. Disclosure of privileged information in ruling on claim of privilege in chambers.

(a) Subject to subdivision (b), the presiding officer may not require disclosure of information claimed to be privileged under this division in order to rule on the claim of privilege; provided, however, that in any hearing conducted pursuant to subdivision (c) of Section 1524 of the Penal Code in which a claim of privilege is made and the court determines that there is no other feasible means to rule on the validity of such claim other than to require disclosure, the court shall proceed in accordance with subdivision (b).

(b) When a court is ruling on a claim of privilege under Article 9 (commencing with Section 1040) of Chapter 4 (official information and identity of informer) or under Section 1060 (trade secret) and is unable to do so without requiring disclosure of the information claimed to be privileged, the court may require the person from whom disclosure is sought or the person authorized to claim the privilege, or both, to disclose the information in chambers out of the presence and hearing of all persons except the person authorized to claim the privilege and such other persons as the person authorized to claim the privilege is willing to have present. If the judge determines that the information is privileged, neither he nor any other person may ever disclose, without the consent of a person authorized to permit disclosure, what was disclosed in the course of the proceedings in chambers.

§916. Exclusion of information subject to claim of privilege.

(a) The presiding officer, on his own motion or on the motion of any party, shall exclude information that is subject to a claim of privilege under this division if:

(1) The person from whom the information is sought is not a person authorized to claim the privilege; and

(2) There is no party to the proceeding who is a person authorized to claim the privilege.

(b) The presiding officer may not exclude information under this section if:

(1) He is otherwise instructed by a person authorized to permit disclosure; or

(2) The proponent of the evidence establishes that there is no person authorized to claim the privilege in existence.

§917. Presumption of confidentiality.

Whenever a privilege is claimed on the ground that the matter sought to be disclosed is a communication made in confidence in the course of the lawyer-client, physician-patient, psychotherapist-patient, clergyman-penitent, or husband-wife relationship, the communication is presumed to have been made in confidence and the opponent of the claim of privilege has the burden of proof to establish that the communication was not confidential.

§918. Effect of error in disallowing claim of privilege.

A party may predicate error on a ruling disallowing a claim of privilege only if he is the holder of the privilege, except that a party may predicate error on a ruling disallowing a claim of privilege by his spouse under Section 970 or 971.

§919. Erroneous disclosure of privileged information.

(a) Evidence of a statement or other disclosure of privileged information is inadmissible against a holder of the privilege if:

(1) A person authorized to claim the privilege claimed it but nevertheless disclosure erroneously was required to be made; or

(2) The presiding officer did not exclude the privileged information as required by Section 916.

(b) If a person authorized to claim the privilege claimed it, whether in the same or a prior proceeding, but nevertheless disclosure erroneously was required by the presiding officer to be made, neither the failure to refuse to disclose nor the failure to seek review of the order of the presiding officer requiring disclosure indicates consent to the disclosure or constitutes a waiver and, under these circumstances, the disclosure is one made under coercion.

§920. No implied repeal of any other statute.

Nothing in this division shall be construed to repeal by implication any other statute relating to privileges.

CHAPTER 4

PARTICULAR PRIVILEGES

ARTICLE 1

PRIVILEGE OF DEFENDANT IN CRIMINAL CASE

§930. Privilege not to be called as a witness and not to testify.

To the extent that such privilege exists under the Constitution of the United States or the State of California, a defendant in a criminal case has a privilege not to be called as a witness and not to testify.

ARTICLE 2

PRIVILEGE AGAINST SELF-INCRIMINATION

§940. Privilege against self-incrimination.

To the extent that such privilege exists under the Constitution of the United States or the State of California, a person has a privilege to refuse to disclose any matter that may tend to incriminate him.

ARTICLE 3

LAWYER-CLIENT PRIVILEGE

§950. "Lawyer," defined.

As used in this article, "lawyer" means a person authorized, or reasonably believed by the client to be authorized, to practice law in any state or nation.

§951. "Client," defined.

As used in this article, "client" means a person who, directly or through an authorized representative, consults a lawyer for the purpose of retaining the lawyer or securing legal service or advice from him in his professional capacity, and includes an incompetent (a) who himself so consults the lawyer or (b) whose guardian or conservator so consults the lawyer in behalf of the incompetent.

© 1992 by J., B. & L. Gould
Printed in the U.S.A.   EP

§952. "Confidential communication between client and lawyer," defined.

As used in this article, "confidential communication between client and lawyer" means information transmitted between a client and his lawyer in the course of that relationship and in confidence by a means which, so far as the client is aware, discloses the information to no third persons other than those who are present to further the interest of the client in the consultation or those to whom disclosure is reasonably necessary for the transmission of the information or the accomplishment of the purpose for which the lawyer is consulted, and includes a legal opinion formed and the advice given by the lawyer in the course of that relationship.

§953. "Holder of the privilege," defined.

As used in this article, "holder of the privilege" means:

(a) The client when he has no guardian or conservator.

(b) A guardian or conservator of the client when the client has a guardian or conservator.

(c) The personal representative of the client if the client is dead.

(d) A successor, assign, trustee in dissolution, or any similar representative of a firm, association, organization, partnership, business trust, corporation, or public entity that is no longer in existence.

§954. Lawyer-client privilege.

Subject to Section 912 and except as otherwise provided in this article, the client, whether or not a party, has a privilege to refuse to disclose, and to prevent another from disclosing, a confidential communication between client and lawyer if the privilege is claimed by:

(a) The holder of the privilege;

(b) A person who is authorized to claim the privilege by the holder of the privilege; or

(c) The person who was the lawyer at the time of the confidential communication, but such person may not claim the privilege if there is no holder of the privilege in existence or if he is otherwise instructed by a person authorized to permit disclosure.

The relationship of attorney and client shall exist between a law corporation as defined in Article 10 (commencing with Section 6160) of Chapter 4 of Division 3 of the Business and Professions Code and the persons to whom it renders professional services, as well as between such persons and members of the State Bar employed by such corporation to render services to such persons. The word "persons" as used in this subdivision includes partnerships, corporations, associations and other groups and entities.

§955. Lawyer required to claim privilege.

The lawyer who received or made a communication subject to the privilege under this article shall claim the privilege whenever he is present when the communication is sought to be disclosed and is authorized to claim the privilege under subdivision (c) of Section 954.

§956. Crime or fraud; no privilege.

There is no privilege under this article if the services of the lawyer were sought or obtained to enable or aid anyone to commit or plan to commit a crime or a fraud.

§957. Deceased client; no privilege.

There is no privilege under this article as to a communication relevant to an issue between parties all of whom claim through a deceased client, regardless of whether the claims are by testate or intestate succession or by inter vivos transaction.

§958. Breach of duty; lawyer-client relationship.

There is no privilege under this article as to a communication relevant to an issue of breach, by the lawyer or by the client, of a duty arising out of the lawyer-client relationship.

§959. Lawyer as attesting witness; no privilege.

There is no privilege under this article as to a communication relevant to an issue concerning the intention or competence of a client executing an attested document of which the lawyer is an attesting witness, or concerning the execution or attestation of such a document.

§960. Deceased client's intention concerning deed of conveyance, will or other writing.

There is no privilege under this article as to a communication relevant to an issue concerning the intention of a client, now deceased, with respect to a deed of conveyance, will, or other writing, executed by the client, purporting to affect an interest in property.

§961. Validity of deed of conveyance, will or other writing.

There is no privilege under this article as to a communication relevant to an issue concerning the validity of a deed of conveyance, will, or other writing, executed by a client, now deceased, purporting to affect an interest in property.

§962. Joint clients; no privilege.

Where two or more clients have retained or consulted a lawyer upon a matter of common interest, none of them, nor the successor in interest of any of them, may claim a privilege under this article as to a communication made in the course of that relationship when such communication is offered in a civil proceeding between one of such clients (or his successor in interest) and another of such clients (or his successor in interest).

ARTICLE 4

PRIVILEGE NOT TO TESTIFY AGAINST SPOUSE

§970. Privilege not to testify against spouse.

Except as otherwise provided by statute, a married person has a privilege not to testify against his spouse in any proceeding.

§971. Privilege not to be called as a witness against spouse by adverse party.

Except as otherwise provided by statute, a married person whose spouse is a party to a proceeding has a privilege not to be called as a witness by an adverse party to that proceeding without the prior express consent of the spouse having the privilege under this section unless the party calling the spouse does so in good faith without knowledge of the marital relationship.

§972. When spousal privilege not applicable.

A married person does not have a privilege under this article in:

(a) A proceeding brought by or on behalf of one spouse against the other spouse.

(b) A proceeding to commit or otherwise place his or her spouse or his or her spouse's property, or both, under the control of another because of the spouse's alleged mental or physical condition.

(c) A proceeding brought by or on behalf of a spouse to establish his or her competence.

(d) A proceeding under the Juvenile Court Law, Chapter 2 (commencing with Section 200) of Part 1 of Division 2 of the Welfare and Institutions Code.

(e) A criminal proceeding in which one spouse is charged with:

(1) A crime against the person or property of the other spouse or of a child, parent, relative, or cohabitant of either, whether committed before or during marriage.

(2) A crime against the person or property of a third person committed in the course of committing a crime against the person or property of the other spouse, whether committed before or during marriage.

(3) Bigamy.

(4) A crime defined by Section 270 or 270a of the Penal Code.

(f) A proceeding resulting from a criminal act which occurred prior to legal marriage of the spouses to each other regarding knowledge acquired prior to that marriage if prior to the legal marriage the witness spouse was aware that his or her spouse had been arrested for or had been formally charged with the crime or crimes about which the spouse is called to testify.

(g) A proceeding brought against the spouse by a former spouse so long as the property and debts of the marriage have not been adjudicated, or in order to establish, modify, or enforce a child, family or spousal support obligation arising from the marriage to the former spouse; in a proceeding brought against a spouse by the other parent in order to establish, modify, or enforce a child support obligation for a child of a nonmarital relationship of the spouse; or in a proceeding brought against a spouse by the guardian of a child of that spouse in order to establish, modify, or enforce a child support obligation of the spouse.

The married person does not have a privilege under this subdivision to refuse to provide information relating to the issues of income, expenses, assets, debts, and employment of either spouse, but may assert the privilege as otherwise provided in this article if other information is requested by the former spouse, guardian, or other parent of the child.

Any person demanding the otherwise privileged information made available by this subdivision, who also has an obligation to support the child for whom an order to establish, modify, or enforce child support is sought, waives his or her marital privilege to the same extent as the spouse as provided in this subdivision.

§973. Waiver of privilege.

(a) Unless erroneously compelled to do so, a married person who testifies in a proceeding to which his spouse is a party, or who testifies against his spouse in any proceeding, does not have a privilege under this article in the proceeding in which such testimony is given.

(b) There is no privilege under this article in a civil proceeding brought or defended by a married person for the immediate benefit of his spouse or of himself and his spouse.

ARTICLE 5

PRIVILEGE FOR CONFIDENTIAL MARITAL COMMUNICATIONS

§980. Privilege for confidential marital communications.

Subject to Section 912 and except as otherwise provided in this article, a spouse (or his guardian or conservator when he has a guardian or conservator), whether or not a party, has a privilege during the marital relationship and afterwards to refuse to disclose, and to prevent another from disclosing, a communication if he claims the privilege and the communication was made in confidence between him and the other spouse while they were husband and wife.

§981. Crime or fraud; no privilege.

There is no privilege under this article if the communication was made, in whole or in part, to enable or aid anyone to commit or plan to commit a crime or a fraud.

§982. Commitment proceeding; no privilege.

There is no privilege under this article in a proceeding to commit either spouse or otherwise place him or his property, or both, under the control of another because of his alleged mental or physical condition.

§983. Competency proceeding; no privilege.

There is no privilege under this article in a proceeding brought by or on behalf of either spouse to establish his competence.

§984. Proceeding brought against spouse by other spouse.

There is no privilege under this article in:

(a) A proceeding brought by or on behalf of one spouse against the other spouse.

(b) A proceeding between a surviving spouse and a person who claims through the deceased spouse, regardless of whether such claim is by testate or intestate succession or by inter vivos transaction.

§985. Criminal proceedings; exceptions to privilege.

There is no privilege under this article in a criminal proceeding in which one spouse is charged with:

(a) A crime committed at any time against the person or property of the other spouse or of a child of either.

(b) A crime committed at any time against the person or property of a third person committed in the course of committing a crime against the person or property of the other spouse.

(c) Bigamy.

(d) A crime defined by Section 270 or 270a of the Penal Code.

§986. Juvenile court proceedings.

There is no privilege under this article in a proceeding under the Juvenile Court Law, Chapter 2 (com-

© 1992 by J., B. & L. Gould
Printed in the U.S.A. EP

mencing with Section 200) of Part 1 of Division 2 of the Welfare and Institutions Code.

§987. Criminal defendant; communication offered in evidence; no privilege.

There is no privilege under this article in a criminal proceeding in which the communication is offered in evidence by a defendant who is one of the spouses between whom the communication was made.

ARTICLE 6

PHYSICIAN-PATIENT PRIVILEGE

§990. "Physician," defined.

As used in this article, "physician" means a person authorized, or reasonably believed by the patient to be authorized, to practice medicine in any state or nation.

§991. "Patient," defined.

As used in this article, "patient" means a person who consults a physician or submits to an examination by a physician for the purpose of securing a diagnosis or preventive, palliative, or curative treatment of his physical or mental or emotional condition.

§992. "Confidential communication between patient and physician," defined.

As used in this article, "confidential communication between patient and physician" means information, including information obtained by an examination of the patient, transmitted between a patient and his physician in the course of that relationship and in confidence by a means which, so far as the patient is aware, discloses the information to no third persons other than those who are present to further the interest of the patient in the consultation or those to whom disclosure is reasonably necessary for the transmission of the information or the accomplishment of the purpose for which the physician is consulted, and includes a diagnosis made and the advice given by the physician in the course of that relationship.

§993. "Holder of the privilege," defined.

As used in this article, "holder of the privilege" means:

(a) The patient when he has no guardian or conservator.

(b) A guardian or conservator of the patient when the patient has a guardian or conservator.

(c) The personal representative of the patient if the patient is dead.

§994. Physician-patient privilege.

Subject to Section 912 and except as otherwise provided in this article, the patient, whether or not a party, has a privilege to refuse to disclose, and to prevent another from disclosing, a confidential communication between patient and physician if the privilege is claimed by:

(a) The holder of the privilege;

(b) A person who is authorized to claim the privilege by the holder of the privilege; or

(c) The person who was the physician at the time of the confidential communication, but such person may not claim the privilege if there is no holder of the privilege in existence or if he is otherwise instructed by a person authorized to permit disclosure.

The relationship of a physician and patient shall exist between a medical or podiatry corporation as defined in the Medical Practice Act and the patient to whom it renders professional services, as well as between such patients and licensed physicians and surgeons employed by such corporation to render services to such patients. The word "persons" as used in this subdivision includes partnerships, corporations, associations, and other groups and entities.

§995. Authority to claim privilege.

The physician who received or made a communication subject to the privilege under this article shall claim the privilege whenever he is present when the communication is sought to be disclosed and is authorized to claim the privilege under subdivision (c) of Section 994.

§996. Exceptions to physician-patient privilege; patient tendering issue of his condition.

There is no privilege under this article as to a communication relevant to an issue concerning the condition of the patient if such issue has been tendered by:

(a) The patient;

(b) Any party claiming through or under the patient;

(c) Any party claiming as a beneficiary of the patient through a contract to which the patient is or was a party; or

(d) The plaintiff in an action brought under Section 376 or 377 of the Code of Civil Procedure for damages for the injury or death of the patient.

§997. Crime or tort; no privilege.

There is no privilege under this article if the services of the physician were sought or obtained to enable or aid anyone to commit or plan to commit a crime or a tort or to escape detection or apprehension after the commission of a crime or a tort.

§998. Criminal proceeding; no privilege.

There is no privilege under this article in a criminal proceeding.

§999. Recovery of damages; no privilege.

There is no privilege under this article as to a communication relevant to an issue concerning the condition of the patient in a proceeding to recover damages on account of the conduct of the patient if good cause for disclosure of the communication is shown.

§1000. Claim through deceased patient; no privilege.

There is no privilege under this article as to a communication relevant to an issue between parties all of whom claim through a deceased patient, regardless of whether the claims are by testate or intestate succession or by inter vivos transaction.

§1001. Breach of duty by physician or patient; no privilege.

There is no privilege under this article as to a communication relevant to an issue of breach, by the physician or by the patient, of a duty arising out of the physician-patient relationship.

§1002. Deceased patient's intention concerning deed of conveyance, will or other writing.

There is no privilege under this article as to a communication relevant to an issue concerning the intention of a patient, now deceased, with respect to a deed of conveyance, will, or other writing, executed by the patient, purporting to affect an interest in property.

§1003. Validity of deed of conveyance, will or other writing.

There is no privilege under this article as to a communication relevant to an issue concerning the validity of a deed of conveyance, will, or other writing, executed by a patient, now deceased, purporting to affect an interest in property.

§1004. Commitment proceeding; no privilege.

There is no privilege under this article in a proceeding to commit the patient or otherwise place him or his property, or both, under the control of another because of his alleged mental or physical condition.

§1005. Competency proceeding; no privilege.

There is no privilege under this article in a proceeding brought by or on behalf of the patient to establish his competence.

§1006. Reports required for public inspection.

There is no privilege under this article as to information that the physician or the patient is required to report to a public employee, or as to information required to be recorded in a public office, if such report or record is open to public inspection.

§1007. Administrative proceedings to terminate right, license, or privilege.

There is no privilege under this article in a proceeding brought by a public entity to determine whether a right, authority, license, or privilege (including the right or privilege to be employed by the public entity or to hold a public office) should be revoked, suspended, terminated, limited, or conditioned.

ARTICLE 7

PSYCHOTHERAPIST-PATIENT PRIVILEGE

§1010. "Psychotherapist," defined.

As used in this article, "psychotherapist" means:

(a) A person authorized, or reasonably believed by the patient to be authorized, to practice medicine in any state or nation who devotes, or is reasonably believed by the patient to devote, a substantial portion of his or her time to the practice of psychiatry.

(b) A person licensed as a psychologist under Chapter 6.6 (commencing with Section 2900) of Division 2 of the Business and Professions Code.

(c) A person licensed as a clinical social worker under Article 4 (commencing with Section 9040) of Chapter 17 of Division 3 of the Business and Professions Code, when he or she is engaged in applied psychotherapy of a nonmedical nature.

(d) A person who is serving as a school psychologist and holds a credential authorizing such service issued by the state.

(e) A person licensed as a marriage, family, and child counselor under Chapter 13 (commencing with Section 4980) of Division 2 of the Business and Professions Code.

(f) A person registered as a psychological assistant who is under the supervision of a licensed psychologist or board certified psychiatrist as required by Section 2913 of the Business and Professions Code, or a person registered as a marriage, family, and child counselor intern who is under the supervision of a licensed marriage, family, and child counselor, a licensed clinical social worker, a licensed psychologist, or a licensed physician certified in psychiatry, as specified in Section 4980.44 of the Business and Professions Code.

(g) A person registered as an associate clinical social worker who is under the supervision of a licensed clinical social worker, a licensed psychologist, or a board certified psychiatrist as required by Section 4996.20 of the Business and Professions Code.

(h) A person exempt from the Psychology Licensing Law pursuant to subdivision (d) of Section 2909 of the Business and Professions Code who is under the supervision of a licensed psychologist or board certified psychiatrist.

(i) A psychological intern as defined in Section 2911 of the Business and Professions Code who is under the supervision of a licensed psychologist or board certified psychiatrist.

(j) A trainee, as defined in subdivision (c) of Section 4980.03 of the Business and Professions Code, who is fulfilling his or her supervised practicum required by subdivision (b) of Section 4980.40 of the Business and Professions Code and is supervised by a licensed psychologist, board certified psychiatrist, a licensed clinical social worker, or a licensed marriage, family, and child counselor.

§1010.5. Educational psychologist-patient privilege.

A communication between a patient and an educational psychologist, licensed under Article 5 (commencing with Section 4986) of Chapter 13 of Division 2 of the Business and Professions Code, shall be privileged to the same extent, and subject to the same limitations, as a communication between a patient and a psychotherapist described in subdivisions (c), (d), and (e) of Section 1010.

§1011. "Patient," defined.

As used in this article, "patient" means a person who consults a psychotherapist or submits to an examination by a psychotherapist for the purpose of securing a diagnosis or preventive, palliative, or curative treatment of his mental or emotional condition or who submits to an examination of his mental or emotional condition for the purpose of scientific research on mental or emotional problems.

§1012. "Confidential communication between patient and psychotherapist," defined.

As used in this article, "confidential communication between patient and psychotherapist" means information, including information obtained by an examination of the patient, transmitted between a patient and his psychotherapist in the course of that relationship and in confidence by a means which, so far as the patient is aware, discloses the information to no third persons other than those who are present to further the interest of the patient in the consultation, or those to whom disclosure is reasonably necessary for the transmission of the information or

© 1992 by J., B. & L. Gould
Printed in the U.S.A.   **EP**

the accomplishment of the purpose for which the psychotherapist is consulted, and includes a diagnosis made and the advice given by the psychotherapist in the course of that relationship.

§1013. "Holder of the privilege," defined.

As used in this article, "holder of the privilege" means:

(a) The patient when he has no guardian or conservator.

(b) A guardian or conservator of the patient when the patient has a guardian or conservator.

(c) The personal representative of the patient if the patient is dead.

§1014. Psychotherapist-patient privilege.

Subject to Section 912 and except as otherwise provided in this article, the patient, whether or not a party, has a privilege to refuse to disclose, and to prevent another from disclosing, a confidential communication between patient and psychotherapist if the privilege is claimed by:

(a) The holder of the privilege.

(b) A person who is authorized to claim the privilege by the holder of the privilege.

(c) The person who was the psychotherapist at the time of the confidential communication, but such person may not claim the privilege if there is no holder of the privilege in existence or if he or she is otherwise instructed by a person authorized to permit disclosure.

The relationship of a psychotherapist and patient shall exist between a psychological corporation as defined in Article 9 (commencing with Section 2995) of Chapter 6.6 of Division 2 of the Business and Professions Code, a marriage, family, and child counseling corporation as defined in Article 6 (commencing with Section 4987.5) of Chapter 13 of Division 2 of the Business and Professions Code, or a licensed clinical social workers corporation as defined in Article 5 (commencing with Section 4998) of Chapter 14 of Division 2 of the Business and Professions Code, and the patient to whom it renders professional services, as well as between those patients and psychotherapists employed by those corporations to render services to those patients. The word "persons" as used in this subdivision includes partnerships, corporations, associations and other groups and entities.

§1014.5. Mental health treatment or counseling of minors under Civil Code §25.9; privilege

Notwithstanding any other provision of law, with respect to situations in which a minor has requested and been given mental health treatment or counseling pursuant to Section 25.9 of the Civil Code, the professional person rendering such mental health treatment or counseling has the psychotherapist-patient privilege.

§1015. Authority to claim privilege.

The psychotherapist who received or made a communication subject to the privilege under this article shall claim the privilege whenever he is present when the communication is sought to be disclosed and is authorized to claim the privilege under subdivision (c) of Section 1014.

§1016. Exceptions to privilege; patient tenders issue of condition.

There is no privilege under this article as to a communication relevant to an issue concerning the mental or emotional condition of the patient if such issue has been tendered by:

(a) The patient;

(b) Any party claiming through or under the patient;

(c) Any party claiming as a beneficiary of the patient through a contract to which the patient is or was a party; or

(d) The plaintiff in an action brought under Section 376 or 377 of the Code of Civil Procedure for damages for the injury or death of the patient.

§1017. Psychotherapist appointed by court or Board of Prison Terms.

(a) There is no privilege under this article if the psychotherapist is appointed by order of a court to examine the patient, but this exception does not apply where the psychotherapist is appointed by order of the court upon the request of the lawyer for the defendant in a criminal proceeding in order to provide the lawyer with information needed so that he or she may advise the defendant whether to enter or withdraw a plea based on insanity or to present a defense based on his or her mental or emotional condition.

(b) There is no privilege under this article if the psychotherapist is appointed by the Board of Prison Terms to examine a patient pursuant to the provisions of Article 4 (commencing with Section 2960) of Chapter 7 of Title 1 of Part 3 of the Penal Code.

§1018. Crime or tort; no privilege.

There is no privilege under this article if the services of the psychotherapist were sought or obtained to enable or aid anyone to commit or plan to commit a crime or a tort or to escape detection or apprehension after the commission of a crime or a tort.

§1019. Claim through deceased patient; no privilege.

There is no privilege under this article as to a communication relevant to an issue between parties all of whom claim through a deceased patient, regardless of whether the claims are by testate or intestate succession or by inter vivos transaction.

§1020. Breach of duty by psychotherapist or patient; no privilege.

There is no privilege under this article as to a communication relevant to an issue of breach, by the psychotherapist or by the patient, or a duty arising out of the psychotherapist-patient relationship.

§1021. Deceased patient's intention concerning deed of conveyance, will or other writing.

There is no privilege under this article as to a communication relevant to an issue concerning the intention of a patient, now deceased, with respect to a deed of conveyance, will, or other writing, executed by the patient, purporting to affect an interest in property.

§1022. Validity of deed of conveyance, will or other writing.

There is no privilege under this article as to a communication relevant to an issue concerning the validity of a deed of conveyance, will, or other writing, executed by a patient, now deceased, purporting to affect an interest in property.

§1023. Sanity proceedings of criminal defendant.

There is no privilege under this article in a proceeding under Chapter 6 (commencing with Section 1367) of Title 10 of Part 2 of the Penal Code initiated at the request of the defendant in a criminal action to determine his sanity.

§1024. Patient dangerous to self or others; no privilege.

There is no privilege under this article if the psychotherapist has reasonable cause to believe that the patient is in such mental or emotional condition as to be dangerous to himself or to the person or property of another and that disclosure of the communication is necessary to prevent the threatened danger.

§1025. Competency proceedings; no privilege.

There is no privilege under this article in a proceeding brought by or on behalf of the patient to establish his competence.

§1026. Reports required for public inspection; privilege.

There is no privilege under this article as to information that the psychotherapist or the patient is required to report to a public employee or as to information required to be recorded in a public office, if such report or record is open to public inspection.

§1027. Patient under 16 who is victim of crime; no privilege.

There is no privilege under this article if all of the following circumstances exist:

(a) The patient is a child under the age of 16.

(b) The psychotherapist has reasonable cause to believe that the patient has been the victim of a crime and that disclosure of the communication is in the best interest of the child.

ARTICLE 8

CLERGYMAN-PENITENT PRIVILEGES

§1030. "Clergyman," defined.

As used in this article, "clergyman" means a priest, minister, religious practitioner, or similar functionary of a church or of a religious denomination or religious organization.

§1031. "Penitent," defined.

As used in this article, "penitent" means a person who has made a penitential communication to a clergyman.

§1032. "Penitential communication," defined.

As used in this article, "penitential communication" means a communication made in confidence, in the presence of no third person so far as the penitent is aware, to a clergyman who, in the course of the discipline or practice of his church, denomination, or organization, is authorized or accustomed to hear such communications and, under the discipline or tenets of his church, denomination, or organization, has a duty to keep such communications secret.

§1033. Privilege of penitent.

Subject to Section 912, a penitent, whether or not a party, has a privilege to refuse to disclose, and to prevent another from disclosing, a penitential communication if he claims the privilege.

§1034. Privilege of clergy.

Subject to Section 912, a clergyman, whether or not a party, has a privilege to refuse to disclose a penitential communication if he claims the privilege.

ARTICLE 8.5

SEXUAL ASSAULT VICTIM-COUNSELOR PRIVILEGE

§1035. "Victim", defined.

As used in this article, "victim" means a person who consults a sexual assault victim counselor for the purpose of securing advice or assistance concerning a mental, physical, or emotional condition caused by a sexual assault.

§1035.2. "Sexual assault victim counselor," defined.

As used in this article, "sexual assault victim counselor" means any of the following:

(a) A person who is engaged in any office, hospital, institution, or center commonly known as a rape crisis center, whose primary purpose is the rendering of advice or assistance to victims of sexual assault and who has received a certificate evidencing completion of a training program in the counseling of sexual assault victims issued by a counseling center that meets the criteria for the award of a grant established pursuant to Section 13837 of the Penal Code and who meets one of the following requirements:

(1) Is a psychotherapist as defined in Section 1010; has a master's degree in counseling or a related field; or has one year of counseling experience, at least six months of which is in rape crisis counseling.

(2) Has 40 hours of training as described below and is supervised by an individual who qualifies as a counselor under paragraph (1). The training, supervised by a person qualified under paragraph (1), shall include, but not be limited to, the following areas: law, medicine, societal attitudes, crisis intervention and counseling techniques, role playing, referral services, and sexuality.

(b) A person who is employed by any organization providing the programs specified in Section 13835.2 of the Penal Code, whether financially compensated or not, for the purpose of counseling and assisting sexual assault victims, and who meets one of the following requirements:

(1) Is a psychotherapist as defined in Section 1010; has a master's degree in counseling or a related field; or has one year of counseling experience, at least six months of which is in rape assault counseling.

(2) Has the minimum training for sexual assault counseling required by guidelines established by the employing agency pursuant to subdivision (c) of Section 13835.10 of the Penal Code, and is supervised by an individual who qualifies as a counselor under paragraph (1). The training, supervised by a person qualified under paragraph (1), shall include, but not

© 1992 by J., B. & L. Gould
Printed in the U.S.A.   EP

be limited to, the following areas: law, victimology, counseling techniques, client and system advocacy, and referral services.

§1035.4. "Confidential communication between the sexual assault counselor and the victim," defined.

As used in this article, "confidential communication between the sexual assault counselor and the victim" means information transmitted between the victim and the sexual assault counselor in the course of their relationship and in confidence by a means which, so far as the victim is aware, discloses the information to no third persons other than those who are present to further the interests of the victim in the consultation or those to whom disclosures are reasonably necessary for the transmission of the information or an accomplishment of the purposes for which the sexual assault counselor is consulted. The term includes all information regarding the facts and circumstances involving the alleged sexual assault and also includes all information regarding the victim's prior or subsequent sexual conduct, and opinions regarding the victim's sexual conduct or reputation in sexual matters.

The court may compel disclosure of information received by the sexual assault counselor which constitutes relevant evidence of the facts and circumstances involving an alleged sexual assault about which the victim is complaining and which is the subject of a criminal proceeding if the court determines that the probative value outweighs the effect on the victim, the treatment relationship, and the treatment services if disclosure is compelled. The court may also compel disclosure in proceedings related to child abuse if the court determines the probative value outweighs the effect on the victim, the treatment relationship, and the treatment services if disclosure is compelled.

When a court is ruling on a claim of privilege under this article, the court may require the person from whom disclosure is sought or the person authorized to claim the privilege, or both, to disclose the information in chambers out of the presence and hearing of all persons except the person authorized to claim the privilege and such other persons as the person authorized to claim the privilege is willing to have present. If the judge determines that the information is privileged and must not be disclosed, neither he or she nor any other person may ever disclose, without the consent of a person authorized to permit disclosure, what was disclosed in the course of the proceedings in chambers.

If the court determines certain information shall be disclosed, the court shall so order and inform the defendant. If the court finds there is a reasonable likelihood that particular information is subject to disclosure pursuant to the balancing test provided in this section, the following procedure shall be followed:

(1) The court shall inform the defendant of the nature of the information which may be subject to disclosure.

(2) The court shall order a hearing out of the presence of the jury, if any, and at the hearing allow the questioning of the sexual assault counselor regarding the information which the court has determined may be subject to disclosure.

(3) At the conclusion of the hearing, the court shall rule which items of information, if any, shall be disclosed. The court may make an order stating what evidence may be introduced by the defendant and the nature of questions to be permitted. The defendant may then offer evidence pursuant to the order of the court. Admission of evidence concerning the sexual conduct of the complaining witness is subject to Sections 352, 782, and 1103.

§1035.6. "Holder of the privilege," defined.

As used in this article, "holder of the privilege" means:

(a) The victim when such person has no guardian or conservator.

(b) A guardian or conservator of the victim when the victim has a guardian or conservator.

(c) The personal representative of the victim if the victim is dead.

§1035.8. Privilege of victim of sexual assault.

A victim of a sexual assault, whether or not a party, has a privilege to refuse to disclose, and to prevent another from disclosing, a confidential communication between the victim and a sexual assault victim counselor if the privilege is claimed by:

(a) The holder of the privilege;

(b) A person who is authorized to claim the privilege by the holder of the privilege; or

(c) The person who was the sexual assault victim counselor at the time of the confidential communication, but such person may not claim the privilege if there is no holder of the privilege in existence or if he is otherwise instructed by a person authorized to permit disclosure.

§1036. Privilege of sexual assault victim counselor.

The sexual assault victim counselor who received or made a communication subject to the privilege under this article shall claim the privilege whenever he is present when the communication is sought to be disclosed and is authorized to claim the privilege under subdivision (c) of Section 1035.8.

§1036.2. "Sexual assault," defined.

As used in this article, "sexual assault" includes all of the following:

(a) Rape, as defined in Section 261 of the Penal Code.

(b) Unlawful sexual intercourse, as defined in Section 261.5 of the Penal Code.

(c) Rape in concert with force and violence, as defined in Section 264.1 of the Penal Code.

(d) Rape of a spouse, as defined in Section 262 of the Penal Code.

(e) Sodomy, as defined in Section 286 of the Penal Code, except a violation of subdivision (e) of that section.

(f) A violation of Section 288 of the Penal Code.

(g) Oral copulation, as defined in Section 288a of the Penal Code, except a violation of subdivision (e) of that section.

(h) Penetration of the genital or anal openings of another person with a foreign object, substance, instrument, or device, as specified in Section 289 of the Penal Code.

(i) Annoying or molesting a child under 18, as defined in Section 647a of the Penal Code.

(j) Any attempt to commit any of the above acts.

ARTICLE 8.7

DOMESTIC VIOLENCE VICTIM-COUNSELOR PRIVILEGE

§1037. "Victim," defined.

As used in this article, "victim" means any person who suffers domestic violence, as defined in Section 1037.7.

§1037.1. "Domestic violence counselor," defined.

As used in this article "domestic violence counselor" means any of the following:

(a) A person who is employed by any organization providing the programs specified in Section 18294 of the Welfare and Institutions Code, whether financially compensated or not, for the purpose of rendering advice or assistance to victims of domestic violence, who has received specialized training in the counseling of domestic violence victims, and who meets one of the following requirements:

(1) Has a master's degree in counseling or a related field; or has one year of counseling experience, at least six months of which is in the counseling of domestic violence victims.

(2) Has at least 40 hours of training as specified in this paragraph and is supervised by an individual who qualifies as a counselor under paragraph (1); or is a psychotherapist, as defined in Section 1010. The training, supervised by a person qualified under paragraph (1), shall include, but need not be limited to, the following areas: history of domestic violence, civil and criminal law as it relates to domestic violence, societal attitudes towards domestic violence, peer counseling techniques, housing, public assistance and other financial resources available to meet the financial needs of domestic violence victims, and referral services available to domestic violence victims.

(b) A person who is employed by any organization providing the programs specified in Section 13835.2 of the Penal Code, whether financially compensated or not, for the purpose of counseling and assisting victims of domestic violence, and who meets one of the following requirements:

(1) Is a psychotherapist as defined in Section 1010; has a master's degree in counseling or a related field; or has one year of counseling experience, at least six months of which is in counseling victims of domestic violence.

(2) Has the minimum training for counseling victims of domestic violence required by guidelines established by the employing agency pursuant to subdivision (c) of Section 13835.10 of the Penal Code, and is supervised by an individual who qualifies as a counselor under paragraph (1). The training, supervised by a person qualified under paragraph (1), shall include, but not be limited to, the following areas: law, victimology, counseling techniques, client and system advocacy, and referral services.

§1037.2. "Confidential communication," defined; disclosure of information.

As used in this article, "confidential communication" means information transmitted between the victim and the counselor in the course of their relationship and in confidence by a means which, so far as the victim is aware, discloses the information to no third persons other than those who are present to further the interests of the victim in the consultation or those to whom disclosures are reasonably necessary for the transmission of the information or an accomplishment of the purposes for which the domestic violence counselor is consulted. It includes all information regarding the facts and circumstances involving all incidences of domestic violence, as well as all information about the children of the victim or abuser and the relationship of the victim with the abuser.

The court may compel disclosure of information received by a domestic violence counselor which constitutes relevant evidence of the facts and circumstances involving a crime allegedly perpetrated against the victim or another household member and which is the subject of a criminal proceeding, if the court determines that the probative value of the information outweighs the effect of disclosure of the information on the victim, the counseling relationship, and the counseling services. The court may compel disclosure if the victim is either dead or not the complaining witness in a criminal action against the perpetrator. The court may also compel disclosure in proceedings related to child abuse if the court determines that the probative value of the evidence outweighs the effect of the disclosure on the victim, the counseling relationship, and the counseling services.

When a court rules on a claim of privilege under this article, it may require the person from whom disclosure is sought or the person authorized to claim the privilege, or both, to disclose the information in chambers out of the presence and hearing of all persons except the person authorized to claim the privilege and such other persons as the person authorized to claim the privilege consents to have present. If the judge determines that the information is privileged and shall not be disclosed, neither he nor she nor any other person may disclose, without the consent of a person authorized to permit disclosure, any information disclosed in the course of the proceedings in chambers.

If the court determines that information shall be disclosed, the court shall so order and inform the defendant in the criminal action. If the court finds there is a reasonable likelihood that any information is subject to disclosure pursuant to the balancing test provided in this section, the procedure specified in subdivisions (1), (2), and (3) of Section 1035.4 shall be followed.

§1037.3. Obligation to report child abuse; no privilege.

Nothing in this article shall be construed to limit any obligation to report instances of child abuse as required by Section 11166 of the Penal Code.

§1037.4. "Holder of the privilege," defined.

As used in this article, "holder of the privilege" means:

(a) The victim when he or she has no guardian or conservator.

(b) A guardian or conservator of the victim when the victim has a guardian or conservator.

§1037.5. Claim of privilege by victim.

A victim of domestic violence, whether or not a party to the action, has a privilege to refuse to disclose, and to prevent another from disclosing, a confidential communication between the victim and a domestic

© 1992 by J., B. & L. Gould
Printed in the U.S.A. **EP**

violence counselor if the privilege is claimed by any of the following persons:

(a) The holder of the privilege.

(b) A person who is authorized to claim the privilege by the holder of the privilege.

(c) The person who was the domestic violence counselor at the time of the confidential communication. However, that person may not claim the privilege if there is no holder of the privilege in existence or if he or she is otherwise instructed by a person authorized to permit disclosure.

§1037.6. Claim of privilege by domestic violence counselor.

The domestic violence counselor who received or made a communication subject to the privilege granted by this article shall claim the privilege whenever he or she is present when the communication is sought to be disclosed and he or she is authorized to claim the privilege under subdivision (c) of Section 1037.5.

§1037.7. Definitions of "domestic violence," "abuse," "family or household member"; other victims.

(a) "Domestic violence" is abuse perpetrated against a family or household member, or against a person as provided in subdivisions (d) and (e).

(b) "Abuse" means intentionally or recklessly causing or attempting to cause bodily injury, or placing another person in reasonable apprehension of imminent serious bodily injury to herself, himself, or another.

(c) "Family or household member" means a spouse, former spouse, parent, child, any other adult person related by consanguinity or affinity within the second degree, or any other person who regularly resides in the household, or who within the last six months regularly resided in the household.

(d) A person who is the parent of a minor child where (1) there exists the presumption that the male parent is the father of any minor child of the female parent pursuant to the Uniform Parentage Act, Part 7 (commencing with Section 7000) of Division 4 of the Civil Code, and (2) one parent has perpetrated abuse as defined in subdivision (b) against the other parent.

(e) A person who is in, or has been in, a dating, courtship, or engagement relationship and abuse as defined in subdivision (b) has been perpetrated against that person by the person with whom they have had a dating, courtship, or engagement relationship.

ARTICLE 9

OFFICIAL INFORMATION AND IDENTITY OF INFORMER

§1040. "Official information," defined; disclosure of information against public interest.

(a) As used in this section, "official information" means information acquired in confidence by a public employee in the course of his or her duty and not open, or officially disclosed, to the public prior to the time the claim of privilege is made.

(b) A public entity has a privilege to refuse to disclose official information, and to prevent another from disclosing official information, if the privilege is claimed by a person authorized by the public entity to do so and:

(1) Disclosure is forbidden by an act of the Congress of the United States or a statute of this state; or

(2) Disclosure of the information is against the public interest because there is a necessity for preserving the confidentiality of the information that outweighs the necessity for disclosure in the interest of justice; but no privilege may be claimed under this paragraph if any person authorized to do so has consented that the information be disclosed in the proceeding. In determining whether disclosure of the information is against the public interest, the interest of the public entity as a party in the outcome of the proceeding may not be considered.

(c) Notwithstanding any other provision of law, the Employment Development Department shall disclose to law enforcement agencies, in accordance with the provisions of subdivision (k) of Section 1095 and subdivision (b) of Section 2714 of the Unemployment Insurance Code, information in its possession relating to any person if an arrest warrant has been issued for the person for commission of a felony.

§1041. Identification of informer; privilege.

(a) Except as provided in this section, a public entity has a privilege to refuse to disclose the identity of a person who has furnished information as provided in subdivision (b) purporting to disclose a violation of a law of the United States or of this state or of a public entity in this state, and to prevent another from disclosing such identity, if the privilege is claimed by a person authorized by the public entity to do so and:

(1) Disclosure is forbidden by an act of the Congress of the United States or a statute of this state; or

(2) Disclosure of the identity of the informer is against the public interest because there is a necessity for preserving the confidentiality of his identity that outweighs the necessity for disclosure in the interest of justice; but no privilege may be claimed under this paragraph if any person authorized to do so has consented that the identity of the informer be disclosed in the proceeding. In determining whether disclosure of the identity of the informer is against the public interest, the interest of the public entity as a party in the outcome of the proceeding may not be considered.

(b) This section applies only if the information is furnished in confidence by the informer to:

(1) A law enforcement officer;

(2) A representative of an administrative agency charged with the administration or enforcement of the law alleged to be violated; or

(3) Any person for the purpose of transmittal to a person listed in paragraph (1) or (2).

(c) There is no privilege under this section to prevent the informer from disclosing his identity.

§1042. Issue of disclosure of identity of informer in criminal proceedings.

(a) Except where disclosure is forbidden by an act of the Congress of the United States, if a claim of privilege under this article by the state or a public entity in this state is sustained in a criminal proceeding, the presiding officer shall make such order or finding of fact adverse to the public entity bringing the proceeding as is required by law upon any issue in the proceeding to which the privileged information is material.

(b) Notwithstanding subdivision (a), where a search is made pursuant to a warrant valid on its face, the public entity bringing a criminal proceeding is not required to reveal to the defendant official information or the identity of an informer in order to establish the legality of the search or the admissibility of any evidence obtained as a result of it.

(c) Notwithstanding subdivision (a), in any preliminary hearing, criminal trial, or other criminal proceeding, any otherwise admissible evidence of information communicated to a peace officer by a confidential informant, who is not a material witness to the guilt or innocence of the accused of the offense charged, is admissible on the issue of reasonable cause to make an arrest or search without requiring that the name or identity of the informant be disclosed if the judge or magistrate is satisfied, based upon evidence produced in open court, out of the presence of the jury, that such information was received from a reliable informant and in his discretion does not require such disclosure.

(d) When, in any such criminal proceeding, a party demands disclosure of the identity of the informant on the ground the informant is a material witness on the issue of guilt, the court shall conduct a hearing at which all parties may present evidence on the issue of disclosure. Such hearing shall be conducted outside the presence of the jury, if any. During the hearing, if the privilege provided for in Section 1041 is claimed by a person authorized to do so or if a person who is authorized to claim such privilege refuses to answer any question on the ground that the answer would tend to disclose the identity of the informant, the prosecuting attorney may request that the court hold an in camera hearing. If such a request is made, the court shall hold such a hearing outside the presence of the defendant and his counsel. At the in camera hearing, the prosecution may offer evidence which would tend to disclose or which discloses the identity of the informant to aid the court in its determination whether there is a reasonable possibility that nondisclosure might deprive the defendant of a fair trial. A reporter shall be present at the in camera hearing. Any transcription of the proceedings at the in camera hearing, as well as any physical evidence presented at the hearing, shall be ordered sealed by the court, and only a court may have access to its contents. The court shall not order disclosure, nor strike the testimony of the witness who invokes the privilege, nor dismiss the criminal proceeding, if the party offering the witness refuses to disclose the identity of the informant, unless, based upon the evidence presented at the hearing held in the presence of the defendant and his counsel and the evidence presented at the in camera hearing, the court concludes that there is a reasonable possibility that nondisclosure might deprive the defendant of a fair trial.

§1043. Discovery or disclosure of peace officer's personnel records.

(a) In any case in which discovery or disclosure is sought of peace officer personnel records or records maintained pursuant to Section 832.5 of the Penal Code or information from those records, the party seeking the discovery or disclosure shall file a written motion with the appropriate court or administrative body upon written notice to the governmental agency which has custody and control of the records. The written notice shall be given at the times prescribed by subdivision (b) of Section 1005 of the Code of Civil Procedure. Upon receipt of the notice the governmental agency served shall immediately notify the individual whose records are sought.

(b) The motion shall include all of the following:

(1) Identification of the proceeding in which discovery or disclosure is sought, the party seeking discovery or disclosure, the peace officer whose records are sought, the governmental agency which has custody and control of the records, and the time and place at which the motion for discovery or disclosure shall be heard.

(2) A description of the type of records or information sought.

(3) Affidavits showing good cause for the discovery or disclosure sought, setting forth the materiality thereof to the subject matter involved in the pending litigation and stating upon reasonable belief that the governmental agency identified has the records or information from the records.

(c) No hearing upon a motion for discovery or disclosure shall be held without full compliance with the notice provisions of this section except upon a showing by the moving party of good cause for noncompliance, or upon a waiver of the hearing by the governmental agency identified as having the records.

§1044. Right of access to medical or psychological history not affected.

Nothing in this article shall be construed to affect the right of access to records of medical or psychological history where such access would otherwise be available under Section 996 or 1016.

§1045. Access to peace officer's investigative records; determinatio of relevance.

(a) Nothing in this article shall be construed to affect the right of access to records of complaints, or investigations of complaints, or discipline imposed as a result of such investigations, concerning an event or transaction in which the peace officer participated, or which he perceived, and pertaining to the manner in which he performed his duties, provided that such information is relevant to the subject matter involved in the pending litigation.

(b) In determining relevance the court shall examine the information in chambers in conformity with Section 915, and shall exclude from disclosure:

(1) Information consisting of complaints concerning conduct occurring more than five years before the event or transaction which is the subject of the litigation in aid of which discovery or disclosure is sought.

(2) In any criminal proceeding the conclusions of any officer investigating a complaint filed pursuant to Section 832.5 of the Penal Code.

(3) Facts sought to be disclosed which are so remote as to make disclosure of little or no practical benefit.

(c) In determining relevance where the issue in litigation concerns the policies or pattern of conduct of the employing agency, the court shall consider whether the information sought may be obtained from other records maintained by the employing agency in the regular course of agency business which would not necessitate the disclosure of individual personnel records.

(d) Upon motion seasonably made by the governmental agency which has custody or control of the records to be examined or by the officer whose

© 1992 by J., B. & L. Gould
Printed in the U.S.A.　　EP

records are sought, and upon good cause showing the necessity thereof, the court may make any order which justice requires to protect the officer or agency from unnecessary annoyance, embarrassment or oppression.

(e) The court shall, in any case or proceeding permitting the disclosure or discovery of any peace officer records requested pursuant to Section 1043, order that the records disclosed or discovered may not be used for any purpose other than a court proceeding pursuant to applicable law.

§1046. Excessive force complaint; access to police report.

In any case, otherwise authorized by law, in which the party seeking disclosure is alleging excessive force by a peace officer in connection with the arrest of that party, the motion shall include a copy of the police report setting forth the circumstances under which the party was stopped and arrested.

§1047. Peace officer records not subject to disclosure.

Records of peace officers, including supervisorial peace officers, who either were not present during the arrest or had no contact with the party seeking disclosure from the time of the arrest until the time of booking, shall not be subject to disclosure.

ARTICLE 10

POLITICAL VOTE

§1050. Privilege as to tenor of vote.

If he claims the privilege, a person has a privilege to refuse to disclose the tenor of his vote at a public election where the voting is by secret ballot unless he voted illegally or he previously made an unprivileged disclosure of the tenor of his vote.

ARTICLE 11

TRADE SECRET

§1060. Privilege of trade secret.

If he or his agent or employee claims the privilege, the owner of a trade secret has a privilege to refuse to disclose the secret, and to prevent another from disclosing it, if the allowance of the privilege will not tend to conceal fraud or otherwise work injustice.

§1061. "Trade secret," defined; procedure to assert trade secret privilege; protective order.

(a) For purposes of this section, and Sections 1062 and 1063:

(1) "Trade secret" means "trade secret," as defined in subdivision (d) of Section 3426.1 of the Civil Code, or paragraph (9) of subdivision (a) of Section 499c of the Penal Code.

(2) "Article" means "article," as defined in paragraph (2) of subdivision (a) of Section 499c of the Penal Code.

(b) In addition to Section 1062, the following procedure shall apply whenever the owner of a trade secret wishes to assert his or her trade secret privilege, as provided in Section 1060, during a criminal proceeding:

(1) The owner of the trade secret shall file a motion for a protective order, or the People may file the motion on the owner's behalf and with the owner's permission. The motion shall include an affidavit based upon personal knowledge listing the affiant's qualifications to give an opinion concerning the trade secret at issue, identifying, without revealing, the alleged trade secret and articles which disclose the secret, and presenting evidence that the secret qualifies as a trade secret under either subdivision (d) of Section 3426.1 of the Civil Code or paragraph (9) of subdivision (a) of Section 499c of the Penal Code. The motion and affidavit shall be served on all parties in the proceeding.

(2) Any party in the proceeding may oppose the request for the protective order by submitting affidavits based upon the affiant's personal knowledge. The affidavits shall be filed under seal, but shall be provided to the owner of the trade secret and to all parties in the proceeding. Neither the owner of the trade secret nor any party in the proceeding may disclose the affidavit to persons other than to counsel of record without prior court approval.

(3) The movant shall, by a preponderance of the evidence, show that the issuance of a protective order is proper. The court may rule on the request without holding an evidentiary hearing. However, in its discretion, the court may choose to hold an in camera evidentiary hearing concerning disputed articles with only the owner of the trade secret, the People's representative, the defendant, and defendant's counsel present. If the court holds such a hearing, the parties' right to examine witnesses shall not be used to obtain discovery, but shall be directed solely toward the question of whether the alleged trade secret qualifies for protection.

(4) If the court finds that a trade secret may be disclosed during any criminal proceeding unless a protective order is issued and that the issuance of a protective order would not conceal a fraud or work an injustice, the court shall issue a protective order limiting the use and dissemination of the trade secret, including, but not limited to, articles disclosing that secret. The protective order may, in the court's discretion, include the following provisions:

(A) That the trade secret may be disseminated only to counsel for the parties, including their associate attorneys, paralegals, and investigators, and to law enforcement officials or clerical officials.

(B) That the defendant may view the secret only in the presence of his or her counsel, or if not in the presence of his or her counsel, at counsel's offices.

(C) That any party seeking to show the trade secret, or articles containing the trade secret, to any person not designated by the protective order shall first obtain court approval to do so:

(i) The court may require that the person receiving the trade secret do so only in the presence of counsel for the party requesting approval.

(ii) The court may require the person receiving the trade secret to sign a copy of the protective order and to agree to be bound by its terms. The order may include a provision recognizing the owner of the trade secret to be a third-party beneficiary of that agreement.

(iii) The court may require a party seeking disclosure to an expert to provide that expert's name, employment history, and any other relevant information to the court for examination. The court shall accept that information under seal, and the information shall not be disclosed by any court except upon termination of the action and upon a showing of good cause to believe the secret has been disseminated by a court-approved expert. The court shall evaluate the expert and determine whether the expert poses a discernible risk of disclosure. The court shall withhold approval if the expert's economic interests place the expert in a competitive position with the victim, unless no other experts are available. The court may interview the expert in camera in aid of its ruling. If the court rejects the expert, it shall state its reasons for doing so on the record and a transcript of those reasons shall be prepared and sealed.

(D) That no articles disclosing the trade secret shall be filed or otherwise made a part of the court record available to the public without approval of the court and prior notice to the owner of the secret. The owner of the secret may give either party permission to accept the notice on the owner's behalf.

(E) Other orders as the court deems necessary to protect the integrity of the trade secret.

(c) A ruling granting or denying a motion for a protective order filed pursuant to subdivision (b) shall not be construed as a determination that the alleged trade secret is or is not a trade secret as defined by subdivision (d) of Section 3426.1 of the Civil Code or paragraph (9) of subdivision (a) of Section 499c of the Penal Code. Such a ruling shall not have any effect on any civil litigation.

(d) A protective order entered by a municipal court pursuant to this section shall remain in effect in a superior court unless that order is amended or vacated for good cause shown.

(e) This section shall have prospective effect only and shall not operate to invalidate previously entered protective orders.

§1062. Exclusion of trade secret information from public in criminal proceeding.

(a) Notwithstanding any other provision of law, in a criminal case, the court, upon motion of the owner of a trade secret, or upon motion by the People with the consent of the owner, may exclude the public from any portion of a criminal proceeding where the proponent of closure has demonstrated a substantial probability that the trade secret would otherwise be disclosed to the public during that proceeding and a substantial probability that the disclosure would cause serious harm to the owner of the secret, and where the court finds that there is no overriding public interest in an open proceeding. No evidence, however, shall be excluded during a criminal proceeding pursuant to this section if it would conceal a fraud, work an injustice, or deprive the People or the defendant of a fair trial.

(b) The motion made pursuant to subdivision (a) shall identify, without revealing, the trade secrets which would otherwise be disclosed to the public. A showing made pursuant to subdivision (a) shall be made during an in camera hearing with only the owner of the trade secret, the People's representative, the defendant, and defendant's counsel present. A court reporter shall be present during the hearing. Any transcription of the proceedings at the in camera hearing, as well as any articles presented at that hearing, shall be ordered sealed by the court and only a court may allow access to its contents upon a showing of good cause. The court, in ruling upon the motion made pursuant to subdivision (a), may consider testimony presented or affidavits filed in any proceeding held in that action.

(c) If, after the in camera hearing described in subdivision (b), the court determines that exclusion of trade secret information from the public is appropriate, the court shall close only that portion of the criminal proceeding necessary to prevent disclosure of the trade secret. Before granting the motion, however, the court shall find and state for the record that the moving party has met its burden pursuant to subdivision (b), and that the closure of that portion of the proceeding will not deprive the People or the defendant of a fair trial.

(d) The owner of the trade secret, the People, or the defendant may seek relief from a ruling denying or granting closure by petitioning a higher court for extraordinary relief.

(e) Whenever the court closes a portion of a criminal proceeding pursuant to this section, a transcript of that closed proceeding shall be made available to the public as soon as practicable. The court shall redact any information qualifying as a trade secret before making that transcript available.

(f) The court, subject to Section 867 of the Penal Code, may allow witnesses who are bound by a protective order entered in the criminal proceeding protecting trade secrets, pursuant to Section 1061, to remain within the courtroom during the closed portion of the proceeding.

§1063. Requests to seal protected articles.

The following provisions shall govern requests to seal articles which are protected by a protective order entered pursuant to Evidence Code Section 1060 or 1061:

(a) The People shall request sealing of articles reasonably expected to be filed or admitted into evidence as follows:

(1) No less than 10 court days before trial, and no less than five court days before any other criminal proceeding, the People shall file with the court a list of all articles which the People reasonably expect to file with the court, or admit into evidence, under seal at that proceeding. That list shall be available to the public. The People may be relieved from providing timely notice upon showing that exigent circumstances prevent that notice.

(2) The court shall not allow the listed articles to be filed, admitted into evidence, or in any way made a part of the court record otherwise open to the public before holding a hearing to consider any objections to the People's request to seal the articles. The court at that hearing shall allow those objecting to the sealing to state their objections.

(3) After hearing any objections to sealing, the court shall conduct an in camera hearing with only the owner of the trade secret contained within those articles, the People's representative, defendant, and defendant's counsel present. The court shall review the articles sought to be sealed, evaluate objections to sealing, and determine whether the People have satisfied the constitutional standards governing public access to articles which are part of the judicial record. The court may consider testimony presented or affidavits filed in any proceeding held in that action. The People, defendant, and the owner of the trade secret may file affidavits based on the affiant's personal knowledge to be considered at that hearing. Those affidavits are to be sealed and not released to the public, but shall be made available to the parties. The court may rule on the request to seal without taking

© 1992 by J., B. & L. Gould
Printed in the U.S.A.   **EP**

testimony. If the court takes testimony, examination of witnesses shall not be used to obtain discovery, but shall be directed solely toward whether sealing is appropriate.

(4) If the court finds that the movant has satisfied appropriate constitutional standards with respect to sealing particular articles, the court shall seal those articles if and when they are filed, admitted into evidence, or in any way made a part of the court record otherwise open to the public. The articles shall not be unsealed absent an order of a court upon a showing of good cause. Failure to examine the court file for notice of a request to seal shall not constitute good cause to consider objections to sealing.

(b) The following procedure shall apply to other articles made a part of the court record:

(1) Where any articles protected by a protective order entered pursuant to Section 1060 or 1061 are filed, admitted into evidence, or in any way made a part of the court record in such a way as to be otherwise open to the public, the People, a defendant, or the owner of a trade secret contained within those articles may request the court to seal those articles.

(2) The request to seal shall be made by noticed motion filed with the court. It may also be made orally in court at the time the articles are made a part of the court record. Where the request is made orally, the movant must file within 24 hours a written description of that request, including a list of the articles which are the subject of that request. These motions and lists shall be available to the public.

(3) The court shall promptly conduct hearings as provided in paragraphs (2), (3), and (4) of subdivision (a). The court shall, pending the hearings, seal those articles which are the subject of the request. Where a request to seal is made orally, the court may conduct hearings at the time the articles are made a part of the court record, but shall reconsider its ruling in light of additional objections made by objectors within two court days after the written record of the request to seal is made available to the public.

(4) Any articles sealed pursuant to these hearings shall not be unsealed absent an order of a court upon a showing of good cause. Failure to examine the court file for notice of a request to seal shall not constitute good cause to consider objections to sealing.

CHAPTER 5

IMMUNITY OF NEWSMAN FROM CITATIONS OF CONTEMPT

§1070. Immunity from contempt for refusal to disclose news source.

(a) A publisher, editor, reporter, or other person connected with or employed upon a newspaper, magazine, or other periodical publication, or by a press association or wire service, or any person who has been so connected or employed, cannot be adjudged in contempt by a judicial, legislative, administrative body, or any other body having the power to issue subpoenas, for refusing to disclose, in any proceeding as defined in Section 901, the source of any information procured while so connected or employed for publication in a newspaper, magazine or other periodical publication, or for refusing to disclose any unpublished information obtained or prepared in gathering, receiving or processing of information for communication to the public.

(b) Nor can a radio or television news reporter or other person connected with or employed by a radio or television station, or any person who has been so connected or employed, be so adjudged in contempt for refusing to disclose the source of any information procured while so connected or employed for news or news commentary purposes on radio or television, or for refusing to disclose any unpublished information obtained or prepared in gathering, receiving or processing of information for communication to the public.

(c) As used in this section, "unpublished information" includes information not disseminated to the public by the person from whom disclosure is sought, whether or not related information has been disseminated and includes, but is not limited to, all notes, outtakes, photographs, tapes or other data of whatever sort not itself disseminated to the public through a medium of communication, whether or not published information based upon or related to such material has been disseminated.

DIVISION 9

EVIDENCE AFFECTED OR EXCLUDED BY EXTRINSIC POLICIES

CHAPTER 1

EVIDENCE OF CHARACTER, HABIT, OR CUSTOM

§1100. Proof of character; opinion evidence, reputation evidence, evidence of conduct.

Except as otherwise provided by statute, any otherwise admissible evidence (including evidence in the form of an opinion, evidence of reputation, and evidence of specific instances of such person's conduct) is admissible to prove a person's character or a trait of his character.

§1101. Evidence of character to prove conduct inadmissible.

(a) Except as provided in this section and in Sections 1102 and 1103, evidence of a person's character or a trait of his or her character (whether in the form of an opinion, evidence of reputation, or evidence of specific instances of his or her conduct) is inadmissible when offered to prove his or her conduct on a specified occasion.

(b) Nothing in this section prohibits the admission of evidence that a person committed a crime, civil wrong, or other act when relevant to prove some fact (such as motive, opportunity, intent, preparation, plan, knowledge, identity, absence of mistake or accident, or whether a defendant in a prosecution for an unlawful sexual act or attempted unlawful sexual act did not reasonably and in good faith believe that the victim consented) other than his or her disposition to commit such an act.

(c) Nothing in this section affects the admissibility of evidence offered to support or attack the credibility of a witness.

§1102. Evidence of character to prove conduct; exceptions in criminal cases.

In a criminal action, evidence of the defendant's character or a trait of his character in the form of an opinion or evidence of his reputation is not made inadmissible by Section 1101 if such evidence is:

(a) Offered by the defendant to prove his conduct in conformity with such character or trait of character.

(b) Offered by the prosecution to rebut evidence adduced by the defendant under subdivision (a).

§1103. Evidence of character of crime victim.

(a) In a criminal action, evidence of the character or a trait of character (in the form of an opinion, evidence of reputation, or evidence of specific instances of conduct) of the victim of the crime for which the defendant is being prosecuted is not made inadmissible by Section 1101 if the evidence is:

(1) Offered by the defendant to prove conduct of the victim in conformity with the character or trait of character.

(2) Offered by the prosecution to rebut evidence adduced by the defendant under paragraph (1).

(b) In a criminal action, evidence of the defendant's character for violence or trait of character for violence (in the form of an opinion, evidence of reputation, or evidence of specific instances of conduct) is not made inadmissible by Section 1101 if the evidence is offered by the prosecution to prove conduct of the defendant in conformity with the character or trait of character and is offered after evidence that the victim had a character for violence or a trait of character tending to show violence has been adduced by the defendant under paragraph (1) of subdivision (a).

(c) (1) Notwithstanding any other provision of this code to the contrary, and except as provided in this subdivision, in any prosecution under Section 261 or 264.1 of the Penal Code, or under Section 286, 288a, or 289 of the Penal Code, or for assault with intent to commit, attempt to commit, or conspiracy to commit a crime defined in any such section, except where the crime is alleged to have occurred in a local detention facility, as defined in Section 6031.4, or in a state prison, as defined in Section 4504, opinion evidence, reputation evidence, and evidence of specific instances of the complaining witness' sexual conduct, or any of such evidence, is not admissible by the defendant in order to prove consent by the complaining witness.

(2) Paragraph (1) shall not be applicable to evidence of the complaining witness' sexual conduct with the defendant.

(3) If the prosecutor introduces evidence, including testimony of a witness, or the complaining witness as a witness gives testimony, and that evidence or testimony relates to the complaining witness' sexual conduct, the defendant may cross-examine the witness who gives the testimony and offer relevant evidence limited specifically to the rebuttal of the evidence introduced by the prosecutor or given by the complaining witness.

(4) Nothing in this subdivision shall be construed to make inadmissible any evidence offered to attack the credibility of the complaining witness as provided in Section 782.

(5) As used in this section, "complaining witness" means the alleged victim of the crime charged, the prosecution of which is subject to this subdivision. *(Amended by Stats 1991 ch 16 §1, eff. 3/18/91.)*

§1104. Character evidence for care or skill inadmissible.

Except as provided in Sections 1102 and 1103, evidence of a trait of a person's character with respect to care or skill is inadmissible to prove the quality of his conduct on a specified occasion.

§1105. Admissibility of habit or custom evidence to prove conduct.

Any otherwise admissible evidence of habit or custom is admissible to prove conduct on a specified occasion in conformity with the habit or custom.

§1106. Plaintiff's sexual behavior in civil action alleging sexual harassment, sexual assault or sexual battery inadmissible.

(a) In any civil action alleging conduct which constitutes sexual harassment, sexual assault, or sexual battery, opinion evidence, reputation evidence, and evidence of specific instances of plaintiff's sexual conduct, or any of such evidence, is not admissible by the defendant in order to prove consent by the plaintiff or the absence of injury to the plaintiff, unless the injury alleged by the plaintiff is in the nature of loss of consortium.

(b) Subdivision (a) shall not be applicable to evidence of the plaintiff's sexual conduct with the alleged perpetrator.

(c) If the plaintiff introduces evidence, including testimony of a witness, or the plaintiff as a witness gives testimony, and the evidence or testimony relates to the plaintiff's sexual conduct, the defendant may cross-examine the witness who gives the testimony and offer relevant evidence limited specifically to the rebuttal of the evidence introduced by the plaintiff or given by the plaintiff.

(d) Nothing in this section shall be construed to make inadmissible any evidence offered to attack the credibility of the plaintiff as provided in Section 783.

§1107. Expert testimony regarding battered women's syndrome admissible.

(a) In a criminal action, expert testimony is admissible by either the prosecution or the defense regarding battered women's syndrome, including the physical, emotional, or mental effects upon the beliefs, perceptions, or behavior of victims of domestic violence, except when offered against a criminal defendant to prove the occurrence of the act or acts of abuse which form the basis of the criminal charge.

(b) The foundation shall be sufficient for admission of this expert testimony if the proponent of the evidence establishes its relevancy and the proper qualifications of the expert witness. Expert opinion testimony on battered women's syndrome shall not be considered a new scientific technique whose reliability is unproven.

(c) For purposes of this section, "abuse" and "domestic violence" are defined as provided in Section 542 of the Code of Civil Procedure for purposes of the Domestic Violence Protection Act.

(d) This section is intended as a rule of evidence only and no substantive change affecting the Penal Code is intended. *(Added by Stats 1991 ch 812 §1, eff. 1/1/92.)*

CHAPTER 2

OTHER EVIDENCE AFFECTED OR EXCLUDED BY EXTRINSIC POLICIES

§1150. Evidence to impeach or support a verdict.

(a) Upon an inquiry as to the validity of a verdict, any otherwise admissible evidence may be received as to statements made, or conduct, conditions, or events

© 1992 by J., B. & L. Gould
Printed in the U.S.A. **EP**

occurring, either within or without the jury room, of such a character as is likely to have influenced the verdict improperly. No evidence is admissible to show the effect of such statement, conduct, condition, or event upon a juror either in influencing him to assent to or dissent from the verdict or concerning the mental processes by which it was determined.

(b) Nothing in this code affects the law relating to the competence of a juror to give evidence to impeach or support a verdict.

§1151. Subsequent remedial or precautionary measures not evidence of negligence or culpability.

When, after occurrence of an event, remedial or precautionary measures are taken, which, if taken previously, would have tended to make the event less likely to occur, evidence of such subsequent measures is inadmissible to prove negligence or culpable conduct in connection with the event.

§1152. Offer to compromise not evidence of liability.

(a) Evidence that a person has, in compromise or from humanitarian motives, furnished or offered or promised to furnish money or any other thing, act, or service to another who has sustained or will sustain or claims that he or she has sustained or will sustain loss or damage, as well as any conduct or statements made in negotiation thereof, is inadmissible to prove his or her liability for the loss or damage or any part of it.

(b) In the event that evidence of an offer to compromise is admitted in an action for breach of the covenant of good faith and fair dealing or violation of subdivision (h) of Section 790.03 of the Insurance Code, then at the request of the party against whom the evidence is admitted, or at the request of the party who made the offer to compromise that was admitted, evidence relating to any other offer or counteroffer to compromise the same or substantially the same claimed loss or damage shall also be admissible for the same purpose as the initial evidence regarding settlement. Other than as may be admitted in an action for breach of the covenant of good faith and fair dealing or violation of subdivision (h) of Section 790.03 of the Insurance Code, evidence of settlement offers shall not be admitted in a motion for a new trial, in any proceeding involving an additur or remittitur, or on appeal.

(c) This section does not affect the admissibility of evidence of any of the following:

(1) Partial satisfaction of an asserted claim or demand without questioning its validity when such evidence is offered to prove the validity of the claim.

(2) A debtor's payment or promise to pay all or a part of his or her preexisting debt when such evidence is offered to prove the creation of a new duty on his or her part or a revival of his or her preexisting duty.

§1152.5. Disclosure of mediation proceedings.

(a) Subject to the conditions and exceptions provided in this section, when persons agree to conduct and participate in a mediation for the purpose of compromising, settling, or resolving a dispute:

(1) Evidence of anything said or of any admission made in the course of the mediation is not admissible in evidence, and disclosure of any such evidence shall not be compelled, in any civil action in which, pursuant to law, testimony can be compelled to be given.

(2) Unless the document otherwise provides, no document prepared for the purpose of, or in the course of, or pursuant to, the mediation, or copy thereof, is admissible in evidence, and disclosure of any such document shall not be compelled, in any civil action in which, pursuant to law, testimony can be compelled to be given.

(b) Subdivision (a) does not limit the admissibility of evidence if all persons who conducted or otherwise participated in the mediation consent to its disclosure.

(c) This section does not apply unless, before the mediation begins, the persons who agree to conduct and participate in the mediation execute an agreement in writing that sets out the text of subdivisions (a) and (b) and states that the persons agree that this section shall apply to the mediation.

(d) This section does not apply where the admissibility of the evidence is governed by Section 4351.5 or 4607 of the Civil Code or by Section 1747 of the Code of Civil Procedure.

(e) Nothing in this section makes admissible evidence that is inadmissible under Section 1152 or any other statutory provision, including, but not limited to, the sections listed in subdivision (d). Nothing in this section limits the confidentiality provided pursuant to Section 65 of the Labor Code.

(f) Paragraph (2) of subdivision (a) does not limit either of the following:

(1) The admissibility of the agreement referred to in subdivision (c).

(2) The effect of an agreement not to take a default in a pending civil action.

§1153. Evidence of plea of guilty or withdrawn plea of guilty by criminal defendant.

Evidence of a plea of guilty, later withdrawn, or of an offer to plead guilty to the crime charged or to any other crime, made by the defendant in a criminal action is inadmissible in any action or in any proceeding of any nature, including proceedings before agencies, commissions, boards, and tribunals.

§1153.5. Evidence of offer for civil resolution of criminal matter.

Evidence of an offer for civil resolution of a criminal matter pursuant to the provisions of Section 33 of the Code of Civil Procedure, or admissions made in the course of or negotiations for the offer shall not be admissible in any action.

§1154. Evidence of offer to settle claim.

Evidence that a person has accepted or offered or promised to accept a sum of money or any other thing, act, or service in satisfaction of a claim, as well as any conduct or statements made in negotiation thereof, is inadmissible to prove the invalidity of the claim or any part of it.

§1155. Evidence of liability insurance inadmissible.

Evidence that a person was, at the time a harm was suffered by another, insured wholly or partially against loss arising from liability for that harm is inadmissible to prove negligence or other wrongdoing.

§1156. Disclosure of records of medical-dental study of in-hospital staff committee.

(a) In-hospital medical or medical-dental staff committees of a licensed hospital may engage in research and medical or dental study for the purpose of reducing morbidity or mortality, and may make findings and recommendations relating to such purpose. Except as provided in subdivision (b), the written records of interviews, reports, statements, or memoranda of such in-hospital medical or medical-dental staff committees relating to such medical or dental studies are subject to Sections 2016 to 2036, inclusive, of the Code of Civil Procedure (relating to discovery proceedings) but, subject to subdivisions (c) and (d), shall not be admitted as evidence in any action or before any administrative body, agency, or person.

(b) The disclosure, with or without the consent of the patient, of information concerning him to such in-hospital medical or medical-dental staff committee does not make unprivileged any information that would otherwise be privileged under Section 994 or 1014; but, notwithstanding Sections 994 and 1014, such information is subject to discovery under subdivision (a) except that the identity of any patient may not be discovered under subdivision (a) unless the patient consents to such disclosure.

(c) This section does not affect the admissibility in evidence of the original medical or dental records of any patient.

(d) This section does not exclude evidence which is relevant evidence in a criminal action.

§1156.1. Disclosure of medical or psychiatric records of quality assurance committee.

(a) A committee established in compliance with Sections 4070 and 5624 of the Welfare and Institutions Code may engage in research and medical or psychiatric study for the purpose of reducing morbidity or mortality, and may make findings and recommendations to the county and state relating to such purpose. Except as provided in subdivision (b), the written records of interviews, reports, statements, or memoranda of such committees relating to such medical or psychiatric studies are subject to Sections 2016 to 2036, inclusive, of the Code of Civil Procedure but, subject to subdivisions (c) and (d), shall not be admitted as evidence in any action or before any administrative body, agency, or person.

(b) The disclosure, with or without the consent of the patient, of information concerning him or her to such committee does not make unprivileged any information that would otherwise be privileged under Section 994 or 1014. However, notwithstanding Sections 994 and 1014, such information is subject to discovery under subdivision (a) except that the identity of any patient may not be discovered under subdivision (a) unless the patient consents to such disclosure.

(c) This section does not affect the admissibility in evidence of the original medical or psychiatric records of any patient.

(d) This section does not exclude evidence which is relevant evidence in a criminal action.

§1157. Proceedings and records of health professional committees exempt from discovery and testimony.

(a) Neither the proceedings nor the records of organized committees of medical, medical-dental, podiatric, registered dietitian, psychological, or veterinary staffs in hospitals, or of a peer review body, as defined in Section 805 of the Business and Professions Code, having the responsibility of evaluation and improvement of the quality of care rendered in the hospi-

tal, or for that peer review body, or medical or dental review or dental hygienist review or chiropractic review or podiatric review or registered dietitian review or veterinary review committees of local medical, dental, dental hygienist, podiatric, dietetic, veterinary, or chiropractic societies, or psychological review committees of state or local psychological associations or societies having the responsibility of evaluation and improvement of the quality of care, shall be subject to discovery.

(b) Except as hereinafter provided, no person in attendance at a meeting of any of those committees shall be required to testify as to what transpired at that meeting.

(c) The prohibition relating to discovery or testimony does not apply to the statements made by any person in attendance at a meeting of any of those committees who is a party to an action or proceeding the subject matter of which was reviewed at that meeting, or to any person requesting hospital staff privileges, or in any action against an insurance carrier alleging bad faith by the carrier in refusing to accept a settlement offer within the policy limits.

(d) The prohibitions in this section do not apply to medical, dental, dental hygienist, podiatric, dietetic, psychological, veterinary, or chiropractic society committees that exceed 10 percent of the membership of the society, nor to any of those committees if any person serves upon the committee when his or her own conduct or practice is being reviewed.

(e) The amendments made to this section by Chapter 1081 of the Statutes of 1983, or at the 1985 portion of the 1985-86 Regular Session of the Legislature, or at the 1990 portion of the 1989-90 Regular Session of the Legislature, do not exclude the discovery or use of relevant evidence in a criminal action.

§1157.5. Proceedings or records of nonprofit medical care foundation or professional standards review organization exempt from discovery and testimony.

Except in actions involving a claim of a provider of health care services for payment for such services, the prohibition relating to discovery or testimony provided by Section 1157 shall be applicable to the proceedings or records of an organized committee of any nonprofit medical care foundation or professional standards review organization which is organized in a manner which makes available professional competence to review health care services with respect to medical necessity, quality of care, or economic justification of charges or level of care.

§1157.6. Proceedings and records of mental health quality assurance committees exempt from discovery and testimony.

Neither the proceedings nor the records of a committee established in compliance with Sections 4070 and 5624 of the Welfare and Institutions Code having the responsibility of evaluation and improvement of the quality of mental health care rendered in county operated and contracted mental health facilities shall be subject to discovery. Except as provided in this section, no person in attendance at a meeting of any such committee shall be required to testify as to what transpired thereat. The prohibition relating to discovery or testimony shall not apply to the statements made by any person in attendance at such a meeting who is a party to an action or proceeding the subject

© 1992 by J., B. & L. Gould
Printed in the U.S.A.   EP

matter of which was reviewed at such meeting, or to any person requesting facility staff privileges.

§1157.7. Proceedings and records of specialty health care services committees exempt from discovery and testimony.

The prohibition relating to discovery or testimony provided in Section 1157 shall be applicable to proceedings and records of any committee established by a local governmental agency to monitor, evaluate, and report on the necessity, quality, and level of specialty health services, including, but not limited to, trauma care services, provided by a general acute care hospital which has been designated or recognized by that governmental agency as qualified to render specialty health care services. The provisions of Chapter 3.5 (commencing with Section 6250) of Division 7 of Title 1 of the Government Code and Chapter 9 (commencing with Section 54950) of Division 2 of Title 5 of the Government Code shall not be applicable to the committee records and proceedings.

§1158. Adult patient's written authorization to inspect and copy medical records.

Whenever, prior to the filing of any action or the appearance of a defendant in an action, an attorney at law or his or her representative presents a written authorization therefor signed by an adult patient, by the guardian or conservator of his or her person or estate, or, in the case of a minor, by a parent or guardian of the minor, or by the personal representative or an heir of a deceased patient, or a copy thereof, a physician and surgeon, dentist, registered nurse, dispensing optician, registered physical therapist, podiatrist, licensed psychologist, osteopath, chiropractor, clinical laboratory bioanalyst, clinical laboratory technologist, or pharmacist or pharmacy, duly licensed as such under the laws of the state, or a licensed hospital, shall make all of the patient's records under his, hers or its custody or control available for inspection and copying by the attorney at law or his, or her, representative, promptly upon the presentation of the written authorization.

No copying may be performed by any medical provider enumerated above, or by an agent thereof, when the requesting attorney has employed a professional photocopier or anyone identified in Section 22451 of the Business and Professions Code as his or her representative to obtain or review the records on his or her behalf. The presentation of the authorization by the agent on behalf of the attorney shall be sufficient proof that the agent is the attorney's representative.

Failure to make such records available, during business hours, within five days after the presentation of the written authorization, may subject the person or entity having custody or control of the records to liability for all reasonable expenses, including attorney's fees, incurred in any proceeding to enforce this section.

All reasonable costs incurred by any person or entity enumerated above in making patient records available pursuant to this section may be charged against the person whose written authorization required the availability of such records.

"Reasonable cost," as used in this section, shall include, but not be limited to, the following specific costs: ten cents ($0.10) per page for standard reproduction of documents of a size 8½ by 14 inches or less;

twenty cents ($0.20) per page for copying of documents from microfilm; actual costs for the reproduction of oversize documents or the reproduction of documents requiring special processing which are made in response to an authorization; reasonable clerical costs incurred in locating and making the records available to be billed at the maximum rate of sixteen dollars ($16) per hour per person, computed on the basis of four dollars ($4) per quarter hour or fraction thereof; actual postage charges; and actual costs, if any, charged to the witness by a third person for the retrieval and return of records held by that third person.

DIVISION 10

HEARSAY EVIDENCE

CHAPTER 1

GENERAL PROVISIONS

§1200. Hearsay rule.

(a) "Hearsay evidence" is evidence of a statement that was made other than by a witness while testifying at the hearing and that is offered to prove the truth of the matter stated.

(b) Except as provided by law, hearsay evidence is inadmissible.

(c) This section shall be known and may be cited as the hearsay rule.

§1201. Multiple hearsay.

A statement within the scope of an exception to the hearsay rule is not inadmissible on the ground that the evidence of such statement is hearsay evidence if such hearsay evidence consists of one or more statements each of which meets the requirements of an exception to the hearsay rule.

§1202. Credibility of hearsay declarant; inconsistent statements.

Evidence of a statement or other conduct by a declarant that is inconsistent with a statement by such declarant received in evidence as hearsay evidence is not inadmissible for the purpose of attacking the credibility of the declarant though he is not given and has not had an opportunity to explain or to deny such inconsistent statement or other conduct. Any other evidence offered to attack or support the credibility of the declarant is admissible if it would have been admissible had the declarant been a witness at the hearing. For the purposes of this section, the deponent of a deposition taken in the action in which it is offered shall be deemed to be a hearsay declarant.

§1203. Hearsay declarant may be cross-examined.

(a) The declarant of a statement that is admitted as hearsay evidence may be called and examined by any adverse party as if under cross-examination concerning the statement.

(b) This section is not applicable if the declarant is (1) a party, (2) a person identified with a party within the meaning of subdivision (d) of Section 776, or (3) a witness who has testified in the action concerning the subject matter of the statement.

(c) This section is not applicable if the statement is one described in Article 1 (commencing with Section

1220), Article 3 (commencing with Section 1235), or Article 10 (commencing with Section 1300) of Chapter 2 of this division.

(d) A statement that is otherwise admissible as hearsay evidence is not made inadmissible by this section because the declarant who made the statement is unavailable for examination pursuant to this section.

§1203.1. Hearsay statements offered at preliminary hearing not subject to cross-examination.

Section 1203 is not applicable if the hearsay statement is offered at a preliminary examination, as provided in Section 872 of the Penal Code.

§1204. Hearsay statement against defendant in criminal action inadmissible.

A statement that is otherwise admissible as hearsay evidence is inadmissible against the defendant in a criminal action if the statement was made, either by the defendant or by another, under such circumstances that it is inadmissible against the defendant under the Constitution of the United States or the State of California.

§1205. No repeal by implication of other hearsay evidence rules.

Nothing in this division shall be construed to repeal by implication any other statute relating to hearsay evidence.

CHAPTER 2

EXCEPTIONS TO THE HEARSAY RULE

ARTICLE 1

CONFESSIONS AND ADMISSIONS

§1220. Admission of party.

Evidence of a statement is not made inadmissible by the hearsay rule when offered against the declarant in an action to which he is a party in either his individual or representative capacity, regardless of whether the statement was made in his individual or representative capacity.

§1221. Adoptive admission by words or other conduct.

Evidence of a statement offered against a party is not made inadmissible by the hearsay rule if the statement is one of which the party, with knowledge of the content thereof, has by words or other conduct manifested his adoption or his belief in its truth.

§1222. Authorized admission.

Evidence of a statement offered against a party is not made inadmissible by the hearsay rule if:

(a) The statement was made by a person authorized by the party to make a statement or statements for him concerning the subject matter of the statement; and

(b) The evidence is offered either after admission of evidence sufficient to sustain finding of such authority or, in the court's discretion as to the order of proof, subject to the admission of such evidence.

§1223. Admission of co-conspirator.

Evidence of a statement offered against a party is not made inadmissible by the hearsay rule if:

(a) The statement was made by the declarant while participating in a conspiracy to commit a crime or civil wrong and in furtherance of the objective of that conspiracy;

(b) The statement was made prior to or during the time that the party was participating in that conspiracy; and

(c) The evidence is offered either after admission of evidence sufficient to sustain a finding of the facts specified in subdivisions (a) and (b) or, in the court's discretion as to the order of proof, subject to the admission of such evidence.

§1224. Statement of declarant whose liability or breach of duty is in issue in civil action.

When the liability, obligation, or duty of a party to a civil action is based in whole or in part upon liability, obligation, or duty of the declarant, or when the claim or right asserted by a party to a civil action is barred or diminished by a breach of duty by the declarant, evidence of a statement made by the declarant is as admissible against the party as it would be if offered against the declarant in an action involving that liability, obligation, duty, or breach of duty.

§1225. Statement of declarant whose right, title or interest is in issue in a civil action.

When a right, title, or interest in any property or claim asserted by a party to a civil action requires a determination that a right, title, or interest exists or existed in the declarant, evidence of a statement made by the declarant during the time the party now claims the declarant was the holder of the right, title, or interest is as admissible against the party as it would be if offered against the declarant in an action involving that right, title, or interest.

§1226. Statement of minor child in action brought for injury to child.

Evidence of a statement by a minor child is not made inadmissible by the hearsay rule if offered against the plaintiff in an action brought under Section 376 of the Code of Civil Procedure for injury to such minor child.

§1227. Statement of deceased in action for wrongful death.

Evidence of a statement by the deceased is not made inadmissible by the hearsay rule if offered against the plaintiff in an action for wrongful death brought under Section 377 of the Code of Civil Procedure.

§1228. Statement of minor child as to sexual abuse for purpose of determining admissibility of defendant's confession.

Notwithstanding any other provision of law, for the purpose of establishing the elements of the crime in order to admit as evidence the confession of a person accused of violating Section 261, 264.1, 285, 286, 288, 288a, 289, or 647a of the Penal Code, a court, in its discretion, may determine that a statement of the complaining witness is not made inadmissible by the hearsay rule if it finds all of the following:

(a) The statement was made by a minor child under the age of 12, and the contents of the statement were included in a written report of a law enforcement official or an employee of a county welfare department.

(b) The statement describes the minor child as a victim of sexual abuse.

© 1992 by J., B. & L. Gould
Printed in the U.S.A.   **EP**

(c) The statement was made prior to the defendant's confession. The court shall view with caution the testimony of a person recounting hearsay where there is evidence of personal bias or prejudice.

(d) There are no circumstances, such as significant inconsistencies between the confession and the statement concerning material facts establishing any element of the crime or the identification of the defendant, that would render the statement unreliable.

(e) The minor child is found to be unavailable pursuant to paragraph (2) or (3) of subdivision (a) of Section 240 or refuses to testify.

(f) The confession was memorialized in a trustworthy fashion by a law enforcement official.

If the prosecution intends to offer a statement of the complaining witness pursuant to this section, the prosecution shall serve a written notice upon the defendant at least 10 days prior to the hearing or trial at which the prosecution intends to offer the statement.

If the statement is offered during trial, the court's determination shall be made out of the presence of the jury. If the statement is found to be admissible pursuant to this section, it shall be admitted out of the presence of the jury and solely for the purpose of determining the admissibility of the confession of the defendant.

ARTICLE 2

DECLARATIONS AGAINST INTEREST

§1230. Declarations against interest.

Evidence of a statement by a declarant having sufficient knowledge of the subject is not made inadmissible by the hearsay rule if the declarant is unavailable as a witness and the statement, when made, was so far contrary to the declarant's pecuniary or proprietary interest, or so far subjected him to the risk of civil or criminal liability, or so far tended to render invalid a claim by him against another, or created such a risk of making him an object of hatred, ridicule, or social disgrace in the community, that a reasonable man in his position would not have made the statement unless he believed it to be true.

ARTICLE 3

PRIOR STATEMENTS OF WITNESSES

§1235. Prior inconsistent statements of witness.

Evidence of a statement made by a witness is not made inadmissible by the hearsay rule if the statement is inconsistent with his testimony at the hearing and is offered in compliance with Section 770.

§1236. Prior consistent statements of witness.

Evidence of a statement previously made by a witness is not made inadmissible by the hearsay rule if the statement is consistent with his testimony at the hearing and is offered in compliance with Section 791.

§1237. Written record of statement.

(a) Evidence of a statement previously made by a witness is not made inadmissible by the hearsay rule if the statement would have been admissible if made by him while testifying, the statement concerns a matter as to which the witness has insufficient present recollection to enable him to testify fully and accurately, and the statement is contained in a writing which:

(1) Was made at a time when the fact recorded in the writing actually occurred or was fresh in the witness' memory;

(2) Was made (i) by the witness himself or under his direction or (ii) by some other person for the purpose of recording the witness' statement at the time it was made;

(3) Is offered after the witness testifies that the statement he made was a true statement of such fact; and

(4) Is offered after the writing is authenticated as an accurate record of the statement.

(b) The writing may be read into evidence, but the writing itself may not be received in evidence unless offered by an adverse party.

§1238. Previous identification.

Evidence of a statement previously made by a witness is not made inadmissible by the hearsay rule if the statement would have been admissible if made by him while testifying and:

(a) The statement is an identification of a party or another as a person who participated in a crime or other occurrence;

(b) The statement was made at a time when the crime or other occurrence was fresh in the witness' memory; and

(c) The evidence of the statement is offered after the witness testifies that he made the identification and that it was a true reflection of his opinion at that time.

ARTICLE 4

SPONTANEOUS, CONTEMPORANEOUS, AND DYING DECLARATIONS

§1240. Spontaneous statement.

Evidence of a statement is not made inadmissible by the hearsay rule if the statement:

(a) Purports to narrate, describe, or explain an act, condition, or event perceived by the declarant; and

(b) Was made spontaneously while the declarant was under the stress of excitement caused by such perception.

§1241. Accompanying statement.

Evidence of a statement is not made inadmissible by the hearsay rule if the statement:

(a) Is offered to explain, qualify, or make understandable conduct of the declarant; and

(b) Was made while the declarant was engaged in such conduct.

§1242. Statement made by dying person.

Evidence of a statement made by a dying person respecting the cause and circumstances of his death is not made inadmissible by the hearsay rule if the statement was made upon his personal knowledge and under a sense of immediately impending death.

ARTICLE 5

STATEMENTS OF MENTAL OR PHYSICAL STATE

§1250. Admissibility of statement of declarant's then existing mental or physical state; inadmissibility of statement or memory or belief.

(a) Subject to Section 1252, evidence of a statement of the declarant's then existing state of mind, emotion, or physical sensation (including a statement of intent, plan, motive, design, mental feeling, pain, or bodily health) is not made inadmissible by the hearsay rule when:

(1) The evidence is offered to prove the declarant's state of mind, emotion, or physical sensation at that time or at any other time when it is itself an issue in the action; or

(2) The evidence is offered to prove or explain acts or conduct of the declarant.

(b) This section does not make admissible evidence of a statement of memory or belief to prove the fact remembered or believed.

§1251. Admissibility of statement of declarant's previously existing mental or physical state when at issue.

Subject to Section 1252, evidence of a statement of the declarant's state of mind, emotion, or physical sensation (including a statement of intent, plan, motive, design, mental feeling, pain, or bodily health) at a time prior to the statement is not made inadmissible by the hearsay rule if:

(a) The declarant is unavailable as a witness; and

(b) The evidence is offered to prove such prior state of mind, emotion, or physical sensation when it is itself an issue in the action and the evidence is not offered to prove any fact other than such state of mind, emotion, or physical sensation.

§1252. Inadmissibility of untrustworthy statements of mental or physical state.

Evidence of a statement is inadmissible under this article if the statement was made under circumstances such as to indicate its lack of trustworthiness.

ARTICLE 6

STATEMENTS RELATING TO WILLS AND TO CLAIMS AGAINST ESTATES

§1260. Statement concerning declarant's will; limitation.

(a) Evidence of a statement made by a declarant who is unavailable as a witness that he has or has not made a will, or has or has not revoked his will, or that identifies his will, is not made inadmissible by the hearsay rule.

(b) Evidence of a statement is inadmissible under this section if the statement was made under circumstances such as to indicate its lack of trustworthiness.

§ 1261. Statement of decedent offered in action against estate; limitation.

(a) Evidence of a statement is not made inadmissible by the hearsay rule when offered in an action upon a claim or demand against the estate of the declarant if the statement was made upon the personal knowledge of the declarant at a time when the

matter had been recently perceived by him and while his recollection was clear.

(b) Evidence of a statement is inadmissible under this section if the statement was made under circumstances such as to indicate its lack of trustworthiness.

ARTICLE 7

BUSINESS RECORDS

§1270. "A business," defined.

As used in this article, "a business" includes every kind of business, governmental activity, profession, occupation, calling, or operation of institutions, whether carried on for profit or not.

§1271. Business records as evidence.

Evidence of a writing made as a record of an act, condition, or event is not made inadmissible by the hearsay rule when offered to prove the act, condition, or event if:

(a) The writing was made in the regular course of a business;

(b) The writing was made at or near the time of the act, condition, or event;

(c) The custodian or other qualified witness testifies to its identity and the mode of its preparation; and

(d) The sources of information and method and time of preparation were such as to indicate its trustworthiness.

§1272. Absence of a record of an act, condition or event.

Evidence of the absence from the records of a business of a record of an asserted act, condition, or event is not made inadmissible by the hearsay rule when offered to prove the nonoccurrence of the act or event, or the nonexistence of the condition, if:

(a) It was the regular course of that business to make records of all such acts, conditions, or events at or near the time of the act, condition, or event and to preserve them; and

(b) The sources of information and method and time of preparation of the records of that business were such that the absence of a record of an act, condition, or event is a trustworthy indication that the act or event did not occur or the condition did not exist.

ARTICLE 8

OFFICIAL RECORDS AND OTHER OFFICIAL WRITINGS

§1280. Official record by public employee.

Evidence of a writing made as a record of an act, condition, or event is not made inadmissible by the hearsay rule when offered to prove the act, condition, or event if:

(a) The writing was made by and within the scope of duty of a public employee;

(b) The writing was made at or near the time of the act, condition, or event; and

(c) The sources of information and method and time of preparation were such as to indicate its trustworthiness.

§1281. Official records of birth, death and marriage.

Evidence of a writing made as a record of a birth, fetal death, death, or marriage is not made inadmis-

© 1992 by J., B. & L. Gould
Printed in the U.S.A.   **EP**

sible by the hearsay rule if the maker was required by law to file the writing in a designated public office and the writing was made and filed as required by law.

§1282. Written finding of presumed death pursuant to Federal Missing Persons Act.

A written finding of presumed death made by an employee of the United States authorized to make such finding pursuant to the Federal Missing Persons Act (56 Stats 143, 1092 and PL 408, Ch 371, 2d Sess 78th Cong; 50 USC App 1001-1016), as enacted or as heretofore or hereafter amended, shall be received in any court, office, or other place in this state as evidence of the death of the person therein found to be dead and of the date, circumstances, and place of his disappearance.

§1283. Official written record by federal employee that person is missing, captured, detained, or dead or alive.

An official written report or record that a person is missing, missing in action, interned in a foreign country, captured by a hostile force, beleaguered by a hostile force, besieged by a hostile force, or detained in a foreign country against his will, or is dead or is alive, made by an employee of the United States authorized by any law of the United States to make such report or record shall be received in any court, office, or other place in this state as evidence that such person is missing, missing in action, interned in a foreign country, captured by a hostile force, beleaguered by a hostile force, besieged by a hostile force, or detained in a foreign country against his will, or is dead or is alive.

§1284. Absence of public record.

Evidence of a writing made by the public employee who is the official custodian of the records in a public office, reciting diligent search and failure to find a record, is not made inadmissible by the hearsay rule when offered to prove the absence of a record in that office.

ARTICLE 9

FORMER TESTIMONY

§1290. "Former testimony," defined.

As used in this article, "former testimony" means testimony given under oath in:

(a) Another action or in a former hearing or trial of the same action;

(b) A proceeding to determine a controversy conducted by or under the supervision of an agency that has the power to determine such a controversy and is an agency of the United States or a public entity in the United States;

(c) A deposition taken in compliance with law in another action; or

(d) An arbitration proceeding if the evidence of such former testimony is a verbatim transcript thereof.

§1291. Admissibility of former testimony; party to former proceeding.

(a) Evidence of former testimony is not made inadmissible by the hearsay rule if the declarant is unavailable as a witness and:

(1) The former testimony is offered against a person who offered it in evidence in his own behalf on the former occasion or against the successor in interest of such person; or

(2) The party against whom the former testimony is offered was a party to the action or proceeding in which the testimony was given and had the right and opportunity to cross-examine the declarant with an interest and motive similar to that which he has at the hearing.

(b) The admissibility of former testimony under this section is subject to the same limitations and objections as though the declarant were testifying at the hearing, except that former testimony offered under this section is not subject to:

(1) Objections to the form of the question which were not made at the time the former testimony was given.

(2) Objections based on competency or privilege which did not exist at the time the former testimony was given.

§1292. Admissibility of foreign testimony; non-party to former proceeding.

(a) Evidence of former testimony is not made inadmissible by the hearsay rule if:

(1) The declarant is unavailable as a witness;

(2) The former testimony is offered in a civil action; and

(3) The issue is such that the party to the action or proceeding in which the former testimony was given had the right and opportunity to cross-examine the declarant with an interest and motive similar to that which the party against whom the testimony is offered has at the hearing.

(b) The admissibility of former testimony under this section is subject to the same limitations and objections as though the declarant were testifying at the hearing, except that former testimony offered under this section is not subject to objections based on competency or privilege which did not exist at the time the former testimony was given.

§1293. Former testimony of minor against parent or guardian at a preliminary examination; proceeding to declare minor a dependent child of the court.

(a) Evidence of former testimony made at a preliminary examination by a minor child who was the complaining witness is not made inadmissible by the hearsay rule if:

(1) The former testimony is offered in a proceeding to declare the minor a dependent child of the court pursuant to Section 300 of the Welfare and Institutions Code.

(2) The issues are such that a defendant in the preliminary examination in which the former testimony was given had the right and opportunity to cross-examine the minor child with an interest and motive similar to that which the parent or guardian against whom the testimony is offered has at the proceeding to declare the minor a dependent child of the court.

(b) The admissibility of former testimony under this section is subject to the same limitations and objections as though the minor child were testifying at the proceeding to declare him or her a dependent child of the court.

(c) The attorney for the parent or guardian against whom the former testimony is offered or, if none, the parent or guardian may make a motion to challenge the admissibility of the former testimony upon a showing that new substantially different issues are present in the proceeding to declare the minor a dependent child than were present in the preliminary examination.

(d) As used in this section, "complaining witness" means the alleged victim of the crime for which a preliminary examination was held.

(e) This section shall apply only to testimony made at a preliminary examination on and after January 1, 1990.

ARTICLE 10

JUDGMENTS

§1300. Conviction of felony; civil actions.

Evidence of a final judgment adjudging a person guilty of a crime punishable as a felony is not made inadmissible by the hearsay rule when offered in a civil action to prove any fact essential to the judgment whether or not the judgment was based on a plea of nolo contendere.

§1301. Judgment against person in action to recover on the indemnity or warranty.

Evidence of a final judgment is not made inadmissible by the hearsay rule when offered by the judgment debtor to prove any fact which was essential to the judgment in an action in which he seeks to:

(a) Recover partial or total indemnity or exoneration for money paid or liability incurred because of the judgment;

(b) Enforce a warranty to protect the judgment debtor against the liability determined by the judgment; or

(c) Recover damages for breach of warranty substantially the same as the warranty determined by the judgment to have been breached.

§1302. Judgment determining liability, obligation or duty of third person.

When the liability, obligation, or duty of a third person is in issue in a civil action, evidence of a final judgment against that person is not made inadmissible by the hearsay rule when offered to prove such liability, obligation, or duty.

ARTICLE 11

FAMILY HISTORY

§1310. Statement of declarant's own family history.

(a) Subject to subdivision (b), evidence of a statement by a declarant who is unavailable as a witness concerning his own birth, marriage, divorce, a parent and child relationship, relationship by blood or marriage, race, ancestry, or other similar fact of his family history is not made inadmissible by the hearsay rule, even though the declarant had no means of acquiring personal knowledge of the matter declared.

(b) Evidence of a statement is inadmissible under this section if the statement was made under circumstances such as to indicate its lack of trustworthiness.

§1311. Statement about family history of another related by blood or marriage or intimately associated with.

(a) Subject to subdivision (b), evidence of a statement concerning the birth, marriage, divorce, death, parent and child relationship, race, ancestry, relationship by blood or marriage, or other similar fact of the family history of a person other than the declarant is not made inadmissible by the hearsay rule if the declarant is unavailable as a witness and:

(1) The declarant was related to the other by blood or marriage; or

(2) The declarant was otherwise so intimately associated with the other's family as to be likely to have had accurate information concerning the matter declared and made the statement (i) upon information received from the other or from a person related by blood or marriage to the other or (ii) upon repute in the other's family.

(b) Evidence of a statement is inadmissible under this section if the statement was made under circumstances such as to indicate its lack of trustworthiness.

§1312. Entries in family Bibles and other family records.

Evidence of entries in family Bibles or other family books or charts, engravings on rings, family portraits, engravings on urns, crypts, or tombstones, and the like, is not made inadmissible by the hearsay rule when offered to prove the birth, marriage, divorce, death, parent and child relationship, race, ancestry, relationship by blood or marriage, or other similar fact of the family history of a member of the family by blood or marriage.

§1313. Reputation among members of family concerning family history.

Evidence of reputation among members of a family is not made inadmissible by the hearsay rule if the reputation concerns the birth, marriage, divorce, death, parent and child relationship, race, ancestry, relationship by blood or marriage, or other similar fact of the family history of a member of the family by blood or marriage.

§1314. Reputation in community concerning family history.

Evidence of reputation in a community concerning the date or fact of birth, marriage, divorce, or death of a person resident in the community at the time of the reputation is not made inadmissible by the hearsay rule.

§1315. Church records concerning family history.

Evidence of a statement concerning a person's birth, marriage, divorce, death, parent and child relationship, race, ancestry, relationship by blood or marriage, or other similar fact of family history which is contained in a writing made as a record of a church, religious denomination, or religious society is not made inadmissible by the hearsay rule if:

(a) The statement is contained in a writing made as a record of an act, condition, or event that would be admissible as evidence of such act, condition, or event under Section 1271; and

(b) The statement is of a kind customarily recorded in connection with the act, condition, or event recorded in the writing.

© 1992 by J., B. & L. Gould
Printed in the U.S.A.   **EP**

§1316. Birth, baptismal, marriage, death certificates.

Evidence of a statement concerning a person's birth, marriage, divorce, death, parent and child relationship, race, ancestry, relationship by blood or marriage, or other similar fact of family history is not made inadmissible by the hearsay rule if the statement is contained in a certificate that the maker thereof performed a marriage or other ceremony or administered a sacrament and:

(a) The maker was a clergyman, civil officer, or other person authorized to perform the acts reported in the certificate by law or by the rules, regulations, or requirements of a church, religious denomination, or religious society; and

(b) The certificate was issued by the maker at the time and place of the ceremony or sacrament or within a reasonable time thereafter.

ARTICLE 12

REPUTATION AND STATEMENTS CONCERNING COMMUNITY HISTORY, PROPERTY INTERESTS, AND CHARACTER

§1320. General community history; reputation.

Evidence of reputation in a community is not made inadmissible by the hearsay rule if the reputation concerns an event of general history of the community or of the state or nation of which the community is a part and the event was of importance to the community.

§1321. Public interest in property; reputation.

Evidence of reputation in a community is not made inadmissible by the hearsay rule if the reputation concerns the interest of the public in property in the community and the reputation arose before controversy.

§1322. Boundary or custom affecting land in community; reputation.

Evidence of reputation in a community is not made inadmissible by the hearsay rule if the reputation concerns boundaries of, or customs affecting, land in the community and the reputation arose before controversy.

§1323. Statement concerning boundary; untrustworthiness.

Evidence of a statement concerning the boundary of land is not made inadmissible by the hearsay rule if the declarant is unavailable as a witness and had sufficient knowledge of the subject, but evidence of a statement is not admissible under this section if the statement was made under circumstances such as to indicate its lack of trustworthiness.

§1324. Character evidence; community opinion.

Evidence of a person's general reputation with reference to his character or a trait of his character at a relevant time in the community in which he then resided or in a group with which he then habitually associated is not made inadmissible by the hearsay rule.

ARTICLE 13

DISPOSITIVE INSTRUMENTS AND ANCIENT WRITINGS

§1330. Writings affecting real or personal property.

Evidence of a statement contained in a deed of conveyance or a will or other writing purporting to affect an interest in real or personal property is not made inadmissible by the hearsay rule if:

(a) The matter stated was relevant to the purpose of the writing.

(b) The matter stated would be relevant to an issue as to an interest in the property; and

(c) The dealings with the property since the statement was made have not been inconsistent with the truth of the statement.

§1331. Ancient writings.

Evidence of a statement is not made inadmissible by the hearsay rule if the statement is contained in a writing more than 30 years old and the statement has been since generally acted upon as true by persons having an interest in the matter.

ARTICLE 14

COMMERCIAL, SCIENTIFIC, AND SIMILAR PUBLICATIONS

§1340. Published compilations used in course of business.

Evidence of a statement, other than an opinion, contained in a tabulation, list, directory, register, or other published compilation is not made inadmissible by the hearsay rule if the compilation is generally used and relied upon as accurate in the course of a business as defined in Section 1270.

§1341. Publications proving facts of general notoriety and interest.

Historical works, books of science or art, and published maps or charts, made by persons indifferent between the parties, are not made inadmissible by the hearsay rule when offered to prove facts of general notoriety and interest.

ARTICLE 15

DECLARANT UNAVAILABLE AS WITNESS

§1350. Serious felony proceeding; death or kidnapping of declarant.

(a) In a criminal proceeding charging a serious felony, evidence of a statement made by a declarant is not made inadmissible by the hearsay rule if the declarant is unavailable as a witness, and all of the following are true:

(1) There is clear and convincing evidence that the declarant's unavailability was knowingly caused by, aided by, or solicited by the party against whom the statement is offered for the purpose of preventing the arrest or prosecution of the party and is the result of the death by homicide or the kidnapping of the declarant.

(2) There is no evidence that the unavailability of the declarant was caused by, aided by, solicited by, or procured on behalf of, the party who is offering the statement.

(3) The statement has been memorialized in a tape recording made by a law enforcement official, or in a written statement prepared by a law enforcement official and signed by the declarant and notorized in the presence of the law enforcement official, prior to the death or kidnapping of the declarant.

(4) The statement was made under circumstances which indicate its trustworthiness and was not the result of promise, inducement, threat, or coercion.

(5) The statement is relevant to the issues to be tried.

(6) The statement is corroborated by other evidence which tends to connect the party against whom the statement is offered with the commission of the serious felony with which the party is charged. The corroboration is not sufficient if it merely shows the commission of the offense or the circumstances thereof.

(b) If the prosecution intends to offer a statement pursuant to this section, the prosecution shall serve a written notice upon the defendant at least 10 days prior to the hearing or trial at which the prosecution intends to offer the statement, unless the prosecution shows good cause for the failure to provide that notice. In the event that good cause is shown, the defendant shall be entitled to a reasonable continuance of the hearing or trial.

(c) If the statement is offered during trial, the court's determination shall be made out of the presence of the jury. If the defendant elects to testify at the hearing on a motion brought pursuant to this section, the court shall exclude from the examination every person except the clerk, the court reporter, the bailiff, the prosecutor, the investigating officer, the defendant and his or her counsel, an investigator for the defendant, and the officer having custody of the defendant. Notwithstanding any other provision of law, the defendant's testimony at the hearing shall not be admissible in any other proceeding except the hearing brought on the motion pursuant to this section. If a transcript is made of the defendant's testimony, it shall be sealed and transmitted to the clerk of the court in which the action is pending.

(d) As used in this section, "serious felony" means any of the felonies listed in subdivision (c) of Section 1192.7 of the Penal Code or any violation of Section 11351, 11352, 11378, or 11379 of the Health and Safety Code.

(e) If a statement to be admitted pursuant to this section includes hearsay statements made by anyone other than the declarant who is unavailable pursuant to subdivision (a), those hearsay statements are inadmissible unless they meet the requirements of an exception to the hearsay rule.

DIVISION 11

WRITINGS

CHAPTER 1

AUTHENTICATION AND PROOF OF WRITINGS

ARTICLE 1

REQUIREMENT OF AUTHENTICATION

§1400. Authentication of a writing, defined.
Authentication of a writing means (a) the introduction of evidence sufficient to sustain a finding that it is the writing that the proponent of the evidence claims it is or (b) the establishment of such facts by any other means provided by law.

§1401. Authentication of a writing required.
(a) Authentication of a writing is required before it may be received in evidence.

(b) Authentication of a writing is required before secondary evidence of its content may be received in evidence.

§1402. Accounting for alteration in writing.
The party producing a writing as genuine which has been altered, or appears to have been altered, after its execution, in a part material to the question in dispute, must account for the alteration or appearance thereof. He may show that the alteration was made by another, without his concurrence, or was made with the consent of the parties affected by it, or otherwise properly or innocently made, or that the alteration did not change the meaning or language of the instrument. If he does that, he may give the writing in evidence, but not otherwise.

ARTICLE 2

MEANS OF AUTHENTICATING AND PROVING WRITINGS

§1410. Article not limited.
Nothing in this article shall be construed to limit the means by which a writing may be authenticated or proved.

§1410.5. Graffiti; evidence of vandalism.
(a) For purposes of this chapter, a writing shall include any graffiti consisting of written words, insignia, symbols, or any other markings which convey a particular meaning.

(b) Any writing described in subdivision (a), or any photograph thereof, may be admitted into evidence in an action for vandalism, for the purpose of proving that the writing was made by the defendant.

(c) The admissibility of any fact offered to prove that the writing was made by the defendant shall, upon motion of the defendant, be ruled upon outside the presence of the jury, and is subject to the requirements of Sections 1416, 1417, and 1418.

§1411. Subscribing witness' testimony not required.
Except as provided by statute, the testimony of a subscribing witness is not required to authenticate a writing.

§1412. Use of other evidence when subscribing witness' testimony denies execution of writing.
If the testimony of a subscribing witness is required by statute to authenticate a writing and the subscribing witness denies or does not recollect the execution of the writing, the writing may be authenticated by other evidence.

§1413. Authentication by witness to execution of a writing.
A writing may be authenticated by anyone who saw the writing made or executed, including a subscribing witness.

© 1992 by J., B. & L. Gould
Printed in the U.S.A.   EP

§1414. Authentication by admission of party.

A writing may be authenticated by evidence that:

(a) The party against whom it is offered has at any time admitted its authenticity; or

(b) The writing has been acted upon as authentic by the party against whom it is offered.

§1415. Authentication by genuineness of handwriting.

A writing may be authenticated by evidence of the genuineness of the handwriting of the maker.

§1416. Personal knowledge of handwriting.

A witness who is not otherwise qualified to testify as an expert may state his opinion whether a writing is in the handwriting of a supposed writer if the court finds that he has personal knowledge of the handwriting of the supposed writer. Such personal knowledge may be acquired from:

(a) Having seen the supposed writer write;

(b) Having seen a writing purporting to be in the handwriting of the supposed writer and upon which the supposed writer has acted or been charged;

(c) Having received letters in the due course of mail purporting to be from the supposed writer in response to letters duly addressed and mailed by him to the supposed writer; or

(d) Any other means of obtaining personal knowledge of the handwriting of the supposed writer.

§1417. Comparison of handwriting by trier of fact.

The genuineness of handwriting, or the lack thereof, may be proved by a comparison made by the trier of fact with handwriting (a) which the court finds was admitted or treated as genuine by the party against whom the evidence is offered or (b) otherwise proved to be genuine to the satisfaction of the court.

§1418. Comparison of writing by expert witness.

The genuineness of writing, or the lack thereof, may be proved by a comparison made by an expert witness with writing (a) which the court finds was admitted or treated as genuine by the party against whom the evidence is offered or (b) otherwise proved to be genuine to the satisfaction of the court.

§1419. Writing 30 years old.

Where a writing whose genuineness is sought to be proved is more than 30 years old, the comparison under Section 1417 or 1418 may be made with writing purporting to be genuine, and generally respected and acted upon as such, by persons having an interest in knowing whether it is genuine.

§1420. Authentication by evidence of response to a communication.

A writing may be authenticated by evidence that the writing was received in response to a communication sent to the person who is claimed by the proponent of the evidence to be the author of the writing.

§1421. Authentication by contents of writing.

A writing may be authenticated by evidence that the writing refers to or states matters that are unlikely to be known to anyone other than the person who is claimed by the proponent of the evidence to be the author of the writing.

ARTICLE 3

PRESUMPTIONS AFFECTING ACKNOWLEDGED WRITINGS AND OFFICIAL WRITINGS

§1450. Presumptions affecting burden of proving evidence.

The presumptions established by this article are presumptions affecting the burden of producing evidence.

§1451. Certificate of acknowledgment.

A certificate of the acknowledgment of a writing other than a will, or a certificate of the proof of such a writing, is prima facie evidence of the facts recited in the certificate and the genuineness of the signature of each person by whom the writing purports to have been signed if the certificate meets the requirements of Article 3 (commencing with Section 1180) of Chapter 4, Title 4, Part 4, Division 2 of the Civil Code.

§1452. Official seals.

A seal is presumed to be genuine and its use authorized if it purports to be the seal of:

(a) The United States or a department, agency, or public employee of the United States.

(b) A public entity in the United States or a department, agency, or public employee of such public entity.

(c) A nation recognized by the executive power of the United States or a department, agency, or officer of such nation.

(d) A public entity in a nation recognized by the executive power of the United States or a department, agency, or officer of such public entity.

(e) A court of admiralty or maritime jurisdiction.

(f) A notary public within any state of the United States.

§1453. Official U.S. signatures.

A signature is presumed to be genuine and authorized if it purports to be the signature, affixed in his official capacity, of:

(a) A public employee of the United States.

(b) A public employee of any public entity in the United States.

(c) A notary public within any state of the United States.

§1454. Foreign official signatures; certification.

A signature is presumed to be genuine and authorized if it purports to be the signature, affixed in his official capacity, of an officer, or deputy of an officer, of a nation or public entity in a nation recognized by the executive power of the United States and the writing to which the signature is affixed is accompanied by a final statement certifying the genuineness of the signature and the official position of (a) the person who executed the writing or (b) any foreign official who has certified either the genuineness of the signature and official position of the person executing the writing or the genuineness of the signature and official position of another foreign official who has executed a similar certificate in a chain of such certificates beginning with a certificate of the genuineness of the signature and official position of the person executing the writing. The final statement may be made only by a secretary of an embassy or legation, counsel general, consul, vice consul, consular agent, or other officer in the foreign service of the United States stationed in the nation, authenticated by the seal of his office.

CHAPTER 2

SECONDARY EVIDENCE OR WRITINGS

ARTICLE 1

BEST EVIDENCE RULE

§1500. Best evidence rule.

Except as otherwise provided by statute, no evidence other than the original of a writing is admissible to prove the content of a writing. This section shall be known and may be cited as the best evidence rule.

§1500.5. Computed recorded information or computer programs; printed representation.

Notwithstanding the provisions of Section 1500, a printed representation of computer information or a computer program which is being used by or stored on a computer or computer readable storage media shall be admissible to prove the existence and content of the computer information or computer program.

Computer recorded information or computer programs, or copies of computer recorded information or computer programs, shall not be rendered inadmissible by the best evidence rule. Printed representations of computer information and computer programs will be presumed to be accurate representations of the computer information or computer programs that they purport to represent. This presumption, however, will be a presumption affecting the burden of producing evidence only. If any party to a judicial proceeding introduces evidence that such a printed representation is inaccurate or unreliable, the party introducing it into evidence will have the burden of proving, by a preponderance of evidence, that the printed representation is the best available evidence of the existence and content of the computer information or computer programs that it purports to represent.

§1501. Copy of lost or destroyed writing admissible.

A copy of a writing is not made inadmissible by the best evidence rule if the writing is lost or has been destroyed without fraudulent intent on the part of the proponent of the evidence.

§1502. Copy of unprocurable writing admissible.

A copy of a writing is not made inadmissible by the best evidence rule if the writing was not reasonably procurable by the proponent by use of the court's process or by other available means.

§1503. Copy of writing under control of opponent admissible.

(a) A copy of a writing is not made inadmissible by the best evidence rule if, at a time when the writing was under the control of the opponent, the opponent was expressly or impliedly notified, by the pleadings or otherwise, that the writing would be needed at the hearing, and on request at the hearing the opponent has failed to produce the writing. In a criminal action,

the request at the hearing to produce the writing may not be made in the presence of the jury.

(b) Though a writing requested by one party is produced by another, and is thereupon inspected by the party calling for it, the party calling for the writing is not obliged to introduce it as evidence in the action.

§1504. Copy of writing inexpedient to produce and not closely related to issues.

A copy of a writing is not made inadmissible by the best evidence rule if the writing is not closely related to the controlling issues and it would be inexpedient to require its production.

§1505. Secondary evidence of writings.

If the proponent does not have in his possession or under his control a copy of a writing described in Section 1501, 1502, 1503, or 1504, other secondary evidence of the content of the writing is not made inadmissible by the best evidence rule. This section does not apply to a writing that is also described in Section 1506 or 1507.

§1506. Copy of record in custody of public entity.

A copy of a writing is not made inadmissible by the best evidence rule if the writing is a record or other writing that is in the custody of a public entity.

§1507. Copy of writing recorded in public records; evidence of writing by statute.

A copy of a writing is not made inadmissible by the best evidence rule if the writing has been recorded in the public records and the record or an attested or a certified copy thereof is made evidence of the writing by statute.

§1508. Secondary evidence of writings in public records.

If the proponent does not have in his possession a copy of a writing described in Section 1506 or 1507 and could not in the exercise of reasonable diligence have obtained a copy, other secondary evidence of the content of the writing is not made inadmissible by the best evidence rule.

§1509. Writing consisting of numerous accounts; summaries.

Secondary evidence, whether written or oral, of the content of a writing is not made inadmissible by the best evidence rule if the writing consists of numerous accounts or other writings that cannot be examined in court without great loss of time, and the evidence sought from there is only the general result of the whole; but the court in its discretion may require that such accounts or other writings be produced for inspection by the adverse party.

§1510. Copy of writing available for inspection at the hearing.

A copy of a writing is not made inadmissible by the best evidence rule if the writing has been produced at the hearing and made available for inspection by the adverse party.

§1511. Duplicate of writing admissible.

A duplicate is admissible to the same extent as an original unless (a) a genuine question is raised as to the authenticity of the original or (b) in the circum-

© 1992 by J., B. & L. Gould
Printed in the U.S.A.   EP

stances it would be unfair to admit the duplicate in lieu of the original.

ARTICLE 2

OFFICIAL WRITINGS AND RECORDED WRITINGS

§1530. Copy of writing in custody of public entity.

(a) A purported copy of a writing in the custody of a public entity, or of an entry in such a writing, is prima facie evidence of the existence and content of such writing or entry if:

(1) The copy purports to be published by the authority of the nation or stats, or public entity therein in which the writing is kept;

(2) The office in which the writing is kept is within the United States or within the Panama Canal Zone, the Trust Territory of the Pacific Islands, or the Ryukyu Islands, and the copy is attested or certified as a correct copy of the writing or entry by a public employee, or a deputy of a public employee, having the legal custody of the writing; or

(3) The office in which the writing is kept is not within the United States or any other place described in paragraph (2) and the copy is attested as a correct copy of the writing or entry by a person having authority to make attestation. The attestation must be accompanied by a final statement certifying the genuineness of the signature and the official position of (i) the person who attested the copy as a correct copy or (ii) any foreign official who has certified either the genuineness of the signature and official position of the person attesting the copy or the genuineness of the signature and official position of another foreign official who has executed a similar certificate in a chain of such certificates beginning with a certificate of the genuineness of the signature and official position of the person attesting the copy. Except as provided in the next sentence, the final statement may be made only by a secretary of an embassy or legation, consul general, consul, vice consul, or consular agent of the United States, or a diplomatic or consular official of the foreign country assigned or accredited to the United States. Prior to January 1, 1971, the final statement may also be made by a secretary of an embassy or legation, consul general, consul, vice consul, consular agent, or other officer in the foreign service of the United States stationed in the nation in which the writing is kept, authenticated by the seal of his office. If reasonable opportunity has been given to all parties to investigate the authenticity and accuracy of the documents, the court may, for good cause shown, (i) admit an attested copy without the final statement or (ii) permit the writing or entry in foreign custody to be evidenced by an attested summary with or without a final statement.

(b) The presumptions established by this section are presumptions affecting the burden of producing evidence.

§1531. Certification of copy of a writing.

For the purpose of evidence, whenever a copy of a writing is attested or certified, the attestation or certificate must state in substance that the copy is a correct copy of the original, or of a specified part thereof, as the case may be.

§1532. Official record of a public entity.

(a) The official record of a writing is prima facie evidence of the existence and content of the original recorded writing if:

(1) The record is in fact a record of an office of a public entity; and

(2) A statute authorized such a writing to be recorded in that office.

(b) The presumption established by this section is a presumption affecting the burden of producing evidence.

ARTICLE 3

PHOTOGRAPHIC COPIES OF WRITINGS

§1550. Photographic copies made in the regular course of business.

A photostatic, microfilm, microcard, miniature photographic or other photographic copy or reproduction, or an enlargement thereof, of a writing is as admissible as the writing itself if such copy or reproduction was made and preserved as a part of the records of a business (as defined by Section 1270) in the regular course of such business. The introduction of such copy, reproduction, or enlargement does not preclude admission of the original writing if it is still in existence.

§1551. Photographic or videotape copies where original destroyed or lost.

A print, whether enlarged or not, from a photographic film (including a photographic plate, microphotographic film, photostatic negative, or similar reproduction) of an original writing destroyed or lost after such film was taken or a reproduction from an electronic recording of video images on magnetic surfaces is admissible as the original writing itself if, at the time of the taking of such film or electronic recording, the person under whose direction and control it was taken attached thereto, or to the sealed container in which it was placed and has been kept, or incorporated in the film or electronic recording, a certification complying with the provisions of Section 1531 and stating the date on which, and the fact that, it was so taken under his direction and control.

ARTICLE 4

PRODUCTION OF BUSINESS RECORDS

§1560. Procedures for subpoena duces tecum for business records.

(a) As used in this article:

(1) "Business" includes every kind of business described in Section 1270.

(2) "Record" includes every kind of record maintained by such a business.

(b) Except as provided in Section 1564, when a subpoena duces tecum is served upon the custodian of records or other qualified witness of a business in an action in which the business is neither a party nor the place where any cause of action is alleged to have arisen, and the subpoena requires the production of all or any part of the records of the business, it is sufficient compliance therewith if the custodian or other qualified witness, within five days after the receipt of the subpoena in any criminal action or within the time agreed upon by the party who served

© 1992 by J., B. & L. Gould
Printed in the U.S.A. **EP**

the subpoena and the custodian or other qualified witness, or within 15 days after the receipt of the subpoena in any civil action or within the time agreed upon by the party who served the subpoena and the custodian or other qualified witness, delivers by mail or otherwise a true, legible, and durable copy of all the records described in the subpoena to the clerk of the court or to the judge if there be no clerk or to such other person as described in subdivision (c) of Section 2026 of the Code of Civil Procedure, together with the affidavit described in Section 1561.

(c) The copy of the records shall be separately enclosed in an inner envelope or wrapper, sealed, with the title and number of the action, name of witness, and date of subpoena clearly inscribed thereon; the sealed envelope or wrapper shall then be enclosed in an outer envelope or wrapper, sealed, and directed as follows:

(1) If the subpoena directs attendance in court, to the clerk of such court, or to the judge thereof if there be no clerk.

(2) If the subpoena directs attendance at a deposition, to the officer before whom the deposition is to be taken, at the place designated in the subpoena for the taking of the deposition or at the officer's place of business.

(3) In other cases, to the officer, body, or tribunal conducting the hearing, at a like address.

(d) Unless the parties to the proceeding otherwise agree, or unless the sealed envelope or wrapper is returned to a witness who is to appear personally, the copy of the records shall remain sealed and shall be opened only at the time of trial, deposition, or other hearing, upon the direction of the judge, officer, body, or tribunal conducting the proceeding, in the presence of all parties who have appeared in person or by counsel at the trial, deposition, or hearing. Records which are original documents and which are not introduced in evidence or required as part of the record shall be returned to the person or entity from whom received. Records which are copies may be destroyed.

(e) As an alternative to the procedures described in subdivisions (b), (c), and (d), the subpoenaing party may direct the witness to make the records available for inspection or copying by the party's attorney or the attorney's representative at the witness' business address under reasonable conditions during normal business hours. It shall be the responsibility of the attorney's representative to deliver any copy of the records as directed in the subpoena. (*Amended by Stats 1991 ch 1090 §14, eff. 1/1/92.*)

§1561. Affidavit authenticating records described in subpoena duces tecum.

(a) The records shall be accompanied by the affidavit of the custodian or other qualified witness, stating in substance each of the following:

(1) The affiant is the duly authorized custodian of the records or other qualified witness and has authority to certify the records.

(2) The copy is a true copy of all the records described in the subpoena duces tecum, or pursuant to subdivision (e) of Section 1560 the records were delivered to the attorney or the attorney's representative for copying at the custodian's or witness' place of business, as the case may be.

(3) The records were prepared by the personnel of the business in the ordinary course of business at or near the time of the act, condition, or event.

(b) If the business has none of the records described, or only part thereof, the custodian or other qualified witness shall so state in the affidavit, and deliver the affidavit and such records as are available in the manner provided in Section 1560.

(c) Where the records described in the subpoena were delivered to the attorney or his or her representative for copying at the custodian's or witness' place of business, in addition to the affidavit required by subdivision (a), the records shall be accompanied by an affidavit by the attorney or his or her representative stating that the copy is a true copy of all the records delivered to the attorney or his or her representative for copying.

§1562. Admissibility of copy of records and affidavit.

If the original records would be admissible in evidence if the custodian had been present and testified to the matters stated in the affidavit, and if the requirements of Section 1271 have been met, the copy of the records is admissible in evidence. The affidavit is admissible as evidence of the matters stated therein pursuant to Section 1561 and the matters so stated are presumed true. When more than one person has knowledge of the facts, more than one affidavit may be made. The presumption established by this section is a presumption affecting the burden of producing evidence.

§1563. Reasonable costs for production of business records; witness fees and mileage.

(a) This article shall not be interpreted to require tender or payment of more than one witness fee and one mileage fee or other charge unless there is an agreement to the contrary.

(b) All reasonable costs incurred in a civil proceeding by any witness which is not a party with respect to the production of all or any part of business records the production of which is requested pursuant to a subpoena duces tecum may be charged against the party serving the subpoena duces tecum.

(1) "Reasonable cost," as used in this section, shall include, but not be limited to, the following specific costs: ten cents ($0.10) per page for standard reproduction of documents of a size 8½ by 14 inches or less; twenty cents ($0.20) per page for copying of documents from microfilm; actual costs for the reproduction of oversize documents or the reproduction of documents requiring special processing which are made in response to a subpoena; reasonable clerical costs incurred in locating and making the records available to be billed at the maximum rate of sixteen dollars ($16) per hour per person, computed on the basis of four dollars ($4) per quarter hour or fraction thereof; actual postage charges; and actual costs, if any, charged to the witness by a third person for the retrieval and return of records held by that third person.

(2) The requesting party shall not be required to pay those costs or any estimate thereof prior to the time the records are available for delivery pursuant to the subpoena, but the witness may demand payment of costs pursuant to this section simultaneous with actual delivery of the subpoenaed records, and until such time as payment is made, is under no obligation to deliver the records.

(3) The witness shall submit an itemized statement for the costs to the requesting party setting forth the reproduction and clerical costs incurred by the

© 1992 by J., B. & L. Gould
Printed in the U.S.A.   EP

witness. Upon demand by the requesting party, the witness shall furnish a statement setting forth the actions taken by the witness in justification of the costs.

(4) The requesting party may petition the court in which the action is pending to recover from the witness all or a part of the costs paid to the witness, or to reduce all or a part of the costs charged by the witness, pursuant to this subdivision, on the grounds that such costs were excessive. Upon the filing of the petition the court shall issue an order to show cause and from the time the order is served on the witness the court has jurisdiction over the witness. The court may hear testimony on the order to show cause and if it finds that the costs demanded and collected, or charged but not collected, exceed the amount authorized by this subdivision, it shall order the witness to remit to the requesting party, or reduce its charge to the requesting party by an amount equal to, the amount of the excess. In the event that the court finds the costs excessive and charged in bad faith by the witness, the court shall order the witness to remit the full amount of the costs demanded and collected, or excuse the requesting party from any payment of costs charged but not collected, and the court shall also order the witness to pay the requesting party the amount of the reasonable expenses incurred in obtaining the order including attorney's fees. If the court finds the costs were not excessive, the court shall order the requesting party to pay the witness the amount of the reasonable expenses incurred in defending the petition, including attorney's fees.

(5) If a subpoena is served to compel the production of business records and is subsequently withdrawn, or is quashed, modified or limited on a motion made other than by the witness, the witness shall be entitled to reimbursement pursuant to paragraph (1) for all costs incurred in compliance with the subpoena to the time that the requesting party has notified the witness that the subpoena has been withdrawn or quashed, modified or limited. In the event the subpoena is withdrawn or quashed, if those costs are not paid within 30 days after demand therefor, the witness may file a motion in the court in which the action is pending for an order requiring payment, and the court shall award the payment of expenses and attorney's fees in the manner set forth in paragraph (4).

(6) Where the records are delivered to the attorney or the attorney's representative for inspection or photocopying at the witness' place of business, the only fee for complying with the subpoena shall not exceed fifteen dollars ($15), plus actual costs, if any, charged to the witness by a third person for retrieval and return of records held offsite by the third person. If the records are retrieved from microfilm, the reasonable cost, as defined in paragraph (1), shall also apply.

(c) When the personal attendance of the custodian of a record or other qualified witness is required pursuant to Section 1564, in a civil proceeding, he or she shall be entitled to the same witness fees and mileage permitted in a case where the subpoena requires the witness to attend and testify before a court in which the action or proceeding is pending and to any additional costs incurred as provided by subdivision (b).

§1564. **Request for personal attendance of custodian and production of original records.**

The personal attendance of the custodian or other qualified witness and the production of the original records is not required unless, at the discretion of the requesting party, the subpoena duces tecum contains a clause which reads:

"The personal attendance of the custodian or other qualified witness and the production of the original records are required by this subpoena. The procedure authorized pursuant to subdivision (b) of Section 1560, and Sections 1561 and 1562, of the Evidence Code will not be deemed sufficient compliance with this subpoena."

§1565. **Multiple subpoenas duces tecum.**

If more than one subpoena duces tecum is served upon the custodian of records or other qualified witness and the personal attendance of the custodian or other qualified witness is required pursuant to Section 1564, the witness shall be deemed to be the witness of the party serving the first such subpoena duces tecum.

§1566. **Applicability of article.**

This article applies in any proceeding in which testimony can be compelled.

CHAPTER 3

OFFICIAL WRITINGS AFFECTING PROPERTY

§1600. **Official record of document affecting an interest in property.**

(a) The record of an instrument or other document purporting to establish or affect an interest in property is prima facie evidence of the existence and content of the original recorded document and its execution and delivery by each person by whom it purports to have been executed if:

(1) The record is in fact a record of an office of a public entity; and

(2) A statute authorized such a document to be recorded in that office.

(b) The presumption established by this section is a presumption affecting the burden of proof.

§1601. **Proof of contents of lost or destroyed official records; abstracts of title to real estate.**

(a) Subject to subdivisions (b) and (c), when in any action it is desired to prove the contents of the official record of any writing lost or destroyed by conflagration or other public calamity, after proof of such loss or destruction, the following may, without further proof, be admitted in evidence to prove the contents of such record:

(1) Any abstract of title made and issued and certified as correct prior to such loss or destruction, and purporting to have been prepared and made in the ordinary course of business by any person engaged in the business of preparing and making abstracts of title prior to such loss or destruction; or

(2) Any abstract of title, or of any instrument affecting title, made, issued, and certified as correct by any person engaged in the business of insuring titles or issuing abstracts of title to real estate, whether the same was made, issued, or certified before or after such loss or destruction and whether the same was made from the original records or from abstract and notes, or either, taken from such records in the preparation and upkeeping of its plant in the ordinary course of its business.

(b) No proof of the loss of the original writing is required other than the fact that the original is not known to the party desiring to prove its contents to be in existence.

(c) Any party desiring to use evidence admissible under this section shall give reasonable notice in writing to all other parties to the action who have appeared therein, of his intention to use such evidence at the trial of the action, and shall give all such other parties a reasonable opportunity to inspect the evidence, and also the abstracts, memoranda, or notes from which it was compiled, and to take copies thereof.

§1603. Deed of conveyance of real property.

A deed of conveyance of real property, purporting to have been executed by a proper officer in pursuance of legal process of any of the courts of record of this state, acknowledged and recorded in the office of the recorder of the county wherein the real property therein described is situated, or the record of such deed, or a certified copy of such record, is prima facie evidence that the property or interest therein described was thereby conveyed to the grantee named in such deed. The presumption established by this section is a presumption affecting the burden of proof.

§1604. Certificate of purchase or of location of lands.

A certificate of purchase, or of location, of any lands in this state, issued or made in pursuance of any law of the United States or of this state, is prima facie evidence that the holder or assignee of such certificate is the owner of the land described therein; but this evidence may be overcome by proof that, at the time of the location, or time of filing a pre-emption claim on which the certificate may have been issued, the land was in the adverse possession of the adverse party, or those under whom he claims, or that the adverse party is holding the land for mining purposes.

§1605. Copies and authenticated translations of Spanish title papers.

Duplicate copies and authenticated translations of original Spanish title papers relating to land claims in this state, derived from the Spanish or Mexican governments, prepared under the supervision of the Keeper of Archives, authenticated by the Surveyor-General or his successor and by the Keeper of Archives, and filed with a county recorder, in accordance with Chapter 281 of the Statutes of 1865-66, are admissible as evidence with like force and effect as the originals and without proving the execution of such originals.

© 1992 by J., B. & L. Gould
Printed in the U.S.A.   EP

HEALTH AND SAFETY CODE

DIVISION 1

ADMINISTRATION OF PUBLIC HEALTH

PART 1

STATE DEPARTMENT OF HEALTH SERVICES

CHAPTER 1.11

MANDATED BLOOD TESTING AND CONFIDENTIALITY TO PROTECT PUBLIC HEALTH

§199.21. Liability for negligent disclosure of AIDS test results.

(a) Any person who negligently discloses results of an HIV test, as defined in Section 26, to any third party, in a manner which identifies or provides identifying characteristics of the person to whom the test results apply, except pursuant to a written authorization, as described in subdivision (g), or except as provided in Section 1603.1 or 1603.3 or any other statute that expressly provides an exemption to this section, shall be assessed a civil penalty in an amount not to exceed one thousand dollars ($1,000) plus court costs, as determined by the court, which penalty and costs shall be paid to the subject of the test.

(b) Any person who willfully discloses the results of an HIV test, as defined in Section 26, to any third party, in a manner which identifies or provides identifying characteristics of the person to whom the test results apply, except pursuant to a written authorization, as described in subdivision (g), or except as provided in Section 1603.1 or 1603.3 or any other statute that expressly provides an exemption to this section, shall be assessed a civil penalty in an amount not less than one thousand dollars ($1,000) and not more than five thousand dollars ($5,000) plus court costs, as determined by the court, which penalty and costs shall be paid to the subject of the test.

(c) Any person who willfully or negligently discloses the results of an HIV test, as defined in Section 26, to a third party, in a manner which identifies or provides identifying characteristics of the person to whom the test results apply, except pursuant to a written authorization, as described in subdivision (g), or except as provided in Section 1603.1 or 1603.3 or any other statute that expressly provides an exemption to this section, which results in economic, bodily, or psychological harm to the subject of the test, is guilty of a misdemeanor, punishable by imprisonment in the county jail for a period not to exceed one year or a fine of not to exceed ten thousand dollars ($10,000) or both.

(d) Any person who commits any act described in subdivision (a) or (b) shall be liable to the subject for all actual damages, including damages for economic, bodily, or psychological harm which is a proximate result of the act.

(e) Each disclosure made in violation of this chapter is a separate and actionable offense.

(f) Except as provided in Article 6.9 (commencing with Section 799) of Chapter 1 of Part 2 of the Insurance Code, the results of an HIV test, as defined in Section 26, which identifies or provides identifying characteristics of the person to whom the test results apply, shall not be used in any instance for the determination of insurability or suitability for employment.

(g) "Written authorization," as used in this section, applies only to the disclosure of test results by a person responsible for the care and treatment of the person subject to the test. Written authorization is required for each separate disclosure of the test results, and shall include to whom the disclosure would be made.

(h) Nothing in this section limits or expands the right of an injured subject to recover damages under any other applicable law. Nothing in this section shall impose civil liability or criminal sanction for disclosure of the results of tests performed on cadavers to public health authorities or tissue banks.

(i) Nothing in this section imposes liability or criminal sanction for disclosure of an HIV test, as defined in Section 26, in accordance with any reporting requirement for a diagnosed case of AIDS by the state department or the Centers for Disease Control under the United States Public Health Service.

(j) The state department may require blood banks and plasma centers to submit monthly reports summarizing statistical data concerning the results of tests to detect the presence of viral hepatitis and HIV. This statistical summary shall not include the identity of individual donors or identifying characteristics which would identify individual donors.

(k) "Disclosed," as used in this section, means to disclose, release, transfer, disseminate, or otherwise communicate all or any part of any record orally, in writing, or by electronic means to any person or entity.

(l) When the results of an HIV test, as defined in Section 26, are included in the medical record of the patient who is the subject of the test, the inclusion is not a disclosure for purposes of this section. *(Amended by Stats 1991 ch 963 §2, eff. 1/1/92.)*

CHAPTER 1.12

ACQUIRED IMMUNE DEFICIENCY SYNDROME RESEARCH CONFIDENTIALITY ACT

§199.37. Penalties for violations.

(a) Any person who willfully or maliciously discloses the content of any confidential research record, to any third party, except pursuant to this chapter, shall be assessed a civil penalty in an amount not less than one thousand dollars ($1,000) and not more than five thousand dollars ($5,000) plus court costs, as determined by the court, which penalty and costs shall be paid to the subject of the test.

(b) Any person who maliciously discloses the content of any confidential research record, to a third party, ex- cept pursuant to this chapter, which results in economic, bodily, or psychological harm to the research subject, is guilty of a misdemeanor, punishable by imprisonment in the county jail for a period not to exceed one year or a fine of not to exceed ten thousand dollars ($10,000) or both.

(c) Any person who commits any act described in subdivision (a) or (b) shall be liable to the subject for all actual damages for economic, bodily, or psychological harm which is a proximate result of the act.

(d) Any person who negligently or willfully violates Section 199.36 is guilty of an infraction punishable by a fine of twenty-five dollars ($25).

(e) Each violation of this chapter is a separate and actionable offense.

(f) Nothing in this section limits or expands the right of an injured research subject to recover damages under any other applicable law. *(Added by Stats 1985 ch 1519 §1.)*

DIVISION 7

DEAD BODIES

PART 1

GENERAL PROVISIONS

CHAPTER 3.7

DEATH

ARTICLE 1

UNIFORM DETERMINATION OF DEATH ACT

§7180. Determining death.

(a) An individual who has sustained either (1) irreversible cessation of circulatory and respiratory functions, or (2) irreversible cessation of all functions of the entire brain, including the brain stem, is dead. A determination of death must be made in accordance with accepted medical standards.

(b) This article shall be applied and construed to effectuate its general purpose to make uniform the law with respect to the subject of this article among states enacting it.

(c) This article may be cited as the Uniform Determination of Death Act.

ARTICLE 2

CONFIRMATION OF DEATH

§7181. Cessation of brain function.

When an individual is pronounced dead by determining that the individual has sustained an irreversible cessation of all functions of the entire brain, including the brain stem, there shall be independent confirmation by another physician.

§7182. Direct transplantation of part of donor.

When a part of the donor is used for direct transplantation pursuant to the Uniform Anatomical Gift Act (Chapter 3.5 (commencing with Section 7150)) and the death of the donor is determined by determining that the individual has suffered an irreversible cessation of all functions of the entire brain, including the brain stem, there shall be an independent confirmation of the death by another physician. Neither the physician making the determination of death under Section 7155.5 nor the physician making the independent confirmation shall participate in the procedures for removing or transplanting a part.

CHAPTER 3.9

NATURAL DEATH ACT
(Added by Stats 1991 ch 895 §2, eff. 1/1/92. Former chapter 3.9 repealed by Stats 1991 ch 895 §1, eff. 1/1/92.)

§7191. Penalties regarding withdrawal of life-sustaining procedures.

(a) A physician or other health care provider who willfully fails to transfer the care of a patient in accordance with Section 7190 is guilty of a misdemeanor.

(b) A physician who willfully fails to record a determination of terminal condition or permanent unconscious condition or the terms of a declaration in accordance with Section 7189 is guilty of a misdemeanor.

(c) An individual who willfully conceals, cancels, defaces, or obliterates the declaration of another individual without the declarant's consent or who falsifies or forges a revocation of the declaration of another individual is guilty of a misdemeanor.

(d) An individual who falsifies or forges the declaration of another individual, or willfully conceals or withholds personal knowledge of a revocation under Section 7188, with the intent to cause a withholding or withdrawal of life-sustaining treatment contrary to the wishes of the declarant, and thereby, because of that act, directly causes life-sustaining treatment to be withheld or withdrawn and death to thereby be hastened, shall be subject to prosecution for unlawful homicide as provided in Chapter 1 (commencing with Section 187) of Title 8 of Part 1 of the Penal Code.

(e) A person who requires or prohibits the execution of a declaration as a condition for being insured for, or receiving, health care services is guilty of a misdemeanor.

(f) A person who coerces or fraudulently induces an individual to execute a declaration is guilty of a misdemeanor.

(g) The sanctions provided in this section do not displace any sanction applicable under other law. *(Added by Stats 1991 ch 895 §2, eff. 1/1/92. Former section 7191 repealed by Stats 1991 ch 895 §1, eff. 1/1/92.)*

§7194. *Repealed by Stats 1991 ch 895 §1, eff. 1/1/92. See, now, section 7191 above.*

CHAPTER 4

DISPOSAL OF UNCLAIMED DEAD

§7208. Penalty for offense.

Every person who lawfully disposes, uses, or sells the body of an unclaimed dead person, or who violates any provision of this chapter is guilty of a misdemeanor.

DIVISION 8

CEMETERIES

PART 1

GENERAL PROVISIONS

CHAPTER 2

VANDALISM

§8101. Punishment.

Every person is guilty of a crime and punishable by imprisonment in the state prison or by imprisonment in the county jail for not exceeding one year, who maliciously does any of the following:

(a) Destroys, cuts, mutilates, effaces, or otherwise injures, tears down, or removes any tomb, monument, memorial, or marker in a cemetery, or any gate, door, fence, wall, post or railing, or any inclosure for the

© 1992 by J., B. & L. Gould
Printed in the U.S.A.   EP

protection of a cemetery or mortuary or any property in a cemetery or mortuary.

(b) Obliterates any grave, vault, niche, or crypt.

(c) Destroys, cuts, breaks or injures any mortuary building or any building, statuary, or ornamentation within the limits of a cemetery.

(d) Disturbs, obstructs, detains or interferes with any person carrying or accompanying human remains to a cemetery or funeral establishment, or engaged in a funeral service, or an interment.

PART 3

PRIVATE CEMETERIES

CHAPTER 2

OPERATION AND MANAGEMENT

ARTICLE 5

OPERATION OF CREMATORIES

§8342. Prohibiting requirement of casket.

No crematory shall make or enforce any rules requiring that human remains be placed in a casket before cremation or that human remains be cremated in a casket, nor shall a crematory refuse to accept human remains for cremation for the reason that they are not in a casket. Every director, officer, agent or representative of a crematory who violates this section is guilty of a misdemeanor. Nothing in this section shall be construed to prohibit the requiring of some type of container or disposal unit.

DIVISION 10

UNIFORM CONTROLLED SUBSTANCES ACT

CHAPTER 1

GENERAL PROVISIONS AND DEFINITIONS

§11000. Naming division.

This division shall be known as the "California Uniform Controlled Substances Act."

§11001. Definitions.

Unless the context otherwise requires, the definitions in this chapter govern the construction of this division.

§11002. Administer defined.

"Administer" means the direct application of a controlled substance, whether by injection, inhalation, ingestion, or any other means, to the body of a patient for his immediate needs or to the body of a research subject by any of the following:

(a) A practitioner or, in his presence, by his authorized agent.

(b) The patient or research subject at the direction and in the presence of the practitioner.

§11003. Agent defined.

"Agent" means an authorized person who acts on behalf of or at the direction of a manufacturer, distributor, or dispenser. It does not include a common or contract carrier, public warehouseman, or employee of the carrier or warehouseman.

§11004. Attorney General defined.

"Attorney General" means the Attorney General of the State of California.

§11005. Board of Pharmacy defined.

"Board of Pharmacy" means the California State Board of Pharmacy.

§11006.5. Concentrated cannabis defined.

"Concentrated cannabis" means the separated resin, whether crude or purified, obtained from marijuana.

§11007. Controlled substance defined.

"Controlled substance," unless otherwise specified, means a drug, substance, or immediate precursor which is listed in any schedule in Section 11054, 11055, 11056, 11057, or 11058. *(Added by Stats 1987 ch 1174 §1.)*

§11008. Customs broker defined.

"Customs broker" means a person in this state who is authorized to act as a broker for any of the following:

(a) A person in this state who is licensed to sell, distribute, or otherwise possess any controlled substance.

(b) A person in any other state who ships any controlled substance into this state.

(c) A person in this state or any other state who ships or transfers any controlled substance through this state.

§11009. Deliver or delivery defined.

"Deliver" or "delivery" means the actual, constructive, or attempted transfer from one person to another of a controlled substance, whether or not there is an agency relationship.

§11010. Dispense defined.

"Dispense" means to deliver a controlled substance to an ultimate user or research subject by or pursuant to the lawful order of a practitioner, including the prescribing, furnishing, packaging, labeling, or compounding necessary to prepare the substance for that delivery.

§11011. Dispenser defined.

"Dispenser" means a practitioner who dispenses.

§11012. Distribute defined.

"Distribute" means to deliver other than by administering or dispensing a controlled substance.

§11013. Distributor defined.

"Distributor" means a person who distributes. The term distributor also includes warehousemen handling or storing controlled substances and customs brokers.

§11014. Drug defined.

"Drug" means (a) substances recognized as drugs in the official United States Pharmacopoeia, official Homeopathic Pharmacopoeia of the United States, or official National Formulary, or any supplement to any of them; (b) substances intended for use in the diagnosis, cure, mitigation, treatment, or prevention of disease in man or animals; (c) substances (other than food) intended to affect the structure or any function of the body of man or animals; and (d) substances intended for use as a component of any article specified in subdivision (a), (b), or (c) of this section. It does not include devices or their components, parts, or accessories.

§11014.5. Drug paraphernalia defined.

(a) "Drug paraphernalia" means all equipment, products and materials of any kind which are designed for use or marketed for use, in planting, propagating, cultivating, growing, harvesting, manufacturing, compounding, converting, producing, processing, preparing, testing, analyzing, packaging, repackaging, storing, containing, concealing, injecting, ingesting, inhaling, or otherwise introducing into the human body a controlled substance in violation of this division. It includes, but is not limited to:

(1) Kits designed for use or marketed for use in planting, propagating, cultivating, growing, or harvesting of any species of plant which is a controlled substance or from which a controlled substance can be derived.

(2) Kits designed for use or marketed for use in manufacturing, compounding, converting, producing, processing, or preparing controlled substances.

(3) Isomerization devices designed for use or marketed for use in increasing the potency of any species of plant which is a controlled substance.

(4) Testing equipment designed for use or marketed for use in identifying, or in analyzing the strength, effectiveness, or purity of controlled substances.

(5) Scales and balances designed for use or marketed for use in weighing or measuring controlled substances.

(6) Containers and other objects designed for use or marketed for use in storing or concealing controlled substances.

(7) Hypodermic syringes, needles, and other objects designed for use or marketed for use in parenterally injecting controlled substances into the human body.

(8) Objects designed for use or marketed for use in ingesting, inhaling, or otherwise introducing marijuana, cocaine, hashish, or hashish oil into the human body, such as:

(A) Carburetion tubes and devices.

(B) Smoking and carburetion masks.

(C) Roach clips, meaning objects used to hold burning material, such as a marijuana cigarette, that has become too small or too short to be held in the hand.

(D) Miniature cocaine spoons, and cocaine vials.

(E) Chamber pipes.

(F) Carburetor pipes.

(G) Electric pipes.

(H) Air-driven pipes.

(I) Chillums.

(J) Bongs.

(K) Ice pipes or chillers.

(b) For the purposes of this section, the phrase "marketed for use" means advertising, distributing, offering for sale, displaying for sale, or selling in a manner which promotes the use of equipment, products, or materials with controlled substances.

(c) In determining whether an object is drug paraphernalia, a court or other authority may consider, in addition to all other logically relevant factors, the following:

(1) Statements by an owner or by anyone in control of the object concerning its use.

(2) Instructions, oral or written, provided with the object concerning its use for ingesting, inhaling, or otherwise introducing a controlled substance into the human body.

(3) Descriptive materials accompanying the object which explain or depict its use.

(4) National and local advertising concerning its use.

(5) The manner in which the object is displayed for sale.

(6) Whether the owner, or anyone in control of the object, is a legitimate supplier of like or related items to the community, such as a licensed distributor or dealer of tobacco products.

(7) Expert testimony concerning its use.

(d) If any provision of this section or the application thereof to any person or circumstance is held invalid, it is the intent of the Legislature that the invalidity shall not affect other provisions or applications of the section which can be given effect without the invalid provision or application and to this end the provisions of this section are severable.

§11015. Definition of Federal bureau.

"Federal bureau" means the Bureau of Narcotics and Dangerous Drugs of the United States Department of Justice, or its successor agency.

§11016. Furnish defined.

"Furnish" has the same meaning as provided in Section 4048.5 of the Business and Professions Code.

§11017. Manufacturer defined.

"Manufacturer" has the same meaning as provided in Section 4034 of the Business and Professions Code.

§11018. Marijuana defined.

"Marijuana" means all parts of the plant Cannabis sativa L., whether growing or not; the seeds thereof; the resin extracted from any part of the plant; and every compound, manufacture, salt, derivative, mixture, or preparation of the plant, its seeds or resin. It does not include the mature stalks of the plant, fiber produced from the stalks, oil or cake made from the seeds of the plant, any other compound, manufacture, salt, derivative, mixture, or preparation of the mature stalks (except the resin extracted therefrom), fiber, oil, or cake, or the sterilized seed of the plant which is incapable of germination.

§11019. Narcotic drug defined.

"Narcotic drug" means any of the following, whether produced directly or indirectly by extraction from substances of vegetable origin, or independently by means of chemical synthesis, or by a combination of extraction and chemical synthesis:

(a) Opium and opiate, and any salt, compound, derivative, or preparation of opium or opiate.

(b) Any salt, compound, isomer, or derivative, whether natural or synthetic, of the substances referred to in subdivision (a), but not including the isoquinoline alkaloids of opium.

(c) Opium poppy and poppy straw.

(d) Coca leaves and any salt, compound, derivative, or preparation of coca leaves, but not including decocainized coca leaves or extractions of coca leaves which do not contain cocaine or ecgonine.

(e) Cocaine, whether natural or synthetic, or any salt, isomer, derivative, or preparation thereof.

(f) Ecgonine, whether natural or synthetic, or any salt, isomer, derivative, or preparation thereof.

© 1992 by J., B. & L. Could
Printed in the U.S.A.   EP

(g) Acetylfentanyl, the thiophene analog thereof, derivatives of either, and any salt, compound, isomer, or preparation of acetylfentanyl or the thiophene analog thereof. *(Amended by Stats 1985 ch 1098 §1.)*

§11020. Opiate defined.

"Opiate" means any substance having an addiction-forming or addiction-sustaining liability similar to morphine or being capable of conversion into a drug having addiction-forming or addiction-sustaining liability. It does not include, unless specifically designated as controlled under Chapter 2 (commencing with Section 11053) of this division, the dextrorotatory isomer of 3-methoxy-n-methylmorphinan and its salts (dextromethorphan). It does include its racemic and levorotatory forms.

§11021. Opium poppy defined.

"Opium poppy" means the plant of the species Papaver somniferum L., except its seeds.

§11022. Person defined.

"Person" means individual, corporation, government or governmental subdivision or agency, business trust, estate, trust, partnership, or association, or any other legal entity.

§11023. Pharmacy defined.

"Pharmacy" has the same meaning as provided in Section 4035 of the Business and Professions Code.

§11024. Physician, dentist, podiatrist, pharmacist, veterinarian defined.

"Physician," "dentist," "podiatrist," "pharmacist", and "veterinarian" mean persons who are licensed to practice their respective professions in this state.

§11025. Poppy straw defined.

"Poppy straw" means all parts, except the seeds, of the opium poppy, after mowing.

§11026. Practitioner defined.

"Practitioner" means any of the following:

(a) A physician, dentist, veterinarian, podiatrist, or pharmacist acting within the scope of a project authorized under Article 18 (commencing with Section 429.70) of Chapter 2 of Part 1 of Division 1, or registered nurse acting within the scope of a project authorized under Article 18 (commencing with Section 429.70) of Chapter 2 of Part 1 of Division 1, or physician's assistant acting within the scope of a project authorized under Article 18 (commencing with Section 429.70) of Chapter 2 of Part 1 of Division 1.

(b) A pharmacy, hospital, or other institution licensed, registered, or otherwise permitted to distribute, dispense, conduct research with respect to or to administer a controlled substance in the course of professional practice or research in this state.

(c) A scientific investigator, or other person licensed, registered or otherwise permitted to distribute, dispense, conduct research with respect to or to administer a controlled substance in the course of professional practice or research in this state. *(Amended by Stats 1986 ch 1042 §1.)*

§11027. Prescription defined.

"Prescription" means an oral order for a controlled substance given individually for the person(s) for whom prescribed, directly from the prescriber to the furnisher or indirectly by means of a written order of the prescriber.

§11029. Production defined.

"Production" includes the manufacture, planting, cultivation, growing, or harvesting of a controlled substance.

§11030. Ultimate user defined.

"Ultimate user" means a person who lawfully possesses a controlled substance for his own use or for the use of a member of his household or for administering to an animal owned by him or by a member of his household.

§11031. Wholesaler defined.

"Wholesaler" has the same meaning as provided in Section 4038 of the Business and Professions Code.

§11032. Use of terms narcotics, restricted dangerous drugs and marijuana.

Whenever reference is made to the term "narcotics" in any provision of law outside of this division, unless otherwise expressly provided, it shall be construed to mean controlled substances classified in Schedules I and II, as defined in this division. Whenever reference is made to "restricted dangerous drugs" outside of this division, unless otherwise expressly provided, it shall be construed to mean controlled substances classified in Schedules III and IV. Whenever reference is made to the term "marijuana" in any provision of law outside of this division, unless otherwise expressly provided, it shall be construed to mean marijuana as defined in this division.

§11033. Isomer defined.

As used in this division, except as otherwise defined, the term "isomer" includes optical and geometrical (diastereomeric) isomers. *(Added by Stats 1985 ch 21 §2.)*

CHAPTER 2

STANDARDS AND SCHEDULES

§11053. Designated names.

The controlled substances listed or to be listed in the schedules in this chapter are included by whatever official, common, usual, chemical, or trade name designated.

§11054. Schedule I of controlled substances.

(a) The controlled substances listed in this section are included in Schedule I.

(b) Opiates. Unless specifically excepted or unless listed in another schedule, any of the following opiates, including their isomers, esters, ethers, salts, and salts of isomers, esters, and ethers whenever the existence of those isomers, esters, ethers, and salts is possible within the specific chemical designation:

(1) Acetylmethadol.
(2) Allylprodine.
(3) Alphacetylmethadol.
(4) Alphameprodine.
(5) Alphamethadol.
(6) Benzethidine.
(7) Betacetylmethadol.
(8) Betameprodine.
(9) Betamethadol.

(10) Betaprodine.
(11) Clonitazene.
(12) Dextromoramide.
(13) Diampromide.
(14) Diethylthiambutene.
(15) Difenoxin.
(16) Dimenoxadol.
(17) Dimepheptanol.
(18) Dimethylthiambutene.
(19) Dioxaphetyl butyrate.
(20) Dipipanone.
(21) Ethylmethylthiambutene.
(22) Etonitazene.
(23) Etoxeridine.
(24) Furethidine.
(25) Hydroxypethidine.
(26) Ketobemidone.
(27) Levomoramide.
(28) Levophenacylmorphan.
(29) Morpheridine.
(30) Noracymethadol.
(31) Norlevorphanol.
(32) Normethadone.
(33) Norpipanone.
(34) Phenadoxone.
(35) Phenampromide.
(36) Phenomorphan.
(37) Phenoperidine.
(38) Piritramide.
(39) Proheptazine.
(40) Properidine.
(41) Propiram.
(42) Racemoramide.
(43) Tilidine.
(44) Trimeperidine.
(45) Any substance which contains any quantity of acetylfentanyl (N[1-phenethyl-4-piperidinyl]acetanilide) or a derivative thereof.
(46) Any substance which contains any quantity of the thiophene analog of acetylfentanyl (N-[1(2-(2-thienyl)ethyl]-4-piperidinyl]acetanilide) or a derivative thereof.
(47) 1-Methyl-4-Phenyl-4-Propionoxypiperidine (MP-PP).
(48) 1-(2-Phenethyl)-4-Phenyl-4-Acetyloxypiperidine (PEPAP).
(c) Opium derivatives. Unless specifically excepted or unless listed in another schedule, any of the following opium derivatives, its salts, isomers, and salts of isomers whenever the existence of those salts, isomers, and salts of isomers is possible within the specific chemical designation:
(1) Acetorphine.
(2) Acetyldihydrocodeine.
(3) Benzylmorphine.
(4) Codeine methylbromide.
(5) Codeine-N-Oxide.
(6) Cyprenorphine.
(7) Desomorphine.
(8) Dihydromorphine.
(9) Drotebanol.
(10) Etorphine (except hydrochloride salt).
(11) Heroin.
(12) Hydromorphinol.
(13) Methyldesorphine.
(14) Methyldihydromorphine.
(15) Morphine methylbromide.
(16) Morphine methylsulfonate.
(17) Morphine-N-Oxide.

(18) Myrophine.
(19) Nicocodeine.
(20) Nicomorphine.
(21) Normorphine.
(22) Pholcodine.
(23) Thebacon.
(d) Hallucinogenic substances. Unless specifically excepted or unless listed in another schedule, any material, compound, mixture, or preparation, which contains any quantity of the following hallucinogenic substances, or which contains any of its salts, isomers, and salts of isomers whenever the existence of those salts, isomers, and salts of isomers is possible within the specific chemical designation (for purposes of this subdivision only, the term "isomer" includes the optical, position, and geometric isomers):
(1) 4-bromo-2,5-dimethoxy-amphetamine—Some trade or other names: 4-bromo-2,5-dimethoxy-alpha-methylphenethylamine; 4-bromo-2,5-DMA.
(2) 2,5-dimethoxyamphetamine—Some trade or other names: 2,5-dimethoxy-alpha-methylphenethylamine; 2,5-DMA.
(3) 4-methoxyamphetamine—Some trade or other names: 4- methoxy-alpha-methylphenethylamine, para-methoxyamphetamine, PMA.
(4) 5-methoxy-3,4-methylenedioxy-amphetamine.
(5) 4-methyl-2,5-dimethoxy-amphetamine—Some trade or other names: 4-methyl-2,5-dimethoxy-alpha-methylphenethylamine; "DOM"; and "STP".
(6) 3,4-methylenedioxy amphetamine.
(7) 3,4,5-trimethoxy amphetamine.
(8) Bufotenine—Some trade or other names: 3- (beta-Dimethylaminoethyl)-5-hydroxyindole; 3-(2-dimethylaminoethyl)-5 indolol; N,N-dimethylserolonin, 5-hydroxy-N,N-dimethyltryptamine; mappine.
(9) Diethyltrypatamine—Some trade or other names: N,N- Diethyltryptamine; DET.
(10) Dimethyltryptamine—Some trade or other names: DMT.
(11) Ibogaine—Some trade or other names: 7-Ethyl-6,6beta, 7,8,9,10,12,13-octahydro-2-methoxy-6,9-methano-5H-pyrido [1',2':1,2] azepino [5,4-b] indole; Tabernanthe iboga.
(12) Lysergic acid diethylamide.
(13) Marijuana.
(14) Mescaline.
(15) Peyote—Meaning all parts of the plant presently classified botanically as Lophophora williamsii Lemaire, whether growing or not, the seeds thereof, any extract from any part of such plant, and every compound, manufacture, salts, derivative, mixture, or preparation of such plant, its seeds or extracts (interprets 21 U.S.C. Sec. 812(c), Schedule 1(c)(12)).
(16) N-ethyl-3-piperidyl benzilate.
(17) N-methyl-3-piperidyl benzilate.
(18) Psilocybin.
(19) Psilocyn.
(20) Tetrahydrocannabinols. Synthetic equivalents of the substances contained in the plant, or in the resinous extractives of Cannabis, sp. and/or synthetic substances, derivatives, and their isomers with similar chemical structure and pharmacological activity such as the following: delta 1 cis or trans tetrahydrocannabinol, and their optical isomers; delta 6 cis or trans tetrahydrocannabinol, and their optical isomers; delta 3,4 cis or trans tetrahydrocannabinol, and its optical isomers.

(Since nomenclature of these substances is not internationally standardized, compounds of these

© 1992 by J., B. & L. Gould
Printed in the U.S.A.   **EP**

structures, regardless of numerical designation of atomic positions covered).

(21) Ethylamine analog of phencyclidine—Some trade or other names: N-ethyl-1-phenyl-cyclohexylamine, (1-phenylcyclohexyl) ethylamine, N-(1- phenylcyclohexyl)ethylamine, cyclohexamine, PCE.

(22) Pyrrolidine analog of phencyclidine—Some trade or other names: 1-(1-phenylcyclohexyl)-pyrrolidine, PCPy, PHP.

(23) Thiophene analog of phencyclidine—Some trade or other names: 1[1-(2 thienyl)-cyclohexyl]-piperidine,2-thienyl analog of phencyclidine, TPCP, TCP.

(e) Depressants. Unless specifically excepted or unless listed in another schedule, any material, compound, mixture, or preparation which contains any quantity of the following substances having a depressant effect on the central nervous system, including its salts, isomers, and salts of isomers whenever the existence of those salts, isomers, and salts of isomers is possible within the specific chemical designation:

(1) Mecloqualone.

(2) Methaqualone.

(f) Unless specifically excepted or unless listed in another schedule, any material, compound, mixture, or preparation which contains any quantity of the following substances having a stimulant effect on the central nervous system, including its isomers:

(1) Cocaine base.

(2) Fenethylline, including its salts.

(3) N-Ethylamphetamine, including its salts.
(Amended by Stats 1987 ch 1174 §1.5.)

§11055. Schedule II of controlled substances.

(a) The controlled substances listed in this section are included in Schedule II.

(b) Any of the following substances, except those narcotic drugs listed in other schedules, whether produced directly or indirectly by extraction from substances of vegetable origin, or independently by means of chemical synthesis, or by combination of extraction and chemical synthesis:

(1) Opium and opiate, and any salt, compound, derivative, or preparation of opium or opiate, with the exception of naloxone hydrochloride (N-allyl-14-hydroxy-nordihydromorphinone hydrochloride), but including the following:

(A) Raw opium.

(B) Opium extracts.

(C) Opium fluid extracts.

(D) Powdered opium.

(E) Granulated opium.

(F) Tincture of opium.

(G) Apomorphine.

(H) Codeine.

(I) Ethylmorphine.

(J) Hydrocodone.

(K) Hydromorphone.

(L) Metopon.

(M) Morphine.

(N) Oxycodone.

(O) Oxymorphone.

(P) Thebaine.

(2) Any salt, compound, isomer, or derivative, whether natural or synthetic, of the substances referred to in paragraph (1), but not including the isoquinoline alkaloids of opium.

(3) Opium poppy and poppy straw.

(4) Coca leaves and any salt, compound, derivative, or preparation of coca leaves, but not including decocainized coca leaves or extractions which do not contain cocaine or ecgonine.

(5) Concentrate of poppy straw (the crude extract of poppy straw in either liquid, solid, or powder form which contains the phenanthrene alkaloids of the opium poppy).

(6) Cocaine, except as specified in Section 11054.

(7) Ecgonine, whether natural or synthetic, or any salt, isomer, derivative, or preparation thereof.

(c) Opiates. Unless specifically excepted or unless in another schedule, any of the following opiates, including its isomers, esters, ethers, salts, and salts of isomers, esters, and ethers whenever the existence of those isomers, esters, ethers, and salts is possible within the specific chemical designation, dextrorphan and levopropoxyphene excepted:

(1) Alfentanil.

(2) Alphaprodine.

(3) Anileridine.

(4) Bezitramide.

(5) Bulk dextropropoxyphene (nondosage forms).

(6) Dihydrocodeine.

(7) Diphenoxylate.

(8) Fentanyl.

(9) Isomethadone.

(10) Levomethorphan.

(11) Levorphanol.

(12) Metazocine.

(13) Methadone.

(14) Methadone-Intermediate 4-cyano-2-dimethyl-amino-4, 4- diphenyl butane.

(15) Moramide-Intermediate, 2-methyl-3-morpholino-1, 1- diphenylpropane-carboxylic acid.

(16) Pethidine (meperidine).

(17) Pethidine-Intermediate-A, 4-cyano-1-methyl-4-phenylpiperidine.

(18) Pethidine-Intermediate-B, ethyl-4- phenyl-piperidine-4-carboxylate.

(19) Pethidine-Intermediate-C, 1-methyl-4-phenyl-piperidine-4- carboxylic acid.

(20) Phenazocine.

(21) Piminodine.

(22) Racemethorphan.

(23) Racemorphan.

(24) Sufentanil.

(d) Stimulants. Unless specifically excepted or unless listed in another schedule, any material, compound, mixture, or preparation which contains any quantity of the following substances having a stimulant effect on the central nervous system:

(1) Amphetamine, its salts, optical isomers, and salts of its optical isomers.

(2) Methamphetamine, its salts, isomers, and salts of its isomers.

(3) Dimethylamphetamine (N,N-dimethylamphetamine), its salts, isomers, and salts of its isomers.

(4) N-ethylmethamphetamine (N-ethyl, N-methyl-amphetamine), its salts, isomers, and salts of its isomers.

(5) Phenmetrazine and its salts.

(6) Methylphenidate.

(e) Depressants. Unless specifically excepted or unless listed in another schedule, any material, compound, mixture, or preparation which contains any quantity of the following substances having a depressant effect on the central nervous system, including its salts, isomers, and salts of isomers whenever the existence of those salts, isomers, and salts of isomers is possible within the specific chemical designation:

(1) Amobarbital.

(2) Pentobarbital.

(3) Phencyclidines, including the following:

(A) 1-(1-phenylcyclohexyl) piperidine (PCP).

(B) 1-(1-phenylcyclohexyl) morpholine (PCM).

(C) Any analog of phencyclidine which is added by the Attorney General by regulation pursuant to this paragraph.

The Attorney General, or his or her designee, may, by rule or regulation, add additional analogs of phencyclidine to those enumerated in this paragraph after notice, posting, and hearing pursuant to Chapter 3.5 (commencing with Section 11340) of Part 1 of Division 3 of Title 2 of the Government Code. The Attorney General shall, in the calendar year of the regular session of the Legislature in which the rule or regulation is adopted, submit a draft of a proposed bill to each house of the Legislature which would incorporate the analogs into this code. No rule or regulation shall remain in effect beyond January 1 after the calendar year of the regular session in which the draft of the proposed bill is submitted to each house. However, if the draft of the proposed bill is submitted during a recess of the Legislature exceeding 45 calendar days, the rule or regulation shall be effective until January 1 after the next calendar year.

(4) Secobarbital.

(5) Glutethimide.

(f) Immediate precursors. Unless specifically excepted or unless listed in another schedule, any material, compound, mixture, or preparation which contains any quantity of the following substances:

(1) Immediate precursor to amphetamine and methamphetamine:

(A)* Phenylacetone. Some trade or other names: phenyl-2 propanone; P2P; benzyl methyl ketone; methyl benzyl ketone.

(2) Immediate precursors to phencyclidine (PCP):

(A) 1-phenylcyclohexylamine.

(B) 1-piperidinocyclohexane carbonitrile (PCC).

(g) Hallucinogenic substances. Any of the following hallucinogenic substances: dronabinol (synthetic) in sesame oil and encapsulated in a soft gelatin capsule in a drug product approved by the federal Food and Drug Administration. *(Amended by Stats 1988 ch 712 §1, eff. 8/29/88.)*

*So in original. No subpar. (B) enacted.

§11056. Schedule III of controlled substances.

(a) The controlled substances listed in this section are included in Schedule III.

(b) Stimulants. Unless specifically excepted or unless listed in another schedule, any material, compound, mixture, or preparation which contains any quantity of the following substances having a stimulant effect on the central nervous system, including its salts, isomers (whether optical, position, or geometric), and salts of those isomers whenever the existence of those salts, isomers, and salts of isomers is possible within the specific chemical designation:

(1) Those compounds, mixtures, or preparations in dosage unit form containing any stimulant substances listed in Schedule II which compounds, mixtures, or preparations were listed on August 25, 1971, as excepted compounds under Section 1308.32 of Title 21 of the Code of Federal Regulations, and any other drug of the quantitative composition shown in that list for

those drugs or which is the same except that it contains a lesser quantity of controlled substances.

(2) Benzphetamine.

(3) Chlorphentermine.

(4) Clortermine.

(5) Mazindol.

(6) Phendimetrazine.

(c) Depressants. Unless specifically excepted or unless listed in another schedule, any material, compound, mixture, or preparation which contains any quantity of the following substances having a depressant effect on the central nervous system:

(1) Any compound, mixture, or preparation containing any of the following:

(A) Amobarbital

(B) Secobarbital

(C) Pentobarbital

or any salt thereof and one or more other active medicinal ingredients which are not listed in any schedule.

(2) Any suppository dosage form containing any of the following:

(A) Amobarbital

(B) Secobarbital

(C) Pentobarbital

or any salt of any of these drugs and approved by the federal Food and Drug Administration for marketing only as a suppository.

(3) Any substance which contains any quantity of a derivative of barbituric acid or any salt thereof.

(4) Chlorhexadol.

(5) Lysergic acid.

(6) Lysergic acid amide.

(7) Methyprylon.

(8) Sulfondiethylmethane.

(9) Sulfonethylmethane.

(10) Sulfonmethane.

(d) Nalorphine.

(e) Narcotic drugs. Unless specifically excepted or unless listed in another schedule, any material, compound, mixture, or preparation containing any of the following narcotic drugs, or their salts calculated as the free anhydrous base or alkaloid, in limited quantities as set forth below:

(1) Not more than 1.8 grams of codeine per 100 milliliters or not more than 90 milligrams per dosage unit, with an equal or greater quantity of an isoquinoline alkaloid of opium.

(2) Not more than 1.8 grams of codeine per 100 milliliters or not more than 90 milligrams per dosage unit, with one or more active, nonnarcotic ingredients in recognized therapeutic amounts.

(3) Not more than 300 milligrams of dihydrocodeinone per 100 milliliters or not more than 15 milligrams per dosage unit, with a fourfold or greater quantity of an isoquinoline alkaloid of opium.

(4) Not more than 300 milligrams of dihydrocodeinone per 100 milliliters or not more than 15 milligrams per dosage unit, with one or more active nonnarcotic ingredients in recognized therapeutic amounts. Additionally, oral liquid preparations of dihydrocodeinone containing the above specified amounts may not contain as its nonnarcotic ingredients two or more antihistamines in combination with each other.

(5) Not more than 1.8 grams of dihydrocodeine per 100 milliliters or not more than 90 milligrams per dosage unit, with one or more active nonnarcotic ingredients in recognized therapeutic amounts.

© 1992 by J., B. & L. Gould
Printed in the U.S.A.   **EP**

(6) Not more than 300 milligrams of ethylmorphine per 100 milliliters or not more than 15 milligrams per dosage unit, with one or more active, nonnarcotic ingredients in recognized therapeutic amounts.

(7) Not more than 500 milligrams of opium per 100 milliliters or per 100 grams or not more than 25 milligrams per dosage unit, with one or more active, nonnarcotic ingredients in recognized therapeutic amounts.

(8) Not more than 50 milligrams of morphine per 100 milliliters or per 100 grams, with one or more active, nonnarcotic ingredients in recognized therapeutic amounts.

(f) Anabolic steroids and chorionic gonadotropin. Any material, compound, mixture, or preparation containing chorionic gonadotropin or an anabolic steroid, including, but not limited to, the following:

(1) Androisoxazole.
(2) Androstenediol.
(3) Bolandiol.
(4) Bolasterone.
(5) Boldenone.
(6) Chlormethandienone.
(7) Clostebol.
(8) Dihydromesterone.
(9) Ethylestrenol.
(10) Fluoxymesterone.
(11) Formyldienolone.
(12) 4-Hydroxy-19-nortestosterone.
(13) Mesterolone.
(14) Methandriol.
(15) Methandrostenolone.
(16) Methenolone.
(17) 17-Methyltestosterone.
(18) Methyltrienolone.
(19) Nandrolone.
(20) Norbolethone.
(21) Norethandrolone.
(22) Normethandrolone.
(23) Oxandrolone.
(24) Oxymestrone.
(25) Oxymetholone.
(26) Quinbolone.
(27) Stanolone.
(28) Stanozolol.
(29) Stenbolone.
(30) Testosterone.
(31) Trenbolone.
(32) Chorionic Gonadotropin, (HGC).

(g) Ketamine. Any material, compound, mixture, or preparation containing ketamine. *(Amended by Stats 1991 ch 294 §1, eff 1/1/92.)*

§11057. Schedule IV of controlled substances.

(a) The controlled substances listed in this section are included in Schedule IV.

(b) Schedule IV shall consist of the drugs and other substances, by whatever official name, common or usual name, chemical name, or brand name designated, listed in this section.

(c) Narcotic drugs. Unless specifically excepted or unless listed in another schedule, any material, compound, mixture, or preparation containing any of the following narcotic drugs, or their salts calculated as the free anhydrous base or alkaloid, in limited quantities as set forth below:

(1) Not more than 1 milligram of difenoxin and not less than 25 micrograms of atropine sulfate per dosage unit.

(2) Dextropropoxyphene (alpha-(+)-4-dimethyl-amino-1,2-diphenyl-3- methyl-2-propionoxybutane).

(d) Depressants. Unless specifically excepted or unless listed in another schedule, any material, compound, mixture, or preparation which contains any quantity of the following substances, including its salts, isomers, and salts of isomers whenever the existence of those salts, isomers, and salts of isomers is possible within the specific chemical designation:

(1) Barbital.
(2) Chloral betaine.
(3) Chloral hydrate.
(4) Chlordiazepoxide.
(5) Clonazepam.
(6) Clorazepate.
(7) Diazepam.
(8) Ethchlorvynol.
(9) Ethinamate.
(10) Flurazepam.
(11) Lorazepam.
(12) Mebutamate.
(13) Meprobamate.
(14) Methohexital.
(15) Methylphenobarbital (Mephobarbital).
(16) Oxazepam.
(17) Paraldehyde.
(18) Petrichoral.
(19) Phenobarbital.
(20) Prazepam.

(e) Fenfluramine. Any material, compound, mixture, or preparation which contains any quantity of the following substances, including its salts, isomers (whether optical, position, or geometric), and salts of those isomers, whenever the existence of those salts, isomers, and salts of isomers is possible:

(1)* Fenfluramine.

(f) Stimulants. Unless specifically excepted or unless listed in another schedule, any material, compound, mixture, or preparation which contains any quantity of the following substances having a stimulant effect on the central nervous system, including its salts, isomers (whether optical, position, or geometric), and salts of those isomers is possible within the specific chemical designation:

(1) Diethylpropion.
(2) Phentermine.
(3) Pemoline (including organometallic complexes and chelates thereof).
(4) Pipradrol.
(5) SPA ((—)-1-dimethylamino-1,2-diphenylethane).

(g) Other substances. Unless specifically excepted or unless listed in another schedule, any material, compound, mixture or preparation which contains any quantity of the following substances, including its salts:

(1)* Pentazocine. *(Amended by Stats 1985 ch 290 §2.)*
So in original. No par. (2) enacted.

§11058. Schedule V of controlled substances.

(a) The controlled substances listed in this section are included in Schedule V.

(b) Schedule V shall consist of the drugs and other substances, by whatever official name, common or usual name, chemical name, or brand name designated, listed in this section.

(c) Narcotic drugs containing nonnarcotic active medicinal ingredients. Any compound, mixture, or preparation containing any of the following narcotic drugs, or their salts calculated as the free anhydrous base or alkaloid, in limited quantities as set forth below, which shall include one or more nonnarcotic active medicinal ingredients in sufficient proportion to confer upon the compound, mixture, or preparation valuable medicinal qualities other than those possessed by narcotic drugs alone:

(1) Not more than 200 milligrams of codeine per 100 milliliters or per 100 grams.

(2) Not more than 100 milligrams of dihydrocodeine per 100 milliliters or per 100 grams.

(3) Not more than 100 milligrams of ethylmorphine per 100 milliliters or per 100 grams.

(4) Not more than 2.5 milligrams of diphenoxylate and not less than 25 micrograms of atropine sulfate per dosage unit.

(5) Not more than 100 milligrams of opium per 100 milliliters or per 100 grams.

(6) Not more than 0.5 milligram of difenoxin and not less than 25 micrograms of atropine sulfate per dosage unit.

(d) Buprenorphine. *(Amended by Stats 1986 ch 63 §1.)*

CHAPTER 3

REGULATION AND CONTROL

ARTICLE 1

REPORTING

§11100. Report transactions; exceptions; punishment.

(a) Any manufacturer, wholesaler, retailer, or other person who sells, transfers, or otherwise furnishes any of the following substances to any person in this state shall submit a report to the Department of Justice of all of those transactions:

(1) Phenyl-2-propanone.
(2) Methylamine.
(3) Ethylamine.
(4) D-lysergic acid.
(5) Ergotamine tartrate.
(6) Diethyl malonate.
(7) Malonic acid.
(8) Ethyl malonate.
(9) Barbituric acid.
(10) Piperidine.
(11) N-acetylanthranilic acid.
(12) Pyrrolidine.
(13) Phenylacetic acid.
(14) Anthranilic acid.
(15) Morpholine.
(16) Ephedrine.
(17) Pseudoephedrine.
(18) Norpseudoephedrine.
(19) Phenylpropanolamine.
(20) Propionic anhydride.
(21) Isosafrole.
(22) Safrole.
(23) Piperonal.
(24) Thionylchloride.
(25) Benzyl cyanide.
(26) Ergonovine maleate.
(27) N-methylephedrine.
(28) N-ethylephedrine.
(29) N-methypseudoephedrine.
(30) N-ethylpseudoephedrine.

(31) Chloroephedrine.
(32) Chloropseudoephedrine.
(33) Any of the substances listed by the Department of Justice in regulations promulgated pursuant to subdivision (b).

(b) The Department of Justice may adopt rules and regulations in accordance with Chapter 3.5 (commencing with Section 11340) of Part 1 of Division 3 of Title 2 of the Government Code that add substances to subdivision (a) if the substance is a precursor to a controlled substance and delete substances from subdivision (a). However, no regulation adding or deleting a substance shall have any effect beyond March 1 of the year following the calendar year during which the regulation was adopted.

(c)(1) Any manufacturer, wholesaler, retailer, or other person shall, prior to selling, transferring, or otherwise furnishing any substance specified in subdivision (a) to a person in this state, require proper identification from the purchaser.

(2) For the purposes of this subdivision, "proper identification" means a valid motor vehicle operator's license or other official and valid state-issued identification of the purchaser which contains a photograph of the purchaser, and includes the residential or mailing address of the purchaser, other than a post office box number, the motor vehicle license number of any motor vehicle owned or operated by the purchaser, a letter of authorization from the business for which any substance specified in subdivision (a) is being furnished, which includes the business license number and address of the business, a full description of how the substance is to be used, and the signature of the purchaser. The person selling, transferring, or otherwise furnishing any substance specified in subdivision (a) shall affix his or her signature as a witness to the signature and identification of the purchaser.

(3) A violation of this subdivision is a misdemeanor.

(d) Any manufacturer, wholesaler, retailer, or other person who sells, transfers, or otherwise furnishes a substance specified in subdivision (a) to a person in this state shall, not less than 21 days prior to delivery of the substance, submit a report of the transaction, which includes the identification information specified in subdivision (c), to the Department of Justice. However, the Department of Justice may authorize the submission of the reports on a monthly basis with respect to repeated, regular transactions between the furnisher and the recipient involving the same substance if the Department of Justice determines that either of the following exist:

(1) A pattern of regular supply of the substance exists between the manufacturer, wholesaler, retailer, or other person who sells, transfers, or otherwise furnishes such substance and the recipient of the substance.

(2) The recipient has established a record of utilization of the substance for lawful purposes.

(e) This section shall not apply to any of the following:

(1) Any pharmacist or other authorized person who sells or furnishes a substance upon the prescription of a physician, dentist, podiatrist, or veterinarian.

(2) Any physician, dentist, podiatrist, or veterinarian who administers or furnishes a substance to his or her patients.

(3) Any manufacturer or wholesaler licensed by the California State Board of Pharmacy who sells,

© 1992 by J., B. & L. Gould
Printed in the U.S.A.   **EP**

transfers, or otherwise furnishes a substance to a licensed pharmacy, physician, dentist, podiatrist, or veterinarian.

(4) Any sale, transfer, furnishing, or receipt of any drug which contains ephedrine, pseudoephedrine, norpseudoephedrine, or phenylpropanolamine and which is lawfully sold, transferred, or furnished over the counter without a prescription pursuant to the federal Food, Drug, and Cosmetic Act (21 U.S.C. Sec. 301 et seq.) or regulations adopted thereunder.

(f)(1) Any person specified in subdivision (d) who does not submit a report as required by that subdivision or who knowingly submits a report with false or fictitious information shall be punished by imprisonment in the county jail not exceeding six months, by a fine not exceeding five thousand dollars ($5,000), or by both the fine and imprisonment.

(2) Any person specified in subdivision (d) who has previously been convicted of a violation of paragraph (1) shall, upon a subsequent conviction thereof, be punished by imprisonment in the state prison, or by imprisonment in the county jail not exceeding one year, by a fine not exceeding one hundred thousand dollars ($100,000), or by both the fine and imprisonment.

(g)(1) It is unlawful for any manufacturer, wholesaler, retailer, or other person to sell, transfer, or otherwise furnish a substance specified in subdivision (a) to a person under 18 years of age.

(2) It is unlawful for any person under 18 years of age to possess a substance specified in subdivision (a).

(3) A violation of this subdivision is a misdemeanor. *(Amended by Stats 1989 ch 1133 §1, eff. 1/1/90.)*

§11100.05. Impose drug cleanup fine.

(a) In addition to any fine or imprisonment imposed under subdivision (f) of Section 11100 or subdivision (f) of Section 11106 of the Health and Safety Code, the following drug cleanup fine shall be imposed:

(1) Ten thousand dollars ($10,000) for violations described in paragraph (1) of subdivision (f) of Section 11100.

(2) One hundred thousand dollars ($100,000) for violations described in paragraph (2) of subdivision (f) of Section 11100.

(3) Ten thousand dollars ($10,000) for violations described in subdivision (f) of Section 11106.

(b) At least once a month, all fines collected under this section shall be transferred to the State Treasury for deposit in the Clandestine Drug Lab Clean-up Account. The transmission to the State Treasury shall be carried out in the same manner as fines collected for the state by a county. *(Added by Stats 1987 ch 1295 §1.)*

§11100.1. Report on receiving substances from outside sources; punishment for failure to report.

(a) Any manufacturer, wholesaler, retailer, or other person who receives from a source outside of this state any substance specified in subdivision (a) of Section 11100 shall submit a report of that transaction to the Department of Justice 21 days in advance of receipt of the substance. However, the Department of Justice may authorize the submission of reports within 72 hours after the actual physical receipt of a specified substance with respect to repeated transactions between a furnisher and a recipient involving the same substance, if the Department of Justice determines that the recipient has established a record of utilization of the substance for lawful purposes. This section does not apply to any person whose prescribing or dispensing activities are subject to the reporting requirements set forth in Section 11164.

(b)(1) Any person specified in subdivision (a) who does not submit a report as required by that subdivision shall be punished by imprisonment in the county jail not exceeding six months, by a fine not exceeding five thousand dollars ($5,000), or by both that fine and imprisonment.

(2) Any person specified in subdivision (a) who has been previously convicted of a violation of subdivision (a) who subsequently does not submit a report as required by subdivision (a) shall be punished by imprisonment in the state prison, or by imprisonment in the county jail not exceeding one year, by a fine not exceeding one hundred thousand dollars ($100,000), or by both that fine and imprisonment. *(Amended by Stats 1989 ch 1133 §2, eff. 1/1/90.)*

§11101. Reporting form.

The State Department of Justice shall provide a common reporting form for the substances in Section 11100 which contains at least the following information:

(a) Name of the substance.

(b) Quantity of the substance sold, transferred, or furnished.

(c) The date the substance was sold, transferred, or furnished.

(d) The name and address of the person buying or receiving such substance.

(e) The name and address of the manufacturer, wholesaler, retailer, or other person selling, transferring, or furnishing such substance.

§11102. Adopt regulations.

The Department of Justice may adopt all regulations necessary to carry out the provisions of this part.

§11103. Reports of theft or loss; discrepancies.

The theft or loss of any substance regulated pursuant to Section 11100 discovered by any licensee or any person regulated by the provisions of this chapter shall be reported to the Department of Justice within three days after such discovery.

Any difference between the quantity of any substance regulated pursuant to Section 11100 received and the quantity shipped shall be reported to the Department of Justice within three days of the receipt of actual knowledge of the discrepancy.

Any report made pursuant to this section shall also include the name of the common carrier or person who transports the substance and date of shipment of the substance.

§11104. Providing §11100(a) substances for unlawful manufacturing; punishment.

Any manufacturer, wholesaler, retailer, or other person who sells, transfers, or otherwise furnishes any of the substances listed in subdivision (a) of Section 11100 with knowledge or the intent that the recipient will use the substance to unlawfully manufacture a controlled substance is guilty of a felony.

§11105. Making false statements in report; penalty.

(a) It is unlawful for any person to knowingly make a false statement in connection with any report or record required under this article.

(b)(1) Any person who violates this section shall be punished by imprisonment in the state prison, or by imprisonment in the county jail not exceeding one year, or by a fine not exceeding five thousand dollars ($5,000), or by both such fine and imprisonment.

(2) Any person who has been previously convicted of violating this section and who subsequently violates this section shall be punished by imprisonment in the state prison for two, three, or four years, or by a fine not exceeding one hundred thousand dollars ($100,000), or by both such fine and imprisonment.

§11106. Permit in order to conduct business; exceptions; application fee.

(a) Any manufacturer, wholesaler, retailer, or other person who sells, transfers, or otherwise furnishes any substance specified in subdivision (a) of Section 11100 to a person in this state or who receives from a source outside of the state any substance specified in subdivision (a) of Section 11100 shall obtain a permit for the conduct of that business from the Department of Justice. However, no permit shall be required of any manufacturer, wholesaler, retailer, or other person for the sale, transfer, furnishing, or receipt of any drug which contains ephedrine, pseudo-ephedrine, norpseudoephedrine, or phenylpropanolamine and which is lawfully sold, transferred, or furnished over the counter without a prescription or by a prescription pursuant to the federal Food, Drug, and Cosmetic Act (21 U.S.C. Sec. 301 et seq.) or regulations adopted thereunder.

(b) Applications for permits shall be filed in writing and signed by the applicant, and shall set forth the name of the applicant, the business in which the applicant is engaged, the business address of the applicant, and a full description of any substance sold, transferred, or otherwise furnished, or received.

(c) The department may grant permits on forms prescribed by it, which shall be effective for not more than one year from the date of issuance. Applications and permits shall be uniform throughout the state, on forms prescribed by the department.

(d) Each applicant shall pay at the time of filing an application for a permit a fee determined by the department which shall not exceed the application processing costs of the department.

(e) A permit granted pursuant to this article may be renewed one year from the date of issuance, and annually thereafter, upon the filing of a renewal application and the payment of a permit renewal fee not to exceed the application processing costs of the department.

(f) Selling, transferring, or otherwise furnishing, or receiving any substance specified in subdivision (a) of Section 11100 without a permit, is a misdemeanor or a felony.

(g)(1) No person under 18 years of age shall be eligible for a permit under this section.

(2) No business for which a permit has been issued shall employ a person under 18 years of age in the capacity of a manager, agent, or representative.

(h)(1) An applicant for an initial permit shall submit with the application two sets of 10-print fingerprint cards for each individual acting in the capacity of an owner, manager, agent, or representative for the applicant.

(2) In the event of subsequent changes in ownership, management, or employment, the applicant shall submit two sets of 10-print fingerprint cards for each individual not previously fingerprinted under this section. *(Amended by Stats 1989 ch 1133 §3, eff. 1/1/90.)*

§11107. Identification required for purchase of chemical apparatus and reagents; definitions.

(a) Any manufacturer, wholesaler, retailer, or other person who sells to any person in this state any laboratory glassware or apparatus, any chemical reagent or solvent, or any combination thereof, where the value of the goods sold in the transaction exceeds one hundred dollars ($100) and the payment for the goods is made in cash or by cashiers check shall do the following:

(1) Require proper purchaser identification as specified in paragraph (2) of subdivision (c) of Section 11100. The person selling, transferring, or otherwise furnishing the goods specified in this section shall enter the proper purchaser identification information onto the bill of sale or a legible copy of the bill of sale and shall also affix his or her signature as witness to the identification of the purchaser.

(2) Retain the bill of sale or the legible copy of the bill of sale containing the purchaser identification information for three years in a readily presentable manner, and present the bill of sale or the legible copy of the bill of sale containing the purchaser identification information upon demand by any law enforcement officer or authorized representative of the Attorney General.

(b) A violation of this section is a misdemeanor.

(c) For the purposes of this section, the following terms have the following meanings:

(1) "Laboratory glassware" includes, but is not limited to, condensors, flasks, separatory funnels, and beakers.

(2) "Apparatus" includes, but is not limited to, heating mantles, ring stands, and rheostats.

(3) "Chemical reagent" means a chemical that reacts chemically with one or more precursors, but does not become part of the finished product.

(4) "Chemical solvent" means a chemical that does not react chemically with a precursor or reagent and does not become part of the finished product. A "chemical solvent" helps other chemicals mix, cools chemical reactions, and cleans the finished product. *(Added by Stats 1989 ch 1133 §4, ef. 1/1/90.)*

§11107.1. Identification required for purchase of certain chemical reagents.

(a) Any manufacturer, wholesaler, retailer, or other person who sells to any person in this state any quantity of sodium cyanide, potassium cyanide, cyclohexanone, bromobenzene, magnesium turnings, mercuric choloride, sodium metal, lead acetate, paladium black, red phosphorous, Refrigerant 11, Refrigerant 12, sodium acetate, or acetic anhydride shall do the following:

(1) Require proper purchaser identification as specified in paragraph (2) of subdivision (c) of Section 11100. The person selling, transferring, or otherwise furnishing the substances specified in this section shall enter the proper purchaser identification information onto the bill of sale or a legible copy of the bill

© 1992 by J., B. & L. Gould
Printed in the U.S.A.   **EP**

of sale and shall also affix his or her signature as witness to the identification of the purchaser.

(2) Retain the bill of sale or the legible copy of the bill of sale containing the purchaser identification information for three years in a readily presentable manner, and present the bill of sale or the legible copy of the bill of sale containing the purchaser identification information upon demand by any law enforcement officer or authorized representative of the Attorney General.

(b) A violation of this section is a misdemeanor. *(Amended by Stats 1990 ch 352 §1, eff. 1/1/91.)*

ARTICLE 2

LICENSES; CUSTOMS BROKERS AND WAREHOUSES

§11122. Storage of controlled substance in licensed warehouse.

(a) A controlled substance shall be stored only in a warehouse which is licensed by the Board of Pharmacy.

(b) This section shall not apply to any of the following:

(1) Any pharmacy or other person who is licensed or authorized by this state to sell or furnish the controlled substance upon the written prescription of a practitioner, as defined in subdivision (a) of Section 11026.

(2) Any practitioner, as defined in subdivision (a) of Section 11026, who possesses a controlled substance for administration to his or her patients.

(3) Any licensed laboratory in this state which is authorized to receive and use the controlled substance.

(4) Any licensed hospital in this state.

(5) Any person who obtains the controlled substance upon the prescription of a practitioner, as defined in subdivision (a) of Section 11026, for his or her personal use.

(6) Any agent or employee of any licensed manufacturer or wholesaler who possesses the controlled substance for display purposes or furnishes controlled substances as a sample at no cost to a licensed pharmacist or practitioner, as defined in subdivision (a) of Section 11026.

(7) A manufacturer licensed pursuant to Section 26685 of this code or Section 4084 or 4084.6 of the Business and Professions Code.

(8) A wholesaler licensed pursuant to Section 4084 or 4084.6 of the Business and Professions Code.

(9) Any emergency medical technician-II, emergency medical technician-paramedic, or mobile intensive care nurse, certified or authorized pursuant to Division 2.5 (commencing with Section 1797) to provide prehospital limited advanced life support or advanced life support as part of a local emergency medical services system, who, in a secure manner and according to policies and procedures established by the local emergency medical services agency as part of the local emergency medical services plan, transports, stores, or administers controlled substances acting within his or her scope of practice.

(10) Any emergency medical response or transport unit which has been approved by the local emergency medical services agency and is operating as part of the local emergency medical services system according to policies and procedures established by the local medical services agency for the emergency medical treatment and transport of patients, upon which, controlled

substances authorized by the scope of practice of the prehospital personnel approved to staff the unit are stored or transported in a secure manner according to policies and procedures established by the local emergency medical services agency. *(Amended by Stats 1986 ch 1042 §4.)*

§11123. Issuing warehouse license; regulations.

(a) Upon application, the Board of Pharmacy may issue a license to store controlled substances to a warehouseman who maintains a warehouse suitable for the proper storage of the controlled substances.

(b) The Board of Pharmacy shall by regulation establish security measures in order to prevent unauthorized persons from gaining access to any area, place or premises in which controlled substances are stored, kept or maintained. Prior to the issuance of a license under this article, the Board of Pharmacy shall inspect an applicant's establishment to determine compliance with security regulations adopted by the Board of Pharmacy.

(c) As a condition to the granting of the license, the warehouseman shall agree to comply with the provisions of this division and any rules and regulations which are adopted by the Board of Pharmacy.

§11124. Maintain inventory of stored controlled substances.

On or before the effective date of this chapter, each licensed warehouseman shall make a complete and accurate record of all stocks of such controlled substances on hand. Thereafter, a current inventory shall be kept and preserved for at least two years from the date of making such inventory. Records and inventories shall contain such information as shall be provided by the rules and regulations promulgated by the Board of Pharmacy.

Such records shall be submitted in summary form to the Board of Pharmacy on or before July 1, 1973, and every two years thereafter.

The Board of Pharmacy shall have the right to inspect such records at the business office of the licensee at any time during business hours.

§11125. Warehouseman to file bond with Board of Pharmacy.

Each warehouseman who applies for a license to store a controlled substance shall execute and file with the Board of Pharmacy a bond to the state as a condition to the granting of the license. The bond shall secure the faithful performance of the warehouseman of his obligations under the laws of the state and the rules and regulations which are adopted pursuant to this division and such additional obligations which he may assume under a contract with the depositor of the drug. The Board of Pharmacy may prescribe the form, amount, terms, and conditions of the bond.

§11127. Application; power to issue and renew licenses.

(a) The provisions of this article shall apply only to licenses issued by the Board of Pharmacy for warehouses which store controlled substances.

(b) The Board of Pharmacy shall have authority to issue licenses for warehouses which store controlled substances. Such licenses shall be issued in accordance with the provisions of this chapter and regulations adopted by the board pursuant thereto. All licenses issued by the Board of Pharmacy shall expire one year from the date of issue. Licenses may be renewed upon application and payment of the renewal fees if the application for renewal is made within the 30-day period prior to the date of expiration. Persons whose licenses have expired shall immediately cease the activity requiring a license, but the Board of Pharmacy shall accept applications for renewal during the 30-day period following the date of expiration if they are accompanied by the new license fee. In no case shall a license be renewed where the application is received more than 30 days after the date of expiration.

(c) Each application for a new or renewal license shall be accompanied by a fee which shall be fixed by the Board of Pharmacy at an amount not to exceed two hundred dollars ($200). The application shall be made upon a form furnished by the Board of Pharmacy. It shall contain such information concerning the background of the applicant and his experience which the Board of Pharmacy may prescribe, in addition to any other information required by law.

§11128. Licenses not transferable.

(a) Licenses issued by the Board of Pharmacy shall not be transferable.

(b) In the event of a change of name, not involving a change of ownership, or a change of address of the licensee, the license shall be returned to the board for cancellation, and a new license application form shall be submitted. The Board of Pharmacy shall cancel the returned license and issue a new license for the unexpired term without fee.

§11129. Suspension or revocation of license.

(a) Any license issued may be suspended or revoked by the Board of Pharmacy. The Board of Pharmacy may refuse to issue a license to any applicant for the reasons set forth in subdivision (b).

The proceedings under this chapter shall be conducted in accordance with Chapter 5 (commencing with Section 11500) of Part 1 of Division 3 of Title 2 of the Government Code, and the Board of Pharmacy shall have all the powers granted therein.

(b) The Board of Pharmacy may deny a license if the applicant does or has done any of the following:

(1) Fails to meet the qualifications established by the Board of Pharmacy pursuant to this chapter for the issuance of the license applied for.

(2) Was previously the holder of a license issued under this chapter which has been revoked and never reissued or was suspended and the terms of the suspension have not been fulfilled.

(3) Has committed any act which, if committed by any licensee, would be grounds for the suspension or revocation of a license issued pursuant to this chapter.

(4) Has committed any act involving dishonesty, fraud, or deceit whereby another is injured or the applicant has benefited.

(5) Has acted in the capacity of a licensed person under this division without having a license therefor.

(6) Has entered a plea of guilty or nolo contendere to, or has been found guilty or convicted of, a felony or a crime involving moral turpitude and the time for appeal has elapsed or the judgment of conviction has been affirmed on appeal, irrespective of an order granting probation following the conviction or suspending the imposition of sentence, or of a subsequent order under the provisions of Section 1203.4 of the Penal Code allowing the person to withdraw his plea of guilty and to enter a plea of not guilty, setting

aside the plea or verdict of guilty, or dismissing the accusation, information, or indictment.

(7) Violated any of the provisions of this division.

§11130. Disciplinary actions for violations by licensee.

The Board of Pharmacy may suspend, revoke, or take other disciplinary action against a license as provided in this chapter if the licensee does any of the following:

(a) Violates any section of this division which relates to his licensed activities.

(b) Is convicted of any felony.

(c) Violates any of the regulations promulgated by the Board of Pharmacy pursuant to this chapter.

(d) Has misrepresented a material fact in obtaining a license.

(e) Aids or abets an unlicensed person to evade the provisions of this division.

(f) Fails to make and keep records showing his transactions as a licensee, or fails to have such records available for inspection by the Board of Pharmacy for a period of not less than three years after completion of any transaction to which the records refer, or refuses to comply with a written request of the Board of Pharmacy to make such records available for inspection.

(g) Violates or attempts to violate the provisions of this division relating to the particular activity for which he is licensed.

(h) Fails to send a copy of the monthly reporting form to the Board of Pharmacy as required by the provisions of this chapter.

§11131. Suspension or revocation of license upon conviction.

A plea or verdict of guilty or a conviction following a plea of nolo contendere is deemed to be a conviction within the meaning of this chapter. The Board of Pharmacy may order the license suspended or revoked, or may decline to issue a license, when the time for appeal has elapsed, the judgment of conviction has been affirmed on appeal, or an order granting probation is made suspending the imposition of sentence, irrespective of a subsequent order under the provisions of Section 1203.4 of the Penal Code allowing such person to withdraw his plea of guilty and to enter a plea of not guilty, setting aside the verdict of guilty, or dismissing the accusation, information, or indictment.

§11132. Forms of disciplinary action.

The Board of Pharmacy may take disciplinary action against any licensee, after a hearing as provided in this chapter, by any of the following:

(a) Imposing probation upon terms and conditions to be set forth by the Board of Pharmacy.

(b) Suspending the license.

(c) Revoking the license.

§11133. Investigation or disciplinary proceedings upon expiration, suspension or surrender of license.

The expiration or suspension of a license by operation of law or by order or decision of the board or a court, or the voluntary surrender of a license by a licensee, shall not deprive the Board of Pharmacy of jurisdiction to proceed with any investigation of, or action or disciplinary proceedings against, the licensee, or to render a decision suspending or revoking the license.

© 1992 by J., B. & L. Gould
Printed in the U.S.A.   **EP**

§11134. Time limitations.

All accusations against licensees shall be filed within three years after the act or omission alleged as the ground for disciplinary action.

§11135. Suspension or revocation of additional licenses.

When any license has been revoked or suspended following a hearing under the provisions of this chapter, any additional license issued under this chapter in the name of the licensee may also be revoked or suspended by the Board of Pharmacy.

§11136. Time period for reinstating suspended or revoked license.

After suspension of the license upon any of the grounds set forth in this chapter, the Board of Pharmacy may reinstate the license upon proof of compliance by the applicant with all provisions of the decision as to reinstatement. After revocation of a license upon any of the grounds set forth in this chapter, the license shall not be reinstated or reissued within a period of one year after the effective date of revocation.

ARTICLE 3

REGISTRATION OF DEALERS AND USERS OF PIPERIDINE

§11140. System of registration; regulations; violations.

(a) The sheriff of each county, in accordance with regulations of the Attorney General, shall maintain a system of registration for persons who sell, purchase, or possess piperidine within the incorporated or unincorporated territory of the county. The regulations of the Attorney General shall prescribe uniform criteria for the issuance of registrations under this article, and shall include a standardized application form and the form of certificates evidencing registration. It shall be unlawful for any person to knowingly sell, purchase, or possess piperidine without having a valid and subsisting registration pursuant to this section. It shall be unlawful for any person to knowingly sell piperidine to, or to purchase piperidine from, any other person who does not possess a valid and subsisting registration to engage in the transaction.

(b) A person convicted of a second or subsequent violation of this section shall be punished by imprisonment in the county jail for a period of six months or by imprisonment in the state prison.

(c) The sheriff shall require registrants to comply with the reasonable conditions of registration as may be required by regulations of the Attorney General to prevent diversion of piperidine for the unlawful manufacture of phencyclidine. The sheriff may revoke the registration of any registrant who fails to comply with a condition of registration.

(d) The sheriff may require a fee for each registration under this section for the purpose of defraying the costs of administering this article. The fees shall not exceed one hundred dollars ($100).

(e) Nothing in this section shall require a person registered to sell, purchase, or possess piperidine in one county to obtain additional registration in order to sell, purchase, or possess piperidine in another county. (*Amended by Stats 1990 ch 350 §5, eff. 1/1/91.*)

CHAPTER 4

PRESCRIPTIONS

ARTICLE 1

REQUIREMENTS OF PRESCRIPTIONS

§11150. Authorization to issue prescriptions.

No person other than a physician, dentist, podiatrist, or veterinarian, or pharmacist acting within the scope of a project authorized under Article 18 (commencing with Section 429.70) of Chapter 2 of Part 1 of Division 1, or registered nurse acting within the scope of a project authorized under Article 18 (commencing with Section 429.70) of Chapter 2 of Part 1 of Division 1, or physician's assistant acting within the scope of a project authorized under Article 18 (commencing with Section 429.70) of Chapter 2 of Part 1 of Division 1 or out-of-state prescriber pursuant to Section 4008 of the Business and Professions Code shall write or issue a prescription.

§11150.6. Classification of methaqualone.

Notwithstanding Section 11150.5 or subdivision (a) of Section 11054, methaqualone, it* salts, isomers, and salts of its isomers shall be deemed to be classified in Schedule I for the purposes of this chapter.
So in original. Probably should be "its".

§11151. Prescriptions written by unlicensed person authorized to practice.

A prescription written by an unlicensed person lawfully practicing medicine pursuant to Section 2065 of the Business and Professions Code, shall be filled only at a pharmacy maintained in the hospital which employs such unlicensed person.

§11152. Prescription requirement.

No person shall write, issue, fill, compound, or dispense a prescription that does not conform to this division.

§11153. Issuing prescription for controlled substances.

(a) A prescription for a controlled substance shall only be issued for a legitimate medical purpose by an individual practitioner acting in the usual course of his or her professional practice. The responsibility for the proper prescribing and dispensing of controlled substances is upon the prescribing practitioner, but a corresponding responsibility rests with the pharmacist who fills the prescription. Except as authorized by this division, the following are not legal prescriptions: (1) an order purporting to be a prescription which is issued not in the usual course of professional treatment or in legitimate and authorized research; or (2) an order for an addict or habitual user of controlled substances, which is issued not in the course of professional treatment or as part of an authorized methadone maintenance program, for the purpose of providing the user with controlled substances, sufficient to keep him or her comfortable by maintaining customary use.

(b) Any person who knowingly violates this section shall be punished by imprisonment in the state prison or in the county jail not exceeding one year, or by a fine not exceeding twenty thousand dollars ($20,000), or by both a fine and imprisonment.

(c) No provision of the amendments to this section enacted during the second year of the 1981-82 Regular Session shall be construed as expanding the scope of practice of a pharmacist.

§11153.5. Furnishing controlled substances for illegitimate purposes; violations.

(a) No wholesaler or manufacturer, or agent or employee of a wholesaler or manufacturer, shall furnish controlled substances for other than legitimate medical purposes.

(b) Anyone who violates this section knowing or having a conscious disregard for the fact, that the controlled substances are for other than a legitimate medical purpose shall be punishable by imprisonment in the state prison, or in the county jail not exceeding one year, or by a fine not exceeding twenty thousand dollars ($20,000), or by both a fine and imprisonment.

(c) Factors to be considered in determining whether a wholesaler or manufacturer, or agent or employee of a wholesaler or manufacturer, furnished controlled substances knowing or having a conscious disregard for the fact that the controlled substances are for other than legitimate medical purposes shall include, but not be limited to, whether the use of controlled substances was for purposes of increasing athletic ability or performance, the amount of controlled substances furnished, the previous ordering pattern of the customer (including size and frequency of orders), the type and size of the customer, and where and to whom the customer distributes the product. *(Amended by Stats 1988 ch 918 §5, eff. 1/1/89.)*

§11154. Restrictions for administering prescriptions.

(a) Except in the regular practice of his or her profession, no person shall knowingly prescribe, administer, dispense, or furnish a controlled substance to or for any person or animal which is not under his or her treatment for a pathology or condition other than addiction to a controlled substance, except as provided in this division.

(b) No person shall knowingly solicit, direct, induce, aid, or encourage a practitioner authorized to write a prescription to unlawfully prescribe, administer, dispense, or furnish a controlled substance.

§11155. Physicians who surrender controlled substance privileges.

Any physician, who by court order or order of any state or governmental agency, or who voluntarily surrenders his controlled substance privileges, shall not possess, administer, dispense, or prescribe a controlled substance unless and until such privileges have been restored, and he has obtained current registration from the appropriate federal agency as provided by law.

§11156. Prohibiting prescription to addicts.

No person shall prescribe for or administer, or dispense a controlled substance to an addict or habitual user, or to any person representing himself as such, except as permitted by this division.

§11157. False prescriptions.

No person shall issue a prescription that is false or fictitious in any respect.

§11158. Dispensing prescriptions for schedule II, III, IV and V substances.

(a) Except as provided in Section 11159 or in subdivision (b) of this section, no controlled substance classified in Schedule II shall be dispensed without a prescription meeting the requirements of this chapter. Except as provided in Section 11159 or when dispensed directly to an ultimate user by a practitioner, other than a pharmacist or pharmacy, no controlled substance classified in Schedule III, IV, or V may be dispensed without a prescription meeting the requirements of this chapter.

(b) A practitioner specified in Section 11150 may dispense directly to an ultimate user a controlled substance classified in Schedule II in an amount not to exceed a 72-hour supply for the patient in accordance with directions for use given by the dispensing practitioner only where the patient is not expected to require any additional amount of the controlled substance beyond the 72 hours. Practitioners dispensing drugs pursuant to this subdivision shall meet the requirements of subdivision (f) of Section 11164.

(c) Except as otherwise prohibited or limited by law, a practitioner specified in Section 11150, may administer controlled substances in the regular practice of his or her profession.

§11159. Order for controlled substance use by hospital patient.

An order for controlled substances for use by a patient in a county or licensed hospital shall be exempt from all requirements of this article, but shall be in writing on the patient's record, signed by the prescriber, dated, and shall state the name and quantity of the controlled substance ordered and the quantity actually administered. The record of such orders shall be maintained as a hospital record for a minimum of seven years.

§11159.1. Order for controlled substances in clinics.

An order for controlled substances furnished to a patient in a clinic which has a permit issued pursuant to Article 3.5 (commencing with Section 4063) of Chapter 9 of Division 2 of the Business and Professions Code, except an order for a Schedule II controlled substance, shall be exempt from the prescription requirements of this article but shall be in writing on the patient's record, signed by the prescriber, dated, and shall state the name and quantity of the controlled substance ordered and the quantity actually furnished. The record of the order shall be maintained as a clinic record for a minimum of seven years. This section shall apply only to a clinic that has obtained a permit under the provisions of Article 3.5 (commencing with Section 4063) of Chapter 9 of Division 2 of the Business and Professions Code.

Clinics that furnish controlled substances shall be required to keep a separate record of the furnishing of those drugs which shall be available for review and inspection by all properly authorized personnel.

§11161. Issuing prescription blanks; unauthorized possession; violations.

(a) Prescription blanks shall be issued by the Department of Justice in serially numbered groups of not more than 100 forms each in triplicate, and shall be furnished to any practitioner authorized to write a prescription for controlled substances classified in

© 1992 by J., B. & L. Gould
Printed in the U.S.A. **EP**

Schedule II. The Department of Justice may charge a fee for the prescription blanks, not to exceed the actual costs of printing and distribution. The prescription blanks shall not be transferable. The Department of Justice shall not, during any 30-day period, issue more than 100 triplicate prescription blanks to any authorized practitioner, until written justification has been received and approved by the Department of Justice. Any person possessing a triplicate prescription blank otherwise than as provided in this section is guilty of a misdemeanor.

(b) When a practitioner is named in a warrant of arrest or is charged in an accusatory pleading with a felony violation of Section 11153, 11154, 11156, 11157, 11170, 11173, 11350, 11351, 11352, 11353, 11353.5, 11377, 11378, 11378.5, 11379, 11379.5, or 11379.6, the court in which the accusatory pleading is filed or the magistrate who issued the warrant of arrest shall, upon the motion of a law enforcement agency which is supported by reasonable cause, issue an order which requires the practitioner to surrender to the clerk of the court all triplicate prescription blanks in the practitioner's possession at a time set in the order and shall direct the Department of Justice to withhold prescription blanks from the practitioner. The law enforcement agency obtaining the order shall notify the Department of Justice of this order. Except as provided in subdivisions (c) and (f) of this section, the order shall remain in effect until further order of the court. Any practitioner possessing prescription blanks in violation of the order is guilty of a misdemeanor.

(c) The order provided by subdivision (b) shall be vacated if the court or magistrate finds that the underlying violation or violations are not supported by reasonable cause at a hearing held within two court days after the practitioner files and personally serves upon the prosecuting attorney and the law enforcement agency that obtained the order, a notice of motion to vacate the order with any affidavits on which the practitioner relies. At the hearing, the burden of proof, by a preponderance of the evidence, is on the prosecution. Evidence presented at the hearing shall be limited to the warrant of arrest with supporting affidavits, the motion to require the defendant to surrender all triplicate prescription blanks with supporting affidavits, the sworn complaint together with any documents or reports incorporated by reference thereto which if based on information and belief state the basis for the information, or any other documents of similar reliability as well as affidavits and counter affidavits submitted by the prosecution and defense. Granting of the motion to vacate the order is no bar to prosecution of the alleged violation or violations.

(d) The defendant may elect to challenge the order issued under subdivision (b) at the preliminary examination. At that hearing, the evidence shall be limited to that set forth in subdivision (c) and any other evidence otherwise admissible at the preliminary examination.

(e) If the practitioner has not moved to vacate the order issued under subdivision (b) of this section by the time of the preliminary examination and he or she is held to answer on the underlying violation or violations, the practitioner shall be precluded from afterwards moving to vacate the order. If the defendant is not held to answer on the underlying charge or charges at the conclusion of the preliminary examination, the order issued under subdivision (b) shall be vacated.

(f) Notwithstanding subdivision (e), any practitioner who is diverted pursuant to Chapter 2.5 (commencing with Section 1000) of Title 7 of Part 2 of the Penal Code may file a motion to vacate the order issued under subdivision (b). *(Amended by Stats 1988 ch 639 §1, eff. 1/1/89.)*

§11162. Format and contents of prescription blanks.

The prescription blanks shall be printed on distinctive paper, the serial number of the group being shown on each form, and each form being serially numbered. The prescription blanks shall bear the preprinted name, address, and category of professional licensure of the practitioner to whom they are issued, and the federal registry number for controlled substances. *(Amended by Stats 1988 ch 398 §1, eff. 1/1/89.)*

§11162.5. Counterfeit prescription blanks; penalty.

(a) Every person who counterfeits a prescription blank purporting to be an official prescription blank prepared and issued pursuant to Section 11161, or knowingly possesses more than three such counterfeited prescription blanks, shall be punished by imprisonment in the state prison or by imprisonment in the county jail for not more than one year.

(b) Every person who knowingly possesses three or fewer counterfeited prescription blanks purporting to be official prescription blanks prepared and issued pursuant to Section 11161, shall be guilty of a misdemeanor punishable by imprisonment in the county jail not exceeding six months, or by a fine not exceeding one thousand dollars ($1,000), or by both.

§11163. One prescription group per prescriber.

Not more than one such prescription group shall in any case be issued or furnished by the Department of Justice to the same prescriber at one time.

§11164. Regulations to comply with in issuing prescriptions for schedule II, III, IV and V controlled substances.

Except as provided in Section 11167, no person shall prescribe a controlled substance, nor shall any person fill, compound, or dispense such a prescription unless it complies with the requirements of this section.

(a) Each prescription for a controlled substance classified in Schedule II shall be wholly written in ink or indelible pencil in the handwriting of the prescriber upon the official prescription form issued by the Department of Justice. Each prescription shall be prepared in triplicate, signed, and dated by the prescriber, and shall contain the name and address of the person for whom the controlled substance is prescribed, the name, quantity, and strength of the controlled substance prescribed, directions for use, and the address, category of professional licensure, and the federal controlled substance registration number of the prescriber. The original and duplicate of the prescription shall be delivered to the pharmacist filling the prescription. The duplicate shall be retained by the pharmacist and the original, properly endorsed by the pharmacist with the name and address of the pharmacy, the pharmacy's state license number, the date the prescription was filled and the signature of the pharmacist, shall be transmitted to the Department of Justice at the end of the month in which the prescription was filled. Upon receipt of an incompletely prepared official prescription form of the Department of Justice, the pharmacist may enter on the face of the prescription the address of the patient.

(b) Each prescription for a controlled substance classified in Schedule III, IV, or V, except as authorized by subdivision (c), shall be subject to the following requirements:

(1) The prescription shall be signed and dated by the prescriber and shall contain the name of the person for whom the controlled substance is prescribed, the name and quantity of the controlled substance prescribed, and directions for use. With respect to prescriptions for controlled substances classified in Schedules III and IV, the signature, date, and information required by this paragraph shall be wholly written in ink or indelible pencil in the handwriting of the prescriber.

(2) In addition, the prescription shall contain the name, address, telephone number, category of professional licensure, and federal controlled substance registration number of the prescriber. The information required by this paragraph shall be either preprinted upon the prescription blank, typewritten, rubber stamped, or printed by hand. Notwithstanding any provision in this section, the prescriber's address, telephone number, category of professional licensure, or federal controlled substances registration number need not appear on the prescription if that information is readily retrievable in the pharmacy.

(3) The prescription shall also contain the address of the person for whom the controlled substance is prescribed. If the prescriber does not specify this address on the prescription, the pharmacist filling the prescription or an employee acting under the direction of the pharmacist shall write or type the address on the prescription or maintain this information in a readily retrievable form in the pharmacy.

(c) Any controlled substance classified in Schedule III, IV, or V may be dispensed upon an oral prescription, which shall be reduced to writing by the pharmacist filling the prescription or by any other person expressly authorized by provisions of the Business and Professions Code. The date of issue of the prescription and all the information required for a written prescription by subdivision (b) shall be included in the written record of the prescription. The pharmacist need not reduce to writing the address, telephone number, license classification, or federal registry number of the prescriber or the address of the patient if that information is readily retrievable in the pharmacy. Pursuant to authorization of the prescriber, any employee of the prescriber on behalf of the prescriber may orally transmit a prescription for a controlled substance classified in Schedule III, IV, or V, if in these cases the written record of the prescription required by this subdivision specifies the name of the employee of the prescriber transmitting the prescription.

(d) The use of commonly used abbreviations shall not invalidate an otherwise valid prescription.

(e) Notwithstanding any provision of subdivisions (b) and (c), prescriptions for a controlled substance classified in Schedule V may be for more than one person in the same family with the same medical need.

(f) In addition to the prescriber's record required by Section 11190, any practitioner dispensing a controlled substance classified in Schedule II in accordance with subdivision (b) of Section 11158 shall prepare a written record thereof on the official forms issued by the Department of Justice, pursuant to

Section 11161, and shall transmit the original to the Department of Justice in accordance with any rules that the department may adopt for completion and transmittal of the forms. *(Amended by Stats 1991 ch 592 §1, eff. 1/1/92.)*

§11166. Time limit for filling prescriptions classified in Schedule II; forged, mutilated, or altered prescriptions.

No person shall fill a prescription for a controlled substance classified in Schedule II which is tendered to him after the seventh day following the date of issue. No person shall knowingly fill a mutilated or forged or altered prescription for a controlled substance except for the addition of the address of the person for whom the controlled substance is prescribed as provided by paragraph (3) of subdivision (b) of Section 11164. *(Amended by Stats 1985 ch 630 §1.)*

§11167. Issuing Schedule II controlled substances in the event of an epidemic, accident or calamity; maintain record.

In the event of an epidemic or accident or calamity, any controlled substance classified in Schedule II may be dispensed upon an oral prescription if failure to issue such a prescription might result in loss of life or intense suffering. Prior to filling such a prescription, the pharmacist shall reduce it to writing. The date of issue of the prescription and all the information required for a written prescription by Section 11164 shall be included in such written record of the prescription.

Additionally, in such an emergency a prescriber may issue a written prescription for a controlled substance classified in Schedule II upon a form other than the official prescription form issued by the Department of Justice. However, such a prescription shall in all other respects comply with the requirements of subdivision (a) of Section 11164.

When an emergency oral or written prescription is issued pursuant to this section, the prescriber shall within 72 hours submit the prescription in the form required by Section 11164 to the pharmacy or pharmacist filling the prescription. If the prescriber does not provide such a prescription within 72 hours, the pharmacist filling the emergency prescription shall, within 144 hours of the time the prescription was filled, so inform the Department of Justice, and in addition, shall maintain for three years a written, readily retrievable record identifying (1) the prescriber; (2) the name, strength, and quantity of the controlled substance dispensed; (3) the circumstances under which the emergency prescription was filled; and (4) the date and method of notifying the Department of Justice, including the name or names of any departmental agents to whom oral notice was furnished.

§11167.5. Oral prescription for patient in licensed skilled nursing or intermediate care facility.

(a) When failure to issue a prescription for a controlled substance classified in Schedule II to a patient in a licensed skilled nursing facility, an intermediate care facility, or a licensed home health agency providing hospice care would, in the opinion of the prescriber, present an immediate hazard to the patient's health and welfare or result in intense suffering to the patient, the prescription may be dispensed upon an oral prescription. Prior to filling the

© 1992 by J., B. & L. Gould
Printed in the U.S.A. **EP**

prescription, the pharmacist shall reduce it to writing in ink or indelible pencil in the handwriting of the pharmacist upon an official prescription form issued by the Department of Justice for that purpose. The prescriptions shall be prepared in triplicate and shall contain the date the prescription was orally transmitted by the prescriber, the name of the person for whom the prescription was authorized, the name and address of the licensed facility or home health agency providing hospice care in which that person is a patient, the name and quantity of the controlled substance prescribed, the directions for use, and the name, address, category of professional licensure, and federal controlled substance registration number of the prescriber. The duplicate shall be retained by the pharmacist, and the triplicate shall be forwarded to the prescriber by the end of the month in which the prescription was issued. The original shall be properly endorsed by the pharmacist with the pharmacy's state license number, the signature of the pharmacist, the name and address of the pharmacy, and the signature of the person who received the controlled substances for the licensed facility or home health agency providing hospice care and shall be forwarded by the pharmacist to the Department of Justice at the end of the month in which the prescription was filled. Upon request, a skilled nursing facility, intermediate care facility, or licensed home health agency providing hospice care shall make available to the dispensing pharmacist copies of signed telephone orders, chart orders, or related documentation substantiating an oral prescription transaction under this section.

(b) For the purposes of this section, "hospice care" means interdisciplinary health care which is designed to alleviate the physical, emotional, social, and spiritual discomforts of an individual who is experiencing the last phases of a terminal disease and to provide supportive care for the primary care person and the family of the patient under hospice care. *(Amended by Stats 1988 ch 398 §3, eff. 1/1/89.)*

§11168. Retain prescription book.

The prescription book containing the prescriber's copies of prescriptions issued shall be retained by the prescriber which shall be preserved for three years.

§11169. Prescribing codeine and paregoric.

When codeine, or dihydrocodeinone or tincture opii camphorata (paregoric) is not combined with other medicinal ingredients, it shall be prescribed on the official triplicate blanks.

§11170. Prescribing for self use.

No person shall prescribe, administer, or furnish a controlled substance for himself.

§11171. Conditions for prescribing, etc.

No person shall prescribe, administer, or furnish a controlled substance except under the conditions and in the manner provided by this division.

§11172. Antedating or postdating.

No person shall antedate or postdate a prescription.

§11173. Obtaining controlled substances by fraud, deceit, misrepresentations.

(a) No person shall obtain or attempt to obtain controlled substances, or procure or attempt to procure the administration of or prescription for con-trolled substances, (1) by fraud, deceit, misrepresentation, or subterfuge; or (2) by the concealment of a material fact.

(b) No person shall make a false statement in any prescription, order, report, or record, required by this division.

(c) No person shall, for the purpose of obtaining controlled substances, falsely assume the title of, or represent himself to be, a manufacturer, wholesaler, pharmacist, physician, dentist, veterinarian, registered nurse, physician's assistant, or other authorized person.

(d) No person shall affix any false or forged label to a package or receptacle containing controlled substances.

§11174. False information; name or address.

No person shall, in connection with the prescribing, furnishing, administering, or dispensing of a controlled substance, give a false name or false address.

§11175. Noncomplying prescriptions.

No person shall obtain or possess a prescription that does not comply with this division, nor shall any person obtain a controlled substance by means of a prescription which does not comply with this division or possess a controlled substance obtained by such a prescription.

§11179. Retaining prescriptions on file.

A person who fills a prescription shall keep it on file for at least three years from the date of filling it.

§11180. Compliance of prescription for controlled substance.

No person shall obtain or possess a controlled substance obtained by a prescription that does not comply with this division.

ARTICLE 2

PRESCRIBER'S RECORD

§11190. Duties of practitioner; keep records.

Every practitioner, other than a pharmacist, who issues a prescription, or dispenses or administers a controlled substance classified in Schedule II shall make a record that, as to the transaction, shows all of the following:

(a) The name and address of the patient.

(b) The date.

(c) The character, including the name and strength, and quantity of controlled substances involved.

The prescriber's record shall show the pathology and purpose for which the prescription is issued, or the controlled substance administered, prescribed, or dispensed. *(Amended by Stats 1988 ch 398 §4, eff. 1/1/89.)*

§11191. Time period for preserving records.

The record shall be preserved for three years.

Every person who violates any provision of this section is guilty of a misdemeanor.

§11192. Use of prima facie evidence.

In a prosecution for a violation of Section 11190, proof that a defendant received or has had in his possession at any time a greater amount of controlled substances than is accounted for by any record required by law or that the amount of controlled substances possessed by a defendant is a lesser amount than is accounted for by any record required by law is prima facie evidence of a violation of the section.

ARTICLE 3

COPIES OF PRESCRIPTIONS

§11195. Receipt given to pharmacist when prescription is taken by officer.

Whenever the pharmacist's copy of a controlled substance prescription is removed by a peace officer, agent of the Attorney General, or inspector of the Board of Pharmacy, or investigator of the Division of Investigation of the Department of Consumer Affairs for the purpose of investigation or as evidence, the officer or inspector or investigator shall give to the pharmacist a receipt in lieu thereof.

ARTICLE 4

REFILLING PRESCRIPTIONS

§11200. Restrictions in refilling prescriptions.

No person shall dispense or refill a controlled substance prescription more than six months after the date thereof or cause a prescription for a Schedule III or IV substance to be refilled in an amount in excess of a 120-day supply, unless renewed by the prescriber. No prescription for a Schedule II substance may be refilled. *(Amended by Stats 1991 ch 592 §2, eff. 1/1/92.)*

§11201. Refilling with unavailable prescriber.

A prescription for a controlled substance, except those in Schedule II, may be refilled without the prescriber's authorization if the prescriber is unavailable to authorize the refill and if, in the pharmacist's professional judgment, failure to refill the prescription might present an immediate hazard to the patient's health and welfare or might result in intense suffering. The pharmacist shall refill only a reasonable amount sufficient to maintain the patient until the prescriber can be contacted. The pharmacist shall note on the reverse side of the prescription the date and quantity of the refill and that the prescriber was not available and the basis for his judgment to refill the prescription without the prescriber's authorization. The pharmacist shall inform the patient that the prescription was refilled without the prescriber's authorization, indicating that the prescriber was not available and that, in the pharmacist's professional judgment, failure to provide the drug might result in an immediate hazard to the patient's health and welfare or might result in intense suffering. The pharmacist shall inform the prescriber within a reasonable period of time. Prior to refilling a prescription pursuant to this section, the pharmacist shall make every reasonable effort to contact the prescriber.

The prescriber shall not incur any liability as the result of a refilling of a prescription pursuant to this section.

ARTICLE 5

PHARMACISTS' RECORDS

§11205. Maintain prescription file.

The owner of a pharmacy or any person who purchases a controlled substance upon federal order forms

as required pursuant to the provisions of the Federal "Comprehensive Drug Abuse Prevention and Control Act of 1970," (P.L. 91—513, 84 Stat. 1236), relating to the importation, exportation, manufacture, production, compounding, distribution, dispensing, and control of controlled substances, and who sells controlled substances obtained upon such federal order forms in response to prescriptions shall maintain and file such prescriptions in a separate file apart from noncontrolled substances prescriptions. Such files shall be preserved for a period of three years.

§11206. Information on transaction record.

Filed prescriptions shall constitute a transaction record that, together with information that is readily retrievable in the pharmacy pursuant to Section 11164 shall show or include the following:

(a) The name(s) and address of the patient(s).

(b) The date.

(c) The character, including the name and strength, quantity, and directions for use of the controlled substance involved.

(d) The name, address, telephone number, category of professional licensure, and the federal controlled substance registration number of the prescriber. *(Amended by Stats 1988 ch 398 §5, eff. 1/1/89.)*

§11207. Prescriptions prepared, etc., by registered or intern pharmacists.

No person other than a registered pharmacist under the laws of this state or an intern pharmacist, as defined in Section 4038.1 of the Business and Professions Code, who is under the personal supervision of a pharmacist, shall compound, prepare, fill or dispense a prescription for a controlled substance.

§11208. Prima facie evidence.

In a prosecution under this division, proof that a defendant received or has had in his possession at any time a greater amount of controlled substances than is accounted for by any record required by law or that the amount of controlled substances possessed by the defendant is a lesser amount than is accounted for by any record required by law is prima facie evidence of guilt.

§11209. Delivery of controlled substances; receipts.

(a) No person shall deliver Schedule II, III, or IV controlled substances to a pharmacy or pharmacy receiving area, nor shall any person receive controlled substances on behalf of a pharmacy unless, at the time of delivery, a pharmacist or authorized receiving personnel signs a receipt showing the type and quantity of the controlled substances received. Any discrepancy between the receipt and the type or quantity of controlled substances actually received shall be reported to the delivering wholesaler or manufacturer by the next business day after delivery to the pharmacy.

(b) The delivery receipt and any record of discrepancy shall be maintained by the wholesaler or manufacturer for a period of three years.

(c) A violation of this section is a misdemeanor.

(d) Nothing in this section shall require a common carrier to label a package containing controlled substances in a manner contrary to federal law or regulation. *(Amended by Stats 1988 ch 918 §6, eff. 1/1/89.)*

© 1992 by J., B. & L. Gould
Printed in the U.S.A.   **EP**

CHAPTER 5

USE OF CONTROLLED SUBSTANCES

ARTICLE 1

LAWFUL MEDICAL USE OTHER THAN TREATMENT OF ADDICTS

§11210. Authorized projects for prescribing, etc., controlled substances.

A physician, surgeon, dentist, veterinarian, or podiatrist, or pharmacist acting within the scope of a project authorized under Article 18 (commencing with Section 429.70) of Chapter 2 of Part 1 of Division 1, or registered acting within the scope of a project authorized under Article 18 (commencing with Section 429.70) of Chapter 2 of Part 1 of Division 1, or physician's assistant acting within the scope of a project authorized under Article 18 (commencing with Section 429.70) of Chapter 2 of Part 1 of Division 1 may prescribe for, furnish to, or administer controlled substances to his patient when the patient is suffering from a disease, ailment, injury, or infirmities attendant upon old age, other than addiction to a controlled substance.

The physician, surgeon, dentist, veterinarian, or podiatrist, or pharmacist acting within the scope of a project authorized under Article 18 (commencing with Section 429.70) of Chapter 2 of Part 1 of Division 1, or registered nurse acting within the scope of a project authorized under Article 18 (commencing with Section 429.70) of Chapter 2 of Part 1 of Division 1, or physician's assistant acting within the scope of a project authorized under Article 18 (commencing with Section 429.70) of Chapter 2 of Part 1 of Division 1 shall prescribe, furnish, or administer controlled substances only when in good faith he believes the disease, ailment, injury, or infirmity, requires such treatment.

The physician, surgeon, dentist, veterinarian, or podiatrist, or pharmacist acting within the scope of a project authorized under Article 18 (commencing with Section 429.70) of Chapter 2 of Part 1 of Division 1, or registered nurse acting within the scope of a project authorized under Article 18 (commencing with Section 429.70) of Chapter 2 of Part 1 of Division 1, or physician's assistant acting within the scope of a project authorized under Article 18 (commencing with Section 429.70) of Chapter 2 of Part 1 of Division 1 shall prescribe, furnish, or administer controlled substances only in such quantity and for such length of time as are reasonably necessary.

§11211. Hospital supply for emergency cases.

In order to provide a supply of controlled substances as may be necessary to handle emergency cases, any hospital which does not employ a resident pharmacist and which is under the supervision of a licensed physician, may purchase controlled substances on federal order forms for such institution, under the name of such hospital, such supply to be made available to a registered nurse for administration to patients in emergency cases, upon direction of a licensed physician.

§11212. Use of controlled substances for research, instruction or analysis.

Persons who, under applicable federal laws or regulations, are lawfully entitled to use controlled substances for the purpose of research, instruction, or analysis, may lawfully obtain and use for such purposes those substances classified in paragraphs (45) and (46) of subdivision (b) of Section 11054 of the Health and Safety Code, upon registration with and approval by the California Department of Justice for use of those substances in bona fide research, instruction, or analysis.

That research, instruction, or analysis shall be carried on only under the auspices of the individual identified by the registrant as responsible for the research. Complete records of receipts, stocks at hand, and use of these controlled substances shall be kept.

The Department of Justice may withdraw approval of the use of such substances at any time. The department may obtain and inspect at any time the records required to be maintained by this section. *(Added by Stats 1985 ch 1098 §1.5.)*

§11213. Approval for use in research, instruction or analysis; records kept.

Persons who, under applicable federal laws or regulations, are lawfully entitled to use controlled substances for the purpose of research, instruction, or analysis, may lawfully obtain and use for such purposes such substances as are defined as controlled substances in this division, upon approval for use of such controlled substances in bona fide research, instruction, or analysis by the Research Advisory Panel established pursuant to Sections 11480 and 11481.

Such research, instruction, or analysis shall be carried on only under the auspices of the head of a research project which has been approved by the Research Advisory Panel pursuant to Section 11480 or Section 11481. Complete records of receipts, stocks at hand, and use of these controlled substances shall be kept.

ARTICLE 2

TREATMENT OF ADDICTS FOR ADDICTION

§11215. Authorization to administer narcotics.

(a) Except as provided in subdivision (b), any narcotic controlled substance employed in treating an addict for addiction shall be administered by:

(1) A physicianand* surgeon.

*So in original. Probably should be "physician and".

(2) A registered nurse acting under the instruction of a physician and surgeon.

(3) A physician assistant licensed pursuant to Chapter 7.7 (commencing with Section 3500) of Division 2 of the Business and Professions Code acting under the patient-specific authority of his or her physician and surgeon supervisor approved pursuant to Section 3515 of the Business and Professions Code.

(b) When acting under the direction of a physician and surgeon, the following persons may administer methadone or other controlled substances orally in the treatment of an addict for addiction to a controlled substance:

(1) A psychiatric technician licensed pursuant to Chapter 10 (commencing with Section 4500) of Division 2 of the Business and Professions Code.

(2) A vocational nurse licensed pursuant to Chapter 6.5 (commencing with Section 2840) of Division 2 of the Business and Professions Code.

(3) A pharmacist licensed pursuant to Chapter 9 (commencing with Section 4000) of Division 2 of the Business and Professions Code.

(c) Except as permitted in this section, no person shall order, permit, or direct any other person to administer a narcotic controlled substance to a person being treated for addiction to a controlled substance. *(Amended by Stats 1991 ch 176 §1, eff. 1/1/92.)*

§11216. *Repealed by Stats 1991 ch 176 §2, eff. 1/1/92.*

§11217. Allowable facilities for treatment.

No person shall treat an addict for addiction to a narcotic drug except in one of the following:

(a) An institution approved by the State Department of Mental Health, and where the patient is at all times kept under restraint and control.

(b) A city or county jail.

(c) A state prison.

(d) A facility designated by a county and approved by the State Department of Mental Health pursuant to Division 5 (commencing with Section 5000) of the Welfare and Institutions Code.

(e) A state hospital.

(f) A county hospital.

(g) A facility licensed by the State Department of Alcohol and Drug Programs pursuant to Division 10.5 (commencing with Section 11750).

(h) A facility as defined in subdivision (a) or (b) of Section 1250 and Section 1250.3.

Methadone in the continuing treatment of addiction to a controlled substance shall be used only in those programs licensed by the State Department of Alcohol and Drug Programs pursuant to Article 3 (commencing with Section 11875) of Chapter 1 of Part 3 of Division 10.5 on either an inpatient or outpatient basis, or both.

This section does not apply during emergency treatment, or where the patient's addiction is complicated by the presence of incurable disease, serious accident, or injury, or the infirmities of old age.

Neither this section nor any other provision of this division shall be construed to prohibit the maintenance of a place in which persons seeking to recover from addiction to a controlled substance reside and endeavor to aid one another and receive aid from others in recovering from such addiction, nor does this section or such division prohibit such aid, provided that no person is treated for addiction in such place by means of administering, furnishing, or prescribing of controlled substances. The preceding sentence is declaratory of preexisting law.

Neither this section or any other provision of this division shall be construed to prohibit short-term methadone detoxification treatment in a controlled setting approved by the director and pursuant to rules and regulations of the director. Facilities and treatment approved by the director under this paragraph shall not be subject to approval or inspection by the Medical Board of California, nor shall persons in such facilities be required to register with, or report the termination of residence with, the police department or sheriff's office. *(Amended by Stats 1989 ch 886 §98, eff. 1/1/90.)*

§11217.5. Treatment in office or medical facility by physician.

Notwithstanding the provisions of Section 11217, a licensed physician and surgeon may treat an addict for addiction in any office or medical facility which, in the professional judgment of such physician and sur-

geon, is medically proper for the rehabilitation and treatment of such addict. Such licensed physician and surgeon may administer to an addict, under his direct care, those medications and therapeutic agents which, in the judgment of such physician and surgeon, are medically necessary, provided that nothing in this section shall authorize the administration of any narcotic drug.

§11218. Allowable amounts of controlled substances for first 15 days of treatment.

A physician treating an addict for addiction shall not prescribe for or furnish the addict more than any one of the following amounts of controlled substances during each of the first 15 days of such treatment:

(a) Eight grains of opium.

(b) Four grains of morphine.

(c) Six grains of Pantopon.

(d) One grain of Dilaudid.

(e) Four hundred milligrams of isonipecaine (Demerol).

(f) One hundred eighty milligrams of methadone.

§11219. Allowable amounts of controlled substances after 15 days of treatment.

After 15 days of treatment the physician shall not prescribe for or furnish to the addict more than any one of the following amounts of controlled substances during each day of such treatment:

(a) Four grains of opium.

(b) Two grains of morphine.

(c) Three grains of Pantopon.

(d) One-half grain of Dilaudid.

(e) Two hundred milligrams of isonipecaine (Demerol).

(f) One hundred eighty milligrams of methadone.

§11220. Discontinuing treatment with narcotics.

At the end of 30 days from the first treatment, the prescribing or furnishing of controlled substances, except methadone, shall be discontinued.

§11221. Physician to furnish treatment report to Attorney General.

The physician prescribing, furnishing, or administering any narcotic controlled substance in the treatment of an addict for addiction shall within five days after the first treatment report by registered mail, over his signature, to the Attorney General stating the name and address of the patient, and the name and quantities of narcotic controlled substances prescribed.

The report shall state the progress of the patient under the treatment.

The physician shall in the same manner further report on the 15th day of the treatment and on the 30th day of the treatment, and thereafter shall make such further reports as are requested in writing by the Attorney General.

§11222. Duty to provide medical aid to arrested person.

In any case in which a person is taken into custody by arrest or other process of law and is lodged in a jail or other place of confinement, and there is reasonable cause to believe that such person is addicted to a controlled substance, it is the duty of the person in charge of the place of confinement to provide the person so confined with medical aid as necessary to

© 1992 by J., B. & L. Gould
Printed in the U.S.A.   **EP**

ease any symptoms of withdrawal from the use of controlled substances.

In any case in which a person, who is participating in a methadone maintenance program, is incarcerated in a jail or other place of confinement, he shall, in the discretion of the director of such program, be entitled to continue in such program until conviction.

ARTICLE 3

PHYSICIANS' REPORTS
(Repealed by Stats 1985 ch 1098 §1.5.)

ARTICLE 3

VETERINARIANS
(Renumbered from Article 4 by Stats 1985 ch 1098 §2.)

§11240. No prescribing, etc. to humans.

No veterinarian shall prescribe, administer, or furnish a controlled substance for himself or any other human being.

§11241. Information included on prescription.

A prescription written by a veterinarian shall state the kind of animal for which ordered and the name and address of the owner or person having custody of the animal.

ARTICLE 4

SALE WITHOUT PRESCRIPTION
(Renumbered from Article 5 by Stats 1985 ch 1098 §3.)

§11250. Retail sale of controlled substances to physicians, etc., by pharmacists.

No prescription is required in case of the sale of controlled substances at retail in pharmacies by pharmacists to any of the following:

(a) Physicians.

(b) Dentists.

(c) Podiatrists.

(d) Veterinarians.

(e) Pharmacists acting within the scope of a project authorized under Article 18 (commencing with Section 429.70) of Chapter 2 of Part 1 of Division 1 or registered nurses acting within the scope of a project authorized under Article 18 (commencing with Section 429.70) of Chapter 2 of Part 1 of Division 1, or physician's assistants acting within the scope of a project authorized under Article 18 (commencing with Section 429.70) of Chapter 2 of Part 1 of Division 1.

In any sale mentioned in this article, there shall be executed any written order that may otherwise be required by federal law relating to the production, importation, exportation, manufacture, compounding, distributing, dispensing, or control of controlled substances.

§11251. Sales at wholesale.

No prescription is required in case of sales at wholesale by pharmacies, jobbers, wholesalers and manufacturers to any of the following:

(a) Pharmacies as defined in the Business and Professions Code.

(b) Physicians.

(c) Dentists.

(d) Podiatrists.

(e) Veterinarians.

(f) Other jobbers, wholesalers or manufacturers.

(g) Pharmacists acting within the scope of a project authorized under Article 18 (commencing with Section 429.70) of Chapter 2 of Part 1 of Division 1, or registered nurses acting within the scope of a project authorized under Article 18 (commencing with Section 429.70) of Chapter 2 of Part 1 of Division 1, or physician's assistants acting within the scope of a project authorized under Article 18 (commencing with Section 429.70) of Chapter 2 of Part 1 of Division 1.

§11252. Written orders or blank forms required.

All wholesale jobbers, wholesalers, and manufacturers, mentioned in this division shall keep, in a manner readily accessible, the written orders or blank forms required to be preserved pursuant to federal law relating to the production, importation, exportation, manufacture, compounding, distributing, dispensing, or control of controlled substances.

§11253. Preservation of written orders and blank forms.

The written orders or blank forms shall be preserved for at least three years after the date of the last entry made.

§11255. Order, etc. for future delivery as a sale.

The taking of any order, or making of any contract or agreement, by any traveling representative or employee of any person for future delivery in this state, of any controlled substance constitutes a sale within the meaning of this division.

§11256. Copy of order for delivery to be sent to Attorney General.

Within 24 hours after any purchaser in this state gives any order for a controlled substance classified in Schedule II to, or makes any contract or agreement for purchases from or sales by, an out-of-state wholesaler or manufacturer of any controlled substances for delivery in this state, the purchaser shall forward to the Attorney General by registered mail a true and correct copy of the order, contract, or agreement.

ARTICLE 5

CANNABIS THERAPEUTIC RESEARCH PROGRAM
(Repealed by Stats 1984 ch 417, eff. 6/30/89.)

CHAPTER 6

OFFENSES AND PENALTIES

ARTICLE 1

OFFENSES INVOLVING CONTROLLED SUBSTANCES FORMERLY CLASSIFIED AS NARCOTICS

§11350. Unlawful possession; punishment.

(a) Except as otherwise provided in this division, every person who possesses (1) any controlled substance specified in subdivision (b) or (c), or paragraph (1) of subdivision (f) of Section 11054, specified in paragraph (14), (15), or (20) of subdivision (d) of Section 11054, or specified in subdivision (b), (c), or (g) of

Section 11055, or (2) any controlled substance classified in Schedule III, IV, or V which is a narcotic drug, unless upon the written prescription of a physician, dentist, podiatrist, or veterinarian licensed to practice in this state, shall be punished by imprisonment in the state prison.

(b) Except as otherwise provided in this division, every person who possesses any controlled substance specified in subdivision (e) of Section 11054 shall be punished by imprisonment in the county jail for not more than one year or in the state prison.

(c) Except as otherwise provided in this division, whenever a person who possesses any of the controlled substances specified in subdivision (a) or (b), the judge may, in addition to any punishment provided for pursuant to subdivision (a) or (b), assess against that person a fine not to exceed seventy dollars ($70) with proceeds of this fine to be used in accordance with Section 1463.23 of the Penal Code. The court shall, however, take into consideration the defendant's ability to pay, and no defendant shall be denied probation because of his or her inability to pay the fine permitted under this subdivision.

(d) Except in unusual cases in which it would not serve the interest of justice to do so, whenever a court grants probation pursuant to a felony conviction under this section, in addition to any other conditions of probation which may be imposed, the following conditions of probation shall be ordered:

(1) For a first offense under this section, a fine of at least one thousand dollars ($1,000) or community service.

(2) For a second or subsequent offense under this section, a fine of at least two thousand dollars ($2,000) or community service.

(3) If a defendant does not have the ability to pay the minimum fines specified in paragraphs (1) and (2), community service shall be ordered in lieu of the fine. *(Amended by Stats 1991 ch 257 §1, eff. 1/1/92.)*

§11351. Unlawful possession for sale; punishment.

Except as otherwise provided in this division, every person who possesses for sale or purchases for purposes of sale (1) any controlled substance specified in subdivision (b), (c), or (e) of Section 11054, specified in paragraph (14), (15), or (20) of subdivision (d) of Section 11054, or specified in subdivision (b), (c), or (g) of Section 11055, or (2) any controlled substance classified in Schedule III, IV, or V which is a narcotic drug, shall be punished by imprisonment in the state prison for two, three, or four years. *(Amended by Stats 1987 ch 970 §2.)*

§11351.5. Sale of cocaine; punishment.

Except as otherwise provided in this division, every person who possesses for sale or purchases for purposes of sale cocaine base which is specified in paragraph (1) of subdivision (f) of Section 11054, shall be punished by imprisonment in the state prison for a period of three, four, or five years. *(Amended by Stats 1987 ch 1174 §3.)*

§11352. Unlawful transportation, sale, administration, giving away; punishment.

(a) Except as otherwise provided in this division, every person who transports, imports into this state, sells, furnishes, administers, or gives away, or offers to transport, import into this state, sell, furnish, ad-

minister, or give away, or attempts to import into this state or transport (1) any controlled substance specified in subdivision (b), (c), or (e), or paragraph (1) of subdivision (f) of Section 11054, specified in paragraph (14), (15), or (20) of subdivision (d) of Section 11054, or specified in subdivision (b), (c), or (g) of Section 11055, or (2) any controlled substance classified in Schedule III, IV, or V which is a narcotic drug, unless upon the written prescription of a physician, dentist, podiatrist, or veterinarian licensed to practice in this state, shall be punished by imprisonment in the state prison for three, four, or five years.

(b) Notwithstanding the penalty provisions of subdivision (a), any person who transports for sale any controlled substances specified in subdivision (a) within this state from one county to another noncontiguous county shall be punished by imprisonment in the state prison for three, six, or nine years. *(Amended by Stats 1989 ch 1102 §1, eff. 1/1/90.)*

§11352.5. Fine and imprisonment for selling heroin.

The court shall impose a fine not exceeding fifty thousand dollars ($50,000), in the absence of a finding that the defendant would be incapable of paying such a fine, in addition to any term of imprisonment provided by law for any of the following persons:

(1) Any person who is convicted of violating Section 11351 of the Health and Safety Code by possessing for sale 14.25 grams or more of a substance containing heroin.

(2) Any person who is convicted of violating Section 11352 of the Health and Safety Code by selling or offering to sell 14.25 grams or more of a substance containing heroin.

(3) Any person convicted of violating Section 11351 of the Health and Safety Code by possessing heroin for sale or convicted of violating Section 11352 of the Health and Safety Code by selling or offering to sell heroin, and who has one or more prior convictions for violating Section 11351 or Section 11352 of the Health and Safety Code.

§11353. Adult using minor to violate provisions; penalty.

Every person 18 years of age or over, (a) who in any voluntary manner solicits, induces, encourages, or intimidates any minor with the intent that the minor shall violate any provision of this chapter or Section 11550 with respect to either (1) a controlled substance which is specified in subdivision (b), (c), or (e), or paragraph (1) of subdivision (f) of Section 11054, specified in paragraph (14), (15), or (20) of subdivision (d) of Section 11054, or specified in subdivision (b), (c), or (g) of Section 11055, or (2) any controlled substance classified in Schedule III, IV, or V which is a narcotic drug, (b) who hires, employs, or uses a minor to unlawfully transport, carry, sell, give away, prepare for sale, or peddle any such controlled substance, or (c) who unlawfully sells, furnishes, administers, gives, or offers to sell, furnish, administer, or give, any such controlled substance to a minor, shall be punished by imprisonment in the state prison for a period of three, six, or nine years. *(Amended by Stats 1990 ch 1664 §1.5, eff. 1/1/91.)*

§11353.1. Adult using minor to violate provisions; additional penalty.

(a) Notwithstanding any other provision of law, any person 18 years of age or over who is convicted of

© 1992 by J., B. & L. Gould
Printed in the U.S.A.   **EP**

a violation of Section 11353, in addition to the punishment imposed for that conviction, shall receive an additional punishment as follows:

(1) If the offense involved heroin, cocaine, cocaine base, or any analog of these substances and occurred upon the grounds of, or within, a church or synagogue, a playground, a public or private youth center, or public swimming pool, during hours in which the facility is open for business, classes, or school-related programs, or at any time when minors are using the facility, the defendant shall, as a full and separately served enhancement to any other enhancement provided in paragraph (3), be punished by imprisonment in the state prison for one year.

(2) If the offense involved heroin, cocaine, cocaine base, or any analog of these substances and occurred upon, or within 1,000 feet of, the grounds of any public or private elementary, vocational, junior high, or high school, during hours that the school is open for classes or school-related programs, or at any time when minors are using the facility where the offense occurs, the defendant shall, as a full and separately served enhancement to any other enhancement provided in paragraph (3), be punished by imprisonment in the state prison for two years.

(3) If the offense involved a minor who is at least four years younger than the defendant, the defendant shall, as a full and separately served enhancement to any other enhancement provided in this subdivision, be punished by imprisonment in the state prison for one, two, or three years, at the discretion of the court.

(b) The additional punishment provided in this section shall not be imposed unless the allegation is charged in the accusatory pleading and admitted by the defendant or found to be true by the trier of fact.

(c) The additional punishment provided in this section shall be in addition to any other punishment provided by law and shall not be limited by any other provision of law.

(d) Notwithstanding any other provision of law, the court may strike the additional punishment provided for in this section if it determines that there are circumstances in mitigation of the additional punishment and states on the record its reasons for striking the additional punishment.

(e) As used in this section the following definitions shall apply:

(1) "Playground" means any park or recreational area specifically designed to be used by children which has play equipment installed, including public grounds designed for athletic activities such as baseball, football, soccer, or basketball, or any similar facility located on public or private school grounds, or on city, county, or state parks.

(2) "Youth center" means any public or private facility that is primarily used to host recreational or social activities for minors, including, but not limited to, private youth membership organizations or clubs, social service teenage club facilities, video arcades, or similar amusement park facilities.

(3) "Video arcade" means any premises where 10 or more video game machines or devices are operated, and where minors are legally permitted to conduct business.

(4) "Video game machine" means any mechanical amusement device, which is characterized by the use of a cathode ray tube display and which, upon the insertion of a coin, slug, or token in any slot or receptacle attached to, or connected to, the machine, may be operated for use as a game, contest, or amusement.

(5) "Within 1,000 feet of the grounds of any public or private elementary, vocational, junior high, or high school" means any public area or business establishment where minors are legally permitted to conduct business which is located within 1,000 feet of any public or private elementary, vocational, junior high, or high school.

(f) This section does not require either that notice be posted regarding the proscribed conduct or that the applicable 1,000-foot boundary limit be marked. *(Amended by Stats 1990 ch 1663 §1; ch 1664 §2; ch 1665 §1, eff. 1/1/91.)*

§11353.5. Adult sale to minor or on school grounds; punishment.

Except as authorized by law, any person 18 years of age or older who unlawfully prepares for sale upon school grounds or a public playground, a church or a synagogue, or sells or gives away a controlled substance, other than a controlled substance described in Section 11353 or 11380, to a minor upon the grounds of, or within, any school, public playground, church, or synagogue providing instruction in kindergarten, or any of grades 1 to 12, inclusive, during hours in which those facilities are open for classes or school-related programs, or at any time when minors are using the facility where the offense occurs, or upon the grounds of a public playground during the hours in which school-related programs for minors are being conducted, or at any time when minors are using the facility where the offense occurs, shall be punished by imprisonment in the state prison for five, seven, or nine years. Application of this section shall be limited to persons at least five years older than the minor to whom he or she prepares for sale, sells, or gives away a controlled substance. *(Amended by Stats 1990 ch 1663 §2; ch 1664 §3; ch 1665 §2, eff. 1/1/91.)*

§11353.6. Juvenile Drug Trafficking and Schoolyard Act.

(A) This section shall be known and may be cited as the Juvenile Drug Trafficking and Schoolyard Act of 1988.

(b) Any person 18 years of age or over who is convicted of a violation of Section 11351.5 or of Section 11352 or 11379.6, as those sections apply to paragraph (1) of subdivision (f) of Section 11054 or a conspiracy to commit such offense, where such violation takes place upon the grounds of, or within 1,000 feet of, a public or private elementary, vocational, junior high school or high school, shall receive an additional punishment of 3, 4, or 5 years at the court's discretion.

(c) Any person 18 years of age or older who is convicted of a violation pursuant to subdivision (b) which involves a minor who is at least four years younger than that person shall, as a full and separately served enhancement to that provided in subdivision (b), be punished by imprisonment in the state prison for 3, 4, or 5 years at the court's discretion.

(d) The additional terms provided in this section shall not be imposed unless the allegation is charged in the accusatory pleading and admitted or found to be true by the trier of fact.

(e) The additional terms provided in this section shall be in addition to any other punishment provided by law and shall not be limited by any other provision of law.

© 1992 by J., B. & L. Gould
Printed in the U.S.A. **EP**

(f) Notwithstanding any other provision of law, the court may strike the additional punishment for the enhancements provided in this section if it determines that there are circumstances in mitigation of the additional punishment and states on the record its reasons for striking the additional punishment. *(Amended by Stats 1988 ch 1248 §1, eff. 1/1/89.)*

§11353.7. Sale of controlled substance to minor in public park.

Except as authorized by law, and except as provided otherwise in Sections 11353.1, 11353.6, and 11380.1 with respect to playgrounds situated in a public park, any person 18 years of age or older who unlawfully prepares for sale in a public park, including units of the state park system and state vehicular recreation areas, or sells or gives away a controlled substance to a minor under the age of 14 years in a public park, including units of the state park system and state vehicular recreation areas, during hours in which the public park, including units of the state park system and state vehicular recreation areas, is open for use, with knowledge that the person is a minor under the age of 14 years, shall be punished by imprisonment in the state prison for three, six, or nine years. *(Amended by Stats 1990 ch 1665 §3, eff. 1/1/91.)*

§11354. Minor soliciting minor to violate provisions.

(a) Every person under the age of 18 years who in any voluntary manner solicits, induces, encourages, or intimidates any minor with the intent that the minor shall violate any provision of this chapter or Section 11550, who hires, employs, or uses a minor to unlawfully transport, carry, sell, give away, prepare for sale, or peddle (1) any controlled substance specified in subdivision (b), (c), or (e), or paragraph (1) of subdivision (f) of Section 11054, specified in paragraph (14), (15), or (20) of subdivision (d) of Section 11054, or specified in subdivision (b), (c), or (g) of Section 11055, or (2) any controlled substance classified in Schedule III, IV, or V which is a narcotic drug, or who unlawfully sells, furnishes, administers, gives, or offers to sell, furnish, administer, or give, any such controlled substance to a minor shall be punished by imprisonment in the state prison.

(b) This section is not intended to affect the jurisdiction of the juvenile court. *(Amended by Stats 1987 ch 970 §5.)*

§11355. Unlawful sale, transportation, pursuant to agreement; punishment.

Every person who agrees, consents, or in any manner offers to unlawfully sell, furnish, transport, administer, or give (1) any controlled substance specified in subdivision (b), (c), or (e), or paragraph (1) of subdivision (f) of Section 11054, specified in paragraph (13), (14), (15), or (20) of subdivision (d) of Section 11054, or specified in subdivision (b), (c), or (g) of Section 11055, or (2) any controlled substance classified in Schedule III, IV, or V which is a narcotic drug to any person, or who offers, arranges, or negotiates to have any such controlled substance unlawfully sold, delivered, transported, furnished, administered, or given to any person and who then sells, delivers, furnishes, transports, administers, or gives, or offers, arranges, or negotiates to have sold, delivered, transported, furnished, administered, or given to any

person any other liquid, substance, or material in lieu of any such controlled substance shall be punished by imprisonment in the county jail for not more than one year, or in the state prison. *(Amended by Stats 1987 ch 970 § 6.)*

§11356. Felony offense and offense punishable as a felony defined.

As used in this article "felony offense", and "offense punishable as a felony" refer to an offense for which the law prescribes imprisonment in the state prison as either an alternative or the sole penalty, regardless of the sentence the particular defendant received.

§11356.5. Punishment based on value of controlled substance.

Any person convicted of a violation of Section 11351, 11352, 11379.5, or 11379.6 insofar as the latter section relates to phencyclidine or any of its analogs which is specified in paragraph (21), (22), or (23) of subdivision (d) of Section 11054 or in paragraph (3) of subdivision (e) of Section 11055, who, as part of the transaction for which he or she was convicted, has induced another to violate Section 11351, 11352, 1379.5, or 11379.6 insofar as the latter section relates to phencyclidine or its analogs, shall be punished by an additional one year in prison if the value of the controlled substance involved in the transaction for which the person was convicted exceeds five hundred thousand dollars ($500,000), by an additional two years in prison if the value of the controlled substance involved in the transaction for which the person was convicted exceeds two million dollars ($2,000,000), or by an additional three years in prison if the value of the controlled substance involved in the transaction for which the person was convicted exceeds five million dollars ($5,000,000). For purposes of this section, "value of the controlled substance" means the retail price to the user. *(Amended by Stats 1985 ch 3 §2.)*

ARTICLE 2

MARIJUANA

§11357. Unlawful possession; punishment.

(a) Except as authorized by law, every person who possesses any concentrated cannabis shall be punished by imprisonment in the county jail for a period of not more than one year or by a fine of not more than five hundred dollars ($500), or by both such fine and imprisonment, or shall be punished by imprisonment in the state prison.

(b) Except as authorized by law, every person who possesses not more than 28.5 grams of marijuana, other than concentrated cannabis, is guilty of a misdemeanor and shall be punished by a fine of not more than one hundred dollars ($100). Notwithstanding other provisions of law, if such person has been previously convicted three or more times of an offense described in this subdivision during the two-year period immediately preceding the date of commission of the violation to be charged, the previous convictions shall also be charged in the accusatory pleading and, if found to be true by the jury upon a jury trial or by the court upon a court trial or if admitted by the person, the provisions of Sections 1000.1 and 1000.2 of the Penal Code shall be applicable to him, and the court shall divert and refer him for education, treatment, or rehabilitation, without a court hearing or

© 1992 by J., B. & L. Gould
Printed in the U.S.A.   EP

determination or the concurrence of the district attorney, to an appropriate community program which will accept him. If the person is so diverted and referred he shall not be subject to the fine specified in this subdivision. If no community program will accept him, the person shall be subject to the fine specified in this subdivision. In any case in which a person is arrested for a violation of this subdivision and does not demand to be taken before a magistrate, such person shall be released by the arresting officer upon presentation of satisfactory evidence of identity and giving his written promise to appear in court, as provided in Section 853.6 of the Penal Code, and shall not be subjected to booking.

(c) Except as authorized by law, every person who possesses more than 28.5 grams of marijuana, other than concentrated cannabis, shall be punished by imprisonment in the county jail for a period of not more than six months or by a fine of not more than five hundred dollars ($500), or by both such fine and imprisonment.

(d) Except as authorized by law, every person 18 years of age or over who possesses not more than 28.5 grams of marijuana, other than concentrated cannabis, upon the grounds of, or within, any school providing instruction in kindergarten or any of grades 1 through 12 during hours the school is open for classes or school-related programs is guilty of a misdemeanor and shall be punished by a fine of not more than five hundred dollars ($500), or by imprisonment in the county jail for a period of not more than 10 days, or both.

(e) Except as authorized by law, every person under the age of 18 who possesses not more than 28.5 grams of marijuana, other than concentrated cannabis, upon the grounds of, or within, any school providing instruction in kindergarten or any of grades 1 through 12 during hours the school is open for classes or school-related programs is guilty of a misdemeanor and shall be subject to the following dispositions:

(1) A fine of not more than two hundred fifty dollars ($250), upon a finding that a first offense has been committed.

(2) A fine of not more than five hundred dollars ($500), or commitment to a juvenile hall, ranch, camp, forestry camp, or secure juvenile home for a period of not more than 10 days, or both, upon a finding that a second or subsequent offense has been committed.

§11358. Planting, cultivating, processing; punishment.

Every person who plants, cultivates, harvests, dries, or processes any marijuana or any part thereof, except as otherwise provided by law, shall be punished by imprisonment in the state prison.

§11359. Penalty for possessing to sell.

Every person who possesses for sale any marijuana, except as otherwise provided by law, shall be punished by imprisonment in the state prison.

§11360. Transportation, importation, sale, or gift of marijuana; penalty.

(a) Except as otherwise provided by this section or as authorized by law, every person who transports, imports into this state, sells, furnishes, administers, or gives away, or offers to transport, import into this state, sell, furnish, administer, or give away, or attempts to import into this state or transport any marijuana shall be punished by imprisonment in the state prison for a period of two, three or four years.

(b) Except as authorized by law, every person who gives away, offers to give away, transports, offers to transport, or attempts to transport not more than 28.5 grams of marijuana, other than concentrated cannabis, is guilty of a misdemeanor and shall be punished by a fine of not more than one hundred dollars ($100). In any case in which a person is arrested for a violation of this subdivision and does not demand to be taken before a magistrate, such person shall be released by the arresting officer upon presentation of satisfactory evidence of identity and giving his written promise to appear in court, as provided in Section 853.6 of the Penal Code, and shall not be subjected to booking.

§11361. Employment of or sale to minor by adult; punishment.

(a) Every person 18 years of age or over who hires, employs, or uses a minor in unlawfully transporting, carrying, selling, giving away, preparing for sale, or peddling any marijuana, who unlawfully sells, or offers to sell, any marijuana to a minor, or who furnishes, administers, or gives, or offers to furnish, administer, or give any marijuana to a minor under 14 years of age, or who induces a minor to use marijuana in violation of law shall be punished by imprisonment in the state prison for a period of three, five, or seven years.

(b) Every person 18 years of age or over who furnishes, administers, or gives, or offers to furnish, administer, or give, any marijuana to a minor 14 years of age or older shall be punished by imprisonment in the state prison for a period of three, four, or five years. *(Amended by Stats 1986 ch 1035 § 2.)*

§11361.5. Destruction of arrest and conviction records after 2 years; exceptions.

(a) Records of any court of this state, any public or private agency that provides services upon referral under Section 1000.2 of the Penal Code, or of any state agency or local public agency pertaining to the arrest or conviction of any person for a violation of subdivision (b), (c), (d), or (e) of Section 11357 or subdivision (b) of Section 11360, shall not be kept beyond two years from the date of the conviction, or from the date of the arrest if there was no conviction, except with respect to a violation of subdivision (e) of Section 11357 the records shall be retained until the offender attains the age of 18 years at which time the records shall be destroyed as provided in this section. Any court or agency having custody of the records shall provide for the timely destruction of the records in accordance with subdivision (c). The requirements of this subdivision do not apply to records of any conviction occurring prior to January 1, 1976, or records of any arrest not followed by a conviction occurring prior to that date.

(b) This subdivision applies only to records of convictions and arrests not followed by conviction occurring prior to January 1, 1976, for any of the following offenses:

(1) Any violation of Section 11357 or a statutory predecessor thereof.

(2) Unlawful possession of a device, contrivance, instrument, or paraphernalia used for unlawfully smoking marijuana, in violation of Section 11364, as it existed prior to January 1, 1976, or a statutory predecessor thereof.

(3) Unlawful visitation or presence in a room or place in which marijuana is being unlawfully smoked or used, in violation of Section 11365, as it existed prior to January 1, 1976, or a statutory predecessor thereof.

(4) Unlawfully using or being under the influence of marijuana, in violation of Section 11550, as it existed prior to January 1, 1976, or a statutory predecessor thereof.

Any person subject to an arrest or conviction for those offenses may apply to the Department of Justice for destruction of records pertaining to the arrest or conviction if two or more years have elapsed since the date of the conviction, or since the date of the arrest if not followed by a conviction. The application shall be submitted upon a form supplied by the Department of Justice and shall be accompanied by a fee, which shall be established by the department in an amount which will defray the cost of administering this subdivision and costs incurred by the state under subdivision (c), but which shall not exceed thirty-seven dollars and fifty cents ($37.50). The application form shall be made available at every local police or sheriff's department and from the Department of Justice and may require that information which the department determines is necessary for purposes of identification.

The department may request, but not require, the applicant to include a self-administered fingerprint upon the application. If the department is unable to sufficiently identify the applicant for purposes of this subdivision without the fingerprint or without additional fingerprints, it shall so notify the applicant and shall request the applicant to submit any fingerprints which may be required to effect identification, including a complete set if necessary, or, alternatively, to abandon the application and request a refund of all or a portion of the fee submitted with the application, as provided in this section. If the applicant fails or refuses to submit fingerprints in accordance with the department's request within a reasonable time which shall be established by the department, or if the applicant requests a refund of the fee, the department shall promptly mail a refund to the applicant at the address specified in the application or at any other address which may be specified by the applicant. However, if the department has notified the applicant that election to abandon the application will result in forfeiture of a specified amount which is a portion of the fee, the department may retain a portion of the fee which the department determines will defray the actual costs of processing the application, provided the amount of the portion retained shall not exceed ten dollars ($10).

Upon receipt of a sufficient application, the Department of Justice shall destroy records of the department, if any, pertaining to the arrest or conviction in the manner prescribed by subdivision (c) and shall notify the Federal Bureau of Investigation, the law enforcement agency which arrested the applicant, and, if the applicant was convicted, the probation department which investigated the applicant and the Department of Motor Vehicles, of the application. Each state or local agency receiving a notice from the Department of Justice shall destroy records of the agency, if any, pertaining to the arrest or conviction specified in the notice, in the manner prescribed by subdivision (c). The application form and the notices from the department to the agencies specified in this subdivision shall be destroyed by the department or

agency, as the case may be, at the time the other records of the arrest or conviction are destroyed.

(c) Destruction of records of arrest or conviction pursuant to subdivision (a) or (b) shall be accomplished by permanent obliteration of all entries or notations upon the records pertaining to the arrest or conviction, and the record shall be prepared again so that it appears that the arrest or conviction never occurred. However, where (1) the only entries upon the record pertain to the arrest or conviction and (2) the record can be destroyed without necessarily effecting the destruction of other records, then the document constituting the record shall be physically destroyed.

(d) Notwithstanding subdivision (a) or (b), written transcriptions of oral testimony in court proceedings and published judicial appellate reports are not subject to this section. Additionally, no records shall be destroyed pursuant to subdivision (a) if the defendant or a codefendant has filed a civil action against the peace officers or law enforcement jurisdiction which made the arrest or instituted the prosecution and if the agency which is the custodian of those records has received a certified copy of the complaint in the civil action, until the civil action has finally been resolved. Immediately following the final resolution of the civil action, records subject to subdivision (a) shall be destroyed pursuant to subdivision (c) if more than two years have elapsed from the date of the conviction or arrest without conviction.

(e) Costs incurred by local agencies in complying with the provisions of subdivision (c) shall be reimbursed as provided in Section 2231 of the Revenue and Taxation Code.

§11361.7. Records subject to destruction to be considered inaccurate; prohibiting alteration of records by public agency; questions on criminal record.

(a) Any record subject to destruction or permanent obliteration pursuant to Section 11361.5, or more than two years of age, or a record of a conviction for an offense specified in subdivision (a) or (b) of Section 11361.5 which became final more than two years previously, shall not be considered to be accurate, relevant, timely, or complete for any purposes by any agency or person. The provisions of this subdivision shall be applicable for purposes of the Privacy Act of 1974 (5 U.S.C. Section 552a) to the fullest extent permissible by law, whenever any information or record subject to destruction or permanent obliteration under Section 11361.5 was obtained by any state agency, local public agency, or any public or private agency that provides services upon referral under Section 1000.2 of the Penal Code, and is thereafter shared with or disseminated to any agency of the federal government.

(b) No public agency shall alter, amend, assess, condition, deny, limit, postpone, qualify, revoke, surcharge, or suspend any certificate, franchise, incident, interest, license, opportunity, permit, privilege, right, or title of any person because of an arrest or conviction for an offense specified in subdivision (a) or (b) of Section 11361.5, or because of the facts or events leading to such an arrest or conviction, on or after the date the records of such arrest or conviction are required to be destroyed by subdivision (a) of Section 11361.5, or two years from the date of such conviction or arrest without conviction with respect to arrests and convictions occurring prior to January 1, 1976. As

© 1992 by J., B. & L. Gould
Printed in the U.S.A. **EP**

used in this subdivision, "public agency" includes, but is not limited to, any state, county, city and county, city, public or constitutional corporation or entity, district, local or regional political subdivision, or any department, division, bureau, office, board, commission or other agency thereof.

(c) Any person arrested or convicted for an offense specified in subdivision (a) or (b) of Section 11361.5 may, two years from the date of such a conviction, or from the date of the arrest if there was no conviction, indicate in response to any question concerning his prior criminal record that he was not arrested or convicted for such offense.

(d) The provisions of this section shall be applicable without regard to whether destruction or obliteration of records has actually been implemented pursuant to Section 11361.5.

§11362. Felony offense and punishable as a felony defined.

As used in this article, "felony offense," and offense "punishable as a felony" refer to an offense for which the law prescribes imprisonment in the state prison as either an alternative or the sole penalty, regardless of the sentence the particular defendant received.

ARTICLE 3

PEYOTE

§11363. Punishment for planting, cultivating and processing peyote.

Every person who plants, cultivates, harvests, dries, or processes any plant of the genus Lophophora, also known as peyote, or any part thereof shall be punished by imprisonment in the county jail for a period of not more than one year or the state prison.

ARTICLE 4

MISCELLANEOUS OFFENSES AND PROVISIONS

§11364. Possession of device, instrument, or paraphernalia, for injecting or smoking substance; punishment.

It is unlawful to possess an opium pipe or any device, contrivance, instrument, or paraphernalia used for unlawfully injecting or smoking (1) a controlled substance specified in subdivision (b), (c), or (e), or paragraph (1) of subdivision (f) of Section 11054, specified in paragraph (14), (15), or (20) of subdivision (d) of Section 11054, specified in subdivision (b) or (c) of Section 11055, or specified in paragraph (2) of subdivision (d) of Section 11055, or (2) a controlled substance which is a narcotic drug classified in Schedule III, IV, or V. *(Amended by Stats 1990 ch 544 §1; ch 1664 §4, eff. 1/1/91.)*

§11364.5. Minors, exclusion from place of business dealing in drug paraphernalia; license revoked or denied for violation.

(a) Except as authorized by law, no person shall maintain or operate any place of business in which drug paraphernalia is kept, displayed or offered in any manner, sold, furnished, transferred or given away unless such drug paraphernalia is completely and wholly kept, displayed or offered within a separate room or enclosure to which persons under the age of 18 years not accompanied by a parent or legal guardian are excluded. Each entrance to such a room or enclosure shall be signposted in reasonably visible and legible words to the effect that drug paraphernalia is kept, displayed or offered in such room or enclosure and that minors, unless accompanied by a parent or legal guardian, are excluded.

(b) Except as authorized by law, no owner, manager, proprietor or other person in charge of any room or enclosure, within any place of business, in which drug paraphernalia is kept, displayed or offered in any manner, sold, furnished, transferred or given away shall permit or allow any person under the age of 18 years to enter, be in, remain in or visit such room or enclosure unless such minor person is accompanied by one of his or her parents or by his or her legal guardian.

(c) Unless authorized by law, no person under the age of 18 years shall enter, be in, remain in or visit any room or enclosure in any place of business in which drug paraphernalia is kept, displayed or offered in any manner, sold, furnished, transferred or given away unless accompanied by one of his or her parents or by his or her legal guardian.

(d) As used in this section, "drug paraphernalia" means all equipment, products, and materials of any kind which are intended for use or designed for use, in planting, propagating, cultivating, growing, harvesting, manufacturing, compounding, converting, producing, processing, preparing, testing, analyzing, packaging, repackaging, storing, containing, concealing, injecting, ingesting, inhaling, or otherwise introducing into the human body a controlled substance. "Drug paraphernalia" includes, but is not limited to, all of the following:

(1) Kits intended for use or designed for use in planting, propagating, cultivating, growing or harvesting of any species of plant which is a controlled substance or from which a controlled substance can be derived.

(2) Kits intended for use or designed for use in manufacturing, compounding, converting, producing, processing, or preparing controlled substances.

(3) Isomerization devices intended for use or designed for use in increasing the potency of any species of plant which is a controlled substance.

(4) Testing equipment intended for use or designed for use in identifying, or in analyzing the strength, effectiveness or purity of controlled substances.

(5) Scales and balances intended for use or designed for use in weighing or measuring controlled substances.

(6) Diluents and adulterants, such as quinine hydrochloride, mannitol, mannite, dextrose, and lactose, intended for use or designed for use in cutting controlled substances.

(7) Separation gins and sifters intended for use or designed for use in removing twigs and seeds from, or in otherwise cleaning or refining, marijuana.

(8) Blenders, bowls, containers, spoons, and mixing devices intended for use or designed for use in compounding controlled substances.

(9) Capsules, balloons, envelopes, and other containers intended for use or designed for use in packaging small quantities of controlled substances.

(10) Containers and other objects intended for use or designed for use in storing or concealing controlled substances.

(11) Hypodermic syringes, needles, and other objects intended for use or designed for use in parenterally injecting controlled substances into the human body.

(12) Objects intended for use or designed for use in ingesting, inhaling, or otherwise introducing marijuana, cocaine, hashish, or hashish oil into the human body, such as the following:

(A) Metal, wooden, acrylic, glass, stone, plastic, or ceramic pipes with or without screens, permanent screens, hashish heads, or punctured metal bowls.

(B) Water pipes.

(C) Carburetion tubes and devices.

(D) Smoking and carburetion masks.

(E) Roach clips, meaning objects used to hold burning material, such as a marijuana cigarette that has become too small or too short to be held in the hand.

(F) Miniature cocaine spoons, and cocaine vials.

(G) Chamber pipes.

(H) Carburetor pipes.

(I) Electric pipes.

(J) Air-driven pipes.

(K) Chillums.

(L) Bongs.

(M) Ice pipes or chillers.

(e) In determining whether an object is drug paraphernalia, a court or other authority may consider, in addition to all other logically relevant factors, the following:

(1) Statements by an owner or by anyone in control of the object concerning its use.

(2) Prior convictions, if any, of an owner, or of anyone in control of the object, under any state or federal law relating to any controlled substance.

(3) Direct or circumstantial evidence of the intent of an owner, or of anyone in control of the object, to deliver it to persons whom he or she knows, or should reasonably know, intend to use the object to facilitate a violation of this section. The innocence of an owner, or of anyone in control of the object, as to a direct violation of this section shall not prevent a finding that the object is intended for use, or designed for use, as drug paraphernalia.

(4) Instructions, oral or written, provided with the object concerning its use.

(5) Descriptive materials, accompanying the object which explain or depict its use.

(6) National and local advertising concerning its use.

(7) The manner in which the object is displayed for sale.

(8) Whether the owner, or anyone in control of the object, is a legitimate supplier of like or related items to the community, such as a licensed distributor or dealer of tobacco products.

(9) The existence and scope of legitimate uses for the object in the community.

(10) Expert testimony concerning its use.

(f) This section shall not apply to any of the following:

(1) Any pharmacist or other authorized person who sells or furnishes drug paraphernalia described in paragraph (11) of subdivision (d) upon the prescription of a physician, dentist, podiatrist or veterinarian.

(2) Any physician, dentist, podiatrist or veterinarian who furnishes or prescribes drug paraphernalia described in paragraph (11) of subdivision (d) to his or her patients.

(3) Any manufacturer, wholesaler or retailer licensed by the California State Board of Pharmacy to sell or transfer drug paraphernalia described in paragraph (11) of subdivision (d).

(g) Notwithstanding any other provision of law, including Section 11374, violation of this section shall not constitute a criminal offense, but operation of a business in violation of the provisions of this section shall be grounds for revocation or nonrenewal of any license, permit, or other entitlement previously issued by a city, county, or city and county for the privilege of engaging in such business and shall be grounds for denial of any future license, permit, or other entitlement authorizing the conduct of such business or any other business, if the business includes the sale of drug paraphernalia.

§11364.7. Drug paraphernalia; punishment.

(a) Any person who delivers, furnishes, or transfers, possesses with intent to deliver, furnish, or transfer, or manufactures with the intent to deliver, furnish, or transfer, drug paraphernalia, knowing, or under circumstances where one reasonably should know, that it will be used to plant, propagate, cultivate, grow, harvest, compound, convert, produce, process, prepare, test, analyze, pack, repack, store, contain, conceal, inject, ingest, inhale, or otherwise introduce into the human body a controlled substance, except as provided in subdivision (b), in violation of this division, is guilty of a misdemeanor.

(b) Any person who manufactures with intent to deliver, furnish, or transfer drug paraphernalia knowing, or under circumstances where one reasonably should know, that it will be used to plant, propagate, cultivate, grow, harvest, manufacture, compound, convert, produce, process, prepare, test, analyze, pack, repack, store, contain, conceal, inject, ingest, inhale, or otherwise introduce into the human body cocaine, cocaine base, heroin, phencyclidine, or methamphetamine in violation of this division shall be punished by imprisonment in the county jail for not more than one year, or in the state prison.

(c) Any person 18 years of age or over who violates subdivision (a) by delivering, furnishing, or transferring drug paraphernalia to a person under 18 years of age who is at least three years his or her junior is guilty of a misdemeanor and shall be punished by imprisonment in the county jail for not more than one year, a fine of not more than one thousand ($1,000), or by both a fine and imprisonment.

(d) The violation, or the causing or the permitting of a violation, of subdivision (a), (b), or (c) by a holder of a business or liquor license issued by a city, county, or city and county, or by the State of California, and in the course of the licensee's business shall be grounds for the revocation of that license.

(e) All drug paraphernalia defined in Section 11014.5 is subject to forfeiture and may be seized by any peace officer pursuant to Section 11471.

(f) If any provision of this section or the application thereof to any person or circumstance is held invalid, it is the intent of the Legislature that the invalidity shall not affect other provisions or applications of this section which can be given effect without the invalid provision or application and to this end the provisions of this section are severable. *(Amended by Stats 1991 ch 573 §1, eff. 1/1/92.)*

© 1992 by J., B. & L. Gould
Printed in the U.S.A.   **EP**

§11365. Presence in place where controlled substance is used; punishment.

(a) It is unlawful to visit or to be in any room or place where any controlled substances which are specified in subdivision (b), (c), or (e), or paragraph (1) of subdivision (f) of Section 11054, specified in paragraph (14), (15), or (20) of subdivision (d) of Section 11054, or specified in subdivision (b) or (c) or paragraph (2) of subdivision (d) of Section 11055, or which are narcotic drugs classified in Schedule III, IV, or V, are being unlawfully smoked or used with knowledge that such activity is occurring.

(b) This section shall apply only where the defendant aids, assists, or abets the perpetration of the unlawful smoking or use of a controlled substance specified in subdivision (a). This subdivision is declaratory of existing law as expressed in People v. Cressey (1970) 2 Cal. 3d 836. *(Amended by Stats 1991 ch 551 §1, eff. 1/1/92.)*

§11366. Opening or maintaining place for selling substance.

Every person who opens or maintains any place for the purpose of unlawfully selling, giving away, or using any controlled substance which is (1) specified in subdivision (b), (c), or (e), or paragraph (1) of subdivision (f) of Section 11054, specified in paragraph (13), (14), (15), or (20) of subdivision (d) of Section 11054, or specified in subdivision (b), (c), paragraph (1) or (2) of subdivision (d), or paragraph (3) of subdivision (e) of Section 11055, or (2) which is a narcotic drug classified in Schedule III, IV, or V, shall be punished by imprisonment in the county jail for a period of not more than one year or the state prison. *(Amended by Stats 1991 ch 492 §1, eff. 1/1/92.)*

§11366.5. Providing place for distribution of controlled substances; punishment.

(a) Any person who has under his or her management or control any building, room, space, or enclosure, either as an owner, lessee, agent, employee, or mortgagee, who knowingly rents, leases, or makes available for use, with or without compensation, the building, room, space, or enclosure for the purpose of unlawfully manufacturing, storing, or distributing any controlled substance for sale or distribution shall be punished by imprisonment in the county jail for not more than one year, or in the state prison.

(b) Any person who has under his or her management or control any building, room, space, or enclosure, either as an owner, lessee, agent, employee, or mortgagee, who knowingly allows the building, room, space, or enclosure to be fortified to suppress law enforcement entry in order to further the sale of any amount of cocaine base as specified in paragraph (1) of subdivision (f) of Section 11054, cocaine as specified in paragraph (6) of subdivision (b) of Section 11055, heroin, phencyclidine, amphetamine, methamphetamine, or lysergic acid diethylamide and who obtains excessive profits from the use of the building, room, space, or enclosure shall be punished by imprisonment in the state prison for two, three, or four years.

(c) Any person who violates subdivision (a) after previously being convicted of a violation of subdivision (a) shall be punished by imprisonment in the state prison for two, three, or four years.

(d) For the purposes of this section, "excessive profits" means the receipt of consideration of a value

substantially higher than fair market value. *(Amended by Stats 1987 ch 1174 § 4.)*

§11366.6. Use of structure to suppress law enforcement entry.

Any person who utilizes a building, room, space, or enclosure specifically designed to suppress law enforcement entry in order to sell, manufacture, or possess for sale any amount of cocaine base as specified in paragraph (1) of subdivision (f) of Section 11054, cocaine as specified in paragraph (6) of subdivision (b) of Section 11055, heroin, phencyclidine, amphetamine, methamphetamine, or lysergic acid diethylamide shall be punished by imprisonment in the state prison for three, four, or five years. *(Amended by Stats 1987 ch 1174 §5.)*

§11366.7. Sale of materials used to manufacture controlled substances.

(a) This section shall apply to the following:

(1) Any chemical or drug.

(2) Any laboratory apparatus or device.

(b) Any retailer or wholesaler who sells any item in paragraph (1) or (2) of subdivision (a) with knowledge or the intent that it will be used to unlawfully manufacture, compound, convert, process, or prepare a controlled substance for unlawful sale or distribution, shall be punished by imprisonment in the county jail for not more than one year, or in the state prison. *(Amended by Stats 1990 ch 350 §6, eff. 1/1/91.)*

§11367. Peace officers immune from prosecution.

All duly authorized peace officers, while investigating violations of this division in performance of their official duties, and any person working under their immediate direction, supervision or instruction, are immune from prosecution under this division.

§11368. Forgery of prescription.

Every person who forges or alters a prescription or who issues or utters an altered prescription, or who issues or utters a prescription bearing a forged or fictitious signature for any narcotic drug, or who obtains any narcotic drug by any forged, fictitious, or altered prescription, or who has in possession any narcotic drug secured by a forged, fictitious, or altered prescription, shall be punished by imprisonment in the county jail for not less than six months nor more than one year, or in the state prison. *(Amended by Stats 1990 ch 43 §1, eff. 1/1/91.)*

§11369. Notification of deportation agency.

When there is reason to believe that any person arrested for a violation of Section 11350, 11351, 11351.5, 11352, 11353, 11355, 11357, 11359, 11360, 11361, 11363, 11366, 11368 or 11550, may not be a citizen of the United States, the arresting agency shall notify the appropriate agency of the United States having charge of deportation matters. *(Amended by Stats 1991 ch 573 §2, eff. 1/1/92.)*

§11370. Prohibition of probation or suspended sentence.

(a) Any person convicted of violating Section 11350, 11351, 11351.5, 11352, 11353, 11355, 11357, 11359, 11360, 11361, 11363, 11366, or 11368, or of committing any offense referred to in those sections, shall not, in any case, be granted probation by the trial court or have the execution of the sentence imposed upon him or her suspended by the court, if he or she has been previously convicted of any offense described in subdivision (c).

(b) Any person who was 18 years of age or over at the time of the commission of the offense and is convicted for the first time of selling, furnishing, administering, or giving a controlled substance which is (1) specified in subdivision (b), (c), (e), or paragraph (1) of subdivision (f) of Section 11054, specified in paragraph (14), (15), or (20) of subdivision (d) of Section 11054, or specified in subdivision (b) or (c) of Section 11055, or (2) which is a narcotic drug classified in Schedule III, IV, or V, to a minor or inducing a minor to use such a controlled substance in violation of law shall not, in any case, be granted probation by the trial court or have the execution of the sentence imposed upon him or her suspended by the court.

(c) Any previous conviction of any of the following offenses, or of an offense under the laws of another state or of the United States which, if committed in this state, would have been punishable as such an offense, shall render a person ineligible for probation or suspension of sentence pursuant to subdivision (a) of this section:

(1) Any felony offense described in this division involving a controlled substance specified in subdivision (b), (c), (e), or paragraph (1) of subdivision (f) of Section 11054, specified in paragraph (13), (14), (15), or (20) of subdivision (d) of Section 11054, or specified in subdivision (b) or (c) of Section 11055.

(2) Any felony offense described in this division involving a narcotic drug classified in Schedule III, IV, or V.

(d) The existence of any previous conviction or fact which would make a person ineligible for suspension of sentence or probation under this section shall be alleged in the information or indictment, and either admitted by the defendant in open court, or found to be true by the jury trying the issue of guilt or by the court where guilt is established by a plea of guilty or nolo contendere or by trial by the court sitting without a jury. *(Amended by Stats 1986 ch 1044 §13.5.)*

§11370.1. Punishment for possession of controlled substances.

(a) Notwithstanding Section 11350 or 11377 or any other provision of law, every person who unlawfully possesses any amount of a substance containing cocaine base, a substance containing cocaine, a substance containing heroin, a substance containing methamphetamine, a crystalline substance containing phencyclidine, a liquid substance containing phencyclidine, plant material containing phencyclidine, or a hand-rolled cigarette treated with phencyclidine while armed with a loaded, operable firearm is guilty of a felony punishable by imprisonment in the state prison for two, three, or four years.

As used in this subdivision, "armed with" means having available for immediate offensive or defensive use.

(b) Except as provided in Section 1000 of the Penal Code, any person who is convicted under this section shall be ineligible for diversion under Chapter 2.5 (commencing with Section 1000) of Title 6 of Part 2 of the Penal Code. *(Amended by Stats 1991 ch 469 §1, eff. 1/1/92.)*

§11370.2. Enhanced sentences for repeat drug offenders.

(a) Any person convicted of a violation of, or of a conspiracy to violate, Section 11351, 11351.5, or 11352 shall receive, in addition to any other punishment authorized by law, including Section 667.5 of the Penal Code, a full, separate, and consecutive three-year term for each prior felony conviction of, or for each prior felony conviction of a conspiracy to violate, Section 11351, 11351.5, 11352, 11378, 11378.5, 11379, 11379.5, 11379.6, 11380, 11380.5, or 11383, whether or not the prior conviction resulted in a term of imprisonment.

(b) Any person convicted of a violation of, or of a conspiracy to violate, Section 11378.5, 11379.5, 11379.6, 11380.5, or 11383 shall receive, in addition to any other punishment authorized by law, including Section 667.5 of the Penal Code, a full, separate, and consecutive three-year term for each prior felony conviction of, or for each prior felony conviction of conspiracy to violate, Section 11351, 11351.5, 11352, 11378, 11378.5, 11379, 11379.5, 11379.6, 11380, 11380.5, or 11383, whether or not the prior conviction resulted in a term of imprisonment.

(c) Any person convicted of a violation of, or of a conspiracy to violate, Section 11378 or 11379 with respect to any substance containing a controlled substance specified in paragraph (1) or (2) of subdivision (d) of Section 11055 shall receive, in addition to any other punishment authorized by law, including Section 667.5 of the Penal Code, a full, separate, and consecutive three-year term for each prior felony conviction of, or for each prior felony conviction of conspiracy to violate, Section 11351, 11351.5, 11352, 11378, 11378.5, 11379, 11379.5, 11379.6, 11380, 11380.5, or 11383, whether or not the prior conviction resulted in a term of imprisonment.

(d) The enhancements provided for in this section shall be pleaded and proven as provided by law.

(e) The conspiracy enhancements provided for in this section shall not be imposed unless the trier of fact finds that the defendant conspirator was substantially involved in the planning, direction, execution, or financing of the underlying offense. *(Amended by Stats 1989 chs 1245 §1, 1326 §1.5, eff. 1/1/90.)*

§11370.4. Enhanced punishment for possession of large amounts of heroin or cocaine.

(a) Any person convicted of a violation of, or of a conspiracy to violate, Section 11351, 11351.5, or 11352 with respect to a substance containing heroin, cocaine base as specified in paragraph (1) of subdivision (f) of Section 11054, or cocaine as specified in paragraph (6) of subdivision (b) of Section 11055 shall receive an additional term as follows:

(1) Where the substance exceeds three pounds by weight, the person shall receive an additional term of three years.

(2) Where the substance exceeds 10 pounds by weight, the person shall receive an additional term of five years.

(3) Where the substance exceeds 25 pounds by weight, the person shall receive an additional term of 10 years.

(4) Where the substance exceeds 100 pounds by weight, the person shall receive an additional term of 15 years.

The conspiracy enhancements provided for in this paragraph shall not be imposed unless the trier of fact

© 1992 by J., B. & L. Gould
Printed in the U.S.A.   EP

finds that the defendant conspirator was substantially involved in the planning, direction, execution, or financing of the underlying offense.

(b) Any person convicted of a violation of, or of conspiracy to violate, Section 11378, 11378.5, 11379, or 11379.5 with respect to a substance containing methamphetamine, amphetamine, phencyclidine (PCP) and its analogs shall receive an additional term as follows:

(1) Where the substance exceeds three pounds by weight, or nine gallons by liquid volume, the person shall receive an additional term of three years.

(2) Where the substance exceeds 10 pounds by weight, or 33⅓ gallons by liquid volume, the person shall receive an additional term of five years.

(3) Where the substance exceeds 25 pounds by weight, or 62½ gallons by liquid volume, the person shall receive an additional term of 10 years.

In computing the quantities involved in this subdivision, plant or vegetable material seized shall not be included.

The conspiracy enhancements provided for in this paragraph shall not be imposed unless the trier of fact finds that the defendant conspirator was substantially involved in the planning, direction, execution, or financing of the underlying offense.

(c) The additional terms provided in this section shall not be imposed unless the allegation that the weight of the substance containing heroin, cocaine base as specified in paragraph (1) of subdivision (f) of Section 11054, cocaine as specified in paragraph (6) of subdivision (b) of Section 11055, methamphetamine, amphetamine, or phencyclidine (PCP) and its analogs exceeds the amounts provided in this section is charged in the accusatory pleading and admitted or found to be true by the trier of fact.

(d) The additional terms provided in this section shall be in addition to any other punishment provided by law.

(e) Notwithstanding any other provision of law, the court may strike the additional punishment for the enhancements provided in this section if it determines that there are circumstances in mitigation of the additional punishment and states on the record its reasons for striking the additional punishment. *(Amended by Stats 1989 chs 1245 §2, 1326 §2.5, eff. 1/1/90.)*

§11370.6. Possession of money or negotiable instruments.

(a) Every person who possesses any moneys or negotiable instruments in excess of one hundred thousand dollars ($100,000) which have been obtained as the result of the unlawful sale, possession for sale, transportation, manufacture, offer for sale, or offer to manufacture any controlled substance listed in Section 11054, 11055, 11056, 11057, or 11058, with knowledge that the moneys or negotiable instruments have been so obtained, and any person who possess any moneys or negotiable instruments in excess of one hundred thousand dollars ($100,000) which are intended by that person for the unlawful purchase of any controlled substance listed in Section 11054, 11055, 11056, 11057, or 11058 and who commits an act in substantial furtherance of the unlawful purchase, shall be punished by imprisonment in the county jail for a term not to exceed one year, or by imprisonment in the state prison for two, three, or four years.

(b) In consideration of the constitutional right to counsel afforded by the Sixth Amendment to the United States Constitution and Section 15 of Article 1 of the California Constitution, when a case charged under subdivision (a) involves an attorney who accepts a fee for representing a client in a criminal investigation or proceeding, the prosecution shall additionally be required to prove that the moneys or negotiable instruments were accepted by the attorney with the intent to participate in the unlawful conduct described in subdivision (a) or to disguise or aid in disguising the source of the funds or the nature of the criminal activity.

(c) In determning the guilt or innocence of a person charged under subdivision (a), the trier of fact may consider the following in addition to any other relevant evidence:

(1) The lack of gainful employment by the person charged.

(2) The expert opinion of a qualified controlled substances expert as to the sources of the assets.

(3) The existence of documents or ledgers that indicate sales of controlled substances. *(Added by Stats 1988 ch 267 §1, eff. 1/1/89.)*

§11371. Punishments for violations of Sections 11153, 11154, 11155 and 11156.

Any person who shall knowingly violate any of the provisions of Section 11153, 11154, 11155, or 11156 with respect to (1) a controlled substance specified in subdivision (b), (c), or (d) of Section 11055, or (2) a controlled substance specified in paragraph (1) of subdivision (b) of Section 11056, or (3) a controlled substance which is a narcotic drug classified in Schedule III, IV, or V, or who in any voluntary manner solicits, induces, encourages or intimidates any minor with the intent that such minor shall commit any such offense, shall be punished by imprisonment in the state prison or in a county jail not exceeding one year, or by a fine not exceeding twenty thousand dollars ($20,000), or by both such fine and imprisonment.

§11371.1. Punishments for violations of Sections 11173 and 11174.

Any person who shall knowingly violate any of the provisions of Section 11173 or 11174 with respect to (1) a controlled substance specified in subdivision (b), (c), or (d) of Section 11055, or (2) a controlled substance specified in paragraph (1) of subdivision (b) of Section 11056, or (3) a controlled substance which is a narcotic drug classified in Schedule III, IV, or V, or who in any voluntary manner solicits, induces, encourages or intimidates any minor with the intent that such minor shall commit any such offense, shall be punished by imprisonment in the state prison, or in a county jail not exceeding one year.

§11372. Fines in addition to prison terms.

(a) In addition to the term of imprisonment provided by law for persons convicted of violating Section 11350, 11351, 11351.5, 11352, 11353, 11355, 11359, 11360, or 11361, the trial court may impose a fine not exceeding twenty thousand dollars ($20,000) for each such offense. In no event shall such fine be levied in lieu of or in substitution for the term of imprisonment provided by law for any of such offenses.

(b) Any person receiving an additional term pursuant to paragraph (1) of subdivision (a) of Section 11370.4, may, in addition, be fined an amount not exceeding one million dollars ($1,000,000) for each such offense.

(c) Any person receiving an additional term pursuant to paragraph (2) of subdivision (a) of Section 11370.4, may, in addition, be fined an amount not to exceed four million dollars ($4,000,000) for each such offense.

(d) Any person receiving an additional term pursuant to paragraph (3) of subdivision (a) of Section 11370.4, may, in addition, be fined by amount not to exceed eight million dollars ($8,000,000) for each such offense.

(e) The court shall make a finding, prior to the imposition of the fines authorized by subdivision (b) to (e), inclusive, that there is a reasonable expectation that the fine, or a substantial portion thereof, could be collected within a reasonable period of time, taking into consideration the defendant's income, earning capacity, and financial resources. *(Amended by Stats 1987 ch 656 §1.)*

§11372.5. Laboratory analysis fee.

(a) Every person who is convicted of a violation of Section 11350, 11351, 11351.5, 11352, 11355, 11358, 11359, 11361, 11363, 11364, 11368, 11375, 11377, 11378, 11378.5, 11379, 11379.5, 11379.6, 11380, 11380.5, 11382, 11383, 11390, 11391, or 11550 or subdivision (a) or (c) of Section 11357, or subdivision (a) of Section 11360 of this code, or Section 4230 of the Business and Professions Code shall pay a criminal laboratory analysis fee in the amount of fifty dollars ($50) for each separate offense. The court shall increase the total fine necessary to include this increment.

With respect to those offenses specified in this subdivision for which a fine is not authorized by other provisions of law, the court shall, upon conviction, impose a fine in an amount not to exceed fifty dollars ($50), which shall constitute the increment prescribed by this section and which shall be in addition to any other penalty prescribed by law.

(b) The county treasurer shall maintain a criminalistics laboratories fund. The sum of fifty dollars ($50) shall be deposited into the fund for every conviction under Section 11350, 11351, 11351.5, 11352, 11355, 11358, 11359, 11361, 11363, 11364, 11368, 11375, 11377, 11378, 11378.5, 11379, 11379.5, 11379.6, 11380, 11380.5, 11382, 11383, 11390, 11391, or 11550, subdivision (a) or (c) of Section 11357, or subdivision (a) of Section 11360 of this code, or Section 4230 of the Business and Professions Code, in addition to fines, forfeitures, and other moneys which are transmitted by the courts to the county treasurer pursuant to Section 11502. The deposits shall be made prior to any transfer pursuant to Section 11502. The county may retain an amount of this money equal to its administrative cost incurred pursuant to this section. Moneys in the criminalistics laboratories fund shall, except as otherwise provided in this section, be used exclusively to fund (1) costs incurred by criminalistics laboratories providing microscopic and chemical analyses for controlled substances, in connection with criminal investigations conducted within both the incorporated or unincorporated portions of the county, (2) the purchase and maintenance of equipment for use by these laboratories in performing the analyses, and (3) for continuing education, training, and scientific development of forensic scientists regularly employed by these laboratories. Moneys in the criminalistics laboratory fund shall be in addition to any allocations pursuant to existing law. As used in this section, "criminalistics laboratory" means a laboratory operated by, or under contract with, a city, county, or other public agency, including a criminalistics laboratory of the Department of Justice, (1) which has not less than one regularly employed forensic scientist engaged in the analysis of solid-dose controlled substances, and (2) which is registered as an analytical laboratory with the Drug Enforcement Administration of the United States Department of Justice for the possession of all scheduled controlled substances. In counties served by criminalistics laboratories of the Department of Justice, amounts deposited in the criminalistics laboratories fund, after deduction of appropriate and reasonable county overhead charges attributable to the collection thereof, shall be paid by the county treasurer once a month to the Controller for deposit into the State General Fund, and shall be excepted from the expenditure requirements otherwise prescribed by this subdivision.

The county treasurer shall, at the conclusion of each fiscal year, determine the amount of any funds remaining in the special fund established pursuant to this section after expenditures for that fiscal year have been made for the purposes herein specified. The county treasurer shall annually distribute those surplus funds in accordance with the allocation scheme for distribution of fines and forfeitures set forth in Section 11502. *(Amended by Stats 1986 ch 1044 §19.5.)*

§11372.7. Fee and fund for drug program.

(a) Except as otherwise provided in subdivision (b) or (e) each person who is convicted of a violation of this chapter shall pay a drug program fee in an amount not to exceed one hundred dollars ($100) for each separate offense. The court shall increase the total fine, if necessary, to include this increment, which shall be in addition to any other penalty prescribed by law.

(b) The court shall determine whether or not the person who is convicted of a violation of this chapter has the ability to pay a drug program fee. If the court determines that the person has the ability to pay, the court may set the amount to be paid and order the person to pay that sum to the county in a manner that the court believes is reasonable and compatible with the person's financial ability. In its determination of whether a person has the ability to pay, the court shall take into account the amount of any fine imposed upon that person and any amount that person has been ordered to pay in restitution. If the court determines that the person does not have the ability to pay a drug program fee, the person shall not be required to pay a drug program fee.

(c) The county treasurer shall maintain a drug program fund. For every drug program fee assessed and collected pursuant to subdivisions (a) and (b), an amount equal to this assessment shall be deposited into the fund for every conviction pursuant to this chapter, in addition to fines, forfeitures, and other moneys which are transmitted by the courts to the county treasurer pursuant to Sections 11372.5 and 11502. These deposits shall be made prior to any transfer pursuant to Section 11502. Amounts deposited in the drug program fund shall be allocated by the administrator of the county's drug program to drug abuse programs in the schools and the com-

© 1992 by J., B. & L. Gould
Printed in the U.S.A.   EP

munity, subject to the approval of the board of supervisors, as follows:

(1) The moneys in the fund shall be allocated through the planning process established pursuant to Sections 11983, 11983.1, 11983.2, and 11983.3.

(2) A minimum of 33 percent of the fund shall be allocated to primary prevention programs in the schools and the community. Primary prevention programs developed and implemented under this article shall emphasize cooperation in planning and program implementation among schools and community drug abuse agencies, and shall demonstrate coordination through an interagency agreement among county offices of education, school district, and the county drug program administrator. These primary prevention programs may include:

(A) School- and classroom-oriented programs, including, but not limited to, programs designed to encourage sound decisionmaking, an awareness of values, an awareness of drugs and their effects, enhanced self-esteem, social and practical skills that will assist students toward maturity, enhanced or improved school climate and relationships among all school personnel and students, and furtherance of cooperative efforts of school- and community-based personnel.

(B) School- or community-based nonclassroom alternative programs, or both, including, but not limited to, positive peer group programs, programs involving youth and adults in constructive activities designed as alternatives to drug use, and programs for special target groups, such as women, ethnic minorities, and other high-risk, high-need populations.

(C) Family-oriented programs, including, but not limited to, programs aimed at improving family relationships and involving parents constructively in the education and nurturing of their children, as well as in specific activities aimed at preventing drug abuse.

(d) Moneys deposited into a county drug program fund pursuant to this section shall supplement, and shall not supplant, any local funds made available to support the county's drug abuse prevention and treatment efforts.

(e) Five percent of the money allocated to primary prevention programs in schools and communities within the county pursuant to paragraph (2) of subdivision (c) shall be used for the purpose of conducting an annual evaluation. The annual evaluation shall be conducted by the office of the county superintendent of schools in counties where the program is operating in a single county or in the office of the county superintendent of schools in the county designated as the lead county in counties where the program is operating as a consortium of counties. The evaluation shall contain the following:

(1) A needs assessment evaluation which provides specific data regarding the problem to be resolved.

(2) A written report of the planning process outlining the deliberations, considerations, and conclusions following a review of the needs assessment.

(3) An end of fiscal year accountability evaluation that will indicate the program's continuing ability to reach appropriate program beneficiaries, deliver the appropriate benefits, and use funds appropriately.

(4) An impact evaluation charged with the task of assessing the effectiveness of the program. Guidelines for the evaluation report format and the timeliness for the submission of the report shall be developed by the State Department of Education. Each county shall submit an evaluation report annually to the State Department of Education and the State Department of Education shall write and submit a report to the Legislature and Governor.

(f) This section shall not apply to any person convicted of a violation of subdivision (b) of Section 11357 of the Health and Safety Code. *(Amended by Stats 1987 ch 621 §4.5.)*

§11373. Treatment or education as a condition of probation.

Whenever any person is granted probation by the trial court after conviction for possession of any controlled substance, such trial court shall, as a condition of probation, order such person to secure education or treatment from a local community agency designated by such court, if such service is available and the person is likely to benefit from the service.

If such defendant is a minor, the trial court shall also order his or her parents or guardian to participate in such education or treatment to the extent the court determines will aid the education or treatment of the minor.

If a minor is found by a juvenile court to have been in possession of any controlled substance, in addition to any other order it may make, such juvenile court shall order the minor to receive education or treatment from a local community agency designated by such court, if such service is available and the person is likely to benefit from the service, and it shall also order his or her parents or guardian to participate in such education or treatment to the extent the court determines will aid the education or treatment of the minor.

§11374. Punishments for violations of this division.

Every person who violates or fails to comply with any provision of this division, except one for which a penalty is otherwise in this division specifically provided, is guilty of a misdemeanor punishable by a fine in a sum not less than thirty dollars ($30) nor more than five hundred dollars ($500), or by imprisonment for not less than 15 nor more than 180 days, or by both.

§11374.5. Unlawful disposal of hazardous substances.

(a) Any manufacturer of a controlled substance who disposes of any hazardous substance that is a controlled substance or chemical used in the manufacture of a controlled substance in violation of any law regulating the disposal of hazardous substances or hazardous waste is guilty of a public offense punishable by imprisonment in the state prison for two, three, or four years or in the county jail not exceeding one year.

(b) As used in this section:

(1) "Dispose" means to abandon, deposit, intern, or otherwise discard as a final action after use has been achieved or a use is no longer intended.

(2) "Hazardous substance" has the meaning as set forth in Section 25316. *(Added by Stats 1986 ch 1031 §1.)*

§11375. Punishments for possession and sale of controlled substances.

(a) As to the substances specified in subdivision (c), this section, and not Sections 11377, 11378, 11379, and 11380, shall apply.

(b) Every person who possesses for sale, or who sells, any substance specified in subdivision (c) shall be punished by imprisonment in the county jail for a period of not more than one year or state prison.

(c) This section shall apply to any material, compound, mixture, or preparation containing any of the following substances:

(1) Chlordiazepoxide.
(2) Clonazepam.
(3) Clorazepate.
(4) Diazepam.
(5) Flurazepam.
(6) Lorazepam.
(7) Mebutamate.
(8) Oxazepam.
(9) Prazepam.
(10) Temazepam.
(11) Halazepam.
(12) Alprazolam.
(13) Propoxyphene.
(14) Diethylpropion.
(15) Phentermine.
(16) Pemoline.
(17) Fenfluramine.

ARTICLE 5

OFFENSES INVOLVING CONTROLLED SUBSTANCES FORMERLY CLASSIFIED AS RESTRICTED DANGEROUS DRUGS

§11377. Punishments for possession of controlled substance.

(a) Except as otherwise provided in subdivision (b) or in Article 7 (commencing with Section 4211) of Chapter 9 of Division 2 of the Business and Professions Code, every person who possesses any controlled substance which is (1) classified in Schedule III, IV, or V, and which is not a narcotic drug, except subdivision (g) of Section 11056, (2) specified in subdivision (d) of Section 11054, except paragraphs (13), (14), (15), and (20) of subdivision (d), (3) specified in paragraph (2) or (3) of subdivision (f) of Section 11054, or (4) specified in subdivision (d), (e), or (f) of Section 11055, unless upon the prescription of a physician, dentist, podiatrist, or veterinarian, licensed to practice in this state, shall be punished by imprisonment in the county jail for a period of not more than one year or the state prison.

(b) Any person who violates subdivision (a) by unlawfully possessing a controlled substance specified in subdivision (f) of Section 11056, and who has not previously been convicted of such a violation involving a controlled substance specified in subdivision (f) of Section 11056, is guilty of a misdemeanor.

(c) In addition to any fine assessed under subdivision (b), the judge may assess a fine not to exceed seventy dollars ($70) against any person who violates subdivision (a), with the proceeds of this fine to be used in accordance with Section 1463.23 of the Penal Code. The court shall, however, take into consideration the defendant's ability to pay, and no defendant shall be denied probation because of his or her inability to pay the fine permitted under this subdivision. (*Amended by Stats 1991 ch 294 §2, eff. 1/1/92.*)

§11378. Punishment for possession of controlled substances for sale.

Except as otherwise provided in Article 7 (commencing with Section 4211) of Chapter 9 of Division 2 of the Business and Professions Code, every person who possesses for sale any controlled substance which is (1) classified in Schedule III, IV, or V and which is not a narcotic drug, except subdivision (g) of Section 11056, (2) specified in subdivision (d) of Section 11054, except paragraphs (13), (14), (15), (20), (21), (22), and (23) of subdivision (d), (3) specified in paragraph (2) or (3) of subdivision (f) of Section 11054, or (4) specified in subdivision (d), (e), or (f), except paragraph (3) of subdivision (e) and subparagraphs (A) and (B) of paragraph (2) of subdivision (f), of Section 11055, shall be punished by imprisonment in the state prison. (*Amended by Stats 1991 ch 294 §3, eff. 1/1/92.*)

§11378.5. Punishment for possession of PCP.

Except as otherwise provided in Article 7 (commencing with Section 4211) of Chapter 9 of Division 2 of the Business and Professions Code, every person who possesses for sale phencyclidine or any analog or any precursor of phencyclidine which is specified in paragraph (21), (22), or (23) of subdivision (d) of Section 11054 or in paragraph (3) of subdivision (e) or in subdivision (f), except subparagraph (A) of paragraph (1) of subdivision (f), of Section 11055, shall be punished by imprisonment in the state prison for a period of three, four, or five years. (*Amended by Stats 1985 ch 3 §5.*)

§11379. Transportation and distribution of controlled substances.

(a) Except as otherwise provided in subdivision (b) and in Article 7 (commencing with Section 4211) of Chapter 9 of Division 2 of the Business and Professions Code, every person who transports, imports into this state, sells, furnishes, administers, or gives away, or offers to transport, import into this state, sell, furnish, administer, or give away, or attempts to import into this state or transport any controlled substance which is (1) classified in Schedule III, IV, or V and which is not a narcotic drug, except subdivision (g) of Section 11056, (2) specified in subdivision (d) of Section 11054, except paragraphs (13), (14), (15), (20), (21), (22), and (23) of subdivision (d), (3) specified in paragraph (2) or (3) of subdivision (f) of Section 11054, or (4) specified in subdivision (d) or (e), except paragraph (3) of subdivision (e), or specified in subparagraph (A) of paragraph (1) of subdivision (f), of Section 11055, unless upon the prescription of a physician, dentist, podiatrist, or veterinarian, licensed to practice in this state, shall be punished by imprisonment in the state prison for a period of two, three, or four years.

(b) Notwithstanding the penalty provisions of subdivision (a), any person who transports for sale any controlled substances specified in subdivision (a) within this state from one county to another noncontiguous county shall be punished by imprisonment in the state prison for three, six, or nine years. (*Amended by Stats 1991 ch 294 §4, eff. 1/1/92.*)

§11379.2. Punishment for possession of ketamine.

Except as otherwise provided in Article 7 (commencing with Section 4211) of Chapter 9 of Division 2 of the Business and Professions Code, every person who possesses for sale or sells any controlled sub-

© 1992 by J., B. & L. Gould
Printed in the U.S.A.   EP

stance specified in subdivision (g) of Section 11056 shall be punished by imprisonment in the county jail for a period of not more than one year or in the state prison. (*Added by Stats 1991 ch 294 §5, eff. 1/1/92.*)

§11379.5. Transportation or distribution of PCP.

(a) Except as otherwise provided in subdivision (b) and in Article 7 (commencing with Section 4211) of Chapter 9 of Division 2 of the Business and Professions Code, every person who transports, imports into this state, sells, furnishes, administers, or gives away, or offers to transport, import into this state, sell, furnish, administer, or give away, or attempts to import into this state or transport phencyclidine or any of its analogs which is specified in paragraph (21), (22), or (23) of subdivision (d) of Section 11054 or in paragraph (3) of subdivision (e) of Section 11055, or its precursors as specified in subparagraph (A) or (B) of paragraph (2) of subdivision (f) of Section 11055, unless upon the prescription of a physician, dentist, podiatrist, or veterinarian licensed to practice in this state, shall be punished by imprisonment in the state prison for a period of three, four, or five years.

(b) Notwithstanding the penalty provisions of subdivision (a), any person who transports for sale any controlled substances specified in subdivision (a) within this state from one county to another noncontiguous county shall be punished by imprisonment in the state prison for three, six, or nine years. (*Amended by Stats 1989 ch 1102 §3, eff. 1/1/90.*)

§11379.6. Manufacture of controlled substances.

(a) Except as otherwise provided by law, every person who manufactures, compounds, converts, produces, derives, processes, or prepares, either directly or indirectly by chemical extraction or independently by means of chemical synthesis, any controlled substance specified in Section 11054, 11055, 11056, 11057, or 11058 shall be punished by imprisonment in the state prison for three, five, or seven years and by a fine not exceeding fifty thousand dollars ($50,000).

(b) Except as otherwise provided by law, every person who offers to perform an act which is punishable under subdivision (a) shall be punished by imprisonment in the state prison for three, four, or five years.

(c) All fines collected pursuant to subdivision (a) shall be transferred to the State Treasury for deposit in the Clandestine Drug Lab Clean-up Account, as established by Section 5 of Chapter 1295 of the Statutes of 1987. The transmission to the State Treasury shall be carried out in the same manner as fines collected for the state by the county. (*Amended by Stats 1989 ch 1024 §1, eff. 1/1/90.*)

§11379.8. Enhanced sentence for possession of large amounts.

(a) Any person convicted of a violation of subdivision (a) of Section 11379.6 with respect to any substance containing a controlled substance which is specified in paragraph (21), (22), or (23) of subdivision (d) of Section 11054, or in paragraph (1) or (2) of subdivision (d) or in paragraph (3) of subdivision (e) or in paragraph (2) of subdivision (f) of Section 11055 shall receive an additional term as follows:

(1) Where the substance exceeds three gallons of liquid by volume or one pound of solid substances by weight, the person shall receive an additional term of three years.

(2) Where the substance exceeds 10 gallons by liquid volume or three pounds of solid substance by weight, the person shall receive an additional term of five years.

(3) Where the substance exceeds 25 gallons of liquid volume or 10 pounds of solid substance by weight, the person shall receive an additional term of 10 years.

In computing the quantities involved in this subdivision, plant or vegetable material seized shall not be included.

(b) The additional terms provided in this section shall not be imposed unless the allegation that the controlled substance exceeds the amounts provided in this section is charged in the accusatory pleading and admitted or found to be true by the trier of fact.

(c) The additional terms provided in this section shall be in addition to any other punishment provided by law.

(d) Notwithstanding any other provision of law, the court may strike the additional punishment for the enhancements provided in this section if it determines that there are circumstances in mitigation of the additional punishment and states on the record its reasons for striking the additional punishment. (*Amended by Stats 1986 ch 80 §3.*)

§11380. Incitement to violate controlled substance laws.

(a) Every person 18 years of age or over who violates any provision of this chapter involving controlled substances which are (1) classified in Schedule III, IV, or V and which are not narcotic drugs or (2) specified in subdivision (d) of Section 11054, except paragraphs (13), (14), (15), and (20) of subdivision (d), specified in paragraph (2) or (3) or subdivision (f) of Section 11054, or specified in subdivision (d), (e), or (f) of Section 11055, by the use of a minor as agent, who solicits, induces, encourages, or intimidates any minor with the intent that the minor shall violate any provision of this article involving those controlled substances or who unlawfully furnishes, offers to furnish, or attempts to furnish those controlled substances to a minor shall be punished by imprisonment in the state prison for a period of three, six, or nine years.

(b) Nothing in this section applies to a registered pharmacist furnishing controlled substances pursuant to a prescription. (*Amended by Stats 1990 ch 1164 §5, 1665 §5, eff. 1/1/91.*)

§11380.1. Incitement to violate controlled substance laws: additional penalty.

(a) Notwithstanding any other provision of law, any person 18 years of age or over who is convicted of a violation of Section 11380, in addition to the punishment imposed for that conviction, shall receive an additional punishment as follows:

(1) If the offense involved phencyclidine (PCP), methamphetamine, or any analog of these substances and occurred upon the grounds of, or within, a church or synagogue, a playground, a public or private youth center, or a public swimming pool, during hours in which the facility is open for business, classes, or school-related programs or at any time when minors are using the facility, the defendant shall, as a full and separately served enhancement to any other enhance-

ment provided in paragraph (3) of this subdivision, be punished by imprisonment in the state prison for one year.

(2) If the offense involved phencyclidine (PCP), methamphetamine or any analog of these substances and occurred upon, or within 1,000 feet of, the grounds of any public or private elementary, vocational, junior high school, or high school, during hours that the school is open for classes or school-related programs, or at any time when minors are using the facility where the offense occurs, the defendant shall, as a full and separately served enhancement to any other enhancement provided in paragraph (3), be punished by imprisonment in the state prison for two years.

(3) If the offense involved a minor who is at least four years younger than the defendant, the defendant shall, as a full and separately served enhancement to any other enhancement provided in this subdivision, be punished by imprisonment in the state prison for one, two, or three years, at the discretion of the court.

(b) The additional punishment provided in this section shall not be imposed unless the allegation is charged in the accusatory pleading and admitted by the defendant or found to be true by the trier of fact.

(c) The additional punishment provided in this section shall be in addition to any other punishment provided by law and shall not be limited by any other provision of law.

(d) Notwithstanding any other provision of law, the court may strike the additional punishment provided for in this section if it determines that there are circumstances in mitigation of the additional punishment and states on the record its reasons for striking the additional punishment.

(e) The definitions contained in subdivision (e) of Section 11353.1 shall apply to this section.

(f) This section does not require either that notice be posted regarding the proscribed conduct or that the applicable 1,000-foot boundary limit be marked. *(Added by Stats 1990 ch 1663 §3; ch 1664 §6; ch 1665 §6, eff. 1/1/91.)*

§11380.5. *Amended by Stats 1990 ch 28; repealed by ch 1664 §7; ch 1665 §7, eff. 1/1/91.*

§11381. Felony offense and punishable as a felony defined.

As used in this article "felony offense" and offense "punishable as a felony" refer to an offense for which the law prescribes imprisonment in the state prison as either an alternative or the sole penalty, regardless of the sentence the particular defendant received.

§11382. Transportation and distribution of non-narcotic controlled substances.

Every person who agrees, consents, or in any manner offers to unlawfully sell, furnish, transport, administer, or give any controlled substance which is (1) classified in Schedule III, IV, or V and which is not a narcotic drug, or (2) specified in subdivision (d) of Section 11054, except paragraphs (13), (14), (15), and (20) of subdivision (d), or specified in subdivision (d), (e), or (f) of Section 11055, to any person, or offers, arranges, or negotiates to have any such controlled substance unlawfully sold, delivered, transported, furnished, administered, or given to any person and then sells, delivers, furnishes, transports, administers, or gives, or offers, or arranges, or negotiates to have sold, delivered, transported, furnished, administered, or

given to any person any other liquid, substance, or material in lieu of any such controlled substance shall be punished by imprisonment in the county jail for not more than one year, or in the state prison. *(Amended by Stats 1985 ch 3 §11.)*

§11382.5. Identifying mark required for legal sale or distribution.

All controlled substances in Schedules I, II, III, IV, and V, in solid or capsule form, except for such controlled substances in the possession or inventory of a wholesaler, retailer, or pharmacist on January 1, 1975, shall not be sold, furnished, or distributed in this state unless they have on the controlled substance if in solid form, or on the capsule if in capsule form, an identifying device, insignia, or mark of the manufacturer of such controlled substance. However, the exception for such controlled substances in the possession or inventory of a wholesaler, retailer, or pharmacist shall not be available to any wholesaler, retailer, or pharmacist under the control or jurisdiction of a manufacturer of controlled substances.

This section shall not apply to a pharmacist who, in accordance with applicable state law, compounds such controlled substance in the course of his practice as a pharmacist for direct dispensing by him upon a prescription of any person licensed to prescribe such controlled substances.

ARTICLE 6

PRECURSORS OF METHAMPHETAMINE AND PHENCYCLIDINE

§11383. Possession of substances with intent to manufacture methamphetamine.

(a) Any person who possesses both methylamine and phenyl-2-propanone (phenylacetone) at the same time with the intent to manufacture methamphetamine, or who possesses both ethylamine and phenyl-2-propanone (phenylacetone) at the same time with the intent to manufacture N-ethylamphetamine, is guilty of a felony and shall be punished by imprisonment in the state prison for two, four, or six years.

(b) Any person who possesses at the same time any of the following combinations, or a combination product thereof, with intent to manufacture phencyclidine (PCP) or any of its analogs specified in paragraph (22) of subdivision (d) of Section 11054 or paragraph (3) of subdivision (e) of Section 11055 is guilty of a felony and shall be punished by imprisonment in the state prison for two, four, or six years:

(1) Piperidine and cyclohexanone.

(2) Pyrrolidine and cyclohexanone.

(3) Morpholine and cyclohexanone.

(c) Any person who possesses at the same time any of the following combinations, or a combination product thereof, with intent to manufacture methamphetamine or any of its analogs specified in subdivision (d) of Section 11055 is guilty of a felony and shall be punished by imprisonment in the state prison for two, four, or six years:

(1) Ephedrine, pseudoephedrine, norpseudoephedrine, N-methylephedrine, N-ethylephedrine, N-methylpseudoephedrine, N-ethylpseudoephedrine, or phenylpropanolamine, plus hydriodic acid.

(2) Ephedrine, pseudoephedrine, norpseudoephedrine, N-methylephedrine, N-ethylephedrine, N-methylpseudoephedrine, N-ethylpseudoephedrine,

© 1992 by J., B. & L. Gould
Printed in the U.S.A.   **EP**

or phenylpropanolamine, thionyl chloride and hydrogen gas.

(3) Ephedrine, pseudoephedrine, norpseudoephedrine, N-methylephedrine, N-ethylephedrine, N-methylpseudoephedrine, N-ethylpseudoephedrine, or phenylpropanolamine, plus phosphorus pentachloride and hydrogen gas.

(4) Ephedrine, pseudoephedrine, norpseudoephedrine, N-methylephedrine, N-ethylephedrine, N-methylpseudoephedrine, N-ethylpseudoephedrine, chloroephedrine and chloropseudoephedrine, or phenylpropanolamine, plus any "reducing" agent.

(d) For purposes of this section, "reducing" means a chemical reaction in which hydrogen combines with another substance or in which oxygen is removed from a substance.

(e) For purposes of this section, possession of the optical, positional, or geometric isomer of any of the compounds listed in this section shall be deemed to be possession of the derivative substance.

(f) For purposes of this section, possession of immediate precursors sufficient for the manufacture of methylamine, ethylamine, phenyl-2-propanone, piperidine, cyclohexanone, pyrrolidine, morpholine, ephedrine, pseudoephedrine, norpseudophedrine, N-methylephedrine, N-ethylephedrine, phenylpropanolamine, hydriodic acid, thionyl chloride, or phosphorus pentachloride shall be deemed to be possession of such a derivative substance. Additionally, possession of any compound or mixture containing piperidine, cyclohexanone, pyrrolidine, or morpholine ephedrine, pseudoephedrine, norpseudoephedrine, N-methylephedrine, N-ethylephedrine, phenylpropanolamine, hydriodic acid, thionyl chloride, or phosphorus pentachloride shall be deemed to be possession of the substance.

(g) Subdivisions (a), (b), (c), (e), and (f) do not apply to drug manufacturers licensed by this state or person authorized by regulation of the Board of Pharmacy to possess those substances or combinations of substances. (*Amended by Stats 1990 ch 1591 §1, eff. 1/1/91.*)

§11384. Authorization of possession for lawful purposes.

The Board of Pharmacy shall, by regulation, authorize such persons to possess any combinations of substance specified in subdivision (a) or (b) of Section 11383 as it determines need and will use such substance for a lawful purpose.

ARTICLE 7

MUSHROOMS
(Added by Stats 1985 ch 1264 §2.)

§11390. Cultivation of spores or mycelium capable of producing controlled substance.

Except as otherwise authorized by law, every person who, with intent to produce a controlled substance specified in paragraph (18) or (19) of subdivision (d) of Section 11054, cultivates any spores or mycelium capable of producing mushrooms or other material which contains such a controlled substance shall be punished by imprisonment in the county jail for a period of not more than one year or in the state prison. *(Added by Stats 1985 ch 1264 §2.)*

§11391. Transportation or distribution of controlled spores or mycelium.

Except as otherwise authorized by law, every person who transports, imports into this state, sells, furnishes, gives away, or offers to transport, import into this state, sell, furnish, or give away any spores or mycelium capable of producing mushrooms or other material which contain a controlled substance specified in paragraph (18) or (19) of subdivision (d) of Section 11054 for the purpose of facilitating a violation of Section 11390 shall be punished by imprisonment in the county jail for a period of not more than one year or in the state prison. *(Added by Stats 1985 ch 1264 §2.)*

§11392. Exceptions for research purposes.

Spores or mycelium capable of producing mushrooms or other material which contains psilocyn or psyoclyin may be lawfully obtained and used for bona fide research, instruction, or analysis, if not in violation of federal law, and if the research, instruction, or analysis is approved by the Research Advisory Panel established pursuant to Sections 11480 and 11481. *(Added by Stats 1985 ch 1264 §2.)*

CHAPTER 6.5

ANALOGS
(Added by Stats 1988 ch 712 §4, eff. 8/29/88.)

§11400. Legislative findings on analogs of controlled substances.

The Legislature finds and declares that the laws of this state which prohibit the possession, possession for sale, offer for sale, sale, manufacturing, and transportation of controlled substances are being circumvented by the commission of those acts with respect to analogs of specified controlled substances which have, are represented to have, or are intended to have effects on the central nervous system which are substantially similar to, or greater than, the controlled substances classified in Sections 11054 and 11055 of which they are analogs. These analogs have been synthesized by so-called "street chemists" and imported into this state from other jurisdictions as precursors to, or substitutes for, controlled substances, due to the nonexistence of applicable criminal penalties. These analogs present grave dangers to the health and safety of the people of this state. Therefore, it is the intent of the Legislature that a controlled substance analog as defined in Section 11401 be considered identical, for purposes of the penalties and punishment specified in Chapter 6 (commencing with Section 11350), to the controlled substance in Section 11054 or 11055 of which it is an analog. *(Added by Stats 1988 ch 712 §4, eff. 8/29/88.)*

§11401. Controlled substance analogs: treatment and definitions.

(a) A controlled substance analog shall, for the purposes of Chapter 6 (commencing with Section 11350), be treated the same as the controlled substance classified in Section 11054 or 11055 of which it is an analog.

(b) Except as provided in subdivision (c), the term "controlled substance analog" means either of the following:

(1) A substance the chemical structure of which is substantially similar to the chemical structure of a

controlled substance classified in Section 11054 or 11055.

(2) A substance which has, is represented as having, or is intended to have a stimulant, depressant, or hallucinogenic effect on the central nervous system that is substantially similar to, or greater than, the stimulant, depressant, or hallucinogenic effect on the central nervous system of a controlled substance classified in Section 11054 or 11055.

(c) The term "controlled substance analog" does not mean any of the following:

(1) Any substance for which there is an approved new drug application as defined under Section 505 of the federal Food, Drug, and Cosmetic Act (21 U.S.C. Sec. 355) or which is generally recognized as safe and effective for use pursuant to Sections 501, 502, and 503 of the federal Food, Drug, and Cosmetic Act (21 U.S.C. Secs. 351, 352, and 353) and 21 C.F.R. Section 330 et seq.

(2) With respect to a particular person, any substance for which an exemption is in effect for investigational use for that person under Section 505 of the federal Food, Drug, and Cosmetic Act (21 U.S.C. Sec. 355), to the extent that the conduct with respect to that substance is pursuant to the exemption.

(3) Any substance, before an exemption as specified in paragraph (2) takes effect with respect to the substance, to the extent the substance is not intended for human consumption. *(Added by Stats 1988 ch 712 §4, eff. 8/29/88.)*

CHAPTER 7

BUREAU OF NARCOTIC ENFORCEMENT

§11450. Employment of staff by Justice Department for carrying out responsibilities under this division.

The Attorney General may, in conformity with the State Civil Service Act, Part 2 (commencing with Section 18500), Division 5, Title 2 of the Government Code, employ such agents, chemists, clerical, and other employees as are necessary for the conduct of the affairs of the Department of Justice in carrying out its responsibilities specified in this division.

§11453. Employment of physician to examine controlled substance users.

The Department of Justice may employ a physician to interview and examine any patient for whom any controlled substance classified in Schedule I, II, or III has been prescribed or to whom any such controlled substance has been furnished or administered, or who is an habitual user of such a controlled substance, or who has a previous addiction record to a substance listed as a controlled substance classified in Schedule I, II, or III.

The patient shall submit to the interview and examination and shall not in any manner hinder or impede it.

The physician employed by the Department of Justice to conduct the interview and examination shall report the results of the examination and interview to the department.

The physician so employed may testify in any action brought under this division or in any administrative hearing conducted under the Medical Practice Act or the Osteopathic Act and his or her testimony is not privileged.

Every person who violates any provision of this section is guilty of a misdemeanor.

§11454. Expenditures and repayment.

The Attorney General and the agents appointed by him, when authorized so to do by the Attorney General, may expend such sums as the Attorney General deems necessary in the purchase of controlled substances for evidence and in the employment of operators to obtain evidence.

The sums so expended shall be repaid to the officer making the expenditures upon claims approved by the Attorney General and subject to postaudit by the Department of Finance. The claims when approved shall be paid out of the funds appropriated or made available by law for the support or use of the Department of Justice.

CHAPTER 8

SEIZURE AND DISPOSITION

§11470. Substances and materials subject to forfeiture.

The following are subject to forfeiture:

(a) All controlled substances which have been manufactured, distributed, dispensed, or acquired in violation of this division.

(b) All raw materials, products and equipment of any kind which are used, or intended for use, in manufacturing, compounding, processing, delivering, importing, or exporting any controlled substance in violation of this division.

(c) All property except real property or a boat, airplane, or any vehicle which is used, or intended for use, as a container for property described in subdivision (a) or (b).

(d) (1) All books, computers, records, and research products and materials, including formulas, microfilm, tapes, data, computer programs, and software which are used, or intended for use, in violation of this division.

(2) Any firearm or other weapon, device, or ammunition subject to Title 2 (commencing with Section 12000) of Part 4 of the Penal Code which is used in any manner to facilitate or which is possessed or used in the commission of a violation of this division.

(e) (1) The interest of any registered owner of a boat, airplane, or any vehicle, which has been used in any manner to facilitate the possession for sale or sale of, or a violation of Section 11379.6 or 11383 involving, 7.125 grams or more of a substance containing either heroin or cocaine base, as specified in paragraph (1) of subdivision (f) of Section 11054, 14.25 grams or more of a substance containing a Schedule I controlled substance except marijuana, peyote, or psilocybin, five pounds dry weight or more of marijuana, peyote, or psilocybin, 14.25 grams or more of a substance containing cocaine, as specified in paragraph (6) of subdivision (b) of Section 11055, or methamphetamine, or 14.25 grams or more of a substance containing a Schedule II controlled substance. However, an interest not to exceed ten thousand dollars ($10,000) in a vehicle which may be lawfully driven on the highway with a class 3 or 4 license, as prescribed in Section 12804 of the Vehicle Code, which is a community property asset of a person who is a registered owner of the vehicle other than the person whose conduct renders the vehicle subject to forfeiture, and which is

© 1992 by J., B. & L. Gould
Printed in the U.S.A. **EP**

the sole class 3 or 4 vehicle available to that registered owner's immediate family, shall not be subject to forfeiture. The exemption from forfeiture provided by this subdivision shall not apply if pursuant to subdivision (e) of Section 11488.5 the trier of fact finds the person claiming the exemption knew or should have known of the unlawful use of the property.

(2) The interest of any person in a license described in Section 23393, 23394, or 23396 of the Business and Professions Code when the licensed premises were used or intended to be used, with the actual knowledge and willful consent of the licensee, to facilitate any violation of Sections 11351, 11351.5, 11355, 11359, 11360, 11378, 11378.5, 11379, 11379.5, 11379.6, and 11382 of this code, or Section 182 of the Penal Code, insofar as the offense involves the manufacture, sale, possession for sale, offer for sale, or offer to manufacture, a controlled substance, or conspiracy to commit at least one of those offenses.

(f) All moneys, negotiable instruments, securities, or other things of value furnished or intended to be furnished by any person in exchange for a controlled substance, all proceeds traceable to such an exchange, and all moneys, negotiable instruments, or securities, which were used or intended to be used to facilitate any violation of Section 11351, 11351.5, 11352, 11355, 11359, 11360, 11378, 11378.5, 11379, 11379.5, 11379.6, or 11382 of this code, or Section 182 of the Penal Code, insofar as the offense involves manufacture, sale, possession for sale, offer for sale, or offer to manufacture, or conspiracy to commit at least one of those offenses, if the exchange, violation, or other conduct which is the basis for the forfeiture occurred within five years of the seizure of the property, or the filing of a complaint under this chapter, or the issuance of an order of forfeiture of the property, whichever comes first.

(g) Real property related to a violation, whether charged or not, of Section 11366, 11366.5, 11366.6, or 11379.6. However, an interest not to exceed one hundred thousand dollars ($100,000) in real property which is used as a family residence and which is owned by two or more persons shall not be subject to forfeiture. The exemption from forfeiture provided by this subdivision shall not apply if pursuant to subdivision (e) of Section 11488.5 the trier of fact finds the person claiming the exemption knew or should have known of the unlawful use of the property.

(h) All right, title, and interest in any property described in this section shall vest in the state upon commission of the act giving rise to forfeiture under this chapter.

The operation of the special vesting rule established by this subdivision shall be limited to circumstances where its application will not defeat the claim of any person, including a bona fide purchaser or encumbrancer who, pursuant to Section 11488.5 or 11488.6, establishes an interest in the property seized, which interest arose prior to the seizure or the filing of the complaint for forfeiture pursuant to this chapter, whichever occurs first, notwithstanding that the interest in the property being claimed was acquired from a person whose property interest would otherwise have been subject to divestment pursuant to this subdivision.

This section shall remain in effect only until January 1, 1994, and as of that date is repealed. *(Amended by Stats 1990 ch 1200 §1, eff. 1/1/91 only until 1/1/94. See other section 11470 below.)*

§11470. Substances and materials subject to forfeiture.

The following are subject to forfeiture:

(a) All controlled substances which have been manufactured, distributed, dispensed, or acquired in violation of this division.

(b) All raw materials, products and equipment of any kind which are used, or intended for use, in manufacturing, compounding, processing, delivering, importing, or exporting any controlled substance in violation of this division.

(c) All property which is used, or intended for use, as a container for property described in subdivision (a) or (b).

(d) All books, records, and research products and materials, including formulas, microfilm, tapes, and data which are used, or intended for use, in violation of this division.

(e) The interest of any registered owner of a boat, airplane, or any vehicle other than an implement of husbandry, as defined in Section 36000 of the Vehicle Code, which has been used as an instrument to facilitate the possession for sale or sale of 14.25 grams or more of heroin, or a substance containing 14.25 grams or more of heroin or 28.5 grams or more of Schedule I controlled substances except marijuana, peyote, or psilocybin; 10 pounds dry weight or more of marijuana, peyote, or psilocybin; 14.25 grams or more of cocaine base specified in paragraph (1) of subdivision (f) of Section 11054; or 28.5 grams or more of cocaine as specified in paragraph (6) of subdivision (b) of Section 11055 or methamphetamine; or a substance containing 14.25 grams or more of cocaine base as specified in paragraph (1) of subdivision (f) of Section 11054; or 28.5 grams or more of cocaine as specified in paragraph (6) of subdivision (b) of Section 11055 or methamphetamine; or 14.25 grams or more of a substance containing cocaine base as specified in paragraph (1) of subdivision (f) of Section 11054; or 57 grams or more of a substance containing cocaine as specified in paragraph (6) of subdivision (b) of Section 11055 or methamphetamine; or 28.5 grams or more of Schedule II controlled substances and the defendant has been convicted of a violation of Section 11351, 11351.5, 11352, 11353, 11359, 11360, 11361, 11378, 11378.5, 11379, 11379.5, or 11379.6, or a conspiracy to commit any such violation and the vehicle was used in the commission of the crime for which the conviction was obtained. No interest in a vehicle which may be lawfully driven on the highway with a class 3 or class 4 license, as prescribed in Section 12804 of the Vehicle Code, may be forfeited under this subdivision if there is a community property interest in the vehicle by a person other than the defendant and the vehicle is the sole class 3 or class 4 vehicle available to the defendant's immediate family.

(f) All moneys, negotiable instruments, securities, or other things of value furnished or intended to be furnished by any person in exchange for a controlled substance in violation of Section 11351, 11351.5, 11352, 11355, 11359, 11360, 11378, 11378.5, 11379, 11379.5, 11379.6, or 11382 of this code, or Section 182 of the Penal Code, insofar as the offense involves manufacture, sale, possession for sale, offer for sale, or offer to manufacture, or conspiracy to commit at least one of those offenses, all proceeds traceable to such an exchange, and all moneys, negotiable instruments, or securities used or intended to be used to facilitate any violation of Section 11351, 11351.5,

11352, 11355, 11359, 11360, 11378, 11378.5, 11379, 11379.5, 11379.6, or 11382 of this code, or Section 182 of the Penal Code, insofar as the offense involves manufacture, sale, possession for sale, offer for sale, or offer to manufacture, or conspiracy to commit at least one of those offenses, provided that the individual is arrested and convicted, for any of the offenses enumerated in this subdivision, and provided further that, the exchange, violation, or other conduct which is the basis for the forfeiture occurred within five years of the arrest leading to the conviction of an of the offenses enumerated in this subdivision.

(g) The real property of any property owner who is convicted of violating Section 11366, 11366.5, or 11366.6 with respect to that property. However, property which is used as a family residence or for other lawful purposes, or which is owned by two or more persons, one of whom had no knowledge of its unlawful use, shall not be subject to forfeiture.

This section shall become operative January 1, 1989, unless the act enacting this section or a later enacted statute provides otherwise. *(Added by Stats 1986 ch 1044 §25.7; amended by Stats 1987 ch 1174 §8. Repealed by Stats 1988 ch 1492 §§2, 16, eff. only until 1/1/94. See other section 11470 above.)*

§11470.1. Recovery of expenses arising from seizure of controlled substances.

(a) The expenses of seizing, eradicating, destroying, or taking remedial action with respect to, any controlled substance or its precursors shall be recoverable from:

(1) Any person who manufactures or cultivates a controlled substance or its precursors in violation of this division.

(2) Any person who aids and abets or who knowingly profits in any manner from the manufacture or cultivation of a controlled substance or its precursors on property owned, leased, or possessed by the defendant, in violation of this division.

(b) The expenses of taking remedial action with respect to any controlled substance or its precursors shall also be recoverable from any person liable for the costs of that remedial action under Chapter 6.8 (commencing with Section 25300) of Division 20 of the Health and Safety Code.

(c) It shall not be necessary to seek or obtain a criminal conviction prior to the entry of judgment for the recovery of expenses. However, if criminal charges are pending against the defendant for the unlawful manufacture or cultivation of any controlled substance or its precursors, an action brought pursuant to this section shall, upon a defendant's request, be continued while the criminal charges are pending.

(d) The action may be brought by the district attorney, county counsel, city attorney, the State Department of Health Services, or Attorney General. All expenses recovered pursuant to this section shall be remitted to the law enforcement agency which incurred them.

(e) (1) The burden of proof as to liability shall be on the plaintiff and shall be by a preponderance of the evidence in an action alleging that the defendant is liable for expenses pursuant to paragraph (1) of subdivision (a). The burden of proof as to liability shall be on the plaintiff and shall be by clear and convincing evidence in an action alleging that the defendant is liable for expenses pursuant to paragraph (2) of subdivision (a). The burden of proof as to the amount of expenses recoverable shall be on the plaintiff and shall be by a preponderance of the evidence in any action brought pursuant to subdivision (a).

(2) Notwithstanding paragraph (1), for any person convicted of a criminal charge of the manufacture or cultivation of a controlled substance or its precursors there shall be a presumption affecting the burden of proof that that person is liable.

(f) Only expenses which meet the following requirements shall be recoverable under this section:

(1) The expenses were incurred in seizing, eradicating, or destroying the controlled substance or its precursors or in taking remedial action with respect to a hazardous substance. These expenses may not include any costs incurred in use of the herbicide paraquat.

(2) The expenses were incurred as a proximate result of the defendant's manufacture or cultivation of a controlled substance in violation of this division.

(3) The expenses were reasonably incurred.

(g) For purposes of this section, "remedial action" shall have the meaning set forth in Section 25322.

(h) For the purpose of discharge in bankruptcy, a judgment for recovery of expenses under this section shall be deemed to be a debt for willful and malicious injury by the defendant to another entity or to the property of another entity.

(i) Notwithstanding Section 526 of the Code of Civil Procedure, the plaintiff may be granted a temporary restraining order or a preliminary injunction, pending or during trial, to restrain the defendant from transferring, encumbering, hypothecating, or otherwise disposing of any assets specified by the court, if it appears by the complaint that the plaintiff is entitled to the relief demanded and it appears that the defendant may dispose of those assets to thwart enforcement of the judgment.

(j) The Legislature finds and declares that civil penalties for the recovery of expenses incurred in enforcing the provisions of this division shall not supplant criminal prosecution for violation of those provisions, but shall be a supplemental remedy to criminal enforcement.

(k) Any testimony, admission, or any other statement made by the defendant in any proceeding brought pursuant to this section, or any evidence derived from the testimony, admission, or other statement, shall not be admitted or otherwise used in any criminal proceeding arising out of the same conduct.

(*l*) No action shall be brought or maintained pursuant to this section against a person who has been acquitted of criminal charges for conduct which may be the basis for an action under this section if, in the criminal action, there has been a finding of factual innocence by the court pursuant to standards set forth in subdivision (b) of Section 851.8 of the Penal Code. *(Amended by Stats 1986 ch 1031 §1.5.)*

§11470.2. Petition for recovery of expenses by prosecuting attorney.

(a) In lieu of a civil action for the recovery of expenses as provided in Section 11470.1, the prosecuting attorney in a criminal proceeding may, upon conviction of the underlying offense, seek the recovery of all expenses recoverable under Section 11470.1 from:

(1) Any person who manufactures or cultivates a controlled substance or its precursors in violation of this division.

© 1992 by J., B. & L. Gould
Printed in the U.S.A.   **EP**

(2) Any person who aids and abets or who knowingly profits in any manner from the manufacture or cultivation of a controlled substance or its precursors on property owned, leased, or possessed by the defendant, in violation of this division. The trier of fact shall make an award of expenses, if proven, which shall be enforceable as any civil judgment. If probation is granted, the court may order payment of the expenses as a condition of probation. All expenses recovered pursuant to this section shall be remitted to the law enforcement agency which incurred them.

(b) The prosecuting attorney may, in conjunction with the criminal proceeding, file a petition for recovery of expenses with the superior court of the county in which the defendant has been charged with the underlying offense. The petition shall allege that the defendant had manufactured or cultivated a controlled substance in violation of Division 10 (commencing with Section 11000) of the Health and Safety Code and that expenses were incurred in seizing, eradicating, or destroying the controlled substance or its precursors. The petition shall also state the amount to be assessed. The prosecuting attorney shall make service of process of a notice of that petition to the defendant.

(c) The defendant may admit to or deny the petition for recovery of expenses. If the defendant admits the allegations of the petition, the court shall rule for the prosecuting attorney and enter a judgment for recovery of the expenses incurred.

(d) If the defendant denies the petition or declines to admit to it, the petition shall be heard in the superior court in which the underlying criminal offense will be tried and shall be promptly heard following the defendant's conviction on the underlying offense. The hearing shall be held either before the same jury or before a new jury in the discretion of the court, unless waived by the consent of all parties.

(e) At the hearing, the burden of proof as to the amount of expenses recoverable shall be on the prosecuting attorney and shall be by a preponderance of the evidence.

(f) For the purpose of discharge in bankruptcy, a judgment for recovery of expenses under this section shall be deemed to be a debt for willful and malicious injury by the defendant to another entity or to the property of another entity.

§11470.3. Forfeiture of minors' property.

(a) Section 11470 shall be applicable to property owned by, or in the possession of, minors.

(b) The procedures for the forfeiture of property that comes within Section 11470 shall be applicable to minors.

(c) Notwithstanding the provisions of this chapter, if a petition has been filed alleging that the minor is a person described in Section 602 of the Welfare and Institutions Code because of a violation which is the basis for the seizure and forfeiture of property under this chapter, any related forfeiture hearing shall be continued until the adjudication of the petition. The forfeiture hearing shall not be conducted in juvenile court. *(Added by Stats 1988 ch 1358 §2, eff. 1/1/89.)*

§11470.4. Person under jurisdiction of juvenile court.

The provisions of this chapter apply to any minor who has been found to be a person described in Section 602 of the Welfare and Institutions Code because of a

violation of Section 11351, 11351.5, 11352, 11355, 11366, 11366.5, 11366.6, 11378.5, 11379, 11379.5, 11379.6, or 11382. *(Added by Stats 1988 ch 1249 §1, eff. 1/1/89.)*

§11471. Conditions for seizure without process.

Property subject to forfeiture under this division may be seized by any peace officer upon process issued by any court having jurisdiction over the property. Seizure without process may be made if any of the following situations exist:

(a) The seizure is incident to an arrest or a search under a search warrant.

(b) The property subject to seizure has been the subject of a prior judgment in favor of the state in a criminal injunction or forfeiture proceeding based upon this division.

(c) There is probable cause to believe that the property is directly or indirectly dangerous to health or safety.

(d) There is probable cause to believe that the property was used or is intended to be used in violation of this division.

§11471.1. Forfeiture of license to sell alcohol.

(a)* Notwithstanding any other provision of this division, a license described in Section 23393, 23394, or 23396 of the Business and Professions Code which is subject to forfeiture under this division may be seized by any peace officer only pursuant to the order of a court issued pursuant to Section 25375 of the Business and Professions Code. *(Added by Stats 1989 ch 1195 §1.4, eff. 1/1/90.)*

So in original. No subd. (b) has been enacted.

§11471.5. Notification of Franchise Tax Board.

A peace officer making a seizure pursuant to Section 11471 shall notify the Franchise Tax Board where there is reasonable cause to believe that the value of the seized property exceeds five thousand dollars ($5,000). *(Added by Stats 1987 ch 924 §1.5.)*

§11472. Issuance of warrants for search and seizure.

Controlled substances and any device, contrivance, instrument, or paraphernalia used for unlawfully using or administering a controlled substance, which are possessed in violation of this division, may be seized by any peace officer and in the aid of such seizure a search warrant may be issued as prescribed by law.

§11473. Destruction of seized property upon conviction.

Except as provided in Section 11473.3, all seizures under provisions of this chapter, except seizures of vehicles, boats, or airplanes, as specified in subdivision (e) of Section 11470, or seizures of moneys, negotiable instruments, securities, or other things of value as specified in subdivisions (c), (d), and (f) of Section 11470, shall, upon conviction of the owner or defendant, be ordered destroyed by the court in which conviction was had. *(Amended by Stats 1989 ch 1195 §1.5, eff. 1/1/90 only until 1/1/94. See other section 11473 below.)*

§11473. Destruction of seized property upon conviction.

All seizures under provisions of this chapter, except seizures of vehicles, boats, or airplanes, as specified in subdivision (e) of Section 11470, or seizures of moneys, negotiable instruments, securities, or other things of value as specified in subdivision (f) of Section 11470, shall, upon conviction of the owner or defendant, be ordered destroyed by the court in which conviction was had. *(Repealed by Stats 1988 ch 1492 §§3, 16, eff. 1/1/89 only until 1/1/94. See other section 11473 above.)*

§11473.1. Proceeds from sale of forfeited vehicle.

All seizures under provisions of this chapter of vehicles which may be lawfully driven upon the highway which a class 3 or class 4 license shall, upon conviction of the defendant, be ordered sold by the court in which conviction was had and the proceeds distributed pursuant to Section 11489. *(Repealed by Stats 1988 ch 1492 §§4, 16, eff. 1/1/89 only until 1/1/94.)*

§11473.2. Placement of seized vehicles in law enforcement programs.

All seizures under provisions of this chapter of vehicles, boats, or airplanes may, upon declaration, or judgment of forfeiture, be placed in the name of the law enforcement agency for use in its law enforcement program. A certified copy of the declaration, or judgment of forfeiture issued by the court as a result of the proceeding, filed with the Department of Motor Vehicles, appropriate federal agency, or other appropriate registry, shall constitute authority for the government entity to convey clear title in its own name for use in its law enforcement program. *(Amended by Stats 1988 ch 1492 §5, eff. 1/1/89 only until 1/1/94. See other section 11473.2 below.)*

§11473.2. Placement of seized vehicles in law enforcement programs.

All seizures under provosions of this chapter of vehicles, boats, or airplanes, excluding vehicles which may be lawfully driven upon the highway with a class 3 or class 4 license, may, upon conviction of the defendant, be placed in the name of the law enforcement agency for use in its law enforcement program. A certified of the judgment of forfeiture issued by the court as a result of the proceeding, filed with the Department of Motor Vehicles, appropriate federal agency, or other appropriate registry, shall continue authority for the government entity to convey clear title in its own name for use in its law enforcement program. *(Repealed by Stats 1988 ch 1492 §§5, 16, eff. 1/1/89 only until 1/1/94. See other section 11473.2 above.)*

§11473.3. Utilization of seized vehicles in law enforcement programs.

(a) When authorized by a final judgment of forfeiture or by a declaration of forfeiture issued pursuant to subdivision (j) of Section 11488.4, items of property seized or subject to forfeiture, but not seized, pursuant to subdivision (b), (c), or (d) of Section 11470 may be utilized by the law enforcement agency in its law enforcement program.

(b) A certified copy of the judgment of forfeiture issued by the court or a declaration of forfeiture issued pursuant to subdivision (j) of Section 11488.4 as a result of the forfeiture proceedings shall serve to vest title to any property specified in subdivision (a) in the law enforcement agency.

(c) The same authority with respect to transfer or sale of property as is specified in Section 11473.2 shall apply to property subject to this section. *(Amended by Stats 1988 ch 1492 §6, eff. 1/1/89 only until 1/1/94. See other section 11473.3 below.)*

§11473.3. Utilization of seized vehicles in law enforcement programs.

(a) When authorized by a final judgment of forfeiture or by a declaration of forfeiture issued pursuant to subdivision (j) of Section 11488.4, items of property seized or subject to forfeiture, but not seized, pursuant to subdivision (b), (c), or (d) of Section 11470 may be utilized by the law enforcement agency in its law enforcement program.

(b) A certified copy of the judgment of forfeiture issued by the court or a declaration of forfeiture issued pursuant to subdivision (j) of Section 11488.4 as a result of the forfeiture proceedings shall serve to vest title to any property specified in subdivision (a) in the named law enforcement agency.

(c) The same authority with respect to transfer or sale of property as is specified in Section 11473.2 shall apply to property subject to this section. *(Repealed by Stats 1988 ch 1492 §§6, 16, eff. 1/1/89 only until 1/1/94. See other section 11473.3 above.)*

§11473.5. Destruction of controlled substances and materials when there is no conviction.

All seizures of controlled substances, instruments, or paraphernalia used for unlawfully using or administering a controlled substance which are in possession of any city, county, or state official as found property, or as the result of a case in which no trial was had or which has been disposed of by way of dismissal or otherwise than by way of conviction, shall be destroyed by order of the court, unless the court finds that the controlled substances, instruments, or paraphernalia were lawfully possessed by the defendant.

§11474. Procedure for court order to destroy seized property.

A court order for the destruction of controlled substances, instruments, or paraphernalia pursuant to the provisions of Section 11473 or 11473.5 may be carried out by a police or sheriff's department or by the Department of Justice. The court order shall specify the agency responsible for the destruction. Controlled substances, instruments, or paraphernalia not in the possession of the designated agency at the time the order of the court is issued shall be delivered to the designated agency for destruction in compliance with the order.

§11475. Forfeiture of Schedule I controlled substances.

Controlled substances listed in Schedule I that are possessed, transferred, sold, or offered for sale in violation of this division are contraband and shall be seized and summarily forfeited to the state. Controlled substances listed in Schedule I, which are seized or come into the possession of the state, the owners of which are unknown, are contraband and shall be summarily forfeited to the state.

§11476. Forfeiture of controlled substance-producing plants.

Species of plants from which controlled substances in Schedules I and II may be derived which have been

© 1992 by J., B. & L. Gould
Printed in the U.S.A.   **EP**

planted or cultivated in violation of this division, or of which the owners or cultivators are unknown, or which are wild growths, may be seized and summarily forfeited to the state.

§11477. Forfeiture of unregistered plants.

The failure, upon demand by a peace officer of the person in occupancy or in control of land or premises upon which the species of plants are growing or being stored, to produce an appropriate registration, or proof that he is the holder thereof, constitutes authority for the seizure and forfeiture of the plants.

§11478. Lawful use of marijuana for research purposes.

Marijuana may be provided by the Attorney General to the heads of research projects which have been registered by the Attorney General, and which have been approved by the research advisory panel pursuant to Section 11480.

The head of the approved research project shall personally receipt for such quantities of marijuana and shall make a record of their disposition. The receipt and record shall be retained by the Attorney General. The head of the approved research project shall also, at intervals and in the manner required by the research advisory panel, report the progress or conclusions of the research project.

§11479. Destruction of large amounts of hazardous or controlled substances.

Notwithstanding Sections 11473.5 and 11474, at any time after seizure by a law enforcement agency of a suspected controlled substance, that amount in excess of 10 pounds in gross weight may be destroyed without a court order by the chief of the law enforcement agency or a designated subordinate. Destruction shall not take place pursuant to this section until all of the following requirements are satisfied:

(a) At least five random and representative samples have been taken, for evidentiary purposes, from the total amount of suspected controlled substances to be destroyed. These samples shall be in addition to the 10 pounds required above. When the suspected controlled substance consists of growing or harvested marijuana plants, at least one 10 pound sample (which may include stalks, branches, or leaves) and five representative samples consisting of leaves or buds shall be retained for evidentiary purposes from the total amount of suspected controlled substances to be destroyed.

(b) Photographs have been taken which reasonably demonstrate the total amount of the suspected controlled substance or container of the suspected controlled substance to be destroyed.

(c) The gross weight of the suspected controlled substance has been determined, either by actually weighing the suspected controlled substance, or by estimating that weight after dimensional measurement of the total suspected controlled substance.

(d) The chief of the law enforcement agency has determined that it is not reasonably possible to preserve the suspected controlled substance in place, or to remove the suspected controlled substance to another location. In making this determination, the difficulty of transporting and storing the suspected controlled substance to another site and the storage facilities may be taken into consideration.

Subsequent to any destruction of a suspected controlled substance pursuant to this section, an affidavit shall be filed within 30 days in the court which has jurisdiction over any pending criminal proceedings pertaining to that suspected controlled substance, reciting the applicable information required by subdivisions (a), (b), (c), and (d) together with information establishing the location of the suspected controlled substance, and specifying the date and time of the destruction. In the event that there are no criminal proceedings pending which pertain to that suspected controlled substance, the affidavit may be filed in any court within the county which would have jurisdiction over a person against whom such criminal charges might be filed. *(Amended by Stats 1989 ch 1072 §1, eff. 1/1/90.)*

§11479.1. Destruction of large amounts of PCP.

(a) Notwithstanding the provisions of Sections 11474, 11474.5, and 11479, at any time after seizure by a law enforcement agency and identification by a forensic chemist or criminalist of phencyclidine, or an analog thereof, that amount in excess of one gram of a crystalline substance containing phencyclidine or its analog, 10 milliliters of a liquid substance containing phencyclidine or its analog, two grams of plant material containing phencyclidine or its analog, or five hand-rolled cigarettes treated with phencyclidine or its analog, may be destroyed without a court order by the chief of the law enforcement agency or a designated subordinate. Destruction shall not take place pursuant to this section until all of the following requirements are satisfied:

(1) At least one gram of a crystalline substance containing phencyclidine or its analog, 10 milliliters of a liquid substance containing phencyclidine or its analog, two grams of plant material containing phencyclidine or its analog, or five hand-rolled cigarettes treated with phencyclidine or its analog have been taken as samples from the phencyclidine or analog to be destroyed.

(2) Photographs have been taken which reasonably demonstrate the total amount of phencyclidine or its analog to be destroyed.

(3) The gross weight of the phencyclidine or its analog has been determined by actually weighing the phencyclidine or analog.

(b) Subsequent to any destruction of phencyclidine or its analog, an affidavit shall be filed within 30 days in the court which has jurisdiction over any pending criminal proceedings pertaining to that phencyclidine or its analog, reciting the applicable information required by paragraphs (1), (2), and (3) of subdivision (a), together with information establishing the location of the phencyclidine or analog and specifying the date and time of the destruction. In the event that there are no criminal proceedings pending which pertain to that phencyclidine or analog, the affidavit may be filed in any court within the county which would have jurisdiction over a person against whom such criminal charges might be filed.

§11479.2. Destruction of large amount of suspected controlled substance other than marijuana.

Notwithstanding the provisions of Sections 11473, 11473.5, 11474, 11479, and 11479.1, at any time after seizure by a law enforcement agency of a suspected controlled substance, except marijuana, any amount, as determined by the court, in excess of 57 grams may, by court order, be destroyed by the chief of a law enforcement agency or a designated subordinate. Destruction shall not take place pursuant to this section until all of the following requirements are satisfied:

(a) At least five random and representative samples have been taken, for evidentiary purposes, from the total amount of suspected controlled substances to be destroyed. Those samples shall be in addition to the 57 grams required above and each sample shall weigh not less than one gram at the time the sample is collected.

(b) Photographs have been taken which reasonably demonstrate the total amount of the suspected controlled substance to be destroyed.

(c) The gross weight of the suspected controlled substance has been determined, either by actually weighing the suspected controlled substance or by estimating such weight after dimensional measurement of the total suspected controlled substance.

(d) In cases involving controlled substances suspected of containing cocaine or methamphetamine, an analysis has determined the qualitative and quantitative nature of the suspected controlled substance.

(e) The law enforcement agency with custody of the controlled substance sought to be destroyed has filed a written motion for the order of destruction in the court which has jurisdiction over any pending criminal proceeding in which a defendant is charged by accusatory pleading with a crime specifically involving the suspected controlled substance sought to be destroyed. The motion shall, by affidavit of the chief of the law enforcement agency or designated subordinate, recite the applicable information required by subdivisions (a), (b), (c), and (d), together with information establishing the location of the suspected controlled substance and the title of any pending criminal proceeding as defined in this subdivision. The motion shall bear proof of service upon all parties to any pending criminal proceeding. No motion shall be made when a defendant is without counsel until the defendant has entered his or her plea to the charges.

(f) The order for destruction shall issue pursuant to this section upon the motion and affidavit in support of the order, unless within 20 days after application for the order, a defendant has requested, in writing, a hearing on the motion,* Within 10 days after the filing of that request, or a longer period of time upon good cause shown by either party, the court shall conduct a hearing on the motion in which each party to the motion for destruction shall be permitted to call and examine witnesses. The hearing shall be recorded. Upon conclusion of the hearing, if the court finds that the defendant would not be prejudiced by the destruction, it shall grant the motion and make an order for destruction. In making the order, the court shall ensure that the representative samples to be retained are of sufficient quantities to allow for qualitative analyses by both the prosecution and the defense. Any order for destruction pursuant to this section shall include the applicable information required by subdivisions (a), (b), (c), (d), and (e) and the name of the agency responsible for the destruction. Unless waived, the order shall provide for a 10-day delay prior to destruction in order to allow expert analysis of the controlled substance by the defense.

*So in original. The comma probably should be a period.

Subsequent to any destruction of a suspected controlled substance pursuant to this section, an affidavit shall be filed within 30 days in the court which ordered destruction stating the location of the retained, suspected controlled substance and specifying the date and time of destruction.

This section does not apply to seizures involving hazardous chemicals or controlled substances in mixture or combination with hazardous chemicals. *(Amended by Stats 1986 ch 1031 §3.)*

§11479.5. Disposal of one ounce or less of controlled substances.

Notwithstanding Sections 11473.5 and 11474, at any time after seizure by a law enforcement agency of a suspected hazardous chemical believed to have been used or intended to have been used in the unlawful manufacture of controlled substances, that amount in excess of one fluid ounce of liquid, or one avoirdupois ounce if solid, of each different type of suspected hazardous chemical and its container, may be disposed of without a court order by the seizing agency. For the purposes of this section, "hazardous chemical" means any material that is believed by the chief of the law enforcement agency to be toxic, carcinogenic, explosive, corrosive, or flammable, and that is believed by the chief of the law enforcement agency to have been used or intended to have been used in the unlawful manufacture of controlled substances.

Destruction pursuant to this section of suspected hazardous chemicals or suspected hazardous chemicals and controlled substances in combination, shall not take place until all of the following requirements are met:

(a) At least a one ounce sample is taken from each different type of suspected hazardous chemical to be destroyed.

(b) At least a one ounce sample has been taken from each container of a mixture of a suspected hazardous chemical with a suspected controlled substance.

(c) Photographs have been taken which reasonably demonstrate the total amount of suspected controlled substances and suspected hazardous chemicals to be destroyed.

(d) The gross weight or volume of the suspected hazardous chemical seized has been determined.

Subsequent to any disposal of a suspected hazardous chemical and its container pursuant to this section, the law enforcement agency involved shall maintain records concerning the details of its compliance with, and reciting the applicable information required by subdivisions (a), (b), (c), and (d), together with the information establishing the location of the suspected hazardous chemical and its container, and specifying the date and time of the disposal.

Subsequent to any destruction of a suspected controlled substance in combination with a hazardous chemical pursuant to this section, an affidavit shall be filed within 30 days in the court which has jurisdiction over any pending criminal proceedings pertaining to the suspected controlled substance, reciting the applicable information required by subdivisions (a), (b), (c), and (d).

A law enforcement agency responsible for the disposal of any hazardous chemical shall comply with the provisions of Chapter 6.5 (commencing with Section 25100) of Division 20 of the Health and Safety Code, as well as all applicable state and federal statutes and regulations. *(Added by Stats 1989 ch 1072 §2, eff. 1/1/90.)*

© 1992 by J., B. & L. Gould
Printed in the U.S.A.   EP

§11480. Research into marijuana and hallucinogenic drugs.

The Legislature finds that there is a need to encourage further research into the nature and effects of marijuana and hallucinogenic drugs and to coordinate research efforts on such subjects.

There is a Research Advisory Panel which consists of a representative of the State Department of Health Services, a representative of the California State Board of Pharmacy, a representative of the Attorney General, a representative of the University of California who shall be a pharmacologist, a physician, or a person holding a doctorate degree in the health sciences, a representative of a private university in this state who shall be a pharmacologist, a physician, or a person holding a doctorate degree in the health sciences, a representative of a statewide professional medical society in this state who shall be engaged in the private practice of medicine and shall be experienced in treating controlled substance dependency, a representative appointed by and serving at the pleasure of the Governor who shall have experience in drug abuse, cancer, or controlled substance research and who is either a registered nurse, licensed pursuant to Chapter 6 (commencing with Section 2700) of Division 2 of the Business and Professions Code, or other health professional. The Governor shall annually designate the private university and the professional medical society represented on the panel. Members of the panel shall be appointed by the heads of the entities to be represented, and they shall serve at the pleasure of the appointing power.

The Research Advisory Panel shall appoint two special members to the Research Advisory Panel, who shall serve at the pleasure of the Research Advisory Panel only during the period Article 6 (commencing with Section 11260) of Chapter 5 remains effective. The additional members shall be physicians and surgeons, and who are board certified in oncology, ophthalmology, or psychiatry.

The panel shall annually select a chairman from among its members.

The panel may hold hearings on, and in other ways study, research projects concerning marijuana or hallucinogenic drugs in this state. Members of the panel shall serve without compensation, but shall be reimbursed for any actual and necessary expenses incurred in connection with the performance of their duties.

The panel may approve research projects, which have been registered by the Attorney General, into the nature and effects of marijuana or hallucinogenic drugs, and shall inform the Attorney General of the head of the approved research projects which are entitled to receive quantities of marijuana pursuant to Section 11478.

The panel may withdraw approval of a research project at any time, and when approval is withdrawn shall notify the head of the research project to return any quantities of marijuana to the Attorney General.

The panel shall report annually to the Legislature and the Governor those research projects approved by the panel, the nature of each research project, and, where available, the conclusions of the research project.

§11481. Research Advisory Panel's hearings and report.

The Research Advisory Panel may hold hearings on, and in other ways study, research projects concerning the treatment of abuse of controlled substances.

The panel may approve research projects, which have been registered by the Attorney General, concerning the treatment of abuse of controlled substances and shall inform the chief of such approval. The panel may withdraw approval of a research project at any time and when approval is withdrawn shall so notify the chief.

The panel shall, annually and in the manner determined by the panel, report to the Legislature and the Governor those research projects approved by the panel, the nature of each research project, and where available, the conclusions of the research project.

§11483. Permissibility of methadone treatment program.

No provision of this division shall be construed to prohibit the establishment and effective operation of a methadone maintenance treatment program licensed pursuant to Article 4 (commencing with Section 11885) of Chapter 1 of Part 3 of Division 10.5.

§11485. Notice of and disposal of seized property; disposition of profits.

Any peace officer of this state who, incident to a search under a search warrant issued for a violation of Section 11358 with respect to which no prosecution of a defendant results, seizes personal property suspected of being used in the planting, cultivation, harvesting, drying, processing, or transporting of marijuana, shall, if the seized personal property is not being held for evidence or destroyed as contraband, and if the owner of the property is unknown or has not claimed the property, provide notice regarding the seizure and manner of reclamation of the property to any owner or tenant of real property on which the property was seized. In addition, this notice shall be posted at the location of seizure and shall be published at least once in a newspaper of general circulation in the county in which the property was seized. If, after 90 days following the first publication of the notice, no owner appears and proves his or her ownership, the seized personal property shall be deemed to be abandoned and may be disposed of by sale to the public at public auction as set forth in Article 1 (commencing with Section 2080) of Chapter 4 of Title 6 of Part 4 of Division 3 of the Civil Code, or may be disposed of by transfer to a government agency or community service organization. Any profit from the sale or tranfer of the property shall be expended for investigative services with respect to crimes involving marijuana. *(Added by Stats 1985 ch 1563 §2.)*

§11488. Procedure for seized property.

(a) Any peace officer of this state, incident or subsequent to making or attempting to make an arrest for a violation of Section 11351, 11351.5, 11352, 11355, 11359, 11360, 11378, 11378.5, 11379, 11379.5, 11379.6, 11382 or 11383 of this code, or Section 182 of the Penal Code insofar as the offense involves manufacture, sale, purchase for the purpose of sale, possession for sale or offer to manufacture or sell, or conspiracy to commit one of those offenses, may seize any item subject to forfeiture under Section 11470.

(b) The peace officer shall also notify the Franchise Tax Board of a seizure where there is reasonable cause to believe that the value of the seized property exceeds five thousand dollars ($5,000).

(c) Receipts for property seized pursuant to this section shall be delivered to any person out of whose possession such property was seized, in accordance with Section 1412 of the Penal Code. In the event property seized was not seized out of anyone's possession, receipt for the property shall be delivered to the individual in possession of the premises at which the property was seized or, if the individual is not present on the premises, the receipt shall be left in a prominent place at the premises.

(d) There shall be a presumption affecting the burden of proof that the person to whom a receipt for property was issued is the owner thereof. This presumption may, however, be rebutted at the forfeiture hearing specified in Section 11488.5. *(Amended by Stats 1989 ch 1195 §2, eff. 1/1/90 only until 1/1/94. See other section 11488 below.)*

§11488. Procedure for seized property.

(a) Any peace officer of this state, subsequent to making or attempting to make an arrest for a violation of Section 11351, 11351.5, 11352, 11355, 11359, 11360, 11378, 11378.5, 11379, 11379.5, 11379.6, or 11382 of this code, or Section 182 of the Penal Code insofar as the offense involves manufacture, sale, purchase for the purpose of sale, possession for sale or offer to manufacture or sell, or conspiracy to commit one of those offenses, may seize any item subject to forfeiture under subdivisions (a) to (f), inclusive, of Section 11470.

The peace officer shall also notify the Franchise Tax Board of a seizure where there is reasonable cause to believe that the value of the seized property exceeds five thousand dollars ($5,000).

(b) Except as provided in this subdivision, the peace officer shall immediately turn over all moneys, negotiable instruments, or other cash equivalents to the superior court of the county in which the defendant has been charged with the underlying or related criminal offense or the superior court of the county in which the property subject to forfeiture has been seized or to the Attorney General or district attorney to hold for that court. Except for property subject to forfeiture pursuant to subdivision (j) of Section 11488.4, these moneys, negotiable instruments, or other cash equivalents shall not be transferred to any other agency, local, state, or federal, except upon court order. The peace officer shall also notify the Franchise Tax Board of a seizure where there is reasonable cause to believe that the value of the seized property exceeds five thousand dollars ($5,000).

This subdivision applies only to the Los Angeles Police Department and the Los Angeles Sheriff's Department and does not apply (1) when the property seized exceeds a value of fifty thousand dollars ($50,000), (2) in any case where the seizure was made in the course of a criminal investigation in which federal law enforcement agents participated, or (3) in any case in which the underlying or related criminal action or proceeding is brought in the federal court.

(c) Receipts for property seized pursuant to this section shall be delivered to any person out of whose possession such property was seized, in accordance with Section 1412 of the Penal Code. In the event property seized was not seized out of anyone's possession, receipt for the property shall be delivered to the individual in possession of the premises at which the property was seized.

(d) There shall be a presumption affecting the burden of proof that the person to whom a receipt for property was issued is the owner thereof. This presumption may, however, be rebutted at the forfeiture hearing specified in Section 11488.5.

This section shall remain in effect only until January 1, 1989, and as of that date is repealed, unless a later enacted statute, which is enacted before January 1, 1989, deletes or extends that date. *(Repealed by Stats 1988 ch 1492 §§7, 16, eff. 1/1/89 only until 1/1/94. See other section 11488 above.)*

§11488.1. Holding of seized property for evidence.

Property seized pursuant to Section 11488 may, where appropriate, be held for evidence. The Attorney General or the district attorney for the jurisdiction involved shall institute and maintain the proceedings. In the County of Los Angeles, in cases where the value of the seized property is twenty-five thousand dollars ($25,000) or less, and the Attorney General, or the district attorney, or both, have declined to institute forfeiture proceedings, the city attorney for the jurisdiction involved, with the consent of the Attorney General, or the district attorney, or both, may institute and maintain the proceedings. *(Amended by Stats 1990 ch 1200 §2, eff. 1/1/91.)*

§11488.2. Procedure for forfeiture of property intended to be exchanged for controlled substance.

Within 15 days after the seizure, if the peace officer does not hold the property seized pursuant to Section 11488 for evidence or if the law enforcement agency for which the peace officer is employed does not refer the matter in writing for the institution of forfeiture proceedings by the Attorney General or the district attorney pursuant to Section 11488.1, the officer shall comply with any notice to withhold issued with respect to the property by the Franchise Tax Board. If no notice to withhold has been issued with respect to the property by the Franchise Tax Board, the officer shall return the property to the individual designated in the receipt therefor or if the property is a vehicle, boat, or airplane, it shall be returned to the registered owner. *(Amended by Stats 1990 ch 1200 §3, eff. 1/1/91.)*

§11488.4. Petition for forfeiture of property intended to exchange for controlled substances.

(a) Except as provided in subdivision (j), if the Attorney General or the district attorney determines that the factual circumstances do warrant that the property seized or subject to forfeiture comes within the provisions of subdivisions (a) to (g), inclusive, of Section 11470, and is not automatically made forfeitable or subject to court order of forfeiture or destruction by another provision of law, the Attorney General or district attorney shall file a complaint for forfeiture with the superior court of the county in which the property subject to forfeiture has been seized or in the county in which the property subject to forfeiture is located. If the complaint alleges that real property is forfeitable, the prosecuting attorney shall cause a lis pendens to be recorded in the office of the county recorder of each county in which the real property is located.

A complaint for forfeiture under this subdivision shall be filed within one year of the seizure of the property which is subject to forfeiture, or within one year of the filing by the Attorney General or district attorney of a lis pendens or other process against the property, whichever is earlier.

© 1992 by J., B. & L. Gould
Printed in the U.S.A.   **EP**

(b) Physical seizure shall not be necessary in order to forfeit property under this chapter. The prosecuting attorney may seek protective orders for any asset pursuant to Section 11492.

(c) The Attorney General or district attorney shall make service of process of the complaint and notice of the initiation of forfeiture proceedings upon every individual designated in a receipt issued for the property seized. In addition, the Attorney General or district attorney shall cause a notice of the seizure, if any, and of the intended forfeiture proceeding, stating that any interested party may file a verified claim with the superior court, as directed by the notice, to be served by personal delivery or by certified mail upon any person who has an interest in the seized property or property subject to forfeiture other than persons designated in a receipt issued for the property seized.

(d) The Attorney General, district attorney, or law enforcement agency which made the seizure shall make an investigation into any right, title, interest, or lien of record with the Department of Motor Vehicles or appropriate federal agency as to a vehicle, boat, or airplane. If the investigation discloses that any person, other than the registered owner, is the legal owner thereof, and the ownership did not arise subsequent to the date and time of arrest or notification of the forfeiture proceedings or seizure of the vehicle, boat, or airplane, the Attorney General or district attorney shall forthwith send a notice to the legal owner at his or her address appearing on the records of the Department of Motor Vehicles or appropriate federal agency.

(e) When a forfeiture action is filed, the notices of the initiation of forfeiture proceedings shall be published once a week for three successive weeks in a newspaper of general circulation in the county where the seizure was made or where the property subject to forfeiture is located.

(f) All notices shall set forth the time within which a claim of interest in the property seized or subject to forfeiture is required to be filed pursuant to Section 11488.5.

(g) (1) No sooner than 10 days after a complaint is filed pursuant to this section, a claimant, who alleges standing based on an interest in the property which arose prior to the seizure or filing of the complaint for forfeiture, whichever occurs first, may move the court for the return of the property named in the claim on the grounds that there is not probable cause to believe that the property is subject to forfeiture pursuant to Section 11470, or is not automatically forfeitable or subject to court order of forfeiture or otherwise subject to destruction by another provision of law. The showing of probable cause may be supported by evidence, prior judicial testimony, deposition, affidavit, or declaration. If the court determines that there is not probable cause to believe that the property is subject to forfeiture it shall order the property returned to the owner thereof unless the property is otherwise lawfully held.

(2) If a complaint is filed pursuant to this section and there is an underlying or related criminal action and the defendant has not pled guilty or nolo contendere, a defendant who is a claimant alleging an interest in the property in the related forfeiture proceeding may move, exclusively pursuant to Section 1538.5 of the Penal Code, for the return of the property on the grounds that there is not probable cause to believe that the property is forfeitable pursuant to Section 11470, or is not automatically made forfeitable

or subject to court order of forfeiture or destruction by another provision of this chapter.

The motion may be made at the preliminary examination or subsequent thereto. If made subsequent to the preliminary examination, the Attorney General or district attorney may submit the record of the preliminary hearing to establish that probable cause exists to believe that the property is subject to forfeiture. If the court determines that there is not probable cause to believe that the property is subject to forfeiture it shall order the property returned to the owner thereof unless the property is otherwise lawfully held.

(h) Within 30 days after a motion for return of property is granted pursuant to subdivision (g), the people may file a petition for writ of mandate or prohibition seeking appellate review of the order.

(i) Except as provided in subdivision (j) of this section and subdivision (d) of Section 11488.5, the People shall have the burden of proving by a preponderance of the evidence that the property is subject to forfeiture as described in Section 11470.

The provisions of the Code of Civil Procedure shall apply to proceedings under this chapter unless otherwise inconsistent with the provisions or procedures set forth in this chapter. However, in a proceeding under this chapter, there shall be no joinder of actions, coordination of actions, except for forfeiture proceedings, or cross-complaints, and the issues shall be limited strictly to questions related to this chapter.

A judgment of forfeiture does not require as a condition precedent thereto, that any defendant be convicted of an offense which made the property subject to forfeiture provided that the facts giving rise to forfeiture occurred within five years of the seizure of the property or within five years of the notification of intention to seek forfeiture. If there is a related criminal action, the issue of forfeiture may be tried in conjunction therewith by agreement of all parties. Trial shall be by jury unless waived by all parties. If there is no related criminal action, the presiding judge of the superior court shall assign the action brought pursuant to this chapter for trial.

(j) The Attorney General or the district attorney of the county in which property is subject to forfeiture under Section 11470 may, pursuant to this subdivision, order forfeiture of personal property not exceeding one hundred thousand dollars ($100,000) in value. The Attorney General or district attorney shall provide notice of proceedings under this subdivision pursuant to subdivisions (c), excluding the provision relating to service of the complaint, (d), (e), and (f), including:

(1) A description of the property.

(2) The appraised value of the property.

(3) The date and place of seizure or location of any property not seized but subject to forfeiture.

(4) The violation of law alleged with respect to forfeiture of the property.

(5) The instructions for filing a claim with the superior court pursuant to Section 11488.5 and time limits for filing a claim. If no claims are timely filed, the Attorney General or the district attorney shall prepare a written declaration of forfeiture of the subject property to the state and dispose of the property in accordance with Section 11489. A written declaration of forfeiture signed by the Attorney General or district attorney under this subdivision shall be deemed to provide good and sufficient title to the forfeited property.

The prosecuting agency ordering forfeiture pursuant to this subdivision shall provide a copy of the declaration of forfeiture to any person listed in the receipt given at the time of seizure and to any person personally served notice of the forfeiture proceedings.

If a claim is timely filed and served, then the Attorney General or district attorney shall file a complaint for forfeiture pursuant to this section within 30 days of the receipt of the claim. The complaint for forfeiture shall then proceed pursuant to other provisions of this chapter, except that no additional notice need be given and no additional claim need be filed.

This section shall remain in effect only until January 1, 1994, and as of that date is repealed. *(Amended by Stats 1990 ch 1200 §4, eff. 1/1/91 only until 1/1/94. See other section 11488.4 below.)*

§11488.4. Petition for forfeiture of property intended to exchange for controlled substances.

(a) Except as provided in subdivision (j), if the Department of Justice or the local governmental entity determines that the factual circumstances do warrant that the moneys, negotiable instruments, securities, or other things of value seized or subject to forfeiture come within the provisions of subdivisions (a) to (g), inclusive, of Section 11470, and are not automatically made forfeitable or subject to court order of forfeiture or destruction by another provision of this chapter, the Attorney General or district attorney shall file a petition of forfeiture with the superior court of the county in which the defendant has been charged with the underlying criminal offense or in which the property subject to forfeiture has been seized or, if no seizure has occurred, in the county in which the property subject to forfeiture is located. If the petition alleges that real property is forfeitable, the prosecuting attorney shall cause a lis pendens to be recorded in the office of the county recorder of each county in which the real property is located.

A petition of forfeiture under this subdivision shall be filed within one year of the seizure of the property which is subject to forfeiture, or within one year of the filing by the Attorney General or district attorney of a lis pendens or other process against the property, whichever is earlier.

(b) Physical seizure of assets shall not be necessary in order to have that particular asset alleged to be forfeitable in a petition under this section. The prosecuting attorney may seek protective orders for any asset pursuant to Section 11492.

(c) The Attorney General or district attorney shall make service of process regarding this petition upon every individual designated in a receipt issued for the property seized. In addition, the Attorney General or district attorney shall cause a notice of the seizure, if any, and of the intended forfeiture proceeding, as well as a notice stating that any interested party may file a verified claim with the superior court of the county in which the property was seized or if the property was not seized, a notice of the initiation of forfeiture proceedings with respect to any interest in the property seized or subject to forfeiture, to be served by personal delivery or by registered mail upon any person who has an interest in the seized property or property subject to forfeiture other than persons designated in a receipt issued for the property seized.

(d) An investigation shall be made by the law enforcement agency as to any claimant to a vehicle, boat, or airplane whose right, title, interest, or lien is of record in the Department of Motor Vehicles or appropriate federal agency. If the law enforcement agency finds that any person, other than the registered owner, is the legal owner thereof, and such ownership did not arise subsequent to the date and time of arrest or notification of the forfeiture proceedings or seizure of the vehicle, boat, or airplane, it shall forthwith send a notice to the legal owner at his or her address appearing on the records of the Department of Motor Vehicles or appropriate federal agency.

(e) When a forfeiture action is filed, the notices shall be published once a week for three successive weeks in a newspaper of general circulation in the county where the seizure was made or where the property subject to forfeiture is located.

(f) All notices shall set forth the time within which a claim of interest in the property seized or subject to forfeiture is required to be filed pursuant to Section 11488.5.

(g) Nothing contained in this chapter shall preclude a person, other than a defendant, claiming an interest in property actually seized from moving for a return of property pursuant to Section 1538.5, 1539, or 1540 of the Penal Code if that person can show standing by proving an interest in the property not assigned subsequent to the seizure or filing of the forfeiture petition.

(h) If there is an underlying or related criminal action, a defendant may move, exclusively pursuant to Section 1538.5 of the Penal Code, for the return of the property on the grounds that there is not probable cause to believe that the property is forfeitable pursuant to subdivisions (a) to (g), inclusive, of Section 11470 and is not automatically made forfeitable or subject to court order of forfeiture or destruction by another provision of this chapter. The motion may be made at the preliminary examination or subsequent thereto. If made subsequent to the preliminary examination, the Attorney General or district attorney may submit the record of the preliminary hearing to establish that probable cause exists to believe that the underlying or related criminal violations have occurred.

Within 15 days after a defendant's motion is granted, the people may file a petition for a writ of mandate or prohibition seeking appellate review of the ruling.

(i) (1) With respect to property described in subdivisions (e) and (g) of Section 11470 for which forfeiture is sought and as to which forfeiture is contested, the state or local governmental entity shall have the burden of proving beyond a reasonable doubt that the property for which forfeiture is sought was used, or intended to be used, to facilitate a violation of one of the offenses enumerated in subdivision (f) or (g) of Section 11470.

(2) In the case of property described in subdivision (f) of Section 11470, except cash, negotiable instruments, or other cash equivalents of a value of not less than twenty-five thousand dollars ($25,000), for which forfeiture is sought and as to which forfeiture is contested, the state or local governmental entity shall have the burden of proving beyond a reasonable doubt that the property for which forfeiture is sought meets the criteria for forfeiture described in subdivision (f) of Section 11470.

(3) In the case of property described in paragraphs (1) or (2), a judgment of forfeiture requires as a condition precedent thereto, that a defendant be convicted

806

© 1992 by J., B. & L. Gould
Printed in the U.S.A.   **EP**

in an underlying or related criminal action of an offense specified in subdivision (f) or (g) of Section 11470 which offense occurred within five years of the seizure of the property subject to forfeiture or within five years of the notification of intention to seek forfeiture. If the defendant is found guilty of the underlying or related criminal offense, the issue of forfeiture shall be tried before the same jury, if the trial was by jury, or tried before the same court, if trial was by court, unless waived by all parties.

(4) In the case of property described in subdivision (f) of Section 11470 that is cash or negotiable instruments of a value of not less than twenty-five thousand dollars ($25,000), the state or local governmental entity shall have the burden of proving by clear and convincing evidence that the property for which forfeiture is sought is such as is described in subdivision (f) of Section 11470. There is no requirement for forfeiture thereof that a criminal conviction be obtained in an underlying or related criminal offense.

(5) If there is an underlying or related criminal action, and a criminal conviction is required before a judgment of forfeiture may be entered, the issue of forfeiture shall be tried in conjunction therewith. Trial shall be by jury unless waived by all parties. If there is no underlying or related criminal action, the presiding judge of the superior court shall assign the action brought pursuant to this chapter for trial.

(j) The Attorney General or the district attorney of the county in which property is subject to forfeiture under Section 11470 may, pursuant to this subdivision, order forfeiture of personal property not exceeding twenty-five thousand dollars ($25,000) in value. The Attorney General or district attorney shall provide notice of proceedings under this subdivision pursuant to subdivisions (c), (d), (e), and (f), including:

(1) A description of the property.

(2) The appraised value of the property.

(3) The date and place of seizure or location of any property not seized but subject to forfeiture.

(4) The violation of law alleged with respect to forfeiture of the property.

(5) The instructions for filing a claim with the Attorney General or the district attorney pursuant to Section 11488.5 and time limits for filing a claim. If no claims are timely filed, the Attorney General or the district attorney shall prepare a written declaration of forfeiture of the subject property to the state and dispose of the property in accordance with Section 11489. A written declaration of forfeiture signed by the Attorney General or district attorney under this subdivision shall be deemed to provide good and sufficient title to the forfeited property.

The prosecuting agency ordering forfeiture pursuant to this subdivision shall provide a copy of the declaration of forfeiture to any person listed in the receipt given at the time of seizure and to any person listed in the receipt given at the time of seizure and to any person personally served notice of the forfeiture proceedings.

If a claim is timely filed, then the Attorney General or district attorney shall file a petition of forfeiture pursuant to this section within 30 days of the receipt of the claim. The petition of forfeiture shall then proceed pursuant to other provisions of this chapter, except that no additional notice need be given and no additional claim need be filed.

(k) If in any underlying or related criminal action or proceeding, in which a petition for forfeiture has been filed pursuant to this section, and a criminal conviction is required before a judgment of forfeiture may be entered, the defendant willfully fails to appear as required there shall be no requirement of a criminal conviction as a prerequisite to forfeiture. In these cases, forfeiture shall be ordered as against the defendant and judgment entered upon default, upon application of the state or local governmental entity. In its application for default, the state or local governmental entity shall be required to give notice to the defendant's attorney of record, if any, in the underlying or related criminal action, and to make a showing of due diligence to locate the defendant. In moving for a default judgment pursuant to this subdivision, the state or local governmental entity shall be required to establish a prima facie case in support of its petition for forfeiture.

(*l*) This section shall remain in effect only until January 1, 1989, and as of that date is repealed, unless a later enacted statute, which is enacted before January 1, 1989, deletes or extends that date. *(Repealed by Stats 1988 ch 1492 §§9, 16, eff. 1/1/89 only until 1/1/94. See other section 11488.4 above.)*

§11488.5. Third party interest.

(a) (1) Any person claiming an interest in the property alleged to be subject to forfeiture may, at any time within 30 days from the date of the first publication of the notice of seizure, if that person was not personally served or served by mail, or within 10 days after receipt of actual notice, file with the superior court, as directed by the notice, a verified claim stating the nature of his or her interest in the property. An endorsed copy of the claim shall be served by the claimant on the Attorney General or district attorney, as appropriate, within 10 days of the filing of the claim. The Judicial Council shall develop and approve official forms for the verified claim that is to be filed pursuant to this section. The official forms shall be drafted in nontechnical language and shall be made available through the office of the clerk of the appropriate court.

(2) Within 30 days of the service of the complaint for forfeiture, a claimant shall file an answer thereto unless for good cause shown, the court extends the time for the filing of the answer.

(b) The property shall remain under control of the law enforcement or prosecutorial agency until the adjudication of the forfeiture hearing.

(c) The claim of the state or a local agency to property subject to forfeiture shall have priority over a claim to the seized or forfeitable property made by the Franchise Tax Board in a notice to withhold issued pursuant to Section 18817 or 26132 of the Revenue and Taxation Code.

(d) If, at the end of the time set forth in paragraph (1) of subdivision (a), there is no claim on file, the court, upon motion, shall declare the property seized or subject to forfeiture pursuant to Section 11470 forfeited to the state. In moving for a default judgment pursuant to this subdivision, the People shall be required to establish a prima facie case in support of its complaint for forfeiture.

(e) (1) If a verified claim and answer are timely filed, the forfeiture proceeding shall be set for hearing pursuant to the rules of the court, but the proceeding shall have priority over other civil cases. A claim and answer shall not be admissible in the proceeding regarding the offense.

(2) The hearing shall be by jury, unless waived by the parties.

(f) Forfeiture shall be ordered when, at the hearing, the People have shown that the property is subject to forfeiture pursuant to Section 11470, in accordance with the burden of proof set forth in subdivision (i) of Section 11488.4.

(g) The forfeiture hearing shall be continued upon motion of the People or a claimant who is concurrently a defendant in a related criminal proceeding until the charge in that proceeding has been resolved in the trial court or the defendant fails to appear. The forfeiture hearing shall be conducted in accordance with Sections 600 to 630, inclusive, of the Code of Civil Procedure if a trial by jury, and by Sections 631 to 636, inclusive, of the Code of Civil Procedure if by the court. Unless the court or jury finds that the property is subject to forfeiture pursuant to Section 11470, the court shall order the property released to the person it determines is entitled thereto.

(h) If the court or jury finds that the property is subject to forfeiture, and finds that a person claiming an interest therein knew or should have known of facts which made the property subject to forfeiture pursuant to Section 11470, the court shall order that the person's interest in the property be forfeited. If the court or jury does not make these findings, the court shall order that the person's interest in the property be returned. The People shall have the burden of proving in accordance with the burden of proof set forth in subdivision (i) of Section 11488.4, that a person claiming an interest knew or should have known of facts which made the property subject to forfeiture pursuant to Section 11470.

(i) All property which was the subject of a forfeiture hearing and which was not released by the court to a claimant shall be declared by the court to be forfeited to the state. Except as provided in Sections 11473.2 and 11473.3, the clerk of the court shall provide for disposition of the forfeited property as set forth in Section 11489. A judgment entered pursuant to this section is not subject to Section 473 of the Code of Civil Procedure.

(j) All property which was the subject of the forfeiture hearing and which was not forfeited shall remain subject to any order to withhold issued with respect to the property by the Franchise Tax Board.

This section shall remain in effect only until January 1, 1994, and as of that date is repealed. *(Amended by Stats 1990 ch 1200 §5, eff. 1/1/91 only until 1/1/94. See other section 11488.5 below.)*

§11488.5. Third party interest.

(a) (1) Any person claiming an interest in the property seized pursuant to Section 11488 may, at any time within 30 days from the date of the first publication of the notice of seizure, if that person was not personally served or served by mail, or within 10 days after receipt of actual notice, file with the superior court of the county in which the defendant has been charged with the underlying or related criminal offense or in which the property was seized or, if there was no seizure, in which the property is located, a verified claim stating his or her interest in the property. A verified copy of the claim shall be served by the claimant on the Attorney General or district attorney, as appropriate.

(2) Any person who claims that the property was assigned to him or to her prior to the seizure or notification of pending forfeiture of the property under this chapter, whichever occurs first, shall file a claim with the court and prosecuting agency pursuant to Section 11488.5 declaring an interest in that property and such interest shall be adjudicated at the forfeiture hearing. The property shall remain under control of the law enforcement or prosecutorial agency until the adjudication of the forfeiture hearing.

(3) The claim of a law enforcement agency to property seized pursuant to Section 11488 or subject to forfeiture shall have priority over a claim to the seized or forfeitable property made by the Franchise Tax Board in a notice to withhold issued pursuant to Section 18817 or 26132 of the Revenue and Taxation Code.

(b) (1) If, at the end of the time set forth in subdivision (a), there is no claim on file, the court, upon motion, shall declare the property seized or subject to forfeiture pursuant to subdivisions (a) to (g), inclusive, of Section 11470 forfeited to the state. In moving for a default judgment pursuant to this subdivision, the state or local governmental entity shall be required to establish a prima facie case in support of its petition for forfeiture.

(2) The clerk of the court shall dispose of the forfeited property as set forth in Section 11489.

(c) (1) If a verified claim is filed, the forfeiture proceeding shall be set for hearing on a day not less than 30 days therefrom, and the proceeding shall have priority over other civil cases. Notice of the hearing shall be given in the same manner as provided in Section 11488.4. Such a verified claim or a claim filed pursuant to subdivision (j) of Section 11488.4 shall not be admissible in the proceedings regarding the underlying or related criminal offense set forth in subdivision (a) of Section 11488.

(2) The hearing shall be by jury, unless waived by consent of all parties.

(d) (1) At the hearing, the state or local governmental entity shall have the burden of establishing, pursuant to subdivision (i) of Section 11488.4, that the owner of any interest in the seized property consented to the use of the property with knowledge that it would be or was used for a purpose for which forfeiture is permitted, in accordance with the burden of proof set forth in subdivision (i) of Section 11488.4.

(2) No interest in the seized property shall be affected by a forfeiture decree under this section unless the state or local governmental entity has proven that the owner of such interest consented to the use of the property with knowledge that it would be or was used for the purpose charged. Forfeiture shall be ordered when, at the hearing, the state or local governmental entity has shown that the assets in question are subject to forfeiture pursuant to Section 11470, in accordance with the burden of proof set forth in subdivision (i) of Section 11488.4.

(e) The forfeiture hearing shall be continued upon motion of the prosecution or the defendant until after a verdict of guilty on any criminal charges specified in this chapter and pending against the defendant have been decided. The forfeiture hearing shall be conducted in accordance with Sections 600 to 630, inclusive, of the Code of Civil Procedure if a trial by jury, and by Sections 631 to 636, inclusive, of the Code of Civil Procedure if by the court. Unless the court or jury finds that the seized property was used for a purpose for which forfeiture is permitted, the court shall order the seized property released to the person it determines is entitled thereto.

© 1992 by J., B. & L. Gould
Printed in the U.S.A.   **EP**

If the court or jury finds that the seized property was used for a purpose for which forfeiture is permitted, but does not find that a person claiming an interest therein, to which the court has determined he or she is entitled, had actual knowledge that the seized property would be or was used for a purpose for which forfeiture is permitted, the court shall order the seized property released to the claimant.

(f) All seized property which was the subject of a contested forfeiture hearing and which was not released by the court to a claimant shall be declared by the court to be forfeited to the state, provided the burden of proof required pursuant to subdivision (i) of Section 11488.4 has been met. Except as provided in Sections 11473.2 and 11473.3, the clerk of the court shall dispose of the forfeited property as set forth in Section 11489.

(g) All seized property which was the subject of the forfeiture hearing and which was not forfeited shall remain subject to any order to withhold issued with respect to the property by the Franchise Tax Board.

(h) This section shall remain in effect only until January 1, 1989, and as of that date is repealed, unless a later enacted statute, which is enacted before January 1, 1989, deletes or extends that date. *(Repealed by Stats 1988 ch 1492 §§12, 16, eff. 1/1/89 only until 1/1/94. See other section 11488.5 above.)*

§11488.6. Relinquishing claims in materials to be exchanged for controlled substances.

(a) If the court or jury at the forfeiture hearing finds that the property is forfeitable pursuant to Section 11470, and further finds that the People have not met its burden of proving that a person holding a valid lien, mortgage, security interest, or interest under a conditional sales contract knew or should have known of facts which would or did make the property subject to forfeiture pursuant to Section 11470 when the interest was acquired, and that person's interest is less than the appraised value of the property, that person may pay to the court the owner's equity, which shall be deemed to be the difference between the appraised value and the amount of the lien, mortgage, security interest, or interest under a conditional sales contract. Upon payment, the People shall relinquish all claims to the property and the court shall enter judgment pursuant to Section 11488.5 against the owner's equity. If the holder of the interest elects not to make payment, the property shall be adjudged forfeited to the state, and the ownership certificate shall be surrendered. The appraised value shall be determined as of the date judgment is entered on a wholesale basis either by agreement between the interestholder and the People, or if they cannot agree, then by the inheritance tax appraiser for the county in which the action is brought. A person holding a valid lien, mortgage, security interest, or interest under a conditional sales contract shall be paid the appraised value of his or her interest in accordance with the provision of Section 11489.

(b) This section shall remain in effect only until January 1, 1994, and as of that date is repealed. *(Amended by Stats 1990 ch 1200 §6, eff. 1/1/91 only until 1/1/94. See other section 11488.6 below.)*

§11488.6. Relinquishing claims in materials to be exchanged for controlled substances.

(a) If the court or jury at the forfeiture hearing finds that the property is forfeitable pursuant to subdivision (e), (f), or (g) of Section 11470, but does not find that a person holding a valid lien, mortgage, security interest, or interest under a conditional sales contract acquired such interest with actual knowledge that the property was to be used for a purpose for which forfeiture is permitted, and the amount due such person is less than the appraised value of the property, such person may pay to the state or the local governmental entity which initiated the forfeiture proceeding the amount of the registered owner's equity, which shall be deemed to be the difference between the appraised value and the amount of the lien, mortgage, security interest, or interest under a conditional sales contract. Upon such payment, the state or local governmental entity shall relinquish all claims to the property. If the holder of the interest elects not to make such payment to the state or local governmental entity, the property shall be deemed forfeited to the state or local governmental entity and the ownership certificate shall be forwarded. The appraised value shall be determined as of the date judgment is entered on a wholesale basis either by agreement between the legal owner and the governmental entity involved, or if they cannot agree, then by the inheritance tax appraiser for the county in which the action is brought. A person holding a valid lien, mortgage, security interest, or interest under a conditional sales contract shall be paid the appraised value of his or her interest in accordance with the provisions of Section 11489.

(b) If the amount due to a person holding a valid lien, mortgage, security interest, or interest under a conditional sales contract is less than the value of the property and the person elects not to make payment to the governmental entity, the property, excluding vehicles identified in Section 11473.2 which a law enforcement agency may place in its own name for use in its law enforcement program, shall be sold at public auction by the Department of General Services or by the local governmental entity which shall provide notice of such sale by one publication in a newspaper published and circulated in the city, community, or locality where the sale is to take place.

(c) The proceeds of sale pursuant to subdivision (b) shall be first distributed in accordance with the provisions of Section 11489. *(Amended by Stats 1988 ch 1492 §§13, 16, eff. 1/1/94. See other section 11488.6 above.)*

§11488.7. Repealed by Stats 1990 ch 1200 §7, eff. 1/1/91.

§11489. Disposition of proceeds from sale of forfeited property.

Notwithstanding Section 11502, and except as otherwise provided in Sections 11473, 11473.2, and 11473.3, in all cases where the property is seized pursuant to this chapter and forfeited to the state or local governmental entity and, where necessary, sold by the Department of General Services or local governmental entity, the money forfeited or the proceeds of sale, and any interest accrued thereon, shall be distributed by the state or local governmental entity as follows:

(a) To the bona fide or innocent purchaser or encumbrancer, conditional sales vendor, or mortgagee of the property, if any, up to the amount of his or her interest in the property, when the court declaring the forfeiture orders a distribution to that person.

(b) The balance, if any, to accumulate, and to be distributed and transferred quarterly in the following manner:

(1) To the state agency or local governmental entity for all expenditures made or incurred by it in connection with the sale of the property, including expenditures for any necessary costs of notice required by Section 11488.4 and any necessary repairs, storage, or transportation of any property seized under this chapter.

(2) Ninety percent of the balance shall be distributed as follows:

(A) Eighty-five percent to the state or local or to the state and local law enforcement agencies that participated in the seizure, allocated between them to reflect the proportionate contribution of each agency.

(B) Fifteen percent to the prosecutorial agency which processes the forfeiture action.

(3) Ten percent of the balance for deposit in the Asset Forfeiture Distribution Fund, which is hereby created, and which shall be administered by the Office of Criminal Justice Planning.

(A) Notwithstanding Section 11340 of the Government Code, one million five hundred thousand dollars ($1,500,000) is hereby continuously appropriated each fiscal year, as adjusted annually by the state and local implicit price deflator, to the State Department of Mental Health for the purposes of Chapter 6 (commencing with Section 5475) of Part 1 of Division 5 of the Welfare and Institutions Code. This subparagraph shall be funded prior to funding subparagraph (B).

(B) After the obligation specified in subparagraph (A) is satisfied, moneys in the Asset Forfeiture Distribution Fund are available for appropriation in the annual Budget Act for the following purposes:

(i) One million dollars ($1,000,000) for the 1991-92 fiscal year to the Los Angeles County Office of Education to fund grants and administer the Gang Risk Intervention Pilot Program as established pursuant to Chapter 5 (commencing with Section 58700) of Part 31 of the Education Code. This clause (i) shall be funded prior to funding clauses (ii) and (iii). This clause (i) shall remain operative only until July 1, 1992, and as of that date is inoperative.

(ii) An amount not to exceed 5 percent of the Asset Forfeiture Distribution Fund to cover administrative costs incurred by the Office of Criminal Justice Planning. Notwithstanding Section 16305.7 of the Government Code, any interest earned or other increment derived from investments made from moneys in the Asset Forfeiture Distribution Fund shall be deposited in the Asset Forfeiture Distribution Fund. This clause (ii) shall be funded prior to funding clause (iii).

(iii) The balance, if any, remaining shall revert to the General Fund on June 30, 1992.

(c) Notwithstanding Item 0820-101-469 of the Budget Act of 1985 (Chapter 111 of the Statutes of 1985), all funds allocated to the Department of Justice pursuant to subparagraph (A) of paragraph (2) of subdivision (b) shall be deposited into the Department of Justice Special Deposit Fund-State Asset Forfeiture Account and used for the law enforcement efforts of the state or for state or local law enforcement efforts pursuant to Section 11493.

All funds allocated to the Department of Justice by the federal government under its Federal Asset Forfeiture program authorized by the Comprehensive Crime Control Act of 1984 may be deposited directly into the Narcotics Assistance and Relinquishment by Criminal Offenders Fund and used for state and local law enforcement efforts pursuant to Section 11493.

Funds which are not deposited pursuant to the above paragraph shall be deposited into the Department of Justice Special Deposit Fund-Federal Asset Forfeiture Account.

(d) All the funds distributed pursuant to paragraph (2) of subdivision (b) shall not supplant any state or local funds that would, in the absence of this subdivision, be made available to support the law enforcement and prosecutorial efforts of these agencies. Funds so distributed shall be used by the law enforcement and prosecutorial agencies exclusively to support law enforcement and prosecutorial efforts of those agencies.

(e) This section shall remain in effect until July 1, 1992, and as of that date is repealed. *(Amended by Stats 1991 ch 641 §§2, 14, eff. 1/1/92 only until 7/1/92. See other sections 11489 below.)*

§11489. Disposition of proceeds from sale of forfeited property.

Notwithstanding Section 11502 and except as otherwise provided in Sections 11473, 11473.2, and 11473.3, in all cases where the property is seized pursuant to this chapter and forfeited to the state or local governmental entity and, where necessary, sold by the Department of General Services or local governmental entity, the money forfeited or the proceeds of sale, and any interest accrued thereon, shall be distributed by the state or local governmental entity as follows:

(a) To the bona fide or innocent purchaser or encumbrancer, conditional sales vendor, or mortgagee of the property, if any, up to the amount of his or her interest in the property, when the court declaring the forfeiture orders a distribution to that person.

(b) The balance, if any, to accumulate, and to be distributed and transferred quarterly in the following manner:

(1) To the state agency or local governmental entity for all expenditures made or incurred by it in connection with the sale of the property, including expenditures for any necessary costs of notice required by Section 11488.4 and any necessary repairs, storage, or transportation of any property seized under this chapter.

(2) Ninety percent of the balance shall be distributed as follows:

(A) Eighty-five percent to the state or local or to the state and local law enforcement agencies that participated in the seizure, allocated between them to reflect the proportionate contribution of each agency.

(B) Fifteen percent to the prosecutorial agency which processes the forfeiture action.

(3) Ten percent of the balance for deposit in the Asset Forfeiture Distribution Fund, which is hereby created, and which shall be administered by the Office of Criminal Justice Planning.

(A) Notwithstanding Section 11340 of the Government Code, one million five hundred thousand dollars ($1,500,000) is hereby continuously appropriated each fiscal year, as adjusted annually by the state and local implicit price deflator, to the State Department of Mental Health for the purposes of Chapter 6 (commencing with Section 5475) of Part 1 of Division 5 of the Welfare and Institutions Code. This subparagraph shall be funded prior to funding subparagraph (B).

© 1992 by J., B. & L. Gould
Printed in the U.S.A.   **EP**

(B) After the obligation specified in subparagraph (A) is satisfied, moneys in the Asset Forfeiture Distribution Fund are available for appropriation in the annual Budget Act for the following purposes:

(i) One million dollars ($1,000,000), in 1989 and 1990 only, to the Los Angeles County Office of Education to fund grants and administer the Gang Risk Intervention Pilot Program as established pursuant to Assembly Bill 3723 of the 1987-88 Regular Session of the Legislature. This clause (i) shall be funded prior to funding clauses (ii) and (iii). This clause (i) shall remain operative only until January 1, 1991, and as of that date is inoperative.

(ii) An amount not to exceed 5 percent of the Asset Forfeiture Distribution Fund to cover administrative costs incurred by the Office of Criminal Justice Planning. Notwithstanding Section 16305.7 of the Government Code, any interest earned or other increment derived from investments made from moneys in the Assets Forfeiture Distribution Fund shall be deposited in the Asset Forfeiture Distribution Fund. This clause (ii) shall be funded prior to funding clause (iii).

(iii) The balance, if any, remaining shall be distributed, as follows:

(I) Eighty-five percent for deposit in the Peace Officers' Training Fund as set forth in Section 13520 of the Penal Code. State agencies shall be entitled to allocations out of the funds generated by this section, in the same manner as provided in Section 13523 of the Penal Code, for drug related training provided to full-time regularly paid peace officers employed by the state, to the extent that there are funds in the Peace Officers' Training Fund generated by this section.

(II) Fifteen percent for financial assistance to provide for a statewide program of education, training, and research for local public prosecutors, which shall be administered by a private nonprofit organization composed of local prosecutors and which provides statewide education, training, and research.

(c) Notwithstanding Item 0820-101-469 of the Budget Act of 1985 (Chapter 111 of the Statutes of 1985), all funds allocated to the Department of Justice pursuant to subparagraph (A) of paragraph (3) of subdivision (b) shall be deposited into the Department of Justice Special Deposit Fund-State Asset Forfeiture Account and used for the law enforcement efforts of the state or for state or local law enforcement efforts pursuant to Section 11493.

All funds allocated to the Department of Justice by the federal government under its Federal Asset Forfeiture program authorized by the Comprehensive Crime Control Act of 1984 may be deposited directly into the Narcotics Assistance and Relinquishment by Criminal Offenders Fund and used for state and local law enforcement efforts pursuant to Section 11493.

Funds which are not deposited pursuant to the above paragraph shall be deposited into the Department of Justice Special Deposit Fund-Federal Asset Forfeiture Account.

(d) All the funds distributed pursuant to paragraph (3) of subdivision (b) shall not supplant any state or local funds that would, in the absence of this subdivision, be made available to support the law enforcement and prosecutorial efforts of these agencies. Funds so distributed shall be used by the law enforcement and prosecutorial agencies exclusively to support law enforcement and prosecutorial efforts of those agencies.

The court shall order the forfeiture proceeds distributed to the state, local, or state and local agencies as provided in this section.

All proceeds from forfeiture proceedings completed after January 1, 1989, shall be distributed in accordance with this section.

(e) This section shall become operative on July 1, 1992.

(f) This section shall remain in effect until January 1, 1994, and as of that date is repealed. *(Added by Stats 1991 ch 641 §3, eff. 1/1/92, oper. 7/1/92. Effective only until 1/1/94. See other sections 11489 above and below.)*

§11489. Disposition of proceeds from sale of forfeited property.

Notwithstanding Section 11502 and except as otherwise provided in Sections 11473 and 11473.2, in all cases where the property is seized pursuant to this chapter and forfeited to the state or local governmental entity and, where necessary, sold by the Department of General Services or local governmental entity, the money forfeited or the proceeds of sale shall be distributed by the state or local governmental entity as follows:

(a) To the bona fide or innocent purchaser, conditional sales vendor, or mortgagee of the property, if any, up to the amount of his or her interest in the property, when the court declaring the forfeiture orders a distribution to that person.

(b) The balance, if any, to accumulate, and to be distributed and transferred quarterly in the following manner:

(1) To the state agency or local governmental entity for all expenditures made or incurred by it in connection with the sale of the property, including expenditures for any necessary repairs, storage, or transportation of any property seized under this chapter.

(2) The remaining funds shall be distributed as follows:

(A) Sixty-five percent to the state, local, or state and local law enforcement entities that participated in the seizure distributed so as to reflect the proportionate contribution of each agency.

(B) Ten percent to the prosecutorial agency which processes the forfeiture action.

(C) Twenty percent to the State Department of Mental Health for deposit in the Mental Health Primary Prevention Fund for primary prevention programs in accordance with Chapter 1083 of the Statutes of 1981. There is hereby created in the State Treasury the Mental Health Primary Prevention Fund. Notwithstanding Section 13340 of the Government Code, the moneys in the Mental Health Primary Prevention Fund are hereby continuously appropriated to the State Department of Mental Health to expend for primary prevention programs in accordance with Chapter 6 (commencing with Section 5475) of Part 1 of Division 5 of the Welfare and Institutions Code. Expenditures may include administrative costs incurred by the department. These administrative costs are not to exceed 5 percent of the fund. Notwithstanding the provisions of Section 16305.7 of the Government Code, any interest earned or other increment derived from investments made from moneys in the fund shall be deposited in the Mental Health Primary Prevention Fund.

(D) Five percent to eligible nonprofit organizations established for the purposes of aiding those seizures and forfeitures. Moneys shall be used to fund the operations of those organizations where it has been determined that information provided by the organization resulted in the seizure of these funds. In all other instances these moneys shall be deposited into the Narcotics Assistance and Relinquishment by Criminal Offenders Fund. The eligibility criteria and amount of funds to be allocated under this subparagraph shall be determined by each county pursuant to county ordinance.

(c) Notwithstanding Item 0820-101-469 of the Budget Act of 1985 (Chapter 111 of the Statutes of 1985), all funds allocated to the Department of Justice pursuant to subparagraph (A) of paragraph (2) of subdivision (b) shall be deposited into the Department of Justice Special Deposit Fund-State Asset Forfeiture Account and used for the law enforcement efforts of the state or for state or local law enforcement efforts pursuant to Section 11493.

All funds allocated to the Department of Justice by the federal government under its Federal Asset Forfeiture program authorized by the Comprehensive Crime Control Act of 1984 may be deposited directly into the Narcotics Assistance and Relinquishment by Criminal Offender Fund and used for state and local law enforcement efforts pursuant to Section 11493.

Funds which are not deposited pursuant to the above paragraph shall be deposited into the Department of Justice Special Deposit Fund-Federal Asset Forfeiture Account.

(d) All the funds distributed to the state or local governmental entity pursuant to subparagraphs (A) and (B) of paragraph (2) of subdivision (b) shall not supplant any state or local funds that would, in the absence of this subdivision, be made available to support the law enforcement and prosecutorial efforts of these agencies.

The court shall order the forfeiture proceeds distributed to the state, local, or state and local governmental entities as provided in this section.

For the purposes of this section, "local governmental entity" means any city, county, or city and county in this state.

All property seized and all proceeds from the sale of property seized pursuant to this chapter prior to October 2, 1985, shall be distributed in accordance with the provisions of this section.

(e) This section shall become operative on January 1, 1994. (Added by Stats 1991 ch 641 §4, eff. 1/1/92, oper. 1/1/94. See other sections 11489 above.)

§11490. Conditions under which division shall not apply.

The provisions of this division relative to forfeiture of vehicles, boats, or airplanes shall not apply to a common carrier, or to an employee acting within the scope of his employment in the enforcement of this division.

§11491. Decisional law unchanged.

Nothing in this chapter shall be construed to extend or change decisional law as it relates to the topic of search and seizure.

§11492. Status quo of property in forfeiture petition.

(a) Concurrent with, or subsequent to, the filing of the complaint, the prosecuting agency may move the superior court for the following pendente lite orders to preserve the status quo or value of the property alleged in the complaint for forfeiture.

(1) An injunction to restrain all interested parties and enjoin them from transferring, encumbering, hypothecating, or otherwise disposing of that property.

(2) Appointment of a receiver to take possession of, care for, manage, and operate the assets and properties so that the property may be maintained and preserved.

(3) Order an interlocutory sale of the property named in the complaint when the property is liable to perish, to waste, or to be significantly reduced in value, or when the expenses of maintaining the property are disproportionate to the value thereof, and the proceeds thereof shall be deposited with the court or as directed by the court pending determination of the forfeiture proceeding.

(b) No preliminary injunction may be granted, receiver appointed, or interlocutory sale ordered without notice to the interested parties and a hearing to determine that the order is necessary to preserve the property named in the complaint, pending the outcome of the proceedings, and that there is probable cause to believe that the property is subject to forfeiture under Section 11470. However, a temporary restraining order may issue pending that hearing pursuant to the provisions of Section 527 of the Code of Civil Procedure.

(c) Notwithstanding any other provision of law, the court in granting these motions may order a surety bond or undertaking to preserve the property interests of the interested parties. (Amended by Stats 1990 ch 1200 §8, eff. 1/1/91.)

§11493. Creation of Narcotics Assistance and Relinquishment by Criminal Offender Fund.

There is hereby created in the General Fund the Narcotics Assistance and Relinquishment by Criminal Offender Fund. The fund shall be administered by an advisory committee which shall be appointed by the Attorney General and which shall be comprised of three police chiefs, three sheriffs, two district attorneys, one private citizen, and the Director of the Division of Law Enforcement of the Department of Justice who shall serve as the executive officer.

The money in the fund shall be available, upon appropriation by the Legislature, for distribution by the advisory committee to local and state law enforcement agencies in support of general narcotic law enforcement efforts.

CHAPTER 9

COLLECTION AND DISPOSITION OF FINES

§11500. Actions by district attorney and Attorney General.

The district attorney, or any person designated by him, of the county in which any violation of this division is committed shall conduct all actions and prosecutions for the violation.

However, the Attorney General, or special counsel employed by the Attorney General for that purpose,

© 1992 by J., B. & L. Gould
Printed in the U.S.A.   EP

may take complete charge of the conduct of such actions or prosecutions. The Attorney General may fix the compensation to be paid for the service and may incur such other expense in connection with the conduct of the actions or prosecutions as he may deem necessary. No attorney employed as special counsel shall receive as compensation more than three thousand five hundred dollars ($3,500) in any one year.

§11501. Recovery of public funds paid for controlled substances during investigation.

The State of California, or any political subdivision thereof, may maintain an action against any person or persons engaged in the unlawful sale of controlled substances for the recovery of any public funds paid over to such person or persons in the course of any investigation of violations of this division. All proceedings under this section shall be instituted in the superior court of the county where the funds were paid over, where the sale was made, or where the defendant resides. Notwithstanding Section 483.010 of the Code of Civil Procedure, in any action under this section, a writ of attachment may be issued, without the showing required by Section 485.010 of the Code of Civil Procedure, in the manner provided by Chapter 5 (commencing with Section 485.010) of Title 6.5 of Part 2 of the Code of Civil Procedure to attach any funds paid over or any other funds on the defendant's person at the time of his arrest.

§11502. Disposition of funds received under this division.

All moneys, forfeited bail, or fines received by any court under this division shall as soon as practicable after the receipt thereof be deposited with the county treasurer of the county in which such court is situated. Amounts so deposited shall be paid at least once a month as follows: 75 percent to the State Treasurer by warrant of the county auditor drawn upon the requisition of the clerk or judge of said court to be deposited in the State Treasury on order of the State Controller; and 25 percent to the city treasurer of the city, if the offense occurred in a city, otherwise to the treasurer of the county in which the prosecution is conducted.

Any money deposited in the State Treasury under the provisions of this section which is determined by the State Controller to have been erroneously deposited therein shall be refunded by him, subject to approval of the State Board of Control prior to the payment of such refund, out of any money in the State Treasury which is available by law for such purpose.

§11503. Fines and forfeitures; collection.

Judges and magistrates who collect fines or forfeitures under this division shall keep a record thereof, and, upon the imposition of any such fine or forfeiture, shall at least monthly transmit a record of it to the county auditor. The county auditor shall transmit a record of the imposition, collection and payment of such fines or forfeitures to the State Controller at the time of transmittal of each warrant to the State Treasurer pursuant to this article.

§11504. Recording of fines levied in lieu of imprisonment.

When an imprisonment has been imposed for a violation of this division, and before the termination of the sentence, the defendant is released by the vaca-

tion of the sentence of imprisonment and the imposition of a fine or forfeiture instead, the fine or forfeiture shall be recorded and accounted for in the same manner as though it had been imposed in the first instance.

§11505. Recording of imprisonment imposed in lieu of fine.

Whenever a fine has been imposed for violation of this division, and before the full payment of the fine a sentence of imprisonment is imposed instead, the imprisonment shall be recorded and accounted for to the county auditor.

§11506. Checking reports.

The State Controller shall check the reports and records received by him with the transmittals of fines and forfeitures and whenever it appears that fines or forfeitures have not been transmitted the county auditor shall and the State Controller may bring suit to enforce their collection or transmittal, or both.

§11507. Liability of judge's bond.

The official bond of any judge or magistrate is liable for his failure to transmit the fines or forfeitures imposed by him under this division.

§11508. Public inspection of judge's records.

The records kept by a judge or magistrate under this division are open to public inspection, and may be checked by the State Controller, the Attorney General, the district attorney of the particular county, or the state bureau.

§11509. *Repealed by Stats 1988 ch 1492 §15, eff. 1/1/89.*

CHAPTER 10

CONTROL OF USERS OF CONTROLLED SUBSTANCES

ARTICLE 1

ADDICTS

§11550. Use of controlled substances prohibited.

(a) No person shall use, or be under the influence of any controlled substance which is (1) specified in subdivision (b), (c), or (e), or paragraph (1) of subdivision (f) of Section 11054, specified in paragraph (14), (15), (21), (22), or (23) of subdivision (d) of Section 11054, specified in subdivision (b) or (c) of Section 11055, or specified in paragraph (1) or (2) of subdivision (d) or in paragraph (3) of subdivision (e) of Section 11055, or (2) a narcotic drug classified in Schedule III, IV, or V, except when administered by or under the direction of a person licensed by the state to dispense, prescribe, or administer controlled substances. It shall be the burden of the defense to show that it comes within the exception. Any person convicted of violating this subdivision is guilty of a misdemeanor and shall be sentenced to serve a term of not less than 90 days or more than one year in the county jail. The court may place a person convicted under this subdivision on probation for a period not to exceed five years and, except as provided in subdivision (c), shall in all cases in which probation is granted require, as a condition thereof, that the person be confined in the county jail for at least 90 days. Other than as provided by subdivision (c), in no event shall the court have the power to absolve a person who violates this subdivision from the obligation of spending at least 90 days in confinement in the county jail.

(b) Any person who (1) is convicted of violating subdivision (a) when the offense occurred within seven years of that person being convicted of two or more separate violations of that subdivision, and (2) refuses to complete a licensed drug rehabilitation program offered by the court pursuant to subdivision (c), shall be punished by imprisonment in the county jail for not less than 180 days nor more than one year. In no event does the court have the power to absolve a person convicted of a violation of subdivision (a) that is punishable under this subdivision from the obligation of spending at least 180 days in confinement in the county jail unless there are no licensed drug rehabilitation programs reasonably available.

For the purpose of this section, a drug rehabilitation program shall not be considered reasonably available unless the person is required to pay no more than the court determines that he or she is reasonably able to pay, in order to participate in the program.

(c) The court may, when it would be in the interest of justice, permit any person convicted of a violation of subdivision (a) punishable under subdivision (a) or (b) to complete a licensed drug rehabilitation program in lieu of part or all of the imprisonment in the county jail. As a condition of sentencing, the court may require the offender to pay all or a portion of the drug rehabilitation program.

In order to alleviate jail overcrowding and to provide recidivist offenders with a reasonable opportunity to seek rehabilitation pursuant to this subdivision, counties are encouraged to include provisions to augment licensed drug rehabilitation programs in their substance abuse proposals and applications submitted to the state for federal and state drug abuse funds.

(d) In addition to any fine assessed under this section, the judge may assess a fine not to exceed seventy dollars ($70) against any person who violates this section, with the proceeds of this fine to be used in accordance with Section 1463.23 of the Penal Code. The court shall, however, take into consideration the defendant's ability to pay, and no defendant shall be denied probation because of his or her inability to pay the fine permitted under this subdivision.

(e) Notwithstanding subdivisions (a) and (b) or any other provision of law, any person who is unlawfully under the influence of cocaine, cocaine base, heroin, methamphetamine, or phencyclidine while in the immediate personal possession of a loaded, operable firearm is guilty of a public offense punishable by imprisonment in county jail for not exceeding one year or in state prison.

As used in this subdivision "immediate personal possession" includes, but is not limited to, the interior passenger compartment of a motor vehicle.

(f) Every person who violates subdivision (e) is punishable upon the second and each subsequent conviction by imprisonment in the state prison for two, three, or four years.

(g) Nothing in this section prevents diversion of a person under Chapter 2.5 (commencing with Section 1000) of Title 6 of Part 2 of the Penal Code unless the person is charged with violating subdivision (b) or (c) of Section 243 of the Penal Code. A person charged

with violating this section by being under the influence of any controlled substance which is specified in paragraph (21), (22), or (23) of subdivision (d) of Section 11054 or in paragraph (3) of subdivision (e) of Section 11055 and with violating either subdivision (b) or (c) of Section 243 of the Penal Code or with a violation of subdivision (e) shall be ineligible for diversion. *(Amended by Stats 1990 ch 1096 §1, eff. 1/1/91, oper. 7/1/91.)*

§11550.1. Probation program in lieu of imprisonment.

(a) Notwithstanding the provisions of Section 11550, as a pilot program applicable solely to Santa Clara County, a court may impose, as conditions of probation for persons convicted of violating Section 11550, in lieu of a term of imprisonment in the county jail, that the person do all of the following:

(1) Participate in an intensive drug treatment program as designated by the court, for not less than 90 days. The court shall consider the need for safety precautions in all drug treatment placements made pursuant to this subdivision.

(2) Be tested regular basis to determine whether the person has recently used a controlled substance.

(3) Pay the costs of the treatment program commensurate with the person's ability to pay.

(4) Complete the intensive drug treatment program in a manner satisfactory to the court.

(5) Such other conditions of probation, in addition to those enumerated, as the court may designate.

(b) If a person fails to successfully complete the program under subdivision (a) and probation is terminated, the court shall impose a term of not less than 90 days, nor more than one year, in the county jail. If a person convicted for a second or subsequent violation of Section 11550 is again granted probation under this section, as a condition thereof that person shall be confined in the county jail for not less than 90 days. No credit for time served in an intensive drug treatment program may be credited toward this 90 day term when the program has not been successfully completed.

(c) This section does not apply to persons where the offense charged involved driving a vehicle while under the influence of a drug or a crime of violence or threatened violence. Any person who has previously participated in a program under this section or has been committed to the California Rehabilitation Center pursuant to Section 3051 of the Welfare and Institutions Code, is ineligible for the program authorized by this section.

(d) Notwithstanding Section 4019 or 2900.5 of the Penal Code, no time served in a drug treatment program pursuant to this section shall be credited against any jail or prison sentence which may be subsequently imposed.

(e) The State of California and the County of Santa Clara shall not be liable for the cost of drug treatment provided pursuant to this section.

(f) This section shall remain in effect only until January 1, 1991, and as of that date is repealed, unless a later statute enacted before January 1, 1991, deletes or extends that date. *(Added by Stats 1988 ch 636 §1, eff. 8/27/88 only until 1/1/91.)*

§11551. Drug testing as a condition of parole.

(a) Whenever any court in this state grants probation to a person who the court has reason to believe is

© 1992 by J., B. & L. Gould
Printed in the U.S.A.   **EP**

or has been a user of controlled substances, the court may require as a condition to probation that the probationer submit to periodic tests by a city or county health officer, or by a physician and surgeon appointed by the city or county health officer with the approval of the Attorney General, to determine, by whatever means is available, whether the probationer is addicted to a controlled substance.

In any case provided for in this subdivision, the city or county health officer, or the physician and surgeon appointed by the city or county health officer with the approval of the Attorney General shall report the results of the tests to the probation officer.

(b) In any case in which a person is granted parole by a county parole board and the person is or has been a user of controlled substances, a condition of the parole may be that the parolee undergo periodic tests as provided in subdivision (a) and that the county or city health officer, or the physician and surgeon appointed by the city or county health officer with the approval of the Attorney General, shall report the results to the board.

(c) In any case in which any state agency grants a parole to a person who is or has been a user of controlled substances, it may be a condition of the parole that the parolee undergo periodic tests as provided in subdivision (a) and that the county or city health officer, or the physician and surgeon appointed by the city or county health officer with the approval of the Attorney General, shall report the results of the tests to such state agency.

(d) The cost of administering tests pursuant to subdivisions (a) and (b) shall be a charge against the county. The cost of administering tests pursuant to subdivision (c) shall be paid by the state.

(e) The state department, in conjunction with the Attorney General, shall issue regulations governing the administering of the tests provided for in this section and providing the form of the report required by this section.

§11552. Administering drug test to arrested person.

In any case in which a person has been arrested for a criminal offense and is suspected of being addicted to a controlled substance, a law enforcement officer having custody of such person may, with the written consent of such person, request the city or county health officer, or physician appointed by such health officer pursuant to Section 11551, to administer to the arrested person a test to determine, by whatever means is available whether the arrested person is addicted to a controlled substance, and such health officer or physician may administer such test to such arrested person.

§11553. Marijuana use not sufficient grounds for administering drug test.

The fact that a person is or has been, or is suspected of being, a user of marijuana is not alone sufficient grounds upon which to invoke Section 11551 or 11552.

This section shall not be construed to limit the discretion of a judge to invoke Section 11551 or 11552 if the court has reason to believe a person is or has been a user of narcotics or drugs other than marijuana.

§11554. State policy toward drug testing.

The rehabilitation of persons addicted to controlled substances and the prevention of continued addiction to controlled substances is a matter of statewide concern. It is the policy of the state to encourage each county and city and county to make use, whenever applicable, of testing procedures to determine addiction to controlled substances or the absence thereof, and to foster research in means of detecting the existence of addiction to controlled substances and in medical methods and procedures for that purpose.

§11555. Attorney General's responsibility to promote this article.

The Attorney General is directed to promote and sponsor the use by agencies of local government of the provisions of this article. The Attorney General may assist such agencies to establish facilities for, and to train personnel to conduct testing procedures pursuant to Section 11551, and may conduct demonstrations thereof for limited periods. For these purposes the Attorney General may procure such medical supplies, equipment, and temporary services of physicians and qualified consultants as may reasonably be necessary. Subject to the availability of funds appropriated for the purpose, the Attorney General may contract with any county or city and county which undertakes to establish facilities and a testing program pursuant to Section 11551, and such contract may provide for payment by the state of such costs of initially establishing and demonstrating such program as the Attorney General may approve.

ARTICLE 2

CONTROLLED SUBSTANCES TREATMENT CONTROL UNITS

§11560. Controlled substance treatment units in prisons.

The Department of Corrections and the Department of the Youth Authority are authorized to establish controlled substances treatment control units in state correctional facilities or training schools or as separate establishments for such study, research, and treatment as may be necessary for control of the addiction or imminent addiction to controlled substances of persons committed to the custody of the Director of Corrections or the Director of the Youth Authority.

§11561. Detention of parolee for controlled substance addiction.

When the Board of Prison Terms concludes that there are reasonable grounds for believing that a man on parole is addicted to, or is in imminent danger of addiction to, controlled substances it may issue an order to detain or place such person in a controlled substance treatment control unit for a period not to exceed 90 days. Such order shall be a sufficient warrant for any peace officer or employee of the Department of Corrections to return to physical custody any such person. Detention pursuant to such order shall not be deemed a suspension, cancellation or revocation of parole until such time as the Board of Prison Terms so orders pursuant to Section 3060 of the Penal Code. A parolee taken into physical custody pursuant to Section 3060 of the Penal Code may be detained in a controlled substance treatment control unit established pursuant to this article.

§11562. Detention of Youth Authority parolee for controlled substance addiction.

When the Youth Authority concludes that there are reasonable grounds for believing that a person committed to its custody, and on parole, is addicted to, or is in imminent danger of addiction to, controlled substances, it may issue an order to detain or place such person in a controlled substance treatment control unit for not to exceed 90 days. Such order shall be a sufficient warrant for any peace officer or employee of the Department of the Youth Authority to return to physical custody any such person. Detention pursuant to such order shall not be deemed a suspension, cancellation, or revocation of parole unless the Youth Authority so orders pursuant to Section 1767.3 of the Welfare and Institutions Code.

With the consent of the Director of Corrections, the Director of the Youth Authority may, pursuant to this section, confine the addicted or potentially addicted person, over 18 years of age, in a controlled substance treatment control unit established by the Department of Corrections.

§11563. Detention of female parolee for controlled substance addiction.

When the Board of Prison Terms concludes that there are reasonable grounds for believing that a woman on parole is addicted to, or is in imminent danger of addiction to, controlled substances, it may issue an order to detain or place such person in a controlled substance treatment control unit for a period not to exceed 90 days. Such order shall be a sufficient warrant for any peace officer or employee of the Department of Corrections to return to physical custody any such person. Detention pursuant to such order shall not be deemed a suspension, cancellation or revocation of parole until such time as the board so orders pursuant to Section 3060 of the Penal Code. A parolee taken into physical custody pursuant to Section 3060, 6043, or 6044 of the Penal Code may be detained in a controlled substance treatment control unit established pursuant to this article.

§11564. Board of Prison Terms' authority does not limit Penal Code.

The authority granted to the Board of Prison Terms and the Youth Authority in no way limits Sections 3060 and 3325 of the Penal Code.

ARTICLE 3

ABATEMENT

§11570. Abatement of buildings deemed nuisances.

Every building or place used for the purpose of unlawfully selling, serving, storing, keeping, manufacturing, or giving away any controlled substance, precursor, or analog specified in this division, and every building or place wherein or upon which those acts take place, is a nuisance which shall be enjoined, abated, and prevented, and for which damages may be recovered, whether it is a public or private nuisance. *(Amended by Stats 1986 ch 1043 §1.5.)*

§11571. Action to abate nuisance by district attorney or citizen of county.

Whenever there is reason to believe that such a nuisance is kept, maintained or exists in any county, the district attorney of the county, in the name of the people, may, or the city attorney of any incorporated city or of any city and county, or any citizen of the state resident in the county, in his or her own name, may, maintain an action to abate and prevent the nuisance and perpetually to enjoin the person conducting or maintaining it, and the owner, lessee, or agent of the building or place, in or upon which the nuisance exists, from directly or indirectly maintaining or permitting the nuisance. *(Amended by Stats 1991 ch 572 §§1, 2, 1196 §7, eff. 1/1/92.)*

§11571.5. Action to abate nuisance by city attorney or prosecutor.

For purposes of this article, an action to abate a nuisance may be taken by the city attorney or city prosecutor of the city within which the nuisance exists, is kept, or is maintained. An action by a city attorney or city prosecutor shall be accorded the same precedence as an action maintained by the district attorney of the county. *(Added by Stats 1986 ch 182 §1.)*

§11572. Complaint to be verified.

Unless filed by the district attorney, or the city attorney of an incorporated city, the complaint in the action shall be verified. *(Amended by Stats 1987 ch 1076 §3.)*

§11573. Temporary writ of injunction.

If the existence of the nuisance is shown in the action to the satisfaction of the court or judge, either by verified complaint or affidavit, the court or judge shall allow a temporary writ of injunction to abate and prevent the continuance or recurrence of the nuisance.

§11573.5. Protection of witnesses.

(a) At the time of application for issuance of a temporary writ pursuant to Section 11573, if proof of the existence of the nuisance depends, in whole or part, upon the affidavits of witnesses who are not peace officers, upon a showing of prior threats of violence or acts of violence by any defendant or other person, the court may issue orders to protect those witnesses, including, but not limited to, nondisclosure of the name, address, or any other information which may identify those witnesses.

(b) A temporary writ issued pursuant to Section 11573 may include closure of the premises pending trial when a prior writ does not result in the abatement of the nuisance. The duration of the writ shall be within the court's discretion. In no event shall the total period of closure pending trial exceed one year. Prior to ruling on a request for closure the court may order that some or all of the rent payments owing to the defendant be placed in an escrow account for a period of up to 90 days or until the nuisance is abated. If the court subsequently orders a closure of the premises, the money in the escrow account shall be used to pay for relocation assistance pursuant to subdivision (d). In ruling upon a request for closure, whether for a defined or undefined duration, the court shall consider all of the following factors:

(1) The extent and duration of the nuisance at the time of the request.

© 1992 by J., B. & L. Gould
Printed in the U.S.A.   **EP**

(2) Prior efforts by the defendant to comply with previous court orders to abate the nuisance.

(3) The nature and extent of any effect which the nuisance has upon other persons, such as residents or businesses.

(4) Any effect of prior orders placing displaced residents' or occupants' rent payments into an escrow account upon the defendant's efforts to abate the nuisance.

(5) The effect of granting the request upon any resident or occupant of the premises who is not named in the action, including the availability of alternative housing or relocation assistance, the pendancy* of any action to evict a resident or occupant, and any evidence of participation by a resident or occupant in the nuisance activity.

*So in original. Probably should be "pendency".

(c) In making an order of closure pursuant to this section, the court may order the premises vacated and may issue any other orders necessary to effectuate the closure. However, all tenants who may be affected by the order shall be provided reasonable notice and an opportunity to be heard at all hearings regarding the closure request prior to the issuance of any order.

(d) In making an order of closure pursuant to this section, the court shall order the defendant to provide relocation assistance to any tenant ordered to vacate the premises, provided the court determines that the tenant was not actively involved in the nuisance activity. The relocation assistance ordered to be paid by the defendant shall be in the amount necessary to cover moving costs, security deposits for utilities and comparable housing, adjustment in any lost rent, and any other reasonable expenses the court may deem fair and reasonable as a result of the court's order.

(e) At the hearing to order closure pursuant to this section, the court may make the following orders with respect to any displaced tenant not actively involved in the nuisance:

(1) Priority for senior citizens, physically handicapped persons, or persons otherwise suffering from a permanent or temporary disability for claims against money for relocation assistance.

(2) Order the local agency seeking closure pursuant to this section to make reasonable attempts to seek additional sources of funds for relocation assistance to displaced tenants, if deemed necessary.

(3) Appoint a receiver to oversee the disbursement of relocation assistance funds, whose services shall be paid from the escrow fund.

(4) Where a defendant has paid relocation assistance pursuant to subdivision (d), the escrow account under subdivision (b) may be released to the defendant and no appointment under paragraph (3) shall be made.

(f) (1) The remedies set forth pursuant to this section shall be in addition to any other existing remedies for nuisance abatement actions, including, but not limited to, the following:

(A) Capital improvements to the property, such as security gates.

(B) Improved interior or exterior lighting.

(C) Security guards.

(D) Posting of signs.

(E) Owner membership in neighborhood or local merchants' associations.

(F) Attending property management training programs.

(G) Making cosmetic improvements to the property.

(2) At all stages of an action brought pursuant to this article, the court has equitable powers to order steps necessary to remedy the problem and enhance the abatement process. (Amended by Stats 1991 ch 247 §1, eff. 1/1/92.)

§11574. Injunction applicant to pay damages if injunction not justified.

On granting the temporary writ the court or judge shall require an undertaking on the part of the applicant to the effect that the applicant will pay to the defendant enjoined such damages, not exceeding an amount to be specified, as the defendant sustains by reason of the injunction if the court finally decides that the applicant was not entitled to the injunction.

§11575. Action's precedence over other actions; exceptions.

The action shall have precedence over all other actions, except criminal proceedings, election contests, hearings on injunctions, and actions to forfeit vehicles under this division.

§11575.5. Evidence to prove a nuisance.

In any action for abatement instituted pursuant to this article, all evidence otherwise authorized by law, including evidence of reputation in a community, as provided in the Evidence Code, shall be admissible to prove the existence of a nuisance. (Added by Stats 1988 ch 1525 §2, eff. 1/1/89.)

§11576. Conditions for dismissing complaint.

If the complaint is filed by a citizen it shall not be dismissed by him or for want of prosecution except upon a sworn statement made by him and his attorney, setting forth the reasons why the action should be dismissed, and by dismissal ordered by the court.

§11577. Substitution of another citizen as plaintiff.

In case of failure to prosecute the action with reasonable diligence, or at the request of the plaintiff, the court, in its discretion, may substitute any other citizen consenting thereto for the plaintiff.

§11578. Plaintiff to pay costs for unjust complaint.

If the action is brought by a citizen and the court finds there was no reasonable ground or cause for the action, the costs shall be taxed against him.

§11579. Order of abatement; payment of costs.

If the existence of the nuisance is established in the action, an order of abatement shall be entered as part of the judgment in the case, and plaintiff's costs in the action are a lien upon the building or place. The lien is enforceable and collectible by execution issued by order of the court.

§11580. Violation of court injunction or order.

A violation or disobedience of the injunction or order for abatement is punishable as a contempt of court by a fine of not less than five hundred dollars ($500) nor more than ten thousand dollars ($10,000), or by imprisonment in the county jail for not less than one nor more than six months, or by both.

A contempt may be based on a violation of any court order including failure to pay relocation assistance. Notwithstanding any other provision of law, any fines assessed for contempt shall first be held by the court and applied to satisfaction of the court's order for relocation assistance pursuant to subdivision (d) of Section 11573.5.

Evidence concerning the duration and repetitive nature of the violations shall be considered by the court in determining the contempt penalties. *(Amended by Stats 1988 ch 1525 §3, eff. 1/1/89.)*

§11581. Order of abatement.

(a) If the existence of the nuisance is established in the action, an order of abatement shall be entered as a part of the judgment, which order shall direct the removal from the dwelling, building, or place of all fixtures, musical instruments, and other movable property used in conducting, maintaining, aiding, or abetting the nuisance and shall direct their sale in the manner provided for the sale of chattels under execution.

(b) (1) The order shall provide for the effectual closing of the dwelling, building, or place against its use for any purpose and for keeping it closed for a period of one year. This subdivision is intended to give priority to closure. Any alternative to closure may be considered only as provided in this section.

(2) In addition, the court may assess a civil penalty not to exceed twenty-five thousand dollars ($25,000) against any or all of the defendants, based upon the severity of the nuisance and its duration.

(3) In establishing the amount of any civil penalty, the court shall consider all of the following factors:

(A) The actions taken by the defendant to mitigate or correct the problem at the dwelling, building, or place or the reasons why the defendant did not take any such action.

(B) The failure of a district attorney or city attorney to serve a notice as required by Section 11571.

(C) Any previous actions brought against the defendant pursuant to this article.

(D) The cost to the agency of investigating and correcting the condition.

(E) Any other factor deemed by the court to be relevant.

(c) (1) If the court finds that any vacancy resulting from closure of the building or place may create a nuisance or that closure is otherwise harmful to the community, in lieu of ordering the building or place closed, the court may order the person who is responsible for the existence of the nuisance, or the person who knowingly permits controlled substances to be unlawfully sold, served, stored, kept, or given away in or from a building or place he or she owns, to pay damages in an amount equal to the fair market rental value of the building or place for one year to the city or county in whose jurisdiction the nuisance is located for the purpose of carrying out their drug prevention and education programs. If awarded to a city, eligible programs may include those developed as a result of cooperative programs among schools, community agencies, and the local law enforcement agency. If awarded to a county, funds shall be used for those programs that are part of the drug program plan, as specified in Section 11983.2. These funds shall not be used to supplant existing city, county, state, or federal resources used for drug prevention and education programs.

(2) For purposes of this subdivision, the actual amount of rent being received for the rental of the dwelling, building, or place, or the existence of any vacancy therein, may be considered, but shall not be the sole determinant of the fair market rental value. Expert testimony may be used to determine the fair market rental value.

(d) This section shall be repealed on January 1, 1996. *(Amended by Stats 1991 ch 247 §2, ch 572 §3, eff. 1/1/92 only until 1/1/96. See other section 11581 below.)*

§11581. Order of abatement.

(a) If the existence of the nuisance is established in the action, an order of abatement shall be entered as a part of the judgment, which order shall direct the removal from the building or place of all fixtures, musical instruments, and other movable property used in conducting, maintaining, aiding, or abetting the nuisance and shall direct their sale in the manner provided for the sale of chattels under execution.

(b) The order shall provide for the effectual closing of the building or place against its use for any purpose, and for keeping it closed for a period of one year. This subdivision is intended to give priority to closure. Any alternative to closure may be considered only as provided in this section.

In addition, the court may assess a civil penalty not to exceed twenty-five thousand dollars ($25,000) against any or all of the defendants, based upon the severity of the nuisance and its duration.

(c) (1) If the court finds that any vacancy resulting from closure of the building or place may create a nuisance or that closure is otherwise harmful to the community, in lieu of ordering the building or place closed, the court may order the person who is responsible for the existence of the nuisance, or the person who knowingly permits controlled substances to be unlawfully sold, served, stored, kept, or given away in or from a building or place he or she owns, to pay damages in an amount equal to the fair market rental value of the building or place for one year to the city or county in whose jurisdiction the nuisance is located for the purpose of carrying out their drug prevention and education programs. If awarded to a city, eligible programs may include those developed as a result of cooperative programs among schools, community agencies, and the local law enforcement agency. If awarded to a county, funds shall be used for those programs that are part of the drug program plan, as specified in Section 11983.2. These funds shall not be used to supplant existing city, county, state, or federal resources used for drug prevention and education programs.

(2) For purposes of this subdivision, the actual amount of rent being received for the rental of the building or place, or the existence of any vacancy therein, may be considered, but shall not be the sole determinant of the fair market rental value. Expert testimony may be used to determine the fair market rental value.

(d) This section shall become operative on January 1, 1996. *(Added by Stats 1991 ch 572 §4, eff. 1/1/92, oper. 1/1/96.)*

§11582. Building under abatement order in court custody.

While the order of abatement remains in effect, the building or place is in the custody of the court.

© 1992 by J., B. & L. Gould
Printed in the U.S.A.   **EP**

§11583. Officer's fees for removal of property.

For removing and selling the movable property, the officer is entitled to charge and receive the same fees as he would for levying upon and selling like property on execution; and for closing the premises and keeping them closed, a reasonable sum shall be allowed by the court.

§11584. Disposition of proceeds from sale of property.

The proceeds of the sale of the movable property shall be applied as follows:

First—To the fees and costs of the removal and sale.

Second—To the allowances and costs of closing and keeping closed the building or place.

Third—To the payment of the plaintiff's costs in the action.

Fourth—The balance, if any, to the owner of the property.

§11585. Disposition of proceeds from sale of building.

If the proceeds of the sale of the movable property do not fully discharge all of the costs, fees, and allowances, the building and place shall then also be sold under execution issued upon the order of the court or judge and the proceeds of the sale shall be applied in like manner.

§11586. Return of building to owner when nuisance abated.

(a) If the owner of the building or place has not been guilty of any contempt of court in the proceedings, and appears and pays all costs, fees, and allowances that are a lien on the building or place and files a bond in the full value of the property conditioned that the owner will immediately abate any nuisance that may exist at the building or place and prevent it from being established or kept thereat within a period of one year thereafter, the court, or judge may, if satisfied of the owner's good faith, order the building or place to be delivered to the owner, and the order of abatement canceled so far as it may relate to the property.

(b) The release of property under the provisions of this division does not release it from any judgment, lien, penalty, or liability to which it may be subject.

§11587. Fine is lien on building in cases of contempt.

Whenever the owner of a building or place upon which the act or acts constituting the contempt have been committed, or the owner of any interest therein, has been guilty of a contempt of court, and fined in any proceedings under this division, the fine is a lien upon the building or place to the extent of his interest in it.

The lien is enforceable and collectible by execution issued by order of the court.

ARTICLE 4

REGISTRATION OF CONTROLLED SUBSTANCE OFFENDERS

§11590. Registration of controlled substance offenders with police.

(a) Except as provided in subdivisions (c) and (d), any person who is convicted in the State of California of any offense defined in Section 11350, 11351, 11351.5, 11352, 11353, 11353.5, 11353.7, 11354, 11355, 11357, 11358, 11359, 11360, 11361, 11363, 11366, 11366.5, 11366.6, 11368, 11378, 11378.5, 11379, 11379.5, 11379.6, 11380, 11380.5, 11383, or 11550, or subdivision (a) of Section 11377, or any person who is discharged or paroled from a penal institution where he or she was confined because of the commission of any such offense, or any person who is convicted in any other state of any offense which, if committed or attempted in this state, would have been punishable as one or more of the above-mentioned offenses, shall within 30 days of his or her coming into any county or city, or city and county in which he or she resides or is temporarily domiciled for that length of time, register with the chief of police of the city in which he or she resides or the sheriff of the county if he or she resides in an unincorporated area.

For persons convicted of an offense defined in Section 11377, 11378, 11379, or 11380, this subdivision shall apply only to offenses involving controlled substances specified in paragraph (12) of subdivision (d) of Section 11054 and paragraph (2) of subdivision (d) of Section 11055, and to analogs of these substances, as defined in Section 11401. For persons convicted of an offense defined in Section 11379 or 11379.5, this subdivision shall not apply if the conviction was for transporting, offering to transport, or attempting to transport a controlled substance.

(b) Any person who is convicted in any federal court of any offense which, if committed or attempted in this state would have been punishable as one or more of the offenses enumerated in subdivision (a) shall within 30 days of his or her coming into any county or city, or city and county in which he or she resides or is temporarily domiciled for that length of time, register with the chief of police of the city in which he or she resides or the sheriff of the county if he or she resides in an unincorporated area.

(c) This section does not apply to a conviction of a misdemeanor under Section 11357, 11360, or 11377.

(d) The registration requirements imposed by this section for the conviction of offenses defined in Section 11353.7, 11366.5, 11366.6, 11377, 11378, 11378.5, 11379, 11379.5, 11379.6, 11380, 11380.5, or 11383, shall apply to any person who commits any of those offenses on and after January 1, 1990. *(Amended by Stats 1990 ch 1417 §2, eff. 9/28/90.)*

§11591. Notification to school authorities of arrest of school employee.

Every sheriff or chief of police, upon the arrest for any of the controlled substance offenses enumerated in Section 11590, or Section 11364, insofar as that section relates to paragraph (12) of subdivision (d) of Section 11054, of any school employee, shall do either of the following:

(1) If such school employee is a teacher in any of the public schools of this state, he or she shall immediately notify by telephone the superintendent of schools of the school district employing such teacher and shall immediately give written notice of the arrest to the Commission for Teacher Preparation and Licensing and to the superintendent of schools in the county wherein such person is employed. Upon receipt of such notice, the county superintendent of schools shall immediately notify the governing board of the school district employing such person.

(2) If such school employee is a nonteacher in any of the public schools of this state, he or she shall

immediately notify by telephone the superintendent of schools of the school district employing such non-teacher and shall immediately give written notice of the arrest to the governing board of the school district employing such person.

(3) If such school employee is a teacher in any private school of this state, he or she shall immediately notify by telephone the private school authority employing such teacher and shall immediately give written notice of the arrest to the private school authority employing such teacher.

§11591.5. Notice to community college authorities of arrest of instructor.

Every sheriff or chief of police, upon the arrest for any of the controlled substance offenses enumerated in Section 11590, or Section 11364, insofar as that section relates to paragraph (9) of subdivision (d) of Section 11054, of any teacher or instructor employed in any community college district shall immediately notify by telephone the superintendent of the community college district employing the teacher or instructor and shall immediately give written notice of the arrest to the Office of the Chancellor of the California Community Colleges. Upon receipt of such notice, the district superintendent shall immediately notify the governing board of the community college district employing the person.

§11592. Notification to parolee of duty to register.

Any person who, on or after the effective date of this section is discharged or paroled from a jail, prison, school, road camp, or other institution where he was confined because of the commission or attempt to commit one of the offenses described in Section 11590 shall, prior to such discharge, parole, or release, be informed of his duty to register under that section by the official in charge of the place of confinement and the official shall require the person to read and sign such form as may be required by the Department of Justice, stating that the duty of the person to register under this section has been explained to him. The official in charge of the place of confinement shall obtain the address where the person expects to reside upon his discharge, parole, or release and shall report such address to the Department of Justice. The official in charge of the place of confinement shall give one copy of the form to the person, and shall send two copies to the Department of Justice, which, in turn, shall forward one copy to the appropriate law enforcement agency having local jurisdiction where the person expects to reside upon his discharge, parole, or release.

§11593. Notification to probationer of duty to register.

Any person who, on or after the effective date of this section is convicted in the State of California of the commission or attempt to commit any of the above-mentioned offenses and who is released on probation or discharged upon payment of a fine shall, prior to such release or discharge, be informed of his duty to register under Section 11590 by the court in which he has been convicted and the court shall require the person to read and sign such form as may be required by the Department of Justice, stating that the duty of the person to register under this section has been explained to him. The court shall obtain the address

where the person expects to reside upon his release or discharge and shall report within three days such address to the Department of Justice. The court shall give one copy of the form to the person, and shall send two copies to the Department of Justice, which, in turn, shall forward one copy to the appropriate law enforcement agency having local jurisdiction where the person expects to reside upon his discharge, parole, or release.

§11594. Registration of convicted persons.

The registration required by Section 11590 shall consist of (a) a statement in writing signed by such person, giving such information as may be required by the Department of Justice, and (b) the fingerprints and photograph of such person. Within three days thereafter the registering law enforcement agency shall forward such statement, fingerprints and photograph to the Department of Justice.

If any person required to register hereunder changes his residence address he shall inform, in writing within 10 days, the law enforcement agency with whom he last registered of his new address. The law enforcement agency shall, within three days after receipt of such information, forward it to the Department of Justice. The Department of Justice shall forward appropriate registration data to the law enforcement agency having local jurisdiction of the new place of residence.

All registration requirements set forth in this article shall terminate five years after the discharge from prison, release from jail or termination of probation or parole of the person convicted. Nothing in this section shall be construed to conflict with the provisions of Section 1203.4 of the Penal Code concerning termination of probation and release from penalties and disabilities of probation.

Any person required to register under the provisions of this section who shall knowingly violate any of the provisions thereof is guilty of a misdemeanor.

The statements, photographs and fingerprints herein required shall not be open to inspection by the public or by any person other than a regularly employed peace or other law enforcement officer.

§11595. Former provisions remain operational.

The provisions of former Article 6 (commencing with Section 11850) of Chapter 7 of Division 10 of this code, which is repealed by the act that adds this article, including Section 11850 as amended by Chapter 796 of the Statutes of 1972, shall remain in effect as to any person who comes within such provisions.

Notwithstanding Section 9605 of the Government Code, the changes which are made in former Section 11850 by Chapter 796 of the Statutes of 1972 shall be effective and operative for the purposes of this section.

CHAPTER 11

EDUCATIONAL PROGRAMS

§11600. Duty of Attorney General and other agencies to carry out educational programs on drug abuse.

The Attorney General, the Board of Pharmacy, and other agencies shall carry out educational programs designed to prevent and deter misuse and abuse of controlled substances. In connection with these programs, he may do all of the following:

© 1992 by J., B. & L. Gould
Printed in the U.S.A.   EP

(a) Promote better recognition of the problems of misuse and abuse of controlled substances within the regulated industry and among interested groups and organizations.

(b) Assist the regulated industry and interested groups and organizations in contributing to the reduction of misuse and abuse of controlled substances.

(c) Consult with interested groups and organizations to aid them in solving administrative and organizational problems.

(d) Assist in the education and training of state and local law enforcement officials in their efforts to control misuse and abuse of controlled substances.

§11601. Attorney General to encourage controlled substance research.

The Attorney General shall encourage research on misuse and abuse of controlled substances. In connection with the research, and in furtherance of the enforcement of this division, he may do all of the following:

(a) Develop new or improved approaches, techniques, systems, equipment and devices to strengthen the enforcement of this division.

(b) Enter into contracts with public agencies, institutions of higher education, and private organizations or individuals for the purpose of conducting demonstrations or special projects which bear directly on misuse and abuse of controlled substances.

§11602. Entering into contracts.

The Attorney General may enter into contracts for educational and research activities without performance bonds.

§11603. Protection of participants in research.

The Attorney General, with the approval of the Research Advisory Panel, may authorize persons engaged in research on the use and effects of controlled substances to withhold the names and other identifying characteristics of individuals who are the subjects of the research. Persons who obtain this authorization are not compelled in any civil, criminal, administrative, legislative, or other proceeding to identify the individuals who are the subjects of research for which the authorization was obtained.

§11604. Legitimate possession of controlled substances by researchers.

The Attorney General, with the approval of the Research Advisory Panel, may authorize the possession and distribution of controlled substances by persons engaged in research. Persons who obtain this authorization are exempt from state prosecution for possession and distribution of controlled substances to the extent of the authorization.

§11605. Survey of drug and alcohol use among pupils in grades 7, 9, 11.

(a) Commencing with the 1991–92 fiscal year, the Attorney General, in consultation with the Governor's Policy Council on Alcohol and Drug Abuse, shall conduct a biennial survey of drug and alcohol use among pupils enrolled in grades 7, 9, and 11. The survey shall assess all of the following:

(1) The frequency and type of substance abuse.

(2) The age of first use and intoxication.

(3) Pertinent attitudes and experiences of pupils.

(4) The experience of pupils with school-based drug and alcohol prevention programs.

(5) As an optional component, the survey may examine the risk factors associated with school dropouts.

(b) The biennial survey shall be based on a statewide sample of pupils enrolled in grades 7, 9, and 11 and shall be consistent with the surveys conducted by the office of the Attorney General in the 1985–86, 1987–88, and 1989–90 fiscal years.

(c) The Attorney General shall release the findings of the survey on or before May of each even-numbered year and shall prepare and distribute a report on the survey to the Legislature, the Governor, the Superintendent of Public Instruction, law enforcement agencies, school districts, and interested members of the general public.

(d) In conducting the survey, the Attorney General shall ensure that the confidentiality of participating school districts and pupils shall be maintained. Pupil questionnaires and answer sheets shall be exempt from the public disclosure requirements prescribed by Chapter 3.5 (commencing with Section 6250) of Division 7 of Title 1 of the Government Code.

(e) Persons reporting data pursuant to the requirements of this article shall not be liable for damages in any action based upon the use or misuse of pupil surveys that are mailed or otherwise transmitted to the Attorney General, or his or her designee.

(f) The requirements prescribed by this article shall continue to be funded with the existing resources of the Attorney General. *(Added by Stats 1990 ch 1332 §1, eff. 1/1/91.)*

CHAPTER 12

CLANDESTINE LABORATORY ENFORCEMENT PROGRAM
(Added by Stats 1986 ch 1029 §1.)

§11640. Legislative findings.

The Legislature finds and declares that there has been a recent and rapid expansion in clandestine laboratories illegally producing a variety of controlled substances. These are increasingly sophisticated operations, frequently located in rural areas or working across jurisdictional lines, which pose substantial dangers to the general public from fire, explosion, and the toxic chemicals involved. The controlled substances these laboratories produce, such as analogs of fentanyl, phencyclidine, and methamphetamine, are extremely difficult to detect and analyze and have caused numerous deaths and serious injuries to those who use them.

The Legislature further finds and declares that, given the number and nature of clandestine laboratories, local law enforcement officials in most jurisdictions lack the training, specialized equipment, and resources to adequately enforce existing law. As a result, the public is increasingly endangered by the laboratories themselves while the controlled substances they produce pose a grave danger to those who use them.

It is the intent of the Legislature in establishing the Clandestine Laboratory Enforcement Program to provide increased funding for special training, equipment, personnel, and financial assistance to state and local law enforcement officials targeted on the investigation and prosecution of clandestine laboratories.

The program shall also increase public awareness of the problems posed by clandestine laboratories and the products they produce. *(Added by Stats 1986 ch 1029 §1.)*

§11641. Establishment of Clandestine Laboratory Enforcement Program.

The Department of Justice shall establish a Clandestine Laboratory Enforcement Program to assist state and local law enforcement and prosecutorial agencies in apprehending and prosecuting persons involved in the unlawful manufacture of controlled substances. *(Added by Stats 1986 ch 1029 §1.)*

§11642. Reimbursement of counties for costs of prosecuting violations.

(a) To the extent moneys are available therefor, the Controller, in accordance with criteria and procedures which shall be adopted by the Department of Justice, may reimburse counties with a population under 1,750,000 for costs of prosecuting violations, attempts to violate, or conspiracies to violate Section 11100, 11100.1, 11104, 11105, 11379.6, or 11383 initiated after January 1, 1987. Funding under this subdivision shall not exceed twenty-five thousand dollars ($25,000) for each prosecution or joint prosecution assisted. All funds allocated to a county under this subdivision shall be distributed by it only to its prosecutorial agency, to be used solely for investigation and prosecution of these offenses. Funds distributed under this subdivision shall not be used to supplant any local funds that would, in the absence of this subdivision, be made available to support the prosecutorial efforts of counties.

Cases wholly financed or reimbursed under any other state or federal program including, but not limited to, the Asset Forfeiture Program (Section 11489), the Major Narcotic Vendors Prosecution Law (Section 13881 of the Penal Code), or the California Career Criminal Apprehension Program (Section 13851 of the Penal Code), shall not be entitled to reimbursement under this subdivision.

(b) To the extent moneys are available therefor, the Controller, in accordance with criteria and procedures which shall be adopted by the Department of Justice, may reimburse counties with a population under 1,750,000 for law enforcement personnel expenses, not exceeding ten thousand dollars ($10,000) per case, incurred in the investigation of violations, attempts to violate, or conspiracies to violate Section 11100, 11100.1, 11104, 11105, 11379.6, or 11383 initiated after January 1, 1987. All funds allocated to a county under this subdivision shall be distributed by it only to its law enforcement agency to be used solely for investigation and detection of these offenses. Funds distributed under this subdivision shall not be used to supplant any local funds that would, in the absence of this subdivision, be made available to support the law enforcement efforts of counties. Cases financed or reimbursed under any other state or federal program, including, but not limited to, the Asset Forfeiture Program, (Section 11489), the California Career Criminal Apprehension Program (Section 13851 of the Penal Code), or the federal Asset Forfeiture Program (21 U.S.C. Sec. 881), shall not be entitled to reimbursement under this subdivision.

(c) (1) To the extent moneys are available therefor, the Controller, in accordance with criteria and procedures which shall be adopted by the Department

of Justice, may reimburse counties with a population under 1,750,000 for costs incurred by, or at the direction of, state or local law enforcement agencies to remove and dispose of or store toxic waste from the sites of laboratories used for the unlawful manufacture of a controlled substance.

(2) The local law enforcement agency or Department of Justice shall notify the local health officer within 24 hours of the seizure of a laboratory used for the unlawful manufacture of a controlled substance. The local health officer shall either:

(A) Make a determination as to whether the site poses an immediate threat to public health and safety, and if so, shall undertake immediate corrective action.

(B) Notify the State Department of Health Services.

As used in this section, "counties" includes any city within a county with a population of less than 1,750,000.

The Department of Justice may adopt emergency regulations consistent with this section and the Administrative Procedure Act. *(Amended by Stats 1991 ch 929 §1, eff. 1/1/92.)*

§11643. Assistance to law enforcement personnel by Bureau of Narcotic Enforcement.

To the extent moneys are available therefor, the Bureau of Narcotic Enforcement in the Department of Justice shall do the following:

(a) In cooperation with the Commission on Peace Officer Standards and Training provide advanced training to state and local law enforcement personnel on the unique skills, such as detection and identification of chemical substances, and safety precautions, such as safe handling, storage, and disposal of toxic substances, necessary to investigate clandestine laboratories illegally manufacturing controlled substances.

(b) Make safety equipment, such as protective clothing and breathing apparatus, available to local law enforcement officials, as needed, on a case-by-case basis in connection with investigation and abatement of laboratories illegally manufacturing controlled substances.

(c) Establish enhanced enforcement teams assigned to the investigation of clandestine laboratories illegally manufacturing controlled substances, particularly targeting cabals operating in multiple local jurisdictions. These teams shall include special agents trained in investigating clandestine laboratories, criminalists to analyze the chemicals involved, auditors to conduct financial investigations and initiate forfeiture proceedings pursuant to Chapter 8 (commencing with Section 11470) where warranted, and analysts to monitor the overall pattern and network of these clandestine laboratories across the state, to develop further cases, and to target law enforcement efforts where needed. *(Added by Stats 1986 ch 1029 §1.)*

§11644. Distribution of informational materials.

To the extent moneys are available therefor, the Crime Prevention Center of the Department of Justice shall prepare and disseminate informational materials on the unique dangers posed by clandestine laboratories and the controlled substances they produce. The Crime Prevention Center shall increase public awareness in areas such as the health dangers created by the laboratories themselves, including how

© 1992 by J., B. & L. Gould
Printed in the U.S.A.   **EP**

to identify and report them, and the unusual effects and dangers of synthetic substances such as analogs of fentanyl, MPPP, phencyclidine, and methamphetamines. *(Added by Stats 1986 ch 1029 §1.)*

§11646. Enforcement of this chapter.

The Attorney General shall adopt rules and regulations for the administration and enforcement of this chapter. *(Added by Stats 1986 ch 1029 §1.)*

§11647. Department of Justice's report to Legislature.

(a) The Crank-Up Task Force Program is hereby created within the Department of Justice as part of the Clandestine Laboratory Enforcement Program with responsibility for establishing, conducting, supporting, and coordinating crank-up task forces composed of state and local law enforcement agencies targeting the investigation, seizure, and cleanup of clandestine laboratories used to manufacture methamphetamine.

(b) The department shall coordinate all investigations undertaken by task forces operating under the Crank-Up Task Force Program with all local agencies having law enforcement responsibilities within the jurisdictions involved. The department also shall solicit participation by appropriate federal agencies with task force investigations whenever possible.

The department's Bureau of Narcotic Enforcement, Bureau of Forensic Services, and Bureau of Organized Crime and Criminal Intelligence shall provide staffing and logistical support for the crank-up task forces, supplying special agents, criminal intelligence analysts, forensic experts, financial auditors, equipment, and funding to the task forces as needed.

(c) Local law enforcement agencies participating in the Crank-Up Task Force Program shall be reimbursed by the department for personnel overtime costs and equipment or supplies required for task force activities. *(Repealed and added by Stats 1990 ch 1417 §§3, 4, eff. 9/28/90.)*

§11648. Annual report on Clandestine Laboratory Program.

The department shall report annually on its activities and on the accomplishments of the Clandestine Laboratory Program to the Legislature and to federal, state, and local law enforcement agencies, as well as to other interested groups. The first report to the Legislature shall be submitted no later than April 1, 1991, and it shall specify the way in which the department's organization and positions relate to the investigation, seizure, and cleanup of clandestine laboratories as of that date. The report shall also include a detailed account of program expenditures. *(Added by Stats 1990 ch 1417 §5, eff. 9/28/90.)*

CHAPTER 13

MISCELLANEOUS

§11650. Actions prior to the effective date of this division.

(a) Prosecution for any violation of law occurring prior to effective date of this division is not affected or abated by this division. If the offense being prosecuted is similar to one set out in Chapter 5 (commencing with Section 11350) of this division, then the penalties

under Chapter 5* (commencing with Section 11350) apply if they are less than those under prior law.
So in original. Probably should be "6".

(b) Civil seizures or forfeitures and injunctive proceedings commenced prior to effective date of this division are not affected by this division.

(c) All administrative proceedings pending under prior laws which are superseded by this division shall be continued and brought to a final determination in accord with the laws and rules in effect prior to effective date of this division. Any substance controlled under prior law which is not listed within Schedules I through V, is automatically controlled without further proceedings and shall be listed in the appropriate schedule.

(d) This division applies to violations of law, seizures and forfeiture, injunctive proceedings, administrative proceedings and investigations which occur on or after the effective date of this division.

§11651. Prior provisions remain in effect.

Any orders and regulations promulgated pursuant to any law affected by this division and in effect on the effective date of this division, not in conflict with it continue in effect until modified, superseded, or repealed.

DIVISION 10.1

IMITATION CONTROLLED SUBSTANCES ACT

CHAPTER 1

GENERAL PROVISIONS AND DEFINITIONS

§11670. Title.

This division shall be known as the "California Imitation Controlled Substances Act."

§11671. Definitions valid for this chapter.

Unless the context otherwise requires, the definitions in this chapter govern the construction of this division.

§11672. Controlled substance defined.

"Controlled substance" means a substance as defined in Section 11007.

§11673. Distribute defined.

"Distribute" means the actual, constructive, or attempted transfer, delivery, or dispensing to another of an imitation controlled substance.

§11674. Manufacture defined.

"Manufacture" means the production, preparation, compounding, processing, encapsulating, packaging or repackaging, labeling or relabeling, of an imitation controlled substance.

§11675. Imitation controlled substance, defined.

"Imitation controlled substance" means (a) a product specifically designed or manufactured to resemble the physical appearance of a controlled substance, such that a reasonable person of ordinary knowledge would not be able to distinguish the imitation from the controlled substance by outward appearances, or (b) a product, not a controlled substance, which, by representations made and by dosage unit appearance, including color, shape, size, or markings, would lead a reasonable person to believe that, if ingested, the product would have a stimulant or depressant effect similar to or the same as that of one or more of the controlled substances included in Schedules I through V, inclusive, of the Uniform Controlled Substances Act, pursuant to Chapter 2 (commencing with Section 11053) of Division 10.

§11676. This division not to restrict other remedies.

The provisions of this division are cumulative, and shall not be construed as restricting any remedy, provisional or otherwise, provided by law for the benefit of any party.

CHAPTER 2

OFFENSES AND PENALTIES

§11680. Penalties for possession of imitation controlled substances.

Any person who knowingly manufactures, distributes, or possesses with intent to distribute, an imitation controlled substance is guilty of a misdemeanor and shall, if convicted, be subject to imprisonment for not more than six months in the county jail or a fine of not more than one thousand dollars ($1,000), or both such imprisonment and fine.

§11681. Distribution of imitation controlled substance to minor.

Any person 18 year of age or over who violates Section 11680 by knowingly distributing an imitation controlled substance to a person under 18 years of age is guilty of a misdemeanor and shall, if convicted, be subject to imprisonment for not more than one year in the county jail or a fine of not more than two thousand dollars ($2,000), or both such imprisonment and fine. Upon a second or subsequent conviction of this offense, the person shall be subject to imprisonment for not more than one year in the county jail and a fine of not less than six thousand dollars ($6,000).

§11682. Distribution of imitation controlled substances for research.

No civil or criminal liability shall be imposed by virtue of this division on any person registered under the California Uniform Controlled Substances Act who manufactures, distributes, or possesses an imitation controlled substance for use by a practitioner, as defined in Section 11026, in the course of lawful professional practice or research.

§11683. Imitation controlled substances; forfeiture.

All imitation controlled substances shall be subject to forfeiture in accordance with the procedures set forth in Chapter 8 (commencing with Section 11470) of Division 10.

DIVISION 11

EXPLOSIVES

PART 1

HIGH EXPLOSIVES

CHAPTER 2

ENFORCEMENT

§12020. Personnel.

The chief and the issuing authority, as defined in Sections 12003 and 12007, respectively, shall in their areas of jurisdiction enforce the provisions of this part and the regulations adopted by the State Fire Marshal pursuant to this part.

Any peace officer, as defined in Sections 830.1, 830.2, and subdivisions (a), (e), (k), and (l) of Section 830.3 of the Penal Code, and those officers listed in Section 830.6 of the Penal Code while acting in the course and scope of their employment as peace officers may enforce the provisions of this part. (Amended by Stats 1990 ch 82 §2, eff. 5/3/90; ch 1695 §3, eff. 1/1/91.)

CHAPTER 3

GENERAL

§12082. Sale of explosives to minors.

No explosives shall be sold, furnished, or given away to any person under 21 years of age, whether such person is acting for himself or for another person, nor shall any such person be eligible to obtain any permit to receive explosives governed by the provisions of this part.

The reference to "under 21 years of age" in this section is unaffected by Section 1 of Chapter 1748 of the Statutes of 1971 or any other provision of that chapter.

§12083. Authorization to enter explosive plant.

With the exception of the chief, the owner, a person authorized to enter by the owner, or the owner's agent, no person shall enter any explosive manufacturing plant, magazine, or vehicle containing explosives.

§12084. Firearms discharged near explosive plant.

No person shall willfully discharge any firearm within 500 feet of any magazine or any explosive manufacturing plant.

§12085. Violations of regulations.

No person shall make, possess, or transport any explosive in a manner prohibited by this part or prohibited by any ordinance of a city, county, or city and county, or prohibited by the laws or regulations governing a harbor in those areas where such ordinance, laws, or regulations apply.

§12086. Theft or loss of explosives.

Any theft or loss of explosives, whether from a storage magazine, a vehicle in which they are being transported, or from a site on which they are being used, or from any other location, shall immediately be reported by the person having control of such ex-

© 1992 by J., B. & L. Gould
Printed in the U.S.A.   EP

plosives to the local police or county sheriff. The local police or county sheriff shall immediately transmit a report of such theft or loss of explosives to the State Bureau of Criminal Identification and Investigation at Sacramento.

§12087. Proper disposing or destroying of explosives.

No person shall abandon or otherwise dispose of any explosives in any manner which might, as the result of such abandonment or disposal, create any danger or threat of danger to life or property. Any person in possession or control of explosives required in the performance of his duties shall, when the need for such explosives no longer exists, either return the explosives to the source from which the explosives were obtained, or to an appropriate issuing authority for disposal or shall destroy the explosives in a safe manner so as not to make them available to persons who might obtain them and use them in a manner prejudicial to the safety of life and property. Magazines or temporary magazines used for storage purposes in any area where blasting is required shall, when the need for such storage no longer exists and the explosives have been removed or disposed of as above required, be removed or demolished, or signs, indicating the presence of explosives in such magazines or on the premises on which such magazines are located, shall be removed or effectively obliterated, and the issuing authority who issued the storage permit shall be immediately notified of the action taken.

§12088. Marking contents of packages.

The contents of a package containing explosives shall be plainly marked on the outside of the package at the time the package is delivered for transportation.

It is unlawful for any person to deliver, or to cause to be delivered, to any carrier for transportation any explosive under any false or deceptive marking, description, invoice, shipping order, or other declaration.

CHAPTER 4

PERMITS

§12101. Application for permit; expiration.

(a) No person shall do any one of the following without first having made application for and received a permit in accordance with this section:

(1) Manufacture explosives.
(2) Sell, furnish, or give away explosives.
(3) Receive, store, or possess explosives.
(4) Transport explosives.
(5) Use explosives.
(6) Operate a terminal for handling explosives.
(7) Park or leave standing any vehicle carrying explosives, except when parked or left standing in or at a safe stopping place designated as such by the Department of the California Highway Patrol under Division 14 (commencing with Section 31600) of the Vehicle Code.

(b) Application for a permit shall be made to the appropriate issuing authority.

(c) (1) A permit shall be obtained from the issuing authority having the responsibility in the area where the activity, as specified in subdivision (a), is to be conducted.

(2) If the person holding a valid permit for the use or storage of explosives desires to purchase or receive explosives in a jurisdiction other than that of intended use or storage, the person shall first present the permit to the issuing authority in the jurisdiction of purchase or receipt for endorsement. The issuing authority may include any reasonable restrictions or conditions which the authority finds necessary for the prevention of fire and explosion, the preservation of life, safety, or the control and security of explosives within the authority's jurisdiction. If, for any reason, the issuing authority refuses to endorse the permit previously issued in the area of intended use or storage, the authority shall immediately notify both the issuing authority who issued the permit and the Department of Justice of the fact of the refusal and the reasons for the refusal.

(3) Every person who sells, gives away, delivers, or otherwise disposes of explosives to another person shall first be satisfied that the person receiving the explosives has a permit valid for that purpose. When the permit to receive explosives indicates that the intended storage or use of the explosives is other than in that area in which the permittee receives the explosives, the person who sells, gives away, delivers, or otherwise disposes of the explosives shall insure that the permit has been properly endorsed by a local issuing authority and, further, shall immediately send a copy of the record of sale to the issuing authority who originally issued the permit in the area of intended storage or use. The issuing authority in the area in which the explosives are received or sold shall not issue a permit for the possession, use, or storage of explosives in an area not within the authority's jurisdiction.

(d) In the event any person desires to receive explosives for use in an area outside of this state, a permit to receive the explosives shall be obtained from the State Fire Marshal.

(e) A permit may include any restrictions or conditions which the issuing authority finds necessary for the prevention of fire and explosion, the preservation of life, safety, or the control and security of explosives.

(f) A permit shall remain valid only until the time when the act or acts authorized by the permit are performed, but in no event shall the permit remain valid for a period longer than one year from the date of issuance of the permit.

(g) Any valid permit which authorizes the performance of any act shall not constitute authorization for the performance of any act not stipulated in the permit.

(h) An issuing authority shall not issue a permit authorizing the transportation of explosives pursuant to this section if the display of placards for that transportation is required by Section 27903 of the Vehicle Code, unless the driver possesses a license for the transportation of hazardous materials issued pursuant to Division 14.1 (commencing with Section 32000 of the Vehicle Code, or the explosives are a hazardous waste or extremely hazardous waste, as defined in Sections 25117 and 25115 of the Health and Safety Code, and the transporter is currently registered as a hazardous waste hauler pursuant to Section 25163 of the Health and Safety Code.

(i) An issuing authority shall not issue a permit pursuant to this section authorizing the handling or storage of class A or B explosives in a building, unless the building has caution placards which meet the

© 1992 by J., B. & L. Gould
Printed in the U.S.A.   **EP**

standards established pursuant to subdivision (g) of Section 12081. *(Amended by Stats 1990 ch 734 §3, eff. 1/1/91.)*

§12102.1. Disposing of certain powders.

Any person who sells, gives, delivers or otherwise disposes of 20 pounds or less of smokeless powder, or one pound or less of black sporting powder, shall first obtain a statement from the person who purchases or otherwise receives such powder, which statement shall include:

(a) The name, address and birth date of the person purchasing or receiving the powder.

(b) The purpose for which the powder is intended to be used, handled, stored, or possessed.

(c) The type and amount of the powder.

(d) The signature of the person purchasing or receiving the powder.

(e) The driver's license number, selective service card number, or other identifying information concerning the person purchasing or receiving the powder.

Any person furnishing a fictitious name or address or knowingly furnishing an incorrect birth date and any person violating any of the provisions of this section is guilty of a misdemeanor.

CHAPTER 5

SALE OR OTHER DISPOSITION

§12120. Permit for selling or disposing of explosives.

No person shall knowingly sell, give away, deliver, or otherwise dispose of any explosive to any person who does not possess a valid permit as required pursuant to Section 12101.

The provisions of this section and subdivisions (e) and (f) of Section 12122 do not apply to transactions by the Department of Defense or to the transactions of an agency or organization acting pursuant to contract with the Department of Defense.

CHAPTER 6

STORAGE

§12150. Container for explosives.

Except for explosives kept only at an explosive manufacturing plant, no person shall possess, keep, or store any explosive which is not completely encased in a tight metal, wooden, or fiber container, or a container approved by the Interstate Commerce Commission.

No person having any explosives in his possession or control shall under any circumstances permit or allow any grains or particles of such explosives to be or remain on the outside of, or about, the containers in which such explosives are kept.

CHAPTER 7

ILLEGAL USE OR POSSESSION

§12303. Lawful possession of an explosive defined.

"Lawful possession of an explosive," as used in this chapter, means possessing explosives in accordance with the stated purpose and conditions of a valid permit obtained pursuant to the provisions of this part, unless such person is specifically excepted from the permit requirements by the provisions of this part.

§12305. Illegal possession.

Every person not in the lawful possession of an explosive who knowingly has any explosive in his possession is guilty of a felony.

CHAPTER 9

PENALTIES

§12400. Misdemeanor violations.

Except as provided in Chapter 7 (commencing with Section 12302), Part 1, Division 11 of the Health and Safety Code, every person who violates any provision of this part, or violates any regulation adopted by the State Fire Marshal pursuant to this part, is guilty of a misdemeanor, punishable by a fine of not more than one thousand dollars ($1,000), or by imprisonment for not more than six months, or by both such fine and imprisonment.

§12401. Felony violations.

Every person who is found guilty of a felony as specified in this part is punishable by imprisonment in the state prison, or in a county jail not exceeding one year, or by fine not exceeding ten thousand dollars ($10,000), or by both such fine and imprisonment.

PART 2

FIREWORKS AND PYROTECHNIC DEVICES

CHAPTER 7

VIOLATIONS

§12676. Sale or transfer.

It is unlawful for any person to sell, transfer, give, deliver, or otherwise convey title of any dangerous fireworks, including fireworks kits, to any person in this state who does not possess and present to the seller or donor for inspection at the time of transfer, a valid permit to receive, use, or transport dangerous fireworks as provided in this part.

§12679. Storage, etc., near flammable liquids.

It is unlawful for any person to store, sell, or discharge any type of fireworks in or within 100 feet of a location where gasoline or any other flammable liquids are stored or dispensed.

§12680. Fireworks near people.

It is unlawful for any person to place, throw, discharge or ignite, or fire dangerous fireworks at any person or group of persons where there is a likelihood of injury to any such person.

§12684. Use of emergency signaling device.

It is unlawful for any person to use or discharge any registered emergency signaling device in any manner other than that permitted by the instructions for use.

§12685. Public display.

It is unlawful for any person to conduct a public display without possessing a valid permit for this purpose.

© 1992 by J., B. & L. Gould
Printed in the U.S.A. **EP**

§12688. Advertisement for sale of fireworks.

It is unlawful for any person to advertise to sell or transfer any class of fireworks, including agricultural and wildlife fireworks or model rocket engines, unless he possesses a valid license or permit.

§12689. Sale to minors.

(a) It is unlawful for any person to sell, give, or deliver any dangerous fireworks to any person under 18 years of age.

(b) It is unlawful for any person who is a retailer to sell or transfer any safe and sane fireworks to a person who is under 16 years of age.

(c) Except as otherwise provided in subdivision (d), it is unlawful for any person who is a retailer to sell or transfer to a person under the age of 18 any rocket, rocket propelled projectile launcher, or similar device containing any explosive or incendiary material whether or not the device is designed for emergency or distance signaling purposes. It is also unlawful for a minor to possess such a device unless he or she has the written permission of, or is accompanied by, his or her parent or guardian while it is in his or her possession.

(d) Model rocket products including model rockets, launch systems, and model rocket motors designed, sold, and used for the purpose of propelling recoverable model rockets may be sold or transferred pursuant to regulations, adopted by the State Fire Marshal which the Fire Marshal determines are reasonably necessary to carry out the requirements of this part.

CHAPTER 8

PENALTIES

§12700. Misdemeanor penalties.

Except as provided in Section 12702, any person who violates any provision of this part, or any regulations issued pursuant to this part, is guilty of a misdemeanor, and upon conviction shall be punished by a fine of not less than five hundred dollars ($500) nor more than one thousand dollars ($1,000), or by imprisonment in the county jail for not exceeding one year, or by both such fine and imprisonment.

§12701. Daily offenses.

A person is guilty of a separate offense for each day during which he commits, continues, or permits a violation of this part, or any provision of, or any order, regulation issued pursuant to this part.

§12702. Violations regarding minors.

Notwithstanding the provisions of Section 12700:

(a) Any person who violates this part by selling, giving, or delivering any dangerous fireworks to any person under 18 years of age is guilty of a misdemeanor and upon a first conviction shall be punished as prescribed in Section 12700.

(b) Upon any second or subsequent conviction of the offense, the person shall be punished by the penalties of a fine of not less than five hundred dollars ($500) nor more than one thousand dollars ($1,000) and by imprisonment in the county jail for one year. The person shall not be granted probation and the execution of the sentence imposed upon the person shall not be suspended by the court.

(c) Any person who violates this part involving any dangerous fireworks item, as defined in Section 12505, or any combination of any dangerous fireworks items, having the total net weight of explosive material of 7,500 grains or more, is guilty of a public offense, and upon conviction thereof shall be punished by imprisonment in the state prison, or in the county jail for not more than one year, or by a fine of not more than five thousand dollars ($5,000), or by both the fine and imprisonment. *(Amended by Stats 1990 ch 350 §7, eff. 1/1/91.)*

DIVISION 20

MISCELLANEOUS HEALTH AND SAFETY PROVISIONS

CHAPTER 5

MISCELLANEOUS PENAL PROVISIONS

§24800. Neglect of duties.

Every person charged with the performance of any duty under the laws of this State relating to the preservation of the public health, who willfully neglects or refuses to perform the same, is guilty of a misdemeanor.

CHAPTER 6.5

HAZARDOUS WASTE CONTROL

ARTICLE 6

TRANSPORTATION

§25163. Transporting hazardous wastes.

(a) (1) Except as otherwise provided in subdivisions (b), (c), and (f), it is unlawful for any person to carry on, or engage in, the transportation of hazardous wastes, unless the person holds a valid registration issued by the department, and it shall be unlawful for any person to transfer custody of a hazardous waste to a transporter who does not hold a valid registration issued by the department. A person who holds a valid registration issued by the department pursuant to this section is a registered hazardous waste transporter, for purposes of this chapter. Any registration issued by the department to a transporter of hazardous waste is not transferable from the person to whom it was issued to any other person.

(2) Any person who transports hazardous waste in a vehicle shall have a valid registration issued by the department in his or her possession while transporting the hazardous waste. The registration certificate shall be shown upon demand to any representative of the department, officer of the Department of the California Highway Patrol, any local health officer, or any public officer designated by the department. Any person registered pursuant to this section may obtain additional copies of the registration from the department upon the payment of a fee of two dollars ($2) for each copy requested, in accordance with Section 12196 of the Government Code.

(3) Commencing January 1, 1986, the hazardous waste information required and collected for registration pursuant to this subdivision shall be recorded and maintained in the management information system

© 1992 by J., B. & L. Gould
Printed in the U.S.A. **EP**

operated by the Department of the California Highway Patrol.

(b) Persons transporting only septic tank, cesspool, seepage pit, or chemical toilet waste that does not contain a hazardous waste originating from other than the body of a human or animal and who hold an unrevoked registration issued by the health officer or the health officer's authorized representative pursuant to Chapter 6 (commencing with Section 25000) are exempt from the requirements of subdivision (a).

(c) Persons transporting hazardous wastes to a permitted hazardous waste facility for transfer, treatment, recycling, or disposal, which wastes do not exceed a total volume of five gallons or do not exceed a total weight of 50 pounds, are exempt from the requirements of subdivisions (a) and (e) and from the requirements of Section 25160 concerning possession of the manifest while transporting hazardous waste, upon meeting all of the following conditions:

(1) The hazardous wastes are transported in closed containers and packed in a manner that prevents the containers from tipping, spilling, or breaking during the transporting.

(2) Different hazardous waste materials are not mixed within a container during the transporting.

(3) If the hazardous waste is extremely hazardous waste or acutely hazardous waste, the extremely hazardous waste or acutely hazardous waste was not generated in the course of any business, and is not more than 2.2 pounds.

(4) The person transporting the hazardous waste is the producer of that hazardous waste, and the person produces no more than 100 kilograms of hazardous waste in any month.

(5) The person transporting the hazardous waste does not accumulate more than a total of 1,000 kilograms of hazardous waste onsite at any one time.

(d) Any person registered as a hazardous waste transporter pursuant to subdivision (a) is not subject to the registration requirements of Chapter 6 (commencing with Section 25000), but shall comply with the terms, conditions, orders, and directions as the health officer or the health officer's authorized representative may deem necessary for the protection of human health and comfort, and shall otherwise comply with the requirements for statements as provided in Section 25007. Violations of those requirements of Section 25007 shall be punished as provided in Section 25010. Proof of registration pursuant to subdivision (a) shall be submitted by mail or in person to the local health officer in the city or county in which the registered hazardous waste transporter will be conducting the activities described in Section 25001.

(e) It is unlawful for any person to transport hazardous waste in any truck, trailer, semitrailer, vacuum tank or cargo tank not inspected by the Department of the California Highway Patrol or to transport hazardous waste in any container, other than a container packaged pursuant to United States Department of Transportation regulations, which has not been inspected by the Department of the California Highway Patrol, or in a rolloff bin which has not been inspected, certified, and maintained in compliance with subdivisions (b) and (c) of Section 25169.1.

(f) Any person authorized to collect solid waste, as defined in Section 40191 of the Public Resources Code, who unknowingly transports hazardous waste to a solid waste facility, as defined in Section 40194 of the Public Resources Code, incidental to the collection of solid waste is not subject to the provisions of subdivisions (a) and (e).

(g) This section shall remain in effect only until January 1, 1995, and as of that date is repealed, unless a later enacted statute, which is enacted before January 1, 1995, deletes or extends that date. *(Amended by Stats 1991 ch 1084 §1, eff. 1/1/92 only until 1/1/95. See other section 25163 below.)*

§25163. Transporting hazardous wastes.

(a) (1) Except as otherwise provided in subdivisions (b), (c), and (f), it is unlawful for any person to carry on, or engage in, the transportation of hazardous wastes, unless the person holds a valid registration issued by the department, and it shall be unlawful for any person to transfer custody of a hazardous waste to a transporter who does not hold a valid registration issued by the department. A person who holds a valid registration issued by the department pursuant to this section is a registered hazardous waste transporter, for purposes of this chapter. Any registration issued by the department to a transporter of hazardous waste is not transferable from the person to whom it was issued to any other person.

(2) Any person who transports hazardous waste in a vehicle shall have a valid registration issued by the department in his or her possession while transporting the hazardous waste. The registration certificate shall be shown upon demand to any representative of the department, officer of the Department of the California Highway Patrol, any local health officer, or any public officer designated by the department. Any person registered pursuant to this section may obtain additional copies of the registration from the department upon the payment of a fee of two dollars ($2) for each copy requested, in accordance with Section 12196 of the Government Code.

(3) The hazardous waste information required and collected for registration pursuant to this subdivision shall be recorded and maintained in the management information system operated by the Department of the California Highway Patrol.

(b) Persons transporting only septic tank, cesspool, seepage pit, or chemical toilet waste that does not contain a hazardous waste originating from other than the body of a human or animal and who hold an unrevoked registration issued by the health officer or the health officer's authorized representative pursuant to Chapter 6 (commencing with Section 25000) are exempt from the requirements of subdivision (a).

(c) Persons transporting hazardous wastes to a permitted hazardous waste facility for transfer, treatment, recycling, or disposal, which wastes do not exceed a total volume of five gallons or do not exceed a total weight of 50 pounds, are exempt from the requirements of subdivisions (a) and (e) and from the requirements of Section 25160 concerning possession of the manifest while transporting hazardous waste, upon meeting all of the following conditions:

(1) The hazardous wastes are transported in closed containers and packed in a manner that prevents the containers from tipping, spilling, or breaking during the transporting.

(2) Different hazardous waste materials are not mixed within a container during the transporting.

© 1992 by J., B. & L. Gould
Printed in the U.S.A.   **EP**

(3) If the hazardous waste is extremely hazardous waste or acutely hazardous waste, the extremely hazardous waste or acutely hazardous waste was not generated in the course of any business, and is not more than 2.2 pounds.

(4) The person transporting the hazardous waste is the producer of that hazardous waste, and the person produces no more than 100 kilograms of hazardous waste in any month.

(5) The person transporting the hazardous waste does not accumulate more than a total of 1,000 kilograms of hazardous waste onsite at any one time.

(d) Any person registered as a hazardous waste transporter pursuant to subdivision (a) is not subject to the registration requirements of Chapter 6 (commencing with Section 25000), but shall comply with the terms, conditions, orders, and directions as the health officer or the health officer's authorized representative may deem necessary for the protection of human health and comfort, and shall otherwise comply with the requirements for statements as provided in Section 25007. Violations of those requirements of Section 25007 shall be punished as provided in Section 25010. Proof of registration pursuant to subdivision (a) shall be submitted by mail or in person to the local health officer in the city or county in which the registered hazardous waste transporter will be conducting the activities described in Section 25001.

(e) It is unlawful for any person to transport hazardous waste in any truck, trailer, semitrailer, vacuum tank, or cargo tank not inspected by the Department of the California Highway Patrol or to transport hazardous waste in any container, other than a container packaged pursuant to United States Department of Transportation regulations, which has not been inspected by the Department of the California Highway Patrol.

(f) Any person authorized to collect solid waste, as defined in Section 40191 of the Public Resources Code, who unknowingly transports hazardous waste to a solid waste facility, as defined in Section 40194 of the Public Resources Code, incidental to the collection of solid waste is not subject to the provisions of subdivisions (a) and (e).

(g) This section shall become operative January 1, 1995. *(Added by Stats 1991 ch 1084 §2, eff. 1/1/92, oper. 1/1/95. See other section 25163 above.)*

CHAPTER 6.8

HAZARDOUS SUBSTANCE ACCOUNT

ARTICLE 2

DEFINITIONS

§25323.6. Unknowingly transporting hazardous waste.

Any person who unknowingly transports hazardous waste to a solid waste facility pursuant to the exemption provided in subdivision (f) of Section 25163 shall not be considered a responsible party for purposes of this chapter solely because of the act of transporting the waste. Nothing in this section shall affect the liability of this person for his or her negligent acts. *(Added by Stats 1990 ch 659 §2, eff. 1/1/91.)*

This page intentionally left blank.

© 1992 by J., B. & L. Gould
Printed in the U.S.A.   **EP**

CALIFORNIA RULES OF COURT

TITLE ONE

APPELLATE RULES

DIVISION I

RULES RELATING TO THE SUPREME COURT AND COURTS OF APPEAL

CHAPTER 1

RULES ON APPEAL

PART V

APPEALS IN CRIMINAL CASES

Rule 30. Rules governing criminal appeals.

The rules governing appeals from the superior court in civil cases shall be applicable to appeals from the superior court in criminal cases except where express provision is made to the contrary, or where the application of a particular rule would be clearly impracticable or inappropriate.

Rule 31. Notice of appeal.

(a) [Time of filing] In the cases provided by law, an appeal is taken by filing a written notice of appeal with the clerk of the superior court within 60 days after the rendition of the judgment or the making of the order. A notice of appeal filed prior to the time prescribed therefor is premature but may, in the discretion of the reviewing court for good cause, be treated as filed immediately after the rendition of the judgment or the making of the order.

Whenever a notice of appeal is received by the clerk of the superior court after the expiration of the period prescribed for filing such notice, the clerk shall mark it "Received (date) but not filed" and advise the party seeking to file the notice that it was received but not filed because the period for filing notice of appeal had elapsed.

If the attorney for a defendant either files a notice of appeal for the defendant or assists the defendant in filing it, the attorney shall serve a copy on the court reporter, lead reporter, or reporting supervisor, and file proof of the service; but the attorney's failure to do so does not affect the validity of the appeal. The reporter shall begin work on the transcript immediately upon being served with a copy of the notice of appeal or upon notice from the clerk, whichever is earlier. (*As amended effective July 1, 1990; previously amended effective Jan. 1, 1951, Jan. 1, 1959, Jan. 1, 1961, Sept. 15, 1961, Nov. 13, 1968, and Jan. 1, 1972.*)

(b) [Form of notice] If the appeal is by the defendant the notice shall be signed by him or by his attorney, and if the appeal is by the People, the notice shall be signed by the district attorney, his deputy, or other counsel for the People. The notice shall be sufficient if it states in substance that the party appeals from a specified judgment or order or a particular part thereof, and shall be liberally construed in favor of its sufficiency. The notice need not specify the court to which the appeal is taken, and, except when judgment of death was pronounced, a notice shall be deemed to be an appeal to the Court of Appeal for the district.

(c) [Notification by clerk] The clerk of the superior court shall forthwith transmit a copy of the notice of appeal and a copy of the sequential list of reporters made pursuant to rule 980.4 to the clerk of the reviewing court and mail a notification of the filing of the notice of appeal to each party other than the appellant. The notification shall state the number and title of the case and the date the notice of appeal was filed. The failure of the clerk to mail such notice or to give such notification shall not affect the validity of the appeal. (*As amended effective Jan. 1, 1992; adopted effective July 1, 1964; and previously amended effective Jan. 1, 1972.*)

(d) [Guilty or nolo contendere plea (subdivision effective January 1, 1992)] If a judgment of conviction is entered upon a plea of guilty or nolo contendere, the defendant shall, within 60 days after the judgment is rendered, file as an intended notice of appeal the statement required by section 1237.5 of the Penal Code; but the appeal shall not be operative unless the trial court executes and files the certificate of probable cause required by that section. Within 20 days after the defendant files the statement the trial court shall execute and file either a certificate of probable cause or an order denying a certificate and shall forthwith notify the parties of the granting or denial of the certificate.

If the appeal from a judgment of conviction entered upon a plea of guilty or nolo contendere is based solely upon grounds (1) occurring after entry of the plea which do not challenge its validity or (2) involving a search or seizure, the validity of which was contested pursuant to section 1538.5 of the Penal Code, the provisions of section 1237.5 of the Penal Code requiring a statement by the defendant and a certificate of probable cause by the trial court are inapplicable, but the appeal shall not be operative unless the notice of appeal states that it is based upon such grounds.

The time for preparing, certifying, and filing the record on appeal or for filing an agreed statement shall begin when the appeal becomes operative. (*As amended effective January 1, 1992.*)

Rule 32. Stay of execution and bail on appeal.

(a) [Stay of execution] An application to the reviewing court for a stay of execution of a judgment of conviction on an appeal pending therein shall include a showing that proper application for a stay was made to the superior court, and that the superior court unjustifiably refused to grant the stay. Pending a ruling on the application, the reviewing court may order the execution of the judgment stayed, and if it so orders it shall notify the trial court pursuant to rule 56(d).

(b) [Bail] An application to the reviewing court for bail or to reduce bail on an appeal pending therein shall be made on such notice to the district attorney and the Attorney General as the court may determine, and shall include a showing that proper application for bail or a reduction of bail was made to the superior court and that such court unjustifiably denied the application.

Rule 33. Contents of record on appeal from judgment or order on motion for new trial; noncapital cases.

(a) [Normal record] If the appeal is taken by the defendant from a judgment of conviction, or if the appeal is taken by the People from an order granting a motion for a new trial, the record on appeal, except as stated in this rule, shall include the following (which shall constitute the normal record):

(1) A clerk's transcript, containing copies of (a) the notice of appeal, any certificate of probable cause executed and filed by the court, and any request for additional record and any order made pursuant thereto; (b) the indictment, information or accusation with any amendments; (c) any demurrer; (d) any motion for a new trial, with supporting and opposing memoranda and affidavits; (e) all minutes of the court relating to the action; (f) the verdict; (g) the judgment or order appealed from and any abstract of judgment—commitment; (h) written instructions given or refused indicating on each instruction the party requesting it; (i) all written communications, formal or informal, between the court and the jury or any individual jurors; (j) any written opinion of the court. If the appeal is by the defendant, the clerk's transcript shall also include copies of (k) each written motion made by defendant and denied in whole or in part, with supporting and opposing memoranda and related affidavits, search warrants and returns, and the transcript of any preliminary examination or grand jury hearing related thereto; (l) the report of the probation officer; (m) copies of certified records of a court or of the Department of Corrections that were introduced in evidence to prove a prior conviction or prior prison term.

(2) A reporter's transcript of (a) the oral proceedings taken on the trial of the cause, including jury instructions, and proceedings at the time of sentencing, granting of probation, or other dispositional hearing, but excluding the voir dire examination of jurors and opening statements; (b) the oral proceedings on the hearing of the motion for a new trial, and on the entry of any plea other than a plea of not guilty; (c) any oral opinion of the court. If the appeal is by the defendant, the reporter's transcript shall also contain (d) the oral proceedings on any motion made by defendant under section 1538.5 of the Penal Code and denied in whole or in part; (e) closing arguments to the jury, comments on the evidence by the court before the jury, and all communications to and from the jury after instructions have been given whether or not denominated as questions or instructions.

(3) To be transmitted as originals upon request by the reviewing court as provided in rule 10; any exhibit admitted in evidence or rejected. (*As amended effective Jan. 1, 1992; previously amended effective Jan. 1, 1966, Jan. 1, 1968, Nov. 13, 1968, July 1, 1971, Jan. 1, 1976, July 1, 1976, Jan. 1, 1982, Jan. 1, 1984, and Jan. 1, 1990.*)

(b) [Request for additional record] The People may request inclusion in the record on an appeal by the People of any item that would be included on an appeal by the defendant. Either party may request the inclusion in the record of any of the following:

(1) In the clerk's transcript: any motion made by the defendant that was granted or any motion made by the People, with supporting and opposing memoranda and affidavits.

(2) In the reporter's transcript: (a) proceedings on the voir dire examination of jurors; (b) opening statements; (c) oral proceedings on motions other than those enumerated in subdivision (a).

(3) To be transmitted as originals: any exhibits admitted in evidence or rejected that have not been requested by the reviewing court under subdivision (a).

An application for additional record shall describe the material to be included and state how it may be useful on appeal. The application shall be filed with the notice of appeal or as soon thereafter as is practicable; it shall be deemed denied if it is filed after the record on appeal is transmitted to the reviewing court. The clerk shall immediately present the request to the judge and notify the reporter. The judge, within five days after the filing of the application, shall make an order directing the inclusion in the record of as much of the additional material as, in the judge's opinion, may be proper to present fairly and fully the points relied on by appellant in the application. Any denial of the application in the trial court shall be without prejudice to an application under rule 12. If the judge fails to make any order within five days after the application is filed, the material requested, with the exception of exhibits, shall be included in the clerk's and reporter's transcripts without an order.

(c) [Record where automatic appeal] When a judgment of death has been rendered, preparation and filing of the record is governed by rules 35 and 39.5.

(d) [Subsequent orders] If the judgment is amended or recalled after the transcript is certified, copies of the amended abstract of judgment or other new dispositional order shall be certified and transmitted to the reviewing court, the defendant, the Attorney General, and defendant's counsel on appeal. If the identity of defendant's counsel on appeal is unknown, that copy shall be sent to the reviewing court with a request that it be forwarded to counsel. The amended abstract or other new order is deemed an augmentation of the record on appeal.

Rule 33.5. Confidential in-camera proceedings.

(a) [Marsden hearings] In addition to the normal record required by any other rule, the record on appeal in a criminal action and in an appeal from the juvenile court shall also include a sealed reporter's transcript of hearings held pursuant to *People* v. *Marsden* (1970) 2 Cal.3d 118. The original and two copies of the sealed transcript shall accompany the record upon its transmission to the reviewing court. The chronological index to the reporter's transcript shall refer to the *Marsden* hearing and state "SEALED" or the equivalent.

The clerk of the reviewing court shall send a copy of the transcript to the defendant's or juvenile's counsel on appeal when counsel is appointed or, in the case of retained counsel, when he or she has appeared in the cause.

If the defendant or juvenile raises a *Marsden* issue in his or her brief, the People shall be sent a copy of the transcript upon their motion to receive it. (*As amended effective Jan. 1, 1992; adopted effective July 1, 1990.*)

(b) [Other in-camera proceedings] In addition to the additional record that may be requested under any other rule, the record on appeal in a criminal action and in an appeal from the juvenile court may, upon request and trial court order as provided in rule 33(b), also include:

(1) A sealed, separately paginated reporter's transcript of any confidential in-camera proceeding from which a party was excluded from being represented. The trial judge may order that the transcript be prepared personally by the court reporter who attended the proceeding. The chronological index to

© 1992 by J., B. & L. Gould
Printed in the U.S.A.   **EP**

the reporter's transcript shall refer to the in-camera proceeding and state "SEALED" or the equivalent.

(2) Written materials submitted to the trial court, all or part of which were determined to be confidential and were withheld from a party.

This reporter's transcript and confidential material, if made part of the record, shall be transmitted to the reviewing court in sealed envelopes marked "CONFIDENTIAL—MAY NOT BE EXAMINED WITHOUT COURT ORDER." Unless otherwise ordered by the reviewing court, the materials described in this subdivision may be examined only by a judge of the reviewing court personally. The reviewing court shall permit examination of these materials by parties to whom the information was accessible in the trial court and their attorneys.

Sealed envelopes containing confidential materials shall be securely filed and kept separately from the main file in the cause. (*Adopted effective July 1, 1990.*)

Rule 34. Contents of record on appeal in other noncapital cases.

If the appeal is taken by the People from a judgment on a demurrer to the indictment, information or accusation, or by the defendant or the People from any appealable order other than an order on motion for a new trial, the record on appeal shall include the following:

(1) A clerk's transcript, containing copies of (a) the notice of appeal; (b) the indictment, information or accusation and all pleas; (c) any demurrer; (d) any judgment, and any order appealed from; (e) any motion or notice of motion, the granting or denial of which constitutes the order appealed from; (f) all affidavits filed in support of or in opposition to the motion; (g) the minutes of the court relating to the judgment or order appealed from; and (h) any abstract of judgment—commitment.

(2) Any reporter's transcript of the oral proceedings incident to the order appealed from.

(3) All exhibits admitted in evidence at the proceedings incident to the order appealed from.

Rule 34.5. Ordering transcript upon conviction after trial.

This rule is adopted under Code of Civil Procedure section 269(b).

Notwithstanding rule 35(b) or any other rule, the trial judge shall order the reporter and the clerk to begin preparing the record on appeal immediately after a verdict or finding of guilty of a felony is announced after a trial on the merits, unless the court determines that it is likely that no appeal from the decision will be made.

In determining the likelihood of an appeal, the trial judge shall consider the facts of the case and the following standards:

(1) An appeal is very likely if (a) the defendant has been convicted of a crime for which probation is prohibited or is prohibited except in unusual cases; or (b) the trial involved a contested question of law important to the outcome.

(2) An appeal is less likely if neither of the factors identified in the preceding paragraph was present.

(3) An appeal is unlikely in relatively few cases that are tried to a verdict or finding of guilt.

(4) If the judge is undecided whether an appeal is likely, the judge should order immediate preparation of the record.

The trial judge's determination to order immediate preparation of the record or not to do so is an administrative decision intended to further the efficient operation of the courts. The determination is not intended to affect any substantive or procedural right of either the defendant or the People. The determination shall not be cited to prove or disprove any issue of law or fact in the case and should not, therefore, be reviewable on appeal or by writ. (*As amended effective Jan. 1, 1991; adopted effective Jan. 1, 1991.*)

Rule 35. Preparation, certification, and filing of record.

(a) **[Clerk's transcript]** On the filing of the notice of appeal the clerk shall prepare an original and two clearly legible copies of the clerk's transcript, in the manner and form required by rule 9. On the entry of a judgment of death the clerk shall prepare an original and five copies. The clerk shall append to the original and each copy a certificate that it is correct. An additional copy of the transcript shall be prepared for the district attorney upon the request of the district attorney in noncapital cases. When there is more than one appealing defendant, the clerk shall prepare an additional copy of the transcript for each additional defendant up to a total of two additional copies, except in a case in which a judgment of death has been rendered against one or more of the defendants when an additional copy shall be prepared for each additional defendant not sentenced to death, and two copies for each defendant sentenced to death.

(b) **[Reporter's transcript]** Where a reporter's transcript is required, the clerk, immediately on the filing of the notice of appeal, shall notify the reporter. The notice shall be delivered to the reporter personally or to his or her office or internal mail receptacle; if the reporter is not employed by the court, the notice may be mailed. The reporter shall prepare an original and the same number of clearly legible copies of the reporter's transcript as are required of the clerk's transcript by subdivision (a), in the manner and form required by rule 9, and shall append to the original and each copy a certificate that it is correct. The reporter shall deliver the original and all the copies to the clerk immediately on their completion, and in no case more than 20 days after the filing of the notice of appeal unless the time is extended as provided in subdivision (d).

Portions of the transcript that were prepared during the trial shall not be retyped unless necessary to correct errors. They shall be bound together with transcripts of any portions of the proceedings not previously transcribed and renumbered. If additional copies are needed, they shall be prepared by photocopying or an equivalent process and not by retyping.

One week after the deadline for filing the transcript, the clerk shall accept completed portions of the transcript from the lead reporter in a multi-reporter case even if not all portions of the transcript are completed. The clerk shall pay promptly each reporter who certifies under penalty of perjury that all of his or her portions of the transcript are completed. (*As amended effective Jan. 1, 1992; previously amended effective Jan 1, 1959, July 1, 1971, Jan. 1, 1985, and July 1, 1990.*)

(c) **[Delivery]** As soon as both the clerk's and reporter's transcripts are completed, the clerk shall deliver one copy to each appealing defendant or to the defendant's trial attorney, one copy to the Attorney General, and if a judgment of death has been rendered, one copy to the district attorney, and note the dates of the deliveries on the original. If a judgment of death was not rendered, the clerk shall send the district attorney a notice of delivery of the prosecution's copy to the Attorney General. When the clerk is notified of the appointment or retention of counsel on appeal for a defendant sentenced to death, a copy shall be delivered to counsel on appeal and the date noted on the original. If there are four or more appealing defendants in a case in which a judgment of death has not been rendered against any defendant, the clerk shall make one copy of both transcripts available for use by the defendants or their attorneys as provided in rule 10.

When a judgment of death has been rendered, within the time provided by rule 39.5(d) any party may serve and file a request for correction of these transcripts. If no request for correction is filed within that time, the clerk shall immediately certify on the original transcripts that no objection was made within the time allowed by law and transmit the original transcripts to the reviewing court as provided in subdivision (e). If a proposed correction is filed within that time, the clerk shall promptly, and in no case longer than the time allowed by rule 39.5(d), deliver the original transcripts to the judge, who shall promptly determine the matter and shall also determine which corrections have sufficient potential significance to require that they be furnished to the parties in the form of copies of corrected transcript pages. The original transcripts shall be corrected to reflect all corrections ordered, by strikeover and interlineation where possible. After corrections have been made, the judge shall certify that all objections have been determined, and that the transcripts have been corrected in accordance with such determination, and shall redeliver the transcripts to the clerk.

In a case in which a judgment of death has not been rendered, the original transcripts shall be transmitted to the reviewing court at the same time copies are delivered to the parties. If there are four or more appealing defendants represented by separate counsel in a case in which judgment of death has not been rendered against any defendant, the appellants' copies shall be made available for the use of the appellants as directed by the appellate court. *(As amended effective Jan. 1, 1991; previously amended effective Jan. 1, 1959, July 1, 1971, Jan. 1, 1972, July 1, 1972, Jan. 1, 1983, and July 1, 1983.)*

(d) **[Extensions of time]** The periods allowed by this rule for preparation of the record shall not be extended by the superior court, but on affidavit showing good cause, and, in the case of a reporter's transcript, on certification by the presiding judge of the superior court or a court administrator designated by the presiding judge that the extension is reasonable and necessary in light of the workload of all reporters in the court, the reviewing court may extend time for not exceeding 60 days in the aggregate.

(e) **[Transmission]** The clerk shall transmit the original transcripts to the clerk of the reviewing court forthwith after certification of the individual transcripts pursuant to subdivisions (a) and (b) or, if a judgment of death was rendered against any defendant, after correction pursuant to subdivision (c). Unless a judgment of death has been rendered against any defendant, the district attorney shall deliver to the

clerk a copy of each transcript furnished the district attorney under subdivision (c). The clerk shall transmit to the Attorney General that copy of each transcript. When a judgment of death has been rendered, the clerk shall, instead, transmit to the Attorney General and all parties (1) notices enumerating all corrections ordered and stating a date of certification, and (2) copies of any pages of the corrected transcripts on which there are corrections that the judge determined pursuant to subdivision (c) shall be furnished to the parties in that form. The copies of corrected pages shall ordinarily be xerographic copies of the originals or their equivalent. In those cases, the clerk shall also transmit the copies of the transcripts required by Penal Code section 1218, with copies of pages containing corrections ordered to be furnished in that form inserted, and with a copy of the notice of corrections. The date of transmission of copies to the Attorney General shall be noted on the original transcripts by the clerk of the superior court. All exhibits admitted in evidence or rejected which are made part of the record on appeal by rule 33 or 34 shall be transmitted to the reviewing court as originals as provided in rule 10. If any exhibits were requested by an appellant as provided in subdivision (b) of rule 33, but the superior court failed to make an order pursuant to the request, the exhibits shall be transmitted only on request of the reviewing court.

The probation officer's report, included in the clerk's transcript pursuant to rule 33 (a)(1)(k), shall be included in the parties' copies of the record on appeal as well as in the copy sent to the reviewing court. The reviewing court's copy of the probation officer's report shall be in a sealed envelope marked "Confidential—May Not Be Examined Without Court Order—Probation Officer Report."

If at any time the clerk learns that a document required by rule 33, 34, or 39.5 to be included in the record on appeal was inadvertently omitted, the clerk shall copy the document, and certify and transmit a copy to the reviewing court as an augmentation to the record without the necessity of a court order. The parties shall be given prompt notice of the transmittal and sent copies as provided in this subdivision and in subdivision (c).

If, during the pendency of the appeal, the trial court makes any new order in the case, including, but not limited to, an order affecting the sentence or affecting probation, the clerk shall certify and transmit to the reviewing court and the probation officer a copy of the order as an augmentation of the record. The parties shall be given prompt notice of the transmittal and sent copies as provided in this subdivision and in subdivision (c). *(As amended effective Jan. 1, 1991; previously amended effective Jan. 1, 1961, July 1, 1971, Jan. 1, 1972, Jan. 1, 1983, July 1, 1983, July 1, 1985, and July 1, 1989.)*

(f) **[Stipulation for partial transcript]** If counsel for both defendant and the People stipulate in writing before the preparation of the record is completed that any part of the record is not required for the proper hearing of the appeal, such part shall not be prepared or transmitted to the reviewing court.

(g) **[Supervision of preparation of record]** Each clerk of a Court of Appeal, acting under the supervision of the Administrative Presiding Justice or the Presiding Justice, shall take all appropriate steps to insure that the clerks and reporters of the superior courts perform their duties under this rule promptly.

© 1992 by J., B. & L. Gould
Printed in the U.S.A.   **EP**

This provision shall not affect the superior courts' responsibility for the prompt preparation of records on appeal.

(h) **[Supervision of preparation of record, death penalty cases]** In cases in which judgments of death have been rendered the Clerk of the Supreme Court, acting under the supervision of the Chief Justice shall take all appropriate steps to ensure that the clerk and reporters of the superior court perform their duties under these rules promptly. This provision does not affect the superior court's responsibility for the prompt preparation of records on appeal in capital cases.

Rule 36. Agreed or settled statement.

(a) **[Agreed statement]** The parties may present the appeal on an agreed statement, which shall conform, as far as practicable, to the provisions of rule 6; provided, however, that within 25 days after filing of the notice of appeal an original and 3 copies of the statement shall be filed with the clerk.

(b) **[Settled statement]** If a transcription of any part of the oral proceedings cannot be obtained for any reason, the appellant, as soon as the impossibility of obtaining a transcript is discovered, may serve and file an application for permission to prepare a settled statement in place thereof. The application shall be verified and shall contain a statement of the facts or a certificate of the clerk showing that a reporter's transcript cannot be obtained. The judge shall decide the application within 5 days, and, if the showing is sufficient, shall make an order permitting the preparation of a settled statement. Thereafter the parties shall conform, as far as practicable, to the provisions of rule 7; provided, however, that the statement shall be delivered to the judge for settlement within 30 days after the making of the order, unless the time is extended by the reviewing court, and an original and 3 copies of the statement as settled shall be engrossed and filed with the clerk.

Rule 37. Briefs.

(a) **[Time and service]** The appellant's opening brief shall be served and filed within 40 days after the filing of the record in the reviewing court. The respondent's brief shall be served and filed within 30 days after the filing of the appellant's opening brief. The appellant's reply brief, if any, shall be served and filed within 20 days after filing of the respondent's brief. The time for filing a brief in a criminal case shall not be extended by stipulation of the parties. Every brief of the defendant shall be served on both the district attorney and the Attorney General and, unless the defendant has expressly requested otherwise in writing, a copy shall be sent to the defendant. Counsel's signed statement that a copy of the brief was sent to the defendant or that counsel has the defendant's written request that briefs not be sent to the defendant is adequate proof thereof; the defendant's address need not be given in the statement. All briefs shall be served on the clerk of the superior court for delivery to the judge who presided at the trial, as provided in rule 16(b). (*As amended effective Jan. 1, 1990; previously amended effective July 1, 1983, and July 1, 1987.*)

(b) **[Form]** Briefs may be typewritten or produced by other process of duplication at the option of the party and shall conform, as far as practicable, to the rules governing briefs on appeal in civil cases. (*As amended effective July 1, 1989.*)

(c) **[Length]** A brief or petition for rehearing in an appeal from a judgment of death may not exceed:

Appellant's opening brief	200 pages
Respondent's brief	200 pages
Reply brief	100 pages
Petition for rehearing	50 pages

excluding tables and indices, unless a longer brief is permitted by the Chief Justice for good cause.

A brief or petition for rehearing in an appeal in any other criminal case may not exceed 75 pages, excluding tables and indices, unless a longer brief is permitted by the presiding justice for good cause. (*Adopted effective July 1, 1989.*)

(d) **[Applicability of amendment]** The length limits in subdivision (c) apply to cases in which the appellant's opening brief is filed on or after January 1, 1990. (*Subdivision adopted effective July 1, 1989.*)

Rule 38. Voluntary dismissal of appeal.

An appellant may dismiss his appeal at any time by filing an abandonment thereof, signed by him or his attorney of record. If the record has not yet been filed in the reviewing court, the abandonment shall be filed with the clerk of the superior court, and such filing shall operate to dismiss the appeal and to restore the jurisdiction of the superior court. If the record has been filed in the reviewing court, the abandonment shall be filed in that court, which may order the dismissal and immediate issuance of the remittitur. The clerk of the court in which the abandonment is filed shall immediately notify the adverse party of the filing of the abandonment or the order of dismissal. If the defendant abandons an appeal, the clerk shall notify both the district attorney and the attorney general.

Rule 39. Juvenile appeals.

(a) **[General provision]** The rules governing appeals from the superior court in criminal cases are applicable to all appeals from the juvenile court and any appeal in an action under Civil Code section 232, except where otherwise expressly provided by this rule or rule 39.1, or where the application of a particular rule would be clearly impracticable or inappropriate. This rule does not apply to any action or proceeding heard by a traffic hearing officer, nor to any rehearing or an appeal from a denial of a rehearing following an order by a traffic hearing officer. (*As amended effective Jan. 1, 1991; adopted effective July 1, 1977; and previously amended effective July 1, 1987, and July 1, 1989.*)

(b) **[Notice of appeal; time for filing]** In the cases provided by law, an appeal from the juvenile court is taken by filing with the clerk of that court a written notice of appeal within 60 days after the rendition of the judgment or the making of the order or, in matters heard by a referee, within 60 days after the order of the referee becomes final under rule 1417(c). When an application for a judicial rehearing of a referee order is made and denied under rule 1418, the notice of appeal shall be filed within 60 days after service of the referee's order in accordance with rule 1416(b)(3), or within 30 days after the entry of the order denying the application, whichever time is greater. When a notice of appeal is received, the clerk shall proceed in accordance with rule 31. (*As amended effective Jan. 1, 1991; adopted effective July 1, 1977.*)

(c) [Contents of record on appeal—normal record] The record on appeal shall include the following (which shall constitute the normal record):

(1) A clerk's transcript, containing copies of:

(a) the notice of appeal and any order made pursuant thereto; (b) the petition and any notice of hearing addressed to the minor, the parent, or guardian; (c) any application or motion for rehearing; (d) all minutes of the court relating to the action; (e) the findings of the juvenile court that the minor is within its jurisdiction; (f) the judgment or order appealed from; (g) any report by a probation officer, social worker, or duly appointed guardian ad litem.

(2) A reporter's transcript of the oral proceedings taken at the jurisdiction and disposition hearing, but excluding opening statements and oral arguments.

(3) To be transmitted as originals upon request by the reviewing court as provided in rule 10: any exhibit admitted in evidence or rejected.

(4) Those portions of the clerk's transcript, reporter's transcript, and exhibits incident to the order appealed from, if the appeal is taken from any subsequent order under section 395 or 800. (*As amended effective Jan. 1, 1991; adopted effective July 1, 1977; and previously amended effective July 1, 1985, and July 1, 1989.*)

(d) [Request for additional record] Either party may request the inclusion in the record of any of the following:

(1) In the clerk's transcript: (a) written motions made or notices of motion given by either side, and affidavits filed in support of or in opposition to a motion for rehearing or any other motion; (b) Any written opinion of the juvenile court.

(2) In the reporter's transcript: (a) Proceedings on any prehearing motions; (b) Opening statements; (c) Oral arguments to the court; (d) Any oral opinion of the juvenile court.

(3) To be transmitted as originals: any exhibits admitted in evidence or rejected that have not been requested by the reviewing court under subdivision (c)(3).

A party who desires any additional record shall file with the notice of appeal or as soon thereafter as is practicable an application describing the material desired and the points on which appellant intends to rely which make its inclusion appropriate. The court shall act on the application in accordance with rule 33(b).

(e) [Priority of juvenile appeals] An appeal from the juvenile court or an appeal in an action under Civil Code section 232 shall have precedence over all other cases, as provided by statute.

(f) [Confidentiality—section 300 proceedings] In an appeal under rule 1435(b) or an appeal from an order or judgment under Civil Code section 232, the record on appeal and briefs may be inspected only by court personnel, the parties to the proceeding or their attorneys, and other persons designated by the court. (*As amended effective Jan. 1, 1991; adopted effective July 1, 1977; and previously amended effective July 1, 1981, and July 1, 1987.*)

Rule 39.1. Special rule for dependency and freedom from custody appeals.

(a) [Applicability of rule] This rule applies to any appeal in an action under either Civil Code section 232 or Welfare and Institutions Code section 300.

(b) [Notice of appeal] The clerk shall give notice of the filing of a notice of appeal in accordance with rule 1(b).

(c) [Copies of record on appeal] Notwithstanding rule 35, the clerk shall not deliver copies of the record on appeal to the Attorney General or the district attorney unless that office represents a party.

(d) [Copies of briefs] Notwithstanding rules 16(c) and 37(a), the parties shall not serve briefs on the Attorney General or the district attorney unless that office represents a party.

(e) [Copies to Supreme Court] Notwithstanding rule 44(b)(2)(ii), proof of delivery of seven copies of each brief to the Supreme Court shall not be required.

(f) [Time for filing notice of appeal] Notice of appeal shall be filed within 60 days after the making of an appealable order or, if the matter was heard by a referee who was not sitting as a temporary judge, within 60 days after the order becomes final under rule 1417(c). (*Subdivision adopted effective Jan. 1, 1992.*)

Rule 39.2. Experimental project for Orange County juvenile appeals.

(a) [Applicability] Notwithstanding any other rule to the contrary, this rule applies to appealable orders of the Orange County Superior Court under section 300 et seq. of the Welfare and Institutions Code and to appeals from judgments of the Orange County Superior Court freeing minors from parental custody and control under Civil Code section 232. (*As amended effective Jan. 1 1992; adopted effective Jan. 1, 1989.*)

(b) [Appealability] Extraordinary writs are encouraged to review orders in child custody proceedings. If a writ is sought after such an order, an appeal will be deemed to be an inadequate remedy.

(c) [Record on appeal] Immediately on the filing of the notice of appeal, the clerk shall assemble the record on appeal by (1) notifying the court reporter by telephone and in writing to prepare a reporter's transcript and to deliver the transcript to the clerk no more than 20 days after the notice of appeal is filed, and (2) preparing the clerk's transcript under rule 35(a).

The record on appeal shall include all portions of a dependency case of which the court has taken judicial notice.

Immediately on completion of the transcripts, the clerk shall certify the record as correct, hand carry it to the reviewing court, and transmit copies to the attorneys for appellant, respondent, the minor, and the express mail service of the United States Postal Service.

(d) [Augmentation and correction of the record] Augmentation or correction of the record shall be done under rule 12. Preparation of a supplemental transcript pursuant to an order under this subdivision shall be given highest priority. The procedures described in subdivision (c) shall be followed when applicable.

(e) [Appellate procedure] The judges and clerks of the superior and reviewing courts shall adopt procedures to identify clearly the record and expedite all processing of a case to which this rule applies. The clerks of the courts shall provide data required to assist the Judicial Council in evaluating the effectiveness of this rule.

(f) [Briefs] To permit determination within the time required by Code of Civil Procedure section 45, the appellant's opening brief shall be served and filed within 30 days after the filing of the record in the reviewing court.

The respondent's brief shall be served and filed within 30 days after the filing of the appellant's open-

© 1992 by J., B. & L. Gould
Printed in the U.S.A.   **EP**

ing brief. The minor's opening brief and appellant's reply brief, if any, shall be served and filed within 20 days after filing of the respondent's brief. Briefs shall conform to rule 37(b).

(g) [Argument and submission] Oral argument shall be held no later than 60 days after appellant's reply brief is filed or is due to be filed. If oral argument is waived, the case shall be deemed submitted as of the sixtieth day after appellant's reply brief is filed.

(h) [Extensions of time] Only the reviewing court may grant extensions of time to prepare the record or to serve and file briefs. The court shall require an exceptional showing of good cause before granting any extension. The trial court shall not grant any extensions of time.

(i) [Expiration of this rule] This rule expires January 1, 1993. *(As adopted effective January 1, 1989, effective only until 1/1/93.)*

Rule 39.3. Appeal from Juvenile Court Denial of Authorization For Abortion Without Parental Consent.

(a) [Applicability] This rule applies to appeals from judgments entered under Health and Safety Code section 25958, notwithstanding any other rule to the contrary.

(b) [Counsel on appeal] Unless otherwise ordered by the reviewing court, counsel who represented the petitioner in juvenile court at the hearing on her petition, or who was appointed by the juvenile court after a hearing at which she was not represented, shall continue to represent her throughout the appeal.

(c) [Notice of appeal] An appeal is not premature if it is filed after the decision is announced, even if the judgment is not yet entered.

An appeal is commenced by filing a notice of appeal as provided in rule 1(a). There is no fee for filing the notice of appeal. The notice shall include a telephone number or numbers at which counsel can be reached within eight hours. The clerk of the superior court shall immediately notify the clerk of the reviewing court by telephone that the appeal has been filed, and the clerk of the reviewing court shall set a hearing for a date within five court days of the telephone notification. The clerk of the superior court shall promptly give counsel oral notice by telephone or personally if counsel is present of the date, time, and place of the hearing. The clerk of the reviewing court shall mail written notice to counsel for appellant.

(d) [Record on appeal] The record on appeal shall consist of the following:

(1) A clerk's transcript consisting of the original or a certified copy of the superior court clerk's file, containing all documents filed in the proceeding, admitted in evidence, or offered in evidence but rejected. Any document containing the petitioner's true name or facts from which her identity could reasonably be deduced shall be sealed from public inspection.

(2) The original or a certified copy of the electronic sound recording and a certified transcript of the sound recording (unless that transcript is waived by the reviewing court) or a reporter's transcript, or both. A "certified transcript of the sound recording" is a transcript of the recording supported by an affidavit that the transcript is a full, true, and correct transcription of the recording. The reviewing court may rely upon the transcript or the electronic sound recording or both and may accept counsel's or petitioner's written or oral statement, under penalty of perjury, to

clarify any unintelligible or ambiguous parts of the record.

Immediately upon the filing of the notice of appeal, the clerk shall assemble the record on appeal by (1) preparing the clerk's transcript; (2) preparing a copy of the sound recording, if required; (3) directing the preparation of a transcript of the sound recording, if required; and (4) directing the court reporter to prepare reporter's transcript, if required. The entire record shall be completed within two court days or within a shorter time ordered by the reviewing court. The record on appeal shall immediately be hand carried to the reviewing court or transmitted by any method no less expeditious than the express mail service of the United States Postal Service. A copy of the completed record shall be transmitted immediately to the attorney for appellant. Neither the trial court nor the reviewing court may extend the time for completing and transmitting the record on appeal. The record shall comply as to form with the requirements of rule 9, except that no index shall be required.

(e) [Briefs and grounds for appeal] The appellant may submit a statement of points, authorities, and argument in letter form not later than the second court day after the notice of appeal is filed, but shall not be deemed in default for failure to do so. Counsel shall be prepared to furnish citations to the record at the time of hearing on appeal to support any factual statements made in a letter or made orally.

(f) [Hearing and decision] The appeal shall be heard or, if oral argument is waived, submitted within five court days after the filing of the notice of appeal. Notice of the time and place of hearing shall be mailed to counsel, as required by statute, and shall also be given by telephone to the clerk of the superior court as provided in subdivision (c). Notice shall not be mailed to the appellant personally except at an address to which she has expressly requested it be sent.

The decision of the Court of Appeal is final forthwith as to that court. A certified copy of the opinion shall be mailed immediately to the trial court, counsel for the appellant, and the appellant if she has given an address for its receipt. In its discretion, the court may issue an order stating its decision authorizing or not authorizing the abortion without parental consent, provided it files a reasoned opinion within one court day of the order in compliance with article VI, section 14 of the Constitution. In order to prevent mootness or the frustration of the relief granted, a remittitur shall issue on the decision forthwith, notwithstanding lack of finality in the Supreme Court.

A certified copy of the order or opinion on appeal is evidence of the appellant's compliance with Health and Safety Code section 25958 and of the minor's receipt of a court's order authorizing an abortion without parental consent. Reliance on them constitutes good faith under Health and Safety Code section 25958.

(g) [Petition for review] If the Court of Appeal denies authorization for an abortion without parental consent, and a petition is filed in the Supreme Court for review, the clerk of the Court of Appeal shall forthwith transmit to the clerk of the Supreme Court all papers on file in the cause. Notwithstanding the provisions of rule 28, the Supreme Court may order review of the Court of Appeal decision within 15 days after receiving the file and may extend the time for an additional 30 days.

(h) [Confidentiality] The record on appeal and the briefs may be inspected only by court personnel, parties to the proceeding and their attorneys, and other persons specifically authorized by the court.

DIVISION II

RULES ON APPEAL TO THE SUPERIOR COURT

CHAPTER 4

APPEALS FROM MUNICIPAL AND JUSTICE COURTS IN CRIMINAL CASES

Rule 181. Definitions.

The definitions in rule 136 apply to this chapter unless the context otherwise requires.

Rule 182. Written notice of appeal.

(a) [Time for filing] An appeal in a criminal case from a judgment or appealable order of a municipal or justice court is taken by filing with the clerk of that court a written notice of appeal signed by the appellant or appellant's attorney. The notice shall specify the judgment or order or part thereof from which the appeal is taken. The notice shall be liberally construed in favor of its sufficiency.

The notice of appeal shall be filed within 30 days after the rendition of the judgment or the making of the order; but if the defendant is committed before final judgment for insanity or narcotics addiction or indeterminately as a mentally disordered sex offender, the notice of appeal shall be filed within 30 days after the commitment.

If the notice of appeal is not filed within the time prescribed, the appeal shall be void and of no effect. A notice received after the expiration of the time prescribed shall be marked by the clerk "Received (date) but not filed", and the clerk shall advise the party seeking to file the notice that it was received but not filed because the period for filing had elapsed.

A notice of appeal filed prior to the time prescribed is premature but may, in the discretion of the reviewing court for good cause, be treated as filed immediately after the rendition of the judgment or the making of the order.

References in this subdivision to the clerk apply to the judge of a justice court, in the absence of a clerk.

(b) [Notification by clerk] The clerk of the trial court, or the judge thereof if there is no clerk, shall forthwith mail a notification of the filing of the notice of appeal to each party other than the appellant. The notification shall state the number and title of the case and the date the notice of appeal was filed. The failure of the clerk or judge to give such notification shall not affect the validity of the appeal.

Rule 183. Record on appeal to Superior Court.

(a) The record on an appeal to a Superior Court from a municipal or an inferior court in a criminal case shall consist of the following items, or so many thereof as may exist in the particular case:

1. The complaint;

2. The plea or pleas of the defendant;

3. All written instructions given, or requested and refused;

4. The verdict, or if a jury was waived, the entry of such waiver in the minutes or docket, and the finding of the court upon the issues;

5. Any written motion or notice of motion for new trial, in arrest of judgment or to dismiss or otherwise terminate the action, or the entry in the minutes or docket of any oral motion to the same effect, and the order of the court thereon;

6. Any demurrer to the complaint, and the order of the court thereon;

7. All other minutes of the court relating to the action;

8. The judgment, and the order appealed from, if the appeal is from an order;

9. The notice of appeal;

10. Any statement or transcript on appeal, or both, settled and certified by the trial judge as hereinafter provided for in rules 184 and 187;

11. All exhibits, instructions, orders, affidavits, papers and documents properly referred to and identified in such statement or transcript, as provided in rule 184;

12. If the appeal is from an order made after judgment, items 2, 3, 4, 5, 6, and 7 may be omitted, and the record shall include any written motion and any written notice of motion, the denial or granting of which is the order appealed from, or the entry in the minutes or docket of any such oral motion, and all minutes of the court relating to such motion.

(b) The matters included in the foregoing item 1 to 9 inclusive, 11 and 12 of subdivision (a), or so many of them as may be pertinent to the appeal taken, shall be prepared by the clerk of the trial court, or by the judge thereof if there is no clerk. The notice of appeal, matters appearing in the minutes or docket of the trial court and any other part of the record, the original of which it is not possible to transmit to the superior court, shall be copied as provided in subdivision (a) of rule 9 and the copies made part of the record on appeal; but the originals of all other matters shall be included in the record. As soon as the statement on appeal, including the transcript, if any, has been settled and certified, or the right of the appellant to have a statement settled and certified shall have terminated, as elsewhere provided in these rules, the clerk of the trial court, or the judge thereof if there is no clerk, shall forthwith transmit the record on appeal, with his certificate that the parts thereof are originals or copies, as the case may be, to the clerk of the superior court to which the appeal is taken.

Rule 184. Statement or transcript.

(a) Where a consideration of the evidence or any part thereof, or of any proceedings which do not otherwise constitute a part of the record on appeal as defined in rule 183, is necessary to a determination of the appeal, the same must be set forth in a statement on appeal settled and certified as provided in these rules, and if not so set forth, it shall be presumed that they were such as to support the judgment or order appealed from. If all or any part of such evidence or other proceedings was reported by an official reporter, the appellant may give notice in his proposed statement that he intends to file a reporter's transcript of the evidence and proceedings so reported, and to make the same a part of the statement, and if he gives such notice he may omit any other statement of the evidence and proceedings so reported from his proposed statement.

(b) In every such statement the appellant shall specify the grounds on which he intends to rely upon appeal and set forth so much of the evidence and other

© 1992 by J., B. & L. Gould
Printed in the U.S.A.   **EP**

proceedings as are necessary for a decision upon said grounds. Said grounds of appeal shall be stated with sufficient particularity to apprise the court and the opposing party of the rulings or other matters of which the appellant intends to complain, but this may be done by any general description calling attention to the points to be made, without specifying each separate ruling or other matter to be complained of. If one of said grounds of appeal is insufficiency of the evidence, the particulars in which it is insufficient shall also be stated, unless a reporter's transcript containing the whole thereof is to be made a part of the statement. No ground of appeal not so specified shall be considered by the superior court unless it shall appear to the satisfaction of said Court that the record on appeal fairly and fully presents the evidence and other proceedings necessary for a decision thereon.

(c) It shall not be necessary in any such statement or transcript to copy any exhibit, instruction, order, affidavit, paper or document on file with the trial court, but the same may be merely referred to by any designation sufficient to identify it. If any point is to be made on appeal as to the giving, refusal or modification of instructions, it shall be necessary to show by said statement of transcript whether any oral instructions were given and, if so, what they were, and by whom requested, and if the written instructions included in the record under rule 183 do not show by whom requested, or what modifications were made in instructions given as modified, these facts shall be set forth in the statement.

(d) An appellant who desires to have a statement settled shall, within 15 days after filing notice of appeal, serve on the respondent and file with the trial court a proposed statement on appeal. If in such proposed statement appellant gives notice that a reporter's transcript is to be filed and made a part thereof, as provided in subdivision (a) of this rule, appellant may file, within 15 days after the filing of the proposed statement, a transcript of the evidence or other proceedings reported by an official reporter, certified by that reporter to be correct, and shall within five days after such filing, notify the respondent thereof. Any such transcript, when settled and certified as provided in rule 187, shall become a part of the statement. If the transcript is not filed or notice is not given of its filing within the time limited by these rules or any lawful extension thereof, the appellant's right to have the transcripts settled and certified as a part of the statement shall terminate and the trial court shall proceed upon the other parts of the proposed statement as provided in rule 187. If the failure to file such transcript in time results from the refusal, failure or inability of the reporter to make all or any part of the transcript, the appellant may, within five days after expiration of the time for filing such transcript, move the trial court for leave to file amendments to the statement to cover the matters originally proposed to be in the transcript. If the trial court grants the motion, the appellant shall serve and file amendments within 15 days after the making of the order and such amendments and the original statement shall be settled and certified as provided in rule 187. If the appellant fails to serve and file a proposed statement on appeal within the time limited by these rules, or any lawful extension thereof, the right to have a statement settled and certified shall forthwith terminate.

Rule 185. Amendments to statement or transcript.

The respondent may within 15 days after such statement is filed, or notice is given of the filing of such transcript, serve on the appellant and file proposed amendments to the statement or transcript, or both.

Rule 185.5. Counsel on appeal.

(a) **[Standards for appointment]** On application of an indigent defendant-appellant, the appellate department shall appoint counsel on appeal for a defendant convicted of a misdemeanor who is subject to incarceration or a fine of more than $500 (including penalty and other assessments), or who is likely to suffer significant adverse collateral consequences as a result of the conviction. A defendant is "subject to" incarceration or a fine if the incarceration or fine is in a sentence, or is a condition of probation, or may be ordered if the defendant violates probation. The court may appoint counsel on appeal for other indigent defendants. A defendant who was represented by appointed counsel in the trial court is presumed to be indigent; other defendants may establish their indigency as in the Courts of Appeal. (*Adopted effective July 1, 1991.*)

(b) **[Application; duty of trial counsel]** If defense trial counsel believes that the client is indigent and will file an appeal, counsel shall prepare for the defendant's signature and file in the trial court an application to the appellate department for appointment of counsel. The application shall include a declaration of indigency supported by evidence of representation in the trial court by appointed counsel or by evidence of indigency in the form required in the Court of Appeal for the district where the court is located. The trial court clerk shall transmit the application to the appellate department along with the record on appeal. A defendant-appellant may, however, apply directly to the appellate department for appointment of counsel after the record on appeal is filed.

The appellate department may take a reasonable time to reconfirm that the defendant-appellant still seeks appointment of counsel or to confirm the facts stated in the application. (*Adopted effective July 1, 1991.*)

Rule 186. Extensions of time and relief from default.

(a) **[Extensions of time]** The court from which the appeal is taken, or a judge thereof, may for good cause shown by affidavit make an order granting not more than a total of 15 days additional to the time limited in these rules for serving and filing the statement, or for filing the transcript and giving notice thereof, or for proposing amendments thereto, or for engrossing the statement or transcript, or both, and presenting the same for certification. The superior court to which an appeal is taken, or if the appeal is to be heard in an appellate department, the presiding judge thereof, may, for good cause shown by affidavit, further extend the time for doing any act required by these rules, except required by these rules, except the time for filing the notice of appeal. Every such extension shall be made upon application as provided in rule 137 before the time extended, including any previous extensions thereof, has expired.

(b) **[Relief from default]** The superior court may for good cause relieve a party from a default occasioned by any failure to comply with these rules, except failure to give timely notice of appeal.

© 1992 by J., B. & L. Gould
Printed in the U.S.A.   **EP**

Rule 187. Settlement of statement or transcript.

Upon the filing of such proposed amendments or the expiration of the time for filing them, the trial judge shall forthwith fix a time for settlement of the statement or transcript, or both, which time shall be as early as the business of the court will permit, either in chambers or in open court, and cause notice to be mailed, at least five days before the time fixed, to each party, or, if any party appears by attorney, then to the attorney, if the mailing address of the party or attorney appears in the files of the case in which the appeal is taken. The trial judge shall at the time fixed, or any other time to which the matter may be continued, settle the statement or transcript, or both, and the amendments proposed, if any, correcting, altering, or rewriting the statement or transcript, or both, as may be necessary to make it set forth fairly and truly the evidence and proceedings relating to the specified grounds of appeal or the matters set forth by the appellant in support of it.

The appellant's specifications of grounds of appeal shall not in any case be eliminated from the settled statement. At the time of settlement the judge may direct the appellant to engross the statement or transcript, or both, as settled. Thereupon the appellant shall engross the statement or transcript, or both, as corrected and settled and present it to the judge for certification within five days from the date of settlement, and if the appellant fails to do so within that period or any lawful extension, the right to have the statement or transcript settled or certified shall terminate. If a statement or transcript is settled and engrossed, if engrossment is ordered, the trial judge shall certify its correctness. A judge may settle and certify the statement or transcript after or before ceasing to be the trial judge. If the trial judge dies, is removed from office, becomes disqualified, or is absent from the state at the time for settling or certifying a statement or transcript, it may be settled or certified by any other judge of the court qualified to act.

The clerk of the trial court shall promptly mail copies of the statement, as settled and certified by the judge, to counsel for the parties and to unrepresented parties, unless the judge certifies that the statement proposed and filed by the appellant was settled without significant change. (As amended effective July 1, 1989.)

Rule 188. Abandonment of appeal.

An appellant may at any time abandon his appeal by filing a written abandonment thereof. Such abandonment shall be filed in the trial court if the record has not yet been filed in the superior court, or in the superior court if the record has been filed in that court. Upon the filing of a written abandonment in the trial court the jurisdiction of that court shall thereby be restored and it shall at once take such proceedings as may be necessary to enforce its judgment or order as if no such appeal had been taken. Upon the filing of such abandonment in the superior court, that court shall dismiss the appeal and issue its remittitur forthwith.

Rule 189. Additions to record.

On a sufficient showing by affidavit, or otherwise, that evidence was taken or proceedings were had in the trial court or that papers are there on file which are material to a disposition of the appeal and are not included in the record on appeal, and a showing of good cause why the same have not been included in said record, the superior court may authorize the trial judge to make a further certificate as to such evidence or other proceedings or papers, and direct the same, when so certified, to be added to the record.

Rule 190. Hearings and dismissals.

Appeals to the superior court in criminal cases shall be calendared, argued and determined, notice of hearings shall be given, and petitions for rehearing and answers thereto shall be filed and acted upon as prescribed in the rules adopted by the Judicial Council for appellate departments of the superior court.

If the appeal is not brought to a hearing within the time limited, or the appellant otherwise fails to prosecute it with diligence, or if the appeal is irregular in any substantial respect, the superior court may, on motion of the respondent or on its own motion, after written notice to the appellant, order it dismissed.

Rule 191. Remittiturs.

(a) **[Issuance and transmission]** Upon the expiration of the period during which a transfer may be ordered, unless a new trial is to be had in the superior court, the clerk of the superior court shall remit to the court from which the appeal was taken a certified copy of the judgment of the superior court and of its opinion, if any, and also all the original exhibits, orders, affidavits, papers and documents which were sent to said superior court in connection with said appeal, except the statement or transcript on appeal and the notice of appeal. After such certified copy of the judgment has been remitted to the court below, the superior court has no further jurisdiction of the appeal or of the proceedings thereon, and the lower court shall make all orders necessary to carry its judgment or order into effect or otherwise proceed in conformity to the decision on appeal.

(b) **[Issuance forthwith]** The court may direct the immediate issuance of the remittitur on stipulation of the parties.

(c) **[Stay of issuance]** The court, for good cause, may stay the issuance of the remittitur for a reasonable period.

(d) **[Recall of remittitur]** A remittitur may be recalled by order of the court on its own motion, on motion after notice supported by affidavits, or on stipulation setting forth the facts which would justify the granting of a motion.

DIVISION III

SENTENCING RULES FOR THE SUPERIOR COURTS

CHAPTER 1

GENERAL PROVISIONS

Rule 401. Authority.

The rules in this division are adopted pursuant to Penal Code section 1170.3 and pursuant to the authority granted to the Judicial Council by the Constitution, article VI, section 6, to adopt rules for court administration, practice and procedure.

© 1992 by J., B. & L. Gould
Printed in the U.S.A.   EP

Rule 403. Application of rules.

These rules apply only to criminal cases in superior courts in which the defendant is convicted of one or more offenses punishable as a felony by a determinate sentence imposed pursuant to chapter 4.5 (commencing with §1170) of Title 7 of Part 2 of the Penal Code.

Rule 405. Applicable definitions.

As used in this division, unless the context otherwise requires:

(a) "These rules" means the rules in this division.

(b) "Base term" is the determinate prison term selected from among the three possible terms prescribed by statute or the determinate prison term prescribed by law if a range of three possible terms is not prescribed.

(c) "Enhancement" means additional term of imprisonment added to the base term.

(d) "Aggravation" or "circumstances in aggravation" means facts which justify the imposition of the upper prison term referred to in section 1170(b).

(e) "Mitigation" or "circumstances in mitigation" means facts which justify the imposition of the lower of three authorized prison terms or facts which justify the court in declining to impose an enhancement when the court has discretion not to impose it. (*As amended effective Jan. 1, 1991; previously amended effective July 28, 1977.*)

(f) "Sentence choice" means the selection of any disposition of the case which does not amount to a dismissal, acquittal, or grant of a new trial. (*As amended effective Jan. 1, 1991.*)

(g) "Section" means a section of the Penal Code.

(h) "Imprisonment" means confinement in a state prison.

(i) "Charged" means charged in the indictment or information.

(j) "Found" means admitted by the defendant or found to be true by the trier of fact upon trial.

Rule 406. Reasons.

(a) **[How given]** If the sentencing judge is required to give reasons for a sentence choice, the judge shall state in simple language the primary factor or factors that support the exercise of discretion or, if applicable, state that the judge has no discretion. The statement need not be in the language of these rules. It shall be delivered orally on the record.

(b) **[When reasons required]** Sentence choices that generally require a statement of a reason include: (1) granting probation; (2) imposing a prison sentence and thereby denying probation; (3) declining to commit to the Youth Authority an eligible juvenile found amenable for treatment; (4) selecting a term other than the middle statutory term for either an offense or an enhancement; (5) imposing consecutive sentences; (6) imposing full consecutive sentences under section 667.6(c) rather than consecutive terms under section 1170.1(a), when the court has that choice; (7) striking or staying the punishment for an enhancement; (8) imposing both weapons and injury enhancements on a single count under section 1170.1(e); (9) waiving a restitution fine; (10) not committing an eligible defendant to the California Rehabilitation Center. (*Adopted effective Jan. 1, 1991.*)

Rule 407. Rules of construction.

As used in these rules:

(a) "Shall" is mandatory, "should" is advisory, "may" is permissive.

(b) The past, present, and future tenses include the others.

(c) The singular includes the plural. (*As amended effective Jan. 1, 1991.*)

Rule 408. Criteria not exclusive; sequence not significant.

(a) The enumeration in these rules of some criteria for the making of discretionary sentencing decisions does not prohibit the application of additional criteria reasonably related to the decision being made. Any such additional criteria shall be stated on the record by the sentencing judge.

(b) The order in which criteria are listed does not indicate their relative weight or importance.

Rule 409. Consideration of criteria.

Relevant criteria enumerated in these rules shall be considered by the sentencing judge, and shall be deemed to have been considered unless the record affirmatively reflects otherwise.

CHAPTER 2

PROVISIONS APPLICABLE TO ALL SENTENCING DECISIONS

Rule 410. General objectives of sentencing.

General objectives of sentencing include:

(a) Protecting society.

(b) Punishing the defendant.

(c) Encouraging the defendant to lead a law abiding life in the future and deterring him from future offenses.

(d) Deterring others from criminal conduct by demonstrating its consequences.

(e) Preventing the defendant from committing new crimes by isolating him for the period of incarceration.

(f) Securing restitution for the victims of crime.

(g) Achieving uniformity in sentencing.

Because in some instances these objectives may suggest inconsistent dispositions, the sentencing judge shall consider which objectives are of primary importance in the particular case.

The sentencing judge should be guided by statutory statements of policy, the criteria in these rules, and the facts and circumstances of the case.

CHAPTER 3

PROBATION

Rule 411. Presentence investigations and reports.

(a) **[Eligible defendant]** If the defendant is eligible for probation, the court shall refer the matter to the probation officer for a presentence investigation and report. Waivers of the presentence report should not be accepted except in unusual circumstances.

(b) **[Ineligible defendant]** Even if the defendant is not eligible for probation, the court should refer the matter to the probation officer for a presentence investigation and report.

(c) **[Supplemental reports]** The court shall order a supplemental probation officer's report in preparation for sentencing proceedings that occur a significant period of time after the original report was prepared.

(d) [Purpose of presentence investigation report] Probation officers' reports are used by judges in determining the appropriate length of a prison sentence and by the Department of Corrections in deciding upon the type of facility and program in which to place a defendant, and are also used in deciding whether probation is appropriate. Section 1203c requires a probation officer's report on every person sentenced to prison; ordering the report before sentencing in probation-ineligible cases will help ensure a well-prepared report. (*Adopted effective Jan.1, 1991; formerly Rule 418.*)

Rule 411.5. Probation officer's presentence investigation report.

(a) [Contents] A probation officer's presentence investigation report in a felony case shall include at least the following:

(1) A face sheet showing at least: (i) the defendant's name and other identifying data; (ii) the case number; (iii) the crime of which the defendant was convicted; (iv) the date of commission of the crime, the date of conviction, and any other dates relevant to sentencing; (v) the defendant's custody status; and (vi) the terms of any agreement upon which a plea of guilty was based.

(2) The facts and circumstances of the crime and the defendant's arrest, including information concerning any co-defendants and the status or disposition of their cases. The source of all such information shall be stated.

(3) A summary of the defendant's record of prior criminal conduct, including convictions as an adult and sustained petitions in juvenile delinquency proceedings. Records of an arrest or charge not leading to a conviction or the sustaining of a petition shall not be included unless supported by facts concerning the arrest or charge.

(4) Any statement made by the defendant to the probation officer, or a summary thereof, including the defendant's account of the circumstances of the crime.

(5) Information concerning the victim of the crime, including: (i) the victim's statement or a summary thereof, if available; (ii) the amount of the victim's loss, and whether or not it is covered by insurance; and (iii) any information required by law.

(6) Any relevant facts concerning the defendant's social history, including but not limited to those categories enumerated in Penal Code section 1203.10, organized under appropriate subheadings including, whenever applicable, "Family," "Education," "Employment and income," "Military," "Medical/psychological," "Record of substance abuse or lack thereof, " and any other relevant subheadings.

(7) Collateral information, including written statements from: (i) official sources such as defense and prosecuting attorneys, police (subsequent to any police reports used to summarize the crime), probation and parole officers who have had prior experience with the defendant, and correctional personnel who observed the defendant's behavior during any period of presentence incarceration; and (ii) interested persons, including family members and others who have written letters concerning the defendant.

(8) An evaluation of factors relating to disposition. This section shall include: (i) a reasoned discussion of the defendant's suitability and eligibility for proba-

tion, and if probation is recommended, a proposed plan including recommendation for the conditions of probation and any special need for supervision; (ii) if a prison sentence is recommended or is likely to be imposed, a reasoned discussion of aggravating and mitigating factors affecting the sentence length; and (iii) a discussion of the defendant's ability to make restitution, pay any fine or penalty which may be recommended, or satisfy any special conditions of probation which are proposed. Discussions of factors affecting suitability for probation and affecting the sentence length shall refer to any sentencing rule directly relevant to the facts of the case, but no rule shall be cited without a reasoned discussion of its relevance and relative importance.

(9) The probation officer's recommendation. When requested by the sentencing judge or by standing instructions to the probation department, the report shall include recommendations concerning the length of any prison term that may be imposed, including the base term, the imposition of concurrent or consecutive sentences, and the imposition or striking of the additional terms for enhancements charged and found.

(10) Detailed information of presentence time spent by the defendant in custody; including the beginning and ending dates of the period(s) of custody; the existence of any other sentences imposed on the defendant during the period of custody; the amount of good behavior, work, or participation credit to which the defendant is entitled; and whether the sheriff or other officer holding custody, the prosecution, or the defense wishes a hearing be held for the purposes of denying good behavior, work, or participation credit.

(11) A statement of mandatory and recommended restitution, restitution fines, other fines, and costs to be assessed against the defendant, including chargeable probation services and attorney fees under section 987.8 when appropriate, findings concerning the defendant's ability to pay, and a recommendation whether any restitution order shall become a judgment under section 1203(j) if unpaid.

(b) [Format] The report shall be on paper 8½ by 11 inches in size and shall follow the sequence set out in subdivision (a) to the extent possible.

(c) [Sources] The source of all information shall be stated. Any person who has furnished information included in the report shall be identified by name or official capacity unless a reason is given for not disclosing the person's identity. (*As amended effective Jan. 1, 1991; adopted effective July 1, 1981; formerly Rule 419.*)

Rule 412. Reasons. Agreement to punishment as reason and as abandonment of certain claims.

(a) [Defendant's agreement as reason] It is an adequate reason for a sentence or other disposition that the defendant, personally and by counsel, has expressed agreement that it be imposed and the prosecuting attorney has not expressed an objection to it. The agreement and lack of objection shall be recited on the record.

(b) [Agreement to sentence abandons 654 claim] By agreeing to a specified prison term personally and by counsel, a defendant who is sentenced to that term or a shorter one abandons any claim that a component of the sentence violates section 654's prohibition of double punishment, unless that claim is

© 1992 by J., B. & L. Gould
Printed in the U.S.A. **EP**

asserted at the time the agreement is recited on the record. (*Adopted effective Jan. 1, 1991.*)

Rule 413. Probation eligibility when probation is limited.

(a) **[Consideration of eligibility]** The court shall determine whether the defendant is eligible for probation.

(b) **[Probation in unusual cases]** If the defendant comes under a statutory provision prohibiting probation "except in unusual cases where the interests of justice would best be served," or a substantially equivalent provision, the court should apply the criteria in subdivision (c) to evaluate whether the statutory limitation on probation is overcome; and if it is, the court should then apply the criteria in rule 414 to decide whether to grant probation.

(c) **[Facts showing unusual case]** The following facts may indicate the existence of an unusual case in which probation may be granted if otherwise appropriate:

(1) (Facts relating to basis for limitation on probation) A fact or circumstance indicating that the basis for the statutory limitation on probation, although technically present, is not fully applicable to the case, including:

(i) The fact or circumstance giving rise to the limitation on probation is, in this case, substantially less serious than the circumstances typically present in other cases involving the same probation limitation, and the defendant has no recent record of committing similar crimes or crimes of violence.

(ii) The current offense is less serious than a prior felony conviction that is the cause of the limitation on probation, and the defendant has been free from incarceration and serious violation of the law for a substantial time before the current offense.

(2) (Facts limiting defendant's culpability) A fact or circumstance not amounting to a defense, but reducing the defendant's culpability for the offense, including:

(i) The defendant participated in the crime under circumstances of great provocation, coercion, or duress not amounting to a defense, and the defendant has no recent record of committing crimes of violence.

(ii) The crime was committed because of a mental condition not amounting to a defense, and there is a high likelihood that the defendant would respond favorably to mental health care and treatment that would be required as a condition of probation.

(iii) The defendant is youthful or aged, and has no significant record of prior criminal offenses. (*Adopted effective Jan. 1, 1991.*)

Rule 414. Criteria affecting probation.

Criteria affecting the decision to grant or deny probation include:

(a) Facts relating to the crime, including:

(1) The nature, seriousness, and circumstances of the crime as compared to other instances of the same crime.

(2) Whether the defendant was armed with or used a weapon.

(3) The vulnerability of the victim.

(4) Whether the defendant inflicted physical or emotional injury.

(5) The degree of monetary loss to the victim.

(6) Whether the defendant was an active or passive participant.

(7) Whether the crime was committed because of an unusual circumstance, such as great provocation, which is unlikely to recur.

(8) Whether the manner in which the crime was carried out demonstrated criminal sophistication or professionalism on the part of the defendant.

(9) Whether the defendant took advantage of a position of trust or confidence to commit the crime.

(b) Facts relating to the defendant, including:

(1) Prior record of criminal conduct; whether as an adult or a juvenile, including the recency and frequency of prior crimes; and whether the prior record indicates a pattern of regular or increasingly serious criminal conduct.

(2) Prior performance on probation or parole and present probation or parole status.

(3) Willingness to comply with the terms of probation.

(4) Ability to comply with reasonable terms of probation as indicated by the defendant's age, education, health, mental faculties, history of alcohol or other substance abuse, family background and ties, employment and military service history, and other relevant factors.

(5) The likely effect of imprisonment on the defendant and his or her dependents.

(6) The adverse collateral consequences on the defendant's life resulting from the felony conviction.

(7) Whether the defendant is remorseful.

(8) The likelihood that if not imprisoned the defendant will be a danger to others. (*As amended and relettered effective Jan. 1, 1991.*)

Rule 416. Criteria affecting probation in unusual cases.

(*Rule repealed effective Jan. 1, 1991.*)

Rule 418. Presentence investigations and reports.

(*Amended and renumbered as rule 411, effective Jan. 1, 1991.*)

Rule 419. Probation officer's presentence investigation report.

(*Amended and renumbered as rule 411.5, effective Jan. 1, 1991.*)

CHAPTER 4

AGGRAVATION, MITIGATION, AND ENHANCEMENT

Rule 420. Selection of base term of imprisonment.

(a) When a sentence of imprisonment is imposed, or the execution of a sentence of imprisonment is ordered suspended, the sentencing judge shall select the upper, middle, or lower term on each count for which the defendant has been convicted, as provided in section 1170(b) and these rules. The middle term shall be selected unless imposition of the upper or lower term is justified by circumstances in aggravation or mitigation.

(b) Circumstances in aggravation and mitigation shall be established by a preponderance of the evidence. Selection of the upper term is justified only if, after a consideration of all the relevant facts, the circumstances in aggravation outweigh the circumstances in mitigation. The relevant facts are included in the case record, the probation officer's report, other reports and statements properly received, statements in aggravation or mitigation, and any further evidence introduced at the sentencing hearing. Selection of the lower term is justified only if, considering the same facts, the circumstances in mitigation outweigh the circumstances in aggravation.

(c) To comply with section 1170(b), a fact charged and found as an enhancement may be used as a reason for imposing the upper term only if the court has discretion to strike the punishment for the enhancement and does so. The use of a fact of an enhancement to impose the upper term of imprisonment is an adequate reason for striking the additional term of imprisonment, regardless of the effect on the total term.

(d) A fact that is an element of the crime shall not be used to impose the upper term.

(e) The reasons for selecting the upper or lower term shall be stated orally on the record, and shall include a concise statement of the ultimate facts which the court deemed to constitute circumstances in aggravation or mitigation justifying the term selected. (*As amended and renumbered effective Jan. 1, 1991; previously amended effective July 28, 1977; formerly Rule 439.*)

Rule 421. Circumstances in aggravation.

Circumstances in aggravation include:

(a) Facts relating to the crime, whether or not charged or chargeable as enhancements, including the fact that:

(1) The crime involved great violence, great bodily harm, threat of great bodily harm, or other acts disclosing a high degree of cruelty, viciousness, or callousness.

(2) The defendant was armed with or used a weapon at the time of the commission of the crime.

(3) The victim was particularly vulnerable.

(4) The defendant induced others to participate in the commission of the crime or occupied a position of leadership or dominance of other participants in its commission.

(5) The defendant induced a minor to commit or assist in the commission of the crime.

(6) The defendant threatened witnesses, unlawfully prevented or dissuaded witnesses from testifying, suborned perjury, or in any other way illegally interfered with the judicial process.

(7) The defendant was convicted of other crimes for which consecutive sentences could have been imposed but for which concurrent sentences are being imposed.

(8) The manner in which the crime was carried out indicates planning, sophistication, or professionalism.

(9) The crime involved an attempted or actual taking or damage of great monetary value.

(10) The crime involved a large quantity of contraband.

(11) The defendant took advantage of a position of trust or confidence to commit the offense.

(b) Facts relating to the defendant, including the fact that:

(1) The defendant has engaged in violent conduct which indicates a serious danger to society.

(2) The defendant's prior convictions as an adult or sustained petitions in juvenile delinquency proceedings are numerous or of increasing seriousness.

(3) The defendant has served a prior prison term.

(4) The defendant was on probation or parole when the crime was committed.

(5) The defendant's prior performance on probation or parole was unsatisfactory.

(c) Any other facts statutorily declared to be circumstances in aggravation. (*As amended effective Jan. 1, 1991.*)

Rule 423. Circumstances in mitigation.

Circumstances in mitigation include:

(a) Facts relating to the crime, including the fact that:

(1) The defendant was a passive participant or played a minor role in the crime.

(2) The victim was an initiator of, willing participant in, or aggressor or provoker of the incident.

(3) The crime was committed because of an unusual circumstance, such as great provocation, which is unlikely to recur.

(4) The defendant participated in the crime under circumstances of coercion or duress, or the criminal conduct was partially excusable for some other reason not amounting to a defense.

(5) The defendant, with no apparent predisposition to do so, was induced by others to participate in the crime.

(6) The defendant exercised caution to avoid harm to persons or damage to property, or the amounts of money or property taken were deliberately small, or no harm was done or threatened against the victim.

(7) The defendant believed that he or she had a claim or right to the property taken, or for other reasons mistakenly believed that the conduct was legal.

(8) The defendant was motivated by a desire to provide necessities for his or her family or self.

(b) Facts relating to the defendant, including the fact that:

(1) The defendant has no prior record, or an insignificant record of criminal conduct, considering the recency and frequency of prior crimes.

(2) The defendant was suffering from a mental or physical condition that significantly reduced culpability for the crime.

(3) The defendant voluntarily acknowledged wrongdoing prior to arrest or at an early stage of the criminal process.

(4) The defendant is ineligible for probation and but for the ineligibility would have been granted probation.

(5) The defendant made restitution to the victim.

(6) The defendant's prior performance on probation or parole was satisfactory. (*As amended effective Jan. 1, 1991.*)

Rule 424. Consideration of applicability of section 654.

Prior to determining whether to impose either concurrent or consecutive sentences on all counts on which the defendant was convicted, the court shall determine whether the proscription in section 654 against multiple punishments for the same act or omission requires a stay of imposition of sentence on some of the counts. (*Adopted effective Jan. 1, 1991.*)

Rule 425. Criteria affecting concurrent or consecutive sentences.

Criteria affecting the decision to impose consecutive rather than concurrent sentences include:

(a) **[Criteria relating to crimes]** Facts relating to the crimes, including whether or not:

© 1992 by J., B. & L. Gould
Printed in the U.S.A.   **EP**

(1) The crimes and their objectives were predominantly independent of each other.

(2) The crimes involved separate acts of violence or threats of violence.

(3) The crimes were committed at different times or separate places, rather than being committed so closely in time and place as to indicate a single period of aberrant behavior.

(b) [Other criteria and limitations] Any circumstances in aggravation or mitigation may be considered in deciding whether to impose consecutive rather than concurrent sentences, except (i) a fact used to impose the upper term, (ii) a fact used to otherwise enhance the defendant's prison sentence, and (iii) a fact that is an element of the crime shall not be used to impose consecutive sentences. (*As amended effective Jan. 1, 1991.*)

Rule 426. Violent sex crimes.

(a) [Multiple violent sex crimes] When a defendant has been convicted of multiple violent sex offenses as defined in section 667.6, the sentencing judge shall determine whether the crimes involved separate victims or the same victim on separate occasions.

(1) (Different victims) If the crimes were committed against different victims, a full, separate, and consecutive term shall be imposed for a violent sex crime as to each victim, under section 667.6(d).

(2) (Same victim, separate occasions) If the crimes were committed against a single victim, the sentencing judge shall determine whether the crimes were committed on separate occasions. In determining whether there were separate occasions, the sentencing judge shall consider whether, between the commission of one sex crime and another, the defendant had a reasonable opportunity to reflect upon his or her actions and nevertheless resumed sexually assaultive behavior. A full, separate, and consecutive term shall be imposed for each violent sex offense committed on a separate occasion under section 667.6(d).

(b) [Same victim, same occasion; other crimes] If the defendant has been convicted of multiple crimes, including at least one violent sex crime, as defined in section 667.6, or if there have been multiple violent sex crimes against a single victim on the same occasion and the sentencing court has decided to impose consecutive sentences, the sentencing judge shall then determine whether to impose a full, separate, and consecutive sentence under section 667.6(c) for the violent sex crime or crimes in lieu of including the violent sex crimes in the computation of the principal and subordinate terms under section 1170.1(a). A decision to impose a fully consecutive sentence under section 667.6(c) is an additional sentence choice which requires a statement of reasons separate from those given for consecutive sentences, but which may repeat the same reasons. The sentencing judge is to be guided by the criteria listed in rule 425, which incorporates rules 421 and 423, as well as any other reasonably related criteria as provided in rule 408. (*Adopted effective Jan. 1, 1991.*)

Rule 428. Criteria affecting imposition of enhancements.

(a) [Imposing or not imposing enhancement] No reason need be given for imposing a term for an enhancement that was charged and found true.

If the judge has statutory discretion to strike the additional term for an enhancement, the court may consider and apply any of the circumstances in mitigation enumerated in these rules or, pursuant to rule 408, any other reasonable circumstances in mitigation that are present.

The judge should not strike the allegation of the enhancement.

(b) [Choice from among three possible terms] When the defendant is subject to an enhancement that was charged and found true for which three possible terms are specified by statute, the middle term shall be imposed unless there are circumstances in aggravation or mitigation or unless, under statutory discretion, the judge strikes the additional term for the enhancement.

The upper term may be imposed for an enhancement only when there are circumstances in aggravation that relate directly to the fact giving rise to the enhancement. The lower term may be imposed based upon any of the circumstances in mitigation enumerated in these rules or, under rule 408, any other reasonable circumstances in mitigation that are present. (*Adopted effective Jan. 1, 1991.*)

CHAPTER 5

PROCEDURAL PROVISIONS

Rule 431. Proceedings at sentencing to be reported.

All proceedings at the time of sentencing shall be reported.

Rule 433. Matters to be considered at time set for sentencing.

(a) In every case, at the time set for sentencing pursuant to section 1191, the sentencing judge shall hold a hearing at which the judge shall:

(1) Hear and determine any matters raised by the defendant pursuant to section 1201.

(2) Determine whether a defendant who is eligible for probation should be granted or denied probation, unless consideration of probation is expressly waived by the defendant personally and by counsel.

(b) If the imposition of sentence is to be suspended during a period of probation after a conviction by trial, the trial judge shall make factual findings as to circumstances which would justify imposition of the upper or lower term if probation is later revoked, based upon evidence admitted at the trial.

(c) If a sentence of imprisonment is to be imposed, or if the execution of a sentence of imprisonment is to be suspended during a period of probation, the sentencing judge shall:

(1) Hear evidence in aggravation and mitigation, and determine, pursuant to section 1170(b), whether to impose the upper, middle or lower term; and set forth on the record the facts and reasons for imposing the upper or lower term.

(2) Determine whether any additional term of imprisonment provided for an enhancement charged and found shall be stricken.

(3) Determine whether the sentences shall be consecutive or concurrent if the defendant has been convicted of multiple crimes.

(4) Determine any issues raised by statutory prohibitions on the dual use of facts and statutory

limitations on enhancements, as required in rules 441 and 447.

(5) Pronounce the court's judgment and sentence, stating the terms thereof and giving reasons for those matters for which reasons are required by law.

(d) All these matters shall be heard and determined at a single hearing unless the sentencing judge otherwise orders in the interests of justice.

(e) When a sentence of imprisonment is imposed under subdivision (c) or under rule 435, the sentencing judge shall inform the defendant, pursuant to section 1170(c), of the parole period provided by section 3000 to be served after expiration of the sentence in addition to any period of incarceration for parole violation.

Rule 435. Sentencing upon revocation of probation.

(a) When the defendant violates the terms of probation or is otherwise subject to revocation of probation, the sentencing judge may make any disposition of the case authorized by statute. (As amended effective Jan. 1, 1991.)

(b) Upon revocation and termination of probation pursuant to section 1203.2, when the sentencing judge determines that the defendant shall be committed to prison:

(1) If the imposition of sentence was previously suspended, the judge shall impose judgment and sentence after considering any findings previously made and hearing and determining the matters enumerated in rule 433(c).

The length of the sentence shall be based on circumstances existing at the time probation was granted, and subsequent events may not be considered in selecting the base term nor in deciding whether to strike or specifically not order the additional punishment for enhancements charged and found.

(2) If the execution of sentence was previously suspended, the judge shall order that the judgment previously pronounced be in full force and effect and that the defendant be committed to the custody of the Director of Corrections for the term prescribed in that judgment.

Rule 437. Statements in aggravation and mitigation.

(a) Statements in aggravation and mitigation referred to in section 1170(b) shall be filed and served at least four days prior to the time set for sentencing pursuant to section 1191 or the time set for pronouncing judgment upon revocation of probation pursuant to section 1203.2(c) if imposition of sentence was previously suspended.

(b) A party seeking consideration of circumstances in aggravation or mitigation may file and serve a statement pursuant to section 1170(b) and this rule.

(c) A statement in aggravation or mitigation shall include:

(1) A summary of facts which the party relies upon as circumstances in aggravation or mitigation justifying imposition of the upper or lower term.

(2) Notice of intention to dispute facts or offer evidence in aggravation or mitigation at the sentencing hearing. The statement shall generally describe the evidence to be offered, including a description of any documents and the name and expected substance of the testimony of any witnesses. No evidence in aggravation or mitigation may be introduced at the sentencing hearing unless it was described in the statement, or unless its admission is permitted by the sentencing judge in the interests of justice.

(d) Assertions of fact in a statement in aggravation or mitigation shall be disregarded unless they are supported by the record in the case, the probation officer's report or other reports properly filed in the case, or other competent evidence.

(e) **[Disputed facts]** In the event the parties dispute the facts upon which the conviction rested, the court shall conduct a presentence hearing and make appropriate corrections, additions, or deletions in the presentence probation report or order a revised report. (*Subdivision adopted effective Jan. 1, 1991.*)

Rule 439. Selection of base term of imprisonment.
(*Amended and renumbered as rule 420, effective Jan. 1, 1991.*)

Rule 440. Procedures on pleas of guilty specifying the punishment, or when no objection to proposed punishment.
(*Rule repealed effective Jan. 1, 1991; see rule 412(a).*)

Rule 441. Dual use of facts; prohibited use of facts.
(*Rule repealed effective Jan. 1, 1991; see rule 420.*)

Rule 443. Reasons by sentencing judge.
(*Rule repealed effective Jan. 1, 1991; see rule 406(a).*)

Rule 445. Procedure in striking enhancements.
(*Rule repealed effective Jan. 1, 1991; see rule 428(a).*)

Rule 447. Limitations on enhancements.

No finding of an enhancement shall be stricken or dismissed because imposition of the term is either prohibited by law or exceeds limitations on the overall aggregate term, such as limits on subordinate terms, the double-the-base-term limitation, or limitations on the imposition of multiple enhancements. The sentencing judge shall impose sentence for the aggregate term of imprisonment computed without reference to those prohibitions and limitations, and shall thereupon stay execution of so much of the term as is prohibited or exceeds the applicable limit. The stay shall become permanent upon the defendant's service of the portion of the sentence not stayed. (*As amended effective Jan. 1, 1991; previously amended effective July 28, 1977.*)

Rule 449. Sentencing on multiple counts.
(*Repealed effective Jan. 1, 1991.*)

Rule 451. Sentence consecutive to indeterminate term or to term in other jurisdiction.

(a) When a defendant is sentenced under section 1170 and the sentence is to run consecutively to a sentence imposed under section 1168 in the same or another proceeding, the judgment shall specify the determinate term imposed under section 1170 computed without reference to the indeterminate sentence, shall order that the determinate term shall be served consecutive to the sentence under section 1168, and shall identify the proceedings in which the indeterminate sentence was imposed. The term under section 1168, and the date of its completion or parole date, and the sequence in which the sentences are

© 1992 by J., B. & L. Gould
Printed in the U.S.A. **EP**

deemed served, will be determined by correctional authorities as provided by law.

(b) When a defendant is sentenced under section 1170 and the sentence is to run consecutively to a sentence imposed by a court of the United State or of another state or territory, the judgment shall specify the determinate term imposed under section 1170 computed without reference to the sentence imposed by the other jurisdiction, shall order that the determinate term shall be served commencing upon the completion of the sentence imposed by the other jurisdiction, and shall identify the other jurisdiction and the proceedings in which the other sentence was imposed.

Rule 452. Determinate sentence consecutive to prior determinate sentence.

If a determinate sentence is imposed pursuant to section 1170.1(a) consecutive to one or more determinate sentences imposed previously in the same court or in other courts, the court in the current case shall pronounce a single aggregate term, as defined in section 1170.1(a), stating the result of combining the previous and current sentences. In those situations:

(1) The sentences on all determinately sentenced counts in all of the cases on which a sentence was or is being imposed shall be combined as though they were all counts in the current case.

(2) The judge in the current case shall make a new determination of which count, in the combined cases, represents the principal term, as defined in section 1170.1(a).

(3) Discretionary decisions of the judges in the previous cases shall not be changed by the judge in the current case. Such decisions include the decision that other than the middle term was justified by circumstances in mitigation or aggravation, making counts in prior cases concurrent with or consecutive to each other, or the decision that circumstances in mitigation justified striking the punishment for an enhancement. (*Adopted effective Jan. 1, 1991.*)

Rule 453. Commitments to nonpenal institutions.

When a defendant is convicted of a crime for which sentence could be imposed under section 1170 and the court orders that he be committed:

(a) To the California Youth Authority pursuant to Welfare and Institutions Code section 1731.5, the order of commitment shall specify the term of imprisonment to which the defendant would have been sentenced. The term shall be determined as provided by sections 1170 and 1170.1 and these rules, as though a sentence of imprisonment were to be imposed.

(b) As a mentally disordered sex offender pursuant to Welfare and Institutions Code section 6316, the order of commitment shall specify the maximum term of commitment, computed as provided in section 6316.1 of that code.

Rule 470. Notification of appeal rights.

After imposing sentence or making an order deemed to be a final judgment in a criminal case upon conviction after trial, or after imposing sentence following a revocation of probation, except where the revocation is after the defendant's admission of viola-

tion of probation, the court shall advise the defendant of his or her right to appeal, of the necessary steps and time for taking an appeal, and of the right of an indigent defendant to have counsel appointed by the reviewing court. A reporter's transcript of the proceedings required by this rule shall be forthwith prepared and certified by the reporter and filed with the clerk. (*As amended and renumbered effective Jan. 1, 1991.*)

Rule 472. Determination of presentence custody time credit.

At the time of sentencing, the court shall cause to be recorded on the judgment or commitment the total time in custody to be credited upon the sentence under Penal Code section 2900.5. Upon referral of the defendant to the probation officer for an investigation and report under Penal Code section 1203(a) or 1203(f), or upon setting a date for sentencing in the absence of a referral, the court shall direct the sheriff, probation officer, or other appropriate person to report to the court and notify the defendant or defense counsel and prosecuting attorney within a reasonable time prior to the date set for sentencing as to the number of days that defendant has been in custody and for which he or she may be entitled to credit. Any challenges to the report shall be heard at the time of sentencing. (*As amended and renumbered effective Jan. 1, 1991.*)

Rule 490. Setting date for execution of death sentence.

(a) **[Open session of court; notice required]** A date for execution of a judgment of death under section 1193 or section 1227 of the Penal Code shall be set at a public session of the court at which the defendant and the people may be represented.

At least 10 days before the session of court at which the date will be set, the court shall mail notice of the time and place of the proceeding by first-class mail, postage prepaid, to the Attorney General, the district attorney, the defendant at the prison address, the defendant's counsel or, if none is known, counsel who most recently represented the defendant on appeal or in postappeal legal proceedings, and the executive director of the California Appellate Project in San Francisco. The clerk shall file a certificate of mailing copies of the notice. The court shall not hold the proceeding or set an execution date unless the record contains a clerk's certificate showing that the notices required by this subdivision were timely mailed.

Unless otherwise provided by statute, the defendant does not have a right to be present in person. (*As amended effective July 1, 1990; adopted effective July 1, 1989.*)

(b) **[Selection of date; notice]** If, at the announced session of court, the court sets a date for execution of the judgment of death, the court shall mail certified copies of the order setting the date to the warden of the state prison and to the Governor, as required by statute; and shall also, within five days of the making of the order, mail by first-class mail, postage prepaid, certified copies of the order setting the date to each of the person required to be given notice by subdivision (a). The clerk shall file a certificate of mailing copies of the order. (*Adopted effective July 1, 1989.*)

This page intentionally left blank.

© 1992 by J., B. & L. Gould
Printed in the U.S.A. **EP**

VEHICLE CODE

DIVISION 2

ADMINISTRATION

CHAPTER 4

ADMINISTRATION AND ENFORCEMENT

ARTICLE 1

LAWFUL ORDERS AND INSPECTIONS

§2800. Compliance with traffic officers.

It is unlawful to willfully fail or refuse to comply with any lawful order, signal, or direction of any peace officer, as defined in Chapter 4.5 (commencing with Section 830) of Title 3 of Part 2 of the Penal Code, when that peace officer is in uniform and is performing duties under any of the provisions of this code, or to refuse to submit to any lawful inspection under this code.

§2800.1. Willfully fleeing from peace officer.

Any person who, while operating a motor vehicle and with the intent to evade, willfully flees or otherwise attempts to elude a pursuing peace officer's motor vehicle, is guilty of a misdemeanor if all of the following conditions exist:

(a) The peace officer's motor vehicle is exhibiting at least one lighted red lamp visible from the front and the person either sees or reasonable* should have seen the lamp.
*So in original. Probably should be "reasonably".

(b) The peace officer's motor vehicle is sounding a siren as may be reasonably necessary.

(c) The peace officer's motor vehicle is distinctively marked.

(d) The peace officer's motor vehicle is operated by a peace officer, as defined in Chapter 4.5 (commencing with Section 830) of Title 3 of Part 2 of the Penal Code, and that peace officer is wearing a distinctive uniform. (Amended by Stats 1988 ch 504 §1, eff. 8/22/88.)

§2800.2. Driving with disregard for safety.

If a person flees or attempts to elude a pursuing peace officer in violation of Section 2800.1 and the pursued vehicle is driven in a willful or wanton disregard for the safety of persons or property, the person driving the vehicle, upon conviction, shall be punished by imprisonment in the state prison, by imprisonment in the county jail for not more than one year, or by a fine of not less than one hundred seventy dollars ($170) nor more than two thousand dollars ($2,000), or by both that fine and imprisonment. (Added by Stats 1988 ch 504 §3, eff. 8/22/88.)

§2800.3. Fleeing from officer causing injury or death.

Whenever willful flight or attempt to elude a pursuing peace officer in violation of Section 2800.1 proximately causes death or serious bodily injury to any person, the person driving the pursued vehicle, upon conviction, shall be punished by imprisonment in the state prison for two, three, or four years or by imprisonment in the county jail for not more than one year, or by a fine of not less than one thousand dollars

($1,000) nor more than ten thousand dollars ($10,000), or by both that fine and imprisonment.

For purposes of this section, "serious bodily injury" has the same meaning as defined in paragraph (5) of subdivision (f) of Section 243 of the Penal Code. (Amended by Stats 1991 ch 656 §1, eff. 1/1/92.)

§2801. Compliance with firemen.

It is unlawful to willfully fail or refuse to comply with any lawful order, signal, or direction of any member of any fire department, paid, volunteer, or company operated, when wearing the badge or insignia of a fireman and when in the course of his duties he is protecting the personnel and fire department equipment.

DIVISION 3

REGISTRATION OF VEHICLES AND CERTIFICATES OF TITLE

CHAPTER 1

ORIGINAL AND RENEWAL OF REGISTRATION; ISSUANCE OF CERTIFICATES OF TITLE

ARTICLE 4

EVIDENCES OF REGISTRATION

§4462. Presentation and examination of registration or identification card.

(a) The driver of a motor vehicle shall present the registration or identification card or other evidence of registration of any or all vehicles under his immediate control for examination upon demand of any peace officer.

(b) No person shall display upon a vehicle, nor present to any peace officer, any registration card, identification card, temporary receipt, license plate, device issued pursuant to Section 4853, or permit not issued for such vehicle or not otherwise lawfully used thereon under this code. (Amended by Stats 1988 ch 640 §1, eff. 1/1/89.)

§4462.5. Misdemeanor violations.

Every person who commits a violation of subdivision (b) of Section 4462, with intent to avoid compliance with vehicle registration requirements of Article 1 (commencing with Section 4000) of Chapter 1 or Article 1 (commencing with Section 5600) of Chapter 2, is guilty of a misdemeanor. (Added by Stats 1988 ch 640 §2, eff. 1/1/89.)

§4463. Penalty for alteration or falsification of evidence of ownership, etc.

(a) Every person who, with intent to prejudice, damage, or defraud, commits any of the following acts is guilty of a felony and upon conviction thereof shall be punished by imprisonment in the state prison for 16 months, two or three years, or by imprisonment in the county jail for not more than one year:

(1) Alters, forges, counterfeits, or falsifies any certificate of ownership, registration card, certificate, license, license plate, device issued pursuant to Section 4853, special plate, or permit provided for by this code or any comparable certificate of ownership, registration card, certificate, license, license plate,

device comparable to that issued pursuant to Section 4853, special plate, or permit provided for by any foreign jurisdiction, or alters, forges, counterfeits, or falsifies any such document, device, or plate with intent to represent it as issued by the department, or alters, forges, counterfeits, or falsifies with fraudulent intent any endorsement of transfer on a certificate of ownership or other document evidencing ownership, or with fraudulent intent displays or causes or permits to be displayed or have in his or her possession any blank, incomplete, canceled, suspended, revoked, altered, forged, counterfeit, or false certificate of ownership, registration card, certificate, license, license plate, device issued pursuant to Section 4853, special plate, or permit.

(2) Utters, publishes, passes, or attempts to pass, as true and genuine, any false, altered, forged, or counterfeited matter listed in subdivision (a) knowing it to be false, altered, forged, or counterfeited.

(b) Every person who, with intent to prejudice, damage, or defraud, commits any of the following acts is guilty of a misdemeanor, and upon conviction thereof shall be punished by imprisonment in the county jail for six months or by a fine of not less than five hundred dollars ($500) or more than one thousand dollars ($1,000), or by both that fine and imprisonment, which penalty shall not be suspended:

(1) Forges, counterfeits, or falsifies any disabled person placard or any comparable placard relating to parking privileges for disabled persons provided for by any foreign jurisdiction, or forges, counterfeits, or falsifies any disabled person placard with intent to represent it as issued by the department.

(2) Passes, or attempts to pass, as true and genuine, any false, forged, or counterfeit disabled person placard knowing it to be false, forged, or counterfeited.

(3) Acquires, possesses, sells, or offers for sale a genuine or counterfeit disabled person placard.

(c) Every person who, with fraudulent intent, displays or causes or permits to be displayed any forged, counterfeit, or false disabled person placard, is guilty of a misdemeanor, and upon conviction thereof shall be punished by imprisonment in the county jail for six months or by a fine of not less than five hundred dollars ($500) or more than one thousand dollars ($1,000), or by both that fine and imprisonment, which penalty shall not be suspended.

(d) No person shall lend any disabled person placard issued to him or her, nor shall any person knowingly permit its use by one not entitled to it. A disabled person placard holder may permit another person to use the placard for the purpose of transporting the disabled person for whom the placard was issued. A violation of this subdivision is a misdemeanor.

(e) For purposes of subdivision (b), (c), or (d), "disabled person placard" means a placard issued pursuant to Section 22511.5 or 22511.9. (*Amended by Stats 1991 ch 630 §1, eff. 1/1/92.*)

§4463.5. Decorative or facsimile license plate.

(a) No person shall manufacture or sell a decorative or facsimile license plate of a size substantially similar to the license plate issued by the department.

(b) Notwithstanding subdivision (a), the director may authorize the manufacture and sale of decorative or facsimile license plates for special events or media productions.

(c) A violation of this section is a misdemeanor punishable by a fine of not less than five hundred dollars ($500). (*Added by Stats 1986 ch 859 §1.*)

ARTICLE 12

SURRENDER OF REGISTRATION DOCUMENTS AND LICENSE PLATES

§5500. Delivery of certificate of ownership, etc. before disassembling vehicle.

(a) Any person, other than a licensed dismantler, desiring to disassemble a vehicle of a type required to be registered under this code, either partially or totally, with the intent to use as parts only, to reduce to scrap, or to construct another vehicle shall deliver to the department the certificate of ownership, the registration card, and the license plates last issued to the vehicle before dismantling may begin.

(b) Any person who is convicted of violating subdivision (a) shall be punished upon a first conviction by imprisonment in the county jail for not less than five days or more than six months, or by a fine of not less than fifty dollars ($50) or more than five hundred dollars ($500), or by both that fine and imprisonment; and, upon a second or any subsequent conviction, by imprisonment in the county jail for not less than 30 days or more than one year, or by a fine of not less than two hundred fifty dollars ($250) or more than one thousand ($1,000), or by both that fine and imprisonment. (*Amended by Stats 1985 ch 1022 §4.*)

DIVISION 4

SPECIAL ANTITHEFT LAWS

CHAPTER 1

REPORTS OF STOLEN VEHICLES

§10500. Police report on theft; information on recovery of vehicle.

(a) Every peace officer, upon receiving a report based on reliable information that any vehicle registered under this code has been stolen, taken, or driven in violation of Section 10851, or that license plates for any vehicle have been lost or stolen, shall, immediately after receiving that information, report the information to the Department of Justice Stolen Vehicle System. An officer, upon receiving information of the recovery of any vehicle which has been previously reported as stolen, taken, or driven in violation of Section 10851, or of the recovery of plates which have been previously reported as lost or stolen, shall immediately report the fact of the recovery to the Department of Justice Stolen Vehicle System. At the same time, the recovering officer shall advise the Department of Justice Stolen Vehicle System and the original reporting police agency of the location and condition of the vehicle or license plates recovered. The original reporting police agency, upon receipt of the information from the recovering officer, shall, within 48 hours, excluding weekends and holidays, notify the reporting party of the location and condition of the recovered vehicle.

(b) If the recovered vehicle is subject to parking or storage charges, Section 10652.5 applies. (*Amended by Stats 1990 ch 337 §1, eff. 1/1/91.*)

© 1992 by J., B. & L. Gould
Printed in the U.S.A.   EP

§10501. False report; punishment for previous conviction.

(a) It is unlawful for any person to make or file a false or fraudulent report of theft of a vehicle required to be registered under this code with any law enforcement agency with intent to deceive.

(b) If a person has been previously convicted of a violation of subdivision (a), he or she is punishable by imprisonment in the state prison for 16 months, or two or three years, or in a county jail for not to exceed one year.

§10502. Report of embezzlement; issue of arrest warrant by owner.

The owner or legal owner of a vehicle registered under this code which has been stolen or embezzled may notify the Department of the California Highway Patrol of the theft or embezzlement but in the event of an embezzlement may make the report only after having procured the issuance of a warrant for the arrest of the person charged with such embezzlement.

Every owner or legal owner who has given any such notice shall notify the Department of the California Highway Patrol of a recovery of the vehicle.

§10503. Notification of report to Department of Motor Vehicles.

The Department of Justice upon receiving notice under this chapter that a vehicle has been stolen, or taken or driven in violation of Section 10851, or that a vehicle reported stolen, or taken or driven in violation of Section 10851 has been recovered, shall notify the Department of Motor Vehicles of the reported theft, taking or driving, or recovery.

§10504. Identification of stolen vehicle by Department of Motor Vehicles; notification to Department of Justice.

The department upon receiving a report of a stolen vehicle, or of a vehicle taken or driven in violation of Section 10851, shall place an appropriate notice in the electronic file system which will identify such vehicles during the processing of new certificates of registration, ownership, or registration and ownership. When such vehicles are thus identified, processing shall be discontinued and the Department of Justice shall be notified. New certificates shall not be issued until cleared by the Department of Justice. Notices shall remain in the Department of Motor Vehicles system until a Department of Justice deletion is received.

A report of a stolen vehicle, or of a vehicle taken or driven in violation of Section 10851, is effective for a period of not less than one year from the date first reported or longer as the department may determine.

CHAPTER 3

ALTERATION OR REMOVAL OF NUMBERS

§10750. Authorization to alter vehicle numbers.

(a) No person shall intentionally deface, destroy, or alter the motor number, other distinguishing number, or identification mark of a vehicle required or employed for registration purposes without written authorization from the department, nor shall any person place or stamp any serial, motor, or other number or mark upon a vehicle, except one assigned thereto by the department.

(b) This section does not prohibit the restoration by an owner of the original vehicle identification number when the restoration is authorized by the department, nor prevent any manufacturer from placing in the ordinary course of business numbers or marks upon new motor vehicles or new parts thereof.

§10751. Manufacturer's or identification number; postseizure hearing; notice of impoundment.

(a) No person shall knowingly buy, sell, offer for sale, receive, or have in his or her possession, any vehicle, or component part thereof, from which any serial or identification number, including, but not limited to, any number used for registration purposes, that is affixed by the manufacturer to the vehicle or component part, in whatever manner deemed proper by the manufacturer, has been removed, defaced, altered, or destroyed, unless the vehicle or component part has attached thereto an identification number assigned or approved by the department in lieu of the manufacturer's number.

(b) Whenever a vehicle described in subdivision (a), including a vehicle assembled with any component part which is in violation of subdivision (a), comes into the custody of a peace officer, it shall be destroyed, sold, or otherwise disposed of under the conditions as provided in an order by the court having jurisdiction. No court order providing for disposition shall be issued unless the person from whom the property was seized, and all claimants to the property whose interest or title is on registration records in the Department of Motor Vehicles, are provided a postseizure hearing by the court having jurisdiction within 90 days after the seizure. This subdivision shall not apply with respect to a seized vehicle or component part used as evidence in any criminal action or proceeding. Nothing in this section shall, however, preclude the return of a seized vehicle or a component part to the owner by the seizing agency following presentation of satisfactory evidence of ownership and, if determined necessary, upon the assignment of an identification number to the vehicle or component part by the department.

(c) Whenever a vehicle described in subdivision (a) comes into the custody of a peace officer, the person from whom the property was seized, and all claimants to the property whose interest or title is on registration records in the Department of Motor Vehicles, shall be notified within five days, excluding Saturdays, Sundays, and holidays, after the seizure, of the date, time, and place of the hearing required in subdivision (b). The notice shall contain the information specified in subdivision (d).

(d) Whenever a peace officer seizes a vehicle described in subdivision (a), the person from whom the property was seized shall be provided a notice of impoundment of the vehicle which shall serve as a receipt and contain the following information:

(1) Name and address of person from whom the property was seized.

(2) A statement that the vehicle seized has been impounded for investigation of a violation of Section 10751 of the California Vehicle Code and that the property will be released upon a determination that the serial or identification number has not been removed, defaced, altered, or destroyed, or upon the presentation of satisfactory evidence of ownership of the vehicle or a component part, if no other person claims an interest in the property; otherwise, a hear-

ing regarding the disposition of the vehicle shall take place in the proper court.

(3) A statement that the person from whom the property was seized, and all claimants to the property whose interest or title is on registration records in the Department of Motor Vehicles, will receive written notification of the date, time, and place of the hearing within five days, excluding Saturdays, Sundays, and holidays, after the seizure.

(4) Name and address of the law enforcement agency where evidence of ownership of the vehicle or component part may be presented.

(5) A statement of the contents of Section 10751 of the Vehicle Code.

(e) A hearing on the disposition of the property shall be held by the municipal or justice court within 90 days after the seizure. The hearing shall be before the court without a jury.

(1) If the evidence reveals either that the serial or identification number has not been removed, defaced, altered, or destroyed or that the number has been removed, defaced, altered, or destroyed but satisfactory evidence of ownership has been presented to the seizing agency or court, the property shall be released to the person entitled thereto. Nothing in this section precludes the return of the vehicle or a component part to a good faith purchaser following presentation of satisfactory evidence of ownership thereof upon the assignment of an identification number to the vehicle or component part by the department.

(2) If the evidence reveals that the identification number has been removed, defaced, altered, or destroyed, and satisfactory evidence of ownership has not been presented, the vehicle shall be destroyed, sold, or otherwise disposed of as provided by court order.

(3) At the hearing, the seizing agency has the burden of establishing that the serial or identification number has been removed, defaced, altered, or destroyed and that no satisfactory evidence of ownership has been presented.

(f) This section does not apply to a scrap metal processor engaged primarily in the acquisition, processing, and shipment of ferrous and nonferrous scrap, and who receives dismantled vehicles from licensed dismantlers, licensed junk collectors, or licensed junk dealers as scrap metal for the purpose of recycling the dismantled vehicles for their metallic content, the end product of which is the production of material for recycling and remelting purposes for steel mills, foundries, smelters, and refiners. (Amended by Stats 1991 ch 13 §25, eff. 2/13/91.)

§10752. Unlawful possession or sale of vehicle serial or identification number.

(a) No person shall, with intent to prejudice, damage, injure, or defraud, acquire, possess, sell, or offer for sale any genuine or counterfeit manufacturer's serial or identification number from or for, or purporting to be from or for, a vehicle or component part thereof.

(b) No person shall, with intent to prejudice, damage, injure, or defraud, acquire, possess, sell, or offer for sale any genuine or counterfeit serial or identification number issued by the department, the Department of the California Highway Patrol, or the vehicle registration and titling agency of any foreign jurisdiction which is from or for, or purports to be from or for, a vehicle or component part thereof.

(c) Every person convicted of a violation of subdivision (a) or (b) shall be punished by imprisonment in the state prison, or in the county jail for not less than 90 days nor more than one year, and by a fine of not less than two hundred fifty dollars ($250) nor more than five thousand dollars ($5,000). (Amended by Stats 1985 ch 623 §2.)

CHAPTER 4

THEFT AND INJURY OF VEHICLES

§10850. Applicability of this chapter.

The provisions of this chapter apply to vehicles upon the highways and elsewhere throughout the State.

§10851. Theft or unlawful use or taking of a vehicle.

(a) Any person who drives or takes a vehicle not his or her own, without the consent of the owner thereof, and with intent either to permanently or temporarily to deprive the owner thereof of his or her title to or possession of the vehicle, whether with or without intent to steal the vehicle, or any person who is a party or an accessory to or an accomplice in the driving or unauthorized taking or stealing, is guilty of a public offense and, upon conviction thereof, shall be punished by imprisonment in the state prison for two, three, or four years or a fine of not more than ten thousand dollars ($10,000), or both, or by imprisonment in the county jail not to exceed one year or a fine of not more than one thousand dollars ($1,000), or both.

(b) Any person who, having been convicted of two previous misdemeanor violations of subdivision (a), former paragraph (3) of Section 487 of the Penal Code, involving an automobile, Section 487h of the Penal Code, or Section 10851 of the Vehicle Code or any combination of those offenses as misdemeanors, is subsequently convicted of a violation of subdivision (a) is punishable for the subsequent conviction by imprisonment in the state prison for two, three, or four years.

(c) If the vehicle is (1) an ambulance, as defined in subdivision (a) of Section 165, (2) a distinctively marked vehicle of a law enforcement agency or fire department, taken while the ambulance or vehicle is on an emergency call and this fact is known to the person driving or taking, or any person who is party or an accessory to or an accomplice in the driving or unauthorized taking or stealing, or (3) a vehicle which has been modified for the use of a disabled veteran or any other disabled person and which displays a distinguishing license plate or placard issued pursuant to Section 22511.5 or 22511.9 and this fact is known or should reasonably have been known to the person driving or taking, or any person who is party or an accessory in the driving or unauthorized taking or stealing, the offense is a felony punishable by imprisonment in the state prison for two, four, or six years and by a fine of not more than ten thousand dollars ($10,000).

(d)(1) Except in unusual cases where the interests of justice would best be served if the person is granted probation, probation shall not be granted to any person who is convicted of a felony violation of subdivision (a), (b), or (c), and who has been previously convicted of two or more felony violations of the offense set forth

© 1992 by J., B. & L. Gould
Printed in the U.S.A.   EP

in subdivision (a) or (c), the offense set forth in former paragraph (3) of Section 487 of the Penal Code, involving a vehicle, or the offense set forth in Section 487h of the Penal Code, or who has been previously convicted of one felony violation of any of those offenses and at least two misdemeanor violations of those offenses.

(2) If the court grants probation under paragraph (1), it shall specify on the court record the reason or reasons for that order.

(e) In any prosecution for a violation of subdivision (a) or (c), the consent of the owner of a vehicle to its taking or driving shall not in any case be presumed or implied because of the owner's consent on a previous occasion to the taking or driving of the vehicle by the same or a different person.

(f) The existence of any fact which makes subdivision (c) applicable shall be alleged in the accusatory pleading, and either admitted by the defendant in open court, or found to be true by the jury trying the issue of guilt or by the court where guilt is established by plea of guilty or nolo contendere or by trial by the court sitting without a jury.

(g) This section shall remain in effect only until January 1, 1993, and as of that date is repealed, unless a later enacted statute, which is enacted before January 1, 1993, deletes or extends that date. *(Amended by Stats 1990 ch 1564 §2, eff. 9/30/90 only until 1/1/93. See other section 10851 below.)*

§10851. Theft or unlawful use or taking of a vehicle.

(a) Any person who drives or takes a vehicle not his or her own, without the consent of the owner thereof, and with intent either to permanently or temporarily deprive the owner thereof of his or her title to or possession of the vehicle, whether with or without intent to steal the vehicle, or any person who is a party or an accessory to or an accomplice in the driving or unauthorized taking or stealing, is guilty of a public offense and, upon conviction thereof, shall be punished by imprisonment in the county jail for not more than one year or in the state prison or by a fine of not more than five thousand dollars ($5,000), or by both the fine and imprisonment.

(b) If the vehicle is (1) an ambulance, as defined in subdivision (a) of Section 165, (2) a distinctively marked vehicle of a law enforcement agency or fire department, taken while the ambulance or vehicle is on an emergency call and this fact is known to the person driving or taking or any person who is party or an accessory to or an accomplice in the driving or unauthorized taking or stealing, or (3) a vehicle which has been modified for the use of a disabled veteran or any other disabled person and which displays a distinguishing license plate or placard issued pursuant to Section 22511.5 or 22511.9 and this fact is known or should reasonably have been known to the person driving or taking, or any person who is party or an accessory in the driving or unauthorized taking or stealing, the offense is a felony punishable by imprisonment in the state prison for two, three, or four years or by a fine of not more than ten thousand dollars ($10,000), or by both the fine and imprisonment.

(c) In any prosecution for a violation of subdivision (a) or (b), the consent of the owner of a vehicle to its taking or driving shall not in any case be presumed or implied because of the owner's consent on a previous occasion to the taking or driving of the vehicle by the same or a different person.

(d) The existence of any fact which makes subdivision (b) applicable shall be alleged in the accusatory pleading, and either admitted by the defendant in open court, or found to be true by the jury trying the issue of guilt or by the court where guilt is established by plea of guilty or nolo contendere or by trial by the court sitting without a jury. *(Added by Stats 1989 ch 930 §11.1, eff. 1/1/93. See other section 10851 above.)*

§10851.5. Punishment for theft of binder chains.

Any person who takes binder chains, required under regulations adopted pursuant to Section 31510, having a value of four hundred dollars ($400) or less which chains are not his own, without the consent of the owner thereof, and with intent either permanently or temporarily to deprive the owner thereof of his title to or possession of the binder chains whether with or without intent to steal the same, or any person who is a party or accessory to or an accomplice in the unauthorized taking or stealing is guilty of a misdemeanor, and upon conviction thereof shall be punished by imprisonment in the county jail for not less than six months or by a fine of not less than one thousand dollars ($1,000) or by both such fine and imprisonment. The consent of the owner of the binder chain to its taking shall not in any case be presumed or implied because of such owner's consent on a previous occasion to the taking of the binder chain by the same or a different person.

§10852. Damaging, tampering with, or destroying vehicle parts.

No person shall either individually or in association with one or more other persons, wilfully injure or tamper with any vehicle or the contents thereof or break or remove any part of a vehicle without the consent of the owner.

§10853. Tampering with vehicle with intent to commit malicious mischief.

No person shall with intent to commit any malicious mischief, injury, or other crime, climb into or upon a vehicle whether it is in motion or at rest, nor shall any person attempt to manipulate any of the levers, starting mechanism, brakes, or other mechanism or device of a vehicle while the same is at rest and unattended, nor shall any person set in motion any vehicle while the same is at rest and unattended.

§10854. Unauthorized use of a vehicle.

Every person having the storage, care, safe-keeping, custody, or possession of any vehicle of a type subject to registration under this code who, without the consent of the owner, takes, hires, runs, drives, or uses the vehicle or who takes or removes any part thereof is guilty of a misdemeanor and upon conviction shall be punished by a fine of not exceeding one thousand dollars ($1,000) or by imprisonment in the county jail for not exceeding one year or by both.

§10855. Failure to return leased or rented vehicle.

Whenever any person who has leased or rented a vehicle wilfully and intentionally fails to return the vehicle to its owner within five days after the lease or rental agreement has expired, that person shall be presumed to have embezzled the vehicle.

DIVISION 6

DRIVERS' LICENSES

CHAPTER 1

ISSUANCE OF LICENSES, EXPIRATION, AND RENEWAL

ARTICLE 1

PERSONS REQUIRED TO BE LICENSED, EXEMPTIONS, AND AGE LIMITS

§12500. Driving unlawful without license.

(a) No person shall drive a motor vehicle upon a highway, unless the person then holds a driver's license issued under this code, except those persons who are expressly exempted under this code.

(b) No person shall drive any motorcycle, motor-driven cycle, or motorized bicycle upon a highway, unless the person then holds a driver's license or endorsement issued under this code for that class, except those persons who are expressly exempted under this code, or those persons specifically authorized to operate motorized bicycles with class 3 or class C licenses as specified in subdivision (g) of Section 12804.9.

(c) No person shall drive a motor vehicle or combination of vehicles that is not of a type for which the person is licensed.

(d) No person shall drive a motor vehicle in or upon any offstreet parking facility, unless the person then holds a driver's license of the appropriate class or certification to operate the vehicle. As used in this subdivision, "offstreet parking facility" means any offstreet facility held open for use by the public for parking vehicles and includes any publicly owned facilities for offstreet parking, and privately owned facilities for offstreet parking where no fee is charged for the privilege to park and which are held open for the common public use of retail customers. (Amended by Stats 1990 ch 1359 §3, eff. 1/1/91.)

§12501. Persons not required to obtain driver's license.

The following persons are not required to obtain a driver's license:

(a) An officer or employee of the United States, while operating a motor vehicle owned or controlled by the United States on the business of the United States, except when the motor vehicle being operated is a commercial motor vehicle, as defined in Section 15210.

(b) Any person while driving or operating implements of husbandry incidentally operated or moved over a highway, except as provided in Section 36300 or 36305.

(c) Any person driving or operating an off-highway motor vehicle subject to identification, as defined in Section 38012, while driving or operating such motor vehicle as provided in Section 38025. Nothing in this subdivision authorizes operation of a motor vehicle by a person without a valid driver's license upon any offstreet parking facility, as defined in subdivision (c)

of Section 12500. (Amended by Stats 1990 ch 1360 §10, eff. 1/1/91.)

§12512.5. Issuance of motorcycle driver's license to minor.

Notwithstanding any other provision of law, no driver's license shall be issued to any person under the age of 18 years authorizing that person to operate any two-wheel motorcycle without satisfactory completion of a motorcyclist rider training program approved by the Commissioner of the California Highway Patrol pursuant to Section 2932.

This section shall become operative on January 1, 1988. (Added by Stats 1986 ch 753 §1.)

§12515. Minimum age for employment as driver.

(a) No person under the age of 18 years shall be employed for compensation by another for the purpose of driving a motor vehicle on the highways.

(b) No person under the age of 21 years shall be employed for compensation by another to drive, and no person under the age of 21 years may drive a motor vehicle, as defined in Section 34500 or subdivision (b) of Section 15210, that is engaged in interstate commerce, or any motor vehicle that is engaged in the interstate or intrastate transportation of hazardous material, as defined in Section 353. (Amended by Stats 1988 ch 1509 §5, eff. 1/1/89.)

§12516. Minimum age for operation of school bus.

It is unlawful for any person under the age of 18 years to drive a school bus transporting pupils to or from school.

ARTICLE 3

ISSUANCE AND RENEWAL OF LICENSES

§12810. Traffic violation point count; allocation of points.

In determining the violation point count, the following shall apply:

(a) Any conviction of failure to stop in the event of an accident in violation of Section 20001 or 20002 shall be given a value of two points.

(b) Any conviction of a violation of Section 23152 or 23153 shall be given a value of two points.

(c) Any conviction of reckless driving shall be given a value of two points.

(d) Any conviction of a violation of subdivision (c) of Section 192 of the Penal Code, or of Section 2800.2, subdivision (b) of Section 21651, subdivision (b) of Section 22348, subdivision (a) of Section 23109, subdivision (c) of Section 23109, or Section 31602 of this code, shall be given a value of two points.

(e) Except as provided in subdivision (g), any other traffic conviction involving the safe operation of a motor vehicle upon the highway shall be given a value of one point.

(f) Any accident in which the operator is deemed by the department to be responsible shall be given a value of one point.

(g) A violation of paragraph (1), (2), (3), or (5) of subdivision (b) of Section 40001 shall not result in a violation point count being given to the driver if the driver is not the owner of the vehicle.

(h) A conviction for only one violation arising from one occasion of arrest or citation shall be counted in

© 1992 by J., B. & L. Gould
Printed in the U.S.A.   EP

determining the violation point count for the purposes of this section.

(i) Any conviction of a violation of Section 14601, 14601.1, 14601.2, or 14601.3 shall be given a value of two points.

(j) Any conviction of a violation of Section 27360 within a 37-month period shall be given a value of one point. *(Amended by Stats 1991 ch 13 §29, eff. 2/13/91; ch 1223 §2, eff. 1/1/92.)*

§12810.2. Exception for seat belt law violation.

Notwithstanding subdivision (d) of Section 12810, no violation point count shall be given for a conviction of a violation of Section 27315 to determine if the person convicted is a negligent driver for purposes of Section 12809, or 13359. *(Amended by Stats 1985 ch 1361 §1.)*

§12810.5. Negligent operator.

(a) Except as otherwise provided in subdivision (b), any person whose driving record shows a violation point count of four or more points in 12 months, six or more points in 24 months, or eight or more points in 36 months shall be prima facie presumed to be a negligent operator of a motor vehicle. In applying this subdivision to a driver, if the person requests and appears at a hearing conducted by the department, the department shall give due consideration to the amount of use or mileage traveled in the operation of a motor vehicle.

(b) (1) Any class 1, class 2, class A, or class B licensed driver, except persons holding certificates pursuant to Section 2512, 12517, 12519, 12519.5, 12523, or 12523.5, or an endorsement issued pursuant to paragraph (2) or (4) of subdivision (a) of Section 15278, who is presumed to be a negligent operator pursuant to subdivision (a), and who requests and appears at a hearing and is found to have a driving record violation point count of six or more points in 12 months, eight or more points in 24 months, or 10 or more points in 36 months is presumed to be a prima facie negligent operator. However, the higher point count shall not apply if the department reasonably determines that four or more points in 12 months, six or more points in 24 months, or eight or more points in 36 months are attributable to the driver's operation of a vehicle requiring only a class 3 or class C license, and not requiring a certificate or endorsement, or a class 4 or class M license.

(2) For purposes of this subdivision, each point assigned pursuant to Section 12810 shall be valued at one and one-half times the value otherwise required by that section for each violation reasonably determined by the department to be attributable to the driver's operation of a vehicle requiring a class 1 or class 2 or class A or class B license, or requiring any certificate or endorsement described in this section.

(c) The department may require a negligent operator whose driving privilege is suspended or revoked pursuant to this section to submit proof of financial responsibility as defined in Section 16430. The proof of financial responsibility shall be filed on or before the date of reinstatement following the suspension or revocation. The proof of financial responsibility shall be maintained with the department for three years following that date of reinstatement.

(d) This section shall remain in effect only until January 1, 1993, and as of that date is repealed, unless a later enacted statute which is enacted before January 1, 1993, deletes or extends that date. *(Amended by Stats 1991 ch 928 §20, eff. 10/14/91 only until 1/1/93. See other section 12810.5 below.)*

§12810.5. Negligent operator.

(a) Except as otherwise provided in subdivision (b), any person whose driving record shows a violation point count of four or more points in 12 months, six or more points in 24 months, or eight or more points in 36 months shall be prima facie presumed to be a negligent operator of a motor vehicle. In applying this subdivision to a driver, if the person requests and appears at a hearing conducted by the department, the department shall give due consideration to the amount of use or mileage traveled in the operation of a motor vehicle.

(b) (1) Any class 1, class 2, class A, or class B licensed driver, except persons holding certificates pursuant to Section 2512, 12517, 12519, 12523, or 12523.5, or an endorsement issued pursuant to paragraph (2) or (4) of subdivision (a) of Section 15278, who is presumed to be a negligent operator pursuant to subdivision (a), and who requests and appears at a hearing and is found to have a driving record violation point count of six or more points in 12 months, eight or more points in 24 months, or 10 or more points in 36 months is presumed to be a prima facie negligent operator. However, the higher point count shall not apply if the department reasonably determines that four or more points in 12 months, six or more points in 24 months, or eight or more points in 36 months are attributable to the driver's operation of a vehicle requiring only a class 3 or class C license, and not requiring a certificate or endorsement, or a class 4 or class M license.

(2) For purposes of this subdivision, each point assigned pursuant to Section 12810 shall be valued at one and one-half times the value otherwise required by that section for each violation reasonably determined by the department to be attributable to the driver's operation of a vehicle requiring a class 1 or class 2 or class A or class B license, or requiring any certificate or endorsement described in this section.

(c) The department may require a negligent operator whose driving privilege is suspended or revoked pursuant to this section to submit proof of financial responsibility, as defined in Section 16430, on or before the date of reinstatement following the suspension or revocation. The proof of financial responsibility shall be maintained with the department for three years following that date of reinstatement.

(d) This section shall become operative on January 1, 1993. *(Added by Stats 1991 ch 928 §21, eff. 10/14/91, oper. 1/1/93.)*

CHAPTER 2

SUSPENSION OR REVOCATION OF LICENSES

ARTICLE 2

SUSPENSION OR REVOCATION BY COURT

§13200. Penalty for speeding or reckless driving.

Whenever any person licensed under this code is convicted of a violation of any provision of this code relating to the speed of vehicles or a violation of Section 23103 the court may, unless this code makes mandatory a revocation by the department, suspend the privilege of the person to operate a motor vehicle for a period of not to exceed 30 days upon a first conviction, for a period of not to exceed 60 days upon a second conviction, and for a period of not to exceed six months upon a third or any subsequent conviction.

§13200.5. Penalty for driving over 100 miles per hour.

Whenever any person licensed under this code is convicted of a violation of subdivision (b) of Section 22348, the court may, unless this code makes mandatory a revocation by the department, suspend the privilege of the person to operate a motor vehicle for a period of not to exceed 30 days.

§13201. Further offenses resulting in suspension.

A court may suspend, for not more than six months, the privilege of any person to operate a motor vehicle upon conviction of any of the following offenses:

(a) Failure of the driver of a vehicle involved in an accident to stop or otherwise comply with Section 20002.

(b) Reckless driving proximately causing bodily injury to any person under Section 23104.

(c) Failure of the driver of a vehicle to stop at a railway grade crossing as required by Section 22452.

(d) Evading a peace officer in violation of Section 2800.1 or 2800.2, or in violation of Section 2800.3 if the person's license is not revoked for that violation pursuant to paragraph (3) of subdivision (a) of Section 13351. *(Amended by Stats 1991 ch 656 §2, eff. 1/1/92.)*

§13202. Controlled substance offenses.

(a) A court may suspend or order that the department revoke in which case the department shall revoke the privilege of any person to operate a motor vehicle upon conviction of any offense related to controlled substances as defined in Division 10 (commencing with Section 11000) of the Health and Safety Code when the use of a motor vehicle was involved in, or incidental to, the commission of the offense.

(b) A court shall order that the department revoke and the department shall revoke the privilege of any person to operate a motor vehicle upon conviction of a violation of Section 11350, 11351, 11352, 11353, 11357, 11359, 11360, or 11361 of the Health and Safety Code when a motor vehicle was involved in, or incidental to, the commission of such offense.

(c) The period of time for suspension or the period after revocation during which the person may not apply for a license shall be determined by the court, but in no event shall such period exceed three years from the date of conviction. *(Amended by Stats 1984 ch 1635 §93.)*

§13202.5. Suspension of license for conviction of a minor for alcohol or marijuana offenses.

(a) For each conviction of a person for any offense specified in subdivision (d), committed while the person was under the age of 21 years, but 13 years of age or older, the court shall suspend the person's driving privilege for one year. If the person convicted does not yet have the privilege to drive, the court shall order the department to delay issuing the privilege to drive for one year subsequent to the time the person be-

comes legally eligible to drive. However, if there is no further conviction for any offense specified in subdivision (d) in a 12-month period after the conviction, the court, upon petition of the person affected, may modify the order imposing the delay of the privilege. For each successive offense, the court shall suspend the person's driving privilege for those possessing a license or delay the eligibility for those not in possession of a license at the time of their conviction for one additional year.

As used in this section, the term "conviction" includes the findings in juvenile proceedings specified in Section 13105.

(b) Whenever the court suspends driving privileges pursuant to subdivision (a), the court in which the conviction is had shall require all driver's licenses held by the person to be surrendered to the court. The court shall within 10 days following the conviction transmit certified abstract of the conviction, together with any driver's licenses surrendered, to the department.

(c) (1) After a court has issued an order suspending or delaying driving privileges pursuant to subdivision (a), the court, upon petition of the person affected, may review the order and may impose restrictions on the person's privilege to drive based upon a showing of a critical need to drive.

(2) As used in this section, "critical need to drive" means the circumstances which are required to be shown for the issuance of a junior permit pursuant to Section 12513.

(3) The restriction shall remain in effect for the balance of the period of suspension or restriction in this section. The court shall notify the department of any modification within 10 days of the order of modification.

(d) This section applies to violations involving controlled substances or alcohol contained in the following provisions:

(1) Article 7 (commencing with Section 4211) of Chapter 9 of Division 2 of, and Sections 25658, 25658.5, 25661, and 25662 of, the Business and Professions Code.

(2) Division 10 (commencing with Section 11000) of the Health and Safety Code.

(3) Section 191.5, paragraph (3) of subdivision (c) of Section 192, subdivision (c) or (d) of Section 192.5, and subdivision (f) of Section 647 of the Penal Code.

(4) Section 23103 when subject to Section 23103.5, Section 23140, and Article 2 (commencing with Section 23152) of Chapter 12 of Division 11 of this code.

(e) Suspension, restriction, or delay of driving privileges pursuant to this section shall be in addition to any penalty imposed upon conviction of any violation specified in subdivision (d). *(Amended by Stats 1990 ch 1696 §3; ch 1697 §4, eff. 1/1/91.)*

ARTICLE 3

SUSPENSION AND REVOCATION BY DEPARTMENT

§13350. Revocation and renewal of driving privileges.

(a) The department shall immediately revoke the privilege of any person to drive a motor vehicle upon receipt of a duly certified abstract of the record of any court showing that the person has been convicted of any of the following crimes or offenses:

© 1992 by J., B. & L. Gould
Printed in the U.S.A.   EP

(1) Failure of the driver of a vehicle involved in an accident resulting in injury or death to any person to stop or otherwise comply with Section 20001.

(2) Any felony in the commission of which a motor vehicle is used, except as provided for in Section 13351, 13352, or 13357.

(3) Reckless driving causing bodily injury.

(b) If a person is convicted of a violation of Section 23152 punishable under Section 23170 or 23175, or a violation of Section 23153 punishable under Section 23190, including a violation of paragraph (3) of subdivision (c) of Section 192 of the Penal Code as provided in Section 193.7 of that code, the court shall, at the time of surrender of the driver's license or temporary permit, require the defendant to sign an affidavit in a form provided by the department acknowledging his or her understanding of the revocation required by paragraph (5), (6) or (7) of subdivision (a) of Section 13352 and an acknowledgment of his or her designation as an habitual traffic offender. A copy of this affidavit shall be transmitted with the license or temporary permit to the department within the prescribed 10 days.

(c) The department shall not reinstate the privilege revoked under subdivision (a) until the expiration of one year after the date of revocation and until the person whose privilege was revoked gives proof of ability to respond in damages as defined in Section 16430. *(Amended by Stats 1991 ch 656 §3, eff. 1/1/92.)*

§13350.5. Vehicular homicide conviction deemed to be DWI conviction.

Notwithstanding Section 13350, for the purposes of this article, conviction of a violation of paragraph (3) of subdivision (c) of Section 192 of the Penal Code is a conviction of a violation of Section 23153. *(Amended by Stats 1991 ch 656 §4, eff. 1/1/92.)*

§13351. Crimes resulting in automatic revocation of license.

(a) The department shall immediately revoke the privilege of any person to drive a motor vehicle upon receipt of a duly certified abstract of the record of any court showing that the person has been convicted of any of the following crimes or offenses:

(1) Manslaughter resulting from the operation of a motor vehicle except when convicted under paragraph (2) of subdivision (c) of Section 192 of the Penal Code.

(2) Upon conviction of three or more violations of Section 20001, 20002, 23103, or 23104 within a period of 12 months from the time of the first offense to the third or subsequent offense, or upon a combination of three or more convictions of violations within a like period.

(3) Violation of Section 191.5 of the Penal Code or of Section 2800.3 causing serious bodily injury resulting in a serious impairment of physical condition, including, but not limited to, loss of consciousness, concussion, serious bone fracture, protracted loss or impairment of function of any bodily member or organ, and serious disfigurement.

(b) The department shall not reinstate the privilege revoked under subdivision (a) until the expiration of three years after the date of revocation and until the person whose privilege was revoked gives proof of ability to respond in damages as defined in

Section 16430. *(Amended by Stats 1991 ch 656 §5, eff. 1/1/92.)*

§13352. Suspension or revocation for driving while under the influence; motor vehicle speed contest.

(a) The department shall immediately suspend or revoke, or record the court-administered suspension or revocation of, the privilege of any person to operate a motor vehicle upon receipt of a duly certified abstract of the record of any court showing that the person has been convicted of a violation of Section 23152 or 23153 or subdivision (a) of Section 23109, or upon receipt of a report of a judge of the juvenile court, a juvenile traffic hearing officer, or a referee of a juvenile court showing that the person has been found to have committed a violation of Section 23152 or 23153 or subdivision (a) of Section 23109. For purposes of this section, suspension or revocation shall be as follows:

(1) Upon a conviction or finding of a violation of Section 23152 punishable under Section 23160, the privilege shall be suspended for a period of six months if the court orders the department to suspend the privilege, or if the court does not grant probation, or if the offense occurred in a vehicle requiring a driver with a class 1 or class 2 driver's license or with a certificate specified in Section 12804.1. However, where (A) the driving privilege is required to be suspended by this paragraph due to the violation having occurred in vehicles requiring a class 1 or class 2 driver's license, and (B) the court grants probation and imposes the condition specified in subdivision (b) of Section 23161, the department shall issue the person a class 3 driver's license restricted in the same manner and subject to the same conditions as specified in subdivision (e) of Section 13352.5. If the person gives proof of ability to respond in damages as defined in Section 16430, the department shall issue the restricted license upon receipt of an abstract of record from the court pursuant to Section 1803 certifying that the court has granted probation to the person on conditions which include the condition specified in subdivision (b) of Section 23161.

(2) Upon a conviction or finding of a violation of Section 23153 punishable under Section 23180, the privilege shall be suspended for a period of one year. The privilege shall not be reinstated until the person gives proof of ability to respond in damages as defined in Section 16430.

(3) Except as provided in Section 13352.5, upon a conviction or finding of a violation of Section 23152 punishable under Section 23165, the privilege shall be suspended for 18 months. The privilege shall not be reinstated until the person gives proof of ability to respond in damages as defined in Section 16430.

(4) Except as provided in Section 13352.5, upon a conviction or finding of a violation of Section 23153 punishable under Section 23185, the privilege shall be revoked for a period of three years. The privilege shall not be reinstated until evidence satisfactory to the department establishes that no grounds exist which would authorize the refusal to issue a license and until the person gives proof of ability to respond in damages as defined in Section 16430.

(5) Upon a conviction or finding of a violation of Section 23152 punishable under Section 23170, the privilege shall be revoked for a period of three years. The privilege shall not be reinstated until the person files proof of ability to respond in damages as defined

in Section 16430 and gives proof satisfactory to the department of successful completion, subsequent to the most recent underlying conviction, of an 18-month program or, if available in the county of the person's residence or employment, a 30-month program licensed pursuant to Chapter 9 (commencing with Section 11836) of Part 2 of Division 10.5 of the Health and Safety Code. The court shall advise the person at the time of sentencing that completion of an 18-month program or a 30-month program is required in order to become eligible for a California driver's license. The court shall also advise the person that after the completion of 24 months of the revocation period, the person may apply to the court for an order granting a restricted driver's license, subject to the following conditions:

(A) The person has satisfactorily completed, subject to the current underlying conviction, either of the following:

(i) A licensed 18-month program pursuant to Section 11836 of the Health and Safety Code.

(ii) The initial 18 months of a licensed 30-month program, if available in the county of the person's residence or employment, pursuant to Section 11836 of the Health and Safety Code.

(B) The person agrees, as a condition of the restriction, to continue satisfactory participation in the 30-month program, if applicable, and to have installed and maintained, as described in Section 23235, an ignition interlock device.

(C) The person provides proof of responsibility to respond in damages as defined in Section 16430.

(D) The person has not applied for and received such an order in conjunction with the current underlying conviction or a prior conviction for violation of Section 23103, 23152, or 23153, if the prior conviction was within the previous seven years.

(E) Any individual convicted of a violation of Section 23152 punishable under Section 23170 may also, at any time after sentencing, petition the court for referral to an 18-month program or, if available in the county of the person's residence or employment, a 30-month program licensed pursuant to Chapter 9 (commencing with Section 11836) of Part 2 of Division 10.5 of the Health and Safety Code. Unless good cause is shown, the court shall order the referral.

(6) Upon a conviction or finding of a violation of Section 23153 punishable under Section 23190, the privilege shall be revoked for a period of five years. The privilege shall not be reinstated until evidence satisfactory to the department establishes that no grounds exist which would authorize the refusal to issue a license and until the person gives proof of ability to respond in damages as defined in Section 16430 and gives proof satisfactory to the department of successful completion, subsequent to the most recent underlying conviction, of a 30-month program, if available in the county of the person's residence or employment or, if not available, an 18-month program licensed pursuant to Chapter 9 (commencing with Section 11836) of Part 2 of Division 10.5 of the Health and Safety Code. The court shall advise the person at the time of sentencing that completion of the 18-month or 30-month program, as applicable, is required in order to become eligible for a California driver's license. The court shall also advise the person that after the completion of 24 months of the revocation period, the person may apply to the court for an order granting

a restricted driver's license, subject to the following conditions:

(A) (i) The person has satisfactorily completed, subject to the current underlying conviction, the 18-month program or the initial 18 months of a licensed 30-month program, as applicable, pursuant to Section 11836 of the Health and Safety Code.

(ii) The person agrees, as a condition of the restriction, to continue satisfactory participation in the 30-month program, if applicable, and to have installed and maintained, as described in Section 23235, an ignition interlock device.

(iii) The person provides proof of responsibility to respond in damages as defined in Section 16430.

(iv) The person has not applied for and received such an order in conjunction with the current underlying conviction or a prior conviction for a violation of Section 23103, 23152, or 23153, if the prior conviction was within the previous seven years.

(B) Any individual convicted of a violation of Section 23153 punishable under Section 23190 may also, at any time after sentencing, petition the court for referral to an 18-month program or, if available in the county of the person's residence or employment, a 30-month program licensed pursuant to Chapter 9 (commencing with Section 11836) of Part 2 of Division 10.5 of the Health and Safety Code. Unless good cause is shown, the court shall order the referral.

(7) Upon a conviction or finding of a violation of Section 23152 punishable under Section 23175, the privilege shall be revoked for a period of four years. The privilege shall not be reinstated until evidence satisfactory to the department establishes that no grounds exist which would authorize the refusal to issue a license and until the person gives proof of ability to respond in damages as defined in Section 16430 and gives proof satisfactory to the department of successful completion, subsequent to the most recent underlying conviction, of an 18-month program or, if available in the county of the person's residence or employment, a 30-month program licensed pursuant to Chapter 9 (commencing with Section 11836) of Part 2 of Division 10.5 of the Health and Safety Code. The court shall advise the person at the time of sentencing that completion of an 18-month program or a 30-month program, as applicable, is required in order to become eligible for a California driver's license. The court shall also advise the person that after the completion of 24 months of the revocation period, the person may apply to the court for an order granting a restricted driver's license, subject to the following conditions:

(A) The person has satisfactorily completed, subject to the current underlying conviction, the initial 18 months of a licensed 30-month program pursuant to Section 11836 of the Health and Safety Code.

(B) The person agrees, as a condition of the restriction, to continue satisfactory participation in the 30-month program, if applicable, and to have installed and maintained, as described in Section 23235, an ignition interlock device.

(C) The person provides proof of responsibility to respond in damages as defined in Section 16430.

(D) The person has not applied for and received such an order in conjunction with the current underlying conviction or a prior conviction for violation of Section 23103, 23152, or 23153, if the prior conviction was within the previous seven years.

© 1992 by J., B. & L. Gould
Printed in the U.S.A. **EP**

(E) Any individual convicted of a violation of Section 23152 punishable under Section 23175 may also, at any time after sentencing, petition the court for referral to an 18-month program or, if available in the county of the person's residence or employment, a 30-month program licensed pursuant to Chapter 9 (commencing with Section 11836) of Part 2 of Division 10.5 of the Health and Safety Code. Unless good cause is shown, the court shall order the referral.

(8) Upon a conviction or finding of a violation of subdivision (a) of Section 23109 punishable under subdivision (e) of that section, the privilege shall be suspended for a period of 90 days to six months, if and as ordered by the court.

(9) Upon a conviction or finding of a violation of subdivision (a) of Section 23109 punishable under subdivision (f) of that section, the privilege shall be suspended for a period of six months, if the court orders the department to suspend the privilege. The privilege shall not be reinstated until the person gives proof of ability to respond in damages as defined in Section 16430.

(b) For the purpose of paragraphs (2) to (9), inclusive, of subdivision (a), the finding of the juvenile court judge, the juvenile traffic hearing officer, or the referee of a juvenile court of a commission of a violation of Section 23152 or 23153 or subdivision (a) of Section 23109, as specified in subdivision (a) of this section, is a conviction.

(c) Each judge of a juvenile court, juvenile traffic hearing officer, or referee of a juvenile court shall immediately report the findings specified in subdivision (a) to the department.

(d) A conviction of an offense in any state, territory, or possession of the United States, the District of Columbia, the Commonwealth of Puerto Rico, or the Dominion of Canada which, if committed in this state, would be a violation of Section 23152, is a conviction of Section 23152 for purposes of this section, and such a conviction of an offense which, if committed in this state, would be a violation of Section 23153, is a conviction of Section 23153 for purposes of this section. The department shall suspend or revoke the privilege to operate a motor vehicle pursuant to this section upon receiving notice of such a conviction.

(e) Whenever the driving privilege is restricted, suspended, or revoked pursuant to this section, the department shall not issue a restricted driver's license or reinstate the driving privilege unless the person gives proof of ability to respond in damages as defined in Section 16430 and maintains that proof for three years. If, at any time during that three-year period, a person who is required to maintain that proof fails to maintain that proof, the department shall suspend that person's driving privilege until the proof of ability to respond in damages is again given to the department. *(Amended by Stats 1991 ch 209 §1, eff. 1/1/92.)*

§13352.2. Conviction of a juvenile for violation of §§23152, 23153 outside of the State of California.

Any finding of a juvenile court judge, juvenile traffic hearing officer, or referee of a juvenile court of a commission of an offense in any state, territory, possession of the United States, the District of Columbia, the Commonwealth of Puerto Rico, or the Dominion of Canada which, if committed in this state, would be a violation of Section 23152, is a conviction of Section 23152 for the purposes of Sections 13352, 13352.3, and

13352.5, and the finding of a juvenile court judge juvenile traffic hearing officer, or referee of a juvenile court of a commission of an offense which, if committed in this state, would be a violation of Section 23153 is a conviction of Section 23153 for the purposes of Sections 13352, 13352.3, and 13352.5.

§13352.3. Revocation of license of a minor convicted for violation of §§23152, 23153.

(a) Notwithstanding any other provision of law, excepting paragraphs (6) and (7) of subdivision (a) of Section 12814.6, subdivisions (b), (c), and (d) of Section 13352, and Sections 13352.2 and 13367, the department shall immediately revoke the privilege to operate a motor vehicle of any person upon receipt of a duly certified abstract of the record of any court showing that the person was convicted of a violation of Section 23152 or 23153 while under 18 years of age, or upon receipt of a report of a judge of the juvenile court, a juvenile traffic hearing officer, or a referee of a juvenile court showing that the person has been found to have committed a violation of Section 23152 or 23153.

(b) The term of the revocation shall be until the person reaches 18 years of age, for one year, or for the period prescribed for restriction, suspension, or revocation specified in subdivision (a) of Section 13352, whichever is longer. The privilege shall not be reinstated until the person gives proof of ability to respond in damages as defined in Section 16430.

§13352.5. Participation in alcohol program.

(a) Unless ordered to do so by the court upon a finding that the terms and conditions of probation were violated, the department shall not suspend, pursuant to paragraph (3) of subdivision (a) of Section 13352, but shall restrict the privilege of any person to operate a motor vehicle upon a conviction or finding that the person violated Section 23152, but only if the court has certified to the department that the court has granted probation to the person on conditions which include the conditions specified in subdivision (b) of Section 23166, the court has restricted the privilege to operate a motor vehicle as provided in that subdivision, and the person gives proof of ability to respond in damages as defined in Section 16430 to the department.

(b) Unless ordered to do so by the court upon a finding that the terms and conditions of probation were violated, the department shall not revoke, pursuant to paragraph (4) of subdivision (a) of Section 13352, but shall suspend for one year and, thereafter, restrict for two additional years, the privilege of any person to operate a motor vehicle upon a conviction or finding that the person violated Section 23153, but only if the court has certified to the department that the court has granted probation to the person on conditions which include the conditions specified in subdivision (b) of Section 23186, the court has ordered the department to suspend the privilege to operate a motor vehicle as provided in that subdivision, and the person gives proof of ability to respond in damages as defined in Section 16430 to the department.

(c) Subdivisions (a) and (b) do not apply to a person who has been referred or rereferred into a program approved pursuant to Chapter 9 (commencing with Section 11837) of Part 2 of Division 10.5 of the Health and Safety Code within four years after the person ceases his or her prior participation in such a program. The four-year period shall commence either on the date the person successfully completes the program or on the date on which the person's driving privilege was suspended or revoked by the department for failure to comply with the program's rules and regulations, whichever is later. With respect to any person convicted of a violation of Section 23152 or 23153 subsequent to the commencement of a four-year period, that person's eligibility to participate in the program again for purposes of this section shall be determined on the basis of the date on which the person is alleged to have committed that offense.

(d) The restriction of the driving privilege under subdivision (a) shall become effective 30 days from the date on which the person consented to participate in the program specified in subdivision (a), excluding any time of imprisonment ordered by the court, but only if the person presents evidence satisfactory to the department that he or she is participating in the program specified in subdivision (b) of Section 23166, gives proof of ability to respond in damages as defined in Section 16430, and pays fees to the department of fifteen dollars ($15) upon application for the restricted license and twenty dollars ($20) upon completion of the treatment program or upon application for an unrestricted license, whichever is sooner. If the person fails to apply for a restricted license, fails to give proof of ability to respond in damages as defined in Section 16430, or if the person fails to show evidence of participation within 30 days, excluding the time of imprisonment ordered by the court, the department shall suspend the driving privilege of the person for the time prescribed in paragraph (3) of subdivision (a) of Section 13352.

(e) The restriction of the driving privilege under subdivision (b) shall become effective 30 days from the end of the period of suspension, but only if the person presents evidence satisfactory to the department that he or she is participating in the program specified in subdivision (b) of Section 23186, gives proof of ability to respond in damages as defined in Section 16430, and pays fees to the department of fifteen dollars ($15) upon application for the restricted license and twenty dollars ($20) upon completion of the treatment program or upon application for an unrestricted license, whichever is sooner. If the person fails to apply for a restricted license, fails to give proof of ability to respond in damages as defined in Section 16430, or if the person fails to show evidence of participation within 30 days from the end of the period of suspension, excluding any time of imprisonment ordered by the court to be served after the end of the period of suspension, the department shall revoke the driving privilege of the person for the time prescribed in paragraph (4) of subdivision (a) of Section 13352.

(f) The driving privilege restricted under subdivision (a) or (b) shall be limited to the hours for driving to and from the place of employment and during the course of employment and driving to and from activities required in an alcohol treatment program specified in subdivision (b) of Section 23166 or subdivision (b) of Section 23186. The department may set forth the times and days of restricted operation established by the court either on a special restricted license or upon the usual license form. Whenever the driving privilege is restricted under subdivision (a) or (b), proof of ability to respond in damages as defined in Section 16430 shall be maintained for three years. If the person maintains proof of ability to respond in damages as defined in Section 16430, the restriction

shall continue in full force and effect until the person presents evidence satisfactory to the department that the person has completed the alcohol treatment program. Except as provided in Section 23168, in no event shall the length of the restriction for a person subject to subdivision (a) be less than the total time of restriction specified in subdivision (b) of Section 23166. In no event shall the total time of suspension and restriction for a person subject to subdivision (b) be less than the applicable period of revocation under paragraph (4) of subdivision (a) of Section 13352.

(g) Except as provided in this subdivision, the department shall suspend or revoke the driving privilege for the time prescribed in paragraph (3) or (4) of subdivision (a) of Section 13352, 60 days from the date that the department notifies the person and the court of the intended action pursuant to subdivision (a) of Section 11837.1 of the Health and Safety Code, or the date ending the additional time ordered by the court under this subdivision, whichever is later. If the person presents evidence satisfactory to the department that the court of jurisdiction has consented to the person's reinstatement in the program and gives proof of ability to respond in damages as defined in Section 16430, the department shall continue in effect the restriction granted under subdivision (c), unless the person has previously been reinstated in the program on two or more occasions, in which case the department shall suspend or revoke the driving privilege for the time prescribed in paragraph (3) or (4) of subdivision (a) of Section 13352. The evidence shall be presented within 45 days of the notice from the department of the intended action or such additional time, not to exceed an additional 45 days, for the determination as is required, ordered, and transmitted to the department by the court, which additional time is not caused by any action or failure to act by the person.

(h) All abstracts of record showing a conviction that are forwarded to the department pursuant to Section 1803 shall state whether the court has granted probation to the person on conditions which include the conditions specified in subdivision (b) of Section 23166 or subdivision (b) of Section 23186 and state the date on which the person consented to participate in the program.

(i) The department, in cooperation with the State Department of Alcohol and Drug Programs, shall adopt such regulations as it deems necessary to implement this section.

(j) This section does not apply to persons whose offense occurred in a vehicle requiring a driver with a class 1 or class 2 driver's license or with a certificate specified in Section 12804.1. (*Amended by Stats 1988 ch 1453 §5, eff. 1/1/89.*)

§13353. Implied consent for chemical testing of blood, breath or urine.

(a) If any person refuses the officer's request to submit to, or fails to complete, a chemical test or tests pursuant to Section 23157, upon receipt of the officer's sworn statement that the officer had reasonable cause to believe the person had been driving a motor vehicle in violation of Section 23152 or 23153 and that the person had refused to submit to, or did not complete, the test or tests after being requested by the officer, the department shall (1) suspend the person's privilege to operate a motor vehicle for a period of one year, (2) revoke the person's privilege to operate a

© 1992 by J., B. & L. Gould
Printed in the U.S.A.   **EP**

motor vehicle for a period of two years if the refusal occurred within seven years of (A) a separate violation of Section 23103 as specified in Section 23103.5, Section 23152, or Section 23153 of this code, or Section 191.5 or paragraph (3) of subdivision (c) of Section 192 of the Penal Code, which resulted in a conviction, or (B) a suspension or revocation of the person's privilege to operate a motor vehicle pursuant to this section or Section 13353.2 for an offense which occurred on a separate occasion, or (3) revoke the person's privilege to operate a motor vehicle for a period of three years if the refusal occurred within seven years of (A) two or more separate violations of Section 23103 as specified in Section 23103.5, Section 23152, or Section 23153 of this code, or Section 191.5 of* paragraph (3) of subdivision (c) of Section 192 of the Penal Code, which resulted in convictions, (B) two or more suspensions or revocations of the person's privilege to operate a motor vehicle pursuant to this section or Section 13353.2 for offenses which occurred on separate occasions, or (C) any combination of two or more of those convictions or administrative suspensions or revocations. The officer's sworn statement shall be submitted pursuant to Section 23158.2 on a form furnished or approved by the department. The suspension or revocation shall not become effective until 45 days after the giving of written notice thereof, or until the end of any stay of the suspension or revocation, as provided for in Section 13558.

*So in original. Probably should be "or".

(b) The notice of the order of suspension or revocation under this section shall be served on the person by a peace officer pursuant to Section 23157. The notice of the order of suspension or revocation shall be on a form provided by the department. If the notice of the order of suspension or revocation has not been served by the peace officer pursuant to Section 23157, the department shall immediately notify the person in writing of the action taken.

(c) Upon receipt of the officer's sworn statement, the department shall review the record. For purposes of this section, the scope of the administrative review shall cover the issues of whether the peace officer had reasonable cause to believe the person had been driving a motor vehicle in violation of Section 23152 or 23153, whether the person was placed under arrest, whether the person refused to submit to, or did not complete, the test or tests after being requested by a peace officer, and whether, except for the persons described in subdivision (a) of Section 23157 who are incapable of refusing, the person had been told that his or her driving privilege would be suspended or revoked if he or she refused to submit to, or did not complete, the test or tests.

(d) The person may request an administrative hearing pursuant to Section 13558. Except as provided in subdivision (e) of Section 13558, the request for an administrative hearing does not stay the order of suspension or revocation.

(e) This section shall remain in effect only until January 1, 1992, and as of that date is repealed. (Amended by Stats 1990 ch 431 §1.7, eff. 7/26/90 only until 1/1/92. See other sections 13353 below.)

§13353. Implied consent for chemical testing of blood, breath or urine.

(a) If any person refuses the officer's request to submit to, or fails to complete, a chemical test or tests pursuant to Section 23157, upon receipt of the officer's sworn statement that the officer had reasonable cause to believe the person had been driving a motor vehicle in violation of Section 23152 or 23153 and that the person had refused to submit to, or did not complete, the test or tests after being requested by the officer, the department shall (1) suspend the person's privilege to operate a motor vehicle for a period of one year, (2) revoke the person's privilege to operate a motor vehicle for a period of two years if the refusal occurred within seven years of (A) a separate violation of Section 23103 as specified in Section 23103.5, Section 23152, or Section 23153 of this code, or Section 191.5 or paragraph (3) of subdivision (c) of Section 192 of the Penal Code, which resulted in a conviction, or (B) a suspension or revocation of the person's privilege to operate a motor vehicle pursuant to this section or Section 13353.2 for an offense which occurred on a separate occasion, or (3) revoke the person's privilege to operate a motor vehicle for a period of three years if the refusal occurred within seven years of (A) two or more separate violations of Section 23103 as specified in Section 23103.5, Section 23152, or Section 23153 of this code, or Section 191.5 or paragraph (3) of subdivision (c) of Section 192 of the Penal Code, or any combination thereof, which resulted in convictions, (B) two or more suspensions or revocations of the person's privilege to operate a motor vehicle pursuant to this section or Section 13353.2 for offenses which occurred on separate occasions, or (C) any combination of two or more of those convictions or administrative suspensions or revocations. The officer's sworn statement shall be submitted pursuant to Section 23158.2 on a form furnished or approved by the department. The suspension or revocation shall not become effective until 45 days after the giving of written notice thereof, or until the end of any stay of the suspension or revocation, as provided for in Section 13558.

(b) The notice of the order of suspension or revocation under this section shall be served on the person by a peace officer pursuant to Section 23157. The notice of the order of suspension or revocation shall be on a form provided by the department. If the notice of the order of suspension or revocation has not been served by the peace officer pursuant to Section 23157, the department shall immediately notify the person in writing of the action taken.

(c) Upon receipt of the officer's sworn statement, the department shall review the record. For purposes of this section, the scope of the administrative review shall cover the issues of whether the peace officer had reasonable cause to believe the person had been driving a motor vehicle in violation of Section 23152 or 23153, whether the person was placed under arrest, whether the person refused to submit to, or did not complete, the test or tests after being requested by a peace officer, and whether, except for the persons described in subdivision (a) of Section 23157 who are incapable of refusing, the person had been told that his or her driving privilege would be suspended or revoked if he or she refused to submit to, or did not complete, the test or tests.

(d) The person may request an administrative hearing pursuant to Section 13558. Except as provided in subdivision (e) of Section 13558, the request for an administrative hearing does not stay the order of suspension or revocation.

(e) If any person who was driving a commercial motor vehicle, as defined in Section 15210, refuses the officer's request to submit to, or fails to complete, a chemical test or tests pursuant to Section 23157, upon receipt of the officer's sworn statement that the officer had reasonable cause to believe the person had been driving a commercial motor vehicle, as defined in Section 15210, in violation of Section 23152 or 23153 and that the person had refused to submit to, or did not complete, the test or tests after being requested by the officer, the department shall suspend or revoke the person's privilege to operate a commercial motor vehicle for the period specified in Section 13352 for conviction of a violation of Section 23152, including any applicable enhancement for convictions of other separate offenses, as specified in that section. The officer's sworn statement shall be submitted on a form furnished or approved by the department. Subdivisions (b), (c), and (d) apply to actions taken under this subdivision.

(f) This section shall become operative on January 1, 1992, and shall remain operative until the director determines that federal regulations adopted pursuant to the Commercial Motor Vehicle Safety Act of 1986 (49 U.S.C. Sec. 2701 et seq.) contained in Section 383.51 or 391.15 of Title 49 of the Code of Federal Regulations do not require the state to suspend a person's commercial driver's license if that person refuses to submit to testing of his or her blood for the concentration of alcohol therein.

(g) The director shall submit a notice of the determination under subdivision (f) to the Secretary of State, and this section shall be repealed upon the receipt of that notice by the Secretary of State. *(Amended by Stats 1990 ch 431 §2, eff. 7/26/90, oper. 1/1/92, eff. until receipt of notice under subd. (g) by the Secretary of State. See other sections 13353 above and below.)*

§13353. Implied consent for chemical testing of blood, breath or urine.

(a) If any person refuses the officer's request to submit to, or fails to complete, a chemical test or tests pursuant to Section 23157, upon receipt of the officer's sworn statement that the officer had reasonable cause to believe the person had been driving a motor vehicle in violation of Section 23152 or 23153 and that the person had refused to submit to, or did not complete, the test or tests after being requested by the officer, the department shall (1) suspend the person's privilege to operate a motor vehicle for a period of one year, (2) revoke the person's privilege to operate a motor vehicle for a period of two years if the refusal occurred within seven years of a separate violation of Section 23103 as specified in Section 23103.5, Section 23152, or Section 23153 of this code, or Section 191.5 or paragraph (3) of subdivision (c) of Section 192 of the Penal Code, which resulted in a conviction, or if the person's privilege to operate a motor vehicle has been previously suspended or revoked pursuant to this section or Section 13353.2 for an offense which occurred on a separate occasion, or (3) revoke the person's privilege to operate a motor vehicle for a period of three years if the refusal occurred within seven years of (A) two or more separate violations of Section 23103 as specified in Section 23103.5, Section 23152, or Section 23153 of this code, or Section 191.5 or paragraph (3) of subdivision (c) of Section 192 of the Penal Code, or any combination thereof, which resulted in convictions, (B) two or more previous suspensions or revocations of the person's privilege to operate a motor vehicle pursuant to this section or

Section 13353.2 for offenses which occurred on separate occasions, or (C) any combination of two or more of those convictions or administrative suspensions or revocations. The officer's sworn statement shall be submitted pursuant to Section 23158.2 on a form furnished or approved by the department. The suspension or revocation shall not become effective until 45 days after the giving of written notice thereof, or until the end of any stay of the suspension or revocation, as provided for in Section 13558.

(b) The notice of the order of suspension or revocation under this section shall be served on the person by a peace officer pursuant to Section 23157. The notice of the order of suspension or revocation shall be on a form provided by the department. If the notice of the order of suspension or revocation has not been served by the peace officer pursuant to Section 23157, the department shall immediately notify the person in writing of the action taken.

(c) Upon receipt of the officer's sworn statement, the department shall review the record. For purposes of this section, the scope of the administrative review shall cover the issues of whether the peace officer had reasonable cause to believe the person had been driving a motor vehicle in violation of Section 23152 or 23153, whether the person was placed under arrest, whether the person refused to submit to, or did not complete, the test or tests after being requested by a peace officer, and whether, except for the persons described in subdivision (a) of Section 23157 who are incapable of refusing, the person had been told that his or her driving privilege would be suspended or revoked if he or she refused to submit to, or did not complete, the test or tests.

(d) The person may request an administrative hearing pursuant to Section 13558. Except as provided in subdivision (e) of Section 13558, the request for an administrative hearing does not stay the order of suspension.

(e) This section shall become operative only upon the receipt by the Secretary of State of the notice specified in subdivision (g) of Section 13353, as added by Section 4 of Chapter 1460 of the Statutes of 1989. *(Amended by Stats 1990 ch 431 §3, eff. 7/26/90, oper. upon receipt of notice under subd. (g) in 2nd section 13353 by Secretary of State. See other sections 13353 above.)*

§13353.2. Suspension of license.

(a) The department shall immediately suspend the privilege of any person to operate a motor vehicle if the person was driving or was in actual physical control of a motor vehicle when the person had 0.08 percent or more, by weight, of alcohol in his or her blood.

(b) The notice of the order of suspension under this section shall be served on the person by a peace officer pursuant to Section 23158.5. The notice of the order of suspension shall be on a form provided by the department. If the notice of the order of suspension has not been served upon the person by the peace officer pursuant to Section 23158.5, upon the receipt of the report of a peace officer submitted pursuant to Section 23158.2, the department shall mail written notice of the order of the suspension to the person at the last known address shown on the department's records and, if the address of the person provided by the peace officer's report differs from the address of record, to that address.

© 1992 by J., B. & L. Gould
Printed in the U.S.A.　　**EP**

(c) The notice of the order of suspension shall clearly specify the reason and statutory grounds for the suspension, the effective date of the suspension, the right of the person to request an administrative hearing, the procedure for requesting an administrative hearing, and the date by which a request for an administrative hearing shall be made in order to receive a determination prior to the effective date of the suspension.

(d) The department shall make a determination of the facts in subdivision (a) on the basis of the report of a peace officer submitted pursuant to Section 23158.2. The determination of the facts, after administrative review pursuant to Section 13557, by the department is final, unless an administrative hearing is held pursuant to Section 13558 and any judicial review of the administrative determination after the hearing pursuant to Section 13559 is final.

(e) The determination of the facts in subdivision (a) is a civil matter which is independent of the determination of the person's guilt or innocence, shall have no collateral estoppel effect on a subsequent criminal prosecution, and shall not preclude the litigation of the same or similar facts in the criminal proceeding. If a person is acquitted of criminal charges relating to a determination of facts under subdivision (a), the department shall immediately reinstate the person's privilege to operate a motor vehicle if the department has suspended it administratively pursuant to subdivision (a), and the department shall return or reissue for the remaining term any driver's license which has been taken from the person pursuant to Section 23158.5 or otherwise. No fee shall be imposed pursuant to Section 14905 for the return or reissuing of a driver's license pursuant to this subdivision. The disposition of a suspension action under this section does not affect any action to suspend or revoke the person's privilege to operate a motor vehicle under any other provision of this code, including, but not limited to, Section 13352 or 13353, or Chapter 3 (commencing with Section 13800). (Amended by Stats 1990 ch 431 §4, eff. 7/26/90.)

§13353.3. Suspension of license; time of effect.

(a) An order of suspension of a person's privilege to operate a motor vehicle pursuant to Section 13353.2 shall become effective 45 days after the person is served with the notice pursuant to Section 23158.5 or subdivision (b) of Section 13353.2.

(b) The period of suspension of a person's privilege to operate a motor vehicle under Section 13353.2 is as follows:

(1) Except as provided in Section 13353.6, if the person has not been convicted of a separate violation of Section 23103 as specified in Section 23103.5, Section 23152, or Section 23153 of this code, or Section 191.5 or paragraph (3) of subdivision (c) of Section 192 of the Penal Code, or the person has not been administratively determined to have refused chemical testing pursuant to Section 13353 or to have been driving with an excessive concentration of alcohol pursuant to Section 13353.2 on a separate occasion, which offense or occurrence occurred within seven years of the occasion in question, the person's privilege to operate a motor vehicle shall be suspended for four months.

(2) If the person has been convicted of one or more separate violations of Section 23103 as specified in Section 23103.5, Section 23152, or Section 23153 of

this code, or Section 191.5 or paragraph (3) of subdivision (c) of Section 192 of the Penal Code, or the person has been administratively determined to have refused chemical testing pursuant to Section 13353 or to have been driving with an excessive concentration of alcohol pursuant to Section 13353.2 on a separate occasion, which offense or occasion occurred within seven years of the occasion in question, the person's privilege to operate a motor vehicle shall be suspended for one year.

(c) If a person's privilege to operate a motor vehicle is suspended pursuant to Section 13353.2 and the person is convicted of a violation of Section 23152 or 23153, including a violation described in Section 23156, arising out of the same occurrence, both the suspension under Section 13353.2 and the suspension or revocation under Section 13352 shall be imposed, except that, notwithstanding Section 13354, the periods of suspension or revocation shall run concurrently, and the total period of suspension or revocation shall not exceed the longer of the two suspension or revocation periods. This subdivision shall not affect a suspension or revocation pursuant to Section 13353 for refusal to submit to chemical testing or the imposition of consecutive periods of suspension or revocation pursuant to Section 13354 for that refusal. (Amended by Stats 1990 ch 431 §5, eff. 7/26/90.)

§13353.4. Nonrestoration of driving privilege.

(a) Except as provided in subdivision (b) of Section 13353.6 or Section 13353.7, the driving privilege shall not be restored, and no restricted or hardship permit to operate a motor vehicle shall be issued, to a person during the suspension or revocation period specified in Section 13353 or 13353.3.

(b) The privilege to operate a motor vehicle shall not be restored after a suspension or revocation pursuant to Section 13352, 13353, or 13353.2 until all applicable reinstatement fees, including the fees prescribed in Section 14905, have been paid and the person gives proof of financial responsibility as defined in Section 16430 to the department.

(c) The privilege to operate a motor vehicle shall not be restored after a suspension or revocation pursuant to Section 13352 until the person gives proof satisfactory to the department of completion of a program approved pursuant to Section 23161 or completion of a program licensed pursuant to Chapter 9 (commencing with Section 11836) of Part 2 of Division 10.5 of the Health and Safety Code for any other person whose driving privilege is suspended or revoked pursuant to Section 13352.

(d) For purposes of this section, completion of a program is the satisfactory completion of all program service requirements approved pursuant to program licensure, and any other court-imposed conditions, as evidenced by a certificate of completion issued by the licensed program. (Amended by Stats 1991 ch 990 §1, eff. 10/14/91.)

§13353.6. Reissuance of commercial driver's license after suspension.

(a) If the person's driver's license is a commercial driver's license, as defined in Section 15210, and if the person has not had a separate violation of Section 23103 as specified in Section 23103.5, Section 23152, or Section 23153 of this code, or Section 191.5 or paragraph (3) of subdivision (c) of Section 192 of the Penal Code which resulted in a conviction, and if the person's privilege to operate a motor vehicle has not been previously suspended or revoked pursuant to Section 13353 or 13353.2 for an offense which occurred on a separate occasion, notwithstanding Section 13551, the department shall, upon receiving the officer's sworn statement and the receipt of the person's driver's license and after review pursuant to subdivision (d) of Section 13353.2, suspend the person's privilege to operate a motor vehicle for 30 days, and then reissue the person a commercial driver's license with restrictions, as follows:

(1) The restricted commercial driver's license shall authorize the operation of a motor vehicle only to and from, and in the course and scope of, the person's employment.

(2) The term of the restricted license is 30 days after the date that the order of suspension is effective pursuant to Section 13353.3 until six months after that date.

(b) The person may be issued an unrestricted commercial driver's license after the term of restriction under this section.

(c) This section applies only to the holder of a commercial driver's license who was not operating a commercial vehicle, as defined in Section 15210, at the time of the offense. *(Amended by Stats 1990 ch 431 §7, eff. 7/26/90.)*

§13353.7. Restricted license.

(a) Subject to subdivision (c) and except as provided in Section 13353.6 for persons who have commercial driver's licenses, if the person whose driving privilege has been suspended under Section 13353.2 has not been convicted of, or found to have committed, a separate violation of Section 23103 as specified in Section 23103.5, Section 23152, or Section 23153 of this code, or Section 191.5 or paragraph (3) of subdivision (c) of Section 192 of the Penal Code, and if the person's privilege to operate a motor vehicle has not been suspended or revoked pursuant to Section 13353 or 13353.2 for an offense which occurred on a separate occasion within seven years of the occasion in question and, if the person subsequently enrolls in a program described in subdivision (b) of Section 23161, that person may apply to the department for a restricted driver's license limited to travel to and from the activities required by the program. After receiving proof of enrollment in the program, and if the person has not been arrested subsequent to the offense for which the person's driving privilege has been suspended under Section 13353.2 for a violation of Section 23103 as specified in Section 23103.5, Section 23152, or Section 23153 of this code, or Section 191.5 or paragraph (3) of subdivision (c) of Section 192 of the Penal Code, and if the person's privilege to operate a motor vehicle has not been suspended or revoked pursuant to Section 13353 or 13353.2 for an offense which occurred on a separate occasion, notwithstanding Section 13551, the department shall, after review pursuant to Section 13557, suspend the person's privilege to operate a motor vehicle for 30 days and then issue the person a restricted driver's license under the following conditions:

(1) The program shall report any failure to participate in the program to the department and shall certify successful completion of the program to the department.

(2) The person gives proof of financial responsibility as defined in Section 16430.

(3) The restricted driver's license authorizes the operation of a motor vehicle only to and from the activities required under the program.

(4) If any person who has been issued a restricted license under this section fails at any time to participate in the program, the department shall suspend the restricted license immediately. The department shall give notice of the suspension under this paragraph in the same manner as prescribed in subdivision (b) of Section 13353.2 for the period specified in Section 13353.3, which is effective upon receipt by the person.

(5) On or after 60 days after the effective date of the restricted license, and upon notification of successful completion of the program, the department may issue an unrestricted driver's license to the person.

(b) If the court of jurisdiction in a criminal action arising out of the same offense orders the department to suspend or revoke the person's privilege to operate a motor vehicle or does not grant probation after conviction of that offense, notwithstanding subdivision (a), the department shall suspend or revoke the person's privilege pursuant to the order of the court or Section 13352.

(c) If the holder of a commercial driver's license was operating a commercial vehicle, as defined in Section 15210, at the time of the violation which resulted in the suspension of that person's driving privilege under Section 13353.2, the department shall, pursuant to this section, if the person is otherwise eligible, issue the person a class C driver's license restricted in the same manner and subject to the same conditions as specified in subdivision (a).

(d) This section does not apply to a person whose driving privilege has been suspended or revoked pursuant to the order of the court or Section 13353 or 13353.2 for an offense which occurred on a separate occasion, or as a result of a conviction of a separate violation of Section 23103, as specified in Section 23103.5, Section 23152, or Section 23153, which violation occurred within seven years of the offense in question. This subdivision shall be operative only so long as a one-year suspension of the driving privilege for a second or subsequent occurrence or offense, with no restricted or hardship licenses permitted, is required by Section 408 or 410 of Title 23 of the United States Code. *(Amended by Stats 1990 ch 216 §116, eff. 1/1/91; ch 431 §8, eff. 7/26/90.)*

§13354. License suspension to run consecutively with sanctions of conviction.

(a) Notwithstanding Section 13366, if (1) an abstract of conviction is received by the department for an offense which requires the department to restrict, suspend, or revoke the privilege to operate a motor vehicle of a person after conviction or finding of a violation pursuant to Section 13352 or 13352.5, (2) there is a suspension of that person's privilege to operate a motor vehicle already in effect for refusal to consent to, or for failure to complete, a chemical test pursuant to Section 13353 or a suspension already in effect for driving with an excessive alcohol content in the person's blood pursuant to Section 13353.2, (3) that suspension is administratively final and resulted from the same arrest, and (4) the sentencing court orders these restrictions, suspensions, revocations, or a combination thereof to run consecutively, then the restriction, suspension, or revocation resulting from the conviction or finding pursuant to Section 13352 or

© 1992 by J., B. & L. Gould
Printed in the U.S.A.　EP

13352.5 shall commence after the suspension already in effect pursuant to Section 13353 or 13353.2 has terminated, except as provided in subdivision (c) of Section 13353.3.

(b) Notwithstanding Section 13366, if (1) the department is required to suspend a person's privilege to operate a motor vehicle for refusal to consent to, or for failure to complete, a chemical test pursuant to Section 13353 or to suspend a person's privilege to operate a motor vehicle for driving with an excessive alcohol content in the person's blood pursuant to Section 13353.2, (2) there is a restriction, suspension, or revocation of the person's privilege to operate a motor vehicle already in effect for a conviction or finding of a violation pursuant to Section 13352 or 13352.5 which resulted from the same arrest, and (3) the sentencing court orders these restrictions, suspensions, revocations, or a combination thereof to run consecutively, then the suspension for refusal to consent to, or for failure to complete, the chemical test pursuant to Section 13353 or the suspension of that person's privilege to operate a motor vehicle already in effect for driving with an excessive alcohol content in the person's blood pursuant to Section 13353.2 shall commence after the restriction, suspension, or revocation already in effect pursuant to Section 13352 or 13352.5 has terminated, except as provided in subdivision (c) of Section 13353.3.

(c) The purpose of this section is to require that any suspension under Section 13353 or 13353.2 and any restriction, suspension or revocation under Section 13352 or 13352.5 resulting from the same arrest are cumulative and shall be imposed consecutively, if so ordered by the court. *(Amended and renumbered by 1989 ch 1460 §6, eff. 7/1/90; formerly §13353.1.)*

§13355. License suspension for driving over 100 miles per hour.

The department shall immediately suspend the privilege of any person to operate a motor vehicle upon receipt of a duly certified abstract of the record of any court showing that the person has been convicted of a violation of subdivision (b) of Section 22348, or upon a receipt of a report of a judge of a juvenile court, a juvenile traffic hearing officer, or a referee of a juvenile court showing that the person has been found to have committed a violation of subdivision (b) of Section 22348 under the following conditions and for the periods, as follows:

(a) Upon a conviction or finding of an offense under subdivision (b) of Section 22348 which occurred within three years of a prior offense resulting in a conviction of an offense under subdivision (b) of Section 22348, the privilege shall be suspended for a period of six months, or the privilege shall be restricted for six months to necessary travel to and from the person's place of employment and, if driving a motor vehicle is necessary to perform the duties of the person's employment, restricted to driving within the person's scope of employment.

(b) Upon a conviction or finding of an offense under subdivision (b) of Section 22348 which occurred within five years of two or more prior offenses resulting in convictions of offenses under subdivision (b) of Section 22348, the privilege shall be suspended for a period of one year, or the privilege shall be restricted for one year to necessary travel to and from the person's place of employment and, if driving a motor vehicle is necessary to perform the duties of the person's employment,

restricted to driving within the person's scope of employment.

§13357. License revocation or suspension for auto theft.

Upon the recommendation of the court the department shall suspend or revoke the privilege to operate a motor vehicle of any person who has been found guilty of a violation of Section 10851.

§13359. Grounds for license suspension or revocation.

The department may suspend or revoke the privilege of any person to operate a motor vehicle upon any of the grounds which authorize the refusal to issue a license.

§13360. Suspension or revocation for violating restrictions of license.

Upon receiving satisfactory evidence of any violation of the restrictions of a driver's license, the department may suspend or revoke the same.

§13361. Offenses which may result in license suspension.

The department may suspend the privilege of any person to operate a motor vehicle upon receipt of a duly certified abstract of the record of any court showing that the person has been convicted of any of the following crimes or offenses:

(a) Failure to stop in the event of an accident resulting in damage to property only, or otherwise failing to comply with the requirements of Section 20002.

(b) A second or subsequent conviction of reckless driving.

(c) Manslaughter resulting from the operation of a motor vehicle as provided in paragraph (2) of subdivision (c) of Section 192 of the Penal Code.

In any case under this section the department is authorized to require proof of ability to respond in damages as defined in Section 16430. *(Amended by Stats 1985 ch 6 §3.)*

CHAPTER 4

VIOLATION OF LICENSE PROVISIONS

§14601. Penalties for driving with a license revoked or suspended for negligent or reckless driving.

(a) No person shall drive a motor vehicle at any time when that person's driving privilege is suspended or revoked for reckless driving in violation of Section 23103 or 23104, any reason listed in subdivision (a) or (c) of Section 12806 authorizing the department to refuse to issue a license, negligent or incompetent operation of a motor vehicle as prescribed in subdivision (e) of Section 12809, or negligent operation as prescribed in Section 12810, and when the person so driving has knowledge of the suspension or revocation. Knowledge shall be presumed if notice has been given by the department to the person. The presumption established by this subdivision is a presumption affecting the burden of proof.

(b) Any person convicted under this section shall be punished as follows:

(1) Upon a first conviction, by imprisonment in the county jail for not less than five days or more than six

months and by fine of not less than three hundred dollars ($300) or more than one thousand dollars ($1,000).

(2) If the offense occurred within five years of a prior offense which resulted in a conviction of a violation of this section or Section 14601.1 or 14601.2, by imprisonment in the county jail for not less than 10 days or more than one year and by fine of not less than five hundred dollars ($500) or more than two thousand dollars ($2,000).

(c) If the offense occurred within five years of a prior offense which resulted in a conviction of a violation of this section or Section 14601.1 or 14601.2 and is granted probation, the court shall impose as a condition of probation that the person be confined in the county jail for at least 10 days.

(d) Nothing in this section prohibits a person from driving a motor vehicle, which is owned or utilized by the person's employer, during the course of employment on private property which is owned or utilized by the employer, except an offstreet parking facility as defined in subdivision (c) of Section 12500. (Amended by Stats 1987 ch 321 §8.)

§14601.1. Penalties for driving with license revoked or suspended for other reasons.

(a) No person shall drive a motor vehicle when his or her driving privilege is suspended or revoked for any reason other than those listed in Section 14601 or 14601.2 and when the person so driving has knowledge of the suspension or revocation. Knowledge shall be presumed if notice has been given by the department to the person. The presumption established by this subdivision is a presumption affecting the burden of proof.

(b) Any person convicted under this section shall be punished as follows:

(1) Upon a first conviction, by imprisonment in the county jail for not more than six months or by a fine of not less than three hundred dollars ($300) or more than one thousand dollars ($1,000), or by both that fine and imprisonment.

(2) If the offense occurred within five years of a prior offense which resulted in a conviction of a violation of this section or Section 14601 or 14601.2, by imprisonment in the county jail for not less than five days or more than one year and by a fine of not less than five hundred dollars ($500) or more than two thousand dollars ($2,000).

(c) Nothing in this section prohibits a person from driving a motor vehicle, which is owned or utilized by the person's employer, during the course of employment on private property which is owned or utilized by the employer, except an offstreet parking facility as defined in subdivision (c) of Section 12500. (Amended by Stats 1986 ch 1306 §10.)

§14601.2. Penalties for driving with license revoked or suspended for driving while under the influence.

(a) No person shall drive a motor vehicle at any time when that person's driving privilege is suspended or revoked for a conviction of a violation of Section 23152 or 23153, and when the person so driving has knowledge of the suspension or revocation.

(b) Except in full compliance with the restriction, no person shall drive a motor vehicle at any time when that person's driving privilege is restricted pursuant to Article 2 (commencing with Section 23152) of Chapter 12 of Division 11, and when the person so driving has knowledge of the restriction.

(c) Knowledge of suspension or revocation of the driving privilege shall be presumed if notice has been given by the department to the person and knowledge of restriction of the driving privilege shall be presumed if notice has been given by the court to the person. The presumption established by this subdivision is a presumption affecting the burden of proof.

(d) Any person convicted of a violation of this section shall be punished as follows:

(1) Upon a first conviction, by imprisonment in the county jail for not less than 10 days or more than six months and by a fine of not less than three hundred dollars ($300) or more than one thousand dollars ($1,000), unless the person has been designated an habitual traffic offender under subdivision (b) of Section 23170 or subdivision (b) of Section 23175, in which case the person shall, in addition, be sentenced as provided in paragraph (3) of subdivision (e) of Section 14601.3.

(2) If the offense occurred within five years of a prior offense which resulted in a conviction of a violation of this section or Section 14601, by imprisonment in the county jail for not less than 30 days or more than one year and by a fine of not less than five hundred dollars ($500) or more than two thousand dollars ($2,000), unless the person has been designated an habitual traffic offender under subdivision (b) of Section 23170 or subdivision (b) of Section 23175, in which case the person shall, in addition, be sentenced as provided in paragraph (3) of subdivision (e) of Section 14601.3.

(e) If any person is convicted of a first offense under this section and is granted probation, the court shall impose as a condition of probation that the person be confined in the county jail for at least 10 days.

(f) If the offense occurred within five years of a prior offense which resulted in a conviction of a violation of this section or Section 14601 and is granted probation, the court shall impose as a condition of probation that the person be confined in the county jail for at least 30 days.

(g) If any person is convicted of a second or subsequent offense which results in a conviction of this section within seven years, but over five years, of a prior offense which resulted in a conviction of a violation of this section or Section 14601 or 14601.1 and is granted probation, the court shall impose as a condition of probation that the person be confined in the county jail for at least 10 days.

(h) Nothing in this section prohibits a person who is participating in, or has completed, an alcohol or drug rehabilitation program from driving a motor vehicle, which is owned or utilized by the person's employer, during the course of employment on private property which is owned or utilized by the employer, except an offstreet parking facility as defined in subdivision (c) of Section 12500.

(i) Nothing in this section prohibits a person with a suspended license from driving a motor vehicle when emergency medical service is needed immediately. (Amended by Stats 1989 ch 1460 §17, eff. 7/1/90.)

§14601.3. Procedures and penalties for habitual traffic offenders.

(a) It is unlawful for a person whose driving privilege has been suspended or revoked to accumulate a driving record history which results from driv-

© 1992 by J., B. & L. Gould
Printed in the U.S.A.   EP

ing during the period of suspension or revocation. A person who violates this subdivision is designated an habitual traffic offender.

For purposes of this section, a driving record history means any of the following, if the driving occurred during any period of suspension or revocation which resulted from a conviction of an offense or offenses of driving under the influence of alcohol or drugs, or both, or from negligent driving:

(1) Two or more convictions within a 12-month period of an offense given a violation point count of two pursuant to Section 12810.

(2) Three or more convictions within a 12-month period of an offense given a violation point count of one pursuant to Section 12810.

(3) Three or more accidents within a 12-month period that are subject to the reporting requirements of Section 16000.

(4) Any combination of convictions or accidents, as specified in paragraphs (1) to (3), inclusive, which results during any 12-month period in a violation point count of three or more pursuant to Section 12810.

(b) Knowledge of suspension or revocation of the driving privilege shall be presumed if notice has been given by the department to the person. The presumption established by this subdivision is a presumption affecting the burden of proof.

(c) The department, within 30 days of receipt of a duly certified abstract of the record of any court or accident report which results in a person being designated an habitual traffic offender, may execute and transmit by mail a notice of that designation to the office of the district attorney having jurisdiction over the location of the person's last known address as contained in the department's records.

(d) (1) The district attorney, within 30 days of receiving the notice required in subdivision (c), shall inform the department of whether or not the person will be prosecuted for being an habitual traffic offender.

(2) Notwithstanding any other provision of this section, any habitual traffic offender designated under subdivision (b) of Section 23170 or subdivision (b) of Section 23175 who is convicted of violating Section 14601.2 shall be sentenced as provided in paragraph (3) of subdivision (e).

(e) Any person convicted under this section of being an habitual traffic offender shall be punished as follows:

(1) Upon a first conviction, by imprisonment in the county jail for 30 days and by a fine of one thousand dollars ($1,000).

(2) Upon a second or any subsequent offense within seven years of a prior conviction under this section, by imprisonment in the county jail for 180 days and by a fine of two thousand dollars ($2,000).

(3) Any habitual traffic offender designated under Section 193.7 of the Penal Code or under subdivision (b) of Section 23170, subdivision (b) of Section 23175, or subdivision (b) of Section 23190 who is convicted of a violation of Section 14601.2 shall be punished by imprisonment in the county jail for 180 days and by a fine of two thousand dollars ($2,000). The penalty in this paragraph shall be consecutive to that imposed for the violation of any other law. *(Amended by Stats 1990 ch 44 §4, eff. 1/1/91.)*

§14601.4. Causing injury while driving with suspended or revoked license.

(a) It is unlawful for any person, while driving a vehicle with a license suspended or revoked pursuant to Section 14601.2 to do any act forbidden by law or neglect any duty imposed by law in the driving of the vehicle, which act or neglect proximately causes bodily injury to any person other than the driver. In proving the person neglected any duty imposed by law in the driving of the vehicle, it is not necessary to prove that any specific section of this code was violated.

(b) Any person convicted under this section shall be imprisoned in the county jail and shall not be released upon work release, community service, or any other release program before the minimum period of imprisonment, prescribed in Section 14601.2, is served. If a person is convicted of such an offense and is granted probation, the court shall require that the person convicted serve at least the minimum time of imprisonment, as specified in those sections, as a term or condition of probation. *(Added by Stats 1988 ch 1254 §4, eff. 1/1/89.)*

§14602. Impounding a motor vehicle.

(a) (1) Whenever a person is convicted of any of the following offenses committed while driving a motor vehicle of which he or she is the owner, the court, at the time sentence is imposed on the person, may order the motor vehicle impounded for a period of not more than six months for a first conviction, and not more than 12 months for a second or subsequent conviction:

(A) Driving with a suspended or revoked driver's license.

(B) A violation of Section 2800.2 resulting in an accident or Section 2800.3, if either violation occurred within seven years of one or more separate convictions for a violation of any of the following:

(i) Section 23103, if the vehicle involved in the violation was driven at a speed of 100 or more miles per hour.

(ii) Section 23152.

(iii) Section 23153.

(iv) Section 191.5 of the Penal Code.

(v) Subdivision (c) of Section 192 of the Penal Code.

(2) The cost of keeping the vehicle is a lien on the vehicle pursuant to Chapter 6.5 (commencing with Section 3067) of Title 14 of Part 4 of Division 3 of the Civil Code.

(b) Notwithstanding subdivision (a), any motor vehicle impounded pursuant to this section which is subject to a chattel mortgage, conditional sale contract, or lease contract shall be released by the court to the legal owner upon the filing of an affidavit by the legal owner that the chattel mortgage, conditional sale contract, or lease contract is in default and shall be delivered to the legal owner upon payment of the accrued cost of keeping the vehicle. *(Amended by Stats 1991 ch 1048 §2, eff. 1/1/92.)*

§14602.5. Driving M1, M2 motor vehicle while privilege suspended, etc.; impoundment.

(a) Whenever a person is convicted for driving any class M1 or M2 motor vehicle, while his or her driving privilege has been suspended or revoked, of which vehicle he or she is the owner, or of which the owner permitted the operation, knowing the person's driving privilege was suspended or revoked, the court may, at the time sentence is imposed on the person, order the motor vehicle impounded in any manner as the court may determine, for a period not to exceed six months for a first conviction, and not to exceed 12 months for a second or subsequent conviction. For the purposes of this section, a "second or subsequent conviction" includes a conviction for any offense described in this section. The cost of keeping the vehicle shall be a lien on the vehicle, pursuant to Chapter 6.5 (commencing with Section 3067) of Title 14 of Part 4 of Division 3 of the Civil Code.

(b) Notwithstanding subdivision (a), any motor vehicle impounded pursuant to this section which is subject to a chattel mortgage, conditional sale contract, or lease contract shall, upon the filing of an affidavit by the legal owner that the chattel mortgage, conditional sale contract, or lease contract is in default, be released by the court to the legal owner, and shall be delivered to him or her upon payment of the accrued cost of keeping the motor vehicle. (*Added by Stats 1990 ch 1359 §5, eff. 1/1/91.*)

§14605. Operation of motor vehicle in a parking facility without driver certification.

(a) No person who owns or is in control of a motor vehicle shall cause or permit another person to operate the vehicle within or upon an offstreet parking facility if the person has knowledge that the driver does not have a driver's license of the appropriate class or certification to operate the vehicle.

(b) No operator of an offstreet parking facility shall hire or retain in his employment an attendant whose duties involve the operating of motor vehicles unless such attendant, at all times during such employment, is licensed as a driver under the provisions of this code.

(c) As used in this section, "offstreet parking facility" means any offstreet facility held open for use by the public for parking vehicles and includes all publicly owned facilities for offstreet parking, and privately owned facilities for offstreet parking where no fee is charged for the privilege to park and which are held open for the common public use of retail customers.

§14606. Requirements for employment of person to drive a motor vehicle.

(a) No person shall employ or hire any person to drive a motor vehicle nor shall he knowingly permit or authorize the driving of a motor vehicle, owned by him or under his control, upon the highways by any person unless the person is then licensed for the appropriate class of vehicle to be driven.

(b) Whenever any person employs or hires any person, including a subhauler, to drive a class 1 or class 2 vehicle, the employer shall ascertain that such person has in his possession a medical certificate as provided in subdivision (c) of Section 12804 which has been issued within two years prior to the date of such employment or hiring. Whenever such person fails to qualify for such a medical certificate on reexamination, the employer shall report such failure to the department.

§14607. Driving by an unlicensed minor.

No person shall cause or knowingly permit his child, ward, or employee under the age of 18 years to drive a motor vehicle upon the highways unless such child, ward, or employee is then licensed under this code.

§14610. Prohibited uses of driver's license.

(a) It is unlawful for any person:

(1) To display or cause or permit to be displayed or have in his possession any canceled, revoked, suspended, fictitious, fraudulently altered, or fraudulently obtained driver's license.

(2) To lend his driver's license to any other person or knowingly permit the use thereof by another.

(3) To display or represent any driver's license not issued to him as being his license.

(4) To fail or refuse to surrender to the department upon its lawful demand any driver's license which has been suspended, revoked or canceled.

(5) To permit any unlawful use of a driver's license issued to him.

(6) To do any act forbidden or fail to perform any act required by this division.

(7) To photograph, photostat, duplicate, or in any way reproduce any driver's license or facsimile thereof in such a manner that it could be mistaken for a valid license, or to display or have in his possession any such photograph, photostat, duplicate, reproduction, or facsimile unless authorized by the provisions of this code.

(8) To alter any driver's license in any manner not authorized by this code.

(b) For purposes of this section, "driver's license" includes a temporary permit to operate a motor vehicle. (*Amended by Stats 1990 ch 44 §5, eff. 1/1/91.*)

§14610.1. Manufacure or sale of document similiar to driver's license prohibited.

(a) No person shall manufacture or sell an identification document of a size and form substantially similar to the drivers' licenses issued by the department.

(b) A violation of this section is a misdemeanor punishable by a fine of not less than five hundred dollars $500). (*Added by Stats 1990 ch 170 §2, eff. 1/1/91.*)

§14610.5. Dishonesty in driving examination.

(a) It is unlawful for any person to do any of the following:

(1) Sell, offer for sale, distribute, or use any crib sheet or cribbing device that contains the answers to any examination administered by the department for any class of driver's license, permit, or certificate.

(2) Impersonate or allow the impersonation of an applicant for any class of driver's license, permit, or certificate for the purpose of fraudulently qualifying the applicant for any class of driver's license, permit, or certificate.

(b) A first conviction under this section is punishable as an infraction; a second or subsequent conviction is punishable as a misdemeanor. (*Added by Stats 1986 ch 960.*)

DIVISION 6.5

MOTOR VEHICLE TRANSACTIONS WITH MINORS

CHAPTER 1

DRIVER'S LICENSE REQUIREMENTS

§15500. Unlicensed minor may not purchase or obtain motor vehicle.

It is unlawful for any minor who does not possess a valid driver's license issued under this code to order, purchase or lease, attempt to purchase or lease, contract to purchase or lease, accept, or otherwise obtain, any vehicle of a type subject to registration.

© 1992 by J., B. & L. Gould
Printed in the U.S.A.   EP

§15501. **Minor may not present false or fradulent license.**

It is unlawful for any minor to present or offer to any person offering for sale or lease or to give or otherwise furnish thereto any motor vehicle of a type subject to registration, a driver's license which is false, fraudulent, or not actually his own for the purpose of ordering, purchasing or leasing, attempting to purchase or lease, contracting to purchase or lease, accepting, or otherwise obtaining such a vehicle.

DIVISION 7

FINANCIAL RESPONSIBILITY LAW

CHAPTER 1

COMPULSORY FINANCIAL RESPONSIBILITY

ARTICLE 1

FINANCIAL RESPONSIBILITY

§16028. **Evidence of financial responsibility for vehicle.**

(a) Every person who drives a motor vehicle required to be registered in this state upon a highway, or who drives a moped upon the highway, shall, when requested by a peace officer pursuant to subdivision (c) or (d), provide evidence of financial responsibility for the vehicle.

Except as otherwise provided in this subdivision and subdivisions (e) and (f), any person who violates this subdivision is guilty of an infraction and shall be punished for each offense by a fine of ninety-five dollars ($95) and an additional penalty assessment of twenty-five dollars ($25). If (1) the citation is issued pursuant to subdivision (c) on a notice to appear for violation of Section 23152, and (2) the driver is convicted of violating Section 23152, then the penalty upon conviction for violation of subdivision (a) is a fine of two hundred dollars ($200) and an additional penalty assessment of sixty dollars ($60). Each defendant shall be fined and assessed a penalty assessment in the amount specified in this section, upon conviction, unless the court determines that in the interests of justice the fine and the penalty assessment should be reduced. Any reduction of the fine and penalty assessment shall be in the same proportion and the court shall state the reasons for reducing the fine and assessment on the record.

In lieu of the fine and penalty assessment otherwise assessable under this subdivision, the court may permit the defendant to perform community service designated by the court.

(b) (1) For purposes of this section, "evidence of financial responsibility" shall be in writing and means any of the following:

(A) The name of the insurance or surety company which issued the automobile liability policy, motor vehicle liability policy, or bond meeting the requirements of Section 16056, in effect for the vehicle, and the number of the insurance policy or surety bond.

(B) If the owner is a self-insurer as provided in Section 16052 or a depositor as provided in Section 16054.2, the certificate or deposit number issued by the department.

(C) An insurance covering note, as specified in Section 382 of the Insurance Code.

(D) A showing that the vehicle is owned or leased by, or under the direction of, the United States or any public entity, as defined in Section 811.2 of the Government Code.

(2) For purposes of this section, "evidence of financial responsibility" also includes the identifying symbol issued to a highway carrier by the Public Utilities Commission pursuant to Section 3543 of the Public Utilities Code and displayed on the motor vehicle.

(3) For purposes of this section, "evidence of financial responsibility in writing" may be satisfied by writing the name of the insurance company or surety company and the policy number or surety bond number on the motor vehicle registration card issued by the Department of Motor Vehicles.

(c) Whenever a notice to appear is issued for any alleged violation of this code, except a violation specified in Chapter 9 (commencing with Section 22500) of Division 11 or any local ordinance adopted pursuant thereto, the cited driver shall furnish written evidence of financial responsibility, as defined by subdivision (b), upon request of the peace officer issuing the citation. The peace officer shall request and write the driver's evidence of financial responsibility on the notice to appear, except where the peace officer is unable to write the driver's evidence of financial responsibility on the notice to appear due to an emergency that requires his or her presence elsewhere. If the cited driver fails to provide evidence of financial responsibility at the time the notice to appear is issued, the peace officer may issue the driver a notice to appear for violation of subdivision (a). The notice to appear for violation of subdivision (a) shall be written on the same citation form as the original violation.

(d) Whenever a peace officer is summoned to the scene of an accident, the driver of any motor vehicle which is in any manner involved in the accident, shall furnish written evidence of financial responsibility as defined by subdivision (b), upon the request of the peace officer making the report. If the driver fails to provide evidence of financial responsibility when requested, the peace officer may issue the driver a notice to appear for violation of subdivision (a).

(e) A person cited in a notice to appear for violation of subdivision (a) may personally appear before the clerk of the court, as designated in the notice to appear, and provide written evidence of financial responsibility in a form consistent with Section 16028.4 showing that the driver was in compliance with Section 16020 at the time the notice to appear for violating subdivision (a) was issued. In lieu of a personal appearance, the person may submit written evidence of financial responsibility by mail to the court. Upon receipt by the clerk of written evidence of financial responsibility in a form consistent with Section 16028.4, further proceedings on the notice to appear for the violation of subdivision (a) of Section 16028 shall be dismissed, subject to Section 16031.

(f) If a driver cited for a violation of subdivision (a) is, at the time of issuance of the notice to appear, driving a motor vehicle owned, operated, or leased by the employer of the driver and driven with the permission of the employer, this section and Sections 16031 and 16032 apply to the employer rather than the driver. In that case, the notice to appear shall be issued to the employer, rather than the driver, and the driver may sign the notice to appear on behalf of the employer and shall notify the employer of the citation within five days after the issuance thereof.

© 1992 by J., B. & L. Gould
Printed in the U.S.A. **EP**

(g) Penalty assessments collected pursuant to subdivision (a) shall he deposited in the county's Courthouse Temporary Construction Fund established pursuant to Section 76001, 76002, 76003, 76004, 76005, or 76006 of the Government Code.

(h) Any penalty assessment imposed pursuant to any other provision of law shall not be imposed on the additional penalty assessment provided in subdivision (a).

(i) This section shall remain in effect only until January 1, 1991, and as of that date is repealed, unless a later enacted statute, which is enacted before January 1, 1991, deletes or extends that date. *(Amended by Stats 1990 ch 888 §2, eff. 9/14/90 only until 1/1/91.)*

§16029. False evidence of financial responsibility.

(a) Except as provided in subdivision (c) of this section, any person who provides false evidence of financial responsibility (1) when requested by a peace officer pursuant to subdivision (c) of Section 16028 or (2) to the clerk of the court as permitted by subdivision (d) of Section 16028, including an expired or canceled insurance policy, bond or certificate or deposit number, is guilty of a misdemeanor punishable by a fine not exceeding five hundred dollars ($500) or imprisonment in the county jail not exceeding 30 days, or by both that fine and imprisonment. The court shall additionally suspend the driver's license of any person convicted of a violation of this subdivision for a period of one year commencing upon the date of the conviction, in accordance with Sections 13206 and 13207. Driver's licenses surrendered to the court pursuant to this section shall be transmitted by the court, together with the required report of the conviction, to the department within 10 days of the conviction. Upon conclusion of the period of suspension, the department shall not return the driver's license until the licensee establishes proof of financial responsibility as prescribed by Section 16034.

(b) However, in lieu of suspending a person's driving privileges pursuant to subdivision (a), the court shall restrict the person's driving privileges to driving that is required in the person's course of employment, if driving of a motor vehicle is necessary in order to perform the duties of the person's primary employment. The restriction shall remain in effect for the period of suspension otherwise required by subdivision (a). The court shall provide for endorsement of the restriction on the person's driver's license, and violation of the restriction constitutes a violation of Section 14603 and grounds for suspension or revocation of the license under Section 13360.

(c) This section does not apply to a driver who is driving a motor vehicle owned, operated, or leased by the employer of the driver and driven with the permission of the employer.

(d) This section shall remain in effect only until January 1, 1991, and as of that date is repealed, unless a later enacted statute, which is enacted before January 1, 1991, deletes or extends that date. *(Amended by Stats 1989 ch 1465 §11, eff. 1/1/90 only until 1/1/91.)*

DIVISION 10

ACCIDENTS AND ACCIDENT REPORTS

CHAPTER 1

ACCIDENTS AND ACCIDENT REPORTS
(Chapter heading added by Stats 1989 ch 281 §2, eff. 1/1/90 only until 1/1/91.)

§20001. Driver must stop at scene of accident.

(a) The driver of any vehicle involved in an accident resulting in injury to any person, other than himself or herself, or in death of any person shall immediately stop the vehicle at the scene of the accident and shall fulfill the requirements of Sections 20003 and 20004.

(b) (1) Except as provided in paragraph (2), any violation of subdivision (a) shall be punished by imprisonment in the state prison, or in the county jail for not to exceed one year or by fine of not to exceed ten thousand dollars ($10,000), or by both.

(2) Any violation of subdivision (a) which results in death or permanent serious injury, shall be punished by imprisonment in the state prison for two, three, or four years, or in the county jail for not to exceed one year or by a fine of not to exceed ten thousand dollars ($10,000), or by both.

As used in this paragraph, "permanent, serious injury," means loss or permanent impairment of function of any bodily member or organ. *(Amended by Stats 1988 ch 1207 §1, eff. 1/1/89.)*

§20002. Driver's duties in an accident.

(a) The driver of any vehicle involved in an accident resulting in damage to any property, including vehicles, shall immediately stop the vehicle at the scene of the accident and shall then and there do one of the following:

(1) Locate and notify the owner or person in charge of that property of the name and address of the driver and owner of the vehicle involved and, upon locating the driver of any other vehicle involved or the owner or person in charge of any damaged property, upon being requested, present his or her driver's license, vehicle registration, and evidence of financial responsibility as specified in subparagraph (B) of paragraph (2) to the other driver, property owner, or person in charge of that property. The information presented shall include the current residence address of the driver and of the registered owner. If the registered owner of an involved vehicle is present at the scene, he shall also, upon request, present his driver's license information, if available, or other valid identification to the other involved parties.

(2) If a traffic or police officer is present at the scene of an accident and a police report is made, each driver involved in the accident shall, unless rendered incapable, exchange with any other driver or property owner involved in the accident and present at the scene, all of the following information:

(A) Driver's name and current residence address, driver's license number, vehicle identification number, and name and current residence address of registered owner.

(B) Evidence of financial responsibility, as specified in Section 16021. If the financial responsibility of a person is a form of insurance, then that person shall,

© 1992 by J., B. & L. Gould
Printed in the U.S.A.   EP

unless rendered incapable, supply the name and address of the insurance company.

(3) Leave in a conspicuous place on the vehicle or other property damaged a written notice giving the name and address of the driver and of the owner of the vehicle involved and a statement of the circumstances thereof and shall without unnecessary delay notify the police department of the city wherein the collision occurred or, if the collision occurred in unincorporated territory, the local headquarters of the Department of the California Highway Patrol.

(b) Any person who parks a vehicle which, prior to the vehicle again being driven, becomes a runaway vehicle and is involved in an accident resulting in damage to any property, attended or unattended, shall comply with the requirements of this section relating to notification and reporting and shall, upon conviction thereof, be liable to the penalties of this section for failure to comply with the requirements.

(c) (1) Any person failing to comply with all the requirements of paragraph (1) or (3) of subdivision (a), or subdivision (b) is guilty of a misdemeanor and, upon conviction thereof, shall be punished by imprisonment in the county jail for not to exceed six months or by a fine of not to exceed one thousand dollars ($1,000), or by both.

(2) Any person who willfully fails to comply with the requirements of paragraph (2) of subdivision (a) shall be guilty of an infraction punishable by a fine not to exceed two hundred fifty dollars ($250). *(Amended by Stats 1991 ch 1103 §2, eff. 1/1/92.)*

§20003. Driver's duties in accident resulting in death or injury.

(a) The driver of any vehicle involved in an accident resulting in injury to or death of any person shall also give his or her name, current residence address, the registration number of the vehicle he or she is driving, and the name and current residence address of the owner to the person struck or the driver or occupants of any vehicle collided with and shall give the information to any traffic or police officer at the scene of the accident and shall render to any person injured in the accident reasonable assistance, including the transportation or the making arrangements for the transportation of that person to a physician, surgeon, or hospital for medical or surgical treatment if it is apparent that treatment is necessary or if that transportation is requested by the injured person.

(b) Any driver subject to the provisions of subdivision (a) shall also, upon being requested, exhibit his or her driver's license, if available, to the person struck or to the driver or occupants of any vehicle collided with and to any traffic or police officer at the scene of the accident. *(Amended by Stats 1991 ch 1103 §3, eff. 1/1/92.)*

§20008. Driver's duty to report accident to authorities.

(a) The driver of a vehicle, other than a common carrier vehicle, involved in any accident resulting in injuries to or death of any person shall within 24 hours after the accident make or cause to be made a written report of the accident to the Department of the California Highway Patrol or, if the accident occurred within a city, to either the Department of the California Highway Patrol or the police department of the city in which the accident occurred. If the agency which receives the report is not responsible for investigating

the accident, it shall immediately forward the report to the law enforcement agency which is responsible for investigating the accident.

On or before the fifth day of each month, every police department which received a report during the previous calendar month of an accident which it is responsible for investigating shall forward the report or a copy thereof to the main office of the Department of the California Highway Patrol at Sacramento.

(b) The owner or driver of a common carrier vehicle involved in any such accident shall make a like report to the Department of the California Highway Patrol on or before the 10th day of the month following the accident.

§20016. Transporting persons injured on highways.

Any peace officer, any member of an organized fire department or fire protection district, any employee of the Department of Transportation assigned to maintenance operations, or any member of the California Highway Patrol may transport or arrange for the transportation of any person injured in an accident upon any highway to a physician and surgeon or hospital, if the injured person does not object to such transportation. Any officer, member, or employee exercising ordinary care and precaution shall not be liable for any damages due to any further injury or for any medical, ambulance, or hospital bills incurred in behalf of the injured party.

§20018. Policy to provide assistance to disabled motorists.

Every law enforcement agency having traffic law enforcement responsibility as specified in subdivision (a) of Section 830.1 and in subdivision (a) of Section 830.2 of the Penal Code shall develop, adopt, and implement a written policy for its officers to provide assistance to disabled motorists on highways within its primary jurisdiction. A copy of the policy shall be available to the public upon request. *(Added by Stats 1985 ch 1203.)*

DIVISION 11

RULES OF THE ROAD

CHAPTER 1

OBEDIENCE TO AND EFFECT OF TRAFFIC LAWS

ARTICLE 4

OPERATION OF BICYCLES

§21200. Rights and duties of riders; driving under influence.

Every person riding a bicycle upon a highway has all the rights and is subject to all the provisions applicable to the driver of a vehicle by this division, including, but not limited to, provisions dealing with driving under the influence or alcoholic beverages or drugs, and by Division 10 (commencing with Section 20000), Section 27400, Division 16.7 (commencing with Section 39000), Division 17 (commencing with Section 40000), and Division 18 (commencing with Section 42000), except those provisions which by their very nature can have no application. *(Amended by Stats 1985 ch 1013.)*

§21200.5. Violation and penalty for riding under influence of alcohol and drugs.

Notwithstanding Section 21200, it is unlawful for any person to ride a bicycle upon a highway while under the influence of an alcoholic beverage or any drug, or under the combined influence of an alcoholic beverage and any drug. Any person arrested for a violation of this section may request to have a chemical test made of the person's blood, breath, or urine for the purpose of determining the alcoholic or drug content of that person's blood, and, if so requested, the arresting officer shall have the test performed. A conviction of a violation of this section shall be punished by a fine of not more than two hundred fifty dollars ($250). Violations of this section are subject to Section 13202.5. *(Amended by Stats 1990 ch 1697 §5, eff. 1/1/91.)*

§21202. Rules for operating bicycle on roadway.

(a) Any person operating a bicycle upon a roadway at a speed less than the normal speed of traffic moving in the same direction at such time shall ride as close as practicable to the right-hand curb or edge of the roadway except under any of the following situations:

(1) When overtaking and passing another bicycle or vehicle proceeding in the same direction.

(2) When preparing for a left turn at an intersection or into a private road or driveway.

(3) When reasonably necessary to avoid conditions (including, but not limited to, fixed or moving objects, vehicles, bicycles, pedestrians, animals, surface hazards, or substandard width lanes) that make it unsafe to continue along the right-hand curb or edge, subject to the provisions of Section 21656. For purposes of this section, a "substandard width lane" is a lane that is too narrow for a bicycle and a vehicle to travel safely side by side within the lane.

(b) Any person operating a bicycle upon a roadway of a highway, which highway carries traffic in one direction only and has two or more marked traffic lanes, may ride as near the left-hand curb or edge of such roadway as practicable.

§21203. Rider hitching onto vehicle.

No person riding upon any motorcycle, motorized bicycle, bicycle, coaster, roller skates, sled, or toy vehicle shall attach the same or himself to any streetcar or vehicle on the roadway.

§21204. Separate seats for passengers; helmets; penalty for violation.

(a) No person operating a bicycle upon a highway shall ride other than upon or astride a permanent and regular seat attached thereto.

(b) No operator shall allow a person riding as a passenger, and no person shall ride as a passenger, on a bicycle upon a highway other than upon or astride a separate seat attached thereto. If the passenger is four years of age or younger, or weighs 40 pounds or less, the seat shall have adequate provision for retaining the passenger in place and for protecting the passenger from the moving parts of the bicycle.

(c) No person operating a bicycle upon a highway shall allow any person who is four years of age or younger, or weighs 40 pounds or less, to ride as a passenger on a bicycle unless that passenger is wearing a helmet meeting the standards of the American

National Standards Institute (ANSI Z 90.4 bicycle helmet standards) or of the Snell Memorial Foundation's 1984 Standard for Protective Headgear for Use in Bicycling.

(d) For purposes of this section, "wearing a helmet" means having a helmet of good fit fastened securely upon the head with the helmet straps.

(e) The first violation of subdivision (c) by any person shall be dismissed by a court if the person charged produces proof that a helmet meeting the standards prescribed in subdivision (c) has been purchased for use by the passenger four years of age or younger, or weighing 40 pounds or less.

(f) Notwithstanding any other provision of law, any violation of subdivision (c) is an infraction punishable by a fine, including all penalty assessments and court costs imposed on the convicted person, of not more than twenty dollars ($20). *(Amended by Stats 1986 ch 58 §1.)*

§21210. Parking bicycles.

No person shall leave a bicycle lying on its side on any sidewalk, or shall park a bicycle on a sidewalk in any other position, so that there is not an adequate path for pedestrian traffic. Local authorities may, by ordinance or resolution, prohibit bicycle parking in designated areas of the public highway, provided that appropriate signs are erected.

CHAPTER 2

TRAFFIC SIGNS, SIGNALS, AND MARKINGS

ARTICLE 1

ERECTION AND MAINTENANCE

§21352. Use of traffic control devices on state highways for public safety.

The Department of Transportation may erect stop signs at any entrance to any state highway and whenever the department determines that it is necessary for the public safety and the orderly and efficient use of the highways by the public, the department may erect and maintain, or cause to be erected and maintained, on any state highway any traffic control signal or any official traffic control device regulating or prohibiting the turning of vehicles upon the highway, allocating or restricting the use of specified lanes or portions of the highway by moving vehicular traffic, establishing crosswalks at or between intersections, or restricting use of the right-of-way by the public for other than highway purposes.

ARTICLE 3

OFFENSES RELATING TO TRAFFIC DEVICES

§21461. Driver to obey traffic control devices.

(a) It shall be unlawful for any driver of a vehicle to fail to obey any sign or signal erected or maintained to indicate and carry out the provisions of this code or any local traffic ordinance or resolution adopted pursuant to a local traffic ordinance, or to fail to obey any device erected or maintained pursuant to Section 21352.

(b) The provisions of subdivision (a) shall not apply to acts constituting violations under Chapter 9 (commencing with Section 22500) of this division or to acts constituting violations of any local traffic ordinance

© 1992 by J., B. & L. Gould
Printed in the U.S.A.   EP

adopted pursuant to Chapter 9 (commencing with Section 22500).

§21461.5. Pedestrians to obey traffic control devices.

It shall be unlawful for any pedestrian to fail to obey any sign or signal erected or maintained to indicate or carry out the provisions of this code or any local traffic ordinance or resolution adopted pursuant to a local traffic ordinance, or to fail to obey any device erected or maintained pursuant to Section 21352.

§21464. Violation for interrupting traffic devices; exceptions.

(a) No person shall without lawful authority deface, injure, attach any material or substance to, knock down, or remove, nor shall any person shoot at, any official traffic control device, traffic guidepost, traffic signpost, or historical marker placed or erected as authorized or required by law, nor shall any person without such authority deface, injure, attach any material or substance to, or remove, nor shall any person shoot at, any inscription, shield, or insignia on any such device, guide, or marker.

(b) No person shall use, nor shall any vehicle, other than an authorized emergency vehicle, be equipped with, any device capable of sending a signal that interrupts or changes the sequence patterns of an official traffic control signal unless that device or use is authorized by the Department of Transportation pursuant to Section 21350 or by local authorities pursuant to Section 21351.

(c) Any willful violation of subdivision (a) or (b) which results in injury to, or the death of, a person is punishable by imprisonment in the state prison, or imprisonment in a county jail for a period of not more than six months, and by a fine of not less than five thousand dollars ($5,000) nor more than ten thousand dollars ($10,000).

(d) Any willful violation of subdivision (a) or (b) which does not result in injury to, or the death of, a person is punishable by a fine of not more than three thousand dollars ($3,000).

(e) The court shall allow the offender to perform community service designated by the court in lieu of all or part of any fine imposed under this section. *(Amended by Stats 1990 ch 447 §1, eff. 1/1/91.)*

§21465. Unofficial traffic control devices.

No person shall place, maintain, or display upon, or in view of, any highway any unofficial sign, signal, device, or marking, or any sign, signal, device, or marking which purports to be or is an imitation of, or resembles, an official traffic control device or which attempts to direct the movement of traffic or which hides from view any official traffic control device.

CHAPTER 3

DRIVING, OVERTAKING, AND PASSING

ARTICLE 2

ADDITIONAL DRIVING RULES

§21700. Driving obstruction.

No person shall drive a vehicle when it is so loaded, or when there are in the front seat such number of persons as to obstruct the view of the driver to the front

or sides of the vehicle or as to interfere with the driver's control over the driving mechanism of the vehicle.

§21702. Driving hours limited.

(a) No person shall drive upon any highway any vehicle designed or used for transporting persons for compensation for more than 10 consecutive hours nor for more than 10 hours spread over a total of 15 consecutive hours. Thereafter, such person shall not drive any such vehicle until eight consecutive hours have elapsed.

Regardless of aggregate driving time, no driver shall drive for more than 10 hours in any 24-hour period unless eight consecutive hours off duty have elapsed.

(b) No person shall drive upon any highway any vehicle designed or used for transporting merchandise, freight, materials or other property for more than 12 consecutive hours nor for more than 12 hours spread over a total of 15 consecutive hours. Thereafter, such person shall not drive any such vehicle until eight consecutive hours have elapsed.

Regardless of aggregate driving time, no driver shall drive for more than 12 hours in any 24-hour period unless eight consecutive hours off duty have elapsed.

(c) This section does not apply in any case of casualty or unavoidable accident or an act of God.

(d) In computing the number of hours under this section, any time spent by a person in driving such a vehicle outside this state shall, upon the vehicle entering this state, be included.

(e) Any person who violates any provision of this section is guilty of a misdemeanor and is punishable by a fine of not less than one hundred dollars ($100) nor more than one thousand dollars ($1,000) for each offense.

(f) This section shall not apply to the driver of a vehicle which is subject to the provisions of Section 34500.

§21703. Closely following.

The driver of a motor vehicle shall not follow another vehicle more closely than is reasonable and prudent, having due regard for the speed of such vehicle and the traffic upon, and the condition of, the roadway.

§21706. Following emergency vehicle within 300 feet.

No motor vehicle, except an authorized emergency vehicle, shall follow within 300 feet of any authorized emergency vehicle being operated under the provisions of Section 21055.

This section shall not apply to a police or traffic officer when serving as an escort within the purview of Section 21057.

§21710. Coasting on down grade.

The driver of a motor vehicle when traveling on down grade upon any highway shall not coast with the gears of such vehicle in neutral.

CHAPTER 5

PEDESTRIANS' RIGHTS AND DUTIES

§21955. Pedestrian crossings.

Between adjacent intersections controlled by traffic control signal devices or by police officers, pedestrians shall not cross the roadway at any place except in a crosswalk.

§21957. Hitchhiking in a roadway.

No person shall stand in a roadway for the purpose of soliciting a ride from the driver of any vehicle.

CHAPTER 6

TURNING AND STOPPING AND TURNING SIGNALS

§22107. Turning signals and movement.

No person shall turn a vehicle from a direct course or move right or left upon a roadway until such movement can be made with reasonable safety and then only after the giving of an appropriate signal in the manner provided in this chapter in the event any other vehicle may be affected by the movement.

§22108. Signal duration.

Any signal of intention to turn right or left shall be given continuously during the last 100 feet traveled by the vehicle before turning.

CHAPTER 7

SPEED LAWS

Article 1

GENERALLY

§22348. Violation for exceeding 100 miles per hour on highway; designated lanes for certain vehicles.

(a) Notwithstanding subdivision (b) of Section 22351, no person shall drive a vehicle upon a highway with a speed limit established pursuant to Section 22349 or 22356 at a speed greater than that speed limit.

(b) Any person who drives a vehicle upon a highway at a speed greater than 100 miles per hour is guilty of an infraction punishable, as follows:

(1) Upon a first conviction of a violation of this subdivision, by a fine of not to exceed five hundred dollars ($500). The court may also suspend the privilege of the person to operate a motor vehicle for a period not to exceed 30 days pursuant to Section 13200.5.

(2) Upon a conviction under this subdivision of an offense which occurred within three years of a prior offense resulting in a conviction of an offense under this subdivision, by a fine of not to exceed five hundred dollars ($500). The person's privilege to operate a motor vehicle shall be suspended by the Department of Motor Vehicles pursuant to Subdivision (a) of Section 13355.

(3) Upon a conviction under this subdivision of an offense which occurred within five years of two or more prior offenses resulting in convictions of offenses under this subdivision, by a fine of not to exceed five hundred dollars ($500). The person's privilege to operate a motor vehicle shall be suspended by the Department of Motor Vehicles pursuant to subdivision (b) of Section 13355.

(c) Any vehicle subject to Section 22406 shall be driven in a lane designated pursuant to Section 21655, or if no lane has been so designated, in the right-hand lane for traffic or as close as practicable to the right-hand edge or curb. When overtaking and passing another vehicle proceeding in the same direction, the drivers shall use either the designated lane, the lane to the immediate left of the right-hand lane, or the right-hand lane for traffic as permitted under this code. If, however, specific lane or lanes have not been designated on a divided highway having four or more clearly marked lanes for traffic in one direction, any such vehicle may also be driven in the lane to the immediate left of the right-hand lane, unless otherwise prohibited under this code. This subdivision does not apply to a driver who is preparing for a left- or right-hand turn or who is in the process of entering into or exiting from a highway or to a driver who is required necessarily to drive in a lane other than the right-hand lane to continue on his or her intended route. (Amended by Stats 1987 ch 25 §1, eff. 5/28/87, ch 72 §2, eff. 6/30/87.)

§22350. Observe safe speed for road conditions.

No person shall drive a vehicle upon a highway at a speed greater than is reasonable or prudent having due regard for weather, visibility, the traffic on, and the surface and width of, the highway, and in no event at a speed which endangers the safety of persons or property.

§22351. Violation of basic speed law.

(a) The speed of any vehicle upon a highway not in excess of the limits specified in Section 22352 or established as authorized in this code is lawful unless clearly proved to be in violation of the basic speed law.

(b) The speed of any vehicle upon a highway in excess of the prima facie speed limits in Section 22352 or established as authorized in this code is prima facie unlawful unless the defendant establishes by competent evidence that the speed in excess of said limits did not constitute a violation of the basic speed law at the time, place and under the conditions then existing.

§22352. Application of prima facie speed limits.

The prima facie limits are as follows and shall be applicable unless changed as authorized in this code and, if so changed, only when signs have been erected giving notice thereof:

(a) Fifteen miles per hour:

(1) When traversing a railway grade crossing, if during the last 100 feet of the approach to the crossing the driver does not have a clear and unobstructed view of the crossing and of any traffic on the railway for a distance of 400 feet in both directions along the railway. This subdivision does not apply in the case of any railway grade crossing where a human flagman is on duty or a clearly visible electrical or mechanical railway crossing signal device is installed but does not then indicate the immediate approach of a railway train or car.

(2) When traversing any intersection of highways if during the last 100 feet of the driver's approach to the intersection the driver does not have a clear and unobstructed view of the intersection and of any traffic upon all of the highways entering the intersection for a distance of 100 feet along all those highways, except at an intersection protected by stop signs or yield right-of-way signs or controlled by official traffic control signals.

(3) On any alley.

(b) Twenty-five miles per hour:

© 1992 by J., B. & L. Gould
Printed in the U.S.A.   **EP**

(1) On any highway other than a state highway, in any business or residence district unless a different speed is determined by local authority under procedures set forth in this code.

(2) When passing a school building or the grounds thereof, contiguous to a highway and posted with a standard "SCHOOL" warning sign, while children are going to or leaving the school either during school hours or during the noon recess period. The prima facie limit shall also apply when passing any school grounds which are not separated from the highway by a fence, gate or other physical barrier while the grounds are in use by children and the highway is posted with a standard "SCHOOL" warning sign.

(3) When passing a senior center or other facility primarily used by senior citizens, contiguous to a street other than a state highway and posted with a standard "SENIOR" warning sign. A local authority is not required to erect any sign pursuant to this paragraph until donations from private sources covering those costs are received and the local agency makes a determination that the proposed signing should be implemented. A local authority may, however, utilize any other funds available to it to pay for the erection of those signs. *(Amended by Stats 1990 ch 441 §1; ch 542 §1, eff. 1/1/91.)*

ARTICLE 2

OTHER SPEED LAWS

§22406. Maximum speed for designated vehicles.

No person shall drive any of the following vehicles on a highway at a speed in excess of 55 miles per hour:

(a) A motortruck or truck tractor having three or more axles or any motortruck or truck tractor drawing any other vehicle.

(b) A passenger vehicle or bus drawing any other vehicle.

(c) A schoolbus transporting any school pupil.

(d) A farm labor vehicle when transporting passengers.

(e) A vehicle transporting explosives.

(f) A trailer bus, as defined in Section 636. *(Amended by Stats 1988 ch 843 §5, eff. 1/1/89.)*

CHAPTER 8

SPECIAL STOPS REQUIRED

§22454. Stopping for schoolbus.

(a) The driver of any vehicle upon meeting or overtaking from either direction any schoolbus equipped with signs as required in this code, which has stopped for the purpose of receiving or discharging any schoolchildren and displays a flashing red light signal visible from front and rear, shall bring the vehicle to a stop immediately before passing the schoolbus and shall not proceed past the schoolbus until the red flashing signal ceases operation.

(b) The driver of a vehicle upon a highway with separate roadways need not stop upon meeting or passing a schoolbus which is upon the other roadway. The driver of a vehicle need not stop upon meeting or passing a schoolbus when the schoolbus is stopped at an intersection where traffic is controlled by a traffic officer or official traffic control signal, or when the schoolbus is stopped at a place where traffic is controlled by a traffic officer or official traffic control signal.

(c) (1) If a vehicle was observed overtaking a schoolbus in violation of subdivision (a), and the driver of the schoolbus witnessed the violation, the driver may, within 24 hours, report the violation and furnish the vehicle license plate number and description and the time and place of the violation to the local law enforcement agency having jurisdiction of the offense. That law enforcement agency shall issue a letter of warning prepared in accordance with paragraph (2) with respect to the alleged violation to the registered owner of the vehicle. The issuance of a warning letter under this paragraph shall not be entered on the driving record of the person to whom it is issued, but does not preclude the imposition of any other applicable penalty.

(2) The Attorney General shall prepare and furnish to every law enforcement agency in the state a form letter for purposes of paragraph (1), and the law enforcement agency may issue those letters in the exact form prepared by the Attorney General. The Attorney General may charge a fee to any law enforcement agency which requests a copy of the form letter to recover the costs of preparing and providing that copy.

(d) This section also applies to a roadway upon private property. *(Amended by Stats 1990 ch 1296 §1, eff. 1/1/91.)*

§22454.5. First and subsequent violations.

Notwithstanding Section 42001, a person convicted of a first violation of Section 22454 shall be punished by a fine of not less than one hundred fifty dollars ($150) or more than two hundred fifty dollars ($250). A person convicted of a second separate violation of Section 22454 shall be punished by a fine of not less than five hundred dollars ($500) or more than one thousand dollars ($1,000). If a person is convicted of a third or subsequent violation of Section 22454 and the offense occurred within three years of two or more separate violations of Section 22454, the Department of Motor Vehicles shall suspend the person's privilege to operate a motor vehicle for one year. *(Amended by Stats 1990 ch 1296 §2, eff. 1/1/91.)*

§22514. Parking near fire hydrants.

No person shall stop, park, or leave standing any vehicle within 15 feet of a fire hydrant except as follows:

(a) If the vehicle is attended by a licensed driver who is seated in the front seat and who can immediately move such vehicle in case of necessity.

(b) If the local authority adopts an ordinance or resolution reducing that distance. If the distance is less than 10 feet total length when measured along the curb or edge of the street, the distance shall be indicated by signs or markings.

(c) If the vehicle is owned or operated by a fire department and clearly marked as a fire department vehicle. *(Amended by Stats 1987 ch 488 §1.)*

§22520.5. Rules for selling or vending along freeways.

(a) No person shall solicit, display, sell, offer for sale, or otherwise vend or attempt to vend any merchandise or service while being wholly or partly within any of the following:

(1) The right-of-way of any freeway, including any on ramp, off ramp, or roadway shoulder which lies within the right-of-way of the freeway.

(2) Any roadway or adjacent shoulder within 500 feet of a freeway off ramp or on ramp.

(3) Any sidewalk within 500 feet of a freeway off ramp or on ramp, when vending or attempting to vend to vehicular traffic.

(b) Subdivision (a) does not apply to a roadside rest area or vista point located within a freeway right-of-way which is subject to Section 22520.6, to a tow truck or service vehicle rendering assistance to a disabled vehicle, or to a person issued a permit to vend upon the freeway pursuant to Section 670 of the Streets and Highways Code.

(c) A violation of this section is an infraction. A second or subsequent conviction of a violation of this section is a misdemeanor. *(Amended by Stats 1988 ch 924 §10, eff. 1/1/89.)*

§22523. Penalties for abandoning vehicle.

(a) No person shall abandon a vehicle upon any highway.

(b) No person shall abandon a vehicle upon public or private property without the express or implied consent of the owner or person in lawful possession or control of the property.

(c) Any person convicted of a violation of this section shall be punished by a fine of not less than one hundred dollars ($100) and shall provide proof that the costs of removal and disposition of the vehicle have been paid. No part of any fine imposed shall be suspended. The fine may be paid in installments if the court determines that the defendant is unable to pay the entire amount in one payment.

(d) Proof that the costs of removal and disposition of the vehicle have been paid shall not be required if proof is provided to the court that the vehicle was stolen prior to abandonment. That proof may consist of a police report or other evidence acceptable to the court.

(e) The costs required to be paid for the removal and disposition of any vehicle determined to be abandoned pursuant to Section 22669 shall not exceed those for towing and seven days of storage. This subdivision does not apply if the registered owner or legal owner has completed and returned to the lienholder a "Declaration of Opposition" form within the time specified in Section 22851.8. *(Amended by Stats 1990 ch 111 §1, eff. 1/1/91.)*

§22526. Anti-Gridlock Act.

(a) A driver of a vehicle shall not enter an intersection or marked crosswalk, notwithstanding any official traffic control signal indication to proceed, unless there is sufficient space on the other side of the intersection or marked crosswalk to accommodate the vehicle driven without obstructing the through passage of vehicles from either side.

(b) A driver of a vehicle which is making a turn at an intersection who is facing a steady circular yellow or yellow arrow signal shall not enter the intersection or marked crosswalk unless there is sufficient space on the other side of the intersection or marked crosswalk to accommodate the vehicle driven without obstructing the through passage of vehicles from either side.

(c) A local authority may post appropriate signs at the entrance to intersections indicating the prohibition in subdivisions (a) and (b).

(d) A violation of this section is a parking violation and is not a violation of law relating to the safe operation of vehicles.

(e) This section shall be known and may be cited as the Anti-Gridlock Act of 1987. *(Added by Stats 1987 ch 739 §1.)*

CHAPTER 10

REMOVAL OF PARKED AND ABANDONED VEHICLES

ARTICLE 1

AUTHORITY TO REMOVE VEHICLES

§22650. Unauthorized removal of vehicle prohibited.

It is unlawful for any peace officer or any unauthorized person to remove any unattended vehicle from a highway to a garage or to any other place, except as provided in this code.

(a) Those law enforcement and other agencies identified in this chapter as having the authority to remove vehicles shall also have the authority to provide hearings in compliance with the provisions of Section 22852. During these hearings the storing agency shall have the burden of establishing the authority for, and the validity of, the removal.

(b) Nothing in this section shall be deemed to prevent a review or other action as may be permitted by the laws of this state by a court of competent jurisdiction.

§22651. Conditions under which vehicle may be removed.

Any peace officer, as defined in Chapter 4.5 (commencing with Section 830) of Title 3 of Part 2 of the Penal Code; or any regularly employed and salaried employee, who is engaged in directing traffic or enforcing parking laws and regulations, of a city or a county in which a vehicle is located, may remove a vehicle located within the territorial limits in which the officer or employee may act, under any of the following circumstances:

(a) When any vehicle is left unattended upon any bridge, viaduct, or causeway or in any tube or tunnel where the vehicle constitutes an obstruction to traffic.

(b) When any vehicle is parked or left standing upon a highway in a position so as to obstruct the normal movement of traffic or in a condition so as to create a hazard to other traffic upon the highway.

(c) When any vehicle is found upon a highway or any public lands and a report has previously been made that the vehicle has been stolen or a complaint has been filed and a warrant thereon issued charging that the vehicle has been embezzled.

(d) When any vehicle is illegally parked so as to block the entrance to a private driveway and it is impractical to move the vehicle from in front of the driveway to another point on the highway.

(e) When any vehicle is illegally parked so as to prevent access by firefighting equipment to a fire hydrant and it is impracticable to move the vehicle from in front of the fire hydrant to another point on the highway.

(f) When any vehicle, except any highway maintenance or construction equipment, is stopped, parked, or left standing for more than four hours upon the

© 1992 by J., B. & L. Gould
Printed in the U.S.A.   EP

right-of-way of any freeway which has full control of access and no crossings at grade and the driver, if present, cannot move the vehicle under its own power.

(g) When the person or persons in charge of a vehicle upon a highway or any public lands are, by reason of physical injuries or illness, incapacitated to an extent so as to be unable to provide for its custody or removal.

(h) When an officer arrests any person driving or in control of a vehicle for an alleged offense and the officer is, by this code or other law, required or permitted to take, and does take, the person into custody.

(i) (1) When any vehicle, other than a rented vehicle, is found upon a highway or any public lands, or is removed pursuant to any subdivision of this section, and it is known to have been issued five or more notices of parking violation over a period of five or more days, to which the owner or person in control of the vehicle has not responded to the agency responsible for processing notices of parking violation or the registered owner of the vehicle is known to have been issued five or more notices for failure to pay or failure to appear in court for traffic violations for which no certificate has been issued by the magistrate or clerk of the court hearing the case showing that the case has been adjudicated or concerning which the registered owner's record has not been cleared pursuant to Chapter 6 (commencing with Section 41500) of Division 17, the vehicle may be impounded until that person furnishes to the impounding law enforcement agency evidence of his or her identity and an address within this state at which he or she can be located and satisfactory evidence that bail has been deposited for all notices of parking violation issued for the vehicle or all traffic violations of the registered owner have been cleared, or both. A notice of parking violation issued for an unlawfully parked vehicle shall be accompanied by a warning that repeated violations may result in the impounding of the vehicle. In lieu of requiring satisfactory evidence that the bail has been deposited, the impounding law enforcement agency may, in its discretion, issue a notice to appear for the offenses charged, as provided in Article 2 (commencing with Section 40500) of Chapter 2 of Division 17. In lieu of either furnishing satisfactory evidence that the bail has been deposited or accepting the notice to appear, that person may demand to be taken without unnecessary delay before a magistrate within the county in which the offenses charged are alleged to have been committed and who has jurisdiction of the offenses and is nearest or most accessible with reference to the place where the vehicle is impounded. Evidence of current registration shall be produced after a vehicle has been impounded or a notice to appear for violation of subdivision (a) of Section 4000 shall be issued to that person.

(2) A vehicle shall be released to the legal owner, as defined in Section 370, if the legal owner does all of the following:

(A) Pays the cost of towing and storing the vehicle.

(B) Submits evidence of payment of fees as provided in Section 9561.

(C) Completes an affidavit in a form acceptable to the impounding law enforcement agency stating that the vehicle was not in possession of the legal owner at the time of occurrence of the offenses relating to standing or parking. A vehicle released to a legal owner under this subdivision is a repossessed vehicle for purposes of disposition or sale. The impounding agen-

cy shall have a lien on any surplus that remains upon sale of the vehicle to which the registered owner is or may be entitled, as security for the deposit of bail for all notices of parking violations issued for the vehicle. The legal owner shall promptly remit to, and deposit with, the agency responsible for processing notices of parking violations from that surplus, on receipt thereof, bail for all notices of parking violations issued for the vehicle.

(j) When any vehicle is found illegally parked and there are no license plates or other evidence of registration displayed, the vehicle may be impounded until the owner or person in control of the vehicle furnishes the impounding law enforcement agency evidence of his or her identity and an address within this state at which he or she can be located.

(k) When any vehicle is parked or left standing upon a highway for 72 or more consecutive hours in violation of a local ordinance authorizing removal.

(l) When any vehicle is illegally parked on a highway in violation of any local ordinance forbidding standing or parking and the use of a highway, or a portion thereof, is necessary for the cleaning, repair, or construction of the highway, or for the installation of underground utilities, and signs giving notice that the vehicle may be removed are erected or placed at least 24 hours prior to the removal by local authorities pursuant to the ordinance.

(m) Wherever the use of the highway, or any portion thereof, is authorized by local authorities for a purpose other than the normal flow of traffic or for the movement of equipment, articles, or structures of unusual size, and the parking of any vehicle would prohibit or interfere with that use or movement, and signs giving notice that the vehicle may be removed are erected or placed at least 24 hours prior to the removal by local authorities pursuant to the ordinance.

(n) Whenever any vehicle is parked or left standing where local authorities, by resolution or ordinance, have prohibited parking and have authorized the removal of vehicles. No vehicle may be removed unless signs are posted giving notice of the removal.

(o) (1) When any vehicle is found upon a highway, any public lands, or an offstreet parking facility with a registration expiration date in excess of one year before the date it is found on the highway, public lands, or the offstreet parking facility. However, if the vehicle is occupied, only a peace officer, as defined in Chapter 4.5 (commencing with Section 830) of Title 3 of Part 2 of the Penal Code, may remove the vehicle. For purposes of this subdivision, the vehicle shall be released to the owner or person in control of the vehicle only after the owner or person furnishes the storing law enforcement agency with proof of current registration and a currently valid driver's license to operate the vehicle.

(2) As used in this subdivision, "offstreet parking facility" means any offstreet facility held open for use by the public for parking vehicles and includes any publicly owned facilities for offstreet parking, and privately owned facilities for offstreet parking where no fee is charged for the privilege to park and which are held open for the common public use of retail customers.

(p) When the peace officer issues the driver of a vehicle a notice to appear for a violation of Section 12500, 14601, 14601.1, or 14601.2 and there is no passenger in the vehicle who has a valid driver's license and authorization to operate the vehicle. Any vehicle so removed from the highway or any public lands shall not be released to the registered owner or his or her agent, except upon presentation of the registered owner's or his or her agent's currently valid driver's license to operate the vehicle and proof of current vehicle registration, or upon order of a court.

(q) Whenever any vehicle is parked for more than 24 hours on a portion of highway which is located within the boundaries of a common interest development, as defined in subdivision (c) of Section 1351 of the Civil Code, and signs, as required by Section 22658.2, have been posted on that portion of highway providing notice to drivers that vehicles parked thereon for more than 24 hours will be removed at the owner's expense, pursuant to a resolution or ordinance adopted by the local authority.

(r) When any vehicle is illegally parked and blocks the movement of a legally parked vehicle. *(Amended by Stats 1991 ch 90 §68, eff. 6/30/91; ch 189 §40, eff. 7/29/91.)*

§22651.1. Storage facility; acceptance of bank cards.

Persons operating or in charge of any storage facility where vehicles are stored pursuant to Section 22651 shall accept a valid bank credit card or cash for payment of towing and storage by the registered owner, legal owner, or the owner's agent claiming the vehicle. In addition, persons operating or in charge of the storage facility shall have sufficient funds on the premises to accommodate and make change in a reasonable monetary transaction.

Credit charges for towing and storage services shall comply with Section 1748.1 of the Civil Code. Law enforcement agencies may include the costs of providing for payment by credit when agreeing with a towing or storage provider on rates. *(Amended by Stats 1990 ch 309 §2, eff. 1/1/91.)*

§22651.2. Removal of vehicle by peace officer.

(a) Any peace officer, as defined in Chapter 4.5 (commencing with Section 830) of Title 3 of Part 2 of the Penal Code; or any regularly employed and salaried employee, who is engaged in directing traffic or enforcing parking laws and regulations, of a city or a county in which a vehicle is located, may remove a vehicle located within the territorial limits in which the officer or employee may act when the vehicle is found upon a highway or any public lands, and if all of the following requirements are satisfied:

(1) Because of the size and placement of signs or placards on the vehicle, it appears that the primary purpose of parking the vehicle at that location is to advertise to the public an event or function on private property or on public property hired for a private event or function to which the public is invited.

(2) The vehicle is known to have been previously issued a notice of parking violation which was accompanied by a notice warning that an additional parking violation may result in the impoundment of the vehicle.

(3) The registered owner of the vehicle has been mailed a notice advising of the existence of the parking violation and that an additional violation may result in the impoundment of the vehicle.

(b) Subdivision (a) does not apply to a vehicle bearing any sign or placard advertising any business or enterprise carried on by or through the use of that vehicle.

(c) Section 22852 applies to the removal of any vehicle pursuant to this section. *(Added by Stats 1990 ch 73 §1, eff. 1/1/91.)*

§22651.3. Procedure for removing vehicles from offstreet parking facilities.

(a) Any peace officer, as that term is defined in Chapter 4.5 (commencing with Section 830) of Title 3 of Part 2 of the Penal Code, or any regularly employed and salaried employee, who is engaged in directing traffic or enforcing parking laws and regulations, of a city or a county in which any vehicle, other than a rented vehicle, is located may remove the vehicle from an offstreet public parking facility located within the territorial limits in which the officer or employee may act when the vehicle is known to have been issued five or more notices of parking violation over a period of five or more days, to which the owner or person in control of the vehicle has not responded or when any vehicle is illegally parked so as to prevent the movement of a legally parked vehicle.

A notice of parking violation issued to a vehicle which is registered in a foreign jurisdiction or is without current California registration and is known to have been issued five or more notices of parking violation over a period of five or more days shall be accompanied by a warning that repeated violations may result in the impounding of the vehicle.

(b) The vehicle may be impounded until the owner or person in control of the vehicle furnishes to the impounding law enforcement agency evidence of his or her identity and an address within this state at which he or she can be located and furnishes satisfactory evidence that bail has been deposited for all notices of parking violation issued for the vehicle. In lieu of requiring satisfactory evidence that the bail has been deposited, the impounding law enforcement agency may, in its discretion, issue a notice to appear for the offenses charged, as provided in Article 2 (commencing with Section 40500) of Chapter 2 of Division 17. In lieu of either furnishing satisfactory evidence that the bail has been deposited or accepting the notice to appear, the owner or person in control of the vehicle may demand to be taken without unnecessary delay before a magistrate within the county in which the offenses charged are alleged to have been committed and who has jurisdiction of the offenses and is nearest or most accessible with reference to the place where the vehicle is impounded.

(c) Evidence of current registration shall be produced after a vehicle has been impounded or a notice to appear for violation of subdivision (a) of Section 4000 shall be issued to the owner or person in control of the vehicle. *(Amended by Stats 1988 ch 619 §2, eff. 1/1/89.)*

§22651.4. Peace officer may impound vehicle and its cargo.

Any peace officer, as defined in Chapter 4.5 (commencing with Section 830) of Title 3 of Part 2 of the Penal Code, may impound a vehicle and its cargo pursuant to Section 34517. *(Added by Stats 1991 ch 707 §1, eff. 1/1/92.)*

§22651.5. Removal of vehicle with activated alarm device.

Any peace officer, as defined in Chapter 4.5 (commencing with Section 830) of Title 3 of Part 2 of the Penal Code, may, upon the complaint of any person,

© 1992 by J., B. & L. Gould
Printed in the U.S.A.   **EP**

remove a vehicle parked within a residence or business district from a highway or from public or private property if an alarm device has been activated within the vehicle, the peace officer is unable to locate the owner of the vehicle within 45 minutes from the time of arrival at the vehicle's location, and the alarm device has not been silenced prior to removal.

Upon removal of a vehicle from a highway or from public or private property pursuant to this section, the peace officer ordering the removal shall immediately report the removal and the location to which the vehicle is removed to the Stolen Vehicle System of the Department of Justice. *(Amended by Stats 1991 ch 928 §29, eff. 10/14/91.)*

§22651.7. Use of device to immobilize vehicles with outstanding parking violations.

In addition to, or as an alternative to, removal, any peace officer, as defined in Chapter 4.5 (commencing with Section 830) of Title 3 of Part 2 of the Penal Code; or any regularly employed and salaried employee who is engaged in directing traffic or enforcing parking laws and regulations, of a city or county in which a vehicle is located may immobilize the vehicle with a device designed and manufactured for the immobilization of vehicles, on a highway located within the territorial limits in which the officer or employee may act if the vehicle is found upon the highway and is known to have been issued five or more notices of parking violation over a period of five or more days to which the owner or person in control of the vehicle has not responded or the registered owner of the vehicle is known to have been issued five or more notices for failure to pay or failure to appear in court for traffic violations for which no certificate has been issued by the magistrate or clerk of the court hearing the case showing that the case has been adjudicated or concerning which the registered owner's record has not been cleared pursuant to Chapter 6 (commencing with Section 41500) of Division 17. The vehicle may be immobilized until that person furnishes to the immobilizing law enforcement agency evidence of his or her identity and an address within this state at which he or she can be located and satisfactory evidence that bail has been deposited for all notices of parking violation issued for the vehicle or all traffic violations of the registered owner have been cleared, or both. A notice of parking violation issued to the vehicle shall be accompanied by a warning that repeated violations may result in the impounding or immobilizing of the vehicle. In lieu of requiring satisfactory evidence that the bail has been deposited, the immobilizing law enforcement agency may, in its discretion, issue a notice to appear for the offenses charged, as provided in Article 2 (commencing with Section 40500) of Chapter 2 of Division 17. In lieu of either furnishing satisfactory evidence that the bail has been deposited or accepting the notice to appear, that person may demand to be taken without unnecessary delay before a magistrate within the county in which the offenses charged are alleged to have been committed and who has jurisdiction of the offenses and is nearest or most accessible with reference to the place where the vehicle is immobilized. Evidence of current registration shall be produced after a vehicle has been immobilized or a notice to appear for violation of subdivision (a) of Section 4000 shall be issued to that person. *(Amended by Stats 1991 ch 90 §69, eff. 6/30/91; ch 189 §41, eff. 7/29/91.)*

§22651.8. Satisfactory evidence of payment of parking violation.

For purposes of paragraph (1) of subdivision (i) of Section 22651 and Section 22651.7, "satisfactory evidence" includes, but is not limited to, a copy of a receipt issued by the department pursuant to subdivision (a) of Section 4760 for the payment of notices of parking violations appearing on the department's records at the time of payment. The processing agency shall, within 72 hours of receiving that satisfactory evidence, update its records to reflect the payments made to the department. If the processing agency does not receive the amount of the parking penalties and administrative fees from the department within four months of the date of issuance of that satisfactory evidence, the processing agency may revise its records to reflect that no payments were received for the notices of parking violation. *(Added by Stats 1991 ch 587 §2, eff. 1/1/92, oper. 7/1/92.)*

§22652. Removal of vehicle unlawfully parked in disabled person's reserved space.

Any peace officer, as defined in Chapter 4.5 (commencing with Section 830) of Title 3 of Part 2 of the Penal Code, or any regularly employed and salaried employee engaged in directing traffic or enforcing parking laws and regulations of a city or county, may remove any vehicle from a stall or space designated for physically handicapped persons pursuant to Section 22511.7 or 22511.8, located within the jurisdictional limits in which the officer or employee is authorized to act, if the vehicle is parked in violation of Section 22507.8 and if the police or sheriff's department or the Department of the California Highway Patrol has been notified.

In a privately or publicly owned or operated off-street parking facility, this section applies only to those stalls and spaces if the posting requirements under subdivisions (a) and (d) of Section 22511.8 have been complied with and if the stalls or spaces are clearly signed or marked. *(Amended by Stats 1985 ch 1041 §11.)*

§22652.5. Liability for vehicle removed from disabled person's space.

The owner or person in lawful possession of an offstreet parking facility, or any local authority owning or operating an offstreet parking facility, who causes a vehicle to be removed from the parking facility pursuant to Section 22511.8, or any state, city, or county employee, is not civilly liable for the removal if the police or sheriff's department in whose jurisdiction the offstreet parking facility or the stall or space is located or the Department of the California Highway Patrol has been notified prior to the removal.

§22653. Removal of a vehicle from private property by a peace officer.

(a) Any peace officer, as that term is defined in Chapter 4.5 (commencing with Section 830) of Title 3 of Part 2 of the Penal Code, other than an employee directing traffic or enforcing parking laws and regulations, may remove a vehicle from private property located within the territorial limits in which the officer is empowered to act, when a report has previously been made that the vehicle has been stolen or a complaint has been filed and a warrant thereon issued charging that the vehicle has been embezzled.

(b) Any peace officer, as that term is defined in Chapter 4.5 (commencing with Section 830) of Title 3 of Part 2 of the Penal Code, may, after a reasonable period of time, remove a vehicle from private property located within the territorial limits in which the officer is empowered to act, if the vehicle has been involved in, and left at the scene of, a traffic accident and no owner is available to grant permission to remove the vehicle. This subdivision does not authorize the removal of a vehicle where the owner has been contacted and has refused to grant permission to remove the vehicle.

(c) Any peace officer as that term is defined in Chapter 4.5 (commencing with Section 830) of Title 3 of Part 2 of the Penal Code, may, at the request of the property owner or person in lawful possession of any private property, remove a vehicle from private property located within the territorial limits in which the officer is empowered to act when an officer arrests any person driving or in control of a vehicle for an alleged offense and the officer is, by this code or other law required or authorized to take, and does take the person arrested before a magistrate without unnecessary delay. *(Amended by Stats 1985 ch 912 §3.)*

§22654. Conditions under which peace officer may move a vehicle.

(a) Whenever any peace officer, as that term is defined in Chapter 4.5 (commencing with Section 830) of Title 3 of Part 2 of the Penal Code, or other employee directing traffic or enforcing parking laws and regulations, finds a vehicle standing upon a highway, located within the territorial limits in which the officer or employee is empowered to act, in violation of Sections 22500 and 22504, the officer or employee may move the vehicle or require the driver or other person in charge of the vehicle to move it to the nearest available position off the roadway or to the nearest parking location, or may remove and store the vehicle if moving it off the roadway to a parking location is impracticable.

(b) Whenever the officer or employee finds a vehicle standing upon a street, located within the territorial limits in which the officer or employee is empowered to act, in violation of a traffic ordinance enacted by local authorities to prevent flooding of adjacent property, he or she may move the vehicle or require the driver or person in charge of the vehicle to move it to the nearest available location in the vicinity where parking is permitted.

(c) Any state, county, or city authority charged with the maintenance of any highway may move any vehicle which is disabled or abandoned or which constitutes an obstruction to traffic from the place where it is located on a highway to the nearest available position on the same highway as may be necessary to keep the highway open or safe for public travel. In addition, employees of the Department of Transportation may remove any disabled vehicle which constitutes an obstruction to traffic on a freeway from the place where it is located to the nearest available location where parking is permitted; and, if the vehicle is unoccupied, the department shall comply with the notice requirements of subdivision (d).

(d) Any state, county, or city authority charged with the maintenance or operation of any highway, highway facility, or public works facility, in cases necessitating the prompt performance of any work on or service to the highway, highway facility, or public works facility, may move to the nearest available location where parking is permitted, any unattended vehicle which obstructs or interferes with the performance of the work or service or may remove and store the vehicle if moving it off the roadway to a location where parking is permitted would be impracticable. If the vehicle is moved to another location where it is not readily visible from its former parked location or it is stored, the person causing the movement or storage of the vehicle shall immediately, by the most expeditious means, notify the owner of the vehicle of its location. If for any reason the vehicle owner cannot be so notified, the person causing the vehicle to be moved or stored shall immediately, by the most expeditious means, notify the police department of the city in which the vehicle was parked, or, if the vehicle had been parked in an unincorporated area of a county, notify the sheriff's department and nearest office of the California Highway Patrol in that county. No vehicle may be removed and stored pursuant to this subdivision unless signs indicating that no person shall stop, park, or leave standing any vehicle within the areas marked by the signs because the work or service would be done, were placed at least 24 hours prior to the movement or removal and storage.

(e) Whenever any peace officer finds a vehicle parked or standing upon a highway in a manner so as to obstruct necessary emergency services, or the routing of traffic at the scene of a disaster, the officer may move the vehicle or require the driver or other person in charge of the vehicle to move it to the nearest available parking location. If the vehicle is unoccupied, and moving the vehicle to a parking location is impractical, the officer may store the vehicle pursuant to Sections 22850 and 22852 and subdivision (a) or (b) of Section 22853. If the vehicle so moved or stored was otherwise lawfully parked, no moving or storage charges shall be assessed against or collected from the driver or owner.

§22655. Removal by peace officer of vehicle involved in hit-and-run accident.

(a) When any peace officer, as that term is defined in Chapter 4.5 (commencing with Section 830) of Title 3 of Part 2 of the Penal Code, has reasonable cause to believe that a motor vehicle on a highway or on private property open to the general public onto which the public is explicitly or implicitly invited, located within the territorial limits in which the officer is empowered to act, has been involved in a hit-and-run accident, and the operator of the vehicle has failed to stop and comply with the provisions of Sections 20002 to 20006, inclusive, the officer may remove the vehicle from the highway or from public or private property for the purpose of inspection.

(b) Unless sooner released, the vehicle shall be released upon the expiration of 48 hours after such removal from the highway or private property upon demand of the owner. When determining the 48-hour period, weekends, and holidays shall not be included.

(c) Notwithstanding subdivision (b), when a motor vehicle to be inspected pursuant to subdivision (a) is a commercial vehicle, any cargo within the vehicle may be removed or transferred to another vehicle.

This section shall not be construed to authorize the removal of any vehicle from an enclosed structure on private property which is not open to the general public.

© 1992 by J., B. & L. Gould
Printed in the U.S.A.　　EP

§22655.3. Storage of vehicle used to flee officer.

Any peace officer, as defined in Chapter 4.5 (commencing with Section 830) of Title 3 of Part 2 of the Penal Code, pursuing a fleeing or evading person in a motor vehicle may remove and store, or cause to be removed and stored, any vehicle used in violation of Section 2800.1 or 2800.2 from property other than that of the registered owner of the vehicle for the purposes of investigation, identification, or apprehension of the driver if the driver of the vehicle abandons the vehicle and leaves it unattended. All towing and storage fees for a vehicle removed under this section shall be paid by the owner, unless the vehicle was stolen or taken without permission.

No vehicle shall be impounded under this section if the driver is arrested before arrival of the towing equipment or if the registered owner is in the vehicle.

As used in this section "remove and store a vehicle" means that the peace officer may cause the removal of a vehicle to, and storage of a vehicle in, a private lot where the vehicle may be secured by the owner of the facility or by the owner's representative.

This section is not intended to change current statute and case law governing searches and seizures. *(Amended and renumbered by Stats 1988 ch 160 §181, eff. 1/1/89; formerly §22651.7.)*

§22655.5. Removal of vehicle used in commission of a crime.

(a) A peace officer, as defined in Chapter 4.5 (commencing with Section 830) of Title 3 of Part 2 of the Penal Code, may remove a motor vehicle from the highway or from public or private property within the territorial limits in which the officer may act, if the peace officer has probable cause to believe either of the following:

(1) That the vehicle was used in the commission of a public offense.

(2) That the vehicle is itself evidence which tends to show that a crime has been committed or that the vehicle contains evidence, which cannot readily be removed, which tends to show that a crime has been committed.

(b) Notwithstanding Section 3068 of the Civil Code or Section 22851 of this code, the following apply with respect to a vehicle removed pursuant to this section:

(1) The owner of the vehicle is not liable for any resulting towing and storage fees unless the vehicle was used by the alleged perpetrator of the crime with the express or implied permission of the owner of the vehicle.

(2) The owner of a stolen vehicle that is removed and held for investigatory or prosecution purposes, or for use as an exhibit in a judicial proceeding, is not liable for any resulting towing and storage fees.

(3) Any towing and storage charges for a vehicle for which the owner is not liable pursuant to paragraph (2) shall be paid by the public agency employer of the peace officer who ordered the removal and storage of the vehicle or the prosecuting agency which ordered the storage of the vehicle.

(c) In any prosecution of the crime for which a vehicle was impounded pursuant to this section, the prosecutor may request, and the court may order, the perpetrator of the crime, if convicted, to pay the costs of towing and storage of the vehicle.

(d) Nothing in this section exempts the public agency whose employee ordered the removal of the vehicle pursuant to subdivision (a) from the notification requirements of Section 22852.

(e) This section shall remain in effect only until January 1, 1993, and as of that date is repealed, unless a later enacted statute, which is enacted before January 1, 1993, deletes or extends that date. *(Amended by Stats 1990 ch 1515 §1, eff. 1/1/91 only until 1/1/93. See other section 22655.5 below.)*

§22655.5. Removal of vehicle used in commission of a crime.

A peace officer, as defined in Chapter 4.5 (commencing with Section 830) of Title 3 of Part 2 of the Penal Code, may remove a motor vehicle from the highway or from public or private property within the territorial limits in which the officer may act under the following circumstances:

(a) When any vehicle is found upon a highway or public or private property and a peace officer has probable cause to believe that the vehicle was used as the means of committing a public offense.

(b) When any vehicle is found upon a highway or public or private property and a peace officer has probable cause to believe that the vehicle is itself evidence which tends to show that a crime has been committed or that the vehicle contains evidence, which cannot readily be removed, which tends to show that a crime has been committed.

(c) Notwithstanding Section 3068 of the Civil Code or Section 22851 of this code, no lien shall attach to a vehicle removed under this section unless the vehicle was used by the alleged perpetrator of the crime with the express or implied permission of the owner of the vehicle.

(d) In any prosecution of the crime for which a vehicle was impounded pursuant to this section, the prosecutor may request, and the court may order, the perpetrator of the crime, if convicted, to pay the costs of towing and storage of the vehicle.

(e) This section shall become operative on January 1, 1993. *(Added by Stats 1990 ch 1515 §2, eff. 1/1/91, oper. 1/1/93.)*

§22656. Removal of vehicle from right-of-way of any rail line.

Any peace officer, as that term is defined in Chapter 4.5 (commencing with Section 830) of Title 3 of Part 2 of the Penal Code, may remove a vehicle from the right-of-way of a railroad, street railway, or light rail line located within the territorial limits in which the officer is empowered to act if the vehicle is parked or abandoned upon any track or within 7½ feet of the nearest rail. *(Amended by Stats 1988 ch 18 §1, eff. 1/1/89.)*

§22658. Procedure for removal of vehicle from private property.

(a) Except as provided in Section 22658.2, the owner or person in lawful possession of any private property may, subsequent to notifying, by telephone or, if impractical, by the most expeditious means available, the city police or county sheriff, whichever is appropriate, cause the removal of a vehicle parked on the property to the nearest public garage under any of the following circumstances:

(1) There is displayed, in plain view at all entrances to the property, a sign not less than 17 by 22 inches in size, with lettering not less than one inch in height, prohibiting public parking and indicating that

vehicles will be removed at the owner's expense, and containing the telephone number of the local traffic law enforcement agency, and the sign may also indicate that a citation may also be issued for the violation.

(2) The vehicle has been issued a notice of parking violation, and 96 hours have elapsed since the issuance of that notice.

(3) The vehicle is on private property and lacks an engine, transmission, wheels, tires, doors, windshield, or any other major part or equipment necessary to operate safely on the highways, the owner or person in lawful possession of the private property has notified the city police or county sheriff, as appropriate, and 24 hours have elapsed since that notification.

(4) The lot or parcel upon which the vehicle is parked is improved with a single-family dwelling.

(b) The person causing removal of the vehicle shall, if the person knows or is able to ascertain from the registration records of the Department of Motor Vehicles the name and address of the registered and legal owner of the vehicle, immediately give, or cause to be given, notice in writing to the registered and legal owner of the fact of the removal, the grounds for the removal, and indicate the place to which the vehicle has been removed. If the vehicle is stored in a public garage, a copy of the notice shall be given to the proprietor of the garage. The notice provided for in this section shall include the amount of mileage on the vehicle at the time of removal. If the person does not know and is not able to ascertain the name of the owner or for any other reason is unable to give the notice to the owner as provided in this section, the person causing removal of the vehicle shall comply with the requirements of subdivision (c) of Section 22853 relating to notice in the same manner as applicable to an officer removing a vehicle from private property.

(c) This section does not limit or affect any right or remedy which the owner or person in lawful possession of private property may have by virtue of other provisions of law authorizing the removal of a vehicle parked upon private property.

(d) The owner of a vehicle removed from private property pursuant to subdivision (a) may recover for any damage to the vehicle resulting from any intentional or negligent act of any person causing the removal of, or removing, the vehicle.

(e) Any owner or person in lawful possession of any private property, or an "association" pursuant to Section 22658.2, causing the removal of a vehicle parked on that property is liable for double the storage or towing charges whenever there has been a failure to comply with paragraph (1), (2), or (3) of subdivision (a) or to state the grounds for the removal of the vehicle if requested by the legal or registered owner of the vehicle as required by subdivision (f).

(f) Any owner or person in lawful possession of any private property, or an "association" pursuant to Section 22658.2, causing the removal of a vehicle parked on that property shall state the grounds for the removal of the vehicle if requested by the legal or registered owner of that vehicle. Any towing company that removes a vehicle from private property with the authorization of the property owner or the property owner's agent shall not be held responsible in any situation relating to the validity of the removal. Any towing company that removes the vehicle under this section shall be responsible for (1) any damage to the

vehicle in the transit and subsequent storage of the vehicle and (2) the removal of a vehicle other than the vehicle specified by the owner or other person in lawful possession of the private property.

(g) Possession of any vehicle under this section shall be deemed to arise when a vehicle is removed from private property and is in transit.

(h) A towing company may impose a charge of not more than one-half of the regular towing charge for the towing of a vehicle at the request of the owner of private property or that owner's agent pursuant to this section if the owner of the vehicle or the owner's agent returns to the vehicle before it is removed from the private property. The regular towing charge may only be imposed after the vehicle has been removed from the property and is in transit.

(i) A charge for towing or storage, or both, of a vehicle under this section is excessive if the charge is greater than that which would have been charged for towing or storage, or both, made at the request of a law enforcement agency under an agreement between the law enforcement agency and a towing company in the city or county in which is located the private property from which the vehicle was, or was attempted to be, removed.

If a request to release a vehicle is made within eight hours from the time the vehicle is brought into the storage facility, regardless of the calendar date, the storage charge shall be for only one day. Not more than one day's storage charge may be required for any vehicle released the same day that it is stored.

(j) Any person who charges a vehicle owner a towing, service, or storage charge at an excessive rate, as described in subdivision (i), is liable to the vehicle owner for four times the amount charged.

(k) Persons operating or in charge of any storage facility where vehicles are stored pursuant to this section shall accept a valid bank credit card or cash for payment of towing and storage by a registered owner or the owner's agent claiming the vehicle. In addition, persons operating or in charge of the storage facility shall have sufficient moneys on the premises to accommodate, and make change in, a reasonable monetary transaction.

Credit charges for towing and storage services shall comply with Section 1748.1 of the Civil Code. Law enforcement agencies may include the costs of providing for payment by credit when making agreements with towing companies as described in subdivision (i).

(*l*) (1) A towing company shall not remove a vehicle from private property without first obtaining written authorization from the property owner or lessee, or an employee or agent thereof, who shall be present at the time of removal. General authorization to remove vehicles at the towing company's discretion shall not be delegated to a towing company or its affiliates except in the case of a vehicle unlawfully parked within 15 feet of a fire hydrant or in a fire lane, or in a manner which interferes with any entrance to, or exit from, the private property.

(2) If a towing company removes a vehicle without written authorization and that vehicle is unlawfully parked within 15 feet of a fire hydrant or in a fire lane, or in a manner which interferes with any entrance to, or exit from, the private property, the towing company shall take, prior to the removal of that vehicle, a photograph of the vehicle which clearly indicates that parking violation. The towing company shall keep one copy of the photograph taken pursuant to this para-

© 1992 by J., B. & L. Gould
Printed in the U.S.A.   EP

graph, and shall present that photograph to the owner or an agent of the owner, when that person claims the vehicle.

(3) Any towing company, or any affiliate of a towing company, which removes a vehicle from private property without first obtaining written authorization from the property owner or lessee, or an employee or agent thereof, who is present at the time of removal, except as permitted by paragraph (1), is liable to the owner of the vehicle for four times the amount of the towing and storage charges, in addition to any applicable criminal penalty, for a violation of paragraph (1). *(Amended by Stats 1991 ch 711 §3; ch 1004 §4, eff. 1/1/92.)*

§22658.1. Procedure when fence is damaged during removal of a vehicle.

(a) Any towing company that, in removing a vehicle, cuts, removes, otherwise damages, or leaves open a fence without the prior approval of the property owner or the person in charge of the property shall then and there do either of the following:

(a)* Locate and notify the owner or person in charge of the property of the damage or open condition of the fence, the name and address of the towing company, and the license, registration, or identification number of the vehicle being removed.

(2) Leave in a conspicuous place on the property the name and address of the towing company, and the license, registration, or identification number of the vehicle being removed, and shall without unnecessary delay, notify the police department of the city in which the property is located, or if the property is located in unincorporated territory, either the sheriff or the local headquarters of the Department of the California Highway Patrol, of that information and the location of the damaged or opened fence.

(b) Any person failing to comply with all the requirements of this section is guilty of an infraction. *(Added by Stats 1985 ch 608 §1.)*
*So in original. Probably should be "(1)".

§22658.2. Removal of vehicle by common interest development association.

(a) Except as provided in subdivision (b), an "association", as defined in subdivision (a) of Section 1351 of the Civil Code, of a common interest development, as defined in subdivision (c) of Section 1351 of the Civil Code, may cause the removal of a vehicle parked on that property to the nearest public garage if all of the following requirements are satisfied:

(1) A sign not less than 17 by 22 inches in size with lettering not less than one inch in height appears at each entrance to the common interest development and contains both of the following:

(A) A statement that public parking is prohibited and all vehicles not authorized to park on the common interest development will be removed at the owner's expense.

(B) The telephone number of the local traffic law enforcement agency.

The sign may also indicate that a citation may be issued for the violation.

(2) If the identity of the registered owner of the vehicle is known or readily ascertainable, the president of the association or his or her designee shall, within a reasonable time, notify the owner of the removal by first-class mail. If the identity of the owner of the vehicle is not known or ascertainable, the presi-

dent of the association or his or her designee shall comply with subdivision (c) of Section 22853.

(3) The president of the association or his or her designee, gives or causes to be given, notice of the removal to the local traffic law enforcement agency immediately after the vehicle has been removed. The notice shall include a description of the vehicle, the license plate number, and the address from where the vehicle was removed.

(b) The association may cause the removal without notice of any vehicle parked in a marked fire lane, within 15 feet of a fire hydrant, in a parking space designated for handicapped without proper authority, or in a manner which interferes with any entrance to, or exit from, the common interest development or any separate interest contained therein.

(c) Notwithstanding Section 1708 of the Civil Code, the association shall not be liable for any damages incurred by the vehicle owner because of the removal of a vehicle in compliance with this section or for any damage to the vehicle caused by the removal. However, the owner of a vehicle removed pursuant to this section may recover for any damage to the vehicle which results from any intentional or negligent act of the association or any person causing the removal of, or removing, the vehicle.

(d) Notwithstanding any other provision of law, subdivisions (f) to (k), inclusive, of Section 22658 apply to the removal of vehicles pursuant to this section. *(Added by Stats 1986 ch 1262.)*

§22659. Removal of vehicle from state property.

Any officer of the California State Police or any person duly authorized by the state agency in possession of property owned by the state, or rented or leased from others by the state and any officer of the California State Police providing policing services to property of a district agricultural association may, subsequent to giving notice to the city police or county sheriff, whichever is appropriate, cause the removal of a vehicle from such property to the nearest public garage, under any of the following circumstances:

(a) When the vehicle is illegally parked in locations where signs are posted giving notice of violation and removal.

(b) When an officer arrests any person driving or in control of a vehicle for an alleged offense and the officer is by this code or other law required to take the person arrested before a magistrate without unnecessary delay.

(c) When any vehicle is found upon such property and report has previously been made that the vehicle has been stolen or complaint has been filed and a warrant thereon issued charging that the vehicle has been embezzled.

(d) When the person or persons in charge of a vehicle upon such property are by reason of physical injuries or illness incapacitated to such an extent as to be unable to provide for its custody or removal.

The person causing removal of such vehicle shall comply with the requirements of Sections 22852 and 22853, relating to notice.

§22669. Procedure for removal of abandoned vehicles.

(a) Any peace officer, as that term is defined in Chapter 4.5 (commencing with Section 830) of Title 3 of Part 2 of the Penal Code, or any other employee of the state, county, or city designated by an agency or department of the state or the board of supervisors or city council to perform this function, in the territorial limits in which the officer or employee is authorized to act, who has reasonable grounds to believe that the vehicle has been abandoned, as determined pursuant to Section 22523, may remove the vehicle from a highway or from public or private property.

(b) Any person performing a franchise or contract awarded pursuant to subdivision (a) of Section 22710, may remove a vehicle from a highway or place to which it has been removed pursuant to subdivision (c) of Section 22654 or from public or private property, after a determination by a peace officer, as that term is defined in Chapter 4.5 (commencing with Section 830) of Title 3 of Part 2 of the Penal Code, or other designated employee of the state, county, or city in which the vehicle is located that the vehicle is abandoned, as determined pursuant to Section 22523.

(c) A state, county, or city employee, other than a peace officer or employee of a sheriff's department or a city police department, designated to remove vehicles pursuant to this section may do so only after he or she has mailed or personally delivered a written report identifying the vehicle and its location to the office of the Department of the California Highway Patrol located nearest to the vehicle.

(d) Motor vehicles which are parked, resting, or otherwise immobilized on any highway or public right-of-way and which lack an engine, transmission, wheels, tires, doors, windshield, or any other part or equipment necessary to operate safely on the highways of this state, are hereby declared a hazard to public health, safety, and welfare and may be removed immediately upon discovery by a peace officer or other designated employee of the state, county, or city. *(Amended by Stats 1987 ch 1133 §4.)*

CHAPTER 12

PUBLIC OFFENSES

ARTICLE 1

DRIVING OFFENSES

§23103. Reckless driving: definition and penalties.

(a) Any person who drives any vehicle upon a highway in willful or wanton disregard for the safety of persons or property is guilty of reckless driving.

(b) Any person who drives any vehicle in any off-street parking facility, as defined in subdivision (d) of Section 12500, in willful or wanton disregard for the safety of persons or property is guilty of reckless driving.

(c) Persons convicted of the offense of reckless driving shall be punished by imprisonment in the county jail for not less than five days nor more than 90 days or by a fine of not less than one hundred forty-five dollars ($145) nor more than one thousand dollars ($1,000), or by both fine and imprisonment, except as provided in Section 23104. *(Amended by Stats 1991 ch 928 §30.5, eff. 10/14/91.)*

§23103.5. Guilty or nolo contendere plea for reckless driving.

(a) When the prosecution agrees to a plea of guilty or nolo contendere to a charge of a violation of Section 23103 in satisfaction of, or as a substitute for, an original charge of a violation of Section 23152, the prosecution shall state for the record a factual basis for the satisfaction or substitution, including whether or not there had been consumption of any alcoholic beverage or ingestion or administration of any drug, or both, by the defendant in connection with the offense. The statement shall set forth the facts which show whether or not there was a consumption of any alcoholic beverage or the ingestion or administration of any drug by the defendant in connection with the offense.

(b) The court shall advise the defendant, prior to the acceptance of the plea offered pursuant to a factual statement pursuant to subdivision (a), of the consequences of a conviction of a violation of Section 23103 as set forth in subdivision (c).

(c) If the court accepts the defendant's plea of guilty or nolo contendere to a charge of a violation of Section 23103 and the prosecutor's statement under subdivision (a) states that there was consumption of any alcoholic beverage or the ingestion or administration of any drugs by the defendant in connection with the offense, the resulting conviction shall be a prior offense for the purposes of Section 23165, 23170, 23175, 23185, 23190 or 23200, as specified in those sections.

(d) The court shall notify the Department of Motor Vehicles of each conviction of Section 23103 which shall be a prior offense for purposes of Section 23165, 23170, 23175, 23185, 23190, or 23200, as provided in this section. *(Amended by Stats 1988 chs 939 §1; ch 1273 §2, eff. 1/1/89, oper. 7/1/89.)*

§23104. Penalties for reckless driving resulting in bodily injury.

(a) Except as provided in subdivision (b), whenever reckless driving of a vehicle proximately causes bodily injury to any person other than the driver, the person driving the vehicle shall, upon conviction thereof, be punished by imprisonment in the county jail for not less than 30 days nor more than six months or by a fine of not less than two hundred twenty dollars ($220) nor more than one thousand dollars ($1,000), or by both the fine and imprisonment.

(b) Any person convicted of reckless driving which proximately causes great bodily injury, as defined in Section 12022.7 of the Penal Code, to any person other than the driver, who previously has been convicted of a violation of Section 23103, 23104, 23109, 23152, or 23153 shall be punished by imprisonment in the state prison, by imprisonment in the county jail for not less than 30 days nor more than six months or by a fine of not less than two hundred twenty dollars ($220) nor more than one thousand dollars ($1,000) or by both the fine and imprisonment.

§23109. Penalties for vehicular speed contests.

(a) No person shall engage in any motor vehicle speed contest on a highway. As used in this section, a motor vehicle speed contest includes a motor vehicle race against another vehicle, a clock, or other timing device. For purposes of this section, an event in which the time to cover a prescribed route of more than 20 miles is measured, but where the vehicle does not exceed the speed limits, is not a speed contest.

(b) No person shall aid or abet in any motor vehicle speed contest on any highway.

(c) No person shall engage in any motor vehicle exhibition of speed on a highway, and no person shall

© 1992 by J., B. & L. Gould
Printed in the U.S.A.　　EP

aid or abet in any motor vehicle exhibition of speed on any highway.

(d) No person shall for the purpose of facilitating or aiding or as an incident to any motor vehicle speed contest or exhibition upon a highway in any manner obstruct or place any barricade or obstruction or assist or participate in placing any barricade or obstruction upon any highway.

(e) Any person convicted of a violation of subdivision (a) shall be punished by imprisonment in the county jail for not less than 24 hours nor more than 90 days or by a fine of not less than three hundred fifty-five dollars ($355) nor more than one thousand dollars ($1,000) or both that fine and imprisonment. The person's privilege to operate a motor vehicle shall be subject to suspension as provided in subdivision (a) of Section 13352. The person's privilege to operate a motor vehicle may be restricted for 90 days to six months to necessary travel to and from that person's place of employment and, if driving a motor vehicle is necessary to perform the duties of the person's employment, restricted to driving in that person's scope of employment. This subdivision does not interfere with the court's power to grant probation in a suitable case.

(f) Any person convicted of a violation of subdivision (a) for an offense which occurred within five years of the date of a prior offense which resulted in a conviction of a violation of subdivision (a) shall be punished by imprisonment in the county jail for not less than four days nor more than six months and by a fine of not less than five hundred dollars ($500) nor more than one thousand dollars ($1,000). Additionally, the Department of Motor Vehicles shall either suspend the person's privilege to operate a motor vehicle, as provided in subdivision (a) of Section 13352, or the person's privilege to operate a motor vehicle shall be restricted for six months to necessary travel to and from that person's place of employment and, if driving a motor vehicle is necessary to perform the duties of the person's employment, restricted to driving in that person's scope of employment. This subdivision does not interfere with the court's power to grant probation in a suitable case.

(g) If the court grants probation to any person punishable under subdivision (f), in addition to the provisions of subdivision (f) and any other terms and conditions imposed by the court, which may include a fine, the court shall impose as a condition of probation that the person be confined in the county jail for not less than 48 hours nor more than six months. The person's privilege to operate a motor vehicle shall also be suspended by the Department of Motor Vehicles pursuant to subdivision (a) of Section 13352 or shall be restricted pursuant to subdivision (f).

(h) If any person is convicted of a violation of subdivision (a) and the vehicle used in the violation is registered to that person, the vehicle may be impounded at the registered owner's expense for not less than one day nor more than 30 days.

(i) Any person who violates subdivision (b), (c), or (d) of this section shall upon conviction thereof be punished by imprisonment in the county jail for not more than 90 days or by fine of not more than five hundred dollars ($500) or by both that fine and imprisonment.

(j) If a person's privilege to operate a motor vehicle is restricted by a court pursuant to this section, the court shall clearly mark the restriction and the dates of the restriction on that person's driver's license and

promptly notify the Department of Motor Vehicles of the terms of the restriction in a manner prescribed by the department. The Department of Motor Vehicles shall place that restriction in the person's records in the Department of Motor Vehicles and enter the restriction on any license subsequently issued by the Department of Motor Vehicles to that person during the period of the restriction.

(k) The court may order that any person convicted under this section, who is to be punished by imprisonment in the county jail, be imprisoned on days other than days of regular employment of the person, as determined by the court.

(l) This section shall be known and may be cited as the Louis Friend Memorial Act.

§23109.5. Penalties for second conviction for engaging in a vehicular speed contest.

(a) In any case charging a violation of subdivision (a) of Section 23109 and where the offense occurs within five years of one or more prior offenses which resulted in conviction of violation of subdivision (a) of Section 23109, the court shall not strike any prior conviction of those offenses for purposes of sentencing in order to avoid imposing, as part of the sentence or term of probation, the minimum time of imprisonment, as provided in subdivision (f) of Section 23109, or for purposes of avoiding revocation, suspension, or restriction of the privilege to operate a motor vehicle, as provided in Section 13352 or 23109.

(b) In any case charging a violation of subdivision (a) of Section 23109, the court shall obtain a copy of the driving record of the person charged from the Department of Motor Vehicles and may obtain any records from the Department of Justice or any other source to determine if one or more prior convictions of the person for violation of subdivision (a) of Section 23109 have occurred within five years of the charged offense.

§23110. Throwing substances or objects at vehicle prohibited.

(a) Any person who throws any substance at a vehicle or any occupant thereof on a highway is guilty of a misdemeanor.

(b) Any person who with intent to do great bodily injury maliciously and wilfully throws or projects any rock, brick, bottle, metal or other missile, or projects any other substance capable of doing serious bodily harm at such vehicle or occupant thereof is guilty of a felony and upon conviction shall be punished by imprisonment in the state prison.

§23111. Throwing cigarettes, matches, etc., on highways.

No person in any vehicle and no pedestrian shall throw or discharge from or upon any road or highway or adjoining area, public or private, any lighted or nonlighted cigarette, cigar, match, or any flaming or glowing substance. This section shall be known as the Paul Buzzo Act.

§23112. Depositing substances and objects on highways.

(a) No person shall throw or deposit, nor shall the registered owner or the driver, if such owner is not then present in the vehicle, aid or abet in the throwing or depositing upon any highway any bottle, can, garbage, glass, nail, offal, paper, wire, any substance likely to injure or damage traffic using the highway, or any noisome, nauseous, or offensive matter of any kind.

(b) No person shall place, deposit or dump, or cause to be placed, deposited or dumped, any rocks, refuse, garbage, or dirt in or upon any highway, including any portion of the right-of-way thereof, without the consent of the state or local agency having jurisdiction over the highway.

§23112.5. Depositing hazardous material on highway.

Any person who dumps, spills, or causes the release of hazardous material, as defined by Section 353, or hazardous waste, as defined by Section 25117 of the Health and Safety Code, upon any highway shall notify the Department of the California Highway Patrol or the agency having traffic jurisdiction for that highway of the dump, spill, or release, as soon as the person has knowledge of the dump, spill, or release and notification is possible. Any person who is convicted of a violation of this section shall be punished by a mandatory fine of not less than two thousand dollars ($2,000). *(Amended by Stats 1990 ch 429 §1, eff. 1/1/91.)*

§23113. Person who deposits substance on highway must remove it.

(a) Any person who drops, dumps, deposits, places, or throws, or causes or permits to be dropped, dumped, deposited, placed, or thrown, upon any highway or street any material described in Section 23112 or in subdivision (d) of Section 23114 shall immediately remove the material or cause the material to be removed.

(b) If the person fails to comply with subdivision (a), the governmental agency responsible for the maintenance of the street or highway on which the material has been deposited may remove the material and collect, by civil action, if necessary, the actual cost of the removal operation in addition to any other damages authorized by law from the person made responsible under subdivision (a).

(c) A member of the Department of the California Highway Patrol may direct a responsible party to remove the aggregate material described in subdivision (d) of Section 23114 from a highway when that material has escaped or been released from a vehicle. *(Amended by Stats 1989 chs 1360 §158, 125 §1, eff. 7/12/89.)*

§23114. Provisions to prevent spilling loads on highways.

(a) No vehicle shall be driven or moved on any highway unless the vehicle is so constructed, covered, or loaded as to prevent any of its contents or load other than clear water or feathers from live birds from dropping, sifting, leaking, blowing, spilling, or otherwise escaping from the vehicle.

(b) (1) Aggregate material shall only be carried in the cargo area of a vehicle. The cargo area shall not contain any holes, cracks, or openings through which that material may escape, regardless of the degree to which the vehicle is loaded, except as provided in paragraph (2).

(2) Every vehicle used to transport aggregate materials, regardless of the degree to which the vehicle is loaded, shall be equipped with all of the following:

(A) Properly functioning seals on any openings used to empty the load, including, but not limited to, bottom-dump release gates and tailgates.

(B) Splash flaps behind every tire, or set of tires, regardless of position on the truck, truck tractor, or trailer.

(C) Center flaps at a location to the rear of each bottom/dump release gate as to trucks or trailers equipped with bottom/dump release gates. The center flap may be positioned directly behind the bottom/dump release gate and in front of the rear axle of the vehicle, or it may be positioned to the rear of the rear axle in line with the splash flaps required behind the tires. The width of the center flap shall extend not more than one inch from one sidewall to the opposite sidewall of the inside tires and shall extend to within five inches of the pavement surface, and shall be not less than 24 inches from the bottom edge to the top edge of that center flap.

(D) Fenders starting at the splash flap with the leading edge of the fenders extending forward at least six inches beyond the center of the axle which cover the tops of tires not already covered by the truck, truck tractor, or trailer body.

(E) Complete enclosures on all vertical sides of the cargo area, including, but not limited to, tailgates.

(F) Shed boards designed to prevent aggregate materials from being deposited on the vehicle body during top loading.

(c) Vehicles comprised of full rigid enclosures are exempt only from subparagraphs (C) and (F) of paragraph (2) of subdivision (b).

(d) For purposes of this section, "aggregate material" means rock fragments, pebbles, sand, dirt, gravel, cobbles, crushed base, asphalt, and other similar materials.

(e) (1) On and after September 1, 1990, in addition to subdivisions (a) and (b), no vehicle shall transport any aggregate material upon a highway unless the material is covered.

(2) Vehicles transporting loads composed entirely of asphalt material are exempt only from the provisions of this section requiring that loads be covered.

(3) Vehicles transporting loads composed entirely of petroleum coke material shall not be required to cover their loads if they are loaded using safety procedures, specialized equipment, and a chemical surfactant designed to prevent materials from blowing, spilling, or otherwise escaping from the vehicle.

(4) Vehicles transporting loads of aggregate materials shall not be required to cover their loads if the load, where it contacts the sides, front, and back of the cargo container area, remains six inches from the upper edge of the container area, and if the load does not extend, at its peak, above any part of the upper edge of the cargo container area.

(5) The requirements of this subdivision shall become operative on September 1, 1990. *(Amended by Stats 1989 chs 125 §2, eff. 7/12/89, 533 §12, eff. 1/1/90.)*

§23115. Vehicles for transporting rubbish.

(a) No vehicle loaded with garbage, swill, cans, bottles, wastepapers, ashes, refuse, trash, or rubbish, or any other noisome, nauseous, or offensive matter, or anything being transported to a dump site for disposal shall be driven or moved upon any highway unless the load is totally covered in a manner which

© 1992 by J., B. & L. Gould
Printed in the U.S.A.   **EP**

will prevent the load or any part of the load from spilling or falling from the vehicle.

(b) This section does not prohibit a rubbish vehicle from being without cover while in the process of acquiring its load if no law, administrative regulation, or local ordinance requires that it be covered in those circumstances.

This section does not apply to any vehicle engaged in transporting wet waste fruit or vegetable matter, or waste products from a food processing establishment. *(Amended by Stats 1988 ch 1486 §4, eff. 1/1/89, oper. 9/1/90.)*

§23116. Transporting minor in cargo space of a truck.

(a) No person driving a motortruck shall transport any minor under the age of 12 years in the back of the motortruck in a space intended for any load on the vehicle on a highway unless the space is enclosed to a height of 46 inches extending vertically from the floor, the vehicle has installed means of preventing the minor from being discharged, or the minor is secured to the vehicle in a manner which will prevent the minor from being thrown, falling, or jumping from the vehicle.

(b) This section does not apply to the transportation of a minor under the age of 12 years in the back of the motortruck when the minor is accompanied by an adult over the age of 18 years in the back of the motortruck.

§23117. Transporting animals in cargo space of a truck.

(a) No person driving a motor vehicle shall transport any animal in the back of the vehicle in a space intended for any load on the vehicle on a highway unless the space is enclosed or has side and tail racks to a height of at least 46 inches extending vertically from the floor, the vehicle has installed means of preventing the animal from being discharged, or the animal is cross tethered to the vehicle, or is protected by a secured container or cage, in a manner which will prevent the animal from being thrown, falling, or jumping from the vehicle.

(b) This section does not apply to any of the following;

(1) The transportation of livestock.

(2) The transportation of a dog whose owner either owns or is employed by a ranching or farming operation who is traveling on a road in a rural area or who is traveling to and from a livestock auction.

(3) The transportation of a dog for purposes associated with ranching or farming. *(Added by Stats 1987 ch 224 §1.)*

§23120. Operation of motor vehicle when glasses obstruct vision.

No person shall operate a motor vehicle while wearing glasses having a temple width of one-half inch or more if any part of such temple extends below the horizontal center of the lens so as to interfere with lateral vision.

§23127. Operation of motor vehicle on trails or paths.

No person shall operate an unauthorized motor vehicle on any state, county, city, private, or district hiking or horseback riding trail or bicycle path that is clearly marked by an authorized agent or owner with signs at all entrances and exits and at intervals of not more than one mile indicating no unauthorized motor vehicles are permitted on the hiking or horseback riding trail, or bicycle path, except bicycle paths which are contiguous or adjacent to a roadway dedicated solely to motor vehicle use.

For the purpose of this section "unauthorized motor vehicle" means any motor vehicle that is driven upon a hiking or horseback riding trail without the written permission of an agent or the owner of the trail or path.

This section does not apply to the operation of an authorized emergency or maintenance vehicle on a hiking or horseback riding trail or bicycle path whenever necessary in furtherance of the purpose for which the vehicle has been classed as an authorized emergency vehicle. Any person who violates this section is guilty of a misdemeanor.

ARTICLE 1.5

JUVENILE OFFENSES INVOLVING ALCOHOL
(Added by Stats 1986 ch 1105.)

§23140. Minor driving under the influence.

(a) It is unlawful for a person under the age of 18 years who has 0.05 percent or more, by weight, of alcohol in his or her blood to drive a vehicle.

(b) A person may be found to be in violation of subdivision (a) if the person was, at the time of driving, under the age of 18 years and under the influence of, or affected by, an alcoholic beverage regardless of whether a chemical test was made to determine that person's blood-alcohol concentration and if the trier of fact finds that the person had consumed an alcoholic beverage and was driving a vehicle while having a concentration of 0.05 percent or more, by weight, of alcohol in his or her blood.

(c) Notwithstanding any provision of law to the contrary, upon a finding that a person has violated this section, the clerk of court, or judge if there is no clerk, shall prepare within 10 days after the finding and immediately forward to the department an abstract of the record of the court in which the finding is made. That abstract shall be a public record and available for public inspection in the same manner as other records reported under Section 1803. *(Amended by Stats 1989 ch 1465 §5, eff. 1/1/90.)*

§23141. Alcohol education program for violators of §23140.

Any person found to have committed a violation of Section 23140 shall be required to participate in an alcohol education program. The court shall require the minor to participate in an alcohol education program or a community service program which provides an alcohol education component unless the court finds that the minor, or the minor's parent or parents, is unable to pay required fees for the program, there is no appropriate program located in the county, or other specific circumstances justify failure to impose this requirement.

§23142. Programs for minors who drive while intoxicated.

If any person is found to have violated Section 23140 and is also found to have violated Section 23152 or 23153, in addition to, and not as an alternative to, the requirements of Section 23154 or any other provision of Article 2 (commencing with Section 23152), that person shall be required to participate in the alcohol education program or the alcohol rehabilitation program required by this article.

§23143. Fees.

Notwithstanding Section 34.10 of the Civil Code, if the court finds it just and reasonable, the court may order the parent or parents of a minor who is ordered to participate in an alcohol education program or a community service program which provides an alcohol education component pursuant to this article, to pay the required fees for the program. *(Added by Stats 1986 ch 1105 §1.)*

§23144. Failure to complete program.

(a) The court may order the department to suspend, revoke, or delay issuance of, and the department, when so ordered, shall suspend, revoke, or delay issuance of the driving privileges of any person convicted of a violation of Section 23140 under both of the following circumstances:

(1) The court has required the person to participate in an alcohol education program or a community service program pursuant to Section 23141, except those persons excluded from participation in a program for reasons specified in Section 23141.

(2) The person fails to show proof of completion of the program as required by the court.

(b) The suspension, revocation, or delay in issuance shall remain in effect until the earlier of either of the following:

(1) The person shows proof of completion of the program satisfactory to the court, and the court orders the department to terminate the suspension, revocation, or delay in issuance of driving privileges.

(2) The date the person reaches the age of 21 years. *(Added by Stats 1988 ch 223 §1, eff. 1/1/89.)*

ARTICLE 2

OFFENSES INVOLVING ALCOHOL AND DRUGS

§23152. Prohibition of driving under the influence of alcohol or drugs.

(a) It is unlawful for any person who is under the influence of an alcoholic beverage or any drug, or under the combined influence of an alcoholic beverage and any drug, to drive a vehicle.

(b) It is unlawful for any person who has 0.08 percent or more, by weight, of alcohol in his or her blood to drive a vehicle.

For purposes of this subdivision, percent, by weight, of alcohol in a person's blood shall be based upon grams of alcohol per 100 milliliters of blood or grams of alcohol per 210 liters of breath.

In any prosecution under this subdivision, it is a rebuttable presumption that the person had 0.08 percent or more, by weight, of alcohol in his or her blood at the time of driving the vehicle if the person had 0.08 percent or more, by weight, of alcohol in his or her blood at the time of the performance of a chemical test within three hours after the driving.

(c) It is unlawful for any person who is addicted to the use of any drug to drive a vehicle. This subdivision shall not apply to a person who is participating in a methadone maintenance treatment program approved pursuant to Article 3 (commencing with Sec-

tion 4350) of Chapter 1 of Part 1 of Division 4 of the Welfare and Institutions Code.

(d) This section shall remain in effect only until January 1, 1992, and as of that date is repealed. *(Amended by Stats 1990 ch 708 §1, eff. 1/1/91 only until 1/1/92. See other sections 23152 below.)*

§23152. Prohibition of driving under the influence of alcohol or drugs.

(a) It is unlawful for any person who is under the influence of an alcoholic beverage or any drug, or under the combined influence of an alcoholic beverage and any drug, to drive a vehicle.

(b) It is unlawful for any person who has 0.08 percent or more, by weight, of alcohol in his or her blood to drive a vehicle.

For purposes of this subdivision, subdivision (d), and, Section 34501.1, percent, by weight, of alcohol in a person's blood shall be based upon grams of alcohol per 100 milliliters of blood or grams of alcohol per 210 liter's of breath.

In any prosecution under this subdivision, it is a rebuttable presumption that the person had 0.08 percent or more, by weight, of alcohol in his or her blood at the time of driving the vehicle if the person had 0.08 percent or more, by weight, of alcohol in his or her blood at the time of the performance of a chemical test within three hours after the driving.

(c) It is unlawful for any person who is addicted to the use of any drug to drive a vehicle. This subdivision shall not apply to a person who is participating in a methadone maintenance treatment program approved pursuant to Article 3 (commencing with Section 4350) of Chapter 1 of Part 1 of Division 4 of the Welfare and Institutions Code.

(d) It is unlawful for any person who has 0.04 percent or more, by weight, of alcohol in his or her blood to drive a commercial motor vehicle, as defined in Section 15210.

In any prosecution under this subdivision, it is a rebuttable presumption that the person had 0.04 percent or more, by weight, of alcohol in his or her blood at the time of driving the vehicle if the person had 0.04 percent or more, by weight, of alcohol in his or her blood at the time of the performance of a chemical test within three hours after the driving.

(e) This section shall become operative on January 1, 1992, and shall remain operative until the director determines that federal regulations adopted pursuant to the Commercial Motor Vehicle Safety Act of 1986 (49 U.S.C. Sec. 2701 et seq.) contained in Section 383.51 or 391.15 of Title 49 of the Code of Federal Regulations do not require the state to prohibit operation of commercial vehicles when the operator has a concentration of alcohol in his or her blood of 0.04 percent by weight or more.

(f) The director shall submit a notice of the determination under subdivision (e) to the Secretary of State, and this section shall be repealed upon the receipt of that notice by the Secretary of State. *(Added by Stats 1989 ch 1114 §25, eff. 1/1/90, oper. 1/1/92 only until receipt of notice by Secretary of State. See other sections 23152 above and below.)*

§23152. Prohibition of driving under the influence of alcohol or drugs.

(a) It is unlawful for any person who is under the influence of an alcoholic beverage or any drug, or under the combined influence of an alcoholic beverage and any drug, to drive a vehicle.

© 1992 by J., B. & L. Gould
Printed in the U.S.A.   **EP**

(b) It is unlawful for any person who has 0.08 percent or more, by weight, of alcohol in his or her blood to drive a vehicle.

For purposes of this subdivision, percent, by weight, of alcohol in a person's blood shall be based upon grams of alcohol per 100 milliliters of blood or grams of alcohol per 210 liters of breath.

In any prosecution under this subdivision, it is a rebuttable presumption that the person had 0.08 percent or more, by weight, of alcohol in his or her blood at the time of driving the vehicle if the person had 0.08 percent or more, by weight, of alcohol in his or her blood at the time of the performance of a chemical test within three hours after the driving.

(c) It is unlawful for any person who is addicted to the use of any drug to drive a vehicle. This subdivision shall not apply to a person who is participating in a methadone maintenance treatment program approved pursuant to Article 3 (commencing with Section 4350) of Chapter 1 of Part 1 of Division 4 of the Welfare and Institutions Code.

(d) This section shall become operative only upon the receipt by the Secretary of State of the notice specified in subdivision (f) of Section 23152, as added by Section 25 of Chapter 1114 of the Statutes of 1989. *(Amended by Stats 1990 ch 708 §2, eff 1/1/91, oper. upon receipt of notice by Secretary of State. See other sections 23152 above.)*

§23153. Injury caused while driving under the influence.

(a) It is unlawful for any person, while under the influence of an alcoholic beverage or any drug, or under the combined influence of an alcoholic beverage and any drug, to drive a vehicle and, when so driving, do any act forbidden by law or neglect any duty imposed by law in the driving of the vehicle, which act or neglect proximately causes bodily injury to any person other than the driver.

(b) It is unlawful for any person, while having 0.08 percent or more, by weight, of alcohol in his or her blood to drive a vehicle and, when so driving, do any act forbidden by law or neglect any duty imposed by law in the driving of the vehicle, which act or neglect proximately causes bodily injury to any person other than the driver.

For purposes of this subdivision, percent, by weight, of alcohol in a person's blood shall be based upon grams of alcohol per 100 milliliters of blood or grams of alcohol per 210 liters of breath.

In any prosecution under this subdivision, it is a rebuttable presumption that the person had 0.08 percent or more, by weight, of alcohol in his or her blood at the time of driving the vehicle if the person had 0.08 percent or more, by weight, of alcohol in his or her blood at the time of the performance of a chemical test within three hours after the driving.

(c) In proving the person neglected any duty imposed by law in the driving of the vehicle, it is not necessary to prove that any specific section of this code was violated.

(d) This section shall remain in effect only until January 1, 1992, and as of that date is repealed. *(Amended by Stats 1990 ch 708 §3, eff. 1/1/91 only until 1/1/92. See other sections 23153 below.)*

§23153. Injury caused while driving under the influence.

(a) It is unlawful for any person, while under the influence of an alcoholic beverage or any drug, or under the combined influence of an alcoholic beverage and any drug, to drive a vehicle and, when so driving, do any act forbidden by law or neglect any duty imposed by law in the driving of the vehicle, which act or neglect proximately causes bodily injury to any person other than the driver.

(b) It is unlawful for any person, while having 0.08 percent or more, by weight, of alcohol in his or her blood to drive a vehicle and, when so driving, do any act forbidden by law or neglect any duty imposed by law in the driving of the vehicle, which act or neglect proximately causes bodily injury to any person other than the driver.

For purposes of this subdivision and subdivision (d), percent, by weight, of alcohol in a person's blood shall be based upon grams of alcohol per 100 milliliters of blood or grains of alcohol per 210 liters of breath.

In any prosecution under this subdivision, it is a rebuttable presumption that the person had 0.08 percent or more, by weight, of alcohol in his or her blood at the time of driving the vehicle if the person had 0.08 percent or more, by weight, of alcohol in his or her blood at the time of the performance of a chemical test within three hours after the driving.

(c) In proving the person neglected any duty imposed by law in the driving of the vehicle, it is not necessary to prove that any specific section of this code was violated.

(d) It is unlawful for any person, while having 0.04 percent or more, by weight, of alcohol in his or her blood to drive a commercial motor vehicle, as defined in Section 15210, and, when so driving, do any act forbidden by law or neglect any duty imposed by law in the driving of the vehicle, which act or neglect proximately causes bodily injury to any person other than the driver.

In any prosecution under this subdivision, it is a rebuttable presumption that the person had 0.04 percent or more, by weight, of alcohol in his or her blood at the time of driving the vehicle if the person had 0.04 percent or more, by weight, of alcohol in his or her blood at the time of performance of a chemical test within three hours after the driving.

(e) This section shall become operative on January 1, 1992, and shall remain operative until the director determines that federal regulations adopted pursuant to the Commercial Motor Vehicle Act of 1986 (49 U.S.C. Sec. 2701 et seq.) contained in Section 383.51 or 391.15 of Title 49 of the Code of Federal Regulations do not require the state to prohibit operation of commercial vehicles when the operator has a concentration of alcohol in his or her blood of 0.04 percent by weight or more.

(f) The director shall submit a notice of the determination under subdivision (e) to the Secretary of State, and this section shall be repealed upon the receipt of that notice by the Secretary of State. *(Added by Stats 1989 ch 1114 §30, eff. 1/1/90, oper. 1/1/92 only until receipt of notice by Secretary of State. See other sections 23153 above and below.)* .

§23153. Injury caused while driving under the influence.

(a) It is unlawful for any person, while under the influence of an alcoholic beverage or any drug, or under the combined influence of an alcoholic beverage and any drug, to drive a vehicle and, when so driving, do any act forbidden by law or neglect any duty imposed by law in the driving of the vehicle, which act or

© 1992 by J., B. & L. Gould
Printed in the U.S.A.   **EP**

neglect proximately causes bodily injury to any person other than the driver.

(b) It is unlawful for any person, while having 0.08 percent or more, by weight, of alcohol in his or her blood to drive a vehicle and, when so driving, do any act forbidden by law or neglect any duty imposed by law in the driving of the vehicle, which act or neglect proximately causes bodily injury to any person other than the driver.

For purposes of this subdivision, percent, by weight, of alcohol in a person's blood shall be based upon grams of alcohol per 100 milliliters of blood or grams of alcohol per 210 liters of breath.

In any prosecution under this subdivision, it is a rebuttable presumption that the person had 0.08 percent or more, by weight, of alcohol in his or her blood at the time of driving the vehicle if the person had 0.08 percent or more, by weight, of alcohol in his or her blood at the time of the performance of a chemical test within three hours after the driving.

(c) In proving the person neglected any duty imposed by law in the driving of the vehicle, it is not necessary to prove that any specific section of this code was violated.

(d) This section shall become operative only upon the receipt by the Secretary of State of the notice specified in subdivision (f) of Section 23153, as added by Section 30 of Chapter 1114 of the Statutes of 1989. *(Amended by Stats 1990 ch 708 §4, eff. 1/1/91, oper. upon receipt of notice by Secretary of State. See other sections 23153 above.)*

§23154. Participation by juveniles in alcohol or drug education program.

(a) Whenever, in any county specified in subdivision (b), a judge of a juvenile court, a juvenile traffic hearing officer, or referee of a juvenile court finds that a person has committed a first violation of Section 23152 or 23153, the person shall be required to participate in and successfully complete an alcohol or drug education program, or both of those programs, as designated by the court. The expense of the person's attendance in the program shall be paid by the person's parents or guardian so long as the person is under the age of 18 years, and shall be paid by the person thereafter. However, in approving the program, each county shall require the program to provide for the payment of the fee for the program in installments by any person who cannot afford to pay the full fee at the commencement of the program and shall require the program to provide for the waiver of the fee for any person who is indigent, as determined by criteria for indigency established by the board of supervisors. Whenever it can be done without substantial additional cost, each county shall require that the program be provided for juveniles at a separate location from, or at a different time of day than, alcohol and drug education programs for adults.

(b) This section applies only in those counties that have one or more alcohol or drug education programs certified by the county alcohol program administrator and approved by the board of supervisors.

§23155. Blood alcohol level as evidence.

(a) Upon the trial of any criminal action, or preliminary proceeding in a criminal action, arising out of acts alleged to have been committed by any person while driving a vehicle while under the influence of an alcoholic beverage in violation of sub-

division (a) of Section 23152 or subdivision (a) of Section 23153, the amount of alcohol in the person's blood at the time of the test as shown by chemical analysis of that person's blood, breath, or urine shall give rise to the following presumptions affecting the burden of proof:

(1) If there was at that time less than 0.05 percent by weight of alcohol in the person's blood, it shall be presumed that the person was not under the influence of an alcoholic beverage at the time of the alleged offense.

(2) If there was at that time 0.05 percent or more but less than 0.08 percent by weight of alcohol in the person's blood, that fact shall not give rise to any presumption that the person was or was not under the influence of an alcoholic beverage, but the fact may be considered with other competent evidence in determining whether the person was under the influence of an alcoholic beverage at the time of the alleged offense.

(3) If there was at that time 0.08 percent or more by weight of alcohol in the person's blood, it shall be presumed that the person was under the influence of an alcoholic beverage at the time of the alleged offense.

(b) Percent by weight of alcohol in the blood shall be based upon grams of alcohol per 100 milliliters of blood.

(c) This section shall not be construed as limiting the introduction of any other competent evidence bearing upon the question whether the person ingested any alcoholic beverage or was under the influence of an alcoholic beverage at the time of the alleged offense. *(Amended by Stats 1989 ch 479 §5, eff. 1/1/90, oper. only until 1/1/92. See other sections 23155 below.)*

§23155. Blood alcohol level as evidence.

(a) Upon the trial of any criminal action, or preliminary proceeding in a criminal action, arising out of acts alleged to have been committed by any person while driving a vehicle while under the influence of an alcoholic beverage in violation of subdivision (a) of Section 23152 or subdivision (a) of Section 23153, the amount of alcohol in the person's blood at the time of the test as shown by chemical analysis of that person's blood, breath, or urine shall give rise to the following presumptions affecting the burden of proof:

(1) If there was at that time less than 0.05 percent by weight of alcohol in the person's blood, it shall be presumed that the person was not under the influence of an alcoholic beverage at the time of the alleged offense.

(2) If there was at that time 0.05 percent or more but less than 0.08 percent by weight of alcohol in the person's blood, that fact shall not give rise to any presumption that the person was or was not under the influence of an alcoholic beverage, but the fact may be considered with other competent evidence in determining whether the person was under the influence of an alcoholic beverage at the time of the alleged offense.

(3) If there was at that time 0.05 percent or more by weight of alcohol in the person's blood, it shall be presumed that the person was under the influence of an alcoholic beverage at the time of the alleged offense.

(b) Percent by weight of alcohol in the person's blood shall be based upon grams of alcohol per 100 milliliters of blood or grams of alcohol per 210 liters of breath.

(c) This section shall not be construed as limiting the introduction of any other competent evidence bearing upon the question whether the person ingested any alcoholic beverage or was under the influence of an alcoholic beverage at the time of the alleged offense.

© 1992 by J., B. & L. Gould
Printed in the U.S.A.   EP

(d) This section shall become operative on January 1, 1992, and shall remain operative until the director determines that federal regulations adopted pursuant to the Commercial Motor Vehicle Safety Act of 1986 (49 U.S.C. Sec. 2701 et seq.) contained in Section 383.51 or 391.15 of Title 49 of the Code of Federal Regulations do not require the state to prohibit operation of commercial vehicles when the operator has a concentration of alcohol in his or her blood of 0.04 percent by weight or more.

(e) The director shall submit a notice of the determination under subdivision (d) to the Secretary of State, and this section shall be repealed upon the receipt of that notice by the Secretary of State. *(Added by Stats 1989 ch 1114 §35, eff. 1/1/90, oper. 1/1/92 only until receipt of notice by Secretary of State. See other sections 23155 above and below.)*

§23155. Blood alcohol level as evidence.

(a) Upon the trial of any criminal action, or preliminary proceeding in a criminal action, arising out of acts alleged to have been committed by any person while driving a vehicle while under the influence of an alcoholic beverage in violation of subdivision (a) of Section 23152 or subdivision (a) of Section 23153, the amount of alcohol in the person's blood at the time of the test as shown by chemical analysis of that person's blood, breath, or urine shall give rise to the following presumptions affecting the burden of proof:

(1) If there was at that time less than 0.05 percent by weight of alcohol in the person's blood, it shall be presumed that the person was not under the influence of an alcoholic beverage at the time of the alleged offense.

(2) If there was at that time 0.05 percent or more but less than 0.08 percent by weight of alcohol in the person's blood, that fact shall not give rise to any presumption that the person was or was not under the influence of an alcoholic beverage, but the fact may be considered with other competent evidence in determining whether the person was under the influence of an alcoholic beverage at the time of the alleged offense.

(3) If there was at that time 0.08 percent or more by weight of alcohol in the person's blood, it shall be presumed that the person was under the influence of an alcoholic beverage at the time of the alleged offense.

(b) Percent by weight of alcohol in the person's blood shall be based upon grams of alcohol per 100 milliliters of blood.

(c) This section shall not be construed as limiting the introduction of any other competent evidence bearing upon the question whether the person ingested any alcoholic beverage or was under the influence of an alcoholic beverage at the time of the alleged offense.

(d) This section shall become operative only upon the receipt by the Secretary of State of the notice specified in subdivision (e) of Section 23155, as added by Section 35 of Senate Bill 1119 of the 1989-90 Regular Session. *(Added by Stats 1989 ch 1114 §37, eff. 1/1/90, oper. upon receipt by Secretary of State of notice specified in subd. (e) of Section 23155, as added by Stats 1989 ch 1114 §35. See other sections 23155 above.)*

§23156. Prior vehicular manslaughter conviction.

(a) For the purposes of this article, a separate offense which resulted in a conviction of a violation of Section 191.5 or paragraph (3) of subdivision (c) of Section 192 of the Penal Code is a separate offense of a violation of Section 23153.

(b) This section shall remain in effect only until January 1, 1992, and as of that date is repealed. *(Amended by Stats 1989 ch 1114 §38, eff. 1/1/90 only until 1/1/92. See other section 23156 below.)*

§23156. Prior vehicular manslaughter conviction.

(a) For the purposes of this article, a separate offense which resulted in a conviction of a violation of subdivision (f) of Section 655 of the Harbors and Navigation Code or of Section 191.5 or paragraph (3) of subdivision (c) of Section 192 of the Penal Code is a separate offense of a violation of Section 23153.

(b) For the purposes of this article and Section 13352, a separate offense which resulted in a conviction of a violation of subdivision (b), (c), (d), or (e) of Section 655 of the Harbors and Navigation Code is a separate violation of Section 23152.

(c) This section shall become operative on January 1, 1992. *(Added by Stats 1989 ch 1114 §39, eff. 1/1/90, oper. 1/1/92. See other section 23156 above.)*

§23157. Implied consent for chemical testing.

(a) (1) Any person who drives a motor vehicle is deemed to have given his or her consent to chemical testing of his or her blood, breath, or urine for the purpose of determining the alcoholic content of his or her blood, and to have given his or her consent to chemical testing of his or her blood or urine for the purpose of determining the drug content of his or her blood, if lawfully arrested for any offense allegedly committed in violation of Section 23152 or 23153. The testing shall be incidental to a lawful arrest and administered at the direction of a peace officer having reasonable cause to believe the person was driving a motor vehicle in violation of Section 23152 or 23153. The person shall be told that his or her failure to submit to, or the failure to complete, the required chemical testing will result in a fine, mandatory imprisonment if the person is convicted of a violation of Section 23152 or 23153, and (A) the suspension of the person's privilege to operate a motor vehicle for a period of one year, (B) the revocation of the person's privilege to operate a motor vehicle for a period of two years if the refusal occurs within seven years of a separate violation of Section 23103 as specified in Section 23103.5, Section 23152, or Section 23153 of this code, or Section 191.5 or paragraph (3) of subdivision (c) of Section 192 of the Penal Code which resulted in a conviction, or if the person's privilege to operate a motor vehicle has been suspended or revoked pursuant to Section 13353 or 13353.2 for an offense which occurred on a separate occasion, or (C) the revocation of the person's privilege to operate a motor vehicle for a period of three years if the refusal occurs within seven years of two or more separate violations of Section 23103 as specified in Section 23103.5, Section 23152, or Section 23153 of this code, or Section 191.5 or paragraph (3) of subdivision (c) of Section 192 of the Penal Code, or any combination thereof, which resulted in convictions, or if the person's privilege to operate a motor vehicle has been suspended or revoked two or more times pursuant to Section 13353 or 13353.2 for offenses which occurred on separate occasions, or if there is any combination of those convictions or administrative suspensions or revocations.

(2) (A) If the person is lawfully arrested for driving under the influence of an alcoholic beverage, the person has the choice of whether the test shall be of his or her blood, breath, or urine, and the officer shall advise the person that he or she has that choice. If the person arrested either is incapable, or states that he or she is incapable, of completing any chosen test, the person shall submit to the person's choice of the remaining tests or test, and the officer shall advise the person that the person has that choice.

(B) If the person is lawfully arrested for driving under the influence of any drug or the combined influence of an alcoholic beverage and any drug, the person has the choice of whether the test shall be of his or her blood, breath, or urine, and the officer shall advise the person that he or she has that choice.

(C) A person who chooses to submit to a breath test may also be requested to submit to a blood or urine test if the officer has reasonable cause to believe that the person was driving under the influence of any drug or the combined influence of an alcoholic beverage and any drug and if the officer has a clear indication that a blood or urine test will reveal evidence of the person being under the influence. The officer shall state in his or her report the facts upon which that belief and that clear indication are based. The person has the choice of submitting to and completing a blood or urine test, and the officer shall advise the person that he or she is required to submit to an additional test and that he or she may choose a test of either blood or urine. If the person arrested either is incapable, or states that he or she is incapable, of completing either chosen test, the person shall submit to and complete the other remaining test.

(3) If the person is lawfully arrested for an offense allegedly committed in violation of Section 23152 or 23153, and, because of the need for medical treatment, the person is first transported to a medical facility where it is not feasible to administer a particular test of, or to obtain a particular sample of, the person's blood, breath, or urine, the person has the choice of those tests which are available at the facility to which that person has been transported. In such an event, the officer shall advise the person of those tests which are available at the medical facility and that the person's choice is limited to those tests which are available.

(4) The officer shall also advise the person that he or she does not have the right to have an attorney present before stating whether he or she will submit to a test or tests, before deciding which test or tests to take, or during administration of the test or tests chosen, and that, in the event of refusal to submit to a test or tests, the refusal may be used against him or her in a court of law.

(5) Any person who is unconscious or otherwise in a condition rendering him or her incapable of refusal is deemed not to have withdrawn his or her consent and a test or tests may be administered whether or not the person is told that his or her failure to submit to, or the noncompletion of, the test or tests will result in the suspension or revocation of his or her privilege to operate a motor vehicle. Any person who is dead is deemed not to have withdrawn his or her consent and a test or tests may be administered at the direction of a peace officer.

(b) Any person who is afflicted with hemophilia is exempt from the blood test required by this section.

(c) Any person who is afflicted with a heart condition and is using an anticoagulant under the direction

of a licensed physician and surgeon is exempt from the blood test required by this section.

(d) A person lawfully arrested for any offense allegedly committed while the person was driving a motor vehicle in violation of Section 23152 or 23153 may request the arresting officer to have a chemical test made of the arrested person's blood, breath, or urine for the purpose of determining the alcoholic content of that person's blood, and, if so requested, the arresting officer shall have the test performed.

(e) If the person, who has been arrested for a violation of Section 23152 or 23153, refuses or fails to complete a chemical test or tests, or requests that a blood or urine test be taken, the peace officer, acting on behalf of the department, shall serve the notice of the order of suspension or revocation of the person's privilege to operate a motor vehicle personally on the arrested person. The notice shall be on a form provided by the department.

(f) If the peace officer serves the notice of the order of suspension or revocation of the person's privilege to operate a motor vehicle, the peace officer shall take possession of any driver's license issued by this state which is held by the person. The temporary driver's license shall be an endorsement on the notice of the order of suspension and shall be valid for 45 days from the date of arrest.

(g) The peace officer shall immediately forward a copy of the completed notice of suspension or revocation form, a copy of the citation, and any driver's license taken into possession under subdivision (b), with the report required by Section 23158.2, to the department. If the person submitted to a blood or urine test, the peace officer shall cause the results of the chemical test to be forwarded to the department within 20 calendar days of the date of the arrest. *(Amended by Stats 1990 ch 431 §15, eff. 7/26/90.)*

§23157.5. Chemical testing; advice.

(a) In addition to the requirements of Section 23157, a person who chooses to submit to a breath test shall be advised before or after the test that the breath-testing equipment does not retain any sample of the breath and that no breath sample will be available after the test which could be analyzed later by the person or any other person.

(b) The person shall also be advised that, because no breath sample is retained, the person will be given an opportunity to provide a blood or urine sample that will be retained at no cost to the person so that there will be something retained that may be subsequently analyzed for the alcoholic content of the person's blood. If the person completes a breath test and wishes to provide a blood or urine sample to be retained, the sample shall be collected and retained in the same manner as if the person had chosen a blood or urine test initially.

(c) The person shall also be advised that the blood or urine sample may be tested by either party in any criminal prosecution. The failure of either party to perform this test shall place no duty upon the opposing party to perform the test nor affect the admissibility of any other evidence of the alcoholic content of the blood of the person arrested.

(d) No failure or omission to advise pursuant to this section shall affect the admissibility of any evidence of the alcoholic content of the blood of the person arrested. *(Amended by Stats 1986 ch 1107 §1.)*

© 1992 by J., B. & L. Gould
Printed in the U.S.A.   EP

§23158. Chemical testing procedures.

(a) Only a licensed physician and surgeon, registered nurse, licensed vocational nurse, duly licensed clinical laboratory technologist or clinical laboratory bioanalyst, unlicensed laboratory personnel regulated pursuant to Sections 1242, 1242.5, and 1246 of the Business and Professions Code, or certified paramedic acting at the request of a peace officer may withdraw blood for the purpose of determining the alcoholic content therein. This limitation does not apply to the taking of breath specimens. An emergency call for paramedic services takes precedence over a peace officer's request for a paramedic to withdraw blood for determining its alcoholic content. A certified paramedic shall not withdraw blood for this purpose unless authorized by his or her employer to do so.

(b) The person tested may, at his own expense, have a licensed physician and surgeon, registered nurse, licensed vocational nurse, duly licensed clinical laboratory technologist or clinical laboratory bioanalyst, unlicensed laboratory personnel regulated pursuant to Sections 1242, 1242.5, and 1246 of the Business and Professions Code, or any other person of his or her own choosing administer a test in addition to any test administered at the direction of a peace officer for the purpose of determining the amount of alcohol in the person's blood at the time alleged as shown by chemical analysis of his or her blood, breath, or urine. The failure or inability to obtain an additional test by a person does not preclude the admissibility in evidence of the test taken at the direction of a peace officer.

(c) Upon the request of the person tested, full information concerning the test taken at the direction of the peace officer shall be made available to the person or the person's attorney.

(d) Notwithstanding any other provision of law, no licensed physician and surgeon, registered nurse, licensed vocational nurse, duly licensed clinical laboratory technologist or clinical laboratory bioanalyst, unlicensed laboratory personnel regulated pursuant to Sections 1242, 1242.5, and 1246 of the Business and Professions Code, or certified paramedic, or hospital, laboratory, or clinic employing or utilizing the services of the licensed physician and surgeon, registered nurse, licensed vocational nurse, duly licensed laboratory technologist or clinical laboratory bioanalyst, unlicensed laboratory personnel regulated pursuant to Sections 1242, 1242.5, and 1246 of the Business and Professions Code, or certified paramedic, owning or leasing the premises on which tests are performed, shall incur any civil or criminal liability as a result of administering of a blood test in a reasonable manner in a hospital, medical laboratory, or medical clinic environment, according to accepted medical practices, without violence by the person administering the test, and when requested in writing by a peace officer to administer the test.

(e) If the test given under Section 23157 is a chemical test of urine, the person tested shall be given such privacy in the taking of the urine specimen as will ensure the accuracy of the specimen and, at the same time, maintain the dignity of the individual involved.

(f) The department, in cooperation with the State Department of Health Services or any other appropriate agency, shall adopt uniform standards for the withdrawal, handling, and preservation of blood samples prior to analysis.

(g) As used in this section, "certified paramedic" does not include any employee of a fire department.

(h) Consent, waiver of liability, or the offering to, acceptance by, or refusal of consent or waiver of liability by the person on whom a test is administered, is not an issue or relevant to the immunity from liability for medical personnel or the medical facility under subdivision (d). *(Amended by Stats 1989 ch 80 §1, eff. 1/1/90.)*

§23158.2. Filing of report.

(a) If a peace officer arrests any person for a violation of Section 23152 or 23153, the peace officer shall immediately forward to the department a sworn report of all information relevant to the enforcement action, including information which adequately identifies the arrested person, a statement of the officer's grounds for belief that the person violated Section 23152 or 23153, a report of the results of any chemical tests which were conducted on the person or the circumstances constituting a refusal to submit to or complete the chemical testing pursuant to Section 23157, a copy of any notice to appear under which the person was released from custody, and, if immediately available, a copy of the complaint filed with the court. For purposes of this section and subdivision (g) of Section 23157, "immediately" means on or before the end of the fifth ordinary business day following the arrest.

(b) The peace officer's sworn report shall be made on forms furnished or approved by the department. *(Amended by Stats 1990 ch 431 §16, eff. 7/26/90.)*

§23158.5. Peace officer filing notice.

(a) If the chemical test results for a person, who has been arrested for a violation of Section 23152 or 23153, show that the person has 0.08 percent or more, by weight, of alcohol in the person's blood, the peace officer, acting on behalf of the department, shall serve a notice of order of suspension of the person's privilege to operate a motor vehicle personally on the arrested person.

(b) If the peace officer serves the notice of order of suspension, the peace officer shall take possession of any driver's license issued by this state which is held by the person. When the officer takes possession of a valid driver's license, the officer shall issue, on behalf of the department, a temporary driver's license. The temporary driver's license shall be an endorsement on the notice of the order of suspension and shall be valid for 45 days from the date of arrest.

(c) The peace officer shall immediately forward a copy of the completed notice of order of suspension form, and any driver's license taken into possession under subdivision (b), with the report required by Section 23158.2, to the department. For purposes of this section, "immediately" means on or before the end of the fifth ordinary business day following the arrest. *(Amended by Stats 1990 ch 431 §17, eff. 7/26/90.)*

§23159. Chemical testing refusal or failure to complete; enhanced penalty.

(a) If any person is convicted of a violation of Section 23152 or 23153, and at the time of the arrest leading to that conviction that person willfully refused a peace officer's request to submit to, or willfully failed to complete, the chemical test or tests pursuant to Section 23157, the court shall impose the following penalties:

(1) If the person is convicted of a first violation of Section 23152, notwithstanding any other provision of subdivision (a) of Section 23161, the terms and conditions of probation shall include the conditions in paragraph (1) of subdivision (a) of Section 23161.

(2) If the person is convicted of a first violation of Section 23153, the punishment prescribed in this article shall be enhanced by an imprisonment of 48 continuous hours in the county jail, whether or not probation is granted and no part of which may be stayed, unless the person is sentenced to, and incarcerated in, the state prison and the execution of that sentence is not stayed.

(3) If the person is convicted of a second violation of Section 23152, punishable under Section 23165, or a second violation of Section 23153, punishable under Section 23185, the punishment prescribed in this article shall be enhanced by an imprisonment of 96 hours in the county jail, whether or not probation is granted and no part of which may be stayed, unless the person is sentenced to, and incarcerated in, the state prison and execution of that sentence is not stayed.

(4) If the person is convicted of a third violation of Section 23152, punishable under Section 23170, the punishment prescribed in this article shall be enhanced by an imprisonment of 10 days in the county jail, whether or not probation is granted and no part of which may be stayed.

(5) If the person is convicted of a fourth or subsequent violation of Section 23152, punishable under Section 23175, the punishment prescribed in this article shall be enhanced by imprisonment of 18 days in the county jail, whether or not probation is granted and no part of which may be stayed.

(b) The willful refusal or failure to complete the chemical test required pursuant to Section 23157 shall be pled and proven. *(Added by Stats 1985 ch 735 §6.)*

§23159.5. Written consent to tests.

(a) On or after January 1, 1990, the Department of Motor Vehicles shall not issue or renew a driver's license to any person unless the person consents in writing to submit to a chemical test or tests of that person's blood, breath, or urine pursuant to Section 23157 when requested to do so by a peace officer.

(b) All application forms for driver's license or driver's license renewal notices processed after January 1, 1990, shall include a requirement that the applicant sign the following declaration as a condition of licensure:

"I agree to submit to a chemical test of my blood, breath, or urine for the purpose of determining the alcohol or drug content of my blood when testing is requested by a peace officer acting in accordance with Section 23157 of the Vehicle Code."

(c) The Department of Motor Vehicles is not, incident to this section, required to maintain, copy, or store any information other than that to be incorporated into the standard application form. *(Added by Stats 1988 ch 1415 §8, eff. 1/1/89.)*

§23160. Penalty; first conviction.

(a) If any person is convicted of a first violation of Section 23152, that person shall be punished by imprisonment in the county jail for not less than 96 hours, at least 48 hours of which shall be continuous, nor more than six months and by a fine of not less than three hundred ninety dollars ($390) nor more than one thousand dollars ($1,000).

(b) The court shall order that any person punished under subdivision (a), who is to be punished by imprisonment in the county jail, be imprisoned on days other than days of regular employment of the person, as determined by the court. If the court determines that 48 hours of continuous imprisonment would interfere with the person's work schedule, the court shall allow the person to serve the imprisonment whenever the person is normally scheduled for time off from work. The court may make this determination based upon a representation from the defendant's attorney or upon an affidavit or testimony from the defendant.

(c) Except as provided in Section 23161, the court shall order the Department of Motor Vehicles to suspend the privilege to operate a motor vehicle of a person punished under this section for six months pursuant to paragraph (1) of subdivision (a) of Section 13352. *(Amended by Stats 1990 ch 286 §1, eff. 1/1/91.)*

§23161. Conditions of probation; first conviction.

(a) Except as provided in subdivision (f), if the court grants probation to any person punished under Section 23160, in addition to the provisions of Section 23206 and any other terms and conditions imposed by the court, the court shall impose as a condition of probation that the person be subject to one of the following:

(1) Be confined in the county jail for at least 48 hours but not more than six months and pay a fine of at least three hundred ninety dollars ($390) but not more than one thousand dollars ($1,000). The court may order the Department of Motor Vehicles to suspend the privilege to operate a motor vehicle pursuant to paragraph (1) of subdivision (a) of Section 13352 when this condition of probation is imposed.

(2) Pay a fine of at least three hundred ninety dollars ($390) but not more than one thousand dollars ($1,000) and, if the person gives proof of ability to respond in damages as defined in Section 16430 to the Department of Motor Vehicles, have the privilege to operate a motor vehicle restricted for 90 days to necessary travel to and from that person's place of employment and to and from the program described in subdivision (b) and, if driving a motor vehicle is necessary to perform the duties of the person's employment, restricted to driving in that person's scope of employment. Whenever the driving privilege is restricted under this section, proof of ability to respond in damages as defined in Section 16430 shall be maintained for three years.

(b) (1) Each county shall, through the county alcohol program administrator, determine its ability to establish, through public or private resources, a program, which is self-supporting through fees collected from program participants, of alcohol or drug education and counseling services, of at least three months' duration and totaling at least 30 hours of direct education and counseling services, which shall be authorized by each county and licensed by, and operated under general regulations established by, the State Department of Alcohol and Drug Programs. A county which shows the State Department of Alcohol and Drug Programs that it has insufficient resources, insufficient potential program participants, or other material disadvantages is not required to establish such a program.

(2) The State Department of Alcohol and Drug Programs may license an alcohol or drug education

© 1992 by J., B. & L. Gould
Printed in the U.S.A.   EP

program that is less than 30 hours in length in any county where the board of supervisors has provided the showing pursuant to paragraph (1), and the State Department of Alcohol and Drug Programs has upheld that showing. The shorter program is subject to all other applicable regulations developed by that state department pursuant to paragraph (3) of subdivision (b) of Section 11837.4.

(3) Except as provided in paragraph (4), in any county where the board of supervisors has approved, and the State Department of Alcohol and Drug Programs has licensed, a program or programs described in paragraph (1) or (2), the court shall also impose as a condition of probation that the driver shall participate in, and successfully complete, an alcohol or drug education and counseling program, or both of these programs, in the driver's county of residence or employment, as designated by the court.

(4) For persons who are active duty personnel in the United States Navy or Marine Corps, the court shall, unless the defendant requests otherwise, impose as a condition of probation that the driver shall participate in, and successfully complete, the Navy Alcohol Drug Safety Action Program rather than a program described in paragraph (1) or (2).

(c) Each county which has approved an alcohol or drug education program or programs and which is licensed by the State Department of Alcohol and Drug Programs shall make provision for persons who can document current inability to pay the program fee, in order to enable those persons to participate. The county shall require that the program report the failure of a person referred to the program to enroll in the program to the referring court.

(d) In order to assure effectiveness of the alcohol or drug education and counseling program, the county shall provide, as appropriate, services to ethnic minorities, women, youth, or any other group that has particular needs related to the program.

(e) (1) Any person required to successfully complete an alcohol or drug education and counseling program as a condition of probation shall enroll in the program and, except when enrollment is required in a program that is required to report failures to enroll to the court, shall furnish proof of the enrollment to the court within the period of time and in the manner specified by the court. The person shall also participate in and successfully complete the program and, shall furnish proof of successful completion within the period of time and in the manner specified by the court. The court shall revoke the person's probation pursuant to Section 23207, except for good cause shown, for the failure to comply with this paragraph.

(2) An alcohol or drug education and counseling program shall report to the court within the period of time and in the manner specified by the court any person who fails to successfully complete the program.

(3) The court, in establishing the reporting requirements in this subdivision, shall consult with the county alcohol program administrator. The county alcohol program administrator shall coordinate the reporting requirements with the Department of Motor Vehicles and the State Department of Alcohol and Drug Programs. That reporting shall ensure that all persons who, after being ordered to attend and complete a program, may be identified for either (1) failure to enroll in, or failure to successfully complete, the program, or (2) successful completion of the program as ordered.

(f) Notwithstanding subdivision (a), if the offense occurred in a vehicle requiring a driver with a class 1 or class 2 driver's license or with a certificate issued pursuant to Section 12804.1, the court shall upon conviction order the department to suspend the driver's privilege pursuant to paragraph (1) of subdivision (a) of Section 13352. *(Amended by Stats 1991 ch 19 §1, eff. 4/1/91.)*

§23165. Penalty; second offense within seven years.

If any person is convicted of a violation of Section 23152 and the offense occurred within seven years of a separate violation of Section 23103 as specified in Section 23103.5 which occurred on or after January 1, 1982, 23152, or 23153, which resulted in a conviction, that person shall be punished by imprisonment in the county jail for not less than 90 days nor more than one year and by a fine of not less than three hundred ninety dollars ($390) nor more than one thousand dollars ($ 1,000). The person's privilege to operate a motor vehicle shall be suspended by the Department of Motor Vehicles pursuant to paragraph (3) of subdivision (a) of Section 13352. *(Amended by Stats 1986 ch 1117 §2.)*

§23166. Conditions of probation; second offense within seven years.

If the court grants probation to any person punished under Section 23165, in addition to the provisions of Section 23206 and any other terms and conditions imposed by the court, the court shall impose as conditions of probation that the person be subject to either subdivision (a) or (b), as follows:

(a) Be confined in the county jail for at least 10 days but not more than one year and pay a fine of at least three hundred ninety dollars ($390) but not more than one thousand dollars ($1,000). The person's privilege to operate a motor vehicle shall be suspended by the Department of Motor Vehicles pursuant to paragraph (3) of subdivision (a) of Section 13352.

(b) All of the following:

(1) Be confined in the county jail for at least 48 hours but not more than one year.

(2) Pay a fine of at least three hundred ninety dollars ($390) but not more than one thousand dollars ($1,000).

(3) If the person gives proof of ability to respond in damages as defined in Section 16430 to the Department of Motor Vehicles, have the privilege to operate a motor vehicle be restricted by the Department of Motor Vehicles pursuant to Section 13352.5, for one year, to necessary travel to and from that person's place of employment and to and from the applicable treatment program described in paragraph (4), and if driving a motor vehicle is necessary to perform the duties of the person's employment, restricted to driving in that person's scope of employment. The Department of Motor Vehicles shall not suspend the person's privilege to operate a motor vehicle under Section 13352, as provided in Section 13352.5, unless the offense occurred in a vehicle requiring a driver with a class 1 or class 2 driver's license or with a certificate specified in Section 12804.1.

(4) Either of the following:

(A) Participate, for at least 18 months subsequent to the underlying conviction and in a manner satisfactory to the court, in a program licensed pursuant to Chapter 9 (commencing with Section 11836) of Part 2 of Division 10.5 of the Health and Safety Code, as designated by the court. The program shall provide for persons who cannot afford the program fee pursuant to paragraph (2) of subdivision (a) of Section 11837.4 of the Health and Safety Code in order to enable those persons to participate.

(B) Participate, for at least 30 months subsequent to the underlying conviction and in a manner satisfactory to the court, in a program licensed pursuant to Chapter 9 (commencing with Section 11836) of Part 2 of Division 10.5 of the Health and Safety Code. A person ordered to treatment pursuant to this subparagraph shall apply to the court or to a board of review, as designated by the court, at the conclusion of the program to obtain the court's order of satisfaction. Only upon the granting of that order of satisfaction by the court may the program issue its certificate of successful completion and report the completion to the Department of Motor Vehicles. A failure to obtain an order of satisfaction at the conclusion of the program is a violation of probation. In order to enable all required persons to participate, each person shall pay the program costs commensurate with the person's ability to pay as determined pursuant to Section 11837.4 of the Health and Safety Code. No condition of probation required pursuant to this subparagraph is a basis for reducing any other probation requirement or for avoiding the mandatory license revocation provisions of paragraph (5) of subdivision (a) of Section 13352. *(Amended by Stats 1991 ch 209 §2, eff. 1/1/92.)*

§23167. Additional penalty for violation of probation; second offense.

Notwithstanding the provisions of Section 23207, if any person has been granted probation under the conditions of subdivision (b) of Section 23166 and fails at any time to participate successfully in the treatment program described in paragraph (4) of that subdivision, the court shall revoke or terminate the probation, and the court may revoke or terminate the probation if the person failed to comply with any other term or condition of probation, and the court shall proceed under either of the following provisions:

(a) Revoke suspension of sentence and proceed as provided in subdivision (c) of Section 1203.2 of the Penal Code and order the Department of Motor Vehicles to suspend the person's privilege to operate a motor vehicle pursuant to paragraph (3) of subdivision (a) of Section 13352 from the date of the order revoking or terminating probation.

(b) Grant a new term of probation on the condition that the person be confined in the county jail for at least 30 days and order the Department of Motor Vehicles to suspend the person's privilege to operate a motor vehicle pursuant to paragraph (3) of subdivision (a) of Section 13352 from the date of the new grant of probation.

§23168. Petition to remove restrictions.

(a) Any person, except as provided in subdivision (b), who has been granted probation under the conditions of subdivision (b) of Section 23166, may, after six months have elapsed since the commencement of participation in the treatment program, petition the court to have the restriction on that person's privilege to operate a motor vehicle removed, and the court may, for good cause shown, order the Department of Motor Vehicles to remove the restrictions upon a showing that the person has successfully participated in the

treatment program and complied with the terms and conditions of probation and has given proof of ability to respond in damages as defined in Section 16430.

(b) Regardless of the type of vehicle used in committing the offense, this section shall not apply to persons holding a class 1 or 2 license or to a person holding a class 3 license who is required to have a certificate under any provision of this code. *(Amended by Stats 1987 ch 726 §7.)*

§23170. Penalty; third offense within seven years.

(a) If any person is convicted of a violation of Section 23152 and the offense occurred within seven years of two separate violations of Section 23103 as specified in Section 23103.5 which occurred on or after January 1, 1982, 23152, or 23153, or any combination thereof, which resulted in convictions, that person shall be punished by imprisonment in the county jail for not less than 120 days nor more than one year and by a fine of not less than three hundred ninety dollars ($390) nor more than one thousand dollars ($1,000). The person's privilege to operate a motor vehicle shall be revoked as required in paragraph (5) of subdivision (a) of Section 13352. The court shall require the person to surrender his or her driver's license to the court in accordance with Section 13550.

(b) Any person convicted of a violation of Section 23152 punishable under this section shall be designated as an habitual traffic offender for a period of three years, subsequent to the conviction. The person shall be advised of this designation pursuant to subdivision (b) of Section 13350. *(Amended by Stats 1988 ch 1415 §9, eff. 1/1/89.)*

§23171. Conditions of probation when punished under §23170.

(a) If the court grants probation to any person punished under Section 23170, in addition to the provisions of Section 23206 and any other terms and conditions imposed by the court, the court shall impose as conditions of probation that the person be confined in the county jail for at least 120 days but not more than one year and pay a fine of at least three hundred ninety dollars ($390) but not more than one thousand dollars ($1,000). The person's privilege to operate a motor vehicle shall be revoked by the Department of Motor Vehicles pursuant to paragraph (5) of subdivision (a) of Section 13352.

(b) In addition to subdivision (a), if the court grants probation to any person punished under Section 23170, the court, may, in its discretion, order as a condition of probation that the person participate, for at least 30 months subsequent to the underlying conviction and in a manner satisfactory to the court, in a program licensed pursuant to Chapter 9 (commencing with Section 11836) of Part 2 of Division 10.5 of the Health and Safety Code. In lieu of the minimum term of imprisonment specified in subdivision (a), the court shall impose as a condition of probation under this subdivision that the person be confined in the county jail for at least 30 days but not more than one year. The court shall not order the treatment prescribed by this subdivision unless the person makes a specific request and shows good cause for the order, whether or not the person has previously completed a treatment program pursuant to paragraph (4) of subdivision (b) of Section 23166 or paragraph (4) of subdivision (b) of Section 23186. A person ordered to

© 1992 by J., B. & L. Gould
Printed in the U.S.A.   EP

treatment pursuant to this subdivision shall apply to the court or to a board of review, as designated by the court, at the conclusion of the program to obtain the court's order of satisfaction. Only upon the granting of that order of satisfaction by the court may the program issue its certificate of successful completion and report the completion to the Department of Motor Vehicles. A failure to obtain an order of satisfaction at the conclusion of the program is a violation of probation. In order to enable all required persons to participate, each person shall pay the program costs commensurate with the person's ability to pay as determined pursuant to Section 11837.4 of the Health and Safety Code. No condition of probation required pursuant to this subdivision is a basis for reducing any other probation requirement in this section or Section 23206 or for avoiding the mandatory license revocation provisions of paragraph (5) of subdivision (a) of Section 13352.

(c) In addition to the provisions of Section 23206 and subdivision (a), if the court grants probation to any person punished under Section 23170 who has not previously completed a treatment program pursuant to paragraph (4) of subdivision (b) of Section 23166 or paragraph (4) of subdivision (b) of Section 23186, and unless the person is ordered to participate in and complete a program under subdivision (b), the court shall impose as a condition of probation that the person participate, for at least 18 months and in a manner satisfactory to the court, in a program licensed pursuant to Chapter 9 (commencing with Section 11836) of Part 2 of Division 10.5 of the Health and Safety Code, as designated by the court. Any person who has previously completed a 12-month or 18-month program licensed pursuant to Chapter 9 (commencing with Section 11836) of Part 2 of Division 10.5 of the Health and Safety Code shall not be eligible for referral pursuant to this subdivision unless a 30-month licensed program is not available for referral in the county of the person's residence or employment. The program shall provide for persons who cannot afford the program fee pursuant to paragraph (2) of subdivision (a) of Section 11837.4 of the Health and Safety Code in order to enable those persons to participate. No condition of probation required pursuant to this subdivision is a basis for reducing any other probation requirement in this section or Section 23206 or for avoiding the mandatory license revocation provisions of paragraph (5) of subdivision (a) of Section 13352. *(Amended by Stats 1991 ch 990 §2, eff. 10/14/91.)*

§23175. Penalty; fourth or more offense within seven years.

(a) If any person is convicted of a violation of Section 23152 and the offense occurred within seven years of three or more separate violations of Section 23103, as specified in Section 23103.5, or Section 23152 or 23153, or any combination thereof, which resulted in convictions, that person shall be punished by imprisonment in the state prison, or in the county jail for not less than 180 days nor more than one year, and by a fine of not less than three hundred ninety dollars ($390) nor more than one thousand dollars ($1,000). The person's privilege to operate a motor vehicle shall be revoked by the Department of Motor Vehicles pursuant to paragraph (7) of subdivision (a) of Section 13352.

(b) Any person convicted of a violation of Section 23152 punishable under this section shall be designated as an habitual traffic offender for a period of three years, subsequent to the conviction. The person shall be advised of this designation pursuant to subdivision (b) of Section 13350. *(Amended by Stats 1991 ch 1091 §160, eff. 1/1/92.)*

§23176. Conditions of probation when punished under §23175.

(a) If the court grants probation to any person punished under Section 23175, in addition to the provisions of Section 23206 and any other terms and conditions imposed by the court, the court shall impose as conditions of probation that the person be confined in the county jail for at least 180 days but not more than one year and pay a fine of at least three hundred ninety dollars ($390) but not more than one thousand dollars ($1,000). The person's privilege to operate a motor vehicle shall be revoked by the Department of Motor Vehicles pursuant to paragraph (7) of subdivision (a) of Section 13352.

(b) In addition to subdivision (a), if the court grants probation to any person punished under Section 23175, the court may, in its discretion, order as a condition of probation that the person participate, for at least 30 months subsequent to the underlying conviction and in a manner satisfactory to the court, in a program licensed pursuant to Chapter 9 (commencing with Section 11836) of Part 2 of Division 10.5 of the Health and Safety Code. In lieu of the minimum term of imprisonment in subdivision (a), the court shall impose as a condition of probation under this subdivision that the person be confined in the county jail for at least 30 days but not more than one year. The court shall not order the treatment prescribed by this subdivision unless the person makes a specific request and shows good cause for the order, whether or not the person has previously completed a treatment program pursuant to paragraph (4) of subdivision (b) of Section 23166 or paragraph (4) of subdivision (b) of Section 23186. A person ordered to treatment pursuant to this subdivision shall apply to the court or to a board of review, as designated by the court, at the conclusion of the program to obtain the court's order of satisfaction. Only upon the granting of that order of satisfaction by the court may the program issue its certificate of successful completion and report the completion to the Department of Motor Vehicles. A failure to obtain an order of satisfaction at the conclusion of the program is a violation of probation. In order to enable all required persons to participate, each person shall pay the program costs commensurate with the person's ability to pay as determined pursuant to Section 11837.4 of the Health and Safety Code. No condition of probation required pursuant to this subdivision is a basis for reducing any other probation requirement in this section or Section 23206 or for avoiding the mandatory license revocation provisions of paragraph (7) of subdivision (a) of Section 13352.

(c) In addition to the provisions of Section 23206 and subdivision (a), if the court grants probation to any person punished under Section 23175 who has not previously completed a treatment program pursuant to paragraph (4) of subdivision (b) of Section 23166 or paragraph (4) of subdivision (b) of Section 23186, and unless the person is ordered to participate in, and complete, a program under subdivision (b), the court shall impose as a condition of probation that the person participate, for at least 18 months and in a manner satisfactory to the court, in a program licensed pursuant to Chapter 9 (commencing with Section 11836) of Part 2 of Division 10.5 of the Health and Safety Code, as designated by the court. Any person who has previously completed a 12-month or 18-month program licensed pursuant to Chapter 9 (commencing with Section 11836) of Part 2 of Division 10.5 of the Health and Safety Code shall not be eligible for referral pursuant to this subdivision unless a 30-month iicensed program is not available for referral in the county of the person's residence or employment. No condition of probation required pursuant to this subdivision is a basis for reducing any other probation requirement in this section or Section 23206 or for avoiding the mandatory license revocation provisions of paragraph (7) of subdivision (a) of Section 13352. *(Amended by Stats 1991 ch 990 §3, eff. 10/14/91.)*

§23180. Penalty; first conviction, violation of §23153.

If any person is convicted of a first violation of Section 23153, that person shall be punished by imprisonment in the state prison, or in the county jail for not less than 90 days nor more than one year, and by a fine of not less than three hundred ninety dollars ($390) nor more than one thousand dollars ($1,000). The person's privilege to operate a motor vehicle shall be suspended by the Department of Motor Vehicles pursuant to paragraph (2) of subdivision (a) of Section 13352.

§23181. Conditions of probation; first conviction.

(a) If the court grants probation to any person punished under Section 23180, in addition to the provisions of Section 23206 and any other terms and conditions imposed by the court, the court shall impose as a condition of probation that the person be confined in the county jail for at least five days but not more than one year and pay a fine of at least three hundred ninety dollars ($390) but not more than one thousand dollars ($1,000). The person's privilege to operate a motor vehicle shall be suspended by the Department of Motor Vehicles pursuant to paragraph (2) of subdivision (a) of Section 13352.

(b)(1) In any county where the county alcohol program administrator has certified, and the board of supervisors has approved, such a program or programs, the court shall also impose as a condition of probation that the driver shall participate in, and successfully complete, an alcohol or drug education and counseling program, established pursuant to subdivision (b) of Section 23161, as designated by the court.

(2) In any county where the board of supervisors has approved and the State Department of Alcohol and Drug programs has licensed such a program or programs, the court shall also impose as a condition of probation that the driver participate in, and successfully complete, an alcohol or drug education and counseling program, or both of these programs, in the driver's county of residence or employment, as designated by the court.

(c) Each county which has approved an alcohol or drug education program or programs and which is licensed by the State Department of Alcohol and Drug Programs shall make provision for persons who can document current inability to pay the program fee, in

order to enable those persons to participate. The county shall require that the program report the failure of a person referred to the program to enroll in the program to the referring court.

(d) In order to assure effectiveness of the alcohol or drug education and counseling program, the county shall provide, as appropriate, services to ethnic minorities, women, youth, or any other group that has particular needs related to the program.

(e) (1) Any person required to successfully complete an alcohol or drug education and counseling program as a condition of probation shall enroll in the program and, except when enrollment is required in a program that is required to report failures to enroll to the court, shall furnish proof of the enrollment to the court within the period of time and in the manner specified by the court. The person shall also participate in and successfully complete the program and shall furnish proof of successful completion within the period of time and in the manner specified by the court. The court shall revoke the person's probation pursuant to Section 23207, except for good cause shown, for the failure to comply with this paragraph.

(2) An alcohol or drug education and counseling program shall report to the court within the period of time and in the manner specified by the court any person who fails to successfully complete the program.

(3) The court, in establishing the reporting requirements in this subdivision, shall consult with the county alcohol program administrator. The county alcohol program administrator shall coordinate the reporting requirements with the Department of Motor Vehicles and the State Department of Alcohol and Drug Programs. That reporting shall ensure that all persons who, after being ordered to attend and complete a program, may be identified for either (1) failure to enroll in, or failure to successfully complete, the program, or (2) successful completion of the program as ordered. *(Amended by Stats 1989 ch 803 §7, eff. 1/1/90.)*

§23182. Multiple victims; enhanced penalty.

Any person who proximately causes bodily injury or death to more than one victim in any one instance of driving in violation of Section 23153 of this code or in violation of Section 191.5 or paragraph (3) of subdivision (c) of Section 192 of the Penal Code, shall, upon a felony conviction, receive an enhancement of one year in the state prison for each additional injured victim. The enhanced sentence provided for in this section shall not be imposed unless the fact of the bodily injury to each additional victim is charged in the accusatory pleading and admitted or found to be true by the trier of fact. The maximum number of one year enhancements which may be imposed pursuant to this section is three.

Notwithstanding any other provision of law, the court may strike the enhancements provided in this section if it determines that there are circumstances in mitigation of the additional punishment and states on the record its reasons for striking the additional punishment. *(Amended by Stats 1988 ch 1264 §1, eff. 1/1/89.)*

§23185. Penalty; second offense within seven years.

If any person is convicted of a violation of Section 23153 and the offense occurred within seven years of a separate violation of Section 23103 as specified in

© 1992 by J., B. & L. Gould
Printed in the U.S.A.   **EP**

Section 23103.5, 23152, or 23153 which resulted in a conviction, that person shall be punished by imprisonment in the state prison, or in the county jail for not less than 120 days nor more than one year, and by a fine of not less than three hundred ninety dollars ($390) nor more than five thousand dollars ($5,000). The person's privilege to operate a motor vehicle shall be revoked by the Department of Motor Vehicles pursuant to paragraph (4) of subdivision (a) of Section 13352. *(Amended by Stats 1988 ch 939 §2; ch 1273 §4, eff. 7/1/89. Former §23185 repealed by Stats 1986 ch 1117.)*

§23186. Conditions of probation when punished under §23185.

If the court grants probation to any person punished under Section 23185, in addition to the provisions of Section 23206 and any other terms and conditions imposed by the court, the court shall impose as conditions of probation that the person be subject to all of the provisions of either subdivision (a) or (b), as follows:

(a) Be confined in the county jail for at least 120 days and pay a fine of at least three hundred ninety dollars ($390) but not more than five thousand dollars ($5,000). The person's privilege to operate a motor vehicle shall be revoked by the Department of Motor Vehicles pursuant to paragraph (4) of subdivision (a) of Section 13352.

(b) All of the following:

(1) Be confined in the county jail for at least 30 days but not more than one year.

(2) Pay a fine of at least three hundred ninety dollars ($390) but not more than one thousand dollars ($1,000).

(3) Pursuant to Section 13352.5, have the privilege to operate a motor vehicle be suspended for one year by the Department of Motor Vehicles and, after that one-year period, if the person gives proof of ability to respond in damages as defined in Section 16430 to the Department of Motor Vehicles, have the privilege restricted by the Department of Motor Vehicles for two additional years to necessary travel to and from that person's place of employment, and to and from the treatment program described in paragraph (4) and, if driving a motor vehicle is necessary to perform the duties of the person's employment, restricted to driving in that person's scope of employment. The Department of Motor Vehicles shall not revoke the person's privilege to operate a motor vehicle under Section 13352, as provided in Section 13352.5, unless the offense occurred in a vehicle requiring a driver with a class 1 or class 2 driver's license or with a certificate specified in Section 12804.1.

(4) Either of the following:

(A) Participate, for at least 18 months subsequent to the underlying conviction and in a manner satisfactory to the court, in a program licensed pursuant to Chapter 9 (commencing with Section 11836) of Part 2 of Division 10.5 of the Health and Safety Code, if available in the county of the person's residence or employment, as designated by the court. The program shall provide for persons who cannot afford the program fee pursuant to paragraph (2) of subdivision (a) of Section 11837.4 of the Health and Safety Code in order to enable those persons to participate.

(B) Participate, for at least 30 months subsequent to the underlying conviction and in a manner satisfactory to the court, in a program licensed pursuant to

Chapter 9 (commencing with Section 11836) of Part 2 of Division 10.5 of the Health and Safety Code, if available in the county of the person's residence or employment. A person ordered to treatment pursuant to this subparagraph shall apply to the court or to a board of review, as designated by the court, at the conclusion of the program to obtain the court's order of satisfaction. Only upon the granting of that order of satisfaction by the court may the program issue its certificate of completion and report the completion to the Department of Motor Vehicles. A failure to obtain an order of satisfaction at the conclusion of the program is a violation of probation. In order to enable all required persons to participate, each person shall pay the program costs commensurate with the person's ability to pay as determined pursuant to Section 11837.4 of the Health and Safety Code. No condition of probation required pursuant to this subparagraph is a basis for reducing any other probation requirement or for avoiding the mandatory license revocation provisions of paragraph (5) of subdivision (a) of Section 13352. *(Amended by Stats 1991 ch 990 §4, eff. 10/14/91.)*

§23187. Added penalty for violation of probation; second offense.

Notwithstanding the provisions of Section 23207, if any person has been granted probation under the conditions of subdivision (b) of Section 23186 and fails at any time to participate successfully in the treatment program described in paragraph (4) of that subdivision, the court shall revoke or terminate the probation, and the court may revoke or terminate the probation if the person failed to comply with any other term or condition of probation, and the court shall proceed under either of the following provisions:

(a) Revoke suspension of sentence and proceed as provided in subdivision (c) of Section 1203.2 of the Penal Code and order the Department of Motor Vehicles to revoke the person's privilege to operate a motor vehicle pursuant to paragraph (4) of subdivision (a) of Section 13352 from the date of the order revoking or terminating probation.

(b) Grant a new term of probation on the condition that the person be confined in the county jail for at least 90 days and order the Department of Motor Vehicles to suspend the person's privilege to operate a motor vehicle pursuant to paragraph (4) of subdivision (a) of Section 13352 from the date of the new grant of probation.

§23190. Penalty; third offense within seven years.

(a) If any person is convicted of a violation of Section 23153 and the offense occurred within seven years of two or more separate violations of Section 23103, as specified in Section 23103.5, or Section 23152 or 23153, or any combination of these violations, which resulted in convictions, that person shall be punished by imprisonment in the state prison for a term of two, three, or four years and by a fine of not less than one thousand fifteen dollars ($1,015) nor more than five thousand dollars ($5,000). The person's privilege to operate a motor vehicle shall be revoked by the Department of Motor Vehicles pursuant to paragraph (6) of subdivision (a) of Section 13352.

(b) Any person convicted of Section 23153 punishable under this section shall be designated as an habitual traffic offender for a period of three years, subsequent to the conviction. The person shall be advised of this designation pursuant to subdivision (b) of Section 13350. *(Amended by Stats 1991 ch 1091 §161, eff. 1/1/92.)*

§23191. Conditions of probation when punished under §23190.

(a) If the court grants probation to any person punished under Section 23190, in addition to the provisions of Section 23206 and any other terms and conditions imposed by the court, the court shall impose as conditions of probation that the person be confined in the county jail for at least one year, that the person pay a fine of at least three hundred ninety dollars ($390) but not more than five thousand dollars ($5,000), and that the person make restitution or reparation pursuant to Section 1203.1 of the Penal Code. The person's privilege to operate a motor vehicle shall be revoked by the Department of Motor Vehicles pursuant to paragraph (6) of subdivision (a) of Section 13352.

(b) In addition to the provisions of Section 23206 and subdivision (a), if the court grants probation to any person punished under Section 23190, the court shall impose as a condition of probation that the person complete, subsequent to the underlying conviction and in a manner satisfactory to the court, an 18-month program or, if available in the county of the person's residence or employment, a 30-month program licensed pursuant to Chapter 9 (commencing with Section 11836) of Part 2 of Division 10.5 of the Health and Safety Code, as designated by the court. In lieu of the minimum term of imprisonment in subdivision (a), the court shall impose as a minimum condition of probation under this subdivision that the person be confined in the county jail for at least 30 days but not more than one year. Except as provided in subdivision (b), if the court grants probation under this section, the court shall order the treatment prescribed by this subdivision, whether or not the person has previously completed a treatment program pursuant to paragraph (4) of subdivision (b) of Section 23166 or paragraph (4) of subdivision (b) of Section 23186. A person ordered to treatment pursuant to this subdivision shall apply to the court or to a board of review, as designated by the court, at the conclusion of the program to obtain the court's order of satisfaction. Only upon the granting of that order of satisfaction by the court may the program issue its certificate of successful completion and report the completion to the Department of Motor Vehicles. A failure to obtain an order of satisfaction at the conclusion of the program is a violation of probation. In order to enable all required persons to participate, each person shall pay the program costs commensurate with the person's ability to pay as determined pursuant to Section 11837.4 of the Health and Safety Code. No condition of probation required pursuant to this subdivision is a basis for reducing any other probation requirement in this section or Section 23206 or for avoiding the mandatory license revocation provisions of paragraph (6) of subdivision (a) of Section 13352. *(Amended by Stats 1991 ch 209 §3, eff. 1/1/92.)*

§23194. Driving under the influence with a minor.

(a) If any person is convicted of a violation of Section 23152 and a minor under 14 years of age was a passenger in the vehicle at the time of the offense, the court shall impose the following penalties in addition to any other penalty prescribed in this article:

(1) If the person is convicted of a violation of Section 23152 punishable under Section 23160, the punishment prescribed in this article shall be enhanced by an imprisonment of 48 continuous hours in the county jail, whether or not probation is granted, no part of which shall be stayed.

(2) If a person is convicted of a violation of Section 23152 punishable under Section 23165, the punishment prescribed in this article shall be enhanced by an imprisonment of 10 days in the county jail, whether or not probation is granted, no part of which may be stayed.

(3) If a person is convicted of a violation of Section 23152 punishable under Section 23170, the punishment prescribed in this article shall be enhanced by an imprisonment of 30 days in the county jail, whether or not probation is granted, no part of which may be stayed.

(4) If a person is convicted of a violation of Section 23152 which is punished as a misdemeanor under Section 23175, the punishment prescribed in this article shall be enhanced by an imprisonment of 90 days in the county jail, whether or not probation is granted, no part of which may be stayed.

(b) The driving of a vehicle in which a minor under 14 years of age was a passenger shall be pled and proven.

(c) No punishment enhancement shall be imposed pursuant to this section if the person is also convicted of a violation of Section 273a of the Penal Code arising out of the same facts and incident. *(Added by Stats 1989 ch 1023 §1, eff. 1/1/90.)*

§23195. Impoundment of vehicle.

(a) Except as provided in subdivision (b), the interest of any registered owner of a motor vehicle which has been used in the commission of a violation of Section 23152 or 23153 for which the owner was convicted, is subject to impoundment as provided in this section. Upon conviction the court may order the vehicle impounded at the registered owner's expense for not less than one nor more than 30 days.

If the offense occurred within five years of a prior offense which resulted in conviction of a violation of Section 23152 or 23153, the prior conviction shall also be charged in the accusatory pleading and if admitted or found to be true by the jury upon a jury trial or by the court upon a court trial, the court shall, except in an unusual case where the interests of justice would best be served by not ordering impoundment, order the vehicle impounded at the registered owner's expense for not less than one nor more than 30 days.

If the offense occurred within five years of two or more prior offenses which resulted in convictions of violations of Section 23152 or 23153, the prior convictions shall also be charged in the accusatory pleading and if admitted or found to be true by the jury upon a jury trial or by the court upon a court trial, the court shall, except in an unusual case where the interests of justice would best be served by not ordering impoundment, order the vehicle impounded at the registered owner's expense for not less than one nor more than 90 days.

For purposes of this section the court may consider in the interests of justice factors such as whether impoundment of the vehicle would result in a loss of employment of the offender or the offender's family,

© 1992 by J., B. & L. Gould
Printed in the U.S.A.   EP

impair the ability of the offender or the offender's family to attend school or obtain medical care, result in the loss of the vehicle because of inability to pay impoundment fees, or unfairly infringe upon community property rights or any other facts the court finds relevant. When no impoundment is ordered in an unusual case pursuant to this section, the court shall specify on the record and shall enter in the minutes the circumstances indicating that the interests of justice would best be served by such a disposition.

(b) No vehicle which may be lawfully driven on the highway with a class 3 or class 4 driver's license, as specified in Section 12804, is subject to impoundment under this section if there is a community property interest in the vehicle owned by a person other than the defendant and the vehicle is the sole vehicle available to the defendant's immediate family which may be operated on the highway with a class 3 or class 4 driver's license.

§23196. Alcohol penalty assessment.

(a) Except as otherwise provided in subdivision (c), any person convicted of a violation of Section 23152 or 23153 shall, in addition to any other fine, assessment, or imprisonment imposed pursuant to law, pay an alcohol abuse education and prevention penalty assessment in an amount not to exceed fifty dollars ($50) for deposit and distribution pursuant to Section 1463.25 of the Penal Code.

(b) The payment of the penalty assessment under this section shall be ordered upon conviction of a person of a violation of Section 23152 or 23153 irrespective of any other proceeding and, if probation is granted, the payment of the penalty assessment shall also be ordered as a condition of probation, except in unusual cases which are subject to subdivision (d) of Section 1464 of the Penal Code.

(c) The court shall determine if the defendant has the ability to pay a penalty assessment. If the court determines that the defendant has the ability to pay a penalty assessment, the court may set the amount to be paid and order the defendant to pay that sum to the county in the manner in which the court believes reasonable and compatible with the defendant's financial ability. In making a determination of whether a defendant has the ability to pay, the court shall take into account the amount of any fine imposed upon the defendant and any amount the defendant has been ordered to pay in restitution. If the court determines that the defendant does not have the ability to pay a penalty assessment, the defendant shall not be required to pay a penalty assessment.

(d) Five percent of the funds allocated to primary prevention programs to the school and the communities pursuant to subdivision (a) of Section 11802 of the Health and Safety Code shall be used to conduct an annual evaluation. The annual evaluation shall be conducted by the office of the county superintendent of schools in counties where the program is operating in a single county or in the office of the county superintendent of schools in the county designated as the lead county in counties where the program is operating as a consortium of counties. The evaluation shall contain the following:

(1) A needs assessment evaluation which provides specific data regarding the problem to be resolved.

(2) A written report of the planning process outlining the deliberations, considerations, and conclusions following a review of the needs assessment.

(3) An end of fiscal year accountability evaluation that will indicate the program's continuing ability to reach appropriate program beneficiaries, deliver the appropriate benefits, and use funds appropriately.

(4) An impact evaluation charged with the task of assessing the effectiveness of the program. Guidelines for the evaluation report format and the timeliness for the submission of the report shall be developed by the State Department of Education. Each county shall submit an evaluation report annually to the State Department of Education and the State Department of Education shall write and submit a report to the Legislature and Governor. (Amended by Stats 1987 ch 621 §6.5.)

§23197. Conditional sentence.

(a) Except as provided in subdivision (c), an order to pay any fine, restitution, or assessment, imposed as a condition of the grant of probation or as part of a judgment of conditional sentence for a violation of Section 23152 or 23153, may be enforced in the same manner provided for the enforcement of money judgments.

(b) A willful failure to pay any fine, restitution, or assessment during the term of probation, is a violation of the terms and conditions of probation.

(c) If an order to pay a fine as a condition of probation is stayed, a writ of execution shall not be issued, and any failure to pay the fine is not willful, until the stay is removed. (Added by Stats 1989 ch 1297 §17, eff. 10/1/89. Former §23197 repealed by Stats 1989 ch 1297 §16, eff. 10/1/89.)

§23198. Vehicle declared a nuisance.

(a) (1) Upon its own motion or upon motion of the prosecutor in a criminal action for a violation of any of the following offenses, the court with jurisdiction over the offense, notwithstanding Section 86 of the Code of Civil Procedure and any other provision of law otherwise prescribing the jurisdiction of the court based upon the value of the property involved, may declare the motor vehicle driven by the defendant to be a nuisance if the defendant is the registered owner of the vehicle:

(A) A violation of Section 191.5 or paragraph (3) of subdivision (c) of Section 192 of the Penal Code.

(B) A violation of Section 23152 which occurred within seven years of two or more separate offenses of Section 191.5 or paragraph (3) of subdivision (c) of Section 192 of the Penal Code, or Section 23152 or 23153, or any combination thereof, which resulted in convictions.

(C) A violation of Section 23153 which occurred within seven years of one or more separate offenses of Section 191.5 or paragraph (3) of subdivision (c) of Section 192 of the Penal Code, or Section 23152 or 23153, which resulted in convictions.

(2) The court or the prosecutor shall give notice of the motion to the defendant, and the court shall hold a hearing before a motor vehicle may be declared a nuisance under this section.

(b) Except as provided in subdivision (g), upon the conviction of the defendant and at the time of pronouncement of sentence, the court with jurisdiction over the offense shall order any vehicle declared to be a nuisance pursuant to subdivision (a) to be sold. Any vehicle ordered to be sold pursuant to this subdivision shall be surrendered to the sheriff of the county or the chief of police of the city in which the violation occurred. The officer to whom the vehicle is surrendered shall promptly ascertain from the department the names and addresses of all legal and registered owners of the vehicle and, within five days of receiving that information, shall send by certified mail a notice to all legal and registered owners of the vehicle other than the defendant, at the addresses obtained from the department, informing them that the vehicle has been declared a nuisance and will be sold or otherwise disposed of pursuant to this section and of the approximate date and location of the sale or other disposition. The notice shall also inform any legal owner of its right to conduct the sale pursuant to subdivision (c).

(c) Any legal owner which in the regular course of its business conducts sales of repossessed or surrendered motor vehicles may take possession and conduct the sale of the vehicle declared to be a nuisance if it notifies the officer to whom the vehicle is surrendered of its intent to conduct the sale within 15 days of the mailing of the notice pursuant to subdivision (b). Sale of the vehicle pursuant to this subdivision may be conducted at the time, in the manner, and on the notice usually given by the legal owner for the sale of repossessed or surrendered vehicles. The proceeds of any sale conducted by the legal owner shall be disposed of as provided in subdivision (e).

(d) If the legal owner does not notify the officer to whom the vehicle is surrendered of its intent to conduct the sale as provided in subdivision (c), the officer shall offer the vehicle for sale at public auction within 60 days of receiving the vehicle. At least 10 days but not more than 20 days prior to the sale, not counting the day of sale, the officer shall give notice of the sale by advertising once in a newspaper of general circulation published in the city or county, as the case may be, in which the vehicle is located, which notice shall contain a description of the make, year, model, identification number, and license number of the vehicle and the date, time, and location of the sale. For motorcycles, the engine number shall also be included. If there is no newspaper of general circulation published in the county, notice shall be given by posting a notice of sale containing the information required by this subdivision in three of the most public places in the city or county in which the vehicle is located, and at the place where the vehicle is to be sold, for 10 consecutive days prior to and including the day of the sale.

(e) The proceeds of a sale conducted pursuant to this section shall be disposed of in the following priority:

(1) To satisfy the costs of the sale, including costs incurred with respect to the taking and keeping of the vehicle pending sale.

(2) To the legal owner in an amount to satisfy the indebtedness owed to the legal owner remaining as of the date of sale, including accrued interest or finance charges and delinquency charges.

(3) To the holder of any subordinate lien or encumbrance on the vehicle to satisfy any indebtedness so secured if written notification of demand is received before distribution of the proceeds is completed. The holder of a subordinate lien or encumbrance, if requested, shall reasonably furnish reasonable proof of its interest and, unless it does so on request, is not entitled to distribution pursuant to this paragraph.

(4) To any other person who can establish an interest in the vehicle, including a community property interest, to the extent of his or her provable interest.

(5) If the vehicle was forfeited as a result of a felony violation of Section 191.5 of the Penal Code, or of Section 23153 which resulted in serious bodily injury to any person other than the defendant, the balance, if any, to the city or county in which the violation occurred, to be deposited in its general fund.

(6) Except as provided in paragraph (5), the balance, if any, to the city or county in which the violation occurred, to be expended for community-based adolescent substance abuse treatment services.

The person conducting the sale shall disburse the proceeds of the sale as provided in this subdivision, and provide a written accounting regarding the disposition to all persons entitled to or claiming a share of the proceeds, within 15 days after the sale is conducted.

(f) If the vehicle to be sold under this section is not of the type that can readily be sold to the public generally, the vehicle shall be destroyed or donated to an eleemosynary institution.

(g) No vehicle shall be sold pursuant to this section in either of the following circumstances:

(1) The vehicle is stolen, unless the identity of the legal and registered owners of the vehicle cannot be reasonably ascertained.

(2) The vehicle is owned by another, or there is a community property interest in the vehicle owned by a person other than the defendant and the vehicle is the only vehicle available to the defendant's immediate family which may be operated on the highway with a class 3 or class 4 driver's license.

(h) The Legislature finds and declares it to be the public policy of this state that no policy of insurance shall afford benefits which would alleviate the financial detriment suffered by any person as a direct or indirect result of a confiscation of a vehicle pursuant to this section. *(Amended by Stats 1989 ch 635 §1, eff. 1/1/90.)*

§23199. Suspension of driving privilege; postponement.

If any person is convicted of a violation of Section 23152 or 23153 and is sentenced to one year in the county jail or more than one year in state prison under Section 23165, 23166, 23170, 23171, 23175, 23176, 23180, 23181, 23182, 23185, 23186, 23190, or 23191, the court may postpone the suspension of the person's driving privilege until the term of imprisonment is served. *(Added by Stats 1990 ch 431 §18, eff. 7/26/90.)*

§23200. Striking separate convictions prohibited.

(a) In any case charging a violation of Section 23152 or 23153 and the offense occurred within seven years of one or more separate violations of Section 23103 as specified in Section 23103.5 which occurred on or after January 1, 1982, 23152, or 23153, or any combination thereof, which resulted in convictions, the court shall not strike any separate conviction of those offenses for purposes of sentencing in order to avoid imposing, as part of the sentence or term of probation, the minimum time of imprisonment and the minimum fine, as provided in this chapter, or for purposes of avoiding revocation, suspension, or restriction of the privilege to operate a motor vehicle, as provided in this code.

© 1992 by J., B. & L. Gould
Printed in the U.S.A.   EP

(b) In any case charging a violation of Section 23152 or 23153, the court shall obtain a copy of the driving record of the person charged from the Department of Motor Vehicles and may obtain any records from the Department of Justice or any other source to determine if one or more separate violations of Section 23103 as specified in Section 23103.5 which occurred on or after January 1, 1982, 23152, or 23153, or any combination thereof, which resulted in convictions, have occurred within seven years of the charged offense. The court may obtain, and accept as rebuttable evidence, a printout from the Department of Motor Vehicles of the driving record of the person charged, maintained by electronic and storage media pursuant to Section 1801 for the purpose of proving those separate violations.

(c) If any separate convictions of violations of Section 23152 or 23153 are reported to have occurred within 10 years of the charged offense, the court shall notify each court where any of the separate convictions occurred for the purpose of enforcing terms and conditions of probation pursuant to Section 23207. *(Amended by Stats 1986 ch 1117 §10.)*

§23201. Lawful use of drugs.

The fact that any person charged with driving under the influence of any drug or the combined influence of alcoholic beverages and any drug in violation of Section 23152 or 23153 is or has been entitled to use the drug under the laws of this state shall not constitute a defense against any violation of the sections.

§23202. Prohibition against suspending or dismissing proceedings due to participation in treatment program.

(a) In any case in which a person is charged with a violation of Section 23152 or 23153, prior to acquittal or conviction, the court shall not suspend or stay the proceedings for the purpose of allowing the accused person to attend or participate, nor shall the court consider dismissal of or entertain a motion to dismiss the proceedings because the accused person attends or participates during that suspension, in any one or more education, training, or treatment programs, including, but not limited to, a driver improvement program, a treatment program for persons who are habitual users of alcohol or other alcoholism program, a program designed to offer alcohol services to problem drinkers, an alcohol or drug education program, or a treatment program for persons who are habitual users of drugs or other drug-related program.

(b) This section shall not apply to any attendance or participation in any education, training, or treatment programs after conviction and sentencing, including attendance or participation in any of those programs as a condition of probation granted after conviction when permitted pursuant to this article.

§23203. Notification of driving restrictions and probation.

(a) If a person's privilege to operate a motor vehicle is restricted by a court pursuant to this article, the court shall clearly mark the restriction and the dates of the restriction on each of that person's operator's licenses and promptly notify the Department of Motor Vehicles of the terms of the restriction in a manner prescribed by the department. The department shall place that restriction on the person's records in the department and enter the restriction on any license subsequently issued by the department to that person during the period of the restriction.

(b) If the court removes a restriction before the end of the previously specified term pursuant to Section 23168, the court shall so mark the person's operator's license in a manner prescribed by the department and promptly notify the department of the removal of the restriction.

(c) If a person is placed on probation pursuant to this article, the court shall promptly notify the Department of Motor Vehicles of the probation and probationary term and conditions in a manner prescribed by the department. The department shall place the fact of probation and the probationary term and conditions on the person's records in the department.

§23204. Surrender of operator's license due to suspension or revocation.

If a person's privilege to operate a motor vehicle is required ordered to be suspended or revoked by the Department of Motor Vehicles pursuant to other provisions of this code upon the conviction of an offense of this article, that person shall surrender each and every operator's license of that person to the court upon conviction. At the time of sentencing, if the court grants probation on terms which permit the person to retain his or her driving privilege, the court may return the person's operator's license to that person. The court shall transmit the license or licenses required to be suspended or revoked to the Department of Motor Vehicles pursuant to Section 13550, and the court shall notify the department.

This section does not apply to an administrative proceeding by the Department of Motor Vehicles to suspend or revoke the driving privilege of any person pursuant to other provisions of law. *(Amended by Stats 1986 ch 1117 §11.)*

§23205. Court order for presentence investigations.

(a) Upon any conviction of a violation of Section 23152 or 23153, any judge of the court may order a presentence investigation to determine whether a person convicted of the violation would benefit from one or more education, training, or treatment programs, and the court may order suitable education, training, or treatment for the person, in addition to imposing any penalties required by this code.

(b) In determining whether to require, as a condition of probation, the participation in a program pursuant to subdivision (b) of Section 23161, subdivision (b) of Section 23166, subdivision (b) of Section 23171, subdivision (b) of Section 23176, subdivision (b) of Section 23181, subdivision (b) of Section 23186, or subdivision (b) of Section 23191, the court may consider any relevant information about the person made available pursuant to a presentence investigation, which is permitted but not required by subdivision (a), or other screening procedure. No such information shall be furnished to the court, however, by any person who also provides services in a privately operated, approved program or who has any direct interest in a privately operated, approved program. In addition, the court shall obtain from the Department of Motor Vehicles a copy of the person's driving record to determine whether the person is eligible to participate in an approved program pursuant to the provisions of this article.

(c) The Judicial Council shall adopt a standard form for use by all courts, defendants, and alcohol or drug education programs in certifying to the court that the person (1) has enrolled within the specified time period, and (2) has successfully completed any program required by Section 23161 or 23181.

§23206. Sentencing; terms and revocations of probation.

(a) If any person is convicted of a violation of Section 23152 or 23153, the court shall not stay or suspend pronouncement of sentencing, and shall pronounce sentence in conjunction with the conviction in a reasonable time, including time for receipt of any presentence investigation report ordered pursuant to Section 23205.

(b) If any person is convicted of a violation of Section 23152 or 23153 and is granted probation, the terms and conditions of probation shall include, but not be limited to the following:

(1) Notwithstanding Section 1203a of the Penal Code, a period of probation not less than three nor more than five years; provided, however, that if the maximum sentence provided for the offense may exceed five years in the state prison, the period during which the sentence may be suspended and terms of probation enforced may be for a longer period than three years but may not exceed the maximum time for which sentence of imprisonment may be pronounced.

(2) A requirement that the person shall not drive a vehicle with any measurable amount of alcohol in his or her blood.

(3) A requirement that the person, if arrested for a violation of Section 23152 or 23153, shall not refuse to submit to a chemical test of his or her blood, breath, or urine, pursuant to Section 23157, for the purpose of determining the alcoholic content of his or her blood.

(4) A requirement that the person shall not commit any criminal offense.

(c) The court shall not absolve a person who is convicted of a violation of Section 23152 or 23153 from the obligation of spending the minimum time in confinement, if any, or of paying the minimum fine provided in this article.

(d) In addition to any other provision of law, if any person violates paragraph (3) of subdivision (b), or violates paragraph (2) of subdivision (b) and the person had a blood alcohol concentration of over 0.04 percent as determined by a chemical test, the court shall revoke or terminate the person's probation as provided by Section 23207, regardless of any other proceeding, and shall only grant a new term of probation of not more than five years on the added condition that the person be confined in the county jail for not less than 48 hours for each of these violations of probation, except in unusual cases where the interests of justice would best be served if this additional condition were not imposed. (*Amended by Stats 1986 ch 1117 §12.*)

§23206.1. Blood-alcohol content specified.

In addition to any other provision of this code, if any person is convicted of a violation of Section 23152 or 23153, the court shall consider a concentration of alcohol in the person's blood of 0.20 percent or more, by weight, or the refusal of the person to take a chemical test as a special factor which may justify enhancing the penalties in sentencing, in determining whether to grant probation, and, if probation is granted, in determining additional or enhanced terms and conditions of probation. (*Amended and renumbered by Stats 1986 ch 248 §241; formerly §23206.5.*)

§23206.5. Sentence for second DWI conviction.

(a) If any person is convicted of a violation of Section 23152 or 23153 and the offense was a second or subsequent offense punishable under Section 23165, 23170, 23175, 23185, or 23190, the court shall require that any term of imprisonment that is imposed include at least one period of not less than 48 consecutive hours of imprisonment or, in the alternative and notwithstanding Section 4024.2 of the Penal Code, that the person serve not less than 10 days of community service.

(b) Notwithstanding any other provision of law, except Section 2900.5 of the Penal Code, unless the court expressly finds in the circumstances that the punishment inflicted would be cruel or unusual punishment prohibited by Section 17 of Article I of the California Constitution, no court or person to whom a person is remanded for execution of sentence shall release, or permit the release of, a person from the requirements of subdivision (a), including, but not limited to, any work-release program, weekend service of sentence program, diversion or treatment program, or otherwise.

(c) For purposes of this section, "imprisonment" means confinement in a jail, in a minimum security facility, or in an inpatient rehabilitation facility, as provided in Part 1309 (commencing with Section 1309.1) of Title 23 of the Code of Federal Regulations.

(d) This section shall become operative only if, and upon the date of the certification by, the Department of Motor Vehicles to the Secretary of State that California has submitted a completed application for federal Title 408 grant programs funds pursuant to that Part 1309. (*Amended by Stats 1990 ch 431 §19, eff. 7/26/90.*)

§23207. Conditions of revocation of probation.

Except as otherwise expressly provided in this article, if a person has been convicted of a violation of Section 23152 or 23153 and the court has suspended execution of the sentence for that conviction and has granted probation, and during the time of that probation, the person is found by the court to have violated a term or condition of that probation required by any provision of this article, the court shall revoke the suspension of sentence, revoke or terminate probation, and shall proceed in the manner provided in subdivision (c) of Section 1203.2 of the Penal Code.

§23208. Driving vehicle at least 30 miles per hour over speed limit: additional punsihment.

(a) Any person who drives a vehicle 30 or more miles per hour over the maximum, prima facie, or posted speed limit on a freeway, or 20 or more miles per hour over the maximum, prima facie, or posted speed limit on any other street or highway, and in a manner prohibited by Section 23103 during the commission of a violation of Section 23152 or 23153 shall, in addition to the punishment prescribed for that person upon conviction of a violation of Section 23152 or 23153, be punished by an additional and consecutive term of 60 days in the county jail.

(b) If the court grants probation or suspends the execution of sentence, it shall require as a condition of probation or suspension that the defendant serve 60

© 1992 by J., B. & L. Gould
Printed in the U.S.A.   **EP**

days in the county jail, in addition and consecutive to any other sentence prescribed by this chapter.

(c) On a first conviction under this section, the court shall order the driver to participate in, and successfully complete, an alcohol or drug education and counseling program, or both an alcohol and a drug education and counseling program. Except in unusual cases where the interests of justice would be served, a finding making this section applicable to a defendant shall not be stricken pursuant to Section 1385 of the Penal Code or any other provision of law. If the court decides not to impose the additional and consecutive term, it shall specify on the court record the reasons for that order.

(d) The additional term provided in this section shall not be imposed unless the facts of driving in a manner prohibited by Section 23103 and driving the vehicle 30 or more miles per hour over the maximum, prima facie, or posted speed limit on a freeway, or 20 or more miles per hour over the maximum, prima facie, or posted speed limit on any other street or highway, are charged in the accusatory pleading and admitted or found to be true by the trier of fact. A finding of driving in that manner shall be based on facts in addition to the fact that the defendant was driving while under the influence of alcohol, any drug, or both, or with a specified percentage of alcohol in the blood. *(Added by Stats 1990 ch 568 §1, eff. 1/1/91.)*

§23209. Limited challenges to separate convictions.

Only one challenge shall be permitted to the constitutionality of a separate conviction of a violation of Section 14601, 14601.2, 23152, or 23153, which was entered in a separate proceeding. When a proceeding to declare a separate judgment of conviction constitutionally invalid has been held, a determination by the court that the separate conviction is constitutional precludes any subsequent attack on constitutional grounds in a subsequent prosecution in which the same separate conviction is charged. In addition, any determination that a separate conviction is unconstitutional precludes any allegation or use of that separate conviction in any judicial or administrative proceeding, and the department shall strike that separate conviction from its records. Pursuant to Section 1803, the court shall report to the Department of Motor Vehicles any determination upholding a conviction on constitutional grounds and any determination that a conviction is unconstitutional.

This section shall not preclude a subsequent challenge to a conviction if, at a later time, a subsequent statute or appellate court decision having retroactive application affords any new basis to challenge the constitutionality of the conviction.

§23210. Other jurisdictions' convictions.

A conviction of an offense in any state, territory, or possession of the United States, the District of Columbia, the Commonwealth of Puerto Rico, or the Dominion of Canada which, if committed in this state, would be a violation of Section 23152 or 23153 of this code, or Section 191.5 or paragraph (3) of subdivision (c) of Section 192 of the Penal Code, is a conviction of Section 23152 or 23153 of this code, or Section 191.5 or paragraph (3) of subdivision (c) of Section 192 of the Penal Code for the purposes of this code. *(Amended by Stats 1990 ch 431 §20, eff. 7/26/90.)*

§23211. Treatment programs; economic interest of court employees.

A court shall not order or refer any person to any program, including an alcohol or drug education program or a program approved pursuant to Chapter 9 (commencing with Section 11837) of Part 2 of Division 10.5 of the Health and Safety Code, or to a provider of such a program, in which any employee of the court has a direct or indirect economic interest.

§23212. Dismissal, substitution, or striking of charges.

When an allegation of a violation of Section 23152 is dismissed by the court, an allegation of a different or lesser offense is substituted for an allegation of a violation of Section 23152, or an allegation of a separate conviction is dismissed or stricken, the court shall specify on the record its reason or reasons for the order. The court shall also specify on the record whether the dismissal, substitution, or striking was requested by the prosecution and whether the prosecution concurred in or opposed the dismissal, substitution, or striking.

When the prosecution makes a motion for a dismissal or substitution, or for the striking of a separate conviction, the prosecution shall submit a written statement which shall become part of the court record and which gives the reasons for the motion. The reasons shall include, but need not be limited to, problems of proof, the interests of justice, why another offense is more properly charged, if applicable, and any other pertinent reasons. If the reasons include the "interests of justice", the written statement shall specify all of the factors which contributed to this conclusion.

§23213. Patient in rehabilitation facility; registration of vehicle.

No patient or other person residing in a social rehabilitation facility licensed pursuant to Chapter 3 (commencing with Section 1500) of Division 2 of the Health and Safety Code for the rehabilitation of persons who have abused alcohol or drugs, shall have a motor vehicle registered in the name of that patient or person on or near the premises of that facility unless the patient or person has an operator's license issued pursuant to this code which is not suspended or revoked.

§23215. Offenses occurring other than on highways.

The department may, but shall not be required to, provide patrol or enforce the provisions of Section 23152 for offenses which occur other than upon a highway.

§23216. References for purposes of enhancement.

(a) The provisions of Sections 2, 6, 7, and 10 expressly apply to the provisions of this article, and, further, for any recidivist or enhancement purpose, reference to an offense by section number is a reference to the provisions contained in that section, insofar as they were renumbered by Chapter 940 of the Statutes of 1981 without substantive change, and those provisions shall be construed as restatements and continuations thereof and not as new enactments.

(b) Any reference in the provisions of this code to a separate violation of Section 23152 shall include a separate offense under Section 23102 or 23105, as those sections read prior to January 1, 1982.

(c) Any reference in the provisions of the Vehicle Code to a separate violation of Section 23153 shall include a separate offense under Section 23101 or 23106 as those sections read prior to January 1, 1982.

(d) The provisions of this section are to be given retroactive effect.

§23217. Legislative findings.

The Legislature finds and declares that some repeat offenders of the prohibition against driving under the influence of alcohol or drugs, when they are addicted or when they have too much alcohol in their systems, may be escaping the intent of the Legislature to punish the offender with progressively greater severity if the offense is repeated one or more times within a seven-year period. This situation may occur when a conviction for a subsequent offense occurs before a conviction is obtained on an earlier offense.

The Legislature further finds and declares that the timing of court proceedings should not permit a person to avoid aggravated mandatory minimum penalties for multiple separate offenses occurring within a seven-year period. It is the intent of the Legislature to provide that a person be subject to enhanced mandatory minimum penalties for multiple offenses within a period of seven years, regardless of whether the convictions are obtained in the same sequence as the offenses had been committed.

Nothing in this section requires consideration of judgment of conviction in a separate proceeding which is entered after the judgment in the present proceeding, except as it relates to violation of probation.

Nothing in this section or the amendments to Section 23165, 23170, 23175, 23185, 23190, 23200, or 23202 made by Chapter 1205 of the Statutes of 1984 affects the penalty for a violation of Section 23152 or 23153 occurring prior to January 1, 1985. *(Amended by Stats 1986 ch 1117 §13.)*

§23220. Driving while drinking.

No person shall drink any alcoholic beverage while driving a motor vehicle upon any highway.

§23221. Drinking inside motor vehicle.

No person shall drink any alcoholic beverage while in a motor vehicle upon a highway.

§23222. Possession of alcoholic beverage receptacle or marijuana while driving.

(a) No person shall have in his or her possession on his or her person, while driving a motor vehicle upon a highway, any bottle, can, or other receptacle, containing any alcoholic beverage which has been opened, or a seal broken, or the contents of which have been partially removed.

(b) Except as authorized by law, every person who possesses, while driving a motor vehicle upon a highway, not more than one avoirdupois ounce of marijuana, other than concentrated cannabis as defined by Section 11006.5 of the Health and Safety Code, is guilty of a misdemeanor and shall be punished by a fine of not more than one hundred dollars ($100). Notwithstanding any other provision of law, if the person has been previously convicted three or more times of an offense described in this subdivision during the two-year period immediately preceding the date of commission of the violation to be charged, the previous

convictions shall also be charged in the accusatory pleading and, if found to be true by the jury upon a jury trial or by the court upon a court trial or if admitted by the person, Sections 1000.1 and 1000.2 of the Penal Code are applicable to the person, and the court shall divert and refer the person for education, treatment, or rehabilitation, without a court hearing or determination or the concurrence of the district attorney, to an appropriate community program which will accept the person. If the person is so diverted and referred, the person is not subject to the fine specified in this subdivision. In any case in which a person is arrested for a violation of this subdivision and does not demand to be taken before a magistrate, the person shall be released by the arresting officer upon presentation of satisfactory evidence of identity and giving his or her written promise to appear in court, as provided in Section 40500, and shall not be subjected to booking.

§23223. Possession of opened alcoholic container.

No person shall have in his or her possession on his or her person, while in a motor vehicle upon a highway, any bottle, can, or other receptacle, containing any alcoholic beverage which has been opened, or a seal broken, or the contents of which have been partially removed.

§23224. Possession of alcoholic beverage in vehicle by persons under 21.

(a) No person under the age of 21 years shall knowingly drive any motor vehicle carrying any alcoholic beverage, unless the person is accompanied by a parent, responsible adult relative, any other adult designated by the parent, or legal guardian for the purpose of transportation of an alcoholic beverage, or is employed by a licensee under the Alcoholic Beverage Control Act (Division 9 (commencing with Section 23000) of the Business and Professions Code), and is driving the motor vehicle during regular hours and in the course of the person's employment. If the driver was unaccompanied, he or she shall have a complete defense if he or she was following, in a timely manner, the reasonable instructions of his or her parent, legal guardian, responsible adult relative, or adult designee relating to disposition of the alcoholic beverage.

(b) No passenger in any motor vehicle who is under the age of 21 years shall knowingly possess or have under that person's control any alcoholic beverage, unless the passenger is accompanied by a parent, legal guardian, responsible adult relative, any other adult designated by the parent, or legal guardian for the purpose of transportation of an alcoholic beverage, or is employed by a licensee under the Alcoholic Beverage Control Act (Division 9 (commencing with Section 23000) of the Business and Professions Code), and possession or control is during regular hours and in the course of the passenger's employment. If the passenger was unaccompanied, he or she shall have a complete defense if he or she was following, in a timely manner, the reasonable instructions of his or her parent, legal guardian, responsible adult relative or adult designee relating to disposition of the alcoholic beverage.

(c) If the vehicle used in any violation of subdivision (a) or (b) is registered to an offender who is under the age of 21 years, the vehicle may be impounded at the owner's expense for not less than one day nor more than 30 days for each violation.

© 1992 by J., B. & L. Gould
Printed in the U.S.A.   EP

(d) Any person under 21 years of age convicted of a violation of this section is subject to Section 13202.5. *(Amended by Stats 1990 ch 1697 §6, eff. 1/1/91.)*

§23225. Storage of opened alcoholic container.

It is unlawful for the registered owner of any motor vehicle, or the driver if the registered owner is not then present in the vehicle, to keep in a motor vehicle, when the vehicle is upon any highway, any bottle, can, or other receptacle containing any alcoholic beverage which has been opened, or a seal broken, or the contents of which have been partially removed, unless the container is kept in the trunk of the vehicle, or kept in some other area of the vehicle not normally occupied by the driver or passengers, if the vehicle is not equipped with a trunk. A utility compartment or glove compartment shall be deemed to be within the area occupied by the driver and passengers.

This section shall not apply to the living quarters of a housecar or camper.

§23226. Keeping opened container in passenger compartment.

It is unlawful for any person to keep in the passenger compartment of a motor vehicle, when the vehicle is upon any highway, any bottle, can, or other receptacle containing any alcoholic beverage which has been opened, or a seal broken, or the contents of which have been partially removed.

This section shall not apply to the living quarters of a housecar or camper.

§23229. Exceptions for possession of alcoholic beverages.

(a) Except as provided in Section 23229.1, Sections 23221 and 23223 do not apply to passengers in any bus, taxicab or limousine for hire licensed to transport passengers pursuant to the Public Utilities Code or proper local authority, or the living quarters of a housecar or camper.

(b) Except as provided in Section 23229.1, Section 23225 does not apply to the driver or owner of a bus, taxicab or limousine for hire licensed to transport passengers pursuant to the Public Utilities Code or proper local authority.

(c) This section shall become operative on July 1, 1989. *(Added by Stats 1988 ch 1105 §7, oper. 7/1/89. Former section 23229 repealed by Stats 1988 ch 1105 §6, eff. 7/1/89.)*

§23229.1. Possession of alcoholic beverages by passengers under 21.

(a) Subject to subdivision (b), Sections 23223 and 23225 do not apply to any charter-party carrier of passengers, as defined in Section 5360 of the Public Utilities Code, operating a limousine for hire when the driver of the vehicle transports any passenger under the age of 21.

(b) For purposes of subdivision (a), it is not a violation of Section 23225 for any charter-party carrier of passengers operating a limousine for hire which is licensed pursuant to the Public Utilities Code to keep any bottle, can, or other receptacle containing any alcoholic beverage in a locked utility compartment within the area occupied by the driver and passengers.

(c) In addition to the requirements of Section 1803, every clerk of a court, or judge if there is no clerk, in which any driver in subdivision (a) was convicted of a violation of Section 23225 shall prepare within ten days after conviction, and immediately forward to the Public Utilities Commission at its office in San Francisco, an abstract of the record of the court covering the case in which the person was convicted. If sentencing is not pronounced in conjunction with the conviction, the abstract shall be forwarded to the commission within 10 days after sentencing, and the abstract shall be certified, by the person required to prepare it, to be true and correct.

For the purposes of this subdivision, a forfeiture of bail is equivalent to a conviction.

(d) This section shall become operative on July 1, 1989. *(Added by Stats 1988 ch 1105 §8, oper. 7/1/89.)*

CHAPTER 13

VEHICULAR CROSSINGS

ARTICLE 1

GENERAL PROVISIONS

§23253. Persons at vehicular crossings must obey officers.

All persons in or upon any vehicular crossing must at all times comply with any lawful order, signal, or direction by voice or hand of any member of the California Highway Patrol or an employee of the Department of Transportation who is a peace officer.

ARTICLE 2

TOWING ON VEHICULAR CROSSINGS

§23270. Towing vehicles on vehicular crossing.

(a) No person shall commence to tow any vehicle or other object on any vehicular crossing unless authorized to do so by the Department of Transportation and unless the towing is done by means of a tow truck as defined in Section 615. No person, other than a member of the California Highway Patrol or an employee of the Department of Transportation, shall, by means of pushing with another vehicle, propel any vehicle or object on a vehicular crossing. No person, other than an employee of the Department of Transportation, shall, on any vehicular crossing, tow any vehicle or other object except a vehicle or object constructed and designed to be towed by a vehicle of a type similar to that being used for this purpose.

(b) The California Transportation Commission shall, by regulation, establish the maximum towing fee which may be charged by any person authorized to tow a vehicle pursuant to subdivision (a). No authorized person shall charge a fee for towing a vehicle which is in excess of the maximum fee established by the California Transportation Commission.

(c) The Director of Transportation may grant a special permit to any person to tow any vehicle or object over and completely across any vehicular crossing when in his or her judgment the towing vehicle is so constructed and equipped that the vehicle or object can be towed across the vehicular crossing without endangering persons or property and without interrupting the orderly traffic across the vehicular crossing.

(d) The prohibitions of this section shall apply only on those vehicular crossings upon which a towing service is maintained by the Department of Transportation. *(Amended by Stats 1990 ch 216 §119, eff. 1/1/91.)*

ARTICLE 3

TOLLS AND OTHER CHARGES

§23301. Tolls charged to vehicles.

Every vehicle which enters into or upon any vehicular crossing immediately becomes liable for such tolls and other charges as may from time to time be prescribed by the California Transportation Commission.

§23302. Evading toll a criminal offense.

It is unlawful for any person to refuse to pay or to evade or attempt to evade the payment of such tolls or other charges. It is prima facie evidence of a violation of this section for any person to enter upon any vehicular crossing without lawful money of the United States in his immediate possession in an amount sufficient to pay the prescribed tolls due from such person.

ARTICLE 4

SPECIAL TRAFFIC REGULATIONS

§23330. Things prohibited on vehicular crossing.

Except where a special permit has been obtained from the Department of Transportation under the provisions of Article 6 (commencing with Section 35780) of Chapter 5 of Division 15, none of the following shall be permitted on any vehicular crossing:

(a) Animals while being led or driven, even though tethered or harnessed.

(b) Bicycles or motorized bicycles, unless the department by signs indicates that either bicycles or motorized bicycles, or both, are permitted upon all or any portion of the vehicular crossing.

(c) Vehicles having a total width of vehicle or load exceeding 102 inches.

(d) Vehicles carrying items prohibited by regulations promulgated by the Department of Transportation.

§23331. Pedestrians prohibited except on sidewalks.

Pedestrians shall not be permitted upon any vehicular crossing, unless unobstructed sidewalks of more than three feet in width are constructed and maintained and signs indicating that pedestrians are permitted are in place.

§23332. Trespassing on vehicular crossing.

It is unlawful for any person to be upon any portion of a vehicular crossing which is not intended for public use without the permission of the Department of Transportation. This section does not apply to a person engaged in the operation, maintenance, or repair of a vehicular crossing or any facility thereon nor to any person attempting to effect a rescue.

§23333. Stopping, standing, or parking on vehicular crossing.

No vehicle shall stop, stand, or be parked in or upon any vehicular crossing except:

(a) When necessary to avoid injury or damage to persons or property.

(b) When necessary for the repair, maintenance or operation of a publicly owned toll bridge.

(c) In compliance with the direction of a member of the California Highway Patrol or an employee of the Department of Transportation who is a peace officer or with the direction of a sign or signal.

(d) In such places as may be designated by the Director of Transportation.

DIVISION 16.5

OFF-HIGHWAY VEHICLES

CHAPTER 5

OFF-HIGHWAY VEHICLE OPERATING RULES

ARTICLE 1

TRAFFIC SIGNS, SIGNALS, AND MARKINGS

§38301. Violation of special regulations.

It is unlawful to operate a vehicle in violation of special regulations whcih have been promulgated by the governmental agency having jurisdiction over public lands, including, but not limited to, regulations governing access, routes of travel, plants, wildlife, wildlife habitat, water resources, and historical sites.

§38301.5. Prohibiting entry into mountain fire district.

Every person convicted of violating a local ordinance which is adopted by a city with a population over 2,000,000 persons pursuant to Section 38301 and which prohibits entry into all or portions of an area designated by ordinance as a mountain fire district shall be punished as follows:

(a) Except as provided in subdivisions (b) and (c), the offense is an infraction punishable by a fine not exceeding one hundred fifty dollars ($150).

(b) For a second offense committed within one year of a prior violation for which there was a conviction punishable under subdivision (a), the offense is punishable as an infraction by a fine not exceeding two hundred fifty dollars ($250).

(c)(1) For a third or subsequent offense committed within one year of two or more prior violations for which there were convictions punishable under this section, the offense is punishable as a misdemeanor by a fine not exceeding one thousand dollars ($1,000) or by imprisonment in the county jail not exceeding 90 days, or by both that fine and imprisonment. Additionally, the court may order impoundment of the vehicle used in the offense under the following conditions:

(A) The person convicted under this subdivision is the owner of the vehicle.

(B) The vehicle is subject to Section 38010.

(2) The period of impoundment imposed pursuant to this subdivision shall be not less than one day nor more than 30 days. The impoundment shall be at the owner's expense.

ARTICLE 5

RECKLESS DRIVING

§38316. Reckless driving of off-highway vehicle.

(a) It is unlawful for any person to drive any off-highway motor vehicle with a willful and wanton disregard for the safety of other persons or property.

© 1992 by J., B. & L. Gould
Printed in the U.S.A.   **EP**

(b) Any person who violates this section shall, upon conviction thereof, be punished by imprisonment in the county jail for not less than five days nor more than 90 days or by fine of not less than fifty dollars ($50) nor more than five hundred dollars ($500) or by both such fine and imprisonment, except as provided in Section 38317.

§38317. Reckless driving resulting in bodily injury.

Whenever reckless driving of an off-highway motor vehicle proximately causes bodily injury to any person, the person driving the vehicle shall, upon conviction thereof, be punished by imprisonment in the county jail for not less than 30 days nor more than six months or by fine of not less than one hundred dollars ($100) nor more than one thousand dollars ($1,000) or by both such fine and imprisonment.

§38318. Throwing substances or discharging firearm at off-highway motor vehicle.

(a) Any person who throws any substance at an off-highway motor vehicle or occupant thereof is guilty of a misdemeanor and shall be punished pursuant to Section 42002 by a fine of not more than one thousand dollars ($1,000) or by imprisonment in the county jail for not more than six months, or by both the fine and imprisonment.

(b) Any person who, with intent to do great bodily injury, maliciously and willfully throws or projects any rock, brick, bottle, metal, or other missile, projects any other substance capable of doing serious bodily harm, or discharges a firearm at an off-highway motor vehicle or occupant therof is guilty of a felony.

§38318.5. Maliciously interfering with use of vehicle.

(a) Any person who maliciously removes or alters trail, danger, or directional markers or signs provided for the safety or guidance of off-highway motor vehicles is guilty of a misdemeanor and shall be punished pursuant to Section 42002 by a fine of not more than one thousand dollars ($1,000) or by imprisonment in the county jail for not more than six months, or by both the fine and imprisonment.

(b) Any person who, with intent to do great bodily injury (1) proximately causes great bodily injury to any person as a result of acts prohibited by subdivision (a), or (2) erects or places any cable, chain, rope, fishing line, or other similar material which is unmarked or intentionally placed, or both, for malicious purpose is guilty of a felony.

(c) Any person convicted under subdivision (a) or (b) shall, if the violation proximately causes one or more adverse environmental impacts, also be liable in civil damages for the cost of mitigation, restoration, or repair thereof, in addition to any other liability imposed by law.

ARTICLE 6

LITTERING AND ENVIRONMENTAL PROTECTION

§38319. Damage caused by operation of vehicle.

No person shall operate, nor shall an owner permit the operation of, an off-highway motor vehicle in a manner likely to cause malicious or unnecessary damage to the land, wildlife, wildlife habitat or vegetative resources.

§38320. Illegal dumping.

(a) No person shall throw or deposit, nor shall the registered owner or the driver, if such owner is not then present in the vehicle, aid or abet in the throwing or depositing, upon any area, public or private, any bottle, can, garbage, glass, nail, offal, paper, wire, any substance likely to injure or kill wild or domestic animal or plant life or damage traffic using such area, or any noisome, nauseous or offensive matter of any kind.

(b) No person shall place, deposit or dump, or cause to be placed, deposited or dumped, any rocks or dirt in or upon any area, public or private, without the consent of the property owner or public agency having jurisdiction over the area.

(c) Any person who violates this section shall, upon conviction thereof, be punished by a fine of not less than fifty dollars ($50). No part of such fine shall be suspended. The court may permit the fine required by this section to be paid in installments if the court determines that the defendant is unable to pay the fine in one lump sum.

DIVISION 17

OFFENSES AND PROSECUTION

CHAPTER 1

OFFENSES

ARTICLE 1

VIOLATION OF CODE

§40000.26. Violation of §34501.12; penalty.

A violation of subdivision (d) of Section 34501.12, relating to inspections, is a misdemenator and not an infraction. This section shall become operative on January 1, 1992. (*Added by Stats 1988 ch 1586 §14, oper. 1/1/92.*)

§40000.28. Misdemeanor upon conviction of three or more violations.

Any offense which would otherwise be an infraction is a misdemeanor if a defendant has been convicted of three or more violations of this code or any local ordinance adopted pursuant to this code within the 12-month period immediately preceding the commission of the offense and such prior convictions are admitted by the defendant or alleged in the accusatory pleading. For this purpose, a bail forfeiture shall be deemed to be a conviction of the offense charged.

This section shall have no application to violations by pedestrians.

ARTICLE 3

PROCEDURE ON PARKING VIOLATIONS

§40202. Attach notice of violation to vehicle.

(a) If a vehicle is unattended during the time of the violation, the peace officer or person authorized to enforce parking laws and regulations shall securely attach to the vehicle a notice of parking violation setting forth the violation, including reference to the section of this code or of the local ordinance or federal statute or regulation so violated, the approximate time thereof, and the location where the violation occurred and fixing a time and place for appearance by the registered owner or the lessee or renter to answer the notice of parking violation. The notice of parking violation shall also set forth the vehicle license number and registration expiration date, the last four digits of the vehicle identification number, if that number is visible through the windshield, the color of the vehicle, and, if possible, the make of the vehicle.

(b) The notice of parking violation shall be attached to the vehicle either under the windshield wiper or in another conspicuous place upon the vehicle so as to be easily observed by the person in charge of the vehicle upon the return of that person.

(c) Once the issuing officer has prepared the notice of parking violation and has attached it to the vehicle as provided in subdivision (a), the officer shall file the notice with the processing agency. Any person, including the issuing officer and any member of the officer's department or agency, or any peace officer who alters, conceals, modifies, nullifies, or destroys, or causes to be altered, concealed, modified, nullified, or destroyed the face of the remaining original or any copy of a citation that was retained by the officer, for any reason, before it is filed with the processing agency or with a person authorized to receive the deposit of the parking penalty, is guilty of a misdemeanor.

(d) If, after a copy of the notice of parking violation is attached to the vehicle, the issuing officer determines that, in the interest of justice, the notice of parking violation should be dismissed, the issuing agency may recommend, in writing, that the charges be dismissed. The recommendation shall cite the reasons for the recommendation and shall be filed with the processing agency.

(e) If the processing agency makes a finding that there are grounds for dismissal, the finding shall be entered on the record and the notice of parking violation shall be canceled pursuant to paragraph (1) of subdivision (a) of Section 40215.

(f) Under no circumstances shall a personal relationship with any officer, public official, or law enforcement agency be grounds for dismissal. *(Amended by Stats 1990 ch 1004 §1, eff. 1/1/91.)*

§40203. Written notice.

The notice of parking violation shall be accompanied by a written notice of the parking penalty due for that violation and the address of the person authorized to receive a deposit of the parking penalty, to whom payments may be sent, and a statement in bold print that payments of the parking penalty for the parking violation may be sent through the mail. *(Added by Stats 1986 ch 939 §15.)*

CHAPTER 2

PROCEDURE ON ARRESTS

ARTICLE 1

ARRESTS

§40300.5. Conditions for arrest without warrant.

Notwithstanding any other provision of law, a peace officer may, without a warrant, arrest a person who is (1) involved in a traffic accident or (2) observed by the peace officer in or about a vehicle which is obstructing a roadway, when the officer has reasonable cause to believe that the person had been driving while under the influence of an alcoholic beverage or any drug, or under the combined influence of an alcoholic beverage and any drug.

§40300.6. Interpretation.

Section 40300.5 shall be liberally interpreted to further safe roads and the control of driving while under the influence of an alcoholic beverage or any drug in order to permit arrests to be made pursuant to that section within a reasonable time and distance away from the scene of a traffic accident.

The enactment of this section during the 1985-86 Regular Session of the Legislature does not constitute a change in, but is declaratory of, the existing law. *(Added by Stats 1986 ch 584 §1.)*

§40301. Procedure upon arrest.

Except as provided in this chapter, whenever a person is arrested for any violation of this code declared to be a felony, he shall be dealt with in like manner as upon arrest for the commission of any other felony.

§40302. Appearance before magistrate.

Whenever any person is arrested for any violation of this code, not declared to be a felony, the arrested person shall be taken without unnecessary delay before a magistrate within the county in which the offense charged is alleged to have been committed and who has jurisdiction of the offense and is nearest or most accessible with reference to the place where the arrest is made in any of the following cases:

(a) When the person arrested fails to present his driver's license or other satisfactory evidence of his identity for examination.

(b) When the person arrested refuses to give his written promise to appear in court.

(c) When the person arrested demands an immediate appearance before a magistrate.

(d) When the person arrested is charged with violating Section 23152.

§40302.5. Arrest of minor.

Whenever any person under the age of 18 years is taken into custody in connection with any traffic infraction case, and he is not taken directly before a magistrate, he shall be delivered to the custody of the probation officer. Unless sooner released, the probation officer shall keep the minor in the juvenile hall pending his appearance before a magistrate. When a minor is cited for an offense not involving the driving of a motor vehicle, the minor shall not be taken into custody pursuant to subdivision (a) of Section 40302 solely for failure to present a driver's license.

§40303.5. Notice to correct violation for specified infractions.

Whenever any person is arrested for any of the following offenses, the arresting officer shall permit the arrested person to execute a notice containing a promise to correct the violation in accordance with the provisions of Section 40610 unless the arresting officer finds that any of the disqualifying conditions specified in subdivision (b) of Section 40610 exist:

© 1992 by J., B. & L. Gould
Printed in the U.S.A.   EP

(a) Any registration infraction set forth in Division 3 (commencing with Section 4000), except subdivision (a) of Section 5204.

(b) Any driver's license infraction set forth in Division 6 (commencing with Section 12500), and subdivision (a) of Section 12951, relating to possession of driver's license.

(c) Section 21201, relating to bicycle equipment.

(d) Any infraction involving equipment set forth in Division 12 (commencing with Section 24000), Division 13 (Commencing with Section 29000), Division 14.8 (commencing with Section 34500), Division 16 (commencing with Section 36000), Division 16.5 (commencing with Section 38000), and Division 16.7 (commencing with Section 39000). *(Amended by Stats 1989 ch 729 §3, oper. 7/1/90.)*

§40304. Discretionary action procedure.

Whenever any person is arrested by any member of the California Highway Patrol for any violation of any state law regulating the operaion of vehicles or the use of the highways declared to be a misdemeanor but which offense is not specified in this code, he shall, in the judgment of the arresting officer, either be given a 10-day notice to appear in the manner provided in this chapter or be taken without unnecessary delay before a magistrate within the county in which the offense charged is alleged to have been committed and who has jurisdiction of the offense and is nearest or most accessible with reference to the place where the arrest is made, or, upon demand of the person arrested, before a magistrate in the judicial district in which the offense is alleged to have been committed.

§40304.5. Arrest on warrant; bail.

Notwithstanding any other provision of law, whenever any person is taken into custody for bail to be collected on two or fewer outstanding warrants for failure to appear on a citation for a parking offense or a traffic infraction, the person shall be provided the opportunity immediately to post bail, and shall not be booked, photographed, or fingerprinted, nor shall an arrest record be made, when the amount of bail required to be paid on the warrant may be ascertained by reference to the face thereof or to a fixed schedule of bail, unless and until all of the following requirements have been exhausted:

(a) If the person has sufficient cash in his or her possession, that person shall be given the opportunity immediately to post bail with the person in charge of the jail or his or her designee.

(b) If the person does not have sufficient cash in his or her possession, that person shall be informed of his or her rights and given the opportunity to do all of the following:

(1) Make not less than three completed telephone calls to obtain bail. The person shall be permitted the use of the police or sheriff's department telephone to make not less than three completed local or collect long-distance telephone calls to obtain bail.

(2) Have not less than three hours in which to arrange for the deposit of bail.

§40305. Arrest of nonresident.

Whenever a nonresident is arrested for violating any section of this code while driving a motor vehicle and does not furnish satisfactory evidence of identity and an address within this State at which he can be located, he may, in the discretion of the arresting officer, be taken immediately before a magistrate within the county where the offense charged is alleged to have been committed, and who has jurisdiction over the offense and is nearest or most accessible with reference to the place where the arrest is made. If the magistrate is not available at the time of the arrest and the arrested person is not taken before any other person authorized to receive a deposit of bail, and if the arresting officer does not have the authority or is not required to take the arrested person before a magistrate or other person authorized to receive a deposit of bail by some other provision of law, the nonresident shall be released from custody upon giving a written promise to appear as provided in Article 2 (commencing with Section 40500).

§40306. Procedure before magistrate; misdemeanor or infraction.

(a) Whenever a person is arrested for a misdemeanor or an infraction and is taken before a magistrate, the arresting officer shall file with the magistrate a complaint stating the offense with which the person is charged.

(b) The person taken before a magistrate shall be entitled to at least five days continuance of his case in which to plead and prepare for trial and the person shall not be required to plead or be tried within the five days unless he waives such time in writing or in open court.

(c) The person taken before a magistrate shall thereupon be released from custody upon his own recognizance or upon such bail as the magistrate may fix.

§40307. Options when magistrate unavailable.

When an arresting officer attempts to take a person arrested for a misdemeanor or infraction of this code before a magistrate and the magistrate or person authorized to act for him is not available, the arresting officer shall take the person arrested, without unnecessary delay, before:

(a) The clerk of the magistrate who shall admit him to bail in accordance with a schedule fixed as provided in Section 1269b of the Penal Code, or

(b) The officer in charge of the most accessible county or city jail or other place of detention within the county who shall admit him to bail in accordance with a schedule fixed as provided in Section 1269b of the Penal Code or may, in lieu of bail, release the person on his written promise to appear as provided in subdivisions (a) through (f) of Section 853.6 of the Penal Code.

Whenever a person is taken into custody pursuant to subdivision (a) of Section 40302 and is arrested for a misdemeanor or infraction of this code pertaining to the operation of a motor vehicle, the officer in charge of the most accessible county or city jail or other place of detention within the county may detain the person arrested for a reasonable period of time, not to exceed two hours, in order to verify his identity.

§40311. Arraignment.

Whenever a person is arrested under authority of a warrant, the court to which such person is taken shall, with his consent, have jurisdiction to arraign him at that time for any other alleged violation of this code or an ordinance relating to traffic offenses for which he has been issued a written notice to appear in court, notwithstanding the fact that the time for appearance specified in such notice has not yet arrived.

§40312. Arrest prohibition; receipt for fine.

A peace officer shall not arrest, on the basis of an outstanding warrant arising from a violation of this code, any person who presents to the peace officer a receipt, from a proper official of the court, indicating that the person has paid the fine for the violation that caused the warrant to be issued. The receipt shall contain sufficient information to identify the name and number of the court issuing the receipt, the date the case was adjudicated or the fine was paid, the case number or docket number, and the violations disposed of.

ARTICLE 2

RELEASE UPON PROMISE TO APPEAR

§40500. Notice.

(a) Whenever a person is arrested for any violation of this code not declared to be a felony, or for a violation of an ordinance of a city or county relating to traffic offenses and he is not immediately taken before a magistrate, as provided in this chapter, the arresting officer shall prepare in triplicate a written notice to appear in court or before a person authorized to receive a deposit of bail, containing the name and address of the person, the license number of his vehicle, if any, the name and address, when available, of the registered owner or lessee of the vehicle, the offense charged and the time and place when and where he shall appear.

(b) The Judicial Council shall prescribe the form of the notice to appear.

(c) Nothing in this section requires the law enforcement agency or the arresting officer issuing the notice to appear to inform any person arrested pursuant to this section of the amount of bail required to be deposited for the offense charged.

(d) Once the arresting officer has prepared the written notice to appear, and has delivered a copy to the arrested person, the officer shall deliver the remaining original and all copies of the notice to appear as provided by Section 40506.

Any person, including the arresting officer and any member of the officer's department or agency, or any peace officer, who alters, conceals, modifies, nullifies, or destroys, or causes to be altered, concealed, modified, nullified, or destroyed, the face side of the remaining original or any copy of a citation that was retained by the officer, for any reason, before it is filed with the magistrate or with a person authorized by the magistrate or judge to receive a deposit of bail, is guilty of a misdemeanor.

If, after an arrested person has signed and received a copy of a notice to appear, the arresting officer or other officer of the issuing agency, determines that, in the interest of justice, the citation or notice should be dismissed, the arresting agency may recommend, in writing, to the magistrate or judge that the case be dismissed. The recommendation shall cite the reasons for the recommendation and be filed with the court.

If the magistrate or judge makes a finding that there are grounds for dismissal, the finding shall be entered on the record and the infraction or misdemeanor dismissed.

Under no circumstances shall a personal relationship with any officer, public official, or law enforcement agency be grounds for dismissal. (*Amended by Stats 1987 ch 72 §4.*)

§40503. Notice on speeding charge.

Every notice to appear or notice of violation and every complaint or information charging a violation of any provision of this code regulating the speed of vehicles upon a highway shall specify the approximate speed at which the defendant is alleged to have driven and exactly the prima facie or maximum speed limit applicable to the highway at the time and place of the alleged offense and shall state any other speed limit alleged to have been exceeded is applicable to the particular type of vehicle or combination of vehicles operated by the defendant.

§40504. Delivery of notice to appear.

(a) The officer shall deliver one copy of the notice to appear to the arrested person and the arrested person in order to secure release must give his written promise to appear in court or before a person authorized to receive a deposit of bail by signing two copies of the notice which shall be retained by the officer. Thereupon the arresting officer shall forthwith release the person arrested from custody.

(b) Any person who signs a written promise to appear with a false or fictitious name is guilty of a misdemeanor regardless of the disposition of the charge upon which he was originally arrested.

§40505. Contents of copy of notice.

Whenever any traffic or police officer delivers a notice to appear or notice of violation charging an offense under this code to any person, it shall include all information set forth upon the copy of the notice filed with a magistrate and no traffic or police officer shall set forth on any notice filed with magistrate or attach thereto or accompany the notice with any written statement giving information or containing allegations which have not been delivered to the person receiving the notice to appear or notice of violation.

§40506. Filing copy of notice.

The officer shall, as soon as practicable, file a copy of the notice with the magistrate or before a person authorized by the magistrate or judge to receive a deposit of bail specified therein, and a copy with the commissioner, chief of police, sheriff or other superior officer of the arresting officer.

§40508. Violating promise to appear.

(a) Any person willfully violating his or her written promise to appear or a lawfully granted continuance of his or her promise to appear in court or before a person authorized to receive a deposit of bail is guilty of a misdemeanor regardless of the disposition of the charge upon which he or she was originally arrested.

(b) Any person willfully failing to pay a lawfully imposed fine for a violation of any provision of this code or a local ordinance adopted pursuant to this code within the time authorized by the court and without lawful excuse having been presented to the court on or before the date the fine is due is guilty of a misdemeanor regardless of the full payment of the fine after such time.

(c) If a person convicted of an infraction fails to pay a fine or any installment thereof within the time

© 1992 by J., B. & L. Gould
Printed in the U.S.A.   EP

authorized by the court, the court may, except as otherwise provided in this subdivision, impound the person's driver's license and order the person not to drive for a period not to exceed 30 days. Before returning the license to the person, the court shall endorse on the reverse side of the license that the person was ordered not to drive, the period for which that order was made, and the name of the court making the order. If a defendant with a class 3 or 4 driver's license satisfies the court that impounding his or her driver's license and ordering the defendant not to drive will affect his or her livelihood, the court shall order that the person limit his or her driving for a period not to exceed 30 days to driving that is essential in the court's determination to the person's employment, including the person's driving to and from his or her place of employment if other means of transportation are not reasonably available. The court shall provide for the endorsement of the limitation on the person's license. The impounding of the license and ordering the person not to drive or the order limiting the person's driving does not constitute a suspension of the license, but a violation of the order constitutes contempt of court. *(Amended by Stats 1987 ch 726 §10.)*

§40514. Warrant.

No warrant shall issue on the charge for the arrest of a person who has given his written promise to appear in court or before a person authorized to receive a deposit of bail, unless he has violated the promise, the lawfully granted continuance of his promise, or has failed to deposit bail, to appear for arraignment, trial or judgment, or to comply with the terms and provisions of the judgment, as required by law.

§40515. Warrant for violation or continuance of promise to appear.

(a) When a person signs a written promise to appear or is granted a continuance of his promise to appear at the time and place specified in the written promise to appear or the continuance thereof, and has not posted bail, the magistrate may issue and have delivered for execution a warrant for his arrest within 20 days after his failure to appear before the magistrate, or if the person promises to appear before an officer authorized to accept bail other than a magistrate and fails to do so on or before the date on which he promised to appear, then, within 20 days after the delivery of the written promise to appear by the officer to a magistrate having jurisdiction over the offense.

(b) When the person violates his promise to appear before an officer authorized to receive bail other than a magistrate, the officer shall immediately deliver to a magistrate having jurisdiction over the offense charged the written promise to appear and the complaint, if any, filed by the arresting officer.

ARTICLE 3

NOTICE OF VIOLATION

§40600. Contents of notice; reasonable cause for issuance.

(a) Notwithstanding any other provision of law, a peace officer who has successfully completed a course or courses of instruction, approved by the Commission on Peace Officer Standards and Training, in the investigation of traffic accidents may prepare in triplicate, on a form approved by the Judicial Council, a written notice of violation when the peace officer has reasonable cause to believe that any person involved in a traffic accident has violated a provision of this code not declared to be a felony or a violation of a local ordinance and the violation was a factor in the occurrence of the traffic accident.

(b) A notice of violation shall contain the name and address of the person, the license number of the person's vehicle, if any, the name and address, when available, of the registered owner or lessee of the vehicle, the offense charged, and the time and place when and where the person may appear in court or before a person authorized to receive a deposit of bail. The time specified shall be at least 10 days after the notice of violation is delivered.

(c) The preparation and delivery of a notice of violation is not an arrest.

(d) For purposes of this article, a peace officer will be deemed to have reasonable cause to issue a written notice of violation if, as a result of the officer's investigation, the officer has evidence, either testimonial or real, or a combination of testimonial and real, that would be sufficient to issue a written notice to appear if the officer had personally witnessed the events investigated.

(e) As used in this section, "peace officer" means any person specified under Section 830.1 or 830.2 of the Penal Code, with the exception of members of the California National Guard.

(f) This article has no application to the procedures specified in Article 2 (commencing with Section 40500).

(g) This section applies to the procedures specified in Chapter 2.5 (commencing with Section 40650), except that the notice of violation shall be as set forth and approved by the Traffic Adjudication Board. *(Amended by Stats 1987 ch 191 §1.)*

§40601. Place specified for appearance.

The place specified in the notice of violation shall be any of the following:

(a) Before a magistrate within the county in which the offense charged is alleged to have been committed and who has jurisdiction of the offense and is nearest or most accessible with reference to the place where the offense charged is alleged to have been committed.

(b) Upon demand of the person receiving the notice of violation, before a municipal court judge or other magistrate having jurisdiction of the offense at the county seat of the county in which the offense is alleged to have been committed. This subdivision applies only if the person arrested resides, or the person's principal place of employment is located, closer to the county seat than to the municipal court or other magistrate nearest or most accessible to the place where the arrest is made.

(c) Before a person authorized to receive a deposit of bail.

The clerk and deputy clerks of the municipal and justice courts are persons authorized to receive bail in accordance with a schedule of bail approved by the judges of those courts.

(d) Before the juvenile court, a juvenile court referee, or a juvenile traffic hearing officer within the county in which the offense charged is alleged to have been committed, if the person receiving the notice of violation appears to be under the age of 18 years. The juvenile court shall by order designate the proper person before whom the appearance is to be made.

If the place specified in the notice of violation is within a district or city and county where a department of the municipal court is to hold a night session within a period of not more than 10 days after the notice of violation is delivered, the notice of violation shall contain, in addition to the above, a statement notifying the person receiving the notice that the person may appear before such a night session of the court.

§40602. Delivering notice.

The officer shall deliver one copy of the notice of violation to the person named therein.

§40604. Issuance of warrant for arrest.

Before any warrant for arrest may issue following the filing of a complaint charging the offense for which the written notice of violation was issued pursuant to Section 40600, a notice of the filing of the complaint shall be issued and served upon the person charged with the offense by personal delivery or by certified mail, postage prepaid and return receipt requested, addressed to the person at the address shown in the accident report. The notice shall contain the name and address of the person, the license number of the vehicle involved, the name and address, when available, of the registered owner or lessee of the vehicle, the offense shown on the written notice of violation, and the approximate time of the commission of the offense. The notice shall inform the person that, unless he appears in the court designated in the notice within 10 days after the service of the notice and answers the charges against him, a warrant will issue for his arrest. Proof of service shall be made by the affidavit of any person over 18 years of age making the service showing the time, place, and manner of service and facts showing that the service was made in accordance with this section. If service is made by mail, no warrant for arrest may issue unless the proof of service includes evidence satisfactory to the court establishing actual delivery to the person by a signed return receipt or other evidence.

ARTICLE 4
NOTICE TO CORRECT VIOLATION

§40614. Misdemeanor to sign false or fictitious name.

Any person who signs a notice to correct or a certificate of correction with a false or fictitious name is guilty of a misdemeanor.

§40616. Misdemeanor for willfully failing to correct or deliver proof.

Any person willfully violating a written promise to correct or willfully failing to deliver proof of correction of violation is guilty of a misdemeanor. Proof of correction may consist of a certification by an authorized representative of one of the following agencies that the alleged violation has been corrected:

(a) Brake, lamp, smog device, or muffler violations may be certified as corrected by any station licensed to inspect and certify for the violation pursuant to Article 8 (commencing with Section 9889.15) of Chapter 20.3 of Division 3 of the Business and Professions Code and Section 27150.2.

(b) Driver license and registration violations may be certified as corrected by the Department of Motor Vehicles or by any clerk or deputy clerk of a court.

(c) Any violation may be certified as corrected by a police department, the California Highway Patrol, sheriff, marshal, or other law enforcement agency regularly engaged in enforcement of the Vehicle Code.

CHAPTER 3

ILLEGAL EVIDENCE

§40800. Officer's vehicle and uniform.

Every traffic officer on duty for the exclusive or main purpose of enforcing the provisions of Division 10 or 11 of this code shall wear a full distinctive uniform, and if the officer while so on duty uses a motor vehicle, it must be painted a distinctive color specified by the commissioner.

This section does not apply to an officer assigned exclusively to the duty of investigating and securing evidence in reference to any theft of a vehicle or failure of a person to stop in the event of an accident or violation of Section 23109 or in reference to any felony charge, or to any officer engaged in serving any warrant when the officer is not engaged in patrolling the highways for the purpose of enforcing the traffic laws.

§40801. Prohibiting use of speed traps.

No peace officer or other person shall use a speed trap in arresting, or participating or assisting in the arrest of, any person for any alleged violation of this code nor shall any speed trap be used in securing evidence as to the speed of any vehicle for the purpose of an arrest or prosecution under this code.

§40802. Definition of "speed trap".

A "speed trap" is either of the following:

(a) A particular section of a highway measured as to distance and with boundaries marked, designated, or otherwise determined in order that the speed of a vehicle may be calculated by securing the time it takes the vehicle to travel the known distance.

(b) A particular section of a highway with a prima facie speed limit provided by this code or by local ordinance pursuant to paragraph (1) of subdivision (b) of Section 22352, or established pursuant to Section 22354, 22357, 22358, or 22358.3, which speed limit is not justified by an engineering and traffic survey conducted within five years prior to the date of the alleged violation, and where enforcement involves the use of radar or other electronic devices which measure the speed of moving objects. This subdivision does not apply to local streets and roads.

For purposes of this section, local streets and roads shall be defined by the latest functional usage and federal-aid system maps as submitted to the Federal Highway Administration. When these maps have not been submitted, the following definition shall be used: A local street or road primarily provides access to abutting residential property and shall meet the following three conditions:

(1) Roadway width of not more than 40 feet.

(2) Not more than one-half mile of uninterrupted length. Interruptions shall include official traffic control devices as defined in Section 445.

(3) Not more than one traffic lane in each direction. *(Amended by Stats 1991 ch 459 §1, eff. 1/1/92. Section 40802 as amended by Stats 1986 §2 was repealed by Stats 1991 ch 459 §2, eff. 1/1/92.)*

© 1992 by J., B. & L. Gould
Printed in the U.S.A.   **EP**

§40803. Evidence regarding speed traps.

(a) No evidence as to the speed of a vehicle upon a highway shall be admitted in any court upon the trial of any person for an alleged violation of this code when the evidence is based upon or obtained from or by the maintenance or use of a speed trap.

(b) In any prosecution under this code of a charge involving the speed of a vehicle, where enforcement involves the use of radar or other electronic devices which measure the speed of moving objects, the prosecution shall establish, as part of its prima facie case, that the evidence or testimony presented is not based upon a speed trap as defined in subdivision (b) of Section 40802.

(c) When a traffic and engineering survey is required pursuant to subdivision (b) of Section 40802, evidence that a traffic and engineering survey has been conducted within five years of the date of the alleged violation or evidence that the offense was committed on a local street or road as defined in subdivision (b) of Section 40802 shall constitute a prima facie case that the evidence or testimony is not based upon a speed trap as defined in subdivision (b) of Section 40802. (Amended by Stats 1991 ch 459 §3, eff. 1/1/92.)

§40804. Testimony regarding speed traps.

(a) In any prosecution under this code upon a charge involving the speed of a vehicle, any officer or other person shall be incompetent as a witness if the testimony is based upon or obtained from or by the maintenance or use of a speed trap.

(b) Every officer arresting, or participating or assisting in the arrest of, a person so charged while on duty for the exclusive or main purpose of enforcing the provisions of Divisions 10 and 11 is incompetent as a witness if at the time of such arrest he was not wearing a distinctive uniform, or was using a motor vehicle not painted the distinctive color specified by the commissioner.

This section does not apply to an officer assigned exclusively to the duty of investigating and securing evidence in reference to any theft of a vehicle or failure of a person to stop in the event of an accident or violation of Section 23109 or in reference to any felony charge or to any officer engaged in serving any warrant when the officer is not engaged in patrolling the highways for the purpose of enforcing the traffic laws.

§40805. Admitting speed trap evidence.

Every court shall be without jurisdiction to render a judgment of conviction against any person for a violation of this code involving the speed of a vehicle if the court admits any evidence or testimony secured in violation of, or which is inadmissible under this article.

§40806. Officer or witness reports.

In the event a defendant charged with an offense under this code pleads guilty, the trial court shall not at any time prior to pronouncing sentence receive or consider any report, verbal or written, of any police or traffic officer or witness of the offense without fully informing the defendant of all statements in the report or statement of witnesses, or without giving the defendant an opportunity to make answer thereto or to produce witnesses in rebuttal, and for such purpose the court shall grant a continuance before pronouncing sentence if requested by the defendant.

CHAPTER 7

ARREST QUOTAS

§41600. Arrest quota, defined.

For purposes of this chapter, "arrest quota" means any requirement regarding the number of arrests made, or the number of citations issued, by a peace officer, or the proportion of such arrests made and citations issued by a peace officer relative to the arrests made and citations issued by another peace officer or group of officer.

§41601. Citation, defined.

For purposes of this chapter, "citation" means a notice to appear, notice of violation, or notice of parking violation.

§41602. Prohibiting use of arrest quota.

No state or local agency employing peace officers engaged in the enforcement of this code or any local ordinance adopted pursuant to this code, may establish any policy requiring any peace officer to meet an arrest quota.

§41603. Criteria for evaluating peace officer's performance.

No state or local agency employing peace officers engaged in the enforcement of this code shall use the number of arrests or citations issued by a peace officer as the sole criterion for promotion, demotion, dismissal, or the earning of any benefit provided by the agency. Any such arrests or citations, and their ultimate dispositions, may only be considered in evaluating the overall performance of a peace officer. Such an evaluation may include, but shall not be limited to, criteria such as attendance, punctuality, work safety, complaints by citizens, commendations, demeanor, formal training, and professional judgment.

CHAPTER 8

CONSOLIDATED DISPOSITION

§41610. Consolidated disposition of offenses.

(a) Whenever any person who is in custody enters a guilty plea to any infraction or misdemeanor under this code and there is outstanding any warrant of arrest for a violation of this code or a local ordinance adopted pursuant to this code that is filed in any court within the same county, the defendant may elect to enter a guilty plea to any of these charged offenses of which the court has a record, except offenses specified in subdivision (b). The court shall sentence the defendant for each of the offenses for which a guilty plea has been entered pursuant to this section, and shall notify the appropriate court or department in each affected judicial district of the disposition. After receiving that notice of disposition, the court in which each complaint was filed shall prepare and transmit to the department any certification required by applicable provisions of Section 40509 as if the court had heard the case.

(b) Subdivision (a) does not authorize entry of a guilty plea as specified in that subdivision to any offense for which a notice of parking violation has been issued, nor to any offense specified in Section 14601.2, 14601.3, 20002, 23103, 23104, 23152, or 23153, subdivision (a) of Section 14601, or subdivision (a) of Section 14601.1.

DIVISION 18

PENALTIES AND DISPOSITION OF FEES, FINES, AND FORFEITURES

CHAPTER 1

PENALTIES

ARTICLE 1

PUBLIC OFFENSES

§42000. Penalty for felony offense.

Unless a different penalty is expressly provided by this code, every person convicted of a felony for a violation of any provision of this code shall be punished by a fine of not less than one thousand dollars ($1,000) or more than ten thousand dollars ($10,000) or by imprisonment in the state prison or by both such fine and imprisonment.

§42000.1. Fine for driving over 100 miles per hour.

Notwithstanding Section 42001, every person convicted of an infraction for a violation described in subdivision (b) of Section 22348 shall be punished by a fine not exceeding five hundred dollars ($500).

§42000.5. Infraction for speeding violations.

Every person convicted of an infraction for a violation of Section 22350, 22406, or 22407 while operating a bus, motor truck, or truck tractor having three or more axles, or any motor truck or truck tractor drawing any other vehicle, shall be punished by a fine not exceeding one hundred dollars ($100) for a first conviction, except that if the person has exceeded the specified speed limit by 10 miles per hour or more, the fine shall not exceed two hundred dollars ($200) for a first conviction, and not exceeding three hundred dollars ($300) for a second or subsequent conviction. *(Amended by Stats 1989 ch 980 §1, eff. 1/1/90.)*

§42001. Punishment for infractions and certain misdemeanors.

(a) Except as provided in Section 42000.5, 42001.1, 42001.2, 42001.3, 42001.5, 42001.7, 42001.8, 42001.9, 42001.11, or 42001.12, or subdivision (b) or (c) of this section, or Article 2 (commencing with Section 42030), every person convicted of an infraction for a violation of this code or of any local ordinance adopted pursuant to this code shall be punished as follows:

(1) By a fine not exceeding one hundred dollars ($100).

(2) For a second infraction occurring within one year of a prior infraction which resulted in a conviction, a fine not exceeding two hundred dollars ($200).

(3) For a third or any subsequent infraction occurring within one year of two or more prior infraction which resulted in convictions, a fine not exceeding two hundred fifty dollars ($250).

(b) Every person convicted of a misdemeanor violation of Section 2800, 2801, or 2803, insofar as they affect failure to stop and submit to inspection of equipment or for an unsafe condition endangering any person, shall be punished as follows:

(1) By a fine not exceeding fifty dollars ($50) or imprisonment in the county jail not exceeding five days.

(2) For a second conviction with a period of one year, a fine not exceeding one hundred dollars ($100) or imprisonment in the county jail not exceeding 10 days, or both that fine and imprisonment.

(3) For a third or any subsequent conviction within a period of one year, a fine not exceeding five hundred dollars ($500) or imprisonment in the county jail not exceeding six months, or both that fine and imprisonment.

(c) A pedestrian convicted of an infraction for a violation of this code or of any local ordinance adopted pursuant to this code shall be punished by a fine not exceeding fifty dollars ($50). *(Amended by Stats 1991 ch 13 §66, eff. 2/13/91.)*

§42001.5. Parking in space designated for disabled persons.

Every person convicted of an infraction for a violation of Section 22507.8 shall be punished by a fine of not less than one hundred dollars ($100). No part of any fine imposed shall be suspended, except that the court may suspend the imposition of the fine ff the person convicted possessed at the time of the offense, but failed to display, a valid distinguishing license plate or placard issued pursuant to Section 22511.5. The fine may be paid in installments if the court determines that the defendant is unable to pay the entire amount in one payment. *(Amended by Stats 1991 ch 630 §2, eff. 1/1/92.)*

§42001.7. Fine for littering.

(a) Every person convicted of a violation of Section 23111 or 23112, or subdivision (a) of Section 23113, shall be punished by a mandatory fine of not less than one hundred dollars ($100) nor more than one thousand dollars ($1,000) upon a first conviction, by a mandatory fine of not less than five hundred dollars ($500) nor more than one thousand dollars ($1,000) upon a second conviction, and by a mandatory fine of not less than seven hundred fifty dollars ($750) nor more than one thousand dollars ($1,000) upon a third or subsequent conviction.

In no case may the court order imprisonment in the county jail for a violation punishable under this subdivision, unless imprisonment is ordered pursuant to Section 166 of the Penal Code.

(b) The court shall, in addition to the fines imposed pursuant to subdivision (a), order the offender to pick up litter or clean up graffiti at a time and place within the jurisdiction of the court as follows:

(1) For a first conviction punished pursuant to subdivision (a), the court shall require the offender to pick up litter or clean up graffiti for not less than eight hours.

(2) For a second conviction punished pursuant to subdivision (a), the court shall require the offender to pick up litter or clean up graffiti for not less than 16 hours.

(3) For a third or subsequent conviction punished pursuant to subdivision (a), the court shall require the offender to pick up litter or clean up graffiti for not less than 24 hours.

(c) It is the intent of the Legislature that persons convicted of highway littering be required to bear the penalty for their actions. Therefore, the court may not suspend the mandatory fines required by subdivision

© 1992 by J., B. & L. Gould
Printed in the U.S.A.   EP

(a) except in unusual cases where the interest of justice would best be served by suspension of the fine. If the court suspends imposition of any fine required by subdivision (a), it shall, as a condition of that suspension, require the offender to pick up litter or clean up graffiti at a time and place within the jurisdiction of the court for not less than eight hours for every one hundred dollars ($100) of fine suspended. The court may not suspend the order to pick up litter or clean up graffiti required by this subdivision or subdivision (b) except in unusual cases where the interest of justice would best be served by suspension of that order. *(Amended by Stats 1990 ch 982 §1, eff. 1/1/91.)*

§42002. Punishment regarding general misdemeanors.

Unless a different penalty is expressly provided by this code, every person convicted of a misdemeanor for a violation of any of the provisions of this code shall be punished by a fine of not exceeding one thousand dollars ($1,000) or by imprisonment in the county jail for not exceeding six months, or by both such fine and imprisonment.

§42002.4. Removing manufacturer's serial number from vehicle.

A violation of Section 10751 shall be punished by imprisonment in the county jail not exceeding six months if the value of the property does not exceed four hundred dollars ($400), and by imprisonment in the county jail not exceeding one year if the value of the property is more than four hundred dollars ($400). *(Added by Stats 1990 ch 408 §2, eff. 1/1/91.)*

This page intentionally left blank.

© 1992 by J., B. & L. Gould
Printed in the U.S.A.   EP

WELFARE AND INSTITUTIONS CODE

DIVISION 2

CHILDREN

ARTICLE 1

GENERAL PROVISIONS

§200. Short title.

This chapter shall be known and may be cited as the "Arnold-Kennick Juvenile Court Law".

§201. Construction of chapter.

The provisions of this chapter, insofar as they are substantially the same as existing statutory provisions relating to the same subject matter, shall be construed as restatements and continuations thereof, and not as new enactments.

§202. Purpose of chapter.

(a) The purpose of this chapter is to provide for the protection and safety of the public and each minor under the jurisdiction of the juvenile court and to preserve and strengthen the minor's family ties whenever possible, removing the minor from the custody of his or her parents only when necessary for his or her welfare or for the safety and protection of the public. When removal of a minor is determined by the juvenile court to be necessary, reunification of the minor with his or her family shall be a primary objective. When the minor is removed from his or her own family, it is the purpose of this chapter to secure for the minor custody, care, and discipline as nearly as possible equivalent to that which should have been given by his or her parents. This chapter shall be liberally construed to carry out these purposes.

(b) Minors under the jurisdiction of the juvenile court who are in need of protective services shall receive care, treatment and guidance consistent with their best interest and the best interest of the public. Minors under the jurisdiction of the juvenile court as a consequence of delinquent conduct shall, in conformity with the interests of public safety and protection, receive care, treatment and guidance which is consistent with their best interest, which holds them accountable for their behavior, and which is appropriate for their circumstances. This guidance may include punishment that is consistent with the rehabilitative objectives of this chapter. If a minor has been removed from the custody of his or her parents, family preservation and family reunification are appropriate goals for the juvenile court to consider when determining the disposition of a minor under the jurisdiction of the juvenile court as a consequence of delinquent conduct when those goals are consistent with his or her best interests and the best interests of the public.

(c) It is also the purpose of this chapter to reaffirm that the duty of a parent to support and maintain a minor child continues, subject to the financial ability of the parent to pay, during any period in which the minor may be declared a ward of the court and removed from the custody of the parent.

(d) Juvenile courts and other public agencies charged with enforcing, interpreting, and administering the juvenile court law shall consider the safety and protection of the public and the best interests of the minor in all deliberations pursuant to this chapter.

Participants in the juvenile justice system shall hold themselves accountable for its results. They shall act in conformity with a comprehensive set of objectives established to improve system performance in a vigorous and ongoing manner.

(e) As used in this chapter, "punishment" means the imposition of sanctions which include the following:

(1) Payment of a fine by the minor.

(2) Rendering of compulsory service without compensation performed for the benefit of the community by the minor.

(3) Limitations on the minor's liberty imposed as a condition of probation or parole.

(4) Commitment of the minor to a local detention or treatment facility, such as a juvenile hall, camp, or ranch.

(5) Commitment of the minor to the Department of the Youth Authority.

"Punishment," for the purposes of this chapter, does not include retribution. *(Amended by Stats 1989 ch 569 §1, eff. 9/20/89.)*

§202.5. Duties of probation officer.

The duties of the probation officer, as described in this chapter with respect to minors alleged or adjudged to be described by Section 300, whether or not delegated pursuant to Section 272, shall be deemed to be social service as defined by Section 10051, and subject to the administration, supervision and regulations of the State Department of Social Services.

§203. Order adjudging minor ward of court.

An order adjudging a minor to be a ward of the juvenile court shall not be deemed a conviction of a crime for any purpose, nor shall a proceeding in the juvenile court be deemed a criminal proceeding.

§204. Transmitting information on arrest of minor.

The Department of Justice shall not knowingly transmit to any person or agency any information relating to an arrest or taking into custody of a minor at the time of such arrest or taking into custody unless such information also includes the disposition resulting therefrom.

"Disposition", as used herein, includes a release of such minor from custody without the filing of an accusatory pleading or the filing of a petition under the provisions of this chapter, a determination of the issue of wardship by the juvenile court, or a determination by the juvenile court that such minor is not a fit subject to be dealt with under the provisions of this chapter.

This section shall not be construed to prohibit the Department of Justice from transmitting fingerprints or photographs of a minor to a law enforcement agency for the purpose of obtaining identification of the minor or from requesting from such agency the history of the minor.

This section shall not be construed to prohibit the Department of Justice from transmitting any information relating to an arrest or taking into custody of a minor received by said bureau prior to the effective date of this section.

§205. Consideration of religious beliefs in placements.

All commitments to institutions or for placement in family homes under this chapter shall be, so far as practicable, either to institutions or for placement in family homes of the same religious belief as that of the person so committed or of his parents or to institutions affording opportunity for instruction in such religious belief.

§206. Segregated facilities for dependent children from wards of court.

Persons taken into custody and persons alleged to be within the description of Section 300, or persons adjudged to be such and made dependent children of the court pursuant to this chapter solely upon that ground, shall be provided by the board of supervisors with separate facilities segregated from persons either alleged or adjudged to come within the description of Section 601 or 602 except as provided in Section 16514. Separate segregated facilities may be provided in the juvenile hall or elsewhere.

The facilities required by this section shall, with regard to minors alleged or adjudged to come within Section 300, be nonsecure.

For the purposes of this section, the term "secure facility" means a facility which is designed and operated so as to insure that all entrances to, and exits from, the facility are under the exclusive control of the staff of the facility, whether or not the person being detained has freedom of movement within the perimeters of the facility, or which relies on locked rooms and buildings, fences, or physical restraints in order to control behavior of its residents. The term "nonsecure facility" means a facility that is not characterized by the use of physically restricting construction, hardware, and procedures and which provides its residents access to the surrounding community with minimal supervision. A facility shall not be deemed secure due solely to any of the following conditions: (1) the existence within the facility of a small room for the protection of individual residents from themselves or others; (2) the adoption of regulations establishing reasonable hours for residents to come and go from the facility based upon a sensible and fair balance between allowing residents free access to the community and providing the staff with sufficient authority to maintain order, limit unreasonable actions by residents, and to ensure that minors placed in their care do not come and go at all hours of the day and night or absent themselves at will for days at a time; and (3) staff control over ingress and egress no greater than that exercised by a prudent parent. The State Department of Social Services may adopt regulations governing the use of small rooms pursuant to this section.

No minor described in this section may be held in temporary custody in any building that contains a jail or lockup for the confinement of adults, unless, while in the building, the minor is under continuous supervision and is not permitted to come into or remain in contact with adults in custody in the building. In addition, no minor who is alleged to be within the description of Section 300 may be held in temporary custody in a building that contains a jail or lockup for the confinement of adults, unless the minor is under the direct and continuous supervision of a peace officer or other child protective agency worker, as specified in Section 11165.9 of the Penal Code, until temporary custody and detention of the minor is assumed pursuant to Section 309. However, if a child protective agency worker is not available to supervise the minor as certified by the law enforcement agency which has custody of the minor, a trained volunteer may be

directed to supervise the minor. The volunteer shall be trained and function under the auspices of the agency which utilizes the volunteer. The minor may not remain under the supervision of the volunteer for more than three hours. A county which elects to utilize trained volunteers for the temporary supervision of minors shall adopt guidelines for the training of the volunteers which guidelines shall be approved by the State Department of Social Services. Each county which elects to utilize trained volunteers for the temporary supervision of minors shall report annually to the department on the number of volunteers utilized, the number of minors under their supervision, and the circumstances under which volunteers were utilized.

No record of the detention of such a person shall be made or kept by any law enforcement agency or the Department of Justice as a record of arrest. *(Amended by Stats 1989 ch 913 §2, eff. 1/1/90.)*

§207. Facilities for care and detention.

(a) No minor shall be detained in any jail, lockup, juvenile hall, or other secure facility who is taken into custody solely upon the ground that he or she is a person described by Section 601 or adjudged to be such or made a ward of the juvenile court solely upon that ground, except as provided in subdivision (b). If any such minor, other than a minor described in subdivision (b), is detained, he or she shall be detained in a sheltered-care facility or crisis resolution home as provided for in Section 654, or in a nonsecure facility provided for in subdivision (a), (b), (c), or (d) of Section 727.

(b) A minor taken into custody upon the ground that he or she is a person described in Section 601, or adjudged to be a ward of the juvenile court solely upon that ground, may be held in a secure facility, other than a facility in which adults are held in secure custody, in any of the following circumstances:

(1) For up to 12 hours after having been taken into custody for the purpose of determining if there are any outstanding wants, warrants, or holds against the minor in cases where the arresting officer or probation officer has cause to believe that the wants, warrants, or holds exist.

(2) For up to 24 hours after having been taken into custody, in order to locate the minor's parent or guardian as soon as possible and to arrange the return of the minor to his or her parent or guardian.

(3) For up to 24 hours after having been taken into custody, in order to locate the minor's parent or guardian as soon as possible and to arrange the return of the minor to his or her parent or guardian, whose parent or guardian is a resident outside of the state wherein the minor was taken into custody, except that the period may be extended to no more than 72 hours when the return of the minor cannot reasonably be accomplished within 24 hours due to the distance of the parents or guardian from the county of custody, difficulty in locating the parents or guardian, or difficulty in locating resources necessary to provide for the return of the minor.

(c) Any minor detained in juvenile hall pursuant to subdivision (b) may not be permitted to come or remain in contact with any person detained on the basis that he or she has been taken into custody upon the ground that he or she is a person described in Section 602 or adjudged to be such or made a ward of the juvenile court upon that ground.

© 1992 by J., B. & L. Gould
Printed in the U.S.A.   EP

(d) Minors detained in juvenile hall pursuant to Sections 601 and 602 may be held in the same facility provided they are not permitted to come or remain in contact within that facility.

(e) Every county shall keep a record of each minor detained under subdivision (b), the place and length of time of the detention, and the reasons why the detention was necessary. Every county shall report this information to the Department of the Youth Authority on a monthly basis, on forms to be provided by that agency.

The Youth Authority shall not disclose the name of the detainee, or any personally identifying information contained in reports sent to the Youth Authority under this subdivision. *(Amended by Stats 1986 ch 1271 §2.)*

§207.1. Lockups used for temporary, secure detention of minors.

(a) No court, judge, referee, peace officer, or employee of a detention facility shall knowingly detain any minor in a jail or lockup, except as provided in subdivision (b) or (d).

(b) Any minor who is alleged to have committed an offense described in subdivision (b) of Section 707, whose case is transferred to a court of criminal jurisdiction pursuant to Section 707.1 after a finding is made that he or she is not a fit and proper subject to be dealt with under the juvenile court law, may be detained in a jail or other secure facility for the confinement of adults, if all of the following conditions are met:

(1) The juvenile court judge makes a finding at the conclusion of the fitness hearing that the minor's further detention in the juvenile hall would endanger the safety of the public or would be detrimental to the other minors in the juvenile hall.

(2) Contact between the minor and adults in the facility is restricted in accordance with Section 208.

(3) The minor is adequately supervised.

(4) The adult facility has been approved by the Youth Authority as an appropriate place for the detention of minors so transferred.

(c) A minor who is found not to be a fit and proper subject to be dealt with under the juvenile court law shall, upon the conclusion of the fitness hearing, be entitled to be released on bail or on his or her own recognizance upon the same circumstances, terms, and conditions as an adult who is alleged to have committed the same offense.

(d) A minor 14 years of age or older who is taken into temporary custody by a peace officer on the basis of being a person described by Section 602, and who, in the reasonable belief of the peace officer, presents a serious security risk of harm to self or others, may be securely detained in a law enforcement facility that contains a lockup for adults, if all of the following conditions are met:

(1) The minor is held in temporary custody for the purpose of investigating the case, facilitating release of the minor to a parent or guardian, or arranging transfer of the minor to an appropriate juvenile facility.

(2) The minor is detained in the law enforcement facility for a period that does not exceed six hours except as provided in subdivision (g).

(3) The minor is informed at the time he or she is securely detained of the purpose of the secure detention, of the length of time the secure detention is expected to last, and of the maximum six-hour period the secure detention is authorized to last. In the event an extension is granted pursuant to subdivision (g), the minor shall be informed of the length of time the extension is expected to last.

(4) Contact between the minor and adults confined in the facility is restricted in accordance with Section 208.

(5) The minor is adequately supervised.

(6) A log or other written record is maintained by the law enforcement agency showing the offense which is the basis for the secure detention of the minor in the facility, the reasons and circumstances forming the basis for the decision to place the minor in secure detention, and the length of time the minor was securely detained.

Any other minor who is taken into temporary custody by a peace officer on the basis that the minor is a person described by Section 602, may be taken to a law enforcement facility that contains a lockup for adults and may be held in temporary custody in the facility for the purposes of investigating the case, facilitating the release of the minor to a parent or guardian, or arranging for the transfer of the minor to an appropriate juvenile facility. However, while in the law enforcement facility, the minor may not be securely detained and shall be supervised in a manner so as to ensure that there will be no contact with adults in custody in the facility. If the minor is held in temporary, nonsecure custody within such a facility, the peace officer shall exercise one of the dispositional options authorized by Sections 626 and 626.5 without unnecessary delay and, in every case, within six hours.

As used in this subdivision, "law enforcement facility" includes a police station or a sheriff's station, but does not include a jail, as defined in subdivision (i).

(e) The Department of the Youth Authority shall assist law enforcement agencies, probation departments, and courts with the implementation of this section by doing all of the following:

(1) The Department of the Youth Authority shall advise each law enforcement agency, probation department, and court affected by this section as to its existence and effect.

(2) The Department of the Youth Authority shall inquire of the official in charge of each jail or lockup that reported the confinement of a minor in calendar year 1984 or 1985 as to whether the jail or lockup may be used for the future confinement of any minor pursuant to subdivision (b), and if the Department of the Youth Authority is informed that the jail or lockup may be so used, it shall inspect the jail or lockup and determine whether it is an appropriate place for the secure detention of minors in conformity with the requirements of law.

(3) The Department of the Youth Authority shall make available and shall, upon request, provide technical assistance to each governmental agency that reported the confinement of a minor in a jail or lockup in calendar year 1984 or 1985. The purpose of this technical assistance is to develop alternatives to the use of jails or lockups for the confinement of minors. These alternatives may include secure or nonsecure facilities located apart from an existing jail or lockup; improved transportation or access to juvenile halls or other juvenile facilities; and other programmatic alternatives recommended by the Department of the Youth Authority. The technical assistance shall take

such form as the Department of the Youth Authority deems appropriate for effective compliance with this section.

(f) The Department of the Youth Authority may exempt a county that does not have a juvenile hall, or may exempt an offshore law enforcement facility, from compliance with this section for a reasonable period of time, until July 1, 1991, for the purpose of allowing the county or the facility to develop alternatives to the use of jails and lockups for the confinement of minors if all of the following conditions are met:

(1) The county or the facility submits a written request to the Department of the Youth Authority for an extension of time to comply with this section.

(2) The Department of the Youth Authority agrees to make available, and the county or the facility agrees to accept, technical assistance to develop alternatives to the use of jails and lockups for the confinement of minors during the period of the extension.

(3) The county or the facility requesting the extension submits to the Department of the Youth Authority a written plan for full compliance with this section by September 1, 1987.

(g) (1) Under the limited conditions of inclement weather, acts of God, or natural disasters that result in the temporary unavailability of transportation, an extension of the six-hour maximum period of detention set forth in paragraph (2) of subdivision (d) may be granted to a county by the Department of the Youth Authority. The extensions may only be granted by the Department of the Youth Authority on an individual, case-by-case basis. If the extension is granted, the detention of minors under those conditions shall not exceed the duration of the special conditions, plus a period reasonably necessary to accomplish transportation of the minor to a suitable juvenile facility, not to exceed six hours after the restoration of available transportation.

A county that receives an extension under this paragraph shall comply with the requirements set forth in subdivision (d). The county shall also provide a written report to the Department of the Youth Authority that specifies when the inclement weather, act of God, or natural disaster ceased to exist, when transportation availability was restored, and when the minor was delivered to a suitable juvenile facility. In the event that the minor was detained for a period in excess of 24 hours, the Department of the Youth Authority shall verify the information contained in the report.

(2) Under the limited condition of temporary unavailability of transportation, an extension of the six-hour maximum period of detention set forth in paragraph (2) of subdivision (d) may be granted by the Department of the Youth Authority to an offshore law enforcement facility. The extension may only be granted by the Department of the Youth Authority on an individual, case-by-case basis. If the extension is granted, the detention of minors under those conditions shall only extend until the next available mode of transportation can be arranged.

An offshore law enforcement facility that receives an extension under this paragraph shall comply with the requirements set forth in subdivision (d). The facility shall also provide a written report to the Department of the Youth Authority that specifies when the next mode of transportation became available, and when the minor was delivered to a suitable juvenile facility. In the event that the minor was detained for a period in excess of 24 hours, the Department of the Youth Authority shall verify the information contained in the report.

(3) At least annually, the Department of the Youth Authority shall review and report on extensions sought and granted under this subdivision. If, upon that review, the Department of the Youth Authority determines that a county has sought one or more extensions resulting in the excessive confinement of minors in adult facilities, or that a county is engaged in a pattern and practice of seeking extensions, it shall require the county to submit a detailed explanation of the reasons for the extensions sought and an assessment of the need for a conveniently located and suitable juvenile facility. Upon receiving this information, the Department of the Youth Authority shall make available, and the county shall accept, technical assistance for the purpose of developing suitable alternatives to the confinement of minors in adult lockups. Based upon the information provided by the county, the Department of the Youth Authority may also place limits on, or refuse to grant, future extensions requested by the county under this subdivision.

(h) Any county that did not have a juvenile hall on January 1, 1987, may establish a special purpose juvenile hall, as defined by the Department of the Youth Authority, for the detention of minors for a period not to exceed 96 hours. Any county that had a juvenile hall on January 1, 1987, may, in addition to the juvenile hall, also establish a special purpose juvenile hall. The Department of the Youth Authority shall prescribe minimum standards for any such facility.

(i) (1) As used in this chapter, "jail" means any building which contains a locked facility administered by a law enforcement or governmental agency, the purpose of which is to detain adults who have been charged with violations of criminal law and are pending trial, or to hold convicted adult criminal offenders sentenced for less than one year.

(2) As used in this chapter, "lockup" means any locked room or secure enclosure under the control of a sheriff or other peace officer which is primarily for the temporary confinement of adults upon arrest.

(3) As used in this section "offshore law enforcement facility" means a sheriff's station containing a lockup for adults that is located on an island located at least 22 miles from the California coastline.

(j) Nothing in this section shall be deemed to prevent a peace officer or employee of an adult detention facility or jail from escorting a minor into the detention facility or jail for the purpose of administering an evaluation, test, or chemical test pursuant to Section 23157 of the Vehicle Code, if all of the following conditions are met:

(1) The minor is taken into custody by a peace officer on the basis of being a person described by Section 602 and there is no equipment for the administration of the evaluation, test, or chemical test located at a juvenile facility within a reasonable distance of the point where the minor was taken into custody.

(2) The minor is not locked in a cell or room within the adult detention facility or jail, is under the continuous, personal supervision of a peace officer or employee of the detention facility or jail, and is not permitted to come in contact or remain in contact with in-custody adults.

© 1992 by J., B. & L. Gould
Printed in the U.S.A.   EP

(3) The evaluation, test, or chemical test administered pursuant to Section 23157 of the Vehicle Code is performed as expeditiously as possible, so that the minor is not unnecessarily delayed within the adult detention facility or jail. Upon completion of the evaluation, test, or chemical test, the minor shall be removed from the detention facility or jail as soon as reasonably possible. No minor shall be held in custody in an adult detention facility or jail under the authority of this paragraph for a period in excess of two hours. *(Amended by Stats 1991 ch 721 §1, eff. 1/1/92.)*

§207.5. Misrepresentation to secure admission to facility.

Every person who misrepresents or falsely identifies himself or herself either verbally or by presenting any fraudulent written instrument to any probation officer, or to any superintendent, director, counselor, or employee of a juvenile hall, home, ranch, or camp for the purpose of securing admission to the premises or grounds of any such juvenile hall, home, ranch, or camp, or to gain access to any minor detained therein, and who would not otherwise qualify for admission or access thereto, is guilty of a misdemeanor.

§208. Prohibition against contact of minor.

(a) When any person under 18 years of age is detained in or sentenced to any institution in which adults are confined, it shall be unlawful to permit such person to come or remain in contact with such adults.

(b) No person who is a ward or dependent child of the juvenile court who is detained in or committed to any state hospital or other state facility shall be permitted to come or remain in contact with any adult person who has been committed to any state hospital or other state facility as a mentally disordered sex offender under the provisions of Article 1 (commencing with Section 6300) of Chapter 2 of Part 2 of Division 6, or with any adult person who has been charged in an accusatory pleading with the commission of any sex offense for which registration of the convicted offender is required under Section 290 of the Penal Code and who has been committed to any state hospital or other state facility pursuant to Section 1026 or 1370 of the Penal Code.

(c) As used in this section, "contact" does not include participation in supervised group therapy or other supervised treatment activities, participation in work furlough programs, or participation in hospital recreational activities which are directly supervised by employees of the hospital, so long as living arrangements are strictly segregated and all precautions are taken to prevent unauthorized associations.

§208.5. Exception.

Notwithstanding any other provision of law, in any case in which a minor who is detained in or committed to a county institution established for the purpose of housing juveniles attains the age of 18 prior to or during the period of detention or confinement he or she may be allowed to come or remain in contact with those juveniles until the age of 19, at which time he or she, upon the recommendation of the probation officer, shall be delivered to the custody of the sheriff for the remainder of the time he or she remains in custody, unless the juvenile court orders continued detention in a juvenile facility. The person shall be advised of his or her ability to petition the court for continued detention in a juvenile facility at the time of his or her

attainment of the age of 19. Notwithstanding any other provision of law, the sheriff may allow such a person to come into and remain in contact with other adults in the county jail or in any other county correctional facility in which he or she is housed. *(Amended by Stats 1986 ch 676 §1.)*

§209. Inspecting place as suitable for confinement of minors.

(a) The judge of the juvenile court of a county, or, if there is more than one such judge, any of the judges of the juvenile court shall, at least annually, inspect any jail, juvenile hall, or lockup which, in the preceding calendar year, was used for confinement, for more than 24 hours, of any minor. The judge shall note in the minutes of the court whether the jail, juvenile hall, or lockup is a suitable place for confinement of minors.

The Department of the Youth Authority shall likewise conduct an annual inspection of each jail, juvenile hall, lockup, or special purpose juvenile hall situated in this state which, during the preceding calendar year, was used for confinement, for more than 24 hours, of any minor.

If either a judge of the juvenile court or the department, after inspection of a jail, juvenile hall, or lockup, finds that it is not being operated and maintained as a suitable place for the confinement of minors, the juvenile court or the department shall give notice of its finding to all persons having authority to confine minors pursuant to this chapter and commencing 60 days thereafter the jail, juvenile hall, or lockup shall not be used for confinement of minors until such time as the judge or department, as the case may be, finds, after reinspection of the jail, juvenile hall, or lockup that the conditions which rendered the facility unsuitable have been remedied, and the facility is a suitable place for confinement of minors.

The custodian of each jail, juvenile hall, and lockup shall make such reports as may be required by the department or the juvenile court to effectuate the purposes of this section.

(b) The Department of the Youth Authority may inspect any law enforcement facility which contains a lockup for adults and which it has reason to believe may not be in compliance with the requirements of subdivision (d) of Section 207.1 or with the certification requirements or standards adopted under Section 210.2. A judge of the juvenile court shall conduct an annual inspection, either in person or through a delegated member of the appropriate county or regional juvenile justice commission, of any law enforcement facility which contains a lockup for adults which, in the preceding year, was used for the secure detention of any minor.

If either the judge or the department finds after inspection that the facility is not being operated and maintained in conformity with the requirements of subdivision (d) of Section 207.1 or with the certification requirements or standards adopted under Section 210.2, the juvenile court or the department shall give notice of its finding to all persons having authority to securely detain minors in the facility, and, commencing 60 days thereafter, the facility shall not be used for the secure detention of a minor until such time as the judge or the department, as the case may be, finds, after reinspection, that the conditions which rendered the facility unsuitable have been remedied, and the facility is a suitable place for the confinement of minors in conformity with all requirements of law.

The custodian of each law enforcement facility which contains a lockup for adults shall make any report as may be required by the department or by the juvenile court to effectuate the purpose of this subdivision.

(c) The department shall collect annual data on the number, place, and duration of confinements of minors in jails and lockups, as defined in subdivision (i) of Section 207.1, and shall annually publish this information in the form as it deems appropriate for the purpose of providing public information on continuing compliance with the requirements of Section 207.1. *(Amended by Stats 1990 ch 1078 §2, eff. 1/1/91.)*

§210. Minimum standards for juvenile halls.

The Youth Authority shall adopt minimum standards for the operation and maintenance of juvenile halls for the confinement of minors.

Any violation of such standards shall render a juvenile hall unsuitable for the confinement of minors for purposes of Section 209.

§210.1. Guidelines for operating nonsecure placement facilities.

The Youth Authority shall develop guidelines for the operation and maintenance of nonsecure placement facilities for persons alleged or found to be persons coming within the terms of Section 601 or 602.

§210.2. Standards for temporary confinement of minors in adult lock-ups.

(a) The Department of the Youth Authority shall adopt regulations establishing standards for law enforcement facilities which contain lockups for adults and which are used for the temporary, secure detention of minors upon arrest under subdivision (d) of Section 207.1. The standards shall identify appropriate conditions of confinement for minors in law enforcement facilities, including standards for places within a police station or sheriff's station where minors may be securely detained; standards regulating contact between minors and adults in custody in lockup, booking, or common areas; standards for the supervision of minors securely detained in these facilities; and any other related standard as the department deems appropriate to effectuate compliance with subdivision (d) of Section 207.1.

(b) Every person in charge of a law enforcement facility which contains a lockup for adults and which is used in any calendar year for the secure detention of any minor shall certify annually that the facility is in conformity with the regulations adopted by the department under subdivision (a). The certification shall be endorsed by the sheriff or chief of police of the jurisdiction in which the facility is located and shall be forwarded to and maintained by the department. The department may provide forms and instructions to local jurisdictions to facilitate compliance with this requirement. *(Amended by Stats 1986 ch 1271 §5.)*

§211. Prohibiting commitment of person under 16 years to state prison.

No person under the age of 16 years shall be committed to a state prison or be transferred thereto from any other institution.

§212. Fees and expenses.

There shall be no fee for filing a petition under this chapter nor shall any fees be charged by any public officer for his services in filing or serving papers or for the performance of any duty enjoined upon him by this chapter, except where the sheriff transports a person to a state institution. If the judge of the juvenile court orders that a ward or dependent child go to a state institution without being accompanied by an officer or that a ward or dependent child be taken to an institution by the probation officer of the county or parole officer of the institution or by some other suitable person, all expenses necessarily incurred therefor shall be allowed and paid in the same manner and from the same funds as such expenses would be allowed and paid were such transportation effected by the sheriff.

§213. Disobedience or interference with lawful court order as contempt.

Any willful disobedience or interference with any lawful order of the juvenile court or of a judge or referee thereof constitutes a contempt of court.

§213.5. Ex parte orders for protection of minor.

(a) During the pendency of any proceeding to declare a minor child a dependent child of the juvenile court, upon application in the manner provided by Section 527 of the Code of Civil Procedure, the juvenile court may issue ex parte orders (1) enjoining any parent, guardian, or member of the minor child's household from molesting, attacking, striking, sexually assaulting, or battering the minor child or any other minor child in the household; (2) excluding any parent, guardian, or member of the minor child's household from the dwelling of the person who has care, custody, and control of the child upon the same showing as is necessary under the provisions of this chapter relating to dependent children to remove a minor from the custody and control of his or her parents or guardians; and (3) enjoining a parent, guardian, or member of the minor child's household from specified behavior including contacting, threatening, or disturbing the peace of the minor, which the court determines is necessary to effectuate orders under paragraph (1) or (2). In the case in which a temporary restraining order is granted without notice, the matter shall be made returnable on an order requiring cause to be shown why the order should not be granted, on the earliest day that the business of the court will permit, but not later than 15 days or, if good cause appears to the court, 20 days from the date the temporary restraining order is granted. The court may, on the motion of the person seeking the restraining order, or on its own motion, shorten the time for service on the person to be restrained of the order to show cause. Any hearing pursuant to this statute may be held simultaneously with the regularly scheduled hearings held in proceedings to declare a minor a dependent child of the juvenile court pursuant to Section 300.

(b) The juvenile court may issue, upon notice and a hearing, any of the orders set forth in subdivision (a). Any restraining order granted pursuant to this subdivision shall remain in effect, in the discretion of the court, not to exceed one year, unless otherwise terminated by the court, extended by mutual consent of all parties to the restraining order, or extended by further order of the court on the motion of any party to the restraining order.

(c) The juvenile court may issue an order made pursuant to subdivision (a) or (b) excluding a person from a residence or dwelling only when the evidence

© 1992 by J., B. & L. Gould
Printed in the U.S.A.   **EP**

affirmatively shows facts sufficient for the court to ascertain that the person seeking the order has a right under color of law to possession of the premises.

In the case of the issuance of an ex parte order, the affidavit in support of the application for the order shall affirmatively show facts sufficient for the court to ascertain that the person seeking the order has a right under color of law to possession of the premises.

(d) Any order issued pursuant to subdivision (a) or (b) shall state on its face the date of expiration of the order.

(e) The juvenile court shall order any designated person or attorney to mail a copy of any order, or extension, modification, or termination thereof, granted pursuant to subdivision (a) or (b), by the close of the business day on which the order, extension, modification, or termination was granted, and any subsequent proof of service thereof, to each local law enforcement agency designated by the person seeking the restraining order or his or her attorney having jurisdiction over the residence of the person who has care, custody, and control of the minor child and such other locations where the court determines that acts of domestic violence or abuse against the minor child or children are likely to occur. Each appropriate law enforcement agency shall make available through an existing system for verification, information as to the existence, terms, and current status of any order issued pursuant to subdivision (a) or (b) to any law enforcement officer responding to the scene of reported domestic violence or abuse.

(f) Any willful and knowing violation of any order granted pursuant to subdivision (a) or (b) shall be a misdemeanor punishable under Section 273.6 of the Penal Code. *(Added by Stats 1989 ch 1409 §2, eff. 1/1/90.)*

§214. Failure to appear.

In each instance in which a provision of this chapter authorizes the execution by any person of a written promise to appear or to have any other person appear before the probation officer or before the juvenile court, any willful failure of such promissor to perform as promised constitutes a misdemeanor and is punishable as such if at the time of the execution of such written promise the promissor is given a copy of such written promise upon which it is clearly written that failure to appear or to have any other person appear as promised is punishable as a misdemeanor.

§215. Definitions.

As used in this chapter, unless otherwise specifically provided, the term "probation officer" shall mean the juvenile probation officer or the person who is both the juvenile probation officer and the adult probation officer, and shall include any social worker in a county welfare department when supervising dependent children of the juvenile court pursuant to Section 272 by order of the court under Section 300, and the term "department of probation" shall mean the department of juvenile probation or the department wherein the services of juvenile and adult probation are both performed.

§216. Inapplicability to fugitive from justice.

This chapter shall not apply:

(a) To any person who violates any law of this state defining a crime, and is at the time of such violation under the age of 18 years, if such person thereafter flees from this state. Any such person may be proceeded against in the manner otherwise provided by law for proceeding against persons accused of crime. Upon the return of such person to this state by extradition or otherwise, proceedings shall be commenced in the manner provided for in this chapter.

(b) To any person who violates any law of another state defining a crime, and is at the time of such violation under the age of 18 years, if such person thereafter flees from that state into this state. Any such person may be proceeded against as an adult in the manner provided in Chapter 4 (commencing with Section 1547) of Title 12 of Part 2 of the Penal Code. The magistrate shall, for purposes of detention, detain such person in juvenile hall if space is available. If no space is available in juvenile hall, the magistrate may detain such person in the county jail.

§217. Use of unclaimed bicycles or toys for juvenile programs.

The board of supervisors of any county or the governing body of any city may by ordinance provide that any bicycles or toys, or both, in the possession of the sheriff of the county or in the possession of the police department of the city which have been unclaimed for a period of at least 60 days may, instead of being sold at public auction to the highest bidder pursuant to the provisions of Section 2080.5 of the Civil Code, be turned over to the probation officer, to the welfare department of the county, or to any charitable or nonprofit organization which is authorized under its articles of incorporation to participate in a program or activity designed to prevent juvenile delinquency and which is exempt from income taxation under federal or state law, or both, for use in any program or activity designed to prevent juvenile delinquency. *(Amended by Stats 1986 ch 865 §1.)*

§218. Compensation of court-appointed counsel.

In any case in which, pursuant to this chapter, the court appoints counsel to represent any person who desires but is unable to employ counsel, counsel shall receive a reasonable sum for compensation and for necessary expenses, the amount of which shall be determined by the court, to be paid out of the general fund of the county.

§219. Workers' compensation benefits for ward injured in rehabilitative work without pay.

The board of supervisors of a county may provide a ward of the juvenile court engaged in rehabilitative work without pay, under an assignment by order of the juvenile court to a work project in a county department, with workers' compensation benefits for injuries sustained while performing such rehabilitative work, in accordance with Section 3364.55 of the Labor Code.

§220. Obtaining abortions in juvenile facilities.

No condition or restriction upon the obtaining of an abortion by a female detained in any local juvenile facility, pursuant to the Therapeutic Abortion Act (Chapter 11 (commencing with Section 25950), Division 20 of the Health and Safety Code), other than those contained in that act, shall be imposed. Females found to be pregnant and desiring abortions, shall be permitted to determine their eligibility for an abortion pursuant to law, and if determined to be eligible, shall be permitted to obtain an abortion.

For the purposes of this section, "local juvenile facility" means any city, county, or regional facility used for the confinement of female juveniles for more than 24 hours.

The rights provided for females by this section shall be posted in at least one conspicuous place to which all females have access.

§221. Personal hygiene, birth control, and family planning services for females in juvenile facilities.

(a) Any female confined in a state or local juvenile facility shall upon her request be allowed to continue to use materials necessary for (1) personal hygiene with regard to her menstrual cycle and reproductive system and (2) birth control measures as prescribed by her physician.

(b) Any female confined in a state or local juvenile facility shall upon her request be furnished by the confining state or local agency with information and education regarding prescription birth control measures.

(c) Family planning services shall be offered to each and every woman inmate at least 60 days prior to a scheduled release date. Upon request any woman inmate shall be furnished by the confining state or local agency with the services of a licensed physician, or she shall be furnished by the confining state or local agency or by any other agency which contracts with the confining state or local agency, with services necessary to meet her family planning needs at the time of her release.

(d) For the purposes of this section, "local juvenile facility" means any city, county, or regional facility used for the confinement of juveniles for more than 24 hours.

This section shall become operative on January 1, 1988.

§222. Right to pregnancy services.

Any female in the custody of a local juvenile facility shall have the right to summon and receive the services of any physician and surgeon of her choice in order to determine whether she is pregnant. If she is found to be pregnant, she is entitled to a determination of the extent of the medical services needed by her and to the receipt of such services from the physician and surgeon of her choice. Any expenses occasioned by the services of a physician and surgeon whose services are not provided by the facility shall be borne by such female.

For the purpose of this section, "local juvenile facility" means any city, county, or regional facility used for the confinement of juveniles for more than 24 hours.

The rights provided for females by this section shall be posted in at least one conspicuous place to which all female wards have access.

§224. Maintenance of current child welfare, mental health, and probation programs.

(a) To ensure maintenance of effort on current child welfare, mental health, and probation programs, and the avoidance of inappropriate reliance on institutionalized care, the Health and Welfare Agency and the Youth and Adult Correctional Agency shall, until January 1, 1997, report annually to the appropriate committees of the Legislature as specified in subdivision (b).

(b) The Health and Welfare Agency shall report annually to the Legislature data on welfare supervised and probation supervised foster care caseloads, which shall include, but not be limited to, all of the following:

(1) The number of cases opened during the year and the percentage of increase or decrease over the previous year.

(2) The number of minors in foster family homes, in group homes, and in other facilities and the percentage of increase or decrease over the previous year.

(3) The number of minors in out-of-county and out-of-state placements and the percentage of increase or decrease over the previous year.

(4) The number of families receiving voluntary, in-home, supervision and the percentage of increase or decrease of those caseloads over the previous year.

(5) The number of minors reunified with their families, the number of terminations, the number of children receiving family preservation services pursuant to Section 16500.5, the number of adoptions, and the number of cases closed for other reasons.

(6) The number of minors, including those adjudicated pursuant to Sections 300 and 600 and those minors who were not so adjudicated, who were placed in state hospitals and private psychiatric facilities and the percentage of increase or decrease over the previous year.

(7) When available, the number of minors in foster care who have been in foster care previously.

(8) When available, the number of minors who have been referred to the Emergency Response program previously and the number of previous referrals for these minors.

(9) The average length of stay of minors in out-of-home placements.

(c) The Youth and Adult Correctional Agency shall, utilizing any available information, including, but not limited to, data supplied by the Department of Justice and the Chief Probation Officers Association, report annually to the appropriate committees of the Legislature on all of the following:

(1) The number of minors adjudicated as court wards pursuant to Sections 601 and 602 and the percentage of increase or decrease over the previous year.

(2) The number of minors committed to Department of the Youth Authority facilities during the year, the commitment offenses by category, both felony and misdemeanor, and the percentage of increase or decrease by category over the previous year.

(3) The number of minors rejected for commitment by the Department of the Youth Authority pursuant to Section 736 and the percentage of increase or decrease over the previous year.

(4) The number of court wards in county juvenile halls, camps, and ranches and the percentage of increase or decrease over the previous year.

(5) The average length of stay for placements in juvenile halls, camps and ranches, and Department of the Youth Authority facilities.

(d) This section shall remain in effect only until January 1, 1997, and as of that date is repealed, unless a later enacted statute, which is enacted before January 1, 1997, deletes or extends that date. *(Added by Stats 1991 ch 91 §10, eff. 6/30/91 only until 1/1/97. This section shall become inoperative 60 days following the date on which the Commission on State Mandates adopts an estimated statewide cost of reimbursement, or following the date on which the first such judicial determination becomes final.)*

© 1992 by J., B. & L. Gould
Printed in the U.S.A.   **EP**

ARTICLE 2

COMMISSIONS AND COMMITTEES

§225. Juvenile justice commission.

In each county there shall be a juvenile justice commission consisting of not less than 7 and no more than 15 citizens. Two or more of the members shall be persons who are between 14 and 21 years of age, provided there are available persons between 14 and 21 years of age who are able to carry out the duties of a commission member in a manner satisfactory to the appointing authority. Each person serving as a member of a probation committee immediately prior to September 15, 1961, shall be a member of the juvenile justice commission and shall continue to serve as such until such time as his or her term of appointment as a member of the probation committee would have expired under any prior provision of law. Upon a vacancy occurring in the membership of the commission and upon the expiration of the term of office of any member, a successor shall be appointed by the presiding judge of the superior court with the concurrence of the judge of the juvenile court or, in a county having more than one judge of the juvenile court, with the concurrence of the presiding judge of the juvenile court for a term of four years. When a vacancy occurs for any reason other than the expiration of a term of office, the appointee to fill such vacancy shall hold office for the unexpired term of his or her predecessor.

Appointments may be made by the presiding judge of the superior court, in the same manner designated in this section for the filling of vacancies, to increase the membership of a commission to the maximum of 15 in any county which has a commission with a membership of less than 15 members.

In any county in which the membership of the commission, on the effective date of amendments to this section enacted at the 1971 Regular Session of the Legislature, exceeds the maximum number permitted by this section, no additional appointments shall be made until the number of commissioners is less than the maximum number permitted by this section. In any case, such county's commission membership shall, on or after January 1, 1974, be no greater than the maximum permitted by this section.

§225.05. Department of the Youth Authority task force.

(a) The Department of the Youth Authority shall convene a task force to identify and recommend methods of achieving better coordination of, and savings, in the continuum of correctional, rehabilitative, and preventive services for youthful offenders, including status offenders adjudicated pursuant to Section 601 and delinquents adjudicated pursuant to Sections 602 and 707. The department shall report on the findings and recommendations of the task force to the Legislature no later than January 15, 1992.

(b) The task force shall develop recommendations for achieving the following:

(1) The use of local community corrections options, including innovative methods of providing delinquency prevention and treatment programs.

(2) Innovative, intensive programs for wards committed to the Department of the Youth Authority facilities.

(3) Coordination with state and local programs which provide treatment and services to youthful offenders.

(4) Restructuring current state and local juvenile justice funding mechanisms in order to provide fiscal and program incentives for the utilization of local juvenile justice treatment and services, including, but not limited to, the utilization of a negotiated net amount or rate model pursuant to Section Article 3 (commencing with Section 5700) of Chapter 2 of Part 1, for payment of costs associated with commitment of wards to the Department of the Youth Authority facilities.

(5) (A) Appropriate funding of juvenile justice programs contained in county realignment under Section 17602, including all of the following provisions:

(i) Article 25.4 (commencing with Section 894) of Chapter 2 of Division 2.

(ii) Article 5.5 (commencing with Section 1790) of Chapter 1 of Division 2.5.

(iii) Article 7 (commencing with Section 1805) of Chapter 1 of Division 2.5.

(iv) Article 10 (commencing with Section 1900) of Chapter 1 of Division 2.5.

(B) The task force shall recommend both short-term and long-term funding solutions for the programs specified in subparagraph (A), including recommendations for appropriate state and local agency responsibility for determining funding levels, program administration, oversight, and evaluation.

(c) The task force shall be composed of persons knowledgeable in delinquency prevention programs, juvenile justice issues, and alternative juvenile justice models, including representatives of the Department of the Youth Authority, the State Department of Social Services, the Chief Probation Officers Association, the County Supervisors Association of California, the County Welfare Directors Association, the Juvenile Court Judges of California, and county and private nonprofit agencies involved with juvenile justice services. In developing its recommendations, the task force shall consult with representatives of providers of group home care for delinquent minors. *(Added by Stats 1991 ch 91 §11, eff. 6/30/91; amended by Stats 1991 ch 611 §7, eff. 10/7/91. This section shall become inoperative 60 days following the date on which the Commission on State Mandates adopts an estimated statewide cost of reimbursement, or following the date on which the first such judicial determination becomes final.)*

§226. Regional juvenile justice commission.

In lieu of county juvenile justice commissions, the boards of supervisors of two or more adjacent counties may agree to establish a regional juvenile justice commission consisting of not less than eight citizens, and having a sufficient number of members so that their appointment may be equally apportioned between the participating counties. Two or more of the members shall be persons who are between 14 and 21 years of age, provided there are available persons between 14 and 21 years of age who are able to carry out the duties of a commission member in a manner satisfactory to the appointing authority. The presiding judge of the superior court with the concurrence of the judge of the juvenile court or, in a county having more than one judge of the juvenile court, with the concurrence of the presiding judge of the juvenile court of each of the participating counties shall appoint an equal number of members to the regional justice commission and they shall hold office for a term of four years. Of those first appointed, however, if the number appointed be an even number, half shall serve for a term of two years and half shall serve for a term of four years and if the number of members first appointed be an odd number, the greater number nearest half shall serve for a term of two years and the remainder shall serve for a term of four years. The respective terms of the members first appointed shall be determined by lot as soon as possible after their appointment. Upon a vacancy occurring in the membership of the commission and upon the expiration of the term of office of any member, a successor shall be appointed by the presiding judge of the superior court with the concurrence of the judge of the juvenile court or, in a county having more than one judge of the juvenile court, with the concurrence of the presiding judge of the juvenile court of the county which originally appointed such vacating or retiring member. When a vacancy occurs for any reason other than the expiration of a term of office, the appointee shall hold office for the unexpired term of his or her predecessor.

§227. Notice of appointment of members.

The clerk of the court of the appointing judge shall immediately notify each person appointed a member of a county or regional juvenile justice commission and thereupon such person shall appear before the appointing judge and qualify by taking an oath faithfully to perform the duties of a member of the juvenile justice commission. The qualification of each member shall be entered in the juvenile court record.

§228. Officers.

A juvenile justice commission shall elect a chairman and vice chairman annually.

§229. Inspection of institutions.

It shall be the duty of a juvenile justice commission to inquire into the administration of the juvenile court law in the county or region in which the commission serves. For this purpose the commission shall have access to all publicly administered institutions authorized or whose use is authorized by this chapter situated in the county or region, shall inspect such institutions no less frequently than once a year, and may hold hearings. A judge of the juvenile court shall have the power to issue subpoenas requiring attendance and testimony of witnesses and production of papers at hearings of the commission.

A juvenile justice commission shall annually inspect any jail or lockup within the county which in the preceding calendar year was used for confinement for more than 24 hours of any minor. It shall report the results of such inspection together with its recommendations based thereon, in writing, to the juvenile court and to the Youth Authority.

§229.5. Administration of group homes.

Notwithstanding any other provision of law, a juvenile justice commission may inquire into the nonconfidential aspects of the administration of group homes receiving placements by order of the juvenile court or courts in the county or region in which the commission serves whose use is authorized by this chapter, and may report thereon to the State Department of Social Services, the presiding judge of the juvenile court or courts, and the chief probation officer of the county or counties. *(Added by Stats 1987 ch 228 §1.)*

§230. Recommendation of changes.

A juvenile justice commission may recommend to any person charged with the administration of any of the provisions of this chapter such changes as it has concluded, after investigation, will be beneficial. A commission may publicize its recommendations.

§231. Reimbursement for expenses.

Members of a juvenile justice commission shall be reimbursed for their actual and necessary expenses incurred in the performance of their duties. Such reimbursement shall be made by the county of appointment or, in lieu of such actual and necessary expenses the board of supervisors may provide that the members of the commission shall be paid not to exceed the sum of twenty-five dollars ($25) per meeting not exceeding two meetings per month. In the case of a regional justice commission, the duty of reimbursement shall be divided among the participating counties in the manner prescribed by agreement of the boards of supervisors.

§232. Cooperation between community agencies.

The board of supervisors may by ordinance provide for the establishment, support, and maintenance of one or more agencies or departments to cooperate with and assist in coordinating on a countywide basis the work of those community agencies engaged in activities designed to prevent juvenile and adult delinquency; and such agencies or departments may cooperate with any such public or community committees, agencies, or councils at their invitation.

§233. Establish delinquency prevention commission.

The board of supervisors may by ordinance provide for the establishment, support, and maintenance of a delinquency prevention commission, composed of not fewer than seven citizens, to coordinate on a countywide basis the work of those governmental and nongovernmental organizations engaged in activities designed to prevent juvenile delinquency. If the board so elects, it may designate the juvenile justice commission, or any other committee or council appointed pursuant to Section 232 or 235, to serve in such capacity.

The commission may receive funds from governmental and nongovernmental sources to hire an executive secretary and necessary staff and to defray needed administrative expenses. The board of supervisors may direct any county department to provide necessary staff service to the commission. The commission may expend its funds on specific projects designed to accomplish its objectives.

Members of the delinquency prevention commission shall be appointed by the board of supervisors to serve a term of four years, and they shall be reimbursed for their actual and necessary expenses incurred in the performance of their duties. Upon a vacancy occurring in the membership of the commission and upon the expiration in the term of office of any member, a successor shall be appointed by the board of supervisors. When a vacancy occurs for any reason other than the expiration of a term of office, the appointee to fill such vacancy shall hold office for the unexpired term of his or her predecessor.

The board of supervisors may appoint initial members to any delinquency prevention commission created after the effective date of the amendment made to this section at the 1973-74 Regular Session of the Legislature to hold office for the following terms: one-half of the membership of an even-numbered com-

© 1992 by J., B. & L. Gould
Printed in the U.S.A.   EP

mission for a term of two years and one-half plus one of the membership of an odd-numbered commission for a term of two years. The remaining initial members and the term of office of each successor appointed to fill a vacancy occurring on the expiration of a term thereafter shall be four years.

For a delinquency prevention commission existing on the effective date of the amendment made to this section at the 1973-74 Regular Session of the Legislature the board of supervisors may at any time upon the expiration of all the members' terms of office appoint members to hold office for the following terms: one-half of the membership of an even-numbered commission for a term of two years and one-half plus one of the membership of an odd-numbered commission for a term of two years. The remaining members and the term of office of each successor appointed to fill a vacancy occurring on the expiration of a term thereafter shall be four years.

Notwithstanding the preceding provisions of this section, the board of supervisors shall appoint two or more persons who are between 14 and 21 years of age to membership on a delinquency prevention commission, provided there are available persons between 14 and 21 years of age who are able to carry out the duties of a commission member in a manner satisfactory to the appointing authority.

§233.5. Responsibility re publication and distribution of indecent or pornographic materials.

In a county having a population of over 6,000,000, the board of supervisors may assign the responsibility for assisting and advising the board and other county officers concerning the publication and distribution of allegedly indecent or pornographic materials and such other related duties as the board may determine proper to the delinquency prevention commission established pursuant to Section 233.

§234. Establish delinquency prevention agency or department.

The board of supervisors may by ordinance provide for the establishment, support, and maintenance of a delinquency prevention agency or department, or may assign delinquency prevention duties to any existing county agency, or department. Any such agency or department may engage in activities designed to prevent juvenile and adult delinquency, including rendering direct and indirect services to persons in the community, and may cooperate with any other agency of government in carrying out its purposes.

§235. Establish public councils or committees.

The juvenile court and the probation department of any county may establish, or assist in the establishment of, any public council or committee having as its object the prevention of juvenile delinquency and may cooperate with, or participate in, the work of any such councils or committees for the purpose of preventing or decreasing juvenile delinquency, including the improving of recreational, health, and other conditions in the community affecting juvenile welfare.

§236. Juvenile delinquency prevention services.

Notwithstanding any other provision of law, probation departments may engage in activities designed to prevent juvenile delinquency. These activities include rendering direct and indirect services to persons in the community. Probation departments shall not be limited to providing services only to those persons on probation being supervised under Section 330 or 654, but may provide services to any juveniles in the community.

ARTICLE 3

PROBATION COMMISSION

§240. Population of counties; membership.

In counties having a population in excess of 6,000,000 in lieu of a county juvenile justice commission, there shall be a probation commission consisting of not less than seven members who shall be appointed by the same authority as that authorized to appoint the probation officer in that county. (Amended by Stats 1987 ch 228 §3.)

§241. Members continuing in office.

The members of a probation commission appointed and holding office under prior provisions of law on January 1, 1977, shall continue in office and shall be members of the probation commission created hereby for the same term as that for which they were appointed. (Amended by Stats 1987 ch 228 §4.)

§241.1. Determining status of a minor.

(a) Whenever a minor appears to come within the description of both Section 300 and Section 601 or 602, the county probation department and the county welfare department shall, pursuant to a jointly developed written protocol described in subdivision (b), initially determine which status will serve the best interests of the minor and the protection of society. The recommendations of both departments shall be presented to the juvenile court with the petition which is filed on behalf of the minor, and the court shall determine which status is appropriate for the minor.

(b) The probation department and the welfare department in each county shall jointly develop a written protocol to ensure appropriate local coordination in the assessment of a minor described in subdivision (a), and the development of recommendations by these departments for consideration by the juvenile court. These protocols shall require, which requirements shall not be limited to, consideration of the nature of the referral, the age of the minor, the prior record of the minor's parents for child abuse, the prior record of the minor for out-of-control or delinquent behavior, the parents' cooperation with the minor's school, the minor's functioning at school, the nature of the minor's home environment, and the records of other agencies which have been involved with the minor and his or her family. The protocols also shall contain provisions for resolution of disagreements between the probation and welfare departments regarding the need for dependency or ward status and provisions for determining the circumstances under which a new petition should be filed to change the minor's status.

(c) Nothing in this section shall be construed to authorize the filing of a petition or petitions, or the entry of an order by the juvenile court, to make a minor simultaneously both a dependent child and a ward of the court. (Added by Stats 1989 ch 1441 §1, eff. 1/1/90.)

§242. Term of office.

The members of the probation commission shall hold office for four years and until their successors are appointed and qualify. Of those first appointed, however, one shall hold office for one year, two for two years, two for three years, and two for four years; and the respective terms of the members first appointed shall be determined by lot as soon as possible after their appointment. When a vacancy occurs in a probation commission by expiration of the term of office of any member thereof, his or her successor shall be appointed to hold office for the term of four years. When a vacancy occurs for any other reason the appointee shall hold office for the unexpired term of his or her predecessor. *(Amended by Stats 1987 ch 228 §5.)*

§243. Advisory capacity of commission.

The probation commission shall function in an advisory capacity to the probation officer. *(Amended by Stats 1987 ch 228 §6.)*

ARTICLE 4

THE JUVENILE COURT

§245. Jurisdiction of court.

Each superior court shall exercise the jurisdiction conferred by this chapter, and while sitting in the exercise of such jurisdiction, shall be known and referred to as the juvenile court.

§245.5. Powers.

In addition to all other powers granted by law, the juvenile court may direct all such orders to the parent, parents, or guardian of a minor who is subject to any proceedings under this chapter as the court deems necessary and proper for the best interests of or for the rehabilitation of the minor. These orders may concern the care, supervision, custody, conduct, maintenance, and support of the minor, including education and medical treatment. *(Amended by Stats 1990 ch 182 §6, eff. 1/1/91.)*

§246. Designate judges to hear cases.

In counties having more than one judge of the superior court, the presiding judge of such court or the senior judge if there is no presiding judge shall annually, in the month of January, designate one or more judges of the superior court to hear all cases under this chapter during the ensuing year, and he shall, from time to time, designate such additional judges as may be necessary for the prompt disposition of the judicial business before the juvenile court.

In all counties where more than one judge is designated as a judge of the juvenile court, the presiding judge of the superior court shall also designate one such judge as presiding judge of the juvenile court.

§247. Appointment of referees.

The judge of the juvenile court, or in counties having more than one judge of the juvenile court, the presiding judge of the juvenile court or the senior judge if there is no presiding judge, may appoint one or more referees to serve on a full-time or part-time basis. A referee shall serve at the pleasure of the appointing judge, and unless the appointing judge makes his order terminating the appointment of a referee, such referee shall continue to serve as such until the appointment of his successor. Except as otherwise pro-

vided by law, the amount and rate of compensation to be paid referees shall be fixed by the board of supervisors. Every referee first appointed on or after January 1, 1977, shall have been admitted to practice law in this state and, in addition, shall have been admitted to practice law in this state for a period of not less than five years or in any other state and this state for a combined period of not less than 10 years. Nothing in this section shall be construed to apply to the qualifications of any referee first appointed prior to January 1, 1977.

§247.5. Disqualify referee; reassignment.

The provisions of Sections 170 and 170.6 of the Code of Civil Procedure shall apply to a referee, provided, that the presiding judge of the juvenile court shall if the motion is granted reassign the matter to another referee or to a judge of the juvenile court.

§248. Hearing cases; furnishing findings and order.

A referee shall hear such cases as are assigned to him or her by the presiding judge of the juvenile court, with the same powers as a judge of the juvenile court, except that a referee shall not conduct any hearing to which the state or federal constitutional prohibitions against double jeopardy apply unless all of the parties thereto stipulate in writing that the referee may act in the capacity of a temporary judge. A referee shall promptly furnish to the presiding judge of the juvenile court and the minor, if the minor is 14 or more years of age or if younger has so requested, and shall serve upon the minor's attorney of record and the minor's parent or guardian or adult relative and the attorney of record for the minor's parent or guardian or adult relative a written copy of his or her findings and order and shall also furnish to the minor, if the minor is 14 or more years of age or if younger has so requested, and to the parent or guardian or adult relative, with the findings and order, a written explanation of the right of such persons to seek review of the order by the juvenile court. Service, as provided in this section, shall be by mail to the last known address of such persons or to the address designated by such persons appearing at the hearing before the referee.

§248.5. Service of findings and orders.

All written findings and orders of the court shall be served by the clerk of the court personally or by first-class mail within three judicial days of their issuance on the petitioner, the minor or the minor's counsel, the parent or the parent's counsel, and the guardian or the guardian's counsel. *(Added by Stats 1990 ch 1530 §2, eff. 1/1/91.)*

§249. Approval of order removing minor from home.

No order of a referee removing a minor from his home shall become effective until expressly approved by a judge of the juvenile court.

§250. Commencement and duration; force and effect of orders.

Except as provided in Section 251, all orders of a referee other than those specified in Section 249 shall become immediately effective, subject also to the right of review as hereinafter provided, and shall continue in full force and effect until vacated or modified upon rehearing by order of the judge of the juvenile court.

© 1992 by J., B. & L. Gould
Printed in the U.S.A.　　**EP**

In a case in which an order of a referee becomes effective without approval of a judge of the juvenile court, it becomes final on the expiration of the time allowed by Section 252 for application for rehearing, if application therefor is not made within such time and if the judge of the juvenile court has not within such time ordered a rehearing pursuant to Section 253.

Where a referee sits as a temporary judge, his or her orders become final in the same manner as orders made by a judge.

§251. Judge's approval of orders.

The judge of the juvenile court, or in counties having more than one judge of the juvenile court, the presiding judge of the juvenile court may establish requirements that any or all orders of referees shall be expressly approved by a judge of the juvenile court before becoming effective.

§252. Application for rehearing; grant or denial.

At any time prior to the expiration of 10 days after service of a written copy of the order and findings of a referee, a minor or his parent or guardian may apply to the juvenile court for a rehearing. Such application may be directed to all or to any specified part of the order or findings, and shall contain a statement of the reasons such rehearing is requested. If all of the proceedings before the referee have been taken down by an official reporter, the judge of the juvenile court may, after reading the transcript of such proceedings, grant or deny such application. If proceedings before the referee have not been taken down by an official reporter, such application shall be granted as of right. If an application for rehearing is not granted, denied, or extended within 20 days following the date of its receipt, it shall be deemed granted. However, the court, for good cause, may extend such period beyond 20 days, but not in any event beyond 45 days, following the date of receipt of the application, at which time the application for rehearing shall be deemed granted unless it is denied within such period. All decisions to grant or deny the application, or to extend the period, shall be expressly made in a written minute order with copies provided to the minor or his parent or guardian, and to the attorneys of record.

§253. Rehearing on judge's motion.

A judge of the juvenile court may, on his own motion made within 20 judicial days of the hearing before a referee, order a rehearing of any matter heard before a referee.

§254. Rehearing conduct.

All rehearings of matters heard before a referee shall be before a judge of the juvenile court and shall be conducted de novo.

§255. Appointment of traffic hearing officers.

The judge of the juvenile court, or in counties having more than one judge of the juvenile court the presiding judge of the juvenile court or the senior judge if there is no presiding judge, may appoint one or more persons of suitable experience, who may be judges of the municipal court or justices of the justice court or a probation officer or assistant or deputy probation officers, to serve as traffic hearing officers on a full-time or part-time basis. A hearing officer shall serve at the pleasure of the appointing judge, and unless the appointing judge makes his order terminating the appointment of a hearing officer, such hearing officer shall continue to serve as such until the appointment of his successor. The board of supervisors shall determine whether any compensation shall be paid to hearing officers, not otherwise employed by a public agency or holding another public office, and shall establish the amounts and rates thereof. An appointment of a probation officer, assistant probation officer, or deputy probation officer as a traffic hearing officer may be made only with the consent of the probation officer.

§256. Officer to hear and dispose of cases.

Subject to the orders of the juvenile court, a traffic hearing officer may hear and dispose of any case in which a minor under the age of 18 years as of the date of the alleged offense is charged with (1) any violation of the Vehicle Code not declared to be a felony, (2) a violation of subdivision (m) of Section 602 of the Penal Code, (3) a violation of the Fish and Game Code not declared to be a felony, (4) a violation of any of the equipment and registration provisions of the Harbors and Navigation Code, (5) a violation of any provision of an ordinance of a city, county, or local agency relating to traffic offenses, or to nontraffic offenses regarding loitering, curfew, or evasion of fares on a public transportation system, as defined by Section 99211 of the Public Utilities Code, (6) a violation of Section 27176 of the Streets and Highways Code, (7) a violation of Section 640 or 640a of the Penal Code, (8) a violation of the rules and regulations established pursuant to Sections 5003 and 5008 of the Public Resources Code, (9) a violation of Section 33211.6 of the Public Resources Code, (10) a violation of Section 25658, 25658.5, 25661, or 25662 of the Business and Professions Code, (11) a violation of subdivision (f) of Section 647 of the Penal Code, (12) a misdemeanor violation of Section 594 of the Penal Code, involving defacing property with paint or any other liquid, or (13) any infraction. *(Amended by Stats 1991 ch 493 §1, 1202 §8, eff. 1/1/92.)*

§256.5. Arrest warrant for minor for failure to appear.

A traffic hearing officer may request the juvenile court judge or referee to issue a warrant of arrest against a minor who is issued and signs a written notice to appear for any violation listed in Section 256 and who fails to appear at the time and place designated in the notice. The juvenile court judge or referee may issue and have delivered for execution a warrant of arrest against a minor within 20 days after the minor's failure to appear as promised or within 20 days after the minor's failure to appear after a lawfully granted continuance of his or her promise to appear. *(Added by Stats 1991 ch 1202 §9, eff. 1/1/92.)*

§257. Conduct of hearing.

With the consent of the minor, a hearing before a traffic hearing officer, or a hearing before a referee or a judge of the juvenile court, where the minor is charged with a traffic offense or a nontraffic offense as specified in this section, may be conducted upon an exact legible copy of a written notice given pursuant to Article 2 (commencing with Section 40500) of Chapter 2 of Division 17 or Section 41103 of the Vehicle Code, or an exact legible copy of a written notice given pursuant to Chapter 5C (commencing with Section 853.6) of Title 3 of Part 2 of the Penal Code when the offense charged is a violation listed in Section 256, in

© 1992 by J., B. & L. Gould
Printed in the U.S.A. **EP**

lieu of a petition as provided in Article 16 (commencing with Section 650). *(Amended by Stats 1991 ch 493 §2, 1202 §10, eff. 1/1/92.)*

§258. Alternatives if minor guilty of traffic violation.

(a) Upon a hearing conducted in accordance with Section 257, and upon either an admission by the minor of the commission of a violation charged, or a finding that the minor did in fact commit the violation, the judge, referee, or traffic hearing officer may do any of the following:

(1) Reprimand the minor and take no further action.

(2) Request the probation officer to commence a proceeding as provided in Article 16 (commencing with Section 650).

(3) Direct that the probation officer undertake a program of supervision of the minor for a period not to exceed six months, in addition to or in place of the following orders.

(4) Order that the minor pay a fine up to the amount that an adult would pay for the same violation, unless the violation is otherwise specified within this section, in which case the fine shall not exceed two hundred fifty dollars ($250). This fine may be levied in addition to or in place of the following orders and the court may waive any or all of this fine, if the minor is unable to pay. In determining the minor's ability to pay, the court shall not consider the ability of the minor's family to pay.

(5) Make any or all of the following orders with respect to a traffic violation which is not charged as a felony:

(A) That the driving privileges of the minor be suspended or restricted as provided in the Vehicle Code or, notwithstanding Section 13203 of the Vehicle Code or any other provision of law, when the Vehicle Code does not provide for the suspension or restriction of driving privileges, that, in addition to any other order, the driving privileges of the minor be suspended or restricted for a period of not to exceed 30 days.

(B) That the minor attend traffic school over a period not to exceed 60 days.

(C) That the minor produce satisfactory evidence that the vehicle or its equipment has been made to conform with the requirements of the Vehicle Code pursuant to Section 40150 of the Vehicle Code.

(D) That the minor perform community service work in a public entity or any private nonprofit entity, for not more than 50 hours over a period of 60 days, during times other than his or her hours of school attendance or employment. Work performed pursuant to this subparagraph shall not exceed 30 hours during any 30-day period. The time frames established by this subparagraph shall not be modified except in unusual cases where the interests of justice would best be served. When the order to work is made by a referee or a traffic hearing officer, it shall be approved by a judge of the juvenile court.

For the purposes of this subparagraph, a judge, referee, or traffic hearing officer shall not, without the consent of the minor, order the minor to perform work with a private nonprofit entity that is affiliated with any religion.

(6) Make any or all of the following orders with respect to a violation of the Fish and Game Code which is not charged as a felony:

(A) That the fishing or hunting license involved be suspended or restricted.

(B) That the minor work in a park or conservation area for a total of not to exceed 20 hours over a period not to exceed 30 days, during times other than his or her hours of school attendance or employment.

(C) That the minor forfeit, pursuant to Section 12157 of the Fish and Game Code, any device or apparatus designed to be, and capable of being, used to take birds, mammals, fish, reptiles, or amphibia and which was used in committing the violation charged. The judge, referee, or traffic hearing officer shall, if the minor committed an offense which is punishable under Section 12008 of the Fish and Game Code, order the device or apparatus forfeited pursuant to Section 12157 of the Fish and Game Code.

(7) If the violation charged is of an ordinance of a city, county, or local agency relating to loitering, curfew, or fare evasion on a public transportation system, as defined by Section 99211 of the Public Utilities Code, or is a violation of Section 640 or 640a of the Penal Code, make the order that the minor shall perform community service for a total time not to exceed 20 hours over a period not to exceed 30 days, during times other than his or her hours of school attendance or employment.

(b) The judge, referee, or traffic hearing officer shall retain jurisdiction of the case until all orders made under this section have been fully complied with. *(Amended by Stats 1991 ch 1202 §11, eff. 1/1/92.)*

§259. *Repealed by Stats 1991 ch 1202 §12, eff. 1/1/92.*

§259.1. *Repealed by Stats 1991 ch 1202 §13, eff. 1/1/92.*

§260. Written report of findings and orders.

A traffic hearing officer shall promptly furnish a written report of his findings and orders to the clerk of the juvenile court. The clerk of the juvenile court shall promptly transmit an abstract of such findings and orders to the Department of Motor Vehicles.

§261. Orders immediately effective.

Subject to the provisions of Section 262, all orders of a traffic hearing officer shall be immediately effective.

§262. Setting aside or modifying orders; rehearing.

Upon motion of the minor or his parent or guardian for good cause, or upon his own motion, a judge of the juvenile court may set aside or modify any order of a traffic hearing officer, or may order or himself conduct a rehearing. If the minor or parent or guardian has made a motion that the judge set aside or modify the order or has applied for a rehearing, and the judge has not set aside or modified the order or ordered or conducted a rehearing within 10 days after the date of the order, the motion or application shall be deemed denied as of the expiration of such period.

§263. Transferring case to county of minor's residence.

At any time prior to the final disposition of a hearing pursuant to Section 257, the judge, referee, or traffic hearing officer may, on motion of the minor, his parent, or guardian, or on its own motion, transfer the case to the county of the minor's residence for further proceedings pursuant to Sections 258, 260, 261, and 262.

© 1992 by J., B. & L. Gould
Printed in the U.S.A.   **EP**

§264. Statewide or regional conferences.

At the direction and under the supervision of the Judicial Council, judges of the juvenile courts and juvenile court referees shall meet from time to time in statewide or regional conferences, to discuss problems arising in the course of administration of this chapter, for the purpose of improving the administration of justice in the juvenile courts. Actual and necessary expenses incurred by a judge or referee in attending any such conference shall be a charge upon the county.

§265. Rules of practice and procedure.

The Judicial Council shall establish rules governing practice and procedure in the juvenile court not inconsistent with law.

ARTICLE 5

PROBATION OFFICERS

§270. Nomination and appointment of probation officers, deputies, and assistants.

Except as provided in Section 69906 of the Government Code, there shall be in each county the offices of probation officer, assistant probation officer, and deputy probation officer. A probation officer shall be appointed in every county.

Probation officers in any county shall be nominated by the juvenile justice commission or regional juvenile justice commission of such county in such manner as the judge of the juvenile court in that county shall direct, and shall then be appointed by such judge.

The probation officer may appoint as many deputies or assistant probation officers as he desires; but such deputies or assistant probation officers shall not have authority to act until their appointments have been approved by a majority vote of the members of the juvenile justice commission, and by the judge of the juvenile court. The term of office of each such deputy or assistant probation officer shall expire with the term of the probation officer who appointed him, but the probation officer, with the written approval of the majority of the members of the juvenile justice commission and of the judge of the juvenile court, may, in his discretion, revoke and terminate any such appointment at any time.

Probation officers may at any time be removed by the judge of the juvenile court for good cause shown; and the judge of the juvenile court may in his discretion at any time remove any such probation officer with the written approval of a majority of the members of the juvenile justice commission.

§271. Application of charter and provisions re appointment and tenure for probation officers, etc.

In counties having charters which provide a method of appointment and tenure of office for probation officers, assistant probation officers, deputy probation officers, and the superintendent, matron, and other employees of the juvenile hall, such charter provisions shall control as to such matters, and in counties which have established or hereafter establish merit or civil service systems governing the methods of, appointment and the tenure of office of, probation officers, assistant probation officers, deputy probation officers, and of the superintendents, matrons and other employees of the juvenile hall, the provisions of such merit or civil service systems shall control as to

such matter; but in all other counties, such matters shall be controlled exclusively by the provisions of this code.

§272. Delegation of duties concerning dependent children.

(a) The board of supervisors may delegate to the county welfare department all or part of the duties of the probation officer concerning dependent children described in Section 300.

(b) The board of supervisors may also delegate to those persons within the county welfare department performing child welfare services the probation officer's right of access to state summary criminal history information pursuant to Section 11105 of the Penal Code as is necessary to carry out its duties concerning children reasonably believed to be described by Section 300. The information shall include any current incarceration, the location of any current probation or parole, any current requirement that the individual register pursuant to Section 290 or 457.1 of the Penal Code, or pursuant to Section 11140 or 11590 of the Health and Safety Code, and any history of offenses involving abuse or neglect of, or violence against, a child, or convictions of any offenses involving violence, sexual offenses, the abuse or illegal possession, manufacture, or sale of alcohol or controlled substances, and any arrest for which the person is released on bail or on his or her own recognizance.

(c) Notwithstanding subdivision (a), a social worker in a county welfare department may perform the duties specified by Section 306. *(Amended by Stats 1990 ch 1530 §3, eff. 1/1/91.)*

§273. Employment of psychiatrists, psychologists, etc.

The probation officer may, within budgetary limitations established by the board of supervisors, employ such psychiatrists, psychologists, and other clinical experts as are required to assist in determining appropriate treatment of minors within the jurisdiction of the juvenile court and in the implementation of such treatment.

§274. Bonds of probation officers, deputies, and assistants.

Each probation officer and each assistant and deputy probation officer receiving an official salary shall furnish a bond in the sum of not more than two thousand dollars ($2,000) and approved by the judge of the juvenile court, conditioned for the faithful discharge of the duties of his office. If such bonds, or any of them, are furnished by a surety company licensed to transact business in the state, the premium thereon shall be paid out of the county treasury. In the event the probation officer, assistants and deputies are included as covered employees in a master bond pursuant to Sections 1481 and 1481.1 of the Government Code, the individual bonds prescribed above shall not be required.

§275. Books and accounts, vouchers; audit.

For the purpose of handling the reimbursement and other payments provided for in this chapter, the probation officer or other county officer designated by the board of supervisors of the county shall keep suitable books and accounts and shall give and keep suitable receipts and vouchers. The auditor of the county shall audit such books and accounts annually, or at least biennially if so ordered by the board of supervisors upon the recommendation of the county auditor, on a fiscal year basis ending June 30 and shall make a report thereon to the judge of the court and to the supervisors of the county prior to the 31st day of the next succeeding month of January.

§276. Powers and duties: re receipt, etc., of moneys.

In addition to the powers and duties of the probation officer elsewhere prescribed in this chapter, he is authorized to receive money, give his receipt therefor, deposit or invest such money as soon as practicable in the county treasury, in a commercial bank account designated and approved for such a purpose by the board of supervisors, or in investment certificates or share accounts issued by a savings and loan association doing business in this state, insured by the Federal Savings and Loan Insurance Corporation and designated and approved for such purpose by the board of supervisors, and direct the disbursement thereof, in any of the following instances:

(a) Money payable to spouse or child in an action for divorce, separate maintenance, or similar action, together with court costs and attorney's fees, upon order of a court of competent jurisdiction. Instead of designating the probation officer to act as court trustee for the receipt and disbursement of money payable to a spouse or child under this subdivision, the court may designate in its order a bonded employee of the court to act as court trustee for that purpose.

(b) Money payable to or on behalf of a ward or dependent child of the juvenile court or a person concerning whom a petition has been filed in the juvenile court. The probation officer may petition the court for approval of any past or prospective disbursement.

(c) Money payable to, by, or on behalf of probationers under the supervision of the probation officer. The probation officer may petition the court for approval of any past or prospective disbursement.

(d) Money payable to a child, wife, or indigent parent when it has been alleged or claimed that there has been a violation of either Section 270, 270a, or 270c of the Penal Code and the matter has been referred to the probation officer by the district attorney.

(e) Gifts of money made to the county to assist in the prevention or correction of delinquency or crime when the donor requests the probation officer to disburse such funds for such purposes and the board of supervisors accepts the gift upon such conditions.

(f) Other similar cases.

In addition to the foregoing, the probation officer is authorized to receive money payable to the county when ordered to do so by a court of competent jurisdiction. Such money shall be deposited or invested in the same manner as the other items set forth in this section.

If a bank account or savings and loan association investment certificate or share account is authorized pursuant to this section, the probation officer must pay into the county treasury all money collected by him or under his control during the preceding month that is payable into the treasury in conformity with Section 24353 of the Government Code.

§277. Authorizing sale of ward's articles of handiwork.

The probation officer may authorize the sale of articles of handiwork made by wards under the jurisdiction of the probation officer to the public at probation institutions, in public buildings, at fairs, or on property operated by nonprofit associations. The cost of any county materials or other property consumed in the manufacture of articles shall be paid for out of funds received from the sale of the articles. The remainder of any funds received from the sale of the articles shall be placed in the ward's trust account pursuant to subdivision (b) of Section 276.

§278. Delegating function to auditor, etc.

The board of supervisors may delegate to the auditor or other county officer any of the functions of the probation officer authorized by Section 276 and required by Sections 1685 to 1687, inclusive, of the Code of Civil Procedure.

§279. Service charge.

The board of supervisors may impose a service charge at a uniform rate sufficient to defray the cost of services of the probation officer or other officer designated to act as trustee, not exceeding 2 percent of the amount collected, in addition to the payments made under subdivision (a), (c), (d), or (f) of Section 276.

The service charge imposed in relation to payments under subdivision (c) of Section 276 shall be imposed only for payments made by probationers, and the service charge imposed in relation to payments made under subdivision (f) of Section 276 shall be imposed only for cases similar to those listed in subdivision (a), (c), or (d) of that section.

When the payments are ordered by the court, the payment of the service charge shall be included in the order. All proceeds shall be deposited in the general fund of the county.

§280. Presence in court; duties.

Except where waived by the probation officer, judge, or referee and the minor, the probation officer shall be present in court to represent the interests of each person who is the subject of a petition to declare that person to be a ward or dependent child upon all hearings or rehearings of his or her case, and shall furnish to the court such information and assistance as the court may require. If so ordered, the probation officer shall take charge of that person before and after any hearing or rehearing.

It shall be the duty of the probation officer to prepare for every hearing on the disposition of a case as provided by Section 356, 358, 358.1, 361.5, 364, 366, 366.2, or 366.21 as is appropriate for the specific hearing, or, for a hearing as provided by Section 702, a social study of the minor, containing such matters as may be relevant to a proper disposition of the case. The social study shall include a recommendation for the disposition of the case. (Amended by Stats 1987 ch 1485 §2.)

§281. Investigation and preparation of reports and recommendations.

The probation officer shall upon order of any court in any matter involving the custody, status, or welfare of a minor or minors, make an investigation of appropriate facts and circumstances and prepare and file

© 1992 by J., B. & L. Gould
Printed in the U.S.A.   EP

with the court written reports and written recommendations in reference to such matters. The court is authorized to receive and consider the reports and recommendations of the probation officer in determining any such matter.

§281.5. Placing minor with relative.

If a probation officer determines to recommend to the court that a minor alleged to come within Section 300, 601, or 602, or adjudged to come within Section 300, 601, or 602 should be removed from the physical custody of his parent or guardian, the probation officer shall give primary consideration to recommending to the court that the minor be placed with a relative of the minor, if such placement is in the best interests of the minor and will be conducive to reunification of the family.

§282. Report of qualifications of society, etc., receiving custody of ward or dependent child.

At any time the judge of the juvenile court may, and upon the request of the county board of supervisors shall, require the probation officer to examine into and report to the court upon the qualifications and management of any society, association, or corporation, other than a state institution, which applies for or receives custody of any ward or dependent child of the juvenile court. No probation officer, however, shall, under authority of this section, enter any institution without its consent. If such consent is refused, commitments to that institution shall not be made.

§283. Powers and authority.

Every probation officer, assistant probation officer, and deputy probation officer shall have the powers and authority conferred by law upon peace officers listed in Section 830.5 of the Penal Code.

§284. Periodic reports to Youth Authority.

All probation officers shall make such special and periodic reports to the Youth Authority as the authority may require and upon forms furnished by the authority.

§285. Periodic reports to the Bureau of Criminal Statistics.

All probation officers shall make such periodic reports to the Bureau of Criminal Statistics as the bureau may require and upon forms furnished by the bureau, provided that no names or social security numbers shall be transmitted regarding any proceeding under Section 300 or 601.

§286. Continuance in office.

Any person lawfully appointed to serve as a probation officer or assistant or deputy probation officer prior to the effective date of this section shall continue in his office or employment as if appointed in the manner prescribed by this article.

ARTICLE 6

DEPENDENT CHILDREN — JURISDICTION

§300. Persons within jurisdiction of juvenile court.

Any minor who comes within any of the following descriptions is within the jurisdiction of the juvenile court which may adjudge that person to be a dependent child of the court:

(a) The minor has suffered, or there is a substantial risk that the minor will suffer, serious physical harm inflicted nonaccidentally upon the minor by the minor's parent or guardian. For the purposes of this subdivision, a court may find there is a substantial risk of serious future injury based on the manner in which a less serious injury was inflicted, a history of repeated inflictions of injuries on the minor or the minor's siblings, or a combination of these and other actions by the parent or guardian which indicate the child is at risk of serious physical harm. For purposes of this subdivision, "serious physical harm" does not include reasonable and age-appropriate spanking to the buttocks where there is no evidence of serious physical injury.

(b) The minor has suffered, or there is a substantial risk that the minor will suffer, serious physical harm or illness, as a result of the failure or inability of his or her parent or guardian to adequately supervise or protect the minor, or the willful or negligent failure of the minor's parent or guardian to adequately supervise or protect the minor from the conduct of the custodian with whom the minor has been left, or by the willful or negligent failure of the parent or guardian to provide the minor with adequate food, clothing, shelter, or medical treatment, or by the inability of the parent or guardian to provide regular care for the minor due to the parent's or guardian's mental illness, developmental disability, or substance abuse. No minor shall be found to be a person described by this subdivision solely due to the lack of an emergency shelter for the family. Whenever it is alleged that a minor comes within the jurisdiction of the court on the basis of the parent's or guardian's willful failure to provide adequate medical treatment or specific decision to provide spiritual treatment through prayer, the court shall give deference to the parent's or guardian's medical treatment, nontreatment, or spiritual treatment through prayer alone in accordance with the tenets and practices of a recognized church or religious denomination, by an accredited practitioner thereof, and shall not assume jurisdiction unless necessary to protect the minor from suffering serious physical harm or illness. In making its determination, the court shall consider (1) the nature of the treatment proposed by the parent or guardian (2) the risks to the minor posed by the course of treatment or nontreatment proposed by the parent or guardian (3) the risk, if any, of the course of treatment being proposed by the petitioning agency, and (4) the likely success of the courses of treatment or nontreatment proposed by the parent or guardian and agency. The minor shall continue to be a dependent child pursuant to this subdivision only so long as is necessary to protect the minor from risk of suffering serious physical harm or illness.

(c) The minor is suffering serious emotional damage, or is at substantial risk of suffering serious emotional damage, evidenced by severe anxiety, depression, withdrawal, or untoward aggressive behavior toward self or others, as a result of the conduct of the parent or guardian or who has no parent or guardian capable of providing appropriate care. No minor shall be found to be a person described by this subdivision if the willful failure of the parent or guardian to provide adequate mental health treatment is based on a sincerely held religious belief and if a less intrusive judicial intervention is available.

(d) The minor has been sexually abused, or there is a substantial risk that the minor will be sexually abused, as defined in Section 11165.1 of the Penal Code, by his or her parent or guardian or a member of his or her household, or the parent or guardian has failed to adequately protect the minor from sexual abuse when the parent or guardian knew or reasonably should have known that the minor was in danger of sexual abuse.

(e) The minor is under the age of five and has suffered severe physical abuse by a parent, or by any person known by the parent, if the parent knew or reasonably should have known that the person was physically abusing the minor. For the purposes of this subdivision, "severe physical abuse" means any of the following: any single act of abuse which causes physical trauma of sufficient severity that, if left untreated, would cause permanent physical disfigurement, permanent physical disability, or death; any single act of sexual abuse which causes significant bleeding, deep bruising, or significant external or internal swelling; or more than one act of physical abuse, each of which causes bleeding, deep bruising, significant external or internal swelling, bone fracture, or unconsciousness. A minor may not be removed from the physical custody of his or her parent or guardian on the basis of a finding of severe physical abuse unless the probation officer has made an allegation of severe physical abuse pursuant to Section 332.

(f) The minor's parent or guardian has been convicted of causing the death of another child through abuse or neglect.

(g) The minor has been left without any provision for support; the minor's parent has been incarcerated or institutionalized and cannot arrange for the care of the minor; or a relative or other adult custodian with whom the child resides or has been left is unwilling or unable to provide care or support for the child, the whereabouts of the parent is unknown, and reasonable efforts to locate the parent have been unsuccessful.

(h) The minor has been freed for adoption from one or both parents for 12 months by either relinquishment or termination of parental rights or an adoption petition has not been granted.

(i) The minor has been subjected to an act or acts of cruelty by the parent or guardian or a member of his or her household, or the parent or guardian has failed to adequately protect the minor from an act or acts of cruelty when the parent or guardian knew or reasonably should have known that the minor was in danger of being subjected to an act or acts of cruelty.

(j) The minor's sibling has been abused or neglected, as defined in subdivision (a), (b), (d), (e), or (i), and there is a substantial risk that the minor will be abused or neglected, as defined in those subdivisions. The court shall consider the circumstances surrounding the abuse or neglect of the sibling, the age and gender of each child, the nature of the abuse or neglect of the sibling, the mental condition of the parent or guardian, and any other factors the court considers probative in determining whether there is a substantial risk to the minor.

It is the intent of the Legislature in enacting this section to provide maximum protection for children who are currently being physically, sexually, or emotionally abused, being neglected, or being exploited, and to protect children who are at risk of that harm.

This protection includes provision of a full array of social and health services to help the child and family and to prevent reabuse of children. That protection shall focus on the preservation of the family whenever possible. Nothing in this section is intended to disrupt the family unnecessarily or to intrude inappropriately into family life, to prohibit the use of reasonable methods of parental discipline, or to prescribe a particular method of parenting. Further, nothing in this section is intended to limit the offering of voluntary services to those families in need of assistance but who do not come within the descriptions of this section. To the extent that savings accrue to the state from child welfare services funding obtained as a result of the enactment of the act that enacted this section, those savings shall be used to promote services which support family maintenance and family reunification plans, such as client transportation, out-of-home respite care, parenting training, and the provision of temporary or emergency in-home caretakers and persons teaching and demonstrating homemaking skills. The Legislature further declares that a physical disability, such as blindness or deafness, is no bar to the raising of happy and well-adjusted children and that a court's determination pursuant to this section shall center upon whether a parent's disability prevents him or her from exercising care and control.

As used in this section "guardian" means the legal guardian of the child. *(Amended by Stats 1991 ch 1203 §1.5, eff. 1/1/92. Section 300, as amended by Stats 1989 §4, was repealed by Stats 1991 ch 1203 §2, eff. 1/1/92.)*

§300.1. Family reunification services not provided.

Notwithstanding subdivision (e) of Section 361 and Section 16507, family reunification services shall not be provided to a minor adjudged a dependent pursuant to subdivision (h) of Section 300. *(Added by Stats 1987 ch 1485 §6.)*

§300.5. Spiritual treatment of minor.

In any case in which a minor is alleged to come within the provisions of Section 300 on the basis that he or she is in need of medical care, the court, in making such finding, shall give consideration to any treatment being provided to the minor by spiritual means through prayer alone in accordance with the tenets and practices of a recognized church or religious denomination by an accredited practitioner thereof.

§301. Program of supervision of minor.

(a) In any case in which a probation officer after investigation of an application for petition or other investigation he or she is authorized to make, determines that a minor is within the jurisdiction of the juvenile court or will probably soon be within that jurisdiction, the probation officer may, in lieu of filing a petition or subsequent to dismissal of a petition already filed, and with consent of the minor's parent or guardian, undertake a program of supervision of the minor. If a program of supervision is undertaken, the probation officer shall attempt to ameliorate the situation which brings the minor within, or creates the probability that the minor will be within, the jurisdiction of Section 300 by providing or arranging to contract for all appropriate child welfare services pursuant to Sections 16506 and 16507.3, within the time periods specified in those sections. No further

© 1992 by J., B. & L. Gould
Printed in the U.S.A.   EP

child welfare services shall be provided subsequent to these time limits. If the family has refused to cooperate with the services being provided, the probation officer may file a petition with the juvenile court pursuant to Section 332. Nothing in this section shall be construed to prevent the probation officer from filing a petition pursuant to Section 332 when otherwise authorized by law.

(b) The program of supervision of the minor undertaken pursuant to this section may call for the minor to obtain care and treatment for the misuse of, or addiction to, controlled substances from a county mental health service or other appropriate community agency.

(c) Probation departments in counties designated by the department as pilot projects for in-home care programs, pursuant to Section 18964, may place, and shall designate, a projected number of children to be referred each year in these projects. *(Amended and renumbered from section 330 by Stats 1991 ch 1203 §4, eff. 1/1/92. Former section 301 renumbered to section 302.)*

§302. Parental rights.

(a) A juvenile court may assume jurisdiction over a child described in Section 300 regardless of whether the child was in the physical custody of both parents or was in the sole legal or physical custody of only one parent at the time that the events or conditions occurred that brought the child within the jurisdiction of the court.

(b) Unless their parental rights have been terminated, both parents shall be notified of all proceedings involving the child. In any case where the probation officer is required to provide a parent or guardian with notice of a proceeding at which the probation officer intends to present a report, the probation officer shall also provide both parents, whether custodial or noncustodial, or any guardian, or the counsel for the parent or guardian a copy of the report prior to the hearing, either personally or by first-class mail. The probation officer shall not charge any fee for providing a copy of a report required by this subdivision.

(c) When a minor is adjudged a dependent of the juvenile court, any issues regarding custodial rights between his or her parents shall be determined solely by the juvenile court, as specified in Sections 304, 361.2, and 362.4, so long as the minor remains a dependent of the juvenile court. *(Amended and renumbered from section 301 by Stats 1991 ch 1203 §3, eff. 1/1/92.)*

§303. Jurisdiction retained.

The court may retain jurisdiction over any person who is found to be a dependent child of the juvenile court until the ward or dependent child attains the age of 21 years. *(Amended by Stats 1987 ch 1485 §7.)*

§304. Exclusion of superior court.

When a minor has been adjudged a dependent child of the juvenile court pursuant to subdivision (c) of Section 360, no other division of any superior court may hear proceedings pursuant to Section 4600 of the Civil Code regarding the custody of the minor. While the minor is a dependent child of the court all issues regarding his or her custody shall be heard by the juvenile court. In deciding issues between the parents or between a parent and a guardian regarding custody

of a minor who has been adjudicated a dependent of the juvenile court, the juvenile court may review any records that would be available to the domestic relations division of a superior court hearing such a matter. The juvenile court, on its own motion, may issue an order directed to either of the parents enjoining any action specified in paragraph (2) or (3) of subdivision (a) of Section 4359 of the Civil Code. The Judicial Council shall adopt forms for these restraining orders. These form orders shall not be confidential and shall be enforceable in the same manner as any other order issued pursuant to Section 4359 of the Civil Code.

This section shall not be construed to divest the domestic relations division of a superior court from hearing any issues regarding the custody of a minor when that minor is no longer a dependent of the juvenile court. *(Amended by Stats 1989 ch 137 §1, eff. 1/1/90.)*

ARTICLE 7

DEPENDENT CHILDREN — TEMPORARY CUSTODY AND DETENTION

§305. Taking minor into temporary custody without warrant.

Any peace officer may, without a warrant, take into temporary custody a minor:

(a) When the officer has reasonable cause for believing that the minor is a person described in Section 300, and, in addition, that the minor has an immediate need for medical care, or the minor is in immediate danger of physical or sexual abuse, or the physical environment or the fact that the child is left unattended poses an immediate threat to the child's health or safety. In cases in which the child is left unattended, the peace officer shall first attempt to contact the child's parent or guardian to determine if the parent or guardian is able to assume custody of the child. If the parent or guardian cannot be contacted, the peace officer shall notify a social worker in the county welfare department to assume custody of the child.

(b) Who is in a hospital and release of the minor to a parent poses an immediate danger to the child's health or safety.

(c) Who is a dependent child of the juvenile court, or concerning whom an order has been made under Section 319, when the officer has reasonable cause for believing that the minor has violated an order of the juvenile court or has left any placement ordered by the juvenile court.

(d) Who is found in any street or public place suffering from any sickness or injury which requires care, medical treatment, hospitalization, or other remedial care. *(Amended by Stats 1988 ch 701 §2, eff. 8/29/88; ch 1075 §1, eff. 1/1/89.)*

§306. Duty of social worker to take temporary custody of minor.

Any social worker in a county welfare department, while acting within the scope of his or her regular duties under the direction of the juvenile court and pursuant to subdivision (b) of Section 272, may do all of the following:

(a) Receive and maintain, pending investigation, temporary custody of a minor who is described in Section 300, and who has been delivered by a peace officer.

(b) Take into and maintain temporary custody of, without a warrant, a minor who has been declared a dependent child of the juvenile court under Section 300 or who the social worker has reasonable cause to believe is a person described in subdivision (b) or (g) of Section 300, and the social worker has reasonable cause to believe that the minor has an immediate need for medical care or is in immediate danger of physical or sexual abuse or the physical environment poses an immediate threat to the child's health or safety.

Before taking a minor into custody a social worker shall consider whether there are any reasonable services available to the worker which, if provided to the minor's parent, guardian, caretaker, or to the minor, would eliminate the need to remove the minor from the custody of his or her parent, guardian, or caretaker. In addition, the social worker shall also consider whether a referral to public assistance pursuant to Chapter 2 (commencing with Section 11200) of Part 3, Chapter 7 (commencing with Section 14000) of Part 3, Chapter 1 (commencing with Section 17000) of Part 5, and Chapter 10 (commencing with Section 18900) of Part 6, of Division 9 would eliminate the need to take temporary custody of the minor. If those services are available they shall be utilized. *(Amended by Stats 1989 ch 408 §2, eff. 1/1/90.)*

§307. Alternative dispositions of minors.

A peace officer or probation officer who takes a minor into temporary custody under the provisions of Section 305 shall thereafter proceed as follows:

(a) The officer may release the minor.

(b) The officer may prepare in duplicate a written notice for the parent or parents of the minor to appear with the minor before the probation officer of the county in which the minor was taken into custody at a time and place specified in the notice. The notice shall also contain a concise statement of the reasons the minor was taken into custody. The officer shall deliver one copy of the notice to the minor and a parent, guardian, or responsible relative of the minor and may require the minor and the parent, guardian, or relative to sign a written promise that he or she shall appear at the time and place designated in the notice. Upon the execution of the promise to appear, the officer shall immediately release the minor. The officer shall, as soon as practicable, file one copy of the notice with the probation officer.

(c) The officer may take the minor without unnecessary delay before the probation officer of the county in which the minor was taken into custody, or in which the minor resides, or in which the acts take place or the circumstances exist which are alleged to bring the minor within the provisions of Section 300, and deliver the minor into the custody of the probation officer.

In determining which disposition of the minor shall be made, the officer shall give preference to the alternative which least interferes with the parents' or guardians' custody of the minor if this alternative is compatible with the safety of the minor. The officer shall also consider the needs of the minor for the least restrictive environment and the protective needs of the community.

§307.4. Written statements.

(a) Any peace officer, probation officer, or social worker who takes into temporary custody pursuant to Sections 305 to 307, inclusive, a minor who comes within the description of Section 300 shall immediately inform, through the most efficient means available, the parent, guardian, or responsible relative, that the minor has been taken into protective custody and that a written statement is available which explains the parent's or guardian's procedural rights and the preliminary stages of the dependency investigation and hearing. The Judicial Council shall, in consultation with the County Welfare Directors Association of California, adopt a form for the written statement, which shall be in simple language and shall be printed and distributed by the county. The written statement shall be made available for distribution through all public schools, probation offices, and appropriate welfare offices. It shall include, but is not limited to, the following information:

(1) The conditions under which the minor will be released, hearings which may be required, and the means whereby further specific information about the minor's case and conditions of confinement may be obtained.

(2) The rights to counsel, privileges against self-incrimination, and rights to appeal possessed by the minor, and his or her parents, guardians, or responsible relative.

(b) If a good faith attempt was made at notification, the failure on the part of the peace officer, probation officer, or social worker to notify the parent or guardian that the written information required by subdivision (a) is available shall be considered to be due to circumstances beyond the control of the peace officer, probation officer, or social worker, and shall not be construed to permit a new defense to any juvenile or judicial proceeding or to interfere with any rights, procedures, or investigations accorded under any other law. *(Added by Stats 1986 ch 386 §1.)*

§307.5. Taking minor to community service program.

Notwithstanding the provisions of Section 307, an officer who takes a minor suspected of being a person described in Section 300 into temporary custody pursuant to subdivision (a) of Section 305 may, in a case where he or she deems that it is in the best interest of the minor and the public, take the minor to a community service program for abused or neglected children. Organizations or programs receiving referrals pursuant to this section shall have a contract or an agreement with the county to provide shelter care or counseling. Employees of a program receiving referrals pursuant to this section are "child care custodians" for the purpose of the requirements of Section 11165.7 of the Penal Code. The receiving organization shall a take immediate steps to notify the minor's parent, guardian, or a responsible relative of the place to which the minor was taken. *(Amended by Stats 1989 ch 913 §5, eff. 1/1/90.)*

§308. Rights of minor taken into custody.

(a) When a peace officer or social worker takes a minor into custody pursuant to this article, he or she shall take immediate steps to notify the minor's parent, guardian, or a responsible relative that the minor is in custody and the place where he or she is being held, except that, upon order of the juvenile court, the parent or guardian shall not be notified of the exact whereabouts of the minor. The court shall issue such an order only upon a showing that notifying the parent or guardian of the exact whereabouts would

© 1992 by J., B. & L. Gould
Printed in the U.S.A.   EP

endanger the child or his or her foster family or that the parent or guardian is likely to flee with the child. However, if it is impossible or impracticable to obtain a court order authorizing nondisclosure prior to the detention hearing, and if the peace officer or social worker has a reasonable belief that the minor or his or her foster family would be endangered by the disclosure of the minor's exact whereabouts, or that the disclosure would cause the custody of the minor to be disturbed, the peace officer or social worker may refuse to disclose the place where the minor is being held. The county welfare department shall make a diligent and reasonable effort to ensure regular telephone contact between the parent and a child of any age, prior to the detention hearing, unless that contact would be detrimental to the child. The initial telephone contact shall take place as soon as practicable, but no later than five hours after the child is taken into custody. The court shall review any such decision not to disclose the place where the minor is being held at the detention hearing, and shall conduct that review within 24 hours upon the application of a parent, guardian, or a responsible relative.

(b) Immediately after being taken to a place of confinement pursuant to this article and, except where physically impossible, no later than one hour after he or she has been taken into custody, a minor 10 years of age or older shall be advised that he or she has the right to make at least two telephone calls from the place where he or she is being held, one call completed to his or her parent, guardian, or a responsible relative, and another call completed to an attorney. The calls shall be at public expense, if the calls are completed to telephone numbers within the local calling area, and in the presence of a public officer or employee. Any public officer or employee who willfully deprives a minor taken into custody of his or her right to make these telephone calls is guilty of a misdemeanor. *(Amended by Stats 1990 ch 320 §1, eff. 1/1/91.)*

§309. Investigation when minor taken into custody; release.

(a) Upon delivery to the probation officer of a minor who has been taken into temporary custody under this article, the probation officer shall immediately investigate the circumstances of the minor and the facts surrounding the minor's being taken into custody and attempt to maintain the minor with the minor's family through the provision of services. The probation officer shall immediately release the minor to the custody of the minor's parent, guardian, or responsible relative unless one or more of the following conditions exist:

(1) The minor has no parent, guardian, or responsible relative; or the minor's parent, guardian, or responsible relative is not willing to provide care for the minor.

(2) Continued detention of the minor is a matter of immediate and urgent necessity for the protection of the minor and there are no reasonable means by which the minor can be protected in his or her home or the home of a responsible relative.

(3) There is substantial evidence that a parent, guardian, or custodian of the minor is likely to flee the jurisdiction of the court.

(4) The minor has left a placement in which he or she was placed by the juvenile court.

(b) In any case in which there is reasonable cause for believing that a minor who is under the care of a physician or surgeon or a hospital, clinic, or other medical facility and cannot be immediately moved is a person described in Section 300, the minor shall be deemed to have been taken into temporary custody and delivered to the probation officer for the purposes of this chapter while the minor is at the office of the physician or surgeon or the medical facility.

(c) If the minor is not released to his or her parent or guardian, the minor shall be deemed detained for purposes of this chapter. *(Amended by Stats 1989 ch 913 §6, eff. 1/1/90.)*

§310. Release conditional on written promise to appear.

As a condition for the release of such minor, the probation officer may require such minor or his parent, guardian, or relative, or both, to sign a written promise that either or both of them will appear before the probation officer at a suitable place designated by the probation officer at a specified time.

§311. Petition for retention of custody of minor; notice to parents.

(a) If the probation officer determines that the minor shall be retained in custody, he shall immediately file a petition pursuant to Section 332 with the clerk of the juvenile court who shall set the matter for hearing on the detention hearing calendar. The probation officer shall thereupon notify each parent or each guardian of the minor of the time and place of the hearing if the whereabouts of each parent or guardian can be ascertained by due diligence, and the probation officer shall serve those persons entitled to notice of the hearing under the provisions of Section 335 with a copy of the petition and notify these persons of the time and place of the detention hearing. This notice may be given orally and shall be given in this manner if it appears that the parent does not read.

(b) In the hearing the minor, parents or guardians have a privilege against self-incrimination and have a right to confrontation by, and cross-examination of, any person examined by the court as provided in Section 319.

§312. Notice to counsel.

Upon reasonable notification by counsel representing the minor, his parents or guardian, the clerk of the court shall notify such counsel of the hearings in the manner provided for notice to the parent or guardian of the minor under this chapter.

§313. Maximum time minor may be held in custody without petition.

(a) Whenever a minor is taken into custody by a peace officer or probation officer, except when such minor willfully misrepresents himself as 18 or more years of age, such minor shall be released within 48 hours after having been taken into custody, excluding nonjudicial days, unless within said period of time a petition to declare him a dependent child has been filed pursuant to the provisions of this chapter.

(b) Whenever a minor who has been held in custody for more than six hours by the probation officer is subsequently released and no petition is filed, the probation officer shall prepare a written explanation of why the minor was held in custody for more than six hours. The written explanation shall be prepared within 72 hours after the minor is released from custody and filed in the record of the case. A copy of the written explanation shall be sent to the parents, guardian, or other person having care or custody of the minor.

§314. Minor willfully misrepresenting age.

When a minor willfully misrepresents himself to be 18 or more years of age when taken into custody by a peace officer or probation officer, and this misrepresentation effects a material delay in investigation which prevents the filing of a petition pursuant to the provisions of this chapter, such petition or complaint shall be filed within 48 hours from the time his true age is determined, excluding nonjudicial days. If, in such cases, the petition is not filed within the time prescribed by this section, the minor shall be immediately released from custody.

§315. Detention hearing.

If a minor has been taken into custody under this article and not released to a parent or guardian, the juvenile court shall hold a hearing (which shall be referred to as a "detention hearing") to determine whether the minor shall be further detained. This hearing shall be held as soon as possible, but in any event before the expiration of the next judicial day after a petition to declare the minor a dependent child has been filed. If the hearing is not held within the period prescribed by this section, the minor shall be released from custody. *(Added by Stats 1987 ch 1485 §17.)*

§316. Information to and rights to counsel of minor.

Upon his or her appearance before the court at the detention hearing, each parent or guardian and the minor, if present, shall first be informed of the reasons why the minor was taken into custody, the nature of the juvenile court proceedings, and the right of each parent or guardian and any minor to be represented at every stage of the proceedings by counsel. *(Added by Stats 1987 ch 1485 §19.)*

§317. Appointment of counsel when unable to pay; conflict of interest.

(a) When it appears to the court that a parent or guardian of the minor desires counsel but is unable to afford and cannot for that reason employ counsel, the court may appoint counsel.

(b) When it appears to the court that a parent or guardian of the minor is unable to afford and cannot for that reason employ counsel, and the minor has been placed in out-of-home care, or the petitioning agency is recommending that the minor be placed in out-of-home care, the court shall appoint counsel, unless the court finds that the parent or guardian has made a knowing and intelligent waiver of counsel.

(c) In any case in which it appears to the court that the minor would benefit from the appointment of counsel the court shall appoint counsel for the minor. Counsel for the minor may be a county counsel, district attorney, public defender, or other member of the bar, provided that the counsel does not represent another party or county agency whose interests conflict with the minor's. The fact that the district attorney represents the minor in a proceeding pursuant to Section 300 as well as conducts a criminal investigation or files a criminal complaint or information arising from the same or reasonably related set of facts as the proceeding pursuant to Section 300 is not in and of itself a conflict of interest. The court shall determine if representation of both the petitioning agency and the minor constitutes a conflict of interest. If the court finds there is a conflict of interest, separate counsel shall be appointed for the minor. The court may fix the compensation to be paid by the county for the services of appointed counsel, if counsel is not a county counsel, district attorney, or public defender.

(d) The counsel appointed by the court shall represent the parent, guardian, or minor at the detention hearing and at all subsequent proceedings before the juvenile court. Counsel shall continue to represent the parent or minor unless relieved by the court upon the substitution of other counsel or for cause. The representation shall include representing the parent or the minor in termination proceedings and in those proceedings relating to the institution or setting aside of a legal guardianship.

(e) The counsel for the minor shall be charged in general with the representation of the minor's interests. To that end, counsel shall make such further investigations as he or she deems necessary to ascertain the facts, including the interviewing of witnesses, and he or she shall examine and cross-examine witnesses in both the adjudicatory and dispositional hearings; he or she may also introduce and examine his or her own witnesses, make recommendations to the court concerning the minor's welfare, and participate further in the proceedings to the degree necessary to adequately represent the minor. In any case in which the minor is four years of age or older, counsel shall interview the minor to determine the minor's wishes and to assess the minor's well-being. In addition, counsel shall investigate the interests of the minor beyond the scope of the juvenile proceeding and report to the court other interests of the minor that may need to be protected by the institution of other administrative or judicial proceedings. The court shall take whatever appropriate action is necessary to fully protect the interests of the minor.

(f) Notwithstanding any other provision of law, counsel shall be given access to all records relevant to the case which are maintained by state or local public agencies. Counsel shall be given access to records maintained by hospitals or by other medical or nonmedical practitioners or by child care custodians, in the manner prescribed by Section 1158 of the Evidence Code. *(Added by Stats 1987 ch 1485 §21, eff. 1/1/89. Former §317 repealed by Stats 1987 ch 1485 §20.)*

§318. *Repealed by Stats 1987 ch 1485 §§23, 53, 54, eff. 1/1/89.*

§318.5. Representation.

In a juvenile court hearing, where the parent or guardian is represented by counsel, the county counsel or district attorney shall, at the request of the juvenile court judge, appear and participate in the hearing to represent the petitioner. *(Amended and renumbered from section 318 by Stats 1987 ch 56 §181.)*

§319. Initial petition hearing proceedings.

At the initial petition hearing the court shall examine the minor's parents, guardians, or other persons having relevant knowledge and hear the relevant evidence as the minor, the minor's parents or guardians, the petitioner, or their counsel desires to present.

© 1992 by J., B. & L. Gould
Printed in the U.S.A.   **EP**

The court may examine the minor, as provided in Section 350.

The probation officer shall report to the court on the reasons why the minor has been removed from the parent's custody; the need, if any, for continued detention; on the available services and the referral methods to those services which could facilitate the return of the minor to the custody of the minor's parents or guardians; and whether there are any relatives who are able and willing to take temporary custody of the minor. The court shall order the release of the minor from custody unless a prima facie showing has been made that the minor comes within Section 300 and any of the following circumstances exist:

(a) There is a substantial danger to the physical health of the minor or the minor is suffering severe emotional damage, and there are no reasonable means by which the minor's physical or emotional health may be protected without removing the minor from the parents' or guardians' physical custody.

(b) There is substantial evidence that a parent, guardian, or custodian of the minor is likely to flee the jurisdiction of the court.

(c) The minor has left a placement in which he or she was placed by the juvenile court.

(d) The minor indicates an unwillingness to return home, if the minor has been physically or sexually abused by a person residing in the home.

The court shall also make a determination on the record as to whether reasonable efforts were made to prevent or eliminate the need for removal of the minor from his or her home and whether there are available services which would prevent the need for further detention. Services to be considered for purposes of making this determination are case management, counseling, emergency shelter care, emergency in-home caretakers, out-of-home respite care, teaching and demonstrating homemakers, parenting training, transportation, and any other child welfare services authorized by the State Department of Social Services pursuant to Chapter 5 (commencing with Section 16500) of Part 4 of Division 9. The court shall also review whether the social worker has considered whether a referral to public assistance services pursuant to Chapter 2 (commencing with Section 11200) of Part 3, Chapter 7 (commencing with Section 14000) of Part 3, Chapter 1 (commencing with Section 17000) of Part 5, and Chapter 10 (commencing with Section 18900) of Part 6, of Division 9 would have eliminated the need to take temporary custody of the minor or would prevent the need for further detention. If the minor can be returned to the custody of his or her parent or guardian through the provision of those services, the court shall place the minor with his or her parent or guardian and order that the services shall be provided. If the minor cannot be returned to the custody of his or her parent or guardian, the court shall determine if there is a relative who is able and willing to care for the child. Where the first contact with the family has occurred during an emergency situation in which the child could not safely remain at home, even with reasonable services being provided, the court shall make a finding that the lack of preplacement preventive efforts were reasonable. Whenever a court orders a minor detained, the court shall state the facts on which the decision is based, shall specify why the initial removal was necessary, and shall order services to be provided as soon as possible to reunify the minor and his or her family if appropriate.

When the minor is not released from custody the court may order that the minor shall be placed in the suitable home of a relative or in an emergency shelter or other suitable licensed place or a place exempt from licensure designated by the juvenile court or in an appropriate certified family home whose license is pending and all the prelicense requirements for such a placement have been met as subdivision (e) of Section 361.2 for a period not to exceed 15 judicial days.

As used in this section, "relative" means an adult who is related to the minor by blood or affinity, including all relatives whose status is preceded by the words "step," "great," "great-great," or "grand." However, only the following relatives shall be given preferential treatment for placement of the minor: an adult who is a grandparent, aunt, uncle, or a sibling of the minor. *(Amended by Stats 1990 ch 1530 §4, eff. 1/1/91.)*

§319.1. Minors needing special mental health treatment.

When the court finds a minor to be a person described by Section 300, and believes that the minor may need specialized mental health treatment while the minor is unable to reside in his or her natural home, the court shall notify the director of the county mental health department in the county where the minor resides. The county mental health department shall perform the duties required under Section 5697.5 for all those minors.

Nothing in this section shall restrict the provisions of emergency psychiatric services to those minors who are involved in dependency cases and have not yet reached the point of adjudication or disposition, nor shall it operate to restrict evaluations at an earlier stage of the proceedings or to restrict orders removing the minor from a detention facility for psychiatric treatment. *(Added by Stats 1985 ch 1286 §1.6.)*

§321. Rehearing for absence of notice.

When a hearing is held under the provisions of this article and no parent or guardian of the minor is present and no parent or guardian has had actual notice of the hearing, a parent or guardian of the minor may file an affidavit setting forth the facts with the clerk of the juvenile court and the clerk shall immediately set the matter for rehearing at a time within 24 hours, excluding Sundays and nonjudicial days from the filing of the affidavit. Upon the rehearing, the court shall proceed in the same manner as upon the original hearing.

If the minor, a parent or guardian or the minor's attorney or guardian ad litem, if either one or the other has been appointed by the court, requests evidence of the prima facie case, a rehearing shall be held within three judicial days to consider evidence of the prima facie case. If the prima facie case is not established, the minor shall be released from detention.

In lieu of a requested rehearing, the court may set the matter for trial within 10 days.

When the court ascertains that the rehearing cannot be held within three judicial days because of the unavailability of a witness, a reasonable continuance may be granted for a period not to exceed five judicial days.

§322. Continuance for one day.

Upon motion of the minor or a parent or guardian of such minor, the court shall continue any hearing or rehearing held under the provisions of this article for one day, excluding Sundays and nonjudicial days.

§323. Order to reappear; specified time and place.

Upon any hearing or rehearing under the provisions of this article, the court may order such minor or any parent or guardian of such minor who is present in court to again appear before the court, the probation officer or the county financial evaluation officer at a time and place specified in said order. *(Amended by Stats 1985 ch 1485 §7.)*

§324. Custody in foreign county; proceedings.

Whenever any minor is taken into temporary custody under the provisions of this article in any county other than the county in which the minor is alleged to be within or to come within the jurisdiction of the juvenile court, which county is referred to herein as the requesting county, the officer who has taken the minor into temporary custody may notify the law enforcement agency in the requesting county of the fact that the minor is in custody. When a law enforcement officer, of such requesting county files a petition pursuant to Section 332 with the clerk of the juvenile court of his respective county and secures a warrant therefrom, he shall forward said warrant, or a telegraphic copy thereof to the officer who has the minor in temporary custody as soon as possible within 48 hours, excluding Sundays and nonjudicial days, from the time said juvenile was taken into temporary custody. Thereafter an officer from said requesting county shall take custody of the minor within five days, in the county in which the minor is in temporary custody, and shall take the minor before the juvenile court judge who issued the warrant, or before some other juvenile court of the same county without unnecessary delay. If the minor is not brought before a judge of the juvenile court within the period prescribed by this section, he must be released from custody.

ARTICLE 8

**DEPENDENT CHILDREN —
COMMENCEMENT OF PROCEEDINGS**

§325. Filing petition.

A proceeding in the juvenile court to declare a minor a dependent child of the court is commenced by the filing with the court, by the probation officer, of a petition, in conformity with the requirements of this article.

§326. Appointment of guardian ad litem.

For the purposes of Child Abuse Prevention and Treatment Act grants to states (Public Law 93-247), in all cases in which there is filed a petition based upon alleged neglect or abuse of the minor, or in which a prosecution is initiated under the Penal Code arising from neglect or abuse of the minor, the probation officer or a social worker who files a petition under this chapter shall be the guardian ad litem to represent the interests of the minor in proceedings under this chapter, unless the court shall appoint another adult as guardian ad litem. However, the guardian ad litem shall not be the attorney responsible for presenting evidence alleging child abuse or neglect in judicial proceedings. No bond shall be required from any guardian ad litem acting under this section.

§327. Proper court.

Either the juvenile court in the county in which a minor resides or in the county where the minor is found or in the county in which the acts take place or the circumstances exist which are alleged to bring such minor within the provisions of Section 300, is the proper court to commence proceedings under this chapter.

§328. Determination whether child welfare services should be offered or proceedings commenced.

Whenever the probation officer has cause to believe that there was or is within the county, or residing therein, a person described in Section 300, the probation officer shall immediately make any investigation he or she deems necessary to determine whether child welfare services should be offered to the family and whether proceedings in the juvenile court should be commenced. If the probation officer determines that it is appropriate to offer child welfare services to the family, the probation officer shall make a referral to these services pursuant to Chapter 5 (commencing with Section 16500) of Part 4 of Division 9.

However, this section does not require an investigation by the probation officer with respect to a minor delivered or referred to any agency pursuant to Section 307.5.

The probation officer shall interview any minor four years of age or older who is a subject of an investigation, and who is in juvenile hall or other custodial facility, or has been removed to a foster home, to ascertain the minor's view of the home environment. If proceedings are commenced, the probation officer shall include the substance of the interview in any written report submitted at an adjudicatory hearing, or if no report is then received in evidence, the probation officer shall include the substance of the interview in the social study required by Section 358. *(Amended by Stats 1987 ch 1485 §25.)*

§328.3. Written notification of decision.

Whenever any officer refers or delivers a minor pursuant to Section 307.5, the agency to which the minor is referred shall immediately make such investigation as it deems necessary to determine what disposition of the referral or delivery should be made. If the referral agency does not initiate a service program on behalf of a minor referred to the agency within 20 calendar days, or initiate a service program on behalf of a minor delivered to the agency within 10 calendar days, that agency shall immediately notify the referring officer of that decision in writing. The referral agency shall retain a copy of that written notification for 30 days.

§329. Application to probation officer to commence proceedings.

Whenever any person applies to the probation officer to commence proceedings in the juvenile court, such application shall be in the form of an affidavit alleging that there was or is within the county, or residing therein, a minor within the provisions of Section 300, and setting forth facts in support thereof. The probation officer shall immediately make such investigation as he deems necessary to determine whether proceedings in the juvenile court should be commenced. If the probation officer does not take action under Section 330 and does not file a petition in the juvenile court within three weeks after such application, he shall endorse upon the affidavit of applicant his decision not to proceed further and his

© 1992 by J., B. & L. Gould
Printed in the U.S.A.   **EP**

reasons therefor and shall immediately notify the applicant of the action taken or the decision rendered by him under this section. The probation officer shall retain the affidavit and his endorsement thereon for a period of 30 days after such notice to applicant.

§330. *Amended and renumbered to section 301 by Stats 1991 ch 1203 §4, eff. 1/1/92.*

§331. Failure to file petition to commence juvenile court proceedings.

When any person has applied to the probation officer, pursuant to Section 329, to commence juvenile court proceedings and the probation officer fails to file a petition within three weeks after such application, such person may, within one month after making such application, apply to the juvenile court to review the decision of the probation officer, and the court may either affirm the decision of the probation officer or order him to commence juvenile court proceedings.

§331.5. Review of decision.

When any officer has referred or delivered a minor to an agency pursuant to Section 307.5, and that agency does not initiate a service program for the minor within the time periods required by Section 328.3, the referring agency may, within 10 court days following receipt of the notification from the referral agency, apply to the probation officer for a review of that decision.

§332. Verification and contents of petition.

A petition to commence proceedings in the juvenile court to declare a minor a ward or a dependent child of the court shall be verified and shall contain all of the following:

(a) The name of the court to which it is addressed.

(b) The title of the proceeding.

(c) The code section and the subdivision under which the proceedings are instituted. If it is alleged that the minor is a person described by subdivision (e) of Section 300, the petition shall include an allegation pursuant to that section.

(d) The name, age, and address, if any, of the minor upon whose behalf the petition is brought.

(e) The names and residence addresses, if known to the petitioner, of both parents and any guardian of the minor. If there is no parent or guardian residing within the state, or if his or her place of residence is not known to the petitioner, the petition shall also contain the name and residence address, if known, of any adult relative residing within the county, or, if there is none, the adult relative residing nearest to the location of the court.

(f) A concise statement of facts, separately stated, to support the conclusion that the minor upon whose behalf the petition is being brought is a person within the definition of each of the sections and subdivisions under which the proceedings are being instituted.

(g) The fact that the minor upon whose behalf the petition is brought is detained in custody or is not detained in custody, and if he or she is detained in custody, the date and the precise time the minor was taken into custody.

(h) A notice to the father, mother, spouse, or other person liable for support of the minor child, of all of the following: (1) Section 903 makes that person, the estate of that person, and the estate of the minor child, liable for the cost of the care, support, and mainte-nance of the minor child in any county institution or any other place in which the child is placed, detained, or committed pursuant to an order of the juvenile court; (2) Section 903.1 makes that person, the estate of that person, and the estate of the minor child, liable for the cost to the county of legal services rendered to the minor or the parent by a private attorney or a public defender appointed pursuant to the order of the juvenile court; (3) Section 903.2 makes that person, the estate of that person, and the estate of the minor child, liable for the cost to the county of the probation supervision of the minor child by the probation officer pursuant to the order of the juvenile court; and (4) the liabilities established by these sections are joint and several. *(Amended by Stats 1990 ch 1530 §5, eff. 1/1/91.)*

§332.5. Proceedings in demonstration counties.

A petition to commence proceedings in the juvenile court of a demonstration county to declare a minor a dependent child of the court shall be verified and must contain:

(a) The name of the court to which the same is addressed.

(b) The title of the proceeding.

(c) The code section or sections and subdivision or subdivisions under which the proceedings are instituted.

(d) The name, age, and address, if any, of the minor upon whose behalf the petition is brought.

(e) The name or names and residence address, if known to the petitioner, of all parents or guardians of such minor. If there is no parent or guardian residing within the state, or if his place of residence is not known to the petitioner, the petition must also contain the name and residence address, if known, of any adult relative residing within the county, or, if there be none, the adult relative residing nearest to the location of the court.

(f) A concise statement of facts, separately stated, to support the conclusion that the minor upon whose behalf the petition is being brought is a person within the definition of Section 300 or 302.

(g) The fact that the minor upon whose behalf the petition is brought is detained in custody or is not detained in custody, and if he is detained in custody, the date and the precise time the minor was taken into custody.

§333. Unverified petition; dismissal.

Any petition filed in juvenile court to commence proceedings pursuant to this chapter that is not verified may be dismissed without prejudice by such court.

§334. Setting petition for hearing; time.

Upon the filing of the petition, the clerk of the juvenile court shall set the same for hearing within 30 days, except that in the case of a minor detained in custody at the time of the filing of the. petition, the petition must be set for hearing within 15 judicial days from the date of the order of the court directing such detention.

§335. Notice of hearing; issuance.

(a) Upon the filing of the petition, the clerk of the juvenile court shall issue a notice, to which shall be attached a copy of the petition, and he or she shall cause the same to be served upon the minor, if the minor is 10 or more years of age, and upon each of the persons described in subdivision (e) of Section 332 whose residence addresses are set forth in the petition and thereafter before the hearing upon all such persons whose residence addresses become known to the clerk. The clerk shall issue a copy of the petition to the attorney for the minor's parent or guardian and to the district attorney, if the district attorney has notified the clerk of the court that he or she wishes to receive the petition, containing the time, date, and place of the hearing.

(b) If the minor is a ward of a guardian appointed pursuant to the Probate Code, the clerk of the juvenile court shall notify the probate department of the superior court which appointed the guardian of the proceedings in the juvenile court. The probation department or counsel for the minor, if any, may petition the probate department of the superior court to have the guardian removed pursuant to Chapter 9 (commencing with Section 2650) of Part 4 of Division 4 of the Probate Code. *(Amended by Stats 1988 ch 1075 §2, eff. 1/1/89.)*

§336. Contents of notice of hearing.

The notice shall contain all of the following:

(a) The name and address of the person to whom the notice is directed.

(b) The date, time, and place of the hearing on the petition.

(c) The name of the minor upon whose behalf the petition has been brought.

(d) Each section and subdivision under which the proceeding has been instituted.

(e) A statement that the parent or guardian or adult relative to whom notice is required to be given, and the minor, are entitled to have an attorney present at the hearing on the petition, and that, if the parent or guardian or an adult relative is indigent and cannot afford an attorney, and desires to be represented by an attorney, the parent or guardian or adult relative shall promptly notify the clerk of the juvenile court, and that in the event counsel or legal assistance is furnished by the court, the parent or guardian or adult relative shall be liable to the county, to the extent of his, her, or their financial ability, for all or a portion of the cost thereof.

(f) A statement that the parent or guardian or responsible relative may be liable for the costs of support of the minor in a county institution. *(Amended by Stats 1987 ch 1485 §28.)*

§337. Service of notice.

(a) Except as provided in subdivision (b), if the minor is detained the clerk of the juvenile court shall cause the notice and copy of the petition to be served on all persons required to receive such notice and copy of the petition, either personally or by certified mail with request for return receipt, as soon as possible after filing of the petition and at least five days prior to the time set for hearing, unless such hearing is set less than five days from the filing of the petition, in which case, such notice and copy of the petition shall be served at least 24 hours prior to the time set for hearing.

(b) If the minor is detained, and all persons entitled to notice were present at the detention hearing, the clerk of the juvenile court shall cause the notice and copy of the petition to be served on all persons required to receive the notice and copy of the petition,

either personally or by first-class mail, as soon as possible after the filing of the petition and at least five days prior to the time set for hearing, unless the hearing is set less than five days from the filing of the petition, in which case the notice and copy of the petition shall be served at least 24 hours prior to the time set for the hearing.

(c) If the minor is not detained the clerk of the juvenile court shall cause the notice and copy of the petition to be served on all persons required to receive such notice and copy of the petition, either personally or by first-class mail, at least 10 days prior to the time set for hearing. If such person is known to reside outside of the county, the clerk of the juvenile court shall mail the notice and copy of the petition by first-class mail, to such person, as soon as possible after filing of the petition and at least 10 days before the time set for hearing. Failure to respond to the notice shall in no way result in arrest or detention. In the instance of failure to appear after notice by first-class mail, the court shall direct that the notice and copy of the petition is to be personally served on all persons required to receive such notice and copy of the petition. Personal service of the notice and copy of the petition outside of the county at least 10 days before the time set for hearing is equivalent to such service by first-class mail. Service may be waived by any person by a voluntary appearance entered in the minutes of the court or by a written waiver of service filed with the clerk of the court at or prior to the hearing.

§338. Issuance of citation.

In addition to the notice provided in Sections 335 and 336 the juvenile court may issue its citation directing any parent or guardian of the person concerning whom a petition has been filed to appear at the time and place set for any hearing or financial evaluation under the provisions of this chapter, including a hearing under the provisions of Section 257, and directing any person having custody or control of the minor concerning whom the petition has been filed to bring such minor with him or her. The notice shall in addition state that a parent or guardian may be required to participate in a counseling program with the minor concerning whom the petition has been filed. Personal service of such citation shall be made at least 24 hours before the time stated therein for such appearance. *(Amended by Stats 1985 ch 1485 §9.)*

§339. Arrest warrant against parent, guardian, etc.

In case such citation cannot be served, or the person served fails to obey it, or in any case in which it appears to the court that the citation will probably be ineffective, a warrant of arrest may issue on the order of the court either against the parent, or guardian, or the person having the custody of the minor, or with whom the minor is living.

§340. Arrest warrant against minor.

Whenever a petition has been filed in the juvenile court alleging that a minor comes within Section 300 and praying for a hearing thereon, or whenever any subsequent petition has been filed praying for a hearing in the matter of the minor and it appears to the court that the circumstances of his or her home environment may endanger the health, person, or welfare of the minor, or whenever a dependent minor has run away from his or her court ordered placement, a

© 1992 by J., B. & L. Gould
Printed in the U.S.A.   **EP**

protective custody warrant may be issued immediately for the minor. *(Amended by Stats 1987 ch 1485 §29.)*

§340.5. Parents of dependent child; threatening social worker.

(a) Whenever pursuant to Article 10 (commencing with Section 360) a social worker is assigned to provide child welfare services, family reunification services, or other services to a dependent child of the juvenile court, the juvenile court may, for good cause shown and after an ex parte hearing, issue its order restraining the parents of the dependent child from threatening the social worker, or any member of the social worker's family, with physical harm.

(b) For purposes of this section, "good cause" means at least one threat of physical harm to the social worker, or any member of the social worker's family, made by the person who is to be the subject of the restraining order, with the apparent ability to carry out the threat.

(c) Violation of a restraining order issued pursuant to this section shall be punishable as contempt. *(Added by Stats 1991 ch 980 §1, eff. 1/1/92.)*

§341. Issuing subpoenas.

Upon request of the probation officer, district attorney, the minor or the minor's parent, guardian, or custodian, or upon its own motion, the court or the clerk of the court, or an attorney, pursuant to Section 1985 of the Code of Civil Procedure shall issue subpoenas requiring attendance and testimony of witnesses and production of papers at any hearing under the provisions of this chapter. When a person attends a juvenile court hearing as a witness upon a subpoena at its discretion, the court may by an order on its minutes, direct the county auditor to draw his warrant upon the county treasurer in favor of such witness for witness fees in the amount and manner prescribed by Section 68093 of the Government Code. Such fees are county charges.

§342. Filing a subsequent petition.

In any case in which a minor has been found to be a person described by Section 300 and the petitioner alleges new facts or circumstances, other than those under which the original petition was sustained, sufficient to state that the minor is a person described in Section 300, the petitioner shall file a subsequent petition. This section does not apply if the jurisdiction of the juvenile court has been terminated prior to the new allegations.

All procedures and hearings required for an original petition are applicable to a subsequent petition filed under this section. *(Amended by Stats 1988 ch 1075 §3.)*

ARTICLE 9

DEPENDENT CHILDREN — HEARINGS

§345. Special or separate session.

All cases under this chapter shall be heard at a special or separate session of the court, and no other matter shall be heard at such a session. No person on trial, awaiting trial, or under accusation of crime, other than a parent, guardian, or relative of the minor, shall be permitted to be present at any such session, except as a witness.

Cases in which the minor is detained and the sole allegation is that the minor is a person described in Section 300 shall be granted precedence on the calendar of the court for the day on which the case is set for hearing. *(Amended by Stats 1987 ch 1485 §31.)*

§346. Exclusion of public.

Unless requested by a parent or guardian and consented to or requested by the minor concerning whom the petition has been filed, the public shall not be admitted to a juvenile court hearing. The judge or referee may nevertheless admit such persons as he deems to have a direct and legitimate interest in the particular case or the work of the court.

§347. Duties of court reporter.

At any juvenile court hearing conducted by a juvenile court judge, an official court reporter shall, and at any such hearing conducted by a juvenile court referee, the official reporter, as directed by the court, may take down in shorthand all the testimony and all of the statements and remarks of the judge and all persons appearing at the hearing; and, if directed by the judge, or requested by the person on whose behalf the petition was brought, or by his parent or legal guardian, or the attorneys of such persons, he must, within such reasonable time after the hearing of the petition as the court may designate, write out the same or such specific portions thereof as may be requested in plain or legible long-hand or by typewriter or other printing machine and certify to the same as being correctly reported and transcribed, and when directed by the court, file the same with the clerk of the court. Unless otherwise directed by the judge, the costs of writing out and transcribing all or any portion of the reporter's short-hand notes shall be paid in advance at the rates fixed for transcriptions in a civil action by the person requesting the same.

§348. Application of provisions relating to variance and amendment of pleadings.

The provisions of Chapter 8 (commencing with Section 469) of Title 6 of Part 2 of the Code of Civil Procedure relating to variance and amendment of pleadings in civil actions shall apply to petitions and proceedings under this chapter, to the same extent and with the same effect as if proceedings under this chapter were civil actions.

§349. Parties present at hearing; right to representation.

A minor who is the subject of a juvenile court hearing and any person entitled to notice of the hearing under the provisions of Section 335, is entitled to be present at such hearing. Any such minor and any such person has the right to be represented at such hearing by counsel of his own choice.

§350. Judge's control of proceedings.

(a) The judge of the juvenile court shall control all proceedings during the hearings with a view to the expeditious and effective ascertainment of the jurisdictional facts and the ascertainment of all information relative to the present condition and future welfare of the person upon whose behalf the petition is brought. Except where there is a contested issue of fact or law, the proceedings shall be conducted in an informal nonadversary atmosphere with a view to obtaining the maximum cooperation of the minor upon whose behalf the petition is brought and all persons interested in his or her welfare with such provisions as the court may make for the disposition and care of the minor.

(b) The testimony of a minor may be taken in chambers and outside the presence of the minor's parent or parents, if the minor's parent or parents are represented by counsel, the counsel is present and any of the following circumstances exist:

(1) The court determines that testimony in chambers is necessary to ensure truthful testimony.

(2) The minor is likely to be intimidated by a formal courtroom setting.

(3) The minor is afraid to testify in front of his or her parent or parents.

After testimony in chambers, the parent or parents of the minor may elect to have the court reporter read back the testimony or have the testimony summarized by counsel for the parent or parents.

The testimony of a minor also may be taken in chambers and outside the presence of the guardian or guardians of a minor under the circumstances specified in this subdivision.

(c) At any hearing in which the probation department bears the burden of proof, after the presentation of evidence on behalf of the probation department has been closed, the court, on motion of the minor, parent or guardian, or on its own motion, shall order whatever action the law requires of it if the court, upon weighing the evidence then before it, finds that the probation department has not met its burden. That action includes, but is not limited to, the dismissal of the petition and release of the minor at a jurisdictional hearing, the return of the minor at an out-of-home review held prior to the permanency planning hearing, or the termination of jurisdiction at an in-home review. If the motion is not granted, the minor, parent, or guardian may offer evidence without first having reserved that right. *(Amended by Stats 1987 ch 1485 §32.)*

§351. *Amended and renumbered to section 318 by Stats 1986 ch 1122.*

§351.5. Petitioner's counsel.

In a juvenile court hearing in a demonstration county the district attorney or county counsel shall, with the consent or at the request of the juvenile court judge or welfare department, represent the petitioner and shall assist in the ascertaining and presenting of the evidence.

§352. Continuance of hearing.

(a) Upon request of counsel for the parent, guardian, minor, or petitioner, the court may continue any hearing under this chapter beyond the time limit within which the hearing is otherwise required to be held, provided that no continuance shall be granted that is contrary to the interest of the minor. In considering the minor's interests, the court shall give substantial weight to a minor's need for prompt resolution of his or her custody status, the need to provide children with stable environments, and the damage to a minor of prolonged temporary placements.

Continuances shall be granted only upon a showing of good cause and only for that period of time shown to be necessary by the evidence presented at the hearing on the motion for the continuance. Neither a stipulation between counsel nor the convenience of the parties is in and of itself a good cause. Further, neither a pending criminal prosecution nor family law matter shall be considered in and of itself as good cause. Whenever any continuance is granted, the facts proven which require the continuance shall be entered upon the minutes of the court.

In order to obtain a motion for a continuance of the hearing, written notice shall be filed at least two court days prior to the date set for hearing, together with affidavits or declarations detailing specific facts showing that a continuance is necessary, unless the court for good cause entertains an oral motion for continuance.

(b) Notwithstanding any other provision of law, if a minor has been removed from the parents' or guardians' custody, no continuance shall be granted that would result in the dispositional hearing, held pursuant to Section 361, being completed longer than 60 days after the hearing at which the minor was ordered removed or detained, unless the court finds that there are exceptional circumstances requiring such a continuance. The facts supporting such a continuance shall be entered upon the minutes of the court. In no event shall the court grant continuances that would cause the hearing pursuant to Section 361 to be completed more than six months after the hearing pursuant to Section 319.

(c) In any case in which the parent, guardian, or minor is represented by counsel and no objection is made to an order continuing any such hearing beyond the time limit within which the hearing is otherwise required to be held, the absence of such an objection shall be deemed a consent to the continuance. The consent does not affect the requirements of subdivision (a). *(Amended by Stats 1986 ch 1122 §8.)*

§353. Reading of petition.

At the beginning of the hearing on a petition filed pursuant to Article 8 (commencing with Section 325) of this chapter, the judge or clerk shall first read the petition to those present. Upon request of any parent, guardian, or adult relative, counsel for the minor, or the minor, if he or she is present, the judge shall explain any term of allegation contained therein and the nature of the hearing, its procedures, and possible consequences. The judge shall ascertain whether the parent, guardian, or adult relative and, when required by Section 317, the minor have been informed of their right to be represented by counsel, and if not, the judge shall advise those persons, if present, of the right to have counsel present and where applicable, of the right to appointed counsel. If such a person is unable to afford counsel and desires to be represented by counsel, the court shall appoint counsel in accordance with Section 317. The court shall continue the hearing for not to exceed seven days, as necessary to make an appointment of counsel, or to enable counsel to acquaint himself or herself with the case, or to determine whether the parent or guardian or adult relative is unable to afford counsel at his or her own expense, and shall continue the hearing as necessary to provide reasonable opportunity for the minor and the parent or guardian or adult relative to prepare for the hearing. *(Amended by Stats 1989 ch 913 §7, eff. 1/1/90.)*

§353.5. Reading of the petition in a demonstration county.

In a demonstration county, at the beginning of the hearing on a petition filed pursuant to Article 8 (com-

© 1992 by J., B. & L. Gould
Printed in the U.S.A.   EP

mencing with Section 325) of this chapter, the judge or clerk shall first read the petition to those present and upon request of the minor upon whose behalf the petition has been brought or upon the request of any parent, relative or guardian, the judge shall explain any term or allegation contained therein and the nature of the hearing, its procedures, and possible consequences. The judge shall ascertain whether the minor and his parent or guardian or adult relative, as the case may be, has been informed of the right of the minor and parents or guardian to be represented by counsel, and if not, the judge shall advise the minor and such person, if present, of the right to have counsel present and where applicable, of the right to appointed counsel. Before proceeding further, the court, in a case in which the minor is alleged to be within the provisions of Section 300 or 302, shall first comply with the provisions of Section 318.5. The court shall continue the hearing for not to exceed seven days, as necessary to make an appointment of counsel, or to enable counsel to acquaint himself with the case, or to determine whether the parent or guardian or adult relative is unable to afford counsel at his own expense, and shall continue the hearing as necessary to provide reasonable opportunity for the minor and the parent or guardian or adult relative to prepare for the hearing.

§354. Continuance of hearing on petition.

Except where a minor is in custody, any hearing on a petition filed pursuant to Article 8 (commencing with Section 325) of this chapter may be continued by the court for not more than 10 days in addition to any other continuance authorized in this chapter whenever the court is satisfied that an unavailable and necessary witness will be available within such time.

§355. Questions to be determined; evidence.

At the jurisdictional hearing, the court shall first consider only the question whether the minor is a person described by Section 300, and for this purpose, any matter or information relevant and material to the circumstances or acts which are alleged to bring him or her within the jurisdiction of the juvenile court is admissible and may be received in evidence. However, proof by a preponderance of evidence, legally admissible in the trial of civil cases must be adduced to support a finding that the minor is a person described by Section 300. If the parent or guardian is not represented by counsel at the hearing, it shall be deemed that objections that could have been made to the evidence were made. *(Amended by Stats 1987 ch 1485 §34.)*

§355.1. Injury as result of neglectful acts.

(a) Where the court finds, based upon competent professional evidence, that an injury, injuries, or detrimental condition sustained by a minor, of such a nature as would ordinarily not be sustained except as the result of the unreasonable or neglectful acts or omissions of either parent, the guardian, or other person who has the care or custody of the minor, that evidence shall be prima facie evidence that the minor is a person described by subdivision (a), (b), or (d) of Section 300.

(b) Proof that either parent, the guardian, or other person who has the care or custody of a minor who is the subject of a petition filed under Section 300, has physically abused, neglected, or cruelly treated another minor shall be admissible in evidence.

(c) The presumption created by subdivision (a) constitutes a presumption affecting the burden of producing evidence.

(d) Testimony by a parent, guardian, or other person who has the care or custody of the minor made the subject of a proceeding under Section 300 shall not be admissible as evidence in any other action or proceeding. *(Amended by Stats 1987 ch 1485 §35.)*

§356. Finding.

After hearing the evidence, the court shall make a finding, noted in the minutes of the court, whether or not the minor is a person described by Section 300 and the specific subdivisions of Section 300 under which the petition is sustained. If it finds that the minor is not such a person, it shall order that the petition be dismissed and the minor be discharged from any detention or restriction theretofore ordered. If the court finds that the minor is such a person, it shall make and enter its findings and order accordingly. *(Added by Stats 1986 ch 1122 §9.)*

§356.5. Duties and responsibilities of child advocate.

A child advocate appointed by the court to represent the interests of a dependent child in a proceeding under this chapter shall have the same duties and responsibilities as a guardian ad litem and shall be trained by and function under the auspices of a court appointed special advocate guardian ad litem program, formed and operating under the guidelines established by the National Court Appointed Special Advocate Association. *(Amended by Stats 1985 ch 1341 §2.)*

§357. Order placing minor in psychopathic ward of county hospital.

Whenever the court, before or during the hearing on the petition, is of the opinion that the minor is mentally ill or if the court is in doubt concerning the mental health of any such person, the court may order that such person be held temporarily in the psychopathic ward of the county hospital or hospital whose services have been approved and/or contracted for by the department of health of the county, for observation and recommendation concerning the future care, supervision, and treatment of such person.

§358. Evidence on question of proper disposition.

(a) After finding that a minor is a person described in Section 300, the court shall hear evidence on the question of the proper disposition to be made of the minor. Prior to making a finding required by this section, the court may continue the hearing on its own motion, the motion of the parent or guardian, or the motion of the minor, as follows:

(1) If the minor is detained during the continuance, and the probation officer is not alleging that subdivision (b) of Section 361.5 is applicable, the continuance shall not exceed 10 judicial days. The court may make such order for detention of the minor or for the minor's release from detention, during the period of continuance, as is appropriate.

(2) If the minor is not detained during the continuance, the continuance shall not exceed 30 days after the date of the finding pursuant to Section 356. However, the court may, for cause, continue the hearing for an additional 15 days.

(3) If the probation officer is alleging that subdivision (b) of Section 361.5 is applicable, the court shall continue the proceedings for a period not to exceed 30 days. The probation officer shall notify each parent of the content of subdivision (b) of Section 361.5 and shall inform each parent that if the court does not order reunification a permanency planning hearing will be held, and that his or her parental rights may be terminated within the time frames specified by law.

(b) Before determining the appropriate disposition, the court shall receive in evidence the social study of the minor made by the probation officer, any study or evaluation made by a child advocate appointed by the court, and such other relevant and material evidence as may be offered. In any judgment and order of disposition, the court shall specifically state that the social study made by the probation officer and the study or evaluation made by the child advocate appointed by the court, if there be any, has been read and considered by the court in arriving at its judgment and order of disposition. Any social study or report submitted to the court by the probation officer shall include the individual child's case plan developed pursuant to Section 16501.1.

(c) If the court finds that a minor is described by subdivision (h) of Section 300 or that subdivision (b) of Section 361.5 may be applicable, the court shall conduct the dispositional proceeding pursuant to subdivision (c) of Section 361.5. *(Amended by Stats 1991 ch 1203 §5, eff. 1/1/92.)*

§358.1. Social studies.

Each social study or evaluation made by a probation officer or child advocate appointed by the court, required to be received in evidence pursuant to Section 358 shall include, but not be limited to, a factual discussion of each of the following subjects:

(a) Whether the county welfare department or probation officer has considered child protective services, as defined in Chapter 5 (commencing with Section 16500) of Part 4 of Division 9, as a possible solution to the problems at hand, and has offered these services to qualified parents if appropriate under the circumstances.

(b) What plan, if any, for return of the child is recommended to the court by the county welfare department or probation officer.

(c) Whether the best interests of the minor will be served by granting reasonable visitation rights with the minor to his or her grandparents, in order to maintain and strengthen the minor's family relationships.

(d) Whether the subject child appears to be a person who is eligible to be considered for further court action to free the child from parental custody and control. *(Amended by Stats 1989 ch 913 §8, eff. 1/1/90.)*

§359. Minor dangerous to self or others from use of narcotics or drugs.

Whenever a minor who appears to be a danger to himself or others as a result of the use of narcotics (as defined in Section 11001 of the Health and Safety Code), or a restricted dangerous drug (as defined in Section 11901 of the Health and Safety Code), is brought before any judge of the juvenile court, the judge may continue the hearing and proceed pursuant to this section. The court may order the minor taken to a facility designated by the county and approved by the State Department of Mental Health as a facility for 72-hour treatment and evaluation. Thereupon the provisions of Section 11922 of the Health and Safety Code shall apply, except that the professional person in charge of the facility shall make a written report to the court concerning the results of the evaluation of the minor.

If the professional person in charge of the facility for 72-hour evaluation and treatment reports to the juvenile court that the minor is not a danger to himself or others as a result of the use of narcotics or restricted dangerous drugs or that the minor does not require 14-day intensive treatment, or if the minor has been certified for not more than 14 days of intensive treatment and the certification is terminated, the minor shall be released if the juvenile court proceedings have been dismissed; referred for further care and treatment on a voluntary basis, subject to the disposition of the juvenile court proceedings; or returned to the juvenile court, in which event the court shall proceed with the case pursuant to this chapter.

Any expenditure for the evaluation or intensive treatment of a minor under this section shall be considered an expenditure made under Part 2 (commencing with Section 5600) of Division 5, and shall be reimbursed by the state as are other local expenditures pursuant to that part.

ARTICLE 10

DEPENDENT CHILDREN — JUDGMENTS AND ORDERS

§360. Alternatives.

After receiving and considering the evidence on the proper disposition of the case, the juvenile court may enter judgment as follows:

(a) If the court finds that the minor is a person described by Section 300, it may, without adjudicating the minor a dependent child of the court, order that services be provided to keep the family together and place the minor and the minor's parent or guardian under the supervision of the probation officer for a time period consistent with Section 301.

(b) If the family subsequently is unable or unwilling to cooperate with the services being provided, the probation officer may file a petition with the juvenile court pursuant to Section 332 alleging that a previous petition has been sustained and that disposition pursuant to subdivision (a) has been ineffective in ameliorating the situation requiring the child welfare services. Upon hearing the petition, the court shall order either that the petition shall be dismissed or that a new disposition hearing shall be held pursuant to subdivision (c).

(c) If the court finds that the minor is a person described by Section 300, it may order and adjudge the minor to be a dependent child of the court. *(Amended by Stats 1991 ch 1203 §6, eff. 1/1/92.)*

§360.5. Entry of judgment by court.

After receiving and considering the evidence on the proper disposition of the case, the juvenile court of a demonstration county may enter judgment as follows:

(a) If the court has found that the minor is a person described in Section 300, it may, without adjudging such minor a dependent child of the court, order that services be provided to keep the family together and place the minor and his parents or guardians under

© 1992 by J., B. & L. Gould
Printed in the U.S.A.   EP

the supervision of the probation officer or social worker in a county welfare department designated pursuant to Section 272 for a period not to exceed six months.

(b) If the court has found that the minor is a person described by Section 300, it may order and adjudge the minor to be a dependent child of the court.

§361. Limitation of parental control by court.

(a) In all cases in which a minor is adjudged a dependent child of the court on the ground that the minor is a person described by Section 300, the court may limit the control to be exercised over the dependent child by any parent or guardian and shall by its order clearly and specifically set forth all such limitations. Any limitation on the right of the parent or guardian to make educational decisions for the child shall be specifically addressed in the court order. The limitations shall not exceed those necessary to protect the child.

(b) No dependent child shall be taken from the physical custody of his or her parents or guardian or guardians with whom the child resides at the time the petition was initiated unless the juvenile court finds clear and convincing evidence of any of the following:

(1) There is a substantial danger to the physical health of the minor or would be if the minor was returned home, and there are no reasonable means by which the minor's physical health can be protected without removing the minor from the minor's parents' or guardians' physical custody. The fact that a minor has been adjudicated a dependent child of the court pursuant to subdivision (e) of Section 300 shall constitute prima facie evidence that the minor cannot be safely left in the custody of the parent or guardian with whom the minor resided at the time of injury.

(2) The parent or guardian of the minor is unwilling to have physical custody of the minor, and the parent or guardian has been notified that if the minor remains out of their physical custody for the period specified in Section 366.25 or 366.26, the minor may be declared permanently free from their custody and control.

(3) The minor is suffering severe emotional damage, as indicated by extreme anxiety, depression, withdrawal, or untoward aggressive behavior toward self or others, and there are no reasonable means by which the minor's emotional health may be protected without removing the minor from the physical custody of his or her parent or guardian.

(4) The minor has been sexually abused by a parent, guardian, or member of his or her household, or other person known to his or her parent, and there are no reasonable means by which the minor can be protected from further sexual abuse without removing the minor from his or her parent or guardian, or the minor does not wish to return to his or her parent or guardian.

(5) The minor has been left without any provision for his or her support, or a parent who has been incarcerated or institutionalized cannot arrange for the care of the minor, or a relative or other adult custodian with whom the child has been left by the parent is unwilling or unable to provide care or support for the child and the whereabouts of the parent is unknown and reasonable efforts to locate him or her have been unsuccessful.

(c) The court shall make a determination as to whether reasonable efforts were made to prevent or to eliminate the need for removal of the minor from his or her home or, if the minor is removed for one of the reasons stated in paragraph (5) of subdivision (b), whether it was reasonable under the circumstances not to make any such efforts. The court shall state the facts on which the decision to remove the minor is based.

(d) The court shall make all of the findings required by subdivision (a) of Section 366 in either of the following circumstances:

(1) The minor has been taken from the custody of his or her parents or guardians and has been living in an out-of-home placement pursuant to Section 319.

(2) The minor has been living in a voluntary out-of-home placement pursuant to Section 16507.4. *(Amended by Stats 1990 ch 182 §7, eff. 1/1/91.)*

§361.2. Placing minor in custody of parent.

(a) When a court orders removal of a minor pursuant to Section 361, the court shall first determine whether there is a parent of the minor, with whom the minor was not residing at the time that the events or conditions arose that brought the minor within the provisions of Section 300, who desires to assume custody of the minor. If such a parent requests custody the court shall place the minor with the parent unless it finds that placement with that parent would be detrimental to the minor.

If the court places the minor with such a parent it may do either of the following:

(1) Order that such parent become legal and physical custodian of the child. The court may also provide reasonable visitation by the noncustodial parent. The court shall then terminate its jurisdiction over the minor. The custody order shall continue unless modified by a subsequent order of the superior court. The order of the juvenile court shall be filed in any domestic relation proceeding between the parents.

(2) Order that the parent assume custody subject to the supervision of the juvenile court. In such a case the court may order that reunification services be provided to the parent or guardian from whom the minor is being removed, or the court may order that services be provided solely to the parent who is assuming physical custody in order to allow that parent to retain later custody without court supervision, or that services be provided to both parents, in which case the court shall determine, at review hearings held pursuant to Section 366, which parent, if either, shall have custody of the minor.

(b) When the court orders removal pursuant to Section 361, the court shall order the care, custody, control, and conduct of the minor to be under the supervision of the probation officer who may place the minor in any of the following:

(1) The home of a relative, including a noncustodial parent.

(2) A foster home in which the child has been placed before an interruption in foster care, if that placement is in the best interest of the child and space is available.

(3) A suitable licensed community care facility.

(4) With a foster family agency to be placed in a suitable licensed foster family home or certified family home which has been certified by the agency as meeting licensing standards.

(5) A home or facility in accordance with the federal Indian Child Welfare Act.

(c) If the minor is taken from the physical custody of the minor's parents or guardians and unless the minor is placed with relatives, the minor shall be placed in foster care in the county of residence of the minor's parents or guardians in order to facilitate reunification of the family.

In the event that there are no appropriate placements available in the parents' or guardians' county, a placement may be made in an appropriate place in another county, preferably a county located adjacent to the parents' or guardians' community of residence.

Nothing in this section shall be interpreted as requiring multiple disruptions of the minor's placement corresponding to frequent changes of residence by the parents or guardians. In determining whether the minor should be moved, the probation officer will take into consideration the potential harmful effects of disrupting the placement of the minor and the parents' or guardians' reason for the move.

(d) Whenever the probation officer must change the placement of the minor and is unable to find a suitable placement within the county and must place the minor outside the county, no such placement shall be made until he or she has served written notice on the parents or guardians at least 14 days prior to the placement, unless the child's health or well-being is endangered by delaying the action or would be endangered if prior notice were given. The notice shall state the reasons which require placement outside the county. The parents or guardians may object to the placement not later than seven days after receipt of the notice and, upon objection the court shall hold a hearing not later than five days after the objection and prior to the placement. The court shall order out-of-county placement if it finds that the minor's particular needs require placement outside the county.

(e) Where the court has ordered a minor placed under the supervision of the probation officer and the probation officer has found that the needs of the child cannot be met in any available licensed or exempt facility, including emergency shelter, the minor may be placed in a suitable family home that has filed a license application with the State Department of Social Services, if all of the following certification conditions are met:

(1) A preplacement home visit is made by the probation officer to determine the suitability of the family home.

(2) The probation officer verifies to the licensing agency in writing that the home lacks any deficiencies which would threaten the physical health, mental health, safety, or welfare of the minor.

(3) The probation officer notifies the licensing agency of the proposed placement and determines that the foster family home applicant has filed specific license application documents prior to and after the placement of the minor. If the license is subsequently denied, the minor shall be removed from the home immediately. The denial of the license constitutes a withdrawal of the certification.

(f) Where the court has ordered removal of the child from the physical custody of his or her parents pursuant to Section 361, the court shall consider whether the family ties and best interest of the minor will be served by granting visitation rights to the minor's grandparents. The court shall clearly specify those rights to the supervising probation officer. *(Amended by Stats 1987 ch 1022 §8.)*

§361.3. Parental loss of custody; subsequent placement.

(a) In any case in which a child is removed from the physical custody of his or her parents pursuant to

Section 361, preferential consideration shall be given to a request by a relative of the child for placement of the child with the relative. In determining whether such a placement is appropriate, the probation officer and court shall consider the ability of the relative to provide a secure and stable environment for the child. Factors to be considered in that assessment include, but are not limited to, the good moral character of the relative; the ability of the relative to exercise proper and effective care and control of the child; the ability of the relative to provide a home and the necessities of life for the child; which relative is most likely to protect the child from his or her parents; which relative is most likely to facilitate visitation with the child's other relatives and to facilitate reunification efforts with the parents; and the best interests of the child. In this regard, the Legislature declares that a physical disability, such as blindness or deafness, is no bar to the raising of children, and a probation officer's determination as to the ability of a disabled relative to exercise care and control should center upon whether the relative's disability prevents him or her from exercising care and control.

(b) In any case in which more than one appropriate relative requests preferential consideration pursuant to this section, the probation officer and the court, in determining which relative should receive preferential consideration, shall consider the best interests of the child, and which of the relatives is most likely to protect the child from his or her parents, to facilitate visitation with the child's other relatives, and to facilitate reunification efforts with the parents. Consideration shall also be given to attempting to place siblings and stepsiblings in the same home if such a placement is found to be in their best interests.

(c) For purposes of this section:

(1) "Preferential consideration" means that the relative seeking placement shall be the first placement to be considered and investigated.

(2) "Relative" means an adult who is a grandparent, aunt, uncle, or sibling. *(Amended by Stats 1989 ch 913 §9, eff. 1/1/90.)*

§361.5. Provision of child welfare services.

(a) Except as provided in subdivision (b), whenever a minor is removed from a parent's or guardian's custody, the juvenile court shall order the probation officer to provide child welfare services to the minor and the minor's parents or guardians for the purpose of facilitating reunification of the family within a maximum time period not to exceed 12 months. The court also shall make findings pursuant to subdivision (a) of Section 366. When counseling or other treatment services are ordered, the parent shall be ordered to participate in those services, unless the parent's participation is deemed by the court to be inappropriate or potentially detrimental to the child. Services may be extended up to an additional six months if it can be shown that the objectives of the service plan can be achieved within the extended time period. Physical custody of the minor by the parents or guardians during the 18-month period shall not serve to interrupt the running of the period.

Except in cases where, pursuant to subdivision (b), the court does not order reunification services, the court shall inform the parent or parents of Section 366.25 or 366.26 and shall specify that the parent's or parents' parental rights may be terminated.

© 1992 by J., B. & L. Gould
Printed in the U.S.A.   EP

(b) Reunification services need not be provided to a parent described in this subdivision when the court finds, by clear and convincing evidence, any of the following:

(1) That the whereabouts of the parents is unknown. A finding pursuant to this paragraph shall be supported by an affidavit or by proof that a reasonably diligent search has failed to locate the parent. The posting or publication of notices is not required in such a search.

(2) That the parent is suffering from a mental disability that is described in Section 232 of the Civil Code and that renders him or her incapable of utilizing those services.

(3) That the minor had been previously adjudicated a dependent pursuant to any subdivision of Section 300 as a result of physical or sexual abuse, that following that adjudication the minor had been removed from the custody of his or her parent or guardian pursuant to Section 361, that the minor has been returned to the custody of the parent or parents or guardian or guardians from whom the minor had been taken originally, and that the minor is being removed pursuant to Section 361, due to additional physical or sexual abuse. However, this section is not applicable if the jurisdiction of the juvenile court has been dismissed prior to the additional abuse.

(4) That the parent of the minor has been convicted of causing the death of another child through abuse or neglect.

(5) That the minor was brought within the jurisdiction of the court under subdivision (e) of Section 300 because of the conduct of that parent.

(c) In deciding whether to order reunification in any case in which this section applies, the court shall hold a dispositional hearing. The probation officer shall prepare a report which discusses whether reunification services shall be provided. When it is alleged, pursuant to paragraph (2) of subdivision (b), that the parent is incapable of utilizing services due to mental disability, the court shall order reunification services unless competent evidence from mental health professionals establishes that, even with the provision of services, the parent is unlikely to be capable of adequately caring for the child within 12 months.

When paragraph (3), (4), or (5), inclusive, of subdivision (b) is applicable, the court shall not order reunification unless it finds that, based on competent testimony, those services are likely to prevent reabuse or continued neglect of the child or that failure to try reunification will be detrimental to the child because the child is closely and positively attached to that parent. The probation officer shall investigate the circumstances leading to the removal of the minor and advise the court whether there are circumstances which indicate that reunification is likely to be successful or unsuccessful and whether failure to order reunification is likely to be detrimental to the child.

The failure of the parent to respond to previous services, the fact that the child was abused while the parent was under the influence of drugs or alcohol, a past history of violent behavior, or testimony by a competent professional that the parent's behavior is unlikely to be changed by services are among the factors indicating that reunification services are unlikely to be successful. The fact that a parent or guardian is no longer living with an individual who severely abused the minor may be considered in deciding that reunification services are likely to be successful, provided that the court shall consider any pattern of behavior on the part of the parent that has exposed the child to repeated abuse.

(d) If reunification services are not ordered pursuant to paragraph (1) of subdivision (b) and the whereabouts of a parent become known within six months of the out-of-home placement of the minor, the court shall order the probation officer to provide family reunification services in accordance with this subdivision. However, the time limits specified in subdivision (a) and Section 366.25 are not tolled by the parent's absence.

(e) (1) If the parent or guardian is incarcerated or institutionalized, the court shall order reasonable services unless the court determines those services would be detrimental to the minor. In determining detriment, the court shall consider the age of the child, the degree of parent-child bonding, the length of the sentence, the nature of the treatment, the nature of crime or illness, the degree of detriment to the child if services are not offered and, for minors 10 years of age or older, the minor's attitude toward the implementation of family reunification services, and any other appropriate factors. Reunification services are subject to the 18-month limitation imposed in subdivision (a). Services may include, but shall not be limited to, all of the following:

(A) Maintaining contact between parent and child through collect phone calls.

(B) Transportation services, where appropriate.

(C) Visitation services, where appropriate.

(D) Reasonable services to extended family members or foster parents providing care for the child if the services are not detrimental to the child.

An incarcerated parent may be required to attend counseling, parenting classes, or vocational training programs as part of the service plan if these programs are available.

(2) The presiding judge of the juvenile court of each county may convene representatives of the county welfare department, the sheriff's department, and other appropriate entities for the purpose of developing and entering into protocols for ensuring the notification, transportation, and presence of an incarcerated or institutionalized parent at all court hearings involving proceedings affecting the minor pursuant to Section 2625 of the Penal Code.

(3) Notwithstanding any other provision of law, if the incarcerated parent is a woman seeking to participate in the community treatment program operated by the Department of Corrections pursuant to Chapter 4 (commencing with Section 3410) of Title 2 of Part 3 of the Penal Code, the court shall determine whether the parent's participation in a program is in the child's best interest and whether it is suitable to meet the needs of the parent and child.

(f) If a court, pursuant to paragraph (2), (3), (4), or (5) of subdivision (b), does not order reunification services, it shall conduct a hearing pursuant to Section 366.25 or 366.26 within 120 days of the dispositional hearing. However, the court shall not schedule a hearing so long as the other parent is being provided reunification services pursuant to subdivision (a). The court may continue to permit the parent to visit the minor unless it finds that visitation would be detrimental to the minor.

(g) Whenever a court orders that a hearing shall be held pursuant to Section 366.25 or 366.26 it shall direct the agency supervising the child and the licensed county adoption agency, or the State Department of Social Services when it is acting as an adoption agency in counties which are not served by a county adoption agency, to prepare an assessment which shall include:

(1) Current search efforts for an absent parent or parents.

(2) A review of the amount of and nature of any contact between the minor and his or her parents since the time of placement.

(3) An evaluation of the minor's medical, developmental, scholastic, mental, and emotional status.

(4) A preliminary assessment of the eligibility and commitment of any identified prospective adoptive parent or guardian, particularly the caretaker, to include a social history including screening for criminal records and prior referrals for child abuse or neglect, the capability to meet the minor's needs, and the understanding of the legal and financial rights and responsibilities of adoption and guardianship.

(5) The relationship of the minor to any identified prospective adoptive parent or guardian, the duration and character of the relationship, the motivation for seeking adoption or guardianship, and a statement from the minor, if the minor is 10 years of age or older, concerning placement and the adoption or guardianship.

(6) An analysis of the likelihood that the minor will be adopted if parental rights are terminated. *(Amended by Stats 1991 ch 820 §3, eff. 1/1/92.)*

§362. Court orders for welfare of minor.

(a) When a minor is adjudged a dependent child of the court on the ground that the minor is a person described by Section 300, the court may make any and all reasonable orders for the care, supervision, custody, conduct, maintenance, and support of the minor, including medical treatment, subject to further order of the court.

(b) When a minor is adjudged a dependent child of the court, on the ground that the minor is a person described by Section 300 and the court orders that a parent or guardian shall retain custody of the minor subject to the supervision of the probation officer, the parents or guardians shall be required to participate in child welfare services or services provided by an appropriate agency designated by the court.

(c) The juvenile court may direct any and all reasonable orders to the parents or guardians of the minor who is the subject of any proceedings under this chapter as the court deems necessary and proper to carry out the provisions of this section, including orders to appear before a county financial evaluation officer. Such an order may include a direction to participate in a counseling or education program, including, but not limited to, a parent education and parenting program operated by a community college, school district, or other appropriate agency designated by the court. A foster parent or relative with whom the minor is placed may be directed to participate in such a program in cases in which the court deems participation is appropriate and in the child's best interest. The program in which a parent or guardian is required to participate shall be designed to eliminate those conditions that led to the court's finding that the minor is a person described by Section 300. *(Amended by Stats 1986 ch 1120 §9; ch 1122 §14.)*

§362.1. Parents' or guardians' visitation rights.

In order to maintain ties between the parent and minor, and to provide information relevant to deciding if, and when, to return a minor to the custody of his or her parent or guardian, every order placing a minor in foster care, and ordering reunification services, shall provide for visitation between the parent or guardian and the minor. Visitation shall be as frequent as possible, consistent with the well-being of the minor. *(Added by Stats 1986 ch 1122 §15.)*

§362.3. Citation directing parents or guardians to attend hearing.

In addition to the notice provided in Sections 332 and 335, the juvenile court may issue its citation directing any parent, guardian, or foster parent of the person concerning whom a petition has been filed to appear at the time and place set for any hearing under the provisions of this chapter, and directing any person having custody or control of the minor concerning whom the petition has been filed to bring the minor with him or her. The notice shall, in addition, state that a parent, guardian, or foster parent may be required to participate in a counseling or education program with the minor concerning whom the petition has been filed. Personal service of the citation shall be made at least 24 hours before the time stated therein for the appearance.

§362.4. Order to enjoin parents from taking action to nullify or dissolve marriage after entry of custody order.

When the juvenile court terminates its jurisdiction over a minor who has been adjudged a dependent child of the juvenile court prior to the minor's attainment of the age of 18 years, and proceedings for the declaration of the nullity or dissolution of the marriage, or for legal separation, of the minor's parents, or proceedings to establish the paternity of the minor child brought under the Uniform Parentage Act (Part 7 (commencing with Section 7000) of Division 4 of the Civil Code), are pending in the superior court of any county, or an order has been entered with regard to the custody of that minor, the juvenile court on its own motion, may issue an order directed to either of the parents enjoining any action specified in paragraph (2) or (3) of subdivision (a) of Section 4359 of the Civil Code or determining the custody of, or visitation with, the child.

Any order issued pursuant to this section shall continue until modified or terminated by a subsequent order of the superior court. The order of the juvenile court shall be filed in the proceeding for nullity, dissolution, or legal separation, or in the proceeding to establish paternity, at the time the juvenile court terminates its jurisdiction over the minor, and shall become a part thereof.

If no action is filed or pending relating to the custody of the minor in the superior court of any county, the juvenile court order may be used as the sole basis for opening a file in the superior court of the county in which the parent, who has been given custody, resides. The court may direct the parent or the clerk of the juvenile court to transmit the order to the clerk of the superior court of the county in which the order is to be filed. The clerk of the superior court shall, immediately upon receipt, open a file, without a filing fee, and assign a case number.

The clerk of the superior court shall, upon the filing of any juvenile court custody order, send by first-class

© 1992 by J., B. & L. Gould
Printed in the U.S.A.   **EP**

mail a copy of the order with the case number to the juvenile court and to the parents at the address listed on the order.

The Judicial Council shall adopt forms for any custody or restraining order issued under this section. These form orders shall not be confidential. *(Amended by Stats 1989 ch 137 §2, eff. 1/1/90.)*

§362.5. Care and supervision of dependent child in demonstration county.

When a minor is adjudged a dependent child of the juvenile court of a demonstration county, on the ground that he is a person described by Section 300 or 302, the court may make any and all reasonable orders for the care, supervision, custody, conduct, maintenance, and support of such minor, including medical treatment, subject to further order of the court.

The court may order the care, custody, control and conduct of such minor to be under the supervision of the probation officer or social worker in a county welfare department of a demonstration county designated pursuant to Section 272 or, if the minor is removed from the custody of his parents or guardians pursuant to Section 361.5, the court may commit such minor to the care, custody and control of:

(a) Some reputable person of good moral character who consents to such commitment.

(b) Some association, society, or corporation embracing within its objects the purpose of caring for such minors, with the consent of such association, society, or corporation.

(c) The probation officer or social worker, to be boarded out or placed in some suitable family home or suitable private institution, subject to the requirements of Chapter 2 (commencing with Section 1250) or Chapter 3 (commencing with Section 1500) of Division 2 of the Health and Safety Code; provided, however, that pending action by the State Department of Social Services, the placement of a minor in a home certified as meeting minimum standards for boarding homes by the probation officer or social worker shall be legal for all purposes.

(d) Any other public agency organized to provide care for needy or neglected children.

When a minor is adjudged a dependent child of the court, on the ground that he is a person described by Section 300 and the court orders that a parent or guardian shall retain custody of such minor subject to the supervision of the probation officer or social worker, the parent or guardian may be required, and may be ordered, to participate in a counseling program designated by the court. When a minor is adjudged a dependent child of the court on the ground that he is a person described by subdivision (d) of Section 300 and the court orders that a parent or guardian shall retain custody of such minor subject to the supervision of the probation officer or social worker, the parent or guardian shall be required to participate in a counseling program designated by the court.

§363. Reduction of public assistance for parent or guardian of child in unfit home.

If the parent or person legally responsible for the care of any minor who is found to be a person described in Section 300 receives public assistance or care, any portion of which is attributable to the minor, a copy of the order of the court providing for the removal of the minor from his or her home shall be furnished to the appropriate social services official, who shall reduce the public assistance and care furnished the parent or other person by the amount attributable to the minor. *(Amended by Stats 1988 ch 701 §4, eff. 8/29/88.)*

§364. Supervision of minor not removed from parent's custody.

(a) Every hearing in which an order is made placing a minor under the supervision of the juvenile court pursuant to Section 300 and in which the minor is not removed from the physical custody of his or her parent or guardian shall be continued to a specific future date not to exceed six months after the date of the original dispositional hearing. The continued hearing shall be placed on the appearance calendar. The court shall advise all persons present of the date of the future hearings, of their rights to be present, and to be represented by counsel.

(b) At least 10 calendar days prior to the hearing, the probation officer shall file a supplemental report with the court describing the services offered to the family and the progress made by the family in eliminating the conditions or factors requiring court supervision. The probation officer shall also make a recommendation regarding the necessity of continued supervision. A copy of this report shall be furnished to all parties at least 10 calendar days prior to the hearing.

(c) After hearing any evidence presented by the probation officer, the parent, the guardian, or the minor, the court shall determine whether continued supervision is necessary. The court shall terminate its jurisdiction unless the probation department establishes by a preponderance of evidence that the conditions still exist which would justify initial assumption of jurisdiction under Section 300, or that such conditions are likely to exist if supervision is withdrawn. Failure of the parent or guardian to participate regularly in any court ordered treatment program shall constitute prima facie evidence that the conditions which justified initial assumption of jurisdiction still exist and that continued supervision is necessary.

(d) If the court retains jurisdiction it shall continue the matter to a specified date, not more than six months from the time of the hearing, at which point the court shall again follow the procedure specified in subdivision (c).

(e) In any case in which the court has ordered that a parent or guardian shall retain physical custody of a minor subject to supervision by a probation officer, and the probation officer subsequently receives a report of acts or circumstances which indicate that there is reasonable cause to believe that the minor is a person described in subdivision (a), (d), or (e) of Section 300, the probation officer shall commence proceedings under this chapter. If, as a result of the proceedings required, the court finds that the minor is a person described in subdivision (a), (d), or (e) of Section 300, the court shall remove the minor from the care, custody, and control of the minor's parent or guardian and shall commit the minor to the care, custody, and control of the probation officer pursuant to Section 361. *(Amended by Stats 1989 ch 913 §11, eff. 1/1/90.)*

§365. Reports by probation officer or other agency concerning minors committed to its care.

The court may require the probation officer or any other agency to render such periodic reports concerning minors committed to its care, custody, and control under the provisions of Section 362 as the court may deem necessary or desirable. The court may require that the probation officer, or any other public agency organized to provide care for needy or neglected children, shall perform such visitation and make such periodic reports to the courts concerning minors committed under such provisions as the court may deem necessary or desirable.

§366. Review by court of status of dependent child.

(a) The status of every dependent child in foster care shall be reviewed periodically as determined by the court but no less frequently than once every six months, as calculated from the date of the original dispositional hearing, until the hearing described in Section 366.25 or 366.26 is completed. The court shall determine the continuing necessity for and appropriateness of the placement, the extent of compliance with the case plan, and the extent of progress which has been made toward alleviating or mitigating the causes necessitating placement in foster care, and shall project a likely date by which the child may be returned to the home or placed for adoption or legal guardianship.

(b) Subsequent to the hearing periodic reviews of each child in foster care shall be conducted pursuant to the requirements of Sections 366.3 and 16503. *(Amended by Stats 1989 ch 913 §12, eff. 1/1/90.)*

§366.1. Supplemental reports; contents.

Each supplemental report required to be filed pursuant to Section 366 shall include, but not be limited to, a factual discussion of each of the following subjects:

(a) Whether the county welfare department or probation officer has considered child protective services, as defined in Chapter 5 (commencing with Section 16500) of Part 4 of Division 9, as a possible solution to the problems at hand, and has offered those services to qualified parents if appropriate under the circumstances.

(b) What plan, if any, for return of the child is recommended to the court by the county welfare department or probation officer.

(c) Whether the subject child appears to be a person who is eligible to be considered for further court action to free the child from parental custody and control.

(d) What actions, if any, have been taken by the parent to correct the problems which caused the child to be made a dependent child of the court. *(Amended by Stats 1987 ch 1485 §41.)*

§366.2. Procedure of status review hearing.

(a) Every hearing conducted by the juvenile court reviewing the status of a dependent child shall be placed on the appearance calendar. The court shall advise all persons present at the hearing of the date of the future hearing, of their right to be present and represented by counsel.

(b) Except as provided in Section 366.3, notice of the hearing shall be mailed by the probation officer to the same persons as in the original proceeding, to the minor's parent or guardian, to the foster parents, community care facility, or foster family agency having physical custody of the minor in the case of a minor removed from the physical custody of his or her parent or guardian, and to the counsel of record, by certified mail addressed to the last known address of the person to be notified, or shall be personally served on those persons, not earlier than 30 days nor later than 15 days preceding the date to which the hearing was continued.

(c) At least 10 calendar days prior to the hearing the probation officer shall file a supplemental report with the court regarding the services offered to the family, the progress made, and, where relevant, the prognosis for return of the minor to the physical custody of his or her parent or guardian, and make his or her recommendation for disposition. The probation officer shall provide the parent or parents with a copy of the report, including his or her recommendation for disposition, at least 10 calendar days prior to the hearing. In the case of a minor removed from the physical custody of his or her parent or guardian, the probation officer shall provide a summary of his or her recommendation for disposition to the counsel for the minor, any court appointed child advocate, foster parents, community care facility, or foster family agency having the physical custody of the minor at least 10 calendar days before the hearing.

(d) Prior to any hearing involving a minor in the physical custody of a community care facility or foster family agency that may result in the return of the minor to the physical custody of his or her parent or guardian, or in adoption or the creation of a legal guardianship, the facility or agency shall file with the court a report containing its recommendation for disposition. Prior to any such hearing involving a minor in the physical custody of a foster parent, the foster parent may file with the court a report containing its recommendation for disposition. The court shall consider any such report and recommendation prior to determining any disposition.

(e) The court shall proceed as follows at the review hearing: The court shall order the return of the minor to the physical custody of his or her parents or guardians unless, by a preponderance of the evidence, it finds that the return of the child would create a substantial risk of detriment to the physical or emotional well-being of the minor. The probation department shall have the burden of establishing that detriment. The failure of the parent or guardian to participate regularly in any court-ordered treatment programs shall constitute prima facie evidence that return would be detrimental. In making its determination, the court shall review the probation officer's report and shall consider the efforts or progress, or both, demonstrated by the parent or guardian and the extent to which he or she cooperated and availed himself or herself of services provided; shall make appropriate findings; and where relevant, shall order any additional services reasonably believed to facilitate the return of the minor to the custody of his or her parent or guardian. The court shall also inform the parent or guardian that if the minor cannot be returned home by the next review hearing, a proceeding pursuant to Section 232 of the Civil Code may be instituted. This section does not apply in a case where, pursuant to Section 361.5, the court has ordered that reunification services shall not be provided.

(f) This section shall apply only to minors made dependents of the court pursuant to subdivision (c) of Section 360 prior to January 1, 1989. *(Amended by Stats 1987 ch 1485 §42.)*

© 1992 by J., B. & L. Gould
Printed in the U.S.A.   EP

§366.21. Procedure of status review hearing; notice.

(a) Every hearing conducted by the juvenile court reviewing the status of a dependent child shall be placed on the appearance calendar. The court shall advise all persons present at the hearing of the date of the future hearing, of their right to be present and represented by counsel.

(b) Except as provided in Section 366.23 and subdivision (a) of Section 366.3, notice of the hearing shall be mailed by the probation officer to the same persons as in the original proceeding, to the minor's parent or guardian, to the foster parents, community care facility, or foster family agency having physical custody of the minor in the case of a minor removed from the physical custody of his or her parent or guardian, and to the counsel of record, by certified mail addressed to the last known address of the person to be notified, or shall be personally served on those persons, not earlier than 30 days nor later than 15 days preceding the date to which the hearing was continued.

The notice shall contain a statement regarding the nature of the hearing to be held and any change in the custody or status of the minor being recommended by the supervising agency. The notice to the foster parent shall indicate that the foster parent may attend all hearings or may submit any information he or she deems relevant to the court in writing.

(c) At least 10 calendar days prior to the hearing the probation officer shall file a supplemental report with the court regarding the services provided or offered to the parents to enable them to assume custody, the progress made, and, where relevant, the prognosis for return of the minor to the physical custody of his or her parent or guardian, and make his or her recommendation for disposition. If the recommendation is not to return the minor to a parent, the report shall specify why the return of the minor would be detrimental to the minor. The probation officer shall provide the parent or parents with a copy of the report, including his or her recommendation for disposition, at least 10 calendar days prior to the hearing. In the case of a minor removed from the physical custody of his or her parent or guardian, the probation officer shall provide a summary of his or her recommendation for disposition to the counsel for the minor, any court appointed child advocate, foster parents, community care facility, or foster family agency having the physical custody of the minor at least 10 calendar days before the hearing.

(d) Prior to any hearing involving a minor in the physical custody of a community care facility or foster family agency that may result in the return of the minor to the physical custody of his or her parent or guardian, or in adoption or the creation of a legal guardianship, the facility or agency shall file with the court a report containing its recommendation for disposition. Prior to any such hearing involving a minor in the physical custody of a foster parent, the foster parent may file with the court a report containing its recommendation for disposition. The court shall consider any such report and recommendation prior to determining any disposition.

(e) At the review hearing held six months after the initial dispositional hearing, the court shall order the return of the minor to the physical custody of his or her parents or guardians unless, by a preponderance of the evidence, it finds that the return of the child would create a substantial risk of detriment to the physical or emotional well-being of the minor. The probation department shall have the burden of establishing that detriment. The failure of the parent or guardian to participate regularly in any court-ordered treatment programs shall constitute prima facie evidence that return would be detrimental. In making its determination, the court shall review the probation officer's report, shall review and consider the report and recommendations of any child advocate appointed pursuant to Section 356.5, and shall consider the efforts or progress, or both, demonstrated by the parent or guardian and the extent to which he or she cooperated and availed himself or herself of services provided; shall make appropriate findings pursuant to subdivision (a) of Section 366; and where relevant, shall order any additional services reasonably believed to facilitate the return of the minor to the custody of his or her parent or guardian. The court shall also inform the parent or guardian that if the minor cannot be returned home by the next review hearing, a proceeding pursuant to Section 366.26 may be instituted. This section does not apply in a case where, pursuant to Section 361.5, the court has ordered that reunification services shall not be provided.

If the minor was removed initially under subdivision (g) of Section 300 and the court finds by clear and convincing evidence that the whereabouts of the parent are still unknown, or the parent has failed to contact and visit the child, the court may schedule a hearing pursuant to Section 366.26 within 120 days. If the court finds by clear and convincing evidence that the parent has been convicted of a felony indicating parental unfitness, the court may schedule a hearing pursuant to Section 366.26 within 120 days.

If the minor had been placed under court supervision with a previously noncustodial parent pursuant to Section 361.2, the court shall determine whether supervision is still necessary. The court may terminate supervision and transfer permanent custody to that parent, as provided for by paragraph (1) of subdivision (a) of Section 361.2.

In all other cases, the court shall direct that any reunification services previously ordered shall continue to be offered to the parent or guardian, provided that the court may modify the terms and conditions of those services. If the child is not returned to his or her parent or parents, the court shall determine whether reasonable services have been provided or offered to the parent or parents which were designed to aid the parent or parents overcome the problems which led to the initial removal and the continued custody of the minor. The court shall order that those services be initiated or continued.

(f) At the review hearing held 12 months after the initial dispositional hearing, the court shall order the return of the minor to the physical custody of his or her parent or guardian unless, by a preponderance of the evidence, it finds that return of the child would create a substantial risk or detriment to the physical or emotional well-being of the minor. The probation department shall have the burden of establishing that detriment. The court shall also determine whether reasonable services have been provided or offered to the parent or parents which were designed to aid the parent or parents to overcome the problems which led to the initial removal and continued custody of the minor. The failure of the parent or guardian to participate regularly in any court-ordered treatment programs shall constitute prima facie evidence that return would be detrimental. In making its determination, the court shall review the probation officer's report and shall consider the efforts or progress, or both, demonstrated by the parent or guardian and the extent to which he or she cooperated and availed himself or herself of services provided. If the minor is not returned to a parent or guardian, the court shall specify the factual basis for its conclusion that return would be detrimental. The court also shall make a finding pursuant to subdivision (a) of Section 366.

(g) If a minor is not returned to the custody of a parent or guardian at the hearing held pursuant to subdivision (f), the court shall do one of the following:

(1) Continue the case for up to six months for another review hearing, provided that the hearing shall occur within 18 months of the date the child was originally taken from the physical custody of his or her parent or guardian. The court shall continue the case only if it finds that there is a substantial probability that the minor will be returned to the physical custody of his or her parent or guardian within six months or that reasonable services have not been provided to the parent or parents. The court shall inform the parent or guardian that if the minor cannot be returned home by the next review hearing, a permanent plan shall be developed at that hearing. The court shall not order that a hearing pursuant to Section 366.26 be held unless there is clear and convincing evidence that reasonable services have been provided or offered to the parents.

(2) Order that the minor remain in long-term foster care, if the court finds by clear and convincing evidence, based upon the evidence already presented to it, that the minor is not adoptable and has no one willing to accept legal guardianship.

(3) Order that a hearing be held within 120 days, pursuant to Section 366.26.

(h) In any case in which the court orders that a hearing pursuant to Section 366.26 shall be held it shall also order the termination of reunification services to the parent. The court shall continue to permit the parent to visit the minor pending the hearing unless it finds that visitation would be detrimental to the minor.

(i) Whenever a court orders that a hearing pursuant to Section 366.26 shall be held, it shall direct the agency supervising the child and the licensed county adoption agency, or the State Department of Social Services when it is acting as an adoption agency in counties which are not served by a county adoption agency, to prepare an assessment which shall include:

(1) Current search efforts for an absent parent or parents.

(2) A review of the amount of and nature of any contact between the minor and his or her parents since the time of placement.

(3) An evaluation of the minor's medical, developmental, scholastic, mental, and emotional status.

(4) A preliminary assessment of the eligibility and commitment of any identified prospective adoptive parent or guardian, particularly the caretaker, to include a social history including screening for criminal records and prior referrals for child abuse or neglect, the capability to meet the minor's needs, and the understanding of the legal and financial rights and responsibilities of adoption and guardianship.

(5) The relationship of the minor to any identified prospective adoptive parent or guardian, the duration and character of the relationship, the motivation for seeking adoption or guardianship, and a statement from the minor, if the minor is 10 years of age or older, concerning placement and the adoption or guardianship.

(6) An analysis of the likelihood that the minor will be adopted if parental rights are terminated.

(j) This section shall apply to minors made dependents of the court pursuant to subdivision (c) of Section 360 on or after January 1, 1989. *(Amended by Stats 1989 ch 913 §13, eff. 1/1/90.)*

§366.22. Return of minor to parents' custody.

(a) When a case has been continued pursuant to paragraph (1) of subdivision (g) of Section 366.21, the court, at the 18-month hearing, shall order the return of the minor to the physical custody of his or her parent or guardian unless, by a preponderance of the evidence, it finds that return of the child would create a substantial risk of detriment to the physical or emotional well-being of the minor. The probation department shall have the burden of establishing the detriment. The failure of the parent or guardian to participate regularly in any court-ordered treatment programs shall constitute prima facie evidence that return would be detrimental. In making its determination, the court shall review the probation officer's report and shall review and consider the report and recommendations of any child advocate appointed pursuant to Section 356.6 and shall consider the efforts or progress, or both, demonstrated by the parent or guardian and the extent to which he or she cooperated and availed himself or herself of services provided. If the minor is not returned to a parent or guardian, the court shall specify the factual basis for its conclusion that return would be detrimental.

If the minor is not returned to a parent or guardian at the 18-month hearing, the court shall develop a permanent plan. The court shall order that a hearing be held pursuant to Section 366.26 in order to determine whether adoption, guardianship, or long-term foster care is the most appropriate plan for the minor. However, if the court finds by clear and convincing evidence, based on the evidence already presented to it that the minor is not adoptable and has no one willing to accept legal guardianship, the court may order that the minor remain in long-term foster care. The hearing shall be held no later than 120 days from the date of the 18-month hearing. The court shall also order termination of reunification services to the parent. The court shall continue to permit the parent to visit the minor unless it finds that visitation would be detrimental to the minor. The court shall determine whether reasonable services have been offered or provided to the parent or guardian.

(b) Whenever a court orders that a hearing pursuant to Section 366.26 shall be held, it shall direct the agency supervising the child and the licensed county adoption agency, or the State Department of Social Services when it is acting as an adoption agency in counties which are not served by a county adoption agency, to prepare an assessment which shall include:

(1) Current search efforts for an absent parent or parents.

(2) A review of the amount of and nature of any contact between the minor and his or her parents or other members of his or her extended family since the time of placement. Although the extended family of each minor shall be reviewed on a case-by-case basis,

© 1992 by J., B. & L. Gould
Printed in the U.S.A.   EP

"extended family" for the purposes of this paragraph shall include, but not be limited to, the minor's siblings, grandparents, aunts, and uncles.

(3) An evaluation of the minor's medical, developmental, scholastic, mental, and emotional status.

(4) A preliminary assessment of the eligibility and commitment of any identified prospective adoptive parent or guardian, particularly the caretaker, to include a social history including screening for criminal records and prior referrals for child abuse or neglect, the capability to meet the minor's needs, and the understanding of the legal and financial rights and responsibilities of adoption and guardianship.

(5) The relationship of the minor to any identified prospective adoptive parent or guardian, the duration and character of the relationship, the motivation for seeking adoption or guardianship, and a statement from the minor, if the minor is 10 years of age or older, concerning placement and the adoption or guardianship.

(6) An analysis of the likelihood that the minor will be adopted if parental rights are terminated. *(Amended by Stats 1991 ch 820 §4, eff. 1/1/92.)*

§366.23. Notification of minor's relatives of termination of parental rights.

(a) Whenever a juvenile court schedules a hearing pursuant to Section 366.26 regarding a minor, it shall direct that the fathers, presumed and alleged, and mother of the minor, the minor, if 10 years of age or older, and any counsel of record, shall be notified of the time and place of the proceedings and advised that they may appear. The notice shall also advise them of the right to counsel, the nature of the proceedings, and of the requirement that at the proceedings the court shall select and implement a plan of adoption, legal guardianship, or long-term foster care for the minor. In all cases where a parent has relinquished his or her child for the purpose of adoption, no notice need be given to that parent. Service of the notice shall be completed at least 45 days before the date of the hearing, except in those cases where notice by publication is ordered in which case the service of the notice shall be completed at least 30 days before the date of the hearing. If the petitioner is recommending termination of parental rights, all persons entitled to receive notice shall also be notified by first-class mail of the recommendation at least 15 days before the scheduled hearing.

(b) Notice to the parent of the hearing may be given in any of the following manners:

(1) Personal service to the parent named in the notice.

(2) Delivery to a competent person who is at least 18 years of age at the parent's usual place of residence or business, and thereafter mailed to the parent named in the notice by first-class mail at the place where the notice was delivered.

(3) If the place of residence is outside the state, service may be made in the manner prescribed in paragraph (1) or (2), or by certified mail, return receipt requested.

(4) If the recommendation of the petitioner is limited to legal guardianship or long-term foster care, service may be made by first-class mail to the parent's usual place of residence or business.

(5) If the father or mother of the minor or any person alleged to be or claiming to be the father or mother cannot, with reasonable diligence, be served

as provided for in paragraph (1), (2), (3), or (4) or if his or her place of residence is not known, the probation officer shall file an affidavit with the court at least 75 days before the date of the hearing, stating the name of the father or mother or alleged father or mother and his or her place of residence, if known, setting forth the efforts that have been made to locate and serve the parent.

(A) If the court determines that there has been due diligence in attempting to locate and serve the parent, and the petitioner limits the recommendation to legal guardianship or long-term foster care, the court shall order that notice be given to the grandparents of the minor, if there are any and if their residences and relationships to the minor are known, by first-class mail of the time and place of the proceedings and that they may appear. In any case where the residence of the parent or alleged parent becomes known, notice shall immediately be served upon the parent or alleged parent as set forth in paragraph (1), (2), (3), or (4).

(B) If the court determines that there has been due diligence in attempting to locate and serve the parent and the petitioner does not limit the recommendation to legal guardianship or long-term foster care, the court shall order that service to the parent be by certified mail, return receipt requested, to the parent's counsel of record, if any. If the parent does not have counsel of record, the court shall order that the service be made by publication of a citation requiring the father or mother, or alleged father or mother, to appear at the time and place stated in the citation, and that the citation be published in a newspaper designated as most likely to give notice to the father or mother. Publication shall be made once a week for four successive weeks. In case of service by certified mail on the counsel of record or publication where the residence of a parent or alleged parent becomes known, notice shall immediately be served upon the parent or alleged parent as set forth in paragraph (1), (2), or (3). When service by certified mail on the counsel of record or publication is ordered, service of a copy of the notice in the manner provided for in paragraph (1), (2), or (3) is equivalent to service by certified mail on the counsel of record or publication. In any case where service by certified mail on the counsel of record or publication is ordered, the court shall also order that notice be given to the grandparents of the minor, if there are any and if their residences and relationships to the minor are known, by first-class mail of the time and place of the proceedings and that they may appear.

If the identity of one or both of the parents or alleged parents of the minor is unknown or if the name of either or both of his or her parents or alleged parents is uncertain, then that fact shall be set forth in the affidavit and the court, if ordering publication, shall order the published citation to be directed to either the father or the mother, or both, of the minor, and to all persons claiming to be the father or mother of the minor naming and otherwise describing the minor.

(6) Notwithstanding paragraphs (1) to (5), inclusive, if the parent is present at the hearing at which the court schedules a hearing pursuant to Section 366.26 regarding the minor, the court shall advise the parent of the time and place of the proceedings, their right to counsel, the nature of the proceedings, and of the requirement that at the proceedings the court select and implement a plan of adoption, legal guard-

ianship, or long-term foster care for the minor. The court shall order the parent to appear for the proceedings and then direct that the parent be noticed thereafter by first-class mail to the parent's usual place of residence or business only.

(7) Notwithstanding paragraphs (1) to (5), inclusive, whenever the whereabouts of a parent is not known at the time the court schedules a hearing pursuant to Section 366.26 regarding a minor, and the petitioner presents to the court an affidavit setting forth the name of the parent and the efforts that have been made to locate the parent, the court shall order that the notice for the parent be as set forth in subparagraph (A) or (B) of paragraph (5).

(c) Notice to the minor, if 10 years of age or older, and to any counsel of record, of the hearing shall be by first-class mail.

(d) Service is deemed complete at the time the notice is personally delivered to the party named in the notice, or 10 days after the notice has been placed in the mail, or at the expiration of the time prescribed by the order for publication, whichever occurs first. *(Amended by Stats 1989 ch 913 §15, eff. 1/1/90.)*

§366.25. Permanency planning hearing.

(a) In order to provide stable, permanent homes for children, a court shall, if the minor cannot be returned home pursuant to subdivision (e) of Section 366.2, conduct a hearing to make a determination regarding the future status of the minor no later than 12 months after the original dispositional hearing in which the child was removed from the custody of his or her parent, parents, or guardians, and in no case later than 18 months from the time of the minor's original placement pursuant to Section 319 or 16507.4 and periodically, but no less frequently than once each 18 months, thereafter during the continuation of foster care. The hearing may be combined with the six months' review as provided for in Section 366. In the case of a minor who comes within subdivision (b) of Section 361.5 and for whom the court has found that reunification services should not be provided, a hearing shall be held pursuant to Section 361.5.

(b) Notice of the proceeding to conduct the review shall be mailed by the probation officer to the same persons as in an original proceeding, to the minor's present custodian, and to the counsel of record, by certified mail addressed to the last known address of the person to be notified, or shall be personally served on those persons not earlier than 30 days, nor later than 15 days prior to the date the review is to be conducted.

(c) Except in cases where permanency planning is conducted pursuant to Section 361.5, the court shall first determine at the hearing whether the minor should be returned to his or her parent or guardian, pursuant to subdivision (e) of Section 366.2. If the minor is not returned to the custody of his or her parent or guardian the court shall determine whether there is a substantial probability that the minor will be returned to the physical custody of his or her parent or guardian within six months. If the court so determines it shall set another review hearing for not more than six months, which shall be a hearing pursuant to this section.

(d) If the court determines that the minor cannot be returned to the physical custody of his or her parent or guardian and that there is not a substantial probability that the minor will be returned within six

months, the court shall develop a permanent plan for the minor. In order to enable the minor to obtain a permanent home the court shall make the following determinations and orders:

(1) If the court finds that it is likely that the minor can or will be adopted, the court shall authorize the appropriate county or state agency to proceed to free the minor from the custody and control of his or her parents or guardians pursuant to Section 232 of the Civil Code unless the court finds that any of the following conditions exist:

(A) The parents or guardians have maintained regular visitation and contact with the minor and the minor would benefit from continuing this relationship.

(B) A minor 10 years of age or older objects to termination of parental rights.

(C) The minor's foster parents, including relative caretakers, are unable to adopt the minor because of exceptional circumstances which do not include an unwillingness to accept legal responsibility for the minor, but are willing and capable of providing the minor with a stable and permanent environment and the removal of the minor from the physical custody of his or her foster parents would be seriously detrimental to the emotional well-being of the minor.

(2) If the court finds that it is not likely that the minor can or will be adopted or that one of the conditions in subparagraph (A), (B), or (C) of paragraph (1) applies, the court shall order the appropriate county department to initiate or facilitate the placement of the minor in a home environment that can be reasonably expected to be stable and permanent. This may be accomplished by initiating legal guardianship proceedings or long-term foster care. Legal guardianship shall be considered before long-term foster care, if it is in the best interests of the child and if a suitable guardian can be found. When the minor is in a foster home and the foster parents, including relative caretakers, are willing and capable of providing a stable and permanent environment, the minor shall not be removed from the home if the removal would be seriously detrimental to the emotional well-being of the minor because the minor has substantial psychological ties to the foster parents. The court shall also make orders for visitation with the parents or guardians unless the court finds by a preponderance of evidence that the visitation would be detrimental to the physical or emotional well-being of the minor.

(3) (A) If the court finds that it is not likely that the minor can or will be adopted, that there is no suitable adult available to become the legal guardian of the minor, and that there are no suitable foster parents except certified homes available to provide the minor with a stable and permanent environment, the court may order the care, custody, and control of the minor transferred from the county welfare department or probation department to a licensed foster family agency. The court shall consider the written recommendation of the county welfare director or chief probation officer regarding the suitability of such a transfer. The transfer shall be subject to further court orders.

(B) The licensed foster family agency shall only use a suitable licensed or other family home which has been certified by the agency as meeting licensing standards. When the care, custody, and control has been transferred to a foster family agency, it shall be responsible for supporting the minor and for providing appropriate services to the minor, including those

© 1992 by J., B. & L. Gould
Printed in the U.S.A.　EP

services ordered by the court. Responsibility for support of the minor shall not in and of itself create liability on the part of the foster family agency to third persons injured by the minor. Those minors whose care, custody, and control are transferred to a foster family agency shall not be eligible for foster care maintenance payments or child welfare services, except for emergency response services pursuant to Section 16504.

(C) Subsequent reviews for these minors shall be conducted every six months by the court. The licensed foster family agency shall be required to submit reports for each minor in its care, custody, and control to the court concerning the continuing appropriateness and extent of compliance with the minor's permanent plan, the extent of compliance with the case plan, and the type and adequacy of services provided to the minor.

(e) The proceeding for the appointment of a guardian for a minor who is a dependent child of the juvenile court shall be in the juvenile court. The court shall receive into evidence a report and recommendation concerning the proposed guardianship. The report shall include, but not be limited to, a discussion of all of the following:

(1) A social history of the proposed guardian, including screening for criminal records and prior referrals for child abuse or neglect.

(2) A social history of the minor, including an assessment of any identified developmental, emotional, psychological, or educational needs, and the capability of the proposed guardian to meet those needs.

(3) The relationship of the minor to the proposed guardian, the duration and character of the relationship, the motivation for seeking guardianship rather than adoption, the proposed guardian's long-term commitment to provide a stable and permanent home for the minor, and a statement from the minor concerning the proposed guardianship.

(4) The plan, if any, for the natural parents for continued involvement with the minor.

(5) The proposed guardian's understanding of the legal and financial rights and responsibilities of guardianship.

The report shall be read and considered by the court prior to ruling on the petition for guardianship, and this shall be reflected in the minutes of the court. The person preparing the report may be called and examined by any party to the proceeding.

(f) Physical custody of a minor by his or her parents or guardians for insubstantial periods during the 12-month period prior to a permanency planning hearing shall not serve to interrupt the running of those periods.

(g) Notwithstanding any other provision of law, the application of any person who, as a foster parent, including relative caretakers, has cared for a dependent child for whom the court has approved a permanent plan for adoption, or who has been freed for adoption, shall be given preference with respect to that child over all other applications for adoptive placement if the agency making the placement determines that the child has substantial emotional ties to the foster parent and removal from the foster parent would be seriously detrimental to the child's well-being.

As used in this subdivision, "preference" means that the application shall be processed and, if satisfactory, the family study shall be completed before the processing of the application of any other person for the adoptive placement of the child.

(h) Subsequent hearings need not be held if (1) the child has been freed for adoption and placed in the adoptive home identified in the previous hearing and is awaiting finalization of the adoption or (2) the child is the ward of a guardian.

(i) This section applies to minors adjudged dependent children of the juvenile court pursuant to subdivision (c) of Section 360 prior to January 1, 1989.

(j) An order by the court that authorizes the filing of a petition to terminate parental rights pursuant to Section 232 or that authorizes the initiation of guardianship proceedings is not an appealable order but may be the subject of review by extraordinary writ. *(Amended by Stats 1989 ch 913 §16, eff. 1/1/90.)*

§366.26. Termination of parental rights and placement of minor in foster care pending adoption.

(a) This section applies to minors who are adjudged dependent children of the juvenile court pursuant to subdivision (c) of Section 360 on or after January 1, 1989. The procedures specified herein are the exclusive procedures for conducting these hearings; Section 4600 of the Civil Code is not applicable to these proceedings. For minors who are adjudged dependent children of the juvenile court pursuant to subdivision (c) of Section 360 on or after January 1, 1989, this section and Sections 221.20, 222.10, and 7017 of the Civil Code specify the exclusive procedures for permanently terminating parental rights with regard to, or establishing legal guardianship of, the minor while the minor is a dependent child of the juvenile court.

(b) At the hearing, which shall be held in juvenile court for all minors who are dependents of the juvenile court, the court, in order to provide stable, permanent homes for these minors, shall review the report as specified in Section 361.5, 366.21, or 366.22, shall indicate that the court has read and considered it, shall receive other evidence that the parties present, and then shall do one of the following:

(1) Permanently sever the parent or parents' rights and order that the child be placed for adoption.

(2) Without permanently terminating parental rights, identify adoption as the permanent placement goal and order that efforts be made to locate an appropriate adoptive family for the minor for a period not to exceed 60 days.

(3) Without permanently terminating parental rights, appoint a legal guardian for the minor and issue letters of guardianship.

(4) Order that the minor be placed in long-term foster care, subject to the regular review of the juvenile court.

In choosing among the above alternatives the court shall proceed pursuant to subdivision (c).

(c) At the hearing the court shall proceed pursuant to one of the following procedures:

(1) The court shall terminate parental rights only if it determines by clear and convincing evidence that it is likely that the minor will be adopted. If the court so determines, the findings pursuant to subdivision (b) of Section 361.5 that reunification services shall not be offered, or the findings pursuant to subdivision (e) of Section 366.21 that the whereabouts of a parent have been unknown for six months or that the parent

has failed to visit or contact the child for six months or that the parent has been convicted of a felony indicating parental unfitness, or pursuant to Section 366.21 or Section 366.22 that a minor cannot or should not be returned to his or her parent or guardian, shall then constitute a sufficient basis for termination of parental rights unless the court finds that termination would be detrimental to the minor due to one of the following circumstances:

(A) The parents or guardians have maintained regular visitation and contact with the minor and the minor would benefit from continuing the relationship.

(B) A minor 10 years of age or older objects to termination of parental rights.

(C) The child is placed in a residential treatment facility, adoption is unlikely or undesirable, and continuation of parental rights will not prevent finding the child a permanent family placement if the parents cannot resume custody when residential care is no longer needed.

(D) The minor is living with a relative or foster parent who is unable or unwilling to adopt the minor because of exceptional circumstances, which do not include an unwillingness to accept legal responsibility for the minor, but who is willing and capable of providing the minor with a stable and permanent environment and the removal of the minor from the physical custody of his or her relative or foster parent would be detrimental to the emotional well-being of the minor.

(2) The court shall not terminate parental rights if at each and every hearing at which the court was required to consider reasonable efforts or services, the court has found that reasonable efforts were not made or that reasonable services were not offered or provided.

(3) If the court finds that termination of parental rights would not be detrimental to the minor pursuant to paragraph (1) and that the minor has a probability for adoption but is difficult to place for adoption and there is no identified or available prospective adoptive parent, the court may identify adoption as the permanent placement goal and without terminating parental rights, order that efforts be made to locate an appropriate adoptive family for the minor for a period not to exceed 60 days. During this 60-day period, the public agency responsible for seeking adoptive parents, for each child shall, to the extent possible, contact other private and public adoption agencies regarding the availability of the child for adoption. At the expiration of this period, another hearing shall be held and the court shall proceed pursuant to paragraph (1), (3), or (4) of subdivision (b). For purposes of this section, a minor may only be found to be difficult to place for adoption if there is no identified or available prospective adoptive parent for the minor because of the minor's membership in a sibling group, or the presence of a diagnosed medical, physical, or mental handicap, or the minor is the age of seven years or more.

(4) If the court finds that adoption of the minor or termination of parental rights is not in the interests of the minor, or that one of the conditions in subparagraph (A), (B), (C), or (D) of paragraph (1) or in paragraph (2) applies, the court shall either order that the present caretakers or other appropriate persons shall become legal guardians of the minor or order that the minor remain in long-term foster care. Legal guardianship shall be considered before long-term foster care, if it is in the best interests of the child and if a suitable guardian can be found. When the minor is living with a relative or a foster parent who is willing and capable of providing a stable and permanent environment, but not willing to become a legal guardian, the minor shall not be removed from the home if the court finds the removal would be seriously detrimental to the emotional well-being of the minor because the minor has substantial psychological ties to the relative caretaker or foster parents. The court shall also make an order for visitation with the parents or guardians unless the court finds by a preponderance of the evidence that the visitation would be detrimental to the physical or emotional well-being of the minor.

(5) If the court finds that the child should not be placed for adoption, that legal guardianship shall not be established, and that there are no suitable foster parents except exclusive-use homes available to provide the minor with a stable and permanent environment, the court may order the care, custody, and control of the minor transferred from the county welfare department or probation department to a licensed foster family agency. The court shall consider the written recommendation of the county welfare director or chief probation officer regarding the suitability of such a transfer. The transfer shall be subject to further court orders.

The licensed foster family agency shall place the minor in a suitable licensed or exclusive-use home which has been certified by the agency as meeting licensing standards. The licensed foster family agency shall be responsible for supporting the minor and for providing appropriate services to the minor, including those services ordered by the court. Responsibility for the support of the minor shall not, in and of itself, create liability on the part of the foster family agency to third persons injured by the minor. Those minors whose care, custody, and control are transferred to a foster family agency shall not be eligible for foster care maintenance payments or child welfare services, except for emergency response services pursuant to Section 16504.

(d) The proceeding for the appointment of a guardian for a minor who is a dependent of the juvenile court shall be in the juvenile court. If the court finds pursuant to this section that legal guardianship is the appropriate permanency plan, it shall appoint the legal guardian and issue letters of guardianship. The assessment prepared pursuant to subdivision (g) of Section 361.5, subdivision (i) of Section 366.21, and subdivision (b) of Section 366.22 shall be read and considered by the court prior to the appointment, and this shall be reflected in the minutes of the court. The person preparing the assessment may be called and examined by any party to the proceeding.

(e) At the beginning of any proceeding pursuant to this section, if the minor or the parents are not being represented by previously retained or appointed counsel, the court shall proceed as follows:

(1) The court shall consider whether the interests of the minor require the appointment of counsel. If the court finds that the interests of the minor do require such protection, the court shall appoint counsel to represent the minor. If the court finds that the interests of the minor require the representation of counsel, counsel shall be appointed whether or not the minor is able to afford counsel. The minor shall not be present in court unless the minor so requests or the court so orders.

© 1992 by J., B. & L. Gould
Printed in the U.S.A.   EP

(2) If a parent appears without counsel and is unable to afford counsel, the court shall appoint counsel for the parent, unless this representation is knowingly and intelligently waived. The same counsel shall not be appointed to represent both the minor and his or her parent. The public defender or private counsel may be appointed as counsel for the parent.

(3) Private counsel appointed under this section shall receive a reasonable sum for compensation and expenses, the amount of which shall be determined by the court. The amount shall be paid by the real parties in interest, other than the minor, in such proportions as the court deems just. However, if the court finds that any of the real parties in interest are unable to afford counsel, the amount shall be paid out of the general fund of the county.

(f) The court may continue the proceeding for not to exceed 30 days as necessary to appoint counsel, and to enable counsel to become acquainted with the case.

(g) At all termination proceedings, the court shall consider the wishes of the child and shall act in the best interests of the child.

The testimony of the minor may be taken in chambers and outside the presence of the minor's parent or parents if the minor's parent or parents are represented by counsel, the counsel is present, and any of the following circumstances exist:

(1) The court determines that testimony in chambers is necessary to ensure truthful testimony.

(2) The minor is likely to be intimidated by a formal courtroom setting.

(3) The minor is afraid to testify in front of his or her parent or parents.

After testimony in chambers, the parent or parents of the minor may elect to have the court reporter read back the testimony or have the testimony summarized by counsel for the parent or parents.

The testimony of a minor also may be taken in chambers and outside the presence of the guardian or guardians of a minor under the circumstances specified in this subdivision.

(h) Any order of the court permanently terminating parental rights under this section shall be conclusive and binding upon the minor person, upon the parent or parents and upon all other persons who have been served with citation by publication or otherwise as provided in this chapter. After making such an order, the court shall have no power to set aside, change, or modify it, but nothing in this section shall be construed to limit the right to appeal the order.

(i) If the court, by order or judgment declared the minor free from the custody and control of both parents, or one parent if the other no longer has custody and control, the court shall at the same time order the minor referred to a licensed county adoption agency for adoptive placement by the agency. However, no petition for adoption may be heard until the appellate rights of the natural parents have been exhausted. The licensed county adoption agency shall be responsible for the care and supervision of the minor and shall be entitled to the exclusive care and control of the minor at all times until a petition for adoption is granted.

(j) Notwithstanding any other provision of law, the application of any person who, as a relative caretaker or foster parent, has cared for a dependent child for whom the court has approved a permanent plan for adoption, or who has been freed for adoption, shall be given preference with respect to that child over all other applications for adoptive placement if the agency making the placement determines that the child has substantial emotional ties to the relative caretaker or foster parent and removal from the relative caretaker or foster parent would be seriously detrimental to the child's well-being.

As used in this subdivision, "preference" means that the application shall be processed and, if satisfactory, the family study shall be completed before the processing of the application of any other person for the adoptive placement of the child.

(k) An order by the court directing that a hearing pursuant to this section be held is not an appealable order, but may be the subject of review by extraordinary writ. (*Amended by Stats 1991 ch 820 §5, eff. 1/1/92.*)

§366.3. Jurisdiction of court over minor pending adoption.

(a) If a juvenile court orders a permanent plan of adoption or legal guardianship pursuant to Section 366.25 or 366.26, the court shall retain jurisdiction over the minor until the minor is adopted or the legal guardianship is established. The status of the minor shall be reviewed every six months to ensure that the adoption or guardianship is completed as expeditiously as possible. When the adoption of the minor has been granted, the court shall terminate its jurisdiction over the minor. The court may continue jurisdiction over the minor as a dependent minor of the juvenile court following the establishment of a legal guardianship or may terminate its dependency jurisdiction and retain jurisdiction over the minor as a ward of the guardianship established pursuant to Section 366.25 or 366.26 and as authorized by Section 366.4. Following a termination of parental rights the parent or parents shall not be a party to, or receive notice of, any subsequent proceedings regarding the minor.

(b) If the court has dismissed dependency jurisdiction following the establishment of a legal guardianship and the legal guardianship is subsequently revoked or otherwise terminated, the county department of social services or welfare department shall notify the juvenile court of this fact. The court may vacate its previous order dismissing dependency jurisdiction over the minor.

Notwithstanding Section 1601 of the Probate Code, the proceedings to terminate a guardianship which has been granted pursuant to Section 366.25 or 366.26 shall be held in the juvenile court, unless the termination is due to the emancipation or adoption of the minor. If the petition to terminate guardianship is granted, the juvenile court may resume dependency jurisdiction over the minor, and may order the county department of social services or welfare department to develop a new permanent plan, which shall be presented to the court within 60 days of the termination.

Unless the parental rights of the child's parent or parents have been terminated, they shall be notified that the guardianship has been revoked or terminated and shall be entitled to participate in the new permanency planning hearing. The court shall try to place the minor in another permanent placement. At the hearing, the parents may be considered as custodians but the minor shall not be returned to the parent or parents unless they prove, by a preponderance of the evidence, that reunification is the best alternative for the minor. The court may, if it is in the interests of the minor, order that reunification services again be provided to the parent or parents.

(c) If the minor is in a placement other than a preadoptive home or the home of a legal guardian and jurisdiction has not been dismissed, the status of the minor shall be reviewed every six months. This review may be conducted by the court or an appropriate local agency; the court shall conduct the review upon the request of the minor's parents or guardian or of the minor and shall conduct the review 18 months after the hearing held pursuant to Section 366.26 and every 18 months thereafter. The reviewing body shall inquire about the progress being made to provide a permanent home for the minor and shall determine the appropriateness of the placement, the continuing appropriateness and extent of compliance with the permanent plan for the child, the extent of compliance with the case plan, and the adequacy of services provided to the child. The review shall also include a determination of the services needed to assist a child who is 16 years of age or older make the transition from foster care to independent living.

Each licensed foster family agency shall submit reports for each minor in its care, custody, and control to the court concerning the continuing appropriateness and extent of compliance with the minor's permanent plan, the extent of compliance with the case plan, and the type and adequacy of services provided to the minor.

Unless their parental rights have been permanently terminated, the parent or parents of the minor are entitled to receive notice of, participate in, those hearings. It shall be presumed that continued care is in the interests of the minor, unless the parent or parents prove, by a preponderance of the evidence, that further efforts at reunification are the best alternative for the minor. In those cases, the court may order that further reunification services be provided to the parent or parents for a period not to exceed six months. *(Amended by Stats 1990 ch 1530 §8, eff. 1/1/91.)*

§366.4. Administration of minor's estate.

Any minor for whom a guardianship has been established resulting from the selection or implementation of a permanent plan pursuant to Section 366.25 or 366.26 is within the jurisdiction of the juvenile court. For those minors, Part 2 (commencing with Section 1500) of Division 4 of the Probate Code, relating to guardianship, shall not apply. If no specific provision of this code or the California Rules of Court is applicable, the provisions applicable to the administration of estates under Part 4 (commencing with Section 2100) of Division 4 of the Probate Code govern so far as they are applicable to like situations. *(Added by Stats 1990 ch 1530 §9, eff. 1/1/91.)*

§367. Detention of dependent child pending disposition.

(a) Whenever a person has been adjudged a dependent child of the juvenile court and has been committed or otherwise disposed of as provided in this chapter for the care of dependent children of the juvenile court, the court may order that said dependent child be detained in a suitable place designated as the court seems fit until the execution of the order of commitment or of other disposition.

(b) In any case in which a minor is detained for more than 15 days pending the execution of the order of commitment or of any other disposition, the court shall periodically review the case to determine whether the delay is reasonable. Such periodic reviews shall be held at least every 15 days, commencing from the time the minor was initially detained pending the execution of the order of commitment or of any other disposition, and during the course of each review court shall inquire regarding the action taken by the probation department to carry out its order, the reasons for the delay, and the effect of the delay upon the minor.

§368. Transfer of dependent child out of state.

In a case where the residence of a dependent child of the juvenile court is out of the state and in another state or foreign country, or in a case where such minor is a resident of this state but his parents, relatives, guardian, or person charged with his custody is in another state, the court may order such minor sent to his parents, relatives, or guardian, or to the person charged with his custody, or, if the minor is a resident of a foreign country, to an official of a juvenile court of such foreign country or an agency of such country authorized to accept the minor, and in such case may order transportation and accommodation furnished, with or without an attendant, as the court deems necessary. If the court deems an attendant necessary, the court may order the probation officer or other suitable person to serve as such attendant. The probation officer shall authorize the necessary expenses of such minor and of the attendant and claims therefor shall be audited, allowed and paid in the same manner as other county claims.

§369. Provision of medical, surgical, dental, or other remedial care to person in custody.

(a) Whenever any person is taken into temporary custody under Article 7 (commencing with Section 305) and is in need of medical, surgical, dental, or other remedial care, the probation officer may, upon the recommendation of the attending physician and surgeon or, if the person needs dental care and there is an attending dentist, the attending dentist, authorize the performance of the medical, surgical, dental, or other remedial care. The probation officer shall notify the parent, guardian, or person standing in loco parentis of the person, if any, of the care found to be needed before that care is provided, and if the parent, guardian, or person standing in loco parentis objects, such care shall be given only upon order of the court in the exercise of its discretion.

(b) Whenever it appears to the juvenile court that any person concerning whom a petition has been filed with the court is in need of medical, surgical, dental, or other remedial care, and that there is no parent, guardian, or person standing in loco parentis capable of authorizing or willing to authorize the remedial care or treatment for that person, the court, upon the written recommendation of a licensed physician and surgeon or, if the person needs dental care, a licensed dentist, and after due notice to the parent, guardian, or person standing in loco parentis, if any, may make an order authorizing the performance of the necessary medical, surgical, dental, or other remedial care for that person.

(c) Whenever a dependent child of the juvenile court is placed by order of the court within the care and custody or under the supervision of the probation officer of the county in which the dependent child resides and it appears to the court that there is no

© 1992 by J., B. & L. Gould
Printed in the U.S.A.   EP

parent, guardian, or person standing in loco parentis capable of authorizing or willing to authorize medical, surgical, dental, or other remedial care or treatment for the dependent child, the court may, after due notice to the parent, guardian, or person standing in loco parentis, if any, order that the probation officer may authorize the medical, surgical, dental, or other remedial care for the dependent child, by licensed practitioners, as may from time to time appear necessary.

(d) Whenever it appears that a minor otherwise within subdivision (a), (b), or (c) requires immediate emergency medical, surgical, or other remedial care in an emergency situation, that care may be provided by a licensed physician and surgeon or, if the minor needs dental care in an emergency situation, by a licensed dentist, without a court order and upon authorization of a probation officer. The probation officer shall make reasonable efforts to obtain the consent of, or to notify, the parent, guardian, or person standing in loco parentis prior to authorizing emergency medical, surgical, dental, or other remedial care. "Emergency situation," for the purposes of this subdivision means a minor requires immediate treatment for the alleviation of severe pain or an immediate diagnosis and treatment of an unforeseeable medical, surgical, dental, or other remedial condition or contagious disease which if not immediately diagnosed and treated, would lead to serious disability or death.

(e) In any case in which the court orders the performance of any medical, surgical, dental, or other remedial care pursuant to this section, the court may also make an order authorizing the release of information concerning that care to probation officers, parole officers, or any other qualified individuals or agencies caring for or acting in the interest and welfare of the minor under order, commitment, or approval of the court.

(f) Nothing in this section shall be construed as limiting the right of a parent, guardian, or person standing in loco parentis, who has not been deprived of the custody or control of the minor by order of the court, in providing any medical, surgical, dental, or other remedial treatment recognized or permitted under the laws of this state.

(g) The parent of any person described in this section may authorize the performance of medical, surgical, dental, or other remedial care provided for in this section notwithstanding his or her age or marital status. In nonemergency situations the parent authorizing the care shall notify the other parent prior to the administration of such care. (Amended by Stats 1990 ch 566 §1, eff. 1/1/91.)

§370. Employment of psychiatrists, psychologists and other clinical experts to determine appropriate treatment.

The juvenile court may, in any case before it in which a petition has been filed as provided in Article 7 (commencing with Section 305), order that the probation officer obtain the services of such psychiatrists, psychologists, or other clinical experts as may be required to assist in determining the appropriate treatment of the minor and as may be required in the conduct or implementation of such treatment. Payment for such services shall be a charge against the county.

ARTICLE 11

DEPENDENT CHILDREN — TRANSFER OF CASES BETWEEN COUNTIES

§375. Transferral of case to another county.

Whenever a petition is filed in the juvenile court of a county other than the residence of the person named in the petition, or whenever, subsequent to the filing of a petition in the juvenile court of the county where such minor resides, the residence of the person who would be legally entitled to the custody of such minor were it not for the existence of a court order issued pursuant to this chapter is changed to another county, the entire case may be transferred to the juvenile court of the county wherein such person then resides at any time after the court has made a finding of the facts upon which it has exercised its jurisdiction over such minor, and the juvenile court of the county wherein such person then resides shall take jurisdiction of the case upon the receipt and filing with it of such finding of the facts and an order transferring the case.

§376. Payment of expenses arising from transfer and support.

The expense of the transfer and all expenses in connection with the transfer and for the support and maintenance of such person shall be paid from the county treasury of the court ordering the transfer until the receipt and filing of the finding and order of transfer in the juvenile court of the transferee county.

The judge shall inquire into the financial condition of such person and of the parent, parents, guardian, or other person charged with his support and maintenance, and if he finds such person, parent, parents, guardian, or other person able, in whole or in part, to pay the expense of such transfer, he shall make a further order requiring such person, parent, parents, guardian, or other person to repay to the county such part, or all, of such expense of transfer as, in the opinion of the court, is proper. Such repayment shall be made to the probation officer who shall keep suitable accounts of such expenses and repayments and shall deposit all such collections in the county treasury.

§377. Information contained in order of transfer.

Whenever a case is transferred as provided in Section 375, the order of transfer shall recite each and all of the findings, orders, or modification of orders that have been made in the case, and shall include the name and address of the legal residence of the parent or guardian of the minor. All papers contained in the file shall be transferred to the county where such person resides. A copy of the order of transfer and of the findings of fact as required in Section 375 shall be kept in the file of the transferring county.

§378. Precedence in court of order of transfer.

Whenever an order of transfer from another county is filed with the clerk of any juvenile court, the clerk shall place the transfer order on the calendar of the court, and it shall have precedence over all actions and civil proceedings not specifically given precedence by other provisions of law and shall be heard by the court at the earliest possible moment following the filing of the order.

§379. Parties in action; right to appeal.

In any action under the provisions of this article in which the residence of a minor person is determined, both the county in which the court is situated and any other county which, as a result of the determination of residence, might be determined to be the county of residence of the minor person, shall be considered to be parties in the action and shall have the right to appeal any order by which residence of the minor person is determined.

§380. Residence of dependent child in county other than that of legal residence.

Any person adjudged to be a dependent child of the juvenile court may be permitted by order of the court to reside in a county other than the county of his legal residence, and the court shall retain jurisdiction over such person.

Whenever a dependent child of the juvenile court is permitted to reside in a county other than the county of his legal residence, he may be placed under the supervision of the probation officer of the county of actual residence, with the consent of such probation officer. The dependent child shall comply with the instructions of such probation officer and upon failure to do so shall be returned to the county of his legal residence for further hearing and order of the court.

ARTICLE 12

DEPENDENT CHILDREN — MODIFICATION OF JUVENILE COURT JUDGMENTS AND ORDERS

§385. Changing, modifying or setting aside court order.

Any order made by the court in the case of any person subject to its jurisdiction may at any time be changed, modified, or set aside, as the judge deems meet and proper, subject to such procedural requirements as are imposed by this article.

§386. Changing, modifying or setting aside order without notice.

No order changing, modifying, or setting aside a previous order of the juvenile court shall be made either in chambers, or otherwise, unless prior notice of the application therefor has been given by the judge or the clerk of the court to the probation officer and to the minor's counsel of record, or, if there is no counsel of record, to the minor and his parent or guardian.

§387. Removal of minor from custody of parent must be preceded by noticed hearing.

An order changing or modifying a previous order by removing a minor from the physical custody of a parent, guardian, relative, or friend and directing placement in a foster home, or commitment to a private or county institution, shall be made only after noticed hearing upon a supplemental petition.

(a) The supplemental petition shall be filed by the probation officer in the original matter and shall contain a concise statement of facts sufficient to support the conclusion that the previous disposition has not been effective in the rehabilitation or protection of the minor.

(b) Upon the filing of the supplemental petition, the clerk of the juvenile court shall immediately set the same for hearing within 30 days, and the probation officer shall cause notice thereof to be served upon the

persons and in the manner prescribed by Sections 335 and 337.

(c) An order for the detention of the minor pending adjudication of the petition may be made only after a hearing is conducted pursuant to Article 7 (commencing with Section 305).

§388. Petition to change order declaring a child a dependent child.

Any parent or other person having an interest in a child who is a dependent child of the juvenile court or the child himself through a properly appointed guardian may, upon grounds of change of circumstance or new evidence, petition the court in the same action in which the child was found to be a dependent child of the juvenile court for a hearing to change, modify, or set aside any order of court previously made or to terminate the jurisdiction of the court. The petition shall be verified and, if made by a person other than the child, shall state the petitioner's relationship to or interest in the child and shall set forth in concise language any change of circumstance or new evidence which are alleged to require such change of order or termination of jurisdiction.

If it appears that the best interests of the child may be promoted by the proposed change of order or termination of jurisdiction, the court shall order that a hearing be held and shall give prior notice, or cause prior notice to be given, to such persons and by such means as prescribed by Section 386, and, in such instances as the means of giving notice is not prescribed by such sections, then by such means as the court prescribes.

§389. Petition to seal records.

(a) In any case in which a petition has been filed with a juvenile court to commence proceedings to adjudge a person a dependent child of the court, in any case in which a person is cited to appear before a probation officer or is taken before a probation officer pursuant to Section 307, or in any case in which a minor is taken before any officer of a law enforcement agency, the person or the county probation officer may, five years or more after the jurisdiction of the juvenile court has terminated as to the person, or, in a case in which no petition is filed, five years or more after the person was cited to appear before a probation officer or was taken before a probation officer pursuant to Section 307 or was taken before any officer of a law enforcement agency, or, in any case, at any time after the person has reached the age of 18 years, petition the court for sealing of the records, including records of arrest, relating to the person's case, in the custody of the juvenile court and probation officer and any other agencies, including law enforcement agencies, and public officials as petitioner alleges, in his petition, to have custody of such records. The court shall notify the district attorney of the county and the county probation officer, if he is not the petitioner of the petition, and such district attorney or probation officer or any of their deputies or any other person having relevant evidence may testify at the hearing on the petition. If, after hearing, the court finds that since such termination of jurisdiction or action pursuant to Section 307, as the case may be, he has not been convicted of a felony or of any misdemeanor involving moral turpitude and that rehabilitation has been attained to the satisfaction of the court, it shall order sealed all records, papers, and exhibits in the

© 1992 by J., B. & L. Gould
Printed in the U.S.A.   **EP**

person's case in the custody of the juvenile court, including the juvenile court record, minute book entries, and entries on dockets, and other records relating to the case in the custody of such other agencies and officials as are named in the order. Thereafter, the proceedings in such case shall be deemed never to have occurred, and the person may properly reply accordingly to any inquiry about the events, records of which are ordered sealed. The court shall send a copy of the order to each agency and official named therein directing the agency to seal its records and five years thereafter to destroy the sealed records. Each such agency and official shall seal records in its custody as directed by the order, shall advise the court of its compliance, and thereupon shall seal the copy of the court's order for sealing of records that it or he received. The person who is the subject of records sealed pursuant to this section may petition the superior court to permit inspection of the records by persons named in the petition, and the superior court may so order. Otherwise, except as provided in subdivision (b), such records shall not be open to inspection.

(b) In any action or proceeding based upon defamation, a court, upon a showing of good cause, may order any records sealed under this section to be opened and admitted into evidence. The records shall be confidential and shall be available for inspection only by the court, jury, parties, counsel for the parties, and any other person who is authorized by the court to inspect them. Upon the judgment in the action or proceeding becoming final, the court shall order the records sealed.

(c) Five years after a juvenile court record has been sealed, the court shall order the destruction of the sealed juvenile court record unless for good cause the court determines that the juvenile court record shall be retained. Any other agency in possession of sealed records shall destroy their records five years after the records were ordered sealed.

§390. Grounds for dismissal of petition.

A judge of the juvenile court in which a petition was filed, at any time before the minor reaches the age of 21 years, may dismiss the petition or may set aside the findings and dismiss the petition if the court finds that the interests of justice and the welfare of the minor require the dismissal, and that the parent or guardian of the minor is not in need of treatment or rehabilitation. (Amended by Stats 1987 ch 1485 §50.)

ARTICLE 13

DEPENDENT CHILDREN — APPEALS

§395. Appeals of judgments.

A judgment in a proceeding under Section 300 may be appealed from in the same manner as any final judgment, and any subsequent order may be appealed from as from an order after judgment; but no such order or judgment shall be stayed by the appeal, unless, pending the appeal, suitable provision is made for the maintenance, care, and custody of the person alleged or found to come within the provisions of Section 300, and unless the provision is approved by an order of the juvenile court. The appeal shall have precedence over all other cases in the court to which the appeal is taken.

A judgment or subsequent order entered by a referee shall become appealable whenever proceedings pursuant to Section 252, 253, or 254 have become

completed or, if proceedings pursuant to Section 252, 253, or 254 are not initiated, when the time for initiating the proceedings has expired.

An appellant unable to afford counsel, shall be provided a free copy of the transcript in any appeal.

The record shall be prepared and transmitted immediately after filing of the notice of appeal, without advance payment of fees. If the appellant is able to afford counsel, the county may seek reimbursement for the cost of the transcripts under subdivision (c) of Section 68511.3 of the Government Code as though the appellant had been granted permission to proceed in forma pauperis. (Amended by Stats 1986 ch 823 §4.)

ARTICLE 13.5

FOSTER CARE OF CHILDREN

§396. Policy of Legislature on foster care.

It is the policy of the Legislature that foster care should be a temporary method of care for the children of this state, that children have a right to a normal home life, that reunification with the natural parent or parents or another alternate permanent living situation such as adoption or guardianship are more suitable to a child's well-being than is foster care, and that this state has a responsibility to attempt to ensure that children are given the chance to have a happy and healthy life, and that, to the extent possible, the current practice of moving children receiving foster care services from one foster home to another until they reach the age of majority should be discontinued.

§397. Report by county welfare department or probation department to State Department of Social Services.

In order to carry out the policy stated in Section 396, each county welfare department or probation department shall report to the State Department of Social Services, in the frequency and format determined by the department, foster care characteristic data and care information deemed essential by the department to establish a foster care information system. The report shall include, but not be limited to, elements that identify the factors necessitating foster care placement, the appropriateness of the placement, and the case goal or objective such as reunification, adoption, guardianship, or long-term foster care placement.

§398. Report by department to Speaker of the Assembly and Senate Rules Committee.

The department shall report to the Speaker of the Assembly and the Senate Rules Committee on the current status of children placed in foster care. The report shall be submitted on October 1, 1981, and shall include, in addition to the current status of children in foster care, an analysis of foster care service plans in relation to the policy set forth in Section 396.

§399. Right of minor to make statement to court.

Any minor being considered for placement in a foster home shall have the right to make a brief statement to the court making a decision on placement. The court may disregard any preferences expressed by the minor. The minor's right to make a statement shall not be limited to the initial placement, but shall continue for any proceedings concerning continued placement or a decision to return to parental custody.

ARTICLE 13.6

SERIOUS HABITUAL OFFENDERS

§500. Findings by Legislature.

The Legislature hereby finds that a substantial and disproportionate amount of serious crime is committed by a relatively small number of chronic juvenile offenders commonly known as serious habitual offenders. In enacting this article, the Legislature intends to support increased efforts by the juvenile justice system comprised of law enforcement, district attorneys, probation departments, juvenile courts, and schools to identify these offenders early in their careers, and to work cooperatively together to investigate and record their activities, prosecute them aggressively by using vertical prosecution techniques, sentence them appropriately, and to supervise them intensively in institutions and in the community. The Legislature further supports increased interagency efforts to gather comprehensive data and actively disseminate it to the agencies in the juvenile justice system, to produce more informed decisions by all agencies in that system, through organizational and operational techniques that have already proven their effectiveness in selected counties in this and other states. *(Added by Stats 1986 ch 1441 §1.)*

§501. Creation of Serious Habitual Offender Program.

(a) There is hereby established in the Office of Criminal Justice Planning a program of financial assistance for law enforcement, district attorneys, probation departments, juvenile courts, and schools, designated the Serious Habitual Offender Program. All funds appropriated to the Office of Criminal Justice Planning for the purposes of this article shall be administered and disbursed by the executive director of that office, and shall, to the greatest extent feasible, be coordinated or consolidated with federal funds that may be made available for these purposes.

(b) From moneys appropriated therefor, the Executive Director of the Office of Criminal Justice Planning may allocate and award funds to agencies in which programs are established in substantial compliance with the policies and criteria set forth in this article. Awards made to individual agencies shall not exceed three years in duration. An agency receiving an award shall provide matching funds at an increasing rate each year; the rate shall be as determined by the Office of Criminal Justice Planning for that agency.

(c) Allocation and award of funds for the purposes of this article shall be made upon application by a district attorney, a local law enforcement agency, a probation department, or a school district, that has been approved by the appropriate governing board of the particular agency. The applicant agency shall use the funds to create an information gathering and analysis unit responsible for the identification of serious habitual offenders and for the dissemination of information about the activities of those offenders to the juvenile justice system. This unit shall participate in the planning, support, and assistance of activities required in Sections 503 to 506, inclusive. Funds disbursed under this article shall not supplant local funds that would, in absence of the program established by this article, be made available to support the juvenile justice system. Local grant awards made under the program shall not be subject to review

as specified in Section 14780 of the Government Code. *(Amended by Stats 1989 ch 1356 §1, eff. 1/1/90.)*

§502. Qualification for program.

(a) An individual shall be the subject of the efforts of programs established pursuant to this article who has been previously adjudged a ward pursuant to Section 602 and is described in any of the following paragraphs:

(1) Has accumulated five total arrests, three arrests for crimes chargeable as felonies and three arrests within the preceding 12 months.

(2) Has accumulated 10 total arrests, two arrests for crimes chargeable as felonies and three arrests within the preceding 12 months.

(3) Has been arrested once for three or more burglaries, robberies, or sexual assaults within the preceding 12 months.

(4) Has accumulated 10 total arrests, eight or more arrests for misdemeanor crimes of theft, assault, battery, narcotics or controlled substance possession, substance abuse, or use or possession of weapons, and has three arrests within the preceding 12 months.

(b) Arrests for infractions or conduct described in Section 601 shall not be utilized in determining whether an individual is described in subdivision (a). All arrests used in determining eligibility for selection for program participation that did not result in a sustained petition shall be certified by the prosecutor as having been provable.

(c) In applying the selection criteria set forth above, a program may elect to limit its efforts to persons described in one or more of the categories listed in subdivision (a), or specified felonies, if crime statistics demonstrate that the persons so identified present a particularly serious problem in the county, or that the incidence of the felonies so specified present a particularly serious problem in the county. *(Added by Stats 1986 ch 1441 §1.)*

§503. Policies of programs under this article.

Programs funded under this article shall adopt and pursue the following policies:

(a) Each participating law enforcement agency shall do all of the following:

(1) Gather data on identified serious habitual offenders.

(2) Compile data into usable format for law enforcement, prosecutors, probation officer, schools, and courts pursuant to interagency agreement.

(3) Regularly update data and disseminate data to juvenile justice system agencies, as needed.

(4) Establish local policies in cooperation with the prosecutor, the probation officer, schools, and the juvenile court regarding data collection, arrest, and detention of serious habitual offenders.

(5) Provide support and assistance to other agencies engaged in the program.

(b) Each participating district attorney's office shall do all of the following:

(1) File petitions based on the most serious provable offenses of each arrest of a serious habitual offender.

(2) Use all reasonable prosecutorial efforts to resist the release, where appropriate, of the serious habitual offender at all stages of the prosecution.

(3) Seek an admission of guilt on all offenses charged in the petition against the offender. The only cases in which the prosecutor may request the court

© 1992 by J., B. & L. Gould
Printed in the U.S.A.   EP

to reduce or dismiss the charges shall be cases in which the prosecutor decides there is insufficient evidence to prove the people's case, the testimony of a material witness cannot be obtained or a reduction or dismissal will not result in a substantial change in sentence. In those cases, the prosecutor shall file a written declaration with the court stating the specific factual and legal basis for such a reduction or dismissal and the court shall make specific findings on the record of its ruling and the reasons therefor.

(4) Vertically prosecute all cases involving serious habitual offenders, whereby the prosecutor who makes the initial filing decision or appearance on such a case shall perform all subsequent court appearances on that case through its conclusion, including the disposition phase.

(5) Make all reasonable prosecutorial efforts to persuade the court to impose the most appropriate sentence upon such an offender at the time of disposition. As used in this paragraph, "most appropriate sentence" means any disposition available to the juvenile court.

(6) Make all reasonable prosecutorial efforts to reduce the time between arrest and disposition of the charge.

(7) Act as liaison with the court and other criminal justice agencies to establish local policies regarding the program and to ensure interagency cooperation in the planning and implementation of the program.

(8) Provide support and assistance to other agencies engaged in the program.

(c) Each participating probation department shall do all of the following:

(1) Cooperate in gathering data for use by all participating agencies pursuant to interagency agreement.

(2) Detain minors in custody who meet the detention criteria set forth in Section 628.

(3) Consider the data relating to serious habitual offenders when making all decisions regarding the identified individual and include relevant data in written reports to the court.

(4) Use all reasonable efforts to file violations of probation pursuant to Section 777 in a timely manner.

(5) Establish local policies in cooperation with law enforcement, the district attorney, schools, and the juvenile court regarding the program and provide support and assistance to other agencies engaged in the program.

(d) Each participating school district shall do all of the following:

(1) Cooperate in gathering data for use by all participating agencies pursuant to interagency agreement. School district access to records and data shall be limited to that information that is otherwise authorized by law.

(2) Report all crimes that are committed on campus by serious habitual offenders to law enforcement.

(3) Report all violations of probation committed on campus by serious habitual offenders to the probation officer or his or her designee.

(4) Provide educational supervision and services appropriate to serious habitual offenders attending schools.

(5) Establish local policies in cooperation with law enforcement, the district attorney, probation and the juvenile court regarding the program and provide support and assistance to other agencies engaged in the program.

(e) On or before March 1, 1988, the Office of Criminal Justice Planning shall submit a written report to the Legislature regarding achievement of program goals. Specifically, the report shall do all of the following:

(1) Document the amount of serious crime committed by a relatively small number of serious habitual offenders.

(2) Provide statistical documentation regarding the total number of juveniles in the program, the types of offenses committed, the manner in which cases are disposed, and a statistical profile of the average juvenile who qualifies for the program.

(3) Evaluate program costs.

(4) Review new operational and organizational techniques used in gathering and disseminating information, in prosecution and in monitoring and supervising serious habitual offenders.

(5) Compare this program and its effectiveness with the techniques and methods used prior to the implementation of the program. *(Added by Stats 1986 ch 1441 §1.)*

§504. Inspection of juvenile court records.

The judge of the juvenile court shall authorize the inspection of juvenile court records, probation and protective services records, district attorney records, school records, and law enforcement records by the participating law enforcement agency charged with the compilation of the data relating to serious habitual offenders into the format used by all participating agencies. *(Added by Stats 1986 ch 1441 §1.)*

§505. Interagency agreement outlining role in program.

Within three months of implementation of the program, all participating agencies in a county shall execute a written interagency agreement outlining their role in the program, including the duties they will perform, the duties other agencies will perform for and with them, and the categories of information to be collected and the plan for its distribution and use. All participating agencies will meet no less than once each month to plan, implement, and refine the operation of the program and to exchange information about individuals subject to the program or other related topics. *(Amended by Stats 1989 ch 1356 §2, eff. 1/1/90.)*

§506. Check of adults' juvenile criminal histories.

Law enforcement agencies and district attorneys participating in programs funded pursuant to this article shall adopt procedures to require a check of juvenile criminal history of all adults whose cases are presented to the district attorney's office for filing. The juvenile criminal history shall be considered by the district attorney in the charging decision and establishing the district attorney's position on the appropriate plea and sentence. *(Added by Stats 1986 ch 1441 §1.)*

ARTICLE 14

WARDS — JURISDICTION

§601. Persons under court jurisdiction due to inability of parents to control.

(a) Any person under the age of 18 years who persistently or habitually refuses to obey the reasonable and proper orders or directions of his parents, guardian, or custodian, or who is beyond the control of such person, or who is under the age of 18 years when he violated any ordinance of any city or county of this state establishing a curfew based solely on age is within the jurisdiction of the juvenile court which may adjudge such person to be a ward of the court.

(b) If a school attendance review board determines that the available public and private services are insufficient or inappropriate to correct the habitual truancy of the minor, or to correct the minor's persistent or habitual refusal to obey the reasonable and proper orders or directions of school authorities, or if the minor fails to respond to directives of a school attendance review board or to services provided, the minor is then within the jurisdiction of the juvenile court which may adjudge such person to be a ward of the court; provided, that it is the intent of the Legislature that no minor who is adjudged a ward of the court pursuant solely to this subdivision shall be removed from the custody of the parent or guardian except during school hours.

§601.1. Persons under court jurisdiction due to inability of school authorities to control.

(a) Any person under the age of 18 years who persistently or habitually refuses to obey the reasonable and proper orders or directions of school authorities, and is thus beyond the control of those authorities, or who is a habitual truant from school within the meaning of any law of this state, shall, prior to any referral to the juvenile court of the county, be referred to a school attendance review board pursuant to Section 48263 of the Education Code, or to a truancy mediation program pursuant to Section 601.3 of this code, or to both a school attendance review board and a truancy mediation program if both have been established in the county.

(b) In addition to any other orders authorized by law, when, after an initial referral as required by subdivision (a), a minor is adjudged a ward of the court on the ground that he or she is a person described in Section 601 by reason of habitual truancy, the court may order the minor to participate in a specified community service or educational program sponsored by either a public or private agency. The minor's participation in the program shall be limited to non-school hours. The court may order the probation officer to pick up and deliver the minor to the program designated by the court on the days that the minor is ordered to participate in the program.

To the extent practically feasible, such a minor shall not be permitted to come or remain in contact with minors ordered to participate in the program as a result of conduct described in Section 602. In no case may the court order that the minor be detained in any program overnight. *(Amended by Stats 1985 ch 667 §1.)*

§601.2. Failure of parents to respond to directives of school attendance review board.

In the event that a parent or guardian or person in charge of a minor described in Section 601.1 fails to respond to directives of the school attendance review board or to services offered on behalf of the minor, the school attendance review board shall direct that the minor be referred to the probation department or to the county welfare department under Section 300, and the school attendance review board may require the school district to file a complaint against the parent, guardian, or other person in charge of such minor as provided in Section 48291 or Section 48454 of the Education Code.

§601.3. Authorization of official to meet with parents of truant minor.

(a) If the district attorney or the probation officer receives notice from the school district pursuant to subdivision (b) of Section 48260.6 of the Education Code that a minor continues to be classified as a truant after the parents or guardians have been notified pursuant to subdivision (a) of Section 48260.5 of the Education Code, or if the district attorney or the probation officer receives notice from the school attendance review board pursuant to subdivision (a) of Section 48263.5 of the Education Code that a minor continues to be classified as a truant after review and counseling by the school attendance review board, the district attorney or the probation officer may request the parents or guardians and the child to attend a meeting in the district attorney's office or at the probation department to discuss the possible legal consequences of the minor's truancy.

(b) Notice of a meeting to be held pursuant to this section shall contain all of the following:

(1) The name and address of the person to whom the notice is directed.

(2) The date, time, and place of the meeting.

(3) The name of the minor classified as a truant.

(4) The section pursuant to which the meeting is requested.

(5) Notice that the district attorney may file a criminal complaint against the parents or guardians pursuant to Section 48293 of the Education Code for failure to compel the attendance of the minor at school.

(c) Notice of a meeting to be held pursuant to this section shall be served at least five days prior to the meeting on each person required to attend the meeting. Service shall be made personally or by certified mail with request for return receipt.

(d) At the commencement of the meeting authorized by this section, the district attorney or the probation officer shall advise the parents or guardians and the child that any statements they make could be used against them in subsequent court proceedings.

(e) Upon completion of the meeting authorized by this section, the probation officer or district attorney after consultation with the probation officer may file a petition pursuant to Section 601 if the district attorney or the probation officer determines that available community resources cannot resolve the truancy problem, or if the pupil or the parents or guardians of the pupil, or both, have failed to respond to services provided or to the directives of the school, the school attendance review board, the probation officer, or the district attorney.

(f) The truancy mediation program authorized by this section may be established by the district attorney or by the probation officer. The district attorney and the probation officer shall coordinate their efforts and shall cooperate in determining which office is best able to operate a truancy mediation program in their county pursuant to this section. *(Amended by Stats 1991 ch 1202 §14, eff. 1/1/92.)*

© 1992 by J., B. & L. Gould
Printed in the U.S.A.   **EP**

§601.4. Jurisdiction of juvenile court over parent of truant minor.

(a) The juvenile court judge may be assigned to sit as a municipal court judge to hear any complaint alleging that a parent, guardian, or other person having control or charge of a minor has violated Section 48293 of the Education Code. The jurisdiction of the juvenile court granted by this section shall not be exclusive and the charge may be prosecuted instead in a municipal or justice court. However, upon motion, that action shall be transferred to the juvenile court.

(b) Notwithstanding Section 737 of the Penal Code, a violation of Section 48293 of the Education Code may be prosecuted pursuant to subdivision (a), by written complaint filed in the same manner as an infraction may be prosecuted in a municipal or justice court. The juvenile court judge, sitting as a municipal court judge, may coordinate the action involving the minor with any action involving the parent, guardian, or other person having control or charge of the minor. Both matters may be heard and decided at the same time unless the parent, guardian, other person having control or charge of the minor, or any member of the press or public objects to closed hearing of the proceedings charging violation of Section 48293 of the Education Code. *(Amended by Stats 1989 ch 1117 §5, eff. 1/1/90.)*

§602. Who is within jurisdiction of juvenile court.

Any person who is under the age of 18 years when he violates any law of this state or of the United States or any ordinance of any city or county of this state defining crime other than an ordinance establishing a curfew based solely on age, is within the jurisdiction of the juvenile court, which may adjudge such person to be a ward of the court.

§603. Prerequisite for trial in juvenile court.

No court shall have jurisdiction to conduct a preliminary examination or to try the case of any person upon an accusatory pleading charging such person with the commission of a public offense or crime when such person was under the age of 18 years at the time of the alleged commission thereof unless the matter has first been submitted to the juvenile court by petition as provided in Article 7 (commencing with Section 650), and said juvenile court has made an order directing that such person be prosecuted under the general law.

§603.5. Jurisdiction of juvenile court in cases of Vehicle Code violations.

(a) Notwithstanding any other provision of law, in counties which adopt the provisions of this section, jurisdiction over the case of a minor alleged to have committed only a violation of the Vehicle Code classified as an infraction or a violation of a local ordinance involving the driving, parking, or operation of a motor vehicle, is with the municipal or justice court, except that the municipal or justice court may refer to the juvenile court for adjudication, cases involving a minor who has been adjudicated a ward of the juvenile court, or who has other matters pending in the juvenile court. An alleged violation of subdivision (a) or (b) of Section 40508 of the Vehicle Code may be referred to the juvenile court for adjudication.

(b) Notwithstanding this article or Articles 15 (commencing with Section 625) to 21 (commencing with Section 800), inclusive, of this chapter, except as otherwise provided in this section, all cases specified in subdivision (a) shall be governed by the general law applicable to violations of the Vehicle Code.

The provisions of this section shall apply only in a county in which the board of supervisors, with the concurrence of the presiding judges of the superior, municipal, and justice courts, adopts a resolution making the section applicable in the county.

§604. Suspension of proceedings and certification.

(a) Whenever a case is before any court upon an accusatory pleading and it is suggested or appears to the judge before whom the person is brought that the person charged was, at the date the offense is alleged to have been committed, under the age of 18 years, the judge shall immediately suspend all proceedings against the person on the charge; he or she shall examine into the age of the person, and if, from the examination, it appears to his or her satisfaction that the person was at the date the offense is alleged to have been committed under the age of 18 years, he or she shall immediately certify all of the following to the juvenile court of the county:

(1) That the person (naming him or her) is charged with a crime (briefly stating its nature).

(2) That the person appears to have been under the age of 18 years at the date the offense is alleged to have been committed, giving the date of birth of the person when known.

(3) That proceedings have been suspended against the person on the charge by reason of his or her age, with the date of the suspension.

The judge shall attach a copy of the accusatory pleading to the certification.

(b) When a court certifies a case to the juvenile court pursuant to subdivision (a), it shall be deemed that jeopardy has not attached by reason of the proceedings prior to certification, but the court may not resume proceedings in the case, nor may a new proceeding under the general law be commenced in any court with respect to the same matter unless the juvenile court has found that the minor is not a fit subject for consideration under the juvenile court law and has ordered that proceedings under the general law resume or be commenced.

(c) The certification and accusatory pleading shall be promptly transmitted to the clerk of the juvenile court. Upon receipt thereof, the clerk of the juvenile court shall immediately notify the probation officer who shall immediately proceed in accordance with Article 16 (commencing with Section 650).

§605. Suspension of statute of limitations.

Whenever a petition is filed in a juvenile court alleging that a minor is a person within the description of Section 602, and while the case is before the juvenile court, the statute of limitations applicable under the general law to the offense alleged to bring the minor within such description is suspended.

§606. Liability of minor to prosecution after filing petition.

When a petition has been filed in a juvenile court, the minor who is the subject of the petition shall not thereafter be subject to criminal prosecution based on the facts giving rise to the petition unless the juvenile court finds that the minor is not a fit and proper subject to be dealt with under this chapter and orders that criminal proceedings be resumed or instituted against him.

§607. Limits to which juvenile court may retain jurisdiction.

(a) The court may retain jurisdiction over any person who is found to be a ward or dependent child of the juvenile court until the ward or dependent child attains the age of 21 years, except as provided in subdivisions (b), (c), and (d).

(b) The court may retain jurisdiction over any person who is found to be a person described in Section 602 by reason of the commission of any of the offenses listed in subdivision (b) of Section 707 until that person attains the age of 25 years if the person was committed to the Department of the Youth Authority.

(c) The court shall not discharge any person from its jurisdiction who has been committed to the Department of the Youth Authority so long as the person remains under the jurisdiction of the Department of the Youth Authority, including periods of extended control ordered pursuant to Section 1800.

(d) The court may retain jurisdiction over any person described in Section 602 by reason of the commission of any of the offenses listed in subdivision (b) of Section 707 who has been confined in a state hospital or other appropriate public or private mental health facility pursuant to Section 702.3 until that person has attained the age of 25 years, unless the court which committed the person finds, after notice and hearing, that the person's sanity has been restored.

(e) The court may retain jurisdiction over any person while that person is the subject of a warrant for arrest issued pursuant to Section 663. (*Amended by Stats 1988 ch 713 §1, eff. 1/1/89.*)

§608. Determination of person's age by dental examination.

In any case in which a person is alleged to be a person described in Section 601 or 602, or subdivision (a) of Section 604, and the age of the person is at issue and the court finds that a scientific or medical test would be of assistance in determining the age of the person, the court may consider ordering an examination of the minor using the method described in "The Permanent Mandibular Third Molar" from the Journal of Forensic Odonto-Stomatology, Vol. 1: No. 1: January-June 1983. (*Added by Stats 1990 ch 749 §1, eff. 1/1/91.*)

ARTICLE 15

WARDS — TEMPORARY CUSTODY AND DETENTION

§625. Grounds on which peace officer may take minor into temporary custody.

A peace officer may, without a warrant, take into temporary custody a minor:

(a) Who is under the age of 18 years when such officer has reasonable cause for believing that such minor is a person described in Section 601 or 602, or

(b) Who is a ward of the juvenile court or concerning whom an order has been made under Section 636 or 702, when such officer has reasonable cause for believing that person has violated an order of the juvenile court or has escaped from any commitment ordered by the juvenile court, or

(c) Who is under the age of 18 years and who is found in any street or public place suffering from any sickness or injury which requires care, medical treatment, hospitalization, or other remedial care.

In any case where a minor is taken into temporary custody on the ground that there is reasonable cause for believing that such minor is a person described in Section 601 or 602, or that he has violated an order of the juvenile court or escaped from any commitment ordered by the juvenile court, the officer shall advise such minor that anything he says can be used against him and shall advise him of his constitutional rights, including his right to remain silent, his right to have counsel present during any interrogation, and his right to have counsel appointed if he is unable to afford counsel.

§625.1. Administering voluntary chemical tests to minors.

Any minor who is taken into temporary custody pursuant to subdivision (a) of Section 625, when the peace officer has reasonable cause for believing the minor is a person described in Section 602, or pursuant to subdivision (b) or (c) of Section 625, may be requested to submit to voluntary chemical testing of his or her urine for the purpose of determining the presence of alcohol or illegal drugs. The peace officer shall inform the minor that the chemical test is voluntary. The results of this test may be considered by the court in determining the disposition of the minor pursuant to Section 706 or 777. Unless otherwise provided by law, the results of such a test shall not be the basis of a petition filed by the prosecuting attorney to declare the minor a person described in Section 602, nor shall it be the basis for such a finding by a court pursuant to Section 702. (*Added by Stats 1989 ch 1117 §6, eff. 1/1/90.*)

§625.2. Informing minor of rights before chemical testing.

(a) Before administering the chemical test pursuant to Section 625.1, the peace officer shall give the following admonition: "I am asking you to take a voluntary urine test to test for the presence of drugs or alcohol in your body. You have the right to refuse to take the test. If you do not take the test, it cannot be used as the basis for filing any additional charges against you. It can be used by a court for the purpose of sentencing. You have the right to telephone your parent or guardian before you decide whether or not to take this test."

(b) The admonition in subdivision (a) shall not be given when a chemical test is administered pursuant to Section 23157 of the Vehicle Code. (*Added by Stats 1989 ch 1117 §7, eff. 1/1/90.*)

§626. Peace officer's alternatives upon taking a minor into custody.

An officer who takes a minor into temporary custody under the provisions of Section 626 may do any of the following:

(a) Release the minor.

(b) Deliver or refer the minor to a public or private agency with which the city or county has an agreement or plan to provide shelter care, counseling, or diversion services to minors so delivered.

(c) Prepare in duplicate a written notice to appear before the probation officer of the county in which the minor was taken into custody at a time and place

© 1992 by J., B. & L. Gould
Printed in the U.S.A.　　EP

specified in the notice. The notice shall also contain a concise statement of the reasons the minor was taken into custody. The officer shall deliver one copy of the notice to the minor or to a parent, guardian, or responsible relative of the minor and may require the minor or the minor's parent, guardian, or relative, or both, to sign a written promise to appear at the time and place designated in the notice. Upon the execution of the promise to appear, the officer shall immediately release the minor. The officer shall, as soon as practicable, file one copy of the notice with the probation officer.

(d) Take the minor without unnecessary delay before the probation officer of the county in which the minor was taken into custody, or in which the minor resides, or in which the acts take place or the circumstances exist which are alleged to bring the minor within the provisions of Section 601 or 602, and deliver the custody of the minor to the probation officer. The peace officer shall prepare a concise written statement of the probable cause for taking the minor into temporary custody and the reasons the minor was taken into custody and shall provide the statement to the probation officer at the time the minor is delivered to the probation officer. In no case shall the officer delay the delivery of the minor to the probation officer for more than 24 hours if the minor has been taken into custody without a warrant on the belief that the minor has committed a misdemeanor.

In determining which disposition of the minor to make, the officer shall prefer the alternative which least restricts the minor's freedom of movement, provided that alternative is compatible with the best interests of the minor and the community. (Amended by Stats 1989 ch 878 §1, eff. 1/1/90.)

§626.5. Means for peace officer to bring minor to attention of juvenile court.

If an officer who takes a minor into temporary custody under the provisions of Section 625 determines that the minor should be brought to the attention of the juvenile court, he or she shall thereafter take one of the following actions:

(a) He or she may prepare in duplicate a written notice to appear before the probation officer of the county in which the minor was taken in custody at a time and place specified in the notice. The notice shall also contain a concise statement of the reasons the minor was taken into custody. The officer shall deliver one copy of the notice to the minor or to a parent, guardian, or responsible relative of the minor and may require the minor or his or her parent, guardian, or relative, or both, to sign a written promise that either or both will appear at the time and place designated in the notice. Upon the execution of the promise to appear, the officer shall immediately release the minor. The officer shall, as soon as practicable, file one copy of the notice with the probation officer.

(b) He or she may take the minor without unnecessary delay before the probation officer of the county in which the minor was taken into custody, or in which the minor resides, or in which the acts took place or the circumstances exist which are alleged to bring the minor within the provisions of Section 601 or 602, and deliver the custody of the minor to the probation officer. The peace officer shall prepare a concise written statement of the probable cause for taking the minor into temporary custody and the reasons the minor was taken into custody and shall provide that

statement to the probation officer at the time the minor is delivered to the probation officer. In no case shall he or she delay the delivery of the minor to the probation officer for more than 24 hours if the minor has been taken into custody without a warrant on the belief that he or she has committed a misdemeanor.

In determining which disposition of the minor he or she will make, the officer shall prefer the alternative which least restricts the minor's freedom of movement, provided that alternative is compatible with the best interests of the minor and the community. (Amended by Stats 1989 ch 878 §2, eff. 1/1/90.)

§627. Notification of parent or guardian; minor's right to make telephone calls.

(a) When an officer takes a minor before a probation officer at a juvenile hall or to any other place of confinement pursuant to this article, he shall take immediate steps to notify the minor's parent, guardian, or a responsible relative that such minor is in custody and the place where he is being held.

(b) Immediately after being taken to a place of confinement pursuant to this article and, except where physically impossible, no later than one hour after he has been taken into custody, the minor shall be advised and has the right to make at least two telephone calls from the place where he is being held, one call completed to his parent or guardian, a responsible relative, or his employer, and another call completed to an attorney. The calls shall be at public expense, if the calls are completed to telephone numbers within the local calling area, and in the presence of a public officer or employee. Any public officer or employee who willfully deprives a minor taken into custody of his right to make such telephone calls is guilty of a misdemeanor.

§627.5. Notification of minor as to constitutional rights.

In any case where a minor is taken before a probation officer pursuant to the provisions of Section 626 and it is alleged that such minor is a person described in Section 601 or 602, the probation officer shall immediately advise the minor and his parent or guardian that anything the minor says can be used against him and shall advise them of the minor's constitutional rights, including his right to remain silent, his right to have counsel present during any interrogation, and his right to have counsel appointed if he is unable to afford counsel. If the minor or his parent or guardian requests counsel, the probation officer shall notify the judge of the juvenile court of such request and counsel for the minor shall be appointed pursuant to Section 634.

§628. Conditions preventing minor from being released into parent's custody.

(a) Upon delivery to the probation officer of a minor who has been taken into temporary custody under the provisions of this article, the probation officer shall immediately investigate the circumstances of the minor and the facts surrounding his being taken into custody and shall immediately release such minor to the custody of his parent, guardian, or responsible relative unless one or more of the following conditions exist:

(1) The minor is in need of proper and effective parental care or control and has no parent, guardian, or responsible relative; or has no parent, guardian, or

responsible relative willing to exercise or capable of exercising such care or control; or has no parent, guardian, or responsible relative actually exercising such care or control.

(2) The minor is destitute or is not provided with the necessities of life or is not provided with a home or suitable place of abode.

(3) The minor is provided with a home which is an unfit place for him by reason of neglect, cruelty, depravity or physical abuse of either of his parents, or of his guardian or other person in whose custody or care he is.

(4) Continued detention of the minor is a matter of immediate and urgent necessity for the protection of the minor or reasonable necessity for the protection of the person or property of another.

(5) The minor is likely to flee the jurisdiction of the court.

(6) The minor has violated an order of the juvenile court.

(7) The minor is physically dangerous to the public because of a mental or physical deficiency, disorder or abnormality.

(b) In any case in which there is reasonable cause for believing that a minor who is under the care of a physician or surgeon or a hospital, clinic, or other medical facility and cannot be immediately moved is a person described in subdivision (d) of Section 300, the minor shall be deemed to have been taken into temporary custody and delivered to the probation officer for the purposes of this chapter while he is at the office of the physician or surgeon or such medical facility.

§628.1. Conditions and procedure for release of minor.

If the minor meets one or more of the criteria for detention under Section 628, but the probation officer believes that 24-hour secure detention is not necessary in order to protect the minor or the person or property of another, or to ensure that the minor does not flee the jurisdiction of the court, the probation officer shall proceed according to this section.

Unless one of the conditions described in paragraph (1), (2), or (3) of subdivision (a) of Section 628 exists, the probation officer shall release such minor to his parent, guardian, or responsible relative on home supervision. As a condition for such release, the probation officer shall require the minor to sign a written promise that he understands and will observe the specific conditions of home supervision release. Such conditions may include curfew and school attendance requirements related to the protection of the minor or the person or property of another, or to the minor's appearances at court hearings. A minor who violates a specific condition of home supervision release which he has promised in writing to obey may be taken into custody and placed in secure detention, subject to court review at a detention hearing.

A minor on home supervision shall be entitled to the same legal protections as a minor in secure detention, including a detention hearing.

§629. Promise to appear.

As a condition for the release of such minor, the probation officer may require such minor or his parent, guardian, or relative, or both, to sign a written promise that either or both of them will appear before the probation officer at the juvenile hall or other suitable place designated by the probation officer at a specified time.

§630. Petition to retain minor in custody.

(a) If the probation officer determines that the minor shall be retained in custody, he shall immediately proceed in accordance with Article 16 (commencing with Section 650) to cause the filing of a petition pursuant to Section 656 with the clerk of the juvenile court who shall set the matter for hearing on the detention calendar. Immediately upon filing the petition with the clerk of the juvenile court, if the minor is alleged to be a person described in Section 601 or 602, the probation officer or the prosecuting attorney, as the case may be, shall serve such minor with a copy of the petition and notify him of the time and place of the detention hearing. The probation officer, or the prosecuting attorney, as the case may be, shall thereupon notify each parent or each guardian of the minor of the time and place of such hearing if the whereabouts of each parent or guardian can be ascertained by due diligence. Such notice may be given orally.

(b) In such hearing the minor has a privilege against self-incrimination and has a right to confrontation by, and cross-examination of, any person examined by the court as provided in Section 635.

§630.1. Notification of counsel regarding hearings.

Upon reasonable notification by counsel representing the minor, his parents or guardian, the clerk of the court shall notify such counsel of the hearings in the manner provided for notice to the parent or guardian of the minor under this chapter.

§631. Limitation on retention of minor without petition.

(a) Except as provided in subdivision (b), whenever a minor is taken into custody by a peace officer or probation officer, except when the minor willfully misrepresents himself or herself as 18 or more years of age, the minor shall be released within 48 hours after having been taken into custody, excluding nonjudicial days, unless within that period of time a petition to declare the minor a ward has been filed pursuant to this chapter or a criminal complaint against the minor has been filed in a court of competent jurisdiction.

(b) Except when the minor represents himself or herself as 18 or more years of age, whenever a minor is taken into custody by a peace officer or probation officer without a warrant on the belief that the minor has committed a misdemeanor that does not involve violence, the threat of violence, or possession or use of a weapon, and if the minor is not currently on probation or parole, the minor shall be released within 48 hours after having been taken into custody, excluding nonjudicial days, unless a petition has been filed to declare the minor to be a ward of the court and the minor has been ordered detained by a judge or referee of the juvenile court pursuant to Section 635. In all cases involving the detention of a minor pursuant to this subdivision, any decision to detain the minor more than 24 hours shall be subject to written review and approval by a probation officer who is a supervisor as soon as possible after it is known that the minor will be detained more than 24 hours. However, if the initial decision to detain the minor more than 24 hours is

© 1992 by J., B. & L. Gould
Printed in the U.S.A.   EP

made by a probation officer who is a supervisor, the decision shall not be subject to review and approval.

(c) Whenever a minor who has been held in custody for more than 24 hours by the probation officer is subsequently released and no petition is filed, the probation officer shall prepare a written explanation of why the minor was held in custody for more than 24 hours. The written explanation shall be prepared within 72 hours after the minor is released from custody and filed in the record of the case. A copy of the written explanation shall be sent to the parents, guardian, or other person having care or custody of the minor. *(Amended by Stats 1989 ch 686 §1, eff. 1/1/90.)*

§631.1. Procedure when minor misrepresents age.

When a minor willfully misrepresents himself to be 18 or more years of age when taken into custody by a peace officer or probation officer, and this misrepresentation effects a material delay in investigation which prevents the filing of a petition pursuant to the provisions of this chapter or the filing of a criminal complaint against him in a court of competent jurisdiction within 48 hours, such petition or complaint shall be filed within 48 hours from the time his true age is determined, excluding nonjudicial days. If, in such cases, the petition or complaint is not filed within the time prescribed by this section, the minor shall be immediately released from custody.

§632. Detention hearing.

(a) Except as provided in subdivision (b), unless sooner released, a minor taken into custody under the provisions of this article shall, as soon as possible but in any event before the expiration of the next judicial day after a petition to declare the minor a ward or dependent child has been filed, be brought before a judge or referee of the juvenile court for a hearing to determine whether the minor shall be further detained. Such a hearing shall be referred to as a "detention hearing."

(b) Whenever a minor is taken into custody without a warrant on the belief that he or she has committed a misdemeanor not involving violence, a threat of violence, or possession or use of weapons, if the minor is not currently on probation or parole, he or she shall be brought before a judge or referee of the juvenile court for hearing as soon as possible, but no later than 48 hours after having been taken into custody, excluding nonjudicial days, after a petition to declare the minor a ward has been filed. In all cases involving the detention of a minor pursuant to this subdivision where the minor will not be brought before the judge or referee of the juvenile court within 24 hours, the decision not to bring the minor before the judge or referee within 24 hours shall be subject to written review and approval by a probation officer who is a supervisor as soon as possible after it is known that the minor will not be brought before the judge or referee within 24 hours. However, if the decision not to bring the minor before the judge or referee within 24 hours is made by a probation officer who is a supervisor, the decision shall not be subject to review and approval.

(c) If the minor is not brought before a judge or referee of the juvenile court within the period prescribed by this section, he or she shall be released from custody. *(Amended by Stats 1989 ch 686 §2, eff. 1/1/90.)*

§633. Notification of minor and parent regarding procedure.

Upon his appearance before the court at the detention hearing, such minor and his parent or guardian, if present, shall first be informed of the reasons why the minor was taken into custody, the nature of the juvenile court proceedings, and the right of such minor and his parent or guardian to be represented at every stage of the proceedings by counsel.

§634. Provision of counsel by court.

When it appears to the court that the minor or his parent or guardian desires counsel but is unable to afford and cannot for that reason employ counsel, the court may appoint counsel. In a case in which the minor is alleged to be a person described in Section 601 or 602, the court shall appoint counsel for the minor if he appears at the hearing without counsel, whether he is unable to afford counsel or not, unless there is an intelligent waiver of the right of counsel by the minor; and, in the absence of such waiver, if the parent or guardian does not furnish counsel and the court determines that the parent or guardian has the ability to pay for counsel, the court shall appoint counsel at the expense of the parent or guardian. In any case in which it appears to the court that there is such a conflict of interest between a parent or guardian and child that one attorney could not properly represent both, the court shall appoint counsel, in addition to counsel already employed by a parent or guardian or appointed by the court to represent the minor or parent or guardian. In a county where there is no public defender the court may fix the compensation to be paid by the county for service of such appointed counsel.

§634.6. Continuity of counsel.

Any counsel upon entering an appearance on behalf of a minor shall continue to represent that minor unless relieved by the court upon the substitution of other counsel or for cause.

§635. Conditions for retention of minor in court custody.

The court will examine such minor, his parent, guardian, or other person having relevant knowledge, hear such relevant evidence as the minor, his parent or guardian or their counsel desires to present, and, unless it appears that such minor has violated an order of the juvenile court or has escaped from the commitment of the juvenile court or that it is a matter of immediate and urgent necessity for the protection of such minor or reasonably necessary for the protection of the person or property of another that he be detained or that such minor is likely to flee to avoid the jurisdiction of the court, the court shall make its order releasing such minor from custody.

The circumstances and gravity of the alleged offense may be considered, in conjunction with other factors, to determine whether it is a matter of immediate and urgent necessity for the protection of the minor or reasonably necessary for the protection of the person or property of another that the minor be detained.

§635.1. Provision of mental health treatment.

When the court finds a minor to be a person described by Section 602 and believes the minor may need specialized mental health treatment while the minor is unable to reside in his or her natural home, the court shall notify the director of the county mental health department in the county where the minor resides. The county mental health department shall perform the duties required under Section 5697.5 for all those minors.

Nothing in this section shall restrict the provision of emergency psychiatric services to those minors who have not yet reached the point of adjudication or disposition, nor shall it operate to restrict evaluations at an earlier stage of the proceedings or to restrict the use of Sections 4011.6 and 4011.8 of the Penal Code. *(Added by Stats 1985 ch 1286 §2.)*

§636. Order for detention in juvenile hall.

If it appears upon the hearing that such minor has violated an order of the juvenile court or has escaped from a commitment of the juvenile court or that it is a matter of immediate and urgent necessity for the protection of such minor or reasonably necessary for the protection of the person or property of another that he be detained or that such minor is likely to flee to avoid the jurisdiction of the court, the court may make its order that such minor be detained in the juvenile hall or other suitable place designated by the juvenile court for a period not to exceed 15 judicial days and shall enter said order together with its findings of fact in support thereof in the records of the court. The circumstances and gravity of the alleged offense may be considered, in conjunction with other factors, to determine whether it is a matter of immediate and urgent necessity for the protection of the minor or the person or property of another that the minor be detained.

If the court finds that the criteria of Section 628.1 are applicable, the court may, and after the operative date of that section the court shall, place the minor on home supervision for a period not to exceed 15 judicial days, and shall enter such order together with its findings of fact in support thereof in the records of the court. If the court releases the minor on home supervision, the court may continue, modify, or augment any conditions of release previously imposed by the probation officer, or may impose new conditions on a minor released for the first time. If there are new or modified conditions, the minor shall be required to sign a written promise to obey such conditions pursuant to Section 628.1.

§636.2. Nonsecure detention facilities.

The probation officer may operate and maintain nonsecure detention facilities, or may contract with public or private agencies offering such services, for those minors who are not considered escape risks and are not considered a danger to themselves or to the person or property of another. Criteria to be considered for detention in such facilities shall include, but not be limited to: (a) the nature of the offense, (b) the minor's previous record including escapes from secure detention facilities, (c) lack of criminal sophistication, and (d) the age of the minor. A minor detained in such facilities who leaves the same without permission may be housed in a secure facility following his apprehension, pending a detention hearing pursuant to Section 632.

§637. Conditions for rehearing due to absence of notice.

When a hearing is held under the provisions of this article and no parent or guardian of such minor is present and no parent or guardian has had actual notice of the hearing, a parent or guardian of such minor may file his affidavit setting forth such facts with the clerk of the juvenile court and the clerk shall immediately set the matter for rehearing at a time within 24 hours, excluding Sundays and nonjudicial days from the filing of the affidavit. Upon the rehearing, the court shall proceed in the same manner as upon the original hearing.

If the minor or, if the minor is represented by an attorney, the minor's attorney, requests evidence of the prima facie case, a rehearing shall be held within three judicial days to consider evidence of the prima facie case. If the prima facie case is not established, the minor shall be released from detention.

When the court ascertains that the rehearing cannot be held within three judicial days because of the unavailability of a witness, a reasonable continuance may be granted for a period not to exceed five judicial days.

§638. Motion for continuance.

Upon motion of the minor or a parent or guardian of such minor, the court shall continue any hearing or rehearing held under the provisions of this article for one day, excluding Sundays and nonjudicial days.

§639. Order to minor or parent to reappear in court.

Upon any hearing or rehearing under the provisions of this article, the court may order such minor or any parent or guardian of such minor who is present in court to again appear before the court or the probation officer or the county financial evaluation officer at a time and place specified in said order. *(Amended by Stats 1985 ch 1485 §11.)*

§641. Minor taken in custody by county other than requesting county.

Whenever any minor is taken into temporary custody under the provisions of this article in any county other than the county in which the minor is alleged to be within or to come within the jurisdiction of the juvenile court, which county is referred to herein as the requesting county, the officer who has taken the minor into temporary custody may notify the law enforcement agency in the requesting county of the fact that the minor is in custody. When a law enforcement officer, of such requesting county files a petition pursuant to Section 656 with the clerk of the juvenile court of his respective county and secures a warrant therefrom, he shall forward said warrant, or a telegraphic copy thereof to the officer who has the minor in temporary custody as soon as possible within 48 hours, excluding Sundays and nonjudicial days, from the time said juvenile was taken into temporary custody. Thereafter an officer from said requesting county shall take custody of the minor within five days, in the county in which the minor is in temporary custody, and shall take the minor before the juvenile court judge who issued the warrant, or before some other juvenile court of the same county without unnecessary delay. If the minor is not brought before a judge of the juvenile court within the period prescribed by this section, he must be released from custody.

© 1992 by J., B. & L. Gould
Printed in the U.S.A. **EP**

ARTICLE 16

WARDS — COMMENCEMENT OF PROCEEDINGS

§650. Procedure to declare minor ward of the court.

(a) Juvenile court proceedings to declare a minor a ward of the court pursuant to Section 601 are commenced by the filing of a petition by the probation officer except as specified in subdivision (b).

(b) Juvenile court proceedings to declare a minor a ward of the court pursuant to subdivision (e) of Section 601.3 may be commenced by the filing of a petition by the probation officer or the district attorney after consultation with the probation officer.

(c) Juvenile court proceedings to declare a minor a ward of the court pursuant to Section 602 are commenced by the filing of a petition by the prosecuting attorney. *(Amended by Stats 1991 ch 1202 §15, eff. 1/1/92.)*

§651. Location of proceedings.

Proceedings under this chapter may be commenced either in the juvenile court for the county in which a minor resides, or in which a minor is found, or in which the circumstances exist or acts take place to bring a minor within the provisions of Section 601 or Section 602.

§652. Investigation as to whether proceedings warranted.

Whenever the probation officer has cause to believe that there was or is within the county, or residing therein, a person within the provisions of Section 601 or 602, the probation officer shall immediately make such investigation as he or she deems necessary to determine whether proceedings in the juvenile court should be commenced. However, this section does not require an investigation by the probation officer with respect to a minor delivered or referred to an agency pursuant to subdivision (b) of Section 626.

§652.5. Investigation as to necessary disposition of minor.

Whenever an officer refers or delivers a minor pursuant to subdivision (b) of Section 626, the agency to which the minor is referred or delivered shall immediately make such investigation as that agency deems necessary to determine what disposition of the minor that agency shall make and shall initiate a service program for the minor when appropriate.

The service program for any minor referred or delivered to the agency for any act described in Section 602 shall include constructive assignments that will help the minor learn to be responsible for his or her actions. The assignments may include, but not be limited to, requiring the minor to repair damaged property or to make other appropriate restitution, or requiring the minor to participate in an educational or counseling program. The minor or his or her parent or guardian may be required to reimburse the agency for all or part of the cost of the service program if he or she has the financial ability to pay.

If the referral agency does not initiate a service program on behalf of a minor referred to the agency within 20 calendar days, or initiate a service program on behalf of a minor delivered to the agency within 10 days, that agency shall immediately notify the refer-

ring officer of that decision in writing. The referral agency shall retain a copy of that written notification for 30 days. *(Amended by Stats 1990 ch 258 §1, eff. 1/1/91.)*

§653. Application to commence proceedings.

Whenever any person applies to the probation officer or the district attorney in accordance with subdivision (e) of Section 601.3, to commence proceedings in the juvenile court, the application shall be in the form of an affidavit alleging that there was or is within the county, or residing therein, a minor within the provisions of Section 601 and setting forth facts in support thereof. The probation officer or the district attorney in consultation with the probation officer shall immediately make such investigation as he or she deems necessary to determine whether proceedings in the juvenile court should be commenced. *(Amended by Stats 1991 ch 1202 §16, eff. 1/1/92.)*

§653.1. Delivery of affidavit.

Notwithstanding Section 653, in the case of an affidavit alleging that the minor committed an offense described in Section 602, the probation officer shall cause the affidavit to be immediately taken to the prosecuting attorney if it appears to the probation officer that the minor has been referred to the probation officer for any violation of an offense listed in subdivision (b) of Section 707 and that offense was allegedly committed when the minor was 16 years of age or older. If the prosecuting attorney decides not to file a petition, he or she may return the affidavit to the probation officer for any other appropriate action. *(Added by Stats 1987 ch 1499 §4.)*

§653.5. Determination as to whether proceedings should be commenced.

(a) Whenever any person applies to the probation officer to commence proceedings in the juvenile court, the application shall be in the form of an affidavit alleging that there was or is within the county, or residing therein, a minor within the provisions of Section 602, or that a minor committed an offense described in Section 602 within the county, and setting forth facts in support thereof. The probation officer shall immediately make any investigation he or she deems necessary to determine whether proceedings in the juvenile court shall be commenced.

(b) Except as provided in subdivision (c), if the probation officer determines that proceedings pursuant to Section 650 should be commenced to declare a person to be a ward of the juvenile court on the basis that he or she is a person described in Section 602, the probation officer shall cause the affidavit to be taken to the prosecuting attorney.

(c) Notwithstanding the provisions of subdivision (b), the probation officer shall cause the affidavit to be taken within 48 hours to the prosecuting attorney in all of the following cases:

(1) If it appears to the probation officer that the minor has been referred to the probation officer for any violation of an offense listed in subdivision (b) of Section 707.

(2) If it appears to the probation officer that the minor is under 16 years of age at the date of the offense and that the offense constitutes a second felony referral to the probation officer.

(3) If it appears to the probation officer that the minor was 16 years of age or older at the date of the

offense and that the offense constitutes a felony referral to the probation officer.

(4) If it appears to the probation officer that the minor has been referred to the probation officer for the sale or possession for sale of a controlled substance as defined in Chapter 2 (commencing with Section 11053) of Division 10 of the Health and Safety Code.

(5) If it appears to the probation officer that the minor has been referred to the probation officer for a violation of Section 11350 or 11377 of the Health and Safety Code where the violation takes place at a public or private elementary, vocational, junior high school, or high school, or a violation of Section 245.5, 626.9, or 626.10 of the Penal Code.

(6) If it appears to the probation officer that the minor has been referred to the probation officer for a violation of Section 186.22 of the Penal Code.

(7) If it appears to the probation officer that the minor has previously been placed in a program of informal probation pursuant to Section 654.

(8) If it appears to the probation officer that the minor has committed an offense in which the restitution owed to the victim exceeds one thousand dollars ($1,000). For purposes of this paragraph, the definition of "victim" in paragraph (1) of subdivision (a) of Section 729.6 and "restitution" in subdivision (d) of Section 729.6 shall apply.

(9) If it appears to the probation officer that the minor was 14 years of age or older at the date of the offense and the offense for which the referral was made constitutes a violation of Section 487h of the Penal Code or Section 10851 of the Vehicle Code.

Except for offenses listed in paragraph (5), the provisions of subdivision (c) shall not apply to a narcotics and drug offense set forth in Section 1000 of the Penal Code.

The prosecuting attorney shall within his or her discretionary power institute proceedings in accordance with his or her role as public prosecutor pursuant to subdivision (b) of Section 650 and Section 26500 of the Government Code. However, if it appears to the prosecuting attorney that the affidavit was not properly referred, that the offense for which the minor was referred should be charged as a misdemeanor, or that the minor may benefit from a program of informal supervision, he or she shall refer the matter to the probation officer for whatever action the probation officer may deem appropriate.

(d) In all matters where the minor is not in custody and is already a ward of the court or a probationer under Section 602, the prosecuting attorney, within five judicial days of receipt of the affidavit from the probation officer, shall institute proceedings in accordance with his or her role as public prosecutor pursuant to subdivision (b) of Section 650 of this code and Section 26500 of the Government Code, unless it appears to the prosecuting attorney that the affidavit was not properly referred or that the offense for which the minor was referred requires additional substantiating information, in which case he or she shall immediately notify the probation officer of what further action he or she is taking.

(e) This section shall remain in effect only until January 1, 1993, and as of that date is repealed, unless a later enacted statute, which is enacted before January 1, 1993, deletes or extends that date.
(Amended by Stats 1989 ch 930 §12, 1117 §8.1, eff. 1/1/90 only until 1/1/93. See other section 653.5 below.)

§653.5. Determination as to whether proceedings should be commenced.

(a) Whenever any person applies to the probation officer to commence proceedings in the juvenile court, the application shall be in the form of an affidavit alleging that there was or is within the county, or residing therein, a minor within the provisions of Section 602, or that a minor committed an offense described in Section 602 within the county, and setting forth facts in support thereof. The probation officer shall immediately make any investigation he or she deems necessary to determine whether proceedings in the juvenile court shall be commenced.

(b) Except as provided in subdivision (c), if the probation officer determines that proceedings pursuant to Section 650 should be commenced to declare a person to be a ward of the juvenile court on the basis that he or she is a person described in Section 602, the probation officer shall cause the affidavit to be taken to the prosecuting attorney.

(c) Notwithstanding the provisions of subdivision (b), the probation officer shall cause the affidavit to be taken within 48 hours to the prosecuting attorney in all of the following cases:

(1) If it appears to the probation officer that the minor has been referred to the probation officer for any violation of an offense listed in subdivision (b) of Section 707.

(2) If it appears to the probation officer that the minor is under 16 years of age at the date of the offense and that the offense constitutes a second felony referral to the probation officer.

(3) If it appears to the probation officer that the minor was 16 years of age or older at the date of the offense and that the offense constitutes a felony referral to the probation officer.

(4) If it appears to the probation officer that the minor has been referred to the probation officer for the sale or possession for sale of a controlled substance as defined in Chapter 2 (commencing with Section 11053) of Division 10 of the Health and Safety Code.

(5) If it appears to the probation officer that the minor has been referred to the probation officer for a violation of Section 11350 or 11377 of the Health and Safety Code where the violation takes place at a public or private elementary, vocational, junior high school, or high school, or a violation of Section 245.5, 626.9, or 626.10 of the Penal Code.

(6) If it appears to the probation officer that the minor has been referred to the probation officer for a violation of Section 186.22 of the Penal Code.

(7) If it appears to the probation officer that the minor has previously been placed in a program of informal probation pursuant to Section 654.

(8) If it appears to the probation officer that the minor has committed an offense in which the restitution owed to the victim exceeds one thousand dollars ($1,000). For purposes of this paragraph, the definition of "victim" in paragraph (1) of subdivision (a) of Section 729.6 and "restitution" in subdivision (d) of Section 729.6 shall apply.

Except for offenses listed in paragraph (5), the provisions of subdivision (c) shall not apply to a narcotics and drug offense set forth in Section 1000 of the Penal Code.

The prosecuting attorney shall within his or her discretionary power institute proceedings in accordance with his or her role as public prosecutor pursuant to subdivision (b) of Section 650 and Section 26500 of

© 1992 by J., B. & L. Gould
Printed in the U.S.A.   EP

the Government Code. However, if it appears to the prosecuting attorney that the affidavit was not properly referred, that the offense for which the minor was referred should be charged as a misdemeanor, or that the minor may benefit from a program of informal supervision, he or she shall refer the matter to the probation officer for whatever action the probation officer may deem appropriate.

(d) In all matters where the minor is not in custody and is already a ward of the court or a probationer under Section 602, the prosecuting attorney, within five judicial days of receipt of the affidavit from, the probation officer, shall institute proceedings in accordance with his or her role as public prosecutor pursuant to subdivision (b) of Section 650 of this code and Section 26500 of the Government Code, unless it appears to the prosecuting attorney that the affidavit was not properly referred or that the offense for which the minor was referred requires additional substantiating information, in which case he or she shall immediately notify the probation officer of what further action he or she is taking.

(e) This section shall become operative on January 1, 1993, unless a later enacted statute, which is enacted before January 1, 1993, changes that date. *(Added by Stats 1989 ch 930 §12.2, 1117 §8.3, eff. 1/1/90, oper. 1/1/93. See other section 653.5 above.)*

§653.7. Decision not to proceed further; reasons.

If the probation officer does not take action under Section 654 and does not file a petition in juvenile court within 21 court days after the application, or in the case of an affidavit alleging that a minor committed an offense described in Section 602 or alleging that a minor is within Section 602, does not cause the affidavit to be taken to the prosecuting attorney within 21 court days after the application, he or she shall endorse upon the affidavit of the applicant the decision not to proceed further and the reasons therefor and shall immediately notify the applicant of the action taken or the decision rendered by him or her under this section. The probation officer shall retain the affidavit and the endorsement thereon for a period of 30 court days after the notice to the applicant.

§654. Preventative programs of supervision.

In any case in which a probation officer, after investigation of an application for a petition or any other investigation he or she is authorized to make concludes that a minor is within the jurisdiction of the juvenile court or will probably soon be within that jurisdiction, the probation officer may, in lieu of filing a petition to declare a minor a dependent child of the court or a minor or a ward of the court under Section 601 or requesting that a petition be filed by the prosecuting attorney to declare a minor a ward of the court under subdivision (e) of Section 601.3 or Section 602 and with consent of the minor and the minor's parent or guardian, delineate specific programs of supervision for the minor, for not to exceed six months, and attempt thereby to adjust the situation which brings the minor within the jurisdiction of the court or creates the probability that the minor will soon be within that jurisdiction. Nothing in this section shall be construed to prevent the probation officer from filing a petition or requesting the prosecuting attorney to file a petition at any time within the six-month period or a 90-day period thereafter. If the probation officer determines that the minor has not involved

himself or herself in the specific programs within 60 days, the probation officer shall immediately file a petition or request that a petition be filed by the prosecuting attorney. However, when in the judgment of the probation officer the interest of the minor and the community can be protected, the probation officer shall make a diligent effort to proceed under this section.

The program of supervision of the minor undertaken pursuant to this section may call for the minor to obtain care and treatment for the misuse of or addiction to controlled substances from a county mental health service or other appropriate community agency.

The program of supervision shall require the parents or guardians of the minor to participate with the minor in counseling or education programs, including, but not limited to, parent education and parenting programs operated by community colleges, school districts, or other appropriate agencies designated by the court if the program of supervision is pursuant to the procedure prescribed in Section 654.2.

Further, this section shall authorize the probation officer with consent of the minor and the minor's parent or guardian to provide the following services in lieu of filing a petition:

(a) Maintain and operate sheltered-care facilities, or contract with private or public agencies to provide these services. The placement shall be limited to a maximum of 90 days. Counseling services shall be extended to the sheltered minor and his or her family during this period of diversion services. The minor and his or her parents may be required to make full or partial reimbursement for the services rendered the minor and his or her family during the diversion process. Referrals for sheltered-care diversion may be made by the minor, his or her family, schools, any law enforcement agency, or any other private or public social service agency.

(b) Maintain and operate crisis resolution homes, or contract with private or public agencies offering these services. Residence at these facilities shall be limited to 20 days during which period individual and family counseling shall be extended the minor and his or her family. Failure to resolve the crisis within the 20-day period may result in the minor's referral to a sheltered-care facility for a period not to exceed 90 days. Referrals shall be accepted from the minor, his or her family, schools, law enforcement or any other private or public social service agency. The minor, his or her parents, or both, may be required to reimburse the county for the cost of services rendered at a rate to be determined by the county board of supervisors.

(c) Maintain and operate counseling and educational centers, or contract with private and public agencies, societies, or corporations whose purpose is to provide vocational training or skills. The centers may be operated separately or in conjunction with crisis resolution homes to be operated by the probation officer. The probation officer shall be authorized to make referrals to the appropriate existing private or public agencies offering similar services when available.

At the conclusion of the program of supervision undertaken pursuant to this section, the probation officer shall prepare and maintain a followup report of the actual program measures taken. *(Amended by Stats 1991 ch 1202 §17, eff. 1/1/92.)*

§654.1. Program of supervision for minor charged with driving under the influence.

(a) Notwithstanding Section 654 or any other provision of law, in any case in which a minor has been charged with a violation of Section 23140 or 23152 of the Vehicle Code, the probation officer may, in lieu of requesting that a petition be filed by the prosecuting attorney to declare the minor a ward of the court under Section 602, proceed in accordance with Section 654 and delineate a program of supervision for the minor. However, the probation officer shall cause the citation for a violation of Section 23140 or 23152 of the Vehicle Code to be heard and disposed of by the judge, referee, or traffic hearing officer pursuant to Sections 257 and 258 as a condition of any program of supervision.

(b) Nothing in this section shall be construed to prevent the probation officer from requesting the prosecuting attorney to file a petition to declare the minor a ward of the court under Section 602 for a violation of Section 23140 or 23152 of the Vehicle Code. However, when in the judgment of the probation officer, the interest of the minor and the community can be protected by adjudication of a violation of Section 23140 or 23152 of the Vehicle Code in accordance with subdivision (a), the probation officer shall proceed under subdivision (a). *(Added by Stats 1988 ch 1258 §1, eff. 1/1/89.)*

§654.2. When a petition is filed to declare a minor a ward of the court.

(a) If a petition has been filed by the prosecuting attorney to declare a minor a ward of the court under Section 602, the court may, without adjudging the minor a ward of the court and with the consent of the minor and the minor's parents or guardian, continue any hearing on a petition for six months and order the minor to participate in a program of supervision as set forth in Section 654. Fifteen days prior to the conclusion of the program of supervision undertaken pursuant to this section, the probation officer shall submit to the court a follow-up report of the minor's participation in the program. The minor and the minor's parents or guardian shall be ordered to appear at the conclusion of the six-month period. If the minor successfully completes the program of supervision, the court shall order the petition be dismissed. If the minor has not successfully completed the program of supervision, proceedings on the petition shall proceed.

(b) If the minor is eligible for Section 654 supervision, and the probation officer believes the minor would benefit from a program of supervision pursuant to this section, the probation officer may, in referring the affidavit described in Section 653.5 to the prosecuting attorney, recommend informal supervision as provided in this section. *(Added by Stats 1989 ch 1117 §11, eff. 1/1/90.)*

§654.3. Minors ineligible for programs of supervision.

No minor shall be eligible for the program of supervision set forth in Section 654 or 654.2 in the following cases, except in an unusual case where the interests of justice would best be served and the court specifies on the record the reasons for its decision:

(a) A petition alleges that the minor has violated an offense listed in subdivision (b) of Section 707.

(b) A petition alleges that the minor has sold or possessed for sale a controlled substance as defined in Chapter 2 (commencing with Section 11053) of Division 10 of the Health and Safety Code.

(c) A petition alleges that the minor has violated Section 11350 or 11377 of the Health and Safety Code where the violation takes place at a public or private elementary, vocational, junior high school, or high school, or a violation of Section 245.5, 626.9, or 626.10 of the Penal Code.

(d) A petition alleges that the minor has violated Section 186.22 of the Penal Code.

(e) The minor has previously participated in a program of supervision pursuant to Section 654.

(f) The minor has previously been adjudged a ward of the court pursuant to Section 602.

(g) A petition alleges that the minor has violated an offense in which the restitution owed to the victim exceeds one thousand dollars ($1,000). For purposes of this paragraph, the definition of "victim" in paragraph (1) of subdivision (a) of Section 729.6 and "restitution" in subdivision (d) of Section 729.6 shall apply. *(Added by Stats 1989 ch 1117 §12, eff. 1/1/90.)*

§654.4. Required participation in alcohol or drug education program.

Any minor who is placed in a program of supervision set forth in Section 654 or 654.2 for a violation of an offense involving the unlawful possession, use, sale, or other furnishing of a controlled substance, as defined in Chapter 2 (commencing with Section 11053) of Division 10 of the Health and Safety Code, or for violating subdivision (f) of Section 647 of the Penal Code or Section 23140 or 23152 of the Vehicle Code, shall be required to participate in and successfully complete an alcohol or drug education program from a county mental health agency or other appropriate community program. *(Added by Stats 1989 ch 1117 §13, eff. 1/1/90.)*

§654.6. Program of supervision: requirements.

A program of supervision pursuant to Section 654 or 654.2 for any minor described in Section 602 shall include constructive assignments that will help the minor learn to be responsible for his or her actions. The assignments may include, but not be limited to, requiring the minor to perform at least 10 hours of community service, requiring the minor to repair damaged property or to make other appropriate restitution, or requiring the minor to participate in an educational or counseling program. The minor or his or her parent or guardian may be required to reimburse the agency for all or part of the cost of the program of supervision if he or she has the financial ability to pay. *(Added by Stats 1990 ch 258 §2, eff. 1/1/91.)*

§655. Review of decision not to declare minor a ward of the court.

(a) When any person has applied to the probation officer, pursuant to Section 653, to request commencement of juvenile court proceedings to declare a minor a ward of the court under Section 602 and the probation officer does not cause the affidavit to be taken to the prosecuting attorney pursuant to Section 653 within 21 court days after such application, the applicant may, within 10 court days after receiving notice of the probation officer's decision not to file a petition, apply to the prosecuting attorney to review the decision of the probation officer, and the prosecuting attorney may either affirm the decision of the

© 1992 by J., B. & L. Gould
Printed in the U.S.A.   EP

probation officer or commence juvenile court proceedings.

(b) When any person has applied to the probation officer or the district attorney, pursuant to Section 653, to commence juvenile court proceedings to declare a minor a dependent child of the court or a ward of the court under Section 601 and the probation officer or district attorney fails to file a petition within 21 court days after making such application, the applicant may, within 10 court days after receiving notice of the probation officer's or district attorney's decision not to file a petition, apply to the juvenile court to review the decision of the probation officer or district attorney, and the court may either affirm the decision of the probation officer or district attorney or order him or her to commence juvenile court proceedings.

(c) Nothing in subdivision (b) shall be construed so as to allow district attorneys to file a petition to make a minor a ward of the court under Section 601, except as specifically allowed by Section 653 in accordance with subdivision (e) of Section 601.3. *(Amended by Stats 1991 ch 1202 §18, eff. 1/1/92.)*

§655.5. Review of decision not to initiate service program.

When an officer has referred or delivered a minor pursuant to subdivision (b) of Section 626, and the referral agency does not initiate a service program for the minor within the time periods required by Section 652.5, the referring agency may within 10 court days following receipt of the notification by the referral agency, apply to the probation officer for a review of that decision.

§656. Contents of petition to commence proceedings in juvenile court.

A petition to commence proceedings in the juvenile court to declare a minor a ward of the court shall be verified and shall contain all of the following:

(a) The name of the court to which it is addressed.

(b) The title of the proceeding.

(c) The code section and subdivision under which the proceedings are instituted.

(d) The name, age, and address, if any, of the minor upon whose behalf the petition is brought.

(e) The names and residence addresses, if known to petitioner, of both of the parents and any guardian of the minor. If there is no parent or guardian residing within the state, or if his or her place of residence is not known to petitioner, the petition shall also contain the name and residence address, if known, of any adult relative residing within the county, or, if there are none, the adult relative residing nearest to the location of the court.

(f) A concise statement of facts, separately stated, to support the conclusion that the minor upon whose behalf the petition is being brought is a person within the definition of each of the sections and subdivisions under which the proceedings are being instituted.

(g) The fact that the minor upon whose behalf the petition is brought is detained in custody or is not detained in custody, and if he or she is detained in custody, the date and the precise time the minor was taken into custody.

(h) A notice to the father, mother, spouse, or other person liable for support of the minor child, that: (1) Section 903 makes that person, the estate of that person, and the estate of the minor child, liable for the cost of the care, support, and maintenance of the minor

child in any county institution or any other place in which the child is placed, detained, or committed pursuant to an order of the juvenile court; (2) Section 903.1 makes that person, the estate of that person, and the estate of the minor child, liable for the cost to the county of legal services rendered to the minor by a private attorney or a public defender appointed pursuant to the order of the juvenile court; (3) Section 903.2 makes that person, the estate of that person, and the estate of the minor child, liable for the cost to the county of the probation supervision of the minor child by the probation officer pursuant to the order of the juvenile court; and (4) the liabilities established by these sections are joint and several.

(i) In a proceeding alleging that the minor comes within Section 601, notice to the parent, guardian, or other person having control or charge of the minor that failure to comply with the compulsory school attendance laws is an infraction, which may be charged and prosecuted before the juvenile court judge sitting as a municipal court judge. In those cases, the petition shall also include notice that the parent, guardian, or other person having control or charge of the minor has the right to a hearing on the infraction before a judge different than the judge who has heard or is to hear the proceeding pursuant to Section 601. The notice shall explain the provisions of Section 170.6 of the Code of Civil Procedure.

(j) If a proceeding is pending against a minor child for a violation of paragraph (7) of subdivision (a) of Section 640 of the Penal Code, a notice to the parent or legal guardian of the minor that if the minor is found to have violated that provision that (1) any community service which may be required of the minor may be performed in the presence, and under the direct supervision, of the parent or legal guardian pursuant to subdivision (b) of Section 640 of the Penal Code; and (2) if the minor is personally unable to pay any fine levied for the violation of paragraph (7) of subdivision (a) of Section 640 of the Penal Code, that the parent or legal guardian of the minor shall be liable for payment of the fine pursuant to that paragraph. *(Amended by Stats 1990 ch 1530 §10, eff. 1/1/91.)*

§656.1. Specification of felony or misdemeanor.

Any petition alleging that the minor is a person described by Section 602 shall specify as to each count whether the crime charged is a felony or a misdemeanor.

§656.2. Minor alleged to have committed felony.

(a) In any case in which a minor is alleged to have committed an act which would have been a felony if committed by an adult, the probation officer shall obtain a statement from the victim, the parent or guardian of the victim if the victim is a minor, or if the victim has died, the victim's next of kin, concerning the offense which shall be included in the social study made by the probation officer and submitted to the court pursuant to Section 706 and shall advise those persons as to the time and place of the disposition hearing. The probation officer shall also provide the victim with information concerning the victim's right to an action for civil damages against the minor and his or her parents and the victim's opportunity to be compensated from the restitution fund. The information shall be in the form of written material prepared by the Judicial Council and shall be provided to each victim for whom the probation officer has a current mailing address.

(b) Notwithstanding any other provision of law, the persons from whom the probation officer is required to obtain a statement pursuant to subdivision (a) shall have the right to attend the disposition hearing conducted pursuant to Section 702 and, subject to the court's discretion, to express their views concerning the offense and disposition of the case. *(Added by Stats 1989 ch 569 §3, eff. 9/20/89. Former §656.2 repealed by Stats 1989 ch 569 §2, eff. 9/20/89.)*

§656.5. Dismissal due to lack of verification.

Any petition filed in juvenile court to commence proceedings pursuant to this chapter that is not verified may be dismissed without prejudice by such court.

§657. Setting time for hearing of petition.

(a) Upon the filing of the petition, the clerk of the juvenile court shall set the same for hearing within 30 days, except as follows:

(1) In the case of a minor detained in custody at the time of the filing of the petition, the petition must be set for hearing within 15 judicial days from the date of the order of the court directing such detention.

(2) In the case of a minor not before the juvenile court at the time of the filing of the petition and for whom a warrant of arrest has been issued pursuant to Section 663, the hearing on the petition shall be stayed until the minor is brought before the juvenile court on the warrant of arrest. The clerk of the juvenile court shall set the petition for hearing within 30 days of the minor's initial appearance in juvenile court on the petition, except that in the case of a minor detained in custody, the petition shall be set for hearing within 15 judicial days from the date of the order of the court directing such detention.

(b) At the detention hearing, or any time thereafter, a minor who is alleged to come within the provisions of Section 601 or 602, may, with the consent of counsel, admit in court the allegations of the petition and waive the jurisdictional hearing.

§658. Procedure for filing petition or supplemental petition.

(a) Except as provided in subdivision (b), upon the filing of the petition, the clerk of the juvenile court shall issue a notice, to which shall be attached a copy of the petition, and he shall cause the same to be served upon the minor, if the minor is eight or more years of age, and upon each of the persons described in subdivision (e) of Section 656 whose residence addresses are set forth in said petition and thereafter before the hearing upon all such persons whose residence addresses become known to the clerk. The clerk shall issue a copy of the petition, to the minor's attorney and to the district attorney, if the district attorney has notified the clerk of the court that he wishes to receive such petition, containing the time, date, and place of the hearing.

(b) Upon the filing of a supplemental petition where the minor has been declared a ward of the court or a probationer under Section 602 in the original matter, the clerk of the juvenile court shall issue a notice, to which shall be attached a copy of the petition, and he or she shall cause the notice to be served upon the minor, if the minor is eight or more years of age, and upon each of the persons described in subdivision

(e) of Section 656 whose residence addresses are set forth in the supplemental petition and thereafter known to the clerk. The clerk shall issue a copy of the supplemental petition to the minor's attorney, and to the district attorney if the probation officer is the petitioner, or, to the probation officer if the district attorney is the petitioner, containing the time, date, and place of the hearing. *(Amended by Stats 1986 ch 757 §4.)*

§659. Contents of notice of petition.

The notice must contain:

(a) The name and address of the person to whom the notice is directed.

(b) The date, time, and place of the hearing on the petition.

(c) The name of the minor upon whose behalf the petition has been brought.

(d) Each section and subdivision under which the proceeding has been instituted.

(e) A statement that the minor and his or her parent or guardian or adult relative, as the case may be, to whom notice is required to be given, are entitled to have an attorney present at the hearing on the petition, and that, if the parent or guardian or such adult relative is indigent and cannot afford an attorney, and the minor or his or her parent or guardian or such adult relative desires to be represented by an attorney, such parent or guardian or adult relative shall promptly notify the clerk of the juvenile court, and that in the event counsel or legal assistance is furnished by the court, the parent or guardian or adult relative shall be liable to the county, to the extent of his, her, or their financial ability, for all or a portion of the cost thereof.

(f) A statement that the parent or parents or responsible relative or guardian may be liable for the costs of support of the minor in a county institution. *(Amended by Stats 1985 ch 1485 §12.)*

§660. Procedure of service of petition.

(a) Except as provided in subdivision (b), if the minor is detained, the clerk of the juvenile court shall cause the notice and copy of the petition to be served on all persons required to receive such notice and copy of the petition, either personally or by certified mail with request for return receipt, as soon as possible after filing of the petition and at least five days prior to the time set for hearing, unless such hearing is set less than five days from the filing of the petition, in which case, such notice and copy of the petition shall be served at least 24 hours prior to the time set for hearing.

(b) If the minor is detained, and all persons entitled to notice, were present at the detention hearing, the clerk of the juvenile court shall cause the notice and copy of the petition to be served on all persons required to receive the notice and copy of the petition, either personally or by first-class mail, as soon as possible after the filing of the petition and at least five days prior to the time set for hearing, unless the hearing is set less than five days from the filing of the petition, in which case the notice and copy of the petition shall be served at least 24 hours prior to the time set for the hearing.

(c) If the minor is not detained, the clerk of the juvenile court shall cause the notice and copy of the petition to be served on all persons required to receive such notice and copy of the petition, either personally or by first-class mail, at least 10 days prior to the time

© 1992 by J., B. & L. Gould
Printed in the U.S.A.   EP

set for hearing. If such person is known to reside outside of the county, the clerk of the juvenile court shall mail the notice and copy of the petition, by first-class mail, to such person, as soon as possible after the filing of the petition and at least 10 days before the time set for hearing. Failure to respond to the notice shall in no way result in arrest or detention. In the instance of failure to appear after notice by first-class mail, the court shall direct that the notice and copy of the petition is to be personally served on all persons required to receive such notice and copy of the petition. Personal service of the notice and copy of the petition outside of the county at least 10 days before the time set for hearing is equivalent to such service by first-class mail. Service may be waived by any person by a voluntary appearance entered in the minutes of the court or by a written waiver of service filed with the clerk of the court at or prior to the hearing.

(d) For purposes of this section, service on the minor's attorney shall constitute service on the minor's parent or guardian.

§661. Order to parent to appear.

In addition to the notice provided in Sections 658 and 659, the juvenile court may issue its citation directing any parent, guardian, or foster parent of the person concerning whom a petition has been filed to appear at the time and place set for any hearing or financial evaluation under the provisions of this chapter, including a hearing under the provisions of Section 257, and directing any person having custody or control of the minor concerning whom the petition has been filed to bring the minor with him or her. The notice shall in addition state that a parent, guardian, or foster parent may be required to participate in a counseling or education program with the minor concerning whom the petition has been filed. If the proceeding is one alleging that the minor comes within the provisions of Section 601, the notice shall in addition contain notice to the parent, guardian, or other person having control or charge of the minor that failure to comply with the compulsory school attendance laws is an infraction, which may be charged and prosecuted before the juvenile court judge sitting as a municipal court judge. In those cases, the notice shall also include notice that the parent, guardian, or other person having control or charge of the minor has the right to a hearing on the infraction before a judge different than the judge who has heard or is to hear the proceeding pursuant to section 601. The notice shall explain the provisions of Section 170.6 of the Code of Civil Procedure. Personal service of the citation shall be made at least 24 hours before the time stated therein for the appearance. *(Amended by Stats 1985 ch 120 §4; ch 1485 §14.)*

§662. Warrant of arrest for parent or guardian of minor.

In case such citation cannot be served, or the person served fails to obey it, or in any case in which it appears to the court that the citation will probably be ineffective, a warrant of arrest may issue on the order of the court either against the parent, or guardian, or the person having the custody of the minor, or with whom the minor is.

§663. Warrant of arrest for minor.

Whenever a petition has been filed in the juvenile court alleging that a minor comes within the provi-

sions of Section 601 or 602 of this code and praying for a hearing thereon, or whenever any subsequent petition has been filed praying for a hearing in the matter of said minor and it appears to the court that the conduct and behavior of the said minor may endanger the health, person, welfare, or property of himself or others, or that the circumstances of his home environment may endanger the health, person, welfare or property of said minor, a warrant of arrest may be issued immediately for the minor.

§664. Subpoenas for hearing.

Upon request of the probation officer, district attorney, the minor or the minor's parent, guardian, or custodian, the court or the clerk of the court shall issue, and, on the court's own motion, it may issue subpoenas requiring attendance and testimony of witnesses and production of papers at any hearing under the provisions of this chapter. When a person attends a juvenile court hearing as a witness upon a subpoena at its discretion, the court may by an order on its minutes, direct the county auditor to draw his warrant upon the county treasurer in favor of such witness for witness fees in the amount and manner prescribed by Section 68093 of the Government Code. The fees are county charges.

ARTICLE 17

WARDS — HEARINGS

§675. Hearing must be at separate session.

(a) All cases under the provisions of this chapter shall be heard at a special or separate session of the court, and no other matter shall be heard at that session. Except as provided in subdivision (b), no person on trial, awaiting trial, or under accusation of crime, other than a parent, guardian, or relative of the minor, shall be permitted to be present at any such session, except as a witness.

(b) Hearings for two or more minors may be heard upon the same rules of joinder, consolidation, and severance as apply to trials in a court of criminal jurisdiction.

§676. Admission of public and interested persons to hearing.

(a) Unless requested by the minor concerning whom the petition has been filed and any parent or guardian present, the public shall not be admitted to a juvenile court hearing. Nothing in this section shall preclude the attendance of up to two family members of a prosecuting witness for the support of that witness, as authorized by Section 868.5 of the Penal Code. The judge or referee may nevertheless admit those persons he or she deems to have a direct and legitimate interest in the particular case or the work of the court. However, except as provided in subdivision (b), members of the public shall be admitted, on the same basis as they may be admitted to trials in a court of criminal jurisdiction, to hearings concerning petitions filed pursuant to Section 602 alleging that a minor is a person described in Section 602 by reason of the violation of any one of the following offenses:

(1) Murder.

(2) Arson of an inhabited building.

(3) Robbery while armed with a dangerous or deadly weapon.

(4) Rape with force or violence or threat of great bodily harm.

(5) Sodomy by force, violence, duress, menace, or threat of great bodily harm.

(6) Oral copulation by force, violence, duress, menace, or threat of great bodily harm.

(7) Any offense specified in Section 289 of the Penal Code.

(8) Kidnapping for ransom.

(9) Kidnapping for purpose of robbery.

(10) Kidnapping with bodily harm.

(11) Assault with intent to murder or attempted murder.

(12) Assault with a firearm or destructive device.

(13) Assault by any means of force likely to produce great bodily injury.

(14) Discharge of a firearm into an inhabited or occupied building.

(15) Any offense described in Section 1203.09 of the Penal Code.

(16) Any offense described in Section 12022.5 of the Penal Code.

(17) Any felony offense in which a minor personally used a weapon listed in subdivision (a) of Section 12020 of the Penal Code.

(18) Burglary of an inhabited dwelling house or trailer coach, as defined in Section 635 of the Vehicle Code, or the inhabited portion of any other building, if the minor previously has been adjudged a ward of the court by reason of the commission of any offense listed in this section, including an offense listed in this paragraph.

(19) Any felony offense described in Section 136.1 or 137 of the Penal Code.

(20) Any offense as specified in Sections 11351, 11351.5, 11352, 11378, 11378.5, 11379, and 11379.5 of the Health and Safety Code.

(21) Criminal street gang activity which constitutes a felony pursuant to Section 186.22 of the Penal Code.

(22) Manslaughter as specified in Section 192 of the Penal Code.

(23) Drive-by shooting or discharge of a weapon from or at a motor vehicle as specified in Sections 246, 247, and 12034 of the Penal Code.

(24) Any crime committed with an assault weapon, as defined in Section 12276 of the Penal Code, including possession of an assault weapon as specified in subdivision (b) of Section 12280 of the Penal Code.

(b) Where the petition filed alleges that the minor is a person described in Section 602 by reason of the commission of rape with force or violence or great bodily harm; sodomy by force, violence, duress, menace, or threat of great bodily harm; oral copulation by force, violence, duress, menace, or threat of great bodily harm; or any offense specified in Section 289 of the Penal Code, members of the public shall not be admitted to the hearing in either of the following instances:

(1) Upon a motion for a closed hearing by the district attorney, who shall make the motion if so requested by the victim.

(2) During the victim's testimony, if, at the time of the offense the victim was under 16 years of age.

(c) The name of a minor found to have committed one of the offenses listed in subdivision (a) shall not be confidential, unless the court, for good cause, so orders.

(d) Notwithstanding Sections 827 and 828 and subject to subdivisions (e) and (f), when a petition is sustained for any offense listed in subdivision (a), the charging petition, the minutes of the proceeding, and the orders of adjudication and disposition of the court that are contained in the court file shall be available for public inspection. Nothing in this subdivision shall be construed to authorize public access to any other documents in the court file.

(e) The probation officer or any party may petition the juvenile court to prohibit disclosure to the public of any file or record. The juvenile court shall prohibit the disclosure if it appears that the harm to the minor, victims, witnesses, or public from the public disclosure outweighs the benefit of public knowledge.

(f) Nothing in this section shall be applied to limit the disclosure of information as otherwise provided for by law. *(Amended by Stats 1990 ch 246 §2, eff. 1/1/91.)*

§677. Presence at hearing of court reporter.

At any juvenile court hearing conducted by a juvenile court judge, an official court reporter shall, and at any such hearing conducted by a juvenile court referee, the official reporter, as directed by the court, may take down in shorthand all the testimony and all of the statements and remarks of the judge and all persons appearing at the hearing; and, if directed by the judge, or requested by the person on whose behalf the petition was brought, or by his parent or legal guardian, or the attorneys of such persons, he must, within such reasonable time after the hearing of the petition as the court may designate, write out the same or such specific portions thereof as may be requested in plain and legible longhand or by typewriter or other printing machine and certify to the same as being correctly reported and transcribed, and when directed by the court, file the same with the clerk of the court. Unless otherwise directed by the judge, the costs of writing out and transcribing all or any portion of the reporter's shorthand notes shall be paid in advance at the rates fixed for transcriptions in a civil action by the person requesting the same.

§678. Application of Code of Civil Procedure.

The provisions of Chapter 8 (commencing with Section 469) of Title 6 of Part 2 of the Code of Civil Procedure relating to variance and amendment of pleadings in civil actions shall apply to petitions and proceedings under this chapter, to the same extent and with the same effect as if proceedings under this chapter were civil actions.

§679. Who is entitled to be present at hearing.

A minor who is the subject of a juvenile court hearing and any person entitled to notice of the hearing under the provisions of Section 658, is entitled to be present at such hearing. Any such minor and any such person has the right to be represented at such hearing by counsel of his own choice or, if unable to afford counsel, has the right to be represented by counsel appointed by the court.

§680. Purpose and procedure of hearing.

The judge of the juvenile court shall control all proceedings during the hearings with a view to the expeditious and effective ascertainment of the jurisdictional facts and the ascertainment of all information relative to the present condition and future welfare of the person upon whose behalf the petition is brought. Except where there is a contested issue of fact or law, the proceedings shall be conducted in an informal nonadversary atmosphere with a view to obtaining the

© 1992 by J., B. & L. Gould
Printed in the U.S.A.   EP

maximum cooperation of the minor upon whose behalf the petition is brought and all persons interested in his welfare with such provisions as the court may make for the disposition and care of such minor.

§681. Appearance of prosecuting attorney.

(a) In a juvenile court hearing which is based upon a petition that alleges that the minor upon whose behalf the petition is being brought is a person within the description of Section 602, the prosecuting attorney shall appear on behalf of the people of the State of California.

(b) In a juvenile court hearing which is based upon a petition that alleges that the minor upon whose behalf the petition is being brought is a person within the description of Section 601 and the minor who is the subject of the hearing is represented by counsel, the prosecuting attorney may, with the consent or at the request of the juvenile court judge, or at the request of the probation officer with the consent of the juvenile court judge, appear and participate in the hearing to assist in the ascertaining and presenting of the evidence. Where the petition in a juvenile court proceeding alleges that a minor is a person described in subdivision (a), (b), or (d) of Section 300, and either of the parents, or the guardian, or other person having care or custody of the minor, or who resides in the home of the minor, is charged in a pending criminal prosecution based upon unlawful acts committed against the minor, the prosecuting attorney shall, with the consent or at the request of the juvenile court judge, represent the minor in the interest of the state at the juvenile court proceeding. The terms and conditions of such representation shall be with the consent or approval of the judge of the juvenile court.

§682. Continuance of trial beyond time limit.

(a) To continue any hearing relating to proceedings pursuant to Section 601 or 602 beyond the time limit within which the hearing is otherwise required to be heard, a written notice shall be filed and served on all parties to the proceeding at least two court days before the hearing sought to be continued, together with affidavits or declarations detailing specific facts showing good cause for the continuance.

(b) A continuance shall be granted only upon a showing of good cause and only for that period of time shown to be necessary by the moving party at the hearing on the motion. Neither stipulation of the parties nor convenience of the parties is, in and of itself, good cause. Whenever any continuance is granted, the facts which require the continuance shall be entered into the minutes.

(c) Notwithstanding subdivision (a), a party may make a motion for a continuance without complying with the requirements of that subdivision. However, unless the moving party shows good cause for failure to comply with those requirements, the court shall deny the motion.

(d) In any case in which the minor is represented by counsel and no objection is made to an order continuing any such hearing beyond the time limit within which the hearing is otherwise required to be held, the absence of such an objection shall be deemed a consent to the continuance. (Amended by Stats 1990 ch 1508 §1, eff. 1/1/91.)

§700. Reading of petition.

At the beginning of the hearing on a petition filed pursuant to Article 16 (commencing with Section 650) of this chapter, the judge or clerk shall first read the petition to those present and upon request of the minor upon whose behalf the petition has been brought or upon the request of any parent, relative or guardian, the judge shall explain any term of allegation contained therein and the nature of the hearing, its procedures, and possible consequences. The judge shall ascertain whether the minor and his parent or guardian or adult relative, as the case may be, has been informed of the right of the minor to be represented by counsel, and if not, the judge shall advise the minor and such person, if present, of the right to have counsel present and where applicable, of the right to appointed counsel. The court shall appoint counsel to represent the minor if he appears at the hearing without counsel, whether he is unable to afford counsel or not, unless there is an intelligent waiver of the right of counsel by the minor; and, in the absence of such waiver, if the parent or guardian does not furnish counsel and the court determines that the parent or guardian has the ability to pay for counsel, the court shall appoint counsel at the expense of the parent or guardian. The court shall continue the hearing for not to exceed seven days, as necessary to make an appointment of counsel, or to enable counsel to acquaint himself with the case, or to determine whether the parent or guardian or adult relative is unable to afford counsel at his own expense, and shall continue the hearing as necessary to provide reasonable opportunity for the minor and the parent or guardian or adult relative to prepare for the hearing.

§700.1. Motion to suppress evidence gained by unlawful search and seizure.

Any motion to suppress as evidence any tangible or intangible thing obtained as a result of an unlawful search or seizure shall be heard prior to the attachment of jeopardy and shall be heard at least five judicial days after receipt of notice by the people unless the people are willing to waive a portion of this time.

If the court grants a motion to suppress prior to the attachment of jeopardy over the objection of the people, the court shall enter a judgment of dismissal as to all counts of the petition except those counts on which the prosecuting attorney elects to proceed pursuant to Section 701.

If, prior to the attachment of jeopardy, opportunity for this motion did not exist or the person alleged to come within the provisions of the juvenile court law was not aware of the grounds for the motion, that person shall have the right to make this motion during the course of the proceeding under Section 701.

§700.2. Informing parent of right to open hearing.

Upon his or her appearance before the juvenile court on a complaint charging violation of Section 48293 of the Education Code, the juvenile court shall inform the parent, guardian, or other person having control or charge of the minor of the right to an open hearing and of the right to have a hearing on the complaint before a judge different than the judge who has heard or is to hear the proceeding pursuant to Section 601. The provisions of Section 170.6 of the Code of Civil Procedure shall be explained to the parent, guardian, or other person having control or charge of the minor.

§700.5. Repealed by Stats 1990 ch 1508 §2, eff. 1/1/91.

§701. Questions to be determined at hearing.

At the hearing, the court shall first consider only the question whether the minor is a person described by Section 300, 601, or 602. The admission and exclusion of evidence shall be pursuant to the rules of evidence established by the Evidence Code and by judicial decision. Proof beyond a reasonable doubt supported by evidence, legally admissible in the trial of criminal cases, must be adduced to support a finding that the minor is a person described by Section 602, and a preponderance of evidence, legally admissible in the trial of civil cases, must be adduced to support a finding that the minor is a person described by Section 300 or 601. When it appears that the minor has made an extrajudicial admission or confession and denies the same at the hearing, the court may continue the hearing for not to exceed seven days to enable the prosecuting attorney to subpoena witnesses to attend the hearing to prove the allegations of the petition. If the minor is not represented by counsel at the hearing, it shall be deemed that objections that could have been made to the evidence were made.

§701.1. Failure to find cause for prosecution.

At the hearing, the court, on motion of the minor or on its own motion, shall order that the petition be dismissed and that the minor be discharged from any detention or restriction therefore ordered, after the presentation of evidence on behalf of the petitioner has been closed, if the court, upon weighing the evidence then before it, finds that the minor is not a person described by Section 601 or 602. If such a motion at the close of evidence offered by the petitioner is not granted, the minor may offer evidence without first having reserved that right.

§702. Finding of the court.

After hearing the evidence, the court shall make a finding, noted in the minutes of the court, whether or not the minor is a person described by Section 300, 601, or 602. If it finds that the minor is not such a person, it shall order that the petition be dismissed and the minor be discharged from any detention or restriction theretofore ordered. If the court finds that the minor is such a person, it shall make and enter its findings and order accordingly, and shall then proceed to hear evidence on the question of the proper disposition to be made of the minor. Prior to doing so, it may continue the hearing, if necessary, to receive the social study of the probation officer, to refer the minor to a juvenile justice community resource program as defined in Article 5.2 (commencing with Section 1784) of Chapter 1 of Division 2.5, or to receive other evidence on its own motion or the motion of a parent or guardian for not to exceed 10 judicial days if the minor is detained during the continuance. If the minor is not detained, it may continue the hearing to a date not later than 30 days after the date of filing of the petition. The court may, for good cause shown continue the hearing for an additional 15 days, if the minor is not detained. The court may make such order for detention of the minor or his or her release from detention, during the period of the continuance, as is appropriate.

If the minor is found to have committed an offense which would in the case of an adult be punishable alternatively as a felony or a misdemeanor, the court shall declare the offense to be a misdemeanor or felony.

§702.3. Plea or finding of insanity.

Notwithstanding any other provision of law:

(a) When a minor denies, by a plea of not guilty by reason of insanity, the allegations of a petition filed pursuant to Section 602 of the Welfare and Institutions Code, and also joins with that denial a general denial of the conduct alleged in the petition, he or she shall first be subject to a hearing as if he or she had made no allegation of insanity. If the petition is sustained or if the minor denies the allegations only by reason of insanity, then a hearing shall be held on the question of whether the minor was insane at the time the offense was committed.

(b) If the court finds that the minor was insane at the time the offense was committed, the court, unless it appears to the court that the minor has fully recovered his or her sanity, shall direct that the minor be confined in a state hospital for the care and treatment of the mentally disordered or any other appropriate public or private mental health facility approved by the community program director, or the court may order the minor to undergo outpatient treatment as specified in Title 15 (commencing with Section 1600) of Part 2 of the Penal Code. The court shall transmit a copy of its order to the community program director or his or her designee. If the allegations of the petition specifying any felony are found to be true, the court shall direct that the minor be confined in a state hospital or other public or private mental health facility approved by the community program director for a minimum of 180 days, before the minor may be released on outpatient treatment. Prior to making the order directing that the minor be confined in a state hospital or other facility or ordered to undergo outpatient treatment, the court shall order the community program director or his or her designee to evaluate the minor and to submit to the court within 15 judicial days of the order his or her written recommendation as to whether the minor should be required to undergo outpatient treatment or committed to a state hospital or another mental health facility. If, however, it shall appear to the court that the minor has fully recovered his or her sanity the minor shall be remanded to the custody of the probation department until his or her sanity shall have been finally determined in the manner prescribed by law. A minor committed to a state hospital or other facility or ordered to undergo outpatient treatment shall not be released from confinement or the required outpatient treatment unless or until the court which committed him or her shall, after notice and hearing, in the manner provided in Section 1026.2 of the Penal Code, find and determine that his or her sanity has been restored.

(c) When the court, after considering the placement recommendation for the community program director required in subdivision (b), orders that the minor be confined in a state hospital or other public or private mental health facility, the court shall provide copies of the following documents which shall be taken with the minor to the state hospital or other treatment facility where the minor is to be confined:

(1) The commitment order, including a specification of the charges.

(2) The computation or statement setting forth the maximum time of commitment in accordance with Section 1026.5 and subdivision (e).

© 1992 by J., B. & L. Gould
Printed in the U.S.A. **EP**

(3) A computation or statement setting forth the amount of credit, if any, to be deducted from the maximum term of commitment.

(4) State Summary Criminal History information.

(5) Any arrest or detention reports prepared by the police department or other law enforcement agency.

(6) Any court-ordered psychiatric examination or evaluation reports.

(7) The community program director's placement recommendation report.

(d) The procedures set forth in Sections 1026, 1026.1, 1026.2, 1026.3, 1026.4, 1026.5, and 1027 of the Penal Code, and in Title 15 (commencing with Section 1600) of Part 2 of the Penal Code, shall be applicable to minors pursuant to this section, except that, in cases involving minors, the probation department rather than the sheriff, shall have jurisdiction over the minor.

(e) No minor may be committed pursuant to this section for a period longer than the jurisdictional limits of the juvenile court, pursuant to Section 607, unless, at the conclusion of the commitment, by reason of a mental disease, defect, or disorder, he or she represents a substantial danger of physical harm to others, in which case the commitment for care and treatment beyond the jurisdictional age may be extended by proceedings in superior court in accordance with and under the circumstances specified in subdivision (b) of Section 1026.5 of the Penal Code.

(f) The provision of a jury trial in superior court on the issue of extension of commitment shall not be construed to authorize the determination of any issue in juvenile court proceedings to be made by a jury. *(Amended by Stats 1989 ch 625 §3, eff. 1/1/90.)*

§702.5. Privileges against self-incrimination and to examine witnesses.

In any hearing conducted pursuant to Section 701 or 702 to determine whether a minor is a person described in Section 601 or 602, the minor has a privilege against self-incrimination and has a right to confrontation by, and cross-examination of, witnesses.

§704. Observation and diagnosis at Youth Authority Center.

(a) If the court has determined that a minor is a person described by Section 602, or if the court has determined that a minor is a person described by Section 601 and a supplemental petition for commitment of such minor to the Youth Authority has been filed pursuant to Section 777, and such minor is otherwise eligible for commitment to the Youth Authority, the court, if it concludes that a disposition of the case in the best interest of the minor requires such observation and diagnosis as can be made at a diagnostic and treatment center of the Youth Authority, may continue the hearing and order that such minor be placed temporarily in such a center for a period not to exceed 90 days, with the further provision in such order that the Director of the Youth Authority report to the court its diagnosis and recommendations concerning the minor within the 90-day period.

(b) The Director of Youth Authority shall, within the 90 days, cause the minor to be observed and examined and shall forward to the court his diagnosis and recommendation concerning such minor's future care, supervision, and treatment.

(c) The Youth Authority shall accept such person if there is in effect a contract made pursuant to Section 1752.1 and if it believes that the person can be materially benefited by such diagnostic and treatment services, and if the Director of the Youth Authority certifies that staff and institutions are available. No such person shall be transported to any facility under the jurisdiction of the Youth Authority until the director has notified the referring court of the place to which said person is to be transported and the time at which he can be received.

(d) The probation officer of the county in which an order is made placing a minor in a diagnostic and treatment center pursuant to this section, or any other peace officer designated by the court, shall execute the order placing such minor in the center or returning him therefrom to the court. The expense of such probation officer or other peace officer incurred in executing such order is a charge upon the county in which the court is situated.

§705. Determination that minor is mentally disordered.

Whenever the court, before or during the hearing on the petition, is of the opinion that the minor is mentally disordered or if the court is in doubt concerning the mental health of any such person, the court may proceed as provided in Section 6550 of this code or Section 4011.6 of the Penal Code.

§706. Disposition of minor.

After finding that a minor is a person described in Section 601 or 602, the court shall hear evidence on the question of the proper disposition to be made of the minor. The court shall receive in evidence the social study of the minor made by the probation officer and such other relevant and material evidence as may be offered, and in any judgment and order of disposition, shall state the social study made by the probation officer has been read and considered by the court.

§706.5. Social study by officer as evidence.

In any case where foster care placement is being considered, or has been made, each social study made by a probation officer, required to be received in evidence pursuant to Section 706, shall include, but not be limited to, the factual material listed in subdivisions (a) and (b) of Section 358.1. *(Added by Stats 1989 ch 569 §4, eff. 9/20/89.)*

§707. Suitability of minor for department programs.

(a) In any case in which a minor is alleged to be a person described in Section 602 by reason of the violation, when he or she was 16 years of age or older, of any criminal statute or ordinance except those listed in subdivision (b), upon motion of the petitioner made prior to the attachment of jeopardy the court shall cause the probation officer to investigate and submit a report on the behavioral patterns and social history of the minor being considered for a determination of unfitness. Following submission and consideration of the report, and of any other relevant evidence which the petitioner or the minor may wish to submit, the juvenile court may find that the minor is not a fit and proper subject to be dealt with under the juvenile court law if it concludes that the minor would not be amenable to the care, treatment, and training program available through the facilities of the juvenile court, based upon an evaluation of the following criteria:

(1) The degree of criminal sophistication exhibited by the minor.

(2) Whether the minor can be rehabilitated prior to the expiration of the juvenile court's jurisdiction.

(3) The minor's previous delinquent history.

(4) Success of previous attempts by the juvenile court to rehabilitate the minor.

(5) The circumstances and gravity of the offense alleged to have been committed by the minor.

A determination that the minor is not a fit and proper subject to be dealt with under the juvenile court law may be based on any one or a combination of the factors set forth above, which shall be recited in the order of unfitness. In any case in which a hearing has been noticed pursuant to this section, the court shall postpone the taking of a plea to the petition until the conclusion of the fitness hearing, and no plea which may already have been entered shall constitute evidence at the hearing.

(b) Subdivision (c) shall be applicable in any case in which a minor is alleged to be a person described in Section 602 by reason of the violation, when he or she was 16 years of age or older, of one of the following offenses:

(1) Murder.

(2) Arson of an inhabited building.

(3) Robbery while armed with a dangerous or deadly weapon.

(4) Rape with force or violence or threat of great bodily harm.

(5) Sodomy by force, violence, duress, menace, or threat of great bodily harm.

(6) Lewd or lascivious act as provided in subdivision (b) of Section 288 of the Penal Code.

(7) Oral copulation by force, violence, duress, menace, or threat of great bodily harm.

(8) Any offense specified in Section 289 of the Penal Code.

(9) Kidnapping for ransom.

(10) Kidnapping for purpose of robbery.

(11) Kidnapping with bodily harm.

(12) Assault with intent to murder or attempted murder.

(13) Assault with a firearm or destructive device.

(14) Assault by any means of force likely to produce great bodily injury.

(15) Discharge of a firearm into an inhabited or occupied building.

(16) Any offense described in Section 1203.09 of the Penal Code.

(17) Any offense described in Section 12022.5 of the Penal Code.

(18) Any felony offense in which the minor personally used a weapon listed in subdivision (a) of Section 12020 of the Penal Code.

(19) Any felony offense described in Section 136.1 or 137 of the Penal Code.

(20) Manufacturing, compounding, or selling one-half ounce or more of any salt or solution of a controlled substance specified in subdivision (e) of Section 11055 of the Health and Safety Code.

(21) Any violent felony, as defined in subdivision (c) of Section 667.5 of the Penal Code, which would also constitute a felony violation of subdivision (b) of Section 186.22 of the Penal Code.

(22) Escape, by the use of force or violence, from any county juvenile hall, home, ranch, camp, or forestry camp in violation of subdivision (b) of Section 871 where great bodily injury is intentionally inflicted upon an employee of the juvenile facility during the commission of the escape.

(23) Torture as described in Sections 206 and 206.1 of the Penal Code.

(24) Aggravated mayhem as described in Section 205 of the Penal Code.

(c) With regard to a minor alleged to be a person described in Section 602 by reason of the violation, when he or she was 16 years of age or older, of any of the offenses listed in subdivision (b), upon motion of the petitioner made prior to the attachment of jeopardy the court shall cause the probation officer to investigate and submit a report on the behavioral patterns and social history of the minor being considered for a determination of unfitness. Following submission and consideration of the report, and of any other relevant evidence which the petitioner or the minor may wish to submit the minor shall be presumed to be not a fit and proper subject to be dealt with under the juvenile court law unless the juvenile court concludes, based upon evidence, which evidence may be of extenuating or mitigating circumstances, that the minor would be amenable to the care, treatment, and training program available through the facilities of the juvenile court based upon an evaluation of each of the following criteria:

(1) The degree of criminal sophistication exhibited by the minor.

(2) Whether the minor can be rehabilitated prior to the expiration of the juvenile court's jurisdiction.

(3) The minor's previous delinquent history.

(4) Success of previous attempts by the juvenile court to rehabilitate the minor.

(5) The circumstances and gravity of the offenses alleged to have been committed by the minor.

A determination that the minor is a fit and proper subject to be dealt with under the juvenile court law shall be based on a finding of amenability after consideration of the criteria set forth above, and findings therefor recited in the order as to each of the above criteria that the minor is fit and proper under each and every one of the above criteria. In making a finding of fitness, the court may consider extenuating or mitigating circumstances in evaluating each of the above criteria. In any case in which a hearing has been noticed pursuant to this section, the court shall postpone the taking of a plea to the petition until the conclusion of the fitness hearing and no plea which may already have been entered shall constitute evidence at the hearing.

(d) If, subsequent to a finding that a minor is an unfit subject to be dealt with under the juvenile court law, the minor is convicted in a court of criminal jurisdiction of an offense listed in subdivision (b) of this section or listed in paragraph (24) of subdivision (c) of Section 1192.7 of the Penal Code, the finding of unfitness which preceded the conviction is applicable to the violation of any law or ordinance defining crime which is alleged to have been committed subsequent to the conviction if the violation would otherwise cause the minor to be a person described in Section 602. The probation officer shall not be required to investigate or submit a report regarding the fitness of a minor for any such subsequent charge. This subdivision shall not be construed to affect the right to appellate review of a finding of unfitness or the duration of the jurisdiction of the juvenile court as specified in Section 607. *(Amended by Stats 1991 ch 303 §1, eff. 1/1/92.)*

© 1992 by J., B. & L. Gould
Printed in the U.S.A.　　**EP**

§707.1. Minors declared unfit subjects for juvenile law.

(a) If the minor is declared not a fit and proper subject to be dealt with under the juvenile court law, the district attorney, or other appropriate prosecuting officer may file an accusatory pleading against the minor in a court of criminal jurisdiction. The case shall proceed from that point according to the laws applicable to a criminal case. If a prosecution has been commenced in another court but has been suspended while juvenile court proceedings are being held, it shall be ordered that the proceedings upon that prosecution shall resume.

(b) (1) The juvenile court may order that a minor alleged to have committed an offense described in subdivision (b) of Section 707 and who has been declared not a fit and proper subject to be dealt with under the juvenile court law be delivered to the custody of the sheriff upon a finding that the presence of the minor in the juvenile hall would endanger the safety of the public or be detrimental to the other inmates detained in the juvenile hall. Other minors declared not fit and proper subjects to be dealt with under the juvenile court law, if detained, shall remain in the juvenile hall pending final disposition by the criminal court or until they attain the age of 18, whichever occurs first.

(2) Upon attainment of the age of 18 such a person who is detained in juvenile hall shall be delivered to the custody of the sheriff unless the court finds that it is in the best interests of the person and the public that he or she be retained in juvenile hall. If a hearing is requested by the person, the transfer shall not take place until after the court has made its findings.

(3) When a person under 18 years of age is detained pursuant to this section in a facility in which adults are confined the detention shall be in accordance with the conditions specified in subdivision (b) of Section 207.1.

(4) A minor found not a fit and proper subject to be dealt with under the juvenile court law shall, upon the conclusion of the fitness hearing, be entitled to release on bail or on his or her own recognizance on the same circumstances, terms, and conditions as an adult alleged to have committed the same offense. *(Amended by Stats 1986 ch 1271 §6.)*

§707.2. Evaluation of minor by Youth Authority.

Prior to sentence, the court of criminal jurisdiction may remand the minor to the custody of the Youth Authority for not to exceed 90 days for the purpose of evaluation and report concerning his amenability to training and treatment offered by the Youth Authority. No minor who was under the age of 18 years when he committed any criminal offense and who has been found not a fit and proper subject to be dealt with under the juvenile court law shall be sentenced to the state prison unless he has first been remanded to the custody of the Youth Authority for evaluation and report pursuant to this section.

The need to protect society, the nature and seriousness of the offense, the interests of justice, the suitability of the minor to the training and treatment offered by the Youth Authority, and the needs of the minor shall be the primary considerations in the court's determination of the appropriate disposition for the minor.

§707.4. Report of failure to convict.

In any case arising under this article in which there is no conviction in the criminal court, the clerk of the criminal court shall report such disposition to the juvenile court, to the probation department, to the law enforcement agency which arrested the minor for the offense which resulted in his remand to criminal court, and to the Department of Justice. Unless the minor has had a prior conviction in a criminal court, the clerk of the criminal court shall deliver to the clerk of the juvenile court all copies of the minor's record in criminal court and shall obliterate the minor's name from any index or minute book maintained in the criminal court. The clerk of the juvenile court shall maintain the minor's criminal court record as provided by Article 22 (commencing with Section 825) of this chapter until such time as the juvenile court may issue an order that they be sealed pursuant to Section 781.

§708. Treatment and evaluation for controlled substance abuse.

Whenever a minor who appears to be a danger to himself or herself or others as a result of the use of controlled substances (as defined in Division 10 (commencing with Section 11000) of the Health and Safety Code), is brought before any judge of the juvenile court, the judge may continue the hearing and proceed pursuant to this section. The court may order the minor taken to a facility designated by the county and approved by the State Department of Mental Health as a facility for 72-hour treatment and evaluation. Thereupon the provisions of Section 5343 of the Welfare and Institutions Code shall apply, except that the professional person in charge of the facility shall make a written report to the court concerning the results of the evaluation of the minor.

If the professional person in charge of the facility for 72-hour evaluation and treatment reports to the juvenile court that the minor is not a danger to himself or herself or others as a result of the use of controlled substances or that the minor does not require 14-day intensive treatment, or if the minor has been certified for not more than 14 days of intensive treatment and the certification is terminated, the minor shall be released if the juvenile court proceedings have been dismissed; referred for further care and treatment on a voluntary basis, subject to the disposition of the juvenile court proceedings; or returned to the juvenile court, in which event the court shall proceed with the case pursuant to this chapter.

Any expenditure for the evaluation or intensive treatment of a minor under this section shall be considered an expenditure made under Part 2 (commencing with Section 5600) of Division 5, and shall be reimbursed by the state as are other local expenditures pursuant to that part.

ARTICLE 18

WARDS — JUDGMENTS AND ORDERS

§725. Judgment of probation or of minor as ward of the court.

After receiving and considering the evidence on the proper disposition of the case, the court may enter judgment as follows:

(a) If the court has found that the minor is a person described by Section 601 or 602, by reason of the commission of an offense other than any of the offenses set forth in Section 654.3, it may, without adjudging the minor a ward of the court, place the minor on probation, under the supervision of the probation officer, for a period not to exceed six months. The minor's probation shall include the conditions required in Section 729.2 except in any case in which the court makes a finding and states on the record its reasons that any of those conditions would be inappropriate. If the offense involved the unlawful possession, use, or furnishing of a controlled substance, as defined in Chapter 2 (commencing with Section 11053) of Division 10 of the Health and Safety Code, a violation of subdivision (f) of Section 647 of the Penal Code, or a violation of Section 25662 of the Business and Professions Code, the minor's probation shall include the conditions required by Section 729.10. If the minor fails to comply with the conditions of probation imposed, the court may order and adjudge the minor to be a ward of the court.

(b) If the court has found that the minor is a person described by Section 601 or 602, it may order and adjudge the minor to be a ward of the court. *(Amended by Stats 1989 chs 936 §2, 1117 §14, eff. 1/1/90.)*

§725.5. Additional considerations.

In determining the judgment and order to be made in any case in which the minor is found to be a person described in Section 602, the court shall consider, in addition to other relevant and material evidence, (1) the age of the minor, (2) the circumstances and gravity of the offense committed by the minor, and (3) the minor's previous delinquent history.

§726. Limitation of parental control.

In all cases wherein a minor is adjudged a ward or dependent child of the court, the court may limit the control to be exercised over such ward or dependent child by any parent or guardian and shall by its order clearly and specifically set forth all such limitations, but no ward or dependent child shall be taken from the physical custody of a parent or guardian unless upon the hearing the court finds one of the following facts:

(a) That the parent or guardian is incapable of providing or has failed or neglected to provide proper maintenance, training, and education for the minor.

(b) That the minor has been tried on probation in such custody and has failed to reform.

(c) That the welfare of the minor requires that his custody be taken from his parent or guardian.

In any case in which the minor is removed from the physical custody of his parent or guardian as the result of an order of wardship made pursuant to Section 602, the order shall specify that the minor may not be held in physical confinement for a period in excess of the maximum term of imprisonment which could be imposed upon an adult convicted of the offense or offenses which brought or continued the minor under the jurisdiction of the juvenile court.

As used in this section and in Section 731, "maximum term of imprisonment" means the longest of the three time periods set forth in paragraph (2) of subdivision (a) of Section 1170 of the Penal Code, but without the need to follow the provisions of subdivision (b) of Section 1170 of the Penal Code or to consider time for good behavior or participation pursuant to Sections 2930, 2931, and 2932 of the Penal Code, plus enhancements which must be proven if pled.

If the court elects to aggregate the period of physical confinement on multiple counts, or multiple petitions, including previously sustained petitions adjudging the minor a ward with Section 602, the "maximum term of imprisonment" shall be specified in accordance with subdivision (a) of Section 1170.1 of the Penal Code.

If the charged offense is a misdemeanor or a felony not included within the scope of Section 1170 of the Penal Code, the "maximum term of imprisonment" is the longest term of imprisonment prescribed by law.

"Physical confinement" means placement in a juvenile hall, ranch, camp, forestry camp or secure juvenile home pursuant to Section 730, or in any institution operated by the Youth Authority.

Nothing in this section shall be construed to limit the power of the court to retain jurisdiction over a minor and to make appropriate orders pursuant to Section 727 for the period permitted by Section 607.

§727. Care and supervision of minor.

(a) When a minor is adjudged a ward of the court on the ground that he or she is a person described by Section 601 or Section 602 the court may make any and all reasonable orders for the care, supervision, custody, conduct, maintenance, and support of the minor, including medical treatment, subject to further order of the court.

In the discretion of the court, a ward may be ordered to be on probation without supervision of the probation officer. The court, in so ordering, may impose on the ward any and all reasonable conditions of behavior as may be appropriate under this disposition. A minor who has been adjudged a ward of the court on the basis of the commission of any of the offenses described in subdivision (b) of Section 707, Section 459 of the Penal Code, or subdivision (a) of Section 11350 of the Health and Safety Code, shall not be eligible for probation without supervision of the probation officer. A minor who has been adjudged a ward of the court on the basis of the commission of any offense involving the sale or possession for sale of a controlled substance, except misdemeanor offenses involving marijuana as specified in Chapter 2 (commencing with Section 11053) of Division 10 of the Health and Safety Code, or of an offense in violation of Section 12220 of the Penal Code, shall be eligible for probation without supervision of the probation officer only when the court determines that the interests of justice would best be served and states reasons on the record for that determination.

In all other cases, the court shall order the care, custody, and control of the minor to be under the supervision of the probation officer who may place the minor in any of the following:

(1) The home of a relative.

(2) A suitable licensed community care facility.

(3) With a foster family agency to be placed in a suitable licensed foster family home or certified family home which has been certified by the agency as meeting licensing standards.

(b) Where the court has ordered a specific minor placed under the supervision of the probation officer and the probation officer has found that the needs of the child cannot be met in any available licensed or exempt facility, including emergency shelter, the minor may be placed in a suitable family home that has filed a license application with the State Department of Social Services, provided that all the following certification conditions are met:

© 1992 by J., B. & L. Gould
Printed in the U.S.A.   **EP**

(1) A preplacement home visit is made by the probation officer to determine the suitability of the family home.

(2) The probation officer verifies to the licensing agency in writing that the home lacks any deficiencies which would threaten the physical health, mental health, safety, or welfare of the minor.

(3) The probation officer notifies the licensing agency of the proposed placement and determines that the foster family home applicant has filed specific license application documents prior to and after the placement of the minor. If the license is subsequently denied, the minor shall be removed from the home immediately. The denial of the license constitutes a withdrawal of the certification.

When a minor has been adjudged a ward of the court on the ground that he or she is a person described in Section 601 or 602 and the court finds that notice has been given in accordance with Section 661, and when the court orders that a parent or guardian shall retain custody of that minor either subject to or without the supervision of the probation officer, the parent or guardian may be required to participate with that minor in a counseling or education program including, but not limited to, parent education and parenting programs operated by community colleges, school districts or other appropriate agencies designated by the court.

(c) The juvenile court may direct any and all reasonable orders to the parents and guardians of the minor who is the subject of any proceedings under this chapter as the court deems necessary and proper to carry out the provisions of subdivisions (a) and (b), including orders to appear before a county financial evaluation officer.

When counseling or other treatment services are ordered for the minor, the parent, guardian, or foster parent shall be ordered to participate in those services, unless participation by the parent, guardian, or foster parent is deemed by the court to be inappropriate or potentially detrimental to the child. (*Amended by Stats 1989 ch 936 §3, eff. 1/1/90.*)

§727.1. Placement facility must be licensed by Youth Authority.

(a) Unless otherwise authorized by law, the court may not order the placement of a minor who is adjudged a ward of the court on the basis that he or she is a person described by either Section 601 or 602 in a private residential facility or program that provides 24-hour supervision, in any state, unless the residential facility or program is licensed for the placement of minors by an agency of the state or states in which the minor will be placed or operates under and is inspected pursuant to standards comparable to those developed by the Youth Authority for similar facilities or programs.

(b) The court shall find, in its order of placement, that the residential facility or program is licensed or operates as required by subdivision (a). The court shall review each such placement for compliance with the requirements of subdivision (a) at least once a year. (*Added by Stats 1986 ch 798 §1.*)

§727.5. Minor to perform community service.

If a minor is found to be a person described in Section 601, the court may order the minor to perform community service, including, but not limited to, graffiti cleanup, for a total time not to exceed 20 hours over a period not to exceed 30 days, during a time other than his or her hours of school attendance or employment. (*Added by Stats 1991 ch 1202 §19, eff. 1/1/92.*)

§728. Minor convicted of vandalism must repair damage.

If a minor is found to be a person described in Section 602 by reason of the commission of vandalism, and the court does not remove the minor from the physical custody of the parent or guardian, the court as a condition of probation, except in any case in which the court makes a finding and states on the record its reasons that such condition would be inappropriate, shall require the minor to wash, paint, repair or replace the defaced, damaged or destroyed property, or otherwise make restitution to the property owner. If restitution is found to be inappropriate, the court, except in any case in which the court makes a finding and states on the record its reasons that such condition would be inappropriate, shall require the minor to perform specified community service. Nothing in this section shall be construed to limit the authority of a juvenile court to provide conditions of probation.

§729. Restitution for battery.

If a minor is found to be a person described in Section 602 by reason of the commission of a battery on _____ described in Penal Code Section 243.5, and the court does not remove the minor from the physical custody of the parent or guardian, the court as a condition of probation, except in any case in which the court makes a finding and states on the record its reasons that such condition would be inappropriate, shall require the minor to make restitution to the victim of the battery. If restitution is found to be inappropriate, the court, except in any case in which the court makes a finding and states on the record its reasons that such condition would be inappropriate, shall require the minor to perform specified community service. Nothing in this section shall be construed to limit the authority of a juvenile court to provide conditions of probation.

§729.1. Repair of damage to transit vehicle.

(a) If a minor is found to be a person described in Section 602 by reason of the commission of a crime which takes place on a public transit vehicle, and the court does not remove the minor from the physical custody of the parent or guardian, the court as a condition of probation, except in any case in which the court makes a finding and states on the record its reasons that the condition would be inappropriate, shall require the minor to wash, paint, repair or replace the damaged or destroyed property, or otherwise make restitution to the property owner. If restitution is found to be inappropriate, the court, except in any case in which the court makes a finding and states on the record its reasons that the condition would be inappropriate, shall require the minor to perform specified community service. Nothing in this section shall be construed to limit the authority of a juvenile court to provide conditions of probation.

(b) As used in subdivision (a), "public transit vehicle" means any motor vehicle, street car, trackless trolley, bus, shuttle, light rail system, rapid transit system, subway, train, taxi cab, or jitney, which transports members of the public for hire. (*Amended and renumbered from section 729 by Stats 1986 ch 248 §247.*)

© 1992 by J., B. & L. Gould
Printed in the U.S.A. **EP**

§729.2. Requirements of minor.

If a minor is found to be a person described in Section 601 or 602 and the court does not remove the minor from the physical custody of the parent or guardian, the court as a condition of probation, except in any case in which the court makes a finding and states on the record its reasons that that condition would be inappropriate, shall:

(a) Require the minor to attend a school program approved by the probation officer without absence.

(b) Require the parents or guardian of the minor to participate with the minor in a counseling or education program, including, but not limited to, parent education and parenting programs operated by community colleges, school districts, or other appropriate agencies designated by the court or the probation department, unless the minor has been declared a dependent child of the court pursuant to Section 300 or a petition to declare the minor a dependent child of the court pursuant to Section 300 is pending.

(c) Require the minor to be at his or her legal residence between the hours of 10:00 p.m. and 6:00 a.m. unless the minor is accompanied by his or her parent or parents, legal guardian or other adult person having the legal care or custody of the minor. *(Added by Stats 1989 ch 1117 §15, eff. 1/1/90.)*

§729.3. Testing of minor.

If a minor is found to be a person described in Section 601 or 602 and the court does not remove the minor from the physical custody of his or her parent or guardian, the court, as a condition of probation, may require the minor to submit to urine testing upon the request of a peace officer or probation officer for the purpose of determining the presence of alcohol or drugs. *(Added by Stats 1989 ch 1117 §16, eff. 1/1/90.)*

§729.6. Who receives restitution.

(a) If a minor is found to be a person described in Section 602, the court shall require as a condition of probation, that the minor make restitution as follows:

(1) To the victim, if the crime involved a victim. For purposes of this section, "victim" shall include the immediate surviving family of the actual victim in homicide cases. Payments shall be made to the Restitution Fund to the extent that the victim has received assistance pursuant to Article 1 (commencing with Section 13959) of Chapter 5 of Part 4 of Division 3 of Title 2 of the Government Code.

(2) To the Restitution Fund, if the crime did not involve a victim.

(b) If the court finds, and states its reasons for the finding on the record, that there are compelling and extraordinary reasons why restitution should not be required as provided in subdivision (a), the court shall require, as a condition of probation, that the minor perform specified community services.

(c) The court may avoid imposing the requirement of community service as a condition of probation only if it finds, and states its reasons for the finding on the record, that there are compelling and extraordinary reasons not to require community service in addition to its finding as to why restitution pursuant to subdivision (a) should not be required.

(d) For purposes of paragraph (1) of subdivision (a), "restitution" means full or partial payment for the value of stolen or damaged property, medical expenses, and wages or profits lost due to injury or to time spent as a witness or in assisting the police or prosecution, which losses were caused by the minor as a result of committing the offense for which he or she was found to be a person described in Section 602. The value of stolen or damaged property shall be the replacement cost of like property, or the actual cost of repairing the property when repair is possible. Restitution collected pursuant to this section shall be credited to any other judgments obtained by the victim against the minor arising out of the offense for which the minor was found to be a person described in Section 602.

(e) For purposes of paragraph (2) of subdivision (a), the amount of restitution to be paid to the Restitution Fund shall be set at the discretion of the court and commensurate with the seriousness of the offense; but shall not exceed one thousand dollars ($1,000) if the person is found to have committed a felony; and shall not exceed one hundred dollars ($100) if the person is found to have committed a misdemeanor.

(f) Nothing in this section shall be construed to limit the authority of the court to grant or deny probation or provide conditions of probation.

§729.7. Plan for settlement of restitution.

At the request of the victim, the probation officer shall assist in mediating a service contract between the victim and the minor under which the amount of restitution owed to the victim by the minor pursuant to Section 729.6 may be paid by performance of specified services. If the court approves of the contract, the court may make performance of services under the terms of the contract a condition of probation. Successful performance of service shall be credited as payment of restitution in accordance with the terms of the contract approved by the court.

§729.8. Community service for possession of drugs on school grounds.

(a) If a minor is found to be a person described in Section 602 by reason of the unlawful possession, use, sale, or other furnishing of a controlled substance, as defined in Chapter 2 (commencing with Section 11053) of the Health and Safety Code an imitation controlled substance as defined in Section 11675 of the Health and Safety Code, or toluene or a toxic, as described in Section 381 of the Penal Code, upon the grounds of any school providing instruction in kindergarten, or any of grades 1 to 12, inclusive, or any church or synagogue, playground, public or private youth center, or public swimming pool, during hours in which these facilities are open for business, classes, or school-related activities or programs, or at any time when minors are using the facility, the court, as a condition of business, classes, or school-related activities or programs, or at any time when minors are using the facility, the court, as a condition of probation, except in any case in which the court makes a finding and states on the record its reasons that the condition would be inappropriate, shall require the minor to perform not more than 100 hours of community service.

(b) The definitions contained in subdivision (e) of Section 11351.1 shall apply to this section.

(c) As used in this section, "community service" means any of the following:

(1) Picking up litter along public streets or highways.

(2) Cleaning up graffiti on school grounds or any public property.

(3) Performing services in a drug rehabilitation center. *(Amended by Stats 1990 ch 1664 §8, eff. 1/1/91.)*

© 1992 by J., B. & L. Gould
Printed in the U.S.A. **EP**

§729.9. Ban on controlled substance use as condition of probation.

If a minor is found to be a person described in Section 602 by reason of the commission of an offense involving the unlawful possession, use, sale, or other furnishing of a controlled substance, as defined in Chapter 2 (commencing with Section 11053) of Division 10 of the Health and Safety Code, and, unless it makes a finding that this condition would not serve the interests of justice, the court, when recommended by the probation officer, shall require, as a condition of probation, in addition to any other disposition authorized by law, that the minor shall not use or be under the influence of any controlled substance and shall submit to drug and substance abuse testing as directed by the probation officer. If the minor is required to submit to testing and has the financial ability to pay all or part of the costs associated with that testing, the court shall order the minor to pay a reasonable fee, which shall not exceed the actual cost of the testing. *(Added by Stats 1987 ch 879 §2.)*

§729.10. Participation of minor in alcohol and controlled substance education program.

(a) Whenever, in any county specified in subdivision (b), a judge of a juvenile court or referee of a juvenile court finds a minor to be a person described in Section 602 by reason of the commission of an offense involving the unlawful possession, use, sale, or other furnishing of a controlled substance, as defined in Chapter 2 (commencing with Section 11053) of Division 10 of the Health and Safety Code, or for violating subdivision (f) of Section 647 of the Penal Code, or Section 25662 of the Business and Professions Code, the minor shall be required to participate in, and successfully complete, an alcohol or drug education program, or both of those programs, as designated by the court. The expense of the person's attendance in the program shall be paid by the person's parents or guardian so long as the person is under the age of 18 years, and shall be paid by the person thereafter. The court shall consider the financial capacity of the person, or the person's parents or guardian, to pay the expense of the person's attendance in the program, and is authorized to waive all or part of the payment of the fee upon a finding of insufficient financial capacity to incur the cost of the fee. However, in approving the program, each county shall require the program to provide for the payment of the fee for the program in installments by any person who cannot afford to pay the full fee at the commencement of the program because of the person's income, earning capacity, or financial resources, and shall require the program to provide for the waiver of the fee for any person who is indigent, as determined by criteria for indigency established by the board of supervisors. Whenever it can be done without substantial additional cost, each county shall require that the program be provided for juveniles at a separate location from, or at a different time of day than, alcohol and drug education programs for adults.

(b) This section applies only in those counties that have one or more alcohol or drug education programs certified by the county alcohol program administrator and approved by the board of supervisors. *(Added by Stats 1989 ch 1117 §17, eff. 1/1/90.)*

§729.11. Juvenile Offender Substance Abuse Treatment Program.

(a) There is hereby established within the Office of Criminal Justice Planning, a demonstration program known as the "Juvenile Offender Substance Abuse Treatment Program." The goal of the demonstration program shall be to provide substance abuse intervention options for the juvenile courts.

(b) The Office of Criminal Justice Planning shall establish a county probation department demonstration project in at least three counties which shall be selected from among those counties submitting applications to the office. The demonstration projects shall be limited to the treatment of delinquent youth who have been assessed to be substance dependent or in imminent danger of substance dependence. Eligible youth will be those over which the juvenile court has retained jurisdiction pursuant to Section 602.

(c) The goals and functions of each demonstration project shall include, but are not limited to, all of the following:

(1) Development of substance assessment screening instruments at each project to be used at intake to classify the juvenile for possible placement in the program.

(2) Intensive in-custody substance abuse programs, including drug and alcohol education, individual and group counseling, family counseling, job training, self-esteem and personal motivation, life skills, and a volunteer mentor support network.

(d) Wards placed in custody shall be assigned to substance intervention team staff trained in program elements based on a reduced caseload.

(e) All wards who complete an in-custody substance abuse program or those placed directly on probation by the courts who require substance abuse intervention shall be transferred to an intensive aftercare or maximum supervision probation caseload. Wards assigned to these intensive caseloads may be required to meet intensive surveillance standards, including antidrug testing, day reporting, frequent contact with the probation officer, frequent contact with a therapist, and participation in designated community service substance prevention work projects for selected youth.

During this period of supervision, program elements, similar to those provided within juvenile custodial facilities, shall be established in the community for individual probationers, and their families, by designated intervention team staff. The "intervention team staff" shall include a probation officer, a treatment counselor, an educator, and job counselor.

(f) The development of the programs specified in subdivisions (c), (d), and (e) shall be in consultation with the county drug and alcohol administrator to assure appropriate program standards and to assure that the program is not duplicative, and that it is coordinated with California's Drug and Alcohol Abuse Master Plan, as specified in Section 11998.1 of the Health and Safety Code.

(g) The Office of Criminal Justice Planning shall submit a final evaluation of the demonstration projects to the Legislature within six months after the completion of the two-year demonstration project. The selected demonstration projects shall cooperate with the Office of Criminal Justice Planning in the writing of the final evaluation.

(h) The demonstration program shall be a two-year program and is contingent upon the availability and receipt of federal Anti-Drug Abuse Act funding. The first-year funding of the program shall be appropriated from moneys received by the Office of Criminal Justice Planning pursuant to the federal

Anti-Drug Abuse Act of 1988 (Public Law 100-690). The second year of funding the program shall be provided by the selected demonstration program projects. *(Added by Stats 1991 ch 482 §2, eff. 10/4/91.)*

§730. Care and supervision of ward of the court.

When a minor is adjudged a ward of the court on the ground that he is a person described by Section 602, the court may order any of the types of treatment referred to in Section 727, and as an additional alternative, may commit the minor to a juvenile home, ranch, camp or forestry camp. If there is no county juvenile home, ranch, camp or forestry camp within the county, the court may commit the minor to the county juvenile hall.

When such ward is placed under the supervision of the probation officer or committed to his care, custody and control, the court may make any and all reasonable orders for the conduct of such ward including the requirement that he go to work and earn money for the support of his dependents or to effect reparation and in either case that he keep an account of his earnings and report the same to the probation officer and apply such earnings as directed by the court. The court may impose and require any and all reasonable conditions that it may determine fitting and proper to the end that justice may be done and the reformation and rehabilitation of the ward enhanced.

§730.5. Fine against minor.

When a minor is adjudged a ward of the court on the ground that he or she is a person described in Section 602, in addition to any of the orders authorized by Section 726, 727, 730, or 731, the court may levy a fine against the minor up to the amount that could be imposed on an adult for the same offense, if the court finds that the minor has the financial ability to pay the fine. Section 1464 of the Penal Code applies to fines levied pursuant to this section. *(Amended by Stats 1988 ch 99 §2, eff. 1/1/89.)*

§730.6. Restitution fine.

(a) When a minor is found to be a person described in Section 602, in addition to any other disposition authorized by law, the court shall levy a restitution fine which shall be deposited in the Restitution Fund, the proceeds of which shall be distributed pursuant to subdivision (b) of Section 13967 of the Government Code.

(b) The restitution fine imposed pursuant to this section shall be in the form of a penalty assessment in accordance with Section 1464 of the Penal Code. In addition, if the person is found to be a person described in Section 602 by reason of the commission of one or more felony offenses, the court shall impose a separate and additional restitution fine of not more than one thousand dollars ($1,000). In setting the amount of the fine for felony offenses, the court shall consider any relevant factors including, but not limited to, the seriousness and gravity of the offense and the circumstances of its commission, any economic gain derived by the minor as a result of the offense, and the extent to which others suffered losses as a result of the offense. Such losses may include pecuniary losses to the victim or his or her dependents as well as intangible losses, such as psychological harm caused by the offense.

(c) The restitution fine shall be imposed in every case in which a minor is found to be a person described in Section 602. Such restitution fine shall be in addition to any other disposition or fine imposed and shall be imposed regardless of the minor's present ability to pay. Except as provided in this section, under no circumstances shall the court fail to impose the separate and additional restitution fine in felony cases required by this section. This fine shall not be subject to penalty assessments pursuant to Section 1464 of the Penal Code. In a case in which the minor is a person described in Section 602 by reason of having committed a felony offense, if the court finds that there are compelling and extraordinary reasons, the court may waive imposition of the restitution fine. When such a waiver is granted, the court shall state on the record all reasons supporting the waiver.

(d) In any case in which the minor is ordered to pay restitution as a condition of probation, the order to pay the restitution fine may be stayed pending the successful completion of probation, and thereafter the stay shall become permanent.

(e) If the restitution fine has been stayed pending successful completion of probation, upon revocation of probation and imposition of sentence the stay shall be lifted. The amount of the restitution fine shall be offset by any restitution payments actually made as a condition of probation. However, probation shall not be revoked for failure of a person to make restitution pursuant to Section 729.6 as a condition of probation unless the court determines that the person has willfully failed to pay or failed to make sufficient bona fide efforts to legally acquire the resources to pay.

(f) At its discretion, the board of supervisors of any county may impose a fee to cover the actual administrative cost of collecting the restitution fine, not to exceed 10 percent of the amount ordered to be paid, to be added to the restitution fine and included in the order of the court, the proceeds of which shall be deposited in the general fund of the county. *(Amended by Stats 1988 ch 975 §4, eff. 1/1/89.)*

§731. Requirements of ward of court; limits on physical detention.

When a minor is adjudged a ward of the court on the ground that he or she is a person described by Section 602, the court may order any of the types of treatment referred to in Sections 727 and 730 and, in addition, may order the ward to make restitution, to pay a fine up to the amount of two hundred fifty dollars ($250) for deposit in the county treasury if the court finds that the minor has the financial ability to pay the fine, or to participate in uncompensated work programs or the court may commit the ward to a sheltered-care facility or may order that the ward and his or her family or guardian participate in a program of professional counseling as arranged and directed by the probation officer as a condition of continued custody of such minor or may commit the minor to the Department of the Youth Authority.

A minor committed to the Department of the Youth Authority may not be held in physical confinement for a period of time in excess of the maximum period of imprisonment which could be imposed upon an adult convicted of the offense or offenses which brought or continued the minor under the jurisdiction of the juvenile court. Nothing in this section limits the power of the Youthful Offender Parole Board to retain the minor on parole status for the period permitted by Section 1769.

© 1992 by J., B. & L. Gould
Printed in the U.S.A.   EP

§731.1. Payment of restitution to victim.

(a) When a minor is committed to the Youth Authority, in lieu of imposing all or a portion of the restitution fine required by Section 730.6, the court shall order restitution to be paid to the victim in cases in which the victim has suffered economic loss as a result of the minor's criminal conduct. For purposes of this section, "victim" shall include the immediate surviving family of the actual victim in homicide cases. For purposes of this section, "restitution" means payment described in subdivision (d) of Section 729.6.

(b) A restitution order imposed pursuant to this section shall identify the losses to which it pertains and may be enforced in a manner provided for the enforcement of money judgments. The making of a restitution order pursuant to this section shall not affect the right of a victim to recovery from the Restitution Fund as provided by law, except to the extent that restitution is actually collected pursuant to the order. Restitution collected pursuant to this section shall be credited to any other judgments obtained by the victim against the minor arising out of the offense for which the minor was found to be a person described in Section 602.

(c) If the court finds that there are compelling and extraordinary reasons, the court may waive imposition of restitution. When such a waiver is granted, the court shall state on the record all reasons supporting the waiver. *(Added by Stats 1988 ch 181 §1, eff. 1/1/89.)*

§731.5. Additional penalty for petty theft.

In addition to the provisions of Section 731, if a minor's conduct constitutes a violation of Section 490.5 of the Penal Code, the court may require the minor to perform public services designated by the court.

§732. Ascertainment that institution can receive minor.

Before a minor is conveyed to any state or county institution pursuant to this article, it shall be ascertained from the superintendent thereof that such person can be received.

§733. Who may not be committed to Youth Authority.

No ward of the juvenile court who is under the age of eight years, and no such ward who is suffering from any contagious, infectious, or other disease which would probably endanger the lives or health of the other inmates of any state school shall be committed to the Youth Authority.

§734. Ward must be in condition to benefit from treatment.

No ward of the juvenile court shall be committed to the Youth Authority unless the judge of the court is fully satisfied that the mental and physical condition and qualifications of the ward are such as to render it probable that he will be benefited by the reformatory educational discipline or other treatment provided by the Youth Authority.

§735. Summary of facts to be sent to director.

Accompanying the commitment papers, the court shall send to the Director of the Youth Authority a summary of all the facts in the possession of the court, covering the history of the ward committed and a statement of the mental and physical condition of the ward.

§736. Acceptance by Youth Authority of persons committed to it.

(a) The Youth Authority shall accept a person committed to it pursuant to this article if it believes that the person can be materially benefited by its reformatory and educational discipline, and if it has adequate facilities to provide that care. No person subject to this section shall be transported to any facility under the jurisdiction of the Youth Authority until the director thereof has notified the committing court of the place to which that person is to be transported and the time at which he or she can be received.

(b) The Youth Authority shall also accept a person committed to it pursuant to this article, provided that the Director of the Youth Authority certifies that staff and institutions are available (1) if he is a borderline psychiatric or borderline mentally deficient case, (2) if he or she is a sex deviate unless he is of a type whose presence in the community, under parole supervision, would present a menace to the public welfare, or (3) if he or she suffers from a primary behavior disorder. No person subject to this section shall be transported to any facility under the jurisdiction of the Youth Authority until the director thereof has notified the committing court of the place to which that person is to be transported and the time at which he can be received. To implement the administration of this paragraph, the Director of the Youth Authority and the Director of Mental Health shall, at least annually, confer and establish policy with respect to the types of cases which should be the responsibility of each department.

§737. Order for detention in detention home.

(a) Whenever a person has been adjudged a ward of the juvenile court and has been committed or otherwise disposed of as provided in this chapter for the care of wards of the juvenile court, the court may order that the ward be detained in the detention home, or in the case of a ward of the age of 18 years or more, in the county jail or otherwise as the court deems fit until the execution of the order of commitment or of other disposition.

(b) In any case in which a minor is detained for more than 15 days pending the execution of the order of commitment or of any other disposition, the court shall periodically review the case to determine whether the delay is reasonable. These periodic reviews shall be held at least every 15 days, commencing from the time the minor was initially detained pending the execution of the order of commitment or of any other disposition, and during the course of each review the court shall inquire regarding the action taken by the probation department to carry out its order, the reasons for the delay, and the effect of the delay upon the minor.

§738. Return of nonresident minor to home state or country.

In a case where the residence of a minor placed on probation under the provisions of Section 725 or of a ward of the juvenile court is out of the state and in another state or foreign country, or in a case where such minor is a resident of this state but his parents, relatives, guardian, or person charged with his custody is in another state, the court may order such minor sent to his parents, relatives, or guardian, or to the person charged with his custody, or, if the minor is a resident of a foreign country, to an official of a juvenile court of such foreign country or an agency of such country authorized to accept the minor, and in such case may order transportation and accommodation furnished, with or without an attendant, as the court deems necessary. If the court deems an attendant necessary, the court may order the probation officer or other suitable person to serve as such attendant. The probation officer shall authorize the necessary expenses of such minor and of the attendant and claims therefor shall be audited, allowed and paid in the same manner as other county claims.

§739. Provision of medical, surgical, dental, or other care.

(a) Whenever any person is taken into temporary custody under Article 15 (commencing with Section 625) and is in need of medical, surgical, dental, or other remedial care, the probation officer may, upon the recommendation of the attending physician and surgeon or, if the person needs dental care and there is an attending dentist, the attending dentist, authorize the performance of that medical, surgical, dental, or other remedial care. The probation officer shall notify the parent, guardian, or person standing in loco parentis of the person, if any, of the care found to be needed before the care is provided, and if the parent, guardian, or person standing in loco parentis objects, such care shall be given only upon order of the court in the exercise of its discretion.

(b) Whenever it appears to the juvenile court that any person concerning whom a petition has been filed with the court is in need of medical, surgical, dental, or other remedial care, and that there is no parent, guardian, or person standing in loco parentis capable of authorizing or willing to authorize the remedial care or treatment for that person, the court, upon the written recommendation of a licensed physician and surgeon or, if the person needs dental care, a licensed dentist, and after due notice to the parent, guardian, or person standing in loco parentis, if any, may make an order authorizing the performance of the necessary medical, surgical, dental, or other remedial care for that person.

(c) Whenever a ward of the juvenile court is placed by order of the court within the care and custody or under the supervision of the probation officer of the county in which the ward resides and it appears to the court that there is no parent, guardian, or person standing in loco parentis capable of authorizing or willing to authorize medical, surgical, dental, or other remedial care or treatment for the ward, the court may, after due notice to the parent, guardian, or person standing in loco parentis, if any, order that the probation officer may authorize the medical, surgical, dental, or other remedial care for the ward by licensed practitioners, as may from time to time appear necessary.

(d) Whenever it appears that a minor otherwise within subdivision (a), (b), or (c) requires immediate emergency medical, surgical, or other remedial care in an emergency situation, that care may be provided by a licensed physician and surgeon or, if the minor needs dental care in an emergency situation, by a licensed dentist, without a court order and upon authorization of a probation officer. The probation officer shall make reasonable efforts to obtain the consent of, or to notify, the parent, guardian, or person standing in loco parentis prior to authorizing emergency medical, surgical,

dental, or other remedial care. "Emergency situation," for the purposes of this subdivision means a minor requires immediate treatment for the alleviation of severe pain or an immediate diagnosis and treatment of an unforeseeable medical, surgical, dental, or other remedial condition or contagious disease which if not immediately diagnosed and treated, would lead to serious disability or death.

(e) In any case in which the court orders the performance of any medical, surgical, dental, or other remedial care pursuant to this section, the court may also make an order authorizing the release of information concerning that care to probation officers, parole officers, or any other qualified individuals or agencies caring for or acting in the interest and welfare of the minor under order, commitment, or approval of the court.

(f) Nothing in this section shall be construed as limiting the right of a parent, guardian, or person standing in loco parentis, who has not been deprived of the custody or control of the minor by order of the court, in providing any medical, surgical, dental, or other remedial treatment recognized or permitted under the laws of this state.

(g) The parent of any person described in this section may authorize the performance of medical, surgical, dental, or other remedial care provided for in this section notwithstanding his or her age or marital status. In nonemergency situations the parent authorizing the care shall notify the other parent prior to the administration of such care. *(Amended by Stats 1990 ch 566 §2, eff. 1/1/91.)*

§740. Placement of minor in home county facility.

(a) Any minor adjudged to be a ward of the court on the basis that he or she is a person described in Section 602 and who is placed in a community care facility shall be placed in such a facility within his or her county of residence, unless he or she has identifiable needs requiring specialized care which cannot be provided in a local facility, or unless his or her needs dictate physical separation from his or her family.

(b) Within 30 days after the placement of a minor adjudged to be a ward of the court on the basis that he or she is a person described in Section 602 in any community care facility outside the ward's county of residence, the probation officer of the county making the placement, or in the case of a Youth Authority ward, the parole officer in charge of his or her case, shall send written notice of the placement, including the name of the ward, the juvenile record of the ward (including any known prior offenses), and the ward's county of residence, to the probation officer of the county in which the community care facility is located; with regard to this requirement, it is the intention of the Legislature that the probation officer of the county making the placement, or in the case of a Youth Authority ward, the parole officer in charge of his or her case, shall make his or her best efforts to send, or to hand deliver, the notice at the same time the placement is made. When such a placement is terminated, the probation officer of the county making the placement, or in the case of a Youth Authority ward, the parole officer in charge of his or her case, shall send notice thereof to any person or agency receiving notification of the placement.

(c) A minor, the parent or guardian of any minor, and counsel representing a minor or the parent or

© 1992 by J., B. & L. Gould
Printed in the U.S.A. **EP**

guardian of a minor may petition the juvenile court for the review of any placement decision concerning the minor made by the probation officer pursuant to subdivision (a). The petition shall state the petitioner's relationship to the minor and shall set forth in concise language the grounds on which the review is sought. The court shall order that a hearing shall be held on the petition and shall give prior notice, or cause prior notice to be given, to such persons and by such means as prescribed by Section 776, and, in instances in which the means of giving notice is not prescribed by that section, then by such means as the court prescribes.

(e)* If a minor is placed in a community care facility out of his or her county of residence and is then arrested and placed in juvenile hall pending a jurisdictional hearing, the county of residence shall pay to the probation department of the county of placement all reasonable costs resulting directly from the minor's stay in the juvenile hall, provided that these costs exceed one hundred dollars ($100).
*So in original. Probably should be "(d)".

(e) If, as a result of the hearing in subdivision (d), the minor is remanded back to his or her county of residence, the county of residence shall pay to the probation department of the county of placement, in addition to any payment made pursuant to subdivision (d), all reasonable costs resulting directly from transporting the minor to the county of residency, provided that these costs exceed one hundred dollars ($100).

(f) Claims made by the probation department in the county of placement, to the county of residence, pursuant to subdivisions (d) and (e), shall be paid within 30 days of the submission of these claims and the probation department in the county of placement shall bear the remaining expense.

(g) As used in this section, "community care facility" shall be defined as provided in Section 1502 of the Health and Safety Code. *(Amended by Stats 1991 ch 1202 §20, eff. 1/1/92.)*

§741. Employment of medical professionals to determine appropriate treatment of a minor.

The juvenile court may, in any case before it in which a petition has been filed as provided in Article 16 (commencing with Section 650), order that the probation officer obtain the services of such psychiatrists, psychologists, physicians and surgeons, dentists, optometrists, audiologists, or other clinical experts as may be required to assist in determining the appropriate treatment of the minor and as may be required in the conduct or implementation of the treatment. Payment for the services shall be a charge against the county.

Whenever diagnosis or treatment pursuant to this section is due to, or related to, drug or alcohol use, the cost thereof shall be considered for the use of funds made available to the county from state or federal sources for the purpose of providing care and treatment for drug- and alcohol-related illness or for drug or alcohol abuse. *(Amended by Stats 1991 ch 482 §3, eff. 10/4/91.)*

§742. Notification of victim regarding outcome of case.

Upon the request of an alleged victim of a crime, the probation officer shall, within 60 days of the final disposition of a case within which a petition has been filed pursuant to Section 602, inform that person by letter of the final disposition of the case. "Final disposition" means dismissal, acquittal, or findings made pursuant to this article. If the court orders that restitution shall be made to the victim of a crime, the amount, terms, and conditions thereof shall be included in the information provided pursuant to this section.

ARTICLE 19

WARDS — TRANSFER OF CASES BETWEEN COUNTIES

§750. Transfer of case to another county.

Whenever a petition is filed in the juvenile court of a county other than the residence of the person named in the petition, or whenever, subsequent to the filing of a petition in the juvenile court of the county where such minor resides, the residence of the person who would be legally entitled to the custody of such minor were it not for the existence of a court order issued pursuant to this chapter is changed to another county, the entire case may be transferred to the juvenile court of the county wherein such person then resides at any time after the court has made a finding of the facts upon which it has exercised its jurisdiction over such minor, and the juvenile court of the county wherein such person then resides shall take jurisdiction of the case upon the receipt and filing with it of such finding of the facts and an order transferring the case.

§751. Payment of expenses of transfer.

The expense of the transfer and all expenses in connection with the transfer and for the support and maintenance of such person shall be paid from the county treasury of the court ordering the transfer until the receipt and filing of the finding and order of transfer in the juvenile court of the transferee county.

The judge shall inquire into the financial condition of such person and of the parent, parents, guardian, or other person charged with his support and maintenance, and if he finds such person, parent, parents, guardian, or other person able, in whole or in part, to pay the expense of such transfer, he shall make a further order requiring such person, parent, parents, guardian, or other person to repay to the county such part, or all, of such expense of transfer as, in the opinion of the court, is proper. Such repayment shall be made to the probation officer who shall keep suitable accounts of such expenses and repayments and shall deposit all such collections in the county treasury.

§752. Certified copy of file to be sent to person's county of residence.

Whenever a case is transferred as provided in Section 750, a certified copy of the file may be made and forwarded to the county where the person resides and shall include the name and address of the legal residence of the parent or guardian of the minor. A certified copy shall be deemed to be the same as the original. The original court file may be kept in the files of the transferring county.

§753. Precedence in court of order of transfer.

Whenever an order of transfer from another county is filed with the clerk of any juvenile court, the clerk shall place the transfer order on the calendar of the court, and it shall have precedence over all actions and civil proceedings not specifically given precedence by other provisions of law and shall be heard by the court at the earliest possible moment following the filing of the order.

§754. County in which court is situated and minor's county of residence both parties in action.

In any action under the provisions of this article in which the residence of a minor person is determined, both the county in which the court is situated and any other county which, as a result of the determination of residence, might be determined to be the county of residence of the minor person, shall be considered to be parties in the action and shall have the right to appeal any order by which residence of the minor person is determined.

§755. Retention of jurisdiction.

Any person placed on probation by the juvenile court or adjudged to be a ward of the juvenile court may be permitted by order of the court to reside in a county other than the county of his legal residence, and the court shall retain jurisdiction over such person.

Whenever a ward of the juvenile court is permitted to reside in a county other than the county of his legal residence, he may be placed under the supervision of the probation officer of the county of actual residence, with the consent of such probation officer. The ward shall comply with the instructions of such probation officer and upon failure to do so shall be returned to the county of his legal residence for further hearing and order of the court.

ARTICLE 20

WARDS — MODIFICATION OF JUVENILE COURT JUDGMENTS AND ORDERS

§775. Changeability of court orders.

Any order made by the court in the case of any person subject to its jurisdiction may at any time be changed, modified, or set aside, as the judge deems meet and proper, subject to such procedural requirements as are imposed by this article.

§776. Court orders not to be changed without notice.

No order changing, modifying, or setting aside a previous order of the juvenile court shall be made either in chambers, or otherwise, unless prior notice of the application therefor has been given by the judge or the clerk of the court to the probation officer and prosecuting attorney and to the minor's counsel of record, or, if there is no counsel of record, to the minor and his parent or guardian.

§777. Removal of minor from custody of parents and subsequent placement.

An order changing or modifying a previous order by removing a minor from the physical custody of a parent, guardian, relative, or friend and directing placement in a foster home, or commitment to a private institution or commitment to a county institution, or an order changing or modifying a previous order by directing commitment to the Youth Authority shall be made only after noticed hearing upon a supplemental petition.

(a) The supplemental petition shall be filed as follows:

(1) By the probation officer where a minor has been declared a ward of the court or a probationer under Section 601 in the original matter and shall contain a concise statement of facts sufficient to support the conclusion that the previous disposition has not been effective in the rehabilitation or protection of the minor.

(2) By the probation officer or the prosecuting attorney, after consulting with the probation officer, if the minor is a court ward or probationer under Section 602 in the original matter and the supplemental petition alleges a violation of a condition of probation not amounting to a crime. The petition shall contain a concise statement of facts sufficient to support the conclusion that the previous disposition has not been effective in the rehabilitation or protection of the minor. The petition shall be filed by the prosecuting attorney, after consulting with the probation officer, if a minor has been declared a ward or probationer under Section 602 in the original matter and the petition alleges a violation of a condition of probation amounting to a crime. The petition shall contain a concise statement of facts sufficient to support the conclusion that the previous disposition has not been effective in the rehabilitation or protection of the minor.

(3) Where the probation officer is the petitioner pursuant to paragraph (2), if prior to the attachment of jeopardy at the time of the jurisdictional hearing it appears to the prosecuting attorney that the minor is not a person described by subdivision (a) or that the supplemental petition was not properly charged, the prosecuting attorney may make a motion to dismiss the supplemental petition and may request that the matter be referred to the probation officer for whatever action the prosecuting attorney or probation officer may deem appropriate.

(b) Notwithstanding the provisions of subdivision (a), if the petition alleges a violation of a condition of probation and is for the commitment of a minor to a county juvenile institution for a period of 30 days or less, or for a less restrictive disposition, it is not necessary to allege and prove that the previous disposition has not been effective in the rehabilitation or protection of the minor. However, before any period of commitment in excess of 15 days is ordered, the court shall determine and consider the effect that an extended commitment period would have on the minor's schooling, including possible loss of credits, and on any current employment of the minor. In order to make such a commitment the court must, however, find that the commitment is in the best interest of the minor. The provisions of this subdivision may not be utilized more than twice during the time the minor is a ward of the court.

(c) Upon the filing of a supplemental petition, the clerk of the juvenile court shall immediately set the same for hearing within 30 days, and the probation officer shall cause notice of it to be served upon the persons and in the manner prescribed by Sections 658 and 660.

(d) An order for the detention of the minor pending adjudication of the petition may be made only after a hearing is conducted pursuant to Article 15 (commencing with Section 625) of this chapter.

(e) The filing of a supplemental petition and the hearing thereon shall not be required for the commitment of a minor to a county institution for a period of

© 1992 by J., B. & L. Gould
Printed in the U.S.A.   EP

30 days or less pursuant to an original or a previous order imposing a specified time in custody and staying the enforcement of the order subject to subsequent violation of a condition or conditions of probation, provided that in order to make the commitment, the court finds at a hearing that the minor has violated a condition of probation. *(Amended by Stats 1989 ch 1117 §18, eff. 1/1/90.)*

§778. Petition to change order or terminate court's jurisdiction.

Any parent or other person having an interest in a child who is a ward of the juvenile court or the child himself through a properly appointed guardian may, upon grounds of change of circumstance or new evidence, petition the court in the same action in which the child was found to be a ward of the juvenile court for a hearing to change, modify, or set aside any order of court previously made or to terminate the jurisdiction of the court. The petition shall be verified and, if made by a person other than the child, shall state the petitioner's relationship to or interest in the child and shall set forth in concise language any change of circumstance or new evidence which are alleged to require such change of order or termination of jurisdiction.

If it appears that the best interests of the child may be promoted by the proposed change of order or termination of jurisdiction, the court shall order that a hearing be held and shall give prior notice, or cause prior notice to be given, to such persons and by such means as prescribed by Sections 776 and 779, and, in such instances as the means of giving notice is not prescribed by such sections, then by such means as the court prescribes.

§779. Change of order of commitment.

The court committing a ward to the Youth Authority may thereafter change, modify, or set aside the order of commitment. Ten days' notice of the hearing of the application therefor shall be served by United States mail upon the Director of the Youth Authority. In changing, modifying, or setting aside such order of commitment, the court shall give due consideration to the effect thereof upon the discipline and parole system of the Youth Authority or of the correctional school in which the ward may have been placed by the Youth Authority. Except as in this section provided, nothing in this chapter shall be deemed to interfere with the system of parole and discharge now or hereafter established by law, or by rule of the Youth Authority, for the parole and discharge of wards of the juvenile court committed to the Youth Authority, or with the management of any school, institution, or facility under the jurisdiction of the Youth Authority. Except as in this section provided, nothing in this chapter shall be deemed to interfere with the system of transfer between institutions and facilities under the jurisdiction of the Youth Authority.

However, before any inmate of a correctional school may be transferred to a state hospital, he shall first be returned to a court of competent jurisdiction and, after hearing, may be committed to a state hospital for the insane in accordance with law.

§780. Persons unsuitable for retention in Youth Authority facilities.

If any person who has been committed to the Youth Authority appears to be an improper person to be received by or retained in any institution or facility under the jurisdiction of the Youth Authority or to be so incorrigible or so incapable of reformation under the discipline of any institution or facility under the jurisdiction of the Youth Authority as to render his or her retention detrimental to the interests of the Youth Authority, the Youthful Offender Parole Board may order the return of such person to the committing court. However, the return of any person to the committing court does not relieve the Department of the Youth Authority of any of its duties or responsibilities under the original commitment, and such commitment continues in full force and effect until it is vacated, modified, or set aside by order of the court.

When any such person is so returned to the committing court, his or her transportation shall be made, and the compensation therefor paid, as provided for the execution of an order of commitment.

§781. Order to seal records.

(a) In any case in which a petition has been filed with a juvenile court to commence proceedings to adjudge a person a ward of the court, in any case in which a person is cited to appear before a probation officer or is taken before a probation officer pursuant to Section 626, or in any case in which a minor is taken before any officer of a law enforcement agency, the person or the county probation officer may, five years or more after the jurisdiction of the juvenile court has terminated as to the person, or, in a case in which no petition is filed, five years or more after the person was cited to appear before a probation officer or was taken before a probation officer pursuant to Section 626 or was taken before any officer of a law enforcement agency, or, in any case, at any time after the person has reached the age of 18 years, petition the court for sealing of the records, including records of arrest, relating to the person's case, in the custody of the juvenile court and probation officer and any other agencies, including law enforcement agencies, and public officials as the petitioner alleges, in his or her petition, to have custody of the records. The court shall notify the district attorney of the county and the county probation officer, if he or she is not the petitioner, and the district attorney or probation officer or any of their deputies or any other person having relevant evidence may testify at the hearing on the petition. If, after hearing, the court finds that since the termination of jurisdiction or action pursuant to Section 626, as the case may be, he or she has not been convicted of a felony or of any misdemeanor involving moral turpitude and that rehabilitation has been attained to the satisfaction of the court, it shall order all records, papers, and exhibits in the person's case in the custody of the juvenile court sealed, including the juvenile court record, minute book entries, and entries on dockets, and other records relating to the case in the custody of the other agencies and officials as are named in the order. In any case in which a ward of the juvenile court is subject to the registration requirements set forth in Section 290 of the Penal Code, a court, in ordering the sealing of the juvenile records of the person, also shall provide in the order that the person is relieved from the registration requirement and for the destruction of all registration information in the custody of the Department of Justice and other agencies and officials. Notwithstanding any other provision of law, the court shall not order the person's records sealed in any case in which the person has been found by the juvenile court to have committed an offense listed in subdivision (b) of Section 707 until at least three years have elapsed since commission of the offense listed in subdivision (b) of Section 707. Once the court has ordered the person's records sealed, the proceedings in the case shall be deemed never to have occurred, and the person may properly reply accordingly to any inquiry about the events, the records of which are ordered sealed. The court shall send a copy of the order to each agency and official named therein, directing the agency to seal its records and stating the date thereafter to destroy the sealed records. Each such agency and official shall seal the records in its custody as directed by the order, shall advise the court of its compliance, and thereupon shall seal the copy of the court's order for sealing of records that it, he, or she received. The person who is the subject of records sealed pursuant to this section may petition the superior court to permit inspection of the records by persons named in the petition, and the superior court may so order. Otherwise, except as provided in subdivision (b), the records shall not be open to inspection.

(b) In any action or proceeding based upon defamation, a court, upon a showing of good cause, may order any records sealed under this section to be opened and admitted into evidence. The records shall be confidential and shall be available for inspection only by the court, jury, parties, counsel for the parties, and any other person who is authorized by the court to inspect them. Upon the judgment in the action or proceeding becoming final, the court shall order the records sealed.

(c)(1) Subdivision (a) does not apply to Department of Motor Vehicles records of any convictions for offenses under the Vehicle Code or any local ordinance relating to the operation, stopping and standing, or parking of a vehicle where the record of any such conviction would be a public record under Section 1808 of the Vehicle Code. However, if a court orders a case record containing any such conviction to be sealed under this section, and if the Department of Motor Vehicles maintains a public record of such a conviction, the court shall notify the Department of Motor Vehicles of the sealing and the department shall advise the court of its receipt of the notice.

Notwithstanding any other provision of law, subsequent to the notification, the Department of Motor Vehicles shall allow access to its record of convictions only to the subject of the record and to insurers which have been granted requester code numbers by the department. Any insurer to which such a record of conviction is disclosed, when such a conviction record has otherwise been sealed under this section, shall be given notice of the sealing when the record is disclosed to the insurer. The insurer may use the information contained in the record for purposes of determining eligibility for insurance and insurance rates for the subject of the record, and the information shall not be used for any other purpose nor shall it be disclosed by an insurer to any person or party not having access to the record.

(2) This subdivision shall not be construed as preventing the sealing of any record which is maintained by any agency or party other than the Department of Motor Vehicles.

(3) This subdivision shall not be construed as affecting the procedures or authority of the Department of Motor Vehicles for purging department records.

(d) Unless for good cause the court determines that the juvenile court record shall be retained, the court shall order the destruction of a person's juvenile court records that are sealed pursuant to this section as follows: five years after the record was ordered sealed, if the person who is the subject of the record was alleged or adjudged to be a person described by Section 601; or when the person who is the subject of the record reaches the age of 38 if the person was alleged or adjudged to be a person described by Section 602. Any other agency in possession of sealed records may destroy its records five years after the record was ordered sealed. (Amended by Stats 1986 ch 277 §1.)

§782. Conditions for dismissal of petition.

A judge of the juvenile court in which a petition was filed, at any time before the minor reaches the age of 21 years, may dismiss the petition or may set aside the findings and dismiss the petition if the court finds that the interests of justice and the welfare of the minor require such dismissal, or if it finds that the minor is not in need of treatment or rehabilitation. The court shall have jurisdiction to order such dismissal or setting aside of the findings and dismissal regardless of whether the minor is, at the time of such order, a ward or dependent child of the court.

§783. Filing of adjudication with Department of Motor Vehicles.

An adjudication that a minor violated any of the provisions enumerated in subdivision (d) of Section 13202.5 of the Vehicle Code shall be reported to the Department of Motor Vehicles at its office in Sacramento within 10 days of the adjudication pursuant to Section 1803 of the Vehicle Code. (Amended by Stats 1988 ch 1254 §5, eff. 1/1/89.)

§784. Filing abstract of record with Department of Motor Vehicles.

Notwithstanding any other provision of law, upon any adjudication that a minor violated any provision of law for which a report would be required under Section 1803 of the Vehicle Code, including any determination that because of the act the minor is a person described in Section 601 or 602 or that a program of supervision should be instituted for the minor, the clerk shall, not more than 30 days after the violation and in no case later than 10 days after the adjudication, prepare an abstract of the record, certify the abstract to be true and correct, and immediately forward the abstract to the Department of Motor Vehicles. The record shall be a public record subject to disclosure in the same manner as reports made under Section 1803 of the Vehicle Code. (Added by Stats 1989 ch 1465 §6, eff. 1/1/90.)

ARTICLE 21

WARDS — APPEALS

§800. Appeal; motion to suppress.

(a) A judgment in a proceeding under Section 601 or 602 may be appealed from, by the minor, in the same manner as any final judgment, and any subsequent order may be appealed from, by the minor, as from an order after judgment. Pending appeal of the order or judgment, the granting or refusal to order release shall rest in the discretion of the juvenile court.

© 1992 by J., B. & L. Gould
Printed in the U.S.A.   EP

The appeal shall have precedence over all other cases in the court to which the appeal is taken.

A ruling on a motion to suppress pursuant to Section 700.1 shall be reviewed on appeal even if the judgment is predicated upon an admission of the allegations of the petition.

A judgment or subsequent order entered by a referee shall become appealable whenever proceedings pursuant to Section 252, 253, or 254 have become completed or, if proceedings pursuant to Section 252, 253, or 254 are not initiated, when the time for initiating the proceedings has expired.

(b) An appeal may be taken by the people from any of the following:

(1) A ruling on a motion to suppress pursuant to Section 700.1 even if the judgment is a dismissal of the petition or any count or counts of the petition. However, no appeal by the people shall lie as to any count which, if the people are successful, will be the basis for further proceedings subjecting any person to double jeopardy.

(2) An order made after judgment entered pursuant to Section 777.

(3) An order modifying the jurisdictional finding by reducing the degree of the offense or modifying the offense to a lesser offense.

(4) An order or judgment dismissing or otherwise terminating the action before the minor has been placed in jeopardy, or where the minor has waived jeopardy. If, pursuant to this paragraph, the people prosecute an appeal of the decision or any review of that decision, it shall be binding upon the people and they shall be prohibited from refiling the case which was appealed.

(5) The imposition of an unlawful order at a dispositional hearing, whether or not the court suspends the execution of the disposition.

(c) Nothing contained in this section shall be construed to authorize an appeal from an order granting probation. Instead, the people may seek appellate review of any grant of probation, whether or not the court imposes disposition, by means of a petition for a writ of mandate or prohibition which is filed within 60 days after probation is granted. The review of any grant of probation shall include review of any order underlying the grant of probation.

(d) An appellant unable to afford counsel, shall be provided a free copy of the transcript in any appeal.

(e) The record shall be prepared and transmitted immediately after filing of the notice of appeal, without advance payment of fees. If the appellant is able to afford counsel, the county may seek reimbursement for the cost of the transcripts under subdivision (c) of Section 68511.3 of the Government Code as though the appellant had been granted permission to proceed in forma pauperis.

(f) All appeals shall be initiated by the filing of notice of appeal in conformity with the requirements of Section 1240.1 of the Penal Code. (*Amended by Stats 1991 ch 649 §1, eff. 1/1/92.*)

ARTICLE 22

WARDS AND DEPENDENT CHILDREN — RECORDS

§825. Record of superior court's findings.
The order and findings of the superior court in each case under the provisions of this chapter shall be

entered in a suitable book or other form of written record which shall be kept for that purpose and known as the "juvenile court record."

§826. Destruction of records by probation officer.

(a) After five years from the date on which the jurisdiction of the juvenile court over a minor is terminated, the probation officer may destroy all records and papers in the proceedings concerning the minor.

The juvenile court record, which includes all records and papers, any minute book entries, dockets and judgment dockets, shall be destroyed by order of the court as follows: when the person who is the subject of the record reaches the age of 28 years, if the person was alleged or adjudged to be a person described by Section 300, when the person who is the subject of the record reaches the age of 21 years, if the person was alleged or adjudged to be a person described by Section 601, or when the person reaches the age of 38 years if the person was alleged or adjudged to be a person described by Section 602, unless for good cause the court determines that the juvenile record shall be retained, or unless the juvenile court record is released to the person who is the subject of the record pursuant to this section.

Any person who is the subject of a juvenile court record may by written notice request the juvenile court to release the court record to his or her custody. Wherever possible, the written notice shall include the person's full name, the person's date of birth, and the juvenile court case number. Any juvenile court receiving the written notice shall release the court record to the person who is the subject of the record five years after the jurisdiction of the juvenile court over the person has terminated, if the person was alleged or adjudged to be a person described by Section 300, or when the person reaches the age of 21 years, if the person was alleged or adjudged to be a person described by Section 601, unless for good cause the court determines that the record shall be retained. Exhibits shall be destroyed as provided under Sections 1418, 1418.5, and 1419 of the Penal Code. For the purpose of this section "destroy" means destroy or dispose of for the purpose of destruction. The proceedings in any case in which the juvenile court record is destroyed or released to the person who is the subject of the record pursuant to this section shall be deemed never to have occurred, and the person may reply accordingly to any inquiry about the events in the case.

(b) If an individual whose juvenile court record has been destroyed or released under subdivision (a) discovers that any other agency still retains a record, the individual may file a petition with the court requesting that the records be destroyed. The petition will include the name of the agency and the type of record to be destroyed. The court shall order that such records also be destroyed unless for good cause the court determines to the contrary. The court shall send a copy of the order to each agency and each agency shall destroy records in its custody as directed by the order, and shall advise the court of its compliance. The court shall then destroy the copy of the petition, the order, and the notice of compliance from each agency. Thereafter, the proceedings in such case shall be deemed never to have occurred.

(c) Juvenile court records in juvenile traffic matters, which include all records and papers, any minute book entries, dockets and judgment dockets, may be destroyed after five years from the date on which the jurisdiction of the juvenile court over a minor is terminated, or when the minor reaches the age of 21 years, if the person was alleged or adjudged to be a person described by Section 601. Prior to such destruction the original record may be microfilmed or photocopied. Every such reproduction shall be deemed and considered an original; and a transcript, exemplification or certified copy of any such reproduction shall be deemed and considered a transcript, exemplification or certified copy, as the case may be, of the original. *(Amended by Stats 1990 ch 698 §1, eff. 1/1/91.)*

§826.5. Destruction of records and papers.

(a) Notwithstanding the provisions of Section 826, at any time before a person reaches the age when his or her records are required to be destroyed, the judge or clerk of the juvenile court or the probation officer may destroy all records and papers, the juvenile court record, any minute book entries, dockets, and judgment dockets in the proceedings concerning the person as a minor if the records and papers, juvenile court record, any minute book entries, dockets, and judgment dockets are microfilmed or photocopied prior to destruction. Exhibits shall be destroyed as provided under Sections 1418, 1418.5, and 1419 of the Penal Code.

(b) Every reproduction shall be deemed and considered an original. A transcript, exemplification, or certified copy of any reproduction shall be deemed and considered a transcript, exemplification, or certified copy, as the case may be, of the original.

§826.6. Notification of minor regarding rights.

(a) Any minor who is the subject of a petition that has been filed in juvenile court to adjudge the minor a dependent child or a ward of the court shall be given written notice by the clerk of the court upon disposition of the petition or the termination of jurisdiction of the juvenile court of all of the following:

(1) The statutory right of any person who has been the subject of juvenile court proceedings to petition for sealing of the case records.

(2) The statutory provisions regarding the destruction of juvenile court records and records of juvenile court proceedings retained by state or local agencies.

(3) The statutory right of any person who has been the subject of juvenile court proceedings to have his or her juvenile court record released to him or her in lieu of its destruction.

(b) In any juvenile case where a local welfare department, probation department, or district attorney is responsible for notifying the minor of the dismissal, release, or termination of the case, the agency shall provide written notice to the minor of the information specified in subdivision (a) upon the dismissal, release, or termination of the case.

(c) A written form providing the information described in this section shall be prepared by the clerk of the court and shall be made available to juvenile court clerks, probation departments, welfare departments, and district attorneys.

§827. Inspection of reports and petitions.

(a) Except as provided in Section 828, a petition filed in any juvenile court proceeding, reports of the probation officer, and all other documents filed in any such case or made available to the probation officer in making his or her report, or to the judge, referee or other hearing officer, and thereafter retained by the probation officer, judge, referee, or other hearing officer, may be inspected only by court personnel, the district attorney, the minor who is the subject of the proceeding, his or her parents or guardian, the attorneys for the parties, and such other persons as may be designated by court order of the judge of the juvenile court upon filing a petition therefor. Child protective agencies, as defined in Section 11165.9 of the Penal Code, also shall be entitled to inspect these documents upon the filing of a declaration under penalty of perjury stating that access to these documents is necessary and relevant in connection with and in the course of a criminal investigation or a proceeding brought to declare a person a dependent child or ward of the juvenile court.

Any records or reports relating to a matter within the jurisdiction of the juvenile court prepared by or released by the court, a probation department, or the county department of social services, any portion of those records or reports, and information relating to the contents of those records or reports, shall not be disseminated by the receiving agencies to any persons or agencies, other than those persons or agencies authorized to receive documents pursuant to this section. Further, any of those records or reports, any portion of those records or reports, and information relating to the contents of those records or reports, shall not be made attachments to any other documents without the prior approval of the presiding judge of the juvenile court, unless they are used in connection with and in the course of a criminal investigation or a proceeding brought to declare a person a dependent child or ward of the juvenile court.

(b) (1) While the Legislature reaffirms its belief that juvenile court records, in general, should be confidential, it is the intent of the Legislature in enacting this subdivision to provide for a limited exception to juvenile court record confidentiality in cases involving serious acts of violence. Further, it is the intent of the Legislature that even in these selected cases dissemination of juvenile court records be as limited as possible, consistent with the need to work with a pupil in an appropriate fashion, and the need to protect potentially vulnerable school staff and other pupils over whom school staff exercise direct supervision and responsibility.

(2) Notwithstanding subdivision (a), written notice that a minor enrolled in a public school in kindergarten or grades 1 to 12, inclusive, has been found by a court of competent jurisdiction to have used, sold, or possessed narcotics or a controlled substance or to have committed any crime listed in paragraphs (1) to (15), inclusive, or (17) to (19), inclusive, of subdivision (b) of Section 707 shall be provided by the court, within seven days, to the superintendent of the school district of attendance, which information shall be expeditiously transmitted to any teacher, counselor, or administrator with direct supervisorial or disciplinary responsibility over the minor who the superintendent or his or her designee, after consultation with the principal at the school of attendance, believes needs this information to work with the pupil in an appropriate fashion, to avoid being needlessly vulnerable or to protect other persons from needless vulnerability. Any information received by a teacher, counselor, or administrator under this subdivision shall be received in confidence for the limited purpose

© 1992 by J., B. & L. Gould
Printed in the U.S.A.　　EP

for which it was provided and shall not be further disseminated by the teacher, counselor, or administrator. An intentional violation of the confidentiality provisions of this section is a misdemeanor punishable by a fine not to exceed five hundred dollars ($500).

(3) If a minor is removed from public school as a result of the court's finding described in subdivision (b) the superintendent shall maintain the information in a confidential file and shall defer transmittal of the information received from the court until the minor is returned to public school. If the minor is returned to a school district other than the one from which the minor came, the parole or probation officer having jurisdiction over the minor shall so notify the superintendent of the last district of attendance who shall transmit the notice received from the court to the superintendent of the new district of attendance.

(c) Each probation report filed with the court concerning a minor whose record is subject to dissemination pursuant to subdivision (b) shall include on the face sheet the school at which the minor is currently enrolled. The county superintendent shall provide the court with a listing of all of the schools within each school district, within the county, along with the name and mailing address of each district superintendent.

(d) Each notice sent by the court pursuant to subdivision (b) shall be stamped with the instruction: "Destroy This Record 12 Months After The Minor Returns To Public School. Unlawful Dissemination of This Information Is A Misdemeanor." No information transmitted by the superintendent pursuant to subdivision (b) shall be transmitted by the superintendent or by any teacher, counselor, or administrator to any other person more than 12 months after receipt of the original notice from the court or more than 12 months after the minor returns to public school, whichever occurs last. Any information received from the court shall be destroyed by school authorities 12 months after its receipt from the court or 12 months after the minor returns to public school, whichever occurs last. At any time after the date by which a record required to be destroyed by this section should have been destroyed, the minor or his or her parent or guardian shall have the right to make a written request to the principal of the school that the minor's school records be reviewed to ensure that the record has been destroyed. Upon completion of any requested review and no later than 30 days after the request for the review was received, the principal or his or her designee shall respond in writing to the written request and either shall confirm that the record has been destroyed or, if the record has not been destroyed, shall explain why destruction has not yet occurred and shall specify the date by which the record will be destroyed.

(e) Except as provided in paragraph (2) of subdivision (b), no liability shall attach to any person who transmits or fails to transmit any notice or information required under subdivision (b). *(Amended by Stats 1991 ch 1202 §21, eff. 1/1/92.)*

§828. Disclosure to another agency of information regarding taking a minor into custody.

(a) Except as provided in Sections 389 and 781 of this code or Section 1203.45 of the Penal Code, any information gathered by a law enforcement agency relating to the taking of a minor into custody may be disclosed to another law enforcement agency, including a school district police or security department, or to any person or agency which has a legitimate need

for the information for purposes of official disposition of a case. When the disposition of a taking into custody is available, it shall be included with any information disclosed.

A court shall consider any information relating to the taking of a minor into custody, if the information is not contained in a record which has been sealed, for purposes of determining whether adjudications of commission of crimes as a juvenile warrant a finding that there are circumstances in aggravation pursuant to Section 1170 of the Penal Code or to deny probation.

(b) When a law enforcement agency has been notified pursuant to Section 1155 that a minor has escaped from a secure detention facility, the law enforcement agency shall release the name of, and any descriptive information about, the minor to a person who specifically requests this information. The law enforcement agency may release the information on the minor without a request to do so if it finds that release of the information would be necessary to assist in recapturing the minor or that it would be necessary to protect the public from substantial physical harm. *(Amended by Stats 1990 ch 776 §1, eff. 1/1/91.)*

§828.1. Disclosure to school personnel of violent or drug-related crime information.

(a) While the Legislature reaffirms its belief that juvenile criminal records, in general, should be confidential, it is the intent of the Legislature in enacting this section to provide for a limited exception to that confidentiality in cases involving serious acts of violence. Further, it is the intent of the Legislature that even in these selected cases the dissemination of juvenile criminal records be as limited as possible, consistent with the need to work with a student in an appropriate fashion, and the need to protect potentially vulnerable school staff and other students over whom the school staff exercises direct supervision and responsibility.

(b) Notwithstanding subdivision (a) of Section 828, a school district police or security department may provide written notice to the superintendent of the school district that a minor enrolled in a public school maintained by that school district, in kindergarten or any of grades 1 to 12, inclusive, has been found by a court of competent jurisdiction to have illegally used, sold, or possessed a controlled substance as defined in Section 11007 of the Health and Safety Code or to have committed any crime listed in paragraphs (1) to (15), inclusive, or paragraphs (17) to (19), inclusive, of subdivision (b) of Section 707. The information may be expeditiously transmitted to any teacher, counselor, or administrator with direct supervisorial or disciplinary responsibility over the minor, who the superintendent or his or her designee, after consultation with the principal at the school of attendance, believes needs this information to work with the student in an appropriate fashion, to avoid being needlessly vulnerable or to protect other persons from needless vulnerability.

(c) Any information received by a teacher, counselor, or administrator pursuant to this section shall be received in confidence for the limited purpose for which it was provided and shall not be further disseminated by the teacher, counselor, or administrator. An intentional violation of the confidentiality provisions of this section is a misdemeanor, punishable by a fine not to exceed five hundred dollars ($500). *(Added by Stats 1990 ch 776 §2, eff. 1/1/91.)*

§829. Review of court records by Board of Prison Terms.

Notwithstanding any other provision of law, the Board of Prison Terms, in order to evaluate the suitability for release of a person before the board, shall be entitled to review juvenile court records which have not been sealed, concerning the person before the board, if those records relate to a case in which the person was found to have committed an offense which brought the person within the jurisdiction of the juvenile court pursuant to Section 602.

§830. Disclosure of information among members of child abuse team.

Notwithstanding any other provision of law, members of a multidisciplinary personnel team engaged in the prevention, identification, and treatment of child abuse may disclose and exchange information and writings to and with one another relating to any incidents of child abuse that may also be a part of a juvenile court record or otherwise designated as confidential under state law if the member of the team having that information or writing reasonably believes it is generally relevant to the prevention, identification, or treatment of child abuse. All discussions relative to the disclosure or exchange of any such information or writings during team meetings are confidential and, notwithstanding any other provision of law, testimony concerning any such discussion is not admissable in any criminal, civil, or juvenile court proceeding.

As used in this section, "child abuse" has the same meaning as defined in Section 18951.

As used in this section, "multidisciplinary personnel team" means any team of three or more persons, as specified in Section 18951, the members of which are trained in the prevention, identification, and treatment of child abuse and are qualified to provide a broad range of services related to child abuse. *(Amended by Stats 1989 ch 86 §1, eff. 1/1/90.)*

ARTICLE 22.5

HOME SUPERVISION

§840. Home supervision program in each county.

There shall be in each county probation department a program of home supervision to which minors described by Section 628.1 shall be referred. Home supervision is a program in which persons who would otherwise be detained in the juvenile hall are permitted to remain in their homes pending court disposition of their cases, under the supervision of a deputy probation officer, probation aide, or probation volunteer.

§841. Duties of person assigned to home supervision.

The duties of a deputy probation officer, or a probation aide, a community worker or a volunteer under the supervision of a deputy probation officer, assigned to home supervision are to assure the minor's appearance at probation officer interviews and court hearings and to assure that the minor obeys the conditions of his or her release and commits no public offenses pending final disposition of his or her case. A deputy probation officer, probation aide, or community worker assigned to home supervision shall have a caseload of no more than 10 minors. However, if the county probation department employs a method of home supervision which includes electronic surveillance, the caseload shall be no more than 15 minors. Whenever possible, a minor shall be assigned to a deputy probation officer, probation aide, community worker, or volunteer who resides in the same community as the minor. *(Amended by Stats 1991 ch 155 §1, eff. 1/1/92.)*

§842. Probation volunteer defined.

A probation volunteer is a person who donates personal services to the probation department and probationers without compensation. A probation aide or a community worker may receive compensation for such services. Probation aides, community workers and volunteers shall not qualify for peace officer status pursuant to Section 830.5 of the Penal Code.

ARTICLE 23

WARDS AND DEPENDENT CHILDREN — JUVENILE HALLS

§850. Maintenance of juvenile hall.

The board of supervisors in every county shall provide and maintain, at the expense of the county, in a location approved by the judge of the juvenile court or in counties having more than one judge of the juvenile court, by the presiding judge of the juvenile court, a suitable house or place for the detention of wards and dependent children of the juvenile court and of persons alleged to come within the jurisdiction of the juvenile court. Such house or place shall be known as the "juvenile hall" of the county. Wherever, in any provision of law, reference is made to detention homes for juveniles, such reference shall be deemed and construed to refer to the juvenile halls provided for in this article.

§851. Juvenile hall not a penal institution.

The juvenile hall shall not be in, or connected with, any jail or prison, and shall not be deemed to be nor be treated as a penal institution. It shall be conducted in all respects as nearly like a home as possible.

§852. Management of hall.

The juvenile hall shall be under the management and control of the probation officer.

§853. Superintendent and staff.

The board of supervisors shall provide for a suitable superintendent to have charge of the juvenile hall, and for such other employees as may be needed for its efficient management, and shall provide for payment, out of the general fund of the county, of suitable salaries for such superintendent and other employees.

§854. Appointment of officers and staff.

The superintendent and other employees of the juvenile hall shall be appointed by the probation officer, pursuant to a civil service or merit system, and may be removed, for cause, pursuant to such system.

§855. List of hall's expenses.

The probation officer shall keep a classified list of expenses for the operation of the juvenile hall and shall file a duplicate copy with the county board of supervisors.

© 1992 by J., B. & L. Gould
Printed in the U.S.A.   EP

§856. Public schools in connection with juvenile hall.

The board of supervisors may provide for the establishment of a public elementary school and of a public secondary school in connection with any juvenile hall, juvenile house, day center, juvenile ranch, or juvenile camp, for the education of the children in such facilities.

§862. Detention of juveniles committed by federal court.

In addition to those juveniles specified in Section 850, the probation officer may receive and detain in the county juvenile hall any juvenile committed thereto by process or order issued under the authority of the United States until such juvenile is discharged according to law as if he had been committed under process issued under the authority of this state, provided, that, in the absence of a valid detention order issued by a federal court, such detention shall not exceed three judicial days. Juveniles detained pursuant to this section shall have all the rights, powers, privileges, and duties, and shall receive the same treatment, afforded juveniles detained pursuant to the laws of this state. The board of supervisors of a county may contract with the United States for reimbursement of the county's cost incurred in the support of such juvenile.

§870. Jointly operated juvenile hall.

Two or more counties may, pursuant to Article 1 (commencing with Section 6500) of Chapter 5 of Division 7 of Title 1 of the Government Code, establish and operate a joint juvenile hall. A joint juvenile hall shall be under the management and control of the probation officers of the participating counties, acting jointly, or of one of such probation officers, as provided by the agreement among the counties, and shall be in the charge of a superintendent selected pursuant to a civil service or merit system. A joint juvenile hall shall be operated in the manner prescribed by this chapter for juvenile halls.

A county participating in the maintenance of a joint juvenile hall pursuant to this section need not maintain a separate juvenile hall.

§871. Escape.

(a) Any person under the custody of a probation officer or any peace officer in a county juvenile hall, or committed to a county juvenile home, ranch, camp, or forestry camp, or any person being transported to or from a county juvenile hall, home, ranch, camp, or forestry camp, who escapes or attempts to escape from that place or during transportation to or from that place, is guilty of a misdemeanor, punishable by imprisonment in the county jail not exceeding one year.

(b) Any person who commits any of the acts described in subdivision (a) by use of force or violence shall be punished by imprisonment in a county jail for not more than one year or by imprisonment in the state prison. *(Amended by Stats 1985 ch 1283 §1.)*

§871.5. Transporting contraband material into facility.

(a) Except as authorized by law, or when authorized by the person in charge of any county juvenile hall, home, ranch, camp or forestry camp, or by an officer of any such juvenile hall, home, or camp empowered by the person in charge to give such an authorization, any person who knowingly brings or sends into, or who knowingly assists in bringing into, or sending into, any county juvenile hall, home, ranch, camp, or forestry camp, or any person who while confined in such an institution possesses therein, any controlled substance, the possession of which is prohibited by Division 10 (commencing with Section 11000) of the Health and Safety Code, any firearm, weapon, or explosive of any kind, or any tear gas or tear gas weapon shall be punished by imprisonment in a county jail for not more than one year or by imprisonment in the state prison.

(b) Except as otherwise authorized in the manner provided in subdivision (a), any person who knowingly uses tear gas or uses a tear gas weapon in an institution or camp specified in subdivision (a) is guilty of a felony.

(c) A sign shall be posted at the entrance of each county juvenile hall, home, ranch, camp, or forestry camp specifying the conduct prohibited by this section and the penalties therefor.

(d) Except as otherwise authorized in the manner provided in subdivision (a), any person who knowingly brings or sends into, or who knowingly assists in bringing into, or sending into, any county juvenile hall, home, ranch, camp, or forestry camp, or any person who while confined in such an institution knowingly possesses therein, any alcoholic beverage shall be guilty of a misdemeanor.

(e) This section shall not be construed to preclude or in any way limit the applicability of any other law proscribing a course of conduct also proscribed by this section. *(Amended by Stats 1985 ch 515 §1.)*

§872. Transfers due to overcrowding of facilities.

Where there is no juvenile hall in the county of residence of minors, or when the juvenile hall becomes unfit or unsafe for detention of minors, the presiding or sole juvenile court judge may, with the recommendation of the probation officer of the sending county and the consent of the probation officer of the receiving county, by written order filed with the county clerk, designate the juvenile hall of any county in the state for the detention of an individual minor for not to exceed 60 days. The court may at any time modify or vacate such order and shall require notice of the transfer to be given to the parent or guardian. The county of residence of a minor so transferred shall reimburse the receiving county for costs and liability as agreed upon by the two counties in connection with such order.

The Department of the Youth Authority shall establish a maximum population limit for each juvenile hall in this state.

As used in this section, the terms "unfit" and "unsafe" shall include a condition in which a juvenile hall is considered by the juvenile court judge, the probation officer of that county, or the Department of the Youth Authority to be too crowded for the proper and safe detention of minors.

ARTICLE 23.5

WARDS — TEAM CAMPS
(Added by Stats 1988 ch 1307 §2, eff. 1/1/89 only until 1/1/94.)

§875. Legislative intent.

In order to combat the growing influence of youth gangs and youth gang-related activity, it is the intent of the Legislature to enact a program which incorporates the individual and social values and mutual support system developed through team sports, provides meaningful educational opportunities for juvenile wards, including counseling on drugs and drug rehabilitation, and serves to provide an effective peer group alternative for members of youth gangs. In enacting this program, the Legislature finds and declares all of the following:

(a) The majority of wards placed in juvenile facilities are or have been members of youth gangs. In Los Angeles County alone, it is estimated that at least 75 percent of the wards confined to probation camps have been gang members. In many cases, these juveniles have been involved in the sale or use of controlled substances.

(b) The abatement of the use of controlled substances and the reduction of juvenile gang-related crimes are of paramount importance to the people of the State of California.

(c) Many of these wards have both academic potential and good athletic ability.

(d) Through participation in team sports in a camp atmosphere, juvenile wards will learn the concept of individual accomplishment as a contribution to a team goal, and cooperation with others to gain a positive self-image as well as gain the ability to resist peer group pressure. These concepts are crucial to the development of individual self-esteem, so necessary to these individuals to effect the desired changes in their behavior, to realize their potential, academically and athletically, and to reduce the influence of youth gang and youth gang-related activity.

(e) There are several model programs for juveniles in Los Angeles County, including Camp Kilpatrick and Lynwood, which provide good examples of the positive role that sports and individual counseling can have in providing meaningful opportunities and mutual support systems for young people. *(Added by Stats 1988 ch 1307 §2, eff. 1/1/89 only until 1/1/94.)*

§875.1. Pilot project.
There is hereby established a pilot project which shall be known as the California TEAM (Together Each Achieves More) Sports Camp Program. The project shall be administered by the office of Criminal Justice Planning or its designee. *(Added by Stats 1988 ch 1307 §2, eff. 1/1/89 only until 1/1/94.)*

§875.2. Funding for TEAM program.
Pursuant to this article, the chief probation officer of a county, with the approval of the board of supervisors, may apply to the office of Criminal Justice Planning for funding to implement a program in the form of a sports camp. Applications shall be made in accordance with guidelines established by the Office of Criminal Justice Planning in accordance with this article. *(Added by Stats 1988 ch 1307 §2, eff. 1/1/89 only until 1/1/94.)*

§875.3. Selection of locations.
The office of Criminal Justice Planning shall select at least three counties. At least one county from the northern region, one county from the southern San Joaquin Valley region, and one county from the southern region shall be selected from those applying and eligible for funding pursuant to guidelines established pursuant to this article. Eligibility shall be established on the basis of need, but counties having the highest juvenile felony statistics and the highest average juvenile probation caseloads shall be given priority for funding. *(Added by Stats 1988 ch 1307 §2, eff. 1/1/89 only until 1/1/94.)*

§875.4. Components of program.
Each county selected for participation in this project shall implement a residential sports camp program for delinquent wards of the juvenile court pursuant to Section 602 which shall contain the following components:

(a) Emphasis on academics, physical fitness, and the development of specific sports skills.

(b) A special academic program geared to high school graduation and college preparation, and including a tutorial program for each ward.

(c) An athletic program to be administered by camp staff and instructed by certified and qualified coaching staff, to emphasize physical fitness, discipline, and the development of skills pertinent to a specific sport, as well as a counseling program regarding the detrimental effects of drugs on athletes.

(d) The teams from each camp program may compete, to the maximum extent possible, in regularly organized high school sports.

(e) Any other components prescribed by office of Criminal Justice Planning guidelines.

For purposes of this article, the office of Criminal Justice Planning shall coordinate activities with the sheriffs department in each of the counties selected for TEAM camps. In addition to selecting at least three TEAM camps, and in cooperation with the sheriff and the chief probation officer, the office of Criminal Justice Planning also shall establish one early intervention TEAM facility in one of the counties selected for juveniles who are first time offenders, but who have not been sentenced to probation camp or to the California Youth Authority. This facility shall otherwise meet the component requirement set forth in this section. *(Added by Stats 1988 ch 1307 §2, eff. 1/1/89 only until 1/1/94.)*

§875.5. Duties of probation officer.
The probation officers assigned to the camp shall also do all of the following:

(a) Assist in enrolling wards from the camps into the appropriate community school.

(b) Assist in securing further educational opportunities for wards, including, but not limited to, securing college scholarships or other financial aid.

(c) Provide such support, counseling, and supervision after graduation from the camp as is necessary to help ensure that the ward will not return to drug-related or gang activity. *(Added by Stats 1988 ch 1307 §2, eff. 1/1/89 only until 1/1/94.)*

§875.6. Evaluation report to Governor and Legislature.
Three years after TEAM camps have been funded pursuant to this article, the office of Criminal Justice Planning shall submit an evaluation report, together with recommendations, to the Governor and the Legislature. The report shall evaluate the progress of the program. The report shall compare recidivism rates between delinquent wards of the juvenile court pursuant to Section 602 who have participated in the TEAM camp program and those who have participated in regular probation camps, since the objective of the TEAM camp program is to reduce

© 1992 by J., B. & L. Gould
Printed in the U.S.A. **EP**

recidivism of the participants by 50 percent compared to other wards who are placed in Youth Authority facilities. The report shall also cite examples of academic or athletic achievements of county wards who participate in the TEAM camp program. If the program fails to reduce recidivism by 30 percent, it shall be deemed to be a failure. The report shall also discuss ways and means to achieve further educational opportunities for Youth Authority and county wards, the effectiveness of the TEAM sports camp concept in helping reduce recidivism into gang and drug-related activity, and the feasibility of implementing TEAM sports camps or similar programs statewide. *(Added by Stats 1988 ch 1307 §2, eff. 1/1/89 only until 1/1/94.)*

§875.7. Repeal of article.

This article shall remain operative only until January 1, 1994, and as of that date is repealed unless a later enacted statute, which is enacted before January 1, 1994, deletes or extends that date. *(Added by Stats 1988 ch 1307 §2, eff. 1/1/89 only until 1/1/94.)*

ARTICLE 24

WARDS AND DEPENDENT CHILDREN — JUVENILE HOMES, RANCHES AND CAMPS

§880. Purpose of establishment of juvenile homes, ranches, or camps.

In order to provide appropriate facilities for the housing of wards of the juvenile court in the counties of their residence or in adjacent counties so that such wards may be kept under direct supervision of said court, and in order to more advantageously apply the salutary effect of home and family environment upon them, and also in order to secure a better classification and segregation of such wards according to their capacities, interests, and responsiveness to control and responsibility, and to give better opportunity for reform and encouragement of self-discipline in such wards, juvenile homes, ranches, or camps may be established, as provided in this article.

§881. Establishment of homes and camps.

The board of supervisors of any county may, by ordinance, establish juvenile homes, ranches, camps, or forestry camps, within or without the county, to which persons made wards of the court on the ground of fitting the description in Section 602 may be committed. As far as possible, the provisions of this chapter relating to commitments to the probation officer shall apply to commitments to such juvenile homes, except that where any ward proves to be unfit to remain in any such home, in the opinion of the superintendent or director thereof, said superintendent or director shall make recommendation to the probation department for consideration for other commitment. Complete operation and authority for the administration shall be vested in the county.

§881.5. Funding for homes and camps.

(a) If, during the 1991-92 fiscal year, a county receives funds pursuant to Section 17602, the county reduces the capacity of its juvenile homes, ranches, camps, or forestry camps below the capacity for those facilities during the 1990-91 fiscal year, and if during the 12-month period subsequent to the month of reduc-

tion, or any subsequent 12-month period, there is an increase of commitments from the county's juvenile court to the Department of the Youth Authority above the number of the commitments during the 1990-91 fiscal year, the county shall contribute to the Department of the Youth Authority an amount equivalent to the actual cost, as determined by the Department of the Youth Authority, of increasing capacity to the fiscal year 1990-91 level or by an amount equal to the increase in commitments from the juvenile court to the Department of the Youth Authority, whichever is more. Any reduction shall be applied to the next payment or payments to which the county is otherwise entitled.

(b) Any county that provides juvenile home, ranch, or camp space to another county pursuant to contract shall not have its entitlement reduced pursuant to this section if it reduces its capacity based on a reduction in the amount of space provided pursuant to the contract.

(c) This section shall not be applicable to a reduction in capacity occurring as a result of an act of God.

(d) This section shall not apply to the County of Alameda if its board of supervisors adopts a resolution on or before June 26, 1991, stating its intent to close a juvenile camp prior to September 1, 1991.

(e) As used in this section, "juvenile home, ranch, camp, or forestry camp" means those facilities established pursuant to Article 24 (commencing with Section 880) of Chapter 2 of Part 1 of Division 2 of the Welfare and Institutions Code. *(Added by Stats 1991 ch 91 §12, eff. 6/30/91. This section shall become inoperative 60 days following the date on which the Commission on State Mandates adopts an estimated statewide cost of reimbursement, or following the date on which the first such judicial determination becomes final.)*

§882. Management.

Such juvenile homes, ranches, camps or forestry camps shall be in charge of a superintendent or director and may be established in conjunction with the probation department, or in any manner determined by the county board of supervisors. Such superintendent or director and other persons employed at such homes or camps shall be appointed by the probation officer, subject to confirmation by the board of supervisors, of the county establishing such homes or camps.

§883. Required labor for wards in camps.

The wards committed to such homes, ranches, camps, or forestry camps may be required to labor on the buildings and grounds thereof, on the making of forest roads for fire prevention or fire fighting, on forestation or reforestation of public lands, or on the making of firetrails or firebreaks, or to perform any other work or engage in any studies or activities on or off of the grounds of such homes, ranches, camps, or forestry camps prescribed by the probation department, subject to such approval as the county board of supervisors by ordinance requires.

Such wards may not be required to labor in fire suppression when under the age of 16 years.

Wards between the ages of 16 years and 18 years may be required to labor in fire suppression if all of the following conditions are met:

(a) The parent or guardian of the ward has given permission for such labor by the ward.

(b) The ward has completed 80 hours of training in forest fire fighting and fire safety, including, but not limited to, the handling of equipment and chemicals, survival techniques, and first aid.

Whenever any ward committed to such camp is engaged in fire prevention work or the suppression of existing fires, he or she shall be subject to worker's compensation benefits to the same extent as a county employee, and the board of supervisors shall provide and cover any such ward committed to such camp while performing such service, with accident, death and compensation insurance as is otherwise regularly provided for employees of the county.

§884. Payment of wages to wards.

The board of supervisors may provide for the payment of wages and pay such wages from the treasury of such county to the wards for the work they do, the sums earned to be paid in reparation, or to the parents or dependents of the ward, or to the ward himself, in such manner and in such proportions as the court directs.

§885. Standards.

(a) The Youth Authority shall adopt and prescribe the minimum standards of construction, operation, programs of education, and training and qualifications of personnel for such juvenile homes, ranches, camps, or forestry camps.

(b) The Youth Authority shall conduct an annual inspection of each juvenile home, ranch, camp, or forestry camp situated in this state which, during the preceding calendar year, was used for confinement of any minor for more than 24 hours. If the Youth Authority, after such inspection, finds that the juvenile home, ranch, camp, or forestry camp is not in compliance with the standards adopted pursuant to subdivision (a) of this section, the Youth Authority shall give notice of its findings to all persons having authority to confine minors in such facilities and commencing 60 days thereafter such juvenile home, ranch, camp, or forestry camp shall not be used for confinement of any minor until such time as the department finds, after reinspection of the facility, that the conditions which rendered the facility unsuitable have been remedied, and such facility is a suitable place for the confinement of minors.

(c) The custodian of each juvenile home, ranch, camp, or forestry camp shall make such reports as may be required by the Youth Authority to effectuate the purposes of this section.

§886. Limits on population.

No juvenile home, ranch, camp, or forestry camp established pursuant to the provisions of this article shall receive or contain more than 100 children at any one time.

§886.5. Expanded capacity of facilities.

Notwithstanding Section 886, a juvenile home, ranch, camp, or forestry camp may receive or contain a maximum of 125 children at any one time if the county has submitted a request for approval for expanded capacity to the Department of the Youth Authority demonstrating a consistent need for juvenile home, ranch, camp, or forestry camp placements which exceeds the beds available in the county, and the department has approved that request. Any request from a county to expand the capacity of a juvenile home, ranch, camp, or forestry camp pursuant to this section shall certify that the facility to be expanded will continue to meet the minimum standards adopted and prescribed pursuant to Section 885 during the period of expanded capacity. The department shall approve any such request only after confirming by inspection of the facility sought to be expanded that the expansion will not result in overcrowding of structures and that the facility will comply with the minimum standards during its period of expanded capacity. *(Amended by Stats 1988 ch 975 §5, eff. 1/1/89.)*

§888. Acceptance of children from another county.

Any county establishing a juvenile home, ranch, or camp under the provisions of this article may, by mutual agreement, accept children committed to that home, ranch, or camp by the juvenile court of another county in the state. Two or more counties may, by mutual agreement, establish juvenile homes or camps, and the rights granted and duties imposed by this article shall devolve upon those counties acting jointly. The provisions of this article shall not apply to any juvenile hall.

§889. Operation of public schools in juvenile facilities.

The board of education shall provide for the administration and operation of public schools in any juvenile home, hall, day center, ranch, camp, regional youth educational facility, or Orange County youth correctional center in existence and providing services prior to the effective date of the amendments to this section made by the Statutes of 1989, established pursuant to Article 2.5 (commencing with Section 48645) of Chapter 4 of Part 27 of the Education Code, or Article 9 (commencing with Section 1850) of Chapter 1 of Division 2.5 of the Welfare and Institutions Code. *(Amended by Stats 1989 ch 929 §3, eff. 1/1/90.)*

§891. State assistance for construction of juvenile facilities.

(a) From any state moneys made available to it for that purpose, the Youth Authority shall share in the cost pursuant to this article of the construction of juvenile homes, juvenile ranch camps, or forestry camps established after July 1, 1957, and for construction at existing juvenile homes, ranches, camps, or forestry camps, by counties which apply therefor.

(b) "Construction," as used in this section, includes construction of new buildings and acquisition of existing buildings and initial equipment of any such buildings; and, to the extent provided for in regulations adopted by the Department of the Youth Authority, remodeling of existing buildings owned by the county, to serve as a juvenile home or to serve the purposes of a juvenile ranch camp or forestry camp, and initial equipment thereof. "Construction" also includes payments made by a county under any lease-purchase agreement or similar arrangement authorized by law and payments for the necessary repair or improvements of property which is leased from the federal government or other public entity without cost to the county for a term of not less than 10 years. It does not include architects' fees or the cost of land acquisition.

(c) The amount of state assistance which shall be provided to any county shall not exceed 50 percent of the project cost approved by the Youth Authority, and,

© 1992 by J., B. & L. Gould
Printed in the U.S.A.   **EP**

in no event shall it exceed three thousand dollars ($3,000) per bed unit of the new juvenile home, juvenile ranch, camp, or forestry camp or per bed unit added to an existing juvenile home, juvenile ranch camp, or forestry camp, as the case may be. The construction project shall be deemed to have as many bed units as the number of persons it is designed to accommodate, not exceeding 100 bed units for any one project.

(d) Application for state assistance for construction funds under this article shall be made to the Youth Authority in the manner and form prescribed by the Youth Authority. The Youth Authority shall prescribe the time and manner of payment of state assistance, if granted.

§892. State assistance for border check facilities.

(a) From any state moneys made available to it for that purpose, the Youth Authority shall provide state assistance pursuant to this section to defray, in whole or in part, the cost of construction of border check station facilities by any city which applies therefor.

"City" as used in this section means any city with a population in excess of 500,000 as determined by the last decennial census, all or part of the boundaries of which are contiguous with the boundaries of a foreign country adjoining this state.

(b) "Construction," as used in this section, includes construction of new buildings and acquisition of existing buildings and initial equipment of any such buildings to serve as a border check station facility. It does not include the cost of land acquisition.

(c) The amount of state assistance which shall be provided to any city shall not exceed 100 percent of the project cost approved by the Youth Authority, and, in no event shall it exceed one hundred thousand dollars ($100,000) for any one project.

(d) Application for state assistance for construction funds under this section shall be made to the Youth Authority in the manner and form prescribed by the Youth Authority. The Youth Authority shall prescribe the time and manner of payment of state assistance, if granted.

(e) The Youth Authority shall adopt and prescribe the minimum standards of construction for such border check station facility. No city shall be entitled to receive any state funds provided for in this section unless and until the minimum standards and qualifications referred to in this section are complied with by such city. Type and standards of construction shall be approved by the city architect's office, city department of public works, or such city department having jurisdiction over public construction.

§893. Special education schools in juvenile facilities.

(a) The board of supervisors of any county with a population of five million or more may provide and maintain a school or schools at a juvenile home, ranch or camp for the purpose of meeting the special educational needs of wards and dependent children of the juvenile court. Such school or schools shall be conducted in such a manner and under such conditions as will minister to the specific individualized educational and training needs of each ward and dependent child in furtherance of the objective of assisting each of them, as much as possible, to fulfill his potential to be a contributing, law-abiding member of society. In the

event the board of supervisors determines that such objective may be promoted as well as or better by provision of educational and training services by a qualified private organization, the board of supervisors on behalf of the county may enter into annual contracts, with or without options to renew, for the provision of such services by such an organization.

(b) The Legislature hereby finds and determines that there are persons whose educational and vocational backgrounds and personal leadership qualities peculiarly fit them to instruct and train wards of the court in promotion of the aforesaid objective, but who lack certification qualifications. Accordingly, the probation officer is hereby authorized to certify to the county board of education and the Superintendent of Public Instruction that a person employed or to be employed by the probation officer or by an organization retained by contract to provide vocational training or vocational training courses at or in connection with the school or schools is peculiarly fit to provide wards of the court such vocational training in promotion of the aforesaid objective.

Such certification shall specify the type or types of service the person is qualified to provide. Upon filing of such certification, such person shall be deemed to be a certificated employee for purposes of authorizing him to provide the services described in the certificate and for apportionment purposes.

(c) The individual school or schools shall have a maximum enrollment of 100 students.

(d) The county superintendent of schools shall report on behalf of the county the average daily attendance for the schools and classes maintained by the county in such school or schools in the manner provided in Sections 41601 and 84701 of the Education Code and other provisions of law.

(e) The Superintendent of Public Instruction shall compute the amount of allowance to be made to the county by reasons of the average daily attendance at such school or schools by multiplying the average daily attendance by the foundation program amount for a high school district which has an average daily attendance of 301 or more during the fiscal year, and shall make allowances based thereon and shall apportion to the county, the allowances so computed in the same manner and at the same times as would be done with respect to allowances and apportionments to the county school service fund.

ARTICLE 24.5

REGIONAL YOUTH EDUCATIONAL FACILITIES

§894. Pilot facilities.

In order to provide a sentencing alternative for the juvenile courts, one or more pilot regional youth educational facilities shall be established as short-term intensive residential programs to which primarily 16- and 17-year-old minor juvenile court wards not committed to the Youth Authority who fit the description in Section 602 may be committed. Participating minors shall be those who are awaiting out-of-home placement in county juvenile halls, educationally behind in school, educable, able to participate in vocational activities, and able to participate in work projects. Each facility shall provide a short-term intensive educational experience, including program elements such as competency-based education services, assessment for learning disabilities including visual perceptual screening and treatment, remedial individual educational plans for diagnosed learning disabilities, electronic and computer education, physical education, vocational and industrial arts and training, job training and experience, character education, victim awareness, and restitution. Wards who complete the short-term intensive program who need continuing services shall be transferred to local facilities for up to 60 days of additional education and training. Following institutional placement, all wards in the program shall receive intensive supervision by a probation officer in their county of residence for a minimum of 120 days. Intensive supervision means a 10 to 15 person caseload per deputy probation officer.

§895. Criteria for selecting counties of location.

(a) From any state moneys made available to it for that purpose, the Youth Authority shall assist counties in the establishment of pilot regional youth educational facilities. Interested counties that agree to provide matching funds or resources, in compliance with standards established by the department, may enter agreements with the Youth Authority to establish these facilities. The facilities shall be operated by participating counties, either solely or under a joint powers agreement. The counties may contract with private agencies to provide job training consultation or other services.

(b) The Youth Authority shall develop selection criteria for participating counties to include, but not be limited to, all of the following factors:

(1) Eligible target population.

(2) Demonstrated ability to administer the program.

(3) Facility capability.

(4) Financial ability to provide matching funds or resources.

(5) Demonstrated need for the program.

(6) Ability to meet regional needs.

(7) Ability to provide specified program elements.

§896. Performance standards; standards of personnel.

(a) The Youth Authority shall establish minimum performance standards for programs of education and training and for qualifications of personnel for all youth educational facilities in the program, including local continuation and intensive supervision components. These standards and qualifications shall be designed to achieve program goals such as an increase in the educational level of participants, better community protection and offender accountability, and preparation of participants to return to the community as responsible and productive members.

(b) The Youth Authority shall conduct an initial inspection and an annual inspection thereafter of each regional youth educational facility. In addition, the Youth Authority may conduct such other inspections as it deems necessary. If the Youth Authority, after inspection, finds that a facility is not in compliance with the standards adopted pursuant to subdivision (a), the Youth Authority shall give notice of its findings to all persons having authority to confine minors in that regional facility. Commencing 60 days thereafter, that regional youth educational facility shall not be used for confinement of any minor until such time as the Youth Authority finds, after reinspection of the facility, that the conditions which rendered the facility

unsuitable have been remedied and that the facility is a suitable place for the confinement of minors.

(c) The custodian of each regional youth educational facility shall make such reports as may be required by the Youth Authority to effectuate the purposes of this section.

§897. Establishment of facility capacity.

The capacity of each regional youth educational facility shall be established pursuant to Sections 886 and 886.5.

§898. Citizens advisory committee.

The participating counties shall appoint a citizens advisory committee with a membership drawn from law enforcement, judiciary, probation, education, corrections, business, and the general public, whose function is to review the goals, objectives, and programs of each youth educational facility and provide input to the facility.

§898.5. Study and report on effect on reducing recidivism.

The Youth Authority shall conduct a study of the effectiveness of the pilot program authorized by this article in reducing recidivism, and shall report thereon to the Legislature no later than January 1, 1989. *(Amended by Stats 1987 ch 92 §1.)*

§899. *Repealed by Stats 1989 ch 468 §1, eff. 1/1/90.*

ARTICLE 25

SUPPORT OF WARDS AND DEPENDENT CHILDREN

§900. Funds for support and maintenance of minor.

(a) If it is necessary that provision be made for the expense of support and maintenance of a ward or dependent child of the juvenile court or of a minor person concerning whom a petition has been filed in accordance with the provisions of this chapter, the order providing for the care and custody of such ward, dependent child or other minor person shall direct that the whole expense of support and maintenance of such ward, dependent child or other minor person, up to the amount of twenty dollars ($20) per month be paid from the county treasury and may direct that an amount up to any maximum amount per month established by the board of supervisors of the county be so paid. The board of supervisors of each county is hereby authorized to establish, either generally or for individual wards or dependent children or according to classes or groups of wards or dependent children, a maximum amount which the court may order the county to pay for such support and maintenance. All orders made pursuant to the provisions of this section shall state the amounts to be so paid from the county treasury, and such amounts shall constitute legal charges against the county.

(b) This section is applicable to a minor who is the subject of a program of supervision undertaken by the probation department pursuant to Section 330 or 654 and who is temporarily placed out of his home by the probation department, with the approval of the court and the minor's parent or guardian, for a period not to exceed seven days.

© 1992 by J., B. & L. Gould
Printed in the U.S.A. EP

§901. Maximum cost for support of ward.

No order for payment shall be made in a sum in excess of the actual cost of supporting and maintaining the ward, dependent child or other minor person.

§902. Payment of additional costs of support of ward.

If it is found that the maximum amount established by the board of supervisors of the county is insufficient to pay the whole expense of support and maintenance of a ward, dependent child, or other minor person, the court may order and direct that such additional amount as is necessary shall be paid out of the earnings, property, or estate of such ward, dependent child, or other minor person, or by the parents or guardian of such ward, dependent child, or other minor person, or by any other person liable for his support and maintenance, to the county officers designated by the board of supervisors who shall in turn pay it to the person, association, or institution that, under court order, is caring for and maintaining such ward, dependent child, or other minor person.

§903. Liability for costs of support.

(a) A parent of a minor, the estate of a parent, and the estate of the minor, shall be liable for the reasonable costs of support of the minor while the minor is placed, or detained in, or committed to, any institution or other place pursuant to Section 625 or pursuant to an order of the juvenile court. However, a county shall not levy charges for the costs of support of a minor detained pursuant to Section 625 unless, at the detention hearing, the juvenile court determines that detention of the minor should be continued, the petition for the offense for which the minor is detained is subsequently sustained, or the minor agrees to a program of supervision pursuant to Section 654. The liability of these persons and estates shall be a joint and several liability.

(b) It shall be the responsibility of a county to demonstrate to any person against whom it seeks to enforce the liability established by this section, that the charges it seeks to impose are limited to the reasonable costs of support of the minor and that these charges exclude any costs of incarceration, treatment, or supervision for the protection of society and the minor and the rehabilitation of the minor. Except in those placements of a minor in which an AFDC-FC grant is made, the county shall separately itemize the cost of each major component, such as food, clothing, and medical expense, contained within the costs of support of the minor, for any person against whom the county seeks to impose liability under this section. An AFDC-FC grant shall be considered a separate, indivisible component item of the cost of support of a minor. Nothing in this section shall preclude the district attorney from seeking reimbursement of AFDC-FC costs pursuant to Section 11350.

(c) It is the intent of the Legislature in enacting this subdivision to protect the fiscal integrity of the county, to protect persons against whom the county seeks to impose liability from excessive charges, to ensure reasonable uniformity throughout the state in the level of liability being imposed, and to ensure that liability is imposed only on persons with the ability to pay. In evaluating a family's financial ability to pay under this section, the county shall take into consideration the family income, the necessary obligations of the family, and the number of persons dependent upon this income. Except in those placements of a minor in which an AFDC-FC grant is made, and except as provided in paragraphs (1), (2), and (3), "costs of support" as used in this section means only actual costs incurred by the county for food and food preparation, clothing, personal supplies, and medical expenses, not to exceed a combined maximum cost of fifteen dollars ($15) per day, except that:

(1) The maximum cost of fifteen dollars ($15) per day shall be adjusted every third year beginning January 1, 1988, to reflect the percentage change in the calendar year annual average of the California Consumer Price Index, All Urban Consumers, published by the Department of Industrial Relations, for the three-year period.

(2) No cost for medical expenses shall be imposed by the county until the county has first exhausted any eligibility the minor may have under private insurance coverage, standard or medically indigent Medi-Cal coverage, and the Robert W. Crown California Children's Services Act (Article 2 (commencing with Section 248) of Chapter 2 of Part 1 of Division 1 of the Health and Safety Code).

(3) In calculating the cost of medical expenses, the county shall not charge in excess of 100 percent of the AFDC fee for service average Medi-Cal payment for that county for that fiscal year as calculated by the State Department of Health Services; however, if a minor has extraordinary medical or dental costs that are not met under any of the coverages listed in paragraph (2), the county may impose these additional costs. *(Amended by Stats 1991 ch 110 §19, 137 §1, eff. 1/1/92.)*

§903.1. Liability for costs of legal services rendered to minor.

The father, mother, spouse, or other person liable for the support of a minor, the estate of such a person, and the estate of the minor, shall be liable for the cost to the county of legal services rendered to the minor by the public defender pursuant to an order of the juvenile court, or for the cost to the county for the legal services rendered to the minor by an attorney in private practice appointed pursuant to an order of the juvenile court. The father, mother, spouse, or other person liable for the support of a minor and the estate of any such person shall also be liable for any cost to the county of legal services rendered directly to the father, mother, or spouse, of the minor or any other person liable for the support of the minor, in a dependency proceeding by the public defender pursuant to an order of the juvenile court, or by an attorney in private practice appointed pursuant to order of the juvenile court. The liability of such persons (in this article called relatives) and estates shall be a joint and several liability.

§903.2. Liability for costs of supervision of minor.

The juvenile court may require that the father, mother, spouse, or other person liable for the support of a minor person, the estates of such persons, and the estate of such minor person, shall be liable for the cost to the county of the probation supervision of the minor person pursuant to the order of the juvenile court, by the probation officer. The liability of such persons (in this article called relatives) and estates shall be a joint and several liability.

§903.3. Liability for cost of sealing records.

The father, mother, spouse, or other person liable for the support of a minor person, the person himself if an adult, or the estates of such persons shall, unless indigent, be liable for the cost to the county for the sealing of any traffic infraction or traffic misdemeanor records pertaining to such person pursuant to this chapter. The liability of such persons and estates shall be a joint and several liability.

§903.4. Support of juveniles in out-of-home care.

(a) The Legislature finds that even though Section 903 establishes parental liability for the cost of the care, support, and maintenance of a child in a county institution or other place in which the child is placed, detained, or committed pursuant to an order of the juvenile court, the collection of child support for juveniles who have been placed in out-of-home care as dependents or wards of the juvenile court under Sections 300, 601, and 602 has not been pursued routinely and effectively.

It is the purpose of this section to substantially increase income to the state and to counties through court-ordered parental reimbursement for the support of juveniles who are in out-of-home placement. In this regard, the Legislature finds that the costs of collection will be offset by the additional income derived from the increased effectiveness of the parental support program.

(b) In any case in which a child is or has been declared a dependent child or a ward of the court pursuant to Section 300, 601, or 602, the juvenile court shall order any agency which has expended moneys or incurred costs on behalf of the child pursuant to a detention or placement order of the juvenile court, to submit to the district attorney, within 30 days, in the form of a declaration, a statement of its costs and expenses for the benefit, support, and maintenance of the child.

(c)(1) The district attorney may petition the superior court to issue an order to show cause why an order should not be entered for continuing support and reimbursement of the costs of the support of any minor described in Section 903.

Any order entered as a result of the order to show cause shall be enforceable in the same manner as any other support order entered by the courts of this state at the time it becomes due and payable.

In any case in which the district attorney has received a declaration of costs or expenses from any agency, the declaration shall be deemed an application for assistance pursuant to Section 11475.1.

(2) The order to show cause shall inform the parent of all of the following facts:

(A) He or she has been sued.

(B) If he or she wishes to seek the advice of an attorney in this matter, it should be done promptly so that his or her financial declaration and written response, if any, will be filed on time.

(C) He or she has a right to appear personally and present evidence in his or her behalf.

(D) His or her failure to appear at the order to show cause hearing, personally or through his or her attorney, may result in an order being entered against him or her for the relief requested in the petition.

(E) Any order entered could result in the garnishment of wages, taking of money or property to enforce the order, or being held in contempt of court.

(F) Any party has a right to request a modification of any order issued by the superior court in the event of a change in circumstances.

(3) Any existing support order shall remain in full force and effect unless the superior court modifies that order pursuant to subdivision (f).

(4) The district attorney shall not be required to petition the court for an order for continuing support and reimbursement if, in the opinion of the district attorney, it would not be appropriate to secure such an order. The district attorney shall not be required to continue collection efforts for any order if, in the opinion of the district attorney, it would not be appropriate or cost effective to enforce the order.

(d)(1) In any case in which an order to show cause has been issued and served upon a parent for continuing support and reimbursement of costs, a completed income and expense declaration shall be filed with the court by the parent; a copy of it shall be delivered to the district attorney at least five days prior to the hearing on the order to show cause.

(2) Any person authorized by law to receive a parent's financial declaration or information obtained therefrom, who knowingly furnishes the declaration or information to a person not authorized by law to receive it, is guilty of a misdemeanor.

(e) If a parent has been personally served with the order to show cause and no appearance is made by the parent, or an attorney in his or her behalf, at the hearing on the order to show cause, the court may enter an order for the principal amount and continuing support in the amount demanded in the petition.

If the parent appears at the hearing on the order to show cause, the court may enter an order for the amount the court determines the parent is financially able to pay.

(f) The court shall have continuing jurisdiction to modify any order for continuing support entered pursuant to this section.

(g) As used in this section, "parent" includes any person specified in Section 903, the estate of any such person, and the estate of the minor person.

(h) The district attorney may contract with another county agency for the performance of any of the duties required by this section.

§903.45. Financial evaluations of parental liability.

(a) The board of supervisors may designate a county financial evaluation officer pursuant to Section 27750 of the Government Code to make financial evaluations of parental liability for reimbursement pursuant to Sections 903, 903.1, 903.2, 903.3, and other reimbursable costs allowed by law, as set forth in this section.

(b) In any county where a board of supervisors has designated a county financial evaluation officer, the juvenile court shall, at the close of the disposition hearing, order any person liable for the cost of support, pursuant to Section 903, the cost of legal services as provided for in Section 903.1 or probation costs as provided for in Section 903.2, or any other reimbursable costs allowed under this code, to appear before the financial evaluation officer for a financial evaluation of his or her ability to pay those costs; and if the responsible person is not present at the disposition hearing, the court shall cite him or her to appear for such a financial evaluation.

© 1992 by J., B. & L. Gould
Printed in the U.S.A.   EP

If the county financial evaluation officer determines that a person so responsible has the ability to pay all or part of the costs, the county financial evaluation officer shall petition the court for an order requiring the person to pay that sum to the county. In evaluating a person's ability to pay under this section, the county financial evaluation officer and the court shall take into consideration the family's income, the necessary obligations of the family, and the number of persons dependent upon this income. Any person appearing for a financial evaluation shall have the right to dispute the county financial evaluation officer's determination, in which case he or she shall be entitled to a hearing before the juvenile court. The county financial evaluation officer at the time of the financial evaluation shall advise such a person of his or her right to a hearing and of his or her rights pursuant to subdivision (c).

At the hearing, any person so responsible for costs shall be entitled to have, but shall not be limited to, the opportunity to be heard in person, to present witnesses and other documentary evidence, to confront and cross-examine adverse witnesses, to disclosure of the evidence against him or her, and to receive a written statement of the findings of the court. The person shall have the right to be represented by counsel, and, when the person is unable to afford counsel, the right to appointed counsel. If the court determines that the person has the ability to pay all or part of the costs, including the costs of any counsel appointed to represent the person at the hearing, the court shall set the amount to be reimbursed and order him or her to pay that sum to the county in a manner in which the court believes reasonable and compatible with the person's financial ability.

If such person or persons, after having been ordered to appear before the county financial evaluation officer, have been given proper notice and fail to appear as ordered, the county financial evaluation officer shall recommend to the court that he, she, or they be ordered to pay the full amount of such costs. Proper notice to him, her, or them shall contain all of the following:

(1) That he, she or they have a right to a statement of such costs as soon as it is available.

(2) His, her, or their procedural rights under Section 27755 of the Government Code.

(3) The time limit within which his, her, or their appearance is required.

(4) A warning that if he, she, or they fail to appear before the county financial evaluation officer, such officer will recommend that the court order him, her, or them to pay such costs in full.

If the county financial evaluation officer determines that such person or persons have the ability to pay all or a portion of these costs, with or without terms, and he, she, or they concur in this determination and agree to the terms of payments, the county financial evaluation officer, upon his or her written evaluation and such person's or persons' written agreement, shall petition the court for an order requiring him, her, or them to pay that sum to the county in a manner which is reasonable and compatible with his, her, or their financial ability. This order may be granted without further notice to such person or persons, provided a copy of the order is served on him, her, or them by mail.

However, if the county financial evaluation officer cannot reach an agreement with such person or persons with respect to either the liability for the costs,

the amount of such costs, his, her or their ability to pay the same, or the terms of payment, the matter shall be deemed in dispute and referred by the county financial evaluation officer back to the court for a hearing.

(c) At any time prior to the satisfaction of a judgment entered pursuant to this section, a person against whom the judgment was entered may petition the rendering court to modify or vacate the judgment on the basis of a change in circumstances relating to his or her ability to pay the judgment.

(d) Execution may be issued on the order in the same manner as on a judgment in a civil action, including any balance remaining unpaid at the termination of the court's jurisdiction over the minor. *(Amended by Stats 1985 ch 1485 §15.1.)*

§903.5. Liability for costs of out-of-home care.

In addition to the requirements of Section 903.4, and notwithstanding any other provision of law, the parent or other person legally liable for the support of a minor, who voluntarily places the minor in 24-hour out-of-home care, shall be liable for the cost of the minor's care, support, and maintenance when the minor receives Aid to Families with Dependent Children-Foster Care (AFDC-FC), Supplemental Security Income-State Supplementary Program (SSI-SSP), or county-only funds. As used in this section "parent" includes any person specified in Section 903. Whenever the county welfare department or the placing agency determines that a court order would be advisable and effective, the department or the agency shall notify the district attorney, who shall proceed pursuant to Section 903.4.

§903.6. Distribution of funds.

Funds collected pursuant to Sections 903, 903.4, and 903.5 shall be distributed in the following manner:

(a) If the program through which the minor is placed is a county-funded program, the county shall retain 100 percent of the funds collected. For the purposes of this subdivision, programs funded in whole or part with county justices system subvention program funds shall be considered to be 100 percent county funded.

(b) If the program through which the minor is placed is funded partially with state or federal funds, the amounts collected shall be distributed by the State Department of Social Services pursuant to Section 11457 and incentives shall be paid pursuant to Sections 15200.1, 15200.2, and 15200.3.

§903.7. Establishment of Foster Children and Parent Training Fund.

(a) There is in the State Treasury the Foster Children and Parent Training Fund, the moneys contained in which shall be used exclusively for the purposes set forth in this section.

(b) For each fiscal year beginning with fiscal year 1981-82, except as provided in Sections 15200.1, 15200.2, and 15200.3, the State Department of Social Services shall determine the amount equivalent to the state share of collections attributable to the enforcement of parental fiscal liability pursuant to Sections 903, 903.4, and 903.5. On July 1, 1982, and every three months thereafter, the department shall notify the Chancellor of the Community Colleges, the Department of Finance, and the Superintendent of Public

Instruction of the above-specified amount. The State Department of Social Services shall authorize the quarterly transfer of any portion of this amount for any particular fiscal year exceeding three million seven hundred fifty thousand dollars ($3,750,000) to the Treasurer for deposit in the Foster Children and Parent Training Fund.'

(c) If sufficient moneys are available in the Foster Children and Parent Training Fund, up to one million dollars ($1,000,000) shall be allocated for the support of foster parent training programs conducted in community colleges. The maximum amount authorized to be allocated pursuant to this subdivision shall be adjusted annually by a cost-of-living increase each year based on the percentage given to discretionary education programs. Funds for the training program shall be provided in a separate budget item in that portion of the Budget Act pertaining to the Chancellor of the California Community Colleges, to be deposited in a separate bank account by the Chancellor of the California Community Colleges.

The chancellor shall use these funds exclusively for foster parent training, as specified by the chancellor in consultation with the California State Foster Parents Association and the State Department of Social Services.

The plans for each foster parent training program shall include the provision of training to facilitate the development of foster family homes and small family homes to care for no more than six children who have special mental, emotional, developmental, or physical needs.

The State Department of Social Services shall facilitate the participation of county welfare departments in the foster parent training program. The State Foster Parents Association, or the local chapters thereof, and the State Department of Social Services shall identify training participants and shall advise the chancellor on the form, content, and methodology of the training program. Funds shall be paid monthly to the foster parent training program until the maximum amount of funds authorized to be expended for that program is expended. No more than 10 percent or seventy-five thousand dollars ($75,000) of these moneys, whichever is greater, shall be used for administrative purposes; of the 10 percent or seventy-five thousand dollars ($75,000), no more than ten thousand dollars ($10,000) shall be expended to reimburse the State Department of Social Services for its services pursuant to this paragraph.

(d) Beginning with fiscal year 1983-84, and each fiscal year thereafter, after all allocations for foster parent training in community colleges have been made, any moneys remaining in the Foster Children and Parent Training Fund may be allocated for foster children services programs pursuant to Chapter 11.3 (commencing with Section 42920) of Part 24 of the Education Code.

(e) The Controller shall transfer moneys from the Foster Children and Parent Training Fund to the Chancellor of the Community Colleges and the Superintendent of Public Instruction as necessary to fulfill the requirements of subdivisions (c) and (d).

After the maximum amount authorized in any fiscal year has been transferred to the Chancellor of the Community Colleges and the Superintendent of Public Instruction, the Controller shall transfer any remaining funds to the General Fund for expenditure for any public purpose.

§904. Determination of charges.

The monthly or daily charge, not to exceed cost, for care, support, and maintenance of minor persons placed or detained in or committed to any institution by order of a juvenile court, the cost of legal services referred to by Section 903.1, the cost of probation supervision referred to by Section 903.2, and the cost of sealing records referred to by Section 903.3 shall be determined by the board of supervisors.

§911. Time limit on order for payment.

No order for payment from the county treasury of the expense of support and maintenance of a ward or dependent child of the juvenile court shall be effective for more than 12 months, and no order for payment from the county treasury of the expense of support and maintenance of a minor person concerning whom a verified petition has been filed in accordance with the provision of this chapter, other than a ward or dependent child of the court, shall be effective for more than one month. Upon all hearings of the case of any ward or dependent child of the juvenile court, the case shall be continued on the calendar, but in no instance to exceed 12 months.

When any ward of the juvenile court is, with the consent of the juvenile court of the county committing him and the officer in charge of the state school to which he was committed or in which he is confined, placed in a boarding home, foster home, or work home, but continues to be under the supervision of such state school, the county may reimburse the boarding home, foster home, or work home in an amount adequate for the maintenance of the ward, but not to exceed twenty-five dollars ($25) per month.

§912. Payment of state by county for persons committed.

For each person hitherto committed to the Youth Authority, the county from which he is committed shall pay the state at the rate of twenty-five dollars ($25) per month for the time such person so committed remains in such state school or in any camp or farm colony, custodial institution, or other institution under the direct supervision of the Youth Authority to which such person may be transferred, in the Deuel Vocational Institution, or in any boarding home, foster home, or other private or public institution in which he is placed by the Youth Authority, on parole or otherwise, and cared for and supported at the expense of the Youth Authority.

The Youth Authority shall present to the county, not more frequently than monthly, a claim for the amount due the state under this section, which the county shall process and pay pursuant to the provisions of Chapter 4 (commencing with Section 29700) of Division 3 of Title 3 of the Government Code.

§913. Contract of county with custodian.

When any person has been adjudged to be a ward or dependent child of the juvenile court, and the court has made an order committing such person to the care of any association, society, or corporation, embracing within its objects the purpose of caring for or obtaining homes for such persons, the county in which such person has been committed may contract with such custodian, for the supervision, investigation, and rehabilitation of such person by such custodian, and may, pursuant to such contract, pay to it an amount determined by mutual agreement, not to exceed the cost to such custodian of such service.

© 1992 by J., B. & L. Gould
Printed in the U.S.A.   EP

§914. Expense for support and maintenance defined.

As used in this article, "expense for support and maintenance" includes the reasonable value of any medical services furnished to the ward or dependent child at the county hospital or at any other county institution, or at any private hospital or by any private physician with the approval of the juvenile court of the county concerned, and the reasonable value of the support of the ward or dependent child at any juvenile hall established pursuant to the provisions of Article 23 (commencing with Section 850) of this chapter or the reasonable value of the ward's support at any forestry camp, juvenile home, ranch, or camp established within or without the county pursuant to the provisions of Article 24 (commencing with Section 880) of this chapter.

ARTICLE 26

WORK FURLOUGHS

§925. Article; where operative.

The provisions of this article shall be operative in any county in which the board of supervisors by ordinance finds, on the basis of employment conditions, the state of juvenile detention facilities, and other pertinent circumstances, that the operation of this article in that county is feasible. In such ordinance the board shall prescribe whether the probation officer or any official in charge of a county juvenile detention facility shall perform the functions of the juvenile work furlough administrator. The board of supervisors may also terminate the operativeness of this article in the county if it finds by ordinance that, because of changed circumstances, the operation of this article in that county is no longer feasible.

§926. Continuation of employment for wards of juvenile court.

When a minor is adjudged a ward of the juvenile court and committed to a county juvenile home, ranch, camp, or forestry camp, the juvenile work furlough administrator may, if he concludes that such person is a fit subject therefor, direct that such person be permitted to continue in his regular employment, if that is compatible with the requirements of Section 928, or may authorize the person to secure employment for himself in the county, unless the court at the time of commitment has ordered that such person not be granted work furloughs.

§927. Employment of ward of juvenile court.

(a) If the juvenile work furlough administrator so directs that the minor be permitted to continue in his or her regular employment, the administrator shall arrange for a continuation of that employment when possible without interruption. If the minor does not have regular employment, and the administrator has authorized the minor to secure employment for himself or herself, the minor may do so, and the administrator may assist the minor in doing so. Any employment so secured must be suitable for the minor and must be at a wage at least as high as the prevailing wage for similar work in the area where the work is performed and in accordance with the prevailing working conditions in the area. In no event may any such employment be permitted where there is a labor dispute in the establishment in which the minor is, or is to be, employed.

(b) If the minor does not have regular employment, the juvenile work furlough administrator may authorize the minor to apply for placement in a local job training program, and the administrator may assist him or her in doing so. The program may include, but shall not be limited to, job training assistance as provided through the Job Training Partnership Act (Public Law 97-300; 29 U.S.C. Sec. 1501 et seq.). *(Amended by Stats 1989 ch 48 §2, eff. 1/1/90.)*

§928. Confinement of ward while not employed.

Whenever the minor is not employed and between the hours or periods of employment, he shall be confined in a juvenile detention facility unless the court or administrator directs otherwise.

§929. Disposition of minor's earnings.

The earnings of the minor shall be collected by the juvenile work furlough administrator, and it shall be the duty of the minor's employer to transmit such wages to the administrator at the latter's request. Earnings levied upon pursuant to Chapter 5 (commencing with Section 706.010) of Division 2 of Title 9 of Part 2 of the Code of Civil Procedure shall not be transmitted to the administrator. If the administrator has requested transmittal of earnings prior to levy, such request shall have priority. When an employer transmits such earnings to the administrator pursuant to this section the employer shall have no liability to the minor for such earnings. From such earnings the administrator shall pay the minor's board and personal expenses, both inside and outside the juvenile detention facility, and shall deduct so much of the costs of administration of this article as is allocable to such minor. If sufficient funds are available after making the foregoing payments, the administrator may, with the consent of the minor, pay, in whole or in part, the preexisting debts of the minor. Any balance shall be retained until the minor's discharge and thereupon shall be paid to the minor.

§930. Violation of conditions of work furlough.

In the event the minor violates the conditions laid down for his conduct, custody, or employment, the juvenile work furlough administrator may order termination of work furloughs for such minor.

ARTICLE 27

4-HOUR SCHOOLS

§940. Establishment and purpose of 24-hour schools.

The board of supervisors in every county may provide and maintain, at the expense of the county, in a location approved by the judge of the juvenile court, or in counties having more than one judge of the juvenile court, by the presiding judge of the juvenile court, a 24-hour school. The school shall be established to provide education and training for minors in accordance with the provisions of Article 1 (commencing with Section 48600) of Chapter 4 of Part 27 of the Education Code.

§941. Management of school.

The 24-hour school shall be under the management and control of the probation officer.

§942. Staff of school.

The board of supervisors shall provide for a suitable superintendent to have charge of the 24-hour school, and for such other employees as may be needed for its efficient management, and shall provide for payment, out of the general fund of the county, of suitable salaries for such superintendent and other employees.

§943. Employment of school staff.

The superintendent and other employees of the 24-hour school shall be appointed by the probation officer, pursuant to a civil service or merit system, and may be removed, for cause, pursuant to such system.

§944. List of school expenses.

The probation officer shall keep a classified list of expenses for the operation of the 24-hour school and shall file a duplicate copy with the county board of supervisors.

§945. School's licensing.

A 24-hour school shall be considered a children's institution for licensing purposes and shall be licensed by the department of social welfare of the county in which the 24-hour school is located.

ARTICLE 28

ADJUSTMENT SCHOOLS

§960. Authority of governing board.

This article shall be construed in conformity with the intent as well as the expressed provisions thereof, and the governing board of any adjustment school may do all those lawful acts that it deems necessary to promote the prosperity of the adjustment school, or to promote the well-being and education of all minors entrusted to its charge. (Added by Stats 1987 ch 1452 §534.)

§961. Governing article.

The terms and provisions of Article 25 (commencing with Section 900) of Chapter 2 of Part 1 of Division 2 and Section 579 shall, so far as applicable, govern and control proceedings under this article. (Added by Stats 1987 ch 1452 §534.)

§962. Organization and maintenance of schools.

The boards of supervisors or other governing bodies of counties and cities and counties may organize, establish, equip, and maintain, including the purchase of suitable sites and the construction of suitable buildings, adjustment schools in each county or city and county for the purpose of furnishing to minors under the age of 18 years pursuant to this article, care, custody, education, training, and adjustment to good citizenship, which shall be continuous and uninterrupted during the period the minors remain in school. (Added by Stats 1987 ch 1452 §534.)

§963. Maintenance of school by two or more counties.

The boards of supervisors of two or more counties may by regularly adopted resolutions or ordinances duly entered on the minutes or proceedings of their respective boards, unite in the organization, establishment, equipment, and maintenance of adjustment schools for the respective counties. In that event, the schools shall be located in one or more of the counties as shall be mutually agreed upon and designated in the resolutions or ordinances. (Added by Stats 1987 ch 1452 §534.)

§964. Government and management of school.

If adjustment schools are organized by only one county or city and county, the government and management shall be vested in a governing board which shall be either the board of education, or similar school governing body, or the county probation committee of the juvenile court, or a board of trustees composed of seven members selected from both the board of education and the probation committee, as may be determined or chosen in the exercise of sound discretion by the board of supervisors or other governing body of the county or city and county. (Added by Stats 1987 ch 1452 §534.)

§965. Government of school run jointly by two or more counties.

If the adjustment schools are organized by the joint action of two or more counties, the boards of supervisors of the counties may by concerted action by duly adopted resolutions entrust the government and management to a governing board, which shall be any of the following:

(a) The board of education of the county in which at least one adjustment school is located.

(b) The probation committee of the juvenile court of the county in which at least one adjustment school is located.

(c) A board of trustees composed of seven members who shall represent all of the counties and each of whom may be selected from either the county board of education or the probation committee of the juvenile court of his or her respective county as shall be determined in the joint resolutions of the boards of supervisors. (Added by Stats 1987 ch 1452 §534.)

§966. Trustees' term of office.

If a board of trustees is chosen to govern and manage the adjustment school the term of office of the trustees shall be six years, except that of the seven trustees first selected, two shall hold office for two years, two shall hold office for four years, and three shall hold office for six years. Each of the two-, four-, and six-year terms shall be assigned by lot to each of the seven trustees. (Added by Stats 1987 ch 1452 §534.)

§967. Rules and regulations of school.

The governing board shall make all needful rules and regulations for the transaction of business and for the management and government of the adjustment school under its jurisdiction, and it shall see that proper care, custody, education, and training are provided for the minors under its care, to the end that the minors shall be adjusted to good citizenship and prepared to become honorable, self-supporting members of society. (Added by Stats 1987 ch 1452 §534.)

§968. Contracts and appropriations.

The governing board shall make all contracts for the organization, establishment, including the purchase of a suitable site and the construction of suitable buildings, equipment, operation, and maintenance of the adjustment school that may be necessary or advisable. In no event shall the amount of money appropriated for any such purpose or other limitation prescribed by law or by order of the governing board, be exceeded or violated. (Added by Stats 1987 ch 1452 §534.)

© 1992 by J., B. & L. Gould
Printed in the U.S.A.　　EP

§969. Interest by school employees in contracts.

No member of the governing board, nor officer, nor employee of any adjustment school shall be interested, personally, directly, or indirectly, in any contract, purchase, or sale made, or in any business carried on in behalf of the school. Any money paid on the contracts or sales may be recovered by a civil suit, and the governing board upon the proof of such interest shall remove from office immediately the member, officer, or employee. *(Added by Stats 1987 ch 1452 §534.)*

§970. School superintendent.

The governing board of the adjustment school shall appoint a superintendent, not of its own number, who shall be a person qualified by training and experience for the character of work to be performed at the adjustment school, and who shall hold office at the pleasure of the governing board. *(Added by Stats 1987 ch 1452 §534.)*

§971. Specifications of officer and staff positions.

The governing board shall determine the number, title duties, and terms of office of all other officers and employees and shall fix their salaries, and that of the superintendent. *(Added by Stats 1987 ch 1452 §534.)*

§972. Superintendent's oath and bonds.

The superintendent of the adjustment school shall, before entering upon the discharge of his or her duties, make and file with the governing board an oath that he or she will faithfully and impartially discharge his or her duties. The superintendent shall also file with the governing board a bond, running to the State of California in a sum the board may determine, and with sureties to be approved by the board, conditioned upon the faithful performance of his or her duties. The premium of the bond shall be a part of the cost of maintaining the adjustment school. *(Added by Stats 1987 ch 1452 §534.)*

§973. Custody of school property by superintendent.

The superintendent, after making and filing the bond, shall, subject to the direction of the governing board, be invested with the custody of the lands, buildings, and all other property pertaining to or under the control of the adjustment school. The superintendent shall account to the governing board in the manner it may require for all property entrusted to the superintendent and for all money received by him or her as superintendent of the adjustment school, or for any of the minors entrusted to its care. *(Added by Stats 1987 ch 1452 §534.)*

§974. Appointment of officers and staff by superintendent.

The superintendent shall also, subject to the direction of the governing board, appoint all officers and employees of the adjustment school, who shall hold office at the pleasure of the superintendent. The superintendent shall exercise the supervisory, executive, and managing powers that are conferred upon him or her by the governing board. *(Added by Stats 1987 ch 1452 §534.)*

§975. Location of residences of superintendent and staff.

The superintendent shall reside in the adjustment school or one of the adjustment schools under his or her jurisdiction and shall be furnished suitable quarters, furniture, food supplies, and laundry for himself or herself and his or her family. The governing board may make similar provision for other officers and employees that the interests of the adjustment school may in its judgment require to reside on the premises. *(Added by Stats 1987 ch 1452 §534.)*

§976. Commitment of minors to school.

The adjustment school shall receive into its care, custody, and control all boys and girls under 18 years of age who are committed to it by order of the juvenile court of the county or city and county maintaining or contributing to the maintenance of the adjustment school. *(Added by Stats 1987 ch 1452 §534.)*

§977. Term of custody.

Any minor who has been committed to the care, custody, and control of any adjustment school shall remain in the school for the duration of the period provided in the order of commitment, or until further order of the juvenile court. *(Added by Stats 1987 ch 1452 §534.)*

§978. Annual review of commitment orders.

The juvenile court shall review the order of commitment at least once each year, and upon review the court may continue, terminate, or modify the order of commitment. *(Added by Stats 1987 ch 1452 §534.)*

§979. Court order to revoke commitment.

If at any time in the opinion of the superintendent of the adjustment school the further detention of the minor is detrimental to the interests of the school, the minor may immediately, upon order of the superintendent, be returned to the committing court, and the court may revoke its previous order, and proceedings may be resumed where they were suspended when the commitment was made. *(Added by Stats 1987 ch 1452 §534.)*

§980. Board's determination of conduct of school.

The governing board of any adjustment school shall cause the school to be conducted as may seem best calculated to carry out the intentions of this article. *(Added by Stats 1987 ch 1452 §534.)*

§981. Content of school's course of study.

There shall be organized a course of study, corresponding as far as practicable with the course of study in the public schools of the state. *(Added by Stats 1987 ch 1452 §534.)*

§982. Vocational training.

There shall be provided in the adjustment school the proper facilities and equipment for vocational and trade training, in addition to other public school education or training that may be determined upon by the governing board. Vocational or trade training education shall be given to each minor while under the care of the adjustment school, to the end that he or she may upon discharge be qualified for honorable and self-supporting employment. *(Added by Stats 1987 ch 1452 §534.)*

§983. Payment for minor's support and maintenance.

Any order of the juvenile court committing a minor to the care, custody, and control of an adjustment school may provide the expense of his or her support and maintenance by directing that the expense be paid in whole or in part by his or her parent, guardian, or other person liable for his or her support and maintenance. *(Added by Stats 1987 ch 1452 §534.)*

§984. Who bears expenses of school.

If the adjustment school is organized, established, equipped, and maintained by only one county or city and county, the entire expense of the school shall be borne by the county or city and county, and the board of supervisors, or other governing body of the county or city and county shall make due and annual provision therefor. The necessary items of expense shall be set forth in the annual budget of the county or city and county. *(Added by Stats 1987 ch 1452 §534.)*

§985. Who bears expenses of school run jointly by two or more counties.

If an adjustment school is organized, established, equipped, and maintained by two or more counties, the initial expense of organizing, establishing, and equipping the school shall be apportioned between each of the counties on a pro rata basis in the ratio that the number of children of school age residing in each county bears to the number of children of school age residing in all of the counties. *(Added by Stats 1987 ch 1452 §534.)*

§986. Who pays maintenance expenses of school run jointly by two or more counties.

The annual expense of maintaining the school by two or more counties, shall be apportioned between the counties on a pro rata basis in the ratio that the average daily enrollment of minors placed in the school from each county during the preceding year bears to the total average daily enrollment in the school from all of the counties during the year. *(Added by Stats 1987 ch 1452 §534.)*

§987. Bond filed by officers who handle money or supplies.

The governing board shall require any officer entrusted with money belonging to an adjustment school or to any of the minors entrusted to its care, or any officer placed in a position of trust and responsibility in the custody of property or in the handling of supplies belonging to the school, to file with the board a bond with sureties approved by the board and in a sum that it may determine, conditioned upon the faithful performance of the duties required, and upon the faithful accounting of all money and property coming into his or her hands or under his or her control by virtue of his or her office. The premiums on the bonds shall be a part of the cost of maintaining the adjustment school. *(Added by Stats 1987 ch 1452 §534.)*

CHAPTER 3

INSTITUTIONS FOR DELINQUENTS

ARTICLE 1

ESTABLISHMENT AND GENERAL GOVERNMENT

§1000. Jurisdiction of Department of the Youth Authority.

The Department of the Youth Authority has jurisdiction over all educational training and treatment institutions now or hereafter established and maintained in the State as correctional schools for the reception of wards of the juvenile court and other persons committed to the department.

§1000.5. Whittier State School renamed Fred C. Nelles School for Boys.

Where in any law of this State the name "Whittier State School" appears it shall hereafter be understood to mean and shall be construed to refer to Fred C. Nelles School for Boys.

§1000.7. Definition of terms.

As used in this chapter, "Youth Authority", "Authority" and "the Authority" mean and refer to the Department of the Youth Authority and "Board" means and refers to the Youthful Offender Parole Board.

§1001. Government of institutions.

The general government and supervision of each such institution is vested in the Youth Authority.

§1001.5. Punishment for having contraband materials in Youth Authority facility.

(a) Except when authorized by law, or when authorized by the person in charge of an institution or camp administered by the Youth Authority, or by an officer of the institution or camp empowered by the person in charge of the institution or camp to give that authorization, any person who knowingly brings or sends into, or who knowingly assists in bringing into, or sending into, any institution or camp, or the grounds belonging to any institution or camp, administered by the Youth Authority, or any person who, while confined in the institution or camp knowingly possesses therein, any controlled substance, the possession of which is prohibited by Division 10 (commencing with Section 11000) of the Health and Safety Code; any alcoholic beverage; any firearm, weapon or explosive of any kind; or any tear gas or tear gas weapon shall be punished by imprisonment in a county jail for not more than one year or by imprisonment in the state prison.

(b) Except as otherwise authorized in the manner provided in subdivision (a), any person who knowingly uses tear gas or uses a tear gas weapon in any institution or camp specified in subdivision (a) is guilty of a felony.

(c) This section shall not be construed to preclude or in any way limit the applicability of any other law proscribing a course of conduct also proscribed by this section. *(Amended by Stats 1985 ch 515 §2.)*

§1001.7. Trespassing on Youth Authority facility grounds by ex-convicts at night.

Every person who, having been previously convicted of a felony and confined in any state prison in this state, without the consent of the officer in charge of any California Youth Authority institution comes upon the grounds of any such institution, or lands belonging or adjacent thereto, in the nighttime, and who refuses or fails to leave upon being requested to do so by an employee of the institution, is guilty of a misdemeanor.

§1002. Powers of Youth Authority.

The Youth Authority may do all lawful acts which it deems necessary to effectuate the purposes for

© 1992 by J., B. & L. Gould
Printed in the U.S.A.   EP

which such schools are established, and to promote the well-being, education and reformation of the inmates thereof; but the authority shall not incur any indebtedness in excess of the moneys appropriated or otherwise made available for the use of such schools.

§1003. Authority's control of institution property.

The authority shall have charge of the land, buildings, apparatus, tools, stock, provisions and other property belonging to each such institution.

§1004. Responsibilities of authority to persons committed.

The authority shall have charge of the persons committed to or confined in each such institution, and shall provide for their care, supervision, education, training, employment, discipline, and government. It shall exercise its powers toward the correction of their faults, the development of their characters, and the promotion of their welfare.

§1006. Land purchased for site of Preston School of Industry.

The land purchased for the site of Preston School of Industry shall be used exclusively for the occupancy and purposes of the school.

§1008. Deportation of aliens committed to Youth Authority.

The Youth Authority shall cooperate with the United States Bureau of Immigration in arranging for the deportation of all aliens who are committed to it.

§1009. Nonresidents committed to Youth Authority.

The Youthful Offender Parole Board may order the return of nonresident persons committed to the Department of the Youth Authority or confined in institutions or facilities subject to the jurisdiction of the department to the states in which they have legal residence. Whenever any public officer (other than an officer or employee of the Youth Authority) receives from any private source any moneys to defray the cost of such transportation, he or she shall immediately transmit such moneys to the Youth Authority. All such moneys, together with any moneys received directly by the authority from private sources for transportation of nonresidents, shall be deposited by the Youth Authority in the State Treasury, in augmentation of the current appropriation for the support of the Youth Authority.

§1009.1. Refunding of unused money.

When, pursuant to Section 1009, money is received by the Department of the Youth Authority from private sources to defray the cost of transportation for the return of a nonresident committed to it and the nonresident is not returned or the money received exceeds the cost of such transportation, the department shall refund to such private sources such money or such excess money, as the case may be.

§1009.2. Making payment pursuant to §1009.1.

The fiscal officer of the Department of the Youth Authority shall make payment of any refund pursuant to Section 1009.1 if the Director of the Youth Authority prepares a voucher which sets forth the facts which pertain to the refund and authorizes its payment.

§1009.3. Withdrawal of funds in State Treasury which are to be refunded.

If any money which is to be refunded has been deposited in the State Treasury, the State Controller, upon receipt of a claim which is filed by the Department of the Youth Authority, shall draw his warrant for the payment of the refund from the fund to which the money was credited.

§1009.4. Retention of small refunds.

If the Director of the Youth Authority finds that the amount of any refund is less than three dollars ($3), he may retain such amount, unless demand for the payment of such refund is made within six months after the determination that a refund is due. If such demand is made, the refund shall be paid.

§1010. Definition of resident of state.

In determining residence for purposes of transportation, a person who has lived continuously in this State for a period of one year and who has not acquired a residence in another State by living continuously therein for at least one year subsequent to his residence in this State shall be deemed to be a resident of this State. Time spent in a public institution or on parole therefrom shall not be counted in determining the matter of residence in this or another State. In determining the residence of a ward of the juvenile court committed to the Youth Authority or confined in any institution under its jurisdiction, due consideration shall be given to the residence of the parents of such ward, and if either one or both parents of the ward are residents of this State the ward shall also be deemed a resident of this State.

§1011. Payment of expenses for transporting wards.

All expenses incurred in returning such persons to other States shall be paid by this State, but the expense of returning residents of this State shall be borne by the States making the returns.

The cost and expense incurred in effecting the transportation of such persons shall be paid from the funds appropriated for that purpose, or, if necessary, from the money appropriated for the care of such persons upon vouchers approved by the State Board of Control.

§1015. Personal property of deceased ward of Youth Authority.

Whenever any person confined in any state institution subject to the jurisdiction of the Youth Authority dies, and any personal funds or property of such person remains in the hands of the Director of the Youth Authority, and no demand is made upon said director by the owner of the funds or property or his legally appointed representative, all money and other personal property of such decedent remaining in the custody or possession of the Director of the Youth Authority shall be held by him for a period of one year from the date of death of the decedent, for the benefit of the heirs, legatees, or successors in interest of such decedent.

Upon the expiration of said one-year period, any money remaining unclaimed in the custody or possession of the director shall be delivered by him to the State Treasurer for deposit in the Unclaimed Property Fund under the provisions of Article 1 of Chapter 6 of Title 10 of Part 3 of the Code of Civil Procedure.

Upon the expiration of said one-year period, all personal property and documents of the decedent, other than cash, remaining unclaimed in the custody or possession of the director shall be disposed of as follows:

(a) All deeds, contracts or assignments shall be filed by the director with the public administrator of the county of commitment of the decedent;

(b) All other personal property shall be sold by the director at public auction, or upon a sealed-bid basis, and the proceeds of the sale delivered by him to the State Treasurer in the same manner as is herein provided with respect to unclaimed money of the decedent. If he deems it expedient to do so, the director may accumulate the property of several decedents and sell the property in such lots as he may determine, provided that he makes a determination as to each decedent's share of the proceeds;

(c) If any personal property of the decedent is not salable at public auction, or upon a sealed-bid basis, or if it has no intrinsic value, or if its value is not sufficient to justify the deposit of such property in the State Treasury, the director may order it destroyed;

(d) All other unclaimed personal property of the decedent not disposed of as provided in paragraphs (a), (b), or (c) hereof, shall be delivered by the director to the State Controller for deposit in the State Treasury under the provisions of Article 1 of Chapter 6 of Title 10 of Part 3 of the Code of Civil Procedure.

§1016. Unclaimed property of escapee, parolee, or discharged ward.

Whenever any person confined in any state institution subject to the jurisdiction of the Youth Authority escapes, or is discharged or paroled from such institution, and any personal funds or property of such person remains in the hands of the Director of the Youth Authority, and no demand is made upon said director by the owner of the funds or property or his legally appointed representative, all money and other intangible personal property of such person, other than deeds, contracts, or assignments, remaining in the custody or possession of the Director of the Youth Authority shall be held by him for a period of seven years from the date of such escape, discharge, or parole, for the benefit of such person or his successors in interest; provided, however, that unclaimed personal funds or property of paroled minors may be exempted from the provisions of this section during the period of their minority and for a period of one year thereafter, at the discretion of the director.

Upon the expiration of said seven-year period, any money and other intangible personal property, other than deeds, contracts or assignments, remaining unclaimed in the custody or possession of the director shall be subject to the provisions of Chapter 7 of Title 10 of Part 3 of the Code of Civil Procedure. Upon the expiration of one year from the date of such escape, discharge, or parole:

(a) All deeds, contracts, or assignments shall be filed by the director with the public administrator of the county of commitment of such person;

(b) All tangible personal property other than money, remaining unclaimed in his custody or possession, shall be sold by the director at public auction, or upon a sealed-bid basis, and the proceeds of the sale shall be held by him subject to the provisions of Section 1752.8 of this code, and subject to the provisions of Chapter 7 of Title 10 of Part 3 of the Code of Civil Procedure. If he deems it expedient to do so, the director may accumulate the property of several in-

mates and may sell the property in such lots as he may determine, provided that he makes a determination as to each inmate's share of the proceeds.

If any tangible personal property covered by this section is not salable at public auction or upon a sealed-bid basis, or if it has no intrinsic value, or if its value is not sufficient to justify its retention by the director to be offered for sale at public auction or upon a sealed-bid basis at a later date, the director may order it destroyed.

§1017. Public notice of disposition.

Before any money or other personal property or documents are delivered to the State Treasurer, State Controller, or public administrator, or sold at auction or upon a sealed-bid basis, or destroyed, under the provisions of Section 1015, and before any personal property or documents are delivered to the public administrator, or sold at auction or upon a sealed-bid basis, or destroyed, under the provisions of Section 1016, of this code, notice of said intended disposition shall be posted at least 30 days prior to the disposition, in a public place at the institution where the disposition is to be made, and a copy of such notice shall be mailed to the last known address of the owner or deceased owner at least 30 days prior to such disposition. The notice prescribed by this section need not specifically describe each item of property to be disposed of.

§1018. Schedule describing money and property delivered.

At the time of delivering any money or other personal property to the State Treasurer or State Controller under the provisions of Section 1015 or of Chapter 7 of Title 10 of Part 3 of the Code of Civil Procedure, the director shall deliver to the State Controller a schedule setting forth a statement and description of all money and other personal property delivered, and the name and last known address of the owner or deceased owner.

§1019. State not liable for destroyed property.

When any personal property has been destroyed as provided in Section 1015 or 1016, no suit shall thereafter be maintained by any person against the State or any officer thereof for or on account of such property.

§1020. Applications of §§1015 and 1016.

Notwithstanding any other provision of law, the provisions of Sections 1015 and 1016 shall apply (1) to all money and other personal property delivered to the State Treasurer or State Controller prior to the effective date of said sections, which would have been subject to the provisions thereof if they had been in effect on the date of such delivery; and (2) to all money and personal property delivered to the State Treasurer or State Controller prior to the effective date of the 1961 amendments to said sections, as said provisions would have applied on the date of such delivery if, on said date of delivery, the provisions of Chapter 1809, Statutes of 1959, had not been in effect.

ARTICLE 3

SUPERINTENDENTS

§1049. Appointment, duties, and remuneration.

Subject to provisions of law relating to the State civil service, the Youth Authority may appoint, define

© 1992 by J., B. & L. Gould
Printed in the U.S.A.   EP

the duties, and fix the salary of the superintendent or executive officer of each institution under this chapter.

§1050. Qualifications.

The superintendent of the institutions under this chapter shall be persons of high moral character, specially qualified for the position.

ARTICLE 4

EMPLOYEES

§1075. Appointment and payment of employees.

The Youth Authority shall, in accordance with law, appoint all officers and employees required at the institutions under this chapter, and shall fix their remuneration.

§1076. Youth Authority officers have powers of peace officers.

The superintendent, assistant superintendent, supervisor, or any employee having custody of wards, of each institution of the Department of the Youth Authority, and any transportation officer of the Department of the Youth Authority, shall have the powers and authority of peace officers listed in Section 830.5 of the Penal Code.

§1077. Meals and subsistence for employees.

At the request of one or more employees of any institution under this chapter, the authority may, at its option, provide, within the grounds of any institution, meals and subsistence for employees who do not reside within the institution, or living facilities, meals and subsistence for employees who reside within the institution. The authority may make a reasonable charge for all facilities taken by or furnished to employees, to be determined by the State Board of Control, and to be deducted from the salary of the employee. No employee shall be compelled to eat his meals at the institution, nor shall he be charged for meals or facilities not furnished to or taken by him. No employee shall be discriminated against in any manner whatsoever because he elects to eat his meals outside the institution grounds.

The provisions of this section apply only to those employees who are not officers and who receive gross salaries as specified by the salary scales of the State Personnel Board, and do not apply to those employees who are officers of an institution or who receive a cash salary plus maintenance for self and family as provided by the salary scales of the State Personnel Board.

ARTICLE 6

CONDUCT, EDUCATION, AND DISCIPLINE

§1120. Intent of Legislature.

(a) It is the intent of the Legislature to insure an appropriate educational program for wards committed to the Department of the Youth Authority. The objective of such program shall be to improve the academic, vocational, and life survival skills of each ward so as to enable such wards to return to the community as productive citizens.

(b) The department shall assess the educational needs of each ward upon commitment and at least annually thereafter until released on parole. The ini-

tial assessment shall include a projection of the academic, vocational, and psychological needs of the ward and shall be used both in making a determination as to the appropriate educational program for the ward and as a measure of progress in subsequent assessments of the educational development of the ward.

The educational program of the department shall be responsive to the needs of all wards, including those who are educationally handicapped or limited-English speaking wards.

(c) The statewide educational program of the department shall include, but shall not be limited to, all of the following courses of instruction:

(1) Academic preparation in the areas of verbal communication skills, reading, writing, and arithmetic.

(2) Vocational preparation including vocational counseling, training in marketable skills, and job placement assistance.

(3) Life survival skills, including preparation in the areas of consumer economics, family life, and personal and social adjustment.

All of the aforementioned courses of instruction shall be offered at each institution within the jurisdiction of the department except camps and those institutions whose primary function is the initial reception and classification of wards. At such camps and institutions the educational program shall take into consideration the purpose and function of the camp and institutional program.

(d) The department shall report to the Legislature and the Superintendent of Public Instruction by February 1, 1980, on the department's assessment of and plan to improve its educational program, including, but not limited to, the training needs of its educational staff, a statement of departmental priorities with regard to its educational program, compliance with state and federal laws with regard to teaching credentials and staffing patterns within its educational program, and plans to implement the provisions of this section.

§1120.5. Maintenance of division of instruction.

At each institution under this chapter the Youth Authority shall organize and maintain a division of instruction and such other divisions as it deems necessary and advisable in the conduct of the school.

§1121. Chief of division of instruction.

The chief of each such division of instruction shall be well trained in modern school administration.

§1122. Courses in division of instruction.

Such divisions of instruction shall have jurisdiction over all courses of instruction. Such courses shall include academic and vocational training, and shall be subject to the approval of the State Superintendent of Public Instruction.

§1123. Director shall provide information about AIDS.

Subject to the availability of adequate state funding for these purposes, the Director of the Youth Authority shall provide all wards at each penal institution within the jurisdiction of the department, including camps, with information about behavior that places a person at high risk for contracting the human immunodeficiency virus (HIV), and about the prevention of transmission of acquired immune deficiency syndrome (AIDS). The director shall provide all wards, who are within one month of release or being placed on parole, with information about agencies and facilities that provide testing, counseling, medical, and support services for AIDS victims. Information about AIDS prevention shall be solicited by the director from the State Department of Health Services, the county health officer, or local agencies providing services to persons with AIDS. The Director of Health Services, or his or her designee, shall approve protocols pertaining to the information to be disseminated, and the training to be provided, under this section. *(Added by Stats 1988 ch 1301 §3, eff. 1/1/89.)*

§1124. Sale of goods or services; primary purpose of instruction.

Each institution under this chapter may manufacture, repair, and assemble products or may raise produce, for use in the institution or in any other State institution or for sale to or pursuant to contract with the public. The primary purpose of all instruction, discipline and industries shall be to benefit the inmates of the several schools and to qualify them for honorable employment and good citizenship. Moneys received from sales or contracts made or entered into under this section shall be used first to defray the expenses of the industry, including wages paid to the wards working in the industry. The wages shall be set by the director. Moneys in excess of those used to support the industry shall be deposited in the "Benefit Fund" as defined in Section 1752.5.

§1125. Inmate's retention of items of his own handiwork.

Each inmate of an institution under this chapter shall be permitted to keep for his own use all articles of handiwork and other finished products suitable primarily for personal use, as determined by the director, which have been fabricated by the inmate.

§1125.5. Maintenance by inmates of access roads.

When any public road is a principal means of access to the Preston School of Industry the Department of the Youth Authority, with the consent of the Department of Finance, may arrange with the California Highway Commission or the board of supervisors of the county in which the road is located for the employment of the inmates of the school in the improvement or maintenance of the road, under supervision of the officers of the school and without compensation to the inmates so employed.

ARTICLE 7

ESCAPES

§1152. Criminality of aiding escape.

(a) Any person who without the use of force or violence willfully assists any parolee of the Department of the Youth Authority whose parole has been revoked, any escapee, any ward confined to a Department of the Youth Authority institution or facility, or who is being transported to or from that institution or facility, or any person in the lawful custody of any officer or person to escape or in an attempt to escape from a Department of the Youth Authority institution or facility, or custody, is guilty of a misdemeanor.

(b) Any person who with the use of force or violence willfully assists any parolee of the Department of the

Youth Authority whose parole has been revoked, any escapee, any ward confined to a Department of the Youth Authority institution or facility, or who is being transported to or from that institution or facility, or any person in the lawful custody of any officer or person to escape or in an attempt to escape from a Department of the Youth Authority institution or facility, or custody, is punishable by imprisonment in the state prison for a term of 16 months, two, or three years or in the county jail for a term not exceeding one year. *(Amended by Stats 1991 ch 687 §1, eff. 1/1/92.)*

§1154. Fees and expenses for returning escaped inmates.

Whenever any person who has escaped from any institution or facility under the jurisdiction of the Youth Authority is returned by a sheriff or probation officer, the sheriff or probation officer shall be paid the same fees and expenses as are allowed such officers by law for the transportation of persons to institutions or facilities under the jurisdiction of the Youth Authority.

§1155. Notification of police of escaped minor.

The person in charge of any secure detention facility, including, but not limited to, a prison, a juvenile hall, a county jail, or any institution under the jurisdiction of the California Youth Authority, shall promptly notify the chief of police of the city in which the facility is located, or the sheriff of the county if the facility is located in an unincorporated area, of an escape by a person in its custody. The person in charge of any secure detention facility under the jurisdiction of the Department of Corrections or the Youth Authority shall release the name of, and any descriptive information about, any person who has escaped from custody to other law enforcement agencies or to other persons if the release of the information would be necessary to assist in recapturing the person or would be necessary to protect the public from substantial physical harm. *(Amended by Stats 1986 ch 359 §3.)*

ARTICLE 8

PAROLES AND DISMISSALS

§1176. Grant of parole.

When, in the opinion of the Youthful Offender Parole Board, any person committed to or confined in any such school deserves parole according to regulations established for the purpose, and it will be to his or her advantage to be paroled, the board may grant parole under such conditions as it deems best. A reputable home or place of employment shall be provided for each person so paroled.

§1177. Honorable discharge.

When any person so paroled has proved his or her ability for honorable self-support, the Youthful Offender Parole Board shall give him or her honorable discharge. Any person on parole who violates the conditions of his or her parole may be returned to the Youth Authority.

§1178. Grant of honorable discharge and recording of reasons.

The Youthful Offender Parole Board may grant honorable discharge to any person committed to or confined in any such school. The reason for such discharge shall be entered in the records.

© 1992 by J., B. & L. Gould
Printed in the U.S.A.   **EP**

§1179. Release of honorably discharged persons carries release from all penalties; person ineligible to become peace officer.

(a) All persons honorably discharged from control of the Youthful Offender Parole Board shall thereafter be released from all penalties or disabilities resulting from the offenses for which they were committed, including, but not limited to, any disqualification for any employment or occupational license, or both, created by any other provision of law. However, such a person shall not be eligible for appointment as a peace officer employed by any public agency if his or her appointment would otherwise be prohibited by Section 1029 of the Government Code.

(b) Notwithstanding the provisions of subdivision (a), such a person may be appointed and employed as a peace officer by the Department of the Youth Authority if (1) at least five years have passed since his or her honorable discharge, and the person has had no misdemeanor or felony convictions except for traffic misdemeanors since he or she was honorably discharged by the Youthful Offender Parole Board, or (2) the person was employed as a peace officer by the Department of the Youth Authority on or before January 1, 1983. No person who is under the jurisdiction of the Department of the Youth Authority shall be admitted to an examination for a peace officer position with the department unless and until the person has been honorably discharged from the jurisdiction of the department by the Youthful Offender Parole Board.

(c) Upon the final discharge or dismissal of any such person, the Youth Authority shall immediately certify the discharge or dismissal in writing, and shall transmit the certificate to the court by which the person was committed. The court shall thereupon dismiss the accusation and the action pending against that person.

§1180. Providing information about parolees to police.

The Department of the Youth Authority shall provide, within 10 days, upon request to the chief of police of a city or the sheriff of a county information available to the department, including actual, glossy photographs, no smaller than 3⅛ x 3⅛ inches in size, and, in conjunction with the Department of Justice, fingerprints concerning persons then on parole who are or may be residing or temporarily domiciled in that city or county. *(Amended by Stats 1986 ch 600 §6.)*

ARTICLE 9

FINANCES

§1200. Payment of duly appropriated funds to State Controller.

The Controller of the State shall, on requisition of any of the institutions under this chapter, duly audited by him, draw his warrant on the State Treasurer for any moneys duly appropriated to pay for the necessary expenditures in the establishment and maintenance of such school, and the State Treasurer shall pay the same from the appropriations provided therefor.

§1201. Payments to be made by committed person's home county.

For each person committed to any state school the county from which he was committed shall make

payments to the state as provided in Section 911 of this code.

ARTICLE 10

THE CALIFORNIA YOUTH TRAINING SCHOOL

§1250. Establishment of California Youth Training School.

There is hereby established an institution for the confinement of males under the custody of the Director of Corrections and the Youth Authority to be known as the Herman G. Stark Youth Training School. *(Amended by Stats 1989 ch 555 §1, eff. 1/1/90.)*

§1251. Purpose of youth training center.

The Herman G. Stark Youth Training School shall be an intermediate security type institution. Its primary purpose shall be to provide custody, care, industrial, vocational and other training, guidance and reformatory help for young men, too mature to be benefited by the programs of correctional schools for juveniles and too immature in crime for confinement in prisons. *(Amended by Stats 1989 ch 555 §2, eff. 1/1/90.)*

§1252. Who may be confined in youth training school.

There may be transferred to and confined in the Herman G. Stark Youth Training School any male subject to the custody, control and discipline of the Youth Authority, whom the Youth Authority believes will be benefited by confinement in such an institution. Whenever by reason of any law governing the commitment of a person to the Youth Authority or to an institution under the jurisdiction of the Youth Authority such a person is deemed not to be a person convicted of a crime, the transfer or placement of such a person in the Herman G. Stark Youth Training School shall not affect the status or rights of the person and shall not be deemed to constitute a conviction of a crime. *(Amended by Stats 1989 ch 555 §3, eff. 1/1/90.)*

§1253. Rules and regulations for Youth Training School.

The Youth Authority shall make rules and regulations for the government of the Herman G. Stark Youth Training School and the management of its affairs. *(Amended by Stats 1989 ch 555 §4, eff. 1/1/90.)*

§1254. Appointment of superintendent and staff.

The Youth Authority shall appoint, subject to civil service, a superintendent for the Herman G. Stark Youth Training School, and such officers and employees as may be necessary, and shall fix their compensation. *(Amended by Stats 1989 ch 555 §5, eff. 1/1/90.)*

§1255. Construction of school facility.

The Youth Authority shall construct and equip, in accordance with law, suitable buildings, structures, and facilities for the Herman G. Stark Youth Training School. *(Amended by Stats 1989 ch 555 §6, eff. 1/1/90.)*

§1256. Youth Authority's powers and duties regarding school.

The Youth Authority shall have the same powers, duties, and responsibilities in respect to the Herman G. Stark Youth Training School and the persons confined therein that the Youth Authority has in respect to institutions established for persons committed to the Youth Authority under Division 2.5 of this code and in respect to such persons, except that the Youth Authority shall have no power to parole, discharge, grant leave of absence to, or otherwise release from the Herman G. Stark Youth Training School any person under the custody of the Director of Corrections and transferred to and confined in the Herman G. Stark Youth Training School, or to transfer any such person from the Herman G. Stark Youth Training School to any other institution whatever, except to return him to the custody of the Director of Corrections.

Except as otherwise provided in this article, the provisions of Part 3 of the Penal Code continue to apply to all persons in the custody of the Director of Corrections who are transferred by the Adult Authority to the Herman G. Stark Youth Training School, so far as such provisions may be applicable. (*Amended by Stats 1989 ch 555 §7, eff. 1/1/90.*)

§1258. Construction for sale of moveable houses by inmates.

The Director of the Youth Authority, in connection with industrial training at the Herman G. Stark Youth Training School, Chino, California, may provide suitable materials and facilities for use by persons confined in the school in the construction of houses which can be moved which, upon their completion, shall be sold to the public upon competitive bids. Proceeds derived from the sale of any such house shall be deposited in the General Fund. Construction shall be limited to not more than one each calendar year and the size shall not exceed one thousand two hundred fifty (1,250) square feet. (*Amended by Stats 1989 ch 555 §8, eff. 1/1/90.*)

CHAPTER 4

INTERSTATE COMPACT ON JUVENILES

§1300.3. Out-of-state Confinement Amendment.

The Out-of-state Confinement Amendment to the Interstate Compact on Juveniles is hereby enacted into law and entered into by this state with all other states legally joining therein in the law substantially as follows:

(a) Whenever the duly constituted judicial or administrative authorities in a sending state shall determine that confinement of a probationer or reconfinement of a parolee is necessary or desirable, said officials may direct that the confinement or reconfinement be in an appropriate institution for delinquent juveniles within the territory of the receiving state, such receiving state to act in that regard solely as agent for the sending state.

(b) Escapees and absconders who would otherwise be returned pursuant to Article V of the compact may be confined or reconfined in the receiving state pursuant to this amendment. In any such case the information and allegations required to be made and furnished in a requisition pursuant to such article shall be made and furnished, but in place of the demand pursuant to Article V, the sending state shall request confinement or reconfinement in the receiving state. Whenever applicable, detention orders as provided in Article V may be employed pursuant to this paragraph preliminary to disposition of the escapee or absconder.

(c) The confinement or reconfinement of a parolee, probationer, escapee, or absconder pursuant to this amendment shall require the concurrence of the appropriate judicial or administrative authorities of the receiving state.

(d) As used in this amendment: (1) "sending state" means sending state as that term is used in Article VII of the compact or the state from which a delinquent juvenile has escaped or absconded within the meaning of Article V of the compact; (2) "receiving state" means any state, other than the sending state, in which a parolee, probationer, escapee, or absconder may be found, provided that said state is a party to this amendment.

(e) Every state which adopts this amendment shall designate at least one of its institutions for delinquent juveniles as a "compact institution" and shall confine persons therein as provided in paragraph (a) hereof unless the sending and receiving state in question shall make specific contractual arrangements to the contrary. All states party to this amendment shall have access to "compact institutions" at all reasonable hours for the purpose of inspecting the facilities thereof and for the purpose of visiting such of said state's delinquents as may be confined in the institution.

(f) Persons confined in "compact institutions" pursuant to the terms of this compact shall at all times be subject to the jurisdiction of the sending state and may at any time be removed from said "compact institution" for transfer to an appropriate institution within the sending state, for return to probation or parole, for discharge, or for any purpose permitted by the laws of the sending state.

(g) All persons who may be confined in a "compact institution" pursuant to the provisions of this amendment shall be treated in a reasonable and humane manner. The fact of confinement or reconfinement in a receiving state shall not deprive any person so confined or reconfined of any rights which said person would have had if confined or reconfined in an appropriate institution of the sending state; nor shall any agreement to submit to confinement or reconfinement pursuant to the terms of this amendment be construed as a waiver of any right which the delinquent would have had if he had been confined or reconfined in any appropriate institution of the sending state except that the hearing or hearings, if any, to which a parolee, probationer, escapee, or absconder may be entitled (prior to confinement or reconfinement) by the laws of the sending state may be had before the appropriate judicial or administrative officers of the receiving state. In this event, said judicial and administrative officers shall act as agents of the sending state after consultation with appropriate officers of the sending state.

(h) Any receiving state incurring costs or other expenses under this amendment shall be reimbursed in the amount of such costs or other expenses by the sending state unless the states concerned shall specifically otherwise agree. Any two or more states party to this amendment may enter into supplementary agreements determining a different allocation of costs as among themselves.

© 1992 by J., B. & L. Gould
Printed in the U.S.A. **EP**

(i) This amendment shall take initial effect when entered into by any two or more states party to the compact and shall be effective as to those states which have specifically enacted this amendment.

Rules and regulations necessary to effectuate the terms of this amendment may be promulgated by the appropriate officers of those states which have enacted this amendment.

§1300.4. Rendition Amendment to the Interstate Compact on Juveniles.

The Rendition Amendment to the Interstate Compact on Juveniles is hereby enacted into law and entered into by this state with all other states legally joining therein in the law substantially as follows:

(a) This amendment shall provide additional remedies and shall be binding only as among and between those party states which specifically execute the same.

(b) All provisions and procedures of Article V and VI of the Interstate Compact on Juveniles shall be construed to apply to any juvenile charged with being a delinquent by reason of a violation of any criminal law. Any juvenile, charged with being a delinquent by reason of violating any criminal law, shall be returned to the requesting state upon a requisition to the state where the juvenile may be found. A petition in such case shall be filed in a court of competent jurisdiction in the requesting state where the violation of criminal law is alleged to have been committed. The petition may be filed regardless of whether the juvenile has left the state before or after the filing of the petition. The requisition described in Article V of the compact shall be forwarded by the judge of the court in which the petition has been filed. *(Added by Stats 1988 ch 608 §1, eff. 1/1/89.)*

§1300.5. Confinement of juvenile in compact institution in another party state.

In addition to any institution in which the authorities of this state may otherwise confine or order the confinement of a delinquent juvenile, such authorities may, pursuant to the Out-of-state Confinement Amendment to the Interstate Compact on Juveniles, confine or order the confinement of a delinquent juvenile in a compact institution within another party state.

§1302. Cooperation to facilitate proper administration of compact.

The compact administrator shall cooperate with all departments, agencies and officers of this State and its subdivisions in facilitating the proper administration of the compact or of any supplementary agreement or agreements entered into by this State thereunder.

§1305. Payment of fee to counsel.

Any judge who appoints counsel or a guardian ad litem pursuant to the provisions of the compact may fix a fee in a reasonable amount, to be paid out of funds available for disposition by the court.

§1306. Enforcement of compact.

The courts, departments, agencies, and officers of this State and its subdivisions shall enforce this compact and shall do all things appropriate to the effectuation of its purposes and intent which may be within their respective jurisdictions.

§1307. Delinquent juvenile defined.

The term "delinquent juvenile" as used in the Interstate Compact on Juveniles shall include those persons subject to the jurisdiction of the juvenile court within the meaning of Section 602 of this code.

DIVISION 2.5

YOUTHS

CHAPTER 1

THE YOUTH AUTHORITY

ARTICLE 1

GENERAL PROVISIONS AND DEFINITIONS

§1706. Research of administration of vitamins, minerals and amino acids; analysis of hair and blood.

(a) Notwithstanding Section 3502 of the Penal Code, research involving the administration of vitamins, minerals, and amino acids to wards and involving analysis of the subject's hair and blood may be conducted provided that the following conditions exist:

(1) The Department of the Youth Authority approves the research after making a determination pursuant to Section 3515 of the Penal Code.

(2) The research subjects have given informed consent under Section 3521 of the Penal Code.

(3) The substances administered in the research are limited to those which are approved by the federal Food and Drug Administration and which do not require a physician's prescription.

(4) The substances are administered only within three times the Recommended Dietary Allowance established by the National Research Council in effect on the effective date of this act under the supervision of a physician.

(5) The withdrawal of blood shall be performed only before commencement and following the conclusion of the research and shall be withdrawn in a medically approved manner. Only a physician, registered nurse, licensed vocational nurse, licensed medical technician, or licensed phlebotomist may withdraw blood specimens for the purposes of this section.

(b) Protocols for the research conducted under this section, and its implementation, shall be subject to review and approval by a research oversight committee. Membership of the committee shall include at least two physicians not employed or on contract to the Department of the Youth Authority or the Department of Corrections, the Chief of Medical Services of the Department of the Youth Authority, a representative from the State Department of Health Services, at least two persons with extensive background in research competent to critique the proposal outlined in this section and assist in its implementation, and a person representing the wards to be selected by the State Public Defender's Office.

(c) As used in this section, "ward" means persons who are committed to the Department of the Youth Authority who are 18 years of age or older.

(d) The Department of the Youth Authority shall not conduct any investigation under this section of a new drug, as defined in Section 201 of the federal Food,

Drug and Cosmetic Act (21 U.S.C. Sec. 321) without approval from the federal Food and Drug Administration.

(e) This section shall remain in effect only until January 1, 1995, and as of that date is repealed, unless a later enacted statute, which becomes effective on or before January 1, 1995, deletes or extends that date. *(Added by Stats 1989 ch 1367 §2, eff. 10/2/89 only until 1/1/95.)*

ARTICLE 2

DEPARTMENT OF THE YOUTH AUTHORITY

§1710. Creation of Department of the Youth Authority.

There is in the Youth and Adult Correctional Agency a Department of the Youth Authority.

§1711. Creation of office of Director of Youth Authority.

The Director of the Youth Authority shall be appointed by the Governor with the advice and consent of the Senate. He or she shall hold office at the pleasure of the Governor but before the director may be removed, the procedures set forth in Section 5051 of the Penal Code shall be followed. He or she shall receive an annual salary provided for by Chapter 6 (commencing with Section 11550) of Part 1 of Division 3 of Title 2 of the Government Code, and shall devote his or her entire time to the duties of his or her office.

§1712. Authorities and duties of Director.

(a) All powers, duties, and functions pertaining to the care and treatment of wards provided by any provision of law and not specifically and expressly assigned to the Youthful Offender Parole Board shall be exercised and performed by the director. The director shall be the appointing authority for all civil service positions of employment in the department. The director may delegate the powers and duties vested in him or her by law, in accordance with Section 7.

(b) The director is authorized to make and enforce all rules appropriate to the proper accomplishment of the functions of the Department of the Youth Authority. Such rules shall be promulgated and filed pursuant to Chapter 4.5 (commencing with Section 11371) of Part 1 of Division 3 of Title 2 of the Government Code, and shall, to the extent practical, be stated in language that is easily understood by the general public.

(c) The Department of the Youth Authority shall maintain, publish, and make available to the general public, a compendium of rules and regulations promulgated by the department pursuant to this section.

(d) The following exceptions to the procedures specified in this section shall apply to the Department of the Youth Authority:

(1) The department may specify an effective date that is any time more than 30 days after the rule or regulation is filed with the Secretary of State; provided that no less than 20 days prior to such effective date, copies of the rule or regulation shall be posted in conspicuous places throughout each institution and shall be mailed to all persons or organizations who request them.

(2) The department may rely upon a summary of the information compiled by a hearing officer; pro-

vided that the summary and the testimony taken regarding the proposed action shall be retained as part of the public record for at least one year after the adoption, amendment, or repeal.

§1713. Qualifications and hiring of Director.

(a) The Director of the Youth Authority shall have wide and successful administrative experience in youth or adult correctional programs embodying rehabilitative or delinquency prevention concepts.

(b) The Governor may request the State Personnel Board to use extensive recruitment and merit selection techniques and procedures to provide a list of persons qualified for appointment as Director of the Youth Authority. The Governor may appoint any person from such list of qualified persons or may reject all names and appoint another person who meets the requirements of this section.

§1714. Cooperation between Board and Director.

(a) It is the intention of the Legislature that the Youthful Offender Parole Board and the Director of the Youth Authority shall cooperate with each other in the establishment of the classification, transfer, discipline, training, and treatment policies of the Department of the Youth Authority, to the end that the objectives of the state youth correctional system can best be attained. The director and the board shall, not less than four times each calendar year, meet for the purpose of discussion of classification, transfer, discipline, training, and treatment policies and problems, and for the purpose of discussion of policies relating to the functions and duties of the board, and it is the intent of the Legislature that whenever possible there shall be agreement on these subjects; however in order to maintain responsibility for the secure and orderly administration of the Youth Authority, the Director of the Youth Authority shall have the final right to determine the policies on classification, transfer, discipline, training and treatment, and the board shall have the final right to determine the policies on its duties and functions.

(b) The Director of the Youth Authority may transfer persons confined in one institution or facility of the Department of the Youth Authority to another. The Youthful Offender Parole Board may request the director to transfer a person who is under the jurisdiction of the department pursuant to Section 1731.5 if, after review of the case history in the course of routine procedures, such transfer is deemed advisable for the further diagnosis and treatment of the ward. The director shall as soon as practicable comply with such request, provided that, if facilities are not available he or she shall report that fact to the board and shall make the transfer as soon as facilities become available; provided further, that if in the opinion of the director such transfer would endanger security he or she may report that fact to the board and refuse to make such transfer.

§1715. Reimbursement of radiologic technologists.

From funds available for the support of the Youth Authority, the director may reimburse persons employed by the authority and certified as radiologic technologists pursuant to Chapter 7.4 (commencing with Section 25660) of Division 20 of the Health and Safety Code for the fees incurred both in connection

© 1992 by J., B. & L. Gould
Printed in the U.S.A. **EP**

with the obtaining of such certification since July 1, 1971, and with regard to the renewal thereof.

ARTICLE 2.5

YOUTHFUL OFFENDER PAROLE BOARD

§1716. Youthful Offender Parole Board.

(a) There is in the Youth and Adult Correctional Agency a Youthful Offender Parole Board, which shall be composed of seven members, each of whom shall be appointed by the Governor, with the advice and consent of the Senate, for a term of four years and until the appointment and qualification of his or her successor, and who shall devote their entire time to its work.

(b) The individuals who were members of the Youth Authority Board immediately prior to the effective date of this section, other than the individual who was Director of the Department of the Youth Authority and Chairman of the Youth Authority Board, shall continue in their respective terms of office as members of the Youthful Offender Parole Board. The term of the member appointed to the term commencing March 15, 1976 shall expire March 15, 1980. The terms of the two members appointed to the terms commencing March 15, 1977 shall expire March 15, 1981. The terms of the two members appointed to the terms commencing March 15, 1978 shall expire March 15, 1982. The terms of the two members appointed to the terms commencing March 15, 1979 shall expire March 15, 1983. The members shall be eligible for reappointment and shall hold office until the appointment and qualification of their successors, with the term of each new appointee to commence on the expiration date of the term of his or her predecessor.

(c) All appointments to a vacancy occurring by reason of any cause other than the expiration of a term shall be for the unexpired term. Each member shall hold office until the appointment and qualification of his or her successor.

(d) If the Senate, in lieu of failing to confirm, finds that it cannot consider all or any of the appointments to the Youthful Offender Parole Board adequately because the amount of legislative business and the probable duration of the session does not permit, it may adopt a single house resolution by a majority vote of all members elected to the Senate to that effect and requesting the resubmission of the unconfirmed appointment or appointments at a succeeding session of the Legislature, whether regular or extraordinary, convening on or after a date fixed in the resolution. This resolution shall be filed immediately after its adoption in the office of the Secretary of State and the appointee or appointees affected shall serve subject to later confirmation or rejection by the Senate.

§1717. Members of Youthful Offender Parole Board.

(a) Persons appointed to the Youthful Offender Parole Board shall have a broad background in and ability for appraisal of youthful law offenders and delinquents, the circumstances of delinquency for which committed, and the evaluation of the individual's progress toward reformation. Insofar as practicable, members shall be selected who have a varied and sympathetic interest in youth correction work including persons widely experienced in the fields of corrections, sociology, law, law enforcement, and education.

(b) The selection of persons and their appointment by the Governor and confirmation by the Senate shall reflect as nearly as possible a cross section of the racial, sexual, economic, and geographic features of the state.

(c) One member of the board shall be designated as chairman by the Governor. The chairman shall be the administrative head of the board and shall exercise all duties and functions necessary to insure that the responsibilities of the board are successfully discharged. He or she shall be the appointing authority for all civil service positions of employment in the board.

§1718. Payment of Chairman and members of the board.

(a) The Chairman and members of the board shall receive an annual salary as provided for by Chapter 6 (commencing with Section 11550) of Part 1 of Division 3 of Title 2 of the Government Code and their actual necessary traveling expenses to the same extent as is provided for other state offices.

(b) The Governor may remove any member of the board for misconduct, incompetency or neglect of duty after a full hearing by the Board of Corrections.

§1719. Powers and duties of Youthful Offender Parole Board.

The following powers and duties shall be exercised and performed by the Youthful Offender Parole Board as such, or may be delegated to a panel, member, or case hearing representative as provided in Section 1721: return of persons to the court of commitment for redisposition by the court, discharge of commitment, orders to parole and conditions thereof, revocation or suspension of parole, recommendation for treatment program, determination of the date of next appearance, return of nonresident persons to the jurisdiction of the state of legal residence.

§1720. Review of cases by board.

(a) The case of each ward shall be heard by the board immediately after the case study of the ward has been completed and at such other times as is necessary to exercise the powers or duties of the board.

(b) The board shall periodically review the case of each ward for the purpose of determining whether existing orders and dispositions in individual cases should be modified or continued in force. These reviews shall be made as frequently as the board considers desirable and shall be made with respect to each ward at intervals not exceeding one year.

(c) The ward shall be entitled to notice if his or her annual review hearing is delayed beyond one year after the previous annual review hearing. The ward shall be informed of the reason for the delay and of the date the review hearing is to be held.

(d) Failure of the board to review the case of a ward within 15 months of a previous review shall not of itself entitle the ward to discharge from the control of the Youth Authority but shall entitle him or her to petition the superior court of the county from which he or she was committed for an order of discharge, and the court shall discharge him or her unless the court is satisfied as to the need for further control.

§1721. Policies of the board.

(a) The Youthful Offender Parole Board shall adopt policies governing the performance of its functions by the full board, or, pursuant to delegation, by panels, or referees. Whenever the board performs its functions meeting en banc in either public or executive sessions to decide matters of policy, at least four members shall be present and no such action shall be valid unless it is concurred in by a majority vote of those present.

(b) Case hearing representatives may be employed to participate with the board in the hearing of cases and to whom authority may be delegated as provided in this section.

(c) The board may delegate its authority to hear, consider, and act upon cases to members or case hearing representatives, sitting either on a panel or as a referee. A panel may consist of two or more members, a member and a case hearing representative, or two case hearing representatives. Two members of a panel shall constitute a quorum, and no action of the panel shall be valid unless concurred in by a majority vote of those present.

(d) When delegating its authority, the board may condition finality of the decision of the panel or referee to whom authority is delegated on concurrence of a member or members of the board. In determining whether, in any case, it shall delegate its authority and the extent of such delegation, the board shall take into account the degree of complexity of the issues presented by the case.

(e) The board shall adopt rules under which a person under the jurisdiction of the Youth Authority or other persons, as specified in such rules, may appeal any decision of a case hearing representative. The board shall consider and act upon the appeal in accordance with such rules.

§1722. Rules and regulations.

(a) Any rules and regulations, including any resolutions and policy statements, promulgated by the Youthful Offender Parole Board, shall be promulgated and filed pursuant to Chapter 3.5 (commencing with Section 11340) of Part 1 of Division 3 of Title 2 of the Government Code, and shall, to the extent practical, be stated in language that is easily understood by the general public.

(b) The board shall maintain, publish, and make available to the general public, a compendium of its rules and regulations, including any resolutions and policy statements, promulgated pursuant to this section.

(c) The following exception to the procedures specified in this section shall apply to the board: The chairperson may specify an effective date that is any time more than 30 days after the rule or regulation is filed with the Secretary of State; provided that no less than 20 days prior to that effective date, copies of the rule or regulation shall be posted in conspicuous places throughout each institution and shall be mailed to all persons or organizations who request them.

§1723. Authority to grant parole; delegation of other authority.

(a) Except as provided in Section 1721, every order granting and revoking parole and issuing final discharges to any person under the jurisdiction of the Youth Authority shall be made by the Youthful Offender Parole Board and the board may not delegate the making of such decisions to any other body or person.

(b) All other powers conferred to the Youthful Offender Parole Board may be exercised through subordinates or delegated to the Department of the Youth Authority under rules established by the board. Any person subjected to an order of such subordinates or of the department pursuant to such delegation may petition the board for review. The board may review such orders under appropriate rules and regulations.

§1724. Board's limitations in expenditures.

The Youthful Offender Parole Board is limited in its expenditures to funds specifically made available for its use.

§1725. Youth Authority Board abolished.

The Youthful Offender Parole Board shall succeed to and shall exercise and perform all powers and duties granted to, exercised by, and imposed upon the Youth Authority Board. The Youth Authority Board is abolished.

§1726. Employees of Youthful Offender Parole Board.

(a) Such employees of the Youthful Offender Parole Board as are needed to carry out its functions shall be selected and appointed pursuant to the State Civil Service Act.

(b) All officers and employees of the Department of the Youth Authority who on the effective date of this section are serving in the state civil service, other than as temporary employees, as part of the direct staff of the Youth Authority Board, including, but not limited to, those officers and employees performing the functions of administrative officer, case hearing representative, and case hearing coordinator, shall be transferred to the Youthful Offender Parole Board. The status, positions, and rights of such persons shall not be affected by the transfer and shall be retained by them as officers and employees of the Youthful Offender Parole Board pursuant to the State Civil Service Act.

§1727. Authority of Chairman to issue subpoenas.

The Chairman of the Youthful Offender Parole Board shall have the authority of a head of a department set forth in subdivision (e) of Section 11181 of the Government Code to issue subpoenas as provided in Article 2 (commencing with Section 11180) of Chapter 2 of Division 3 of Title 2 of the Government Code. The board shall adopt regulations on the policies and guidelines for the issuance of subpoenas.

ARTICLE 3

COMMITMENTS TO YOUTH AUTHORITY

§1730. Certification of approval to Governor.

(a) No person may be committed to the Authority until the Authority has certified in writing to the Governor that it has approved or established places of preliminary detention and places for examination and study of persons committed, and has other facilities and personnel sufficient for the proper discharge of its duties and functions.

(b) Before certification to the Governor as provided in subsection (a), a court shall, upon conviction of a person under 21 years of age at the time of his apprehension, deal with him without regard to the provisions of this chapter.

© 1992 by J., B. & L. Gould
Printed in the U.S.A.   EP

§1731. Determine age.

When in any criminal proceeding in a court of this State a person has been convicted of a public offense for which the court has power under this chapter to commit to the Authority, the court shall determine whether the person was less than 21 years of age at the time of the apprehension from which the criminal proceeding resulted. Proceedings in a juvenile court in respect to a juvenile are not criminal proceedings as that phrase is used in this chapter.

§1731.5. Commitment to Authority; qualifications.

(a) After certification to the Governor as provided in this article, a court may commit to the authority any person convicted of a public offense who comes within paragraphs (1), (2), and (3), or paragraphs (1), (2), and (4), below:

(1) Is found to be less than 21 years of age at the time of apprehension.

(2) Is not convicted of first degree murder, committed when that person was 18 years of age or older, or sentenced to death, imprisonment for life, imprisonment for 90 days or less, or the payment of a fine, or after having been directed to pay a fine, defaults in the payment thereof, and is subject to imprisonment for more than 90 days under the judgment.

(3) Is not granted probation.

(4) Was granted probation and probation is revoked and terminated.

(b) The Youth Authority shall accept a person committed to it pursuant to this article if it believes that the person can be materially benefited by its reformatory and educational discipline, and if it has adequate facilities to provide that care.

(c) Any person under the age of 21 years who is not committed to the authority pursuant to this section may be transferred to the authority by the Director of Corrections with the approval of the Director of the Youth Authority. In sentencing a person under the age of 21 years, the court may order that the person shall be transferred to the custody of the Youth Authority pursuant to this subdivision. When the court makes such an order and the Youth Authority fails to accept custody of the person, the person shall be returned to court for resentencing. The transfer shall be solely for the purposes of housing the inmate, allowing participation in the programs available at the institution by the inmate, and allowing Youth Authority parole supervision of the inmate, who, in all other aspects shall be deemed to be committed to the Department of Corrections and shall remain subject to the jurisdiction of the Director of Corrections and the Board of Prison Terms. Notwithstanding subdivision (b) of Section 2900 of the Penal Code, the Director of the Department of Corrections, with the concurrence of the Director of the Youth Authority, may designate a facility under the jurisdiction of the Director of the Youth Authority as a place of reception for any person described in this subdivision.

The Director of the Youth Authority shall have the same powers with respect to an inmate transferred pursuant to this subdivision as if the inmate had been committed or transferred to the Youth Authority either under the Arnold-Kennick Juvenile Court Law or subdivision (a).

The duration of the transfer shall extend until the Director of the Youth Authority orders the inmate returned to the Department of Corrections, the inmate is ordered discharged by the Board of Prison Terms, or the inmate reaches the age of 25 years, whichever first occurs. *(Amended by Stats 1987 ch 354 §1.)*

§1731.6. Temporary placement; observation; acceptance.

(a) In any county in which there is in effect a contract made pursuant to Section 1752.1, if a court has determined that a person comes within the provisions of Section 1731.5 and concludes that a proper disposition of the case requires such observation and diagnosis as can be made at a diagnostic and treatment center of the Youth Authority, the court may continue the hearing and order that such person be placed temporarily in such a center for a period not to exceed 90 days, with the further provision in such order that the Director of the Youth Authority report to the court its diagnosis and recommendations concerning the person within the 90-day period.

(b) The Director of the Youth Authority shall, within the 90 days, cause the person to be observed and examined and shall forward to the court his diagnosis and recommendation concerning such person's future care, supervision, and treatment.

(c) The Youth Authority shall accept such person if it believes that the person can be materially benefited by such diagnostic and treatment services and if the Director of the Youth Authority certifies that staff and institutions are available. No such person shall be transported to any facility under the jurisdiction of the Youth Authority until the director has notified the referring court of the place to which such person is to be transported and the time at which he can be received.

(d) Notwithstanding the provisions of subdivision (c), the Youth Authority shall accept without cost to the county any persons remanded pursuant to Section 707.2.

(e) The sheriff of the county in which an order is made placing a person in a diagnostic and treatment center pursuant to this section, or any other peace officer designated by the court, shall execute the order placing such person in the center or returning him therefrom to the court. The expense of such sheriff or other peace officer incurred in executing such order is a charge upon the county in which the court is situated.

§1732. Prohibit commitment to Authority of 18-year-old sex offender.

No person convicted of violating Section 261, Section 264.1, subdivision (b) of Section 288, Section 289, or of sodomy or oral copulation by force, violence, duress, menace or threat of great bodily harm as provided in Section 286 or 288a of the Penal Code committed when that person was 18 years of age who has previously been convicted of any such felony shall be committed to the Youth Authority. This section does not prohibit the adjournment of criminal proceedings pursuant to Division 3 (commencing with Section 3000) or Division 6 (commencing with Section 6000) of the Welfare and Institutions Code. *(Amended by Stats 1989 ch 555 §9, eff. 1/1/90.)*

§1732.4. *Repealed by Stats 1991 ch 721 §2, eff. 1/1/92.*

§1732.5. No commitment to Authority for serious felony.

Notwithstanding any other provision of law, no person convicted of murder, rape or any other serious felony, as defined in Section 1192.7 of the Penal Code, committed when he or she was 18 years of age or older shall be committed to Youth Authority.

The provisions of this section shall not be amended by the Legislature except by statute passed in each house by rollcall vote entered in the journal, two-thirds of the membership concurring, or by a statute that becomes effective only when approved by the electors.

§1732.7. Commitment for minor offenses.

A person who is convicted of a public offense for which the maximum penalty provided by law is imprisonment for not more than 90 days, and who is found to be less than 21 years of age at the time of his apprehension, may be committed to the Authority only if it is brought to the court's knowledge that the person has been previously convicted of a public offense or has been a ward of the juvenile court by reason of a public offense and the court is satisfied that society will best be protected by commitment to the Authority.

§1733. License revoked or suspended.

Nothing in this chapter prevents a court from revoking or suspending any license issued to the defendant under any law of this State where such revocation or suspension is otherwise provided for.

§1735. Confinement for unpaid fine.

If the court sentences a person under 21 years of age at the time of his apprehension to the payment of a fine and the fine is not paid, the court may either remit the fine in whole or in part, or commit him to confinement for a length of time permitted by the statutes relating to imprisonment for failure to pay fines. But such confinement may be only in a place approved by the Authority.

§1736. Juvenile court; commitment to Authority.

The juvenile court may in its discretion commit persons subject to its jurisdiction to the Authority, and the Authority may in its discretion accept such commitments.

§1737. Recall commitment; resentence.

When a person has been committed to the custody of the authority, if it is deemed warranted by a diagnostic study and recommendation approved by the director, the judge who ordered the commitment or, if the judge is not available, the presiding or sole judge of the court, within 120 days of the date of commitment on his or her own motion, or the court, at any time thereafter upon recommendation of the director, may recall the commitment previously ordered and resentence the person as if he or she had not previously been sentenced. The time served while in custody of the authority shall be credited toward the term of any person resentenced pursuant to this section.

As used in this section, "time served while in custody of the authority" means the period of time during which the person was physically confined in a state institution by order of the Youth Authority or the Youthful Offender Parole Board.

§1737.1. Convict's return to committing court.

Whenever any person who has been convicted of a public offense in adult court and committed to and accepted by the Youth Authority appears to the Youth-ful Offender Parole Board, either at the time of his or her first appearance before the board or thereafter, to be an improper person to be retained by the Youth Authority, or to be so incorrigible or so incapable of reformation under the discipline of the Youth Authority as to render his or her detention detrimental to the interests of the Youth Authority and the other persons committed thereto, the board may order the return of such a person to the committing court. The court may then commit the person to a state prison or sentence him or her to a county jail as provided by law for punishment of the offense of which he or she was convicted. The maximum term of imprisonment for a person committed to a state prison under this section shall be a period equal to the maximum term prescribed by law for the offense of which he or she was convicted less the period during which he or she was under the control of the Youth Authority. This section shall not apply to commitments from juvenile court.

As used in this section "period during which he or she was under the control of the Youth Authority" means the period of time during which he or she was physically confined in a state institution by order of the Youth Authority or Youthful Offender Parole Board.

§1737.5. Effect of commitment to Authority.

A commitment to the Authority is a judgment within the meaning of Chapter 1 of Title 8 of Part 2 of the Penal Code, and is appealable.

§1738. Disposition after commitment.

When the court commits a person to the authority the court may order him conveyed to some place of detention approved or established by the authority or may direct that he be left at liberty until otherwise ordered by the authority under such conditions as in the court's opinion will insure his submission to any orders which the authority may issue. No such person shall be transported to any facility under the jurisdiction of the Youth Authority until the director has notified the sheriff of the county of the committing court of the place to which said person is to be transported and the time at which he can be received.

§1739. Right to appeal.

(a) The right of a person who has been convicted of a public offense to a new trial or to an appeal from the judgment of conviction shall not be affected by anything in this chapter.

(b) When a person who has been convicted and committed to the Authority appeals from the conviction, the execution of the commitment to the Authority shall not be stayed by the taking of the appeal except as provided in subsection (c). The person so committed shall remain subject to the control of the Authority, until final disposition of the appeal.

(c) A person convicted and committed to the Authority may be admitted to bail under the provisions of Section 1272 of the Penal Code, or in the discretion of the court, may be left at liberty, under such conditions as in the court's opinion will insure his cooperation in reasonable expedition of the appellate proceedings and his submission to the control of the Authority at the proper time.

§1740. Copy of commitment order to Authority.

When a court commits a person to the Authority such court shall at once forward to the Authority a certified copy of the order of commitment.

© 1992 by J., B. & L. Gould
Printed in the U.S.A.   EP

§1741. Report on case history.

The judge before whom the person was tried and committed, the district attorney or other official who conducted the prosecution, and the probation officer of the county, shall obtain and with the order of commitment furnish to the authority, in writing, all information that can be given in regard to the career, habits, degree of education, age, nationality, parentage and previous occupations of such person, together with a statement to the best of their knowledge as to whether such person was industrious, and of good character, the nature of his associates and his disposition.

The reports required by this section shall be made upon forms furnished by the authority or according to an outline furnished by it.

When a person has been committed to the authority, the court and the prosecuting and police authorities and other public officials shall make available to the authority all pertinent data in their possession in respect to the case.

ARTICLE 4

POWERS AND DUTIES OF YOUTH AUTHORITY

§1752.82. Payment of restitution fine.

Whenever an adult or minor is committed to or housed in a Youth Authority facility and he or she owes restitution to a victim or a restitution fine imposed pursuant to Section 13967 of the Government Code or pursuant to Section 730.6 or 731.1 of this code, the director may deduct a reasonable amount not to exceed 20 percent from the wages of that adult or minor and the amount so deducted, exclusive of the costs of administering this section, which shall be retained by the director, shall be transferred to the State Board of Control for deposit in the Restitution Fund in the State Treasury in the case of a restitution fine, or, in the case of a restitution order, and upon the request of the victim, shall be paid directly to the victim. Any amount so deducted shall be credited against the amount owing on the fine or to the victim. The committing court shall be provided a record of any such payments. *(Amended by Stats 1988 ch 181 §2, eff. 1/1/89.)*

§1752.83. Deduct funds for destruction of public property.

(a) It is the intent of the Legislature that wards of the Youth Authority be held accountable for intentional damage and destruction of public property committed while they are confined in Youth Authority facilities. To that end, and notwithstanding the provisions of Sections 1752.8 and 1752.81, the Youth Authority may deduct from a ward's trust fund any amounts that are necessary to pay for intentional damage to public property caused by the ward while confined within an institution or other facility of the Youth Authority.

(b) The Youth Authority shall utilize the procedures in its regulations for disciplinary actions to determine whether the damage or destruction was intentionally caused by the ward and, if so, to determine the amount to be deducted to pay for the damage or destruction.

(c) Funds that are deducted shall remain with the Youth Authority and shall be used to repair or replace the public property damaged or destroyed as provided for in the Budget Act for that fiscal year. *(Amended*

and renumbered by Stats 1986 ch 248 §248; formerly §1752.82.)

§1752.85. Funds from sale of articles of handiwork.

The Director of the Youth Authority may authorize the sale of articles of handiwork made by wards under the jurisdiction of the authority to the public at Youth Authority institutions, in public buildings, at fairs, or on property operated by nonprofit associations. The cost of any state property used for the manufacture of articles shall be paid for out of funds received from the sale of the articles. The remainder of any funds received from the sale of the articles shall be placed in the ward's trust account pursuant to Section 1752.8 of the Welfare and Institutions Code.

§1753.3. Transferring wards to local facility.

(a) The Director of the Youth Authority may enter into an agreement with a city, county, or city and county, to permit transfer of wards in the custody of the Director of the Youth Authority to an appropriate facility of the city, county, or city and county, if the official having jurisdiction over the facility has consented. The agreement shall provide for contributions to the city, county, or city and county toward payment of costs incurred with reference to the transferred wards.

(b) When an agreement entered into pursuant to subdivision (a) is in effect with respect to a particular local facility, the Director of the Youth Authority may transfer wards and parole violators to the facility.

(c) Notwithstanding subdivision (b), the Director of the Youth Authority may deny placement in a local facility to a parole violator who was committed to the Youth Authority for the commission of any offense set forth in subdivision (b) of Section 707.

(d) Wards transferred to those facilities are subject to the rules and regulations of the facility in which they are confined, but remain under the legal custody of the Department of the Youth Authority. *(Amended by Stats 1988 ch 1608 §6, eff. 1/1/89.)*

§1753.4 Placement of parole violators; reimbursement rate.

(a) Pursuant to Section 1753.3 the Director of the Youth Authority may enter into a long-term agreement not to exceed 20 years with a city, county, or city and county to place parole violators in a facility which is specially designed and built for the incarceration of parole violators and state youth authority wards.

(b) The agreement shall provide that persons providing security at the facilities shall be peace officers who have completed the minimum standards for the training of local correctional peace officers established under Section 6035 of the Penal Code.

(c) In determining the reimbursement rate pursuant to an agreement entered into pursuant to subdivision (a), the director shall take into consideration the costs incurred by the city, county, or city and county for services and facilities provided, and any other factors which are necessary and appropriate to fix the obligations, responsibilities, and rights of the respective parties.

(d) The Director of the Youth Authority, to the extent possible, shall select city, county, or city and county facilities in areas where medical, food, and other support services are available from nearby existing prison facilities.

(e) The Director of the Youth Authority, with the approval of the Department of General Services, may enter into an agreement to lease state property for a period not in excess of 20 years to be used as the site for a facility operated by a city, county, or city and county authorized by this section.

(f) No agreement may be entered into under this section unless the cost per ward in the facility is no greater than the average costs of keeping a ward in a comparable Youth Authority facility, as determined by the Director of the Youth Authority. *(Amended by Stats 1987 ch 1450 §12.)*

§1753.6. Delivery of ward's child in county hospital.

In any case in which a ward of the Youth Authority is temporarily released from actual confinement in an institution of the authority and placed in a county hospital for purposes of delivery of her child, the authority may reimburse the county for the actual cost of services rendered by the county hospital to the newborn infant of the ward.

§1753.7. Family planning services provided for confined females.

(a) Any female confined in a Department of the Youth Authority facility shall, upon her request, be allowed to continue to use materials necessary for (1) personal hygiene with regard to her menstrual cycle and reproductive system and (2) birth control measures as prescribed by her physician.

(b) Any female confined in a Department of the Youth Authority facility shall upon her request be furnished by the department with information and education regarding prescription birth control measures.

(c) Family planning services shall be offered to each and every female confined in a Department of Youth Authority facility at least 60 days prior to a scheduled release date. Upon request any such female shall be furnished by the department with the services of a licensed physician or she shall be furnished by the department or by any other agency which contracts with the department with services necessary to meet her family planning needs at the time of her release.

§1756. Transfer of mentally disordered to state hospitals.

Notwithstanding any other provision of law, if, in the opinion of the Director of the Youth Authority, the rehabilitation of any mentally disordered, or developmentally disabled person confined in a state correctional school may be expedited by treatment at one of the state hospitals under the jurisdiction of the State Department of Mental Health or the State Department of Developmental Services, the Director of the Youth Authority shall certify that fact to the director of the appropriate department who may authorize receipt of the person at one of the hospitals for care and treatment. Upon notification from the director that the person will no longer benefit from further care and treatment in the state hospital, the Director of the Youth Authority shall immediately send for, take, and receive the person back into a state correctional school. Any person placed in a state hospital under this section who is committed to the authority shall be released from the hospital upon termination of his or her commitment unless a petition for detention of that person is filed under the provisions of Part 1 (commencing with Section 5000) of Division 5.

§1760.7. Reports on adult and juvenile probation.

The director shall investigate, examine, and make reports upon adult and juvenile probation.

The director may establish standards for the performance of probation duties, and upon request consult with and make investigations and recommendations to probation officers, probation committees, juvenile justice commissions, and to judges of the superior courts, including such judges as are designated juvenile court judges of any county.

The director may also, upon request, consult with, make investigations for, and recommendations to probation officers, probation committees, juvenile justice commissions, and to judges of the superior courts, including such judges as are designated juvenile court judges of any county, to aid them in the operation and maintenance of their juvenile halls.

§1763. Written records.

The authority shall keep written records of all examinations and of the conclusions predicated thereon and of all orders concerning the disposition or treatment of every person subject to its control. After five years from the date on which the jurisdiction of the authority over a ward is terminated the authority may destroy such records. For the purposes of this section "destroy" means destroy or dispose of for the purpose of destruction.

§1764. Disclosure of information.

Notwithstanding any other provision of law, any of the following information in the possession of the Youth Authority regarding persons 16 years of age or older who were committed to the Youth Authority by a court of criminal jurisdiction, or who were committed to the Department of Corrections and were subsequently transferred to the Youth Authority, shall be disclosed to any member of the public, upon request, by the director or his or her designee:

(a) The name and age of the person.

(b) The court of commitment and the offense that was the basis of commitment.

(c) The date of commitment.

(d) Any institution where the person is or was confined.

(e) The actions taken by any paroling authority regarding the person, which relate to parole dates.

(f) The date the person is scheduled to be released to the community, including release to a reentry work furlough program.

(g) The date the person was placed on parole.

(h) The date the person was discharged from the jurisdiction of the Youth Authority and the basis for the discharge.

(i) In any case where the person has escaped from any institution under the jurisdiction of the Youth Authority, a physical description of the person and the circumstances of the escape.

The provisions of this section shall not be construed to authorize the release of any information which could place any individual in personal peril; which could threaten Youth Authority security; or which is exempt from disclosure pursuant to the California Public Records Act (Chapter 3.5 (commencing with Section 6250) of Division 7 of Title 1 of the Government Code). *(Amended by Stats 1989 chs 624 §3.5, 1048 §1, eff. 1/1/90.)*

© 1992 by J., B. & L. Gould
Printed in the U.S.A.　　EP

§1764.1. Release of information for offenses under §676.

Notwithstanding any other provision of law, the director or his or her designee may release the information described in Section 1764 regarding a person committed to the Youth Authority by a juvenile court for an offense described in subdivision (a) of Section 676, to any member of the public who requests the information, unless the court has ordered confidentiality under subdivision (c) of Section 676. *(Amended by Stats 1989 chs 624 §4, 1048 §2, eff. 1/1/90.)*

§1764.2. *Repealed by Stats 1990 ch 216 §122, eff. 1/1/91.*

§1764.3. Notification of release date of youth committed to Youth Authority.

(a) Whenever a person is committed to the Youth Authority by a court of criminal jurisdiction, or is committed to the Department of Corrections and subsequently transferred to the Youth Authority, for a conviction of a violent felony listed in subdivision (c) of Section 667.5 of the Penal Code, the director or his or her designee shall, with respect to that person, provide all notices that would be required to be provided by the Board of Prison Terms or the Department of Corrections pursuant to Sections 3058.6 and 3058.8 of the Penal Code, if that person were confined in their respective institutions.

(b) In order to be entitled to receive from the department, pursuant to subdivision (a), the notice set forth in Section 3058.8 of the Penal Code, the requesting party shall keep the department informed of his or her current mailing address.

(c) The notice required under this section shall be provided within 10 days of release with respect to persons committed to the Youth Authority by a court of criminal jurisdiction. *(Added by Stats 1989 ch 624 §6, eff. 1/1/90.)*

§1766. Authority of youthful offender parole board.

When a person has been committed to the Youth Authority, the Youthful Offender Parole Board may

(a) Permit him his liberty under supervision and upon such conditions as it believes best designed for the protection of the public.*

(b) Order his or her confinement under such conditions as it believes best designed for the protection of the public, except that a person committed to the Youth Authority pursuant to Sections 731 or 1731.5 may not be held in physical confinement for a total period of time in excess of the maximum period of imprisonment which could be imposed upon an adult convicted of the offense or offenses which brought the minor under the jurisdiction of the juvenile court, or which resulted in the commitment of the young adult to the Youth Authority. Nothing in this subdivision limits the power of the board to retain the minor or the young adult on parole status for the period permitted by Sections 1769, 1770, and 1771;

(c) Order reconfinement or renewed release under supervision as often as conditions indicate to be desirable;

(d) Revoke or modify any order except an order of discharge as often as conditions indicate to be desirable;

(e) Modify an order of discharge if conditions indicate that such modification is desirable and when such modification is to the benefit of the person committed to the authority;

(f) Discharge him or her from its control when it is satisfied that such discharge is consistent with the protection of the public.

So in original. Probably should be a semicolon.

§1766.1. Payment of restitution fine.

When permitting an adult or minor committed to the Youth Authority his or her liberty pursuant to subdivision (a) of Section 1766, the Youthful Offender Parole Board shall impose as a condition thereof that the adult or minor pay in full any restitution fine or restitution order imposed pursuant to Section 13967 of the Government Code or Section 730.6 or 731.1 of this code. Payment shall be in installments set in an amount consistent with the adult's or minor's ability to pay. *(Amended by Stats 1988 ch 181 §3, eff. 1/1/89.)*

§1767. Hearing to consider release on parole.

Upon request, written notice of any hearing to consider the release on parole of any person under the control of the Youth Authority for the commission of a crime or committed to the authority as a person described in Section 602 shall be sent by the Youthful Offender Parole Board at least 30 days before the hearing to any victim of a crime committed by the person, or to the next of kin of the victim if the victim has died. The requesting party shall keep the board apprised of his or her current mailing address.

The victim or next of kin has the right to appear, personally or by counsel, at the hearing and to adequately and reasonably express his or her views concerning the crime and the person responsible. The board, in deciding whether to release the person on parole, shall consider the statements of victims and next of kin made pursuant to this section and shall include in its report a statement of whether the person would pose a threat to public safety if released on parole.

The provisions of this section shall not be amended by the Legislature except by statute passed in each house by rollcall vote entered in the journal, two-thirds of the membership concurring, or by a statute that becomes effective only when approved by the electors.

§1767.1. Considering parole of person under 18 years of age.

At least 30 days before the Youthful Offender Parole Board meets to review or consider the parole of any person under 18 years of age who has been committed to the control of the Department of the Youth Authority for the commission of any offense described in subdivision (b) of Section 707, the board shall send written notice of hearing to each of the following persons: the judge of the court which committed the person to the authority, the attorney for the person, the district attorney of the county from which the person was committed, the law enforcement agency that investigated the case, and, where he or she has filed a request for such notice with the board, the victim or next of kin of the victim of the offense for which the person was committed to the authority. The notice to the victim or next of kin of the victim shall be sent to the last mailing address on file with the board.

Each of the persons so notified shall have the right to submit a written statement to the board at least 10 days prior to the scheduled hearing for the board's consideration at the hearing. Nothing in this subdivision shall be construed to permit any person so notified to attend the hearing.

§1767.2. Conditions for granting probation or parole.

Every order granting probation or parole to any person under the control of the Authority who has been convicted of any of the offenses enumerated in Section 290 of the Penal Code shall require as a condition of such probation or parole that such person totally abstain from the use of alcoholic liquor or beverages.

§1767.3. Suspend, cancel, or revoke parole; return to custody.

(a) The Youthful Offender Parole Board may suspend, cancel, or revoke any parole and may order returned to custody of the department any person committed to it who is on parole.

(b) The written order of the chairperson of the board is a sufficient warrant for any peace officer to return to the custody of the department any person committed to it who is on parole or who has been permitted his or her liberty on condition.

(c) The written order of the Director of the Department of the Youth Authority is a sufficient warrant for any peace officer to return to the custody of the department, pending further proceedings before the Youthful Offender Parole Board or the Board of Prison Terms, any person committed to, or in the custody of, the department who is on parole or who has been permitted his or her liberty upon condition, or for any peace officer to return to the custody of the department any person who has escaped from the custody of the department or from any institution or facility in which he or she has been placed by the department.

(d) All peace officers shall execute the orders in like manner as a felony warrant. *(Amended by Stats 1988 ch 160 §186, eff. 1/1/89.)*

§1767.4. Expenses incurred upon return to custody.

Whenever any person paroled by the Youthful Offender Parole Board is returned to the department upon the order of the board by a peace officer or probation officer, the officer shall be paid the same fees and expenses as are allowed such officers by law for the transportation of persons to institutions or facilities under the jurisdiction of the department.

§1767.5. Care of paroled person; payment of expenses.

The authority may pay any private home for the care of any person committed to the authority and paroled by the Youthful Offender Parole Board to the custody of the private home (including both persons committed to the authority under this chapter and persons committed to it by the juvenile court) at a rate to be approved by the Department of Finance. Payments for such care of paroled persons may be made from funds available to the authority for such purpose, or for the support of the institution or facility under the jurisdiction of the authority from which the person has been paroled.

§1767.6. Copy of reports in parole revocation proceedings.

In parole revocation proceedings, a parolee or his attorney shall receive a copy of any police, arrest, and crime reports pertaining to such proceedings. Portions of such reports containing confidential information need not be disclosed if the parolee or his attorney has been notified that confidential information has not been disclosed.

§1767.7. Revolving fund for payment of expenses.

A sum may be withdrawn by the authority from the funds available for the support of the authority without at the time furnishing vouchers and itemized statements. This sum shall be used as a revolving fund for payments for the care of persons paroled to private homes as provided in Section 1767.5. At the close of each fiscal year, or at any other time, upon demand of the Department of Finance the money so drawn shall be accounted for and substantiated by vouchers and itemized statements submitted to and audited by the State Controller.

§1767.8. Hearing to consider parole release of rape or murder offender.

In the case of any person under the control of the Youth Authority for the commission of any offense of rape in violation of subdivision (2) or subdivision (3) of Section 261 of the Penal Code, or murder, written notice of any hearing to consider the release on parole of the person shall be sent by the Youthful Offender Parole Board to the following persons at least 30 days before the hearing: the judge of the court by whom the person was committed to the authority, the attorney for the person, the district attorney of the county from which the person was committed, and the law enforcement agency which investigated the case. The board shall also send written notice to the victim of the rape or the next of kin of the person murdered if he or she requests notice from the board and keeps it apprised of his or her current mailing address.

§1767.9. Considering parole of person over age 18.

At least 30 days before the Youthful Offender Parole Board meets to review or consider the parole of any person over 18 years of age who has been committed to the control of the Youth Authority for the commission of any offense described in subdivision (b) of Section 707, the board shall send written notice thereof to each of the following persons: the judge of the court which committed the person to the authority, the attorney for the person, the district attorney of the county from which the person was committed, the law enforcement agency that investigated the case, and, where he or she has filed a request for such notice with the board, the victim or next of kin of the victim of the offense for which the person was committed to the authority. The burden shall be on the requesting party to keep the board apprised of his or her current mailing address.

Each of the persons so notified shall have the right to submit a written statement to the board at least 10 days prior to the scheduled hearing for the board's consideration at the hearing. Nothing in this subdivision shall be construed to permit any person so notified to attend the hearing.

At the hearing the presiding officer shall state findings and supporting reasons for the decision of the board. The findings and reasons shall be reduced to writing, and shall be made available for inspection by

© 1992 by J., B. & L. Gould
Printed in the U.S.A.   EP

members of the public no later than 30 days from the date of the hearing.

§1768.7. Penalty for escape or attempt to escape.

(a) Any person committed to the authority who escapes or attempts to escape from the institution or facility in which he or she is confined, who escapes or attempts to escape while being conveyed to or from such an institution or facility, who escapes or attempts to escape while outside or away from such an institution or facility under custody of Youth Authority officials, officers, or employees, or who, with intent to abscond from the custody of the Youth Authority, fails to return to such an institution or facility at the prescribed time while outside or away from the institution or facility on furlough or temporary release, is guilty of a felony.

(b) Any offense set forth in subdivision (a) which is accomplished by force or violence is punishable by imprisonment in the state prison for a term of two, four, or six years. Any offense set forth in subdivision (a) which is accomplished without force or violence is punishable by imprisonment in the state prison for a term of 16 months, two or three years or in the county jail not exceeding one year.

(c) For purposes of this section, "committed to the authority" means a commitment to the Youth Authority pursuant to Section 731 or 1731.5; a remand to the custody of the Youth Authority pursuant to Section 707.2; a placement at the Youth Authority pursuant to Section 704, 1731.6, or 1753.1; or a transfer to the custody of the Youth Authority pursuant to subdivision (c) of Section 1731.5. (Amended by Stats 1985 ch 1283 §2.)

§1768.8. Punishment for assault or battery on individual not confined.

(a) An assault or battery by any person confined in an institution under the jurisdiction of the Youth Authority upon the person of any individual who is not confined therein shall be punishable by a fine not exceeding two thousand dollars ($2,000), or by imprisonment in the county jail not exceeding one year, or by both a fine and imprisonment.

(b) An assault or battery by any person confined in an institution under the jurisdiction of the Youth Authority upon the person of any individual who is not confined therein, which inflicts serious bodily injury upon the victim, is punishable by imprisonment in the state prison for two, three, or four years, or in county jail for not more than one year. (Amended by Stats 1989 ch 995 §1, eff. 1/1/90.)

§1768.9. Blood tests to detect AIDS or AIDS-related complex.

(a) Notwithstanding any other provision of law, a person under the jurisdiction or control of the Department of the Youth Authority is obligated to submit to a test for the probable causative agent of AIDS upon a determination of the chief medical officer of the facility that clinical symptoms of AIDS or AIDS-related complex, as recognized by the Centers for Disease Control, is present in the person. In the event that the subject of the test refuses to submit to such a test, the department may seek a court order to require him or her to submit to the test.

(b) Prior to ordering a test pursuant to subdivision (a), the chief medical officer shall ensure that the subject of the test receives pretest counseling. The counseling shall include:

(1) Testing procedures, effectiveness, reliability, and confidentiality.

(2) The mode of transmission of HIV.

(3) Symptoms of AIDS and AIDS-related complex.

(4) Precautions to avoid exposure and transmission.

The chief medical officer shall also encourage the subject of the test to undergo voluntary testing prior to ordering a test. The chief medical officer shall also ensure that the subject of the test receives posttest counseling.

(c) The following procedures shall apply to testing conducted under this section:

(1) The withdrawal of blood shall be performed in a medically approved manner. Only a physician, registered nurse, licensed vocational nurse, licensed medical technician, or licensed phlebotomist may withdraw blood specimens for the purposes of this section.

(2) The chief medical officer shall order that the blood specimens be transmitted to a licensed medical laboratory which has been approved by the State Department of Health Services for the conducting of AIDS testing, and that tests, including all readily available confirmatory tests, be conducted thereon for medically accepted indications of exposure to or infection with HIV.

(3) The subject of the test shall be notified face-to-face as to the results of the test.

(d) All counseling and notification of test results shall be conducted by one of the following:

(1) A physician and surgeon who has received training in the subjects described in subdivision (b).

(2) A registered nurse who has received training in the subjects described in subdivision (b).

(3) A psychologist who has received training in the subjects described in subdivision (b) and who is under the purview of either a registered nurse or physician and surgeon who has received training in the subjects described in subdivision (b).

(4) A licensed social worker who has received training in the subjects described in subdivision (b) and who is under the purview of either a registered nurse or physician and surgeon who has received training in the subjects described in subdivision (b).

(5) A trained volunteer counselor who has received training in the subjects described in subdivision (b) and who is under the supervision of either a registered nurse or physician and surgeon who has received training in the subjects described in subdivision (b).

(e) The Department of the Youth Authority shall provide medical services appropriate for the diagnosis and treatment of those infected with HIV.

(f) The Department of the Youth Authority may operate separate housing facilities for wards and inmates who have tested positive for HIV infection and who continue to engage in activities which transmit HIV. These facilities shall be comparable to those of other wards and inmates with access to recreational and educational facilities, commensurate with the facilities available in the institution.

(g) Notwithstanding any other provision of law, the chief medical officer of a facility of the Department of the Youth Authority may do all of the following:

(1) Disclose results of a test for the probable causative agent of AIDS to the superintendent or ad-

ministrator of the facility where the test subject is confined.

(2) When test results are positive, inform the test subject's known sexual partners or needle contacts in a Department of the Youth Authority facility of the positive results, provided that the test subject's identity is kept confidential. All wards and inmates who are provided with this information shall be provided with the counseling described in subdivision (b).

(3) Include the test results in the subject's confidential medical record which is to be maintained separate from other case files and records.

(h) Actions taken pursuant to this section shall not be subject to subdivisions (a) to (c), inclusive, of Section 199.21 of the Health and Safety Code. In addition, the requirements of subdivision (a) of Section 199.22 of the Health and Safety Code shall not apply to testing performed pursuant to this section. *(Repealed and added by Stats 1989 ch 765 §§3, 4, eff. 1/1/90.)*

§1769. Discharge of persons committed to Youth Authority by juvenile court.

(a) Every person committed to the Department of the Youth Authority by a juvenile court shall, except as provided in subdivision (b), be discharged upon the expiration of a two-year period of control or when the person reaches his or her 21st birthday, whichever occurs later, unless an order for further detention has been made by the committing court pursuant to Article 6 (commencing with Section 1800).

(b) Every person committed to the Department of the Youth Authority by a juvenile court who has been found to be a person described in Section 602 by reason of the violation of any of the offenses listed in subdivision (b) of Section 707, shall be discharged upon the expiration of a two-year period of control or when the person reaches his or her 25th birthday, whichever occurs later, unless an order for further detention has been made by the committing court pursuant to Article 6 (commencing with Section 1800).

§1770. Discharge when convicted of misdemeanor.

Every person convicted of a misdemeanor and committed to the authority shall be discharged upon the expiration of a two-year period of control or when the person reaches his 23rd birthday, whichever occurs later, unless an order for further detention has been made by the committing court pursuant to Article 6 (commencing with Section 1800).

§1771. Discharge when convicted of felony.

Every person convicted of a felony and committed to the authority shall be discharged when such person reaches his 25th birthday, unless an order for further detention has been made by the committing court pursuant to Article 6 (commencing with Section 1800) or unless a petition is filed under Article 5 of this chapter. In the event such a petition under Article 5 is filed, the authority shall retain control until the final disposition of the proceeding under Article 5.

§1772. Definition and effect of honorable discharge.

(a) Every person honorably discharged from control by the Youthful Offender Parole Board who has not, during the period of control by the authority been placed by the authority in a state prison shall thereafter be released from all penalties and disabilities

resulting from the offense or crime for which he or she was committed, and every person discharged may petition the court which committed him or her, and the court may upon such petition set aside the verdict of guilty and dismiss the accusation or information against the petitioner who shall thereafter be released from all penalties and disabilities resulting from the offense or crime for which he or she was committed, including, but not limited to, any disqualification for any employment or occupational license, or both, created by any other provision of law. However, such a person shall not be eligible for appointment as a peace officer employed by any public agency if his or her appointment would otherwise be prohibited by Section 1029 of the Government Code.

(b) Notwithstanding the provisions of subdivision (a), such person may be appointed and employed as a peace officer by the Department of the Youth Authority if (1) at least five years have passed since his or her honorable discharge, and the person has had no misdemeanor or felony convictions except for traffic misdemeanors since he or she was honorably discharged by the Youthful Offender Parole Board, or (2) the person was employed as a peace officer by the Department of the Youth Authority on or before January 1, 1983. No person who is under the jurisdiction of the Department of the Youth Authority shall be admitted to an examination for a peace officer position with the department unless and until the person has been honorably discharged from the jurisdiction of the department by the Youthful Offender Parole Board.

(c) Every person discharged from control by the Youthful Offender Parole Board shall be informed of this privilege in writing at the time of discharge.

"Honorably discharged" as used in this section means and includes every person whose discharge is based upon a good record on parole.

ARTICLE 6

EXTENDED DETENTION OF DANGEROUS PERSONS

§1800. Petition court for order to extend detention.

Whenever the Youthful Offender Parole Board determines that the discharge of a person from the control of the Youth Authority at the time required by Section 1766, 1769, 1770, 1770.1, or 1771, as applicable, would be physically dangerous to the public because of the person's mental or physical deficiency, disorder, or abnormality, the board, through its chairman, shall request the prosecuting attorney to petition the committing court for an order directing that the person remain subject to the control of the authority beyond that time. The petition shall be filed at least 90 days before the time of discharge otherwise required. The petition shall be accompanied by a written statement of the facts upon which the board bases its opinion that discharge from control of the Youth Authority at the time stated would be physically dangerous to the public, but no such petition shall be dismissed nor shall an order be denied merely because of technical defects in the application.

The prosecuting attorney shall promptly notify the Youthful Offender Parole Board of a decision not to file a petition.

© 1992 by J., B. & L. Gould
Printed in the U.S.A.   EP

§1801. Notice and hearing; court order to continue treatment or discharge.

If a petition is filed with the court for an order as provided in Section 1800, the court shall notify the person whose liberty is involved, and, if the person is a minor, his or her parent or guardian (if that person can be reached, and, if not, the court shall appoint a person to act in the place of the parent or guardian) of the application, and shall afford the person an opportunity to appear in court with the aid of counsel and of process to compel attendance of witnesses and production of evidence. When the person is unable to provide his or her own counsel, the court shall appoint counsel to represent him or her.

If after a full hearing the court is of the opinion that discharge of the person would be physically dangerous to the public because of his or her mental or physical deficiency, disorder, or abnormality, the court shall order the Youth Authority to continue the treatment of the person. If the court is of the opinion that discharge of the person from continued control of the authority would not be physically dangerous to the public, the court shall order the person to be discharged from control of the authority.

§1801.5. Demand for jury trial after hearing.

If the person is ordered returned to the Youth Authority following a hearing by the court, the person, or his or her parent or guardian on the person's behalf, may, within 10 days after the making of such order, file a written demand that the question of whether he or she is physically dangerous to the public be tried by a jury in the superior court of the county in which he or she was committed. Thereupon, the court shall cause a jury to be summoned and to be in attendance at a date stated, not less than four days nor more than 30 days from the date of the demand for a jury trial. The court shall submit to the jury the question: Is the person physically dangerous to the public because of his mental or physical deficiency, disorder, or abnormality. The court's previous order entered pursuant to Section 1801 shall not be read to the jury, nor alluded to in such trial. The person shall be entitled to all rights guaranteed under the federal and state constitutions in criminal proceedings. The trial shall require a unanimous jury verdict, employing the standard of proof beyond a reasonable doubt.

§1801.6. Costs chargeable when venue changed.

When the venue of a proceeding under this chapter is changed, costs of the proceeding are chargeable as provided in Section 1037 of the Penal Code. (*Added by Stats 1988 ch 235 §2, eff. 1/1/89.*)

§1802. File new application for continued detention.

When an order for continued detention is made as provided in Section 1801, the control of the authority over the person shall continue, subject to the provisions of this chapter, but, unless the person is previously discharged as provided in Section 1766, the Youthful Offender Parole Board shall, within two years after the date of such order in the case of persons committed by the juvenile court, or within two years after the date of such order in the case of persons committed after conviction in criminal proceedings, file a new application for continued detention in accordance with the provisions of Section 1800 if continued detention is deemed necessary. Such applications may be

repeated at intervals as often as in the opinion of the board may be necessary for the protection of the public, except that the department shall have the power, in order to protect other persons in the custody of the department to transfer the custody of any person over 21 years of age to the Director of Corrections for placement in the appropriate institution.

Each person shall be discharged from the control of the authority at the termination of the period stated in this section unless the board has filed a new application and the court has made a new order for continued detention as provided above in this section.

§1803. Appeal of court order.

An order of the committing court made pursuant to this article is appealable by the person whose liberty is involved in the same manner as a judgment in a criminal case. The appellate court may affirm the order of the lower court, or modify it, or reverse it and order the appellant to be discharged. Pending appeal, the appellant shall remain under the control of the authority.

DIVISION 3

NARCOTIC ADDICTS

CHAPTER 1

COMMITMENT AND TREATMENT OF NARCOTIC ADDICTS

ARTICLE 1

ADMINISTRATION

§3001. Purpose of detention, treatment and rehabilitation facility.

The narcotic detention, treatment and rehabilitation facility referred to herein shall be one within the Department of Corrections whose principal purpose shall be the receiving, control, confinement, employment, education, treatment and rehabilitation of persons under the custody of the Department of Corrections or any agency thereof who are or have been addicted to narcotics or who by reason of repeated use of narcotics are in imminent danger of becoming addicted.

§3002. Punishment for escape or attempted escape.

Every person committed pursuant to this chapter or former Chapter 11 (commencing with Section 6399) of Title 7 of the Penal Code who escapes or attempts to escape from lawful custody is guilty of a crime punishable by imprisonment in the state prison. This section does not apply to unauthorized absence from a halfway house.

§3008. Copy of officer's report to department.

When a court commits a person to the custody of the Director of Corrections pursuant to this chapter, the court shall immediately after making the order of commitment, mail to the Department of Corrections, at the facility to which the person committed is delivered, a copy of such reports as the probation officer may have made relative to such person.

§3009. Definition of narcotic addict.

A "narcotic addict", as used in this division refers to any person, adult or minor, who is addicted to the unlawful use of any narcotic as defined in Division 10 of the Health and Safety Code, except marijuana.

ARTICLE 2

INVOLUNTARY COMMITMENT OF PERSONS CONVICTED OF A CRIME

§3050. Proceedings for commitment upon conviction in municipal or justice court.

Upon conviction of a defendant of any crime in a municipal or justice court, or following revocation of probation previously granted, whether or not sentence has been imposed, if it appears to the judge that the defendant may be addicted or by reason of repeated use of narcotics may be in imminent danger of becoming addicted to narcotics, such judge shall adjourn the proceedings or suspend the imposition or execution of the sentence, certify the defendant to the superior court and order the district attorney to file a petition for a commitment of the defendant to the Director of Corrections for confinement in the narcotic detention, treatment and rehabilitation facility.

Upon the filing of such a petition, the superior court shall order the defendant to be examined by one physician. At the request of the defendant, the court shall order the defendant to be examined by a second physician. At least one day before the time of the examination as fixed by the court order, a copy of the petition and order for examination shall be personally delivered to the defendant. A written report of the examination by the physician or physicians shall be delivered to the court, and if the report is to the effect that the person is not addicted nor in imminent danger of addiction, it shall so certify and return the defendant to the municipal or justice court which certified such defendant to the superior court for such further proceedings as the judge of such municipal or justice court deems warranted. If the report is to the effect that the defendant is addicted or is by reason of the repeated use of narcotics in imminent danger of addiction, further proceedings shall be conducted in compliance with Sections 3104, 3105, 3106, and 3107.

If, after a hearing, the judge finds that the defendant is a narcotic addict, or is by reason of the repeated use of narcotics in imminent danger of becoming addicted thereto, and is not ineligible for the program under the application of Section 3052, he or she shall make an order committing such defendant to the custody of the Director of Corrections for confinement in the facility until such time as he or she is discharged pursuant to Article 5 (commencing with Section 3200), except as this chapter permits earlier discharge. If, upon the hearing, the judge shall find that the defendant is not a narcotic addict and is not in imminent danger of becoming addicted to narcotics, the judge shall so certify and return the defendant to the municipal or justice court which certified the defendant to the superior court for such further proceedings as the judge of the municipal or justice court deems warranted.

If a person committed pursuant to this section is dissatisfied with the order of commitment, he or she may within 10 days after the making of such order, file a written demand for a jury trial in compliance with Section 3108.

§3051. Proceedings for commitment upon conviction in superior court.

Upon conviction of a defendant for any crime in any superior court, or following revocation of probation previously granted, and upon imposition of sentence, if it appears to the judge that the defendant may be addicted or by reason of repeated use of narcotics may be in imminent danger of becoming addicted to narcotics the judge shall suspend the execution of the sentence and order the district attorney to file a petition for commitment of the defendant to the Director of Corrections for confinement in the narcotic detention, treatment, and rehabilitation facility unless, in the opinion of the judge, the defendant's record and probation report indicate such a pattern of criminality that he or she does not constitute a fit subject for commitment under this section.

Upon the filing of such a petition, the court shall order the defendant to be examined by one physician; provided, that the examination may be waived by a defendant if the defendant has been examined in accordance with Section 1203.03 of the Penal Code and such examination encompassed whether defendant is addicted or is in imminent danger of addiction, and if the defendant is represented by counsel and competent to understand the effect of such waiver. At the request of the defendant, the court shall order the defendant to be examined by a second physician. At least one day before the time of the examination as fixed by the court order, a copy of the petition and order for examination shall be personally delivered to the defendant. A written report of the examination by the physician or physicians shall be delivered to the court, and if the report is to the effect that the person is not addicted nor in imminent danger of addiction, it shall so certify and return the defendant to the department of the superior court which directed the filing of the petition for the ordering of the execution of the sentence. Such court may, unless otherwise prohibited by law, modify such sentence or suspend the imposition of such sentence. If the report is to the effect that the defendant is addicted or is by reason of the repeated use of narcotics in imminent danger of addiction, further proceedings shall be conducted in compliance with Sections 3104, 3105, 3106, and 3107.

If, after a hearing, the judge finds that the defendant is a narcotic addict, or is by reason of the repeated use of narcotics in imminent danger of becoming addicted to narcotics, the judge shall make an order committing such person to the custody of the Director of Corrections for confinement in the facility until such time as he or she is discharged pursuant to Article 5 (commencing with Section 3200), except as this chapter permits earlier discharge. If, upon the hearing, the judge shall find that the defendant is not a narcotic addict and is not in imminent danger of becoming addicted to narcotics, the judge shall so certify and return the defendant to the department of the superior court which directed the filing of the petition for the ordering of execution of sentence. Such court may, unless otherwise prohibited by law, modify such sentence or suspend the imposition of such sentence.

If a person committed pursuant to this section is dissatisfied with the order of commitment, he or she may within 10 days after the making of such order file a written demand for a jury trial in compliance with Section 3108.

§3052. Inapplicability of provisions.

(a) Sections 3050 and 3051 shall not apply to any of the following:

(1) Persons convicted of any offense for which the provisions of Section 667.6 of the Penal Code apply, or

© 1992 by J., B. & L. Gould
Printed in the U.S.A.   **EP**

any offense described in Chapter 1 (commencing with Section 450) of Title 13 of Part 1 of such code; or any person convicted of committing or attempting to commit any violent felony as defined in subdivision (c) of Section 667.5 of the Penal Code.

(2) Persons whose sentence is enhanced pursuant to subdivision (b) of Section 12022 of the Penal Code, or Section 12022.3, 12022.5, 12022.6, 12022.7, or 12022.8 of such code; or persons whose sentence is subject to the provisions of Section 3046 of the Penal Code; or persons whose conviction results in a sentence which, in the aggregate, exclusive of any credit that may be earned pursuant to Article 2.5 (commencing with Section 2930) of Chapter 7 of Title 1 of Part 3 of the Penal Code, exceeds six years' imprisonment in state prison; or persons found to come under the provisions of Section 1203.06 of the Penal Code.

(b) Notwithstanding the provisions of subdivision (a) of this section or Section 3053, the fact a person comes within Section 1203.07 of the Penal Code does not mean that he or she may not be committed and treated.

§3053. Unfit subject for confinement.

(a) If at any time following receipt at the facility of a person committed pursuant to this article, the Director of Corrections concludes that the person, because of excessive criminality or for other relevant reason, is not a fit subject for confinement or treatment in such narcotic detention, treatment and rehabilitation facility, he shall return the person to the court in which the case originated for such further proceedings on the criminal charges as that court may deem warranted.

(b) A person committed pursuant to this article who is subsequently committed to the Director of Corrections pursuant to Section 1168 or 1170 of the Penal Code shall not be a fit subject for treatment pursuant to this article. The court committing the person to the Director of Corrections pursuant to Section 1168 or 1170 of the Penal Code shall immediately notify the court which originally committed the person pursuant to this article. Upon receipt of such person committed pursuant to Section 1168 or 1170 of the Penal Code or upon notification of such commitment, whichever is sooner, the Director of Corrections shall notify the court which committed the person pursuant to this article of such subsequent commitment. Upon receipt of notification of such subsequent commitment the court which had committed the person pursuant to this article shall automatically terminate the commitment and shall promptly set for hearing the matter of further proceedings on the criminal charges.

(c) If the defendant was originally committed pursuant to Section 3050 or 3051, the committing court, if the criminal proceedings were conducted in another court, shall notify that court which adjourned its criminal proceedings or suspended sentence in such case pending the civil commitment. In such event, that criminal court shall then promptly set for hearing the matter of the sentencing of the defendant upon the conviction which subsequently resulted in the original civil commitment.

§3054. No requirement to register as narcotics offender.

A person committed to the custody of the Director of Corrections pursuant to this article is not required to register pursuant to Article 4 (commencing with

Section 11590) of Chapter 10 of Division 10 of the Health and Safety Code.

ARTICLE 3

INVOLUNTARY COMMITMENT OF PERSONS NOT CONVICTED OF A CRIME

§3100. Petition for commitment of probationer.

Anyone who believes that a person is addicted to the use of narcotics or by reason of the repeated use of narcotics is in imminent danger of becoming addicted to their use or any person who believes himself to be addicted or about to become addicted may report such belief to the district attorney, under oath, who may, when there is probable cause, petition the superior court for a commitment of such person to the Director of Corrections for confinement in the narcotic detention, treatment and rehabilitation facility. As used in this article the term "person" includes any person who is released on probation by any court of this state.

§3100.6. Admission to hospital or institution to test for addiction.

Any peace officer or health officer who has reasonable cause to believe that a person is addicted to the use of narcotics or by reason of the repeated use of narcotics is in imminent danger of becoming addicted to their use may take the person, for his best interest and protection, to the county hospital or other suitable medical institution designated by the board of supervisors of the county.

Upon written application of the peace officer or health officer, the physician or superintendent in charge of the designated hospital or institution may admit the person believed to be addicted to the use of narcotics or in imminent danger of becoming addicted to their use. The application shall state the circumstances under which the person's condition was called to the officer's attention, shall state the date, time and place of taking the person into custody and shall state the facts upon which the officer has reasonable cause to believe that the person is addicted to the use of narcotics or by reason of the repeated use of narcotics is in imminent danger of becoming addicted to their use. The application shall be signed by the officer, and a copy of the application shall be presented to the person prior to his admittance to the hospital or institution.

Within 24 hours of admittance, a physician shall conduct an examination to determine whether the person is addicted to the use of narcotics or by reason of the repeated use of narcotics is in imminent danger of becoming addicted to their use and may provide the person with medical aid as necessary to ease any symptoms of the withdrawal from the use of narcotics.

If, after examination, the physician does not believe that the person is addicted to the use of narcotics or by reason of the repeated use of narcotics is in imminent danger of becoming addicted to their use, he shall immediately report his belief to the physician or superintendent in charge of the hospital or institution, who shall discharge the person immediately.

If, after examination, the physician believes that further examination is necessary to determine whether the person is addicted to the use of narcotics or by reason of the repeated use of narcotics is in imminent danger of addiction to their use, he shall prepare an affidavit which states that he has examined the person and has such belief. The physician or superintendent in charge of the hospital or institution thereupon shall have the power to detain the person for not more than an additional 48 hours for further examination.

If, after such further examination, the physician does not believe that the person is addicted to the use of narcotics or by reason of the repeated use of narcotics is in imminent danger of becoming addicted to their use, he shall immediately report his belief to the physician or superintendent in charge of the hospital or institution, who shall discharge the person immediately.

If, after such examination, or further examination, the physician believes that the person is addicted to the use of narcotics or by reason of the repeated use of narcotics is in imminent danger of becoming addicted to their use, he shall prepare an affidavit which states that he has examined the person and has such belief, and which states the time and date of admission to the hospital or institution and the time and date of the examination and, if appropriate, the further examination. The physician or superintendent in charge of the hospital or institution thereupon shall report such belief to the district attorney, who may petition the superior court for a commitment of the person to the Director of Corrections for confinement in the narcotic detention and rehabilitation facility.

Unless the petition of the district attorney, accompanied by the affidavit of the examining physician, is filed in the superior court within 72 hours after admittance to the hospital or institution, excluding Saturdays, Sundays and judicial holidays, the physician or superintendent in charge shall discharge the person immediately.

No evidence of violations of Sections 11350, 11357, and 11550 of the Health and Safety Code found during the examination authorized by this section shall be admissible in any criminal proceeding against the person.

§3101. Unlawfully adjudging person as narcotic addict.

Every person who knowingly contrives to have any person adjudged a narcotic addict under this article unlawfully or improperly, is guilty of a misdemeanor.

§3102. Order for examination and confinement.

Upon the filing of a proper petition pursuant to Section 3100, the court shall order the person sought to be committed to be examined by two physicians. Upon the filing of a proper petition pursuant to Section 3100.6, accompanied by the affidavit of the examining physician, the court need not order the person sought to be committed to be examined by any other physician or physicians. The court may also order that the person be confined pending hearing in a county hospital or other suitable institution designated by the board of supervisors of the county if the petition is accompanied by the affidavit of a physician alleging that the physician has examined such person within 72 hours prior to the filing of the petition, excluding Saturdays, Sundays, and judicial holidays, and has concluded that, unless confined, such person is likely to injure himself or herself, or others, or become a menace to the public. In any case in which a person is so ordered to be confined, the person in charge of the institution shall provide the person ordered confined with medical aid as necessary to ease any symptoms of withdrawal from the use of narcotics. Such medical aid

shall not be administered by a peace officer who is not licensed as a physician and surgeon.

§3102.5. Contents of petition filed.

The petition filed pursuant to Section 3100 of this code shall contain the following:

(a) The name, title and address of the petitioner.

(b) The name of the person who is believed to be a narcotic addict, or who because of repeated use of narcotics is in imminent danger of becoming addicted thereto.

(c) Statements supporting the belief that the person alleged to be addicted is in fact addicted or in imminent danger of addiction.

(d) The address, telephone number (if any), birth date, birthplace, age, sex, marital status, occupation, and a physical description of the person believed to be a narcotic addict.

(e) A statement that the person believed to be a narcotic addict or in imminent danger of addiction is in need of care, supervision and treatment at the narcotic detention, treatment and rehabilitation facility of the State of California.

§3103. Delivery of petition and order for examination.

At least one day before the time of the examination as fixed by the court order, a copy of the petition and order for examination shall be personally delivered to the person.

§3103.5. Physicians' examination.

Upon an order by the court that a person be examined, the court shall appoint two physicians to examine the person to determine whether the person is addicted to narcotics or in imminent danger of becoming addicted thereto.

A written report of the examination by the physicians shall be delivered to the court, and if the report is to the effect that the person is not addicted nor in imminent danger of addiction, it shall order the petition dismissed.

§3104. Right to representation by counsel.

If the report is to the effect that the person is addicted or is by reason of the repeated use of narcotics in imminent danger of addiction, the person shall be taken before the judge, who shall then inform him of his right to be represented by counsel, to make a defense to the petition, to produce witnesses in his behalf, and to cross-examine witnesses. If he is financially unable to employ counsel the judge shall appoint counsel to represent him, and in a county where there is no public defender or where the judge finds that the public defender has properly refused to represent the person, the judge shall fix the compensation to be paid by the county for such services. The judge shall by order fix such time and place for the hearing in open court as will give a reasonable opportunity for the production and examination of witnesses.

§3105. Issuing subpoenas.

The court may issue subpoenas for attendance of witnesses at the hearing and the person sought to be committed shall have the right to have subpoenas issued for such purpose.

§3106. Addiction determined by court.

At the hearing, the court shall determine whether the person is addicted to the use of narcotics or is by reason of the repeated use of narcotics in imminent

© 1992 by J., B. & L. Gould
Printed in the U.S.A.   EP

danger of addiction. The court shall compel the attendance of the physicians who conducted the examination required by Section 3050, 3051, 3100.6 or 3102, who shall testify as to the result of the examination, unless the presence of the physicians is waived and it is stipulated that their affidavit or report may be received in evidence.

§3106.5. Petition denied or commitment ordered.

If the court determines that the person is not addicted to the use of narcotics, or in imminent danger of addiction, the petition shall be denied. If the court determines that the person is addicted to the use of narcotics or is by reason of the repeated use of narcotics in imminent danger of addiction, the court shall order the person committed to the custody of the Director of Corrections, until such time as he is discharged in accordance with Article 5 of this chapter, except as provided in Section 3109.

§3107. Hearing waived.

Hearing may be waived by consent of the person, expressed in open court or in writing by the person after the arraignment required by Section 3104 and after consultation with counsel.

§3108. Right to jury trial after order of commitment.

If the person so committed or any friend in his behalf is dissatisfied with the order of commitment, he may within 10 days after the making of such order, file a written demand that the question of his addiction or imminent danger of addiction be tried by a jury in the superior court of the county in which he was committed. Thereupon, the court shall cause a jury to be summoned and to be in attendance at a date stated, not less than 4 days nor more than 30 days from the date of the demand for a jury trial. The court shall submit to the jury the question: Is the person addicted to the use of narcotics or is he by reason of the repeated use of narcotics in imminent danger of addiction? The order of commitment entered pursuant to Sections 3050, 3051, or 3106.5 shall not be read to the jury, nor alluded to in such trial. The trial shall be had as provided by law for the trial of civil cases and the petition shall be dismissed unless a verdict that the person is addicted or in imminent danger of addiction is found by at least three-fourths of the jury.

The person committed shall be awarded all his constitutional rights including, but not limited to, his right to counsel, his right to notice of the nature of the proceedings brought against him, his right to the process of the court to compel the attendance of witnesses in his behalf, and his right to be confronted with witnesses.

§3109. Discharge when unfit for confinement or treatment.

(a) If at any time following receipt at the facility of a person committed pursuant to this article, the Director of Corrections concludes that such person is not, because of excessive criminality or for other relevant reason, a fit subject for confinement or treatment in a facility of the Department of Corrections, the director may order such person discharged.

(b) A person committed pursuant to this article who is subsequently committed to the Director of Corrections pursuant to Section 1168 or 1170 of the Penal Code shall not be a fit subject for treatment pursuant to this article and shall be ordered discharged.

§3110. No requirement to register as narcotic offender.

A person committed to the custody of the Director of Corrections pursuant to this article is not required to register pursuant to Article 4 (commencing with Section 11590) of Chapter 10 of Division 10 of the Health and Safety Code.

§3111. Public officers' immunity from liability.

In the performance of acts and duties required by this article, any peace officer, health officer, physician, superintendent of an institution or district attorney shall have the same immunity from liability as is provided for public officers in Sections 820.2 and 821.6 of the Government Code.

ARTICLE 4

RELEASE IN OUTPATIENT STATUS

§3150. Establishment of Narcotic Addict Evaluation Authority.

(a) Membership. There is in the Youth and Adult Correctional Agency a Narcotic Addict Evaluation Authority, hereafter referred to in this article as the "authority". The authority shall be composed of seven members, each of whom shall be appointed by the Governor, for a term of four years and until the appointment and qualification of his successor. Members shall be eligible for reappointment. The chairman of the authority shall be designated by the Governor from time to time. The terms of the members first appointed to the authority shall expire as follows: one on January 15, 1965, one on January 15, 1966, one on January 15, 1967, and one on January 15, 1968. The terms of the three members first appointed to the authority pursuant to amendments to this section enacted at the 1979-80 Regular Session of the Legislature shall expire as follows: one on January 15, 1983, one on January 15, 1984, and one on January 15, 1985. Their successors shall hold office for terms of four years, each term to commence on the expiration date of the term of the predecessor. The Governor shall fill every vacancy for the balance of the unexpired term. Insofar as practicable, persons appointed to the authority shall have a broad background in law, sociology, law enforcement, medicine, or education, and shall have a deep interest in the rehabilitation of narcotic addicts.

(b) Duties. Each member of the authority shall devote such time to the duties of his or her office as required for performance of his or her duties and shall be entitled to an annual salary of nine thousand five hundred dollars ($9,500) for attendance upon business of the authority. The chairman shall be entitled to an annual salary of ten thousand dollars ($10,000). In addition, each member shall be allowed actual expenses incurred in the discharge of his duties, including travel expenses.

(c) The authority shall maintain its headquarters at the California Rehabilitation Center and shall be provided with necessary office space, equipment and services from funds appropriated to the California Rehabilitation Center.

(d) The authority shall meet at the center or its branches at such times as may be necessary for a full and complete study of the cases of all patients who are certified by the Director of Corrections to the authority as having recovered from addiction or imminent danger of addiction to such an extent that release in an outpatient status is warranted. Other times and places of meetings may also be fixed by the authority. Where the authority performs its functions by meeting en banc in either public or executive sessions to decide matters of general policy, at least three members shall be present, and no such action shall be valid unless it is concurred in by a majority vote of those present. The authority may meet and transact business in panels. Each authority panel shall consist of at least two members of the authority. Two members of the authority shall constitute a quorum for the transaction of business of a panel. No action shall be valid unless concurred in by a majority of the members present.

(e) Members of other similar boards may be assigned to hear cases and make recommendations to the authority. Such recommendations shall be made in accordance with policies established by a majority of the total membership of the authority.

§3151. Release in outpatient status.

After an initial period of observation and treatment, and subject to the rules and policies established by the Director of Corrections, whenever a person committed under Article 2 or Article 3 of this chapter has recovered from his addiction or imminent danger of addiction to such an extent that, in the opinion of the Director of Corrections, release in an outpatient status is warranted, the director shall certify such fact to the authority. If the director has not so certified within the preceding 12 months, in the anniversary month of the commitment of any person committed under this chapter his case shall automatically be referred to the authority for consideration of the advisability of release in outpatient status. Upon any such certification by the director or such automatic certification, the authority may release such person in an outpatient status subject to all rules and regulations adopted by the authority, and subject to all conditions imposed by the authority, whether of general applicability or restricted to the particular person released in outpatient status, and subject to being retaken and returned to inpatient status as prescribed in such rules, regulations, or conditions. The supervision of such persons while in an outpatient status shall be administered by the Department of Corrections. Such persons are not subject to the provisions of Penal Code Section 2600.

A single member of the authority may by written or oral order suspend the release in outpatient status of such a person and cause him to be retaken, until the next meeting of the authority. The written order of any member of the authority shall be a sufficient warrant for any peace officer to return such persons to physical custody.

It is hereby made the duty of all peace officers to execute any such order in like manner as ordinary criminal process.

§3152. Rules regarding outpatient status.

The rules for persons in outpatient status shall include but not be limited to close supervision of the person after release from the facility, periodic and surprise testing for narcotic use, counseling and return to inpatient status at the California Rehabilitation Center or its branches at the discretion of the authority, if from the reports of agents of the Department of Corrections or other information including reports of law enforcement officers as to the conduct of the person, the authority concludes that it is for the best interests of the person and society that this be done.

§3152.5. Outpatient revocation proceedings.

In outpatient revocation proceedings, an outpatient or his attorney shall receive a copy of any police, arrest, and crime reports pertaining to such proceedings. Portions of such reports containing confidential information need not be disclosed if the outpatient or his attorney has been notified that confidential information has not been disclosed.

§3153. Halfway houses as pilot projects.

The Director of Corrections is authorized to establish one or more halfway houses in large metropolitan areas as pilot projects in order to determine the effectiveness of such control on the addict's rehabilitation, particularly upon his release from the narcotic detention and treatment facility. Rules and regulations governing the operation of such halfway houses shall be established by the Director of Corrections and shall provide for control of the earnings of persons assigned to such halfway houses during their residence there, from which shall be deducted such charges for maintenance as the Director of Corrections may prescribe.

§3154. Participation in methadone maintenance project.

A person released in an outpatient status from the California Rehabilitation Center may, with the approval of the Department of Corrections and the Narcotic Addict Evaluation Authority, voluntarily participate in a methadone maintenance project approved under Section 11876 of the Health and Safety Code.

Participation in a methadone maintenance project shall not be construed to break the abstention from the use of narcotics for the purpose of Section 3200.

§3155. Payment upon release.

In addition to any other payment to which he or she is entitled by law, each person who has been committed to the custody of the Director of Corrections pursuant to this chapter shall, upon his or her release, be paid the sum of two hundred dollars ($200), from such appropriations that may be made available for the purposes of this section.

The director may prescribe rules and regulations (a) to limit or eliminate any payments provided for in this section to persons who have not been confined at least six consecutive months prior to their release in instances where the director determines that such a payment is not necessary for the rehabilitation of the prisoner, and (b) to establish procedures for the payment of the sum of the two hundred dollars ($200) within the first 60 days of a prisoner's release.

The provisions of this section shall not be applicable if the person is released to the custody of another state or to the custody of the federal government, nor shall they apply to persons discharged pursuant to Section 3109 who subsequently, as a result of such discharge, are committed to state prison.

§3156. Authority's rules and regulations.

(a) Any rules and regulations, including any resolutions and policy statements, promulgated by the authority, shall be promulgated and filed pursuant to Chapter 3.5 (commencing with Section 11340) of Part

© 1992 by J., B. & L. Gould
Printed in the U.S.A. EP

1 of Division 3 of Title 2 of the Government Code, and shall, to the extent practical, be stated in language that is easily understood by the general public.

(b) The authority shall maintain, publish, and make available to the general public, a compendium of its rules and regulations, including any resolutions and policy statements, promulgated pursuant to this section.

(c) The following exceptions to the procedures specified in this section apply to the authority: The chairman may specify an effective date that is any time more than 30 days after the rule or regulation is filed with the Secretary of State; provided that no less than 20 days prior to that effective date, copies of the rule or regulation shall be posted in conspicuous places throughout each institution and shall be mailed to all persons or organizations who request them.

§3157. Issuing subpoenas.

The Chairman of the Narcotic Addict Evaluation Authority shall have the authority of a head of a department set forth in subdivision (e) of Section 11181 of the Government Code to issue subpoenas as provided in Article 2 (commencing with Section 11180) of Chapter 2 of Division 3 of Title 2 of the Government Code. The authority shall adopt regulations on the policies and guidelines for the issuance of regulations.

ARTICLE 5

DISCHARGE OF NARCOTIC ADDICTS

§3200. Recommendation for discharge.

(a) If at any time the Director of Corrections is of the opinion that a person committed pursuant to Article 3 (commencing with Section 3100) while in outpatient status has abstained from the use of narcotics, other than as medically prescribed in a methadone program pursuant to Section 3154, for at least six consecutive months and has otherwise complied with the conditions of his or her release, the director shall recommend to the Narcotic Addict Evaluation Authority that such person be discharged from the program. If the authority concurs in the opinion of the director, it shall discharge such person from the program.

(b) If at any time the director is of the opinion that a person committed for a period of 24 months, or less, pursuant to Article 2 (commencing with Section 3050) while in outpatient status has abstained from the use of narcotics, other than as medically prescribed in a methadone program pursuant to Section 3154, for at least 12 consecutive months and has otherwise complied with the conditions of his or her release, or if at any time the director is of the opinion that a person committed for a period of more than 24 months pursuant to Article 2 (commencing with Section 3050) while in outpatient status has abstained from the use of narcotics, other than as medically prescribed in a methadone program pursuant to Section 3154, for at least 16 consecutive months and has otherwise complied with the conditions of his or her release, the director shall so advise the Narcotic Addict Evaluation Authority. If the authority concurs in the opinion of the director, it shall file with the superior court of the county in which the person was committed a certificate alleging such facts and recommending to the court the discharge of the person from the program. The authority shall serve a copy of such certificate upon the district attorney of the county. Upon the filing of such certificate, the court shall discharge the person from the program. The court may, unless otherwise

prohibited by law, modify the sentence, dismiss the criminal charges of which such person was convicted, or suspend further proceedings, as it deems warranted in the interests of justice. Where such person was certified to the superior court from a municipal or justice court, the person shall be returned to such court, which may dismiss the original charges. In any case where the criminal charges are not dismissed and the person is sentenced thereon, time served in custody while under commitment pursuant to Article 2 (commencing with Section 3050) shall be credited on such sentence. Such dismissal shall have the same force and effect as a dismissal under Section 1203.4 of the Penal Code, except the conviction is a prior conviction for purposes of Division 10 (commencing with Section 11000) of the Health and Safety Code.

§3201. Maximum term of commitment.

(a) Except as otherwise provided in subdivisions (b) and (c) of this section, if a person committed pursuant to this chapter has not been discharged from the program prior to expiration of 16 months, the Director of Corrections shall, on the expiration of such period, return him or her to the court from which he or she was committed, which court shall discharge him or her from the program and order him or her returned to the court in which criminal proceedings were adjourned, or the imposition of sentence suspended, prior to his or her commitment or certification to the superior court.

(b) Any other provision of this chapter notwithstanding, in any case in which a person was committed pursuant to Article 3 (commencing with Section 3100), such person shall be discharged no later than 12 months after his or her commitment.

(c) Any person committed pursuant to Article 2 (commencing with Section 3050), whose execution of sentence in accordance with the provisions of Section 1170 of the Penal Code was suspended pending a commitment pursuant to Section 3051, who has spent, pursuant to this chapter, a period of time in confinement or in custody, excluding any time spent on outpatient status, equal to that which he or she would have otherwise spent in state prison had sentence been executed, including application of good behavior and participation credit provisions of Article 2.5 (commencing with Section 2930) of Chapter 7 of Title 1 of Part 3 of the Penal Code, shall, upon reaching such accumulation of time, be released on parole under the jurisdiction of the Narcotic Addict Evaluation Authority subject to all of the conditions imposed by the authority and subject to the provisions of Article 1 (commencing with Section 3000) of Chapter 8 of Title 1 of Part 3 of the Penal Code. A person on parole who violates the rules, regulations or conditions imposed by the authority shall be subject to being retaken and returned to the California Rehabilitation Center as prescribed in such rules, regulations, or conditions and in accordance with the provisions of Sections 3151 and 3152. At the termination of this period of parole supervision or of custody in the California Rehabilitation Center, the person shall be returned by the Director of Corrections to the court from which such person was committed, which court shall discharge him or her from the program and order him or her returned to the court which suspended execution of such person's sentence to state prison. Such court, notwithstanding any other provision of law, shall suspend or terminate further proceedings in the interest of justice, modify the sentence in the same manner as if the commitment had been recalled pursuant to subdivision (d) of Section 1170 of the Penal Code, or order execution of the suspended sentence. Upon the ordering of the execution of such sentence, the term imposed shall be deemed to have been served in full.

Except as otherwise provided in the preceding paragraph, or as otherwise provided in Section 3200, the period of commitment, including outpatient status, for persons committed pursuant to Section 3051, which commitment is subsequent to a criminal conviction for which execution of sentence to state prison is suspended, shall equal the term imposed under Section 1170 of the Penal Code, notwithstanding good time and participation credit provisions of Article 2.5 (commencing with Section 2930) of Chapter 7 of Title 1 of Part 3 of such code. Upon reaching such period of time, such person shall be released on parole under the jurisdiction of the Narcotic Addict Evaluation Authority subject to all of the conditions imposed by the authority and subject to the provisions of Article 1 (commencing with Section 3000) of Chapter 8 of Title 1 of Part 3 of the Penal Code. A person on parole who violates the rules, regulations, or conditions imposed by the authority shall be subject to being retaken and returned to the California Rehabilitation Center as prescribed in such rules, regulations, or conditions and in accordance with the provisions of Sections 3151 and 3152. At the termination of this period of parole supervision or of custody in the California Rehabilitation Center the person shall be returned by the Director of Corrections to the court from which he or she was committed, which court shall discharge such person from the program and order him or her returned to the court which suspended execution of the person's sentence to state prison. Such court, notwithstanding any other provision of law, shall suspend or terminate further proceedings in the interest of justice, modify the sentence in the same manner as if the commitment had been recalled pursuant to subdivision (d) of Section 1170 of the Penal Code, or order execution of the suspended sentence. Upon the ordering of the execution of such sentence, the term imposed shall be deemed to have been served in full.

Nothing in this section shall preclude a person who has been discharged from the program from being recommitted under the program, irrespective of the periods of time of any previous commitments.

DIVISION 5

COMMUNITY MENTAL HEALTH SERVICES

PART 1

THE LANTERMAN-PETRIS-SHORT ACT

CHAPTER 2

INVOLUNTARY TREATMENT

ARTICLE 1

DETENTION OF MENTALLY DISORDERED PERSONS FOR EVALUATION AND TREATMENT

§5150. Detention of mentally disordered persons for evaluation and treatment.

When any person, as a result of mental disorder, is a danger to others, or to himself or herself, or gravely disabled, a peace officer, member of the attending staff, as defined by regulation, of an evaluation facility designated by the county, designated members of a mobile crisis team provided by Section 5651.7, or other professional person designated by the county may, upon probable cause, take, or cause to be taken, the person into custody and place him or her in a facility designated by the county and approved by the State Department of Mental Health as a facility for 72-hour treatment and evaluation.

Such facility shall require an application in writing stating the circumstances under which the person's condition was called to the attention of the officer, member of the attending staff, or professional person, and stating that the officer, member of the attending staff, or professional person has probable cause to believe that the person is, as a result of mental disorder, a danger to others, or to himself or herself, or gravely disabled. If the probable cause is based on the statement of a person other than the officer, member of the attending staff, or professional person, such person shall be liable in a civil action for intentionally giving a statement which he or she knows to be false.

§5150.1. Interference with peace officer or jailer.

No peace officer seeking to transport, or having transported, a person to a designated facility for assessment under Section 5150, shall be instructed by mental health personnel to take the person to, or keep the person at, a jail solely because of the unavailability of an acute bed, nor shall the peace officer be forbidden to transport the person directly to the designated facility. No mental health employee from any county, state, city, or any private agency providing Short-Doyle psychiatric emergency services shall interfere with a peace officer performing duties under Section 5150 by preventing the peace officer from entering a designated facility with the person to be assessed, nor shall any employee of such an agency require the peace officer to remove the person without assessment as a condition of allowing the peace officer to depart.

"Peace officer" for the purposes of this section also means a jailer seeking to transport or transporting a person in custody to a designated facility for assessment consistent with Section 4011.6 or 4011.8 of the Penal Code and Section 5150. *(Added by Stats 1985 ch 1286.)*

§5151. Detention period.

If the facility for 72-hour treatment and evaluation admits the person, it may detain him for evaluation and treatment for a period not to exceed 72 hours, excluding Saturdays, Sundays, and holidays if evaluation and treatment services cannot reasonably be made available on those days. The certification by the department is subject to renewal every two years. The department shall adopt regulations defining criteria for determining whether a facility can reasonably be expected to make evaluation and treatment services available on Saturdays, Sundays, and holidays.

Prior to admitting a person to the facility for 72-hour treatment and evaluation pursuant to Section 5150, the professional person in charge of the facility or his or her designee shall assess the individual in person to determine the appropriateness of the involuntary detention.

If in the judgment of the professional person in charge of the facility providing evaluation and treatment, or his or her designee, the person can be proper-

© 1992 by J., B. & L. Gould
Printed in the U.S.A. **EP**

ly served without being detained, he or she shall be provided evaluation, crisis intervention, or other inpatient or outpatient services on a voluntary basis.

Nothing in this section shall be interpreted to prevent a peace officer from delivering individuals to a designated facility for assessment under Section 5150. Furthermore, the preadmission assessment requirement of this section shall not be interpreted to require peace officers to perform any additional duties other than those specified in Sections 5150.1 and 5150.2. *(Amended by Stats 1986 ch 323.)*

§5152. Evaluation, treatment, release.

(a) Each person admitted to a facility for 72-hour treatment and evaluation under the provisions of this article shall receive an evaluation as soon after he or she is admitted as possible and shall receive whatever treatment and care his or her condition requires for the full period that he or she is held. The person shall be released before 72 hours have elapsed only if, the psychiatrist directly responsible for the person's treatment believes, as a result of his or her personal observations, that the person no longer requires evaluation or treatment. If any other professional person who is authorized to release the person, believes the person should be released before 72 hours have elapsed, and the psychiatrist directly responsible for the person's treatment objects, the matter shall be referred to the medical director of the facility for the final decision. However, if the medical director is not a psychiatrist, he or she shall appoint a designee who is a psychiatrist. If the matter is referred, the person shall be released before 72 hours have elapsed only if the psychiatrist making the final decision believes, as a result of his or her personal observations, that the person no longer requires evaluation or treatment.

(b) Persons who have been detained for evaluation and treatment shall be released, referred for further care and treatment on a voluntary basis, certified for intensive treatment, or a conservator or temporary conservator shall be appointed pursuant to this part as required.

(c) Persons who have been detained for evaluation and treatment, who are receiving medications as a result of their mental illness, shall be given, as soon as possible after detention, written and oral information about the probable effects of the medication by a person designated by the mental health facility where the person is detained. The State Department of Mental Health shall develop and promulgate written materials on the effects of medications, for use by county mental health programs as disseminated or as modified by the county mental health program, addressing the probable effects and the possible side effects of the medication. The following information shall be given orally to the patient:

(1) The nature of the mental illness, or behavior, that is the reason the medication is being given or recommended.

(2) The likelihood of improving or not improving without the medications.

(3) Reasonable alternative treatments available.

(4) The name and type, frequency, amount, and method of dispensing the medications, and the probable length of time that the medications will be taken.

The fact that the information has or has not been given shall be indicated in the patient's chart. If the information has not been given, the designated person shall document in the patient's chart the justification

for not providing the information. A failure to give information about the probable effects and possible side effects of the medication shall not constitute new grounds for release. *(Amended by Stats 1985 ch 1288; Stats 1986 ch 872.)*

§5152.1. Notice to peace officer and health director.

The professional person in charge of the facility providing 72-hour evaluation and treatment, or his or her designee, shall notify the county mental health director or the director's designee and the peace officer who makes the written application Pursuant to Section 5150 or a person who is designated by the law enforcement agency that employs the peace officer, when the person has been released after 72-hour detention, when the person is not detained, or when the person is released before the full period of allowable 72-hour detention if all of the following conditions apply:

(a) The peace officer requests such notification at the time he or she makes the application and the peace officer certifies at that time in writing that the person has been referred to the facility under circumstances which, based upon an allegation of facts regarding actions witnessed by the officer or another person, would support the filing of a criminal complaint.

(b) The notice is limited to the person's name, address, date of admission for 72-hour evaluation and treatment, and date of release.

If a police officer, law enforcement agency, or designee of the law enforcement agency, possesses any record of information obtained pursuant to the notification requirements of this section, the officer, agency, or designee shall destroy that record two years after receipt of notification.

§5152.2. Method of notification.

Each law enforcement agency within a county shall arrange with the county mental health director a method for giving prompt notification to peace officers pursuant to Section 5152.1.

§5153. Officer to apprehend in plain clothes.

Whenever possible, officers charged with apprehension of persons pursuant to this article shall dress in plain clothes and travel in unmarked vehicles.

DIVISION 6

ADMISSIONS AND JUDICIAL COMMITMENTS

PART 2

JUDICIAL COMMITMENTS

CHAPTER 2

COMMITMENT CLASSIFICATION

ARTICLE 2

MENTALLY RETARDED PERSONS

§6500. Commitment of dangerous persons.

On and after July 1, 1971, no mentally retarded person may be committed to the State Department of Developmental Services pursuant to this article, unless he or she is a danger to himself or herself or others. For the purposes of this article, dangerousness to self or others shall be considered to include, but not be limited to, a finding of incompetence to stand trial pursuant to the provisions of Chapter 6 (commencing with Section 1367) of Title 10 of Part 2 of the Penal Code when the defendant has been charged with murder, mayhem, aggravated mayhem, a violation of Section 207 or 209 of the Penal Code in which the victim suffers intentionally inflicted great bodily injury, robbery perpetrated by torture or by a person armed with a dangerous or deadly weapon or in which the victim suffers great bodily injury, a violation of subdivision (b) of Section 451 of the Penal Code, a violation of subdivision (2) or (3) of Section 261 of the Penal Code, a violation of Section 459 of the Penal Code in the first degree, assault with intent to commit murder, a violation of Section 220 of the Penal Code in which the victim suffers great bodily injury, a violation of Section 12303.1, 12303.3, 12308, 12309, or 12310 of the Penal Code, or if the defendant has been charged with a felony involving death, great bodily injury, or an act which poses a serious threat of bodily harm to another person.

Any order of commitment made pursuant to this article shall expire automatically one year after the order of commitment is made. This section shall not be construed to prohibit any party enumerated in Section 6502 from filing subsequent petitions for additional periods of commitment. In the event such subsequent petitions are filed, the procedures followed shall be the same as with an initial petition for commitment.

In any proceedings conducted under the authority of this article the alleged mentally retarded person shall be informed of his or her right to counsel by the court; and if the person does not have an attorney for the proceedings the court shall immediately appoint the public defender or other attorney to represent him or her. The person shall pay the cost for such legal service if he or she is able to do so. At any judicial proceeding under the provisions of this article, allegations that a person is mentally retarded and a danger to himself or herself or to others shall be presented by the district attorney for the county unless the board of supervisors, by ordinance or resolution, delegates such authority to the county counsel. *(Amended by Stats 1989 ch 897 §47, eff. 1/1/90.)*

§6502. Petition for commitment.

A petition for the commitment of a mentally retarded person to the State Department of Developmental Services may be filed in the superior court of the county in which such person is physically present. The following persons may request the person authorized to present allegations pursuant to Section 6500 to file a petition for commitment:

(a) The parent, guardian, conservator, or other person charged with the support of the mentally retarded person.

(b) The probation officer.

(c) The Youth Authority.

(d) Any person designated for that purpose by the judge of the court.

(e) The Director of Corrections.

(f) The regional center director or his designee.

Such request shall state the petitioner's reasons for supposing the person to be eligible for admission thereto, and shall be verified by affidavit.

§6503. Time and place to hear petition.

The court shall fix a time and place for the hearing of the petition. The time for the hearing shall be set no more than 60 days after the filing of the petition. The court may grant a continuance only upon a showing of good cause. The hearing may, in the discretion of the court, be held at any place which the court deems proper, and which will give opportunity for the production and examination of witnesses.

§6504. Due notice of hearing.

In all cases the court shall require due notice of the hearing of the petition to be given to the alleged mentally retarded person. Whenever a petition is filed, the court shall require such notice of the hearing of the petition as it deems proper to be given to any parent, guardian, conservator, or other person charged with the support of the person mentioned in the petition.

§6504.5. Written report of evaluation.

Wherever a petition is filed pursuant to this article, the court shall appoint the director of a regional center for the developmentally disabled established under Division 4.5 of this code, or the designee of the director, to examine the alleged mentally retarded person.

Within 15 judicial days after his appointment, the regional center director or designee shall submit to the court in writing a report containing his evaluation of the alleged mentally retarded person. The report shall contain a recommendation of a facility or facilities in which the alleged developmentally disabled person may be placed.

The report shall include a description of the least restrictive residential placement necessary to achieve the purposes of treatment.

§6505. Order for apprehension and delivery to court.

Whenever the court considers it necessary or advisable, it may cause an order to issue for the apprehension and delivery to the court of the alleged mentally retarded person, and may have the order executed by any peace officer.

§6506. Order for custody, care and treatment pending hearing.

Pending the hearing, the court may order that the alleged dangerous mentally retarded person may be left in the charge of his or her parent, guardian, conservator, or other suitable person, or placed in a state hospital for the developmentally disabled or in the county psychiatric hospital. Prior to the issuance of an order under this section, the regional center shall recommend to the court a suitable person or facility to care for the alleged mentally retarded person.

Pending the hearing the court may order that the person receive necessary habilitation, care, and treatment, including medical and dental treatment.

Orders made pursuant to this section shall expire at the time set for the hearing pursuant to Section 6503. If the court upon a showing of good cause grants a continuance of the hearing on the matter, it shall order that the person be detained pursuant to this section until the hearing on the petition is held.

§6507. Subpoena of witnesses.

The court shall inquire into the condition or status of the alleged mentally retarded person. For this purpose it may by subpoena require the attendance before

© 1992 by J., B. & L. Gould
Printed in the U.S.A.   **EP**

it of a physician who has made a special study of mental retardation and is qualified as a medical examiner, and of a clinical psychologist, or of two such physicians, or of two such psychologists, to examine the person and testify concerning his mentality. The court may also by subpoena require the attendance of such other persons as it deems advisable, to give evidence.

§6509. Order of commitment for treatment.

If the court finds that the person is mentally retarded, and that he is a danger to himself or to others, the court may make an order that the person be committed to the State Department of Developmental Services for suitable treatment and habilitation services. Suitable treatment and habilitation services is defined as the least restrictive residential placement necessary to achieve the purposes of treatment. Care and treatment of a person committed to the State Department of Developmental Services may include placement in any state hospital, any licensed community care facility as defined in Section 1504, or any health facility as defined in Section 1250. The court shall hold a hearing as to the available placement alternatives and consider the report of the regional center director or designee submitted pursuant to Section 6504.5. After hearing all the evidence the court shall order that the person be committed to that placement which the court finds to be the most appropriate alternative. The court, however, may commit a mentally retarded person who is not a resident of this state under Section 4460 for the purpose of transportation of such person to the state of his legal residence pursuant to Section 4461. The State Department of Developmental Services shall receive the person committed to it and shall place the person in the placement ordered by the court.

If the Department of Developmental Services decides that a change in placement is necessary, it shall notify in writing the court of commitment, the district attorney and the attorney of record for the person and the regional center of such decision at least 15 days in advance of the proposed change in placement. The court may hold a hearing and (1) approve or disapprove of the change, or (2) take no action in which case the change shall be deemed approved. At the request of the district attorney or of the attorney for the person, a hearing shall be held.

§6511. Contriving to adjudge mentally retarded.

Any person who knowingly contrives to have any person adjudged mentally retarded under the provisions of this article, unlawfully or improperly, is guilty of a misdemeanor.

§6512. Juvenile court proceedings regarding mentally retarded.

If, when a boy or girl is brought before a juvenile court under the juvenile court law, it appears to the court, either before or after adjudication, that the person is mentally retarded, or if, on the conviction of any person of crime by any court it appears to the court that the person is mentally retarded, the court may adjourn the proceedings or suspend the sentence, as the case may be, and direct some suitable person to take proceedings under this article against the person before the court, and the court may order that, pending the preparation, filing, and hearing of the petition, the person before the court be detained in a place of safety,

or be placed under the guardianship of some suitable person, on his entering into a recognizance for the appearance of the person upon trial or under conviction when required. If, upon the hearing of the petition, or upon a subsequent hearing, the person upon trial or under conviction is not found to be mentally retarded, the court may proceed with the trial or impose sentence, as the case may be.

CHAPTER 7

DUTIES OF PEACE OFFICERS

§6800. Duties regarding indigent committed persons.

All peace officers and other persons having similar duties relating to judicially committed poor persons shall see that all poor and indigent committed persons within their respective municipalities are speedily granted the relief conferred by this part. When so ordered by a superior court judge, they shall see that such committed persons are, without unnecessary delay, transferred to the proper state hospitals provided for their care and treatment. Before sending a person to any such hospital, they shall see that he is in a state of bodily cleanliness and comfortably clothed with clean clothes. The department may by order direct that any person whom it deems unsuitable therefor shall not be employed as an attendant for any committed person. After the patient has been delivered to the proper officers of the hospital, the care and custody of the county or municipality from which he is sent ceases.

CHAPTER 8

MENTALLY DISORDERED PERSONS CHARGED WITH CRIME

§6825. Procedures.

The procedures for handling mentally disordered persons charged with the commission of public offenses are provided for in Section 1026 of the Penal Code and in Chapter 6 (commencing with Section 1365), Title 10, Part 2 of the Penal Code.

DIVISION 7

MENTAL INSTITUTIONS

CHAPTER 2

STATE HOSPITALS FOR THE MENTALLY DISORDERED

§7275. Persons liable for patient's care.

The husband, wife, father, mother, or children of a patient in a state hospital for the mentally disordered, the estates of such persons, and the guardian or conservator and administrator of the estate of such patient shall cause him to be properly and suitably cared for and maintained, and shall pay the costs and charges of his transportation to a state institution. The husband, wife, father, mother, or children of a patient in a state hospital for the mentally disordered and the administrators of their estates, and the estate of such person shall be liable for his care, support, and maintenance in a state institution of which he is a patient. The liability of such persons and estates shall be a joint and several liability, and such liability shall exist whether the person has become a patient of a state institution pursuant to the provisions of this code or pursuant to the provisions of Sections 1026, 1368, 1369, 1370, and 1372 of the Penal Code.

This section does not impose liability for the care of mentally retarded persons in state hospitals.

§7325. Apprehension of patient escapee.

When any patient committed by a court to a state hospital or other institution on or before June 30, 1969, or when any patient who is judicially committed on or after July 1, 1969, or when any patient who is involuntary* detained pursuant to Part 1 (commencing with Section 5000) of Division 5 escapes from any state hospital, any hospital or facility operated by or under the Veteran's** Administration of the United States government, or any facility designated by a county pursuant to such Part 1, or any facility into which the patient has been placed by his or her conservator appointed pursuant to Chapter 3 (commencing with Section 5350), Part 1, Division 5, of this code, or when a judicially committed patient's return from leave of absence has been authorized or ordered by the State Department of Mental Health, or the State Department of Developmental Services, or the facility of the Veteran's** Administration, any peace officer, upon written request of the state hospital, veterans' facility, or the facility designated by a county, or the patient's conservator appointed pursuant to Chapter 3 (commencing with Section 5350), Part 1, Division 5, of this code, shall without the necessity of a warrant or court order, or any officer or employee of the State Department of Mental Health, or of the State Department of Developmental Services, designated to perform such duties may, apprehend, take into custody and deliver him or her to the state hospital or to a facility of the Veterans'** Administration, or the facility designated by a county, or to any person or place authorized by the State Department of Mental Health, or by the State Department of Developmental Services, or by the Veterans'** Administration, or the local director of the county mental health program of the county in which is located the facility designated by the county, or the patient's conservator appointed pursuant to Chapter 3 (commencing with Section 5350), Part 1, Division 5, of this code, as the case may be, to receive him or her. Every officer or employee of the State Department of Mental Health, or of the State Department of Developmental Services, designated to apprehend or return such patients shall have the powers and privileges of peace officers so far as necessary to enforce the provisions of this section.

As used in this section, "any peace officer" means the persons specified in Section 830.1 of the Penal Code.

The written notification of the escape required by this section shall include the name and physical description of the patient, his or her home address, the degree of dangerousness of the patient and any additional information which is necessary to apprehend and return the patient. Any officer or employee of a state hospital, hospital or facility operated by or under the Veterans'** Administration, or any facility designated by a county pursuant to Part 1 (commencing with Section 5000) of Division 5 shall provide any peace officer with any information concerning any patient who escapes from such hospital or facility in order to assist in the apprehension and return of the patient.

The person in charge of such hospital or facility, or his or her designee, may provide telephonic notification of the escape to the law enforcement agency of the county or city in which the hospital or facility is located. If such notification is given, the time and date of notification, the person notified, and the person making the notification shall be noted in the written notification required by this section.
*So in original. Probably should be "involuntarily".
**So in original. Probably should be "Veterans".

§7325.5. Information needed to apprehend escapee not guilty by reason of insanity.

Notwithstanding Section 5328, information regarding a person's name, reason for commitment, age, physical description, and any other information which the medical director of the treatment facility considers essential in aiding apprehension of the escapee shall be released if the person has escaped from a state mental health facility, and the person was committed to the state mental health facility by a court after being found not guilty by reason of insanity pursuant to Section 1026 of the Penal Code, unable to stand trial due to mental condition pursuant to Section 1370 of the Penal Code, or a mentally disordered sex offender pursuant to Division 6 (commencing with Section 6000).

§7326. Willfully assisting committed patient to escape.

Any person who willfully assists any judicially committed or remanded patient of a state hospital or other public or private mental health facility to escape, to attempt to escape therefrom, or to resist being returned from a leave of absence shall be punished by imprisonment in the state prison, a fine of not more than ten thousand dollars ($10,000), or both such imprisonment and fine; or by imprisonment in a county jail for a period of not more than one year, a fine of not more than two thousand dollars ($2,000), or both such imprisonment and fine.

§7327. Fees and expenses for delivery of patients.

Every peace officer who is designated in and pursuant to Section 7325 delivers or assists in the delivery of a patient to a state hospital or other place designated by a state hospital shall be entitled to receive from the state hospital such fees and expenses as are payable to sheriffs for conveyance of patients to state hospitals.

DIVISION 8

MISCELLANEOUS

CHAPTER 3

FIREARMS

§8100. Possession by mental patient.

(a) A person shall not have in his or her possession or under his or her custody or control, or purchase or receive, or attempt to purchase or receive, any firearms whatsoever or any other deadly weapon, if on or after January 1, 1992, he or she has been admitted to a facility and is receiving inpatient treatment and, in the opinion of the attending health professional who is primarily responsible for the patient's treatment of

© 1992 by J., B. & L. Gould
Printed in the U.S.A.   EP

a mental disorder, is a danger to self or others, as specified by Section 5150, 5250, or 5300, even though the patient has consented to that treatment. A person is not subject to this subdivision once he or she is discharged from the facility.

(b) (1) A person shall not have in his or her possession or under his or her custody or control, or purchase or receive, or attempt to purchase or receive, any firearms whatsoever or any other deadly weapon for a period of six months whenever, on or after January 1, 1992, he or she communicates to a licensed psychotherapist, as defined in subdivisions (a) to (e), inclusive, of Section 1010 of the Evidence Code, a serious threat of physical violence against a reasonably identifiable victim or victims. The six-month period shall commence from the date that the licensed psychotherapist reports to the local law enforcement agency the identity of the person making the communication. The prohibition provided for in this subdivision shall not apply unless the licensed psychotherapist notifies a local law enforcement agency of the threat by that person. The person, however, may own, possess, have custody or control over, or receive or purchase any firearm if a superior court, pursuant to paragraph (3) and upon petition of the person, has found, by a preponderance of the evidence, that the person is likely to use firearms or other deadly weapons in a safe and lawful manner.

(2) Upon receipt of the report from the local law enforcement agency pursuant to subdivision (c) of Section 8105, the Department of Justice shall notify by certified mail, return receipt requested, a person subject to this subdivision of the following:

(A) That he or she is prohibited from possessing, having custody or control over, receiving, or purchasing any firearm or other deadly weapon for a period of six months commencing from the date that the licensed psychotherapist reports to the local law enforcement agency the identity of the person making the communication. The notice shall state the date when the prohibition commences and ends.

(B) That he or she may petition a court, as provided in this subdivision, for an order permitting the person to own, possess, control, receive, or purchase a firearm.

(3) Any person who is subject to paragraph (1) may petition the superior court of his or her county of residence for an order that he or she may own, possess, have custody or control over, receive, or purchase firearms. At the time the petition is filed, the clerk of the court shall set a hearing date and notify the person, the Department of Justice, and the district attorney. The people of the State of California shall be the respondent in the proceeding and shall be represented by the district attorney. Upon motion of the district attorney, or upon its own motion, the superior court may transfer the petition to the county in which the person resided at the time of the statements, or the county in which the person made the statements. Within seven days after receiving notice of the petition, the Department of Justice shall file copies of the reports described in Section 8105 with the superior court. The reports shall be disclosed upon request to the person and to the district attorney. The district attorney shall be entitled to a continuance of the hearing to a date of not less than 14 days after the district attorney is notified of the hearing date by the clerk of the court. Notwithstanding any other provision of law, declarations, police reports, including criminal history information, and any other material

and relevant evidence that is not excluded under Section 352 of the Evidence Code, shall be admissible at the hearing under this paragraph. If the court finds by a preponderance of the evidence that the person would be likely to use firearms in a safe and lawful manner, the court shall order that the person may have custody or control over, receive, possess, or purchase firearms. A copy of the order shall be submitted to the Department of Justice. Upon receipt of the order, the department shall delete any reference to the prohibition against firearms from the person's state summary criminal history information.

(c) "Discharge," for the purposes of this section, does not include a leave of absence from a facility.

(d) "Attending health care professional," as used in this section, means the licensed health care professional primarily responsible for the person's treatment who is qualified to make the decision that the person has a mental disorder and has probable cause to believe that the person is a danger to self or others.

(e) "Deadly weapon," as used in this section and in Sections 8101, 8102, and 8103, means any weapon, the possession or concealed carrying of which is prohibited by Section 12020 of the Penal Code.

(f) "Danger to self," as used in subdivision (a), means a voluntary person who has made a serious threat of, or attempted, suicide with the use of a firearm or other deadly weapon.

(g) A violation of subdivision (a) of, or paragraph (1) of subdivision (b) of, this section shall be a public offense, punishable by imprisonment in the state prison, or in a county jail for not more than one year, by a fine not exceeding one thousand dollars ($1,000), or by both that imprisonment and fine.

(h) The prohibitions set forth in this section shall be in addition to those set forth in Section 8103.

(i) Any person admitted and receiving treatment prior to January 1, 1992, shall be governed by this section, as amended by Chapter 1090 of the Statutes of 1990, until discharged from the facility. (*Amended by Stats 1991 ch 951 §9, 952 §5, eff. 1/1/92.*)

§8101. Penalty for giving deadly weapon to mental patient.

Any person who shall knowingly supply, sell, give, or allow possession or control of any firearm or deadly weapon to any person described in Section 8100 or 8103 shall be punishable by imprisonment in a state prison, or in a county jail for a period of not exceeding one year, by a fine of not exceeding one thousand dollars ($1,000), or by both such fine and imprisonment. "Deadly weapon", as used in this section, has the meaning prescribed by Section 8100. (*Amended by Stats 1985 ch 1324 §3.*)

§8102. Confiscating firearm from mental patient.

(a) Whenever a person who has been detained or apprehended for examination of his or her mental condition or who is a person described in Section 8100 or 8103, is found to own, have in his or her possession or under his or her control, any firearm whatsoever, or any other deadly weapon, the firearm or other deadly weapon shall be confiscated by any law enforcement agency or peace officer, who shall retain custody of the firearm or other deadly weapon.

"Deadly weapon," as used in this section, has the meaning prescribed by Section 8100.

(b) Upon confiscation of any firearm or other deadly weapon from a person who has been detained or apprehended for examination of his or her mental condition, the peace officer or law enforcement agency shall notify the person of the procedure for the return of any firearm or other deadly weapon which has been confiscated.

Where the person is released without judicial commitment, the professional person in charge of the facility, or his or her designee, shall notify the person of the procedure for the return of any firearm or other deadly weapon which may have been confiscated.

Health facility personnel shall notify the confiscating law enforcement agency upon release of the detained person, and shall make a notation to the effect that the facility provided the required notice to the person regarding the procedure to obtain return of any confiscated firearm.

(c) Upon the release of a person without judicial commitment as described in subdivision (b), the confiscating law enforcement agency shall have 10 days, unless good cause is shown, to initiate a petition in the superior court for a hearing to determine whether the return of a firearm or other deadly weapon would be likely to result in endangering the person or others, and to send a notice advising the person of his or her right to a hearing on this issue.

(d) The law enforcement agency shall inform the person that he or she has 30 days to respond to the court clerk to confirm his or her desire for a hearing, and that the failure to respond will result in a default order forfeiting the confiscated firearm or weapon. For the purpose of this subdivision, the person's last known address shall be the address provided to the law enforcement officer by the person at the time of the person's detention or apprehension.

(e) If the person responds and requests a hearing, the court clerk shall set a hearing, no later than 30 days from receipt of the request. The court clerk shall notify the person and the district attorney of the date, time, and place of the hearing.

(f) If the person does not respond within 30 days of the notice, the law enforcement agency may file a petition for order of default.

(g) If the law enforcement agency does not initiate proceedings within the 10-day period, it shall make the weapon available for return. *(Amended by Stats 1991 ch 866 §8, eff. 1/1/92.)*

§8103. Certificate for possession; prohibiting possession.

(a) (1) No person who after October 1, 1955, has been adjudicated by a court of any state to be a danger to others as a result of mental disorder or mental illness, or who has been adjudicated to be a mentally disordered sex offender, shall purchase or receive, or attempt to purchase or receive, or have in his or her possession, custody, or control any firearm or any other deadly weapon unless there has been issued to the person a certificate by the court of adjudication upon release from treatment or at a later date stating that the person may possess a firearm or any other deadly weapon without endangering others, and the person has not, subsequent to the issuance of the certificate, again been adjudicated by a court to be a danger to others as a result of a mental disorder or mental illness.

(2) The court shall immediately notify the Department of Justice of the court order finding the individual to be a person described in paragraph (1). The court shall also notify the Department of Justice of any certificate issued as described in paragraph (1).

(b) (1) No person who has been found, pursuant to Section 1026 of the Penal Code or the law of any other state or the United States, not guilty by reason of insanity of murder, mayhem, a violation of Section 207 or 209 of the Penal Code in which the victim suffers intentionally inflicted great bodily injury, robbery in which the victim suffers great bodily injury, a violation of Section 451 or 452 of the Penal Code involving a trailer coach, as defined in Section 635 of the Vehicle Code, or any dwelling house, a violation of subdivision (2) or (3) of Section 261 of the Penal Code, a violation of Section 459 of the Penal Code in the first degree, assault with intent to commit murder, a violation of Section 220 of the Penal Code in which the victim suffers great bodily injury, a violation of Section 12303.1, 12303.2, 12303.3, 12308, 12309, or 12310 of the Penal Code, or of a felony involving death, great bodily injury, or an act which poses a serious threat of bodily harm to another person, or a violation of the law of any other state or the United States which includes all the elements of any of the above felonies as defined under California law, shall purchase or receive, or attempt to purchase or receive, or have in his or her possession or under his or her custody or control any firearm or any other deadly weapon.

(2) The court shall immediately notify the Department of Justice of the court order finding the person to be a person described in paragraph (1).

(c) (1) No person who has been found, pursuant to Section 1026 of the Penal Code or the law of any other state or the United States, not guilty by reason of insanity of any crime other than those described in subdivision (b) shall purchase or receive, or attempt to purchase or receive, or shall have in his or her possession, custody, or control any firearm or any other deadly weapon unless the court of commitment has found the person to have recovered sanity, pursuant to Section 1026.2 of the Penal Code or the law of any other state or the United States.

(2) The court shall immediately notify the Department of Justice of the court order finding the person to be a person described in paragraph (1). The court shall also notify the Department of Justice when it finds that the person has recovered his or her sanity.

(d) (1) No person found by a court to be mentally incompetent to stand trial, pursuant to Section 1370 or 1370.1 of the Penal Code or the law of any other state or the United States, shall purchase or receive, or attempt to purchase or receive, or shall have in his or her possession, custody, or control any firearm or any other deadly weapon, unless there has been a finding with respect to the person of restoration to competence to stand trial by the committing court, pursuant to Section 1372 of the Penal Code or the law of any other state or the United States.

(2) The court shall immediately notify the Department of Justice of the court order finding the person to be mentally incompetent as described in paragraph (1). The court shall also notify the Department of Justice when it finds that the person has recovered his or her competence.

(e) (1) No person who has been placed under conservatorship by a court, pursuant to Section 5350 or the law of any other state or the United States, because the person is gravely disabled as a result of a mental disorder or impairment by chronic alcoholism shall

© 1992 by J., B. & L. Gould
Printed in the U.S.A.   EP

purchase or receive, or attempt to purchase or receive, or shall have in his or her possession, custody, or control any firearm or any other deadly weapon while under the conservatorship if, at the time the conservatorship was ordered or thereafter, the court which imposed the conservatorship found that possession of a firearm or any other deadly weapon by the person would present a danger to the safety of the person or to others. Upon placing any person under conservatorship, and prohibiting firearm or any other deadly weapon possession by the person the court shall notify the person of this prohibition.

(2) The court shall immediately notify the Department of Justice of the court order placing the person under conservatorship and prohibiting firearm or any other deadly weapon possession by the person as described in paragraph (1). The notice shall include the date the conservatorship was imposed and the date the conservatorship is to be terminated. If the conservatorship is subsequently terminated before the date listed in the notice to the Department of Justice or the court subsequently finds that possession of a firearm or any other deadly weapon by the person would no longer present a danger to the safety of the person or others, the court shall immediately notify the Department of Justice.

(3) All information provided to the Department of Justice pursuant to paragraph (2) shall be kept confidential, separate, and apart from all other records maintained by the department, and shall be used only to determine eligibility to purchase or possess firearms or other deadly weapons. Any person who knowingly furnishes any such information for any other purpose is guilty of a misdemeanor. All such information concerning any person shall be destroyed upon receipt by the Department of Justice of notice of the termination of conservatorship as to that person pursuant to paragraph (2).

(f) (1) No person who has been (A) taken into custody as provided in Section 5150 because that person is a danger to himself, herself, or to others, (B) assessed within the meaning of Section 5151, and (C) admitted to a designated facility within the meaning of Sections 5151 and 5152 because that person is a danger to himself, herself, or others, shall own, possess, control, receive, or purchase, or attempt to own, possess, control, receive, or purchase any firearm for a period of five years after the person is released from the facility. A person described in the preceding sentence, however, may own, possess, control, receive, or purchase, or attempt to own, possess, control, receive, or purchase any firearm if, at or prior to being released, the person is certified by the professional person in charge of the facility or his or her designee to be a person who is likely to use firearms in a safe and lawful manner or if the superior court has, pursuant to paragraph (4), upon petition of the person, found, by a preponderance of the evidence, that the person is likely to use firearms in a safe and lawful manner.

(2) For each person subject to this subdivision, the facility shall immediately, on the date of admission, submit a report to the Department of Justice, on a form prescribed by the department, containing information which includes, but is not limited to, the identity of the person and the legal grounds upon which the person was admitted to the facility.

Any report prescribed by this subdivision shall be confidential, except for purposes of the court proceedings described in this subdivision and for determining the eligibility of the person to own, possess, control, receive, or purchase a firearm. The state summary criminal history may state that the person is prohibited from owning, possessing, controlling, receiving, or purchasing a firearm under this subdivision or any other provision of law.

(3) Prior to, or concurrent with, the discharge, the facility shall inform a person subject to this subdivision that he or she is prohibited from owning, possessing, controlling, receiving, or purchasing any firearm for a period of five years. Simultaneously, the facility shall inform the person that he or she may petition a court, as provided in this subdivision, for an order permitting the person to own, possess, control, receive, or purchase a firearm.

(4) Any person who is subject to paragraph (1) may petition the superior court of his or her county of residence for an order that he or she may own, possess, control, receive, or purchase firearms. At the time the petition is filed, the clerk of the court shall set a hearing date and notify the person, the Department of Justice, and the district attorney. The People of the State of California shall be the respondent in the proceeding and shall be represented by the district attorney. Upon motion of the district attorney, or on its own motion, the superior court may transfer the petition to the county in which the person resided at the time of his or her detention, the county in which the person was detained, or the county in which the person was evaluated or treated. Within seven days after receiving notice of the petition, the Department of Justice shall file copies of the reports described in Section 8103 with the superior court. The reports shall be disclosed upon request to the person and to the district attorney. The district attorney shall be entitled to a continuance of the hearing to a date of not less than 14 days after the district attorney was notified of the hearing date by the clerk of the court. Notwithstanding any other provision of law, declarations, police reports, including criminal history information, and any other material and relevant evidence which is not excluded under Section 352 of the Evidence Code, shall be admissible at the hearing under this section. If the court finds by a preponderance of the evidence that the person would be likely to use firearms in a safe and lawful manner, the court may order that the person may own, control, receive, possess, or purchase firearms. A copy of the order shall be submitted to the Department of Justice. Upon receipt of the order, the Department of Justice shall delete any reference to the prohibition against firearms from the person's state summary criminal history information.

(g) (1) No person who has been certified for intensive treatment under Section 5250, 5260, or 5270.15 shall own, possess, control, receive, or purchase, or attempt to own, possess, control, receive, or purchase any firearm for a period of five years.

Any person who meets the criteria contained in subdivision (e) or (f) who is released from intensive treatment shall nevertheless, if applicable, remain subject to the prohibition contained in subdivision (e) or (f).

(2) For each person certified for intensive treatment under paragraph (1), the facility shall immediately submit a report to the Department of Justice, on a form prescribed by the department, containing information regarding the person, including, but not limited to, the legal identity of the person and the legal

grounds upon which the person was certified. Any report submitted pursuant to this paragraph shall only be used for the purposes specified in paragraph (2) of subdivision (f).

(3) Prior to, or concurrent with, the discharge of each person certified for intensive treatment under paragraph (1), the facility shall inform the person of that information specified in paragraph (3) of subdivision (f).

(4) Any person who is subject to the prohibition contained in paragraph (1) may fully invoke the provisions of paragraph (4) of subdivision (f).

(h) For all persons identified in subdivisions (f) and (g), facilities shall report to the Department of Justice as specified in those subdivisions, except facilities shall not report persons under subdivision (g) if the same persons previously have been reported under subdivision (f).

Additionally, all facilities shall report to the Department of Justice upon the discharge of persons from whom reports have been submitted pursuant to subdivision (f) or (g).

(i) Every person who owns or possesses or has under his or her custody or control, or purchases or receives, or attempts to purchase or receive, any firearm or any other deadly weapon in violation of this section is guilty of a felony which is punishable by imprisonment in the state prison, or in the county jail for not more than one year, and which is subject to subdivision (b) of Section 17 of the Penal Code.

(j) "Deadly weapon," as used in this section, has the meaning prescribed by Section 8100. *(Amended by Stats 1991 ch 955 §10, eff. 1/1/92.)*

§8104. Availability of identifying records.

The State Department of Mental Health shall maintain in a convenient central location and shall make available to the Department of Justice those records which the State Department of Mental Health has in its possession which are necessary to identify persons who come within the provisions of Section 8100 or 8103. These records shall be made available to the Department of Justice upon request. The Department of Justice shall make such requests only with respect to its duties with regard to applications for permits for, or the purchase or transfer of, explosives as defined in Section 12000 of the Health and Safety Code, devices defined in Section 12001 of the Penal Code, machineguns as defined in Section 12200 of the Penal Code, short-barreled shotguns or short-barreled rifles as defined in Section 12020 of the Penal Code, assault weapons as defined in Section 12276 of the Penal Code, and destructive devices as defined in Section 12301 of the Penal Code. These records shall not be furnished or made available to any person unless the department determines that disclosure of any information in the records is necessary to carry out its duties with respect to applications for permits for, or the purchase or transfer of, explosives, destructive devices, devices as defined in Section 12001 of the Penal Code, short-barreled shotguns, short-barreled rifles, assault weapons, and machineguns. *(Amended by Stats 1990 ch 1090 §5, eff. 1/1/91.)*

§8105. Information available to Department of Justice.

(a) The Department of Justice shall request each public and private mental hospital, sanitarium, and institution to submit to the department that information which the department deems necessary to identify those persons who are within the provisions of subdivision (a) of Section 8100, in order to carry out its duties in relation to firearms, destructive devices, and explosives.

(b) Upon request of the Department of Justice pursuant to subdivision (a), each public and private mental hospital, sanitarium, and institution shall submit to the department that information which the department deems necessary to identify those persons who are within the provisions of subdivision (a) of Section 8100, in order to carry out its duties in relation to firearms, destructive devices, and explosives.

(c) A licensed psychotherapist shall immediately report to a local law enforcement agency the identity of a person subject to subdivision (b) of Section 8100. Upon receipt of the report, the local law enforcement agency, on a form prescribed by the Department of Justice, shall immediately notify the department of the person who is subject to subdivision (b) of Section 8100.

(d) (1) Except as provided in paragraph (2), all information provided to the Department of Justice pursuant to this section shall be kept confidential, separate, and apart from all other records maintained by the department, and shall be used by the department only to determine eligibility to acquire, carry, and possess firearms, destructive devices, and explosives.

(2) Except for purposes of the court proceedings described in subdivision (b) of Section 8100 and for determining the eligibility of the person to acquire, carry, and possess firearms, destructive devices, and explosives, all information provided to the Department of Justice pursuant to this subdivision shall be kept confidential, separate, and apart from all other records maintained by the department. The information shall be used solely for the purposes of the court proceedings described in subdivision (b) of Section 8100 and by the department only to determine the eligibility of persons to acquire, carry, and possess firearms, destructive devices, and explosives.

(e) Reports shall not be required or requested under this section where the same person has been previously reported pursuant to section 8103 or 8104. *(Amended by Stats 1991 ch 951 §10, eff. 1/1/92.)*

DIVISION 9

PUBLIC SOCIAL SERVICES

PART 3

AID AND MEDICAL ASSISTANCE

CHAPTER 11

ELDER ABUSE AND DEPENDENT ADULT CIVIL PROTECTION ACT
(Chapter heading amended by Stats 1991 ch 774 §1, eff. 1/1/92.)

ARTICLE 2

DEFINITIONS

§15610. Definitions.

As used in this chapter:

(a) "Elder" means any person residing in this state, 65 years of age or older.

© 1992 by J., B. & L. Gould
Printed in the U.S.A.   **EP**

(b) (1) "Dependent adult" means any person residing in this state, between the ages of 18 and 64, who has physical or mental limitations which restrict his or her ability to carry out normal activities or to protect his or her rights including, but not limited to, persons who have physical or developmental disabilities or whose physical or mental abilities have diminished because of age.

(2) "Dependent adult" includes any person between the ages of 18 and 64 who is admitted as an inpatient to a 24-hour health facility, as defined in Sections 1250, 1250.2, and 1250.3 of the Health and Safety Code.

(c) "Physical abuse" means all of the following:

(1) Assault, as defined in Section 240 of the Penal Code.

(2) Battery, as defined in Section 242 of the Penal Code.

(3) Assault with a deadly weapon or force likely to produce great bodily injury, as defined by Section 245 of the Penal Code.

(4) Unreasonable physical constraint, or prolonged or continual deprivation of food or water.

(5) Sexual assault, which means any of the following:

(A) Sexual battery, as defined in Section 243.4 of the Penal Code.

(B) Rape, as defined in Section 261 of the Penal Code.

(C) Rape in concert, as described in Section 264.1 of the Penal Code.

(D) Incest, as defined in Section 285 of the Penal Code.

(E) Sodomy, as defined in Section 286 of the Penal Code.

(F) Oral copulation, as defined in Section 288a of the Penal Code.

(G) Penetration of a genital or anal opening by a foreign object, as defined in Section 289 of the Penal Code.

(6) Use of a physical or chemical restraint or psychotropic medication under any of the following conditions:

(A) For punishment.

(B) For a period significantly beyond that for which the restraint or medication was authorized pursuant to the instructions of a physician licensed in the State of California, who is providing medical care to the elder or dependent adult at the time the instructions are given.

(C) For any purpose not consistent with that authorized by the physician.

(d) "Neglect" means the negligent failure of any person having the care or custody of an elder or a dependent adult to exercise that degree of care which a reasonable person in a like position would exercise. Neglect includes, but is not limited to, all of the following:

(1) Failure to assist in personal hygiene, or in the provision of food, clothing, or shelter.

(2) Failure to provide medical care for physical and mental health needs. No person shall be deemed neglected or abused for the sole reason that he or she voluntarily relies on treatment by spiritual means through prayer alone in lieu of medical treatment.

(3) Failure to protect from health and safety hazards.

(4) Failure to prevent malnutrition.

(e) "Abandonment" means the desertion or willful foresaking of an elder or a dependent adult by anyone having care or custody of that person under circumstances in which a reasonable person would continue to provide care and custody.

(f) "Fiduciary abuse" means a situation in which any person who has the care or custody of, or who stands in a position of trust to, an elder or a dependent adult, takes, secretes, or appropriates their money or property, to any use or purpose not in the due and lawful execution of his or her trust.

(g) "Abuse of an elder or a dependent adult" means physical abuse, neglect, intimidation, cruel punishment, fiduciary abuse, abandonment, isolation, or other treatment with resulting physical harm or pain or mental suffering, or the deprivation by a care custodian of goods or services which are necessary to avoid physical harm or mental suffering.

(1) For purposes of this subdivision, "isolation" includes any of the following:

(A) Acts intentionally committed for the purpose of preventing, and that do serve to prevent, an elder or dependent adult from receiving his or her mail or telephone calls.

(B) Telling a caller or prospective visitor that an elder or dependent adult is not present, or does not wish to talk with the caller, or does not wish to meet with the visitor, where the statement is false, is contrary to the express wishes of the elder or the dependent adult, whether he or she is competent or not, and is made for the purpose of preventing the elder or dependent adult from having contact with family, friends, or concerned persons.

(C) False imprisonment, as defined in Section 236 of the Penal Code.

(D) Physical restraint of an elder or dependent adult, for the purpose of preventing the elder or dependent adult from meeting with visitors.

(2) The acts set forth in paragraph (1) shall be subject to a rebuttable presumption that they do not constitute isolation if they are performed pursuant to the instructions of a physician licensed to practice medicine in the State of California, who is caring for the elder or dependent adult at the time the instructions are given, and who gives the instructions as part of his or her medical care.

(3) The acts set forth in paragraph (1) shall not constitute isolation if they are performed in response to a reasonably perceived threat of danger to property or physical safety.

(h) "Care custodian" means an administrator or an employee, except persons who do not work directly with elders or dependent adults as part of their official duties, including members of support staff and maintenance staff, of any of the following public or private facilities when the facilities provide care for elders or dependent adults:

(1) Twenty-four-hour health facilities, as defined in Sections 1250, 1250.2, and 1250.3 of the Health and Safety Code.

(2) Clinics.

(3) Home health agencies.

(4) Adult day health care centers.

(5) Secondary schools which serve 18- to 22-year-old dependent adults and postsecondary educational institutions which serve dependent adults or elders.

(6) Sheltered workshops.

(7) Camps.

(8) Community care facilities, as defined by Section 1502 of the Health and Safety Code and residential care facilities for the elderly, as defined in Section 1569.2 of the Health and Safety Code.

(9) Respite care facilities.

(10) Foster homes.

(11) Regional centers for persons with developmental disabilities.

(12) State Department of Social Services and State Department of Health Services licensing divisions.

(13) County welfare departments.

(14) Offices of patients' rights advocates.

(15) Office of the long-term care ombudsman.

(16) Offices of public conservators and public guardians.

(17) Any other protective or public assistance agency which provides health services or social services to elders or dependent adults.

(i) "Health practitioner" means a physician and surgeon, psychiatrist, psychologist, dentist, resident, intern, optometrist, podiatrist, chiropractor, licensed nurse, dental hygienist, licensed clinical social worker, marriage, family, and child counselor, or any other person who is currently licensed under Division 2 (commencing with Section 500) of the Business and Professions Code, any emergency medical technician I or II, paramedic, a person certified pursuant to Division 2.5 (commencing with Section 1797) of the Health and Safety Code, a psychological assistant registered pursuant to Section 2913 of the Business and Professions Code, a marriage, family, and child counselor trainee, as defined in subdivision (c) of Section 4980.03 of the Business and Professions Code, or an unlicensed marriage, family, and child counselor intern registered under Section 4980.44 of the Business and Professions Code, state or county public health or social service employee who treats an elder or a dependent adult for any condition, a coroner, or a religious practitioner who diagnoses, examines or treats elders or dependent adults.

(j) "Adult protective services agency" means a county welfare department, except persons who do not work directly with elders or dependent adults as part of their official duties, including members of support staff and maintenance staff.

(k) "Adult protective services" means those preventive and remedial activities performed on behalf of elders and dependent adults who are unable to protect their own interests; harmed or threatened with harm; caused physical or mental injury due to the action or inaction of another person or their own action due to ignorance, illiteracy, incompetence, mental limitation or poor health; lacking in adequate food, shelter, or clothing; exploited of their income and resources; or deprived of entitlement due them.

(l) "Goods and services which are necessary to avoid physical harm or mental suffering" include, but are not limited to, all of the following:

(1) The provision of medical care for physical and mental health needs.

(2) Assistance in personal hygiene.

(3) Possessing adequate clothing.

(4) Adequately heated and ventilated shelter.

(5) Protection from health and safety hazards.

(6) Protection from malnutrition, under those circumstances where the results include, but are not limited to, malnutrition and deprivation of necessities or physical punishment.

(7) Transportation and assistance necessary to secure any of the needs set forth in paragraphs (1) to (6) above.

(m) "Investigation" means that activity necessary to determine the validity of a report of elder or dependent adult abuse, neglect, or abandonment.

(n) "Long-term care ombudsman" means the State Long-Term Care Ombudsman, long-term care ombudsmen of the Department of Aging, and persons acting in the capacity of ombudsman coordinators as described in Chapter 9 (commencing with Section 9700) of Division 8.5.

(o) "Developmentally disabled person" means a person with a developmental disability specified by or as described in subdivision (a) of Section 4512.

(p) "Mental suffering" means deliberately subjecting a person to fear, agitation, confusion, severe depression, or other forms of serious emotional distress, through threats, harassment, or other forms of intimidating behavior.

(q) "Patient's rights advocate" means a person who has no direct or indirect clinical or administrative responsibility for the patient, and who shall be responsible for ensuring that laws, regulations, and policies on the rights of the patient are observed.

(r) "Local law enforcement agency" means a city police or county sheriff's department, or a county probation department, except persons who do not work directly with elders or dependent adults as part of their official duties, including members of support staff and maintenance staff. *(Amended by Stats 1991 ch 197 §1, eff. 1/1/92.)*

ARTICLE 4

REPORTS OF ABUSE

§15632. Persons required to report elder abuse; statement of knowledge of section 15630.

(a) Any person who enters into employment on or after January 1, 1986, as a care custodian, health practitioner, or with an adult protective services agency or a local law enforcement agency, prior to commencing his or her employment and as a prerequisite to that employment shall sign a statement on a form, which shall be provided by the prospective employer, to the effect that he or she has knowledge of Section 15630 and will comply with its provisions. The signed statement shall be retained by the employer.

(b) Agencies or facilities that employ persons required to make reports pursuant to Section 15630, who were employed prior to January 1, 1986, shall inform those persons of their responsibility to make reports by delivering to them a copy of the statement specified in subdivision (c).

(c) The statement shall be in the following form:

California state law REQUIRES care custodians, health practitioners, and employees of adult protective services agencies and local law enforcement agencies to report physical abuse of elders and dependent adults.

Those professionals must report physical abuse under the following circumstances:

(1) When the reporter has observed an incident that reasonably appears to be physical abuse.

(2) When the reporter has observed a physical injury where the nature of the injury, its location on the body, or the repetition of the injury, clearly indicates that physical abuse has occurred.

© 1992 by J., B. & L. Gould
Printed in the U.S.A.   EP

(3) When the reporter is told by an elder or a dependent adult that he or she has experienced behavior constituting physical abuse.

The report must be made immediately, or as soon as possible, by telephone to either the long-term care ombudsman coordinator or to a local law enforcement agency when the abuse is alleged to have occurred in a long-term care facility, or to either the county adult protective services agency or to a local law enforcement agency when the abuse is alleged to have occurred anywhere else, and must be followed by a written report within two working days. The report must include:

(1) The name of the person making the report.

(2) The name, age, and present location of the elder or dependent adult.

(3) The names and addresses of family members or other persons responsible for the elder or dependent adult's care, if known.

(4) The nature and extent of the person's condition.

(5) Any information that led the reporter to suspect that abuse has occurred.

(6) The date of the incident.

State law also PERMITS the reporting of other types of abuse of elders and dependent adults, such as neglect, intimidation, fiduciary abuse, abandonment, isolation, or other treatment that results in physical harm, pain, or mental suffering. These reports may be made when the reporter has actual knowledge or reasonably suspects that abuse has occurred. If the conduct involves criminal activity not constituting physical abuse, it may be immediately reported to a law enforcement agency.

The law provides that care custodians, health practitioners, or employees of adult protective services agencies or local law enforcement agencies shall not incur either civil or criminal liability for any report they are required or permitted to make under this law.

However, failure to report physical abuse of an elder or dependent adult is a misdemeanor, punishable by not more than six months in the county jail or by a fine of not more than one thousand dollars ($1,000), or by both fine and imprisonment.

Reports made under this law are confidential and may be disclosed only to the agencies specified. Violation of the confidentiality provisions is also a misdemeanor, punishable by not more than six months in the county jail, by a fine of not more than five hundred dollars ($500), or by both fine and imprisonment.

The following is the exact text of portions of the elder and dependent adult abuse reporting law which pertain to the responsibilities of professionals who are required to report abuse of elders and dependent adults:

CONDITIONS UNDER WHICH REPORTING OF PHYSICAL ABUSE IS REQUIRED:

Subdivision (a) of Section 15630 of the Welfare and Institutions Code:

"(a) (1) Any elder or dependent adult care custodian, health practitioner, or employee of a county adult protective services agency or a local law enforcement agency, who in his or her professional capacity or within the scope of his or her employment, either has observed an incident that reasonably appears to be physical abuse, has observed a physical injury where the nature of the injury, its location on the body, or the repetition of the injury, clearly indicates that physical abuse has occurred, or is told by an elder or dependent adult that he or she has experienced be-

havior constituting physical abuse, shall report the known or suspected instance of physical abuse either to the long-term care ombudsman coordinator or to a local law enforcement agency when the physical abuse is alleged to have occurred in a long-term care facility, or to either the county adult protective services agency or to a local law enforcement agency when the physical abuse is alleged to have occurred anywhere else, immediately or as soon as possible by telephone, and shall prepare and send a written report thereof within two working days.

(2) The reports required by this section should contain the following information unless the information is unavailable by the person reporting:

(A) The name, address, telephone number, and occupation of the person reporting.

(B) The name and address of the victim.

(C) The date, time, and place of the incident.

(D) Other details, including the reporter's observations and beliefs concerning the incident.

(E) Any statement relating to the incident made by the victim.

(F) The name of any individuals believed to have knowledge of the incident.

(G) The name of the individuals believed to be responsible for the incident and their connection to the victim."

CONDITIONS UNDER WHICH REPORTING OF ABUSE IS PERMITTED:

Subdivision (b) of Section 15630 of the Welfare and Institutions Code:

"(b) Any care custodian, health practitioner, or employee of an adult protective services agency or local law enforcement agency who has knowledge of or reasonably suspects that other types of elder or dependent adult abuse have been inflicted upon an elder or dependent adult or that his or her emotional well-being is endangered in any other way, may report the known or suspected instance of abuse either to a long-term care ombudsman coordinator when the abuse is alleged to have occurred in a long-term care facility, or to the county adult protective services agency when the abuse is alleged to have occurred anywhere else. If the conduct involves criminal activity not already covered by subdivision (a), it may be immediately reported to the appropriate law enforcement agency."

PROFESSIONALS WHO ARE REQUIRED TO REPORT PHYSICAL ABUSE OF ELDERS AND DEPENDENT ADULTS:

(a) Care custodians, as defined by subdivision (h) of Section 15610 of the Welfare and Institutions Code:

"(h) 'Care custodian' means an administrator or an employee, except persons who do not work directly with elders or dependent adults as part of their official duties, including members of support staff and maintenance staff, of any of the following public or private facilities when the facilities provide care for elders or dependent adults:

(1) Twenty-four hour health facilities, as defined in Sections 1250, 1250.2, and 1250.3 of the Health and Safety Code.

(2) Clinics.

(3) Home health agencies.

(4) Adult day health care centers.

(5) Secondary schools which serve 18- to 22-year-old dependent adults and postsecondary educational institutions which serve dependent adults or elders.

(6) Sheltered workshops.

(7) Camps.

(8) Community care facilities, as defined by Section 1502 of the Health and Safety Code and residential care facilities for the elderly, as defined in Section 1569.2 of the Health and Safety Code.

(9) Respite care facilities.

(10) Foster homes.

(11) Regional centers for persons with developmental disabilities.

(12) State Department of Social Services and State Department of Health Services licensing divisions.

(13) County welfare departments.

(14) Offices of patients' rights advocates.

(15) Office of the long-term care ombudsman.

(16) Offices of public conservators and public guardians.

(17) Any other protective or public assistance agency which provides health services or social services to elders or dependent adults."

(b) Health practitioners, as defined by subdivision (i) of Section 15610 of the Welfare and Institutions Code:

"(i) 'Health practitioner' means a physician and surgeon, psychiatrist, psychologist, dentist, resident, intern, podiatrist, chiropractor, licensed nurse, dental hygienist, licensed clinical social worker, marriage, family and child counselor, or any other person who is currently licensed under Division 2 (commencing with Section 500) of the Business and Professions Code, any emergency medical technician I or II, paramedic, a person certified pursuant to Division 2.5 (commencing with Section 1797) of the Health and Safety Code, a psychological assistant registered pursuant to Section 2913 of the Business and Professions Code, a marriage, family and child counselor trainee, as defined in subdivision (c) of Section 4980.03 of the Business and Professions Code, or an unlicensed marriage, family and child counselor intern registered under Section 4980.44 of the Business and Professions Code, state or county public health or social service employee who treats an elder or a dependent adult for any condition, a coroner, or a religious practitioner who diagnoses, examines or treats elders or dependent adults."

(c) Employees of adult protective services agencies, as defined by subdivision (j) of Section 15610 of the Welfare and Institutions Code:

"(j) 'Adult protective services agency' means a county welfare department, except persons who do not work directly with elders or dependent adults as part of their official duties, including members of support staff and maintenance staff."

(d) Employees of local law enforcement agencies, as defined by subdivision (r) of Section 15610 of the Welfare and Institutions Code:

"(r) 'Local law enforcement agency' means a city police or county sheriffs department, or a county probation department, except persons who do not work directly with elders or dependent adults as part of their official duties, including members of support staff and maintenance staff."

DEFINITION OF "ELDER":

Subdivision (a) of Section 15610 of the Welfare and Institutions Code:

"(a) 'Elder' means any person residing in this state, 65 years of age or older."

DEFINITION OF "DEPENDENT ADULT":

Subdivision (b) of Section 15610 of the Welfare and Institutions Code:

"(b) (1) 'Dependent adult' means any person residing in this state, between the ages of 18 and 64, who has physical or mental limitations which restrict his or her ability to carry out normal activities or to protect his or her rights including, but not limited to, persons who have physical or developmental disabilities or whose physical or mental abilities have diminished because of age.

(2) 'Dependent adult' includes any person between the ages of 18 and 64 who is admitted as an inpatient to a 24-hour health facility, as defined in Sections 1250, 1250.2, and 1250.3 of the Health and Safety Code."

DEFINITION OF "ABUSE OF AN ELDER OR A DEPENDENT ADULT":

Subdivision (g) of Section 15610 of the Welfare and Institutions Code:

"(g) 'Abuse of an elder or a dependent adult' means physical abuse, neglect, intimidation, cruel punishment, fiduciary abuse, abandonment, isolation, or other treatment with resulting physical harm or pain or mental suffering, or the deprivation by a care custodian of goods and services which are necessary to avoid physical harm or mental suffering.

(1) For purposes of this subdivision, 'isolation' includes any of the following:

(A) Acts intentionally committed for the purpose of preventing, and that do serve to prevent, an elder or dependent adult from receiving his or her mail or telephone calls.

(B) Telling a caller or prospective visitor that an elder or dependent adult is not present, or does not wish to talk with the caller, or does not wish to meet with the visitor, where the statement is false, is contrary to the express wishes of the elder or the dependent adult, whether he or she is competent or not, and is made for the purpose of preventing the elder or dependent adult from having contact with family, friends, or concerned persons.

(C) False imprisonment, as defined in Section 236 of the Penal Code.

(D) Physical restraint of an elder or dependent adult, for the purpose of preventing the elder or dependent adult from meeting with visitors.

(2) The acts set forth in paragraph (1) shall be subject to a rebuttable presumption that they do not constitute isolation if they are performed pursuant to the instructions of a physician licensed to practice medicine in the State of California, who is caring for the elder or dependent adult at the time the instructions are given, and who gives the instructions as part of his or her medical care.

(3) The acts set forth in paragraph (1) shall not constitute isolation if they are performed in response to a reasonably perceived threat of danger to property or physical safety."

DEFINITION OF "PHYSICAL ABUSE":

Subdivision (c) of Section 15610 of the Welfare and Institutions Code:

"(c) 'Physical abuse' means all of the following:

(1) Assault, as defined in Section 240 of the Penal Code.

(2) Battery, as defined in Section 242 of the Penal Code.

(3) Assault with a deadly weapon or force likely to produce great bodily injury, as defined by Section 245 of the Penal Code.

(4) Unreasonable physical constraint, or prolonged or continual deprivation of food or water.

© 1992 by J., B. & L. Gould
Printed in the U.S.A.   EP

(5) Sexual assault, which means any of the following:

(A) Sexual battery, as defined in Section 243.4 of the Penal Code.

(B) Rape, as defined in Section 261 of the Penal Code.

(C) Rape in concert, as described in Section 264.1 of the Penal Code.

(D) Incest, as defined in Section 285 of the Penal Code.

(E) Sodomy, as defined in Section 286 of the Penal Code.

(F) Oral copulation, as defined in Section 288a of the Penal Code.

(G) Penetration of a genital or anal opening by a foreign object, as defined in Section 289 of the Penal Code.

(6) Use of a physical or chemical restraint or psychotropic medication under any of the following conditions:

(A) For punishment.

(B) For a period significantly beyond that for which the restraint or medication was authorized pursuant to the instructions of a physician licensed in the State of California, who is providing medical care to the elder or dependent adult at the time the instructions are given.

(C) For a purpose other than that authorized by the physician.*

*So in original. Probably should have closing quotation marks following "physician.".

(d) The cost of printing, distribution, and filing of these statements shall be borne by the employer.

(e) On and after January 1, 1987, when a person is issued a state license or certificate to engage in a profession or occupation the members of which are required to make a report pursuant to Section 15630, the state agency issuing the license or certificate shall send a statement substantially similar to the one contained in subdivision (c) to the person at the same time as it transmits the document indicating licensure or certification to the person.

(f) As an alternative to the procedure required by subdivision (e), a state agency may cause the required statement to be printed on all application forms for a license or certificate printed on or after January 1, 1987.

(g) The retention of statements required by subdivision (a), and the delivery of statements required by subdivision (b) shall be the full extent of the employer's duty pursuant to this section. The failure of any employee or other person associated with the employer to report physical abuse of elders or dependent adults or otherwise meet the requirements of this chapter shall be the sole responsibility of that person. The employer or facility shall incur no civil or other liability for the failure of those persons to comply with the requirements of this chapter. *(Amended by Stats 1990 ch 435 §2, eff. 1/1/91.)*

This page intentionally left blank.

© 1992 by J., B. & L. Gould
Printed in the U.S.A. **EP**

CA Penal Code Handbook—Index

(All references are to sections or rules of the following: Penal Code (P.); Business and Professions Code (B.P.); Evidence Code (E.); Health and Safety Code - Controlled Substances (H.S.); Rules of Court (R.); Vehicle Code (V.); and Welfare and Institutions Code - Juvenile Court Law (W.I.).)

© 1992 by J., B. & L. Gould
Printed in the U.S.A. **EP**

© 1992 by J., B. & L. Gould
Printed in the U.S.A.   **EP**

© 1992 by J., B. & L. Gould
Printed in the U.S.A. **EP**

© 1992 by J., B. & L. Gould
Printed in the U.S.A.   **EP**

© 1992 by J., B. & L. Gould
Printed in the U.S.A. **EP**

© 1992 by J., B. & L. Gould
Printed in the U.S.A.   **EP**

© 1992 by J., B. & L. Gould
Printed in the U.S.A. **EP**

intent to sell narcotics, H.S.11351,
H.S.11370.2, H.S.11370.4
intent to sell restricted dangerous drugs,
H.S.11378
narcotics, H.S.11350
paraphernalia *(See Paraphernalia)*
peyote *(See also Marijuana; Restricted
Dangerous Drugs)*, H.S.11363
punishment for, H.S. 11370.1
Possession of money derived from sale,
H.S.11370.6
Possession without prescription, B.P.4230
Prescriptions; forging, H.S.11368
Prohibition of use as condition of probation,
W.I.729.9
Quantity; sentencing, P.1170.73
Restricted dangerous drugs
—H.S.11377 to 11383
incitement of minor, H.S.11380, H.S.11380.1
ketamine *(See Ketamine)*
phencyclidine (PCP) *(See Phencyclidine (PCP))*
possession, H.S.11377
sale, H.S.11378 to 11379.5
Sale to minor; public park, H.S.11353.7
Sale to prison inmate, P.4573.9
Schedule I, H.S.11054
Schedule II, H.S.11055
Schedule III, H.S.11056
Schedule IV, H.S.11057
Schedule V, H.S.11058
Seizure, H.S.11471, H.S.11472
Use prohibited on probation, P.1203.1ab
Violations
probation; minimum sentence, P.1203.076
(See also DUI)

CONVERSION OF REAL ESTATE
Grand theft, P.487b
Petty theft, P.487c

CONVEYANCES
Fraudulent, P.531, P.531a

CONVICT(S)
Foreign, importing, P.173
Interfering with while working, P.2790
(See also Prisoner(s))

CONVICT-MADE GOODS
Handiwork, P.2813, P.4026
Sale outside California, P.2880 to 2891
advertising, P.2886
disinfection, P.2884
labeling, P.2881 to 2883
Unlawful sale, P.2812

CONVICTION
Judgment; hearsay exception, E.1300
Second
punishment, P.666.5

COPY
Collateral writing, E.1504
Lost or destroyed writing, E.1501
Photographic or videotape; original destroyed or
lost, E.1551
writings, E.1550, E.1551
Record in custody; public entity, E.1506
Recorded writing, E.1507
Records; admissibility, E.1562
Unavailable writing, E.1502
Writing; at hearing, E.1510
certification, E.1531
Writing in control of other party, E.1503
Writing in official custody, E.1530

CORDLESS TELEPHONE
Intercepting communications, P.632.6

CORPORAL INJURY
Inflicting on child, P.273d, P.11165.4
Inflicting on spouse, P.273.5

CORPORATE SEALS
Forgery, P.472

CORPORATIONS
Proceedings against, P.1390 to 1397

CORRECTIONAL INDUSTRY PRODUCTS
Purchase, P.4497.50–4497.56

CORRECTIONAL INSTITUTION
Defined, P.7502

CORRECTIONAL OFFICERS, PERSONNEL
Authority to carry firearms, P.830.5
Definition, P.6031.5
Duties, P.830.55
Minimum standards, P.6035

CORRECTIONAL TRAINING FACILITY
—P.2045 to 2045.6

CORRECTIONS COMPACTS
—P.11184 to 11197
Enforcement, P.11192

CORRECTIONS TRAINING FUND
—P.6040 to 6044
Creation, P.6040
State aid, P.6041, P.6042

CORRUPT SPORTING PRACTICES
—P.337b to 337e

CORRUPTION
—P.92 to 100

CORRUPTLY
Defined, P.7

COSTS
Ability to pay, P.1203.1e, P.1203.1f
Administrative; prisoner permitted to continue
regular employment, P.1209
Change of venue, P.1037
Child abuse counseling, P.1000.17
Community treatment programs, P.3422, P.3424
Counsel, P.987.2 to 987.9
County industrial farms, P.4121 to 4123
Court, defraying, P.1463.22
Incarceration, P.1203.1c, P.1203.1d
Probation, P.1203.1b
Unlawful liquor sale actions, P.11203

COUNCILMEN
Bribing, P.165

COUNSEL
Appeal; fees, P.1241
Compensation, assigned, P.987.2 to 987.9
Corporation, P.1396
Minor, W.I.317 to 318.5
Number to be heard in appeal, P.1254
Number who may argue cause, P.1095
Obtaining, time, P.860
On appeal, R.185.5
Preliminary examination, P.987.1
Representing defendant in capital case, P.686.1
Representation at hearing on certificate of
rehabilitation, P.4852.04, P.4852.08
Right, P.987
at parole hearing, P.3041.7
Special, P.936, P.936.5
grand jury, P.936.7
Trial date; scheduling, P.1048.1

COUNSELING
Defined, P.7502
Substance abuse, P.1203.096

© 1992 by J., B. & L. Gould
Printed in the U.S.A. **EP**

© 1992 by J., B. & L. Gould
Printed in the U.S.A.   EP

© 1992 by J., B. & L. Gould
Printed in the U.S.A. **EP**

© 1992 by J., B. & L. Gould
Printed in the U.S.A. **EP**

© 1992 by J., B. & L. Gould
Printed in the U.S.A. **EP**

© 1992 by J., B. & L. Gould
Printed in the U.S.A.   **EP**

© 1992 by J., B. & L. Gould
Printed in the U.S.A.   **EP**

© 1992 by J., B. & L. Gould
Printed in the U.S.A. **EP**

© 1992 by J., B. & L. Gould
Printed in the U.S.A.   **EP**

© 1992 by J., B. & L. Gould
Printed in the U.S.A. **EP**

© 1992 by J., B. & L. Gould
Printed in the U.S.A.   **EP**

© 1992 by J., B. & L. Gould
Printed in the U.S.A.   **EP**

© 1992 by J., B. & L. Gould
Printed in the U.S.A.   **EP**

Doctor, B.P.2054
Medical license applicant, B.P.584
Vocational nurse applicant, B.P.2886, B.P.2887
(See also False personation)

IMPORTING
Foreign convicts, P.173

IMPOUNDED DOMESTIC ANIMAL
Care, P.597e

IMPRISONMENT(S)
Base term, P.1170, R.420
Civil rights violation, P.422.6 to 422.9
Credits, P.2930 to 2935
False, P.210.5, P.236, P.237
Felony; discharging firearm in vehicle,
P.12022.55
Female prisoners, P.3200 to 3409
Life, P.3046
Mandatory; firearm offenses, P.1203.095
Minimum, P.3049
Terms, commencement, P.2900 to 2903

IMPROPER MATTER
Basis of opinion testimony, E.803

IN-CUSTODY INFORMANT
—P.1127a

INCARCERATION
Payment of costs, P.1203.01

INCENDIARY MATERIAL
—P.12301

INCEST
—P.285

INCESTUOUS MARRIAGES
Solemnizing, P.359

INCOMPETENCY
Commitment, P.1370.3 to 1371
Effect, P.1367
Inquiry into, P.1367 to 1375.5
Recovery from, P.1372
Trial, P.1369
Verdict, P.1370.1
Witness; no defense, P.122

INCOMPLETE CREDIT CARD
Possession, P.484i

INCONSISTENT CONDUCT
Witness, E.769

INCONSISTENT STATEMENT
Witness, E.769
evidence, E.770

INCRIMINATING TESTIMONY
Compelling, P.1324, P.1324.1
(See also Self-incrimination)

INDECENT EXPOSURE
—P.314

INDEMNITY
Hearing, P.4902, P.4903
Person entitled to; judgment; hearsay exception,
E.1301
Persons erroneously convicted and pardoned,
P.4900 to 4906

INDIAN(S) *(See Native Americans)*

INDICTMENT/INFORMATION
Definitions, P.889
Disclosing fact, P.168
Finding and presentment of information, P.940
to 945
Form, P.951
Offenses prosecuted by, P.682
Setting aside, P.995 to 999a
Superior court prosecutions by, P.737, P.738
Time for filing, P.739
Transmission, P.1029

INDIGENT DEFENDANT
Appeal, P.1240.1
Funds provided for investigators and
preparation of defense, P.987.9

INDIGENT PARTY
Return to place of arrest, P.686.5

INDUSTRIAL FARMS
—P.4100 to 4137
(See also County industrial farms)

INDUSTRIAL PROPERTY
Trespassing or loitering, P.552 to 555.5

INDUSTRIAL ROAD CAMPS
Transfer to, P.19b

INFANT
False pretenses re birth, P.156
Substitution of one for another, P.157

INFERENCE
Defined, E.600

INFERIOR COURT
Appeals, P.1466 to 1469
Bail provisions, P.1458, P.1459
Criminal jurisdiction, P.1462
Disposition of fines and forfeitures, P.1462.3,
P.1463 to 1464, P.1464.8
Docket, P.1428
Issuance of arrest warrant, P.1427
Judgment; how rendered, P.1445
Pleas; procedure, P.1429, P.1429.5
Proceedings, P.1427 to 1464
Pronouncing judgment; time, P.1449

INFLICTING INJURY ON
Child, resulting in traumatic condition, P.273d
Spouse, P.273s

**INFLICTING PHYSICAL AND MENTAL
SUFFERING**
Caretaker of dependent adult, P.367a

INFLUENCING TESTIMONY
—P.137

INFORMANT
Identity; privilege, E.1040 to 1047
In-custody, P.1127a

INFORMATION *(See Disclosure;
Indictment/information)*

INFORMATION CENTER
Violent crime *(See Violent Crime Information
Center)*

INFORMED CONSENT
Behavioral research, P.3501, P.3502, P.3521
Organic therapy, P.2672 to 2674

INFRACTION(S)
Applicability of misdemeanor provisions, P.19.7
Arrest for; release of person, P.853.5
How distinguished, P.17
Offenses constituting, P.19.8
Petty theft, P.490.1
Punishment, P.19.2
Trial, P.1042.5

INHUMAN TRANSPORTATION
Animals, P.597a

INHUMANITY TO
Prisoners, P.147

INITIAL SENTENCING
—P.1170 to 1170.95
Aggregate consecutive terms, P.1170.1
Uniformity; rules, P.1170.3

INJURIES
Reports by hospitals, P.11160 to 11162

INJURING
Aircraft, P.625b
Animal; while hunting, P.384h

© 1992 by J., B. & L. Gould
Printed in the U.S.A.   **EP**

© 1992 by J., B. & L. Gould
Printed in the U.S.A.   **EP**

© 1992 by J., B. & L. Gould
Printed in the U.S.A.   **EP**

© 1992 by J., B. & L. Gould
Printed in the U.S.A.   **EP**

© 1992 by J., B. & L. Gould
Printed in the U.S.A. **EP**

© 1992 by J., B. & L. Gould
Printed in the U.S.A.   **EP**

© 1992 by J., B. & L. Gould
Printed in the U.S.A.   **EP**

© 1992 by J., B. & L. Gould
Printed in the U.S.A.　EP

**PRACTICE OF MEDICINE WITHOUT
LICENSE**
—B.P.2052
Risking bodily harm, B.P.2053
PRELIMINARY EXAMINATION
Counsel, P.987.1
PRELIMINARY FACT
—E.400
Determination, E.405
 procedure, E.402
 relevancy, personal knowledge, authenticity
  disputed, E.403
PRELIMINARY HEARING
Hearsay statements, E.1203.1
Presence of defendant, P.1043.5
PRELIMINARY INVESTIGATIONS
—P.1001.52
PRESCRIPTIONS
Blanks, B.P.4390.1
Controlled substance
 possession without, B.P.4230
Dangerous devices, B.P.4227.2
Dangerous drugs
 exceptions, B.P.4227, B.P.4227.1
 labeling containers, B.P.4228
 refilling, B.P.4229, B.P.4229.5
False representation over telephone, B.P.4390.5
Forged, B.P.4390
PRESENTENCE CUSTODY TIME CREDIT
Determination, R.472
PRESIDING OFFICER
Defined, E.905
PRESTON SCHOOL OF INDUSTRY
—W.I.1006
PRESUMPTION(S)
Affecting burden of producing evidence; defined,
 E.603
 effect of, E.604
Affecting burden of proof; defined, E.605
 effect of, E.606
Affecting writings, E.1450 to 1454
Ancient document, E.643
Burden of proof, E.660 to 669.5
Ceremonial marriage, E.663
Classification, E.601
Conclusive, E.620 to 624
 establishment, E.620
Conveyance of property, E.642
Date of writing, E.640
Death of person, E.667
Defined, E.600
Delivery of money, E.631
Delivery of object, E.632
Effect of in criminal action; reasonable doubt,
 E.607
Estoppel, E.623, E.624
Facts in written instrument, E.622
Intent of act, E.665
Judgment of court; rights of parties, E.639
Judicial jurisdiction, E.666
Local ordinances; residential construction,
 E.669.5
Negligence, E.669
Obligation delivered to debtor, E.633
Official duty performed, E.664
Owner of legal title, E.662
Ownership, possession, E.637
Ownership of property, E.638
Possession of obligation, E.635
Possession of order, E.634

Printed materials, E.645.1
Publication of public authority, E.644
Publication of reports of cases, E.645
Receipt of later installment, E.636
Receipt of later rent, E.636
Receipt of letter properly mailed, E.641
Res ipsa loquitur, E.646
Return of process server, E.647
Standards of conduct for public employees,
 E.669.1
Unlawful intent, E.668
PRETRIAL DIVERSION
Traffic violations, P.1001.40
**PRIMARILY CLERICAL OR
ADMINISTRATIVE**
Defined, P.13518
PRINCIPALS
Parties to crime, P.31
PRINTED MATERIAL
Presumption, E.645.1
PRISON(S)
Access to, by grand jury, P.921
Canteen, P.5005
Conditions; inquiry by grand jury, P.919
Construction, P.7000 to 7009
 bond act, P.7100 to 7434
 environmental assessment study, P.7011,
  P.7012
Definitions, P.6081, P.6082
Demolishing, P.4600
Personnel; appointment, P.6050 to 6055
Public transportation services, P.6356
Report of deaths, P.5021
Rules and regulations for administration, P.5058
Sites
 master plan, P.7003.5
State; control over, P.5054
Terms; enhancement, P.667 to 669
Visitor services, P.6350 to 6355
PRISON INDUSTRIES REVOLVING FUND
—P.2806, P.2811, P.2816, P.2817
PRISON INDUSTRY AUTHORITY
—P.2800 to 2817
Board of directors, P.2802, P.2803
 expenses, P.2804
Establishment, P.2800
Jurisdiction and power, P.2805, P.2807, P.2808
Purposes, P.2801
PRISONER LITERACY ACT
—P.2053
PRISONERS
Access to computer systems, P.2702
AIDS test
 appeal to superior court, P.7516.5
 chief medical officer's decision
  appeal, P.7513, P.7515
 chief medical officer's responsibilities, P.7503
 confidentiality, P.7517
 counseling for inmates, law enforcement
  officers, P.7514
 definitions
  AIDS, P.7502
  bodily fluids, P.7502
  correctional institution, P.7502
  counseling, P.7502
  HIV defined, P.7502
  HIV test, P.7502
  inmate, P.7502
  law enforcement employee, P.7502
  minor, P.7502

© 1992 by J., B. & L. Gould
Printed in the U.S.A.   **EP**

© 1992 by J., B. & L. Gould
Printed in the U.S.A. **EP**

© 1992 by J., B. & L. Gould
Printed in the U.S.A.   **EP**

© 1992 by J., B. & L. Gould
Printed in the U.S.A.   **EP**

© 1992 by J., B. & L. Gould
Printed in the U.S.A. **EP**

© 1992 by J., B. & L. Gould
Printed in the U.S.A.   EP

© 1992 by J., B. & L. Gould
Printed in the U.S.A.   **EP**

© 1992 by J., B. & L. Gould
Printed in the U.S.A.   **EP**

© 1992 by J., B. & L. Gould
Printed in the U.S.A. **EP**

© 1992 by J., B. & L. Gould
Printed in the U.S.A. **EP**

© 1992 by J., B. & L. Gould
Printed in the U.S.A.   **EP**

New Publications from Gould

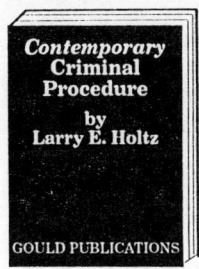

Contemporary Criminal Procedure
by Larry E. Holtz

A new and innovative approach to the study of modern constitutional criminal procedure. Through a distinctive **Question - Answer - Rationale** format, Mr. Holtz removes the guesswork in, and tedious search for, "today's" law. The text dissects and analyzes pertinent court cases in the law of *Arrest, Search and Seizure, Investigative Detentions (Stop-and-Frisk), Motor Vehicle Stops, Interviews, Confessions and Miranda, Identification Procedures, and Law-Enforcement Civil Liability.* Available in hardcover 3-ring looseleaf binder or softcover bound edition. Approx. 700 pages.

Supervision Handbook
by Mario J. Ferrari

A hands-on manual. Subjects covered include the following: Traits of Leadership; Maintaining Discipline; Developing Cooperation; Principles of On-The-Job Instruction; Common Sense About Training; Handling Complaints and Grievances; Understanding Human Behavior; Principles of Public Speaking; The Supervisor's Responsibility for Public Relations; Job Planning — Budgeting Time and Effort; The Supervisor's Responsibility for Safety; Basic Concepts of Organization and Management; and A Model for "Grass Roots" Field Supervision. Approx. 175 pages.

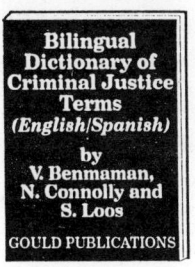

Bilingual Dictionary of Criminal Justice Terms (English/Spanish)
by Virginia Benmaman, Norma Connolly and Scott Loos

A current, comprehensive collection defined in both English and Spanish reflecting significant Penal Code offenses and Criminal Procedure terms. Includes flow charts on the nature of offenses and arrest to conviction procedures. Approx. 250 pages.

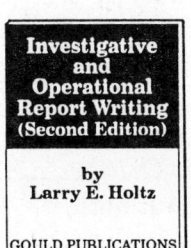

Investigative and Operational Report Writing (Second Edition)
by Larry E. Holtz

A welcome addition to any law enforcement or security officer's arsenal. **Investigative and Operational Report Writing** is a compact and easy-to-read, quick-reference guide for any professional who must document his or her actions and observations in an official report, with the possibility of thereafter testifying in court from that report. In ten easy steps, Mr. Holtz demonstrates how any report can be improved, providing the professional in the field with the means to not only substantially professionalize official reporting but to easily begin turning out Investigative or Operational Reports which are clear, concise, and perfectly understandable. Compact pocket size 5½ x 8½. Approx. 50 pages.

(order form on reverse side)

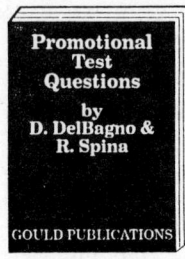

Promotional Test Questions
by D. DelBagno and R. Spina

A practical, in-depth study guide consisting of approximately 2,000 multiple choice questions and answers. This manual will increase the efficiency and effectiveness of the law enforcement professional and is indispensable in preparation for promotion examinations. Approx. 420 pages.

United States Code Unannotated
All 50 Titles — Up-to-date

A compilation of all 50 titles of the Federal Statutes unannotated. Each law is individually indexed and each volume is arranged for proficient use with related U.S.C. Titles. All statutory changes are incorporated into text. Each volume is replaced annually by a complete, new, up-to-date volume. No more pocket parts. No more supplements. No more interleaving. No more outdated laws. Volume One includes: Titles 9, 15, 17, 28, and 35. Available in softcover bound or looseleaf format. Each volume is approximately 1,300 pages; 7 x 10.

☐ *Contemporary* **Criminal Procedure** *by Holtz* ☐ looseleaf ☐ softcover .... $ 34.95

☐ **Supervision Handbook** *by Ferrari* .... $ 14.95

☐ **Bilingual Dictionary of Criminal Justice Terms** *(English/Spanish)*
    by Benmaman, Connolly and Loos .... $ 17.95

☐ **Investigative & Operational Report Writing 2nd Ed.** *by Holtz* .... $ 6.95

☐ **Promotional Test Questions** *by DelBagno and Spina* .... $ 19.95

☐ **United States Code Unannotated** ☐ looseleaf ☐ softcover .... $ 395.00

☐ Please send me a catalogue with complete listings

☐ I have enclosed my check or money order in the amount of $ _____ (including shipping & handling and applicable sales tax). Shipping & handling is $4.00 for the first item; $3.00 for the second item, and $2.00 for each additional item; $39 for United States Code Unannotated (U.S.C.U.™).

Charge to my: ☐ MasterCard ☐ VISA • **1-800-847-6502** • $15.00 minimum per order

Card # _____ Exp. Date _____

AUTHORIZED SIGNATURE (required) _____ *Tel.* (   ) _____

Name (please type or print) _____

Street Address (No P.O. Boxes, Please) _____ *Apt. / Suite #* _____

City _____ *State* _____ *Zip Code* _____

Quantity discounts available • Prices subject to change without notice

Gould Publications 199/300 State Street, Binghamton, NY 13901-2782

GOULD'S QUICK FIND LOCATOR™

HOW TO USE: Bend the edge and follow the arrow to the corresponding black mark.

◀ **Penal Code**

◀ **Business and Professions Code**

◀ **Evidence Code**

◀ **Health and Safety Code**

◀ **Rules of Court**

◀ **Vehicle Code**

◀ **Welfare and Institutions Code**

◀ **Index**